PETERSON'S
INTERNSHIPS
2000

PETERSON'S 2000

Internships

The Largest Source of Internships Available

20th edition

Peterson's
Thomson Learning™

Australia • Canada • Denmark • Japan • Mexico • New Zealand • Philippines
Puerto Rico • Singapore • South Africa • Spain • United Kingdom • United States

About Peterson's

Peterson's is the country's largest educational information/communications company, providing the academic, consumer, and professional communities with books, software, and online services in support of lifelong education access and career choice. Well-known references include Peterson's annual guides to private schools, summer programs, colleges and universities, graduate and professional programs, financial aid, international study, adult learning, and career guidance. Peterson's Web site at petersons.com is the only comprehensive—and most heavily traveled—education resource on the Internet. The site carries all of Peterson's fully searchable major databases and includes financial aid sources, test-prep help, job postings, direct inquiry and application features, and specially created Virtual Campuses for every accredited academic institution and summer program in the U.S. and Canada that offers in-depth narratives, announcements, and multimedia features.

Visit Peterson's Education Center on the Internet (World Wide Web) at www.petersons.com

Editorial inquiries concerning this book should be addressed to the editor at Peterson's, P.O. Box 2123, Princeton, New Jersey 08543-2123.

ISSN 1082-2577
ISBN 0-7689-0261-4

Printed in the United States of America

10 9 8 7 6 5 4 3 2 1

TABLE OF CONTENTS

How to Use This Book

Internships 2000 is a comprehensive directory of internship opportunities across the United States and abroad; the guide provides detailed, pertinent, annually updated information on tens of thousands of short-term positions available in numerous career areas.

Listings are categorized according to the type of company or organization that sponsors the internship. Most sponsors offer positions in career areas that extend beyond their specific field, so you should use the **Field of Interest Index** to find the types of programs that interest you. For example, this index will allow you to find a public relations position at an accounting firm or an accounting position at a public relations firm.

To help you make the most effective use of *Internships 2000*, entries contain the following groups of information.

What You'll Find in the Profiles

1. General Information
In this section you will find a brief description of the organization and its purpose and data on its size and the number of internship applications received each year.

2. Internships Available
Provides information about the type and number of positions available, basic job descriptions, duration of the internships, salaries, training, eligibility requirements, and whether international applicants are accepted.

3. Benefits
Provides information about the benefits available to interns, including training, housing, meal plans, health plans, whether an intern may arrange for *college credit through his or her own college or university, permanent employment opportunities, and placement services.

4. International Internships
Provides location of organization's internship placement opportunities outside the United States.

5. Contact
Includes the name, address, telephone number, and, when available, fax number and e-mail and World Wide Web addresses of the contact for the organization's internship program. Make special note of any application directions listed here to increase your chances for a positive response from the internship sponsor.

*College credit arrangements must be made prior to the student's participation in the internship.

GENERAL COMPANY
123 Main Street
Urban Center, NJ 08543

❶ **General Information** Entrepreneurial database publishing and communications company specializing in education and career reference books. Established 1966. Number of employees: 200. Number of internship applications received each year: 50. Division of Unified Corporation, Atlanta, Georgia.

❷ **Internships Available** ▶ *2 public relations interns:* responsibilities include drafting and disseminating press releases, establishing media contacts. Duration is 8 weeks. Paid. Candidates should have word processing skills, either Apple or IBM. Open to college sophomores, college juniors, college seniors. ▶ *35 data editors:* responsibilities include reviewing survey data for internal consistency, resolving discrepant data with respondents over the phone, data entry. Duration is 6 months. $6 per hour. Open to college sophomores. International applications accepted.

❸ **Benefits** Formal training, opportunity to attend seminars/workshops, and free parking. Sponsor is willing to complete any necessary paperwork required for an intern to receive educational credit. Possibility of full-time employment. Placement assistance provided, including letters of recommendation, names of contacts. Housing provided at $95 per week. Meals provided at no cost.

❹ **International Internships** Available in Paris, France; Madrid, Spain.

❺ **Contact** Call or write to Internship Coordinator, P.O. Box 2123, Urban Center, New Jersey 08543. In-person interview required. Phone: 609-555-1212. Fax: 609-555-0923. E-mail: coord@gc.com. World Wide Web: http://www.gc.com. Application deadline: May 15.

A Note on International Internships

"Exciting Jobs Overseas," "Hundreds of Positions Worldwide: All Fields"—the ads sound great. Do your thing in another country. See the world. Maybe—but before you've gone too far, a closer look might be in order. What is an "international" career and what do *you* want from it? Are you interested in business, government, the United Nations, nonprofit voluntary groups? Do you want to teach, undertake research, be a part of management, or assist in the needs of developing countries? And, perhaps most important of all, do you want to advance your career in the

United States, or do you want to pursue an international career in the fullest sense of the word by spending most of your working life in other countries? If you are honest with yourself in answering questions such as these, you will be a long way toward realizing your goal.

Far too many people seem to think that a strong interest in international work or some past foreign travel experience is sufficient to launch an international career. Unfortunately, this thinking can lead to a rude awakening.

First of all, you should think about the potential international applications of your chosen profession. Then, in addition to the training and preparation necessary to do your job, you should think about the additional preparation needed for an international career. What kind of language skills will you need? Do you have the ability to work with people of many different cultural backgrounds?

In addition to checking the new **International Internships** section in the profiles and using the listings in the new **International Internships Index**, be a bit creative in making use of the **Employer Index.** While the opportunities listed in the **International Internships Index** are exclusively international in nature, many other employers listed in *Internships 2000* offer experiences with an international dimension. You can also find international opportunities in the **Field of Interest Index** under the International category.

The international dimension of every field of human endeavor expands as the world grows more interdependent, and challenging opportunities exist for the individual interested in an international career. Whether one's working life develops in a single country overseas, in a series of assignments in different countries, or in the United States with only occasional overseas travel, one or more international internship experiences will give you that all-important head start on an international career.

Some organizations accept interns of any age or academic level. Others limit their internships based on the academic level of the applicant. The **Academic Level Required Index** identifies organizations that have indicated the academic level(s) that are required for their internships. These may or may not be minimum requirements. An organization may indicate one or all of the options available, from high school student through college graduate.

If you are looking for an internship so that you have relevant experience to put on your resume, but whether you are going to be paid is still a concern, use the **Paid Internships Index** to find all of the organizations that are willing to pay for your talents and skills. Keep in mind that an unpaid internship will still give you valuable experience and will enhance your resume.

If you already have enough experience to know that you are on the right career path, check out the **Possibility of Permanent Employment Index** to find organizations that indicate they have an interest in keeping their best interns on the job on a full-time basis.

About the Data

The information in these listings was collected during the spring and summer of 1999 through questionnaire mailings and telephone interviews with representatives of each of the sponsoring organizations. Although every entry has been completely updated, you should be aware that changes in the data may occur after the publication of the book; contact the sponsors directly for the most current information on their internship program.

Peterson's does not make any claim concerning the hiring policies or practices of sponsoring organizations in this book.

The Internship Experience

by Jay Heflin and Richard Thau

There's a "catch-22" dominating today's job market. Employers tend to hire experienced personnel only, leaving non-experienced college students little opportunity to break in. Fortunately, a way around this obstacle is gaining popularity: internships.

After interning with a company, many individuals will be invited to become a part of the permanent staff. In today's highly competitive job-seeking market, a diploma from an outstanding institution no longer guarantees a job. Today's companies seek seasoned professionals, even for their entry-level positions. Internship programs can provide this unique experience.

"Had I not done an internship, I certainly would never be where I am today, or gotten my first job," proclaims Steve Schanwald in a *Chicago Tribune* article. According to the article, Schanwald, the marketing and broadcasting director for the Chicago Bulls, attributes much of his success to a summer internship in the sports marketing department at the University of

---

INTERN PROFILE

Heather Sapp, 20; intern with the Atlanta Committee for the Olympic Games

During the summer of 1996, I had the honor of being a part of the Summer Olympic Games in Atlanta. I worked in the International Ticketing Office of the Olympic Family Hotel.

While working in the office, I had the opportunity to interact with people from all over the world, putting my French and Spanish language skills to good use. And since the Olympic Family Hotel was also the International Olympic Committee Headquarters, I frequently saw and dealt with many famous people, including heads of state.

My duties included some menial tasks, such as faxing and answering the telephone, but I also got to do some protocol work. The office was responsible for the distribution and allocation of complimentary tickets and required the person who delivered them to be skilled in the protocol pertaining to accreditation categories. On other occasions, I served as a hostess at the VIP entrance to various sporting events.

This internship experience is one that I will long remember. And as an international relations major, I know that the Olympics was a truly first-class summer internship.

INTERN PROFILE

Jeff Kessler, 21; intern at The Polling Company

The Polling Company does polls, surveys, focus groups, and analysis for conservative political candidates and for businesses. Because it's such a small office (4 full-time employees and 3 interns), I actually got to do a lot of substantial work and not just run errands.

The other interns and I interviewed groups of congressional legislative assistants on technology policy. I also administered a poll at the College Republican National Convention, tabulated the results, and wrote up a summary that I submitted to my company.

I feel that this internship gave me, a conservative political science major, an idea of what really goes on behind the scenes in a career I wish to pursue. Even though the job involved some "grunt" work, on the whole it was a wonderful experience.

Maryland. The internship helped him secure his first professional position as the director of sports promotions at the U.S. Air Force Academy.

Education Over a Paycheck

With some internships, the payoff is not reflected in the paycheck but in the valuable experience gained by working in a professional environment. In an article in *USA Today*, Telia Cummings talks about her experience while working with the staff of ABC's *Nightline*. "The 12-week internship cost me about $1,500, including $150 to the University of Akron in Ohio to administer my one-credit internship. I also paid $15 to $25 a week for subways from downtown Washington to the Maryland suburbs."

Was it worth it? Without a doubt. Cummings said she had to skimp a lot on the necessities of life, was dependent on her friends' charity a few times for loans, and took full advantage of leftovers from *Nightline*'s catered dinners on Thursdays, "all with no regrets," the article states. Cummings explains that this internship "was a once-in-a-lifetime chance" and she decided early on that the experience would be worth the sacrifice.

During her internship, as described in the article, Cummings' responsibilities included "sitting in on tapings, attending White House briefings, and meeting pros like host Ted Koppel." Ms. Cummings saw these tasks and what she learned from them as more important than taking a job only for financial gain and having no interest in pursuing it further.

While gaining valuable, hands-on experience is what matters most to interns such as Cummings, career management expert Victor Lindquist warns students to use good judgment when deciding to take an internship that does not pay. Lindquist says "some corporations exploit the eagerness and innocence" of novice employees.

Let Curiosity Be Your Guide

Carrie Schwartz used an internship for its most basic purpose: to test career possibilities.

Schwartz was a student at the University of Washington and after graduation was planning to attend medical school. Yet still she was curious about the industry of her major, psychology. To satisfy her curiosity, she took an internship in the mental health center of Harbor View Hospital in Seattle, Washington.

"It was very interesting," she says. Schwartz recalls "preparing the learning materials that dealt with the patient's specific issues, that were going to be circulated during his or her session. I also assisted in the scoring of patients' psychological tests and helped in interpreting those scores. One of my most interesting jobs was videotaping the sessions a patient would have with their doctors, and one of the most challenging of my duties was assisting with the charting of a patient's

---

INTERN PROFILE

Jennifer Young, 21; intern with *The Journal Newspaper*

As an intern at The Journal Newspaper *in Fairfax, Virginia, I worked with* The Fairfax Journal, The Alexandria Journal, *and* The Arlington Journal. *All are daily newspapers that cover local news in Virginia and Washington, D.C.*

My job was that of a reporter. On my first day, I was assigned to cover a murder. I went to the location of the crime, talked to people who lived nearby, and then wrote up a front-page story.

Right from the start I was kept busy writing stories that ranged from covering a senior day-care event to fireworks regulations in the area. Whenever there was a story that needed to be covered, I was assigned to it.

Working for these newspapers provided me with the opportunity to put my experience as an editor with the Duke Chronicle *to good use.*

INTERN PROFILE

Jen Lee, 21; intern at Mt. Sinai Medical Center

As a senior at the College of William and Mary, I spent two summers interning at the Mount Sinai Medical Center in New York City. Working in a molecular hematology lab, the majority of my research involved the gene therapy of the beta-globin gene, which is implicated in diseases such as sickle cell anemia and beta-thalassemia.

In addition to teaching me various techniques in molecular biology, the internship also provided access to scientists who are at the top of their fields. Every week there were seminars and meetings featuring prominent scientists from all over the world speaking about their research.

During the first summer, I spent most of my time learning the different procedures used in the lab. I worked with a postdoctoral fellow who served as a mentor. During the second summer, I was given my own research problem and was responsible for all aspects of the project.

---

progress." All the patients Schwartz had contact with were a part of the hospital's outpatient program. These individuals were referred by the court to the hospital for medical care as well as therapy sessions. "The work was so interesting," Schwartz says, "that I almost decided to go to graduate school for psychology, but I finally decided to stick to my original plan, attending medical school." She says that "if it hadn't been for the lure of medical school, I would have definitely taken the job they offered me."

Sponsors Value Interns

Working as an intern is a job and should never be considered a donation or hand-out from the company. In fact, the exact opposite is true. To most sponsors, the value of an internship program is often greater to them than to their interns. Since economic tides are ever-changing and governmental intervention and support wanes with every budget cut, many organizations cannot operate without the involvement of interns.

Students who intern for Hidden Villa Environmental Education Program in Los Altos Hills, California, are instrumental in keeping the organic farm running. Chris Overington, Hidden Villa's manager, says, " The students get real hands-on experience being on the farm. They spend about 30 hours total each week working the land and teaching preschool to sixth-grade children about how to care for and maintain a working organic farm. They

---

INTERN PROFILE

Steve Williams, 20; intern with Geotecnia y Cimientos, S.A.

Growing up in southern California, it was natural for me to take Spanish in high school. Drawing on my linguistic ability, I decided to join the International Honors Program at Duke University and intern at Geotecnia, a civil engineering company in Madrid, Spain.

Geotecnia gave me the opportunity to experience two sides of a large engineering firm. In the office, I helped draft surveying maps, translated reports, fixed computer problems, and prepared graphs and charts. I even headed one of the many work sites for the Madrid Metro. It was fascinating to learn about the extensive work that goes into developing an intricate public transportation system like this one.

Interning in Spain combined the best of both worlds: learning the language and culture while receiving practical work experience. I'm confident that this experience will help me in the future.

---

in them. The *Chicago Tribune* reports, "For Motorola's six internships in its Northbrook, Illinois–based Automotive and Industrial group, more than 500 engineering students applied." It goes on to state that "Kraft recruiters interviewed 150 candidates for 11 Kraft USA marketing spots. Sidley and Austin received more than 1,000 resumes and coordinated 500 law school on-campus interviews for 47 jobs."

A Win-Win Combination

Despite the competition, internships are a crucial element in educational training. Not only does a student receive practical knowledge about a current major or career interest, but companies also get a chance to improve their bottom line. Perhaps the term "synergy" best describes the mutual benefit that the sponsors and the intern bring to one another. No matter what you call it, internships have become an integral part of a higher learning experience. And as demands for more well-rounded graduates increase, the need for internships will surely rise as well.

Jay Heflin and Richard Thau are freelance business writers from New York City.

---

also attend classes themselves for about 5 hours a week. Here they are instructed on the techniques of successfully running a farm." Hidden Villa interns are the backbone of the farm. If they don't do their job, the farm will not be as productive.

"Our interns are an integral part of the staff," says Sheryl Berger, public relations manager for the Alley Theatre in Houston, Texas. "In fact, they do the same thing as the rest of the staff. As a nonprofit, we're always understaffed."

Berger has 7 part-time interns, each of whom commits 15 to 20 hours per week for a minimum of eight weeks. "'The more you put in, the more you get out,' I always tell them," says Berger. Perhaps as a result of her exhortations, her interns have moved on to other arts organizations throughout Texas. These include the Houston Ballet, the Grand 1894 Opera House, Pace Theatricals, and the Texas Institute for Arts and Education. "Now I have contacts at all these organizations," Berger says contentedly.

A Prized Commodity

Be prepared for fierce competition when interviewing for an internship; it has become a buyer's market. Just as the number of internship programs is increasing, so is the number of students who wish to take part

---

INTERN PROFILE

Jennifer Russell, 20; intern with Barefoot Films

Ever since elementary school, I have been interested in film and broadcasting. For several months, I was able to combine these two interests in an internship with Barefoot Films, a television commercial production company in Decatur, Georgia. As an English major, I hope to blend my classroom and job experience into a career in either film or broadcasting.

At Barefoot, I worked both in the company's office and on the set. When in the office, I was an assistant to the company's president. My duties included answering the telephone, data entry, and researching sites for possible commercial shoots. When on the set, I sometimes acted as a script supervisor and took notes on the scenes as they were filmed. At other times, I was a production assistant, running errands and helping out where needed. Working at Barefoot films allowed me greater insight into this interesting and diverse field.

What Sponsors Seek in an Intern

by Jay Heflin and Richard Thau

The road to a career is more like a maze: choosing a college, picking a major, vying for class standing, constructing a resume, and finally scheduling interviews. Most students wishing to enter the workplace are put through their paces long before they sign on with an employer. It can be very stressful. And to make matters worse, some students find themselves with jobs that they know very little about.

Graduating students usually discover that choosing a job is bewildering and aggravating. But there is something that can teach a student the fundamentals of career life: an internship.

"College graduates who have served internships

David Reynolds, Human Resource Specialist, Wolf Creek Nuclear Operating Corporation, Burlington, Kansas

"We look for candidates who have a unique interest in power generation," states David Reynolds, Human Resources Specialist with Wolf Creek Nuclear Operating Corporation, a commercial nuclear electric power generating station. His company employs, at about $10.50 an hour, junior and senior college students for one semester.

But interest is not the only requirement to secure an internship at Wolf Creek, as Mr. Reynolds explains. "Grades and the student's major are also important. We look for engineering students who have a GPA above a 2.5 or 2.7, something above average."

receive, on average, higher starting salaries and more job offers than those with no internship experience," adds Maury Hanigan, president of New York-based Hanigan Consulting Group, a firm that studies the internship programs of Fortune 500 companies.

Indeed, internships can be the most impressive item on a student's resume. It shows real experience and the ability to accomplish more than digesting college classroom theories. In some instances, participating in an internship will put a particular person ahead of the competition and can be the deciding factor in securing paid employment later.

Amy Leahy, Intern Coordinator, Omicon Cable, Hamtramck, Michigan

"Enthusiastic" is the way Amy Leahy describes the interns she hires. "Experience is something we give them [the interns] in return," she adds. Ms. Leahy works with Omicon Cable, a public access cable company. Her company employs local programming interns of college or even high school level.

"We want to show the person interested in pursuing this career that it is not a 9 to 5 job and also that it could be for anyone," says Leahy. Interns who work at Omicon Cable are not paid for the first semester; if they decide to stay on, they receive a small monthly stipend.

Corporations know the advantages of hiring interns. In today's competitive economy, companies can no longer afford to spend valuable recruiting time on unknown entities. Internships allow a company to "test" a prospective employee nearly risk-free. A lot more can be learned about a person's work habits and attitudes within a three-month semester internship than in a number of half-hour interviews. It is common to find companies hiring 80 to 90 percent of their interns for full-time positions after graduation.

Companies also favor interns because they help to improve the bottom line. While most interns are paid a nominal stipend, their take-home pay is usually

Catherine Councill, President, Maryland Film Office, Baltimore, Maryland

Catherine Councill at the Maryland Film Office believes in giving high school graduates a chance to learn a career. Her company markets the state of Maryland to film companies, enticing them to do their shooting there. "We like to bring the people on board who show the greatest amount of enthusiasm during the interview," she says.

But being a high school graduate isn't the only qualification required to interview with Ms. Councill's company. "Normally we like to have interns who are studying marketing or communication. That way they know the lingo that accompanies the marketing field."

Marya Warshaw, Director, Gowanus Arts Exchange, Brooklyn, New York

For Marya Warshaw at the Gowanus Arts Exchange, experience is needed to fill one of her internship slots. "For our arts administration intern," she explains, "we look for someone who has worked before. Especially on the technical side, it's hard to teach someone all that needs to be done and still get a show off the ground."

Gowanus' internships are as short as eight weeks or as long as a full year. The longer "experience required" positions are paid. "We try to be very accommodating [on both the time availability and salary] because having interns on our crew is very valuable, for us as well as for them."

nowhere near what it would cost a company to employ someone full-time. "Some companies find investing in summer internships more cost effective than straight recruiting," stated Roger Muller, Placement Director at Northwestern University.

What do sponsors seek in an intern? The answer to this question is simple: It varies. Seemingly there are just as many different, specific qualifications needed to land an internship as there are companies within the broad scope of corporate America. No single criterion, such as grades, job experience, or major, can encapsulate what companies seek in their prospective interns. Each corporation has specific needs, and those needs must be filled by interns with specific skills.

Interest, Not Just Grades

"Good grades and related job experience are important. But we also look at what school activities they [prospective interns] participate in," said Kim Hendershot, personnel specialist at Burns and McDonnell in Kansas City, Missouri, an engineering consulting firm that hires about 30 paid interns each year.

Hendershot said the company considers school activities so important because they give insight about a student: "Belonging to the Greek system or being a member of an organization that is related to their discipline can often tell us more about a student than can be reflected in their grades or job experience."

Another company that considers school activities and personal interests in addition to grades and related job experience is *The Nation* magazine. "Grades and majors aren't as big a deal as interest in progressive causes

and knowledge of such current events," said Sandy Wood, a staffer at *The Nation* in charge of recruiting interns.

The Nation employs 7 interns in New York and 1 in Washington, D.C. While at the magazine, interns must complete four "assignments" that require that they assist the publication's editors and columnists. "Their tasks on the assignments vary widely," said Mr. Wood. "There are some secretarial duties and research to be done. But the biggest part they play is fact checking and assisting the publicity director with news releases."

Desire, Experience, and Grades

Still, there are companies that consider a candidate's grade point average as important as interpersonal skills and interests.

Jennifer Craig, the marketing director at Union Station, a mall in Indianapolis, said, "Careful attention to detail and a grade point average of at least 3.0" are required to intern with her company. Responsibilities for an intern include implementing special events, creating press releases, and assisting with programs that will enhance gross sales.

Craig went on to say that "qualified individuals for an internship program at Union Station should display a high drive, a willingness to be flexible, and related experience." Union Station employs 2 interns each year. Each intern is paid a weekly stipend of about $100.

Just as Craig said a related background in the field of marketing is important to becoming an intern in her company, so did Jeanine Triolo, marketing manager with *Vibe* Magazine in New York City. "If they're majoring in marketing, I'd be more inclined to hire them,"

THE MEXICAN MUSEUM

Yalonda Perez, Intern Coordinator, Mexican Museum, San Francisco, California

At the Mexican Museum in San Francisco, California, possessing previous experience with the correct educational background can help secure an internship position. "Our interns are usually undergraduates majoring in art history or Latino history or graduate students with work experience," says Ms. Perez, an employee with the Museum.

Her museum accepts students into a wide range of internship programs. They range from curatorial to outreach programs. These positions are not paid, but the work completed does count toward college credit for the intern.

she said. "They are taught the fundamentals of marketing in school and are ready to apply what they've learned. I don't have to teach them anything; we can get right to work on projects that need to be accomplished for the magazine."

Triolo also sees availability of the intern's time as a crucial factor when considering who to hire. "I need someone for at least three or four days a week. We have projects lasting between fourteen and twenty days, and for [the interns] to get the best education possible about life in the marketing world, they have to see the project through all the way, from beginning to deadline."

Even though some companies view grades, majors, or school activities as important factors, there are some institutions that place special emphasis on an interview. Others are less strict. Terry Denson, chief of the Public Service Corps Placement Unit for the City of New York's Department of Personnel, says they have no grade requirement. His service usually places 1,000 students out of 1,200 applicants into paying summer work within the city's government. "Almost everyone is guaranteed a job," Mr. Denson stated.

The Universal Trait

Amid numerous company needs and intern qualifications, there was one universal trait that all internship sponsors hoped to see in internship candidates: a winning attitude. Possessing the desire to succeed is key to unlocking any door of opportunity.

Council for Court Excellence

Priscilla Skillman, Program Analyst, Council for Court Excellence, Washington, D.C.

To be an intern at the Council for Court Excellence, the student has to be a triple threat: interested, experienced, and knowledgeable. "We require that our interns have an interest in public policy, a strong academic background, and be able to provide writing samples of past work," reports Priscilla Skillman, Program Analyst for the firm. Her group is a nonprofit, nonpartisan civic organization working to improve the administration of justice in local and federal courts.

Interns are not paid, but the experienced gained is immeasurable. "Our interns are usually with us for one semester," says Ms. Skillman, "but we would be delighted to have them stay longer." Skillman's firm accepts 1 to 3 interns per semester to assist in the development of selected projects.

Jay Heflin and Richard Thau are freelance business writers from New York City.

Interning at the Smithsonian

The Smithsonian Institution is known to visitors for its outstanding museums and exhibits. An intern, on the other hand, has opportunities that range beyond the obvious. In addition to internships that involve working with exhibits and displays at the better-known Smithsonian museums, many opportunities exist either behind-the-scenes at these organizations or in other, less well-known branches of the Smithsonian. As such, interns get to explore a side of the Smithsonian the public rarely sees and have a rewarding and unique educational experience—whether it's doing research in Central America at the Smithsonian Tropical Research Institute or planning exhibits at the National Museum of Art.

The internship positions themselves may be hard to find. In most cases, departments and divisions are responsible for their own internship program, which means that a prospective intern might need to research and contact a number of different offices in order to find the right opportunity. But the internships are there—more than 700 of them each year. Most are available in the Washington, D.C., area, but others are available in New York, Boston, and Panama—locations one does not normally consider the Smithsonian's domain.

Interns have been an important part of the workings of the Smithsonian since the 1960s. During the summer, when most internships are available, interns augment the 7,000-employee workforce by as much as 10 percent. But it is not just the numbers that are important. Interns serve a crucial ongoing role. "They bring a lot of new blood into the Smithsonian," says Allison Wickens, Intern Services Program Specialist at the Center for Museum Studies. The relationship is good for the intern, too. "The benefit of the internship is that you get to know the people in the organization," says Wickens, herself a three-time intern at the Smithsonian. In many cases, the internship includes an orientation to various museums and departments that are part of the Smithsonian. As a result of getting to know the organization, many interns, like Wickens, return for additional internship assignments and eventually regular employment. According to Wickens, there is another group of interns—college students, mostly—who are looking for research or museum experience but not necessarily permanent employment.

History and Scope

That the Smithsonian should offer internships seems a natural extension of its long record of research and education. The Institution was founded in 1846 by an act of Congress, following a substantial donation by the British scientist James Smithson, who envisioned an organization "for the increase and diffusion of knowledge among men." Federal appropriations and private donations have supported the Smithsonian through the years.

The Smithsonian offers internships in nearly every discipline in which it is involved, covering specialties beyond the range of a traditional museum, such as history, art, culture, botany, and zoology. This results in some unexpected opportunities for interns. Many agencies and departments operate in support of the Smithsonian's public activities, offering opportunities for interns.

At the Smithsonian's Division of Architectural History and Historic Preservation, which oversees affairs relating to the preservation and history of Institution buildings, interns work with original architectural drawings, photographs, memoranda, and other architectural documents. "A lot of prospective interns confuse it with an architectural [design] experience. It's really architectural history," says Sabina Wiedenhoeft, Intern Coordinator and Architectural History Specialist. "Most interns do research projects."

Some interns are researching material for a book on the Smithsonian's Arts and Industries building, which dates back to 1881. Some are investigating the history of museum design and the influence it might have had on the design of the Arts and Industries building, while others are preparing material about the design of the building itself. But interns do more than research architecture during their 10-week stay. "We try to familiarize them with all the Smithsonian museums," says Wiedenhoeft of the division's interns.

Other Smithsonian units function for long periods of time in relative obscurity. On the Smithsonian's Joseph Henry Papers project, interns assist in preparing a fifteen-volume edition of the papers of Joseph Henry, an eminent American physicist and the first Secretary of the Smithsonian Institution.

According to Mark Rothenberg, Editor and Internship Coordinator for the project, interns have been a vital part of the project since its inception in 1967. "We often get applicants who are looking for a museum experience," rather than individuals interested in the kind of historical research with which the project is concerned, Rothenberg says. "But there are always many more qualified applicants than there are positions," he adds.

From time to time, the project has been favored by as many as 6 or 7 interns at once. Rothenberg estimates that over the years interns have accounted for 10 to 20 percent of the project's total work force. Most interns on the project seek to sharpen research skills in preparation for a career in historical research.

Each intern is given a general task and a thematic task. A general task might include scouring nineteenth-century newspapers for references to the Smithsonian, specifically references to the intellectual and cultural life surrounding the Institution in Henry's day. A thematic task might consist of researching science education in the nineteenth century by consulting secondary sources such as Henry's lecture notes.

In 1997, interns on the Joseph Henry Papers project were involved in preparing material used in the celebration of Henry's 200th birthday, a rare public aspect of the project.

There are also internship opportunities at the well-known branches of the Smithsonian. At the National Museum of American Art, there are 20 to 25 positions for college juniors and seniors and graduate students with a background in American history, art history, or studio art. Interns work closely with curatorial and training departments and, in some cases, receive a stipend.

Similarly, most interns at the National Museum of African Art (home to more than 7,000 items, with collections in art of northern and sub-Saharan Africa) are required to have art and art history training in African art. Opportunities exist in curatorial, preservation, exhibits, and public relations departments. The National Museum of African Art receives more than 100 applications each year for its handful of positions.

Eligibility, Application, and Compensation

Although 60 to 70 percent of interns at the Smithsonian are undergraduates, there are plenty of positions for recent college graduates, graduate students, and career-changers in addition to a few positions for high school students. Most positions require an interest or course work in the subject area in which the intern will work.

Interns who are uncertain about an area of study are encouraged to contact the Center for Museum Studies, which serves as the central administrative office for internships at the Smithsonian. This office can offer general information about the kinds of internships that are available, but by no means can it offer a comprehensive picture. Individuals who have identified a particular museum or department at which they want to intern should contact the corresponding office directly (see offices list below).

About 30 percent of the internships offer a stipend. Each is arranged at the discretion of the individual department or museum and depends upon the availability of funding, which varies from year to year.

Stipend values can go as high as those at the National Air and Space Museum, where interns may earn $3500 per one-semester internship.

On the other hand, most positions offer the possibility of academic credit in conjunction with a college or university. In many cases, the internship is structured to this end. For instance, the National Museum of American Art hosts an advanced program that offers academic credit for interns with 12 credit hours of graduate academic course work in art history. The semester-long internship features more than twenty-five workshops in art history, conservation, registration, and other related topics. There is an extensive required reading list and an oral examination. The intern receives a letter grade upon successful completion of the program.

Summary

Whatever their assignment—behind-the-scenes or otherwise—interns at the Smithsonian engage in structured, focused learning in addition to education about the Institution in general. Internships at the Smithsonian are designed and intended to complement an intern's educational and career goals. There is perhaps no other organization of this magnitude that embraces the idea of internships and nurtures its interns in quite the same manner. One is certainly hard-pressed to find another organization so vibrant in education about culture, nature, science, and technology.

The following is a comprehensive list of the departments within the Smithsonian that offer internships. For those interested in one or more of these internship positions, a separate inquiry should be made to the Intern Coordinator at each site.

Anacostia Museum
FP, MRC 520
1901 Fort Place, SE
Washington, D.C. 20560

Architectural History and Historic Preservation
Arts and Industries Building
Suite 2263, MRC 417
900 Jefferson Drive, SW
Washington, D.C. 20560

Archives of American Art
331 BAL MRC 216
8th and F Streets, NW
Washington, D.C. 20560

Archives of American Art, New York City
1285 Avenue of the Americas, Lobby
New York, NY 10019

Arthur M. Sackler Gallery and Freer Gallery of Art
Room 2034, MRC 707
950 Jefferson Drive, SW
Washington, D.C. 20560

Center for African American History and Culture
Arts and Industries Building
Suite 1130, MRC 431
900 Jefferson Drive, SW
Washington, D.C. 20560

Center for Folklife Programs and Cultural Studies
Suite 2600, MRC 914
955 L'Enfant Plaza
Washington, D.C. 20560

Center for Museum Studies
Arts and Industries Building
Suite 2235, MRC 427
900 Jefferson Drive, SW
Washington, D.C. 20560

Conservation Analytical Laboratory
MSC F2011, MRC 534
Washington, D.C. 20560

Conservation and Research Center
1500 Remount Road
Front Royal, VA 22630

Cooper-Hewitt Museum
2 East 91st Street
New York, NY 10128

Engineering and Design Services
955 L'Enfant Plaza
Suite 3230, MRC 908
Washington, D.C. 20560

Friends of the National Zoo
National Zoological Park
Communications
3000 Block of Connecticut Avenue, NW
Washington, D.C. 20008

Hirshhorn Museum and Sculpture Garden
Room 410, MRC 350
7th and Independence, SW
Washington, D.C. 20560

Horticulture Services Division
Arts and Industries Building
Suite 2282, MRC 420
900 Jefferson Drive, SW
Washington, D.C. 20560

Institutional Studies Office
Arts and Industries Building
Suite 1271, MRC 405
900 Jefferson Drive, SW
Washington, D.C. 20560

International Center
Ripley Center
Room 3123, MRC 705
950 Jefferson Drive, SW
Washington, D.C. 20560

Joseph Henry Papers
Arts and Industries Building
Suite 2188, MRC 429
900 Jefferson Drive, SW
Washington, D.C. 20560

National Air and Space Museum
Room 3743, MRC 305
601 Independence Avenue, SW
Washington, D.C. 20560

National Collections (OR)
Arts and Industries Building
Suite 3101, MRC 410
900 Jefferson Drive, SW
Washington, D.C. 20560

National Museum of African Art
Room 2150, MRC 708
950 Independence Avenue, SW
Washington, D.C. 20560

National Museum of American Art
Room 270, MRC 210
8th and G Streets, NW
Washington, D.C. 20560

National Museum of American History
Room 1040, MRC 605
12th and Constitution Ave, NW
Washington, D.C. 20560

National Museum of the American Indian
Suite 7103, MRC 934
470 L'Enfant Plaza
Washington, D.C. 20560

National Museum of Natural History
Room 210, MRC 158
10th and Constitution Avenue, NW
Washington, D.C. 20560

Research Training Program
Room W411, MRC 166
10th and Constitution Avenue, NW
Washington, D.C. 20560

National Portrait Gallery
Room 195, MRC 213
8th and F Street, NW
Washington, D.C. 20560

National Postal Museum
Room 196A, MRC 570
2 Massachusetts Avenue, NE
Washington, D.C. 20560

National Zoological Park
Administration
3000 Block of Connecticut Avenue, NW
Washington, D.C. 20008

National Zoological Park
Office of Human Resources
3000 Block of Connecticut Avenue, NW
Washington, D.C. 20008

Office of Equal Employment and Minority Affairs
MRC 921
955 L'Enfant Plaza
Washington, D.C. 20560

Office of Exhibits Central
Room 3f11, MRC 808
1111 N. Capitol Street
Washington, D.C. 20560

Office of Fellowships and Grants
Suite 7000, MRC 902
955 L'Enfant Plaza
Washington, D.C. 20560

Office of the General Counsel
Room 302, MRC 012
1000 Jefferson Drive, SW
Washington, D.C. 20560

Office of Government Relations
Room 220, MRC 019
1000 Jefferson Drive, SW
Washington, D.C. 20560

Office of Human Resources
Suite 2100, MRC 912
955 L'Enfant Plaza
Washington, D.C. 20560

Office of Information Technology
Arts and Industries Building
Suite 2224, MRC 433
900 Jefferson Drive, SW
Washington, D.C. 20560

Office of Membership and Development
Arts and Industries Building
Suite 1481, MRC 439
900 Jefferson Drive, SW
Washington, D.C. 20560

Office of Imaging, Printing, and Photographic
    Services
American History Building
Room CB054, MRC 644
12th and Constitution Avenue, NW
Washington, D.C. 20560

Office of Public Affairs
Arts and Industries Building
Room 2410, MRC 421
900 Jefferson Drive, SW
Washington, D.C. 20560

Office of the Smithsonian Institution Archives
Arts and Industries Building
Suite 2135, MRC 414
900 Jefferson Drive, SW
Washington, D.C. 20560

Office of Sponsored Projects
Suite 7400, MRC 903
955 L'Enfant Plaza
Washington, D.C. 20560

Product Development and Product Licensing
Suite 8000, MRC 951
955 L'Enfant Plaza
Washington, D.C. 20560

Smithsonian Astrophysical Observatory
Mail Stop 83
60 Garden Street
Cambridge, MA 02138

Smithsonian Environmental Research Center
Box 28
Edgewater, MD 21037

Smithsonian Institution Libraries
Natural History Building
Room 28, MRC 154
10th and Constitution Avenue, NW
Washington, D.C. 20560

Smithsonian Office of Education
Intern Coordinator
Arts and Industries Building
Suite 1163, MRC 402
900 Jefferson Drive, SW
Washington, D.C. 20560

Smithsonian Press/Smithsonian Productions
Suite 7100, MRC 950
470 L'Enfant Plaza
Washington, D.C. 20560

Smithsonian Institution Retail
Suite 8000, MRC 951
955 L'Enfant Plaza
Washington, D.C. 20560

Smithsonian Institution Traveling Exhibition Service
Ripley Center
Room 3146, MRC 706
950 Jefferson Drive, SW
Washington, D.C. 20560

Smithsonian Tropical Research Institute
Unit 0948
APO AA 34002-0948

The Smithsonian Associates
Ripley Center
Room 3077, MRC 701
950 Jefferson Drive, SW
Washington, D.C. 20560

Interning Within the Computer Industry

by Jay Heflin and Richard Thau

Fifty years ago, Howard Aiken, a computer engineer, thought a total of six computers would meet all the tallying needs of the United States. He couldn't have been more wrong. Today, there are millions of personal computers and workstations worldwide that perform duties deemed impossible back then. The abilities of computers have far exceeded anyone's expectation, allowing boundless opportunities for the professional as well as the student. Paul Jankovic, President of Southeastern Internship Association, a company providing internship information to college directors and staff members, says, "Computer internships are obviously on the rise." He explains that "most companies are purchasing more computer equipment because they are relying on them to handle an increasing amount of the work load. This growth creates more jobs for people who are knowledgeable in computers and thus allows more interns." Jankovic's company has experienced this trend firsthand. "We've nearly doubled our computer inventory," he says, "and now we have more interns working for us than in the past."

Recently, 5 computer science interns worked with Lockheed Sanders Incorporated, a firm that designs and develops advanced defense electronics. "I began my internship researching the Web and writing pages on the Web program HTML," says Jeff Lee, who interned with Lockheed during the summer. "Now I'm writing test programs on Java and also assisting in the writing of a new application for the Web."

Another intern with Lockheed is Joe Wagovich. He works with the company's mainframes. "When I started the internship, I was working with the hardware simulation VHDL," Wagovich states, "Now, I've just started writing programs on Visual C++." Wagovich says that he learned the basics of Visual C++ while studying at the University of Virginia. "School was a good start," he explains, "but I've learned so much more about the program with the hands-on experience I've gained by participating in the internship."

Working on the Web and with computer hardware are just two of the opportunities that await the intern. Other examples of jobs for interns in other companies include working with software design engineers whose responsibilities might be writing and editing software programs. Interns can also work as system engineers and assist in the development of object-oriented software programs. Work on a company's mainframe might also be available to college interns. Examples of some of these tasks are troubleshooting or designing a company's network, training users in the use of the company's system, or helping define the needs for internal users of a PC.

Best Bets

Computer science majors have demanding assignment and classroom schedules that leave very little time to participate in, let alone interview for, an internship. But as the author of the book *Opportunities in Computer Systems Careers* (NTC Publishing Group, 1996), Julie Kling Burns, states, "[There is] one kind of work that should be pursued wholeheartedly. Any computer-related work experience you gain [as an] undergraduate will be useful to you." Employers like hiring college graduates who have computer-related work experience in entry-level positions. "Professionals in the computer industry cannot stress enough the benefits of working on an internship," Burns says.

Where Do You Look?

In addition to books such as this, university career placement centers offer information about computer internships. Here a student can discover intern opportunities on the local, national, and global level and also become connected with internship service programs that can assist in placing a student into a company-sponsored program.

One such company is the Philadelphia Center, a firm that focuses on placing about 700 undergraduates into internship programs nationwide. Explains Executive Director Steven E. Brooks, "after students qualify [with the correct major and acceptable grades] within their own university to become intern candidates, they then apply to our company and will be set up for interviews for interning with sponsor companies."

After a student is placed by Brooks' firm, the intern commences on a "learning plan." This plan outlines the objectives the intern wishes to accomplish. "Periodically," says Brooks, "the intern and a member of the sponsor company will be interviewed by our company to see how well the student is attaining the goals that were set at the onset of the internship. Sometimes those goals change once the intern has had an opportunity to experience his or her major in the workplace."

Professional computer societies also may have information about internship opportunities. George R. Eggert, CSP, executive director for the Institute for Certification of Computer Professionals (ICCP) says in the introduction of Burns' book that "professional computer societies were created to help entry-level personnel and beginning professionals to boost their careers." Societies like the ICCP or the Associate Computer Professional (ACP) "allow students to better define their goals," states Eggert, "and get a firm grasp on their educational and professional development. Organizations like the Association of Computing Management allow students to interact with professionals who have been successful in this ever-changing [computer] field."

Winning Criteria

As in other fields, the requirements for a person's acceptance as an intern within the computer industry varies from company to company. But one prerequisite seems to be universal: formal training. Attendance at a four-year university or college and having a grade point average of at least 2.7 is deemed necessary for a candidate for an internship program within the computer field. But computer internships are not exclusive to upperclass students only; students completing their sophomore year can become eligible for candidacy in most internship programs.

Also, computer internships are not limited to computer science majors. In many cases, marketing, education, or social sciences majors will qualify a student for a computer internship. Knowledge of programs like autoCAD, WordPerfect, UNIX, and C++ can also improve a candidate's chances.

The Message

Computers are being utilized more and more every day. An internship in the computer world allows an individual valuable experience and education that can lead to a number of careers in an increasing number of industries. The message is clear: the opportunities for the computer intern are infinite. New and challenging positions for computer personnel are being created every day, in every business, in every part of the world.

Jay Heflin and Richard Thau are freelance business writers from New York City.

International Applicants for U.S. Internships

by Robert M. Sprinkle and Elizabeth Chazottes

In an effort to provide as accurate guidance as possible for students from outside the United States, each employer listed in *Internships 2000* has been asked if applications will be accepted from international students. Peterson's has also asked if the employer is willing to undertake the necessary steps—either directly with the U.S. Immigration and Naturalization Service (INS) or through an educational exchange organization—to make it possible for the student to secure a proper U.S. visa that will allow legal employment while in the United States.

There are significant penalties for employers who hire foreign nationals illegally. Foreign nationals can be deported and barred from returning to the United States for violating their visa status. If an employer in the United States offers you an internship, make certain that both you *and* the employer know and follow the requirements of U.S. law *before* you leave home.

Passports

In order to secure a U.S. visa that permits employment in an internship, you must have a valid passport from your own country. Your passport must be valid for six months beyond the date on which you expect to leave the United States. A number of countries have special "passport validity" agreements with the United States under which a passport is considered to be valid for six months beyond the expiration date stated in the passport. In order to avoid last-minute problems, you should contact U.S. consular officials as early as possible to determine the exact requirement for your country.

Visas

Unlike many countries, the United States does not control the activities of noncitizens by the use of work permits, residence permits, or police registration. Instead, what an individual may or may not do while in the United States depends entirely on the specific type of visa granted. As a result, the United States has the world's most complex visa system—there are currently forty-six different kinds of nonimmigrant visas! (Although an individual may be a full-time student in his/her own country, a "student" visa for admission to the United States applies *only* to people attending an American school for full-time study. Thus, the three kinds of student visas cannot be used by a student coming to the United States for only an internship experience.)

As a general rule, there are only four U.S. visas that are likely to be suitable for students coming to the United States for employment in an internship:

H-2B "Temporary Worker": U.S. companies may use this visa to temporarily employ skilled or unskilled foreign nationals in positions for which there is a temporary need and for which qualified U.S. workers are unavailable. There is a two-step process involved. First, a "temporary labor" certification must be requested from the state employment service office serving the area in which the proposed employment is offered. Once it is processed by the state office, the request is forwarded to the U.S. Department of Labor's regional office so that a final determination can be made. The employer must demonstrate: (a) that a real job exists (i.e., not a job made up to suit the particular background of the foreign national); (b) that substantial efforts have been made to fill the job with a U.S. citizen; (c) that no qualified U.S. citizens can be found for the job; and (d) that the job to be filled is of a one-time, seasonal, peak-load, or intermittent nature. Once the labor certification is approved, a visa petition must then be filed by the employer with the INS. There are also annual limits on the number of H-2B admissions permitted. Once the limit is attained, no new petitions are accepted by INS until the next fiscal year (October 1).

H-3 "Trainee": This visa is used by U.S. companies to bring foreign employees to the U.S. to participate in established company training programs. A "temporary labor" certification is not required. The employer must submit the H-3 application to the Immigration Service District Office that covers the area in which the person will work. The application must include a detailed training plan to show what the trainee will do in the U.S., including how much time will be spent in "classroom and other instruction" and how much time will be devoted to "on-the-job training." Information on the position the individual will fill when he or she returns to his or her home country is also required. The company must demonstrate that the training is provided with the intent to employ the individual abroad upon completion of training or to provide skills that will increase the value of the individual to a foreign business. Any productive work must be incidental to the training program. The employer must also substantiate that the training program provides knowledge or experience that is unavailable in the individual's own country.

J-1 "Exchange Visitor": The J-1 visa may be used only by individuals who are participants in a program specifically approved by the U.S. Information Agency. There are fourteen different J-1 categories, each with its own specific rules and regulations. Approved programs are granted only to U.S. sponsoring organizations, such as U.S. government agencies, schools and universities, hospitals, companies, and private educational exchange organizations. Each sponsor is granted a specific "program description" that specifies the activities permitted for participants in the sponsor's program.

Special Note: Unlike all other U.S. visa categories administered by the Immigration Service, the U.S. Information Agency (USIA) has primary responsibility for the regulations governing the use of the J-1 "Exchange Visitor" visa. While the information in this article is accurate as of the publication date, the U.S. Congress has mandated the merger of USIA into the Department of State, effective October 1, 1999. The exchange visitor program will then fall under the direction of the Bureau for Educational and Cultural Affairs (or it's equivalent) at the Department of State. You should seek updated information from U.S. consular officials overseas and/or from the individual J-1 sponsoring organizations.

Of the fourteen J-1 categories, the "trainee" and "summer travel/work" categories are suitable for most international students coming to the U.S. for paid internships. The principal trainee exchange organizations for students are the International Association of Students in Economics and Business Management (AIESEC), the International Association for the Exchange of Students for Technical Experience (IAESTE), and the Council on International Educational Exchange (CIEE). The maximum length of practical training time per program is eighteen months.

Several organizations have been granted J-1 authorizations for "summer travel/work" programs. These permit university students to work in any job they may find during the summer months (November to February for students from the Southern Hemisphere). No extensions of visas are permitted, and changes to other J-1 visa categories are not allowed. Pre-placements are required for 50 percent of the participants, and students should check with the U.S. sponsoring organization about specific requirements. The Council on International Educational Exchange (CIEE) is the largest of these programs, but several other programs also operate summer travel/work programs.

In some cases, an individual coming to the United States on the J-1 visa may be subject to the "two-year foreign residence requirement" as the result of a "skills list" that the person's home country has asked USIA to establish for its citizens. If the person's field is included on the "skills list" for his/her country, it will generally be necessary for the individual to return to his/her country for a minimum of two years before coming back to the United States on most of the nonimmigrant visas or as a "permanent resident." Most European countries do not have skills lists, but many other countries do, and if return to the United States within a two-year period is of concern, specific information should be sought from U.S. consular officials.

J-1 Program Sponsors

Trainee Exchange Programs

AIESEC/US
135 West 50th Street, 17th Floor
New York, New York 10020
212-757-3774
Fax: 212-757-4062
E-mail: aiesec@us.aiesec.org
World Wide Web: http://www.us.aiesec.org

Association for International Practical Training and
    IAESTE-US
10400 Little Patuxent Parkway, Suite 250
Columbia, Maryland 21044-3510
410-997-2200
410-997-2883
Fax: 410-992-3924
E-mail: exchanges@aipt.org
pinpoint@aipt.org (for placements)
World Wide Web: http://www.aipt.org

American-Scandinavian Foundation
15 East 65th Street
New York, New York 10021
212-879-9779
Fax: 212-249-3444
E-mail: training@amscan.org
World Wide Web: http://www.amscan.org

CDS International
871 United Nations Plaza, 1st Floor
New York, New York 10017-1814
212-497-3500
Fax: 212-497-3535
E-mail: info@cdsintl.org
World Wide Web: http://www.cdsintl.org

Council on International Educational Exchange
205 East 42nd Street
New York, New York 10017
212-822-2600
Fax: 212-822-2699
E-mail: info@councilexchanges.org
World Wide Web: http//:www.ciee.org

InterExchange, Inc.
161 Sixth Avenue
New York, New York 10013
212-924-0446
Fax: 212-924-0575
E-mail: info@interexchange.org
World Wide Web: http://www.interexchange.org

MAST International
University of Minnesota
1954 Buford Avenue, Room 240
St. Paul, Minnesota 55108-6197
612-624-3740
Fax: 612-625-7031
E-mail: mast@coa1.agoff.umn.edu
World Wide Web: http://mast.agri.umn.edu

Ohio International Agricultural and Horticultural Intern
  Program
700 Ackerman Road, Suite 360
Columbus, Ohio 43202
614-292-7720
Fax: 614-688-8611
E-mail: mchrisma@pop.service.ohio-state.edu

Sister Cities International
1300 Pennsylvania Avenue, NW
Washington, D.C. 20004
202-312-1200
Fax: 202-312-1201
E-mail: info@sister-cities.org
World Wide Web: http://www.sister-cities.org

YMCA International Program Services
71 West 23rd Street, Suite 1904
New York, New York 10010
212-727-8800
Fax: 212-727-8814
E-mail: ips@ymcanyc.org

Summer Travel/Work Programs

Council on International Educational Exchange
(see address in preceding listing)

InterExchange, Inc.
(see address in preceding listing)

YMCA International Program Services
(see address in preceding listing)

Work Experience USA
2330 Marinship Way, Suite 250
Sausalito, California 94965
415-339-2728
Fax: 415-339-2744
E-mail: workexperienceusa@compuserve.com
World Wide Web: http://www.workexperienceusa.com

Q "International Cultural Exchange Visitor": The "Q" visa allows the employer to apply to INS for permission to hire a person from another country who is over 18 years of age for a period of not more than fifteen months to undertake prearranged employment or training and to share or demonstrate his or her own culture with Americans. A frequently cited example of a major "Q" employer is the EPCOT Center at Walt Disney World in Florida. Another example would be a museum or a department of a museum devoted to the art and culture of the student's home country.

The "cultural component" must be an integral part of the employment or training offered. The employer must demonstrate that the individual to be hired is fully able to communicate with Americans about his or her culture as well as being fully qualified for the work aspects of the position. Substantial documentation is required as part of the employer's application.

Visa Procedures

If an employer's applications for an H-2B, H-3, or Q visa are successful, the District Office of the Immigration and Naturalization Service will advise the U.S. Embassy in the student's country. The student can then secure the visa and travel to the U.S. In the case of the J-1 visa, the sponsoring organization that has agreed to include the student issues a U.S. government document called an IAP-66 (a "Certificate of Eligibility"). The IAP-66 is sent to the student to use to apply for the J-1 visa in his or her country.

Upon entering the United States, the admitting Immigration Inspector issues a Form I-94 (Arrival/Departure Record) to H-2B, H-3, and Q visa holders that notes the specific visa granted and the date when the "Permit to Stay" expires. J-1 visa holders are issued a Permit to Stay with the notation "D/S" (for duration of status). This means that J-1 trainees may remain in the U.S. as long as they are engaged in their training program or until the end date of their IAP-66, plus 30 days. The I-94 form (and IAP-66 for the J-1 trainee) is the only documentation needed for the student to proceed to the workplace and take up the assignment.

Employment Eligibility Verification

U.S. law requires employers to examine documentation proving that persons hired are either citizens of the United States or noncitizens legally authorized for employment during their stay in the United States.

Essentially, the law requires that within three business days after a person is hired, the employer must *physically examine* documentation that (a) establishes proof of the new employee's identity and (b) establishes that the person is either a U.S. citizen or is a noncitizen who has the legal right to be employed in the United States. The law and the related regulations, administered by INS, require that a record of the verification process be maintained in the employer's files for a period of three years after the date of hiring. For this purpose, the INS has developed the I-9 Form.

Virtually all kinds of employment are covered, from a full-time job with a large employer such as IBM to mowing grass on a regular basis for your next-door neighbor. Certainly, all of the jobs listed in *Internships 2000* will require you and your employer to complete the I-9 form. The I-9 form is in two parts. The top half must be filled out by the employee—you. You then present the form, together with your documentation, to your employer, who will complete the bottom half of the form.

Social Security Number

In most cases, you will find it necessary to secure a Social Security number. It is widely used in the United States as a basic identification number—and in most automated payroll systems, in university enrollment systems, and for transactions such as opening a bank account.

Individuals entering the U.S. on the F, J, M, and Q visas are usually exempt from the U.S. Social Security Tax, but those entering on other visas (such as H-2B or H-3) can expect to have the tax withheld from their pay.

While it is possible to apply for a Social Security number at an American Embassy or Consulate General, it is often four to six months before the individual receives the number. Since Social Security regulations require an in-person application, it is usually better to take care of this matter after arrival in the United States. Normally, numbers are issued within four to six weeks after the application has been submitted to a local Social Security office.

It will be important for you to provide full documentation that clearly shows that you have a visa that permits employment. The Social Security official to whom you submit your application will want to see your passport, your I-94 form, visa documents (such as the triplicate copy of the IAP-66), and any documents related to your work placement. If you do not present the proper documentation, a Social Security card marked "Not Valid for Employment" will be issued.

Income Tax

As a general rule, individuals coming to the United States on any of the visas discussed in this article will be subject to U.S. income tax (and possibly state and local income tax) on the money they earn while in the country. H-2B workers are required to obtain a Certificate of Compliance, or Sailing Permit, before departure from the U.S. The Sailing Permit is evidence that they have paid whatever taxes may be due the U.S. government. H-3, J-1, and Q visa holders are exempt from this requirement. However, they are not exempt from filing an income tax "return." Between January 1 and April 15 of the year

following your employment, you will have to submit an income tax return (Form 1040EZ or Form 1040) to the IRS. The 1040EZ is used if you have no dependents, earned less than $50,000 of income, and have no travel expense deductions. If you have remained in the country from one year to the next, you also must submit a Form 8843 to verify your nonresident status. Tax regulations and procedures are not simple, and you should seek help from your employer and/or your sponsoring organization if you are participating in a J-1 program. You may also wish to secure a copy of IRS Publication 519, "U.S. Tax Guide for Aliens," which is available free of charge from the Internal Revenue Service.

Full-Time Students at U.S. Schools

Individuals enrolled at U.S. colleges and universities for full-time academic study are usually admitted on the basis of the F-1 (student), M-1 (student), or student category of the J-1 visa. In each case, internship employment may be possible before graduation, after graduation, or both. When such employment may take place, the length of time allowed and what the employment is called (practical training, curricular practical training, academic training) depend on the specific visa and circumstances of the individual student. A number of schools in the United States offer academic courses—usually known as cooperative education programs—that combine periods of study with periods of practical training employment. Under certain conditions, students from other countries who are enrolled as regular, full-time students in a cooperative education program are allowed to undertake the practical training assignments (usually paid) in the same manner as American students. For information on enrollment in cooperative education programs and the American colleges and universities that offer these opportunities, contact:

Cooperative Education Association
8640 Guilford Road, Suite 215
Columbia, Maryland 21046
Telephone: 410-290-3666
Fax: 410-290-7084
World Wide Web: http://www.ceainc.org

Whether enrolled in a cooperative education program, whether before or after graduation, and regardless of the type of visa (M-1, F-1, or J-1) the student remains under the legal sponsorship of his or her college, university, or (in the case of some J-1 students) Exchange Visitor Program sponsor. Thus, assistance with proper arrangements for periods of practical training must be sought from the international student adviser at the student's school.

Visa Violations or Overstays

Important changes to U.S. immigration laws have taken effect and more changes are ahead. All international visitors, trainees, and temporary work visa holders will be affected by these laws. It is extremely important that you know exactly what you are permitted to do on the type of visa you have been granted and how long you are permitted to remain in the United States. If you have any questions about this, please check with your program sponsor, employer, or the INS. If your program ends early, you are not permitted to remain in the United States. You must either return home upon completion of your internship or work program or take the steps necessary to legally remain in the United States. Recent changes in immigration laws have been passed with severe penalties for foreign nationals who overstay their visas or who violate their status. You could be barred from returning to the U.S. for 10 years or longer if you violate your visa status, even unintentionally.

In Conclusion

Most countries of the world have very strict regulations regarding employment for noncitizens in order to protect job opportunities for their own citizens. The United States is no different, especially in periods of high unemployment. What is different, however, is the U.S. system of visas and the rules and regulations that apply to each type (and subtype) of visa. The process of securing a proper visa takes a good deal of time (sometimes as long as four to six months) and can often be frustrating. Thus, it is wise to contact prospective employers as early as possible so that the employer has sufficient time to undertake the paperwork involved. If you have applied to or have been accepted by an organization such as AIESEC or IAESTE, make that fact known to the employer as each sponsoring organization has its own internal procedures that must be followed. With careful advance preparation, however, most students will be able to cope with the complexities of the U.S. legal system.

Robert M. Sprinkle is the Executive Director, Emeritus, of the Association for International Practical Training, and has written numerous articles on international practical training, overseas employment, and student travel.

Elizabeth Chazottes is the Executive Director and CEO of the Association for International Practical Training.

How to Apply for an Internship

There is more involved in getting an internship than simply making contact with an internship sponsor. Each step—resume and cover letter, learning contract, interview, and follow-up—is important and requires a lot of planning and preparation.

The Resume

When you prepare your resume, remember that it is going to be quickly scanned by the potential employer. Your resume has to be designed so that it will bring the employer's eye to key words that satisfy his or her professional needs.

A resume should be an accurate representation of your past achievements and future goals. The idea is to reflect your energy and ambition by listing activities, employment experience, and achievements; cooperative attitude by highlighting any clubs or sports you participated in; and orderly and businesslike mind with a crisp, neat resume.

The resume should be well organized, easy to read and understand, concise, and one page in length. Don't overcrowd your resume: leave one-inch margins on all four sides; leave sufficient white space between items; avoid thick paragraphs. Bullets are helpful in calling attention to important points on your resume. Personal information such as age, weight, and health isn't appropriate. Remember to include the following:

1. Basic identification—Name, current address (school and permanent are necessary), phone number.

2. Education—Most current education, degrees earned, anticipated graduation date, major and minor areas of study, and course topics, if desired.

3. Related experience—The work, study, campus, or community activities in chronological order that have given you experience important to your internship goals. This section may be divided into work and activities subject areas and is generally a good catch-all for other internships or nonpaying work experience such as campus or community positions that require more actual work and commitment than social or athletic organizations require.

4. Honors and achievements—Listing these highlights your accomplishments and shows that you have outside interests.

5. References—Indicate that you will provide these upon request. Have a typed list of names, addresses, and telephone numbers of people who have agreed to provide recommendations for you, as well as copies of any recommendation letters you have already received. Remember to take this list with you on every interview.

When in doubt as to how you should style your resume, your best bet is to stick with a conventional resume that presents all the information neatly and concisely, grouped in categories and presented in chronological order. It is more important to spend extra time on proofreading and editing your resume for content rather than worrying about style. Use the sample resume that follows as your guide.

Resumes don't necessarily have to be typeset. Neatly typed, high-quality photocopies are acceptable to most employers as are resumes composed on a personal computer. If you're not confident of your resume-writing skills, have your resume reviewed by a counselor, campus placement officer, or professional acquaintance who has experience in this area.

The Cover Letter

The cover letter is a personal introduction, so try to make yours a unique reflection of your personality. A cover letter also offers a chance to build on your resume by expanding on any past experience that suits the particular internship for which you are applying.

The cover letter should be neatly typed on good paper that matches the color and style of your resume. Consult the sample cover letter that follows as you write your own cover letters. Include the following information:

1. Your address

2. The sponsor's name, title, and address

3. The date

4. A paragraph stating your purpose in writing the letter and your interest in the position offered

5. A paragraph highlighting those qualifications and interests related to the position that appear on your resume

6. A paragraph on the follow-up action that you plan to take and how and when you can be reached for an interview

7. Thank you

The Interview

Most listings in this book state whether an in-person interview is required. In an interview, employers do more than check your overall appearance and attitude. They want to hear you speak about your abilities, career objectives, strengths, weaknesses, and potential contributions to their company. Do not underestimate your competition, and remember that making excuses or apologies for yourself will not improve your chances for success in an interview.

The interview is also your opportunity to ask some questions. You are, after all, looking for valuable insights into a career as well as investing your time and effort. The following points will help you prepare for your interview.

1. It is very important to learn as much as possible about the company or organization where you are applying. Talk to any employees of the company whom you might know, research the company through the local Chamber of Commerce, and look through professional or trade publications as well as local newspapers to learn about new company developments.

2. Think about the questions you will be asked:
   - Why do you want to work for our company?
   - What qualifies you to work here?
   - What are your personal/work strengths and weaknesses, and how do you hope to utilize/improve them?
   - Why did you choose our company over others?
   - What are your professional goals; how will you apply them as you work and after your internship?
   - What do you expect to gain and learn from your internship?

3. Review your personal qualifications and be able to explain them.

4. Always take extra copies of your resume, references, and correspondence with the intern coordinator with you to the interview in case you are asked for additional copies or need to refer to them for clarification. Package them neatly in a folder or briefcase so you can easily find what you need and don't walk in with a fistful of papers.

5. Think of meaningful questions you want to ask the sponsor.

6. Develop a learning contract.

When you walk into the interview, dressed neatly, with your learning contract, resume, and any other necessary materials in order, remember to:

- Keep good eye contact.
- Be a good listener.
- Answer questions directly.
- Ask for clarification of questions when necessary. Keep your responses positive, reinforcing your specific interests and qualifications.
- Question the employer on anything that confuses you concerning the internship and discuss your learning contract.
- Speak on personal topics only if asked.
- Inquire about follow-up procedures: should you call next week or wait for further notification?
- Sincerely thank the interviewer and offer times that you will be available should any further questions arise.

Within a week after the interview, follow up with a thank-you letter reaffirming your interest in the position. Remember to mention the date of your interview and the position for which you interviewed. In this letter you might also want to clarify or reiterate any important questions you were asked.

The Learning Contract

A learning contract, though not a necessary or traditional step, could help you get the most out of your internship whether or not you are interning for credit. The contract is, in a sense, the syllabus of your internship. It can help guarantee that you get the most out of your internship by defining and refining your goals and those of your employer from the very beginning. Therefore, a learning contract must be a mutual agreement of goals between your internship sponsor and you—and your school, if you are a student.

Work through a rough draft of your learning contract and bring it to your interview where you can then work out the specifics. If your employer doesn't know what a learning contract is, leave a copy after the interview so that he or she can study it.

Specifics of the learning contract:

1. General identification of intern, direct supervisor, college adviser if applicable, dates of internship duration.

2. Responsibilities—Basic job duties, not just a title but the expected day-to-day or project plans. Also describe how your direct supervisor will assist you and monitor your progress.

3. Learning objectives—What do you want to learn through your duties? Use specific statements—lofty "I want to become a professional" phrases provide no real information and tell the employer you have little understanding of your needs or plans for fulfilling them.

4. Criteria for evaluation—Will you receive college credit, salary, or final evaluation? What will your work evaluation be based upon? Who will conduct the evaluation?

5. Signatures of parties involved to validate the agreement—the intern, the sponsor, and, if necessary, the college or placement adviser monitoring the internship.

In Conclusion

The entire process of identifying an internship, applying for it, and interviewing can take several weeks or more. Remember to start planning for your internship early. Not only will you spare yourself the anxiety of last-minute scrambling, but you will also stand a better chance of securing a competitive internship.

Sample Cover Letter

4225 Cypress Avenue
Indianapolis, IN 36221
March 1, 1999

Mr. Frederick Goland
Personnel Director
Midwest Public Relations
Suite 21
112 Jefferson Street
Carmel, IN 36241

Dear Mr. Goland:

As my senior year at Indiana University approaches, I feel it's necessary for me to supplement my education with practical experience. When researching area public relations firms in the Career Development Office at Indiana University recently, I found that Midwest Public Relations offers creative internships and that my qualifications match your eligibility requirements.

As my enclosed resume indicates, my studies and work experience revolve around journalism and administration. As a writer/editor for *The Hoosier*, I've written more than thirty articles on various topics ranging from sports and entertainment to editorial commentary. I also developed my computer skills and was instrumental in the purchase and implementation of the newspaper's first computer-layout system. As a manager and administrator, I was able to successfully direct a 15-person writing staff by assigning story ideas, balancing deadlines, and giving the paper its overall editorial direction.

After graduation, my career plans include working for a public relations firm such as yours. I think that my desire to succeed, coupled with my education and work background, will enable me to excel in this field. If possible, I would like to speak with you to learn more about the creative internship you offer at Midwest. I will call you later this month about arranging a meeting, should you not contact me before then.

Thank you for your time and consideration.

Sincerely,

John Simonson

John Simonson

Sample Resume

JOHN SIMONSON
4225 Cypress Avenue
Indianapolis, Indiana 36221
317-655-9001

EDUCATION

Candidate for Bachelor of Arts, June 2000
Indiana University
English literature major; business minor
Relevant course work:
> Advertising Theory
> English Media
> Creative Writing I & II
> Beginning Journalism

RELATED EXPERIENCE

Writer/Associate Editor, The Hoosier, student newspaper. Duties include writing and editing articles, computer layout, pasteup, and assisting the supervision of a 36-page, twice-weekly newspaper. Spring 1997–present

Administrative Assistant, Theatre-by-the-Bay. Assisted in all aspects of office administration for a small summer stock theater. Handled mailing lists, wrote press releases and promotional copy, and developed computer skills. Summers 1997–98

Computer Lab Assistant, IU Business College. Oversaw student use of business computer systems, provided assistance, and logged usage reports. Fall 1996–Spring 1997

HONORS AND ACHIEVEMENTS

Hall Government Association, Secretary 1996
Dean's List, Fall 1996, Spring 1997, Spring 1998, Fall 1998
Short story, "Don't Look Back," published in the Graduate Literary Review, Spring 1998
Meals on Wheels Volunteer, Christmas 1996
Intramural wrestling champion, Winter 1996

REFERENCES

Available upon request

ACCOMMODATIONS AND FOODSERVICES

GENERAL

AMELIA ISLAND PLANTATION
PO Box 3000
Amelia Island, Florida 32035-3000

General Information 1,330 acre internationally recognized, gated resort/residential community located in northeast Florida offering miles of sandy beach and many amenities. Established in 1974. Number of employees: 1,100. Number of internship applications received each year: 1,000.

Internships Available ▶ *3–6 culinary interns:* responsibilities include gaining hands-on experience in a wide variety of culinary situations through a rotation that includes banquets, pastry, and restaurants. Candidates should have ability to work independently, ability to work with others, college courses in field, plan to pursue career in field, own transportation, knife skills, customer service skills, fluency in conversational English (speaking, reading, writing, and understanding). Duration is flexible. $8 per hour. Open to college juniors, college seniors, graduate students. ▶ *1 floral intern:* responsibilities include sales, inventory, and opening and closing duties of the plantation florist; processing and delivering of orders; and set up and tear-down of product. Candidates should have ability to work with others, college courses in field, experience in the field, personal interest in the field, self-motivation, own transportation, customer service skills, valid driver's license, good driving record, ability to lift at least 25 pounds, one year experience in a floral/retail shop preferred, fluency in conversational English (speaking, reading, writing, and understanding). Duration is minimum of 16 weeks. $225 per week housing stipend. Open to college juniors, college seniors, graduate students. ▶ *4–8 golf level I and turf management interns:* responsibilities include working as a golf level I intern (assisting guests, members, owners, and employees in golf experience) or as a turf management intern (mowing greens, collars, tees, fairways and roughs, raking sand bunkers, and changing cups). Candidates should have ability to work independently, knowledge of field, strong interpersonal skills, own transportation, customer service skills, valid driver's license, a good driving record, basic knowledge of golf, fluency in conversational English (speaking, reading, writing, and understanding). Duration is 16–32 weeks. $5.15 per hour plus tips. Open to college juniors, college seniors, graduate students. ▶ *1 graphics intern:* responsibilities include working at the in-house print shop, printing all of the one and two-color materials for the resort, including brochures, flyers, forms, menus, newsletters, booklets, invitations, cards, calendars, posters, and advertisements. Candidates should have ability to work independently, college courses in field, computer skills, editing skills, writing skills, own transportation, customer service skills, fluency in conversational English (speaking, reading, writing, and understanding). Duration is minimum of 16 weeks. $225 per week housing stipend. Open to college juniors, college seniors, graduate students. ▶ *2–4 lodging and rooms management/ housekeeping interns:* responsibilities include working as either a lodging intern (rotating through transportation, bell service, and hotline departments to the front desk/reservations departments) or as rooms management/ housekeeping intern assisting with daily activities including inspecting rooms and public areas, ordering supplies, and other duties. Candidates should have ability to work with others, college courses in field, knowledge of field, self-motivation, own transportation, customer service skills, valid driver's license, good driving record, fluency in conversational English (speaking, reading, writing, and understanding). Duration is minimum of 16 weeks. $225 per week housing stipend. Open to college juniors, college seniors, graduate students. ▶ *1–2 nature science interns:* responsibilities include assisting Nature Science program manager in providing social and group guests, club members, properly owners, employees and the community with nature programs; working closely with local animal sanctuaries in animal rescues on property. Candidates should have college courses in field, knowledge of field, oral communication skills, personal interest in the field, self-motivation, own transportation, customer service skills, fluency in conversational English (speaking, reading, writing, and understanding). Duration is minimum of 16 weeks. $225 per week housing stipend. Open to college juniors, college seniors, graduate students. ▶ *Promotions intern:* responsibilities include working closely with the marketing, conference services, sales, and graphics departments in implementation of new promotions, programs, events, and individual projects (especially with restaurants, golf, tennis, florist, recreation, fitness center, and holiday/special events). Candidates should have ability to work independently, declared college major in field, knowledge of field, oral communication skills, self-motivation, strong interpersonal skills, written communication skills, good time-management and problem-solving skills, valid driver's license, own transportation, knowledge of QuarkXpress preferred, fluency in conversational English (speaking, reading, writing, and understanding). Duration is minimum of 16 weeks. $225 per week housing stipend. Open to college juniors, college seniors, graduate students. ▶ *1 public relations intern:* responsibilities include researching, writing, producing, distributing, and mailing of press releases; updating media mailing list and collection of "clip reports;" responding to editorial requests; preparation of press kits; responding to slide requests; hosting/entertaining visiting writers; and any other "pop-up" projects. Candidates should have ability to work with others, college courses in field, knowledge of field, self-motivation, written communication skills, own transportation, experience/ training in media and community relations and publicity or marketing desirable, creative graphic or photography skills are a plus, must be fluent in conversational English (speaking, reading, writing, and understanding). Duration is minimum of 16 weeks. $225 per week housing stipend. Open to college juniors, college seniors, graduate students. ▶ *6–15 recreation interns:* responsibilities include participation in program design, implementation and evaluation or children's programs and group events, guest relations, major projects, pool maintenance, and minor facilities upkeep. Candidates should have ability to work with others, college courses in field, knowledge of field, self-motivation, own transportation, fluency in conversational English (speaking, reading, writing, and understanding), and customer service skills. First aid, CPR, and life saving certificates preferred. Duration is minimum of 16 weeks. $225 per week housing stipend. Open to college juniors, college seniors, graduate students. ▶ *3–4 special events interns:* responsibilities include assisting in the planning, set-up, tear down, and evaluation of

theme parties. Candidates should have ability to work with others, college courses in field, organizational skills, plan to pursue career in field, self-motivation, own transportation, customer service skills, detail oriented, experience using a day planner, fluency in conversational English (speaking, reading, writing, and understanding). Duration is minimum of 16 weeks. $225 per week housing stipend. Open to college juniors, college seniors, graduate students. ▶ *1 staff development intern:* responsibilities include assisting with training classes and job fairs; inputting and analyzing data; conducting software classes for beginners; helping with mailings, meetings, and special projects. Candidates should have analytical skills, college courses in field, computer skills, oral communication skills, self-motivation, writing skills, written communication skills, customer service skills, fluency in conversational English (speaking, reading, writing, and understanding). Duration is minimum of 16 weeks. $225 per week housing stipend. Open to college juniors, college seniors. ▶ *1–2 tennis interns:* responsibilities include court maintenance, pro shop duties, tennis instruction, racquet stringing, organization, and implementation of tournaments. Candidates should have ability to work independently, college courses in field, knowledge of field, plan to pursue career in field, own transportation, customer service skills, 4.5 level of tennis playing ability, ability to string racquets, fluency in conversational English (speaking, reading, writing, and understanding). Duration is 16–32 weeks. $5.15 per hour; additional pay for giving lessons. Open to college juniors, college seniors, graduate students. International applications accepted.
Benefits Formal training, free meals, job counseling, on-the-job training, opportunity to attend seminars/workshops, possible full-time employment, willing to act as a professional reference, willing to complete paperwork for educational credit, willing to provide letters of recommendation, housing packages available to limited number of students, assistance in locating housing provided to others, use of amenities/property at a discounted rate.
Contact Write, call, fax, or e-mail Barbara Ross, Internship Coordinator. Phone: 904-277-5904. Fax: 904-277-5994. E-mail: intern@aipfl.com. Telephone interview required. Applicants must submit a formal organization application, cover letter, resume, academic transcripts, four personal references, 2 academic and 2 professional references, 3 writing samples for promotions, public relations, and graphics positions. Application deadline: March 15 for summer (recommended), July 1 for fall (recommended), November 15 for spring (recommended). World Wide Web: http://www.aipfl.com.

THE BALSAMS GRAND RESORT HOTEL
Route 26
Dixville Notch, New Hampshire 03576-9710

General Information Four-star, historic hotel on 15,000 acres; interns lead wide variety of activities for guests of all ages. Established in 1866. Number of employees: 450. Number of internship applications received each year: 40.
Internships Available ▶ *1–4 recreation interns:* responsibilities include daily activity programming, promotion, and leadership for adults and families; weekly journal; special project; guiding hikes, walks, and leading tours; working in all aspects of resort's recreational services. Candidates should have declared college major in field, organizational skills, plan to pursue career in field, self-motivation, strong interpersonal skills, strong leadership ability. Duration is 12–14 weeks. stipend; hourly wage for overtime. Open to college juniors, college seniors.
Benefits Free housing, free meals, on-the-job training, opportunity to attend seminars/workshops, tuition assistance, willing to act as a professional reference, willing to complete paperwork for educational credit, willing to provide letters of recommendation.
Contact Write, call, fax, or e-mail Katherine Everett, Recreation Director. Phone: 603-255-3400. Fax: 603-255-4221. E-mail: thebalsams@aol.com. In-person interview recommended. Applicants must submit a formal organization application, cover letter, resume, academic transcripts, letter of recommendation, at least

3 personal references. Application deadline: April 30 for summer, December 1 for winter. World Wide Web: http://www.thebalsams.com.

BONAVENTURE HOTEL & SUITES
404 South Figueroa Street
Los Angeles, California 90071

General Information Hotel. Number of employees: 700. Unit of Interstate Hotel Corporation, Pittsburgh, Pennsylvania. Number of internship applications received each year: 75.
Internships Available ▶ *Accounting interns:* responsibilities include assisting the department with general office work, compiling and researching information, and attending department meetings. Candidates should have ability to work with others, computer skills, knowledge of field, office skills, oral communication skills, organizational skills, personal interest in the field, self-motivation. Duration is 2–6 months. Open to college freshmen, college sophomores, college juniors, college seniors, recent college graduates, graduate students, individuals reentering the workforce. ▶ *Catering department interns:* responsibilities include assisting in the planning of events, completing general office work, compiling and researching information. Candidates should have ability to work with others, computer skills, office skills, oral communication skills, organizational skills, research skills, written communication skills, major in hotel management, business, or communications preferred. Duration is minimum of 2 eight-hour shifts for 10- to 15-week school-year program; minimum of 3 eight-hour shifts for 12- to 15-week summer program. Open to college freshmen, college sophomores, college juniors, college seniors, recent college graduates, graduate students, individuals re-entering the workforce and career changers only if enrolled in a college program. ▶ *Convention services department interns.* responsibilities include communicating with customers, planning events, and compiling and researching information. Candidates should have ability to work with others, computer skills, office skills, oral communication skills, organizational skills, research skills, written communication skills, major in hotel management, business, or communications preferred. Duration is minimum of 2 eight-hour shifts for 10- to 15-week school-year program; minimum of 3 eight-hour shifts for 12- to 15-week summer program. Open to college freshmen, college sophomores, college juniors, college seniors, recent college graduates, graduate students, individuals re-entering the workforce and career changers only if enrolled in a college program. ▶ *Food and beverage interns:* responsibilities include assisting outlet managers with organizing and implementing marketing concepts, developing new marketing and promotional strategies, and researching and tracking; sales promotion and follow-up to generate new business. Candidates should have office skills, oral communication skills, organizational skills, research skills, written communication skills, marketing skills and some knowledge of food and beverage required; major in hotel restaurant management, business, or communications preferred. Duration is minimum of 2 eight-hour shifts for 10- to 15-week school-year program; minimum of 3 eight-hour shifts for 12- to 15-week summer program. Open to college freshmen, college sophomores, college juniors, college seniors, recent college graduates, graduate students, individuals re-entering the workforce and career changers only if enrolled in a college program. ▶ *Human resources interns:* responsibilities include helping to plan and coordinate hotel-sponsored events, create and implement incentive programs for associates, screen applicants and check references for recruitment, manage associate accounts, and coordinate associate benefits such as discounts or worker's compensation. Candidates should have computer skills, office skills, oral communication skills, organizational skills, strong interpersonal skills, written communication skills, major in hotel management, business, or communications preferred. Duration is minimum of 2 eight-hour shifts for 10- to 15-week school-year program; minimum of 3 eight-hour shifts for 12- to 15-week summer program. Open to recent high school graduates, college freshmen, college sophomores, college juniors, college seniors, recent college graduates, graduate students, individuals re-entering the workforce and career changers only if enrolled in a college program. ▶ *Sales and marketing interns:* responsibili-

Bonaventure Hotel & Suites (continued)

ties include attending weekly sales meetings; researching competitive analyses; telemarketing to potential clients; accessing group sales files; reviewing group sales, tour, travel, and corporate files for potential business; creating sales flyers. Candidates should have computer skills, office skills, oral communication skills, organizational skills, research skills, strong interpersonal skills, written communication skills, good marketing skills; aptitude for sales; major in hotel management, business, communications, sociology, or psychology preferred. Duration is minimum of 2 eight-hour shifts for 10- to 15-week school-year program; minimum of 3 eight-hour shifts for 12- to 15-week summer program. Open to college freshmen, college sophomores, college juniors, college seniors, recent college graduates, graduate students, individuals re-entering the workforce and career changers only if enrolled in a college program. All positions are unpaid. International applications accepted.

Benefits Formal training, free meals, on-the-job training, opportunity to attend seminars/workshops, possible full-time employment, travel reimbursement, willing to act as a professional reference, willing to complete paperwork for educational credit.

International Internships Available.

Contact Write, call, or fax Vincente Jaramillo, Human Resources Coordinator, 404 South Figueroa Street, Los Angeles, California 90071. Phone: 213-612-4843. Fax: 213-612-4849. In-person interview recommended. Applicants must submit a cover letter, resume, three personal references. Applications are accepted continuously.

THE CLUB AT SEABROOK ISLAND
1002 Landfall Way
Johns Island, South Carolina 29455

General Information Private, residential resort community. Established in 1971. Number of employees: 300. Number of internship applications received each year: 30.

Internships Available ▶ *8 recreation interns:* responsibilities include working in all areas of the Recreation Department, including Kids Club, rental office and fitness center, lifeguarding, teen and family programs, and poolside activities. Candidates should have knowledge of field, organizational skills, personal interest in the field, self-motivation, strong interpersonal skills, strong leadership ability. Duration is May to September. $400 per month. Open to college seniors. International applications accepted.

Benefits Formal training, free housing, free meals, job counseling, names of contacts, on-the-job training, opportunity to attend seminars/workshops, possible full-time employment, willing to act as a professional reference, willing to complete paperwork for educational credit, willing to provide letters of recommendation.

Contact Write, fax, or e-mail Scott D. Raisley, Director of Recreation, 1002 Landfall Way, Johns Island, South Carolina 29455. Fax: 843-768-7524. E-mail: seabrook98@aol.com. In-person interview recommended. Applicants must submit a cover letter, resume, three personal references. Applications are accepted continuously. World Wide Web: http://www.seabrookresort.com.

CROWNE PLAZA RESORT
130 Shipyard Drive
Hilton Head Island, South Carolina 29928

General Information Resort hotel. Established in 1993. Number of employees: 12. Division of Bass Hotels and Resorts, Atlanta, Georgia. Number of internship applications received each year: 50.

Internships Available ▶ *12–17 leisure activities interns:* responsibilities include programming activities, bike and bean chair rentals, poolside activities, health and fitness memberships, conference and group recreational activities. Candidates should have ability to work independently, computer skills, declared college major in field, experience in the field, knowledge of field, oral communication skills, plan to pursue career in field, self-motivation, strong interpersonal skills, strong leadership ability, written communication skills, experience in recreation field (preferred). Duration is 3 months. $7 per hour. Open to col-

lege sophomores, college juniors, college seniors, recent college graduates. International applications accepted.

Benefits Formal training, free meals, housing at a cost, job counseling, on-the-job training, opportunity to attend seminars/workshops, possible full-time employment.

International Internships Available.

Contact Write, call, or fax Melissa Lone, Director of Leisure Activities, 130 Shipyard Drive, Hilton Head, South Carolina 29928. Phone: 843-842-2400 Ext. 7612. Fax: 843-842-9975. In-person interview recommended. Applicants must submit a formal organization application, resume, three personal references. Applications are accepted continuously.

GRAND MARAIS HOTEL COMPANY
310 East Highway 61, PO Box 667
Grand Marais, Minnesota 55604-0667

General Information Hospitality company including four motels in a unique destination—wilderness area. Established in 1987. Number of employees: 50. Number of internship applications received each year: 75.

Internships Available ▶ *3–6 front office-guest services interns:* responsibilities include reservations, guest check-in and out; front desk selling, balancing day's business, guest relations, using variety of office equipment, assisting in facilities' management tasks, cross-training in other departments to understand inter-department relationship, assisting in training new staff, staff scheduling, revising procedures, possible assignments in accounting and human resource areas. Candidates should have office skills, oral communication skills, self-motivation, strong interpersonal skills, strong leadership ability, business and/or human resource interest and/or courses helpful. Duration is minimum 12 months. $6.25 per hour starting wage with possible merit-performance raises. Open to college juniors, college seniors, recent college graduates, graduate students, career changers, individuals reentering the workforce. International applications accepted.

Benefits On-the-job training, opportunity to attend seminars/workshops, possible full-time employment, willing to act as a professional reference, willing to complete paperwork for educational credit, willing to provide letters of recommendation, discounts to area activities (skiing, canoeing, mountain bike rentals), use of property pool and spas, discounted housing available.

Contact Write, fax, or e-mail Darcie Peet, Co-Owner, 310 South Highway 61 PO Box 667, Grand Marais, Minnesota 55604-0667. Fax: 218-387-2307. E-mail: gmhotel@att.com. Telephone interview required. Applicants must submit a cover letter, resume (describing hobbies, sports, outside interests, awards, recognition, volunteer work),two personal references from former supervisors. Applications are accepted continuously.

HYATT REGENCY MINNEAPOLIS
1300 Nicollet Mall
Minneapolis, Minnesota 55403

General Information Hotel frequented mainly by business and business convention travelers in downtown Minneapolis, Minnesota. Number of employees: 335. Unit of Hyatt Hotels Corporation, Chicago, Illinois. Number of internship applications received each year: 75.

Internships Available ▶ *2 food and beverage interns:* responsibilities include working with line, supervisory, and management employees. Duration is 3-6 months in summer and fall. ▶ *2 room interns:* responsibilities include working with line, supervisory, and management employees. Duration is dependent on school's requirements. All positions paid. Open to college freshmen, college sophomores, college juniors, college seniors, recent college graduates, graduate students. International applications accepted.

Benefits Formal training, free meals, job counseling, names of contacts, possible full-time employment, willing to complete paperwork for educational credit.

Contact Write Lauri Larson, Employment Coordinator. In-person interview required. Applicants must submit a formal organization application, cover letter, resume, two personal references. Applications are accepted continuously.

KIAWAH ISLAND RESORT
12 Kiawah Beach Drive
Kiawah, South Carolina 29455

General Information 10,000-acre resort that caters to business groups and family vacationers. Number of employees: 350. Number of internship applications received each year: 50.
Internships Available ▶ *14 recreation interns:* responsibilities include working in 5 different areas of recreation department, completing a special project, meeting with department heads/supervisors, and going on a field trip. Candidates should have major in recreation preferred. Duration is 12–15 weeks. $150 per week. Open to college juniors, college seniors, recent college graduates, graduate students. International applications accepted.
Benefits Formal training, job counseling, names of contacts, willing to complete paperwork for educational credit, willing to provide letters of recommendation, housing provided (electricity and water are the responsibility of the intern).
Contact Write, call, or fax John Girault, Activities Director. Phone: 843-768-2745. Fax: 843-768-6022. Telephone interview required. Applicants must submit a cover letter, resume, 3 work or school references. Applications are accepted continuously.

LITCHFIELD BEACH & GOLF RESORT
PO Drawer 320
Pawleys Island, South Carolina 29585

General Information Golf company that owns or operates eight golf courses, three resorts, and one of top five U.S. tennis resorts. Established in 1971. Number of employees: 950. Number of internship applications received each year: 30.
Internships Available ▶ *8 recreation interns:* responsibilities include leadership of guest activities (children and adults), administrative duties, guest services, implementing group and special events, promotion/marketing, recreation programs and activities. Candidates should have college degree in related field, knowledge of field, self-motivation, strong interpersonal skills, strong leadership ability. Duration is 15 weeks. $150 per week. Open to college juniors, college seniors. International applications accepted.
Benefits Formal training, housing at a cost, job counseling, meals at a cost, names of contacts, on-the-job training, opportunity to attend seminars/workshops, possible full-time employment, travel reimbursement, tuition assistance, willing to act as a professional reference, willing to complete paperwork for educational credit, willing to provide letters of recommendation, worker's compensation, use of recreational facilities.
Contact Write, call, fax, or e-mail Kambra Chopp, Assistant Recreation Director, PO Drawer 320, Pawleys Island, South Carolina 29585. Phone: 803-237-3000 Ext. 5572. Fax: 803-237-3282. E-mail: litchfld@sccoast.net. In-person interview recommended. Applicants must submit a formal organization application, cover letter, resume, academic transcripts, two letters of recommendation. Application deadline: April 18 for summer. World Wide Web: http://www.litchfieldbeach.com.

SNOW MOUNTAIN RANCH
PO Box 169
Winter Park, Colorado 80482

General Information YMCA conference center and family resort. Established in 1907. Number of employees: 200. Branch of YMCA of the Rockies, Estes Park, Colorado. Number of internship applications received each year: 15.
Internships Available ▶ *2–6 adventure education instructors:* responsibilities include facilitating adventure/outdoor based programs including low/high elements challenge course, environmental education, climbing wall, and day hike interpretations. Candidates should have ability to work with others, college courses in field, knowledge of field, plan to pursue career in field, strong leadership ability, BS/BA degree in environmental education, adventure education, environmental science or related field preferred; current first aid and adult/child CPR required. Duration is 1–3 semesters. Position available as unpaid or at $145 per week. Open to college sophomores, college juniors, college seniors, recent college graduates, graduate students, individuals reentering the workforce. ▶ *1 chaplain's assistant:* responsibilities include supporting the office of the Chaplain in providing leadership in the development of the religious and spiritual life and activities at Snow Mountain Ranch. Candidates should have computer skills, declared college major in field, experience in the field, office skills, oral communication skills, plan to pursue career in field, strong interpersonal skills, strong leadership ability, writing skills, driver's license; previous experience leading and participating in church activities; musical background preferred. Duration is 1–2 semesters. Position available as unpaid or at $145 per week. Open to college seniors, recent college graduates, graduate students. ▶ *1–2 conference associates:* responsibilities include managing and administrating conference resources to the effect of efficient communication and negotiation of services to meet group needs. Candidates should have college degree in related field, office skills, oral communication skills, organizational skills, plan to pursue career in field, self-motivation, strong interpersonal skills, strong leadership ability, driver's license and acceptable driving record. Duration is 1–3 semesters. Position available as unpaid or at $145 per week. Open to recent college graduates, graduate students, law students, career changers, individuals reentering the workforce. ▶ *1 craft shop supervisor:* responsibilities include providing supervision and guidance to staff and guests when director is not present and teaching crafts to the guests and staff who visit the craft shop. Candidates should have organizational skills, personal interest in the field, self-motivation, strong interpersonal skills, strong leadership ability. Duration is May to August/September. Position available as unpaid or at $145 per week. Open to college juniors, college seniors, recent college graduates, graduate students, law students, career changers, individuals reentering the workforce. ▶ *2 family programs assistants:* responsibilities include developing, marketing, and implementing family programs for the guests of Snow Mountain Ranch. Candidates should have ability to work independently, knowledge of field, organizational skills, plan to pursue career in field, strong interpersonal skills, strong leadership ability, guitar skills helpful; first aid and CPR certification required, lifeguard certification helpful. Duration is 1 summer. Position available as unpaid or at $145 per week. Open to college juniors, college seniors, recent college graduates. ▶ *1–5 food and beverage interns:* responsibilities include working on various assignments. Candidates should have ability to work independently, ability to work with others, college degree in related field, experience in the field, organizational skills, personal interest in the field, plan to pursue career in field, self-motivation, strong interpersonal skills, strong leadership ability. Duration is 1–3 semesters. Position available as unpaid or at $145–$160 per week. Open to college juniors, college seniors, recent college graduates. ▶ *10–13 front desk attendants:* responsibilities include ensuring the satisfaction of all potential and actual guests over the telephone and in person, as well as accounting for all income during assigned shift. Candidates should have college courses in field, computer skills, office skills, oral communication skills, plan to pursue career in field, strong interpersonal skills, strong leadership ability, fundamental math skills. Duration is 1–2 semesters. $145 per week. Open to recent high school graduates, college freshmen, college sophomores, college juniors, college seniors, recent college graduates, graduate students, law students, career changers, individuals reentering the workforce. ▶ *1–2 human resources associates:* responsibilities include assisting with the daily operations of the Human Resources Office by completing secretarial, receptionist, and driving duties. Candidates should have declared college major in field, organizational skills, plan to pursue career in field, strong interpersonal skills, strong leadership ability, writing skills, driver's license with acceptable driving record. Duration is 1–2 semesters. Position available as unpaid or at $145 per week. Open to college juniors, college seniors, recent college graduates, graduate students, law students. ▶ *1 recreation supervisor:* responsibilities include training, scheduling, and general supervision of recreation staff and facilities. Candidates should have declared college major in field, knowledge of field, organizational skills, strong interpersonal skills, strong

Snow Mountain Ranch (continued)

leadership ability, current certifications in Lifeguard Training, Lifeguard Training Instructor, American Canoeing Basic Paddlers, First Aid, and CPR; minimum 3 years lifeguarding and pool supervisory experience. Duration is 1–3 semesters. Position available as unpaid or at $145–$170 per week. Open to college freshmen, college sophomores, college juniors, college seniors, recent college graduates, graduate students. ▶ *2 staff activities coordinators:* responsibilities include developing, implementing, and evaluating activities for co-workers on their time off. Candidates should have ability to work independently, oral communication skills, organizational skills, plan to pursue career in field, strong interpersonal skills, strong leadership ability, written communication skills, driver's license and acceptable driving record. Duration is 1–2 semesters. Position available as unpaid or at $145 per week. Open to college seniors, recent college graduates, graduate students, law students.

Benefits Formal training, free housing, free meals, job counseling, on-the-job training, opportunity to attend seminars/workshops, possible full-time employment, willing to act as a professional reference, willing to complete paperwork for educational credit, willing to provide letters of recommendation, free use of recreation facilities on-site.

Contact Write, call, fax, or e-mail Julie Watkins, Human Resources Director. Phone: 970-887-2152. Fax: 303-449-6781. E-mail: jfuqua@snowmtnranch.org. Telephone interview required. Applicants must submit a formal organization application, cover letter, resume, 3 letters of recommendation on YMCA forms (provided). Applications are accepted continuously. World Wide Web: http://www.ymcarockies.org.

SOUTH SEAS PLANTATION
PO Box 194
Captiva Island, Florida 33924

General Information Full-service destination resort property. Established in 1970. Number of employees: 700. Division of MeriStar Hotels and Resorts, Washington, District of Columbia. Number of internship applications received each year: 300.

Internships Available ▶ *5–15 culinary interns:* responsibilities include working with chefs in three restaurants. Candidates should have ability to work independently, ability to work with others, experience in the field, oral communication skills, organizational skills, self-motivation. Duration is 6 months. $6 per hour. Open to recent high school graduates, college freshmen, college sophomores, college juniors, college seniors, recent college graduates, graduate students, law students, career changers, individuals reentering the workforce. ▶ *5–8 front desk/lodging interns.* Candidates should have ability to work independently, analytical skills, computer skills, editing skills, experience in the field, oral communication skills, organizational skills, research skills, self-motivation, strong interpersonal skills, writing skills. Duration is 9 months. $7 per hour plus commissions. Open to recent high school graduates, college freshmen, college sophomores, college juniors, college seniors, recent college graduates, graduate students, law students, career changers, individuals reentering the workforce. ▶ *15–20 housekeeping interns:* responsibilities include servicing and cleaning resort units. Candidates should have ability to work independently, ability to work with others, knowledge of field, oral communication skills, organizational skills, self-motivation. Duration is 9 months minimum. $7 per hour. Open to recent high school graduates, college freshmen, college sophomores, college juniors, college seniors, recent college graduates, graduate students, law students, career changers, individuals reentering the workforce. ▶ *5–10 landscaping interns:* responsibilities include manicuring and taking care of greenhouse, nursery stock, trees, and shrubs; maintaining interiorscapes; cleaning streets and grounds. Candidates should have ability to work independently, college courses in field, experience in the field, oral communication skills, personal interest in the field, self-motivation, strong interpersonal skills. Duration is 9 months minimum. $7 per hour plus incentive. Open to recent high school graduates, college freshmen, college sophomores, college juniors, college seniors, recent college graduates, graduate students, career changers, individuals reentering the workforce. ▶ *20–50 server interns:* responsibilities include carrying trays and waiting on guests. Candidates should have ability to work independently, oral communication skills, organizational skills, self-motivation, strong interpersonal skills, strong leadership ability. Duration is 6 months. $8 per hour. Open to recent high school graduates, college freshmen, college sophomores, college juniors, college seniors, recent college graduates, graduate students, law students, career changers, individuals reentering the workforce. International applications accepted.

Benefits Job counseling, names of contacts, on-the-job training, opportunity to attend seminars/workshops, possible full-time employment, willing to complete paperwork for educational credit, willing to provide letters of recommendation, attendance at AHMA management classes, guest service and alcohol certification training, housing provided at $75-$150 biweekly, meals provided at a small cost.

Contact Write, call, fax, or e-mail Bonnie Zeidler, Employment Specialist. Phone: 941-472-7588. Fax: 941-472-7648. E-mail: bonnie.zeidler@ssrc.com. In-person interview recommended. Applicants must submit a formal organization application, cover letter, resume. Applications are accepted continuously.

WILD DUNES RESORT
5801 Palmetto Drive
Isle of Palms, South Carolina 29451

General Information Resort providing service excellence, first-rate accommodations, recreation, and meeting facilities. Established in 1976. Number of employees: 700. Subsidiary of Lowe Enterprises, Los Angeles, California. Number of internship applications received each year: 200.

Internships Available ▶ *20–24 recreation interns:* responsibilities include running kids camps, activities, beach services, pool attendant, and corporate recreation office work; completing a special project, attending meetings, and completing financial worksheets; shadow program; and intern exchange program. Candidates should have ability to work independently, experience in the field, oral communication skills, self-motivation, strong interpersonal skills, strong leadership ability. Duration is 13-15 weeks (40-45 hours per week). $200 per month and if WSI certified, extra money for teaching swimming lessons. Open to college juniors, college seniors, recent college graduates, graduate students, college freshman and sophomores may be considered depending on school. International applications accepted.

Benefits Formal training, free housing, meals at a cost, names of contacts, on-the-job training, opportunity to attend seminars/workshops, possible full-time employment, willing to act as a professional reference, willing to complete paperwork for educational credit, willing to provide letters of recommendation, employee discounts, access to all amenities, nationally accredited internship site through Resort and Commercial Recreation Association (RCRA).

Contact Write, call, fax, or e-mail Eric M. Carlson, Recreation and Internship Director. Phone: 800-845-8880 Ext. 2171. Fax: 843-886-2195. E-mail: ecarlson@wilddunes.com. Telephone interview required. Applicants must submit a formal organization application, cover letter, resume, three personal references, three letters of recommendation, photo (optional). Applications are accepted continuously. World Wide Web: http://www.wilddunes.com.

ADMINISTRATIVE AND SUPPORT SERVICES

EMPLOYMENT SERVICES

AMERICAN ASSOCIATION OF OVERSEAS STUDIES
151 West 82nd Street, #4E
New York, New York 10024-5534

General Information International placement service working with over 200 universities and 150 preparatory and high schools to place 100 students annually in business, law, theater, communications/media, sciences, journalism, politics, arts/museums, psychology, women's studies, music, fashion, and food and wine. Established in 1984. Number of employees: 1. Affiliate of Anglo International Education Consultants, London, United Kingdom. Number of internship applications received each year: 50.

Internships Available ▶ *60–100 interns:* responsibilities include various duties according to the internship. Candidates should have ability to work independently, computer skills, office skills, oral communication skills, organizational skills, personal interest in the field, self-motivation, strong interpersonal skills, writing skills, enthusiasm, willingness to help. Duration is 1–6 months. Unpaid. Open to high school students, high school seniors, recent high school graduates, college freshmen, college sophomores, college juniors, college seniors, recent college graduates, graduate students, law students, career changers. International applications accepted.

Benefits Free meals, housing at a cost, job counseling, names of contacts, opportunity to attend seminars/workshops, willing to act as a professional reference, willing to complete paperwork for educational credit, willing to provide letters of recommendation.

International Internships Available in London, United Kingdom.

Contact Write, call, fax, or e-mail Ms. Janet Kollek Evans, Director, 151 West 82nd Street, New York, New York 10024-5534. Phone: 212-724-0804. E-mail: aaos2000@hotmail.com. Telephone interview required. Applicants must submit a formal organization application, personal reference, two letters of recommendation. Applications are accepted continuously. Fees: $200. World Wide Web: http://www.worldwide.edu/uk/aaos/.

AMERICAN SLAVIC STUDENT INTERNSHIP SERVICE AND TRAINING CORPORATION (ASSIST)
221 East Market Street, PMB 254
Iowa City, Iowa 52245

General Information Firm that organizes internships in Russia for students of Russian language and international relations. Established in 1992. Number of internship applications received each year: 50.

Internships Available ▶ *English teachers:* responsibilities include teaching English to individuals or groups of students of various ages and ability levels in schools, cooperatives, and institutes in Moscow or St. Petersburg. Candidates should have experience in teaching English helpful, knowledge of Russian language desirable. Open to individuals 18 years of age and older. ▶ *Accountants:* responsibilities include helping Russian companies maintain their books. Candidates should have computer skills, 3 years of Russian language recommended, not required; account-

ing experience or training helpful. Open to individuals 18 years of age and older. ▶ *Advertising specialists:* responsibilities include consulting Russian firms about advertising their products in Western markets. Candidates should have 3 years of Russian language recommended, not required; familiarity with advertising and economics. Open to individuals 18 years or older. ▶ *Editors:* responsibilities include checking and editing translations for English language magazines. Candidates should have 3 years of Russian language recommended, not required; editing experience helpful. Open to individuals 18 years of age and older. ▶ *Journalists:* responsibilities include writing articles for Russian and English newspapers and magazines. Candidates should have ability to write in Russian, prior journalism experience. Open to individuals 18 years and older. ▶ *Marketing consultants:* responsibilities include consulting and marketing to Russian firms. Candidates should have 3 years of Russian language recommended, not required; knowledge of economics. Open to individuals 18 years and older. ▶ *Translators:* responsibilities include translating documents from Russian to English and from English to Russian and translating negotiations. Candidates should have excellent command of Russian language. Open to individuals 18 years and older. Duration for all positions is flexible. All positions are unpaid. International applications accepted.

Benefits Possible full-time employment, willing to complete paperwork for educational credit, willing to provide letters of recommendation, stipend provided, housing with families included in fees for program.

Contact Write, call, fax, or e-mail Christopher Mattison, Director. Phone: 319-354-6693. Fax: 319-354-6693. E-mail: assistusa@aol.com. Telephone interview required. Applicants must submit a formal organization application, cover letter, resume, 2 language references and 2 personal references. Applications are accepted continuously. Fees: $25. World Wide Web: http://www.glasnet.ru/~assistm/index.html.

ASSOCIATION FOR INTERNATIONAL PRACTICAL TRAINING (AIPT), STUDENT EXCHANGES PROGRAM/IAESTE
10400 Little Patuxent Parkway, Suite 250
Columbia, Maryland 21044-3510

General Information International citizen exchange organization that arranges on-the-job training exchanges for students and young professionals in a variety of fields in more than 60 countries. Established in 1950. Number of employees: 34.

Internships Available ▶ *50–150 student exchanges/IAESTE interns:* responsibilities include training in a field of choice ranging from technical fields to hospitality/tourism. Candidates should have ability to work independently, college courses in field, self-motivation, international interest, experience in field preferred. Duration is 1–18 months. varied according to host employer. Open to college freshmen, college sophomores, college juniors, college seniors, graduate students, law students. International applications accepted.

Benefits Formal training, free housing, free meals, health insurance, housing at a cost, meals at a cost, on-the-job training, opportunity to attend seminars/workshops, willing to complete paperwork for educational credit.

Association for International Practical Training (AIPT), Student Exchanges Program/IAESTE (continued)

International Internships Available.

Contact Write, fax, or e-mail Customer Service Representative. Fax: 410-992-3924. E-mail: aipt@aipt.org. No phone calls. Telephone interview required. Applicants must submit a formal organization application, cover letter, resume, academic transcripts, portfolio, personal reference, essay. Application deadline: December 16 for IAESTE; continuous for other programs. Fees: $50. World Wide Web: http://www.aipt.org.

BOSTON UNIVERSITY INTERNATIONAL PROGRAMS
232 Bay State Road
Boston, Massachusetts 02215

General Information Boston University's Division of International Programs offers internship in China, Great Britain, Spain, Russia, France, Australia, Germany, Ireland, Israel, and Washington, DC. The programs combine academic course work with a full-time internship and each program awards 16-20 semester hours of credit. Established in 1984. Number of employees: 16. Unit of Boston University, Boston, Massachusetts. Number of internship applications received each year: 800.

Internships Available ▶ *15–25 interns (Beijing, China):* responsibilities include working in any of the following fields: advertising and public relations, the arts, business and economics, health and human services, hospitality administration, journalism, film and television, politics, and pre-law. Candidates should have oral communication skills, personal interest in the field, self-motivation, written communication skills, four semesters or equivalent of college-level Chinese. Open to college juniors, college seniors, recent college graduates. ▶ *10–30 interns (Dresden, Germany):* responsibilities include working in any of the following fields: business and economics, engineering, film and television, health and human services, and journalism. Candidates should have oral communication skills, personal interest in the field, self-motivation, written communication skills, five semesters or equivalent of college-level German. Open to college juniors, college seniors, recent college graduates. ▶ *15–25 interns (Dublin, Ireland):* responsibilities include working in any of the following fields: advertising and public relations, the arts, business and economics, health and human services, hospitality administration, journalism, film and television, politics, and pre-law. Candidates should have oral communication skills, personal interest in the field, self-motivation, written communication skills. Open to college juniors, college seniors, recent college graduates. ▶ *5–20 interns (Haifa, Israel):* responsibilities include working in any of the following fields: archaeology, business, computer technologies, education, international trade, medical services, public relations, social work, and women's studies. Candidates should have oral communication skills, personal interest in the field, self-motivation, written communication skills. Open to college sophomores, college juniors, college seniors, recent college graduates. ▶ *175–230 interns (London, England):* responsibilities include working in any of the following fields: advertising, marketing and public relations, the arts, film and television, journalism, management, finance and economics, pre-law, politics and international relations, Europe and politics in the emerging European Union, and psychology and social policy. Candidates should have oral communication skills, personal interest in the field, self-motivation, written communication skills. Open to college sophomores, college juniors, college seniors, recent college graduates. ▶ *15–25 interns (Madrid, Spain):* responsibilities include working in any of the following fields: advertising and public relations, the arts, business and economics, health and human services, hospitality administration, journalism, film, and television, politics, prelaw, and Teaching English to Speakers of Foreign Languages (TEFL). Candidates should have oral communication skills, personal interest in the field, self-motivation, written communication skills, five semesters or equivalent of college-level Spanish. Open to college juniors, college seniors, recent college graduates. ▶ *10–30 interns (Moscow, Russia Federation):* responsibilities include working in any of the following fields: advertising and public relations, the arts, business and

economics, health and human services, hospitality administration, journalism, film and television, politics, and pre-law. Candidates should have oral communication skills, personal interest in the field, self-motivation, written communication skills, four semesters or equivalent of college-level Russian. Open to college sophomores, college juniors, college seniors, recent college graduates. ▶ *40–60 interns (Paris, France):* responsibilities include working in any of the following fields: advertising and public relations, the arts, business and economics, health and human services, hospitality administration, journalism, film and television, politics, and pre-law. Candidates should have oral communication skills, personal interest in the field, self-motivation, written communication skills, four semesters or equivalent of college-level French. Open to college sophomores, college juniors, college seniors, recent college graduates. ▶ *70 interns (Sydney, Australia):* responsibilities include working in any of the following fields: advertising and public relations, the arts, business and economics, health and human services, hospitality administration, journalism, film and television, politics, and pre-law. Candidates should have oral communication skills, personal interest in the field, self-motivation, written communication skills. Open to college juniors, college seniors, recent college graduates. ▶ *30–50 interns (Washington, D.C.):* responsibilities include working in any of the following fields: advertising and public relations, the arts, business and economics, health and human services, hospitality administration, journalism, film and television, politics, and pre-law. Candidates should have oral communication skills, personal interest in the field, self-motivation, written communication skills. Open to college juniors, college seniors. Duration for all positions is 1 semester. All positions are unpaid. International applications accepted.

Benefits Formal training, willing to complete paperwork for educational credit, academic credit for internship.

International Internships Available in Sydney, Australia; Beijing, China; Paris, France; Dresden, Germany; Dublin, Ireland; Haifa, Israel; Moscow, Russian Federation; Madrid, Spain; London, United Kingdom.

Contact Write, call, fax, or e-mail Division of International Programs. Phone: 617-353-9888. Fax: 617-353-5402. E-mail: abroad@bu.edu. Applicants must submit a formal organization application, academic transcripts, two letters of recommendation, approval of participation from home institution, 1-2 writing samples (depending on program), in-person interview (telephone acceptable) recommended for some programs. Application deadline: March 15 for fall, March 1 for summer, October 15 for spring. Fees: $40. World Wide Web: http://www.bu.edu/abroad.

CITY OF NEW YORK DEPARTMENT OF CITYWIDE ADMINISTRATIVE SERVICES
1 Center Street, 24th Floor
New York, New York 10007

General Information Internship referral and placement service that provides paid internships for college students eligible for the Public Service Corps program. The service provides an opportunity for students to work in fields related to their career interest, to learn about city government, and to become personally involved in the delivery of city services. The service has both an academic credit and a volunteer component. Established in 1966. Number of employees: 9. Number of internship applications received each year: 1,200.

Internships Available ▶ *1–5 Public Service Corps placement interns:* responsibilities include interviewing and assigning applicants, developing and evaluating intern assignments, and acting as liaison with participating agencies. Candidates should have ability to work independently, computer skills, office skills, oral communication skills, strong interpersonal skills. $6–$7 per hour. ▶ *30–50 accounting aides:* responsibilities include examining books and records of financial operations. Candidates should have ability to work independently, college courses in field, computer skills, knowledge of field, personal interest in the field, plan to pursue career in field. $7–$9 per hour. ▶ *100–200 administrative aides:* responsibilities include performing a variety of responsibilities related to the management of the daily opera-

tions of an agency. Candidates should have ability to work independently, ability to work with others, computer skills, office skills, oral communication skills, research skills, written communication skills. $6–$8 per hour. ▶ *10–20 caseworker assistants:* responsibilities include assisting in interviewing and counseling individuals and maintaining records in hospitals. Candidates should have ability to work independently, ability to work with others, analytical skills, college courses in field, computer skills, knowledge of field, oral communication skills, organizational skills, personal interest in the field, plan to pursue career in field, strong leadership ability, writing skills. $6–$8 per hour. ▶ *200–500 clerical aides:* responsibilities include typing, filing, answering phones, and performing other clerical office functions. Candidates should have computer skills, office skills, oral communication skills, strong interpersonal skills, writing skills. $6–$7 per hour. ▶ *20–40 community workers:* responsibilities include assisting neighborhood organizations in housing, social, and economic programs. Candidates should have computer skills, knowledge of field, oral communication skills, personal interest in the field, strong interpersonal skills, strong leadership ability, writing skills. $6–$8 per hour. ▶ *30–60 legal assistants:* responsibilities include performing research, report writing, and court liaison activities. Candidates should have ability to work independently, analytical skills, college courses in field, computer skills, knowledge of field, oral communication skills, organizational skills, plan to pursue career in field, research skills, self-motivation, strong interpersonal skills, writing skills. $10–$12 per hour. ▶ *20–30 personnel assistants:* responsibilities include assisting in interviewing, making phone inquiries for references and surveys, report writing, record keeping, and related administrative functions. Candidates should have ability to work independently, computer skills, oral communication skills, organizational skills, strong interpersonal skills, written communication skills. $6–$7 per hour. ▶ *40–60 recreation leaders:* responsibilities include working with community youths and supervising trips, games, arts and crafts, and sports. Candidates should have ability to work independently, oral communication skills, personal interest in the field, strong interpersonal skills, strong leadership ability. $6–$8 per hour. ▶ *60–100 research aides:* responsibilities include assisting in obtaining and evaluating data. Candidates should have ability to work independently, analytical skills, computer skills, declared college major in field, oral communication skills, organizational skills, personal interest in the field, research skills, self-motivation, writing skills. $6–$8 per hour. ▶ *100–150 teaching assistants:* responsibilities include aiding teachers in working with children, youths, or adults in day care. Candidates should have ability to work independently, analytical skills, computer skills, declared college major in field, experience in the field, knowledge of field, oral communication skills, organizational skills, plan to pursue career in field, research skills, strong interpersonal skills, writing skills. $6–$8 per hour. Duration for all positions is either 1 summer session (July 1-August 31) or 1 academic session (September 1-May 31). Open to college freshmen, college sophomores, college juniors, college seniors. International applications accepted.
Benefits On-the-job training, opportunity to attend seminars/workshops, possible full-time employment, willing to complete paperwork for educational credit.
Contact Write Terry Denson, Chief, Public Service Corps Placement Unit. No phone calls. In-person interview required. Applicants must submit a formal organization application, cover letter, resume, academic transcripts. Applications are accepted continuously. World Wide Web: http://www.ci.nyc.ny.us/.

COLLEGE WORKS PAINTING
2601 Elliot Avenue, Suite 2150
Seattle, Washington 98121

General Information Organization providing training and financial support to organize and operate an independent house-painting business. Established in 1997. Number of employees: 310. Number of internship applications received each year: 1,500.
Internships Available ▶ *120 branch managers:* responsibilities include recruiting and training a 6-9 person team; marketing, pricing, and selling services; production, quality and cost control;

collections; and promoting ethical business practices; positions also available in Oregon and Washington. Duration is April-September (part-time in spring, full-time in summer). $7,000 per duration of internship. Open to college freshmen, college sophomores, college juniors, college seniors.
Benefits Formal training, free meals, job counseling, names of contacts, on-the-job training, opportunity to attend seminars/workshops, possible full-time employment, willing to complete paperwork for educational credit, willing to provide letters of recommendation, scholarships, trips to Cabo San Lucas, special training workshops for top producers.
Contact Write, call, fax, or e-mail Michael Profant, Vice President, 2601 Elliot Avenue, Suite 2150, Seattle, Washington 98121. Phone: 888-450-9675. Fax: 206-956-8454. E-mail: swpainting@aol.com. In-person interview required. Applicants must submit a formal organization application, resume. Application deadline: April 1. World Wide Web: http://www.collegeworks.com.

DYNAMY
27 Sever Street
Worcester, Massachusetts 01609

General Information Nine-month internship program for students exploring their career interests. Interns complete a three-week Outward Bound course and a series of three 9-11 week internships during the program. Established in 1969. Number of employees: 14. Number of internship applications received each year: 60.
Internships Available ▶ *40 interns:* responsibilities include completing 1 to 3 internships (areas include business, education, government, radio, TV, theater, social service, fine arts, medicine, restaurant/hotel management, retail, and environmental science), meeting weekly with a Dynamy Internship year adviser, and participating in community service activities and a 3-week outdoor education program. Candidates should have ability to work independently, oral communication skills, self-motivation, strong interpersonal skills, strong leadership ability. Duration is 4–9 months. Unpaid. Open to individuals ages 17-22.
Benefits Formal training, housing at a cost, job counseling, opportunity to attend seminars/workshops, tuition assistance, willing to act as a professional reference, willing to provide letters of recommendation, up to 12 college credits available through Clark University.
Contact Write, call, fax, or e-mail Mr. David Rynick, Executive Director. Phone: 508-755-2571. Fax: 508-755-4692. E-mail: dynamy@neasc.org. In-person interview required. Applicants must submit a formal organization application, two writing samples, three letters of recommendation. Application deadline: December 1. Fees: $10,250. World Wide Web: http://www.dynamy.org.

EDUCATIONAL PROGRAMMES ABROAD (EPA)
137 North Park Street
Kalamazoo, Michigan 49007

General Information Program that offers internships in London, Bonn, Brussels, Madrid, Paris, or Melbourne. Established in 1977.
Internships Available ▶ *Interns:* responsibilities include working in national or regional government, various businesses, social services, health administration, medical research, media, or environmental organizations in London, Bonn, Brussels, Madrid, Paris, or Melbourne. Duration is 1 semester or summer. Unpaid. Open to college juniors, college seniors, recent college graduates, graduate students, law students.
Benefits Housing at a cost, meals at a cost, willing to complete paperwork for educational credit.
International Internships Available in Melbourne, Australia; Brussels, Belgium; Paris, France; Bonn, Germany; Madrid, Spain; London, United Kingdom.
Contact Write, call, fax, or e-mail Eleanor Krawutschke, U.S. Director. Phone: 616-382-0139. Fax: 616-382-5222. E-mail: epainterns@aol.com. Applicants must submit a formal organization application, academic transcripts, writing sample, letter of recommendation. Application deadline: March 1 for summer, May 1 for fall, November 15 for spring. World Wide Web: http://www.studyabroad.com/.

EXPLORATIONS IN TRAVEL, INC.
1922 River Road
Guilford, Vermont 05301

General Information   Organization that provides travel opportunities and volunteer placments for students and adults. Established in 1990. Number of employees: 3.

Internships Available   ▶ *1–5 agricultural/conservation volunteers (New Zealand):* responsibilities include working on small farms, teaching in schools, working with environmental and conservation organizations. Candidates should have ability to work independently, ability to work with others, oral communication skills, self-motivation. Duration is flexible. Open to high school seniors, recent high school graduates, college freshmen, college sophomores, college juniors, college seniors, recent college graduates, graduate students, career changers, individuals reentering the workforce. ▶ *1–5 animal shelter volunteers (Puerto Rico):* responsibilities include working with an animal shelter/clinic in Puerto Rico caring for dogs, cats, and horses, and assisting veterinarian. Candidates should have ability to work independently, ability to work with others, personal interest in the field, self-motivation, Spanish language skills useful. Duration is flexible. Open to recent high school graduates, college freshmen, college sophomores, college juniors, college seniors, recent college graduates, graduate students, career changers, individuals reentering the workforce, retired persons. ▶ *1–5 environmental education/conservation volunteers (Mexico):* responsibilities include teaching environmental education to student and community members in Mexico, assisting with field research on environmental changes to conservation areas. Candidates should have ability to work independently, ability to work with others, self-motivation, Spanish language skills useful. Duration is flexible. Open to recent high school graduates, college freshmen, college sophomores, college juniors, college seniors, recent college graduates, graduate students, career changers, individuals reentering the workforce, retired persons. ▶ *1–5 environmental/conservation project volunteers (Ecuador):* responsibilities include working on environmental and conservation projects. Candidates should have ability to work independently, ability to work with others, self-motivation, Spanish language skills. Duration is flexible. Open to recent high school graduates, college freshmen, college sophomores, college juniors, college seniors, recent college graduates, graduate students, career changers, individuals reentering the workforce, retired persons. ▶ *1–5 rainforest conservation volunteers (Australia):* responsibilities include working in a tropical research center which focuses on the study, care, and rehabilitation of flying foxes in Australia; rainforest protection activism opportunity also available. Candidates should have ability to work independently, oral communication skills, self-motivation, strong interpersonal skills. Duration is flexible. Open to college freshmen, college sophomores, college juniors, college seniors, recent college graduates, graduate students, career changers, individuals reentering the workforce, retired persons. ▶ *1–5 rainforest reserve volunteers (Costa Rica):* responsibilities include working with a small rainforest reserve in Costa Rica, including trail maintenance, tree planting, connection with local school and students. Candidates should have ability to work independently, ability to work with others, self-motivation, Spanish language skills. Duration is flexible. Open to recent high school graduates, college freshmen, college sophomores, college juniors, college seniors, recent college graduates, graduate students, career changers, individuals reentering the workforce, retired persons. ▶ *1–5 rainforest reserve volunteers (Puerto Rico):* responsibilities include working with a small rainforest reserve in Puerto Rico; trail maintenance, reforestation projects, receiving visiting eco-tourist groups. Candidates should have ability to work independently, self-motivation, strong interpersonal skills. Duration is flexible. Open to high school seniors, recent high school graduates, college freshmen, college sophomores, college juniors, college seniors, recent college graduates, graduate students, career changers, individuals reentering the workforce, retired persons. ▶ *1–5 rainforest/conservation volunteers (Belize):* responsibilities include working with a research and education facility in the rainforests of Belize; assisting with field research, trail maintenance, construction, gardening, community workshops.

Candidates should have ability to work independently, ability to work with others, self-motivation. Duration is flexible. Open to recent high school graduates, college freshmen, college sophomores, college juniors, college seniors, recent college graduates, graduate students, career changers, individuals reentering the workforce, retired persons. ▶ *1–5 sea turtle project volunteers (Costa Rica and Mexico):* responsibilities include working with an environmental organization which focuses on protecting beaches and monitoring sea turtles, night patrols of beaches, and documenting turtle activity. Candidates should have ability to work independently, ability to work with others, personal interest in the field, self-motivation, Spanish language skills useful. Duration is flexible, from April to August. Open to recent high school graduates, college freshmen, college sophomores, college juniors, college seniors, recent college graduates, graduate students, career changers, individuals reentering the workforce, retired persons. ▶ *1–5 teaching assistant volunteers (Costa Rica):* responsibilities include working with rural elementary and secondary schools in Costa Rica including teaching English and other subjects and organizing recreational activities. Candidates should have ability to work independently, oral communication skills, self-motivation, strong interpersonal skills. Duration is flexible. Open to recent high school graduates, college freshmen, college sophomores, college juniors, college seniors, recent college graduates, graduate students, career changers, individuals reentering the workforce, retired persons. ▶ *1–5 teaching assistant volunteers (Ecuador):* responsibilities include working with rural elementary and secondary schools in Ecuador including teaching English and other subjects and organizing recreational activities. Candidates should have ability to work independently, oral communication skills, self-motivation, strong interpersonal skills. Duration is flexible. Open to recent high school graduates, college freshmen, college sophomores, college juniors, college seniors, recent college graduates, graduate students, career changers, individuals reentering the workforce, retired persons. ▶ *1–5 volunteers (Samoa):* responsibilities include working with projects related to sustainable tourism, wildlife conservation, tree projects, community-based tourism projects. Candidates should have ability to work independently, ability to work with others, self-motivation. Duration is flexible. Open to recent high school graduates, college freshmen, college sophomores, college juniors, college seniors, recent college graduates, graduate students, career changers, individuals reentering the workforce, retired persons. ▶ *1–5 wildlife rescue volunteers (Costa Rica):* responsibilities include working with an environmental education center and wildlife rehabilitation. Candidates should have ability to work independently, ability to work with others, self-motivation, Spanish language skills useful. Duration is flexible (one month minimum). Open to recent high school graduates, college freshmen, college sophomores, college juniors, college seniors, recent college graduates, graduate students, career changers, individuals reentering the workforce, retired persons. All positions are unpaid. International applications accepted.

Benefits   Health insurance, housing at a cost, meals at a cost, names of contacts, willing to act as a professional reference, willing to complete paperwork for educational credit, willing to provide letters of recommendation, opportunity for language study.

International Internships   Available in Belize; Costa Rica; Ecuador; Mexico; New Zealand; Puerto Rico.

Contact   Write, call, fax, or e-mail John Lee, Volunteer Coordinator. Phone: 802-257-0152. Fax: 802-257-2784. E-mail: explore@sover.net. Telephone interview required. Applicants must submit a formal organization application, cover letter, resume, two letters of recommendation, placement fee of $600—$950 upon acceptance. Applications are accepted continuously. Fees: $35. World Wide Web: http://www.exploretravel.com.

GEORGIA GOVERNOR'S INTERN PROGRAM
245 State Capitol
Atlanta, Georgia 30334

General Information   Internship program that offers hands-on experience working with state and nonprofit agencies. Established in 1971. Number of employees: 3. Unit of Governor's Office, Atlanta, Georgia. Number of internship applications received each year: 500.

Internships Available ▶ *200–300 interns.* Candidates should have ability to work with others, college courses in field, computer skills, office skills, oral communication skills, personal interest in the field, strong leadership ability. Duration is 10–13 weeks. stipend of $375-$2000 per internship depending on year of school and number of hours worked. Open to college juniors, college seniors, graduate students, law students.

Benefits Formal training, opportunity to attend seminars/ workshops, tuition assistance, willing to provide letters of recommendation.

Contact Write, call, or fax Mr. Ryan Tucker, Director. Phone: 404-656-3804. Fax: 404-651-5110. In-person interview required. Applicants must submit a formal organization application, resume. Application deadline: April 7 for summer, July 9 for fall, October 8 for spring. World Wide Web: http://www.ganet.org/gov.

HANDS ON ATLANTA
1605 Peachtree Street, Suite 100
Atlanta, Georgia 30309

General Information Nonprofit, volunteer organization that organizes more than 250 flexible volunteer opportunities per month and matches 20,000 volunteer members to these opportunities. Established in 1989. Number of employees: 32. Affiliate of City Cares of America, New York, New York. Number of internship applications received each year: 20.

Internships Available ▶ *2–4 development interns:* responsibilities include assisting with grant writing, individual and corporate giving, and special events related to fund-raising. Candidates should have ability to work independently, analytical skills, computer skills, editing skills, oral communication skills, organizational skills, personal interest in the field, research skills, self-motivation, strong interpersonal skills, writing skills. ▶ *7–12 program management interns:* responsibilities include working directly with volunteers to meet critical community needs; interns can choose program area such as education, homelessness, or housing. Candidates should have ability to work independently, computer skills, editing skills, oral communication skills, organizational skills, personal interest in the field, self-motivation, strong interpersonal skills, strong leadership ability, writing skills. ▶ *2–4 special events interns:* responsibilities include assisting in planning and implementing special events including event logistics, public relations, and advertising. Candidates should have computer skills, editing skills, oral communication skills, organizational skills, personal interest in the field, self-motivation, strong interpersonal skills, strong leadership ability, writing skills. Duration for all positions is 10 weeks. All positions are unpaid. Open to college freshmen, college sophomores, college juniors, college seniors, recent college graduates, graduate students, law students, career changers, individuals reentering the workforce. International applications accepted.

Benefits Formal training, on-the-job training, opportunity to attend seminars/workshops, possible full-time employment, willing to act as a professional reference, willing to complete paperwork for educational credit, willing to provide letters of recommendation.

Contact Write, call, fax, or e-mail Jessica Kirkwood, Director of Community Programs. Phone: 404-872-2252 Ext. 20. Fax: 404-872-2251. E-mail: jkirkwood@handsonatlanta.com. In-person interview required. Applicants must submit a cover letter, resume, two writing samples, two personal references. Applications are accepted continuously. World Wide Web: http://www. handsonatlanta.com.

INTERN AMERICA, INC.
217 East 86th Street, Suite 133
New York, New York 10028

General Information Professional placement organization that provides unpaid internships in the United States to international and U.S. candidates. Established in 1997. Number of employees: 2.

Internships Available ▶ *Interns:* responsibilities include working in a tailor-made internship based on individual's education or experience; fields include architecture, art, communications, computers, education, engineering, entertainment, fashion, finance, government, hospitality, import/export, health care, international trade, law, marketing, public affairs, public relations, social work, and travel/tourism. Candidates should have ability to work independently, college courses in field, computer skills, experience in the field, knowledge of field, office skills, oral communication skills, personal interest in the field, research skills, self-motivation, strong interpersonal skills, written communication skills, advanced-level English language skills for international students. Duration is minimum of 4 weeks. Unpaid. Open to college freshmen, college sophomores, college juniors, college seniors, recent college graduates, graduate students, law students, career changers, junior professionals. International applications accepted.

Benefits Job counseling, on-the-job training, willing to act as a professional reference, willing to complete paperwork for educational credit, willing to provide letters of recommendation, information on housing provided, packet awarded at end of internship with new resume including internship experience, letters of reference from Intern America and the host company, certificate of completion.

Contact Write, call, fax, or e-mail Shannon Randolph, Executive Director, 217 East 86th Street, Suite 133, New York, New York 10028. Phone: 212-744-5132. Fax: 212-744-3106. E-mail: contact@internamerica.com. In-person interview recommended. Applicants must submit a formal organization application, cover letter, resume, writing sample, $950 fee for a minimum of four weeks and $200 for each additional week upon acceptance. Applications are accepted continuously. World Wide Web: http:// www.internamerica.com.

INTERN EXCHANGE INTERNATIONAL LTD.
130 Harold Road
Woodmere, New York 11598

General Information Organization offering travel to London and the opportunity to participate in career-based internships, arts activities, special interest activities, and cultural trips/tours. Established in 1987. Number of employees: 1. Number of internship applications received each year: 150.

Internships Available ▶ *5–10 resident assistants (London):* responsibilities include supervising interns studying in London. Candidates should have background in journalism, theater, film/video, photography, psychology, business, or fashion and design. stipend. Open to college seniors, recent college graduates, graduate students, must be at least 20 years of age. ▶ *120–150 student travel-interns (London):* responsibilities include interning in any of the following academic areas: archaeology, architecture, art history/appreciation, business (banking/finance, marketing), communications, government and politics, health sciences, journalism, prelaw, premed, social services, film, photography, fashion and design, and community service. Candidates should have ability to work independently, oral communication skills, personal interest in the field, self-motivation, strong interpersonal skills. Unpaid. Open to individuals ages 16-18. Duration for all positions is 31 days in June-July. International applications accepted.

Benefits On-the-job training, willing to provide letters of recommendation, cultural trips available, housing provided for resident assistants.

International Internships Available in London, United Kingdom.

Contact Write, call, fax, or e-mail Lynn Ann Weinstein or Nina Miller Glickman, M.Ed, Directors. Phone: 516-374-3939. Fax: 516-374-2104. E-mail: internexchange@compuserve.com. Applicants must submit a formal organization application, academic transcripts, writing sample, fee of approximately $4,895 and deposit of $450 upon acceptance for student-travel interns only, 1-2 letters of recommendation (depending on field). Applications are accepted continuously. Fees: $50. World Wide Web: http://www.internexchange.com.

INTERNSHIP PROGRAMS/AUSTRALIA
4361 Eastwood Drive
Santa Maria, California 93455-3917

General Information Program created to provide international students access to custom-designed comprehensive internships in Australia in a wide range of fields including, but not limited to: business/finance, communications, law, politics, the arts, social work, biology, computers, and ecotourism. Established in 1985. Number of employees: 2. Unit of Global Education Designs, Pty. Ltd., Brisbane, Australia. Number of internship applications received each year: 200.
Internships Available ▶ *1–100 professional development interns:* responsibilities include working in public and private sectors in Australia; internships custom-designed to meet interests and needs of interns. Candidates should have ability to work independently, knowledge of field, personal interest in the field, plan to pursue career in field, self-motivation, strong interpersonal skills. Duration is 6–78 weeks. Unpaid. Open to high school seniors, recent high school graduates, college freshmen, college sophomores, college juniors, college seniors, recent college graduates, graduate students, law students, career changers, individuals reentering the workforce. International applications accepted.
Benefits Formal training, housing at a cost, meals at a cost, names of contacts, on-the-job training, opportunity to attend seminars/workshops, willing to act as a professional reference, willing to complete paperwork for educational credit, willing to provide letters of recommendation.
International Internships Available in Australia.
Contact Write, call, fax, or e-mail Robert/Barbara Yoshioka, Managing Consultants. Phone: 800-704-4880. Fax: 800-704-4880. E-mail: ryb20z@impulse.net. Applicants must submit a formal organization application, cover letter, resume, academic transcripts. Applications are accepted continuously. Fees: $500. World Wide Web: http://www.advc.com/internships.

INTERNSHIPS INTERNATIONAL
1116 Cowper Drive
Raleigh, North Carolina 27608

General Information Placement service for quality, unpaid internships in London, Paris, Florence, Dublin, Budapest, Santiago, Stuttgart, Melbourne, Shanghai, Bangkok and Viet Nam, and Nairobi. Established in 1994. Number of employees: 2. Number of internship applications received each year: 50.
Internships Available ▶ *Interns:* responsibilities include all fields as requested by interns. Duration is 6 weeks to 6 months. Unpaid. Open to college seniors, recent college graduates, graduate students, law students, career changers. International applications accepted.
Benefits Professional internship.
International Internships Available in Melbourne, Australia; Santiago, Chile; Shanghai, China; Paris, France; Stuttgart, Germany; Budapest, Hungary; Dublin, Ireland; Florence, Italy; Nairobi, Kenya; Bangkok, Thailand; London, United Kingdom; Viet Nam.
Contact Write, call, fax, or e-mail Judy Tilson, Director. Phone: 919-832-1575. Fax: 919-834-7170. E-mail: intintl@aol.com. In-person interview recommended. Applicants must submit a formal organization application, cover letter, resume, academic transcripts, two letters of recommendation, photo. Applications are accepted continuously. World Wide Web: http://www.rtpnet.org/~intintl.

JEWISH VOCATIONAL SERVICE
111 Prospect Street
East Orange, New Jersey 07017

General Information Service providing career/vocational counseling and job placement assistance, including college selection to men and women in career transition, those returning to the workforce, or recent college graduates. Established in 1939. Number of employees: 70. Number of internship applications received each year: 5.

Internships Available ▶ *6 career/education counseling, rehab, and emigre interns (2 of each):* responsibilities include assisting with assessment, group counseling sessions, support groups, and interviews; helping keep library up to date; attending staff meetings and workshops; and dealing with placement and unemployed clients. Candidates should have college courses in field, computer skills, experience in the field, personal interest in the field, strong interpersonal skills. Duration is 4–12 months. Unpaid. Open to recent college graduates, graduate students, career changers. International applications accepted.
Benefits Formal training, job counseling, names of contacts, on-the-job training, opportunity to attend seminars/workshops, possible full-time employment, willing to complete paperwork for educational credit, willing to provide letters of recommendation.
Contact Write, fax, or e-mail Ms. Linda Zamer, Director of Career, Counseling, and Placement. Fax: 973-674-7773. E-mail: lzamer@jvsnj.org. No phone calls. In-person interview required. Applicants must submit a cover letter, resume, two personal references. Applications are accepted continuously. World Wide Web: http://www.jvsnj.org.

JOB CORPS
200 Constitution Avenue, NW, N-4507
Washington, District of Columbia 20210

General Information Employment and training center. Established in 1964. Number of employees: 31. Division of United States Department of Labor, Washington, District of Columbia. Number of internship applications received each year: 50.
Internships Available ▶ *4–6 interns:* responsibilities include acting as knowledgeable consultants in working with professional staff. Candidates should have ability to work independently, analytical skills, computer skills, experience in the field, knowledge of field, oral communication skills, research skills, self-motivation, strong interpersonal skills, written communication skills. Duration is one year to 18 months. $32,000–$44,000 per year. Open to recent college graduates, graduate students. International applications accepted.
Benefits Names of contacts, on-the-job training, opportunity to attend seminars/workshops, travel reimbursement, willing to complete paperwork for educational credit, willing to provide letters of recommendation.
Contact Write, call, fax, or e-mail John Chowning, Intern Coordinator. Phone: 202-219-5556 Ext. 133. Fax: 202-219-5183. E-mail: chowningj@doleta.gov. In-person interview recommended. Applicants must submit a formal organization application, cover letter, resume, academic transcripts, two personal references, three letters of recommendation. Applications are accepted continuously.

MOGPA MINNESOTA ORGANIZATION FOR GLOBAL PROFESSIONAL ASSIGNMENTS
678 Lake Pine Drive
Shoreview, Minnesota 55126

General Information Company that provides bilingual college students or recent graduates, pursuing a career in business, engineering, science or technology, with 6-to-12-month work assignments in Asia with American, Japanese and Chinese companies. Established in 1993. Number of employees: 5. Number of internship applications received each year: 100.
Internships Available ▶ *Business-related fields interns:* responsibilities include entry-level work for American, Japanese, or Chinese company in Japan or China in the fields of business administration, international business, accounting, finance, management, marketing, etc. Candidates should have college courses in field, oral communication skills, plan to pursue career in field, written communication skills, ability to speak fluent English and either Japanese, Mandarin, or Cantonese. Open to college juniors, college seniors, recent college graduates, graduate students, U.S. citizens or permanent residents or Japanese or Chinese citizens who go/went to school in the U.S. ▶ *Computer-related fields interns:* responsibilities include entry-level work for an American, Japanese, or Chinese company located in Japan or China in the fields of information systems/technology,

computer science, computer programming, software, etc. Candidates should have college courses in field, oral communication skills, plan to pursue career in field, written communication skills, ability to speak fluent English and either Japanese Cantonese, or Mandarin. Open to college juniors, college seniors, recent college graduates, graduate students, U.S. citizens or permanent residents or Japanese or Chinese citizens who go/went to school in the U.S. ▶ *Engineering-related fields interns:* responsibilities include entry-level work for an American, Japanese, or Chinese company in Japan or China in the fields of chemical engineering, mechanical engineering, electrical engineering, etc. Candidates should have college courses in field, oral communication skills, plan to pursue career in field, written communication skills, ability to speak fluent English and either Japanese, Mandarin, or Cantonese. Open to college juniors, college seniors, recent college graduates, graduate students, U.S. citizens or permanent residents or Japanese, or Chinese citizens who go/went to school in the US. Duration for all positions is 6–12 months. All positions paid at negotiated with individual companies. International applications accepted.

Benefits Housing at a cost, job counseling, possible full-time employment, willing to complete paperwork for educational credit, assistance in obtaining visas and housing.

International Internships Available in China; Japan.

Contact Write, call, fax, or e-mail Yvette N. Forrer, Communications Director, 678 Lake Pine Drive, Shoreview, Minnesota 55126. Phone: 651-481-0583. Fax: 651-481-0592. E-mail: mogpa@aol.com. In-person interview recommended. Applicants must submit a formal organization application, cover letter, resume, academic transcripts, writing sample, three letters of recommendation, 3 short essays, demonstrated proficiency in an Asian language. Fees: $75. World Wide Web: http://www.mogpa.com.

MOUNTBATTEN INTERNSHIP PROGRAMME
50 East 42nd Street, Suite 2000
New York, New York 10017-5405

General Information Exchange visitor program providing one-year professional internships for British, New Zealand, and Australian citizens in New York and for U.S. citizens only in London, UK. Established in 1984. Number of employees: 14. Number of internship applications received each year: 100.

Internships Available ▶ *6–15 internships in London, UK:* responsibilities include general, entry-level work in various fields such as clerical, administrative, research, paralegal, analytical, and information technology. Duration is 12 months beginning in October. $1,000 per month. Open to recent college graduates, graduate students, law students, career changers, only those who are U.S. citizens. ▶ *100–150 internships in New York:* responsibilities include general entry level work in management, business, commerce and finance with clerical, administrative, research, paralegal, analytical, and information technology duties. Duration is 1 year beginning in January, May, or September. $940 month, plus free housing. Open to recent college graduates, graduate students, law students, career changers, only those who are citizens of Great Britain, Australia, or New Zealand (no US citizens). Candidates for all positions should have computer skills, office skills, oral communication skills, self-motivation, strong interpersonal skills, written communication skills. International applications accepted.

Benefits Formal training, health insurance, housing at a cost, job counseling, on-the-job training, opportunity to attend seminars/workshops, willing to act as a professional reference, willing to complete paperwork for educational credit, willing to provide letters of recommendation, limited tuition assistance.

International Internships Available in London, United Kingdom.

Contact Write, call, fax, or e-mail Ellen S. Lautz, Administrative Director, 50 East 42nd Street, Suite 200, New York, New York 10017. Phone: 212-557-5380. Fax: 212-557-5383. E-mail: elautz@mountbatten.org. In-person interview required. Applicants must submit a formal organization application, resume, academic transcripts, three personal references, three letters of recommendation, personal statement (esssay form), 1 to 2 writing samples. Application deadline: May 10 for internships in London. Fees: $50. World Wide Web: http://www.mountbatten.org.

NATIONAL CONSORTIUM FOR GRADUATE DEGREES FOR MINORITIES IN ENGINEERING AND SCIENCE, INC.
PO Box 537
Notre Dame, Indiana 46556

General Information Organization that matches students who are interested in graduate degrees in engineering and science with employer sponsors; over 75 companies and over 80 universities participate. Established in 1976. Number of employees: 12. Number of internship applications received each year: 800.

Internships Available ▶ *40 Ph.D. fellowships in engineering and science (20 each):* responsibilities include working on engineering and science projects. $12,000 living stipend per year towards graduate school tuition and fees. Open to students obtaining Ph.D. in either engineering or science. ▶ *200 master's fellowships in engineering:* responsibilities include working on engineering projects. $6,000 living stipend per year towards graduate school tuition and fees. Open to students obtaining master's degree in engineering. Duration for all positions is 1-3 summers.

Benefits Housing at a cost, on-the-job training, travel reimbursement.

Contact Write, call, fax, or e-mail Valerie Washington, Staff Assistant. Phone: 219-631-7771. Fax: 219-287-1486. E-mail: gem.l@nd.edu. Applicants must submit a formal organization application, academic transcripts, three letters of recommendation. Application deadline: December 1. World Wide Web: http://www.nd.edu/~gem/.

OFFICE OF FELLOWSHIPS & GRANTS, SMITHSONIAN INSTITUTION
955 L'Enfant Plaza, Suite 7000
Washington, District of Columbia 20560

General Information Office that offers fellowships and internships for research and study in fields that are actively pursued by the museums and research organizations of the Institution. Number of internship applications received each year: 150.

Internships Available ▶ *15 James E. Webb Minority Graduate interns:* responsibilities include interning in the areas of business and public administration. $400 per week. ▶ *30–40 Minority Internship Program interns:* responsibilities include participating in research or museum-related activities in one of the many museums or departments of the Smithsonian Institution. $300 per week. ▶ *20 Native American Internship Program interns:* responsibilities include participating in research or museum activities related to Native-American studies. $300 per week. Duration for all positions is 10 weeks.

Benefits Opportunity to attend seminars/workshops, travel reimbursement, willing to complete paperwork for educational credit, willing to provide letters of recommendation.

Contact Write, call, or e-mail Ms. Pamela Hudson, Academic Program Specialist. Phone: 202-287-3271. E-mail: siofg@ofg.si.edu. Application deadline: February 15 for James E. Webb Minority Graduate and Minority Internship Program, March 1 for summer Native American Program, July 1 for fall Native American Program, November 1 for spring Native American Program. World Wide Web: http://www.si.edu/research+study.

OFFICE OF INTERNSHIPS AND EXPERIENTIAL EDUCATION
Taft Hall, The University of Rhode Island
Kingston, Rhode Island 02881

General Information Internship office that administers full-time, 15-credit, academic internship program and serves as information and referral source for part-time, some out-of-state and some international placements, and service learning opportunities. Established in 1975. Number of employees: 3. Unit of University of Rhode Island, Feinstein Center for Service Learning, Kingston, Rhode Island. Number of internship applications received each year: 250.

Internships Available ▶ *600 interns.* Candidates should have ability to work independently, oral communication skills, plan to pursue career in field, self-motivation, strong interpersonal skills,

Office of Internships and Experiential Education (continued)

written communication skills. Duration is 1 semester. Unpaid. Open to college juniors, college seniors. International applications accepted.

Benefits Opportunity to attend seminars/workshops, willing to act as a professional reference, willing to complete paperwork for educational credit, willing to provide letters of recommendation.

International Internships Available in Dominican Republic; Dublin, Ireland.

Contact Write, call, fax, or e-mail Ms. Lynn Gaulin, Director. Phone: 401-874-2160. Fax: 401-874-4573. E-mail: lga5668u@postoffice.uri.edu. In-person interview required. Applicants must submit a formal organization application, academic transcripts, 1-2 letters of recommendation, telephone interview acceptable for non-URI students. Application deadline: April 1 for summer, June 1 for fall, November 1 for spring. World Wide Web: http://www.uri.edu/univcol/u_uya.htm.

PARTNERS INTERNSHIP PROGRAM–AUGSBURG COLLEGE
2211 Riverside Avenue
Minneapolis, Minnesota 55454

General Information Organization that places undergraduates in nonprofit agencies where they are managers of specific self-contained projects for the purpose of introducing students to the opportunities in the nonprofit sector. Established in 1990. Number of employees: 1. Unit of Augsburg College, Minneapolis, Minnesota. Number of internship applications received each year: 100.

Internships Available ▶ *25–30 interns:* responsibilities include working in nonprofit organizations in Minnesota, Wisconsin, and North Dakota in all areas related to nonprofit activities. Candidates should have ability to work independently, analytical skills, computer skills, editing skills, office skills, oral communication skills, organizational skills, personal interest in the field, research skills, self-motivation, strong interpersonal skills, strong leadership ability, writing skills. Duration is 10 weeks. $8 per hour. Open to college freshmen, sophomores, and juniors who are only currently enrolled students in any Minnesota, Wisconsin, or North Dakota college or university.

Benefits Opportunity to attend seminars/workshops, travel reimbursement, comprehensive internship experience, educational and professional growth.

Contact Write or call Rosangelica Aburto, Program Director. Phone: 612-330-1575. Applicants must submit a resume. Application deadline: May 1 for summer.

PUBLIC SERVICE CORPS, NEW YORK CITY, DEPARTMENT OF CITYWIDE ADMINISTRATIVE SERVICES
1 Centre Street, Room 2435
New York, New York 10007

General Information Agency that provides internship opportunities throughout city agencies. Established in 1966. Number of employees: 11. Division of Department of Citywide Administrative Services, New York, New York. Number of internship applications received each year: 1,000.

Internships Available ▶ *600–700 Federal Work-Study Program interns:* responsibilities include working in a broad range of fields including government administration, creative arts, social work, health care, research, education, computer science, economic development, finance, accounting, labor relations, transportation, and management. Duration is to be determined by each school. $6–$12 per hour for federally funded college work-study students. Open to undergraduates, graduate students, and law students who are eligible for federal work-study program. ▶ *Academic credit/volunteer interns:* responsibilities include working in a broad range of fields including government administration, creative arts, social work, health care, research, education, computer science, economic development, finance, accounting, labor relations, transportation, and management. Duration is flexible. Unpaid. Open to college freshmen, college sophomores,

college juniors, college seniors, graduate students, law students. Candidates for all positions should have specific college courses and/or skills by internship.

Benefits Opportunity to attend seminars/workshops, willing to complete paperwork for educational credit, experience in public service, credit can be arranged with college approval.

Contact Write, call, or fax Ms. Marjorie Jelin, Director. Phone: 212-669-3255. Fax: 212-669-3633. In-person interview required. Applicants must submit a formal organization application. Applications are accepted continuously.

RHODE ISLAND COMMISSION ON STATE GOVERNMENT INTERNSHIPS
Room 8AA State House
Providence, Rhode Island 02903

General Information Program intended to give Rhode Island students attending out-of-state schools an opportunity to get hands-on training relating to their majors. Established in 1969. Number of employees: 5. Number of internship applications received each year: 250.

Internships Available ▶ *12–20 art interns.* Duration is 8–12 weeks. Position available as unpaid or paid. ▶ *Business school/secretarial students.* Candidates should have computer skills, organizational skills, personal interest in the field. Duration is 8 weeks. Unpaid. Open to individuals reentering the workforce. ▶ *30–40 business/finance interns.* Duration is 8–12 weeks. Position available as unpaid or paid. ▶ *30–40 city or town solicitors.* Duration is 8–12 weeks. Position available as unpaid or paid. ▶ *20 education interns.* Duration is 8–12 weeks. Position available as unpaid or paid. ▶ *Health interns.* Duration is 8–12 weeks. Position available as unpaid or paid. ▶ *High school interns.* Candidates should have analytical skills, oral communication skills, personal interest in the field, self-motivation. Duration is 1 month. Unpaid. Open to high school students. ▶ *50–100 legal interns.* Duration is 8–12 weeks. $100 per week. ▶ *100 legislation interns.* Duration is 8–12 weeks. Position available as unpaid or paid. ▶ *40 miscellaneous interns.* Duration is 8–12 weeks. Position available as unpaid or paid. ▶ *40 programming/data entry interns.* Duration is 8–12 weeks. Position available as unpaid or paid. International applications accepted.

Benefits Formal training, job counseling, opportunity to attend seminars/workshops, possible full-time employment, willing to complete paperwork for educational credit, willing to provide letters of recommendation.

Contact Write, call, fax, or e-mail Mr. Robert W. Gemma, Executive Director. Phone: 401-222-6782. Fax: 401-222-6142. E-mail: rgemma@rilin.state.ri.us. In-person interview required. Application deadline: May 15 for summer; continuous for all other positions. World Wide Web: http://www.rilin.state.ri.us.

RHODE ISLAND STATE GOVERNMENT INTERN PROGRAM
Room 8AA, State House Building
Providence, Rhode Island 02903

General Information Program that places college, graduate, and law students into Rhode Island's government agencies for internships. Established in 1969. Number of employees: 5. Number of internship applications received each year: 400.

Internships Available ▶ *200 education interns:* responsibilities include working in a state government agency such as the Department of Health, the Department of Education, or the Attorney General's office. Duration is 8–12 weeks. Unpaid. ▶ *200 summer interns:* responsibilities include working in a state government agency such as the Department of Health, the Department of Education, or the Attorney General's office. Duration is 8 weeks. $100 per week. International applications accepted.

Benefits Job counseling, names of contacts, opportunity to attend seminars/workshops, possible full-time employment, willing to complete paperwork for educational credit, willing to provide letters of recommendation.

Contact Write, fax, or e-mail Mr. Robert W. Gemma, Executive Director. Fax: 401-222-6142. E-mail: rgemma@rilin.state.ri.us. In-person interview required. Application deadline: May 15. World Wide Web: http://www.rilin.state.ri.us.

RHODE ISLAND STUDENT EMPLOYMENT NETWORK
560 Jefferson Boulevard
Warwick, Rhode Island 02886

General Information Statewide year-round clearinghouse for student employment and experiential education. Established in 1971. Number of employees: 1. Unit of Rhode Island Higher Education Assistance Authority, Warwick, Rhode Island. Number of internship applications received each year: 800.
Internships Available ▶ *300–500 Rhode Island interns:* responsibilities include various duties depending on where the intern is placed. Duration is 1–2 semesters. Position available as unpaid or paid. Open to college freshmen, college sophomores, college juniors, college seniors, graduate students, law students.
Benefits Job counseling, names of contacts, willing to complete paperwork for educational credit, willing to provide letters of recommendation.
Contact Write, call, or e-mail Student Services Unit. Phone: 401-736-1180. E-mail: ctotoro@ids.net. In-person interview recommended. Program registration. Applications are accepted continuously. World Wide Web: http://www.riheaa.org.

UNITED STATES ARMY RECRUITING COMMAND
1307 Third Avenue
Fort Knox, Kentucky 40121-2726

General Information US Army Recruiting Command conducts recruiting of health care professionals for the Army Meidcal Department. Unit of United States Department of the Army, Washington, District of Columbia. Number of internship applications received each year: 65.
Internships Available ▶ *60 advanced general dentistry interns.* Candidates should have ability to work with others, oral communication skills, research skills, strong interpersonal skills, strong leadership ability, written communication skills. Duration is October 1 to September 30. $3,400 per month. Open to senior dental students, dental school graduates within 3 years after graduation. ▶ *5–10 clinical psycology interns.* Candidates should have analytical skills, college degree in related field, oral communication skills, strong interpersonal skills, strong leadership ability, written communication skills. Duration is 1 year. $35,000 to $40,000 per year. Open to graduate students. ▶ *10 dietetics interns.* Candidates should have computer skills, oral communication skills, strong interpersonal skills, strong leadership ability, written communication skills. Duration is September to May. $2,400 per month. Open to college seniors, recent college graduates, graduate students. ▶ *6 occupational therapy interns.* Candidates should have computer skills, oral communication skills, strong interpersonal skills, strong leadership ability, written communication skills. Duration is 7 months. $2,400 per month. Open to college seniors, recent college graduates, graduate students.
Benefits Formal training, health insurance, meals at a cost, opportunity to attend seminars/workshops, possible full-time employment, travel reimbursement, tuition assistance, willing to complete paperwork for educational credit, on-post housing or a housing allowance, a subsistence allowance.
Contact Write, call, fax, or e-mail Maj. Martha A. Davis, Program Manager (dietetics, occupational therapy), Capt. Leslie Randolph-Moss, Program Manager (clinical psychology), 1307 Third Avenue, Attn.: RCRO-HS-SVD (for dietetics and occupational therapy), Attn.: RCRO-HS-MS (for clinical psychology), Fort Knox, Kentucky 40121. Phone: 502-626-0360. Fax: 502-626-0923. E-mail: martha.davis@usarec.army.mil or leslie.randolph-moss@usarec.army.mil. In-person interview required. Applicants must submit a formal organization application, cover letter, resume, academic transcripts, three letters of recommendation, other materials as specificed by specific position. Application deadline: January 15 for clinical psychology positions, February 1 for fall

(dietetics and occupational therapy positions), May 1 for winter and summer (dietetics and occupational therapy positions). World Wide Web: http://www.goarmy.com.

UNIVERSITY OF NORTH CAROLINA INSTITUTE OF GOVERNMENT, SUMMER INTERN PROGRAM
Campus Box 3330, Knapp Building, University of North Carolina
Chapel Hill, North Carolina 27599-3330

General Information Program that allows students to live, learn, and work together through internships in the Raleigh area in a variety of fields including museums and cultural organizations, parks and recreation, the arts, and government offices. Established in 1962. Number of internship applications received each year: 300.
Internships Available ▶ *20 interns.* Candidates should have oral communication skills, personal interest in the field, strong interpersonal skills, writing skills. Duration is 10 weeks. $270 per week. Open to college sophomores, college juniors, college seniors.
Benefits Housing at a cost, meals at a cost, on-the-job training, willing to complete paperwork for educational credit, willing to provide letters of recommendation, networking opportunities, field trips, access to campus facilities, worker's compensation, opportunity to attend seminars.
Contact Write, call, fax, or e-mail Ms. Lisa Podhajsky, Program Manager. Phone: 919-966-4347. Fax: 919-962-0654. E-mail: podhajsky@iogmail.iog.unc.edu. In-person interview required. Applicants must submit a formal organization application, resume, academic transcripts, two letters of recommendation, 1 cover letter/essay. Application deadline: January 28. World Wide Web: http://ncinfo.iog.unc.edu/intern.html.

VOLUNTEERS FOR PEACE
PO Box 202
Belmont, Vermont 05730

General Information Placement service that places North Americans in 1500 work camps worldwide. Established in 1981. Number of employees: 3. Number of internship applications received each year: 500.
Internships Available ▶ *1,200–1,400 international work campers:* responsibilities include living with an international group of 12-20 persons and becoming involved in a community service project. Candidates should have ability to work with others, organizational skills, self-motivation, strong interpersonal skills, intercultural experience. Duration is 2 to 3 weeks each program; interns normally register for multiple camps. Unpaid. Open to individuals age 15 or over. International applications accepted.
Benefits Free housing, meals at a cost, opportunity to attend seminars/workshops, willing to complete paperwork for educational credit, inexpensive international experience.
International Internships Available.
Contact Write, call, fax, or e-mail Mr. Peter Coldwell, Director. Phone: 802-259-2759. Fax: 802-259-2922. E-mail: vfp@vfp.org. Applicants must submit a formal organization application, resume, $195 for room and board upon acceptance. Applications are accepted continuously. World Wide Web: http://www.vfp.org.

THE WASHINGTON CENTER FOR INTERNSHIPS AND ACADEMIC SEMINARS
2000 M Street, NW, Suite 750
Washington, District of Columbia 20036-3307

General Information Center that provides off-campus full-time internships and 1–2 week academic seminars in all fields for students from more than 750 colleges and universities. Established in 1975. Number of employees: 50. Number of internship applications received each year: 1,200.
Internships Available ▶ *50 College Plus One interns:* responsibilities include varied duties depending on student's interests and expertise. Candidates should have analytical skills, office skills, oral communication skills, plan to pursue career in field, self-

The Washington Center for Internships and Academic Seminars (continued)
motivation, written communication skills. Duration is 10–12 weeks. Position available as unpaid or paid. Open to recent college graduates, graduate students, law students. ▶ *50 Law Plus One interns:* responsibilities include varied law-related duties depending upon student's interests. Candidates should have analytical skills, knowledge of field, office skills, oral communication skills, plan to pursue career in field, written communication skills. Duration is 10 weeks in the summer. Position available as unpaid or paid. Open to law students. ▶ *30 North American Free Trade Agreement (NAFTA) Program interns:* responsibilities include varied duties related to bi- or tri-lateral trade issues between U.S., Canada, and Mexico. Candidates should have analytical skills, knowledge of field, office skills, oral communication skills, personal interest in the field, written communication skills. Duration is 10–15 weeks. minimum $2000 financial assistance guaranteed and applied toward housing. Open to college juniors, college seniors, graduate students. ▶ *50 diversity in Congress program interns:* responsibilities include being placed in Congressional offices; general staff work. Candidates should have ability to work with others, analytical skills, office skills, oral communication skills, self-motivation, written communication skills. Duration is 10–15 weeks. $2000 minimum guaranteed financial assistance applied toward housing. Open to college juniors, college seniors, graduate students. ▶ *50 environment interns:* responsibilities include varied duties related to environmental issues. Candidates should have analytical skills, knowledge of field, office skills, oral communication skills, self-motivation, written communication skills, major in any field related to environment. Duration is 10–15 weeks. guaranteed minimum financial assistance of $1000 applied toward housing. Open to college juniors, college seniors, graduate students. ▶ *10–25 federal government interns:* responsibilities include working for federal government agencies, such as Commerce, Interior, and EPA on various projects and initiatives. Candidates should have computer skills, oral communication skills, organizational skills, research skills, written communication skills. Duration is 10–15 weeks. $4,500–$6,000 per semester. Open to college juniors, college seniors. ▶ *500 general intern:* responsibilities include working in American studies, arts management, business, communications, computer science, consumer advocacy, environment, government affairs, health and science, international relations/studies, labor relations/studies, law, politics/public policy, public administration, social work, urban studies, or women's studies. Candidates should have analytical skills, office skills, oral communication skills, organizational skills, self-motivation, written communication skills. Duration is 10–15 weeks. Position available as unpaid or at $1000—$6000 per semester depending on placement. Open to college juniors, college seniors, recent college graduates, graduate students, law students. ▶ *50 mass communications interns:* responsibilities include working in journalism, public relations, public affairs, or advertising. Candidates should have college courses in field, knowledge of field, oral communication skills, plan to pursue career in field, self-motivation, written communication skills. Duration is 10–15 weeks. guaranteed financial assistance of $1000 minimum applied toward housing. Open to college juniors, college seniors, graduate students. ▶ *25 minority leaders fellowship program interns:* responsibilities include variety of tasks for students in any major field, with an emphasis on quantitative and analytical skills. Candidates should have analytical skills, office skills, oral communication skills, self-motivation, strong leadership ability, written communication skills. Duration is 10–15 weeks. all program and housing fees paid (minimum value = $5500). Open to college juniors, college seniors, graduate students. ▶ *50*

nonprofit leaders interns: responsibilities include working for a nonprofit organization, such as an advocacy group, or trade or professional associations. Candidates should have ability to work with others, analytical skills, office skills, oral communication skills, self-motivation, written communication skills. Duration is 10–15 weeks. guaranteed financial assistance of $1000 minimum applied toward housing. Open to college juniors, college seniors, graduate students. ▶ *50 study abroad in DC interns:* responsibilities include varied duties with an international component possibly involving the use of foreign language and cultural skills. Candidates should have office skills, oral communication skills, organizational skills, self-motivation, written communication skills. Duration is 10–15 weeks. Position available as unpaid or paid. Open to college juniors, college seniors, graduate students. ▶ *50 women in public policy interns:* responsibilities include varied duties related to public policy. Candidates should have ability to work independently, ability to work with others, analytical skills, office skills, oral communication skills, self-motivation, written communication skills. Duration is 10–15 weeks. guaranteed financial assistance of $1000 minimum applied toward housing. Open to college juniors, college seniors, graduate students. International applications accepted.

Benefits Formal training, housing at a cost, names of contacts, opportunity to attend seminars/workshops, possible full-time employment, willing to act as a professional reference, willing to complete paperwork for educational credit, willing to provide letters of recommendation, financial aid available in certain fields and student discounts for certain services.

Contact Write, call, fax, or e-mail Dr. Eugene J. Alpert, Vice President for Academic Affairs. Phone: 800-486-8921. Fax: 202-336-7609. E-mail: info@twc.edu. Applicants must submit a formal organization application, resume, academic transcripts, two letters of recommendation, short essay on topic related to internship request area. Application deadline: March 15 for summer, June 15 for fall, November 15 for spring. Fees: $60. World Wide Web: http://www.twc.edu.

Y.E.S. TO JOBS
1416 North La Brea Avenue, PO Box 3390
Hollywood, California 90028

General Information Program designed to introduce minority high school students to career opportunities behind the scenes in the entertainment industry. Established in 1987. Number of employees: 3. Number of internship applications received each year: 800.

Internships Available ▶ *150–250 interns:* responsibilities include various duties as entry level assistants working in the entertainment industry. Candidates should have computer skills, oral communication skills, personal interest in the field, self-motivation, strong interpersonal skills, written communication skills. Duration is 10 weeks. Paid. Open to high school students, high school seniors, individuals 16-18 years old.

Benefits Formal training, job counseling, names of contacts, on-the-job training, opportunity to attend seminars/workshops, willing to complete paperwork for educational credit, willing to provide letters of recommendation.

Contact Write, fax, or e-mail Jaleesa Hazzard, Executive Director, 1416 North La Brea Avenue, PO Box 3390, Hollywood, California 90028. Fax: 323-856-2613. E-mail: yestojobs@aol.com. No phone calls. In-person interview required. Applicants must submit a formal organization application. Application deadline: April 1 for summer.

ARTS, ENTERTAINMENT, AND RECREATION

GENERAL

AMELIA WELLNESS CENTER
869 Sadler Road, Suite 5
Fernandina Beach, Florida 32034

General Information Health and fitness club. Established in 1987. Number of employees: 25. Number of internship applications received each year: 75.
Internships Available ► *1–2 interns:* responsibilities include acting as manager-on-duty, group fitness leader, and customer service representative; fitness assessment; exercise prescription; promotion; advertising and selling fitness programs offered by club. Candidates should have computer skills, oral communication skills, personal interest in the field, self-motivation, strong interpersonal skills, strong leadership ability, writing skills. Duration is 3–4 years. $300–$600 per month. Open to college seniors, recent college graduates, graduate students. International applications accepted.
Benefits Names of contacts, on-the-job training, possible full-time employment, willing to act as a professional reference, willing to complete paperwork for educational credit, willing to provide letters of recommendation.
Contact E-mail Doug Lane, Owner, 869 Sadler Road, Suite 5, Fernandina Beach, Florida 32034. E-mail: awc@net-magic.net. Telephone interview required. Applicants must submit a cover letter, resume. Applications are accepted continuously. World Wide Web: http://www.ameliawellness.nu.

AMERICANS FOR THE ARTS
1000 Vermont Avenue, NW, 12th Floor
Washington, District of Columbia 20005

General Information National organization of groups and individuals dedicated to advancing the arts and culture in communities across the United States; works with cultural organizations, arts and business leaders, and patrons to provide leadership, advocacy, visibility, professional development and research, and information that will advance support for the arts and culture. Established in 1972. Number of employees: 15. Number of internship applications received each year: 70.
Internships Available ► *2 interns:* responsibilities include duties relating to community arts, membership, communication, research, and arts education and/or national arts advocacy. Candidates should have ability to work independently, computer skills, experience in the field, oral communication skills, organizational skills, written communication skills. Duration is flexible. Position available as unpaid or paid. Open to college juniors, college seniors, recent college graduates, graduate students, individuals reentering the workforce. International applications accepted.
Benefits Job counseling, names of contacts, opportunity to attend seminars/workshops, willing to complete paperwork for educational credit, willing to provide letters of recommendation.
Contact Write, call, fax, or e-mail Melissa Palarea, Internship Coordinator. Phone: 202-371-2830. Fax: 202-371-0424. E-mail: mpalarea@artsusa.org. In-person interview recommended. Applicants must submit a cover letter, resume. Applications are accepted continuously. World Wide Web: http://www.artsusa. org.

ANDERSON RANCH ARTS CENTER
Box 5598
Snowmass Village, Colorado 81615

General Information Arts center that offers workshops in painting and drawing, printmaking, ceramics, sculpture, woodworking, furniture design, photography, interdisciplinary studies, and children's studies; winter programs include a studio residency internship program. Established in 1966. Number of employees: 15. Number of internship applications received each year: 200.
Internships Available ► *20 summer assistants:* responsibilities include working in all areas of Anderson Ranch, assisting workshop instructors and class participants, preparation of materials, maintenance, cleaning, and various duties. Candidates should have experience in the field. Duration is May to August/September. monthly stipend. Open to recent college graduates, graduate students.
Benefits Free housing, free meals, opportunity to attend seminars/workshops, willing to act as a professional reference, willing to provide letters of recommendation.
Contact Write, call, or fax Ketty Herb, Program Administrator. Phone: 970-923-3181. Fax: 970-923-3871. Telephone interview required. Applicants must submit a formal organization application, cover letter, resume, portfolio, three personal references. Application deadline: March 16.

APERTURE FOUNDATION
20 East 23rd Street
New York, New York 10010

General Information Not-for-profit organization devoted to the promotion of photography as a unique form of expression through publication, exhibition, and educational programs. Established in 1952. Number of employees: 31. Number of internship applications received each year: 500.
Internships Available ► *2 Burden Gallery interns:* responsibilities include assisting in exhibition organization, manning the desk during public hours (promoting sales, showing limited-edition portfolios), opening and closing the gallery, shipping and receiving original work, generating promotion (exhibitions, openings, and special events), darkroom maintenance and work, assisting with invitation mailings and opening receptions. Candidates should have computer skills, office skills, oral communication skills, personal interest in the field, strong interpersonal skills, written communication skills. Open to college juniors, college seniors, recent college graduates, graduate students. ► *2 Director's office interns:* responsibilities include acting as liaison between Director's office and other departments; locating and requesting review copies of books, periodicals, and videos; maintaining the library; maintaining a database; and assisting with the preparation of important meetings. Candidates should have ability to work independently, office skills, organizational skills, strong interpersonal skills, writing skills. Open to college juniors, college seniors, recent college graduates, graduate students. ► *2 Paul Strand archive interns:* responsibilities include

Aperture Foundation (continued)

maintaining ongoing file of Strand material in print and other related material; organizing, cataloging and preserving Aperture collection of artwork and photographs; inventorying and organizing book library; exhibition preparation work (Burden Gallery and Traveling Exhibitions); administration of copyright and permissions for use of photographs by Paul Strand; assembly, distribution, and recordkeeping of limited editions and portfolios; darkroom and on-camera copy work. Candidates should have ability to work independently, ability to work with others, office skills, organizational skills, personal interest in the field, research skills. Open to college juniors, college seniors, recent college graduates, graduate students. ► *2 design interns:* responsibilities include preparing files for color output, creating mechanicals, sizing art, scanning and placing photographs, conceptual design on selected projects, and general office support. Candidates should have ability to work independently, computer skills, office skills, personal interest in the field, strong interpersonal skills. Open to college juniors, college seniors, recent college graduates, graduate students. ► *2 development interns:* responsibilities include compilation of proposal packets (research, writing, and editing), updating donor listings, assisting with the annual appeal, assisting with board and donor relations, assisting with special events, maintaining the development database, assisting with the coordination of Work-Scholar Program. Candidates should have oral communication skills, organizational skills, personal interest in the field, research skills, strong interpersonal skills, writing skills. Open to college juniors, college seniors, recent college graduates, graduate students. ► *6 editorial interns:* responsibilities include researching pictures and texts, reviewing manuscripts and portfolios, contacting outside sources to request artwork for reproduction, proofreading, compiling copy for catalogues and book jackets, some darkroom work, some development and publicity support, and registering copyrights. Candidates should have ability to work independently, editing skills, experience in the field, organizational skills, strong interpersonal skills, writing skills. Open to college juniors, college seniors, recent college graduates, graduate students, law students. ► *2 foreign rights interns:* responsibilities include interfacing with foreign distributors and publishers, assisting with contracts and licensing agreements, arranging coeditions of Aperture books with publishers worldwide, identifying new publishing partners, preparing for the Frankfurt Book Fair, organizing pricing of books for potential foreign copublications. Candidates should have ability to work independently, computer skills, office skills, organizational skills, personal interest in the field, writing skills. Open to college juniors, college seniors, recent college graduates, graduate students. ► *2 marketing and circulation interns:* responsibilities include preparing sales materials, updating and mailing media kits, maintaining contact with distributors and sales representatives, creating and placing advertisements, selling ad space, maintaining the database, and producing direct mail. Candidates should have ability to work independently, computer skills, office skills, organizational skills, personal interest in the field, writing skills. Open to college juniors, college seniors, recent college graduates, graduate students. ► *2 production interns:* responsibilities include acting as liaison with outside companies, checking quotes and mechanicals, writing purchase orders, organizing and packaging original materials for transport, assisting with color corrections and some designing, and organizing information for invoicing, distribution, and billing. Candidates should have knowledge of field, office skills, organizational skills, plan to pursue career in field, strong interpersonal skills. Open to college juniors, college seniors, recent college graduates, graduate students. ► *2 publicity interns:* responsibilities include maintaining publicity books, assisting in the preparation of materials, creating first draft press releases, circulating reviews to sales representatives, updating files and mailing lists, research, assisting in promotion projects, and permissions. Candidates should have ability to work independently, office skills, organizational skills, personal interest in the field, strong interpersonal skills, writing skills. Open to college juniors, college seniors, recent college graduates, graduate students, law students. ► *2 traveling exhibition interns:* responsibilities include maintaining files on correspondence and venues contacted,

researching potential venues, keeping the mailing list of potential venues up to date, assisting in the creation of exhibition kits, and mailing the kits to potential venues, coordinating exhibitions, maintaining the museum/gallery database, assisting with Burden Gallery openings. Candidates should have ability to work independently, oral communication skills, organizational skills, personal interest in the field, strong interpersonal skills, writing skills. Open to college juniors, college seniors, recent college graduates, graduate students. Duration for all positions is minimum of 6 months. All positions paid at $250 per month. International applications accepted.

Benefits Possible full-time employment, willing to act as a professional reference, willing to complete paperwork for educational credit, willing to provide letters of recommendation, print upon completion of internship.

Contact Write, call, fax, or e-mail Maria Decsey, Work-Scholar Coordinator. Phone: 212-505-5555. Fax: 212-979-7759. E-mail: mdecsey@aperture.org. In-person interview recommended. Applicants must submit a cover letter, resume, two writing samples. Applications are accepted continuously. World Wide Web: http://www.aperture.org.

APPLE ART GALLERY
49 Jobs Lane
Southampton, New York 11968

General Information Art gallery showing only the owner's work. Established in 1998. Number of employees: 2. Division of Apple Graphics and Advertising of Merrick, Inc., Merrick, New York. Number of internship applications received each year: 40.

Internships Available ► *3–10 gallery assistants:* responsibilities include interacting with clients, selling art, organizing, answering questions, answering the telephone, and credit card sales. Candidates should have ability to work independently, oral communication skills, personal interest in the field, self-motivation, strong interpersonal skills, strong leadership ability, reliability, timeliness, and honesty. Duration is flexible. Position available as unpaid or at 5% commission on each piece an intern sells. Open to high school students, high school graduates, college freshmen, college sophomores, college juniors, college seniors, recent college graduates, graduate students, law students, career changers, individuals reentering the workforce. International applications accepted.

Benefits On-the-job training, possible full-time employment, willing to act as a professional reference, willing to complete paperwork for educational credit, willing to provide letters of recommendation.

Contact Write or e-mail Allison Schneider, Partner, 2314 Merrick Road, Merrick, New York 11566. E-mail: perezowitz@aol.com. No phone calls. In-person interview recommended. Applicants must submit a cover letter, resume, photograph. Applications are accepted continuously.

ARTISTS SPACE
38 Greene Street, 3rd Floor
New York, New York 10013

General Information Nonprofit organization that supports emerging, under-recognized, and unaffiliated artists in the visual arts, including video, performance, architecture, and design. Established in 1973. Number of employees: 7. Number of internship applications received each year: 70.

Internships Available ► *1 artists file intern:* responsibilities include assisting Artist File Coordinator through updating database of artists, conducting appointments in the file, troubleshooting with the database, and possible Web site assistance if applicable. Candidates should have computer skills, personal interest in the field, self-motivation, strong interpersonal skills, strong art background, strong Macintosh skills. ► *1 curatorial intern:* responsibilities include working closely with curator and artists, reviewing artists' work, and assisting with events and exhibitions. Candidates should have ability to work independently, computer skills, personal interest in the field, self-motivation, strong art background. ► *Operations interns:* responsibilities include assisting with day-to-day operations of the gallery, working with Intern

Coordinator, participating in special projects, and dealing with past and present exhibitions. Candidates should have ability to work independently, computer skills, organizational skills, personal interest in the field, self-motivation, strong interpersonal skills. Duration for all positions is flexible. All positions are unpaid. Open to college freshmen, college sophomores, college juniors, college seniors, recent college graduates, graduate students. International applications accepted.
Benefits Job counseling, on-the-job training, willing to act as a professional reference, willing to complete paperwork for educational credit, willing to provide letters of recommendation, possibility of exhibiting samples of work, access to all NYC galleries and museums.
Contact Write, call, fax, or e-mail Ms. Tara McDowell, Internship/Volunteer Coordinator. Phone: 212-226-3970. Fax: 212-966-1434. E-mail: t.mcdowell@artistsspace.org. In-person interview recommended. Applicants must submit a formal organization application, cover letter, resume, two personal references. Applications are accepted continuously. World Wide Web: http://www.artistsspace.org.

ASIAN AMERICAN ARTS CENTRE
26 Bowery Street, 3rd Floor
New York, New York 10013

General Information Multipurpose facility that offers ongoing visual arts exhibitions of contemporary Asian-American and other culturally diverse arts as well as rehearsals/workshops. Established in 1974. Number of employees: 3. Number of internship applications received each year: 5.
Internships Available ▶ *1 curatorial intern:* responsibilities include working closely with the director, researching and organizing exhibitions. Candidates should have college courses in field, editing skills, knowledge of field, oral communication skills, personal interest in the field, strong interpersonal skills, written communication skills. Duration is 3 months or more. ▶ *1 development assistant:* responsibilities include researching funding resources, writing grant proposals, and assisting in preparing grants. Candidates should have editing skills, research skills, strong interpersonal skills, strong leadership ability, writing skills, written communication skills. Duration is 3 months or more. ▶ *2–3 gallery assistants:* responsibilities include various tasks depending on intern's abilities and interests. Candidates should have computer skills, knowledge of field, organizational skills, personal interest in the field, strong interpersonal skills, writing skills. Duration is 6–7 months. All positions are unpaid. Open to college freshmen, college sophomores, college juniors, college seniors, recent college graduates, graduate students. International applications accepted.
Benefits On-the-job training, willing to complete paperwork for educational credit, general training, opportunity to learn working processes in all areas of art and art administration.
Contact Write Mr. Robert Lee, Director, 26 Bowery Street, 3rd Floor, New York, New York 10013. In-person interview required. Applicants must submit a cover letter, resume. Applications are accepted continuously.

BARBARA STRASEN
1724 South Pacific Avenue
San Pedro, California 90731

General Information Freelance visual artist who makes paintings (often combined with photography, mixed media, and installations) for exhibition and sale to galleries and museums nationally and internationally. Number of employees: 2. Number of internship applications received each year: 10.
Internships Available ▶ *1–3 studio assistants/interns:* responsibilities include painting under tutelage, canvas building, preparation imagery research, literary research, professional correspondence, framing and presenting artwork, and manufacturing 2-D and 3-D components of artwork. Candidates should have ability to work independently, ability to work with others, college courses in field, oral communication skills, personal interest in the field, research skills. Duration is flexible. Unpaid. Open

to college seniors, recent college graduates, graduate students, career changers. International applications accepted.
Benefits Formal training, job counseling, names of contacts, on-the-job training, willing to act as a professional reference, willing to complete paperwork for educational credit, willing to provide letters of recommendation, use of research facilities.
Contact Write Ms. Barbara Strasen, Artist. No phone calls. In-person interview recommended. Applicants must submit a cover letter, resume, three letters of recommendation. Applications are accepted continuously.

BETSEY JOHNSON
498 Seventh Avenue, 21st Floor
New York, New York 10018

General Information Fashion designer showroom. Established in 1978. Number of employees: 60. Number of internship applications received each year: 100.
Internships Available ▶ *3–4 design interns:* responsibilities include assisting design team with fabric resourcing, arts and crafts, and running errands. ▶ *4–5 sales interns:* responsibilities include assisting sales executives and customer relations, compiling sketch and swatch booklets, typing line sheets and letters, filing, and running errands. Duration for all positions is flexible. All positions are unpaid. Open to recent high school graduates, college freshmen, college sophomores, college juniors, college seniors, recent college graduates. International applications accepted.
Benefits Possible full-time employment, willing to complete paperwork for educational credit, willing to provide letters of recommendation.
Contact Write or fax Joanna Levy, Internship Coordinator (sales), Mandy Black, Internship Coordinator (design). Fax: 212-244-0855. In-person interview recommended. Applicants must submit a cover letter, resume. Applications are accepted continuously.

BLAZING ADVENTURES
Box 5068
Snowmass Village, Colorado 81615

General Information Organization providing outdoor adventure tours. Established in 1979. Number of employees: 100. Number of internship applications received each year: 12.
Internships Available ▶ *1–2 group services interns:* responsibilities include assisting groups of guests with reservations in a knowledgeable and professional manner, resolving customer service issues and any operational problems, and utilizing the telephones and computers extensively to perform these responsibilities (all under the supervision of the group services director). Candidates should have computer skills, office skills, oral communication skills, organizational skills, self-motivation, strong interpersonal skills, written communication skills. ▶ *4–5 main office summer interns:* responsibilities include assisting guests with reservations in a knowledgeable and professional manner, resolving customer service issues and any operational problems, and utilizing the telephones and computers extensively to perform these responsibilities (all under the supervision of the office manager). Candidates should have computer skills, office skills, oral communication skills, organizational skills, self-motivation, strong interpersonal skills. Duration for all positions is May 15-August 31. All positions paid at $150 per week plus 2% sales commission. Open to college freshmen, college sophomores, college juniors, college seniors, recent college graduates, graduate students, law students, career changers, individuals reentering the workforce. International applications accepted.
Benefits Formal training, housing at a cost, job counseling, on-the-job training, possible full-time employment, willing to act as a professional reference, willing to complete paperwork for educational credit, willing to provide letters of recommendation.
Contact Write, call, fax, or e-mail Laurie Harris, Manager. Phone: 970-923-4544. Fax: 970-923-4994. E-mail: blazing@rof.net. Telephone interview required. Applicants must submit a formal organization application, resume, personal reference, 3-4 letters of recommendation. Application deadline: continuous, but May 1 preferred. World Wide Web: http://www.blazingadventures.com.

BRICK WALL MANAGEMENT
648 Amsterdam Avenue, #4A
New York, New York 10025

General Information Music artist management. Established in 1996. Number of employees: 2. Number of internship applications received each year: 50.
Internships Available ▶ *1–3 general interns:* responsibilities include general office administration. Candidates should have ability to work independently, computer skills, office skills, oral communication skills, organizational skills, personal interest in the field, plan to pursue career in field, research skills, strong interpersonal skills, writing skills. Duration is 3–5 months. Unpaid. Open to college freshmen, college sophomores, college juniors, college seniors, recent college graduates, career changers. International applications accepted.
Benefits On-the-job training, willing to act as a professional reference, willing to provide letters of recommendation.
Contact Write, fax, or e-mail Anthony Daddabbo. Fax: 212-724-0849. E-mail: bweast@bwmgmt.com. No phone calls. In-person interview recommended. Applicants must submit a cover letter, resume. Applications are accepted continuously. World Wide Web: http://www.brickwallmgmt.com.

BRISTOL-MYERS SQUIBB- CENTER FOR HEALTH AND FITNESS
1 Squibb Drive
New Brunswick, New Jersey 08903

General Information Corporate employee health and fitness center. Number of internship applications received each year: 6.
Internships Available ▶ *1–2 health and fitness interns:* responsibilities include working with participants to complete fitness assessments and exercise prescriptions, assisting in operation of facility and opening/closing routines. Candidates should have ability to work independently, college courses in field, oral communication skills, personal interest in the field, self-motivation, strong interpersonal skills, CPR certification. Duration is 1 semester. Unpaid. Open to college freshmen, college sophomores, college juniors, college seniors, recent college graduates. International applications accepted.
Benefits Names of contacts, possible full-time employment, willing to act as a professional reference, willing to provide letters of recommendation.
Contact Write or call Sharon Combes-Kelemen, Supervisor of Health and Fitness, 1 Squibb Lane, New Brunswick, New Jersey 08903. Phone: 732-519-3900. In-person interview required. Applicants must submit a resume, academic transcripts. Applications are accepted continuously.

CAMPBELL SOUP COMPANY, HEALTH AND FITNESS CENTER
One Campbell Road
Camden, New Jersey 08103

General Information Health and fitness center for World Headquarter's employees, spouses, and retirees. Number of internship applications received each year: 10.
Internships Available ▶ *Interns:* responsibilities include working directly with exercise physiologists to assist in the administration, planning, and implementation of all health and fitness services programs by doing fitness evaluations, development of fitness programs, floor supervision, and class leadership. Candidates should have declared college major in field, personal interest in the field, strong interpersonal skills. Unpaid. Open to college juniors, college seniors. International applications accepted.
Benefits Names of contacts, on-the-job training, willing to act as a professional reference, willing to complete paperwork for educational credit, willing to provide letters of recommendation.
Contact Write, call, fax, or e-mail Bill Craig, Manager, Health and Fitness Center, One Campbell Place, Box 84, Camden, New Jersey 08103. Phone: 609-342-3940. Fax: 609-968-2984. E-mail: bill_craig@campbellsoup.com. In-person interview recommended. Applicants must submit a cover letter, resume. Applications are accepted continuously.

CAROL BANCROFT AND FRIENDS
PO Box 266, 121 Dodgingtown Road
Bethel, Connecticut 06801

General Information Organization that specializes in art for children's and young adults' publications, represents over 50 artists, and acts as an agent for illustrators. Established in 1973. Number of employees: 2. Number of internship applications received each year: 10.
Internships Available ▶ *1 promotional assistant:* responsibilities include assembling promotion packets, packaging and logging art on loan to clients, original art retrieving, caring for artist samples, and performing general clerical tasks. Candidates should have ability to work independently, knowledge of field, oral communication skills, organizational skills, personal interest in the field, plan to pursue career in field, self-motivation. Duration is flexible. Unpaid. Open to college freshmen, college sophomores, college juniors, college seniors, recent college graduates, individuals reentering the workforce. International applications accepted.
Benefits Names of contacts, on-the-job training, opportunity to attend seminars/workshops, willing to act as a professional reference, willing to complete paperwork for educational credit, willing to provide letters of recommendation, stipend upon completion of internship.
Contact Write, call, or fax Carol Bancroft, Artist Agent. Phone: 203-748-4823. Fax: 203-748-5481. In-person interview required. Applicants must submit a cover letter, resume. Applications are accepted continuously.

CASTILLO CULTURAL CENTER
500 Greenwich Street, #201
New York, New York 10013

General Information Independent multicultural arts center housing off-off-Broadway Castillo Theatre, a laboratory for developmental theater, extensive inner-city youth programs, and book publishing. Established in 1983. Number of employees: 25. Division of Community Literacy Research Project, Inc., New York, New York. Number of internship applications received each year: 75.
Internships Available ▶ *10–15 community literacy research project/ nonprofit management interns:* responsibilities include assisting in cultivation research, volunteer recruitment, marketing, and fundraising. Candidates should have ability to work independently, oral communication skills, self-motivation, strong interpersonal skills. Duration is minimum 3 months (preferred); one weeknight or daytime weekend shift per week. Open to college freshmen, college sophomores, college juniors, college seniors, recent college graduates, graduate students, law students, career changers, individuals reentering the workforce. ▶ *2–4 public relations/ marketing interns:* responsibilities include working with skilled publicist promoting off-off-Broadway theater and nonprofit development programs for inner-city youth; hands-on experience dealing with major media outlets in the largest media market in the U.S.; weekly house staff (ushering) assignment and weekly support shift part of internship requirement. Candidates should have ability to work independently, computer skills, office skills, oral communication skills, personal interest in the field, strong interpersonal skills, English language skills required. Duration is minimum 3 months (preferred) including weekday hours. Open to college freshmen, college sophomores, college juniors, college seniors, recent college graduates, graduate students, career changers, individuals reentering the workforce. ▶ *3–6 theater costume design/construction and wardrobe interns:* responsibilities include working with resident designer at the Castillo Theatre; costume construction, makeup, wardrobe; qualified interns may participate in design; weekly house staff (ushering) and weekly support shift part of internship requirement. Candidates should have ability to work independently, ability to work with others, experience in the field, oral communication skills, personal interest in the field, self-motivation. Duration is

minimum 3 months; evenings and weekends preferred. Open to college freshmen, college sophomores, college juniors, college seniors, recent college graduates, graduate students, career changers, individuals reentering the workforce. ▶ *3–6 theater lighting design and engineering interns:* responsibilities include working with resident designer to produce lighting for Castillo Theatre; electrics, engineering; qualified interns may assist in design; weekly house staff (ushering) and weekly support shift part of internship requirement. Candidates should have ability to work independently, ability to work with others, experience in the field, oral communication skills, personal interest in the field, self-motivation. Duration is minimum 3 months (preferred) evenings and weekends only. Open to recent high school graduates, college freshmen, college sophomores, college juniors, college seniors, recent college graduates, graduate students, career changers, individuals reentering the workforce. ▶ *3–6 theater management and administration interns:* responsibilities include working with managing director of growing off-off-Broadway theater; hands-on experience in scheduling, budget mangement, staff development, audience building, volunteer recruitment, and theatrical and event production; weekly house staff (ushering) assignment and weekly support shift as part of internship requirement. Candidates should have computer skills, office skills, organizational skills, personal interest in the field, self-motivation, strong interpersonal skills. Duration is minimum 3 months (preferred); flexible am/pm hours. Open to college freshmen, college sophomores, college juniors, college seniors, recent college graduates, graduate students, law students, career changers, individuals reentering the workforce. ▶ *4–8 theater production assistants/stage hands:* responsibilities include assisting producers and stage managers at the Castillo Theatre; attendance at rehearsals required; weekly house staff assignments and a weekly support shift part of internship requirement. Candidates should have ability to work independently, computer skills, oral communication skills, organizational skills, personal interest in the field, strong interpersonal skills. Duration is minimum 3 months (preferred); evenings and some weekends. Open to college freshmen, college sophomores, college juniors, college seniors, recent college graduates, graduate students, career changers, individuals reentering the workforce. ▶ *4–8 theater set construction and scenic painting interns:* responsibilities include working with resident designer to produce sets for Castillo Theatre productions; research, construction, scenic painting; qualified interns may assist in design; weekly house staff (ushering) and weekly support shift part of internship requirement. Candidates should have ability to work independently, ability to work with others, experience in the field, oral communication skills, personal interest in the field, self-motivation, theater experience preferred. Duration is minimum 3 months (preferred); flexible hours including evenings. Open to recent high school graduates, college freshmen, college sophomores, college juniors, college seniors, recent college graduates, career changers, individuals reentering the workforce. ▶ *2–4 theater sound design and engineering interns:* responsibilities include working with resident designer at Castillo Theatre; research, sound engineering; weekly staff (ushering) and weekly support shift part of internship requirement. Candidates should have ability to work independently, ability to work with others, oral communication skills, personal interest in the field, research skills, self-motivation. Duration is minimum 3 months (preferred); flexible hours evenings and weekends. Open to college freshmen, college sophomores, college juniors, college seniors, recent college graduates, graduate students, career changers, individuals reentering the workforce. ▶ *4–8 video design and engineering interns:* responsibilities include hands-on experience in cinematography, lighting, audio, and video editing in a fast-paced creative environment; weekly house staff (ushering) and weekly support shift part of internship requirement. Candidates should have ability to work independently, ability to work with others, computer skills, experience in the field, oral communication skills, self-motivation. Duration is minimum 3 months (preferred); flexible hours. Open to college freshmen, college sophomores, college juniors, college seniors, recent college graduates, graduate students, career changers, individuals reentering the workforce. All positions are unpaid. International applications accepted.

Benefits Names of contacts, on-the-job training, opportunity to attend seminars/workshops, willing to act as a professional reference, willing to complete paperwork for educational credit, willing to provide letters of recommendation, credit available for most positions.
Contact Write, call, fax, or e-mail Gail Elberg, Internship Coordinator. Phone: 212-941-5800. Fax: 212-941-8340. E-mail: castilloth@aol.com. Telephone interview required. Applicants must submit a cover letter, resume. Applications are accepted continuously. World Wide Web: http://www.castillo.org.

CENTER FOR PHOTOGRAPHY AT WOODSTOCK
59 Tinker Street
Woodstock, New York 12498

General Information Nonprofit arts organization dedicated to promoting excellence in photography and the related arts through exhibition, publication, and education. Number of employees: 4. Number of internship applications received each year: 30.
Internships Available ▶ *1 arts administration intern:* responsibilities include working in the Center's galleries as an administrative assistant, exploring programs and exhibitions, and assisting in the production of the *Center Quarterly* and other publications. Duration is 3 months. ▶ *4 photography workshop interns/assistants:* responsibilities include assisting in Woodstock Photography Workshops program, a summer and fall of workshops involving nationally recognized artists. Staff handles publicity, hospitality, event facilitation, program documentation, and various administrative duties. Duration is 4 months (June-September). Candidates for all positions should have experience in the field, personal interest in the field, strong interpersonal skills. All positions are unpaid. International applications accepted.
Benefits Formal training, names of contacts, opportunity to attend seminars/workshops, possible full-time employment, travel reimbursement, willing to complete paperwork for educational credit, willing to provide letters of recommendation, use of darkrooms, $3000 tuition remission for photography workshop internships.
Contact Write or fax Kathleen Kenyon, Associate Director. Fax: 914-679-6337. In-person interview required. Resume, portfolio, 2 personal references for photography workshop internships. Application deadline: March/April for personal interviews (photography workshop). World Wide Web: http://users.aol.com/epwphoto.

CIRCLE IN THE SQUARE THEATRE SCHOOL
1633 Broadway
New York, New York 10019-6795

General Information Theater school preparing tomorrow's working actors with professional training. Established in 1961. Number of employees: 23. Number of internship applications received each year: 5.
Internships Available ▶ *1 assistant stage manager.* Candidates should have ability to work independently, experience in the field, strong interpersonal skills, willingness to perform all theater-related work. Duration is September to June. Open to recent college graduates, graduate students, career changers, individuals reentering the workforce. ▶ *1 theater school assistant:* responsibilities include scheduling and monitoring auditions, acting as production assistant for school projects, performing administrative tasks, and specifically helping with creation of study guides. Candidates should have computer skills, office skills, oral communication skills, research skills, strong interpersonal skills, written communication skills. All positions are unpaid. International applications accepted.
Benefits On-the-job training, willing to complete paperwork for educational credit, willing to provide letters of recommendation.
Contact Write Dr. Rhonda Dodd, Associate Director of School. E-mail: circleinthesquare@juno.com. No phone calls. In-person interview required. Applicants must submit a cover letter, resume. Applications are accepted continuously. World Wide Web: http://www.circlesquare.org.

CITYARTS, INC.
525 Broadway, Suite 700
New York, New York 10012

General Information CityArts is a 30-year-old nonprofit organization dedicated to the creation of public artworks that are responsive to the needs of individual communities throughout New York City. Established in 1968. Number of employees: 2. Number of internship applications received each year: 60.

Internships Available ▶ *10–20 artist assistants:* responsibilities include working at the mural site, supervising young participants, and assisting the artist in all phases of the project from workshop to wall. Candidates should have ability to work with others, personal interest in the field, strong leadership ability, some interest in working with children. Duration is dependent on project availability. ▶ *1–4 clerical interns:* responsibilities include providing general office support such as phones, errands, filing. Candidates should have computer skills, office skills, oral communication skills, organizational skills, strong interpersonal skills. Duration is dependent on students' availability. ▶ *1–4 fundraising interns:* responsibilities include researching corporate and foundation sources, preparing grant applications and support materials, helping with fund-raising events, and assisting in planning fund-raising strategies. Candidates should have analytical skills, oral communication skills, organizational skills, research skills, self-motivation, writing skills. Duration is dependent on students' availability. ▶ *1–2 marketing/promotions interns:* responsibilities include developing marketing strategies for CityArts' products and services, researching markets, and creating promotional materials. Candidates should have ability to work independently, computer skills, personal interest in the field, research skills, self-motivation, writing skills. Duration is dependent on students' availability. ▶ *1–4 public relations interns:* responsibilities include organizing and monitoring CityArts mailing list, updating and expanding press contact lists, preparing press releases, and researching possibilities for media coverage. Candidates should have computer skills, editing skills, oral communication skills, self-motivation, written communication skills. Duration is dependent on students' availability. All positions are unpaid. Open to high school students, high school seniors, recent high school graduates, college freshmen, college sophomores, college juniors, college seniors, recent college graduates, graduate students, law students, career changers, individuals reentering the workforce. International applications accepted.

Benefits Formal training, willing to act as a professional reference, willing to complete paperwork for educational credit, willing to provide letters of recommendation.

Contact Write or call Ms. Tsipi Ben-Haim, Executive Director, 525 Broadway, Suite 700, New York, New York 10012. Phone: 212-966-0377. In-person interview recommended. Applicants must submit a cover letter, resume. Applications are accepted continuously. World Wide Web: http://www.cityarts.org.

COLORADO COUNCIL ON THE ARTS
750 Pennsylvania Street
Denver, Colorado 80203-3699

General Information State arts agency that awards grants to arts organizations and artists and promotes the arts in Colorado. Established in 1967. Number of employees: 8. Unit of State of Colorado, Department of Higher Education, Denver, Colorado. Number of internship applications received each year: 12.

Internships Available ▶ *1 Arts in Public Places intern:* responsibilities include assisting director in administration of program. Candidates should have ability to work independently, college courses in field, computer skills, oral communication skills, personal interest in the field, written communication skills. ▶ *1 artist promotion intern:* responsibilities include helping to develop and arrange promotional opportunities for artists. ▶ *1 communications intern:* responsibilities include developing and monitoring agency communications, including press releases, newsletter, brochures, and Web site. Candidates should have ability to work independently, college courses in field, computer skills, oral communication skills, personal interest in the field, written communication skills. Duration for all positions is 3–12 months. All positions are unpaid. Open to college freshmen, college sophomores, college juniors, college seniors, recent college graduates, graduate students, career changers. International applications accepted.

Benefits Job counseling, names of contacts, opportunity to attend seminars/workshops, willing to complete paperwork for educational credit, willing to provide letters of recommendation.

Contact Write or e-mail Internship Coordinator, 750 Pennsylvania Street, Denverq, Colorado 80203-3699. E-mail: coloarts@artswire.org. No phone calls. In-person interview recommended. Applicants must submit a cover letter, resume. Applications are accepted continuously. World Wide Web: http://www.state.co.us/gov_dir/a.

COMMUNITY ARTS ADMINISTRATION INTERNSHIP PROGRAM, NORTH CAROLINA ARTS COUNCIL
Department of Cultural Resources
Raleigh, North Carolina 27601-2807

General Information Council that works to enrich the cultural life of the state by nurturing and supporting excellence in the arts and providing opportunities for every North Carolinian to experience the arts. Established in 1974. Number of employees: 24. Division of North Carolina Arts Council/Department of Cultural Resources, Raleigh, North Carolina. Number of internship applications received each year: 35.

Internships Available ▶ *4 interns:* responsibilities include grants writing, fund-raising, financial management, interagency relationships, programming, planning, community arts administration, organizational structure. Candidates should have ability to work independently, college courses in field, oral communication skills, organizational skills, personal interest in the field, plan to pursue career in field, self-motivation, strong interpersonal skills, strong leadership ability. Duration is 3 months. $1,000 per month. Open to recent college graduates, career changers, individuals reentering the workforce. International applications accepted.

Benefits Possible full-time employment, willing to provide letters of recommendation.

Contact Write, call, fax, or e-mail Viola Bullock, Arts in Community Program Assistant. Phone: 919-733-7897 Ext. 29. Fax: 919-715-5406. E-mail: vbullock@ncacmail.dcr.state.nc.us. Applicants must submit a formal organization application, cover letter, resume, in-person interview for persons accepted. Application deadline: May 1 for September-June of following year. World Wide Web: http://www.ncarts.org.

CONNIE ROGERS INC., CURATORIAL CONSULTANTS
152 East 94th Street
New York, New York 10128

General Information Art consulting firm that assembles large art collections, primarily contemporary, for major corporations and advises on acquisitions in impressionist and modern art for private collections. Established in 1979. Number of employees: 3.

Internships Available ▶ *3 interns:* responsibilities include performing administrative tasks, working with slide archives, photo documenting, cataloging art, and inventorying. Candidates should have analytical skills, computer skills, office skills, organizational skills, personal interest in the field, research skills. Duration is flexible. Unpaid. Open to college sophomores, college juniors, college seniors, recent college graduates, graduate students, career changers, individuals reentering the workforce.

Benefits Job counseling, names of contacts, on-the-job training, possible full-time employment, willing to complete paperwork for educational credit, willing to provide letters of recommendation, invitations to art gallery openings.

Contact Write or call Ms. Connie Rogers, Principal. Phone: 212-410-3492. Applicants must submit a cover letter, resume, call to follow up letter. Applications are accepted continuously.

CORNERSTONE HEALTH & FITNESS
Box 1308
Doylestown, Pennsylvania 18901

General Information Health and fitness center. Established in 1995. Number of employees: 60. Number of internship applications received each year: 30.
Internships Available ▶ *2–6 student interns:* responsibilities include fitness assessment, exercise prescription, nutrition counseling, exercise programming for special populations, project development, facility management, program administration, marketing, customer service, and attending lectures. Candidates should have declared college major in field, knowledge of field, oral communication skills, plan to pursue career in field, strong interpersonal skills, strong leadership ability, current CPR certification, personal liability insurance. Duration is variable as deemed appropriate through university requirements. Unpaid. Open to college sophomores, college juniors, college seniors, graduate students. International applications accepted.
Benefits Formal training, job counseling, names of contacts, on-the-job training, opportunity to attend seminars/workshops, possible full-time employment, willing to act as a professional reference, willing to complete paperwork for educational credit, willing to provide letters of recommendation.
Contact Write, call, or fax Nancy Zambraski, Internship Coordinator, PO Box 1308, Doylestown, Pennsylvania 18901. Phone: 215-794-3700. Fax: 215-794-3922. In-person interview required. Applicants must submit a cover letter, resume, three personal references. Applications are accepted continuously.

CORPORATE FITNESS WORKS
18558 Office Park Drive
Montgomery Village, Maryland 20886

General Information A health promotion and fitness management firm that customizes health promotion programs for businesses, government agencies, and office park developers. Services range from providing on-site wellness/fitness management, health risk appraisals, health fairs, health screenings, facility design/layout, equipment purchase, and program consulting. Established in 1988. Number of employees: 6. Number of internship applications received each year: 100.
Internships Available ▶ *1–30 fitness specialists:* responsibilities include administering physical fitness assessments, developing individualized programs, supervising the exercise room, teaching classes or clinics, and assisting with the center newsletter. Candidates should have college courses in field, computer skills, declared college major in field, organizational skills, strong interpersonal skills. Duration is 12–16 weeks. Unpaid. Open to college juniors, college seniors, recent college graduates, graduate students. International applications accepted.
Benefits Formal training, job counseling, names of contacts, on-the-job training, opportunity to attend seminars/workshops, possible full-time employment, willing to act as a professional reference, willing to complete paperwork for educational credit, willing to provide letters of recommendation.
Contact Fax or e-mail Kelley Monahan, Internship Administrator, 18558 Office Park Drive, Montgomery Village, Maryland 20886. Fax: 301-417-0651. E-mail: kmonahan@corporatefitnessworks.com. No phone calls. Applications are accepted continuously. World Wide Web: http://www.corporatefitnessworks.com.

CREATIVE TIME, INC.
307 Seventh Avenue, Suite 1904
New York, New York 10001

General Information Public arts organization presenting multidisciplinary artworks in the public setting in and around New York City. Established in 1973. Number of employees: 5. Number of internship applications received each year: 75.
Internships Available ▶ *1 Web assistant:* responsibilities include developing Web site to reflect current and upcoming programming and maintaining and expanding Web archives. Candidates should have ability to work independently, computer skills, organizational skills, personal interest in the field, research skills,

self-motivation, Macintosh experience preferred, but not required. ▶ *1–4 general administrative assistants:* responsibilities include assisting staff with general office duties for hands-on experience with the basic functions of art administration, programming, and development; includes assisting with preparation of proposals for funding, maintaining membership records, conducting correspondence, and helping with special events. Candidates should have ability to work independently, computer skills, office skills, personal interest in the field, self-motivation, written communication skills. ▶ *10 on-site assistants:* responsibilities include assisting visual and performing artists, architects, and site manager to assemble and dismantle art exhibitions; overseeing exhibition hours, greeting and informing public, maintaining site, assisting sound-and-light technicians and performers during performances; collecting tickets; and seating audience. Candidates should have ability to work independently, personal interest in the field, self-motivation, strong interpersonal skills. ▶ *1 public relations assistant:* responsibilities include helping to organize each show and opening, sending out press releases and announcements, answering telephones, typing correspondence, taking reservations for performance series, updating mailing lists, and distributing posters. Candidates should have ability to work independently, computer skills, editing skills, office skills, oral communication skills, personal interest in the field, self-motivation, writing skills. Duration for all positions is flexible. All positions are unpaid. Open to college freshmen, college sophomores, college juniors, college seniors, recent college graduates, graduate students. International applications accepted.
Benefits Job counseling, names of contacts, possible full-time employment, willing to complete paperwork for educational credit, willing to provide letters of recommendation, hands-on art experience.
Contact Write or call Ms. Jennifer Charron, Internships Coordinator. Phone: 212-206-6674. In person interview recommended. Applicants must submit a cover letter, resume. Applications are accepted continuously. World Wide Web: http://www.creativetime.org.

CULTUREFINDER, INC.
850 Seventh Avenue, Suite 703
New York, New York 10019-5230

General Information Leading Web site for arts information on the Web and AOL covering Broadway, theater, classical music, opera, dance, jazz and the visual arts. Established in 1995. Number of employees: 19. Number of internship applications received each year: 150.
Internships Available ▶ *1 business development intern:* responsibilities include working with business development, sales, marketing, and other departments as needed. This intern will have broad exposure to the entire business and will work on projects as needed by these departments. Candidates should have computer skills, office skills, organizational skills, self-motivation, strong interpersonal skills. Duration is 12–15 weeks. Position available as unpaid or paid. Open to college freshmen, college sophomores, college juniors, college seniors, recent college graduates. ▶ *1 editorial intern:* responsibilities include working with our editorial staff on developing editorial content from regular weekly publishing to special project developoment. You will have the opportunity to write and learn online publishing. Candidates should have computer skills, editing skills, personal interest in the field, self-motivation, strong interpersonal skills, writing skills. Duration is 12–15 weeks. Position available as unpaid or at up to $100 per week. Open to college freshmen, college sophomores, college juniors, college seniors, recent college graduates. ▶ *1 event listings/ticketing intern:* responsibilities include working in our calendar department to help develop our national weekly event listings, learning the dynamics of our day-to-day online ticketing operations, and working on individual projects. Candidates should have ability to work independently, computer skills, organizational skills, personal interest in the field, writing skills. Duration is 12–15 weeks. Position available as unpaid or paid. Open to college freshmen, college sophomores, college juniors, college seniors, recent college graduates. ▶ *2 production assistants:* responsibilities include assisting the producer

CultureFinder, Inc. (continued)

with day-to-day publishing responsibilities on the Web and AOL including editing text and graphics. Candidates should have ability to work independently, computer skills, knowledge of field, oral communication skills, organizational skills, personal interest in the field, self-motivation, written communication skills, proactive approach; interest and/or experience in the arts highly recommended. Duration is 3 months. stipend. Open to college freshmen, college sophomores, college juniors, college seniors, recent college graduates, graduate students, career changers, individuals reentering the workforce. ▶ *1 production intern:* responsibilities include day-to-day online publishing on the Web and AOL, as well as project work in our production department. Candidates should have computer skills, knowledge of field, self-motivation, HTML plus Photoshop. Duration is 12–15 weeks. Position available as unpaid or at up to $100 per week. Open to college freshmen, college sophomores, college juniors, college seniors, recent college graduates. International applications accepted.

Benefits Names of contacts, on-the-job training, willing to act as a professional reference, willing to complete paperwork for educational credit, willing to provide letters of recommendation.

Contact Fax or e-mail Andrea Gerson, Internship Coordinator. Fax: 212-765-4277. E-mail: cfintern@aol.com. No phone calls. In-person interview recommended. Applicants must submit a cover letter, resume. Application deadline: April 30 for summer, July 15 for fall, December 15 for spring. World Wide Web: http://www.culturefinder.com (AOL Keyword: culturefinder).

DACTYL FOUNDATION FOR THE ARTS AND HUMANITIES
64 Grand Street
New York, New York 10013

General Information Not-for-profit organization that offers opportunities and awards in the fields of visual arts, film, theory, music, poetry, and lectures. Established in 1996. Number of employees: 5. Number of internship applications received each year: 25.

Internships Available ▶ *4–10 intern/gallery assistants:* responsibilities include working as gallery attendant, updating database, event planning, telephone work, and assisting the managing director in public relations, fund-raising, membership, and general operating support. Candidates should have computer skills, knowledge of field, office skills, oral communication skills, self-motivation, written communication skills. Position available as unpaid or at hourly pay for evening events. Open to recent high school graduates, college freshmen, college sophomores, college juniors, college seniors, recent college graduates, graduate students. International applications accepted.

Benefits On-the-job training, travel reimbursement, willing to act as a professional reference, willing to complete paperwork for educational credit, willing to provide letters of recommendation.

Contact Write, call, fax, or e-mail Carrie Spafford, Managing Director. Phone: 212-219-2344. Fax: 212-226-7320. E-mail: email@dactyl.org. In-person interview required. Applicants must submit a cover letter, resume. Applications are accepted continuously. World Wide Web: http://www.dactyl.org.

DAVID FINDLAY, JR. FINE ART
41 East 57th Street, Suite 1115
New York, New York 10022-1908

General Information American 19th- and early 20th-century painting and sculpture gallery. Established in 1870. Number of employees: 2. Number of internship applications received each year: 30.

Internships Available ▶ *2–3 fall and winter interns:* responsibilities include working on projects involving aspects of the gallery's operations including administrative tasks, inventories, photographing paintings, catalog layout and research, organizing artist's files, researching master paintings, developing marketing programs for particular works, exhibitions, and scheduling. Duration is flexible. Open to college freshmen, college sophomores, college juniors, college seniors, recent college graduates, gradu-

ate students, career changers. ▶ *3 summer interns:* responsibilities include working on projects involving aspects of the gallery's operations including administrative tasks, inventories, photographing paintings, catalog layouts and research, organizing artist files, researching master paintings, developing marketing programs for particular works, exhibitions, and scheduling. Duration is 1 month. Open to college freshmen, college sophomores, college juniors, college seniors, recent college graduates, graduate students. Candidates for all positions should have computer skills, oral communication skills, personal interest in the field, research skills, writing skills, written communication skills. All positions are unpaid. International applications accepted.

Benefits Job counseling, names of contacts, willing to complete paperwork for educational credit, willing to provide letters of recommendation, paid lunch.

Contact Write, call, fax, or e-mail Anne Wayson, Assistant Director, 41 East 57th Street, Suite 1115, New York, New York 10022-1908. Phone: 212-486-7660. Fax: 212-980-2650. E-mail: gallery@findlayart.com. In-person interview required. Applicants must submit a cover letter, resume. Applications are accepted continuously. World Wide Web: http://www.findlayart.com.

THE DAY OF THE CHILD WORLD CONCERT, INC.
155 South Palm Canyon Drive, Suite A25
Palm Springs, California 92262

General Information Children's charity entertainment company. Established in 1998. Number of employees: 4.

Internships Available ▶ *1–3 administration directors:* responsibilities include performing office duties including computer work. Candidates should have ability to work independently, computer skills, office skills, self-motivation, writing skills. Duration is flexible. Position available as unpaid or paid. Open to high school students, high school seniors, recent high school graduates, college freshmen, college sophomores, college juniors, college seniors, recent college graduates, graduate students, career changers, individuals reentering the workforce.

Benefits Formal training, job counseling, names of contacts, on-the-job training, possible full-time employment, willing to act as a professional reference, willing to complete paperwork for educational credit, willing to provide letters of recommendation.

Contact Fax or e-mail Robert Cipriano, President, 155 South Palm Canyon Drive, Suite A25, Palm Springs, California 92262. Fax: 760-320-0095. E-mail: 1congroup@earthlink.net. In-person interview recommended. Applicants must submit a cover letter, writing sample, two personal references, letter of recommendation. Applications are accepted continuously.

THE DIRECTOR'S COMPANY
311 West 43rd, Suite 307
New York, New York 10036

General Information Theater that specializes in the development of the director. Established in 1980. Number of employees: 4.

Internships Available ▶ *2–3 interns:* responsibilities include performing general office duties and working on projects during rehearsals. Candidates should have ability to work with others, computer skills, experience in the field, self-motivation, writing skills, written communication skills. Duration is 3 months minimum. Position available as unpaid or paid. Open to high school seniors, recent high school graduates, college freshmen, college sophomores, college juniors, college seniors, recent college graduates, graduate students. International applications accepted.

Benefits Opportunity to attend seminars/workshops, possible full-time employment, willing to complete paperwork for educational credit, willing to provide letters of recommendation.

Contact Write or fax Sarah Orth, Internship Coordinator. Fax: 212-246-5882. No phone calls. In-person interview recommended. Applicants must submit a cover letter, resume. Applications are accepted continuously.

DISABLED SPORTS USA- FAR WEST
PO Box 9780
Truckee, California 96162

General Information An organization that provides high challenge sports to people with physical, cognitive, or developmental disabilities. Established in 1967. Number of employees: 50. Program of Disabled Sports USA- Far West, Citrus Heights, California. Number of internship applications received each year: 20.

Internships Available ▶ *2 Tahoe Adaptive Ski School winter interns:* responsibilities include involvement in all aspects of an adaptive ski program; attending clinics; assisting and teaching lessons; working on outreach, fund-raising, and other administrative projects. Candidates should have ability to work independently, computer skills, oral communication skills, strong interpersonal skills, written communication skills, strong intermediate alpine skiing abilities. Duration is December to April (4 days per week). Open to college sophomores, college juniors, college seniors, recent college graduates, graduate students, career changers, individuals reentering the workforce. ▶ *1–3 program assistants for executive offices:* responsibilities include recreation program design and implementation/administration, client registration and follow-up, volunteer and equipment coordination. Candidates should have ability to work independently, ability to work with others, office skills, oral communication skills, organizational skills, written communication skills. Duration is June to August, 3 to 4 days per week. Open to college sophomores, college juniors, college seniors, recent college graduates, graduate students, law students, career changers. ▶ *Summer interns:* responsibilities include leading and assisting with white water rafting, waterskiing, and the Donner Lake camp-outs summer programs. Candidates should have oral communication skills, organizational skills, strong interpersonal skills, strong leadership ability, background in camping, waterskiing, or rafting helpful. Duration is June to August (3 days per week). Open to college sophomores, college juniors, college seniors, recent college graduates, graduate students, career changers, individuals reentering the workforce. All positions are unpaid. International applications accepted.

Benefits Formal training, housing at a cost, meals at a cost, names of contacts, on-the-job training, opportunity to attend seminars/workshops, possible full-time employment, willing to act as a professional reference, willing to complete paperwork for educational credit, willing to provide letters of recommendation, skiing priveleges, $100 per month stipend.

Contact Write, call, fax, or e-mail Katherine Hayes Rodriguez, Program Director, PO Box 9780, Truckee, California 96162. Phone: 530-581-4161. Fax: 530-581-3127. E-mail: dsusatahoe@truckee.net. In-person interview recommended. Applicants must submit a formal organization application, cover letter, resume, three personal references, written response to 6 questions. Application deadline: April 15 for summer, October 31 for winter/spring. World Wide Web: http://www.dsusafw.org.

FRANKLIN FURNACE ARCHIVE, INC.
45 John Street, Suite 611
New York, New York 10038-3706

General Information Production entity focused primarily on getting performance art on the World Wide Web. Established in 1976. Number of employees: 4. Number of internship applications received each year: 100.

Internships Available ▶ *1–1,000 volunteers:* responsibilities include working with artists, fund-raising and development, administration, technical assistance, Web site maintenance and development, production assistance (cable TV/film), and archiving/cataloging of artists' information. Candidates should have love of contemporary art. Duration is flexible. Unpaid. Open to high school students, high school seniors, recent high school graduates, college freshmen, college sophomores, college juniors, college seniors, recent college graduates, graduate students, law students, career changers, individuals reentering the workforce. International applications accepted.

Benefits Job counseling, names of contacts, on-the-job training, opportunity to attend seminars/workshops, willing to act as a professional reference, willing to complete paperwork for educational credit, willing to provide letters of recommendation.

Contact Write, call, fax, or e-mail Harley Spiller, Internship Coordinator. Phone: 212-766-2606. Fax: 212-766-2740. E-mail: harley@franklinfurnace.org. Applicants must submit a cover letter, resume, in-person interview recommended (telephone or e-mail interview acceptable). Applications are accepted continuously. World Wide Web: http://www.franklinfurnace.org.

GREATER LYNN YMCA
20 Neptune Boulevard
Lynn, Massachusetts 01902

General Information Organization that provides health and recreation services to the residents of Lynn and surrounding communities. Established in 1873. Number of employees: 25.

Internships Available ▶ *1 active older adult assistant:* responsibilities include developing senior program in aquatics and fitness areas. Duration is 12 months. ▶ *1–2 aquatic assistants:* responsibilities include promoting and marketing aquatic program for all ages. Duration is 10 months. ▶ *1 fitness assistant:* responsibilities include assisting fitness directors with aerobic classes and fitness assessments. Candidates should have knowledge of field, oral communication skills, personal interest in the field, plan to pursue career in field, strong interpersonal skills. Duration is 12 months. Open to college freshmen, college sophomores, college juniors, college seniors, recent college graduates. ▶ *1–3 youth counselors:* responsibilities include supervising and planning new youth program which includes school-age drop-in, high school drop-in, and formal aquatic and fitness classes. Duration is 10 months. All positions are unpaid. International applications accepted.

Benefits Names of contacts, possible full-time employment, willing to complete paperwork for educational credit, willing to provide letters of recommendation.

Contact Write or call Elaine V. Kurkul, Branch Director. Phone: 781-581-3105. In-person interview required. Applications are accepted continuously.

HEADLANDS CENTER FOR THE ARTS
Building 944, Fort Barry
Sausalito, California 94965

General Information Interdisciplinary art center that provides residencies across the country and abroad for artists from the Bay Area, commissions artists to develop unique functional spaces in its quarters (which is a 1907 former army barracks building), and provides programs for the public, including art talks, open houses, and publications. Established in 1982. Number of employees: 12. Number of internship applications received each year: 50.

Internships Available ▶ *2–4 interns:* responsibilities include assisting artists in redeveloping spaces or researching and creating a slide library; performing administrative duties including slide library documentation, publicity, membership management, and events coordination; building duties, including research and construction; assisting national and international artists-in-residence periodically in constructing installations and special projects; and processing residency applications. Candidates should have ability to work independently, ability to work with others, computer skills, office skills, organizational skills, plan to pursue career in field. Duration is flexible, typically 6 weeks. Unpaid. Open to college seniors, recent college graduates, graduate students. International applications accepted.

Benefits Free housing, meals at a cost, opportunity to attend seminars/workshops, willing to complete paperwork for educational credit, willing to provide letters of recommendation, free attendance at all activities, readings, and art talks.

Contact Write, call, fax, or e-mail Ms. Holly Blake, Residency Manager. Phone: 415-331-2784. Fax: 415-331-3857. E-mail: holly@headlands.org. In-person interview recommended. Applicants must submit a cover letter, resume. Applications are accepted continuously.

THE INSTITUTE FOR UNPOPULAR CULTURE
1850 Union Street, Suite 1523
San Francisco, California 94123

General Information   Nonprofit organization devoted to fostering and promoting obscure, subversive art. Established in 1989. Number of employees: 3. Number of internship applications received each year: 30.

Internships Available ▶ *5–10 interns:* responsibilities include various clerical duties, writing, graphic design and layout, fundraising, research, and use of numerous computer programs. Internships are designed to meet interests of individual intern. Candidates should have ability to work independently, office skills, personal interest in the field, research skills, self-motivation, writing skills. Duration is flexible. Unpaid. Open to college freshmen, college sophomores, college juniors, college seniors, recent college graduates, graduate students, law students, career changers, individuals reentering the workforce. International applications accepted.

Benefits Job counseling, names of contacts, on-the-job training, possible full-time employment, willing to act as a professional reference, willing to complete paperwork for educational credit, willing to provide letters of recommendation.

Contact Write, call, or fax Kate Colby, Internship Coordinator. Phone: 415-986-4382. Fax: 415-986-4354. Telephone interview required. Applicants must submit a cover letter, resume. Applications are accepted continuously.

INTERNATIONAL SCULPTURE CENTER
14 Fairgrounds Road, Suite B
Hamilton, New Jersey 08619

General Information   Nonprofit art organization dedicated to contemporary sculpture; publishes Sculpture magazine, holds sculpture conference biennially, provides services and support to the field of sculpture and to sculptors. Established in 1960. Number of employees: 15. Number of internship applications received each year: 50.

Internships Available ▶ *1–2 conference interns:* responsibilities include assisting Conference Director. Candidates should have ability to work independently, analytical skills, computer skills, editing skills, office skills, oral communication skills, organizational skills, personal interest in the field, research skills, self-motivation, strong interpersonal skills, strong leadership ability, writing skills, knowledge or experience in field helpful. Open to college seniors, recent college graduates, graduate students. ▶ *1–2 management interns:* responsibilities include working in the President's office and on marketing and development projects. Candidates should have ability to work independently, analytical skills, computer skills, editing skills, knowledge of field, office skills, oral communication skills, organizational skills, personal interest in the field, research skills, self-motivation, strong interpersonal skills, strong leadership ability, writing skills. Open to college seniors, recent college graduates, graduate students, MBA candidates preferred. Duration for all positions is 1–2 semesters. All positions available as unpaid or at stipend sometimes available. International applications accepted.

Benefits Willing to complete paperwork for educational credit, willing to provide letters of recommendation, attendance at local art events.

Contact E-mail Elizabeth Ries, Assistant to the President, 14 Fairgrounds Road, Suite B, Hamilton, New Jersey 08619. Fax: 609-689-1061. E-mail: elizabeth@sculpture.org. No phone calls. In-person interview recommended. Applicants must submit a cover letter, resume. World Wide Web: http://www.sculpture.org.

J. E. JASEN STUDIO
36 East Tenth Street
New York, New York 10003-6219

General Information   Studio that designs and produces enamel art objects. Established in 1979. Number of internship applications received each year: 20.

Internships Available ▶ *1 art studio intern:* responsibilities include working in studio. Candidates should have knowledge of field, oral communication skills, personal interest in the field, self-motivation. Duration is 10 weeks. Unpaid. Open to recent high school graduates, college freshmen, college sophomores, college juniors, college seniors, recent college graduates, graduate students, career changers, individuals reentering the workforce. International applications accepted.

Benefits Opportunity to attend seminars/workshops, willing to act as a professional reference, willing to complete paperwork for educational credit, willing to provide letters of recommendation. **Contact** Write, call, or fax Ms. June Jasen, Owner. Phone: 212-674-6113. Fax: 212-777-6375. In-person interview recommended. Applicants must submit a cover letter, resume, portfolio. Applications are accepted continuously.

KENTUCKY STATE PARKS, DIVISION OF RECREATION & INTERPRETATION
Capitol Plaza Tower, 11th Floor, 500 Mero Street
Frankfort, Kentucky 40601

General Information   Provider of recreational and leisure opportunities for visitors to the commonwealth while protecting and promoting historical, cultural, and natural resources. Established in 1924. Number of employees: 225. Number of internship applications received each year: 12.

Internships Available ▶ *8–12 naturalists:* responsibilities include planning, organizing, implementing, and evaluating interpretive programs; inspecting and maintaining hiking trails; researching new and various trends in the field of recreation and interpretation; other projects as assigned. Candidates should have ability to work independently, college courses in field, computer skills, declared college major in field, knowledge of field, oral communication skills, organizational skills, personal interest in the field, plan to pursue career in field, research skills, self-motivation, strong interpersonal skills, strong leadership ability, writing skills, minimum 2.25 GPA at time of application, valid driver's license. ▶ *15–24 recreation leaders:* responsibilities include planning, organizing, implementing, and evaluating recreational and interpretive programs for park visitors; researching new and various trends in the field of parks and recreation; inspection of various recreational facilities and special projects as assigned. Candidates should have ability to work independently, college courses in field, computer skills, declared college major in field, office skills, oral communication skills, organizational skills, personal interest in the field, plan to pursue career in field, research skills, self-motivation, strong interpersonal skills, strong leadership ability, writing skills, minimum 2.25 GPA at time of application, valid driver's license. Duration for all positions is minimum of 20 hours per week. All positions available as unpaid or at $5 per hour. Open to college juniors, college seniors, graduate students, college sophomores who are registered for junior year. International applications accepted.

Benefits Formal training, meals at a cost, names of contacts, on-the-job training, opportunity to attend seminars/workshops, possible full-time employment, willing to act as a professional reference, willing to complete paperwork for educational credit, willing to provide letters of recommendation.

Contact Write, call, fax, or e-mail Cynthia Howard-Cottongim, Assistant Director of Recreation. Phone: 502-564-2172. Fax: 502-564-0224, 564-9015. E-mail: cynthia_hcottongim@mail.state.ky.us. In-person interview required. Applicants must submit a formal organization application, cover letter, resume, academic transcripts, two personal references, two letters of recommendation, division application and work agreement. Application deadline: April 1 for summer, August 1 for fall, December 1 for spring.

LEO CASTELLI GALLERY
59 East 79th Street
New York, New York 10021

General Information   Art gallery representing American and European contemporary artists. Established in 1957. Number of employees: 7. Number of internship applications received each year: 75.

Internships Available ▶ *2 photo archive/general assistants:* responsibilities include assisting in the Photo Archive Department and being a general gallery assistant. Candidates should have ability to work with others, organizational skills, personal interest in the field, strong interpersonal skills. Duration is 3–4 months. Unpaid. Open to college freshmen, college sophomores, college juniors, college seniors, recent college graduates, graduate students. International applications accepted.
Benefits Willing to complete paperwork for educational credit, willing to provide letters of recommendation.
Contact Write or fax Amy Poll, Director. Fax: 212-249-5220. In-person interview required. Applicants must submit a cover letter, resume. Application deadline: May 1 for summer.

LOS ANGELES MUNICIPAL ART GALLERY
4804 Hollywood Boulevard
Los Angeles, California 90027

General Information City-run gallery supporting the southern California art community and its artists. Established in 1971. Number of employees: 45. Division of Cultural Affairs Department, Los Angeles, California. Number of internship applications received each year: 30.
Internships Available ▶ *3–6 education interns:* responsibilities include working as gallery educators while evaluating and exploring the potential of art galleries and museums as educational sources. Candidates should have ability to work independently, college courses in field, computer skills, oral communication skills, personal interest in the field, research skills, self-motivation, strong interpersonal skills, writing skills. Duration is 3–4 months. Unpaid. Open to recent high school graduates, college freshmen, college sophomores, college juniors, college seniors, recent college graduates, graduate students, career changers, individuals reentering the workforce, college graduates who are interested in museum education. International applications accepted.
Benefits Names of contacts, opportunity to attend seminars/workshops, willing to act as a professional reference, willing to complete paperwork for educational credit, willing to provide letters of recommendation, formal training in museum education.
Contact Write, call, fax, or e-mail Ms. Sara L. Cannon, Education Coordinator. Phone: 213-485-4581. Fax: 213-485-8396. E-mail: cadmet@earthlink.net. In-person interview recommended. Applicants must submit a formal organization application, cover letter, resume. Application deadline: May 1 for summer, August 1 for fall, December 1 for spring.

LOWER MANHATTAN CULTURAL COUNCIL
5 World Trade Center, Suite 9235
New York, New York 10048

General Information Manhattan arts council serving artists and audiences; offers free public performances, exhibitions, programs and services; provides visual and new media arts residencies; administers public regrant funds, and supports arts education. Established in 1973. Number of employees: 11. Number of internship applications received each year: 50.
Internships Available ▶ *1 arts programs and services assistant:* responsibilities include assisting in one or more of these areas: World Views artist residency program, visual arts services, Thundergulch new media arts programs, performing arts programs, services festivals, art education, regrant fund administration, public relations, and marketing and fund-raising. Duration is flexible. Position available as unpaid or paid. Open to high school students, high school seniors, recent high school graduates, college freshmen, college sophomores, college juniors, college seniors, recent college graduates, graduate students, law students, career changers, individuals reentering the workforce. International applications accepted.
Benefits Job counseling, names of contacts, opportunity to attend seminars/workshops, possible full-time employment, travel reimbursement, willing to act as a professional reference, willing to complete paperwork for educational credit, willing to provide letters of recommendation, complimentary tickets to many New York City performances.

Contact Write, call, or fax Ms. Tricia Mire, Internship Coordinator, 5 World Trade Center, Suite 923B, New York, New York 10048. Phone: 212-432-0900 Ext. 213. Fax: 212-432-3646. In-person interview recommended. Applicants must submit a cover letter, resume. Applications are accepted continuously.

MAGNUM PHOTOS, INC.
151 West 25th Street, 5th Floor
New York, New York 10001

General Information Cooperative photo agency with active editorial, archive, corporate, and advertising departments; archive contains over 1 million pictures representing 55 photographers. Established in 1947. Number of employees: 18. Number of internship applications received each year: 250.
Internships Available ▶ *1–6 interns:* responsibilities include working in department on different projects, assisting in production, taking part in basic office duties, and performing some computer work, editing, and archive research. Candidates should have ability to work independently, ability to work with others, plan to pursue career in field, research skills, self-motivation. Duration is 3–4 months. Position available as unpaid or paid. Open to recent high school graduates, college freshmen, college sophomores, college juniors, college seniors, recent college graduates, graduate students, career changers, individuals reentering the workforce. International applications accepted.
Benefits Possible full-time employment, willing to complete paperwork for educational credit, willing to provide letters of recommendation, use of after-hour darkroom and portfolio views, transportation reimbursement (airfare not included).
International Internships Available in Paris, France; Tokyo, Japan; London, United Kingdom.
Contact Write, call, fax, or e-mail Kim Bourus, Executive Administrator. Phone: 212-929-6000. Fax: 212-929-9325. E-mail: kim@magnumphotos.com. In-person interview recommended. Applicants must submit a cover letter, resume. Applications are accepted continuously.

MARYLAND ART PLACE
218 West Saratoga Street
Baltimore, Maryland 21201

General Information Nonprofit regional art center exhibiting the work of contemporary artists in all media. Established in 1981. Number of employees: 4. Number of internship applications received each year: 20.
Internships Available ▶ *6 programming/development interns:* responsibilities include assisting staff with programming, fund-raising, installation of exhibitions, performing administrative duties and public relations work; archiving electronic database work, maintaining Web site, and slide library duties. Candidates should have office skills, oral communication skills, personal interest in the field, self-motivation, writing skills. Duration is 1–2 semesters. Unpaid. Open to college freshmen, college sophomores, college juniors, college seniors, recent college graduates, graduate students.
Benefits Formal training, opportunity to attend seminars/workshops, willing to complete paperwork for educational credit, willing to provide letters of recommendation, acquisition of marketable skills.
Contact Write, call, or e-mail Julie Cavnor, Assistant Director. Phone: 410-962-8565. E-mail: map@charm.net. In-person interview required. Applicants must submit a cover letter, resume, personal reference. Application deadline: May 15 for summer, July 15 for fall, November 15 for spring. World Wide Web: http://www.MDartplace.org.

MIX: NEW YORK LESBIAN AND GAY EXPERIMENTAL FILM/VIDEO FESTIVAL
29 John Street, Suite 132
New York, New York 10038

General Information Film festival, presenting 11-day series of screening in November of each year in New York City. MIX organizes other screenings at sister festivals in Mexico and Brazil,

MIX: New York Lesbian and Gay Experimental Film/Video Festival (continued)
as well as during U.S. college tour. Established in 1987. Number of employees: 3. Number of internship applications received each year: 40.

Internships Available ▶ *3–5 festival assistants:* responsibilities include assisting festival director and coordinator in all matters relating to production of festival, including making dubs, communicating with filmakers, advertisers, grantmakers, and curators. Candidates should have office skills, oral communication skills, organizational skills, personal interest in the field, strong interpersonal skills, written communication skills. Duration is 6 months in summer or fall. Open to recent high school graduates, college freshmen, college sophomores, college juniors, college seniors, recent college graduates. ▶ *1–2 hospitality assistants:* responsibilities include assisting hospitality coordinator in dealing with festival guests, filmakers, and donors; communicating perks of attending festival; working with donors to secure premiums for guests; providing information to guests; helping with accommodations; and handing out complimentary tickets. Candidates should have office skills, oral communication skills, organizational skills, personal interest in the field, strong interpersonal skills. Duration is 5 months, in summer or fall. Open to college freshmen, college sophomores, college juniors, college seniors. All positions are unpaid. International applications accepted.

Benefits Names of contacts, on-the-job training, opportunity to attend seminars/workshops, possible full-time employment, willing to act as a professional reference, willing to complete paperwork for educational credit, willing to provide letters of recommendation.

Contact Write, call, fax, or e-mail Jonathon Aubry, Festival Coordinator. Phone: 212-571-5155. Fax: 212-571-5155. E-mail: info@mixnyc.org. In-person interview recommended. Applicants must submit a cover letter, resume, two personal references. Applications are accepted continuously. World Wide Web: http://www.mixnyc.org.

MYRON MELNICK STUDIO
3001 Welton Street
Denver, Colorado 80205

General Information Visual artist's in-house gallery, containing an extensive collection of pop art, abstract hand-cast paper sculptures, and monoprints. Established in 1979. Number of employees: 4. Number of internship applications received each year: 50.

Internships Available ▶ *1 curator:* responsibilities include organizing and curating a large art collection. Candidates should have ability to work independently, analytical skills, computer skills, editing skills, office skills, organizational skills, personal interest in the field, research skills, writing skills, fine arts majors/graduates. ▶ *1–3 studio assistants:* responsibilities include working in the studio in connection with a hands-on experience creating artwork. Candidates should have ability to work independently, ability to work with others, analytical skills, personal interest in the field, self-motivation, fine arts majors/graduates. Duration for all positions is flexible. All positions paid at negotiable. Open to college seniors, recent college graduates, graduate students.

Benefits Formal training, job counseling, names of contacts, opportunity to attend seminars/workshops, possible full-time employment, willing to complete paperwork for educational credit, willing to provide letters of recommendation, free housing (possible).

Contact Write, call, or fax Mr. Myron Melnick, Artist. Phone: 303-292-3131. Fax: 303-292-3131. In-person interview recommended. Applications are accepted continuously.

NEW DRAMATISTS
424 West 44th Street
New York, New York 10036

General Information Nonprofit workshop for playwrights; dedicated to finding gifted playwrights and giving them time, space, and tools to develop their craft to fulfill their potential and make lasting contributions to the theater. Established in 1949. Number of employees: 7. Number of internship applications received each year: 100.

Internships Available ▶ *1 development/administrative intern:* responsibilities include assisting in fund-raising projects, grant proposal writing, and bookkeeping. ▶ *2 literary management interns:* responsibilities include communicating directly with member playwrights and getting involved with ScriptShare (a national script distribution service) and International Playwrights Exchange Program. ▶ *1 public relations/special events intern:* responsibilities include writing press releases and newsletter articles, designing a variety of communications materials, organizing mass mailings, and arranging publicity friendly fund-raising events. ▶ *2 stage management/casting interns:* responsibilities include managing more than one stage, setting up and planning auditions, assisting member playwrights in the smooth running of rehearsals and readings, and regulating all maintenance and behind-the-scenes activities. Candidates for all positions should have ability to work independently, oral communication skills, self-motivation, strong interpersonal skills, written communication skills. Duration for all positions is 3 months (minimum). All positions are unpaid. Open to high school students, high school seniors, recent high school graduates, college freshmen, college sophomores, college juniors, college seniors, recent college graduates, graduate students, law students, career changers, individuals reentering the workforce. International applications accepted.

Benefits Willing to complete paperwork for educational credit, complimentary tickets to Broadway and off-Broadway productions.

Contact Write, call, fax, or e-mail Mr. Stephen Haff, Internship Coordinator. Phone: 212-757-6960 Ext. 20. Fax: 212-265-4738. E-mail: newdram@aol.com. In-person interview required. Applicants must submit a cover letter, resume. Applications are accepted continuously.

NEW YORK CITY PERCENT FOR ART PROGRAM
330 West 42nd Street, 14th Floor
New York, New York 10036

General Information Government art organization that commissions artwork for city-owned property. Established in 1982. Number of employees: 2. Unit of New York City Department of Cultural Affairs, New York, New York. Number of internship applications received each year: 120.

Internships Available ▶ *2–5 program assistants:* responsibilities include answering requests, processing artists' applications, assisting with research, and preparing correspondence. Candidates should have ability to work with others, office skills, oral communication skills, personal interest in the field, self-motivation, written communication skills. Duration is flexible. Unpaid. Open to recent high school graduates, college freshmen, college sophomores, college juniors, college seniors, recent college graduates, graduate students, career changers, individuals reentering the workforce, retirees. International applications accepted.

Benefits Job counseling, names of contacts, opportunity to attend seminars/workshops, travel reimbursement, willing to complete paperwork for educational credit, willing to provide letters of recommendation.

Contact Write or call Cathie Behrend, Deputy Director. Phone: 212-643-7791. In-person interview recommended. Applicants must submit a cover letter, resume. Applications are accepted continuously. World Wide Web: http://www.ci.nyc.ny.us.

PERA CLUB
PER 200, PO Box 52025
Phoenix, Arizona 85072

General Information Recreation facility for public utility company, providing park facility for programming, large scale special events, fitness, sports programs, private parties, business functions, and rental groups. Established in 1952. Number of employees: 3,500. Unit of Salt River Project, Tempe, Arizona. Number of internship applications received each year: 15.

Internships Available ▶ *1–2 coordinator interns:* responsibilities include working as a full-time staff member with the same

responsibilities as coordinators (store, maintenance, fitness, office, booking, pool, and other operations). Duration is flexible. $75 per week. Open to college freshmen, college sophomores, college juniors, college seniors, recent college graduates, graduate students. International applications accepted.
Benefits Names of contacts, opportunity to attend seminars/workshops, willing to complete paperwork for educational credit, willing to provide letters of recommendation, use of facility (store, fitness center, pool).
Contact Write, call, or fax Ms. Marcia Beat, Associate Club Manager. Phone: 602-236-5782. Fax: 602-236-5920. E-mail: mrbeat1@yahoo.com. In-person interview recommended. Applicants must submit a formal organization application, resume. Applications are accepted continuously.

PUBLIC ARTS FOR PUBLIC SCHOOLS, DIVISION OF SCHOOL FACILITIES
28-11 Queens Plaza North
Long Island City, New York 11101

General Information Curator of 1200 artworks in New York City public schools, including murals, paintings, sculptures, stained glass, and graphics from 1850 to the present. Established in 1989. Number of employees: 3. Unit of New York City Board of Education, New York, New York. Number of internship applications received each year: 5.
Internships Available ▶ *1–2 assistant registrars:* responsibilities include inspection and evaluation of condition of artwork throughout New York City schools in cooperation with curator; creation of condition reports; data entry; and incidental art handling. Candidates should have computer skills, office skills, organizational skills, research skills, background in art history and/or studio art. Duration is flexible (minimum 4 months, one day per week). Unpaid. Open to college freshmen, college sophomores, college juniors, college seniors, recent college graduates, graduate students. International applications accepted.
Benefits Formal training, on-the-job training, willing to act as a professional reference, willing to complete paperwork for educational credit, willing to provide letters of recommendation, opportunities to meet major public artists, introduction to conservation community.
Contact Write Gregory Frux, Project Manager. In-person interview required. Applicants must submit a cover letter, resume. Applications are accepted continuously.

SALZMAN INTERNATIONAL
716 Sanchez Street
San Francisco, California 94114

General Information Agency for freelance illustrators working in communicating arts such as publishing and advertising. Established in 1982. Number of employees: 3. Number of internship applications received each year: 50.
Internships Available ▶ *1–3 administrative assistants/office staff members:* responsibilities include daily clerical duties and working in all aspects of marketing and managing the careers of 15 artists. Candidates should have ability to work independently, office skills, oral communication skills, organizational skills, self-motivation, written communication skills. Duration is 3–6 months. Unpaid. Open to recent high school graduates, college freshmen, college sophomores, college juniors, college seniors, recent college graduates, graduate students, career changers, individuals reentering the workforce. International applications accepted.
Benefits Job counseling, names of contacts, on-the-job training, opportunity to attend seminars/workshops, possible full-time employment, willing to complete paperwork for educational credit, willing to provide letters of recommendation.
Contact Write Mr. Richard Salzman, Artist Representative. In-person interview recommended. Applicants must submit a cover letter. Applications are accepted continuously.

SAN FRANCISCO ART COMMISSION GALLERY
401 Van Ness Avenue
San Francisco, California 94102

General Information Municipal art gallery exhibiting a broad range of Bay Area contemporary art. Established in 1970. Number of employees: 2. Unit of San Francisco Art Commission, San Francisco, California. Number of internship applications received each year: 35.
Internships Available ▶ *1–4 gallery assistants:* responsibilities include working with staff and assisting in all areas of gallery operations. Duration is 6 weeks to 6 months. Unpaid.
Benefits Willing to complete paperwork for educational credit, willing to provide letters of recommendation.
Contact Write, call, fax, or e-mail Internship Coordinator. Phone: 415-554-6080. Fax: 415-252-2595. E-mail: sfacg@earthlink.net. In-person interview required. Applicants must submit a cover letter, resume. Applications are accepted continuously. World Wide Web: http://www.postfun.com/sfac/.

SCULPTURE MAGAZINE
1529 18th Street, NW
Washington, District of Columbia 20009

General Information Nonprofit art organization dedicated to contemporary sculpture; publishes Sculpture magazine, holds sculpture conference biennially, provides services and support to the field of sculpture and to sculptors. Established in 1960. Number of employees: 15. Unit of International Sculpture Magazine, Hamilton, New Jersey. Number of internship applications received each year: 50.
Internships Available ▶ *1–2 publications interns:* responsibilities include researching, compiling information for publication, clerical tasks, and small writing projects. Candidates should have ability to work independently, knowledge of field, organizational skills, research skills, written communication skills. Duration is 4–12 months. Unpaid. Open to college juniors, college seniors, recent college graduates, graduate students. International applications accepted.
Benefits Willing to complete paperwork for educational credit, willing to provide letters of recommendation, attendance at local art events.
Contact Write or e-mail Twylene Moyer, Managing Editor. E-mail: sculpt@dgsys.com. No phone calls. In-person interview recommended. Applicants must submit a cover letter, resume. Applications are accepted continuously. World Wide Web: http://www.sculpture.org.

S F CAMERAWORK
115 Natoma Street
San Francisco, California 94105-3703

General Information Nonprofit artists' organization whose purpose is to stimulate dialogue, encourage inquiry, and communicate ideas about contemporary photography through an exhibition program, a bookstore, a lecture series, and a biannual magazine. Established in 1974. Number of employees: 4. Number of internship applications received each year: 90.
Internships Available ▶ *3–4 interns:* responsibilities include performing administrative duties and assisting with the installation of exhibitions. Candidates should have college courses in field, computer skills, knowledge of field, office skills, strong interpersonal skills, writing skills. Duration is 4 months minimum. Unpaid. Open to recent high school graduates, college freshmen, college sophomores, college juniors, college seniors, recent college graduates, graduate students, individuals reentering the workforce. International applications accepted.
Benefits Formal training, job counseling, names of contacts, on-the-job training, opportunity to attend seminars/workshops, willing to act as a professional reference, willing to complete paperwork for educational credit, willing to provide letters of recommendation.
Contact Write, call, fax, or e-mail Mr. Rodrigo Diaz, Gallery Manager. Phone: 415-764-1001. Fax: 415-764-1003. E-mail: sfcamera@sfcamerawork.org. In-person interview required.

S F Camerawork (continued)

Applicants must submit a cover letter, resume. Applications are accepted continuously. World Wide Web: http://www.sfcamerawork.org.

SONY MUSIC ENTERTAINMENT INC.
550 Madison Avenue
New York, New York 10022

General Information   Music entertainment corporation including CBS records, Columbia and Epic records, and new labels such as The Work Group, 550 Music, and Crave. Number of employees: 1,756. Division of Sony, Inc, Japan. Number of internship applications received each year: 1,000.

Internships Available ▶ *Summer associates (New York headquarters):* responsibilities include opportunities for first-year law student in legal copyright, and/or business affairs department; first year MBA opportunities in finance, accounting, and information technology. Candidates should have ability to work independently, computer skills, oral communication skills, organizational skills, plan to pursue career in field, self-motivation, strong interpersonal skills, strong leadership ability, written communication skills. $160-$200/day (commensurate with experience). Open to minority (African-American, Latino, Asian, American Indian) first-year MBA or first-year law students. ▶ *50–60 summer interns (NY/Santa Monica,CA):* responsibilities include working in promotions, publicity, retail marketing, artists and repertoire (A&R), A&R administration, business, affairs, accounting, or MIS. Candidates should have ability to work with others, office skills, oral communication skills, organizational skills, personal interest in the field, minimum 3.0 GPA in declared major, prior work experience a plus, computer knowledge a plus. $8 per hour. Open to minority (African-American, Latino, Asian, American Indian) undergraduate college students; college seniors considered only if returning to school in fall. ▶ *9 summer interns (sales and distribution branches):* responsibilities include working with sales representatives, progressive music marketing representative, marketing manager, sales manager, and branch manager. Candidates should have ability to work with others, computer skills, oral communication skills, organizational skills, personal interest in the field, self-motivation, minimum 3.0 GPA in declared major, record industry experience desired, one year retail or other music industry experience a plus, car required. $8 per hour. Open to minority (African-American, Latino, Asian, American Indian) undergraduate college students; college seniors considered only if returning to school in fall. Duration for all positions is 10 weeks.

Benefits Job counseling, opportunity to attend seminars/workshops, possible full-time employment, willing to act as a professional reference, willing to provide letters of recommendation, travel reimbursement possible for second application interview invitees, access to on-site employee store, possible promotional freebies, housing provided for engineering interns who are relocated to manufacturing facilities outside of New York.

Contact Write or fax Department 13—5, 550 Madison Avenue, New York, New York 10022. Fax: 212-833-7151. No phone calls. In-person interview required. Applicants must submit a cover letter, resume. Application deadline: March 31 for undergraduates, December 31 for first-year law and first-year MBA students. World Wide Web: http://www.sony.com.

SOUTHERN EXPOSURE
401 Alabama Street
San Francisco, California 94110

General Information   Nonprofit artists' organization providing opportunities for noncommercial activity, challenging artists to exhibit work in a supportive and open environment. Established in 1974. Number of employees: 4. Unit of Project Artaud, San Francisco, California. Number of internship applications received each year: 20.

Internships Available ▶ *2–3 artists in education interns:* responsibilities include facilitating and administering a hands-on education program for schools and youth organizations, which consists

of workshops on relevant aesthetic and social issues; serving as an artist's classroom assistant, program coordinator, artist's liaison, program developer, and fundraiser. Candidates should have oral communication skills, personal interest in the field, strong interpersonal skills, strong leadership ability. ▶ *2–3 arts administration interns:* responsibilities include working in the areas of membership development/coordination, publicity/public relations, graphic design, Web site design/maintenance, and grants management. Candidates should have computer skills, office skills, organizational skills, self-motivation, strong interpersonal skills, writing skills. ▶ *2 curatorial interns:* responsibilities include working with the curatorial committee, a group of 8–12 diverse and active Bay Area artists and coordinating, managing and processing all exhibition proposals; attending all monthly meetings of the curatorial committee. Candidates should have computer skills, office skills, oral communication skills, organizational skills, strong interpersonal skills, writing skills. ▶ *1–2 installation/exhibition coordinators:* responsibilities include assisting in the facilitation and installation of monthly visual arts exhibitions and acting as liaison between artists and staff; serving as volunteer coordinator and recruiter, assistant to exhibition installation, assistant to presentation coordination, technical assistant, event staffer, and fundraiser. Candidates should have ability to work independently, computer skills, oral communication skills, organizational skills, self-motivation, strong interpersonal skills, written communication skills. Duration for all positions is 1 summer or minimum of 6 months during academic year (minimum of 6 hours per week). All positions are unpaid. Open to college freshmen, college sophomores, college juniors, college seniors, recent college graduates, graduate students, career changers. International applications accepted.

Benefits Job counseling, names of contacts, willing to complete paperwork for educational credit, willing to provide letters of recommendation.

Contact Write, call, fax, or e-mail Lynne Cooney, Internship Program Coordinator. Phone: 415-863-2141. Fax: 415-863-1841. E-mail: soex@soex.org. In-person interview recommended. Applicants must submit a cover letter, resume. Applications are accepted continuously. World Wide Web: http://www.soex.org.

STEEN ART STUDY
961 East California Boulevard 329
Pasadena, California 91106-4057

General Information   Independent art historian and educator who performs research; is involved in publishing, curating, and lecturing; and conducts classes and study trips. Established in 1983. Number of employees: 1. Number of internship applications received each year: 5.

Internships Available ▶ *1 intern:* responsibilities include assisting in research, conducting classes, and curatorial and registrar work on a private collection. Candidates should have ability to work independently, ability to work with others, college courses in field, computer skills, office skills, oral communication skills, plan to pursue career in field, research skills, self-motivation, written communication skills. Duration is 1 year. Unpaid. International applications accepted.

Benefits Formal training, job counseling, names of contacts, opportunity to attend seminars/workshops, possible full-time employment, willing to complete paperwork for educational credit, willing to provide letters of recommendation.

Contact Write, call, fax, or e-mail Mr. Ronald E. Steen, Art Historian and Art Educator. Phone: 323-681-6343. Fax: 626-681-6343. E-mail: steenartstudy@fmsn.com. In-person interview recommended. Applications are accepted continuously.

TRURO CENTER FOR THE ARTS AT CASTLE HILL
PO Box 756
Truro, Massachusetts 02666

General Information   Summer art school offering a wide range of workshops in painting, printmaking, drawing, sculpture, writing, photography, book arts, metal, and clay taught by well-established artists and crafts people. Established in 1971. Number of employees: 6. Number of internship applications received each year: 20.

Internships Available ▶ *1–12 general interns:* responsibilities include assisting in daily maintenance of buildings and grounds, preparing studios for workshops, mixing clay and glazes, doing odd jobs connected with special public events, and assisting in office work. Candidates should have ability to work independently, oral communication skills, self-motivation, strong interpersonal skills. Duration is 1–2 months. Unpaid. Open to high school seniors, recent high school graduates, college freshmen, college sophomores, college juniors, college seniors, recent college graduates, graduate students, law students, career changers, individuals reentering the workforce. International applications accepted.

Benefits Willing to complete paperwork for educational credit, willing to provide letters of recommendation, opportunity to attend seminars/workshops with leading artists.

Contact Write, call, fax, or e-mail Mary Stackhouse, Director. Phone: 508-349-7511. Fax: 508-349-7513. E-mail: castlehill@capecod.net. In-person interview recommended. Application deadline: June 1 for summer.

VISUAL ART EXCHANGE
325 Blake Street
Raleigh, North Carolina 27601

General Information Nonprofit arts organization open to emerging and professional artists of all levels; offering art programs, exhibits, workshops; maintains a gallery in downtown Raleigh. Established in 1980. Number of internship applications received each year: 8.

Internships Available ▶ *1–3 gallery interns:* responsibilities include assisting Executive Director with all aspects of arts management or with special projects including preparing promotional materials, hanging shows, and planning special events. Duration is flexible. Unpaid. Open to high school students, high school seniors, recent high school graduates, college freshmen, college sophomores, college juniors, college seniors, recent college graduates, graduate students, law students, career changers, individuals reentering the workforce.

Benefits Formal training, job counseling, names of contacts, opportunity to attend seminars/workshops, willing to complete paperwork for educational credit, willing to provide letters of recommendation.

Contact Write, call, or fax Executive Director. Phone: 919-828-7834. Fax: 919-828-7834. In-person interview recommended. Applicants must submit a cover letter, resume. Applications are accepted continuously.

VISUAL STUDIES WORKSHOP
31 Prince Street
Rochester, New York 14607

General Information Center for the study of the visual image, especially the photographic image; projects include an exhibition program and a research center; educational programs including an M.F.A. program; offices of the journal *AFTERIMAGE*; a publishing program; a print shop; a bookstore; a gallery; and a media center. Established in 1969. Number of employees: 11. Number of internship applications received each year: 100.

Internships Available ▶ *1 AFTERIMAGE intern:* responsibilities include learning critical writing, news reporting, and production. ▶ *2 exhibitions program interns:* responsibilities include working in curating, exhibitions, gallery management, and a traveling exhibition service. ▶ *2 media center interns:* responsibilities include assisting with video equipment access and performing research and public relations tasks for lecture screening series. ▶ *2 research center interns:* responsibilities include assisting in print collection management, cataloging, and exhibition preparation and installation. ▶ *2 special graphics interns:* responsibilities include working on book design, production, distribution, and media projects. Duration for all positions is 1 semester. All positions are unpaid. International applications accepted.

Benefits Opportunity to attend seminars/workshops, willing to complete paperwork for educational credit, access to photo, film, video, and book collections.

Contact Write, call, or fax Ms. Catherine Higgins, Administrative Assistant. Phone: 716-442-8676. Fax: 716-442-1992. Applicants must submit a cover letter, resume, three letters of recommendation. Applications are accepted continuously.

WALT DISNEY WORLD, COMPANY
Walt Disney World College Program, PO Box 10,900
Lake Buena Vista, Florida 32830-0090

General Information Hospitality and entertainment industry comprising 14 resorts, 4 theme parks, 3 water parks, and numerous recreational venues; over 1,500 different types of jobs support the operation of the resort. Established in 1971. Number of employees: 55,000. Number of internship applications received each year: 50,000.

Internships Available ▶ *Attractions cast members interns:* responsibilities include greeting guests, operating ride systems, giving long narrations, assisting guests on and off the rides, custodial duties, and cash handling. Candidates should have ability to work independently, oral communication skills, self-motivation, strong interpersonal skills, script memorization ability. Duration is spring (January-May); summer (June-August); fall (September-December). $6 per hour. Open to college freshmen, college sophomores, college juniors, college seniors, graduate students. ▶ *Culinary assistants:* responsibilities include assisting in food preparation for guest meals by mixing, peeling and dicing, grillwork, and sandwich and salad preparations. Candidates should have ability to work independently, ability to work with others, oral communication skills, organizational skills, personal interest in the field, formal education required for some culinary positions. Duration is spring (January-May); summer (June-August); fall (September-December). $6 per hour. Open to college freshmen, college sophomores, college juniors, college seniors, recent college graduates. ▶ *Custodial cast members:* responsibilities include answering guest questions, emptying trash cans, cleaning restrooms, sweeping park areas, and assisting with busing and cleaning restaurants. Candidates should have ability to work independently, oral communication skills, organizational skills, self-motivation, strong interpersonal skills. Duration is spring (January-May); summer (June-August); fall (September-December). $6 per hour. Open to college freshmen, college sophomores, college juniors, college seniors, graduate students. ▶ *Full-service food and beverage cast members:* responsibilities include greeting, assigning, and seating guests; handling cash, preparing food, rolling silverware into linens, folding napkins, and some custodial duties. Candidates should have ability to work independently, oral communication skills, organizational skills, self-motivation, strong interpersonal skills, written communication skills. Duration is spring (January-May); summer (June-August); fall (September-December). $6 per hour. Open to college freshmen, college sophomores, college juniors, college seniors, graduate students. ▶ *Hospitality cast members:* responsibilities include working in one of Disney's themed resorts or campgrounds, in such roles as guest services, bell services, or front desk operations. Candidates should have ability to work independently, knowledge of field, oral communication skills, organizational skills, personal interest in the field, self-motivation, strong interpersonal skills, strong leadership ability, written communication skills, major in the hospitality field. Duration is 6 months. $6 per hour. Open to college freshmen, college sophomores, college juniors, college seniors, graduate students. ▶ *Housekeeping cast members:* responsibilities include making beds, dusting, cleaning bathrooms, and putting out fresh towels; lifting, bending, and pulling; attending regular informal meetings with hotel management. Candidates should have ability to work independently, organizational skills, personal interest in the field, self-motivation, strong interpersonal skills, major in the hospitality field. Duration is spring (January-May); summer (June-August); fall (September-December). $6 per hour. Open to college freshmen, college sophomores, college juniors, college seniors, graduate students. ▶ *Lifeguarding cast members:* responsibilities include monitoring guests' safety as they swim, keeping the

Walt Disney World, Company (continued)

pool areas clean, and answering questions in any of Disney's pools, marinas, or water parks; Disney conducts the certification process. Candidates should have ability to work independently, oral communication skills, personal interest in the field, self-motivation, strong interpersonal skills, strong leadership ability, previous certification helpful. Duration is spring (January-May); summer (June-August); fall (September-December). $6 per hour. Open to college freshmen, college sophomores, college juniors, college seniors, graduate students. ► *Merchandise cast members:* responsibilities include working in any of Disney's theme parks, resorts, or downtown Disney area; answering guest questions, stocking shelves, ringing up merchandise, and cleaning work areas; may also work in wheelchair and stroller rental areas. Candidates should have ability to work independently, oral communication skills, organizational skills, self-motivation, strong interpersonal skills. Duration is spring (January-May); summer (June-August); fall (September-December). $6 per hour. Open to college freshmen, college sophomores, college juniors, college seniors, graduate students. ► *Park greeters:* responsibilities include serving as the first point of contact for guests inside all parks, validating guests' tickets, greeting guests, and giving out maps and general information. Candidates should have ability to work independently, oral communication skills, self-motivation, strong interpersonal skills, comfort with high-volume interaction. Duration is spring (January-May); summer (June-August); fall (September-December). $6 per hour. Open to college freshmen, college sophomores, college juniors, college seniors, graduate students. ► *Quick-service food and beverage interns:* responsibilities include serving guests at over 240 restaurants, fast food counters, and snack bars; rotating different stations while filling orders, cashiering, cleaning, stocking, preparing, and assembling food items. Candidates should have ability to work independently, oral communication skills, self-motivation, strong interpersonal skills. Duration is spring (January-May); summer (June-August); fall (September-December). $6 per hour. Open to college freshmen, college sophomores, college juniors, college seniors, graduate students. ► *Recreation cast members:* responsibilities include handling ticket sales and towel rentals, keeping marinas and water parks clean, and answering guest questions. Candidates should have ability to work independently, oral communication skills, self-motivation, strong interpersonal skills, interest in working outdoors. Duration is spring (January-May); summer (June-August); fall (September-December). $6 per hour. Open to college freshmen, college sophomores, college juniors, college seniors, graduate students. ► *Transportation cast members:* responsibilities include assisting guests on and off boats, trams, and monorails; keeping transportation lines moving smoothly, as well as answering guest questions and giving information while guests are waiting. Candidates should have ability to work independently, oral communication skills, self-motivation, strong interpersonal skills, valid driver's license. Duration is spring (January-May); summer (June-August); fall (September-December). $6 per hour. Open to college freshmen, college sophomores, college juniors, college seniors, graduate students. International applications accepted.

Benefits Housing at a cost, job counseling, names of contacts, on-the-job training, opportunity to attend seminars/workshops, willing to complete paperwork for educational credit, willing to provide letters of recommendation, transportation provided from on-site housing to work location.

Contact Call Allen Rejonis, Manager, Marketing College Recruiting, Walt Disney World College Program PO Box 10,900, Lake Buena Vista, Florida 32830-0090. Phone: 407-934-6656. Applicants must submit a formal organization application, attendance at recruitment presentation at one of over 200 colleges/universities nationwide (consult Web site for dates and locations). Application deadline: between September and November for spring positions; between February and April for summer/fall positions. World Wide Web: http://www.careermosaic.com/cm/wdw/wdw1.html.

WARD-NASSE GALLERY
178 Prince Street
New York, New York 10012

General Information Nonprofit, artist-administered alternative space dedicated to the presentation of visual, spoken, and performing arts. Established in 1970. Number of employees: 1. Number of internship applications received each year: 10.
Internships Available ► *2–5 interns:* responsibilities include organizing exhibits; installing art; assisting with press, advertisements, sales, and financial matters; opening and closing the gallery; general office duties; and working on a special project if desired. Candidates should have ability to work with others, personal interest in the field. Duration is 3 months to 1 year. Unpaid. Open to recent high school graduates, college freshmen, college sophomores, college juniors, college seniors, recent college graduates, graduate students, law students, career changers, individuals reentering the workforce. International applications accepted.
Benefits Job counseling, names of contacts, on-the-job training, possible full-time employment, travel reimbursement, willing to complete paperwork for educational credit, willing to provide letters of recommendation, possibility of sales commissions.
Contact Write or call Mr. Harry Nasse, Executive Director. Phone: 212-925-6951. In-person interview required. Applicants must submit a cover letter. Applications are accepted continuously. World Wide Web: http://www.wardnasse.org.

WOMEN'S STUDIO WORKSHOP
PO Box 489
Rosendale, New York 12472

General Information Studio arts programs offering specialized studios in intaglio, papermaking, photography, screenprinting, offset, letterpress, book arts, and ceramics. Established in 1974. Number of employees: 7. Number of internship applications received each year: 40.
Internships Available ► *3 studio interns:* responsibilities include maintaining studio facilities and assisting artists in residence and instructors. Candidates should have ability to work independently, ability to work with others, college courses in field, knowledge of field, self-motivation. Duration is 3 months minimum. Position available as unpaid or at $75 per month (September—May only). Open to college juniors, college seniors, recent college graduates, graduate students. International applications accepted.
Benefits Formal training, free housing, opportunity to attend seminars/workshops, willing to complete paperwork for educational credit.
Contact Write or call Ms. Ann Kalmbach, Executive Director. Phone: 914-658-9133. In-person interview recommended. Applicants must submit a cover letter, resume, portfolio, 3 personal references or letters of recommendation. Application deadline: March 15 for summer, November 1 for spring. World Wide Web: http://www.wsworkshop.org.

MUSEUMS, HISTORICAL SITES, ZOOS, AND NATURE PARKS

ACADIA NATIONAL PARK
PO Box 177
Bar Harbor, Maine 04609

General Information Resource protection and resource-based recreation/educational agency. Established in 1916. Number of employees: 150. Unit of National Park Service, Washington, District of Columbia. Number of internship applications received each year: 35.

Internships Available ▶ *2 environmental education interns:* responsibilities include working with park education staff in presenting natural and cultural history curriculum-based programs for grades 3 through 6, both in the classroom and at the park. Custom programs and special projects related to environmental education possible. Candidates should have ability to work independently, ability to work with others, knowledge of field, oral communication skills, personal interest in the field. Duration is 10 weeks in spring or fall. Position available as unpaid or at $100 per week. Open to recent high school graduates, college freshmen, college sophomores, college juniors, college seniors, recent college graduates, graduate students, career changers, individuals reentering the workforce. International applications accepted.
Benefits Formal training, free housing, job counseling, on-the-job training, opportunity to attend seminars/workshops, willing to act as a professional reference, willing to complete paperwork for educational credit, willing to provide letters of recommendation.
Contact Write, call, fax, or e-mail Cynthia Ocel, Education Coordinator, PO Box 177, Bar Harbor, Maine 04609. Phone: 207-288-5459. Fax: 207-288-5507. E-mail: cynthia_ocel@nps.gov. Telephone interview required. Applicants must submit a cover letter, resume, three personal references. Application deadline: March 1 for spring, July 10 for fall. World Wide Web: http://www.nps.gov/acad.

AGATE FOSSIL BEDS NATIONAL MONUMENT
301 River Road
Harrison, Nebraska 69346-2734

General Information National monument set aside for mammalian paleontological resources and Captain James H. Cook's Oglala Lakota Sioux Native American artifacts collection; set in a mixed prarie high plains ecosystem with extensive wetlands. Established in 1965. Number of employees: 13. Unit of National Park Service, Washington, District of Columbia. Number of internship applications received each year: 5.
Internships Available ▶ *1–2 SCA interns:* responsibilities include various tasks depending upon specific research interpretation, and/or management needs. Candidates should have ability to work independently, analytical skills, computer skills, organizational skills, strong interpersonal skills, writing skills. Duration is 3 months (usually in summer). $2,500 per duration of internship. Open to recent high school graduates, college freshmen, college sophomores, college juniors, college seniors, recent college graduates, graduate students, law students, law school graduates, career changers, individuals reentering the workforce. ▶ *Volunteers-in-Parks interns:* responsibilities include interpreting for public and/or performing curatorial duties, library research, resource management, and general clerical duties. Candidates should have ability to work independently, computer skills, oral communication skills, personal interest in the field, strong interpersonal skills, writing skills. Duration is flexible (at least 1 month). Unpaid. Open to individuals 18 or older. International applications accepted.
Benefits Formal training, free housing, job counseling, on-the-job training, opportunity to attend seminars/workshops, willing to act as a professional reference, willing to complete paperwork for educational credit, willing to provide letters of recommendation, 2 trailer pads with full hookups, reimbursement for mileage, small stipend for meals, 3 bedroom house available for occupancy, tuition assistance and health insurance supported if funds are available.
Contact Write, call, fax, or e-mail Dr. Ruthann Knudson, Acting Volunteer Coordinator. Phone: 308-668-2211. Fax: 308-668-2318. E-mail: agfo_ranger_activities@nps.gov. Telephone interview required. Applicants must submit a formal organization application, cover letter, resume, three personal references. Applications are accepted continuously. World Wide Web: http://www.nps.gov/agfo/.

AIRMEN MEMORIAL MUSEUM
5211 Auth Road
Suitland, Maryland 20746

General Information Small museum with library and archives, focusing on enlisted history of the United States Air Force and its predecessor organizations. Established in 1986. Number of employees: 4. Affiliate of Air Force Sergeants Association, Suitland, Maryland. Number of internship applications received each year: 80.
Internships Available ▶ *2 fall and spring interns:* responsibilities include various tasks relating to museum professions. Candidates should have ability to work independently, college courses in field, computer skills, experience in the field, knowledge of field, oral communication skills, personal interest in the field, research skills, strong interpersonal skills, writing skills. Duration is 10 weeks. approximately $1,500 for the duration of the internship. Open to college freshmen, college sophomores, college juniors, college seniors, recent college graduates. ▶ *1 summer intern:* responsibilities include various tasks relating to museum professions. Candidates should have ability to work independently, college courses in field, college degree in related field, computer skills, experience in the field, knowledge of field, oral communication skills, plan to pursue career in field, research skills, self-motivation, strong interpersonal skills, writing skills. Duration is 12 weeks. approximately $4,000 for the duration of the internship. Open to graduate students. International applications accepted.
Benefits Formal training, on-the-job training, possible full-time employment, willing to act as a professional reference, willing to complete paperwork for educational credit, willing to provide letters of recommendation.
Contact Write James D. Staton, Chief Executive Officer, 5211 Auth Road, Suitland, Maryland 20746. No phone calls. In-person interview required. Applicants must submit a cover letter, resume, academic transcripts, writing sample, letter of recommendation. Application deadline: April for summer, June for fall, November for spring.

ALBANY INSTITUTE OF HISTORY AND ART
125 Washington Avenue
Albany, New York 12210-2296

General Information Museum dedicated to collecting, preserving, interpreting, and promoting interest in the history, art, and culture of Albany and the upper Hudson Valley Region through collections, exhibitions, education programs, library, research projects, publications, and other programs offered to the general public. Established in 1791. Number of employees: 40. Number of internship applications received each year: 50.
Internships Available ▶ *1–2 curatorial interns:* responsibilities include researching projects related to works of art, historical objects, and exhibitions; basic accessioning and cataloguing tasks; conducting inventory control; condition reporting; proofreading, permanent collection record photography, slide labeling, and filing. Candidates should have ability to work independently, ability to work with others, computer skills, plan to pursue career in field, research skills, self-motivation. Duration is 1 semester. Open to college seniors, recent college graduates, graduate students. ▶ *1–2 development/fund-raising interns:* responsibilities include providing support services including conducting research, updating records in the database, assisting with mailings, and aiding with foundation, corporate, and individual proposal preparation. Candidates should have ability to work with others, computer skills, office skills, organizational skills, personal interest in the field, writing skills. Duration is flexible. Open to college seniors, recent college graduates, graduate students, career changers, individuals reentering the workforce. ▶ *1–3 education interns:* responsibilities include developing educational material or programs related to the collections. Candidates should have ability to work independently, knowledge of field, oral communication skills, strong interpersonal skills, written communication skills. Duration is 1–2 semesters. Open to high school students, high school seniors, recent high school graduates, college freshmen, college sophomores, college juniors, college seniors, recent college graduates, graduate students. ▶ *2–3*

Albany Institute of History and Art (continued)

library interns: responsibilities include arranging and describing library collections including books, maps, photographs, and manuscripts; accessioning, cataloging, and inventorying of collections. Candidates should have computer skills, oral communication skills, organizational skills, research skills, self-motivation, written communication skills. Duration is 1 semester. Open to college juniors, college seniors, recent college graduates, graduate students. ▶ *1–2 museum shop interns:* responsibilities include conducting sales transactions using cash register and credit card terminal; greeting and assisting customers in shop and over the phone; receiving, pricing and stocking merchandise; participating in inventory. Candidates should have ability to work independently, organizational skills, strong interpersonal skills. Duration is flexible. Open to college freshmen, college sophomores, college juniors, college seniors. ▶ *1–2 public relations interns:* responsibilities include maintaining brochure racks; scanning newspapers and magazines for publicity clippings; distributing flyers, posters, and calendars to local points of interest; researching and developing mailing lists; assisting in mailing projects; writing publicity reports; researching and writing press material; making follow-up calls to reporters; assisting at openings and receptions; doing audience research; compiling statistical data. Candidates should have computer skills, office skills, plan to pursue career in field, strong interpersonal skills, writing skills. Duration is usually one term or semester. Open to college juniors, college seniors, recent college graduates, graduate students, individuals reentering the workforce. All positions are unpaid.
Benefits Names of contacts, willing to complete paperwork for educational credit, willing to provide letters of recommendation.
Contact Write Gail Kendall, Director of Finance and Administration. In-person interview required. Applicants must submit a cover letter, resume. Applications are accepted continuously.

ALLEGHENY PORTAGE RAILROAD NATIONAL HISTORIC SITE
110 Federal Park Road
Gallitzin, Pennsylvania 16641

General Information The first railroad to cross the Allegheny Mountains. Built in the 1830's, it used 10 incline planes to connect both ends of the Pennsylvania Mainline Canal. Established in 1964. Number of employees: 35. Unit of United States National Park Service, Washington, District of Columbia. Number of internship applications received each year: 2.
Internships Available ▶ *1–2 curatorial aides:* responsibilities include cataloguing, photographing, preparing items for storage, general conservation, record keeping, and inventories. Candidates should have ability to work independently, ability to work with others, computer skills, experience in the field, organizational skills, personal interest in the field. Open to college freshmen, college sophomores, college juniors, college seniors, recent college graduates, graduate students. ▶ *1–5 interpretive aides:* responsibilities include working in the contact station, performing guided talks and walks, and preparing brochures. Candidates should have oral communication skills, personal interest in the field, strong interpersonal skills. Open to high school seniors, recent high school graduates, college freshmen, college sophomores, college juniors, college seniors, recent college graduates, individuals reentering the workforce. ▶ *1–4 resource management aides:* responsibilities include monitoring water, flora, and fauna and performing vegetation studies, reforestation, and other projects. Candidates should have ability to work independently, college courses in field, experience in the field, personal interest in the field, research skills, written communication skills. Open to college freshmen, college sophomores, college juniors, college seniors, recent college graduates, graduate students, career changers, individuals reentering the workforce. Duration for all positions is flexible. All positions are unpaid. International applications accepted.
Benefits Formal training, free housing, job counseling, on-the-job training, willing to complete paperwork for educational credit, willing to provide letters of recommendation, limited reimbursement of travel and meal expenses.

Contact Write, call, or e-mail Chuck Smith, Chief, Interpretation and Education. Phone: 814-886-6156. E-mail: alpo_interpretation@nps.gov. Applicants must submit a formal organization application, 2-3 personal references. Applications are accepted continuously. World Wide Web: http://www.nps.gov/alpo.

ALLEN MEMORIAL ART MUSEUM, OBERLIN COLLEGE
87 North Main Street
Oberlin, Ohio 44074-1161

General Information Museum holding a collection ranging the entire history of art with strengths in the areas of 17th-century Dutch and Flemish painting, European art of the late 19th and early 20th centuries, contemporary American art, and Old Master and Japanese prints. Established in 1917. Number of employees: 20. Department of Oberlin College, Oberlin, Ohio. Number of internship applications received each year: 25.
Internships Available ▶ *1 education intern:* responsibilities include daily operation of Museum's education office, assisting in training and overseeing of student docent corps, conducting tours and workshops, contributing to written and interpretive materials, coordinating programming and publicity. Candidates should have computer skills, knowledge of field, oral communication skills, organizational skills, plan to pursue career in field, strong interpersonal skills, written communication skills, B.A. in art history. Duration is 12.5 months. $15,000 per duration of internship. Open to recent college graduates, graduate students. International applications accepted.
Benefits Health insurance, names of contacts, on-the-job training, possible full-time employment, tuition assistance, willing to act as a professional reference, willing to provide letters of recommendation, life insurance, paid vacation, and sick leave.
Contact Write, fax, or e-mail Education Coordinator. Fax: 440-775-6841. E-mail: sharonf.patton@oberlin.edu. No phone calls. In-person interview recommended. Applicants must submit a cover letter, resume, three letters of recommendation. Application deadline: May 31 for internship beginning in August. World Wide Web: http://www.oberlin.edu/wwwmap/allen_art.html.

ALTERNATIVE MUSEUM
594 Broadway, Suite 402
New York, New York 10012-3234

General Information Contemporary art museum providing a forum for art that addresses social and humanitarian issues. Established in 1975. Number of employees: 3. Number of internship applications received each year: 60.
Internships Available ▶ *10 interns:* responsibilities include performing general gallery work such as organization and presentation of exhibitions and public receptions; art handling; and performing administrative work, word processing, and research. Candidates should have ability to work independently, computer skills, office skills, oral communication skills, self-motivation, writing skills. Duration is 3–10 months. Unpaid. Open to high school seniors, college freshmen, college sophomores, college juniors, college seniors, recent college graduates, graduate students. International applications accepted.
Benefits Possible full-time employment, willing to complete paperwork for educational credit, willing to provide letters of recommendation.
Contact Write, call, or fax Elisa White, Curatorial Assistant. Phone: 212-966-4444. Fax: 212-226-2158. In-person interview required. Applicants must submit a cover letter, resume, 2-3 letters of recommendation. Applications are accepted continuously.

ANACOSTIA MUSEUM AND CENTER FOR AFRICAN AMERICAN HISTORY AND CULTURE
900 Jefferson Drive, SW, A&I-1130, MRC 431
Washington, District of Columbia 20560

General Information Museum and center devoted to increasing public understanding and awareness of the historical experiences and cultural expressions of people of African descent and heritage living in the Americas. Established in 1967. Number of employees: 25. Unit of Smithsonian Institution, Washington, District of Columbia. Number of internship applications received each year: 60.

Internships Available ▶ *3–6 education, research, and public programs interns:* responsibilities include research, data base acquisition, interacting with visitors, working Internet, on-line word processing, and occasional site visitation in Washington, D.C. area. Candidates should have computer skills, oral communication skills, research skills, self-motivation, written communication skills. Duration is 6 weeks to 2 months. Position available as unpaid or paid. Open to college sophomores, college juniors, college seniors, graduate students. International applications accepted.

Benefits Names of contacts, on-the-job training, opportunity to attend seminars/workshops, willing to complete paperwork for educational credit, willing to provide letters of recommendation. **Contact** Write, call, or fax Intern Coordinator, 900 Jefferson Drive, SW, A&I—1130, MRC 431, Washington, District of Columbia 20560. Phone: 202-357-4500. Fax: 202-357-2636. Applicants must submit a formal organization application, cover letter, resume, academic transcripts, three letters of recommendation, statement of interest. Applications are accepted continuously. World Wide Web: http://www.si.edu.

ANASAZI HERITAGE CENTER
27501 Highway 184
Dolores, Colorado 81323

General Information Archaeology museum with extensive curatorial facilities, a data management program for sites, and state-of-the-art exhibits. Established in 1988. Number of employees: 9. Unit of Bureau of Land Management, Washington, District of Columbia. Number of internship applications received each year: 50.

Internships Available ▶ *1 curatorial assistant:* responsibilities include assisting the curator with a variety of collections management activities. Candidates should have analytical skills, college courses in field, computer skills, experience in the field, organizational skills, plan to pursue career in field. Duration is 8 weeks. $50 per week. Open to college sophomores, college juniors, college seniors, recent college graduates, graduate students, career changers. ▶ *1 interpretive assistant:* responsibilities include assisting in a variety of routine and specialized tasks. Candidates should have college courses in field, computer skills, experience in the field, organizational skills, personal interest in the field, plan to pursue career in field. Duration is 8-week period from June to August. stipend of $50 per week. Open to college sophomores, college juniors, college seniors, graduate students, career changers. International applications accepted.

Benefits Formal training, free housing, job counseling, names of contacts, opportunity to attend seminars/workshops, willing to complete paperwork for educational credit, willing to provide letters of recommendation. **Contact** Write Ms. Susan Thomas, Internship Coordinator. Telephone interview required. Applicants must submit a cover letter, resume. Application deadline: April 1 for summer. World Wide Web: http://www.co.blm.gov/ahchmepge.htm.

THE ANDY WARHOL MUSEUM
117 Sandusky Street
Pittsburgh, Pennsylvania 15212

General Information Museum that features extensive permanent collections of art and archives, and presents the work of one of the most influential American artists of the second half of the 20th century. Established in 1994. Number of employees: 64. Unit of Carnegie Institute, Pittsburgh, Pennsylvania. Number of internship applications received each year: 300.

Internships Available ▶ *1–2 archives interns:* responsibilities include assisting with all aspects of archival collection including inventory, exhibitions, research, and special projects as assigned by the archivist. Candidates should have computer skills, knowledge of field, office skills, organizational skills, personal interest in the field, self-motivation. Open to high school students,

high school seniors, recent high school graduates, college freshmen, college sophomores, college juniors, college seniors, recent college graduates, graduate students, law students, career changers, individuals reentering the workforce. ▶ *1–2 curatorial department interns:* responsibilities include assisting with day-to-day operations and special projects including research, exhibitions, and publications. Candidates should have computer skills, editing skills, office skills, research skills, written communication skills. Open to high school students, high school seniors, recent high school graduates, college freshmen, college sophomores, college juniors, college seniors, recent college graduates, graduate students, law students, career changers, individuals reentering the workforce. ▶ *Education department interns.* Candidates should have oral communication skills, personal interest in the field, self-motivation, strong interpersonal skills, strong leadership ability. Open to high school students, high school seniors, recent high school graduates, college freshmen, college sophomores, college juniors, college seniors, recent college graduates, graduate students, law students, career changers, individuals reentering the workforce. ▶ *1 film and video intern:* responsibilities include administrative and research duties. Duration for all positions is flexible. All positions are unpaid. International applications accepted.

Benefits Job counseling, names of contacts, opportunity to attend seminars/workshops, possible full-time employment, willing to complete paperwork for educational credit, willing to provide letters of recommendation, lectures and special events. **Contact** Write Rachel Baron, Administrative Assistant. No phone calls. In-person interview recommended. Applicants must submit a cover letter, resume. Applications are accepted continuously. World Wide Web: http://www.warhol.org/warhol.

ANGELINA NATIONAL FOREST
710 North First Street, Room 100
Lufkin, Texas 75901

General Information National forest offering multiple uses including recreation, wildlife, timber, soil, and water resources. Number of employees: 23. Unit of National Forests and Grasslands in Texas, Lufkin, Texas. Number of internship applications received each year: 5.

Internships Available ▶ *2–3 volunteer campground hosts:* responsibilities include greeting campers, informing visitors of campground rules, assisting in cleaning, and maintaining the area. Candidates should have ability to work independently, oral communication skills, self-motivation, strong interpersonal skills. Duration is 3 months. ▶ *Volunteers:* responsibilities include assisting with recreation or wildlife habitat management, maintaining campgrounds and hiking trails, and assisting with various other duties. Candidates should have experience in the field, oral communication skills, plan to pursue career in field, written communication skills. All positions are unpaid.

Benefits Formal training, job counseling, names of contacts, opportunity to attend seminars/workshops, willing to complete paperwork for educational credit, willing to provide letters of recommendation, free campsite for volunteer campground hosts. **Contact** Write Mr. Glenn Donahoe, District Ranger. In-person interview recommended. Applicants must submit a cover letter, resume. Applications are accepted continuously.

ANTIETAM NATIONAL BATTLEFIELD
PO Box 158
Sharpsburg, Maryland 21782

General Information Preserves and protects the site of the Battle of Antietam and provides information about the battle of Antietam or Sharpsburg. Established in 1890. Number of employees: 40. Number of internship applications received each year: 15.

Internships Available ▶ *Volunteers in the Park (VIP):* responsibilities include staffing the information desk, assisting librarian/historian as library aide, accessioning books, manuscripts, conducting research, and assisting researchers/visitors with research. Duration is flexible. Unpaid. Open to people of all ages. International applications accepted.

Antietam National Battlefield (continued)

Benefits Formal training, willing to complete paperwork for educational credit, protection for on-the-job injury, limited reimbursement of travel and meal expenses.
Contact Write, call, fax, or e-mail Anita Bartlinski, Personnel. Phone: 301-432-5124. Fax: 301-432-4590. E-mail: anita_bartlinski@ nps.gov. In-person interview required. Applicants must submit a cover letter, resume. Applications are accepted continuously. World Wide Web: http://www.nps.gov/anti.

ARCHITECTURAL HISTORY AND HISTORIC PRESERVATION, SMITHSONIAN INSTITUTION
Arts and Industries Building, Room 2263, MRC 417
Washington, District of Columbia 20560

General Information Office that integrates the architectural history of Smithsonian buildings with their preservation, conducts research on history of all Institution buildings, reviews proposed changes which affect historical integrity of buildings, and possesses holdings and records relating to the design and construction of Institution buildings. Established in 1986. Number of employees: 6. Division of Smithsonian Institution, Washington, District of Columbia. Number of internship applications received each year: 40.
Internships Available ▶ *1–2 architectural history interns:* responsibilities include integrating original documentation, such as correspondence and memoranda, architectural drawings, photographs, and other architectural materials to explore architectural history of the Smithsonian buildings. Candidates should have ability to work independently, analytical skills, college courses in field, research skills, writing skills. Duration is 10 weeks. Position available as unpaid or paid. Open to college freshmen, college sophomores, college juniors, college seniors, recent college graduates, graduate students. International applications accepted.
Benefits Job counseling, names of contacts, opportunity to attend seminars/workshops, willing to complete paperwork for educational credit, willing to provide letters of recommendation.
Contact Write, call, or e-mail Intern Coordinator. Phone: 202-357-2571. E-mail: ahhpmx@sivm.si.edu. Applicants must submit a cover letter, resume, academic transcripts, writing sample, two letters of recommendation. Application deadline: April 1 for summer. World Wide Web: http://www.si.edu.

ARCHIVE OF FOLK CULTURE, AMERICAN FOLKLIFE CENTER, LIBRARY OF CONGRESS
Washington, District of Columbia 20540-4610

General Information National archive of folk music, ethnomusicology, and folklore. Established in 1928. Number of employees: 16. Number of internship applications received each year: 40.
Internships Available ▶ *4–8 interns:* responsibilities include performing bibliographic and reference work, reader service, cataloging, photocopying, accessioning, filing, and working on a special project that will benefit both the intern and the Archive. Candidates should have ability to work with others, computer skills, experience in the field, office skills, personal interest in the field, written communication skills. Duration is 200-1000 hours or more. Unpaid. Open to recent high school graduates, college freshmen, college sophomores, college juniors, college seniors, recent college graduates, graduate students, career changers, individuals reentering the workforce. International applications accepted.
Benefits Job counseling, names of contacts, on-the-job training, opportunity to attend seminars/workshops, willing to act as a professional reference, willing to complete paperwork for educational credit, willing to provide letters of recommendation.
Contact Write, call, fax, or e-mail Ann Hoog, Folklife Specialist (Reference). Phone: 202-707-5510. Fax: 202-707-2076. E-mail: folklife@loc.gov. In-person interview recommended. Applicants must submit a cover letter, resume. Applications are accepted continuously. World Wide Web: http://lcweb.loc.gov/folklife.

ARCHIVES OF AMERICAN ART, SMITHSONIAN INSTITUTION
901 D Street, SW, Suite 704
Washington, District of Columbia 20560

General Information Organization that collects the personal papers of American artists, art dealers, and critics and makes them available to historians and students. Established in 1954. Number of employees: 30. Number of internship applications received each year: 80.
Internships Available ▶ *2 interns:* responsibilities include research on a variety of staff projects. Duration is flexible. Unpaid. Open to college juniors, college seniors, recent college graduates, graduate students, career changers, individuals reentering the workforce. International applications accepted.
Benefits Formal training, job counseling, names of contacts, opportunity to attend seminars/workshops, willing to complete paperwork for educational credit, willing to provide letters of recommendation.
Contact Write or e-mail Ms. Liza Kirwin, Southeast Regional Collector, 901 D Street, SW, Suite 704, Washington, District of Columbia 20560. E-mail: lkirwin@sivm.si.edu. Applicants must submit a cover letter, resume, two letters of recommendation, Smithsonian application (available at: www.si.edu/cms/iosi. htm#contents). Applications are accepted continuously. World Wide Web: http://www.si.edu/artarchives.

ART INSTITUTE OF CHICAGO
111 South Michigan Avenue
Chicago, Illinois 60603

General Information Art institute that collects, preserves, exhibits, and interprets for the public one of the finest collections of visual arts in the nation. Established in 1879.
Internships Available ▶ *Interns:* responsibilities include performing special projects and research in curatorial and administrative departments. Duration is flexible. Position available as unpaid or paid. Open to college juniors, college seniors, graduate students.
Benefits Job counseling, names of contacts, willing to act as a professional reference, willing to complete paperwork for educational credit, willing to provide letters of recommendation, membership privileges.
Contact Write, call, or fax Laura M. Elk, Internship Coordinator. Phone: 312-629-9420. Fax: 312-857-0141. In-person interview recommended. Applicants must submit a cover letter, resume. Applications are accepted continuously. World Wide Web: http://www.artic.edu/aic/firstpage.html.

BADLANDS NATIONAL PARK
PO Box 6
Interior, South Dakota 57750

General Information Organization that protects park resources and provides enjoyment and education for park visitors. Established in 1939. Number of employees: 50. Number of internship applications received each year: 70.
Internships Available ▶ *2–3 Enos Mills Nature Education interns:* responsibilities include preparing and presenting guided walks and talks, staffing visitor center, coordinating special events. Candidates should have ability to work with others, computer skills, oral communication skills, plan to pursue career in field, self-motivation, writing skills. Duration is May 23 to August 20. $1000 reimbursement of expenses. Open to college sophomores, college juniors, college seniors, recent college graduates, graduate students, law students, career changers, individuals reentering the workforce. ▶ *1–2 John C. Clark Paleontological Educational interns:* responsibilities include preparing and presenting interpretive programs on paleontology to park visitors. Candidates should have declared college major in field, oral communication skills, research skills, self-motivation, strong interpersonal skills. Duration is 13 weeks. $1,000 per duration of internship. Open to college sophomores, college juniors, college seniors, recent college graduates, graduate students, career changers. ▶ *2–4 fall nature education interns:* responsibilities include preparing and

presenting school programs on geology, ecology, or history; staffing visitor center; writing and school activity preparation. Candidates should have ability to work independently, college courses in field, oral communication skills, strong interpersonal skills, written communication skills. Duration is September to November. $1000 reimbursement of expenses plus uniforms. Open to college juniors, college seniors, recent college graduates, graduate students, law students, career changers, individuals reentering the workforce. ▶ *1 library internship:* responsibilities include cataloging library books, slides, and museum objects in database. Candidates should have ability to work independently, ability to work with others, computer skills, knowledge of field, office skills, self-motivation. Duration is September to November. $500 reimbursement of expenses. Open to college freshmen, college sophomores, college juniors, college seniors, recent college graduates, graduate students, law students, career changers, individuals reentering the workforce, librarians on sabbatical. ▶ *2–10 mini-internships:* responsibilities include submitting proposal for project relating to Badlands National Park at least 8 weeks prior to proposed start date. Candidates should have ability to work independently, computer skills, personal interest in the field, research skills, self-motivation, writing skills. Duration is 8 weeks (year round). Unpaid. Open to college freshmen, college sophomores, college juniors, college seniors, recent college graduates, graduate students, law students, career changers, individuals reentering the workforce, teachers on sabbatical. ▶ *1–4 spring education interns:* responsibilities include preparing and presenting programs in schools on geology, ecology, or history; staffing visitor center; developing lesson plans; leading guided walks. Candidates should have ability to work independently, college courses in field, oral communication skills, plan to pursue career in field, strong interpersonal skills, written communication skills. Duration is March 1 to May 23. $1000 reimbursement of expenses plus uniforms. Open to college juniors, college seniors, recent college graduates, graduate students, law students, career changers, individuals reentering the workforce. ▶ *1–2 winter education interns:* responsibilities include developing lesson plans, children's materials, exhibits, and related curricula-based activities; staffing visitor center; creative writing. Candidates should have ability to work independently, ability to work with others, plan to pursue career in field, research skills, written communication skills. Duration is December to February. $1000 reimbursement of expenses. Open to college seniors, recent college graduates, graduate students, career changers, teachers on sabbatical. International applications accepted.
Benefits Formal training, free housing, job counseling, on-the-job training, opportunity to attend seminars/workshops, willing to act as a professional reference, willing to complete paperwork for educational credit, willing to provide letters of recommendation, worker's compensation.
Contact Write, call, fax, or e-mail Marianne Mills, Chief, Resource Education. Phone: 605-433-5245. Fax: 605-433-5248. E-mail: badl_interpretation@nps.gov. Applicants must submit a formal organization application, cover letter, writing sample, three personal references, letter of recommendation. Application deadline: January 15 for spring, March 15 for summer, July 1 for fall. World Wide Web: http://www.nps.gov/badl/.

BALTIMORE MUSEUM OF INDUSTRY
1415 Key Highway
Baltimore, Maryland 21230

General Information History museum that preserves and interprets Baltimore's and Maryland's rich industrial heritage focusing on education and archival holdings and collections that include a steam tug and working machinery. Established in 1981. Number of employees: 55. Number of internship applications received each year: 15.
Internships Available ▶ *1–3 archives interns:* responsibilities include processing holdings and working on cleaning and documenting archives. ▶ *1 curatorial intern:* responsibilities include performing historical research on artifacts and processing. ▶ *1–5 education interns:* responsibilities include helping to research, plan, and implement Museum educational programs with emphasis on interactive activities for children. ▶ *1 exhibits intern:*

responsibilities include helping design and build exhibits. ▶ *1 public relations intern:* responsibilities include helping with mailings and daily operation of public relations office. ▶ *1–3 research interns:* responsibilities include performing historical research for Museum files. Duration for all positions is flexible. All positions are unpaid. Open to college freshmen, college sophomores, college juniors, college seniors, recent college graduates, graduate students, law students, career changers, individuals reentering the workforce. International applications accepted.
Benefits Possible full-time employment, willing to complete paperwork for educational credit, willing to provide letters of recommendation.
Contact Write, call, or fax Ms. Jeannine Finton, Coordinator of Educational Programs. Phone: 410-727-4808. Fax: 410-727-4869. In-person interview required. Applicants must submit a cover letter, resume. Applications are accepted continuously.

BALTIMORE ZOO
Druid Hill Park
Baltimore, Maryland 21217

General Information Zoo involved in education, conservation, research, and recreation. Established in 1876. Number of employees: 150.
Internships Available ▶ *Behavioral research interns:* responsibilities include data collection by animal observation, summarizing data, inputing into computer spreadsheet program, some processing and graphing, training other observers, collecting plant materials for animals, assembling enrichment items for animals, and research. Candidates should have computer skills, personal interest in the field, TB test (may be required); Lotus 1-2-3 skills; major in biology or psychology. Duration is October-May, February-September, or June-January. Open to college juniors, college seniors. ▶ *Departmental interns:* responsibilities include working in horticulture, education, membership, financial analysis, special events, marketing, public relations, herpetology, aviculture, and mammalogy. Candidates should have personal interest in the field, TB test (may be required). Duration is either 1 semester, 1 summer, or 1 month at midterm break. Open to college freshmen, college sophomores, college juniors, college seniors. All positions are unpaid.
Benefits Names of contacts, willing to complete paperwork for educational credit, willing to provide letters of recommendation, discounts at all concessions, free parking.
Contact Call Internships at the Zoo, Volunteer Department. Phone: 410-396-7623. Fax: 410-396-6464. In-person interview recommended. Applicants must submit a formal organization application, academic transcripts, three letters of recommendation, 150- to 200-word essay. Applications are accepted continuously.

BEAVER LAKE NATURE CENTER
East Mud Lake Road
Baldwinsville, New York 13027

General Information A 580-acre park with a 200-acre lake and 10 miles of trails established to enhance visitors' understanding and appreciation of the natural world. Established in 1970. Number of employees: 12. Unit of Onondaga County Parks, Syracuse, New York. Number of internship applications received each year: 50.
Internships Available ▶ *4 naturalist interns:* responsibilities include presenting a wide range of on-site interpretive programs to students and youth or family groups and assisting with exhibit production and program development. Candidates should have knowledge of field, oral communication skills, personal interest in the field, self-motivation, strong interpersonal skills. Duration is 3 months minimum. $100–$135 per week. Open to college juniors, college seniors, recent college graduates. International applications accepted.
Benefits Free housing, job counseling, names of contacts, on-the-job training, opportunity to attend seminars/workshops, possible full-time employment, willing to act as a professional reference, willing to provide letters of recommendation.

Beaver Lake Nature Center (continued)

Contact Write, call, or fax Mr. Greg Smith, Park Naturalist. Phone: 315-638-2519. Fax: 315-638-1488. In-person interview recommended. Applicants must submit a cover letter, resume, three personal references. Applications are accepted continuously.

BLUE RIDGE PARKWAY
400 BB&T Building, One Pack Square
Asheville, North Carolina 28801

General Information Scenic and recreational route connecting Shenandoah National Park and Great Smoky Mountains National Park. Established in 1935. Number of employees: 1. Unit of United States National Park Service, Washington, District of Columbia. Number of internship applications received each year: 25.

Internships Available ▶ *1–2 interpreters:* responsibilities include operating visitor centers, giving guided walks and talks, doing independent projects. Candidates should have experience in the field, oral communication skills, personal interest in the field, strong interpersonal skills. Duration is flexible. Unpaid.

Benefits Job counseling, willing to complete paperwork for educational credit, willing to provide letters of recommendation.

Contact Write or call Mr. Phil Noblitt, Volunteer Coordinator. Phone: 828-271-4779 Ext. 242. E-mail: phil_noblitt@nps.gov. Applications are accepted continuously. World Wide Web: http://www.nps.gov/blri/.

BOOKER T. WASHINGTON NATIONAL MONUMENT
12130 Booker T. Washington Highway
Hardy, Virginia 24101

General Information National park service site where Booker T. Washington was born in 1856; focuses on interpretive programs about the influence of slavery on Washington's life. Established in 1956. Number of employees: 13. Unit of United States National Park Service, Washington, District of Columbia.

Internships Available ▶ *1 costumed interpreter:* responsibilities include presenting interpretive programs to the general public. Candidates should have ability to work independently, oral communication skills, personal interest in the field, strong interpersonal skills, writing skills. Open to high school students, high school seniors, recent high school graduates, college freshmen, college sophomores, college juniors, college seniors, recent college graduates, graduate students, law students, career changers, individuals reentering the workforce. ▶ *1 information desk receptionist:* responsibilities include greeting visitors, explaining primary theme of park story, explaining available programs and facilities, and operating book sales area. Candidates should have ability to work independently, computer skills, oral communication skills, personal interest in the field, strong interpersonal skills. All positions are unpaid.

Benefits Job counseling, willing to complete paperwork for educational credit.

Contact Write or e-mail Ms. Alice Hanawalt, Volunteers-In-Parks Coordinator. E-mail: alice_hanawalt@nps.gov. In-person interview required. Applications are accepted continuously.

BOSTON MUSEUM OF SCIENCE FELLOWSHIP PROGRAM
Science Park
Boston, Massachusetts 02114-1099

General Information Museum whose mission is to stimulate interest in and further understanding of science and technology and their importance to individuals and society. Established in 1830. Number of employees: 300. Number of internship applications received each year: 100.

Internships Available ▶ *2 education fellows:* responsibilities include working with the staff of the Programs Division to learn and present science education programs for museum visitors and school groups; assisting in the organization and maintenance of the teaching spaces and equipment; pursuing independent projects developed in conjunction with the fellow's manager. Candidates should have college degree in related field, experi-

ence in the field, oral communication skills, plan to pursue career in field, self-motivation, strong interpersonal skills. Duration is 1 year. $11 per hour. Open to college seniors, recent college graduates, graduate students, career changers, individuals reentering the workforce. International applications accepted.

Benefits Health insurance, on-the-job training, possible full-time employment.

Contact Write, fax, or e-mail Sherlyn Pang, Senior Recruiter. Fax: 617-589-0362. E-mail: jobs@mos.org. No phone calls. In-person interview required. Applicants must submit a cover letter, resume, three personal references. Application deadline: June 1. World Wide Web: http://www.mos.org.

BRIDGER–TETON NATIONAL FOREST, KEMMERER RANGER DISTRICT
PO Box 31
Kemmerer, Wyoming 83101

General Information National forest area encompassing over 300,000 acres between Jackson Hole, Wyoming, and the Wasatch Mountains of Utah; includes more than 250 miles of trails. Number of employees: 10. Number of internship applications received each year: 20.

Internships Available ▶ *Backcountry hospitality lake hosts:* responsibilities include being stationed at Lake Alice to oversee campsite and fishing camp usage, interacting with visitors to the lake facilities, obtaining demographic information, maintaining lake and trails. Candidates should have ability to work independently, ability to work with others, oral communication skills, personal interest in the field, self-motivation, good physical condition. Duration is 2 months (July and August). Unpaid. Open to college juniors, college seniors, recent college graduates, graduate students, career changers. ▶ *1–2 backcountry patrol and trail maintenance interns:* responsibilities include patrolling trails, helping rebuild and maintain trails, interacting with trail users, and providing information. Candidates should have ability to work independently, ability to work with others, knowledge of field, personal interest in the field, self-motivation, good physical condition. Duration is 2 months (July and August). Unpaid. Open to college juniors, college seniors, recent college graduates, graduate students, law students, career changers. ▶ *1–3 campground hosts:* responsibilities include greeting visitors, providing information, and maintaining the campsite. Candidates should have ability to work independently, oral communication skills, self-motivation, strong interpersonal skills. Duration is 4–5 months. Position available as unpaid or paid. Open to recent college graduates, graduate students, career changers, retirees. International applications accepted.

Benefits Free housing, job counseling, names of contacts, on-the-job training, opportunity to attend seminars/workshops, travel reimbursement, willing to complete paperwork for educational credit, willing to provide letters of recommendation.

Contact Write or call Mr. Jerry Rustad, Natural Resources Specialist. Phone: 307-877-4415. Applicants must submit a formal organization application, two personal references. Applications are accepted continuously.

BROOKFIELD ZOO
3300 South Golf Road
Brookfield, Illinois 60513

General Information Zoo that strives to enhance appreciation of the earth's biological heritage and to help visitors achieve a sustainable relationship with the natural world through conservation. Established in 1934. Number of employees: 400. Number of internship applications received each year: 200.

Internships Available ▶ *1–4 education department interns:* responsibilities include involvement in school programs, casual visitor program, community outreach, public programs, and accessibility for the disabled. Candidates should have college courses in field, oral communication skills, plan to pursue career in field, self-motivation, strong interpersonal skills. Open to college juniors, college seniors, recent college graduates, graduate students. ▶ *10–15 interns:* responsibilities include working in areas of graphic arts/design, marketing, public relations, education, audio-visual and photographic services, animal nutrition, publications, and exhibit design. Candidates should have ability to work independently, ability to work with others, college courses in field, oral communication skills, self-motivation, written communication skills. Open to college juniors, college seniors, recent college graduates, graduate students, career changers, individuals reentering the workforce. ▶ *15–25 zookeeper interns:* responsibilities include working in all aspects of captive animal management, including exhibit/enclosure maintenance, animal husbandry, diet preparation, record keeping, and observations duties. Candidates should have ability to work independently, ability to work with others, college courses in field, knowledge of field, plan to pursue career in field, self-motivation. Open to college juniors, college seniors, recent college graduates, graduate students. Duration for all positions is 6–12 weeks. All positions are unpaid. International applications accepted.

Benefits On-the-job training, opportunity to attend seminars/workshops, willing to act as a professional reference, willing to complete paperwork for educational credit, willing to provide letters of recommendation, hands-on experience with exotic, native, and domestic animals in all aspects of captive animal management.

Contact Write or fax Ms. Jan Rizzo, Intern Program Coordinator. Fax: 708-485-0986. No phone calls. In-person interview required. Applicants must submit a formal organization application, cover letter, resume, academic transcripts, two letters of recommendation. Application deadline: February 1 for summer, August 1 for fall, December 1 for winter. Fees: $15.

THE BROOKLYN MUSEUM OF ART
200 Eastern Parkway
Brooklyn, New York 11238

General Information Art museum with a collection of more than two million items and a program of exhibitions, educational activities, and community events; collection ranges from ancient to contemporary art. Established in 1823. Number of employees: 225. Number of internship applications received each year: 100.

Internships Available ▶ *1 New York City Museum School intern:* responsibilities include researching, preparing, and teaching NYCMS students, preparing teaching materials, and assisting with administrative work. Candidates should have ability to work independently, computer skills, office skills, oral communication skills, strong interpersonal skills, written communication skills. Duration is September to June. ▶ *1–8 community and public programs interns:* responsibilities include assisting in the development and execution of permanent collection, special exhibition, and non-collection based programs for adult audiences; assisting with the museum's presentation of gallery talks, seminars, workshops, and lectures and with the production of film, video, music, dance, poetry and performance art programs; and research, logistical support, outreach, and production of writing materials. Candidates should have ability to work independently, oral communication skills, plan to pursue career in field, strong interpersonal skills, strong leadership ability, written communication skills. Duration is September to June (full-time). ▶ *1–2 learning center interns:* responsibilities include researching, developing, and maintaining multimedia resources for children, teachers, and family; teaching school groups in the museum's galleries. Candidates should have ability to work independently, computer skills, oral communication skills, strong interpersonal skills, written communication skills. Duration is September to June. ▶ *5–8 school, youth, and family programs interns:* responsibilities include researching, preparing, and teaching daily school group and family programs in a particular area of the museum's permanent collection; preparing teaching materials related to special exhibitions; assisting in researching, writing, and producing a wide variety of materials for children, teachers, and families. Candidates should have ability to work independently, oral communication skills, plan to pursue career in field, self-motivation, strong interpersonal skills, strong leadership ability, written communication skills. Duration is September to June. All positions paid at $12,000 per duration of internship. Open to recent college graduates, career changers. International applications accepted.

Benefits Formal training, on-the-job training, opportunity to attend seminars/workshops, willing to act as a professional reference, willing to complete paperwork for educational credit, willing to provide letters of recommendation.

Contact Write, call, or fax Internship Coordinator, Education Department. Phone: 718-638-5000 Ext. 230. Fax: 718-783-6501. In-person interview recommended. Applicants must submit a cover letter, resume, personal reference, two letters of recommendation. Application deadline: February 15.

BROOKS MUSEUM OF ART
1934 Poplar Avenue, Overton Park
Memphis, Tennessee 38104

General Information Fine arts museum whose collection spans from the ancient to the contemporary. Established in 1917. Number of employees: 64. Number of internship applications received each year: 20.

Internships Available ▶ *1–2 curatorial interns:* responsibilities include assisting curator with research of collections. Candidates should have ability to work independently, college courses in field, computer skills, research skills, written communication skills. Duration is 1 semester. Open to college juniors, college seniors, recent college graduates, graduate students. ▶ *1 media/public relations intern:* responsibilities include writing press releases, assisting in media outreach/contact, and supporting public relations staff. Candidates should have ability to work independently, oral communication skills, self-motivation, strong interpersonal skills, written communication skills. Duration is June to August. Open to college juniors, college seniors, recent college graduates. ▶ *1–3 registrar's office interns:* responsibilities include assisting in general office work, helping upkeep collections, and preparing exhibits. Candidates should have ability to work independently, computer skills, declared college major in field, organizational skills, plan to pursue career in field, research skills. Duration is 1 semester. Open to college seniors, recent college graduates, graduate students. All positions are unpaid. International applications accepted.

Benefits On-the-job training, willing to complete paperwork for educational credit, willing to provide letters of recommendation.

Contact Write Charles Beegle, Director of Internships. Phone: 901-722-3504. Fax: 901-722-3522. In-person interview required. Applicants must submit a cover letter, resume. Applications are accepted continuously. World Wide Web: http://www.brooksmuseum.org.

BUFFALO BILL HISTORICAL CENTER
720 Sheridan Avenue
Cody, Wyoming 82414

General Information Organization with four museums that advances knowledge of the western United States. Established in 1917. Number of employees: 70. Number of internship applications received each year: 30.

Internships Available ▶ *3–4 Native American interns:* responsibilities include working in curatorial or education departments, working with objects or teaching. Candidates should have ability to work independently, ability to work with others, college courses in field, personal interest in the field, self-motivation. Duration is 3 months. $1,000 per month. Open to college sophomores, college juniors, college seniors, recent college graduates, graduate students. ▶ *6–8 general interns:* responsibilities include working in various departments at any of four BBHC museums, according to museum's needs and intern's desire and ability. Candidates should have ability to work independently, ability to work with others, personal interest in the field, self-motivation, research and computer skills helpful. Duration is 3-month average. Position available as unpaid or at $1,000 per month. Open to college juniors, college seniors, recent college graduates, graduate students. International applications accepted.

Benefits On-the-job training, opportunity to attend seminars/workshops, willing to act as a professional reference, willing to complete paperwork for educational credit, willing to provide letters of recommendation, stipends for some internships.

Buffalo Bill Historical Center (continued)

Contact Write, call, fax, or e-mail Sharon Schroeder, Director of Education. Phone: 307-578-4005. Fax: 307-587-5714. E-mail: schroder@wavecom.net. Applicants must submit a formal organization application, academic transcripts, three letters of recommendation. Application deadline: four months prior to start date. World Wide Web: http://www.bbhc.org.

BUFFALO NATIONAL RIVER
402 North Walnut, Suite 136
Harrison, Arkansas 72601

General Information National river that conserves and interprets an area containing unique scenic and scientific features and preserves a free-flowing stream in an important segment of the Buffalo River for the benefit and enjoyment of present and future generations. Established in 1972. Number of employees: 75. Unit of United States National Park Service, Washington, District of Columbia. Number of internship applications received each year: 2.

Internships Available ▶ *1 interpretation intern:* responsibilities include performing visitor center program development and presentation, school outreach, and other resource-oriented duties. Candidates should have ability to work independently, ability to work with others, college courses in field, oral communication skills, personal interest in the field, writing skills. Duration is 12 weeks. Unpaid. Open to college sophomores, college juniors, college seniors. International applications accepted.

Benefits Formal training, job counseling, names of contacts, willing to complete paperwork for educational credit, willing to provide letters of recommendation, possible reimbursement of in-park travel expenses.

Contact Write Volunteer/Intern Coordinator. In-person interview recommended. Applicants must submit a cover letter, resume. Application deadline: January 1 for spring, July 1 for fall.

CABRILLO NATIONAL MONUMENT
1800 Cabrillo Memorial Drive
San Diego, California 92106-3601

General Information Agency that seeks to preserve park scenery, natural and historical objects, and wildlife. Established in 1913. Number of employees: 20. Unit of United States National Park Service, Washington, District of Columbia. Number of internship applications received each year: 15.

Internships Available ▶ *1–2 park ranger interns:* responsibilities include developing and presenting interpretive programs, introducing film presentations, conducting nature walks, and assisting with education programs and natural resource management projects. Candidates should have ability to work independently, oral communication skills, personal interest in the field, self-motivation, strong interpersonal skills, written communication skills. Duration is 1 semester. Unpaid. Open to college freshmen, college sophomores, college juniors, college seniors, graduate students. International applications accepted.

Benefits Formal training, job counseling, names of contacts, on-the-job training, opportunity to attend seminars/workshops, willing to complete paperwork for educational credit, willing to provide letters of recommendation, aid on the application process provided.

Contact Write John Golda, Internship Coordinator. In-person interview recommended. Applicants must submit a formal organization application. Applications are accepted continuously. World Wide Web: http://www.nps.gov/cabr.

CALAVERAS BIG TREES STATE PARK
22708 Broadway Street
Columbia, California 95310

General Information State park established to protect two groves of Giant Sequoia (largest trees in the world); located in the central Sierra Nevada, California. Established in 1931. Number of employees: 26. District of California Department of Parks & Recreation, Sacramento, California. Number of internship applications received

Internships Available ▶ *2 interns:* responsibilities include conducting interpretive programs, operating and maintaining all equipment, conducting sales of merchandise, working with volunteers and paid staff; working in visitor center. Candidates should have ability to work independently, analytical skills, college courses in field, computer skills, knowledge of field, oral communication skills, plan to pursue career in field, research skills, self-motivation, strong interpersonal skills, written communication skills. Duration is 3 months (June-September). $195 per month. Open to college freshmen, college sophomores, college juniors, college seniors, recent college graduates, graduate students. International applications accepted.

Benefits Free housing, job counseling, names of contacts, on-the-job training, opportunity to attend seminars/workshops, willing to complete paperwork for educational credit, willing to provide letters of recommendation.

Contact Write, call, fax, or e-mail Bruce Thomsen, District Interpretive Specialist. Phone: 209-532-0150. Fax: 209-532-5064. E-mail: calavera@goldrush.com. In-person interview recommended. Applicants must submit a cover letter, resume. Application deadline: February 15 for summer.

CALIFORNIA DEPARTMENT OF PARKS AND RECREATION, INDIAN GRINDING ROCK STATE HISTORIC PARK
14881 Pine Grove-Volcano Road
Pine Grove, California 95665

General Information A 135-acre historic park preserving an outcropping of marbleized limestone with some 1185 mortar holes; the Chaw'se Regional Indian Museum, also located in the park, features an outstanding collection of Sierra Nevada Indian artifacts. Established in 1968. Number of employees: 3. Unit of Calaveras District, Columbia, California. Number of internship applications received each year: 25.

Internships Available ▶ *1–2 park aides:* responsibilities include conducting guided walks, public talks, and campfire programs; operating museum sales counter and conducting museum archives work; performing housekeeping and light maintenance duties; and conducting oral history tape recordings and research on Sierra Nevada Indian culture. Candidates should have college courses in field, experience in the field, oral communication skills, strong interpersonal skills, demonstrated ability to work effectively with volunteers, multi-cultural groups, and the Native American community. Duration is 3 months. Unpaid. Open to college sophomores, college juniors, college seniors, recent college graduates, graduate students.

Benefits Free housing, opportunity to attend seminars/workshops, willing to complete paperwork for educational credit.

Contact Write or call Mr. Curt Kraft, Supervising Park Ranger. Phone: 209-296-7488. In-person interview recommended. Applicants must submit a formal organization application, resume, 3 personal refences or letters of recommendation. Applications are accepted continuously.

CALIFORNIA DEPARTMENT OF PARKS AND RECREATION, OLD TOWN SAN DIEGO STATE HISTORIC PARK
4002 Wallace Street
San Diego, California 92110

General Information Historic park that offers a variety of educational activities such as tours, museums, artifacts, crafts, cooking, and a demonstration of the 1821-1872 period. Number of employees: 20. Unit of California State Parks, Sacramento, California. Number of internship applications received each year: 30.

Internships Available ▶ *1–2 adobe builders:* responsibilities include plastering and building adobe walls in the historic park. Candidates should have ability to work with others, knowledge of field, organizational skills, plan to pursue career in field, self-motivation. Duration is 3–6 months. Open to recent high school graduates, career changers, individuals reentering the workforce. ▶ *1–3 curatorial assistants:* responsibilities include assisting curatorial staff in care, maintenance, cataloging, and processing of artifacts and museum displays. Candidates should have ability to work with others, knowledge of field, organizational skills, plan to pursue career in field, self-motivation. Duration is 3–6 months. Open to college freshmen, college sophomores, college juniors, college seniors, recent college graduates, graduate students. ▶ *1–3 display developers:* responsibilities include developing new historic/interpretive displays for the public and maintaining and updating existing displays. Candidates should have ability to work independently, experience in the field, organizational skills, plan to pursue career in field, research skills. Duration is 3–6 months. Open to college freshmen, college sophomores, college juniors, college seniors, recent college graduates, graduate students. ▶ *1–3 groundskeeping interns:* responsibilities include working with groundskeeping staff to develop and maintain historically accurate gardens in the park. Candidates should have ability to work independently, ability to work with others, knowledge of field, personal interest in the field, self-motivation. Duration is 3–6 months. Open to high school seniors, recent high school graduates, college freshmen, college sophomores, college juniors, college seniors, recent college graduates, graduate students, individuals reentering the workforce. ▶ *5–10 historic skills demonstrators:* responsibilities include demonstrating historic skills such as candlemaking, cooking, leather tooling, soapmaking, and blacksmithing to the public. Candidates should have experience in the field, oral communication skills, personal interest in the field, strong interpersonal skills. Duration is 6–9 months. Open to high school students, high school seniors, recent high school graduates. ▶ *5–10 historic tour guides:* responsibilities include presenting tours to school children focusing on the 1800's era history and its relation to the historic park. Candidates should have knowledge of field, oral communication skills, plan to pursue career in field, strong interpersonal skills. Duration is 3–6 months. Open to recent high school graduates, college freshmen, college sophomores, college juniors, college seniors, recent college graduates, graduate students, career changers. ▶ *1–3 maintenance assistants:* responsibilities include assisting maintenance staff in facility maintenance, operation, repair, and development. Candidates should have ability to work with others, experience in the field, organizational skills, plan to pursue career in field. Duration is 3–6 months. Open to high school students, high school seniors, recent high school graduates, career changers, individuals reentering the workforce. ▶ *1–3 park-aid interns:* responsibilities include contacting public, conducting historic tours, collecting fees, operating visitor center, and performing resource management. Candidates should have experience in the field, oral communication skills, plan to pursue career in field, self-motivation, strong interpersonal skills. Duration is 3–6 months. Open to recent high school graduates, college freshmen, college sophomores, college juniors, college seniors, recent college graduates, graduate students, individuals reentering the workforce. ▶ *1–2 public relations/advertising interns:* responsibilities include advertising park events through various forms of the media, developing media contacts and lists, writing advertising copy, and transferring to a computer. Candidates should have ability to work independently, computer skills, knowledge of field, oral communication skills, strong interpersonal skills, written communication skills. Duration is 3–6 months. Open to college freshmen, college sophomores, college juniors, college seniors, recent college graduates. ▶ *1–2 receptionists:* responsibilities include answering phones, providing general information to the public. Candidates should have ability to work with others, office skills, oral communication skills, organizational skills, plan to pursue career in field. Duration is 3–6 months. Open to high school students, high school seniors, recent high school graduates, career changers, individuals reentering the workforce. ▶ *1–3 volunteer coordinator assistants:* responsibilities include working with Volunteer Coordinator in developing and coordinating interpretive events and organizing volunteer activities. Candidates should have organizational skills, plan to pursue career in field, self-motivation, strong interpersonal skills. Duration is 3–6 months. Open to college freshmen, college sophomores, college juniors, college seniors, recent college graduates, graduate students. All positions are unpaid. International applications accepted.

Benefits Formal training, job counseling, names of contacts, on-the-job training, opportunity to attend seminars/workshops, willing to act as a professional reference, willing to complete paperwork for educational credit, willing to provide letters of recommendation, worker's compensation, possibility of seasonal part-time employment.
Contact Write, call, or fax Steffani Jarrett, State Park Superintendent. Phone: 619-220-5424. Fax: 619-220-5421. In-person interview required. Applicants must submit a formal organization application, resume, writing sample, three personal references. Applications are accepted continuously.

CALLAWAY GARDENS
PO Box 2000
Pine Mountain, Georgia 31822-2000

General Information Horticulture display garden and resort with conservatories, nature trails, lodging, golf, tennis, and man-made beach. Established in 1952. Number of employees: 1,200. Number of internship applications received each year: 50.
Internships Available ▶ *1 education intern:* responsibilities include conducting and assisting with education programs in home horticulture and natural history. Candidates should have experience in the field, knowledge of field, oral communication skills, strong interpersonal skills. Duration is 6 months in spring or summer. $6 per hour. Open to college freshmen, college sophomores, college juniors, college seniors, recent college graduates, graduate students, college juniors, seniors, graduate students preferred. ▶ *4 education interns:* responsibilities include conducting and assisting with education programs in home horticulture and natural history. Candidates should have experience in the field, knowledge of field, oral communication skills, strong interpersonal skills. Duration is 3 months in summer. $6 per hour. Open to college freshmen, college sophomores, college juniors, college seniors, recent college graduates, graduate students, college juniors, seniors, graduate students preferred. ▶ *4 horticulture interns:* responsibilities include performing manual labor and equipment operation in grounds maintenance, conservatories, greenhouses, trails, and the vegetable garden. Candidates should have college courses in field, experience in the field, knowledge of field. Duration is 3 months in summer. $6 per duration of internship. Open to college freshmen, college sophomores, college juniors, college seniors, graduate students, college juniors, seniors, graduate students preferred. International applications accepted.
Benefits Formal training, free housing, meals at a cost, possible full-time employment, willing to complete paperwork for educational credit, willing to provide letters of recommendation, opportunity to attend classes and field trips.
Contact Write, call, fax, or e-mail Kathryne Hayden, Intern Registrar. Phone: 706-663-5146. Fax: 706-663-6720. E-mail: kfhayde@callawaygardens.com. Applicants must submit a formal organization application, cover letter, resume, three letters of recommendation. Application deadline: January 15 for 6-month internship (March-August), February 15 for summer. World Wide Web: http://www.callawaygardens.com.

CAMBRIDGE HISTORICAL SOCIETY
159 Brattle Street
Cambridge, Massachusetts 02138-3300

General Information Museum that emphasizes the history of Cambridge, Massachusetts. Established in 1905. Number of employees: 2. Number of internship applications received each year: 12.
Internships Available ▶ *1 curatorial intern:* responsibilities include cataloging collections. Candidates should have ability to work independently, college courses in field, knowledge of field, organizational skills, personal interest in the field, writing skills. ▶ *1 education intern:* responsibilities include giving house and neighborhood tours and developing interpretive programs about Cambridge and/or Cambrigians. Candidates should have computer skills, knowledge of field, oral communication skills, personal interest in the field, research skills, strong interpersonal skills, written communication skills. ▶ *1 museum management intern:*

Cambridge Historical Society (continued)

responsibilities include assisting in all aspects of the museum management office, including public relations, public programs, and financial matters. Candidates should have analytical skills, computer skills, organizational skills, personal interest in the field, writing skills, written communication skills. ▶ *1 research intern:* responsibilities include corresponding with individuals seeking historical information, and conducting research for the museum. Candidates should have ability to work independently, computer skills, knowledge of field, oral communication skills, research skills, self-motivation, written communication skills. Duration for all positions is flexible. All positions are unpaid. Open to college sophomores, college juniors, college seniors, recent college graduates, graduate students, career changers.

Benefits Job counseling, names of contacts, on-the-job training, willing to act as a professional reference, willing to complete paperwork for educational credit, willing to provide letters of recommendation, informal training.

Contact Write, call, fax, or e-mail Aurore Eaton, Executive Director. Phone: 617-547-4252. Fax: 617-661-1623. E-mail: camhistory@aol.com. In-person interview recommended. Applicants must submit a cover letter, resume, personal reference. Applications are accepted continuously.

CAPITAL CHILDREN'S MUSEUM
800 Third Street, NE
Washington, District of Columbia 20002

General Information Research and development institution involved with innovative educational methods for children and comprised of 3 main departments: Capitol Children's Museum (hands-on, interactive museum), Options School (for at-risk children grades 5-8), and Media Arts Center (video, animation, and computers). Established in 1979. Number of employees: 80. Number of internship applications received each year: 200.

Internships Available ▶ *1–2 Media Arts Center interns:* responsibilities include creating animation and video projects, teaching children 2-D and 3-D animation video camps and classes, and creating videos for public relations purposes. Candidates should have computer skills, ability to work with children in an encouraging and supportive way. Duration is one summer, January break, or May term. Open to college sophomores, college juniors, college seniors, recent college graduates, graduate students. ▶ *1–2 Options School teaching aides:* responsibilities include working with at-risk 5th-8th graders in Options Public Charter School located on Museum's 4th floor. Candidates should have ability to work independently, self-motivation, strong interpersonal skills. Open to college juniors, college seniors, recent college graduates, graduate students, graduate students majoring in reading, counseling, or other specific educational areas. ▶ *4–8 Renaissance Camp interns:* responsibilities include teaching, gathering research materials, preparing 5 classes in hands-on art and science subjects for 4-8 one-week-long day camps for children 6-12 years; includes training in skills and concepts in alternative education. Candidates should have ability to work independently, oral communication skills, strong interpersonal skills, experience with ages 6-12; basic knowledge of art and science topics helpful. Duration is mid-June to mid-July; mid-July to mid-August; or mid-June to mid-August. Open to college freshmen, college sophomores, college juniors, college seniors, recent college graduates, graduate students, career changers. ▶ *2 World Wide Web page interns:* responsibilities include managing cooperative teams of children throughout the Web page production process. Candidates should have familiarity with Internet, PC (Windows 95), and Macintosh platforms, HTML+, and Photoshop or Paintshop programs. Duration is 2 months. Open to college sophomores, college juniors, college seniors, recent college graduates, graduate students. ▶ *1–2 animation interns:* responsibilities include assisting in all phases of animation, including 2-D and 3-D, instruction, and post production. Candidates should have ability to work with others, personal interest in the field, desire to teach and assist children in accomplishing their goals. Duration is mid-June to mid-July or mid-July to mid-August. Open to college sophomores, college juniors, college seniors, recent college graduates, graduate students. ▶ *1 chemical science center*

educator: responsibilities include teaching and demonstrating chemical experiments; guiding children in hands-on chemistry; developing new hands-on activities; helping with chemistry-based art projects; creating curricular outlines for summer camps and short classes. Candidates should have knowledge of field, personal interest in the field. Duration is one summer, January break, or May term. Open to college sophomores, college juniors, college seniors, recent college graduates, graduate students. ▶ *1–2 development department interns:* responsibilities include donor prospect research, working with database, and writing grant proposals. Duration is one summer, semester, January break, or May term. Open to college sophomores, college juniors, college seniors, recent college graduates, graduate students. ▶ *1–2 educational outreach interns:* responsibilities include teaching interactive science classes, developing classes for schools, and developing educational packets for teachers and parents. Candidates should have computer skills, ability to deal with groups of children. Duration is one summer, January break, or May term. Open to college sophomores, college juniors, college seniors, recent college graduates, graduate students. ▶ *1 exhibit design and graphics intern:* responsibilities include developing exhibits, artwork, graphic arts, painting murals, hanging pictures, repairing murals, designing brochures, and making displays. Duration is one summer, January break, or May term. Open to college sophomores, college juniors, college seniors, recent college graduates, graduate students. ▶ *1 public relations intern:* responsibilities include promoting Museum with press releases, public service announcements, and brochures; obtaining media coverage; coordinating events; and developing original media outlet contacts. Candidates should have ability to work independently, ability to work with others, computer skills, writing skills. Duration is one summer, semester, January break, or May term. Open to college sophomores, college juniors, college seniors, recent college graduates, graduate students, career changers. ▶ *1 volunteer coordinator intern:* responsibilities include developing outreach projects; meeting the needs of volunteers; helping to orient young teens, adults, and senior citizens; attending internship fairs; working with court-appointed community service clients. Candidates should have computer skills, oral communication skills, organizational skills, strong interpersonal skills. Duration is one summer, May term, or January break. Open to college sophomores, college juniors, college seniors, recent college graduates, graduate students. All positions are unpaid. International applications accepted.

Benefits On-the-job training, possible full-time employment, willing to act as a professional reference, willing to complete paperwork for educational credit, willing to provide letters of recommendation.

Contact Write, call, or fax Ms. Susan Albers, Volunteer Coordinator. Phone: 202-675-4124. Fax: 202-675-4140. Telephone interview required. Applicants must submit a formal organization application, cover letter, resume. Applications are accepted continuously.

CARLSBAD CAVERNS NATIONAL PARK
3225 National Parks Highway
Carlsbad, New Mexico 88220

General Information Park consisting of 47,000 acres of Chihuahuan desert and more than 85 caves; established to conserve resources and to provide for understanding, appreciation, and enjoyment of park resources. Established in 1923. Number of employees: 100. Unit of United States Department of Interior, Washington, District of Columbia. Number of internship applications received each year: 100.

Internships Available ▶ *1 WWW computer specialist:* responsibilities include assisting with the development of park's Web site. Candidates should have ability to work independently, computer skills, experience in the field, knowledge of field, self-motivation, writing skills. Duration is flexible. Open to individuals at least 18 years old with necessary skills. ▶ *1 education assistant/artist:* responsibilities include working with the Junior Ranger program and interpreting the park resources for children and other visitors, and creating artwork and illustrating for park publications. Candidates should have ability to work independently, ability to work with others, oral communication skills, personal interest in the field, writing skills, interest in working with the public. Duration is June-August. Open to recent high school graduates, college freshmen, college sophomores, college juniors, college seniors, recent college graduates, graduate students. ▶ *1 education program developer:* responsibilities include developing original, hands-on interdisciplinary programs based on standards for various academic levels. Candidates should have ability to work independently, college degree in related field, editing skills, experience in the field, written communication skills. Duration is June-August. Open to recent college graduates, graduate students, career changers, individuals reentering the workforce. ▶ *1 historian assistant:* responsibilities include assisting the park historian with oral history transcripts, research, and filing. Candidates should have ability to work independently, office skills, organizational skills, personal interest in the field, research skills, writing skills. Duration is flexible. Open to individuals 18 years or older with interest in history. ▶ *1–2 park photographers:* responsibilities include taking photos of assigned subjects to update the park's slide and photo collection and assisting with the slide file and database. Candidates should have ability to work independently, computer skills, experience in the field, office skills, organizational skills, self-motivation. Duration is flexible. Open to college seniors, recent college graduates, graduate students, career changers, individuals reentering the workforce. ▶ *1–2 visitor services assistants:* responsibilities include working with the public, answering questions, and providing visitor assistance while staffing the information desk; roving cave trails; and presenting cave orientations. Candidates should have ability to work with others, experience in the field, oral communication skills, personal interest in the field, self-motivation. Duration is flexible (2 months minimum). Open to individuals 18 years or older with interest in working with the public. ▶ *1–2 wildlife research assistants:* responsibilities include assisting in bird monitoring programs, conducting point counts to estimate cowbird abundance, conducting nest searches to measure the breeding success and brood parasitism rates on neotropical migrant species. Candidates should have ability to work independently, experience in the field, knowledge of field, research skills, self-motivation. Duration is April-August. Open to college juniors, college seniors, recent college graduates, graduate students. All positions are unpaid. International applications accepted.

Benefits Job counseling, on-the-job training, opportunity to attend seminars/workshops, willing to complete paperwork for educational credit, protection from tort claims, worker's compensation for on-the-job injuries.

Contact Write, call, fax, or e-mail Volunteer Coordinator. Phone: 505-785-2232. Fax: 505-785-2302. E-mail: cave_interpretation@nps.gov. Telephone interview required. Applicants must submit a cover letter, resume. Applications are accepted continuously. World Wide Web: http://www.nps.gov/cave.

CATOCTIN MOUNTAIN PARK
6602 Foxville Road
Thurmont, Maryland 21788-1598

General Information Park dedicated to the preservation and protection of historical objects and wildlife. Established in 1936. Number of employees: 40. Unit of United States National Park Service, Washington, District of Columbia. Number of internship applications received each year: 24.

Internships Available ▶ *1–7 cabin camp hosts:* responsibilities include providing people with assistance, performing office duties, and checking cabins. Candidates should have ability to work independently, office skills, oral communication skills, personal interest in the field, strong interpersonal skills. Duration is 1 month. Open to college juniors, college seniors, recent college graduates, graduate students, law students, career changers, individuals reentering the workforce. ▶ *1–5 campground hosts:* responsibilities include answering questions for visitors, maintaining campground, and keeping track of how many campsites are open. Candidates should have ability to work independently, oral communication skills, personal interest in the field, self-motivation, strong interpersonal skills. Duration is 1 month. Open to college juniors, college seniors, recent college gradu-

ates, graduate students, law students, career changers, individuals reentering the workforce. ▶ *1–4 resource education interns:* responsibilities include providing visitor services and interpretive programs. Candidates should have ability to work independently, oral communication skills, personal interest in the field, self-motivation, strong interpersonal skills. Duration is 10–12 weeks. Open to high school seniors, recent high school graduates, college freshmen, college sophomores, college juniors, college seniors, recent college graduates, graduate students, law students, career changers, individuals reentering the workforce. ▶ *1–4 resource management interns:* responsibilities include performing education, vegetation, water quality, and wildlife studies. Candidates should have ability to work independently, ability to work with others, knowledge of field, oral communication skills, personal interest in the field, written communication skills. Duration is 10–12 weeks. Open to high school students, high school seniors, recent high school graduates, college freshmen, college sophomores, college juniors, college seniors, recent college graduates, graduate students, law students, career changers, individuals reentering the workforce. All positions are unpaid. International applications accepted.

Benefits Free housing, willing to complete paperwork for educational credit, willing to provide letters of recommendation.

Contact Write Chief Ranger. Telephone interview required. Applicants must submit a resume. Application deadline: March 1 for summer, August 1 for fall; continuous for cabin camp hosts and campground hosts. World Wide Web: http://www.nps.gov/cato/.

CENTER FOR MUSEUM STUDIES, SMITHSONIAN INSTITUTION
900 Jefferson Drive, SW, Suite 2235
Washington, District of Columbia 20560-0427

General Information Central referral service for internships in Smithsonian departments and offices in projects emphasizing museum methods and current practices in the field. Established in 1846. Number of employees: 6,000. Number of internship applications received each year: 700.

Internships Available ▶ *600–700 interns:* responsibilities include assisting in any of 50 museums, research institutes, or offices, including curatorial, education, collections management, public relations, exhibit design and production, museum registration, and scientific research. Candidates should have oral communication skills, personal interest in the field, self-motivation, written communication skills. Duration is flexible. Position available as unpaid or paid. Open to recent high school graduates, college freshmen, college sophomores, college juniors, college seniors, recent college graduates, graduate students, law students, career changers, individuals reentering the workforce, individuals 16 or older. International applications accepted.

Benefits Job counseling, names of contacts, opportunity to attend seminars/workshops, willing to act as a professional reference, willing to complete paperwork for educational credit, willing to provide letters of recommendation, discounts at museum shops and cafeteria, possibility of stipends for some positions.

Contact Write, call, or e-mail Elena Piquer Mayberry, Experiential Programs Manager. Phone: 202-357-3102. E-mail: siintern@cms.si.edu. Applicants must submit a formal organization application, academic transcripts, writing sample, two letters of recommendation, 5 copies of all materials. Application deadline: February 15 for summer, June 15 for fall, October 15 for winter/spring. World Wide Web: http://www.si.edu/cms/iosi.htm.

CHICAGO BOTANIC GARDEN
1000 Lake Cook Road
Glencoe, Illinois 60022-0400

General Information Botanical garden containing horticultural displays that promote understanding of plants, gardening, and natural resource conservation. Established in 1965. Number of employees: 200. Unit of Chicago Horticultural Society. Number of internship applications received each year: 100.

Internships Available ▶ *3 conservation ecology interns:* responsibilities include conservation management, plant identification,

Chicago Botanic Garden (continued)

planting, weeding, seed collection, field surveys, maintenance, propagation, and research. Candidates should have ability to work independently, ability to work with others, declared college major in field, knowledge of field, plan to pursue career in field, familiarity with Illinois flora helpful. Duration is 3 months. $6 per hour. Open to college freshmen, college sophomores, college juniors, college seniors, recent college graduates, graduate students. ▶ *1–5 education and programming interns:* responsibilities include assisting in planning, implementation, and evaluation of education, visitor, or community programs for all ages. Candidates should have college courses in field, experience in the field, oral communication skills, self-motivation, strong interpersonal skills, strong leadership ability. Duration is 3–6 months. $6 per hour. Open to college freshmen, college sophomores, college juniors, college seniors, recent college graduates, graduate students. ▶ *Graphic design volunteers:* responsibilities include working on design team on a variety of projects. Candidates should have ability to work independently, ability to work with others, computer skills, editing skills, experience in the field, written communication skills. Duration is 3–12 months. Unpaid. Open to college freshmen, college sophomores, college juniors, college seniors, recent college graduates, graduate students, career changers. ▶ *2 horticultural therapy interns:* responsibilities include assisting with horticultural therapy program development, presenting workshops, evaluating programs, maintenance, garden design, and working with groups in plant-related activities. Candidates should have ability to work with others, declared college major in field, knowledge of field, oral communication skills, plan to pursue career in field. Duration is 6 months. $6 per hour. Open to college freshmen, college sophomores, college juniors, college seniors, recent college graduates, graduate students. ▶ *4–6 horticulture interns:* responsibilities include gaining experience in horticulture and public garden operations and administration. Candidates should have ability to work independently, ability to work with others, declared college major in field, knowledge of field, plan to pursue career in field. Duration is flexible (3-12 months). $6 per hour. Open to college freshmen, college sophomores, college juniors, college seniors, recent college graduates, graduate students. ▶ *1 integrated pest management intern:* responsibilities include assisting with weed, disease, and insect control, monitoring and identifying pests and recommending control measures, applying proper controls, assisting with special projects, and keeping accurate records. Candidates should have ability to work independently, ability to work with others, college courses in field, knowledge of field, personal interest in the field, Illinois pesticide applicators license (training provided). Duration is 3 months. $6 per hour. Open to college freshmen, college sophomores, college juniors, college seniors, recent college graduates, graduate students. ▶ *1 native plant research intern:* responsibilities include assisting with field surveys of indigenous plants, pollination biology studies on rare species, collection of voucher speciments for the Herbarium, and collection of seed and living material for research projects. Candidates should have ability to work independently, ability to work with others, analytical skills, declared college major in field, knowledge of field, personal interest in the field, research skills. Duration is 9 months. $6 per hour. Open to college freshmen, college sophomores, college juniors, college seniors, recent college graduates, graduate students. ▶ *1 plant breeding intern:* responsibilities include assisting in developing new ornamental plants through breeding and selection; performing hand-pollinations, recording data, collecting seeds, accessioning plants, maintaining living plant collection, and conducting tissue culture research. Candidates should have ability to work independently, analytical skills, declared college major in field, knowledge of field, plan to pursue career in field, research skills. Duration is 6–9 months. $6 per hour. Open to college freshmen, college sophomores, college juniors, college seniors, recent college graduates, graduate students. ▶ *1 plant propagation intern:* responsibilities include gaining experience in propagation nursery and greenhouse ornamental landscape and native plants, maintaining propagules, conducting inventory, and keeping accurate computer records. Candidates should have ability to work independently, ability to work with others, declared col-

lege major in field, knowledge of field, plan to pursue career in field. Duration is 12 months. $6 per hour. Open to college freshmen, college sophomores, college juniors, college seniors, recent college graduates, graduate students. ▶ *1 plant records intern:* responsibilities include assisting collections management department with accessioning, mapping, labeling, researching new and rare plants, entering data, creating computerized maps, generating plant lists, producing display labels, and recordkeeping to track living plant collection. Candidates should have ability to work independently, ability to work with others, computer skills, declared college major in field, knowledge of field, personal interest in the field. Duration is 3–6 months. $6 per hour. Open to college freshmen, college sophomores, college juniors, college seniors, recent college graduates, graduate students. International applications accepted.

Benefits Formal training, free housing, job counseling, names of contacts, on-the-job training, opportunity to attend seminars/workshops, possible full-time employment, willing to act as a professional reference, willing to complete paperwork for educational credit, willing to provide letters of recommendation. **Contact** Write, call, fax, or e-mail Ms. Aviva Levavi, Internship Coordinator. Phone: 847-835-8263. Fax: 847-835-1635. E-mail: alevavi@chicagobotanic.org. Applicants must submit a formal organization application, resume, academic transcripts, three letters of recommendation, essay. Application deadline: March 1. World Wide Web: http://www.chicago-botanic.org.

CHICAGO CHILDREN'S MUSEUM
Navy Pier, 700 East Grand, Suite 127
Chicago, Illinois 60611-3428

General Information Interactive children's museum that inspires creative and interactive learning and leads children to the discovery and love of learning. Established in 1982. Number of employees: 100. Number of internship applications received each year: 300.

Internships Available ▶ *1–2 community service interns:* responsibilities include developing curriculum for school and community outreach for teachers, children, and parents. Candidates should have computer skills, oral communication skills, organizational skills, strong interpersonal skills, strong leadership ability, written communication skills. Open to college sophomores, college juniors, college seniors, recent college graduates, graduate students. ▶ *1 development intern:* responsibilities include researching potential donors and assisting in creating fund-raising proposals. Candidates should have computer skills, research skills, strong interpersonal skills, written communication skills. Open to college sophomores, college juniors, college seniors, recent college graduates, graduate students, individuals reentering the workforce. ▶ *2–3 education interns:* responsibilities include planning workshops, developing educational programs, and facilitating activities. Candidates should have computer skills, organizational skills, self-motivation, strong interpersonal skills. Open to college sophomores, college juniors, college seniors, recent college graduates, graduate students. ▶ *1 exhibits intern:* responsibilities include researching products and services, keylining exhibit labels, and creating temporary displays. Candidates should have editing skills, research skills, written communication skills. Open to college sophomores, college juniors, college seniors, recent college graduates, graduate students, individuals reentering the workforce. ▶ *1–2 human resource interns:* responsibilities include performing duties relating to all aspects of the volunteer program including recruitment, training, retention, and recognition. Candidates should have analytical skills, computer skills, oral communication skills, organizational skills, strong interpersonal skills, written communication skills. Open to college juniors, college seniors, recent college graduates, graduate students. ▶ *3 marketing interns:* responsibilities include soliciting membership and assisting in social events and public relations/marketing. Candidates should have analytical skills, computer skills, office skills, oral communication skills, strong interpersonal skills, written communication skills. Open to college sophomores, college juniors, college seniors, recent college graduates, graduate students, individuals reentering the workforce. Duration for all positions is 3 months. All positions are unpaid. International applications accepted.

Benefits Job counseling, willing to complete paperwork for educational credit, willing to provide letters of recommendation, $100 travel stipend.

Contact Write, call, fax, or e-mail Phyllis Barker, Director of Volunteer and Intern Services. Phone: 312-464-7652. Fax: 312-527-9082. E-mail: phyllisb@chichildrensmuseum.org. In-person interview recommended. Applicants must submit a resume, writing sample, two personal references. Application deadline: January 30 for winter/spring, June 1 for summer, September 30 for fall.

CHILDREN'S MUSEUM OF INDIANAPOLIS
PO Box 3000
Indianapolis, Indiana 46206

General Information Museum that strives to enrich the lives of children by creating excellent exhibits, programs, and experiences that share knowledge, stimulate imagination, kindle curiosity, and affirm the joy of lifelong learning. Established in 1925. Number of employees: 400. Number of internship applications received each year: 200.

Internships Available ▶ *60–70 interns:* responsibilities include performing customized duties that match the intern's interests and the museum's needs. Candidates should have ability to work independently, oral communication skills, organizational skills, self-motivation, strong interpersonal skills. Duration is 1 semester. Unpaid. Open to college freshmen, college sophomores, college juniors, college seniors, recent college graduates, graduate students. International applications accepted.

Benefits Formal training, housing at a cost, job counseling, names of contacts, on-the-job training, opportunity to attend seminars/workshops, possible full-time employment, willing to act as a professional reference, willing to complete paperwork for educational credit, willing to provide letters of recommendation.

Contact Write, call, fax, or e-mail Suzanne Mandel, Manager, Recruiting Services. Phone: 317-334-3302. Fax: 317-920-2047. E-mail: suzannem@childrensmuseum.org. In-person interview required. Applicants must submit a cover letter, resume, portfolio for graphic design internships, telephone interview acceptable if applicant is located more than 2 hours from Indianapolis. Applications are accepted continuously. World Wide Web: http://www.childrensmuseum.org.

THE CLOISTERS
Fort Tryon Park
New York, New York 10040

General Information Museum devoted to the art of medieval Europe with a collection including architectural fragments, sculptures, frescoes, illuminated manuscripts, tapestries, stained glass, medieval metal works, and paintings. Established in 1938. Number of employees: 60. Branch of Metropolitan Museum of Art, New York, New York. Number of internship applications received each year: 300.

Internships Available ▶ *8 interns:* responsibilities include teaching day campers (ages 4–12) about medieval art and giving gallery talks on a specialized topic to the general public. Candidates should have ability to work independently, college courses in field, knowledge of field, oral communication skills, personal interest in the field, research skills, self-motivation, strong interpersonal skills. Duration is 9 weeks. $2,250 per duration of internship. Open to college freshmen, college sophomores, college juniors, college seniors. International applications accepted.

Benefits Names of contacts, on-the-job training, opportunity to attend seminars/workshops, willing to complete paperwork for educational credit, willing to provide letters of recommendation.

Contact Write or call Dr. Nancy Wu, Summer Internship Coordinator/Assistant Museum Educator. Phone: 212-650-2280. Contact the department for an application flyer prior to submitting a formal application, academic transcripts, 2 letters of

recommendation, and completing an in-person interview. Application deadline: February 1 for summer. World Wide Web: http://www.metmuseum.org.

COLONIAL NATIONAL HISTORICAL PARK
PO Box 210
Yorktown, Virginia 23690

General Information National historical park that preserves, protects, and interprets the site of the first permanent English settlement in the New World (Jamestown) and the site of the last major battle of the American Revolutionary War (Yorktown). Established in 1930. Number of employees: 80. Unit of United States National Park Service, Washington, District of Columbia. Number of internship applications received each year: 10.

Internships Available ▶ *1 cataloging intern:* responsibilities include cataloging artifacts. Candidates should have ability to work independently, ability to work with others, analytical skills, college courses in field, experience in the field, office skills, organizational skills. Duration is 4–6 weeks. Position available as unpaid or paid. Open to college juniors, college seniors, recent college graduates, graduate students. ▶ *1 computer intern:* responsibilities include creating and organizing computer files to track information and working with the park's Division of Building and Historical Preservation. Candidates should have ability to work independently, ability to work with others, computer skills, office skills, organizational skills. Duration is flexible. Unpaid. Open to high school students, high school seniors, recent high school graduates, college freshmen, college sophomores, college juniors, college seniors, recent college graduates, graduate students, individuals reentering the workforce. ▶ *4–6 division of historical interpretations:* responsibilities include historical research and preparing and presenting interpretive programs; internship can be tailored to meet the intern's needs and the park's interests. Candidates should have college courses in field, editing skills, knowledge of field, oral communication skills, personal interest in the field, research skills, strong interpersonal skills, writing skills. Duration is 9–12 weeks. Position available as unpaid or paid. Open to college freshmen, college sophomores, college juniors, college seniors, recent college graduates, graduate students. ▶ *1 furniture survey intern:* responsibilities include preparing paperwork for furniture survey of items on exhibit and in storage. Candidates should have ability to work with others, analytical skills, college courses in field, computer skills, knowledge of field, office skills, organizational skills, research skills. Duration is 4–6 weeks. Position available as unpaid or paid. ▶ *1 landscape architect:* responsibilities include working closely with park landscape architect on a variety of projects relating to, but not exclusively, historic landscape inventory, landscape maintenance plans, design projects, and historic documentation. Candidates should have ability to work independently, analytical skills, computer skills, declared college major in field, knowledge of field, oral communication skills, plan to pursue career in field, research skills, self-motivation, strong interpersonal skills, written communication skills. Duration is 3 months to 1 semester. Unpaid. Open to college juniors, college seniors, recent college graduates, graduate students, only those who are in a lanscape architecture architecture degree program. ▶ *1 preservation through housekeeping intern:* responsibilities include housekeeping in museum storage area, two historic houses, and museum exhibits. Candidates should have ability to work independently, knowledge of field, personal interest in the field, strong interpersonal skills. Duration is 4–6 weeks. Unpaid. Open to college freshmen, college sophomores, college juniors, college seniors, recent college graduates, graduate students. International applications accepted.

Benefits Formal training, free housing, names of contacts, on-the-job training, opportunity to attend seminars/workshops, willing to act as a professional reference, willing to complete paperwork for educational credit, willing to provide letters of recommendation, stipends may be available.

Contact Write, fax, or e-mail Volunteer Coordinator, PO Box 210, Yorktown, Virginia 83690. Phone: 757-898-3400. Fax: 757-898-6346. E-mail: peggie_gaul@nps.gov. In-person interview recommended. Applicants must submit a cover letter, resume,

Colonial National Historical Park *(continued)*

academic transcripts. Application deadline: March 25 for summer, July 1 for fall, October 1 for spring. World Wide Web: http://www.nps.gov/colo/.

THE COLONIAL WILLIAMSBURG FOUNDATION
PO Box 1776
Williamsburg, Virginia 23187-1776

General Information Living history museum that interprets the lives and times of 18th-century Williamsburg and colonial Virginia residents. Established in 1926. Number of employees: 3,600. Number of internship applications received each year: 100.
Internships Available ▶ *5–15 interns:* responsibilities include working in such areas as architecture, architectural research, archives and records, historic trades programs, decorative arts administration, historic research, interpretive education, program development, and personnel. Candidates should have ability to work independently, computer skills, organizational skills, personal interest in the field, written communication skills, experience and/or college courses in field. Duration is 2–12 months. Unpaid. Open to college juniors, college seniors, recent college graduates, graduate students, career changers.
Benefits Willing to complete paperwork for educational credit.
Contact Write, call, or fax Ms. Peggy McDonald Howells, Manager, Museum Professional Services, PO Box 1776, Wililamsburg, Virginia 23187-1776. Phone: 757-220-7211. Fax: 757-565-8744. In-person interview recommended. Applicants must submit a cover letter, resume, 1 to 2 personal references, 1 to 2 letters of recommendation. Applications are accepted continuously. World Wide Web: http://www.history.org.

COLORADO DIVISION OF PARKS AND RECREATION, TRINIDAD LAKE STATE PARK
32610 Highway 12
Trinidad, Colorado 81082

General Information Organization overseeing Trinidad Lake State Park, located in the Purgatoire River Valley among pinion/juniper forests, whose goals are to ensure safety, provide resource protection, and enforce administrative regulations and laws. Established in 1980. Number of employees: 3. Unit of Colorado Division of Parks & Recreation, Denver, Colorado. Number of internship applications received each year: 15.
Internships Available ▶ *1 intern:* responsibilities include working in various areas of Colorado State Park operations including interpretation, research, programming, public safety, resource protection, revenue collection, visitor contact, conducting surveys, maintenance, and attending management meetings. Candidates should have ability to work independently, ability to work with others, oral communication skills, plan to pursue career in field, self-motivation, writing skills. Duration is 2–6 months. Position available as unpaid or paid. Open to college freshmen, college sophomores, college juniors, college seniors.
Benefits Formal training, housing at a cost, job counseling, names of contacts, opportunity to attend seminars/workshops, possible full-time employment, willing to complete paperwork for educational credit, willing to provide letters of recommendation, leadership skills.
Contact Write or e-mail Mr. Brad Henley, Senior Ranger. E-mail: tdadlake@rmi.net. No phone calls. In-person interview recommended. Applicants must submit a resume. Application deadline: April 1 for summer, August 1 for winter. World Wide Web: http://www.coloradoparks.org.

COLORADO HISTORICAL SOCIETY
1300 Broadway
Denver, Colorado 80203

General Information Educational institution that collects, preserves, and interprets the history and prehistory of Colorado and the West. Established in 1879. Number of employees: 100. Division of State of Colorado, Department of Higher Education, Denver, Colorado. Number of internship applications received each year: 150.

Internships Available ▶ *Interns:* responsibilities include working in education, publications, public service, books and manuscripts, decorative/fine arts, material culture, photography, design and production, or the historian's office. Candidates should have ability to work independently, ability to work with others, college courses in field, organizational skills, personal interest in the field, self-motivation. Duration is up to 1 year. Unpaid. Open to college freshmen, college sophomores, college juniors, college seniors, recent college graduates, graduate students. International applications accepted.
Benefits Job counseling, names of contacts, possible full-time employment, willing to complete paperwork for educational credit, willing to provide letters of recommendation.
Contact Write or fax Jennifer Adams, Administrative Assistant III. Fax: 303-866-4464. No phone calls. In-person interview recommended. Applicants must submit a cover letter, resume, two letters of recommendation. Applications are accepted continuously.

COLORADO STATE PARKS, STEAMBOAT LAKE STATE PARK
PO Box 750
Clark, Colorado 80428

General Information State park reservoir for camping, fishing, water sports, winter recreation, wildlife, and hunting. Established in 1967. Number of employees: 15. Unit of Colorado Division of Parks & Recreation, Denver, Colorado. Number of internship applications received each year: 40.
Internships Available ▶ *1 environmental education/interpretation specialist:* responsibilities include developing, scheduling, promoting, and conducting environmental education and interpretive programs to be presented at Steamboat Lake and Pearl Lake State Parks and the local community. Candidates should have ability to work independently, declared college major in field, oral communication skills, organizational skills, plan to pursue career in field, self-motivation, valid driver's license, willingness to work weekends, holidays, and evening shifts. Duration is 5 months from May-September (40 hours per week). $7 per hour. ▶ *2–4 seasonal park rangers:* responsibilities include supervising the safety of park visitors, enforcing rules and regulations, patrolling park area, and performing public relations, interpretive programs, maintenance, and office and administrative duties. Candidates should have ability to work independently, declared college major in field, oral communication skills, self-motivation, strong interpersonal skills, valid driver's license, willingness to work weekends, holidays, and evening shifts, successful completion of personal background investigation. Duration is 5 months from May-September (40 hours per week). $7 per hour. ▶ *1 winter intern:* responsibilities include visitor center operation, public relations, interpretation/environmental education, snow removal, maintenance, administrative tasks, and assisting with patrol functions by foot, motor vehicle, and snow mobile. Candidates should have ability to work independently, declared college major in field, oral communication skills, plan to pursue career in field, self-motivation, strong interpersonal skills, valid driver's license, willingness to work weekends and holidays, current CPR first aid certification. Duration is December to April (flexible). Unpaid. Open to college juniors, college seniors, recent college graduates, individuals at least 21 years old.
Benefits Formal training, housing at a cost, names of contacts, on-the-job training, opportunity to attend seminars/workshops, possible full-time employment, willing to act as a professional reference, willing to complete paperwork for educational credit, willing to provide letters of recommendation.
Contact Write, call, fax, or e-mail Mr. David Meline, Park Ranger. Phone: 970-879-3922. Fax: 970-879-8258. E-mail: steambt@csn.net. In-person interview recommended. Applicants must submit a formal organization application. Application deadline: March 15 for summer (suggested deadline), November 15 for winter (suggested deadline). World Wide Web: http://www.coloradoparks.org/steamboat.

CONTEMPORARY ART MUSEUM
PO Box 66
Raleigh, North Carolina 27602-0066

General Information Nonprofit art museum that presents new and innovative works by regional, national, and international artists and designers through a schedule of diverse exhibitions that explore aesthetic cultural and ideological issues. Established in 1983. Number of employees: 4. Number of internship applications received each year: 10.

Internships Available ▶ *1 curatorial intern:* responsibilities include assisting the curator of exhibitions with aspects of planning, research, and implementation of the exhibition schedule. Candidates should have computer skills, declared college major in field, knowledge of field, research skills, strong interpersonal skills, writing skills. Duration is 1–2 semesters. Open to college juniors, college seniors, recent college graduates, graduate students, career changers, individuals reentering the workforce. ▶ *1–2 education interns:* responsibilities include assisting in the development of educational programs for exhibitions, community outreach, and working on special educational projects with local high schools and middle schools. Candidates should have college courses in field, computer skills, oral communication skills, organizational skills, personal interest in the field, written communication skills. Duration is 1–2 semesters. Open to college sophomores, college juniors, college seniors, recent college graduates, graduate students, career changers, individuals reentering the workforce. ▶ *1–2 marketing interns:* responsibilities include working with a membership committee, performing public relations work, assisting the development director, and assisting with all phases of marketing. Candidates should have computer skills, oral communication skills, personal interest in the field, strong interpersonal skills, written communication skills. Duration is 1 semester. Open to college sophomores, college juniors, college seniors, recent college graduates, graduate students, career changers, individuals reentering the workforce. All positions available as unpaid or paid. International applications accepted.

Benefits Opportunity to attend seminars/workshops, possible full-time employment, willing to act as a professional reference, willing to complete paperwork for educational credit, willing to provide letters of recommendation.

Contact Write or call Courtenay Bailey-Murcko, Director of Development. Phone: 919-836-0088. In-person interview recommended. Applicants must submit a cover letter, resume, three personal references, three letters of recommendation, 2—3 writing samples. Applications are accepted continuously. World Wide Web: http://www.camnc.org.

COOPER-HEWITT NATIONAL DESIGN MUSEUM, SMITHSONIAN INSTITUTION
2 East 91st Street
New York, New York 10128

General Information Museum serving as a resource for architects, designers, studio artists, craftpeople, and scholars; the nearly quarter-million object collection includes decorative arts, drawings and prints, textiles and wallcoverings, and an extensive library. Established in 1897. Number of employees: 128. Number of internship applications received each year: 50.

Internships Available ▶ *1 Lippincott & Margulies summer intern:* responsibilities include working in the Museum's holdings of drawings and prints, archives, and related collections. Candidates should have commitment to a career in design or design history/criticism. Duration is 10 weeks. $2,500 per duration of internship. ▶ *Peter Krueger summer interns:* responsibilities include assisting on special projects for a specific curatorial, educational, or administrative department and participating in daily museum activities. Candidates should have career consideration in art history, design, museum studies, or museum education. Duration is 10 weeks. $2,500 per duration of internship. ▶ *Smithsonian Institution minority interns.* Duration is 10 weeks. Position available as unpaid or at stipend available. ▶ *Academic year interns:* responsibilities include researching and producing exhibits, administering and planning classes and tours, cataloging and managing collections, and library management. Duration is flexible. Unpaid. ▶ *1–12 volunteer interns:* responsibilities include learning about the programs, policies, procedures, and operations of the National Design Museum and of museums in general. Duration is 10 weeks. Unpaid. Open to college freshmen, college sophomores, college juniors, college seniors, recent college graduates, graduate students. International applications accepted.

Benefits Opportunity to attend seminars/workshops, willing to complete paperwork for educational credit, willing to provide letters of recommendation, stipend available for minority intern program.

Contact Write or fax Intern Coordinator. Fax: 212-860-6909. In-person interview recommended. Applicants must submit a cover letter, resume, academic transcripts, two letters of recommendation. Application deadline: March 31. World Wide Web: http://www.si.edu/ndm/.

DANFORTH MUSEUM OF ART
123 Union Avenue
Framingham, Massachusetts 01702

General Information Community museum that presents changing exhibits, many drawn from its permanent collection; operates an art school with 70 courses for adults and children; offers Junior Gallery experiences, workshops, and curriculum kits to teachers and students. Established in 1975. Number of employees: 16. Number of internship applications received each year: 50.

Internships Available ▶ *1–3 curatorial assistants:* responsibilities include assisting director with research, formation of archives, packing/unpacking art work, and exhibition installation. Candidates should have college courses in field, computer skills, knowledge of field, knowledge of Microsoft Word. Duration is 1 semester (8-10 hours per week). ▶ *1–3 development and marketing interns:* responsibilities include donor information processing and research, benefit events, grant research and writing, and drafting public relations and marketing brochures. Candidates should have computer skills, knowledge of field, personal interest in the field. Duration is 1 semester (8 to 10 hours per week). ▶ *2–3 education interns:* responsibilities include assisting education coordinator in school outreach, scheduling guided tours, docent training, developing Art on the Move curriculum kits, and conducting student tours. Candidates should have knowledge of Word. Duration is 1 semester (8 to 10 hours per week). All positions are unpaid. Open to college juniors, college seniors, recent college graduates, graduate students, career changers.

Benefits On-the-job training, willing to act as a professional reference, willing to complete paperwork for educational credit, willing to provide letters of recommendation, job lists provided when available.

Contact Write, call, or fax Ronald L. Crusan, Director, 125 Union Avenue, Framingham, Massachusetts 01702. Phone: 508-620-0050. Fax: 508-872-5542. In-person interview recommended. Applicants must submit a cover letter, resume, academic transcripts. Applications are accepted continuously.

D. C. BOOTH HISTORIC NATIONAL FISH HATCHERY
423 Hatchery Circle
Spearfish, South Dakota 57783

General Information Historic federal fish hatchery with museum and archives of fish culture. Established in 1896. Number of employees: 15. Unit of U.S. Fish and Wildlife Service, Washington, District of Columbia. Number of internship applications received each year: 10.

Internships Available ▶ *1–2 archives aides:* responsibilities include assisting with archival processing and storage and research. Candidates should have ability to work independently, knowledge of field, research skills, self-motivation, written communication skills. Open to high school seniors, recent high school graduates, college freshmen, college sophomores, college juniors, college seniors, recent college graduates, graduate students, career changers, individuals reentering the workforce. ▶ *1–2 museum aides:* responsibilities include assisting with collection care, pest

D. C. Booth Historic National Fish Hatchery (continued)
management, preservation maintenance, monitoring environmental conditions, cataloging, photographing, and aiding in conservation. Candidates should have ability to work independently, college courses in field, knowledge of field, self-motivation, written communication skills. Open to college freshmen, college sophomores, college juniors, college seniors, recent college graduates, graduate students, career changers, individuals reentering the workforce. Duration for all positions is 2–6 months. All positions available as unpaid or at dependent on funding. International applications accepted.
Benefits Free housing, names of contacts, on-the-job training, possible full-time employment, willing to complete paperwork for educational credit, willing to provide letters of recommendation.
Contact Write, call, fax, or e-mail Ms. Randi Sue Smith, Curator. Phone: 605-642-7730. Fax: 605-642-2336. E-mail: randi_smith@ fws.gov. Applicants must submit a cover letter, resume, two personal references. Application deadline: March 15 for summer; continuous for other positions. World Wide Web: http:// www.fws.gov/r6dcbth/dcbooth.html.

DECATUR HOUSE
748 Jackson Place, NW
Washington, District of Columbia 20006

General Information Historic house museum located near the White House that interprets its residents' history, 1819 to 1956. Established in 1956. Number of employees: 12. Unit of National Trust for Historic Preservation, Washington, District of Columbia. Number of internship applications received each year: 20.
Internships Available ▶ *1–2 curatorial assistants:* responsibilities include assisting curator of collections with cataloging, caring for and maintaining museum's collection, and aiding in exhibit preparation, installment, and coordination. Candidates should have computer skills, personal interest in the field, self-motivation, strong interpersonal skills, writing skills. Duration is at least 6-8 weeks. Open to college sophomores, college seniors, recent college graduates, graduate students, career changers. ▶ *1–3 education assistants:* responsibilities include assisting curator of education with school group tours, developing educational materials, and working with tour guides to learn museum and collections. Candidates should have computer skills, experience in the field, knowledge of field, personal interest in the field, strong interpersonal skills, written communication skills. Duration is 3 months. Open to college seniors, recent college graduates, graduate students, career changers. ▶ *1–3 research interns:* responsibilities include researching certain areas pertaining to Decatur House collection and its occupants and utilizing on-site materials and local organizations to gather research information. Candidates should have ability to work with others, college courses in field, college degree in related field, knowledge of field, research skills, self-motivation, written communication skills. Duration is at least 6-8 weeks. Open to college seniors, recent college graduates, graduate students, career changers. All positions are unpaid. International applications accepted.
Benefits Names of contacts, on-the-job training, opportunity to attend seminars/workshops, willing to complete paperwork for educational credit, willing to provide letters of recommendation, membership after 30 hours' service, opportunity to become immersed in the workings of a medium historic house museum.
Contact Write, call, fax, or e-mail Ms. Molly Neal, Director of Collections and Programs. Phone: 202-842-0918. Fax: 202-842-0030. E-mail: decatur_house@nthp.org. In-person interview recommended. Applicants must submit a cover letter, resume, two letters of recommendation. Application deadline: January 1 for spring (suggested deadline), May 1 for summer (suggested deadline), October 1 for winter; suggested deadlines; but applications are accepted year-round.

DELTA AREA STATE PARKS
PO Box 682
Delta Junction, Alaska 99737

General Information District that includes 5 recreation sites, 1 historical park, salmon and trout fishing, and numerous campgrounds and serves as a main access point for the Interior. Established in 1975. Number of employees: 3. Branch of Alaska Division of Parks and Outdoor Recreation, Anchorage, Alaska. Number of internship applications received each year: 15.
Internships Available ▶ *2–3 ranger assistants:* responsibilities include janitorial and park maintenance, camper registration, offering visitor information, conducting firewood sales and distribution, and visitor center staffing. Candidates should have ability to work independently, oral communication skills, organizational skills, self-motivation, strong interpersonal skills. Duration is 6–12 weeks. Unpaid. Open to recent high school graduates, college juniors, college seniors, recent college graduates, graduate students, career changers. International applications accepted.
Benefits Free housing, on-the-job training, opportunity to attend seminars/workshops, possible full-time employment, willing to act as a professional reference, willing to complete paperwork for educational credit, willing to provide letters of recommendation, meal stipend.
Contact Write, fax, or e-mail Mr. Brooks Ludwig, Ranger. Fax: 907-895-5043. E-mail: brooks_ludwig@dnr.state.ak.us. Applicants must submit a formal organization application, cover letter, resume, academic transcripts, three personal references. Application deadline: February 28 for summer.

DENALI NATIONAL PARK AND PRESERVE
PO Box 9
Denali Park, Alaska 99755

General Information National park serving to preserve, protect, and interpret the natural and cultural history of 6 million acres, recognized for its wildlife and North America's tallest peak Mt. McKinley. Established in 1917. Number of employees: 70. Unit of United States National Park Service, Washington, District of Columbia. Number of internship applications received each year: 300.
Internships Available ▶ *1–2 backcountry volunteers:* responsibilities include issuing bear-resistant food containers to backcountry users, advising visitors of safe hiking and minimum impact techniques, issuing permits at VAC, conducting backcountry patrols, and special projects. Candidates should have ability to work independently, computer skills, knowledge of field, oral communication skills, personal interest in the field, self-motivation, strong interpersonal skills. Open to college seniors, recent college graduates, graduate students, career changers, individuals reentering the workforce. ▶ *1–2 interpretive naturalists:* responsibilities include preparing and presenting educational programs and providing information at the Visitor Center (VAC). Candidates should have ability to work independently, computer skills, knowledge of field, oral communication skills, organizational skills, personal interest in the field, self-motivation, strong interpersonal skills, strong leadership ability, writing skills. Open to recent college graduates, graduate students, career changers. ▶ *1–2 resource management volunteers:* responsibilities include assisting researchers and resource managers in a variety of field and office work. Candidates should have ability to work independently, knowledge of field, organizational skills, personal interest in the field, research skills, self-motivation, strong interpersonal skills, written communication skills. Open to recent college graduates, graduate students, career changers. Duration for all positions is 1 summer (May 15-September 1). All positions are unpaid. International applications accepted.
Benefits Formal training, job counseling, on-the-job training, daily stipend of $10.
Contact Write, call, fax, or e-mail Jamie Lasell, VIP Coordinator. Phone: 907-683-2294. Fax: 907-683-9623. E-mail: jamie_lasell@ nps.gov. Applicants must submit a resume. Application deadline: March 15. World Wide Web: http://www.nps.gov/dena.

DENVER ART MUSEUM
100 West 14th Avenue Parkway
Denver, Colorado 80204

General Information Art museum with world collection (Asian, PreColumbian, Spanish Colonial, American Indian, American,

European, and African) and special emphasis on museum education and outreach. Number of employees: 100. Number of internship applications received each year: 15.

Internships Available ▶ *5–8 museum education interns:* responsibilities include applying research to educational tasks such as didactic exhibitions; performing outreach to culturally diverse individuals; assisting school, family, and adult programs; and teaching youth and adults in Museum galleries. Candidates should have computer skills, knowledge of field, oral communication skills, personal interest in the field, strong interpersonal skills, written communication skills. Duration is 3–12 months. Unpaid. Open to college juniors, college seniors, recent college graduates, graduate students, career changers, individuals reentering the workforce. International applications accepted.

Benefits Formal training, opportunity to attend seminars/workshops, possible full-time employment, willing to complete paperwork for educational credit, willing to provide letters of recommendation.

Contact Write or call Christine Deal, Education Administrator. Phone: 303-640-2953. In-person interview recommended. Applicants must submit a formal organization application, cover letter, resume, academic transcripts, three personal references, letter of recommendation. Applications are accepted continuously.

DENVER BOTANIC GARDENS
909 York Street
Denver, Colorado 80206

General Information Urban botanic gardens headquartered on 23 acres within 2 miles of downtown Denver with additional property located in the foothills (6,000–8,000 feet), montane (8,000–10,000 feet), and alpine (above timberline) zones. Established in 1951. Number of employees: 100. Number of internship applications received each year: 30.

Internships Available ▶ *5–6 applied horticulture interns:* responsibilities include working with garden professionals. Candidates should have ability to work with others, college courses in field, knowledge of field, personal interest in the field. Duration is 10 weeks. $2,000 per duration of internship (approximate). Open to college juniors, college seniors, graduate students, older students returning to school. International applications accepted.

Benefits Names of contacts, opportunity to attend seminars/workshops, possible full-time employment, willing to complete paperwork for educational credit, willing to provide letters of recommendation.

Contact Write, fax, or e-mail Ms. Paula D. Ogilvie, Education Specialist. Fax: 303-370-8196. E-mail: ogilviep@botanicgardens.org. Applicants must submit a formal organization application, resume, academic transcripts, three letters of recommendation. Application deadline: February 17. World Wide Web: http://www.botanicgardens.org.

DESCANSO GARDENS
1418 Descanso Drive
La Canada Flintridge, California 91011

General Information Botanical garden with special emphasis on camellia, rose, and native plants. Established in 1947. Number of employees: 48. Number of internship applications received each year: 10.

Internships Available ▶ *5 summer interns.* Candidates should have ability to work with others, college courses in field, declared college major in field, knowledge of field, plan to pursue career in field. Duration is 10 weeks. $6 per hour. Open to college juniors, college seniors, recent college graduates.

Benefits Willing to complete paperwork for educational credit, willing to provide letters of recommendation, opportunity to learn the functions of a botanic garden, hands-on experience.

Contact Write, call, or fax Ms. Robin Sease, Manager of Public Programming. Phone: 818-952-7787. Fax: 818-949-7982. Applicants must submit a cover letter, resume, three letters of recommendation. Application deadline: February 28 for summer.

DETROIT INSTITUTE OF ARTS
5200 Woodward Avenue
Detroit, Michigan 48202-4094

General Information Institute that preserves, collects, and displays works of art and furthers the understanding and appreciation of the visual arts. Established in 1885. Number of employees: 270. Number of internship applications received each year: 80.

Internships Available ▶ *3–4 high school placement interns:* responsibilities include participation in authorized school field experience of short duration and in conjunction with authorized school programs. Unpaid. ▶ *1 museum diversity intern:* responsibilities include assisting in museum departments on tasks matching the intern's educational background and work experience. Duration is up to 11 months. Paid. Open to graduate students. ▶ *4–6 professional/graduate interns:* responsibilities include working with curators and museum personnel in assuming responsibilities equivalent to those of entry level professional staff. Duration is 10–12 months. Position available as unpaid or paid. ▶ *1–2 undergraduate field studies interns:* responsibilities include assisting in various museum departments on a single project or varied duties, ranging from general office work to research, according to intern's qualifications and interests. Duration is flexible. Unpaid. International applications accepted.

Benefits Job counseling, names of contacts, on-the-job training, opportunity to attend seminars/workshops, willing to complete paperwork for educational credit, willing to provide letters of recommendation.

Contact Write, call, fax, or e-mail Gina Alexander Granger, Assistant Educator. Phone: 313-833-1858. Fax: 313-833-7355. E-mail: granger@dia.ci.detroit.mi.us. Applicants must submit a cover letter, resume, letter of recommendation. Applications are accepted continuously. World Wide Web: http://www.dia.org.

DISCOVERY CREEK CHILDREN'S MUSEUM OF WASHINGTON
5125 MacArthur Boulevard, NW, Suite 10
Washington, District of Columbia 20016

General Information Museum focusing on environmental and art education, located on 12-acre site that includes the only remaining one-room schoolhouse in Washington, D.C. Established in 1993. Number of employees: 8. Number of internship applications received each year: 20.

Internships Available ▶ *5–10 education interns:* responsibilities include assisting with development and teaching of Museum's school and weekend public programs utilizing live wildlife, art activities, and outdoor exploration; helping lead art projects, science experiments, outdoor hikes, and activities, including canoeing, white water rafting, and wildlife demonstrations. Candidates should have ability to work independently, oral communication skills, organizational skills, personal interest in the field, research skills, self-motivation, strong interpersonal skills, strong leadership ability, written communication skills. Duration is 1 month to 1 year. Position available as unpaid or paid. Open to college freshmen, college sophomores, college juniors, college seniors, recent college graduates, graduate students, career changers, individuals reentering the workforce. International applications accepted.

Benefits Names of contacts, on-the-job training, willing to act as a professional reference, willing to complete paperwork for educational credit, willing to provide letters of recommendation.

Contact Write, call, or fax Intern Coordinator. Phone: 202-364-3111. Fax: 202-364-3114. In-person interview recommended. Applicants must submit a formal organization application, cover letter, resume, academic transcripts, two letters of recommendation, writing sample may be required. Applications are accepted continuously. World Wide Web: http://www.discoverycreek.org.

THE DRAWING CENTER
35 Wooster Street
New York, New York 10013

General Information   Not-for-profit arts institution focusing on the presentation of contemporary and historic drawing, with an emphasis on providing opportunities for emerging and under-recognized artists. Established in 1977. Number of employees: 13. Number of internship applications received each year: 100.

Internships Available   ► *1–2 development assistants:* responsibilities include assisting the director of development, research, and preparing grant proposals; researching prospective donors, maintaining donor database, and tracking gifts. Candidates should have college courses in field, computer skills, research skills, self-motivation, written communication skills. Duration is 3 months. Open to college juniors, college seniors, graduate students. ► *2 education assistants:* responsibilities include assisting the educator in preparation and administration for the Schools Program and assisting during Schools Program session. Candidates should have ability to work with others, computer skills, knowledge of field, organizational skills, plan to pursue career in field, research skills, self-motivation. Open to college freshmen, college sophomores, college juniors, college seniors, recent college graduates, graduate students, individuals interested in the arts. ► *6–10 general assistants:* responsibilities include assisting in all phases of gallery operations including installation of exhibitions and administration and research regarding exhibitions, publications, fund-raising, maintaining the slide registry, and organizing and preparing for public programming. Candidates should have ability to work independently, college courses in field, computer skills, oral communication skills, organizational skills, self-motivation. Duration is 3 months. Open to college freshmen, college sophomores, college juniors, college seniors, recent college graduates, graduate students. All positions available as unpaid or at $6–$10 per hour. International applications accepted.

Benefits   Willing to act as a professional reference, willing to complete paperwork for educational credit, willing to provide letters of recommendation, professional references provided upon satisfactory completion of internships, opportunity to attend a variety of programs including lectures, readings, panel discussions, and artists' talks. The Drawing Center is able to share salaries with sponsoring schools for students who participate in federal work-study programs.

Contact   Write, call, fax, or e-mail Ms. Katie Dyer, Assistant to the Director. Phone: 212-219-2166. Fax: 212-966-2976. E-mail: drawcent@drawingcenter.org. In-person interview recommended. Applicants must submit a formal organization application, resume, two personal references. Applications are accepted continuously.

EDSEL & ELEANOR FORD HOUSE
1100 Lake Shore Road
Grosse Point Shore, Michigan 48236

General Information   The historic home of auto pioneer Edsel Ford and his family. It is an historic house museum designed by Albert Kahn and set on 87 acres of lake-front property designed by Jens Jensen.

Internships Available   ► *Curatorial and collection care interns:* responsibilities include inventory, registration, and care of art objects. Candidates should have interest in museum field, art history background. ► *Marketing and public relations interns:* responsibilities include writing press releases and assisting with media relations and special events. Candidates should have interest in museum field. Duration for all positions is flexible. All positions are unpaid. Open to college freshmen, college sophomores, college juniors, college seniors, graduate students.

Contact   Write, fax, or e-mail Director Human Resources, 1100 Lake Shore Road, Grosse Point Shore, Michigan 48236. Fax: 313-884-5977. E-mail: dboucke@fordhouse.org. No phone calls. Applicants must submit a cover letter, resume, portfolio. Applications are accepted continuously. World Wide Web: http://www.fordhouse.org.

FAIRCHILD TROPICAL GARDEN
10901 Old Cutler Road
Miami, Florida 33156

General Information   Botanical garden of 83 acres specializing in palms, cycads, tropical flowering trees, shrubs, and vines and promoting education, research, and conservation. Established in 1938. Number of employees: 57. Number of internship applications received each year: 20.

Internships Available   ► *2 student interns:* responsibilities include working closely with supervisor (curator, horticulturist, or nursery manager) in the Conservatory with palms and cycads, in the flowering tree section, or in the plant records department. Candidates should have ability to work independently, ability to work with others, declared college major in field, plan to pursue career in field, ability to work in subtropical climate. Duration is 10 weeks. Paid. Open to college seniors, recent college graduates, graduate students, young professionals. International applications accepted.

Benefits   Names of contacts, on-the-job training, opportunity to attend seminars/workshops, possible full-time employment, willing to complete paperwork for educational credit, willing to provide letters of recommendation, hands-on experience.

Contact   Write, fax, or e-mail Internship Coordinator. Phone: 305-667-1651 Ext. 3315. Fax: 305-661-8953. E-mail: ftgarden@juno.com. Applicants must submit a formal organization application, 3 personal references or letters of recommendation. Application deadline: March 15 for summer. World Wide Web: http://www.ftg.org.

FELLOWS RIVERSIDE GARDENS
123 McKinley Avenue
Youngstown, Ohio 44509

General Information   An 11-acre public display garden. Established in 1891. Number of employees: 5. Unit of Mill Creek Metropolitan Park District, Youngstown, Ohio. Number of internship applications received each year: 6.

Internships Available   ► *2 gardeners:* responsibilities include maintaining plants with opportunity to focus on specific area of interest and offering educational assistance in classes and programs. Candidates should have major in horticulture, biology, or sciences preferred. Duration is 10–35 weeks. $5 per hour. Open to college freshmen, college sophomores, college juniors, college seniors, recent college graduates. International applications accepted.

Benefits   Job counseling, names of contacts, opportunity to attend seminars/workshops, willing to complete paperwork for educational credit, willing to provide letters of recommendation, workers' compensation coverage.

Contact   Write or call Mr. Keith Kaiser, Assistant Horticulture Director. Phone: 330-740-7116. In-person interview recommended. Applicants must submit a formal organization application, resume, two personal references, two letters of recommendation. Application deadline: April 1 for summer. World Wide Web: http://www.cboss.com/millcreek.

FILOLI
86 Canada Road
Woodside, California 94062

General Information   Early 20th-century country estate with a 16-acre formal garden. Number of employees: 30.

Internships Available   ► *2 garden apprentices:* responsibilities include performing public garden maintenance including mowing, blowing, edging, caring for displays, pruning, and greenhouse work. Duration is 6 months (40 hours per week). ► *5 garden interns:* responsibilities include performing public garden maintenance including mowing, blowing, edging, caring for displays, pruning, and greenhouse work. Duration is 10 weeks in spring, summer, or fall (40 hours per week). Candidates for all positions should have major in horticulture, public garden management, landscape maintenance, landscape preservation, landscape architecture, environmental studies, botany, or biology. All positions paid at $6 per hour. Open to college freshmen, college sophomores, college juniors, college seniors, recent college graduates, graduate students. International applications accepted.

Benefits Formal training, opportunity to attend seminars/workshops, willing to complete paperwork for educational credit. **Contact** Write, call, fax, or e-mail Ms. Lucy Tolmach, Director of Horticulture. Phone: 650-364-8300 Ext. 214. Fax: 650-366-7836. E-mail: filoli@earthlink.net. In-person interview recommended. Applicants must submit a formal organization application, cover letter, academic transcripts, three personal references. Application deadline: January 14 for spring (March—May), March 31 for summer (June—August), July 16 for fall (September—November), August 14 for for 6-month (January—June) apprenticeship. World Wide Web: http://www.filoli.org.

FISHERMEN'S BEND RECREATION SITE
PO Box 785
Mill City, Oregon 97360

General Information Multiple resource management agency involved in the operation and maintenance of one multiple use recreation site and four small recreation sites. Established in 1964. Number of employees: 6. Field office of Bureau of Land Management, Salem District, Salem, Oregon. Number of internship applications received each year: 2.

Internships Available ▶ *2–3 park rangers:* responsibilities include park maintenance and public relations. Candidates should have ability to work independently, ability to work with others, oral communication skills, personal interest in the field, self-motivation, willingness to work outdoors under variable conditions. Duration is 3–4 months. Position available as unpaid or at weekly subsistence pay at $100 per week. Open to recent high school graduates, college freshmen, college sophomores, college juniors, college seniors, recent college graduates, individuals reentering the workforce.

Benefits Free housing, on-the-job training, opportunity to attend seminars/workshops, willing to complete paperwork for educational credit, willing to provide letters of recommendation, field trips. **Contact** Write, call, fax, or e-mail J.B. Grant, Park Manager. Phone: 503-897-2406. Fax: 503-897-2406. E-mail: jgrant@or.blm.gov. Telephone interview required. Applicants must submit a resume, personal reference. Application deadline: January 1 for spring, March 1 for summer, July 1 for fall.

FLORIDA PARK SERVICE, KORESHAN STATE HISTORIC SITE
PO Box 7
Estero, Florida 33928

General Information Organization that offers programs of cultural interest to the public. Number of employees: 11. Unit of Florida Division of Parks and Recreation, Tallahasee, Florida. Number of internship applications received each year: 1.

Internships Available ▶ *1 actor/drama intern:* responsibilities include researching Koreshan drama, documenting their drama and presentation in living history format (1894-1920s). Candidates should have ability to work independently, oral communication skills, strong interpersonal skills. Unpaid. ▶ *1 archaeologist:* responsibilities include planning and conducting primary archaeological surveys in the park's Natural Historic District and compiling the results into format usable by management to make decisions. Candidates should have analytical skills, college courses in field, oral communication skills, research skills, self-motivation, writing skills. Unpaid. ▶ *1 architect:* responsibilities include preparing drawings of park buildings and other structures, inspecting buildings for structural analysis, and recommending conservation/stabilization/restoration treatments. Candidates should have ability to work independently, college courses in field, organizational skills, research skills, self-motivation, written communication skills. Unpaid. Open to college freshmen, college sophomores, college juniors, college seniors, recent college graduates, graduate students, individuals reentering the workforce. ▶ *1 artist:* responsibilities include exhibit designs, preparing graphics, painting murals and signs, preparing advertising designs for special events, and making replicas of garden concrete ornaments.

Candidates should have ability to work independently, experience in the field, personal interest in the field, self-motivation, written communication skills. Unpaid. ▶ *1 grant writer:* responsibilities include researching prospective grant sources, planning and preparing grant applications, and developing a support base for the park. Candidates should have college courses in field, computer skills, oral communication skills, organizational skills, writing skills. Unpaid. Open to college freshmen, college sophomores, college juniors, college seniors, recent college graduates, graduate students. ▶ *1 historic preservationist:* responsibilities include cataloging and conserving papers and artifacts. Candidates should have ability to work independently, personal interest in the field, research skills, self-motivation, writing skills, written communication skills. Unpaid. Open to college freshmen, college sophomores, college juniors, college seniors, recent college graduates, graduate students, individuals reentering the workforce. ▶ *1 interpreter:* responsibilities include providing historical knowledge to visitors and answering questions. Candidates should have ability to work independently, oral communication skills, personal interest in the field, self-motivation, strong interpersonal skills. Unpaid. Open to high school seniors, college freshmen, college sophomores, college juniors, college seniors, recent college graduates, graduate students, career changers, individuals reentering the workforce. ▶ *1 landscape specialist/horticulturist:* responsibilities include researching and documenting historic landscape of Koreshan Settlement, collecting seeds, propagation and planting. Candidates should have ability to work independently, ability to work with others, knowledge of field, personal interest in the field, research skills, self-motivation. Position available as unpaid or paid. Open to recent high school graduates, college freshmen, college sophomores, college juniors, college seniors, recent college graduates, individuals reentering the workforce. ▶ *1 maintenance worker:* responsibilities include mowing and trimming grass and maintaining facilities and grounds of the historic site. Candidates should have ability to work independently, ability to work with others, self-motivation. Unpaid. Open to recent high school graduates, college freshmen, college sophomores, college juniors, college seniors, career changers, individuals reentering the workforce, retirees. ▶ *1 management assistant:* responsibilities include working with assistant park manager to handle a wide variety of duties pertaining to daily operation of the park, recruiting, coordinating and scheduling volunteer activities, preparing requisitions, purchase orders, correspondence, and other admininstration. Candidates should have college courses in field, computer skills, oral communication skills, organizational skills, strong interpersonal skills, writing skills. Unpaid. Open to college freshmen, college sophomores, college juniors, college seniors, recent college graduates. ▶ *1 musician:* responsibilities include compiling musical history of Koreshans, preparing advertising, planning, and playing at special events and concerts. Candidates should have ability to work independently, ability to work with others, experience in the field, personal interest in the field, self-motivation. Unpaid. ▶ *1 resource management specialist:* responsibilities include preparing natural communities for prescribed burns, surveying Estero River, making recommendations and implementing resource management plans and actions such as exotic removal, erosion control, vegetation surveys, spider surveys, and gopher tortoises surveys. Candidates should have ability to work independently, ability to work with others, self-motivation. Unpaid. Open to high school seniors, recent high school graduates, college freshmen, college sophomores, college juniors, college seniors, recent college graduates, individuals reentering the workforce. Duration for all positions is flexible. International applications accepted.

Benefits Job counseling, names of contacts, on-the-job training, possible full-time employment, willing to complete paperwork for educational credit, willing to provide letters of recommendation.

Contact Write, call, fax, or e-mail Ezell Givens, Assistant Park Manager. Phone: 941-992-0311. Fax: 941-992-1607. E-mail: bj.koresh@juno.com. In-person interview recommended. Applicants must submit a formal organization application, resume. Applications are accepted continuously. World Wide Web: http://www.dep.state.fl.us/parks.

FLORISSANT FOSSIL BEDS NATIONAL MONUMENT
PO Box 185
Florissant, Colorado 80816

General Information National park providing interpretive services to the public while managing 6000-acre site containing Ponderosa pine forests, grassy wildflower meadows, and 35-million-year-old plant and insect fossils. Established in 1969. Number of employees: 18. Unit of United States National Park Service, Washington, District of Columbia. Number of internship applications received each year: 25.

Internships Available ▶ *3–5 interpretive division interns:* responsibilities include preparing and presenting programs for large and small groups on natural resources, conservation, and environmental ethics; conducting guided walks and tours to points of interest; and interpreting the natural features of the area. Candidates should have knowledge of field, oral communication skills, plan to pursue career in field, strong interpersonal skills. Duration is 12 weeks. Open to recent high school graduates, college freshmen, college sophomores, college juniors, college seniors, recent college graduates, graduate students, law students, career changers, individuals reentering the workforce. ▶ *Paleontological/education interns:* responsibilities include fossil collection and curation; assisting with excation, inventory, and monitoring of sites; database development; self-directed research; and assisting the education program by doing outreach education in the community. Candidates should have college courses in field, experience in the field, oral communication skills, written communication skills. Duration is August 15 to November 15. Open to college juniors, college seniors, recent college graduates, graduate students, individuals reentering the workforce. ▶ *2–4 paleontology interns:* responsibilities include fossil collection and curation; assisting with excavation, inventory, and monitoring of sites; database development; self-directed research. Candidates should have college courses in field, knowledge of field, personal interest in the field, plan to pursue career in field. Duration is 12 weeks. Open to college sophomores, college juniors, college seniors, recent college graduates, graduate students, law students, career changers, individuals reentering the workforce. All positions are unpaid. International applications accepted.

Benefits Formal training, free housing, job counseling, names of contacts, on-the-job training, opportunity to attend seminars/workshops, willing to act as a professional reference, willing to complete paperwork for educational credit, willing to provide letters of recommendation, uniforms provided, $60 per week stipend.

Contact Write, call, fax, or e-mail Ms. Linda Lutz-Ryan, Park Ranger. Phone: 719-748-3253. Fax: 719-748-3164. E-mail: linda_lutz-ryan@nps.gov. Telephone interview required. Applicants must submit a cover letter, resume, two personal references. Application deadline: March 20 for summer, June 20 for fall. World Wide Web: http://www.nps.gov/flfo.

FOOTHILLS ART CENTER
809 15th Street
Golden, Colorado 80401

General Information Nonprofit 501c3 visual art museum/gallery. Established in 1968. Number of employees: 7. Number of internship applications received each year: 5.

Internships Available ▶ *1–2 interns:* responsibilities include general arts administration assistance, organizing and hanging shows, artist contact, membership contact, some clerical work. Candidates should have ability to work independently, ability to work with others, college courses in field, computer skills, office skills, organizational skills, personal interest in the field, plan to pursue career in field, written communication skills. Duration is 10-40 hours per week. Unpaid. Open to college juniors, college seniors, recent college graduates, graduate students, career changers. International applications accepted.

Benefits Job counseling, names of contacts, on-the-job training, opportunity to attend seminars/workshops, willing to act as a professional reference, willing to complete paperwork for educational credit, willing to provide letters of recommendation.

Contact Write, call, or fax Elizabeth Mader, Director Operations/Carol Dickinson, Executive Director, 809 15th Street, Golden, Colorado 80401. Phone: 303-279-3922. Fax: 303-279-9470. In-person interview recommended. Applicants must submit a cover letter, resume, three personal references. Applications are accepted continuously. World Wide Web: http://www.foothillsartcenter.org.

FORT LARAMIE NATIONAL HISTORIC SITE
HC72 Box 389
Fort Laramie, Wyoming 82212

General Information Restored military outpost in southeastern Wyoming, near the Laramie Mountains, about 100 miles north of Cheyenne. Established in 1938. Number of employees: 18. Unit of United States National Park Service, Washington, District of Columbia.

Internships Available ▶ *1–5 interpretation volunteers:* responsibilities include interacting with visitors and preparing and presenting information on surroundings. Candidates should have ability to work independently, knowledge of field, oral communication skills, strong interpersonal skills, written communication skills. Duration is 1 summer. Unpaid. Open to college freshmen, college sophomores, college juniors, college seniors, recent college graduates.

Benefits Formal training.

Contact Write, fax, or e-mail Administrative Officer. Fax: 307-837-2120. E-mail: fola_superintendent@nps.gov. No phone calls. Applicants must submit a formal organization application, resume, academic transcripts. Applications are accepted continuously.

FORT LARNED NATIONAL HISTORIC SITE
RR 3
Larned, Kansas 67550

General Information Historic site dedicated to interpreting life along the Santa Fe Trail in 1868, featuring living history activities in ten buildings. Established in 1966. Number of employees: 14. Unit of United States National Park Service, Washington, District of Columbia. Number of internship applications received each year: 3.

Internships Available ▶ *1–2 interpretation interns:* responsibilities include guiding tours, assisting in the visitor center, manning living history stations, researching, and working with museum collection. Candidates should have ability to work independently, computer skills, oral communication skills, personal interest in the field, self-motivation, strong interpersonal skills. Open to college juniors, college seniors, recent college graduates, graduate students, career changers, individuals reentering the workforce. ▶ *1–2 museum interns.* Candidates should have ability to work independently, ability to work with others, computer skills, oral communication skills, personal interest in the field, self-motivation. Open to college juniors, college seniors, recent college graduates, graduate students, individuals reentering the workforce. Duration for all positions is flexible. All positions are unpaid.

Benefits Formal training, job counseling, names of contacts, on-the-job training, travel reimbursement, willing to complete paperwork for educational credit, willing to provide letters of recommendation.

Contact Write, call, or e-mail Mr. Steve Linderer, Superintendent. Phone: 316-285-6911. E-mail: fols_superintendent@nps.gov. In-person interview recommended. Applicants must submit a cover letter. Application deadline: April 25 for summer. World Wide Web: http://www.nps.gov/fols/.

FORT NECESSITY NATIONAL BATTLEFIELD
1 Washington Parkway
Farmington, Pennsylvania 15437

General Information Site commemorating the start of the French and Indian War in 1754. Established in 1931. Number of employees: 22. Unit of United States National Park Service, Washington, District of Columbia. Number of internship applications received each year: 5.

Internships Available ▶ *1–3 administrative aides:* responsibilities include monitoring/reviewing expenditures and financial reports, filing, word processing, and preparing travel documents. Candidates should have oral communication skills, personal interest in the field, strong interpersonal skills. Open to high school seniors, recent high school graduates, college freshmen, college sophomores, college juniors, college seniors, recent college graduates, individuals reentering the workforce. ▶ *1–2 curatorial aides:* responsibilities include cataloguing, photographing, preparing items for storage, general conservation, record keeping, and inventories. Candidates should have ability to work independently, ability to work with others, computer skills, experience in the field, organizational skills, personal interest in the field. Open to college freshmen, college sophomores, college juniors, college seniors, recent college graduates, graduate students. ▶ *1–5 interpretive aides:* responsibilities include working in the contact station, performing guided talks and walks, and preparing brochures. Candidates should have ability to work with others, oral communication skills, personal interest in the field, strong interpersonal skills. Open to high school seniors, recent high school graduates, college freshmen, college sophomores, college juniors, college seniors, recent college graduates, graduate students. ▶ *1–3 resource management aides:* responsibilities include monitoring flora and fauna, performing reforestation and other projects, and monitoring water. Candidates should have ability to work independently, college courses in field, experience in the field, personal interest in the field, research skills, written communication skills. Open to college freshmen, college sophomores, college juniors, college seniors, recent college graduates, graduate students. Duration for all positions is flexible. All positions are unpaid. International applications accepted.

Benefits Formal training, free housing, job counseling, on-the-job training, willing to complete paperwork for educational credit, willing to provide letters of recommendation, limited reimbursement for meals and travel.

Contact Write, call, or e-mail Mr. Chuck Smith, Chief, Interpretation and Education. Phone: 724-329-5512. E-mail: fone_interpretation@nps.gov. Applicants must submit a formal organization application, three personal references. Applications are accepted continuously. World Wide Web: http://www.nps.gov/fone.

FOSSIL BUTTE NATIONAL MONUMENT
PO Box 592
Kemmerer, Wyoming 83101

General Information Preserves paleontological sites and related geological phenomena; provides for the display and interpretation of scientific specimens. Established in 1972. Number of employees: 7. Unit of United States National Park Service, Washington, District of Columbia. Number of internship applications received each year: 10.

Internships Available ▶ *2 interpretation-resource management interns:* responsibilities include staffing information desk and presenting interpretive programs; labor intensive conservation projects such as trail maintenance, stream erosion projects; cultural and natural resource management projects that may include preparation of specimens and organization of museum collections, wildlife and plant surveys, and documentation of archeological sites; preparation and presentation of programs to school groups including guided hikes. Candidates should have knowledge of field, oral communication skills, personal interest in the field, self-motivation, strong interpersonal skills. Open to recent high school graduates, college freshmen, college sophomores, college juniors, college seniors, recent college graduates, graduate students, law students, career changers, individuals reentering the workforce. ▶ *1–2 paleontology interns:* responsibilities include fossil collection and preparation. Candidates should have ability to work independently, ability to work with others, declared college major in field, oral communication skills, personal interest in the field, self-motivation. Open to college freshmen, college sophomores, college juniors, college seniors, recent col-

lege graduates, graduate students. Duration for all positions is 12 weeks. All positions are unpaid. International applications accepted.

Benefits Formal training, free housing, names of contacts, on-the-job training, willing to complete paperwork for educational credit, willing to provide letters of recommendation, $50 stipend.

Contact Write, call, or e-mail Marcia D. Fagnant, Park Ranger. Phone: 307-877-4455. E-mail: marcia_fagnant@nps.gov. Telephone interview required. Applicants must submit a formal organization application. Application deadline: March 15 for spring and summer, July 1 for fall. Fees: $1. World Wide Web: http://www.nps.gov/fobu.

FRANKLIN D. ROOSEVELT LIBRARY
511 Albany Post Road
Hyde Park, New York 12538

General Information Library and museum containing the papers, books, and personal memorabilia of President Franklin D. Roosevelt, the papers of his wife, Anna Eleanor Roosevelt, and many of his political associates and contemporaries. Established in 1941. Number of employees: 25. Unit of Office of Presidential Libraries, National Archives & Records Administration, Washington, District of Columbia. Number of internship applications received each year: 40.

Internships Available ▶ *7–8 William R. Emerson interns:* responsibilities include organizing and automating archival materials, making indices, finding aids and databases, digitizing documents and photographs, and assisting with other archival and museum projects. Candidates should have ability to work with others, college courses in field, computer skills, personal interest in the field, research skills, written communication skills. Duration is 6-8 weeks during summer. $200 per week. Open to college freshmen, college sophomores, college juniors, college seniors, recent college graduates. International applications accepted.

Benefits On-the-job training, willing to complete paperwork for educational credit, willing to provide letters of recommendation.

Contact Write or e-mail Mr. Raymond Teichman, Supervisory Archivist. E-mail: library@roosevelt.nara.gov. In-person interview recommended. Applicants must submit a formal organization application, cover letter, resume, academic transcripts, two letters of recommendation. Application deadline: April 1. World Wide Web: http://www.academic.marist.edu/fdr.

FREDERICKSBURG AND SPOTSYLVANIA NATIONAL MILITARY PARK
120 Chatham Lane
Fredericksburg, Virginia 22405

General Information National historic park whose main objective is to preserve and interpret 4 major Civil War battles and related Civil War structures. Established in 1927. Number of employees: 50. Agency of National Park Service, Washington, District of Columbia. Number of internship applications received each year: 25.

Internships Available ▶ *1–2 administrative assistants:* responsibilities include conducting various federal government budget and personnel activities. Candidates should have ability to work with others, computer skills, office skills, personal interest in the field, self-motivation. Open to recent high school graduates, college freshmen, college sophomores, college juniors, college seniors, recent college graduates, career changers. ▶ *2 curatorial assistants:* responsibilities include cataloging and recordkeeping associated with museum objects and other projects such as exhibit guides. Candidates should have ability to work independently, knowledge of field, organizational skills, personal interest in the field, self-motivation. Open to college juniors, college seniors, recent college graduates, graduate students. ▶ *4 historical interpreters:* responsibilities include assisting visitors at information desk and park library and providing walking tours. Candidates should have knowledge of field, oral communication skills, personal interest in the field, self-motivation, strong interpersonal skills. Open to college juniors, college seniors, recent college graduates, graduate students. ▶ *3 historical researchers:* responsibilities include indexing manuscripts, writing brochures, and assisting

Fredericksburg and Spotsylvania National Military Park (continued)
with various other historical and cultural resource management projects. Candidates should have ability to work independently, knowledge of field, personal interest in the field, research skills, self-motivation, writing skills. Open to college juniors, college seniors, recent college graduates, graduate students. ▶ *1–2 natural resource assistants:* responsibilities include monitoring water quality, agricultural pests, fire, weather, and/or gypsy moths. Candidates should have ability to work independently, college courses in field, personal interest in the field, self-motivation. Open to college juniors, college seniors, recent college graduates, graduate students. ▶ *2 restoration assistants:* responsibilities include working on various projects related to the preservation or restoration of historic structures. Candidates should have ability to work with others, experience in the field. Open to recent high school graduates, college freshmen, college sophomores, college juniors, college seniors, recent college graduates, career changers, individuals reentering the workforce. Duration for all positions is 2–4 months. All positions are unpaid. International applications accepted.
Benefits Formal training, job counseling, names of contacts, on-the-job training, travel reimbursement, tuition assistance, willing to complete paperwork for educational credit, willing to provide letters of recommendation, possibility of seasonal employment, free housing provided except in summer (summer housing generally limited to historical interpreter interns only).
Contact Write, call, fax, or e-mail Mr. Gregory A. Mertz, Supervisory Historian. Phone: 540-373-6124. Fax: 540-654-5521. E-mail: greg_mertz@nps.gov. In-person interview recommended. Applicants must submit a formal organization application. Applications are accepted continuously. World Wide Web: http://www.nps.gov/frsp or http://www.sep.nps.gov.

FRIENDSHIP HILL NATIONAL HISTORIC SITE
RD 1, Box 149-A
Point Marion, Pennsylvania 15474

General Information Site located along the Monongahela River that contains the home of Albert Gallatin, Secretary of the Treasury under Presidents Jefferson and Madison. Established in 1981. Number of employees: 8. Unit of National Park Service, Washington, District of Columbia. Number of internship applications received each year: 2.
Internships Available ▶ *1–2 curatorial aides:* responsibilities include cataloguing, photographing, preparing items for storage, general conservation, record keeping, and inventories. Candidates should have ability to work independently, ability to work with others, computer skills, experience in the field, organizational skills, personal interest in the field. Open to college freshmen, college sophomores, college juniors, college seniors, recent college graduates, graduate students. ▶ *1–5 interpretive aides:* responsibilities include working in the contact station, performing guided talks and walks, and preparing brochures. Candidates should have oral communication skills, personal interest in the field, strong interpersonal skills. Open to high school seniors, recent high school graduates, college freshmen, college sophomores, college juniors, college seniors, recent college graduates, individuals reentering the workforce. ▶ *1–4 resource management aides:* responsibilities include monitoring water, flora, and fauna, and performing vegetation studies, reforestation, and other projects. Candidates should have ability to work independently, college courses in field, experience in the field, personal interest in the field, research skills, written communication skills. Open to college freshmen, college sophomores, college juniors, college seniors, recent college graduates, graduate students, career changers, individuals reentering the workforce. Duration for all positions is flexible. All positions are unpaid. International applications accepted.
Benefits Formal training, free housing, job counseling, on-the-job training, willing to complete paperwork for educational credit, willing to provide letters of recommendation, limited reimbursement of travel and meal expenses.
Contact Write, call, or e-mail Mr. Chuck Smith, Chief, Interpretation and Education. Phone: 724-725-9190. E-mail: frhi_interpretation@nps.gov. Applicants must submit a formal

organization application, two personal references. Applications are accepted continuously. World Wide Web: http://www.nps.gov/frhi/.

FULLER MUSEUM OF ART
455 Oak Street
Brockton, Massachusetts 02301

General Information Art museum and museum school with permanent collection and rotating exhibits whose mission is to serve as an educational and cultural institution to the region. Established in 1969. Number of employees: 12. Number of internship applications received each year: 10.
Internships Available ▶ *Administrative interns:* responsibilities include assisting the director in researching available sources of foundation and grant income and obtaining corporate support, researching for present and upcoming exhibitions, book reviewing, lobbying, planning meeting sessions, and assisting the business manager in budget preparation and control and a wide range of business-related activities. ▶ *Curatorial/registration interns:* responsibilities include surveying and researching the permanent collection for various purposes (education, condition, reports, preliminary cataloging, insurance, and restoration) and researching particular artists or works. ▶ *Education interns:* responsibilities include assisting in researching exhibits for creation of teacher materials and guides, cataloging museum slide collection. ▶ *Museum school interns:* responsibilities include assisting the coordinator in a variety of tasks. ▶ *Public relations interns:* responsibilities include assisting in writing news releases and public service announcements, promoting all Fuller Museum exhibits and events, writing and editing quarterly newsletters, and maintaining accurate and up-to-date art listings and calendar of events in all area newspapers. Duration for all positions is 1 semester. All positions are unpaid. Open to college freshmen, college sophomores, college juniors, college seniors, recent college graduates, graduate students, law students, career changers, individuals reentering the workforce.
Benefits Willing to provide letters of recommendation, opportunity to research, study, and be part of an organization serving the community.
Contact Write or fax Douglas Hyland, Director. Fax: 508-587-6191. No phone calls. In-person interview required. Applicants must submit a cover letter, resume. Applications are accepted continuously.

GALLERY ARCHIVES, NATIONAL GALLERY OF ART
Washington, District of Columbia 20565

General Information Archives responsible for the long-term care of historical records of the National Gallery of Art including files, photographs, and architectural drawings. Number of employees: 4. Number of internship applications received each year: 15.
Internships Available ▶ *1–2 archivist interns:* responsibilities include arranging and describing historical records, developing database for architectural records, providing assistance to researchers, writing guides describing historical records, and assisting with preservation. Candidates should have ability to work independently, oral communication skills, plan to pursue career in field, strong interpersonal skills, written communication skills. Duration is minimum 30 hours per week for 12 weeks. Unpaid. Open to college seniors, recent college graduates, graduate students. International applications accepted.
Benefits Formal training, job counseling, names of contacts, on-the-job training, opportunity to attend seminars/workshops, willing to act as a professional reference, willing to complete paperwork for educational credit, willing to provide letters of recommendation.
Contact Write, fax, or e-mail Maygene Daniels, Chief, Gallery Archives. Fax: 202-842-6948. E-mail: gallery-archives@nga.gov. In-person interview recommended. Applicants must submit a cover letter, resume, academic transcripts, two letters of recommendation. Applications are accepted continuously. World Wide Web: http://www.nga.gov.

GRANT-KOHRS RANCH NHS
210 Missouri Avenue
Deer Lodge, Montana 59722

General Information National historic site committed to the preservation and interpretation of cattle ranching and westward expansion. Established in 1972. Number of employees: 21. Unit of National Park Service, Washington, District of Columbia.
Internships Available ▶ *1–3 museum technicians:* responsibilities include museum housekeeping, monitoring, and environmental control. Candidates should have ability to work independently, college courses in field, computer skills, knowledge of field, plan to pursue career in field. Duration is 6–12 weeks. $10 per hour. Open to graduate students. International applications accepted.
Benefits Job counseling, on-the-job training, willing to act as a professional reference, willing to complete paperwork for educational credit, willing to provide letters of recommendation.
Contact Write, call, fax, or e-mail Chris Ford, Curator, 210 Missouri Avenue, Deer Lodge, Montana 59722. Phone: 406-846-3268. Fax: 406-846-3962. E-mail: chris_ford@nps.gov. Applicants must submit a formal organization application. Application deadline: April 2 for summer. World Wide Web: http://www.nps.gov/grko.

GREENBURGH NATURE CENTER
99 Dromore Road
Scarsdale, New York 10583

General Information Nature center that provides exhibits and programs for all ages on natural history and the environment; 33-acre site includes woods, pond, field, orchid, nature trails, and cultivated lawns and gardens; indoor exhibits include petting zoo with over 140 live animals, greenhouse with botanical exhibits on plant adaptation room, and changing natural history exhibits. Established in 1975. Number of employees: 12. Number of internship applications received each year: 30.
Internships Available ▶ *1 naturalist intern:* responsibilities include planning and leading educational activities for a wide variety of audiences, working with and directing the activities of volunteers, preparing bulletin board displays, designing and constructing exhibits, writing articles for newsletter or brochure, preparing audio-visual materials, caring for and handling plants and live animals, checking trails and exhibits, changing program announcements and other weekly professional chores, and completing a project arranged with supervisor. Candidates should have ability to work independently, oral communication skills, personal interest in the field, research skills, strong interpersonal skills. Duration is 12 weeks. $120 per week. Open to college freshmen, college sophomores, college juniors, college seniors, recent college graduates, graduate students. International applications accepted.
Benefits Free housing, job counseling, names of contacts, on-the-job training, opportunity to attend seminars/workshops, willing to complete paperwork for educational credit, willing to provide letters of recommendation.
Contact Write, call, fax, or e-mail Mary Gillick, Naturalist. Phone: 914-723-3470. Fax: 914-725-6599. E-mail: gbhntr@aol.com. In-person interview recommended. Applicants must submit a formal organization application, resume, three personal references. Applications are accepted continuously. World Wide Web: http://www.townlink.net/gnc.

HALEAKALA NATIONAL PARK
PO Box 369
Makawao, Hawaii 96768

General Information One of 374 National Park Service units set aside to preserve and conserve the scenery, natural and historic objects, and wildlife for future generations. Established in 1916. Number of employees: 60. Number of internship applications received each year: 150.
Internships Available ▶ *1–2 endangered species management interns:* responsibilities include monitoring traplines for predators of endangered species, monitoring endangered species, computer data entry, and other duties. Candidates should have ability to work independently, ability to work with others, college courses in field, computer skills, oral communication skills, ability to work at high elevation on steep slopes in extreme weather conditions. Position available as unpaid or at $60 per week dependent on funding. Open to college sophomores, college juniors, college seniors, recent college graduates, graduate students. ▶ *1–2 interpretive interns:* responsibilities include working at two information stations handling book sales; issuing backcountry cabin permits, answering phones, and providing informal 20-minute interpretive talks; presenting formal educational interpretation. Candidates should have ability to work independently, computer skills, oral communication skills, personal interest in the field, strong interpersonal skills. Position available as unpaid or at $60 per week dependent on funding. Open to college juniors, college seniors, recent college graduates, career changers, individuals reentering the workforce. ▶ *1–2 vegetation management and feral animal control interns:* responsibilities include assisting with various resources management projects including planting native species; control and removal of alien vegetation; inspection, maintenance, and repair of feral animal control fences and traplines; vegetation monitoring. Candidates should have ability to work with others, self-motivation, written communication skills, ability to work in remote field sites. Position available as unpaid or at $60 per week dependent on funding. Open to college sophomores, college juniors, college seniors, recent college graduates, graduate students. Duration for all positions is 3 months minimum.
Benefits Formal training, opportunity to attend seminars/workshops, possible full-time employment, willing to complete paperwork for educational credit, willing to provide letters of recommendation.
Contact Write or e-mail Volunteer Coordinator. E-mail: hale_interpretation@nps.gov. Applicants must submit a resume, academic transcripts. Applications are accepted continuously. World Wide Web: http://www.nps.gov/hale.

HARPERS FERRY NATIONAL HISTORICAL PARK
PO Box 65
Harpers Ferry, West Virginia 25425

General Information Park whose mission is to preserve and protect the natural and cultural resources of the Harpers Ferry area including natural heritage, transportation, water powered industry, John Brown's raid, the Civil War, and African-American history for the education of current and future generations. Established in 1944. Number of employees: 125. Unit of United States National Park Service, Washington, District of Columbia. Number of internship applications received each year: 10.
Internships Available ▶ *1–3 archeological research assistants:* responsibilities include assisting with prior, current, and future projects involving both field and lab work; digging and labeling; documentation and research. Candidates should have ability to work independently, ability to work with others, computer skills, knowledge of field, personal interest in the field. Duration is 6–12 weeks. Open to high school students, high school seniors, recent high school graduates, college freshmen, college sophomores, college juniors, college seniors, recent college graduates, graduate students, law students, career changers, individuals reentering the workforce. ▶ *1–6 curatorial/collections management assistants:* responsibilities include documenting, cataloging, and inventory control of primary and secondary source materials; care and maintenance of artifact collections with proper curatorial methods; performing research duties and assisting outside researchers. Candidates should have computer skills, declared college major in field, plan to pursue career in field, research skills, self-motivation, written communication skills. Duration is 6 weeks. Open to high school seniors, recent high school graduates, college freshmen, college sophomores, college juniors, college seniors, recent college graduates, graduate students, individuals reentering the workforce. ▶ *1–6 period exhibits interns:* responsibilities include assisting in management and operation of 19th century exhibits, special events with living history groups, and the educational program. Candidates should have ability to work with others, college courses in field, oral communication skills, research skills, written communica-

Harpers Ferry National Historical Park (continued)

tion skills, knowledge of 19th century history. Duration is 6–24 weeks. Open to high school seniors, college freshmen, college sophomores, college juniors, college seniors, recent college graduates, graduate students, individuals reentering the workforce. ▶ *1–3 visitor services assistants:* responsibilities include assisting in the operation of visitor information desks, museum tours, and special event organization. These tasks involve frequent public contact and/or special research projects. Candidates should have ability to work with others, oral communication skills, organizational skills, personal interest in the field, self-motivation, strong interpersonal skills. Duration is 6–24 weeks. Open to college freshmen, college sophomores, college juniors, college seniors, recent college graduates, graduate students. All positions are unpaid. International applications accepted.
Benefits Free housing, job counseling, names of contacts, on-the-job training, opportunity to attend seminars/workshops, travel reimbursement, willing to act as a professional reference, willing to complete paperwork for educational credit, willing to provide letters of recommendation.
Contact Write, call, fax, or e-mail David Fox, Volunteer Coordinator. Phone: 304-535-6282. Fax: 304-535-2912. E-mail: david_fox@nps. gov. In-person interview recommended. Applicants must submit a formal organization application, cover letter, resume. Applications are accepted continuously. World Wide Web: http://www. nps.gov/hafe/hf_visit.htm.

HENRY FORD MUSEUM & GREENFIELD VILLIAGE
20900 Oakwood Boulevard, PO Box 1970
Dearborn, Michigan 48121-1970

General Information The largest indoor and outdoor museum in the world providing unique educational experiences based on authentic objects, stories, and lives from America's traditions of ingenuity, resourcefulness, and innovation.
Internships Available ▶ *1 intern:* responsibilities include updating the media list database, accompanying the media "on location" at Museum and Village, answering telephones, writing media alerts, and assisting with mailings. Duration is 1 semester (summer, fall, winter, spring). Unpaid. Open to college freshmen, college sophomores, college juniors, college seniors, recent college graduates, graduate students.
Benefits Willing to complete paperwork for educational credit.
Contact Write Kimberly Johnson, Publicity Assistant, 20900 Oakwood Boulevard, PO Box 1970, Dearborn, Michigan 48121-1970. No phone calls. Applicants must submit a cover letter, resume. Applications are accepted continuously. World Wide Web: http://www.hfmgv.org.

THE HERMITAGE
4580 Rachel's Lane
Hermitage, Tennessee 37076

General Information Organization that presents the home of Andrew Jackson to visitors. Established in 1889. Number of employees: 80. Number of internship applications received each year: 200.
Internships Available ▶ *8 historical archaeology interns:* responsibilities include participating in all phases of field excavation and laboratory processing of finds. Duration is 5 weeks in summer. $1,250 per duration of internship. ▶ *6 historical archaeology interns (non-archaelogy majors):* responsibilities include participating in all phases of field excavation and laboratory processing of finds. Duration is 2 weeks. $500 per duration of internship. Open to college freshmen, college sophomores, college juniors, college seniors, recent college graduates, graduate students. International applications accepted.
Benefits Free housing, free meals, job counseling, names of contacts, willing to complete paperwork for educational credit, willing to provide letters of recommendation.
Contact Write or call Dr. Larry McKee, Director of Archaeology. Phone: 615-889-2941. Fax: 615-889-9289. E-mail: lmckeeherm@ aol.com. Applicants must submit a cover letter, resume, two personal references. Application deadline: April 10. World Wide Web: http://www.thehermitage.com.

HIRSHHORN MUSEUM & SCULPTURE GARDEN
Smithsonian Institution, Room 410, MRC 350
Washington, District of Columbia 20560

General Information Museum of 19th- and 20th-century paintings, sculptures, and graphics emphasizing 20th-century and contemporary art. Established in 1974. Number of employees: 60. Number of internship applications received each year: 60.
Internships Available ▶ *Conservation interns.* Candidates should have declared college major in field, knowledge of field, plan to pursue career in field. Duration is 10 weeks. Position available as unpaid or paid. Open to college juniors, college seniors, recent college graduates, graduate students. ▶ *Exhibition and design interns.* Candidates should have experience in the field, plan to pursue career in field. Duration is 10 weeks. Unpaid. Open to college juniors, college seniors, recent college graduates, graduate students. ▶ *Graduate interns.* Candidates should have declared college major in field. Duration is 1 semester. Unpaid. Open to graduate students. ▶ *Photography interns.* Candidates should have college courses in field, experience in the field, plan to pursue career in field. Duration is 10 weeks. Unpaid. Open to college sophomores, college juniors, college seniors, recent college graduates, graduate students. ▶ *Public programs interns:* responsibilities include assisting in curatorial, education, publications, or public affairs division. Candidates should have ability to work with others, college courses in field, computer skills, experience in the field, oral communication skills, research skills, written communication skills. Duration is 10 weeks. Unpaid. Open to college juniors, college seniors, recent college graduates, graduate students. ▶ *Undergraduate interns:* responsibilities include working in a specific department of the museum and participating in a series of seminars on the museum's collection and organization. Candidates should have college courses in field, organizational skills, research skills, writing skills. Duration is 10 weeks. Unpaid. Open to college juniors, college seniors, recent college graduates, graduate students. International applications accepted.
Benefits Opportunity to attend seminars/workshops, willing to act as a professional reference, willing to complete paperwork for educational credit, willing to provide letters of recommendation.
Contact Write or fax Teresia Bush, Intern Coordinator, Smithsonian Institution, Room 410, MRC 350, Washington, District of Columbia 20560. Fax: 202-786-2682. No phone calls. Applicants must submit a cover letter, resume, academic transcripts. Application deadline: March 1 for summer, June 1 for fall, November 1 for spring.

HISTORIC DEERFIELD
Box 321
Deerfield, Massachusetts 01342

General Information Nonprofit museum dedicated to promoting the understanding and appreciation of New England history, architecture, and decorative arts. Established in 1954. Number of employees: 100. Number of internship applications received each year: 25.
Internships Available ▶ *6–10 summer fellows:* responsibilities include studying early American history and material culture, visiting other museums in New Zealand and beyond, receiving training as guides and as interpreters of history to the general public, and researching and writing a paper. Candidates should have ability to work independently, oral communication skills, self-motivation, strong interpersonal skills, written communication skills. Duration is mid-June to mid-August. Unpaid. Open to college sophomores, college juniors, college seniors.
Benefits Meals at a cost, opportunity to attend seminars/workshops, willing to complete paperwork for educational credit, archaeological digs, touring various historic sites, all program tuition costs covered (must only pay room and board, for which financial aid is available).
Contact Write, fax, or e-mail Kenneth Hafertepe, Director of Academic Programs. Fax: 413-774-4175. E-mail: sfp@historic-deerfield.org. No phone calls. Applicants must submit a formal organization application, academic transcripts, two letters of

recommendation, personal statement explaining interest in internship. Application deadline: April 1. Fees: $15. World Wide Web: http://www.historic-deerfield.org.

THE HOLDEN ARBORETUM
9500 Sperry Road
Kirtland, Ohio 44094

General Information 3,100-acre museum of wood plants intended for educational and scientific purposes. Established in 1931. Number of employees: 82. Number of internship applications received each year: 100.
Internships Available ▶ *1 conservation intern:* responsibilities include maintaining conservation collections. Candidates should have ability to work independently, ability to work with others, college courses in field, knowledge of field, personal interest in the field, self-motivation. Duration is 3 months. $6 per hour. ▶ *1 education intern:* responsibilities include teaching and producing educational materials. Candidates should have ability to work independently, college courses in field, computer skills, knowledge of field, office skills, oral communication skills, personal interest in the field, plan to pursue career in field, self-motivation, strong interpersonal skills, writing skills. Duration is 1 year. $6–$7 per hour. ▶ *7 horticultural maintenance/production interns:* responsibilities include caring for horticultural collections and gardens. Candidates should have ability to work independently, ability to work with others, college courses in field, plan to pursue career in field, self-motivation. Duration is 3 months. $6 per hour. ▶ *1 horticultural therapy intern:* responsibilities include working with special populations and teaching. Candidates should have ability to work independently, ability to work with others, college courses in field, personal interest in the field, plan to pursue career in field, self-motivation. Duration is 6 months. $6 per hour. ▶ *1 horticulture intern:* responsibilities include keeping plant records and horticultural collections. Candidates should have ability to work independently, ability to work with others, college courses in field, computer skills, knowledge of field, office skills, plan to pursue career in field, self-motivation. Duration is 1 year. $6–$7 per hour. ▶ *1 landscape gardening intern:* responsibilities include maintaining intensive horticulture plantings on a 5-acre estate within the arboretum. Candidates should have ability to work independently, ability to work with others, college courses in field, personal interest in the field, plan to pursue career in field. Duration is 3–5 months. $6 per hour. Open to college freshmen, college sophomores, college juniors, college seniors, recent college graduates, graduate students. International applications accepted.
Benefits Formal training, housing at a cost, job counseling, names of contacts, possible full-time employment, willing to complete paperwork for educational credit, willing to provide letters of recommendation.
Contact Write, call, fax, or e-mail Greg J. Wright, Intern Coordinator. Phone: 440-256-1110. Fax: 440-256-1655. E-mail: educ@pop.holdenarb.org. Applicants must submit a cover letter, resume, three personal references. Application deadline: February 1. World Wide Web: http://www.holdenarb.org.

HOPEWELL FURNACE NATIONAL HISTORIC SITE
2 Mark Bird Lane
Elverson, Pennsylvania 19520

General Information Historic site preserving a 19th-century ironmaking community and a 200,000-object museum collection on 848 acres. Established in 1938. Number of employees: 17. Unit of United States National Park Service, Washington, District of Columbia. Number of internship applications received each year: 45.
Internships Available ▶ *4 education coordinator assistants:* responsibilities include assisting the education coordinator in planning, developing, and implementing a variety of education programs for a wide range of ages and interests. Candidates should have ability to work independently, ability to work with others, computer skills, knowledge of field, self-motivation, writing skills. Duration is 90 days. Open to recent high school graduates, college freshmen, college sophomores, college juniors, college

seniors, recent college graduates, graduate students, career changers, individuals reentering the workforce. ▶ *1–3 farm assistant/collier apprentices:* responsibilities include routine livestock care often in historic costume and/or historic charcoal making often in historic costume; qualified candidate will be trained. Candidates should have ability to work independently, ability to work with others, oral communication skills, organizational skills, self-motivation. Duration is 2 weeks to 4 months. Open to recent high school graduates, college freshmen, college sophomores, college juniors, college seniors, recent college graduates. ▶ *2–3 history interpretation interns:* responsibilities include making living history presentations and cultural demonstrations, developing programs, and performing educational programming. Candidates should have knowledge of field, oral communication skills, personal interest in the field, self-motivation, strong interpersonal skills. Duration is 200 hours. Open to recent high school graduates, college freshmen, college sophomores, college juniors, college seniors, recent college graduates, graduate students, law students, career changers, individuals reentering the workforce. ▶ *2–3 museum/curatorial management interns:* responsibilities include cataloging, archival preservation, photography preservation, and environmental monitoring. Candidates should have ability to work independently, computer skills, personal interest in the field, research skills, self-motivation, written communication skills. Duration is 200 hours. Open to recent high school graduates, college freshmen, college sophomores, college juniors, college seniors, recent college graduates, graduate students, law students, career changers, individuals reentering the workforce. ▶ *2–3 research historians:* responsibilities include conducting program-specific research using on-site archives to provide biographical/occupational data on individuals represented in living history program. Candidates should have ability to work independently, computer skills, knowledge of field, personal interest in the field, research skills, written communication skills. Duration is 200 hours minimum. Open to recent high school graduates, college freshmen, college sophomores, college juniors, college seniors, recent college graduates, graduate students, law students, career changers, individuals reentering the workforce. ▶ *1–2 visitor center assistants:* responsibilities include serving as front line contact for visitors, collecting and accounting for fees and association sales, operating cash registers, running audio/visual programs, and other duties as assigned. Candidates should have ability to work independently, oral communication skills, personal interest in the field, strong interpersonal skills. Duration is 4–6 weeks. Open to high school seniors, recent high school graduates, college freshmen, college sophomores, college juniors, college seniors, recent college graduates, individuals reentering the workforce. All positions are unpaid. International applications accepted.
Benefits Formal training, free housing, job counseling, on-the-job training, opportunity to attend seminars/workshops, willing to act as a professional reference, willing to complete paperwork for educational credit, willing to provide letters of recommendation, guidance through federal government hiring practices, $5 per day meal reimbursement, mileage reimbursement.
Contact Write, call, fax, or e-mail Mr. Frank Hebblethwaite, Supervisory Historian.TDD: 610-582-2093. Phone: 610-582-8773 Ext. 202. Fax: 610-582-2768. E-mail: hofu_superintendent@nps. gov. Telephone interview required. Applicants must submit a formal organization application, cover letter, resume, three personal references. Applications are accepted continuously. World Wide Web: http://www.nps.gov/hofu/index.html.

HORTICULTURE SERVICES DIVISION, SMITHSONIAN INSTITUTION
Arts and Industries Building, 900 Jefferson Drive, SW, Room 2282
Washington, District of Columbia 20560-0420

General Information Division of the Smithsonian that conducts research and organizes education and exhibit programs in practical and historical horticulture. Provides horticultural exhibits,

Horticulture Services Division, Smithsonian Institution (continued)
landscape design, and interior plant rotation for all Smithsonian buildings. Division of Smithsonian Institution, Washington, District of Columbia.
Internships Available ▶ *Interns:* responsibilities include assisting on special projects or working in normal horticultural activities such as historic gardens design and maintenance, supplying tropical plants for special events, doing greenhouse and nursery work, maintaining collections of rare and historical plants. Candidates should have ability to work independently, ability to work with others, coursework relating to horticulture, museum plant collections, entomology, landscaping, museology, or other disciplines relevant to work of the division. Duration is 10–16 weeks. Position available as unpaid or at limited stipend is available infrequently. Open to individuals who have taken college or university courses within the year prior to start of internship. International applications accepted.
Benefits On-the-job training, opportunity to attend seminars/workshops, willing to complete paperwork for educational credit.
Contact Write or call Intern Program. Phone: 202-357-1928. Specific application materials (sent after request by phone or mail). Application deadline: 3 months prior to proposed start date. World Wide Web: http://www.si.edu.

THE HUDSON RIVER MUSEUM OF WESTCHESTER
511 Warburton Avenue
Yonkers, New York 10701

General Information General community museum interpreting art, history, and science. Established in 1922. Number of employees: 40. Number of internship applications received each year: 30.
Internships Available ▶ *1–2 curatorial interns:* responsibilities include completing projects and cataloging archives. Duration is flexible. Open to high school students, high school seniors, recent high school graduates, college freshmen, college sophomores, college juniors, college seniors, recent college graduates, graduate students, law students, career changers, individuals reentering the workforce. ▶ *1–3 data entry clerks:* responsibilities include entering mailing lists into database. Candidates should have ability to work independently, computer skills, office skills, self-motivation, touch typing skills. Duration is flexible. Open to high school students, high school seniors, recent high school graduates, college freshmen, college sophomores, college juniors, college seniors, recent college graduates, graduate students, law students, law school graduates, career changers, individuals reentering the workforce. ▶ *1–2 development interns:* responsibilities include working on direct mail, grants, and prospect research. Duration is flexible. Open to high school students, high school seniors, recent high school graduates, college freshmen, college sophomores, college juniors, college seniors, recent college graduates, graduate students, law students, career changers, individuals reentering the workforce. ▶ *1–3 landscapers:* responsibilities include raking, watering, planting, and maintaining the grounds. Candidates should have ability to work independently, ability to work with others, self-motivation. Duration is flexible (April to October). Open to high school students, high school seniors, recent high school graduates, college freshmen, college sophomores, college juniors, college seniors, recent college graduates, graduate students, law students, law school graduates, career changers, individuals reentering the workforce. ▶ *1–2 museum shop interns:* responsibilities include assisting with buying, displays, inventory, and sales. Duration is flexible. Open to high school students, high school seniors, recent high school graduates, college freshmen, college sophomores, college juniors, college seniors, recent college graduates, graduate students, law students, career changers, individuals reentering the workforce. ▶ *1–2 public relations interns:* responsibilities include drafting press releases, brochures, and written materials. Duration is flexible. Open to high school students, high school seniors, recent high school graduates, college freshmen, college sophomores, college juniors, college seniors, recent college graduates, graduate students, law students, career changers, individuals reentering the workforce. All positions are unpaid. International applications accepted.

Benefits Job counseling, names of contacts, possible full-time employment, willing to complete paperwork for educational credit, willing to provide letters of recommendation.
Contact Write, call, fax, or e-mail Zoe Lindsay, Public Relations Associate. Phone: 914-963-4550. Fax: 914-963-8558. E-mail: hrm@hrm.org. In-person interview recommended. Applicants must submit a cover letter, resume. Applications are accepted continuously. World Wide Web: http://www.hrm.org.

INDEPENDENT CURATORS INTERNATIONAL (ICI)
799 Broadway, Suite 205
New York, New York 10003

General Information International nonprofit traveling exhibition service specializing in contemporary art. Established in 1975. Number of employees: 10. Number of internship applications received each year: 30.
Internships Available ▶ *1 development intern:* responsibilities include assisting in planning benefit dinner and donor events; researching individual, foundation, and corporate prospects; and preparing grant applications and other proposals. Candidates should have ability to work independently, computer skills, office skills, organizational skills, strong interpersonal skills, written communication skills. Duration is 8–12 weeks. Open to college sophomores, college juniors, college seniors, recent college graduates, graduate students, law students, career changers. ▶ *1–2 exhibitions interns:* responsibilities include assisting with maintenance of files and records; preparing checklists, condition reports, installation instructions, and catalog information; and collecting and maintaining visual materials. Candidates should have ability to work independently, computer skills, knowledge of field, office skills, oral communication skills, organizational skills. Duration is minimum of 3 months (minimum of 15 hours per week). Open to college sophomores, college juniors, college seniors, recent college graduates, graduate students, career changers. ▶ *1 registration intern:* responsibilities include assisting with maintenance of files and records; preparation of registration forms and installation instructions. Candidates should have ability to work independently, ability to work with others, computer skills, knowledge of field, office skills, oral communication skills, organizational skills, personal interest in the field, written communication skills. Duration is minimum of 3 months (minimum of 15 hours per week). Open to college sophomores, college juniors, college seniors, recent college graduates, graduate students, career changers. All positions are unpaid. International applications accepted.
Benefits Willing to complete paperwork for educational credit, willing to provide letters of recommendation, stipend sometimes available, reimbursement of local travel expenses.
Contact Write, fax, or e-mail Liz Moya, Executive Assistant. Fax: 212-477-4781. E-mail: info@ici-exhibitions.org. No phone calls. In-person interview recommended. Applicants must submit a cover letter, resume, letter of recommendation, two letters of recommendation. Applications are accepted continuously. World Wide Web: http://www.ici-exhibitions.org.

INSTITUTE OF CONTEMPORARY ART
118 South 36th Street
Philadelphia, Pennsylvania 19104

General Information Art museum that provides a forum for innovative art of the present and recent past through pioneering exhibitions, scholarship, publications, and educational programs. Established in 1963. Number of employees: 8. Unit of University of Pennsylvania, Philadelphia, Pennsylvania. Number of internship applications received each year: 30.
Internships Available ▶ *1 assistant volunteer coordinator:* responsibilities include assisting with recruiting, training, and placement of volunteers; managing volunteers at special events; maintaining records. Candidates should have ability to work independently, computer skills, office skills, oral communication skills, organizational skills, strong interpersonal skills. Duration is 1–2 semesters. Open to college juniors, college seniors, recent college graduates, career changers, individuals reentering the workforce. ▶ *1–2 business administration interns:* responsibilities

include assisting business manager in marketing, office procedures, data entry, and filing. Candidates should have computer skills, office skills, organizational skills, self-motivation. Duration is 1–2 semesters. Open to college sophomores, college juniors, college seniors, recent college graduates, career changers. ▶ *1 curatorial intern:* responsibilities include researching, coordinating slides, and assisting with mailings. Candidates should have ability to work independently, editing skills, organizational skills, research skills, self-motivation, writing skills, major in art history preferred. Duration is 1–2 semesters. Open to college juniors, college seniors, recent college graduates, graduate students. ▶ *1–2 development interns:* responsibilities include assisting with grant writing, membership, special events, database, mailings, research funding, and marketing. Candidates should have computer skills, office skills, organizational skills, self-motivation, writing skills. Duration is year-round or shorter. Open to college sophomores, college juniors, college seniors, recent college graduates, career changers. ▶ *1 public relations intern:* responsibilities include maintaining clipping file, coordinating press packages, and writing press releases and promotional articles. Candidates should have ability to work independently, computer skills, office skills, oral communication skills, organizational skills, written communication skills, experience in field helpful. Duration is year-round or shorter. Open to college freshmen, college sophomores, college juniors, college seniors, recent college graduates, graduate students, career changers, individuals reentering the workforce. All positions are unpaid.

Benefits On-the-job training, possible full-time employment, willing to complete paperwork for educational credit, willing to provide letters of recommendation.

Contact Write, call, or fax Ms. Rilice Lefton, Director of Volunteer Services. Phone: 215-898-7108. Fax: 215-898-5050. In-person interview recommended. Applicants must submit a cover letter. Applications are accepted continuously. World Wide Web: http://www.upenn.edu/ica.

INSTITUTIONAL STUDIES OFFICE, SMITHSONIAN INSTITUTION
Arts and Industries Building, 900 Jefferson Drive, SW, Room 1271
Washington, District of Columbia 20560-0405

General Information A pan-Institutional resource dedicated to the scientific study of the characteristics, attitudes, opinions, and experiences of the Smithsonian's varied publics. Unit of Smithsonian Institution, Washington, District of Columbia.

Internships Available ▶ *ISO interns:* responsibilities include collaborating with staff on data collection, analysis, and presentation in connection with studies of museum visitors and program participants, and working on independent research projects. Candidates should have ability to work independently, social science background and some coursework in research methods helpful. Duration is minimum of 2 months. Unpaid. International applications accepted.

Benefits Willing to complete paperwork for educational credit.
Contact Write, call, or fax Director. Phone: 202-786-2232. Fax: 202-786-2648. Applicants must submit a formal organization application, academic transcripts, personal reference, essay. Applications are accepted continuously. World Wide Web: http://www.si.edu.

INTERNATIONAL CENTER, SMITHSONIAN INSTITUTION
Quad 3123
Washington, District of Columbia 20560-0705

General Information A grouping of different units and activities which conducts the Smithsonian's international programs, supports activities abroad, and coordinates international interests, particularly those that don't fall within the scope of a single museum or bureau. Unit of Smithsonian Institution, Washington, District of Columbia.

Internships Available ▶ *Interns:* responsibilities include assisting in the development and maintenance of projects sponsored by the various units, research, writing, editing, scheduling, database maintenance, and light office work. Candidates should have background in international affairs, nature conservancy, or environmental studies relevant to some projects, familiarity with word processing and other computer programs is desirable. Duration is minimum of 2 months (full-time). Unpaid. International applications accepted.

Benefits Willing to complete paperwork for educational credit.
Contact Write, call, or fax Internship Coordinator. Phone: 202-357-2519. Fax: 202-786-2557. Applicants must submit a formal organization application, academic transcripts, personal reference, essay. Applications are accepted continuously. World Wide Web: http://www.si.edu.

IRON MISSION STATE PARK
635 North Main Street
Cedar City, Utah 84720

General Information State park museum that preserves Southwestern pioneer memorabilia and transportation and farming equipment. Established in 1973. Number of employees: 3. Division of Utah Department of Parks and Recreation, Salt Lake City, Utah. Number of internship applications received each year: 5.

Internships Available ▶ *1–2 museum aides:* responsibilities include assisting curator in cataloging and preserving artifacts. Candidates should have computer skills, organizational skills, research skills, writing skills, written communication skills. Duration is 10–14 weeks. Position available as unpaid or at $50 per week. Open to college sophomores, college juniors, college seniors, recent college graduates, graduate students. International applications accepted.

Benefits Names of contacts, on-the-job training, opportunity to attend seminars/workshops, willing to act as a professional reference, willing to complete paperwork for educational credit, willing to provide letters of recommendation.

Contact Write, call, fax, or e-mail Todd Prince, Park Manager. Phone: 435-586-9290. Fax: 435-865-6830. E-mail: nrdpr.ironmiss@state.ut.us. Applicants must submit a formal organization application, cover letter, resume. Application deadline: January 15 for spring, March 15 for summer, July 1 for fall, October 1 for winter.

ISLE ROYALE NATIONAL PARK
800 East Lakeshore Drive
Houghton, Michigan 49931

General Information Wilderness park containing historic and cultural resources located on the largest island in Lake Superior; features 165 miles of hiking trails and is home to moose, wolves, foxes, and a variety of water fowl including loons, great blue herons, and ducks. Established in 1940. Number of employees: 100. Unit of National Park Service, Washington, District of Columbia. Number of internship applications received each year: 75.

Internships Available ▶ *1 assistant purser:* responsibilities include assisting the purser in NPS vessel RANGER III on voyages to and from Isle Royale, assisting with visitor information and interpretive programs, issuing backcountry permits and collecting fees. Candidates should have computer skills, oral communication skills, organizational skills, personal interest in the field, self-motivation, strong interpersonal skills. ▶ *1–2 backcountry campground host/ranger assistants:* responsibilities include living and working in a remote backcountry campground; assisting Ranger division by checking camping permits, providing information to visitors, conducting interpretive programs, providing first aid and emergency assistance, and campground maintenance. Candidates should have ability to work independently, experience in the field, oral communication skills, plan to pursue career in field, self-motivation, strong interpersonal skills. ▶ *1 interpretive resource center manager:* responsibilities include locating and providing information and materials for park staff in support of interpretive program, managing park library, maintaining audio-visual equipment and slide collection. Candidates should have ability to work with others, computer skills, office skills, personal interest in the field, self-motivation, written com-

Isle Royale National Park (continued)

munication skills. ▶ *1 photo/darkroom volunteer:* responsibilities include operating darkroom, maintaining park historic photo collection, documentary photographs and slides of park projects and operations; copying historic photos, designing brochures. Candidates should have ability to work independently, computer skills, experience in the field, organizational skills, self-motivation, ability to independently operate photo darkroom. ▶ *1–2 resource management technicians:* responsibilities include assisting with air, water quality, and acid rain monitoring; field sampling; inventory and monitoring of bird populations; compiling backcountry camping permit data; location and removal of exotic plant species; assisting with field research. Candidates should have ability to work independently, college courses in field, experience in the field, personal interest in the field, research skills, written communication skills. ▶ *1–3 visitor center assistants:* responsibilities include general staffing of visitor center; collecting fees, issuing camping permits, trip planning, greeting and orienting visitors, meeting ferry boats, conducting interpretive programs, hikes, selling books. Candidates should have computer skills, office skills, oral communication skills, personal interest in the field, self-motivation, strong interpersonal skills. Duration for all positions is 3 months (June-August). All positions are unpaid. Open to recent high school graduates, college freshmen, college sophomores, college juniors, college seniors, recent college graduates, graduate students, law students, career changers, individuals reentering the workforce. International applications accepted.

Benefits Formal training, free housing, job counseling, names of contacts, on-the-job training, possible full-time employment, willing to complete paperwork for educational credit, willing to provide letters of recommendation, uniform, meal reimbursement.

Contact Write, call, or e-mail Ms. Elizabeth Valencia, Volunteer Coordinator. Phone: 906-487-7153. E-mail: liz_valencia@nps. gov. Applicants must submit a formal organization application. Application deadline: March 15. World Wide Web: http://www. nps.gov/isro/.

ISLIP ART MUSEUM
50 Irish Lane
East Islip, New York 11730

General Information Art museum emphasizing contemporary and avant-garde works and mixed media installations. Established in 1971. Number of employees: 10. Number of internship applications received each year: 10.

Internships Available ▶ *1–2 assistant curators:* responsibilities include assisting with all curatorial functions and gallery sittings. Candidates should have computer skills, plan to pursue career in field, research skills, strong interpersonal skills, writing skills. Duration is flexible. Unpaid. Open to college freshmen, college sophomores, college juniors, college seniors, recent college graduates, graduate students. ▶ *1–2 director's assistants:* responsibilities include assisting in fund development, research, and special projects. Candidates should have ability to work independently, plan to pursue career in field, self-motivation, strong interpersonal skills. Position available as unpaid or paid. Open to recent high school graduates, college freshmen, college sophomores, college juniors, college seniors, recent college graduates, graduate students, career changers. ▶ *1–2 museum school assistants:* responsibilities include helping with art classes at museum and other museum programs. Candidates should have ability to work independently, oral communication skills, self-motivation, strong interpersonal skills. Unpaid.

Benefits Job counseling, names of contacts, willing to complete paperwork for educational credit, willing to provide letters of recommendation.

Contact Write Ms. Mary Lou Cohalan, Director. No phone calls. In-person interview required. Applicants must submit a cover letter, resume. Applications are accepted continuously.

JAMESTOWN-YORKTOWN FOUNDATION
PO Box 1607
Williamsburg, Virginia 23187-1607

General Information Educational institution that operates Jamestown Settlement and the Yorktown Victory Center, museums that preserve and interpret the first English settlement in the New World and the story of the American Revolution. Established in 1956. Number of employees: 400. Number of internship applications received each year: 50.

Internships Available ▶ *1 curatorial intern:* responsibilities include assisting with various curatorial projects. Candidates should have ability to work with others, editing skills, research skills, self-motivation, writing skills, written communication skills. $5 per hour. Open to recent college graduates, graduate students. ▶ *1 education intern:* responsibilities include assisting with educational programs. Candidates should have ability to work independently, ability to work with others, knowledge of field, oral communication skills, plan to pursue career in field, written communication skills. $5 per hour. Open to recent college graduates, graduate students. ▶ *1 marketing intern:* responsibilities include assisting with marketing programs. Candidates should have ability to work with others, knowledge of field, oral communication skills, plan to pursue career in field, self-motivation, written communication skills. $5 per hour. Open to college juniors, college seniors, recent college graduates, graduate students. ▶ *1 research intern:* responsibilities include researching selected topics. Candidates should have ability to work with others, plan to pursue career in field, research skills, strong leadership ability, writing skills. Position available as unpaid or at $5 per hour. Open to college seniors, recent college graduates, graduate students. Duration for all positions is 3 months.

Benefits Formal training, opportunity to attend seminars/ workshops, possible full-time employment, willing to act as a professional reference, willing to complete paperwork for educational credit, willing to provide letters of recommendation.

Contact Write Grace F. Van Divender, Training and Special Services Manager. Applicants must submit a formal organization application, cover letter, resume, three letters of recommendation. Applications are accepted continuously.

JEWEL CAVE NATIONAL MONUMENT
RR 1, Box 60 AA
Custer, South Dakota 57730

General Information Organization that administers and manages the natural resources of Jewel Cave. Established in 1908. Number of employees: 42. Unit of National Park Service, Washington, District of Columbia. Number of internship applications received each year: 20.

Internships Available ▶ *1–2 cave management interns:* responsibilities include resources management, including cave management; hydrology studies, such as water sampling and dye tracing; and working with computer/GIS systems. Candidates should have computer skills, oral communication skills, personal interest in the field, self-motivation, written communication skills, caving experience. Duration is 1 year. Position available as unpaid or at $100 stipend (per week). Open to college freshmen, college sophomores, college juniors, college seniors, recent college graduates, graduate students. ▶ *2–3 interpreter volunteers:* responsibilities include researching, preparing and presenting scenic or historic cave tours and a variety of surface programs; working at the information desk; answering public information requests; and possibly other projects which may include: assisting with production of interpretive publications, resource management projects, photography, library work. Candidates should have ability to work independently, oral communication skills, personal interest in the field, self-motivation, strong interpersonal skills, educational background in related area ,such as geology, environmental education, recreational resource management, or natural history. Duration is 1 summer (generally, May 25 to August 31). Position available as unpaid or at $10 stipend (per work day). Open to college freshmen, college sophomores, college juniors, college seniors, recent college graduates, graduate students, career changers. International applications accepted.

Benefits Formal training, free housing, job counseling, names of contacts, on-the-job training, willing to act as a professional reference, willing to complete paperwork for educational credit, willing to provide letters of recommendation.

Contact Write or fax Ms. Karen Rosga, Chief of Interpretation, RR1, Box 60 AA, Custer, South Dakota 57730. Fax: 605-673-3294. Telephone interview required. Applicants must submit a formal organization application, cover letter, resume, academic transcripts, two personal references. Application deadline: March 25 for interpreter positions (summer), July 15 for interpreter positions (fall), October 15 for cave management positions. World Wide Web: http://www.nps.gov/jeca.

JOHNSTOWN FLOOD NATIONAL MONUMENT
733 Lake Road
South Fork, Pennsylvania 15956

General Information Memorial preserving the ruins of the South Fork Dam which burst on May 31, 1889 and caused one of the worst disasters in American history. Number of employees: 10. Unit of United States National Park Service, Washington, District of Columbia. Number of internship applications received each year: 2.

Internships Available ▶ *1–2 curatorial aides:* responsibilities include cataloguing, photographing, preparing items for storage, general conservation, record keeping, and inventories. Candidates should have ability to work independently, ability to work with others, computer skills, experience in the field, organizational skills, personal interest in the field. Open to college freshmen, college sophomores, college juniors, college seniors, recent college graduates, graduate students. ▶ *1–5 interpretive aides:* responsibilities include working in the contact station, performing guided talks and walks, and preparing brochures. Candidates should have oral communication skills, personal interest in the field, strong interpersonal skills. Open to high school seniors, recent high school graduates, college freshmen, college sophomores, college juniors, college seniors, recent college graduates, individuals reentering the workforce. ▶ *1–4 resource management aides:* responsibilities include monitoring water, flora, and fauna and performing vegetation studies, reforestation, and other projects. Candidates should have ability to work independently, college courses in field, experience in the field, personal interest in the field, research skills, written communication skills. Open to college freshmen, college sophomores, college juniors, college seniors, recent college graduates, graduate students, career changers, individuals reentering the workforce. Duration for all positions is flexible. All positions are unpaid. International applications accepted.

Benefits Formal training, job counseling, on-the-job training, willing to complete paperwork for educational credit, willing to provide letters of recommendation, limited reimbursement of travel and meal expenses.

Contact Write, call, or e-mail Chuck Smith, Chief, Interpretation and Education, 733 Lake Road, South Fork, Pennsylvania 15956. Phone: 814-495-4643. E-mail: jofl_interpretation@nps.gov. Applicants must submit a formal organization application, 2-3 personal references. Applications are accepted continuously. World Wide Web: http://www.nps.gov/alpo.

JOSHUA TREE NATIONAL PARK
74485 National Park Drive
Twentynine Palms, California 92277

General Information National park in southern California desert that provides protection of cultural and natural resources of the Mojave and Colorado deserts. Established in 1936. Number of employees: 65. Number of internship applications received each year: 10.

Internships Available ▶ *Interpreters/volunteers:* responsibilities include operating the visitor center, assisting in field studies, and conducting walking tours. Duration is 3 months. Unpaid. Open to U.S. citizens 18 or older.

Benefits Formal training, job counseling, willing to complete paperwork for educational credit, willing to provide letters of recommendation.

Contact Write, call, fax, or e-mail Mr. Joe Zarki, Chief of Interpretation. Phone: 760-367-5500. Fax: 760-367-6392. E-mail: joe_zarki@nps.gov. Applicants must submit a cover letter, resume. Applications are accepted continuously. World Wide Web: http://www.nps.gov/jotr/.

THE J. PAUL GETTY TRUST
1200 Getty Center Drive
Los Angeles, California 90049-1687

General Information Art museum of European art before 1900 and photography; research institute for the history of art and humanities; conservation institute; education institute; grant program. Established in 1953. Number of employees: 1,200. Number of internship applications received each year: 700.

Internships Available ▶ *20 Getty graduate interns:* responsibilities include working in one of the Getty programs. Candidates should have ability to work with others, college degree in related field, knowledge of field, plan to pursue career in field, research skills, writing skills. Duration is 9–12 months. $13,837 for 9 months; $20,000 for 12 months. Open to graduate students. ▶ *10–15 Getty multicultural undergraduate summer interns:* responsibilities include working with a mentor on specific projects in one of the Getty programs, possibly including work in administration, information technology, conservation, curatorial research, education, grantmaking, library and resource collections, public affairs, public programs, or publications. Duration is 10 weeks (June-August). $3,000 per duration of internship. Open to undergraduates who either reside in or attend college in the Los Angeles area. International applications accepted.

Benefits Health insurance, job counseling, names of contacts, on-the-job training, opportunity to attend seminars/workshops, willing to provide letters of recommendation, educational travel stipend.

Contact Write, call, fax, or e-mail graduate program at 310-440-7331 or fax 310-440-7750; undergraduate program at 310-440-7129 or fax 310-440-7703. E-mail: interns@getty.edu. In-person interview recommended. Applicants must submit a formal organization application, cover letter, academic transcripts, two letters of recommendation. Application deadline: January 1 for graduate interns, March 1 for undergraduate interns. World Wide Web: http://www.getty.edu.

JUDAH L. MAGNES MUSEUM
2911 Russell Street
Berkeley, California 94705

General Information Jewish art museum that preserves and collects historical Jewish objects and contemporary fine art on Jewish themes or by Jewish artists and houses the Blumenthal Rare Book Manuscript Library and the Western Jewish History Center. Established in 1962. Number of employees: 15. Number of internship applications received each year: 10.

Internships Available ▶ *1–10 interns:* responsibilities include working in all departments including registration/collections care; fine arts including painting, sculpture, and graphics; public relations; publications; the Blumenthal Rare Book and Manuscript Library; or the Western Jewish History Center archives of the 13 Western states. Candidates should have ability to work independently, ability to work with others, analytical skills, knowledge of field, organizational skills, plan to pursue career in field. Duration is 4–12 months. Unpaid. Open to college seniors, recent college graduates, graduate students, career changers, individuals reentering the workforce.

Benefits Names of contacts, opportunity to attend seminars/workshops, willing to complete paperwork for educational credit, willing to provide letters of recommendation.

Contact Write, call, or fax Marni Welch, Registrar. Phone: 510-549-6955. Fax: 510-849-3650. In-person interview recommended. Applicants must submit a cover letter, resume. Applications are accepted continuously. World Wide Web: http://www.ftgi.com/iar/comp/283.html.

KANSAS STATE HISTORICAL SOCIETY
6425 Southwest Sixth Avenue
Topeka, Kansas 66615-1099

General Information   Society that collects, preserves, and interprets Kansas history. Established in 1875. Number of employees: 140. Number of internship applications received each year: 10.

Internships Available   ▶ *1 Lela Barnes intern:* responsibilities include managing archives and manuscript records. Candidates should have ability to work independently, computer skills, organizational skills, plan to pursue career in field, research skills, written communication skills. Duration is 10 weeks. $1,800 per duration of internship. ▶ *3–5 interns:* responsibilities include working in the archaeology, archives, or education department, the historical preservation office, or the Kansas Museum of History. Candidates should have ability to work independently, ability to work with others, computer skills, oral communication skills, research skills, written communication skills. Duration is 6–10 weeks. Unpaid. Open to college juniors, college seniors, graduate students. International applications accepted.

Benefits   Job counseling, names of contacts, possible full-time employment, willing to complete paperwork for educational credit, willing to provide letters of recommendation.

Contact   Write, call, fax, or e-mail Dr. David Haury, Assistant Director. Phone: 785-272-8681 Ext. 201. Fax: 785-272-8682. E-mail: dhaury@kshs.org. In-person interview recommended. Applicants must submit a formal organization application, cover letter, resume, academic transcripts, letter of recommendation. Application deadline: April 15 for summer, June 15 for fall, November 15 for spring. World Wide Web: http://www.kshs.org.

KOHL CHILDREN'S MUSEUM
165 Green Bay Road
Wilmette, Illinois 60091

General Information   A not-for-profit cultural institution which provides children, their families and teachers with an array of hands-on learning experiences. Established in 1985. Number of employees: 65. Number of internship applications received each year: 75.

Internships Available   ▶ *1 Kohl/McCormick teaching awards intern:* responsibilities include assisting with program evaluation, strategic planning, and award event details. Candidates should have computer skills, oral communication skills, organizational skills, self-motivation, strong interpersonal skills, written communication skills. Duration is 8–12 weeks. Open to college sophomores, college juniors, college seniors, recent college graduates, graduate students, career changers. ▶ *1 Women's Board (Development) intern:* responsibilities include fund-raising proposals, special events, Board relations, and the Women's Board Benefit. Candidates should have ability to work independently, oral communication skills, organizational skills, research skills, strong interpersonal skills, written communication skills. Duration is 8–12 weeks. Open to college freshmen, college sophomores, college juniors, college seniors, recent college graduates, graduate students, career changers. ▶ *1 communications intern:* responsibilities include helping plan and implement publicity for exhibits, education programs, and special events; drafting press releases; conducting research on untapped markets; assisting with graphic design for publications; and maintaining clip and photo archives. Candidates should have ability to work independently, computer skills, plan to pursue career in field, strong interpersonal skills, writing skills, knowledge of graphic education design computer programs. Duration is 8–12 weeks. Open to college sophomores, college juniors, college seniors, recent college graduates, graduate students, career changers. ▶ *1 computer technology intern:* responsibilities include diagnosing hardware and software problems in MAC-based computers, aiding in the planning and implementation of an upcoming Internet connection for our computer exhibit. Candidates should have ability to work independently, analytical skills, computer skills, experience in the field, knowledge of field, self-motivation. Duration is 8–12 weeks. Open to college freshmen, college sophomores, college juniors, college seniors, recent college graduates, graduate

students, career changers. ▶ *1–2 development interns:* responsibilities include working on fund-raising proposals, special events, board relations, annual benefit, golf outing, and membership drives. Candidates should have computer skills, office skills, oral communication skills, research skills, self-motivation, written communication skills. Duration is flexible. Open to college sophomores, college juniors, college seniors, recent college graduates, graduate students, career changers. ▶ *1–4 education department interns:* responsibilities include providing curricular and facilitation support for school field trip workshops, outreach programs, and teacher/parent workshops; helping with material preparation, research, and general department duties. Candidates should have oral communication skills, personal interest in the field, plan to pursue career in field, self-motivation, strong interpersonal skills, strong leadership ability. Duration is 8–12 weeks. Open to college freshmen, college sophomores, college juniors, college seniors, recent college graduates, graduate students, career changers. ▶ *1 exhibits intern:* responsibilities include assisting in the planning, production, and maintenance of interactive environments for children. Candidates should have ability to work independently, computer skills, personal interest in the field, research skills, strong interpersonal skills, written communication skills. Duration is 8–12 weeks. Open to college sophomores, college juniors, college seniors, recent college graduates, graduate students, career changers. ▶ *1 human resources/administrative/operations intern:* responsibilities include assisting in updating policy and operations manuals and developing forms for human resource use. Candidates should have ability to work independently, computer skills, oral communication skills, strong interpersonal skills, written communication skills. Duration is 8–12 weeks. Open to college freshmen, college sophomores, college juniors, college seniors, recent college graduates, graduate students, career changers. ▶ *1–2 special events interns:* responsibilities include coordinating family programs, researching new ideas, developing activities, and assisting in implementation of various events. Candidates should have oral communication skills, organizational skills, self-motivation, strong interpersonal skills, written communication skills. Duration is 8–12 weeks. Open to college freshmen, college sophomores, college juniors, college seniors, recent college graduates, graduate students, career changers. ▶ *1 volunteer department intern:* responsibilities include assisting in creating community connections at local schools and universities; helping with department events, recruitment, and orientation. Candidates should have ability to work independently, computer skills, oral communication skills, strong interpersonal skills, written communication skills. Duration is 8–12 weeks. Open to college sophomores, college juniors, college seniors, recent college graduates, graduate students, career changers. All positions are unpaid. International applications accepted.

Benefits   Job counseling, on-the-job training, opportunity to attend seminars/workshops, possible full-time employment, willing to complete paperwork for educational credit, willing to provide letters of recommendation.

Contact   Write, call, fax, or e-mail Ms. Lee Kite, Director of Volunteer/Intern Services. Phone: 847-256-6056. Fax: 847-256-5438. E-mail: kcm165@aol.com. In-person interview recommended. Applicants must submit a formal organization application, cover letter, resume, three personal references. Application deadline: May 1 for summer, July 1 for fall, December 1 for winter. World Wide Web: http://www.kohlchildrensmuseum.org.

KRESGE ART MUSEUM
Michigan State University
East Lansing, Michigan 48824

General Information   Art museum that collects, preserves, exhibits, and interprets works of art of all periods. Established in 1959. Number of employees: 7. Unit of Michigan State University, East Lansing, Michigan. Number of internship applications received each year: 30.

Internships Available   ▶ *1 museum intern:* responsibilities include learning all facets of museum work including exhibit development, grant writing, registration, and publicity. Duration is 10 months. $13,000 per duration of internship. International applications accepted.

Benefits Health insurance, job counseling, names of contacts, opportunity to attend seminars/workshops, travel reimbursement, willing to provide letters of recommendation, inexpensive faculty housing.
Contact Write Ms. Carol Fisher, Education Coordinator. Application deadline: March 15. World Wide Web: http://www.msu.edu/unit/kamuseum.

LASSEN VOLCANIC NATIONAL PARK
PO Box 100, 38050 Highway 36 East
Mineral, California 96063-0100

General Information National park with the mission of preserving and protecting the park's natural resources and providing for the continued enjoyment of the lands. Established in 1916. Number of employees: 108. Number of internship applications received each year: 20.
Internships Available ▶ *1–2 interpretive aides:* responsibilities include assisting with winter naturalist programs; working with slide, photo, and museum collections; and recording wildlife sightings. Candidates should have ability to work independently, oral communication skills, self-motivation, strong interpersonal skills, strong leadership ability. Duration is 3 months in winter (January through March). Open to recent high school graduates, college freshmen, college sophomores, college juniors, college seniors, recent college graduates, graduate students, career changers, individuals reentering the workforce. ▶ *1–4 interpretive aides:* responsibilities include supporting junior ranger with living history and field interpretive programs and helping in the visitor center. Candidates should have ability to work independently, oral communication skills, personal interest in the field, self-motivation, strong interpersonal skills. Duration is 3 months in summer (June through August). Open to recent high school graduates, college freshmen, college sophomores, college juniors, college seniors, recent college graduates, graduate students, career changers, individuals reentering the workforce. ▶ *1 librarian:* responsibilities include reaccessing 2 small libraries having a collection of 2000 books, computerizing books, preparing catalog and check-out cards, recataloging and updating books, and updating technical file. Candidates should have ability to work independently, college courses in field, computer skills, declared college major in field, knowledge of field, office skills, organizational skills, personal interest in the field, plan to pursue career in field, research skills, self-motivation, written communication skills. Duration is flexible. Open to recent high school graduates, college freshmen, college sophomores, college juniors, college seniors, recent college graduates, graduate students, career changers, individuals reentering the workforce. ▶ *1 museum technician:* responsibilities include assisting with museum cataloging and curatorial tasks of historical, archival, and botanical collections. Candidates should have ability to work independently, ability to work with others, computer skills, experience in the field, organizational skills, personal interest in the field, research skills, written communication skills. Duration is flexible. Open to recent high school graduates, college freshmen, college sophomores, college juniors, college seniors, recent college graduates, graduate students, career changers, individuals reentering the workforce. ▶ *1–3 resource management aides:* responsibilities include working either independently of or in direct support of resource management staff on defined field project work, computer database entry, and other projects. Candidates should have ability to work independently, computer skills, knowledge of field, research skills, self-motivation, written communication skills. Duration is 3 months in summer (June through August). Open to college freshmen, college sophomores, college juniors, college seniors, recent college graduates, graduate students, career changers. All positions are unpaid. International applications accepted.
Benefits Formal training, free housing, names of contacts, willing to complete paperwork for educational credit, willing to provide letters of recommendation, possible reimbursement for some expenses.
Contact Write, call, or fax Nancy Bailey, Volunteers in Parks Coordinator. Phone: 530-595-4444 Ext. 5133. Fax: 530-595-3408. In-person interview recommended. Applicants must submit a

formal organization application, two personal references. Application deadline: March 1 for summer, October 1 for winter.

LIBRARY OF CONGRESS JUNIOR FELLOWS PROGRAM
Library of Congress, LM-642
Washington, District of Columbia 20540-4600

General Information Library that collects, preserves, and serves material from a wide range of disciplines including history, area studies, film, fine arts, literature, and music. Established in 1800. Number of employees: 5,000. Unit of United States Federal Government, Washington, District of Columbia.
Internships Available ▶ *Junior fellows:* responsibilities include assisting in selected divisions to reduce arrearage, producing finding aids and bibliographic records, preparing materials for preservation and service, and doing bibliographical research. Duration is 2-3 months in summer (40 hours per week). $300 per week. Open to college juniors, college seniors, recent college graduates, graduate students. International applications accepted.
Contact Write, call, fax, or e-mail Junior Fellows Program Coordinator, Library Services. Phone: 202-707-5330. Fax: 202-707-6269. E-mail: jrfell@loc.gov. Applicants must submit academic transcripts, letter of recommendation, cover letter indicating area(s) of interest, resume or Application for Federal Employment (SF 171). Application deadline: April 15. World Wide Web: http://lcweb.loc.gov/rr/jrfell/.

LONGWOOD GARDENS
PO Box 501
Kennett Square, Pennsylvania 19348

General Information Horticultural display garden for the education and enjoyment of the public. Established in 1954. Number of employees: 300. Number of internship applications received each year: 150.
Internships Available ▶ *2 arboriculture interns:* responsibilities include assisting the arborist crew in maintaining the tree collection. Refer to Web site. ▶ *1 computer graphics intern:* responsibilities include producing computer generated depictions and drawings of Longwood Gardens structures. Refer to Web site. ▶ *1 continuing education intern:* responsibilities include assisting with continuing education program. Refer to Web site. ▶ *Curatorial interns:* responsibilities include assisting curator in daily activities. Refer to Web site. ▶ *4 greenhouse production interns:* responsibilities include working with production crops and unusual crops. Refer to Web site. ▶ *2 grounds keeping interns:* responsibilities include various duties. Refer to Web site. ▶ *10 indoor display interns:* responsibilities include maintaining display garden. Refer to Web site. ▶ *2 integrated pest management interns:* responsibilities include assisting integrated pest manager. Refer to Web site. ▶ *1 lanscape design intern:* responsibilities include various duties. Refer to Web site. ▶ *1 nursery intern:* responsibilities include general nursery work. Refer to Web site. ▶ *10 outdoor display interns:* responsibilities include maintenance of annuals and perennials in seasonal sections of the garden; weeding, mulching, watering, pruning, staking, and fertilizing; working with herbs, bulbs, ground covers, vegetables, fruits, and roses. Refer to Web site. ▶ *1 performing arts intern:* responsibilities include assisting with publicity/marketing for 350-event program. Refer to Web site. ▶ *1 student programs intern:* responsibilities include working with students. Refer to Web site. ▶ *2 visitor education interns:* responsibilities include interpreting gardens. Refer to Web site. All positions paid at $5 per hour.
Benefits Formal training, free housing, job counseling, names of contacts, opportunity to attend seminars/workshops, willing to complete paperwork for educational credit, willing to provide letters of recommendation.
Contact Write, call, fax, or e-mail Mr. David J. Foresman, Student Programs Coordinator. Phone: 610-388-1000 Ext. 501. Fax: 610-388-2908. E-mail: studentprograms@longwoodgardens.org. Applicants must submit a formal organization application, resume, academic transcripts, statement of professional objectives. Applica-

Longwood Gardens (continued)

tion deadline: February 1 for summer and fall, November 1 for winter and spring. World Wide Web: http://www.longwoodgardens.org.

THE MARITIME AQUARIUM AT NORWALK
10 North Water Street
Norwalk, Connecticut 06854

General Information An aquarium, maritime museum, and educational center which encourages and excites appreciation of science, the interrelationship of global ecology and natural and cultural events as they relate to Long Island Sound. Established in 1988. Number of employees: 80. Number of internship applications received each year: 300.
Internships Available ▶ *5 maritime aquarium educators:* responsibilities include a rotation through 3 different departments (Education, Aquarium, and Volunteers), participating in a variety of jobs from preparing seal food to helping teach educational programs. Candidates should have ability to work independently, oral communication skills, personal interest in the field, research skills, self-motivation, strong interpersonal skills, strong leadership ability, written communication skills. Duration is minimum 6 weeks. Unpaid. Open to high school students, high school seniors, recent high school graduates, college freshmen, college sophomores, college juniors, college seniors, recent college graduates, graduate students, individuals at least 16 years old. International applications accepted.
Benefits Names of contacts, on-the-job training, possible full-time employment, willing to act as a professional reference, willing to complete paperwork for educational credit, willing to provide letters of recommendation.
Contact Write, fax, or e-mail Lauren Sikorski, Intern Coordinator. Fax: 203-838-5416. E-mail: intern.coor@aol.com. No phone calls. In-person interview recommended. Applicants must submit a formal organization application, cover letter, resume, academic transcripts, writing sample, three letters of recommendation. Applications are accepted continuously.

MEADOWSIDE NATURE CENTER
5100 Meadowside Lane
Rockville, Maryland 20855

General Information Nature center located within a 2700-acre regional park outside of Washington, DC. Established in 1927. Number of employees: 5. Unit of Maryland National Capital Park and Planning Commission, Department of Parks, Silver Spring, Maryland. Number of internship applications received each year: 20.
Internships Available ▶ *1–2 naturalist interns:* responsibilities include developing and presenting interpretive programs for diverse audiences including conservation clubs and special events, assisting with field studies and maintenance of wildlife and heritage gardens, rehabilitated animal display, and other exhibits. Candidates should have college courses in field, oral communication skills, personal interest in the field, self-motivation, strong interpersonal skills. Duration is 14–16 weeks. hourly minimum wage. Open to college freshmen, college sophomores, college juniors, college seniors, recent college graduates, graduate students, law students, career changers, individuals reentering the workforce. International applications accepted.
Benefits Formal training, housing at a cost, on-the-job training, opportunity to attend seminars/workshops, willing to act as a professional reference, willing to complete paperwork for educational credit, willing to provide letters of recommendation, outings to other park facilities, park housing available.
Contact Write, call, or fax Ms. Sara Staples, Intern Coordinator. Phone: 301-924-4141. Fax: 301-924-1034. In-person interview recommended. Applicants must submit a cover letter, resume, evidence of academic coursework. Application deadline: March 1 for summer, June 1 for winter, October 1 for spring.

THE METROPOLITAN MUSEUM OF ART
1000 Fifth Avenue
New York, New York 10028-0198

General Information Art museum that emphasizes encyclopedic collection of master works of art. Established in 1870. Number of employees: 2,500. Number of internship applications received each year: 450.
Internships Available ▶ *Interns:* responsibilities include varied duties for college and graduate students interested in art museum and related careers. Both full- and part-time positions are available for the summer as well as the academic year. Please contact the Education Department for further information. Candidates should have ability to work with others, computer skills, oral communication skills, written communication skills, background in art history, knowledge of foreign languages. Position available as unpaid or paid. Open to college freshmen, college sophomores, college juniors, college seniors, recent college graduates, graduate students. International applications accepted.
Benefits Meals at a cost, on-the-job training, willing to complete paperwork for educational credit, letters of recommendation provided if appropriate.
Contact Write, call, fax, or e-mail Education Department. Phone: 212-570-3710. Fax: 212-570-3782. E-mail: mma-ed@interport.net. In-person interview required. Applicants must submit a cover letter, resume, academic transcripts, two letters of recommendation, essay of not more than 500 words which states reason for application and career goals, list of art history and other relevant courses taken. Application deadline: contact "Internship Programs" for exact dates. World Wide Web: http://www.metmuseum.org/.

THE MEXICAN MUSEUM
Building D, Fort Mason Center
San Francisco, California 94123

General Information Art museum dedicated to the visual expression of Mexican and Latin American people. The museum collects pre-Hispanic, colonial, popular art, Mexican, and Latino/Chicano fine art. Established in 1975. Number of employees: 12. Number of internship applications received each year: 20.
Internships Available ▶ *1–2 art registration interns:* responsibilities include working on research and art registration procedures. Candidates should have ability to work with others, college degree in related field, knowledge of field, organizational skills, self-motivation. Duration is 1–6 months. Open to college seniors, recent college graduates, graduate students, individuals reentering the workforce. ▶ *2–3 education interns:* responsibilities include assisting with school tours, Family Sunday, and archiving. Candidates should have ability to work independently, computer skills, office skills, oral communication skills, organizational skills, self-motivation, strong interpersonal skills. Duration is 1–3 months. Open to college juniors, college seniors, recent college graduates, graduate students, career changers, individuals reentering the workforce. ▶ *3 museum interns:* responsibilities include working in one of the following areas: curatorial, education, development, registration, or public relations. Candidates should have oral communication skills, organizational skills, personal interest in the field, plan to pursue career in field, self-motivation, strong interpersonal skills. Duration is 1–6 months. Open to college juniors, college seniors, recent college graduates, graduate students, individuals reentering the workforce. All positions are unpaid. International applications accepted.
Benefits Formal training, on-the-job training, opportunity to attend seminars/workshops, willing to act as a professional reference, willing to complete paperwork for educational credit.
Contact Write, call, fax, or e-mail Olivia Armas, Education Coordinator. Phone: 415-202-9700. Fax: 415-441-7683. E-mail: olivia@mexicanmuseum.org. In-person interview required. Applicants must submit a formal organization application, cover letter, resume, writing sample, letter of recommendation. Applications are accepted continuously.

MILWAUKEE PUBLIC MUSEUM
800 West Wells Street
Milwaukee, Wisconsin 53233

General Information Natural and human history museum. Established in 1882. Number of employees: 140. Number of internship applications received each year: 60.
Internships Available ▶ *1–3 anthropology interns:* responsibilities include collections work in the following areas: American Indian, Africa, Pacific Islands, Central and South America. Candidates should have ability to work independently, ability to work with others, analytical skills, college courses in field, computer skills, office skills, organizational skills, plan to pursue career in field, research skills, self-motivation, writing skills. Duration is 1–3 months. Open to college sophomores, college juniors, college seniors, recent college graduates, graduate students. ▶ *1–3 education interns:* responsibilities include presenting educational programs to groups and performing collection research and program development. Candidates should have ability to work independently, college courses in field, oral communication skills, organizational skills, personal interest in the field, self-motivation, strong interpersonal skills. Duration is 1–3 months. Open to college sophomores, college juniors, college seniors, recent college graduates, graduate students. ▶ *1–3 exhibit programs interns:* responsibilities include assisting in the production of various components of permanent and temporary exhibits, the installation of special exhibits, and upkeep of exhibits. Candidates should have ability to work independently, college courses in field, experience in the field, plan to pursue career in field. Duration is 1–2 semesters. Open to college juniors, college seniors, recent college graduates. ▶ *1–2 history interns:* responsibilities include working on collections from colonial America, European societies, North Africa, Middle East, classical civilizations, Asia, and specific areas in textiles and military weapons. Candidates should have ability to work independently, analytical skills, college courses in field, computer skills, editing skills, office skills, organizational skills, plan to pursue career in field, research skills, self-motivation, writing skills. Duration is 1–3 months. Open to college seniors, graduate students. ▶ *1–3 marketing interns:* responsibilities include working in public relations, communications, advertising, and journalism. Candidates should have ability to work independently, college courses in field, computer skills, editing skills, knowledge of field, office skills, oral communication skills, organizational skills, self-motivation, strong interpersonal skills, writing skills. Duration is 1–3 months. Open to college sophomores, college juniors, college seniors, recent college graduates. ▶ *1–2 zoology interns:* responsibilities include assisting with collections maintenance, lab work, and local fieldwork. Candidates should have ability to work independently, analytical skills, college courses in field, computer skills, knowledge of field, plan to pursue career in field, research skills, self-motivation, written communication skills. Duration is 1–3 months. Open to college juniors, college seniors, recent college graduates, graduate students. All positions are unpaid. International applications accepted.
Benefits Job counseling, names of contacts, on-the-job training, opportunity to attend seminars/workshops, willing to complete paperwork for educational credit, willing to provide letters of recommendation.
Contact Write, call, fax, or e-mail Ms. Dawn Scher Thomae, Museum Internship Coordinator. Phone: 414-278-6157. Fax: 414-278-6100. E-mail: thomae@mpm.edu. In-person interview recommended. Applicants must submit a cover letter, resume. Application deadline: March 1 for summer, November 1 for spring.

THE MINNEAPOLIS INSTITUTE OF ARTS
2400 Third Avenue, South
Minneapolis, Minnesota 55404

General Information Art museum that emphasizes collection of master works of art in the areas of painting, sculpture, decorative arts, prints, drawings, photography, textiles, and Asian, African, Oceanic, and Native-American arts. Established in 1883. Number of employees: 200. Number of internship applications received each year: 75.
Internships Available ▶ *1–2 curatorial interns:* responsibilities include assisting in preparation of object files and occasionally researching and writing gallery and catalog materials. Candidates should have ability to work with others, college courses in field, declared college major in field, organizational skills, research skills, writing skills. Open to college freshmen, college sophomores, college juniors, college seniors, recent college graduates, graduate students, career changers, individuals reentering the workforce. ▶ *2–3 development interns:* responsibilities include assisting department in various capacities relating to fund-raising. Candidates should have computer skills, knowledge of field, office skills, oral communication skills, research skills, written communication skills. Open to college freshmen, college sophomores, college juniors, college seniors, recent college graduates, graduate students. ▶ *5–10 education interns:* responsibilities include assisting in preparation of teaching materials for use in schools and researching and writing gallery and catalog materials. Candidates should have ability to work independently, computer skills, editing skills, plan to pursue career in field, research skills, writing skills. Open to college freshmen, college sophomores, college juniors, college seniors, recent college graduates, graduate students. ▶ *3–5 library interns:* responsibilities include working on various projects relating to library exhibitions such as museum object files. Candidates should have college courses in field, computer skills, experience in the field, organizational skills, strong interpersonal skills, written communication skills. Open to college freshmen, college sophomores, college juniors, college seniors, recent college graduates, graduate students, career changers, individuals reentering the workforce. ▶ *1–2 marketing/ communications interns:* responsibilities include compiling press clippings and other various duties and opportunities. Candidates should have ability to work with others, college courses in field, computer skills, editing skills, experience in the field, written communication skills. Open to college freshmen, college sophomores, college juniors, college seniors. ▶ *1 registration intern:* responsibilities include working on various projects including inventory of parts of a collection. Candidates should have ability to work with others, college courses in field, experience in the field, office skills, organizational skills, plan to pursue career in field. Open to college freshmen, college sophomores, college juniors, college seniors, recent college graduates, graduate students. Duration for all positions is dependent on project requirements. All positions are unpaid. International applications accepted.
Benefits Names of contacts, opportunity to attend seminars/workshops, possible full-time employment, willing to complete paperwork for educational credit, willing to provide letters of recommendation.
Contact Write, call, fax, or e-mail Treden P. Wagoner, Intern Coordinator. Phone: 888-642-2787 Ext. 3189. Fax: 612-870-3004. E-mail: twagoner@artsmia.org. Applicants must submit a formal organization application, cover letter, resume, academic transcripts, two letters of recommendation, writing samples and interviews may be required. Application deadline: March 1 for summer, June 1 for fall/winter, October 1 for winter/spring. World Wide Web: http://www.artsMIA.org.

MINNESOTA MUSEUM OF AMERICAN ART
75 West Fifth Street, Landmark Center, Suite 505
St. Paul, Minnesota 55102

General Information Art museum that collects, preserves, enriches, and educates the community on 19th- and 20th-century American art. Established in 1927. Number of employees: 8. Number of internship applications received each year: 50.
Internships Available ▶ *1 curatorial assistant:* responsibilities include assisting curator with didactics, gallery installation and research. Candidates should have computer skills, knowledge of field, research skills, writing skills. Open to recent college graduates, graduate students. ▶ *1 development assistant:* responsibilities include performing office duties and assisting department in development research. Candidates should have ability to work

Minnesota Museum of American Art (continued)

independently, editing skills, research skills, strong interpersonal skills, writing skills. Open to college juniors, college seniors, recent college graduates, graduate students, career changers. ▶ *1 public relations/marketing assistant:* responsibilities include assisting PR coordinator with writing and distributing press releases and other publications. Candidates should have ability to work independently, computer skills, editing skills, office skills, oral communication skills, organizational skills, self-motivation, writing skills. Open to college juniors, college seniors, recent college graduates, graduate students, career changers. Duration for all positions is 3 months. All positions are unpaid. International applications accepted.

Benefits Opportunity to attend seminars/workshops, willing to complete paperwork for educational credit, willing to provide letters of recommendation, 50% discount on art classes and catalogs, complimentary museum membership.

Contact Write, call, fax, or e-mail Alisa Hacker, Community Services Coordinator, 75 West Fifth Street Landmark Center, Suite 505, St. Paul, Minnesota 55102. Phone: 651-292-4367. Fax: 651-292-4340. E-mail: mmaa@mtn.org. In-person interview recommended. Applicants must submit a formal organization application, cover letter, resume, academic transcripts. Applications are accepted continuously. World Wide Web: http://www.mtn.org/MMAA/.

THE MINNESOTA ZOO
13000 Zoo Boulevard
Apple Valley, Minnesota 55124

General Information Conservation organization and facility whose goal is to help people realize the importance of animals and their impact on the world. Established in 1977. Number of employees: 300. Number of internship applications received each year: 80.

Internships Available ▶ *10–30 animal management interns:* responsibilities include caring for exotic and domestic animals; preparing diets; cleaning exhibits; learning techniques of zoo animal management; observing, reporting, and evaluating animal behavior; responding to animal emergencies; observing medical procedures; and effectively communicating with visitors on animal-related questions. Candidates should have college courses in field, oral communication skills, strong interpersonal skills. Open to college juniors, college seniors. ▶ *2–4 education interns:* responsibilities include teaching in the informal setting of a zoo, handling animals for interpretive demonstrations, developing effective presentations, responding to questions from diverse audiences, structuring lesson plans, developing curriculum, working effectively with students and zoo education staff, and becoming environmental interpreters. Candidates should have college courses in field, oral communication skills, plan to pursue career in field, strong interpersonal skills, written communication skills. Open to college juniors, college seniors. ▶ *1–2 horticulture interns:* responsibilities include assisting with horticulture projects throughout the Zoo, and assisting in maintenance of greenhouse plants. Candidates should have ability to work independently, college courses in field, plan to pursue career in field, self-motivation, strong interpersonal skills. Open to college juniors, college seniors. ▶ *1–2 information management interns:* responsibilities include software and LAN support, and database and Internet management. Candidates should have analytical skills, college courses in field, computer skills, oral communication skills, strong interpersonal skills. Open to college juniors, college seniors. ▶ *2–4 marketing interns:* responsibilities include working with media crews, writing and mailing press releases, promoting special events, writing and editing articles for membership, and working with sales department. Candidates should have ability to work with others, college courses in field, oral communication skills, strong interpersonal skills, written communication skills. Open to college juniors, college seniors. ▶ *1–4 veterinary technician interns:* responsibilities include performing lab work, assisting and observing animal medical procedures, and assisting veterinarian with routine procedures. Candidates should have college courses in field, oral communication skills, plan to pursue career in field, strong interpersonal skills, written communica-

tion skills. Open to college juniors, college seniors, current students in veterinary medical training program. Duration for all positions is 10-14 weeks (30-40 hours per week). All positions are unpaid.

Benefits Willing to complete paperwork for educational credit, willing to provide letters of recommendation.

Contact Write, call, fax, or e-mail Teri Weitz, Personnel Officer. Phone: 612-431-9212. Fax: 612-431-9211. E-mail: teri.weitz@state. mn.us. Applicants must submit a formal organization application, cover letter, resume, academic transcripts, letter of recommendation. Application deadline: March 1 for summer, August 1 for fall, October 1 for winter, December 1 for spring. World Wide Web: http://www.mnzoo.com.

MONTANA FISH, WILDLIFE, AND PARKS, REGION 7, MAKOSHIKA STATE PARK
1301 Snyder Avenue, PO Box 1242
Glendive, Montana 59330

General Information State park that preserves and protects an area of natural scenic beauty and ecological significance for the benefit of the public. Established in 1953. Number of employees: 4. Division of Montana Department of Fish, Wildlife, and Parks, Helena, Montana. Number of internship applications received each year: 5.

Internships Available ▶ *1 interpreter/paleontologist:* responsibilities include performing general duties related to park management; developing trails, campfire lectures, and youth program. Candidates should have college courses in field, computer skills, oral communication skills, writing skills, written communication skills. Duration is 12 weeks. $6 per hour. Open to college sophomores, college juniors, college seniors. International applications accepted.

Benefits Health insurance, on-the-job training, possible full-time employment, willing to complete paperwork for educational credit, willing to provide letters of recommendation.

Contact Write or call Mr. Chris Lorentz, Park Manager, 1301Snyder Avenue, PO Box 1242, Glendive, Montana 59330. Phone: 406-365-6256. Telephone interview required. Applicants must submit a cover letter, resume, academic transcripts. Application deadline: March 15 for summer.

THE MONTCLAIR ART MUSEUM
3 South Mountain Avenue
Montclair, New Jersey 07042

General Information Art museum with a permanent collection spanning 3 centuries of American art with strengths in 19th-century American landscapes, Hudson River School, and American impressionist paintings in addition to a Native-American collection of almost 4000 objects representing nearly every North American indigenous culture. Established in 1914. Number of employees: 30.

Internships Available ▶ *1 Schering-Plough intern:* responsibilities include overseeing the functioning of all aspects of the museum. Candidates should have computer skills, oral communication skills, personal interest in the field, plan to pursue career in field, writing skills. Duration is September-May (minimum of 2 days per week). Position available as unpaid or at $4000 stipend for living expenses for duration of internship. ▶ *Collections management interns:* responsibilities include assisting registrar in care and cataloging of collections. Duration is 1 summer. Unpaid. ▶ *Communications interns:* responsibilities include assisting media coordinator and director of communications in various tasks relating to production of publications, press releases, advertising flyers, and updating press lists. Duration is 1 summer. Unpaid. ▶ *Curatorial interns:* responsibilities include assisting curator of collections. Duration is 1 summer. Unpaid. ▶ *Development interns:* responsibilities include assisting in prospect and donor research and grant writing. Duration is 1 summer. Unpaid. ▶ *Education interns:* responsibilities include assisting in training docents, scheduling tours, developing educational programs, and working with art school. Candidates should have computer skills, oral communication skills, organizational skills, research skills, strong interpersonal skills, writing skills. Duration is 1 summer.

Unpaid. ▶ *Exhibit design/installation interns:* responsibilities include assisting exhibit designer in preparing and installing exhibitions, fabricating casework, and crating artifacts. Duration is 1 summer. Unpaid. Open to college freshmen, college sophomores, college juniors, college seniors, graduate students. International applications accepted.
Benefits Names of contacts, willing to complete paperwork for educational credit, willing to provide letters of recommendation.
Contact Write Tara Belluscio, Director of Education. No phone calls. Applicants must submit a cover letter, resume. Application deadline: March 30 for summer, May 1 for Schering-Plough internship.

MONTSHIRE MUSEUM OF SCIENCE
One Montshire Road
Norwich, Vermont 05055

General Information Science museum that uses materials and devices, natural objects, exhibits, live animals, and indoor/outdoor settings as catalysts in experiencing science and encouraging observation, curiosity, intuition, problem-solving, and imagination. Established in 1974. Number of employees: 26. Number of internship applications received each year: 16.
Internships Available ▶ *1 Internet and education intern:* responsibilities include developing bibliography of global Internet resources. Candidates should have ability to work independently, computer skills, experience in the field, oral communication skills, strong interpersonal skills. Duration is 15 weeks. $600 stipend. Open to college juniors, college seniors, recent college graduates, graduate students, career changers. ▶ *3 environmental education interns:* responsibilities include planning, development, and teaching in environmental day camps. Candidates should have personal interest in the field, strong interpersonal skills, ability to work with children. Duration is 10 weeks summer only. $1000 stipend. Open to college sophomores, college juniors, college seniors, recent college graduates. ▶ *2 exhibit/design fabrication interns:* responsibilities include researching, designing, constructing, and refining exhibits. Candidates should have ability to work independently, oral communication skills, research skills, written communication skills. Duration is 15 weeks. $600 stipend. Open to college juniors, college seniors, recent college graduates, graduate students, career changers. ▶ *1 land management intern:* responsibilities include following master plan and management objectives for 100-acre property, doing trail and grounds work. Candidates should have ability to work independently, personal interest in the field, self-motivation, ability to operate chain saw. Duration is 15 weeks. $600 stipend. Open to college juniors, college seniors, recent college graduates, graduate students, career changers. ▶ *1 membership and development intern:* responsibilities include development and coordination of annual fund, major gifts, and planned giving programs; working with Montshire Associates, a local forum for business, education, and government; providing support for family and individual members. Candidates should have ability to work independently, oral communication skills, organizational skills, strong interpersonal skills, written communication skills. Duration is 15 weeks. $600 stipend. Open to college juniors, college seniors, recent college graduates, graduate students, career changers. ▶ *1 public relations intern:* responsibilities include working in the various avenues of communication. Candidates should have editing skills, oral communication skills, plan to pursue career in field, research skills, strong interpersonal skills, written communication skills. Duration is 15 weeks. $600 stipend. Open to college juniors, college seniors, recent college graduates, graduate students, career changers. ▶ *4 science education interns:* responsibilities include teaching a variety of science and ecology classes to preschoolers, school children, teachers, and families; participating in environmental camps, overnights, and demonstrations; developing curricula; interpreting exhibits, outreach programs, teacher workshops, and courses. Candidates should have ability to work independently, personal interest in the field, strong interpersonal skills, interest in working with children and adults. Duration is 15 weeks. $600 stipend. Open to college juniors, college seniors, recent college graduates, career changers.

Benefits Free housing, on-the-job training, opportunity to attend seminars/workshops, willing to complete paperwork for educational credit, willing to provide letters of recommendation.
Contact Write, call, fax, or e-mail Ms. Amy VanderKooi, Museum Educator. Phone: 802-649-2200. Fax: 802-649-3637. E-mail: montshire@valley.net. In-person interview recommended. Applicants must submit a formal organization application, cover letter, resume, writing and art sample for exhibit/design interns, writing sample for public relations interns. Applications are accepted continuously. World Wide Web: http://www.valley.net/~mms/.

MOORES CREEK NATIONAL BATTLEFIELD
40 Patriots Hall Drive
Currie, North Carolina 28435

General Information Preserves the site of the Revolutionary War Battle of Moores Creek. Established in 1926. Number of employees: 6. Unit of United States National Park Service, Washington, District of Columbia. Number of internship applications received each year: 4.
Internships Available ▶ *1–4 visitor use assistants:* responsibilities include performing interpretation, managing resources, and conducting historical research. Candidates should have college courses in field, computer skills, knowledge of field, oral communication skills, personal interest in the field, strong interpersonal skills. Duration is year-round. Unpaid. Open to high school seniors, recent high school graduates, college freshmen, college sophomores, college juniors, college seniors. International applications accepted.
Benefits Names of contacts, travel reimbursement, willing to complete paperwork for educational credit, experience in a national park.
Contact Write, call, fax, or e-mail Linda L. Brown, Lead Park Ranger. Phone: 910-283-5591. Fax: 910-283-5351. E-mail: linda_brown@nps.gov. In-person interview recommended. Applicants must submit a resume, two personal references. Applications are accepted continuously. World Wide Web: http://www.gov.nps.mocr.

MORRIS ARBORETUM OF THE UNIVERSITY OF PENNSYLVANIA
9414 Meadowbrook Avenue
Philadelphia, Pennsylvania 19118

General Information University arboretum that emphasizes teaching, research, and outreach programs. Established in 1932. Number of employees: 50. Unit of University of Pennsylvania, Philadelphia, Pennsylvania. Number of internship applications received each year: 50.
Internships Available ▶ *1 arborist intern:* responsibilities include working in all phases of tree care. Candidates should have ability to work with others, personal interest in the field, climbing experience. Open to college juniors, college seniors, recent college graduates. ▶ *1 education intern:* responsibilities include working closely with education staff and volunteer guides to develop workshops for experienced guides and training sessions to recruit new guides; supervising school tour program, running special programs for school children, and developing specialized tours for the public; and helping coordinator prepare adult-education course brochure by selecting course topics and instructors and writing promotional copy for the brochures. Candidates should have ability to work independently, college courses in field, computer skills, editing skills, experience in the field, oral communication skills, self-motivation, strong interpersonal skills, written communication skills. Open to college seniors, recent college graduates, graduate students, career changers, individuals reentering the workforce. ▶ *1 flora of Pennsylvania intern:* responsibilities include working in a major herbarium and creating a modern flora using computerized systems. Candidates should have ability to work independently, analytical skills, college courses in field, computer skills, knowledge of field, personal interest in the field, plan to pursue career in field, research skills, self-motivation, written communication skills. Open to college seniors, recent college graduates, graduate students, career changers, individuals reentering the workforce. ▶ *1 horticultural*

Morris Arboretum of the University of Pennsylvania (continued)

intern: responsibilities include assisting arboretum horticulturists in all phases of garden development and care and supervising gardening activities of volunteers and part-time staff. Candidates should have ability to work independently, ability to work with others, knowledge of field, organizational skills, personal interest in the field, self-motivation. Open to college juniors, college seniors, recent college graduates, graduate students, career changers, individuals reentering the workforce. ► *1 plant protection intern:* responsibilities include assisting the arboretum's plant pathologist with the Integrated Pest Management (IPM) program. Candidates should have ability to work independently, analytical skills, college courses in field, personal interest in the field, research skills, self-motivation. Open to college seniors, recent college graduates, graduate students, career changers, individuals reentering the workforce. ► *1 propagation intern:* responsibilities include assisting propagator in the development of plant production and propagation schemes. Candidates should have ability to work independently, ability to work with others, college courses in field, knowledge of field, organizational skills, personal interest in the field, self-motivation. Open to college seniors, recent college graduates, graduate students, career changers, individuals reentering the workforce. ► *1 rosarian intern:* responsibilities include working with experienced horticulturist to plan, plant, and maintain Arbaretum's rose garden display. Candidates should have ability to work independently, ability to work with others, college courses in field, knowledge of field, personal interest in the field, self-motivation. Open to college juniors, college seniors, recent college graduates, graduate students, career changers, individuals reentering the workforce. ► *1 urban forestry intern:* responsibilities include working on community landscape consultation projects. Candidates should have college courses in field, computer skills, editing skills, oral communication skills, organizational skills, personal interest in the field, self-motivation, strong interpersonal skills, writing skills. Open to college seniors, recent college graduates, graduate students, career changers, individuals reentering the workforce. Duration for all positions is 1 year. All positions paid at $7 per hour. International applications accepted.
Benefits Formal training, health insurance, on-the-job training, opportunity to attend seminars/workshops, tuition assistance, willing to act as a professional reference, willing to complete paperwork for educational credit, willing to provide letters of recommendation.
Contact Write, call, fax, or e-mail Ms. Jan McFarlan, Education Coordinator. Phone: 215-247-5777 Ext. 156. Fax: 215-247-7862. E-mail: jlm@pobox.upenn.edu. Telephone interview required. Applicants must submit a cover letter, resume, academic transcripts, three letters of recommendation. Application deadline: February 15 for June start date. World Wide Web: http://www.upenn.edu/morris/.

MOUNT DESERT ISLAND HISTORICAL SOCIETY
2 Oak Hill Road, PO Box 653
Mount Desert, Maine 04660

General Information Society that manages a musuem and archive, offers educationla programs, acts as a voice for historic preservation on Mt. Desert Island, and publishes an annual history journal. Established in 1931. Number of employees: 1. Number of internship applications received each year: 10.
Internships Available ► *1 assistant to the Director:* responsibilities include assisting with tours of museum, cataloging, collection care, research assistance, and program development assistance. Candidates should have computer skills, oral communication skills, personal interest in the field, research skills, strong interpersonal skills, written communication skills. Duration is 3 weeks (June 1 to August 31). $1,000 stipend including free housing ($2,000 without housing). Open to college freshmen, college sophomores, college juniors, college seniors, recent college graduates, graduate students. International applications accepted.
Benefits Free housing, willing to act as a professional reference, willing to complete paperwork for educational credit, will-

ing to provide letters of recommendation, opportunity to gain basic experience in small musuem management.
Contact Write, call, or e-mail Jaylene Roths, Director. Phone: 207-244-5043. E-mail: jroths@acadia.net. In-person interview recommended. Applicants must submit a cover letter, resume. Application deadline: March 1.

MOUNT ROGERS NATIONAL RECREATION AREA
3714 Highway 16
Marion, Virginia 24354

General Information National recreation area conducting multiple-use management of public natural resources. Number of employees: 30. Unit of George Washington and Jefferson National Forests, Roanoke, Virginia. Number of internship applications received each year: 10.
Internships Available ► *1 GIS/GPS specialist:* responsibilities include mapping forest resources such as trails, roads, and streams with a Global Positioning System unit; preparing maps and other products using Geographic Information System technology. Candidates should have ability to work independently, college courses in field, computer skills, knowledge of field, self-motivation, writing skills. Duration is flexible. Open to college freshmen, college sophomores, college juniors, college seniors, recent college graduates, graduate students, law students, career changers. ► *1–2 backcountry horse rangers:* responsibilities include providing wilderness education, documenting use of resources, and performing trail maintenance. Candidates should have ability to work independently, oral communication skills, personal interest in the field, self-motivation, strong interpersonal skills. Duration is 2-6 months from May to October. Open to recent high school graduates, college freshmen, college sophomores, college juniors, college seniors, recent college graduates, graduate students, law students, career changers, individuals reentering the workforce. ► *4–8 backcountry rangers:* responsibilities include providing wilderness education, documenting use of resources, and performing trail maintenance. Candidates should have ability to work independently, oral communication skills, personal interest in the field, self-motivation, strong interpersonal skills. Duration is 2-6 months from May to October. Open to recent high school graduates, college freshmen, college sophomores, college juniors, college seniors, recent college graduates, graduate students, law students, career changers, individuals reentering the workforce. ► *1–2 environmental education specialists:* responsibilities include providing environmental education programs in local schools. Candidates should have ability to work independently, oral communication skills, self-motivation, strong interpersonal skills, written communication skills. Duration is 1-4 months from March to June. Open to recent high school graduates, college freshmen, college sophomores, college juniors, college seniors, recent college graduates, graduate students, law students, career changers, individuals reentering the workforce. ► *1 interpreter:* responsibilities include providing programs for visitors. Candidates should have ability to work independently, oral communication skills, organizational skills, self-motivation, strong interpersonal skills, writing skills. Duration is 2-6 months from May to October. Open to recent high school graduates, college freshmen, college sophomores, college juniors, college seniors, recent college graduates, graduate students, law students, career changers, individuals reentering the workforce. ► *1–2 mountain bike patrol interns:* responsibilities include mountain bike patroling and maintaining Virginia Creeper National Recreation Trail. Candidates should have ability to work independently, oral communication skills, personal interest in the field, self-motivation, strong interpersonal skills. Duration is 2-6 months from May to October. Open to recent high school graduates, college freshmen, college sophomores, college juniors, college seniors, recent college graduates, graduate students, law students, career changers, individuals reentering the workforce. ► *2–4 recreation aides:* responsibilities include performing recreation area cleanup, operations, and maintenance. Candidates should have ability to work independently, ability to work with others, self-motivation. Duration is 2-6 months from May to October. Open to recent high school graduates, college freshmen, college sophomores,

college juniors, college seniors, recent college graduates, graduate students, law students, career changers, individuals reentering the workforce. ▶ *2–4 trail maintenance workers:* responsibilities include working on a crew performing trail maintenance throughout the 150,000-acre Mount Rogers NRA. Candidates should have ability to work with others, personal interest in the field, self-motivation, strong leadership ability. Duration is 2-6 months from May to October. Open to recent high school graduates, college freshmen, college sophomores, college juniors, college seniors, recent college graduates, graduate students, law students, career changers, individuals reentering the workforce. ▶ *1–2 visitor center staff:* responsibilities include staffing visitor center during busy season. Candidates should have ability to work independently, office skills, oral communication skills, self-motivation, strong interpersonal skills. Duration is 2-6 months from May to October. Open to recent high school graduates, college freshmen, college sophomores, college juniors, college seniors, recent college graduates, graduate students, law students, career changers, individuals reentering the workforce. All positions available as unpaid or at $5–$10 per day. International applications accepted.
Benefits Free housing, names of contacts, on-the-job training, opportunity to attend seminars/workshops, willing to act as a professional reference, willing to complete paperwork for educational credit, willing to provide letters of recommendation, free campsites available, backcountry cabin may be available for some positions.
Contact Write, call, fax, or e-mail Mr. Tim Eling, Volunteer Coordinator. Phone: 540-783-5196. Fax: 540-783-5504. E-mail: teling/r8_gwjeff_mtrogers@fs.fed.us. Applicants must submit a formal organization application, cover letter. Applications are accepted continuously.

MOUNT RUSHMORE NATIONAL MEMORIAL
PO Box 268
Keystone, South Dakota 57751

General Information National Park Service site that commemorates the first 150 years of American democracy with a meeting carving of four important presidents' faces. Established in 1925. Number of employees: 70. Number of internship applications received each year: 10.
Internships Available ▶ *1–2 interpretation interns:* responsibilities include developing and presenting interpretive talks and guided walks, staffing information desk, performing informal roving interpretation, assisting speaker at evening program, and assisting with special events and museum curator research. Candidates should have ability to work with others, oral communication skills, personal interest in the field, self-motivation, written communication skills. Duration is 12 to 16 weeks in fall, winter, and spring. Open to college students in a related field. ▶ *1 museum intern:* responsibilities include accessioning and cataloging, database management, preventive conservation, museum storage and security, exhibit planning, and possibly collections research. Candidates should have ability to work with others, college courses in field, organizational skills, plan to pursue career in field, research skills, written communication skills. Duration is 12 to 16 weeks in fall, winter, and spring. Open to recent college graduates, graduate students, career changers, college students actively enrolled in museum studies for academic credit. ▶ *2–3 resource management and visitor protection interns:* responsibilities include assisting with visitor services; monitoring trails, climbing areas, and boundaries. Candidates should have ability to work independently, ability to work with others, oral communication skills, personal interest in the field, self-motivation. Duration is 12–16 weeks. Open to college students. All positions paid at stipend of $50 per week. International applications accepted.
Benefits Formal training, free housing, job counseling, meals at a cost, on-the-job training, willing to complete paperwork for educational credit, willing to provide letters of recommendation, potential seasonal job opportunities with the National Park Service, limited reimbursement for some expenses.
International Internships Available.

Contact Write or call James G. Popovich, Chief of Interpretation. Phone: 605-574-3114. Telephone interview required. Applicants must submit a cover letter, resume, three personal references. Applications are accepted continuously. World Wide Web: http://www.nps.gov/moru.

THE MUSEUM OF MODERN ART
11 West 53rd Street
New York, New York 10019

General Information Art museum with collection of modern and contemporary art. Established in 1929. Number of employees: 600. Number of internship applications received each year: 800.
Internships Available ▶ *12-month interns:* responsibilities include attending summer lecture series and a professional conference, and assisting on projects based on Museum requirements, projects may be in the director's office, curatorial departments, development, education and research support, exhibition and collection support, marketing and communications, or administrative departments. Candidates should have personal interest in the field, plan to pursue career in field, recently completed bachelor's or master's program. Duration is full-time for 12 months beginning in September. depends on available funding, includes standard health and vacation benefits and additional $1,000 for travel expenses and registration. Open to recent college graduates, U.S. citizens or permanent residents. ▶ *Fall interns:* responsibilities include assisting on projects based on museum requirements, projects may be in the director's office, curatorial departments, development, education and research support, exhibition and collection support, marketing and communications, retail and operations, or administrative departments. Candidates should have college courses in field, personal interest in the field. Duration is 2 days per week for 12 weeks. Open to college juniors, college seniors, graduate students, international students, and beginning professionals. ▶ *Spring interns:* responsibilities include assisting on projects based on museum requirements, projects may be in the director's office, curatorial departments, development, education and research support, exhibition and collection support, marketing and communications, retail and operations, or administrative departments. Candidates should have college courses in field, personal interest in the field. Duration is minimum 2 days per week for 12 weeks. Open to college juniors, college seniors, graduate students, individuals reentering the workforce, international students, and beginning professionals. ▶ *Summer interns:* responsibilities include attending lecture series and assisting on projects based on museum requirements, projects may be in the director's office, curatorial departments, development, education and research support, exhibition and collection support, marketing and communications, retail and operations, or administrative departments. Candidates should have college courses in field, personal interest in the field. Duration is full-time for 9 weeks. Position available as unpaid or at $2,000 awarded based on available funding. Open to college juniors, college seniors, recent college graduates, graduate students. International applications accepted.
Benefits On-the-job training, opportunity to attend seminars/workshops, possible full-time employment, health insurance for 12-month program only.
Contact Write or e-mail Internship Coordinator, 11 West 53 Street, New York, New York 10019. E-mail: moma_internship@moma.org. In-person interview recommended. Applicants must submit a formal organization application, resume, academic transcripts, two letters of recommendation. Application deadline: January 28 for summer, June 30 for 12-month program, June 30 for fall, November 19 for spring. World Wide Web: http://www.moma.org.

MUSEUM OF ARTS AND SCIENCES
1040 Museum Boulevard
Daytona Beach, Florida 32114

General Information Museum of art, science, and history that emphasizes the conservation of and education about its permanent collections in the areas of American art, Cuban art, African art, French art, Chinese art, decorative arts, and Indian and Persian

Museum of Arts and Sciences (continued)

miniatures, as well as the prehistory of Florida. Established in 1954. Number of employees: 23. Number of internship applications received each year: 20.
Internships Available ▶ *1 anthropology intern.* Candidates should have college courses in field, computer skills, knowledge of field, organizational skills, research skills, writing skills. Duration is minimum 6 weeks; 2-month commitment preferred. ▶ *1–3 collections department registrar assistants:* responsibilities include research, cataloging, object handling. Candidates should have college courses in field, computer skills, organizational skills, personal interest in the field, research skills, self-motivation. Duration is June to September (flexible). ▶ *1–2 decorative art curatorial interns.* Candidates should have college courses in field, computer skills, organizational skills, personal interest in the field, research skills, writing skills. Duration is minimum 6 weeks; 2-month commitment preferred. ▶ *1 education assistant:* responsibilities include cataloging and research. Candidates should have college courses in field, computer skills, knowledge of field, organizational skills, research skills, writing skills. Duration is minimum 6 weeks; 2-month commitment preferred. ▶ *1 environmentalist assistant.* Candidates should have college courses in field, computer skills, knowledge of field, organizational skills, research skills, writing skills. Duration is minimum 6 weeks; 2-month commitment preferred. ▶ *1–2 fine art curatorial interns.* Candidates should have college courses in field, computer skills, organizational skills, personal interest in the field, research skills, writing skills. Duration is minimum 6 weeks; 2-month commitment preferred. ▶ *2 museum education interns.* Duration is minimum 6 weeks; 2-month commitment preferred. ▶ *1 paleontology intern.* Candidates should have college courses in field, computer skills, knowledge of field, organizational skills, research skills, writing skills. Duration is minimum 6 weeks; 2-month commitment preferred. All positions are unpaid. Open to college freshmen, college sophomores, college juniors, college seniors, recent college graduates, graduate students. International applications accepted.
Benefits Formal training, names of contacts, possible full-time employment, willing to complete paperwork for educational credit, willing to provide letters of recommendation.
Contact Write, call, fax, or e-mail Mr. Anthony Knight, Curator of Education. Phone: 904-255-0285. Fax: 904-255-5040. E-mail: j2p@aol.com. In-person interview required. Applicants must submit a cover letter, resume. Application deadline: May 1 for summer. World Wide Web: http://www.moas.org.

MUSEUM OF CONTEMPORARY ART
220 East Chicago Avenue
Chicago, Illinois 60611

General Information Contemporary art museum focusing on international, multimedia work from 1945 to present; maintains permanent collection of over 2000 works and over 3000 artist books. Established in 1967. Number of employees: 190. Number of internship applications received each year: 200.
Internships Available ▶ *3 collections and exhibitions interns:* responsibilities include assisting Director with daily operations of collections management, exhibition organization and tours, research, contracts, and budget management. Candidates should have ability to work independently, ability to work with others, computer skills, office skills, organizational skills, research skills. ▶ *3–4 curatorial interns:* responsibilities include assisting curatorial staff with research and preparing artists' biographies and handling correspondence, general research inquiries, and daily departmental activities. Candidates should have knowledge of field, organizational skills, personal interest in the field, research skills, written communication skills. ▶ *1–2 development interns:* responsibilities include conducting research, developing lists of prospects, sending proposals in the area of restricted fundraising, and assisting with grant writing. Candidates should have organizational skills, personal interest in the field, research skills, self-motivation, written communication skills. ▶ *1–2 editorial interns:* responsibilities include assisting museum editor and designer in all phases of production of museum gallery and working on invitations and calendar, including proofreading and

basic editing. Candidates should have computer skills, editing skills, knowledge of field, organizational skills, written communication skills. ▶ *2 education interns:* responsibilities include assisting in art historical research and providing on-site support for outreach program, public lectures, MCA library, and docent training sessions. Candidates should have computer skills, office skills, oral communication skills, organizational skills, research skills, strong interpersonal skills. ▶ *1 graphic design intern:* responsibilities include developing and producing materials related to MCA's graphic needs, including exhibition catalogues, gallery signage, and brochures. Candidates should have ability to work independently, ability to work with others, college courses in field, computer skills, knowledge of field, organizational skills. ▶ *1 library intern:* responsibilities include organizing library resources by sorting and labeling books. Candidates should have ability to work independently, computer skills, office skills, organizational skills, personal interest in the field, written communication skills. ▶ *3–4 marketing interns:* responsibilities include conducting research on prospective audience markets, assisting in analysis of demographic admissions, and working in database. Candidates should have oral communication skills, organizational skills, personal interest in the field, research skills, strong interpersonal skills, writing skills. ▶ *1–2 performance programs interns:* responsibilities include assisting Director in various aspects of producing MCA programs in performance art, dance, music, literature, and video/film. Candidates should have ability to work with others, college courses in field, knowledge of field, oral communication skills, organizational skills. ▶ *1 photo archives intern:* responsibilities include assisting library staff in the slide library by sorting, relabeling, and organizing. Candidates should have computer skills, knowledge of field, office skills, organizational skills, personal interest in the field, self-motivation. ▶ *3–4 public relations interns:* responsibilities include assisting in planning and implementing publicity; writing press releases, public service announcements, and media alerts; and conducting visitor surveys. Candidates should have ability to work independently, office skills, oral communication skills, organizational skills, written communication skills. ▶ *1 special events/hospitality intern:* responsibilities include maintaining special events calendar, organizing on-site problem solving, offering creative input, and assisting with planning and coordinating events. Candidates should have ability to work with others, computer skills, knowledge of field, oral communication skills, organizational skills, strong interpersonal skills. Duration for all positions is 3 months (16 hours per week). All positions are unpaid. Open to college freshmen, college sophomores, college juniors, college seniors, recent college graduates, graduate students. International applications accepted.
Benefits Formal training, job counseling, names of contacts, opportunity to attend seminars/workshops, willing to complete paperwork for educational credit, willing to provide letters of recommendation, opportunity to attend staff events, receptions, meetings, lecture series, access to MCA job boards.
Contact Write, call, or fax Ms. Heather Convey, Internship Coordinator. Phone: 312-280-2660. Fax: 312-397-4095. In-person interview recommended. Applicants must submit a formal organization application, cover letter, resume, two letters of recommendation. Application deadline: March 15 for summer, July 15 for fall, November 15 for winter/spring. World Wide Web: http://www.mcachicago.org.

THE MUSEUM OF FINE ARTS, HOUSTON
PO Box 6826
Houston, Texas 77265-6826

General Information Museum dedicated to serving all people by pursuing excellence in art through collection, exhibition, and education. Established in 1900. Number of employees: 250. Number of internship applications received each year: 80.
Internships Available ▶ *5 summer interns:* responsibilities include working in various curatorial and administrative departments. Candidates should have personal interest in the field, research skills, writing skills. Duration is 10 weeks. $2,500 per duration of internship. Open to college sophomores, college juniors, college seniors.

Benefits Job counseling, names of contacts, willing to act as a professional reference, willing to complete paperwork for educational credit, willing to provide letters of recommendation. **Contact** Write, call, or fax Lara Fieldbinder, Administrative Assistant. Phone: 713-639-7320. Fax: 713-639-7707. In-person interview required. Applicants must submit a resume, academic transcripts, letter of recommendation, one-page essay describing applicant's interest in internship. Application deadline: January 31. World Wide Web: http://www.mfah.org.

MUSEUM OF SCIENCE
Science Park
Boston, Massachusetts 02114

General Information Museum designed to stimulate interest in science and technology and further understanding of their importance to individuals and society. Established in 1830. Number of employees: 450.
Internships Available ▶ *Science and non-science interns:* responsibilities include writing and editing print materials, working with the public and school groups, and serving in a variety of departments within the Museum. Duration is 3-12 months in winter/spring and summer/fall periods. Position available as unpaid or at $6–$7 per hour. Open to recent high school graduates, college freshmen, college sophomores, college juniors, college seniors, recent college graduates, graduate students, career changers, individuals reentering the workforce, high school seniors who have volunteered at the museum. International applications accepted.
Benefits Names of contacts, on-the-job training, opportunity to attend seminars/workshops, possible full-time employment, willing to act as a professional reference, willing to complete paperwork for educational credit, meals at a discount, informal job counseling.
Contact Write, call, fax, or e-mail Ms. Sandra Smith, Intern Coordinator, Community Relations. Phone: 617-589-0314. Fax: 617-589-0454. E-mail: ssmith@mos.org. In-person interview recommended. Applicants must submit a cover letter, resume, two letters of recommendation, 2 writing samples for publication and media relations positions. Application deadline: March 1 for summer; continuous for fall/spring positions. World Wide Web: http://www.mos.org.

THE MUSEUM OF TELEVISION AND RADIO
25 West 52nd Street
New York, New York 10019

General Information Museum that collects, preserves, and exhibits radio and television programs. Established in 1975. Number of employees: 180. Number of internship applications received each year: 150.
Internships Available ▶ *2–4 curatorial department interns:* responsibilities include compiling information about programs and individuals significant in the history of the media, listening to and reviewing programs in the museum's collection, and drafting correspondence. Candidates should have editing skills, organizational skills, research skills, self-motivation, writing skills, written communication skills. Duration is flexible. ▶ *1 development department intern:* responsibilities include researching sources of corporate/individual underwriting, coordinating department activities, and preparing press kits. Candidates should have ability to work independently, computer skills, oral communication skills, organizational skills, research skills, written communication skills. Duration is May to August. Open to college freshmen, college sophomores, college juniors, college seniors, recent college graduates, graduate students, career changers. ▶ *2–3 education department interns:* responsibilities include assisting in the research, preparation, and teaching of group presentations and scheduling groups for education programs. Candidates should have computer skills, oral communication skills, personal interest in the field, strong interpersonal skills, written communication skills. Duration is according to need. Open to college freshmen, college sophomores, college juniors, college seniors, recent college graduates, graduate students. ▶ *1 exhibitions/seminars intern:* responsibilities include assisting the coordinator

in implementing special projects and with preliminary panelist contact. Candidates should have ability to work independently, computer skills, oral communication skills, organizational skills, research skills, written communication skills. Duration is according to need. Open to college freshmen, college sophomores, college juniors, college seniors, recent college graduates, graduate students. ▶ *1–4 library services department interns:* responsibilities include watching videotapes, listening to audio tapes, using microfilm and reference sources to research facts, and indexing. Candidates should have computer skills, editing skills, research skills, self-motivation, written communication skills. Duration is according to need. ▶ *1–2 public relations department interns:* responsibilities include working closely with the staff on routine duties (typing, filing, photocopying) and long-term projects (press releases, telephone projects, organization of exhibition openings, and press conferences). Candidates should have ability to work independently, office skills, organizational skills, research skills, written communication skills. Duration is according to need. ▶ *1 publications department intern:* responsibilities include proofreading, light copy editing, photocopying, trafficking copy, and handling phone contact with designers and printers. Candidates should have college courses in field, computer skills, editing skills, organizational skills, written communication skills. Duration is according to need. Open to college freshmen, college sophomores, college juniors, college seniors, recent college graduates, graduate students. ▶ *1–4 research service department interns.* Candidates should have analytical skills, editing skills, knowledge of field, research skills, written communication skills. Duration is according to need. All positions are unpaid.
Benefits Formal training, opportunity to attend seminars/workshops, willing to complete paperwork for educational credit, willing to provide letters of recommendation.
Contact Call, fax, or e-mail Shannon Slon Simon, Internship Coordinator. Phone: 212-621-6600. Fax: 212-621-6700. E-mail: ssimon@mtr.org. In-person interview recommended. Applicants must submit a cover letter, resume, writing sample, two letters of recommendation. Application deadline: April 15 for summer; continuous for fall and winter. World Wide Web: http://www.mtr.org.

MUSKEGON MUSEUM OF ART
296 West Webster Avenue
Muskegon, Michigan 49440

General Information Art museum that collects and exhibits ancient through contemporary American, European, and Asian artwork including paintings, prints, drawings, sculpture, glass, and photography. Established in 1912. Number of employees: 12. Unit of Muskegon Public Schools, Muskegon, Michigan. Number of internship applications received each year: 10.
Internships Available ▶ *2–5 collections management interns:* responsibilities include working with the Registrar to learn aspects of collection data management, data entry, inventory, label production, condition reports, exhibit installation, loans, and art accessions. Candidates should have ability to work independently, ability to work with others, computer skills, editing skills, office skills, oral communication skills, research skills, self-motivation. Open to recent high school graduates, college freshmen, college sophomores, college juniors, college seniors, recent college graduates, career changers, individuals reentering the workforce. ▶ *1–2 curatorial interns:* responsibilities include conducting in-depth research on selected areas of the permanent collection, and exhibition training. Candidates should have ability to work independently, analytical skills, computer skills, editing skills, oral communication skills, organizational skills, research skills, self-motivation, strong interpersonal skills, writing skills. Open to college juniors, college seniors, recent college graduates, career changers. ▶ *1–2 education interns:* responsibilities include interpretation of selected portions of the permanent collection; writing didactic labels, exhibit brochures, and family gallery guides; organizing programming and art stations; working with the Museum Docent program in-museum tours and classroom outreach. Candidates should have computer skills, editing skills, oral communication skills, research skills, strong

Muskegon Museum of Art (continued)

interpersonal skills, writing skills. Open to recent high school graduates, college freshmen, college sophomores, college juniors, college seniors, recent college graduates, career changers, individuals reentering the workforce. ▶ *1 gift shop intern:* responsibilities include working with manager, buying and selling museum merchandise, doing inventory and budget, creating design and layout, and working on some advertising. Candidates should have computer skills, oral communication skills, personal interest in the field, self-motivation. Open to college freshmen, college sophomores, college juniors, college seniors, recent college graduates, career changers, individuals reentering the workforce. ▶ *1 public relations and development intern:* responsibilities include coordinating communications, media relations, general museum communications, visitor services, marketing, special projects, grant preparation, campaign and membership development. Candidates should have computer skills, editing skills, oral communication skills, organizational skills, personal interest in the field, research skills, strong interpersonal skills, writing skills. Open to college juniors, college seniors, recent college graduates, career changers. Duration for all positions is flexible. All positions are unpaid. International applications accepted.

Benefits Job counseling, on-the-job training, opportunity to attend seminars/workshops, willing to act as a professional reference, willing to complete paperwork for educational credit, willing to provide letters of recommendation, assistance with preparing application.

Contact Write, call, or fax Babs Vaughan, Registrar. Phone: 616-720-2575. Fax: 616-720-2585. In-person interview required. Applicants must submit a formal organization application, resume, academic transcripts, letter of recommendation. Applications are accepted continuously.

MYSTIC SEAPORT MUSEUM
75 Greenmanville Avenue, PO Box 6000
Mystic, Connecticut 06355

General Information Maritime museum on 17 acres with outdoor orientation, 3 tall ships, maritime artifacts, paintings, small craft, and exhibitions. Established in 1929. Number of employees: 400. Number of internship applications received each year: 50.

Internships Available ▶ *10–12 museum studies interns:* responsibilities include weekly field trips to neighboring museums for behind-the-scenes tours, 4 days per week in a work project in a specialized area, and participating in seminars on aspects of museum studies. Candidates should have oral communication skills, personal interest in the field, self-motivation, strong interpersonal skills, written communication skills. Duration is 10 weeks in summer. limited stipends available. Open to college juniors, college seniors, recent college graduates, graduate students, law students, career changers. International applications accepted.

Benefits Formal training, housing at a cost, on-the-job training, opportunity to attend seminars/workshops, possible full-time employment, willing to act as a professional reference, willing to complete paperwork for educational credit, willing to provide letters of recommendation.

Contact Write, call, fax, or e-mail Ms. Katrina Bercaw, Associate Director of Administration, Munson Institute, 75 Greenmanville Avenue, PO Box 6000, Mystic, Connecticut 06355-0990. Phone: 860-572-5359 Ext. 4. Fax: 860-572-5329. E-mail: munson@mysticseaport.org. In-person interview recommended. Applicants must submit a formal organization application, resume, academic transcripts, three letters of recommendation. Application deadline: March 30 for summer. World Wide Web: http://www.mysticseaport.org.

NATIONAL BUILDING MUSEUM
401 F Street, NW
Washington, District of Columbia 20001

General Information Museum whose exhibitions and educational programs interpret the worlds of engineering and architectural design, environmental and urban planning, building crafts and materials, and historic preservation. Established in 1980. Number of employees: 35. Number of internship applications received each year: 50.

Internships Available ▶ *8–15 student interns:* responsibilities include working in one of the following departments: exhibitions, collections, education, public affairs, development, or administration. Candidates should have ability to work independently, ability to work with others, oral communication skills, personal interest in the field, self-motivation, written communication skills. Duration is flexible. Unpaid. Open to high school seniors, college freshmen, college sophomores, college juniors, college seniors, graduate students. International applications accepted.

Benefits Names of contacts, opportunity to attend seminars/workshops, willing to complete paperwork for educational credit, willing to provide letters of recommendation, weekly intern enrichment program for summer interns, complimentary member benefits.

Contact Write, call, fax, or e-mail Michael Kruelle, Volunteer and Visitor Services Coordinator, 401 F Street, Washington, District of Columbia 20001. Phone: 202-272-2448. Fax: 202-272-2564. E-mail: mkruelle@nbm.org. In-person interview recommended. Applicants must submit a formal organization application, academic transcripts, two letters of recommendation. Applications are accepted continuously. World Wide Web: http://www.nbm.org.

NATIONAL MUSEUM OF AFRICAN ART, SMITHSONIAN INSTITUTION
Quad
Washington, District of Columbia 20560-0708

General Information A major research and reference center and the only national museum in the United States dedicated to the collection, exhibition, conservation, and study of African art. Unit of Smithsonian Institution, Washington, District of Columbia.

Internships Available ▶ *Interns:* responsibilities include assisting museum staff in the following departments: administration, conservation, curatorial, education, exhibition and design, photo archives, public affairs, or registration. Candidates should have background in art history, museum studies, anthropology, or related disciplines. Duration is 10-week minimum (20 hours per week) in fall, spring or summer. Unpaid. Open to college freshmen, college sophomores, college juniors, college seniors, recent college graduates, graduate students, individuals interested in exploring museum professions. International applications accepted.

Benefits Willing to complete paperwork for educational credit.

Contact Write, call, or fax Internship Coordinator. Phone: 202-357-4600 Ext. 224. Fax: 202-357-4879. Applicants must submit a formal organization application, academic transcripts, personal reference, essay. Application deadline: February 15 for summer, June 15 for fall, October 15 for spring. World Wide Web: http://www.si.edu/nmafa/.

NATIONAL MUSEUM OF THE AMERICAN INDIAN, SMITHSONIAN INSTITUTION
470 L'Enfant Plaza, Suite 7103
Washington, District of Columbia 20560-0934

General Information Museum dedicated to the preservation, study and exhibition of the life, languages, literature, history and arts of the Native peoples of the Western Hemisphere. Unit of Smithsonian Institution, Washington, District of Columbia.

Internships Available ▶ *1 conservation intern.* Candidates should have strong interest in conservation and academic background in anthropology, history, journalism, museum studies, fine arts, chemistry, biology, or botany. Duration is 1 year. stipend. Open to college juniors, college seniors, Native peoples of the Americas and Hawaii (target audience for this position). ▶ *Interns:* responsibilities include projects that vary by department and range from museum operations to research; typical project activities are installing exhibits, cataloging photos, creating visitor guides, developing press kits, or editing label text. Duration is

10-week sessions in winter (January to March), spring (March to May), summer (June to August), and fall (October to December). Position available as unpaid or at a limited number of stipends, targeted primarily at American Indian, Native Hawaiian and Alaska Native students. International applications accepted.

Benefits Willing to complete paperwork for educational credit, guided work/research internship provides students with museum practice and program development experience.

Contact Write, call, or e-mail Training Coordinator, Cultural Resources Center (CCS), 4220 Silver Hill Road, Suitland, Maryland 20746. Phone: 301-238-6624. E-mail: interns@ic.si. edu. Applicants must submit academic transcripts, personal reference, essay, application (available on Web site or by mail request). Application deadline: 3 months prior to proposed start date. World Wide Web: http://www.si.edu/nmai.

NATIONAL MUSEUM OF AMERICAN ART SMITHSONIAN INSTITUTION
MRC 210, Room 270, 8th and G Streets, NW
Washington, District of Columbia 20560-0210

General Information Museum that acquires, preserves, studies, and exhibits American painting, sculpture, graphic arts, photography, and folk art. Established in 1829. Number of employees: 150. Division of Smithsonian Institution, Washington, District of Columbia. Number of internship applications received each year: 100.

Internships Available ▶ *10–15 graduate interns:* responsibilities include performing duties in the general museum training program. Duration is 1–2 semesters. Position available as unpaid or at possible stipend. Open to college seniors, recent college graduates, graduate students, law students. ▶ *8–10 summer interns:* responsibilities include performing duties in the curatorial, design and production, and educational departments. Duration is 8 weeks. Position available as unpaid or at possible stipend-amount may vary each year. Open to college juniors, college seniors, recent college graduates. Candidates for all positions should have ability to work with others, analytical skills, organizational skills, plan to pursue career in field, research skills, writing skills, minimum "B" average in academic studies. International applications accepted.

Benefits Formal training, job counseling, names of contacts, opportunity to attend seminars/workshops, willing to provide letters of recommendation, stipend available for some positions, willing to complete any necessary paperwork required for an intern to receive educational credit (pending formal arrangement with sponsoring university or college).

Contact Write, call, fax, or e-mail Judith Houston, Intern Program Officer, MRC 210, Room 270, 8th and G Streets, NW, Washington, District of Columbia 20560-0210. Phone: 202-357-2714. Fax: 202-786-2607. E-mail: jhouston@nmaa.si.edu. Applicants must submit a formal organization application, cover letter, resume, academic transcripts, three letters of recommendation. Application deadline: March 1 for summer. World Wide Web: http://www.nmaa.si.edu.

NATIONAL MUSEUM OF AMERICAN HISTORY
14th Street and Constitution Avenue, NW, Room 1040
MRC 0605
Washington, District of Columbia 20560-0605

General Information Museum that investigates, interprets, collects, preserves, exhibits, and honors the heritage of the American people. Established in 1964. Number of employees: 300. Unit of Smithsonian Institution, Washington, District of Columbia. Number of internship applications received each year: 350.

Internships Available ▶ *35–100 interns:* responsibilities include assisting in scholarly research, museum practices, and developing professional skills in a variety of career fields. Contact office for list of current projects. Candidates should have personal interest in the field, various skills, depending on project. Duration is 8 weeks minimum, up to 1 year. Unpaid. Open to high school students, high school seniors, recent high school graduates, college freshmen, college sophomores, college juniors, college seniors, recent college graduates, graduate students, law students, career changers, individuals reentering the workforce. International applications accepted.

Benefits Formal training, job counseling, names of contacts, opportunity to attend seminars/workshops, willing to complete paperwork for educational credit, willing to provide letters of recommendation.

Contact Write, call, or e-mail Allison Wickens, Acting Internship Coordinator. Phone: 202-357-1606. E-mail: intern@nmah.si.edu. In-person interview recommended. Applicants must submit a formal organization application, academic transcripts, two letters of recommendation, personal essay as outlined on the application. Applications are accepted continuously. World Wide Web: http://www.si.edu/nmah/interns.

NATIONAL MUSEUM OF NATURAL HISTORY, SMITHSONIAN INSTITUTION
Room CE214, MRC 158, 10th and Constitution Avenue, NW
Washington, District of Columbia 20560-0158

General Information Museum that employs curatorial and scientific staff to collect specimens and conduct research and field observations in the natural sciences. Established in 1984. Number of employees: 22. Number of internship applications received each year: 200.

Internships Available ▶ *Natural science interns:* responsibilities include beginning and completing a project assigned and supervised by curator. Duration is 1–3 months. Unpaid. Open to college freshmen, college sophomores, college juniors, college seniors, graduate students. International applications accepted.

Benefits Opportunity to attend seminars/workshops, willing to complete paperwork for educational credit, willing to provide letters of recommendation.

Contact Write or fax Magda Schremp, Internship Coordinator, Room CE 214, MRC 158 10th and Constitution Avenue, NW, Washington, District of Columbia 20560-0158. Phone: 202-357-3045. Fax: 202-786-2778. Applicants must submit a formal organization application, 500-to 1000-word essay on how internships will affect career goals, 2 academic references. Application deadline: March 15 for summer.

THE NATIONAL MUSEUM OF WOMEN IN THE ARTS
1250 New York Avenue, NW
Washington, District of Columbia 20005

General Information Art museum whose permanent collection (renaissance to present), temporary exhibits, and education programs recognize the achievements of women artists. Established in 1981. Number of employees: 50. Number of internship applications received each year: 100.

Internships Available ▶ *1 Coca–Cola intern:* responsibilities include working in any of the following departments: accounting, administration, corporate development, curatorial, education, exhibition design and production, library and resource center research, membership, national programs, publications, public relations, registrar, retail operations, or special events. Candidates should have college courses in field, knowledge of field, oral communication skills, organizational skills, personal interest in the field, research skills, strong interpersonal skills, written communication skills, plan to pursue museum career, prior experience (exhibition design and production), minimum GPA of 3.5. Duration is 1 summer (June to August), 1 fall, 1 winter (12 weeks). $1,500 per duration of internship. Open to college juniors, college seniors, recent college graduates, graduate students. ▶ *1 Lebovitz intern:* responsibilities include working in any of the following departments: accounting, administration, corporate development, curatorial, education, exhibition design and production, library and resource center research, membership, national programs, publications, public relations, registrar, retail operations, or special events. Candidates should have ability to work with others, computer skills, editing skills, knowledge of field, oral communication skills, personal interest

The National Museum of Women in the Arts (continued)

in the field, research skills, self-motivation, writing skills, plan to pursue career in art, prior experience (exhibition design and production), minimum GPA of 3.5. Duration is September-December. $1,500 per duration of internship. Open to college juniors, college seniors, recent college graduates. ▶ *12–14 general interns:* responsibilities include working in any of the following departments: accounting, administration, corporate development curatorial, education, exhibition design and production, library and resource center research, membership, national programs, publications, public relations, registrar, retail operations, or special events. Candidates should have ability to work with others, computer skills, knowledge of field, oral communication skills, organizational skills, personal interest in the field, research skills, writing skills, prior experience (exhibition design and production), minimum GPA of 3.0. Duration is 12 weeks. Unpaid. Open to college juniors, college seniors, graduate students. International applications accepted.

Benefits Formal training, opportunity to attend seminars/workshops, possible full-time employment, willing to complete paperwork for educational credit, willing to provide letters of recommendation, art history course on women artists (fall and winter only), tours of exhibits in Washington, DC featuring women artists.

Contact Write, call, or fax Ms. Andrea Leifer-Schless, Volunteer Coordinator, Department of Education, 1250 New York Avenue, SW, Washington, District of Columbia 20005. Phone: 800-222-7270. Fax: 202-393-3234. Applicants must submit a cover letter, resume, academic transcripts, personal reference, letters of recommendation including one personal letter and one academic letter, applicants for Coca-Cola and Lebovitz internships must submit one writing sample (1-2 pages) in addition to other requirements. Application deadline: March 15 for summer, June 15 for fall, October 30 for winter. World Wide Web: http://www.nmwa.org.

NATIONAL PARK SERVICE BLACK CANYON OF THE GUNNISON NATIONAL MONUMENT AND CURECANTI NATIONAL RECREATION AREA
102 Elk Creek
Gunnison, Colorado 81230

General Information Recreation area that preserves resources, provides public recreational activities , and educates the public on natural and historical aspects of area. Established in 1916. Number of employees: 30. Number of internship applications received each year: 20.

Internships Available ▶ *1–3 environmental education interns:* responsibilities include providing curriculum-based environmental education programming for preschool through 12th grade. Candidates should have ability to work independently, knowledge of field, oral communication skills, self-motivation, strong interpersonal skills. Duration is 12 weeks. Open to college freshmen, college sophomores, college juniors, college seniors, recent college graduates. ▶ *1–3 interpreters:* responsibilities include researching, developing, and presenting interpretative talks for guided walks, demonstrations, and boat tours on a variety of topics based on park themes. Candidates should have ability to work independently, computer skills, knowledge of field, oral communication skills, strong interpersonal skills. Duration is 12–15 weeks. Open to college freshmen, college sophomores, college juniors, college seniors, recent college graduates. ▶ *1 museum technician:* responsibilities include cataloging and conservative care for cultural and natural history specimens. Candidates should have ability to work independently, computer skills, office skills, self-motivation, writing skills. Duration is 12–15 weeks. Open to college seniors, recent college graduates, graduate students. All positions paid at $1,200–$1,500 per duration of internship. International applications accepted.

Benefits Job counseling, names of contacts, willing to complete paperwork for educational credit, willing to provide letters of recommendation, stipend provided, housing provided if available.

Contact Write Schelle Frye, Volunteer Coordinator. No phone calls. Applicants must submit a cover letter, resume. Applications are accepted continuously. World Wide Web: http://www.nps.gov/blca.

NATIONAL PARK SERVICE OZARK NATIONAL SCENIC RIVERWAYS
PO Box 490
Van Buren, Missouri 63965

General Information Park that conserves outstanding examples of the natural and cultural resources of the United States for the benefit and enjoyment of present and future generations. Established in 1964. Number of employees: 85. Unit of United States National Park Service, Washington, District of Columbia. Number of internship applications received each year: 5.

Internships Available ▶ *1–2 archival assistants:* responsibilities include assisting in cataloging and organizing archival material at Ozark National Scenic Riverways. Duration is flexible. ▶ *1–2 landscape architects:* responsibilities include updating public land records; developing public sign proposals, plans, and drawings for public park facilities, trails, etc.; reviewing scenic easements, rights of way, and park boundaries. Duration is May-September. ▶ *1–2 museum assistants:* responsibilities include accessioning, cataloging, and handling museum objects. Duration is flexible. ▶ *2 natural resources interns:* responsibilities include assisting in monitoring waterways, conducting bacteria sampling, lab work, and other natural resource duties. Duration is flexible. All positions are unpaid. Open to college juniors, college seniors, recent college graduates, graduate students.

Benefits Formal training, job counseling, willing to complete paperwork for educational credit, willing to provide letters of recommendation, dormitory/shared apartment available rent free on limited basis.

Contact Write, call, or fax Debbie Wisdom, Personnel Specialist. Phone: 573-323-8800. Fax: 573-323-8840. In-person interview recommended. Applicants must submit a resume. Applications are accepted continuously. World Wide Web: http://www.nps.gov/ozar/.

NATIONAL PORTRAIT GALLERY, SMITHSONIAN INSTITUTION
Old Patent Office Building, 8th and G Streets, NW, Room 195
Washington, District of Columbia 20001

General Information Free public museum for the exhibition and study of portraiture and statuary depicting men and women who have made significant contributions to the history, development, and culture of the people of the United States and the artists who created such works. Established in 1962. Unit of Smithsonian Institution, Washington, District of Columbia.

Internships Available ▶ *Interns:* responsibilities include assistance with varied projects depending on needs of the departments as well as intern's skills and interests. Duration is typically, at least 3 months (20 hours per week). Unpaid. International applications accepted.

Benefits Willing to complete paperwork for educational credit.

Contact Write, call, or fax Internships Coordinator, Education Department, Room 195, Washington, District of Columbia 20560-0210. Phone: 202-357-2920 Ext. 8. Fax: 202-357-1830. Applicants must submit a formal organization application, academic transcripts, personal reference, essay. Application deadline: April 30 for summer; continuous for other times of year. World Wide Web: http://www.npg.si.edu/.

NATIONAL POSTAL MUSEUM, SMITHSONIAN INSTITUTION
MRC 570
Washington, District of Columbia 20560-0570

General Information One of the largest and most comprehensive collections of stamps and philatelic materials in the world, housing six major galleries. Unit of Smithsonian Institution, Washington, District of Columbia.

Internships Available ▶ *10 interns:* responsibilities include working with professional staff on current projects relating to exhibits, education, collections, curatorship, and membership/public affairs. Duration is flexible. Unpaid. Open to undergraduates and some high school students. International applications accepted.

Benefits Job counseling, names of contacts, opportunity to attend seminars/workshops, willing to complete paperwork for educational credit.

Contact Write, call, fax, or e-mail Esther Washington, Program Manager, Education Department—MRC 570, Washington, District of Columbia 20560-0570. Phone: 202-357-2861. Fax: 202-633-9393. E-mail: ewashington@npm.si.edu. Applicants must submit a formal organization application, academic transcripts, personal reference, essay. Applications are accepted continuously. World Wide Web: http://www.si.edu/postal/.

NATIONAL TROPICAL BOTANICAL GARDENS
PO Box 340
Lawai, Hawaii 96765

General Information Nonprofit scientific and education organization consisiting of 5 gardens and 3 preserves in Hawaii and Florida. Established in 1964. Number of employees: 60. Number of internship applications received each year: 50.

Internships Available ▶ *2–20 interns:* responsibilities include courses and hands-on experience in plant science and horticulture programs, including grounds and nursery. Candidates should have knowledge of field, personal interest in the field, plan to pursue career in field, self-motivation, strong interpersonal skills, courses in botany, horticulture, or related fields. Duration is 10–12 weeks. minimum wage to $6-$7 per hour. Open to college freshmen, college sophomores, college juniors, college seniors, recent college graduates, graduate students. International applications accepted.

Benefits Formal training, health insurance, housing at a cost, on-the-job training, opportunity to attend seminars/workshops, willing to complete paperwork for educational credit.

Contact Write or e-mail Dr. Gaugau Tavana, National Tropical Botanical Garden Headquarters, Education Department. E-mail: tavana@ntbg.org. No phone calls. Applicants must submit a formal organization application, cover letter, academic transcripts, two letters of recommendation. Application deadline: April 30 for fall, November 30 for spring/summer.

NATIONAL ZOOLOGICAL PARK, FRIENDS OF THE
NATIONAL ZOO, SMITHSONIAN INSTITUTION
3001 Connecticut Avenue, NW
Washington, District of Columbia 20008

General Information Zoo with various exhibits including a giant panda exhibit, a cheetah conservation station, an Amazonian rain forest exhibit, and a Komodo dragon hatchling exhibit. Established in 1889. Number of employees: 300. Number of internship applications received each year: 500.

Internships Available ▶ *1 animal behavior research trainee:* responsibilities include collecting and analyzing basic behavioral data, primarily using animals on and off exhibit at the National Zoo or the Conservation and Research Center. Duration is 12 weeks. $2,400–$3,000 per duration of internship. Open to college freshmen, college sophomores, college juniors, college seniors, recent college graduates. ▶ *1 animal records trainee:* responsibilities include developing and describing methods for identification of individual animals in the Zoo while working under the supervision of the program advisor, curators, and keepers. Duration is 12 weeks. $2,400–$3,000 per duration of internship. Open to college freshmen, college sophomores, college juniors, college seniors, recent college graduates. ▶ *1 genetics research trainee:* responsibilities include application of genetic methods such as DNA fingerprinting to population biology and conservation problems. Duration is 12 weeks. $2,400–$3,000 per duration of internship. Open to college freshmen, college sophomores, college juniors, college seniors, recent college graduates. ▶ *Human resources interns:* responsibilities include assisting Director with daily office operations; responding to Director's telephone and mail inquiries regarding vacancies and internships, and sending out the appropriate information; updating and maintaining personnel files and distributing reports to departments on a weekly and monthly basis; and updating and taking employee ID badges. Candidates should have computer skills, oral communication skills, organizational skills, writing skills, interest in field of human resources management, ability to lift 25 pounds, driver's license and clean motor vehicle record. Duration is summer, fall, spring. Unpaid. ▶ *1 husbandry/exhibit interpretation research trainee:* responsibilities include studying the effects of management practices (enclosure design, diet, social grouping, etc.) on zoo animal performance and exhibit effectiveness; participation in zoo animal husbandry and public interpretation programs focusing on collection of specimens. Duration is 12 weeks. $2,400–$3,000 per duration of internship. Open to college freshmen, college sophomores, college juniors, college seniors, recent college graduates. ▶ *1 landscaping trainee:* responsibilities include assisting the horticulturalist in developing effective habitats, exhibits, and educational displays; performing plant research, data recording, and field work. Duration is 12 weeks. $2,400–$3,000 per duration of internship. Open to college freshmen, college sophomores, college juniors, college seniors, recent college graduates. ▶ *3 membership interns:* responsibilities include supervising Summer Safari day camp, interviewing keepers and Zoo staff to compile animal and exhibit fact sheets, reviewing videotapes in Membership Department Library and writing a synopsis for teacher reference, writing a collection of PawPrints articles, developing interactive children's activities for camp and workshop. Candidates should have computer skills, oral communication skills, organizational skills, writing skills, interest in field of education, ability to lift 25 pounds, driver's license and clean motor vehicle record. Duration is summer. Position available as unpaid or paid. ▶ *1 nutrition research trainee:* responsibilities include participation in studies evaluating dietary adequacy, nutrient utilization, foraging strategies, and/or reproductive performance (including milk analyses). Duration is 12 weeks. $2,400–$3,000 per duration of internship. Open to college freshmen, college sophomores, college juniors, college seniors, recent college graduates. ▶ *1 public affairs trainee:* responsibilities include assisting in developing, implementing, and evaluating programs, written materials, and/or electronic multimedia productions. Candidates should have computer skills, desire to develop support for multicultural audiences of the zoo. Duration is 12 weeks. $2,400–$3,000 per duration of internship. Open to college freshmen, college sophomores, college juniors, college seniors, recent college graduates. ▶ *1 reproductive physiology research trainee:* responsibilities include participating in collection, evaluation, and storage of semen and embryos and working with in vitro fertilization and hormone analysis. Duration is 12 weeks. $2,400–$3,000 per duration of internship. Open to college freshmen, college sophomores, college juniors, college seniors, recent college graduates. ▶ *1 veterinary pathology research trainee:* responsibilities include investigating ongoing pathological problems of zoo animals. Duration is 12 weeks. $2,400–$3,000 per duration of internship. Open to veterinary college students who have completed sophomore year. ▶ *1 zoo animal medicine research trainee:* responsibilities include participating in ongoing program and methods in the care of zoo animals. Duration is 12 weeks. $2,400–$3,000 per duration of internship. Open to veterinary college students who have completed sophomore year. International applications accepted.

Benefits Opportunity to attend seminars/workshops.

Contact Write FONZ Traineeship Program, FONZ Human Resources, National Zoological Park, 3001 Connecticut Avenue, NW, Washington, District of Columbia 2008. Applicants must submit a formal organization application, academic transcripts, two letters of recommendation, 500- to 1000-word statement of interest, 15-20 black and white prints or color slides for zoo photography interns. Application deadline: February 28 for spring FONZ human resources positions, March 15 for FONZ membership positions, March 1 for summer FONZ human resources positions, 12/31 for zoo traineeships, June 30 for fall FONZ human resources positions, December 31 for zoo traineeships. World Wide Web: http://www.fonz.org.

THE NAVAL HISTORICAL CENTER
Washington Navy Yard, Building 76
Washington, District of Columbia 20374

General Information Museum that undertakes historical research and writing, archival management, documentary editing, museum exhibits, educational and public programs, collections management, and library services for the Navy and the public. Established in 1801. Number of employees: 90. Unit of Department of the Navy, Washington, District of Columbia. Number of internship applications received each year: 30.

Internships Available ▶ *1–6 archival interns:* responsibilities include processing and cataloging documents, answering public inquiries, and assisting researchers. Candidates should have ability to work independently, analytical skills, organizational skills, personal interest in the field, research skills, self-motivation. Duration is 120–800 hours. Open to college freshmen, college sophomores, college juniors, college seniors, recent college graduates, graduate students, career changers, individuals reentering the workforce. ▶ *1–4 art curator interns:* responsibilities include supporting the organizing of the Navy's art collection as well as researching and writing for the collection's exhibit program. Candidates should have ability to work with others, college courses in field, computer skills, knowledge of field, research skills, written communication skills. Duration is 120–800 hours. Open to college freshmen, college sophomores, college juniors, college seniors, recent college graduates, graduate students, career changers, individuals reentering the workforce. ▶ *1–4 conservation interns:* responsibilities include assisting with conservation projects and independent artifact care. Candidates should have ability to work independently, ability to work with others, organizational skills, personal interest in the field, appreciation of artifacts. Duration is 120–800 hours. Open to college juniors, college seniors, recent college graduates, graduate students, career changers, individuals reentering the workforce. ▶ *1–4 copyediting interns:* responsibilities include editing publications for the printed products of the branches, including books, booklets, brochures, and magazines. Candidates should have ability to work independently, computer skills, editing skills, organizational skills, self-motivation, written communication skills. Duration is 120–800 hours. Open to college juniors, college seniors, recent college graduates, graduate students, career changers. ▶ *1–10 curator interns:* responsibilities include assisting the museum curator with research and developing an exhibition script or text for publications. Candidates should have ability to work independently, research skills, strong interpersonal skills, writing skills. Duration is 120–800 hours. Open to high school seniors, recent high school graduates, college freshmen, college sophomores, college juniors, college seniors, recent college graduates, graduate students, career changers, individuals reentering the workforce. ▶ *1–5 design interns:* responsibilities include making models, preparing shop drawings, type design, graphic photography, photo silkscreening, mounting photographs, and assisting in matting, framing, and installation. Candidates should have ability to work with others, college courses in field, computer skills, experience in the field. Duration is 120–800 hours. Open to high school seniors, recent high school graduates, college freshmen, college sophomores, college juniors, college seniors, recent college graduates, graduate students, career changers, individuals reentering the workforce. ▶ *1–4 education interns:* responsibilities include working independently and with the Director of Education to conceive, develop, and implement education programs directly relating to the museum's collection. Candidates should have ability to work independently, personal interest in the field, research skills, strong interpersonal skills, written communication skills. Duration is 120–800 hours. Open to college juniors, college seniors, recent college graduates, graduate students, career changers, individuals reentering the workforce. ▶ *3–20 historian interns:* responsibilities include historical research and writing for the branches dealing with post-1945 U.S. Naval history, U.S. commissioned ships, and aviation history of the U.S. Navy. Candidates should have ability to work independently, analytical skills, college courses in field, research skills, writing skills. Duration is 120–800 hours. Open to college freshmen, college sophomores, college juniors, college seniors,

recent college graduates, graduate students, career changers, individuals reentering the workforce. ▶ *2 library interns:* responsibilities include all aspects of library work. Candidates should have ability to work independently, ability to work with others, computer skills, organizational skills, personal interest in the field, research skills. Duration is 120–800 hours. Open to college freshmen, college sophomores, college juniors, college seniors, recent college graduates, graduate students, career changers. ▶ *1–6 public relations interns:* responsibilities include writing press releases and public service announcements, developing mailing lists, and creating and implementing strategies to increase the awareness of The Navy Museum nationally and locally. Candidates should have ability to work independently, editing skills, oral communication skills, organizational skills, writing skills. Duration is 120–800 hours. Open to college freshmen, college sophomores, college juniors, college seniors, recent college graduates, graduate students, career changers, individuals reentering the workforce. ▶ *2–10 registrarial interns:* responsibilities include collections management of the Navy's artifact collection, including accessioning, cataloging, and identifying artifacts. Candidates should have ability to work independently, ability to work with others, computer skills, organizational skills, research skills, self-motivation. Duration is 3–10 weeks. Open to high school seniors, recent high school graduates, college freshmen, college sophomores, college juniors, college seniors, recent college graduates, graduate students, career changers, individuals reentering the workforce. All positions available as unpaid or at $400 per duration of internship. International applications accepted.

Benefits On-the-job training, willing to act as a professional reference, willing to complete paperwork for educational credit, willing to provide letters of recommendation, small stipend.

Contact Write, call, fax, or e-mail Dr. Edward M. Furgol, Curator. Phone: 202-433-6901. Fax: 202-433-8200. E-mail: efurgol@nhc.navy.mil. In-person interview recommended. Applicants must submit a formal organization application, academic transcripts, writing sample, letter of recommendation, portfolio for design interns. Applications are accepted continuously. World Wide Web: http://www.history.navy.mil.

NEW YORK BOTANICAL GARDEN
200th Street and Southern Boulevard
Bronx, New York 10458-5126

General Information Internationally recognized center for botanical research, dedicated to environmental education and the conservation of plant diversity; operations at this facility include scientific research, horticulture, and education. Established in 1891. Number of employees: 500.

Internships Available ▶ *2–3 Bronx green-up interns:* responsibilities include implementing programs in community gardening and composting, and supporting the development of school garden lessons and curriculum. Candidates should have ability to work independently, knowledge of field, oral communication skills, personal interest in the field, self-motivation, strong interpersonal skills. Duration is variable (according to funding). variable (according to funding). Open to college freshmen, college sophomores, college juniors, college seniors, recent college graduates. ▶ *5–7 Everett public service internship program positions:* responsibilities include working on community outreach, research, education projects. Candidates should have college courses in field, computer skills, knowledge of field, oral communication skills, personal interest in the field, plan to pursue career in field, research skills, strong interpersonal skills, strong leadership ability. Duration is 8–10 weeks. $200 per week. Open to college freshmen, college sophomores, college juniors, college seniors, recent college graduates, graduate students. ▶ *1–7 botanical science interns:* responsibilities include working side by side with prominent scientists in areas such as economic botany, systematic botany, molecular systematics, and the Harding Laboratory, Library and Herbarium, the largest in the Western Hemisphere, with six million plant specimens. Candidates should have college courses in field, experience in the field, knowledge of field, personal interest in the field, plan to pursue career in field, research skills. Duration is variable (according to funding).

variable (according to funding). Open to college freshmen, college sophomores, college juniors, college seniors, recent college graduates, graduate students. ▶ *16 horticulture interns:* responsibilities include assisting gardeners, curators, and managers in the care of plants, gardens, collection and records. Candidates should have ability to work independently, ability to work with others, college courses in field, knowledge of field, plan to pursue career in field, self-motivation, strong interpersonal skills. Duration is 6–8 months. Position available as unpaid or at $8 per hour. Open to college freshmen, college sophomores, college juniors, college seniors, recent college graduates.
Contact Write, call, fax, or e-mail Lourdes Reyes, Human Resources Coordinator. Phone: 718-817-8872. Fax: 718-220-6504. E-mail: lreyes@nybg.org. In-person interview recommended. Applicants must submit a cover letter, resume, academic transcripts, personal reference. Application deadline: March 31 for horticulture positions and Everett positions; continuous for other positions. World Wide Web: http://www.nybg.org.

NORLANDS LIVING HISTORY CENTER
290 Norlands Road
Livermore, Maine 04253

General Information Museum that brings to life the daily activities of 19th-century rural New England through role playing, hands-on experience, and demonstrations performed in historic buildings. Established in 1974. Number of employees: 19. Unit of Washburn-Norlands Foundation, Livermore, Maine. Number of internship applications received each year: 12.
Internships Available ▶ *2–4 agricultural interns:* responsibilities include performing 19th-century farm activities, working with school groups, working with livestock, and maintaining site. Candidates should have ability to work independently, oral communication skills, personal interest in the field, self-motivation, strong interpersonal skills. $50 per week; increases to $75 a week after 3 months, to $100 a week after 6 months. Open to recent high school graduates, college freshmen, college sophomores, college juniors, college seniors, recent college graduates, graduate students, law students, career changers, individuals reentering the workforce. ▶ *1 archival intern:* responsibilities include researching, organizing, and maintaining the archives; working with visiting scholars. Candidates should have ability to work independently, computer skills, organizational skills, personal interest in the field, research skills, self-motivation. $50 per week; increases to $75 a week after 3 months, to $100 a week after 6 months. Open to college juniors, college seniors, recent college graduates, graduate students, law students, career changers, librarians and teachers. ▶ *1 curatorial intern:* responsibilities include working in an 1870s mansion that has recently undergone major restoration, maintaining collections. Candidates should have ability to work independently, ability to work with others, computer skills, organizational skills, research skills, self-motivation. $50 per week; increases to $75 a week after 3 months, to $100 a week after 6 months. Open to college juniors, college seniors, recent college graduates, graduate students, career changers. ▶ *2–4 interpretation/education interns:* responsibilities include guiding tours and groups, working as living-history interpreter for hands-on educational programs, possibility of working with lifestock and site maintenance. Candidates should have oral communication skills, organizational skills, personal interest in the field, self-motivation, strong interpersonal skills, strong leadership ability. $50 per week; increases to $75 a week after 3 months, to $100 a week after 6 months. Open to college juniors, college seniors, recent college graduates, graduate students, law students, career changers, individuals reentering the workforce, retired teachers, history buffs, and individuals with farming backgrounds. Duration for all positions is 2–6 months. International applications accepted.
Benefits Free housing, possible full-time employment, willing to act as a professional reference, willing to complete paperwork for educational credit, willing to provide letters of recommendation, attendance at college level Adult Live-in "70 hours in 1870" free-of-charge.
Contact Write, call, or fax Judith Bielecki, Executive Director. Phone: 207-897-4366. Fax: 207-897-4963. In-person interview

recommended. Applicants must submit a formal organization application, cover letter, resume, 2-page essay, 3 letters of recommendation or personal references. Applications are accepted continuously. World Wide Web: http://www.norlands.org.

NORTH CAROLINA MUSEUM OF ART
2110 Blue Ridge Road
Raleigh, North Carolina 27607-6494

General Information Art museum with collections ranging from ancient through contemporary; strengths in American and Old Masters paintings, particularly Dutch, Flemish, and Italian. Established in 1956. Number of employees: 100. Number of internship applications received each year: 25.
Internships Available ▶ *1 curatorial department intern:* responsibilities include researching under the direction of the curator. Candidates should have ability to work independently, analytical skills, college degree in related field, computer skills, experience in the field, organizational skills, plan to pursue career in field, research skills, self-motivation, written communication skills. Duration is minimum of 2-3 months. Open to graduate students. ▶ *1 design department intern:* responsibilities include assisting the head exhibition designer. Candidates should have ability to work independently, college courses in field, computer skills, experience in the field, plan to pursue career in field, self-motivation. Duration is 2–3 months. Open to college juniors, college seniors, recent college graduates, graduate students. ▶ *1 development office intern:* responsibilities include devising and maintaining tracking system for travel program participation and correlation to giving history. Candidates should have ability to work independently, computer skills, knowledge of field, office skills, oral communication skills, organizational skills, personal interest in the field, self-motivation, strong interpersonal skills, strong leadership ability, written communication skills. Duration is 2–3 months. Open to college juniors, college seniors, recent college graduates, graduate students. ▶ *3 education department interns:* responsibilities include researching and writing on objects in collection; slide library work, including research, labeling, and filing; assisting with studio art classes; and assisting museum programmers in planning, coordinating, and implementing educational programs. Candidates should have ability to work independently, college courses in field, computer skills, knowledge of field, office skills, oral communication skills, organizational skills, personal interest in the field, research skills, self-motivation, strong interpersonal skills, strong leadership ability, written communication skills. Duration is 2-3 months minimum. Open to college juniors, college seniors, recent college graduates, graduate students. ▶ *3 educational outreach interns:* responsibilities include researching and writing on objects in the collection; slide library work, including research, labeling, and filing; assisting with studio art classes; assisting museum programmers in planning and implementing programs; making contact with special populations and minorities; calling outreach volunteers; and compiling outreach data. Candidates should have ability to work independently, college courses in field, computer skills, knowledge of field, oral communication skills, organizational skills, personal interest in the field, research skills, self-motivation, strong interpersonal skills, written communication skills. Duration is 2–3 months. Open to college juniors, college seniors, recent college graduates, graduate students. ▶ *1 registration department intern:* responsibilities include recordkeeping in regard to the permanent collection. Candidates should have ability to work independently, college courses in field, computer skills, knowledge of field, office skills, organizational skills, personal interest in the field, research skills, self-motivation, written communication skills. Duration is 1 semester. Open to college juniors, college seniors, recent college graduates, graduate students. All positions are unpaid. International applications accepted.
Benefits Travel reimbursement, willing to complete paperwork for educational credit, free admission to museum events (lectures, films, concerts).
Contact Write or call Cynthia Dopko, Office Manager, Education Department. Phone: 919-839-6262 Ext. 2143. In-person interview recommended. Applicants must submit a cover letter,

North Carolina Museum of Art (continued)

resume, academic transcripts. Application deadline: April 1 for summer, July 1 for fall, November 1 for winter/spring.

NORTH CAROLINA STATE PARKS AND RECREATION, CLIFFS OF THE NEUSE STATE PARK
345-A Park Entrance Road
Seven Springs, North Carolina 28578

General Information Park serving the people of North Carolina and protecting a unique area of scientific value and scenic beauty. Established in 1945. Number of employees: 5. Unit of North Carolina State Park System, Raleigh, North Carolina. Number of internship applications received each year: 6.

Internships Available ► *1 museum/librarian/researcher:* responsibilities include working in park museum cataloging slides, conducting research on cliff deposits, and writing papers on findings. Open to college juniors, college seniors, recent college graduates, graduate students. ► *Researchers:* responsibilities include collecting and cataloging a plant collection of flora found in the park to be stored in the park's herbarium. Open to college seniors, recent college graduates, graduate students. Candidates for all positions should have ability to work independently, college courses in field, knowledge of field, oral communication skills, personal interest in the field, research skills. Duration for all positions is 4 months. All positions are unpaid. International applications accepted.

Benefits Free housing, names of contacts, possible full-time employment, willing to complete paperwork for educational credit, willing to provide letters of recommendation.

Contact Write or call Mr. Daniel Smith, Park Superintendent. Phone: 919-778-6234. In-person interview required. Applications are accepted continuously.

NORTH CAROLINA STATE PARKS AND RECREATION, HANGING ROCK STATE PARK
PO Box 278
Danbury, North Carolina 27016

General Information State park that strives to preserve and protect an area of scenic and natural beauty and provide a recreational area for the public. Established in 1936. Number of employees: 11. Unit of North Carolina Division of Parks and Recreation, Raleigh, North Carolina. Number of internship applications received each year: 5.

Internships Available ► *1 assistant ranger:* responsibilities include park operations and interpretation. Candidates should have college courses in field, knowledge of field, oral communication skills, self-motivation, strong interpersonal skills. Duration is 7 months. Position available as unpaid or at $7 per hour. Open to college freshmen, college sophomores, college juniors, college seniors, recent college graduates. ► *1 lifeguard:* responsibilities include lifeguarding lake. Candidates should have knowledge of field, oral communication skills, self-motivation, strong interpersonal skills, American Red Cross certification. Duration is 3 months. $7 per hour. Open to high school seniors, recent high school graduates, college freshmen, college sophomores, college juniors, college seniors, recent college graduates. ► *1 naturalist/interpreter:* responsibilities include presenting natural and cultural interpretive programs to park visitors. Candidates should have ability to work independently, college courses in field, knowledge of field, oral communication skills, strong interpersonal skills. Duration is 3-6 months (40 hours per week). Unpaid. Open to college juniors, college seniors, recent college graduates, graduate students. ► *1 park attendant:* responsibilities include maintaining and operating campgrounds, and resource management. Candidates should have knowledge of field, oral communication skills, personal interest in the field, self-motivation, strong interpersonal skills. Duration is 6 months. Position available as unpaid or at $6 per hour. Open to college freshmen, college sophomores, college juniors, college seniors. ► *1 resource management specialist:* responsibilities include working on assigned resource management problems and issues; some research may be involved. Candidates should have ability to work independently, declared college major in field, experience in the field, research skills, strong interpersonal skills, written communication skills. Duration is 3-6 months (40 hours per week). Unpaid. Open to college juniors, college seniors, recent college graduates, graduate students. International applications accepted.

Benefits Housing at a cost, names of contacts, possible full-time employment, willing to complete paperwork for educational credit, willing to provide letters of recommendation.

Contact Write, call, fax, or e-mail Mr. Tommy R. Wagoner, Park Superintendent, PO Box 278, Danbury, North Carolina 27015. Phone: 336-593-8480. Fax: 336-593-9166. E-mail: ncs1220@ interpath.com. In-person interview recommended. Applicants must submit a formal organization application, resume. Application deadline: February 1 for spring, March 1 for summer.

NORTH CAROLINA STATE PARKS AND RECREATION, JOCKEY'S RIDGE STATE PARK
West Carolina Drive
Nags Head, North Carolina 27959

General Information Park providing high-quality management of scenic, ecological, and cultural values for public benefit. Established in 1975. Number of employees: 16. Unit of North Carolina State Park System, Raleigh, North Carolina. Number of internship applications received each year: 50.

Internships Available ► *2 assistant rangers:* responsibilities include planning and providing public education. Candidates should have ability to work with others, knowledge of field, oral communication skills, personal interest in the field, research skills, strong interpersonal skills. Duration is 3 months for 1 assistant and 6 months for other assistant. $7 per hour. ► *2 volunteer/ naturalist interns:* responsibilities include planning and providing public education. Candidates should have ability to work with others, college courses in field, knowledge of field, oral communication skills, personal interest in the field, research skills. Duration is flexible. Unpaid. Open to high school students, high school seniors, recent high school graduates, college freshmen, college sophomores, college juniors, college seniors, recent college graduates, graduate students, law students, career changers, individuals reentering the workforce. International applications accepted.

Benefits Names of contacts, on-the-job training, possible full-time employment, willing to act as a professional reference, willing to complete paperwork for educational credit, willing to provide letters of recommendation, free housing for volunteers working over 16 hours per week.

Contact Write or call Mr. John Fullwood, Park Ranger II, PO Box 592, Nags Head, North Carolina 27959. Phone: 252-441-7132. In-person interview recommended. Applicants must submit a formal organization application, cover letter. Application deadline: March 1 for summer, July 1 for fall.

NORTH CAROLINA STATE PARKS AND RECREATION, JORDAN LAKE STATE RECREATION AREA
280 State Park Road
Apex, North Carolina 27502

General Information Park preserving a unique area of scenic significance and natural beauty and providing recreational enjoyment. Established in 1980. Number of employees: 31. Unit of North Carolina State Park System, Raleigh, North Carolina. Number of internship applications received each year: 1.

Internships Available ► *1–4 assistant park rangers:* responsibilities include providing information to guests, registering campers, supervising other summer help and ticket booth operations, and performing all tasks necessary in park operations. Candidates should have ability to work independently, college courses in field, declared college major in field, oral communication skills, plan to pursue career in field, self-motivation, strong interpersonal skills. Duration is 4–6 months. Position available as unpaid or at $7 per hour. Open to college freshmen, college sophomores, college juniors, college seniors, recent college graduates, individuals reentering the workforce.

Benefits Formal training, names of contacts, possible full-time employment, willing to complete paperwork for educational credit, willing to provide letters of recommendation.
Contact Write or call Mr. Mike Seigh, Park Superintendent. Phone: 919-362-0586. In-person interview required. Applicants must submit a formal organization application, resume. Application deadline: March 31 for summer.

NORTH CAROLINA STATE PARKS AND RECREATION, MEDOC MOUNTAIN STATE PARK
4400 Medoc Mountain Road
Enfield, North Carolina 27823

General Information Park preserving an area of natural beauty and botanical significance. Established in 1974. Number of employees: 6. Unit of North Carolina State Park System, Raleigh, North Carolina. Number of internship applications received each year: 1.
Internships Available ▶ *1–2 volunteers:* responsibilities include working as an interpreter or park attendant. Candidates should have knowledge of field, plan to pursue career in field, self-motivation, strong interpersonal skills. Duration is 3–6 months. Unpaid. Open to college freshmen, college sophomores, college juniors, college seniors, recent college graduates, graduate students, career changers, must be 18 years of age or older. International applications accepted.
Benefits On-the-job training, opportunity to attend seminars/workshops, possible full-time employment, willing to complete paperwork for educational credit, willing to provide letters of recommendation.
Contact Write, call, or e-mail Mr. Lyndon Sutton, Superintendent, PO Box 400, Hollister, North Carolina 27844. Phone: 252-445-2280. E-mail: medocmtn@coastalnct.com. In person interview required. Applicants must submit a formal organization application, resume. Application deadline: March 1 for summer.

NORTH CAROLINA STATE PARKS AND RECREATION, MOUNT JEFFERSON STATE PARK
Jefferson, North Carolina 28640

General Information State park that preserves and protects an area of scenic beauty and environmental and ecological significance. Number of employees: 8. Unit of North Carolina State Park System, Raleigh, North Carolina. Number of internship applications received each year: 15.
Internships Available ▶ *1 archaeological researcher:* responsibilities include researching archaeology of the river area. Candidates should have ability to work independently, ability to work with others, analytical skills, college courses in field, computer skills, editing skills, knowledge of field, personal interest in the field, research skills, self-motivation, writing skills. Position available as unpaid or at $7 per hour. Open to college juniors, college seniors, recent college graduates, graduate students, North Carolina residents. ▶ *1–2 environmental education specialists:* responsibilities include developing student environmental programs. Candidates should have ability to work independently, college courses in field, computer skills, editing skills, knowledge of field, oral communication skills, personal interest in the field, research skills, self-motivation, strong interpersonal skills, writing skills. Position available as unpaid or at $7 per hour. Open to college sophomores, college juniors, college seniors, recent college graduates, graduate students, career changers, North Carolina residents. ▶ *1 interpretive specialist:* responsibilities include developing programs for schools and evening visitors and making field identifications. Candidates should have ability to work independently, analytical skills, college courses in field, computer skills, editing skills, knowledge of field, office skills, oral communication skills, organizational skills, personal interest in the field, research skills, self-motivation, strong interpersonal skills, writing skills. Position available as unpaid or at $7 per hour. Open to college sophomores, college juniors, college seniors, recent college graduates, graduate students, career changers, North Carolina residents. ▶ *1 mapping intern:* responsibilities include mapping park using computer GIS system and database management. Candidates should have ability to work independently,

analytical skills, college courses in field, computer skills, editing skills, knowledge of field, organizational skills, personal interest in the field, research skills, self-motivation, strong interpersonal skills, writing skills. Position available as unpaid or at $7 per hour. Open to college juniors, college seniors, graduate students, North Carolina residents. ▶ *1 natural heritage researcher:* responsibilities include floristics inventory, documenting endangered species, and identifying species recognized as endangered. Candidates should have ability to work independently, analytical skills, college courses in field, computer skills, editing skills, knowledge of field, organizational skills, personal interest in the field, research skills, self-motivation, strong interpersonal skills, writing skills. Position available as unpaid or at $7 per hour. Open to college juniors, college seniors, recent college graduates, graduate students, career changers, North Carolina residents. ▶ *1 park photographer:* responsibilities include photographing flora and fauna of the park. Candidates should have ability to work independently, knowledge of field, personal interest in the field, self-motivation, strong interpersonal skills. Unpaid. Open to recent high school graduates, college freshmen, college sophomores, college juniors, college seniors, recent college graduates, graduate students, career changers, North Carolina residents. Duration for all positions is flexible. International applications accepted.
Benefits Free housing, names of contacts, possible full-time employment, willing to complete paperwork for educational credit, willing to provide letters of recommendation.
Contact Write, call, fax, or e-mail Mr. Jay Wild, Superintendent. Phone: 336-982-2587. Fax: 336-982-3943. E-mail: moje@skybest.com. In-person interview recommended. Applicants must submit a cover letter, resume. Application deadline: January 31 for paid interns; continuous for volunteer interns. World Wide Web: http://www.ncsparks.net.

NORTH CAROLINA STATE PARKS AND RECREATION, NEW RIVER STATE PARK
1477 Wagoner Access Road, PO Box 48
Jefferson, North Carolina 28640

General Information Recreational park that seeks to preserve and protect an area of scenic beauty and environmental and ecological significance. Established in 1976. Number of employees: 22. Unit of North Carolina State Park System, Raleigh, North Carolina. Number of internship applications received each year: 15.
Internships Available ▶ *1–3 archaeological researchers:* responsibilities include researching and documenting archaeology of the river area. Candidates should have ability to work independently, ability to work with others, analytical skills, college courses in field, computer skills, editing skills, knowledge of field, personal interest in the field, research skills, self-motivation, writing skills, written communication skills. Duration is 4–10 months. Position available as unpaid or at $7 per hour. Open to college juniors, college seniors, recent college graduates, graduate students. ▶ *1–2 environmental education specialists:* responsibilities include developing student environmental programs. Candidates should have ability to work independently, college courses in field, computer skills, editing skills, knowledge of field, oral communication skills, personal interest in the field, research skills, self-motivation, strong interpersonal skills, writing skills. Duration is 3–10 months. Position available as unpaid or at $7 per hour. Open to college sophomores, college juniors, college seniors, recent college graduates, graduate students, career changers, North Carolina residents. ▶ *2–4 exhibit and publications specialists:* responsibilities include design, layout, and construction of new exhibits and publications for park interpretive programs and materials. Candidates should have ability to work independently, analytical skills, college courses in field, computer skills, editing skills, knowledge of field, organizational skills, personal interest in the field, research skills, self-motivation, strong interpersonal skills, writing skills, desktop publishing skills preferred. Duration is 3–10 months. Position available as unpaid or at $7 per hour. Open to college freshmen, college sophomores, college juniors, college seniors, recent college graduates, individuals reentering the workforce. ▶ *1–4 interpretive specialists:* responsibili-

North Carolina State Parks and Recreation, New River State Park (continued)

ties include developing school and evening group programs and identifying species in the field. Candidates should have ability to work independently, analytical skills, college courses in field, computer skills, editing skills, knowledge of field, office skills, oral communication skills, organizational skills, personal interest in the field, research skills, self-motivation, strong interpersonal skills, writing skills. Duration is 3–10 months. Position available as unpaid or at $7 per hour. Open to college sophomores, college juniors, college seniors, recent college graduates, graduate students, career changers. ▶ *1–4 mapping interns:* responsibilities include mapping the state park using GIS software and GPS devices. Candidates should have ability to work independently, analytical skills, college courses in field, computer skills, editing skills, knowledge of field, organizational skills, personal interest in the field, research skills, self-motivation, strong interpersonal skills, writing skills. Duration is 4–6 months. Position available as unpaid or at $7 per hour. Open to college juniors, college seniors, recent college graduates, graduate students, career changers. ▶ *1–2 natural heritage researchers:* responsibilities include identifying and documenting endangered species and performing floristics or faunal inventory. Candidates should have ability to work independently, analytical skills, college courses in field, computer skills, editing skills, knowledge of field, organizational skills, personal interest in the field, research skills, self-motivation, strong interpersonal skills, writing skills. Duration is 3–12 months. Position available as unpaid or at $7 per hour. Open to college juniors, college seniors, recent college graduates, graduate students, career changers. ▶ *1–2 park photographers:* responsibilities include photographing flora and fauna of the state park. Candidates should have ability to work independently, knowledge of field, personal interest in the field, self-motivation, strong interpersonal skills. Duration is 3 months. Unpaid. Open to recent high school graduates, college freshmen, college sophomores, college juniors, college seniors, recent college graduates, graduate students, career changers. ▶ *1–3 river user surveyors:* responsibilities include conducting survey of river water levels to ensure safe use by rafters and canoers. Candidates should have ability to work independently, analytical skills, college courses in field, computer skills, knowledge of field, office skills, personal interest in the field, research skills, self-motivation, strong interpersonal skills, writing skills. Duration is 3–6 months. Position available as unpaid or at $7 per hour. Open to college juniors, college seniors, recent college graduates, graduate students. ▶ *5–10 trails construction technicians:* responsibilities include design, layout, and construction of hiking trails using hand tools and natural materials; supervision of volunteer and court-assigned laborers. Candidates should have ability to work independently, personal interest in the field, self-motivation, strong interpersonal skills. Duration is 3–10 months. Position available as unpaid or at $7 per hour. Open to recent high school graduates, college freshmen, college sophomores, college juniors, college seniors, recent college graduates, graduate students, career changers, individuals reentering the workforce. International applications accepted.
Benefits Free housing, job counseling, names of contacts, possible full-time employment, willing to act as a professional reference, willing to complete paperwork for educational credit, willing to provide letters of recommendation, paid internships for North Carolina residents only.
Contact Write, call, fax, or e-mail Mr. Jay Wild, Superintendent. Phone: 336-982-2587. Fax: 336-982-3943. E-mail: neri@skybest. com. In-person interview recommended. Applicants must submit a resume, academic transcripts, three personal references, letter of recommendation. Application deadline: January 31 for paid; continuous for volunteer interns. World Wide Web: http://www.ncsparks.net.

NORTH CAROLINA STATE PARKS AND RECREATION, PETTIGREW STATE PARK
2252 Lakeshore Road
Creswell, North Carolina 27928

General Information State park whose goal is to preserve and protect unique state natural areas and provide public enjoyment.

Established in 1939. Number of employees: 8. Unit of North Carolina State Park System, Raleigh, North Carolina. Number of internship applications received each year: 5.
Internships Available ▶ *1–2 general utility workers:* responsibilities include working with the administrative staff, maintenance staff, and generally doing what needs to be done. Candidates should have ability to work independently, ability to work with others, personal interest in the field. Duration is March to September (40 hours per week). $7 per hour. Open to recent high school graduates, college freshmen, college sophomores, college juniors, college seniors, individuals reentering the workforce. ▶ *1–2 naturalists:* responsibilities include conducting aquatic plant surveys, rare plant species surveys, and new plant experimentation. Candidates should have personal interest in the field, plan to pursue career in field. Duration is flexible. Unpaid. Open to college sophomores, college juniors, college seniors. ▶ *1 park attendant:* responsibilities include maintaining grounds and facilities. Candidates should have ability to work independently, ability to work with others, personal interest in the field, plan to pursue career in field, valid driver's license. Duration is 3 months in summer. $6 per hour. Open to recent high school graduates, individuals 18 years of age. ▶ *1 volunteer:* responsibilities include performing various duties around the park. Candidates should have ability to work independently, ability to work with others, personal interest in the field, plan to pursue career in field, self-motivation. Duration is flexible. Unpaid. Open to college freshmen, college sophomores, college juniors, college seniors, recent college graduates, graduate students. International applications accepted.
Benefits Names of contacts, possible full-time employment, willing to act as a professional reference, willing to complete paperwork for educational credit, willing to provide letters of recommendation, free camping.
Contact Write, call, or e-mail Mr. Sid Shearin, Superintendent. Phone: 252-797-4475. E-mail: pettigrew_sp@coastalnet.com. In-person interview recommended. Applications are accepted continuously.

NORTH CAROLINA STATE PARKS AND RECREATION, RAVEN ROCK STATE PARK
3009 Raven Rock Road
Lillington, North Carolina 27546

General Information State park that conserves and protects natural resources and provides opportunities for recreation and environmental education. Established in 1970. Number of employees: 5. Unit of North Carolina Department of Environment and Natural Resources, Raleigh, North Carolina. Number of internship applications received each year: 1.
Internships Available ▶ *1 facilities and grounds intern:* responsibilities include assisting in the routine maintenance of park facility and grounds. Candidates should have ability to work independently, ability to work with others, self-motivation. Duration is 3–4 months. ▶ *1 natural resource interpreter:* responsibilities include utilizing interpretive materials on a rotating basis to provide information on the park's natural resources. Candidates should have ability to work independently, oral communication skills, personal interest in the field, research skills, self-motivation, written communication skills. Duration is flexible. ▶ *1 trail maintenance intern:* responsibilities include assisting staff in maintenance of hiking and bridle trails, trimming overgrowth and fallen trees from trail path, and maintaining water bars, footbridges, trail blazes, signs, and markers. Candidates should have ability to work independently, ability to work with others, self-motivation. Duration is 3–4 months. All positions are unpaid. Open to recent high school graduates, college freshmen, college sophomores, college juniors, college seniors, recent college graduates, graduate students, law students, career changers, individuals reentering the workforce. International applications accepted.
Benefits Names of contacts, possible full-time employment, willing to complete paperwork for educational credit, willing to provide letters of recommendation.
Contact Write, call, fax, or e-mail Eric Folk, Park Ranger 1. Phone: 910-893-4888. Fax: 910-814-2200. E-mail: ravenroc@foto. infi.net. In-person interview required. Applicants must submit a

formal organization application. Applications are accepted continuously. World Wide Web: http://ils.unc.edu/parkproject/ncparks.htm.

OFFICE OF EXHIBITS CENTRAL, SMITHSONIAN INSTITUTION
MRC 808, 1111 North Capitol Street, NE
Washington, District of Columbia 20560

General Information Office that supports museums and bureaus throughout the Smithsonian in the areas of exhibition design, script writing and editing, and all phases of exhibit production. Established in 1975. Number of employees: 40. Unit of Smithsonian Institution, Washington, District of Columbia. Number of internship applications received each year: 50.
Internships Available ▶ *Design interns:* responsibilities include preparing presentation sketches and scale drawings for exhibition designs. Candidates should have ability to work independently, computer skills, plan to pursue career in field, self-motivation, courses or background in design or graphic arts. ▶ *Editing interns:* responsibilities include proofreading, working with type, editing exhibit scripts, and writing captions. Candidates should have college courses in field, editing skills, research skills, strong interpersonal skills, writing skills. ▶ *Exhibit coordinator assistants:* responsibilities include budgeting analysis, project scheduling and formatting, and general administrative tasks. Candidates should have ability to work with others, computer skills, office skills, writing skills. ▶ *Fabrications interns:* responsibilities include performing tasks such as cabinetry, sheet plastics work, painting and staining, building crates, and packing artifacts. Candidates should have ability to work independently, self-motivation, experience with woodworking tools or machinery, experience with painting or refinishing walls/furniture. ▶ *Graphics interns:* responsibilities include interpreting and implementing drawings and layouts, mixing inks, silkscreening, and mounting photographs. Candidates should have ability to work independently, computer skills, self-motivation, courses or experience in graphic arts. ▶ *Model-making interns:* responsibilities include making models and replicas, freeze-dry and traditional taxidermy, and fabrication of custom mounts and brackets. Candidates should have ability to work independently, self-motivation, courses or background in art, sculpture or model-making. Duration for all positions is 3 months. All positions are unpaid. Open to college freshmen, college sophomores, college juniors, college seniors. International applications accepted.
Benefits On-the-job training, opportunity to attend seminars/workshops, willing to act as a professional reference, willing to complete paperwork for educational credit.
Contact Write Timothy Smith, Intern Coordinator, MRC 808 1111 North Capitol Street, NE, Washington, District of Columbia 20560. Applicants must submit a formal organization application, academic transcripts, two letters of recommendation, essay. Application deadline: February 15 for summer, June 15 for fall, October 15 for spring. World Wide Web: http://www.si.edu.

OFFICE OF HISTORIC ALEXANDRIA
PO Box 178, City Hall
Alexandria, Virginia 22313

General Information Office involved with the preservation of historic sites, artifacts, and records and the enhancement and preservation of the cultural diversity of Alexandria; provides programs to bring people and business to the city. Established in 1983. Number of employees: 70. Unit of City of Alexandria, Alexandria, Virginia. Number of internship applications received each year: 40.
Internships Available ▶ *6–8 Alexandria archaeology interns:* responsibilities include assisting with exhibitions and public programs. Candidates should have college courses in field, computer skills, experience in the field, knowledge of field, personal interest in the field, strong interpersonal skills. Open to high school seniors, college freshmen, college sophomores, college juniors, college seniors, recent college graduates, graduate students. ▶ *4 Black History Resource Center interns:* responsibilities include assisting with interpretation and public programs.

Candidates should have oral communication skills, plan to pursue career in field, strong interpersonal skills, written communication skills. Open to high school students, high school seniors, college freshmen, college sophomores, college juniors, college seniors, recent college graduates, graduate students. ▶ *4 Ft. Ward Museum interns:* responsibilities include cataloging. Candidates should have editing skills, knowledge of field, plan to pursue career in field, research skills, writing skills. Open to college sophomores, college juniors, college seniors, recent college graduates, graduate students. ▶ *4 Gadsby's Tavern Museum interns:* responsibilities include assisting with interpretation and public programs. Candidates should have college courses in field, knowledge of field, oral communication skills, plan to pursue career in field, writing skills. Open to high school seniors, college freshmen, college sophomores, college juniors, college seniors, recent college graduates, graduate students. ▶ *4 Lyceum interns:* responsibilities include assisting with exhibitions and public programs. Candidates should have college courses in field, oral communication skills, personal interest in the field, strong interpersonal skills, written communication skills. Open to high school seniors, college freshmen, college sophomores, college juniors, college seniors, recent college graduates, graduate students, individuals reentering the workforce. ▶ *2 archives interns:* responsibilities include preparing and finding records and cataloging the collection of archival materials relating to history of the city. Candidates should have college courses in field, computer skills, knowledge of field, plan to pursue career in field, written communication skills. Open to college juniors, college seniors, recent college graduates, graduate students. Duration for all positions is 6–8 weeks. All positions are unpaid. International applications accepted.
Benefits Formal training, job counseling, names of contacts, on-the-job training, opportunity to attend seminars/workshops, willing to act as a professional reference, willing to complete paperwork for educational credit, willing to provide letters of recommendation.
Contact Write, call, fax, or e-mail Ms. Jean Taylor Federico, Director. Phone: 703-838-4554. Fax: 703-838-6451. E-mail: jean.federico@ci.alexandria.va.us. In-person interview recommended. Applicants must submit a cover letter, resume, three personal references, three letters of recommendation. Applications are accepted continuously. World Wide Web: http://ci.alexandria.va.us/oha.

OFFICE OF IMAGING, PRINTING, AND PHOTOGRAPHIC SERVICES, SMITHSONIAN INSTITUTION
American History Building, Room CG054
Washington, District of Columbia 20560-0644

General Information Central photographic unit in support of the Smithsonian's research and publications, for museum's collections, for documenting the Institution's history, and for the needs of the public. Unit of Smithsonian Institution, Washington, District of Columbia.
Internships Available ▶ *Electronic imaging interns:* responsibilities include assisting staff in scanning photographic images and cataloging them into the master database, digital restoration, retouching, printing, and conversion of photo CD images. Candidates should have interest in photography, knowledge of professional type cameras and lighting equipment, knowledge of Internet and America Online. Duration is 3–9 weeks. ▶ *Photo studio assistants:* responsibilities include assisting photographers in studio, special event, or electronic photo assignments; working on preparation, execution, and post-production of all projects. Candidates should have basic camera equipment of their own (camera, lenses and flash) and interest in photography. Duration is 6–8 weeks. All positions are unpaid. International applications accepted.
Benefits Willing to complete paperwork for educational credit.
Contact Write, call, or fax Lori Aceto. Phone: 202-786-2707. Fax: 202-357-1853. Applicants must submit a formal organization application, academic transcripts, portfolio, personal reference. Applications are accepted continuously. World Wide Web: http://photo2.si.edu.

OFFICE OF MEMBERSHIP AND DEVELOPMENT, SMITHSONIAN INSTIUTION
1000 Jefferson Drive
Washington, District of Columbia 20560-0035

General Information Office that generates private financial support for the Smithsonian Institution through individual, corporate, and foundation fundraising, as well as membership and gift programs. Unit of Smithsonian Institution, Washington, District of Columbia.
Internships Available ► *Interns:* responsibilities include research on prospect identification and assisting with special projects such as those involved with corporation and foundation giving, the Women's Committee, and the prospect/donor database system. Candidates should have background in fundraising, marketing, grant writing, museum studies or public relations; familiarity with word processing programs and IBM PCs; and strong research, writing, and organizational skills. Duration is minimum of 1 semester or summer term (at least 20 hours per week). Unpaid. International applications accepted.
Benefits On-the-job training, willing to complete paperwork for educational credit.
Contact Write, call, or fax Internship Coordinator. Phone: 202-357-4300. Fax: 202-786-2516. Applicants must submit a formal organization application, resume, academic transcripts, two letters of recommendation, short essay describing interest in internship. Application deadline: April 1 for summer; applications are reviewed throughout the year, but these deadlines are recommended, August 1 for fall, December 1 for winter/spring. World Wide Web: http://www.si.edu.

OFFICE OF THE CURATOR, SUPREME COURT OF THE UNITED STATES
1 First Street, NE
Washington, District of Columbia 20543

General Information Office that records and preserves the history of the Supreme Court; creates the historical exhibits in the building; develops, catalogues, and preserves the collections of the Court; offers private tours and lectures. Established in 1973. Number of employees: 6. Unit of United States Supreme Court, Washington, District of Columbia. Number of internship applications received each year: 150.
Internships Available ► *2–8 curatorial interns:* responsibilities include conducting lectures and tours for visitors and assisting with curatorial projects; cataloguing photographs, papers, and memorabilia; assisting with the development and installation of exhibits; researching and responding to public information requests. Duration is 12 weeks (1-5 positions); or 3 weeks, mid-December to first week in January (1-3 positions). $9 per hour. ► *8–10 curatorial interns (course credit only):* responsibilities include conducting lectures and tours for visitors and assisting with curatorial projects; cataloguing photographs, papers, and memorabilia; assisting with the development and installation of exhibits; researching and responding to public information requests. Duration is 1 semester. Unpaid. Candidates for all positions should have computer skills, office skills, oral communication skills, research skills, strong interpersonal skills, written communication skills. Open to college sophomores, college juniors, college seniors, recent college graduates, graduate students.
Benefits Opportunity to attend seminars/workshops, willing to complete paperwork for educational credit, willing to provide letters of recommendation, training in curatorial work, museum procedures, and public speaking.
Contact Write or call Jane Yarborough, Visitor Programs Coordinator. Phone: 202-479-3298. In-person interview recommended. Applicants must submit a formal organization application, cover letter, resume, writing sample, three personal references, three letters of recommendation. Application deadline: March 1 for summer (May-August), July 1 for fall (September-December), November 1 for winter (January-May).

OLD POST OFFICE TOWER, NATIONAL PARK SERVICE
900 Ohio Drive, SW
Washington, District of Columbia 20042-2000

General Information Historical building located near Congress offering views from the observation deck and supplying educational opportunities. Established in 1984. Number of employees: 12. Unit of National Park Service, Washington, District of Columbia. Number of internship applications received each year: 10.
Internships Available ► *1 full-time intern:* responsibilities include researching and developing new interpretive programs for the visiting public school outreach programs and Internet projects; research paper on the management of National Parks is required. Candidates should have oral communication skills, research skills, self-motivation, strong interpersonal skills, writing skills. Open to high school students, high school seniors, recent high school graduates, college freshmen, college sophomores, college juniors, college seniors, recent college graduates. ► *1–3 part-time interns:* responsibilities include working in a national park providing visitor services and developing programs for area schools. Candidates should have ability to work independently, college courses in field, oral communication skills, personal interest in the field, research skills, self-motivation, strong interpersonal skills, writing skills. Duration is flexible. Open to high school students, recent high school graduates, college freshmen, college sophomores, college juniors, college seniors. All positions are unpaid. International applications accepted.
Benefits Job counseling, names of contacts, opportunity to attend seminars/workshops, possible full-time employment, willing to complete paperwork for educational credit, willing to provide letters of recommendation, assistance completing the SF-171 form (government application for employment) provided, internship time qualifies as previous federal employment when applying for government jobs.
Contact Write, call, or fax Stan Cofield, Site Manager. Phone: 202-606-8691. Fax: 202-208-4918. In-person interview recommended. Applicants must submit a cover letter, resume. Application deadline: February 1 for spring, May 1 for summer, October 1 for winter. World Wide Web: http://www.nps.gov/opot.

OLYMPIC NATIONAL PARK
600 East Park Avenue
Port Angeles, Washington 98362

General Information National park managing 923,000 acres of coast, rain forest, and mountains. Established in 1938. Number of employees: 140. Number of internship applications received each year: 300.
Internships Available ► *8–9 backcountry rangers:* responsibilities include assisting park rangers with various tasks including visitor contacts, providing information to the public, patrolling trails and roads, operating backcountry stations, minor trail maintenance, various resource management projects, light maintenance, and search-and-rescue operations. Candidates should have ability to work independently, ability to work with others, oral communication skills, personal interest in the field. Duration is 1–3 months. $50 per month. Open to college freshmen, college sophomores, college juniors, college seniors, recent college graduates, graduate students, law students, career changers, individuals reentering the workforce. ► *14 campground hosts:* responsibilities include assisting area park rangers with operations and light maintenance of campgrounds in a designated location within the park. Candidates should have ability to work independently, ability to work with others, oral communication skills, personal interest in the field, access to recreation vehicle or trailer. Duration is usually June to Labor Day. Unpaid. Open to college seniors, recent college graduates, graduate students, career changers, individuals reentering the workforce. ► *4–8 eduction rangers:* responsibilities include assisting with daily operations of a major visitor center, providing environmental education programs to local schools, conducting nature walks and talks, planning exhibits, and assisting with search-and-rescue. Candidates should have ability to work independently, computer skills, oral communication skills, strong interpersonal skills, strong leadership

ability, written communication skills. Duration is 3–4 months. $100 per month. Open to college freshmen, college sophomores, college juniors, college seniors, recent college graduates, graduate students. ▶ *4–6 natural resource management interns:* responsibilities include aiding park scientists and resource managers in a variety of projects, including fish and other wildlife studies, wilderness revegetation, conducting plant ecology research, monitoring programs, and collecting and inputting resource data. Candidates should have ability to work independently, ability to work with others, college courses in field, oral communication skills, personal interest in the field, written communication skills. Duration is 2–5 months. $100 per month. Open to college freshmen, college sophomores, college juniors, college seniors, recent college graduates, graduate students. ▶ *1–3 wilderness information center interns:* responsibilities include developing a working knowledge of park wilderness destinations, regulations, and "Leave No Trace" outdoor skills; issuing camping reservations and permits; answering phone and mail. Candidates should have ability to work independently, ability to work with others, oral communication skills, strong leadership ability, written communication skills. Duration is April to September. $50 per month. Open to college freshmen, college sophomores, college juniors, college seniors, recent college graduates, graduate students, law students, career changers, individuals reentering the workforce. International applications accepted.
Benefits Free housing, job counseling, names of contacts, opportunity to attend seminars/workshops, willing to complete paperwork for educational credit, willing to provide letters of recommendation.
Contact Write Volunteer Coordinator. Applicants must submit a formal organization application, resume. Application deadline: April 15 for natural resource management, campground host, and summer education rangers, October 1 for winter education rangers; continuous for all others. World Wide Web: http://www.nps.gov/olym.

ORLANDO MUSEUM OF ART
2416 North Mills Avenue
Orlando, Florida 32803

General Information Museum featuring public programs and activities that interpret its permanent collections and special exhibitions. Established in 1924. Number of employees: 40. Number of internship applications received each year: 20.
Internships Available ▶ *3 education development interns:* responsibilities include performing activities tailored to the needs of the department that plans museum programs. Candidates should have ability to work independently, computer skills, knowledge of field, oral communication skills, organizational skills, strong interpersonal skills, knowledge of pre-Columbian, African, or contemporary American art helpful. Duration is 2 months minimum. Unpaid. Open to college sophomores, college juniors, college seniors, recent college graduates, graduate students.
Benefits Formal training, names of contacts, on-the-job training, opportunity to attend seminars/workshops, willing to complete paperwork for educational credit, willing to provide letters of recommendation.
Contact Write Ms. Susan Rosoff, Curator of Education, 2416 North Mills Avenue, Orlando, Florida 23803. No phone calls. In-person interview recommended. Applicants must submit a cover letter, resume, letter of recommendation. Applications are accepted continuously. World Wide Web: http://www.OMArt.org.

PASADENA HISTORICAL MUSEUM
470 West Walnut Street
Pasadena, California 91103

General Information Museum operating an historic 1905 mansion, a museum of Finnish folk art, and a library archive building. Established in 1924. Number of employees: 10. Number of internship applications received each year: 1.
Internships Available ▶ *1 assistant educator:* responsibilities include maintaining accurate publicity lists, updating docent training materials, recruiting and training volunteers, and updat-

ing membership lists. Candidates should have ability to work independently, office skills, oral communication skills, organizational skills, self-motivation, strong interpersonal skills, strong leadership ability. Duration is flexible. ▶ *1 research library intern:* responsibilities include learning the care and preservation of documents, books, and photographs; researching reference questions; and assisting in cataloging materials. Candidates should have ability to work independently, analytical skills, computer skills, personal interest in the field, research skills, self-motivation. Duration is 3–6 months. All positions are unpaid. Open to high school students, high school seniors, recent high school graduates, college freshmen, college sophomores, college juniors, college seniors, recent college graduates, graduate students, law students, career changers, individuals reentering the workforce. International applications accepted.
Benefits Formal training, names of contacts, on-the-job training, willing to complete paperwork for educational credit, willing to provide letters of recommendation.
Contact Write or fax Ms. Linda Koci, Administrative Director. Fax: 626-577-1662. No phone calls. In-person interview required. Applicants must submit a cover letter, resume, two personal references. Applications are accepted continuously.

PEABODY ESSEX MUSEUM
East India Square
Salem, Massachusetts 01970

General Information Museam of art, architecture,and culture. Established in 1799. Number of employees: 120. Number of internship applications received each year: 100.
Internships Available ▶ *9–15 museum educators:* responsibilities include assisting with educational programming; helping to produce the Museum's most popular public program "Eerie Events". Candidates should have ability to work independently, computer skills, knowledge of field, oral communication skills, writing skills, written communication skills. Duration is by arrangement. Unpaid. Open to college freshmen, college sophomores, college juniors, college seniors, recent college graduates, graduate students. International applications accepted.
Benefits Formal training, job counseling, names of contacts, opportunity to attend seminars/workshops, willing to act as a professional reference, willing to complete paperwork for educational credit, willing to provide letters of recommendation.
Contact Write, call, fax, or e-mail Employee Relations, East India Square, Salem, Massachusetts 01970. Phone: 978-745-9500. Fax: 978-741-8793. E-mail: pem@pem.org. In-person interview recommended. Applicants must submit a cover letter, resume, academic transcripts. Applications are accepted continuously. World Wide Web: http://www.pem.org.

PEGGY GUGGENHEIM COLLECTION
Dursoduro 701
Venice 30123 Italy

General Information Art museum founded at the death of Peggy Guggenheim, exhibiting collection of masterworks of the first half of the 20th century. Established in 1980. Number of employees: 20. Unit of Solomon R. Guggenheim Foundation, New York, New York. Number of internship applications received each year: 500.
Internships Available ▶ *90–110 interns:* responsibilities include coordinating operation of the galleries of the museum during opening times including preparation and staffing of the galleries as well as temporary exhibitions. Candidates should have plan to pursue career in field, art history or art-related background, some working knowledge of Italian helpful. Duration is 1–3 months. $750–$800 per month. Open to college freshmen, college sophomores, college juniors, college seniors, recent college graduates, graduate students. International applications accepted.
Benefits Opportunity to attend seminars/workshops, willing to complete paperwork for educational credit, willing to provide letters of recommendation.

Peggy Guggenheim Collection (continued)
Contact Write, call, or fax Chiara Barbieri, Studentship Coordinator. Applicants must submit a formal organization application, more specific materials sent with application. Application deadline: December 1.

PENNSBURY MANOR
400 Pennsbury Memorial Road
Morrisville, Pennsylvania 19067

General Information Historic site of William Penn's reconstructed home. Number of employees: 20. Unit of Pennsylvania Historical and Museum Commission, Harrisburg, Pennsylvania. Number of internship applications received each year: 10.
Internships Available ▶ *1 Alice Hemenway Memorial intern:* responsibilities include doing curatorial/research work, developing educational programs, or doing horticultural work. Candidates should have personal interest in the field, plan to pursue career in field. Duration is flexible. Paid. Open to college juniors, college seniors, recent college graduates, graduate students, career changers, individuals reentering the workforce. ▶ *1 PHMC intern:* responsibilities include doing research/curatorial work, developing educational programs, or doing horticultural work. Candidates should have college courses in field, knowledge of field, personal interest in the field, plan to pursue career in field. Duration is 12-15 weeks in summer. $6 per hour. Open to those who live in or attend school in Pennsylvania; must have student status for the semester before and after internship. ▶ *Interns (for credit or experience):* responsibilities include doing curatorial/research work, developing educational programs, or doing horticultural work. Candidates should have personal interest in the field. Duration is flexible. Unpaid. International applications accepted.
Benefits On-the-job training, willing to act as a professional reference, willing to complete paperwork for educational credit, willing to provide letters of recommendation.
Contact Write Mary Ellyn Kunz, Director of Interpretation. In-person interview recommended. Applicants must submit a formal organization application, cover letter, resume, academic transcripts. Application deadline: December 15 for summer PHMC position; continuous for others. World Wide Web: http://www.Pennsburymanor.org.

PENNSYLVANIA HISTORICAL AND MUSEUM COMMISSION
PO Box 1026
Harrisburg, Pennsylvania 17108-1026

General Information Public history and museum agency for the Commonwealth of Pennsylvania. Established in 1913. Number of employees: 500. Number of internship applications received each year: 200.
Internships Available ▶ *30 interns:* responsibilities include completing a variety of assignments in history, historic preservation, museums, archives, architecture, communications, and related fields. Candidates should have ability to work independently, computer skills, oral communication skills, research skills, strong interpersonal skills, written communication skills. Duration is 10–15 weeks. $6 per hour. Open to Pennsylvania residents or students attending a Pennsylvania college (applicants must be returning to class at conclusion of internship).
Benefits Formal training, job counseling, names of contacts, possible full-time employment, travel reimbursement, willing to act as a professional reference, willing to complete paperwork for educational credit, willing to provide letters of recommendation, interesting work and preprofessional experience, willing to provide supervision for academic credit.
Contact Write, call, fax, or e-mail Linda Shopes, Historian and Internship Coordinator. Phone: 717-772-3257. Fax: 717-787-4822. E-mail: lshopes@phmc.pa.us. In-person interview required. Applicants must submit a formal organization application, academic transcripts. Application deadline: December 15 for summer. World Wide Web: http://www.phmc.pa.us.

PENNSYLVANIA STATE PARKS, GIFFORD PINCHOT STATE PARK
2200 Rosstown Road
Lewisberry, Pennsylvania 17339

General Information State park covering 2300 acres including a 340-acre lake. Located near the state capitol, Gettysburg Battlefield, the Amish country, and Reading outlet malls. The park offers camping, boating, fishing, hiking, swimming, picnicking, hunting, winter activities, and environmental education. Number of employees: 50. Number of internship applications received each year: 1.
Internships Available ▶ *1–2 park naturalist assistants:* responsibilities include assisting with guided walks and creating and advertising campfire program. Duration is 4 months in the summer. Unpaid. Open to college freshmen, college sophomores, college juniors, college seniors.
Benefits Formal training, job counseling, names of contacts, opportunity to attend seminars/workshops, travel reimbursement, willing to complete paperwork for educational credit, willing to provide letters of recommendation.
Contact Write, call, fax, or e-mail Park Manager. Phone: 717-432-5011. Fax: 717-432-0367. E-mail: gpinchot.sp@a1.dcnr.state.pa.us. In-person interview required. Applicants must submit a cover letter, resume. Application deadline: March 1. World Wide Web: http://www.dcnr.state.pa.us.

PENNSYLVANIA STATE PARKS, GREENWOOD FURNACE STATE PARK
RR 2 Box 118
Huntingdon, Pennsylvania 16652-9006

General Information State park offering a full range of camping and activities including a visitor center offering historical interpretation of the former iron furnace. Established in 1929. Number of employees: 30. Unit of Bureau of State Parks, Harrisburg, Pennsylvania. Number of internship applications received each year: 3.
Internships Available ▶ *Interpretation interns:* responsibilities include operating visitor center/gift shop; visitor contact; conducting programs on environmental, historical, and cultural topics (including hikes, talks, demonstrations, living history reenactments); historical and environmental research. All training provided. Candidates should have computer skills, oral communication skills, personal interest in the field, self-motivation, strong interpersonal skills. Duration is flexible; dependent upon student's academic needs. Unpaid. Open to high school students, high school seniors, recent high school graduates, college freshmen, college sophomores, college juniors, college seniors, recent college graduates, graduate students, individuals reentering the workforce. International applications accepted.
Benefits Job counseling, names of contacts, opportunity to attend seminars/workshops, willing to complete paperwork for educational credit, willing to provide letters of recommendation, housing may be available, worker's compensation coverage, service effectiveness training.
Contact Write, call, fax, or e-mail Paul T. Fagley, Cultural Interpreter. Phone: 814-667-1805. Fax: 814-667-1802. E-mail: greenwoodfurn.sp@a1.dcnr.state.pa.us. In-person interview recommended. Applicants must submit a formal organization application, cover letter, resume. Applications are accepted continuously.

PICTURED ROCKS NATIONAL LAKESHORE
PO Box 40
Munising, Michigan 49862-0040

General Information Recreation area that strives to protect natural and cultural resources. Established in 1966. Number of employees: 30. Unit of United States National Park Service, Washington, District of Columbia. Number of internship applications received each year: 20.
Internships Available ▶ *1 biological technician:* responsibilities include researching and documenting flora, fauna, and other natural resources. Candidates should have ability to work

independently, computer skills, knowledge of field. Duration is 4–5 months. Open to college seniors, recent college graduates, graduate students. ▶ *1 sociological researcher:* responsibilities include conducting research and surveys on visitor use, impacts, and preferences in the lakeshore. Candidates should have ability to work independently, ability to work with others, knowledge of field, oral communication skills, self-motivation. Duration is May 1–October 1. Open to college juniors, college seniors, recent college graduates, graduate students. All positions are unpaid. International applications accepted.

Benefits Free housing, job counseling, names of contacts, willing to complete paperwork for educational credit, willing to provide letters of recommendation.

Contact Write Ms. Sherry L. Tunteri, Administrative Manager. Applicants must submit a cover letter, resume, academic transcripts, three personal references. Applications are accepted continuously. World Wide Web: http://www.nps.gov/piro.

PITTSBURGH CIVIC GARDEN CENTER
1059 Shady Avenue
Pittsburgh, Pennsylvania 15232

General Information Horticultural education center stressing gardening, floral design, and the environment. Established in 1935. Number of employees: 14. Number of internship applications received each year: 10.

Internships Available ▶ *3–6 interns:* responsibilities include assisting in all aspects of maintaining gardens and children's programming. Candidates should have ability to work independently, declared college major in field, plan to pursue career in field, self-motivation, strong interpersonal skills. Duration is 10–16 weeks. $6 per hour. Open to college juniors, college seniors, recent college graduates, graduate students.

Benefits Formal training, on-the-job training, opportunity to attend seminars/workshops, willing to act as a professional reference, willing to complete paperwork for educational credit, willing to provide letters of recommendation.

Contact Write, call, fax, or e-mail Ms. Marjorie A. Radebaugh, Horticulture/Education Director. Phone: 412-441-4442. Fax: 412-665-2368. E-mail: garden@trfn.clpgh.org. In-person interview required. Applicants must submit a formal organization application, cover letter, academic transcripts, three letters of recommendation. Application deadline: January 31 for spring/summer. World Wide Web: http://trfn.clpgh.org/garden.

THE POETRY PROJECT AT ST. MARK'S CHURCH
131 East 10th Street
New York, New York 10003

General Information Literary center with an arts program featuring readings, performances, workshops, and publications. Established in 1966. Number of employees: 11. Number of internship applications received each year: 35.

Internships Available ▶ *1–5 interns:* responsibilities include filing, researching archives, updating archives and documentation, assisting with market research, preparing and distributing publications, organizing tape and video archives, updating and mailing membership lists, and documenting ongoing programs and events. Candidates should have ability to work with others, college courses in field, editing skills, office skills, personal interest in the field, plan to pursue career in field, research skills, self-motivation, writing skills. Duration is 1 semester. Unpaid. Open to high school students, recent high school graduates, college freshmen, college sophomores, college juniors, college seniors, recent college graduates. International applications accepted.

Benefits Opportunity to attend seminars/workshops, willing to act as a professional reference, willing to complete paperwork for educational credit, willing to provide letters of recommendation, opportunity to attend literary events, use of research facilities, work-study funds.

Contact Write or e-mail Ms. Marcella Durand, Program Coordinator. E-mail: poproj@artomatic.com. In-person interview recommended.

Applicants must submit a cover letter, resume. Applications are accepted continuously. World Wide Web: http://www.poetryproject.com.

REDWOOD NATIONAL AND STATE PARK
1111 Second Street
Crescent City, California 95531

General Information National park that protects coastal Redwood forest and stream ecosystem. Established in 1968. Number of employees: 150. Unit of United States National Park Service, Washington, District of Columbia. Number of internship applications received each year: 50.

Internships Available ▶ *1–4 camp host interns:* responsibilities include compiling visitor statistics; maintaining bulletin boards; greeting visitors and providing information; minor unskilled maintenance; may provide initial first aid and accident scene management prior to arrival of emergency response team. Candidates should have computer skills, strong interpersonal skills, ability to obtain Standard First Aid/CPR certification; good knowledge of park rules, regulations and policies; ability to operate two-way radios. Duration is 1–6 months. Unpaid. Open to recent high school graduates, career changers, individuals reentering the workforce. ▶ *3–4 environmental education specialist interns:* responsibilities include conducting programs during the day and occasionally in the evening at either Howland Hill or Wolf Creek Outdoor School; curriculum focuses on the coast redwood forest communities, tidepools (Howland Hill only), prairies, and cultural history. Candidates should have own transportation. Duration is mid-March to mid-June and Labor Day to mid-November. food stipend. ▶ *Interpretation (guide) specialist interns:* responsibilities include providing visitor services at visitor center; planning, researching, and presenting interpretive presentations, including talks, tours, and hikes to varied audiences. Candidates should have college courses in field, oral communication skills, writing skills. Position available as unpaid or at $5–$7 per day. ▶ *Librarian interns:* responsibilities include assisting the reorganization of park library and assisting in the ongoing maintenance of library. Candidates should have ability to work independently, computer skills, office skills, basic knowledge of library operations, including the Dewey Decimal System. Unpaid. ▶ *Park protection ranger interns:* responsibilities include greeting visitors and answering questions, providing a wide variety of information on park facilities and activities, natural and cultural history. Candidates should have computer skills, knowledge of field, office skills, oral communication skills, strong interpersonal skills. Unpaid. ▶ *Resource management technician interns.* Candidates should have college courses in field. Unpaid. Open to college freshmen, college sophomores, college juniors, college seniors. ▶ *Trail crew interns:* responsibilities include cutting brush manually with a variety of hard tools; installing and cleaning water bars on trails; felling trees with hand saws; routine construction of wooden and stone bridges; clearing culverts and drainage ditches; placing signs and installing fence posts; incidental motor vehicle operation. Candidates should have ability to work independently, ability to work with others, good knowledge of hand tools; ability to handle uneven, steep terrain carrying heavy loads; ability to handle isolation. Duration is 8–10 weeks. Unpaid. Open to recent high school graduates, college freshmen, college sophomores, college juniors, college seniors, recent college graduates, career changers. ▶ *Visitor services specialist interns:* responsibilities include staffing park information centers, answering visitor questions, handling sales of educational items, responding to radio and telephone calls and providing educational information; completion of one or more interpretive-related assignments. Candidates should have knowledge of field, personal interest in the field, strong interpersonal skills, money handling skills; basic understanding of the National Park Service; CPR/first aid knowledge helpful. Duration is 1–4 months. Unpaid. ▶ *1–2 volunteer coordinator assistant interns.* Unpaid. Open to recent high school graduates, college freshmen, college sophomores, college juniors, college seniors, recent college graduates, graduate students, law students, career changers, individuals reentering the workforce. International applications accepted.

Redwood National and State Park (continued)
Benefits Job counseling, names of contacts, on-the-job training, willing to complete paperwork for educational credit, willing to provide letters of recommendation, uniform provided.
Contact Write or call Cathy Morris, Volunteer Coordinator. Phone: 707-464-6101 Ext. 5068. In-person interview recommended. Applicants must submit a formal organization application. Applications are accepted continuously.

REYNOLDA HOUSE MUSEUM OF AMERICAN ART
Reynolda Road, PO Box 11765
Winston-Salem, North Carolina 27116-1765

General Information Historic house/art museum emphasizing interdisciplinary learning in American art, music, and literature; collection includes American paintings, prints, and sculpture. Established in 1964. Number of employees: 38. Number of internship applications received each year: 35.
Internships Available ▶ *Additional education interns:* responsibilities include assisting coordinator of education in scheduling, leading tours, development and implementation of public programs, and special research projects. Candidates should have ability to work independently, ability to work with others, college degree in related field, computer skills, oral communication skills, written communication skills. Duration is September through August. stipend of $15,000 per year. Open to recent college graduates, graduate students. ▶ *3–4 education interns:* responsibilities include leading school tours, working with special needs groups, and performing general research and an independent research project. Candidates should have ability to work independently, ability to work with others, oral communication skills, organizational skills, personal interest in the field, written communication skills. Duration is 1 semester. Unpaid. Open to college juniors, college seniors, recent college graduates, graduate students. ▶ *1 public relations intern:* responsibilities include writing copy and conducting program outreach. Candidates should have ability to work independently, ability to work with others, computer skills, oral communication skills, personal interest in the field, written communication skills. Duration is summer. Unpaid. Open to college juniors, recent college graduates, individuals reentering the workforce. International applications accepted.
Benefits Job counseling, names of contacts, opportunity to attend seminars/workshops, possible full-time employment, willing to act as a professional reference, willing to complete paperwork for educational credit, willing to provide letters of recommendation.
Contact Write or call Ms. Marjorie Northup, Assistant Director for Programs, Reynolds Road, PO Box 11765, Winston-Salem, North Carolina 27116-1765. Phone: 336-725-5325. In-person interview recommended. Applicants must submit a formal organization application, cover letter, resume, two letters of recommendation. Application deadline: May 12 for 1-year paid position, July 1 for fall, December 1 for spring.

RHODE ISLAND HISTORICAL SOCIETY
110 Benevolent Street
Providence, Rhode Island 02906

General Information History museum that collects Rhode Island objects, documents, and memorabilia and plans exhibitions about Rhode Island history. Established in 1822. Number of employees: 30. Number of internship applications received each year: 25.
Internships Available ▶ *1–4 collections' care interns:* responsibilities include cataloging objects and assisting in data entry, registration duties, and exhibition installations. Candidates should have ability to work independently, computer skills, declared college major in field, knowledge of field, oral communication skills, research skills, strong interpersonal skills, writing skills. Duration is 1 semester. Unpaid. Open to college juniors, college seniors, recent college graduates, graduate students, career changers. International applications accepted.

Benefits Formal training, willing to act as a professional reference, willing to complete paperwork for educational credit, willing to provide letters of recommendation.
Contact Write, call, or fax Ms. Linda Eppich, Chief Curator. Phone: 401-331-8575. Fax: 410-751-2307. In-person interview recommended. Applicants must submit a formal organization application, cover letter, resume, letter of recommendation. Application deadline: April 1 for summer; at least 2 months prior to start of internship for academic year.

ROCK BRIDGE MEMORIAL STATE PARK
5901 South Highway 163
Columbia, Missouri 65203

General Information Recreational state park of 2200 acres known for its cave systems, hiking and biking trails, and wild area. Established in 1967. Number of employees: 8. Unit of Department of Natural Resources, Division of State Parks, Jefferson City, Missouri. Number of internship applications received each year: 1.
Internships Available ▶ *1–3 naturalists:* responsibilities include leading tours and programs and conducting research. Candidates should have ability to work independently, oral communication skills, organizational skills, self-motivation, strong interpersonal skills. Duration is 3 months. Position available as unpaid or at $6 to $8 per hour or stipend. Open to recent high school graduates, college freshmen, college sophomores, college juniors, college seniors, recent college graduates, graduate students, law students, career changers, individuals reentering the workforce. ▶ *Park aides:* responsibilities include helping with general maintenance duties, greeting visitors, and performing light office duties. Candidates should have ability to work independently, computer skills, editing skills, office skills, oral communication skills, personal interest in the field, self-motivation, strong interpersonal skills, strong leadership ability, writing skills. Duration is flexible. Unpaid. Open to high school students, high school seniors, recent high school graduates, college freshmen, college sophomores, college juniors, college seniors, recent college graduates, graduate students, law students, career changers, individuals reentering the workforce. ▶ *1–10 stewardship interns:* responsibilities include removing old fences and cedar trees and prescribed burning in the park. Candidates should have ability to work with others, research skills. Duration is flexible. Position available as unpaid or at $6 per hour. Open to high school students, high school seniors, recent high school graduates, college freshmen, college sophomores, college juniors, college seniors, recent college graduates, graduate students, law students, career changers, individuals reentering the workforce. ▶ *1 volunteer coordinator:* responsibilities include coordinating volunteers working in park, including those who work with the Friends of Rock Bridge. Candidates should have oral communication skills, self-motivation, strong interpersonal skills, strong leadership ability, ability to handle responsibility of up to 10 persons' safety in adverse wilderness conditions. Duration is flexible. $6 to $8 per hour or stipend. ▶ *3–8 wild cave tour leaders:* responsibilities include leading groups on tours of wilderness caves. Duration is 6–7 months. Unpaid. Open to college freshmen, college sophomores, college juniors, college seniors, recent college graduates, graduate students, law students. International applications accepted.
Benefits Possible full-time employment, willing to complete paperwork for educational credit, willing to provide letters of recommendation.
Contact Write or e-mail Mr. Scott W. Schulte, Superintendent. E-mail: dsprock@mail.dnr.state.mo.us. No phone calls. In-person interview recommended. Applicants must submit a cover letter, resume, three personal references. Applications are accepted continuously.

ROTUNDA GALLERY
33 Clinton Street
Brooklyn, New York 11201

General Information Contemporary visual art gallery. Established in 1981. Number of employees: 3. Unit of Brooklyn Informa-

tion and Culture (BRIC), Brooklyn, New York. Number of internship applications received each year: 5.
Internships Available ▶ *5 interns.* Candidates should have ability to work independently, office skills, oral communication skills, personal interest in the field, self-motivation, strong interpersonal skills. Duration is 1 semester. Unpaid. Open to college juniors, college seniors, recent college graduates, graduate students, individuals reentering the workforce, working artists. International applications accepted.
Benefits On-the-job training, willing to act as a professional reference, willing to complete paperwork for educational credit, willing to provide letters of recommendation.
Contact Write, call, fax, or e-mail Meridith McNeal, Director of Education. Phone: 718-875-4047. Fax: 718-488-0609. E-mail: rotunda@brooklynx.org. In-person interview recommended. Applicants must submit a cover letter, resume. Applications are accepted continuously. World Wide Web: http://www.brooklynx.org.

SAGAMORE INSTITUTE, INC.
PO Box 146, Sagamore Road
Raquette Lake, New York 13436

General Information Nonprofit national historic site offering public tours and programs in regional culture and outdoor and environmental education. Established in 1972. Number of employees: 15. Number of internship applications received each year: 150.
Internships Available ▶ *3 acting/performance interpretation interns:* responsibilities include performing play (4 performances per week), interpreting camp's history, and leading public tours in character. Candidates should have ability to work with others, analytical skills, oral communication skills, strong interpersonal skills, acting skills and experience, liberal arts education. Duration is June 15-September 5 and September 5-October 31 desirable. $75-$100 per week stipend. Open to college juniors, college seniors, recent college graduates, graduate students, career changers, individuals who are Irish and between ages 18 and 25. ▶ *3 historic interpreters:* responsibilities include leading public tours of National Registered Historic Site; interpreting architectural, socio-economic, regional, and national land-use history. Candidates should have analytical skills, college courses in field, oral communication skills, strong interpersonal skills, strong leadership ability, writing skills. Duration is June 15-September 5 and/or September 5-October 31. $75—$100 per week stipend. Open to college juniors, college seniors, recent college graduates, graduate students, career changers, individuals reentering the workforce. ▶ *2 management interns:* responsibilities include assisting innkeeper, registrar and bookshop/craft shop. Candidates should have ability to work independently, office skills, oral communication skills, organizational skills, strong interpersonal skills, retail experience desirable. Duration is June 15-September 5 and/or September 5-October 31. $75—$100 per week stipend. Open to college freshmen, college sophomores, college juniors, college seniors, recent college graduates, graduate students. ▶ *1 oral historian:* responsibilities include managing and developing archives of resident artisans and families and assisting with public interpretation. Candidates should have ability to work independently, declared college major in field, knowledge of field, oral communication skills, research skills, strong interpersonal skills. Duration is June 15-September 5 and/or September 5-October 31. $75—$100 per week stipend. Open to college juniors, college seniors, recent college graduates, graduate students. ▶ *2 outdoor environmental educators:* responsibilities include assisting guiding staff with environmental education program for wide variety of ages. Candidates should have experience in the field, oral communication skills, self-motivation, strong interpersonal skills, strong leadership ability, first aid/CPR certifications; water safety instruction/wilderness first responder certification desirable. Duration is June 15-September 5 and/or September 5-October 31. $75—$100 per week stipend. Open to college juniors, college seniors, recent college graduates, graduate students. ▶ *1 theatre technician intern:* responsibilities include managing visitor's center performance space for multiple use, lighting/sound design and

run, and some changeovers. Candidates should have ability to work independently, computer skills, experience in the field, oral communication skills, strong interpersonal skills, basic carpentry skills, liberal arts education (preferred). Duration is June 15-September 5 and Setember 5-October 15 desirable. $75-$100 per week stipend. Open to college sophomores, college juniors, college seniors, recent college graduates, graduate students, career changers. ▶ *1 tour supervisor:* responsibilities include managing tours and training. Candidates should have analytical skills, college degree in related field, oral communication skills, strong interpersonal skills, strong leadership ability, writing skills, teaching/interpretive experience. Duration is June 15-September 5 and/or September 5-October 31. $100 per week stipend. Open to recent college graduates, graduate students, career changers. International applications accepted.
Benefits Formal training, free housing, free meals, job counseling, on-the-job training, opportunity to attend seminars/workshops, willing to act as a professional reference, willing to complete paperwork for educational credit, willing to provide letters of recommendation.
Contact Write, call, fax, or e-mail Dr. Michael Wilson, Sagamore Associate Director, 9 Kiwassa Road, Saranac Lake, New York 12983. Phone: 518-891-1718. Fax: 518-891-2561. E-mail: mwilson@northnet.org. In-person interview recommended. Applicants must submit a cover letter, resume, three personal references, one expository writing sample. Application deadline: May 1 for summer (mid-June to early September), July 31 for fall (September to October). World Wide Web: http://www.sagamore.org.

THE SAINT LOUIS ART MUSEUM–SUMMER INTERNSHIP PROGRAM
1 Fine Arts Drive, Forest Park
St. Louis, Missouri 63110-1380

General Information Comprehensive, free public art museum with diverse collection from cultures worldwide, strong educational programs, and a regular schedule of special exhibitions. Established in 1879. Number of employees: 160. Number of internship applications received each year: 30.
Internships Available ▶ *1 Romare Bearden Minority Museum fellow:* responsibilities include giving public lectures, researching and writing on collection and/or special exhibitions, and other responsibilities contingent upon the Fellow's background and the Museum's current programs. Candidates should have ability to work with others, college courses in field, oral communication skills, plan to pursue career in field, research skills, major and/or at least 1 year graduate work in art education, art history, anthropology, museum studies, area studies, archaeology, or related field (no studio artists). Duration is 1 year. includes full benefits and travel budget (please telephone for information on salaries). Open to graduate students, career changers, those with at least one year of graduate school by starting date. ▶ *3-4 summer interns:* responsibilities include researching, giving public gallery talks, writing synopses of works in the collection for public use, conducting visitor surveys, preparing teacher workshop materials, researching potential acquisitions and future exhibitions, attending staff meetings, and performing various responsibilities in the education and curatorial departments and museum library. Candidates should have college courses in field, declared college major in field, research skills, self-motivation, writing skills, major in art education, art history, anthropology, museum studies, archaeology, or related field (no studio artists). Duration is 2 months full- or part-time, in June and July. Unpaid. Open to college seniors, graduate students, recent college graduates planning to attend graduate school, St. Louis city or county residents. ▶ *1-5 volunteer interns (education department):* responsibilities include talks, customer service in the resource center, researching and writing materials for use by kindergarten to 12th grade teachers, researching for teacher workshops and gallery. Candidates should have ability to work independently, ability to work with others, college courses in field, computer skills, research skills, writing skills. Duration is variable, usually a regular schedule for one semester (3 to 20 hours per week). Unpaid. Open to college juniors, college seniors, graduate students. International applications accepted.

The Saint Louis Art Museum–Summer Internship Program (continued)

Benefits Names of contacts, opportunity to attend seminars/workshops, willing to complete paperwork for educational credit, willing to provide letters of recommendation, assistance with resume preparation, health benefits, and travel reimbursement for Romare Bearden fellowships only.
Contact Write, call, fax, or e-mail Dr. Elizabeth Vallance, Director of Education. Phone: 314-721-0072 Ext. 264. Fax: 314-721-4911. E-mail: vallance@slam.org. Applicants must submit a cover letter, resume, academic transcripts, 1 writing sample in a humanities area (research positions), cover letter indicating exact dates and times of availability to work, names and phone numbers of 3 professional or academic references. Application deadline: February 1 for summer, continuous for other positions, March 1 for Bearden fellows. World Wide Web: http://www.slam.org.

SAM HOUSTON NATIONAL FOREST
394 FM1375 West
New Waverly, Texas 77358

General Information National forest focusing on natural resource management. Established in 1905. Number of employees: 38. Unit of United States Department of Agriculture, National Forest Service, Lufkin, Texas. Number of internship applications received each year: 30.
Internships Available ▶ *1–2 botany interns:* responsibilities include surveying and mapping sensitive plant populations and taking botanical inventories. Candidates should have ability to work independently, ability to work with others, knowledge of field, personal interest in the field, self-motivation. Unpaid. ▶ *1–10 wildlife biology interns:* responsibilities include working with threatened and endangered species and on wildlife habitat improvement projects. Candidates should have ability to work independently, oral communication skills, personal interest in the field, self-motivation, strong interpersonal skills. Position available as unpaid or paid. Duration for all positions is flexible. Open to high school students, high school seniors, recent high school graduates, college freshmen, college sophomores, college juniors, college seniors, recent college graduates, graduate students, law students, career changers, individuals reentering the workforce. International applications accepted.
Benefits Formal training, on-the-job training, opportunity to attend seminars/workshops, willing to complete paperwork for educational credit, willing to provide letters of recommendation.
Contact Write, call, fax, or e-mail Ms. Dawn K. Carrie, Wildlife Biologist. Phone: 409-344-6205 Ext. 222. Fax: 409-344-2123. E-mail: carrie_dawn/r8_tx@fs.fed.us. In-person interview recommended. Applicants must submit a cover letter, resume, two personal references. Applications are accepted continuously.

SAN JOSE MUSEUM OF ART
110 South Market Street
San Jose, California 95113

General Information Art museum that focuses on 20th century art with exhibitions, education programs, collections, publications, art school, and outreach programs. Established in 1969. Number of employees: 40. Number of internship applications received each year: 50.
Internships Available ▶ *8–10 interns:* responsibilities include working in areas of education, marketing, development, and curatorial (project based). Candidates should have ability to work independently, computer skills, oral communication skills, plan to pursue career in field, self-motivation, writing skills. Duration is flexible. Unpaid. Open to recent high school graduates, college freshmen, college sophomores, college juniors, college seniors, recent college graduates, graduate students, individuals reentering the workforce. International applications accepted.
Benefits On-the-job training, possible full-time employment, willing to act as a professional reference, willing to complete paperwork for educational credit, willing to provide letters of recommendation, opportunity to work on specific museum project and observe general museum operation.

Contact Write, fax, or e-mail Margaret Maynard, Curator of Education, Interpretation. Fax: 408-288-6588. E-mail: margie@sjmusart.org. No phone calls. In-person interview recommended. Applicants must submit a cover letter, resume, personal reference, letter of recommendation. Applications are accepted continuously. World Wide Web: http://www.sjmusart.org.

SAWTOOTH NATIONAL FOREST, FAIRFIELD RANGER DISTRICT
102 First Street East
Fairfield, Idaho 83327

General Information National forest committed to maintaining the land and enabling people to enjoy the environment. Established in 1905. Number of employees: 11. Unit of United States Forest Service, Washington, District of Columbia.
Internships Available ▶ *1 range management volunteer:* responsibilities include assisting with range trend evaluation, range structural improvement, and noxious weed control. Duration is 2 months. ▶ *1 trail maintenance/construction volunteer:* responsibilities include maintaining trails, taking inventory, and putting up signs. Duration is 1–3 months. Open to college sophomores, college juniors, college seniors. Candidates for all positions should have ability to work independently, ability to work with others, oral communication skills, plan to pursue career in field, self-motivation. All positions are unpaid.
Benefits Formal training, free housing, job counseling, on-the-job training, willing to complete paperwork for educational credit, willing to provide letters of recommendation.
Contact Write Mr. Joe Miczulski, Recreation Forester, PO Box 189, Fairfield, Idaho 83327. No phone calls. In-person interview recommended. Applicants must submit a cover letter, resume, two personal references. Applications are accepted continuously.

SCIENCE CENTER OF NEW HAMPSHIRE
PO Box 173
Holderness, New Hampshire 03245

General Information The mission of the Science Center is to advance understanding of ecology by exploring New Hampshire's natural world. Established in 1966. Number of employees: 35. Number of internship applications received each year: 40.
Internships Available ▶ *1 island caretaker intern:* responsibilities include caretaking, working with visitors, natural history interpretation. Candidates should have ability to work independently, oral communication skills, self-motivation, strong interpersonal skills, ability to deal with unusual living arrangment (on island for most of summer). Duration is mid-June to Labor Day (minimum of 5 nights per week on island). ▶ *4–5 summer education/animal care interns:* responsibilities include 15 minute animal presenations ("mini talks") to general public; some work on special events and projects, helping care for live animal collection, working with docents, rotation in our Science Center Day Camp. Candidates should have ability to work independently, ability to work with others, oral communication skills, self-motivation, strong interpersonal skills, courses in environmental education, education, or natural sciences. Duration is June 1 to August 30. All positions paid at $90 per week plus housing. Open to college juniors, college seniors, recent college graduates, graduate students, career changers, individuals reentering the workforce. International applications accepted.
Benefits Free housing, names of contacts, on-the-job training, opportunity to attend seminars/workshops, willing to act as a professional reference, willing to complete paperwork for educational credit, willing to provide letters of recommendation.
Contact Write, fax, or e-mail Amy Yeakel, Director of Education. Fax: 603-968-2229. E-mail: scnh@lr.net. In-person interview recommended. Applicants must submit a formal organization application, cover letter, resume, personal reference. Application deadline: February 1 for summer (June 1 to August 30). World Wide Web: http://www.sciencectrofnh.org.

SIUSLAW NATIONAL FOREST, WALDPORT RANGER DISTRICT–CAPE PERPETUA SCENIC AREA
PO Box 274
Yachats, Oregon 97498

General Information Visitor center containing individual displays that interpret cultural and natural history, including forest environments, old growth, marine biology, and archaeology. Established in 1967. Number of employees: 5. Unit of United States Forest Service, Washington, District of Columbia. Number of internship applications received each year: 20.
Internships Available ▶ *1–2 naturalist interns:* responsibilities include giving nature walks, nature talks, coordinating and giving campfire programs, fee collection, maintenance, and trailwork. Candidates should have ability to work independently, computer skills, oral communication skills, strong interpersonal skills, written communication skills. Duration is 90–100 days. $8 per hour. Open to college freshmen, college sophomores, college juniors, college seniors. ▶ *1–2 naturalist volunteers:* responsibilities include giving nature walks, nature talks, coordinating and giving campfire programs, fee collection, maintenance, and trailwork. Candidates should have ability to work independently, computer skills, oral communication skills, self-motivation, strong interpersonal skills, written communication skills. Duration is flexible. Unpaid. Open to high school students, high school seniors, recent high school graduates, college freshmen, college sophomores, college juniors, college seniors, recent college graduates, graduate students, law students, career changers, individuals reentering the workforce. International applications accepted.
Benefits Formal training, names of contacts, on-the-job training, willing to act as a professional reference, willing to complete paperwork for educational credit, willing to provide letters of recommendation, meal stipend ($5 per day) for volunteers, free housing when available, housing at a cost for paid positions.
Contact Write, call, or fax Kristine Cochrane, Scenic Area Manager. Phone: 541-547-3289. Fax: 541-547-4616. In-person interview recommended. Applicants must submit a cover letter, resume, academic transcripts, three personal references. Application deadline: March 31 for summer, August 15 for fall; continuous for other positions.

THE SMITHSONIAN ASSOCIATES
1100 Jefferson Drive, SW, Room 3077
Washington, District of Columbia 20560-0701

General Information Educational and cultural outreach arm of the Smithsonian Institution which creates and administers special programs and educational activities as well as providing membership services. Unit of Smithsonian Institution, Washington, District of Columbia. Number of internship applications received each year: 75.
Internships Available ▶ *Interns:* responsibilities include researching and planning educational programs for children and adults or working in any of the other departments such as public affairs, national outreach, marketing/membership, study tours, young associates, Discovery Theater, or administration. Candidates should have strong interest in TSA's mission and in educational programming and willingness to travel. Duration is flexible. Unpaid. Open to college freshmen, college sophomores, college juniors, college seniors, graduate students. International applications accepted.
Benefits Opportunity to attend seminars/workshops, willing to complete paperwork for educational credit, hands-on learning experience.
Contact Write or e-mail Marcia H. Gregory, Volunteer Coordinator. E-mail: volunof@tsa.si.edu. In-person interview recommended. Applicants must submit a formal organization application, writing sample, cover letter explaining areas of interest and proposed dates of availability, 2 letters of recommendation from professors. Applications are accepted continuously. World Wide Web: http://www.si.edu/tsa/rap.

SMITHSONIAN CENTER FOR MATERIALS RESEARCH AND EDUCATION
4210 Silver Hill Road
Suitland, Maryland 20746

General Information Specialized center for research and training in the conservation and technical study of Smithsonian objects and related materials. Unit of Smithsonian Institution, Washington, District of Columbia.
Internships Available ▶ *Conservation interns:* responsibilities include participation in a variety of projects and activities coordinated with appropriate staff conservators. Duration is 1 academic year. Open to advanced students enrolled in graduate conservation training programs that require the student to have a year of such experience. ▶ *Preprogram interns:* responsibilities include participation in a variety of projects and activities coordinated with appropriate staff conservators. Candidates should have coursework in art history, studio art and chemistry (highly recommended). Duration is 6–12 months. Open to individuals seeking experience to enhance their qualifications for entry into a graduate conservation training program. ▶ *Research interns:* responsibilities include participation in a variety of projects and activities coordinated with appropriate staff conservators. Duration is 3 months (minimum). Open to undergraduate and graduate students in the appropriate disciplines relevant to materials conservation. ▶ *Summer interns:* responsibilities include participation in a variety of projects and activities coordinated with appropriate staff conservators. Duration is 10 weeks (June to mid-August). Open to students enrolled in graduate conservation training programs or those with equivalent education and experience. All positions available as unpaid or at stipends sometimes available on a very limited basis. International applications accepted.
Benefits Formal training, on-the-job training, opportunity to attend seminars/workshops, willing to complete paperwork for educational credit.
Contact Write, call, or fax Francine Lewis, Internship Coordinator. Phone: 301-230-3700 Ext. 102. Fax: 301-238-3709. Application materials, which vary by type of internship, can be requested by mail or phone. Application deadline: February 1 for summer interns, preprogram interns and conservation interns; continuous applications for research interns. World Wide Web: http://www.si.edu/scmre/index.html.

SMITHSONIAN INSTITUTION ARCHIVES
Arts and Industries Building, 900 Jefferson Drive, SW, Room 2135
Washington, District of Columbia 20560-0414

General Information Repository for documents of historic value about the Smithsonian. Unit of Smithsonian Institution, Washington, District of Columbia.
Internships Available ▶ *Interns:* responsibilities include working as an apprentice to a staff specialist in the areas of archiving, institutional history, oral history, or national collections. Candidates should have prior course work in American history, humanities, museum studies, collections management or the sciences (desirable, but not a pre-requisite). Duration is 10 weeks. Position available as unpaid or at stipend may be offered if funds are available. Open to college freshmen, college sophomores, college juniors, college seniors, graduate students. International applications accepted.
Benefits Formal training, on-the-job training, opportunity to attend seminars/workshops, willing to complete paperwork for educational credit.
Contact Write, call, or fax Internship Coordinator. Phone: 202-357-1420. Fax: 202-357-2395. Applicants must submit academic transcripts, personal reference, essay, application (which can be downloaded from Web site). Application deadline: March 1 for summer, July 1 for fall, November 1 for spring. World Wide Web: http://www.si.edu/organiza/offices/archive/start.htm.

SMITHSONIAN INSTITUTION LIBRARIES
NHB 24, MRC 154, 10th and Constitution Avenue
Washington, District of Columbia 20560

General Information System of branch libraries that contains hard-bound volumes, rare books, current journals, and manuscripts. Number of internship applications received each year: 50.
Internships Available ▶ *Collection management interns.* ▶ *Planning and administration interns.* ▶ *Research services interns.* ▶ *Systems and technical services interns.* Duration for all positions is flexible. All positions are unpaid. Open to college freshmen, college sophomores, college juniors, college seniors, recent college graduates, graduate students. International applications accepted.
Benefits Job counseling, names of contacts, opportunity to attend seminars/workshops, willing to complete paperwork for educational credit, willing to provide letters of recommendation.
Contact Write, call, or fax Internship Coordinator. Phone: 202-357-1851. Fax: 202-357-4532. In-person interview recommended. Applicants must submit a cover letter, resume. Applications are accepted continuously. World Wide Web: http://www.sil.si.edu.

THE SOCIETY FOR THE PRESERVATION OF NEW ENGLAND ANTIQUITIES
141 Cambridge Street
Boston, Massachusetts 02114

General Information Museum of cultural history that preserves, interprets, and collects buildings, landscapes, and objects reflecting New England life from the 17th-century to the present. Established in 1910. Number of employees: 50. Number of internship applications received each year: 100.
Internships Available ▶ *2–6 interns:* responsibilities include working with collections, archaeology, archives, education, public relations and research departments on current and special projects in museum interpretation, social history, architectural history, and landscape and agricultural history. Duration is flexible. Unpaid. Open to college freshmen, college sophomores, college juniors, college seniors, recent college graduates, graduate students, career changers, individuals reentering the workforce.
Benefits Opportunity to attend seminars/workshops, willing to complete paperwork for educational credit, willing to provide letters of recommendation.
Contact Write or fax Ms. Anne Grady, Research Historian. Fax: 617-227-9204. No phone calls. In-person interview recommended. Applicants must submit a formal organization application, cover letter, resume, three personal references. Application deadline: May 1 for summer; continuous deadlines for other times of year. World Wide Web: http://www.spnea.org.

SOLOMON R. GUGGENHEIM MUSEUM
1071 Fifth Avenue
New York, New York 10128

General Information Internationally oriented museum of modern and contemporary art. Established in 1959. Number of employees: 350. Unit of Solomon R. Guggenheim Foundation, New York, New York. Number of internship applications received each year: 600.
Internships Available ▶ *25–30 interns:* responsibilities include participating 2 or more days a week on a schedule that includes field trips, seminars, and learning about the various functions of the museum and the art field in general. Duration is 4 months in spring or fall. Unpaid. ▶ *20–25 summer interns:* responsibilities include participating 5 days a week on a full-time schedule that includes field trips, seminars, and learning about the various functions of the museum and the art field in general. Duration is 9 mid-June to mid-August. Position available as unpaid or paid. Candidates for all positions should have computer skills, declared college major in field, office skills, plan to pursue career in field, research skills, writing skills. Open to college juniors, college seniors, recent college graduates, graduate students. International applications accepted.
Benefits Opportunity to attend seminars/workshops, possible full-time employment, willing to act as a professional reference, willing to complete paperwork for educational credit, some stipends may be available for graduate-level students.
International Internships Available in Bilbao, Spain.
Contact Write, fax, or e-mail Allison M. Derusha, Education Program Coordinator. Fax: 212-423-3634. E-mail: aderusha@ guggenheim.org. In-person interview recommended. Applicants must submit a cover letter, resume, academic transcripts, writing sample, two letters of recommendation. Application deadline: February 15 for summer, July 15 for fall, November 15 for spring. World Wide Web: http://www.guggenheim.org.

SOUTHERN OHIO MUSEUM AND CULTURAL CENTER
PO Box 990, 825 Gallia Street
Portsmouth, Ohio 45662

General Information Art museum that presents 10-month schedule of changing, temporary exhibitions primarily in the visual arts in addition to performing arts and films and offers classes, workshops, and special programs. Established in 1979. Number of employees: 7. Number of internship applications received each year: 5.
Internships Available ▶ *1 exhibit curator:* responsibilities include assisting in organizing exhibitions, making contacts, and following up with paperwork. Candidates should have computer skills, oral communication skills, organizational skills, research skills, strong interpersonal skills, written communication skills. Open to recent college graduates, graduate students. ▶ *1 public relations assistant:* responsibilities include assisting in publicizing museum programs, preparation of newsletters and news releases, and some graphic arts work. Candidates should have computer skills, editing skills, oral communication skills, strong interpersonal skills, writing skills. Open to college juniors, college seniors, recent college graduates, graduate students. Duration for all positions is 3 months minimum. All positions are unpaid.
Benefits Names of contacts, opportunity to attend seminars/ workshops, possible full-time employment, travel reimbursement, willing to complete paperwork for educational credit, willing to provide letters of recommendation.
Contact Write, fax, or e-mail Ms. Kay Bouyack, Administrative Director or Ms. Sara Johnson, Director of Planning. Fax: 740-354-4090. E-mail: somuseum@aol.com. No phone calls. In-person interview required. Applicants must submit a cover letter, resume, two personal references. Applications are accepted continuously.

SOUTH STREET SEAPORT MUSEUM
207 Front Street
New York, New York 10038

General Information Maritime history museum, located in a 12-block historic district in downtown Manhattan, that interprets the role of the seaport in the development of the city, the state, and the nation through education programs, exhibitions, and the preservation of buildings and ships. Established in 1967. Number of employees: 100. Number of internship applications received each year: 150.
Internships Available ▶ *Interns:* responsibilities include working in any of the following areas: archaeology, education, fundraising/development, maritime crafts, marketing/special events, printing and stationers shop, schooner *Lettie G. Howard*, ship restoration and maintenance, collections management, exhibit research, library, membership, publications, tour marketing, schooner *Pioneer*, boat building. Duration is flexible. Unpaid. Open to high school students, high school seniors, recent high school graduates, college freshmen, college sophomores, college juniors, college seniors, recent college graduates, graduate students, career changers, individuals reentering the workforce. International applications accepted.
Benefits Formal training, on-the-job training, opportunity to attend seminars/workshops, possible full-time employment, willing to act as a professional reference, willing to complete paperwork for educational credit, willing to provide letters of recommendation.
Contact Write, call, or fax Ms. Patricia Sands, Director of Volunteer Programs. Phone: 212-748-8727. Fax: 212-748-8610.

In-person interview required. Applicants must submit a resume. Applications are accepted continuously. World Wide Web: http://www.southstseaport.org.

SPRINGFIELD ARMORY NATIONAL HISTORIC SITE/ NATIONAL PARK SERVICE
1 Armory Square
Springfield, Massachusetts 01105-1299

General Information Site commemorating the critical role Springfield Armory played in the nation's military history; preserves, researches, and interprets the firearms collection, archives, library, and structures; provides the story of technological developments of the Armory complex and their impacts on civilization. Established in 1974. Number of employees: 14. Unit of National Park Service, Washington, District of Columbia. Number of internship applications received each year: 10.

Internships Available ▶ *1–2 archives summer interns:* responsibilities include organizing, boxing, and cataloging archives; housekeeping and environmental monitoring. Candidates should have analytical skills, computer skills, oral communication skills, organizational skills, research skills, written communication skills. Duration is 12 weeks (minimum of 30 hours per week). Unpaid. Open to college freshmen, college sophomores, college juniors, college seniors. ▶ *1–2 collections management interns:* responsibilities include environmental monitoring; housekeeping, including cleaning exhibits; using the collection management database, Automated National Catalog System (ANCS). Candidates should have ability to work with others, computer skills, editing skills, self-motivation, writing skills. Duration is 2 semesters, 240 hours minimum. Position available as unpaid or paid. Open to college juniors, college seniors, recent college graduates, graduate students, law students, career changers, individuals reentering the workforce. ▶ *1–2 conservation interns:* responsibilities include rehousing archaeological collection; cleaning and housing paper, metal, and wood materials. Candidates should have ability to work with others, computer skills, editing skills, self-motivation, writing skills. Duration is 1 semester. Position available as unpaid or paid. Open to college juniors, college seniors, recent college graduates, graduate students, law students, career changers, individuals reentering the workforce. ▶ *1–3 interpretive program assistants:* responsibilities include assisting with development of museum exhibits and public programs, testing curriculum-based education programs. Candidates should have ability to work independently, oral communication skills, self-motivation, strong interpersonal skills, writing skills. Duration is 120 hours. Position available as unpaid or paid. Open to college juniors, college seniors, recent college graduates, graduate students, law students, career changers, individuals reentering the workforce. ▶ *4–6 library/archives interns:* responsibilities include cataloging new books, rehousing archives, participating in housekeeping, and making phase boxes for historic books. Candidates should have analytical skills, computer skills, oral communication skills, organizational skills, research skills, written communication skills. Duration is 1 semester, 120 hours minimum. Unpaid. Open to college juniors, college seniors, recent college graduates, graduate students, law students, career changers, individuals reentering the workforce. ▶ *1–2 maintenance resource evaluators:* responsibilities include gathering and entering data into the inventory assessment program, entering reports and evaluating the maintenance program. Candidates should have ability to work with others, computer skills, editing skills, self-motivation, writing skills. Duration is 8–10 weeks. Position available as unpaid or paid. Open to college juniors, college seniors, recent college graduates, graduate students, law students, career changers, individuals reentering the workforce. ▶ *1 market plan developer:* responsibilities include creating a plan to publicize the Historic Site and available services and programs. Candidates should have oral communication skills, organizational skills, strong interpersonal skills, strong leadership ability, writing skills. Duration is flexible, minimum of 10 hours per week. Position available as unpaid or paid. Open to college juniors, college seniors, recent college graduates, graduate students, law students, career changers, individuals reentering the workforce. ▶ *4–6 oral history interns:* responsibilities include transcribing, compiling, and cataloging

information on the 100 oral histories into the parks database; intern will need to read *Transcribing and Editing Oral History* by Willa K. Baum. Candidates should have ability to work independently, computer skills, editing skills, knowledge of field, organizational skills, ability to understand elderly voices on audio tape. Duration is 1 semester, 120 hours minimum. Unpaid. Open to college juniors, college seniors, recent college graduates, graduate students, law students, career changers, individuals reentering the workforce. ▶ *1 promotional development intern:* responsibilities include creating brochures, flyers, and other non-personal materials for the public and schools; researching and developing concepts with park rangers. Candidates should have ability to work independently, computer skills, knowledge of field, personal interest in the field, strong leadership ability, writing skills. Duration is flexible, minimum of 10 hours per week. Unpaid. Open to college juniors, college seniors, recent college graduates, graduate students, law students, career changers, individuals reentering the workforce. ▶ *1–2 research assistants:* responsibilities include researching publications, archives, microfilm, or newspapers for park staff or outside researchers. Candidates should have ability to work independently, ability to work with others, analytical skills, computer skills, research skills, written communication skills. Duration is 1 semester, 120 hours minimum. Unpaid. Open to college juniors, college seniors, recent college graduates, graduate students, law students, career changers, individuals reentering the workforce. International applications accepted.

Benefits Formal training, names of contacts, on-the-job training, opportunity to attend seminars/workshops, willing to act as a professional reference, willing to complete paperwork for educational credit, willing to provide letters of recommendation, worker's compensation, local travel expenses (mileage).

Contact Write, call, fax, or e-mail Joanne Gangi, Chief of Visitor Services, Volunteer Parks Program Coordinator. Phone: 413-734-8551. Fax: 413-747-8062. E-mail: joanne_gangi@nps.gov. In-person interview required. Applicants must submit a cover letter, resume, writing sample, two personal references, security background check required. Application deadline: July 1 for fall and January winter break, November 1 for spring and summer. World Wide Web: http://www.nps.gov/spar.

SPRINGFIELD LIBRARY AND MUSEUMS
220 State Street
Springfield, Massachusetts 01103

General Information Administrative organization for the Springfield libraries and 4 separate museums. Established in 1857. Number of employees: 275. Number of internship applications received each year: 10.

Internships Available ▶ *1 curatorial assistant (art):* responsibilities include assisting in various duties depending on interests. Candidates should have ability to work independently, ability to work with others, computer skills, declared college major in field, knowledge of field, oral communication skills, plan to pursue career in field, research skills, written communication skills. Open to college seniors, graduate students. ▶ *1 curatorial assistant (science):* responsibilities include cataloguing natural history collections, exhibit preparation, possibly some animal care. Candidates should have ability to work independently, ability to work with others, computer skills, declared college major in field, knowledge of field, plan to pursue career in field. Open to college juniors, college seniors, graduate students. ▶ *1 public relations intern:* responsibilities include writing press releases, writing for a variety of audiences, and performing various other publicity-related duties. Candidates should have ability to work independently, ability to work with others, college courses in field, computer skills, editing skills, oral communication skills, plan to pursue career in field, research skills, writing skills. Open to college seniors, graduate students. Duration for all positions is 1 semester. All positions are unpaid.

Benefits Job counseling, on-the-job training, willing to act as a professional reference, willing to complete paperwork for educational credit, willing to provide letters of recommendation.

Contact Write Ms. Sara Orr, Publicist. No phone calls. In-person interview required. Applicants must submit a cover letter, resume,

Springfield Library and Museums (continued)
academic transcripts, writing sample may be required. Applications are accepted continuously. World Wide Web: http://www.quadrangle.org.

STATEN ISLAND INSTITUTE OF ARTS AND SCIENCES
75 Stuyvesant Place
Staten Island, New York 10301-1998

General Information Organization that focuses on Staten Island and its people and has strong collections in these subjects. Established in 1881. Number of employees: 50. Number of internship applications received each year: 75.
Internships Available ▶ *2 archival assistants:* responsibilities include working on special research projects requiring direct involvement with original material (including artifacts and archival holdings such as oral and written personal histories, documents, photographs, leaflets, fliers, and memoirs); identifying and locating appropriate artifacts, archival holdings, and materials relating to the material culture and contributions of working-class people on Staten Island. Candidates should have ability to work independently, personal interest in the field, research skills, self-motivation. Duration is 15 weeks. Open to high school seniors, recent high school graduates, college freshmen, college sophomores, college juniors, college seniors, recent college graduates, individuals reentering the workforce. ▶ *1 art collections intern:* responsibilities include inventorying, cataloging, and storing art collection objects, entering into database art collection objects, marking museum objects with permanent identification numbers, tracking incoming donations to the permanent collection, completing condition reports for incoming loans, updating incoming loan files, assisting with installation and removal of exhibits, and other assigned collections-related duties. Candidates should have ability to work independently, ability to work with others, organizational skills, self-motivation. Duration is flexible, 2 days per week (4 hours per day preferred). Open to high school seniors, recent high school graduates, college freshmen, college sophomores, college juniors, college seniors. ▶ *1 marketing intern:* responsibilities include assisting in preparation of media and newsletter mailings, distribution of printed materials, and direct marketing of group programs and public events through direct contact with tourism professionals and community groups. Candidates should have ability to work with others, computer skills, editing skills, organizational skills, personal interest in the field, self-motivation, writing skills. Duration is flexible. Open to college freshmen, college sophomores, college juniors, college seniors, recent college graduates, graduate students, career changers, individuals reentering the workforce. ▶ *2 science assistants:* responsibilities include performing various duties within the science department. Possible areas of work include archaeology collection, entomology, botany, zoology, data entry, geology, Staten Island paleontology, mounted bird collection, herbarium, and myxomycete collection. Candidates should have ability to work independently, college courses in field, computer skills, experience in the field, personal interest in the field, self-motivation. Duration is flexible. Open to college freshmen, college sophomores, college juniors, college seniors, recent college graduates. All positions are unpaid. International applications accepted.
Benefits Formal training, job counseling, possible full-time employment, willing to complete paperwork for educational credit, willing to provide letters of recommendation.
Contact Write, call, or fax Ms. Peggy Hammerle-McGuire, Vice President of Collections. Phone: 718-727-1135. Fax: 718-273-5683. In-person interview required. Applicants must submit a cover letter, resume, academic transcripts. Applications are accepted continuously.

STATEN ISLAND ZOO, EDUCATION DEPARTMENT
614 Broadway
Staten Island, New York 10310

General Information Zoological park focusing on the goals of conservation, education, and recreation in order to present exotic animals to the public. Established in 1936. Number of employees: 34. Unit of Staten Island Zoo, Staten Island, New York. Number of internship applications received each year: 50.
Internships Available ▶ *1 camp art teacher:* responsibilities include teaching art programs and creating curriculum. Duration is 3 months. $250 per week. Open to college juniors, college seniors. ▶ *1 camp recreation teacher:* responsibilities include teaching recreation and creating curriculum. Duration is 3 months. $250 per week. Open to college juniors, college seniors, recent college graduates. ▶ *1 camp science teacher:* responsibilities include teaching science programs and creating curriculum. Duration is 3 months. $250 per week. Open to college juniors, college seniors, recent college graduates. ▶ *1 zoomobile teacher:* responsibilities include teaching outreach programs with live animals, feeding and taking care of animals in education department. Duration is 9 months. $372 per week. Open to recent college graduates, graduate students. International applications accepted.
Benefits Job counseling, names of contacts, opportunity to attend seminars/workshops, willing to complete paperwork for educational credit, willing to provide letters of recommendation.
Contact Write, call, or fax Assistant Director of Education. Phone: 718-442-3174. Fax: 718-981-8711. In-person interview required. Applicants must submit a cover letter, resume. Application deadline: February 25 for summer, June 30 for fall. World Wide Web: http://www.statenislandzoo.org.

STONES RIVER NATIONAL BATTLEFIELD
3501 Old Nashville Highway
Murfreesboro, Tennessee 37129-3094

General Information Organization geared towards preserving the national battlefield site and providing for the study of the Battle of Stones River. Established in 1927. Number of employees: 9. Unit of United States National Park Service, Washington, District of Columbia. Number of internship applications received each year: 50.
Internships Available ▶ *1 clerical assistant:* responsibilities include performing office work, including filing and data entry. Candidates should have computer skills, editing skills, knowledge of field, office skills, organizational skills. Duration is 8–10 weeks. Open to recent high school graduates, college freshmen, college sophomores, college juniors, college seniors, recent college graduates, graduate students, career changers, individuals reentering the workforce. ▶ *1 historian:* responsibilities include conducting historical research. Candidates should have college courses in field, computer skills, knowledge of field, oral communication skills, research skills, written communication skills. Duration is flexible. Open to recent college graduates, graduate students, career changers, individuals reentering the workforce. ▶ *1 interpreter:* responsibilities include preparing and presenting interpretive programs and operating the visitor's center. Candidates should have knowledge of field, oral communication skills, personal interest in the field, strong interpersonal skills, written communication skills. Duration is flexible. Open to recent high school graduates, college freshmen, college sophomores, college juniors, college seniors, recent college graduates, graduate students, career changers, individuals reentering the workforce. ▶ *1 library assistant:* responsibilities include cataloging and classifying library. Candidates should have computer skills, knowledge of field, office skills, organizational skills. Duration is flexible. Open to college juniors, college seniors, recent college graduates, graduate students, career changers, individuals reentering the workforce. ▶ *1 maintenance worker:* responsibilities include maintaining trails, including spreading woodchips and clearing debris. Candidates should have ability to work independently, knowledge of field, organizational skills, personal interest in the field, self-motivation. Duration is flexible. Open to recent high school graduates, college freshmen, college sophomores, college juniors, college seniors, recent college graduates, graduate students, career changers, individuals reentering the workforce. ▶ *Museum curators:* responsibilities include caring for museum collection. Candidates should have analytical skills, computer skills, knowledge of field, organizational skills, research skills. Duration is flexible. Open to college juniors, college seniors, recent college gradu-

ates, graduate students, career changers, individuals reentering the workforce. ▶ *1 natural resource management technician:* responsibilities include biological monitoring, taking plant census, and eradicating exotic species. Candidates should have ability to work independently, analytical skills, college courses in field, research skills, self-motivation. Duration is flexible. Open to college juniors, college seniors, recent college graduates, graduate students, career changers, individuals reentering the workforce. All positions are unpaid.
Benefits Formal training, job counseling, on-the-job training, opportunity to attend seminars/workshops, willing to complete paperwork for educational credit, willing to provide letters of recommendation, worker's compensation.
Contact Write, call, fax, or e-mail Bettie C. Cook, VIP Coordinator. Phone: 615-893-9501. Fax: 615-893-9508. E-mail: stri_administration@nps.gov. In-person interview recommended. Applicants must submit a formal organization application, two personal references. Applications are accepted continuously. World Wide Web: http://www.nps.gov/stri.

STRONG MUSEUM
1 Manhattan Square
Rochester, New York 14607

General Information Public educational institution that collects, preserves, and interprets historic artifacts, manuscripts, and other materials that depict everyday life in America after 1820, emphasizing the Northeast during the era of industrialization. Established in 1982. Number of employees: 160. Number of internship applications received each year: 40.
Internships Available ▶ *2 summer interns:* responsibilities include working in one of the following: collections, library, research, exhibit design, administration, finance, conservation or education departments. Candidates should have ability to work independently, declared college major in field, oral communication skills, plan to pursue career in field, self-motivation, strong interpersonal skills, written communication skills. Duration is 12 weeks. $4,000 per duration of internship. ▶ *Volunteer interns:* responsibilities include working in one of the following: collections, library, research, administration, conservation, education or guest services. Candidates should have ability to work independently, oral communication skills, self-motivation, strong interpersonal skills, writing skills. Duration is 10–12 weeks. Unpaid. Open to college sophomores, college juniors, college seniors, recent college graduates, graduate students.
Benefits Names of contacts, on-the-job training, opportunity to attend seminars/workshops, willing to complete paperwork for educational credit, willing to provide letters of recommendation.
Contact Write, call, or fax Kathleen S. Dengler, Director, Human Resources. Phone: 716-263-2700. Fax: 716-263-2493. Applicants must submit a formal organization application, cover letter, resume, two personal references, three letters of recommendation. Application deadline: December 1 for summer. World Wide Web: http://www.strongmuseum.org.

SUNSET CRATER VOLCANO, WALNUT CANYON, AND WUPATKI NATIONAL MONUMENTS
Route 3, Box 149
Flagstaff, Arizona 86004

General Information Three national monuments managed by the National Park Service including a volcano, cliff dwellings, and pueblo archaeological sites; provides for visitor enjoyment, education, and resource protection. Number of employees: 50. Unit of Flagstaff Area National Monuments, Flagstaff, Arizona. Number of internship applications received each year: 100.
Internships Available ▶ *10–20 environmental education/interpretation/ visitor services interns:* responsibilities include staffing visitor center; developing and conducting interpretive programs for park visitors; developing and conducting environmental education programs for school groups; creating educational displays and publications; roving trails and making visitor contacts to discourage theft and vandalism of natural and cultural resources; preparing equipment for wildfire management; assisting in first aid and emergency situations. Candidates should have oral com-

munication skills, personal interest in the field, self-motivation, strong interpersonal skills, written communication skills. Duration is 3–6 months. Open to recent high school graduates, college freshmen, college sophomores, college juniors, college seniors, recent college graduates, graduate students, career changers, individuals reentering the workforce. ▶ *1–2 maintenance interns:* responsibilities include providing maintenance of park facilities including janitorial services, trail maintenance, trash collection, painting, minor repairs, and other physical labor duties as skills allow. Candidates should have ability to work independently, ability to work with others, experience in the field, personal interest in the field, self-motivation, ability to do physical labor. Duration is 3–6 months. Open to high school seniors, recent high school graduates, college freshmen, college sophomores, college juniors, college seniors, recent college graduates, graduate students, career changers, individuals reentering the workforce. ▶ *1–5 resource management interns:* responsibilities include assisting in studying and protecting cultural and natural resources; performing curatorial work; roving archaeological sites; conducting scientific studies; assisting in planning efforts; entering data on computer; and assisting interpretive staff in preparing educational material. Candidates should have analytical skills, experience in the field, knowledge of field, personal interest in the field, research skills, self-motivation. Duration is 3–6 months. Open to college freshmen, college sophomores, college juniors, college seniors, recent college graduates, graduate students, individuals reentering the workforce. ▶ *1 volunteer coordinator:* responsibilities include assisting in coordinating the volunteer program for three national monuments; recruiting volunteers; reviewing applications and routing to appropriate supervisors; maintaining records, managing funds; coordinating recognition events, and providing training assistance. Candidates should have ability to work independently, oral communication skills, organizational skills, self-motivation, strong interpersonal skills, written communication skills. Duration is 6–12 months. Open to college freshmen, college sophomores, college juniors, college seniors, recent college graduates, graduate students, career changers, individuals reentering the workforce. All positions are unpaid. International applications accepted.
Benefits Formal training, free housing, job counseling, names of contacts, on-the-job training, opportunity to attend seminars/workshops, willing to act as a professional reference, willing to complete paperwork for educational credit, willing to provide letters of recommendation, coverage for on-the-job injury or tort claim, uniform provided.
Contact Write, call, fax, or e-mail Anita Davis, Volunteer Coordinator. Phone: 520-526-0502. Fax: 520-714-0565. E-mail: anita_davis@nps.gov. Telephone interview required. Applicants must submit a formal organization application, cover letter, resume, three personal references. Applications are accepted continuously. World Wide Web: http://www.nps.gov/sucr.

THEODORE ROOSEVELT NATIONAL PARK
315 Second Avenue, PO Box 7
Medora, North Dakota 58645

General Information National park preserving the Little Missouri Badlands and 70,000 acres that are home to a variety of wildlife including bison, elk, wild horses, and variety birds. Established in 1947. Number of employees: 50. Number of internship applications received each year: 20.
Internships Available ▶ *2 biological science technicians:* responsibilities include performing resource management duties including exotic pest control and wildlife surveys. Candidates should have ability to work independently, ability to work with others, oral communication skills, research skills, self-motivation, written communication skills. Open to college freshmen, college sophomores, college juniors, college seniors, recent college graduates, graduate students, career changers, individuals reentering the workforce. ▶ *3–5 interpretive volunteers:* responsibilities include working at the information desk, presenting information to the public at talks and formal evening programs, leading guided nature hikes, and undertaking special projects that employ the skills of the volunteer. Candidates should have ability to work independently, ability to work with others, oral communication skills, organizational

Theodore Roosevelt National Park (continued)

skills, self-motivation, written communication skills. Open to college freshmen, college sophomores, college juniors, college seniors, recent college graduates, graduate students, individuals reentering the workforce. Duration for all positions is 2–3 months. All positions paid. International applications accepted. **Benefits** Formal training, free housing, job counseling, names of contacts, on-the-job training, willing to complete paperwork for educational credit, willing to provide letters of recommendation, subsistence pay.
Contact Write or call Bruce Kaye, Chief of Interpretation. Phone: 701-623-4466. Telephone interview required. Applicants must submit a cover letter, resume, two personal references. Application deadline: February 15 for spring/summer.

TIMPANOGOS CAVE NATIONAL MONUMENT
RR 3 Box 200
American Fork, Utah 84003

General Information National monument encompassing 250 acres consisting of 3 caves linked by manmade tunnels in the canyon walls of American Fork Canyon. Established in 1922. Number of employees: 10. Unit of United States National Park Service, Washington, District of Columbia. Number of internship applications received each year: 25.
Internships Available ▶ *1 administrative support intern:* responsibilities include answering phones, typing, filing, and performing other office work. Candidates should have ability to work with others, experience in the field, oral communication skills, self-motivation, written communication skills. Duration is flexible. Open to college sophomores, college juniors, college seniors. ▶ *1 cave management intern:* responsibilities include conducting tours of caves, maintaining the area, gathering data on the caves, and mapping and surveying caves. Candidates should have ability to work with others, college courses in field, knowledge of field, oral communication skills, written communication skills. Duration is flexible. Open to college sophomores, college juniors, college seniors, recent college graduates. ▶ *1 visitor center intern:* responsibilities include greeting visitors, conducting interpretive programs, providing information, and operating cash register. Candidates should have ability to work with others, knowledge of field, oral communication skills, self-motivation, written communication skills. Duration is 4 months. Open to college sophomores, college juniors, college seniors. All positions are unpaid. International applications accepted.
Benefits Formal training, job counseling, names of contacts, willing to complete paperwork for educational credit, willing to provide letters of recommendation, necessary equipment/supervision provided, stipend possible.
Contact Write, call, fax, or e-mail Mr. Mike Gosse, Chief Ranger. Phone: 801-756-5239. Fax: 801-756-5661. E-mail: michael_gosse@ nps.gov. In-person interview recommended. Applicants must submit a cover letter, resume. Application deadline: March 15. World Wide Web: http://www.nps.gov.

TONGASS NATIONAL FOREST, ADMIRALTY NATIONAL MONUMENT
8461 Old Dairy Road
Juneau, Alaska 99801

General Information National monument and wilderness dedicated to preserving natural, cultural, geological, historical, scientific, recreational, wildlife, and wilderness resources and monitoring and protecting a coastal, temperate rain forest. Established in 1978. Number of employees: 8. Unit of United States Forest Service, Washington, District of Columbia. Number of internship applications received each year: 60.
Internships Available ▶ *1–2 wilderness rangers:* responsibilities include backcountry monitoring of wilderness campsites, cabins, and recreation sites; conducting campsite cleanup; and assisting with visitor contact and wilderness education. Candidates should have ability to work with others, oral communication skills, personal interest in the field, self-motivation. Duration is

1 summer. Unpaid. Open to college juniors, college seniors, recent college graduates, graduate students, law students, career changers.
Benefits Free housing, free meals, job counseling, names of contacts, travel reimbursement, willing to complete paperwork for educational credit, willing to provide letters of recommendation.
Contact Write, call, or e-mail Mr. John Neary, Wilderness Assistant. Phone: 907-790-7481. E-mail: jneary/r10@fs.fed.us. In-person interview recommended. Applicants must submit a formal organization application. Application deadline: March 1.

TRAILSIDE MUSEUMS AND WILDLIFE CENTER
Palisades Interstate Park Commission
Bear Mountain, New York 10911

General Information Large park and recreational facility that promotes conservation of natural resources and provides space for outdoor recreation, home to non-releasable native New York wildlife; also performs wildlife rehabilitation. Established in 1927. Number of internship applications received each year: 10.
Internships Available ▶ *6 zookeeper assistants:* responsibilities include providing care for permanently injured or orphaned park wildlife in zoo setting under the supervision of a park ranger/zookeeper. Candidates should have ability to work independently, ability to work with others, oral communication skills, plan to pursue career in field, self-motivation. Duration is Mid May–mid August (4 positions) or end August–mid November (2 positions). Unpaid. Open to college freshmen, college sophomores, college juniors, college seniors. International applications accepted.
Benefits Formal training, names of contacts, on-the-job training, possible full-time employment, willing to act as a professional reference, willing to complete paperwork for educational credit, willing to provide letters of recommendation.
Contact Write, call, fax, or e-mail Ms. Jennifer Verstraete, Head Zookeeper. Phone: 914-786-2701 Ext. 278. Fax: 914-786-2776. E-mail: uncl@icu.com. In-person interview recommended. Applicants must submit a resume. Applications are accepted continuously. World Wide Web: http://www.trailsidenewyork. com.

TUCSON CHILDREN'S MUSEUM
PO Box 2609
Tucson, Arizona 85702-2609

General Information Museum that offers fun and learning through interactive programs and exhibits. Established in 1991. Number of employees: 15. Number of internship applications received each year: 10.
Internships Available ▶ *1–5 Spanish translators:* responsibilities include translating museum signs into Spanish and assisting with school group tours. Candidates should have ability to work independently, oral communication skills, self-motivation, strong interpersonal skills, writing skills, fluency in Spanish. Open to high school seniors, recent high school graduates, college freshmen, college sophomores, college juniors, college seniors, individuals reentering the workforce. ▶ *1–3 education interns:* responsibilities include planning and implementing museum workshops, designing educational materials for museum exhibits, and conducting tours for school groups. Candidates should have ability to work independently, analytical skills, editing skills, knowledge of field, oral communication skills, organizational skills, personal interest in the field, research skills, self-motivation, strong interpersonal skills, strong leadership ability, writing skills. Open to college freshmen, college sophomores, college juniors, college seniors, recent college graduates. ▶ *1 graphic artist:* responsibilities include designing brochures, newsletters, and museum signs, and possibly painting murals. Candidates should have ability to work independently, ability to work with others, knowledge of field, organizational skills, personal interest in the field, self-motivation, writing skills. Open to high school seniors, recent high school graduates, college freshmen, college sophomores, college juniors, college seniors. ▶ *1–2 marketing interns:* responsibilities include developing a marketing portfolio for the museum and marketing museum memberships. Candidates

should have ability to work independently, college courses in field, computer skills, knowledge of field, oral communication skills, organizational skills, personal interest in the field, self-motivation, strong interpersonal skills, strong leadership ability, writing skills. Open to college freshmen, college sophomores, college juniors, college seniors, recent college graduates, graduate students. ▶ *1–2 public relations interns:* responsibilities include writing public service announcements for events at the museum and keeping calendar listings in newspapers and magazines current. Candidates should have ability to work independently, ability to work with others, computer skills, editing skills, knowledge of field, office skills, oral communication skills, organizational skills, personal interest in the field, self-motivation, writing skills. Open to high school seniors, recent high school graduates, college freshmen, college sophomores, college juniors, college seniors, individuals reentering the workforce. Duration for all positions is 1–2 semesters. All positions are unpaid. International applications accepted.

Benefits Formal training, job counseling, names of contacts, opportunity to attend seminars/workshops, willing to act as a professional reference, willing to complete paperwork for educational credit, willing to provide letters of recommendation.

Contact Write, fax, or e-mail Connie Espinoza, Education Specialist. Fax: 520-792-0639. E-mail: tuchimu@azstarnet.com. No phone calls. In-person interview recommended. Applicants must submit a formal organization application, cover letter, resume, two personal references, two letters of recommendation. Applications are accepted continuously.

UCR/CALIFORNIA MUSEUM OF PHOTOGRAPHY
University of California, Riverside
Riverside, California 92521

General Information Laboratory for exploring the art history, social history, and technology of photography and related media. Established in 1973. Number of employees: 13. Number of internship applications received each year: 75.

Internships Available ▶ *1–3 museum assistants:* responsibilities include assisting with educational programs and exhibitions installation, and performing administrative, collections, curatorial, or marketing and publications duties. Duration is 3 months minimum. Unpaid. International applications accepted.

Benefits Job counseling, willing to complete paperwork for educational credit, willing to provide letters of recommendation.

Contact Write, fax, or e-mail Jonathan Green, Director. Fax: 909-787-4797. E-mail: jgreen@citrus.ucr.edu. No phone calls. In-person interview recommended. Applicants must submit a cover letter, resume, portfolio. Applications are accepted continuously. World Wide Web: http://www.cmp.ucr.edu.

U.S. HOLOCAUST MEMORIAL MUSEUM
100 Raoul Wallenberg Place, SW
Washington, District of Columbia 20024-2126

General Information Leading institution for the documentation, study, and interpretation of Holocaust history. Established in 1993. Number of employees: 400. Branch of United States Holocaust Memorial Council, Washington, District of Columbia. Number of internship applications received each year: 200.

Internships Available ▶ *1–2 academic publications interns:* responsibilities include reviewing submitted memoirs, articles and books for possible publication, assisting in production of the museum's journal *Holocaust and Genocide Studies.* Candidates should have ability to work independently, editing skills, research skills, writing skills, European language skills. Duration is 12 weeks. Position available as unpaid or paid. Open to college sophomores, college juniors, college seniors, recent college graduates, graduate students, career changers, individuals reentering the workforce. ▶ *1 archives intern:* responsibilities include translating and summarizing Estonian wartime trial records. Candidates should have college courses in field, computer skills, knowledge of field, research skills, writing skills, European language skills. Duration is 10–12 weeks. Unpaid. Open to college sophomores, college juniors, college seniors, recent college graduates, graduate students, career changers, individuals reentering the workforce.

▶ *1 collections intern:* responsibilities include assisting with research projects and catalog holdings of the museum's collections. Candidates should have ability to work independently, ability to work with others, computer skills, research skills, writing skills. Duration is 12 weeks. Unpaid. Open to college sophomores, college juniors, college seniors, recent college graduates, graduate students, career changers. ▶ *1 education intern:* responsibilities include assisting with the development of various educational projects including teacher resources. Candidates should have ability to work independently, ability to work with others, computer skills, knowledge of field, research skills, writing skills. Duration is 10–12 weeks. Unpaid. Open to college sophomores, college juniors, college seniors, recent college graduates, graduate students, career changers. ▶ *1–2 international programs interns:* responsibilities include assisting with the development of programs sponsored by the museum throughout the world. Candidates should have computer skills, knowledge of field, oral communication skills, strong interpersonal skills, written communication skills, knowledge of eastern European language helpful. Duration is 10–12 weeks. Unpaid. Open to college sophomores, college juniors, college seniors, recent college graduates, graduate students, career changers. ▶ *1 membership intern:* responsibilities include assisting with the development and maintenance of the membership program. Candidates should have computer skills, office skills, oral communication skills, strong interpersonal skills, written communication skills. Duration is 8–10 weeks. Unpaid. Open to college sophomores, college juniors, college seniors, recent college graduates, graduate students, career changers. ▶ *1 museum administration intern:* responsibilities include assisting with the behind-the-scenes administration of a national museum. Candidates should have office skills, oral communication skills, strong interpersonal skills, writing skills. Duration is 10–12 weeks. Unpaid. Open to college sophomores, college juniors, college seniors, recent college graduates, graduate students, career changers. ▶ *1 photo archive department intern:* responsibilities include maintaining archives of Holocaust photographs. Candidates should have ability to work independently, ability to work with others, analytical skills, computer skills, organizational skills, research skills. Duration is 12 weeks. Unpaid. Open to college sophomores, college juniors, college seniors, recent college graduates, graduate students, career changers. ▶ *2–4 research interns:* responsibilities include assisting senior research scholars. Candidates should have ability to work independently, ability to work with others, computer skills, editing skills, research skills, writing skills. Duration is 12 weeks. Unpaid. Open to college sophomores, college juniors, college seniors, recent college graduates, graduate students, law students, career changers, individuals reentering the workforce. ▶ *1 visitor services intern:* responsibilities include assisting in various public service areas, including gallery floor and learning center, and doing research on measures to improve the operation of gallery services. Candidates should have oral communication skills, strong interpersonal skills, strong leadership ability. Duration is 12 weeks. Unpaid. Open to college sophomores, college juniors, college seniors, recent college graduates, graduate students, career changers. ▶ *1 volunteer services intern:* responsibilities include assisting with the development of a volunteer program for a diverse constituency. Candidates should have ability to work independently, computer skills, oral communication skills, strong interpersonal skills, writing skills. Duration is 12 weeks. Unpaid. Open to college sophomores, college juniors, college seniors, recent college graduates, graduate students, career changers. International applications accepted.

Benefits Formal training, job counseling, names of contacts, on-the-job training, opportunity to attend seminars/workshops, willing to act as a professional reference, willing to complete paperwork for educational credit, willing to provide letters of recommendation.

Contact Write, call, or fax Intern Office. Phone: 202-479-9738. Fax: 202-488-6568. Telephone interview required. Applicants must submit a formal organization application, cover letter, resume, academic transcripts, two letters of recommendation.

Application deadline: March 15 for summer, June 15 for fall, October 15 for winter/spring. World Wide Web: http://www. ushmm.org.

VEGA STATE PARK
PO Box 186
Collbran, Colorado 81624

General Information Public recreation area. Established in 1972. Number of employees: 2. Unit of Colorado State Parks, Denver, Colorado. Number of internship applications received each year: 10.

Internships Available ▶ *1–2 environmental educators:* responsibilities include developing and presenting a variety of interpretive activities and community outreach programs. Candidates should have ability to work independently, oral communication skills, organizational skills, self-motivation, strong interpersonal skills, written communication skills. Position available as unpaid or at $7 per hour. Open to high school seniors, recent high school graduates, college freshmen, college sophomores, college juniors, college seniors, recent college graduates, graduate students, career changers, individuals reentering the workforce. ▶ *1–4 seasonal park rangers:* responsibilities include learning and performing natural resource law enforcement, maintenance, selling passes and permits, providing information to the public, riding along with other agencies, attending public meetings, and learning the administrative aspects of park management. Candidates should have ability to work independently, oral communication skills, self-motivation, strong interpersonal skills, written communication skills. $5.28 per hour if under 21 years old (no law enforcement commission); $6.58 per hour 21 and over. Open to individuals 18 or over for non-commissioned position; 21 or older for commissioned position. Duration for all positions is 1 summer. International applications accepted.

Benefits Formal training, free housing, job counseling, on-the-job training, willing to complete paperwork for educational credit, willing to provide letters of recommendation.

Contact Write, call, fax, or e-mail Mr. Kevin Tobey, Park Manager. Phone: 970-487-3407. Fax: 970-487-3404. E-mail: vega@csn.net. In-person interview recommended. Applicants must submit a formal organization application, three personal references. Applications are accepted continuously.

VIRGINIA MUSEUM OF FINE ARTS
2800 Grove Avenue
Richmond, Virginia 23221-2466

General Information State supported museum that houses a collection of original works of art and sponsors a variety of art programs. Established in 1936. Number of employees: 193. Number of internship applications received each year: 70.

Internships Available ▶ *1–2 art reference librarians:* responsibilities include assisting staff in implementation of auxiliary services provided to museum staff, scholars, students, and the public. Candidates should have ability to work with others, computer skills, knowledge of field, organizational skills, personal interest in the field, self-motivation. Open to college juniors, college seniors, recent college graduates, graduate students. ▶ *1–2 arts administration interns:* responsibilities include assisting in the research, planning, and coordination of a variety of ongoing educational programs, resources, and services. Candidates should have ability to work independently, computer skills, organizational skills, research skills, self-motivation, writing skills. Open to college juniors, college seniors, recent college graduates, graduate students. ▶ *1–4 curatorial interns:* responsibilities include researching, cataloging, and working on permanent and special exhibitions. Candidates should have ability to work independently, college courses in field, computer skills, organizational skills, research skills, self-motivation, writing skills. Open to college seniors, recent college graduates, graduate students. ▶ *1 docent program intern:* responsibilities include assisting staff with administration and collections research needs in the tour services office. Candidates should have ability to work with others, computer skills, oral communication skills, organizational skills, research

skills, self-motivation, writing skills. Open to college juniors, college seniors, recent college graduates, graduate students. ▶ *1 grants and research intern:* responsibilities include assisting with researching sources for funding and developing proposals to foundations and corporations. Candidates should have ability to work independently, computer skills, organizational skills, plan to pursue career in field, research skills, writing skills. Open to college juniors, college seniors, recent college graduates. ▶ *1–2 marketing and public affairs interns:* responsibilities include assisting staff with publicizing and marketing special exhibitions, programs, and events. Candidates should have computer skills, declared college major in field, office skills, self-motivation, writing skills. Open to college juniors, college seniors, recent college graduates, graduate students. ▶ *1–2 membership interns:* responsibilities include assisting staff with general operating services, activities, and benefits. Candidates should have ability to work with others, computer skills, office skills, oral communication skills, organizational skills, self-motivation. Open to college juniors, college seniors, recent college graduates, graduate students. ▶ *1 photographic resources intern:* responsibilities include assisting staff with documentation of works of art from permanent collection and various daily operational services. Candidates should have computer skills, knowledge of field, organizational skills, research skills, self-motivation, strong interpersonal skills. Open to college juniors, college seniors, recent college graduates, graduate students. ▶ *1–2 research projects interns:* responsibilities include researching Museum's collection and producing new or updating existing documentation. Candidates should have ability to work independently, ability to work with others, college courses in field, computer skills, research skills, writing skills. Open to college juniors, college seniors, recent college graduates, graduate students. ▶ *6–7 school and family programs interns:* responsibilities include researching and producing materials for school and adult activities and working on special events and programs. Candidates should have ability to work with others, computer skills, office skills, oral communication skills, organizational skills, plan to pursue career in field, research skills, self-motivation, writing skills. Open to college juniors, college seniors, recent college graduates, graduate students. ▶ *1 statewide educational resources intern:* responsibilities include assisting staff with the development of traveling exhibitions, research, inspection and repair of media resources, and general office support. Candidates should have ability to work independently, ability to work with others, computer skills, office skills, organizational skills, research skills, self-motivation, writing skills. Open to college juniors, college seniors, recent college graduates, graduate students. ▶ *2–3 visitor services interns:* responsibilities include assisting with staffing information and special events ticket desks; providing customer services related to permanent galleries. Candidates should have computer skills, office skills, oral communication skills, organizational skills, strong interpersonal skills, writing skills. Open to college juniors, college seniors, recent college graduates. Duration for all positions is 1 semester. All positions are unpaid. International applications accepted.

Benefits Willing to act as a professional reference, willing to complete paperwork for educational credit, willing to provide letters of recommendation.

Contact Write, call, or e-mail David Pittman, Internship Coordinator. Phone: 804-367-0885. Fax: 804-367-9393. E-mail: dpittman@vmfa. state.va.us. In-person interview recommended. Applicants must submit a cover letter, resume, academic transcripts, writing sample, two letters of recommendation. Application deadline: March 15 for summer, August 15 for fall, November 15 for spring. World Wide Web: http://www.vmfa.state.va.us.

WADSWORTH ATHENEUM
600 Main Street
Hartford, Connecticut 06103-2990

General Information Fine arts museum housing a collection with strengths in 19th-century American painting, Renaissance and Baroque European painting, European and American decorative arts, the Amistad Foundation Collection of African-American art and artifacts, and the Nutting Collection of Colonial American furniture. Established in 1842. Number of employees: 150. Number of internship applications received each year: 100.

Internships Available ▶ *1 business office intern:* responsibilities include performing office duties. Candidates should have computer skills. ▶ *1 curatorial intern:* responsibilities include conducting research on permanent collection, labeling objects, and cataloging entries. Candidates should have computer skills, knowledge of field, research skills, written communication skills. ▶ *1 design and installation intern:* responsibilities include assisting with 2- and 3-dimensional designs within the organization. Candidates should have ability to work with others, knowledge of field, personal interest in the field. ▶ *1 development intern:* responsibilities include fund-raising, writing grants, learning how to solicit corporate contributions/individual patrons, conducting market research, and building databases. Candidates should have ability to work independently, computer skills, office skills, organizational skills, self-motivation. ▶ *1 education intern:* responsibilities include assisting in implementing public programs including lectures, concerts, films, symposia, teachers' workshops, and children's programs; writing educational material such as gallery handouts and slide programs; grant writing; and surveying educational programs. Candidates should have ability to work independently, computer skills, office skills, organizational skills, research skills, written communication skills. ▶ *1 library intern:* responsibilities include serving museum staff and the public. Candidates should have computer skills, office skills, self-motivation. ▶ *1 membership intern:* responsibilities include assisting in membership drives, organizing membership activities and exhibition openings, and coordinating publication of membership materials. Candidates should have ability to work with others, computer skills, office skills, oral communication skills, strong interpersonal skills, written communication skills. ▶ *1 museum shop intern:* responsibilities include assisting in retail facility within museum. Candidates should have ability to work with others, oral communication skills. ▶ *1 photographic services intern:* responsibilities include maintaining museum's extensive slide holdings, handling all slide loans to staff and public, processing all requests regarding rights and reproductions, planning photo shoots, and filing and maintaining photographic archives. Candidates should have ability to work independently, office skills, organizational skills. ▶ *1 public information intern:* responsibilities include assisting public relations staff with writing press releases. Candidates should have computer skills, editing skills, written communication skills. ▶ *1 registrar intern:* responsibilities include maintaining provenance files on permanent collections, making accession cards, and researching objects for inventory. Candidates should have computer skills, office skills, oral communication skills, written communication skills. Duration for all positions is flexible. All positions are unpaid. Open to college freshmen, college sophomores, college juniors, college seniors, recent college graduates, graduate students, career changers, individuals reentering the workforce. International applications accepted.

Benefits Job counseling, names of contacts, opportunity to attend seminars/workshops, possible full-time employment, willing to complete paperwork for educational credit, willing to provide letters of recommendation, opportunity to attend all museum education programs.

Contact Write or call Ms. Amy Milner, Internship Coordinator. Phone: 860-278-2670 Ext. 312. In-person interview recommended. Applicants must submit a cover letter, resume, academic transcripts, two letters of recommendation. Application deadline: April 30 for summer, August 30 for fall/winter, December 31 for spring. World Wide Web: http://www.wadsworthatheneum.org.

THE WALTERS ART GALLERY
600 North Charles Street
Baltimore, Maryland 21201

General Information Art museum containing the collections amassed by William and Henry Walters; collection represents 5000 years: from ancient Egypt to 1900, including the art of Asia. Established in 1931. Number of employees: 130. Number of internship applications received each year: 100.

Internships Available ▶ *2–3 curatorial interns:* responsibilities include performing duties determined by the curators of medieval art, Renaissance and Baroque art, Asian art, and manuscripts and rare books; research cataloging; and working on permanent and special exhibitions. Candidates should have college degree in related field, computer skills, organizational skills, research skills, writing skills. Duration is 1–2 semesters. Open to college juniors, college seniors, recent college graduates, graduate students. ▶ *1–3 installation/preparation interns:* responsibilities include assisting in preparation and installation of temporary exhibitions. Candidates should have ability to work independently, ability to work with others, analytical skills, computer skills, experience in the field, organizational skills. Duration is 1–2 semesters. Open to college juniors, college seniors, recent college graduates, graduate students. ▶ *2–4 marketing interns:* responsibilities include promoting special exhibitions and tours. Candidates should have analytical skills, computer skills, organizational skills, research skills, strong interpersonal skills, writing skills. Duration is 1–2 semesters. Open to college juniors, college seniors, recent college graduates, graduate students. ▶ *1–2 membership interns:* responsibilities include working on annual giving and membership campaigns. Candidates should have ability to work independently, analytical skills, computer skills, oral communication skills, organizational skills, strong interpersonal skills. Duration is 1–2 semesters. Open to college juniors, college seniors, recent college graduates, graduate students. ▶ *1–5 public programs interns:* responsibilities include producing and promoting public programs and designing family activity guides. Candidates should have ability to work independently, computer skills, oral communication skills, organizational skills, strong interpersonal skills. Duration is 1–2 semesters. Open to college sophomores, college juniors, college seniors. ▶ *1–2 public relations interns:* responsibilities include working on public, community, and media relations projects. Candidates should have ability to work independently, computer skills, editing skills, oral communication skills, writing skills. Duration is 1 semester. Open to college juniors, college seniors, recent college graduates, graduate students. ▶ *1–3 registrar interns:* responsibilities include updating catalog cards and learning methods of collection management and inventory control via computer. Candidates should have ability to work independently, analytical skills, computer skills, experience in the field, organizational skills, written communication skills. Duration is 8–10 weeks. Open to college juniors, college seniors, recent college graduates, graduate students. ▶ *1–2 research library interns:* responsibilities include cataloging and user services. Candidates should have ability to work independently, computer skills, organizational skills, personal interest in the field, research skills, written communication skills. Duration is 1–2 semesters. Open to college juniors, college seniors, recent college graduates, graduate students. ▶ *2–3 special events interns:* responsibilities include working on special events in conjunction with exhibitions, special interest groups, and the community. Candidates should have ability to work independently, computer skills, oral communication skills, organizational skills, strong interpersonal skills, written communication skills. Duration is 1 semester. Open to college sophomores, college juniors, college seniors, recent college graduates. ▶ *1–2 student/tour programs interns:* responsibilities include researching and writing materials for tours for school and adult groups and producing resource materials for teachers. Candidates should have ability to work independently, college courses in field, computer skills, research skills, writing skills. Duration is 1–2 semesters. Open to college juniors, college seniors, recent college graduates, graduate students. All positions are unpaid. International applications accepted.

Benefits On-the-job training, opportunity to attend seminars/workshops, willing to complete paperwork for educational credit, willing to provide letters of recommendation.

Contact Write, call, or e-mail Mr. John J. Shields, Manager of Docent and Internship Programs. Phone: 410-547-9000. E-mail: jshields@thewalters.org. Telephone interview required. Applicants must submit a cover letter, resume, academic transcripts, two letters of recommendation. Application deadline: April 15 for summer, July 15 for fall, November 1 for spring.

WHITNEY MUSEUM OF AMERICAN ART
945 Madison Avenue
New York, New York 10021

General Information Museum dedicated to 20th-century American art and contemporary artists. Established in 1930. Number of employees: 210. Number of internship applications received each year: 125.

Internships Available ▶ *Interns:* responsibilities include working in a variety of areas including curatorial, branch museums, communications and public relations, development, education, film and video, library, publications, information services, exhibitions, and collections management. Candidates should have ability to work with others, college courses in field, computer skills, office skills, research skills, self-motivation. Duration is 2–4 months. Unpaid. Open to college sophomores, college juniors, college seniors, graduate students. International applications accepted.

Benefits On-the-job training, opportunity to attend seminars/workshops, possible full-time employment, willing to complete paperwork for educational credit, willing to provide letters of recommendation, discounts at museum and facilities, limited stipends may be available.

Contact Write Ms. Hillary Blass, Human Resources Manager. No phone calls. In-person interview required. Applicants must submit a cover letter, resume, academic transcripts, personal reference, letter of recommendation, one-page statement of purpose. Application deadline: March 1 for summer; continuous for spring/fall. World Wide Web: http://www.echonyc.com/~whitney.

WILDLIFE PRAIRIE PARK
3826 North Taylor Road, RR 2, Box 50
Peoria, Illinois 61615

General Information Wildlife park that encompasses 2000 acres of grazing land, lakes, and forests and presents wild animals native to Illinois. Number of employees: 35. Number of internship applications received each year: 50.

Internships Available ▶ *3–4 education interns:* responsibilities include greeting school groups and assisting with various interpretive programs such as the Outdoor Classroom, guiding tours, presenting daily interpretive programs to the general public, assisting with special events, performing certain opening and closing procedures, trail monitoring, and completing a special project. Candidates should have biology and environmental interests. Duration is 12 weeks. Position available as unpaid or paid. Open to college juniors, college seniors, recent college graduates, graduate students.

Benefits Free housing, possible full-time employment, willing to complete paperwork for educational credit, leadership skills.

Contact Write, call, fax, or e-mail Ms. Bonnie Cannon, Internship Coordinator, 3826 North Taylor Road, RR 2 Box 50, Peoria, Illinois 61615. Phone: 309-676-0998. Fax: 309-676-7783. E-mail: wppark@aol.com. Applicants must submit a cover letter, resume. Application deadline: February 27 for summer. World Wide Web: http://www.wildlifepark.org.

WIND CAVE NATIONAL PARK
RR1 Box 190
Hot Springs, South Dakota 57747

General Information National park that preserves and protects an exceptional maze-cave with a rare cave formation called ""boxwork" and maintains a beautiful mixed-grass prairie complete with representative wildlife. Established in 1903. Number of employees: 60. Unit of United States National Park Service, Washington, District of Columbia. Number of internship applications received each year: 50.

Internships Available ▶ *4 interpretation park rangers:* responsibilities include preparing and presenting interpretive programs including cave tours, visitor center demonstrations, and prairie hikes. Candidates should have ability to work independently, oral communication skills, personal interest in the field, self-motivation, strong interpersonal skills. Duration is 3–5 months.

$35–$75 per week. Open to college sophomores, college juniors, college seniors, recent college graduates, graduate students, law students, career changers.

Benefits Formal training, free housing, job counseling, names of contacts, willing to complete paperwork for educational credit, willing to provide letters of recommendation, uniform allowance, meal stipend.

Contact Write, call, or e-mail Ms. Kathy Steichen, Assistant Chief Interpreter. Phone: 605-745-4600. E-mail: kathy_steichen@nps.gov. Telephone interview required. Applicants must submit a formal organization application, cover letter, resume, academic transcripts. Application deadline: March 1 for summer, July 1 for fall, November 1 for spring.

WINTERTHUR MUSEUM, GARDEN AND LIBRARY
Winterthur, Delaware 19735

General Information Complete community for the presentation, preservation and exploration of American arts and historic structures; naturalistic garden; research library and academic center. Established in 1951. Number of employees: 425. Number of internship applications received each year: 30.

Internships Available ▶ *1 arborist intern:* responsibilities include assisting arborists in maintaining health and vigor of the trees throughout Winterthur garden; learning good arboricultural techniques and safety practices. Duration is 2 months (June to August). $6 per hour. ▶ *7 horticulture interns:* responsibilities include assisting the horticulturist of a particular garden and/or plant group; working with and under the guidance of a horticulturist or production supervisor in continually maintaining the design of the garden or plant group by practicing good horticulture techniques. Duration is 3 months (June-September). $6 per hour. Candidates for all positions should have ability to work with others, knowledge of field, personal interest in the field. Open to college freshmen, college sophomores, college juniors, college seniors. International applications accepted.

Benefits Meals at a cost, opportunity to attend seminars/workshops, possible full-time employment, willing to complete paperwork for educational credit, willing to provide letters of recommendation, field trips, safety training.

Contact Write, call, or fax Kay Collins, Employment Manager. Phone: 302-888-4830. Fax: 302-888-4956. In-person interview required. Applicants must submit a formal organization application, cover letter, resume. Application deadline: March 1.

WOMEN'S HISTORY AND RESOURCE CENTER
1734 N Street, NW
Washington, District of Columbia 20036

General Information Archives and library devoted to women's history with an emphasis on women in volunteerism. Unit of General Federation of Women's Clubs, Washington, District of Columbia.

Internships Available ▶ *Interns:* responsibilities include working with books and archival mateials, researching answers to reference inquiries, assisting researchers, receiving training for archival computer project tasks. Candidates should have strong interest in archives, women's history, and volunteerism. Duration is fall, spring, or summer (flexible hours). Unpaid. Open to college freshmen, college sophomores, college juniors, college seniors, graduate students, individuals reentering the workforce. International applications accepted.

Benefits Willing to complete paperwork for educational credit, small stipend at completion of internship.

Contact Write, fax, or e-mail Korina Adkins, Director, 1734 N Street, NW, Washington, District of Columbia 20036. Fax: 202-835-0246. E-mail: whrc@gfwc.org. Applicants must submit a resume. Applications are accepted continuously. World Wide Web: http://www.gfwc.org/whrc.htm.

YESHIVA UNIVERSITY MUSEUM
2520 Amsterdam Avenue
New York, New York 10033

General Information Museum that preserves, exhibits, and interprets Jewish life, art history, and culture through multidisciplinary exhibitions, contemporary shows, and scholarly catalogs. Established in 1973. Number of employees: 10. Unit of Yeshiva University, New York, New York. Number of internship applications received each year: 25.

Internships Available ▶ *1 curatorial intern:* responsibilities include research, cataloging, and exhibitions. Candidates should have ability to work independently, ability to work with others, computer skills, editing skills, office skills, research skills, writing skills. Duration is 3 months minimum. Open to high school students, high school seniors, recent high school graduates, college freshmen, college sophomores, college juniors, college seniors, recent college graduates, graduate students, individuals reentering the workforce. ▶ *2 education interns:* responsibilities include conducting youth programs and art workshops for visiting school groups (after training). Candidates should have ability to work independently, ability to work with others, office skills, oral communication skills, written communication skills. Duration is 2–12 months. Open to high school students, college freshmen, college sophomores, college juniors, college seniors, graduate students, individuals reentering the workforce. ▶ *1 registration intern:* responsibilities include collections research and recordkeeping. Candidates should have ability to work independently, ability to work with others, computer skills, editing skills, office skills, research skills, writing skills. Duration is 3 months minimum. Open to high school students, college freshmen, college sophomores, college juniors, college seniors, graduate students, individuals reentering the workforce. All positions are unpaid. International applications accepted.

Benefits Job counseling, names of contacts, opportunity to attend seminars/workshops, willing to complete paperwork for educational credit, willing to provide letters of recommendation.

Contact Write or fax Ms. Randi Glickberg, Administrator. Fax: 212-960-5406. In-person interview required. Applicants must submit a cover letter, resume, 2 personal references/letters of recommendation. Applications are accepted continuously. World Wide Web: http://www.yu.edu/museum/.

PERFORMING ARTS COMPANIES

THE ACTING COMPANY–GROUP I ACTING COMPANY, INC.
420 West 42nd Street, Third Floor
New York, New York 10036-6809

General Information Professional touring classical repertory theater. Established in 1972. Number of employees: 10. Number of internship applications received each year: 20.

Internships Available ▶ *2 development interns:* responsibilities include performing administrative fund-raising duties. Candidates should have ability to work independently, computer skills, office skills, oral communication skills, organizational skills, personal interest in the field. Duration is 1–2 semesters. Open to college freshmen, college sophomores, college juniors, college seniors, recent college graduates. ▶ *1 office intern:* responsibilities include performing administrative duties. Candidates should have ability to work independently, computer skills, organizational skills, personal interest in the field, self-motivation, written communication skills. Duration is 1–2 semesters. Open to recent high school graduates, college freshmen, college sophomores, college juniors, college seniors, recent college graduates, graduate students. ▶ *1–2 stage management interns:* responsibilities include assisting with rehearsals. Candidates should have ability to work independently, computer skills, oral communication skills, organizational skills, plan to pursue career in field, written com-

munication skills. Duration is 4 months (mid-September to mid-January). Open to recent high school graduates, college freshmen, college sophomores, college juniors, college seniors, recent college graduates. All positions paid at $50 per week. International applications accepted.

Benefits Job counseling, names of contacts, on-the-job training, possible full-time employment, willing to act as a professional reference, willing to complete paperwork for educational credit, willing to provide letters of recommendation.

Contact Write or fax Ms. Daryl Samuel, General Manager, PO Box 898, Times Square Station, New York, New York 10108-0898. Fax: 212-714-2643. In-person interview recommended. Applicants must submit a cover letter, resume, writing sample. Applications are accepted continuously. World Wide Web: http://www.theactingcompany.org.

ACTOR'S THEATRE OF LOUISVILLE
316 West Main Street
Louisville, Kentucky 40202

General Information Regional repertory theater that produces 30 or more shows a season including three major festivals. Number of employees: 200.

Internships Available ▶ *22 acting apprentices:* responsibilities include working with afternoon production crew and evening running crew; some acting opportunities on mainstage, with guaranteed casting in apprentice projects. ▶ *1 apprentice company management intern.* ▶ *1 casting intern.* ▶ *1 community relations and company management intern.* ▶ *2–5 costume interns.* ▶ *2–4 directing interns:* responsibilities include some design opportunities on apprentice projects. ▶ *1 festival intern.* ▶ *1–2 lighting and sound interns.* ▶ *2 literary interns.* ▶ *1 production management intern.* ▶ *2 public relations/marketing interns.* ▶ *3 stage management interns.* Duration for all positions is flexible. All positions are unpaid. Open to college freshmen, college sophomores, college juniors, college seniors, recent college graduates, graduate students, career changers, individuals reentering the workforce. International applications accepted.

Benefits Names of contacts, opportunity to attend seminars/workshops, possible full-time employment, willing to complete paperwork for educational credit, willing to provide letters of recommendation.

Contact Write, call, or fax Director of the Apprentice/Intern Company. Phone: 502-584-1265. Fax: 502-561-3300. In-person interview required. Applicants must submit a cover letter, resume, academic transcripts, portfolio, two letters of recommendation. Application deadline: April 15 for summer. World Wide Web: http://www.actorstheatre.org.

ALLEY THEATRE
615 Texas Avenue
Houston, Texas 77002

General Information Theater presenting plays of merit performed by a company of actors for a subscription audience. Established in 1947. Number of employees: 80. Number of internship applications received each year: 100.

Internships Available ▶ *1 casting intern:* responsibilities include interacting with artistic staff. Candidates should have ability to work independently, analytical skills, computer skills, editing skills, knowledge of field, office skills, oral communication skills, organizational skills, plan to pursue career in field, research skills, self-motivation, strong interpersonal skills, written communication skills. Duration is 3–9 months. Unpaid. Open to college seniors, recent college graduates, graduate students, career changers. ▶ *2 company managers:* responsibilities include interacting with guests. Candidates should have oral communication skills, self-motivation, strong interpersonal skills, written communication skills. Duration is 3 months (20 hours per week). Unpaid. Open to college seniors, recent college graduates, graduate students, career changers. ▶ *1 costumes/wigs intern:* responsibilities include assisting shop manager and wigmaster. Candidates should have ability to work independently, knowledge of field, plan to pursue career in field, research skills, self-motivation, strong interpersonal skills. Duration is 3–9 months. Position avail-

Alley Theatre (continued)

able as unpaid or at $200 per week. Open to college seniors, recent college graduates, graduate students, career changers. ▶ *1 development intern:* responsibilities include performing fund-raising tasks. Candidates should have computer skills, office skills, organizational skills, personal interest in the field, self-motivation, strong interpersonal skills, writing skills. Duration is September-December, December-March, or March-June (20 hours per week). Unpaid. Open to college seniors, recent college graduates, graduate students, career changers. ▶ *1 dramaturgy intern:* responsibilities include reading new plays. Candidates should have ability to work independently, analytical skills, computer skills, personal interest in the field, research skills, self-motivation, writing skills. Duration is 3 months (20 hours per week). Unpaid. Open to college seniors, recent college graduates, graduate students, career changers. ▶ *1 general manager intern:* responsibilities include performing elements of production. Candidates should have ability to work independently, computer skills, office skills, organizational skills, plan to pursue career in field, written communication skills. Duration is September-December, December-March, or March-June (20 hours per week). Unpaid. Open to college seniors, recent college graduates, graduate students, career changers. ▶ *1 lighting intern:* responsibilities include operating Prestige 3000. Candidates should have ability to work independently, ability to work with others, college courses in field, computer skills, knowledge of field, self-motivation. Duration is 3–9 months. Position available as unpaid or at $200 per week. Open to college seniors, recent college graduates, graduate students, career changers. ▶ *1 marketing intern:* responsibilities include devising advertising strategies. Candidates should have computer skills, knowledge of field, office skills, oral communication skills, organizational skills, personal interest in the field, research skills, self-motivation, strong interpersonal skills, writing skills. Duration is 8-10 weeks (20 hours per week). Unpaid. Open to college seniors, recent college graduates, graduate students, career changers. ▶ *1 props intern.* Candidates should have ability to work independently, analytical skills, knowledge of field, personal interest in the field, research skills, self-motivation, strong interpersonal skills. Duration is 3 months. Position available as unpaid or at $200 per week. Open to college seniors, recent college graduates, graduate students, career changers, individuals reentering the workforce. ▶ *1 public relations intern:* responsibilities include writing press releases. Candidates should have computer skills, editing skills, office skills, oral communication skills, organizational skills, personal interest in the field, research skills, self-motivation, strong interpersonal skills, writing skills. Duration is 3 months (20 hours per week). Unpaid. Open to college seniors, recent college graduates, graduate students, career changers. ▶ *1 sound intern:* responsibilities include running sound for shows. Candidates should have ability to work independently, ability to work with others, analytical skills, knowledge of field, organizational skills, plan to pursue career in field, research skills. Duration is 3–9 months. Position available as unpaid or at $200 per week. Open to college seniors, recent college graduates, graduate students, career changers. ▶ *1 technical directing intern:* responsibilities include assisting the technical director. Candidates should have computer skills, knowledge of field, plan to pursue career in field, research skills, self-motivation, strong interpersonal skills. Duration is 3–9 months. Position available as unpaid or at $200 per week. Open to college seniors, recent college graduates, graduate students, career changers. International applications accepted.

Benefits Names of contacts, possible full-time employment, willing to complete paperwork for educational credit, willing to provide letters of recommendation, flexible hours.

Contact Write Ms. Bettye Fitzpatrick, Director of Interns. In-person interview recommended. Applicants must submit a formal organization application, cover letter, resume, three letters of recommendation. Application deadline: February 1 for spring, July 1 for fall, October 1 for winter.

ALLIANCE THEATRE COMPANY
Robert W. Woodruff Arts Center, 1280 Peachtree Street, NE
Atlanta, Georgia 30309

General Information Theater company offering a diverse 11-play season of contemporary plays, musical theater, world and regional premieres, and classics in its 784-seat mainstage and 200-seat studio theaters; also offers 2 children's theater productions. Established in 1966. Number of employees: 125. Division of Woodruff Arts Center, Atlanta, Georgia. Number of internship applications received each year: 25.

Internships Available ▶ *1 properties intern:* responsibilities include assisting with fabrications and purchase of properties; load-in, strike, and return of properties' items; maintenance of props work and storage areas; and inventory control in props storage and supplies. Candidates should have ability to work independently, ability to work with others, knowledge of field, plan to pursue career in field, self-motivation. Duration is 9 months. $210 per week, plus overtime after 40 hours. Open to recent college graduates, graduate students, career changers. ▶ *1 scenery intern:* responsibilities include helping to fabricate/construct scenic elements and technical requirements of each set design; installing and striking scenic elements; loading and unloading materials as well as scenery. Candidates should have ability to work independently, ability to work with others, experience in the field, personal interest in the field, self-motivation. Duration is 9 months. $210 per week, plus overtime after 40 hours. Open to recent college graduates, graduate students, career changers, individuals reentering the workforce. ▶ *1 sound intern:* responsibilities include assisting with realization of sound plots, recording and editing of materials, loading in sound equipment, operating sound equipment, maintaining records of sound production information. Candidates should have ability to work independently, ability to work with others, college courses in field, experience in the field, self-motivation. Duration is 9 months. $210 per week, plus overtime after 40 hours. Open to recent college graduates, graduate students, career changers, individuals reentering the workforce. ▶ *3 stage management interns:* responsibilities include performing clerical work, maintaining rehearsal halls during rehearsal, assisting with all rehearsals, preparation and distribution of rehearsal and performance notes, operating backstage positions. Candidates should have ability to work with others, experience in the field, office skills, organizational skills, plan to pursue career in field. Duration is 8–9 months. $210 per week, plus overtime after 40 hours. Open to recent college graduates, graduate students. ▶ *1 stage operations intern:* responsibilities include assisting with installation, running, and striking of all productons; assisting with all repertory changeovers, load-in, running, and load-out of all stages; assisting with maintenance of stage house and rigging. Candidates should have ability to work independently, ability to work with others, experience in the field, personal interest in the field, self-motivation. Duration is 9 months. $210 per week, plus overtime after 40 hours. Open to recent college graduates, graduate students, career changers, individuals reentering the workforce.

Benefits Job counseling, names of contacts, on-the-job training, possible full-time employment, willing to act as a professional reference, willing to provide letters of recommendation.

Contact Write, call, or fax Mr. Steve Lindsley, Production Coordinator. Phone: 404-733-4776. Fax: 404-733-4625. In-person interview recommended. Applicants must submit a formal organization application, cover letter, resume, three personal references, two letters of recommendation. Application deadline: May 14 for production positions, June 7 for administration positions.

AMERICAN CONSERVATORY THEATER
30 Grant Avenue
San Francisco, California 94108

General Information One of the nation's largest and most active resident professional theaters. Established in 1967. Number of employees: 500. Number of internship applications received each year: 75.

Internships Available ▶ *Artistic staff associates:* responsibilities include working with the directors and artistic staff in the publications, casting, and literary departments. Candidates should have ability to work independently, analytical skills, computer skills, editing skills, experience in the field, office skills, oral communication skills, organizational skills, plan to pursue career in field, research skills, strong interpersonal skills, written communication skills. Duration is 2–10 months. Unpaid. Open to college freshmen, college sophomores, college juniors, college seniors, recent college graduates, graduate students, career changers. ▶ *1 costume rental intern:* responsibilities include maintaining large stock of period costumes; organizing and creating a unified look for business, personal, and theatrical rentals; and furnishing rehearsal costumes for mainstage theater productions. Candidates should have ability to work independently, college courses in field, computer skills, experience in the field, office skills, oral communication skills, organizational skills, plan to pursue career in field, research skills, self-motivation, strong interpersonal skills, written communication skills. Duration is 9–10 months. $165 per week. Open to college freshmen, college sophomores, college juniors, college seniors, recent college graduates, graduate students, career changers, individuals reentering the workforce. ▶ *1 costume shop intern:* responsibilities include assisting in costume shop, shopping, stitching, and various costume building; duties as determined by the shop manager. Candidates should have ability to work independently, ability to work with others, college courses in field, computer skills, editing skills, experience in the field, office skills, oral communication skills, organizational skills, plan to pursue career in field, research skills, self-motivation, strong leadership ability, writing skills. Duration is 9–10 months. $165 per week. Open to college freshmen, college sophomores, college juniors, college seniors, recent college graduates, individuals reentering the workforce. ▶ *1 lighting design intern:* responsibilities include assisting the lighting design associate in maintaining all records necessary for upkeep of the repertory plot and inventory, drafting designs for special effects, assisting the designers in hanging and focusing lights, and supervising technical rehearsals. Candidates should have ability to work independently, ability to work with others, college courses in field, computer skills, experience in the field, office skills, oral communication skills, organizational skills, plan to pursue career in field, research skills, self-motivation, strong leadership ability, written communication skills. Duration is 9–10 months. $165 per week. Open to recent college graduates, graduate students. ▶ *1 makeup and wig construction intern:* responsibilities include working under the direction of the theater's wigmaster in the repertory shop and on special projects. Candidates should have ability to work independently, ability to work with others, analytical skills, knowledge of field, oral communication skills, organizational skills, plan to pursue career in field, research skills, self-motivation, practical experience in related field, college degree in related field preferred. Duration is 9–10 months. $165 per week. Open to college freshmen, college sophomores, college juniors, college seniors, recent college graduates, graduate students, career changers, individuals reentering the workforce. ▶ *1 marketing/public relations associate:* responsibilities include learning day-to-day operations, writing, proofreading, photo production, developing and executing signage and posters, and maintaining the database. Candidates should have ability to work independently, analytical skills, college courses in field, computer skills, editing skills, experience in the field, office skills, oral communication skills, organizational skills, plan to pursue career in field, research skills, self-motivation, strong interpersonal skills, strong leadership ability, written communication skills. Duration is 2 months (minimum). Unpaid. Open to college sophomores, college juniors, college seniors, recent college graduates, graduate students. ▶ *1–2 production interns: show only:* responsibilities include assistance on show-specific production work. Candidates should have ability to work independently, college courses in field, computer skills, editing skills, experience in the field, office skills, oral communication skills, plan to pursue career in field, research skills, strong interpersonal skills, written communication skills. Duration is 1–2 months. $165 per week. Open to college freshmen, college

juniors, college seniors, recent college graduates, career changers, individuals reentering the workforce. ▶ *1 production management intern:* responsibilities include assisting the production management team in operation of production departments. The intern learns about season schedule, budget planning, contracts, design development, and day-to-day production operations. Candidates should have ability to work independently, analytical skills, college courses in field, computer skills, editing skills, experience in the field, office skills, oral communication skills, organizational skills, plan to pursue career in field, research skills, self-motivation, strong interpersonal skills, written communication skills. Duration is 8–10 months. $165 per week. Open to college seniors, recent college graduates, graduate students, career changers. ▶ *1 properties intern:* responsibilities include creation and fabrication of hand props and set dressings for mainstage productions. Candidates should have ability to work independently, analytical skills, college courses in field, experience in the field, office skills, oral communication skills, organizational skills, plan to pursue career in field, research skills, self-motivation, strong interpersonal skills, written communication skills. Duration is 9–10 months. $165 per week. Open to college freshmen, college sophomores, college juniors, college seniors, recent college graduates, graduate students, career changers. ▶ *1 scenic design intern:* responsibilities include working under the direction of the design associate and the technical supervisor to learn the specific techniques and construction methods developed by the theater staff; emphasis on drafting and mold building. Candidates should have ability to work independently, ability to work with others, college courses in field, computer skills, knowledge of field, office skills, oral communication skills, organizational skills, plan to pursue career in field, research skills, written communication skills. Duration is 9–10 months. $165 per week. Open to college freshmen, college sophomores, college juniors, college seniors, recent college graduates. ▶ *1 sound design intern:* responsibilities include assisting the repertory designer in mounting each production. Candidates should have ability to work independently, college courses in field, computer skills, experience in the field, office skills, oral communication skills, organizational skills, plan to pursue career in field, research skills, self-motivation, strong interpersonal skills, writing skills. Duration is 9–10 months. $165 per week. Open to recent college graduates, graduate students. ▶ *2–3 stage management interns:* responsibilities include assisting in the development/production of shows. Candidates should have ability to work independently, analytical skills, college courses in field, computer skills, editing skills, experience in the field, office skills, oral communication skills, organizational skills, plan to pursue career in field, research skills, self-motivation, strong interpersonal skills, strong leadership ability, written communication skills. Duration is 8–10 months. $165 per week. Open to college freshmen, college sophomores, college juniors, college seniors, recent college graduates, graduate students, career changers, individuals reentering the workforce. **Benefits** Formal training, job counseling, names of contacts, on-the-job training, opportunity to attend seminars/workshops, possible full-time employment, willing to act as a professional reference, willing to complete paperwork for educational credit, willing to provide letters of recommendation, assistance with resume preparation. **Contact** Write Ms. Susan West, Intern Coordinator. No phone calls. Applicants must submit a formal organization application, cover letter, resume, writing sample, three letters of recommendation. Application deadline: April 15 for production positions; continuous for artistic positions. Fees: $10. World Wide Web: http://www.act-sfbay.org.

THE AMERICAN PLACE THEATRE
111 West 46th Street
New York, New York 10036

General Information Theater producing the work of American writers which strives for an uncompromising commitment to unconventional and daring plays. Established in 1963. Number of employees: 28. Number of internship applications received each year: 400.

The American Place Theatre (continued)

Internships Available ▶ *4 administrative assistants:* responsibilities include assisting staff with day-to-day functions of office. Candidates should have ability to work independently, computer skills, editing skills, office skills, oral communication skills, organizational skills, self-motivation, strong interpersonal skills, writing skills. Duration is flexible. Open to college juniors, college seniors, recent college graduates, graduate students. ▶ *1 assistant to artistic director:* responsibilities include assisting artistic director in script evaluations, fund-raising, correspondence, and daily maintenance of activities schedule. Candidates should have ability to work independently, analytical skills, college courses in field, computer skills, editing skills, knowledge of field, office skills, oral communication skills, organizational skills, plan to pursue career in field, research skills, self-motivation, strong interpersonal skills, writing skills. Duration is one academic year. Open to college seniors, recent college graduates, graduate students, career changers, individuals reentering the workforce. ▶ *3 education interns:* responsibilities include assisting education directors in the coordination and creative planning of 3 education programs: Urban Writes, Literature to Life, and Teacher's Place. Candidates should have ability to work independently, analytical skills, college courses in field, computer skills, knowledge of field, office skills, oral communication skills, organizational skills, personal interest in the field, self-motivation, strong interpersonal skills, writing skills, interest in production/stage management. Duration is one academic year. Open to college seniors, recent college graduates, graduate students. ▶ *1–2 fund-raising interns:* responsibilities include assisting the Director of Development in tracking funders and writing grants. Candidates should have ability to work independently, ability to work with others, computer skills, editing skills, office skills, organizational skills, personal interest in the field, research skills, writing skills. Duration is 1 semester. Open to college seniors, recent college graduates, graduate students, individuals reentering the workforce. ▶ *2–4 literary interns:* responsibilities include assisting Artistic Director in reading and processing incoming submissions and with new play development programs. Candidates should have ability to work independently, ability to work with others, analytical skills, college courses in field, computer skills, office skills, oral communication skills, organizational skills, personal interest in the field, research skills, self-motivation, writing skills, interest in playwriting or dramaturgy. Duration is 1 semester. Open to college juniors, college seniors, recent college graduates, graduate students. ▶ *2 production interns:* responsibilities include assisting production manager in rehearsal and running of productions. Candidates should have ability to work independently, ability to work with others, college courses in field, computer skills, experience in the field, office skills, oral communication skills, organizational skills, plan to pursue career in field, self-motivation, written communication skills. Open to college juniors, college seniors, recent college graduates, graduate students. All positions available as unpaid or paid. International applications accepted.

Benefits Job counseling, names of contacts, on-the-job training, opportunity to attend seminars/workshops, possible full-time employment, travel reimbursement, willing to act as a professional reference, willing to complete paperwork for educational credit, willing to provide letters of recommendation.
Contact Write, fax, or e-mail Internship Director. Fax: 212-391-4019. E-mail: pfontana@americanplacetheatre.org. No phone calls. In-person interview recommended. Applicants must submit a cover letter, resume, three letters of recommendation. Applications are accepted continuously. World Wide Web: http://www.americanplacetheatre.org.

AMERICAN REPERTORY THEATRE
64 Brattle Street
Cambridge, Massachusetts 02138

General Information Fully professional resident theater company at Harvard University's Loeb Drama Center in Cambridge that produces a 5-play mainstage season, a New Stages series, and a number of special events using a permanent ensemble of actors, directors, designers, technicians, and administrators performing in repertory. Established in 1979. Number of employees: 60. Unit of Harvard University, Cambridge, Massachusetts. Number of internship applications received each year: 20.

Internships Available ▶ *1 artistic management intern:* responsibilities include assisting in company management/casting office. Candidates should have ability to work independently, oral communication skills, self-motivation, strong interpersonal skills, written communication skills. Duration is flexible. Open to college freshmen, college sophomores, college juniors, college seniors, graduate students. ▶ *1 box office intern:* responsibilities include assisting staff in the sale and processing of tickets and performing general customer services and computer work. Candidates should have ability to work independently, computer skills, office skills, strong interpersonal skills. Duration is flexible. Open to college freshmen, college sophomores, college juniors, college seniors, recent college graduates, graduate students. ▶ *1 costume shop intern:* responsibilities include assisting in all phases of construction process. Candidates should have ability to work independently, knowledge of field, organizational skills, self-motivation. Duration is 12 weeks. Open to college freshmen, college sophomores, college juniors, college seniors, graduate students. ▶ *1 fund-raising intern:* responsibilities include researching prospects, working with volunteer committees, maintaining records, and helping with special events and telethons. Candidates should have office skills, oral communication skills, personal interest in the field, strong interpersonal skills, written communication skills. Duration is flexible. Open to college freshmen, college sophomores, college juniors, college seniors, recent college graduates, graduate students, career changers, individuals reentering the workforce. ▶ *1 house management intern:* responsibilities include assisting in front-of-house operations management and learning concession/gift shop procedures. Candidates should have ability to work independently, office skills, oral communication skills, self-motivation, strong interpersonal skills. Duration is flexible. Open to recent high school graduates, college freshmen, college sophomores, college juniors, college seniors, recent college graduates, individuals reentering the workforce. ▶ *1 literary management intern:* responsibilities include assisting with events, dramaturgical research, critical evaluation of scripts, and gathering research material. Candidates should have ability to work independently, computer skills, office skills, self-motivation, writing skills. Duration is flexible. Open to college freshmen, college sophomores, college juniors, college seniors, recent college graduates, graduate students, career changers. ▶ *1 marketing/public relations intern:* responsibilities include assisting in planning and execution of audience studies and ticket sales initiatives. Candidates should have office skills, oral communication skills, strong interpersonal skills, writing skills. Duration is 12 weeks. Open to college freshmen, college sophomores, college juniors, college seniors, recent college graduates, graduate students. ▶ *1 production management intern:* responsibilities include assisting with budget and monitoring expenditures. Candidates should have ability to work independently, oral communication skills, self-motivation, strong interpersonal skills, written communication skills. Duration is flexible. Open to college freshmen, college sophomores, college juniors, college seniors, recent college graduates, graduate students. ▶ *1 running crew intern:* responsibilities include assisting with stage management, lighting, wardrobe, sound, or properties. Candidates should have strong interpersonal skills. Duration is 8–10 weeks. Open to college freshmen, college sophomores, college juniors, college seniors, recent college graduates, graduate students. ▶ *1 scene shop intern:* responsibilities include assisting in budgeting, scheduling, construction, finishing, and installation of scenery and property. Candidates should have ability to work independently, oral communication skills, self-motivation, strong interpersonal skills, written communication skills. Duration is 12 weeks. Open to college freshmen, college sophomores, college juniors, college seniors, recent college graduates, graduate students. ▶ *1 stage management intern:* responsibilities include assisting in all aspects of the production process. Candidates should have ability to work independently, ability to work with others, knowledge of field, self-motivation, strong leadership ability. Duration is 8–12 weeks. Open to college freshmen, college sophomores, college juniors, college seniors, recent college graduates, graduate students. ► *1 voice coach intern:* responsibilities include assisting vocal coach. Candidates should have college courses in field, knowledge of field, personal interest in the field. Duration is 6 weeks minimum. Open to recent college graduates, graduate students. All positions are unpaid. International applications accepted.

Benefits Names of contacts, on-the-job training, willing to act as a professional reference, willing to complete paperwork for educational credit, willing to provide letters of recommendation.
Contact Write or call Dax Kiger, Coordinator of Internship Programs, Loeb Drama Center. Phone: 617-495-2668. Fax: 617-495-2668 Ext. 8836. E-mail: kiger@fas.harvard.edu. In-person interview recommended. Applicants must submit a cover letter, resume, two personal references. Applications are accepted continuously. World Wide Web: http://www.amrep.org.

AMERICAN STAGE
211 Third Street South
St. Petersburg, Florida 33731

General Information Nonprofit residential professional theater mandated as an arts agency to provide theater productions and related educational and outreach programs to the citizens of west central Florida. Established in 1977. Number of employees: 13. Number of internship applications received each year: 100.
Internships Available ► *1–2 administrative interns:* responsibilities include performing general administrative, fund-raising, and box office work. Duration is flexible. Position available as unpaid or paid. ► *2–4 technical interns:* responsibilities include working in carpentry and costume shops and running shows. Duration is 10 months. $150 per week. Open to college freshmen, college sophomores, college juniors, college seniors, recent college graduates, graduate students.
Benefits Job counseling, names of contacts, willing to complete paperwork for educational credit, willing to provide letters of recommendation.
Contact Write Mr. Tom Block, Operations Manager. No phone calls. In-person interview required. Applicants must submit a cover letter, resume. Applications are accepted continuously.

AMERICAN STAGE FESTIVAL (THE YOUNG COMPANY)
14 Court Street
Nashua, New Hampshire 03060

General Information Nationally recognized professional theater in southern New Hampshire with a 500-seat house producing 5 mainstage and 5 children's shows and staged readings from May to September. Established in 1971. Number of employees: 25. Number of internship applications received each year: 500.
Internships Available ► *20 actors:* responsibilities include performing in 5 children's shows, understudying, and assisting with mainstage. Candidates should have knowledge of field, oral communication skills, plan to pursue career in field, self-motivation. Unpaid. ► *2 administrative interns:* responsibilities include assisting company manager and management staff. Candidates should have knowledge of field, oral communication skills, organizational skills, plan to pursue career in field, written communication skills. $50 per week. ► *1 costumer:* responsibilities include designing and constructing costumes. Candidates should have knowledge of field, plan to pursue career in field. $50 per week. ► *2 directing interns:* responsibilities include assisting with mainstage. Candidates should have knowledge of field, oral communication skills, plan to pursue career in field, strong interpersonal skills, written communication skills. Unpaid. ► *1 lighting intern:* responsibilities include assisting with mainstage shows and design. Candidates should have knowledge of field, plan to pursue career in field. $50 per week. ► *2 marketing interns:* responsibilities include helping with marketing. Candidates should have knowledge of field, oral communication skills, plan to pursue career in field, written communication skills. $50 per week. ► *1 properties intern:* responsibilities include assisting property master on all shows, acting as property manager for Young Company. Candidates should have knowledge of field, plan to pursue career in field. $50 per week. ► *4 stage managers:*

responsibilities include assisting stage managers of mainstage and Young Company. Candidates should have ability to work with others, knowledge of field, oral communication skills, plan to pursue career in field. Unpaid. ► *2 technical director/designers:* responsibilities include assisting with set and prop design and construction. Candidates should have plan to pursue career in field. $50 per week. Duration for all positions is June 1 to August 31. Open to recent high school graduates, college freshmen, college sophomores, college juniors, college seniors, recent college graduates. International applications accepted.
Benefits Free housing, on-the-job training, opportunity to attend seminars/workshops, willing to act as a professional reference, willing to complete paperwork for educational credit, willing to provide letters of recommendation, EMC credit for performers and assistant stage managers.
Contact Write or fax Scott Severance, Director of Youth Programs. Fax: 603-889-2336. No phone calls. Telephone interview required. Applicants must submit a cover letter, resume. Application deadline: April 15. World Wide Web: http://www.americanstagefestival.org.

ARDEN THEATRE COMPANY
40 North Second Street
Philadelphia, Pennsylvania 19106

General Information Theater company whose mission is to tell the greatest stories by the greatest storytellers of all time. Established in 1988. Number of employees: 25. Number of internship applications received each year: 100.
Internships Available ► *6 apprentices:* responsibilities include general office assistance, production assistance, box office work, marketing, and fund-raising. Duration is 8 months. $250 per week. ► *3 artistic assistants:* responsibilities include assisting artistic office staff. Duration is flexible. Unpaid. ► *2 development assistants:* responsibilities include assisting development staff in all areas of fund-raising. Duration is flexible. Unpaid. ► *3 marketing assistants:* responsibilities include assisting staff in all areas of marketing. Duration is flexible. Unpaid. ► *15–20 production assistants:* responsibilities include assisting stage and production managers, and working in the areas of lighting, sound, props, costumes, and sets. Duration is August to June. Unpaid. Open to high school students, high school seniors, recent high school graduates, college freshmen, college sophomores, college juniors, college seniors, recent college graduates, graduate students, law students, career changers, individuals reentering the workforce.
Benefits Formal training, job counseling, names of contacts, opportunity to attend seminars/workshops, possible full-time employment, willing to complete paperwork for educational credit, willing to provide letters of recommendation.
Contact Write or fax Lesley Moore, Intern Coordinator. Fax: 215-922-7011. No phone calls. In-person interview recommended. Applicants must submit a cover letter, resume. Applications are accepted continuously.

ARENA STAGE
1101 Sixth Street, SW
Washington, District of Columbia 20024

General Information One of the world's leading resident theater companies consisting of a core of resident artists, craftspeople, theater technicians, and administrators who seek to illuminate the human experience through the highest professional standard of theater art; 8-play season runs mid-August through mid-June. Established in 1950. Number of employees: 180. Number of internship applications received each year: 300.
Internships Available ► *8–10 administration interns:* responsibilities include assisting the executive director, external affairs director, or business/personnel office or working with communications, development, fund-raising, information systems, casting/productions office, sales office, or operations director. Candidates should have knowledge of field, office skills, oral communication skills, organizational skills, strong interpersonal skills, writing skills. Duration is 3–9 months. Open to college freshmen, college sophomores, college juniors, college seniors, recent college graduates, graduate students, career changers. ► *7–11 artistic*

Arena Stage (continued)

interns: responsibilities include assisting in directing, dramaturgy/literary management, casting/production, and arts in education/playwriting. Candidates should have analytical skills, college courses in field, experience in the field, organizational skills, research skills, writing skills. Duration is 6 weeks (directing), 4–9 months (all others). ▶ *2–3 living stage interns:* responsibilities include assisting in administration or production of Living Stage (social outreach theater). Candidates should have knowledge of field, personal interest in the field, strong interpersonal skills, written communication skills, commitment to children and theater for social change. Duration is 3–9 months. Open to college freshmen, college sophomores, college juniors, college seniors, recent college graduates, graduate students, career changers. ▶ *11–22 production interns:* responsibilities include assisting with company management, costumes, lighting, production management, properties, scene painting, set construction, sound, or stage management. Candidates should have ability to work independently, college courses in field, experience in the field, plan to pursue career in field, strong interpersonal skills. Duration is 4–9 months. Open to college freshmen, college sophomores, college juniors, college seniors, recent college graduates, graduate students, career changers. All positions paid at $120 per week. International applications accepted.
Benefits Job counseling, names of contacts, opportunity to attend seminars/workshops, possible full-time employment, willing to act as a professional reference, willing to complete paperwork for educational credit, willing to provide letters of recommendation, modest stipend.
Contact Write, call, fax, or e-mail Ms. A. Lorraine Robinson, Intern Coordinator. Phone: 202-554-9066. Fax: 202-488-4056. E-mail: arenastalr@aol.com. Telephone interview required. Applicants must submit a cover letter, resume, academic transcripts, writing sample, two letters of recommendation. Application deadline: March 1 for summer, May 1 for fall, October 1 for spring. World Wide Web: http://www.arenastage.org.

ASH LAWN–HIGHLAND SUMMER FESTIVAL
1941 James Monroe Parkway
Charlottesville, Virginia 22902-8722

General Information Summer festival producing 2 operas and 1 musical theater production for a total of 28 performances; hosts additional musical and theatrical productions for all ages. Established in 1978. Number of employees: 60. Unit of College of William and Mary, Williamsburg, Virginia. Number of internship applications received each year: 20.
Internships Available ▶ *1 administrative intern:* responsibilities include maintaining databases, organizing fund-raising mailings, designing summer festival programs, providing general office support. Duration is flexible. Open to high school seniors, recent high school graduates, college freshmen, college sophomores, college juniors, college seniors, recent college graduates, graduate students. ▶ *1 arts management intern:* responsibilities include working in administrative office, with production staff, and in the costume shop and box office. Duration is flexible. Open to college freshmen, college sophomores, college juniors, college seniors, recent college graduates, graduate students. ▶ *1 development intern:* responsibilities include composing development materials and fund-raising strategies, and expanding and maintaining databases. Duration is flexible. Open to college juniors, college seniors, recent college graduates, graduate students. ▶ *1 marketing intern:* responsibilities include developing marketing strategies and contacts, researching, organizing and updating grant information, and assisting with grant writing. Duration is flexible. Open to college freshmen, college sophomores, college juniors, college seniors, recent college graduates, graduate students. ▶ *1 press intern:* responsibilities include composing press releases and calendar listings, organizing press databases, developing contacts with area newspapers, magazines, and both radio and television stations. Duration is one summer. Open to college freshmen, college sophomores, college juniors, college seniors, recent college graduates, graduate students. ▶ *1 production intern:* responsibilities include scene painting, scene shifting, lighting design,

theatrical sewing, and carpentry. Duration is one summer. Open to high school seniors, recent high school graduates, college freshmen, college sophomores, college juniors, college seniors, recent college graduates, graduate students. All positions are unpaid. International applications accepted.
Benefits Free housing, job counseling, names of contacts, willing to complete paperwork for educational credit, willing to provide letters of recommendation, hands-on experience in the operation and production of professional opera company.
Contact Write, call, fax, or e-mail Mr. Brooke Joyce, Assistant to the General Manager. Phone: 804-293-4500. Fax: 804-293-0736. E-mail: summerfestival@avenue.org. Applicants must submit a cover letter, resume. Applications are accepted continuously. World Wide Web: http://monticello.avenue.gen.va.us/Arts/Ashlawn/ashl2.html.

ATLANTIC THEATER COMPANY
336 West 20th Street
New York, New York 10011

General Information Nonprofit off-Broadway acting ensemble dedicated to producing new theater and featuring a distinctive acting technique. Established in 1985. Number of employees: 11. Number of internship applications received each year: 25.
Internships Available ▶ *2–4 development/marketing interns:* responsibilities include marketing, fund-raising, and organizing development and benefits. Candidates should have ability to work independently, ability to work with others, computer skills, organizational skills, self-motivation, writing skills. Duration is flexible. Open to college freshmen, college sophomores, college juniors, college seniors, recent college graduates, graduate students. ▶ *3 office interns:* responsibilities include managing house and box office and performing public relations and general office work. Candidates should have editing skills, office skills, oral communication skills, organizational skills, self-motivation, strong interpersonal skills, writing skills. Duration is September 1-May 31. Open to college freshmen, college sophomores, college juniors, college seniors, recent college graduates. ▶ *10 production interns:* responsibilities include working on lighting, sets, props, and costumes, and running crew for all productions. Candidates should have knowledge of field. Duration is September 1-May 31. Open to college freshmen, college sophomores, college juniors, college seniors, recent college graduates. All positions are unpaid. International applications accepted.
Benefits Names of contacts, willing to complete paperwork for educational credit, willing to provide letters of recommendation.
Contact Write or fax Freda Farrell, Company Manager. Fax: 212-645-8755. No phone calls. In-person interview recommended. Applicants must submit a cover letter, resume. Applications are accepted continuously.

A TRAVELING JEWISH THEATRE
323 Geary Street, Suite 415
San Francisco, California 94102

General Information A professional nonprofit theater ensemble writing and performing original works based on Jewish tradition and themes and reaching out to people from all backgrounds. Established in 1978. Number of employees: 3. Number of internship applications received each year: 3.
Internships Available ▶ *1–4 interns:* responsibilities include assisting with all aspects of arts administration from production, education, marketing, and special events coordination to volunteer recruitment and the upkeep of donor database and mailing lists and serving as a liaison between the theater and outside community. Candidates should have computer skills, office skills, oral communication skills, personal interest in the field, strong interpersonal skills. Duration is flexible. Unpaid. International applications accepted.
Benefits Job counseling, names of contacts, on-the-job training, opportunity to attend seminars/workshops, possible full-time employment, willing to act as a professional reference, willing to complete paperwork for educational credit, willing to provide letters of recommendation.

Contact Write, call, fax, or e-mail Karen Stahr, Marketing Director, 323 Geary Street Suite 415, San Francisco, California 94102. Phone: 415-399-1809 Ext. 302. Fax: 415-399-1844. E-mail: mail@atjt.com. In-person interview required. Applicants must submit a cover letter, resume. Applications are accepted continuously. World Wide Web: http://www.atjt.com.

BALLET INTERNATIONALE
502 North Capital Avenue, Suite B
Indianapolis, Indiana 46204

General Information Professional performing ballet company offering home, educational, and tour performances. Established in 1973. Number of employees: 44. Number of internship applications received each year: 10.
Internships Available ▶ *2 development interns:* responsibilities include maintaining lists and helping with campaigns and special events. Candidates should have ability to work independently, computer skills, editing skills, office skills, organizational skills, self-motivation, strong interpersonal skills. Duration is flexible. Unpaid. Open to high school students, high school seniors, recent high school graduates, college freshmen, college sophomores, college juniors, college seniors, recent college graduates, graduate students, law students, career changers, individuals reentering the workforce. ▶ *2 public relations/marketing interns:* responsibilities include writing, organizing, and coordinating various projects. Candidates should have ability to work independently, analytical skills, college courses in field, computer skills, editing skills, office skills, oral communication skills, organizational skills, plan to pursue career in field, research skills, self-motivation, strong interpersonal skills, writing skills. Duration is flexible. Unpaid. Open to recent high school graduates, college freshmen, college sophomores, college juniors, college seniors, recent college graduates, graduate students, career changers. ▶ *1 technical intern:* responsibilities include working backstage and constructing sets and props. Candidates should have ability to work with others, computer skills, organizational skills, plan to pursue career in field, self-motivation. Duration is 16 weeks. Position available as unpaid or at maximum of $200 per week. Open to recent high school graduates, college freshmen, college sophomores, college juniors, college seniors, recent college graduates, graduate students, career changers, individuals reentering the workforce. International applications accepted.
Benefits Formal training, names of contacts, on-the-job training, opportunity to attend seminars/workshops, possible full-time employment, willing to act as a professional reference, willing to complete paperwork for educational credit, willing to provide letters of recommendation.
Contact Write, call, or fax Barbara A. Turner, Managing Director. Phone: 317-637-8979. Fax: 317-637-1637. In-person interview recommended. Applications are accepted continuously. World Wide Web: http://www.balletinternationale.org.

BARROW GROUP
PO Box 5112
New York, New York 10185

General Information Theater performing full-length new works. Established in 1986. Number of employees: 5. Number of internship applications received each year: 12.
Internships Available ▶ *Design interns.* ▶ *Development interns:* responsibilities include grant writing, fund-raising, and publicity. Candidates should have computer skills, oral communication skills, organizational skills, self-motivation, writing skills. ▶ *Dramaturgy interns.* ▶ *General management interns.* Candidates should have computer skills, office skills, oral communication skills, organizational skills, self-motivation, written communication skills. Duration is flexible. ▶ *Literary management interns.* ▶ *Production interns.* All positions are unpaid. International applications accepted.
Benefits Opportunity to attend seminars/workshops, possible full-time employment, willing to complete paperwork for educational credit, willing to provide letters of recommendation.
Contact Write, call, fax, or e-mail Nicole Foster, Managing Director. Phone: 212-522-1421. Fax: 212-522-1402. E-mail: barrowgroup@earthlink.net. In-person interview recommended. Applicants must submit a resume. Applications are accepted continuously.

BATTERY DANCE COMPANY
380 Broadway, 5th Floor
New York, New York 10013-3518

General Information Dance company that tours internationally, works extensively in the public schools, and produces an annual free public dance festival in New York City's financial district; also organizes domestic tours by foreign dance troupes. Established in 1976. Number of employees: 15. Number of internship applications received each year: 30.
Internships Available ▶ *2 administrative assistants:* responsibilities include performing office management duties. Candidates should have ability to work independently, ability to work with others, computer skills, office skills, oral communication skills, personal interest in the field, self-motivation, strong interpersonal skills, written communication skills. ▶ *1 intern:* responsibilities include coordinating contracts and publicity, acting as site liaison, assisting in ad campaign, and administration. Candidates should have ability to work independently, ability to work with others, oral communication skills, personal interest in the field, self-motivation, strong interpersonal skills, written communication skills. Duration for all positions is flexible. All positions are unpaid. Open to high school students, high school seniors, recent high school graduates, college freshmen, college sophomores, college juniors, college seniors, recent college graduates, graduate students, law students, career changers, individuals reentering the workforce. International applications accepted.
Benefits Job counseling, names of contacts, on-the-job training, possible full-time employment, willing to act as a professional reference, willing to complete paperwork for educational credit, willing to provide letters of recommendation, opportunity to attend seminars/workshops and performances.
Contact Write, call, fax, or e-mail Ms. Claire Pannell, Managing Director. Phone: 212-219-3910. Fax: 212-219-3911. E-mail: pannell@bway.net. In-person interview recommended. Applicants must submit a cover letter, resume, writing sample. Applications are accepted continuously. World Wide Web: http://www.batterydanceco.com.

BERKELEY REPERTORY THEATRE
2025 Addison Street
Berkeley, California 94704

General Information Professional, nonprofit theater company that produces mainstage, short-run, and school touring productions. Established in 1968. Number of employees: 50. Number of internship applications received each year: 200.
Internships Available ▶ *1 artistic administration/company management intern:* responsibilities include working with the administrative director and company manager, reading and critiquing scripts, observing rehearsals, and assisting in contacting various artists who work with the theater. Candidates should have computer skills, knowledge of field, office skills, oral communication skills, personal interest in the field, plan to pursue career in field, self-motivation, strong interpersonal skills, written communication skills, basic experience in area of application. Open to college juniors, college seniors, recent college graduates, graduate students. ▶ *1 costumes intern:* responsibilities include participating in costume construction, crafts, repairs, and alterations; assisting with makeup, hair, and wigs; working on stock maintenance; and running wardrobe for some major productions. Candidates should have ability to work independently, ability to work with others, knowledge of field, personal interest in the field, plan to pursue career in field, self-motivation, sewing skills. Open to college juniors, college seniors, recent college graduates, graduate students. ▶ *1 development intern:* responsibilities include assisting with fund-raising campaigns and donations, including direct mail, telefunding, special events, and administration. Candidates should have computer skills, knowledge of field, plan to pursue career in field, research skills, self-

Berkeley Repertory Theatre (continued)

motivation, strong interpersonal skills, writing skills, basic experience in area of application. Open to college juniors, college seniors, recent college graduates, graduate students. ▶ *1 education intern:* responsibilities include assisting the planning of school touring production, arranging student matinees, assisting at teacher in-service seminars and teacher artist workshops, and providing adminstrative help on curriculum study guides. Candidates should have computer skills, oral communication skills, plan to pursue career in field, research skills, self-motivation, strong interpersonal skills, written communication skills, basic experience in area of application. Open to college juniors, college seniors, recent college graduates, graduate students. ▶ *1 lighting/electrics intern:* responsibilities include assisting master electrician in all phases of technical electrics production, including maintenance and repair of the lighting system, hanging and focusing, testing special effects, and lighting. Candidates should have ability to work independently, ability to work with others, knowledge of field, personal interest in the field, plan to pursue career in field, self-motivation, basic experience in area of application. Open to college juniors, college seniors, recent college graduates, graduate students. ▶ *1 literary/dramaturgy intern:* responsibilities include reading and critiquing plays under consideration for the season; assisting the literary manager with processing new scripts; occasionally writing and/or editing materials for programs, newsletters, and study guides; maintaining script library; and possibly serving as production dramaturg. Candidates should have ability to work independently, computer skills, editing skills, knowledge of field, plan to pursue career in field, research skills, writing skills, basic experience in area of application. Open to college juniors, college seniors, recent college graduates, graduate students. ▶ *1 marketing/public relations intern:* responsibilities include working with single ticket and subscription campaigns, telemarketing, direct mail projects, and community outreach. Candidates should have computer skills, editing skills, knowledge of field, organizational skills, plan to pursue career in field, research skills, self-motivation, writing skills, basic experience in area of application. Open to college juniors, college seniors, recent college graduates, graduate students. ▶ *1 properties intern:* responsibilities include working in prop shop and procuring or building all properties for a show. Candidates should have ability to work independently, knowledge of field, plan to pursue career in field, research skills, self-motivation, strong interpersonal skills, basic experience in area of application. Open to college juniors, college seniors, recent college graduates, graduate students. ▶ *1 scenic construction intern:* responsibilities include working with woods, metals, and plastics, and acting as builder, welder, and draftsperson. Candidates should have ability to work independently, ability to work with others, analytical skills, knowledge of field, plan to pursue career in field, self-motivation, ability to use craftmaking tools. Open to college juniors, college seniors, recent college graduates, graduate students. ▶ *1 scenic painting intern:* responsibilities include developing craft projects using sculpting, texture, color matching, and a variety of scenic painting techniques; assisting scenic artists with all productions; and assisting scenic designers in dressing sets. Candidates should have ability to work independently, ability to work with others, knowledge of field, plan to pursue career in field, self-motivation, basic experience in area of application. Open to college juniors, college seniors, recent college graduates, graduate students. ▶ *1 sound intern:* responsibilities include working with audio technician on sophisticated sound system designing, recording, and digital sampling and installing; maintaining and repairing the sound system. Candidates should have ability to work independently, ability to work with others, knowledge of field, plan to pursue career in field, research skills, self-motivation, basic experience in area of application. Open to college juniors, college seniors, recent college graduates, graduate students. ▶ *1 stage management intern:* responsibilities include assisting stage managers in all aspects of their work, including rehearsal process, technical rehearsals, and possibly working with a production through the completion of the run. Candidates should have computer skills, knowledge of field, plan to pursue career in field, self-motivation, strong interpersonal skills, strong leadership ability, basic experi-

ence in area of application. Open to college juniors, college seniors, recent college graduates, graduate students. ▶ *1 theatre administration intern:* responsibilities include assisting in contracting artists, house management, and assorted projects as needed. Candidates should have computer skills, office skills, plan to pursue career in field, strong interpersonal skills, strong leadership ability, writing skills. Open to college seniors, recent college graduates, graduate students, law students, career changers. Duration for all positions is August/September to May/June. All positions paid at $300 per month. International applications accepted.

Benefits Formal training, job counseling, names of contacts, on-the-job training, opportunity to attend seminars/workshops, possible full-time employment, willing to act as a professional reference, willing to complete paperwork for educational credit, willing to provide letters of recommendation, housing provided for a limited number of interns.

Contact Write, call, fax, or e-mail Intern Coordinator. Phone: 510-204-8901 Ext. 222. Fax: 510-841-7711. E-mail: brtprod@berkeleyrep.org. In-person interview recommended. Applicants must submit a cover letter, resume, three personal references, three letters of recommendation, 2 writing samples if applying for the literary internship. Application deadline: April 15. World Wide Web: http://www.berkeleyrep.org.

BILINGUAL FOUNDATION OF THE ARTS
421 North Avenue 19
Los Angeles, California 90031

General Information Bilingual Spanish-English theater company that performs plays by Hispanic and Hispanic-American playwrights and also has a touring children's theater company and teen theater. Established in 1973. Number of employees: 14. Number of internship applications received each year: 10.

Internships Available ▶ *1–2 development/marketing interns:* responsibilities include fund-raising and development. Candidates should have computer skills, personal interest in the field, research skills, strong interpersonal skills, strong leadership ability, writing skills. Duration is 3–12 months. ▶ *1–2 marketing interns:* responsibilities include performing data entry, compiling statistical data, preparing audience surveys, reporting survey results, and assisting in preparation of marketing plan. Candidates should have computer skills, office skills, organizational skills, strong interpersonal skills, written communication skills. Duration is flexible. All positions are unpaid. Open to college seniors, recent college graduates, graduate students, career changers, individuals reentering the workforce.

Benefits On-the-job training, possible full-time employment, willing to provide letters of recommendation.

Contact Write, fax, or e-mail Elena Minor, Managing Director. Fax: 213-225-1250. E-mail: bfateatro@aol.com. No phone calls. Applicants must submit a cover letter, resume. Applications are accepted continuously. World Wide Web: http://www.californiaculture.net/bilingual.

BOARSHEAD: MICHIGAN PUBLIC THEATER
425 South Grand Avenue
Lansing, Michigan 48933

General Information Professional theater with a 6-show season and strong education programs devoted to teaching young people the value of creative art through workshops, professional residencies, a touring production, and 2 in-house productions. Established in 1966. Number of employees: 19. Number of internship applications received each year: 25.

Internships Available ▶ *4–5 acting interns:* responsibilities include performing in 1 touring and 2 in-house shows for children, working in all capacities of theater production, participating in some staged readings, possible roles in 2 mainstage productions, and leading workshops as needed. Candidates should have ability to work with others, experience in the field, plan to pursue career in field, strong interpersonal skills, ability and willingness to work "theater hours" on a daily basis. ▶ *1 stage management intern:* responsibilities include stage managing 2 in-house children's shows, tour managing 1 children's tour, stage managing staged readings, assistant stage managing all 6 mainstage shows, and assisting in the shop when needed. Candidates should have ability to work with others, experience in the field, plan to pursue career in field, self-motivation, strong interpersonal skills, ability to work "theater hours" on a daily basis. Duration for all positions is 9 months. All positions paid at $85 per week. Open to college freshmen, college sophomores, college juniors, college seniors, recent college graduates, graduate students. International applications accepted.

Benefits Formal training, free housing, opportunity to attend seminars/workshops, willing to act as a professional reference, willing to complete paperwork for educational credit, willing to provide letters of recommendation, accumulation of Equity points needed for union memberships.

Contact Write, call, or fax Joe A. Babb, Director of Education. Phone: 517-484-7800 Ext. 105. Fax: 517-484-2564. In-person interview required. Applicants must submit a formal organization application, resume, personal reference, two letters of recommendation, audition (held in Lansing, New York, Philadelphia and Chicago every spring). Application deadline: May 31 for spring.

BOND STREET THEATRE COALITION
2 Bond Street
New York, New York 10012

General Information Theater focusing on original work having a physical style, that tours internationally performing socially relevant material with minimal use of language. Established in 1976. Number of employees: 10. Number of internship applications received each year: 100.

Internships Available ▶ *1 acting intern:* responsibilities include acting as understudy for all roles, standing-in for actors as necessary in rehearsals, attending all rehearsals (as possible), learning all skills (musical, physical, etc.). Candidates should have experience in the field, plan to pursue career in field, self-motivation, strong interpersonal skills, strong physical training or capable of physical training (dance, gymnastics, etc.), musical skills are a plus. Open to college freshmen, college sophomores, college juniors, college seniors, recent college graduates, graduate students. ▶ *1 business intern:* responsibilities include helping to design, implement, produce company projects with Artistic Director and Managing Director. Candidates should have ability to work independently, ability to work with others, computer skills, organizational skills, personal interest in the field, writing skills. Open to college freshmen, college sophomores, college juniors, college seniors, recent college graduates, graduate students, career changers, individuals reentering the workforce. ▶ *1 costume design intern.* Candidates should have ability to work independently, knowledge of field, personal interest in the field, research skills, self-motivation, strong interpersonal skills. Open to college freshmen, college sophomores, college juniors, college seniors, recent college graduates, graduate students, career changers, individuals reentering the workforce. ▶ *1 development intern:* responsibilities include identifying and drafting applications for grants, foundations, and awards. Candidates should have ability to work independently, computer skills, personal interest in the field, research skills, self-motivation, writing skills. Open to college freshmen, college sophomores, college juniors, college seniors, recent college graduates, graduate students, career changers, individuals reentering the workforce. ▶ *1 directing intern:* responsibilities include assisting the Director, dramaturgical functions. Candidates should have oral communication skills, personal interest in the field, plan to pursue career in field, research skills, strong interpersonal skills, writing skills. Open to college freshmen, college sophomores, college juniors, college seniors, recent college graduates, graduate students. ▶ *1 general management intern:* responsibilities include general office management and management/coordination of company projects. Candidates should have ability to work independently, computer skills, office skills, organizational skills, self-motivation, written communication skills. Open to college freshmen, college sophomores, college juniors, college seniors, recent college graduates, graduate students, career changers, individuals reentering the workforce. ▶ *1 press/marketing intern:* responsibilities

include primarily marketing productions to festivals and other venues, both in USA and globally, some press work also. Candidates should have computer skills, oral communication skills, personal interest in the field, self-motivation, strong interpersonal skills, writing skills. Open to college freshmen, college sophomores, college juniors, college seniors, recent college graduates, graduate students, career changers, individuals reentering the workforce. ▶ *1 production intern:* responsibilities include all around production assistance. Candidates should have ability to work independently, experience in the field, organizational skills, personal interest in the field, strong interpersonal skills, versatility, a wide range of interests and abilities in the field. Open to college freshmen, college sophomores, college juniors, college seniors, recent college graduates, graduate students, career changers, individuals reentering the workforce. ▶ *1 set design intern.* Candidates should have ability to work independently, knowledge of field, personal interest in the field, research skills, self-motivation, strong interpersonal skills. Open to college freshmen, college sophomores, college juniors, college seniors, recent college graduates, graduate students, career changers, individuals reentering the workforce. ▶ *1 stage management intern.* Candidates should have ability to work independently, ability to work with others, knowledge of field, organizational skills, personal interest in the field, self-motivation. Open to college freshmen, college sophomores, college juniors, college seniors, recent college graduates, graduate students, career changers. Duration for all positions is open. All positions available as unpaid or paid. International applications accepted.

Benefits Formal training, on-the-job training, opportunity to attend seminars/workshops, willing to complete paperwork for educational credit, willing to provide letters of recommendation, possibility of international travel, possible stipend.

Contact Write, call, fax, or e-mail Joanna Sherman, Artistic Director or Michael Mc Guigan, Managing Director. Phone: 212-254-4614. Fax: 212-254-4614. E-mail: bondst@webspan.net. In-person interview recommended. Applicants must submit a cover letter, resume, photo not required but recommended for acting interns. Applications are accepted continuously. World Wide Web: http://www.bondst.org.

CENTER STAGE
700 North Calvert Street
Baltimore, Maryland 21202

General Information Professional regional theater whose artistic goal is to explore a wide range of dramatic literature and production approaches, from fresh visions of the classics to active support for contemporary writing. Established in 1963. Number of employees: 110. Number of internship applications received each year: 100.

Internships Available ▶ *1 communications intern:* responsibilities include managing the student critics program, generating publicity for the theater's educational programs, producing the in-house newsletter, and assisting with publications, press relations, advertising, and promotions. Candidates should have computer skills, knowledge of field, oral communication skills, self-motivation, strong interpersonal skills, writing skills, desktop publishing skills (QuarkXpress on MAC). Open to recent college graduates, college or graduate students willing to take a year off from college. ▶ *1 company management intern:* responsibilities include assisting with all aspects of company and facilities management, including actor, director, and other theater consultants' contacts, travel arrangements, and accommodations; auditions; management of all theater-owned housing units; and attending to the needs and requirements of visiting artists. Candidates should have ability to work with others, computer skills, oral communication skills, organizational skills, self-motivation. Open to recent college graduates, college or graduate students willing to take a year off from school. ▶ *1 costumes/wardrobe intern:* responsibilities include assisting in costume shop with construction, shopping for shows, and maintenance of stock, as well as assisting with running crew and daily wardrobe maintenance as needed. Opportunities to learn more about crafts or wig maintenance are also available. Candidates should have ability to work with others, knowledge of field, oral com-

Center Stage (continued)

munication skills, organizational skills, self-motivation, fast and accurate sewing skills. Open to recent college graduates, career changers, college or graduate students willing to take a year off from school. ▶ *1 development/fund-raising intern:* responsibilities include active participation in all fund-raising activities, including the annual direct mail and telefunding campaigns, special events, funding research, special projects, and day-to-day booking and acknowledgment of gifts. Candidates should have computer skills, office skills, oral communication skills, organizational skills, self-motivation, strong interpersonal skills. Open to recent college graduates, career changers, college or graduate students willing to take a year off from school. ▶ *1 education/theater for a new generation intern:* responsibilities include assisting in scheduling workshops and other programs for middle and high schools, universities, and colleges; facilitating theater artists' school visits; developing educational and outreach activities and materials; and other special projects. Candidates should have college degree in related field, computer skills, oral communication skills, organizational skills, self-motivation, strong interpersonal skills. Open to recent college graduates, college or graduate students willing to take a year off from school. ▶ *1 electrics intern:* responsibilities include assisting electricians with hanging and focusing, creation of special effects, maintenance of lighting equipment, and running of each show. Candidates should have ability to work with others, computer skills, knowledge of field, oral communication skills, self-motivation. Open to recent college graduates, college or graduate students willing to take a year off from school. ▶ *1 marketing intern:* responsibilities include assisting with market research and ticket promotions, coordinating complimentary gift certficiate program, distributing marketing materials, and working with the on-campus sales team. Candidates should have computer skills, knowledge of field, oral communication skills, self-motivation, strong interpersonal skills, written communication skills. Open to recent college graduates, college or graduate students willing to take a year off from college. ▶ *1 properties intern:* responsibilities include assisting in all aspects of procuring and creating props for each production; this includes carpentry, sculpting, metalwork, sewing, upholstery, painting, drawing, and research. Candidates should have ability to work with others, experience in the field, oral communication skills, research skills, self-motivation. Open to recent college graduates, career changers, college or graduate students willing to take a year off from school. ▶ *1 scenic art intern:* responsibilities include assisting the charge painter in the painting and occasional sculpting of all scenic elements. Candidates should have ability to work with others, experience in the field, oral communication skills, personal interest in the field, self-motivation, painting and drawing skills. Open to recent college graduates, career changers, college or graduate students willing to take a year off from school. ▶ *1 scenic carpentry intern:* responsibilities include working in the scene shop on construction of scenery for six mainstage productions. Candidates should have ability to work independently, ability to work with others, experience in the field, oral communication skills, self-motivation, experience with wood construction and standard shop tools. Open to recent college graduates, college and graduate students willing to take a year off from college. ▶ *1 sound intern:* responsibilities include assisting audio engineers in maintaining and installing equipment and with the running of each show. Candidates should have ability to work with others, computer skills, knowledge of field, oral communication skills, self-motivation. Open to recent college graduates, college or graduate students willing to take a year off from school. ▶ *2 stage management interns:* responsibilities include working in all aspects of stage management, with primary duties in the rehearsal hall and as part of the running crew. Candidates should have computer skills, experience in the field, oral communication skills, organizational skills, self-motivation, strong interpersonal skills. Open to recent college graduates, college or graduate students willing to take year off from school. Duration for all positions is seasonal: August/September to May/June. All positions paid at $80 per week.

Benefits Free housing, job counseling, names of contacts, on-the-job training, opportunity to attend seminars/workshops, pos-

sible full-time employment, willing to complete paperwork for educational credit, willing to provide letters of recommendation, assistance with resume preparation, interview assistance, free e-mail.

Contact Write, call, fax, or e-mail Katharyn Davies, Internship Coordinator. Phone: 410-685-3200 Ext. 330. Fax: 410-539-3912. E-mail: kdavies@centerstage.org. Telephone interview required. Applicants must submit a formal organization application, cover letter, resume, two letters of recommendation, portfolio or writing sample may be required. Applications are accepted continuously. World Wide Web: http://www.centerstage.org.

CENTER THEATER ENSEMBLE AND THE TRAINING CENTER FOR THE WORKING ACTOR, DIRECTOR, AND PLAYWRIGHT
1346 West Devon Avenue
Chicago, Illinois 60660

General Information Not-for-profit Equity theater and training center for actors, directors, and playwrights. Established in 1984. Number of employees: 12. Number of internship applications received each year: 30.

Internships Available ▶ *4 acting interns:* responsibilities include working on administrative tasks and understudying roles. Candidates should have oral communication skills, organizational skills, plan to pursue career in field, self-motivation, strong interpersonal skills, strong leadership ability. ▶ *2 administrative interns:* responsibilities include performing administrative tasks. Candidates should have ability to work independently, office skills, personal interest in the field, self-motivation, strong interpersonal skills, written communication skills. ▶ *4 directing interns:* responsibilities include working on administrative tasks and assisting with directing. Candidates should have ability to work independently, oral communication skills, personal interest in the field, self-motivation, strong interpersonal skills, strong leadership ability. ▶ *2 literary interns:* responsibilities include reading and coordinating submitted plays. Candidates should have ability to work independently, organizational skills, personal interest in the field, research skills, writing skills. ▶ *2 marketing interns:* responsibilities include assisting director. Candidates should have ability to work with others, knowledge of field, organizational skills, self-motivation, writing skills. ▶ *4 technical interns:* responsibilities include assisting designers and stage managers. Candidates should have knowledge of field, organizational skills, personal interest in the field, self-motivation, strong interpersonal skills, strong leadership ability. Duration for all positions is 3–6 months. All positions are unpaid. Open to recent high school graduates, college freshmen, college sophomores, college juniors, college seniors, recent college graduates, graduate students, law students, career changers, individuals reentering the workforce.

Benefits Formal training, job counseling, names of contacts, opportunity to attend seminars/workshops, possible full-time employment, willing to act as a professional reference, willing to complete paperwork for educational credit, willing to provide letters of recommendation.

Contact Write or call Dale Calandra, Intern Coordinator. Phone: 773-508-0200. In-person interview required. Applicants must submit a formal organization application, cover letter, two letters of recommendation. Applications are accepted continuously.

CHEN AND DANCERS
70 Mulberry Street, 2nd Floor
New York, New York 10013

General Information Modern Asian-American dance company that emphasizes education and community activities. Established in 1978. Number of employees: 6. Number of internship applications received each year: 20.

Internships Available ▶ *1–2 administrative assistants:* responsibilities include performing a broad range of office duties. Candidates should have computer skills, personal interest in the field, writing skills. Position available as unpaid or paid. ▶ *1–2 maintenance interns:* responsibilities include painting, refinishing wood benches, performing general maintenance, and production assistance. Unpaid. Duration for all positions is flexible. Open to high school students, high school seniors, recent high school graduates, college freshmen, college sophomores, college juniors, college seniors, recent college graduates, graduate students, law students, career changers, individuals reentering the workforce. International applications accepted.

Benefits Formal training, on-the-job training, willing to complete paperwork for educational credit, willing to provide letters of recommendation.

Contact Write or e-mail Dian Dong, Associate Director. E-mail: info@htchendance.org. No phone calls. In-person interview required. Applicants must submit a cover letter, resume, writing sample, personal reference. Applications are accepted continuously. World Wide Web: http://www.htchendance.org.

THE CHILDREN'S THEATRE COMPANY
2400 Third Avenue South
Minneapolis, Minnesota 55404

General Information North America's largest professional theater for young people and adults dedicated to producing excellence in theater for audiences in the Twin Cities and nationwide. Established in 1964. Number of employees: 90. Number of internship applications received each year: 100.

Internships Available ▶ *3–4 costume construction interns.* Candidates should have ability to work independently, ability to work with others, declared college major in field, experience in the field, oral communication skills, organizational skills. Duration is 3 months minimum. Unpaid. Open to college juniors, college seniors, recent college graduates, graduate students. ▶ *1–2 development interns.* Candidates should have ability to work independently, computer skills, knowledge of field, organizational skills, research skills, written communication skills. Duration is 3 months minimum. Unpaid. Open to college juniors, college seniors, recent college graduates, graduate students. ▶ *2–6 directing interns.* Candidates should have ability to work with others, analytical skills, experience in the field, organizational skills. Duration is 3 months. Unpaid. Open to college seniors, recent college graduates, graduate students. ▶ *Education outreach interns.* Candidates should have ability to work with others, declared college major in field, experience in the field, organizational skills, plan to pursue career in field, strong leadership ability. Duration is 3 months. Unpaid. Open to college seniors, recent college graduates, graduate students. ▶ *2–3 lighting and sound interns:* responsibilities include duties based on applicant's abilities and department needs. Candidates should have ability to work independently, ability to work with others, experience in the field, oral communication skills, organizational skills, plan to pursue career in field. Duration is 3 months minimum. Unpaid. Open to college juniors, college seniors, recent college graduates, graduate students. ▶ *1–2 marketing interns.* Candidates should have computer skills, editing skills, knowledge of field, office skills, organizational skills, written communication skills. Duration is 3 months minimum. Unpaid. Open to college juniors, college seniors, recent college graduates, graduate students. ▶ *6–8 performing apprentices:* responsibilities include acting in productions, classes, and studio theater production. Candidates should have college courses in field, college degree in related field, oral communication skills, plan to pursue career in field, self-motivation, strong interpersonal skills. Duration is 11 months. stipend. Open to college juniors, college seniors, recent college graduates, graduate students. ▶ *1 properties apprentice.* Candidates should have ability to work independently, college degree in related field, declared college major in field, experience in the field, oral communication skills, plan to pursue career in field. Duration is 3 months minimum. stipend. Open to college seniors, recent college graduates, graduate students. ▶ *2–3 properties construction interns.* Candidates should have ability to work independently, declared college major in field, experience in the field, oral communication skills, plan to pursue career in field, self-motivation. Duration is 3 months minimum. Unpaid. Open to college juniors, college seniors, recent college graduates, graduate students. ▶ *1 stage management apprentice:* responsibilities include assisting with preproduction and rehearsals and run of 3–4 mainstage and/or tour productions and stage managing 1–3 studio theater projects. Candidates should have

computer skills, declared college major in field, experience in the field, organizational skills, plan to pursue career in field, strong leadership ability. Duration is 8–10 weeks. stipend. Open to college juniors, college seniors, recent college graduates, graduate students. ▶ *4–5 stage management interns.* Candidates should have ability to work with others, experience in the field, office skills, organizational skills, plan to pursue career in field, strong leadership ability. Duration is 3 months minimum. Unpaid. Open to college juniors, college seniors, recent college graduates, graduate students.

Benefits Formal training, names of contacts, possible full-time employment, willing to complete paperwork for educational credit, willing to provide letters of recommendation.

Contact Write, call, fax, or e-mail Ms. Deb Pearson, Production Associate. Phone: 612-874-0500. Fax: 612-874-8119. E-mail: 102412. 3307@compuserve.com. In-person interview recommended. Applicants must submit a cover letter, resume, portfolio, three letters of recommendation. Applications are accepted continuously. World Wide Web: http://www.childrenstheatre.com.

CHILD'S PLAY TOURING THEATRE
2518 West Armitage Street
Chicago, Illinois 60647

General Information Professional touring children's theater that performs stories and poems written by children and adapted by professional actors and musicians. Established in 1978. Number of employees: 14. Number of internship applications received each year: 30.

Internships Available ▶ *1–3 administrative/public relations interns:* responsibilities include producing newsletter and assisting general manager and office manager. Candidates should have ability to work with others, computer skills, office skills, oral communication skills, research skills, written communication skills. ▶ *1–3 assistants to executive director/producer:* responsibilities include all aspects of running a theater, including board development, fundraising, and marketing. Candidates should have computer skills, oral communication skills, organizational skills. ▶ *1–3 development interns:* responsibilities include researching funding sources and assisting with proposal preparation. Candidates should have computer skills, office skills, oral communication skills, research skills, writing skills. ▶ *1–3 millenium project interns:* responsibilities include overseeing various aspects of the millenium project, including coordinating events, working with other companies or groups, and production work. Candidates should have computer skills, oral communication skills, organizational skills, writing skills. ▶ *3 story readers/coordinators:* responsibilities include reading, categorizing, culling, filing young authors' works, contacting young authors, and helping to script stories. Candidates should have computer skills, office skills, oral communication skills, organizational skills, personal interest in the field, written communication skills. ▶ *2–6 technical interns:* responsibilities include assisting production manager with sets, props, and costumes. Candidates should have ability to work with others, knowledge of field, personal interest in the field, self-motivation. Duration for all positions is flexible. All positions available as unpaid or at an occasional stipend. Open to anyone interested. International applications accepted.

Benefits Names of contacts, opportunity to attend seminars/workshops, possible full-time employment, willing to complete paperwork for educational credit, willing to provide letters of recommendation, reimbursement of work-related travel expenses, lunch allowance (for those who work 20 hours or more per week).

Contact Write, call, fax, or e-mail Ms. June Podagrosi, Executive Producer. Phone: 773-235-8911. Fax: 773-235-5478. E-mail: cptt@sprynet.com. In-person interview recommended. Applicants must submit a formal organization application, resume, 1 or 2 writing samples. Application deadline: May 30 for summer, August 15 for fall, November 30 for spring.

CINCINNATI PLAYHOUSE IN THE PARK
Box 6537
Cincinnati, Ohio 45206

General Information Live theater that presents professional theater productions to the Cincinnati region; the Playhouse is a member of the League of Regional Theaters. Established in 1960. Number of employees: 60. Number of internship applications received each year: 150.
Internships Available ▶ *Administration interns.* ▶ *Limited directing interns.* ▶ *Production interns.* ▶ *Stage management interns.* Duration for all positions is flexible. All positions available as unpaid or paid. Open to college freshmen, college sophomores, college juniors, college seniors, recent college graduates, graduate students.
Benefits Possible full-time employment, willing to complete paperwork for educational credit, willing to provide letters of recommendation.
Contact Write, call, or fax Internship Coordinator. Phone: 513-345-2242. Fax: 513-345-2254. In-person interview required. Applicants must submit a cover letter, resume. Applications are accepted continuously. World Wide Web: http://www.cincyplay.com.

CIRCA '21 DINNER PLAYHOUSE
1828 Third Avenue
Rock Island, Illinois 61201

General Information Theater that produces a year-round season of musicals, modern comedies, a series of children's plays, and special guest artist concerts as well as national tours. Established in 1977. Number of employees: 65. Number of internship applications received each year: 15.
Internships Available ▶ *1–2 public relations interns:* responsibilities include writing copy for ads and press releases and creating flyers, promotional materials, and mailing lists; assisting with group sales. Candidates should have college courses in field, computer skills, personal interest in the field, self-motivation, strong interpersonal skills, written communication skills, artistic skills helpful. Duration is flexible. Open to college juniors, college seniors, recent college graduates. ▶ *1 stage management intern:* responsibilities include assisting resident stage manager with rehearsal duties and functioning as a running crew member. Candidates should have declared college major in field, experience in the field, organizational skills, personal interest in the field, strong interpersonal skills, strong leadership ability. Duration is linked to the production schedule. Open to college juniors, college seniors, recent college graduates, graduate students. ▶ *1–2 technical interns:* responsibilities include assisting in building of scenery and/or painting, maintaining the show, and functioning as a running crew member. Candidates should have ability to work independently, ability to work with others, college courses in field, experience in the field, organizational skills, technical skills. Duration is linked to the production schedule. Open to college sophomores, college juniors, college seniors, recent college graduates. ▶ *1 ticket office intern:* responsibilities include working in ticket sales (individual and group) and handling financial reconciliation of sales. Candidates should have computer skills, oral communication skills, organizational skills, personal interest in the field, strong interpersonal skills. Duration is 6 to 12 weeks or more. Open to college sophomores, college juniors, college seniors, recent college graduates. All positions are unpaid. International applications accepted.
Benefits Job counseling, names of contacts, on-the-job training, possible full-time employment, tuition assistance, willing to act as a professional reference, willing to complete paperwork for educational credit, willing to provide letters of recommendation.
Contact Write Mr. Dennis Hitchcock, Producer. No phone calls. In-person interview recommended. Applicants must submit a cover letter, resume, two letters of recommendation. Applications are accepted continuously. World Wide Web: http://www.circa21.com.

CLASSIC STAGE COMPANY
136 East 13th Street
New York, New York 10003

General Information Nonprofit 171-seat theater dedicated to the reimagination of classics for an American audience; producing a season of 3 plays committed to new directorial or authorial perspectives on the classics. Established in 1967. Number of employees: 54. Number of internship applications received each year: 25.
Internships Available ▶ *2 audience services interns:* responsibilities include assisting in member solicitation, tracking, and related clerical work. Candidates should have ability to work with others, experience in the field, office skills, oral communication skills, strong interpersonal skills, customer service experience preferred. Duration is 6–8 weeks. Position available as unpaid or paid. Open to college seniors, recent college graduates, graduate students. ▶ *2 literary/dramaturgy interns:* responsibilities include reading plays, producing projects, and dramaturgical work. Candidates should have ability to work independently, analytical skills, knowledge of field, plan to pursue career in field, written communication skills. Duration is 1 semester. Unpaid. Open to college seniors, recent college graduates, graduate students. ▶ *3 marketing/development interns:* responsibilities include assisting in research, grant compilation, and related clerical work. Candidates should have ability to work independently, analytical skills, knowledge of field, research skills, writing skills. Duration is 1 semester. Unpaid. Open to college seniors, recent college graduates, graduate students. ▶ *4 production/management interns:* responsibilities include assisting with budget research, acquisition of production needs, actual production work, company and facilities management. Candidates should have ability to work with others, experience in the field, office skills, oral communication skills, organizational skills, self-motivation. Duration is 1 semester. Unpaid. Open to college freshmen, college sophomores, college juniors, college seniors, recent college graduates, graduate students.
Benefits Formal training, job counseling, names of contacts, opportunity to attend seminars/workshops, possible full-time employment, willing to act as a professional reference, willing to complete paperwork for educational credit, willing to provide letters of recommendation, complimentary tickets to off-Broadway productions.
Contact Write or fax Mr. Jason Loewith, Internship Coordinator. Fax: 212-477-7504. No phone calls. In-person interview recommended. Applicants must submit a cover letter, resume. Applications are accepted continuously.

THE CLEVELAND PLAY HOUSE
8500 Euclid Avenue
Cleveland, Ohio 44106

General Information Theater dedicated to the presentation of new and classical plays. Established in 1915. Number of employees: 60. Number of internship applications received each year: 50.
Internships Available ▶ *1–8 assistant directors:* responsibilities include assisting directors during rehearsals. Duration is 6–8 weeks. ▶ *1 business intern:* responsibilities include helping in all areas of business office. Duration is 8–10 weeks. ▶ *2 development interns:* responsibilities include grant writing, telemarketing, and fund-raising. Duration is 2–12 months. ▶ *2 literary interns:* responsibilities include reading and evaluating scripts and assisting dramaturg. Duration is 6 weeks to 9 months. ▶ *4 marketing interns:* responsibilities include assisting in all aspects of marketing. Duration is 2–12 months. ▶ *1 playwriting intern:* responsibilities include assisting literary manager. Duration is 6 weeks to 9 months. ▶ *2 production assistants:* responsibilities include assisting stage managers in rehearsal and performance. Duration is 6 weeks to 9 months. ▶ *6 shop interns:* responsibilities include working with costumes, lights, sound, and props. Duration is 2–9 months. All positions are unpaid. Open to recent college graduates, graduate students.

Benefits Job counseling, possible full-time employment, willing to complete paperwork for educational credit, willing to provide letters of recommendation.
Contact Write, call, fax, or e-mail Mr. David Colacci, Director of Apprentice Program. Phone: 216-795-7000 Ext. 205. Fax: 216-795-7005. E-mail: dchermes@aol.com. Applicants must submit a cover letter, resume, photo. Applications are accepted continuously. World Wide Web: http://www.cleveplayhouse.org.

COLLEGE LIGHT OPERA COMPANY
Highfield Theatre, PO Drawer 906
Falmouth, Massachusetts 02541

General Information Summer stock music theater serving as training ground for all aspects of theater performance and management. Established in 1969. Number of employees: 80. Number of internship applications received each year: 400.
Internships Available ▶ *1 assistant business manager.* Candidates should have ability to work independently, computer skills, experience in the field, office skills, oral communication skills, writing skills. Duration is June 5 to August 30. $1,000 per duration of internship. Open to college freshmen, college sophomores, college juniors, college seniors, recent college graduates. ▶ *2 box office interns:* responsibilities include managing box office. Candidates should have ability to work independently, ability to work with others, experience in the field, office skills, oral communication skills, written communication skills. Duration is June 5 to August 30. $1,000 per duration of internship. Open to high school seniors, recent high school graduates, college freshmen, college sophomores, college juniors, college seniors, graduate students. ▶ *1 cook:* responsibilities include menu planning, food buying and cooking for 80 people in co-op setting. Candidates should have ability to work with others, knowledge of field, organizational skills, personal interest in the field, strong leadership ability. Duration is June 5 to August 30. $3,500–$4,000 per duration of internship. Open to college freshmen, college sophomores, college juniors, college seniors, recent college graduates, career changers, individuals reentering the workforce. ▶ *6 costume crew interns:* responsibilities include assisting with making costumes. Candidates should have ability to work independently, ability to work with others, college courses in field, knowledge of field. Duration is June 5 to August 30. $1,000 per duration of internship. Open to high school seniors, recent high school graduates, college freshmen, college sophomores, college juniors, college seniors, recent college graduates, graduate students. ▶ *18 orchestra musicians:* responsibilities include performing in 9 musicals. Candidates should have ability to work with others, college courses in field, knowledge of field, experience in orchestra work. Duration is June 15 to August 30. $500 per duration of internship. Open to high school seniors, recent high school graduates, college freshmen, college sophomores, college juniors, college seniors, recent college graduates, graduate students. ▶ *1 publicity director.* Candidates should have ability to work independently, experience in the field, oral communication skills, self-motivation, writing skills. Duration is June 5 to August 30. $1,000 per duration of internship. Open to college freshmen, college sophomores, college juniors, college seniors, recent college graduates. ▶ *32 singers/actors:* responsibilities include performing in 9 musicals. Candidates should have ability to work with others, experience in the field, personal interest in the field, self-motivation, strong singing/acting skills. Duration is June 15 to August 30. Unpaid. Open to college freshmen, college sophomores, college juniors, college seniors, recent college graduates, graduate students. ▶ *6 stage crew interns:* responsibilities include assisting with building scenery. Candidates should have ability to work independently, ability to work with others, college courses in field, knowledge of field, experience in set construction, set painting, and lighting. Duration is June 5 to August 30. $1,000 per duration of internship. Open to high school seniors, recent high school graduates, college freshmen, college sophomores, college juniors, college seniors, recent college graduates. International applications accepted.
Benefits Formal training, free housing, free meals, job counseling, names of contacts, on-the-job training, willing to act as a

professional reference, willing to complete paperwork for educational credit, willing to provide letters of recommendation.
Contact Write, call, fax, or e-mail Mr. Robert A. Haslun, Producer, 162 South Cedar Street, Oberlin, Ohio 44074. Phone: 440-774-8485. Fax: 440-775-8642. E-mail: bob.haslun@oberlin.edu. Applicants must submit a formal organization application, resume, two letters of recommendation. Application deadline: March 15 for summer; continuous after March 15 if openings remain. World Wide Web: http://www.capecod.net/cloc.

CONNECTICUT OPERA ASSOCIATION, INC.
226 Farmington Avenue
Hartford, Connecticut 06105

General Information 56-year-old regional opera company offering quality productions, guest artists from both American and international companies, and a resident ensemble. Established in 1942. Number of employees: 8.
Internships Available ▶ *1 development intern:* responsibilities include assisting with fund-raising. Candidates should have some fund-raising experience. ▶ *1–2 marketing interns:* responsibilities include assisting with marketing, sales, and public relations. Candidates should have some marketing experience. ▶ *1 production intern:* responsibilities include assisting with mainstage and resident touring productions. Candidates should have some experience in production. Duration for all positions is flexible. All positions are unpaid. Open to high school students, high school seniors, recent high school graduates, college freshmen, college sophomores, college juniors, college seniors, recent college graduates, graduate students, law students, career changers, individuals reentering the workforce.
Benefits Formal training, job counseling, names of contacts, willing to complete paperwork for educational credit, willing to provide letters of recommendation, complimentary tickets to Connecticut Opera productions.
Contact Write, call, or fax Production Manager. Phone: 860-527-0713. Fax: 860-293-1715. In-person interview required. Applicants must submit a cover letter, resume. Applications are accepted continuously. World Wide Web: http://www.connecticutopera.org.

CORTLAND REPERTORY THEATRE, INC.
37 Franklin Street
Cortland, New York 13045

General Information Professional summer stock theater whose mission is to bring affordable cultural opportunities to a primarily rural area. Established in 1972. Number of employees: 2. Number of internship applications received each year: 250.
Internships Available ▶ *1–3 box office interns:* responsibilities include cashier and phone work, working walk-up box office, selling tickets, and preparing daily reconciliations. Candidates should have analytical skills, office skills, organizational skills, self-motivation, strong interpersonal skills, theater background helpful. Duration is 14 weeks. ▶ *6–7 performing interns:* responsibilities include acting in productions and doing shop duties. Candidates should have ability to work with others, college courses in field, knowledge of field, personal interest in the field, self-motivation. Duration is up to 13 weeks. ▶ *2–3 production interns:* responsibilities include performing props, scenery, costume, light, and sound duties and running crews. Candidates should have ability to work with others, college courses in field, knowledge of field, oral communication skills, self-motivation. Duration is up to 14 weeks. All positions paid at $80 per week. International applications accepted.
Benefits Formal training, free housing, on-the-job training, willing to complete paperwork for educational credit.
Contact Write, fax, or e-mail William V. Morris, Producing Director. Fax: 607-753-0047. E-mail: crt@clarityconnect.com. No phone calls. Applicants must submit a cover letter, resume. Application deadline: April 1 for summer. World Wide Web: http://www.cortlandrep.org.

COURT THEATRE (THE PROFESSIONAL THEATRE AT THE UNIVERSITY OF CHICAGO)
5535 South Ellis Avenue
Chicago, Illinois 60637

General Information Professional residence Equity theater company located on the University of Chicago campus. Established in 1954. Number of employees: 20.

Internships Available ▶ *1 arts management intern:* responsibilities include assisting development, marketing, or business staff. Candidates should have college courses in field, experience in the field, oral communication skills, personal interest in the field, plan to pursue career in field, self-motivation, strong interpersonal skills, written communication skills. Duration is flexible. Open to college freshmen, college sophomores, college juniors, college seniors, graduate students. ▶ *1 casting intern:* responsibilities include developing schedules, assisting in daily communications and general operations, and assisting with organizational research. Candidates should have knowledge of field, oral communication skills, personal interest in the field, plan to pursue career in field, self-motivation, written communication skills. Duration is flexible. Open to college freshmen, college sophomores, college juniors, college seniors, recent college graduates. ▶ *1 costume design intern:* responsibilities include researching, shopping for, and coordinating costume and prop elements. Candidates should have experience in the field, knowledge of field. Duration is 4 months. Open to college juniors, college seniors, graduate students. ▶ *1 directing intern:* responsibilities include researching materials, note-taking during rehearsals, and participating in production meetings. Candidates should have ability to work with others, experience in the field, oral communication skills, plan to pursue career in field, research skills, written communication skills. Duration is 6–14 weeks. Open to graduate students. ▶ *1–3 dramaturgy interns:* responsibilities include researching and writing playnotes. Candidates should have computer skills, editing skills, research skills, writing skills. Duration is 6–14 weeks. Open to college juniors, college seniors, graduate students. ▶ *1–3 education interns:* responsibilities include overseeing high school matinee program. Candidates should have college courses in field, declared college major in field, plan to pursue career in field, strong interpersonal skills, ability to work with children. Duration is 8–10 weeks. ▶ *1–3 literary interns:* responsibilities include reading plays, reviews, and theater publications. Candidates should have experience in the field, knowledge of field, oral communication skills, research skills, writing skills. ▶ *1–3 production assistants:* responsibilities include developing projects with various staff members. Candidates should have experience in the field, knowledge of field, personal interest in the field, plan to pursue career in field. Open to college juniors, college seniors, graduate students. ▶ *1 production management intern:* responsibilities include processing new actor pictures and resumes, maintaining files, and setting up auditions. Candidates should have experience in the field, knowledge of field, plan to pursue career in field, self-motivation. Duration is flexible. Open to college juniors, college seniors, recent college graduates, graduate students. ▶ *1–3 scenic design interns:* responsibilities include drafting, researching, and developing scale models; attending production meetings; and assisting in technical rehearsals. Candidates should have experience in the field, knowledge of field, plan to pursue career in field. Duration is 6–14 weeks. Open to college juniors, college seniors, graduate students. ▶ *2 stage management interns:* responsibilities include working directly with stage manager and assistant stage manager in all areas of preparation and the rehearsal process, including the technical rehearsal; may lead to a paid position. Candidates should have computer skills, knowledge of field, office skills, organizational skills, personal interest in the field, self-motivation. Duration is 6–14 weeks. Open to college seniors, recent college graduates, graduate students. All positions are unpaid.

Benefits On-the-job training, opportunity to attend seminars/workshops, possible full-time employment, willing to act as a professional reference, willing to complete paperwork for educational credit, willing to provide letters of recommendation.

Contact Write Kari Strugala, Intern Coordinator. No phone calls. In-person interview recommended. Applicants must submit a cover letter, resume, two personal references, two letters of recommendation. Applications are accepted continuously.

CREEDE REPERTORY THEATRE
124 North Main Street
Creede, Colorado 81130

General Information Nonprofit theater striving to raise standards of practice, to make the performing arts more accessible to the public, and to promote greater understanding of the performing arts. Established in 1966. Number of employees: 36. Number of internship applications received each year: 500.

Internships Available ▶ *1 business intern:* responsibilities include working with bookkeeping and in advertising, payroll, fundraising, box office, and front-of-house duties. Candidates should have computer skills, office skills, oral communication skills, organizational skills, personal interest in the field, self-motivation, strong interpersonal skills, strong leadership ability, written communication skills. Duration is 4 months. ▶ *3 costume interns:* responsibilities include sewing and maintaining costumes and dressing actors. Candidates should have ability to work independently, personal interest in the field, self-motivation, strong interpersonal skills. Duration is late May to late August. Open to recent high school graduates, college freshmen, college sophomores, college juniors, college seniors, recent college graduates, graduate students, law students, career changers, individuals reentering the workforce. ▶ *1 light/sound intern:* responsibilities include assisting technical director in hanging and changing light plans, and designing and assisting lighting designer during shows and set changeovers. Candidates should have ability to work independently, ability to work with others, analytical skills, experience in the field, knowledge of field, organizational skills, personal interest in the field, self-motivation. Duration is late May to late August. Open to recent high school graduates, college freshmen, college sophomores, college juniors, college seniors, recent college graduates, graduate students, law students, career changers, individuals reentering the workforce. ▶ *2–3 shop/set interns:* responsibilities include building, painting, and assembling sets; conducting set changeovers and backstage scene changes; and running shows by performing crew work. Candidates should have personal interest in the field, self-motivation, strong interpersonal skills. Duration is late May to late August. Open to recent high school graduates, college freshmen, college sophomores, college juniors, college seniors, recent college graduates, graduate students, law students, career changers, individuals reentering the workforce. ▶ *1 stage management intern:* responsibilities include assisting stage manager, functioning as stage manager for 1 show, scheduling, typing, and working backstage. Candidates should have ability to work independently, experience in the field, oral communication skills, organizational skills, self-motivation, strong interpersonal skills, strong leadership ability, written communication skills. Duration is late May to late August. Open to recent high school graduates, college freshmen, college sophomores, college juniors, college seniors, recent college graduates, graduate students, law students, career changers, individuals reentering the workforce. All positions paid at $130 per week.

Benefits Free housing, names of contacts, on-the-job training, possible full-time employment, willing to act as a professional reference, willing to complete paperwork for educational credit, willing to provide letters of recommendation.

Contact Write, call, fax, or e-mail Mr. Richard Baxter, Chief Executive Officer. Phone: 719-658-2540. Fax: 719-658-2343. E-mail: crt@creederep.com. In-person interview recommended. Applicants must submit a cover letter, resume, three personal references. Application deadline: March 1 for summer. World Wide Web: http://www.creederep.com.

DALLAS THEATER CENTER
3636 Turtle Creek Boulevard
Dallas, Texas 75219

General Information Theater committed to supporting the work of the most exciting, daring, and uncompromising artists as well as serving the community through the plays presented and special programs offered. Established in 1959. Number of employees: 75. Number of internship applications received each year: 100.

Internships Available ▶ *1–3 arts administrators:* responsibilities include working in the areas of fund-raising, marketing, development, and general management; assisting department heads in daily operations, special events, and planning. Candidates should have ability to work independently, analytical skills, computer skills, editing skills, office skills, oral communication skills, organizational skills, personal interest in the field, self-motivation, strong interpersonal skills, written communication skills. minimum wage. Open to college freshmen, college sophomores, college juniors, college seniors, recent college graduates, graduate students. ▶ *1 company manager:* responsibilities include assisting in all areas required to maintain efficient company operations, including booking travel, housing, and hospitality arrangements for visiting artists. Candidates should have ability to work independently, computer skills, oral communication skills, organizational skills, personal interest in the field, self-motivation, strong interpersonal skills, written communication skills. minimum wage. Open to college freshmen, college sophomores, college juniors, college seniors, recent college graduates, graduate students. ▶ *2 director/literary managers:* responsibilities include assisting mainstage productions, directing own workshop productions, reading new scripts, gathering and organizing research for mainstage productions, attending local productions, maintaining correspondence with playwrights, and providing administrative assistance. Candidates should have ability to work independently, computer skills, knowledge of field, office skills, oral communication skills, organizational skills, plan to pursue career in field, research skills, self-motivation, strong interpersonal skills, strong leadership ability, written communication skills. minimum wage. Open to college juniors, college seniors, recent college graduates, graduate students. ▶ *6–8 production interns:* responsibilities include assisting with props, costumes, electric, sound, carpentry, scenic art, wardrobe, and stage operations. Candidates should have ability to work independently, ability to work with others, college courses in field, experience in the field, plan to pursue career in field, self-motivation. minimum wage. Open to college freshmen, college sophomores, college juniors, college seniors, recent college graduates, graduate students. ▶ *1 production management intern:* responsibilities include assisting producing manager in overseeing all production related concerns including scheduling and the facilitation of communication between production departments and visiting artists. Candidates should have ability to work independently, ability to work with others, computer skills, office skills, oral communication skills, organizational skills, personal interest in the field, self-motivation. minimum wage. Open to college juniors, college seniors, recent college graduates, graduate students. ▶ *2 stage managers:* responsibilities include working with Equity stage managers in all aspects of their work and being involved in production from the beginning of the rehearsal process through the run of mainstage productions. Candidates should have ability to work independently, ability to work with others, computer skills, editing skills, experience in the field, oral communication skills, organizational skills, self-motivation, strong leadership ability. minimum wage. Open to college freshmen, college sophomores, college juniors, college seniors, recent college graduates, graduate students. Duration for all positions is August to May. International applications accepted.

Benefits On-the-job training, opportunity to attend seminars/workshops, possible full-time employment, willing to act as a professional reference, willing to complete paperwork for educational credit, willing to provide letters of recommendation.

Contact Write, call, or fax Lisa Lawrence Holland, Director, Internship Program. Phone: 214-526-8210 Ext. 281. Fax: 214-521-7666. Applicants must submit a formal organization application, cover letter, resume, three letters of recommendation. Application deadline: May 28 for all positions.

DENVER CENTER THEATRE COMPANY
1050 13th Street
Denver, Colorado 80204

General Information Nonprofit regional theater producing 12 productions in four theaters and tour productions locally, nationally, and internationally. Established in 1978. Number of employees: 400. Unit of Denver Center for the Performing Arts, Denver, Colorado. Number of internship applications received each year: 100.

Internships Available ▶ *1–2 administration/marketing interns:* responsibilities include assisting in various aspects of marketing and communication for nonprofit regional theater. Candidates should have ability to work independently, oral communication skills, personal interest in the field, self-motivation, strong interpersonal skills, written communication skills. Position available as unpaid or paid. Open to college seniors, recent college graduates, graduate students, law students. ▶ *1–2 costume/wigs/wardrobe interns:* responsibilities include running crew assignment involving costume and accessories maintenance and quick change techniques. Candidates should have ability to work with others, personal interest in the field. Position available as unpaid or paid. Open to high school seniors, recent high school graduates, college freshmen, college sophomores, college juniors, college seniors, recent college graduates, graduate students, law students, career changers, individuals reentering the workforce. ▶ *1 lighting design intern:* responsibilities include working with resident and guest professional staff members during the season with a focus on drafting, equipment maintenance, electrics, special effects, and special projects. Candidates should have ability to work with others, knowledge of field, personal interest in the field, self-motivation. Position available as unpaid or paid. Open to college seniors, recent college graduates, graduate students. ▶ *1 literary intern:* responsibilities include participating in the management and presentation of readings, corresponding with playwrights and agents, cataloguing submitted scripts, reading and evaluating new works, and providing dramaturgical research. Candidates should have ability to work independently, ability to work with others, knowledge of field, self-motivation, written communication skills. Position available as unpaid or paid. Open to college seniors, recent college graduates, graduate students, law students, individuals reentering the workforce. ▶ *1 properties intern:* responsibilities include using techniques in welding, vacuforming plastics, painting, carving, furniture construction and upholstery, and other crafts. Candidates should have ability to work with others, knowledge of field, personal interest in the field. Position available as unpaid or paid. Open to college juniors, college seniors, recent college graduates, graduate students. ▶ *1 scene design intern:* responsibilities include drafting, model building, design and technical research in scenic and prop areas, and scene painting. Candidates should have experience in the field, knowledge of field, oral communication skills, plan to pursue career in field, self-motivation, strong interpersonal skills. Duration is 8–10 weeks. Position available as unpaid or paid. Open to college juniors, college seniors, recent college graduates, graduate students. ▶ *1 scene painting intern:* responsibilities include using traditional methods and innovative techniques, assisting the DCTC scenic artists in painting and finishing scenery and technical effects for productions. Candidates should have ability to work with others, knowledge of field, personal interest in the field. Position available as unpaid or paid. Open to high school seniors, recent high school graduates, college juniors, college seniors, recent college graduates, graduate students, career changers, individuals reentering the workforce. ▶ *1 sound intern:* responsibilities include working closely with artistic staff in such areas as live recording sessions, recorded music and effects, and the mixing of vocals and sound during a performance. Candidates should have ability to work with others, knowledge of field, personal interest in the field. Position available as unpaid or paid. Open to college seniors, recent college graduates, graduate students. ▶ *1–3 stage management/production interns:* responsibilities include organizing daily schedules, conducting rehearsals, attending design and production meetings, and focusing on the detail work surrounding productions. Candidates should have ability to work independently, ability to

Denver Center Theatre Company (continued)

work with others, knowledge of field, oral communication skills, plan to pursue career in field, self-motivation. Unpaid. Open to college freshmen, college sophomores, college juniors, college seniors, recent college graduates, graduate students, law students, career changers. ▶ *1 technical production intern:* responsibilities include working in a master/apprentice relationship with the DCTC Technical Director , learning a variety of disciplines, ranging from fiscal management to high tech invention of scenic solutions. Candidates should have ability to work independently, ability to work with others, college courses in field, knowledge of field, organizational skills, personal interest in the field, plan to pursue career in field. Position available as unpaid or paid. Open to college seniors, recent college graduates, graduate students. International applications accepted.
Benefits Formal training, names of contacts, on-the-job training, possible full-time employment, willing to complete paperwork for educational credit, willing to provide letters of recommendation, limited stipends may be available in some departments.
Contact Write, call, fax, or e-mail Dan McNeil, Technical Director, 1101 13th Street, Denver, Colorado 80204. Phone: 303-446-4860. Fax: 303-573-0432. E-mail: dmcneil@star.dcpa.org. Applicants must submit a cover letter, resume. Applications are accepted continuously. World Wide Web: http://www.denvercenter.org.

DODGER THEATRICAL HOLDINGS, INC.
1501 Broadway, Suite 1904
New York, New York 10036

General Information Theatrical partnership that produces Broadway plays and musicals. Established in 1983. Number of employees: 45. Number of internship applications received each year: 50.
Internships Available ▶ *1 administrative intern:* responsibilities include providing office assistance and clerical backup. Candidates should have computer skills, personal interest in the field. Duration is 1 semester. Paid. Open to college freshmen, college sophomores, college juniors, college seniors.
Benefits Possible full-time employment, willing to complete paperwork for educational credit, modest stipend.
Contact Write or fax Ms. Tracy Regan, Human Resources. Fax: 212-398-1723. No phone calls. In-person interview required. Applicants must submit a cover letter, resume. Applications are accepted continuously.

DORSET THEATRE FESTIVAL
Box 570
Dorset, Vermont 05251-0510

General Information Professional nonprofit Equity theater company producing summer seasons of 5 mainstage plays and children's play. Established in 1976. Number of employees: 76. Program of American Theatre Works Inc., Dorset, Vermont. Number of internship applications received each year: 50.
Internships Available ▶ *3–4 arts management interns:* responsibilities include helping with fund-raising, publicity, box office duties, special events planning, and related managerial tasks. Candidates should have experience in the field, organizational skills, plan to pursue career in field, self-motivation, strong interpersonal skills, writing skills. $100–$120 per week. Open to college freshmen, college sophomores, college juniors, college seniors, recent college graduates, graduate students, career changers, individuals reentering the workforce. ▶ *3–5 technical theater interns:* responsibilities include working closely with designers on the costumes, props, sets, and lighting. Candidates should have ability to work independently, ability to work with others, college courses in field, knowledge of field, plan to pursue career in field. $100–$150 per week. Open to college freshmen, college sophomores, college juniors, college seniors, recent college graduates, graduate students, individuals reentering the workforce. Duration for all positions is 3-4 months in summer.
Benefits Free housing, names of contacts, on-the-job training, opportunity to attend seminars/workshops, willing to act as a professional reference, willing to complete paperwork for educational credit, willing to provide letters of recommendation.

Contact Write, call, fax, or e-mail Ms. Jill Charles, Artistic Director. Phone: 802-867-2223. Fax: 802-867-0144. E-mail: theatre@sover.net. In-person interview recommended. Applicants must submit a cover letter, resume, two personal references. Application deadline: April 15. World Wide Web: http://www.theatredirectories.com.

DRAMA LEAGUE
165 West 46th Street, Suite 601
New York, New York 10036

General Information Organization whose purpose is to develop and administer programs that foster the growth of artists and audiences. Established in 1916. Number of employees: 6. Number of internship applications received each year: 50.
Internships Available ▶ *1 administrative intern:* responsibilities include daily mail, receptionist work, special projects (including archival work), and sending out mailings. Candidates should have ability to work independently, computer skills, office skills, oral communication skills, organizational skills, research skills, self-motivation, strong interpersonal skills, writing skills, MS Word, Excel, QuarkXpress. Duration is 12 weeks. $50 per week. Open to college freshmen, college sophomores, college juniors, college seniors.
Benefits Job counseling, names of contacts, opportunity to attend seminars/workshops, possible full-time employment, travel reimbursement, willing to complete paperwork for educational credit, willing to provide letters of recommendation.
Contact Write, fax, or e-mail Jane Ann Crum, Executive Director. Fax: 212-302-2254. E-mail: dlny@echonyc.com. No phone calls. In-person interview recommended. Applicants must submit a cover letter, resume. Application deadline: January 1 for spring, March 1 for summer, June 1 for fall, September 1 for winter. World Wide Web: http://www.echonyc.com/.

EDEN THEATRICAL WORKSHOP, INC.
1570 Gilpin Street
Denver, Colorado 80218

General Information Community theater organization that focuses primarily on social issues-oriented dramas. Established in 1963. Number of employees: 1. Number of internship applications received each year: 6.
Internships Available ▶ *1 administrative assistant:* responsibilities include assisting in every aspect of program including paperwork and artistic projects. Candidates should have ability to work independently, ability to work with others, editing skills, oral communication skills, self-motivation, writing skills, interest in small nonprofit organizations. Duration is flexible. Unpaid. Open to college freshmen, college sophomores, college juniors, college seniors, recent college graduates, graduate students. International applications accepted.
Benefits Free meals, job counseling, names of contacts, possible full-time employment, willing to complete paperwork for educational credit, willing to provide letters of recommendation, reimbursement of incidental expenses.
Contact Write or call Ms. Lucy M. Walker, President/Executive Director. Phone: 303-321-2320. In-person interview recommended. Applicants must submit a cover letter, resume. Applications are accepted continuously.

FAIRFAX SYMPHONY ORCHESTRA
PO Box 1300
Annandale, Virginia 22003

General Information Nonprofit professional symphony orchestra that performs year-round in Northern Virginia and greater metropolitan Washington, D.C. Established in 1956. Number of employees: 4. Number of internship applications received each year: 30.
Internships Available ▶ *1 administrative intern:* responsibilities include assisting executive director and acting as board liaison. Candidates should have ability to work independently, ability to work with others, computer skills, office skills, oral communication skills, organizational skills, self-motivation, strong interpersonal

skills, writing skills, written communication skills. Duration is 8–12 weeks. Unpaid. Open to college juniors, college seniors, recent college graduates, graduate students, individuals reentering the workforce. ▶ *1 database/special projects intern:* responsibilities include assisting with database entry, formatting, reviewing, and updating; and assisting with fund-raising projects and outreach events. Candidates should have ability to work with others, analytical skills, college courses in field, computer skills, office skills, research skills. Duration is 8–12 weeks. Unpaid. Open to college juniors, college seniors, recent college graduates, graduate students. ▶ *1 development intern:* responsibilities include working on fund-raising projects. Candidates should have ability to work independently, analytical skills, college courses in field, computer skills, knowledge of field, office skills, oral communication skills, organizational skills, personal interest in the field, research skills, self-motivation, strong interpersonal skills, writing skills. Duration is 8–24 weeks. Unpaid. Open to college juniors, college seniors, recent college graduates, graduate students, career changers, individuals reentering the workforce. ▶ *1 marketing intern:* responsibilities include assisting with press relations and promotional projects. Candidates should have ability to work independently, ability to work with others, computer skills, declared college major in field, editing skills, experience in the field, office skills, oral communication skills, organizational skills, self-motivation, writing skills. Duration is 8–24 weeks. Unpaid. Open to college juniors, college seniors, recent college graduates, graduate students, career changers, individuals reentering the workforce.
Benefits Job counseling, names of contacts, on-the-job training, opportunity to attend seminars/workshops, possible full-time employment, willing to complete paperwork for educational credit, willing to provide letters of recommendation, tickets to concerts.
Contact Write, fax, or e-mail Philip A. Tukey, Executive Director. Fax: 703-642-7205. E-mail: pat@fairfaxsymphony.org. In-person interview recommended. Applicants must submit a cover letter, resume, personal reference. Applications are accepted continuously. World Wide Web: http://www.fairfaxsymphony.org.

FARGO-MOORHEAD COMMUNITY THEATRE
PO Box 2844
Fargo, North Dakota 58108

General Information Theater providing the Fargo-Moorhead area and surrounding region with high-quality avocational experiences, opportunities, and education; annually presents 5 mainstage productions in addition to children's shows, booked-in productions, a senior adults vaudeville, a biennial playwrights' contest, and a full series of classes for grades K-12 and for special needs adults. Established in 1946. Number of employees: 12. Number of internship applications received each year: 12.
Internships Available ▶ *2 box office interns:* responsibilities include assisting in handling and processing season memberships and ticket reservations, working daily and performance night shifts as required, and assisting in preparation of daily and nightly audits and audience counts. Candidates should have computer skills, office skills, oral communication skills, strong interpersonal skills. ▶ *1–2 children's theater interns:* responsibilities include assisting in supervision and execution of child- or youth-related outreach programs and coordination of youth theater classes. Candidates should have knowledge of field, oral communication skills, personal interest in the field, strong interpersonal skills, ability to work with children and youth. ▶ *2 costuming interns:* responsibilities include assisting in the construction and maintenance of costumes, makeup, and wigs and maintaining cleanliness of work area. Candidates should have ability to work independently, ability to work with others, knowledge of field. ▶ *1 general administration intern:* responsibilities include assisting in computer operation and programming, computerization and updating of mailing lists and box office membership records, preparation and procurement of grants and granting opportunities, and execution of all theater clerical tasks. Candidates should have computer skills, office skills, oral communication skills, writing skills. ▶ *1–2 marketing interns:* responsibilities include assisting in marketing and promotion for all mainstage and children's

theater productions, developing and maintaining solid audience base, and conducting and evaluating audience surveys. Candidates should have ability to work independently, ability to work with others, office skills, self-motivation, writing skills. ▶ *2 scenery and lighting interns:* responsibilities include assisting in construction of sets and properties, removal and breakdown of sets and lights, and maintenance of plant services and equipment. Candidates should have ability to work independently, knowledge of field, oral communication skills, self-motivation, strong interpersonal skills. Duration for all positions is flexible. All positions are unpaid. Open to college freshmen, college sophomores, college juniors, college seniors. International applications accepted.
Benefits Opportunity to attend seminars/workshops, willing to complete paperwork for educational credit, willing to provide letters of recommendation, assistance with resume preparation, leadership skills, use of research facilities.
Contact Write Internship Coordinator. No phone calls. Applicants must submit a cover letter, resume, three personal references. Applications are accepted continuously. World Wide Web: http://www.fargoweb.com/fmc.

52ND STREET PROJECT
500 West 52nd Street, 2nd Floor
New York, New York 10019

General Information Nonprofit organization that serves inner-city children by putting them together with adult actors to create original theater. Established in 1981. Number of employees: 6. Number of internship applications received each year: 25.
Internships Available ▶ *General interns:* responsibilities include working with staff in the areas of marketing, development, business, production, and teaching. Candidates should have computer skills, office skills, personal interest in the field, self-motivation, strong interpersonal skills, strong leadership ability. Duration is flexible. Unpaid. Open to high school seniors, recent high school graduates, college freshmen, college sophomores, college juniors, college seniors, recent college graduates, graduate students. International applications accepted.
Benefits Names of contacts, willing to complete paperwork for educational credit, willing to provide letters of recommendation, weekend or week-long trips to the country with children.
Contact Write, call, fax, or e-mail George Babiak, Production Manager. Phone: 212-333-5252. Fax: 212-333-5598. E-mail: project52@aol.com. Applicants must submit a cover letter, resume. Applications are accepted continuously. World Wide Web: http://www.52project.org.

FIJI COMPANY/PING CHONG AND COMPANY
47 Great Jones Street
New York, New York 10012

General Information Center focusing on contemporary avant-garde theater and art. Established in 1975. Number of employees: 5. Number of internship applications received each year: 1.
Internships Available ▶ *General management interns:* responsibilities include duties tailored to intern's abilities and center's needs. Candidates should have office skills, oral communication skills, personal interest in the field, research skills, strong interpersonal skills, written communication skills. Duration is flexible. Unpaid. Open to college freshmen, college sophomores, college juniors, college seniors, recent college graduates, graduate students, individuals reentering the workforce. International applications accepted.
Benefits Job counseling, willing to complete paperwork for educational credit, willing to provide letters of recommendation, small stipend available.
Contact Write Bruce Allardice, Managing Director. In-person interview recommended. Applicants must submit a cover letter. Applications are accepted continuously.

FLAT ROCK PLAYHOUSE
PO Box 310
Flat Rock, North Carolina 28731

General Information   Theater that produces nine shows annually from May through December. Established in 1952. Number of employees: 70. Number of internship applications received each year: 30.

Internships Available   ▶ *15–18 apprentices/interns:* responsibilities include learning through practical experience and exposure to as many facets of theatre as possible, including acting, technical/design, improvisation, scene design, lighting, costumes, and resume preparation. Candidates should have ability to work with others, knowledge of field, plan to pursue career in field, self-motivation, strong interpersonal skills, prior theatrical experience. Duration is 10–20 weeks. Position available as unpaid or paid. Open to recent high school graduates, college freshmen, college sophomores, college juniors, college seniors, recent college graduates, graduate students, individuals reentering the workforce. International applications accepted.

Benefits   Free housing, free meals, on-the-job training, opportunity to attend seminars/workshops, willing to act as a professional reference, willing to complete paperwork for educational credit, willing to provide letters of recommendation, Equity Membership Candidacy Program.

Contact   Write, call, or e-mail Apprentice Director. Phone: 828-693-0403. E-mail: frp@flatrockplayhouse.org. Applicants must submit a formal organization application, resume, two personal references, in-person audition recommended (video tape acceptable). Application deadline: April 1 for summer. World Wide Web: http://www.flatrockplayhouse.org.

FLORIDA STUDIO THEATRE
1241 North Palm Avenue
Sarasota, Florida 34236

General Information   Professional nonprofit theater that runs a mainstage season of contemporary plays November through August under Actor's Equity Contract, a cabaret club theater with a three-show mainstage program September through December and January through May, and various festivals. Established in 1973. Number of employees: 50. Number of internship applications received each year: 500.

Internships Available   ▶ *4 children's education interns:* responsibilities include organizing and teaching children's acting programs and performing on children's tour. Candidates should have oral communication skills, personal interest in the field, strong interpersonal skills. Duration is October to May. $60 per week. Open to recent college graduates. ▶ *3–4 development or marketing administration interns:* responsibilities include working box office, concessions, public relations, and subscription and membership sales; company management, house management. Candidates should have ability to work independently, ability to work with others, computer skills, office skills, organizational skills, good communcation skills in general. Duration is summer (late May to late August); or year (September to May). pay starts at $40 per week. Open to recent high school graduates, college freshmen, college sophomores, college juniors, college seniors, recent college graduates. ▶ *2 literary management interns:* responsibilities include providing literary assistance to the new play program and script analysis and evaluation. Candidates should have computer skills, office skills, organizational skills, research skills, written communication skills. Duration is May to August. $40 per week. Open to recent high school graduates, college freshmen, college sophomores, college juniors, college seniors, recent college graduates. ▶ *2–3 production interns:* responsibilities include building sets, working with props and costumes, and loading and running shows. Candidates should have ability to work independently, ability to work with others, experience in the field, organizational skills, self-motivation. Duration is 3–12 months. $40 per week. Open to recent high school graduates, college freshmen, college sophomores, college juniors, college seniors, recent college graduates. ▶ *3–4 stage managers:* responsibilities include assisting Equity stage managers with rehearsals and running mainstage productions and cabarets. Candidates should have analytical skills, knowledge of field, organizational skills, strong interpersonal skills, strong leadership ability. Duration is October to May; summer position also available. $40 per week. Open to recent high school graduates, college freshmen, college sophomores, college juniors, college seniors, recent college graduates.

Benefits   Formal training, free housing, possible full-time employment, willing to complete paperwork for educational credit, willing to provide letters of recommendation.

Contact   Write, call, or fax James Ashford, Assistant to Artistic Director. Phone: 941-366-9017. Fax: 941-955-4137. Telephone interview required. Applicants must submit a formal organization application, cover letter, resume, 2-3 personal references, 2-3 letters of recommendation. Application deadline: April 1 for summer; continuous for academic year.

FOOLS COMPANY, INC.
423 West 46th Street
New York, New York 10036-3510

General Information   Not-for-profit cultural and educational organization whose mission is to produce and present innovative and unconventional works and workshops in all areas of the performing arts. Established in 1970. Number of employees: 10. Number of internship applications received each year: 50.

Internships Available   ▶ *5 administration interns:* responsibilities include working in funding, publicity, and public relations for performing arts productions and workshops. Duration is 10 months. ▶ *5 production interns:* responsibilities include assisting with company productions and workshops. Duration is 3–6 months. Candidates for all positions should have ability to work independently, oral communication skills, personal interest in the field, self-motivation, strong interpersonal skills, written communication skills. All positions are unpaid. Open to high school seniors, recent high school graduates, college freshmen, college sophomores, college juniors, college seniors, recent college graduates, graduate students, law students, career changers, individuals reentering the workforce. International applications accepted.

Benefits   Formal training, job counseling, names of contacts, on-the-job training, opportunity to attend seminars/workshops, possible full-time employment, willing to act as a professional reference, willing to complete paperwork for educational credit, willing to provide letters of recommendation, possibility of subsidized housing.

Contact   Write or call Dr. Martin Russell, Artistic Director. Phone: 212-307-6000. In-person interview required. Applicants must submit a cover letter, resume, telephone interview acceptable for international applicants only. Applications are accepted continuously.

GEVA THEATRE
75 Woodbury Boulevard
Rochester, New York 14607

General Information   Theater that strives to present and advance the art of theater so that its artists, audience, and the community can celebrate the human experience through an active participation in this art form. Established in 1972. Number of employees: 45. Number of internship applications received each year: 35.

Internships Available   ▶ *1 education intern:* responsibilities include assisting with education programming. Candidates should have ability to work independently, computer skills, organizational skills, personal interest in the field, research skills, strong interpersonal skills, writing skills. Duration is 9 months. Unpaid. ▶ *1 electrics apprentice:* responsibilities include assisting in running shows. Candidates should have computer skills, experience in the field, office skills, plan to pursue career in field, strong interpersonal skills. Duration is 10 months. $206 per week. Open to recent college graduates. ▶ *1 literary intern:* responsibilities include script analysis and heavy duty play development work. Candidates should have computer skills, knowledge of field, organizational skills, personal interest in the field, writing skills. Duration is 9 months. Position available as unpaid or paid. Open to recent college graduates, graduate students. ▶ *2 stage management apprentices:* responsibilities include assisting in running shows. Candidates should have computer skills, experience in the field, oral communication skills, organizational skills, plan to pursue career in field, self-motivation. Duration is 10 months. $206–$250 per week.

Benefits Job counseling, names of contacts, possible full-time employment, willing to complete paperwork for educational credit, willing to provide letters of recommendation.

Contact Write Skip Greer, Director of Education. In-person interview recommended. Applicants must submit a cover letter, resume. Applications are accepted continuously.

GOODMAN THEATRE
200 South Columbus Drive
Chicago, Illinois 60603

General Information Oldest and largest nonprofit theater in Chicago producing classic and contemporary works. Established in 1925. Number of employees: 95. Number of internship applications received each year: 100.

Internships Available ▶ *1 arts in education intern:* responsibilities include assisting with student matinee performances, writing articles or exercises for study guides, compiling information from student and teacher evaluations, helping to coordinate high school teacher seminars, corresponding with school groups or other community organizations, and assisting with organization of archival material. Candidates should have ability to work independently, computer skills, oral communication skills, organizational skills, personal interest in the field, written communication skills. Duration is 3–4 months. Position available as unpaid or paid. Open to college juniors, college seniors, recent college graduates, graduate students. ▶ *Business administration interns:* responsibilities include assisting with a variety of activities, including routine accounting, travel and housing arrangements for guest artists, and special projects. Candidates should have oral communication skills, written communication skills, basic knowledge of business and clerical procedures. Duration is 3–4 months. Unpaid. Open to college seniors, recent college graduates, graduate students. ▶ *1 casting intern:* responsibilities include scheduling and monitoring auditions, corresponding with actors and agents, and maintaining actor files. Candidates should have ability to work independently, computer skills, office skills, plan to pursue career in field, strong interpersonal skills, written communication skills. Duration is 3–4 months. Unpaid. Open to college juniors, college seniors, recent college graduates, graduate students. ▶ *1 costuming intern:* responsibilities include general costume construction and assisting with office clerical tasks. Candidates should have ability to work independently, knowledge of field, organizational skills, plan to pursue career in field, strong interpersonal skills. Duration is 2 to 3 months in fall/winter only; 20 hours per week minimum. Unpaid. Open to college juniors, college seniors, recent college graduates, graduate students. ▶ *1 development intern:* responsibilities include researching prospective contributors and grants, writing for newsletters and the annual report, developing fund-raising campaigns, and writing solicitation letters. Candidates should have ability to work with others, computer skills, knowledge of field, oral communication skills, plan to pursue career in field, written communication skills. Duration is 3–4 months. Unpaid. Open to college juniors, college seniors, recent college graduates, graduate students. ▶ *1 dramaturgy intern:* responsibilities include researching various subjects for newsletter articles and program notes, assisting with preparation of scripts for rehearsals, maintaining in-house library, working on script changes once play is in production, and assisting with new script reading and evaluation. Candidates should have ability to work independently, computer skills, editing skills, organizational skills, research skills, written communication skills. Duration is 3–4 months. Unpaid. Open to college juniors, college seniors, recent college graduates, graduate students. ▶ *1 electrics intern:* responsibilities include hanging and focusing lights, helping to create special effects, equipment maintenance. Candidates should have ability to work independently, organizational skills, plan to pursue career in field, strong interpersonal skills, knowledge of computerized lighting systems is a plus. Duration is 2 to 3 months in fall/winter only; 20 hours per week minimum. Unpaid. Open to college juniors, college seniors, recent college graduates, graduate students. ▶ *1 literary management intern:* responsibilities include assisting in solicitation and recording of new manuscripts; maintaining extensive script library; analyzing and evaluating solicited manuscripts; corresponding with playwrights, agents, theaters, and play development programs; and researching playwright production histories. Candidates should have ability to work independently, computer skills, editing skills, organizational skills, research skills, written communication skills. Duration is 3–4 months. Unpaid. Open to college juniors, college seniors, recent college graduates, graduate students. ▶ *1 properties intern:* responsibilities include assisting with researching, purchasing, creating, and maintaining scenic elements for a variety of period and contemporary productions. Candidates should have ability to work independently, knowledge of field, organizational skills, plan to pursue career in field, strong interpersonal skills. Duration is 2 to 3 months in fall/winter only; 20 hours per week minimum. Unpaid. Open to college juniors, college seniors, recent college graduates, graduate students. ▶ *1 public relations intern:* responsibilities include assisting in areas of marketing and advertising, proofreading newsletter and program copy, compiling audience survey results, distributing promotional materials, and facilitating special events. Candidates should have ability to work with others, knowledge of field, office skills, plan to pursue career in field, strong interpersonal skills, written communication skills. Duration is 3–4 months. Unpaid. Open to college juniors, college seniors, recent college graduates, graduate students. ▶ *1 scenery intern:* responsibilities include building and installing scenery. Candidates should have knowledge of field, organizational skills, plan to pursue career in field, self-motivation, strong interpersonal skills. Duration is 2 to 3 months in fall/winter only; 20 hours per week minimum. Unpaid. Open to college juniors, college seniors, recent college graduates, graduate students. ▶ *Sound interns:* responsibilities include helping to create sound scores for mainstage and studio productions, and learning advanced procedures for installing, operating, and maintaining sound equipment. Duration is 3–4 months in fall/winter only; 20 hours per week minimum. Unpaid. ▶ *1–2 stage management interns:* responsibilities include assisting stage managers with preproduction preparation and continuing through technical rehearsals, preview weeks, and opening nights. Candidates should have computer skills, knowledge of field, organizational skills, plan to pursue career in field, strong interpersonal skills. Duration is 6–8 weeks or length of production. Position available as unpaid or paid. Open to college seniors, recent college graduates, graduate students. ▶ *1 ticket services intern:* responsibilities include learning the art of customer service, operating the box office computer system, and assisting with the planning of special events. Candidates should have ability to work with others, computer skills, knowledge of field, office skills, plan to pursue career in field, strong interpersonal skills. Duration is 2–3 months. Unpaid. Open to college juniors, college seniors, recent college graduates, graduate students. International applications accepted.

Benefits Job counseling, names of contacts, willing to complete paperwork for educational credit, willing to provide letters of recommendation.

Contact Write Ms. Julie Massey, Intern Coordinator. In-person interview recommended. Applicants must submit a formal organization application, cover letter, resume, two letters of recommendation. Application deadline: March 18 for summer, June 18 for fall, November 5 for winter. World Wide Web: http://www.goodman.theatre.org.

GOODSPEED OPERA HOUSE
Box A
East Haddam, Connecticut 06423

General Information Professional, award-winning theater with a 30-year history of producing musical theater. Established in 1963. Number of employees: 100. Number of internship applications received each year: 500.

Goodspeed Opera House (continued)

Internships Available ▶ *2 carpentry interns:* responsibilities include running crew and building sets. Candidates should have college courses in field. Duration is 1–2 semesters. Unpaid. Open to college freshmen, college sophomores, college juniors, college seniors, graduate students. ▶ *2 electric interns:* responsibilities include running follow spots for production and helping shop build shows. Candidates should have college courses in field. Duration is 1–2 semesters. Unpaid. Open to college freshmen, college sophomores, college juniors, college seniors, graduate students. ▶ *2 props interns:* responsibilities include running crew and building props. Candidates should have college courses in field. Duration is 1–2 semesters. Unpaid. Open to college freshmen, college sophomores, college juniors, college seniors, graduate students. ▶ *1 scenic art intern:* responsibilities include helping the scenic artists paint scenery. Candidates should have college courses in field. Duration is 1–2 semesters. Unpaid. Open to college freshmen, college sophomores, college juniors, college seniors, recent college graduates. ▶ *2–4 stage management interns:* responsibilities include assisting stage manager during rehearsals and performances. Candidates should have ability to work independently, college degree in related field, computer skills, editing skills, knowledge of field, office skills, oral communication skills, organizational skills, plan to pursue career in field, self-motivation, strong interpersonal skills, strong leadership ability, writing skills. Duration is 4–16 weeks. stipend of $200 per wek. Open to recent college graduates. ▶ *2 wardrobe interns:* responsibilities include working in the costume shop and running wardrobe. Candidates should have college courses in field. Duration is 1–2 semesters. Unpaid. Open to college freshmen, college sophomores, college juniors, college seniors, graduate students.

Benefits Free housing, housing at a cost, names of contacts, on-the-job training, opportunity to attend seminars/workshops, willing to complete paperwork for educational credit, willing to provide letters of recommendation.

Contact Write, fax, or e-mail Mr. R. Glen Grusmark, Production Manager, Box A, East Haddam, Connecticut 06243. Fax: 860-873-2480. E-mail: rgrusmark@goodspeed.org. No phone calls. Telephone interview required. Applicants must submit a cover letter, resume, three personal references, proof that credit will be received from educational institution. Applications are accepted continuously. World Wide Web: http://www.goodspeed. org.

HARTFORD STAGE
50 Church Street
Hartford, Connecticut 06103

General Information Stage company that produces top-quality, professional theater for Connecticut's capital city and its surrounding communities; under the direction of Michael Wilson since April 1998, Hartford Stage has deepened its commitment to new works and reinterpretations of classic plays. Established in 1964. Number of employees: 50. Number of internship applications received each year: 50.

Internships Available ▶ *5–7 interns:* responsibilities include performing tasks related to available positions in administration (business, communications and development), production, stage management, production management, company management, and artistic directing, literary management, dramaturgy, and education. Candidates should have ability to work independently, college courses in field, computer skills, experience in the field, office skills, oral communication skills, organizational skills, plan to pursue career in field, research skills, self-motivation, strong interpersonal skills, writing skills. Duration is flexible. Unpaid. Open to college juniors, college seniors, recent college graduates, graduate students. International applications accepted.

Benefits Willing to act as a professional reference, willing to complete paperwork for educational credit, willing to provide letters of recommendation.

Contact Write Intern Coordinator. Fax: 860-525-4420. No phone calls. In-person interview recommended. Applicants must submit a cover letter, resume, two letters of recommendation. Application deadline: April 1 for summer, November 1 for spring.

HOME FOR CONTEMPORARY THEATRE AND ART (HERE)
145 Avenue of the Americas, Ground Floor
New York, New York 10013

General Information Theater and gallery that develops new works. Established in 1986. Number of employees: 50. Number of internship applications received each year: 300.

Internships Available ▶ *1–2 administrative interns.* Candidates should have ability to work independently, ability to work with others, analytical skills, knowledge of field, office skills, organizational skills, self-motivation. Open to college freshmen, college sophomores, college juniors, college seniors, recent college graduates, individuals reentering the workforce. ▶ *1–2 development interns:* responsibilities include assisting the development director in writing grant proposals. Candidates should have ability to work independently, computer skills, editing skills, oral communication skills, research skills, self-motivation, written communication skills. Open to recent high school graduates, college freshmen, college sophomores, college juniors, college seniors, recent college graduates, individuals reentering the workforce. ▶ *1–2 gallery interns:* responsibilities include assisting the gallery director in organizing gallery shows and loading in. Candidates should have oral communication skills, personal interest in the field, strong interpersonal skills, written communication skills. Open to high school students, high school seniors, recent high school graduates, college freshmen, college sophomores, college juniors, college seniors, recent college graduates, individuals reentering the workforce. ▶ *1–2 production interns:* responsibilities include assiting the production manager with running and maintaining 3 theatres; possibility of running tech on shows. Candidates should have ability to work independently, organizational skills, personal interest in the field, self-motivation, strong interpersonal skills. Open to high school students, high school seniors, recent high school graduates, college freshmen, college sophomores, college juniors, college seniors, career changers, individuals reentering the workforce. ▶ *1–2 programming interns:* responsibilities include assisting the programming director in reviewing artists and booking space. Candidates should have ability to work independently, oral communication skills, organizational skills, self-motivation, strong interpersonal skills. Open to high school seniors, recent high school graduates, college freshmen, college sophomores, college juniors, college seniors, recent college graduates, individuals reentering the workforce. ▶ *1–2 publicity/marketing interns.* Candidates should have computer skills, editing skills, oral communication skills, personal interest in the field, self-motivation, strong interpersonal skills, written communication skills. Open to recent high school graduates, college freshmen, college sophomores, college juniors, college seniors, recent college graduates, individuals reentering the workforce. Duration for all positions is flexible. All positions are unpaid. International applications accepted.

Benefits Possible full-time employment, willing to complete paperwork for educational credit, willing to provide letters of recommendation, exposure to a wide range of artistic activity, possibility of travel reimbursement.

Contact Write, fax, or e-mail Kathleen Brown, Internship Coordinator. Fax: 212-647-0257. E-mail: kathleen@here.org. In-person interview recommended. Applicants must submit a cover letter, resume. Applications are accepted continuously. World Wide Web: http://www.HERE.org.

HORSE CAVE THEATRE
Box 215
Horse Cave, Kentucky 42749

General Information Nonprofit repertory theater bringing professional theater to the area at an affordable price while promoting educational outreach programs and student theater workshops. Established in 1976. Number of employees: 10. Number of internship applications received each year: 12.

Internships Available ▶ *3–5 apprentices:* responsibilities include assisting with lighting, scene shop, costumes, props, box office management, sound, or administration. Candidates should have ability to work independently, ability to work with others, knowledge of field, personal interest in the field, self-motivation. Duration is 6 months. pay is commensurate with experience. Open to recent high school graduates, college freshmen, college sophomores, college juniors, college seniors, recent college graduates, graduate students. International applications accepted.
Benefits Free housing, opportunity to attend seminars/workshops, willing to act as a professional reference, willing to provide letters of recommendation.
Contact Write, call, fax, or e-mail Robert Brock, Education Director. Phone: 502-786-1200. Fax: 502-786-5298. E-mail: hctstaff@scrtc.blue.net. In-person interview recommended. Applicants must submit a formal organization application, resume, two letters of recommendation. Application deadline: April 1. World Wide Web: http://www.horsecavetheatre.org.

INDIANA REPERTORY THEATRE
140 West Washington Street
Indianapolis, Indiana 46204

General Information Theater company that produces 6 mainstage and 3 upperstage productions in a season that operates from October to May. Established in 1972. Number of employees: 175. Number of internship applications received each year: 30.
Internships Available ▶ *2 stage management interns:* responsibilities include assisting with rehearsals and backstage. Candidates should have college degree in related field, experience in the field, organizational skills, plan to pursue career in field, self-motivation, strong interpersonal skills. Duration is 9 months. $5.50 per hour (overtime pay after 40 hours).
Benefits Names of contacts, possible full-time employment, willing to complete paperwork for educational credit, willing to provide letters of recommendation.
Contact Write Ms. Jane Robison, General Manager. No phone calls. In-person interview recommended. Applicants must submit a cover letter, resume, three letters of recommendation. Applications are accepted continuously. World Wide Web: http://www.indianarep.com.

JEAN COCTEAU REPERTORY THEATER
Bouwerie Lane Theater, 330 Bowery
New York, New York 10012

General Information Theater specializing in classic plays. Established in 1971. Number of employees: 6.
Internships Available ▶ *General administration interns:* responsibilities include assisting in all areas of general management including marketing, development, and audience services. ▶ *Production interns:* responsibilities include assisting in all areas of production including scenery, properties, costumes, lighting and sound. Duration for all positions is flexible. All positions are unpaid.
Benefits Willing to complete paperwork for educational credit, willing to provide letters of recommendation, small stipend for work-related expenses.
Contact Write, fax, or e-mail Kristen Chirillo, General Manager, Bouwerie Lane Theater 330 Bowery, New York, New York 10012. Fax: 212-777-6151. E-mail: cocteau@jeancocteaurep.org. Submit letter of inquiry and statement of purpose. World Wide Web: http://www.jeancocteaurep.org.

JOHN DREW THEATER OF GUILD HALL
158 Main Street
East Hampton, New York 11937

General Information Performing arts presenter and Equity theater associated with art museum. Number of employees: 20. Unit of Guild Hall of East Hampton, East Hampton, New York. Number of internship applications received each year: 50.
Internships Available ▶ *1 management intern:* responsibilities include assisting publicist and performing general office operations.

Open to college freshmen, college sophomores, college juniors, college seniors. ▶ *1 production management intern:* responsibilities include assisting production manager. Open to college freshmen, college sophomores, college juniors, college seniors. ▶ *1–2 technical interns:* responsibilities include completing general backstage assignments. Open to high school seniors, college freshmen, college sophomores, college juniors. Duration for all positions is one summer. All positions paid at $100 per week.
Benefits Job counseling, names of contacts, willing to complete paperwork for educational credit, willing to provide letters of recommendation.
Contact Write, call, or fax Mr. Leonard Ziemkiewicz, General Manager. Phone: 516-324-4051. Fax: 516-324-2722. In-person interview recommended. Applicants must submit a cover letter, resume. Applications are accepted continuously. World Wide Web: http://www.GuildHall.org.

THE KITCHEN: CENTER FOR VIDEO, MUSIC, DANCE, PERFORMANCE, FILM, AND LITERATURE
512 West 19th Street
New York, New York 10011

General Information International nonprofit organization dedicated to presenting emerging artists and experimental art forms. Established in 1971. Number of employees: 20. Number of internship applications received each year: 200.
Internships Available ▶ *1–8 curatorial interns:* responsibilities include assisting with artist contacts and reviewing and responding to submissions. ▶ *1–12 fund-raising interns:* responsibilities include assisting in grant writing and fund-raising. ▶ *1–5 management/administration interns:* responsibilities include assisting on special projects and in daily office management. ▶ *1–3 marketing interns:* responsibilities include assisting in all aspects of marketing. ▶ *1–2 media services interns:* responsibilities include organizing video archive, performing data entry, and assisting with daily administrative organization, international video distribution, and rotating video installations. ▶ *1–5 technical crew interns:* responsibilities include assisting with maintenance of theater and equipment; working directly with artists to help run shows. Duration for all positions is flexible. All positions available as unpaid or paid. Open to high school students, high school seniors, recent high school graduates, college freshmen, college sophomores, college juniors, college seniors, recent college graduates, graduate students, law students, career changers, individuals reentering the workforce. International applications accepted.
Benefits Formal training, job counseling, names of contacts, willing to complete paperwork for educational credit, willing to provide letters of recommendation, access to video archive, performances, internationally renowned artists, and the New York City art scene.
Contact Write, call, fax, or e-mail Renee Danger-James, Internship Coordinator. Phone: 212-255-5793. Fax: 212-645-4258. E-mail: info@thekitchen.org. Applicants must submit a cover letter, resume. Applications are accepted continuously. World Wide Web: http://www.thekitchen.org.

LA MAMA E.T.C.
74 A East Fourth Street
New York, New York 10003

General Information Experimental theater. Established in 1961. Number of employees: 19. Number of internship applications received each year: 30.
Internships Available ▶ *Stage management interns.* Duration is flexible. Unpaid. Open to high school students, high school seniors, recent high school graduates, college freshmen, college sophomores, college juniors, college seniors, recent college graduates, graduate students, law students, career changers, individuals reentering the workforce. International applications accepted.
Benefits Names of contacts, willing to complete paperwork for educational credit, willing to provide letters of recommendation.
Contact Write, call, fax, or e-mail Marybeth Ward, Intern Coordinator. Phone: 212-254-6468. Fax: 212-254-7597. E-mail:

La Mama E.T.C. (continued)
lamama@lamama.org. Applicants must submit a cover letter, resume. Applications are accepted continuously.

LINCOLN CENTER FOR THE PERFORMING ARTS
70 Lincoln Center Plaza
New York, New York 10023-6583

General Information Producer and presenter of 300 events annually and manager of the Lincoln Center complex. Established in 1956. Number of employees: 500. Number of internship applications received each year: 80.
Internships Available ► *2 arts management interns:* responsibilities include providing assistance on projects to be chosen by the intern in consultation with senior staff members. Candidates should have ability to work independently, analytical skills, computer skills, oral communication skills, plan to pursue career in field, written communication skills. Duration is 12 weeks. $500 per week. Open to graduate students.
Benefits Names of contacts, willing to complete paperwork for educational credit, willing to provide letters of recommendation, tickets to performances.
Contact Write or fax Jay D. Spivack, Director of Human Resources and Labor Relations. Fax: 212-875-5185. No phone calls. In-person interview required. Applicants must submit a cover letter, resume, 1 writing sample (finalists only) and 2 letters of recommendation (finalists only). Application deadline: February 1 for summer. World Wide Web: http://www.lincolncenter.org.

THE LIRA ENSEMBLE
6525 North Sheridan Road, SKY 905
Chicago, Illinois 60626

General Information Professional performing arts company specializing in Polish music, song, and dance. Established in 1965. Number of employees: 3. Number of internship applications received each year: 4.
Internships Available ► *2 assistants to the general manager:* responsibilities include assisting in the management of a professional performance company. Candidates should have ability to work independently, computer skills, office skills, oral communication skills, personal interest in the field, written communication skills. Duration is flexible. Unpaid. Open to college juniors, college seniors, recent college graduates, graduate students, career changers. International applications accepted.
Benefits Job counseling, names of contacts, on-the-job training, opportunity to attend seminars/workshops, possible full-time employment, willing to complete paperwork for educational credit, willing to provide letters of recommendation.
Contact Write, call, or fax Ms. Lucyna Migala, Artistic Director and General Manager, 6525 North Sheridan Road SKY 905, Chicago, Illinois 60626. Phone: 773-508-7040. Fax: 773-508-7043. In-person interview recommended. Applicants must submit a cover letter, resume. Applications are accepted continuously.

MABOU MINES
150 First Avenue
New York, New York 10009

General Information Avant-garde theater company emphasizing the creation of new theater pieces from original texts and the theatrical use of existing texts staged from a specific point of view. Established in 1970. Number of employees: 4. Number of internship applications received each year: 75.
Internships Available ► *1 administrative intern:* responsibilities include assisting in maintaining archives, preparing promotional materials, running errands, handling telephone calls, general filing, computer input, and general office maintenance. Duration is 1 semester. Unpaid. Open to college freshmen, college sophomores, college juniors, college seniors, recent college graduates. International applications accepted.
Benefits Job counseling, opportunity to attend seminars/workshops, willing to complete paperwork for educational credit, willing to provide letters of recommendation, opportunity to accompany artistic directorate to art events.

Contact Write, call, fax, or e-mail Ms. Martha Elliot, Company Manager. Phone: 212-473-0559. Fax: 212-473-2410. E-mail: mabou@thing.net. In-person interview required. Applicants must submit a cover letter, resume. Applications are accepted continuously.

MAINE STATE MUSIC THEATRE
14 Maine Street, Suite 109
Brunswick, Maine 04011

General Information Theater dedicated to polishing, preserving, and producing musical plays and training young theater professionals. Established in 1959. Number of employees: 60. Number of internship applications received each year: 60.
Internships Available ► *4 administrative interns:* responsibilities include working with company management, marketing, box office and house management. Candidates should have ability to work independently, office skills, oral communication skills, organizational skills, strong interpersonal skills. $50 per week. ► *15 performers.* Candidates should have experience in the field. $30 per week. ► *15 technicians:* responsibilities include working in stage management, painting, scenery, props, electronics, and costumes; and building and installing sets. Candidates should have ability to work with others, college courses in field, experience in the field, plan to pursue career in field, self-motivation. $50 per week. Duration for all positions is May to August. Open to recent high school graduates, college freshmen, college sophomores, college juniors, college seniors, recent college graduates, graduate students. International applications accepted.
Benefits Free housing, free meals, names of contacts, on-the-job training, opportunity to attend seminars/workshops, willing to complete paperwork for educational credit, willing to provide letters of recommendation, 13 Equity membership candidate points.
Contact Write, call, fax, or e-mail Ms. Rachel Clarke, Company Manager. Phone: 207-725-8769. Fax: 207-725-1199. E-mail: msmtjobs@blazenetme.net. In-person interview recommended. Applicants must submit a formal organization application, resume, two letters of recommendation. Application deadline: March 31. World Wide Web: http://www.msmt.org.

MANHATTAN CLASS COMPANY
120 West 28th Street, 2nd Floor
New York, New York 10001

General Information Off-Broadway theatre. Established in 1983. Number of employees: 10. Number of internship applications received each year: 20.
Internships Available ► *1 box office intern.* Duration is flexible. ► *5–10 casting interns.* Duration is flexible. ► *1 development intern.* Duration is flexible. ► *5–15 general management interns.* Candidates should have computer skills, editing skills, office skills, oral communication skills, strong interpersonal skills, writing skills. Duration is based on applicant's availability. Open to high school students, high school seniors, recent high school graduates, college freshmen, college sophomores, college juniors, college seniors, recent college graduates, graduate students, career changers, individuals reentering the workforce. ► *1 house management intern.* Duration is flexible. ► *10–20 production interns:* responsibilities include assisting with production of a not-for-profit theater. Candidates should have office skills, oral communication skills, personal interest in the field, strong interpersonal skills, writing skills. Duration is based on applicant's availability. Open to high school seniors, recent high school graduates, college freshmen, college sophomores, college juniors, college seniors, recent college graduates, graduate students, career changers, individuals reentering the workforce. All positions are unpaid. International applications accepted.
Benefits Names of contacts, travel reimbursement, willing to complete paperwork for educational credit, willing to provide letters of recommendation.
Contact Write, fax, or e-mail Jodi Schoenbrun, General Manager. Fax: 212-727-7780. E-mail: mcc@mcctheater.com. In-person interview recommended. Applicants must submit a cover letter,

resume, two personal references. Applications are accepted continuously. World Wide Web: http://www.mcctheater.com/mcc/.

MANHATTAN THEATRE CLUB
311 West 43rd Street, 8th Floor
New York, New York 10036

General Information Nonprofit professional theater with a commitment to developing and producing new works; sponsors a variety of special events including readings of plays-in-progress and a series called Writers-in-Performance. Established in 1970. Number of employees: 50. Number of internship applications received each year: 500.
Internships Available ▶ *8–14 interns:* responsibilities include working in the following departments: casting, fund-raising, general and business management, information systems, literary, marketing, musical theatre, production management, and Writers-in-Performance. Candidates should have ability to work independently, ability to work with others, computer skills, office skills, personal interest in the field, written communication skills. Duration is 1–3 semesters. $115 per week. Open to college freshmen, college sophomores, college juniors, college seniors, recent college graduates, graduate students, career changers. International applications accepted.
Benefits Opportunity to attend seminars/workshops, possible full-time employment, willing to complete paperwork for educational credit, willing to provide letters of recommendation, free and discounted tickets to cultural events in New York City.
Contact Write, fax, or e-mail Paul A. Kaplan Theatre Management Program. Fax: 212-399-4329. E-mail: interns@mtc-nyc.org. No phone calls. In-person interview recommended. Applicants must submit a formal organization application, cover letter, resume, two letters of recommendation. Application deadline: March 1 for summer, July 15 for fall, November 30 for winter/spring. World Wide Web: http://www.mtc-nyc.org.

MCCARTER THEATRE–CENTER FOR THE PERFORMING ARTS
91 University Place
Princeton, New Jersey 08540

General Information Performing arts center producing and presenting world-class artists in drama, music, dance, and special events. Received 1994 Tony Award for outstanding regional theater. Established in 1963. Number of employees: 100. Number of internship applications received each year: 150.
Internships Available ▶ *1 company/production management intern:* responsibilities include coordinating artists' travel and housing arrangements, scheduling use of company car, and tracking company management expenses. Candidates should have ability to work independently, organizational skills, self-motivation, strong interpersonal skills, strong leadership ability. $75 weekly stipend. Open to college juniors, college seniors, recent college graduates, career changers, individuals reentering the workforce. ▶ *1 costumes/wardrobe intern:* responsibilities include planning, building, and maintaining costumes. Candidates should have ability to work independently, ability to work with others, college courses in field, knowledge of field, organizational skills, personal interest in the field, research skills, self-motivation. $75 weekly stipend. Open to college juniors, college seniors, recent college graduates, graduate students, career changers, individuals reentering the workforce. ▶ *1 development intern:* responsibilities include involvement with government, corporate, foundation, and individual solicitations for support. Candidates should have ability to work independently, office skills, organizational skills, research skills, self-motivation, writing skills. $75 weekly stipend. Open to college juniors, college seniors, recent college graduates, graduate students, career changers, individuals reentering the workforce. ▶ *2 directing interns:* responsibilities include administrative work for the office of the Artistic Director, assisting with in-house casting, NY/NJ production coverage, reading of new material for the artistic team, serving as assistant to the director on mainstage production (subject to the Artistic Director's discretion). Candidates should have experience in the

field, organizational skills, personal interest in the field, plan to pursue career in field, self-motivation, strong interpersonal skills, strong leadership ability. $75 weekly stipend. Open to college juniors, college seniors, recent college graduates, graduate students, career changers, individuals reentering the workforce. ▶ *1 house management/special events intern:* responsibilities include full front-of-house management responsibilities including managing service and concessions areas, coordinating usher schedules, assisting receptions, benefits, dinners, and lobby rentals. Candidates should have oral communication skills, organizational skills, strong interpersonal skills, strong leadership ability. $75 weekly stipend. Open to college juniors, college seniors, recent college graduates, graduate students, career changers, individuals reentering the workforce. ▶ *1 literary management intern:* responsibilities include participating in the administration of the Literary Office, script reading, planning and coordinating McCarter's new play festival, organizing playreadings, and occasional dramaturgical research. Candidates should have ability to work with others, editing skills, knowledge of field, oral communication skills, research skills, writing skills. $75 weekly stipend. Open to college juniors, college seniors, recent college graduates, graduate students, career changers, individuals reentering the workforce. ▶ *1 marketing intern:* responsibilities include assisting with press and publicity management, publications management, audience development, graphic design, and group sales. Candidates should have ability to work with others, computer skills, oral communication skills, organizational skills, self-motivation, written communication skills. $75 weekly stipend. Open to college juniors, college seniors, recent college graduates, graduate students, career changers, individuals reentering the workforce. ▶ *1 producing intern:* responsibilities include participating in general management (including personnel, contracts, facilities, and operations), house management, and business management. Candidates should have ability to work with others, computer skills, office skills, oral communication skills, organizational skills, self-motivation. $75 weekly stipend. Open to college juniors, college seniors, recent college graduates, graduate students, career changers, individuals reentering the workforce. ▶ *1 properties intern:* responsibilities include participating in the procurement, construction, set-up, running, and maintenance of props, beginning with the design process and continuing through to strike. Candidates should have ability to work independently, ability to work with others, organizational skills, personal interest in the field, self-motivation. $75 weekly stipend. Open to college juniors, college seniors, recent college graduates, graduate students, career changers, individuals reentering the workforce. ▶ *1 stage management intern:* responsibilities include preparing for and attending rehearsal with shared responsibility for organizing and tracking production needs, communicating with various departments, and maintaining a work environment conducive to the best artistic efforts. Candidates should have college courses in field, knowledge of field, oral communication skills, organizational skills, plan to pursue career in field, self-motivation, strong interpersonal skills, strong leadership ability. $75 weekly stipend. Open to college juniors, college seniors, recent college graduates, graduate students, career changers, individuals reentering the workforce. ▶ *1 technical direction/scene shop intern:* responsibilities include working in all aspects of scenery development for a large proscenium stage operating on a repertory schedule, and participating on changeover and running crews. Candidates should have analytical skills, college courses in field, knowledge of field, organizational skills, self-motivation, strong interpersonal skills, strong leadership ability. $75 weekly stipend. Open to college juniors, college seniors, recent college graduates, graduate students, career changers, individuals reentering the workforce. Duration for all positions is 9–10 months. International applications accepted.

Benefits Free housing, possible full-time employment, willing to act as a professional reference, willing to complete paperwork for educational credit, willing to provide letters of recommendation.

Contact Write, fax, or e-mail Ms. Kathleen Nolan, General Manager. Fax: 609-497-0369. E-mail: knolan@mccarter.org. In-person interview recommended. Applicants must submit a formal organization application, cover letter, resume, two personal references, two letters of recommendation, writing samples (literary position). Application deadline: May 15. World Wide Web: http://www.mccarter.org.

MERRIMACK REPERTORY THEATRE
50 East Merrimack Street
Lowell, Massachusetts 01852

General Information Professional theater producing 7 quality productions from September through May. Established in 1979. Number of employees: 20. Number of internship applications received each year: 30.
Internships Available ▶ *2 administrative interns:* responsibilities include assisting administrative staff with special projects, data entry, answering phones, bulk mailings, and typing. Candidates should have ability to work independently, computer skills, personal interest in the field, self-motivation, strong interpersonal skills. Duration is variable. Unpaid. ▶ *4 production interns:* responsibilities include assisting production staff in areas of stage management, electrics, and scenery. Candidates should have ability to work independently, ability to work with others, knowledge of field, personal interest in the field, self-motivation, strong interpersonal skills. Duration is 9 months. Position available as unpaid or paid. Open to high school students, high school seniors, recent high school graduates, college freshmen, college sophomores, college juniors, college seniors, recent college graduates, graduate students. International applications accepted.
Benefits Free housing, possible full-time employment, willing to act as a professional reference, willing to complete paperwork for educational credit, willing to provide letters of recommendation, 2 free tickets to each production.
Contact Write, call, fax, or e-mail Harriet Sheets, General Manager. Phone: 978-454-6324. Fax: 978-934-0166. E-mail: mrtlowell@aol.com. In-person interview recommended. Applicants must submit a resume, three personal references. Applications are accepted continuously. World Wide Web: http://www.mrtlowell.com.

MILWAUKEE REPERTORY THEATER
108 East Wells Street
Milwaukee, Wisconsin 53202

General Information Major regional theater producing a broad range of classical and contemporary theater pieces. Established in 1953. Number of employees: 150. Number of internship applications received each year: 75.
Internships Available ▶ *14–16 actors:* responsibilities include acting and understudying on projects. Candidates should have college courses in field, knowledge of field, plan to pursue career in field, self-motivation, strong interpersonal skills. Open to college seniors, recent college graduates, graduate students, individuals reentering the workforce, semi-professional actors. ▶ *3 directors:* responsibilities include assisting directors with projects, running understudy rehearsals, and directing readings of new materials. Candidates should have ability to work independently, knowledge of field, oral communication skills, organizational skills, personal interest in the field, plan to pursue career in field, research skills, strong interpersonal skills, strong leadership ability, writing skills. Open to college seniors, recent college graduates, graduate students, individuals reentering the workforce, early career directors. ▶ *1 dramaturgy intern:* responsibilities include reading new scripts, researching projects, and assisting with research for specific productions. Candidates should have ability to work independently, editing skills, knowledge of field, organizational skills, personal interest in the field, research skills, self-motivation, writing skills. Open to college seniors, recent college graduates, graduate students, individuals reentering the workforce, semi-professional dramaturgs or literary managers. Duration for all positions is 1 full season (August to May). All positions are unpaid. International applications accepted.
Benefits Job counseling, opportunity to attend seminars/workshops, willing to act as a professional reference, willing to

complete paperwork for educational credit, willing to provide letters of recommendation, points toward an Equity status.
Contact Write, call, or e-mail Sandy Ernst, Intern Company Director. Phone: 414-224-1761 Ext. 374. E-mail: milwaukrep@aol.com. In-person interview recommended. Applicants must submit a formal organization application, resume, writing sample, three personal references, three letters of recommendation, auditions required for acting internships. Application deadline: April 30.

MONTE BROWN DANCE
1170 Broadway
New York, New York 10001

General Information International 9-member contemporary touring dance company. Established in 1981. Number of employees: 9. Number of internship applications received each year: 5.
Internships Available ▶ *1 administrative intern:* responsibilities include performing duties related to fund-raising, booking, financial management, programming, marketing, attending staff and board meetings, taking turns with the management staff in the general upkeep of the office/studio. Candidates should have interest in dance and enrollment in business program. Duration is 1–2 semesters. Unpaid. Open to college freshmen, college sophomores, college juniors, college seniors, recent college graduates, graduate students.
Benefits Names of contacts, opportunity to attend seminars/workshops, willing to complete paperwork for educational credit, willing to provide letters of recommendation, 3 hours of credit if arranged by student in advance of internship.
Contact Write, fax, or e-mail Managing Director. Phone: 212-251-0789. Fax: 212-251-0743. E-mail: emonted@aol.com. In-person interview required. Applicants must submit a cover letter, resume. Applications are accepted continuously.

THE NEW CONSERVATORY THEATRE CENTER
25 Van Ness Avenue, Lower Lobby
San Francisco, California 94102

General Information Nonprofit theater school and performing arts company for children ages 4-19 emphasizing new and socially aware plays for family audiences; school consists of three educational theater touring companies for youths in grades K-12. Established in 1981. Number of employees: 20. Number of internship applications received each year: 25.
Internships Available ▶ *3 Pride Season interns:* responsibilities include working in production (stage management, design or with assistant directors); program is designed to feature work for and by gay and lesbian artists. Candidates should have ability to work independently, analytical skills, office skills, oral communication skills, personal interest in the field, self-motivation, strong interpersonal skills. Duration is flexible (evening hours). Position available as unpaid or at $6–$7 per hour. Open to college freshmen, college sophomores, college juniors, college seniors. ▶ *1 development intern.* Candidates should have ability to work independently, analytical skills, college courses in field, computer skills, editing skills, office skills, oral communication skills, organizational skills, plan to pursue career in field, research skills, self-motivation, strong interpersonal skills, strong leadership ability, writing skills. Duration is 3–6 months. Position available as unpaid or at $6–$9 per hour. Open to high school students, high school seniors, recent high school graduates, college freshmen, college sophomores, college juniors, college seniors, recent college graduates, graduate students. ▶ *2 general audience interns:* responsibilities include working in production or audience development and marketing. Candidates should have ability to work independently, office skills, oral communication skills, organizational skills, strong interpersonal skills, strong leadership ability. Duration is flexible (evening hours). Position available as unpaid or at $6–$7 per hour. Open to recent high school graduates, college freshmen, college sophomores, college juniors, college seniors, recent college graduates. ▶ *1 marketing and promotion intern.* Candidates should have ability to work independently, college courses in field, computer skills, knowledge

of field, office skills, oral communication skills, personal interest in the field, research skills, self-motivation, strong interpersonal skills, strong leadership ability, writing skills. Duration is 3–9 months. Position available as unpaid or at $7–$9 per hour. ▶ *Teaching assistants.* Candidates should have oral communication skills, strong interpersonal skills, strong leadership ability. Duration is 1–9 months. Position available as unpaid or at $6–$7 per hour. ▶ *1 touring program intern.* Candidates should have ability to work with others, analytical skills, computer skills, office skills, oral communication skills, organizational skills, personal interest in the field, research skills, self-motivation, strong leadership ability, writing skills, written communication skills. Duration is 3–9 months. Position available as unpaid or at $6–$7 per hour. Open to recent high school graduates, college freshmen, college juniors, college seniors, career changers. International applications accepted.

Benefits Opportunity to attend seminars/workshops, possible full-time employment, travel reimbursement, willing to provide letters of recommendation.

Contact Write Mr. Ed Decker, Executive Director. No phone calls. In-person interview recommended. Applications are accepted continuously.

NEW JERSEY SHAKESPEARE FESTIVAL
36 Madison Avenue
Madison, New Jersey 07940

General Information Actor's Equity theater devoted to producing the works of Shakespeare and other classic masterworks. Established in 1962. Number of employees: 250. Number of internship applications received each year: 500.

Internships Available ▶ *2 box office interns:* responsibilities include functioning as junior staff members, dealing with the public, and learning the important and intricate workings of ticketing procedures. Candidates should have ability to work independently, ability to work with others, computer skills, experience in the field, office skills, organizational skills. Duration is flexible. ▶ *3–5 costume design interns:* responsibilities include assisting costume shop supervisor and designers for the productions. Candidates should have ability to work with others, college degree in related field, knowledge of field, personal interest in the field, plan to pursue career in field. Duration is summer (May through August) or fall (August through December). ▶ *2 directing interns:* responsibilities include functioning as house manager for the festival, reporting to the managing director, and dealing with the public. Candidates should have college courses in field, experience in the field, research skills, self-motivation, strong leadership ability. Duration is flexible. ▶ *3–4 house management interns:* responsibilities include assisting on mainstage productions, coaching apprentices on scenes and monologues, and directing projects with non-Equity company members. Candidates should have ability to work independently, ability to work with others, experience in the field, oral communication skills, strong leadership ability, written communication skills, ability to handle the public. Duration is flexible. ▶ *3 lighting design interns:* responsibilities include assisting with mainstage productions and working under the supervision of the master electrician. Candidates should have college courses in field, computer skills, knowledge of field, personal interest in the field. Duration is flexible. ▶ *2 production interns:* responsibilities include assisting with logistical operations, including transporting actors, pricing and purchasing supplies, theater maintenance, and load-ins. Candidates should have ability to work with others, analytical skills, computer skills, office skills, organizational skills, personal interest in the field. Duration is flexible. ▶ *2 props interns:* responsibilities include coordinating and acquiring props for each show and acting as properties manager throughout the season. Candidates should have ability to work with others, experience in the field, personal interest in the field, research skills, painting and craftwork experience. Duration is flexible. ▶ *3–4 set design interns:* responsibilities include assisting with the construction and painting of sets and props for each show. Candidates should have ability to work independently, ability to work with others, college courses in field, knowledge of field, plan to pursue career in field, painting skills, carpentry skills.

Duration is summer (May through August) or fall (August through December). ▶ *1–2 sound design interns:* responsibilities include working directly with resident sound designer and taking responsibility for the operation of sound for each show. Candidates should have ability to work independently, ability to work with others, computer skills, editing skills, knowledge of field, research skills. Duration is flexible. ▶ *6 stage management interns:* responsibilities include assisting Equity stage managers for each show. Candidates should have analytical skills, oral communication skills, organizational skills, plan to pursue career in field, strong interpersonal skills, written communication skills. Duration is summer (May through August) or fall (August through December). ▶ *2–4 technical production interns:* responsibilities include working as part of the team that builds and mounts productions for the festival. Candidates should have ability to work independently, ability to work with others, organizational skills, personal interest in the field, drafting skills. Duration is flexible. ▶ *5 theater administration interns:* responsibilities include working in publicity, development, general management, and/or casting divisions. Candidates should have ability to work independently, ability to work with others, computer skills, office skills, organizational skills, personal interest in the field, writing skills, experience in specific area preferred. Duration is summer (May through August) or fall (August through December). All positions are unpaid. Open to college freshmen, college sophomores, college juniors, college seniors, recent college graduates, graduate students, law students, career changers, individuals reentering the workforce. International applications accepted.

Benefits Formal training, housing at a cost, job counseling, names of contacts, opportunity to attend seminars/workshops, possible full-time employment, willing to complete paperwork for educational credit, willing to provide letters of recommendation.

Contact Write or fax Mr. Joe Discher, Artistic Associate. Fax: 973-408-3361. In-person interview recommended. Applicants must submit a cover letter, resume, three personal references. Application deadline: May 1 for summer, September 1 for fall. World Wide Web: http://www.njshakespeare.org.

NEW STAGE THEATRE
1100 Carlisle Street
Jackson, Mississippi 39202

General Information Professional theater that operates on a letter of agreement with Actor's Equity Association and is committed to providing Mississippi with the best in theater arts. Established in 1967. Number of employees: 20.

Internships Available ▶ *3 tech interns:* responsibilities include assisting with costumes, carpentry, or a combination of electrics and carpentry. Duration is August to May. $140 per week. Open to college juniors, college seniors, recent college graduates, graduate students. International applications accepted.

Benefits Formal training, opportunity to attend seminars/workshops, possible full-time employment, willing to complete paperwork for educational credit, willing to provide letters of recommendation, reimbursement of work-related travel expenses.

Contact Write, call, fax, or e-mail Mr. Keith Black, Production Manager. Phone: 601-948-5836. Fax: 601-948-3538. E-mail: kblack05@sprynet.com. In-person interview required. Applicants must submit a cover letter, resume. Applications are accepted continuously.

NEW YORK CITY BALLET/NYC OPERA
20 Lincoln Center
New York, New York 10023

General Information Ballet and opera companies performing classical and modern repertory. Established in 1948. Number of employees: 220. Unit of City Center of Music and Drama, New York, New York. Number of internship applications received each year: 35.

Internships Available ▶ *1 lighting intern:* responsibilities include assisting resident and guest designers in the execution of lighting designs, drafting, computerized paperwork, focus, directing the crew, and design maintenance. Candidates should have abil-

New York City Ballet/NYC Opera (continued)

ity to work with others, knowledge of field, oral communication skills, organizational skills, plan to pursue career in field. Duration is 7 months. $1,500 per month. Open to recent college graduates, graduate students.
Benefits Formal training, names of contacts, on-the-job training, opportunity to attend seminars/workshops, possible full-time employment, travel reimbursement, willing to act as a professional reference, willing to provide letters of recommendation.
Contact Write, call, fax, or e-mail Mark Stanley, Lighting Director. Phone: 212-870-5658. Fax: 212-870-5651. E-mail: esorrin@nycballet. com. In-person interview required. Applicants must submit a cover letter, resume, portfolio, three letters of recommendation. Application deadline: February 28.

NEW YORK STATE THEATRE INSTITUTE
Russell Sage Campus, 155 River Street
Troy, New York 12180

General Information Professional theater company and statewide arts-in-education program developing one new musical theater production a season for family audiences, and performing a range of classical, modern, contemporary, and new works for school, family, and general audiences. Established in 1976. Number of employees: 32. Number of internship applications received each year: 100.
Internships Available ▶ *20–30 interns:* responsibilities include working in areas of technical theater, arts management, performance, and arts-in-education; participating in the operation of a professional theater. Duration is 5 months. Unpaid. Open to high school seniors, recent high school graduates, college freshmen, college sophomores, college juniors, college seniors, recent college graduates, graduate students, career changers, individuals reentering the workforce. International applications accepted.
Benefits Formal training, job counseling, names of contacts, opportunity to attend seminars/workshops, travel reimbursement, tuition assistance, willing to complete paperwork for educational credit, willing to provide letters of recommendation, academic credit granted by State University of New York at Albany and Russell Sage College.
Contact Write, call, fax, or e-mail Ms. Arlene Leff, Intern Program Administrator, Russell Sage Campus 155 River Street, Troy, New York 12180. Phone: 518-274-3573. Fax: 518-274-3815. E-mail: nysti@capital.net. In-person interview recommended. Application deadline: June 1 for summer, November 1 for spring. World Wide Web: http://www.nysti.org.

NORTH SHORE MUSIC THEATRE
Dunham Road, PO Box 62
Beverly, Massachusetts 01915-0062

General Information Professional theater dedicated to the American musical and programs for young audiences, serving over 300,000 patrons from April through December. Established in 1955. Number of employees: 100. Unit of North Shore Community Arts Foundation, Beverly, Massachusetts. Number of internship applications received each year: 100.
Internships Available ▶ *2 company management interns:* responsibilities include assisting company manager with housing, transportation, and services for Equity companies and concert road groups. Candidates should have office skills, self-motivation, strong interpersonal skills. Open to individuals 21 years of age and older. ▶ *2–4 electrics interns:* responsibilities include hanging and focusing instruments and running follow spots for musicals and concerts. Candidates should have strong interpersonal skills, no fear of heights. Open to individuals 18 years of age and older. ▶ *6–8 production assistants:* responsibilities include working within various departments to gain basic understanding and assisting in various departments with show runs. Candidates should have strong interpersonal skills. Open to individuals 18 years of age and older. ▶ *1 properties intern:* responsibilities include procuring and creating theatrical props and special effects. Candidates should have ability to work independently, ability to work with others, experience in the field, personal interest in the field,

carpentry skills. Open to individuals 18 years of age and older. ▶ *1 scenic art intern:* responsibilities include scenic painting for musicals and concerts; emphasis is on painting 3-dimensional units. Candidates should have ability to work independently, ability to work with others, experience in the field, personal interest in the field. Open to individuals 18 years of age and older. ▶ *2 sound interns:* responsibilities include maintaining equipment, sound setup, and operating wireless microphones for musicals and concerts. Candidates should have experience in the field, knowledge of field, personal interest in the field, plan to pursue career in field, strong interpersonal skills. Open to individuals 18 years of age and older. ▶ *1–2 stage management interns:* responsibilities include assisting Equity stage manager or running crew supervisor in rehearsing and running musicals and children's shows. Candidates should have experience in the field, knowledge of field, personal interest in the field, self-motivation, strong interpersonal skills, strong leadership ability. Open to individuals 18 years of age and older. ▶ *1–2 wardrobe interns:* responsibilities include providing fitting, maintenance, and dressing needs for musicals and concerts. Candidates should have experience in the field, knowledge of field, strong interpersonal skills, sewing skills. Open to individuals 18 years of age and older. Duration for all positions is 4–8 months. All positions paid at $200 per week. International applications accepted.
Benefits Names of contacts, opportunity to attend seminars/workshops, possible full-time employment, willing to complete paperwork for educational credit, willing to provide letters of recommendation, educational stipend, educational seminars.
Contact Write or fax Assistant Production Manager. Fax: 508-922-0768. No phone calls. In-person interview recommended. Applicants must submit a formal organization application, cover letter, resume, three personal references. Applications are accepted continuously. World Wide Web: http://www.nsmt.org.

OMAHA MAGIC THEATRE
325 South 16th Street
Omaha, Nebraska 68102

General Information Professional nonunion theater devoted to research, new performance work, development, and touring of original plays and plays with music. Number of employees: 3. Number of internship applications received each year: 12.
Internships Available ▶ *3 interns:* responsibilities include aiding in all aspects of theater work, including building sets, performing, theater maintenance, and office work. Duration is flexible. Unpaid. International applications accepted.
Benefits Formal training, job counseling, names of contacts, opportunity to attend seminars/workshops, possible full-time employment, willing to complete paperwork for educational credit, willing to provide letters of recommendation.
Contact Write, fax, or e-mail Ms. Jo Ann Schmidman, Artistic Director. Fax: 402-932-6818. E-mail: jschmiem@unomaha.edu. No phone calls. Applicants must submit a resume, three personal references, detailed letter of interest. Applications are accepted continuously.

ORGANIC THEATER COMPANY
1420 Maple Avenue
Evanstown, Illinois 60201

General Information Theater dedicated to plays with depth of character and literary strength. Produces a number of Chicago premiers. Established in 1969. Number of employees: 10. Number of internship applications received each year: 20.
Internships Available ▶ *1 grant writing intern:* responsibilities include evaluating grant materials, researching grant possibilities, and writing grant applications. Candidates should have computer skills, editing skills, writing skills, Microsoft Office '97 skills. Duration is 8–12 weeks. Open to recent college graduates, graduate students. ▶ *1–4 stage management interns:* responsibilities include assisting stage management staff through rehearsals and all performances. Candidates should have ability to work independently, ability to work with others. Duration is 9–15

weeks. Open to recent college graduates, graduate students, career changers. All positions are unpaid. International applications accepted.

Benefits Job counseling, on-the-job training, possible full-time employment, willing to complete paperwork for educational credit, willing to provide letters of recommendation.

Contact Write, fax, or e-mail Nina Jones, Managing Director. Fax: 847-475-9200. E-mail: nina.jones@usa.net. No phone calls. In-person interview recommended. Applicants must submit a cover letter, resume. Application deadline: continuous (after April 15 only).

PAN ASIAN REPERTORY THEATRE
47 Great Jones Street
New York, New York 10012

General Information Professional theater celebrating Asian-American expressiveness, producing new plays, Asian masterworks in translation, and Western classics in non-traditional settings. Established in 1977. Number of employees: 4. Number of internship applications received each year: 50.

Internships Available ▶ *Administrative interns.* Candidates should have ability to work with others, college courses in field, knowledge of field, oral communication skills, personal interest in the field, self-motivation. Duration is 3 months minimum. ▶ *Production interns.* Candidates should have ability to work with others, college courses in field, knowledge of field, personal interest in the field, self-motivation. Duration is flexible. All positions paid. Open to college freshmen, college sophomores, college juniors, college seniors, recent college graduates, graduate students. International applications accepted.

Benefits Names of contacts, tuition assistance, willing to complete paperwork for educational credit, willing to provide letters of recommendation, small stipend.

Contact Write, fax, or e-mail Tisa Chang, Artistic/Producing Director. Fax: 212-505-6014. E-mail: panasian@aol.com. Applicants must submit a cover letter, resume. Applications are accepted continuously. World Wide Web: http://www.panasian.org.

PAPER MILL PLAYHOUSE
Brookside Drive
Millburn, New Jersey 07041

General Information Theater company producing the highest quality productions and accompanying activities. Established in 1938. Number of employees: 100. Number of internship applications received each year: 25.

Internships Available ▶ *1–3 general administration interns:* responsibilities include working with various departments including education, development, fund-raising, marketing, public relations, and casting. Candidates should have ability to work independently, analytical skills, computer skills, editing skills, office skills, oral communication skills, organizational skills, plan to pursue career in field, research skills, self-motivation, strong interpersonal skills, writing skills. Duration is flexible. Unpaid. Open to high school students, high school seniors, recent high school graduates, college freshmen, college sophomores, college juniors, college seniors, recent college graduates, graduate students.

Benefits Formal training, job counseling, on-the-job training, willing to act as a professional reference, willing to complete paperwork for educational credit, willing to provide letters of recommendation.

Contact Write, fax, or e-mail Susan Speidel, Director of Education. Fax: 973-376-0825. E-mail: sspeidel@papermill.org. No phone calls. In-person interview recommended. Applicants must submit a cover letter, resume, two writing samples, three personal references, three letters of recommendation. Applications are accepted continuously. World Wide Web: http://www.papermill.org.

THE PEARL THEATRE COMPANY
80 Saint Mark's Place
New York, New York 10003

General Information Nonprofit classical theatre company. Established in 1982. Number of employees: 7. Number of internship applications received each year: 100.

Internships Available ▶ *1 administrative intern:* responsibilities include assisting in all administrative departments including marketing, development, finance, production, and artistic direction. Candidates should have ability to work independently, computer skills, knowledge of field, office skills, oral communication skills, personal interest in the field, plan to pursue career in field, self-motivation, strong interpersonal skills, writing skills. Duration is August to May. $150—$175 weekly stipend. Open to college juniors, college seniors, recent college graduates, career changers. ▶ *1 costume intern:* responsibilities include assisting costume designer on 5 classical plays and wardrobe maintenance. Candidates should have ability to work independently, ability to work with others, experience in the field, plan to pursue career in field, self-motivation, indestructibly positive attitude, reasonable background in theatrical costumes. Duration is 10 months, full-time. up to $225 weekly stipend. Open to recent college graduates. ▶ *2 stage management interns:* responsibilities include assisting stage manager with 3 to 5 productions, scheduling, prompting, blocking, production meetings, light board, sound and floor managing. Candidates should have ability to work independently, analytical skills, knowledge of field, oral communication skills, organizational skills, plan to pursue career in field, self-motivation, strong interpersonal skills. Duration is 6 to 10 months, full-time. $150—$175 weekly stipend. Open to recent college graduates. International applications accepted.

Benefits Job counseling, names of contacts, on-the-job training, possible full-time employment, willing to act as a professional reference, willing to complete paperwork for educational credit, willing to provide letters of recommendation, Equity membership candidacy points for stage management interns.

Contact Write or fax Jessica Kroll, General Manager. Fax: 212-505-3404. No phone calls. In-person interview recommended. Applicants must submit a cover letter, resume, two writing samples, three personal references. Applications are accepted continuously. World Wide Web: http://www.pearltheatre.org.

PENINSULA PLAYERS
W4351 Peninsula Players Road
Fish Creek, Wisconsin 54212-9799

General Information Professional resident summer theater. Established in 1935. Number of employees: 40. Number of internship applications received each year: 40.

Internships Available ▶ *2–4 administrative interns:* responsibilities include assisting with box office operation, promotion and publicity, accounting, and house management. Candidates should have office skills, oral communication skills, personal interest in the field, strong interpersonal skills, written communication skills. ▶ *6 production interns:* responsibilities include working in areas of costume, carpentry, electrical, design, props, and stage management. Candidates should have ability to work with others, knowledge of field, personal interest in the field, self-motivation. Duration for all positions is 1 summer, June 1 to Labor Day. All positions paid at $50–$75 per week. Open to high school seniors, recent high school graduates, college freshmen, college sophomores, college juniors, college seniors, recent college graduates, graduate students, career changers. International applications accepted.

Benefits Free housing, free meals, possible full-time employment, travel reimbursement, willing to act as a professional reference, willing to complete paperwork for educational credit, willing to provide letters of recommendation.

Contact Write or call Mr. Todd Schmidt, General Manager. Phone: 920-868-3287. Telephone interview required. Applicants must submit a formal organization application, cover letter, resume, two letters of recommendation. Application deadline: May 1. World Wide Web: http://www.peninsulaplayers.com.

PIONEER PLAYHOUSE
840 Stanford Road
Danville, Kentucky 40422

General Information   A summer stock theater producing plays. Established in 1950. Number of employees: 30. Number of internship applications received each year: 50.
Internships Available ▶ *5 acting and technical interns:* responsibilities include assisting in all aspects of play productions. Duration is 1 summer. Unpaid. Open to high school students, high school seniors, recent high school graduates, college freshmen, college sophomores, college juniors, college seniors, recent college graduates, graduate students, law students, career changers, individuals reentering the workforce. International applications accepted.
Benefits   Meals at a cost, willing to complete paperwork for educational credit.
Contact   Write, call, or fax Col. Eben Henson, Producer. Phone: 606-236-2747. Fax: 606-236-2341. $947 tuition plus room and board for high school-level interns; others pay only room and board. Application deadline: May 1.

PITTSBURGH CIVIC LIGHT OPERA
719 Liberty Avenue
Pittsburgh, Pennsylvania 15222

General Information   Producer of Broadway-scale, professional musicals in a 2,837-seat theater during the summer. Established in 1946. Number of employees: 20. Number of internship applications received each year: 50.
Internships Available ▶ *1 summer development apprentice.* Candidates should have computer skills, office skills, oral communication skills, organizational skills, strong interpersonal skills, written communication skills. ▶ *Summer general administration apprentices:* responsibilities include working for the executive director and handling a full range of administrative tasks in company office. Candidates should have computer skills, office skills, oral communication skills, organizational skills, strong interpersonal skills, written communication skills. ▶ *Summer outreach apprentices:* responsibilities include performing general duties such as data entry and assisting with a variety of outreach programs. Candidates should have computer skills, office skills, oral communication skills, organizational skills, strong interpersonal skills, written communication skills. ▶ *1 summer promotion/marketing apprentice:* responsibilities include performing a broad range of tasks such as writing press releases, distributing flyers and posters, and escorting stars on interviews. Candidates should have computer skills, office skills, oral communication skills, organizational skills, strong interpersonal skills, written communication skills. ▶ *1–2 technical apprentices.* Candidates should have computer skills, knowledge of the field, oral communication skills, personal interest in the field, strong interpersonal skills, written communication skills. Duration for all positions is 10 weeks. All positions paid at $75 per week. Open to recent high school graduates, college freshmen, college sophomores, college juniors, college seniors. International applications accepted.
Benefits   Names of contacts, on-the-job training, willing to act as a professional reference, willing to complete paperwork for educational credit, willing to provide letters of recommendation.
Contact   Write or fax Van Kaplan, Executive Producer/General Manager. Fax: 412-281-5339. In-person interview recommended. Applicants must submit a formal organization application, cover letter, resume, two personal references. Application deadline: March 15. World Wide Web: http://www.pittsburghCLO.org.

PLAYHOUSE ON THE SQUARE
51 South Cooper
Memphis, Tennessee 38104

General Information   Nonprofit professional theater with a mission to create challenging, truthful, entertaining, and culturally diverse high-quality theater that reflects, improves, and reaches the present and future community. Established in 1969. Number of employees: 23. Number of internship applications received each year: 300.

Internships Available ▶ *7 acting interns:* responsibilities include acting and technical or administrative work. Candidates should have ability to work with others, knowledge of field, plan to pursue career in field, self-motivation. Open to recent college graduates. ▶ *1 administrative intern:* responsibilities include assisting with clerical duties, box office, house management, and subscription drive. Candidates should have ability to work independently, computer skills, knowledge of field, oral communication skills, self-motivation, strong leadership ability. Open to recent college graduates. ▶ *1 costumes intern:* responsibilities include assisting with costuming. Candidates should have college courses in field, knowledge of field, organizational skills, plan to pursue career in field, self-motivation. Open to recent college graduates. ▶ *2 stage management interns:* responsibilities include assisting with management and technical tasks. Candidates should have ability to work independently, ability to work with others, knowledge of field, organizational skills, self-motivation, strong leadership ability. Open to recent college graduates. ▶ *1 technical/set design intern:* responsibilities include assisting with set construction. Candidates should have ability to work with others, knowledge of field, organizational skills, personal interest in the field, self-motivation. Duration for all positions is 1 year. All positions paid at $100 per week.
Benefits   Free housing, health insurance, job counseling, names of contacts, on-the-job training, possible full-time employment, willing to act as a professional reference, willing to complete paperwork for educational credit, willing to provide letters of recommendation, free utilities, local phone, laundry facilities.
Contact   Write Jackie Nichols, Executive Producer. In-person interview required. Applicants must submit a resume, two letters of recommendation. Applications are accepted continuously.

PORTLAND STAGE COMPANY
PO Box 1458
Portland, Maine 04104

General Information   Resident professional theater producing a 6-play mainstage season and providing numerous other educational and cultural services. Established in 1974. Number of employees: 30. Number of internship applications received each year: 100.
Internships Available ▶ *1 directing/dramaturgy intern:* responsibilities include assisting directors on mainstage productions, conducting dramaturgical research, and assisting artistic staff on day-to-day administrative activities. Candidates should have knowledge of field, plan to pursue career in field, research skills, self-motivation, strong interpersonal skills, writing skills. Open to recent high school graduates, college freshmen, college sophomores, college juniors, college seniors, recent college graduates, graduate students. ▶ *3–5 production interns:* responsibilities include working in carpentry/scene painting, costumes, and electrics/sound props; assisting professionals in their assigned production department with construction, maintenance, and crew management. Candidates should have ability to work independently, ability to work with others, knowledge of field, plan to pursue career in field, self-motivation. Open to recent high school graduates, college freshmen, college sophomores, college juniors, college seniors, recent college graduates, graduate students. ▶ *2 stage management interns:* responsibilities include assisting Equity Stage managers in all areas of production and preproduction. Candidates should have college degree in related field, knowledge of field, plan to pursue career in field, self-motivation, strong interpersonal skills. Open to recent high school graduates, college freshmen, college sophomores, college juniors, college seniors, recent college graduates, graduate students. ▶ *1–2 theater administration interns:* responsibilities include assisting with marketing development company and general arts management activities. Candidates should have ability to work independently, computer skills, oral communication skills, organizational skills, writing skills. Open to recent high school graduates, college freshmen, college sophomores, college juniors, college seniors, recent college graduates, graduate students, career changers. Duration for all positions is September to May. All positions paid.

Benefits Formal training, housing at a cost, opportunity to attend seminars/workshops, possible full-time employment, willing to act as a professional reference, willing to complete paperwork for educational credit, willing to provide letters of recommendation.
Contact Write, call, fax, or e-mail Dawn McAndrews, Director of Education and Outreach. Phone: 207-774-1043. Fax: 207-774-0576. E-mail: portstage@aol.com. Telephone interview required. Applicants must submit a formal organization application, cover letter, resume, writing sample, two letters of recommendation. Application deadline: May 31 for full-season positions; continuous for partial-season positions. World Wide Web: http://www.portlandarts.com/portlandstageco.

PRIMARY STAGES
584 Ninth Avenue
New York, New York 10036

General Information Producer of new American plays. Established in 1985. Number of employees: 6. Number of internship applications received each year: 75.
Internships Available ▶ *1–4 production interns:* responsibilities include assisting the set, lighting, costume, or sound designer in research and implementation of production design. Candidates should have knowledge of field, oral communication skills, personal interest in the field, self-motivation, strong interpersonal skills. Duration is 5 weeks or more. ▶ *1–4 publicity and marketing interns:* responsibilities include assisting publicity/marketing staff in marketing production, special events, and subscription campaigns. Candidates should have oral communication skills, self-motivation, strong interpersonal skills, writing skills. Duration is flexible. ▶ *1–4 stage management interns:* responsibilities include assisting the manager in rehearsals and serving as running crew backstage. Candidates should have knowledge of field, oral communication skills, personal interest in the field, self-motivation, strong interpersonal skills. Duration is 9 weeks or more. All positions are unpaid. Open to college freshmen, college sophomores, college juniors, college seniors, recent college graduates, graduate students, career changers, individuals reentering the workforce. International applications accepted.
Benefits Job counseling, names of contacts, on-the-job training, willing to complete paperwork for educational credit, willing to provide letters of recommendation.
Contact Write, fax, or e-mail Seth Gordon, Associate Producer. Fax: 212-333-2025. E-mail: primary@ix.netcom.com. No phone calls. In-person interview recommended. Applicants must submit a cover letter, resume. Applications are accepted continuously.

PULSE ENSEMBLE THEATRE
432 West 42nd Street
New York, New York 10036

General Information Ensemble theater company that produces mainstage shows, Bare Bones Classic Season (a studio season), and readings of new plays. Established in 1989. Number of employees: 6. Number of internship applications received each year: 40.
Internships Available ▶ *12–20 acting interns:* responsibilities include playing small parts in shows and providing general assistance in the preparation of shows. Candidates should have acting experience or training. Duration is 6 months. Open to high school students, high school seniors, recent high school graduates, college freshmen, college sophomores, college juniors, college seniors, recent college graduates, graduate students, law students, career changers, individuals reentering the workforce. ▶ *2–4 directing interns:* responsibilities include assisting the Director in taking a play from casting through to performance. Candidates should have ability to work independently, ability to work with others, experience in the field, oral communication skills, research skills, strong leadership ability. Duration is 6–8 weeks. Open to recent high school graduates, college seniors, recent college graduates, graduate students, individuals reentering the workforce. ▶ *2–6 fund-raising interns:* responsibilities include finding funding sources, helping to complete grant applications, and helping at fund-raising events. Candidates

should have ability to work independently, computer skills, organizational skills, research skills, writing skills. Duration is 3–12 months. Open to recent college graduates, graduate students, law students, career changers. ▶ *2–4 management interns:* responsibilities include assisting the general manager, organizing volunteer groups, and assisting at the box office. Duration is 6 months. Open to high school students, high school seniors, recent high school graduates, college freshmen, college sophomores, college juniors, college seniors, recent college graduates, graduate students, law students, career changers, individuals reentering the workforce. ▶ *2–4 marketing interns:* responsibilities include typing and distributing publicity and making promotional telephone calls. Duration is 3 months minimum. Open to high school students, high school seniors, recent high school graduates, college freshmen, college sophomores, college juniors, college seniors, recent college graduates, graduate students, law students, career changers, individuals reentering the workforce. ▶ *2–3 production interns:* responsibilities include setting up scenery, working on sound tapes, and running lighting boards. Candidates should have ability to work independently, experience in the field, knowledge of field, organizational skills, personal interest in the field, research skills. Duration is 3 months minimum. Open to high school students, high school seniors, recent high school graduates, college freshmen, college sophomores, college juniors, college seniors, recent college graduates, graduate students, law students, career changers, individuals reentering the workforce. ▶ *1–3 stage management interns:* responsibilities include operating shows and sound and light equipment and setting props. Duration is 3 months minimum. Open to high school students, high school seniors, recent high school graduates, college freshmen, college sophomores, college juniors, college seniors, recent college graduates, graduate students, law students, career changers, individuals reentering the workforce. All positions are unpaid. International applications accepted.
Benefits Formal training, job counseling, on-the-job training, possible full-time employment, willing to complete paperwork for educational credit, willing to provide letters of recommendation, reimbursement for job-related travel.
Contact Write or call Alexa Kelly, Artistic Director. Phone: 212-695-1596. In-person interview recommended. Applicants must submit a cover letter, resume, two letters of recommendation, audition (for acting interns). Application deadline: June 1 for fall, December 1 for spring.

REPERTORIO ESPANOL
138 East 27th Street
New York, New York 10016

General Information Spanish language theater company that presents plays from Spain's Golden Age, contemporary Latin-American classics, and works by new playwrights. Established in 1968. Number of employees: 12. Number of internship applications received each year: 5.
Internships Available ▶ *Interns:* responsibilities include performing duties in the areas of community affairs, media relations, and fund development; preparing press packages for groups and responding to inquiries; arranging rehearsals, changing jets, helping with various production activities. Duration is flexible. Position available as unpaid or paid. Open to recent high school graduates, college freshmen, college sophomores, college juniors, college seniors, recent college graduates. International applications accepted.
Benefits Names of contacts, possible full-time employment, willing to complete paperwork for educational credit, willing to provide letters of recommendation, free tickets to performances.
Contact Write, call, or fax Mr. Felix Arocho, Director of Audience Development. Phone: 212-889-2850. Fax: 212-686-3732. In-person interview recommended. Applicants must submit a cover letter, resume. Applications are accepted continuously.

ROUNDABOUT THEATRE COMPANY, INC.
231 West 39th Street
New York, New York 10018

General Information Nonprofit Broadway theater presenting revivals of classic plays. Established in 1965. Number of employees: 80. Number of internship applications received each year: 100.

Internships Available ▶ *1 business management intern:* responsibilities include assisting with income and expense controls, clerical duties, daily operations, and building management. Candidates should have computer skills, organizational skills. Open to high school students, high school seniors, recent high school graduates, college freshmen, college sophomores, college juniors, college seniors, recent college graduates, graduate students, law students, career changers. ▶ *1 casting intern:* responsibilities include assisting with clerical duties, especially photocopying, and arranging auditions and readings. Candidates should have ability to work with others, organizational skills, strong interpersonal skills, good phone manner. Open to high school students, high school seniors, recent high school graduates, college freshmen, college sophomores, college juniors, college seniors, recent college graduates, graduate students, individuals reentering the workforce. ▶ *2 development interns:* responsibilities include assisting with clerical duties, researching potential donors, and performing specific fund-raising projects. Candidates should have oral communication skills, strong interpersonal skills, written communication skills. Open to high school students, high school seniors, recent high school graduates, college freshmen, college sophomores, college juniors, college seniors, recent college graduates, graduate students. ▶ *1 education intern:* responsibilities include assisting with research and writing of newsletter articles, study guides, and lobby display; assisting with school visits; clerical duties. Candidates should have oral communication skills, organizational skills, written communication skills, attention to detail. Open to high school students, high school seniors, recent high school graduates, college freshmen, college sophomores, college juniors, college seniors, recent college graduates, graduate students, career changers, individuals reentering the workforce. ▶ *1 marketing intern:* responsibilities include assisting with clerical duties, ticket sales, press coverage, public relations, subscriber services, and special events. Candidates should have computer skills, oral communication skills, organizational skills, strong interpersonal skills. Open to high school students, high school seniors, recent high school graduates, college freshmen, college sophomores, college juniors, college seniors, recent college graduates, graduate students, law students, career changers. ▶ *Production interns:* responsibilities include assisting technicians and carpenters with construction, installation, and maintenance of scenery, props, and lighting equipment; assisting in related office work. Candidates should have ability to work with others, experience in the field, organizational skills. Open to high school seniors, recent high school graduates, college freshmen, college sophomores, college juniors, college seniors, recent college graduates, graduate students, career changers. ▶ *2 ticket services interns:* responsibilities include clerical duties, large mailings, some data entry and phone calls. Candidates should have ability to work independently, oral communication skills, organizational skills. Open to high school students, high school seniors, recent high school graduates, college freshmen, college sophomores, college juniors, college seniors, recent college graduates, individuals reentering the workforce. Duration for all positions is flexible. All positions paid at $8–$20 per day.

Benefits Job counseling, names of contacts, possible full-time employment, travel reimbursement, willing to complete paperwork for educational credit, willing to provide letters of recommendation, stipend available.

Contact Write or fax Philip Alexander, Intern Coordinator. Fax: 212-768-8175. In-person interview required. Applicants must submit a cover letter, resume. Application deadline: March 1 for summer, August 1 for fall, November 1 for spring. World Wide Web: http://www.roundabouttheatre.org.

SAN FRANCISCO OPERA
301 Van Ness Avenue
San Francisco, California 94102

General Information Opera producing a season of international opera and regularly presenting premiers of new operas and commissioned works. Established in 1932. Number of employees: 140. Number of internship applications received each year: 100.

Internships Available ▶ *1–2 artistic and musical administration interns:* responsibilities include acting as liaison with artists, managers, and other theaters; conducting research, entering computer data about auditions; organizing audition material; filing confidential artistic information. Candidates should have ability to work independently, computer skills, office skills, organizational skills, strong interpersonal skills. Duration is 12 open. Open to recent high school graduates, college freshmen, college sophomores, college juniors, college seniors, recent college graduates, graduate students, individuals reentering the workforce. ▶ *1–2 costume shop interns:* responsibilities include running errands, shopping for fabrics and materials, maintaining notion inventory, sorting fabric sampler, recording and arranging trimmings, pulling and replacing costumes from stock. Candidates should have ability to work with others, oral communication skills, personal interest in the field, self-motivation. Duration is open. Open to recent high school graduates, college freshmen, college sophomores, college juniors, college seniors, recent college graduates, graduate students, individuals reentering the workforce. ▶ *1–2 development interns:* responsibilities include special events planning, individual and institutional gifts fund-raising, assisting with grant writing, prospect research, fund-raising systems, planned giving, telefunding. Candidates should have office skills, oral communication skills, self-motivation, strong interpersonal skills, writing skills. Duration is open. Open to recent high school graduates, college freshmen, college sophomores, college juniors, college seniors, recent college graduates. ▶ *1–2 finance/accounting interns:* responsibilities include filing and organizing financial documents, reconciling and analyzing accounts, and assisting with special projects. Candidates should have ability to work with others, analytical skills, computer skills, knowledge of field, organizational skills. Duration is open. Open to recent high school graduates, college freshmen, college sophomores, college juniors, college seniors, recent college graduates, graduate students, individuals reentering the workforce. ▶ *1–2 guild activities and events interns:* responsibilities include working with the board of directors; assisting with special events, education and outreach program, volunteer management, and fund-raising development. Candidates should have computer skills, oral communication skills, self-motivation, strong interpersonal skills, written communication skills. Duration is open. Open to recent high school graduates, college freshmen, college sophomores, college juniors, college seniors, recent college graduates, graduate students, individuals reentering the workforce. ▶ *1–2 human resources/labor relations interns:* responsibilities include assistig with recruiting/hiring, health and safety fair, employee training and development, managing personnel records, compensation and benefit coordination, and policies and procedures administration. Candidates should have computer skills, oral communication skills, organizational skills, strong interpersonal skills, written communication skills. Duration is 8–10 open. Open to recent high school graduates, college freshmen, college sophomores, college juniors, college seniors, recent college graduates, graduate students, individuals reentering the workforce. ▶ *1–2 information systems interns:* responsibilities include assisting with data backup and maintenance, equipment and software inventory management, conducting Internet research and file searches, routine network and hardware maintenance, and with Sybase, C++, Powerbuilder, Access, and RPG programming. Candidates should have ability to work independently, ability to work with others, computer skills, knowledge of field, office skills, personal interest in the field, research skills. Duration is open. Open to recent high school graduates, college freshmen, college sophomores, college juniors, college seniors, recent college graduates, graduate students, individuals reentering the workforce. ▶ *1–2 marketing interns:* responsibilities include composing collateral copy; collecting art/images for brochures; compiling information from a variety of sources; editing/proofreading documents and coordinating proofreading throughout organization; placing advertisements or event-related media; and assisting with budgeting, sales reporting, and compiling statistics. Candidates should have ability to work with others, computer skills, editing skills, oral communication skills, writing skills. Duration is open. Open to recent high school graduates, college freshmen, college sophomores, college juniors, college seniors, recent college graduates, graduate students, individuals reentering the workforce. ▶ *1–2 opera center interns:* responsibilities include assisting with events and performances, preparations for Western Opera Theater (national touring company), public relations and marketing, artist services, and with various aspects of the Merola Opera Program (11-week training for young artists). Candidates should have ability to work with others, computer skills, oral communication skills, personal interest in the field, strong interpersonal skills, written communication skills. Duration is open. Open to recent high school graduates, college freshmen, college sophomores, college juniors, college seniors, recent college graduates, graduate students, individuals reentering the workforce. ▶ *1–2 orchestra administration interns:* responsibilities include providing general assistance to the Orchestra Manager by assisting with musicians' employment records, assisting with engaging substitute and extra musicians, assisting with rehearsals and performances, tracking attendance and breaks, and assisting with financial reports. Candidates should have computer skills, oral communication skills, personal interest in the field, strong interpersonal skills, written communication skills. Duration is open. Open to recent high school graduates, college freshmen, college sophomores, college juniors, college seniors, recent college graduates, graduate students, individuals reentering the workforce. ▶ *1–2 production interns:* responsibilities include participating in production meetings, assisting with the design and management of productions from scene shop to stage, creating and manipulating information on department network. Candidates should have ability to work with others, computer skills, personal interest in the field. Duration is open. Open to recent high school graduates, college freshmen, college sophomores, college juniors, college seniors, recent college graduates, graduate students, individuals reentering the workforce. ▶ *1–2 public relations interns:* responsibilities include assisting members of public relations team with daily activities, assisting with mailings and photo distribution; maintaining photo and artist files; assisting during performances, events, and conferences when necessary; maintaining press database. Candidates should have ability to work with others, computer skills, oral communication skills, organizational skills, written communication skills. Duration is open. Open to recent high school graduates, college freshmen, college sophomores, college juniors, college seniors, recent college graduates, graduate students, individuals reentering the workforce. All positions are unpaid. International applications accepted.

Benefits Possible full-time employment, willing to act as a professional reference, willing to complete paperwork for educational credit, willing to provide letters of recommendation, opportunity to attend dress rehearsals.

Contact Write, call, or e-mail Anne Phillippi, Human Resource Assistant/Internship Coordinator. Phone: 415-565-3286. E-mail: aphillippi@sfopera.com. In-person interview recommended. Applicants must submit a formal organization application, resume, 2-3 personal references. Applications are accepted continuously. World Wide Web: http://www.sfopera.com.

SAN JOSE REPERTORY THEATRE
101 Paseo de San Antonio
San Jose, California 95113

General Information Professional theater company that produces all types of theater from new works to classics to musicals in a six-show season running from September to June. Established in 1980. Number of employees: 50. Number of internship applications received each year: 50.

Internships Available ▶ *Interns:* responsibilities include stage management, costumes, lighting design, company management,

and marketing. Candidates should have ability to work independently, experience in the field, organizational skills, strong interpersonal skills. Duration is flexible. Unpaid. Open to recent high school graduates, college freshmen, college sophomores, college juniors, college seniors, recent college graduates. ▶ *Interns:* responsibilities include painting scenic art and production management. Candidates should have ability to work independently, college courses in field, knowledge of field, self-motivation. Position available as unpaid or paid. Open to recent college graduates.

Benefits Job counseling, names of contacts, on-the-job training, possible full-time employment, willing to act as a professional reference, willing to complete paperwork for educational credit, willing to provide letters of recommendation, opportunity to work alongside professionals and become an integral part of production process.

Contact Write or fax Drayton Foltz, Production Manager. Fax: 408-367-7237. No phone calls. In-person interview recommended. Applicants must submit a formal organization application, cover letter, resume, three personal references. Applications are accepted continuously. World Wide Web: http://www.sjrep.com.

SEATTLE OPERA ASSOCIATION
PO Box 9248
Seattle, Washington 98109

General Information Opera company producing 5 full scale operas per season. Established in 1964. Number of internship applications received each year: 30.

Internships Available ▶ *3 assistant direction interns:* responsibilities include observing rehearsals, keeping a "blocking book," walking roles for absent performers, and other duties as determined by the stage director. Candidates should have ability to work independently, experience in the field, knowledge of field, oral communication skills, personal interest in the field, plan to pursue career in field, strong interpersonal skills. Duration is 4 weeks. Open to college seniors, recent college graduates, graduate students, career changers, individuals reentering the workforce. ▶ *5 costume interns:* responsibilities include assisting the Costume Shop Manager in shopping and other duties based on the ability of the intern. Candidates should have ability to work independently, knowledge of field, oral communication skills, personal interest in the field, strong interpersonal skills, ability to sew at an intermediate level. Duration is 6 weeks. Open to high school students, high school seniors, recent high school graduates, college freshmen, college sophomores, college juniors, college seniors, recent college graduates, graduate students, career changers, individuals reentering the workforce, individuals studying fashion design or college theater costume design/construction. ▶ *5 hair and make-up interns.* Candidates should have ability to work independently, knowledge of field, oral communication skills, personal interest in the field, strong interpersonal skills, previous experience in make-up application for stage. Duration is 3 weeks. Open to high school students, high school seniors, recent high school graduates, college freshmen, college sophomores, college juniors, college seniors, recent college graduates, graduate students, career changers, individuals reentering the workforce, those studying wig and make-up application for theater and opera or those studying at salon schools. ▶ *5 music library interns:* responsibilities include working directly with the music librarian, marking scores, and performing other duties as determined by the music librarian. Candidates should have ability to work independently, college courses in field, experience in the field, knowledge of field, personal interest in the field, self-motivation, ability to read music well and in different clefs. Duration is 6–10 weeks. Open to high school seniors, recent high school graduates, college freshmen, college sophomores, college juniors, college seniors, recent college graduates, graduate students, career changers, individuals reentering the workforce. ▶ *Stage management interns:* responsibilities include working as part of the stage management team, taking notes, typing schedules and other paperwork, cueing performers, and other duties as assigned by the stage manager. Candidates should have ability to work independently, computer skills, experience in the field, knowledge of field, office skills, oral

Seattle Opera Association (continued)

communication skills, organizational skills, personal interest in the field, strong interpersonal skills. Duration is 10 weeks. Open to recent high school graduates, college freshmen, college sophomores, college juniors, college seniors, recent college graduates, graduate students, career changers, individuals reentering the workforce. All positions are unpaid. International applications accepted.

Benefits On-the-job training, willing to act as a professional reference, willing to complete paperwork for educational credit, willing to provide letters of recommendation, opportunities to attend rehearsals and coachings and to meet with artists and staff.

Contact Write, call, fax, or e-mail Paula Podemski, Production Supervisor, PO Box 9248, Seattle, Washington 98109. Phone: 206-676-5812. Fax: 206-389-7651. E-mail: opera@seanet.com. In-person interview recommended. Applicants must submit a formal organization application, cover letter, resume, three personal references. Applications are accepted continuously. World Wide Web: http://www.seattleopera.org.

SECOND CITY, INC.
1616 North Wells
Chicago, Illinois 60614

General Information Theater that presents original material written in an improvisational manner. Established in 1959. Number of employees: 150. Number of internship applications received each year: 50.

Internships Available ▶ *2 administrative interns:* responsibilities include mailing promotional and informational material and working on special projects in marketing. Duration is 1 semester or 1 summer. Unpaid. Open to college freshmen, college sophomores, college juniors, college seniors, graduate students. International applications accepted.

Benefits Willing to complete paperwork for educational credit, willing to provide letters of recommendation.

Contact Write, fax, or e-mail Beth Kligerman, Administrative Director. Fax: 312-664-9837. E-mail: bmk1616@aol.com. In-person interview recommended. Applicants must submit a cover letter, resume, two personal references, two letters of recommendation. Applications are accepted continuously. World Wide Web: http://www.secondcity.com.

SHADOW BOX THEATRE
325 West End Avenue, 12B
New York, New York 10023

General Information Theater focusing on children's theater and Arts-in-Education for inner-city children; with home-based theater, in-school and after-school workshop program, and summer touring group. Established in 1967. Number of employees: 3. Number of internship applications received each year: 20.

Internships Available ▶ *1–2 administrative interns:* responsibilities include assisting with telephone bookings, marketing, publicity, general administrative duties. Candidates should have ability to work with others, computer skills, office skills, oral communication skills, organizational skills, written communication skills. Duration is flexible. ▶ *Theater interns:* responsibilities include assisting with technical aspects of theater, house management, box office, and assisting the director. Candidates should have college courses in field, experience in the field, knowledge of field, personal interest in the field, strong interpersonal skills. Duration is flexible (minimum of 8 weeks). All positions are unpaid. Open to college freshmen, college sophomores, college juniors, college seniors.

Benefits Willing to complete paperwork for educational credit, willing to provide letters of recommendation.

Contact Write or fax Marlyn Baum, Managing Director. Fax: 212-724-0767. In-person interview required. Applicants must submit a cover letter, resume, two letters of recommendation. Applications are accepted continuously.

SOCIETY HILL PLAYHOUSE, CENTER FOR THE PERFORMING ARTS, INC.
507 South Eighth Street
Philadelphia, Pennsylvania 19147

General Information Center that presents theater as a social and communicative art, encompasses artistic quality and professional excellence, provides a place where the artist can develop and grow, and serves all segments of the community. Established in 1959. Number of employees: 5. Number of internship applications received each year: 100.

Internships Available ▶ *1 public relations intern:* responsibilities include working with managing and program directors and assisting with fund-raising, production promotions, mailing lists, and group sales. Duration is flexible. ▶ *2 technical interns:* responsibilities include assisting and training with technical director on main stage, second space, and educational theater projects in all areas of technical theater including lighting, setting, and sound. Duration is 6–12 months. All positions are unpaid. International applications accepted.

Benefits Job counseling, names of contacts, opportunity to attend seminars/workshops, possible full-time employment, willing to complete paperwork for educational credit, willing to provide letters of recommendation.

Contact Write, call, or fax Ms. Susan Turlish, Program Director. Phone: 215-923-0210. Fax: 215-923-1789. In-person interview required. Applicants must submit a formal organization application, resume. Applications are accepted continuously. World Wide Web: http://www.erols.com/SHP.

SOHO REPERTORY THEATRE
46 Walker Street
New York, New York 10013

General Information Theater specializing in new and avant-garde plays. Established in 1975. Number of employees: 7.

Internships Available ▶ *Administration interns.* Candidates should have computer skills, office skills, oral communication skills, organizational skills, personal interest in the field, self-motivation. ▶ *Business interns.* Candidates should have computer skills, office skills, oral communication skills, organizational skills, personal interest in the field, self-motivation. ▶ *Development interns.* Candidates should have computer skills, office skills, oral communication skills, organizational skills, personal interest in the field, self-motivation. ▶ *Literary interns.* Candidates should have ability to work independently, analytical skills, personal interest in the field, self-motivation, writing skills, written communication skills. ▶ *Production interns.* Candidates should have computer skills, office skills, oral communication skills, organizational skills, personal interest in the field, self-motivation. Duration for all positions is flexible. All positions are unpaid. Open to college freshmen, college sophomores, college juniors, college seniors, recent college graduates, graduate students, law students, career changers, individuals reentering the workforce.

Benefits Travel reimbursement, willing to complete paperwork for educational credit, willing to provide letters of recommendation.

Contact Write, call, or fax Alexandra Conley, Executive Director. Phone: 212-941-8632. Fax: 212-941-7148. Applicants must submit a cover letter, resume. Applications are accepted continuously. World Wide Web: http://www.sohorep.org.

STAGE ONE: PROFESSIONAL THEATER FOR YOUNG AUDIENCES
501 West Main Street
Louisville, Kentucky 40202

General Information Professional Equity adult theater company performing for young audiences and their teachers and families. Established in 1946. Number of employees: 50. Number of internship applications received each year: 45.

Internships Available ▶ *2 acting interns:* responsibilities include portraying a wide range of characters, and serving as an assistant stage manager. Candidates should have ability to work independently, experience in the field, oral communication skills, self-motivation, strong interpersonal skills. ▶ *1 development intern:*

responsibilities include assisting director of development in securing contributions from individuals, corporations, and foundations; assisting in preparation of grant proposals; and maintaining computer database. Candidates should have analytical skills, computer skills, research skills, strong interpersonal skills, writing skills. ▶ *1 education intern:* responsibilities include leading/ teaching middle and high school drama workshops, writing educational materials for middle/high school students, and providing administrative support for school matinee performances. Candidates should have ability to work independently, ability to work with others, experience in the field, knowledge of field, oral communication skills, written communication skills. ▶ *1 marketing intern:* responsibilities include writing press releases and feature stories, proofing copy, maintaining archives, distributing brochures and posters, box office customer service for no less than two plays, and overseeing and preparing all marketing for State One's Critics' Circle new play series. Candidates should have editing skills, personal interest in the field, self-motivation, writing skills, written communication skills, time management skills. ▶ *1 production intern:* responsibilities include scene shop construction duties, light hangs and focusing, and sound board operation. Candidates should have ability to work independently, experience in the field, personal interest in the field, self-motivation, strong interpersonal skills. Duration for all positions is 4–9 months. All positions paid at $150 per week. Open to recent high school graduates, college freshmen, college sophomores, college juniors, college seniors, recent college graduates, graduate students. International applications accepted. **Benefits** Job counseling, names of contacts, on-the-job training, possible full-time employment, travel reimbursement, willing to act as a professional reference, willing to complete paperwork for educational credit, willing to provide letters of recommendation.
Contact Write, call, or fax Mr. J. Daniel Herring, Associate Producing Director. Phone: 502-589-5946. Fax: 502-588-5910. Applicants must submit a cover letter, resume, three personal references. Applications are accepted continuously. World Wide Web: http://www.stageone.org.

TADA!
120 West 28th Street
New York, New York 10001

General Information Nonprofit children's theater ensemble producing high-quality productions performed by children for family audiences. Established in 1984. Number of employees: 5. Number of internship applications received each year: 15.
Internships Available ▶ *1 arts administrative assistant:* responsibilities include assisting in the running of the office. Candidates should have experience in the field, office skills, research skills, writing skills. Duration is 12 weeks. Unpaid. ▶ *1 assistant director:* responsibilities include working with director and children in rehearsals. Candidates should have experience in the field. Duration is flexible. Unpaid. ▶ *1 assistant stage manager:* responsibilities include assisting stage manager with rehearsals and performances. Candidates should have experience in the field. Duration is 3 months. Paid. ▶ *1 assistant technical director:* responsibilities include helping construct set and props. Candidates should have experience in the field. Duration is flexible. Unpaid. ▶ *1 assistant to designers:* responsibilities include working with set, costume, or lighting designer. Candidates should have experience in the field. Duration is flexible. Unpaid. ▶ *1 box office intern.* Duration is flexible. $6 per hour. ▶ *1 development assistant:* responsibilities include working with development director. Candidates should have knowledge of field. Duration is flexible. Unpaid. ▶ *1 house manager:* responsibilities include dealing with audience. Candidates should have experience in the field. Duration is flexible. $7 per hour. ▶ *3 literary interns:* responsibilities include reading and reviewing scripts. Candidates should have editing skills, writing skills. Duration is flexible. Unpaid. ▶ *1 theater electrician/board operator:* responsibilities include assisting with tech work and performances. Candidates should have experience in the field. Duration is 2 months. Paid. ▶ *1 wardrobe supervisor:* responsibilities include maintaining costumes and working backstage with children. Candidates should have experi-

ence in the field. Duration is 2 months. Paid. Open to college freshmen, college sophomores, college juniors, college seniors. International applications accepted.
Benefits Names of contacts, willing to complete paperwork for educational credit, willing to provide letters of recommendation.
Contact Write, call, fax, or e-mail Julie Renn, Administrative Associate. Phone: 212-627-1732. Fax: 212-243-6736. E-mail: tada@ziplink.net. In-person interview required. Applicants must submit a cover letter, resume. Applications are accepted continuously.

THE THEATER AT MONMOUTH
PO Box 385
Monmouth, Maine 04259

General Information Professional summer theater dedicated to producing classical plays in rotating repertory. Established in 1970. Number of employees: 40. Number of internship applications received each year: 500.
Internships Available ▶ *8–10 actor interns:* responsibilities include acting in mainstage productions and children's show, working backstage, assisting stage manager, and working in office, costume, or scene shop. Duration is 12–20 weeks. $50–$150 per week. ▶ *1–3 costume interns:* responsibilities include engaging in all aspects of costumes, including patterning, cutting, stitching, millinery, garment repair, and alterations. Duration is 8 weeks. $50–$150 per week. ▶ *1–3 office interns:* responsibilities include staffing box office, house management, concessions and gift shop management, performing customer service and data entry. Duration is 14 weeks. $50–$100 per week. ▶ *1 stage management intern:* responsibilities include assisting stage manager in working backstage and full management of children's show. Duration is 13 weeks. $50 per week. ▶ *1–3 technical interns:* responsibilities include engaging all aspects of physical production, including lights and sound, scenery, and props. Duration is 8–14 weeks. $40–$60 per week. Candidates for all positions should have experience in the field, personal interest in the field. Open to recent high school graduates, college freshmen, college sophomores, college juniors, college seniors, recent college graduates, graduate students, law students, career changers, individuals reentering the workforce. International applications accepted.
Benefits Free housing, free meals, names of contacts, willing to complete paperwork for educational credit, willing to provide letters of recommendation.
Contact Write David Greenham, Managing Director. No phone calls. In-person interview recommended. Applicants must submit a cover letter, resume, audition for actor interns. Applications are accepted continuously. World Wide Web: http://www.theateratmonmouth.org.

THEATER FOR THE NEW CITY FOUNDATION, INC.
155 First Avenue
New York, New York 10003

General Information Nonprofit off-Broadway theater that presents 44 shows each season. Established in 1970. Number of employees: 10. Number of internship applications received each year: 50.
Internships Available ▶ *Administrative interns:* responsibilities include assisting executive and administrative director. ▶ *Financial development/fund-raising interns:* responsibilities include writing grants, typing, and performing foundation research and clerical duties. ▶ *Technical interns:* responsibilities include assisting technical director. Duration for all positions is flexible. All positions are unpaid. Open to individuals 17 and older. International applications accepted.
Benefits Possible full-time employment, willing to complete paperwork for educational credit.
Contact Write, call, fax, or e-mail Mr. Jerry Jaffe, Administrator. Phone: 212-254-1109. Fax: 212-979-6570. E-mail: thetheater@aol.com. In-person interview recommended. Applicants must submit a cover letter, resume. Applications are accepted continuously.

THEATRE DE LA JEUNE LUNE
105 First Street North
Minneapolis, Minnesota 55401

General Information Theater company with an interactive, highly physical style of performance. Established in 1978. Number of employees: 82. Number of internship applications received each year: 50.

Internships Available ▶ *3–12 assistant designers:* responsibilities include assisting set, costume, and lighting designers in research and construction. Duration is 6–8 weeks. ▶ *3–6 assistant directors:* responsibilities include keeping up scripts and assisting in blocking and scheduling. Duration is 6–12 weeks. ▶ *3–9 assistant stage managers:* responsibilities include assisting the stage manager in running rehearsals, doing fittings, and scheduling. Duration is 6–18 weeks. ▶ *1–3 business interns:* responsibilities include assisting the finance manager with accounting work reconciliations, balances, and budget. Duration is flexible. ▶ *1–4 development interns:* responsibilities include assisting with mailings, project research, and donor events. Duration is 8–10 weeks. ▶ *1–3 dramaturgical interns:* responsibilities include assisting in writing scripts, keeping updates, and performing research. Duration is flexible. ▶ *1–3 front-of-house interns:* responsibilities include assisting in usher recruitment and front-of-house duties, managing and conducting inventory on concessions, and working the box office. Duration is flexible. ▶ *1–2 music interns:* responsibilities include assisting the composer and music director, providing accompaniment at rehearsals, and copying music. Duration is flexible. ▶ *1–3 properties interns:* responsibilities include locating, arranging, and constructing show props. Duration is 6 weeks. ▶ *3 technical interns:* responsibilities include assisting the technical director in building, drafting, shop organization, and building management. Duration is 3–12 weeks. All positions are unpaid. Open to high school students, high school seniors, recent high school graduates, college freshmen, college sophomores, college juniors, college seniors, recent college graduates, graduate students, law students, career changers, individuals reentering the workforce. International applications accepted.

Benefits Job counseling, names of contacts, opportunity to attend seminars/workshops, possible full-time employment, willing to complete paperwork for educational credit, willing to provide letters of recommendation, tickets.

Contact Write, call, or fax Luverne Seifert, Artistic Associate. Phone: 612-332-3968. Fax: 612-332-0048. In-person interview recommended. Applicants must submit a cover letter, resume. Applications are accepted continuously.

THE THEATRE-STUDIO, INC.
750 Eighth Avenue, Suite 200
New York, New York 10036

General Information Studio theater that focuses on growth of theater arts for the community. Established in 1980. Number of employees: 10. Number of internship applications received each year: 50.

Internships Available ▶ *1–3 administrative assistant interns:* responsibilities include monitoring daily trafficking schedule and logging phone messages, telephone contact work, correspondence, filing, and organizing and monitoring play scripts. Candidates should have ability to work independently, computer skills, oral communication skills, organizational skills, strong interpersonal skills, written communication skills. Duration is 3–6 months. Unpaid. ▶ *1–5 grant researchers:* responsibilities include researching types of grants available to theater production companies, organizing and presenting findings to Artistic Director, and selecting and writing grants. Candidates should have ability to work independently, editing skills, knowledge of field, research skills, written communication skills. Duration is flexible. Position available as unpaid or at varies with funds received. ▶ *1–3 production assistant interns:* responsibilities include teaching two performances per week with such duties as operation of simple sound/light equipment, setting up house, working on set changes and strikes, prop/costume searches, updating fliers and programs, and running errands. Candidates should

have computer skills, knowledge of field, organizational skills, self-motivation, strong interpersonal skills, written communication skills. Duration is 3–6 months. Unpaid. Open to high school students, high school seniors, recent high school graduates, college freshmen, college sophomores, college juniors, college seniors, recent college graduates, graduate students, law students, career changers, individuals reentering the workforce. International applications accepted.

Benefits Formal training, opportunity to attend seminars/workshops, willing to complete paperwork for educational credit, willing to provide letters of recommendation, opportunity to work in a professional production.

Contact Write, call, or fax A. M. Raychel, Producing/Artistic Director. Phone: 212-719-0500. Fax: 212-719-0537. Applicants must submit a cover letter, resume, two writing samples, three personal references, three letters of recommendation, in-person interview within 2 weeks of receipt of application/letter of interest. Applications are accepted continuously.

THEATRE VIRGINIA
2800 Grove Avenue
Richmond, Virginia 23221

General Information Professional theater producing musicals, dramas, comedies, and classics on its mainstage from September to May; provides numerous educational programs and hosts a young playwrights' competition called "New Voices for the Theatre". Established in 1954. Number of employees: 45. Number of internship applications received each year: 50.

Internships Available ▶ *12–20 administrative interns:* responsibilities include working in development, arts administration, ticket operations, marketing/public relations, company management, house management, or education departments. Candidates should have computer skills, oral communication skills, personal interest in the field, self-motivation, strong interpersonal skills, writing skills. Duration is flexible. Open to high school seniors, recent high school graduates, college freshmen, college sophomores, college juniors, college seniors, recent college graduates, graduate students. ▶ *5–10 production interns:* responsibilities include assisting in area of specialization: production assistance, scenic carpentry, properties, scenic artistry, costume production, wardrobe, electrics, or sound. Candidates should have ability to work independently, ability to work with others, knowledge of field, personal interest in the field, self-motivation. Duration is varies. Open to recent high school graduates, college freshmen, college sophomores, college juniors, college seniors, recent college graduates, graduate students. All positions available as unpaid or paid.

Benefits Job counseling, names of contacts, on-the-job training, possible full-time employment, willing to complete paperwork for educational credit, willing to provide letters of recommendation.

Contact Write, call, or fax Eleanor Connor, Director of Education and Outreach. Phone: 804-353-6100. Fax: 804-353-8799. In-person interview recommended. Applicants must submit a cover letter, resume. Application deadline: March 1 for production positions; continuous for administrative positions. World Wide Web: http://www.theatreva.com.

THEATREWORKS
1100 Hamilton Court
Menlo Park, California 94025

General Information Professional nonprofit theater company presenting high-quality live theater that reflects the diversity of its community. Established in 1970. Number of employees: 30. Number of internship applications received each year: 50.

Internships Available ▶ *6–10 administrative interns:* responsibilities include working in the areas of development/events, outreach, ticket services, marketing, or operations. Candidates should have ability to work with others, computer skills, office skills, oral communication skills, organizational skills, personal interest in the field. Duration is 4-8 weeks (20 hours per week). $500 per duration of internship. Open to college freshmen, college sophomores, college juniors, college seniors, recent college graduates, graduate students, law students, career changers, individuals reentering the workforce. ▶ *15–20 artistic interns:* responsibilities include working in the areas of directing, literary, casting, or musical directing. Candidates should have ability to work with others, experience in the field, oral communication skills, personal interest in the field, directing experience required for assistant directors, music theory and piano skills required for assistant music directors. Duration is 4-8 weeks (5-20 hours per week). Position available as unpaid or at $100 per duration of internship. Open to college freshmen, college sophomores, college juniors, college seniors, recent college graduates, graduate students, law students, career changers, individuals reentering the workforce. ▶ *25–30 production interns:* responsibilities include working in the areas of scenic design, scenic/props, costume design, lighting design, sound design, stage management,or production management. Candidates should have ability to work with others, experience in the field, oral communication skills, personal interest in the field, drafting or rendering skills required for design assistant positions. Duration is 4-8 weeks (35 hours per week). $200–$400 per duration of internship. Open to recent high school graduates, college freshmen, college sophomores, college juniors, college seniors, recent college graduates, graduate students, law students, career changers, individuals reentering the workforce.

Benefits Job counseling, names of contacts, on-the-job training, opportunity to attend seminars/workshops, travel reimbursement, willing to act as a professional reference, willing to complete paperwork for educational credit, willing to provide letters of recommendation, complimentary tickets to productions.

Contact Write, fax, or e-mail Ms. Leslie Martinson, Associate Artist. Fax: 650-463-1963. E-mail: interns@theatreworks.org. In-person interview recommended. Applicants must submit a formal organization application, cover letter, resume. Application deadline: February 1 for spring, April 1 for early summer, June 1 for late summer/fall, October 1 for winter. World Wide Web: http://www.theatreworks.org.

TRINITY REPERTORY COMPANY
201 Washington Street
Providence, Rhode Island 02903

General Information Professional regional theater engaging the audience as participants. Established in 1964. Number of employees: 100. Number of internship applications received each year: 50.

Internships Available ▶ *3–6 administration interns:* responsibilities include working in development, general management, house management, and educational outreach. Candidates should have computer skills, oral communication skills, strong interpersonal skills, written communication skills, accounting skills. Duration is August to June. Position available as unpaid or at $50 per week. Open to high school seniors, recent high school graduates, college freshmen, college sophomores, college juniors, college seniors, recent college graduates. ▶ *4–6 production interns:* responsibilities include working in one of several positions in production, stage management, props, costumes, lighting or set construction. Candidates should have college courses in field, experience in the field, oral communication skills, plan to pursue career in field, strong interpersonal skills. Duration is August to June, full-time. $50 per week. Open to recent college graduates. International applications accepted.

Benefits Formal training, job counseling, names of contacts, on-the-job training, opportunity to attend seminars/workshops, possible full-time employment, willing to act as a professional reference, willing to complete paperwork for educational credit, willing to provide letters of recommendation, 2 complimentary tickets for each production, stipend, free housing for year-round interns.

Contact Write, call, or e-mail Nancy Safian, Educational Outreach Coordinator. Phone: 401-521-1100 Ext. 256. E-mail: nsafian@trinityrep.com. In-person interview recommended. Applicants must submit a cover letter, resume, writing sample. Application deadline: May 1 for full-time seasonal interns; continuous for all other positions. World Wide Web: http://www.trinityrep.com.

UNTITLED THEATER COMPANY #61
235 West 102 Street, Suite 16-S
New York, New York 10025

General Information Nonprofit producer of experimental and philosophic plays Off-Off-Broadway. Established in 1992. Number of employees: 3. Number of internship applications received each year: 5.

Internships Available ▶ *1–3 artistic associates:* responsibilities include assisting in the directorial and playwriting aspects of theater, including the position of assistant director and dramaturg. Candidates should have ability to work with others, knowledge of field, oral communication skills, organizational skills, personal interest in the field, research skills, writing skills. Duration is 2 months. Open to college freshmen, college sophomores, college juniors, college seniors, recent college graduates. ▶ *1–5 assistants to the Artistic Director:* responsibilities include assisting the Artistic Director in all areas, including publicity, grant writing, and scheduling. Candidates should have ability to work independently, knowledge of field, office skills, oral communication skills, organizational skills, personal interest in the field, research skills, writing skills. Duration is flexible. Open to high school students, high school seniors, recent high school graduates, college freshmen, college sophomores, college juniors, college seniors, recent college graduates. ▶ *1–3 company managers:* responsibilities include organizing performances, readings, and rehearsals. Candidates should have ability to work independently, ability to work with others, knowledge of field, organizational skills. Duration is flexible. Open to college freshmen, college sophomores, college juniors, college seniors, recent college graduates. ▶ *1–5 stage managers:* responsibilities include supervising all the technical aspects of a production: organizing props, light, and sound. Candidates should have knowledge of field, oral communication skills, organizational skills, personal interest in the field, strong interpersonal skills. Duration is 2 months. Open to high school students, high school seniors, recent high school graduates, college freshmen, college sophomores, college juniors, college seniors, recent college graduates. All positions are unpaid. International applications accepted.

Benefits Names of contacts, on-the-job training, opportunity to attend seminars/workshops, willing to act as a professional reference, willing to complete paperwork for educational credit, willing to provide letters of recommendation.

Contact Write or call Edward Einhorn, Artistic Director, 235 West 102 Street, Suite 16-S, New York, New York 10025. Phone: 212-866-1073. In-person interview recommended. Applicants must submit a cover letter, resume. Applications are accepted continuously. World Wide Web: http://www.geocities.com/Broadway/5705.

VICTORY GARDENS THEATER
2257 North Lincoln Avenue
Chicago, Illinois 60614

General Information World premiere theater emphasizing the development of Chicago playwrights. Established in 1974. Number of employees: 18. Number of internship applications received each year: 30.

Internships Available ▶ *1 administrative intern:* responsibilities include assisting managing director, director of development, and marketing director in daily tasks and projects. Candidates should have ability to work independently, analytical skills, college courses in field, computer skills, editing skills, knowledge of field, office skills, oral communication skills, organizational skills, personal interest in the field, research skills, self-motivation, strong interpersonal skills, writing skills. Duration is 3-5 months (variable). Open to college seniors, recent college graduates, graduate students, individuals reentering the workforce. ▶ *2 artistic interns:* responsibilities include assisting literary manager. Candidates should have ability to work independently, college courses in field, computer skills, editing skills, knowledge of field, office skills, oral communication skills, organizational skills, personal interest in the field, research skills, self-motivation, strong interpersonal skills, writing skills. Duration is 3–6 months. Open to college seniors, recent college graduates, graduate

Victory Gardens Theater (continued)

students, career changers, individuals reentering the workforce. ▶ *3 production interns:* responsibilities include assisting administrative director. Candidates should have ability to work independently, ability to work with others, college courses in field, knowledge of field, plan to pursue career in field, self-motivation, carpentry, electrical, technical theater skills. Duration is 6-8 weeks (variable). Open to recent high school graduates, college freshmen, college sophomores, college juniors, college seniors, recent college graduates, graduate students, law students, career changers, individuals reentering the workforce. All positions are unpaid. International applications accepted.

Benefits Names of contacts, opportunity to attend seminars/workshops, possible full-time employment, willing to complete paperwork for educational credit, willing to provide letters of recommendation.

Contact Write, fax, or e-mail Darcy Hughes, Administrative Assistant. Fax: 773-549-2779. E-mail: vgtheater@aol.com. No phone calls. In-person interview recommended. Applicants must submit a cover letter, resume, two personal references, two letters of recommendation. Applications are accepted continuously. World Wide Web: http://www.victorygardens.org.

VINEYARD THEATER
108 East 15th Street
New York, New York 10003-9689

General Information Theater that specializes in developing and producing new dramatic and musical theater. Established in 1981. Number of employees: 6. Number of internship applications received each year: 20.

Internships Available ▶ *1–2 management interns:* responsibilities include assisting with business, fund-raising, and marketing. Candidates should have ability to work with others, computer skills, office skills, oral communication skills, self-motivation, written communication skills. Unpaid. Open to college freshmen, college sophomores, college juniors, college seniors, recent college graduates, graduate students, career changers. ▶ *1–4 production interns:* responsibilities include assisting with scheduling, rehearsals, and technical work. Candidates should have ability to work independently, personal interest in the field, self-motivation, strong interpersonal skills, strong leadership ability. Position available as unpaid or paid. Open to high school seniors, college freshmen, college sophomores, college juniors, college seniors, recent college graduates, graduate students, career changers, individuals reentering the workforce. Duration for all positions is flexible. International applications accepted.

Benefits Job counseling, names of contacts, willing to complete paperwork for educational credit, willing to provide letters of recommendation.

Contact Write or fax Ms. Laura Ma, General Manager. Fax: 212-353-3803. No phone calls. In-person interview recommended. Applications are accepted continuously.

WALNUT STREET THEATRE
9th and Walnut Streets
Philadelphia, Pennsylvania 19107

General Information Major regional theater. Established in 1809. Number of employees: 50. Number of internship applications received each year: 250.

Internships Available ▶ *4 acting interns (including 2 for African Americans):* responsibilities include performing, teaching youth acting classes, understudying mainstage shows, and acting as readers at auditions. Duration is 9 months. ▶ *1 casting and literary management intern:* responsibilities include assisting casting director in all local and New York auditions; working in literary office reviewing scripts. Duration is 8–10 weeks. ▶ *1 development intern:* responsibilities include assisting the development manager in grantmanship, responding to volunteers for theater, and fund-raising. ▶ *1 general management intern:* responsibilities include assisting the general manager with space management, housing, building maintenance, and agreed contracts. ▶ *1 house management intern:* responsibilities include assisting house manager on all mainstage plays, including lobby duty and tickets. ▶ *1–2*

marketing interns: responsibilities include assisting the marketing staff. ▶ *1 painting intern:* responsibilities include learning extensive scene-painting techniques in a large paint shop operation and working closely with the charge scenic artist in all phases of scene painting. ▶ *1 props intern:* responsibilities include assisting the properties manager in construction and acquisition of props for all productions and learning skills in sewing, upholstery, carpentry, sculpturing, painting, and/or calligraphy. ▶ *1 run crew intern:* responsibilities include moving sets, load-ins, and load-outs. ▶ *2 stage management interns:* responsibilities include assisting in all facets of rehearsals and productions. ▶ *1 subscriptions intern:* responsibilities include phone management, subscription, and ticket exchange. All positions paid at $255 per week.

Benefits Formal training, health insurance, opportunity to attend seminars/workshops, possible full-time employment, willing to act as a professional reference, willing to complete paperwork for educational credit, willing to provide letters of recommendation, job placement opportunities.

Contact Write, call, fax, or e-mail School Director. Phone: 215-574-3550 Ext. 566. Fax: 215-574-3598. E-mail: wstschool@aol.com. In-person interview recommended. Applicants must submit a formal organization application, cover letter, resume, three personal references. Application deadline: May 1 for acting interns; varies for fall positions.

THE WESTERN STAGE
156 Homestead Avenue
Salinas, California 93901

General Information Theater emphasizing the development of artists and new works. Established in 1975. Number of employees: 45. Number of internship applications received each year: 425.

Internships Available ▶ *1 casting intern:* responsibilities include assisting in set-up of season audition tour and local auditions; publicity; assisting in direct casting; maintaining casting files, records, and calendar; script analysis. Candidates should have ability to work independently, ability to work with others, computer skills, oral communication skills, organizational skills, personal interest in the field, self-motivation. Duration is 5–9 months. $500–$700 per month. Open to recent high school graduates, college freshmen, college sophomores, college juniors, college seniors, recent college graduates, graduate students, career changers, individuals reentering the workforce. ▶ *5–10 theater interns:* responsibilities include marketing, management, and design duties. Candidates should have ability to work with others, oral communication skills, personal interest in the field, self-motivation, strong leadership ability, written communication skills. Duration is 3–9 months. $400–$750 per month. Open to recent high school graduates, college freshmen, college sophomores, college juniors, college seniors, recent college graduates, career changers, individuals reentering the workforce.

Benefits Formal training, job counseling, names of contacts, on-the-job training, opportunity to attend seminars/workshops, possible full-time employment, tuition assistance, willing to complete paperwork for educational credit, willing to provide letters of recommendation, scholarships and stipends.

Contact Write, call, fax, or e-mail Melissa Chin, Associate Artistic Director. Phone: 831-755-6987. Fax: 831-755-6954. E-mail: mchin@hartnell.cc.ca.us. In-person interview recommended. Applicants must submit a formal organization application, cover letter, resume, portfolio, two personal references. Applications are accepted continuously. World Wide Web: http://www.westernstage.org.

WESTPORT COUNTRY PLAYHOUSE
25 Powers Court
Westport, Connecticut 06880

General Information Professional summer theater in an historic building. Established in 1931. Number of employees: 50. Number of internship applications received each year: 50.

Internships Available ▶ *1 administrative intern:* responsibilities include assisting general manager in reception, office management, actor housing and transportation, and working with board of directors on fund-raising projects. Candidates should have computer skills, office skills, organizational skills, personal interest in the field, self-motivation, strong interpersonal skills. Duration is 3 months. $150–$250 per week. Open to college freshmen, college sophomores, college juniors, college seniors, recent college graduates. ▶ *1 press intern:* responsibilities include assisting public relations director in writing press releases and ad copy for radio and print, assisting in playbill publication, scheduling critics, and working on special promotional events. Candidates should have computer skills, editing skills, oral communication skills, personal interest in the field, strong interpersonal skills, writing skills. Duration is 3 months. $150–$250 per week. Open to college sophomores, college juniors, college seniors, recent college graduates, graduate students. ▶ *10 technical interns:* responsibilities include rotating duties in electrics, set design and painting, wardrobe, stage management, carpentry, and props. Candidates should have ability to work independently, ability to work with others, college courses in field, knowledge of field, plan to pursue career in field, self-motivation. Duration is 14 weeks. $100 per week. Open to high school seniors, recent high school graduates, college freshmen, college sophomores, college juniors, college seniors, recent college graduates, graduate students, career changers. International applications accepted.

Benefits Free housing, names of contacts, on-the-job training, opportunity to attend seminars/workshops, possible full-time employment, willing to act as a professional reference, willing to complete paperwork for educational credit, willing to provide letters of recommendation, points earned in Actor's Equity Association Membership Candidate Program.

Contact Write, call, fax, or e-mail Ms. Julie A. Monahan, General Manager. Phone: 203-227-5137. Fax: 203-221-7482. E-mail: westportplay@mindspring.com. In-person interview recommended. Applicants must submit a formal organization application, cover letter, resume, two personal references, two letters of recommendation. Applications are accepted continuously. World Wide Web: http://www.westportplayhouse.org.

WILLIAMSTOWN THEATER FESTIVAL
1000 Main Street, PO Box 517
Williamstown, Massachusetts 01267

General Information Summer theater presenting productions of revivals of classics and new works by new playwrights. Established in 1953. Number of employees: 60. Number of internship applications received each year: 600.

Internships Available ▶ *60–70 acting apprenticeships:* responsibilities include taking acting classes and alternate days of crew work. Candidates should have ability to work with others, plan to pursue career in field, self-motivation, strong interpersonal skills, written communication skills. Open to high school students, high school seniors, recent high school graduates, college freshmen, college sophomores, college juniors, college seniors, recent college graduates, graduate students, career changers, individuals reentering the workforce, individuals 17 and over. ▶ *60 administrative and technical interns:* responsibilities include working in any of the following areas: scenic design/scenic art, costume design/construction, lighting design/electrics, sound design/production, scenic carpentry, directing, publications/graphic design, photography, general management, production management, company management, house management, box office, publicity, stage management, literary management/dramaturgy, cabaret management/production. Candidates should have ability to work with others, knowledge of field, organizational skills, self-motivation, strong interpersonal skills. Open to high school students, high school seniors, recent high school graduates, college freshmen, college sophomores, college juniors, college seniors, recent college graduates, graduate students, career changers, individuals reentering the workforce. Duration for all positions is 1 summer (June-August). All positions are unpaid. International applications accepted.

Benefits Housing at a cost, meals at a cost, names of contacts, on-the-job training, opportunity to attend seminars/workshops, willing to act as a professional reference, willing to complete paperwork for educational credit, willing to provide letters of recommendation, opportunity to work with professionals in field.

Contact Write, call, fax, or e-mail Anne Lowrie, Company Manager, 100 East 17th Street, 3rd Floor, New York, New York 10003. Phone: 212-228-2286. Fax: 212-228-9091. E-mail: alowrie@wtfestival.org. In-person interview recommended. Applicants must submit a formal organization application, cover letter, resume, portfolio, two personal references, two letters of recommendation, $30 application fee for the apprentice workshop only. Application deadline: April 16 for acting apprentices; continuous for other positions. World Wide Web: http://www.wtfestival.org.

THE WILMA THEATER
265 South Broad Street
Philadelphia, Pennsylvania 19107

General Information Nonprofit, professional, innovative theater under the artistic direction of Jiri and Blanka Zizka. Established in 1973. Number of employees: 18. Number of internship applications received each year: 75.

Internships Available ▶ *1 artistic fellow:* responsibilities include assisting artistic directors and literary manager/dramaturg, assistant directing, directing understudies and extras, note-taking for directors, and serving as the artistic directors' personal assistant. Candidates should have ability to work independently, ability to work with others, analytical skills, experience in the field, organizational skills, writing skills. Duration is full theater season, August to June. $250 per week. Open to recent college graduates, graduate students. ▶ *1 development intern:* responsibilities include working with development director on grant proposals and reports, researching new prospects, helping coordinate fund-raising events, assisting with correspondence, and maintaining development files. Candidates should have ability to work independently, office skills, oral communication skills, organizational skills, strong interpersonal skills, written communication skills. Duration is flexible. Unpaid. Open to college freshmen, college sophomores, college juniors, college seniors, recent college graduates, graduate students, individuals reentering the workforce. ▶ *1 education intern:* responsibilities include assisting with administration, registration, and promotion of school; coordinating volunteers; assisting with outreach programming; and publicity for all aspects of the department. Candidates should have ability to work independently, personal interest in the field, self-motivation, strong interpersonal skills, written communication skills, sense of humor. Duration is flexible. Unpaid. Open to college freshmen, college sophomores, college juniors, college seniors, recent college graduates. ▶ *1 literary intern:* responsibilities include assisting literary manager/dramaturg with play reading and evaluation, script solicitation and administration, correspondence, and coordination of symposia; performing dramaturgical research for quarterly newsletter. Candidates should have ability to work independently, ability to work with others, analytical skills, editing skills, research skills, writing skills. Duration is flexible. Unpaid. Open to college freshmen, college sophomores, college juniors, college seniors, recent college graduates. ▶ *1–2 marketing/publicity interns:* responsibilities include working with marketing/publicity director, understudying all aspects of theater promotion, graphic design, editing playbill, photographic archiving, analysis of audience, and development of theater literature. Candidates should have ability to work independently, computer skills, oral communication skills, organizational skills, personal interest in the field, written communication skills. Duration is flexible. Unpaid. Open to college freshmen, college sophomores, college juniors, college seniors, recent college graduates, graduate students, individuals reentering the workforce. ▶ *1 production fellow:* responsibilities include working closely with the artistic directors, production manager, technical director, and stage manager. Duties may include set construction, painting, load-in, strike, electrics, lighting, and running crew. Candidates should have ability to work independently, ability to work with others, experience in the field, personal interest in the field, plan to pursue career in field, self-motivation. Duration is full theater season, August to June. $250 per week. Open to recent college graduates, graduate students. ▶ *1 theater management intern:* responsibilities include working with managing director and assistant to managing direc-

The Wilma Theater (continued)

tor, serving as liaison and organizing board meetings, contracting, union relations, and researching funding sources. Candidates should have ability to work independently, experience in the field, office skills, oral communication skills, strong interpersonal skills, strong leadership ability. Duration is flexible. Unpaid. Open to college juniors, college seniors, recent college graduates, graduate students, individuals reentering the workforce. International applications accepted.

Benefits Names of contacts, on-the-job training, possible full-time employment, willing to act as a professional reference, willing to complete paperwork for educational credit, willing to provide letters of recommendation, free tickets, cover letter and resume writing workshops, discounts on studio school classes.

Contact Write, call, fax, or e-mail Char Vandermeer, Education Director. Phone: 215-893-9456 Ext. 101. Fax: 215-893-0895. E-mail: info@wilmatheater.org. Applicants must submit a cover letter, resume, two writing samples, in-person or telephone interview. Applications are accepted continuously. World Wide Web: http://www.wilmatheater.org.

WOLF TRAP FOUNDATION FOR THE PERFORMING ARTS
1624 Trap Road
Vienna, Virginia 22182

General Information Performing arts organization that presents music, dance, theater, opera, and related educational programs. Established in 1971. Number of employees: 65. Number of internship applications received each year: 250.

Internships Available ▶ *1 accounting intern:* responsibilities include assisting in the reporting of all foundation financial activities. Candidates should have ability to work independently, ability to work with others, analytical skills, computer skills, office skills, college courses or practical experience in accounting preferred. Duration is 12 weeks during summer. approximately $205 per week. Open to college freshmen, college sophomores, college juniors, college seniors, recent college graduates, graduate students, career changers. ▶ *2 associates/ membership interns:* responsibilities include providing a variety of special events and activities for foundation members, organizing volunteers, and administrative duties as assigned. Candidates should have ability to work independently, computer skills, office skills, oral communication skills, organizational skills, self-motivation, strong interpersonal skills, strong leadership ability, writing skills. Duration is 12 weeks during summer and spring. approximately $205 per full week. Open to college freshmen, college sophomores, college juniors, college seniors, recent college graduates, graduate students, career changers. ▶ *1 development intern:* responsibilities include researching, organizing, and preparing reports on individual, corporate, and foundation prospects; assisting with telemarketing and direct mail campaigns. Candidates should have ability to work independently, computer skills, editing skills, office skills, oral communication skills, organizational skills, personal interest in the field, research skills, self-motivation, strong interpersonal skills, writing skills. Duration is 12 weeks during summer, fall, and spring. approximately $205 per full week. Open to college freshmen, college sophomores, college juniors, college seniors, recent college graduates, graduate students, career changers. ▶ *1 education intern:* responsibilities include assisting with scheduling and coordination of artist residencies and assisting the staff with daily office operations. Candidates should have ability to work independently, computer skills, editing skills, office skills, oral communication skills, organizational skills, self-motivation, strong interpersonal skills, writing skills. Duration is 12 weeks during summer, fall, and spring. approximately $205 per full week. Open to college freshmen, college sophomores, college juniors, college seniors, recent college graduates, graduate students, career changers. ▶ *1 food and beverage/concessions intern:* responsibilities include assisting with planning and coordination of events. Candidates should have oral communication skills, organizational skills, personal interest in the field, strong interpersonal skills. Duration is 12 weeks during summer. approximately $205 per full week. Open to college freshmen, college sophomores, college juniors, col-

lege seniors, recent college graduates, graduate students, career changers. ▶ *1 group sales/box office intern:* responsibilities include assisting Director of Group Sales in completing daily tasks and projects, including learning to utilize a computerized ticketing system for mail order processing; some marketing and desktop publishing. Candidates should have computer skills, office skills, oral communication skills, organizational skills, strong interpersonal skills, writing skills. Duration is 12 weeks during summer and spring. approximately $205 per full week. Open to college freshmen, college sophomores, college juniors, college seniors, recent college graduates, graduate students, career changers. ▶ *2 human resources interns:* responsibilities include assisting membership with requests, organizing volunteers, updating/maintaining personnel files. Candidates should have ability to work independently, analytical skills, computer skills, editing skills, office skills, oral communication skills, organizational skills, personal interest in the field, research skills, self-motivation, strong interpersonal skills, strong leadership ability, writing skills. Duration is 12 weeks during summer, fall, and spring. approximately $205 per full week. Open to college freshmen, college sophomores, college juniors, college seniors, recent college graduates, graduate students, career changers. ▶ *1 information systems intern:* responsibilities include maintaining and repairing all the systems and networks, including network administration, system maintenance, system upgrade, and Internet connectivity. Candidates should have ability to work independently, college courses in field, computer skills, knowledge of field, personal interest in the field, self-motivation, strong interpersonal skills. Duration is 12 weeks during summer. approximately $205 per full week. Open to college freshmen, college sophomores, college juniors, college seniors, recent college graduates, graduate students. ▶ *6 media relations/graphics design/advertising/publications/marketing/photography interns:* responsibilities include working in media relations, advertising, or publications; performing such tasks as research, writing, and editing. Candidates should have ability to work independently, ability to work with others, computer skills, editing skills, knowledge of field, office skills, oral communication skills, organizational skills, personal interest in the field, research skills, self-motivation, strong leadership ability, written communication skills. Duration is dependent upon position. approximately $205 per full week. Open to college freshmen, college sophomores, college juniors, college seniors, recent college graduates, graduate students, career changers. ▶ *1 opera administration intern (Wolf Trap Opera Company):* responsibilities include attending production meetings, rehearsals, and performances; updating company history, repertoire lists, contact sheets, and mailings lists; and assisting the administrative director and staff in the daily office operations. Candidates should have ability to work independently, computer skills, editing skills, office skills, oral communication skills, organizational skills, personal interest in the field, self-motivation, strong interpersonal skills, strong leadership ability, writing skills. Duration is 12 weeks during summer. approximately $205 per full week. Open to college freshmen, college sophomores, college juniors, college seniors, recent college graduates, graduate students, career changers. ▶ *1 planning and initiatives intern:* responsibilities include coordinating with staff and outside partners on projects such as planning, government relations, long-term commissions, special productions, new series, and cooperative projects with other arts organizations and community partnerships. Candidates should have ability to work independently, computer skills, oral communication skills, organizational skills, strong interpersonal skills, written communication skills. Duration is 12 weeks during summer and fall. approximately $205 per week. ▶ *1 special events intern:* responsibilities include assisting with preparations for donor/cultivation events and assisting the staff with daily office operations. Candidates should have ability to work independently, computer skills, office skills, oral communication skills, organizational skills, personal interest in the field, research skills, self-motivation, strong interpersonal skills, writing skills. Duration is 12 weeks during summer and spring. approximately $205 per week. ▶ *2 special programs interns:* responsibilities include assisting the director in the coordination and execution of activities that support the program, production, and education departments. Candidates should have ability to work independently, computer skills, editing skills, office skills, oral communication skills, organizational skills, personal interest in the field, research skills, self-motivation, strong interpersonal skills, strong leadership ability, writing skills. Duration is 12 weeks during fall and spring. approximately $205 per full week. Open to college freshmen, college sophomores, college juniors, college seniors, recent college graduates, graduate students, career changers, individuals reentering the workforce. ▶ *4 stage management interns (Wolf Trap Opera Company):* responsibilities include assisting stage management team in all aspects of the rehearsal process and running side of stage during performance. Candidates should have ability to work independently, knowledge of field, oral communication skills, plan to pursue career in field, self-motivation, strong interpersonal skills. Duration is 12 weeks during summer. approximately $205 per full week. Open to high school students, high school seniors, recent high school graduates, college freshmen, college sophomores, college juniors, college seniors, recent college graduates, graduate students. ▶ *Technical interns (Wolf Trap Opera Company):* responsibilities include working side by side with professional directors, designers, and technicians in mounting and running each opera; working with props, carpentry, electrics, and costumes. Candidates should have ability to work independently, ability to work with others, knowledge of field, oral communication skills, organizational skills, personal interest in the field, plan to pursue career in field, self-motivation. Duration is 8-10 weeks during summer. approximately $205 per full week. Open to high school students, high school seniors, recent high school graduates, college freshmen, college sophomores, college juniors, college seniors, recent college graduates, graduate students, career changers. International applications accepted.

Benefits Job counseling, opportunity to attend seminars/workshops, possible full-time employment, willing to act as a professional reference, willing to complete paperwork for educational credit, willing to provide letters of recommendation, complimentary performance tickets when possible, opportunity to join in 403 (B) plan.

Contact Write or call Mia De Mezza, Program Manager. Phone: 703-255-1933. In-person interview recommended. Applicants must submit a cover letter, resume, two writing samples, two letters of recommendation. Application deadline: March 15 for summer, July 1 for fall, November 15 for spring. World Wide Web: http://www.wolf-trap.org.

WOMEN'S PROJECT AND PRODUCTIONS
55 West End Avenue
New York, New York 10023

General Information Nonprofit theater organization that seeks to develop and produce original works written and directed by women in the off-Broadway theater and to promote women in the theater nationally. Established in 1978. Number of employees: 3. Number of internship applications received each year: 100.

Internships Available ▶ *1 administrative intern:* responsibilities include assisting office personnel with general administrative duties and working with the managing director on special projects. Candidates should have ability to work with others, computer skills, office skills, oral communication skills, organizational skills, self-motivation. Duration is flexible. Open to high school students, high school seniors, recent high school graduates, college freshmen, college sophomores, college juniors, college seniors, recent college graduates, graduate students, career changers, individuals reentering the workforce. ▶ *1 development assistant:* responsibilities include assisting development director in researching funding sources, drafting development-related correspondence, coordinating mail solicitation, and helping with the ongoing activities of development department. Candidates should have ability to work independently, computer skills, oral communication skills, personal interest in the field, research skills, written communication skills. Duration is 20 hours per week. Open to college freshmen, college sophomores, college juniors, college seniors, recent college graduates, graduate students, career changers, individuals reentering the workforce. ▶ *1 education intern:* responsibilities include teaching, creating lesson plans, and assisting with the final production. Candidates

should have college courses in field, experience in the field, organizational skills, personal interest in the field, strong interpersonal skills. Duration is flexible. Open to college juniors, college seniors, recent college graduates, graduate students, career changers, individuals reentering the workforce. ▶ *2 literary assistants:* responsibilities include reading and evaluating play scripts, assisting in processing scripts and updating artistic files, and assisting literary manager with the reading series and ongoing activities of the literary department. Candidates should have ability to work independently, analytical skills, computer skills, knowledge of field, research skills, written communication skills. Duration is 20 hours per week. Open to college freshmen, college sophomores, college juniors, college seniors, recent college graduates, graduate students, career changers, individuals reentering the workforce. ▶ *1 marketing assistant:* responsibilities include copywriting for programs, helping to prepare mailings, telemarketing, and assisting in writing newsletter. Candidates should have ability to work independently, computer skills, knowledge of field, oral communication skills, organizational skills. Duration is 6 weeks (minimum). Open to college freshmen, college sophomores, college juniors, college seniors, recent college graduates, graduate students, career changers, individuals reentering the workforce. ▶ *1 production intern:* responsibilities include assisting crew during rehearsals or performances of full productions and possibly serving as general production assistant or assisting the director. Candidates should have ability to work independently, experience in the field, self-motivation, strong interpersonal skills, maturity and ability to handle pressure. Duration is 25 to 35 hours per week. Open to college freshmen, college sophomores, college juniors, college seniors, recent college graduates, graduate students, career changers, individuals reentering the workforce. All positions are unpaid. International applications accepted.

Benefits Names of contacts, possible full-time employment, willing to complete paperwork for educational credit, willing to provide letters of recommendation, complimentary tickets to all performances by WPP and to other New York theaters when available.

Contact Write, call, fax, or e-mail Elizabeth Rheinfrank, Assistant to Artistic Director/Intern Coordinator. Phone: 212-765-1706. Fax: 212-765-2024. E-mail: wpp@earthlink.net. In-person interview required. Applicants must submit a cover letter, resume. Applications are accepted continuously. World Wide Web: http://www.womensproject.org.

PERFORMING ARTS, SPECTATOR SPORTS, AND RELATED INDUSTRIES

AMERICAN DANCE FESTIVAL
Box 90772
Durham, North Carolina 27708

General Information Organization that supports modern dance artists through performance, education, and special programs and works to promote dance consciousness in the American public. Established in 1934. Number of employees: 17. Number of internship applications received each year: 60.

Internships Available ▶ *1-2 archives interns:* responsibilities include managing the video collections and summer duplication services, participating in cataloging materials, assisting with reference inquiries, and other processing projects. Candidates should have college courses in field, experience in the field, knowledge of field, organizational skills, research skills, writing skills, knowledge of DOS-based computers, detail-oriented, ability to handle multiple tasks, previous cataloging experience, knowledge of video duplication equipment in an archive

American Dance Festival (continued)

preferred. Duration is late May through late July. $950 stipend per internship. Open to college sophomores, college juniors, college seniors, recent college graduates, graduate students, law students, career changers. ▶ *1 box office intern:* responsibilities include selling single tickets on a computerized box office system, Prologue. Candidates should have ability to work independently, ability to work with others, computer skills, oral communication skills, organizational skills, self-motivation. Duration is late May through late July. stipend of $1100 per internship. Open to college sophomores, college juniors, college seniors, recent college graduates. ▶ *1 community development intern:* responsibilities include working on a variety of tasks and special projects involving the corporate and business community, local government agencies, volunteers, board members, friends, and other community projects. Candidates should have ability to work independently, computer skills, oral communication skills, strong interpersonal skills, written communication skills, public relations experience helpful. Duration is late May through late July. $950 stipend for duration of internship. Open to college sophomores, college juniors, college seniors, recent college graduates, graduate students, law students, career changers. ▶ *1 facilities intern:* responsibilities include facilitating the technical, studio, housing, food, and transportation needs for the entire ADF community. Candidates should have ability to work independently, analytical skills, computer skills, oral communication skills, self-motivation, strong interpersonal skills. Duration is 8–9 weeks. stipend of $1100 per internship. Open to college freshmen, college sophomores, college juniors, college seniors, recent college graduates, graduate students, law students, career changers. ▶ *1 finance intern:* responsibilities include assisting in accounts receivable, cash receipts, accounts payable, grant reports, payroll, and financial reporting. Candidates should have ability to work independently, college courses in field, computer skills, oral communication skills, written communication skills, background or interest in the arts preferred. Duration is late May through late July. stipend of $950 per internship. Open to college sophomores, college juniors, college seniors, recent college graduates. ▶ *1 international programs intern:* responsibilities include working with the International Choreographers Residency Program Director and the ADF Director's office in a wide range of tasks. Candidates should have ability to work independently, computer skills, experience in the field, oral communication skills, self-motivation, strong interpersonal skills, detail oriented, flexibility, desire to work with international artists, fluency in one or more foreign languages strongly recommended. Duration is 8–9 weeks. $950 stipend per internship. Open to college freshmen, college sophomores, college juniors, college seniors, recent college graduates, graduate students, law students, career changers. ▶ *1 performance intern:* responsibilities include administrative coordination of all activities connected with the professional performing companies. Candidates should have ability to work independently, oral communication skills, organizational skills, personal interest in the field, strong interpersonal skills, written communication skills, ability to handle multiple tasks, detail-oriented. Duration is 8–10 weeks. stipend of $950 per internship. Open to college freshmen, college sophomores, college juniors, college seniors, recent college graduates, graduate students, law students, career changers. ▶ *1 press intern.* Candidates should have ability to work independently, computer skills, editing skills, office skills, oral communication skills, organizational skills, personal interest in the field, self-motivation, strong interpersonal skills, writing skills, flexibility, ability to work under pressure, knowledge of Microsoft Word, and dance background helpful. $950 stipend for duration of internship. Open to college sophomores, college juniors, college seniors, recent college graduates, graduate students, career changers, individuals reentering the workforce. ▶ *1 publications intern:* responsibilities include contacting artists for program information; editing, proofing, setting programs in Page Maker 6.0, and coordinating printing and delivery; design work in newspaper advertisements and invitations. Candidates should have computer skills, editing skills, organizational skills, self-motivation, writing skills, written communication skills, responsibility, detail-oriented, ability to work under pressure, experience with Page Maker. Dura-

tion is 8 weeks. stipend of $950 per internship. Open to college freshmen, college sophomores, college juniors, college seniors, recent college graduates, graduate students, career changers. ▶ *School administration interns:* responsibilities include working with an international student body and faculty of over 500 people; maintaining the school's master schedule as well as publishing the daily and weekly calendars; assisting in academic relationships with Duke University; assisting school VIP's; and assigning jobs to scholarship students. Candidates should have ability to work independently, analytical skills, computer skills, experience in the field, oral communication skills, self-motivation, strong interpersonal skills. Duration is 8–9 weeks. $950 stipend per internship. Open to college freshmen, college sophomores, college juniors, college seniors, recent college graduates, graduate students, law students, career changers. ▶ *1 support services intern:* responsibilities include facilitating the technical, studio, housing, food and transportation needs for the entire ADF community; assisting in virtually all aspects of setting up and running an international arts festival. Candidates should have ability to work independently, analytical skills, computer skills, oral communication skills, self-motivation, strong interpersonal skills. Duration is 8–9 weeks. stipend of $1100 per internship. Open to college freshmen, college sophomores, college juniors, college seniors, recent college graduates, graduate students, law students, career changers. International applications accepted. **Benefits** Job counseling, names of contacts, opportunity to attend seminars/workshops, possible full-time employment, willing to complete paperwork for educational credit, willing to provide letters of recommendation, free dance classes, free admission to dance concerts. **Contact** Write, call, fax, or e-mail Jeannie Mellinger, Director of Community Development and Public Affairs. Phone: 919-684-6402. Fax: 919-684-5459. E-mail: adfnc@acpub.duke.edu. Telephone interview required. Applicants must submit a formal organization application, cover letter, resume, 2-3 personal references and 2-3 letters of recommendation, sample of Page Maker skills for publication interns. Application deadline: February 1 for summer. World Wide Web: http://www.americandancefestival. org.

AMERICAN HOCKEY LEAGUE
425 Union Street
West Springfield, Massachusetts 01089

General Information Premiere development league for the National Hockey League. Established in 1936. Number of employees: 12. Number of internship applications received each year: 50.

Internships Available ▶ *1–2 marketing department interns:* responsibilities include assisting the marketing staff in day-to-day marketing operations; servicing league sponsors; assisting in coordination of AHL All-Star Classic; some marketing research; writing. Candidates should have computer skills, editing skills, oral communication skills, personal interest in the field, self-motivation, written communication skills. Duration is 3-4 months (spring/summer/fall semester). Open to college juniors, college seniors, recent college graduates, graduate students. ▶ *1–2 public relations department interns:* responsibilities include servicing local and national media, writing news releases, assisting editor in production of publications, and assisting in day-to-day office duties. Candidates should have computer skills, editing skills, office skills, oral communication skills, personal interest in the field, written communication skills. Duration is 3-4 months (fall/spring/summer semester). Open to college juniors, college seniors, recent college graduates, graduate students, law students. All positions are unpaid.

Benefits Names of contacts, on-the-job training, opportunity to attend seminars/workshops, possible full-time employment, willing to act as a professional reference, willing to complete paperwork for educational credit, willing to provide letters of recommendation, attendance at AHL events.

Contact Write Mr. Christos J. Nikolis, Coordinator, Marketing Services. In-person interview recommended. Applicants must submit a cover letter, resume, two writing samples, two personal references, two letters of recommendation. Application deadline: March 15 for summer, July 1 for fall, November 1 for spring. World Wide Web: http://www.canoe.ca/ahl.

AMERICAN SYMPHONY ORCHESTRA LEAGUE
1156 15th Street, NW, Suite 800
Washington, District of Columbia 20005

General Information National service organization for symphony, chamber, youth, and university orchestras in America working to ensure the artistic, organizational, and financial strength of American orchestras. Established in 1942. Number of employees: 30. Number of internship applications received each year: 115.
Internships Available ▶ *6–8 orchestra management fellowships:* responsibilities include duties while on rotating 15-week assignments at 3 American orchestras, including assisting in orchestra operations, marketing, public relations, development, volunteerism, governance, contract negotiations, financial management, long-range planning, artistic administration, education, and outreach. Candidates should have knowledge of field, personal interest in the field, plan to pursue career in field, strong interpersonal skills, strong leadership ability. Duration is 1 year. $25,000 stipend. Open to college seniors, recent college graduates, graduate students, law students, career changers, individuals reentering the workforce. International applications accepted.
Benefits Formal training, health insurance, job counseling, names of contacts, on-the-job training, opportunity to attend seminars/workshops, travel reimbursement, willing to provide letters of recommendation, access to employment services offered by the League.
Contact Write, call, fax, or e-mail Mr. Jesse Rosen, Vice President, Management Development. Phone: 202-776-0212 Ext. 246. Fax: 202-776-0224. E-mail: jrosen@symphony.org. In-person interview required. Applicants must submit a formal organization application, academic transcripts, three writing samples, three personal references. Application deadline: November 6. Fees: $45. World Wide Web: http://www.symphony.org.

APPEL FARM ARTS AND MUSIC CENTER
457 Shirley Road
Elmer, New Jersey 08318

General Information Fine and performing arts center concentrating on 3 areas: presenting arts (music, dance, theater) to the local community, providing affordable meeting and work space for artists and art organizations, and offering arts education for children through a summer camp. Established in 1960. Number of employees: 18. Number of internship applications received each year: 50.
Internships Available ▶ *1 assistant events coordinator:* responsibilities include house manager for Evening and Family Matinee Series in a 250-seat house, assisting with coordination of 2,000-seat Country Music event and 10,000-seat Arts and Music Festival, tabulating program surveys and reports, miscellaneous other office duties. Candidates should have ability to work independently, oral communication skills, organizational skills, self-motivation, strong interpersonal skills, strong leadership ability. Duration is 3–12 months. $500 per month. Open to recent college graduates, graduate students, individuals reentering the workforce, college seniors if seeking credit. ▶ *1–2 marketing associates:* responsibilities include box office management for 16 plus shows (250-seat house), 3 plus shows (2,000-seat house), 1 show (10,000-seat house); assisting with marketing to radio, press, and audience; tabulating audience surveys and selling ads for program book. Candidates should have ability to work independently, ability to work with others, oral communication skills, organizational skills, self-motivation, written communication skills. Duration is one to three months, with longer internships available. $300 per month. Open to college seniors, recent college graduates, graduate students, individuals reentering the workforce. ▶ *1 outreach coordinator:* responsibilities include coordinating and executing outreach programs with schools and artists, maintaining surveys and records of program, and other miscellaneous office duties. Candidates should have ability to work independently, oral communication skills, organizational skills, strong interpersonal

skills, written communication skills. Duration is 3–6 months. $300 per month. Open to college seniors, recent college graduates, graduate students, individuals reentering the workforce.
Benefits Free housing, free meals, names of contacts, on-the-job training, possible full-time employment, willing to act as a professional reference, willing to complete paperwork for educational credit, willing to provide letters of recommendation.
Contact Write, call, fax, or e-mail Ms. Heather Yelle, Intern Coordinator, PO Box 888, Elmer, New Jersey 08318. Phone: 609-358-2472. Fax: 609-358-6513. E-mail: appelarts@aol.com. Telephone interview required. Applicants must submit a formal organization application, cover letter, resume, three letters of recommendation. Applications are accepted continuously. World Wide Web: http://www.appelfarm.org.

ARCADY MUSIC SOCIETY
PO Box 780
Bar Harbor, Maine 04609

General Information Organization that presents high-quality chamber music. Established in 1980. Number of employees: 2. Number of internship applications received each year: 10.
Internships Available ▶ *1–2 interns:* responsibilities include selling ads, distributing posters, and handling publicity, sales, and artists' housing arrangements. Candidates should have ability to work with others, college courses in field, computer skills, office skills, organizational skills, personal interest in the field. Duration is 3–4 months. $800–$1,000 per duration of internship. Open to college freshmen, college sophomores, college juniors, college seniors, recent college graduates, graduate students, career changers. International applications accepted.
Benefits Free housing, job counseling, names of contacts, willing to provide letters of recommendation, some free meals on concert nights.
Contact Write, call, fax, or e-mail Ms. Melba C. Wilson, Executive Director. Phone: 207-288-3151. Fax: 207-288-3151. E-mail: mwilson@acadia.net. In-person interview recommended. Applicants must submit a cover letter, resume, two personal references. Application deadline: February 1 for summer.

ARCHIVE OF CONTEMPORARY MUSIC
54 White Street
New York, New York 10013

General Information Nonprofit music library and research center, with over one million recordings, dedicated to the collection and preservation of all types of popular music from around the world, 1950 to the present. Established in 1986. Number of employees: 2. Number of internship applications received each year: 75.
Internships Available ▶ *12 interns:* responsibilities include assisting in cataloging, filing press clippings, conducting research, and performing general office duties. Candidates should have ability to work with others, computer skills, knowledge of field, office skills, organizational skills, personal interest in the field, research skills, self-motivation. Duration is flexible. Unpaid. Open to high school students, high school seniors, college freshmen, college sophomores, college juniors, college seniors. International applications accepted.
Benefits Job counseling, opportunity to attend seminars/workshops, willing to complete paperwork for educational credit, willing to provide letters of recommendation, computer training, local transportation costs.
Contact Write, call, fax, or e-mail Mr. Bob George, Director. Phone: 212-226-6967. Fax: 212-226-6540. E-mail: arcmusic@inch.com. In-person interview recommended. Applicants must submit a resume. Applications are accepted continuously. World Wide Web: http://www.arcmusic.org.

BALLET MET
322 Mount Vernon Avenue
Columbus, Ohio 43215

General Information Professional dance company and academy. Established in 1978. Number of employees: 100. Number of internship applications received each year: 150.
Internships Available ▶ *1–4 marketing interns:* responsibilities include working on special events, press coordination marketing, and some design. Candidates should have ability to work independently, computer skills, editing skills, oral communication skills, written communication skills, design experience helpful. Duration is 3 months. Position available as unpaid or paid. Open to college sophomores, college juniors, college seniors. International applications accepted.
Benefits Names of contacts, willing to complete paperwork for educational credit, willing to provide letters of recommendation.
Contact Write, call, fax, or e-mail Brandi Pennington, Marketing Communications Associate. Phone: 614-229-4860 Ext. 163. Fax: 614-229-4858. E-mail: bpennington@balletmet.org. In-person interview recommended. Applicants must submit a cover letter, resume, writing sample. Applications are accepted continuously. World Wide Web: http://www.balletmet.org.

BARRY-HAFT-BROWN ARTISTS AGENCY
165 West 46th Street, Suite 908
New York, New York 10036

General Information Theatrical agency that handles actors for television, film, stage and regional theater. Established in 1988. Number of employees: 2. Number of internship applications received each year: 35.
Internships Available ▶ *1–2 interns:* responsibilities include assisting agents in all aspects of daily activities. Candidates should have computer skills, knowledge of field, office skills, oral communication skills, organizational skills, personal interest in the field, self-motivation, strong interpersonal skills. Duration is 1 summer. Position available as unpaid or at $5 per hour. Open to recent high school graduates, college freshmen, college sophomores, college juniors, college seniors, recent college graduates, graduate students, law students, career changers, individuals reentering the workforce. International applications accepted.
Benefits Formal training, possible full-time employment, willing to complete paperwork for educational credit.
International Internships Available in France; Italy; Russian Federation; Sweden; United Kingdom.
Contact Write Meg Pantera, Agent. In-person interview required. Applicants must submit a cover letter, resume. Applications are accepted continuously.

BOSTON BALLET
19 Clarendon Street
Boston, Massachusetts 02116

General Information Fourth largest dance company in the U.S.; performs a variety of classic story ballets, contemporary ballets, and avant-garde works. Established in 1965. Number of employees: 110. Number of internship applications received each year: 20.
Internships Available ▶ *1–2 Boston Ballet school interns:* responsibilities include exploring arts education and management. Candidates should have ability to work independently, computer skills, office skills, oral communication skills, written communication skills. Open to college sophomores, college juniors, college seniors, recent college graduates, graduate students. ▶ *1 company manager intern:* responsibilities include assisting company manager in applying for visas and coordinating contracts and logistics for visiting artists. Candidates should have ability to work independently, ability to work with others, computer skills, office skills, oral communication skills, organizational skills. Open to college freshmen, college sophomores, college juniors, college seniors. ▶ *2 development interns:* responsibilities include performing corporate research. Candidates should have ability to work independently, ability to work with others, office skills, oral communication skills, organizational skills, research skills. Open to college freshmen,

college sophomores, college juniors, college seniors. ▶ *1 graphic design intern:* responsibilities include assisting in-house graphic designer with various design projects. Candidates should have ability to work with others, computer skills, oral communication skills, personal interest in the field, self-motivation. Open to college sophomores, college juniors, college seniors, recent college graduates, graduate students. ▶ *1 human resource intern:* responsibilities include working directly with the human resources manager to maintain basic benefit accruals, conduct research and market surveys, and implement special projects. Candidates should have ability to work with others, computer skills, office skills, oral communication skills, organizational skills, research skills, writing skills. Open to college sophomores, college juniors, college seniors, recent college graduates, graduate students. ▶ *2 marketing interns:* responsibilities include researching and assisting with promotional material. Candidates should have ability to work with others, office skills, oral communication skills, research skills, writing skills. Open to college freshmen, college sophomores, college juniors, college seniors. ▶ *2 public relations interns:* responsibilities include assisting with organization of press material and filing and updating dancer biographical information. Candidates should have ability to work with others, computer skills, office skills, oral communication skills, writing skills. Open to college freshmen, college sophomores, college juniors, college seniors. ▶ *1 retail/wholesale division intern:* responsibilities include assisting staff in all aspects of the retail/wholesale business, including product development. Candidates should have ability to work with others, computer skills, oral communication skills, organizational skills. Open to college sophomores, college juniors, college seniors, recent college graduates, graduate students. ▶ *1 ticket office intern:* responsibilities include working in customer service and ticket distribution. Candidates should have computer skills, office skills, oral communication skills, self-motivation, strong interpersonal skills. Open to college freshmen, college sophomores, college juniors, college seniors. Duration for all positions is flexible. All positions are unpaid. International applications accepted.
Benefits Names of contacts, opportunity to attend seminars/workshops, possible full-time employment, willing to act as a professional reference, willing to complete paperwork for educational credit, willing to provide letters of recommendation, free performances.
Contact Write, call, or fax Intern Coordinator. Phone: 617-695-6950 Ext. 240. Fax: 617-695-6995. In-person interview recommended. Applicants must submit a cover letter, resume. Applications are accepted continuously. World Wide Web: http://www.boston.com/bostonballet.

BROOKLYN ACADEMY OF MUSIC
30 Lafayette Avenue
Brooklyn, New York 11217-1486

General Information Internationally recognized performing arts center. Established in 1861. Number of employees: 100. Number of internship applications received each year: 200.
Internships Available ▶ *1–2 fund-raising interns:* responsibilities include writing reports and proposals for grants. Candidates should have ability to work independently, computer skills, office skills, organizational skills, writing skills. Duration is flexible. Position available as unpaid or at stipend of $150 per week. ▶ *1 human resources intern.* Duration is varied. Unpaid. Open to college freshmen, college sophomores, college juniors, college seniors, recent college graduates, graduate students, law students, career changers. ▶ *1–2 marketing interns:* responsibilities include providing general administrative support services. Candidates should have ability to work independently, computer skills, office skills, oral communication skills, organizational skills, personal interest in the field, written communication skills. Duration is flexible. Position available as unpaid or at stipend of $150 per week. Open to high school seniors, recent high school graduates, college freshmen, college sophomores, college juniors, college seniors, recent college graduates, graduate students, career changers, individuals reentering the workforce. ▶ *1 production intern:* responsibilities include working with stagehands, technical, and wardrobe personnel to provide administrative support.

Candidates should have ability to work independently, computer skills, office skills, oral communication skills, organizational skills, personal interest in the field, self-motivation, strong interpersonal skills. Duration is flexible. Unpaid. Open to college freshmen, college sophomores, college juniors, college seniors, recent college graduates, graduate students. ▶ *1 rentals intern:* responsibilities include administrative/clerical duties, answering phones, answering questions about renting the theaters, running errands, and proofreading contracts and schedules. Candidates should have ability to work independently, computer skills, office skills, oral communication skills, self-motivation, strong interpersonal skills. Duration is flexible. Unpaid. Open to college freshmen, college sophomores, college juniors, college seniors, recent college graduates, graduate students, career changers. ▶ *1–2 special events interns:* responsibilities include assisting in fund-raising, planning, and execution of events. Candidates should have computer skills, office skills, organizational skills, self-motivation, strong interpersonal skills. Duration is flexible. Position available as unpaid or at stipend of $150 per week. Open to high school students, high school seniors, recent high school graduates, college freshmen, college sophomores, college juniors, college seniors, recent college graduates, graduate students, career changers, individuals reentering the workforce. International applications accepted.

Benefits Names of contacts, possible full-time employment, willing to complete paperwork for educational credit.

Contact Write or fax Liz Sharp, Human Resource Director, 30 Lafayette Avenue, Brooklyn, New York 11217-1485. Fax: 718-636-4179. No phone calls. In-person interview required. Applicants must submit a resume, letter of interest specifying which internship requested and dates of availability. Applications are accepted continuously. World Wide Web: http://www.bam.org.

CARNEGIE HALL
881 Seventh Avenue
New York, New York 10019

General Information Concert hall providing concerts of classical, jazz, and other styles of music. Established in 1891. Number of employees: 100. Number of internship applications received each year: 50.

Internships Available ▶ *1 corporate fund/special events intern:* responsibilities include researching potential corporate donors, comparative studies, assisting with special events projects, general office support. Candidates should have ability to work independently, ability to work with others, computer skills, organizational skills, research skills, strong interpersonal skills, writing skills. Duration is 1 semester. ▶ *1 foundation and government relations intern:* responsibilities include researching potential foundations, writing foundation and government proposals, general office support. Candidates should have ability to work independently, ability to work with others, computer skills, research skills, strong interpersonal skills, writing skills, written communication skills. Duration is 1 semester. ▶ *1 marketing intern:* responsibilities include creating marketing plans, placing advertisements, writing copy and bulletins, handling ticket requests, listing rentals, and providing office support. Candidates should have ability to work independently, computer skills, organizational skills, strong interpersonal skills, writing skills. Duration is 1 semester. ▶ *1 publicity intern:* responsibilities include writing press releases, photo captions, and radio announcements and providing office support. Candidates should have ability to work independently, computer skills, plan to pursue career in field, strong interpersonal skills, writing skills. Duration is 3 to 5 months by semester. All positions paid at minimum wage. Open to college freshmen, college sophomores, college juniors, college seniors, recent college graduates, graduate students, law students, career changers, individuals reentering the workforce. International applications accepted.

Benefits Willing to complete paperwork for educational credit, willing to provide letters of recommendation.

Contact Write or fax Carol Stark, Human Resources Administrator. Fax: 212-581-6539. In-person interview required. Applicants must submit a cover letter, resume, 1-2 writing samples. Application

deadline: April 15 for summer, July 15 for fall, November 15 for spring. World Wide Web: http://www.carnegiehall.org.

CHAMBER MUSIC AMERICA
305 Seventh Avenue, 5th Floor
New York, New York 10001-6008

General Information National service organization for professional chamber music ensembles and presenters. Established in 1978. Number of employees: 13. Number of internship applications received each year: 10.

Internships Available ▶ *1 conferences intern.* Candidates should have ability to work with others, analytical skills. Duration is 6–8 weeks. Open to college freshmen, college sophomores, college juniors, college seniors, graduate students. ▶ *2 magazine interns.* Duration is flexible. Open to college freshmen, college sophomores, college juniors, college seniors. All positions are unpaid.

Benefits Job counseling, names of contacts, opportunity to attend seminars/workshops, possible full-time employment, willing to complete paperwork for educational credit, possible stipends.

Contact Write, call, fax, or e-mail Pauline Willis, Director of Finance and Administration. Phone: 212-242-2022. Fax: 212-242-7955. E-mail: info@chamber-music.org. In-person interview recommended. Applicants must submit a cover letter, resume. Applications are accepted continuously. World Wide Web: http://www.chamber-music.org.

CHARLOTTE WILCOX COMPANY
1560 Broadway, Suite 910
New York, New York 10036

General Information Organization managing Broadway, touring-shows, and undertaking such responsibilities as contracts, budgets, taxes, and union rulings. Established in 1976. Number of employees: 3. Number of internship applications received each year: 25.

Internships Available ▶ *1–2 office assistants:* responsibilities include assisting in general office duties such as filing, phone work, running errands, computer input, typing, and working on special projects. Candidates should have ability to work independently, computer skills, office skills, oral communication skills, personal interest in the field, plan to pursue career in field, research skills, self-motivation, strong interpersonal skills, writing skills. Duration is flexible. stipend of $100 per week. Open to college freshmen, college sophomores, college juniors, college seniors, recent college graduates. International applications accepted.

Benefits Job counseling, names of contacts, on-the-job training, possible full-time employment, willing to act as a professional reference, willing to complete paperwork for educational credit, willing to provide letters of recommendation.

Contact Write or fax Charlotte Wilcox, General Manager. Fax: 212-764-5766. No phone calls. In-person interview recommended. Applicants must submit a cover letter, resume. Applications are accepted continuously.

THE CHORAL ARTS SOCIETY OF WASHINGTON
5225 Wisconsin Avenue, NW, Suite 603
Washington, District of Columbia 20015-2016

General Information 180-member symphonic chorus that performs a season subscription series at the Kennedy Center, in addition to concerts with the National Symphony Orchestra, international tours and recordings. Established in 1965. Number of employees: 8. Number of internship applications received each year: 50.

Internships Available ▶ *1 box office intern:* responsibilities include assisting with ticket sales, bookkeeping, and database management. Candidates should have analytical skills, computer skills, oral communication skills, self-motivation, strong interpersonal skills, written communication skills. ▶ *1 development/fund-raising intern:* responsibilities include assisting with research, computer database management, and proposal writing. Candidates should have computer skills, oral communication skills, self-motivation, strong

The Choral Arts Society of Washington (continued)

interpersonal skills, written communication skills. ▶ *1 outreach coordinator:* responsibilities include coordinating a choral tribute to Dr. Martin Luther King Jr., arranging preconcert lectures for students, and providing area students with complimentary tickets for concerts. Candidates should have oral communication skills, organizational skills, self-motivation, strong interpersonal skills, written communication skills. ▶ *1–2 public relations/marketing interns:* responsibilities include writing press releases, designing brochures, assisting with marketing research and group sales, designing and editing the quarterly newsletter, updating press lists, and photographing and assisting with special events. Candidates should have computer skills, oral communication skills, organizational skills, self-motivation, strong interpersonal skills, written communication skills. ▶ *1 special events coordinator:* responsibilities include planning, soliciting advertisers and donors, and database management. Candidates should have computer skills, oral communication skills, organizational skills, self-motivation, strong interpersonal skills, written communication skills. Duration for all positions is flexible. All positions are unpaid. Open to college sophomores, college juniors, college seniors, recent college graduates, graduate students. International applications accepted.

Benefits Formal training, job counseling, names of contacts, opportunity to attend seminars/workshops, possible full-time employment, willing to act as a professional reference, willing to complete paperwork for educational credit, willing to provide letters of recommendation.

Contact Write or fax Carrie Halpert, Director of Public Relations and Marketing. Fax: 202-244-4244. No phone calls. In-person interview required. Applicants must submit a cover letter, resume, writing sample, three personal references. Applications are accepted continuously. World Wide Web: http://www.choralarts.org.

CITY CENTER
130 West 56th Street
New York, New York 10019

General Information Not-for-profit performing arts center in New York City that presents, co-presents, and commercially rents its mainstage to prominent performing arts groups and other attractions. Established in 1943. Number of employees: 35. Number of internship applications received each year: 30.

Internships Available ▶ *1 development intern:* responsibilities include researching funding prospects; maintaining fund-raising database; writing letters; assisting in the coordination of department mailings, membership renewals, and solicitations; and performing general office duties. Candidates should have ability to work independently, computer skills, research skills, self-motivation, strong interpersonal skills, written communication skills, interest in performing arts, development, and marketing. Duration is flexible. Position available as unpaid or paid. Open to college freshmen, college sophomores, college juniors, college seniors, recent college graduates, graduate students, law students, career changers, individuals reentering the workforce. ▶ *1 marketing intern:* responsibilities include assisting in development/production of City Center's patron guide, season brochure, and photo gallery; maintaining marketing database; general office duties. Candidates should have computer skills, oral communication skills, strong interpersonal skills, written communication skills, sense of humor. Duration is Flexible-fall/spring/summer. varies. Open to college freshmen, college sophomores, college juniors, college seniors, recent college graduates, graduate students, law students. ▶ *1 outreach/education intern:* responsibilities include working with arts groups to coordinate their student performances, creating materials for presentations and workshops, documenting and evaluating the program. Candidates should have knowledge of field, organizational skills, self-motivation, strong interpersonal skills, writing skills. Duration is 1 semester. Position available as unpaid or paid. Open to college freshmen, college sophomores, college juniors, college seniors, recent college graduates, graduate students. International applications accepted.

Benefits Names of contacts, opportunity to attend seminars/workshops, possible full-time employment, willing to act as a professional reference, willing to provide letters of recommendation, stipend available.

Contact Write, fax, or e-mail Joe Chiplock, Associate Manager for Administration. Fax: 212-246-9778. E-mail: jchiplock@citycenter.org. No phone calls. In-person interview required. Applicants must submit a cover letter, resume. Applications are accepted continuously. World Wide Web: http://www.citycenter.org.

COMCAST-SPECTACOR
3601 South Broad Street
Philadelphia, Pennsylvania 19148

General Information Sports and entertainment company that operates the First Union Spectrum/Center facilities, 3 professional sports franchises and a cable broadcast sports network.

Internships Available ▶ *1 accounting intern:* responsibilities include maintaining data files, preparing bank reconciliations, assisting with payroll functions, analyzing G/L accounts, and entering accounts payable invoices in the accounting system. Candidates should have Lotus experience (helpful), ability to meet deadlines. Duration is 1 semester in fall, spring, or summer. Open to college juniors and seniors, or graduate students working for academic credit. ▶ *1 advertising sales intern:* responsibilities include developing new concepts for advertising venues at the First Union Spectrum/Center, assisting staff with research and design for various projects, handling phone inquiries, coordinating promotions and special events, and assisting with client sponsorship agreements. Candidates should have oral communication skills, self-motivation, strong interpersonal skills, written communication skills, ability to use Word, WordPerfect, PowerPoint, and Lotus 123 (preferred). Duration is spring or fall semester. Open to college juniors and seniors, or graduate students working for academic credit. ▶ *1 building public relations intern:* responsibilities include assisting with generating and pitching story ideas to media; assisting with brainstorming, planning, and executing publicity events; assisting with media tours; handling correspondence and assisting with mailings; and keeping a comprehensive record of events. Candidates should have oral communication skills, organizational skills, written communication skills, good phone skills, ability to use WordPerfect 5.1/6.0. Duration is 1 semester in fall, spring, or summer. Open to college juniors and seniors, or graduate students working for academic credit. ▶ *1 electronic media engineering intern:* responsibilities include learning the various computer-controlled systems which operate video, audio, intercom, and electronic message systems throughout the First Union Center; assisting the engineer in event set-up and troubleshooting. Candidates should have basic understanding of electronic circuit theory including video and audio system signals, component-level understanding of DC electronic (helpful). Duration is 1 semester in fall, spring, or summer. Open to 2nd-year technical school student with audio and television major, leading to an associate degree or equivalent. ▶ *1 electronic media intern:* responsibilities include editing and logging highlights from Flyers and 76ers games; assisting producer during game nights; operation of cameras, audio, and editing equipment; and routing switchers and graphics. Candidates should have ability to work independently, communications or television major, at least a Production II prerequisite, ability to do basic editing and production assistant duties. Duration is 1 semester in fall, spring, or summer. Open to college juniors and seniors, or graduate students working for academic credit. ▶ *1 event production intern:* responsibilities include participating in event-related duties, assisting with coordination of amenities for First Union Center tours, assisting event production staff on various projects, and assisting with coordination of vendor functions. Candidates should have oral communication skills, written communication skills, ability to use wordprocessing and spreadsheet applications (Microsoft Word, WordPerfect, Lotus 123, and Excel), good phone skills, and the ability to meet deadlines. Duration is 1 semester in fall, spring, or summer. Open to college juniors and seniors, or graduate students working for academic credit. ▶ *1 event public relations intern:* responsibilities include organizing photo files and show files, handling event-related correspondence, helping to plan and execute publicity events, assisting with mailings, and providing support during events. Candidates should have oral communication skills, organizational skills, written communication skills, good phone skills, ability to use WordPerfect 5.1/6.0, experience with database management (preferred). Duration is 1 semester in fall, spring, or summer. Open to college juniors and seniors, or graduate students working for academic credit. ▶ *2 event services interns:* responsibilities include assisting in promotion of shows and sporting events to group customers, helping to promote and implement the Public Tour program, processing orders, and customer service. Candidates should have oral communication skills, written communication skills, ability to use WordPerfect and Lotus software. Duration is 1 semester in fall, spring, or summer. Open to college juniors and seniors, or graduate students working for academic credit. ▶ *2 graphic services interns:* responsibilities include assisting in design, layout, and production of printed materials; maintaining computer files; assisting with production of game-day materials, and participating in brainstorming on proposed graphics projects. Candidates should have strong Macintosh computer skills along with a working knowledge of QuarkXpress, Illustrator, and PhotoShop. Duration is 1 semester in fall, spring, or summer. Open to college juniors and seniors, or graduate students working for academic credit. ▶ *1 human resources intern:* responsibilities include working with recruiter to promote and administer the internship program, assisting in orientation of interns, maintaining internship files, and screening incoming employment applications and mailing responses to applicants. Candidates should have oral communication skills, organizational skills, written communication skills, ability to use Microsoft Word (or WordPerfect), Excel, and cc:Mail. Duration is 1 semester in fall, spring, or summer. Open to college juniors and seniors, or graduate students working for academic credit. ▶ *2 marketing interns:* responsibilities include promoting shows and sporting events; assisting the security, operations, and promotions departments on days of events, creating post-event marketing summaries, and doing demographic and psychographic market research. Candidates should have oral communication skills, written communication skills, basic knowledge of wordprocessing and spreadsheet applications, computer graphics experience (helpful). Duration is 1 semester in fall, spring, or summer. Open to college juniors and seniors, or graduate students working for academic credit. ▶ *2 operations interns:* responsibilities include assisting with event-related activities, assisting with changeover tasks, and helping to create a production book concerning events held at the First Union Spectrum/Center. Candidates should have ability to use WordPerfect, Microsoft Word, and Excel; ability to adapt to a wide variety of projects; ability to meet deadlines. Duration is 1 semester in fall, spring, or summer. Open to college juniors and seniors, or graduate students working for academic credit. ▶ *1 recruiting intern:* responsibilities include helping to screen employment applications and resumes, handling responses to applicants and updating database, and assisting with interviewing and the coordination of employment paperwork. Candidates should have oral communication skills, organizational skills, written communication skills, ability to use Microsoft Word (or WordPerfect), Excel, and cc:Mail. Duration is 1 semester in fall, spring, or summer. Open to college juniors and seniors or graduate students working for academic credit. ▶ *1 sports' charities intern:* responsibilities include assisting in preparation of Flyers' Wives Fight for Lives Carnival; taking ticket orders; assisting in preparation and coordination of all charity events; coordinating solicitation, mailing, and distribution of Carnival tickets and information; and merchandise and inventory control. Candidates should have strong typing/computer skills, ability to work some nights or weekends. Duration is 1 semester in fall, spring, or summer. Open to college juniors and seniors, or graduate students working for academic credit. ▶ *1 tour guide intern:* responsibilities include leading individuals and groups on informative tours of the First Union Center, providing office support, scheduling tours, telemarketing prospective clients, and assisting in marketing and promoting tours. Candidates should have oral communication skills, strong interpersonal skills, willingness to work some weekends, ability to speak to large groups and to do extensive walking, ability to

use WordPerfect and Lotus software. Duration is 1 semester in fall, spring, or summer. Open to college juniors and seniors, or graduate students working for academic credit. All positions are unpaid.
Benefits Names of contacts, possible full-time employment, willing to complete paperwork for educational credit.
Contact Write Internship Program, Human Resources Department. No phone calls. In-person interview required. Applicants must submit a formal organization application, resume, cover letter indicating reasons for choosing this internship and the qualities or attributes that will help make a contribution, faculty recommendation form (sent with application). Application deadline: at least 2 months prior to the intended start date. World Wide Web: http://www.comcast-spectacor.com.

THE COSTUME COLLECTION
601 West 26th Street, 17th Floor
New York, New York 10001

General Information Organization that introduces students to the New York costume business and to realistic aspects of project design. Established in 1977. Number of employees: 10. Unit of Theater Development Fund, New York, New York. Number of internship applications received each year: 50.
Internships Available ▶ *8 design interns:* responsibilities include completing a design project under the tutelage of top designers. Candidates should have college courses in field, knowledge of field, personal interest in the field, costume design ability. Duration is 7–8 weeks. minimum wage. Open to college freshmen, college sophomores, college juniors, college seniors, recent college graduates, graduate students. International applications accepted.
Benefits Formal training, opportunity to attend seminars/workshops, possible full-time employment, willing to act as a professional reference, willing to complete paperwork for educational credit, willing to provide letters of recommendation.
Contact Write, call, fax, or e-mail Mr. Domingo Rodriguez, Director Emeritus. Phone: 212-989-5855. Fax: 212-206-0922. E-mail: costumes@tdf.org. Applicants must submit a formal organization application, cover letter, resume, 2 examples of color renderings. Application deadline: March 15 for summer. World Wide Web: http://www.tdf.org.

DIXON PLACE
258 Bowery
New York, New York 10012

General Information Organization that nurtures theatre, performance, dance and literary artists by encouraging the development of new work and assists emerging and established artists to explore the creative process by providing a safe, supportive environment. Established in 1986. Number of employees: 13. Number of internship applications received each year: 35.
Internships Available ▶ *1–2 administrative assistants:* responsibilities include preparing monthly calendars, handling press listings and press releases, updating the mailing list, and scheduling artists' rehearsal times. Candidates should have ability to work independently, computer skills, knowledge of field, office skills, self-motivation, strong interpersonal skills. Duration is 1 semester. Unpaid. ▶ *1–2 administrative/technical interns:* responsibilities include preparing monthly calendars, press listings, and press releases; updating the mailing list; scheduling artists' rehearsal time; providing technical assistance for artists; working the box office; hosting shows; and opening and closing the theater. Candidates should have computer skills, experience in the field, oral communication skills, self-motivation, strong interpersonal skills. Duration is 3 months minimum. Position available as unpaid or at $100-$125 per week for occasional long-running shows. ▶ *1–2 technical assistants:* responsibilities include providing technical assistance for artists; setting up light, sound, and video; working the box office; opening and closing the theater; and videotaping performances. Candidates should have experience in the field, oral communication skills, organizational skills, self-motivation, strong interpersonal skills. Duration is 1 semester. Position available as unpaid or at $100 per week for occasional

Dixon Place (continued)

long-running shows. Open to college sophomores, college juniors, college seniors, recent college graduates, graduate students, career changers. International applications accepted.
Benefits Formal training, names of contacts, on-the-job training, willing to complete paperwork for educational credit, willing to provide letters of recommendation.
Contact Write, call, fax, or e-mail Ms. Ellie Covan, Executive Director. Phone: 212-219-3088. Fax: 212-274-9114. E-mail: contact@dixonplace.org. In-person interview recommended. Applicants must submit a cover letter, resume. Application deadline: March 15 for summer, July 1 for fall, November 1 for winter/spring. World Wide Web: http://www.dixonplace.org.

ELITE MODEL MANAGEMENT, CHICAGO
58 West Huron
Chicago, Illinois 60610

General Information Model management. Established in 1982. Number of employees: 20. Unit of Elite Model Management, New York, New York. Number of internship applications received each year: 100.
Internships Available ▶ *3–5 management assistants:* responsibilities include office duties including filing, fax, and phone coverage and assisting model bookers. Candidates should have ability to work independently, ability to work with others, computer skills, office skills, oral communication skills, organizational skills, personal interest in the field, self-motivation, writing skills. Duration is 2-4 months (flexible). Unpaid. Open to recent high school graduates, college freshmen, college sophomores, college juniors, college seniors, recent college graduates.
Benefits On-the-job training, willing to act as a professional reference, willing to complete paperwork for educational credit, willing to provide letters of recommendation.
Contact Write Shannon E. Hill, New Faces Booker. No phone calls. Applicants must submit a cover letter, resume, interview after review of resume. Applications are accepted continuously. World Wide Web: http://www.elitechicago.com.

FLORIDA GRAND OPERA
1200 Coral Way
Miami, Florida 33145

General Information Grand opera producing company presenting 35 performances of 5 grand operas each session in addition to a small-scale touring production and various other performance programs. Established in 1942. Number of employees: 25. Number of internship applications received each year: 100.
Internships Available ▶ *Music interns:* responsibilities include studying, training, and giving frequent professional and educational outreach performances. Candidates should have ability to work with others, oral communication skills, plan to pursue career in field. Duration is flexible. $150–$170 per week. ▶ *4 production interns:* responsibilities include apprenticing with a member of the company's staff in either stage management, costuming, props, or lighting design. Candidates should have ability to work independently, ability to work with others, college courses in field, computer skills, office skills. Duration is flexible. $150–$175 per week. Open to college graduates.
Benefits Free housing, health insurance, opportunity to attend seminars/workshops, possible full-time employment, travel reimbursement, willing to complete paperwork for educational credit, willing to provide letters of recommendation.
Contact Write, call, or fax Mr. Paul Lapinski, Assistant General Manager or Mr. Bernard Uzan, Apprentice Coordinator. Phone: 305-854-1643. Fax: 305-856-1042. Applicants must submit a cover letter, resume, 8x10 photo. Application deadline: August 30 for production positions, October 27 for music positions. World Wide Web: http://www.fgo.org.

FOUNDATION FOR THE ADVANCE OF DANCE, INC.
55 Bethune Street, Suite 630-A
New York, New York 10014

General Information Sponsors Edith Stephen Electric Current Dance Company and young choreographers' scholarships for training, acts as consultant, and presents dance programs and dance workshops throughout the U.S. and Europe. Established in 1970. Number of employees: 3. Number of internship applications received each year: 20.
Internships Available ▶ *1 arts administrator intern:* responsibilities include correspondence and assisting in bookings for the company, including publicity, press releases, and public relations. Duration is flexible. Unpaid. Open to college freshmen, college sophomores, college juniors, college seniors. International applications accepted.
Benefits Job counseling, names of contacts, opportunity to attend seminars/workshops, willing to provide letters of recommendation.
Contact Write, call, or fax Ms. E. Kapel, Arts Administrator. Phone: 212-989-2250. Fax: 212-645-7495. In-person interview recommended. Applicants must submit a resume. Applications are accepted continuously.

GALA CHORUSES
PO Box 65084
Washington, District of Columbia 20035

General Information Association of gay, lesbian, and feminist choruses that produces educational publications, annual conferences, and music festivals. Established in 1982. Number of employees: 5. Number of internship applications received each year: 10.
Internships Available ▶ *1 development assistant:* responsibilities include assisting with writing and the compilation of government and foundation grant proposals, donor research, preparation of background materials, special events planning, and maintenance of donor files. Candidates should have ability to work independently, computer skills, editing skills, oral communication skills, personal interest in the field, written communication skills. Duration is flexible. Open to college juniors, college seniors, recent college graduates, graduate students, career changers. ▶ *1 marketing assistant:* responsibilities include assisting with advertising sales, exhibitor sales, and membership marketing. Candidates should have ability to work independently, editing skills, oral communication skills, personal interest in the field, written communication skills. Duration is flexible. Open to college juniors, college seniors, recent college graduates, graduate students, career changers. ▶ *Membership services assistants:* responsibilities include responding to information requests via telephone, mail, fax, or e-mail. Candidates should have ability to work independently, editing skills, oral communication skills, personal interest in the field, written communication skills. Duration is flexible. Open to college juniors, college seniors, recent college graduates, graduate students, career changers. ▶ *1 publications assistant:* responsibilities include updating organization's annual publications including repertoire listings, diversity guide, membership handbook, and newsletters. Candidates should have college courses in field, editing skills, personal interest in the field, written communication skills. Duration is 2 months in summer. Open to college juniors, college seniors, recent college graduates, career changers. All positions are unpaid. International applications accepted.
Benefits Names of contacts, willing to complete paperwork for educational credit, willing to provide letters of recommendation, hosted housing may be available.
Contact Write, fax, or e-mail Kenneth T. Cole, Executive Director. Fax: 202-467-5831. E-mail: galachorus@aol.com. No phone calls. In-person interview recommended. Applicants must submit a resume. Applications are accepted continuously.

GOLIARD CONCERTS
21-65 41st Street
Astoria, New York 11105

General Information Professional chamber music company presenting an annual concert series in an historic church in Queens, New York, with performances that include chorale, chamber, orchestra, and soloists. Established in 1983. Number of employees: 3. Number of internship applications received each year: 20.

Internships Available ▶ *1–2 arts management interns:* responsibilities include assisting with coordination and fund-raising events, performing clerical work and marketing tasks, and assisting in concerts, festivals, and tour productions. Candidates should have ability to work independently, office skills, oral communication skills, plan to pursue career in field, self-motivation, writing skills. Duration is 3-4 months or longer. $150 per month. Open to college freshmen, college sophomores, college juniors, college seniors, recent college graduates, graduate students. International applications accepted.

Benefits Free housing, job counseling, names of contacts, on-the-job training, opportunity to attend seminars/workshops, possible full-time employment, willing to complete paperwork for educational credit, willing to provide letters of recommendation.

Contact Write, call, or fax Shauna Wilkins, Office Administrator. Phone: 718-728-8927. Fax: 718-728-8927. In-person interview recommended. Applicants must submit a cover letter, resume. Applications are accepted continuously.

GUS GIORDANO JAZZ DANCE CHICAGO
614 Davis Street
Evanston, Illinois 60201

General Information Nonprofit American jazz dance company that tours internationally and nationally and offers local performances in the Chicago area. Established in 1962. Number of employees: 12. Number of internship applications received each year: 5.

Internships Available ▶ *4 interns:* responsibilities include completing light typing assignments, writing press releases and dancers' biographies, performing general administrative work, grant writing, and providing research assistance. Candidates should have ability to work independently, ability to work with others, computer skills, office skills, oral communication skills, written communication skills. Duration is 2–6 months. Unpaid. Open to college freshmen, college sophomores, college juniors, college seniors, recent college graduates, individuals reentering the workforce. International applications accepted.

Benefits On-the-job training, travel reimbursement, willing to act as a professional reference, willing to complete paperwork for educational credit, willing to provide letters of recommendation, workman's compensation insurance.

Contact Write, call, or fax Ben Hodge, Executive Director. Phone: 847-866-6779. Fax: 847-866-9228. In-person interview recommended. Applicants must submit a cover letter, resume, two personal references. Applications are accepted continuously.

HANDEL & HAYDN SOCIETY
300 Massachusetts Avenue
Boston, Massachusetts 02115

General Information Professional orchestra and chorus specializing in period instrument performances of Baroque and classical music. Established in 1815. Number of employees: 12. Number of internship applications received each year: 30.

Internships Available ▶ *1 development intern:* responsibilities include assisting with donor research and correspondence. ▶ *1 marketing department intern:* responsibilities include assisting with press releases and customer services. Duration for all positions is flexible. All positions are unpaid. Open to recent high school graduates, college freshmen, college sophomores, college juniors, college seniors, recent college graduates, graduate students, law students, career changers, individuals reentering the workforce.

Benefits Willing to complete paperwork for educational credit, willing to provide letters of recommendation.

Contact Write, call, fax, or e-mail Ms. Debra Moniz, Director of Finance. Fax: 617-266-4217. E-mail: handlhaydn@aol.com. In-person interview recommended. Applicants must submit a cover letter, resume. Applications are accepted continuously. World Wide Web: http://www.handelandhaydn.org.

JACOB'S PILLOW DANCE FESTIVAL, INC.
PO Box 287
Lee, Massachusetts 01238

General Information Festival presenting ten weeks of dance performances and conducting a professional dance school each summer. Established in 1942. Number of employees: 75. Number of internship applications received each year: 100.

Internships Available ▶ *1 archives/preservation assistant:* responsibilities include working alongside the Director of Preservation in the archives department. Candidates should have computer skills, oral communication skills, organizational skills, personal interest in the field, research skills, self-motivation. Duration is 3 months or longer. stipend of $300. Open to college juniors, college seniors, recent college graduates, graduate students, career changers. ▶ *1 business intern:* responsibilities include assisting business manager. Candidates should have computer skills, office skills, organizational skills, personal interest in the field, self-motivation, strong interpersonal skills. Duration is 3 months. $100 per month. Open to college juniors, college seniors, recent college graduates, graduate students, career changers. ▶ *2 development interns:* responsibilities include fund-raising and grant writing. Candidates should have analytical skills, computer skills, editing skills, organizational skills, personal interest in the field, written communication skills. Duration is 3 months. stipend of $300. Open to college juniors, college seniors, recent college graduates, graduate students, career changers. ▶ *3 marketing/press interns:* responsibilities include working to promote the festival and the school. Candidates should have ability to work independently, ability to work with others, computer skills, personal interest in the field, writing skills. Duration is 3 months. stipend of $300. Open to college juniors, college seniors, recent college graduates, graduate students, career changers. ▶ *1 operations intern:* responsibilities include managing the day-to-day activities of a multi-theater dance festival. Candidates should have oral communication skills, organizational skills, personal interest in the field, self-motivation, strong interpersonal skills. Duration is 3 months. stipend of $300. Open to college freshmen, college sophomores, college juniors, college seniors, recent college graduates, graduate students, individuals reentering the workforce. ▶ *1 programming intern:* responsibilities include coordinating audience enrichment programs. Candidates should have analytical skills, computer skills, organizational skills, personal interest in the field, self-motivation, strong interpersonal skills. Duration is 3 months. stipend of $300. Open to college juniors, college seniors, recent college graduates, graduate students, career changers, individuals reentering the workforce. ▶ *2 school interns:* responsibilities include assisting school coordinator in the daily operation of school programs. Candidates should have computer skills, oral communication skills, personal interest in the field, self-motivation, strong interpersonal skills, written communication skills. Duration is 3 months. stipend of $300. Open to college juniors, college seniors, recent college graduates, graduate students, career changers, individuals reentering the workforce. ▶ *11 technical theater interns:* responsibilities include running crew for 2 theaters. Candidates should have ability to work with others, analytical skills, experience in the field, oral communication skills, personal interest in the field, self-motivation. Duration is 3 months. stipend of $300. Open to college freshmen, college sophomores, college juniors, college seniors, recent college graduates, graduate students, individuals reentering the workforce. ▶ *1 video intern:* responsibilities include Documenting various activities of the season. Candidates should have ability to work independently, ability to work with others, experience in the field, oral communication skills, personal interest in the field, self-motivation. Duration is 3 months. stipend of $300. Open to college juniors, college seniors, recent college graduates, graduate students, career changers. International applications accepted.

Jacob's Pillow Dance Festival, Inc. (continued)

Benefits Free housing, free meals, names of contacts, on-the-job training, opportunity to attend seminars/workshops, willing to act as a professional reference, willing to complete paperwork for educational credit, willing to provide letters of recommendation, opportunity to see dance performances.

Contact Write, fax, or e-mail Debbie Markowitz, Company Manager. Fax: 413-243-4744. E-mail: dmarkowitz.jpdf@taconic.net. Telephone interview required. Applicants must submit a cover letter, resume, two letters of recommendation, a work-related reference, and 2 writing samples (maximum 3 pages) for marketing/press, development, education, and programming applicants. Application deadline: March 6 for summer, September 13 for fall, December 1 for spring.

JENNIFER MULLER/THE WORKS
131 West 24th Street
New York, New York 10011

General Information New York City–based contemporary dance company that does extensive international touring. Established in 1974. Number of employees: 5. Number of internship applications received each year: 15.

Internships Available ▶ *1 accounting intern:* responsibilities include working on general ledger and bookkeeping tasks. Open to college freshmen, college sophomores, college juniors, college seniors, recent college graduates, graduate students, dancers. ▶ *2 administration interns:* responsibilities include assisting managers in day-to-day operations, special events, and fund-raising. Open to college freshmen, college sophomores, college juniors, college seniors, recent college graduates, graduate students. ▶ *1 tour planning intern:* responsibilities include contacting sponsors and travel and hotel bookings. Open to college freshmen, college sophomores, college juniors, college seniors, recent college graduates, graduate students, dancers. Duration for all positions is flexible. All positions are unpaid. International applications accepted.

Benefits Job counseling, possible full-time employment, willing to complete paperwork for educational credit, willing to provide letters of recommendation.

Contact Write Ms. Lynette Muller, Office Manager. In-person interview recommended. Applications are accepted continuously.

THE JOHN F. KENNEDY CENTER FOR THE PERFORMING ARTS
2700 F Street, NW
Washington, District of Columbia 20566

General Information National performing arts center. Established in 1971. Number of internship applications received each year: 550.

Internships Available ▶ *1 Alliance for Arts Education intern:* responsibilities include assisting with national recognition programs for outstanding school administrators and local school boards, administering fellowships, and working with a national network of state organizations. Candidates should have computer skills, knowledge of field, writing skills. Open to college juniors, college seniors, recent college graduates, graduate students. ▶ *1 American College Theater intern:* responsibilities include assisting with technical coordination of ACTF national festival, responding to telephone inquiries, updating mailing lists, and handling national festival ticket distribution. Candidates should have computer skills, oral communication skills, plan to pursue career in field, writing skills. Open to college juniors, college seniors, recent college graduates, graduate students. ▶ *1 Arts Edge intern:* responsibilities include assisting director and staff with research, collection, and organization of information to be disseminated through the Arts Edge Web site. Candidates should have computer skills, knowledge of field, writing skills. Open to college juniors, college seniors, recent college graduates, graduate students. ▶ *1 Friends of Center intern:* responsibilities include working in special events production, volunteer management, retail management, visitor services, and community relations. Candidates should have computer skills, oral communication skills, strong interpersonal skills. Open to college juniors, college seniors,

recent college graduates, graduate students. ▶ *4 National Symphony Orchestra interns:* responsibilities include assisting with organization of special concerts for young people, administering training programs and competitions for high school musicians, fielding phone inquiries, researching programming issues, working with volunteers, and compiling material for NSO education programs. Candidates should have computer skills, knowledge of field, oral communication skills, plan to pursue career in field, writing skills. Open to college juniors, college seniors, recent college graduates. ▶ *2 advertising interns:* responsibilities include providing administrative support and dealing with ad trafficking and placements, broadcast production, editing, and promotional event planning. Candidates should have computer skills, knowledge of field, oral communication skills, plan to pursue career in field, writing skills. Open to college juniors, college seniors, recent college graduates, graduate students. ▶ *5 development interns:* responsibilities include assisting in administration of fund-raising campaigns and working on project research, special projects, membership services, grants, sponsorship, corporate fund, and Circle Fund. Candidates should have ability to work with others, computer skills, oral communication skills, organizational skills, writing skills. Open to college juniors, college seniors, recent college graduates, graduate students. ▶ *5 education interns:* responsibilities include assisting with the administration of arts education events and evaluating programs, workshops, discussions, master classes, and performances. Candidates should have computer skills, oral communication skills, plan to pursue career in field, writing skills. Open to college juniors, college seniors, recent college graduates, graduate students. ▶ *1 production intern:* responsibilities include serving as a production or design assistant for shows and events in the Center's six theater and non-theater spaces. Candidates should have computer skills, experience in the field, knowledge of field, oral communication skills, strong interpersonal skills. Open to college juniors, college seniors, recent college graduates, graduate students. ▶ *1 programming intern:* responsibilities include contract preparation, supernumerary coordination, artist hospitality, and special performance event management. Candidates should have computer skills, organizational skills, plan to pursue career in field, strong interpersonal skills, writing skills. Open to college juniors, college seniors, recent college graduates, graduate students. ▶ *2 youth and family programs interns:* responsibilities include assisting with theater training program, contributing to audience and program development projects, supporting the artistic and production staff, acting as production interns by assisting the stage managers or design assistants, or working with the artistic and production staff. Candidates should have computer skills, knowledge of field, plan to pursue career in field, writing skills. Open to college juniors, college seniors, recent college graduates, graduate students. Duration for all positions is 3–4 months. All positions paid at $650 per month. International applications accepted.

Benefits Formal training, opportunity to attend seminars/workshops, willing to complete paperwork for educational credit, willing to provide letters of recommendation, opportunity to attend performances.

Contact Write, call, or e-mail Danika C. Foster, Internship Program Coordinator, Education Department. Phone: 202-416-8821. E-mail: dcfoster@mail.kennedy-center.org. Applicants must submit a cover letter, resume, academic transcripts, two letters of recommendation, 1- to 3-page writing sample. Application deadline: March 1 for summer, June 15 for fall, November 1 for winter/spring. World Wide Web: http://www.kennedy-center.org.

LYRIC OPERA OF CHICAGO
20 North Wacker Drive, #860
Chicago, Illinois 60606

General Information Organization that engages in the study of opera, music, and the fine arts and sponsors, produces, and encourages opera and musical performances in and about Chicago and elsewhere. Established in 1954. Number of internship applications received each year: 30.

Internships Available ▶ *1 Lyric Opera Center intern:* responsibilities include organizing auditions and road trips; archiving audition materials. Candidates should have ability to work independently, office skills, oral communication skills, organizational skills, strong interpersonal skills, written communication skills. Duration is 3 months in the summer (if needed). Open to recent high school graduates, college freshmen, college sophomores, college juniors, college seniors, recent college graduates, graduate students, career changers, individuals reentering the workforce. ▶ *1–2 artistic/technical interns:* responsibilities include assisting with research, archiving, and scheduling projects. Candidates should have ability to work independently, computer skills, knowledge of field, oral communication skills, plan to pursue career in field, research skills. Duration is flexible (generally during summer). Open to college freshmen, college sophomores, college juniors, college seniors, recent college graduates, graduate students, individuals reentering the workforce. ▶ *1 backstage/production intern:* responsibilities include assisting in backstage activities. Candidates should have experience in the field, oral communication skills, organizational skills, plan to pursue career in field, strong interpersonal skills. Duration is 4 to 6 months from summer to winter (when needed). Open to college freshmen, college sophomores, college juniors, college seniors, recent college graduates, graduate students, individuals reentering the workforce. ▶ *6–10 development/fund-raising interns:* responsibilities include assisting in organizing fund-raising events and processing donor records. Candidates should have ability to work independently, computer skills, oral communication skills, organizational skills, strong interpersonal skills, written communication skills. Duration is flexible. Open to recent high school graduates, college freshmen, college sophomores, college juniors, college seniors, recent college graduates, graduate students, career changers, individuals reentering the workforce. ▶ *1–2 education interns:* responsibilities include assisting with educational outreach programs and administration of education department activities. Candidates should have oral communication skills, organizational skills, plan to pursue career in field, strong interpersonal skills, writing skills. Duration is flexible. Open to recent high school graduates, college freshmen, college sophomores, college juniors, college seniors, recent college graduates, graduate students, individuals reentering the workforce. ▶ *1 finance/administration intern:* responsibilities include assisting with general accounting functions, and business administration. Candidates should have ability to work independently, analytical skills, computer skills, knowledge of field, organizational skills, plan to pursue career in field. Duration is 3-6 months in winter/spring (if needed). Open to college sophomores, college juniors, college seniors, recent college graduates, graduate students, individuals reentering the workforce. ▶ *1 marketing/public relations intern:* responsibilities include assisting in publicity functions. Candidates should have ability to work with others, computer skills, oral communication skills, organizational skills, plan to pursue career in field, writing skills, music/theater background, office experience desirable. Duration is 3 months in spring (if needed). Open to college seniors, recent college graduates, graduate students. All positions are unpaid. International applications accepted.

Benefits Job counseling, names of contacts, opportunity to attend seminars/workshops, possible full-time employment, willing to act as a professional reference, willing to complete paperwork for educational credit, willing to provide letters of recommendation, use of research materials and rehearsal areas, includes travel stipend.

Contact Write, call, fax, or e-mail Stacie Sue Schmidt, Human Resources Services Coordinator. Phone: 312-332-2244 Ext. 499. Fax: 312-419-1082. E-mail: sschmidt@lyricopera.org. In-person interview recommended. Applicants must submit a formal organization application, cover letter, resume. Applications are accepted continuously.

MARK DEGARMO AND DANCERS/DYNAMIC FORMS, INC.
179 East Third Street, Suite #24
New York, New York 10009

General Information Not-for-profit modern dance company. Established in 1985. Number of employees: 1. Number of internship applications received each year: 10.
Internships Available ▶ *1–2 administrative interns:* responsibilities include assisting in dance-related development, bookings, and office work depending on interests and initiative of intern. Candidates should have computer skills, office skills, personal interest in the field, plan to pursue career in field, strong interpersonal skills, written communication skills. Duration is flexible (usually 2-3 months). Unpaid. Open to college juniors, college seniors, recent college graduates, graduate students, career changers, individuals reentering the workforce. International applications accepted.
Benefits Job counseling, names of contacts, on-the-job training, opportunity to attend seminars/workshops, possible full-time employment, willing to act as a professional reference, willing to complete paperwork for educational credit, willing to provide letters of recommendation.
Contact Write, fax, or e-mail Mr. Mark DeGarmo, Artistic Director. Phone: 212-267-8723. Fax: 212-267-8723. E-mail: markdegarmo@hotmail.com. In-person interview recommended. Applicants must submit a cover letter, resume, 1-2 letters of recommendation. Applications are accepted continuously.

METROPOLITAN OPERA GUILD EDUCATION DEPARTMENT
70 Lincoln Center Plaza
New York, New York 10023-6593

General Information Program dedicated to furthering music education in schools and communities across the nation through a variety of activities such as school residencies, lecture series, backstage tours, multimedia resources, and special performances for students at the Metropolitan Opera House. Number of employees: 9. Number of internship applications received each year: 15.
Internships Available ▶ *4 interns:* responsibilities include performing office tasks, managing the box office, editing and producing study materials, and coordinating students in the Opera House. Candidates should have computer skills, experience in the field, office skills, oral communication skills, plan to pursue career in field. Duration is 3 months minimum (15 hours minimum per week). $500 stipend per semester. Open to college freshmen, college sophomores, college juniors, college seniors, recent college graduates, graduate students. International applications accepted.
Benefits Job counseling, opportunity to attend seminars/workshops, willing to complete paperwork for educational credit, willing to provide letters of recommendation.
Contact Write, call, fax, or e-mail Ms. Gretchen Weerheim, Family Programs Coordinator. Phone: 212-769-7022. Fax: 212-769-8519. E-mail: gweerheim@operaed.org. In-person interview required. Applicants must submit a cover letter, resume, three letters of recommendation. Application deadline: May 1 for summer, July 1 for fall, December 1 for spring. World Wide Web: http://www.metguild.org.

MIDLAND CENTER FOR THE ARTS
1801 West St. Andrews
Midland, Michigan 48640

General Information Organization that provides various kinds of entertainment including musical comedy, jazz bands, dance groups, and pop artists. Established in 1943. Number of employees: 75. Number of internship applications received each year: 20.
Internships Available ▶ *2–3 technical production interns:* responsibilities include assisting in the daily activities of the scene shop, including scenery construction and painting; assisting in coordinating all arrangements for Summer Festival events such as hiring

Midland Center for the Arts (continued)

of crews, rental equipment, hospitality and artist transport; working with the technical staff on all technical aspects (light and sound) of events, including all load-ins, strikes, and performances; assisting in proper shop maintenance and repair of equipment as needed; supervising paid and volunteer crews in conjunction with other staff. Candidates should have ability to work independently, ability to work with others, college courses in field, experience in the field, knowledge of field, personal interest in the field. Duration is 10–16 weeks. $5–$6 per hour. Open to college freshmen, college sophomores, college juniors, college seniors, recent college graduates. International applications accepted.

Benefits On-the-job training, possible full-time employment, willing to act as a professional reference, willing to complete paperwork for educational credit, willing to provide letters of recommendation.

Contact Write, fax, or e-mail Mark Turpin, Director of Technical Services. Fax: 517-631-7890. E-mail: turpin@mcfta.org. No phone calls. In-person interview recommended. Applicants must submit a cover letter, resume. Application deadline: March 15 for summer.

MINNESOTA DANCE ALLIANCE
528 Hennepin Avenue, Suite 600
Minneapolis, Minnesota 55403

General Information Service organization for the art of dance in Minnesota. Established in 1979. Number of employees: 5. Number of internship applications received each year: 10.

Internships Available ▶ *Intern assistants to the member programs manager:* responsibilities include helping administer re-granting programs for choreographers and dancers (artist and panelist relations, guidelines, publicity), and assisting with member relations (mailings, database updates). Candidates should have computer skills, organizational skills, personal interest in the field, self-motivation, strong interpersonal skills, written communication skills. ▶ *Intern assistants to the communications manager:* responsibilities include assisting with publicity, press and artist relations, and front-of-house for MDA productions; researching local media; and helping with archival folders and database updates. Candidates should have editing skills, organizational skills, personal interest in the field, self-motivation, strong interpersonal skills, written communication skills. ▶ *Intern assistants to the executive director:* responsibilities include assisting with grant writing and research into funding opportunities, helping prepare final reports, assisting with board meetings and relations, and working on other projects as needed. Candidates should have organizational skills, personal interest in the field, research skills, self-motivation, strong interpersonal skills, written communication skills. ▶ *Intern assistants to the production director:* responsibilities include assisting with the daily operations of studio 6A, and the Dance Alliance's theater (activities range from general maintenance to technical set-up for shows). There is also the opportunity to participate in running shows. Candidates should have ability to work independently, ability to work with others, knowledge of field, personal interest in the field, self-motivation. Duration for all positions is flexible. All positions are unpaid. Open to high school seniors, recent high school graduates, college freshmen, college sophomores, college juniors, college seniors, recent college graduates, graduate students, law students, law school graduates, career changers, individuals reentering the workforce. International applications accepted.

Benefits Names of contacts, on-the-job training, opportunity to attend seminars/workshops, possible full-time employment, willing to complete paperwork for educational credit, willing to provide letters of recommendation.

Contact Write, call, or fax Ms. June Wilson, Executive Director. Phone: 612-340-1900. Fax: 612-340-0910. In-person interview recommended. Applicants must submit a cover letter, resume, two personal references. Applications are accepted continuously.

MISSOURI SYMPHONY SOCIETY
PO Box 1121
Columbia, Missouri 65205

General Information Private nonprofit corporation dedicated to bringing fine music to central Missouri, educating central Missouri youth about music, and preserving and restoring the historic Missouri Theatre. Established in 1970. Number of employees: 4. Number of internship applications received each year: 10.

Internships Available ▶ *1 marketing intern:* responsibilities include marketing the annual "Kids' Koncert" and assisting in marketing the 22 other concerts by copywriting, designing, and performing routine clerical duties. Candidates should have computer skills, office skills, oral communication skills, organizational skills, writing skills. Duration is 10 weeks. Position available as unpaid or paid. Open to college freshmen, college sophomores, college juniors, college seniors, recent college graduates, graduate students, career changers.

Benefits Possible full-time employment, willing to complete paperwork for educational credit, willing to provide letters of recommendation.

Contact Write or fax Laura Mertens, Marketing Director. Fax: 573-449-4214. No phone calls. In-person interview recommended. Applicants must submit a cover letter, resume. Applications are accepted continuously.

MUSIC MOUNTAIN INC.
PO Box 1739
Sharon, Connecticut 06069

General Information Showcase for string quartets and summer chamber music festival; presents 33 concerts from June through September and offers 8 seminars. Established in 1930. Number of employees: 2.

Internships Available ▶ *1 intern:* responsibilities include working in box office, ticket sales, press, publicity, and artist/seminar participant relations. Candidates should have ability to work independently, ability to work with others, strong interpersonal skills, own vehicle. Duration is 3 months. $250 per week. Open to college freshmen, college sophomores, college juniors, college seniors, graduate students, career changers, individuals reentering the workforce.

Benefits Free housing, job counseling, names of contacts, opportunity to attend seminars/workshops, willing to provide letters of recommendation, concerts.

Contact Write, call, fax, or e-mail Mr. Nicholas Gordon, President, Board of Managers. Phone: 860-364-2080. Fax: 860-364-2090. E-mail: ngordon@snet.net. In-person interview recommended. Application deadline: April 30 for summer. World Wide Web: http://www.musicmountain.org.

NASCAR (NATIONAL ASSOCIATION FOR STOCK CAR AUTO RACING)
1801 West International Speedway Boulevard
Daytona Beach, Florida 32114

General Information NASCAR is the governing body over 13 racing divisions, including the NASCAR Winston Cup Series, NASCAR Busch Series and the NASCAR Craftsman Truck Series. Established in 1948. Number of employees: 130. Number of internship applications received each year: 30.

Internships Available ▶ *1–3 special projects interns/trainees:* responsibilities include computer and print research, assisting with magazine layouts, and proposal design. Candidates should have ability to work independently, knowledge of field, research skills, self-motivation, writing skills, background in journalism and computers recommended. Duration is 1 semester in fall and spring, 8 weeks in summer. Paid. Open to college freshmen, college sophomores, college juniors, college seniors, recent college graduates.

Benefits Names of contacts, opportunity to attend seminars/workshops, willing to act as a professional reference, willing to complete paperwork for educational credit, willing to provide letters of recommendation, work-related travel reimbursement and school credit available.

Contact Write, fax, or e-mail Christine Pirozzi, Special Projects Assistant. Fax: 904-947-6712. E-mail: cpirozzi@race.nascar.com. No phone calls. In-person interview recommended. Applicants must submit a cover letter, resume, writing sample (preferred). Application deadline: February 15 for summer, May 15 for fall, October 15 for spring. World Wide Web: http://www.nascar.com.

OPERA COMPANY OF PHILADELPHIA
510 Walnut Street, Suite 1500
Philadelphia, Pennsylvania 19106

General Information Company presenting performances of grand opera in the original language of composition with internationally acclaimed performers and rising young talent, staged at the Academy of Music. Established in 1975. Number of employees: 25. Number of internship applications received each year: 20.

Internships Available ▶ *1 box office intern:* responsibilities include taking subscription and single ticket orders, performing data entry, answering phones, and filing. Candidates should have ability to work with others, computer skills, office skills, oral communication skills. Unpaid. ▶ *1 business office intern:* responsibilities include data entry, accounting, filing, and typing. Candidates should have computer skills, experience in the field, office skills. Unpaid. ▶ *1 development intern:* responsibilities include typing and data entry, filing, recordkeeping, planning special events, scheduling, and acknowledging donors. Candidates should have computer skills, knowledge of field, office skills. Unpaid. ▶ *1–3 education office interns:* responsibilities include coordinating dress rehearsal attendance, corresponding, entering data, maintaining teacher contact, coordinating special events, assisting with general clerical and administrative tasks, researching opera background for educational materials, and some public relations duties. Candidates should have computer skills, editing skills, office skills, personal interest in the field, research skills, writing skills. Position available as unpaid or at $6 per hour. ▶ *1 general administration intern:* responsibilities include answering phones, typing, and filing. Candidates should have ability to work with others, computer skills, office skills, organizational skills, personal interest in the field. Unpaid. ▶ *1 marketing intern:* responsibilities include creating target marketing mailings, researching possible audience members, and designing advertisements. Candidates should have computer skills, office skills, oral communication skills, personal interest in the field, written communication skills. Unpaid. ▶ *1 public relations intern:* responsibilities include assisting with mass mailings; editing and producing press releases, media packages, and newsletters; scheduling press and artists' interviews and conferences; and filing. Candidates should have computer skills, editing skills, office skills, organizational skills, personal interest in the field. Unpaid. Duration for all positions is flexible. Open to anyone with the desire to work with the company. International applications accepted.

Benefits Names of contacts, possible full-time employment, willing to complete paperwork for educational credit, willing to provide letters of recommendation, work-study granted to in-state residents when possible.

Contact Write or call Judy Williams, Assistant Director of Education. Phone: 215-928-2100 Ext. 216. In-person interview recommended. Applicants must submit a cover letter, resume. Applications are accepted continuously. World Wide Web: http://www.operaphilly.com.

OVERLAND ENTERTAINMENT
257 West 52nd Street
New York, New York 10019

General Information Entertainment company that books and produces private corporate events. Established in 1985. Number of employees: 8. Number of internship applications received each year: 75.

Internships Available ▶ *1 entertainment intern:* responsibilities include assisting in the research of event space location and talent availability; maintaining informational computer databases; aiding Director of Sales in researching new clientele; preparing press packages and informational materials for event proposals. Candidates should have ability to work independently, computer skills, oral communication skills, personal interest in the field, research skills, self-motivation. Duration is flexible. Unpaid. Open to college freshmen, college sophomores, college juniors, college seniors, recent college graduates, graduate students. International applications accepted.

Benefits Names of contacts, travel reimbursement, willing to complete paperwork for educational credit, willing to provide letters of recommendation, opportunity to attend special entertainment functions.

Contact Write or fax Leane Jablonski, Internship Coordinator. Fax: 212-262-5229. No phone calls. In-person interview required. Applicants must submit a resume, two personal references. Application deadline: April 15 for summer, July 5 for fall.

PAN AMERICAN MUSICAL ART RESEARCH, INC.
198 Broadway, Room 807
New York, New York 10038

General Information Coordinator and curator of performing arts of South, Central, and North America that provides services such as exchange opportunities, programming, publicity, grant writing, and general management for artists. Established in 1984. Number of employees: 2. Number of internship applications received each year: 6.

Internships Available ▶ *1–2 program assistants:* responsibilities include developing and maintaining database concerning the dance and music artists of the Americas, developing leads to book performances, and maintaining artists' files. Candidates should have computer skills, office skills, oral communication skills, organizational skills, personal interest in the field, some knowledge of the Spanish language. Duration is 1–6 months. Unpaid. Open to college seniors, recent college graduates, graduate students, career changers, individuals reentering the workforce. International applications accepted.

Benefits Housing at a cost, job counseling, names of contacts, on-the-job training, opportunity to attend seminars/workshops, possible full-time employment, travel reimbursement, willing to act as a professional reference, willing to complete paperwork for educational credit, willing to provide letters of recommendation, free lunches, possible commision income on artists' bookings.

International Internships Available in El Salvador; Mexico.

Contact Write, call, fax, or e-mail Jan Michael Hanvik, Executive Director. Phone: 212-267-8723. Fax: 212-267-8723. E-mail: pamarj@aol.com. In-person interview recommended. Applicants must submit a cover letter, resume, 1-2 personal references and letters of recommendation (domestic applicants), 2-3 personal references and letters of recommedation (international applicants). Applications are accepted continuously. World Wide Web: http://www.pamar.com.

PHILADELPHIA FLYERS
3601 South Broad Street
Philadelphia, Pennsylvania 19148

General Information Professional hockey team in the National Hockey League. Unit of Comcast-Spectacor, Philadelphia, Pennsylvania.

Internships Available ▶ *1 community relations intern:* responsibilities include scheduling and arranging Flyers School program, corresponding with elementary schools, handling charitable donation requests, sorting and answering fan mail, sending birthday packages and get well cards, organizing and assisting in team/individual public appearances and promotional events, and data entry. Candidates should have oral communication skills, strong interpersonal skills, written communication skills, ability to use Microsoft Word, WordPerfect, Lotus 123, and Goldmine software (preferred). Duration is 1 semester in fall, spring, or summer. ▶ *1 fan development/youth hockey intern:*

Philadelphia Flyers (continued)

responsibilities include assisting fan development staff on research, design, and brainstorming for proposed projects; assisting in coordination of NHL BREAKOUT event, and performing minimal clerical duties. Candidates should have oral communication skills, written communication skills, interest in sports marketing and/or public relations, hockey background (preferred). Duration is June 1 through July 31. ▶ *2 public relations interns:* responsibilities include assisting with production and distribution of game notes for media, obtaining post-game quotes from participants, organizing publications database and photo files, assisting in coordination of NHL All-Star balloting, assisting with press releases, publicity events, and a variety of projects, and handling daily and weekly press clippings. Candidates should have oral communication skills, organizational skills, written communication skills, ability to use WordPerfect 5.1/6.0, ability with database management (preferred). Duration is 1 semester in fall, spring, or summer. ▶ *1 rink management and development intern:* responsibilities include assisting rink development staff with projects involving facility marketing, public relations, site analysis, and construction-related issues; helping with clerical duties as assigned. Candidates should have oral communication skills, written communication skills, interest in facility management, marketing, group sales and/or public relations, or construction management is preferred. Duration is May 1 through September 1. ▶ *1 sales/marketing intern:* responsibilities include assisting sales/marketing staff with projects and brainstorming sessions, responding to phone inquiries, helping with season ticket database mailings and game-day promotions, maintaining data files, and game-day customer relations. Candidates should have oral communication skills, organizational skills, written communication skills, ability to meet deadlines, friendly manner for customer service contacts, knowledge of WordPerfect (required) and Goldmine (helpful), ability to work game nights and game weekends. Duration is 1 semester in fall, spring, or summer. All positions are unpaid. Open to college juniors and seniors, or graduate students working for academic credit.

Benefits Names of contacts, possible full-time employment, willing to complete paperwork for educational credit, excellent experience in the sports and entertainment industry.

Contact Write Internship Program, Human Resources Department. No phone calls. In-person interview required. Applicants must submit a formal organization application, resume, cover letter indicating reasons for choosing internship and qualities/attributes that will help make a contribution, faculty recommendation form (sent with application). Application deadline: at least 2 months prior to the intended start date. World Wide Web: http://www.comcast-spectacor.com.

PHILADELPHIA PHANTOMS
3601 South Broad Street
Philadelphia, Pennsylvania 19148

General Information The American Hockey League affiliate of the Philadelphia Flyers. Unit of Comcast-Spectacor, Philadelphia, Pennsylvania.

Internships Available ▶ *2 assistants to the Ticketing Manager:* responsibilities include assisting with phone sales, customer service inquiries, and internal data entry/accounting tasks; distributing Phantoms literature at selected events; and working on a variety of promotional projects. Candidates should have oral communication skills, written communication skills, ability to use WordPerfect and Lotus 123 sotfware. ▶ *1 marketing intern:* responsibilities include assisting staff with marketing projects, following up event promotions, and creating post-event marketing summaries; writing and handling press releases and statistics; assisting in day-of-event operations; and coordinating media publicity. Candidates should have ability to use Word, WordPerfect, and Lotus 123. ▶ *1 public relations intern:* responsibilities include writing and handling press releases and statistics, corresponding with season ticket holders, assisting in advertising and printing, coordinating media publicity, and working on various projects with staff. Candidates should have oral communication skills, written communication skills, ability to use Word, WordPerfect, and Lotus 123. Duration for all positions is 1 semester in fall,

spring, or summer. All positions are unpaid. Open to college juniors and seniors or graduate students, working for academic credit.

Benefits Names of contacts, possible full-time employment, willing to complete paperwork for educational credit, excellent experience in the sports and entertainment industry.

Contact Write Internship Program, Human Resources Department. No phone calls. In-person interview required. Applicants must submit a formal organization application, resume, cover letter indicating reasons for choosing a particular internship and the qualities or attributes that will help make a contribution, faculty recommendation form (sent with application). Application deadline: at least 2 months prior to intended start date. World Wide Web: http://www.comcast-spectacor.com.

PHILADELPHIA 76ERS
3601 South Broad Street
Philadelphia, Pennsylvania 19148

General Information Professional basketball team playing in the National Basketball Association (NBA). Unit of Comcast-Spectacor, Philadelphia, Pennsylvania.

Internships Available ▶ *2 box office interns:* responsibilities include processing contracts, processing and mailing season tickets and game day tickets, and handling customer questions and complaints. Candidates should have computer skills, strong interpersonal skills, ability to use Windows 95 programs such as Microsoft Excel and WordPerfect. Duration is 1 semester in spring or fall. ▶ *1 community relations intern:* responsibilities include handling phone inquiries maintaining database files, ordering merchandise for charitable donations, assisting staff with correspondence and special projects, and responding to requests for autographed items, financial donations, tickets, and speaking appearances. Candidates should have organizational skills, strong interpersonal skills, ability to use Microsoft Word and Excel, and WordPerfect (preferred). Duration is 1 semester in fall, spring, or summer. ▶ *2 fan relations interns:* responsibilities include responding to requests for fan club information, selling fan club memberships at home games, and tracking inventory and mailing for fan club. Candidates should have computer skills, organizational skills, strong interpersonal skills, ability to work game days outside normal business hours, proficient in use of the Internet and Microsoft applications (Word, Access, and Excel). Duration is 1 semester in fall or spring. ▶ *1 marketing intern:* responsibilities include following up on promotions/marketing events and advertising, updating the Web site, assisting the Director of Fan Relations, and responding to customer phone inquiries. Candidates should have oral communication skills, written communication skills, ability to use Microsoft Office and the Internet, experience with Pagemaker (desirable), ability to work some game nights and weekends. Duration is 1 semester in fall, spring, or summer. ▶ *1 operations intern:* responsibilities include handling phone inquiries and clerical tasks, assisting coaching and scouting staff, assisting with operation of scouting database, and helping with a variety of duties related to team practices and games. Candidates should have organizational skills, strong interpersonal skills, excellent phone skills, ability to use Microsoft Word and Excel. Duration is 1 semester in fall, spring, or summer. ▶ *1 promotions intern:* responsibilities include following up on event promotions and creating post-event marketing summaries, updating computer kiosks, assisting in game operations/promotional events, and scripting advertising that will appear on Arenavision and message boards. Candidates should have computer skills, oral communication skills, organizational skills, written communication skills, ability to use Microsoft Office applications and WordPerfect and Lotus 123, event production background (preferred). Duration is 1 semester in fall, spring, or summer. ▶ *1 public relations intern:* responsibilities include acting as liaison with media, attending home games (including weekends), assisting with publications, organizing team and individual photo files, organizing mass mailings, handling press clippings, and participating in a variety of public relations projects. Candidates should have oral communication skills, organizational skills, strong interpersonal skills, written communication skills, ability to use Pagemaker, MS Word, WordPerfect, or Lotus 123 software. Duration is 1 semester in fall, spring, or summer. ▶ *1–2 sales interns:* responsibilities include assisting in mass marketing campaigns and in prospecting leads for corporate sales managers; coordinating trade shows, open houses, and off-site presentations; helping with clerical duties, customer service, and phone relations. Candidates should have professional phone skills, attention to detail. Duration is 1 semester in fall, spring, or summer. ▶ *5 statistics interns:* responsibilities include recording, deciphering and logging box scores; updating individual and team statistics as well as play-by-play records for 76ers and other NBA teams; and assisting staff on various projects. Candidates should have computer skills, attention to detail and accuracy with numbers, interest in basketball statistics (preferred). Duration is 1 semester in fall, spring, or summer. All positions are unpaid. Open to college juniors and seniors or graduate students, working for academic credit.

Benefits Names of contacts, possible full-time employment, willing to complete paperwork for educational credit, excellent experience in the sports and entertainment industry.

Contact Write Internship Program, Human Resources Department. No phone calls. In-person interview required. Applicants must submit a formal organization application, resume, cover letter indicating reasons for choosing a particular internship and the qualities/attributes that will help make a contribution, faculty recommendation form (sent with application). Application deadline: at least 2 months prior to the intended start date. World Wide Web: http://www.comcast-spectacor.com.

POSEY SCHOOL OF DANCE, INC.
PO Box 254
Northport, New York 11768

General Information Community school of dance offering education and professional training. Established in 1953. Number of employees: 10. Number of internship applications received each year: 25.

Internships Available ▶ *1 studio manager:* responsibilities include studio management. Candidates should have knowledge of field, oral communication skills, strong interpersonal skills, strong leadership ability, knowledge of dance techniques, ballet, and modern dance. Duration is 10–12 months. Position available as unpaid or at $100–$450 per month. Open to recent college graduates, graduate students, career changers. ▶ *1 summer studio manager:* responsibilities include studio management. Candidates should have knowledge of field, oral communication skills, strong interpersonal skills, strong leadership ability, written communication skills, knowledge of dance techniques, ballet, and modern dance. Duration is 4–5 weeks. $250–$300 per duration of internship. Open to recent college graduates, graduate students, career changers, performers entering education.

Benefits Formal training, job counseling, names of contacts, opportunity to attend seminars/workshops, possible full-time employment, willing to act as a professional reference, willing to complete paperwork for educational credit, willing to provide letters of recommendation, personal introductions.

Contact Write, call, or e-mail Ms. Elsa Posey, President. Phone: 516-757-2700. E-mail: 74534.1660@compuserve.com. Telephone interview required. Applicants must submit a cover letter, resume. Applications are accepted continuously.

QUEENS THEATER IN THE PARK
PO Box 520069
Flushing, New York 11352

General Information Performing arts center. Established in 1989. Number of employees: 40. Number of internship applications received each year: 20.

Internships Available ▶ *1–3 office/stage production interns:* responsibilities include performing work in office, stage, and theater; ushering. ▶ *Stage production interns:* responsibilities include performing work in office, stage, and theater; ushering. Duration for all positions is 1 semester. All positions are unpaid. Open to high school students, high school seniors, recent high school graduates, college freshmen, college sophomores, col-

lege juniors, college seniors, recent college graduates, graduate students, law students, career changers, individuals reentering the workforce.

Benefits Willing to complete paperwork for educational credit.

Contact Write, call, fax, or e-mail Ms. Lois Newhart, General Manager. Phone: 718-760-0064. Fax: 718-760-1972. E-mail: qtiparts@aol.com. In-person interview required. Applicants must submit a cover letter, resume. Applications are accepted continuously. World Wide Web: http://www.queenstheatre.org.

RICHARD FRANKEL PRODUCTIONS
729 7th Avenue, 12th Floor
New York, New York 10019

General Information Independent theatrical production and general management company that general manages and produces plays and musicals, and acts as general manager for other theatrical producers. Established in 1985. Number of employees: 60. Number of internship applications received each year: 500.

Internships Available ▶ *Interns:* responsibilities include assignments under the supervision of the General Manager of one show, compiling daily sales figures, assisting company managers at theater, providing production assistant services for shows in rehearsal and pre-production, and implementing grass-roots marketing campaigns. Candidates should have computer skills, oral communication skills, organizational skills, personal interest in the field, strong interpersonal skills. Duration is 3-4 months full-time (Monday through Friday 10 AM to 6 PM). $100 per week. Open to college freshmen, college sophomores, college juniors, college seniors. International applications accepted.

Benefits Formal training, job counseling, names of contacts, on-the-job training, opportunity to attend seminars/workshops, possible full-time employment, willing to act as a professional reference, willing to complete paperwork for educational credit, willing to provide letters of recommendation.

Contact Write, call, fax, or e-mail Lori Steiger, Internship Coordinator, 729 Seventh Avenue, 12th Floor, New York, New York 10019. Phone: 212-302-5559. Fax: 212-302-8094. E-mail: lori@rfpny.com. In-person interview recommended. Applicants must submit a cover letter, resume, academic transcripts. Applications are accepted continuously. World Wide Web: http://www.rfpny.com.

ROCKPORT CHAMBER MUSIC FESTIVAL
PO Box 312
Rockport, Massachusetts 01966

General Information Four-week festival in June-July presenting chamber music featuring nationally known groups. Established in 1982. Number of employees: 3. Number of internship applications received each year: 10.

Internships Available ▶ *1 summer intern/stage manager:* responsibilities include handling office, selling tickets, and assisting artistic director. Candidates should have ability to work with others, knowledge of field, office skills, oral communication skills, personal interest in the field, self-motivation, strong interpersonal skills, ability to read music well. Duration is 1 month. $800 per month. Open to college freshmen, college sophomores, college juniors, college seniors, recent college graduates.

Benefits Free housing, job counseling, names of contacts, willing to complete paperwork for educational credit, willing to provide letters of recommendation, opportunity to interact with musicians.

Contact Write, fax, or e-mail Madeline and Ted Scharfenstein, General Managers. Fax: 978-546-8459. E-mail: rcmf@shore.net. Telephone interview required. Applicants must submit a cover letter, resume, two letters of recommendation. Application deadline: February 15. World Wide Web: http://www1.shore.net/~persnav/rcmf.htm.

SETTLEMENT MUSIC SCHOOL
416 Queen Street, PO Box 25120
Philadelphia, Pennsylvania 19147-3094

General Information Community school of the arts offering individual and class instruction in music and dance to students regardless of age, background, or ability to pay. Established in 1908. Number of employees: 15. Number of internship applications received each year: 5.

Internships Available ► *1 development intern:* responsibilities include researching possible funding sources, coordinating mailings, and updating databases and spreadsheets. Candidates should have ability to work with others, computer skills, knowledge of field, office skills, oral communication skills, personal interest in the field, research skills, writing skills. ► *1 marketing/public relations intern:* responsibilities include maintaining mailing lists, designing computer graphics, conducting market research, planning special events, and coordinating press relations. Candidates should have ability to work with others, computer skills, office skills, personal interest in the field, writing skills. Duration for all positions is flexible. All positions are unpaid. Open to college freshmen, college sophomores, college juniors, college seniors, recent college graduates, graduate students, law school graduates, career changers, individuals reentering the workforce. International applications accepted.
Benefits Job counseling, willing to act as a professional reference, willing to complete paperwork for educational credit, willing to provide letters of recommendation, free concerts.
Contact Write, fax, or e-mail Ms. Bridget DiFebbo, Development Associate. Fax: 215-551-0483. E-mail: smsdev@smsmusic. org. No phone calls. In-person interview required. Applicants must submit a cover letter, resume. Applications are accepted continuously. World Wide Web: http://www.smsmusic.org.

SPOLETO FESTIVAL USA
PO Box 157
Charleston, South Carolina 29402-0157

General Information Arts festival that produces and presents world-class opera, dance, theater, chamber music, symphonic music, jazz, visual arts, and experimental multimedia works of all kinds. Established in 1977. Number of employees: 14. Number of internship applications received each year: 300.

Internships Available ► *1–2 artist services interns:* responsibilities include assisting with artist transportation, preparing mailings and artist welcome packets, scheduling and set-up of backstage hospitality, answering phones, correspondence, filing, and other administrative tasks. Candidates should have ability to work with others, computer skills, office skills, organizational skills, self-motivation. Duration is 4–6 weeks. ► *5–6 box office interns:* responsibilities include assisting with box office window/telephone sales, program information, ticket collection, and processing mail orders. Candidates should have strong interpersonal skills, strong customer service skills. Duration is 4–5 weeks. ► *1 business office intern:* responsibilities include assisting with recording cash receipts, preparing and recording disbursements, and personnel and payroll operations. Candidates should have computer skills, organizational skills. Duration is 4–5 weeks. ► *2 development interns:* responsibilities include assisting with development report, distribution of contributor benefits, and coordination of special events. Candidates should have ability to work independently, organizational skills, self-motivation, strong interpersonal skills. Duration is 4–5 weeks. ► *2 general administration interns:* responsibilities include assisting office staff with all office duties and assisting chamber music director and rehearsal coordinator. Candidates should have computer skills, office skills, organizational skills, strong interpersonal skills. Duration is 4–5 weeks. ► *1 housing intern:* responsibilities include organizing housing at the College of Charleston, preparing housing lists and forms, overseeing arrival and departure of participants, and working with college staff. Candidates should have ability to work independently, organizational skills, strong interpersonal skills. Duration is 4–5 weeks. ► *13–15 merchandising interns:* responsibilities include assisting with sales of souvenir merchandise. Candidates should have ability to work independently, ability to work with others, organizational skills, self-motivation, strong customer service skills. Duration is 4–5 weeks. ► *6 orchestra management interns:* responsibilities include assisting in the transport and setup of equipment and large instruments for rehearsals and performances. Candidates should have ability to work independently, ability to work with others, self-motivation, knowledge of music helpful, but not required. Duration is 4–5 weeks. ► *30 production interns:* responsibilities include working in stage carpentry and electrics, wardrobe, properties, wigs and makeup, sound, and production administration. Candidates should have ability to work independently, ability to work with others, experience in the field, knowledge of field, self-motivation. Duration is 4–5 weeks. ► *5 public relations interns:* responsibilities include staffing the press room and assisting the press in obtaining interviews, photos, and story information for print, radio, and television coverage. Candidates should have ability to work with others, computer skills, office skills, writing skills. Duration is 4–5 weeks. All positions paid at $225 per week. Open to college freshmen, college sophomores, college juniors, college seniors, recent college graduates, graduate students. International applications accepted.
Benefits Free housing, possible full-time employment, willing to complete paperwork for educational credit, access to performances.
Contact Write, fax, or e-mail Ms. Margaret Summers, Apprentice Program Coordinator. Fax: 843-723-6383. E-mail: msummers@ spoletousa.org. No phone calls. Applicants must submit a formal organization application, cover letter, resume, two letters of recommendation, 2 writing samples (public relations positions only). Application deadline: February 1. World Wide Web: http://www.spoletousa.org.

THE SUCHIN COMPANY
12747 Riverside Drive, Suite 208
Valley Village, California 91607-3333

General Information Personal management company that represents actors, writers, broadcasters, and other entertainment-oriented individuals; advises and counsels with regard to career aspirations. Established in 1979. Number of employees: 3. Number of internship applications received each year: 20.
Internships Available ► *2 personal manager assistants:* responsibilities include updating resumes and biographies of clients, receiving auditions from agents, and coordinating with artist's schedule. Candidates should have office skills, oral communication skills, organizational skills, research skills, self-motivation, strong interpersonal skills. Unpaid. Open to college freshmen, college sophomores, college juniors, college seniors. International applications accepted.
Benefits Job counseling, names of contacts, on-the-job training, opportunity to attend seminars/workshops, willing to complete paperwork for educational credit, willing to provide letters of recommendation.
Contact Write, call, fax, or e-mail Mr. Milton B. Suchin, President. Phone: 818-505-0044. Fax: 818-505-0110. E-mail: starmgri@aol. com. In-person interview required. Applicants must submit a cover letter, resume, two personal references, two letters of recommendation. Applications are accepted continuously.

WASHINGTON PERFORMING ARTS SOCIETY
2000 L Street, NW, Suite 810
Washington, District of Columbia 20036-4907

General Information Nonprofit organization focused on presenting classical music, traditional and contemporary dance, world music, jazz, Latino artforms, gospel, and performance art in concert halls, theaters, schools, senior citizen centers, and embassies throughout the Washington, DC area. Established in 1965. Number of employees: 25. Number of internship applications received each year: 25.
Internships Available ► *1 administrative assistants:* responsibilities include general assistance to the Finance and Administration Department, including general office work, maintenance of databases and spreadsheets, as well as organization and evaluation of new information. Candidates should have computer

skills, office skills, organizational skills, research skills, self-motivation, writing skills. Duration is 1–2 semesters. Position available as unpaid or at $400 per month. Open to college juniors, college seniors, recent college graduates, graduate students, career changers. ▶ *1 development assistant:* responsibilities include researching corporate, foundation, and individual donors, processing mail, assisting with writing of grants and special events, and general office work; some evening hours required. Candidates should have ability to work with others, computer skills, plan to pursue career in field, research skills, writing skills. Duration is 1 semester. $400 per month. Open to college seniors, recent college graduates, graduate students, career changers. ▶ *1 graphic design assistant.* Candidates should have ability to work with others, computer skills, knowledge of field, personal interest in the field, self-motivation, fluency in Quark, knowledge of Photoshop. Duration is 1–2 semesters. $600 per month. Open to college juniors, college seniors, recent college graduates, graduate students, career changers. ▶ *1 programming assistant:* responsibilities include transporting artists, coordinating/booking hotel accomodations, assisting with front of house and ticketing at performances, and general office work. Candidates should have computer skills, knowledge of field, organizational skills,

personal interest in the field, research skills, strong interpersonal skills. Duration is 4–9 months. Unpaid. Open to college seniors, recent college graduates, graduate students, career changers. ▶ *1–2 public relations and marketing assistants:* responsibilities include writing and distributing press releases; writing copy for promotions, sales pieces, and newsletters; assisting with special promotions, direct mail campaigns, list management, and response tracking and analysis; proofing; preparing reviewer kits for concerts; maintaining press kits and department files; and general office work. Candidates should have editing skills, knowledge of field, organizational skills, research skills, self-motivation, writing skills. Duration is 1–2 semesters. $600 per month. Open to college juniors, college seniors, recent college graduates, graduate students, career changers. International applications accepted.

Benefits Names of contacts, willing to complete paperwork for educational credit, willing to provide letters of recommendation.
Contact Write, fax, or e-mail Internship Coordinator. Fax: 202-331-7678. E-mail: wpas@wpas.org. No phone calls. In-person interview recommended. Applicants must submit a cover letter, resume, writing sample, personal reference. Applications are accepted continuously. World Wide Web: http://www.wpas.org.

EDUCATIONAL SERVICES

GENERAL

ACUHO-I (ASSOCIATION OF COLLEGE AND UNIVERSITY HOUSING OFFICERS–INTERNATIONAL)
Riverwatch Tower, 364 West Lane Avenue, Suite C
Columbus, Ohio 43201-1062

General Information Professional educational association for administrators and staff of college and university housing and food-service departments. Established in 1949. Number of internship applications received each year: 175.
Internships Available ▶ *150–175 housing interns:* responsibilities include working in financial management, programming, accounting, operations, residence life, and summer conferences. Candidates should have oral communication skills, organizational skills, plan to pursue career in field, strong interpersonal skills, written communication skills. Duration is 8 weeks (minimum). hourly wage of at least the federal minimum wage. Open to recent college graduates, graduate students. International applications accepted.
Benefits Free housing, opportunity to attend seminars/workshops, willing to act as a professional reference, willing to complete paperwork for educational credit, willing to provide letters of recommendation.
Contact Write, call, fax, or e-mail Cindy Spencer, Internship Committee Chairman, Office of Residential and Greek Life, Conrad Hall, University of Nebraska, Kearney, Nebraska 68849. Phone: 308-865-8519. Fax: 308-865-8714. E-mail: spencerc@unk.edu. Telephone interview required. Applicants must submit a formal organization application, 1-page resume. Application deadline: call or e-mail for deadlines. World Wide Web: http://www.acuho.ohio-state.edu/.

AIM FOR THE HANDICAPPED
945 Danbury Road
Dayton, Ohio 45420

General Information Educational facility that offers specialized education to handicapped children and adults. Established in 1958. Number of employees: 7. Number of internship applications received each year: 15.
Internships Available ▶ *1–3 education department assistants:* responsibilities include teaching handicapped children and adults, setting up programs in schools, working on the newsletter, and performing general office duties. Candidates should have ability to work with others, office skills, oral communication skills, personal interest in the field, self-motivation, written communication skills. Duration is flexible. Open to high school students, high school seniors, recent high school graduates, college freshmen, college sophomores, college juniors, college seniors, recent college graduates, graduate students, career changers, individuals reentering the workforce. ▶ *1 receptionist/executive assistant:* responsibilities include answering multi-line telephone system, bulk mail, word processing, keeping records organized, and possibly working with individuals who have special needs. Candidates should have computer skills, office skills, oral communication skills, organizational skills, self-motivation, written communication skills. Open to recent high school graduates, college freshmen, college sophomores, college juniors, college seniors, recent college graduates, graduate students, law students, career chang-

ers, individuals reentering the workforce. All positions available as unpaid or paid. International applications accepted.
Benefits On-the-job training, possible full-time employment, willing to act as a professional reference, willing to complete paperwork for educational credit, willing to provide letters of recommendation, assistance in locating housing.
Contact Write, call, fax, or e-mail Belinda S. Long, Education Director. Phone: 937-294-4611. Fax: 937-294-3783. E-mail: aimkids@aol.com. In-person interview recommended. Applicants must submit a cover letter, resume, three personal references, three letters of recommendation. Applications are accepted continuously.

AMERICAN ASSOCIATION OF SCHOOL ADMINISTRATORS
1801 North Moore Street
Arlington, Virginia 22209-1813

General Information Association ensuring the highest quality education systems for all learners through the support and development of leadership. Established in 1865. Number of employees: 45. Number of internship applications received each year: 15.
Internships Available ▶ *1 Web site intern:* responsibilities include assisting with basic coding for AASA's Web site and writing short summaries of reports for the Web. Candidates should have computer skills, editing skills, knowledge of field, self-motivation, writing skills, knowledge of HTML coding. Unpaid. Open to college sophomores, college juniors, college seniors, recent college graduates, graduate students. ▶ *1 government relations intern:* responsibilities include assisting government relations staff with preparing information for its work in keeping various levels of government informed about education and conducting research. Candidates should have knowledge of field, personal interest in the field, research skills, self-motivation, strong interpersonal skills, written communication skills. Unpaid. Open to college freshmen, college sophomores, college juniors, college seniors, recent college graduates, graduate students, law students. ▶ *1–2 magazine interns:* responsibilities include writing, editing, and handling various organizational functions within the communications department. Candidates should have computer skills, editing skills, writing skills, college courses in English or journalism. Position available as unpaid or paid. Open to college freshmen, college sophomores, college juniors, college seniors, recent college graduates, graduate students. Duration for all positions is flexible.
Benefits Names of contacts, willing to complete paperwork for educational credit, willing to provide letters of recommendation.
Contact Write, call, fax, or e-mail Ms. Liz Griffin, Managing Editor, The School Administrator Magazine. Phone: 703-875-0753. Fax: 703-528-2146. E-mail: lgriffin@aasa.rog. Telephone interview required. Applicants must submit a cover letter, resume, three writing samples. Application deadline: April 15 for summer, July 15 for fall, October 15 for spring. World Wide Web: http://www.aasa.org.

AMERICAN COUNCIL FOR INTERNATIONAL STUDIES
102 Greenwich Avenue
Greenwich, Connecticut 06830

General Information Institute providing educational/cultural exchanges for high school and college students and interested adults on 15 campuses in Europe, Asia, Australia, Africa, Russia and South America. Established in 1964. Number of employees: 125. Number of internship applications received each year: 100.

Internships Available ▶ *25–40 interns:* responsibilities include attending classes for 4 weeks and working for 10 weeks full time in business (marketing, finance, management), communications (media), fine arts (design and lens media), politics, and theater. Candidates should have minimum 2.5 GPA. Duration is 12–15 weeks. Unpaid. Open to college freshmen, college sophomores, college juniors, college seniors. International applications accepted.

Benefits Formal training, opportunity to attend seminars/workshops, possible full-time employment, willing to complete paperwork for educational credit, willing to provide letters of recommendation, health insurance, housing, and meals provided at $11,340 per semester.

International Internships Available in Shizuoka, Japan; London, United Kingdom.

Contact Write, call, fax, or e-mail Sharman Hedayati, College Division, Director of Admissions. Phone: 800-727-AIFS Ext. 6097. Fax: 203-869-9615. E-mail: info@aifs.com. Applicants must submit a formal organization application, academic transcripts, writing sample, two personal references, tuition payment required upon acceptance. Application deadline: May 15 for fall, November 1 for spring. Fees: $50. World Wide Web: http://www.aifs.com.

AMERICAN UNIVERSITY IN MOSCOW
1800 Connecticut Avenue, NW
Washington, District of Columbia 20009

General Information Educational institute that conducts conferences, seminars, and educational programs for students and leaders in business, politics, and academia in the U.S. and the Commonwealth of Independent States. Established in 1991. Number of employees: 5. Number of internship applications received each year: 50.

Internships Available ▶ *5 assistants to program coordinators:* responsibilities include assisting in all work related to the programs. Candidates should have computer skills, editing skills, office skills, oral communication skills, writing skills. Duration is 1–6 months. Unpaid. Open to recent high school graduates, college freshmen, college sophomores, college juniors, college seniors, recent college graduates. International applications accepted.

Benefits Names of contacts, opportunity to attend seminars/workshops, possible full-time employment, travel reimbursement, willing to complete paperwork for educational credit, willing to provide letters of recommendation.

Contact Write, call, fax, or e-mail Dr. Edward Lozansky, President. Phone: 202-986-6010. Fax: 202-667-4244. E-mail: lozansky@aol.com. Telephone interview required. Applicants must submit a resume. Applications are accepted continuously. World Wide Web: http://www.RussiaHouse.org.

ASHAY: EDUCATIONAL RESOURCES FOR A MULTICULTURAL WORLD
1800 South Robertson Boulevard, Suite 408
Los Angeles, California 90035

General Information Organization that develops educational curriculum designed to help people understand and appreciate human differences from race and ethnicity to sexuality, age, and ability. Established in 1995. Number of employees: 2. Number of internship applications received each year: 10.

Internships Available ▶ *1–3 event planning interns:* responsibilities include helping plan and implement programs to expose people to Ashay and cultivate further involvement, working on small receptions in people's homes and larger special events, overseeing logistics, including invitations and food. Candidates should have ability to work independently, organizational skills, self-motivation, strong interpersonal skills, strong leadership ability. Duration is 3–6 months. Open to college seniors, recent college graduates, graduate students, career changers, individuals reentering the workforce. ▶ *1–2 fund-raising interns:* responsibilities include researching, writing for grants and corporate sponsor-

ships, planning/implementing fund-raising events, and helping with direct mail campaign. Candidates should have ability to work independently, computer skills, organizational skills, research skills, self-motivation, written communication skills. Duration is 4–6 months. Open to college seniors, recent college graduates, graduate students, career changers, individuals reentering the workforce. ▶ *1–3 marketing and promotion interns:* responsibilities include helping to plan and implement teachers focus groups, researching leads for multicultural communication game distribution, identifying conferences at which game can be presented, working to have game included in educational resource catalogs. Candidates should have ability to work independently, organizational skills, research skills, self-motivation, strong interpersonal skills, written communication skills. Duration is 3–6 months. Open to college seniors, recent college graduates, graduate students, career changers. ▶ *1–3 special projects interns:* responsibilities include varied duties depending on intern's skills/interests and project needs. Possible areas include Web master, database design and maintenance, public speaking, outreach and networking, and graphic design. Candidates should have ability to work independently, computer skills, organizational skills, self-motivation, strong interpersonal skills. Duration is 4–6 months. Open to college seniors, recent college graduates, graduate students, career changers. All positions available as unpaid or paid.

Benefits On-the-job training, willing to act as a professional reference, willing to complete paperwork for educational credit, willing to provide letters of recommendation, learning valuable transferable skills.

Contact Write, call, fax, or e-mail Ms. Shifra Teitelbaum, Director, 1800 South Robertson Boulevard, Suite 408, Los Angeles, California 90035. Phone: 310-842-9125. Fax: 310-204-6221. E-mail: ashay@iname.com. In-person interview recommended. Applicants must submit a formal organization application, cover letter, resume, three personal references, two letters of recommendation. Applications are accepted continuously. World Wide Web: http://www.laca.org/ashay.

ASSOCIATED WESTERN UNIVERSITIES, INC.
4190 South Highland Drive, Suite 211
Salt Lake City, Utah 84124

General Information Nonprofit educational consortium linking students, postgraduates, and faculty with fellowship, internship, and sabbatical research opportunities in science and engineering at federal and industrial laboratories. Established in 1959. Number of employees: 30. Number of internship applications received each year: 2,500.

Internships Available ▶ *200–300 graduate fellowships:* responsibilities include conducting research towards master's or doctoral thesis or exploring research and technology career options at a cooperating facility. Candidates should have college courses in field, college degree in related field, computer skills, oral communication skills, research skills, continuous enrollment in a university thesis program is required during tenure. Duration is up to 12 months. stipend of at least $1300 per month. Open to graduate students in science and engineering. ▶ *200–300 postgraduate research fellowships.* Candidates should have ability to work independently, ability to work with others, college degree in related field, oral communication skills, personal interest in the field, research skills. Duration is 1–3 years. stipend paid by the facility. Open to recent bachelor's degree, master's degree, or Ph.D. graduates. ▶ *500–600 student research fellowships:* responsibilities include working in primarily research and applied technology positions under the guidance of experienced scientists and engineers; facilities range from federal to private industry. Candidates should have ability to work with others, college courses in field, computer skills, knowledge of field, oral communication skills, research skills. Duration is 8–16 weeks. $300 per week. Open to college sophomores, college juniors, college seniors, recent college graduates, graduate students. International applications accepted.

Benefits Health insurance, housing at a cost, names of contacts, opportunity to attend seminars/workshops, possible full-time employment, travel reimbursement, tuition assistance, willing to

Associated Western Universities, Inc. (continued)

act as a professional reference, willing to complete paperwork for educational credit, willing to provide letters of recommendation.

Contact Write, call, fax, or e-mail Fellowship Programs Assistant. Phone: 801-273-8900. Fax: 801-277-5632. E-mail: info@awu.org. Applicants must submit a resume, academic transcripts, two letters of recommendation, formal organizational application (can be filled out on-line). Application deadline: February 1 for summer (recommended), March 20 for fall (recommended), October 20 for spring (recommended). World Wide Web: http://www.awu.org.

ASSOCIATION FOR EXPERIENTIAL EDUCATION (AEE)
2305 Canyon Boulevard, Suite 100
Boulder, Colorado 80302

General Information Not-for-profit international professional membership association with roots in adventure education, committed to the development, practice, and evaluation of experiential learning in all settings. Established in 1972. Number of employees: 7. Number of internship applications received each year: 100.

Internships Available ▶ *1–7 administrative interns:* responsibilities include duties that are dependent upon the applicant's experience and interests and the needs of AEE. Candidates should have computer skills, office skills, organizational skills, self-motivation, strong interpersonal skills. Duration is 1-6 months (3-month blocks preferred). ▶ *1–3 publications and marketing interns:* responsibilities include various duties dependent on the applicant's interest and experience, as well as on the needs of AEE. Candidates should have editing skills, research skills, self-motivation, writing skills. Duration is 1 to 12 months (3-month blocks preferred). All positions are unpaid. Open to high school students, high school seniors, recent high school graduates, college freshmen, college sophomores, college juniors, college seniors, recent college graduates, graduate students, law students, career changers, individuals reentering the workforce. International applications accepted.

Benefits Formal training, job counseling, names of contacts, on-the-job training, opportunity to attend seminars/workshops, possible full-time employment, willing to act as a professional reference, willing to complete paperwork for educational credit, willing to provide letters of recommendation.

Contact Write, fax, or e-mail Sharon Heinlen, Executive Director. Fax: 303-440-9581. E-mail: sharon@aee.org. No phone calls. Applicants must submit a formal organization application, cover letter, resume. Applications are accepted continuously. World Wide Web: http://www.aee.org.

AUDUBON CENTER OF THE NORTH WOODS
PO Box 530
Sandstone, Minnesota 55072

General Information Environmental education center that stresses the positive relationship between people and nature. Programs combine natural history, outdoor skills, and ethics and serve youth, college, and adult audiences. Established in 1968. Number of employees: 24. Number of internship applications received each year: 40.

Internships Available ▶ *4–6 environmental education interns:* responsibilities include leading residential programs for children and adults and assisting with eco-tours, outdoor recreation trips, gear care, curriculum development, and maintenance. Candidates should have ability to work independently, ability to work with others, college courses in field, knowledge of field, oral communication skills, self-motivation. Duration is 5–9 months. $280 per month. Open to college seniors, recent college graduates, graduate students. ▶ *4–6 summer environmental education interns:* responsibilities include residential environmental instruction for summer youth camps, dorm supervision, camping/canoeing trips, assistance with teacher workshops and adult/family programs, gear care, and maintenance. Candidates should have ability to work with others, knowledge of field, oral communication skills, personal interest in the field, self-motivation, strong

leadership ability. Duration is 3 months. $280–$400 per month. Open to college sophomores, college juniors, college seniors, recent college graduates, graduate students. ▶ *1–2 wildlife interns:* responsibilities include care/feeding/training of educational raptors and reptiles, educational programming with captive animals, care/feeding of animals in rehabilitation, development of educational materials, and maintenance. Candidates should have ability to work independently, ability to work with others, oral communication skills, organizational skills, personal interest in the field, self-motivation. Duration is 6–12 months. $280 per month. Open to college juniors, college seniors, recent college graduates, graduate students. International applications accepted.

Benefits Formal training, free housing, free meals, names of contacts, on-the-job training, opportunity to attend seminars/workshops, possible full-time employment, willing to act as a professional reference, willing to complete paperwork for educational credit, willing to provide letters of recommendation, graduate credits in environmental education.

Contact Write, call, fax, or e-mail Intern Coordinator. Phone: 320-245-2648. Fax: 320-245-5272. E-mail: audubonl@ecenet.com. In-person interview recommended. Applicants must submit a cover letter, resume, three personal references. Application deadline: April 15 for summer environmental education positions; continuous for other positions. World Wide Web: http://www.audubon-center.com.

BEAVER COLLEGE CENTER FOR EDUCATION ABROAD
Beaver College, CEA, 450 South Easton Road
Glenside, Pennsylvania 19038-3295

General Information College that arranges junior and senior year abroad for transfer credit. Established in 1948. Unit of Beaver College, Glenside, Pennsylvania.

Internships Available ▶ *Study abroad interns (Dublin):* responsibilities include acting as an aide to a member of the Irish Parliament in Dublin. Duration is 1 semester. Open to college juniors, college seniors. ▶ *Study abroad interns (London):* responsibilities include holding positions in public policy, social science, communications, or business. Duration is 1 semester or 1 summer. Open to college juniors, college seniors, recent college graduates for summer only. Candidates for all positions should have ability to work independently, college courses in field, oral communication skills, strong interpersonal skills, written communication skills. All positions are unpaid. International applications accepted.

Benefits Free housing, willing to complete paperwork for educational credit.

International Internships Available in Dublin, Ireland; London, United Kingdom.

Contact Write, call, fax, or e-mail Center for Education Abroad, Program Coordinators, Beaver College CEA, 450 South Easton Road, Glenside, Pennsylvania 19038-3295. Phone: 888-232-8379. Fax: 215-572-2174. E-mail: cea@beaver.edu. In-person interview required. Applicants must submit a formal organization application, resume, academic transcripts, letter of recommendation. Application deadline: April 20 for fall, October 15 for spring. Fees: $35. World Wide Web: http://www.beaver.edu/cea/.

BOSTON UNIVERSITY SARGENT CAMP SCHOOL PROGRAM
36 Sargent Camp Road
Hancock, New Hampshire 03449

General Information Program offering environmental and outdoor education, including initiatives, trust activities, and ropes-course work, for 5th- through 8th-graders. Established in 1912. Number of employees: 18. Unit of Boston University, Boston, Massachusetts. Number of internship applications received each year: 50.

Internships Available ▶ *1 nature center coordinator:* responsibilities include assisting in teaching environmental lessons, providing interns with new ideas or facts for lessons, supervising students in the nature center during free time, creating new

displays and working on the physical appearance of the nature center, and attending most meals. Candidates should have ability to work independently, ability to work with others, oral communication skills, organizational skills, personal interest in the field, research skills, self-motivation. ▶ *15 resident school program interns:* responsibilities include teaching groups of 8–10 students environmental and outdoor education, supervising students, and attending weekly staff meetings. Candidates should have oral communication skills, personal interest in the field, self-motivation, strong interpersonal skills, strong leadership ability. Duration for all positions is 3–9 months. All positions paid at $110–$130 per week. Open to recent high school graduates, college freshmen, college sophomores, college juniors, college seniors, recent college graduates, graduate students, law students, career changers, individuals reentering the workforce.
Benefits Formal training, free housing, free meals, names of contacts, opportunity to attend seminars/workshops, possible full-time employment, willing to complete paperwork for educational credit, willing to provide letters of recommendation, job lists provided when available.
Contact Write, call, or fax Fred Ferreira, School Program Coordinator. Phone: 603-525-3311. Fax: 603-525-4151. In-person interview recommended. Applicants must submit a formal organization application, three letters of recommendation. Application deadline: June 30 for fall, December 12 for winter/spring.

BRADFORD WOODS OUTDOOR CENTER
5040 State Road 67 North
Martinsville, Indiana 46151

General Information Organization that provides environmental education, adventure challenge education, and recreational programming for a variety of populations. Number of employees: 35. Unit of Indiana University Bloomington, Bloomington, Indiana. Number of internship applications received each year: 10.
Internships Available ▶ *Apprentices:* responsibilities include teaching environmental education, leading recreational activities; conducting evening activities during assigned environmental education programs; facilitating group icebreakers, initiatives and ropes/teams course events; and conducting evening activities during assigned adventure recreation, therapeutic and leadership programs. Candidates should have ability to work independently, oral communication skills, self-motivation, strong interpersonal skills, strong leadership ability, written communication skills. Duration is February to May or August to November. $300 monthly stipend. ▶ *Interns.* Candidates should have ability to work independently, ability to work with others, oral communication skills, organizational skills, self-motivation, strong leadership ability. Duration is February to May or August to November. $200 monthly stipend. Open to undergraduate and graduate students majoring in environmental education, outdoor education, adventure/challenge education, biology, and related fields. ▶ *Outdoor instructor interns:* responsibilities include teaching modules in a variety of areas; leading night hikes, campfires, and recreational activities; high ropes courses, climbing wall, canoeing, and back country experiences for junior and high school students and youth at risk. Candidates should have ability to work independently, oral communication skills, self-motivation, strong interpersonal skills, strong leadership ability, written communication skills. Duration is 1 semester. $165–$225 per week. Open to college freshmen, college sophomores, college juniors, college seniors, recent college graduates, graduate students. ▶ *Outdoor instructors:* responsibilities include completing reports, schedules, lessons, or program plans and other paperwork as assigned; teaching environmental education modules; leading recreational activities; conducting evening activities as assigned during environmental education programs; assisting with facilitating group icebreakers, initiatives, ropes/team course events; and conducting evening activities during assigned adventure recreation, therapeutic, and/or leadership programs. Candidates should have ability to work independently, knowledge of field, oral communication skills, strong interpersonal skills, strong leadership ability. Duration is February to May, or

August to November. $165 per week. Open to college freshmen, college sophomores, college juniors, college seniors, recent college graduates, graduate students, career changers. ▶ *5 therapeutic recreation and summer interns:* responsibilities include cabin counseling and general program planning. Candidates should have ability to work independently, oral communication skills, personal interest in the field, self-motivation, strong interpersonal skills. Duration is 1 summer (May to August). $50 stipend. Open to college freshmen, college sophomores, college juniors, college seniors, recent college graduates, graduate students. International applications accepted.
Benefits Free housing, free meals, on-the-job training, worker's ompensation, health and accident insurance provided for some positions.
Contact Write, call, or e-mail Staffing Coordinator. Phone: 765-342-2915. E-mail: bradwood@indiana.edu. In-person interview recommended. Applicants must submit a cover letter, resume, two personal references. Applications are accepted continuously. World Wide Web: http://www.indiana.edu/~bradwood/.

BRECKENRIDGE OUTDOOR EDUCATION CENTER
Box 697
Breckenridge, Colorado 80424

General Information Education center offering year-round wilderness and adventure programs for individuals of all abilities, as well as team building, leadership development, and adaptive skiing opportunities for individuals with disabilities and other special needs, and offers team building program for professionals. Accredited by Association of Experiential Education. Established in 1976. Number of employees: 25. Number of internship applications received each year: 100.
Internships Available ▶ *10 summer wilderness interns:* responsibilities include precourse planning, addressing participants' needs, instructing in all activities, and performing postcourse and participation evaluation. Duration is 4–5 months. $50 per month stipend. ▶ *12 winter interns:* responsibilities include instructing disabled individuals in skiing and working with various adaptive equipment, ski methods, and winter wilderness courses. Duration is 6 months. $50 per month stipend. Candidates for all positions should have CPR and first aid certifications. Open to individuals 21 years old. International applications accepted.
Benefits Formal training, free housing, free meals, names of contacts, possible full-time employment, willing to complete paperwork for educational credit, willing to provide letters of recommendation, ski pass in winter, worker's compensation, athletics club pass.
Contact Write, call, fax, or e-mail Internship Coordinator. Phone: 970-453-6422. Fax: 970-453-4676. E-mail: boec@boec.org. Applicants must submit a cover letter, resume, formal application (please find on Web site). Application deadline: March 31 for summer, September 15 for fall. World Wide Web: http://www.boec.org.

BROOKINGS INSTITUTION–CENTER FOR PUBLIC POLICY EDUCATION (CPPE)
1775 Massachusetts, NW
Washington, District of Columbia 20036

General Information Nonprofit public policy research organization that designs and conducts executive education programs for corporate and government executives. Established in 1917. Number of employees: 250. Number of internship applications received each year: 50.
Internships Available ▶ *1 intern:* responsibilities include working with senior staff members to identify possible topics and speakers for public policy conferences, researching new companies to visit as part of conferences on understanding business policy, working with marketing staff to identify potential companies to attend programs, and performing clerical duties as assigned. Duration is flexible. Unpaid.
Benefits Opportunity to attend seminars/workshops, willing to complete paperwork for educational credit.
Contact Write Ms. Irma Gray, Program Assistant, Center for Public Policy Education. In-person interview recommended.

Brookings Institution–Center for Public Policy Education (CPPE) (continued)
Applicants must submit a resume, writing sample. Applications are accepted continuously. World Wide Web: http://www.brook.edu.

CADRE OF CORPS
1719 24th Street
Sacramento, California 95816

General Information Provider of environmental education, service learning, academic enrichment, and positive recreation activities to children and youth. Established in 1995. Number of employees: 130. Unit of California Conservation Corps, Sacramento, California. Number of internship applications received each year: 118.

Internships Available ▶ *118 Americorps members:* responsibilities include providing environmental education, academic enrichment, service learning opportunities, and positive recreational options to children and youth. Candidates should have ability to work independently, ability to work with others, oral communication skills, self-motivation, strong interpersonal skills, desire to work with children and youth. Duration is 1 year. $6 per hour. Open to recent high school graduates, college freshmen, college sophomores, college juniors, college seniors, recent college graduates, graduate students, individuals reentering the workforce.

Benefits Formal training, health insurance, on-the-job training, opportunity to attend seminars/workshops, possible full-time employment, willing to act as a professional reference, willing to provide letters of recommendation, education award.

Contact Write, call, fax, or e-mail Maggie Coulter, Program Administrator, 1719 24th Street, Sacramento, California 95816. Phone: 916-341-3156. Fax: 916-445-1007. E-mail: maggiec@ccc.ca.gov. Applicants must submit a formal organization application, resume, three personal references, in-person or telephone interview. Application deadline: April 1 for part-time, August 1 for fall. World Wide Web: http://www.ccc.ca.gov.

CATHOLIC UNIVERSITY OF AMERICA, DEPARTMENT OF POLITICS
300 Marist Hall
Washington, District of Columbia 20064

General Information Nonprofit group engaged in research, training, and technical assistance for working-class, ethnic neighborhood organizations in older industrial cities and offering political internships in Washington, D.C.; London, England; and Dublin, Ireland in conjunction with NCUEA. Unit of National Center for Urban Ethnic Affairs, Washington, District of Columbia. Number of internship applications received each year: 500.

Internships Available ▶ *6 British Parliamentary interns:* responsibilities include working closely with parliamentary sponsor performing research, being involved in constituency relations, and acting as a party liaison. Candidates should have knowledge of field, oral communication skills, research skills, self-motivation, strong leadership ability, writing skills. Duration is 1 semester. Open to college juniors, college seniors, recent college graduates, graduate students. ▶ *5 European Parliamentary interns:* responsibilities include working for English-speaking elected officials and administrative officials of the European Union on research projects in conjunction with a European studies semester. Candidates should have knowledge of field, oral communication skills, personal interest in the field, research skills, self-motivation, writing skills. Duration is 1 semester. Open to college juniors, college seniors, recent college graduates, graduate students. ▶ *6 House of Commons interns:* responsibilities include acting as assistant to the members of Parliament, performing research, being involved in constituency relations, and acting as a party liaison. Candidates should have knowledge of field, oral communication skills, personal interest in the field, research skills, self-motivation, writing skills. Duration is 1 semester. Open to college juniors, college seniors, recent college graduates, graduate students. ▶ *15 Irish Parliamentary interns:* responsibilities include working as professional aides to members of the

Irish Parliament by performing research, being involved in constituency relations, acting as a party liaison, and preparing briefing materials while becoming familiar with the Irish Parliament. Candidates should have oral communication skills, personal interest in the field, research skills, self-motivation, strong interpersonal skills, writing skills. Duration is 1 semester. Open to college juniors, college seniors, recent college graduates, graduate students. ▶ *9 London summer interns:* responsibilities include performing duties of research aide in Parliament. Candidates should have knowledge of field, oral communication skills, personal interest in the field, research skills, self-motivation, writing skills. Duration is May to July. Open to college sophomores, college juniors, college seniors, recent college graduates, law students. ▶ *U.S. political interns:* responsibilities include working in government and policy organizations. Duration is 1 semester. Open to college juniors, college seniors, recent college graduates, graduate students. ▶ *Research interns:* responsibilities include acting as research assistants on national policy issues. Duration is 1 semester. Open to college juniors, college seniors, recent college graduates, graduate students. All positions are unpaid. International applications accepted.

Benefits Formal training, opportunity to attend seminars/workshops, possible full-time employment, willing to provide letters of recommendation, university credit.

International Internships Available in Belgium; Germany; Dublin, Ireland; London, United Kingdom.

Contact Write, call, fax, or e-mail Dr. John Kromkowski, Director of Internships. Phone: 202-319-5128. Fax: 202-319-6289. E-mail: kromkowski@cua.edu. Applicants must submit a cover letter, resume, academic transcripts, three letters of recommendation. Applications are accepted continuously. World Wide Web: http://www.cua.edu.

CENTRO DE DISENO ARQUITECTURA Y CONTRUCCION
Apartado Postal 3900
Tegucigalpa Honduras

General Information Private university specializing in architecture and design; committed to investigation and community outreach. Established in 1996. Number of employees: 28. Number of internship applications received each year: 2.

Internships Available ▶ *1 computer services intern:* responsibilities include providing support to users of computer lab; offering training opportunities for students and staff; helping design operational programs; developing database for university operations. Candidates should have ability to work independently, computer skills, knowledge of field, self-motivation, strong interpersonal skills, minimum of intermediate-level Spanish. Duration is 1–3 semesters. Open to college juniors, college seniors, recent college graduates, graduate students, career changers. ▶ *1–2 construction technology interns:* responsibilities include giving workshops on specific construction skills, such as building types, the use of specific materials, and building models. Candidates should have ability to work with others, experience in the field, oral communication skills, personal interest in the field, strong interpersonal skills, minimum of intermediate-level Spanish. Duration is 1–12 weeks. Open to college seniors, recent college graduates, graduate students, career changers, individuals reentering the workforce, people with specific construction skills (carpentry, etc.). ▶ *1 environmental issues intern:* responsibilities include researching laws and compliance alternatives, proposing and developing extension courses, organizing environmental events, preparing training and course materials, helping draft proposals for program needs. Candidates should have ability to work independently, knowledge of field, research skills, self-motivation, written communication skills, minimum of intermediate-level Spanish. Duration is 1–3 semesters. Open to college juniors, college seniors, recent college graduates, graduate students, career changers, individuals reentering the workforce, professionals in the field desiring overseas experience or research opportunities. ▶ *1 librarian:* responsibilities include activities to strengthen library services, managing Internet access and monitoring for topics of interest, soliciting additional library resources. Candidates should have ability to work independently, computer skills, knowledge of field, research skills, self-motivation, minimum of intermediate-level Spanish. Duration is 1–3 semesters. Open to college seniors, recent college graduates, graduate students, career changers, individuals reentering the workforce, professionals in the field desiring overseas experience. ▶ *1 marketing intern:* responsibilities include helping design and write public relations and promotional materials, designing ad campaigns, organizing promotional events, working with student admissions process, investigating need for new degree and extension courses. Candidates should have ability to work with others, computer skills, experience in the field, self-motivation, strong interpersonal skills, minimum of intermediate-level Spanish. Duration is 2–6 months. Open to college seniors, recent college graduates, graduate students, career changers, individuals reentering the workforce, professionals in the field desiring overseas experience. ▶ *1–2 municipal support interns:* responsibilities include helping develop materials to train municipal employees and elected officials on basic urban planning issues. Candidates should have ability to work independently, declared college major in field, knowledge of field, self-motivation, written communication skills, minimum of intermediate-level Spanish. Duration is 1–3 semesters. Open to college seniors, recent college graduates, graduate students, career changers, individuals reentering the workforce, professionals in the field desiring overseas experience or research opportunities. ▶ *1–3 research interns:* responsibilities include locating and translating background materials; participating in testing, experiments, and design; providing logistical support; helping design final reports, and drafting proposals for additional research projects. Candidates should have ability to work independently, ability to work with others, analytical skills, knowledge of field, research skills, minimum of intermediate-level Spanish. Duration is 1–3 semesters. Open to college juniors, college seniors, recent college graduates, graduate students, career changers, individuals reentering the workforce, professionals in the fields of architecture, design, engineering, or construction desiring overseas experience. ▶ *1–3 teaching assistants:* responsibilities include providing support for teachers in workshop settings, helping prepare exercises and materials, evaluating and proposing teaching methods, proposing and developing new courses, and helping draft proposals for program needs. Candidates should have declared college major in field, knowledge of field, oral communication skills, self-motivation, strong interpersonal skills, minimum of intermediate-level Spanish. Duration is 1–3 semesters. Open to college seniors, recent college graduates, graduate students, career changers, architecture or design professionals desiring overseas or teaching experience. ▶ *1–4 urban and regional planning interns:* responsibilities include working with municipal governments to develop plans and offering courses or training on the subject. Candidates should have ability to work with others, declared college major in field, oral communication skills, strong interpersonal skills, written communication skills, minimum of intermediate-level Spanish. Duration is 1–12 months. Open to college seniors, recent college graduates, graduate students, individuals reentering the workforce, professionals in the field desiring overseas experience. All positions available as unpaid or paid. International applications accepted.

Benefits Housing at a cost, meals at a cost, opportunity to attend seminars/workshops, willing to act as a professional reference, willing to complete paperwork for educational credit, willing to provide letters of recommendation, participation in CEDAC courses free of charge.

Contact Write, fax, or e-mail Lorette Pellettiere Calix, Internship Coordinator, TGU-00039, PO Box 025387, Miami, Florida 33102-5387. Phone: 11-. Fax: 011-504-232-6024. E-mail: cedac@sdnhon.org.hn. Applicants must submit a cover letter, resume, academic transcripts, three letters of recommendation, e-mail address if possible. Applications are accepted continuously.

CHILDREN'S NATURE INSTITUTE
1440 Harvard Street
Santa Monica, California 90404

General Information Organization whose mission is to educate young children, families, and teachers in the natural sciences; and to inspire respect, appreciation, and love for the natural environment in all children, with special attention to underserved populations. Established in 1985. Number of employees: 4. Number of internship applications received each year: 5.
Internships Available ▶ *2 marketing/public relations interns:* responsibilities include assisting nonprofit organization in all aspects of marketing and public relations. Candidates should have ability to work independently, knowledge of field, oral communication skills, strong interpersonal skills, written communication skills. Open to college sophomores, college juniors, college seniors, recent college graduates, graduate students, career changers, individuals reentering the workforce. ▶ *1–3 project assistants:* responsibilities include assisting in researching and coordinating educational and other projects for a nonprofit organization. Candidates should have ability to work independently, computer skills, organizational skills, research skills, writing skills. Open to high school seniors, recent high school graduates, college freshmen, college sophomores, college juniors, college seniors, recent college graduates, graduate students, law students, law school graduates, career changers, individuals reentering the workforce. All positions are unpaid. International applications accepted.
Benefits On-the-job training, opportunity to attend seminars/workshops, willing to act as a professional reference, willing to complete paperwork for educational credit, willing to provide letters of recommendation.
Contact Write, call, fax, or e-mail Executive Director. Phone: 310-998-1151. Fax: 310-998-1182. E-mail: chldnature@aol.com. In-person interview recommended. Applicants must submit a cover letter, resume, three personal references. Applications are accepted continuously. World Wide Web: http://www.childrensnatureinst.org.

CHINGACHGOOK YMCA OUTDOOR CENTER
1872 Pilot Knob Road
Kattskill Bay, New York 12844

General Information Outdoor, environmental, and adventure education center in the Adirondacks that teaches school children, college students, families, and adult groups. Established in 1913. Number of employees: 25. Branch of Capital District YMCA, Albany, New York. Number of internship applications received each year: 5.
Internships Available ▶ *2–4 cooks:* responsibilities include preparing meals for cafeteria style dining room with 3-4 others, serving up to 400 persons per meal. Candidates should have ability to work independently, ability to work with others, knowledge of field, strong interpersonal skills. Duration is 7–10 weeks. Position available as unpaid or at $150–$300 per week. Open to recent high school graduates, college freshmen, college sophomores, college juniors, college seniors, recent college graduates, individuals reentering the workforce. ▶ *3–4 outdoor educators:* responsibilities include leading environmental, recreational, adventure and outdoor classes to school children, families, college students, and adults. Candidates should have experience in the field, personal interest in the field, strong interpersonal skills, strong leadership ability. Duration is 8–15 weeks. Position available as unpaid or at $100–$200 per week. Open to recent high school graduates, college freshmen, college sophomores, college juniors, college seniors, recent college graduates. International applications accepted.
Benefits Formal training, free housing, free meals, names of contacts, on-the-job training, opportunity to attend seminars/workshops, possible full-time employment, willing to act as a professional reference, willing to complete paperwork for educational credit.
Contact Write or call Kenis Sweet, Outdoor Center Director. Phone: 518-656-9462. In-person interview recommended. Applicants

Chingachgook YMCA Outdoor Center (continued)

must submit a cover letter, resume, personal reference. Application deadline: March 1 for spring, June 1 for fall.

CHOATE ROSEMARY HALL
333 Christian Street
Wallingford, Connecticut 06492

General Information Secondary school with summer enrichment and credit programs. Established in 1916. Number of employees: 100. Number of internship applications received each year: 100.
Internships Available ▶ *30–35 teaching interns:* responsibilities include teaching in two classes, serving as residential house adviser, and coaching two afternoons per week. Candidates should have ability to work with others, organizational skills, personal interest in the field, plan to pursue career in field, self-motivation, strong leadership ability. Duration is 5 weeks. $1,750–$1,900 per duration of internship. Open to college juniors, college seniors, recent college graduates, graduate students, career changers. International applications accepted.
Benefits Free housing, free meals, names of contacts, on-the-job training, willing to act as a professional reference, willing to provide letters of recommendation, training with two different senior teachers.
Contact Write, call, fax, or e-mail Jim Irzyk, Director of Summer Programs. Phone: 203-697-2365. Fax: 203-697-2519. E-mail: jirzyk@choate.edu. In-person interview recommended. Applicants must submit a formal organization application, cover letter, resume, academic transcripts, two letters of recommendation. Application deadline: March 1 for teaching positions (submissions by January encouraged). World Wide Web: http://www.choate.edu/summer.

THE COLLEGE SETTLEMENT OF PHILADELPHIA AND KUHN DAY CAMP
600 Witmer Road
Horsham, Pennsylvania 19044

General Information Resident and day camp that stresses environmental awareness in all activities including rock climbing, backpacking, outpost camping, and ""regular" camping; offers a residential outdoor school program for schools in the Philadelphia area during the fall and spring. Established in 1922. Number of employees: 8. Number of internship applications received each year: 200.
Internships Available ▶ *50–65 counselors:* responsibilities include living with children and directing activities. Candidates should have ability to work independently, experience in the field, oral communication skills, self-motivation, strong interpersonal skills, strong leadership ability. Duration is 9 weeks (summer only). $1,600–$2,000 per duration of internship. Open to college freshmen, college sophomores, college juniors, college seniors, recent college graduates, graduate students. ▶ *3 lifeguards:* responsibilities include instructing swimming and ensuring safety of recreational program participants. Candidates should have knowledge of field, oral communication skills, strong interpersonal skills, strong leadership ability, lifeguard training required; water safety instruction helpful. Duration is 9 weeks (summer only). $1,800–$2,100 per duration of internship. Open to college sophomores, college juniors, college seniors, recent college graduates, graduate students. ▶ *2 nurses.* Duration is 9 weeks (summer only). $1,600–$2,000 per duration of internship. Open to college juniors, college seniors, recent college graduates, graduate students, career changers. ▶ *5 teachers/naturalists:* responsibilities include teaching small groups of children and leading large group and environmental activities. Candidates should have experience in the field, oral communication skills, personal interest in the field, strong interpersonal skills, strong leadership ability. Duration is 3 months (spring and fall only). $150–$225 per week. ▶ *2 teen adventure leaders:* responsibilities include leading adventure trips with 13- and 14-year-olds. Candidates should have experience in the field, oral communication skills, personal interest in the field, self-motivation, strong interpersonal skills, strong leadership ability. Duration is 9 weeks

(summer only). $2,000 per duration of internship. Open to college seniors, recent college graduates, graduate students, individuals reentering the workforce. International applications accepted.
Benefits Formal training, free housing, free meals, names of contacts, opportunity to attend seminars/workshops, willing to act as a professional reference, willing to complete paperwork for educational credit, willing to provide letters of recommendation.
International Internships Available in Ireland; United Kingdom.
Contact Write, call, fax, or e-mail Andrew Fielding, Program Director, 600 Winter Road, Horsham, Pennsylvania 19044. Phone: 215-542-7974. Fax: 215-542-7457. E-mail: camps@i-bob.com. In-person interview recommended. Applicants must submit a formal organization application, resume, three personal references. Application deadline: January 1 for spring (recommended), May 1 for summer (recommended), August 1 for fall (recommended).

COMMUNITY INFORMATION CENTER
1335 Marine Drive
Astoria, Oregon 97103

General Information Internet and computer training center and regional Web server. Established in 1996. Number of employees: 13. Number of internship applications received each year: 2.
Internships Available ▶ *1–2 instructor assistant/computer lab monitors:* responsibilities include assisting with classes on Internet, World Wide Web, digital imagery, business on Web, and televideo conferencing. Candidates should have ability to work with others, computer skills, oral communication skills, personal interest in the field, self-motivation. Open to high school seniors, recent high school graduates, college freshmen, college sophomores, college juniors, college seniors, recent college graduates, graduate students, career changers, individuals reentering the workforce. ▶ *1–2 research analysts:* responsibilities include gathering and publishing community indicator data on social, economic, and environmental measures on Web site. Candidates should have ability to work independently, ability to work with others, computer skills, oral communication skills, organizational skills, personal interest in the field, research skills, self-motivation, written communication skills. Duration is up to 1 year. Open to college freshmen, college sophomores, college juniors, college seniors, recent college graduates, career changers, individuals reentering the workforce. All positions are unpaid. International applications accepted.
Benefits On-the-job training, willing to act as a professional reference, willing to complete paperwork for educational credit, willing to provide letters of recommendation.
Contact Call or e-mail Link Shadley, Director, 1335 Marine Drive, Astoria, Oregon 97103. Phone: 503-325-8502. E-mail: link@ctrf.net. In-person interview recommended. Applicants must submit a resume. Applications are accepted continuously. World Wide Web: http://www.columbia-pacific.interrain.org.

CORO EASTERN CENTER
42 Broadway, Suite 1827-35
New York, New York 10004

General Information Conducts research, education, and training in public affairs; participants' learning comes from their experiences in field assignments, interviews, and projects with diverse organizations. Established in 1942. Number of employees: 8. Number of internship applications received each year: 100.
Internships Available ▶ *12 Coro Fellows in Public Affairs:* responsibilities include working a minimum of 1600 hours over 9.5 months in 6 field assignments in public relations (government, business, labor unions, nonprofit, media, and political campaigns); dozens of group interviews, 2 projects, 2-3 three-day retreats, and bi-weekly seminars. Candidates should have ability to work independently, analytical skills, computer skills, editing skills, office skills, oral communication skills, organizational skills, personal interest in the field, research skills, self-motivation, strong interpersonal skills, strong leadership ability, writing skills. Duration is September-June. Position available as unpaid or at stipend according to financial need. Open to college seniors,

recent college graduates, graduate students, law students, career changers, individuals reentering the workforce. International applications accepted.

Benefits Formal training, names of contacts, on-the-job training, opportunity to attend seminars/workshops, possible full-time employment, willing to act as a professional reference, willing to complete paperwork for educational credit, willing to provide letters of recommendation, monthly stipends available based on financial need (ranging from $400-$800).

Contact Write, call, fax, or e-mail Yago Northern, Program Manager, 42 Broadway, Suite 1827-35, New York, New York 10004. Phone: 212-248-2935. Fax: 212-248-2970. E-mail: ynorthern@coro.org. In-person interview required. Applicants must submit a formal organization application, academic transcripts, two writing samples, four letters of recommendation, participation (for finalists) in a series of group "exercises" and interviews in late March/early April. Application deadline: February 5. Fees: $50. World Wide Web: http://www.coro.org.

CORO MIDWESTERN
1730 South 11th Street, Suite 102
St. Louis, Missouri 63104

General Information Conducting research, education, and training in public affairs; participants' learning comes from their experiences in field assignments, interviews, and projects with diverse organizations. Established in 1942. Number of employees: 12. Number of internship applications received each year: 100.

Internships Available ▶ *12 Coro fellows in public affairs:* responsibilities include working a minimum of 1600 hours over 9.5 months in 6 field assignments of public affairs (government, business, labor unions, non-profit, media, and political campaigns); dozens of group interviews, 2 projects, 2-3 three-day retreats, and bi-weekly seminars. Candidates should have ability to work independently, analytical skills, computer skills, editing skills, office skills, oral communication skills, organizational skills, personal interest in the field, research skills, self-motivation, strong interpersonal skills, strong leadership ability, writing skills. Duration is September-June. Position available as unpaid or at stipend (based on financial need). Open to college seniors, recent college graduates, graduate students, law students, career changers, individuals reentering the workforce. International applications accepted.

Benefits Formal training, names of contacts, on-the-job training, opportunity to attend seminars/workshops, possible full-time employment, willing to act as a professional reference, willing to complete paperwork for educational credit, willing to provide letters of recommendation, monthly stipends available based on financial need (ranging from $400-$800).

Contact Write, call, fax, or e-mail Liza Cohen, Manager, Fellows Recruitment. Phone: 314-621-3040 Ext. 11. Fax: 314-621-1874. E-mail: coro@inlink.com. Applicants must submit a formal organization application, academic transcripts, two writing samples, four letters of recommendation, participation (for finalists) in a series of group "exercises" and interviews in late March/early April. Application deadline: February 5 for fall. Fees: $50. World Wide Web: http://www.coro.org.

CORO NORTHERN CALIFORNIA
690 Market Street, 11th Floor
San Francisco, California 94104

General Information Conducts research, education, and training in public affairs; participants' learning comes from their experiences in field assignments, interviews, and projects with diverse organization. Established in 1942. Number of employees: 12. Number of internship applications received each year: 100.

Internships Available ▶ *12 Coro Fellows in Public Affairs:* responsibilities include working a minimum of 1600 hours over 9.5 months in 6 field assignments of public affairs (government, business, labor unions, nonprofit, media, and political campaigns); dozens of group interviews, 2 projects, 2-3 three-day retreats, and bi-weekly seminars. Candidates should have ability to work independently, analytical skills, computer skills, editing skills, office skills, oral communication skills, organizational skills,

personal interest in the field, research skills, self-motivation, strong interpersonal skills, strong leadership ability, writing skills. Duration is September-June. Position available as unpaid or paid. Open to college seniors, recent college graduates, graduate students, law students, career changers, individuals reentering the workforce. International applications accepted.

Benefits Formal training, names of contacts, on-the-job training, opportunity to attend seminars/workshops, possible full-time employment, willing to act as a professional reference, willing to complete paperwork for educational credit, willing to provide letters of recommendation, monthly stipends available based on financial need (ranging from $400-$800).

Contact Write, call, fax, or e-mail Gracie Cornejo, Director of Recruitment. Phone: 415-986-0521. Fax: 415-986-5522. E-mail: gcornejo@coro.org. In-person interview required. Applicants must submit a formal organization application, academic transcripts, two writing samples, four letters of recommendation, participation (for finalists) in a series of group "exercises" and interviews in late March/early April. Application deadline: February 5. Fees: $50. World Wide Web: http://www.coro.org.

THE CUSHMAN SCHOOL
592 North East 60th Street
Miami, Florida 33137

General Information Non-denominational, non-discriminatory independent school designed for preschool through 8th grade boys and girls of average and above average development and learning ability. Established in 1924. Number of employees: 50. Number of internship applications received each year: 15.

Internships Available ▶ *2-4 educational interns:* responsibilities include helping with small reading groups, assisting in the writing process, and generating thematic projects. Candidates should have knowledge of field, oral communication skills, personal interest in the field, strong interpersonal skills. Duration is 1 semester. Unpaid. Open to recent college graduates, graduate students. International applications accepted.

Benefits Opportunity to attend seminars/workshops, possible full-time employment, willing to complete paperwork for educational credit, opportunity to teach, stipend of $2000 for U.S. residents, $3000 for foreign residents.

Contact Write, fax, or e-mail Frances Harnage, Assistant to the Head of School. Fax: 305-757-1632. E-mail: fharnage@cushmanschool.net. No phone calls. Applicants must submit a cover letter, resume, photo of applicant. Application deadline: May 1 for spring positions for following year, December 5 for fall positions for following year. World Wide Web: http://www.cushmanschool.net.

DAVIS & COMPANY, INC.
80 Grand Avenue
River Edge, New Jersey 07661

General Information An agency that helps companies improve performance by reaching, engaging, and motivating employees. Services include communication consulting, implementation, training/learning, evaluation, and measurement. It has extensive experience building awareness about key business issues, including organizational change, business strategy, vision, mission, process improvement, and reward and recognition. Established in 1984. Number of employees: 12. Number of internship applications received each year: 200.

Internships Available ▶ *2 interns:* responsibilities include writing short articles for newsletters, preparing press releases, researching articles, organizing media lists, and attending client meetings. It could also entail designing graphics and Web site support. Candidates should have declared college major in field, oral communication skills, plan to pursue career in field, strong interpersonal skills, written communication skills, enthusiasm, good attitude. Duration is 1 semester. $7 per hour. Open to college juniors, college seniors, recent college graduates, graduate students.

Benefits Job counseling, names of contacts, on-the-job training, opportunity to attend seminars/workshops, possible full-

Davis & Company, Inc. (continued)

time employment, travel reimbursement, willing to complete paperwork for educational credit, willing to provide letters of recommendation.

Contact Write, fax, or e-mail Ms. Ellen Van Den Heuvel, Director of Human Resources and Administration. Fax: 201-342-7701. E-mail: ellen.vandenheuvel@davisandco.com. No phone calls. In-person interview required. Applicants must submit a cover letter, resume. Applications are accepted continuously. World Wide Web: http://www.davishays.com.

DOUGLAS RANCH CAMPS
6114 La Salle Avenue, Box 539
Piedmont, California 94611

General Information Children's summer camp, which is private, traditional and old fashioned. It teaches social skills and leadership and has structured sports activities. Established in 1925. Number of employees: 2. Unit of Douglas Ranch Camps, Inc., Carmel Valley, California. Number of internship applications received each year: 50.

Internships Available ▶ *2–5 archery instructors:* responsibilities include teaching archery lessons to children at camp, participating in the overall camp program, and caring for a cabin of 4 to 5 campers. ▶ *2–5 crafts/instructors:* responsibilities include planning, preparing and teaching children a variety of nature and camp crafts; participating in the overall camp program; and caring for a cabin of 4 to 5 children. ▶ *2–5 general camp counselors:* responsibilities include caring for cabin of 4 to 5 campers, teaching sports activities, planning and leading campwide games and programs, and being a positive role model. ▶ *2–5 horseback riding instructors/wranglers:* responsibilities include teaching children horseback riding at camp, basic care and grooming of horses, and caring for a cabin of 4 to 5 campers. ▶ *2–5 riflery instructors:* responsibilities include teaching riflery lessons to children, participating in the overall camp program, and caring for a cabin of 4 to 5 children. ▶ *2–5 swim instructors/lifeguards:* responsibilities include teaching swim lessons to children in camp pool, lifeguarding, teaching waterpolo, and caring for a cabin of 4 to 5 campers. ▶ *2–5 tennis instructors:* responsibilities include teaching tennis lessons to children, supervising games, participating in the overall camp program, and caring for a cabin of 4 to 5 children. Candidates for all positions should have ability to work independently, personal interest in the field, self-motivation, strong interpersonal skills, strong leadership ability. Duration for all positions is summer (8 to 10 weeks). All positions paid at $1,700–$2,300 per duration of internship. Open to college freshmen, college sophomores, college juniors, college seniors, recent college graduates.

Benefits Free housing, free meals, health insurance, on-the-job training, opportunity to attend seminars/workshops, willing to act as a professional reference, willing to complete paperwork for educational credit, willing to provide letters of recommendation.

Contact Write, call, fax, or e-mail Kristen Smith, Assistant Director, 6114 La Salle Avenue, Box 539, Piedmont, California 94611. Phone: 510-339-2706. Fax: 510-339-1932. E-mail: director@douglascamp.com. In-person interview recommended. Applicants must submit a formal organization application, cover letter, two personal references, two letters of recommendation. Application deadline: May 1. World Wide Web: http://www.douglascamp.com.

EDUCATE THE CHILDREN
205 Dey Street
Ithaca, New York 14850

General Information International development organization. Established in 1991. Number of employees: 3. Number of internship applications received each year: 22.

Internships Available ▶ *12 English teaching interns:* responsibilities include teaching and tutoring Nepali children at an English-speaking boarding school in Kathmandu. Candidates should have ability to work with others, experience in the field, strong interpersonal skills, cross-cultural skills, teaching/tutoring skills. Duration is 3 months. Open to individuals at least 20 years of

age. ▶ *1 program assistant:* responsibilities include research, secretarial tasks, newsletter production, and design and execution of promotional campaigns. Candidates should have ability to work independently, computer skills, office skills, oral communication skills, research skills, written communication skills. Duration is flexible. Open to college freshmen, college sophomores, college juniors, college seniors, recent college graduates, graduate students, career changers. All positions are unpaid. International applications accepted.

Benefits On-the-job training, opportunity to attend seminars/workshops, willing to act as a professional reference, willing to complete paperwork for educational credit, willing to provide letters of recommendation, free housing and meals in Nepal.

International Internships Available in Kathmandu, Nepal.

Contact Write or e-mail Kelly Carragee, Program Coordinator, PO Box 414, Ithaca, New York 14850. E-mail: info@etc-nepal.org. In-person interview recommended. Applicants must submit a formal organization application, resume, two personal references. Application deadline: December 1 for spring. Fees: $500. World Wide Web: http://www.etc-nepal.org.

FLORIDA INTERNATIONAL UNIVERSITY
University Park
Miami, Florida 33199

General Information A large multicampus, multicultural university in Miami-Dade County, Florida. Established in 1965. Number of employees: 4,000. Number of internship applications received each year: 10.

Internships Available ▶ *1–2 nutrition interns:* responsibilities include coordinating special health promotion campaigns related to nutrition, one-on-one nutritional counseling, teaching workshops on nutrition and healthy cooking, creating educational materials and marketing tools. Candidates should have ability to work independently, ability to work with others, college courses in field, declared college major in field, knowledge of field, oral communication skills, self-motivation. ▶ *1–2 wellness interns:* responsibilities include coordinating special health promotion campaigns (health fairs), creating educational materials and publicity, performing fitness assessments, one-on-one health education, and teaching workshops on a variety of subjects. Candidates should have ability to work independently, ability to work with others, declared college major in field, knowledge of field, oral communication skills, self-motivation. Duration for all positions is flexible (ideally, January to April or August to December). All positions are unpaid. Open to college freshmen, college sophomores, college juniors, college seniors, recent college graduates, graduate students. International applications accepted.

Benefits Formal training, job counseling, names of contacts, on-the-job training, opportunity to attend seminars/workshops, possible full-time employment, willing to act as a professional reference, willing to complete paperwork for educational credit, willing to provide letters of recommendation.

Contact Write, call, fax, or e-mail Mary M. Munroe, Wellness Coordinator, University Park, HWC 215, Miami, Florida 33199. Phone: 305-348-4020. Fax: 305-348-3336. E-mail: xmunroe@fiu.edu. Telephone interview required. Applicants must submit a cover letter, resume. Applications are accepted continuously. World Wide Web: http://www.fiu.edu/.

FOCUS ON WOMEN PROGRAM, HENRY FORD COMMUNITY COLLEGE
5101 Evergreen Road
Dearborn, Michigan 48128-1495

General Information Comprehensive education program that offers academic women's studies classes, noncredit seminars, assistance to returning adults, and a vocational education tuition payment program. Established in 1974. Number of employees: 5. Unit of Henry Ford Community College, Dearborn, Michigan. Number of internship applications received each year: 5.

Internships Available ▶ *1 program intern.* Candidates should have computer skills, oral communication skills, self-motivation, strong

interpersonal skills, written communication skills. Duration is 6–12 months. Unpaid. Open to college seniors, recent college graduates, graduate students.
Benefits Names of contacts, opportunity to attend seminars/workshops, willing to provide letters of recommendation.
Contact Write, call, fax, or e-mail Internship Coordinator. Phone: 313-845-9629. Fax: 313-317-4158. E-mail: donna@mail.henryford.cc.mi.us. In-person interview recommended. Applications are accepted continuously.

FOOD SERVICE MANAGEMENT INTERNSHIP COMMITTEE
105 Smalley Center, Purdue University
West Lafayette, Indiana 47906-4205

General Information Educational program whose purpose is to introduce aspiring professionals to the food-service industry and to provide on-the-job experience that will better qualify them to assume responsibilities related to college and university food service. Established in 1961. Unit of Association of College and University Housing Officers–International/National Association of College and University Food Services. Number of internship applications received each year: 120.
Internships Available ▶ *55–65 food service management interns:* responsibilities include working with food service employees to develop understanding of personnel, production, service, sanitation,and safety issues; working with professional staff to learn policies and issues affecting decisions in food service, gaining experience in supervision, and planning and coordinating food service functions. Candidates should have ability to work with others, college courses in field, knowledge of field, oral communication skills, organizational skills, personal interest in the field. Duration is 8 weeks. stipend of $1200 plus room and board. Open to college juniors, college seniors, recent college graduates, graduate students. International applications accepted.
Benefits Free housing, free meals, job counseling, names of contacts, on-the-job training, opportunity to attend seminars/workshops, possible full-time employment, willing to act as a professional reference, willing to complete paperwork for educational credit, willing to provide letters of recommendation.
Contact Write, call, fax, or e-mail Sarah C. Johnson, Chairperson. Phone: 765-494-1000. Fax: 765-494-0718. E-mail: sarah.c.johnson.1@purdue.edu. Telephone interview required. Applicants must submit a formal organization application, cover letter, resume, letter of recommendation. Application deadline: January 23 for summer.

4-H FARLEY OUTDOOR EDUCATION CENTER
615 Route 130
Mashpee, Massachusetts 02649

General Information Primarily a day and overnight summer camp for children, with some programs being developed for schools in the spring and fall seasons; strong environmental focus. Established in 1934. Unit of University of Massachusetts Amherst, Amherst, Massachusetts.
Internships Available ▶ *1–2 environmental educators:* responsibilities include organizing, developing, and providing educational activities for children 4-14 years of age. Candidates should have experience in the field, plan to pursue career in field, self-motivation, strong interpersonal skills. Duration is 2 months. approximately $150 per week. Open to college juniors, college seniors, recent college graduates, graduate students, career changers. International applications accepted.
Benefits Free housing, free meals, names of contacts, on-the-job training, travel reimbursement, willing to act as a professional reference, willing to complete paperwork for educational credit, willing to provide letters of recommendation.
Contact Write or e-mail Mr. Michael Campbell, Executive Director. E-mail: 4hfarley@cape.com. No phone calls. In-person interview recommended. Applicants must submit a formal organization application, cover letter, resume, personal reference, letter of recommendation. Applications are accepted continuously. World Wide Web: http://www.umass.edu/umext/camps/c-farley.htm.

THE FULBRIGHT COMMISSION
62 Doughty Street
London WCIN 2LS United Kingdom

General Information Educational exchange between the US and the UK. Established in 1948. Number of employees: 7. Number of internship applications received each year: 15.
Internships Available ▶ *4–8 information officers:* responsibilities include working in U.S. Educational Advisory Service providing information and advice about studying in the USA, project work on events, researching publications and handouts, and some general administrative work. Candidates should have office skills, organizational skills, research skills, self-motivation, strong interpersonal skills, written communication skills. Duration is 3–6 months. Unpaid. ▶ *1–2 information officers:* responsibilities include working in the U.S. Educational Advisory Service providing information and advice about studying in the USA, project work on events, researching publications and handouts, and some general administrative work. Candidates should have office skills, personal interest in the field, research skills, self-motivation, strong interpersonal skills, written communication skills. Duration is 6 months. $8 per hour. Open to college juniors, college seniors, recent college graduates, graduate students. International applications accepted.
Benefits On-the-job training, willing to act as a professional reference, willing to complete paperwork for educational credit, willing to provide letters of recommendation, possible reimbursement of fee for work visa, free lunch, reimbursement for travel in London.
International Internships Available in London, United Kingdom.
Contact Write, call, fax, or e-mail Louise Cook, Director, Educational Advisory Service. Phone: 44-171-539-4401. Fax: 44-171-404-6874. E-mail: lcook@fulbright.co.uk. In-person interview recommended. Applicants must submit a cover letter, resume, names and contact details of two referees. Applications are accepted continuously. World Wide Web: http://www.fulbright.co.uk.

GEORGE WILLIAMS COLLEGE EDUCATIONAL CENTERS
PO Box 210
Williams Bay, Wisconsin 53191

General Information Educational conference center providing outdoor and nontraditional learning experiences and sponsoring regional conferences. Established in 1886. Number of employees: 65. Affiliate of Aurora University, Aurora, Illinois. Number of internship applications received each year: 50.
Internships Available ▶ *4–8 adventure education positions:* responsibilities include facilitating team building and leadership development programs for adolescents, colleges, and adult groups by utilizing trust building, group initiatives, high and low ropes courses, team and individual climbing elements, and off-campus rock climbing. Candidates should have experience in the field, oral communication skills, organizational skills, strong interpersonal skills, strong leadership ability. Duration is March-November. $280–$320 per week. Open to college seniors, recent college graduates, graduate students, career changers. ▶ *Outdoor recreation positions:* responsibilities include coordinating conference groups and leading activities, including sports, games, natural awareness, and orienteering. Candidates should have ability to work independently, ability to work with others, experience in the field, self-motivation, strong leadership ability, waterfront skills, qualified life guard, experience in sailing, canoeing, windsurfing, skiing (downhill or cross country). Duration is 1 summer or 1 winter (12 to 15 weeks each). $150 per week. Open to college seniors, recent college graduates, graduate students. ▶ *7 outdoor/environmental education positions:* responsibilities include coordinating school groups and teaching classes in natural awareness, wetlands, lake study, astronomy, and weather. Candidates should have ability to work with others, organizational skills, personal interest in the field, plan to pursue career in field, self-motivation, strong leadership ability. Duration is September-May. $150–$215 per week. Open to recent college graduates, graduate students. International applications accepted.

George Williams College Educational Centers (continued)

Benefits Formal training, names of contacts, on-the-job training, willing to act as a professional reference, willing to complete paperwork for educational credit, willing to provide letters of recommendation, supplemental medical policy, use of recreational facilities (tennis, golf, waterfront), free room and board for outdoor/environmental education and outdoor recreation positions, room and board at a cost for adventure education positions.
Contact Write, fax, or e-mail Ms. Cathy Coster or Ms. Sharon Wuttke, Associate Directors of Adventure/Outdoor Recreation Education. Fax: 414-245-8549. E-mail: owls@idcnet.com. No phone calls. In-person interview recommended. Applicants must submit a cover letter, resume, three personal references. Applications are accepted continuously.

GLOBAL CAMPUS, UNIVERSITY OF MINNESOTA
102 Nicholson Hall, 216 Pillsbury Drive, SE
Minneapolis, Minnesota 55455-0138

General Information Study abroad program designed to give students an opportunity to accent program curriculum by working as an intern in a variety of fields. Established in 1972. Number of employees: 30. Number of internship applications received each year: 25.
Internships Available ▶ *London interns:* responsibilities include working in one of a variety of fields. Candidates should have oral communication skills, personal interest in the field. Open to college freshmen, college sophomores, college juniors, college seniors, recent college graduates. ▶ *15 Toledo interns:* responsibilities include working in one of a variety of fields. Candidates should have personal interest in the field, strong Spanish language skills. Open to college sophomores, college juniors, college seniors, recent college graduates. ▶ *Venezuela interns:* responsibilities include working in one of a variety of fields. Candidates should have oral communication skills, personal interest in the field, Spanish language skills desirable. Open to college sophomores, college juniors, college seniors, recent college graduates, graduate students. All positions are unpaid. International applications accepted.
Benefits Health insurance, housing at a cost, meals at a cost, on-the-job training, opportunity to attend seminars/workshops, willing to complete paperwork for educational credit, participants earn 15 University of Minnesota semester credits while on the International Program (3 or 6 of those credits go towards the internship).
International Internships Available in Toledo, Spain; London, United Kingdom; Caracas, Venezuela; Merida, Venezuela.
Contact Write, call, fax, or e-mail The Global Campus. Phone: 612-626-9000. Fax: 612-626-8009. E-mail: abroad@umn.edu. Applicants must submit a formal organization application, academic transcripts, letter of recommendation. Application deadline: April 15 for fall (England), July 30 for fall or academic year (Spain), July 1 for fall (Venezuela), July 30 for fall (or academic year (Spain), November 30 for spring (Spain), November 15 for spring (England), November 1 for sping (Venezuela, November 30 for spring (Venezuela). Fees: $50. World Wide Web: http://www.UMabroad.umn.edu/.

GLOBAL CAMPUS, UNIVERSITY OF MINNESOTA, MINNESOTA STUDIES IN INTERNATIONAL DEVELOPMENT (MSID)
102 Nicholson Hall, Pillsbury Drive, SE
Minneapolis, Minnesota 55455-0138

General Information Study abroad program for students and professionals built around grassroots development internships in Ecuador, India, Kenya, and Senegal; fields include agriculture, education, environment, health, microbusiness development, social services, and women in development. Established in 1972. Unit of University of Minnesota, Twin Cities Campus, Minneapolis, Minnesota. Number of internship applications received each year: 70.
Internships Available ▶ *70–100 interns:* responsibilities include working in a non-governmental organization at the grassroots level in the area of intern's choice and completing related

coursework. Candidates should have ability to work independently, analytical skills, personal interest in the field, self-motivation, strong interpersonal skills, intercultural sensitivity and adaptability. Duration is fall semester; or fall semester and January; or academic year. Unpaid. Open to college juniors, college seniors, recent college graduates, graduate students, law students, career changers, individuals reentering the workforce. International applications accepted.
Benefits Opportunity to attend seminars/workshops, willing to complete paperwork for educational credit, up to 45 quarter credits for the internship and related coursework, support services overseas.
International Internships Available in Ecuador; India; Kenya; Senegal.
Contact Write, call, fax, or e-mail The Global Campus. Phone: 612-626-9000. Fax: 612-626-8009. E-mail: umabroad@tc.umn.edu. Applicants must submit a formal organization application, academic transcripts, two writing samples, letter of recommendation. Application deadline: February 15 for priority consideration; April 1 final deadline. Fees: $50. World Wide Web: http://www.umabroad.umn.edu/.

GREAT SMOKY MOUNTAINS INSTITUTE AT TREMONT
9275 Tremont Road
Townsend, Tennessee 37882

General Information Residential environmental education center dedicated to creating environmentally literate students who want to help preserve and protect places such as the Smokies. Established in 1969. Number of employees: 20. Unit of Great Smoky Mountains Natural History Association, Gatlinburg, Tennessee. Number of internship applications received each year: 25.
Internships Available ▶ *1–3 teacher/naturalist interns:* responsibilities include assisting with all aspects of the residential environmental education program. Candidates should have college courses in field, experience in the field, oral communication skills, strong interpersonal skills, written communication skills. Duration is 1 year. Position available as unpaid or paid. Open to college sophomores, college juniors, college seniors, recent college graduates. ▶ *4–6 teacher/naturalists assistants:* responsibilities include working in summer youth camp. Candidates should have ability to work independently, knowledge of field, oral communication skills, personal interest in the field, self-motivation, strong interpersonal skills. Duration is 6–10 weeks. Unpaid. Open to college sophomores, college juniors, college seniors, recent college graduates, graduate students. International applications accepted.
Benefits Formal training, free housing, free meals, job counseling, names of contacts, on-the-job training, opportunity to attend seminars/workshops, possible full-time employment, willing to act as a professional reference, willing to complete paperwork for educational credit, willing to provide letters of recommendation, health insurance for one-year interns (after 90 days of employment).
Contact Write or e-mail Mr. Ken Voorhis, Director. E-mail: gsmit@smokiesnha.org. In-person interview recommended. Applicants must submit a formal organization application, cover letter, resume, three personal references. Application deadline: February 15 for summer, June 1 for fall, September 15 for spring. World Wide Web: http://www.nps.gov/grsm/Tremont.htm.

GULF WIND COUNCIL OF CAMP FIRE BOYS AND GIRLS
1814 Creighton Road
Pensacola, Florida 32504

General Information Organization that provides informal educational opportunities for young persons. Established in 1910. Number of employees: 40. Unit of Camp Fire Boys and Girls, Kansas City, Missouri. Number of internship applications received each year: 20.
Internships Available ▶ *1 Special Sitters project manager:* responsibilities include developing, implementing, and monitoring Special

Sitters project, including performing tasks involving publicity, community outreach, recruitment and training, and matching and referring sitters to families. Duration is flexible. Unpaid. Open to individuals 18 years of age or older. ▶ *1–4 area service team managers:* responsibilities include managing, maintaining, and extending program services. Duration is 11 months. Unpaid. Open to individuals 18 years of age or older. ▶ *5–20 club co-leaders:* responsibilities include facilitating activities tailored to children's needs and interests. Duration is 2 semesters. Unpaid. Open to individuals 18 years of age or older. ▶ *1 self-reliance course coordinator:* responsibilities include recruiting course participants and arranging course sites. Duration is 2 semesters. Unpaid. Open to individuals 18 years of age or older. ▶ *5 self-reliance instructors:* responsibilities include arranging and teaching assigned self-reliance courses. Duration is 2 semesters. Unpaid. Open to individuals 18 years of age or older. ▶ *1 teen pregnancy prevention/abstinence program intern:* responsibilities include assisting program administrator in delivering teen pregnancy programs, such as "Baby, Think It Over;" building an awareness team; providing materials to teens from the resource library; and planning special events. Duration is 1 year. Position available as unpaid or paid. Open to mature individuals of 21 years of age or older. International applications accepted.

Benefits Formal training, names of contacts, opportunity to attend seminars/workshops, possible full-time employment, travel reimbursement, willing to complete paperwork for educational credit, willing to provide letters of recommendation.

Contact Write, call, fax, or e-mail La-Vonne Haven, Executive Director. Phone: 850-476-1760. Fax: 850-476-6614. E-mail: cfgulfwind@juno.com. In-person interview required. Applicants must submit a formal organization application, cover letter, resume, personal and criminal background checks, fingerprint screening, tuberculosis test required. Applications are accepted continuously.

HIDDEN VILLA ENVIRONMENTAL EDUCATION PROGRAM
26870 Moody Road
Los Altos Hills, California 94022

General Information School-year program introducing 4-12-year-olds to the wonders and magic of farms and the natural world. Established in 1970. Number of employees: 10. Unit of The Trust for Hidden Villa, Los Altos Hills, California. Number of internship applications received each year: 40.

Internships Available ▶ *4 environmental education interns:* responsibilities include teaching on a farm, in the wilderness, and in a classroom for 25 hours per week; working on a farm for 10 hours per week; and spending 5 hours per week on special projects and in meetings. Candidates should have oral communication skills, plan to pursue career in field, self-motivation, strong interpersonal skills, strong leadership ability. Duration is 4–9 months. $500 per month. Open to recent high school graduates, college freshmen, college sophomores, college juniors, college seniors, recent college graduates, graduate students, law students, career changers, individuals reentering the workforce. International applications accepted.

Benefits Formal training, free housing, health insurance, job counseling, names of contacts, opportunity to attend seminars/ workshops, willing to complete paperwork for educational credit, willing to provide letters of recommendation, reimbursement for mileage, unlimited farm grown food.

Contact Write, call, or e-mail Internship Coordinator. Phone: 650-949-8643. E-mail: hveep@earthlink.net. Telephone interview required. Applicants must submit a formal organization application, cover letter, resume. Application deadline: April 12 for fall, November 3 for winter/spring. World Wide Web: http://www.home.earthlink.net/~hveep.

HIGHER EDUCATION CONSORTIUM FOR URBAN AFFAIRS, INC.
Mail 36, 1536 Hewitt Avenue
St. Paul, Minnesota 55104-1284

General Information Interdisciplinary college-level study programs in U.S. and abroad, focussed on strategies to address social inequality, incorporating internships, field projects, and independent research. Established in 1971. Number of employees: 6. Number of internship applications received each year: 70.

Internships Available ▶ *25 City Arts interns:* responsibilities include working in one of many Minneapolis-St. Paul arts-related projects combined with seminars that explore the connections between the arts, cultural expression, social change, and the impact of class, race, and gender. Placement based on intern's interests. Candidates should have ability to work with others, analytical skills, oral communication skills, personal interest in the field, self-motivation, written communication skills. Duration is February to May. Position available as unpaid or paid. ▶ *25 Metro Urban Studies Term (MUST) interns:* responsibilities include working in one of many Minneapolis-St.Paul public, nonprofit, or community agencies, combined with seminars that examine issues of social inequality in the urban environment and strategies for change. Placement based on intern's interests. Candidates should have ability to work with others, analytical skills, oral communication skills, personal interest in the field, self-motivation, written communication skills. Duration is September to December. Position available as unpaid or paid. ▶ *15 community interns in Latin America:* responsibilities include working in one of many community agencies based in Quito, Ecuador, combined with seminar and independent project, all focussing on community participation for social change. Placement based on intern's interests. Candidates should have ability to work independently, personal interest in the field, self-motivation, strong interpersonal skills, two years college-level Spanish, ability to speak and comprehend Spanish with confidence. Duration is February to May. Unpaid. Open to college sophomores, college juniors, college seniors. International applications accepted.

Benefits Opportunity to attend seminars/workshops, willing to complete paperwork for educational credit, willing to provide letters of recommendation, full semester of academic credit.

International Internships Available in Quito, Ecuador.

Contact Write, call, fax, or e-mail Ms. Rebecca Rassier, Director of Student Services, Mail 36, 1536 Hewitt Avenue, St. Paul, Minnesota 55104-1284. Phone: 651-646-8832. Fax: 651-659-9421. E-mail: info@hecua.org. Applicants must submit a formal organization application, resume, academic transcripts, two personal references. Application deadline: April 15 for Metro Urban Studies Term, November 1 for community internships in Latin America, December 1 for City Arts. Fees: $75. World Wide Web: http://www.hecua.org.

HORIZONS FOR YOUTH
121 Lakeview Street
Sharon, Massachusetts 02067

General Information Residential environmental education center that works with children. Established in 1938. Number of employees: 20. Number of internship applications received each year: 100.

Internships Available ▶ *1–3 instructors:* responsibilities include developing and teaching outdoor activities related to ecology, environmental science, and group dynamics. Candidates should have ability to work with others, oral communication skills, personal interest in the field, self-motivation, previous work with children. Duration is 12–17 weeks. $180 per week. Open to college sophomores, college juniors, college seniors, recent college graduates, graduate students, law students, career changers. International applications accepted.

Benefits Free housing, free meals, on-the-job training, opportunity to attend seminars/workshops, willing to act as a professional reference, willing to complete paperwork for educational credit, willing to provide letters of recommendation.

Horizons for Youth (continued)

Contact Write, call, fax, or e-mail Mr. Michael Dattilio, Program Director. Phone: 781-828-7550. Fax: 781-784-1287. E-mail: outdoors@horizons.tiac.net. In-person interview recommended. Applicants must submit a formal organization application, cover letter, resume, 3 references. Applications are accepted continuously. World Wide Web: http://www.hfy.org.

THE HOSPITALITY MANAGEMENT TRAINING INSTITUTE
760 Market Street, Suite 1009
San Francisco, California 94102

General Information Hotel/restaurant management college teaching certified management classes with diploma programs, internships, and job placement services worldwide. Established in 1991. Number of employees: 14. Affiliate of American Hotel and Motel Association, Washington, District of Columbia. Number of internship applications received each year: 5.

Internships Available ▶ *2 marketing interns:* responsibilities include placing international phone calls, creating marketing reports, and assisting with update of business plan. Candidates should have college degree in related field, computer skills, bilingual ability. Duration is flexible. Unpaid. Open to recent college graduates, graduate students. International applications accepted.

Benefits Formal training, job counseling, names of contacts, on-the-job training, possible full-time employment, willing to complete paperwork for educational credit, willing to provide letters of recommendation.

International Internships Available in Australia; Paris, France; Tokyo, Japan; London, United Kingdom.

Contact Write or fax Sherris Goodwin, Executive Director. Fax: 415-677-9810. No phone calls. In-person interview recommended. Applicants must submit a formal organization application, cover letter, resume, academic transcripts, three personal references, two letters of recommendation, three letters of recommendation. Applications are accepted continuously.

IACOCCA INSTITUTE, GLOBAL VILLAGE FOR FUTURE LEADERS OF BUSINESS & INDUSTRY
111 Research Drive
Bethlehem, Pennsylvania 18015

General Information Institution of higher learning. Established in 1988. Number of employees: 56. Division of Lehigh University, Bethlehem, Pennsylvania. Number of internship applications received each year: 200.

Internships Available ▶ *Global Village Iacocca interns:* responsibilities include attending all lectures/seminars and other scheduled learning activities, sharing information about your home culture and history with other interns, hosting executive visitors, and producing results on assigned projects. Candidates should have oral communication skills, self-motivation, strong interpersonal skills, strong leadership ability, well-developed personal value system. Duration is 6 weeks (June 27 to August 8). Unpaid. Open to college freshmen, college sophomores, college juniors, college seniors, recent college graduates, graduate students, law students, career changers, young entrepreneurs, family-owned business members, corporate new-hires. International applications accepted.

Benefits Formal training, housing at a cost, job counseling, meals at a cost, names of contacts, on-the-job training, opportunity to attend seminars/workshops, willing to act as a professional reference, willing to complete paperwork for educational credit, willing to provide letters of recommendation.

Contact Write, call, fax, or e-mail M. Frances Schurtz-Leon, Candidate Manager. Phone: 610-758-6887. Fax: 610-758-6550. E-mail: mfs2@lehigh.edu or mfrances@epix.net. Applicants must submit a formal organization application, cover letter, academic transcripts, two letters of recommendation. Applications are accepted continuously. Fees: $50. World Wide Web: http://www.lehigh.edu/~village.

INNER QUEST, INC.
34752 Charles Town Pike
Purcellville, Virginia 20132

General Information Outdoor education organization teaching personal growth and skill development through outdoor adventure activities such as rock climbing, caving, canoeing, kayaking, and challenge courses. Established in 1979. Number of employees: 20. Number of internship applications received each year: 100.

Internships Available ▶ *10 apprentice instructors:* responsibilities include teaching climbing, caving, canoeing, kayaking, and challenge courses. Candidates should have ability to work with others, oral communication skills, strong leadership ability. Duration is 12 weeks. $950 per duration of internship. Open to individuals 18 or older.

Benefits Formal training, possible full-time employment, willing to complete paperwork for educational credit, willing to provide letters of recommendation.

Contact Write, call, fax, or e-mail Sara Smith, Assistant Director. Phone: 540-668-6699. Fax: 540-668-6253. E-mail: rsmith_innerquest@compuserve.com. In-person interview recommended. Applicants must submit a formal organization application, cover letter, resume, three personal references. Applications are accepted continuously.

THE INSTITUTE FOR CENTRAL AMERICAN DEVELOPMENT STUDIES (ICADS)
Department 826, PO Box 025216
Miami, Florida 33102-5216

General Information Study abroad program and international educational institute offering internships and Spanish immersion in Costa Rica, Nicaragua, and Belize. Established in 1986. Number of employees: 23. Number of internship applications received each year: 75.

Internships Available ▶ *15 ICADS summer internship program interns:* responsibilities include acquiring practical field experience in Costa Rica, working on environmental and social justice issues. Candidates should have ability to work independently, personal interest in the field, self-motivation, strong interpersonal skills, strong leadership ability. Duration is 10 weeks. Open to high school seniors, recent high school graduates, college freshmen, college sophomores, college juniors, college seniors, recent college graduates, graduate students, law students, career changers, individuals who want institutional support, but do not require academic credit. ▶ *12 field course in resource management and sustainable development interns:* responsibilities include travel and research in three different ecological zones within Costa Rica. Candidates should have ability to work independently, ability to work with others, personal interest in the field, self-motivation, strong interpersonal skills, strong leadership ability, background/study in either social sciences or environmental subjects. Duration is 3½ month (1 semester). Open to recent high school graduates, college freshmen, college sophomores, college juniors, college seniors, recent college graduates, graduate students. ▶ *25 semester internship and research program interns:* responsibilities include participating in a classroom and a field internship component. (Internships focused on social justice issues can be done in Costa Rica, Nicaragua, or Belize). Candidates should have ability to work independently, personal interest in the field, self-motivation, strong interpersonal skills, strong leadership ability. Duration is 3½ months (1 semester). Open to recent high school graduates, college freshmen, college sophomores, college juniors, college seniors, recent college graduates, graduate students. All positions are unpaid. International applications accepted.

Benefits On-the-job training, opportunity to attend seminars/workshops, willing to act as a professional reference, willing to complete paperwork for educational credit, willing to provide letters of recommendation.

International Internships Available in Belize; Costa Rica; Nicaragua.

Contact Write, call, fax, or e-mail ICADS, Department 826, PO Box 025216, Miami, Florida 33102-5216. Phone: 506-225-0508. Fax: 506-234-1337. E-mail: icads@netbox.com. Applicants must submit a formal organization application, academic transcripts, two letters of recommendation, writing samples (short essays). Application deadline: April 1 for fall semester-long programs, May 1 for summer programs, November 1 for spring semester-long programs. World Wide Web: http://www.icadscr.com.

THE INSTITUTE FOR EARTH EDUCATION
Cedar Cove
Greenville, West Virginia 24945

General Information Designer of educational programs that will help people increase their understanding of, appreciation for, and harmony with the earth's natural systems and communities. Established in 1974. Number of employees: 3. Number of internship applications received each year: 30.
Internships Available ▶ *1–6 earth education interns:* responsibilities include assisting with Earth Education study and tutorials, the living practicum, and development and maintenance of the center; helping with food production and preservation; and assisting in the office. Candidates should have oral communication skills, plan to pursue career in field, self-motivation, strong interpersonal skills, written communication skills, willingness to work hard and follow instructions when needed. ▶ *1 landcare coordinator:* responsibilities include assisting in master planning, housing rehabilitation, trail design, and establishing teepee and treehouse villages; developing wild cave tours; some basic maintenance. Candidates should have ability to work independently, knowledge of field, oral communication skills, personal interest in the field, self-motivation, strong interpersonal skills. ▶ *2–4 organic gardeners:* responsibilities include planning, sowing, harvesting, and preserving organic produce. Candidates should have ability to work independently, ability to work with others, knowledge of field, oral communication skills, personal interest in the field, self-motivation. Duration for all positions is 2–12 months. All positions are unpaid. Open to recent high school graduates, college freshmen, college sophomores, college juniors, college seniors, recent college graduates, graduate students, career changers, individuals reentering the workforce. International applications accepted.
Benefits Formal training, free housing, free meals, job counseling, names of contacts, on-the-job training, opportunity to attend seminars/workshops, willing to act as a professional reference, willing to complete paperwork for educational credit, willing to provide letters of recommendation.
Contact Write, call, fax, or e-mail Internship Coordinator. Phone: 304-832-6404. Fax: 304-832-6077. E-mail: iee1@aol.com. Telephone interview required. Applicants must submit a formal organization application, resume, letter of recommendation. Applications are accepted continuously. World Wide Web: http://www.eartheducation.org.

THE INSTITUTE FOR EXPERIENTIAL LEARNING
1901 Pennsylvania Avenue, NW, Suite 707
Washington, District of Columbia 20006

General Information Institute that works to advance the theory of experiential education through internship programs for graduate and undergraduate students. Established in 1990. Number of employees: 6. Number of internship applications received each year: 400.
Internships Available ▶ *80–100 IEL interns:* responsibilities include participating fully in office life by attending meetings and special events, performing research, writing reports, and preparing briefings. Candidates should have ability to work independently, analytical skills, knowledge of field, office skills, oral communication skills, organizational skills, personal interest in the field, research skills, self-motivation, strong interpersonal skills, strong leadership ability, writing skills. Duration is 10-15 weeks, 4 days per week. Position available as unpaid or at $300–$1,500 per month. Open to college juniors, college seniors, recent college graduates, graduate students, law students, career changers. International applications accepted.
Benefits Formal training, housing at a cost, job counseling, names of contacts, opportunity to attend seminars/workshops, possible full-time employment, willing to act as a professional

reference, willing to complete paperwork for educational credit, willing to provide letters of recommendation, career counseling and professional development.
Contact Write, call, fax, or e-mail Jerrod Wheeler, Program Coordinator, 1901 Pennsylvania Avenue, NW, Suite 707, Washington, District of Columbia 20006. Phone: 202-435-0770. Fax: 202-833-8581. E-mail: info@ielnet.org. Applicants must submit a formal organization application, academic transcripts, three letters of recommendation. Application deadline: April 2 for summer, May 4 for fall, November 24 for spring. Fees: $40. World Wide Web: http://www.ielnet.org.

INSTITUTE FOR INTERNATIONAL COOPERATION AND DEVELOPMENT
PO Box 520
Williamstown, Massachusetts 01267

General Information Nonprofit organization training volunteers for work in Africa and Latin America. The work is carried out with people from local communities within fields of education, health, and small-scale construction. Established in 1987. Number of employees: 5. Number of internship applications received each year: 300.
Internships Available ▶ *10–15 Zambia/India interns:* responsibilities include community work within health, environment, HIV prevention, school education, and preschools. Candidates should have ability to work with others, personal interest in the field, self-motivation. Duration is 12 months. Open to individuals over 18 years. ▶ *10–15 volunteers in Angola:* responsibilities include preventative health care and teaching in schools, and community environmental projects. Candidates should have ability to work with others, personal interest in the field, self-motivation. Duration is 12 months. Open to individuals over 18 year old. ▶ *10–15 volunteers in Brazil:* responsibilities include helping in community construction, collecting information from local people, and working with street children. Duration is 6 months. Open to individuals over 18 years old. ▶ *10–15 volunteers in Mozambique:* responsibilities include teaching in schools for street kids and in vocational schools, teacher training, and village health campaigns. Candidates should have ability to work with others, personal interest in the field, self-motivation. Duration is 18 months. Open to individuals over 18 years old. ▶ *10–15 volunteers in Nicaragua:* responsibilities include helping in construction of a school and a water supply facility, assisting in a preschool, collecting information from the country and the region. Candidates should have ability to work with others, personal interest in the field, self-motivation. Duration is 11 months. Open to individuals over 18 year old. ▶ *10–15 volunteers in Zimbabwe:* responsibilities include working with families in rural villages to provide health care, assisting small-scale farmers in improving food production, and HIV prevention. Candidates should have ability to work with others, personal interest in the field, self-motivation, strong leadership ability. Duration is 12 months. Open to individuals over 18 years old. All positions are unpaid. International applications accepted.
Benefits Job counseling, possible full-time employment, housing, meals, and education are provided with tuition.
Contact Write, call, fax, or e-mail Uli Stosch, Director. Phone: 413-458-9828. Fax: 413-458-3323. E-mail: iicdinfo@berkshire.net. In-person interview recommended. Application deadline: February 1 for spring, August 1 for fall. Fees: $15. World Wide Web: http://www.iicd-volunteer.org.

INSTITUTE FOR LEADERSHIP DEVELOPMENT
275 York Lanes, York University, 4700 Keele Street
Toronto, Ontario M3J 1P3 Canada

General Information United Nations Global Partnership Programme that builds leadership skills in young professionals and entrepreneurs in Canada and around the world through skills enhancement programmes, distance learning and work placements. Established in 1995. Number of employees: 6. Unit of United Nations, New York, New York. Number of internship applications received each year: 700.

Institute for Leadership Development (continued)

Internships Available ▶ *Interns:* responsibilities include a variety of assignments with UN agencies, international institutions, and private sector organizations. Candidates should have ability to work with others, college degree in related field, computer skills, plan to pursue career in field, strong leadership ability, second language skills often required. Duration is 6 to 10 months on average. $700–$1,400 per month. Open to those with a graduate degree or equivalent.

Benefits Health insurance, possible full-time employment, willing to act as a professional reference, willing to provide letters of recommendation, job search support, pre-placement training, and housing at a cost/free housing (depending on placement).

International Internships Available.

Contact Write, call, fax, or e-mail Laura Edgar, Programmes Manager, 275 York Lanes, York University, 4700 Keele Street, Toronto, Ontario M3J 1P3 Canada. Phone: 416-736-2100 Ext. 88704. Fax: 416-736-5693. E-mail: unforum@yorku.ca. In-person interview recommended. Applicants must submit a resume, two letters of recommendation, formal application (must be submitted by mail or courier; faxes and e-mails are not acceptable). Application deadline: May 31 for fall. World Wide Web: http://www.yorku.ca/org/ild.

THE INSTITUTE FOR THE ACADEMIC ADVANCEMENT OF YOUTH/ THE JOHNS HOPKINS UNIVERSITY
3400 North Charles Street
Baltimore, Maryland 21218

General Information Institute that provides academically talented pre-college students the opportunity to take rigorous courses in mathematics, science, computer science, humanities, and writing at college campuses in the United States. Established in 1980. Number of employees: 150. Unit of Johns Hopkins University, Baltimore, Maryland. Number of internship applications received each year: 2,500.

Internships Available ▶ *15 health assistants:* responsibilities include overseeing medication and medical appointments for live-in, pre-college students; contacting parents when necessary, completing reports. Candidates should have oral communication skills, personal interest in the field, self-motivation, strong interpersonal skills, written communication skills. $2000 per 6-week internship. Open to college juniors, college seniors, recent college graduates, graduate students, medical or pre-med students. ▶ *15 office managers:* responsibilities include managing an office, overseeing petty cash account, and supervising office staff at a fast-paced, live-in camp for gifted pre-college students. Candidates should have computer skills, experience in the field, office skills, organizational skills, strong interpersonal skills, strong leadership ability. $3200 per 7-week internship. Open to college juniors, college seniors, recent college graduates, graduate students, business students. ▶ *400 resident assistants:* responsibilities include caring for the needs of live-in, pre-college students, sponsoring and leading daily activities. Candidates should have ability to work with others, oral communication skills, self-motivation, strong interpersonal skills, strong leadership ability. $1800 per 6-week internship. Open to college freshmen, college sophomores, college juniors, college seniors, recent college graduates. ▶ *35 residential program assistants:* responsibilities include answering phones, covering office, purchasing supplies, and conducting recreational activities at a residential camp for gifted pre-college students. Candidates should have computer skills, office skills, oral communication skills, self-motivation, strong interpersonal skills, written communication skills. $1800 per 6-week internship. Open to college juniors, college seniors, recent college graduates, age 21 and over preferred in order to drive rental vehicles. ▶ *400 teaching assistants/laboratory assistants:* responsibilities include supporting instructor with clerical work for the class, tutoring the students, proctoring study hall, and teaching some lessons. Candidates should have college courses in field, oral communication skills, personal interest in the field, strong interpersonal skills, strong leadership ability, written communication skills. $1600 per 6-week internship for teaching assistants; $1800 per 6-week internship for laboratory assistants. Open to college freshmen, college sophomores, college juniors, college seniors, recent college graduates, graduate students, law students. Duration for all positions is late June through early August. International applications accepted.

Benefits Formal training, free housing, free meals, job counseling, names of contacts, on-the-job training, opportunity to attend seminars/workshops, possible full-time employment, willing to act as a professional reference, willing to complete paperwork for educational credit, willing to provide letters of recommendation.

Contact Write, call, fax, or e-mail Summer Employment Opportunities. Phone: 410-516-0053. Fax: 410-516-0093. E-mail: academic@jhunix.hcf.jhu.edu. Telephone interview required. Applicants must submit a formal organization application, cover letter, resume, academic transcripts, three letters of recommendation. Application deadline: January 31 for summer. World Wide Web: http://www.jhu.edu/~gifted/acadprog/jobs.html.

INSTITUTE OF EUROPEAN STUDIES/INSTITUTE OF ASIAN STUDIES
223 West Ohio Street
Chicago, Illinois 60610

General Information Nonprofit organization that has been providing quality study abroad programs since 1950. IES organizes internships for credit as an important part of cultural learning within its academic program. Established in 1950. Number of employees: 37. Number of internship applications received each year: 500.

Internships Available ▶ *London summer interns:* responsibilities include working in government agencies/political parties, Parliament, multinational corporations/British companies, and museums/art galleries. Students also participate in a corresponding academic seminar for a total of 6 credits. Candidates should have solid academic credentials relating to studies or experience in government, business, or the arts. Duration is 6–7 weeks. Unpaid. Open to college juniors, college seniors, graduate students. ▶ *Interns (abroad):* responsibilities include working in government agencies/political parties, business and social services, the arts/museums/theaters, communications/publishing, education/schools, and fashion design in Adelaide, Beijing, Berlin, Freiburg, La Plata, London, Madrid, Milan, Nantes, Paris, Salamanca, Tokyo, and Vienna (Note: not all types available at all locations). Candidates should have minimum GPA of 3.0, proficiency in native language of country of placement. Duration is one semester or full academic year. Unpaid. Open to college sophomores, college juniors, college seniors, graduate students. ▶ *2–3 marketing interns:* responsibilities include working with Vice President of Marketing and Recruitment to review ongoing research projects, developing processes and designs for approaching the marketing questions at hand, and implementing the market research projects. Candidates should have ability to work independently, ability to work with others, analytical skills, computer skills, organizational skills, personal interest in the field, strong critical thinking skills. Duration is 2–3 months. $1,000—$1,500 stipend for full-time interns; prorated share for part-time interns. Open to college sophomores, college juniors, college seniors, recent college graduates. International applications accepted.

Benefits Health insurance, opportunity to attend seminars/workshops, willing to complete paperwork for educational credit, academic credit, housing included in program cost.

International Internships Available in La Plata, Argentina; Adelaide and Canberra, Australia; Vienna, Austria; Beijing, China; Dijon, Nantes, and Paris, France; Berlin and Frieburg, Germany; Milan, Italy; Tokyo, Japan; Madrid and Salamanca, Spain; London, United Kingdom.

Contact Write, call, fax, or e-mail International Education Representative. Phone: 312-944-1750. Fax: 312-944-1448. E-mail: info@iesabroad.org. In-person interview required. Applicants must submit a formal organization application, cover letter, resume, academic transcripts, two letters of recommendation, must first be admitted to academic program; program fee of $7,900—$10,500 for interns abroad upon acceptance, program fee of $3,200 for London summer interns upon acceptance. Application deadline: March 1 for summer (London), May 1 for fall/full year, November 1 for spring. Fees: $25. World Wide Web: http://www.iesabroad.org.

INTERLOCKEN
RFD 2, Box 165
Hillsboro Upper Village, New Hampshire 03244

General Information   Experiential learning center that offers educational summer adventures for young people ages 9-18, an international residential summer camp in New Hampshire, and travel programs in the U.S. and abroad. Established in 1961. Number of employees: 100. Number of internship applications received each year: 200.
Internships Available   ▶ *25–30 camp counselors:* responsibilities include teaching specialty areas and being responsible for living units. Candidates should have self-motivation, strong interpersonal skills, skills for teaching in particular area and experience working with children. Duration is 9 weeks. $1200 to $1600 per 9 weeks. Open to college freshmen, college sophomores, college juniors, college seniors, recent college graduates, graduate students. ▶ *25–30 travel interns:* responsibilities include leading a small group travel adventure in the U.S., Europe, Latin America, Africa, Asia, or the Caribbean. Candidates should have ability to work independently, experience in the field, knowledge of field, self-motivation, strong interpersonal skills, strong leadership ability, experience working with teenagers, willingness to work 24 hours a day 7 days a week. Duration is 4–6 weeks. $1,000–$1,600 per duration of internship. Open to graduate students, minimum age of 24. International applications accepted.
Benefits   Free housing, free meals, names of contacts, willing to act as a professional reference, willing to complete paperwork for educational credit, willing to provide letters of recommendation.
Contact   Write, fax, or e-mail Ms. Judi Wisch, Staffing Coordinator. Fax: 603-478-5260. E-mail: judi@interlocken.org. In-person interview recommended. Applicants must submit a formal organization application, cover letter, resume, three letters of recommendation. Applications are accepted continuously. World Wide Web: http://www.interlocken.org.

INTERNATIONAL FIELD STUDIES
709 College Avenue
Columbus, Ohio 43209

General Information   Nonprofit organization that provides logistical support to get students and educators into the marine biology field. Two programs are offered: marine biology field station in Andros Island, Bahamas, and sailing programs in the northern and central Bahamas. Established in 1970. Number of employees: 4. Number of internship applications received each year: 40.
Internships Available   ▶ *1–3 first-mates:* responsibilities include supporting crew on sailing program. Candidates should have analytical skills, experience in the field, oral communication skills, organizational skills, personal interest in the field, self-motivation, strong interpersonal skills, strong leadership ability. ▶ *1–3 staff interns:* responsibilities include supporting staff at field station. Candidates should have college courses in field, experience in the field, oral communication skills, personal interest in the field, research skills, self-motivation, strong interpersonal skills, mechanical abilities desirable. Duration for all positions is 1–2 years. All positions paid. Open to recent college graduates. International applications accepted.
Benefits   Free meals, opportunity to attend seminars/workshops, possible full-time employment, willing to complete paperwork for educational credit, stipend.
Contact   Write, call, fax, or e-mail Jeffrey Michael, Human Resources Director. Phone: 800-962-3805. Fax: 614-235-9744. E-mail: ifs@infinet.com. In-person interview required. Applicants must submit a cover letter, resume. Applications are accepted continuously. Fees: $495. World Wide Web: http://www.intlfieldstudies.com.

THE INTERNATIONAL PARTNERSHIP FOR SERVICE-LEARNING
815 Second Avenue, Suite 315
New York, New York 10017

General Information   Organization that administers international graduate and undergraduate study-abroad programs, combining academic study with service learning/hands-on community service. Established in 1982. Number of employees: 8. Number of internship applications received each year: 150.
Internships Available   ▶ *100–200 student program interns:* responsibilities include providing service to communities in need, teaching/tutoring at all levels (preschool–adult), providing rehabilitation for mentally or physically handicapped people, or assisting with health care, counseling, recreation, and community development. Candidates should have oral communication skills, personal interest in the field, strong interpersonal skills, written communication skills, minimum score of 550 on the TOEFL (non-native English speakers). Duration is variable. Unpaid. Open to recent high school graduates, college freshmen, college sophomores, college juniors, college seniors, recent college graduates, graduate students, career changers, individuals reentering the workforce. International applications accepted.
Benefits   Housing at a cost, meals at a cost, on-the-job training, opportunity to attend seminars/workshops, willing to act as a professional reference, willing to complete paperwork for educational credit, willing to provide letters of recommendation, academic study and credit.
International Internships   Available in Prague, Czech Republic; Guayaquil and Quito, Ecuador; Montpellier, France; Calcutta, India; Beer-Shera, Israel; Kingston, Jamaica; Guadalajara, Mexico; Manila, Philippines; London and Glasgow, United Kingdom.
Contact   Write, call, fax, or e-mail Dr. Howard A. Berry, President. Phone: 212-986-0989. Fax: 212-986-5039. E-mail: pslny@aol.com. Applicants must submit a formal organization application, academic transcripts, two letters of recommendation, $250 deposit as part of program fees. Application deadline: April 15 for summer, July 15 for fall, November 15 for spring. World Wide Web: http://www.studyabroad.com.

INTERNSHIPS IN FRANCOPHONE EUROPE
26 Rue Cmdt. Mouchette J-108
75014 Paris France

General Information   Semester-long academic program that includes 12 weeks full-time professional experience in French public life, preceded by 5 weeks of intensive preparation. Established in 1988. Number of employees: 4.
Internships Available   ▶ *5–10 interns:* responsibilities include working in various institutions in the public sector and nongovernmental organizations. Candidates should have ability to work independently, ability to work with others, analytical skills, self-motivation, adequate command of French. Duration is 12–17 weeks. Unpaid. Open to college sophomores, college juniors, college seniors, recent college graduates, graduate students. International applications accepted.
Benefits   Formal training, job counseling, opportunity to attend seminars/workshops, tuition assistance, willing to complete paperwork for educational credit, willing to provide letters of recommendation, faculty advising throughout the internship.
Contact   Write, call, fax, or e-mail Timothy Carlson. Phone: 33-1-43-21-78-07. Fax: 33-1-42-79-94-13. E-mail: ifeparis@worldnet.fr. Applicants must submit a formal organization application, resume, academic transcripts, writing sample, two letters of recommendation, other materials specified on Web site. Application deadline: June 1 for fall, November 1 for spring. Fees: $5,950. World Wide Web: http://www.ifeparis.org.

JOHN C. CAMPBELL FOLK SCHOOL
One Folk School Road
Brasstown, North Carolina 28902

General Information   School with one-week sessions throughout the year, teaching crafts; wood, metal, and fiber painting; song/

John C. Campbell Folk School (continued)
dance and musical intruments. Established in 1925. Number of employees: 35. Number of internship applications received each year: 30.
Internships Available ▶ *3–8 work/study interns.* Candidates should have ability to work independently, self-motivation, strong interpersonal skills. Duration is 6–12 weeks. Unpaid. Open to recent high school graduates, college freshmen, college sophomores, college juniors, college seniors, recent college graduates, graduate students, law students, law school graduates, career changers, individuals reentering the workforce.
Benefits Free housing, free meals.
Contact Write or call Hanne Dalsemer, Registrar, 1 Folk School Road, Brasstown, North Carolina 28902. Phone: 828-837-2775. Applicants must submit two personal references, personal statement (1-2 pages). Applications are accepted continuously. Fees: $35. World Wide Web: http://www.folkschool.com.

JOY OUTDOOR EDUCATION CENTER
PO Box 157
Clarksville, Ohio 45113

General Information Private nonprofit organization dedicated to providing quality educational programs for individuals of all ages. Established in 1938. Number of employees: 25. Number of internship applications received each year: 65.
Internships Available ▶ *3–5 experiential educators:* responsibilities include teaching outdoor classes in environment, cultural history, and adventure and supervising the dining hall. Candidates should have knowledge of field, oral communication skills, self-motivation, strong interpersonal skills, strong leadership ability. Duration is September–June; 45-50 hours per week (2 evenings required weekly). $170 per week. Open to college freshmen, college sophomores, college juniors, college seniors, recent college graduates, graduate students, career changers. International applications accepted.
Benefits Formal training, free housing, free meals, names of contacts, opportunity to attend seminars/workshops, possible full-time employment, willing to complete paperwork for educational credit, willing to provide letters of recommendation.
Contact Write, call, fax, or e-mail Ms. Mary Pat Bourne, Director of Outdoor School Program. Phone: 800-300-7094 Ext. 238. Fax: 937-289-3179. E-mail: osp@in-touch.net. In-person interview recommended. Applicants must submit a formal organization application, cover letter, resume, 3-5 personal references. Applications are accepted continuously.

JUILLIARD SCHOOL
60 Lincoln Center Plaza
New York, New York 10023-6590

General Information Specialized professional school for the performing arts. Established in 1905. Number of employees: 550. Number of internship applications received each year: 200.
Internships Available ▶ *4 costume shop interns:* responsibilities include constructing costumes, dyeing, painting, and performing alterations and repairs. Candidates should have ability to work with others, knowledge of field, plan to pursue career in field, self-motivation, sewing experience. Duration is September to May. Open to recent high school graduates, college freshmen, college sophomores, college juniors, college seniors, recent college graduates, graduate students, career changers. ▶ *1 drama division intern:* responsibilities include assisting Manager/Auditions Coordinator in daily administrative and production operations. Candidates should have ability to work independently, computer skills, office skills, oral communication skills, organizational skills, self-motivation, strong interpersonal skills, written communication skills. Duration is September to May. Open to recent high school graduates, college freshmen, college sophomores, college juniors, college seniors, recent college graduates, graduate students, career changers. ▶ *2 electrics interns:* responsibilities include reading light plots and assisting master electricians with hanging, focusing, and maintaining equipment. Candidates should have ability to work with others, knowledge of field, plan to pursue career in field, self-motivation. Duration is September

to May. Open to recent high school graduates, college freshmen, college sophomores, college juniors, college seniors, recent college graduates, graduate students, career changers. ▶ *1 facilities management intern:* responsibilities include assisting the Director of Facilities and Engineering. Candidates should have ability to work independently, computer skills, oral communication skills, organizational skills, plan to pursue career in field, self-motivation, strong interpersonal skills, written communication skills. Duration is September to May. Open to college freshmen, college sophomores, college juniors, college seniors, recent college graduates, graduate students, career changers, individuals reentering the workforce. ▶ *1 intern program intern:* responsibilities include assisting Director with all aspects of managing the program and coordinating the master calendar. Candidates should have ability to work independently, computer skills, oral communication skills, organizational skills, self-motivation, strong interpersonal skills, written communication skills. Duration is September to May. Open to college freshmen, college sophomores, college juniors, college seniors, recent college graduates, graduate students, career changers, individuals reentering the workforce. ▶ *1 production assistant:* responsibilities include working with resident production stage managers on various productions and special events. Candidates should have ability to work independently, computer skills, oral communication skills, organizational skills, self-motivation, strong interpersonal skills. Open to college freshmen, college sophomores, college juniors, college seniors, recent college graduates, graduate students, career changers, individuals reentering the workforce. ▶ *2 props interns:* responsibilities include reviewing script for props breakdown; researching, designing, and constructing prop designs; and running crew assignments. Candidates should have ability to work with others, knowledge of field, plan to pursue career in field, self-motivation. Duration is September to May. Open to recent high school graduates, college freshmen, college sophomores, college juniors, college seniors, recent college graduates, graduate students, career changers. ▶ *2 scene painting interns:* responsibilities include assisting design, layout, scene painting, texturing, sculpturing, and paint shop maintenance. Candidates should have ability to work independently, ability to work with others, knowledge of field, plan to pursue career in field, self-motivation. Duration is September to May. Open to college seniors, recent college graduates, graduate students, career changers. ▶ *1 sound intern:* responsibilities include assisting engineer in recording events, creating sound effects tracks, making repairs, videotaping drama and opera. Candidates should have ability to work independently, ability to work with others, knowledge of field, plan to pursue career in field, self-motivation. Duration is September to May. Open to recent high school graduates, college freshmen, college sophomores, college juniors, college seniors, recent college graduates, graduate students, career changers. ▶ *3 stage carpentry interns:* responsibilities include reading blueprints, specifying materials, designing layout, and constructing scenery. Candidates should have ability to work with others, knowledge of field, plan to pursue career in field, self-motivation, basic carpentry skills. Duration is September to May. Open to recent high school graduates, college freshmen, college sophomores, college juniors, college seniors, recent college graduates, graduate students, career changers. ▶ *6 stage management interns:* responsibilities include assisting production stage managers on opera, drama, and dance productions. Candidates should have ability to work independently, knowledge of field, oral communication skills, plan to pursue career in field, self-motivation, strong interpersonal skills, written communication skills. Duration is September to May. Open to college sophomores, college juniors, college seniors, recent college graduates, graduate students. ▶ *1 vocal arts interns:* responsibilities include assisting the administrators of this division who manage the daily and long-term planning of opera productions, master classes, auditions, and curriculum. Candidates should have ability to work independently, computer skills, oral communication skills, organizational skills, personal interest in the field, self-motivation, strong interpersonal skills. Duration is September to May. Open to college freshmen, college sophomores, college juniors, college seniors, recent college graduates, graduate students, career changers. All positions paid at $226 per week.

Benefits Health insurance, names of contacts, possible full-time employment, willing to complete paperwork for educational credit, willing to provide letters of recommendation.
Contact Write, call, fax, or e-mail Helen Taynton, Intern Director. Phone: 212-799-5000 Ext. 621. Fax: 212-724-0263. E-mail: htaynton@juilliard.edu. In-person interview recommended. Applicants must submit a formal organization application, resume, three letters of recommendation, 250-word statement of expectations of the internship program and how it relates to career goals. Application deadline: June 1. Fees: $15.

KINGSLEY MONTESSORI SCHOOL
30 Fairfield Street
Boston, Massachusetts 02116

General Information Small coeducational day school in an urban location serving children preschool through grade 6 using the Montessori method. Established in 1938. Number of employees: 35. Number of internship applications received each year: 5.
Internships Available ▶ *1 office assistant:* responsibilities include assisting the office manager. Candidates should have office skills, organizational skills, writing skills. Duration is flexible. ▶ *3–4 teaching assistants:* responsibilities include assisting head teacher in the preschool and elementary classroom. Duration is 1 year. Open to individuals enrolled in a Montessori program or an early childhood education program. All positions paid. International applications accepted.
Benefits Names of contacts, opportunity to attend seminars/workshops, possible full-time employment, willing to complete paperwork for educational credit, willing to provide letters of recommendation, life insurance and health benefits.
Contact Write, call, fax, or e-mail Ms. Renee DuChainey-Farkes, Head of School. Phone: 617-536-5984. Fax: 617-536-7507. E-mail: renee@kingsley.org. Applicants must submit a cover letter, resume. Applications are accepted continuously.

LATIN AMERICAN CENTER FOR EXPERIENTIAL EDUCATION
Avenida Bolivar #911, Plaza Bolivar Apto-201, Oficina #7, La Esperilla
Santo Domingo Dominican Republic

General Information Study and internship abroad program. Established in 1998. Number of employees: 3. Number of internship applications received each year: 30.
Internships Available ▶ *3–6 interns:* responsibilities include working in business, anthropology, physical therapy, occupational therapy, natural resource management, nursing, medicine, engineering, pharmacy, sustainable community development, community coordination, education, psychology, social work, or special education. Candidates should have ability to work independently, analytical skills, college degree in related field, computer skills, office skills, oral communication skills, organizational skills, personal interest in the field, plan to pursue career in field, self-motivation, strong interpersonal skills, writing skills, written communication skills, some positions require intermediate or advanced Spanish, others require beginner Spanish. Duration is 1 semester (August to December, January to April, or June to August). Position available as unpaid or at local stipend. Open to college sophomores, college juniors, college seniors, recent college graduates, graduate students, law students, career changers. International applications accepted.
Benefits Formal training, housing at a cost, meals at a cost, names of contacts, on-the-job training, opportunity to attend seminars/workshops, possible full-time employment, willing to act as a professional reference, willing to complete paperwork for educational credit, willing to provide letters of recommendation.
International Internships Available in Santo Domingo, Dominican Republic.
Contact Call, fax, or e-mail James McCoy, Co-Director. Phone: 809-541-9765. Fax: 809-541-9765. E-mail: lacee@codetel.net.do. Applicants must submit a formal organization application, resume, academic transcripts, approval of the student's study abroad advisor. Applications are accepted continuously.

LEARN WELL RESOURCES
3967 Valley Vista
Camino, California 95709

General Information Nonprofit education organization. Established in 1994. Number of employees: 4. Number of internship applications received each year: 3.
Internships Available ▶ *1–2 education program developers:* responsibilities include helping to develop online health and ethics courses. Candidates should have ability to work independently, computer skills, knowledge of field, research skills, self-motivation, writing skills. Duration is 1–2 semesters. Unpaid. Open to graduate students.
Benefits On-the-job training.
Contact Write R. Klimes, President. Applicants must submit a formal organization application, resume. Applications are accepted continuously. World Wide Web: http://www.edx.org.

LITTLE KESWICK SCHOOL, INC.
PO Box 24
Keswick, Virginia 22947

General Information Special education residential school for 30 emotionally disturbed or learning disabled boys ages 7 through 18. Established in 1963. Number of employees: 35. Number of internship applications received each year: 5.
Internships Available ▶ *1–2 interns:* responsibilities include working as a classroom, recreation, or residential aide. Candidates should have ability to work with others, experience in the field, oral communication skills, personal interest in the field, self-motivation, strong interpersonal skills. Duration is 1–2 semesters. Unpaid. Open to college seniors, recent college graduates, graduate students. International applications accepted.
Benefits Formal training, names of contacts, opportunity to attend seminars/workshops, possible full-time employment, willing to complete paperwork for educational credit, willing to provide letters of recommendation.
Contact Write, call, or fax Ms. Terry Columbus, Director. Phone: 804-295-0457. Fax: 804-977-1892. In-person interview required. Applications are accepted continuously. World Wide Web: http://www.avenue.org/lks.

THE LOWELL WHITEMAN SCHOOL
42605 RCR #36
Steamboat Springs, Colorado 80487

General Information College prep boarding and day school for grades 9-12. Established in 1957. Number of employees: 26. Number of internship applications received each year: 150.
Internships Available ▶ *3 interns:* responsibilities include dormitory supervision, activities, and teaching one class. Candidates should have ability to work independently, college degree in related field, self-motivation, strong interpersonal skills, strong leadership ability. Duration is 2 semesters beginning mid-August. $9,000 per duration of internship. Open to recent college graduates, graduate students. International applications accepted.
Benefits Free housing, free meals, health insurance, opportunity to attend seminars/workshops, possible full-time employment, willing to act as a professional reference, willing to complete paperwork for educational credit, willing to provide letters of recommendation.
Contact Write, call, fax, or e-mail Walt Daub, Headmaster. Phone: 970-879-1350. Fax: 970-879-0506. E-mail: daubw@whiteman.edu. In-person interview required. Applicants must submit a cover letter, resume, academic transcripts, three letters of recommendation. Application deadline: April 15. World Wide Web: http://www.whiteman.edu.

MANICE EDUCATION CENTER
PO Box 953
North Adams, Massachusetts 01247

General Information Environmental/wilderness education program serving economically disadvantaged New York City youth through challenging outdoor adventures. Established in

Manice Education Center (continued)

1897. Number of employees: 15. Unit of Christodora, Inc., New York, New York. Number of internship applications received each year: 25.

Internships Available ▶ *4 environmental education interns:* responsibilities include teaching ecology, wilderness, and group leadership skills; facilitating environmental debates; leading science labs and cooperative games; and being responsible for the overnight supervision of 6 students, 4 nights per week. Candidates should have knowledge of field, oral communication skills, personal interest in the field, self-motivation, strong interpersonal skills, strong leadership ability. Duration is 2 months in spring or fall. Open to college sophomores, college juniors, college seniors, recent college graduates, graduate students, career changers. ▶ *4 wilderness leadership interns:* responsibilities include co-leading wilderness expeditions; teaching low-impact wilderness travel skills, general ecology, and interpretation; facilitating environmental debates; leading science labs and cooperative games; and supervising students overnight. Candidates should have experience in the field, oral communication skills, self-motivation, strong interpersonal skills, strong leadership ability. Duration is June 15 to September 2. Open to college sophomores, college juniors, college seniors, recent college graduates, graduate students. All positions paid at $170 per week. International applications accepted.
Benefits Formal training, free housing, free meals, health insurance, job counseling, names of contacts, on-the-job training, possible full-time employment, willing to act as a professional reference, willing to complete paperwork for educational credit, willing to provide letters of recommendation, job lists provided when available, equipment discounts.
Contact Write, fax, or e-mail Mr. Brian Robinson, Director, 666 Broadway, 9th Floor, New York, New York 10012. Fax: 212-353-2052. E-mail: christodora@prodigy.net. No phone calls. In-person interview recommended. Applicants must submit a formal organization application, cover letter, resume, academic transcripts, two personal references, three letters of recommendation. Application deadline: February 1 for spring, March 1 for summer, June 1 for fall.

MANZANO DAY SCHOOL
1801 Central Avenue, NW
Albuquerque, New Mexico 87104-1197

General Information Independent elementary school. Established in 1938. Number of employees: 55. Number of internship applications received each year: 50.
Internships Available ▶ *4–5 camp interns:* responsibilities include teaching environmental subjects to first through fifth graders, developing instructional materials, participating in campfires, and doing light maintenance at camp in Jemas mountains. Duration is 1-2 months in fall. $1,200 per duration of internship. ▶ *2 environmental education interns:* responsibilities include teaching environmental subjects to pre-kindergarten through fifth graders, developing and maintaining instructional materials, participating in camp fires, and doing light maintenance at camp in Jemas mountains. Duration is 2-3 months in fall. $600 per duration of internship. International applications accepted.
Benefits Formal training, free meals, job counseling, names of contacts, possible full-time employment, travel reimbursement, willing to complete paperwork for educational credit, willing to provide letters of recommendation.
Contact Write, call, fax, or e-mail Kay Pickett, Head of School. Phone: 505-243-6659. Fax: 505-243-4711. E-mail: kp@mds.k12.nm.us. In-person interview required. Applicants must submit a cover letter, resume, three personal references, three letters of recommendation. Applications are accepted continuously. World Wide Web: http://www.mds.k12.nm.us.

MARYMOUNT STUDY ABROAD PROGRAM
Marymount College
Tarrytown, New York 10591-3796

General Information Academic program providing opportunity for undergraduate study at universities in central London combined with internships and work experience placements according to individual interests. Established in 1924. Number of employees: 3. Department of Marymount College, Tarrytown, New York. Number of internship applications received each year: 20.
Internships Available ▶ *Australian interns:* responsibilities include working within the Australian House of Parliament. Candidates should have ability to work independently, ability to work with others, college courses in field, self-motivation, written communication skills, major in political science. ▶ *London interns:* responsibilities include working in a variety of fields including fashion design, merchandising, public relations, publishing, art gallery/museums, journalism, communications, British education, or international business. Candidates should have ability to work independently, college courses in field, declared college major in field, oral communication skills, strong interpersonal skills, written communication skills. Duration for all positions is 1 semester. All positions are unpaid. Open to college juniors, college seniors. International applications accepted.
Benefits Job counseling, willing to complete paperwork for educational credit, academic study abroad opportunity.
International Internships Available in Melbourne, Australia; London, United Kingdom.
Contact Write, call, fax, or e-mail Director, Study Abroad Program. Phone: 888-662-4685. Fax: 914-631-3261. E-mail: studyab@mmc.marymt.edu. Applicants must submit a formal organization application, resume, academic transcripts, two personal references, two letters of recommendation, study abroad application. Application deadline: March 10 for Australia fall term, April 15 for London fall or full term, October 15 for spring term. Fees: $40. World Wide Web: http://www.marymt.edu/~studyab/studyab.html.

MCKEEVER ENVIRONMENTAL LEARNING CENTER
55 McKeever Lane
Sandy Lake, Pennsylvania 16145

General Information Resident environmental education center for grades k-12 that specializes in preservice and in-service teacher education. Established in 1974. Number of employees: 10. Department of Slippery Rock University of Pennsylvania, Slippery Rock, Pennsylvania. Number of internship applications received each year: 15.
Internships Available ▶ *2 co-op interns:* responsibilities include assisting in implementing special programs, supervising student teachers, providing alternate evening coverage, overseeing props and program supplies, providing on-line status with rental group activities, and assisting with office support. Candidates should have ability to work independently, oral communication skills, organizational skills, strong interpersonal skills, strong leadership ability. Duration is 12 months. $8 per hour. Open to recent college graduates. International applications accepted.
Benefits Formal training, free housing, job counseling, names of contacts, on-the-job training, opportunity to attend seminars/workshops, travel reimbursement, willing to act as a professional reference, willing to provide letters of recommendation, free meal when working with group.
Contact Write, call, fax, or e-mail Mr. Francis M. Bires, Director. Phone: 724-376-1000. Fax: 724-376-8235. E-mail: info@mckeever.org. In-person interview required. Applicants must submit a formal organization application, cover letter, resume, academic transcripts, three letters of recommendation. Applications are accepted continuously. World Wide Web: http://www.mckeever.org.

MENDOCINO WOODLANDS ENVIRONMENTAL EDUCATION PROGRAM
PO Box 267
Mendocino, California 95460

General Information A 5-day residential outdoor science school for students from grades 4–8 who take part in hands-on learning and exploration of several ecosystems, community living skills, and conservation ethics. Established in 1974. Number of employees: 22. Unit of Mendocino Woodlands Camp Association, Mendocino, California. Number of internship applications received each year: 40.

Internships Available ▶ *1–2 teachers/naturalist interns:* responsibilities include participating in staff training, assisting director with administrative duties, helping supervise counselor staff, assisting with supervision of recreation time, and assisting naturalists teaching in field. Candidates should have oral communication skills, plan to pursue career in field, self-motivation, strong interpersonal skills, strong leadership ability. Duration is 3 months (approximately). $100 per week. Open to recent high school graduates, college freshmen, college sophomores, college juniors, college seniors, recent college graduates, graduate students, career changers, individuals reentering the workforce. International applications accepted.

Benefits Formal training, free housing, free meals, names of contacts, possible full-time employment, willing to complete paperwork for educational credit, will provide a written evaluation.

Contact Write, call, fax, or e-mail Ms. Jeanne Coleman, Director. Phone: 707-937-5755. Fax: 707-937-5415. E-mail: nwca@mcn. org. In-person interview recommended. Applicants must submit a cover letter, resume. Application deadline: December 1. World Wide Web: http://www.mcn.org/1/woodlands/.

MIDDLE EARTH, INC.
299 Jacksonville Road
Warminister, Pennsylvania 18974

General Information Day treatment center and alternative high school. Established in 1973. Number of employees: 10. Number of internship applications received each year: 12.

Internships Available ▶ *3 criminal justice interns:* responsibilities include conducting informal counseling and working with probation officer. Duration is dependent on university requirements. ▶ *3 educational interns:* responsibilities include teaching in classroom setting. Duration is flexible. ▶ *3 social services interns:* responsibilities include working one-on-one with adolescents. Duration is dependent on university requirements. Candidates for all positions should have ability to work independently, oral communication skills, organizational skills, self-motivation, strong interpersonal skills. All positions are unpaid. Open to college freshmen, college sophomores, college juniors, college seniors, graduate students. International applications accepted.

Benefits Names of contacts, opportunity to attend seminars/workshops, possible full-time employment, willing to complete paperwork for educational credit, willing to provide letters of recommendation, lunch provided at no cost.

Contact Write, call, or fax Ms. Elizabeth A. Quigley, Director of Educational Programming. Phone: 215-443-0280. Fax: 215-443-0245. In-person interview recommended. Applications are accepted continuously.

MINIWANCA–AMERICAN YOUTH FOUNDATION
8845 West Garfield Road
Shelby, Michigan 49455

General Information Multi-purpose youth center on the shores of Lake Michigan offering retreat, conference, leadership development, team building, and community building services for a variety of populations. Established in 1924. Number of employees: 13. Unit of American Youth Foundation, St. Louis, Missouri. Number of internship applications received each year: 10.

Internships Available ▶ *3–6 program interns:* responsibilities include assisting in program development and implementation for a variety of populations, facilitating ropes courses and other experience-based activities, providing hospitality for retreats and conferences, assisting in support services for all programs, assisting with administration, marketing, public relations, and evaluations of all programs. Candidates should have experience working with children; CPR and first aid certification (required); lifeguard training (preferred). Duration is 1–2 semesters. $375 per month. Open to individuals at least 18 years of age. International applications accepted.

Benefits Formal training, free housing, health insurance, job counseling, names of contacts, opportunity to attend seminars/

workshops, willing to complete paperwork for educational credit, willing to provide letters of recommendation, meals (when programs are running).

Contact Write, call, fax, or e-mail Elizabeth Potter, Program Director. Phone: 616-861-2262. Fax: 616-861-5244. E-mail: wancapop@oceana.net. In-person interview recommended. Applicants must submit a formal organization application, cover letter, resume, three personal references, letter of recommendation. Applications are accepted continuously. World Wide Web: http://www.ayf.com.

MISS PORTER'S SCHOOL
60 Main Street
Farmington, Connecticut 06032

General Information Independent boarding and day school for girls grades 9-12. Established in 1843. Number of employees: 120. Number of internship applications received each year: 50.

Internships Available ▶ *3–4 teaching interns:* responsibilities include teaching 1-2 sections within discipline, acting as Assistant House Director, and coaching or advising the equivalent of two seasons of activity. Candidates should have ability to work independently, ability to work with others, college courses in field, computer skills, oral communication skills, strong interest in working with adolescents. Duration is 2 semesters. $10,000 per internship. Open to recent college graduates, graduate students. International applications accepted.

Benefits Free housing, free meals, health insurance, job counseling, names of contacts, on-the-job training, opportunity to attend seminars/workshops, possible full-time employment, travel reimbursement, willing to act as a professional reference, willing to complete paperwork for educational credit, willing to provide letters of recommendation, mentorship by teacher.

Contact Write, call, fax, or e-mail Alan Sherman, Director of the New Teacher Program. Phone: 860-409-3693. Fax: 860-409-3515. E-mail: alan_sherman@mps.pvt.k12.ct.us. In-person interview required. Applicants must submit a cover letter, resume, academic transcripts, two letters of recommendation. Applications are accepted continuously. World Wide Web: http://www.mps.pvt.k12.ct.us/.

NAFSA
1307 New York Avenue, NW, 8th Floor
Washington, District of Columbia 20005

General Information Nonprofit membership association that provides training, information, and other educational services to professionals in the field of international educational exchange. Established in 1963.

Internships Available ▶ *Interns:* responsibilities include working on a specific project in areas such as publications, conference, membership, accounting, government, human resources, and international grants program. Duration is flexible. Unpaid. Open to high school students, high school seniors, recent high school graduates, college freshmen, college sophomores, college juniors, college seniors, recent college graduates, graduate students, law students, law school graduates, career changers, individuals reentering the workforce.

Contact Write Director of Human Resources, 1307 New York Avenue, NW, 8th Floor, Washington, District of Columbia 20009-5728. Applicants must submit a cover letter, resume. Applications are accepted continuously. World Wide Web: http://www.nafsa.org.

NATIONAL COALITION OF ALTERNATIVE COMMUNITY SCHOOLS TEACHER EDUCATION PROGRAM
Upattinas Resource Center, 429 Greenridge Road
Glenmoore, Pennsylvania 19343

General Information Coalition that offers internships in alternative education in grades K-12, public and private, with the possibility of international placement. Established in 1993. Number of employees: 1. Affiliate of National Coalition of Alternative

National Coalition of Alternative Community Schools Teacher Education Program (continued)

Community Schools (NCACS), Ann Arbor, Michigan. Number of internship applications received each year: 12.

Internships Available ▶ *10 alternative/experiential teaching interns:* responsibilities include teaching at a self-chosen member school. Candidates should have ability to work independently, oral communication skills, personal interest in the field, self-motivation, strong interpersonal skills. Duration is 1 year. Position available as unpaid or at dependent upon school selected. Open to college seniors, recent college graduates, graduate students, career changers, individuals reentering the workforce. International applications accepted.

Benefits Formal training, job counseling, names of contacts, on-the-job training, opportunity to attend seminars/workshops, possible full-time employment, tuition assistance, willing to act as a professional reference, willing to complete paperwork for educational credit, willing to provide letters of recommendation, some housing depending on placement.

International Internships Available in Yokohama, Japan.

Contact Write, call, fax, or e-mail Ms. Sandra M. Hurst, Director of Teacher Education Program, Upattinas Resource Center, 429 Greenridge Road, Glenmore, Pennsylvania 19343. Phone: 610-458-5138. Fax: 610-458-8688. E-mail: upatinas@chesco.com. In-person interview recommended. Applicants must submit a formal organization application, cover letter, resume, academic transcripts, personal reference, $3000 fee for tuition upon acceptance. Applications are accepted continuously. Fees: $25.

NATIONAL FOUNDATION FOR THE IMPROVEMENT OF EDUCATION
1201 16th Street, NW, Suite 416
Washington, District of Columbia 20036-3207

General Information Education foundation concerned with improving the quality of education that comes from empowering teachers and those who support the teaching/learning process through programs including dropout prevention for at-risk youth, innovative applications of technology for restructuring, and professional development of educators. Established in 1969. Number of employees: 13. Unit of National Education Association, Washington, District of Columbia. Number of internship applications received each year: 20.

Internships Available ▶ *2 research/program interns:* responsibilities include contributing to program development and implementation through research, analysis, and synthesis of information and assisting with some fund-raising, public relations, and support work. Candidates should have ability to work with others, computer skills, office skills, personal interest in the field, research skills, writing skills. Duration is 3–4 months. Unpaid. Open to college sophomores, college juniors, college seniors, recent college graduates, graduate students. International applications accepted.

Benefits Opportunity to attend seminars/workshops, possible full-time employment, willing to provide letters of recommendation.

Contact Write, fax, or e-mail Ms. Lisa Kothari, Internship Coordinator. Fax: 202-822-7779. E-mail: lkothari@nea.org. No phone calls. Applicants must submit a cover letter, resume. Applications are accepted continuously. World Wide Web: http://www.nfie.org.

NATIONAL SCIENCE FOUNDATION
4201 Wilson Boulevard, Suite 315
Arlington, Virginia 22230

General Information Independent agency of the Federal Government established by Congress to promote and advance scientific progress in the United States by funding research and education projects in science and engineering across all disciplines. Established in 1950. Number of employees: 1,300. Number of internship applications received each year: 800.

Internships Available ▶ *Computer specialists GS-5/7:* responsibilities include performing basic analyses, design programming, and maintenance tasks; assisting with the installation or demonstration of new applications software; assisting in troubleshooting

and fact finding data processing problems; or assisting in the preparation of spreadsheets, graphs, and reports. Candidates should have ability to work independently, college degree in related field, computer skills, knowledge of field, office skills, oral communication skills, organizational skills, self-motivation, strong interpersonal skills, strong leadership ability, written communication skills. $25,088–$35,501 per year. Open to recent college graduates, graduate students. ▶ *Office automation clerks:* responsibilities include typing and word-processing, sorting and distributing mail, maintaining files, and assisting office visitors and telephone callers. Candidates should have ability to work independently, computer skills, office skills, oral communication skills, self-motivation, strong interpersonal skills. $18,422–$28,053 per year. Open to high school students, high school seniors, recent high school graduates, college freshmen, college sophomores, college juniors, college seniors, recent college graduates, graduate students, law students, career changers, individuals reentering the workforce. ▶ *Science aides/technicians GS-2/3/4:* responsibilities include performing duties such as collecting, preparing, receiving, reviewing, and verifying documents; maintaining office records; locating and compiling data or information from files and other data sources; and/or performing arithmetic and some mathematical procedures using automated data processing to support the work of the program. Candidates should have ability to work independently, computer skills, office skills, oral communication skills, organizational skills, self-motivation, strong interpersonal skills. $18,422–$28,053 per year. Open to high school students, high school seniors, recent high school graduates, college freshmen, college sophomores, college juniors, college seniors, recent college graduates, graduate students, law students, career changers, individuals reentering the workforce. ▶ *Science assistants, AD-1:* responsibilities include assisting with the technical review and evaluation of proposals; conducting analyses and preparing reports; providing factual information regarding agency objectives, policies and procedures to prospective awardees and institutional representatives; assisting with panel and advisory meetings; or developing computer programs to facilitate program activities. Candidates should have ability to work independently, analytical skills, college courses in field, computer skills, editing skills, knowledge of field, office skills, oral communication skills, organizational skills, personal interest in the field, research skills, self-motivation, strong interpersonal skills, strong leadership ability, writing skills. $22,208 per year. Duration for all positions is summer (through end of September).

Benefits On-the-job training, possible full-time employment, willing to provide letters of recommendation.

Contact Write, call, fax, or e-mail Madalyn Chisley, Personnel Assistant. Phone: 703-306-1185 Ext. 3034. Fax: 703-306-0260. E-mail: mchisley@nsf.gov. Applicants must submit a resume, academic transcripts. Application deadline: April 30 (recommended). World Wide Web: http://www.nsf.gov/oirm.

NATIONAL SOCIETY FOR EXPERIENTIAL EDUCATION
3509 Haworth Drive, Suite 207
Raleigh, North Carolina 27609-7229

General Information Nonprofit education association and resource center that supports colleges and universities, high schools, community agencies, and businesses by helping students learn through meaningful work and service experiences. Established in 1971. Number of employees: 7.

Internships Available ▶ *1 marketing intern:* responsibilities include assisting with plans for marketing publications and services. Candidates should have office skills, oral communication skills, organizational skills, self-motivation, writing skills. ▶ *1 publications intern:* responsibilities include assisting with writing and editing publications. Candidates should have ability to work with others, computer skills, editing skills, research skills, self-motivation, writing skills, written communication skills. ▶ *1 special projects intern:* responsibilities include assisting in a wide variety of duties including assisting in logistics for meetings and training institute, fund-raising, and membership services. Candidates should have ability to work independently, ability to work with

others, oral communication skills, organizational skills, self-motivation, written communication skills. Duration for all positions is flexible. All positions available as unpaid or paid. Open to college freshmen, college sophomores, college juniors, college seniors, recent college graduates, graduate students. International applications accepted.
Benefits Job counseling, names of contacts, willing to complete paperwork for educational credit, willing to provide letters of recommendation, possible membership, publications, stipend.
Contact Write, fax, or e-mail Arie Fennelly, Program Assistant. Fax: 919-787-3381. E-mail: info@nsee.org. No phone calls. In-person interview recommended. Applicants must submit a cover letter, resume, writing sample. Applications are accepted continuously. World Wide Web: http://www.nsee.org.

NEW CANAAN COUNTRY SCHOOL
PO Box 997
New Canaan, Connecticut 06840

General Information Independent elementary school enrolling 575 students in grades Pre-K through 9. Established in 1936. Number of employees: 120. Number of internship applications received each year: 200.
Internships Available ▶ *16 teaching fellowships:* responsibilities include assisting in all areas of program in a self-contained K-6 homeroom. Candidates should have oral communication skills, personal interest in the field, self-motivation, strong interpersonal skills, written communication skills. Duration is September to June. $13,500 taxable stipend. Open to college seniors, recent college graduates, graduate students, career changers. International applications accepted.
Benefits Formal training, health insurance, housing at a cost, job counseling, names of contacts, opportunity to attend seminars/workshops, possible full-time employment, tuition assistance, willing to provide letters of recommendation, possibility of pursuing master's degree at Manhattanville College.
Contact Write Ms. Dana Mallozzi, Fellowship Coordinator. In-person interview required. Applicants must submit a cover letter, resume, academic transcripts, three letters of recommendation. Application deadline: April 1. World Wide Web: http://www.nccs.pvt.k12.ct.us.

NEW CANAAN NATURE CENTER
144 Oenoke Ridge
New Canaan, Connecticut 06840

General Information Environmental education center and sanctuary dedicated to helping people of all ages understand, appreciate, and care for the natural world. Established in 1960. Number of employees: 30. Number of internship applications received each year: 150.
Internships Available ▶ *12–14 summer teachers/naturalists:* responsibilities include planning and team-teaching diverse programs that include the study of natural science, nature crafts, sensory awareness, and general environmental education in day camp setting with groups of up to 14 children (pre-K through 4th grade). Candidates should have experience in the field, oral communication skills, personal interest in the field, strong interpersonal skills. Duration is 11 weeks. Open to college freshmen, college sophomores, college juniors, college seniors, recent college graduates, graduate students, career changers, individuals reentering the workforce. ▶ *2–3 teacher/naturalist interns:* responsibilities include planning and presenting natural science programs for pre-kindergarten through middle school students, teaching selected public programs, and assisting with animal care. Candidates should have ability to work independently, college courses in field, knowledge of field, plan to pursue career in field, strong interpersonal skills. Duration is 9 months (Labor Day to Memorial Day). Open to recent college graduates, graduate students, career changers, individuals reentering the workforce. All positions paid at $220–$240 per week. International applications accepted.
Benefits Formal training, free housing, job counseling, on-the-job training, opportunity to attend seminars/workshops, pos-

sible full-time employment, willing to act as a professional reference, willing to complete paperwork for educational credit, willing to provide letters of recommendation.
Contact Write or fax Mr. Matt Black, Director of School Programs and/Summer Camp. Phone: 203-966-9577. Fax: 203-966-6536. In-person interview recommended. Applicants must submit a cover letter, resume, three personal references. Application deadline: April 1 for summer, continuous for nine-month positions.

19TH DISTRICT INTERNSHIP ASSOCIATION
PO Box 2731
York, Pennsylvania 17405

General Information Non-political, non-partisan community involvement good government initiative to provide financial sponsorship for college students from the 19th Congressional District to work in the Washington office of the District Congressman each summer. Established in 1977. Number of internship applications received each year: 30.
Internships Available ▶ *8 summer internships in Washington:* responsibilities include participating in the routine and not-so-routine duties of the congressional office; students are also given an opportunity to observe government in action and are treated as employees, not student interns. Candidates should have computer skills, office skills, oral communication skills, strong interpersonal skills, written communication skills. Duration is 2 six-week sessions from mid-May through mid-August (2 women and 2 men per each 6-week session). Unpaid. Open to undergraduate students 18 to 22 years of age, who are legal residents of the 19th Congressional District of Pennsylvania; can attend any college or university.
Benefits Free housing, opportunity to attend seminars/workshops, $200 weekly stipend for basic expenses, free shuttle service to and from Union Station (within walking distance of Congressman's office).
Contact Write or call Charles C. Flaharty, Summer Internship Chairperson, PO Box 2731, York, Pennsylvania 17405. Phone: 717-757-6468. Applicants must submit a formal organization application, in-person interview for semi-finalists. Application deadline: January 15 for summer.

NORTHFIELD MOUNT HERMON SUMMER SCHOOL
206 Main Street
Northfield, Massachusetts 01360

General Information Summer coeducational boarding school with a curriculum focusing on enrichment for junior and senior high school students; students come from all over the U.S. and the world. Established in 1961. Number of employees: 110. Number of internship applications received each year: 250.
Internships Available ▶ *35 teaching fellows:* responsibilities include assistant teaching, leading a sport and workshop, assisting with dorm supervision. Candidates should have ability to work independently, college courses in field, personal interest in the field, strong interpersonal skills. Duration is 6 weeks. $2,000 per duration of internship. Open to recent college graduates, graduate students, current college juniors and seniors. International applications accepted.
Benefits Formal training, free housing, free meals, job counseling, names of contacts, possible full-time employment, willing to complete paperwork for educational credit, willing to provide letters of recommendation.
Contact Write, call, fax, or e-mail Debra J. Frank, Associate Director. Phone: 413-498-3290. Fax: 413-498-3112. E-mail: summer_school@nmh.northfield.ma.us. Applicants must submit a formal organization application, cover letter, resume, academic transcripts, two letters of recommendation, either in-person or telephone interview. Application deadline: February 20. World Wide Web: http://www.nmh.northfield.ma.us/summer/.

PACIFIC AND ASIAN AFFAIRS COUNCIL
1633 East-West Road, Building 96-35
Honolulu, Hawaii 96848

General Information Nonprofit organization that has been teaching international studies for over 45 years. It is a member of the World Affairs Council of America and has organized forums featuring speakers such as the Dalai Lama and Bob Dole.
Internships Available ▶ *1–2 assistant program coordinators:* responsibilities include helping to plan educational programs and doing basic office duties. Duration is flexible. Unpaid. Open to college freshmen, college sophomores, college juniors, college seniors.
Contact Write, call, fax, or e-mail Truman Leung, Program Coordinator, 1633 East-West Road, Building 96-35, Honolulu, Hawaii 96848. Phone: 808-944-7784. Fax: 808-944-7785. E-mail: taac@aloha.net. Applicants must submit a cover letter, resume. Applications are accepted continuously. World Wide Web: http://www.aloha.net/~paac.

PARK SCHOOL
171 Goddard Avenue
Brookline, Massachusetts 02146

General Information Independent day school of more than 500 students from nursery through 9th grade. Established in 1888. Number of employees: 100. Number of internship applications received each year: 150.
Internships Available ▶ *8–10 teaching interns:* responsibilities include teaching full-time with a mentor teacher with classroom placements during the year and handling all aspects of teaching, coaching, and play directing. Candidates should have knowledge of field, oral communication skills, self-motivation, strong interpersonal skills, written communication skills. Duration is academic year (9 months). $10,000 per internship plus additional pay for coaching, drama, and after school program help. Open to recent college graduates, graduate students, career changers. International applications accepted.
Benefits Formal training, health insurance, job counseling, names of contacts, opportunity to attend seminars/workshops, tuition assistance, willing to complete paperwork for educational credit, willing to provide letters of recommendation.
Contact Write Ms. Linda Knight, Director of Interns. Applicants must submit a cover letter, resume, academic transcripts, three personal references, in-person interview (held February to May). Applications are accepted continuously. World Wide Web: http://www.parkschool.org.

PEAK PERFORMANCE
PO Box 1867
Big Bear Lake, California 92315-1867

General Information Company that designs and delivers experiential adventure learning for businesses, schools, churches, and families. Established in 1994. Number of employees: 33. Number of internship applications received each year: 50.
Internships Available ▶ *1–4 program specialists:* responsibilities include designing and delivering adventure education programs to varied audiences. Candidates should have ability to work with others, oral communication skills, personal interest in the field, self-motivation, strong interpersonal skills, strong leadership ability. Duration is 1 semester. Position available as unpaid or at $50 per week. Open to college juniors, college seniors, recent college graduates, graduate students, career changers, individuals reentering the workforce. International applications accepted.
Benefits Formal training, free housing, free meals, job counseling, on-the-job training, opportunity to attend seminars/workshops, willing to act as a professional reference, willing to complete paperwork for educational credit, willing to provide letters of recommendation, discounts on equipment.
Contact Write, fax, or e-mail Mark H. Rowland, President. Fax: 909-866-9004. E-mail: peak@bigbear.net. Telephone interview required. Applicants must submit a cover letter, resume, three personal references. Application deadline: October 1 for winter. World Wide Web: http://www.peaktraining.com.

THE PHILADELPHIA CENTER
121 South Broad Street, 7th Floor
Philadelphia, Pennsylvania 19107

General Information Off-campus experiential education program comprised of a full time internship with opportunities in all disciplines, academic seminars, and independent living. Established in 1967. Number of employees: 10. Affiliate of Great Lakes College Association, Inc., Ann Arbor, Michigan. Number of internship applications received each year: 180.
Internships Available ▶ *180–200 interns:* responsibilities include working in numerous fields including communications, business, education, law, government, psychology, social service, science, and arts. Duration is 1 semester. Unpaid. Open to college sophomores, college juniors, college seniors, recent college graduates, graduate students. International applications accepted.
Benefits Formal training, job counseling, names of contacts, on-the-job training, opportunity to attend seminars/workshops, willing to act as a professional reference, willing to complete paperwork for educational credit, willing to provide letters of recommendation, college credit, more than 700 placements from which to choose, program student advisors act as career and academic counselors, networking possibilities.
Contact Write, call, fax, or e-mail Marie Mercaldo, Marketing Director. Phone: 215-735-7300. Fax: 215-735-7373. E-mail: admin@philactr.edu. Applicants must submit a formal organization application, academic transcripts, two letters of recommendation, proof of eligibility for off-campus study (determined by applicant's school), $7560 tuition cost upon acceptance. Applications are accepted continuously. World Wide Web: http://www.libertynet.org/~philactr.

PHILLIPS ACADEMY
180 Main Street
Andover, Massachusetts 01810-4161

General Information Private secondary boarding and day preparatory school. Established in 1778. Number of employees: 550. Number of internship applications received each year: 350.
Internships Available ▶ *10–12 fellowships:* responsibilities include teaching two sections of a departmental offering, acting as house counselor in dormitory, and participating in athletics. Candidates should have ability to work independently, college degree in related field, declared college major in field, knowledge of field, oral communication skills, plan to pursue career in field, self-motivation, strong interpersonal skills, strong leadership ability, written communication skills. Duration is September to June. $15,000 per year. Open to college seniors, recent college graduates, graduate students, career changers. ▶ *25–30 teaching assistants:* responsibilities include assisting the teaching of two courses, running a dormitory, coaching an afternoon activity, chaperoning, and facilitating nearly every facet of boarding school life. Candidates should have oral communication skills, plan to pursue career in field, strong interpersonal skills, written communication skills. Duration is end of June to early August. $2,100 per duration of internship. Open to recent college graduates, graduate students. International applications accepted.
Benefits Free housing, free meals, health insurance, job counseling, names of contacts, on-the-job training, opportunity to attend seminars/workshops, willing to act as a professional reference, willing to provide letters of recommendation, life insurance, dental insurance.
Contact Write, call, or e-mail J. Philip Zaeder, Dean of Faculty. Phone: 978-749-4003. E-mail: ldiamondis@andover.edu. In-person interview required. Applicants must submit a formal organization application, cover letter, resume, academic transcripts, writing sample, personal reference, three letters of recommendation. Application deadline: February 16 for fellowships (September start), March 15 for teaching assistants (June start). World Wide Web: http://www.andover.edu.

PRESIDENTIAL CLASSROOM
119 Oronoco Street
Alexandria, Virginia 22314-2015

General Information Nonprofit, nonpartisan educational organization that brings high school students to Washington, D.C., for 1-week experiential government programs. Established in 1968. Number of employees: 12. Number of internship applications received each year: 200.
Internships Available ▶ *11 program interns:* responsibilities include providing administrative and logistical support. Candidates should have ability to work independently, ability to work with others, oral communication skills, organizational skills, strong interpersonal skills, strong leadership ability. Duration is 5 weeks in the summer, 9 weeks in the winter. Unpaid. Open to college sophomores, college juniors, college seniors, recent college graduates. International applications accepted.
Benefits Formal training, free housing, free meals, job counseling, names of contacts, opportunity to attend seminars/workshops, possible full-time employment, willing to act as a professional reference, willing to complete paperwork for educational credit, willing to provide letters of recommendation, stipend.
Contact Write, call, fax, or e-mail Mr. Christopher Rochette, Program Manager. Phone: 800-441-5400. Fax: 703-548-5728. E-mail: prezintern@aol.com. Telephone interview required. Applicants must submit a formal organization application, two letters of recommendation. Application deadline: April 15 for summer, December 1 for winter. World Wide Web: http://www.presidentialclassroom.org.

PROJECT USE, URBAN SUBURBAN ENVIRONMENTS
PO Box 837, 76 East Front Street
Red Bank, New Jersey 07701-0837

General Information Year-round experiential educational center for children and adults from all backgrounds offering one-to-21 day programs for schools, state agencies, service corps, youth groups, and the general public; activities include initiative games, high ropes courses, backpacking, canoeing, kayaking, and rock climbing. Established in 1970. Number of employees: 50. Number of internship applications received each year: 3.
Internships Available ▶ *1–3 field instructors:* responsibilities include preparing for, conducting, and concluding safe wilderness experiences for all courses. Candidates should have ability to work independently, oral communication skills, personal interest in the field, research skills, self-motivation, strong interpersonal skills, written communication skills, love of outdoors and related activities. Duration is 3 months. $100-$150 per week plus room and board. Open to high school seniors, recent high school graduates, college freshmen, college sophomores, college juniors, college seniors, recent college graduates, graduate students, law students, career changers, individuals reentering the workforce, must be 18 years old. International applications accepted.
Benefits Formal training, free housing, free meals, names of contacts, opportunity to attend seminars/workshops, possible full-time employment, willing to act as a professional reference, willing to complete paperwork for educational credit, willing to provide letters of recommendation.
Contact Write, call, fax, or e-mail Dominique St.-Pierre, Program Director, PO Box 837, 76 East Front Street, Red Bank, New Jersey 07701-0837. Phone: 732-219-7300. Fax: 732-219-7305. E-mail: projectuse@monmouth.com. In-person interview recommended. Applicants must submit a formal organization application, two personal references. Applications are accepted continuously.

RIVER BEND NATURE CENTER
PO Box 186
Faribault, Minnesota 55021

General Information Provider of environmental and natural education programs to school and the community. Established in 1980. Number of employees: 5. Number of internship applications received each year: 100.

Internships Available ▶ *1–2 naturalist interns:* responsibilities include providing natural history programs to the public and children; writing press releases, curriculum, and newsletters; and assisting with land management and maintenance practices. Candidates should have oral communication skills, plan to pursue career in field, self-motivation, strong interpersonal skills, written communication skills. Duration is seasonal. $140 per week. Open to college juniors, college seniors, recent college graduates, graduate students, career changers. International applications accepted.
Benefits Formal training, free housing, job counseling, names of contacts, on-the-job training, opportunity to attend seminars/workshops, willing to act as a professional reference, willing to complete paperwork for educational credit, willing to provide letters of recommendation.
Contact Write or e-mail John Blackmer, Chief Naturalist. E-mail: blackmer@rbnc.org. No phone calls. In-person interview recommended. Applicants must submit a cover letter, resume, three personal references, application packet (must be requested). Application deadline: March 11 for summer, June 8 for school-year position. World Wide Web: http://www.rbnc.org.

ROGERS ENVIRONMENTAL EDUCATION CENTER
PO Box 716
Sherburne, New York 13460

General Information Group of environmental education centers dedicated to teaching the public about natural resources, environmental issues, natural history, and ecological principles. Established in 1967. Number of employees: 5. Unit of New York State Department of Environmental Conservation, Albany, New York. Number of internship applications received each year: 70.
Internships Available ▶ *15–20 naturalist interns:* responsibilities include teaching groups, writing articles, and working on special projects. Candidates should have ability to work with others, college courses in field, oral communication skills, personal interest in the field, self-motivation, written communication skills. Duration is 10–12 weeks. $100 per week. Open to college sophomores, college juniors, college seniors, recent college graduates, graduate students, career changers, individuals reentering the workforce. International applications accepted.
Benefits Formal training, free housing, job counseling, names of contacts, on-the-job training, opportunity to attend seminars/workshops, willing to act as a professional reference, willing to complete paperwork for educational credit, willing to provide letters of recommendation.
Contact Write, call, fax, e-mail, or in person Mr. Fred von Mechow, Environmental Educator II. Phone: 607-674-4017. Fax: 607-674-2655. E-mail: rogers@norwich.net. In-person interview recommended. Applicants must submit a formal organization application, resume, three personal references. Application deadline: February 15 for summer, May 1 for fall, August 1 for winter, December 1 for spring. World Wide Web: http://www.ascent.net/rogers/.

ST. JOHNSBURY ACADEMY
7 Main Street
St. Johnsbury, Vermont 05819

General Information Academy that provides educational programs to 850 students. Established in 1842. Number of employees: 90. Number of internship applications received each year: 275.
Internships Available ▶ *1–4 teaching interns:* responsibilities include teaching 2 sections, increasing to 3 sections in the second semester, living in residence, working closely with a mentor teacher, and observing classes. Candidates should have college degree in related field, computer skills, oral communication skills, plan to pursue career in field, strong leadership ability, written communication skills. Duration is August 15 to June 15. $10,000 per duration of internship. Open to recent college graduates with a minimum 3.0 GPA.
Benefits Formal training, free housing, free meals, health insurance, job counseling, names of contacts, opportunity to attend seminars/workshops, possible full-time employment, tuition assistance, willing to provide letters of recommendation.

St. Johnsbury Academy (continued)

Contact Write, call, fax, or e-mail Mr. Carl-Martin Nelson, Director of Internships. Phone: 802-751-2257. Fax: 802-748-5463. E-mail: sinternships@stj.k12.vt.us. In-person interview required. Applicants must submit a cover letter, resume, academic transcripts, three personal references, three letters of recommendation. Application deadline: April 1.

ST. PAUL'S SCHOOL
325 Pleasant Street
Concord, New Hampshire 03301-2591

General Information Coeducational boarding school that offers college preparatory programs. Established in 1856. Number of employees: 200. Number of internship applications received each year: 150.

Internships Available ▶ *30–35 Advanced Studies Program interns:* responsibilities include offering classroom assistance and dormitory supervision, and supervising recreational activities. Candidates should have college courses in field, oral communication skills, personal interest in the field, self-motivation, strong interpersonal skills. Duration is 5 weeks in summer. $1,500 per duration of internship. Open to college juniors, college seniors, recent college graduates. ▶ *2–4 teaching fellows:* responsibilities include teaching, coaching, and supervising students in dormitories. Candidates should have college courses in field, knowledge of field, oral communication skills, self-motivation, strong interpersonal skills. Duration is 9 months. $15,000 per duration of internship. Open to college seniors, recent college graduates. International applications accepted.

Benefits Formal training, free housing, free meals, job counseling, names of contacts, on-the-job training, opportunity to attend seminars/workshops, possible full-time employment, willing to act as a professional reference, willing to provide letters of recommendation, health insurance for academic year interns.

Contact Write, call, fax, or e-mail Mr. Jeffrey C. Bradley, Director. Phone: 603-229-4777. Fax: 603-229-4767. E-mail: asp@sps.edu. In-person interview required. Applicants must submit a formal organization application, resume, academic transcripts, three letters of recommendation, 2-page personal statement. Application deadline: January 20. World Wide Web: http://www.sps.edu.

SCHUYKILL CENTER FOR ENVIRONMENTAL EDUCATION
8480 Hagy's Mill Road
Philadelphia, Pennsylvania 19128-1998

General Information Environmental education facility presenting programming for kindergarten through graduate school with a yearly audience of 80,000. Established in 1965. Number of employees: 16. Number of internship applications received each year: 28.

Internships Available ▶ *2 education interns:* responsibilities include teaching daily class, assisting education staff, and working on projects. Candidates should have ability to work independently, college courses in field, experience in the field, plan to pursue career in field, self-motivation, previous experience working with children. Duration is 15 weeks. $1,600 per duration of internship. Open to college juniors, college seniors, recent college graduates, graduate students, career changers.

Benefits Formal training, names of contacts, opportunity to attend seminars/workshops, willing to complete paperwork for educational credit, willing to provide letters of recommendation.

Contact Write, call, or fax Gayle Whittle, Environmental Educator. Phone: 215-482-7300. Fax: 215-482-8158. Telephone interview required. Applicants must submit a formal organization application, cover letter, resume, personal reference, letter of recommendation. Applications are accepted continuously. World Wide Web: http://www.schuykillcenter.org.

SMITHSONIAN OFFICE OF EDUCATION
Arts and Industries Building, 900 Jefferson Drive, SW, Suite 2235
Washington, District of Columbia 20560-0427

General Information Office that provides professional development for teachers, publishes information and curriculum materials for schools, and encourages productive relationships between schools and museums. The Office also supports educational efforts within the Smithsonian's various museums, offices, and institutes. Unit of Smithsonian Institution, Washington, District of Columbia.

Internships Available ▶ *Interns:* responsibilities include developing and coordinating educational projects; assisting in the publishing, researching and coordinating development proposals and special events; working on Internet services and other electronic outreach activities. Duration is minimum of 6 weeks, 20 hours per week. Unpaid. International applications accepted.

Benefits Willing to complete paperwork for educational credit.

Contact Write, call, or e-mail Elena Piquer Mayberry, Experiential Programs Manager, 900 Jefferson Drive, SW, Suite 2235, Washington, District of Columbia 20560-0427. Phone: 202-357-3102. E-mail: siintern@cms.si.edu. Applicants must submit a formal organization application, resume, academic transcripts, writing sample, two letters of recommendation. See Web site (www.si.edu/cms/intern.htm) for more specifics. Application deadline: February 15 for summer, June 15 for fall, October 15 for winter/spring. World Wide Web: http://www.educate.si.edu.

SOLOTRON 13, INC.
30 McArthur Boulevard
Buzzards Bay, Massachusetts 02532

General Information Corporation with purpose to establish a complex campus (Institute for Scientific and Environmental Awareness) for the study of educational and scientific pursuit. Established in 1998. Number of employees: 5. Number of internship applications received each year: 30.

Internships Available ▶ *10–15 interns:* responsibilities include assisting in planning, design, and curriculum development of a new interdisciplinary environmental awareness campus on Cape Cod. Candidates should have ability to work independently, ability to work with others, analytical skills, declared college major in field, organizational skills. Duration is flexible. Paid. Open to college juniors, college seniors. International applications accepted.

Benefits Housing at a cost, meals at a cost, on-the-job training, opportunity to attend seminars/workshops, possible full-time employment, willing to complete paperwork for educational credit, willing to provide letters of recommendation.

Contact Fax Duncan Smith-Rhorberg, Student Liaison Contact, 2387 Harvard Mail Center, Cambridge, Massachusetts 02138. Fax: 508-759-2481. Telephone interview required. Applicants must submit a resume, academic transcripts, brief 1-page letter describing how this project will contribute to educational and career objectives. Applications are accepted continuously. World Wide Web: http://www.iseacampus.org.

SPANISH EDUCATION DEVELOPMENT CENTER
1840 Kalorama Road, NW
Washington, District of Columbia 20009

General Information Hispanic nonprofit organization that offers educational programs for children and adults. Established in 1971. Number of employees: 25.

Internships Available ▶ *20–40 English as a Second Language teachers:* responsibilities include leading a small group by implementing teacher's lesson plans, observing and learning selected ESL techniques from the teacher, and working with individual students who have been absent or who need extra assistance. Candidates should have ability to work independently, ability to work with others, oral communication skills, self-motivation. Duration is 12 weeks. Open to college freshmen, college sophomores, college juniors, college seniors, recent college graduates, graduate students, law students. ▶ *8–10 after school teacher aides (Silver Spring,*

Maryland): responsibilities include conducting small group activities with children. Candidates should have ability to work independently, ability to work with others, oral communication skills, self-motivation. Duration is flexible (3:00 PM-6:30 PM, Monday to Friday). Open to high school students, high school seniors, recent high school graduates, college freshmen, college sophomores, college juniors, college seniors, recent college graduates, graduate students, law students. ▶ *10–20 preschool teacher assistants:* responsibilities include helping classroom teacher supervise children; preparing educational materials; interacting with children through stories, games, teaching, and songs; and working with children in small group activities designed either by the teacher or the assistant. Candidates should have ability to work independently, ability to work with others, oral communication skills, self-motivation. Duration is flexible. Open to high school students, high school seniors, recent high school graduates, college freshmen, college sophomores, college juniors, college seniors, recent college graduates, graduate students. ▶ *2–5 proposal writing interns:* responsibilities include performing foundation research and proposal writing. Candidates should have computer skills, editing skills, research skills, writing skills. Duration is flexible. Open to college freshmen, college sophomores, college juniors, college seniors, recent college graduates, graduate students, individuals reentering the workforce. ▶ *6–10 special project assistants:* responsibilities include conducting foundation research, public relations, fund-raising, and material and curriculum development. Candidates should have computer skills, editing skills, research skills, writing skills. Duration is flexible. Open to college freshmen, college sophomores, college juniors, college seniors, recent college graduates, graduate students, individuals reentering the workforce. All positions are unpaid. International applications accepted.

Benefits Formal training, willing to complete paperwork for educational credit, willing to provide letters of recommendation.
Contact Write, call, fax, or e-mail Ms. Doris Estrada, Director, Volunteer Program. Phone: 202-462-8848. Fax: 202-462-6886. E-mail: sedcen@erols.com. In-person interview recommended. Applicants must submit a resume. Applications are accepted continuously.

SPONSORS FOR EDUCATIONAL OPPORTUNITY CAREER PROGRAM
23 Gramercy Park South
New York, New York 10003

General Information Nonprofit organization that provides training, orientation, and summer internships to undergraduate students of color in the areas of accounting, asset management, corporate law, investment banking, and management consulting. Established in 1963. Number of internship applications received each year: 1,500.
Internships Available ▶ *10–15 accounting interns:* responsibilities include working as full member of auditing teams on client engagements; or working in either internal audit division, the comptroller's office, or on the staff of the chief financial officer at a major investment banking firm. Candidates should have ability to work independently, ability to work with others, analytical skills, college courses in field, knowledge of field. Open to college juniors. ▶ *10–15 asset management interns:* responsibilities include working as research assistants to one or more portfolio managers and in marketing to identify potential clients. Candidates should have ability to work independently, ability to work with others, analytical skills, computer skills, knowledge of field, coursework in economics and finance desirable. Open to college juniors; exceptional sophomores may be considered; seniors who will have one semester to complete at the time of the internship may be considered. ▶ *30–35 corporate law interns:* responsibilities include document indexing, distributions, citation checking and document review, working side by side with established attorneys on significant assignments that range from closing of major corporate transactions to pro bono projects. Candidates should have ability to work independently, ability to work with others, analytical skills, oral communication skills, plan to pursue career in field, written communication skills. Open to graduating seniors who plan to attend law school in the fall;

exceptional juniors may be considered. ▶ *125–150 investment banking interns:* responsibilities include working in finance at major investment firm; performing tasks similar to those of full-time analysts. Candidates should have ability to work independently, ability to work with others, analytical skills, computer skills, knowledge of field, coursework in economics and finance desirable. Open to college juniors; exceptional freshmen and sophomores may be considered; seniors who will have one semester to complete at the time of the internship may be considered. ▶ *10–20 management consulting interns:* responsibilities include research for presentations, data analysis, "number cruching" and preparation of presentation documents; interfacing with clients and travel to client offices to conduct on-site analyses. Candidates should have ability to work independently, ability to work with others, analytical skills, knowledge of field, oral communication skills, written communication skills. Open to college juniors; seniors who will have one semester to complete at the time of the internship may be considered. Duration for all positions is minimum 10 weeks in summer. All positions paid at competitive salary. International applications accepted.
Benefits Formal training, job counseling, names of contacts, on-the-job training, opportunity to attend seminars/workshops, possible full-time employment.
International Internships Available in London, United Kingdom.
Contact Write or call Career Program. Phone: 212-979-2040. In-person interview required. Applicants must submit a formal organization application, resume, academic transcripts, writing sample, two letters of recommendation. Application deadline: February 15. World Wide Web: http://www.seo-ny.org.

STREAM (ST. LOUIS REGIONAL EXPERIENTIAL ADVENTURE MOVEMENT)
1315 Ann Avenue
St. Louis, Missouri 63104

General Information Organization that serves youth and adults who work with youth. Established in 1974. Number of employees: 8. Unit of American Youth Foundation, St. Louis, Missouri. Number of internship applications received each year: 5.
Internships Available ▶ *1–4 interns:* responsibilities include planning, conducting, and evaluating programs; offering clerical support; supervising all activities; preparing food; attending sessions, consulting with program director on a major project; and co-leading day and/or overnight trips. Candidates should have ability to work with others, personal interest in the field, major in education, social work, or recreation preferred. Duration is flexible. Unpaid. Open to college freshmen, college sophomores, college juniors, college seniors, recent college graduates. International applications accepted.
Benefits Formal training, names of contacts, on-the-job training, possible full-time employment, willing to act as a professional reference, willing to complete paperwork for educational credit, willing to provide letters of recommendation, meals provided on trips, handicapped accessible facilities.
Contact Write or fax Sandy Franklin, Secretary, 1315 Ann Avenue, St. Louis, Missouri 63104. Fax: 314-772-7542. No phone calls. In-person interview recommended. Applicants must submit a formal organization application, cover letter, resume. Applications are accepted continuously. World Wide Web: http://www. ayf.org.

SUMMER AT HAWTHORNE VALLEY FARM CAMP
327 CR 21C
Ghent, New York 12075

General Information A farm and nature camp experience for children 9-12 on a commercial biodynamic dairy farm. Established in 1972. Number of employees: 25. Unit of Rudolph Steiner Educational and Farm Association, Ghent, New York. Number of internship applications received each year: 75.
Internships Available ▶ *4–5 interns:* responsibilities include taking grade school children on a tour and leading nature activities on a biodynamic farm. Candidates should have ability to work independently, knowledge of field, oral communication skills, organizational skills, personal interest in the field, self-

Summer at Hawthorne Valley Farm Camp (continued)

motivation, strong interpersonal skills, strong leadership ability. Duration is fall and/or spring semester. $200 per month. Open to college freshmen, college sophomores, college juniors, college seniors, recent college graduates, career changers, individuals reentering the workforce, those over 21 (preferably) or those who are mature and experienced at working with children. ▶ *12–15 summer camp counselors:* responsibilities include working with children in an outdoor nature camp/farm setting in a variety or relevant activities. Candidates should have ability to work with others, oral communication skills, personal interest in the field, self-motivation, strong interpersonal skills, strong leadership ability. Duration is end of June to mid-August (8 weeks). $1000 for term of camp. Open to recent high school graduates, college freshmen, college sophomores, college juniors, college seniors, career changers, applicants over 21 years preferred; younger applicants must be mature and experienced with children. International applications accepted.

Benefits Formal training, free housing, free meals, job counseling, on-the-job training, opportunity to attend seminars/workshops, willing to act as a professional reference, willing to complete paperwork for educational credit, willing to provide letters of recommendation.

International Internships Available.

Contact Write, call, fax, or e-mail Ruth Bruns, Executive Director, 327CR 21C, Ghent, New York 12075. Phone: 518-672-4790. Fax: 518-672-7608. E-mail: vsp@taconic.net. In-person interview recommended. Applicants must submit a formal organization application, cover letter, resume, references with observations of applicant with children. Application deadline: January 15 for spring, June 1 for summer camp counselor (hiring begins January and is ususally completed by April 15), August 30 for fall. World Wide Web: http://www.camppage.com/hawthorne.

SUMMERBRIDGE NATIONAL
361 Oak Street
San Francisco, California 94102

General Information Education program that provides free academic enrichment to 5th-9th graders and teaching, mentorship, and tutoring opportunities to high school and college students. Established in 1991. Number of employees: 14. Number of internship applications received each year: 1,300.

Internships Available ▶ *100–160 master teachers:* responsibilities include mentoring young high school and college teacher interns, supporting lesson planning, providing resources, and monitoring teachers. Candidates should have ability to work with others, oral communication skills, organizational skills, strong leadership ability, written communication skills. Duration is mid-June to August. $500–$1,500 per duration of internship. Open to experienced middle school educators. ▶ *500–800 school-year tutors:* responsibilities include providing one-to-one mentoring, teaching, and tutoring to children. Candidates should have ability to work with others, oral communication skills, organizational skills, strong leadership ability, writing skills. Duration is September through May. Position available as unpaid or at $1,500–$2,000 per duration of internship. Open to high school students, high school seniors, college freshmen, college sophomores, college juniors, college seniors, recent college graduates, graduate students. ▶ *800–900 teachers (summer):* responsibilities include planning daily lessons, planning and overseeing special events, and acting as mentors. Candidates should have ability to work with others, oral communication skills, organizational skills, strong leadership ability, writing skills. Duration is 2–3 months. Position available as unpaid or at $500–$2000 per internship; stipend enhancement may be possible upon request. Open to high school students, high school seniors, recent high school graduates, college freshmen, college sophomores, college juniors, college seniors, recent college graduates. International applications accepted.

Benefits Formal training, on-the-job training, opportunity to attend seminars/workshops, possible full-time employment, tuition assistance, willing to act as a professional reference, will-

ing to complete paperwork for educational credit, willing to provide letters of recommendation, room and board for out-of-town interns may be available.

International Internships Available in Hong Kong.

Contact Write, call, fax, or e-mail Office Manager. Phone: 415-865-2970 Ext. 100. Fax: 415-865-2979. E-mail: info@summerbridge.org. In-person interview recommended. Applicants must submit a formal organization application, resume, writing sample, letter of recommendation, general application via Web site. Applications are accepted continuously. World Wide Web: http://www.summerbridge.org.

SUNRISE LAKE OUTDOOR EDUCATION CENTER
7 North 749 Route 59
Bartlett, Illinois 60103

General Information Center whose facilities and programs are specifically designed to serve disabled children and youth, ages 3 to 21, by offering a diverse outdoor education program that provides a high-quality education and recreational experience. Established in 1978. Number of employees: 6. Unit of Northwest Suburban Special Education Organization, Mt. Prospect, Illinois. Number of internship applications received each year: 25.

Internships Available ▶ *2 interns:* responsibilities include working cooperatively with the outdoor education specialist and special education teachers to plan and implement experiential learning activities with all ages and categories of disabled students in the areas of nature awareness, arts, aquatics, and winter activities. Candidates should have ability to work independently, analytical skills, experience in the field, strong interpersonal skills, special education/outdoor education background preferred. Duration is 4–9 months. $250 per week. Open to recent high school graduates, college freshmen, college sophomores, college juniors, college seniors, recent college graduates, graduate students, career changers.

Benefits Job counseling, names of contacts, opportunity to attend seminars/workshops, travel reimbursement, willing to complete paperwork for educational credit, willing to provide letters of recommendation.

Contact Write Mr. John Guarrine, Outdoor Education Specialist. In-person interview recommended. Applicants must submit a formal organization application, cover letter, resume, academic transcripts, three personal references. Applications are accepted continuously.

SUNY CORTLAND CAREER SERVICES/INTERNSHIP OFFICE
State University of New York
Cortland, New York 13045

General Information 4-year liberal arts college. Established in 1868. Number of employees: 1,000. Unit of State University of New York at Albany, Albany, New York. Number of internship applications received each year: 10.

Internships Available ▶ *1 career services intern:* responsibilities include learning all areas of career service, including counseling, career exploration, event planning and implementation, information/library management, experiential education, recruitment, and job search skills and interacting with all levels of administration and students. Candidates should have office skills, oral communication skills, organizational skills, personal interest in the field, strong interpersonal skills, writing skills. Duration is flexible. Unpaid. Open to graduate students, career changers. International applications accepted.

Benefits Formal training, job counseling, names of contacts, opportunity to attend seminars/workshops, willing to complete paperwork for educational credit, willing to provide letters of recommendation, housing at reduced rate possible in summer.

Contact Write or fax Mr. John Shirley, Assistant Director. Fax: 607-753-2937. No phone calls. In-person interview recommended. Applicants must submit a cover letter, resume. Applications are accepted continuously. World Wide Web: http://www.cortland.edu/www/career/.

UNIVERSITY OF GEORGIA, MARINE EXTENSION SERVICE
30 Ocean Science Circle
Savannah, Georgia 31411

General Information Marine education center and aquarium that emphasizes teaching about the coastal environment. Established in 1970. Number of employees: 19. Unit of University of Georgia, Athens, Georgia. Number of internship applications received each year: 30.

Internships Available ► *3 Sea Grant marine education interns:* responsibilities include teaching a wide variety of marine-related topics to K-12 students and adults at location on Skidaway Island. Candidates should have college degree in related field, personal interest in the field, plan to pursue career in field, self-motivation, strong interpersonal skills. Duration is 50 weeks. $200 per week. Open to recent college graduates. International applications accepted.

Benefits Formal training, free housing, job counseling, names of contacts, on-the-job training, opportunity to attend seminars/workshops, travel reimbursement, willing to provide letters of recommendation, some meals provided.

Contact Write or call Ms. Edith Schmidt, Acting Associate Director of Education, Marine Extension Service. Phone: 912-598-2496. Telephone interview required. Applicants must submit a cover letter, resume, academic transcripts, three personal references, three letters of recommendation. Application deadline: May 22 for fall. World Wide Web: http://www.marsci.uga.edu./EXT/MAREX.html.

UNIVERSITY OF IOWA- WOMEN'S ATHLETICS
340 Carver-Hawkeye Arena
Iowa City, Iowa 52242

General Information NCAA Division I athletic program. Established in 1972. Number of employees: 55. Number of internship applications received each year: 20.

Internships Available ► *1–2 academic student services interns:* responsibilities include duties dependent on major. Can include educational programming, career programming, office duties, advising of 2 to 4 student athletes. Candidates should have ability to work with others, oral communication skills, organizational skills, personal interest in the field, research skills, written communication skills. Duration is fall, spring, and/or summer. Unpaid. Open to graduate students. ► *1 compliance assistant:* responsibilities include assisting in daily compliance responsibilities, including policy development, form development, interpretations, self-reports, research, and audits. Candidates should have analytical skills, computer skills, oral communication skills, research skills, self-motivation, written communication skills. Duration is fall, spring, or summer. Unpaid. Open to graduate students, law students. ► *1 event management intern:* responsibilities include coordinating staffing for various sport venues, serving as assistant event manager at various venues, assisting in the development of management manuals and tournament guides. Candidates should have ability to work independently, oral communication skills, organizational skills, strong interpersonal skills, written communication skills. Duration is August to May. Position available as unpaid or at $6 per hour. Open to college seniors, graduate students. ► *1–5 general administration assistants:* responsibilities include assisting in daily administrative tasks, correspondence, research projects, event management duties, and internal audits (compliance). Candidates should have analytical skills, computer skills, oral communication skills, research skills, self-motivation, written communication skills. Duration is fall, spring, or summer. Unpaid. Open to college seniors, recent college graduates, graduate students, law students. ► *1 sports information intern:* responsibilities include aiding in game-day operation of assigned sports, writing and editing weekly releases, maintaining historical data of assigned sports, acting as main contact of sport, and working on design and layout projects for publications. Candidates should have ability to work independently, computer skills, editing skills, oral communication skills, writing skills, interest in sports and public relations. Duration is 1–2 years. Position available as unpaid or paid. Open to college

freshmen, college sophomores, college juniors, college seniors, recent college graduates, graduate students. ► *1–6 sports marketing assistants:* responsibilities include designing and implementing sports marketing plans for individual sports; assisting with newsletters, event promotions, message center operations, and miscellaneous office duties. Candidates should have ability to work with others, computer skills, office skills, oral communication skills, writing skills. Duration is 2–8 semesters. Position available as unpaid or at $5–$8 per hour. Open to college freshmen, college sophomores, college juniors, college seniors, graduate students. International applications accepted.

Benefits On-the-job training, willing to act as a professional reference, willing to complete paperwork for educational credit, willing to provide letters of recommendation.

Contact Write Mary C. Curtis, Associate Athletic Director, 340 Carver Hawkeye Arena, Iowa City, Iowa 52242. Applicants must submit a cover letter, resume, interest survey. Applications are accepted continuously. World Wide Web: http://www.hawkeyesports.com.

UNIVERSITY OF MICHIGAN, SCHOOL OF PUBLIC HEALTH, POPULATION FELLOWS PROGRAMS
109 Observatory
Ann Arbor, Michigan 48109-2029

General Information Program that offers internships and fellowships in population, family planning, reproductive health, and population-environment. Established in 1984. Number of employees: 18. Number of internship applications received each year: 125.

Internships Available ► *5 HBCU/HSI graduate interns:* responsibilities include applied work in international population or population-environment. Candidates should have analytical skills, experience in the field, organizational skills, personal interest in the field, plan to pursue career in field. Duration is 3–6 months. stipend available for duration of internship. Open to individuals with graduate degrees from Historically Black Colleges or Universities or Hispanic-Serving Institutions. ► *10 HBCU/HSI undergraduate interns:* responsibilities include entry-level, professional work in international population and population-environment. Candidates should have analytical skills, oral communication skills, organizational skills, personal interest in the field, strong interpersonal skills, written communication skills. Duration is 10–16 months. professional stipend for duration of internship. Open to juniors and seniors from Historically Black Colleges and Universities or Hispanic-Serving Institutions. ► *20 population fellows:* responsibilities include population, family planning, and reproductive health programming, including program design, implementation, administration, and evaluation. Candidates should have knowledge of field, personal interest in the field, plan to pursue career in field. Duration is 2 years. yearly stipend. Open to individuals with graduate degrees in population-related areas. ► *10 population-environment fellows:* responsibilities include design, implementation, and evaluation of programs that link population, family planning, and reproductive health service delivery with environmental programming. Candidates should have knowledge of field, personal interest in the field, plan to pursue career in field. Duration is 2 years. yearly stipend. Open to individuals with graduate degrees and expertise in population-environment.

Benefits Health insurance, names of contacts, on-the-job training, opportunity to attend seminars/workshops, travel reimbursement, willing to act as a professional reference, willing to provide letters of recommendation.

International Internships Available.

Contact Write, call, fax, or e-mail Population Fellows Program. Phone: 734-763-9456. Fax: 734-647-0643. E-mail: pop.fellows@umich.edu. In-person interview recommended. Applicants must submit a formal organization application, cover letter, resume, academic transcripts, writing sample, three letters of recommendation. Application deadline: February 1 for undergraduate positions, April 1 for fall fellows and graduate interns, November 1 for spring fellows and graduate interns.

UNIVERSITY OF VIRGINIA, MOUNTAIN LAKE BIOLOGICAL STATION
Gilmer Hall
Charlottesville, Virginia 22901

General Information Academic center for teachers and research in field biology. Established in 1939. Number of employees: 6. Academic Research Center/Institute of University of Virginia, Charlottesville, Virginia. Number of internship applications received each year: 150.
Internships Available ▶ *10 interns:* responsibilities include supervised independent research. Candidates should have ability to work independently, ability to work with others, analytical skills, college courses in field, computer skills, oral communication skills, personal interest in the field, plan to pursue career in field, self-motivation, writing skills. Duration is June 1 to August 15. $2500 scholarship. Open to college freshmen, college sophomores, college juniors. International applications accepted.
Benefits Free housing, free meals, housing at a cost, meals at a cost, names of contacts, opportunity to attend seminars/workshops, possible full-time employment, tuition assistance, willing to act as a professional reference, willing to complete paperwork for educational credit, willing to provide letters of recommendation.
Contact Write, call, fax, or e-mail Brenda Christensen, Administrative Assistant, University of Virginia, Gilmer Hall, Charlottesville, Virginia 22901. Phone: 804-982-5486. Fax: 804-982-5626. E-mail: mtlake@virginia.edu. Applicants must submit a formal organization application, academic transcripts, letter of recommendation. Application deadline: March 1. World Wide Web: http://www.virginia.edu/~mtlake.

U.S. ENVIRONMENTAL PROTECTION AGENCY, OFFICE OF ENVIRONMENTAL EDUCATION, NNEMS FELLOWSHIP PROGRAM
401 M Street, SW (1704)
Washington, District of Columbia 20460

General Information The NNEMS Fellowship Program offers undergraduate and graduate students research opportunities nationwide. Established in 1987. Number of internship applications received each year: 250.
Internships Available ▶ *90–100 national network for environmental management studies positions:* responsibilities include research in the areas of environmental policy, regulation, and law; environmental management and administration; environmental science; public relations and communications; and computer programming and development. Candidates should have ability to work independently, ability to work with others, college courses in field, personal interest in the field, research skills, written communication skills, minimum GPA of 3.0 (undergraduates), enrollment in an academic program directly related to pollution abatement and control, one semester of graduate work (graduate students). Duration is full-time summer or part-time school year. $1,654–$2,804 per month. Open to college freshmen, college sophomores, college juniors, college seniors, graduate students.
Benefits On-the-job training, opportunity to attend seminars/workshops, willing to act as a professional reference, willing to provide letters of recommendation, work-related travel reimbursement.
Contact Write, call, fax, or e-mail Sheri Jojokian, Environmental Education Specialist. Phone: 202-260-5283. Fax: 202-260-4095. E-mail: jojokian.sheri@epa.gov. Telephone interview required. Applicants must submit a formal organization application, resume, academic transcripts, 1-page work plan proposal, 1 letter of reference from a professor or advisor, NNEMS Liability Agreement (obtained from Web site or Career Service Center of participating universities). Application deadline: December 20. World Wide Web: http://www.epa.gov/ocepa111/NNEMS/index.html.

VALLEY OF THE MOON BOYS AND GIRLS CLUB
PO Box 780
Sonoma, California 95476

General Information Organization that provides daily, ongoing youth development programs featuring art, scholastics, achievement, health and fitness, environmental education, and leadership development. Established in 1962. Number of employees: 12. Number of internship applications received each year: 1.
Internships Available ▶ *1–2 fitness interns:* responsibilities include assisting in setting up fitness program for individuals. Open to individuals 18 years of age or older. ▶ *Interns:* responsibilities include participating in ongoing programs such as the communications program (working on a radio show or newspaper staff), cultural arts program, drama/theater program, leadership development program, recreation program, education program, and others; may also customize intern program based on major, skills, talents, or interests, as approved by director. Open to individuals 16 years of age or older accepted; individuals 18 years of age or older preferred. Duration for all positions is flexible. All positions available as unpaid or paid. International applications accepted.
Benefits Willing to complete paperwork for educational credit, willing to provide letters of recommendation, possible pay for summer interns.
Contact Write or call Sharon Somogyi, Program Director. Phone: 707-938-8544. In-person interview required. Phone call of interest. Applications are accepted continuously.

VOYAGEUR OUTWARD BOUND SCHOOL
PO Box 450
Ely, Minnesota 55731

General Information Adventure-based school, using wilderness experiences to enhance students self-reliance, compassion, physical fitness, and cooperation. Established in 1964. Number of employees: 135. Unit of Voyageur Outward Bound, Minneapolis, Minnesota. Number of internship applications received each year: 200.
Internships Available ▶ *20–25 interns:* responsibilities include initial field training and support work assignments in all program areas. Candidates should have ability to work with others, self-motivation, strong interpersonal skills, flexibility, sense of humor. Duration is 5–8 weeks. $50 per week stipend. Open to college freshmen, college sophomores, college juniors, college seniors, recent college graduates, graduate students, law students, career changers, individuals reentering the workforce, must be age 21 or older. International applications accepted.
Benefits Free housing, free meals, job counseling, names of contacts, on-the-job training, willing to complete paperwork for educational credit, willing to provide letters of recommendation.
Contact Write, call, or fax Staffing Coordinator. Phone: 218-365-5761. Fax: 218-365-5626. Applicants must submit a formal organization application. Application deadline: March 1. World Wide Web: http://www.vobs.com.

WAHSEGA 4-H CENTER
77 Cloverleaf Trail
Dahlonega, Georgia 30533

General Information Camp that provides outdoor wilderness challenges to school-age children and helps them build a better self-image; places a special emphasis on science and environmental education. Established in 1991. Number of employees: 15. Unit of University of Georgia, Athens, Georgia. Number of internship applications received each year: 50.
Internships Available ▶ *4–8 environmental educators:* responsibilities include teaching environmental education. Candidates should have ability to work independently, oral communication skills, self-motivation, strong interpersonal skills, strong leadership ability. Duration is 8–10 weeks. $190 per week plus room and board. Open to college seniors, recent college graduates, graduate students, career changers, individuals reentering the workforce, individuals with 2 years college if experienced working with youth.

Benefits Formal training, opportunity to attend seminars/ workshops, willing to act as a professional reference, willing to complete paperwork for educational credit, willing to provide letters of recommendation, certification in Project Wild, Project Learning Tree, Project West, American Red Cross Standard First Aid, and CPR.
Contact Write, call, fax, or e-mail Ms. Dawn Garrison, Camp Manager. Phone: 706-864-2050. Fax: 706-867-2901. E-mail: eeewah@ stc.net. In-person interview recommended. Applicants must submit a cover letter, resume. Applications are accepted continuously.

WAVE INC., NATIONAL HEADQUARTERS
525 School Street, SW, Suite 500
Washington, District of Columbia 20024

General Information National education organization that assists at-risk youth by providing dropout prevention and employment training programs to 200 school- and community-based affiliates in 30 states. Established in 1969. Number of employees: 15. Number of internship applications received each year: 20.
Internships Available ▶ *1 desktop publisher/editor intern:* responsibilities include newsletter writing, editing, and desktop publishing. Duration is minimum of 2 semesters. Position available as unpaid or paid. ▶ *1 development intern:* responsibilities include researching prospects and writing proposals and brochures for public relations. Duration is 1 semester. Position available as unpaid or paid. Open to college juniors, college seniors, graduate students. International applications accepted.
Benefits Names of contacts, willing to complete paperwork for educational credit, willing to provide letters of recommendation.
Contact Write, call, or fax Intern Coordinator. Phone: 202-484-0103. Fax: 202 488 7595. In person interview recommended. Applicants must submit a cover letter, resume, three personal references. Applications are accepted continuously.

WILLIAM PENN HOUSE
515 East Capitol Street, SE
Washington, District of Columbia 20003

General Information Quaker seminar and hospitality center, providing educational programs and human service opportunities. Established in 1966. Number of employees: 5. Number of internship applications received each year: 20.
Internships Available ▶ *3 interns:* responsibilities include hospitality and program work. Candidates should have computer skills, office skills, oral communication skills, strong interpersonal skills, writing skills. Duration is 12 months. $400 per month. Open to college freshmen, college sophomores, college juniors, college seniors, recent college graduates, graduate students, career changers. International applications accepted.
Benefits Free housing, free meals, health insurance, on-the-job training, opportunity to attend seminars/workshops, possible full-time employment, willing to act as a professional reference, willing to complete paperwork for educational credit, willing to provide letters of recommendation.
Contact Write, call, or e-mail Errol Hess, Executive Director, 515 East Capitol Street, SE, Washington, District of Columbia 20003. Phone: 202-543-5560. E-mail: dirpennhouse@pennsnet.org. In-person interview recommended. Applicants must submit a cover letter, resume, three personal references. Applications are accepted continuously.

WOLF CREEK OUTDOOR SCHOOL/REDWOOD NATIONAL AND STATE PARKS
PO Box 7
Orrick, California 95555

General Information School for students in grades four through six, offering programs in awareness and value clarification, campfire programs, and old growth, stream, and prairie studies. Established in 1972. Number of employees: 2. Unit of Redwood National and State Parks. Number of internship applications received each year: 30.

Internships Available ▶ *6 environmental education interns:* responsibilities include instructing 4th, 5th, and 6th grade students; leading activities involving environmental education. Duration is 12 weeks. $10 per day. Open to college freshmen, college sophomores, college juniors, college seniors, recent college graduates. International applications accepted.
Benefits Free housing, names of contacts, possible full-time employment, willing to complete paperwork for educational credit, willing to provide letters of recommendation.
Contact Write, call, fax, or e-mail Jay Moeller, Park Ranger/ Director. Phone: 707-822-7611 Ext. 5266. Fax: 707-488-2861. E-mail: jay_moeller@nps.gov. Applicants must submit a formal organization application, cover letter, resume. Applications are accepted continuously. World Wide Web: http://www.nps.gov/ redw/index.html.

WOLVERINE CAMPS OUTDOOR EDUCATION CENTER
Wolverine Camps
Wolverine, Michigan 49799

General Information Residential outdoor education program for grades 5–8. Established in 1968. Number of employees: 8. Number of internship applications received each year: 3.
Internships Available ▶ *1–3 instructors:* responsibilities include teaching classes in natural history, pioneer living, orienteering, survival, and ropes course; performing light maintenance duties; and program planning. Candidates should have ability to work with others, declared college major in field, oral communication skills, plan to pursue career in field, self-motivation, willingness to learn new skills. Duration is 6 months. $100–$125 per week. Open to college seniors.
Benefits Formal training, free housing, free meals, names of contacts, on-the-job training, opportunity to attend seminars/ workshops, possible full-time employment, willing to complete paperwork for educational credit, willing to provide letters of recommendation.
Contact Write Mr. Eric Schupbach. In-person interview recommended. Applicants must submit a resume. Applications are accepted continuously. World Wide Web: http://www. wolverinecamps.com.

WOMEN'S SPORTS FOUNDATION
Eisenhower Park
East Meadow, New York 11554

General Information Nonprofit national education organization that promotes sports and fitness opportunities for girls and women. Established in 1974. Number of employees: 40. Number of internship applications received each year: 100.
Internships Available ▶ *15–45 interns:* responsibilities include researching topics in women's sports, staffing the Information Referral Service and toll-free hotline, assisting staff with projects according to abilities and skills, writing for the newsletter, and planning fund-raising projects and events. Duration is 3–12 months. $350–$600 per month. Open to recent high school graduates, college freshmen, college sophomores, college juniors, college seniors, recent college graduates, graduate students, law students, career changers, individuals reentering the workforce. ▶ *2–6 minority interns:* responsibilities include researching topics in women's sports, staffing the Information Referral Service and toll-free hotline, assisting staff with projects according to abilities and skills, writing for newsletter, and planning fund-raising projects and events. Duration is 3–12 months. $1,000 per month. Open to recent high school graduates, college freshmen, college sophomores, college juniors, college seniors, recent college graduates, graduate students, law students, career changers, individuals reentering the workforce. ▶ *Part-time interns:* responsibilities include researching topics in women's sports, staffing the Information Referral Service and toll-free hotline, assisting staff with projects according to abilities and skills, writing for newsletter, and planning fund-raising projects and events. Duration is 3 months. Unpaid. Open to high school students, high school seniors, recent high school graduates, college freshmen, college sophomores, college juniors, college seniors, recent

Women's Sports Foundation (continued)

college graduates, graduate students, law students, career changers, individuals reentering the workforce. Candidates for all positions should have ability to work independently, computer skills, editing skills, knowledge of field, office skills, oral communication skills, organizational skills, personal interest in the field, research skills, self-motivation, strong interpersonal skills, writing skills. International applications accepted.
Benefits Job counseling, names of contacts, on-the-job training, opportunity to attend seminars/workshops, willing to complete paperwork for educational credit, willing to provide letters of recommendation.
Contact Write, call, fax, or e-mail Jennifer Walter, Educational Services Manager. Phone: 516-542-4700. Fax: 516-542-4716. E-mail: wosportjaw@aol.com. In-person interview recommended. Applicants must submit a formal organization application, resume, two letters of recommendation. Applications are accepted continuously. World Wide Web: http://www.lifetimetv.com/WoSport.

WOODBERRY FOREST SUMMER SCHOOL
Woodberry Station
Woodberry Forest, Virginia 22989

General Information Summer school program that provides developmental, remedial, and advanced credit academic work and enrichment for high school-age students. Established in 1889. Number of employees: 21. Unit of Woodberry Forest School. Number of internship applications received each year: 200.
Internships Available ▶ *20–25 teaching interns:* responsibilities include assisting with classroom instruction, tutoring and reviewing with students, monitoring study hall, supervising dormitories, supervising athletics and fine arts programs, and chaperoning trips. Candidates should have knowledge of field, oral communication skills, self-motivation, strong interpersonal skills, strong leadership ability, written communication skills. Duration is 6 weeks. $1,600 per duration of internship. Open to college juniors, college seniors, recent college graduates, graduate students, career changers, individuals reentering the workforce. International applications accepted.
Benefits Free meals, on-the-job training, willing to complete paperwork for educational credit, willing to provide letters of recommendation.
Contact Write, call, fax, or e-mail Ben Hale, Director. Phone: 540-672-6047. Fax: 540-672-9076. E-mail: wfs_summer@woodberry.org. In-person interview recommended. Applicants must submit a cover letter, resume, academic transcripts, two personal references. Application deadline: March 15. World Wide Web: http://www.woodberry.org.

WOODROW WILSON INTERNATIONAL CENTER FOR SCHOLARS
One Woodrow Wilson Plaza, 1300 Pennsylvania Avenue, NW
Washington, District of Columbia 20004-3027

General Information An international institute for advanced study. Established in 1968. Number of employees: 68. Number of internship applications received each year: 700.
Internships Available ▶ *50–60 research assistants:* responsibilities include searching for source materials at area institutions; analysis and summarization of research materials; compilation of bibliographies; proofreading and editing of written work; clarification of quotations in response to references; and locating and transporting of inter-library loan materials. Candidates should have college courses in field, computer skills, editing skills, office skills, research skills, writing skills. Duration is 3–9 months. Unpaid. Open to college juniors, college seniors, recent college graduates, graduate students, law students. International applications accepted.
Benefits Opportunity to attend seminars/workshops, willing to act as a professional reference, willing to complete paperwork for educational credit, willing to provide letters of recommendation.
Contact Write, call, fax, or e-mail Dr. Bahman Amini, Internship Coordinator. Phone: 202-691-4083. Fax: 202-691-4001. E-mail:

benamini@wwic.si.edu. In-person interview recommended. Applicants must submit a cover letter, resume, academic transcripts, two letters of recommendation. Applications are accepted continuously. World Wide Web: http://www.wwics.si.edu/.

WORLD GAME INSTITUTE
3215 Race Street
Philadelphia, Pennsylvania 19104

General Information Nonprofit research and education organization that educates people on prerogatives and responsibilities of global citizenship through unique interactive workshops, Internet simulations, and K-12 programs on global issues for schools and museums. Established in 1972. Number of employees: 22. Number of internship applications received each year: 100.
Internships Available ▶ *1–2 development/public relations interns:* responsibilities include assisting development director with writing and researching grant proposals, press releases, and other duties. Candidates should have computer skills, editing skills, oral communication skills, research skills, self-motivation, written communication skills. Open to college freshmen, college sophomores, college juniors, college seniors, recent college graduates, graduate students. ▶ *1–2 education interns:* responsibilities include conducting research on methods for global/geographic education and assisting in development of curriculum materials. Candidates should have computer skills, experience in the field, plan to pursue career in field, research skills, writing skills. Open to college juniors, college seniors, recent college graduates, graduate students. ▶ *1 general office assistant:* responsibilities include assisting Office Manager with daily tasks of office, including product order fullfillment, answering phones, copying, faxing, and program material production. Candidates should have ability to work independently, ability to work with others, computer skills, office skills, oral communication skills, written communication skills. Open to high school students, high school seniors, recent high school graduates, college freshmen, college sophomores, individuals reentering the workforce. ▶ *1–5 marketing interns:* responsibilities include working directly with the Director of Marketing Coordinator on market research projects, programming a client database, performing day-to-day marketing responsibilities, copywriting, and other appropriate duties. Candidates should have computer skills, knowledge of field, oral communication skills, organizational skills, self-motivation, written communication skills. Open to college freshmen, college sophomores, college juniors, college seniors, recent college graduates, graduate students. Duration for all positions is flexible. All positions are unpaid. International applications accepted.
Benefits Names of contacts, on-the-job training, opportunity to attend seminars/workshops, possible full-time employment, willing to act as a professional reference, willing to complete paperwork for educational credit, willing to provide letters of recommendation, Pennsylvania work-study students receive stipend.
Contact Write, call, fax, or e-mail Terry Hofer, Internship Coordinator. Phone: 800-220-GAME. Fax: 215-387-3009. E-mail: wgi@worldgame.org. In-person interview recommended. Applicants must submit a cover letter, resume, two personal references, letter of recommendation. Applications are accepted continuously. World Wide Web: http://www.worldgame.org.

WORLDTEACH
Harvard Institute for International Development, 14 Story Street
Cambridge, Massachusetts 02138

General Information Private, nonprofit organization that sends volunteers to teach in Africa, Asia, and Latin America. Established in 1986. Number of employees: 30. Unit of Harvard Institute for International Development, Cambridge, Massachusetts. Number of internship applications received each year: 850.
Internships Available ▶ *20 summer teachers:* responsibilities include teaching English, speaking Chinese, and taking part in cultural exchange with Chinese students. Candidates should have ability to work with others, oral communication skills, strong

interpersonal skills, English fluency. Duration is 1 summer (June to August). Unpaid. Open to college freshmen, college sophomores, college juniors, college seniors, recent college graduates, graduate students, law students. ▶ *250–300 teachers:* responsibilities include primarily teaching English, and also science and mathematics, to students in developing countries. Candidates should have ability to work independently, oral communication skills, strong interpersonal skills, interest in other cultures. Duration is 6–12 months. small monthly stipend (varies from country to country). Open to recent college graduates, graduate students, law students, career changers. International applications accepted.
Benefits Formal training, free housing, health insurance, names of contacts, opportunity to attend seminars/workshops, possible full-time employment, willing to provide letters of recommendation, student loans deferrable, limited, need-based financial aid available to cover the program fee.
International Internships Available in China; Costa Rica; Ecuador; Honduras; Mexico; Namibia.
Contact Write, call, fax, or e-mail Ms. Jodi Hullinger, Director of Recruiting and Admissions, Harvard Institute for International Development 14 Story Street, Cambridge, Massachusetts 02138. Phone: 800-4-Teach-0. Fax: 617-495-1599. E-mail: info@worldteach. org. In-person interview required. Applicants must submit a formal organization application, resume, academic transcripts, 3 essays, 2 personal references or letters of recommendation. Applications are accepted continuously. World Wide Web: http://www.worldteach.org.

WYMAN CENTER
600 Kiwanis Drive
Eureka, Missouri 63025

General Information Education center that focuses on educational readiness; citizenship; self-esteem; self-motivation; leadership; communication; intercultural understanding; environment; and spiritual, ethical, and moral values. Established in 1898. Number of employees: 50. Number of internship applications received each year: 25.
Internships Available ▶ *1–8 program interns:* responsibilities include instructing and facilitating groups in environmental and adventure activities including caving orienting, high and low challenge courses, evening activities, and training and supervising counselors; participating in presentations and outreach programs; and designing curriculum and teaching materials; community-based programs for youth, other positions available in community-based programs for youth, teens, and families. Candidates should have experience in the field, oral communication skills, personal interest in the field, self-motivation, strong interpersonal skills. Duration is flexible. $400–$800 per month. Open to recent high school graduates, college freshmen, college sophomores, college juniors, college seniors, recent college graduates, graduate students, law students, career changers, individuals reentering the workforce. International applications accepted.
Benefits Formal training, free housing, free meals, names of contacts, on-the-job training, opportunity to attend seminars/workshops, possible full-time employment, willing to act as a professional reference, willing to complete paperwork for educational credit, willing to provide letters of recommendation.
Contact Write, fax, or e-mail Claire Wyneken, Vice President. Fax: 636-938-5289. E-mail: wyman@stlouis.missouri.org. No phone calls. In-person interview recommended. Applicants must submit a formal organization application, cover letter, resume, three personal references, child abuse and criminal background checks required. Applications are accepted continuously.

YMCA CAMP BERNIE ENVIRONMENTAL EDUCATION CENTER
327 Turkey Top Road
Port Murray, New Jersey 07865

General Information Resident summer camp and September through June resident outdoor education center where students from New York and New Jersey spend 2–5 days per week in an outdoor setting. Established in 1956. Number of employees: 87.

Branch of YMCA of Ridgewood, Ridgewood, New Jersey. Number of internship applications received each year: 7.
Internships Available ▶ *2–5 interns/outdoor educators:* responsibilities include assisting with planning, leading, and supervising instructional and recreational activities for elementary, junior, and high school students; instructing classes in all areas of environmental and outdoor education; and conducting outdoor education planning and training sessions for teachers, students, and parents. Candidates should have college courses in field, oral communication skills, personal interest in the field, strong interpersonal skills, strong leadership ability. Duration is flexible. $200–$250 per week. Open to college juniors, college seniors, recent college graduates, graduate students, career changers. International applications accepted.
Benefits Formal training, free housing, free meals, on-the-job training, opportunity to attend seminars/workshops, possible full-time employment, travel reimbursement, willing to act as a professional reference, willing to complete paperwork for educational credit, willing to provide letters of recommendation.
Contact Write, call, fax, or e-mail Kirk Weber, Director of Environmental Education. Phone: 908-832-5315. Fax: 908-832-9078. E-mail: campbernie@campbernieymca.org. In-person interview recommended. Applicants must submit a formal organization application, cover letter, resume, three letters of recommendation, 6 personal references. Application deadline: April 1 for summer, November 1 for winter/spring. World Wide Web: http://www.campbernieymca.org.

YMCA CAMP CAMPBELL GARD
4803 Augspurger Road
Hamilton, Ohio 45011

General Information Outdoor education program offering day and resident programming to elementary school children of all ages and abilities. Established in 1926. Number of employees: 30. Unit of Greater Miami Valley YMCA, Hamilton, Ohio.
Internships Available ▶ *2–3 naturalist interns:* responsibilities include assisting with instruction, evening programming, various program tasks, and living history. Candidates should have ability to work independently, ability to work with others, oral communication skills, personal interest in the field, self-motivation, strong leadership ability. Duration is 1 semester. $100 per week. International applications accepted.
Benefits Free housing, free meals, names of contacts, on-the-job training, opportunity to attend seminars/workshops, possible full-time employment, willing to complete paperwork for educational credit, willing to provide letters of recommendation, YMCA membership.
Contact Write, call, fax, or e-mail Ms. Marsha Rolph, Outdoor Education Director. Phone: 513-867-0600. Fax: 513-867-0127. E-mail: campstaff@ccgymca.org. In-person interview recommended. Applicants must submit a formal organization application, cover letter, resume, three personal references. Applications are accepted continuously.

YMCA OF GREATER OKLAHOMA CITY/CAMP CLASSEN
Route 1, Box 46
Davis, Oklahoma 73030-9801

General Information 2440-acre resident camp offering a summer youth camp, school year outdoor education programs, and family programs on weekends, and seeking to help people grow in mind, body, and spirit. Established in 1940. Number of employees: 25. Unit of YMCA of Greater Oklahoma City, Oklahoma City, Oklahoma. Number of internship applications received each year: 10.
Internships Available ▶ *4 program assistants:* responsibilities include assisting in the operation of programs such as nature education, cooperative courses and games, and helping in facility care and development. Candidates should have analytical skills, oral communication skills, personal interest in the field, self-motivation, strong interpersonal skills, love of children and willingness to learn. Duration is 1 summer, spring, or fall. Position available as unpaid or at $100–$206 per week. Open to

YMCA of Greater Oklahoma City/Camp Classen (continued)

recent high school graduates, college freshmen, college sophomores, college juniors, college seniors, recent college graduates, graduate students, career changers, individuals reentering the workforce. International applications accepted.

Benefits Formal training, free housing, free meals, job counseling, names of contacts, on-the-job training, opportunity to attend seminars/workshops, possible full-time employment, willing to act as a professional reference, willing to complete paperwork for educational credit, willing to provide letters of recommendation.

Contact Write, call, or fax Albert McWhorter, Camp Director. Phone: 580-369-2272. Fax: 580-369-2284. In-person interview recommended. Applicants must submit a formal organization application, resume, three personal references. Applications are accepted continuously.

FINANCE AND INSURANCE

GENERAL

AETNA, INC.
151 Farmington Avenue, RSAA
Hartford, Connecticut 06156

General Information Global insurance, financial services, and health care benefits company. Established in 1858. Number of employees: 30,000. Number of internship applications received each year: 2,000.
Internships Available ▶ *20–100 interns:* responsibilities include performing various duties specific to each assignment. Duration is 1 summer. $9–$12 per hour. Open to college freshmen, college sophomores, college juniors, college seniors. International applications accepted.
Benefits Formal training, job counseling, names of contacts, opportunity to attend seminars/workshops, possible full-time employment, travel reimbursement, willing to provide letters of recommendation.
Contact Write or e-mail Intern Coordinator, RSAA. E-mail: jobs@aetna.com. No phone calls. In-person interview required. Applicants must submit a cover letter, resume. Applications are accepted continuously. World Wide Web: http://www.aetna.com.

ALTERNATIVES FEDERAL CREDIT UNION
301 West State Street
Ithaca, New York 14850-5431

General Information Community development financial institution that specializes in services to micro-business, not-for-profit, and low-income members. Established in 1979. Number of employees: 25. Number of internship applications received each year: 70.
Internships Available ▶ *1 PC training intern:* responsibilities include designing and delivering PC training on a small group basis and delivering individual support. Candidates should have computer skills, experience in the field, knowledge of field, oral communication skills, strong interpersonal skills. Duration is 1 semester. ▶ *1 disaster planning intern:* responsibilities include expanding emergency manual into a workable plan. Candidates should have ability to work independently, computer skills, oral communication skills, organizational skills, research skills, self-motivation. Duration is 1 semester. Open to college juniors, college seniors, recent college graduates, graduate students, career changers. ▶ *1 employee benefits intern:* responsibilities include researching and establishing a Section 125 benefits plan, in which each employee may choose the benefits they would most use. Candidates should have ability to work independently, oral communication skills, organizational skills, research skills, written communication skills. Duration is flexible. Open to college juniors, college seniors, recent college graduates, graduate students, law students, career changers, individuals reentering the workforce. ▶ *1 youth entrepreneurship outreach intern:* responsibilities include developing an outreach plan for mini-MBA program involving youths and documenting the program; compiling an adult mentor list; designing a community involvement project; documentation of program; includes guiding and supporting Dollars for Dreams, a youth-run branch serving youth only. Candidates should have self-motivation, strong interpersonal skills. Duration is flexible (Thursday and Friday each week).

Open to high school students, high school seniors, recent high school graduates, college freshmen, college sophomores, college juniors, college seniors, recent college graduates, graduate students, law students, career changers, individuals reentering the workforce. All positions are unpaid. International applications accepted.
Benefits On-the-job training, willing to complete paperwork for educational credit, willing to provide letters of recommendation.
Contact Write, call, fax, or e-mail Ms. Mary Ziegler, Intern Coordinator. Phone: 607-273-3582 Ext. 819. Fax: 607-277-6391. E-mail: mziegler@alternatives.org. Applicants must submit a formal organization application, resume, three personal references. Applications are accepted continuously. World Wide Web: http://www.alternatives.org.

BLUE CROSS BLUE SHIELD OF MARYLAND
10455 Mill Run Circle
Owings Mills, Maryland 21117

General Information Managed care organization (insurance company). Established in 1937. Number of employees: 5,000. Number of internship applications received each year: 300.
Internships Available ▶ *1–5 interns.* Candidates should have office skills, oral communication skills, personal interest in the field, strong interpersonal skills, written communication skills, Microsoft computer software knowledge desirable. Duration is full-time in summer, part-time during academic year. $8—$12 per hour depending on experience. Open to college freshmen, college sophomores, college juniors, college seniors, graduate students. International applications accepted.
Benefits On-the-job training, opportunity to attend seminars/workshops, possible full-time employment, willing to complete paperwork for educational credit.
Contact Write, call, fax, or e-mail Ivanie Myers-Bronson, Intern Recruiter. Phone: 410-998-7772. Fax: 410-998-5313. E-mail: ivanie.myers-bronson@bcbsmd.com. In-person interview required. Applicants must submit a cover letter, resume. Applications are accepted continuously. World Wide Web: http://www.BCBSMD.com.

CHRYSLER FINANCIAL CORPORATION
27777 Franklin Road
Southfield, Michigan 48034-8266

General Information Non-bank financial services company. Number of employees: 700. Unit of Chrysler Corporation, Auburn Hills, Michigan.
Internships Available ▶ *General counsel interns:* responsibilities include some legal research and general office work. ▶ *8–12 interns:* responsibilities include working in computer science or finance departments. Duration for all positions is 3-4 months in summer. All positions paid. Open to college freshmen, college sophomores, college juniors, college seniors.
Contact Write or call Ms. Elena Tuczek, Human Resources. Phone: 248-948-3733. In-person interview required. Applicants must submit a cover letter, resume. Applications are accepted continuously.

CIGNA CORPORATION
1601 Chestnut Street, 2 Liberty Place
Philadelphia, Pennsylvania 19192

General Information Premier global employee benefits provider. Established in 1792. Number of employees: 5,000. Number of internship applications received each year: 1,000.
Internships Available ▶ *100–150 summer interns:* responsibilities include working in actuarial science, risk management, finance, human resources, computer science, computer engineering, or MIS; working on project-based, meaningful assignments; attending luncheons, informational panel discussions, and developmental workshops. Candidates should have analytical skills, oral communication skills, self-motivation, strong interpersonal skills, strong leadership ability, written communication skills. Duration is 10–12 weeks. $11–$15 per hour. Open to college sophomores, college juniors, college seniors, graduate students. International applications accepted.
Benefits Job counseling, names of contacts, on-the-job training, opportunity to attend seminars/workshops, possible full-time employment, willing to complete paperwork for educational credit, willing to provide letters of recommendation, housing stipend.
Contact Write, fax, or e-mail Dianne M. Certo, University Relations Consultant. Fax: 215-761-5516. E-mail: dianne.certo@cigna.com. No phone calls. In-person interview recommended. Applicants must submit a cover letter, resume. Application deadline: March 31. World Wide Web: http://www.cigna.com.

CROWN CAPITAL
540 Pacific Avenue
San Francisco, California 94133

General Information Commercial/real estate investment and mortgage banking organization. Established in 1977. Number of internship applications received each year: 200.
Internships Available ▶ *1–2 interns:* responsibilities include working directly for owner principals, assisting in commercial real estate investment and mortgage banking business. Candidates should have analytical skills, computer skills, personal interest in the field, self-motivation, strong interpersonal skills, writing skills. Duration is 3–12 months. $500 per month. Open to college juniors, college seniors, recent college graduates, graduate students, law students.
Benefits On-the-job training, possible full-time employment, travel reimbursement, willing to act as a professional reference, willing to complete paperwork for educational credit, willing to provide letters of recommendation, working directly with senior principals of the company.
Contact Write or fax David W. Yancey, President. Fax: 415-398-6057. In-person interview recommended. Applicants must submit a cover letter, resume, academic transcripts, SAT scores. Application deadline: February 1 for spring, April 1 for summer, July 1 for fall, November 1 for winter.

FANNIE MAE
3900 Wisconsin Avenue, NW
Washington, District of Columbia 20016

General Information Financial services company, whose mission is to develop the financial products and services that increase the availability and affordability of housing for low-, moderate-, and middle-income Americans. Established in 1938. Number of employees: 2,600. Number of internship applications received each year: 200.
Internships Available ▶ *10–15 summer interns/analysts:* responsibilities include handling professional-level assignments in business units across the company, including financial analysis, market research, systems testing and development, and writing proposals. Candidates should have analytical skills, computer skills, oral communication skills, plan to pursue career in field, written communication skills, 3-5 years of relevant work experience, fluency in English, minimum GPA of 3.3. Duration is 10 weeks. Paid. Open to first-year MBA students specializing in finance, MIS, and/or real estate; first-year MS students specializing in industrial or computer engineering; or first-year MPA or MPP students. International applications accepted.
Benefits Formal training, job counseling, on-the-job training, opportunity to attend seminars/workshops, possible full-time employment, willing to complete paperwork for educational credit, assignment to a peer mentor, possible free housing.
Contact Write, fax, or e-mail Lora McCray, Program Manager, 3900 Wisconsin Avenue, NW, Washington, District of Columbia 20016. Fax: 202-752-3804. E-mail: lora_mccray@fanniemae.com. No phone calls. Applicants must submit a cover letter, resume, writing sample. Application deadline: February 28. World Wide Web: http://www.fanniemae.com.

FEDERAL RESERVE BANK OF CHICAGO
230 South LaSalle Street
Chicago, Illinois 60604

General Information Institution that formulates the nation's monetary policy, supervises and regulates member banks and bank holding companies, acts as the government's bank, and operates nationwide payments mechanism for clearing of checks and the transferring of funds. Established in 1913. Number of employees: 2,000. Unit of The Federal Reserve, Washington, District of Columbia. Number of internship applications received each year: 600.
Internships Available ▶ *45–60 summer interns:* responsibilities include working in internal auditing, supervision and regulation, human resources, operations, communications, automation, or economic research departments on projects for the assigned area; projects with the intern group; participating in several seminars, workshops, and outside activities. Candidates should have analytical skills, computer skills, plan to pursue career in field, self-motivation, strong interpersonal skills, ability to learn quickly. Duration is 1 summer. $8–$16 per hour. Open to college freshmen, college sophomores, college juniors, college seniors, graduate students.
Benefits Job counseling, names of contacts, on-the-job training, opportunity to attend seminars/workshops, possible full-time employment, willing to act as a professional reference, willing to complete paperwork for educational credit, willing to provide letters of recommendation, assistance with resume preparation, interview assistance provided.
Contact Write or fax Intern Coordinator Staffing Division, 230 South LaSalle Streetq, Chicago, Illinois 60604. Fax: 312-913-2682. In-person interview required. Applicants must submit a cover letter, resume. Application deadline: March 1. World Wide Web: http://www.frbchi.org.

THE FRANKLIN
1 Franklin Square
Springfield, Illinois 62713

General Information Life insurance sales company. Established in 1884. Number of employees: 1,000. Subsidiary of American General, Houston, Texas. Number of internship applications received each year: 200.
Internships Available ▶ *Career interns:* responsibilities include life insurance sales, building client relations, and introducing others to sales opportunities. Candidates should have ability to work independently, oral communication skills, personal interest in the field, self-motivation, strong interpersonal skills, written communication skills. Duration is 12 weeks. compensation derived from sales activity and results. Open to college juniors, college seniors, recent college graduates, graduate students, law students, career changers, individuals reentering the workforce. International applications accepted.
Benefits Formal training, job counseling, names of contacts, on-the-job training, opportunity to attend seminars/workshops, willing to act as a professional reference, willing to complete paperwork for educational credit, opportunity for entrepreneurial advancement.
Contact Write, call, fax, or e-mail Patti Sauer, Coordinator. Phone: 217-528-2011 Ext. 2302. Fax: 217-528-6163. In-person interview recommended. Applicants must submit a formal

organization application, cover letter, resume, references and recommendations may be necessary, depending on placement. Applications are accepted continuously. World Wide Web: http://www.thefranklin.com.

INSURANCE SERVICES OFFICE, INC. (ISO)
7 World Trade Center
New York, New York 10048

General Information Organization that collects loss data from property/casualty insurance companies and provides aggregated information and services to insurers, agents, and brokers. Established in 1971. Number of employees: 670. Number of internship applications received each year: 200.
Internships Available ▶ *6–12 actuarial interns:* responsibilities include completing actuarial projects. Candidates should have ability to work independently, computer skills, oral communication skills, personal interest in the field, self-motivation, written communication skills, strong interest in an actuarial career. Duration is 3 months. $450–$600 per week. Open to college juniors.
Benefits On-the-job training, opportunity to attend seminars/workshops, possible full-time employment, holiday pay for summer holidays, retroactive salary increase upon successful completion of actuarial examination during internship.
Contact Write or e-mail Ms. Nancie L. Merritt, Assistant Manager, Recruitment. E-mail: nmerritt@iso.com. No phone calls. In-person interview required. Applicants must submit a formal organization application, cover letter, resume. Application deadline: May 15 for summer. World Wide Web: http://www.ISO.com.

INTERNATIONAL MONETARY FUND
700 19th Street, NW
Washington, District of Columbia 20431

General Information International financial institution, responsible for monitoring the international monetary system. Established in 1946. Number of employees: 2,500. Number of internship applications received each year: 750.
Internships Available ▶ *37 summer interns:* responsibilities include undertaking a research project on a subject set by the employing department and preparing a paper. Candidates should have ability to work independently, analytical skills, college degree in related field, computer skills, knowledge of field, organizational skills, research skills, self-motivation, writing skills, written communication skills. Duration is 13 weeks. $3,000 per month. Open to graduate students in international economics or a related field, preferably at end of third or fourth year in PhD program. International applications accepted.
Benefits Health insurance, opportunity to attend seminars/workshops, possible full-time employment, travel reimbursement.
Contact Write, fax, or e-mail Summer Intern Program, Recruitment Division. Fax: 202-623-7333. E-mail: recruit@imf.org. Applicants must submit a cover letter, resume, academic transcripts, college campus interview during IMF recruitment desirable. Application deadline: January 31. World Wide Web: http://www.imf.org.

J.P. MORGAN
60 Wall Street
New York, New York 10260

General Information Global financial firm which advises on corporate strategy and structure, raises capital, trades a range of financial instruments, and manages investment portfolios. Established in 1854. Number of employees: 8,000. Number of internship applications received each year: 10,000.
Internships Available ▶ *15–20 internal consulting services interns:* responsibilities include documenting business procedures and test controls (audit intern); maintaining financial reporting, infrastructure, and report compilation (financial); investigating demographic trends and assisting in developing training programs (human resources); reviewing workflows and analyzing processes (operations); reengineering technology processes and helping to define technology strategy (technology). Candidates should have ability to work independently, analytical skills, oral com-

munication skills, self-motivation, strong interpersonal skills, strong leadership ability, written communication skills, interest in financial services field. Duration is 10-12 weeks (summer only). $725 per week. ▶ *20–25 internal consulting services/applications delivery interns:* responsibilities include various assignments including designing applications, developing detailed programming specifications, programming and testing new applications, and training users. Candidates should have ability to work independently, analytical skills, computer skills, oral communication skills, self-motivation, strong interpersonal skills, strong leadership ability, written communication skills, interest in financial services industry; working knowledge of at least one programming language (Excel, C, C++, Smalltalk, Visual Basic, Java, or other third-generation language). Duration is 10-12 weeks (summer only). $725 per week. Open to college juniors. ▶ *30–35 investment banking interns:* responsibilities include assisting with financial and company valuation analyses, database maintenance, financial model creation and maintenance, preparation of materials for client presentations. Candidates should have ability to work independently, analytical skills, computer skills, oral communication skills, plan to pursue career in field, self-motivation, strong interpersonal skills, strong leadership ability, written communication skills, quantitative skills, ability to work under pressure. Duration is 10-12 weeks (summer only). $725 per week. Open to college juniors. ▶ *30–35 investment banking interns (MBA):* responsibilities include working primarily with client and product teams on the marketing, structuring, and execution of financial and advisory assignments. Candidates should have ability to work independently, analytical skills, computer skills, knowledge of field, oral communication skills, plan to pursue career in field, self-motivation, strong interpersonal skills, strong leadership ability, written communication skills, self-confidence in working with clients. Duration is 10-12 weeks (summer only). $1,450 per week. Open to MBA students. ▶ *20–25 investment management interns:* responsibilities include working with professionals from both investment and client areas on various assignments, such as conducting research, analyzing portfolio performance, preparing client presentations, and other projects. Candidates should have ability to work independently, analytical skills, computer skills, oral communication skills, plan to pursue career in field, self-motivation, strong interpersonal skills, strong leadership ability, written communication skills, quantitative and technical skills. Duration is 10-12 weeks (summer only). $725 per week. Open to college juniors. ▶ *1–5 investment management interns (MBA):* responsibilities include conducting research for portfolio recommendations; developing valuation methods (research interns); assisting with analyzing, trading, constructing, and monitoring portfolios (portfolio management); creating presentations and publications, providing client service (marketing). Candidates should have ability to work independently, analytical skills, computer skills, knowledge of field, oral communication skills, plan to pursue career in field, self-motivation, strong interpersonal skills, strong leadership ability, written communication skills, quantitative and technical skills for some positions. Duration is 10-12 weeks (summer only). $1,450 per week. Open to MBA students. ▶ *15–20 junior interns:* responsibilities include working in one of the following groups: investment banking, markets, private client, investment management, or internal consulting services. Placements are made based on the intern's skills and interests and on business need. Candidates should have ability to work independently, analytical skills, computer skills, office skills, oral communication skills, organizational skills, plan to pursue career in field, self-motivation, strong interpersonal skills, strong leadership ability, written communication skills, quantitative and qualitative skills, college courses in field preferred. Duration is 10 weeks (summer only). $500 per week (freshmen), $600 per week (sophomores). Open to women, people of color, and people with disabilities, who are college freshmen or sophomores. ▶ *10–15 private client interns:* responsibilities include various assignments including research, financial, and investments analysis; assistance with business maintenance and development; product and sales support. Candidates should have ability to work independently, analytical skills, computer skills, oral communication skills, plan to pursue career in field, self-motivation, strong interpersonal skills, written communication

J.P. Morgan *(continued)*

skills, quantitative and qualitative skills, sound judgment and discretion. Duration is 10-12 weeks (summer only). $725 per week. Open to college juniors. ▶ *20–25 private client interns (MBA):* responsibilities include rotation through several groups: securities sales, investment management, client advisory, generational planning, and credit. Candidates should have ability to work independently, analytical skills, computer skills, knowledge of field, oral communication skills, plan to pursue career in field, self-motivation, strong interpersonal skills, strong leadership ability, written communication skills, judgment and self-confidence in working with clients, ability to work in a fast-paced environment. Duration is 10 weeks (summer only). $1,450 per week. Open to MBA students. ▶ *45–50 sales, trading, and research markets interns:* responsibilities include various assignments including assisting a salesperson in collecting market and client information, working with a trader on a spreadsheet to value and hedge financial instruments, or working with a researcher to assess market trends. Candidates should have ability to work independently, analytical skills, computer skills, oral communication skills, plan to pursue career in field, self-motivation, strong interpersonal skills, strong leadership ability, written communication skills, decision-making skills, critical-thinking skills. Duration is 10-12 weeks (summer only). $725 per week. Open to college juniors. ▶ *30–35 sales, trading, and research markets interns (MBA):* responsibilities include assignments in equities, fixed income, or emerging markets group; could include compiling research, technical analysis, and market commentaries for sales and syndicate desks; assisting traders in managing risk liquidity and interest rate exposure; developing economic, strategic, credit, and risk analysis for investors and the firm; developing news on prospect and stock prices; preparing presentations for clients. Candidates should have ability to work independently, analytical skills, computer skills, knowledge of field, oral communication skills, plan to pursue career in field, self-motivation, strong interpersonal skills, strong leadership ability, written communication skills, quantitative skills, ability to think critically, client focus, self-confidence, ability to work in a fast-paced environment. Duration is 10-12 weeks (summer only). $1,450 per week. Open to MBA students. International applications accepted.
Benefits Meals at a cost, names of contacts, on-the-job training, opportunity to attend seminars/workshops, possible full-time employment, willing to complete paperwork for educational credit, admission to museums.
Contact Write Corporate Recruiting, 60 Wall Street, 40th Floor, New York, New York 10260. No phone calls. In-person interview recommended. Applicants must submit a cover letter, resume, academic transcripts. Application deadline: March 1 for undergraduates, December 31 for MBAs. World Wide Web: http://www.jpmorgan.com.

LUTHERAN BROTHERHOOD
625 Fourth Avenue, South, MS 1385
Minneapolis, Minnesota 56415

General Information A Fortune 500, not-for-profit, financial services company. Established in 1917. Number of employees: 1,300. Unit of Lutheran Brotherhood Home Office, Minneapolis, Minnesota. Number of internship applications received each year: 300.
Internships Available ▶ *100–150 financial services interns:* responsibilities include marketing, financial management training, running appointments with a mentoring district representative, and financial analyses. Candidates should have ability to work independently, oral communication skills, self-motivation, strong interpersonal skills, strong leadership ability, entrepreneurial style. Duration is May to September. Position available as unpaid or at $150 per week plus commissions. Open to college freshmen, college sophomores, college juniors, college seniors, graduate students, law students. International applications accepted.
Benefits Formal training, on-the-job training, opportunity to attend seminars/workshops, possible full-time employment, willing to act as a professional reference, willing to complete

paperwork for educational credit, willing to provide letters of recommendation, licensing reimbursement, expense-paid trip to our Minneapolis home office, business stipend.
Contact Write, call, fax, or e-mail Laura LeVander, Field Recruiting Development Specialist, 625 Fourth Avenue South, MS 1385, Minneapolis, Minnesota 55415. Phone: 800-688-6027. Fax: 612-340-7142. E-mail: levander.laura@luthbro.com. Telephone interview required. Applicants must submit a cover letter, resume, three personal references. Application deadline: May 1. World Wide Web: http://www.luthbro.com.

NATIONAL ASSOCIATION OF PROFESSIONAL SURPLUS LINES OFFICES
6405 North Cosby Avenue, #201
Kansas City, Missouri 64151

General Information Trade association representing the surplus lines segment of the insurance industry. Established in 1975. Number of employees: 5. Number of internship applications received each year: 60.
Internships Available ▶ *6–8 summer interns:* responsibilities include working 4 weeks at a NAPSLO member broker and 5 weeks for a NAPSLO member company. 4 interns are selected to attend the national convention; 1 intern selected for an additional 3-week internship with a broker in London. Candidates should have ability to work with others, computer skills, oral communication skills, plan to pursue career in field, self-motivation, written communication skills. Duration is 9 weeks. $400 per week. Open to college juniors, college seniors, recent college graduates, graduate students. International applications accepted.
Benefits Names of contacts, possible full-time employment, travel reimbursement, willing to complete paperwork for educational credit, reimbursement of housing costs.
International Internships Available in London, United Kingdom.
Contact Write, call, fax, or e-mail Bill Davis, Internship Committee Co- Chairman, 6405 North Cosby Avnenue, #201, Kansas City, Missouri 64151. Phone: 816-741-3910. Fax: 816-741-5409. E-mail: napslo@microlink.net. Applicants must submit a formal organization application, resume, academic transcripts, two personal references. Application deadline: February 1. World Wide Web: http://www.napslo.org.

NEW YORK STOCK EXCHANGE
11 Wall Street
New York, New York 10005

General Information World's largest equities market whose principal business is to manage, develop, and regulate the premier market of trading corporate securities. Established in 1792. Number of employees: 1,500. Number of internship applications received each year: 500.
Internships Available ▶ *35–50 interns:* responsibilities include working as needed in either the accounting, finance, international, CIS, client service, technology, or regulatory department. Candidates should have computer skills, office skills, oral communication skills, organizational skills, strong interpersonal skills, written communication skills. Duration is 10 weeks in summer, June to August. Paid. Open to college sophomores, college juniors.
Benefits On-the-job training, opportunity to attend seminars/workshops, possible full-time employment.
Contact Write or fax Summer Internship Coordinator, Human Resources, Staffing Department, 11 Wall Street, 16th Floor, New York, New York 10005. Fax: 212-656-2050. No phone calls. Telephone interview required. Applicants must submit a cover letter, resume. Application deadline: March 31. World Wide Web: http://www.nyse.com.

PRINCIPAL FINANCIAL GROUP
711 High Street
Des Moines, Iowa 50392-0550

General Information Organization that provides financial services. Established in 1879. Number of employees: 9,000. Number of internship applications received each year: 200.
Internships Available ▶ *2–5 accounting interns:* responsibilities include assisting on accounting projects in a team environment. Candidates should have declared college major in field, plan to pursue career in field, self-motivation, strong interpersonal skills, strong leadership ability. Duration is 3 months. $11 per hour. Open to college sophomores, college juniors, college seniors, graduate students. ▶ *1–2 capital management interns:* responsibilities include researching possible entities of investing and funding. Candidates should have ability to work independently, analytical skills, declared college major in field, plan to pursue career in field, research skills, strong leadership ability. Duration is 3 months. $13–$18 per hour. Open to MBA students only. ▶ *8–10 commercial real estate interns:* responsibilities include assisting in purchasing, underwriting, and liquidating corporate owned property. Candidates should have ability to work independently, analytical skills, college courses in field, plan to pursue career in field, strong interpersonal skills, experience in finance and/or real estate (preferred). Duration is 6–9 months. $11–$12 per hour. Open to college juniors, college seniors. ▶ *30–40 information analyst interns:* responsibilities include application development, database administration, and networking. Candidates should have ability to work independently, declared college major in field, plan to pursue career in field, self-motivation, strong interpersonal skills, strong leadership ability. Duration is 3–12 months. $13 per hour plus housing stipend. Open to college sophomores, college juniors, college seniors.
Benefits Job counseling, on-the-job training, possible full-time employment, willing to act as a professional reference, willing to complete paperwork for educational credit, willing to provide letters of recommendation, housing subsidy for commercial real estate interns.
Contact Write, fax, or e-mail Andrew Zastrow, Human Resources Department. Fax: 515-247-5874. E-mail: zastrow.andrew@principal.com. In-person interview recommended. Applicants must submit a cover letter, resume, academic transcripts, 3 professional references. Application deadline: January 1 for summer (information technology positions), January 31 for summer (undergraduate positions), January 1 for summer (MBA postions); continuous for commercial real estate. World Wide Web: http://www.principal.com.

STATE FARM INSURANCE COMPANIES
3 State Farm Plaza, K-1
Bloomington, Illinois 61791

General Information Insurance company. Established in 1922. Number of employees: 10,000. Number of internship applications received each year: 500.
Internships Available ▶ *33–35 business analyst interns:* responsibilities include two weeks training, ten weeks assigned to a corporate systems area which includes hands-on projects that provide an excellent opportunity to learn more about State Farm systems operations. Candidates should have oral communication skills, strong interpersonal skills, strong leadership ability, written communication skills, major in accounting, insurance, or finance; 6-9 hours of accounting depending on major; minimum GPA of 3.0 overall and in major. ▶ *9–12 corporate accounting interns:* responsibilities include two weeks training, ten weeks assigned to a corporate accounting area which includes hands-on projects that provide an excellent opportunity to learn more about State Farm accounting operations. Candidates should have oral communication skills, strong interpersonal skills, strong leadership ability, written communication skills, major in accounting, insurance, or finance with 12 or more hours of accounting; minimum GPA of 3.2 overall, 3.2 in major courses. ▶ *100 programmer/analyst interns:* responsibilities include two weeks training, ten weeks in an area with real programming assignments; participation in professional and personal development classes. Candidates

should have oral communication skills, strong interpersonal skills, strong leadership ability, written communication skills, major in computer science, management information systems, or mathematics; minimum GPA 3.0; 6-9 hours applied computer science classes (at least 3 hours in COBOL, PL/1, PASCAL, C, C++, or other high level languages). Duration for all positions is one summer. All positions paid at $13 per hour. Open to college sophomores, college juniors, college seniors.
Benefits Formal training, meals at a cost, opportunity to attend seminars/workshops, possible full-time employment, travel reimbursement, willing to complete paperwork for educational credit, possible 401(k) contribution, assistance with locating housing.
Contact Write, call, or e-mail Rodney Litwiller, Human Resources Representative, 3 State Farm Plaza, K—1, Bloomington, Illinois 61791. Phone: 309-763-2822. E-mail: rodney.litwiller.gho5@statefarm.com. In-person interview required. Applicants must submit a formal organization application, resume, academic transcripts, application may be made through college placement office. Application deadline: February 1 for summer. World Wide Web: http://www.statefarm.com.

STATE TEACHERS RETIREMENT SYSTEM OF OHIO (STRS OHIO)
275 East Broad Street
Columbus, Ohio 43215-3771

General Information One of the largest pension funds in the United States, managing assets totaling $50 billion at market value, provides benefits to more than 300,000 public educators. Established in 1920. Number of employees: 505. Number of internship applications received each year: 600.
Internships Available ▶ *1 communications intern (design team):* responsibilities include assisting members of the department in fulfilling their duties; assisting members of the design team in the production of print materials, Web-based communication, and multimedia presentations. Candidates should have ability to work independently, computer skills, declared college major in field, office skills, oral communication skills, organizational skills, plan to pursue career in field, self-motivation, strong interpersonal skills, written communication skills, proficiency in word processing software, experience with Microsoft Word and Macintosh preferred. Open to college juniors, college seniors, recent college graduates, graduate students. ▶ *1 communications intern (editorial team):* responsibilities include assisting members of the department in fulfilling their duties, assisting members of the editorial team in writing brochure copy, newsletter articles, Web-based information, news releases, and other communication materials. Candidates should have ability to work independently, computer skills, declared college major in field, editing skills, office skills, oral communication skills, plan to pursue career in field, research skills, self-motivation, strong interpersonal skills, writing skills, proficiency in word processing software, experience with Microsoft Word and Macintosh preferred. Open to college juniors, college seniors, recent college graduates, graduate students. ▶ *1 equities research assistant:* responsibilities include assisting the manager and equity securities analysts in the fundamental research process to ensure high-quality investment decisions. Candidates should have analytical skills, college courses in field, computer skills, declared college major in field, office skills, oral communication skills, organizational skills, personal interest in the field, plan to pursue career in field, research skills, self-motivation, strong interpersonal skills, strong leadership ability, written communication skills, competence in the use of standard spreadsheet and word processing software. Open to college juniors, college seniors, recent college graduates, graduate students. ▶ *1 finance accounting assistant:* responsibilities include performing general administrative duties for the accounting department, assisting in other areas of finance on an as-needed basis, sorting and distributing mail, responding to telephone inquiries from employers, typing, and distributing correspondence between STRS and employers. Candidates should have computer skills, declared college major in field, office skills, organizational skills, plan to pursue career in field, self-motivation, strong interpersonal skills, knowledge of word process-

State Teachers Retirement System of Ohio (STRS Ohio) (continued)

ing software and other Windows applications preferred. Open to college juniors, college seniors, recent college graduates, graduate students. ▶ *1 fixed income research assistant:* responsibilities include compiling and analyzing data to assist the investment staff in making decisions regarding bond and mortgage investments. Candidates should have ability to work independently, analytical skills, college courses in field, computer skills, declared college major in field, office skills, oral communication skills, organizational skills, personal interest in the field, plan to pursue career in field, research skills, self-motivation, strong interpersonal skills, written communication skills, knowledge of spreadsheet software preferred; computer experience. Open to college juniors, college seniors, recent college graduates, graduate students. ▶ *2 health care intern:* responsibilities include assisting in preparation of research and financial budget plans, and assisting or substituting for health care services staff where needed. Candidates should have ability to work independently, computer skills, declared college major in field, office skills, oral communication skills, organizational skills, plan to pursue career in field, self-motivation, strong interpersonal skills, written communication skills, competence in the use of standard spreadsheet and word processing software. Open to college juniors, college seniors, recent college graduates, graduate students. ▶ *1 international research assistant:* responsibilities include assisting the portfolio manager and country analysts in the fundamental research process to ensure high quality investment decisions. Candidates should have ability to work independently, analytical skills, college courses in field, computer skills, declared college major in field, office skills, oral communication skills, personal interest in the field, plan to pursue career in field, research skills, self-motivation, strong interpersonal skills, competence in the use of standard spreadsheet and word processing software. Open to college juniors, college seniors, recent college graduates, graduate students. ▶ *1 programmer:* responsibilities include designing, coding, testing, modifying, and implementing STRS information systems using Computer Aided Software Engineering (CASE) methodologies. Candidates should have ability to work independently, college courses in field, computer skills, declared college major in field, office skills, organizational skills, personal interest in the field, plan to pursue career in field, research skills, self-motivation, strong interpersonal skills, written communication skills, experience in information technology preferred. Open to college juniors, college seniors, recent college graduates, graduate students. ▶ *1 real estate research assistant:* responsibilities include working on assigned projects to assist the investment staff in acquisition disposition, and asset management decisions. Candidates should have ability to work independently, analytical skills, computer skills, declared college major in field, office skills, oral communication skills, organizational skills, personal interest in the field, plan to pursue career in field, research skills, self-motivation, strong interpersonal skills, written communication skills, working knowledge of application software for word processing, spreadsheets, and databases. Open to college juniors, college seniors, recent college graduates, graduate students, college juniors, seniors, or recent graduates with real estate major. Duration for all positions is 3–4 months. All positions paid at $600–$750 per week. International applications accepted.

Benefits Formal training, free housing, job counseling, on-the-job training, opportunity to attend seminars/workshops, possible full-time employment, travel reimbursement, willing to act as a professional reference, willing to complete paperwork for educational credit, willing to provide letters of recommendation, free fitness center membership.

Contact Write, call, fax, or e-mail Marilyn A. Thomas, Staffing Coordinator. Phone: 614-227-2908. Fax: 614-227-2952. E-mail: thomasm@strsoh.org. In-person interview recommended. Applicants must submit a formal organization application, cover letter, resume, physical and drug screen required, 3 personal/business references. Application deadline: April 30 for summer; continuous for other positions. World Wide Web: http://www.strsoh.org.

WELLS FARGO
420 Montgomery, 11th Floor
San Francisco, California 94163

General Information Full-service bank serving United States businesses and residents. Established in 1852. Number of internship applications received each year: 1,500.

Internships Available ▶ *Auditing/accounting interns:* responsibilities include conducting audits on specific business units, working on the trading floor and trading desk, researching investment mutual growth funds, and performing industry analysis for compliance purposes. Candidates should have ability to work independently, analytical skills, college courses in field, computer skills, knowledge of field, office skills, oral communication skills, personal interest in the field, research skills, self-motivation, strong interpersonal skills, writing skills. Paid. ▶ *6–18 finance interns:* responsibilities include assisting with calculation and development of loan loss factors, analyzing data and budgets, preparing management reports, and financial planning. Candidates should have ability to work independently, analytical skills, college courses in field, computer skills, knowledge of field, oral communication skills, personal interest in the field, research skills, self-motivation, strong interpersonal skills, writing skills. $2,000–$5,000 per month. ▶ *1–3 human resources interns.* Candidates should have ability to work independently, analytical skills, college courses in field, computer skills, knowledge of field, oral communication skills, self-motivation, strong interpersonal skills, writing skills. Paid. ▶ *2–15 information systems interns:* responsibilities include assisting in the analysis, design, development, implementation, maintenance, and modification of business applications and computer systems; supporting vast voice/data communications systems for ATMS; and working with systems professionals using Oracle, Informix or Sybase databases, object-oriented software, C++, MS Windows, MS Office, Perl. Candidates should have ability to work independently, analytical skills, college courses in field, computer skills, knowledge of field, oral communication skills, personal interest in the field, self-motivation, strong interpersonal skills, written communication skills. Paid. ▶ *6–12 lending interns:* responsibilities include working as a credit analyst, handling inquiries, conducting client calls, evaluating credit worthiness, extending sound loans, and participating in the restructuring of high-risk loans. Candidates should have ability to work independently, analytical skills, college courses in field, computer skills, knowledge of field, oral communication skills, personal interest in the field, self-motivation, strong interpersonal skills, writing skills. Paid. ▶ *6–12 marketing interns:* responsibilities include working with product managers to implement a consumer promotion targeted for college students and communicating and coordinating between project management, retail branches, promotional agency, and campus administrators. Candidates should have ability to work independently, analytical skills, college courses in field, computer skills, knowledge of field, oral communication skills, personal interest in the field, self-motivation, strong interpersonal skills, writing skills. Paid. ▶ *1–4 operations interns:* responsibilities include evaluating training programs, developing operational plans and processes, writing business cases, and other related tasks. Candidates should have ability to work independently, analytical skills, college courses in field, computer skills, knowledge of field, oral communication skills, organizational skills, personal interest in the field, research skills, self-motivation, strong interpersonal skills, writing skills. Paid. Duration for all positions is 10–12 weeks. Open to college juniors, college seniors, graduate students.

Benefits Opportunity to attend seminars/workshops, possible full-time employment, travel reimbursement.

Contact Write or call Summer Internship Program, Position #3115. Phone: 800-541-8980. Applicants must submit a resume. Application deadline: April 3 for summer. World Wide Web: http://www.wellsfargosip.jobinfo.com.

HEALTH CARE AND SOCIAL ASSISTANCE

HEALTH-CARE SERVICES

ACCREDITED CARE, INC.
106 West Third Street, Suite 707
Jamestown, New York 14701

General Information Provider of home health-care services.
Internships Available ▶ *1 general intern:* responsibilities include assisting with all aspects of home health care. Duration is flexible; minimum of 2 months. Position available as unpaid or paid. ▶ *1 general office assistant (part-time):* responsibilities include administrative duties. Duration is flexible (minimum of 2 months). Unpaid. Open to high school students, high school seniors, recent high school graduates, college freshmen, college sophomores, college juniors, college seniors, recent college graduates, graduate students, law students, career changers, individuals reentering the workforce. International applications accepted.
Benefits Possible full-time employment, willing to complete paperwork for educational credit, willing to provide letters of recommendation.
Contact Write or call Mr. Fred Press, Director. Phone: 212-517-8110. In-person interview recommended. Applicants must submit a cover letter, resume. Applications are accepted continuously.

ADVOCATE FITNESS
205 Touhy, Suite 110
Park Ridge, Illinois 60068-5881

General Information Health care organization. Established in 1898. Number of employees: 22,000. Branch of Advocate Health Care, Oak Brook, Illinois. Number of internship applications received each year: 100.
Internships Available ▶ *7–8 "site" interns:* responsibilities include various duties, depending on intern's developmental needs and interests. Candidates should have ability to work independently, knowledge of field, organizational skills, self-motivation, strong interpersonal skills. Duration is 400 hours. Position available as unpaid or at $250–$500 per duration of internship. Open to college juniors, college seniors, recent college graduates, graduate students.
Benefits Names of contacts, on-the-job training, opportunity to attend seminars/workshops, possible full-time employment, willing to act as a professional reference, willing to complete paperwork for educational credit, willing to provide letters of recommendation.
Contact Write, call, fax, or e-mail Rebecca Steurer, Exercise Physiologist/Internship Coordinator, BWA Wellness Center, 700 25th Avenue, Bellwood, Illinois 60614. Phone: 708-547-2939. Fax: 708-547-2759. E-mail: fcstaff@ats.bwauto.com. In-person interview recommended. Applicants must submit a resume. Applications are accepted continuously.

AMERICAN CANCER SOCIETY
600 North Jackson Street
Media, Pennsylvania 19063

General Information A nonprofit health organization dedicated to the prevention, control, and eradication of cancer. Serves Bucks, Chester, Delaware, Montgomery, and Philadelphia counties. Established in 1913. Number of employees: 65. Unit of American Cancer Society, Pennsylvania Division, Hershey, Pennsylvania. Number of internship applications received each year: 20.
Internships Available ▶ *Fund-raising interns:* responsibilities include performing community outreach and data collection and writing letters, brochures, and press releases. Candidates should have ability to work independently, computer skills, oral communication skills, strong interpersonal skills, written communication skills. Open to college freshmen, college sophomores, college juniors, college seniors, recent college graduates, graduate students, law students, career changers, individuals reentering the workforce. ▶ *Patient services interns:* responsibilities include performing community outreach and data collection and writing letters, brochures, and press releases. Candidates should have ability to work independently, oral communication skills, personal interest in the field, strong interpersonal skills, written communication skills. Open to college freshmen, college sophomores, college juniors, college seniors, recent college graduates, graduate students, individuals reentering the workforce. ▶ *Public education interns.* Candidates should have organizational skills, personal interest in the field, research skills, strong interpersonal skills, strong leadership ability. Open to college freshmen, college sophomores, college juniors, college seniors. ▶ *Public relations interns:* responsibilities include performing community outreach and data collection and writing letters, brochures, and press releases. Candidates should have ability to work independently, editing skills, oral communication skills, strong interpersonal skills, written communication skills. Open to college freshmen, college sophomores, college juniors, college seniors, graduate students. Duration for all positions is flexible. All positions are unpaid. International applications accepted.
Benefits On-the-job training, opportunity to attend seminars/workshops, possible full-time employment, willing to act as a professional reference, willing to complete paperwork for educational credit, willing to provide letters of recommendation, travel allowance for assigned projects.
Contact Write, call, or fax Debbie Gaynor, Director of Volunteer and Community Development, 1626 Locust Street, Philadelphia, Pennsylvania 19103. Phone: 215-985-5400. Fax: 215-985-5406. In-person interview required. Applicants must submit a formal organization application, cover letter, resume. Applications are accepted continuously.

AMERICAN CORPORATE HEALTH PROGRAMS, INC.
559 West Uwchlan Avenue, Suite 220
Exton, Pennsylvania 19341

General Information Management consulting, fitness center management/staffing, health promotion/disease management. Established in 1976. Number of employees: 75. Number of internship applications received each year: 200.

American Corporate Health Programs, Inc. (continued)

Internships Available ▶ *5–7 corporate fitness interns:* responsibilities include testing and development of exercise prescriptions, participant instruction and supervision, individual counseling, educational display design, recreational and motivational programming, program marketing, and aerobics class instruction. Candidates should have ability to work with others, college courses in field, declared college major in field, personal interest in the field, CPR certification. Duration is 12 weeks or 450 hours. Unpaid. Open to college juniors, college seniors, recent college graduates, graduate students. ▶ *2–3 heatlh promotion interns:* responsibilities include health screenings, event coordination, health promotion planning, program promotion, implementation, and evaluation. Candidates should have ability to work with others, declared college major in field, knowledge of field, personal interest in the field, strong interpersonal skills, CPR certification. Duration is 12 weeks or 450 hours. Position available as unpaid or paid. Open to college juniors, college seniors, recent college graduates, graduate students. ▶ *1–2 sales and marketing interns:* responsibilities include marketing tool creations, sales prospecting, proposal writing, account sales, forecasting, budget management, product/service delivery strategies. Candidates should have computer skills, oral communication skills, organizational skills, research skills, self-motivation, written communication skills. Duration is approximately 450 hours (12 weeks). Position available as unpaid or paid. Open to college juniors, college seniors, recent college graduates, graduate students, career changers.

Benefits Formal training, job counseling, names of contacts, on-the-job training, possible full-time employment, willing to act as a professional reference, willing to complete paperwork for educational credit, willing to provide letters of recommendation.

Contact Write, fax, or e-mail Andrea Kelly, Internship Coordinator, 559 Uwchlan Avenue, Suite 220, Exton, Pennsylvania 19341. Fax: 610-594-9079. E-mail: achpinc@aol.com. Telephone interview required. Applicants must submit a formal organization application, resume. Applications are accepted continuously.

AMERICAN HEART ASSOCIATION NATIONAL CENTER
7272 Greenville Avenue
Dallas, Texas 75231

General Information Largest national nonprofit voluntary health association dedicated to reducing death and disability from cardiovascular disease and stroke. Established in 1924. Number of employees: 400. Number of internship applications received each year: 50.

Internships Available ▶ *2 corporate health interns.* Candidates should have ability to work independently, college courses in field, computer skills, declared college major in field, oral communication skills, organizational skills, plan to pursue career in field, self-motivation, strong interpersonal skills, strong leadership ability, written communication skills. Duration is 10–14 weeks. Unpaid. Open to college juniors, college seniors, graduate students.

Benefits Job counseling, names of contacts, on-the-job training, opportunity to attend seminars/workshops, possible full-time employment, willing to act as a professional reference, willing to complete paperwork for educational credit, willing to provide letters of recommendation.

Contact Write, call, fax, or e-mail Margaret Hawkins, Manager, Corporate Health, 7272 Greenville Avenue, Dallas, Texas 75231. Phone: 214-706-1521. Fax: 214-706-1931. E-mail: mhawkins@heart.org. In-person interview recommended. Applicants must submit a formal organization application, cover letter, resume, academic transcripts, personal reference, three letters of recommendation. Applications are accepted continuously. World Wide Web: http://www.americanheart.org.

AMERICAN HEART ASSOCIATION, PENNSYLVANIA-DELAWARE AFFILIATE
1019 Mumma Road
Camp Hill, Pennsylvania 17011-8835

General Information Organization that strives to reduce disability and death from cardiovascular diseases and strokes. Established in 1949. Number of employees: 95.

Internships Available ▶ *1 account assistant:* responsibilities include assisting in special projects using Excel and dBase software. ▶ *1 communications assistant:* responsibilities include assisting in campaign promotions. ▶ *1 computer hardware/systems technician:* responsibilities include teaching new software and identifying hardware/software needs. Candidates should have computer skills. ▶ *1 development assistant:* responsibilities include assisting in executing development projects. ▶ *1 development research assistant:* responsibilities include researching major corporate donors, foundation donors, and planned giving donors. ▶ *1 human resources assistant:* responsibilities include assisting on specific projects. ▶ *1 program assistant:* responsibilities include assisting in planning and executing community education programs. ▶ *1 research assistant:* responsibilities include assisting on research projects related to public policy and health-related legislation. ▶ *1 training assistant:* responsibilities include assisting in meeting training needs of staff and volunteers and designing model orientation/training programs. Duration for all positions is 3–12 months. All positions are unpaid. Open to college freshmen, college sophomores, college juniors, college seniors. International applications accepted.

Benefits Possible full-time employment, willing to complete paperwork for educational credit.

Contact Write, call, fax, or e-mail Jan Reddy, Director of Personnel. Phone: 717-975-4800 Ext. 116. Fax: 717-975-5597. E-mail: jreddy@heart.org. In-person interview required. Applicants must submit a resume. Applications are accepted continuously. World Wide Web: http://www.ahapa.org.

AMERICAN LUNG ASSOCIATION OF CENTRAL FLORIDA
1333 West Colonial Drive
Orlando, Florida 32804

General Information Nonprofit health organization. Established in 1904. Number of employees: 9. Affiliate of American Lung Association, New York, New York. Number of internship applications received each year: 20.

Internships Available ▶ *Program interns:* responsibilities include coordinating various programs related to lung disease and assisting program director as needed. Candidates should have ability to work independently, knowledge of field, personal interest in the field, self-motivation, strong interpersonal skills. Open to high school seniors, recent high school graduates, college freshmen, college sophomores, college juniors, college seniors, recent college graduates, graduate students, career changers, individuals reentering the workforce, senior citizens. ▶ *Public relations interns:* responsibilities include public relations, media relations, special events, fund-raising. Assignments will be made based on intern's talents and interests. Candidates should have ability to work independently, oral communication skills, self-motivation, strong interpersonal skills, written communication skills. Open to college freshmen, college sophomores, college juniors, college seniors, recent college graduates. Duration for all positions is varies. All positions are unpaid.

Benefits Names of contacts, on-the-job training, opportunity to attend seminars/workshops, possible full-time employment, travel reimbursement, willing to act as a professional reference, willing to complete paperwork for educational credit, willing to provide letters of recommendation.

Contact Write, call, fax, or e-mail Kristel Phillips, Program Director, 1333 West Colonial Drive, Orlando, Florida 32804. Phone: 407-425-5864. Fax: 407-425-2876. E-mail: alacf@gdi.net. In-person interview recommended. Applicants must submit a cover letter, resume. Applications are accepted continuously. World Wide Web: http://www.lungusa.org.

AMERICAN LUNG ASSOCIATION OF THE DISTRICT OF COLUMBIA (ALADC)
475 H Street, NW
Washington, District of Columbia 20001-2617

General Information Voluntary private health association working to prevent lung disease and promote lung health. Established in 1902. Number of employees: 5. Unit of American Lung Association, New York, New York. Number of internship applications received each year: 20.

Internships Available ▶ *1–2 Tobacco and D.C. Thoracic Society interns:* responsibilities include providing staff support in tobacco control and smoking cessation programs, assisting in coordinating and planning D.C. Thoracic Society conferences, information research and database management and producing and distributing program promotional materials. Candidates should have computer skills, office skills, oral communication skills, organizational skills, strong interpersonal skills, written communication skills. ▶ *1–3 athletic events interns:* responsibilities include assisting with the development of ALADC's athletic special events and promotions, assisting with the coordination and implementation of the Fun Run program, planning and developing the Bike Trek program, and recruiting health club involvement with ALADC. Candidates should have computer skills, oral communication skills, personal interest in the field, strong interpersonal skills, written communication skills, physical education background/major preferred. Duration is 4 weeks minimum. Open to high school seniors, recent high school graduates, college freshmen, college sophomores, college juniors, college seniors, recent college graduates, graduate students, career changers, individuals reentering the workforce. ▶ *1–3 creative design interns:* responsibilities include assisting in design and production of ALADCS annual report and newsletter, designing graphics for Bike Trek and Auction marketing, updating Web site, and assisting with design and layout of brochures and other promotional and educational materials. Candidates should have computer skills, office skills, oral communication skills, strong interpersonal skills, written communication skills, desktop publishing and familiarity with Internet and HTML. Duration is 4 weeks minimum. Open to college freshmen, college sophomores, college juniors, college seniors, recent college graduates, graduate students, career changers. ▶ *2–3 marketing interns:* responsibilities include assisting with the development and implementation of marketing plans; conducting market research and analysis, including survey development and implementation; producing and distributing marketing materials; and maintaining marketing contacts database. Candidates should have analytical skills, computer skills, oral communication skills, research skills, strong interpersonal skills, written communication skills. Open to college sophomores, college juniors, college seniors, recent college graduates, graduate students, law students, career changers. ▶ *2–3 program interns:* responsibilities include providing staff support to lung health and asthma education programs, assisting with information research as well as production and distribution of program promotional materials, maintaining program contact records in database and assisting in the coordination of health fairs. Candidates should have computer skills, office skills, oral communication skills, organizational skills, strong interpersonal skills, written communication skills. Duration is 4 weeks minimum. Open to high school seniors, recent high school graduates, college freshmen, college sophomores, college juniors, college seniors, recent college graduates, graduate students, law students, career changers, individuals reentering the workforce. All positions are unpaid. International applications accepted.

Benefits Names of contacts, on-the-job training, opportunity to attend seminars/workshops, willing to act as a professional reference, willing to complete paperwork for educational credit, willing to provide letters of recommendation, reimbursement of expenses while on official assignments.

Contact Write, fax, or e-mail Mr. Rolando Andrewn, Executive Director. Fax: 202-682-5874. E-mail: randrewn@aladc.org. No phone calls. In-person interview recommended. Applicants must submit a cover letter, resume, two personal references. Application deadline: February 15 for summer, September 15 for fall, December 1 for spring.

ANXIETY DISORDERS ASSOCIATION OF AMERICA
11900 Parklawn Drive, Suite 100
Rockville, Maryland 20852-2624

General Information Nonprofit association dedicated to promoting the prevention, treatment, and cure of anxiety disorders. Established in 1980. Number of employees: 12. Number of internship applications received each year: 10.

Internships Available ▶ *2 administrative assistants:* responsibilities include assisting all departments with administrative duties such as typing, filing, copying, large mailings, word processing, and computer work. Candidates should have computer skills, office skills, organizational skills, strong interpersonal skills, writing skills. Duration is 1 semester. Open to recent high school graduates, college freshmen, college sophomores, college juniors, college seniors, career changers. ▶ *1–2 assistant newsletter editors:* responsibilities include assisting in the production of a newsletter, corresponding with advertisers and writers, proofing and editing the newsletter, and other administrative tasks. Candidates should have ability to work independently, ability to work with others, editing skills, self-motivation, written communication skills. Duration is 1 semester. Open to college freshmen, college sophomores, college juniors, college seniors, recent college graduates, graduate students. ▶ *2–4 marketing development interns:* responsibilities include assisting in all areas of marketing and soliciting, maintaining a database, and coordinating mailings. Candidates should have ability to work independently, ability to work with others, knowledge of field, oral communication skills, self-motivation, writing skills. Duration is flexible (16 hours per week). Open to college freshmen, college sophomores, college juniors, college seniors, recent college graduates, graduate students. ▶ *2–4 telecommunications specialists:* responsibilities include developing and maintaining an efficient avenue of obtaining and retaining members of the association; exploring new initiatives for the association. Candidates should have ability to work independently, experience in the field, oral communication skills, strong interpersonal skills. Duration is 1 semester. Open to college freshmen, college sophomores, college juniors, college seniors, recent college graduates, graduate students. All positions are unpaid. International applications accepted.

Benefits Possible full-time employment, willing to act as a professional reference, willing to complete paperwork for educational credit, willing to provide letters of recommendation.

Contact Write, call, fax, or e-mail Carrie Plowden, Intern Coordinator. Phone: 301-231-9259 Ext. 221. Fax: 301-231-7392. E-mail: cplowden@adaa.org. In-person interview required. Applicants must submit a resume. Applications are accepted continuously. World Wide Web: http://www.adaa.org.

ARIZONA HEART INSTITUTE MESA
6335 East Main Street, #4
Mesa, Arizona 85205

General Information Outpatient clinic dedicated to prevention and treatment of heart and vascular diseases. Established in 1975. Number of employees: 17. Division of Arizona Heart Institute, Phoenix, Arizona. Number of internship applications received each year: 25.

Internships Available ▶ *6–8 exercise physiology interns (undergraduate):* responsibilities include completing flow chart of experiences and observations, participating in Phase II and III cardiovascular rehabilitation program, patient education, supervision, and follow-up. Duration is 350–700 hours. Unpaid. ▶ *2 graduate exercise physiology interns (cardiovascular conditioning):* responsibilities include completing flow chart of clinical observations and experiences, participating in operation of Phase II and III cardiovascular rehabilitation program, and supervising and instructing undergraduate interns. Duration is September to December or January to April. $650 per month. Candidates for all positions should have college courses in field, college

Arizona Heart Institute Mesa (continued)

degree in related field, computer skills, knowledge of field, oral communication skills, strong interpersonal skills, current CPR certification. Open to recent college graduates, graduate students. International applications accepted.

Benefits Formal training, on-the-job training, possible full-time employment, willing to act as a professional reference, willing to complete paperwork for educational credit, willing to provide letters of recommendation, occassional free meals and seminars/workshops.

Contact Call or e-mail Andrew Weiler, Program Director Cardiovascular Conditioning, 6335 East Main Street # 4, Mesa, Arizona 85205. Phone: 602-244-9700. E-mail: aweiler@azheart.com. In-person interview required. Applicants must submit a formal organization application, cover letter, resume, academic transcripts, 1-2 letters of recommendation. Applications are accepted continuously. World Wide Web: http://www.azheart.com.

THE BRONX-LEBANON HOSPITAL CENTER
1650 Selwyn Avenue, Suite 8F
Bronx, New York 10457

General Information Largest volunteer, nonprofit, health-care system serving the South and Central Bronx. It has two hospital divisions and more than 30 ambulatory medical practices. Established in 1890. Number of employees: 4,000. Number of internship applications received each year: 500.

Internships Available ▶ *100–200 interns:* responsibilities include assisting as needed in the various hospital departments. Candidates should have ability to work with others, personal interest in the field, desire to assist others, positive attitude. Duration is 6 months (minimum). Unpaid. Open to college freshmen, college sophomores, college juniors, college seniors, graduate students, high school students 14 years or older.

Benefits Free meals, names of contacts, on-the-job training, opportunity to attend seminars/workshops, willing to act as a professional reference, willing to complete paperwork for educational credit, willing to provide letters of recommendation, uniforms.

Contact Write or call The Volunteer Office, 1650 Selwyn Avenue Suite 8F, Bronx, New York 10457. Phone: 718-960-1371. In-person interview required. Applicants must submit a formal organization application, cover letter, resume, academic transcripts, two personal references, letter of recommendation, 6 hours of hospital orientation required. Applications are accepted continuously.

CAMP LA JOLLA
176 C Avenue
Coronado, California 92118

General Information Fitness and weight loss camp. Established in 1979. Number of employees: 86. Number of internship applications received each year: 10.

Internships Available ▶ *3–10 counselors:* responsibilities include working with campers from 7 a.m. to 9 p.m., teaching three physical activity classes per day, and acting as counselor. Candidates should have experience in the field, organizational skills, personal interest in the field, strong interpersonal skills, strong leadership ability. Duration is 8–10 weeks. Position available as unpaid or paid. Open to college freshmen, college sophomores, college juniors, college seniors, recent college graduates, graduate students. International applications accepted.

Benefits Free housing, free meals, names of contacts, on-the-job training, willing to complete paperwork for educational credit, willing to provide letters of recommendation.

Contact Write, call, fax, or e-mail Donna Volpe, Personnel Director, 176 C Avenue, Coronado, California 92118. Phone: 800-825-8746. Fax: 619-435-8188. E-mail: camplj@aol.com. In-person interview recommended. Applicants must submit a formal organization application, personal reference, letter of recommendation. Applications are accepted continuously. World Wide Web: http://www.camplajolla.com.

CHILDREN'S HOSPICE INTERNATIONAL
2202 Mt. Vernon Avenue, Suite 3C
Alexandria, Virginia 22301

General Information Organization that provides advocacy and outreach services for children with life-threatening conditions and their families. Established in 1983. Number of employees: 4. Number of internship applications received each year: 20.

Internships Available ▶ *1–2 interns:* responsibilities include performing office duties, coordinating resources, disseminating information, and working on special projects. Duration is flexible. Unpaid. Open to college freshmen, college sophomores, college juniors, college seniors, recent college graduates, graduate students, law students, career changers, individuals reentering the workforce. International applications accepted.

Benefits Opportunity to attend seminars/workshops, possible full-time employment, willing to complete paperwork for educational credit, willing to provide letters of recommendation.

Contact Write or e-mail Ann Armstrong-Dailey, Founding Director. E-mail: chiorg@aol.com. In-person interview recommended. Applicants must submit a cover letter, resume. Application deadline: March 1 for summer, December 15 for spring. World Wide Web: http://www.chionline.org.

CLINICAL DIRECTORS NETWORK, INC.
54 West 39 Street, 11th Floor
New York, New York 10018

General Information Nonprofit network that arranges conferences, workshops, and training for clinicians research; emphasizes clinical trials, healthcare services, research and development, and finding alternative treatments for AIDS through community programs. Established in 1985. Number of employees: 12. Number of internship applications received each year: 75.

Internships Available ▶ *1 AIDS program intern:* responsibilities include gathering and entering information into the database and assisting at a health center. Candidates should have ability to work independently, college courses in field, personal interest in the field, strong interpersonal skills, computer literacy in IBM-compatible programs, interest in public health and/or public administration. Duration is 1 summer to 1 year. Unpaid. Open to recent high school graduates, college freshmen, college sophomores, college juniors, college seniors, recent college graduates, graduate students. ▶ *2 administrative interns:* responsibilities include setting up conferences, preparing contacts, making hotel arrangements, data entry, and assisting in fundraising events. Candidates should have ability to work independently, analytical skills, office skills, oral communication skills, organizational skills, self-motivation, strong interpersonal skills, written communication skills, computer literacy in IBM-related programs, interest in public health and/or public administration. Duration is year-round. Unpaid. Open to recent high school graduates, college freshmen, college sophomores, college juniors, college seniors, recent college graduates, individuals reentering the workforce. ▶ *1–2 immunizations interns:* responsibilities include assisting coordinator with health centers. Candidates should have ability to work independently, analytical skills, college courses in field, office skills, oral communication skills, personal interest in the field, research skills, self-motivation, strong interpersonal skills, written communication skills, computer literacy in IBM-related programs, interest in public health and/or public administration. Duration is year-round. Position available as unpaid or at $6–$8 per hour. Open to recent high school graduates, college freshmen, college sophomores, college juniors, college seniors, recent college graduates, graduate students. ▶ *1–2 marketing interns:* responsibilities include assisting in the marketing department, research for future conference sponsors, and developing marketing tools. Candidates should have ability to work independently, declared college major in field, office skills, oral communication skills, organizational skills, self-motivation, strong interpersonal skills, written communication skills, computer literacy in IBM-compatible programs, interest in public health and/or public administration. Duration is year-round. Unpaid. Open to college freshmen, college sophomores, college juniors, college seniors, recent college graduates. ▶ *4–6 research programs*

interns: responsibilities include assisting research program coordinator with administrative and research tasks at office and health centers. Candidates should have ability to work independently, analytical skills, oral communication skills, organizational skills, plan to pursue career in field, research skills, self-motivation, strong interpersonal skills, written communication skills, computer literacy in IBM-compatible programs, interest in public health and/or public administration. Duration is year-round. Unpaid. Open to recent high school graduates, college freshmen, college sophomores, college juniors, college seniors, recent college graduates, graduate students. International applications accepted.
Benefits On-the-job training, opportunity to attend seminars/workshops, willing to act as a professional reference, willing to complete paperwork for educational credit, willing to provide letters of recommendation, networking opportunities.
Contact Write, fax, or e-mail Internship Department. Fax: 212-382-0669. E-mail: niga100w@cdc.gov. No phone calls. In-person interview required. Applicants must submit a formal organization application, cover letter, resume, 2-3 letters of recommendation. Applications are accepted continuously. World Wide Web: http://www.CDNetwork.org.

CONOCO WELLNESS
600 North Dairy Ashford, PEO110
Houston, Texas 77079

General Information Oil company wellness center. Established in 1982. Number of employees: 2,500. Division of Conoco Oil, Inc., Houston, Texas.
Internships Available ▶ *2 wellness interns:* responsibilities include facility supervision, orientations, assisting the director with program design, marketing and implementation, Web site maintenance, employee presentations, and administrative responsibilities. Candidates should have college courses in field, computer skills, oral communication skills, self-motivation, written communication skills, declared major in health/wellness related areas. Duration is 16 to 19 weeks or 1 semester. $700 stipend per month. Open to college juniors, college seniors, graduate students. International applications accepted.
Benefits Names of contacts, on-the-job training, willing to act as a professional reference, willing to complete paperwork for educational credit, willing to provide letters of recommendation.
Contact Write, call, or e-mail Donna K. Sullivan, Wellness Director, 600 North Dairy Ashford, Houston, Texas 77079. Phone: 281-293-5211. E-mail: donna.k.sullivan@usa.conoco.com. Telephone interview required. Applicants must submit a formal organization application, resume. Application deadline: February 15 for summer, May 30 for fall, September 15 for spring.

THE EVANGELICAL LUTHERAN GOOD SAMARITAN SOCIETY
4800 West 57th Street
Sioux Falls, South Dakota 57117-5038

General Information Society that provides nursing care and independent living to older persons and others in need. Established in 1922. Number of employees: 250. Number of internship applications received each year: 250.
Internships Available ▶ *5–15 administrator-in-training interns:* responsibilities include learning the role of the administrator in a long-term care retirement facility. Candidates should have ability to work with others, college courses in field, knowledge of field, organizational skills, strong leadership ability. Duration is 6–12 months. $15,000–$20,000 per year. Open to college seniors, recent college graduates, graduate students, law students, career changers. International applications accepted.
Benefits Formal training, health insurance, on-the-job training, opportunity to attend seminars/workshops, possible full-time employment, travel reimbursement, willing to complete paperwork for educational credit, willing to provide letters of recommendation, pension and tax-deferred annuity.
Contact Write, call, fax, or e-mail Dean Mertz, Vice President for Human Development. Phone: 605-362-3100 Ext. 3120. Fax: 605-362-3240. E-mail: dmertz@good-sam.org. In-person interview

required. Applicants must submit a formal organization application, resume, academic transcripts, letter of recommendation. Applications are accepted continuously.

EXTENDICARE HEALTH SERVICES, INC.
105 West Michigan Street
Milwaukee, Wisconsin 53203

General Information Nationwide operator of over 200 long-term care, subacute, and assisted living facilities. Established in 1968. Number of employees: 25,000. Number of internship applications received each year: 100.
Internships Available ▶ *Administrators in training:* responsibilities include preparing to take the licensure exam to become a nursing home administrator. Candidates should have ability to work independently, analytical skills, oral communication skills, organizational skills, plan to pursue career in field, self-motivation, strong interpersonal skills, strong leadership ability, written communication skills, prior experience in the service or health care industry preferred. Duration is 6 months. Paid. Open to college seniors, recent college graduates, graduate students, law students, career changers.
Benefits Health insurance, possible full-time employment, tuition assistance.
Contact Write, fax, or e-mail John Goff, National Recruiter. Fax: 414-908-8143. E-mail: jgoff@extendicare.com. Telephone interview required. Applicants must submit a cover letter, resume, in-person interview (travel expenses paid) for finalists. Applications are accepted continuously.

FEMINIST HEALTH CENTER OF PORTSMOUTH, INC.
559 Portsmouth Avenue, PO Box 456
Greenland, New Hampshire 03840

General Information Free-standing, nonprofit clinic providing the following services: GYN care, primary care, abortions, STD/HIV counselling and testing, pregnancy testing, birth control, health education and community outreach. Established in 1980. Number of employees: 20. Number of internship applications received each year: 5.
Internships Available ▶ *1–5 health care counselors:* responsibilities include information sharing, client interviewing and assessing, communicating effectively and utilizing strong interpersonal skills while working as part of a team in the delivery of care. Candidates should have college courses in field, oral communication skills, personal interest in the field, strong interpersonal skills, pro-choice views. Position available as unpaid or at $6–$9 per hour. Open to college freshmen, college sophomores, college juniors, college seniors, recent college graduates, graduate students, career changers, individuals reentering the workforce.
Benefits Formal training, job counseling, names of contacts, on-the-job training, possible full-time employment, willing to act as a professional reference, willing to complete paperwork for educational credit, willing to provide letters of recommendation.
Contact Write, call, or fax Diana Braun, Executive Director. Phone: 603-436-7588. Fax: 603-431-0451. In-person interview required. Applicants must submit a cover letter, resume, academic transcripts, three personal references, three letters of recommendation. Applications are accepted continuously.

FOUNDATION FOR CONTEMPORARY MENTAL HEALTH
2112 F Street, NW, 404
Washington, District of Columbia 20037

General Information Nonprofit organization furthering understanding of mental health. Established in 1967. Number of internship applications received each year: 100.
Internships Available ▶ *15–20 interns:* responsibilities include working as an entry-level professional in a psychiatric hospital, residential treatment center, or psychiatric day hospital program and attending weekly educational workshops. Candidates should have coursework in abnormal psychology. Duration is 8 weeks.

Unpaid. Open to college juniors, college seniors, recent college graduates, graduate students. International applications accepted.

Benefits Formal training, opportunity to attend seminars/workshops, possible full-time employment, willing to complete paperwork for educational credit, willing to provide letters of recommendation, intensive clinical experience.

Contact Write, call, or fax Hanh Hoang, Administrator, Summer Internship Program. Phone: 202-296-7100. Fax: 202-296-5455. Applicants must submit a formal organization application, cover letter, three letters of recommendation. Application deadline: March 1 for summer.

FRANKFORT REGIONAL MEDICAL CENTER
299 King's Daughters Drive
Frankfort, Kentucky 40601

General Information Hospital/health-care services. Established in 1974. Number of employees: 535. Number of internship applications received each year: 5.

Internships Available ▶ *Interns:* responsibilities include various tasks, depending on the position. Candidates should have ability to work independently, analytical skills, computer skills, declared college major in field, editing skills, office skills, oral communication skills, organizational skills, personal interest in the field, research skills, self-motivation, strong interpersonal skills, writing skills. Unpaid. Open to college seniors.

Benefits Formal training, job counseling, on-the-job training, possible full-time employment, willing to act as a professional reference, willing to complete paperwork for educational credit, willing to provide letters of recommendation.

Contact Write or fax Bev Young, Human Resources Director, 299 King's Daughters Drive, Frankfort, Kentucky 40601. Fax: 502-226-7956. No phone calls. Applicants must submit a formal organization application, cover letter, resume. Applications are accepted continuously. World Wide Web: http://www.frankfortregional.com.

FRONTIER NURSING SERVICE
132 FNS Drive
Wendover, Kentucky 41775

General Information Rural health care provider and midwife educator. Established in 1925. Number of employees: 300. Number of internship applications received each year: 120.

Internships Available ▶ *4 "courier" volunteers:* responsibilities include delivering supplies, hosting dinners, assisting with office work, participating in various community events, acting as teaching aide in local schools, and accompanying health care professionals during daily routine. Candidates should have ability to work independently, ability to work with others, self-motivation, strong interpersonal skills, valid driver's license, access to a car. Duration is 12 weeks. Unpaid. Open to recent high school graduates, college freshmen, college sophomores, college juniors, college seniors, recent college graduates, graduate students, law students, career changers, individuals reentering the workforce, candidates who are 18 or older. International applications accepted.

Benefits Housing at a cost, meals at a cost, opportunity to attend seminars/workshops, willing to complete paperwork for educational credit, willing to provide letters of recommendation.

Contact Write or call Jeremy T. Bush, Courier Coordinator. Phone: 606-672-2317. Telephone interview required. Applicants must submit a formal organization application, three letters of recommendation, $250 room and board fee to be paid by applicant or applicant's college/school (upon acceptance). Applications are accepted continuously.

GOOD SAMARITAN SOCIETY
PO Box 5038
Sioux Falls, South Dakota 57117-5038

General Information Society that provides shelter and services to the frail elderly and others in need, and operates approximately 250 nursing centers and residential facilities throughout the country. Established in 1922. Number of employees: 250. Affiliate of The Evangelical Lutheran Church. Number of internship applications received each year: 300.

Internships Available ▶ *Administrators in training:* responsibilities include operating and administering a long-term care facility. Candidates should have college courses in field, knowledge of field, organizational skills, self-motivation, strong interpersonal skills, strong leadership ability. Duration is 6–12 months. monthly stipend. Open to college seniors, recent college graduates, graduate students, law students, career changers, individuals reentering the workforce. International applications accepted.

Benefits Formal training, health insurance, opportunity to attend seminars/workshops, possible full-time employment, travel reimbursement.

Contact Write, call, fax, or e-mail Dean Mertz, Vice President for Human Development. Phone: 605-362-3100 Ext. 120. Fax: 605-362-3240. E-mail: dmertz@good-sam.org. In-person interview required. Applicants must submit a formal organization application, cover letter, resume, academic transcripts, three personal references. Applications are accepted continuously. World Wide Web: http://www.good-sam.com.

GOULD FARM
Box 157, Gould Road
Monterey, Massachusetts 01245-0157

General Information Gould Farm is a rural residential center providing integrated, structured rehabilitation for adults with psychiatric disorders and a continuum of services through the Boston Area Program. Established in 1913. Number of employees: 45. Number of internship applications received each year: 100.

Internships Available ▶ *2–3 assistant house advisors:* responsibilities include working as house advisors in one of three houses; assisting with Social Security, Medicaid, health insurance, medication, and goal setting. Candidates should have oral communication skills, organizational skills, self-motivation, strong interpersonal skills. Open to college juniors, college seniors, recent college graduates, graduate students, career changers. ▶ *1 community resources workleader:* responsibilities include helping clients to improve social and work skills through activities program. Candidates should have ability to work independently, computer skills, office skills, strong interpersonal skills. Open to college juniors, college seniors, recent college graduates, graduate students, career changers. ▶ *1–2 farm workleaders:* responsibilities include making assignments for animal care, field work, haying, and fencing; working with clients; teaching work habits and skills. Candidates should have ability to work with others, oral communication skills, strong interpersonal skills. Open to college juniors, college seniors, recent college graduates, graduate students. ▶ *1 gardens workleader:* responsibilities include making assignments for maintaining the grounds, teaching work habits and skills, helping clients develop social skills. Candidates should have ability to work with others, oral communication skills, self-motivation. ▶ *1–3 kitchen and roadside store workleaders:* responsibilities include making assignment for meals and operating restaurant; helping clients to improve work habits, work, and social skills. Candidates should have ability to work independently, oral communication skills, strong interpersonal skills. Open to college juniors, college seniors, recent college graduates, graduate students, career changers. ▶ *1–2 volunteer case managers (Boston program):* responsibilities include providing support to clients who have moved on from Gould Farm, facilitating meal preparation and providing rides, leading and supporting work program, assisting with medication, attending meetings and training, organizing and leading activities. Candidates should have oral communication skills, self-motivation, strong interpersonal skills. Open to college juniors, college seniors, recent college graduates, graduate students, career changers. Duration for all positions is 12 months. All positions paid at $250 per month.

Benefits Formal training, free housing, free meals, health insurance, on-the-job training, opportunity to attend seminars/

workshops, possible full-time employment, willing to complete paperwork for educational credit, willing to provide letters of recommendation.
Contact Write, call, fax, or e-mail Ms. Paula Snyder, Human Resources Manager, Box 157 Gould Road, Monterey, Massachusetts 01245-0157. Phone: 413-528-1804. Fax: 413-528-5051. E-mail: gfarm@vgnernet.net. In-person interview recommended. Applicants must submit a cover letter, resume, three letters of recommendation. Applications are accepted continuously. World Wide Web: http://www.gouldfarm.org.

GRACIE SQUARE HOSPITAL
421 East 75th Street
New York, New York 10021

General Information Psychiatric hospital with the following inpatient services: general, geriatric, detoxification, drug/alcohol rehabilitation, Asian, and partial hospitalization program. Established in 1958. Number of employees: 250. Unit of New York Hospital Network, New York, New York. Number of internship applications received each year: 60.
Internships Available ▶ *1–2 psychology externs:* responsibilities include performing psychodiagnostic testing, individual and group psychotherapy, and attending staff meetings. Candidates should have ability to work with others, declared college major in field, oral communication skills, plan to pursue career in field, self-motivation, written communication skills, current enrollment in a graduate program. Duration is September through May. Open to graduate students. ▶ *1–2 psychology intern:* responsibilities include observing clinical process, serving as research assistant, and attending workshops and staff meetings; psychodiagnostic testing and psychotherapy experience commensurate with skills. Candidates should have ability to work with others, oral communication skills, plan to pursue career in field, self-motivation, written communication skills, current enrollment in undergraduate or graduate program. Duration is 10 weeks minimum from May to August; start and end dates flexible. Open to college juniors, graduate students. All positions paid at $2,000 per duration of internship.
Benefits Meals at a cost, on-the-job training, opportunity to attend seminars/workshops, willing to complete paperwork for educational credit, willing to provide letters of recommendation, willing to act as an academic reference.
Contact Write or call Dr. Fran Luckom-Nurnberg, Director, Department of Psychological Services. Phone: 212-434-5378. In-person interview required. Applicants must submit a formal organization application, resume, academic transcripts, writing sample, two personal references. Application deadline: February 28 for summer, September 15 for fall.

GREATER BALTIMORE MEDICAL CENTER
6701 North Charles Street
Baltimore, Maryland 21204

General Information Nonprofit community hospital. Established in 1965. Number of employees: 3,000.
Internships Available ▶ *2 public relations and marketing interns:* responsibilities include assisting with events and publications, distributing literature, setting up displays, picking up materials; and writing articles and news releases. Duration is 3 months. Unpaid. Open to college freshmen, college sophomores, college juniors, college seniors.
Benefits Possible full-time employment, willing to complete paperwork for educational credit, school registration fee paid.
Contact Write or call Vivienne Stearns-Elliott, Director, Community and Media Relations. Phone: 410-828-2132. Applicants must submit a cover letter, resume, writing sample. Applications are accepted continuously.

HEALTH CAREER OPPORTUNITY PROGRAM, RUSK INSTITUTE OF REHABILITATION MEDICINE
New York University Medical Center, 400 East 34th Street, RR 812
New York, New York 10016

General Information Full-service rehabilitation facility. Established in 1948. Number of employees: 1,000. Unit of New York University Medical Center, New York, New York. Number of internship applications received each year: 1,000.
Internships Available ▶ *50–150 interns:* responsibilities include performing tasks related to either a research area or a clinical area such as nursing, rehabilitation medicine, recreation therapy, occupational therapy, physical therapy, and horticultural therapy, and attending lectures, films, demonstrations, and presentations on the various careers in rehabilitation. Candidates should have ability to work independently, oral communication skills, plan to pursue career in field, self-motivation, strong interpersonal skills. Duration is 4 weeks. Position available as unpaid or paid. Open to high school seniors, college freshmen, college sophomores, college juniors, college seniors. International applications accepted.
Benefits Formal training, on-the-job training, opportunity to attend seminars/workshops, willing to provide letters of recommendation, housing provided at $575 for the month of July.
Contact Write Mr. Glenn Goldfinger, Director, HCOP, New York University Medical Center, 560 First Avenue, Greenberg Hall, C-95, New York, New York 10016. No phone calls. Applicants must submit a formal organization application, cover letter. Application deadline: March 1 for summer fellows/interns.

HUMAN SERVICE ALLIANCE
3983 Old Greensboro Road
Winston-Salem, North Carolina 27101

General Information An all-volunteer organization that provides hands-on care for the terminally ill in a home-like, caring setting at no charge. Established in 1987. Number of internship applications received each year: 40.
Internships Available ▶ *8 caregivers:* responsibilities include providing personal care to the terminally ill, keeping records and charts, assisting in upkeep of residential facility, and preparing meals. Candidates should have positive attitude, cooperative nature, and willingness to work in teams. Duration is 2–52 weeks. Unpaid. Open to high school students, high school seniors, recent high school graduates, college freshmen, college sophomores, college juniors, college seniors, recent college graduates, graduate students, law students, career changers, individuals reentering the workforce. International applications accepted.
Benefits Formal training, free housing, free meals, job counseling, on-the-job training, opportunity to attend seminars/workshops, willing to act as a professional reference, willing to complete paperwork for educational credit, willing to provide letters of recommendation.
Contact Write, call, fax, or e-mail Dr. Sanford Danziger, Coordinator of Internships. Phone: 336-761-8745. Fax: 336-722-7882. E-mail: sdanziger@hsa.org. Telephone interview required. Applicants must submit a formal organization application, three personal references, full-length photo. Application deadline: March 15 for summer. World Wide Web: http://www.hsa.org.

INDIAN HEALTH SERVICE
12300 Twinbrook Parkway, Suite 100A
Rockville, Maryland 20852

General Information Provider of health care to over 1.5 million American Indians and Alaska Natives; seeks to elevate health status to the highest level possible. Established in 1955. Number of employees: 375. Number of internship applications received each year: 500.
Internships Available ▶ *1–20 COSTEP externs.* Duration is 120 days. Paid. Open to college juniors, college seniors.

Indian Health Service (continued)

Benefits Job counseling, names of contacts, opportunity to attend seminars/workshops, possible full-time employment, tuition assistance, willing to complete paperwork for educational credit.
Contact Write, call, or fax Vickye Santiago, Intern Coordinator. Phone: 301-443-6197. Fax: 301-443-4815. Applicants must submit a cover letter, resume, academic transcripts. Applications are accepted continuously. World Wide Web: http://www.ihs.gov.

INSTITUTE FOR MENTAL HEALTH INITIATIVES
4545 42nd Street, NW, Suite 311
Washington, District of Columbia 20016

General Information Not-for-profit organization that promotes mental health by making the latest research accessible and understandable to the general public and media industry. Established in 1982. Number of employees: 5. Number of internship applications received each year: 90.
Internships Available ▶ *1–4 mental health interns:* responsibilities include conducting research on mental health topics, assisting with writing of 2 quarterly publications, performing outreach to general public and media community, coordinating workshops and seminars, and some office support/administrative work. Unpaid. ▶ *1–3 public relations interns:* responsibilities include marketing research and business development strategies; assisting in preparation of press releases, promotion material, and media correspondence; assisting in developing relationships with media professionals; and providing assistance for the development of a fund-raising plan. Position available as unpaid or paid. Candidates for all positions should have ability to work independently, ability to work with others, oral communication skills, organizational skills, self-motivation, written communication skills. Duration for all positions is flexible. Open to college freshmen, college sophomores, college juniors, college seniors, recent college graduates, graduate students. International applications accepted.
Benefits Names of contacts, opportunity to attend seminars/workshops, possible full-time employment, willing to complete paperwork for educational credit, willing to provide letters of recommendation.
Contact Write, call, or fax Intern Coordinator. Phone: 202-364-7111. Fax: 202-363-3891. In-person interview recommended. Applicants must submit a cover letter, resume, two personal references, 1- to 2-page writing sample. Application deadline: April 1 for summer. World Wide Web: http://www.imhi.org.

INTERMOUNTAIN PLANNED PARENTHOOD
721 North 29th Street
Billings, Montana 59101

General Information Organization that serves 14,000 patients per year for birth control, cancer screening, treatment for sexually transmitted diseases, counseling, and education; the organization believes in wanted children, loving and approachable parents, decisions based on knowledge, and the right to make those decisions. Established in 1969. Number of employees: 50. Affiliate of Planned Parenthood Federation of America, Washington, District of Columbia. Number of internship applications received each year: 5.
Internships Available ▶ *Interns:* responsibilities include working in education, development, administration, patient services, or other positions. Each position has varying responsibilities, duties, and requirements. Candidates should have ability to work independently, ability to work with others, computer skills, oral communication skills, personal interest in the field, self-motivation. Duration is flexible. Unpaid. Open to high school students, high school seniors, recent high school graduates, college freshmen, college sophomores, college juniors, college seniors, recent college graduates, graduate students, law students, career changers, individuals reentering the workforce. International applications accepted.

Benefits On-the-job training, willing to complete paperwork for educational credit, willing to provide letters of recommendation, basic reproductive healthcare and family planning services provided free after 50 hours of work.
Contact Write, call, fax, or e-mail Tammy Tucker, Volunteer Coordinator. Phone: 406-248-3636. Fax: 406-245-8182. E-mail: tammy_tucker@ppfa.org. Applicants must submit a formal organization application, cover letter, resume. Applications are accepted continuously. World Wide Web: http://www.impp.org.

L & T HEALTH AND FITNESS
7309 Arlington Boulevard #202
Falls Church, Virginia 22042

General Information A premier provider of innovative health and fitness management services. Spectrum of services includes health fitness programming, facility management, facility design consultation, and health promotional services. Established in 1984. Number of employees: 250. Number of internship applications received each year: 50.
Internships Available ▶ *Fitness specialist interns:* responsibilities include learning all aspects of facility management and operations, assisting staff with creation and implementation of health promotion programs, and supervising group and one-on-one fitness activities. Candidates should have ability to work independently, declared college major in field, oral communication skills, personal interest in the field, strong interpersonal skills, writing skills. Duration is minimum of 8-10 weeks, 16-40 hours per week; contract arranged on an individual basis. $100 per week stipend based on full-time (40 hours). Open to college freshmen, college sophomores, college juniors, college seniors, must be enrolled in health/fitness-related degree program. International applications accepted.
Benefits On-the-job training, possible full-time employment, willing to act as a professional reference, willing to provide letters of recommendation.
Contact Write, call, fax, or e-mail Michelle Warren, Intern Coordinator, 7309 Arlington Boulevard, #202, Falls Church, Virginia 22042. Phone: 703-204-1355 Ext. 45. Fax: 703-204-2332. E-mail: michelle_l_warren@email.mobil.com. In-person interview recommended. Applicants must submit a formal organization application, resume. Application deadline: April 10 for summer, July 10 for fall, November 10 for spring. World Wide Web: http://www.ltwell.com.

MACOMB-OAKLAND REGIONAL CENTER, INC.
16200 19 Mile Road, PO Box 380710
Clinton Township, Michigan 48038-0070

General Information Internationally renowned mental health agency providing case management and clinical support services to persons with developmental disabilities and mental illness. Established in 1972. Number of employees: 392. Number of internship applications received each year: 15.
Internships Available ▶ *1–3 occupational therapy interns:* responsibilities include training/in-service; care consultation; assessments and evaluations, program planning and review; providing and monitoring adaptive and functional equipment; resource/liaison with community. Candidates should have ability to work independently, ability to work with others, computer skills, declared college major in field, self-motivation. $14 per hour. Open to college seniors. ▶ *1–3 speech and language pathology interns:* responsibilities include assessment; program planning; training; case consultation, monitor, and review. Candidates should have ability to work independently, ability to work with others, college degree in related field, self-motivation, computer skills helpful. $14 per hour. Open to graduate students. ▶ *1–2 therapeutic recreation specialists:* responsibilities include performing therapeutic recreation assessments; in-service training to consumers and their families, home staff, and other professionals; adapting equipment for consumers independent use; and developing programs and clinical treatments designed to assist in consumer development and independence. Candidates should have ability to work independently, ability to work with others,

computer skills, declared college major in field, self-motivation. Unpaid. Open to college seniors. Duration for all positions is flexible. International applications accepted.

Benefits Formal training, names of contacts, on-the-job training, possible full-time employment, travel reimbursement.

Contact Write or fax Peter J. Lynch, Director of Human Resources. Fax: 810-412-7889. No phone calls. In-person interview recommended. Applicants must submit a formal organization application, cover letter, resume, academic transcripts. Applications are accepted continuously.

NATIONAL ASSOCIATION OF ANOREXIA NERVOSA AND ASSOCIATED DISORDERS (ANAD)
PO Box 7
Highland Park, Illinois 60035

General Information National, nonprofit, educational, and self-help association offering a variety of services to aid anorexics, bulimics, and their families. Established in 1976. Number of employees: 11. Number of internship applications received each year: 70.

Internships Available ▶ *6 interns:* responsibilities include co-authoring a booklet of support group guidelines and steps toward recovery, researching, national hot-line, correspondence with eating disorders sufferers, organizing a national conference, coordinating and administering special projects. Candidates should have ability to work independently, oral communication skills, self-motivation, strong interpersonal skills, written communication skills. Duration is flexible. Unpaid. Open to college juniors, college seniors, recent college graduates, graduate students.

Benefits Willing to complete paperwork for educational credit, willing to provide letters of recommendation.

Contact Write, call, fax, or e-mail Dawn Ries, Administrator. Phone: 847-831-3438. Fax: 847-433-4632. E-mail: anad20@aol.com. Applicants must submit a cover letter, resume. Applications are accepted continuously. World Wide Web: http://members.aol.com/anad20/index.html.

NATIONAL HEALTHY MOTHERS, HEALTHY BABIES
121 North Washington Street, Suite 300
Alexandria, Virginia 22314

General Information Health education coalition concerned with improving the health of women and children by promoting good habits and collaborating with health education programs. Established in 1981. Number of employees: 12. Number of internship applications received each year: 100.

Internships Available ▶ *2–4 program assistants:* responsibilities include providing program and administrative support, research and writing. Candidates should have computer skills, personal interest in the field, writing skills, MS Office experience helpful. Duration is flexible. Unpaid. Open to college freshmen, college sophomores, college juniors, college seniors, recent college graduates, graduate students, law students, career changers, individuals reentering the workforce. International applications accepted.

Benefits Job counseling, names of contacts, opportunity to attend seminars/workshops, travel reimbursement, willing to complete paperwork for educational credit, willing to provide letters of recommendation.

Contact Write, call, fax, or e-mail Laquitta Bowers, Director of Intern Programs. Phone: 703-836-6110 Ext. 225. Fax: 703-836-3470. E-mail: lbowers@hmhb.org. In-person interview recommended. Applicants must submit a cover letter, resume. Applications are accepted continuously. World Wide Web: http://www.hmhb.org.

THE NATIONAL HEMOPHILIA FOUNDATION
116 West 32nd Street, 11th Floor
New York, New York 10001

General Information Foundation dedicated to the treatment and the cure of hemophilia, related bleeding disorders, and complications of those disorders (including HIV infection), and to improving the quality of life of all those affected through the promotion and support of research, education, and other services. Established in 1948. Number of employees: 37. Number of internship applications received each year: 10.

Internships Available ▶ *Interns:* responsibilities include performing duties that fit the needs and interests of the Foundation and the intern. Candidates should have computer skills, oral communication skills, organizational skills, research skills, strong interpersonal skills, writing skills. Duration is flexible. Unpaid. Open to college freshmen, college sophomores, college juniors, college seniors. International applications accepted.

Benefits Possible full-time employment, willing to complete paperwork for educational credit, willing to provide letters of recommendation.

Contact Write, fax, or e-mail Ms. Susan Levitt-Kass, Office Manager. Fax: 212-328-3777. E-mail: slevitt@hemophilia.org. No phone calls. In-person interview required. Applicants must submit a cover letter, resume, academic transcripts, 1-2 writing samples, 1-2 personal references. Applications are accepted continuously. World Wide Web: http://www.hemophilia.org.

NEW YORK OPEN CENTER
83 Spring Street
New York, New York 10012

General Information Center for holistic healing and culture. Established in 1984. Number of employees: 38. Number of internship applications received each year: 10.

Internships Available ▶ *1–2 "Lapis Magazine" management assistants:* responsibilities include marketing, outreach, and occasional filing and organization. Candidates should have computer skills, telephone skills. Duration is 6 months or longer. ▶ *2–4 administrative assistants:* responsibilities include paperwork; meeting deadlines and troubleshooting in reference to health insurance, supplies and track lists; interaction with bookkeeping and vendors; personnel file updating; clerical duties; data entry; and keeping minutes of meetings. Duration is 6 months or longer. Open to high school seniors, recent high school graduates, college freshmen, college sophomores, college juniors, college seniors, recent college graduates, graduate students, law students, career changers, individuals reentering the workforce. ▶ *1–2 assistants to the Volunteer/Intern Coordinator:* responsibilities include updating volunteer files, calling volunteers for special projects, correspondence, coordination and interaction with interns in all other departments; planning social events for volunteers and interns. Duration is 6 months minimum. ▶ *4–6 bookstore management assistants:* responsibilities include merchandise and visual display work, computer programming and data entry, bookkeeping, management and administrative assistance. Duration is 6 months or longer. ▶ *1–2 events coordination management assistants:* responsibilities include maintaining classroom needs and interacting with instructors. Duration is 8–10 weeks. ▶ *2–3 reception management assistants:* responsibilities include fielding calls and connecting them to different departments, fielding patron calls regarding the nature of the Open Center. Duration is 6 months or longer. ▶ *3–4 registration management assistants:* responsibilities include answering customer calls about classes, registration, payment; signing up and entering patrons into classes by way of computer. Duration is 6 months or longer. ▶ *2–3 wellness management assistants:* responsibilities include answering incoming phone calls and booking bodywork appointments for clients; updating and revising schedules to interact with bodywork volunteers, practitioners, and wellness manager; taking cash, checks, and money from clients; preparing bodywork rooms; some clerical work. Duration is 6 months or longer. All positions are unpaid. International applications accepted.

Benefits On-the-job training, opportunity to attend seminars/workshops, possible full-time employment, willing to complete paperwork for educational credit, willing to provide letters of recommendation, free classes at the Open Center.

Contact Write, call, fax, or e-mail Mr. Mark Gerow, Volunteer and Intern Coordinator. Phone: 212-219-2527 Ext. 117. Fax: 212-226-4056. E-mail: nyocvol@aol.com. In-person interview recommended. Applicants must submit a resume, 2 personal references (suggested). Applications are accepted continuously. World Wide Web: http://www.opencenter.org.

NEW YORK PRESBYTERIAN HOSPITAL, WEILL CORNELL WESTCHESTER
21 Bloomingdale Road
White Plains, New York 10605

General Information   Nonprofit and voluntary comprehensive psychiatric facility with inpatient and partial hospitalization and day hospital programs, clinics, and outpatient departments. Established in 1894. Number of employees: 1,000. Number of internship applications received each year: 100.
Internships Available ▶ *1–2 administrative volunteers:* responsibilities include working in an administrative office assisting with daily operations. Candidates should have ability to work independently, computer skills, office skills, oral communication skills, organizational skills, strong interpersonal skills, writing skills. Duration is June to August, full-time. ▶ *10–20 clinical volunteers:* responsibilities include working in an inpatient unit, partial hospitalized program, or day hospital program. Candidates should have ability to work independently, ability to work with others, knowledge of field, oral communication skills, personal interest in the field. Duration is June to August, full-time. ▶ *8–10 research volunteers:* responsibilities include working on a clinical or scientific research project, collecting data, interviewing subjects, and entering data into computer. Candidates should have analytical skills, computer skills, research skills, background in biology or chemistry. Duration is June to August, full time. All positions are unpaid. Open to college sophomores, college juniors, college seniors, recent college graduates. International applications accepted.
Benefits   Opportunity to attend seminars/workshops, possible full-time employment, willing to complete paperwork for educational credit, willing to provide letters of recommendation, participation in an orientation program.
Contact   Write, call, or fax Diane A. Clark, MA, Director of Volunteers. Phone: 914-997-5780. Fax: 914-682-6909. In-person interview recommended. Applicants must submit a formal organization application, resume, one academic and one personal letter of recommendation. Application deadline: April 1.

NORTHWESTERN MEMORIAL HOSPITAL WELLNESS INSTITUTE
240 East Ontario, Suite 400
Chicago, Illinois 60611

General Information   A leading academic medical center serving the entire Chicago area. It is an organization of caregivers who consistently aspire to high standards of quality and cost effectiveness. Established in 1972. Number of employees: 4,000. Number of internship applications received each year: 75.
Internships Available ▶ *1 student intern:* responsibilities include assisting in community education seminars, program coordination; development of speaker biographies and researching educational materials; coordinating corporate wellness programs; locating speakers and implementing program logistics; facilitating employee wellness events; helping with blood drives, incentive programs, and blood pressure screenings. Candidates should have ability to work independently, computer skills, oral communication skills, self-motivation, strong interpersonal skills, written communication skills, good judgement skills in project management. Duration is 8–12 weeks. Unpaid. Open to college seniors, recent college graduates. International applications accepted.
Benefits   Housing at a cost, names of contacts, on-the-job training, opportunity to attend seminars/workshops, possible full-time employment, travel reimbursement, willing to act as a professional reference, willing to complete paperwork for educational credit, willing to provide letters of recommendation.
Contact   Write or fax Leigh Ginther or Sherri Martin, Coordinators, 240 East Ontario, Suite 400, Chicago, Illinois 60611. Fax: 312-926-5444. In-person interview required. Applicants must

submit a cover letter, resume. Applications are accepted continuously. World Wide Web: http://www.NMH.org.

PREVENT BLINDNESS OHIO
1500 West Third Avenue, Suite 200
Columbus, Ohio 43212

General Information   Organization dedicated to preserving sight and preventing blindness through vision screenings, education programs, and support of vision research. Established in 1957. Number of employees: 15. Affiliate of National Society to Prevent Blindness, Schaumburg, Illinois. Number of internship applications received each year: 12.
Internships Available ▶ *3 adult vision screeners:* responsibilities include scheduling vision screenings at corporations, clubs, and industries and assisting with screenings. Candidates should have oral communication skills, personal interest in the field, self-motivation, strong interpersonal skills. Duration is flexible. Position available as unpaid or at $6–$8 per hour. Open to high school students, high school seniors, recent high school graduates, college freshmen, college sophomores, college juniors, college seniors, recent college graduates, graduate students, law school graduates, career changers, individuals reentering the workforce. ▶ *1–3 client follow-up coordinators:* responsibilities include communicating with clients (via mass mailings and phone) to learn information regarding their eye health; documenting testimonials of program success stories via client follow-up contact; maintaining client follow-up database. Candidates should have ability to work independently, computer skills, oral communication skills, personal interest in the field, self-motivation, strong interpersonal skills. Duration is flexible. Position available as unpaid or at $6–$8 per hour. Open to college juniors, college seniors, recent college graduates, graduate students, career changers, individuals reentering the workforce. ▶ *2 development assistants:* responsibilities include assisting director of development with annual campaign, planned giving, fundraising, and follow-up. Candidates should have ability to work independently, ability to work with others, computer skills, oral communication skills, personal interest in the field, self-motivation. Duration is 3–12 months. Position available as unpaid or at $6–$7 per hour. Open to college juniors, college seniors, recent college graduates, career changers, individuals reentering the workforce. ▶ *1 information and referral coordinator:* responsibilities include maintaining and updating information and resource library; researching new education topics; fulfilling client requests for eye health and safety information and resources; maintaining information and referral database. Candidates should have computer skills, office skills, organizational skills, personal interest in the field, research skills, self-motivation. Duration is flexible. Position available as unpaid or at $6–$8 per hour. Open to recent high school graduates, college freshmen, college sophomores, college juniors, college seniors, recent college graduates, graduate students, career changers, individuals reentering the workforce. ▶ *1 legislative-advocacy communication coordinator:* responsibilities include implementing letter-writing campaigns; coordinating visits between volunteers and legislators; tracking activity on advocacy database. Candidates should have computer skills, organizational skills, personal interest in the field, self-motivation, strong interpersonal skills, written communication skills. Duration is 3–12 months. Position available as unpaid or at $6–$8 per hour. Open to college juniors, college seniors, recent college graduates, graduate students, career changers, individuals reentering the workforce. ▶ *2 pre-school vision screeners:* responsibilities include scheduling vision screenings at schools, assisting in screenings, and training others. Candidates should have oral communication skills, personal interest in the field, self-motivation, strong interpersonal skills. Position available as unpaid or at $6–$8 per hour. Open to high school students, high school seniors, recent high school graduates, college freshmen, college sophomores, college juniors, college seniors, recent college graduates, graduate students, law students, career changers, individuals reentering the workforce. ▶ *1 public relations assistant:* responsibilities include assisting public relations director with monthly statewide press kits, sending stories to the media, and writing for quarterly newspaper.

Candidates should have ability to work independently, ability to work with others, oral communication skills, personal interest in the field, self-motivation, written communication skills. Unpaid. Open to high school students, high school seniors, recent high school graduates, college freshmen, college sophomores, college juniors, college seniors, recent college graduates, graduate students, law school graduates, career changers, individuals reentering the workforce. ▶ *1–3 speaker's bureau coordinators:* responsibilities include designing speaker presentations and recruiting speakers for eye health and safety awareness; tracking speaker presentations and activities in volunteer database. Candidates should have ability to work with others, oral communication skills, organizational skills, personal interest in the field, self-motivation, written communication skills. Duration is flexible. Position available as unpaid or at $6–$8 per hour. Open to college juniors, college seniors, recent college graduates, graduate students, career changers, individuals reentering the workforce. ▶ *2 special events assistants:* responsibilities include assisting with planning and implementing of up to 6 special events. Candidates should have ability to work independently, organizational skills, personal interest in the field, self-motivation, strong interpersonal skills. Duration is 3–12 weeks. Unpaid. Open to high school students, high school seniors, recent high school graduates, college freshmen, college sophomores, college juniors, college seniors, recent college graduates, graduate students, law students, career changers, individuals reentering the workforce. ▶ *1–3 volunteer coordinators:* responsibilities include recruiting volunteers and volunteer groups for vision screening, speaker's bureau presentation, and special program activities; maintaining communication via phone and written forms with current volunteers; designing and implementing volunteer recognition program; maintaining volunteer database. Candidates should have oral communication skills, organizational skills, personal interest in the field, self-motivation, strong interpersonal skills. Duration is flexible. Position available as unpaid or at $6–$8 per hour. Open to college juniors, college seniors, recent college graduates, graduate students, career changers, individuals reentering the workforce. International applications accepted.
Benefits Names of contacts, on-the-job training, opportunity to attend seminars/workshops, possible full-time employment, travel reimbursement, willing to act as a professional reference, willing to complete paperwork for educational credit, willing to provide letters of recommendation.
Contact Write, call, fax, or e-mail Ms. Sherill Williams, President, CEO. Phone: 614-464-2020. Fax: 614-481-9670. E-mail: 112020.2634@compuserve.com. In-person interview recommended. Applicants must submit a cover letter, resume. Applications are accepted continuously. World Wide Web: http://www.preventblindness.org.

RUDOLF STEINER FELLOWSHIP FOUNDATION
241 Hungry Hollow Road
Spring Valley, New York 10977

General Information An intergenerational, work-based, long-term care community. Care of the elderly is central, but care is extended to individuals of all ages, including some handicapped persons, in eight supportive work areas. Established in 1966. Number of employees: 40. Number of internship applications received each year: 6.
Internships Available ▶ *6–12 co-worker interns:* responsibilities include participating in direct care of elderly in farm setting, assisting with maintenance chores as needed. Duration is 1–12 months. Paid. Open to recent high school graduates, college freshmen, college sophomores, college juniors, college seniors, recent college graduates, graduate students, law students, career changers, individuals reentering the workforce. ▶ *4–6 rotating community development interns:* Candidates should have ability to work independently, oral communication skills, personal interest in the field, self-motivation, strong interpersonal skills. Duration is 6–12 months. Position available as unpaid or at possible financial support on an individual basis. Open to college sophomores, college juniors, college seniors, recent college graduates, graduate students, law students, career changers. International applications accepted.

Benefits Formal training, free housing, free meals, job counseling, on-the-job training, opportunity to attend seminars/workshops, possible full-time employment, willing to act as a professional reference, willing to complete paperwork for educational credit, willing to provide letters of recommendation.
Contact Write, call, fax, or e-mail Ann Scharff, Administrator, 241 Hungry Hollow Road, Spring Valley, New York 10977. Phone: 914-356-8494. Fax: 914-356-8468. E-mail: fellowship@spyral.net. In-person interview recommended. Applicants must submit a formal organization application, cover letter, resume, two personal references, two letters of recommendation. Applications are accepted continuously.

RUTH SHEETS ADULT CARE CENTER
228 West Edenton Street
Raleigh, North Carolina 27603

General Information Care center specializing in the care of dementia patients, most of whom have been diagnosed with Alzheimer's disease. Established in 1991. Number of employees: 4. Number of internship applications received each year: 12.
Internships Available ▶ *1–2 recreation interns:* responsibilities include implementing and assisting with activities for senior citizens. Candidates should have ability to work independently, oral communication skills, personal interest in the field, strong interpersonal skills, strong leadership ability. ▶ *1–2 social work interns:* responsibilities include performing intake work and keeping progress notes, service notes, and service plans. Candidates should have ability to work independently, personal interest in the field, self-motivation, strong interpersonal skills, strong leadership ability. Duration for all positions is 1 semester. All positions available as unpaid or at $220 per month. Open to college freshmen, college sophomores, college juniors, college seniors.
Benefits Job counseling, meals at a cost, names of contacts, opportunity to attend seminars/workshops, possible full-time employment, travel reimbursement, willing to complete paperwork for educational credit, willing to provide letters of recommendation.
Contact Write, call, or fax Judith A. Shotts, Director. Phone: 919-832-7227. Fax: 919-829-5780. In-person interview recommended. Applicants must submit a resume, two personal references, letter of recommendation. Applications are accepted continuously.

SHEPPARD PRATT HEALTH SYSTEM
6501 North Charles Street
Towson, Maryland 21286

General Information Psychiatric hospital. Established in 1895. Number of employees: 1,800. Number of internship applications received each year: 35.
Internships Available ▶ *1 human resources intern:* responsibilities include recruitment and training in the Human Resources Department. Candidates should have ability to work independently, college degree in related field, knowledge of field, oral communication skills, strong interpersonal skills, written communication skills. Duration is 1 year. $9 per hour. Open to recent college graduates, graduate students. International applications accepted.
Benefits Formal training, job counseling, names of contacts, on-the-job training, opportunity to attend seminars/workshops, possible full-time employment, willing to act as a professional reference, willing to complete paperwork for educational credit, willing to provide letters of recommendation.
Contact E-mail Mary Jeanne Mullen, Senior Human Resources Generalist, 6501 North Charles Street, Baltimore, Maryland 21285-6815. E-mail: mmullen@sheppardpratt.org. In-person interview required. Applicants must submit a formal organization application, cover letter, resume, two letters of recommendation. Application deadline: April 30.

SWEDISH MEDICAL CENTER/HUMAN RESOURCES
747 Broadway
Seattle, Washington 98122

General Information Acute medical care facility. Established in 1910. Number of employees: 5,000.
Internships Available ▶ *Interns:* responsibilities include assisting in various departments of medical center as needed. Positions include epidemiology, nursing (residency), quality improvement, and pastoral care. Candidates should have computer skills, office skills, oral communication skills, personal interest in the field, strong interpersonal skills, health care experience desirable. Duration is flexible. Position available as unpaid or at stipend sometimes available for some positions. Open to college juniors, college seniors, recent college graduates, graduate students. International applications accepted.
Benefits On-the-job training, possible full-time employment, willing to act as a professional reference, willing to complete paperwork for educational credit.
Contact Write, fax, or e-mail Intern Coordinator, Human Resources Department, 747 Broadway, Seattle, Washington 98122. Fax: 206-386-2145. E-mail: employ@swedish.org. No phone calls. In-person interview recommended. Applicants must submit a formal organization application, cover letter, resume, 2-4 personal or professional references/letters of recommendation. Applications are accepted continuously. World Wide Web: http://www.swedish.org.

THOMAS JEFFERSON UNIVERSITY
Eleventh and Walnut Streets
Philadelphia, Pennsylvania 19107

General Information Internationally recognized academic healthcare center with mission of state-of-the-art research, quality education, and quality healthcare. Established in 1824. Number of employees: 10,000. Number of internship applications received each year: 10.
Internships Available ▶ *2–5 human resources interns:* responsibilities include rotation of employee relations and employment divisions, data entry, report production and analyses, applicant tracking, reference checks, surveys. Candidates should have ability to work independently, computer skills, office skills, oral communication skills, organizational skills, personal interest in the field, plan to pursue career in field, self-motivation, strong interpersonal skills. Duration is 1 summer or 1 semester. Unpaid. Open to college juniors, college seniors. International applications accepted.
Benefits Job counseling, on-the-job training, opportunity to attend seminars/workshops, possible full-time employment, willing to act as a professional reference, willing to complete paperwork for educational credit, willing to provide letters of recommendation.
Contact Write, fax, or e-mail Linda C. Mitchell, Manager, Employee Selection and Placement, 201 South 11th Street, 1st Floor, Martin Building, Philadelphia, Pennsylvania 19107. Fax: 215-503-8219. E-mail: gloria.leventhal@mail.tju.edu. No phone calls. In-person interview required. Applicants must submit a formal organization application, resume. Applications are accepted continuously. World Wide Web: http://www.tju.edu/.

UNITED STATES ARMY CENTER FOR HEALTH PROMOTION AND PREVENTIVE MEDICINE
Aberdeen Proving Ground
Aberdeen, Maryland 21010-5422

General Information Organization that provides information and consultative services to leaders charged with responsibility for the occupational and environmental health of military and civilian service members and associated communities worldwide. Established in 1946. Unit of Oak Ridge Associated Universities, Oak Ridge, Tennessee. Number of internship applications received each year: 200.
Internships Available ▶ *Interns:* responsibilities include performing applied research and development in the areas of environmental health engineering programs, projects, and activities. Candidates should have ability to work independently, research skills, self-motivation, strong interpersonal skills, strong leadership ability. Duration is 1–12 months. monthly stipend payment. Open to college freshmen, college sophomores, college juniors, college seniors, recent college graduates, graduate students.
Benefits On-the-job training, opportunity to attend seminars/workshops, possible full-time employment, travel reimbursement.
International Internships Available in Germany.
Contact Write, call, fax, or e-mail Betty Bowling, Program Specialist, Science and Engineering Education, ORISE Mail Stop 36, PO Box 117, Oak Ridge, Tennessee 37831-0117. Phone: 423-576-8503. Fax: 423-241-5219. E-mail: bowlingb@orau.gov. Applicants must submit a formal organization application, resume, academic transcripts, 3 professional references. Applications are accepted continuously. World Wide Web: http://www.orau.gov.

WILDLIFE CARE CENTER
3200 Southwest 4th Avenue
Fort Lauderdale, Florida 33315

General Information Animal hospital. Established in 1969. Number of employees: 28. Number of internship applications received each year: 10.
Internships Available ▶ *2–8 veterinary interns:* responsibilities include assisting the veterinarian. Candidates should have ability to work independently, college courses in field, knowledge of field, oral communication skills, personal interest in the field, plan to pursue career in field, self-motivation, strong interpersonal skills, written communication skills. Unpaid. Open to recent college graduates, graduate students. International applications accepted.
Benefits On-the-job training, possible full-time employment, willing to act as a professional reference, willing to complete paperwork for educational credit, willing to provide letters of recommendation.
Contact Write or fax Dr. Roberta Silfen, Executive Director, 3200 SW 4th Avenue, Fort Lauderdale, Florida 33315. Fax: 954-524-9415. No phone calls. Telephone interview required. Applicants must submit a formal organization application, cover letter, resume, academic transcripts, two personal references, two letters of recommendation. Applications are accepted continuously. World Wide Web: http://www.wildcare.org.

SOCIAL ASSISTANCE

AFFILIATED SANTE GROUP AND THE ROCK CREEK FOUNDATION
1107 Spring Street, Suite #C
Silver Spring, Maryland 20910

General Information A student and volunteer program that meets academic and personal community service needs by helping disabled individuals create individualized, personal solutions to their emotional, job , and life-functioning issues in mainstream society. Established in 1973. Number of employees: 300. Number of internship applications received each year: 200.
Internships Available ▶ *5 business interns:* responsibilities include working with CEO to assist directors of program in policy analysis and marketing. Candidates should have ability to work independently, analytical skills, computer skills, declared college major in field, editing skills, experience in the field, knowledge of field, office skills, oral communication skills, organizational skills, personal interest in the field, plan to pursue career in field, research skills, self-motivation, strong interpersonal skills, strong leadership ability, writing skills. Open to college juniors, college seniors, recent college graduates, graduate students, career changers, individuals reentering the workforce.
▶ *5 computer volunteers/interns:* responsibilities include assessment, evaluation, management, or research. Candidates should have ability to work independently, ability to work with others, analytical skills, computer skills, editing skills, knowledge of field, office skills, organizational skills, personal interest in the field,

self-motivation, writing skills. Open to high school students, high school seniors, recent high school graduates, college freshmen, college sophomores, college juniors, college seniors, recent college graduates, graduate students, career changers, individuals reentering the workforce. ▶ *5 employment consultants:* responsibilities include assisting adults with disabilities to integrate into the community and on the job. Candidates should have ability to work independently, computer skills, knowledge of field, oral communication skills, organizational skills, personal interest in the field, self-motivation, strong interpersonal skills, strong leadership ability, writing skills. Open to college juniors, college seniors, recent college graduates, graduate students, individuals reentering the workforce. ▶ *10 leadership/volunteerism/service learning interns:* responsibilities include working with individuals with disabilities. Candidates should have ability to work independently, computer skills, editing skills, experience in the field, knowledge of field, organizational skills, personal interest in the field, self-motivation, strong interpersonal skills, strong leadership ability, writing skills. Open to high school students, high school seniors, recent high school graduates, college freshmen, college sophomores, college juniors, college seniors, recent college graduates, graduate students, law students, career changers, individuals reentering the workforce. ▶ *5 organizational development interns:* responsibilities include working with directors and staff to conduct surveys on policy, procedures, systems of companies, meetings, and infrastructure. Candidates should have ability to work independently, analytical skills, college courses in field, computer skills, editing skills, knowledge of field, office skills, oral communication skills, organizational skills, personal interest in the field, self-motivation, strong interpersonal skills, strong leadership ability, writing skills. Open to college juniors, college seniors, recent college graduates, graduate students, career changers, individuals reentering the workforce. ▶ *5 psychology interns:* responsibilities include developing and teaching consumer life skills such as community adaptation. Candidates should have ability to work independently, oral communication skills, organizational skills, personal interest in the field, self-motivation, strong interpersonal skills, strong leadership ability, written communication skills. Open to college sophomores, college juniors, college seniors, recent college graduates, graduate students, career changers, individuals reentering the workforce. ▶ *5 public relations/marketing interns:* responsibilities include marketing duties, technical writing, media networking, and special event planning. Candidates should have ability to work independently, analytical skills, computer skills, declared college major in field, editing skills, knowledge of field, organizational skills, personal interest in the field, self-motivation, strong interpersonal skills, strong leadership ability, writing skills. Open to college juniors, college seniors, graduate students. ▶ *5 recreation specialists:* responsibilities include facilitating groups and assisting with community integration and special events. Candidates should have ability to work independently, college courses in field, computer skills, knowledge of field, oral communication skills, organizational skills, personal interest in the field, self-motivation, strong interpersonal skills, strong leadership ability, writing skills. Open to high school seniors, recent high school graduates, college freshmen, college sophomores, college juniors, college seniors, recent college graduates, graduate students, career changers, individuals reentering the workforce, therapeutic recreation majors. ▶ *5 rehabilitation psychology interns:* responsibilities include performing assessments, case management, and attending interdisciplinary team meetings. ▶ *3 research interns:* responsibilities include performing special research projects in behavioral applications, neuropsychology, human relations, and recreation. Candidates should have ability to work independently, analytical skills, college courses in field, computer skills, editing skills, knowledge of field, office skills, organizational skills, personal interest in the field, research skills, self-motivation, strong interpersonal skills, writing skills. Open to recent college graduates, graduate students, career changers. ▶ *10 social work/counseling interns:* responsibilities include case management, facilitating groups, and performing assessments. Candidates should have ability to work independently, knowledge of field, oral communication skills, organizational skills, personal interest in the field, self-motivation, strong

leadership ability, written communication skills. Open to college juniors, college seniors, recent college graduates, graduate students, career changers, individuals reentering the workforce. ▶ *5 student/volunteer career counselors:* responsibilities include assisting staff with interviewing students, surveying satisfaction, updating database for community referrals, and attending seminars/community collaborations. Candidates should have ability to work independently, college courses in field, computer skills, editing skills, experience in the field, knowledge of field, office skills, oral communication skills, organizational skills, personal interest in the field, self-motivation, strong interpersonal skills, strong leadership ability, writing skills. Open to college freshmen, college sophomores, college juniors, college seniors, recent college graduates, graduate students, career changers, individuals reentering the workforce. Duration for all positions is 3 months minimum (2 days weekly). All positions are unpaid. International applications accepted.

Benefits Formal training, housing at a cost, job counseling, names of contacts, on-the-job training, opportunity to attend seminars/workshops, possible full-time employment, willing to act as a professional reference, willing to complete paperwork for educational credit, willing to provide letters of recommendation, possibility of partial parking reimbursement.

Contact Write, call, or fax Ms. Beth Albaneze, Director of Students/Volunteers. Phone: 301-589-8303 Ext. 834. Fax: 301-588-1567. In-person interview recommended. Applicants must submit a formal organization application, cover letter, resume, personal reference, letter of recommendation. Applications are accepted continuously.

ALLIANCE FOR CHILDREN AND FAMILIES POLICY OFFICE
1701 K Street, NW, Suite 200
Washington, District of Columbia 20006-1503

General Information Organization representing voluntary nonprofit agencies across the country, providing a wide range of services to children and families. Established in 1911. Number of employees: 7. Division of Alliance for Children and Families, Milwaukee, Wisconsin. Number of internship applications received each year: 40.

Internships Available ▶ *1–2 graduate fellows:* responsibilities include attending congressional hearings and legislative bill drafting sessions regarding budget, family, and children's issues and writing analytical summaries of these events; following public policy that impacts children and families; participating in coalitions of significant advocacy groups developing legislation/strategy to influence the public policy process; and aiding in the research, writing, and production of publications. Candidates should have ability to work independently, ability to work with others, analytical skills, college courses in field, knowledge of field, personal interest in the field, writing skills. Open to college juniors, college seniors, recent college graduates, graduate students, law students. ▶ *2–3 policy interns:* responsibilities include working on a research project, attending congressional hearings and other governmental meetings, developing FSA policy meetings, writing reports and analyses of proposed legislation, summarizing policy studies, and assisting with administrative functions of office. Candidates should have ability to work independently, analytical skills, college courses in field, knowledge of field, personal interest in the field, writing skills. Duration is flexible. Open to college juniors, college seniors, recent college graduates, graduate students, law students, career changers. All positions are unpaid. International applications accepted.

Benefits Names of contacts, on-the-job training, opportunity to attend seminars/workshops, willing to complete paperwork for educational credit, willing to provide letters of recommendation.

Contact Write, call, fax, or e-mail Carmen Delgado Votaw, Senior Vice President. Phone: 202-223-3447. Fax: 202-331-7476. E-mail: cvotaw@alliance1.org. In-person interview required. Applicants must submit a cover letter, resume, writing sample. Applications are accepted continuously. World Wide Web: http://www.alliance1.org.

ALTERNATIVE HOUSE
2136 Gallows Road, Suite E
Dunn Loring, Virginia 22027

General Information Shelter and outreach program that builds on the innate strengths and resiliency of children, youth, and families through individual, group, and family interaction. Established in 1972. Number of employees: 30. Unit of Alternative House, Inc., Dunn Loring, Virginia. Number of internship applications received each year: 30.

Internships Available ▶ *1–6 Kaleidoscope (shelter for 5-12 year olds) interns:* responsibilities include planning and initiating recreational, educational, and groups activities for children ages 5-12; supervising youth; maintaining documentation of activities; and adhering to professional standards. Candidates should have ability to work independently, oral communication skills, self-motivation, strong interpersonal skills, strong leadership ability, writing skills. Open to recent high school graduates, college freshmen, college sophomores, college juniors, college seniors, recent college graduates, graduate students, law students, career changers, individuals reentering the workforce. ▶ *Emergency teen shelter interns:* responsibilities include planning and initiating recreational, educational, and group activities for youth ages 13-17; supervising youth; maintaining documentation of activities; and adhering to professional standards. Candidates should have oral communication skills, self-motivation, strong interpersonal skills, strong leadership ability, written communication skills. Open to high school seniors, recent high school graduates, college freshmen, college sophomores, college juniors, college seniors, recent college graduates, graduate students, law students, career changers, individuals reentering the workforce. ▶ *1–3 outreach programs interns:* responsibilities include implementing new programs in outreach and teen center programs; planning and initiating recreational, educational, and group activities for youth ages 13-17; networking with poeple within the community and other agencies; and adhering to professional standards. Candidates should have ability to work independently, oral communication skills, self-motivation, strong interpersonal skills, strong leadership ability. Open to college sophomores, college juniors, college seniors, recent college graduates, graduate students, law students, career changers. ▶ *1–3 transitional living program interns:* responsibilities include planning and initiating recreational, educational, and group activities for young adults ages 16-21; maintaining documentation of activities; adhering to professional standards. Candidates should have oral communication skills, self-motivation, strong interpersonal skills, strong leadership ability, writing skills. Open to college sophomores, college juniors, college seniors, recent college graduates, graduate students, law students, career changers. Duration for all positions is 3–12 months. All positions are unpaid. International applications accepted.

Benefits Formal training, possible full-time employment, willing to complete paperwork for educational credit, willing to provide letters of recommendation.

Contact Write, call, or fax Volunteer Coordinator. Phone: 703-820-9039. Fax: 703-820-0788. In-person interview recommended. Applicants must submit a formal organization application, cover letter, resume, three personal references. Application deadline: April 15 for summer, August 1 for fall, December 15 for spring.

AMERICAN ANOREXIA/BULIMIA ASSOCIATION, INC.
165 West 46th Street, Suite 1108
New York, New York 10036

General Information Social service organization that provides services and programs for individuals involved with eating disorders and aids in education, research, and prevention of these illnesses. Established in 1978. Number of employees: 2. Number of internship applications received each year: 50.

Internships Available ▶ *2–3 interns:* responsibilities include outreach work, responding to requests by phone and mail, light clerical and computer work, research, special projects work, and developing a database for the purpose of fund-raising. Candidates should have knowledge of field, office skills, oral communica-

tion skills, personal interest in the field, self-motivation, written communication skills. Duration is 1–2 semesters. Unpaid. Open to college freshmen, college sophomores, college juniors, college seniors, recent college graduates, graduate students.

Benefits Free meals, on-the-job training, opportunity to attend seminars/workshops, travel reimbursement, willing to act as a professional reference, willing to complete paperwork for educational credit.

Contact Write or fax Danielle Gougon, Outreach Director. Fax: 212-278-0698. No phone calls. In-person interview required. Applicants must submit a cover letter, resume. Application deadline: March 1 for summer, November 1 for spring. World Wide Web: http://www.aabainc.org.

AMERICAN FOUNDATION FOR THE BLIND
11 Penn Plaza, Suite 300
New York, New York 10001

General Information Nonprofit organization with offices in Atlanta, Chicago, Dallas, San Francisco, and Washington, DC that serves as the national resource for the public and for local services for blind and visually impaired persons. Established in 1921. Number of employees: 150. Number of internship applications received each year: 5.

Internships Available ▶ *1–3 editorial or communications assistants:* responsibilities include bibliographic research, editing, and writing. Candidates should have ability to work independently, ability to work with others, computer skills, editing skills, organizational skills, written communication skills. Position available as unpaid or at $6—$16 per hour depending on experience (if funding permits). ▶ *1–3 social science research assistants:* responsibilities include conducting policy research and program evaluation. Candidates should have ability to work independently, ability to work with others, computer skills, organizational skills, personal interest in the field, research skills. Position available as unpaid or at $6-$16 per hour depending on experience (if funding permits). Duration for all positions is 1–2 semesters. Open to college juniors, college seniors, recent college graduates, graduate students, law students, career changers, individuals reentering the workforce. International applications accepted.

Benefits Job counseling, names of contacts, on-the-job training, opportunity to attend seminars/workshops, possible full-time employment, willing to act as a professional reference, willing to complete paperwork for educational credit, willing to provide letters of recommendation.

Contact Write, call, fax, or e-mail Dr. Corinne Kirchner, Director of Policy Research and Program Evaluation. Phone: 212-502-7640. Fax: 212-502-7773. E-mail: newyork@afb.net. In-person interview recommended. Applicants must submit a resume, 2 personal references or letters of recommendation, 1 writing sample may be required. Applications are accepted continuously. World Wide Web: http://www.afb.org/afb.

AMERICAN RED CROSS
8111 Gatehouse Road
Falls Church, Virginia 22042

General Information Humanitarian organization which provides relief to victims of disasters and helps people prevent, prepare for, and respond to emergencies. Established in 1881. Number of employees: 1,000. Number of internship applications received each year: 200.

Internships Available ▶ *12–20 Presidential interns for minority students:* responsibilities include working in positions throughout NHQ including finance, government relations, biomedical services, international services, communications, HIV/AIDS education, disaster, and the Holland Laboratory. Candidates should have college courses in field, oral communication skills, personal interest in the field, written communication skills. Duration is 10 weeks. $8 per hour. Open to college freshmen, college sophomores, college juniors, college seniors, graduate students.

Benefits On-the-job training, opportunity to attend seminars/workshops, possible full-time employment, willing to complete paperwork for educational credit, willing to provide letters of recommendation.
Contact Write, fax, or e-mail Debbera Hayward, Senior Director of Diversity, 8111 Gatehouse Road, 6th Floor, Falls Church, Virginia 22042. Fax: 703-206-8572. E-mail: haywardd@usa.redcross.org. No phone calls. In-person interview recommended. Applicants must submit a cover letter, resume. Application deadline: April 9 for summer. World Wide Web: http://www.redcross.org.

ASPIRA ASSOCIATION, INC.
1444 I Street, NW, Suite 800
Washington, District of Columbia 20005

General Information Nonprofit organization devoted to serving Puerto Rican and other Latino youth through leadership development and education. Established in 1961. Number of employees: 13. Number of internship applications received each year: 50.
Internships Available ▶ *2 community service interns:* responsibilities include collecting and synthesizing data on AmeriCorps members and their service performed, creating and disseminating recruitment materials for the following service term, and planning national member and staff meetings. Candidates should have ability to work independently, analytical skills, computer skills, organizational skills, research skills, self-motivation. Duration is 1 to 2 semesters or a 10-week summer term. Position available as unpaid or at $200 weekly stipend for summer only. Open to college juniors, college seniors, recent college graduates, graduate students, law students. ▶ *1–2 dropout prevention interns:* responsibilities include working in dropout prevention on appraisal of project impact, analysis and synthesis of program documentation, and research and development of materials for program support. Candidates should have analytical skills, knowledge of field, organizational skills, personal interest in the field, self-motivation, written communication skills. Duration is 1–2 semesters. Unpaid. Open to college sophomores, college juniors, college seniors, recent college graduates, graduate students, law students. ▶ *3 health policy interns:* responsibilities include researching and developing policy pieces, providing support to the director of education, attending hearings and meetings, and developing analyses. Candidates should have analytical skills, experience in the field, personal interest in the field, research skills, self-motivation, written communication skills. Duration is 1 to 2 semesters (2 school year positions) or 1 summer (one 10-week position). Position available as unpaid or at $200 weekly stipend for summer only. Open to college sophomores, college juniors, college seniors, recent college graduates, graduate students, law students. ▶ *3 legislative analysts:* responsibilities include tracking federal legislation, maintaining contact with congressional offices, attending hearings and meetings, carrying out follow-up actions, and researching a policy issue. Candidates should have analytical skills, experience in the field, personal interest in the field, research skills, self-motivation, written communication skills. Duration is 1-2 semesters (2 school-year positions) or 1 summer (1 10-week position). Position available as unpaid or at $200 weekly stipend for summer only. Open to college sophomores, college juniors, college seniors, recent college graduates, graduate students, law students. ▶ *2 parental leadership interns:* responsibilities include providing support to ASPIRA's Parents for Educational Excellence program through assisting in developing training and implementation manuals. Candidates should have analytical skills, organizational skills, personal interest in the field, research skills, self-motivation, written communication skills. Duration is 1 to 2 semesters or a 10-week summer term. Position available as unpaid or at $200 weekly stipend for summer only. Open to college sophomores, college juniors, college seniors, recent college graduates, graduate students, law students. ▶ *2 program development interns:* responsibilities include assisting in expanding ASPIRA's programs by identifying prospective corporate and foundation sources, writing grant proposals,and providing input and assistance on marketing and program development activities. Candidates should have computer skills, organizational skills, research skills, self-

motivation, strong interpersonal skills, written communication skills. Duration is 1 to 2 semesters or a 10-week summer term. Position available as unpaid or at $200 weekly stipend for summer only. Open to college sophomores, college juniors, college seniors, recent college graduates, graduate students, law students. ▶ *2 youth leadership and community service interns:* responsibilities include assisting in program implementation and evaluation, material development. Candidates should have analytical skills, knowledge of field, organizational skills, personal interest in the field, self-motivation, written communication skills. Duration is 1 to 2 semesters or a 10-week summer term. Position available as unpaid or at $200 weekly stipend for summr only. Open to college sophomores, college juniors, college seniors, recent college graduates, graduate students, law students. International applications accepted.
Benefits Names of contacts, opportunity to attend seminars/workshops, possible full-time employment, willing to complete paperwork for educational credit, willing to provide letters of recommendation, course credit available for school-year interns.
Contact Write, call, fax, or e-mail Manager, Youth Leadership and Community Service. Phone: 202-835-3600. Fax: 202-835-3613. E-mail: info@aspira.org. Applicants must submit a cover letter, resume. Application deadline: February 1 for spring, April 1 for summer, October 1 for fall. World Wide Web: http://www.incacorp.com/aspira.

AUDUBON YMCA
2460 Boulevard of the Generals
Norristown, Pennsylvania 19403

General Information Organization that provides the community with services that promote healthy spirits, minds, and bodies. Established in 1984. Number of employees: 70. Branch of Phoenixville Area YMCA, Phoenixville, Pennsylvania. Number of internship applications received each year: 4.
Internships Available ▶ *5–10 volunteers:* responsibilities include performing office duties and assisting in child care, administration, physical education, or marketing. Candidates should have ability to work independently, office skills, oral communication skills, personal interest in the field, self-motivation, strong interpersonal skills. Duration is flexible. Unpaid. Open to college freshmen, college sophomores, college juniors, college seniors, recent college graduates, graduate students, career changers. International applications accepted.
Benefits Job counseling, names of contacts, on-the-job training, opportunity to attend seminars/workshops, possible full-time employment, willing to complete paperwork for educational credit, willing to provide letters of recommendation.
Contact Write, call, or fax Janet Genuardi, Branch Executive Director. Phone: 610-539-0900. Fax: 610-539-2975. E-mail: janetg@net-thing.net. In-person interview required. Applicants must submit a cover letter, resume, two personal references, two letters of recommendation. Applications are accepted continuously. World Wide Web: http://www.phoenixvilleymca.com.

BEING ALIVE SAN DIEGO
4070 Centre Street
San Diego, California 92103

General Information HIV/AIDS service organization. Established in 1989. Number of employees: 22.
Internships Available ▶ *5–10 childcare assistant:* responsibilities include providing support to childcare coordinator in caring for children. Candidates should have ability to work independently, ability to work with others, college courses in field, oral communication skills, personal interest in the field, plan to pursue career in field, recent tuberculosis test, a criminal index check and fingerprinting, and at least 12 units ECE child development (in order to work unsupervised). Unpaid. Open to college freshmen, college sophomores, college juniors, college seniors. International applications accepted.
Benefits Formal training, job counseling, on-the-job training, opportunity to attend seminars/workshops, possible full-time employment, willing to act as a professional reference, willing to provide letters of recommendation.

Being Alive San Diego (continued)

Contact Write, call, fax, or e-mail Jesus M. Gonzalez, Operations Manager, 4070 Centre Street, San Diego, California 92103. Phone: 619-291-1400. Fax: 619-291-1471. E-mail: rlpiii@pacbell. net. In-person interview recommended. Applicants must submit a formal organization application, cover letter, resume. Applications are accepted continuously. World Wide Web: http://www. beingalive.org.

BERKSHIRE FARM CENTER AND SERVICES FOR YOUTH
Route 22
Canaan, New York 12029

General Information Nonprofit social service agency serving troubled, at-risk adolescents, and their families of New York State. Established in 1886. Number of employees: 350. Number of internship applications received each year: 15.

Internships Available ▶ *10–15 teaching assistants:* responsibilities include assisting teacher in diverse subjects in public junior and high schools. Candidates should have ability to work independently, oral communication skills, plan to pursue career in field, self-motivation, strong interpersonal skills, strong leadership ability, written communication skills, interest in troubled, at-risk adolescent youth. ▶ *20–25 youth counselors/advocates/mentors:* responsibilities include assisting in supervision of troubled adolescents. Candidates should have ability to work with others, plan to pursue career in field, self-motivation, strong interpersonal skills, interest in troubled, at-risk adolescent youth. Duration for all positions is flexible. All positions available as unpaid or at $7 per hour. Open to recent high school graduates, college freshmen, college sophomores, college juniors, college seniors, recent college graduates, graduate students, law students, career changers, individuals reentering the workforce. International applications accepted.

Benefits Formal training, free meals, job counseling, names of contacts, on-the-job training, opportunity to attend seminars/workshops, possible full-time employment, willing to act as a professional reference, willing to complete paperwork for educational credit, willing to provide letters of recommendation.

Contact Write, call, or fax Lawrence "Lari" Brandstein, Director of Volunteer Services. Phone: 518-781-4567 Ext. 322. Fax: 518-781-3710. In-person interview required. Applicants must submit a formal organization application, resume, three personal references. Applications are accepted continuously.

BETHESDA LUTHERAN HOMES AND SERVICES, INC.
700 Hoffmann Drive
Watertown, Wisconsin 53094-6204

General Information Facility that provides residential and training services to individuals with mental retardation. Established in 1904. Number of employees: 700. Number of internship applications received each year: 21.

Internships Available ▶ *1 Camp Matz co-op:* responsibilities include organizing and carrying out goal-oriented, age-appropriate, challenging activities for campers; assisting camp counselors during activities; working with campers one-to-one during activity time; may assist with personal care for campers. Candidates should have declared college major in field, oral communication skills, personal interest in the field, strong interpersonal skills, written communication skills, experience in some volunteer or paid work involving children or adults with developmental disabilities. ▶ *1 chaplaincy representative (co-op position):* responsibilities include providing spiritual nurture for people with mental retardation, leading Bible classes and serving as a chapel aide. Candidates should have ability to work with others, declared college major in field, experience in the field, personal interest in the field, Lutheran background. ▶ *2 nursing student co-ops:* responsibilities include performing nursing duties designed to enhance the student's knowledge of the role of a professional nurse in a facility which provides care and treatment for people who have physical and mental disabilities. Candidates should have ability to work with others,

declared college major in field, experience in the field, personal interest in the field, plan to pursue career in field. ▶ *2 psychology interns:* responsibilities include assisting in preparing resident annual summaries and psychological assessments, preparing and analyzing data collection materials, assisting in the development of behavior treatment programs. Candidates should have ability to work with others, analytical skills, college courses in field, organizational skills, personal interest in the field. ▶ *1 public relations co-op:* responsibilities include writing articles and stories, doing layouts and photographic assignments, constructing displays, giving tours of Bethesda, and assisting with special events as required. Candidates should have computer skills, editing skills, oral communication skills, plan to pursue career in field, self-motivation, writing skills. ▶ *1 student social worker (co-op position):* responsibilities include working directly with residents individually or in groups in social skill development or behavior training; assisting with writing and monitoring Individual Program Plans (in conjunction with an assigned social worker/QMRP). Candidates should have ability to work with others, college courses in field, organizational skills, personal interest in the field, plan to pursue career in field. ▶ *2 student teachers (co-op positions):* responsibilities include working as a team, assisting in organizing and planning classroom activities, seeking materials and preparing for activities outlines in lesson plans, assisting with all record keeping as assigned by the supervising teacher. Candidates should have declared college major in field, experience in the field, personal interest in the field, strong interpersonal skills, strong leadership ability. ▶ *2 volunteer services clerks/Camp Matz (co-op positions):* responsibilities include supervising and coordinating all activities and completing all clerical work for the Servant Event Program at Camp Matz. Candidates should have ability to work independently, ability to work with others, oral communication skills, strong leadership ability, written communication skills, camp experience desirable, Lutheran background. Duration for all positions is 12 weeks in summer. All positions paid at $7 per hour. Open to college juniors, college seniors, graduate students. International applications accepted.

Benefits Formal training, free housing, on-the-job training, opportunity to attend seminars/workshops, possible full-time employment, tuition assistance, willing to act as a professional reference, low cost or free housing may be available.

Contact Write, call, fax, or e-mail Kevin Keller, Coordinator, Outreach Programs and Services. Phone: 800-369-4636 Ext. 525. Fax: 920-261-8441. E-mail: kkeller@blhs.org. In-person interview recommended. Applicants must submit a formal organization application, two personal references, letter of recommendation, cover letter, resume desirable; preference given to Lutheran students. Application deadline: March 1 for summer co-op positions; continuous for chaplaincy and recreation therapist positions. World Wide Web: http://www.bethesdainfo.org.

BIG BROTHERS BIG SISTERS-NIAGARA COUNTY, INC.
86 Park Avenue
Lockport, New York 14094

General Information Nonprofit organization that matches in-risk children, ages 7-15, from single parent homes, with a volunteer adult role model to serve as a friend. Established in 1973. Number of employees: 4. Number of internship applications received each year: 3.

Internships Available ▶ *1 program aide:* responsibilities include assisting with office responsibilities, participating in agency events, planning and implementing agency events, contributing to newsletters, keeping records, and doing clerical work. Candidates should have ability to work independently, ability to work with others, office skills, oral communication skills, organizational skills, personal interest in the field. Duration is flexible. Unpaid. Open to high school students, high school seniors, college freshmen, college sophomores, college juniors, college seniors, recent college graduates, graduate students, career changers, individuals reentering the workforce. International applications accepted.

Benefits Formal training, job counseling, names of contacts, on-the-job training, willing to act as a professional reference, willing to complete paperwork for educational credit, willing to provide letters of recommendation.

Contact Write, call, fax, or e-mail Annemarie C. Bettino, President. Phone: 716-434-1855. Fax: 716-434-2242. E-mail: bbbsnc@buffnet.net. In-person interview required. Applicants must submit a cover letter, resume, academic transcripts. Applications are accepted continuously.

BIG BROTHERS/BIG SISTERS OF AUBURN AND CAYUGA COUNTY
17 Nelson Street
Auburn, New York 13021

General Information Social service agency that recruits, screens, trains, and matches adult mentors with at-risk children; employs professional caseworkers who provide supervision and family support. Established in 1968. Number of employees: 4. Unit of Big Brothers/Big Sisters of America, Philadelphia, Pennsylvania. Number of internship applications received each year: 3.

Internships Available ▶ *1 child caseworker:* responsibilities include supervising self-esteem activities and planning and implementing two large group activities for caseload; clientele is pregnant and/or parenting teens. Candidates should have analytical skills, knowledge of field, organizational skills, personal interest in the field, strong interpersonal skills, written communication skills. Duration is 8 months. Unpaid. Open to college sophomores, college juniors, college seniors, recent college graduates, career changers, individuals reentering the workforce.

Benefits Formal training, names of contacts, opportunity to attend seminars/workshops, travel reimbursement, willing to complete paperwork for educational credit, willing to provide letters of recommendation.

Contact Write Edward H. Bell, Executive Director. No phone calls. In-person interview required. Applications are accepted continuously.

BIG BROTHERS/BIG SISTERS OF BEAVER COUNTY
930 Third Street #2
Beaver, Pennsylvania 15009

General Information Youth development agency that recruits, screens, and supervises adult volunteers in one-to-one mentoring relationships with disadvantaged school-age youth. Established in 1976. Number of employees: 5. Affiliate of Big Brothers/Big Sisters of America, Philadelphia, Pennsylvania. Number of internship applications received each year: 10.

Internships Available ▶ *1–3 caseworker interns:* responsibilities include assisting caseworkers with recruitment, screening, training, supervising volunteers, and fund-raising. Candidates should have ability to work with others, college courses in field, oral communication skills, plan to pursue career in field, self-motivation. Duration is 3 months. Unpaid. Open to college freshmen, college sophomores, college juniors.

Benefits Opportunity to attend seminars/workshops, possible full-time employment, travel reimbursement, willing to complete paperwork for educational credit.

Contact Write, call, or fax Pam Webb, Executive Director. Phone: 724-728-4300. Fax: 724-728-3674. In-person interview required. Applicants must submit a cover letter, resume. Application deadline: August 1 for fall, November 1 for spring.

BIG BROTHERS/BIG SISTERS OF BERRIEN & CASS
1 South Fifth, PO Box 194
Niles, Michigan 49120-0194

General Information Organization that prepares children for the future by enhancing their strengths through new experiences and friendship with qualified mentors. Established in 1967. Number of employees: 5. Affiliate of Big Brothers/Big Sisters of America, Inc, Philadelphia, Pennsylvania. Number of internship applications received each year: 1.

Internships Available ▶ *1 case work assistant:* responsibilities include supervising unmatched clients, conducting volunteer and

client trainings, contributing to the agency newsletter, and membership on the Activities Committee. Candidates should have oral communication skills, plan to pursue career in field, self-motivation, strong interpersonal skills, written communication skills. Duration is 6–12 months. Unpaid. Open to college juniors or seniors majoring in social science or education.

Benefits On-the-job training, willing to complete paperwork for educational credit, willing to provide letters of recommendation.

Contact Write Jeanine Larson, Executive Director. No phone calls. In-person interview required. Applicants must submit a resume, letter of recommendation. Applications are accepted continuously.

BIG BROTHERS/BIG SISTERS OF CENTRAL SUSQUEHANNA VALLEY
356 Market Street
Sunbury, Pennsylvania 17801-2338

General Information Program that matches adult volunteers one-to-one with children needing additional adult companionship, support, guidance and understanding; provides group activities for children and youth. Established in 1982. Number of employees: 3. Affiliate of Big Brothers/Big Sisters of America, Philadelphia, Pennsylvania. Number of internship applications received each year: 2.

Internships Available ▶ *2 adjunct caseworkers:* responsibilities include contacting clients to monitor progress of client matches; writing and recording case notes reports; maintaining records of clients, cases, volunteers, and parents' inquiries; doing routine clerical work; assisting with social and fund-raising functions; and attending group meetings, staff meetings, and board of director meetings. Candidates should have ability to work independently, oral communication skills, personal interest in the field, strong interpersonal skills, written communication skills. Unpaid. Open to college freshmen, college sophomores, college juniors, college seniors. International applications accepted.

Benefits Opportunity to attend seminars/workshops, travel reimbursement, willing to act as a professional reference, willing to complete paperwork for educational credit, willing to provide letters of recommendation.

Contact Write, call, or fax Thomas Groninger, Executive Director. Phone: 570-286-3127. Fax: 570-523-7699. In-person interview recommended. Applicants must submit a formal organization application, resume, three personal references. Applications are accepted continuously.

BIG BROTHERS/BIG SISTERS OF DANVILLE (UNITED WAY)
1225 West Main Street, PO Box 2362
Danville, Virginia 24541

General Information Youth organization that matches role models with children in need and provides recreational and support services. Established in 1973. Number of employees: 2. Affiliate of Big Brothers/Big Sisters of America, Philadelphia, Pennsylvania. Number of internship applications received each year: 1.

Internships Available ▶ *1 caseworker:* responsibilities include monitoring matches between adults and children and assisting in processing applications. Candidates should have ability to work independently, ability to work with others, knowledge of field, self-motivation. Duration is flexible. Open to college juniors, college seniors, recent college graduates. ▶ *1 clerical intern:* responsibilities include updating files on computer, and assisting in correspondence and phone calls. Candidates should have computer skills, office skills, written communication skills. Duration is flexible. Open to recent high school graduates, college freshmen, college sophomores, individuals reentering the workforce. ▶ *1 public relations and fund-raising intern:* responsibilities include assisting in organizing and coordinating fund-raising activities and promotions; and writing newsletters, brochures, and news releases. Candidates should have ability to work independently, computer skills, experience in the field, strong interpersonal skills, written communication skills. Duration is 1 semester. Open to college juniors, college seniors, recent col-

Big Brothers/Big Sisters of Danville (United Way) (continued)

lege graduates. ▶ *1 recreation specialist:* responsibilities include organizing and supervising activities and events for adults and children. Candidates should have ability to work with others, computer skills, knowledge of field, oral communication skills, organizational skills, self-motivation, strong leadership ability. Duration is 1 semester. Open to recent high school graduates, college freshmen, college sophomores, college juniors, college seniors, recent college graduates. All positions are unpaid.
Benefits Names of contacts, willing to complete paperwork for educational credit, willing to provide letters of recommendation.
Contact Write, call, fax, or e-mail Carroll W. Wiles, Executive Director, 1225 West Main Street, PO Box 2362, Danville, Virginia 24541. Phone: 804-792-3700. Fax: 804-791-3187. E-mail: bbbs@ dancom.com. In-person interview required. Applicants must submit a formal organization application, three personal references. Applications are accepted continuously. World Wide Web: http:// www.dpuway.org/bbbs.

BIG BROTHERS/BIG SISTERS OF MERIDEN/ WALLINGFORD
6 Fairfield Boulevard
Wallingford, Connecticut 06492

General Information Nonprofit agency designed to improve the lives of children by providing them with a one-to-one mentoring experience with a professionally screened and supervised volunteer. Established in 1968. Number of employees: 4.
Internships Available ▶ *2 caseworkers:* responsibilities include interviewing; processing; screening; orienting children, parents, and volunteers to program; matching children with volunteers; and supervising matches. Duration is 1 year. Open to recent high school graduates, college freshmen, college sophomores, college juniors, college seniors, recent college graduates, graduate students, law students, career changers, individuals reentering the workforce, must be 18 years or older. ▶ *1 office intern:* responsibilities include administrative duties, including handling and filing paperwork, typing, answering phones, and general office duties. Duration is flexible. Open to high school students, high school seniors, recent high school graduates, college freshmen, college sophomores, college juniors, college seniors, recent college graduates, graduate students, law students, career changers, individuals reentering the workforce. All positions available as unpaid or paid. International applications accepted.
Benefits Job counseling, names of contacts, opportunity to attend seminars/workshops, travel reimbursement, willing to complete paperwork for educational credit, willing to provide letters of recommendation.
Contact Write or call Liz Davis, Executive Director. Phone: 203-269-8200. In-person interview required. Applicants must submit a formal organization application, resume, three personal references. Applications are accepted continuously.

BIG BROTHERS/BIG SISTERS OF NORTH ALABAMA
3322 South Memorial Parkway, Suite 342B
Huntsville, Alabama 35801

General Information Organization that provides friends and role models for children between the ages of 5 and 15 and fosters one-to-one mentoring relationship with adult volunteers. Established in 1982. Number of employees: 4. Number of internship applications received each year: 4.
Internships Available ▶ *1–4 long-term interns:* responsibilities include observing interviews, home visits, and empowerment training of volunteers, children, and their parents; working with staff to process applications to programs; participating in matching children and volunteers; helping to recruit volunteers; and participating in agency fundraisers. Candidates should have ability to work independently, ability to work with others, oral communication skills, plan to pursue career in field, self-motivation, written communication skills. Duration is minimum of 500 hours. Open to college juniors, college seniors. ▶ *1–4 short-term interns:* responsibilities include observing interviews, home visits, and

empowerment training of volunteers, children, and their parents; working with staff to process applications to programs; participating in matching children and volunteers; helping to recruit volunteers; and participating in agency fundraisers. Duration is under 500 hours. Open to high school seniors, recent high school graduates, college freshmen, college sophomores, college juniors, college seniors, individuals reentering the workforce. All positions are unpaid. International applications accepted.
Benefits Names of contacts, willing to complete paperwork for educational credit, willing to provide letters of recommendation.
Contact Write, call, or fax Lahoma Worley, Executive Director. Phone: 256-880-2123. Fax: 256-880-2177. In-person interview required. Applicants must submit a resume, personal reference. Applications are accepted continuously.

BIG BROTHERS/BIG SISTERS OF NORTH CENTRAL OHIO
PO Box 553
Tiffin, Ohio 44883

General Information Organization that makes a positive impact in the lives of children through a professionally supported mentoring relationship with a caring and committed volunteer by enhancing and developing the assets of caring, confidence, and competence in the child's personal and social development. Established in 1980. Number of employees: 4.
Internships Available ▶ *1–3 caseworkers:* responsibilities include supervising matches and processing clients and volunteers, grant writing. Duration is flexible. Unpaid. Open to college freshmen, college sophomores, college juniors, college seniors.
Benefits Names of contacts, willing to act as a professional reference, willing to complete paperwork for educational credit, willing to provide letters of recommendation.
Contact Write or call Kimberly Bash, Executive Director. Phone: 419-448-0112. In-person interview required. Applicants must submit a cover letter, resume. Applications are accepted continuously.

BIG BROTHERS/BIG SISTERS OF RACINE, INC.
824 Sixth Street
Racine, Wisconsin 53403

General Information Organization that seeks to achieve positive development of minors from single-parent homes by pairing them with carefully screened adult volunteers. Established in 1960. Number of employees: 6. Unit of Big Brothers/Big Sisters of America, Philadelphia, Pennsylvania. Number of internship applications received each year: 4.
Internships Available ▶ *2–4 caseworkers/social workers:* responsibilities include performing intake and assessments of clients and volunteers and supervising matches. Candidates should have ability to work independently, college courses in field, oral communication skills, organizational skills, personal interest in the field, written communication skills. Duration is 1–2 months. Unpaid. Open to college freshmen, college sophomores, college juniors, college seniors, recent college graduates, graduate students, career changers, individuals reentering the workforce. International applications accepted.
Benefits Formal training, job counseling, names of contacts, on-the-job training, opportunity to attend seminars/workshops, travel reimbursement, willing to act as a professional reference, willing to complete paperwork for educational credit, willing to provide letters of recommendation.
Contact Write or call Tom Weiss, Executive Director. Phone: 414-637-7625. In-person interview required. Applicants must submit a cover letter, resume. Applications are accepted continuously.

BIG BROTHERS/BIG SISTERS OF ROCK AND WALWORTH COUNTIES
1400 Huebbe Parkway
Beloit, Wisconsin 53511

General Information Organization that matches children ages 6-14 from single parent families with adult role models and provides opportunities for the emotional growth of children.

Established in 1971. Number of employees: 5. Unit of Big Brothers/Big Sisters of America, Philadelphia, Pennsylvania. Number of internship applications received each year: 2.
Internships Available ▶ *1–2 fund-raising coordinators:* responsibilities include planning annual bowling and golf events, writing grant proposals, and general fund-raising. Candidates should have ability to work independently, knowledge of field, oral communication skills, organizational skills, self-motivation, written communication skills. Duration is flexible. Position available as unpaid or at $6–$10 per hour. Open to college freshmen, college sophomores, college juniors, college seniors, recent college graduates, graduate students, law students, career changers, individuals reentering the workforce. ▶ *1–2 general office interns:* responsibilities include billing, data entry, telephoning, and computer input. Candidates should have ability to work with others, computer skills, knowledge of field, office skills, oral communication skills, writing skills. Duration is flexible. Position available as unpaid or paid. Open to recent high school graduates, college freshmen, college sophomores, college juniors, college seniors, recent college graduates, graduate students, career changers, individuals reentering the workforce. ▶ *1–2 marketing coordinators:* responsibilities include performing general agency marketing and creating public service announcements and newsletters. Candidates should have ability to work independently, ability to work with others, computer skills, knowledge of field, oral communication skills, organizational skills, research skills, self-motivation, strong leadership ability, written communication skills. Duration is 12 months. Unpaid. Open to recent high school graduates, college freshmen, college sophomores, college juniors, college seniors, recent college graduates, graduate students, career changers, individuals reentering the workforce. International applications accepted.
Benefits Formal training, names of contacts, opportunity to attend seminars/workshops, travel reimbursement, willing to act as a professional reference, willing to complete paperwork for educational credit, willing to provide letters of recommendation.
Contact Write or call Nancy Mignon, Executive Director, 1400 Huebe Parkway, Beloit, Wisconsin 53511. Phone: 608-362-8223. In-person interview required. Applicants must submit a cover letter, resume, two personal references, two letters of recommendation. Applications are accepted continuously.

BIG BROTHERS BIG SISTERS OF SALEM COUNTY
203 East Broadway
Salem, New Jersey 08079

General Information Organization that provides positive opportunities for growth and development to children and youth at risk through one-to-one matches with volunteers, educational programs, and recreational activities. Established in 1986. Number of employees: 2. Affiliate of Big Brothers/Big Sisters of America, Philadelphia, Pennsylvania. Number of internship applications received each year: 1.
Internships Available ▶ *1 fund developer:* responsibilities include helping plan fundraisers, distributing flyers, and soliciting doorprizes and corporate sponsors. Candidates should have ability to work independently, computer skills, oral communication skills, self-motivation, strong interpersonal skills. Duration is 6–12 months. Open to recent high school graduates, college freshmen, college sophomores, college juniors, college seniors, recent college graduates, graduate students, law students, career changers, individuals reentering the workforce. ▶ *1 program intern:* responsibilities include providing casework services, interviewing children and families, and matching supervision and assistance with recreational and educational activities. Candidates should have computer skills, experience in the field, oral communication skills, strong interpersonal skills, written communication skills. Duration is 12 months. Open to recent high school graduates, college freshmen, college sophomores, college juniors, college seniors, recent college graduates, graduate students, law students, career changers, individuals reentering the workforce. ▶ *1 volunteer recruiter:* responsibilities include creating brochures of information to be distributed throughout the county; calling and writing to local businesses asking for volunteers. Candidates should have ability to work independently, computer skills, oral

communication skills, strong interpersonal skills, strong leadership ability. Duration is 3–6 months. Open to high school seniors, recent high school graduates, college freshmen, college sophomores, college juniors, college seniors, recent college graduates, graduate students, law students, career changers, individuals reentering the workforce. All positions are unpaid. International applications accepted.
Benefits Formal training, job counseling, names of contacts, on-the-job training, opportunity to attend seminars/workshops, possible full-time employment, travel reimbursement, willing to act as a professional reference, willing to complete paperwork for educational credit, willing to provide letters of recommendation.
Contact Write, call, or fax Mr. Greg Munson, Executive Director. Phone: 609-935-8778. Fax: 609-935-3675. In-person interview required. Applicants must submit a cover letter, resume, personal reference, three letters of recommendation. Applications are accepted continuously.

BIG BROTHERS/BIG SISTERS OF SOUTHERN NEVADA
1785 East Sahara Avenue, Suite A-100
Las Vegas, Nevada 89104

General Information Organization that matches children ages 6–14, primarily from single-parent families, with mature, responsible, caring adults and older high school students. Established in 1973. Number of employees: 17. Affiliate of Big Brothers/Big Sisters of America, Philadelphia, Pennsylvania. Number of internship applications received each year: 2.
Internships Available ▶ *1–3 case management and intake interns:* responsibilities include managing a designated case load, interviewing prospective clients and volunteers, and documenting results of interviews. Candidates should have ability to work independently, declared college major in field, oral communication skills, self-motivation, strong interpersonal skills, written communication skills. Duration is 3–12 months. Position available as unpaid or at $10–$11 per hour. Open to college sophomores, college juniors, college seniors, recent college graduates, graduate students, career changers, individuals reentering the workforce. International applications accepted.
Benefits Names of contacts, on-the-job training, opportunity to attend seminars/workshops, possible full-time employment, willing to complete paperwork for educational credit, willing to provide letters of recommendation, mileage reimbursement.
Contact Write, fax, or e-mail Elisabeth Painter, Vice President of Programs. Phone: 702-731-2227 Ext. 414. Fax: 702-737-9209. E-mail: bbbsep@aol.com. No phone calls. In-person interview recommended. Applicants must submit a cover letter, resume, academic transcripts, 2-3 letters of recommendation. Applications are accepted continuously. World Wide Web: http://www.bbbssn.org.

BIG BROTHERS/BIG SISTERS OF THE FOX VALLEY
158 East Chicago Avenue
Elgin, Illinois 60120

General Information Youth development agency that provides programs to enrich young people's lives and match adult volunteers with children from single parent homes. Established in 1980. Number of employees: 7. Number of internship applications received each year: 12.
Internships Available ▶ *1 case worker intern:* responsibilities include interviewing, training, public speaking, surveying, researching, supervising activities, acting as group co-leaders, recruiting youth, and fund-raising. Duration is flexible. Unpaid. Open to high school students, high school seniors, recent high school graduates, college freshmen, college sophomores, college juniors, college seniors, recent college graduates, graduate students, law students, career changers, individuals reentering the workforce. International applications accepted.
Benefits Formal training, names of contacts, possible full-time employment, willing to complete paperwork for educational credit, willing to provide letters of recommendation.

Big Brothers/Big Sisters of the Fox Valley (continued)
Contact Write Ms. Deborah Howe, Executive Director. No phone calls. In-person interview required. Applicants must submit a resume. Applications are accepted continuously.

BIG BROTHERS/BIG SISTERS OF THE MARSHFIELD AREA
PO Box 315
Marshfield, Wisconsin 54449

General Information Organization that serves children from single parent families by providing role models, friends, and positive life experiences. Established in 1967. Number of employees: 3.
Internships Available ▶ *1–2 case managers (social work):* responsibilities include screening volunteers, clients, and parents; processing volunteers and clients; writing individual plans; and assisting in planning and carrying out agency activities and socials. Candidates should have analytical skills, college courses in field, knowledge of field, oral communication skills, strong interpersonal skills, written communication skills. Unpaid. Open to college seniors, recent college graduates, graduate students. ▶ *1–2 marketing interns:* responsibilities include developing marketing campaign strategies and various promotional materials, researching various avenues to use as tools for promotion and advertising. Candidates should have college courses in field, editing skills, knowledge of field, organizational skills, self-motivation, written communication skills. Unpaid. Open to college juniors, college seniors, recent college graduates, graduate students, individuals reentering the workforce. ▶ *1 program development for after school tutoring intern:* responsibilities include developing an after-school tutoring program for low-income students, developing materials, promoting program, and acting as associate director. Candidates should have ability to work with others, oral communication skills, organizational skills, self-motivation, strong leadership ability, written communication skills. Position available as unpaid or at $9–$10 per hour. Open to college juniors, college seniors, recent college graduates, graduate students, career changers. ▶ *1–2 program directors:* responsibilities include pursuing advertising, publications, public service announcements and presentations, and developing new ways to promote program. Candidates should have college courses in field, knowledge of field, personal interest in the field, self-motivation, strong interpersonal skills, strong leadership ability. Unpaid. Open to college juniors, college seniors, recent college graduates, graduate students. Duration for all positions is flexible.
Benefits On-the-job training, opportunity to attend seminars/workshops, travel reimbursement, willing to act as a professional reference, willing to complete paperwork for educational credit, willing to provide letters of recommendation.
Contact Write or call Ms. Leslie Plechaty, Executive Director. Phone: 715-387-6198. Fax: 715-384-7145. In-person interview required. Applicants must submit a cover letter, resume, personal reference, two letters of recommendation. Applications are accepted continuously.

BIG BROTHERS/BIG SISTERS OF THE TULAROSA BASIN
821 Alaska Avenue
Alamogordo, New Mexico 88310

General Information Organization that recruits mature, responsible, caring adults to act as mentors to children. Established in 1988. Number of employees: 4. Unit of Children in Need of Service, Alamogordo, New Mexico.
Internships Available ▶ *1–2 assistant case managers:* responsibilities include working with case files of clients and volunteers and setting up case plans and objectives. Duration is 3 months. Unpaid. ▶ *2 mentor coordinators:* responsibilities include keeping track of case files and 14 local schools involved in program; and recruiting volunteers for program. Duration is minimum of 3 months, during academic school year. Position available as unpaid or paid. Open to college freshmen, college sophomores, college juniors, college seniors, recent college graduates, graduate students, career changers. International applications accepted.

Benefits Names of contacts, opportunity to attend seminars/workshops, possible full-time employment, willing to complete paperwork for educational credit, willing to provide letters of recommendation.
Contact Write, call, fax, or e-mail Leroy Copeland, Executive Director. Phone: 505-434-3652. Fax: 505-434-1031. E-mail: lcope@netmdc.com. In-person interview required. Applicants must submit a cover letter, resume, three letters of recommendation. Applications are accepted continuously.

BIG BROTHERS/BIG SISTERS OF TUSCARAWAS, CARROL, AND HARRISON COUNTIES
151 North Broadway
New Philadelphia, Ohio 44663

General Information Social service organization that matches mature, emotionally stable adults with at-risk children ages 6-14 in order to provide positive role models and friendship. Established in 1981. Number of employees: 6. Number of internship applications received each year: 2.
Internships Available ▶ *1 administrative assistant:* responsibilities include orientation of volunteers, supervising group activities and coordinating, and editing monthly newsletter. Candidates should have ability to work independently, computer skills, editing skills, office skills, oral communication skills, organizational skills. Open to college sophomores, college juniors, college seniors, recent college graduates, graduate students, career changers. ▶ *1 case manager:* responsibilities include interviewing, crisis counseling, compiling documentation, and planning and organizing group activities. Candidates should have ability to work independently, analytical skills, oral communication skills, strong interpersonal skills, written communication skills. Open to college sophomores, college juniors, college seniors, recent college graduates, graduate students, career changers. ▶ *1 marketing/public relations coordinator:* responsibilities include public speaking, graphic arts, and fund-raising. Candidates should have editing skills, oral communication skills, strong interpersonal skills, writing skills. Open to college sophomores, college juniors, college seniors, recent college graduates, graduate students, career changers, individuals reentering the workforce. Duration for all positions is flexible. All positions are unpaid. International applications accepted.
Benefits Names of contacts, on-the-job training, opportunity to attend seminars/workshops, possible full-time employment, travel reimbursement, willing to act as a professional reference, willing to complete paperwork for educational credit, willing to provide letters of recommendation.
Contact Write, call, or e-mail Viola K. Miller, LSW, Executive Director. Phone: 888-364-5965. E-mail: bbbs@tusco.net. In-person interview required. Applicants must submit a cover letter, resume, three personal references. Applications are accepted continuously.

BOSTON YWCA
140 Clarendon Street
Boston, Massachusetts 02116

General Information Organization that raises public awareness of economic security, child care, the health of the young, and world peace. Established in 1875. Number of employees: 100. Unit of YWCA of the USA, New York, New York. Number of internship applications received each year: 50.
Internships Available ▶ *Encore Plus interns:* responsibilities include researching and doing community outreach for the Encore Plus breast and cervical cancer outreach and education program. ▶ *YVC (Youth Voice Collaborative) interns:* responsibilities include instructing youth to use various forms of print and broadcast media. ▶ *Child care center interns:* responsibilities include assisting in the classroom summer program and creative arts programs, and leading parenting workshops. ▶ *Comprehensive adolescent parenting program interns:* responsibilities include leading young parent workshops and working in health and nutrition education. ▶ *External affairs interns:* responsibilities include assisting with research, writing proposals, marketing, public relations, and managing the office. Duration for all positions is flexible. All positions are unpaid. Open to high school students,

high school seniors, recent high school graduates, college freshmen, college sophomores, college juniors, college seniors, recent college graduates, graduate students, law students, career changers, individuals reentering the workforce. International applications accepted.

Benefits Housing at a cost, meals at a cost, on-the-job training, possible full-time employment, willing to act as a professional reference, willing to complete paperwork for educational credit, willing to provide letters of recommendation.

Contact Write, call, or fax Pat Creary, Human Resources Manager. Phone: 617-351-7642. Fax: 617-351-7615. In-person interview required. Applicants must submit a formal organization application, cover letter, resume, three personal references, three letters of recommendation. Applications are accepted continuously.

BOULDER COUNTY AIDS PROJECT
2118 14th Street
Boulder, Colorado 80302

General Information AIDS service organization. Established in 1984. Number of employees: 14. Number of internship applications received each year: 6.

Internships Available ▶ *1–3 agency assistants:* responsibilities include giving administrative assistance to different agency departments. Candidates should have computer skills, office skills, organizational skills, strong interpersonal skills, writing skills, written communication skills. Open to high school seniors, recent high school graduates, college freshmen, college sophomores, college juniors, college seniors, recent college graduates, career changers, individuals reentering the workforce. ▶ *1–3 development associates:* responsibilities include coordinating special events for fund-raising. Candidates should have ability to work independently, oral communication skills, organizational skills, self-motivation, strong interpersonal skills. Open to college freshmen, college sophomores, college juniors, college seniors, recent college graduates, career changers, individuals reentering the workforce. All positions are unpaid.

Benefits On-the-job training, opportunity to attend seminars/workshops, willing to act as a professional reference, willing to complete paperwork for educational credit, willing to provide letters of recommendation.

Contact Write or e-mail Matt Patrick, Executive Director, 2118 14th Street, Boulder, Colorado 80302. E-mail: matt@bcap.org. No phone calls. In-person interview recommended. Applicants must submit a cover letter, resume, two writing samples, two personal references, two letters of recommendation. Applications are accepted continuously. World Wide Web: http://www.bcap.org.

BOYS AND GIRLS CLUB OF ALBANY
21 Delaware Avenue
Albany, New York 12210

General Information Organization that promotes the social, educational, and vocational development of boys and girls by building self-esteem, values, and skills during youth and adolescence. Established in 1891. Number of employees: 28. Unit of Boys and Girls Club of America, Atlanta, Georgia. Number of internship applications received each year: 10.

Internships Available ▶ *1–10 program assistants:* responsibilities include working with children, implementing activities, supervising children, and working with the site director and coordinator. Candidates should have oral communication skills, personal interest in the field, self-motivation, strong interpersonal skills, strong leadership ability. ▶ *1–5 program counselors:* responsibilities include helping youth to achieve and maintain fitness to acquire a broad range of physical skills; to develop a sense of teamwork, cooperation, and fairness; and to lead healthy, active lifestyles. Candidates should have ability to work independently, ability to work with others, knowledge of field, organizational skills, self-motivation, strong leadership ability. Duration for all positions is flexible. All positions are unpaid. Open to high school students, high school seniors, recent high school graduates, college freshmen, college sophomores, college juniors, col-

lege seniors, recent college graduates, graduate students, law students, career changers, individuals reentering the workforce. International applications accepted.

Benefits Names of contacts, on-the-job training, opportunity to attend seminars/workshops, possible full-time employment, willing to complete paperwork for educational credit, willing to provide letters of recommendation.

Contact Write, call, or fax Doretha Holmes, Deputy Executive Director. Phone: 518-462-5528. Fax: 518-462-5540. In-person interview recommended. Applicants must submit a formal organization application, cover letter, resume, two writing samples, three personal references, three letters of recommendation. Applications are accepted continuously.

BOYS AND GIRLS CLUB OF BROCKTON, INC.
233 Warren Avenue
Brockton, Massachusetts 02401-4321

General Information Youth development organization that provides guidance and offers programs to serve youth of disadvantaged circumstances. Established in 1988. Number of employees: 15. Number of internship applications received each year: 5.

Internships Available ▶ *1 fund-raising intern:* responsibilities include assisting in implementing the annual financial development plan, grantwriting, assisting with board and youth fund-raising events, and directing mail campaigns. Candidates should have ability to work independently, analytical skills, organizational skills, personal interest in the field, research skills, self-motivation. Duration is flexible. Open to college sophomores, college juniors, college seniors. ▶ *1–3 health promotion interns:* responsibilities include assisting in supervising teen leaders to plan and implement prevention programs for peers and younger members. Candidates should have ability to work independently, ability to work with others, oral communication skills, personal interest in the field, self-motivation, strong leadership ability. Open to college juniors, college seniors. ▶ *1–5 learning center interns:* responsibilities include helping to coordinate and implement learning center programs in computer learning, homework assistance, tutoring, SAT preparation, career awareness activities; and leading field trips, special activities, and programs. Candidates should have ability to work independently, ability to work with others, oral communication skills, self-motivation, strong leadership ability, written communication skills. Duration is flexible. Open to college freshmen, college sophomores, college juniors, college seniors, individuals reentering the workforce. ▶ *1–3 leisure studies interns:* responsibilities include working with the sports programs in basketball, soccer, volleyball, and baseball; working in the games room; and planning special events. Candidates should have ability to work independently, knowledge of field, oral communication skills, personal interest in the field, strong interpersonal skills, strong leadership ability. Duration is flexible. Open to college freshmen, college sophomores, college juniors, college seniors, individuals reentering the workforce. ▶ *1 marketing intern:* responsibilities include promoting club programs, implementing annual marketing plan, maintaining media relations, organizing membership and volunteer recruitment campaigns, planning and implementing regional campaigns, updating brochures, and assisting with annual newsletter and annual report. Candidates should have ability to work independently, analytical skills, organizational skills, research skills, self-motivation, writing skills. Duration is flexible. Open to college freshmen, college sophomores, college juniors, college seniors. All positions are unpaid. International applications accepted.

Benefits Formal training, names of contacts, possible full-time employment, willing to complete paperwork for educational credit, willing to provide letters of recommendation.

Contact Write, call, or fax Joanne Hoops, Executive Director. Phone: 508-586-3503. Fax: 508-588-2772. In-person interview required. Applicants must submit a resume, personal reference, two letters of recommendation. Application deadline: August 1 for fall; continuous for remainder of year.

BOYS AND GIRLS CLUB OF CLIFTON
822 Clifton Avenue
Clifton, New Jersey 07013

General Information Youth serving organization for boys and girls ages 2½-17. Established in 1958. Number of employees: 80. Unit of Boys and Girls Club of America, Atlanta, Georgia. Number of internship applications received each year: 20.

Internships Available ▶ *9 "School's Out" program supervisors:* responsibilities include implementing care programs from 2:30-6:30 for 35 students ages 6-11. Candidates should have experience in the field, oral communication skills, personal interest in the field, self-motivation, strong interpersonal skills. Duration is 10 months. $7–$8 per hour. ▶ *6–8 after-school program counselors:* responsibilities include acting as group leader for elementary school children, and providing supervision and instruction in the after-school program 3-6:30 daily. Candidates should have college courses in field, experience in the field, oral communication skills, organizational skills, personal interest in the field, self-motivation, strong interpersonal skills. Duration is from September-June. $6–$7 per hour. Open to high school seniors, college freshmen, college sophomores, college juniors, college seniors. ▶ *1 individual service coordinator:* responsibilities include counseling, providing crisis intervention, and implementing tutorial care, parenting, and life skills program. Candidates should have college degree in related field, oral communication skills, organizational skills, self-motivation, written communication skills. Duration is 12 months. up to $25 per hour. Open to graduate students. ▶ *4–6 lifeguards:* responsibilities include lifeguarding pool for all open swims, lessons, swim team, and adult swims. Candidates should have lifeguard training , first aid/CPR certification. Duration is 12 months. $8 per hour. ▶ *1 summer assistant program director:* responsibilities include implementing and supervising summer day camp program; working with staff and children (Monday-Friday) to direct summer program activities. Candidates should have experience in the field, oral communication skills, personal interest in the field, self-motivation, strong interpersonal skills, written communication skills. Duration is June to August. $9 per hour. Open to college juniors, college seniors, recent college graduates. ▶ *6–10 summer group counselors:* responsibilities include supervising and conducting activities for a group of 25 youngsters ages 6-12, overseeing specific age groups in a highly structured camp-at-home program, and performing administrative duties. Candidates should have experience in the field, oral communication skills, personal interest in the field, self-motivation, strong interpersonal skills, strong leadership ability. Duration is June 28-August 20. $6–$7 per hour. Open to high school seniors, college freshmen, college sophomores, college juniors, college seniors. ▶ *1 summer trip program coordinator:* responsibilities include implementing summer trip program for three age groups (6-8, 9-10, 11-16); one trip per week per age group; supervision, chaperoning, and administration of program. Candidates should have ability to work with others, office skills, oral communication skills, personal interest in the field, self-motivation, written communication skills, responsibility, maturity. Duration is June to September. $8–$9 per hour. Open to college juniors, college seniors. ▶ *4–6 water safety instructors:* responsibilities include teaching American Red Cross swim lessons levels I-VII plus safety and life saving classes. Candidates should have experience in the field, current WSI, First Aid, and CPR certifications. Duration is 12 months. $8–$10 per hour. Open to high school seniors, recent high school graduates, college freshmen, college sophomores, college juniors, college seniors, individuals reentering the workforce.

Benefits Formal training, names of contacts, possible full-time employment, willing to complete paperwork for educational credit, willing to provide letters of recommendation, access to Boys and Girls Club of America job listings and career services.

Contact Write, call, fax, or e-mail Robert Foster, Director of Operations. Phone: 973-773-0086. Fax: 973-773-3103. E-mail: bgcclif@jungle.net. In-person interview required. Applicants must submit a resume, two personal references, letter of recommendation. Application deadline: April 15 for summer, August 15 for fall, December 15 for winter/spring. World Wide Web: http://www.boysandgirlsclbclifton.org.

BOYS AND GIRLS CLUB OF COLUMBUS, INC.
115 South Gift Street
Columbus, Ohio 43215

General Information Social development organization that offers educational, physical, social skills, and personal development programs to children ages 6–18. Established in 1948. Number of employees: 20.

Internships Available ▶ *1–2 marketing and development interns:* responsibilities include assisting director of development with full range of duties related to media contacts, special events, and program promotions. Candidates should have ability to work independently, oral communication skills, plan to pursue career in field, strong interpersonal skills, written communication skills. Duration is 3 months to 1 year. Open to college juniors, college seniors, recent college graduates, graduate students. ▶ *1–2 youth group leaders:* responsibilities include providing leadership and working directly with Keystone and Torch clubs that focus on service projects within the club as well as the larger community. Candidates should have ability to work independently, oral communication skills, plan to pursue career in field, self-motivation, strong interpersonal skills. Duration is 9 months. Open to recent high school graduates, college freshmen, college sophomores, college juniors, college seniors, recent college graduates, graduate students. All positions are unpaid. International applications accepted.

Benefits Formal training, names of contacts, on-the-job training, opportunity to attend seminars/workshops, possible full-time employment, willing to complete paperwork for educational credit, willing to provide letters of recommendation.

Contact Write or fax Robert Zuercher, Executive Director. Fax: 614-221-1225. No phone calls. In-person interview required. Applications are accepted continuously.

BOYS AND GIRLS CLUB OF LAKELAND, INC.
PO Box 763
Lakeland, Florida 33802

General Information Organization that helps local, disadvantaged youth to become responsible citizens and leaders. Established in 1939. Number of employees: 27. Unit of Boys and Girls Club of America, Atlanta, Georgia. Number of internship applications received each year: 1.

Internships Available ▶ *1–4 interns:* responsibilities include working with youth ages 6-18 from urban, disadvantaged backgrounds. Candidates should have ability to work independently, ability to work with others, oral communication skills, organizational skills, personal interest in the field, self-motivation. Duration is flexible. Unpaid. Open to high school students, high school seniors, recent high school graduates, college freshmen, college sophomores, college juniors, college seniors, recent college graduates, graduate students, career changers, individuals reentering the workforce. International applications accepted.

Benefits Formal training, job counseling, names of contacts, opportunity to attend seminars/workshops, possible full-time employment, willing to complete paperwork for educational credit, willing to provide letters of recommendation.

Contact Write or call Rex Perry, Executive Director. Phone: 941-686-1719. In-person interview recommended. Applicants must submit a cover letter, resume. Applications are accepted continuously.

BOYS AND GIRLS CLUB OF LARIMER COUNTY
1400 Remington Street
Fort Collins, Colorado 80524

General Information Organization that helps all youth to develop maximum potential by providing personal growth, educational, and recreational programs in an environment of mutual trust and respect. Established in 1987. Number of employees: 12.

Internships Available ▶ *Gameroom/recreation interns:* responsibilities include supervising and assisting full-time staff with playtime and recreational activities for children ages 6-18. ▶ *Learning-lab/computer technicians:* responsibilities include planning, implementing, and coordinating activities of the computer lab with full-time staff for youth ages 6-18. ▶ *Program director interns:* responsibilities include helping full-time staff with the planning and supervision of programs for children ages 6-18. Duration for all positions is flexible. All positions are unpaid. Open to college freshmen, college sophomores, college juniors, college seniors, recent college graduates, graduate students. International applications accepted.

Benefits Names of contacts, opportunity to attend seminars/workshops, possible full-time employment, willing to complete paperwork for educational credit, willing to provide letters of recommendation.

Contact Write or call Joe MacIsaac, Executive Director. Phone: 970-484-5198. In-person interview recommended. Applicants must submit a formal organization application, background check required. Applications are accepted continuously.

BOYS AND GIRLS CLUB OF PLYMOUTH, INC.
PO Box 3479
Plymouth, Massachusetts 02361

General Information Organization that provides area youth with activities designed to build self-esteem, develop leadership skills, and promote positive life choices. Established in 1911. Number of employees: 11. Affiliate of Boys and Girls Club of America, Atlanta, Georgia. Number of internship applications received each year: 6.

Internships Available ▶ *1 junior staff intern:* responsibilities include interacting with children, handling small amounts of money. Candidates should have ability to work with others, oral communication skills, personal interest in the field, self-motivation, patience. Position available as unpaid or at $5 per hour. Open to high school students, high school seniors. ▶ *1–2 youth counselors:* responsibilities include running programs, dealing with children and parents, answering phones, and overseeing recreational activities. Candidates should have ability to work independently, oral communication skills, personal interest in the field, self-motivation, strong interpersonal skills. Position available as unpaid or at $7 per hour. Open to recent high school graduates, college freshmen, college sophomores, college juniors, college seniors, recent college graduates, graduate students, career changers, individuals reentering the workforce. Duration for all positions is 10 months. International applications accepted.

Benefits Names of contacts, on-the-job training, willing to act as a professional reference, willing to complete paperwork for educational credit, willing to provide letters of recommendation.

Contact Write or call Mr. Ron Randall, Executive Director. Phone: 508-746-6070. In-person interview required. Applicants must submit a formal organization application, resume, two letters of recommendation. Applications are accepted continuously.

BOYS AND GIRLS CLUB OF TAMPA BAY, INC.
3020 West Laurel Street
Tampa, Florida 33607

General Information Youth agency with 16 sites in Hillsborough County that serves school-age children after school and all day on school holidays and during the summer by providing educational, athletic, cultural, enrichment, and prevention programs with a focus on the disadvantaged. Established in 1929. Number of employees: 75. Unit of Boys and Girls Club of America, Atlanta, Georgia. Number of internship applications received each year: 3.

Internships Available ▶ *1–3 career program directors:* responsibilities include working with youth on college and career program development goal setting classes, job readiness, and volunteer activities (community service). Candidates should have oral communication skills, personal interest in the field, self-motivation, strong interpersonal skills, strong leadership ability. Duration is 1–2 semesters. Position available as unpaid or at $7–$9 per hour. Open to recent high school graduates, college freshmen, college sophomores, college juniors, college seniors, individuals reentering the workforce, individuals 18 years or older with high school diploma or GED. ▶ *2–14 cultural specialists:* responsibilities include working with small groups of youth to develop singing, musical instrument, dance or artistic talents; auditioning students and working on a show group; working with youth in developing skills in painting, sculpting, and related mediums. Candidates should have ability to work independently, oral communication skills, organizational skills, personal interest in the field, strong interpersonal skills, strong leadership ability. Duration is 1 semester, 1 school year, or 1 summer. Unpaid. Open to recent high school graduates, college freshmen, college sophomores, college juniors, college seniors, recent college graduates, career changers, individuals reentering the workforce, individuals 18 years of age or older. ▶ *2–5 data collection specialists:* responsibilities include obtaining data on club membership, program participation, and attendance from clubs and schools, and entering data into main system and relating it to grant reports. Candidates should have computer skills, research skills, self-motivation, written communication skills. Duration is 1 semester. Position available as unpaid or at $7 per hour. Open to college freshmen, college sophomores, college juniors, college seniors, recent college graduates, graduate students, law students, career changers, individuals reentering the workforce, individuals 18 years of age or older. ▶ *10–19 girls' sports coordinators:* responsibilities include planning and implementing athletic events for females only. Candidates should have oral communication skills, organizational skills, personal interest in the field, strong interpersonal skills, strong leadership ability. Duration is 1–2 semesters. Unpaid. Open to recent high school graduates, college freshmen, college sophomores, college juniors, college seniors, recent college graduates, career changers, individuals 18 years of age or older. ▶ *1–6 outreach program specialists:* responsibilities include delivering outreach and prevention programs to public and private schools and public housing sites, planning and implementing school outreach programs with educational and athletic activities, and conducting county-wide outreach events. Candidates should have ability to work independently, oral communication skills, organizational skills, personal interest in the field, self-motivation, strong interpersonal skills. Duration is 1 semester, 1 school year, or 1 summer. Position available as unpaid or paid. Open to recent high school graduates, college freshmen, college sophomores, college juniors, college seniors, recent college graduates, graduate students, career changers, individuals reentering the workforce, individuals 18 years of age or older. ▶ *10–19 prevention specialists:* responsibilities include conducting group session with school-aged children in violence prevention, drug abuse prevention, AIDS education, peer pressure response, and similar programs. Candidates should have analytical skills, oral communication skills, personal interest in the field, strong interpersonal skills, written communication skills. Duration is 1–2 semesters. Position available as unpaid or at $7 per hour. Open to recent high school graduates, college freshmen, college sophomores, college juniors, college seniors, recent college graduates, career changers, individuals 18 years of age or older. ▶ *1–3 research associates:* responsibilities include researching grant opportunities, collecting data, and assisting with grant writing and monitoring. Candidates should have ability to work independently, editing skills, plan to pursue career in field, research skills, self-motivation, written communication skills. Duration is 1 semester, 1 school year, or 1 summer. Unpaid. Open to college freshmen, college sophomores, college juniors, college seniors, recent college graduates, graduate students, career changers, individuals reentering the workforce, individuals 18 years of age or older. ▶ *1 special events coordinator:* responsibilities include working with management staff to develop and implement special events and fundraisers for Boys and Girls Clubs of Tampa Bay. Candidates should have ability to work independently, organizational skills, personal interest in the field, self-motivation, strong interpersonal skills. Duration is 1 semester, 1 school year, or 1 summer. Unpaid. Open to college freshmen, college sophomores, college juniors, college seniors, recent college graduates, graduate students, career changers, individuals reentering the workforce, individuals 18 years of age or older. ▶ *2 teen services coordinators:* responsibilities include working directly with teens, developing leadership skills, and enhancing their educational pursuit. Candidates should have oral com-

Boys and Girls Club of Tampa Bay, Inc. (continued)

munication skills, strong interpersonal skills, strong leadership ability, written communication skills. Position available as unpaid or at $8–$9 per hour. Open to recent high school graduates, college freshmen, college sophomores, college juniors, college seniors, recent college graduates, graduate students, career changers, individuals reentering the workforce. ▶ *14–28 tutor/homework assistants:* responsibilities include working with children one-to-one and in small groups to improve their academic achievement. Candidates should have ability to work independently, oral communication skills, self-motivation, strong interpersonal skills, written communication skills. Duration is 1 semester. Unpaid. Open to recent high school graduates, college freshmen, college sophomores, college juniors, college seniors, recent college graduates, graduate students, law students, career changers, individuals reentering the workforce, individuals 18 years of age or older. ▶ *7–28 youth development professionals:* responsibilities include assisting in program areas as designated by club director, working with small groups of children on specific programs, coaching, and supervising. Candidates should have ability to work independently, oral communication skills, organizational skills, personal interest in the field, self-motivation, strong interpersonal skills. Duration is 2 semesters. Position available as unpaid or at $7 per hour. Open to recent high school graduates, college freshmen, college sophomores, college juniors, college seniors, recent college graduates, career changers, individuals reentering the workforce, individuals 18 years of age or older. ▶ *14–56 youth development professionals:* responsibilities include coordinating and leading appropriate activities within a group while acting as program assistant to year-round staff. Candidates should have ability to work independently, oral communication skills, organizational skills, personal interest in the field, self-motivation, strong interpersonal skills. Duration is 1 summer or 1 semester. Position available as unpaid or at $7 per hour. Open to recent high school graduates, college freshmen, college sophomores, college juniors, college seniors, recent college graduates, career changers, individuals reentering the workforce, individuals 18 years of age or older. International applications accepted.
Benefits Formal training, job counseling, names of contacts, on-the-job training, opportunity to attend seminars/workshops, possible full-time employment, willing to complete paperwork for educational credit, willing to provide letters of recommendation.
Contact Write, call, fax, or e-mail Lisbeth Moore, Director of Services. Phone: 813-875-5771. Fax: 813-875-5483. E-mail: bmoore@ bgctampa.org. In-person interview required. Applicants must submit a formal organization application, cover letter, resume. Applications are accepted continuously.

BOYS AND GIRLS CLUB OF WESTERN BROOME, INC.
Riverview Drive, PO Box 149
Endicott, New York 13761-0149

General Information Educational/recreational nonprofit organization that provides for the educational, psychological, and physical needs of infants to seniors, with an emphasis on youth development. Established in 1994. Number of employees: 55. Unit of Boys and Girls Club of America, Atlanta, Georgia. Number of internship applications received each year: 1.
Internships Available ▶ *1–2 fall interns:* responsibilities include working with children in an after-school program. Candidates should have ability to work independently, organizational skills, personal interest in the field, strong interpersonal skills, interest in working with young children 6-12 years or adolescents 12-14 years, experience in field desirable. Duration is 10 months. Unpaid. Open to recent high school graduates, college freshmen, college sophomores, college juniors, college seniors, recent college graduates, graduate students, individuals reentering the workforce. ▶ *1 grant writing assistant:* responsibilities include assisting with grant writing to secure funds, working on other projects. Candidates should have computer skills, editing skills, plan to pursue career in field, research skills, self-motivation, written communication skills. Duration is flexible. Unpaid. Open to college sophomores, college juniors, college seniors, recent

college graduates, graduate students, career changers. ▶ *1 older adults intern:* responsibilities include researching and developing psychological/social needs for seniors in community, implementing program, training leaders, and interacting with clients. Candidates should have college courses in field, experience in the field, oral communication skills, plan to pursue career in field, strong interpersonal skills, writing skills. Duration is flexible. Unpaid. Open to recent high school graduates, college freshmen, college sophomores, college juniors, college seniors, recent college graduates, graduate students, career changers, individuals reentering the workforce. ▶ *Summer fun club unit leader/assistants:* responsibilities include planning, organizing, and implementing programs and age-appropriate activities for children in a day camp unit; teaching cooking and crafts; and leading hikes. Candidates should have ability to work with others, personal interest in the field, self-motivation, strong leadership ability. Duration is 2 months. $5 per hour. Open to recent high school graduates, college freshmen, college sophomores, college juniors. International applications accepted.
Benefits Job counseling, names of contacts, on-the-job training, willing to act as a professional reference, willing to complete paperwork for educational credit, willing to provide letters of recommendation.
Contact Write, call, or fax Joanne Cheatham-Valent, Financial Development Director. Phone: 607-754-0225. Fax: 607-754-2801. In-person interview required. Applicants must submit a cover letter, resume, three personal references. Application deadline: March 1 for summer, May 1 for fall. World Wide Web: http:// www.hancock.net/~ebgclub.

BOYS AND GIRLS CLUB OF WORCESTER
2 Ionic Avenue
Worcester, Massachusetts 01608

General Information Organization that provides recreation, physical education, and leadership development activities for youth. Established in 1889. Number of employees: 25. Number of internship applications received each year: 3.
Internships Available ▶ *Youth development interns:* responsibilities include assisting staff with delivery of programs. Candidates should have ability to work independently, oral communication skills, organizational skills, plan to pursue career in field, self-motivation, strong interpersonal skills, strong leadership ability. Duration is flexible. Position available as unpaid or at $6–$8 per hour. Open to high school seniors, recent high school graduates, college freshmen, college sophomores, college juniors, college seniors, recent college graduates. International applications accepted.
Benefits Job counseling, names of contacts, possible full-time employment, willing to complete paperwork for educational credit, willing to provide letters of recommendation.
Contact Write, call, fax, or e-mail Vince Del Monte, Executive Director, 2 Ionic Avenue, Worcester, Massachusetts 01608. Phone: 508-754-2686. Fax: 508-754-2686. E-mail: bgcworc@ worldnet.att.net. In-person interview recommended. Applicants must submit a cover letter, resume, academic transcripts, 5 personal references. Applications are accepted continuously.

BOYS AND GIRLS CLUB OF ZIONSVILLE
1575 Mulberry Street
Zionsville, Indiana 46077

General Information Community center with trained professional staff to run and create diverse programs for youths ages 5-18 focusing on health, physical education, cultural enrichment, citizenship, leadership, and personal adjustment. Established in 1981. Number of employees: 5. Number of internship applications received each year: 4.
Internships Available ▶ *2 interns:* responsibilities include supervising and interacting with youth between the ages of 5 and 18 and running programs designed for youth. Duration is 2 semesters. Position available as unpaid or paid. Open to high school students, high school seniors, recent high school gradu-

ates, college freshmen, college sophomores, college juniors, college seniors, recent college graduates, graduate students. International applications accepted.
Benefits Names of contacts, opportunity to attend seminars/ workshops, willing to provide letters of recommendation.
Contact Write, call, or fax Ms. Cary Bowman, Unit Director. Phone: 317-873-6670. Fax: 317-873-9176. In-person interview recommended. Applicants must submit a formal organization application, cover letter, resume, two personal references, two letters of recommendation. Applications are accepted continuously.

BOYS HOPE GIRLS HOPE NATIONAL OFFICE
12120 Bridgeton Square Drive
Bridgeton, Missouri 63044-2607

General Information National organization that provides family-like homes and college preparatory educational opportunities for at-risk, yet academically capable, boys and girls. Established in 1977. Number of employees: 125. Number of internship applications received each year: 50.
Internships Available ▶ *1–2 administrative interns:* responsibilities include providing administrative support and office support for executive office resource development efforts. Candidates should have ability to work with others, office skills, oral communication skills, written communication skills. Duration is flexible. ▶ *50 tutors:* responsibilities include providing tutoring assistance to boys or girls at a local program. Candidates should have ability to work with others, oral communication skills, strong interpersonal skills. Duration is flexible. ▶ *25–30 volunteer residential counselors:* responsibilities include living with children and other staff, maintaining a structured and stable home environment for up to 8 boys or girls, assuming a mentoring role, assisting students in academics, assisting houseparents in daily home operation, and exploring college and career opportunities with students. Candidates should have oral communication skills, self-motivation, strong interpersonal skills, strong leadership ability. Duration is 12 months. All positions paid at $200 per month. Open to recent college graduates, graduate students, career changers.
Benefits Formal training, free housing, free meals, health insurance, on-the-job training, opportunity to attend seminars/ workshops, possible full-time employment, travel reimbursement, willing to act as a professional reference, willing to complete paperwork for educational credit, willing to provide letters of recommendation.
Contact Write, call, fax, or e-mail Stephanie Welberg, Volunteer Coordinator. Phone: 800-545-2697. Fax: 314-298-1251. E-mail: swelberg@bhgh.org. In-person interview recommended. Applicants must submit a formal organization application, resume, academic transcripts, three personal references. Applications are accepted continuously. World Wide Web: http://www.boyshopegirlshope.org.

BRETHREN VOLUNTEER SERVICE
1451 Dundee Avenue
Elgin, Illinois 60120

General Information Volunteer organization with goals that include working for peace, advocating justice, serving basic human needs, and maintaining the integrity of creation. Established in 1948. Number of employees: 4. Unit of Church of the Brethren, Elgin, Illinois. Number of internship applications received each year: 100.
Internships Available ▶ *80–100 domestic interns/volunteers:* responsibilities include performing duties that vary according to project and volunteer's skills, experience, and interest. Duration is 1 year. Open to recent high school graduates, college freshmen, college sophomores, college juniors, college seniors, recent college graduates, graduate students, law students, career changers. ▶ *6–20 overseas interns/volunteers:* responsibilities include working on one of 34 projects overseas in over 18 countries, including China, France, Germany, the Netherlands, Nigeria, Northern Ireland, Bosnia, and Poland, and performing duties that vary according to project. Duration is 2 years minimum.

Open to college graduates 21 years or older. All positions paid at $45–$65 per month. International applications accepted.
Benefits Free housing, free meals, health insurance, cost of travel expenses to and from project for U.S. positions, life insurance.
International Internships Available in Bosnia and Herzegovina; China; France; Germany; Japan; Netherlands; Nigeria; Poland; United Kingdom.
Contact Write, call, fax, or e-mail Brethren Volunteer Service Recruitment. Phone: 800-323-8039. Fax: 847-742-0278. E-mail: cob.bvs.parti@ecunet.org. Applicants must submit a formal organization application, cover letter, resume, academic transcripts, current photo and essay, $400 for overseas travel. Applications are accepted continuously. Fees: $15. World Wide Web: http://www.brethren.org.

CABBAGE PATCH SETTLEMENT HOUSE
1413 South Sixth Street
Louisville, Kentucky 40208

General Information Independently funded Christian charity serving inner-city, underprivileged clients through day care, family services, recreation, education, and counseling programs. Established in 1910. Number of employees: 30. Number of internship applications received each year: 25.
Internships Available ▶ *1 day care assistant:* responsibilities include assisting in programs and leadership for youth ages 2½ to 6. Candidates should have ability to work with others, knowledge of field, oral communication skills, self-motivation, strong leadership ability. Duration is flexible. Unpaid. Open to college juniors, college seniors, recent college graduates, graduate students, career changers. ▶ *1–5 education aides:* responsibilities include tutoring, supervising study hall for grades 1-12, and teaching college preparation classes for at-risk students. Candidates should have college courses in field, computer skills, oral communication skills, self-motivation, strong interpersonal skills, written communication skills. Duration is flexible (September to May). Unpaid. Open to college seniors, recent college graduates, graduate students. ▶ *1–6 recreation assistants:* responsibilities include planning and leading recreation and outdoor camping programs for youth. Candidates should have knowledge of field, oral communication skills, self-motivation, strong interpersonal skills, strong leadership ability. Duration is 10 weeks. $2,600–$3,000 per duration of internship. Open to college juniors, college seniors, recent college graduates, graduate students. ▶ *1–4 social work aides:* responsibilities include developing proactive social work programs for at-risk youth and their families. Candidates should have college courses in field, computer skills, knowledge of field, oral communication skills, strong interpersonal skills. Duration is flexible. Unpaid. Open to college juniors, college seniors, recent college graduates, graduate students, career changers.
Benefits Job counseling, names of contacts, possible full-time employment, willing to act as a professional reference, willing to complete paperwork for educational credit, willing to provide letters of recommendation.
Contact Write or fax Rod Napier, Director of Programs and Services. Fax: 502-637-9943. No phone calls. In-person interview required. Applicants must submit a cover letter, resume, academic transcripts, three personal references, three letters of recommendation, criminal records check. Application deadline: March 30 for summer, July 30 for fall, November 15 for spring.

CAMP COURAGEOUS OF IOWA
12007 190th Street, PO Box 418
Monticello, Iowa 52310-0418

General Information Year-round camp holding the belief that individuals with disabilities have the right to opportunities found in the world around them. The curriculum challenges those individuals with recreational and educational activities. Established in 1972. Number of employees: 30. Number of internship applications received each year: 30.
Internships Available ▶ *1–15 counselors:* responsibilities include personal care of campers who have disabilities, assisting in leading activities for the same individual, responsible for health and

Camp Courageous of Iowa (continued)

well-being of the campers. Candidates should have ability to work independently, plan to pursue career in field, self-motivation, strong interpersonal skills, strong leadership ability, ability to work with special needs children and adults ranging in age from 3 to 100. Duration is year-round. Position available as unpaid or at $100 monthly stipend. Open to high school seniors, recent high school graduates, college freshmen, college sophomores, college juniors, college seniors, recent college graduates, graduate students, career changers, individuals reentering the workforce. International applications accepted.
Benefits Free housing, free meals, on-the-job training, possible full-time employment, worker's compensation, restricted medical plan.
Contact Write, call, fax, or e-mail Dina S. Grant, Internship Coordinator. Phone: 319-465-5916 Ext. 204. Fax: 319-465-5919. E-mail: camp@campcourageous.org. In-person interview recommended. Applicants must submit a formal organization application, three personal references. Applications are accepted continuously. World Wide Web: http://www.camp@campcourageous.org.

CAMP FIRE BOYS AND GIRLS
PO Box 3275
San Diego, California 92163-1275

General Information Nonprofit organization providing clubs, camping, and self-reliance for youth to develop self-esteem and the skills to function as caring, self-directed individuals. Established in 1929. Number of employees: 8. Unit of Camp Fire Boys and Girls, Kansas City, Missouri. Number of internship applications received each year: 6.
Internships Available ▶ *3 self-reliance instructors:* responsibilities include working with classroom-sized groups of children to deliver a fun, structured, interactive course on self-reliance; scheduling courses; and keeping applicable records. Candidates should have ability to work independently, college courses in field, oral communication skills, self-motivation, strong interpersonal skills. Duration is 1 semester. Position available as unpaid or paid. Open to college juniors, college seniors, recent college graduates, graduate students.
Benefits Formal training, names of contacts, possible full-time employment, willing to complete paperwork for educational credit, willing to provide letters of recommendation.
Contact Write, call, or fax Self-Reliance Program Coordinator. Phone: 619-291-8985. Fax: 619-291-8988. In-person interview required. Applicants must submit a resume, three personal references. Applications are accepted continuously.

CAMP FIRE BOYS AND GIRLS, GEORGIA COUNCIL
100 Edgewood Avenue, Suite 528
Atlanta, Georgia 30303

General Information Youth development organization. Established in 1910. Number of employees: 15. Affiliate of Camp Fire Boys and Girls, Kansas City, Missouri. Number of internship applications received each year: 10.
Internships Available ▶ *1–2 public relations interns:* responsibilities include creating brochures, writing press releases, following up on press contacts, organizing special events. Candidates should have ability to work independently, oral communication skills, self-motivation, strong interpersonal skills, writing skills. Position available as unpaid or at $5 per hour. Open to college freshmen, college sophomores, college juniors, college seniors, recent college graduates, career changers, individuals reentering the workforce.
Benefits Job counseling, on-the-job training, opportunity to attend seminars/workshops, willing to act as a professional reference, willing to complete paperwork for educational credit, willing to provide letters of recommendation, free parking.
Contact Write, fax, or e-mail Linda Woodworth, Communications Director, 100 Edgewood Avenue, Suite 528, Atlanta, Georgia 30303. Fax: 404-527-7139. E-mail: info@campfirega.org. In-person interview recommended. Applicants must submit a formal

organization application, cover letter, resume, three writing samples. Applications are accepted continuously. World Wide Web: http://www.campfirega.org.

CAMP FIRE BOYS AND GIRLS, NORTH OAKLAND COUNCIL
4450 Walton Boulevard, Suite C
Waterford, Michigan 48329

General Information Organization that provides, through a program of informal education, opportunities for youth to realize their potential and to function as caring, self-directed individuals, responsible to themselves and to others. Established in 1910. Number of employees: 5. Unit of Camp Fire Boys and Girls, Kansas City, Missouri.
Internships Available ▶ *Club leaders:* responsibilities include conducting a Camp Fire program for a group of 5-15 children. Candidates should have oral communication skills, organizational skills, self-motivation, strong interpersonal skills, strong leadership ability. Duration is 2 semesters. Unpaid. Open to recent high school graduates, college freshmen, college sophomores, college juniors, college seniors, recent college graduates, individuals reentering the workforce. ▶ *1–15 day camp counselors:* responsibilities include working with a group of 10 campers in a day camp setting on a pre-planned program. Candidates should have oral communication skills, organizational skills, self-motivation, strong interpersonal skills, strong leadership ability. Duration is 4 weeks in the summer. $125 per week. Open to recent high school graduates, college freshmen, college sophomores, college juniors, college seniors, recent college graduates, graduate students, law students, career changers, individuals reentering the workforce. ▶ *1–4 school club leaders:* responsibilities include conducting a pre-planned Camp Fire meeting bi-weekly for youth at risk. Candidates should have oral communication skills, organizational skills, plan to pursue career in field, self-motivation, strong interpersonal skills. Duration is 2 semesters. $7 per hour. Open to high school seniors, recent high school graduates, college freshmen, college sophomores, college juniors, college seniors, recent college graduates, graduate students, law students, career changers, individuals reentering the workforce. International applications accepted.
Benefits Formal training, names of contacts, opportunity to attend seminars/workshops, willing to complete paperwork for educational credit, willing to provide letters of recommendation.
Contact Write, call, fax, or e-mail Ms. Barb Zelinski, Program Director. Phone: 248-618-9050. Fax: 248-618-9052. E-mail: campfireno@aol.com. In-person interview required. Application deadline: May 1 for summer camp.

CAMPHILL SOLTANE
224 Nantmeal Road
Glenmoore, Pennsylvania 19343

General Information Intentional rural community promoting healing in social life, agriculture, the arts, and education with handicapped young adults. Established in 1988. Number of employees: 25. Affiliate of Camphill Association, Glenmoore, Pennsylvania. Number of internship applications received each year: 30.
Internships Available ▶ *10–15 co-worker/orchards assistants/direct care/volunteer co-worker:* responsibilities include working in organic, biodynamic 400-tree orchard pruning, mulching, and learning about biodynamic agriculture. Candidates should have ability to work independently, self-motivation, strong interpersonal skills, strong leadership ability. Duration is 1–12 months. Open to recent high school graduates, college freshmen, college sophomores, college juniors, college seniors, recent college graduates, graduate students, career changers, individuals reentering the workforce. ▶ *5–15 community interns:* responsibilities include performing general duties within the life-sharing community. Candidates should have ability to work independently, self-motivation, strong interpersonal skills, strong leadership ability. Duration is 1–12 months. Open to recent high school graduates, college freshmen, college sophomores, college juniors, college seniors, recent college graduates, graduate students,

career changers, individuals reentering the workforce. ▶ *1 development/fund-raising intern:* responsibilities include research, grant writing, proposal development, database management, record keeping, clerical duties, strategic planning and evaluation, phone solicitation, and brochure preparation. Candidates should have ability to work independently, computer skills, office skills, oral communication skills, organizational skills, personal interest in the field, self-motivation, strong interpersonal skills, strong leadership ability, written communication skills. Duration is 1–3 months. Open to recent high school graduates, college freshmen, college sophomores, college juniors, college seniors, recent college graduates, graduate students, law students, career changers, individuals reentering the workforce. ▶ *2–4 pottery studio assistants:* responsibilities include working with handicapped students coiling, pinching, firing, glazing, developing, and designing products; researching outlets and sales opportunities; and exhibiting at craft fairs. Candidates should have ability to work independently, self-motivation, strong interpersonal skills, strong leadership ability. Duration is 1–12 months. Open to recent high school graduates, college freshmen, college sophomores, college juniors, college seniors, recent college graduates, graduate students, individuals reentering the workforce. ▶ *5–10 special education assistants:* responsibilities include working one-on-one with handicapped students in life skills training, including reading, writing, and money management. Candidates should have ability to work independently, self-motivation, strong interpersonal skills, strong leadership ability. Duration is 1–12 months. Open to recent high school graduates, college freshmen, college sophomores, college juniors, college seniors, recent college graduates, graduate students, law students, career changers, individuals reentering the workforce. ▶ *2–4 weaving studio assistants:* responsibilities include working with handicapped students ages 18–25 weaving, spinning, dyeing natural wools, designing and developing products, and developing outlets and craft fair sales opportunities. Candidates should have ability to work independently, self-motivation, strong interpersonal skills, strong leadership ability. Duration is 1–12 months. Open to recent high school graduates, college freshmen, college sophomores, college juniors, college seniors, recent college graduates, graduate students, career changers, individuals reentering the workforce. All positions are unpaid. International applications accepted.
Benefits Formal training, free housing, free meals, health insurance, names of contacts, on-the-job training, opportunity to attend seminars/workshops, willing to complete paperwork for educational credit, willing to provide letters of recommendation, spending money, health insurance for internships lasting 6 months or longer, possibility of full-time involvement.
Contact Write, call, fax, or e-mail Mr. Cornelius M. Pietzner, Executive Director. Phone: 610-469-0933. Fax: 610-469-1054. E-mail: soltane@aol.com. In-person interview recommended. Applicants must submit a formal organization application. Applications are accepted continuously. World Wide Web: http://www.camphill.soltane.org.

CAMP WOODSON
741 Old U.S. 70
Swannanoa, North Carolina 28778

General Information Year-round therapeutic wilderness camping program for juvenile delinquents. Established in 1976. Number of employees: 19. Division of Youth Services, State of North Carolina, Raleigh, North Carolina. Number of internship applications received each year: 15.
Internships Available ▶ *15 fieldwork interns:* responsibilities include hiking, camping, canoeing, horseback riding, and/or rock climbing with students and staff; assisting with office paperwork such as documentation, treatment plans, and records; and daily counseling of individuals and groups. Candidates should have ability to work independently, oral communication skills, self-motivation, strong interpersonal skills, strong leadership ability. Duration is flexible. Unpaid. Open to college freshmen, college sophomores, college juniors, college seniors, recent

college graduates, graduate students, law students, career changers, individuals reentering the workforce. International applications accepted.
Benefits Formal training, free meals, job counseling, names of contacts, opportunity to attend seminars/workshops, possible full-time employment, willing to complete paperwork for educational credit, willing to provide letters of recommendation, use of equipment.
Contact Write, call, or fax Marilyn Kaylor, Internship Coordinator. Phone: 828-686-5411. Fax: 828-686-7671. In-person interview recommended. Applicants must submit a cover letter, resume, three personal references. Applications are accepted continuously.

CATHOLIC BIG BROTHERS
3300 West Temple Street
Los Angeles, California 90026

General Information Social service organization that provides healthy, male role models to fatherless children. Established in 1925. Number of employees: 13. Affiliate of Big Brothers/Big Sisters of America, Inc, Philadelphia, Pennsylvania. Number of internship applications received each year: 3.
Internships Available ▶ *1 development assistant:* responsibilities include assisting director of development, locating foundations, researching criteria for grant applications, and writing letters to donors. Candidates should have office skills, oral communication skills, organizational skills, research skills, written communication skills. Open to recent high school graduates, college freshmen, college sophomores, college juniors, college seniors, recent college graduates, graduate students, career changers, individuals reentering the workforce. ▶ *Program assistants:* responsibilities include assisting director of programs, keeping records, assuring quality, and planning and follow-up. ▶ *1 public relations assistant:* responsibilities include assisting directors of public relations and recruitment, maintaining relationship with media, creating new sources of recruitment, and writing media releases. Candidates should have office skills, oral communication skills, plan to pursue career in field, strong interpersonal skills, written communication skills. Open to recent high school graduates, college freshmen, college sophomores, college juniors, college seniors, recent college graduates, graduate students, career changers, individuals reentering the workforce. Duration for all positions is flexible. All positions are unpaid.
Benefits Formal training, possible full-time employment, travel reimbursement, willing to complete paperwork for educational credit.
Contact Write, call, fax, or e-mail Stephanie Wilson, Director of Development and Recruitment. Phone: 213-251-9800. Fax: 213-251-9855. E-mail: cbbhip@aol.com. In-person interview required. Applicants must submit a cover letter, resume, writing sample. Applications are accepted continuously.

CATHOLIC CHARITIES FLEMINGTON
6 Park Avenue
Flemington, New Jersey 08822

General Information Multi-service agency providing a wide range of quality mental health and substance abuse services to individuals, families, neighborhoods, and communities. Established in 1982. Number of employees: 35. Number of internship applications received each year: 8.
Internships Available ▶ *6–8 family service office interns:* responsibilities include conducting assessments and case management with an emphasis on family therapy; individual, couples, family, and group counseling. Candidates should have ability to work independently, college courses in field, plan to pursue career in field, strong interpersonal skills, written communication skills. Duration is 3 months for summer internships; 9-12 months for others. Unpaid. Open to recent college graduates, graduate students, college students pursuing master's-level degree for social work or counseling psychology.
Benefits Names of contacts, on-the-job training, possible full-time employment, willing to complete paperwork for educational credit.

Catholic Charities Flemington (continued)

Contact Write, call, or fax Judith Lemezis, Program Director. Phone: 908-782-7905. Fax: 908-782-5934. In-person interview required. Applicants must submit a resume, school referral. Applications are accepted continuously.

CATHOLIC CHARITIES METUCHEN
288 Rues Lane
East Brunswick, New Jersey 08816

General Information Multi-service agency providing a wide range of quality services to individuals, families, neighborhoods, and communities. Established in 1982. Number of employees: 700. Number of internship applications received each year: 55.
Internships Available ► *14 Bridgewater family services office interns:* responsibilities include conducting assessments, and individual, couples, and family therapy. Candidates should have ability to work independently, oral communication skills, plan to pursue career in field, strong interpersonal skills, written communication skills. Duration is 2 semesters. Open to graduate students. ► *1 East Brunswick child/adolescent/partial care program intern:* responsibilities include conducting case management, crisis management, intakes, and individual, family, and group counseling with emphasis on group treatment. Candidates should have oral communication skills, personal interest in the field, strong interpersonal skills, written communication skills. Duration is 2 semesters. Open to college seniors in social work program. ► *3 East Brunswick mental health center interns:* responsibilities include conducting assessments; case management; individual, couples, family, and group counseling. Candidates should have ability to work independently, oral communication skills, personal interest in the field, plan to pursue career in field, strong interpersonal skills, written communication skills. Duration is 2 semesters. Open to second-year MSW students. ► *1 Edison child/adolescent partial care intern:* responsibilities include conducting case management, crisis management, screenings, and individual, family, and group counseling with emphasis on group treatment. Candidates should have ability to work independently, oral communication skills, personal interest in the field, strong interpersonal skills, written communication skills. Open to 1st year MSW students. ► *3 Edison family services office interns:* responsibilities include conducting assessments, case management, and individual, couples, family, and group counseling. Candidates should have ability to work independently, oral communication skills, personal interest in the field, strong interpersonal skills, written communication skills. Duration is 2 semesters. Open to second-year MSW students. ► *1–12 Flemington family services office interns:* responsibilities include conducting assessments; individual, couples, family, and group counseling; case management, with an emphasis on family therapy. Candidates should have ability to work independently, oral communication skills, personal interest in the field, plan to pursue career in field, strong interpersonal skills, written communication skills. Duration is 1–3 semesters. Open to graduate students. ► *7 Perth Amboy skills training program and inner city counseling program interns:* responsibilities include conducting intakes, assessments, and individual, couples, family, and group counseling; and performing traditional office and in-home services in the areas of child neglect/abuse, sexual abuse, juvenile justice or foster families. Candidates should have ability to work independently, oral communication skills, personal interest in the field, plan to pursue career in field, strong interpersonal skills, written communication skills. Duration is 2 semesters. Open to college seniors and graduate students in social work programs. ► *7 Phillipsburg family services office interns:* responsibilities include conducting assessments, and individual, couples, and family counseling. Candidates should have ability to work independently, oral communication skills, plan to pursue career in field, strong interpersonal skills, written communication skills. Duration is 2 semesters. Open to graduate students. All positions are unpaid. International applications accepted.
Benefits Names of contacts, opportunity to attend seminars/workshops, possible full-time employment, willing to complete paperwork for educational credit, willing to provide letters of recommendation.

Contact Write, call, or fax Patricia Moore, Student Coordinator. Phone: 732-257-6100. Fax: 732-651-9834. In-person interview required. Applicants must submit academic transcripts. Applications are accepted continuously.

CATHOLIC CHARITIES USA
1731 King Street, Suite 200
Alexandria, Virginia 22314

General Information National organization that supports local social services organizations. Established in 1910. Number of employees: 50. Number of internship applications received each year: 10.
Internships Available ► *1 legislative intern:* responsibilities include attending Congressional hearings, working with issue coalitions, writing and delivery of materials to Congress, writing for legislative newsletter, administrative assistance. Unpaid. ► *1 loaned executive intern:* responsibilities include attending and reporting about congressional hearings, working with issue coalitions, letter writing and delivery of materials to Congress, calling congressional staff, writing for legislative newsletter, answering correspondence. Unpaid. ► *1 public relations intern:* responsibilities include assisting communications department by writing articles, organizing clipping files, and assisting with information requests and special events. Candidates should have editing skills, oral communication skills, organizational skills, self-motivation, writing skills. Duration is flexible. $6 per hour. Open to college sophomores, college juniors, college seniors, recent college graduates. International applications accepted.
Benefits Opportunity to attend seminars/workshops, possible full-time employment, willing to act as a professional reference, willing to complete paperwork for educational credit, willing to provide letters of recommendation.
Contact Write, call, fax, or e-mail Genna Viozzi, Communications Assistant. Phone: 703-549-1390 Ext. 114. Fax: 703-549-1656. E-mail: gviozzi@catholiccharitiesusa.org. In-person interview required. Applicants must submit a cover letter, resume, two writing samples. Applications are accepted continuously. World Wide Web: http://www.catholiccharitiesusa.org.

CENTER FOR COMMUNICATION RESOURCES
1419 West Blackhawk
Chicago, Illinois 60622

General Information Community-based media arts center with community computer lab, equipment access program, workshops, screening program, and youth instructional programs. Established in 1978. Number of employees: 2. Number of internship applications received each year: 10.
Internships Available ► *Marketing/publicity interns:* responsibilities include marketing and publicity for programs and services. Candidates should have computer skills, office skills, oral communication skills, organizational skills, writing skills. Open to college freshmen, college sophomores, college juniors, college seniors, recent college graduates, graduate students. ► *Video/computer instructors/mentors:* responsibilities include working with youth on computers, Internet, and video production. Candidates should have computer skills, oral communication skills, personal interest in the field, strong interpersonal skills. Open to high school students, high school seniors, recent high school graduates, college freshmen, college sophomores, college juniors, college seniors. Duration for all positions is continuous. All positions are unpaid. International applications accepted.
Benefits Names of contacts, on-the-job training, opportunity to attend seminars/workshops, willing to act as a professional reference, willing to complete paperwork for educational credit, willing to provide letters of recommendation.
Contact Write, call, fax, or e-mail Nalani McClendon, Executive Director, 1419 West Blackhawk Street, Chicago, Illinois 60622. Phone: 773-862-6868. Fax: 773-862-0707. E-mail: ccr@psinet.com. In-person interview recommended. Applicants must submit a cover letter, resume. Applications are accepted continuously. World Wide Web: http://www.bham.net/soe/ccr.

CENTER FOR COMMUNITY SOLUTIONS
4508 Mission Bay Drive
San Diego, California 92109

General Information Community center providing services such as hospital accompaniment for rape survivors, 24-hour sexual assault and domestic violence crisis prevention and intervention, educational programs, and various counseling services. Established in 1969. Number of employees: 35. Number of internship applications received each year: 20.
Internships Available ▶ *10–20 crisis line counselors:* responsibilities include working on 24-hour crisis line for survivors of sexual assault and family violence. Duration is flexible. Unpaid. ▶ *1–15 in-person counseling interns/MFT and social work interns:* responsibilities include in-person counseling for men, women, and their families. Candidates should have college degree in related field, declared college major in field, knowledge of field, oral communication skills, plan to pursue career in field, strong interpersonal skills, written communication skills. Duration is 1 year. Unpaid. Open to graduate students. ▶ *1–4 legal clinic assistants:* responsibilities include assisting with temporary restraining orders and divorce procedures for battered women. Position available as unpaid or paid. Open to law students. ▶ *5–10 safehouse assistants:* responsibilities include helping with emergency shelter for victims of violence. Position available as unpaid or paid. ▶ *5–10 speakers:* responsibilities include speaking on violence against women and other issues. Candidates should have oral communication skills, strong interpersonal skills. Unpaid. Open to college freshmen, college sophomores, college juniors, college seniors, recent college graduates, graduate students, law students, career changers, individuals reentering the workforce. International applications accepted.
Benefits Job counseling, names of contacts, on-the-job training, opportunity to attend seminars/workshops, willing to complete paperwork for educational credit, willing to provide letters of recommendation, therapy training and supervision.
Contact Write or call Verna Griffin-Tabor, Executive Director. Phone: 619-272-5777 Ext. 19. In-person interview required. Applicants must submit a formal organization application, resume, autobiographical statement. Application deadline: June 15 for fall, December 31 for winter/spring.

CHILDREN'S CREATIVE RESPONSE TO CONFLICT
PO Box 271
Nyack, New York 10960

General Information Program established by the New York Quaker Project on Community Conflict to provide specially designed activities in which participants experience ways to examine conflicts and develop solutions. Established in 1972. Number of employees: 6. Number of internship applications received each year: 25.
Internships Available ▶ *2 interns:* responsibilities include facilitating small groups within workshops, helping to gather materials for use with activities, and sharing administrative duties. Candidates should have knowledge of field, oral communication skills, plan to pursue career in field, strong interpersonal skills, ability to work well with children, commitment to nonviolence. Duration is 3–12 months. Unpaid. Open to college seniors, recent college graduates, graduate students, law students, career changers, individuals reentering the workforce. International applications accepted.
Benefits Formal training, on-the-job training, opportunity to attend seminars/workshops, tuition assistance, willing to complete paperwork for educational credit, willing to provide letters of recommendation.
Contact Write, call, fax, or e-mail Priscilla Prutzman, Executive Director. Phone: 914-353-1796. Fax: 914-358-4924. E-mail: ccrcnyack@aol.com. Telephone interview required. Applicants must submit a cover letter, resume. Applications are accepted continuously.

CHILDREN, YOUTH, AND FAMILY COUNCIL
111 North 49th Street, c/o Kirkbride
Philadelphia, Pennsylvania 19139

General Information Coalition of 58 private nonprofit child welfare agencies that advocates for children and families in the child welfare system. Established in 1984. Number of employees: 7. Number of internship applications received each year: 8.
Internships Available ▶ *1 policy analyst:* responsibilities include analyzing policy and developing group positions. Candidates should have computer skills, editing skills, knowledge of field, oral communication skills, research skills, writing skills. Open to college juniors, college seniors, recent college graduates, graduate students. ▶ *Researchers:* responsibilities include researching issues related to child welfare. Candidates should have ability to work independently, computer skills, oral communication skills, research skills, strong interpersonal skills, written communication skills. Open to recent college graduates, graduate students. Duration for all positions is flexible. All positions are unpaid. International applications accepted.
Benefits Formal training, job counseling, names of contacts, on-the-job training, opportunity to attend seminars/workshops, possible full-time employment, travel reimbursement, willing to act as a professional reference, willing to complete paperwork for educational credit, willing to provide letters of recommendation.
Contact Write, call, or fax Margaret Zukoski, Acting Executive Director. Phone: 215-748-4688. Fax: 215-748-4699. In-person interview required. Applicants must submit a resume, writing sample, three personal references. Applications are accepted continuously.

CHRYSALIS: A CENTER FOR WOMEN
2650 Nicollet Avenue South
Minneapolis, Minnesota 55408-1662

General Information Center helping women who are experiencing crisis or transition to lead more successful lives. Established in 1974. Number of employees: 50. Number of internship applications received each year: 100.
Internships Available ▶ *2–3 LAW (Legal Assistance for Women) program interns:* responsibilities include assisting in various capacities; acting as a LAW clinic advocate and information session facilitator; excellent opportunity to gain experience with program development and supervision in nonprofit legal program. Candidates should have ability to work independently, knowledge of field, oral communication skills, personal interest in the field, strong interpersonal skills, comfort with public speaking. Open to college freshmen, college sophomores, college juniors, college seniors, recent college graduates, law students, career changers, individuals reentering the workforce. ▶ *2 chemical dependency interns:* responsibilities include participating in different phases of chemical treatment program, including assessments and individual and group sessions. Candidates should have college courses in field, knowledge of field, personal interest in the field, plan to pursue career in field, strong interpersonal skills. Duration is flexible. Open to graduate students, those enrolled in or graduates of chemical dependency certification program. ▶ *2–3 development interns:* responsibilities include assisting development department in areas of fund-raising, annual appeals, grant writing, and donor research. Candidates should have ability to work independently, computer skills, organizational skills, self-motivation, strong interpersonal skills, writing skills. Open to college freshmen, college sophomores, college juniors, college seniors, recent college graduates, graduate students, career changers, individuals reentering the workforce. ▶ *2–3 family education interns:* responsibilities include providing support in several capacities to children in various stages of development. Candidates should have knowledge of field, oral communication skills, personal interest in the field, self-motivation, strong interpersonal skills. Open to college freshmen, college sophomores, college juniors, college seniors, recent college graduates, career changers, individuals reentering the workforce. ▶ *1–2 marketing and communications interns:* responsibilities include assisting director in areas of community outreach and event planning and coordination; excellent opportunity to learn about nonprofit sec-

Chrysalis: A Center for Women (continued)

tor and develop marketing skills including public speaking. Candidates should have computer skills, editing skills, organizational skills, self-motivation, writing skills. Duration is flexible. Open to college sophomores, college juniors, college seniors, recent college graduates, graduate students, career changers, individuals reentering the workforce. ▶ *3 mental health clinic interns:* responsibilities include participating in all aspects of clinic operations, including intakes and individual, group, and family therapy. Candidates should have college courses in field, knowledge of field, oral communication skills, plan to pursue career in field, strong interpersonal skills. Duration is 9 month minimum, September through June. Open to graduate students. ▶ *2–3 mental health intake interns:* responsibilities include providing phone and in-person intake assessments and referral services to potential mental health clinic clients. Candidates should have ability to work independently, computer skills, knowledge of field, oral communication skills, strong interpersonal skills. Duration is flexible. Open to college freshmen, college sophomores, college juniors, college seniors, recent college graduates. ▶ *10–15 resource counseling interns:* responsibilities include assisting in crisis counseling, helping clients find resources, and helping telephone and walk-in clients. Candidates should have oral communication skills, personal interest in the field, self-motivation, strong interpersonal skills. Duration is flexible. Open to college freshmen, college sophomores, college juniors, college seniors, recent college graduates, graduate students, law students, career changers, individuals reentering the workforce. ▶ *5–10 support group facilitator interns:* responsibilities include meeting weekly with a small group of women who wish to support each other in particular issues such as self-worth, self-empowerment, uncoupling, single motherhood, middle years, and lesbian issues. Candidates should have knowledge of field, oral communication skills, personal interest in the field, self-motivation, strong interpersonal skills. Duration is 1 year minimum. Open to college freshmen, college sophomores, college juniors, college seniors, recent college graduates, graduate students, law students, career changers, individuals reentering the workforce. All positions are unpaid. International applications accepted.
Benefits Formal training, names of contacts, on-the-job training, opportunity to attend seminars/workshops, possible full-time employment, willing to act as a professional reference, willing to complete paperwork for educational credit, willing to provide letters of recommendation.
Contact Write, call, fax, or e-mail Ms. Tiffany Muller, Volunteer Coordinator. Phone: 612-871-0118. Fax: 612-870-2403. E-mail: tmuller@chrysaliswomen.org. In-person interview recommended. Applicants must submit a cover letter, resume, 1 or 2 personal references. Applications are accepted continuously. World Wide Web: http://www.chrysaliswomen.org.

CIRCLE OF NEIGHBORS
One College Center, Box 76000
Colorado Springs, Colorado 80970

General Information Nonprofit community service organization with focus on planning and funding for college-bound students. Established in 1897. Number of employees: 4. Affiliate of Neighbors of Woodcraft, Oregon City, Oregon. Number of internship applications received each year: 25.
Internships Available ▶ *College planning consultants:* responsibilities include explaining the process of college planning, and interviewing candidates for assistance. Candidates should have ability to work independently, oral communication skills, personal interest in the field, self-motivation, strong interpersonal skills, strong leadership ability. Open to high school students, high school seniors, recent high school graduates, college freshmen, college sophomores, college juniors, college seniors, recent college graduates, graduate students, law students, career changers, individuals reentering the workforce, retirees. ▶ *Community service interns:* responsibilities include gathering information on potential applicants for community service projects in their own communities. Candidates should have ability to work independently, oral communication skills, self-motivation, strong interpersonal skills, strong leadership ability. Open to high school students,

high school seniors. Duration for all positions is indefinite. All positions available as unpaid or paid. International applications accepted.
Benefits Formal training, job counseling, names of contacts, on-the-job training, opportunity to attend seminars/workshops, possible full-time employment, tuition assistance, willing to act as a professional reference, willing to complete paperwork for educational credit, willing to provide letters of recommendation.
Contact Write, call, fax, or e-mail Tom Okuto, Manager, One College Center, Box 76000, Colorado Springs, Colorado 80970. Phone: 800-743-4731. Fax: 800-347-4796. E-mail: tomokuto@aol. com. In-person interview recommended. Applicants must submit a cover letter, resume. Applications are accepted continuously. World Wide Web: http://www.circleofneighbors.org.

COMMISSION FOR WOMEN–COUNSELING AND CAREER CENTER
255 North Washington Street
Rockville, Maryland 20850

General Information Commission that advises the county council and agencies of the state and federal governments on issues of concern to women. In addition to advocating equal rights for women, the center helps women gain skills necessary to participate as equals in society. Established in 1972. Number of employees: 10. Department of Montgomery County Government, Rockville, Maryland. Number of internship applications received each year: 10.
Internships Available ▶ *1–3 Commission for Women interns:* responsibilities include researching and preparing reports. Candidates should have ability to work independently, analytical skills, computer skills, editing skills, knowledge of field, oral communication skills, organizational skills, personal interest in the field, research skills, self-motivation, strong interpersonal skills, strong leadership ability, writing skills. Duration is 1 year. Open to college seniors, recent college graduates, graduate students, law students, career changers, individuals reentering the workforce. ▶ *5 counseling and career center interns:* responsibilities include assisting with information and referral services. Candidates should have analytical skills, college degree in related field, computer skills, knowledge of field, oral communication skills, organizational skills, personal interest in the field, research skills, strong interpersonal skills, written communication skills, some counseling experience. Duration is 2 semesters (preferred). Open to second-year graduate students. ▶ *1–5 counseling specialists:* responsibilities include psychosocial and career counseling with short problem-solving approach. Candidates should have ability to work with others, analytical skills, college degree in related field, experience in the field, oral communication skills, plan to pursue career in field, strong interpersonal skills. Duration is 2 semesters (preferred). Open to second-year graduate students enrolled in a master's program. All positions are unpaid. International applications accepted.
Benefits Job counseling, on-the-job training, opportunity to attend seminars/workshops, willing to complete paperwork for educational credit, willing to provide letters of recommendation, supervision for counseling interns and those who need supervision in order to earn certification.
Contact Write, call, or e-mail Ms. Thyra Packett, Program Manager. Phone: 301-279-1869. Fax: 301-279-1318. E-mail: packet@ co.mo.md.us. In-person interview recommended. Applicants must submit a formal organization application, cover letter, resume. Applications are accepted continuously. World Wide Web: http://www.co.mo.md.us/cfw.

COMMUNITY CRISIS CENTER
PO Box 1390
Elgin, Illinois 60121

General Information Center providing immediate, twenty-four hour, caring and professional services in response to requests from individuals and families affected by domestic violence, sexual assault, and other crisis situations. Established in 1975. Number of employees: 76. Number of internship applications received each year: 15.

Internships Available ▶ *4–6 case managers:* responsibilities include crisis intervention on the hotline, individual counseling with an assigned shelter resident client, providing information to walk-in clients. Duration is 400 hours. Open to college seniors. ▶ *1–2 children's workers:* responsibilities include assisting Children's Program staff with individual and group activities with the children in the shelter. Duration is 1 semester (20 hours per week). Open to college sophomores. ▶ *2–4 counselors:* responsibilities include crisis intervention via hotline, individual and group counseling with residents and walk-in clients, family counseling with resident adults and their minor children. Duration is September to May. Open to graduate students. ▶ *2–4 shelter workers:* responsibilities include assisting Resident Case Managers in responding to the needs of the women and children in the shelter. Duration is 1 semester (20 hours per week). Open to college sophomores. Candidates for all positions should have college courses in field, declared college major in field, oral communication skills, strong interpersonal skills, written communication skills. All positions are unpaid.

Benefits Formal training, names of contacts, on-the-job training, opportunity to attend seminars/workshops, possible full-time employment, willing to act as a professional reference, willing to complete paperwork for educational credit, willing to provide letters of recommendation.

Contact Call Maureen Manning-Rosenfeld, MS, LCPC, Director of Client Services. Phone: 847-697-2380. In-person interview required. Applicants must submit a cover letter, resume. Application deadline: March 1 for summer, May 1 for fall, October 1 for spring. World Wide Web: http://www.crisisel.mcs.net.

COMMUNITY HARVEST FOOD BANK
PO Box 10967
Fort Wayne, Indiana 46855

General Information Organization that works to alleviate hunger by collecting and distributing donated foods; operates through a network of 480 agencies in northeast Indiana and Allen County. Established in 1983. Number of employees: 20. Number of internship applications received each year: 2.

Internships Available ▶ *1–2 agency services interns:* responsibilities include working directly with member agencies, handling order placements, invoicing, appointments, and taking care of agency needs; ensuring that office runs smoothly; and helping with on-site monitoring. Candidates should have ability to work independently, ability to work with others, computer skills, office skills, oral communication skills, organizational skills. Duration is ongoing throughout the year. Open to recent high school graduates, college freshmen, college sophomores, college juniors, college seniors, career changers, individuals reentering the workforce. ▶ *1 resource development intern:* responsibilities include database (11,000 names) maintenance and expansion, research of emerging trends in fund-raising (e.g. cause-related marketing), proposal writing and preparation. Candidates should have ability to work independently, computer skills, oral communication skills, personal interest in the field, written communication skills. Duration is 3–12 months. Open to college freshmen, college sophomores, college juniors, college seniors, recent college graduates, graduate students. ▶ *2–3 service learning assistants:* responsibilities include working with students and adults in gardens, assisting with driving, serving lunch to students, keeping records of attendance and product usage, and warehouse distribution of food to member agencies. Candidates should have ability to work independently, computer skills, oral communication skills, personal interest in the field, self-motivation, strong interpersonal skills, strong leadership ability, writing skills. Duration is 3 months. Open to recent high school graduates, college freshmen, college sophomores, college juniors, college seniors, recent college graduates, graduate students, law students, career changers, individuals reentering the workforce. All positions are unpaid.

Benefits On-the-job training, possible full-time employment, willing to act as a professional reference, willing to complete paperwork for educational credit, willing to provide letters of recommendation.

Contact Write, call, or fax Mike Eling, Warehouse Manager. Phone: 219-447-3696. Fax: 219-447-4859. In-person interview recommended. Applicants must submit a cover letter, resume. Applications are accepted continuously.

COMMUNITY MEDIATION CENTER
36 Southgate Court, Suite 102
Harrisonburg, Virginia 22801

General Information Mediation center providing services to individuals, families, organizations, and communities, as well as mediation and conflict resolution training. Established in 1982. Number of employees: 5. Number of internship applications received each year: 15.

Internships Available ▶ *5 case managers:* responsibilities include interviewing clients referred to mediation (by phone or in court) and scheduling cases for mediation. Candidates should have ability to work independently, college courses in field, oral communication skills, personal interest in the field, self-motivation, strong interpersonal skills, written communication skills. Duration is flexible. Unpaid. Open to college juniors, college seniors, recent college graduates, graduate students, law students, career changers. International applications accepted.

Benefits Formal training, names of contacts, on-the-job training, opportunity to attend seminars/workshops, willing to act as a professional reference, willing to complete paperwork for educational credit, willing to provide letters of recommendation.

Contact Write, call, fax, or e-mail Timothy Ruebke, Senior Case Manager. Phone: 540-434-0059. Fax: 540-574-0174. E-mail: mediate@rica.net. In-person interview recommended. Applicants must submit a cover letter, resume. Application deadline: April 1 for summer, July 1 for fall, November 1 for spring. World Wide Web: http://home.rica.net/mediate/.

COMMUNITY YEAR–MHA
1000 Twinbrook Parkway
Rockville, Maryland 20851

General Information Local Americorp service corporation that seeks to tap potential energy and idealism of young adults as resources to address the most pressing social needs of Montgomery County, Maryland. Established in 1992. Number of employees: 3. Unit of Mental Health Association of Montgomery County, Rockville, Maryland.

Internships Available ▶ *15 corps members:* responsibilities include working with people in need from preschool through adults, including handicapped children, chronically mentally ill adults, middle school students with special needs, and senior adults. Candidates should have ability to work with others. Duration is September-July (40 hours per week). $125 per week. Open to individuals between the ages of 17 and 25 who reside in Montgomery County, Maryland. International applications accepted.

Benefits Formal training, health insurance, job counseling, names of contacts, opportunity to attend seminars/workshops, willing to provide letters of recommendation, $4,725 scholarship available.

Contact Write, call, or fax Esther Kaleko-Kravitz, Director. Phone: 301-424-0656 Ext. 147. Fax: 301-738-1030. In-person interview required. Applicants must submit a formal organization application, two personal references. Application deadline: August 31.

COMMON GROUND SANCTUARY
1410 South Telegraph
Bloomfield Hills, Michigan 48302

General Information Comprehensive voluntary counseling and psychiatric assessment services for children, youth and families; residential and non-residential care for people who are in crisis situations. Established in 1974. Number of employees: 217. Number of internship applications received each year: 30.

Internships Available ▶ *1 accountant:* responsibilities include tracking daily receipts and disbursements and performing general ledger, payroll, budgeting, and budget analysis duties. Candidates should have ability to work independently, analytical skills,

Common Ground Sanctuary (continued)

computer skills, experience in the field, organizational skills, self-motivation, strong interpersonal skills, written communication skills. Duration is minimum of 1 semester. Open to recent high school graduates, college freshmen, college sophomores, college juniors, college seniors, career changers, individuals reentering the workforce. ▶ *1 business administrator:* responsibilities include assisting in developing business plans, strategic planning, internal information management, and personnel policies. Candidates should have ability to work independently, analytical skills, experience in the field, office skills, oral communication skills, organizational skills, self-motivation, strong interpersonal skills, strong leadership ability, written communication skills. Duration is minimum of 1 semester. Open to college freshmen, college sophomores, college juniors, college seniors, recent college graduates. ▶ *6 counselors:* responsibilities include directing case load of 2–10 youth and families and providing after-care and advocacy counseling. Candidates should have college courses in field, knowledge of field, oral communication skills, personal interest in the field, self-motivation, strong interpersonal skills, writing skills. Duration is 14–52 weeks. ▶ *4–20 direct care workers:* responsibilities include performing daily supervision, intakes, group counseling, recreational supervision, and teen consultation. Candidates should have personal interest in the field, strong interpersonal skills, written communication skills. Duration is minimum of 1 semester. Open to recent high school graduates, college freshmen, college sophomores, college juniors, college seniors, recent college graduates, law students, career changers, individuals reentering the workforce. ▶ *2 marketing and public relations interns:* responsibilities include assisting in development and implementation of a corporate public relations strategic plan, including written, oral, and media relations, as well as marketing publications. Candidates should have ability to work with others, computer skills, knowledge of field, oral communication skills, personal interest in the field, self-motivation, written communication skills. Duration is 10–52 weeks. Open to high school seniors, recent high school graduates, college freshmen, college sophomores, college juniors, college seniors, recent college graduates, graduate students, individuals reentering the workforce. ▶ *2 victim assistance advocates:* responsibilities include providing advocacy, counseling, and support services to victims of crime, providing education and awareness classes/outreach, supporting research and statistics. Candidates should have ability to work with others, college courses in field, computer skills, knowledge of field, oral communication skills, research skills, self-motivation, written communication skills. Duration is 12–52 weeks. Open to college freshmen, college sophomores, college juniors, college seniors, graduate students. All positions are unpaid. International applications accepted.

Benefits Free meals, opportunity to attend seminars/workshops, possible full-time employment, travel reimbursement, willing to complete paperwork for educational credit, willing to provide letters of recommendation.

Contact Write, fax, or e-mail James A. Perlaki, Director of Community Intervention Services. Fax: 248-456-8147. E-mail: sanctuary6@aol.com. No phone calls. In-person interview required. Applicants must submit a formal organization application, resume, academic transcripts, three personal references. Application deadline: February 1 for spring/summer (recommended deadline), November 1 for winter (recommended deadline).

CORPORATION FOR NATIONAL SERVICE
1201 New York Avenue, NW
Washington, District of Columbia 20525

General Information Federal government corporation in partnership with state and local governments and nonprofit organizations that administers AmeriCorps, Learn and Serve America, and the National Senior Serivce Corps. Established in 1994. Number of employees: 350. Number of internship applications received each year: 150.

Internships Available ▶ *AmeriCorps Education Awards Program interns:* responsibilities include assisting with grant proposal review, selection, and award process; assisting staff with reviewing progress, tracking and supporting current grantees; and

conducting special research on current grantees and program accomplishments. Candidates should have ability to work with others, oral communication skills, written communication skills, ability to learn quickly, good sense of humor, computer skills (useful). ▶ *1 AmeriCorps Leaders intern:* responsibilities include soliciting, researching, and writing articles on service leadership for the newsletter; researching and distributing technical assistance information; facilitating networking efforts; developing leadership contacts database; and initiating a project of own design. Candidates should have ability to work independently, oral communication skills, self-motivation, strong interpersonal skills, strong leadership ability, written communication skills, Desk-top publishing, html, and Filemaker Pro skills (useful). Duration is 10 weeks. Open to college freshmen, college sophomores, college juniors, college seniors, recent college graduates, graduate students. ▶ *1–3 AmeriCorps VISTA interns:* responsibilities include designing, delivering, and tabulating results of evaluations; assisting in the design of training for AmeriCorps*VISTA leaders; recruiting colleges to participate in the VISTA Post-Service Educational Opportunities Program, and expanding the VISTA alumni database. Candidates should have ability to work independently, analytical skills, oral communication skills, organizational skills, personal interest in the field, research skills, strong interpersonal skills, writing skills, written communication skills, knowledge of MS Word helpful. Duration is 10 weeks. Open to college freshmen, college sophomores, college juniors, college seniors, recent college graduates, graduate students. ▶ *AmeriCorps recruitment, selection, and placement interns:* responsibilities include working on a project designed to improve the methods, efficiency, and evaluation of recruitment efforts. Candidates should have ability to work independently, ability to work with others, analytical skills, oral communication skills, research skills, written communication skills, interest in community service, background working with student organizations or admission offices. Duration is 10 weeks in summer. Open to college freshmen, college sophomores, college juniors, college seniors, recent college graduates, graduate students. ▶ *1 AmeriCorps* State, South Cluster office intern:* responsibilities include identifying efforts made between AmeriCorps*State and other Corporation—supported programs to resolve community need, studying interaction between state commissions and their governing bodies, studying state commission feedback on performance and exploring methods of improvement, and gathering and assembling resource guide of program and state commission best practices. Candidates should have ability to work with others, self-motivation, commitment to national service movement, experience in community service helpful, academic background in social work or public administration helpful. Duration is summer. ▶ *1 AmeriCorps*NCCC intern:* responsibilities include supporting the production of a quarterly newsletter, acting as liaison to the field for the development of submissions to the contractor responsible for newsletter layout, and helping maintain NCCC project information. Candidates should have ability to work independently, computer skills, editing skills, organizational skills, self-motivation, writing skills, Microsoft Office experience (useful), area of study in journalism (helpful but not required). Duration is 10 weeks. Open to college freshmen, college sophomores, college juniors, college seniors, recent college graduates, graduate students. ▶ *2–5 Learn and Serve America interns:* responsibilities include developing a program director's manual; enhancing the content of information on the Web, preparing articles for publication, researching program issues, reviewing program portfolios and developing profiles, and filling requests for the field. Candidates should have ability to work independently, ability to work with others, personal interest in the field, self-motivation, writing skills, experience with service-learning (preferred). Duration is 10 weeks. Open to college freshmen, college sophomores, college juniors, college seniors, recent college graduates, graduate students. ▶ *National Senior Service Corps interns:* responsibilities include analyzing and mapping service data, researching questions about Senior Corps programs from Congress, developing program enhancements for foster grandparents, senior companions, and the retired and senior volunteers. Candidates should have ability to work independently, oral communication skills, written communica-

tion skills. Duration is 10 weeks in summer. Open to college freshmen, college sophomores, college juniors, college seniors, recent college graduates, graduate students. ▶ *1–2 congressional and intergovernmental relations interns:* responsibilities include researching policy matters related to national service, supporting key work related to reauthorization legislation, assisting with preparation of materials for the next appropriations cycle, and responding to congressional inquiries. Candidates should have ability to work independently, analytical skills, knowledge of field, office skills, oral communication skills, written communication skills, ability to handle simple math, academic background in political science, public policy, economics, public administration, law, or English. Duration is 10 weeks. Open to college sophomores, college juniors, college seniors, recent college graduates, graduate students. ▶ *1 legal intern:* responsibilities include working on various assignments in the Office of the General Counsel, including legal research, writing memoranda, case preparation, and developing guidelines. Candidates should have experience with legal research and nonprofit service organizations (desirable). Duration is 10 weeks in summer. Open to 1st and 2nd year law students only. ▶ *1 policy research intern:* responsibilities include performing research on policy studies such as enrollment and attrition issues in AmeriCorps, gender bias in national service, and how to promote quality programming in a decentralized structure, doing performance planning, and creating customer service standards. Candidates should have ability to work independently, ability to work with others, analytical skills, college courses in field, computer skills, knowledge of field, research skills, written communication skills, MS Word proficiency (required), knowledge of Excel and SPSS (useful). Duration is 10 weeks. Open to college sophomores, college juniors, college seniors, recent college graduates, graduate students. ▶ *Public affairs interns:* responsibilities include writing press releases and feature articles, assisting with special events such as press conferences, assembling press packets, transcribing speeches, and compiling news clips packages for targeted members of Congress. Candidates should have ability to work with others, research skills, writing skills, academic background in journalism, marketing, or communications (useful). Duration is 10 weeks in summer. Open to college freshmen, college sophomores, college juniors, college seniors, recent college graduates, graduate students. All positions are unpaid.
Benefits On-the-job training, opportunity to attend seminars/ workshops, possible full-time employment, willing to act as a professional reference, willing to provide letters of recommendation.
Contact Write, call, fax, or e-mail Intern Coordinator. Phone: 202-606-5000. Fax: 202-565-2787. E-mail: mliss@cns.gov. Telephone interview required. Applicants must submit a cover letter, resume. Application deadline: March 15 for summer positions; continuous for other positions. World Wide Web: http://www. nationalservice.org/.

COUNTERPOINT SHELTERS AND CRISIS CENTER
715 Inkster Road
Inkster, Michigan 48141

General Information Social service agency that provides a wide range of services including adoption, foster care, drug abuse prevention, and a runaway shelter. Established in 1975. Number of employees: 20. Unit of Starfish Family Services, Inkster, Michigan. Number of internship applications received each year: 40.
Internships Available ▶ *6–10 counseling or group work interns:* responsibilities include working with non-adjudicated teens toward family reunification, helping teens with independent living skills, and performing group work; crisis line and crisis drop-in counseling. Candidates should have ability to work with others, college courses in field, knowledge of field, oral communication skills, plan to pursue career in field, self-motivation, written communication skills. Duration is flexible; minimum 40 hours. Open to college freshmen, college sophomores, college juniors, college seniors, graduate students, career changers. ▶ *1–3 youth assistance group workers.* Candidates should have ability to work independently, college degree in related field, oral communication skills, self-motivation, written communication

skills, group work skills. Duration is ongoing. Open to recent college graduates, law students, career changers. ▶ *10–15 youth care workers/counselors:* responsibilities include managing floor in residential program for 1-10 adolescents, conducting intakes, performing crisis management and individual, family, and group counseling. Candidates should have ability to work independently, ability to work with others, knowledge of field, oral communication skills, plan to pursue career in field, written communication skills. Duration is flexible. Open to college freshmen, college sophomores, college juniors, college seniors. All positions are unpaid. International applications accepted.
Benefits Names of contacts, on-the-job training, opportunity to attend seminars/workshops, possible full-time employment, willing to act as a professional reference, willing to complete paperwork for educational credit, willing to provide letters of recommendation.
Contact Write, call, fax, or e-mail Linda Connolly, Director. Phone: 313-563-5005. Fax: 313-728-3500. E-mail: lconnolly@sfish. org. In-person interview required. Applicants must submit a formal organization application, academic transcripts, personal reference, letter of recommendation, TB tests, criminal records check. Applications are accepted continuously.

DANIEL WEBSTER COUNCIL, BOY SCOUTS: OUTDOOR EDUCATION & OUTREACH DIVISION
571 Holt Avenue
Manchester, New Hampshire 03109

General Information Outdoor adventure education/counseling program for troubled youths. Administers "Learning for Life" program, a national outreach program for at-risk and developmentally disabled youth. Established in 1984. Number of employees: 5. Number of internship applications received each year: 4.
Internships Available ▶ *Intern instructors:* responsibilities include designing and implementing outdoor adventure-based counseling programs. Candidates should have ability to work with others, experience in the field, oral communication skills, personal interest in the field, self-motivation, strong leadership ability. Duration is 9 months (beginning in fall), or 12 months (beginning in summer). Position available as unpaid or paid. Open to recent college graduates, graduate students. International applications accepted.
Benefits Formal training, free housing, names of contacts, opportunity to attend seminars/workshops, possible full-time employment, travel reimbursement, willing to act as a professional reference, willing to complete paperwork for educational credit, willing to provide letters of recommendation, custom-designed internships based upon the interests and needs of the intern, possible stipends for meals during summer.
Contact Write, call, or e-mail John Rainville, Outdoor Education and Outreach Program Specialist. Phone: 603-625-6431. E-mail: jfrain1@aol.com. In-person interview recommended. Applicants must submit a cover letter, resume. Applications are accepted continuously. World Wide Web: http://www.dwcbsa. org.

DEVELOPMENTAL DISABILITIES RESOURCE CENTER
11177 West 8th Avenue
Lakewood, Colorado 80215-5503

General Information Human services agency providing support to people with developmental disabilities.
Internships Available ▶ *Interns:* responsibilities include working as a teacher in special education, as an occupational, physical, or speech therapist; or as a social worker. Duration is flexible. Position available as unpaid or paid. Open to college freshmen, college sophomores, college juniors, college seniors, graduate students.
Contact Write, call, fax, or e-mail Bret Billings, Coordinator of Volunteers and Community Services, 11177 West 8th Avenue, Lakewood, New Jersey 80215-5503. Phone: 303-233-3363. Fax: 303-233-4622. E-mail: bbilling@ddrcco.com. Applicants must submit a resume, cover letter (explaining what work you are

interested in). A formal application will follow. Applications are accepted continuously. World Wide Web: http://www.ddrcco.com.

DUNELAND YMCA
215 Roosevelt Street
Chesterton, Indiana 46304

General Information Community organization that provides programs for all ages, including child care, fitness, senior, and youth programs. Established in 1966. Number of employees: 70. Unit of YMCA of the USA, Chicago, Illinois. Number of internship applications received each year: 25.

Internships Available ▶ *1 adult program coordinator:* responsibilities include identifying program needs and developing adult activities and programs. Candidates should have ability to work independently, oral communication skills, self-motivation, strong interpersonal skills, strong leadership ability. Duration is flexible. $5–$7 per hour. Open to college juniors, college seniors, career changers, individuals reentering the workforce. ▶ *3–5 child care assistants:* responsibilities include supervising school-age children enrolled in YMCA day care and summer care, and working actively with them. Candidates should have ability to work independently, college courses in field, knowledge of field, oral communication skills, strong interpersonal skills. Duration is flexible. $6 per hour. Open to high school seniors, recent high school graduates, college freshmen, college sophomores, college juniors, college seniors, recent college graduates, graduate students, career changers, individuals reentering the workforce. ▶ *4 youth basketball interns:* responsibilities include supervising youth basketball league practices and games, helping to organize teams, and recruiting coaches and referees. Candidates should have ability to work independently, personal interest in the field, self-motivation, strong interpersonal skills. Duration is 4 months in winter. $5 per hour. Open to high school students, high school seniors, recent high school graduates, college freshmen, college sophomores, college juniors, college seniors, recent college graduates, individuals reentering the workforce. ▶ *1 youth development coordinator:* responsibilities include assisting with high school and middle school teen clubs, organizing monthly middle school dances, developing and coordinating youth activities and programs, and coordinating Youth in Government program. Candidates should have ability to work independently, oral communication skills, self-motivation, strong interpersonal skills, strong leadership ability. Duration is 9 months. $5 per hour. Open to college juniors, college seniors, recent college graduates, career changers, individuals reentering the workforce.

Benefits Names of contacts, opportunity to attend seminars/workshops, possible full-time employment, travel reimbursement, willing to complete paperwork for educational credit, willing to provide letters of recommendation, full YMCA membership.

Contact Write, call, or fax Ms. Rose Essary, Executive Director. Phone: 219-926-4204. Fax: 219-926-2603. In-person interview required. Applications are accepted continuously.

EASTER SEALS ROCKY MOUNTAIN VILLAGE
2644 Alvarado Road, PO Box 115
Empire, Colorado 80438

General Information Nonprofit organization which provides services for children and adults with physical and/or mental disabilities. Established in 1951. Number of employees: 7. Program of Easter Seals Colorado, Lakewood, Colorado. Number of internship applications received each year: 5.

Internships Available ▶ *1 program intern:* responsibilities include working with the assistant director to coordinate, develop, and implement programs for summer residential coed camp for people with disabilities. Candidates should have ability to work with others, experience in the field, organizational skills, personal interest in the field, strong interpersonal skills, strong leadership ability. Duration is 1 summer. Unpaid. Open to college freshmen, college sophomores, college juniors, college seniors, recent college graduates, graduate students. ▶ *1 public relations intern:* responsibilities include working with computer specialist

to develop weekly camp newsletter, developing press releases, and working with director of communications for Easter Seals. Candidates should have ability to work independently, ability to work with others, computer skills, experience in the field, writing skills, newsletter/layout skills. Duration is 1 summer. Position available as unpaid or at $125 per week with $200 bonus if entire season completed. Open to recent high school graduates, college freshmen, college sophomores, college juniors, college seniors, recent college graduates, graduate students. ▶ *2 therapeutic recreation interns:* responsibilities include assisting program staff in planning and implementing activities for children and adults with special needs; case study and individual project also required. Candidates should have ability to work with others, declared college major in field, knowledge of field, organizational skills, self-motivation, writing skills. Duration is 1 summer or semester. Unpaid. Open to college juniors, college seniors.

Benefits Free housing, free meals, on-the-job training, willing to act as a professional reference, willing to complete paperwork for educational credit, willing to provide letters of recommendation.

Contact Write, call, or e-mail Ms. Christine Newell, Director of Camping/Recreation, 2644 Alvarado Road, PO Box 115, Empire, Colorado 80438. Phone: 303-569-2333. E-mail: newellc@cess.org. In-person interview recommended. Applicants must submit a formal organization application, cover letter, resume, three letters of recommendation. Applications are accepted continuously. World Wide Web: http://www.eastersealsco.org.

ECUMENICAL SOCIAL MINISTRIES
201 North Weber Street
Colorado Springs, Colorado 80903

General Information Nonprofit human services agency which provides basic emergency services, food, rental assistance, medicine, clothing, etc. Established in 1982. Number of employees: 9. Number of internship applications received each year: 45.

Internships Available ▶ *Accounting interns:* responsibilities include running statistical reports, making out financial statements, working with loan program, and learning data entry, voucher systems, checkbook systems, and the process for acknowledging donations. ▶ *1–10 human resource interns:* responsibilities include assisting clients in seeking employment and career opportunities, and helping individuals develop interviewing techniques, cover letters, etc. Candidates should have ability to work with others, declared college major in field, knowledge of field, oral communication skills, self-motivation, written communication skills. Open to high school seniors, college seniors, recent college graduates, graduate students, career changers, individuals reentering the workforce. ▶ *1–10 social work interns:* responsibilities include assisting low-income families in rent or utilities, and working in direct services to provide assistance in counseling, goal setting, and financial planning. Candidates should have ability to work independently, personal interest in the field, plan to pursue career in field, self-motivation, strong interpersonal skills. Open to high school seniors, college seniors, recent college graduates, graduate students, career changers, individuals reentering the workforce. All positions are unpaid.

Benefits On-the-job training, willing to act as a professional reference, willing to complete paperwork for educational credit, willing to provide letters of recommendation.

Contact Write or call Marcia Hanscom, Volunteer Coordinator. Phone: 719-633-1537. In-person interview required. Applications are accepted continuously.

ELIZABETH STONE HOUSE
PO Box 59
Jamaica Plain, Massachusetts 02130

General Information Emergency shelter for battered women and their children. Residential mental health alternative for women in emotional distress and their children. Transitional housing and economic development programs. Established in 1974. Number of employees: 20. Number of internship applications received each year: 120.

Internships Available ▶ *Administrative/direct service interns:* responsibilities include providing support to outreach coordinator, fund-raiser, administrative coordinator, and direct service staff. Candidates should have ability to work independently, ability to work with others, computer skills, office skills, oral communication skills, organizational skills, personal interest in the field, self-motivation, written communication skills. Duration is flexible. Open to recent high school graduates, college freshmen, college sophomores, college juniors, college seniors, recent college graduates, graduate students, law students, career changers, individuals reentering the workforce. ▶ *Child care interns:* responsibilities include coordinating children's activities with child-care worker and supervisor. Candidates should have ability to work with others, experience in the field, oral communication skills, plan to pursue career in field, self-motivation, strong interpersonal skills. Duration is flexible. Open to college freshmen, college sophomores, college juniors, college seniors, recent college graduates, graduate students, law students, career changers, individuals reentering the workforce. ▶ *5–10 direct service co-advocates:* responsibilities include providing emotional support to women in the program and attending at least 1 weekly house meeting. Candidates should have ability to work independently, personal interest in the field, self-motivation, strong interpersonal skills, strong leadership ability. Duration is minimum of 6 months. Open to college freshmen, college sophomores, college juniors, college seniors, recent college graduates, graduate students, law students, career changers, individuals reentering the workforce. ▶ *Donation interns:* responsibilities include creating holding spaces for donations, coordinating all receiving and distribution of donations to residents, and sending appropriate thank you notes. Candidates should have ability to work independently, oral communication skills, personal interest in the field, self-motivation, written communication skills. Duration is flexible. Open to college freshmen, college sophomores, college juniors, college seniors, recent college graduates, graduate students, law students, career changers, individuals reentering the workforce. All positions are unpaid. International applications accepted.
Benefits On-the-job training, opportunity to attend seminars/workshops, willing to act as a professional reference, willing to complete paperwork for educational credit, willing to provide letters of recommendation.
Contact Write, call, or fax Sylvia Rebay, Outreach and Education Coordinator. Phone: 617-522-3659 Ext. 206. Fax: 617-522-0968. E-mail: stonehse@aol.com. In-person interview recommended. Applicants must submit a formal organization application. Application deadline: May 30 for fall.

THE EMPOWER PROGRAM
6925 Willow Street, NW
Washington, District of Columbia 20012

General Information Nonprofit educational organization that works with youth, ages 10-21, to prevent gender-based violence, such as sexual harassment, sexual assault, dating violence, and bullying. Established in 1992. Number of employees: 19. Number of internship applications received each year: 25.
Internships Available ▶ *5–15 interns:* responsibilities include participation in every aspect of the organization from research, writing, and editing publications to program development, event planning, and fund-raising. Candidates should have oral communication skills, personal interest in the field, self-motivation, strong interpersonal skills, writing skills. Duration is dependent on intern's availability. Unpaid. Open to high school students, high school seniors, recent high school graduates, college freshmen, college sophomores, college juniors, college seniors, recent college graduates, graduate students, law students, career changers, individuals reentering the workforce. International applications accepted.
Benefits Names of contacts, on-the-job training, opportunity to attend seminars/workshops, possible full-time employment, willing to act as a professional reference, willing to complete paperwork for educational credit, willing to provide letters of recommendation.

Contact Write, call, fax, or e-mail Caitlin Finnegan, Program Associate, 6925 Willow Street, NW, Washington, District of Columbia 20012. Phone: 202-882-2800. Fax: 202-882-2543. E-mail: caitlin@empowered.org. In-person interview recommended. Applicants must submit a cover letter, resume, writing sample. Applications are accepted continuously. World Wide Web: http://www.empowered.org.

FAIR ACRES FAMILY YMCA
2600 Grand Avenue
Carthage, Missouri 64836

General Information Nonprofit organization that promotes family harmony and health. Established in 1990. Number of employees: 85.
Internships Available ▶ *1–7 camp counselors:* responsibilities include organizing activities for a group of 15 school-age children and supervising children. Candidates should have ability to work with others, knowledge of field, organizational skills, personal interest in the field. Duration is 13 weeks. $5–$6 per hour. Open to recent high school graduates, college freshmen, college sophomores, college juniors, college seniors. ▶ *1 sports coordinator:* responsibilities include coordinating daily youth and adult sports programs. Candidates should have ability to work independently, ability to work with others, knowledge of field, oral communication skills, personal interest in the field, written communication skills. Duration is flexible. Position available as unpaid or paid. Open to college freshmen, college sophomores, college juniors, college seniors. ▶ *1–5 youth coordinators:* responsibilities include creating and coordinating activities for pre-school through school-age youth. Candidates should have ability to work independently, ability to work with others, knowledge of field, oral communication skills, written communication skills. Duration is 12 months. Position available as unpaid or paid. Open to recent high school graduates, college freshmen, college sophomores, college juniors, college seniors, recent college graduates, career changers. International applications accepted.
Benefits Names of contacts, on-the-job training, opportunity to attend seminars/workshops, possible full-time employment, willing to act as a professional reference, willing to complete paperwork for educational credit, willing to provide letters of recommendation.
Contact Write or call Mike McPherson, Executive Director. Phone: 417-358-1070. In-person interview recommended. Applicants must submit a formal organization application, three personal references, three letters of recommendation. Applications are accepted continuously.

FAMILIES FIRST
1105 West Peachtree Street, NE
Atlanta, Georgia 30357

General Information Private nonprofit social service agency specializing in family and children's services.
Internships Available ▶ *Social work interns:* responsibilities include various tasks including individual and family counseling. Duration is flexible. Unpaid. Open to graduate students.
Benefits Free parking.
Contact Write, fax, or e-mail Tammy Murray, Human Resources, 1105 West Peachtree Street, NE, Atlanta, Georgia 30357. Fax: 404-685-0203. E-mail: tammy@familiesfirst.org. Applicants must submit a cover letter, resume. Applications are accepted continuously. World Wide Web: http://www.familiesfirst.org.

FAMILY SERVICE AGENCY OF SAN MATEO COUNTY
1870 El Camino Real
Burlingame, California 94010

General Information Agency that provides a full range of counseling including individual, couple, group, and family therapy. Established in 1950. Number of employees: 200. Number of internship applications received each year: 30.
Internships Available ▶ *8 interns:* responsibilities include performing individual, couple, family, and group counseling.

Family Service Agency of San Mateo County (continued)
Duration is 9 months (September-May). Open to graduate students. ▶ *Non-licensed counselors:* responsibilities include performing individual, couple, family, and group counseling. Duration is unlimited. Open to post-graduate students. Candidates for all positions should have ability to work independently, oral communication skills, self-motivation, strong interpersonal skills, written communication skills. All positions available as unpaid or paid. International applications accepted.
Benefits Formal training, willing to complete paperwork for educational credit.
Contact Write, call, or fax Doris O'Neal, Coordinator. Phone: 650-692-0555. Fax: 650-363-1401. In-person interview required. Applicants must submit a cover letter, resume. Application deadline: August 31 for graduate students; continuous for post-graduate students.

FAMILY YMCA
465 West Sixth Avenue
Lancaster, Ohio 43130

General Information Nonprofit organization providing fitness, health, social, and recreational opportunities for children, adults, and families. Established in 1920. Number of employees: 62. Number of internship applications received each year: 1.
Internships Available ▶ *1–2 program interns:* responsibilities include assisting with programs in various departments, including aquatics, fitness, gymnastics, non-physical, or office support. Candidates should have ability to work independently, personal interest in the field, self-motivation, strong interpersonal skills, strong leadership ability. Duration is flexible. Position available as unpaid or paid. Open to high school seniors, recent high school graduates, college freshmen, college sophomores, college juniors, college seniors, recent college graduates, graduate students, law students, career changers, individuals reentering the workforce.
Benefits Job counseling, names of contacts, on-the-job training, opportunity to attend seminars/workshops, willing to act as a professional reference, willing to complete paperwork for educational credit, willing to provide letters of recommendation, YMCA membership.
Contact Write or call Maryjane Gard, Program Director. Phone: 740-654-0616. In-person interview required. Applicants must submit a formal organization application, resume, personal reference, high school diploma, academic transcripts, and 1-3 personal references for child care positions. Applications are accepted continuously.

FAMILY YMCA OF LOWER BUCKS COUNTY
601 South Oxford Valley Road
Fairless Hills, Pennsylvania 19030

General Information Association that serves the community by providing facilities to promote healthy bodies, minds, and spirits. Established in 1956. Number of employees: 276. Number of internship applications received each year: 2.
Internships Available ▶ *Aquatics instructors:* responsibilities include teaching aquatics, programming, and lifeguarding. Candidates should have WSI certification. ▶ *Child care assistants:* responsibilities include assisting in the teaching of children and the administration of child care programs. Candidates should have criminal background check/child abuse clearance required. ▶ *Fitness assistants:* responsibilities include assisting the senior physical education director and teaching classes in gymnastics, youth sports, and adult fitness. Candidates should have ability to work with others, personal interest in the field, self-motivation. Duration for all positions is flexible. All positions are unpaid. Open to high school students, high school seniors, recent high school graduates, college freshmen, college sophomores, college juniors, college seniors, recent college graduates, graduate students, law students, career changers, individuals reentering the workforce. International applications accepted.
Benefits Job counseling, names of contacts, opportunity to attend seminars/workshops, possible full-time employment, travel

reimbursement, willing to complete paperwork for educational credit, willing to provide letters of recommendation.
Contact Write or fax Krissi Zigenfus, Physical Director. Fax: 215-946-9329. In-person interview recommended. Applicants must submit a resume, three personal references. Applications are accepted continuously.

FEGS (FEDERATION EMPLOYMENT AND GUIDANCE SERVICE)
80 Vandam Street, 9th Floor
New York, New York 10013

General Information One of the largest not-for-profit human services organizations in the country, providing vocational, educational, and rehabilitation services for clients with physical, psychiatric, and developmental disabilities; provides employment services, vocational rehabilitation, services for high school drop-out prevention, and services for new immigrants. Established in 1934. Number of employees: 2,200. Number of internship applications received each year: 300.
Internships Available ▶ *150–200 interns:* responsibilities include working on special projects as developed and arranged between the intern and the agency. Candidates should have knowledge of field, oral communication skills, organizational skills, personal interest in the field, plan to pursue career in field, strong interpersonal skills, written communication skills. Duration is flexible, preferably 2 semesters. Unpaid. Open to college freshmen, college sophomores, college juniors, college seniors, recent college graduates, graduate students, law students, career changers, individuals reentering the workforce. International applications accepted.
Benefits Formal training, job counseling, on-the-job training, opportunity to attend seminars/workshops, possible full-time employment, willing to act as a professional reference, willing to complete paperwork for educational credit, willing to provide letters of recommendation, extensive training program.
Contact Write or call Ms. Karen Zuckerman, Director of Student Internships. Phone: 212-366-8228. In-person interview required. Applicants must submit a formal organization application, cover letter, resume, two letters of recommendation. Applications are accepted continuously.

FELLOWSHIP OF RECONCILIATION
PO Box 271
Nyack, New York 10960

General Information National interfaith peace and justice organization committed to active nonviolence as a means of personal, social, and political change. Established in 1915. Number of employees: 27. Number of internship applications received each year: 50.
Internships Available ▶ *1 communications intern:* responsibilities include working with the staff of Fellowship, keyboarding, proofreading, researching, and handling correspondence and other assignments. Duration is September to August. Open to persons age 21 and over. ▶ *1 international/interfaith intern:* responsibilities include working with the International/Interfaith Secretary on a range of issues and projects, including organizing national campaigns, coordinating interfaith work camps abroad, and promoting local support for other national efforts. Duration is 1 year. Open to individuals 21 and over. ▶ *1 local group organizing intern:* responsibilities include working with FOR's network of 80 local groups and affiliates, helping in the formation of new groups, preparing informational mailing and resources, organizing gatherings, arranging for speakers, and carrying out other projects to strengthen local FOR organizing. Duration is September to August. Open to persons age 21 and over. ▶ *1 racial/economic justice and youth nonviolence intern:* responsibilities include assisting in outreach to other organizations; coordinating campaigns, the Peacemaker Training Institute, nonviolence education, training programs for adults, and projects related to racial and economic justice issues; managing correspondence; and helping to develop written resources. Dura-

tion is September to August. Open to persons age 21 and over. All positions paid at $650 per month. International applications accepted.

Benefits Free housing, health insurance, opportunity to attend seminars/workshops, willing to act as a professional reference, willing to complete paperwork for educational credit, willing to provide letters of recommendation, 4 weeks vacation and paid holidays.

Contact Write, call, fax, or e-mail Neera Singh, Internship Coordinator. Phone: 914-358-4601 Ext. 31. Fax: 914-358-4924. E-mail: pti@forusa.org. Telephone interview required. Applicants must submit a formal organization application, resume, personal reference. Application deadline: April 1. World Wide Web: http://www.nonviolence.org/for.

FLORENCE CRITTENTON CENTER
234 East Avenue 33
Los Angeles, California 90031-1937

General Information Residential treatment center for abused and neglected teenage girls and teen moms and group home for severely emotionally disturbed adolescents. Provides residents with educational, vocational, parenting, and life skills. Established in 1892. Number of employees: 105. Number of internship applications received each year: 30.

Internships Available ▶ *5–10 cuddlers:* responsibilities include changing, feeding, playing, supervising, and other duties associated with caring for infants and toddlers in our Child Development Center. Candidates should have personal interest in the field, strong interpersonal skills, some knowledge/experience with children preferred. Duration is 2 hours per week for about 3 months. Open to college freshmen, college sophomores, college juniors, college seniors, recent college graduates, graduate students, law students, career changers, individuals reentering the workforce, adults over 18 years of age. ▶ *2–3 readers/storytellers:* responsibilities include reading to residents as well as their infants and toddlers one night a week. Candidates should have oral communication skills, personal interest in the field, self-motivation, strong interpersonal skills, ability to deal with disturbed behavior. Duration is 1 hour per week for approximately 3 months. Open to college freshmen, college sophomores, college juniors, college seniors, recent college graduates, graduate students, law students, career changers, individuals reentering the workforce, adults over 18 years of age. ▶ *20–25 tutors:* responsibilities include working one-on-one with a resident, tutoring on various high school subjects that include math, literacy, English, history, etc. Candidates should have ability to work with others, oral communication skills, personal interest in the field, self-motivation, ability to handle disturbed behavior. Duration is 1 hour per week for approximately 3 months. Open to recent high school graduates, college freshmen, college sophomores, college juniors, college seniors, recent college graduates, graduate students, law students, career changers, individuals reentering the workforce, adults over 18 years of age. ▶ *4–5 workshop coordinators:* responsibilities include conducting workshops/activities with residents on cultural, artistic, athletic, vocational, or clinical topics, varying according to the interests of the volunteer. Candidates should have knowledge of topic/activity. Duration is varied. Open to college freshmen, college sophomores, college juniors, college seniors, recent college graduates, graduate students, law students, career changers, individuals reentering the workforce, adults over 18 years of age. All positions are unpaid. International applications accepted.

Benefits Formal training, on-the-job training, possible full-time employment, willing to act as a professional reference, willing to complete paperwork for educational credit, willing to provide letters of recommendation, experience working with at-risk youth.

Contact Write, call, or fax Kim Knight, Volunteer Services Coordinator, PO Box 31219, Los Angeles, California 90031-1937. Phone: 323-225-4211 Ext. 209. Fax: 323-225-1602. In-person interview required. Applicants must submit a formal organization application, three personal references, TB test, criminal clearance check. Applications are accepted continuously.

FOURTH WORLD MOVEMENT
7600 Willow Hill Drive
Landover, Maryland 20785

General Information International organization which develops partnerships between very poor families and other citizens through civic, educational, and cultural projects. Projects maintained by culturally diverse corps of full-time, long-term volunteers. Established in 1957. Number of employees: 10. Unit of International Movement ATD Fourth World, Pierrelaye, France. Number of internship applications received each year: 100.

Internships Available ▶ *2–6 FWM trainee volunteers:* responsibilities include working on projects emphasizing education, creative expression, and civic involvement undertaken in partnership with families in persistent poverty. Candidates should have ability to work independently, ability to work with others, sense of commitment and community. Duration is 2–20 years. $3,200 to $6,500 per year plus housing and health insurance. Open to those who have completed 3-month FWM internship. ▶ *2–6 FWM volunteer corps interns:* responsibilities include living with and learning from FWM Volunteer Corps members; reading, research, videos, and discussion on poverty issues; manual work to maintain and refurbish FWM Centers; interaction and activities with children and families in poverty. Candidates should have ability to work independently, ability to work with others, patience, willingness to learn, willingness to question what you think you know, sense of humor. Duration is 2–3 months. Unpaid. Open to recent high school graduates, college freshmen, college sophomores, college juniors, college seniors, recent college graduates, graduate students, law students, career changers, individuals reentering the workforce. ▶ *4–12 interns:* responsibilities include living and working with the full-time volunteers at Washington-area center, with shorter stays at the New York center; participating in office and manual work and in programs with poor children and their families; learning the Movement's history and approach through videos, readings, and discussions; planning and evaluating meetings; writing regular reports about their experiences. Candidates should have one year employment or college experience. Duration is 3 months (possible 2 year commitment). Unpaid. Open to U.S. citizens 19 years or older, high school graduates.

Benefits Formal training, free housing, names of contacts, on-the-job training, opportunity to attend seminars/workshops, willing to act as a professional reference, willing to complete paperwork for educational credit, willing to provide letters of recommendation, possibility of long-term commitment internationally, with stipend after internship.

Contact Write or e-mail Jill Cunningham, Internship Coordinator. E-mail: fourthworld@erols.com. No phone calls. In-person interview recommended. Applicants must submit a formal organization application, cover letter, resume, three letters of recommendation, self-addressed stamped envelope (55 cents). Application deadline: May 15 for summer, August 15 for fall, December 15 for spring. Fees: $25. World Wide Web: http://www.atd-fourthworld.org.

FRESH YOUTH INITIATIVES
280 Ft. Washington Avenue #5
New York, New York 10032

General Information Youth service organization. Established in 1993. Number of employees: 8. Number of internship applications received each year: 25.

Internships Available ▶ *5 group leaders:* responsibilities include working directly with client population according to intern's talents, interests, and organizational needs. Candidates should have ability to work independently, analytical skills, computer skills, editing skills, office skills, oral communication skills, personal interest in the field, research skills, self-motivation, strong leadership ability, writing skills. Duration is flexible. Unpaid. Open to recent high school graduates, college freshmen, college sophomores, college juniors, college seniors, recent college graduates, graduate students, career changers, individuals reentering the workforce. International applications accepted.

Fresh Youth Initiatives (continued)

Benefits On-the-job training, opportunity to attend seminars/workshops, willing to act as a professional reference, willing to provide letters of recommendation.

Contact Write, call, fax, or e-mail Rodney M. Fuller, Co-Director. Phone: 212-781-1113. Fax: 212-781-1151. E-mail: freshyi@worldnet.att.net. In-person interview recommended. Applicants must submit a cover letter, resume, personal reference. Applications are accepted continuously.

GEORGIA COUNCIL OF CAMP FIRE BOYS AND GIRLS
100 Edgewood Avenue, NE, Suite 528
Atlanta, Georgia 30303

General Information Organization that provides fun, experiential programs which enable youth to develop into caring, self-directed, and responsible individuals. Established in 1910. Number of employees: 15. Unit of Camp Fire Boys and Girls, Oklahoma City, Oklahoma. Number of internship applications received each year: 10.

Internships Available ▶ *1 administrative assistant:* responsibilities include filing, photocopying, and returning calls and answering requests for information. Candidates should have editing skills, office skills, oral communication skills, strong interpersonal skills, written communication skills. Duration is 5 months. Unpaid. Open to high school seniors, recent high school graduates, college freshmen, college sophomores, college juniors, college seniors, recent college graduates, individuals reentering the workforce. ▶ *1 public relations intern:* responsibilities include writing press releases, designing flyers, and taking photographs. Candidates should have ability to work independently, computer skills, editing skills, writing skills. Duration is 1 semester. Position available as unpaid or paid. Open to college juniors, college seniors, recent college graduates, graduate students, career changers, individuals reentering the workforce. International applications accepted.

Benefits Formal training, names of contacts, on-the-job training, opportunity to attend seminars/workshops, willing to complete paperwork for educational credit, willing to provide letters of recommendation.

Contact Write, call, fax, or e-mail Linda Woodworth, Communications Director. Phone: 404-527-7125 Ext. 135. Fax: 404-527-7139. E-mail: info@campfirega.org. In-person interview recommended. Applicants must submit a cover letter, resume, three writing samples. Applications are accepted continuously. World Wide Web: http://www.campfirega.org.

GIRL SCOUTS OF LIMBERLOST COUNCIL
2135 Spy Run Avenue
Fort Wayne, Indiana 46805

General Information Organization that serves the social and developmental needs of girls ages 5-17. Established in 1958. Number of employees: 23. Unit of Girl Scouts of the USA, New York, New York. Number of internship applications received each year: 2.

Internships Available ▶ *2 youth leaders:* responsibilities include leading troops in central city locations. Candidates should have oral communication skills, personal interest in the field, self-motivation, strong interpersonal skills, strong leadership ability. Duration is 8–12 months. Unpaid. Open to college freshmen, college sophomores, college juniors, college seniors, recent college graduates, graduate students, law students, career changers, individuals reentering the workforce.

Benefits On-the-job training, possible full-time employment, travel reimbursement, willing to act as a professional reference, willing to complete paperwork for educational credit, willing to provide letters of recommendation.

Contact Write, call, or fax Janet Suter, Collaboration Extension and Outreach Director. Phone: 219-422-3417. Fax: 219-422-0084. In-person interview required. Applicants must submit a cover letter, resume, three personal references. Applications are accepted continuously.

GIRL SCOUTS OF PALM GLADES COUNCIL, INC.
2728 Lake Worth Road
Lake Worth, Florida 33461

General Information Organization that strives to instill leadership qualities in young women, develop their self-esteem, to help them to reach their fullest potential and to prepare them to be caring, confident, and resourceful citizens. Established in 1912. Number of employees: 25. Unit of Girl Scouts of the USA, New York, New York. Number of internship applications received each year: 5.

Internships Available ▶ *1 marketing/communications intern:* responsibilities include assisting director of communications with all aspects of public relations, publicity, and promotion media. Candidates should have ability to work independently, college courses in field, oral communication skills, organizational skills, strong interpersonal skills, written communication skills. Duration is one semester minimum. Unpaid. Open to college sophomores, college juniors, college seniors. International applications accepted.

Benefits Job counseling, names of contacts, possible full-time employment, willing to complete paperwork for educational credit, willing to provide letters of recommendation.

Contact Write or fax Lisa Johnson, Director, Marketing and Communications. Fax: 561-547-2169. In-person interview recommended. Applicants must submit a cover letter, resume, writing sample. Applications are accepted continuously. World Wide Web: http://www.palmgladesgirlscouts.org.

GIRL SCOUTS OF SOUTHWESTERN NEW YORK
2661 Horton Road
Jamestown, New York 14701

General Information Organization that provides girls with contemporary, developmental experiences to inspire the highest ideals of character and conduct to foster development into happy, resourceful, and contributing adult women. Established in 1930. Number of employees: 11. Unit of Girl Scouts of the USA, New York, New York. Number of internship applications received each year: 1.

Internships Available ▶ *1–3 outreach managers:* responsibilities include assisting with the delivery of community outreach programs for girls in underserved areas. Candidates should have oral communication skills, organizational skills, personal interest in the field, self-motivation, strong interpersonal skills, strong leadership ability, writing skills, written communication skills. Unpaid. Open to college freshmen, college sophomores, college juniors, college seniors, recent college graduates, graduate students, law students, career changers, individuals reentering the workforce. ▶ *1–2 program assistants:* responsibilities include assisting with the design and delivery of programs for girls ages 5-17. Candidates should have oral communication skills, strong interpersonal skills. Duration is flexible. Unpaid. Open to high school juniors, high school seniors. ▶ *Summer resident camp interns:* responsibilities include administrative, camp direction, unit leading, and a variety of other duties. Candidates should have oral communication skills, organizational skills, personal interest in the field, self-motivation, strong interpersonal skills, strong leadership ability. $6–$9 per hour. Open to high school seniors, recent high school graduates, college freshmen, college sophomores, college juniors, college seniors, recent college graduates, graduate students, law students, career changers. ▶ *1–3 training assistants:* responsibilities include designing and delivering volunteer training to groups of 10-45 adults. Candidates should have oral communication skills, organizational skills, research skills, self-motivation, strong interpersonal skills, strong leadership ability. Unpaid. Open to recent high school graduates, college freshmen, college sophomores, college juniors, college seniors, recent college graduates, graduate students, law students, career changers, individuals reentering the workforce. International applications accepted.

Benefits Names of contacts, opportunity to attend seminars/workshops, possible full-time employment, travel reimbursement, willing to complete paperwork for educational credit, willing to provide letters of recommendation.

Contact Write, call, or fax Lisa Lane-Gniewecki, Executive Director. Phone: 716-665-2225. Fax: 716-661-9704. In-person interview recommended. Applicants must submit a resume. Applications are accepted continuously.

GIRL SCOUTS–RIVERLAND
2710 Quarry Road
LaCrosse, Wisconsin 54601

General Information Organization whose mission is to develop girls ages 5-17 into competent, resourceful, adult citizens. Established in 1912. Number of employees: 26. Unit of Girl Scouts of the USA, New York, New York. Number of internship applications received each year: 1.
Internships Available ▶ *1 MIS intern:* responsibilities include assisting in all MIS operations. Candidates should have ability to work independently, computer skills, oral communication skills, organizational skills, personal interest in the field, strong interpersonal skills. Duration is 2 semesters. $5–$6 per hour. ▶ *1 assistant program director:* responsibilities include managing all program delivery to girls ages 5-17. Candidates should have ability to work independently, editing skills, oral communication skills, organizational skills, self-motivation, strong interpersonal skills, strong leadership ability, written communication skills. Duration is 1–2 semesters. Position available as unpaid or paid. Open to college juniors, recent college graduates. ▶ *1 training assistant:* responsibilities include conducting adult education trainings in the volunteer management system. Candidates should have ability to work independently, computer skills, oral communication skills, organizational skills, self-motivation, strong interpersonal skills, strong leadership ability, written communication skills. Duration is 1–2 semesters. Position available as unpaid or paid. Open to college juniors, recent college graduates. International applications accepted.
Benefits Health insurance, job counseling, names of contacts, opportunity to attend seminars/workshops, possible full-time employment, travel reimbursement, willing to complete paperwork for educational credit, willing to provide letters of recommendation, job lists provided when available.
Contact Write or call Ms. Mary M. Rohrer, Executive Director/CEO. Phone: 608-784-3693. In-person interview recommended. Applications are accepted continuously. World Wide Web: http://www.wi.centuryinter.net/gscouts.

GIRLS INCORPORATED OF GREATER LOWELL
220 Worthen Street
Lowell, Massachusetts 01852

General Information Nonprofit organization that provides after-school programs for girls ages 6–18 in the greater Lowell area. Established in 1945. Number of employees: 10. Affiliate of Girls Incorporated, New York, New York. Number of internship applications received each year: 2.
Internships Available ▶ *1–2 program counselors:* responsibilities include developing and implementing educational, cultural, and recreational programs for girls at least 6 years old. Candidates should have ability to work independently, ability to work with others, personal interest in the field, self-motivation, strong interpersonal skills. Duration is 3–12 months. Unpaid. Open to high school seniors, recent high school graduates, college freshmen, college sophomores, college juniors, college seniors, recent college graduates, graduate students, career changers, individuals reentering the workforce. International applications accepted.
Benefits Formal training, names of contacts, on-the-job training, opportunity to attend seminars/workshops, willing to act as a professional reference, willing to complete paperwork for educational credit, willing to provide letters of recommendation.
Contact Write or call Carol S. Duncan, Executive Director. Phone: 978-458-6529. In-person interview required. Applicants must submit a cover letter, resume. Applications are accepted continuously.

GIRLS INCORPORATED OF METROPOLITAN DALLAS
2040 Empire Central Drive
Dallas, Texas 75235

General Information Nonprofit agency that strives to assist economically disadvantaged girls ages 6-18. Established in 1968. Unit of Girls Incorporated, New York, New York. Number of internship applications received each year: 1.
Internships Available ▶ *1 program assistant:* responsibilities include coordinating programs or Board committees and assisting with executive and management duties. Open to college freshmen, college sophomores, college juniors, college seniors, recent college graduates, graduate students, career changers, individuals reentering the workforce. ▶ *1 public relations assistant:* responsibilities include contacting media, writing press releases, maintaining media list, and assisting with special events. Open to college freshmen, college sophomores, college juniors, college seniors, recent college graduates, graduate students, career changers, individuals reentering the workforce. ▶ *1 special events assistant:* responsibilities include working on major fund-raising event, and working with volunteers, corporate sponsors, and graphic artists/printers. Open to college freshmen, college sophomores, college juniors, college seniors, recent college graduates, graduate students, career changers, individuals reentering the workforce. ▶ *1 volunteer specialist:* responsibilities include interacting with volunteers on all levels, assisting with special events, using computer skills, attending volunteer fairs, mailing information to prospective volunteers. Candidates should have computer skills, office skills, oral communication skills, organizational skills, self-motivation, strong interpersonal skills, written communication skills. Open to college freshmen, college sophomores, college juniors, college seniors, recent college graduates, career changers, individuals reentering the workforce. Duration for all positions is flexible. All positions are unpaid. International applications accepted.
Benefits Names of contacts, opportunity to attend seminars/workshops, possible full-time employment, travel reimbursement, willing to provide letters of recommendation.
Contact Write, call, or fax Lynette Smith, Volunteer Coordinator. Phone: 214-654-4543. Fax: 214-350-8115. In-person interview required. Applicants must submit a formal organization application, cover letter, resume. Applications are accepted continuously.

GOLDEN CRADLE ADOPTION SERVICES
1050 Kings Highway North, Suite 201
Cherry Hill, New Jersey 08034

General Information Private, nonprofit, New Jersey licensed agency that provides adoption and maternity services to men and women faced with an unplanned pregnancy and to infertile couples seeking to build families through adoption. Established in 1980. Number of employees: 12. Number of internship applications received each year: 5.
Internships Available ▶ *1 public relations/marketing intern:* responsibilities include reviewing and revising all marketing materials, and developing short-term and long-range marketing plans for the organization. Candidates should have college courses in field, computer skills, plan to pursue career in field, self-motivation, writing skills. Open to college juniors, college seniors, recent college graduates, graduate students, career changers. ▶ *1–2 research analysts:* responsibilities include gathering and analyzing data to review services and provide improvements for clients. Candidates should have college courses in field, computer skills, research skills, self-motivation, written communication skills. Open to college juniors, college seniors, recent college graduates, graduate students, career changers. ▶ *1–3 social work interns:* responsibilities include handling client case load by following a birthparent or adoptive parent through the adoption process following New Jersey regulations regarding adoption. Candidates should have computer skills, declared college major in field, plan to pursue career in field, strong interpersonal skills, writing skills. Duration for all positions is flexible. All positions are unpaid. International applications accepted.

Golden Cradle Adoption Services (continued)

Benefits Formal training, names of contacts, possible full-time employment, travel reimbursement, willing to complete paperwork for educational credit, willing to provide letters of recommendation.
Contact Write, call, fax, or e-mail Jared N. Rolsky, Executive Director. Phone: 609-667-2229. Fax: 609-667-5437. E-mail: gcadopt@erols.com. In-person interview required. Applications are accepted continuously. World Wide Web: http://www.goldencradle.org.

GRASSROOTS INTERNATIONAL
179 Boylston Street, 4th Floor
Boston, Massachusetts 02130

General Information Organization that provides cash grants and material aid to community organizations for social change in Haiti, Mexico, Eritrea, Brazil, the West Bank, and Gaza strip. Established in 1983. Number of employees: 9. Number of internship applications received each year: 10.
Internships Available ▶ *1 Latin America/Caribbean program assistant:* responsibilities include performing research related to Latin America and the Caribbean. Candidates should have ability to work independently, computer skills, oral communication skills, organizational skills, research skills, writing skills. ▶ *1 communications/media program assistant:* responsibilities include monitoring the international electronic and print media. Candidates should have ability to work independently, analytical skills, computer skills, oral communication skills, organizational skills, research skills. Duration for all positions is 1 semester. All positions are unpaid. Open to college freshmen, college sophomores, college juniors, college seniors, recent college graduates, graduate students, career changers. International applications accepted.
Benefits Formal training, names of contacts, opportunity to attend seminars/workshops, willing to complete paperwork for educational credit, willing to provide letters of recommendation.
Contact Write, call, fax, or e-mail Orson Moon, Administrative Coordinator. Phone: 617-524-1400. Fax: 617-524-5525. E-mail: grassroots@igc.apc.org. In-person interview recommended. Applicants must submit a cover letter, resume, writing sample, 3 character references. Applications are accepted continuously. World Wide Web: http://www.grassrootsonline.org.

GREEN CHIMNEYS CHILDREN'S SERVICES, INC.
Caller Box 719, Doansburg Road
Brewster, New York 10509

General Information Voluntary, nonsectarian multiservice agency and residential treatment center dedicated to basic education for children and daily living skills programs for adults. Established in 1947. Number of employees: 350. Number of internship applications received each year: 30.
Internships Available ▶ *1–6 farm interns:* responsibilities include assisting with farm science, riding, and greenhouse programs; assisting the professional staff with teaching the students while participating in daily chores, daily living skills programs, public programming events, academic studies, horticultural projects, athletics and recreational activities, and other outdoor activities. Candidates should have ability to work independently, experience in the field, oral communication skills, personal interest in the field, strong interpersonal skills, written communication skills. Duration is 3 months minimum; June 1-August 31 for summer, September 1-December 30 for fall, January 3-May 31 for winter/spring. Position available as unpaid or paid. Open to college juniors, college seniors, recent college graduates, graduate students. International applications accepted.
Benefits Free housing, free meals, opportunity to attend seminars/workshops, possible full-time employment, willing to complete paperwork for educational credit, willing to provide letters of recommendation.
Contact Write, call, fax, or e-mail Ms. Jackie Ryan, Intern Coordinator. Phone: 914-279-2995 Ext. 158. Fax: 914-279-2714. E-mail: gchimney@gchimney.org. In-person interview recommended. Applicants must submit a formal organization

application, resume, three personal references. Applications are accepted continuously. World Wide Web: http://www.gchimney.org/~gchimney.

HARDEE COUNTY FAMILY YMCA
610 West Orange Street
Wauchula, Florida 33873

General Information Organization that offers programs to help strengthen local families. Number of employees: 23. Unit of Sarasota Family YMCA, Inc., Sarasota, Florida. Number of internship applications received each year: 2.
Internships Available ▶ *6 child-care workers:* responsibilities include supervising children ages 5-12. Duration is 3 months in summer. minimum wage. Open to high school seniors, recent high school graduates, college freshmen, college sophomores, college juniors, college seniors, recent college graduates, graduate students, law students, career changers, individuals reentering the workforce. International applications accepted.
Benefits Names of contacts, possible full-time employment, willing to complete paperwork for educational credit, willing to provide letters of recommendation.
Contact Write or call Cassandra White, Executive Director. Phone: 941-773-3411. In-person interview required. Applicants must submit a formal organization application, resume, two personal references, 2 professional references, criminal background check required. Applications are accepted continuously.

HARTFORD FOOD SYSTEM
509 Wethersfield Avenue
Hartford, Connecticut 06114

General Information Community food-advocacy organization that develops and operates food programs designed to assist lower-income families. Established in 1978. Number of employees: 7. Number of internship applications received each year: 25.
Internships Available ▶ *1 food policy research assistant:* responsibilities include investigating policies and issues related to food, agriculture, or nutrition. Candidates should have computer skills, oral communication skills, personal interest in the field, self-motivation, writing skills. Duration is 6–12 months. $200–$250 per week. ▶ *4–6 organic farm interns:* responsibilities include general farm duties on a 16-acre community-supported agriculture farm that grows organic produce for and with lower-income urban families. Candidates should have ability to work with others, oral communication skills, personal interest in the field, ability to perform physically hard work. Duration is 2–4 months. $100–$200 per week. Open to college freshmen, college sophomores, college juniors, college seniors, recent college graduates, career changers. International applications accepted.
Benefits Names of contacts, opportunity to attend seminars/workshops, possible full-time employment, travel reimbursement, willing to complete paperwork for educational credit, willing to provide letters of recommendation, stipend, possibility of housing.
Contact Write or call Mr. Mark Winne, Executive Director. Phone: 860-296-9325. In-person interview recommended. Applicants must submit a cover letter, resume, writing sample. Applications are accepted continuously.

HEARIH-CHANDLER FAMILY YMCA OF YMCA OF METROPOLITAN MOBILE, INC.
951 Downtowner Boulevard
Mobile, Alabama 36609

General Information Organization that provides instruction and assistance in the areas of health/wellness, community service, youth, and adult sports, aquatics programming, and child care. Established in 1850. Number of employees: 155. Branch of YMCA of Metropolitan Mobile, Mobile, Alabama. Number of internship applications received each year: 15.
Internships Available ▶ *2–4 administrative interns:* responsibilities include assisting executive director in developing membership appreciation special events, dealing with member service issues, leading customer service training for staff. Candidates

should have oral communication skills, organizational skills, self-motivation, strong interpersonal skills, written communication skills. ▶ *2–4 fitness interns:* responsibilities include assisting fitness director in fitness testing, program implementation, and senior and women's programs. Candidates should have knowledge of field, oral communication skills, self-motivation, strong interpersonal skills, written communication skills. Duration for all positions is as required by intern's school. All positions are unpaid. Open to college freshmen, college sophomores, college juniors, college seniors, recent college graduates, graduate students. International applications accepted.
Benefits On-the-job training, possible full-time employment, willing to act as a professional reference, willing to complete paperwork for educational credit, willing to provide letters of recommendation.
Contact Write or fax Mike Bocuieri, Chief Executive Officer, PO Box 2272, Mobile, Alabama 36652. Fax: 334-438-1174. No phone calls. In-person interview recommended. Applicants must submit a formal organization application, cover letter, resume, personal reference, drug test, criminal background check. Applications are accepted continuously.

HEMLOCK GIRL SCOUT COUNCIL
350 Hale Avenue
Harrisburg, Pennsylvania 17105

General Information Youth services organization that focuses on the growth and development of girls ages 5-17, and the training and support of adults who work with them. Established in 1963. Number of employees: 45. Number of internship applications received each year: 1.
Internships Available ▶ *1–3 field aides:* responsibilities include supporting adults, promoting the delivery of programs, and providing special activities for girls. Duration is flexible. Unpaid. International applications accepted.
Benefits Names of contacts, opportunity to attend seminars/workshops, possible full-time employment, travel reimbursement, willing to complete paperwork for educational credit, willing to provide letters of recommendation.
Contact Write or fax Mr. Randall K. Cline, Executive Director. Fax: 717-234-5097. No phone calls. In-person interview recommended. Applications are accepted continuously. World Wide Web: http://www.hgsc.org.

HERBERT HOOVER BOYS AND GIRLS CLUB
2901 North Grand Avenue
St. Louis, Missouri 63107

General Information Organization that provides educational, sports, personal development, and cultural programs for youth ages 6-18. Established in 1967. Number of employees: 19. Unit of Boys and Girls Club of America, Atlanta, Georgia. Number of internship applications received each year: 40.
Internships Available ▶ *Arts and crafts instructors:* responsibilities include planning and implementing age-appropriate activities in a variety of media with a focus on ethnic art forms. Candidates should have ability to work independently, college courses in field, computer skills, knowledge of field, oral communication skills, organizational skills, self-motivation, strong interpersonal skills. Duration is 3–12 months. $7–$10 per hour. Open to college juniors, college seniors, recent college graduates, graduate students. ▶ *1 computer instructor:* responsibilities include giving computer instruction to youth and assisting in computer club and resource center. Candidates should have ability to work independently, ability to work with others, computer skills, knowledge of field, oral communication skills. Duration is 12 months. $9–$12 per hour. Open to college seniors, recent college graduates, graduate students. ▶ *1–3 tutors:* responsibilities include providing tutoring and homework assistance in resource center. Candidates should have ability to work with others, computer skills, knowledge of field, oral communication skills, strong leadership ability. Duration is 9 months. Position available as unpaid or at $6–$11 per hour. Open to college seniors, recent college graduates, graduate students. ▶ *6–15 youth group counselors:* responsibilities include supervising and planning activities of group summer day camp, providing counseling and guidance as needed to include appropriate age specific programs and support. Candidates should have ability to work independently, college courses in field, organizational skills, plan to pursue career in field, self-motivation, strong leadership ability. Duration is 3 months. $5–$7 per hour. Open to recent high school graduates, college freshmen, college sophomores, college juniors, college seniors, recent college graduates, graduate students, individuals reentering the workforce. International applications accepted.
Benefits Formal training, names of contacts, on-the-job training, possible full-time employment, willing to complete paperwork for educational credit, willing to provide letters of recommendation.
Contact Write, call, or fax Debra M.B. Harris, Unit Director. Phone: 314-652-8300. Fax: 314-652-8007. In-person interview required. Applicants must submit a resume. Application deadline: May 1 for summer, August 1 for fall. World Wide Web: http://www.hhbgc.org.

HILLEL: THE FOUNDATION FOR JEWISH CAMPUS LIFE
1640 Rhode Island Avenue, NW
Washington, District of Columbia 20036

General Information Jewish foundation that promotes religious, social, educational, and recreational student activities, focusing on leadership development. Established in 1923. Number of employees: 55. Number of internship applications received each year: 150.
Internships Available ▶ *1 Arline and David L. Bittker Fellowship:* responsibilities include Jewish identity and awareness programming, networking with Jewish student leaders from around the world, developing leadership programs through conferences, national initiatives, and grants programs; working with students on the Hillel Board of Directors. Candidates should have ability to work independently, oral communication skills, organizational skills, personal interest in the field, plan to pursue career in field, self-motivation, strong interpersonal skills, strong leadership ability, writing skills. Duration is 1 year. $20,000 per year. ▶ *1 Hillel Public Policy Fellow:* responsibilities include overseeing campuses involved in two community service initiatives, training and developing new programs for those students and supervisors, promoting Israel programming and awareness, planning major Jewish public policy conference as well as social justice programming pieces for two other student conferences, and administrating grants for student programs. Candidates should have ability to work independently, computer skills, oral communication skills, organizational skills, personal interest in the field, self-motivation, strong interpersonal skills, strong leadership ability, writing skills. Duration is 1 year. $20,000 per year. ▶ *65–100 Hillel's Steinhardt Jewish Campus Service Corps:* responsibilities include promoting Jewish involvement to previously unaffiliated Jewish students on campus; creating involving programs to encourage Jewish students to interact with other Jews in social, educational, or community service settings; working with Jewish leaders on campus to connect them to their Judaism. Candidates should have ability to work independently, oral communication skills, self-motivation, strong interpersonal skills, strong leadership ability, written communication skills. Duration is 11 months. $18,000–$19,500 per duration of internship. Open to recent college graduates. International applications accepted.
Benefits Formal training, health insurance, names of contacts, on-the-job training, opportunity to attend seminars/workshops, possible full-time employment, willing to act as a professional reference, willing to provide letters of recommendation.
International Internships Available in Montreal, Canada; Quebec, Canada; Toronto, Canada; Jerusalem, Israel; Tel Aviv, Israel.
Contact Write, call, fax, or e-mail Laura Siegel, Assistant Director of Human Resources. Phone: 202-857-6559. Fax: 202-857-6693. E-mail: lsiegel@hillel.org. Telephone interview required. Applicants must submit a formal organization application, resume, academic transcripts, writing sample, two letters of recommendation. Application deadline: March 1. Fees: $25. World Wide Web: http://www.hillel.org.

HOLLYBROOK APARTMENTS–ST. JOSEPH'S VILLA
8000 Brook Road
Richmond, Virginia 23227

General Information Apartment complex that is funded by the federal government and primarily serves persons with physical disabilities. Established in 1980. Number of employees: 2. Number of internship applications received each year: 10.
Internships Available ▶ *1–3 interns:* responsibilities include managing cases, assessing vocations, and coordinating services. Candidates should have ability to work independently, college courses in field, knowledge of field, oral communication skills, self-motivation, strong interpersonal skills, strong leadership ability, written communication skills. Duration is 1 semester. Unpaid. Open to college freshmen, college sophomores, college juniors, college seniors, recent college graduates, graduate students, career changers, individuals reentering the workforce, professionals seeking licensure. International applications accepted.
Benefits Formal training, job counseling, names of contacts, possible full-time employment, willing to complete paperwork for educational credit, willing to provide letters of recommendation.
Contact Write, call, or fax Mary Beth Johnson. Phone: 804-553-3222. Fax: 804-553-3259. In-person interview required. Applicants must submit a formal organization application, cover letter, resume, academic transcripts, three personal references. Applications are accepted continuously.

HOME FREE
3409 Kilmer Lane
Plymouth, Minnesota 55441

General Information Shelter for battered women and their children that provides safe temporary housing, advocacy, information, support, and referrals. Established in 1980. Number of employees: 30. Division of Missions, Inc., Plymouth, Minnesota. Number of internship applications received each year: 10.
Internships Available ▶ *1–3 children's advocates:* responsibilities include providing direct services and recreational activities for children; helping them to express their feelings and needs; assessing children's needs in cooperation with staff and mothers; and modeling non-violent disciplinary options. Candidates should have college courses in field, plan to pursue career in field, self-motivation, strong interpersonal skills. Duration is 100 hours (minimum). Open to high school seniors, recent high school graduates, college freshmen, college sophomores, college juniors, college seniors, recent college graduates, graduate students, career changers, individuals reentering the workforce. ▶ *1–3 community advocacy interns:* responsibilities include providing telephone crisis support to women who have been assaulted by their partners; accompanying to Order for Protection filings and hearings in family court and criminal court; providing other individual and systems advocacy. Candidates should have ability to work independently, analytical skills, computer skills, office skills, oral communication skills, self-motivation, strong interpersonal skills, strong leadership ability, written communication skills. Open to recent high school graduates, college freshmen, college sophomores, college juniors, college seniors, recent college graduates, graduate students, law students, career changers, individuals reentering the workforce. ▶ *1–3 women's advocates:* responsibilities include providing crisis line coverage in the shelter, individual and systems advocacy including the criminal justice system, facilitating cooperative living in the shelter, and providing orientation and support to shelter residents. Candidates should have ability to work independently, office skills, oral communication skills, self-motivation, strong interpersonal skills, strong leadership ability, written communication skills. Duration is 100 hours (minimum). Open to recent high school graduates, college freshmen, college sophomores, college juniors, college seniors, recent college graduates, graduate students, law students, individuals reentering the workforce. All positions are unpaid. International applications accepted.
Benefits Formal training, opportunity to attend seminars/workshops, willing to act as a professional reference, willing to

complete paperwork for educational credit, willing to provide letters of recommendation, reimbursement for work-related mileage.
Contact Write or call Kari Hitchcock, Volunteer Coordinator. Phone: 612-545-7080 Ext. 11. In-person interview required. Applicants must submit a formal organization application, cover letter, resume, three personal references. Applications are accepted continuously.

H.O.M.E. INC.
PO Box 10
Orland, Maine 04472

General Information Corporation dedicated to ""helping people to help themselves" by providing education, an outlet for the sale of crafts, and health care to low-income individuals in addition to job training and housing. Established in 1970. Number of employees: 50. Number of internship applications received each year: 15.
Internships Available ▶ *1 adult volunteer program intern:* responsibilities include clearing land, gathering hay, painting houses, putting up fences, and working on repairs with low-income families. Candidates should have ability to work independently, oral communication skills, self-motivation, strong interpersonal skills, written communication skills. Duration is 6–12 months. Open to high school seniors, recent high school graduates, individuals reentering the workforce. ▶ *2 farm assistants:* responsibilities include working with Cashmere goats, sheep, work horses, and all phases of farm life; traning horses to work as team; gardening; cutting hay; general barn duties. Candidates should have ability to work independently, ability to work with others, experience in the field, knowledge of field, oral communication skills, personal interest in the field, self-motivation, written communication skills, flexibility. Duration is 6–12 months. Open to recent high school graduates, recent college graduates, career changers, individuals reentering the workforce. ▶ *2 house construction interns:* responsibilities include learning construction and carpentry and building homes. Candidates should have ability to work independently, oral communication skills, self-motivation, strong interpersonal skills, willingness to learn and follow instructions. Duration is 3–24 months. Open to recent high school graduates, recent college graduates, career changers, individuals reentering the workforce. ▶ *2 wood harvesting/processing interns:* responsibilities include operating saw and shingle mill and harvesting wood with horses. Candidates should have ability to work independently, oral communication skills, self-motivation, strong interpersonal skills, written communication skills. Duration is 6–24 months. Open to recent high school graduates, individuals reentering the workforce. ▶ *2 woodworking/cabinet makers:* responsibilities include learning cabinetry and woodworking from start to finish. Candidates should have ability to work independently, oral communication skills, self-motivation, strong interpersonal skills, written communication skills. Duration is 6–24 months. Open to recent high school graduates, recent college graduates, career changers, individuals reentering the workforce. All positions are unpaid. International applications accepted.
Benefits Free housing, free meals, opportunity to attend seminars/workshops, possible full-time employment, willing to complete paperwork for educational credit, willing to provide letters of recommendation, possible small stipend after training.
Contact Write, call, or e-mail Fr. Randy Eldridge, OHR, Volunteer Coordinator. Phone: 207-469-7961. E-mail: padre@acadia.net. Applicants must submit a cover letter, resume, two personal references, two letters of recommendation. Application deadline: February 1 for summer, July 1 for fall, November 1 for spring. World Wide Web: http://www.h.o.m.e.coop.net.

THE HOSPITALITY PROGRAM
138 Tremont Street
Boston, Massachusetts 02111

General Information Provider of temporary, affordable accommodations for families of patients receiving treatment in Boston area hospitals. Established in 1983. Number of employees: 8. Number of internship applications received each year: 3.

Internships Available ▶ *1 communications specialist:* responsibilities include working with professional staff in developing communications materials, including brochures and exhibits. ▶ *1 fund-raising specialist:* responsibilities include assisting with and possibly coordinating fund-raising projects. ▶ *1 office specialist:* responsibilities include developing, maintaining, and enhancing databases for mailing lists and assisting with placement process. Candidates for all positions should have ability to work independently, computer skills, office skills, oral communication skills, organizational skills, personal interest in the field, self-motivation, strong interpersonal skills, writing skills. Duration for all positions is flexible. All positions are unpaid. Open to college freshmen, college sophomores, college juniors, college seniors, recent college graduates, graduate students, career changers, individuals reentering the workforce. International applications accepted.

Benefits On-the-job training, willing to act as a professional reference, willing to complete paperwork for educational credit, willing to provide letters of recommendation.

Contact Write, call, or fax Suzanne S. Patterson, Volunteer and Training Coordinator, 138 Tremont Street, Boston, Massachusetts 02111. Phone: 617-482-4338. Fax: 617-482-8431. In-person interview required. Applicants must submit a cover letter, resume, academic transcripts, three personal references. Applications are accepted continuously. World Wide Web: http://www.tiac.net/users/hospprog/.

IMMIGRATION AND REFUGEE SERVICES OF AMERICA
1717 Massachusetts Avenue, NW, Suite 200
Washington, District of Columbia 20036

General Information Nonsectarian network of nonprofit agencies providing direct services and advocacy for migrant individuals and families of all nationalities. Established in 1922. Number of employees: 55. Number of internship applications received each year: 300.

Internships Available ▶ *1 "Hamilton Fish, Jr." Training Center intern:* responsibilities include researching program opportunities related to training professionals who work with the foreign-born; drafting program reports, memoranda and correspondence; identifying Internet resources; attending meetings for training staff; maintaining training database and producing training materials; some clerical support. Candidates should have ability to work independently, computer skills, personal interest in the field, writing skills, interest in education desirable/ability to work well under pressure. $75-$100 monthly stipend. Open to college freshmen, college sophomores, college juniors, college seniors, recent college graduates, graduate students, career changers. ▶ *1 "The Colombia Project" intern:* responsibilities include researching current developments regarding Colombia; assisting in writing, preparation, and mailing of newsletter on Colombia; organizing monthly meetings of Colombia round table; developing and maintaining mailing list of groups/individuals interested in Colombia. Candidates should have ability to work independently, computer skills, personal interest in the field, research skills, writing skills, Spanish language skills preferred, experience with Macintosh computer system. $75-$100 monthly stipend. Open to college freshmen, college sophomores, college juniors, college seniors, recent college graduates, graduate students, career changers. ▶ *1 IRSA's National Refugee Women Project intern:* responsibilities include researching and assisting with recruitment of potential advisory committee members; research of refugee women's reproductive health care, leadership development, cultural orientation, and female circumcision; general administrative support. Candidates should have ability to work independently, computer skills, personal interest in the field, research skills, self-motivation. $75-$100 monthly stipend. Open to college freshmen, college sophomores, college juniors, college seniors, recent college graduates, graduate students, law students, career changers. ▶ *1 International Organization of Migration (IOM) collection department intern:* responsibilities include assisting in database and collection activities for International Organization of Migration Loan Department. Candidates should have computer skills, knowledge of field, background in business management preferred, experience with Paradox database and collection operations helpful. $75-$100 monthly stipend. Open to college juniors, college seniors, recent college graduates, graduate students, career changers. ▶ *6 USCR research interns:* responsibilities include researching current refugee situations for newsletter articles, reports, and annual survey. Areas of research are: Africa, Latin America, Asia, North America, Europe, the former Soviet Union, and the Middle East. Other responsibilities include attending meetings of relevance to region, responding to public inquiries, and some clerical support. Candidates should have ability to work independently, editing skills, research skills, writing skills, computer skills (preferably with Macintosh). $75-$100 monthly stipend. Open to college juniors, college seniors, recent college graduates, graduate students, career changers. ▶ *1 administrative services intern:* responsibilities include assisting in formulating administrative and operational policies and procedures. Candidates should have college courses in field, computer skills, writing skills, interest in learning how to manage a business or nonprofit organization. $75-$100 monthly stipend. Open to college juniors, college seniors, recent college graduates, graduate students, career changers. ▶ *1 communications/media intern:* responsibilities include assisting communications officer in forging links with print, radio, and TV media; assisting media database management; tracking our organization in the news; answering inquiries about our work. Candidates should have ability to work independently, computer skills, oral communication skills, personal interest in the field, writing skills, enthusiasm, positive attitude. $75-$100 monthly stipend. Open to college freshmen, college sophomores, college juniors, college seniors, recent college graduates, graduate students, career changers. ▶ *1 fund-raising/development intern:* responsibilities include researching potential funding sources, assisting direct mailing campaigns, tracking our organization in the news, answering inquiries about our work, attending meetings on behalf of development staff, working with donor management database. Candidates should have ability to work independently, computer skills, personal interest in the field, writing skills, enthusiasm, positive attitude. $75-100 monthly stipend. Open to college freshmen, college sophomores, college juniors, college seniors, recent college graduates, graduate students, career changers. ▶ *1 government liaison intern:* responsibilities include drafting correspondence and making calls related to advocacy efforts; providing written summaries of bills and regulations; drafting informational memos and action alerts to partner agencies; attending Congressional hearings, mark-ups, and briefings; researching legal issues on migration; arranging meetings with Congressional staff; providing clerical support. Candidates should have knowledge of field, personal interest in the field, research skills, writing skills, ability to work well under pressure, graduate-level course work in law (preferred). $75-$100 monthly stipend. Open to college seniors, recent college graduates, graduate students, law students. ▶ *1 program development for direct services to refugees intern:* responsibilities include researching international, national, state, and local program opportunities and policy matters in health care, housing, and other immigrant issues; needs assessment; proposal development; program development; administration and evaluation; general administrative support. Candidates should have computer skills, oral communication skills, personal interest in the field, self-motivation, written communication skills, graduate-level course work in social work (preferred). $75-$100 monthly stipend. Open to college seniors, recent college graduates, graduate students. ▶ *1 refugee mental health program intern:* responsibilities include assisting in preparation of regional mental health conferences, online research, correspondence and editing reports, and general administrative support. Candidates should have computer skills, oral communication skills, personal interest in the field, self-motivation, writing skills. $75-$100 monthly stipend. Open to college freshmen, college sophomores, college juniors, college seniors, recent college graduates, graduate students, career changers. Duration for all positions is 12 weeks minimum. International applications accepted.

Immigration and Refugee Services of America (continued)

Benefits On-the-job training, willing to act as a professional reference, willing to complete paperwork for educational credit, willing to provide letters of recommendation, local travel reimbursement.

Contact Write, call, fax, or e-mail Cathy Chappell-Chambers, Internship Coordinator. Phone: 202-797-2105. Fax: 202-347-2460. E-mail: cchappell@irsa-uscr.org. In-person interview recommended. Applicants must submit a cover letter, resume, two personal references, one 3- to 5-page writing sample. Application deadline: April 15 for summer, August 1 for fall, December 15 for winter/spring. World Wide Web: http://www.refugees.org.

INSTITUTE FOR VICTIMS OF TRAUMA
6801 Market Square Drive
McLean, Virginia 22101

General Information Private, nonprofit organization founded to address the emotional, logistical, and advocacy needs of individuals hurt or affected by political violence. Established in 1987. Number of employees: 2. Unit of World Federation for Mental Health, Alexandria, Virginia. Number of internship applications received each year: 20.

Internships Available ▶ *1 administrative assistant:* responsibilities include business writing and general office maintenance and handling correspondence. Candidates should have ability to work with others, computer skills, personal interest in the field, self-motivation, writing skills, must have own vehicle for transportation. Duration is flexible; 12-15 hours per week. $10–$12 per hour. Open to graduate students, college juniors and seniors with prior internship experience and good references. International applications accepted.

Benefits Names of contacts, opportunity to attend seminars/workshops, willing to complete paperwork for educational credit, willing to provide letters of recommendation, free meals on work days.

Contact Write, fax, or e-mail Dr. Leila F. Dane, Executive Director. Fax: 703-847-0470. E-mail: ivt@micro-neil.com. No phone calls. In-person interview recommended. Applicants must submit a cover letter, resume, academic transcripts, writing sample. Application deadline: May 15 for summer; continuous for other positions. World Wide Web: http://www.micro-neil.com/ivt.

INTERCRISTO
19303 Fremont Avenue North
Seattle, Washington 98133

General Information Christian nonprofit job referral service. Established in 1967. Number of employees: 10. Division of CRISTA MINISTRIES, Seattle, Washington.

Internships Available ▶ *1 telemarketer:* responsibilities include market research and sales work. Candidates should have ability to work independently, ability to work with others, computer skills, oral communication skills, self-motivation. Position available as unpaid or paid. Open to college juniors, college seniors, recent college graduates, graduate students, career changers.

Benefits Possible full-time employment, willing to complete paperwork for educational credit, willing to provide letters of recommendation.

Contact Write or e-mail LisaMarie Hatch, Business and Operations Supervisor. E-mail: lmh@crista.org. In-person interview required. Applicants must submit a formal organization application, three personal references. Applications are accepted continuously. World Wide Web: http://www.jobsinaflash.org.

INTERNATIONAL RESCUE COMMITTEE- ATLANTA RESETTLEMENT OFFICE
4151 Memorial Drive, Suite 201-C
Decatur, Georgia 30032

General Information Nonsecular refugee settlement organization which helps refugees find jobs and accomodation and adjust during their first 90 days in the USA.

Internships Available ▶ *Volunteers:* responsibilities include various tasks working with refugees primarily from Bosnia, Kosovo, Rwanda, and Vietnam. Candidates should have language skills or TOEFL qualification a plus. Duration is flexible. Unpaid. Open to college students or education preferred but not essential.

Contact Write, call, fax, or e-mail Paula McNicholas, Volunteer Coordinator, 4151 Memorial Drive, Suite 201-C, Decatur, Georgia 30032. Phone: 404-292-7731 Ext. 26. Fax: 404-292-5325. E-mail: paula@irc-atlanta.org. Applicants must submit a resume. Applications are accepted continuously. World Wide Web: http://www.irc-atlanta.org.

IOWANA COUNCIL OF CAMP FIRE BOYS AND GIRLS
226 29th Street Drive, SE, Suite E-2
Cedar Rapids, Iowa 52403

General Information Organization that provides informal education opportunities for youth to function as caring, self-directed, responsible individuals and seeks to improve conditions in society that affect youth. Established in 1910. Number of employees: 6. Unit of Camp Fire Boys and Girls, Kansas City, Missouri. Number of internship applications received each year: 1.

Internships Available ▶ *1 alumni search intern:* responsibilities include developing and implementing a plan to locate "lost" Camp Fire alumni in the eastern third of Iowa. Candidates should have ability to work independently, ability to work with others, oral communication skills, organizational skills, self-motivation, written communication skills. Duration is flexible. Open to high school students, high school seniors, recent high school graduates, college freshmen, college sophomores, college juniors, college seniors, recent college graduates, graduate students, law students, career changers, individuals reentering the workforce. ▶ *1 assistant camp director:* responsibilities include assisting with program development and implementation, facility management, marketing, fund-raising, and volunteer management. Candidates should have ability to work independently, oral communication skills, organizational skills, self-motivation, strong interpersonal skills, written communication skills. Duration is 6–12 months. Open to recent high school graduates, college freshmen, college sophomores, college juniors, college seniors, recent college graduates, graduate students, law students, career changers, individuals reentering the workforce. ▶ *1–3 club administrators:* responsibilities include recruiting youth and adult volunteers, providing training, and programming. Candidates should have ability to work independently, organizational skills, self-motivation, strong interpersonal skills, strong leadership ability. Duration is 9–12 months. Open to recent high school graduates, college freshmen, college sophomores, college juniors, college seniors, recent college graduates, graduate students, law students, career changers, individuals reentering the workforce. ▶ *1 grant research intern:* responsibilities include researching grant opportunities for Camp Hitaga and The Iowana Council of Camp Fire; preliminary grant writing. Candidates should have ability to work independently, organizational skills, research skills, self-motivation, written communication skills. Duration is 1–2 semesters. Open to college freshmen, college sophomores, college juniors, college seniors, recent college graduates, graduate students, law students, career changers, individuals reentering the workforce. ▶ *1 marketing (Absolutely Incredible Kid Day) intern:* responsibilities include developing and implementing marketing plan for Absolutely Incredible Kid Day, the 3rd Thursday in March; asking people to write loving letters to children. Candidates should have ability to work independently, organizational skills, self-motivation, strong interpersonal skills, strong leadership ability, written communication skills. Duration is 2–8 months. Open to high school students, high school seniors, recent high school graduates, college freshmen, college sophomores, college juniors, college seniors, recent college graduates, graduate students, law students, career changers, individuals reentering the workforce. ▶ *1 self-reliance administrator:* responsibilities include training self-reliance instructors, scheduling courses, and working with schools. Candidates should have ability to work independently, organizational skills, self-motivation, strong interpersonal skills, strong leadership ability. Duration is 9

months. Open to recent high school graduates, college freshmen, college sophomores, college juniors, college seniors, recent college graduates, graduate students, law students, career changers, individuals reentering the workforce. All positions are unpaid. International applications accepted.
Benefits Names of contacts, possible full-time employment, travel reimbursement, willing to complete paperwork for educational credit, willing to provide letters of recommendation.
Contact Write, call, or fax Dennis Clubb, Executive Director, 226 29th Street Drive, SE Suite E-2, Cedar Rapids, Iowa 52403. Phone: 319-362-8268. Fax: 319-362-7963. In-person interview recommended. Applications are accepted continuously. World Wide Web: http://www.cedar-rapids.net/campfire.

JEWISH FAMILY AND CHILDREN'S SERVICES
1710 Scott Street
San Francisco, California 94115

General Information A multifunction social service and mental health organization that provides multiplicity programs including counseling, homecare, adoptions, and emigrant resettlement. It is the oldest ongoing charity west of the Mississippi. Established in 1850.
Internships Available ▶ *Academic year interns:* responsibilities include working in counseling, homecare, adoptions, or emigrant resettlement. Candidates should have enrollment in a clinical training program. Duration is 1 academic year. Unpaid. Open to 2nd year graduate students or postgraduate students. ▶ *Summer interns:* responsibilities include Jewish communal work. Duration is 10 weeks. $250 per week. Open to Jewish undergraduate students.
Contact Write, call, fax, or e-mail David Reinstein, Internship Coordinator, 1710 Scott Street, San Francisco, California 94115. Phone: 650-591-8991 Ext. 111. Fax: 650-591-1339. E-mail: davidr@jfcs.org. Applicants must submit a cover letter, resume. Application deadline: May 15 for summer, June 30 for academic year. World Wide Web: http://www.jfcs.org.

JOINT ACTION IN COMMUNITY SERVICE (JACS)
3535 Market Street, Suite 12100
Philadelphia, Pennsylvania 19104

General Information Youth service organization that provides support services to students from the Job Corps program. Established in 1967. Number of employees: 4. Branch of Joint Action in Community Service, Washington, District of Columbia. Number of internship applications received each year: 10.
Internships Available ▶ *1–2 client outreach/office assistants:* responsibilities include Contacting former Job Corps students and conducting needs assessments, locating resources for use by staff, and various administrative tasks. Candidates should have ability to work independently, office skills, oral communication skills, self-motivation, strong interpersonal skills, written communication skills. ▶ *2–3 resource center coordinators:* responsibilities include assisting students in the Resource Center (most assistance will be with job searches), conducting needs assessments by phone with former students and researching social services as well as educational, training, and employment opportunities. Candidates should have ability to work independently, computer skills, oral communication skills, self-motivation, strong interpersonal skills, written communication skills. Duration for all positions is 2–12 months. All positions are unpaid. Open to college freshmen, college sophomores, college juniors, college seniors, recent college graduates, graduate students, law students, career changers, individuals reentering the workforce, retirees. International applications accepted.
Benefits Formal training, job counseling, names of contacts, on-the-job training, opportunity to attend seminars/workshops, willing to act as a professional reference, willing to complete paperwork for educational credit, willing to provide letters of recommendation, stipend for travel and meal expenses.
Contact Write, call, fax, or e-mail Eve Barnett, Regional Program Assistant. Phone: 800-782-5227. Fax: 215-596-6335. E-mail: ebarnett@doleta.gov. In-person interview recommended. Applicants must

submit a cover letter, resume, two personal references. Applications are accepted continuously. World Wide Web: http://www.jacsinc.org.

JUVENILE WELFARE BOARD OF PINELLAS COUNTY
6698 68th Avenue North, Suite A
Pinellas Park, Florida 33781-5060

General Information Special taxing district dedicated to children's services which plans, coordinates, and contracts for services, and researches outcomes. Established in 1946. Number of employees: 55. Number of internship applications received each year: 10.
Internships Available ▶ *1–3 research and evaluation center interns:* responsibilities include working as a research assistant. Candidates should have analytical skills, computer skills, editing skills, oral communication skills, organizational skills, personal interest in the field, research skills, self-motivation, strong interpersonal skills, writing skills. Duration is 12 months. $7–$9 per hour. Open to graduate students or responsible undergraduates preferred. International applications accepted.
Benefits Formal training, names of contacts, opportunity to attend seminars/workshops, possible full-time employment, travel reimbursement, willing to complete paperwork for educational credit, willing to provide letters of recommendation.
Contact Write or fax Human Resources. Phone: 727-547-5600. Fax: 727-547-5610. In-person interview required. Cover letter and resume desirable. Applications are accepted continuously.

KIPS BAY BOYS AND GIRLS CLUB
1930 Randall Avenue
Bronx, New York 10473

General Information Club that enhances the quality of life for young people through constructive and structured activities in recreation and skills development. Established in 1915. Number of employees: 80. Number of internship applications received each year: 6.
Internships Available ▶ *1–2 cadet aides:* responsibilities include assisting in the cadet room with children ages 6 to 9, supervising games and reading, and helping with homework. Candidates should have oral communication skills, self-motivation, strong interpersonal skills, strong leadership ability, ability to work well with youth ages 6-9. ▶ *1–2 clerical aides:* responsibilities include assisting at front desk to check-in persons, answering phones, and dispersing information. Candidates should have oral communication skills, self-motivation, strong interpersonal skills, strong leadership ability, written communication skills. Open to college freshmen, college sophomores, college juniors, college seniors. ▶ *1–2 games room aides/recreation aides:* responsibilities include assisting in supervision of the games room. Candidates should have oral communication skills, self-motivation, strong interpersonal skills, strong leadership ability, knowledge of gamesroom games (pool, ping pong, chess, checkers). ▶ *2–3 office aides:* responsibilities include assisting support staff with day-to-day work. Candidates should have computer skills, office skills, oral communication skills, self-motivation, strong interpersonal skills. Open to college juniors, college seniors, recent college graduates. Duration for all positions is October to August. All positions are unpaid. International applications accepted.
Benefits Job counseling, names of contacts, possible full-time employment, willing to complete paperwork for educational credit, willing to provide letters of recommendation.
Contact Write or fax Harold Maldonado, Senior Program Director. Fax: 718-991-2117. In-person interview required. Applicants must submit a resume, personal reference. Applications are accepted continuously.

KOSCIUSKO COMMUNITY YMCA
1401 East Smith Street
Warsaw, Indiana 46580

General Information Organization that provides health, fitness, aquatics, and social services to the community. Established in 1964. Number of employees: 100. Association of YMCA of the USA, Chicago, Illinois.
Internships Available ▶ *1 physical department intern:* responsibilities include organizing classes and programs; marketing; hiring, training, and supervising staff; creating new programs and evaluating current programs; and performing other duties in the physical department. Candidates should have ability to work independently, oral communication skills, organizational skills, self-motivation, strong interpersonal skills, written communication skills. Duration is as needed. Position available as unpaid or paid. Open to college freshmen, college sophomores, college juniors, college seniors, recent college graduates. International applications accepted.
Benefits Formal training, job counseling, names of contacts, opportunity to attend seminars/workshops, possible full-time employment, willing to complete paperwork for educational credit, willing to provide letters of recommendation.
Contact Write, call, or fax Thomas J. Coxey, Director of Health and Physical Education. Phone: 219-269-9622. Fax: 219-269-1396. In-person interview required. Applicants must submit a resume. Applications are accepted continuously.

LACASA/ZACHARIAS CENTER (LAKE COUNTY COUNCIL AGAINST SEXUAL ASSAULT)
4275 Grand Avenue
Gurnee, Illinois 60031

General Information Comprehensive rape crisis center. Established in 1983. Number of employees: 17. Unit of Illinois Coalition Against Sexual Assault (ICASA), Springfield, Illinois. Number of internship applications received each year: 10.
Internships Available ▶ *Clinical interns:* responsibilities include providing client-centered individual and group counseling to non-offending survivors of sexual assault and sexual abuse, ages 3 through adult. Candidates should have college courses in field, experience in the field, oral communication skills, strong interpersonal skills, feminist philosophy. Duration is 10-40 hours per week. Unpaid. Open to graduate students.
Benefits Formal training, on-the-job training, opportunity to attend seminars/workshops, willing to act as a professional reference, willing to complete paperwork for educational credit, willing to provide letters of recommendation.
Contact Call Joanie Dovekas, Director of Clinical Services, 4275 Grand Avenue, Gurnee, Illinois 60031. Phone: 847-244-1187. In-person interview required. Applicants must submit a cover letter, resume, personal reference, successful completion of state-required volunteer training course (40—60 hours). Application deadline: March 1.

LATIN AMERICAN ART RESOURCE PROJECT
7044 Woodville Road
Mt. Airy, Maryland 21771

General Information Development program that teaches poor communities how to make art and artisanry with low-cost local resources. Established in 1994. Number of employees: 6. Number of internship applications received each year: 20.
Internships Available ▶ *1–3 development interns:* responsibilities include working in Honduras or the U.S. combining field work, studio work, and office work. Candidates should have ability to work with others, office skills, organizational skills, personal interest in the field, self-motivation, written communication skills. Open to recent high school graduates, college freshmen, college sophomores, college juniors, college seniors, recent college graduates, graduate students, law students, career changers, individuals reentering the workforce, college graduates preferred. ▶ *1–2 studio interns:* responsibilities include working in Honduras or the U.S. assisting with studio projects in painting and sculpture. Candidates should have ability to work

independently, ability to work with others, personal interest in the field, aptitude for manual skills. Open to recent high school graduates, college freshmen, college sophomores, college juniors, college seniors, recent college graduates, graduate students, law students, career changers, individuals reentering the workforce. Duration for all positions is 3–6 months. All positions are unpaid. International applications accepted.
Benefits Job counseling, names of contacts, on-the-job training, opportunity to attend seminars/workshops, possible full-time employment, willing to act as a professional reference, willing to complete paperwork for educational credit, willing to provide letters of recommendation, tutorials and classes, room and board included in program cost.
International Internships Available in Honduras.
Contact Write, call, fax, or e-mail Mr. William Swetcharnik, Program Director. Phone: 301-831-7286. E-mail: swetcharnik@ hood.edu. In-person interview recommended. Applicants must submit a cover letter, resume, academic transcripts, two personal references, two letters of recommendation, $900 per month participation fee upon acceptance. Applications are accepted continuously. World Wide Web: http://www.hood.edu/academic/art/laarp.

LITTLE BROTHERS–FRIENDS OF THE ELDERLY
355 North Ashland
Chicago, Illinois 60607

General Information National nonprofit voluntary organization committed to relieving isolation and loneliness among the elderly. Established in 1959. Number of employees: 30. Affiliate of International Federation of Little Brothers of the Poor, Paris, France. Number of internship applications received each year: 30.
Internships Available ▶ *1–20 intergenerational visiting program interns:* responsibilities include organizing activities for the elderly, giving daily living assistance, driving, and conducting special summer projects. Candidates should have ability to work independently, college courses in field, knowledge of field, oral communication skills, organizational skills, personal interest in the field, self-motivation, strong interpersonal skills. Duration is 3–9 months. Unpaid. Open to college freshmen, college sophomores, college juniors, college seniors, recent college graduates, graduate students, career changers, individuals reentering the workforce. ▶ *1–2 nonprofit management interns:* responsibilities include undertaking special projects for the Director such as research, evaluation, and planning. Candidates should have ability to work independently, analytical skills, computer skills, editing skills, office skills, oral communication skills, organizational skills, research skills, self-motivation, strong interpersonal skills, written communication skills. Unpaid. Open to college juniors, college seniors, recent college graduates, graduate students, career changers, individuals reentering the workforce. ▶ *1–3 photography interns:* responsibilities include visiting the elderly in their homes, during holiday parties and at special gatherings; photographing the elderly who are visited and/or those who attend the celebrations; taking responsibility for the development of the photographs; identifying and cataloging each shot according to date and whether it is an individual shot or was taken at a Little Brothers event. Candidates should have ability to work independently, oral communication skills, personal interest in the field, self-motivation, strong interpersonal skills. Duration is 3–9 months. Unpaid. Open to college freshmen, college sophomores, college juniors, college seniors, recent college graduates, graduate students, career changers, individuals reentering the workforce. ▶ *1–5 program assistants:* responsibilities include developing and nurturing friendship with diverse elderly individuals and planning and executing various social activities; opportunity for Spanish-speaking student. Candidates should have ability to work independently, knowledge of field, oral communication skills, personal interest in the field, self-motivation, strong interpersonal skills. Duration is 12 months. $600 monthly stipend. Open to college juniors, college seniors, recent college graduates, graduate students, career changers, individuals reentering the workforce. ▶ *1–3 public relations interns:* responsibilities include working in the areas of marketing/public relations, and fund-

raising. Candidates should have ability to work independently, ability to work with others, editing skills, knowledge of field, oral communication skills, personal interest in the field, research skills, self-motivation, writing skills. Duration is 3–12 months. Unpaid. Open to college freshmen, college sophomores, college juniors, college seniors, recent college graduates, graduate students, career changers, individuals reentering the workforce. ▶ *1–2 summer vacation interns:* responsibilities include creating a family atmosphere for elderly, organizing activities, giving daily living assistance, and driving in a country setting. Candidates should have oral communication skills, organizational skills, personal interest in the field, self-motivation, strong interpersonal skills. Duration is June to August (3 months). $150 per week. Open to college freshmen, college sophomores, college juniors, college seniors, recent college graduates, graduate students, career changers, individuals reentering the workforce. International applications accepted.
Benefits Free housing, names of contacts, on-the-job training, opportunity to attend seminars/workshops, possible full-time employment, willing to act as a professional reference, willing to complete paperwork for educational credit, willing to provide letters of recommendation, room and board for summer vacation interns, room for program assistants.
International Internships Available in France; Dublin, Ireland; Acapulco, Mexico.
Contact Write, call, fax, or e-mail Ms. Christine Bertrand, Coordinator of Intergenerational Visiting Program. Phone: 312-455-1000. Fax: 312-455-9674. E-mail: general.chi@littlebrothers.org. In-person interview recommended. Applicants must submit a cover letter, resume, two personal references, two letters of recommendation, 2-3 writing samples for public relations interns. Applications are accepted continuously. World Wide Web: http://www.littlebrothers.org/chicago.

LIVING IN SAFE ALTERNATIVES, INC.—PLAINVILLE GROUP HOME
50 Bank Street
Plainville, Connecticut 06062-2703

General Information Group home setting in a residential community serving the social, emotional, educational and therapeutic needs of abused, abandoned, neglected,and adjudicated adolescent females. Strong focus is on teaching independent living skills. Established in 1972. Number of employees: 17. Division of Living In Safe Alternatives, Inc., Plainville, Connecticut. Number of internship applications received each year: 8.
Internships Available ▶ *1 administrative intern:* responsibilities include assisting program coordinator in developing agency projects, assisting with and observing daily administrative tasks, learning to balance administrative duties with client contact. Candidates should have ability to work independently, computer skills, knowledge of field, research skills, strong interpersonal skills, writing skills. Open to college seniors. ▶ *1 youth work intern:* responsibilities include interaction with and observation of clients, communication with on-duty staff weekly, participation in supervision and one self-directed workshop or group with clients. Candidates should have knowledge of field, oral communication skills, personal interest in the field, self-motivation, strong interpersonal skills, written communication skills. Open to college juniors, college seniors. Duration for all positions is 1 semester. All positions are unpaid.
Benefits Formal training, names of contacts, on-the-job training, opportunity to attend seminars/workshops, possible full-time employment, willing to act as a professional reference, willing to complete paperwork for educational credit, willing to provide letters of recommendation.
Contact Write, call, or fax April E. Morrison, Program Coordinator, 50 Bank Street, Plainville, Connecticut 08062-2703. Phone: 860-747-9930. Fax: 860-793-3221. In-person interview required. Applicants must submit a formal organization application, cover letter, resume, three personal references, letter of recommendation, current physical exam including PPD, police background check. Applications are accepted continuously.

LONG LANE SCHOOL, DEPARTMENT OF CHILDREN AND FAMILIES
PO Box 882
Middletown, Connecticut 06457

General Information Juvenile justice residential treatment facility for youths ages 12–16; provides custody and treatment of juvenile offenders. Established in 1971. Number of employees: 300. Unit of Department of Children and Families, State of Connecticut, Middletown, Connecticut. Number of internship applications received each year: 5.
Internships Available ▶ *2 clinical interns:* responsibilities include supervising counseling and group work. Candidates should have oral communication skills, personal interest in the field, strong interpersonal skills, writing skills. Open to graduate students. ▶ *4 residential interns:* responsibilities include assisting paraprofessional group leader. Candidates should have college courses in field, oral communication skills, personal interest in the field, self-motivation, strong interpersonal skills. Open to college freshmen, college sophomores, college juniors, college seniors, recent college graduates, graduate students. Duration for all positions is flexible. All positions are unpaid.
Benefits Formal training, opportunity to attend seminars/workshops, possible full-time employment, willing to act as a professional reference, willing to complete paperwork for educational credit, willing to provide letters of recommendation.
Contact Write, call, or fax Dr. Patrick Russolillo, Director, Clinical Services. Phone: 860-344-7497. Fax: 860-344-2346. In-person interview required. Applicants must submit a formal organization application, cover letter, resume, personal reference. Applications are accepted continuously.

LUTHERAN SOCIAL SERVICES
4406 Georgia Avenue, NW
Washington, District of Columbia 20011

General Information Multi-faceted social service agency serving the Washington metropolitan area. Established in 1917. Number of employees: 125. Number of internship applications received each year: 8.
Internships Available ▶ *1–2 refugee case aides:* responsibilities include providing direct services to refugee families including airport pick-up, orientation, enrollment in school, application for social and health services, pre-employment training, and English intruction. Candidates should have oral communication skills, personal interest in the field, self-motivation, strong interpersonal skills, cross-cultural sensitivity. Duration is varies; 6 months to 1 year. Open to recent high school graduates, college freshmen, college sophomores, college juniors, college seniors, recent college graduates, career changers, individuals reentering the workforce. ▶ *1 social work aide:* responsibilities include conducting client intakes for emergency assistance, evaluating information to determine needs, making referrals to other agencies, organizing and collaborating with area groups concerned with social needs. Candidates should have ability to work independently, ability to work with others, computer skills, oral communication skills, research skills, written communication skills. Duration is 6 months to 1 year. Open to college freshmen, college sophomores, college juniors, college seniors, career changers. All positions are unpaid. International applications accepted.
Benefits On-the-job training, opportunity to attend seminars/workshops, possible full-time employment, willing to act as a professional reference, willing to complete paperwork for educational credit, willing to provide letters of recommendation.
Contact Write, call, fax, or e-mail Kathy Hadzibajric, Director of Volunteer Services, 4406 Georgia Avenue, NW, Washington, District of Columbia 20011. Phone: 202-723-3000 Ext. 203. Fax: 202-723-3303. E-mail: hadzibajrick@lssnca.org. In-person interview recommended. Applicants must submit a formal organization application, cover letter, resume, three personal references. Applications are accepted continuously. World Wide Web: http://www.lssnca.org/lssnca

LUTHERAN VOLUNTEER CORPS
1226 Vermont Avenue, NW
Washington, District of Columbia 20005

General Information Nonprofit organization that places individuals in full-time volunteer assignments. Placements include: advocy, health, legal, environmental, social services, education, and youth child services. Established in 1979. Number of employees: 81. Unit of Luther Place Memorial Church, Washington, District of Columbia. Number of internship applications received each year: 145.

Internships Available ▶ *80–90 volunteers:* responsibilities include various duties according to position; positions available in nine U.S. cities. Candidates should have ability to work independently, ability to work with others, organizational skills, personal interest in the field, self-motivation, flexibility and maturity. Duration is 1–2 years. $85 monthly stipend. Open to college seniors, recent college graduates, career changers.

Benefits Free housing, free meals, health insurance, names of contacts, on-the-job training, opportunity to attend seminars/workshops, travel reimbursement, willing to act as a professional reference, willing to provide letters of recommendation.

Contact Write, call, fax, or e-mail Dawn Longenecker, Recruitment Coordinator, 1226 Vermont Avenue, Washington, District of Columbia 20005. Phone: 202-387-3222. Fax: 202-667-0037. E-mail: lvc.dc@ecunet.org. Telephone interview required. Applicants must submit a formal organization application, academic transcripts, three personal references, one essay. Application deadline: applications accepted March 1 to June 1 only. World Wide Web: http://www.lvchome.org.

MAINE CENTERS FOR WOMEN, WORK, AND COMMUNITY
Stoddard House, University of Maine at Augusta, 46 University Drive
Augusta, Maine 04330-9410

General Information Program providing a range of comprehensive support, pre-employment, education, training, self-employment, and employment services and resources designed to assist displaced homemakers and single parents in developing marketable skills and in making the transition to economically viable paid employment. Established in 1978. Number of employees: 28. Unit of University of Maine at Augusta, Augusta, Maine. Number of internship applications received each year: 3.

Internships Available ▶ *1–10 interns:* responsibilities include working in program planning and direct service, management information systems assistance, self-employment, workforce literacy, economic and leadership development, and advocacy; may also focus on research and public policies issues relating to women's economic development. Candidates should have ability to work independently, computer skills, knowledge of field, organizational skills, strong interpersonal skills. Duration is 3–12 months. Unpaid. Open to college juniors, college seniors, recent college graduates, graduate students, law students, career changers, individuals reentering the workforce. International applications accepted.

Benefits Job counseling, names of contacts, on-the-job training, opportunity to attend seminars/workshops, willing to complete paperwork for educational credit, willing to provide letters of recommendation, reimbursement for job-related travel expenses.

Contact Write, call, fax, or e-mail Ms. Eloise Vitelli, Associate Director, Stoddard House University of Maine at Augusta, 46 University Drive, Augusta, Maine 04330-9410. Phone: 207-621-3432. Fax: 207-621-3429. E-mail: evitelli@maine.edu. In-person interview required. Applicants must submit a formal organization application, cover letter, resume, 2 personal references or letters of recommendation. Applications are accepted continuously.

MAKE-A-WISH FOUNDATION OF CENTRAL AND SOUTHERN ARIZONA
711 East Northern Avenue
Phoenix, Arizona 85020

General Information Nonprofit organizations that grants wishes to children, age 2½-18, who suffer from life-threatening illnesses.

Internships Available ▶ *1 intern:* responsibilities include assisting staff in all aspects of program administration. Candidates should have ability to work well with children and to interact with volunteers. Duration is flexible. Unpaid. Open to college freshmen, college sophomores, college juniors, college seniors, recent college graduates, graduate students. International applications accepted.

Benefits Names of contacts, on-the-job training, possible full-time employment, willing to complete paperwork for educational credit, willing to provide letters of recommendation, good nonprofit experience.

Contact Write or fax Dr. Judith Bauersfeld, Executive Director, 711 East Northern Avenue, Phoenix, Arizona 85020. Fax: 602-395-0722. Applicants must submit a cover letter, resume. Applications are accepted continuously. World Wide Web: http://www.wish.org/centralaz.

MARYHAVEN CENTER OF HOPE
1010 Route 112
Port Jefferson Station, New York 11776

General Information Not-for-profit, non-sectarian agency committed to serving both children and adults who are mentally and physically challenged by establishing, maintaining, and operating progressive programs and services which are residential, therapeutic, and vocational in nature. The ideal goal is the attainment of normalization in all aspects of life for each individual in its care. Established in 1931. Number of employees: 1,065. Affiliate of Catholic Health Services of Long Island, Melville, New York. Number of internship applications received each year: 40.

Internships Available ▶ *Applied behavior specialist assistants:* responsibilities include following up on behavior plan at sites, reporting to ABS, collecting data, and reporting results. Unpaid. ▶ *Applied behavior specialist interns:* responsibilities include data collection, analysis, and functional assessments. $8 per hour. ▶ *Case managers:* responsibilities include consumer contact; overseeing training in work setting, case notes, and observing consumers during free time activities. Unpaid. ▶ *Home touch coordinators:* responsibilities include tracking goals, billing sheets for monthly services to consumers, petty cash, mileage for staff; liaison between staff, families, and consumers; reviewing documentation for completion and accuracy. Unpaid. ▶ *Personnel specialist interns:* responsibilities include recruiting, clerical tasks, benefit administration, and special projects. $7 per hour. ▶ *Recreational therapist interns:* responsibilities include assisting in running groups, special projects, and outings; needs assessments for individual consumers. Unpaid. ▶ *Social worker interns:* responsibilities include individual sessions, crisis intervention techniques. Unpaid. ▶ *Special education teacher interns:* responsibilities include classroom management; IEP development, leading to special education certification. Unpaid. ▶ *Vocational instructor interns:* responsibilities include assisting in running groups, assisting with Thrift Shop, performing evaluations on consumers, individual assessments for work readiness and skills. Unpaid. ▶ *Vocational rehabilitation counselor interns:* responsibilities include consumer contact, overseeing training in work setting, case notes, and observing consumers during free time activities. Unpaid. Duration for all positions is flexible. International applications accepted.

Benefits Formal training, names of contacts, on-the-job training, opportunity to attend seminars/workshops, possible full-time employment, willing to act as a professional reference, willing to complete paperwork for educational credit, willing to provide letters of recommendation.

Contact Write, call, or fax Elizabeth Schultz, Human Resource Specialist. Phone: 516-474-4120 Ext. 277. Fax: 516-474-0826. In-person interview recommended. Applicants must submit a formal organization application, resume, academic transcripts, personal reference, course curriculum. Applications are accepted continuously.

MASSACHUSETTS SOCIETY OF PREVENTION OF CRUELTY TO CHILDREN–CAPE COD
206 Breed's Hill Road
Hyannis, Massachusetts 02601

General Information Child welfare agency that focuses on the prevention of child abuse and neglect. Established in 1878. Number of employees: 40. Unit of MSPCC, Boston, Massachusetts. Number of internship applications received each year: 5.
Internships Available ▶ *2–3 interns:* responsibilities include providing assistance to home visitors and group leaders, and working with parents and children on developmental and behavioral issues. Candidates should have self-motivation, strong interpersonal skills. Duration is flexible. Open to high school students, high school seniors, recent high school graduates, college freshmen, college sophomores, college juniors, college seniors, recent college graduates, graduate students, law students, career changers, individuals reentering the workforce. ▶ *2–3 social work interns:* responsibilities include visiting homes with families of young children and conducting group and family parenting education. Candidates should have ability to work independently, ability to work with others. Duration is 2 semesters. Open to college juniors, college seniors, recent college graduates, graduate students, career changers, individuals reentering the workforce. All positions are unpaid.
Benefits Formal training, opportunity to attend seminars/workshops, possible full-time employment, travel reimbursement, willing to complete paperwork for educational credit, willing to provide letters of recommendation, group and individual supervisory meetings.
Contact Write, call, or fax Susan Norton, Good Start Director. Phone: 800-272-9722. Fax: 508-790-3988. In-person interview required. Applicants must submit a formal organization application, resume, three personal references, criminal offense record investigation required. Applications are accepted continuously.

MCMAHON SERVICES FOR CHILDREN
305 Seventh Avenue, 9th Floor
New York, New York 10001

General Information Foster care program that provides out-of-home placement services for abused and neglected children and adolescents. Established in 1937. Number of employees: 70. Division of Good Shepherd Services, New York, New York. Number of internship applications received each year: 12.
Internships Available ▶ *3–5 social work assistants:* responsibilities include assisting staff in providing services to children and families, and developing arts and crafts projects. Candidates should have ability to work independently, oral communication skills, personal interest in the field, self-motivation, strong interpersonal skills, written communication skills, valid driver's license, Spanish ability, willingness to do field work, use public transportation, and make inner city home visits. Duration is flexible. Unpaid. Open to college juniors, college seniors, recent college graduates, graduate students.
Benefits Job counseling, opportunity to attend seminars/workshops, travel reimbursement, willing to complete paperwork for educational credit, willing to provide letters of recommendation.
Contact Write, call, or fax Sr. Claire Napoleon, Director of Program Quality. Phone: 212-243-7070 Ext. 237. Fax: 212-243-8085. In-person interview required. Applicants must submit a resume. Application deadline: April 1 for summer.

MEET THE WILDERNESS
PO Box 468
Edwards, Colorado 81632

General Information Nonprofit organization that provides wilderness experiential education to at-risk and underprivileged youth. Established in 1974. Number of employees: 14. Number of internship applications received each year: 4.

Internships Available ▶ *Experiential education guides:* responsibilities include guiding groups of young people on wilderness trips. Candidates should have ability to work independently, experience in the field, knowledge of field, oral communication skills, personal interest in the field, self-motivation, strong interpersonal skills, strong leadership ability. Duration is 2–3 months. Position available as unpaid or paid. Open to college seniors, recent college graduates, graduate students. International applications accepted.
Benefits On-the-job training, willing to act as a professional reference, willing to complete paperwork for educational credit, willing to provide letters of recommendation.
Contact Write or e-mail Tom McCalden, Director, PO Box 468, Edwards, Colorado 81632. E-mail: tmccalden@yahoo.com. No phone calls. Applicants must submit a cover letter, resume. Applications are accepted continuously. World Wide Web: http://www.meetthewilderness.org.

MERCK FAMILY FUND
303 Adams Street
Milton, Massachusetts 02186-4253

General Information Organization committed to the preservation of the environment through protection of eastern ecosystems and sustainable economics, and a concern for socially and economically disadvantaged people, supporting youth, and organizing urban greening projects in Boston, Providence, and New York. Established in 1954. Number of employees: 3. Number of internship applications received each year: 50.
Internships Available ▶ *1–3 grants interns:* responsibilities include evaluating proposals, conducting interviews, preparing summaries, conducting outreach, research, and assisting with office administration; proposals related to sustainable economics, eastern forest ecosystems, urban greening, and youth organizing. Candidates should have oral communication skills, organizational skills, self-motivation, strong interpersonal skills, written communication skills, familiarity with the Foundation's program areas; familiarity with Macintosh computers and Internet research. Duration is 3–8 months. $1200 per month for 4-day work week or $10 per hour for fewer hours. Open to college seniors, recent college graduates, graduate students, law students, career changers. International applications accepted.
Benefits Job counseling, names of contacts, on-the-job training, opportunity to attend seminars/workshops, willing to act as a professional reference, willing to complete paperwork for educational credit, willing to provide letters of recommendation.
Contact Write, fax, or e-mail Susan J. Quass, Fund Administrator. Fax: 617-696-7262. E-mail: merck@merckff.org. No phone calls. Applicants must submit a cover letter, resume, writing sample, list of 3 references. Application deadline: May 1 for summer, August 1 for fall, December 1 for spring. World Wide Web: http://www.merckff.org.

METROPOLITAN YMCA OF THE ORANGES
2 Babcock Place
West Orange, New Jersey 07052

General Information Association that seeks to improve the quality of community life by fostering healthful living, developing responsible leaders and citizens, strengthening the family unit, promoting the quality of all persons, protecting the environment, and uniting community members and community organizations to solve contemporary problems. Established in 1886. Number of employees: 350. Number of internship applications received each year: 10.
Internships Available ▶ *2–3 athletics interns:* responsibilities include developing, teaching, and implementing sports programs. Candidates should have experience in the field, organizational skills, personal interest in the field, strong interpersonal skills, strong leadership ability. Duration is flexible. ▶ *2–3 child care interns:* responsibilities include teaching children ages 6 weeks–5 years. Candidates should have college courses in field, knowledge of field, organizational skills, personal interest in the field, strong interpersonal skills. Duration is flexible. ▶ *2–3 environmental education interns:* responsibilities include developing, teaching,

Metropolitan YMCA of the Oranges (continued)

and implementing programs in environmental education. Candidates should have college courses in field, organizational skills, personal interest in the field, strong interpersonal skills, strong leadership ability. Duration is flexible. ▶ *Marketing/public relations interns:* responsibilities include working directly with Vice President of Marketing and Public Relations to help implement marketing strategies at YMCA branches. Candidates should have ability to work with others, college courses in field, computer skills, editing skills, oral communication skills, writing skills. Duration is 6 months-1 year. All positions available as unpaid or paid. Open to college freshmen, college sophomores, college juniors, college seniors, recent college graduates, graduate students, law students, career changers, individuals reentering the workforce. International applications accepted.

Benefits Names of contacts, opportunity to attend seminars/workshops, possible full-time employment, travel reimbursement, willing to complete paperwork for educational credit, willing to provide letters of recommendation.

Contact Write, call, fax, or e-mail Paula Maliandi, Vice President, Marketing and Public Relations. Phone: 973-325-8881. Fax: 973-325-8771. E-mail: ymcapr@aol.com. In-person interview required. Application deadline: March 1 for summer, October 1 for winter.

METUCHEN-EDISON YMCA
65 High Street
Metuchen, New Jersey 08840

General Information Community-based YMCA that offers membership privileges and programming services to build body, mind, and spirit for all persons in the community. Established in 1921. Number of employees: 250. Number of internship applications received each year: 2.

Internships Available ▶ *2–4 child care classroom teachers:* responsibilities include assisting in day care center, kindergarten class, or pre-school program. Candidates should have oral communication skills, personal interest in the field, strong interpersonal skills, strong leadership ability, written communication skills. Duration is 4 weeks (minimum). Open to high school seniors, recent high school graduates, college freshmen, college sophomores, college juniors, college seniors, recent college graduates, career changers, individuals reentering the workforce. ▶ *1–3 fitness directors:* responsibilities include conducting fitness testing and demonstrating Nautilus, free weight, and cardiorespiratory equipment. Candidates should have knowledge of field, oral communication skills, self-motivation, strong interpersonal skills, strong leadership ability. Duration is flexible. Open to recent high school graduates, college freshmen, college sophomores, college juniors, college seniors, recent college graduates, graduate students, career changers, individuals reentering the workforce. All positions available as unpaid or at $6–$8 per hour. International applications accepted.

Benefits Formal training, names of contacts, on-the-job training, opportunity to attend seminars/workshops, possible full-time employment, travel reimbursement, willing to act as a professional reference, willing to complete paperwork for educational credit, willing to provide letters of recommendation, national YMCA job listings provided.

Contact Write, call, or fax Janice Garbolino, Physical Director. Phone: 732-548-2044. Fax: 732-548-5397. In-person interview required. Applicants must submit a formal organization application, resume, two personal references, criminal background check required. Applications are accepted continuously.

MISSISSIPPI VALLEY GIRL SCOUT COUNCIL
2011 Second Avenue
Rock Island, Illinois 61201

General Information Organization that seeks to inspire girls with the highest ideals of character, conduct, patriotism, and service. Established in 1912. Number of employees: 30. Unit of Girl Scouts of the USA, New York, New York. Number of internship applications received each year: 1.

Internships Available ▶ *1–2 activity center assistants:* responsibilities include working with children K-8 at local schools after

school. Candidates should have knowledge of field, oral communication skills, personal interest in the field, self-motivation, strong interpersonal skills, strong leadership ability. Duration is flexible. $6–$7 per hour. Open to college freshmen, college sophomores, college juniors, college seniors, recent college graduates, career changers, individuals reentering the workforce. ▶ *1 communications specialist:* responsibilities include writing and computerizing monthly and quarterly membership newsletters and coordinating membership requests for further information. Candidates should have ability to work independently, organizational skills, research skills, self-motivation, strong interpersonal skills, written communication skills. Duration is flexible. Position available as unpaid or at $100 per duration of internship. Open to recent high school graduates, college freshmen, college sophomores, college juniors, college seniors. ▶ *1 program intern:* responsibilities include organizing events, researching community organizations. Candidates should have ability to work independently, organizational skills, research skills, self-motivation, strong interpersonal skills, written communication skills. Duration is flexible. Position available as unpaid or at $100 per duration of internship. Open to recent high school graduates, college freshmen, college sophomores, college juniors, college seniors. ▶ *1 social work intern:* responsibilities include researching and implementing programs and designing and coordinating one annual special event. Candidates should have ability to work independently, oral communication skills, self-motivation, strong interpersonal skills, written communication skills. Duration is 10 months. Unpaid. Open to college freshmen, college sophomores, college juniors, college seniors. International applications accepted.

Benefits Formal training, on-the-job training, opportunity to attend seminars/workshops, possible full-time employment, travel reimbursement, willing to complete paperwork for educational credit, willing to provide letters of recommendation.

Contact Write, call, or fax Micki Hankes, Program Manager, 240 Classic Car Court, SW, Suite A, Cedar Rapids, Iowa 52404. Phone: 319-363-8335. Fax: 319-363-1620. In-person interview required. Applicants must submit a formal organization application, cover letter, resume, three personal references. Applications are accepted continuously.

MOHAWK VALLEY COMMUNITY ACTION AGENCY, INC.
207 North James Street
Rome, New York 13440

General Information Community action agency that offers a range of human services programs to benefit low/moderate income families and individuals. Established in 1966. Number of employees: 205. Number of internship applications received each year: 10.

Internships Available ▶ *1–2 public information interns:* responsibilities include working with area news organizations to promote the agency and to educate the public about the various programs and services offered. Candidates should have editing skills, knowledge of field, oral communication skills, research skills, writing skills. Duration is 6–12 months. Unpaid. Open to recent high school graduates, college freshmen, college sophomores, college juniors, college seniors, recent college graduates. International applications accepted.

Benefits Names of contacts, possible full-time employment, travel reimbursement, willing to complete paperwork for educational credit, willing to provide letters of recommendation.

Contact Write, call, or fax Richard E. Weltz, Assistant to Executive Director. Phone: 315-339-5640. Fax: 315-339-2981. In-person interview required. Applicants must submit a formal organization application, resume. Applications are accepted continuously.

MORRIS AREA GIRL SCOUT COUNCIL
1579 Sussex Turnpike
Randolph, New Jersey 07869

General Information Agency that recruits and retains girls and adults into the Girl Scouting organization and provides fun and interesting programs so that girls can become happy, resourceful citizens. Established in 1912. Number of employees: 15. Unit of Girl Scouts of the USA, New York, New York.

Internships Available ▶ *1 clerical aide:* responsibilities include collating and using computer and risograph. Candidates should have ability to work with others, computer skills, office skills, organizational skills, self-motivation, written communication skills. Paid. Open to high school seniors, recent high school graduates, college freshmen, college sophomores, college juniors, college seniors, recent college graduates, individuals reentering the workforce. ▶ *2 field aides:* responsibilities include organizing troops, orienting leaders, and giving support to volunteers. Candidates should have oral communication skills, self-motivation, strong interpersonal skills, strong leadership ability, written communication skills. Paid. Open to college juniors, college seniors, recent college graduates, individuals reentering the workforce. ▶ *1 fund development intern:* responsibilities include researching funding sources and writing proposals. Candidates should have ability to work independently, oral communication skills, organizational skills, strong interpersonal skills, writing skills, written communication skills. Paid. Open to college juniors, college seniors, recent college graduates, individuals reentering the workforce. ▶ *1 special needs aide:* responsibilities include planning programs and conducting meetings for the hearing impaired, physically impaired, and emotionally disturbed. Candidates should have ability to work independently, oral communication skills, organizational skills, personal interest in the field, strong interpersonal skills. Paid. Open to college juniors, college seniors, recent college graduates, graduate students, career changers. Duration for all positions is 3–10 months. International applications accepted.

Benefits Formal training, on-the-job training, possible full-time employment, willing to complete paperwork for educational credit, willing to provide letters of recommendation.

Contact Write, call, fax, or e-mail Martha Krall, Membership Services Director. Phone: 973-927-7722. Fax: 973-927-7683. E-mail: gsboard@magsc.org. In-person interview required. Applicants must submit a resume. Applications are accepted continuously. World Wide Web: http://magsc.org.

MULTIFAITH AIDS PROJECT (MAPS)
1729 Harvard Avenue
Seattle, Washington 98122

General Information Multifaith agency that provides group housing to low income and homeless people with AIDS who are capable of independent living. Established in 1988. Number of employees: 11. Unit of Multifaith Works, Seattle, Washington. Number of internship applications received each year: 10.

Internships Available ▶ *1 short-term intern:* responsibilities include assisting House Manager and office staff. Duration is 2–3 months. Unpaid. ▶ *1 volunteer program coordinator:* responsibilities include volunteer placement, volunteer group projects coordination, volunteer maintenance, Ravenna House coordinator, tracking volunteer hours/projects, administrative duties, and recruitment. Candidates should have ability to work independently, computer skills, oral communication skills, strong interpersonal skills, ability to work comfortably in a non-proselytizing multifaith environment. Duration is 1 year. $10,000 to $15,000 per internship. International applications accepted.

Benefits Formal training, health insurance, job counseling, names of contacts, opportunity to attend seminars/workshops, willing to complete paperwork for educational credit, willing to provide letters of recommendation, assistance with resume preparation.

Contact Write or call Volunteer Program Director. Phone: 206-324-2216. In-person interview recommended. Applicants must submit a cover letter, resume. Application deadline: March 1 for fall.

MY SISTER'S PLACE
PO Box 29596
Washington, District of Columbia 20017

General Information Temporary shelter for battered women and their children; services include children's programs, a 24-hour hotline, support groups, transitional housing, financial assistance, community education, public relations, and administration. Established in 1979. Number of employees: 14. Number of internship applications received each year: 25.

Internships Available ▶ *1–2 SOS center assistants:* responsibilities include supervising children, screening potential clients over the phone, assisting with case management, accompanying clients to court, assisting with support groups, and performing administrative work. Candidates should have college courses in field, knowledge of field, office skills, oral communication skills, personal interest in the field, plan to pursue career in field, self-motivation, strong interpersonal skills, written communication skills. Duration is open. Open to recent high school graduates, college freshmen, college sophomores, college juniors, college seniors, recent college graduates, graduate students, law students, career changers, individuals reentering the workforce. ▶ *1–2 administration interns:* responsibilities include providing general administrative help. Candidates should have ability to work independently, ability to work with others, office skills, self-motivation. Duration is flexible. Open to recent high school graduates, college freshmen, college sophomores, college juniors, college seniors, recent college graduates, graduate students, law students, career changers, individuals reentering the workforce. ▶ *1–2 children's program interns:* responsibilities include assisting in children's program. Candidates should have personal interest in the field, self-motivation, strong interpersonal skills. Open to recent high school graduates, college freshmen, college sophomores, college juniors, college seniors, recent college graduates, graduate students, law students, career changers, individuals reentering the workforce. ▶ *1–2 development and fundraising assistants:* responsibilities include assisting in drafting grant proposals, program development, organizing events, and doing some administrative work, such as data entry. Candidates should have ability to work independently, analytical skills, computer skills, editing skills, office skills, oral communication skills, organizational skills, personal interest in the field, research skills, self-motivation, strong interpersonal skills, writing skills. Duration is open. Open to recent high school graduates, college freshmen, college sophomores, college juniors, college seniors, graduate students, law students, career changers. ▶ *1–2 employment and housing interns:* responsibilities include assisting agency, working directly with residents, and developing resources. Duration is flexible. Open to recent high school graduates, college freshmen, college sophomores, college juniors, college seniors, recent college graduates, graduate students, law students, career changers, individuals reentering the workforce. ▶ *1–5 hotline interns:* responsibilities include answering hotline, assisting residents, and crisis counseling. Candidates should have ability to work independently, ability to work with others, oral communication skills, personal interest in the field, self-motivation. Open to recent high school graduates, college freshmen, college sophomores, college juniors, college seniors, recent college graduates, graduate students, law students, career changers, individuals reentering the workforce. ▶ *1–2 public relations interns:* responsibilities include assisting with community education, events, public speaking, newsletter, governmental research, and public relations. Candidates should have ability to work independently, computer skills, editing skills, office skills, oral communication skills, organizational skills, personal interest in the field, research skills, self-motivation, strong interpersonal skills, writing skills. Duration is flexible. Open to recent high school graduates, college freshmen, college sophomores, college juniors, college seniors, recent college graduates, graduate students, law students, career changers, individuals reentering the workforce. ▶ *1–2 women's advocacy interns:* responsibilities include assisting with direct services to residents and coordinating resources. Candidates should have oral communication skills, plan to pursue career in field, self-motivation, strong interpersonal skills, written communication skills. Duration is flexible. Open to recent high school graduates, college freshmen, college sophomores, college juniors, college seniors, recent college graduates, graduate students, law students, career changers, individuals reentering the workforce. All positions are unpaid.

Benefits Formal training, job counseling, names of contacts, opportunity to attend seminars/workshops, possible full-time

My Sister's Place (continued)

employment, willing to complete paperwork for educational credit, willing to provide letters of recommendation, training in crisis counseling.
Contact Write, call, or fax Ms. Alena Biagas, Director, Volunteer Program. Phone: 202-529-5261. Fax: 202-529-5984. Telephone interview required. Applicants must submit a cover letter, resume. Application deadline: May 15 for summer, August 1 for fall, December 15 for winter.

NATIONAL SPORTS CENTER FOR THE DISABLED
677 Winter Park Drive, PO Box 1290
Winter Park, Colorado 80482

General Information Provides mountain recreational services to children and adults with disabilities. Established in 1970. Number of employees: 54. Unit of Winter Park Recreation Association, Winter Park, Colorado. Number of internship applications received each year: 30.
Internships Available ▶ *5–6 summer instructors:* responsibilities include assessing, planning, implementing, leading, and documenting a wide variety of outdoor recreation activities. Candidates should have college courses in field, knowledge of field, organizational skills, strong interpersonal skills, strong leadership ability. Duration is 3 months. ▶ *5 winter instructors:* responsibilities include assessing and evaluating disabled students, teaching skiing one-on-one, assisting with adaptive equipment lab, administering a weekly program, and assisting with special events and projects. Candidates should have ability to work independently, college courses in field, knowledge of field, organizational skills, strong interpersonal skills. Duration is 1–20 weeks. All positions are unpaid. Open to college juniors, graduate students, career changers. International applications accepted.
Benefits Names of contacts, opportunity to attend seminars/workshops, possible full-time employment, willing to complete paperwork for educational credit, willing to provide letters of recommendation, season pass to resort, uniform, half-price food at the cafeteria, free transportation, eligibility for employee housing at reasonable cost.
Contact Write, call, fax, or e-mail Ms. Georgianne Glass Dominguez, CTRS Operations Manager, Intern Supervisor. Phone: 970-726-1542. Fax: 970-726-4112. E-mail: jbuch@csn.net. In-person interview recommended. Applicants must submit a formal organization application, cover letter, resume. Application deadline: March 1 for summer, August 1 for winter. World Wide Web: http://www.nscd.org/nscd.

NATIONAL STUDENT CAMPAIGN AGAINST HUNGER AND HOMELESSNESS
11965 Venice Boulevard, Suite 408
Los Angeles, California 90066

General Information Coalition of student and community members who are working to end hunger and homelessness through education, service, and organizing; trains students to create or improve service programs, promotes campus and community collaborations, and initiates programs to fight poverty. Number of internship applications received each year: 50.
Internships Available ▶ *2 National Conference interns:* responsibilities include helping to coordinate the Outreach Program and organizing the annual national student conference. Duration is flexible; at least one semester. ▶ *2 food salvage interns:* responsibilities include developing food salvage programs that ensure unused high school and college campus cafeteria food will go to those members of the local community who are in need of it. Duration is flexible; at least one semester. ▶ *2 publication interns:* responsibilities include updating project manuals and developing a series of fact sheets on hunger and homelessness. Duration is flexible; at least one semester. ▶ *2 spring cleanup interns:* responsibilities include publicizing community service work-a-thon to campuses across the country and coordinating fund-raising efforts for the cleanup. Duration is flexible (at least one semester). All positions are unpaid. Open to high school seniors, recent high school graduates, college freshmen, college sophomores, college juniors, college seniors, recent col-

lege graduates, graduate students, career changers, individuals reentering the workforce. International applications accepted.
Benefits Willing to complete paperwork for educational credit, opportunity for meaningful project experience, chance to make a difference in lives of others.
Contact Call or e-mail Julie Miles, Executive Director. Phone: 800-664-8647 Ext. 323. E-mail: nscah@aol.com. In-person interview recommended. Applicants must submit a cover letter, resume. Applications are accepted continuously. World Wide Web: http://www.pirg.org/nscahh.

NCO YOUTH AND FAMILY SERVICES
1305 West Oswego Road
Naperville, Illinois 60540

General Information Licensed child welfare agency providing individual, family, and group counseling; prevention services; crisis programs for runaways; and boys group home. Established in 1971. Number of employees: 17. Number of internship applications received each year: 25.
Internships Available ▶ *1–3 counselor masters:* responsibilities include providing individual, family, and group counseling. Candidates should have ability to work independently, analytical skills, college degree in related field, oral communication skills, strong interpersonal skills, written communication skills. Duration is 9 months (fall to spring). Open to graduate students. ▶ *1–3 prevention interns:* responsibilities include working with other agencies on prevention programs for youths. Candidates should have ability to work independently, declared college major in field, oral communication skills, strong interpersonal skills, strong leadership ability. Duration is flexible. Open to college seniors, recent college graduates. ▶ *2 youth workers:* responsibilities include working on activities with shelter residents. Candidates should have ability to work independently, declared college major in field, oral communication skills, strong interpersonal skills, strong leadership ability. Duration is flexible. Open to college seniors. All positions are unpaid.
Benefits Names of contacts, on-the-job training, opportunity to attend seminars/workshops, possible full-time employment, willing to act as a professional reference, willing to complete paperwork for educational credit, willing to provide letters of recommendation.
Contact Write, call, or fax Ms. Beverly Garrett, Executive Director, 1305 West Oswego Road, Naperville, Illinois 60540. Phone: 630-961-2992. Fax: 630-961-7251. In-person interview required. Applicants must submit a cover letter, resume, three personal references. Application deadline: March 1 for fall counselor masters positions.

NEW HAVEN BOYS AND GIRLS CLUB
253 Columbus Avenue
New Haven, Connecticut 06519

General Information Private nonprofit organization that offers membership, recreation, and certain social services to youths ages 5-19. Established in 1871. Number of employees: 8. Unit of Boys and Girls Club of America, Atlanta, Georgia. Number of internship applications received each year: 4.
Internships Available ▶ *Interns:* responsibilities include working with group clubs, specialty grants, case management, athletics, and social recreation programs. Candidates should have ability to work with others, experience in the field, self-motivation, strong interpersonal skills. Duration is 1 year. $400 to $450 per week (summer). Open to college juniors, college seniors, recent college graduates, graduate students, career changers, individuals of at least 21 years of age. ▶ *1–2 summer camp senior counselors:* responsibilities include handling a group of 30 to 35 youngsters (age range 5—12 years), following planned activities calendar, planning/implementing specialty activities, attendance taking, and conferences with parents when necessary. Candidates should have college courses in field, oral communication skills, self-motivation, strong interpersonal skills, strong leadership ability. Duration is June 26 to August (2 months). $400–$450 per week. Open to college sophomores, college juniors, college seniors, recent college graduates. International applications accepted.

Benefits Names of contacts, willing to complete paperwork for educational credit, willing to provide letters of recommendation. **Contact** Write Jean M. Sheeley, Executive Director. No phone calls. In-person interview required. Applicants must submit a cover letter, resume. Applications are accepted continuously.

NEW HORIZONS FOR COMMUNITY-BOUND INDIVIDUALS, INC.
1340 Southeast 9th Avenue
Hialeah, Florida 33010

General Information Nonprofit organization serving adults with mental retardation by providing recreational, vocational, and medical assistance with in a residential setting.
Internships Available ▶ *Volunteers:* responsibilities include working on adminstration, direct care, accounts, social work, or art therapy (dependent on the volunteers interests and skills). Duration is flexible. Unpaid. Open to anyone interested.
Benefits Possible full-time employment, liability insurance.
Contact Write, call, fax, or e-mail Ed Aldama, Executive Director, 1340 SE 9th Avenue, Hialeah, Florida 33010. Phone: 305-887-1535. Fax: 305-887-4948. E-mail: nuhorizons@earthlink.net. Applicants must submit a resume, personal reference. Applications are accepted continuously. World Wide Web: http://www.nuhorizons.org.

OLD FIRST REFORMED CHURCH
4th and Race Streets
Philadelphia, Pennsylvania 19106

General Information Church with strong community outreach component, including homeless shelter, summer day camp, job program for teenagers, youth hostel, and afterschool program. Established in 1727. Number of employees: 4. Unit of United Church of Christ, Cleveland, Ohio. Number of internship applications received each year: 15.
Internships Available ▶ *5 summer staff interns:* responsibilities include staffing summer day camp or teen jobs program, as well as rotating duty for nightly youth hostel. Candidates should have ability to work with others, oral communication skills, self-motivation, strong interpersonal skills, strong leadership ability, strong ability to work with children. Duration is 2 months. Open to recent high school graduates, college freshmen, college sophomores, college juniors, college seniors, recent college graduates, graduate students, career changers, individuals reentering the workforce. ▶ *1 volunteer:* responsibilities include working with homeless shelter, youth groups, after school childcare program, youth hostel, summer day camp and youth jobs program; generally serving as welcoming presence for inclusive church community. Candidates should have ability to work independently, computer skills, editing skills, office skills, oral communication skills, organizational skills, personal interest in the field, self-motivation, strong interpersonal skills, strong leadership ability, writing skills. Duration is 1 year. Open to college freshmen, college sophomores, college juniors, college seniors, recent college graduates, graduate students, career changers, individuals reentering the workforce. All positions paid at $125 per week. International applications accepted.
Benefits Free housing, job counseling, names of contacts, on-the-job training, opportunity to attend seminars/workshops, willing to act as a professional reference, willing to complete paperwork for educational credit, willing to provide letters of recommendation, catastrophic insurance, free meals for summer interns.
Contact Write, call, or fax Julie Steiner, Program Director. Phone: 215-922-4566. Fax: 215-922-6366. In-person interview recommended. Applicants must submit a formal organization application, cover letter, resume, three personal references, additional application to the United Church of Christ Office of Voluntary Service. Applications are accepted continuously.

OLIVET BOYS AND GIRLS CLUB
1161 Pershing Boulevard
Reading, Pennsylvania 19611

General Information Youth service agency that provides recreation, education, and guidance programs for boys and girls ages 6-18. Established in 1898. Number of employees: 107. Unit of Boys and Girls Club of America, Atlanta, Georgia. Number of internship applications received each year: 1.
Internships Available ▶ *1–3 drug and alcohol education assistants:* responsibilities include assisting with drug and alcohol education programs at the club and in outreach programs, assisting in HIV-AIDS education programs and individual guidance programs at seasonal retreats and at week-long residential camps. Open to college freshmen, college sophomores, college juniors, college seniors. ▶ *1–4 education assistants:* responsibilities include assisting with the planning and operation of homework centers, tutoring and publicizing the center, working with literacy programs, and expanding current computer programs. Candidates should have ability to work with others, computer skills, written communication skills. Open to college freshmen, college sophomores, college juniors, college seniors, recent college graduates, graduate students. ▶ *1–3 physical education assistants:* responsibilities include assisting with the planning and implementation of physical education activities for the facilities including gym and fitness rooms and supervising and maintaining safety levels of all program equipment. Open to college freshmen, college sophomores, college juniors, college seniors. Duration for all positions is 10 weeks. All positions available as unpaid or paid.
Benefits Formal training, names of contacts, opportunity to attend seminars/workshops, possible full-time employment, willing to complete paperwork for educational credit, willing to provide letters of recommendation.
Contact Write Richard G. DeGroote, Assistant Executive Director. In-person interview required. Applicants must submit a resume, letter of recommendation. Applications are accepted continuously.

OVERSEAS SERVICE CORPS OF THE YMCA
101 North Wacker Drive
Chicago, Illinois 60606

General Information Community service organization with local associations worldwide. Established in 1974. Number of employees: 25. Unit of YMCA of the USA, Chicago, Illinois. Number of internship applications received each year: 75.
Internships Available ▶ *25–30 English teachers:* responsibilities include teaching English in a community-based YMCA in Taiwan. Candidates should have knowledge of field, oral communication skills, personal interest in the field, strong interpersonal skills, written communication skills, willingness to live in another culture for 1 year. Duration is 1 year. NT$16,000-$20,000 per month. Open to recent college graduates, graduate students, law students, career changers.
Benefits Free housing, health insurance, names of contacts, possible full-time employment, willing to provide letters of recommendation, orientations in Seattle and Taiwan, return airfare, paid vacation, bonus after year of teaching.
International Internships Available in Taiwan.
Contact Write, call, fax, or e-mail Jann Sterling, Program Assistant. Phone: 312-269-1167. Fax: 312-977-0884. E-mail: jsterling@ymcausa.org. In-person interview required. Applicants must submit a formal organization application, cover letter, academic transcripts, three letters of recommendation. Application deadline: April 15 for fall placement. Fees: $50.

OXFAM AMERICA
26 West Street
Boston, Massachusetts 02111

General Information Nonprofit international agency that funds self-help development and disaster relief projects in Africa, Asia, and the Americas, also produces and distributes educational materials for people in the U.S. on issues of hunger and sustain-

Oxfam America *(continued)*

able development. Established in 1970. Number of employees: 65. Number of internship applications received each year: 1,000.
Internships Available ▶ *30 interns/volunteers:* responsibilities include providing clerical support, computer-based tasks, writing project summaries, and helping with educational campaigns depending on the availability of special projects; no overseas assignments; working in what is essentially an office environment. For more information, e-mail fast@oxfamamerica.org or call 1-800-597-FAST. Candidates should have analytical skills, computer skills, editing skills, office skills, organizational skills, research skills, writing skills, evidence of interest in issues of poverty and hunger, experience or involvement in community or campus events that educate around these issues (preferred). Duration is flexible. Unpaid. Open to high school students, high school seniors, recent high school graduates, college freshmen, college sophomores, college juniors, college seniors, recent college graduates, graduate students, law students, career changers, individuals reentering the workforce. International applications accepted.
Benefits Opportunity to attend seminars/workshops, willing to complete paperwork for educational credit, willing to provide letters of recommendation, oxfam is not able to fund internships or travel, and does not offer priority to volunteers in getting a job with the organization.
Contact Write, call, or e-mail Ms. Diana Hughes, Coordinator of the Volunteer and Intern Program. Phone: 617-728-2468. E-mail: dhughes@oxfamamerica.org. In-person interview recommended. Applicants must submit a cover letter, resume. Applications are accepted continuously. World Wide Web: http://www.oxfamamerica.org.

PATHFINDERS
1614 East Kane Place
Milwaukee, Wisconsin 53202

General Information Organization that provides short-term crisis intervention, counseling, and shelter programs for adolescents ages 11-17. Established in 1970. Number of employees: 30. Unit of The Counseling Center of Milwaukee, Inc., Milwaukee, Wisconsin. Number of internship applications received each year: 30.
Internships Available ▶ *1–20 assistant advocates:* responsibilities include providing direct one-on-one contact with teenage clients, telephone crisis counseling, facilitating groups, performing intake assessments, and general management tasks. Candidates should have ability to work independently, ability to work with others, oral communication skills, personal interest in the field, self-motivation, written communication skills. Duration is 4 months. Open to recent high school graduates, college freshmen, college sophomores, college juniors, college seniors, career changers, individuals reentering the workforce. ▶ *1–4 graduate student therapist interns:* responsibilities include providing direct one-on-one therapy with teenage clients and their families. Candidates should have ability to work independently, oral communication skills, personal interest in the field, strong interpersonal skills, written communication skills. Duration is 1–2 semesters. Open to graduate students. ▶ *1–6 peer advocates:* responsibilities include providing direct one-on-one contact with teenage clients, positive peer role modeling, facilitating groups, and telephone crisis counseling. Candidates should have ability to work independently, oral communication skills, self-motivation, strong interpersonal skills, written communication skills. Duration is 3 months. Open to high school students, high school seniors. All positions are unpaid. International applications accepted.
Benefits Formal training, free meals, names of contacts, opportunity to attend seminars/workshops, possible full-time employment, willing to act as a professional reference, willing to complete paperwork for educational credit, willing to provide letters of recommendation.
Contact Write, call, or fax Lisa Gumm, Program Assistant. Phone: 414-271-1560. Fax: 414-271-1831. In-person interview required. Applicants must submit a formal organization application, two personal references. Application deadline: January 9 for spring, May 15 for summer, August 21 for winter.

PENN LAUREL GIRL SCOUT COUNCIL
1600 Mount Zion Road, PO Box 20159
York, Pennsylvania 17402-0140

General Information Organization that inspires girls with the highest ideals of character, conduct, patriotism, and service to become happy and resourceful citizens. Established in 1961. Number of employees: 50. Unit of Girl Scouts of the USA, New York, New York. Number of internship applications received each year: 250.
Internships Available ▶ *2 business managers:* responsibilities include performing accounting, purchasing, store sales, and marketing functions. Candidates should have ability to work with others, college courses in field, knowledge of field, office skills, organizational skills, self-motivation. $1,800–$2,200 per duration of internship. Open to college sophomores, college juniors, college seniors, recent college graduates. ▶ *30–45 camp counselors:* responsibilities include monitoring the care and well-being of campers and scheduling programs. Candidates should have organizational skills, personal interest in the field, self-motivation, strong interpersonal skills, strong leadership ability. $1,500–$1,900 per duration of internship. Open to recent high school graduates, college freshmen, college sophomores, college juniors, college seniors, recent college graduates, graduate students. ▶ *2 nature specialists:* responsibilities include developing and implementing camp nature program. Candidates should have knowledge of field, oral communication skills, organizational skills, personal interest in the field, strong interpersonal skills. $1,500–$1,900 per duration of internship. Open to college sophomores, college juniors, college seniors, recent college graduates. ▶ *2 nurses:* responsibilities include performing general nursing duties. Candidates should have college degree in related field, experience in the field, organizational skills, strong interpersonal skills, strong leadership ability. salary based on experience and certification/license. Open to recent college graduates, LPN's, RN's, EMT's. Duration for all positions is June 1 to August 15. International applications accepted.
Benefits Formal training, free housing, free meals, health insurance, opportunity to attend seminars/workshops, possible full-time employment, willing to complete paperwork for educational credit, willing to provide letters of recommendation.
Contact Write, call, fax, or e-mail Vicky Miley, Outdoor Program Administrator. Phone: 717-757-3561. Fax: 717-755-1550. E-mail: gsinfo@pennlaurel.org. In-person interview recommended. Applicants must submit a formal organization application, three personal references. Application deadline: December 31 for summer. World Wide Web: http://www.pennlaurel.org.

PHOENIXVILLE AREA YMCA
400 East Pothouse Road
Phoenixville, Pennsylvania 19460

General Information Organization that provides the community with services that promote healthy spirits, minds, and bodies. Established in 1952. Number of employees: 180.
Internships Available ▶ *1–3 aquatic interns:* responsibilities include teaching preschool, youth, and adult swim programs; conducting aquatic fitness and/or therapeutic program; assisting with staff scheduling; assisting with management of outdoor pool complex during summer internship. Candidates should have experience in the field, oral communication skills, personal interest in the field, self-motivation, strong interpersonal skills, strong leadership ability. Duration is summer or 1-3 semesters. Position available as unpaid or at dependent upon experience and certifications. Open to college juniors, college seniors, recent college graduates, graduate students. ▶ *2–5 childcare interns:* responsibilities include assisting with staffing schedules, designing lesson plans for various age groups, assisting in provider care, learning state licensing requirements, developing promotional piece for services offered. Candidates should have college courses in field, plan to pursue career in field, self-motivation, strong interpersonal skills, strong leadership ability, written communication skills. Duration is summer or 1-3 semesters. Position available as unpaid or at dependent upon experience and credits in field. Open to high school seniors, college freshmen, college

sophomores, college juniors, college seniors, recent college graduates, individuals pursuing childcare certificates. ▶ *1–3 community and family recreation interns:* responsibilities include designing lesson plan for outdoor education, designing youth and/or family special events, creating promotional strategy for youth and/or family programs, assisting in day camp program during summer internship. Candidates should have ability to work independently, oral communication skills, personal interest in the field, self-motivation, strong interpersonal skills, strong leadership ability. Duration is summer or 1-3 semesters. Position available as unpaid or at dependent upon experience and related coursework. Open to college freshmen, college sophomores, college juniors, college seniors, recent college graduates. ▶ *1 corporate office intern:* responsibilities include basic accounting, data entry, answering phones, filing, word processing, spread sheets. Candidates should have computer skills, office skills, organizational skills, plan to pursue career in field, self-motivation, strong interpersonal skills. Duration is 1 summer or 1 semester. Position available as unpaid or at $7–$8 per hour. Open to college freshmen, college sophomores, college juniors, college seniors, graduate students. ▶ *1 financial development intern:* responsibilities include entering data into donor database, assisting with fund-raising events, assisting with organizing annual appeal, researching and writing grant proposals. Candidates should have ability to work independently, computer skills, oral communication skills, plan to pursue career in field, research skills, strong interpersonal skills, writing skills. Duration is 1–3 semesters. Position available as unpaid or paid. Open to college juniors, college seniors, graduate students. ▶ *1–3 health and fitness interns:* responsibilities include designing individualized fitness programs, orienting clients on equipment use, developing fitness-related bulletin boards, developing and implementing fitness incentive program, fitness testing. Candidates should have college courses in field, declared college major in field, plan to pursue career in field, self-motivation, strong interpersonal skills, strong leadership ability. Duration is summer or 1-3 semesters. Unpaid. Open to high school seniors, college juniors, college seniors, recent college graduates, graduate students. ▶ *1 public relations intern:* responsibilities include writing press releases, duplication of public relations materials, design of fliers, sign painting, special event decorations. Candidates should have computer skills, editing skills, knowledge of field, self-motivation, strong interpersonal skills, written communication skills. Duration is summer or 1-3 semesters. Position available as unpaid or at $6–$8 per hour. Open to college freshmen, college sophomores, college juniors, college seniors, recent college graduates, graduate students. International applications accepted.

Benefits Job counseling, names of contacts, on-the-job training, opportunity to attend seminars/workshops, possible full-time employment, willing to complete paperwork for educational credit, willing to provide letters of recommendation.

Contact Write, call, fax, or e-mail Linda Petrecca, Human Resources Director. Phone: 610-935-4940. Fax: 610-933-8867. E-mail: lindap@net-thing.net. In-person interview required. Applicants must submit a cover letter, resume, two personal references, two letters of recommendation. Applications are accepted continuously. World Wide Web: http://www.phoenixvilleymca.com.

PRESBYTERIAN CHILD WELFARE AGENCY
116 Buckhorn Lane
Buckhorn, Kentucky 41721

General Information Agency that provides residential care for abused children. Established in 1902. Number of employees: 220.

Internships Available ▶ *2–4 case workers:* responsibilities include working with abused and neglected children. Candidates should have ability to work independently, computer skills, oral communication skills, self-motivation, strong interpersonal skills, strong leadership ability, written communication skills. Duration is 6 months to 2 years. Open to college juniors, college seniors, recent college graduates, graduate students, career changers. ▶ *3–5 child care specialists or social workers:* responsibilities include performing diverse child care duties. Candidates

should have ability to work independently, analytical skills, college courses in field, computer skills, experience in the field, office skills, oral communication skills, plan to pursue career in field, self-motivation, strong interpersonal skills, strong leadership ability, written communication skills. Duration is 6 months to 2 years. Open to college juniors, college seniors, recent college graduates, graduate students, career changers. ▶ *1–3 therapists:* responsibilities include supervising case workers and house parents. Candidates should have ability to work independently, college courses in field, computer skills, knowledge of field, oral communication skills, organizational skills, self-motivation, strong interpersonal skills, strong leadership ability, written communication skills. Duration is 1–2 years. Open to college seniors, recent college graduates, graduate students. All positions available as unpaid or paid. International applications accepted.

Benefits Free housing, job counseling, names of contacts, opportunity to attend seminars/workshops, possible full-time employment, willing to complete paperwork for educational credit, willing to provide letters of recommendation, some expenses.

Contact Write, call, or fax Patti Wilder, Human Resources. Phone: 606-398-7245. Fax: 606-398-7912. In-person interview required. Applicants must submit a resume, personal reference. Applications are accepted continuously.

PRESIDIO COMMUNITY YMCA
360 18th Avenue
San Francisco, California 94121

General Information Community agency serving youth, adults, families, and seniors through a variety of social, recreational, educational, and fitness programs. Established in 1922. Number of employees: 300. Unit of YMCA of San Francisco, San Francisco, California.

Internships Available ▶ *Child care counselors:* responsibilities include assisting with preschool and after-school child care programs. ▶ *Fitness coordinators:* responsibilities include assisting in the development and implementation of fitness programs for teens and seniors. Duration for all positions is minimum of one semester. All positions available as unpaid or paid. Open to college freshmen, college sophomores, college juniors, college seniors, recent college graduates, graduate students, career changers. International applications accepted.

Benefits Formal training, names of contacts, opportunity to attend seminars/workshops, possible full-time employment, willing to complete paperwork for educational credit, willing to provide letters of recommendation.

Contact Write or fax Amy Choi, Human Resources Coordinator. Fax: 415-668-3370. No phone calls. In-person interview required. Applicants must submit a cover letter, resume, three personal references. Applications are accepted continuously. World Wide Web: http://www.presidioymca.org.

PREVENTION PLUS
2284 Old Rex Morrow Road
Morrow, Georgia 30260

General Information Organization currently working with the Insiders Teen Center, a youth-run facility working with at risk youth, parents, community leaders, and agencies.

Internships Available ▶ *Computer specialists:* responsibilities include helping to set up the lab and training. ▶ *Social work/sociology interns:* responsibilities include various tasks depending on the intern's needs and interests. Duration for all positions is flexible. All positions are unpaid.

Contact Write, call, or e-mail Lois Collins, Director, 2284 Old Rex Morrow Road, Morrow, Georgia 30260. Phone: 404-363-9600. E-mail: lcollins@school.com. Applicants must submit a resume, formal work schedule. Applications are accepted continuously.

PROGRAM FOR AID TO VICTIMS OF SEXUAL ASSAULT, INC. (PAVSA)
Building for Women, 32 East First Street, Suite 200
Duluth, Minnesota 55802

General Information Program offering crisis intervention and support advocacy to victims/survivors of sexual assault and their friends and family and sexual assault education to the community, professionals, and schools. Established in 1975. Number of employees: 7. Number of internship applications received each year: 10.
Internships Available ▶ *1–3 advocate interns:* responsibilities include assisting in crisis intervention, assisting in coordinating volunteers, one-to-one advocacy, and systems advocacy. Candidates should have ability to work independently, oral communication skills, organizational skills, self-motivation, strong interpersonal skills. Open to college sophomores, college juniors, college seniors, recent college graduates, graduate students, law students, career changers. ▶ *1–2 researchers:* responsibilities include initiating and completing research project under supervision of staff members and presenting results to staff and community. Candidates should have ability to work independently, computer skills, research skills, self-motivation, strong interpersonal skills, written communication skills. Open to college juniors, college seniors, recent college graduates, graduate students, law students, career changers. Duration for all positions is 3–12 months. All positions are unpaid. International applications accepted.
Benefits Formal training, job counseling, names of contacts, opportunity to attend seminars/workshops, willing to act as a professional reference, willing to complete paperwork for educational credit, willing to provide letters of recommendation.
Contact Write, call, fax, or e-mail Dorie Jenson, Advocacy Coordinator. Phone: 218-726-1442. Fax: 218-720-4890. E-mail: pavsa@cp.duluth.mn.us. In-person interview recommended. Applicants must submit a formal organization application, resume, three personal references, criminal history background check. Applications are accepted continuously.

PROJECT JERICHO FAMILY SERVICES, INC.
877 North Federal Boulevard
Denver, Colorado 80204

General Information Agency that handles foster care (family recruitment and child placement); family and individual therapy; drug/alcohol counseling, therapy and out-patient rehabilitation; and day-treatment educational center for teens. Established in 1988. Number of employees: 80. Number of internship applications received each year: 3.
Internships Available ▶ *1–2 foster care coordinators:* responsibilities include working closely with clients who are in foster-homes, overseeing completion of treatment plan, case documentation, and transportation. Candidates should have ability to work independently, analytical skills, college courses in field, knowledge of field, oral communication skills, organizational skills, personal interest in the field, plan to pursue career in field, self-motivation, strong interpersonal skills, strong leadership ability, writing skills. Position available as unpaid or at $1,000–$1,500 per month. Open to college seniors, recent college graduates, graduate students. ▶ *1–2 teachers or assistant teachers:* responsibilities include teaching or assisting teacher in standard academic activities. Candidates should have college courses in field, editing skills, knowledge of field, oral communication skills, organizational skills, personal interest in the field, plan to pursue career in field, self-motivation, strong interpersonal skills, strong leadership ability, writing skills. Position available as unpaid or at negotiable. Open to college freshmen, college sophomores, college juniors, college seniors, recent college graduates, graduate students. International applications accepted.
Benefits Job counseling, names of contacts, on-the-job training, possible full-time employment, willing to act as a professional reference, willing to complete paperwork for educational credit, willing to provide letters of recommendation.
Contact Write, call, fax, or e-mail David Stang, Executive Director. Phone: 303-573-0331. Fax: 303-573-0398. E-mail: weivel@bwn.net. In-person interview required. Applicants must submit a

formal organization application, cover letter, resume, academic transcripts, three personal references, three letters of recommendation, background check. Applications are accepted continuously. Fees: $60. World Wide Web: http://www.geocities.com/~fostering.

PROJECT OPEN HAND ATLANTA
176 Ottley Drive
Atlanta, Georgia 30324

General Information Meals-on-wheels program for people with AIDS in metro Atlanta. Established in 1988. Number of employees: 25. Number of internship applications received each year: 10.
Internships Available ▶ *1–2 interns:* responsibilities include developing well-rounded view of the overall organization. Areas of concentration would be kitchen rotation and volunteer services. Candidates should have oral communication skills, personal interest in the field, self-motivation, strong interpersonal skills. Duration is flexible. Position available as unpaid or paid. Open to high school students, high school seniors, recent high school graduates, college freshmen, college sophomores, college juniors, college seniors, recent college graduates, graduate students, law students, career changers, individuals reentering the workforce, those 17 years and older. International applications accepted.
Benefits On-the-job training, possible full-time employment, willing to act as a professional reference, willing to complete paperwork for educational credit, willing to provide letters of recommendation.
Contact Write or fax Lee Nagle, Operations Official, 176 Ottley Drive, Atlanta, Georgia 30324. Fax: 404-872-9301. No phone calls. Telephone interview required. Applicants must submit a formal organization application, cover letter, resume, two personal references. Applications are accepted continuously. World Wide Web: http://www.projectopenhand.org.

THE RAPE CRISIS CENTER OF CENTRAL MASSACHUSETTS, INC.
146 West Boylston Drive
Worcester, Massachusetts 01606

General Information Program providing comprehensive services to survivors of sexual assault and their concerned others as well as education geared toward ending violence against women. Established in 1973. Number of employees: 14. Number of internship applications received each year: 10.
Internships Available ▶ *10 counselors:* responsibilities include providing legal and medical advocacy, on-call hotline coverage, face-to-face counseling, and opportunity for facilitating support groups. Duration is 6 months minimum. Unpaid. Open to individuals 18 or older. International applications accepted.
Benefits Formal training, names of contacts, opportunity to attend seminars/workshops, possible full-time employment, travel reimbursement, willing to complete paperwork for educational credit, willing to provide letters of recommendation.
Contact Write, call, or fax Director of Counseling Services. Phone: 508-852-7600. Fax: 508-852-7870. In-person interview required. Volunteer questionnaire. Application deadline: March 31 for spring, August 31 for fall.

RESOURCE CENTER FOR WOMEN
1301 Seminole Boulevard, Suite 150
Largo, Florida 33770

General Information Displaced homemaker and single parent organization providing Pinellas and Pasco county clients with personal and career counseling, preemployment training, personal growth and assertiveness training, decision-making and problem-solving techniques, parenting classes, professional career placement services, and referrals for other services. Established in 1977. Number of employees: 13. Number of internship applications received each year: 10.
Internships Available ▶ *3 assistant intake counselors:* responsibilities include screening clients, scheduling intake counseling appointments, referring clients to available community services,

and assisting with case management and clerical tasks. Duration is flexible. ▶ *1 community development/media representative:* responsibilities include assisting with public relations, preparing news releases and public service announcements, and maintaining speaker's bureau. ▶ *3 community/agency outreach interns:* responsibilities include visiting community sites and interviewing potential clients, distributing material, and providing information and referrals for various needs of clients. ▶ *3 job developer interns:* responsibilities include developing and maintaining a network of job/employment contacts and monitoring placement services files. ▶ *3 personal growth counselor interns:* responsibilities include intake interviews, serving as teaching assistant in career and personal growth classes, referrals to other agencies, short-term individual counseling assistance, and short-term group experience. Duration is flexible. Open to college seniors, recent college graduates. ▶ *1 research assistant:* responsibilities include conducting statistical/demographic research (national/state/local), grant and subject research, and setting up libraries. All positions are unpaid.
Benefits Formal training, job counseling, names of contacts, opportunity to attend seminars/workshops, possible full-time employment, travel reimbursement, willing to complete paperwork for educational credit, willing to provide letters of recommendation.
Contact Write Ms. Dolores K. Benjamin, Executive Director. In-person interview required. Applicants must submit a cover letter, resume, 1-2 personal references. Applications are accepted continuously.

SAFEHOUSE DENVER, INC.
1111 Osage Street, Suite 230
Denver, Colorado 80204

General Information Domestic violence outreach and shelter facility, serving women and children who are victims of domestic violence. Established in 1977. Number of employees: 26. Number of internship applications received each year: 10.
Internships Available ▶ *1–3 outreach advocates:* responsibilities include answering the crisis line, facilitating groups, working on indirect projects, attending staff meetings, and participating in supervisions. Candidates should have oral communication skills, organizational skills, self-motivation, strong interpersonal skills, written communication skills. Duration is 16–25 weeks. ▶ *2–3 shelter advocates:* responsibilities include answering the 24 hour crisis line, maintaining a safe and secure residential facility, and individual case management and advocacy. Candidates should have college courses in field, knowledge of field, self-motivation, strong interpersonal skills. All positions are unpaid. Open to college seniors, recent college graduates, graduate students, career changers. International applications accepted.
Benefits Formal training, on-the-job training, opportunity to attend seminars/workshops, willing to act as a professional reference, willing to provide letters of recommendation.
Contact Call or e-mail Sarah Duensing, Volunteer Coordinator, 1111 Osage Street, Suite 230, Denver, Colorado 80204. Phone: 303-830-2660. E-mail: safehouse-shelter@sni.net. In-person interview required. Applicants must submit a cover letter. Applications are accepted continuously. World Wide Web: http://www.safehouse-denver.com.

ST. ELIZABETH SHELTER
804 Alarid Street
Sante Fe, New Mexico 87501

General Information Homeless shelter providing services to homeless individuals and families. Established in 1986. Number of employees: 26. Number of internship applications received each year: 10.
Internships Available ▶ *5 direct service interns:* responsibilities include taking in homeless guests, supervising evening operation of shelter, maintenance of facilities, writing for newsletter, and assisting with case management. Candidates should have ability to work independently, personal interest in the field, self-motivation, strong interpersonal skills. Duration is 3–12 months. $55–$85 per week. Open to college sophomores, college juniors,

college seniors, recent college graduates, graduate students, law students, career changers, individuals reentering the workforce. International applications accepted.
Benefits Free housing, free meals, health insurance, names of contacts, on-the-job training, possible full-time employment, willing to act as a professional reference, willing to complete paperwork for educational credit, willing to provide letters of recommendation.
Contact Write or call Mr. Hank Hughes, Executive Director. Phone: 505-982-6611. Telephone interview required. Applicants must submit a formal organization application, cover letter, resume, three personal references. Applications are accepted continuously.

ST. JUDE'S RANCH FOR CHILDREN
PO Box 61695
Boulder City, Nevada 89006

General Information Residential therapeutic environment for children with emotional disturbances. Established in 1967. Number of employees: 50. Number of internship applications received each year: 3.
Internships Available ▶ *1 art therapy intern:* responsibilities include working with expressive arts therapists and performing individual and group therapy under direction of certified art therapists to satisfy requirements for degree. Duration is 1–2 semesters. Unpaid. ▶ *2–3 homebound school teacher assistants (paraprofessional):* responsibilities include assisting head teacher in teaching math, English, reading, history, and science at a very basic level. Candidates should have computer skills, knowledge of field, organizational skills, self-motivation, strong interpersonal skills, strong leadership ability. Duration is 9–10 months. $200 per month. Open to recent college graduates, graduate students, career changers. ▶ *1 social work intern:* responsibilities include working with a social worker doing intake calls, updating files, transporting children to doctor and dental appointments, developing social work skills, and increasing knowledge base and experience. Candidates should have college courses in field, oral communication skills, organizational skills, personal interest in the field, self-motivation, strong interpersonal skills. Duration is 1–2 semesters. Unpaid. Open to college seniors, recent college graduates, graduate students. ▶ *2–4 summer recreation program volunteers:* responsibilities include assisting with summer swimming and recreation program, acting as counselors for summer church camp, teaching or enhancing swimming skills and coaching swim team, assisting with summer youth work program on campus, and assisting with tutoring. Candidates should have oral communication skills, organizational skills, personal interest in the field, strong interpersonal skills, strong leadership ability. Duration is 3 months. $200 per month. Open to college juniors, college seniors, recent college graduates, individuals reentering the workforce. International applications accepted.
Benefits Formal training, free housing, free meals, names of contacts, opportunity to attend seminars/workshops, possible full-time employment, willing to complete paperwork for educational credit, willing to provide letters of recommendation.
Contact Write, call, or fax Pat Brewer, Human Resources. Phone: 702-294-7106. Fax: 702-294-7114. In-person interview recommended. Application deadline: February 1 for summer, July 1 for fall.

SALVATION ARMY BOYS AND GIRLS CLUB
3701 R Street
Richmond, Virginia 23223

General Information Nonprofit organization that provides services in education, social recreation, and sports for young persons and senior citizens. Established in 1949. Number of employees: 12. Unit of The Salvation Army, Richmond, Virginia. Number of internship applications received each year: 10.
Internships Available ▶ *6 program aides:* responsibilities include implementing and planning activities in the fields of education, social recreation, sports, and services for senior citizens. Candidates should have ability to work independently, ability to

work with others, computer skills, oral communication skills, organizational skills, strong leadership ability. Duration is flexible. Unpaid. International applications accepted.
Benefits Job counseling, names of contacts, possible full-time employment, willing to complete paperwork for educational credit, willing to provide letters of recommendation.
Contact Call Lawanda Rowe, Executive Assistant. Phone: 804-222-3122. In-person interview required. Applicants must submit a cover letter, resume. Applications are accepted continuously.

SALVATION ARMY BOYS AND GIRLS CLUBS
750 Haywood Road
Asheville, North Carolina 28806

General Information Agency that provides social, cultural, educational, physical, and spiritual development for disadvantaged and at-risk youth. Established in 1989. Number of employees: 14. Unit of The Salvation Army, Atlanta, Georgia. Number of internship applications received each year: 5.
Internships Available ▶ *5–10 athletic assistants/coaches:* responsibilities include assisting athletic director with sports programs for basketball, flag football, and roller hockey, and possibly softball, soccer, or volleyball. Candidates should have ability to work with others, oral communication skills, organizational skills, self-motivation, strong leadership ability. Duration is 3–4 months. ▶ *1–2 cultural/art instructors:* responsibilities include teaching visual and/or performing art to elementary students and/or teenagers. Candidates should have ability to work with others, oral communication skills, organizational skills, personal interest in the field, strong leadership ability, written communication skills. Duration is 2 months. ▶ *3–10 day care counselors:* responsibilities include leading a group of children, ages 5-12, in after school or summer day camp activities and conducting age-appropriate VBS-type devotions. Candidates should have ability to work with others, oral communication skills, organizational skills, self-motivation, strong leadership ability. Duration is one summer or 12 months. All positions available as unpaid or at $6–$8 per hour. Open to high school seniors, recent high school graduates, college freshmen, college sophomores, college juniors, college seniors, recent college graduates, individuals reentering the workforce. International applications accepted.
Benefits Tuition assistance.
Contact Write or fax Wes Sharpe, Executive Director. Fax: 704-258-2113. In-person interview recommended. Applicants must submit a resume. Applications are accepted continuously.

SAN DIEGO YOUTH AND COMMUNITY SERVICES
3255 Wing Street
San Diego, California 92110

General Information Local social service agency that provides innovative responses to emerging social problems. Established in 1970. Number of employees: 180. Number of internship applications received each year: 30.
Internships Available ▶ *2–3 case aides:* responsibilities include providing assistance to agency social workers for children in foster homes. Candidates should have ability to work independently, oral communication skills, self-motivation, strong interpersonal skills, written communication skills. Duration is 3–6 months. Open to recent high school graduates, college freshmen, college sophomores, college juniors, college seniors, recent college graduates, individuals reentering the workforce. ▶ *1–4 counselor interns:* responsibilities include providing general counseling and advocacy services to those in need and maintaining client records. Candidates should have ability to work independently, oral communication skills, personal interest in the field, self-motivation, strong interpersonal skills, written communication skills. Duration is 3–6 months. Open to college juniors, college seniors, recent college graduates, graduate students, career changers, individuals reentering the workforce. ▶ *2–3 delinquency prevention interns:* responsibilities include planning, implementing, and supervising peer education, mediation, and after-school recreational activities for at-risk youth. Candidates should have ability to work independently, oral communication skills, personal

interest in the field, self-motivation, strong interpersonal skills. Duration is 3–6 months. Open to college freshmen, college sophomores, college juniors, college seniors, recent college graduates, graduate students, law students, career changers, individuals reentering the workforce. ▶ *1–2 emergency assistance volunteers:* responsibilities include providing emergency service and case management to homeless adults and families on a walk-in basis. Candidates should have ability to work independently, office skills, oral communication skills, self-motivation, strong interpersonal skills. Duration is 4–6 months. Open to recent high school graduates, college freshmen, college sophomores, college juniors, college seniors, recent college graduates, graduate students, law students, career changers, individuals reentering the workforce. ▶ *1–4 mobile health clinic volunteers:* responsibilities include counseling HIV-positive youth, collecting data, and developing and distributing promotional and educational materials. Candidates should have ability to work independently, oral communication skills, self-motivation, strong interpersonal skills, written communication skills. Duration is 3–6 months. Open to recent high school graduates, college freshmen, college sophomores, college juniors, college seniors, recent college graduates, graduate students, law students, career changers, individuals reentering the workforce. ▶ *5–10 shelter mentors:* responsibilities include general support to at-risk teens including group and individual activities, chores, homework, and administrative support. Candidates should have ability to work independently, oral communication skills, self-motivation, strong interpersonal skills, written communication skills. Duration is 5–6 months. Open to college freshmen, college sophomores, college juniors, college seniors, recent college graduates, graduate students, law students, career changers. ▶ *4–6 teen shelter interns:* responsibilities include supervising shelter residents in chores, homework, recreational trips, group therapy, and reviewing case files. Candidates should have ability to work independently, oral communication skills, personal interest in the field, self-motivation, strong interpersonal skills, written communication skills. Duration is 6 months. Open to college freshmen, college sophomores, college juniors, college seniors, recent college graduates, graduate students, law students, career changers, individuals reentering the workforce. ▶ *5–10 tutors:* responsibilities include tutoring elementary school students in reading and math, working with middle school children during after-school program. Candidates should have ability to work independently, oral communication skills, self-motivation, strong interpersonal skills, written communication skills. Duration is 3–6 months. Open to high school students, high school seniors, recent high school graduates, college freshmen, college sophomores, college juniors, college seniors, recent college graduates, graduate students, law students, career changers, individuals reentering the workforce. All positions are unpaid. International applications accepted.
Benefits Formal training, willing to complete paperwork for educational credit, willing to provide letters of recommendation.
Contact Write, call, or e-mail Stephen Romano, Volunteer Services Team Leader, 3255 Wing Street, San Diego, California 92110. Phone: 619-221-8600. E-mail: sdycs@aol.com. In-person interview recommended. Applicants must submit a cover letter, resume, three personal references. Application deadline: April 15 for summer; continuous for other positions. World Wide Web: http://www.sdycs.org.

SAN DIEGUITO BOYS AND GIRLS CLUBS
PO Box 615
Solana Beach, California 92075

General Information Organization dedicated to sponsoring activities that promote the health, self-esteem, and welfare of youth. Established in 1968. Number of employees: 75. Unit of Boys and Girls Club of America, Atlanta, Georgia.
Internships Available ▶ *1 arts and crafts program assistant:* responsibilities include supervising children, facilitating arts and crafts activities. ▶ *1 education assistant:* responsibilities include teaching children to operate computer programs and supervising children in tutoring programs. ▶ *1 games room assistant:* responsibilities include supervising children; supervising social

recreation games, pool, football, and Ping Pong; answering phones; and dealing with people needing assistance. ▶ *1 marketing/public relations intern:* responsibilities include producing and publishing bimonthly program brochure, and marketing programs through schools and press releases. ▶ *1 physical education assistant:* responsibilities include supervising children and physical education activities. Duration for all positions is 1 summer. All positions available as unpaid or paid. Open to college freshmen, college sophomores, college juniors, college seniors. International applications accepted.
Benefits Names of contacts, opportunity to attend seminars/workshops, possible full-time employment, willing to complete paperwork for educational credit, willing to provide letters of recommendation.
Contact Write or fax Vickie Beaty, Assistant Executive Director. Fax: 619-755-0138. No phone calls. In-person interview required. Applicants must submit a formal organization application, cover letter, resume, two letters of recommendation. Applications are accepted continuously.

SARAH HEINZ HOUSE
East Ohio and Heinz Streets
Pittsburgh, Pennsylvania 15212

General Information Youth recreation center for children ages 7-18. Established in 1901. Number of employees: 55. Affiliate of Boys and Girls Club of America, Atlanta, Georgia. Number of internship applications received each year: 15.
Internships Available ▶ *1–7 day camp counselors:* responsibilities include supervising children, planning and implementing programs or activities, and counseling children. $1,000 per duration of internship. ▶ *1–10 resident camp counselors:* responsibilities include supervising children, planning and implementing programs or activities, and counseling children. $750–$1,000 per duration of internship. Candidates for all positions should have ability to work independently, personal interest in the field, self-motivation, strong interpersonal skills, strong leadership ability. Duration for all positions is June to August. Open to high school seniors, recent high school graduates, college freshmen, college sophomores, college juniors, college seniors, recent college graduates, graduate students, law students, career changers, individuals reentering the workforce. International applications accepted.
Benefits Formal training, on-the-job training, willing to act as a professional reference, willing to complete paperwork for educational credit, willing to provide letters of recommendation, free housing, meals, and health insurance available at resident camp only.
Contact Write, call, or fax Sherri L. Kotwica, Program Director. Phone: 412-231-2377. Fax: 412-231-2428. In-person interview required. Applicants must submit a formal organization application, resume, three personal references. Application deadline: May 31.

SCOTT COUNTY FAMILY YMCA
606 West Second Street
Davenport, Iowa 52801

General Information Organization that puts Judeo-Christian principles into practice through programs which build a healthy spirit, mind, and body for all. Established in 1858. Number of employees: 200. Number of internship applications received each year: 1.
Internships Available ▶ *1–3 adult sports interns:* responsibilities include leading activities and leagues. ▶ *1–3 aquatics interns:* responsibilities include teaching aquatics lessons and water exercise classes. ▶ *1–3 camping interns:* responsibilities include working in day camp, resident camps, outdoor education, and special camps. ▶ *1–3 child care interns.* ▶ *1–3 fitness department interns:* responsibilities include leading classes and offering personal training and corporate fitness consulting. ▶ *1–3 fundraising/marketing interns:* responsibilities include helping with Kids to Camp program, Partners with Youth Campaign, and performing various marketing and promotional duties. ▶ *1–3 youth sports interns.* Duration for all positions is flexible. All positions are

unpaid. Open to high school students, high school seniors, recent high school graduates, college freshmen, college sophomores, college juniors, college seniors, recent college graduates, graduate students, law students, career changers, individuals reentering the workforce. International applications accepted.
Benefits Formal training, names of contacts, opportunity to attend seminars/workshops, possible full-time employment, travel reimbursement, willing to complete paperwork for educational credit, willing to provide letters of recommendation.
Contact Write, call, or fax Ms. Bridget Cullen, Senior Program Director. Phone: 319-359-3733. Fax: 319-322-3876. In-person interview required. Applicants must submit a resume. Applications are accepted continuously.

SE PREVENTION RESOURCE CENTER
512 Gentilly Road
Statesboro, Georgia 30458

General Information Center that acts as a lending library, produces newsletters, and holds workshops and conferences related to substance abuse prevention as it relates to risk and protective factors. Established in 1991. Number of employees: 6. Subsidiary of Pineland MH/MR/SA Community Service Board, Statesboro, Georgia. Number of internship applications received each year: 20.
Internships Available ▶ *2 project evaluation specialists:* responsibilities include learning about basic prevention models, participating in training and community endeavors sponsored by the center, developing and implementing one major evaluation project, and assisting with compilation of pre/post tests and outcome indicators. Candidates should have ability to work with others, organizational skills, research skills, self motivation, writing skills. Duration is August 15 to December 1. Position available as unpaid or at $1,000 per semester. Open to college seniors, graduate students. International applications accepted.
Benefits Formal training, on-the-job training, opportunity to attend seminars/workshops, willing to act as a professional reference, willing to provide letters of recommendation.
Contact Write, call, fax, or e-mail Susan E. Pajari, SE Prevention Resource Center Manager, 512 Gentilly Road, Statesboro, Georgia 30458. Phone: 912-764-2457. Fax: 912-489-8552. E-mail: spajari@bulloch.com. In-person interview required. Applicants must submit a resume. Application deadline: May 1 for summer, August 1 for fall, December 1 for spring.

SERVICE LEAGUE OF SAN MATEO COUNTY
727 Middlefield Road
Redwood City, California 94063

General Information Organization that provides services to San Mateo jail inmates, their families, and those released from jail. Established in 1961. Number of employees: 8. Number of internship applications received each year: 6.
Internships Available ▶ *2–3 assistant release counselors:* responsibilities include interviewing and assisting former inmates and their families with counseling and emergency needs and maintaining computer client records and statistics. Candidates should have computer skills, oral communication skills, organizational skills, plan to pursue career in field, self-motivation, strong interpersonal skills. Duration is 6 months minimum; flexible hours (minimum 8 hours per week). Open to college juniors, college seniors, recent college graduates. ▶ *2 assistants to jail coordinators:* responsibilities include assisting jail coordinators, responding to inmate requests in county jail as appropriate, acting as liaison between inmate and family. Candidates should have ability to work independently, declared college major in field, oral communication skills, organizational skills, self-motivation, strong interpersonal skills, personal interest or knowledge of field, strong sense of self. Duration is 9 months (school year); flexible hours (minimum 8 hours per week). Open to college freshmen, college sophomores, college juniors, college seniors, recent college graduates, individuals age 21 or older. All positions are unpaid.

Service League of San Mateo County (continued)

Benefits On-the-job training, willing to act as a professional reference, willing to complete paperwork for educational credit, willing to provide letters of recommendation.

Contact Write or call Ms. Sherri Auchard, Volunteer Director. Phone: 650-364-4664. Applicants must submit a formal organization application, cover letter, three letters of recommendation, in-person interview required (telephone interview acceptable on occasion). Applications are accepted continuously.

SOUTH BAY COMMUNITY SERVICES
315 4th Avenue, Suite E
Chula Vista, California 91910

General Information Community-based agency providing individual, family, and group counseling in a variety of programs, including juvenile diversion, gang intervention, after school, peer support, domestic violence, runaways, and homeless families, and functioning as short-term shelter for runaway and homeless youths and housing facility for homeless families. Established in 1971. Number of employees: 120. Number of internship applications received each year: 10.

Internships Available ▶ *2–4 KIDZBIZ interns:* responsibilities include helping recruit business mentors from surrounding community to work with youth in developing entrepreneurial skills that will enable them to run their own business; writing for *Infiniti* magazine publication; attending classes. Candidates should have oral communication skills, personal interest in the field, self-motivation, strong interpersonal skills, strong leadership ability, written communication skills. Duration is 6 months minimum. Unpaid. Open to recent college graduates, graduate students, law students, career changers, individuals reentering the workforce. ▶ *1–6 case managers:* responsibilities include providing support, education, and assistance to families struggling with issues of domestic violence and homelessness; interviewing clients; helping residents develop plans for safety and change and monitoring their progress in being accountable and achieving their individual goals. Candidates should have ability to work with others, oral communication skills, personal interest in the field, self-motivation, written communication skills. Duration is 6 months, 10-20 hours per week. Position available as unpaid or paid. Open to college seniors, recent college graduates, graduate students, career changers, individuals reentering the workforce. ▶ *2–4 diversion interns:* responsibilities include interviewing and gathering background information; problem-solving with runaways or their families; keeping appropriate records, documentation, and statistics; and participating in agency activities. Candidates should have ability to work with others, knowledge of field, oral communication skills, personal interest in the field, written communication skills. Duration is 6 months minimum, 20 hours per week. Position available as unpaid or paid. Open to recent college graduates, graduate students, individuals reentering the workforce. ▶ *2–10 literacy tutors:* responsibilities include tutoring or teaching elementary or junior high school students in academic subjects and keeping appropriate records and documentation. Candidates should have ability to work independently, oral communication skills, personal interest in the field, self-motivation, strong interpersonal skills, written communication skills. Duration is year-round. Position available as unpaid or paid. Open to college juniors, college seniors, recent college graduates, graduate students, individuals reentering the workforce. ▶ *2–10 residential volunteers:* responsibilities include assisting at youth and homeless shelters with overall functioning, fostering individual goals and tasks of residents; may include teaching cooking and preparing balanced meals, utilizing the transportation system, interviewing for jobs, communicating with others, budgeting finances, and problem solving skills. Candidates should have ability to work independently, analytical skills, oral communication skills, personal interest in the field, strong interpersonal skills, written communication skills. Duration is 6 months minimum, 10-20 hours per week. Position available as unpaid or paid. Open to college seniors, recent college graduates, graduate students. ▶ *2–8 youth and family counselors:* responsibilities include providing individual, family, and group counseling; case management; writing supporting documenta-

tion; keeping appropriate monthly statistics; and participating in agency community service activities. Candidates should have ability to work independently, ability to work with others, experience in the field, oral communication skills, personal interest in the field, written communication skills. Duration is 6 months minimum, 20 hours per week. Position available as unpaid or paid. Open to recent college graduates, graduate students. International applications accepted.

Benefits Formal training, on-the-job training, opportunity to attend seminars/workshops, possible full-time employment, willing to act as a professional reference, willing to complete paperwork for educational credit, willing to provide letters of recommendation, clinical supervision for marriage-family-child counselors and social work interns, some stipends available.

Contact Write, call, or fax Pam Wright, Clinical Director. Phone: 619-420-3620. Fax: 619-420-8722. In-person interview required. Applicants must submit a resume, three personal references. Applications are accepted continuously.

SOUTHEASTERN NETWORK OF YOUTH AND FAMILY SERVICES
1761 South Lumpkin Street
Athens, Georgia 30606

General Information Regional training and technical assistance provider to youth services professionals.

Internships Available ▶ *1 community development intern.* ▶ *1 marketing intern.* ▶ *1 nonprofit management intern.* ▶ *1 social work intern.* Duration for all positions is flexible. All positions available as unpaid or paid. Open to anyone interested.

Benefits Willing to complete paperwork for educational credit.

Contact Write, call, fax, or e-mail Ms. Gail Kurtz, Executive Director. Phone: 706-354-4568. Fax: 706-353-0026. E-mail: glkurtz@ senetwork.org. Applicants must submit a cover letter, resume. Applications are accepted continuously. World Wide Web: http:// www.senetwork.org.

SOUTH WOOD COUNTY YMCA
211 Wisconsin River Drive
Port Edwards, Wisconsin 54469

General Information Fellowship based on Christian values with a mission to provide facilities, programs, and services that enhance the health and physical well-being of all persons and improve the quality of life for the citizens of southern Wood County. Established in 1958. Number of employees: 100. Number of internship applications received each year: 6.

Internships Available ▶ *1 aquatics assistant:* responsibilities include performing various tasks in the pool area. Candidates should have ability to work independently, experience in the field, oral communication skills, personal interest in the field, self-motivation, strong interpersonal skills, strong leadership ability. Duration is flexible. Position available as unpaid or paid. Open to high school students, high school seniors, recent high school graduates, college freshmen, college sophomores, college juniors, college seniors, recent college graduates, individuals reentering the workforce. ▶ *1 assistant maintenance intern.* Candidates should have ability to work independently, ability to work with others, personal interest in the field, self-motivation. Unpaid. Open to high school students, high school seniors, recent high school graduates, college freshmen, college sophomores, college juniors, college seniors, individuals reentering the workforce. ▶ *1 day care assistant:* responsibilities include caring for children. Candidates should have oral communication skills, organizational skills, personal interest in the field, self-motivation, strong interpersonal skills. Duration is flexible. Position available as unpaid or paid. Open to recent high school graduates, college freshmen, college sophomores, college juniors, college seniors, recent college graduates, individuals reentering the workforce. ▶ *1 office area assistant:* responsibilities include performing various office-related duties. Candidates should have ability to work independently, computer skills, office skills, oral communication skills, personal interest in the field, self-motivation, strong interpersonal skills, writing skills. Unpaid. Open to high school seniors, recent high school graduates, college freshmen, college sophomores, college juniors, college seniors, recent college graduates, individuals reentering the workforce. ▶ *1 physical fitness assistant:* responsibilities include conducting fitness classes and testing. Candidates should have ability to work independently, experience in the field, knowledge of field, oral communication skills, organizational skills, personal interest in the field, self-motivation, strong interpersonal skills, strong leadership ability. Duration is flexible. Position available as unpaid or paid. Open to recent high school graduates, college freshmen, college sophomores, college juniors, college seniors, recent college graduates, individuals reentering the workforce. ▶ *1–2 summer camp assistants:* responsibilities include performing camp-related duties. Candidates should have oral communication skills, personal interest in the field, self-motivation, strong interpersonal skills, strong leadership ability. Duration is flexible. Unpaid. Open to high school students, high school seniors, recent high school graduates, college freshmen, college sophomores, college juniors, college seniors, recent college graduates. ▶ *1 summer special events assistant coordinator.* Candidates should have ability to work independently, oral communication skills, personal interest in the field, research skills, self-motivation, strong interpersonal skills, strong leadership ability, written communication skills. Duration is flexible. Unpaid. Open to high school students, high school seniors, recent high school graduates, college freshmen, college sophomores, college juniors, college seniors, recent college graduates, individuals reentering the workforce. ▶ *1 youth director assistant:* responsibilities include working in youth sports. Candidates should have ability to work independently, oral communication skills, organizational skills, personal interest in the field, self-motivation, strong interpersonal skills, strong leadership ability. Unpaid. Open to high school seniors, recent high school graduates, college freshmen, college sophomores, college juniors, college seniors, recent college graduates, individuals reentering the workforce. International applications accepted.

Benefits Formal training, names of contacts, on-the-job training, opportunity to attend seminars/workshops, possible full-time employment, willing to act as a professional reference, willing to complete paperwork for educational credit, willing to provide letters of recommendation, national YMCA job listings provided, YMCA membership.

Contact Write, call, or fax Donald Franklin, Executive Director. Phone: 715-887-3240. Fax: 715-887-3262. In-person interview recommended. Applicants must submit a cover letter, resume, two personal references. Applications are accepted continuously.

SPECIAL EQUESTRIAN RIDING THERAPY, INC.
PO Box 1098
Agoura Hills, California 91376

General Information Organization providing therapeutic horsemanship for the disabled. Established in 1987. Number of employees: 1. Unit of North American Riding for the Handicapped Association (NARHA), Denver, Colorado. Number of internship applications received each year: 15.

Internships Available ▶ *2 program assistants:* responsibilities include assisting with lessons for disabled riders, horse and tack care, and horse training if qualified. Candidates should have ability to work independently, ability to work with others, oral communication skills, self-motivation, strong leadership ability, written communication skills. Duration is 1–3 months. Unpaid. Open to recent high school graduates, college freshmen, college sophomores, college juniors, college seniors, recent college graduates, graduate students, law students, career changers, individuals reentering the workforce. International applications accepted.

Benefits Formal training, free housing, job counseling, names of contacts, on-the-job training, opportunity to attend seminars/workshops, willing to act as a professional reference, willing to complete paperwork for educational credit, willing to provide letters of recommendation.

Contact Write, call, fax, or e-mail Nora Fischbach, Program Director. Phone: 818-776-6476. Fax: 818-705-2201. E-mail: sert@instanet.com. In-person interview recommended. Applicants must submit a cover letter, resume, two personal references. Applications are accepted continuously. World Wide Web: http://www.instanet.com/~sert.

SPRING LAKE RANCH, INC.
Spring Lake Road
Cuttingsville, Vermont 05738

General Information Therapeutic community for emotionally disturbed adults. Established in 1933. Number of employees: 35. Number of internship applications received each year: 20.

Internships Available ▶ *1–6 work leaders/house advisers:* responsibilities include leading work crews in a safe manner so that residents will have a challenging, meaningful, enjoyable experience; overseeing practical aspects of house residents' lives and giving them support and guidance in reaching their goals; and participating in and contributing to the ranch community. Candidates should have oral communication skills, organizational skills, personal interest in the field, self-motivation, strong interpersonal skills. Duration is 6 months or longer. $150 per week. Open to recent college graduates, graduate students, career changers, individuals reentering the workforce, individuals 21 or older (not necessary to have college degree). International applications accepted.

Benefits Free housing, free meals, health insurance, on-the-job training, opportunity to attend seminars/workshops, possible full-time employment, willing to provide letters of recommendation, vacation and sick time.

Contact Write or call Ms. Lynn McDermott, Personnel. Phone: 802-492-3322. In-person interview recommended. Applicants must submit a resume. Applications are accepted continuously.

STARFIRE COUNCIL OF GREATER CINCINNATI
885 North Bend Road
Cincinnati, Ohio 45224

General Information Organization that enables persons with disabilities to develop their full potential through service to the community, information education, and social interaction. Established in 1993. Number of employees: 15.

Internships Available ▶ *2 outing managers:* responsibilities include designing and implementing recreational and volunteer outings for adults and/or youths with disabilities, leading outings where needed, maximizing potential for members' personal growth through outings. Candidates should have ability to work independently, oral communication skills, organizational skills, personal interest in the field, self-motivation, strong interpersonal skills. Duration is flexible, minimum commitment of 1 academic term or semester. Unpaid. Open to college sophomores, college juniors, college seniors, recent college graduates, graduate students, career changers, individuals reentering the workforce. International applications accepted.

Benefits Job counseling, on-the-job training, opportunity to attend seminars/workshops, possible full-time employment, travel reimbursement, willing to act as a professional reference, willing to complete paperwork for educational credit, willing to provide letters of recommendation.

Contact Write, call, or fax Jim Rogers, Program Director. Phone: 513-242-0584. Fax: 513-242-0587. In-person interview recommended. Applicants must submit a cover letter, resume, three personal references. Applications are accepted continuously.

STARLIGHT CHILDREN'S FOUNDATION OF NY*NJ*CT
1560 Broadway, Suite 600
New York, New York 10036

General Information Starlight brightens the lives of seriously ill children between the ages of 4 and 18 through a variety of programs, which include wish granting and various activities in and out of hospital pediatric wards. Established in 1985. Number of employees: 8. Unit of Starlight Children's Foundation International, Los Angeles, California. Number of internship applications received each year: 100.

Starlight Children's Foundation of NY*NJ*CT (continued)

Internships Available ▶ *1 children's services intern:* responsibilities include maintaining hospital party and outpatient activities programs, scheduling parties and entertainment for parties, distributing outpatient tickets, maintaining donor correspondence, and assisting with granting of wishes. ▶ *1 marketing and event intern:* responsibilities include working closely with fund-raising associate by assisting with the planning and implementation of special events, maintaining donor correspondence, and soliciting various items and donations. The intern also assists with promotions, newsletters, and marketing. Candidates for all positions should have office skills, oral communication skills, organizational skills, self-motivation, strong interpersonal skills, written communication skills. Duration for all positions is 3 months minimum. All positions are unpaid. Open to college sophomores, college juniors, college seniors, recent college graduates. International applications accepted.
Benefits Formal training, on-the-job training, willing to complete paperwork for educational credit, willing to provide letters of recommendation.
Contact Write, call, fax, or e-mail Michaela Potter, Marketing and Volunteer Coordinator. Phone: 212-354-2878. Fax: 212-354-2977. E-mail: michaela@starlightnyc.org. In-person interview recommended. Applicants must submit a formal organization application, cover letter, resume, three personal references. Application deadline: March 31 for summer; continuous for fall and winter. World Wide Web: http://www.starlight.org.

TEEN LINE
PO Box 48750
Los Angeles, California 90048

General Information Organization that provides teen-to-teen hotline and associated community outreach services. Established in 1981. Number of employees: 4. Unit of Cedars-Sinai Medical Center, Los Angeles, California. Number of internship applications received each year: 20.
Internships Available ▶ *2–4 administrative interns:* responsibilities include assisting program manager with all administrative tasks. Candidates should have ability to work independently, computer skills, office skills, self-motivation, strong interpersonal skills, written communication skills. Duration is flexible; minimum of 12 weeks. Open to high school students, high school seniors, college freshmen, college sophomores, college juniors, college seniors, recent college graduates. ▶ *6 resource associates:* responsibilities include facilitating meetings of adolescents and supervising their work on teen hotline. Candidates should have analytical skills, knowledge of field, oral communication skills, organizational skills, personal interest in the field, strong interpersonal skills. Duration is 6 months. Open to graduate students. All positions are unpaid. International applications accepted.
Benefits Formal training, opportunity to attend seminars/workshops, possible full-time employment, willing to complete paperwork for educational credit, willing to provide letters of recommendation.
Contact Write or call Elaine Leader, Executive Director, Teen Line. Phone: 310-855-3401. In-person interview required. Applicants must submit a resume. Applications are accepted continuously.

TEXAS ALLIANCE FOR HUMAN NEEDS
1016 East 12th Street
Austin, Texas 78702

General Information Independent statewide coalition concerned with issues affecting low- and moderate-income individuals in Texas. Established in 1982. Number of employees: 3. Number of internship applications received each year: 80.
Internships Available ▶ *3–6 combination interns.* Candidates should have ability to work independently, ability to work with others, analytical skills, computer skills, oral communication skills, written communication skills. Duration is 3–6 months. Position available as unpaid or paid. Open to college juniors, college seniors, recent college graduates, graduate students, law students, career changers, individuals reentering the workforce. ▶ *1–3 development interns:* responsibilities include direct mail,

major donor solicitation, and grant-writing projects. Candidates should have computer skills, oral communication skills, organizational skills, self-motivation, strong interpersonal skills, written communication skills. Duration is 3–6 months. Position available as unpaid or at a commission in form of percentage of funds raised. Open to college juniors, college seniors, recent college graduates, graduate students, law students, career changers, individuals reentering the workforce. ▶ *1–3 education interns:* responsibilities include writing and distributing educational pieces on poverty issues. Candidates should have ability to work independently, computer skills, oral communication skills, research skills, self-motivation, written communication skills. Duration is 3–6 months. Unpaid. Open to high school seniors, recent high school graduates, college freshmen, college sophomores, college juniors, college seniors, recent college graduates, graduate students, law students, career changers, individuals reentering the workforce. ▶ *2 field interns:* responsibilities include assisting field organizers in developing meetings and literature on low-income/poverty issues. Candidates should have ability to work independently, oral communication skills, organizational skills, strong interpersonal skills, strong leadership ability. Duration is 6–12 months. Unpaid. Open to college juniors, college seniors, recent college graduates, graduate students, law students, career changers, individuals reentering the workforce. ▶ *1 minority health intern:* responsibilities include organizing around and documenting issues impacting the minority communities, serving as liaison to Texas Minority Health Network, and coordinating newsletters and interns. Candidates should have ability to work independently, oral communication skills, organizational skills, personal interest in the field, strong leadership ability, written communication skills. Duration is 6–9 months. $300 per month. ▶ *1–3 newsletter interns:* responsibilities include assisting in preparation of newsletter by researching and writing articles. Candidates should have ability to work independently, analytical skills, editing skills, research skills, self-motivation, writing skills. Duration is 3–6 months. Unpaid. Open to high school seniors, recent high school graduates, college freshmen, college sophomores, college juniors, college seniors, recent college graduates, graduate students, law students, career changers, individuals reentering the workforce. ▶ *1–3 office interns:* responsibilities include answering phone, filing, responding to letters, assembling information packets, and maintaining the computer mailing list. Candidates should have ability to work independently, office skills, oral communication skills, organizational skills, self-motivation, written communication skills. Duration is 3–6 months. Unpaid. Open to high school seniors, recent high school graduates, college freshmen, college sophomores, college juniors, college seniors, recent college graduates, graduate students, law students, career changers, individuals reentering the workforce. ▶ *2–3 research/poverty interns:* responsibilities include researching poverty issues and attending legislative hearings. Candidates should have ability to work independently, analytical skills, computer skills, research skills, writing skills. Duration is 3–6 months. Unpaid. Open to recent high school graduates, college freshmen, college sophomores, college juniors, college seniors, recent college graduates, graduate students, law students, career changers, individuals reentering the workforce. International applications accepted.
Benefits Free housing, job counseling, names of contacts, on-the-job training, opportunity to attend seminars/workshops, willing to act as a professional reference, willing to complete paperwork for educational credit, willing to provide letters of recommendation, health insurance for minority health interns.
Contact Write, call, fax, or e-mail Ms. Jude Filler, Executive Director. Phone: 512-474-5019. Fax: 512-474-5058. E-mail: hn0796@handsnet.org. Telephone interview required. Applicants must submit a cover letter, resume. Applications are accepted continuously. World Wide Web: http://www.main.org/tahn.

TOUCH OF NATURE ENVIRONMENTAL CENTER
Southern Illinois University, Mailcode 6888
Carbondale, Illinois 62901-6888

General Information Spectrum Wilderness Program utilizes wilderness settings, initiative courses, and group processes to help youth-at-risk grow in confidence and self-reliance. Established in 1964. Number of employees: 60. Unit of Southern Illinois University Carbondale, Carbondale, Illinois. Number of internship applications received each year: 20.

Internships Available ▶ *6–12 spectrum interns:* responsibilities include assisting lead and assistant instructors in providing outdoor therapeutic programs for youth at risk. Candidates should have knowledge of field, oral communication skills, plan to pursue career in field, strong interpersonal skills, written communication skills. Duration is 2–6 months. $250–$1,000 per month. Open to high school students, high school seniors, recent high school graduates, college freshmen, college sophomores, college juniors, college seniors, recent college graduates, graduate students, law students, career changers, individuals reentering the workforce. ▶ *1–5 therapeutic recreation interns:* responsibilities include observing in a variety of settings, doing a minimum of 10 assessments and 2 treatment plans, attending a minimum of one administrative meeting, attending all T.R. seminars weekly, co-leading or leading at least one activity per session, attending all staff meetings, performing pre-arranged duties, coordinating evening programs. Candidates should have ability to work independently, ability to work with others, knowledge of field, personal interest in the field, strong interpersonal skills, strong leadership ability, some coursework and experience in the field is desirable. Duration is May 30 to July 31. Position available as unpaid or paid. Open to college sophomores, college juniors, college seniors, recent college graduates, graduate students. International applications accepted.

Benefits Free housing, on-the-job training, possible full-time employment, willing to complete paperwork for educational credit, willing to provide letters of recommendation, meals during program operation.

Contact Write, call, or fax Program Coordinator, Spectrum Wilderness Program. Phone: 618-453-1121. Fax: 618-453-1188. In-person interview recommended. Applicants must submit a formal organization application, cover letter, resume, three personal references. Applications are accepted continuously. World Wide Web: http://www.pso.siu.edu/tonec.

TRAVELERS AID
828 West Peachtree Street, NW, #320
Atlanta, Georgia 30308

General Information Nonprofit social service agency working with people in crisis, preventing homelessness. Established in 1900. Number of employees: 8. Number of internship applications received each year: 10.

Internships Available ▶ *1–3 development associates:* responsibilities include assisting with fund-raising and working on annual campaign. Candidates should have ability to work independently, oral communication skills, personal interest in the field, research skills, self-motivation, written communication skills. Open to college freshmen, college sophomores, college juniors, college seniors, graduate students. ▶ *1–3 volunteer coordinator associates:* responsibilities include helping to coordinate the volunteer program. Candidates should have experience in the field, oral communication skills, self-motivation, strong interpersonal skills, written communication skills. Open to college freshmen, college sophomores, college juniors, college seniors, recent college graduates, graduate students. Duration for all positions is 6–12 months. All positions are unpaid. International applications accepted.

Benefits Names of contacts, on-the-job training, opportunity to attend seminars/workshops, travel reimbursement, willing to act as a professional reference, willing to complete paperwork for educational credit, willing to provide letters of recommendation.

Contact Call, fax, or e-mail Karyn Reasoner, Director, 828 West Peachtree Street, NW, #320, Atlanta, Georgia 30308. Phone: 404-817-7070 Ext. 25. Fax: 404-817-9922. E-mail: kzr@hotmail.com. Applicants must submit a resume, two writing samples, 3 personal references or letters of recommendation, in-person or telephone interview. Applications are accepted continuously.

UCSF AIDS HEALTH PROJECT
Box 0884
San Francisco, California 94143-0884

General Information HIV education, prevention, and counseling. Established in 1984. Number of employees: 127. Unit of University of California, San Francisco, San Francisco, California. Number of internship applications received each year: 80.

Internships Available ▶ *3 HIV counseling and testing interns:* responsibilities include providing phone-bank callers with confidential testing information; risk assessment, disclosure, and HIV counseling at test sites; data entry of CDC demographics and phone bank data. Candidates should have computer skills, office skills, oral communication skills, personal interest in the field, strong interpersonal skills, ability to discuss sexual behavior by telephone. Open to college freshmen, college sophomores, college juniors, college seniors, recent college graduates, graduate students, law students, career changers, individuals reentering the workforce. ▶ *1 behavioral research intern:* responsibilities include data entry from surveys, generating reports and statistical analyses, word processing and library searches with medical library research software, general office work, conducting client interviews. Candidates should have analytical skills, computer skills, office skills, oral communication skills, personal interest in the field, research skills, ability to conduct interviews related to sexual behavior. Open to college freshmen, college sophomores, college juniors, college seniors, recent college graduates, graduate students, law students, law school graduates, career changers, individuals reentering the workforce. ▶ *1 client support services administrative intern:* responsibilities include answering telephones, greeting clients, and acting as receptionist in evening; general office work; data entry. Candidates should have computer skills, office skills, oral communication skills, organizational skills, personal interest in the field, strong interpersonal skills. Open to college freshmen, college sophomores, college juniors, college seniors, recent college graduates, graduate students, law students, career changers, individuals reentering the workforce. ▶ *1 community psychiatric substance abuse services intern:* responsibilities include general office duties, data entry, reception duties, conducting two client intake interviews per week. Candidates should have computer skills, office skills, oral communication skills, organizational skills, personal interest in the field, strong interpersonal skills. Open to college freshmen, college sophomores, college juniors, college seniors, recent college graduates, graduate students, law students, career changers, individuals reentering the workforce. ▶ *1 computer/database intern:* responsibilities include software and hardware troubleshooting, software installation, end-user training, designing and maintaining databases, working as part of MIS team. Candidates should have analytical skills, college courses in field, computer skills, knowledge of field, oral communication skills, organizational skills, personal interest in the field, strong interpersonal skills. Open to college freshmen, college sophomores, college juniors, college seniors, recent college graduates, graduate students, law students, career changers, individuals reentering the workforce. ▶ *2 editorial researcher/writer interns:* responsibilities include library research, writing, proofreading, administrative and other tasks. Candidates should have ability to work independently, ability to work with others, computer skills, personal interest in the field, research skills, writing skills. Open to college freshmen, college sophomores, college juniors, college seniors, recent college graduates, graduate students, law students, career changers, individuals reentering the workforce. ▶ *1 fund-raising and development intern:* responsibilities include participating in solicitation campaign by developing budgets, preparing literature, and other duties; communicating with media; maintaining donor database. Candidates should have computer skills, office skills, oral communication skills, personal interest in the field, strong interpersonal skills, written communication skills. Open to college freshmen, college sophomores, college juniors, college seniors, recent college graduates, graduate students, law students, career changers, individuals reentering the workforce. ▶ *1 marketing intern:* responsibilities include reviewing educational materials, daily sales tracking, writing, and strategy development. Candidates should have college courses in field, computer skills, knowledge

UCSF AIDS Health Project (continued)

of field, office skills, oral communication skills, personal interest in the field, plan to pursue career in field, strong interpersonal skills, written communication skills. Open to college freshmen, college sophomores, college juniors, college seniors, recent college graduates, graduate students, law students, career changers, individuals reentering the workforce. ▶ *1 prevention services administrative intern:* responsibilities include assisting with administrative duties, designing and production of workshops and community events. Candidates should have computer skills, office skills, organizational skills, personal interest in the field, strong interpersonal skills. Open to college freshmen, college sophomores, college juniors, college seniors, recent college graduates, graduate students, law students, career changers, individuals reentering the workforce. ▶ *1 services center operations intern:* responsibilities include general office duties, data entry, producing forms/flyers, part-time reception duties, handling confidential client information. Candidates should have ability to work independently, computer skills, office skills, oral communication skills, self-motivation, strong interpersonal skills, written communication skills. Open to college freshmen, college sophomores, college juniors, college seniors, recent college graduates, graduate students, law students, career changers, individuals reentering the workforce. Duration for all positions is one year from July to June. All positions are unpaid. International applications accepted.

Benefits On-the-job training, opportunity to attend seminars/workshops, willing to act as a professional reference, willing to complete paperwork for educational credit, willing to provide letters of recommendation, housing allowance.

Contact Write, call, fax, or e-mail Susan Sunshine, Staffing Coordinator. Phone: 415-476-3890. Fax: 415-476-3613. E-mail: susan_sunshine.ahp_mcb@quickmail.ucsf.edu. Telephone interview required. Applicants must submit a formal organization application, resume, two writing samples. Application deadline: March 31. World Wide Web: http://www.ucsf-ahp.org.

UNITED JEWISH FEDERATION OF METROWEST
901 Route 10
Whippany, New Jersey 07981-1156

General Information Jewish organization that works to enhance life of Jewish community and to create a future rooted in Jewish religious heritage. Established in 1923. Number of employees: 100. Number of internship applications received each year: 8.

Internships Available ▶ *1 editorial intern:* responsibilities include writing news releases and ad copy, updating bios and media lists, organizing photo files, and contacting lay leaders by phone for information. Duration is June-September. Position available as unpaid or paid. Open to recent high school graduates, college freshmen, college sophomores, college juniors, college seniors, recent college graduates, graduate students, law students, career changers, individuals reentering the workforce, outstanding high school students.

Benefits Willing to complete paperwork for educational credit, willing to provide letters of recommendation.

Contact Write, call, fax, or e-mail Fran Weiss, Senior Writer. Phone: 973-884-4800. Fax: 973-884-7361. E-mail: fweiss@ujfmetrowest.org. In-person interview required. Applicants must submit a resume, writing sample. Applications are accepted continuously. World Wide Web: http://www.ujfmetrowest.org.

UNITED WAY OF HOWARD COUNTY
210 West Walnut
Kokomo, Indiana 46901

General Information Organization that raises and distributes funds for community social service needs. Established in 1929. Number of employees: 15. Number of internship applications received each year: 2.

Internships Available ▶ *1–3 campaign associates:* responsibilities include learning fund-raising techniques and helping to raise $2.5 million during the campaign. Candidates should have ability to work independently, computer skills, office skills, oral communication skills, personal interest in the field, self-motivation,

strong interpersonal skills, strong leadership ability, written communication skills. ▶ *1 communications/marketing associate:* responsibilities include writing press releases and local campaign materials and producing videos. Candidates should have ability to work independently, editing skills, office skills, oral communication skills, self-motivation, strong interpersonal skills, strong leadership ability, written communication skills. ▶ *1 information and referral associate:* responsibilities include working with people who have problems and providing access to appropriate assistance. Candidates should have ability to work independently, computer skills, office skills, oral communication skills, personal interest in the field, self-motivation, strong interpersonal skills, strong leadership ability, written communication skills. ▶ *1 planning/allocations associate:* responsibilities include helping to assess community needs and distributing funds to meet those needs. Candidates should have ability to work independently, computer skills, editing skills, office skills, oral communication skills, self-motivation, strong interpersonal skills, strong leadership ability, written communication skills. Duration for all positions is 3–6 months. All positions are unpaid. Open to high school students, high school seniors, recent high school graduates, college freshmen, college sophomores, college juniors, college seniors, recent college graduates, graduate students, law students, career changers, individuals reentering the workforce, retirees. International applications accepted.

Benefits Job counseling, names of contacts, possible full-time employment, travel reimbursement, willing to complete paperwork for educational credit, willing to provide letters of recommendation.

Contact Write, call, or fax Michael Spear, President. Phone: 765-457-6691. Fax: 765-454-5569. In-person interview required. Applicants must submit a formal organization application, resume. Applications are accepted continuously.

UNITED WAY OF SOUTHEASTERN PENNSYLVANIA
7 Benjamin Franklin Parkway
Philadelphia, Pennsylvania 19103

General Information Fundraising, fund-distributing organization for human services whose Community Services Division links people who need or want to help organizations in the community. Established in 1921. Number of employees: 100. Number of internship applications received each year: 20.

Internships Available ▶ *1 information and referral specialist:* responsibilities include answering phones and responding to caller needs. Candidates should have ability to work independently, ability to work with others, oral communication skills, plan to pursue career in field, written communication skills. Open to college seniors, recent college graduates, graduate students, career changers. ▶ *2 volunteer center aides:* responsibilities include collecting data on agencies using volunteers, referring potential volunteers to agencies, and helping arrange a recognition event or conference. Candidates should have computer skills, oral communication skills, personal interest in the field, self-motivation, strong interpersonal skills. Open to college juniors, college seniors, recent college graduates, graduate students, individuals reentering the workforce. Duration for all positions is year-round. All positions are unpaid. International applications accepted.

Benefits Formal training, on-the-job training, opportunity to attend seminars/workshops, possible full-time employment, willing to complete paperwork for educational credit, willing to provide letters of recommendation.

Contact Write, call, or fax Camara K. Jordan, Manager, Volunteer Centers, United Way Philadelphia Office. Phone: 215-665-2468. Fax: 215-665-2531. In-person interview required. Applicants must submit a cover letter, resume. Applications are accepted continuously.

UNITED WAY OF WACO
PO Box 2027
Waco, Texas 76703

General Information Clearinghouse for pledges that are allocated to member agencies. Established in 1923. Number of employees: 4. Number of internship applications received each year: 4.

Internships Available ▶ *1 intern:* responsibilities include record-keeping, sending out press notices, and assisting in the placing of volunteers in member agencies. Duration is flexible. Unpaid. Open to high school students, high school seniors, recent high school graduates, college freshmen, college sophomores, college juniors, college seniors, recent college graduates, graduate students, law students, career changers, individuals reentering the workforce. International applications accepted.
Benefits Names of contacts, possible full-time employment, willing to complete paperwork for educational credit, willing to provide letters of recommendation.
Contact Write, call, or fax Dorothy Wienecke, Communication Coordinator/Volunteer Center Director. Phone: 254-741-1980. Fax: 254-741-1984. In-person interview recommended. Applicants must submit a resume. Applications are accepted continuously.

UPPER BUCKS YMCA
151 South 14th Street
Quakertown, Pennsylvania 18951

General Information Social service organization that provides programs in health, fitness, aquatics, and child care. Established in 1969. Number of employees: 100. Number of internship applications received each year: 1.
Internships Available ▶ *1 camp counselor:* responsibilities include planning activities and ensuring safety and welfare of campers ages 5-12. Candidates should have oral communication skills, strong interpersonal skills, written communication skills, declared major in education or human services. Duration is 3½ months. $5 per hour. ▶ *2 child care interns:* responsibilities include working in a team-teaching situation and caring for the safety of the children. Candidates should have college courses in field, oral communication skills, plan to pursue career in field, strong interpersonal skills, strong leadership ability, background in early childhood, human services, or education. Duration is 3 months. $6 per hour. ▶ *1 physical instructor:* responsibilities include setting up weight training and fitness programs, supervising workout programs, and coaching children in sports. Candidates should have ability to work independently, ability to work with others, experience in the field, knowledge of field, oral communication skills, personal interest in the field. Duration is flexible. Unpaid. Open to college freshmen, college sophomores, college juniors, college seniors, recent college graduates, graduate students, law students, career changers, individuals reentering the workforce. International applications accepted.
Benefits Names of contacts, opportunity to attend seminars/workshops, possible full-time employment, travel reimbursement, willing to complete paperwork for educational credit, willing to provide letters of recommendation, CPR and first aid training, YMCA membership.
Contact Write, call, or fax Pat Hess, Youth and Family Program Director. Phone: 215-536-8409. Fax: 215-538-2943. In-person interview required. Applications are accepted continuously. Fees: $20.

VA COOL- VIRGINIA CAMPUS OUTREACH OPPORTUNITY LEAGUE
RC Box 26, 28 Westhampton Way, University of Richmond
Richmond, Virginia 23173

General Information Statewide nonprofit organization that works with a network of colleges in Virginia, through students, faculty and staff, to promote and enhance campus-based community service and service learning. Established in 1989. Number of employees: 3.
Internships Available ▶ *2–4 program assistants:* responsibilities include varied duties based on the needs of organization and intern; can include special events planning, production of publications, grant writing, or workshop development. Candidates should have ability to work independently, computer skills, editing skills, oral communication skills, research skills, written communication skills. Unpaid. Open to recent high school graduates, college freshmen, college sophomores, college juniors,

college seniors, recent college graduates, graduate students, law students, career changers. International applications accepted.
Benefits Names of contacts, opportunity to attend seminars/workshops, willing to act as a professional reference, willing to provide letters of recommendation, free parking.
Contact Write, call, or e-mail Tina Coris, Program Director, RC Box 26, 28 Westhampton Way, University of Richmond, Richmond, Virginia 23173. Phone: 804-289-8989. E-mail: ccoris@richmond. edu. In-person interview recommended. Applicants must submit a cover letter, resume. Applications are accepted continuously. World Wide Web: http://www.richmond.edu/~vacool/.

VALLEY YOUTH HOUSE
1615 Northampton Street
Easton, Pennsylvania 18042

General Information Youth house that provides preventative and responsive services for troubled young people, offering emergency shelter, long-term care, counseling, guidance, information, preparation for adulthood, and referral. Established in 1973. Number of employees: 125. Number of internship applications received each year: 40.
Internships Available ▶ *3 administration interns:* responsibilities include performing program audits, assisting in the planning and execution of the Project Child Conference (community conference on child abuse), coordinating community resources, completing agency research, and assisting in agency grant writing. Candidates should have declared college major in field, oral communication skills, organizational skills, self-motivation, strong interpersonal skills, written communication skills. Duration is 1–2 semesters. Open to graduate students. ▶ *8–10 bachelor's-level clinical counseling interns:* responsibilities include becoming familiar with the policies, practices, and protocols of the agency; conducting entry and intake interviews with clients; providing individual counseling; participating in family counseling as an observer; providing ongoing behavior management and client supervision; accompanying clients to appointments and activities; providing direct in-person client services; providing all appropriate and required timely documentation; performing case management; and participating in weekly undergraduate intern group supervision. Candidates should have declared college major in field, oral communication skills, self-motivation, strong interpersonal skills, written communication skills. Duration is 1–2 semesters. Open to college juniors, college seniors. ▶ *10–15 master's- level clinical counseling interns:* responsibilities include performing direct, in-person client service; successfully engaging and maintaining clients through the treatment process; completing adolescent and parent intake interviews and their subsequent dictation; providing individual, parent, family, and group counseling services within the context of office-based or outreach services and according to treatment plans; providing ongoing case coordination; assessing and collecting client fees; completing necessary documentation; and participating in weekly supervision and biweekly group supervision. Candidates should have ability to work independently, declared college major in field, oral communication skills, self-motivation, strong interpersonal skills, written communication skills. Duration is 2 semesters. Open to graduate students. All positions are unpaid. International applications accepted.
Benefits Names of contacts, opportunity to attend seminars/workshops, possible full-time employment, travel reimbursement, willing to act as a professional reference, willing to complete paperwork for educational credit, willing to provide letters of recommendation.
Contact Write, call, or fax Ms. Linda Getz, ACS, LSW, Internship Director. Phone: 610-252-2681. Fax: 610-252-9923. In-person interview required. Applicants must submit a formal organization application, resume. Application deadline: April 30 for summer, July 30 for fall (until slots are filled).

VERY SPECIAL ARTS
1300 Connecticut Avenue, NW, Suite 700
Washington, District of Columbia 20036

General Information Organization that implements art education programs for people with mental and physical disabilities through a network of national and international affiliates. Established in 1974. Number of employees: 50. Number of internship applications received each year: 100.

Internships Available ▶ *1–2 programs interns:* responsibilities include arts administration, assisting with special projects, events management, Internet research, database management, and general administrative assistance with arts administration projects. Candidates should have ability to work independently, ability to work with others, computer skills, oral communication skills, organizational skills, research skills, written communication skills. $650 per month for full-time positions. ▶ *1–5 seasonal interns:* responsibilities include assisting with program administration and special projects, and working in the organization's departments, including program development, national and international affiliate services, communications, development, and Internet research. Candidates should have computer skills, oral communication skills, organizational skills, personal interest in the field, strong interpersonal skills, written communication skills. $650 monthly stipend for full-time positions, prorated for part-time positions. Duration for all positions is 3–6 months. Open to college juniors, college seniors, recent college graduates, graduate students. International applications accepted.

Benefits Possible full-time employment, willing to complete paperwork for educational credit, opportunity to attend Kennedy Center seminars/workshops.

Contact Write, call, fax, or e-mail Ms. Vivian Fong, Director of Human Resources. Phone: 800-933-8721. Fax: 202-737-0725. E-mail: hr@vsarts.org. Telephone interview required. Applicants must submit a cover letter, resume, in-person interview for local applicants. Applications are accepted continuously. World Wide Web: http://www.vsarts.org.

VILLAGE ATLANTA
3965 Roosevelt Highway
College Park, Georgia 30349

General Information Christian rehabilitation program for homeless women and their children providing each family with their own 2-room efficiency apartment during their 6-month stay, a 4-phase therapeutic program to help mothers move towards self-sufficiency and independent living, and a therapeutic child development center for the children. Established in 1938. Number of employees: 20. Unit of Atlanta Union Mission, Atlanta, Georgia. Number of internship applications received each year: 6.

Internships Available ▶ *1–3 child-care providers:* responsibilities include supervising and caring for children in child development center (nursery, preschool, or after school), preparing developmentally appropriate lessons and teaching art and educational activities, and acting as a role model by demonstrating positive interactions and social behavior. Candidates should have ability to work with others, computer skills, experience in the field, oral communication skills, organizational skills, strong leadership ability. Duration is 3–12 months. Open to high school seniors, recent high school graduates, college freshmen, college sophomores, college juniors, college seniors, recent college graduates, graduate students, career changers, individuals reentering the workforce. ▶ *1–3 counseling/social work interns:* responsibilities include providing therapeutic activities that promote the welfare of the clients such as recordkeeping, case management, intake, group and individual therapy, and educational classes. Candidates should have college courses in field, knowledge of field, oral communication skills, strong interpersonal skills, strong leadership ability, written communication skills. Duration is 6–12 months. Open to recent college graduates, graduate students. All positions are unpaid. International applications accepted.

Benefits Free housing, free meals, names of contacts, on-the-job training, opportunity to attend seminars/workshops, possible full-time employment, willing to act as a professional reference, willing to complete paperwork for educational credit, willing to provide letters of recommendation.

Contact Write, call, fax, or e-mail Ruth Goodwin, Program Director. Phone: 404-669-0138. Fax: 404-762-0240. E-mail: rgoodwin@aum-atl.org. In-person interview recommended. Applicants must submit a resume. Applications are accepted continuously. World Wide Web: http://ww.aum-atl.org.

VINCENTIAN SERVICE CORPS–CENTRAL
7800 Natural Bridge
St. Louis, Missouri 63121

General Information Program for lay women and men who want to work with those at an economic disadvantage while living in a community with other members and experiencing a simple lifestyle. Established in 1984. Number of employees: 2. Number of internship applications received each year: 6.

Internships Available ▶ *4 child care workers (infant to kindergarten):* responsibilities include developing relationships with the children and their parents; assisting in planning and executing the daily activities designed for emotional, social, educational, and physical development of assigned children. Candidates should have ability to work with others, knowledge of field, oral communication skills, personal interest in the field, self-motivation. Duration is 1 year, full time. Open to college seniors, recent college graduates, career changers, individuals reentering the workforce, individuals interested in young children. ▶ *10–20 paid volunteers:* responsibilities include working with parishes, schools, clinics, and social service agencies in urban areas. Candidates should have oral communication skills, self-motivation, strong interpersonal skills, desire to experience community. Duration is 1 year. Open to college seniors, recent college graduates, graduate students, career changers. ▶ *6–12 skills trainers:* responsibilities include training and direct care for clients regarding everyday activities, plus helping to maintain the daily household operations; helping clients build social skills. Candidates should have ability to work with others, oral communication skills, personal interest in the field, self-motivation. Duration is 1 year, full time. Open to college seniors, recent college graduates, graduate students, law students, career changers, individuals reentering the workforce, anyone able to work with handicapped people. All positions paid at $100 monthly stipend. International applications accepted.

Benefits Free housing, health insurance, opportunity to attend seminars/workshops, possible full-time employment, travel reimbursement, tuition assistance, willing to complete paperwork for educational credit, $100 monthly food allowance.

International Internships Available in Germany.

Contact Write, call, fax, or e-mail Sr. Mary Catherine Dunn, D.C., Director. Phone: 314-382-2800 Ext. 291. Fax: 314-382-8392. E-mail: vsccentral@juno.com. In-person interview recommended. Applicants must submit a formal organization application, academic transcripts, 5 personal references and 5 letters of recommendation. Application deadline: May 31 for August. World Wide Web: http://www.flash.net/~vscwest.

VISITING NEIGHBORS INC.
665 Broadway, 7th Floor, Suite 701
New York, New York 10012

General Information Organization that fosters independence for senior citizens living in their homes through neighbor assistance and escort and shopping program. Established in 1972. Number of employees: 8. Number of internship applications received each year: 6.

Internships Available ▶ *5 psychology interns:* responsibilities include working with professional staff on small caseload while providing mental stimulation, encouragement, and physical independence to people over 60. Candidates should have analytical skills, oral communication skills, personal interest in the field, strong interpersonal skills, written communication skills. Duration is 6–12 months. Open to college sophomores, college juniors, college seniors, recent college graduates, graduate students, career changers, individuals reentering the workforce.

▶ *4 public relations and communications interns:* responsibilities include working on newsletter and putting together press kit. Candidates should have ability to work independently, oral communication skills, self-motivation, strong interpersonal skills, writing skills. Duration is open. Open to college sophomores, college juniors, college seniors, recent college graduates, graduate students, career changers, individuals reentering the workforce.
▶ *1 social work intern:* responsibilities include working in office, in field with clients, and managing a caseload in size corresponding to intern's level of experience and maturity. Candidates should have oral communication skills, personal interest in the field, self-motivation, strong interpersonal skills, written communication skills. Duration is flexible. Open to college freshmen, college sophomores, college juniors, college seniors, recent college graduates, graduate students, career changers, individuals reentering the workforce. All positions are unpaid. International applications accepted.
Benefits On-the-job training, willing to act as a professional reference, willing to complete paperwork for educational credit, willing to provide letters of recommendation.
Contact Write, call, or fax Ms. Cynthia Maurer, Executive Director. Phone: 212-260-6200. Fax: 212-260-2962. In-person interview required. Applicants must submit a formal organization application, cover letter, 2 (total) personal references and/or letters of recommendation. Applications are accepted continuously.

VOLUNTEER CENTER OF SAN FRANCISCO
425 Jackson Street
San Francisco, California 94111

General Information Organization serving as a clearinghouse for nonprofit agency volunteers. Established in 1946. Number of employees: 23. Number of internship applications received each year: 12.
Internships Available ▶ *1–5 program interns:* responsibilities include various administrative support for one of the following programs: Youth Empowerment, Youth Quest, Linking San Francisco, Board Match, Transitional Volunteer Program, community service, case management, corporate services. Candidates should have computer skills, office skills, oral communication skills, organizational skills, self-motivation, written communication skills. Duration is 1 semester. Unpaid. Open to high school students, recent high school graduates, college freshmen, college sophomores, college juniors, college seniors, recent college graduates, graduate students, career changers, individuals reentering the workforce. International applications accepted.
Benefits Willing to act as a professional reference, willing to complete paperwork for educational credit, willing to provide letters of recommendation, opportunity to gain knowledge of nonprofit sector and make contacts.
Contact Call or e-mail Amy Conn, Office Manager. Phone: 415-982-8999 Ext. 222. E-mail: vcsf@vcsf.org. In-person interview required. Applicants must submit a formal organization application. Applications are accepted continuously. World Wide Web: http://www.vcsf.org.

WASHINGTON COMMUNITY YMCA/YWCA
121 East Main Street
Washington, Iowa 52353

General Information Organization that provides health, recreation, and social programs, including full service child care. Established in 1925. Number of employees: 65.
Internships Available ▶ *1 child care teacher:* responsibilities include teaching preschool. Duration is flexible. ▶ *1 child caregiver:* responsibilities include providing child care. Duration is flexible. ▶ *1 health/fitness intern:* responsibilities include working with individuals and groups on health and wellness. Duration is 6–12 weeks. ▶ *1–2 youth physical programs interns:* responsibilities include setting up, administering, and implementing youth sports for kindergarten through sixth grades. Duration is 6–12 weeks. All positions paid. Open to college freshmen, college sophomores, college juniors, college seniors. International applications accepted.

Benefits Possible full-time employment, willing to complete paperwork for educational credit, willing to provide letters of recommendation.
Contact Write or call Paul Gausmann, Executive Director. Phone: 319-653-2141. In-person interview required. Applicants must submit a formal organization application, cover letter, resume, three letters of recommendation. Applications are accepted continuously.

WASHINGTON, D.C., RAPE CRISIS CENTER
PO Box 34125
Washington, District of Columbia 20043

General Information Private nonprofit agency offering 24-hour crisis counseling, companion services, and community education programs on related issues. Established in 1972. Number of employees: 11. Number of internship applications received each year: 50.
Internships Available ▶ *1–2 administration interns:* responsibilities include coordinating the workshop program, database management, and assisting in planning the Center's annual gala. Candidates should have ability to work with others, office skills, oral communication skills, organizational skills, self-motivation, written communication skills. Duration is flexible. Open to high school seniors, recent high school graduates, college freshmen, college sophomores, college juniors, college seniors, recent college graduates, individuals reentering the workforce. ▶ *2 community education interns:* responsibilities include assisting with coordinating the speaker's bureau, Sexual Assault Awareness Month self-defense classes, and other community education projects; some interns, depending on experience, have the option of being trained to conduct presentations. Candidates should have ability to work with others, knowledge of field, oral communication skills, organizational skills, self-motivation, written communication skills. Duration is flexible (3 months minimum). Open to high school seniors, recent high school graduates, college freshmen, college sophomores, college juniors, college seniors, recent college graduates, graduate students, career changers, individuals reentering the workforce. ▶ *3–5 counseling and advocacy interns:* responsibilities include assisting with volunteer schedule and other volunteer-related projects, attending training sessions for professionals on sexual abuse, and assisting the counseling and advocacy department by working on ongoing projects including updating the referral guide to the library; summer interns can be trained to work on 24-hour crisis hotline. Candidates should have office skills, organizational skills, personal interest in the field, self-motivation, strong interpersonal skills. Duration is flexible (3 months minimum). Open to high school seniors, recent high school graduates, college freshmen, college sophomores, college juniors, college seniors, recent college graduates, career changers, individuals reentering the workforce. ▶ *2 development interns:* responsibilities include assisting with fund-raising projects, including direct mail, phone-a-thons, and special projects and events. Candidates should have ability to work independently, computer skills, office skills, organizational skills, self-motivation, strong interpersonal skills. Duration is flexible (3 months minimum). Open to high school seniors, recent high school graduates, college freshmen, college sophomores, college juniors, college seniors, recent college graduates, career changers, individuals reentering the workforce. All positions are unpaid. International applications accepted.
Benefits Formal training, names of contacts, opportunity to attend seminars/workshops, travel reimbursement, willing to act as a professional reference, willing to complete paperwork for educational credit, willing to provide letters of recommendation.
Contact Write, call, fax, or e-mail Geneive Villamora, Assistant to the Executive Director. Phone: 202-232-0789. Fax: 202-387-3812. E-mail: dcrcc@erols.com. In-person interview recommended. Applicants must submit a formal organization application, cover letter, resume. Application deadline: April 15 for summer, August 15 for fall, December 15 for spring. World Wide Web: http://www.dcrcc.org.

WAYNESBORO YMCA
810 East Main Street
Waynesboro, Pennsylvania 17268

General Information Worldwide fellowship united by a common loyalty to Jesus Christ for the purpose of building Christian personality and a Christian society. Established in 1917. Number of employees: 50. Number of internship applications received each year: 1.

Internships Available ▶ *1–3 assistant aquatic supervisors:* responsibilities include teaching programs for 6-36-month olds, 3-5-year olds, 6-12-year olds, water exercise for adults and seniors, and arthritis water program; performing administrative duties, supervising housekeeping of pool area, maintaining records of swimming lesson participants and keeping monthly statistical summaries. Candidates should have ability to work independently, knowledge of field, personal interest in the field, self-motivation, strong interpersonal skills, certification in CPR, first aid, and lifeguard. Duration is 3–12 months. Position available as unpaid or at $6 per hour. Open to college freshmen, college sophomores, college juniors, college seniors, recent college graduates, graduate students, career changers, individuals reentering the workforce. ▶ *1–2 fitness consultants:* responsibilities include assessing member's fitness status and needs and designing an exercise program to meet their needs, cleaning equipment, and overseeing fitness center. Candidates should have ability to work independently, analytical skills, oral communication skills, personal interest in the field, self-motivation, strong interpersonal skills. Duration is flexible. $5–$6 per hour. Open to college freshmen, college sophomores, college juniors, college seniors, recent college graduates, graduate students, individuals reentering the workforce. ▶ *1–2 group supervisors:* responsibilities include overseeing and assisting in the operation of an after-school program for school-age children. Candidates should have experience in the field, oral communication skills, plan to pursue career in field, strong interpersonal skills, interest in aiding children socially and emotionally. Duration is 9 months. Unpaid. Open to high school seniors, recent high school graduates, college freshmen, college sophomores, college juniors, college seniors, recent college graduates, graduate students, individuals reentering the workforce. International applications accepted.

Benefits Names of contacts, on-the-job training, opportunity to attend seminars/workshops, possible full-time employment, travel reimbursement, willing to complete paperwork for educational credit, willing to provide letters of recommendation.

Contact Write, call, or fax Betsy Metz, Program Director. Phone: 717-762-6012. Fax: 717-762-4368. In-person interview required. Applicants must submit a cover letter, resume. Applications are accepted continuously.

WAYSIDE YOUTH AND FAMILY SUPPORT NETWORK
75 Fountain Street
Framingham, Massachusetts 01702

General Information Organization that provides social services and mental health services for children, teens, and families. Established in 1973. Number of employees: 500. Number of internship applications received each year: 50.

Internships Available ▶ *2 business interns:* responsibilities include performing marketing, fund-raising, and administrative duties. Candidates should have ability to work independently, analytical skills, computer skills, organizational skills, self-motivation, written communication skills. Duration is 6–12 months. Open to college juniors, college seniors, recent college graduates, graduate students. ▶ *10 child care workers:* responsibilities include milieu management (under direction of supervisors), meal preparation, activity planning and implementation, and group work. Candidates should have college courses in field, oral communication skills, self-motivation, strong interpersonal skills, writing skills. Duration is 6 months minimum (16 hours per week). Open to college juniors, college seniors, recent college graduates, individuals reentering the workforce. ▶ *30 counselors:* responsibilities include individual, family, and group counseling; in-home counseling; case management; outreach into communities; assessments; crisis intervention; and quality improvement project. Candidates should have ability to work independently, experience in the field, oral communication skills, self-motivation, strong interpersonal skills, written communication skills. Duration is 9 months minimum (24 hours per week). Open to graduate students. ▶ *2 nurses:* responsibilities include working with teens in the health clinic and working in schools and the community with special needs children. Candidates should have ability to work independently, oral communication skills, self-motivation, strong interpersonal skills, written communication skills. Duration is 6–9 months. Open to RN's or higher. ▶ *2 research assistants:* responsibilities include development of databases, data entry and data analysis, running quality management reports. Candidates should have ability to work independently, analytical skills, computer skills, knowledge of field, research skills, self-motivation, knowledge of database creation. Duration is 6 to 9 months (minimum 6 hours per week). Open to college juniors, college seniors, recent college graduates, graduate students. ▶ *Social workers:* responsibilities include providing individual and group counseling in a mental health clinic. Candidates should have ability to work independently, experience in the field, oral communication skills, self-motivation, strong interpersonal skills, written communication skills. Duration is flexible. Open to graduate students. ▶ *Teachers:* responsibilities include working in an alternative education program. Candidates should have ability to work independently, oral communication skills, organizational skills, personal interest in the field, strong leadership ability, written communication skills. Duration is 2 semesters (6-8 months). Open to college juniors, college seniors, recent college graduates, graduate students. All positions are unpaid. International applications accepted.

Benefits Formal training, opportunity to attend seminars/workshops, possible full-time employment, willing to complete paperwork for educational credit, willing to provide letters of recommendation.

Contact Write or e-mail Betsy Reid, Vice President of Clinical Services. E-mail: ereid@waysideyouth.org. No phone calls. In-person interview required. Applicants must submit a formal organization application, cover letter, resume, three personal references. Applications are accepted continuously.

WEST COUNTY FAMILY YMCA
7777 Edinger Avenue, Suite 210
Huntington Beach, California 92647

General Information Organization that institutes programs that build healthy bodies, minds, and spirits. Established in 1968. Number of employees: 40. Unit of YMCA of Orange County, Costa Mesa, California.

Internships Available ▶ *1–5 Indian agents:* responsibilities include attending parents meetings, parent/child meetings, program events (campouts, trips, parties), and staff meetings. Candidates should have organizational skills, strong interpersonal skills, strong leadership ability, enjoyment of children. Duration is 12 months. Unpaid. ▶ *1–2 public relations/advertisers:* responsibilities include attending local civic and public club meetings, helping to create and establish a strong public relations and advertising campaign for community, and organizing and evaluating fundraisers. Duration is 12 months. Unpaid. ▶ *1–4 sports coordinators:* responsibilities include supervising staff, maintaining equipment, scheduling programs, organizing banquets, and coordinating promotions, evaluations, and advertising. Candidates should have knowledge of field, oral communication skills, organizational skills, strong interpersonal skills, strong leadership ability. Duration is 9 months. Unpaid. Open to recent high school graduates, college freshmen, college sophomores, college juniors, college seniors, recent college graduates, graduate students, law students, career changers, individuals reentering the workforce. ▶ *1–2 summer day camp assistant directors:* responsibilities include organizing and directing summer day camp program for elementary school students; must schedule trips and activities for entire summer; supervision of up to 8 staff members. Candidates should have ability to work with others, experience in the field, office skills, oral communication skills, organizational skills, strong leadership ability. Duration is 4–5 months. Paid.

Open to recent high school graduates, college freshmen, college sophomores, college juniors, college seniors, recent college graduates, graduate students, law students, career changers, individuals reentering the workforce. ▶ *Summer day camp counselors:* responsibilities include supervision of 8-10 elementary school campers on field trips and on-site, planning and organizing activities. Candidates should have ability to work with others, experience in the field, organizational skills, strong leadership ability. Duration is 3 months. Paid. Open to recent high school graduates, college freshmen, college sophomores, college juniors, college seniors, recent college graduates, graduate students, law students, career changers, individuals reentering the workforce. International applications accepted.
Benefits Names of contacts, opportunity to attend seminars/workshops, possible full-time employment, willing to complete paperwork for educational credit, willing to provide letters of recommendation.
Contact Write, call, or fax Francesca Stretch, Intern Coordinator, 7777 Edinger Avenue, Suite 210, Huntington Beach, California 92647. Phone: 714-896-9622. Fax: 714-896-8202. In-person interview recommended. Applicants must submit a formal organization application. Applications are accepted continuously.

WEST ROXBURY/ROSLINDALE YMCA
15 Bellevue Street
West Roxbury, Massachusetts 02132

General Information Social service agency open to all ages whose activities include physical education classes, youth sports, swimming, teen outreach and counseling, adult health and wellness classes, and a licensed child care center. Established in 1911. Number of employees: 150. Unit of Greater Boston YMCA, Boston, Massachusetts. Number of internship applications received each year: 2.
Internships Available ▶ *2–3 Nautilus/fitness instructors:* responsibilities include introducing members to cardiovascular/strength center, teaching fitness classes in aerobics and step-aerobics, or helping with adult leagues in coed volleyball or men's basketball. Candidates should have ability to work with others, knowledge of field, oral communication skills, personal interest in the field, self-motivation, strong leadership ability. Duration is year-round. Position available as unpaid or at $8–$9 per hour. Open to college freshmen, college sophomores, college juniors, college seniors, recent college graduates, graduate students, career changers, individuals reentering the workforce. ▶ *3–8 child care workers:* responsibilities include helping design age-appropriate curriculum, implementing program, communicating with parents, and providing a safe, nurturing environment. Candidates should have ability to work with others, knowledge of field, oral communication skills, personal interest in the field, self-motivation, strong leadership ability. Duration is year-round. Position available as unpaid or at $9–$12 per hour. Open to college freshmen, college sophomores, college juniors, college seniors, recent college graduates, graduate students, career changers, individuals reentering the workforce. ▶ *2–3 physical education instructors:* responsibilities include teaching physical education program for area grammar schools. Candidates should have ability to work with others, college courses in field, knowledge of field, oral communication skills, plan to pursue career in field, strong leadership ability. Duration is flexible. Position available as unpaid or at $8–$12 per hour. ▶ *1–2 youth sports instructors:* responsibilities include teaching youth sports classes in soccer, tee-baseball, basketball, hockey, and tennis. Candidates should have ability to work with others, knowledge of field, oral communication skills, personal interest in the field, self-motivation, strong leadership ability. Duration is year-round. Position available as unpaid or at $8–$9 per hour. Open to college freshmen, college sophomores, college juniors, college seniors, recent college graduates, graduate students, career changers, individuals reentering the workforce.
Benefits Formal training, names of contacts, opportunity to attend seminars/workshops, possible full-time employment, willing to complete paperwork for educational credit, willing to provide letters of recommendation.

Contact Write, call, or fax Marion Kelly, Executive Director. Phone: 617-323-3200. Fax: 617-469-5255. In-person interview required. Applicants must submit a formal organization application, resume, three personal references. Applications are accepted continuously.

WINANT AND CLAYTON VOLUNTEERS
109 East 50th Street
New York, New York 10022

General Information Organization providing community service in Britain on projects dealing with people of all ages and with a variety of needs. Established in 1948. Number of employees: 1. Number of internship applications received each year: 60.
Internships Available ▶ *20 volunteers:* responsibilities include working 40-hour weeks alongside trained social workers in inner-city London; serving a varied population with different needs, including homeless, alcoholics, battered women, children in day care, community drugs team, persons with AIDS, and psychiatric rehabilitation. Candidates should have ability to work independently, oral communication skills, personal interest in the field, self-motivation, strong interpersonal skills, strong leadership ability. Duration is 3 months (mid-June to mid-August). Unpaid. Open to high school seniors, recent high school graduates, college freshmen, college sophomores, college juniors, college seniors, recent college graduates, graduate students, law students, career changers, individuals reentering the workforce, people of all ages 18 and over.
Benefits Formal training, free housing, willing to provide letters of recommendation, $70 per week stipend.
International Internships Available in United Kingdom.
Contact Write, call, or fax Ms. Nanette Rousseau, Coordinator of Volunteers. Phone: 212-378-0271. Fax: 212-378-0281. In-person interview recommended. Applicants must submit a formal organization application, resume, two personal references. Application deadline: January 30. Fees: $35. World Wide Web: http://www.voicenet.com/~mjmcc/.

THE WOMEN'S CENTER
133 Park Street, NE
Vienna, Virginia 22180

General Information Private nonprofit group of professionals offering individual counseling and psychotherapy, career counseling, separation and divorce services, support and therapy groups, legal and financial education, workshops, and educational programs. Established in 1974. Number of employees: 85. Number of internship applications received each year: 50.
Internships Available ▶ *1–2 career services interns:* responsibilities include helping to implement career programs, researching, and assisting with the annual conference and the mentoring program. Duration is 6 months. Open to college freshmen, college sophomores, college juniors, college seniors, recent college graduates, graduate students, career changers. ▶ *2 development interns:* responsibilities include assisting with fund-raising and proposal writing, foundation research, and corporate solicitation. Candidates should have ability to work with others, oral communication skills, personal interest in the field, written communication skills. Duration is 6 months. Open to college freshmen, college sophomores, college juniors, college seniors, recent college graduates, graduate students, career changers. ▶ *3–6 information/intake interns:* responsibilities include assisting callers by providing information and referrals to meet needs, making counseling appointments, and researching community resources. Candidates should have ability to work independently, oral communication skills, strong interpersonal skills, interest in psychology, social work, and/or women's studies. Duration is 6–12 months. Open to college juniors, college seniors, recent college graduates, graduate students, career changers. ▶ *3 public relations interns:* responsibilities include assisting with developing and implementing marketing strategies, publicity, and media contacts for special events; performing research; making press calls; promoting programs; and participating in program planning. Candidates should have ability to work with others, oral communication skills, personal interest in the field, written com-

The Women's Center (continued)

munication skills. Duration is flexible. Open to college freshmen, college sophomores, college juniors, college seniors, recent college graduates, graduate students, career changers. ▶ *14 therapy/clinical interns:* responsibilities include individual and group therapy and assisting with workshop presentation. Some interns also provide counseling. Duration is 8 months. Open to individuals completing master's degree in social work or professional counseling, or a doctorate degree in psychology. All positions are unpaid. International applications accepted.

Benefits On-the-job training, opportunity to attend seminars/workshops, willing to complete paperwork for educational credit.

Contact Write, call, or fax Ms. Gale Gearhart, Director of Administration. Phone: 703-281-2657 Ext. 244. Fax: 703-242-1454. In-person interview required. Applicants must submit a resume. Applications are accepted continuously. World Wide Web: http://www.thewomenscenter.org.

YMCA CAMP POTAWOTAMI
PO Box 38
South Milford, Indiana 46786

General Information Camp that provides educational programs in a Christian environment. Established in 1919. Number of employees: 40. Branch of YMCA of Greater Fort Wayne, Fort Wayne, Indiana. Number of internship applications received each year: 1.

Internships Available ▶ *2 outdoor education specialists:* responsibilities include developing programs, serving as liaisons to schools, working with school groups, and implementing programs. Candidates should have knowledge of field, personal interest in the field, self-motivation, strong interpersonal skills, strong leadership ability. Duration is 4–5 months. Position available as unpaid or at $150–$160 per week. Open to recent high school graduates, college freshmen, college sophomores, college juniors, college seniors, recent college graduates, graduate students, law students, career changers, individuals reentering the workforce. International applications accepted.

Benefits Formal training, free housing, free meals, job counseling, names of contacts, opportunity to attend seminars/workshops, possible full-time employment, travel reimbursement, willing to complete paperwork for educational credit, willing to provide letters of recommendation.

Contact Write, call, fax, or e-mail Sonny Adkins, Executive Director. Phone: 219-351-2525. Fax: 219-351-3915. E-mail: ymcacamp@kuntrynet.com. In-person interview recommended. Applicants must submit a cover letter, resume, three letters of recommendation. Applications are accepted continuously. World Wide Web: http://www.camp-potawotami.org.

YMCA FRIENDSHIP BETWEEN THE AGES-MENTORING PROGRAM
302 West First Street
Duluth, Minnesota 55802

General Information Program that works with youth and families (usually low income, single parent households) to provide adult mentors for children. Established in 1882. Number of employees: 120. Number of internship applications received each year: 5.

Internships Available ▶ *6–8 human services interns:* responsibilities include working with families using interviewing skills, performing casework, maintaining contact with adult volunteers and families, and planning, implementing, and evaluating special programs/activities. Candidates should have ability to work independently, college degree in related field, self-motivation, strong interpersonal skills. Duration is 6–12 months. Unpaid. Open to graduate students. International applications accepted.

Benefits Names of contacts, possible full-time employment, travel reimbursement, willing to complete paperwork for educational credit, willing to provide letters of recommendation, free YMCA membership.

Contact Write or call Mr. Blair Gagne, Program Director. Phone: 218-722-4745 Ext. 125. In-person interview required. Applications are accepted continuously.

YMCA OF GREATER NEW YORK AT GREENKILL OUTDOOR ENVIRONMENTAL EDUCATION CENTER
Big Pond Road, PO Box B
Huguenot, New York 12746

General Information Center that provides outdoor education and other camping/conference-related services to elementary school–age students to help develop teamwork and an understanding of natural resources. Established in 1975. Number of employees: 40. Branch of YMCA of Greater New York, New York, New York. Number of internship applications received each year: 75.

Internships Available ▶ *2–6 naturalists interns:* responsibilities include teaching outdoor environmental education and assisting with operating the residential center. Candidates should have college courses in field, personal interest in the field, plan to pursue career in field, strong interpersonal skills, strong leadership ability. Duration is 8–16 weeks. $50 per week. Open to college juniors, college seniors, recent college graduates, career changers. International applications accepted.

Benefits Formal training, free housing, free meals, names of contacts, on-the-job training, possible full-time employment, willing to complete paperwork for educational credit, willing to provide letters of recommendation, worker's compensation.

Contact Write, call, fax, or e-mail Heather Chadwick, Director, Big Pond Road, PO Box B, Huguenot, New York 12746. Phone: 914-858-2200. Fax: 914-858-7823. E-mail: greenkilloeec@pickeonline.net. In-person interview recommended. Applicants must submit a formal organization application, cover letter, resume, three personal references. Application deadline: January 15 for spring, March 15 for summer, April 15 for fall, October 15 for winter. World Wide Web: http://www.ymcanyc.org.

YMCA OF GREATER TOLEDO, WEST BRANCH
2020 Tremainsville
Toledo, Ohio 43613

General Information Organization that institutes Christian principles through programs that build a healthy spirit, mind, and body for all. Established in 1865. Number of employees: 80. Unit of YMCA of Greater Toledo, Toledo, Ohio. Number of internship applications received each year: 5.

Internships Available ▶ *1–3 outdoor pool manager interns/assistant manager interns:* responsibilities include marketing; budgeting; hiring, supervising, and evaluating a staff of 30–45; and maintaining daily operations and upkeep of pool. Candidates should have ability to work with others, experience in the field, oral communication skills, self-motivation, strong leadership ability. Duration is 5–9 months. $6–$8 per hour. Open to college sophomores, college juniors, college seniors. ▶ *1–2 program director interns:* responsibilities include helping to plan, budget, and manage the program department for youth sports, teens, aquatics, family programming, and fitness; helping prepare flyers, newsletters, and brochures; and performing public relations duties. Candidates should have ability to work with others, experience in the field, oral communication skills, organizational skills, plan to pursue career in field, self-motivation. Duration is 6–9 months. Position available as unpaid or paid. Open to college juniors, college seniors.

Benefits Formal training, names of contacts, opportunity to attend seminars/workshops, possible full-time employment, willing to act as a professional reference, willing to complete paperwork for educational credit, willing to provide letters of recommendation, national YMCA job listings provided.

Contact Write, call, or fax Ms. Diane Nicely, Associate Executive Director. Phone: 419-475-3496. Fax: 419-475-8837. In-person interview recommended. Applicants must submit a formal organization application. Applications are accepted continuously.

YMCA OF GREATER WEST CHESTER
123 North Church Street
West Chester, Pennsylvania 19380

General Information Advocacy and resource organization for the community in relation to women's and children's issues.
Internships Available ▶ *Interns:* responsibilities include assisting program staff in six core areas: Women's Information Network, mentoring, Homeshare, community outreach, recreation and fitness, and the Mothers' Center. Duration is flexible. Unpaid. Open to high school students, high school seniors, recent high school graduates, college freshmen, college sophomores, college juniors, college seniors, recent college graduates, graduate students, law students, law school graduates, career changers, individuals reentering the workforce.
Contact Write, call, or fax Frances Luft, Volunteer Coordinator. Phone: 610-692-3737. Fax: 610-692-5014. Applications are accepted continuously.

YMCA SAFE PLACE SERVICES
1410 South First Street
Louisville, Kentucky 40208

General Information Agency that provides emergency shelter care to teens with serious family problems. Established in 1974. Number of employees: 30. Unit of YMCA of Greater Louisville, Louisville, Kentucky. Number of internship applications received each year: 25.
Internships Available ▶ *2 administrative interns:* responsibilities include assisting in the development of grant and foundation proposals and performing quality assurance studies. Candidates should have computer skills, editing skills, office skills, organizational skills, research skills, writing skills. Duration is 1–2 semesters. Unpaid. Open to college freshmen, college sophomores, college juniors, college seniors, recent college graduates. ▶ *1–2 clerical interns:* responsibilities include filing, typing, and performing computer work. Candidates should have analytical skills, computer skills, office skills, research skills, self-motivation, writing skills. Duration is 1 semester. Unpaid. Open to recent high school graduates, college freshmen, college sophomores, college juniors, college seniors, recent college graduates, graduate students, career changers. ▶ *2–4 social workers/counselors:* responsibilities include counseling individuals, groups, and families; presenting life skills; and conducting informal discussions with youth. Candidates should have ability to work independently, oral communication skills, self-motivation, strong interpersonal skills, written communication skills. Duration is 1–2 semesters. Unpaid. Open to recent college graduates, graduate students. ▶ *4–6 youth workers:* responsibilities include supervising 8-10 youths in meal preparation, chores, and recreation. Candidates should have oral communication skills, self-motivation, strong interpersonal skills, strong leadership ability, written communication skills. Duration is 1 semester. Position available as unpaid or at $7.25-$8.25 per hour. Open to high school seniors, recent high school graduates, college freshmen, college sophomores, college juniors, college seniors, recent college graduates, graduate students, career changers. International applications accepted.
Benefits Formal training, free meals, names of contacts, opportunity to attend seminars/workshops, possible full-time employment, willing to complete paperwork for educational credit, willing to provide letters of recommendation.
International Internships Available in Bombay, India; Dublin, Ireland; Lisburn, United Kingdom.
Contact Write or fax John M. Papanek, Director of Counseling Services. Fax: 502-635-1443. No phone calls. In-person interview required. Applications are accepted continuously.

YMCA TRAINING ALLIANCE
11 East Adams Street, Suite 300
Chicago, Illinois 60603

General Information Nonprofit organization that helps individuals achieve economic and career advancement by providing opportunities to enhance skills and self-esteem through job training and placement, literacy education, and referral services; the

Alliance also works with coalitions on issues relating to economic advancement. Established in 1976. Number of employees: 20. Unit of YMCA of Metropolitan Chicago, Chicago, Illinois. Number of internship applications received each year: 12.
Internships Available ▶ *1–2 employment interns:* responsibilities include assisting individuals in making career decisions and overcoming barriers to employment. Candidates should have computer skills, oral communication skills, organizational skills, self-motivation, strong interpersonal skills, strong leadership ability. Duration is open. Open to college sophomores, college juniors, college seniors, recent college graduates, graduate students, career changers. ▶ *1 fund-raising administration intern:* responsibilities include assisting in researching/writing grant proposals. Candidates should have ability to work independently, computer skills, editing skills, research skills, self-motivation, writing skills. Duration is flexible. Open to college juniors, college seniors, recent college graduates, graduate students, career changers. ▶ *1 research intern:* responsibilities include gathering data and participating in preparing reports to study the effects of training and pre-employment activities on the economic self-sufficiency of low-income individuals. Candidates should have ability to work independently, ability to work with others, analytical skills, computer skills, editing skills, organizational skills, research skills, writing skills. Duration is flexible. Open to college juniors, college seniors, recent college graduates, graduate students, law students, career changers. ▶ *1 working knowledge intern:* responsibilities include tutoring, helping with curriculum development, and publishing a student-written journal. Candidates should have ability to work with others, computer skills, oral communication skills, personal interest in the field, self-motivation, written communication skills. Duration is flexible. ▶ *1 youth program intern:* responsibilities include assisting in development and implementation of youth programs centered around leadership development and youth career development and assisting in program fund-raising. Candidates should have computer skills, organizational skills, personal interest in the field, self-motivation, strong interpersonal skills, writing skills. Duration is open. Open to college sophomores, college juniors, college seniors, recent college graduates, graduate students. All positions are unpaid. International applications accepted.
Benefits Job counseling, possible full-time employment, willing to complete paperwork for educational credit, willing to provide letters of recommendation.
Contact Write, call, or fax Ms. Marcia Medema, Director of Workforce Development. Phone: 312-913-2150 Ext. 32. Fax: 312-913-2157. In-person interview recommended. Applicants must submit a cover letter, resume. Applications are accepted continuously.

YMCA-USO OF THE PIKES PEAK REGION
PO Box 1694
Colorado Springs, Colorado 80901

General Information Organization that runs adult, youth, and children's programs designed to promote personal growth, enhance family relationships, improve physical and mental health, foster leadership abilities, develop specific skills, and to have fun. Established in 1885. Number of employees: 400. Number of internship applications received each year: 25.
Internships Available ▶ *Communications/marketing interns:* responsibilities include developing materials for community-wide celebration of the arts on New Year's Eve, public speaking, and volunteer recruitment. Duration is 8–12 weeks. ▶ *Day camp interns:* responsibilities include developing program for summer day camp. Candidates should have college courses in field, experience in the field, oral communication skills, personal interest in the field, strong interpersonal skills. Duration is 10–12 weeks. ▶ *Fitness/wellness interns:* responsibilities include administering corporate cup program which involves various corporations locally in sports challenges, developing schedules, awards banquets, and events. Candidates should have oral communication skills, personal interest in the field, plan to pursue career in field, self-motivation, strong interpersonal skills, written communication skills. Duration is 3 months. ▶ *Fundraisers:* responsibilities include developing database of donors through research and technical information regarding foundations and grants.

YMCA-USO of the Pikes Peak Region (continued)

Candidates should have knowledge of field, office skills, oral communication skills, research skills, strong interpersonal skills, written communication skills. Duration is flexible. Open to college juniors, college seniors. ▶ *Resident camp program interns:* responsibilities include developing program for resident camp. Candidates should have experience in the field, personal interest in the field, strong interpersonal skills, strong leadership ability. Duration is 8–10 weeks. Open to college juniors, college seniors. ▶ *Youth sports interns:* responsibilities include developing and coordinating youth sports programs for the association or branch. Candidates should have ability to work independently, experience in the field, knowledge of field, personal interest in the field, self-motivation, strong interpersonal skills. Duration is flexible. All positions paid at $200 per month stipend. International applications accepted.

Benefits Possible full-time employment, willing to complete paperwork for educational credit, willing to provide letters of recommendation, free room and board for summer resident camping positions.

Contact Write or e-mail Ms. Gwenda Valentine, Director, Human Resources. E-mail: gvalentine@ppymca.org. No phone calls. In-person interview recommended. Applicants must submit a formal organization application, cover letter, resume, academic transcripts, three personal references, three letters of recommendation. Applications are accepted continuously.

YOUTH AND SHELTER SERVICES, INC.
420 Kellog, PO Box 1628
Ames, Iowa 50010

General Information Organization that exists to help children, youth, and families solve problems, grow, and become self-sufficient, responsible, contributing members of society. Established in 1976. Number of employees: 125. Number of internship applications received each year: 15.

Internships Available ▶ *10–15 residential interns:* responsibilities include supervising residents and monitoring activities, maintaining a non-judgmental attitude, adhering to agency policies and procedures, and listening effectively to residents; providing for the daily maintenance of the house and assuring safe living conditions; answering phones and receiving visitors, updating staff, and writing chore charts. Candidates should have ability to work with others, plan to pursue career in field, strong leadership ability, writing skills. Duration is 4 months in fall, spring,or summer. ▶ *1–2 youth service associates:* responsibilities include adhering to agency policies and procedures, assisting with grade school programs, co-facilitating the parents' nurturing class, assisting with special projects, and developing an activities curriculum. Candidates should have ability to work independently, ability to work with others, computer skills, office skills, personal interest in the field, self-motivation. Duration is flexible. All positions are unpaid. Open to individuals 18 years of age or older. International applications accepted.

Benefits Formal training, names of contacts, opportunity to attend seminars/workshops, possible full-time employment, willing to complete paperwork for educational credit, willing to provide letters of recommendation.

Contact Write, call, fax, or e-mail Heidi Heilskov, Volunteer Coordinator. Phone: 515-232-4331. Fax: 415-233-2440. E-mail: pedept@yss.ames.ia.us. In-person interview recommended. Applicants must submit a formal organization application, cover letter, resume, 2-3 personal references and 2-3 letters of recommendation. Application deadline: April 1 for summer, August 1 for fall, November 1 for spring. World Wide Web: http://www.yss.ames.ia.us.

YOUTH OPPORTUNITIES UPHELD
81 Plantation Street
Worcester, Massachusetts 01604

General Information Nonprofit organization that provides troubled adolescents and families with opportunities to deal with problems in ways that promote development as individuals and as contributing members of society. Established in 1970. Number of employees: 350. Number of internship applications received each year: 150.

Internships Available ▶ *2–4 alternative sentencing project interns:* responsibilities include setting up community service for first-time offenders, filing paperwork, and supervision. Candidates should have ability to work with others, computer skills, oral communication skills, organizational skills, writing skills, written communication skills. Duration is 1–2 semesters. Open to high school seniors, college freshmen, college sophomores, college juniors, college seniors, graduate students. ▶ *10–35 court mentor program interns:* responsibilities include working as an outreach counselor for "court-involved" or at-risk adolescents who are struggling with individual or family problems, filing weekly/monthly reports, attending weekly staff meeting, and organizing activities. Candidates should have ability to work independently, self-motivation, strong interpersonal skills, strong leadership ability. Duration is 6–12 months. Open to college freshmen, college sophomores, college juniors, college seniors, graduate students. ▶ *Educational counselors:* responsibilities include working in an alternative school for troubled adolescents, tutoring, participating in sports or activities, and monitoring behaviors on a daily point sheet. Candidates should have ability to work with others, oral communication skills, organizational skills, personal interest in the field, writing skills. Duration is 4 months minimum. Open to college freshmen, college sophomores, college juniors, college seniors, graduate students. ▶ *8 graduate clinical interns:* responsibilities include performing individual/family counseling, assessments, observations, and therapy sessions. Candidates should have analytical skills, college degree in related field, plan to pursue career in field, strong interpersonal skills. Duration is 8–10 weeks. Open to graduate students. ▶ *Residential counselors:* responsibilities include working in a residential home for troubled adolescents, attending group meetings, working as an advocate to youth, and participating in activities that are set up for youth. Candidates should have oral communication skills, personal interest in the field, self-motivation, strong interpersonal skills. Duration is 4 months minimum. Open to college freshmen, college sophomores, college juniors, college seniors, graduate students. ▶ *2 teen parent counselors:* responsibilities include assisting staff in planning group activities, spending time with teenage mothers, assisting in weekly menu planning, and participating as a positive role model. Candidates should have oral communication skills, personal interest in the field, strong interpersonal skills, written communication skills. Duration is 4 months minimum. Open to college freshmen, college sophomores, college juniors, college seniors, graduate students. All positions are unpaid. International applications accepted.

Benefits Formal training, names of contacts, opportunity to attend seminars/workshops, possible full-time employment, travel reimbursement, willing to act as a professional reference, willing to complete paperwork for educational credit, willing to provide letters of recommendation.

Contact Write, call, or fax Lenore Johnson, Coordinator of Mentoring and Prevention Services. Phone: 508-755-3620 Ext. 337. Fax: 508-849-5631. In-person interview required. Applicants must submit a formal organization application, cover letter, resume, three letters of recommendation, criminal records check required. Applications are accepted continuously. World Wide Web: http://www.youinc.org.

YWCA/DOMESTIC VIOLENCE PREVENTION CENTER
626 Church Street
Lynchburg, Virginia 24504

General Information Organization that serves battered women and their children and seeks to eliminate abuse. Established in 1978. Number of employees: 18. Unit of YWCA of the USA, New York, New York. Number of internship applications received each year: 5.

Internships Available ▶ *1 APA advocate assistant:* responsibilities include overseeing the Batterer's Program to include intake, financial, and attendance management; writing letters to court and appearing at court. Candidates should have ability to work

independently, computer skills, oral communication skills, personal interest in the field, strong interpersonal skills, written communication skills. Duration is 1 October to December 1999. Position available as unpaid or paid. Open to recent college graduates, graduate students, individuals reentering the workforce. ▶ *DVPC interns:* responsibilities include providing casework assistance. Candidates should have ability to work independently, ability to work with others, computer skills, office skills, oral communication skills, personal interest in the field, written communication skills. Duration is 1 semester. Unpaid. Open to college seniors, graduate students, individuals reentering the workforce. International applications accepted.
Benefits Formal training, opportunity to attend seminars/workshops, possible full-time employment, travel reimbursement, willing to complete paperwork for educational credit.
Contact Write, call, or fax Bonnie C. Stewart, DVPC Director. Phone: 804-528-1041. Fax: 804-847-4723. In-person interview required. Applicants must submit a resume. Applications are accepted continuously.

YWCA OF BINGHAMTON/BROOME COUNTY
80 Hawley Street
Binghamton, New York 13901

General Information Organization that strives to empower women and girls and eliminate racism; offers emergency shelter, housing, child care, health and fitness programs, art and multicultural programs. Established in 1892. Unit of YWCA of the USA, New York, New York. Number of internship applications received each year: 15.
Internships Available ▶ *2 child care interns:* responsibilities include providing quality child care to preschool and toddlers. Open to college freshmen, college sophomores, college juniors, college seniors, recent college graduates, graduate students, career changers, individuals reentering the workforce. ▶ *1–2 counselor interns:* responsibilities include working in emergency housing shelter serving women age 16 and older; conducting intake interviews; case management; referrals to area agencies; and assisting women in meeting individual goals. Open to college freshmen, college sophomores, college juniors, college seniors, recent college graduates, graduate students, career changers. ▶ *1–2 outreach interns:* responsibilities include working with housing team to develop speakers bureau and program materials to increase community awareness of housing programs and track program referrals; developing community outreach program. Open to college freshmen, college sophomores, college juniors, college seniors, recent college graduates, graduate students, career changers, individuals reentering the workforce. ▶ *1 recreation intern:* responsibilities include planning, promoting and implementing activities for residents; scheduling guest speakers; developing newsletters and bulletin boards. Open to college freshmen, college sophomores, college juniors, college seniors, recent college graduates, graduate students, career changers, individuals reentering the workforce. Duration for all positions is flexible. All positions are unpaid. International applications accepted.
Benefits Formal training, job counseling, names of contacts, possible full-time employment, willing to complete paperwork for educational credit, willing to provide letters of recommendation.
Contact Write or fax Internship Coordinator. Fax: 607-723-9610. In-person interview recommended. Applicants must submit academic transcripts. Applications are accepted continuously.

YWCA OF CARLISLE
301 G Street
Carlisle, Pennsylvania 17013-1389

General Information Community service agency whose mission is to empower women and girls and to eliminate racism. Established in 1919. Number of employees: 65. Unit of YWCA of the USA, New York, New York. Number of internship applications received each year: 2.
Internships Available ▶ *1–3 interns:* responsibilities include working in all program and service areas. Candidates should have ability to work independently, oral communication skills, plan

to pursue career in field, strong interpersonal skills, written communication skills. Duration is September to December, January to May. Unpaid. Open to college juniors, college seniors. International applications accepted.
Benefits Names of contacts, opportunity to attend seminars/workshops, travel reimbursement, willing to complete paperwork for educational credit, willing to provide letters of recommendation.
Contact Write, call, fax, or e-mail Barbara Kohutiak, Executive Director. Phone: 717-243-3818. Fax: 717-243-3948. E-mail: carywca@pa.net. In-person interview required. Applicants must submit a cover letter, resume, three personal references. Application deadline: March 1 for summer, July 1 for fall, October 1 for spring.

YWCA OF ST. PAUL
198 Western Avenue North
St. Paul, Minnesota 55102-1790

General Information Nonprofit membership-based organization governed by women and dedicated to the advancement of women and families. Established in 1907. Number of employees: 67. Unit of YWCA of the USA, New York, New York. Number of internship applications received each year: 15.
Internships Available ▶ *1–2 5K race coordinators:* responsibilities include assisting with marketing activities; soliciting sponsors, gifts, and food; corresponding with sponsors and runners; organizing and supervising volunteers; and obtaining permits, brochures, and race summaries. Candidates should have ability to work independently, ability to work with others, knowledge of field, oral communication skills, organizational skills, strong leadership ability. Open to college freshmen, college sophomores, college juniors, college seniors, recent college graduates, graduate students, career changers, individuals reentering the workforce. ▶ *1 Operation SMART (science, math and relevant technology) intern:* responsibilities include developing and teaching one 4-week session for 2nd-3rd grade girls and one 8-week session of SMART programs at an outreach site for 4th-6th grade girls; developing and leading Family Math/Science Night. Candidates should have ability to work independently, college courses in field, knowledge of field, oral communication skills, personal interest in the field, research skills, self-motivation, strong interpersonal skills, strong leadership ability. Open to college freshmen, college sophomores, college juniors, college seniors, recent college graduates, graduate students, career changers, individuals reentering the workforce. ▶ *1–2 assistant child care providers:* responsibilities include scheduling and supervising activities and special events; providing a safe and caring atmosphere that promotes learning and enjoyment; maintaining communication with staff, children, and parents; and assisting with billing and invoicing program participants. Candidates should have ability to work independently, oral communication skills, organizational skills, self-motivation, strong interpersonal skills. Open to recent high school graduates, college sophomores, college juniors, college seniors, recent college graduates, career changers, individuals reentering the workforce. ▶ *1 child enrichment center intern:* responsibilities include participating in the children's program by developing and implementing activities appropriate to the curriculum and providing support to the child development specialists. Candidates should have ability to work independently, ability to work with others, analytical skills, experience in the field, personal interest in the field, self-motivation. Open to college freshmen, college sophomores, college juniors, college seniors, recent college graduates, graduate students, career changers, individuals reentering the workforce. ▶ *1 community organizer:* responsibilities include contacting community agencies and developing relationships, creating an organized database of community resources and contacts with those agencies, and working with internal departments. Candidates should have ability to work independently, ability to work with others, office skills, organizational skills, self-motivation. Open to college sophomores, college juniors, college seniors, recent college graduates, career changers, individuals reentering the workforce. ▶ *1 family support services intern:* responsibilities include assisting in the development of family intervention mentoring project for families in transition. Candidates should have ability to work independently,

YWCA of St. Paul (continued)

ability to work with others, analytical skills, computer skills, experience in the field, office skills, oral communication skills, organizational skills, self-motivation, strong leadership ability, written communication skills. Open to college juniors, college seniors, recent college graduates, graduate students, career changers, individuals reentering the workforce. ▶ *1 health and fitness intern:* responsibilities include orienting clients to resources, assisting staff with personal training, and representing the health and fitness center. Candidates should have ability to work independently, college degree in related field, experience in the field, oral communication skills, organizational skills, personal interest in the field, self-motivation, strong interpersonal skills, strong leadership ability. ▶ *1 support services intern:* responsibilities include assisting in monitoring the school attendance of elementary age students who are part of a transitional housing program and maintaining accurate information pertaining to their progress. Candidates should have ability to work independently, college courses in field, computer skills, experience in the field, office skills, oral communication skills, personal interest in the field, self-motivation, strong interpersonal skills, written communication skills. Open to college juniors, college seniors, recent college graduates, graduate students, career changers, individuals reentering the workforce. ▶ *1–3 transitional housing interns:* responsibilities include providing guidance and support to clients, assisting residents with finding resource information, providing information about YWCA and transitional housing programs, and documenting and reporting information to staff. Candidates should have ability to work independently, ability to work with others, analytical skills, computer skills, office skills, oral communication skills, organizational skills, plan to pursue career in field, self-motivation, strong leadership ability, written communication skills. Open to college freshmen, college sophomores, college juniors, college seniors, recent college graduates, graduate students, law students, career changers, individuals reentering the workforce. ▶ *1 volunteer coordinator intern:* responsibilities include recruiting, screening, and training potential volunteers, and assisting with volunteer program management. Candidates should have ability to work independently, computer skills, office skills, oral communication skills, organizational skills, strong interpersonal skills, strong leadership ability, written communication skills. Open to college freshmen, college sophomores, college juniors, college seniors, recent college graduates, career changers, individuals reentering the workforce. Duration for all positions is 3 months (minimum). All positions are unpaid. International applications accepted.

Benefits Names of contacts, on-the-job training, opportunity to attend seminars/workshops, possible full-time employment, travel reimbursement, willing to act as a professional reference, willing to complete paperwork for educational credit, willing to provide letters of recommendation.

Contact Write, call, fax, or e-mail Elizabeth Ellis, Volunteer Coordinator. Phone: 651-222-3741. Fax: 651-222-6307. E-mail: eellis@ywcaofstpaul.org. In-person interview recommended. Applicants must submit a formal organization application, cover letter, resume, three personal references, letter of recommendation, criminal background check paid for by YWCA. Applications are accepted continuously.

YWCA OF WAKE COUNTY, INC.
1012 Oberlin Road
Raleigh, North Carolina 27605

General Information Women's membership organization that provides programs and services to women and families in Wake County. Established in 1923. Number of employees: 145. Affiliate of YMCA of the USA, New York, New York. Number of internship applications received each year: 10.

Internships Available ▶ *1–2 New Horizons program interns:* responsibilities include working with Adolescent Pregnancy Prevention program, helping recruit participants ages 9 to 14 for Boys and Girls Clubs, planning programs and special events, and working with pregnant and parenting teens. Candidates should have ability to work independently, oral communication skills, self-motivation, strong interpersonal skills, strong leader-

ship ability. Duration is 1–4 semesters. Open to high school students, high school seniors, recent high school graduates, college freshmen, college sophomores, college juniors, college seniors, recent college graduates, graduate students, law students, career changers, individuals reentering the workforce. ▶ *1–2 administrative assistants:* responsibilities include assisting with word processing, data entry, and general clerical support. Candidates should have ability to work independently, ability to work with others, computer skills, oral communication skills, self-motivation, written communication skills. Duration is 1–2 semesters. Open to recent high school graduates, college freshmen, college sophomores, college juniors, college seniors, individuals reentering the workforce. ▶ *1 child safety information intern:* responsibilities include presenting a program on "Home Alone" safety to fourth graders. Candidates should have oral communication skills, self-motivation, strong interpersonal skills, strong leadership ability, ability to speak to children at their level. Duration is fall or spring semester. Open to adults interested in providing safety information to children. ▶ *1 communications/editorial intern:* responsibilities include writing articles and promotional material and assisting with word processing and desktop publishing. Candidates should have ability to work independently, computer skills, editing skills, oral communication skills, writing skills. Duration is 1–2 semesters. Open to high school seniors, college freshmen, college sophomores, college juniors, college seniors. ▶ *1 encore plus intern:* responsibilities include teaching women ages 40 and over early detection of breast and cervical cancer, scheduling mammograms and pap smears, and providing emotional support. Candidates should have ability to work independently, analytical skills, computer skills, knowledge of field, oral communication skills, organizational skills, personal interest in the field, self-motivation, strong interpersonal skills, strong leadership ability, written communication skills. Duration is flexible. Open to graduate students. ▶ *1–2 finance/accounting interns:* responsibilities include data entry, accounts receivable, posting and management duties. Candidates should have ability to work independently, computer skills, knowledge of field, office skills, oral communication skills, written communication skills. Duration is 1–2 semesters. Open to recent high school graduates, college freshmen, college sophomores, college juniors, college seniors, recent college graduates, individuals reentering the workforce. ▶ *1 fitness intern:* responsibilities include assisting with scheduling, special events, and marketing the fitness facility. Candidates should have ability to work independently, ability to work with others, knowledge of field, organizational skills, written communication skills. Duration is 1–2 semesters. Open to college juniors, college seniors, recent college graduates. ▶ *1–2 infant/toddler child-care interns:* responsibilities include caring for infants and toddlers using developmentally appropriate activities in a licensed day care center, developing curricula, and performing administrative duties. Candidates should have ability to work independently, ability to work with others, knowledge of field, self-motivation, love of children. Duration is 1 semester. ▶ *1 marketing intern:* responsibilities include assisting with development and implementation of marketing initiatives, coordinating market research, advising on marketing ideas, and coordinating needs for promotional materials. Candidates should have analytical skills, editing skills, oral communication skills, personal interest in the field, writing skills. Duration is 1–2 semesters. Open to high school seniors, college freshmen, college sophomores, college juniors, college seniors. All positions available as unpaid or paid. International applications accepted.

Benefits On-the-job training, opportunity to attend seminars/workshops, willing to act as a professional reference, willing to complete paperwork for educational credit, willing to provide letters of recommendation, discount on fitness membership, mileage reimbursment.

Contact Write, call, fax, or e-mail Ms. Gwen Moragne, Director of Special Projects. Phone: 919-828-3205. Fax: 919-828-4072. E-mail: wakeywca@ipass.net. In-person interview recommended. Applicants must submit a cover letter, resume. Applications are accepted continuously. World Wide Web: http://www.citysearch.com/rdu/ywcawakecounty.

YWCA OF WESTERN NEW YORK
190 Franklin Street
Buffalo, New York 14202

General Information Membership movement of women of diverse beliefs, faiths, and values committed to the empowerment of women. Established in 1870. Number of employees: 300. Number of internship applications received each year: 5.

Internships Available ▶ *2 assistant case managers:* responsibilities include conducting intake interviews, documenting files, scheduling presentations, and facilitating workshops. Unpaid. ▶ *1–5 child care assistants:* responsibilities include assisting in planning activities for children ages 6 weeks-5 years and working cooperatively with teachers and parents. Position available as unpaid or paid. ▶ *2 child care curriculum developers:* responsibilities include developing a curriculum for children ages 6 weeks-12 years in science, math, health, safety, and social studies. Unpaid. ▶ *15 extended day program aides:* responsibilities include developing weekly program plans for children ages 5-12; researching reference articles and organizations; establishing a library system of articles, games, and crafts; and working with children. Position available as unpaid or paid. ▶ *1–2 grant research assistants:* responsibilities include researching funding opportunities and compiling required data. Unpaid. ▶ *1 health and wellness assistant:* responsibilities include teaching fitness classes; marketing programs, outreach events, and demonstrations; and assisting with mailings and filing. Duration is 8–10 weeks. Unpaid. ▶ *1 residence program aide:* responsibilities include performing crisis management, coordinating resident services, recording behavioral data, directing facility supervision services, monitoring medications, and alternating as group team leader. Unpaid. ▶ *1–2 special events/public relations interns:* responsibilities include assisting in the arrangement and promotion of special events and helping with publicity. Candidates should have ability to work independently, computer skills, oral communication skills, organizational skills, research skills, self-motivation, strong interpersonal skills, written communication skills. Unpaid. ▶ *4 teen center program aide interns:* responsibilities include performing outreach, facilitating group discussion and workshops, and communicating with teens about available services. Duration is 16 weeks minimum. Unpaid. International applications accepted.

Benefits Formal training, opportunity to attend seminars/workshops, possible full-time employment, willing to complete paperwork for educational credit, willing to provide letters of recommendation.

Contact Write, call, or fax Connie Downing, Human Resources. Phone: 716-852-6120. Fax: 716-852-1629. In-person interview required. Applicants must submit a cover letter, resume, writing sample, three letters of recommendation. Applications are accepted continuously.

INFORMATION

GENERAL

ACCURACY IN MEDIA
4455 Connecticut Avenue, NW, Suite 330
Washington, District of Columbia 20008

General Information A nonprofit educational organization whose purpose is to monitor bias and inaccuracies in the news media through a newsletter and news column. Established in 1969. Number of employees: 15. Number of internship applications received each year: 50.
Internships Available ▶ *1–2 business/marketing assistants.* Candidates should have analytical skills, computer skills, oral communication skills, personal interest in the field, self-motivation, strong interpersonal skills. ▶ *2 reporters:* responsibilities include reporting and writing news stories for weekly paper that deals with foreign affairs. Candidates should have editing skills, personal interest in the field, research skills, self-motivation, writing skills. ▶ *1 researcher:* responsibilities include researching particular topics and producing a study or report on findings. Candidates should have personal interest in the field, self-motivation, strong interpersonal skills, writing skills. ▶ *1–2 writers:* responsibilities include researching and writing articles for *The Campus Report*. Candidates should have editing skills, personal interest in the field, research skills, self-motivation, strong interpersonal skills, writing skills. Duration for all positions is 6–18 weeks. All positions paid at $125 per week. Open to high school students, high school seniors, recent high school graduates, college freshmen, college sophomores, college juniors, college seniors, recent college graduates, graduate students, law students, career changers, individuals reentering the workforce.
Benefits Opportunity to attend seminars/workshops, possible full-time employment, willing to act as a professional reference, willing to complete paperwork for educational credit, willing to provide letters of recommendation.
Contact Write, fax, or e-mail Mr. Don Irvine, Executive Director, 4455 Conneticut Avenue, NW, Suite 330, Washington, District of Columbia 20008. Fax: 202-364-4098. E-mail: intern@aim.org. No phone calls. In-person interview recommended. Applicants must submit a formal organization application, cover letter, resume, academic transcripts, two writing samples. Application deadline: March 31 for summer, October 31 for spring. World Wide Web: http://www.aim.org/.

BROADCAST ADVERTISING CLUB OF CHICAGO
325 West Huron Street, #403
Chicago, Illinois 60610

General Information Club of 1000 broadcast media executives from ad agencies and stations. Established in 1960. Number of internship applications received each year: 25.
Internships Available ▶ *5–6 interns:* responsibilities include assisting broadcast negotiator or media planner at major advertising agencies or working with broadcast station time salesmen. Candidates should have analytical skills, college courses in field, computer skills, organizational skills, plan to pursue career in field, ability to take direction in a cooperative manner. Duration is 10 weeks in summer (9-5, Monday to Friday). $2,000 per duration of internship. Open to college juniors, college seniors, graduate students, residents of Illinois only.

Benefits Job counseling, on-the-job training, opportunity to attend seminars/workshops, possible full-time employment, willing to act as a professional reference, willing to complete paperwork for educational credit, willing to provide letters of recommendation.
Contact Call or fax Joyce R. Saxon, Treasurer, 325 West Huron Street, #403, Chicago, Illinois 60610. Phone: 312-341-1900 Ext. 249. Fax: 321-440-1970. In-person interview required. Applicants must submit a formal organization application, 500-word essay. Application deadline: March 3.

CENTER FOR INVESTIGATIVE REPORTING, INC.
500 Howard Street, Suite 206
San Francisco, California 94105

General Information Nonprofit organization producing television and print media reports on national and international issues including environment, science, public health, constitutional government-freedom of information, social justice, international affairs, economic and financial issues, and the public trust. Established in 1977. Number of employees: 3. Number of internship applications received each year: 100.
Internships Available ▶ *6–10 interns:* responsibilities include working closely with staff reporters on tasks including research, information organization, story development, and production. Candidates should have analytical skills, oral communication skills, personal interest in the field, plan to pursue career in field, self-motivation, written communication skills. Duration is 6 months. Monthly stipend of $150. Open to college freshmen, college sophomores, college juniors, college seniors, recent college graduates, graduate students, law students, career changers, individuals reentering the workforce. International applications accepted.
Benefits Job counseling, names of contacts, opportunity to attend seminars/workshops, possible full-time employment, willing to complete paperwork for educational credit, willing to provide letters of recommendation.
Contact Write, call, or e-mail Communications Director. Phone: 415-543-1200. E-mail: cir@igc.apc.org. Applicants must submit a cover letter, resume, 2-3 writing samples. Application deadline: May 1 for summer/fall, December 1 for winter/spring. World Wide Web: http://www.muckraker.org.

JAZBO PRODUCTIONS
185 Pier Avenue
Santa Monica, California 90405

General Information Feature film, television, internet, and live stage production company involved in the development of feature films and made-for-television productions for the networks and major studios. Established in 1985. Number of employees: 1. Number of internship applications received each year: 150.
Internships Available ▶ *1–2 interns:* responsibilities include assisting with general office duties and management of scripts, videotapes, and concept treatments; performing story analysis of scripts; and screening/summarizing potential projects. Candidates should have ability to work independently, computer skills, knowledge of field, oral communication skills, self-motivation, written communication skills. Unpaid. Open to college sophomores, college juniors, college seniors, recent college graduates, graduate students, law students, career changers, individuals reentering the workforce.

Benefits Job counseling, names of contacts, on-the-job training, opportunity to attend seminars/workshops, possible full-time employment, willing to act as a professional reference, willing to complete paperwork for educational credit, willing to provide letters of recommendation.
Contact Write, call, or fax Ms. Jill Marti, President. Phone: 310-664-6004. Fax: 310-664-3656. In-person interview recommended. Applicants must submit a formal organization application, cover letter, resume, three personal references, 2-3 professional references. Applications are accepted continuously.

MINORITIES IN BROADCASTING TRAINING PROGRAM/MIBTP
PO Box 39696
Los Angeles, California 90039

General Information Nonprofit organization formed to provide training opportunity to minority college graduates in TV/radio, news reporting, and news management. Established in 1993. Number of internship applications received each year: 250.
Internships Available ▶ *1–2 new management trainees:* responsibilities include learning all aspects of newsroom, learning decision-making process. Candidates should have ability to work independently, experience in the field, oral communication skills, self-motivation, strong interpersonal skills, written communication skills. $5–$8 per hour. Open to graduate students, career changers. ▶ *4–8 reporter trainees:* responsibilities include learning all aspects of newsroom reporting. Candidates should have ability to work independently, oral communication skills, self-motivation, strong interpersonal skills, written communication skills. $5–$6 per hour. Open to college graduates who have been out of school 2 years or more. Duration for all positions is 6–9 months.
Benefits Formal training, job counseling, names of contacts, on-the-job training, possible full-time employment, willing to act as a professional reference, willing to provide letters of recommendation.
Contact E-mail Patrice Williams, PO Box 39696, Los Angeles, California 90039. E-mail: news-trainee@thebroadcaster.com. No phone calls. In-person interview recommended. Applicants must submit a formal organization application, resume, academic transcripts, three personal references, three letters of recommendation, demo tape for reporters. Must request application between January and June by sending $2.00 to cover cost of duplicaton. Specify for which program you want to apply. Application deadline: May for reporter training program, May 30 for news management training program. Fees: $10. World Wide Web: http://www.theBroadcaster.com.

NATIONAL SECURITY AND NATURAL RESOURCES NEWS SERVICE
1100 Connecticut Avenue, NW, Suite 1310
Washington, District of Columbia 20036

General Information Nonprofit news service that works to increase and improve the major news media coverage of military, arms control, and international security stories as well as environmental and natural resources stories. Established in 1990. Number of employees: 10. Unit of Public Education Center, Inc., Washington, District of Columbia. Number of internship applications received each year: 30.
Internships Available ▶ *2–6 National Security News Service journalism and research interns:* responsibilities include assisting reporters with investigative stories on the military and defense industries and environmental issues. Duration is 1 semester. ▶ *2–6 human rights news service interns:* responsibilities include assisting reports with investigative stories about human rights (both foreign and domestic) for eventual publication in the major media. Duration is 2 months. ▶ *2–6 natural resources news service journalism and research interns:* responsibilities include assisting reporters with investigative stories on the environment (both foreign and domestic) for eventual publication in the major news media. Duration is 2 months. Candidates for all positions should have ability to work independently, oral communication skills, personal interest in the field, research skills, writing skills. All positions

are unpaid. Open to college juniors, college seniors, recent college graduates, graduate students. International applications accepted.
Benefits Job counseling, names of contacts, on-the-job training, travel reimbursement, willing to complete paperwork for educational credit, willing to provide letters of recommendation.
Contact Write, call, fax, or e-mail Margaret Savage, Intern Coordinator. Phone: 202-466-4310. Fax: 202-466-4344. E-mail: savage@publicedcenter.org. Applicants must submit a cover letter, resume, writing sample. Application deadline: April 30 for summer, November 30 for spring. World Wide Web: http://www.publicedcenter.org.

PRIMARK
5161 River Road
Bethesda, Maryland 20816

General Information Leading provider of financial intelligence delivered by online and CD-ROM-based research tools. Established in 1968. Number of employees: 450. Number of internship applications received each year: 50.
Internships Available ▶ *3 human resources/administration interns:* responsibilities include day-to-day human resources functions. Candidates should have ability to work independently, computer skills, editing skills, knowledge of field, office skills, oral communication skills, organizational skills, strong interpersonal skills, written communication skills. $7–$11 per hour. Open to high school students, high school seniors, recent high school graduates, college freshmen, college sophomores, college juniors, college seniors, recent college graduates, graduate students, law students, career changers, individuals reentering the workforce. ▶ *1–5 technology interns:* responsibilities include quality control testing; application development; network services providing on-line user help. Candidates should have college courses in field, experience in the field, Visual Basic skills, ACCESS skills, UNIX skills, C programming skills. $8–$15 per hour. Open to recent high school graduates, college freshmen, college sophomores, college juniors, college seniors, recent college graduates, graduate students, law students, career changers, individuals reentering the workforce. Duration for all positions is flexible.
Benefits On-the-job training, opportunity to attend seminars/workshops, possible full-time employment, willing to act as a professional reference, willing to complete paperwork for educational credit.
Contact Write, fax, or e-mail Rachael Mason, Human Resources Generalist. Fax: 301-718-2340. E-mail: rachael.mason@disclosure.com. No phone calls. In-person interview recommended. Applicants must submit a formal organization application, resume. Applications are accepted continuously. World Wide Web: http://www.disclosure.com.

TIME WARNER INC.
75 Rockefeller Plaza, 4th Floor
New York, New York 10019

General Information Media and entertainment industry. Number of employees: 500. Number of internship applications received each year: 100.
Internships Available ▶ *Summer interns:* responsibilities include various tasks depending on the position. Candidates should have ability to work independently, analytical skills, computer skills, office skills, oral communication skills, organizational skills, self-motivation, strong interpersonal skills, writing skills. Duration is 35 hours per week. variable. Open to college freshmen, college sophomores, college juniors, college seniors, recent college graduates, graduate students, law students, career changers.
Benefits On-the-job training, possible full-time employment, willing to act as a professional reference, willing to provide letters of recommendation, in-house summer seminars specifically geared to interns.
Contact Write or fax Karen Mangione, Human Resources Manager. Fax: 212-275-3048. No phone calls. In-person interview required. Applicants must submit a formal organization application, cover letter, resume, personal reference, academic transcripts,

Time Warner Inc. (continued)

writing sample may be required. Applications are accepted continuously. World Wide Web: http://www.timewarner.com.

MOTION PICTURE AND SOUND RECORDING INDUSTRIES

ARCHIVE FILMS/PHOTOS
530 West 25th Street
New York, New York 10001

General Information Stock film and photographic image footage library providing historic motion picture clips and photos to advertising agencies, corporations, TV producers, news broadcasts, documentary makers, and feature films. Established in 1979. Number of employees: 130. Subsidiary of The Image Bank, Dallas, Texas. Number of internship applications received each year: 75.
Internships Available ▶ *1 film acquisition intern:* responsibilities include preparing new collections for acquisition into the library; cleaning, editing, cataloging, labeling, and researching films; transferring films to VHS cassettes. Candidates should have ability to work independently, analytical skills, computer skills, organizational skills, personal interest in the field, research skills, self-motivation. Duration is 2–3 months. Open to recent high school graduates, college freshmen, college sophomores, college juniors, college seniors, recent college graduates. ▶ *1–2 film research interns:* responsibilities include compilation of video cassettes of archival film footage for use in advertising, corporate, broadcast, multimedia, and feature film projects. Candidates should have ability to work independently, analytical skills, college courses in field, computer skills, oral communication skills, organizational skills, plan to pursue career in field, research skills, self-motivation, strong interpersonal skills, writing skills, working knowledge of American and international history and film industry a plus. Duration is 3 months. Open to college freshmen, college sophomores, college juniors, college seniors, recent college graduates, graduate students, career changers. ▶ *Photo digital imaging interns:* responsibilities include researching through photo database and coordinating images with dates throughout the year. Candidates should have ability to work independently, ability to work with others, computer skills, oral communication skills, research skills, writing skills. Duration is 2–3 months. Open to college freshmen, college sophomores, college juniors. ▶ *2–3 photo library interns:* responsibilities include undertaking general photo library projects from filing images to labeling photos; other cataloging projects as directed by manager. Candidates should have ability to work with others, computer skills, oral communication skills, organizational skills, personal interest in the field, self-motivation. Duration is 2–3 months. Open to college juniors, college seniors, recent college graduates, graduate students, law students, career changers. ▶ *1–2 photo research interns:* responsibilities include using File Maker Pro database, Macintosh platform, research in files, organization of files. Candidates should have ability to work independently, ability to work with others, oral communication skills, research skills, knowledge of photographic medium, some background or courses in history helpful. Duration is 2–3 months. Open to college freshmen, college sophomores, college juniors. All positions are unpaid. International applications accepted.
Benefits Formal training, names of contacts, on-the-job training, possible full-time employment, travel reimbursement, willing to complete paperwork for educational credit, willing to provide letters of recommendation, free lunches.
Contact Write or fax Intern Coordinator. Fax: 212-645-2137. No phone calls. In-person interview recommended. Applicants must submit a cover letter, resume. Applications are accepted continuously. World Wide Web: http://www.archivefilms.com.

ASSISTANT DIRECTORS TRAINING PROGRAM
15503 Ventura Boulevard
Encino, California 91436

General Information Training program that provides 400 days of on-the-job training, supplemented by classroom seminars, in the work of second assistant directors. Established in 1965. Number of employees: 2. Unit of Directors Guild- Producer Training Plan, Encino, California. Number of internship applications received each year: 1,000.
Internships Available ▶ *15–20 assistant director trainees:* responsibilities include assisting with administrative procedures in motion picture and television production, attending regular seminars that cover subjects pertinent to second assistant director work, and working with various studio and production companies. Candidates should have ability to work independently, oral communication skills, organizational skills, self-motivation, strong interpersonal skills, stamina. Duration is 400 days. $470–$578 per week. Open to recent high school graduates, college sophomores, college juniors, college seniors, recent college graduates, graduate students, law students, career changers, individuals reentering the workforce. International applications accepted.
Benefits Formal training, health insurance, job counseling, names of contacts, on-the-job training, opportunity to attend seminars/workshops.
Contact Write, call, or e-mail Ms. Kate Tilley-Carroll, Administrator. Phone: 818-386-2545. E-mail: trainingprogram@dgptp.org. Applicants must submit a formal organization application, writing sample. Application deadline: November 15 for internship beginning following June. Fees: $50. World Wide Web: http://www.dgptp.org.

ASSOCIATION OF INDEPENDENT VIDEO AND FILMMAKERS–FOUNDATION FOR INDEPENDENT VIDEO AND FILM
304 Hudson Street, 6th Floor
New York, New York 10013

General Information Trade association of 5000 independent media professionals that provides advocacy and information services. Established in 1975. Number of employees: 10. Number of internship applications received each year: 60.
Internships Available ▶ *2–4 administrative interns:* responsibilities include assisting with research, filing, and data entry. Candidates should have ability to work independently, computer skills, knowledge of field, office skills, oral communication skills, organizational skills, personal interest in the field, research skills, self-motivation, strong interpersonal skills, written communication skills. Duration is year-round (up to 16 hours per week). Unpaid. Open to high school seniors, recent high school graduates, college freshmen, college sophomores, college juniors, college seniors, recent college graduates, graduate students, individuals reentering the workforce. ▶ *1 editorial intern:* responsibilities include assisting the Independent Film and Video Monthly editorial staff; researching and writing. Candidates should have ability to work independently, ability to work with others, computer skills, editing skills, knowledge of field, office skills, research skills, self-motivation, written communication skills. Duration is year-round. $100 per month. Open to college juniors, college seniors, recent college graduates, graduate students, career changers. ▶ *1–2 membership interns:* responsibilities include assisting with research and mailings, including database maintenance. Candidates should have ability to work independently, computer skills, knowledge of field, office skills, research skills, writing skills. Duration is year-round (up to 16 hours per week). Unpaid. Open to college freshmen, college sophomores, college juniors, college seniors, recent college graduates, graduate students, individuals reentering the workforce. International applications accepted.
Benefits Job counseling, names of contacts, opportunity to attend seminars/workshops, willing to act as a professional reference, willing to complete paperwork for educational credit, willing to provide letters of recommendation, membership in AIVF, selection of free publications in library.

Contact Write, fax, or e-mail Michelle Coe, Program and Information Services Director, Paul Power, Managing Editor/contact for editorial position, 304 Hudson Street 6th Floor, New York, New York 10013. Fax: 212-463-8519. E-mail: michelle@aivf.org, independent@aivf.org. No phone calls. In-person interview required. Applicants must submit a formal organization application, cover letter, resume. Applications are accepted continuously. World Wide Web: http://www.AIVF.org.

BEACH ASSOCIATES
200 North Glebe Road, Suite 720
Arlington, Virginia 22203

General Information Video production company that specializes in organizational communications. Established in 1979. Number of employees: 10. Number of internship applications received each year: 20.
Internships Available ▶ *1 marketing assistant intern:* responsibilities include updating marketing materials, researching potential clients, assisting with specialized marketing campaigns, compiling marketing packets, answering phones, typing, running errands, dubbing, faxing, copying, shipping packages, and filing. Candidates should have ability to work with others, college courses in field, computer skills, knowledge of field, office skills, oral communication skills, organizational skills, personal interest in the field, self-motivation, written communication skills. Open to college sophomores, college juniors, college seniors, recent college graduates. ▶ *1 new media intern:* responsibilities include digitizing and editing video, designing and developing WWW pages and CD-ROMS, working on live Webcast events and designing and maintaining promotional materials. Candidates should have ability to work independently, analytical skills, computer skills, declared college major in field, organizational skills, self-motivation. Open to students who will receive college credit for internships. ▶ *1 production assistant intern:* responsibilities include entering scripts, answering the phone, logging and labeling tapes, gripping on ENG and EFP shoots, operating teleprompter, editing, running errands, dubbing, typing, making travel arrangements, faxing, copying, bulking tapes, shipping packages, and filing. Candidates should have ability to work with others, college courses in field, computer skills, knowledge of field, office skills, oral communication skills, organizational skills, personal interest in the field, self-motivation, written communication skills. Open to college sophomores, college juniors, college seniors, recent college graduates. Duration for all positions is 1 semester. All positions are unpaid. International applications accepted.
Benefits Formal training, names of contacts, on-the-job training, opportunity to attend seminars/workshops, willing to complete paperwork for educational credit, willing to provide letters of recommendation, free parking.
Contact Write, call, fax, or e-mail Ms. Kay Leonard, Executive Vice President, General Manager. Phone: 703-812-8813. Fax: 703-812-9710. E-mail: kleonard@beachassociates.com. Telephone interview required. Applicants must submit a cover letter, resume. Applications are accepted continuously. World Wide Web: http://www.beachassociates.com.

BUZZCO ASSOCIATES, INC.
33 Bleecker Street
New York, New York 10012

General Information Traditional animation company with projects ranging from corporate sales films, cable network IDs, network public service announcements, and national and regional commercials. Established in 1985. Number of employees: 5. Number of internship applications received each year: 25.
Internships Available ▶ *1–3 interns:* responsibilities include performing production research and assisting film editorial staff. Candidates should have ability to work with others, plan to pursue career in field, self-motivation. Duration is 1–6 months. Unpaid. Open to high school seniors, recent high school graduates, college freshmen, college sophomores, college juniors, college seniors, recent college graduates, individuals reentering the workforce.

Benefits Job counseling, names of contacts, possible full-time employment, willing to complete paperwork for educational credit, willing to provide letters of recommendation, access to facilities.
Contact Write, call, fax, or e-mail Ms. Candy Kugel, Director, Producer. Phone: 212-473-8800. Fax: 212-473-8891. E-mail: info@buzzzco.com. In-person interview required. Applicants must submit a cover letter. Applications are accepted continuously. World Wide Web: http://www.buzzzco.com.

D'ELIA-WITTKOFSKI PRODUCTIONS
1 Market Street
Pittsburgh, Pennsylvania 15222

General Information Organization that engages in production of corporate industrial videos and some broadcast videos. Established in 1981. Number of employees: 30. Number of internship applications received each year: 20.
Internships Available ▶ *1–3 production interns:* responsibilities include learning equipment and how company operation works, performing some duties of production assistant and associate producer, operating teleprompter, running tapes, getting food for clients, and helping with daily administrative and production tasks. Duration is 2 months (with a review and possible rollover). Paid. Open to recent college graduates.
Benefits Formal training, possible full-time employment, travel reimbursement.
Contact Write or fax Chere Tiller, Operations Coordinator. Fax: 412-391-0185. In-person interview required. Applicants must submit a cover letter, resume. Applications are accepted continuously. World Wide Web: http://www.deliawitt.com.

FEVER FILMS
23 East 10th Street, #PHG
New York, New York 10003

General Information Film distribution, exhibition, and production company, focusing on experimental, independent, and short-form work. Interests include the avant garde, progressive documentary, and lesbian and gay film and video. Established in 1995. Number of employees: 3. Number of internship applications received each year: 50.
Internships Available ▶ *1–2 distribution assistants:* responsibilities include assisting with identifying potential markets for titles; preparing press kits and promotional packets for exhibitors; writing or organizing material about films; maintaining database; inspection of film prints; packing, shipping and logging films; liaison with exhibition venues; and working with Super-8 and 16mm film elements. Candidates should have ability to work independently, office skills, oral communication skills, organizational skills, personal interest in the field, written communication skills. Duration is flexible; seasonal interns or short-term (2-weeks spring break or 3 to 4 weeks in winter). Unpaid. Open to college freshmen, college sophomores, college juniors, college seniors, recent college graduates. International applications accepted.
Benefits Job counseling, names of contacts, on-the-job training, opportunity to attend seminars/workshops, willing to act as a professional reference, willing to complete paperwork for educational credit, willing to provide letters of recommendation, opportunity to meet and work with film and video artists.
Contact Write, fax, or e-mail Stephen Kent Jusick, Founder. Fax: 212-475-1399. E-mail: skj@echonyc.com. In-person interview required. Applicants must submit a cover letter, resume. Applications are accepted continuously. World Wide Web: http://www.geocities.com/SoHo/Lofts/1847.

FILM/VIDEO ARTS
817 Broadway
New York, New York 10003

General Information Nonprofit organization that offers subsidized rates to independent film and video makers, holds classes in multimedia and Web construction, and provides production and postproduction equipment and services in film and video.

Film/Video Arts (continued)

Established in 1968. Number of employees: 15. Number of internship applications received each year: 500.

Internships Available ▶ *1–2 media training interns:* responsibilities include performing administrative responsibilities related to signing students up for classes, publicizing classes, and acting as a teaching assistant in production classes. ▶ *1–8 postproduction interns:* responsibilities include answering phones, admitting clients to postproduction rooms, setting up and troubleshooting video rough edit rooms, and scheduling postproduction rooms. ▶ *1 public relations intern:* responsibilities include assisting public relations director with research, promotion, and special events. ▶ *1–3 vault interns:* responsibilities include checking in rental equipment and preparing rental orders. Duration for all positions is 6 months. All positions are unpaid. Open to college freshmen, college sophomores, college juniors, college seniors, recent college graduates, graduate students, law students, career changers, individuals reentering the workforce. International applications accepted.

Benefits Formal training, opportunity to attend seminars/workshops, possible full-time employment, willing to complete paperwork for educational credit, willing to provide letters of recommendation, opportunity to use equipment and facility for personal noncommercial projects on a standby basis.

Contact Write, call, fax, or e-mail Intern Manager. Phone: 212-673-9361. Fax: 212-475-3467. E-mail: fva@interport.net. In-person interview required. Applicants must submit a formal organization application, cover letter, resume. Applications are accepted continuously. World Wide Web: http://www.fva.com.

HISTORIC FILMS
12 Goodfriend Drive
East Hampton, New York 11937

General Information Historic stock footage library specializing in archival film and musical performances. Established in 1991. Number of employees: 9. Number of internship applications received each year: 50.

Internships Available ▶ *2–3 research assistants:* responsibilities include video research, logging of images, film to tape transfer, and various other duties. Candidates should have ability to work independently, analytical skills, office skills, organizational skills, personal interest in the field, research skills. Duration is 6–10 weeks. Unpaid. Open to recent high school graduates, college freshmen, college sophomores, college juniors, college seniors, recent college graduates, graduate students, career changers, individuals reentering the workforce.

Benefits Names of contacts, possible full-time employment, willing to complete paperwork for educational credit, willing to provide letters of recommendation.

Contact Write, call, or fax Kevin Rice, Internship Coordinator. Phone: 516-329-9200. Fax: 516-329-9260. In-person interview recommended. Applicants must submit a cover letter, resume. Applications are accepted continuously. World Wide Web: http://www.historic.com.

INTERNATIONAL DOCUMENTARY ASSOCIATION
1551 South Robertson Boulevard, Suite 201
Los Angeles, California 90035-4257

General Information Nonprofit organization founded to promote and support the work of nonfiction and documentary film and video makers and promote international understanding through the documentary arts and sciences. Established in 1982. Number of employees: 8. Number of internship applications received each year: 50.

Internships Available ▶ *1–14 interns:* responsibilities include working in special events or administration. Candidates should have ability to work independently, ability to work with others, personal interest in the field. Duration is flexible. Unpaid. Open to high school students, high school seniors, recent high school graduates, college freshmen, college sophomores, college juniors, college seniors, recent college graduates, graduate students, career changers, anyone interested in nonfiction film. International applications accepted.

Benefits Names of contacts, opportunity to attend seminars/workshops, willing to complete paperwork for educational credit, willing to provide letters of recommendation, membership after 30 hours of service.

Contact Write, fax, or e-mail Mr. Amitai B. Aller, Membership Coordinator. Fax: 310-785-9334. E-mail: ida@artnet.net. No phone calls. In-person interview recommended. Applicants must submit a cover letter, resume. Applications are accepted continuously. World Wide Web: http://www.documentary.org.

LEFRAK PRODUCTIONS, INC.
40 West 57th Street, Suite 409
New York, New York 10019

General Information Film and television development company headed by an independent producer. Established in 1980. Number of employees: 5. Number of internship applications received each year: 50.

Internships Available ▶ *5–7 interns:* responsibilities include performing general office work, attending the theater, and looking for new project ideas. Candidates should have ability to work independently, computer skills, knowledge of field, office skills, oral communication skills, organizational skills, plan to pursue career in field, research skills, self-motivation, strong interpersonal skills, written communication skills. Duration is 3 months (flexible). Unpaid. Open to college freshmen, college sophomores, college juniors, college seniors, recent college graduates, graduate students, law students, career changers. International applications accepted.

Benefits Formal training, job counseling, on-the-job training, possible full-time employment, willing to act as a professional reference, willing to complete paperwork for educational credit, willing to provide letters of recommendation.

Contact Call, fax, or e-mail Internship Coordinator. Phone: 212-541-9444. Fax: 212-974-8205. E-mail: lfp@aol.com. In-person interview recommended. Applicants must submit a resume. Application deadline: February 1 for spring, May 1 for summer, November 1 for winter.

LIGHTHOUSE PRODUCTIONS
120 El Camino Drive, Suite 212
Beverly Hills, California 90212

General Information Feature film and television production company. Established in 1974. Number of employees: 2. Number of internship applications received each year: 150.

Internships Available ▶ *2–4 story development interns:* responsibilities include script coverage and general assistant responsibilities (phone, fax, copy machine). Candidates should have analytical skills, office skills, oral communication skills, plan to pursue career in field, writing skills. Duration is 10–15 weeks. Unpaid. Open to college juniors, college seniors, recent college graduates, graduate students. International applications accepted.

Benefits Formal training, job counseling, willing to complete paperwork for educational credit, willing to provide letters of recommendation.

Contact Write or fax Internship Coordinator. Fax: 310-859-7511. No phone calls. In-person interview recommended. Applicants must submit a formal organization application, resume, writing sample. Application deadline: February 1 for spring, May 1 for summer and fall, December 1 for winter.

LOVETT PRODUCTIONS, INC.
155 Sixth Avenue, 10th Floor
New York, New York 10013

General Information Independent production company that produces documentary and reality programming, video news releases, industrials, and independent films. Established in 1989. Number of employees: 5. Number of internship applications received each year: 100.

Internships Available ▶ *2–5 production office assistants:* responsibilities include assisting in all aspects of pre- and postproduction, research, writing, logging, labeling, videotaping, dubbing, and phones. Candidates should have ability to work independently,

oral communication skills, self-motivation, strong interpersonal skills, written communication skills. Duration is 1 semester. Unpaid. International applications accepted.
Benefits Travel reimbursement, willing to complete paperwork for educational credit, stipend for food and transportation ($10 per day), willing to provide references and recommendations based on performance.
Contact Write, call, or fax Rebecca Levi, Office Manager. Phone: 212-242-8999. Fax: 212-242-7347. In-person interview recommended. Applicants must submit a cover letter, resume. Applications are accepted continuously. World Wide Web: http://www.lovettproductions.com.

LUCASFILM LTD. AND LUCAS LICENSING LTD.
PO Box 2009
San Rafael, California 94912

General Information Lucasfilm provides business services for productions by Lucasfilm. Established in 1971. Number of employees: 300. Number of internship applications received each year: 200.
Internships Available ▶ *8–12 interns:* responsibilities include assisting in THX engineering, marketing, licensing (publishing, merchandising, product development), graphic design, human resources, finance, ranch operations departments, or archives. Candidates should have ability to work independently, computer skills, experience in the field, office skills, personal interest in the field, self-motivation. Duration is 10–12 weeks. minimum wage. Open to college juniors, college seniors, graduate students, law students.
Benefits Job counseling, on-the-job training, opportunity to attend seminars/workshops, willing to complete paperwork for educational credit, willing to provide letters of recommendation.
Contact Amy Schafbuch, Employment Manager and Program Specialist, PO Box 2009, San Rafael, California 94912. No phone calls. Telephone interview required. Applicants must submit a formal organization application, resume, academic transcripts, two personal references, answers to questionnaire. Application deadline: March 31 for summer, July 31 for fall, November 30 for spring. World Wide Web: http://www.lucasfilm.com.

MARYLAND FILM OFFICE
217 East Redwood Street, 9th Floor
Baltimore, Maryland 21202

General Information State organization marketing Maryland's film/video industry and locations to the motion picture and television production industry. Established in 1980. Number of employees: 5. Unit of Maryland Department of Business and Economic Development, Baltimore, Maryland. Number of internship applications received each year: 80.
Internships Available ▶ *1–4 marketing interns:* responsibilities include writing, making phone calls, scouting potential film locations, and conducting research. Candidates should have analytical skills, computer skills, editing skills, office skills, oral communication skills, organizational skills, research skills, self-motivation, strong interpersonal skills, writing skills. Duration is 1–2 semesters. Unpaid. Open to recent high school graduates, college freshmen, college sophomores, college juniors, college seniors, recent college graduates, graduate students, career changers, individuals reentering the workforce.
Benefits Job counseling, names of contacts, travel reimbursement, willing to act as a professional reference, willing to complete paperwork for educational credit, willing to provide letters of recommendation.
Contact Write Mr. Michael B. Styer, Director. No phone calls. In-person interview required. Applicants must submit a cover letter, resume. Applications are accepted continuously.

MARY PERILLO, INC.
125 Cedar Street, #8 South
New York, New York 10006

General Information Company that produces film and video products including video art, music and dance performances, music videos, commercials, Sesame Street shorts, and high-end graphics. Established in 1983. Number of employees: 2. Number of internship applications received each year: 150.
Internships Available ▶ *1–2 arts administration interns:* responsibilities include assisting with grant writing, fund-raising, research, and correspondence. ▶ *1–2 production interns:* responsibilities include performing office/library duties, dubbing, and production tasks. Duration for all positions is flexible. All positions are unpaid. Open to college freshmen, college sophomores, college juniors, college seniors, recent college graduates. International applications accepted.
Benefits Names of contacts, possible full-time employment, willing to complete paperwork for educational credit, willing to provide letters of recommendation.
Contact Write, call, fax, or e-mail Ms. Molly Maguire, Office Manager. Phone: 212-608-3943. Fax: 212-240-0407. E-mail: mmmpi@aol.com. In-person interview recommended. Applicants must submit a cover letter, resume. Applications are accepted continuously.

MD WAX/ COURIER FILMS
1560 Broadway, Room 706
New York, New York 10036

General Information Distributor of foreign and independent films. Established in 1983. Number of employees: 2. Unit of Morton Dennis Wax, New York, New York. Number of internship applications received each year: 50.
Internships Available ▶ *1–3 marketing assistants:* responsibilities include creating and implementing marketing plans for films, writing advertising and promotional releases, contacting exhibitors, and providing general office assistance. Candidates should have ability to work independently, computer skills, office skills, oral communication skills, self-motivation, writing skills. Duration is 1–6 months. Unpaid. Open to college freshmen, college sophomores, college juniors, college seniors. International applications accepted.
Benefits On-the-job training, willing to act as a professional reference, willing to complete paperwork for educational credit, willing to provide letters of recommendation.
Contact Write or fax Ms. Sandra Wax, Vice President. Fax: 212-302-5364. No phone calls. Applicants must submit a cover letter, resume. Applications are accepted continuously.

METRO-GOLDWYN-MAYER/UNITED ARTISTS
1350 Sixth Avenue, 24th Floor
New York, New York 10019

General Information Movie company that releases first-run films into the domestic market. Established in 1924. Number of employees: 7. Number of internship applications received each year: 200.
Internships Available ▶ *3–5 MGM/UA interns:* responsibilities include working in publicity and promotions departments. Duration is 1 semester. Unpaid. Open to college freshmen, college sophomores, college juniors, college seniors. International applications accepted.
Benefits Names of contacts, willing to complete paperwork for educational credit, willing to provide letters of recommendation.
Contact Write, call, fax, or e-mail Lisa Zaks, Internship Coordinator, 1350 Sixth Avenue, 25th Floor, New York, New York 10019. Phone: 212-708-0377. Fax: 212-708-0370. E-mail: lzaks@mgm.com. In-person interview required. Applicants must submit a cover letter, resume. Applications are accepted continuously. World Wide Web: http://www.mgm.com.

NASSAU COUNTY OFFICE OF CINEMA AND TELEVISION PROMOTION
1550 Franklin Avenue, Suite 207
Mineola, New York 11501

General Information Film commission that scouts locations and facilitates film production, commercials, videos, and still photography. Established in 1989. Number of employees: 6. Unit

Nassau County Office of Cinema and Television Promotion (continued)
of Nassau County Department of Commerce and Industry, Mineola, New York. Number of internship applications received each year: 30.

Internships Available ▶ *1 data entry intern:* responsibilities include updating and entering data into film database. Candidates should have ability to work with Office Suite program. Open to high school seniors, recent high school graduates, college freshmen, college sophomores, college juniors, college seniors, recent college graduates, graduate students, law students, career changers, individuals reentering the workforce. ▶ *1–4 film coordinators:* responsibilities include contacting clients by phone, scouting locations, researching, updating files, following up on film shoots, and assisting with permit procedures. Candidates should have ability to work independently, oral communication skills, personal interest in the field, self-motivation, strong interpersonal skills. Open to high school seniors, recent high school graduates, college freshmen, college sophomores, college juniors, college seniors, recent college graduates, graduate students, law students, career changers, individuals reentering the workforce. ▶ *3 location photographers:* responsibilities include photographing locations, mansions, and parks. Candidates should have personal interest in the field. Open to recent high school graduates, college freshmen, college sophomores, college juniors, college seniors, recent college graduates, graduate students, law students, career changers, individuals reentering the workforce. Duration for all positions is flexible. All positions are unpaid.

Benefits Formal training, names of contacts, willing to complete paperwork for educational credit, willing to provide letters of recommendation.

Contact Write, call, or fax Ms. Debra Markowitz, Director, Cinema and Television Promotion. Phone: 516-571-3168. Fax: 516-571-4161. In-person interview recommended. Applicants must submit a resume. Applications are accepted continuously. World Wide Web: http://www.co.nassau.ny.us/tv.html.

NORTHWEST FILM CENTER
1219 Southwest Park Avenue
Portland, Oregon 97205

General Information Regional media arts center serving the Northwest with film and video exhibitions, continuing education, artist-in-the-schools programs, and fellowships programs. Established in 1972. Number of employees: 15. Unit of Portland Art Museum, Portland, Oregon. Number of internship applications received each year: 100.

Internships Available ▶ *3–4 education interns:* responsibilities include working at the equipment room desk and assisting with preparations for film classes. Candidates should have ability to work independently, knowledge of field, oral communication skills, organizational skills, strong interpersonal skills, written communication skills. ▶ *1–4 education/equipment interns:* responsibilities include assisting with equipment rental program, and helping students with film and video equipment. Candidates should have ability to work independently, knowledge of field, organizational skills, personal interest in the field, self-motivation, strong interpersonal skills. Open to recent high school graduates, college freshmen, college sophomores, college juniors, college seniors, recent college graduates, graduate students, law students, career changers. ▶ *1–4 public relations assistants:* responsibilities include performing a wide variety of tasks related to public relations. Candidates should have office skills, organizational skills, personal interest in the field, research skills, self-motivation, strong interpersonal skills. Open to recent high school graduates, college freshmen, college sophomores, college juniors, college seniors, recent college graduates, graduate students, law students, career changers, individuals reentering the workforce. Duration for all positions is 1 semester. All positions are unpaid. International applications accepted.

Benefits Names of contacts, opportunity to attend seminars/workshops, willing to complete paperwork for educational credit, willing to provide letters of recommendation, opportunity to attend screenings and events and to take classes.

Contact Write or e-mail Internship Coordinator. E-mail: info@nwfilm.org. In-person interview recommended. Applicants must submit a cover letter, resume. Application deadline: May 15 for summer, August 15 for fall, December 15 for winter. World Wide Web: http://www.nwfilm.org.

OPEN CITY FILMS/ BLOW UP PICTURES
198 Avenue of the Americas
New York, New York 10013

General Information Independent film production company. Established in 1993. Number of employees: 5. Number of internship applications received each year: 750.

Internships Available ▶ *6–10 office assistants:* responsibilities include assisting in all areas of office operations including phones, mailings, script tracking, research, and press kit production. Candidates should have analytical skills, oral communication skills, organizational skills, personal interest in the field, research skills, written communication skills. Duration is 3 months. Unpaid. Open to college freshmen, college sophomores, college juniors, college seniors, recent college graduates, graduate students. International applications accepted.

Benefits Names of contacts, willing to act as a professional reference, willing to complete paperwork for educational credit, willing to provide letters of recommendation.

Contact Write, fax, or e-mail J. P. Travis. Fax: 212-343-1849. E-mail: jp@opencityfilms.com. No phone calls. In-person interview recommended. Applicants must submit a cover letter, resume. Application deadline: April 15 for summer, November 1 for spring.

PARTOS COMPANY
6363 Wilshire Boulevard, Suite 227
Los Angeles, California 90048

General Information Talent and literary agency representing both film and commercial clients including directors, writers, directors of photography, and editors. Established in 1991. Number of employees: 3. Number of internship applications received each year: 100.

Internships Available ▶ *Internet interns:* responsibilities include helping in creation and publication of online magazine, writing and researching articles, graphic design. Candidates should have computer and graphic design skills (not required but helpful). ▶ *1–3 office interns:* responsibilities include filing, handling calls, some running, and the possibility of performing some public relations work. Duration for all positions is flexible. All positions available as unpaid or paid. Open to high school students, high school seniors, recent high school graduates, college freshmen, college sophomores, college juniors, college seniors, recent college graduates, graduate students, law students, career changers, individuals reentering the workforce. International applications accepted.

Benefits Formal training, job counseling, names of contacts, possible full-time employment, travel reimbursement, willing to complete paperwork for educational credit, willing to provide letters of recommendation.

Contact Write, call, fax, or e-mail Internship Coordinator. Phone: 323-951-1320. Fax: 323-951-1324. E-mail: interns@partos.com. In-person interview required. Applicants must submit a cover letter, resume. Applications are accepted continuously. World Wide Web: http://www.partos.com.

PATRIOT PICTURES
2029 Century Park East, Suite 3900
Los Angeles, California 90067

General Information Film production company.
Internships Available ▶ *Interns:* responsibilities include assisting Director of Development in such tasks as research, tracking scripts, preparing publicity materials, project planning, scheduling, and script coverage. Duration is flexible. Unpaid. Open to college freshmen, college sophomores, college juniors, college seniors, recent college graduates, students who can earn academic credit for internship.

Benefits On-the-job training, willing to act as a professional reference, willing to complete paperwork for educational credit, willing to provide letters of recommendation.
Contact Write, fax, or e-mail Tracee Hillyer, Executive Assistant, 2029 Century Park East, Suite 3900, Los Angeles, California 90067. Fax: 310-556-3145. E-mail: michael_mendelsohn@paribas. com. Applicants must submit a resume. Applications are accepted continuously.

PUBLIC INTEREST VIDEO NETWORK
4704 Overbrook Road
Bethesda, Maryland 20816

General Information Media center producing public television documentaries and assisting issue-oriented nonprofit organizations and the government in using the media. Established in 1979. Number of employees: 4. Number of internship applications received each year: 20.
Internships Available ▶ *2 production assistants:* responsibilities include assisting producer/director in field production, production research, and distribution efforts and handling office-related matters. Candidates should have ability to work independently, ability to work with others, computer skills, editing skills, office skills, research skills, self-motivation, written communication skills, media 100 experience a plus. Duration is 3 or more months. Unpaid. Open to college juniors, college seniors, recent college graduates, graduate students, career changers. International applications accepted.
Benefits Formal training, job counseling, names of contacts, possible full-time employment, travel reimbursement, willing to act as a professional reference, willing to complete paperwork for educational credit, willing to provide letters of recommendation, filming on location across the U.S.
Contact Write or call Ms. Elsa D. Newman, Assistant Director/ Attorney. Phone: 301-656-7244. In-person interview recommended. Applicants must submit a cover letter, resume, writing sample, three personal references. Application deadline: February 1 for summer (recommended deadline); continuous for academic year.

RADIO & TELEVISION NEWS DIRECTORS FOUNDATION
1000 Connecticut Avenue, NW, Suite 615
Washington, District of Columbia 20036-5302

General Information Nonprofit foundation. Number of employees: 10. Unit of Radio & Television News Directors Foundation, Washington, District of Columbia. Number of internship applications received each year: 150.
Internships Available ▶ *Capitol Hill interns (summer and spring):* responsibilities include following newsworthy congressional activities and helping to coordinate broadcast coverage of these activities. Candidates should have college courses in field, knowledge of field, personal interest in the field, plan to pursue career in field, self-motivation. Duration is March to May or June to August. $1,000 per month. ▶ *1 Jane Pauley intern:* responsibilities include learning the nuts and bolts of developing local newscasts with an emphasis on producing, writing, and reporting skills. Candidates should have ability to work with others, knowledge of field, oral communication skills, personal interest in the field, plan to pursue career in field, self-motivation. Duration is June to November. $1,120 per month. ▶ *4–6 minority news management interns:* responsibilities include working in a management-related capacity, such as production, the assignment desk, or administration. Candidates should have college courses in field, knowledge of field, personal interest in the field, plan to pursue career in field. Duration is June to November. $1,000–$1,300 per month. Open to recent college graduates.
Benefits Names of contacts, possible full-time employment.
Contact Write, call, or e-mail Dani Browne, Awards and Events Assistant, 1000 Connecticut Avenue, NW, Suite 615, Washington, District of Columbia 20036-5302. Phone: 202-467-5218. E-mail: danib@rtndf.org. Applicants must submit a formal organization application, resume, two letters of recommendation. Application deadline: January 19 for spring Capitol Hill positions, March

1 for summer Capitol Hill, news management, and Jane Pauley positions. World Wide Web: http://www.rtndf.org.

SIMON & GOODMAN PICTURE COMPANY
2095 Broadway, Suite 402
New York, New York 10023

General Information Documentary film company. Established in 1987. Number of employees: 5. Number of internship applications received each year: 200.
Internships Available ▶ *3–6 interns:* responsibilities include assisting the editor and producer with research and miscellaneous office duties. Candidates should have ability to work with others, college courses in field, experience in the field, knowledge of field, office skills, self-motivation. Duration is 1 semester. Unpaid. Open to undergraduate or graduate film students, recent graduates. International applications accepted.
Benefits Names of contacts, on-the-job training, opportunity to attend seminars/workshops, possible full-time employment, willing to act as a professional reference, willing to complete paperwork for educational credit, willing to provide letters of recommendation, possible attendance at film shoots.
Contact Write, fax, or e-mail Internship Coordinator, 2095 Broadway, Sutie 402, New York, New York 10023. Fax: 212-721-0922. E-mail: sgpic@aol.com. No phone calls. In-person interview recommended. Applicants must submit a cover letter, resume. Applications are accepted continuously.

S.O.S. PRODUCTIONS, INC.
753 Harmon Avenue
Columbus, Ohio 43223

General Information Film, audio, video, and postproduction facility that makes television commercials and corporate videos. Established in 1981. Number of employees: 44. Number of internship applications received each year: 50.
Internships Available ▶ *1 audio post-production intern:* responsibilities include recording, editing, and working in sound design. Candidates should have college courses in field, oral communication skills, personal interest in the field, self-motivation, strong interpersonal skills, students must be receiving college credit and must have own vehicle and valid driver's license. Duration is 1 semester. ▶ *1–2 production interns:* responsibilities include setting-up and wrapping video film equipment; understanding the purpose of each production service and the planning and execution phases of the production process; and assisting in building, lighting, and striking sets. Candidates should have college courses in field, oral communication skills, personal interest in the field, self-motivation, strong interpersonal skills, students must be receiving college credit and must have vehicle and valid driver's license. Duration is 10 weeks. All positions paid at $50 per week. Open to college freshmen, college sophomores, college juniors, college seniors.
Benefits Names of contacts, on-the-job training, possible full-time employment, willing to act as a professional reference, willing to complete paperwork for educational credit, willing to provide letters of recommendation, free lunches.
Contact Write or fax Cory Wills, Production Manager. Fax: 614-221-3836. No phone calls. In-person interview required. Applicants must submit a cover letter, resume. Applications are accepted continuously.

STONE VS. STONE
189 Franklin Street, 3rd Floor
New York, New York 10013

General Information Film publishing or studios (independent and cable) with an emphasis on non fiction-based political thriller material and other book projects. Number of internship applications received each year: 50.
Internships Available ▶ *1–3 development interns:* responsibilities include investigative research of stories and characters to be developed for film and book projects. Candidates should have research skills, writing skills, residence in New York City vicinity, writing/research experience preferred. Duration is flexible.

Stone vs. Stone (continued)

Unpaid. Open to college freshmen, college sophomores, college juniors, college seniors, recent college graduates, graduate students, law students, career changers, individuals reentering the workforce.

Benefits Willing to complete paperwork for educational credit, willing to provide letters of recommendation.

Contact Write, call, or e-mail Web Stone, Producer. Phone: 212-941-1200. E-mail: stonesnyc@aol.com. In-person interview required. Applicants must submit a resume, writing sample. Applications are accepted continuously.

TOMMY BOY MUSIC
902 Broadway
New York, New York 10010

General Information Record label. Established in 1981. Number of employees: 95. Number of internship applications received each year: 300.

Internships Available ▶ *1 A and R intern:* responsibilities include copying demo tapes, recycling tapes, and working closely with department coordinator. Unpaid. Open to college freshmen, college sophomores, college juniors, college seniors, graduate students. ▶ *1–2 accounting interns:* responsibilities include filing, data entry, some billing duties, and account analysis. Unpaid. Open to college freshmen, college sophomores, college juniors, college seniors, graduate students. ▶ *1 business affairs intern:* responsibilities include various duties in the legal and business affairs departments. Position available as unpaid or paid. Open to college freshmen, college sophomores, college juniors, college seniors, graduate students. ▶ *1–4 marketing interns:* responsibilities include following up on phone calls, updating lists, and coordinating mailings for various areas of marketing department, including promotions and retail. Candidates should have oral communication skills, strong interpersonal skills. Unpaid. Open to high school students, college freshmen, college sophomores, college juniors, college seniors, graduate students. ▶ *1–3 media interns:* responsibilities include compiling press clippings; collating and mailing press releases. Candidates should have oral communication skills, written communication skills. Unpaid. Open to college freshmen, college sophomores, college juniors, college seniors, graduate students. Duration for all positions is flexible by semester.

Benefits Names of contacts, possible full-time employment, willing to complete paperwork for educational credit, willing to provide letters of recommendation.

Contact Fax or e-mail Karen Tumelty, Quality of Life. Fax: 212-388-8400. E-mail: karen.tumelty@tommyboy.com. No phone calls. In-person interview recommended. Applicants must submit a cover letter, resume, proof that internship is for college credit. Applications are accepted continuously.

WALL STREET MUSIC
1189 East 14 Mile Road
Birmingham, Michigan 48009-2025

General Information Record company specializing in hip-hop, R&B, rap, jazz alternative, and new age music. Established in 1985. Number of employees: 8. Branch of Wall Street Productions, Atlanta, Georgia. Number of internship applications received each year: 80.

Internships Available ▶ *1–2 engineering/production interns:* responsibilities include learning the inner workings of the music production industry using Digidesign random-access multitrack recording software, digital soundfile editors, digital multitrack tape machines, video/audio machine control interfacing, and digital sequencing software during all stages of the audio production chain, and exercising organizational skills. Candidates should have computer skills, declared college major in field, experience in the field, oral communication skills, organizational skills, plan to pursue career in field. Duration is 15–20 weeks. Open to college freshmen, college sophomores, college juniors, college seniors, recent college graduates, graduate students, law students. ▶ *1–2 marketing interns:* responsibilities include assisting in maintaining databases for each marketing area; contact-

ing and negotiating with mailing list brokers; helping prepare international direct-mail campaigns; composing press releases for international newswires; and disseminating press kits for radio, television, and print. Candidates should have ability to work independently, computer skills, oral communication skills, organizational skills, plan to pursue career in field, written communication skills. Duration is 15–20 weeks. Open to college freshmen, college sophomores, college juniors, college seniors, recent college graduates, graduate students, law students. ▶ *1–2 media/artist/public relations interns:* responsibilities include writing news releases, biographies, and fact sheets; compiling and packaging press kits; acquiring performance information regarding artist tours and assisting in promotional mailings to magazines and press; arranging for interviews and promotional events and requesting and cataloging tearsheets from press; electronically pasting up press coverage for press kits; tracking inventory of artists' promotional materials; assisting in follow-up of targeted media personnel; exploring media advertising based upon media plan; helping coordinate record release parties; and interacting with Wall Street artists on all promotional issues. Candidates should have ability to work independently, computer skills, oral communication skills, organizational skills, plan to pursue career in field, written communication skills. Duration is 15–20 weeks. Open to college freshmen, college sophomores, college juniors, college seniors, recent college graduates, graduate students, law students. ▶ *1–2 promotions interns:* responsibilities include promoting new music video releases in conjunction with over 90 music video networks, arranging appearances of artists on video networks, exploring video advertising strategies, seeking out additional video networks throughout the world, maintaining status and contact reports on computer, assisting in contact with retailers and distributors, providing advance notice of new releases, coordinating promotional mailings, determining retailer's need for promotional products, keeping distributors informed of activity of artists, mediating between retailers regarding promotional events, exploring retail co-op advertising, seeking out additional distributor networks, troubleshooting inventory and shipping problems, and maintaining status and contact reports on computer. Candidates should have ability to work independently, computer skills, oral communication skills, organizational skills, plan to pursue career in field, written communication skills. Duration is 5 months. Open to college freshmen, college sophomores, college juniors, college seniors, recent college graduates, graduate students. All positions are unpaid. International applications accepted.

Benefits Job counseling, names of contacts, opportunity to attend seminars/workshops, possible full-time employment, willing to act as a professional reference, willing to complete paperwork for educational credit, willing to provide letters of recommendation, use of company computers for resumes and mass mailings.

Contact Write Mr. Tim Rochon, Vice President, Operations, 1189 East 14 Mile Road, Birmingham, Alabama 48009-2025. In-person interview recommended. Applicants must submit a formal organization application, cover letter, resume, two writing samples. Applications are accepted continuously. World Wide Web: http://www.wallstreetmusic.com.

WOMEN MAKE MOVIES, INC.
462 Broadway, 5th Floor
New York, New York 10013

General Information National women's media organization that facilitates the production, promotion, and distribution of films and videotapes by and about women. Established in 1972. Number of employees: 13. Number of internship applications received each year: 60.

Internships Available ▶ *1–5 distribution assistants:* responsibilities include working in distribution department, maintenance of database and mailing lists of distribution, upkeep of in-house video library, and working in shipping room. Candidates should have ability to work with others, computer skills, office skills, oral communication skills, plan to pursue career in field, written communication skills. ▶ *1 general office assistant:* responsibilities include working with administrative manager. Candidates

should have ability to work with others, computer skills, office skills, oral communication skills, plan to pursue career in field, written communication skills. ▶ *1–2 graphic production assistants:* responsibilities include producing one-sheets and other promotional pieces from templates. Candidates should have ability to work with others, computer skills, knowledge of field, office skills, research skills, written communication skills. ▶ *1–2 production assistants:* responsibilities include upkeep of offices on computer database, organizing the upkeep of resource files, and assisting with the winter and fall workshops. Candidates should have ability to work independently, ability to work with others, computer skills, office skills, oral communication skills, plan to pursue career in field, written communication skills. ▶ *1–3 promotions assistants:* responsibilities include assisting sales and marketing staff with outreach to community-based and academic organizations, writing and proofreading promotinal copy, and designing fliers. Candidates should have ability to work with others, computer skills, editing skills, office skills, oral communication skills, writing skills. Duration for all positions is 1 semester. All positions are unpaid. Open to college freshmen, college sophomores, college juniors, college seniors, recent college graduates, graduate students. International applications accepted. **Benefits** Names of contacts, opportunity to attend seminars/workshops, travel reimbursement, willing to complete paperwork for educational credit, willing to provide letters of recommendation, access to film collection, resource files, and independent filmmaking network.
Contact Write, fax, or e-mail Bernadette Speach, Internship Coordinator. Fax: 212-925-2052. E-mail: info@wmm.com. No phone calls. In-person interview recommended. Applicants must submit a formal organization application, cover letter, resume. Applications are accepted continuously. World Wide Web: http://www.wmm.com.

NEWSPAPER PUBLISHERS

THE ADVOCATE
PO Box 588
Baton Rouge, Louisiana 70821

General Information Publisher of daily newspaper. Established in 1907. Number of employees: 566. Number of internship applications received each year: 50.
Internships Available ▶ *2 reporter interns:* responsibilities include reporting the news. Candidates should have ability to work with others, college degree in related field, experience in the field, self-motivation, writing skills. Duration is 2 years. $11–$13 per hour. Open to college seniors, recent college graduates. International applications accepted.
Benefits Health insurance, possible full-time employment, travel reimbursement, willing to act as a professional reference, willing to provide letters of recommendation.
Contact Write, call, fax, or e-mail Betty Jo Baker, Human Resources Director. Phone: 225-388-0171. Fax: 225-388-0397. E-mail: bjbaker@theadvocate.com. In-person interview required. Applicants must submit a formal organization application, resume, portfolio, writing sample, three personal references. Applications are accepted continuously. World Wide Web: http://www.theadvocate.com.

AKRON BEACON JOURNAL
44 East Exchange Street
Akron, Ohio 44309

General Information Newspaper publishing company. Established in 1839. Number of employees: 700. Unit of Knight Ridder, San Jose, California. Number of internship applications received each year: 100.
Internships Available ▶ *4–5 advertising sales interns:* responsibilities include developing advertising revenues from existing clients,

cold-calling for new business (commissionable), understanding market research and using it to develop sales presentations. Candidates should have ability to work with others, computer skills, declared college major in field, oral communication skills, self-motivation, written communication skills. Duration is flexible (3 months in the summer). $350 per week plus commission. Open to college juniors, college seniors, recent college graduates.
Benefits Formal training, opportunity to attend seminars/workshops, possible full-time employment, travel reimbursement, willing to act as a professional reference, willing to complete paperwork for educational credit, willing to provide letters of recommendation.
Contact Write or fax Nancy Whitehead, Advertising Operations Manager. Fax: 330-996-3299. In-person interview required. Applicants must submit a cover letter, resume. Application deadline: March 15. World Wide Web: http://www.ohio.com.

AMERICAN YOUTH WORK CENTER/YOUTH TODAY
1200 17th Street, NW, 4th Floor
Washington, District of Columbia 20036

General Information A national monthly newspaper for professionals concerned with youth, especially at-risk, out-of-school youth; topics may include child welfare, juvenile justice, child labor, and substance abuse. Established in 1983. Number of employees: 9. Number of internship applications received each year: 100.
Internships Available ▶ *1–3 reporter interns:* responsibilities include gathering and analyzing information, writing short articles, preparing regular features and proofreading copy, covering meetings on Capitol Hill and meetings sponsored by public policy organizations, and performing some administrative duties. Candidates should have ability to work independently, college courses in field, computer skills, editing skills, knowledge of field, office skills, oral communication skills, organizational skills, plan to pursue career in field, research skills, self-motivation, strong interpersonal skills, writing skills. Duration is full-time summer or part-time or full-time year-round. $6 per hour. Open to high school students, high school seniors, recent high school graduates, college freshmen, college sophomores, college juniors, college seniors, recent college graduates, graduate students, career changers. International applications accepted.
Benefits Names of contacts, on-the-job training, opportunity to attend seminars/workshops, possible full-time employment, willing to act as a professional reference, willing to complete paperwork for educational credit, willing to provide letters of recommendation.
International Internships Available in Jamaica.
Contact Write, call, fax, or e-mail Robin Weiss-Castro, Internship Coordinator. Phone: 202-785-0764. Fax: 202-728-0657. E-mail: youthtoday@aol.com. In-person interview recommended. Applicants must submit a cover letter, resume, two writing samples. Applications are accepted continuously.

ANCHORAGE DAILY NEWS
PO Box 149001
Anchorage, Alaska 99514

General Information General circulation daily newspaper. Established in 1946. Number of employees: 530. Unit of McClatchy Newspapers, Sacramento, California. Number of internship applications received each year: 400.
Internships Available ▶ *1 copy editor intern:* responsibilities include layout, headlines, editing. Candidates should have computer skills, editing skills, experience in the field, organizational skills, writing skills, ability to meet deadlines. Duration is 12 weeks, June 1-August 31. Open to college juniors, college seniors, recent college graduates, graduate students, career changers, individuals reentering the workforce. ▶ *1 photographer intern:* responsibilities include acting as general assignment photographer; reporting to photo editor; 40 hours/week, overtime as needed on occasion. Candidates should have ability to work independently, experience in the field, oral communication skills, strong interpersonal skills, written communication skills. Duration is 12 weeks, June 1-August 31 (slightly flexible start/stop dates).

Anchorage Daily News (continued)

Open to college sophomores, college juniors, college seniors, recent college graduates, graduate students, career changers, individuals reentering the workforce. ▶ *2 reporting interns:* responsibilities include acting as general assignment reporter, 40 hours/week plus overtime as occasionally needed; reporting, writing, meeting deadlines; reports to metro or feature editor. Candidates should have college courses in field, experience in the field, oral communication skills, research skills, strong interpersonal skills, writing skills. Duration is 12 weeks. Open to college juniors, college seniors, recent college graduates, graduate students, career changers, individuals reentering the workforce. All positions paid at $10 per hour.

Benefits Job counseling, names of contacts, on-the-job training, opportunity to attend seminars/workshops, possible full-time employment, travel reimbursement, willing to complete paperwork for educational credit, small grant toward getting to and returning from Anchorage, assistance in finding lodging.

Contact Write or call Maryellen Lambert, Office Manager. Phone: 907-257-4315. Applicants must submit a cover letter, resume, portfolio, at least 6 writing samples. Application deadline: January 1 for summer. World Wide Web: http://www.adn.com.

ANN ARBOR NEWS
340 East Huron
Ann Arbor, Michigan 48106-1147

General Information Daily newspaper publisher. Established in 1838. Number of employees: 400. Unit of Newhouse Newspapers. Number of internship applications received each year: 100.

Internships Available ▶ *1–2 photographers:* responsibilities include taking photographs and working in studio. Candidates should have computer skills, knowledge of field, plan to pursue career in field. Duration is 3–6 months. $375 per week. Open to college juniors, college seniors, recent college graduates, graduate students. ▶ *1–2 reporters/copy editors:* responsibilities include performing copy desk work, covering breaking news, and interviewing for features. Candidates should have ability to work with others, editing skills, experience in the field, plan to pursue career in field, writing skills. Duration is 3 months. $380 per week. Open to college sophomores, college juniors, college seniors, recent college graduates. ▶ *1–2 sales representatives:* responsibilities include selling classified or display advertising space to contract advertisers and acting as salespersons during summer. Candidates should have ability to work independently, oral communication skills, personal interest in the field, self-motivation, strong interpersonal skills, written communication skills. Duration is 3 months. $10 per hour. Open to college sophomores, college juniors, college seniors.

Benefits Formal training, on-the-job training, possible full-time employment, willing to act as a professional reference, willing to complete paperwork for educational credit, willing to provide letters of recommendation.

Contact Write Richard Fitzgerald, Metro Editor. Applicants must submit a cover letter, resume, academic transcripts, four writing samples, writing references. Application deadline: January 15 for summer. World Wide Web: http://aa.mlive.com.

ARKANSAS DEMOCRAT-GAZETTE
PO Box 2221
Little Rock, Arkansas 72203

General Information Daily statewide newspaper. Number of employees: 200. Subsidiary of Wehco Media, Little Rock, Arkansas. Number of internship applications received each year: 100.

Internships Available ▶ *2–4 reporting interns:* responsibilities include reporting in the news department or working in the features department. Candidates should have college courses in field, experience in the field, oral communication skills, plan to pursue career in field, writing skills. Duration is May/June to August/September. Paid. Open to college sophomores, college juniors, college seniors. International applications accepted.

Benefits Names of contacts, on-the-job training, possible full-time employment, willing to act as a professional reference, opportunity to gain experience.

Contact Write or e-mail Linda Friedlieb, City Editor, PO Box 2221, Little Rock, Arkansas 72203. E-mail: linda_friedlieb@ardengaz.com. Applicants must submit a cover letter, resume, personal reference, 8-10 writing samples. Application deadline: November 15. World Wide Web: http://www.ardemgaz.com.

THE ATLANTA JOURNAL AND CONSTITUTION
72 Marietta Street, NW
Atlanta, Georgia 30303

General Information Major daily metropolitan newspaper. Number of internship applications received each year: 500.

Internships Available ▶ *News interns:* responsibilities include working in department that matches an intern's area of skill or experience, such as reporting, copy editing, photography, or graphic arts. Candidates should have previous professional daily experience with deadlines, preferably on a newspaper; must have worked on campus newspaper or other publications. Duration is 10 weeks in summer, winter positions possible. $550 per week. Open to college juniors, college seniors, recent college graduates, graduate students.

Benefits Job counseling, opportunity to attend seminars/workshops, possible full-time employment, willing to complete paperwork for educational credit, willing to provide letters of recommendation, mentor system that aids professional growth.

Contact Write or e-mail Angela Tuck, News Personnel Manager. E-mail: atuck@ajc.com. No phone calls. Applicants must submit a resume, personal reference, 500-word essay (see Web site or write for details), copies of 5-10 news clips or samples of photos/graphics/headlines. Application deadline: December 15 for summer. World Wide Web: http://www.ajc.com/internship.

THE BAKERSFIELD CALIFORNIAN
1707 Eye Street
Bakersfield, California 93301

General Information Daily newspaper. Established in 1866. Number of employees: 385. Number of internship applications received each year: 200.

Internships Available ▶ *2–3 interns (new media):* responsibilities include city guide updating and posting news stories to the Web site. Candidates should have knowledge of field, oral communication skills, plan to pursue career in field, self-motivation, written communication skills. Duration is 6 months. $8 per hour. Open to college freshmen, college sophomores, college juniors, college seniors, recent college graduates, graduate students, career changers. ▶ *Marketing interns:* responsibilities include assisting in the marketing research department as well as promotion. Candidates should have ability to work independently, analytical skills, oral communication skills, organizational skills, research skills, written communication skills. Duration is 3–4 months. $10 per hour. Open to college sophomores. ▶ *4 photographers.* Candidates should have experience in the field, knowledge of field, oral communication skills, plan to pursue career in field, self-motivation, written communication skills. Duration is 13 weeks. $340 per week. Open to college freshmen, college sophomores, college juniors, college seniors, recent college graduates, graduate students, career changers. ▶ *4 reporters.* Candidates should have declared college major in field, experience in the field, oral communication skills, self-motivation, strong interpersonal skills, written communication skills. Duration is 13 weeks. $340 per week. Open to college freshmen, college sophomores, college juniors, college seniors, recent college graduates, graduate students, career changers. International applications accepted.

Benefits On-the-job training, possible full-time employment, willing to act as a professional reference, willing to complete paperwork for educational credit, willing to provide letters of recommendation.

Contact Write, call, fax, or e-mail Logan Molen, Assistant Managing Editor/Days, PO Box 440, Bakersfield, California 93302-0440. Phone: 661-395-7373. Fax: 661-395-7519. E-mail: lmolen@bakersfield.com. In-person interview recommended. Applicants must submit a formal organization application, resume, three personal references, five writing samples. Applications are accepted continuously.

BEE PUBLICATIONS
5564 Main Street
Williamsville, New York 14221

General Information Publications agency, including 9 newspapers, that reports on local government, schools, sports, and other community activities in a professional manner. Established in 1879. Number of employees: 60. Number of internship applications received each year: 8.
Internships Available ▶ *1–5 reporters:* responsibilities include rewriting press releases; editing copy; and writing feature, news, and sports stories. Duration is 1 semester. Unpaid. Open to college freshmen, college sophomores, college juniors, college seniors. International applications accepted.
Benefits Formal training, possible full-time employment, willing to complete paperwork for educational credit.
Contact Write, call, fax, or e-mail Mr. David Sherman, Managing Editor. Phone: 716-632-4700. Fax: 716-633-8601. E-mail: beenews@aol.com. In-person interview required. Applicants must submit a cover letter, resume. Applications are accepted continuously.

THE BIRMINGHAM NEWS
2200 Fourth Avenue North
Birmingham, Alabama 35203

General Information Newspaper recognized regionally and nationally for its reporting and commentary. Established in 1888. Unit of Advance Publications, Staten Island, New York. Number of internship applications received each year: 100.
Internships Available ▶ *2 fall sports interns:* responsibilities include working as a beginning sports reporter. Candidates should have ability to work independently, ability to work with others, college courses in field, computer skills, knowledge of field, plan to pursue career in field, research skills, self-motivation, writing skills, minimum B average in course work. Duration is 16 weeks. $325 per week. Open to college sophomores, college juniors, college seniors. ▶ *3 summer advertising interns:* responsibilities include working as a beginning/regular salesperson. Duration is 10–12 weeks. $6 per hour. Open to college sophomores, college juniors. ▶ *4 summer news interns:* responsibilities include working as a beginning reporter. Candidates should have ability to work independently, ability to work with others, college courses in field, computer skills, knowledge of field, plan to pursue career in field, research skills, writing skills, minimum B average in course work. Duration is 10–12 weeks. $325 per week. Open to college sophomores, college juniors.
Benefits Formal training, possible full-time employment, travel reimbursement, willing to complete paperwork for educational credit, willing to provide letters of recommendation.
Contact Write, call, or fax Ms. Carol Nunnelley, Managing Editor (for news internships). Phone: 205-325-2111. Fax: 205-325-2283. Applicants must submit a cover letter, resume, 8-10 writing samples. Application deadline: January 15 for summer, April 15 for fall. World Wide Web: http://www.al.com.

BIRMINGHAM POST-HERALD
2200 Fourth Avenue, North
Birmingham, Alabama 35203-3802

General Information Daily afternoon newspaper in Birmingham, Alabama. Established in 1921. Number of employees: 54. Subsidiary of Scripps Howard Company, Cincinnati, Ohio. Number of internship applications received each year: 100.
Internships Available ▶ *1 copyediting intern:* responsibilities include working as a beginning copy editor. Candidates should have college courses in field, computer skills, editing skills, knowledge of field, plan to pursue career in field. Open to college sophomores, college juniors. ▶ *1 photographic intern:* responsibilities include working as a beginning photographer. Candidates should have ability to work independently, ability to work with

others, college courses in field, knowledge of field, plan to pursue career in field. Open to college freshmen, college sophomores, college juniors. ▶ *2 reporting interns:* responsibilities include working as a beginning reporter. Candidates should have ability to work independently, ability to work with others, computer skills, oral communication skills, plan to pursue career in field, writing skills. Open to college sophomores, college juniors. Duration for all positions is 12 weeks. All positions paid at $300 per week. International applications accepted.
Benefits On-the-job training, possible full-time employment, travel reimbursement, willing to complete paperwork for educational credit, willing to provide letters of recommendation.
Contact Write, fax, or e-mail Becky Gallagher, Public Service Director. Fax: 205-325-2410. E-mail: mailbox@postherald.com. No phone calls. Applicants must submit a cover letter, resume, three personal references, five writing samples. Application deadline: January 31 for summer, May 31 for fall. World Wide Web: http://www.postherald.com.

BOCA RATON NEWS
33 Southeast 3rd Street
Boca Raton, Florida 33432

General Information Daily newspaper covering local community news. Established in 1955. Number of employees: 200. Unit of Knight Ridder, San Jose, California. Number of internship applications received each year: 30.
Internships Available ▶ *Copy editors:* responsibilities include assisting in layout, design, and copy editing. ▶ *Photographer/graphics interns:* responsibilities include taking photographs and processing film. ▶ *Reporters:* responsibilities include researching, interviewing, and writing for local news, business, features, and sports desks. Duration for all positions is flexible. All positions available as unpaid or paid. Open to college freshmen, college sophomores, college juniors, college seniors, recent college graduates, graduate students, career changers. International applications accepted.
Benefits Possible full-time employment, willing to complete paperwork for educational credit, willing to provide letters of recommendation.
Contact Write Ron Smith, Editor-in-Chief. No phone calls. In-person interview recommended. Applicants must submit a formal organization application, cover letter, resume, academic transcripts, three letters of recommendation. Applications are accepted continuously. World Wide Web: http://www.bocaratonnews.com.

THE BOSTON GLOBE
135 Morrissey Boulevard
Boston, Massachusetts 02107

General Information Newspaper. Established in 1872. Number of employees: 2,300. Subsidiary of The New York Times, New York, New York. Number of internship applications received each year: 200.
Internships Available ▶ *2 business summer interns:* responsibilities include accounts payable and payroll (accounting intern); advertising sales (advertising intern). Candidates should have ability to work independently, analytical skills, computer skills, knowledge of field, office skills, oral communication skills, organizational skills, personal interest in the field, self-motivation, strong interpersonal skills, written communication skills. Duration is 13 weeks. $570 per week. Open to college sophomores, college juniors. ▶ *15 editorial summer:* responsibilities include general assignment reporting for 13 interns. There is also 1 editorial design position and 1 photography position. Candidates should have editing skills, writing skills, experience with school newspaper, previous internship at a daily or weekly newspaper. Duration is 1 summer. $575 per week. Open to college sophomores, college juniors. ▶ *3 one-year interns:* responsibilities include advertising sales, advertising design, or circulation. Candidates should have ability to work independently, analytical skills, college degree in related field, computer skills, knowledge of field, office skills, oral communication skills, organizational skills, plan to pursue career in field, self-

The Boston Globe (continued)

motivation, strong interpersonal skills, written communication skills. Duration is 1 year. $24,000–$41,000 per year. Open to recent college graduates. International applications accepted.
Benefits On-the-job training, opportunity to attend seminars/workshops, health insurance for one-year internship.
Contact Write, call, or fax Clare Larson, Human Resources Associate; Daisey Harris, Assistant to the Editor, (617)929-3120, for editorial summer positions, PO Box 2378, Boston, Massachusetts 02107. Phone: 617-929-2795. Fax: 617-929-3376. In-person interview required. Applicants must submit a formal organization application, cover letter, resume. Application deadline: February 25 for business summer and one-year positions, November 12 for editorial summer. World Wide Web: http://www.boston.com/extranet.

BUCKS COUNTY COURIER TIMES
8400 Route 13
Levittown, Pennsylvania 19057

General Information Suburban Philadelphia newspaper with a circulation of over 70,000. Established in 1910. Number of employees: 300. Unit of Calkins Newspapers, Levittown, Pennsylvania. Number of internship applications received each year: 100.
Internships Available ▶ *1 copy editor:* responsibilities include copy editing daily newspaper copy. Candidates should have ability to work with others, analytical skills, computer skills, editing skills, knowledge of field, written communication skills. Duration is 12 weeks (June to August). ▶ *1 feature writer:* responsibilities include writing and editing features. Candidates should have analytical skills, computer skills, editing skills, research skills, strong interpersonal skills, writing skills. Duration is 12 weeks (June to August). ▶ *1 photographer/graphics person:* responsibilities include photo or graphic (computer) work. Candidates should have ability to work with others, analytical skills, organizational skills, personal interest in the field, self-motivation, strong interpersonal skills. Duration is 12 weeks. ▶ *Reporters:* responsibilities include reporting for daily newspaper. Candidates should have analytical skills, personal interest in the field, research skills, self-motivation, strong interpersonal skills, writing skills. Duration is 12 weeks. ▶ *1 sports writer:* responsibilities include writing features covering sports events, and editing. Candidates should have analytical skills, computer skills, editing skills, personal interest in the field, research skills, strong interpersonal skills, writing skills. Duration is 12 weeks (June to August). All positions paid at $365 per week. Open to college juniors, college seniors, recent college graduates, graduate students.
Benefits Names of contacts, willing to complete paperwork for educational credit, willing to provide letters of recommendation, car expenses.
Contact Write, call, fax, or e-mail Carolyn Per, Internship Coordinator. Phone: 215-949-4185. Fax: 215-949-4177. E-mail: cper@calkinsnewspapers.com. In-person interview recommended. Applicants must submit a formal organization application, cover letter, resume, published writing samples. Application deadline: February 1 for summer. World Wide Web: http://www.bcct-gpn.com.

BUFFALO NEWS
1 News Plaza, PO Box 100
Buffalo, New York 14240

General Information Publisher of daily newspaper. Established in 1880. Number of employees: 1,000. Unit of Berkshire Hathaway, Inc., Omaha, Nebraska. Number of internship applications received each year: 100.
Internships Available ▶ *Copy editors:* responsibilities include editing news stories and verifying facts and grammar. Candidates should have college courses in field, editing skills, knowledge of field, writing skills, experience on school newspaper. Duration is one summer (usually 3 months). $316 per week. Open to college juniors, graduate students. ▶ *Photographers:* responsibilities include replacing vacationing staffer. Candidates should have knowledge of field, oral communication skills, written communication skills, experience on school newspaper. Duration is one summer (usually 3 months). $316 per week. Open to college juniors, graduate students. ▶ *Reporters:* responsibilities include replacing vacationing staffer. Candidates should have computer skills, oral communication skills, writing skills, written communication skills, experience on school newspaper. Duration is 3 months. $316 per week. Open to college juniors, graduate students. ▶ *3–4 salespeople:* responsibilities include selling retail advertising. Candidates should have ability to work independently, analytical skills, college courses in field, knowledge of field, office skills, oral communication skills, organizational skills, personal interest in the field, self-motivation, strong interpersonal skills, written communication skills. Duration is June-August. $235 per week. Open to college freshmen, college sophomores, college juniors, college seniors.
Benefits Willing to complete paperwork for educational credit, willing to provide letters of recommendation.
Contact Write Margaret M. Sullivan, Managing Editor. No phone calls. In-person interview required. Applicants must submit a formal organization application, cover letter, resume, 4-6 writing samples. Application deadline: December 1 for summer.

THE BULLETIN
1526 Northwest Hill Street
Bend, Oregon 97701

General Information Flagship paper in group of 9 papers (5 daily and 4 weekly) located in Oregon and California. Established in 1903. Number of employees: 200. Unit of Western Communications Inc., Bend, Oregon. Number of internship applications received each year: 100.
Internships Available ▶ *1–2 copy editors:* responsibilities include entry-level copy editing and page layout. Candidates should have college courses in field, computer skills, editing skills, plan to pursue career in field, writing skills. ▶ *1–4 interns:* responsibilities include substituting for vacationing regular staff members. Candidates should have analytical skills, college courses in field, computer skills, organizational skills, plan to pursue career in field, writing skills. ▶ *1–2 photographers:* responsibilities include entry-level news photography. Candidates should have college courses in field, computer skills, experience in the field, organizational skills, plan to pursue career in field, writing skills, published work samples. ▶ *1–2 reporters:* responsibilities include entry-level news reporting. Candidates should have college courses in field, computer skills, organizational skills, plan to pursue career in field, research skills, writing skills. Duration for all positions is 1 summer (June to September). All positions paid at $1,500 per month. Open to college juniors, college seniors, recent college graduates, graduate students. International applications accepted.
Benefits Job counseling, names of contacts, on-the-job training, opportunity to attend seminars/workshops, possible full-time employment, willing to act as a professional reference, willing to complete paperwork for educational credit, willing to provide letters of recommendation.
Contact Write Mr. John Henrikson, Associate Editor. No phone calls. Telephone interview required. Applicants must submit a cover letter, resume, 4-8 writing samples. Application deadline: March 1. World Wide Web: http://www.bendbulletin.com.

CALLER-TIMES
820 Lower North Broadway
Corpus Christi, Texas 78401

General Information Daily newspaper providing coverage in a 10-county area in southern Texas. Established in 1883. Number of employees: 400. Unit of EW Scripts, Cincinnati, Ohio. Number of internship applications received each year: 40.
Internships Available ▶ *3 newsroom interns.* Candidates should have editing skills, research skills, writing skills. Duration is 10 weeks. $280–$300 per week. Open to college sophomores, college juniors, college seniors.
Benefits Names of contacts, possible full-time employment, willing to provide letters of recommendation.

Contact Write, call, fax, or e-mail Mr. Nick Jimenez, Editorial Page Editor, 520 Lower North Broadway, Corpus Christi, Texas 78401. Phone: 512-886-3787. Fax: 512-886-3732. E-mail: jimenezn@caller.com. In-person interview recommended. Applicants must submit a cover letter, resume, writing sample. Application deadline: January 30. World Wide Web: http://www.caller.com.

CEDAR RAPIDS GAZETTE, INC.
PO Box 511
Cedar Rapids, Iowa 52406

General Information Multi-media company publishing regional newspaper. Established in 1883. Number of employees: 470. Unit of The Gazette Company, Cedar Rapids, Iowa. Number of internship applications received each year: 200.
Internships Available ▶ *2 advertising interns:* responsibilities include working with display and classified advertising; planning and conducting sales presentations; coordinating ad design and layouts. Candidates should have ability to work independently, college courses in field, computer skills, oral communication skills, organizational skills, plan to pursue career in field, written communication skills. Duration is 3 months in summer. $6 per hour. Open to college sophomores, college juniors. ▶ *3–4 news reporting interns:* responsibilities include general reporting responsibilities. Candidates should have ability to work independently, college courses in field, computer skills, knowledge of field, plan to pursue career in field, written communication skills. Duration is 3 months in fall, spring, or summer. $8 per hour. Open to college sophomores, college juniors, college seniors. ▶ *3–4 photo interns:* responsibilities include taking photos for stories in newspaper. Candidates should have ability to work independently, ability to work with others, college courses in field, knowledge of field, oral communication skills, plan to pursue career in field, self-motivation. Duration is 3 months in fall, spring, or summer. $8 per hour. Open to college sophomores, college juniors, college seniors, recent college graduates. ▶ *1 public relations intern:* responsibilities include assisting with "Newspaper in Education" projects and events, attending Editor's coffees, assisting with "In your neighborhood" projects, in-house promotions, and other related efforts. Candidates should have ability to work independently, computer skills, knowledge of field, oral communication skills, personal interest in the field, strong interpersonal skills. Duration is 1 summer. $7 per hour. Open to college sophomores, college juniors. International applications accepted.
Benefits Possible full-time employment, willing to complete paperwork for educational credit, willing to provide letters of recommendation.
Contact Write, fax, or e-mail Patricia Thoms, Human Resources Employment Manager. Fax: 319-368-8834. E-mail: gazcohr@fyiowa.com. No phone calls. Applicants must submit a cover letter, resume. Application deadline: January 1 for summer, March 31 for advertising positions (summer term only), May 1 for fall, October 1 for winter.

COLUMBIA JOURNALISM REVIEW
Journalism Building, Columbia University
New York, New York 10027

General Information National monitor of the news media. Established in 1961. Number of internship applications received each year: 100.
Internships Available ▶ *1–2 interns:* responsibilities include handling phones, photocopying, researching, reporting, writing, and fact checking. Candidates should have ability to work independently, ability to work with others, computer skills, oral communication skills, research skills, written communication skills. Duration is 3–5 months. Unpaid. Open to college freshmen, college sophomores, college juniors, college seniors, recent college graduates, graduate students, career changers, individuals reentering the workforce. International applications accepted.
Benefits Opportunity to attend seminars/workshops, willing to act as a professional reference, willing to complete paperwork for educational credit, willing to provide letters of recommendation, freelance rates for published work.

Contact Write Ms. Gloria Cooper, Managing Editor. Applicants must submit a cover letter, resume, writing sample. Applications are accepted continuously.

CONNECTICUT POST
410 State Street
Bridgeport, Connecticut 06430

General Information Daily newspaper. Established in 1883. Number of employees: 525. Subsidiary of Thomson Newspapers, Stamford, Connecticut. Number of internship applications received each year: 60.
Internships Available ▶ *Interns (news, features, or sports):* responsibilities include performing the duties of a reporter in the news, features, or sports department. Candidates should have editing skills, oral communication skills, plan to pursue career in field, research skills, writing skills. Duration is based on school guidelines. Unpaid. Open to college freshmen, college sophomores, college juniors, college seniors, high school students over age 16.
Benefits On-the-job training, willing to act as a professional reference, willing to complete paperwork for educational credit, willing to provide letters of recommendation.
Contact Write, call, fax, or e-mail Cindy Simoneau, Assistant Managing Editor, 410 State Street, Bridgeport, Connecticut 06604. Phone: 203-330-6391. Fax: 203-367-8158. E-mail: csimoneau.connpost@snet.net. Telephone interview required. Applicants must submit a resume, letter of recommendation, 1 personal reference from an academic advisor, 3-4 writing samples. Applications are accepted continuously.

COURIER–JOURNAL
525 West Broadway
Louisville, Kentucky 40202

General Information Newspaper serving the state of Kentucky and southern Indiana.
Internships Available ▶ *Artists:* responsibilities include helping with layouts, graphics, and illustrations. Candidates should have oral communication skills, personal interest in the field, writing skills, computer skills to work with desktop publishing applications. ▶ *Photographers/photo editors:* responsibilities include photographing news stories and helping with design layout, editing, and developing. Candidates should have ability to work with others, editing skills, oral communication skills, personal interest in the field, research skills, writing skills. ▶ *Reporters and copy editors:* responsibilities include attending weekly meetings and working in all aspects of news reporting. Candidates should have ability to work independently, ability to work with others, computer skills, office skills, oral communication skills, personal interest in the field, research skills, writing skills. Duration for all positions is 12 weeks in summer. All positions paid at $400 per week. Open to college freshmen, college sophomores, college juniors, college seniors, graduate students. International applications accepted.
Benefits Possible full-time employment, travel reimbursement.
Contact Write or call Mr. Mervin Aubespin, Associate Editor/Development. Phone: 502-582-4191. Applicants must submit a cover letter, resume, 6 writing samples. Application deadline: November 15 for summer.

THE DAILY PRESS
7505 Warwick Boulevard
Newport News, Virginia 23607

General Information Daily newspaper. Established in 1896. Number of employees: 550. Unit of Tribune Company, Chicago, Illinois. Number of internship applications received each year: 300.
Internships Available ▶ *4 summer/fall interns:* responsibilities include writing, copy editing, or performing photographic or graphic artist duties. Candidates should have ability to work independently, analytical skills, college courses in field, computer skills, editing skills, knowledge of field, oral communication skills, organizational skills, personal interest in the field, plan to pursue

The Daily Press (continued)

career in field, research skills, self-motivation, strong interpersonal skills, writing skills. Duration is 10 weeks. $390 per week. Open to college sophomores, college juniors, college seniors, recent college graduates, graduate students, career changers. International applications accepted.
Benefits Formal training, job counseling, names of contacts, on-the-job training, opportunity to attend seminars/workshops, possible full-time employment, travel reimbursement, willing to act as a professional reference, willing to complete paperwork for educational credit, willing to provide letters of recommendation, mentoring.
Contact Write, call, fax, or e-mail Sheila Solomon, Staff Development Editor. Phone: 757-247-4646. Fax: 757-244-7437. E-mail: srsolomon@dailypress.com. Telephone interview required. Applicants must submit a cover letter, resume, academic transcripts, portfolio, personal reference, 5 writing samples. Application deadline: December 1. World Wide Web: http://www.hamptonroads.digitalcity.com or www.dailypress.com.

THE DAILY REVIEW
116 Main Street
Towanda, Pennsylvania 18848

General Information Daily newspaper with circulation of 10,000; also publishes "Farmer's Friend", an agricultural weekly paper. Established in 1880. Number of employees: 100. Unit of Times—Shamrock Media Group, Scranton, Pennsylvania. Number of internship applications received each year: 15.
Internships Available ▶ *Reporter interns:* responsibilities include reporting news stories and copy editing. Candidates should have computer skills, office skills, writing skills. Duration is flexible. Unpaid. Open to high school students, high school seniors, recent high school graduates, college freshmen, college sophomores, college juniors, college seniors, recent college graduates, graduate students, law students, career changers, individuals reentering the workforce. International applications accepted.
Benefits Job counseling, names of contacts, on-the-job training, possible full-time employment, willing to complete paperwork for educational credit, willing to provide letters of recommendation.
Contact Write, call, fax, or e-mail Ian Fennell, Managing Editor. Phone: 570-265-1635. Fax: 570-265-4200. E-mail: review@epics.net. In-person interview recommended. Applicants must submit a resume, two personal references. Applications are accepted continuously. World Wide Web: http://www.thedailyreview.com.

THE DALLAS MORNING NEWS
508 Young Street
Dallas, Texas 75202

General Information Daily newspaper. Established in 1885. Number of employees: 2,200. Unit of A. H. Belo Corporation, Dallas, Texas. Number of internship applications received each year: 400.
Internships Available ▶ *5 copy editors.* Candidates should have analytical skills, college courses in field, editing skills, experience in the field, plan to pursue career in field, writing skills. ▶ *1–2 graphic artists.* Candidates should have ability to work with others, college courses in field, computer skills, knowledge of field, self-motivation. ▶ *2 photographers.* Candidates should have ability to work with others, college courses in field, knowledge of field, plan to pursue career in field, self-motivation. ▶ *10–12 reporters.* Candidates should have analytical skills, college courses in field, editing skills, experience in the field, plan to pursue career in field, writing skills. Duration for all positions is 12 weeks. All positions paid at $500 per week. Open to college freshmen, college sophomores, college juniors, college seniors, recent college graduates, graduate students.
Benefits Job counseling, on-the-job training, opportunity to attend seminars/workshops, willing to act as a professional reference, willing to complete paperwork for educational credit, willing to provide letters of recommendation.
Contact Write Vernon Smith, Assistant Managing Editor, Communications Center, PO Box 655237, Dallas, Texas 75265.

Applicants must submit a cover letter, resume, portfolio, three personal references, 500-word biographical essay, 6-10 writing samples. Application deadline: December 1 for summer. World Wide Web: http://www.dallasnews.com.

DELAWARE COUNTY DAILY TIMES
500 Mildred Avenue
Primos, Pennsylvania 19018

General Information Seven-day-per-week newspaper serving Delaware County. Established in 1876. Number of employees: 140. Unit of The Journal Register Company, Trenton, New Jersey. Number of internship applications received each year: 50.
Internships Available ▶ *1–3 reporters:* responsibilities include covering fires, school board meetings, corporate events, and features. Candidates should have ability to work independently, ability to work with others, personal interest in the field, self-motivation, writing skills. Duration is 3 months. $434–$450 per week. Open to college freshmen, college sophomores, college juniors, college seniors, recent college graduates.
Benefits Possible full-time employment, travel reimbursement, willing to act as a professional reference, willing to complete paperwork for educational credit, willing to provide letters of recommendation.
Contact Write, call, fax, or e-mail Linda DeMeglio, Managing Editor. Phone: 610-622-8817. Fax: 610-622-8887. E-mail: newsroom@delcotimes.com. In-person interview recommended. Applicants must submit a cover letter, resume, 3 to 6 writing samples. Application deadline: March 1. World Wide Web: http://www.delcotimes.com.

DEMOCRAT AND CHRONICLE
55 Exchange Boulevard
Rochester, New York 14614

General Information Newspaper that serves the Rochester, New York area. Number of employees: 1,000. Unit of Gannett Co., Inc., Arlington, Virginia.
Internships Available ▶ *1 business reporting intern.* Candidates should have analytical skills, organizational skills, research skills, self-motivation, written communication skills, valid driver's license. ▶ *1 copy editing intern.* Candidates should have analytical skills, editing skills, organizational skills, research skills, self-motivation, written communication skills, valid driver's license. Duration for all positions is 10 weeks during summer. All positions paid at $500 per week.
Benefits On-the-job training, willing to complete paperwork for educational credit.
Contact Write Matt Dudek, Assistant Managing Editor/Administration, Dow Jones Newspaper Fund, PO Box 300, Princeton, New Jersey 08543-0300. No phone calls. Drug test and medical evaluation required; apply through college placement office. Application deadline: deadlines, set by the DOW Jones Newspaper Fund, may be obtained through your college placement director. World Wide Web: http://www.democratandchronicle.com.

DENVER POST CORPORATION
1560 Broadway
Denver, Colorado 80202

General Information Publisher of general circulation newspaper. Established in 1892. Number of employees: 1,400. Number of internship applications received each year: 300.
Internships Available ▶ *3–7 interns:* responsibilities include reporting news, editing copy, graphics, or photography in a department commensurate with intern's skills and interests. Candidates should have computer skills, experience in the field, oral communication skills, organizational skills, plan to pursue career in field, self-motivation, strong interpersonal skills, writing skills. Open to college seniors. ▶ *3–7 reporters.* Candidates should have college courses in field, computer skills, oral communication skills, self-motivation, strong interpersonal skills, writing skills. Open to college juniors, college seniors, graduate

students. Duration for all positions is 10 weeks. All positions paid at $400 per week. International applications accepted.

Benefits On-the-job training, willing to act as a professional reference, willing to complete paperwork for educational credit, willing to provide letters of recommendation, reimbursement for travel while on assignment, health insurance after 30 days.

Contact Write Christopher V. Lopez, Internship Recruiter. Telephone interview required. Applicants must submit a cover letter, resume, portfolio, 3 names of personal references, up to 10 writing samples. Application deadline: December 1 for summer. World Wide Web: http://www.denverpost.com.

DESERET NEWS
30 East First South Street
Salt Lake City, Utah 84111

General Information Daily newspaper. Established in 1850. Number of employees: 165. Number of internship applications received each year: 1.

Internships Available ▶ *4 summer interns:* responsibilities include newspaper reporter duties. Candidates should have declared college major in field, oral communication skills, plan to pursue career in field, research skills, writing skills. Duration is 3 months. $8 per hour. Open to college juniors.

Benefits On-the-job training, possible full-time employment, tuition assistance, willing to complete paperwork for educational credit.

Contact Write Ms. Sharon Thompson, Personnel Director. No phone calls. In-person interview required. Applicants must submit a formal organization application. Applications are accepted continuously. World Wide Web: http://www.desnew.com.

DES MOINES REGISTER
715 Locust Street
Des Moines, Iowa 50309

General Information Daily and Sunday statewide newspaper. Established in 1826. Number of employees: 1,200. Unit of Gannett News Service, Arlington, Virginia. Number of internship applications received each year: 200.

Internships Available ▶ *1 art intern (summer):* responsibilities include producing informational graphics for the daily and Sunday newspaper. Candidates should have ability to work with others, college courses in field, plan to pursue career in field, self-motivation, written communication skills, Macintosh skills. ▶ *3 copy editor interns (summer):* responsibilities include editing copy and stories, writing headlines and doing layouts (2 nightside news copy desk positions; 1 sports copy desk position). Candidates should have ability to work with others, college courses in field, computer skills, editing skills, plan to pursue career in field, self-motivation, layout/design skills. ▶ *1 photo intern (summer):* responsibilities include shooting photos on deadline and for enterprise stories. Candidates should have ability to work with others, college courses in field, computer skills, plan to pursue career in field, self-motivation, strong visual skills. ▶ *5 reporting interns (summer):* responsibilities include reporting stories, both breaking news and enterprise, for the daily and Sunday Register. Candidates should have ability to work with others, college courses in field, plan to pursue career in field, research skills, writing skills, written communication skills. Duration for all positions is 12 weeks. All positions paid at $10 per hour. Open to college juniors, college seniors. International applications accepted.

Benefits Formal training, names of contacts, on-the-job training, opportunity to attend seminars/workshops, possible full-time employment, willing to complete paperwork for educational credit, willing to provide letters of recommendation, reimbursement of work-related travel.

Contact Write Diane E. Graham, Managing Editor/Staff Development, P.O. Box 957, Des Moines, Iowa 50311. No phone calls. Applicants must submit a cover letter, resume, 5-7 writing clips, 2-3 personal references. Application deadline: February 1 for fall. World Wide Web: http://www.desmoinesregister.com.

DETROIT FREE PRESS
600 West Fort Street
Detroit, Michigan 48226

General Information One of the nation's 10 largest newspapers; winner of 8 Pulitzer Prizes. Established in 1831. Number of employees: 290. Unit of Knight Ridder, San Jose, California. Number of internship applications received each year: 450.

Internships Available ▶ *1 Web editor.* ▶ *1 business writer.* ▶ *2 city desk interns.* ▶ *1 entertainment writer.* ▶ *1 features copy editor.* ▶ *1 graphics intern.* ▶ *1 health writer.* ▶ *1 lifestyles writer.* ▶ *1 news copy editor.* ▶ *1 photography intern.* ▶ *1 sports copy editor.* ▶ *1 sports writer.* Duration for all positions is 12 weeks. All positions paid at $498 per week. Open to college sophomores, college juniors, college seniors, recent college graduates, graduate students, career changers. International applications accepted.

Benefits Formal training, job counseling, names of contacts, on-the-job training, opportunity to attend seminars/workshops, possible full-time employment, willing to complete paperwork for educational credit, willing to provide letters of recommendation.

Contact Write Mr. Joe Grimm, Recruiting and Development Editor. In-person interview recommended. Applicants must submit a cover letter, resume, portfolio, three personal references, 6 writing samples. Application deadline: December 1 for summer. World Wide Web: http://www.freep.com/jobspage.

DOW JONES NEWSPAPER FUND
PO Box 300
Princeton, New Jersey 08543-0300

General Information Private foundation that promotes journalism careers. Established in 1959. Number of employees: 4. Number of internship applications received each year: 600.

Internships Available ▶ *12 business reporting interns:* responsibilities include attending a training program; working at a daily newspaper as a business reporter. Candidates should have ability to work independently, ability to work with others, oral communication skills, personal interest in the field, writing skills. Duration is 12 weeks in summer. Open to college sophomores, college juniors. ▶ *100 editing interns:* responsibilities include attending a 1- to 2-week training program and working as a copy editor at daily newspapers, on-line newspapers, and real-time financial news services. Candidates should have ability to work with others, computer skills, editing skills, personal interest in the field, writing skills. Duration is 10 weeks. Open to college juniors, college seniors, graduate students. All positions paid at $275 per week minimum.

Benefits Formal training, $1000 scholarship for those returning to college following the internship, some travel reimbursement.

Contact Write, call, fax, or e-mail Editing Intern Program. Phone: 609-452-2820. Fax: 609-520-5804. E-mail: newsfund@wsj.dowjones.com. Telephone interview required. Applicants must submit a formal organization application, resume, academic transcripts, two personal references, essay. Application deadline: November 15. World Wide Web: http://www.dowjones.com/newsfund.

ELYRIA CHRONICLE–TELEGRAM
225 East Avenue, PO Box 4010
Elyria, Ohio 44035

General Information Daily and Sunday newspaper. Established in 1829. Number of employees: 50. Number of internship applications received each year: 50.

Internships Available ▶ *2 newsroom interns:* responsibilities include reporting and writing. Candidates should have ability to work independently, ability to work with others, plan to pursue career in field, research skills, self-motivation, writing skills. $300 per week. Open to college freshmen, college sophomores, college juniors, college seniors. ▶ *1 photo department intern:* responsibilities include taking photos for paper. Candidates should have ability to work independently, ability to work with others, college courses in field, knowledge of field, plan to pursue career in field, self-motivation. Position available as unpaid or paid. Open to college freshmen, college sophomores, college juniors,

Elyria Chronicle–Telegram (continued)
college seniors, recent college graduates. Duration for all positions is 3 months. International applications accepted.
Benefits Job counseling, names of contacts, possible full-time employment, travel reimbursement, willing to act as a professional reference.
Contact Write, fax, or e-mail Mr. Rudy Dicks, Managing Editor. Fax: 440-329-7282. E-mail: ect@ohio.net. In-person interview required. Applicants must submit a cover letter, resume, three personal references, 5-10 writing samples. Application deadline: March 1 for summer. World Wide Web: http://www.chronicletelegram.com.

EMPIRE STATE WEEKLIES
2010 Empire Boulevard
Webster, New York 14580

General Information Group of weekly community newspapers serving eastern Monroe and western Wayne counties. Established in 1863. Number of employees: 25. Number of internship applications received each year: 8.
Internships Available ▶ *2 editorial interns:* responsibilities include assisting with general editorial duties. Candidates should have editing skills, oral communication skills, personal interest in the field, strong interpersonal skills, writing skills, written communication skills. Duration is 3–6 months. Unpaid. Open to high school seniors, college freshmen, college sophomores, college juniors, college seniors, recent college graduates. International applications accepted.
Benefits Job counseling, on-the-job training, possible full-time employment, willing to complete paperwork for educational credit, willing to provide letters of recommendation.
Contact Write or call Jenifer Calus, Managing Editor. Phone: 716-671-1533. In-person interview recommended. Applicants must submit a cover letter, resume, three writing samples, three personal references. Application deadline: February 15 for spring, April 15 for summer, July 15 for fall.

THE FREE LANCE-STAR
616 Amelia Street
Fredericksburg, Virginia 22401

General Information Local 7-day-per-week newspaper that focuses on local, state, national, and international news. Established in 1885. Number of employees: 385. Number of internship applications received each year: 70.
Internships Available ▶ *1 minority journalism intern:* responsibilities include working general assignment beat, writing, reporting, covering meetings and spot assignments, researching assignments, participating in department meetings, and possibly taking photos. Candidates should have ability to work independently, ability to work with others, editing skills, experience in the field, oral communication skills, writing skills. Duration is 10 weeks. $2,500 per duration of internship. Open to college juniors, college seniors, recent college graduates.
Benefits On-the-job training, possible full-time employment, willing to act as a professional reference, willing to complete paperwork for educational credit, willing to provide letters of recommendation.
Contact Write, call, fax, or e-mail Ms. Lee-Ann Williams, Human Resources Manager. Phone: 540-374-5453. Fax: 540-374-5449. E-mail: hr@flstarweb.com. In-person interview required. Applicants must submit a cover letter, resume, academic transcripts, six writing samples. Application deadline: February 26 for summer. World Wide Web: http://www.flstarweb.com.

THE GAZETTE
30 South Prospect Street
Colorado Springs, Colorado 80903

General Information Daily newspaper. Established in 1872. Number of employees: 500. Unit of Freedom Communications, Irvine, California. Number of internship applications received each year: 100.

Internships Available ▶ *Interns:* responsibilities include various duties from year to year; please refer to Web site for information on number of openings, pay, and types of internships available. Paid. International applications accepted.
Benefits On-the-job training, possible full-time employment.
Contact Write Connie Steele, Newsroom Administrator, PO Box 1779, Colorado Springs, Colorado 80901. In-person interview recommended. Applicants must submit a cover letter, resume, 6 writing samples. Application deadline: January 31 for summer; continuous for all others. World Wide Web: http://www.gazette.com/gaz/intern.html.

HERALD-PRESS
7 North Jefferson Street, PO Box 867
Huntington, Indiana 46750

General Information Community newspaper serving a rural county with a population of 36,000. Established in 1848. Number of employees: 30. Number of internship applications received each year: 10.
Internships Available ▶ *1 newsroom intern:* responsibilities include assisting with reporting, feature writing, and rewriting. Candidates should have college courses in field, plan to pursue career in field, strong interpersonal skills, writing skills. Duration is 3 months. $6 per hour. Open to recent high school graduates, college freshmen, college sophomores, college juniors, college seniors, recent college graduates, graduate students, individuals reentering the workforce, high school students with strong journalism skills.
Benefits Possible full-time employment, willing to complete paperwork for educational credit, willing to provide letters of recommendation, overtime pay and reimbursement for mileage.
Contact Write or e-mail Mr. Mike Perkins, Editor, PO Box 867, Huntington, Indiana 46750. E-mail: hpnews@h-ponline.com. No phone calls. Applicants must submit a cover letter, resume, 3-4 writing samples. Application deadline: March 15 for summer.

HIGH COUNTRY NEWS
Box 1090
Paonia, Colorado 81428

General Information covering the newspaper communities and environment of the Rocky Mountain West, the Great Basin, and the Pacific Northwest with a circulation of 19,000. Established in 1970. Number of employees: 25. Number of internship applications received each year: 50.
Internships Available ▶ *6 interns:* responsibilities include writing news briefs and stories for Western Roundup section, looking for story leads in news releases and newspapers, sorting mail, and answering telephone calls. Candidates should have research skills, self-motivation, strong interpersonal skills, writing skills, knowledge of High Country news and the West. Duration is 4 months. stipend of $100 per month. Open to recent high school graduates, college freshmen, college sophomores, college juniors, college seniors, recent college graduates, graduate students, law students, career changers, individuals reentering the workforce.
Benefits Free housing, on-the-job training, willing to complete paperwork for educational credit, willing to provide letters of recommendation.
Contact Write, call, or e-mail Greg Hanscom, Assistant Editor, PO Box 1090, Paonia, Colorado 81428. Phone: 970-527-4898. E-mail: editor@hcn.org. Telephone interview required. Applicants must submit a cover letter, resume, three writing samples. Application deadline: March 1 for summer (May 1-August 31), June 1 for fall (September 1-December 14), September 1 for spring (January 1-April 30). World Wide Web: http://www.hcn.org.

LAKE CHARLES AMERICAN PRESS
PO Box 2893
Lake Charles, Louisiana 70602

General Information Daily independent and family-owned newspaper. Established in 1895. Number of employees: 200. Number of internship applications received each year: 50.

Internships Available ▶ *1 editorial intern:* responsibilities include newswriting, reporting, feature writing, and working with top editors. Candidates should have declared college major in field, plan to pursue career in field, self-motivation, written communication skills. Duration is 2-3 months in summer. $8 per hour. Open to college freshmen, college sophomores, college juniors, college seniors. International applications accepted.
Benefits Formal training, possible full-time employment, willing to complete paperwork for educational credit, opportunity to work with top editors.
Contact Write, fax, or e-mail Mr. Brett Downer, Editor. Fax: 318-494-4070. E-mail: bdowner@americanpress.com. No phone calls. Applicants must submit a cover letter, resume, 5 writing samples. Application deadline: March 30. World Wide Web: http://www.americanpress.com.

LAS VEGAS REVIEW-JOURNAL
PO Box 70
Las Vegas, Nevada 89125

General Information Daily newspaper with circulation of 180,000. Established in 1905. Number of employees: 730. Unit of Donrey Media Group, Fort Smith, Arkansas. Number of internship applications received each year: 50.
Internships Available ▶ *1-3 reporters:* responsibilities include general assignment reporting. Candidates should have college courses in field, editing skills, research skills, strong interpersonal skills, writing skills. Duration is 3 months in summer. $10 per hour. Open to college juniors, college seniors, recent college graduates, graduate students, journalism majors.
Benefits Names of contacts, possible full-time employment, willing to complete paperwork for educational credit, willing to provide letters of recommendation.
Contact Write, fax, or e-mail Charles Zobell, Managing Editor, PO Box 70, Las Vegas, Nevada 89125-0070. Fax: 702-383-4676. E-mail: charles_zobell@lvrj.com. No phone calls. In-person interview recommended. Applicants must submit a cover letter, resume, writing sample. Application deadline: March 15 for summer. World Wide Web: http://ww.lvrj.com.

LEXINGTON HERALD-LEADER
100 Midland Avenue
Lexington, Kentucky 40508

General Information Pulitzer prize winning newspaper covering central and eastern Kentucky with daily circulation of about 125,000 and Sunday circulation of about 165,000. Number of employees: 550. Unit of Knight Ridder, San Jose, California. Number of internship applications received each year: 200.
Internships Available ▶ *1 copy editing intern:* responsibilities include editing copy and writing headlines. Candidates should have college courses in field, computer skills, editing skills, knowledge of field, writing skills. Duration is 11 weeks (40 hours per week). Open to college freshmen, college sophomores, college juniors, college seniors. ▶ *1 design desk intern:* responsibilities include layout and design. Candidates should have ability to work independently, college courses in field, computer skills, knowledge of field, personal interest in the field. Duration is 11 weeks (40 hours per week). Open to college freshmen, college sophomores, college juniors, college seniors, recent college graduates. ▶ *1 photo intern:* responsibilities include taking photos. Candidates should have ability to work independently, ability to work with others, knowledge of field, personal interest in the field, self-motivation. Duration is 11 weeks in summer (40 hours per week). Open to college freshmen, college sophomores, college juniors, college seniors, recent college graduates, graduate students. ▶ *4 reporting interns:* responsibilities include reporting and writing stories. Candidates should have college courses in field, experience in the field, oral communication skills, personal interest in the field, writing skills. Duration is 11 weeks. Open to college freshmen, college sophomores, college juniors, college seniors, recent college graduates. All positions paid at $370 per week. International applications accepted.
Benefits On-the-job training, opportunity to attend seminars/workshops, possible full-time employment, willing to act as a

professional reference, willing to complete paperwork for educational credit, willing to provide letters of recommendation, reimbursement for mileage and other job-related expenses while on assignment.
Contact Write or e-mail Ms. Liz Caras Petros, Regional Editor. E-mail: lpetros@herald-leader.com. Applicants must submit a cover letter, resume, 5-10 writing samples, telephone interview (for finalists). Application deadline: November 15 for summer. World Wide Web: http://www.kentuckyconnect.com.

LIMA NEWS
3515 Elida Road, PO Box 690
Lima, Ohio 45802-0690

General Information Newspaper. Number of employees: 36. Unit of Freedom Communications, Irvine, California. Number of internship applications received each year: 50.
Internships Available ▶ *2 photographers.* Candidates should have ability to work independently, knowledge of field, plan to pursue career in field, self-motivation, strong interpersonal skills. Duration is 3 months (winter, spring, summer, and fall). Open to college freshmen, college sophomores, college juniors. ▶ *1 reporter.* Duration is 1 summer. Open to college freshmen, college sophomores, college juniors, college seniors, graduate students. All positions paid at $280 per week.
Benefits On-the-job training, possible full-time employment, willing to act as a professional reference, willing to complete paperwork for educational credit.
Contact Write Mr. Jim Krumel, Managing Editor. No phone calls. In-person interview required. Applicants must submit a cover letter, resume, three personal references, three letters of recommendation, 6-10 writing clips. Applications are accepted continuously. World Wide Web: http://www.limanews.com.

LOS ANGELES TIMES
Times Mirror Square
Los Angeles, California 90053

General Information Metropolitan newspaper providing extensive coverage of local, state, national, and foreign news. Established in 1881. Number of employees: 6,500. Unit of Times Mirror, Los Angeles, California. Number of internship applications received each year: 700.
Internships Available ▶ *1-2 business news interns:* responsibilities include working as staff writer. Candidates should have ability to work independently, ability to work with others, computer skills, oral communication skills, research skills, writing skills. Duration is 12-17 weeks. Open to college juniors, college seniors, recent college graduates, graduate students. ▶ *1 copy editing intern:* responsibilities include working as staff copy editor. Candidates should have ability to work independently, ability to work with others, computer skills, editing skills, oral communication skills, research skills. Duration is flexible. Open to college juniors, college seniors, recent college graduates, graduate students. ▶ *1-2 informational graphics interns:* responsibilities include working as staff artist. Candidates should have ability to work independently, ability to work with others, computer skills, editing skills, oral communication skills. Duration is 12-17 weeks. Open to college juniors, college seniors, recent college graduates, graduate students. ▶ *6-8 news interns:* responsibilities include working as staff writer. Candidates should have ability to work independently, ability to work with others, computer skills, editing skills, oral communication skills, research skills, writing skills. Duration is 12-17 weeks. Open to college juniors, college seniors, recent college graduates, graduate students. ▶ *1-3 photo interns:* responsibilities include working as staff photographer. Candidates should have ability to work independently, ability to work with others, computer skills, experience in the field, oral communication skills, self-motivation. Duration is 12-17 weeks. Open to college juniors, college seniors, recent college graduates, graduate students. ▶ *1-3 sports interns:* responsibilities include working as staff writer. Candidates should have ability to work independently, ability to work with others, computer skills, experience in the field, oral communication skills, research skills,

Los Angeles Times (continued)
writing skills. Duration is 12–17 weeks. Open to college juniors, college seniors, graduate students. All positions are unpaid.
Benefits Job counseling, names of contacts, on-the-job training, opportunity to attend seminars/workshops, willing to complete paperwork for educational credit, willing to provide letters of recommendation.
Contact Write or call Stan Allison, Director, Editorial Internships. Phone: 800-283-NEWS Ext. 77123. Applicants must submit a cover letter, resume, samples of previous work. Application deadline: June 1 for fall, October 1 for spring, December 1 for summer. World Wide Web: http://www.latimes.com.

MIDWEST SUBURBAN PUBLISHING
6901 West 159th Street
Tenley Park, Illinois 60477

General Information Publisher of 20 twice-weekly suburban newspapers and a 7-day regional daily, emphasizing local news. Established in 1901. Number of employees: 800. Unit of Hollinger International, Toronto, Canada. Number of internship applications received each year: 75.
Internships Available ▶ *1 Web site intern:* responsibilities include maintaining directories and daily logs; maintaining Web site with daily breaking stories; and light programming. Candidates should have computer skills, HTML experience desirable. ▶ *1 news photographer:* responsibilities include photo assignments, film processing, and printing. Candidates should have background/experience in photography. ▶ *6 news reporters:* responsibilities include writing news and feature stories, possibly including sports writing, depending on intern's interest. Candidates should have major in journalism. Duration for all positions is 10 weeks. All positions paid at $300–$375 per week. Open to college freshmen, college sophomores, college juniors, college seniors. International applications accepted.
Benefits Possible full-time employment, travel reimbursement, willing to complete paperwork for educational credit, willing to provide letters of recommendation.
Contact Write, fax, or e-mail Peter Neill, Editor-in-Chief. Fax: 708-633-5999. E-mail: pneill@interaccess. com. No phone calls. In-person interview recommended. Applicants must submit a cover letter, resume. Applications are accepted continuously. World Wide Web: http://www.dailysouthtown.com.

MILWAUKEE JOURNAL SENTINEL
333 West State Street
Milwaukee, Wisconsin 53203

General Information Publisher of largest newspaper in Wisconsin with daily circulation of 285,000 and Sunday circulation of 490,000. Established in 1837. Number of employees: 1,500. Subsidiary of Journal Communications, Milwaukee, Wisconsin. Number of internship applications received each year: 500.
Internships Available ▶ *2–3 copy editing interns:* responsibilities include copy editing and writing news and feature stories. Candidates should have ability to work independently, ability to work with others, college courses in field, computer skills, editing skills, experience in the field, plan to pursue career in field, research skills, written communication skills. ▶ *1 graphics intern:* responsibilities include completing infographics and illustrations. Candidates should have ability to work independently, ability to work with others, college courses in field, computer skills, editing skills, knowledge of field, plan to pursue career in field, research skills, self-motivation. ▶ *1 photography intern:* responsibilities include taking news and feature photos. Candidates should have ability to work independently, ability to work with others, college courses in field, knowledge of field, plan to pursue career in field, self-motivation. ▶ *6–7 reporting interns:* responsibilities include writing news and feature stories. Candidates should have ability to work independently, ability to work with others, analytical skills, college courses in field, computer skills, editing skills, experience in the field, knowledge of field, plan to pursue career in field, research skills, self-motivation, written communication skills. Duration for all positions is 12 weeks. All positions paid

at $450 per week. Open to college juniors, college seniors, recent college graduates, graduate students. International applications accepted.
Benefits Job counseling, on-the-job training, opportunity to attend seminars/workshops, possible full-time employment, willing to act as a professional reference, willing to complete paperwork for educational credit, willing to provide letters of recommendation, reimbursement for mileage and other job-related expenses while on assignment.
Contact Write Heidi Reuter Lloyd, Senior Editor/Administration. Fax: 414-224-2772. E-mail: hlloyd@onwis.com. No phone calls. Applicants must submit a cover letter, resume, portfolio, three personal references, 5-6 writing samples, in-person or telephone interview. Application deadline: December 1 for summer. World Wide Web: http://www.jsonline.com.

NATIONAL JOURNALISM CENTER
800 Maryland Avenue, NE
Washington, District of Columbia 20002

General Information Organization that provides training to reporters in order to improve the field of investigative reporting. Established in 1977. Number of employees: 9. Unit of Education and Research Institute. Number of internship applications received each year: 300.
Internships Available ▶ *75–80 journalism interns:* responsibilities include researching, reporting, writing, and a few administrative tasks. Candidates should have ability to work independently, analytical skills, editing skills, organizational skills, plan to pursue career in field, research skills, self-motivation, strong interpersonal skills, writing skills. Duration is 12 weeks. $100 per week. Open to college juniors, college seniors, recent college graduates, career changers.
Benefits Housing at a cost, job counseling, names of contacts, opportunity to attend seminars/workshops, willing to act as a professional reference, willing to complete paperwork for educational credit, willing to provide letters of recommendation, access to in-house job bank, resume referral provided.
Contact Write, call, fax, or e-mail Mr. Malcolm Kline, Editor. Phone: 202-544-1333. Fax: 202-546-3489. E-mail: mal@eri-njc. org. In-person interview recommended. Applicants must submit a formal organization application, cover letter, resume, 2-3 writing samples. Application deadline: February 1 for spring, May 1 for summer, September 1 for fall. World Wide Web: http://eri-njc.org.

NEW HAVEN ADVOCATE
One Long Wharf Drive
New Haven, Connecticut 06511-5991

General Information Alternative weekly newspaper. Established in 1975. Number of employees: 26. Unit of New Mass Media, Hatfield, Massachusetts. Number of internship applications received each year: 35.
Internships Available ▶ *2–5 editorial interns:* responsibilities include writing, reporting, and data entry. Candidates should have oral communication skills, research skills, self-motivation, written communication skills. Duration is 3–4 months. Unpaid. Open to high school students, high school seniors, recent high school graduates, college freshmen, college sophomores, college juniors, college seniors, recent college graduates, graduate students, law students, career changers, individuals reentering the workforce.
Benefits Formal training, names of contacts, on-the-job training, travel reimbursement, willing to act as a professional reference, willing to complete paperwork for educational credit, willing to provide letters of recommendation, published writing/clips.
Contact Write or e-mail Carole Bass, Managing Editor. E-mail: cbass@newhavenadvocate.com. No phone calls. In-person interview required. Applicants must submit a cover letter, resume, three writing samples. Applications are accepted continuously. World Wide Web: http://www.newhavenadvocate.com.

THE NEWS-COURIER
PO Box 670
Athens, Alabama 35612

General Information Newspaper. Number of employees: 25. Unit of Community Newspaper Holdings, Inc., Birmingham, Alabama. Number of internship applications received each year: 8.

Internships Available ▶ *1 reporter:* responsibilities include interviews, meeting coverage, writing stories, and some photography. Candidates should have editing skills, organizational skills, plan to pursue career in field, self-motivation, written communication skills. $5–$6 per hour. International applications accepted.

Benefits On-the-job training, possible full-time employment.

Contact Write or fax Ben Sheroan, Publisher, PO Box 670, Athens, Alabama 35612. Fax: 256-233-7753. No phone calls. In-person interview recommended. Applicants must submit a cover letter, resume, three personal references, 5 writing samples. Applications are accepted continuously.

NEWSDAY
235 Pinelawn Road
Melville, New York 11747-4250

General Information Nation's fifth-largest daily newspaper with a circulation of over 760,000. Established in 1945.

Internships Available ▶ *40 reporters, librarians, photographers, graphic interns, and copy editors:* responsibilities include covering spot news, writing features, reporting, taking photographs, library work, on-line Internet research and artwork. Duration is 10 weeks. $530 per week. Open to college juniors, college seniors, graduate students.

Benefits Opportunity to attend seminars/workshops, willing to complete paperwork for educational credit, willing to provide letters of recommendation, travel reimbursement while on assignment.

Contact Write, call, or e-mail Walter Middlebrook, Associate Editor for Recruitment. Phone: 516-843-2637. E-mail: walter.middlebrook@newsday.com. Applicants must submit a formal organization application, cover letter, resume, academic transcripts, three personal references, three letters of recommendation, portfolio (graphics and photography interns), writing samples (reporters, librarians, or editors). Application deadline: May 31 for fall, November 15 for summer, November 8 for spring.

OMAHA WORLD-HERALD COMPANY
1334 Dodge Street
Omaha, Nebraska 68102

General Information Mass circulation newspaper. Established in 1865. Number of employees: 900. Number of internship applications received each year: 50.

Internships Available ▶ *4 advertising interns:* responsibilities include sales, production, and special projects. Candidates should have computer skills, declared college major in field, knowledge of field, personal interest in the field, self-motivation, writing skills. $350 per week. ▶ *4–6 news interns:* responsibilities include writing news and feature stories and editing copy. Candidates should have analytical skills, editing skills, personal interest in the field, self-motivation, writing skills. $350 per week; $1000 scholarship. Duration for all positions is 12 weeks. Open to college juniors, college seniors.

Benefits Formal training, job counseling, on-the-job training, opportunity to attend seminars/workshops, possible full-time employment, willing to act as a professional reference, willing to complete paperwork for educational credit, willing to provide letters of recommendation, some mentoring.

Contact Write, call, or fax Jeff Gauger or Joanne Stewart, news interns. Phone: 402-444-1000. Fax: 402-345-0183. In-person interview recommended. Applicants must submit a cover letter, resume, 4-6 examples of works. Application deadline: November 1 for summer.

THE ORLANDO SENTINEL
633 North Orange Avenue
Orlando, Florida 32801

General Information Newspaper. Established in 1876. Number of employees: 1,300. Unit of Tribune Company, Chicago, Illinois. Number of internship applications received each year: 250.

Internships Available ▶ *4 interns:* responsibilities include working in various areas including reporting, editing, business, photography, features, or graphic arts. Duration is 11 weeks. $500 per week. Open to college seniors, recent college graduates, graduate students, individuals with previous internships in journalism.

Benefits Possible full-time employment, willing to act as a professional reference, willing to complete paperwork for educational credit.

Contact Write Donna Eyring, Deputy Managing Editor. Applicants must submit a cover letter, resume, two personal references, six writing samples. Application deadline: December 15 for summer. World Wide Web: http://www.orlandosentinel.com.

THE PALM BEACH POST
2751 South Dixie Highway
West Palm Beach, Florida 33405

General Information Daily newspaper. Number of employees: 1,200. Unit of Cox Newspapers, Inc., Atlanta, Georgia. Number of internship applications received each year: 400.

Internships Available ▶ *2 photography interns:* responsibilities include working as full-time photographer. Candidates should have ability to work independently, ability to work with others, oral communication skills, self-motivation, former photo internship. Duration is 12–16 weeks. ▶ *3 summer reporting interns-metro or sports:* responsibilities include working in the same capacity as a full-time reporter. Candidates should have ability to work independently, ability to work with others, experience in the field, oral communication skills, plan to pursue career in field, written communication skills. Duration is 10–12 weeks. All positions paid. Open to college freshmen, college sophomores, college juniors, college seniors, graduate students.

Benefits Job counseling, names of contacts, on-the-job training, opportunity to attend seminars/workshops, willing to act as a professional reference, willing to complete paperwork for educational credit, willing to provide letters of recommendation.

Contact Write or call Lynn Kalber, Director of Administration/Newsroom, 2751 South Dixie Highway, West Palm Beach, Florida 33405. Phone: 561-820-4439. Applicants must submit a cover letter, resume, portfolio, writing sample. Application deadline: April 1 for fall, December 1 for summer. World Wide Web: http://www.pbpost.com.

PENSACOLA NEWS JOURNAL
PO Box 12710
Pensacola, Florida 32574

General Information Newspaper on Florida's northwest Gulf Coast with circulation of 65,000 daily and 85,000 Sunday. Number of employees: 77. Number of internship applications received each year: 60.

Internships Available ▶ *Copy editors:* responsibilities include writing headlines, editing copy, and assembling pages for all sections of newspaper. Candidates should have ability to work with others, declared college major in field, editing skills, experience in the field, written communication skills. ▶ *Photographers:* responsibilities include shooting pictures, processing film, and using computer for film editing. Candidates should have ability to work with others, computer skills, declared college major in field, experience in the field, written communication skills, own transportation. ▶ *Reporters:* responsibilities include reporting and writing stories. Candidates should have ability to work independently, declared college major in field, experience in the field, research skills, written communication skills, own transportation. Duration for all positions is 10 weeks in summer. All positions paid. Open to college juniors, college seniors, recent college graduates, graduate students.

Pensacola News Journal (continued)

Benefits Formal training, job counseling, names of contacts, opportunity to attend seminars/workshops, possible full-time employment, willing to complete paperwork for educational credit, job lists provided when available, minority job fairs.
Contact Write or call Bob Bryan, Deputy Managing Editor. Phone: 850-435-8525. In-person interview recommended. Applicants must submit a resume. Application deadline: January 1 for summer.

PEORIA JOURNAL STAR
1 News Plaza
Peoria, Illinois 61643

General Information Newspaper with a circulation of 87,900 Monday–Friday, 106,000 Saturday, and 112,600 Sunday. Established in 1855. Number of employees: 400. Unit of Copley Newspapers, Inc., La Jolla, California. Number of internship applications received each year: 300.
Internships Available ▶ *2 news interns:* responsibilities include reporting assigned stories. Candidates should have ability to work with others, college courses in field, experience in the field, oral communication skills, self-motivation, written communication skills, reporting skills. Duration is 2–4 months. $275 per week. Open to college juniors, college seniors, recent college graduates, graduate students.
Benefits On-the-job training, possible full-time employment, willing to complete paperwork for educational credit, willing to provide letters of recommendation.
Contact Write, fax, or e-mail Jerry McDowell, City Editor. Fax: 309-686-3296. E-mail: jmcdowell@pjstar.com. In-person interview recommended. Applicants must submit a cover letter, resume, 5-10 writing samples, 3-5 personal references. Application deadline: February 15 for summer, July 30 for fall, November 30 for spring. World Wide Web: http://www.pjstar.com.

PHILADELPHIA INQUIRER
PO Box 8263
Philadelphia, Pennsylvania 19101

General Information Major metropolitan newspaper that offers a strong investigative approach to issues and a solid national and foreign report. Established in 1829. Number of employees: 480. Unit of Knight Ridder, San Jose, California. Number of internship applications received each year: 200.
Internships Available ▶ *7 Art Peters Programs interns:* responsibilities include training on copy desk, reporting. Candidates should have ability to work independently, editing skills, plan to pursue career in field, self-motivation, strong interpersonal skills, written communication skills. Duration is 1 summer. $633 per week. Open to college freshmen, college sophomores, college juniors, graduate students (between semesters). ▶ *2 Knight Ridder Minority Specialty Development Program interns:* responsibilities include working with editors and reporters. Candidates should have ability to work independently, computer skills, oral communication skills, research skills, self-motivation, strong interpersonal skills, strong leadership ability, written communication skills. Duration is 1 year. $765 per week. Open to recent college graduates, graduate students. ▶ *Suburban Reporting Program interns:* responsibilities include working in geographic beat areas, to provide stories of government, schools, police, courts, and features. Candidates should have oral communication skills, plan to pursue career in field, self-motivation, strong interpersonal skills, written communication skills. Duration is 2 years. $565 per week. Open to college seniors, recent college graduates, graduate students, working journalists with limited experience. ▶ *1 photojournalism intern:* responsibilities include shooting assignments in news, features, and sports. Candidates should have ability to work independently, analytical skills, experience in the field, oral communication skills, plan to pursue career in field, self-motivation, strong interpersonal skills, strong leadership ability, written communication skills. Duration is 1 summer. $633 per week. Open to college freshmen, college sophomores, college juniors, college seniors, graduate students. International applications accepted.

Benefits Formal training, health insurance, job counseling, names of contacts, opportunity to attend seminars/workshops, possible full-time employment, willing to act as a professional reference, willing to complete paperwork for educational credit, willing to provide letters of recommendation, ongoing evaluations.
Contact Write, call, or e-mail Paul Jablow, Director of Internships, Inquirer Suburban Newsroom, 800 River Road, Conshohocken, Pennsylvania 19428. Phone: 610-313-8104. E-mail: jablowp@phillynews.com. In-person interview recommended. Applicants must submit a resume, portfolio, writing sample, personal reference. Application deadline: January 15 for photojournalism interns, November 15 for Art Peters Program; continuous for suburban reporting program, December 1 for Knight Ridder Minority Specialty Development Program. World Wide Web: http://www.phillynews.com.

PITTSBURGH POST-GAZETTE
34 Boulevard of the Allies
Pittsburgh, Pennsylvania 15222

General Information Publisher of a daily morning newspaper. Established in 1786. Number of employees: 1,400. Unit of Blade Communications, Inc., Toledo, Ohio. Number of internship applications received each year: 300.
Internships Available ▶ *8 academic interns:* responsibilities include working in area of interest to intern. Candidates should have plan to pursue career in field, writing skills. Duration is flexible. Unpaid. Open to high school seniors, recent high school graduates, college freshmen, college sophomores, college juniors, college seniors. ▶ *8 interns:* responsibilities include working in 4 departments: copy editing, news, editorial, and one specialty department such as business, features, or sports. Candidates should have college courses in field, plan to pursue career in field, writing skills. Duration is 13 weeks. $480–$510 per week. Open to college juniors, college seniors, recent college graduates, graduate students. ▶ *Two-year associates:* responsibilities include performing tasks of a full-time employee. Candidates should have college courses in field, editing skills, experience in the field, writing skills. Duration is 2 years. $510 per week. Open to recent college graduates, graduate students, career changers. International applications accepted.
Benefits Formal training, on-the-job training, possible full-time employment, willing to act as a professional reference, willing to complete paperwork for educational credit, willing to provide letters of recommendation, reimbursement of travel expenses on work assignments, full benefit package for 2-year interns only.
Contact Write, fax, or e-mail John Craig, Editor. Fax: 412-263-2014. E-mail: jcraig@post-gazette.com. No phone calls. Applicants must submit a cover letter, resume, three personal references, 5-8 writing samples. Application deadline: December 1 for summer. World Wide Web: http://www.post-gazette.com.

THE PULLIAM FELLOWSHIPS
307 North Pennsylvania
Indianapolis, Indiana 46204

General Information Journalism work-study program for graduating college seniors. Established in 1974. Number of employees: 4. Unit of Central Newspapers, Inc., Phoenix, Arizona. Number of internship applications received each year: 100.
Internships Available ▶ *20 Pulliam fellowships:* responsibilities include reporting and copy editing. Candidates should have ability to work independently, ability to work with others, editing skills, plan to pursue career in field, self-motivation, writing skills. Duration is 10 weeks. $5,500 stipend. Open to college seniors. International applications accepted.
Benefits Job counseling, names of contacts, on-the-job training, opportunity to attend seminars/workshops, possible full-time employment, travel reimbursement, willing to act as a professional reference, willing to provide letters of recommendation, 2 lunches and 1 dinner provided weekly.
Contact Write, call, fax, or e-mail Russell B. Pulliam, Fellowship Director. Phone: 317-633-9121. Fax: 317-630-9549. E-mail: pulliam@starnews.com. Applicants must submit a formal organization application, academic transcripts, three writing samples, three

letters of recommendation, editorial (400-600 words) on any topic, photo of self suitable for reproduction. Application deadline: March 1 for final entries; other early admissions applicants will be considered with later entries, November 15 for early admissions applicants; up to five winners will be notified by December 15. World Wide Web: http://www.starnews.com/pjf.

REGIONAL NEWS
12243 South Harlem Avenue
Palos Heights, Illinois 60463

General Information   Weekly suburban newspaper. Established in 1941. Number of employees: 30. Number of internship applications received each year: 20.
Internships Available ▶ *1 advertising/sales intern:* responsibilities include performing outside and some telephone sales. Candidates should have ability to work independently, ability to work with others, college courses in field, experience in the field, oral communication skills, personal interest in the field, self-motivation. Duration is 13 weeks. $8 per hour plus commission. Open to college juniors, college seniors, recent college graduates, graduate students, career changers with sales experience.
Benefits Job counseling, names of contacts, on-the-job training, possible full-time employment, willing to act as a professional reference, willing to complete paperwork for educational credit, willing to provide letters of recommendation, car allowance.
Contact Write Mr. Charles Richards, Publisher. No phone calls. In-person interview recommended. Applicants must submit a formal organization application, cover letter, resume. Application deadline: April 1 for summer.

THE REPORTER
PO Box 630
Fond du Lac, Wisconsin 54936-0630

General Information   Daily newspaper. Established in 1870. Number of employees: 110. Unit of Thomson Newspapers, Toronto, Ontario, Canada. Number of internship applications received each year: 25.
Internships Available ▶ *2 news interns:* responsibilities include newswriting duties. Candidates should have ability to work independently, ability to work with others, analytical skills, computer skills, self-motivation, writing skills. Duration is 12 weeks. $7 per hour. Open to college sophomores, college juniors, college seniors, recent college graduates, graduate students.
Benefits On-the-job training, possible full-time employment, willing to act as a professional reference, willing to complete paperwork for educational credit, willing to provide letters of recommendation.
Contact Write, call, fax, or e-mail Mr. Harley Buchholz, Associate Editor. Phone: 920-922-4600. Fax: 920-922-5388. E-mail: mail@thereporter.net. In-person interview recommended. Applicants must submit a cover letter, resume, 4-5 writing samples, 2-3 personal references. Application deadline: March 1 for summer.

RICHMOND TIMES-DISPATCH
333 East Grace Street
Richmond, Virginia 23219

General Information   Newspaper with daily circulation of approximately 215,000 and Sunday circulation of 250,000. Established in 1850. Number of employees: 230. Unit of Media General, Richmond, Virginia. Number of internship applications received each year: 180.
Internships Available ▶ *1 graphics intern:* responsibilities include using Macintosh graphics illustration and free-hand illustration in news department. Candidates should have ability to work independently, computer skills, personal interest in the field, self-motivation, strong interpersonal skills, writing skills. Duration is 10 weeks (May to August). ▶ *7 news department editorial interns:* responsibilities include writing, reporting, editing, and processing information. Candidates should have analytical skills, editing skills, plan to pursue career in field, self-motivation, strong interpersonal skills, writing skills. Duration is 10 weeks (May to August). ▶ *1 photo intern:* responsibilities include taking news and feature photographs and conducting photo lab work. Candidates should have ability to work independently, computer skills, knowledge of field, plan to pursue career in field, strong interpersonal skills, writing skills. Duration is 10 weeks (September to November). All positions paid at $400 per week. Open to college juniors, college seniors, recent college graduates, graduate students.
Benefits Job counseling, names of contacts, on-the-job training, possible full-time employment, willing to provide letters of recommendation, opportunity to attend periodic intern meetings that include speakers from the newsroom and other departments.
Contact Write Mr. John Dillon, Deputy Managing Editor, PO Box 85333, Richmond, Virginia 23293. In-person interview recommended. Applicants must submit a cover letter, resume, 5-8 writing samples, 2-3 personal references. Application deadline: January 10 for reporting and graphics positions, June 12 for photo position (fall only). World Wide Web: http://www.gatewayva.com.

ST. PETERSBURG TIMES
490 First Avenue South
St. Petersburg, Florida 33701-4204

General Information   Independent metropolitan daily newspaper covering west-central Florida. Established in 1884.
Internships Available ▶ *Summer interns:* responsibilities include working either in the newsroom, design and graphics, or business departments performing hands-on newspaper tasks. Duration is 10 weeks. Paid. Open to college sophomores, college juniors, college seniors.
Benefits Some scholarships possible.
Contact Write, call, or e-mail Nancy Waclawek (newsroom interns), or Bill Shelton (Human Resources), PO Box 1121, St. Petersburg, Florida 33731. Phone: 727-893-8780. E-mail: shelton@sptimes.com. Applicants must submit a cover letter, resume, 5-6 clips (reporting interns), portfolio samples (art/design/photography interns). Application deadline: December 1. World Wide Web: http://www.sptimes.com.

SAN FRANCISCO BAY GUARDIAN
520 Hampshire Street
San Francisco, California 94110

General Information   San Francisco–based liberal alternative news and arts/entertainment weekly paper. Established in 1966. Number of employees: 125. Number of internship applications received each year: 175.
Internships Available ▶ *3 arts and entertainment journalism interns:* responsibilities include sorting mail and faxes, compiling and writing "superlists," becoming a staff writer for the calendar section, writing preview blurbs and short reviews by pitch or on assignment. Candidates should have ability to work independently, computer skills, oral communication skills, personal interest in the field, plan to pursue career in field, research skills, self-motivation, strong interpersonal skills, writing skills, demonstrable background/interest in either music, theater, or film, knowledge of San Francisco area helpful. Open to college sophomores, college juniors, college seniors, recent college graduates, graduate students. ▶ *8–10 editorial interns:* responsibilities include writing, researching, checking facts, and assisting in the newsroom. Candidates should have ability to work independently, oral communication skills, personal interest in the field, research skills, writing skills. Open to college freshmen, college sophomores, college juniors, college seniors, recent college graduates, graduate students, career changers, individuals reentering the workforce. Duration for all positions is 4 months, 2 days per week. All positions are unpaid. International applications accepted.
Benefits Formal training, job counseling, names of contacts, on-the-job training, opportunity to attend seminars/workshops, willing to act as a professional reference, willing to complete paperwork for educational credit, willing to provide letters of recommendation.

San Francisco Bay Guardian (continued)

Contact Write, call, fax, or e-mail Cassi Feldman, Editorial Coordinator. Phone: 415-255-3100. Fax: 415-255-8762. E-mail: cassi@sfbg.com. In-person interview recommended. Applicants must submit a cover letter, resume, three writing samples. Application deadline: April 15 for summer, August 15 for fall, December 15 for spring. World Wide Web: http://www.sfbg.com.

SAN FRANCISCO CHRONICLE
901 Mission Street
San Francisco, California 94103-2988

General Information Nationally prominent newspaper with daily circulation of 475,000 and Sunday circulation of 592,000.
Internships Available ▶ *2-year interns:* responsibilities include reporting, copy editing, photography, graphics and design or library assignments depending on skills and experience; working as part of regular staff following a brief orientation. Duration is 2 years. $33,000 the first year; $38,000 the second year. Open to college graduates who have been out of school no longer than 1 year prior to start of internship. ▶ *Summer interns:* responsibilities include reporting, copy editing, photography, graphics and design, library assignments depending on the applicant's skills and experience; working as part of regular staff following a brief orientation. Duration is 12 weeks beginning in mid-June. $510 per week. Open to college students or college graduates who have been out of school no longer than 1 year prior to start of internship.
Benefits Hands-on experience system of mentors, comprehensive health benefits after 3 months (2-year interns).
Contact Write Leslie Guevarra, Editorial Hiring and Development, 901 Mission Street, San Francisco, California 94103-2988. Applicants must submit a cover letter, resume, personal reference, clippings, portfolio, or examples of work (dependent upon position). Application deadline: November 15. World Wide Web: http://www.sfgate.com/chronicle/internship/.

SOCIETY OF PROFESSIONAL JOURNALISTS
PO Box 77
Greencastle, Indiana 46135

General Information Organization that serves the professional needs of journalists and students pursuing careers in journalism. Established in 1909. Number of employees: 12. Number of internship applications received each year: 25.
Internships Available ▶ *2 interns:* responsibilities include researching and writing about freedom of information issues. Candidates should have ability to work independently, computer skills, editing skills, research skills, writing skills. Duration is 10 weeks in summer. $400 per week. Open to college juniors, college seniors, recent college graduates, graduate students, law students. International applications accepted.
Benefits Names of contacts, opportunity to attend seminars/workshops, possible full-time employment, willing to complete paperwork for educational credit.
Contact Write, call, fax, or e-mail Pulliam/Kilgore Internships. Phone: 765-653-3333. Fax: 765-653-4631. E-mail: spj@spjhq.org. Applicants must submit a formal organization application, cover letter, resume, 1-3 writing samples. Application deadline: March 3. World Wide Web: http://spj.org.

THE STATE NEWSPAPER
PO Box 1333
Columbia, South Carolina 29202

General Information Newspaper that serves South Carolina with a daily circulation of 140,000. Established in 1801. Number of employees: 600. Unit of Knight Ridder, San Jose, California. Number of internship applications received each year: 250.
Internships Available ▶ *1 copy editor:* responsibilities include editing copy and writing headlines. Candidates should have ability to work independently, college courses in field, editing skills, oral communication skills, plan to pursue career in field, written communication skills. Duration is 10–12 weeks. ▶ *1–2 report-*

ing interns: responsibilities include covering events and writing stories. Candidates should have ability to work independently, oral communication skills, organizational skills, plan to pursue career in field, writing skills. Duration is 8-10 weeks in summer. All positions paid at $325 per week. Open to college sophomores, college juniors.
Benefits Job counseling, names of contacts, possible full-time employment, willing to complete paperwork for educational credit, willing to provide letters of recommendation.
Contact Write Ms. Beverly Dominick, Newsroom Development Manager. No phone calls. Applicants must submit a cover letter, resume, three personal references, five writing samples. Application deadline: December 1 for summer. World Wide Web: http://www.state.com.

THE TAMPA TRIBUNE
202 South Parker Street
Tampa, Florida 33606

General Information Newspaper that publishes an AM edition, Monday to Sunday, with a circulation of about 265,000. Unit of Media General, Richmond, Virginia.
Internships Available ▶ *Interns:* responsibilities include reporting and handling all aspects of news gathering and writing. Duration is 12 weeks. $375 per week. Open to college freshmen, college sophomores, college juniors, college seniors, graduate students.
Benefits On-the-job training, willing to act as a professional reference, willing to provide letters of recommendation, professional experience.
Contact Write, call, or fax Carolyn Bower, Director, Staff Development, PO Box 191, Tampa, Florida 33601. Phone: 813-259-7763. Fax: 813-259-7676. Applicants must submit a formal organization application, cover letter, resume, three personal references, 6-10 writing samples, at least 1 letter of recommendation. Application deadline: November 26.

TOLEDO BLADE
541 North Superior Street
Toledo, Ohio 43660

General Information Publisher of a daily newspaper. Established in 1836. Number of employees: 600. Division of Blade Communications, Inc., Toledo, Ohio. Number of internship applications received each year: 300.
Internships Available ▶ *4 photographers:* responsibilities include taking, processing, and printing pictures. Candidates should have ability to work independently, ability to work with others, computer skills, oral communication skills, personal interest in the field, writing skills, advanced photography skills. ▶ *4–6 reporters:* responsibilities include general assignment reporting. Candidates should have ability to work independently, ability to work with others, computer skills, editing skills, oral communication skills, writing skills. Duration for all positions is 90–120 days. All positions paid at $460 per week. Open to college juniors, college seniors, recent college graduates, graduate students. International applications accepted.
Benefits On-the-job training, possible full-time employment, willing to complete paperwork for educational credit.
Contact Write Frank Craig, Assistant Managing Editor, Administration. No phone calls. In-person interview recommended. Applicants must submit a cover letter, resume, 3 to 6 writing samples. Application deadline: December 30 for summer; continuous for photo interns only. World Wide Web: http://www.toledoblade.com.

THE VILLAGE VOICE
36 Cooper Square
New York, New York 10003

General Information Weekly newspaper that covers the arts. Established in 1955. Number of employees: 250. Number of internship applications received each year: 200.
Internships Available ▶ *15–60 interns:* responsibilities include researching, editing, and answering telephones and the mail.

Candidates should have ability to work independently, computer skills, editing skills, knowledge of field, plan to pursue career in field, research skills, written communication skills. Duration is 3 months (year-round). Unpaid. Open to high school students, high school seniors, recent high school graduates, college freshmen, college sophomores, college juniors, college seniors, recent college graduates, graduate students, law students, career changers, individuals reentering the workforce. International applications accepted.

Benefits Formal training, on-the-job training, opportunity to attend seminars/workshops, possible full-time employment, willing to complete paperwork for educational credit, willing to provide letters of recommendation.

Contact Write, call, or e-mail Frank Ruscitti, Intern Coordinator. Phone: 212-475-3300 Ext. 2300. E-mail: editor@villagevoice.com. Applicants must submit a formal organization application, cover letter, resume, 2-3 writing samples (no poetry or fiction), 1-2 personal references or letters of recommendation. Application deadline: January 31 for spring, March 31 for summer, July 31 for fall, November 30 for winter. World Wide Web: http://www.villagevoice.com.

THE VINDICATOR
PO Box 780
Youngstown, Ohio 44501-0780

General Information Daily newspaper with circulation of about 100,000. Number of internship applications received each year: 40.

Internships Available ▶ *5 interns:* responsibilities include substantive contributions to the daily work of a newspaper in the following areas: reporting, copy desk, photography, and design/graphics. Candidates should have ability to work independently, ability to work with others, computer skills, editing skills, knowledge of field, writing skills. Duration is 12 weeks. $428 per week. Open to college sophomores, college juniors, college seniors.

Contact Write, call, or e-mail Ernest A. Brown, Jr., Intern Coordinator, PO Box 780, Youngstown, Ohio 44501-0780. Phone: 330-747-1471 Ext. 304. E-mail: vindinews@cboss.com. In-person interview required. Applicants must submit a cover letter, resume, three writing samples, two personal references. Application deadline: March 1.

THE WALL STREET JOURNAL
200 Liberty Street
New York, New York 10281

General Information Global daily business paper with circulation of nearly 2 million and a news staff of 500. Established in 1889. Number of employees: 8,500. Unit of Dow Jones & Co., New York, New York. Number of internship applications received each year: 500.

Internships Available ▶ *15–18 summer news reporting interns:* responsibilities include reporting and writing on a daily basis; positions located at bureaus throughout the country. Duration is 10 weeks. $600 per week. Open to college freshmen, college sophomores, college juniors, college seniors, recent college graduates, graduate students.

Benefits Willing to provide letters of recommendation.

International Internships Available in Brussels, Belgium; Hong Kong, China; Tokyo, Japan; London, United Kingdom.

Contact Write Carolyn Phillips, Assistant Managing Editor. Applicants must submit a cover letter, resume, 12 by-line clips. Application deadline: November 24.

THE WASHINGTON POST
1150 15th Street, NW
Washington, District of Columbia 20071

General Information Newspaper publisher. Established in 1877. Number of employees: 3,500. Unit of The Washington Post Co., Washington, District of Columbia. Number of internship applications received each year: 600.

Internships Available ▶ *3–4 copy editors:* responsibilities include working on foreign, national, metro, sports, and business copy desks. Candidates should have ability to work with others, computer skills, editing skills, knowledge of field, personal interest in the field, writing skills. $873 per week. ▶ *1–2 news artists:* responsibilities include producing graphics and maps. Candidates should have ability to work with others, computer skills, editing skills, knowledge of field, research skills, writing skills. $794 per week. ▶ *1–2 page designers:* responsibilities include designing pages for news and features sections. Candidates should have computer skills, editing skills, knowledge of field, oral communication skills, writing skills. $794 per week. ▶ *1 photographer:* responsibilities include shooting photos and working inside the photo department. Candidates should have ability to work independently, ability to work with others, experience in the field, oral communication skills, personal interest in the field. $794 per week. ▶ *12–14 reporters:* responsibilities include reporting and writing stories for metro, business, sports, and style sections. Candidates should have ability to work independently, experience in the field, research skills, strong interpersonal skills, writing skills. $794 per week. Duration for all positions is 12 weeks (June to August). Open to college juniors, college seniors, graduate students. International applications accepted.

Benefits Formal training, job counseling, names of contacts, opportunity to attend seminars/workshops, possible full-time employment, willing to act as a professional reference, willing to provide letters of recommendation, reimbursement of work-related travel expenses.

Contact Write Summer News Program. No phone calls. In-person interview required. Applicants must submit a formal organization application, resume, academic transcripts, portfolio, two letters of recommendation, 6-8 writing samples for photographers' portfolios. Application deadline: November 1. World Wide Web: http://www.washingtonpost.com/intern.

THE WASHINGTON TIMES
3600 New York Avenue, NE
Washington, District of Columbia 20002

General Information Publisher of a daily newspaper. Established in 1982. Number of employees: 500. Number of internship applications received each year: 250.

Internships Available ▶ *1 graphic artist:* responsibilities include page design and production (Quark Xpress) of news and features, production of information graphics, and story illustration. Candidates should have ability to work independently, ability to work with others, college courses in field, computer skills, personal interest in the field, self-motivation. ▶ *1 photographer:* responsibilities include photographing daily news assignments according to newspaper deadlines. Candidates should have ability to work with others, computer skills, declared college major in field, experience in the field, plan to pursue career in field, self-motivation. ▶ *7 reporters:* responsibilities include reporting and writing news and feature stories. Candidates should have ability to work with others, knowledge of field, oral communication skills, plan to pursue career in field, self-motivation, writing skills. Duration for all positions is 8 weeks. All positions paid at $300 per week. Open to college sophomores, college juniors, college seniors. International applications accepted.

Benefits On-the-job training, possible full-time employment, willing to complete paperwork for educational credit.

Contact Write Barbara Taylor, Assistant Managing Editor. Applicants must submit a cover letter, resume, 5-10 writing samples. Application deadline: January 31 for summer.

WINSTON-SALEM JOURNAL
PO Box 3159
Winston-Salem, North Carolina 27102

General Information Daily newspaper emphasizing all-around excellence in form and content. Established in 1897. Number of employees: 484. Unit of Media General, Richmond, Virginia. Number of internship applications received each year: 100.

Internships Available ▶ *1 advertising sales representative:* responsibilities include selling ads. Candidates should have college courses

Winston-Salem Journal (continued)

in field, experience in the field, organizational skills, plan to pursue career in field, strong interpersonal skills. Duration is 8–10 weeks. $275 per week. ▶ *4 news reporter interns:* responsibilities include reporting. Candidates should have college courses in field, experience in the field, personal interest in the field, plan to pursue career in field, self-motivation, writing skills. Duration is 10–12 weeks. $375 per week. ▶ *1 photographer intern:* responsibilities include working in photojournalism department. Candidates should have ability to work independently, college courses in field, experience in the field, personal interest in the field, plan to pursue career in field. Duration is 8–10 weeks. $375 per week. Open to college juniors. International applications accepted.

Benefits On-the-job training, possible full-time employment.
Contact Write, call, fax, or e-mail Mr. Randy Noftle, Director of Human Resources. Phone: 336-727-7330. Fax: 336-727-4096. E-mail: rnoftle@w-s-journal.com. Applicants must submit a formal organization application, cover letter, resume, academic transcripts, three writing samples, two personal references. Application deadline: December 31 for summer.

NEWSPAPER, PERIODICAL, BOOK, AND DATABASE PUBLISHERS

ADAMS MEDIA CORPORATION
260 Center Street
Holbrook, Massachusetts 02343

General Information A diversified publisher of print and electronic products. Career titles include "Job Bank" books (more than one million copies sold) and the "Knock 'em Dead" series (more than two million copies sold). Established in 1981. Number of employees: 60. Number of internship applications received each year: 25.
Internships Available ▶ *1–5 editorial interns:* responsibilities include phone and Internet research, writing company profiles, copy editing, proofreading, database maintenance. Candidates should have ability to work with others, computer skills, editing skills, plan to pursue career in field, research skills, writing skills. Open to recent high school graduates, college freshmen, college sophomores, college juniors, college seniors, recent college graduates, graduate students, career changers, individuals reentering the workforce. ▶ *1–3 graphic design interns:* responsibilities include assisting Managing Editor in the creation of fliers to be used to market books. Candidates should have ability to work with others, computer skills, organizational skills, personal interest in the field, plan to pursue career in field, self-motivation, proficiency in Quark. Open to college freshmen, college sophomores, college juniors, college seniors, recent college graduates, graduate students, career changers, individuals reentering the workforce. Duration for all positions is 1 semester (8 hours per week or more). All positions are unpaid.
Benefits Willing to act as a professional reference, willing to complete paperwork for educational credit, willing to provide letters of recommendation.
Contact Write, call, fax, or e-mail Michelle Roy Kelly, Assistant Managing Editor, 260 Center Street, Holbrook, Massachusetts 02343. Phone: 781-607-5315. Fax: 781-767-2055. E-mail: mkelly@adamsmedia.com. In-person interview required. Applicants must submit a cover letter, resume, proofreading and writing tests for editorial position. Applications are accepted continuously. World Wide Web: http://www.adamsmedia.com.

AGORA, INC.
14 West Mt. Vernon Place
Baltimore, Maryland 21201

General Information International publisher of investment, travel, and health-related consumer publications with affiliated offices in Florida, New Mexico, London, and Paris. Established in 1979. Number of employees: 250. Number of internship applications received each year: 400.
Internships Available ▶ *Agora travel publishing editorial assistants (Ireland):* responsibilities include research, writing, editing, correspondence, and administrative duties. Candidates should have ability to work independently, ability to work with others, computer skills, editing skills, oral communication skills, research skills, written communication skills. $10—$15 per day, or $6 per hour. ▶ *Editorial associates:* responsibilities include research, fact checking, correcting copy, and administrative duties. Candidates should have ability to work independently, ability to work with others, computer skills, oral communication skills, written communication skills. $10—$15 per day, or $6 per hour. ▶ *Human resources interns:* responsibilities include assisting in recruitment, payroll, benefits administration, and administrative duties. Candidates should have ability to work independently, college courses in field, computer skills, knowledge of field, office skills, oral communication skills, personal interest in the field, self-motivation, written communication skills. $10-$15 per day, or $6 per hour. ▶ *Marketing interns:* responsibilities include print buying, customer correspondence, and general administrative duties. Candidates should have ability to work independently, ability to work with others, computer skills, oral communication skills, written communication skills. $10—$15 per day, or $6 per hour. Duration for all positions is 3–6 months. Open to college freshmen, college sophomores, college juniors, college seniors, graduate students. International applications accepted.
Benefits Opportunity to attend seminars/workshops, possible full-time employment, willing to complete paperwork for educational credit, willing to provide letters of recommendation, stipends of varying amounts available.
International Internships Available in Waterford, Ireland.
Contact Write, call, fax, or e-mail Jamie Dembeck, Intern Coordinator. Phone: 410-895-7981. Fax: 410-783-8455. E-mail: jdembeck@agora-inc.com. Applicants must submit a cover letter, resume. Applications are accepted continuously.

AMERICAN VISIONS MAGAZINE
1101 Pennsylvania Avenue, NW, Suite 820
Washington, District of Columbia 20004

General Information Magazine published to promote an understanding and appreciation of African-American history and culture. Established in 1986. Number of employees: 12. Number of internship applications received each year: 30.
Internships Available ▶ *Advertising interns:* responsibilities include typing, correspondence, light filing, tracking ads, data entry, assisting during production process, coordinating information for advertisers, and researching contacts for new advertising prospects. Open to college freshmen, college sophomores, college juniors, college seniors, recent college graduates, graduate students, law students, career changers, individuals reentering the workforce. ▶ *Editorial interns:* responsibilities include researching, corresponding with writers, light filing, proofreading, computer entry, writing press releases, and possibly writing for the magazine. Open to high school students, high school seniors, recent high school graduates, college freshmen, college sophomores, college juniors, college seniors, recent college graduates, graduate students, law students, career changers, individuals reentering the workforce. Duration for all positions is flexible. All positions are unpaid.
Benefits Willing to complete paperwork for educational credit, use of computer facilities.
Contact Write or fax Editorial Assistant. Fax: 202-347-4096. No phone calls. In-person interview recommended. Applicants must submit a cover letter, resume. Applications are accepted continuously. World Wide Web: http://www.americanvisions.com.

ART PAPERS MAGAZINE
PO Box 5748
Atlanta, Georgia 31107

General Information The voice of contemporary art and culture. It delivers provocative and artistic ideas and information to art creators, collectors, professionals, and enthusiasts. Established in 1977. Number of employees: 6. Number of internship applications received each year: 100.

Internships Available ▶ *1 advertising sales assistant:* responsibilities include classified advertising sales and layout, client management, and follow-up. Candidates should have computer skills, editing skills, office skills, research skills, writing skills. ▶ *1 assistant to director:* responsibilities include assisting executive director with facilitating communication between magazine and business community, board of directors relations, grant writing and follow-up, and administrative duties associated with all aspects of magazine production. Candidates should have computer skills, editing skills, office skills, research skills, writing skills. ▶ *1 circulation assistant:* responsibilities include assisting the circulation manager with daily contact with readers from all over the U.S., building relations with national network book stores and galleries; hands-on management of circulation development and direct mail campaigns. Candidates should have computer skills, editing skills, office skills, research skills, writing skills. ▶ *1 editorial assistant:* responsibilities include assisting the editor with copy editing, managing articles through production, and maintaining historical records and archives. Candidates should have computer skills, editing skills, office skills, research skills, writing skills. ▶ *1 finance assistant:* responsibilities include hands-on management of all day-to-day finance-related matters, data entry, and database management. Candidates should have computer skills, editing skills, office skills, research skills, writing skills, knowledge of Excel and Quick Books is a plus. ▶ *1 marketing assistant:* responsibilities include assisting market management with distribution of publicity/press releases to media contacts, organizing promotional events, and developing relationships with corporate sponsors. Candidates should have computer skills, editing skills, office skills, research skills, writing skills. Duration for all positions is 1 semester (minimum). All positions are unpaid. Open to college juniors, college seniors, recent college graduates, graduate students. International applications accepted.

Benefits Willing to act as a professional reference, willing to complete paperwork for educational credit, willing to provide letters of recommendation.

Contact Write, call, fax, or e-mail Ms. Larisa Gray, Executive Director. Phone: 404-588-1837. Fax: 404-588-1836. E-mail: lgray@artpapers.org. In-person interview recommended. Applicants must submit a cover letter, resume, three personal references, 1 writing sample for the editorial position. Applications are accepted continuously. World Wide Web: http://www.artpapers.org.

BARRICADE BOOKS
150 Fifth Avenue, Suite 700
New York, New York 10011

General Information Publishing company. Established in 1991. Number of employees: 5. Number of internship applications received each year: 100.

Internships Available ▶ *1–2 publisher's assistants:* responsibilities include general office support and entry-level editorial and publicity tasks. Candidates should have office skills, oral communication skills, personal interest in the field, self-motivation, writing skills. Duration is 3 months. $25 per day. Open to college sophomores, college juniors, college seniors, recent college graduates, graduate students.

Benefits On-the-job training, willing to act as a professional reference, willing to complete paperwork for educational credit, willing to provide letters of recommendation.

Contact Write, call, fax, or e-mail Jeff Nordstedt, Internship Coordinator. Phone: 212-627-7000. Fax: 212-627-7028. E-mail: barricade@earthlink.net. Applicants must submit a cover letter, resume. Application deadline: May 1 for summer, December 1 for spring. World Wide Web: http://www.barricadebooks.com.

BEACON PRESS
25 Beacon Street
Boston, Massachusetts 02108

General Information Publisher of trade and scholarly nonfiction. Established in 1854. Number of employees: 30. Unit of Unitarian Universalist Association, Boston, Massachusetts. Number of internship applications received each year: 300.

Internships Available ▶ *6–9 open enrollment internships:* responsibilities include working in two departments, completing two major projects, and performing clerical and other duties. Candidates should have ability to work independently, analytical skills, computer skills, office skills, oral communication skills, organizational skills, self-motivation, written communication skills, editing and research skills (helpful). Duration is 12 weeks during the summer or during the month of January. Unpaid. Open to college freshmen, college sophomores, college juniors, college seniors, recent college graduates, graduate students, career changers, individuals reentering the workforce, people of all races. ▶ *6–9 people of color interns.* Candidates should have ability to work independently, analytical skills, computer skills, office skills, oral communication skills, organizational skills, self-motivation, written communication skills. Duration is 3 months from February to May or from September to December. $350–$1,000 per duration of internship. Open to college freshmen, college sophomores, college juniors, college seniors, recent college graduates, graduate students, career changers, individuals reentering the workforce, open only to people of color. International applications accepted.

Benefits Job counseling, names of contacts, on-the-job training, possible full-time employment, willing to complete paperwork for educational credit, willing to provide letters of recommendation.

Contact Write, fax, or e-mail Pat Neblett, Internship Coordinator. Fax: 617-742-2290. E-mail: pneblett@beacon.org. No phone calls. Applicants must submit a cover letter, resume. Application deadline: March 1 for summer, June 1 for fall, October 1 for winter, December 1 for spring.

BIBLICAL ARCHAEOLOGY SOCIETY
4710 41st Street, NW
Washington, District of Columbia 20016

General Information Nonprofit nondenominational, educational organization publishing 3 magazines and producing other media and tours on archaeology and the Bible. Established in 1975. Number of employees: 30. Number of internship applications received each year: 50.

Internships Available ▶ *2 editorial assistants:* responsibilities include clerical duties, letter writing, photo searches, proofreading, corrections to publications, and correspondence. Candidates should have ability to work with others, computer skills, office skills, oral communication skills, research skills, written communication skills. Duration is minimum of one summer or one semester. Position available as unpaid or at $6–$8 per hour. Open to college freshmen, college sophomores, college juniors, college seniors, recent college graduates, graduate students, career changers, individuals reentering the workforce. International applications accepted.

Benefits Names of contacts, on-the-job training, possible full-time employment, travel reimbursement, willing to act as a professional reference, willing to complete paperwork for educational credit, willing to provide letters of recommendation.

Contact Write, fax, or e-mail Judith A. Horowitz, Personnel Manager, 4710 41st Street, NW, Washington, District of Columbia 20016. Fax: 202-364-2636. E-mail: operations@bib-arch.org. In-person interview recommended. Applicants must submit a cover letter, resume, writing sample. Applications are accepted continuously. World Wide Web: http://www.bib-arch.org.

BOSTON MAGAZINE
300 Massachusetts Avenue
Boston, Massachusetts 02115

General Information Publisher of city/regional magazine. Established in 1963. Number of employees: 50. Unit of Metro Corporation, New York, New York. Number of internship applications received each year: 300.
Internships Available ▶ *3 advertising sales interns:* responsibilities include assisting account executives and sales assistant with client contact and management of materials, including soliciting and preparing media packets. ▶ *1–2 art interns:* responsibilities include assisting art director and associate with monthly productions, extensive photo research, and trafficking artwork. ▶ *5–10 editorial interns:* responsibilities include working in direct positions with writers and editors, performing basic research, tracking and calling sources for information, and working on story development. ▶ *5 promotions/special projects interns:* responsibilities include helping in organizing functions sponsored by the magazine, working with the production manager, helping service the various advertising and promotion needs of the manager, and compiling and writing monthly press reports. Duration for all positions is 1 semester. All positions are unpaid. Open to college freshmen, college sophomores, college juniors, college seniors, recent college graduates, graduate students, career changers. International applications accepted.
Benefits Names of contacts, opportunity to attend seminars/workshops, possible full-time employment, willing to complete paperwork for educational credit, willing to provide letters of recommendation.
Contact Write, fax, or e-mail Amy Mazak, Business Coordinator. Fax: 617-262-4925. E-mail: amazak@bostonmagazine.com. No phone calls. In-person interview required. Applicants must submit a cover letter, resume, 1 writing sample for editorial positions. Application deadline: April 15 for summer, August 1 for fall, December 1 for spring. World Wide Web: http://www.bostonmagazine.com.

THE BUREAU OF NATIONAL AFFAIRS, INC.
1250 23rd Street, NW, 4th Floor
Washington, District of Columbia 20037-1164

General Information Private publisher of print and electronic news and specialized news and information services covering developments in business, economics, law, taxation, employee relations, environmental protection, and other public policy issues. Established in 1947. Number of employees: 1,600. Number of internship applications received each year: 100.
Internships Available ▶ *2–4 editorial interns:* responsibilities include clipping the wire service, copy editing, proofreading, and reporting. ▶ *1 legal editorial intern:* responsibilities include clipping the wire service, copyediting, proofreading, reporting, and writing cases. Duration for all positions is 12 weeks. All positions paid. Open to college juniors, college seniors. International applications accepted.
Benefits Formal training, possible full-time employment, willing to complete paperwork for educational credit.
Contact Write, call, or fax Monica Daley, Internship Coordinator. Phone: 202-261-1570. Fax: 202-261-1583. In-person interview recommended. Applicants must submit a cover letter, resume, three writing samples. Applications are accepted continuously. World Wide Web: http://www.bna.com.

CAHNERS BUSINESS INFORMATION
201 King of Prussia Road
Radnor, Pennsylvania 19089

General Information Publisher of business publications. Established in 1860. Number of employees: 700. Unit of Reed-Elsevier, Amsterdam, Netherlands. Number of internship applications received each year: 25.
Internships Available ▶ *1–3 MIS interns:* responsibilities include assisting in Internet projects and Web site development. Candidates should have ability to work independently, computer skills, organizational skills, written communication skills, some experience in computer-related fields. Duration is flexible. ▶ *4–8 editorial interns:* responsibilities include editing and proofreading, writing byline articles, assisting with magazine production, rewriting and editorial research. Candidates should have computer skills, editing skills, oral communication skills, organizational skills, writing skills, experience with desktop publishing programs such as Quark Express, Illustrator, and Photoshop is helpful. Duration is flexible. ▶ *Marketing interns:* responsibilities include assisting in the preparation of questionnaires and promotional mailings, updating promotional and competitive files, and performing research for sales/market reports. Candidates should have ability to work with others, college courses in field, computer skills, office skills, research skills, self-motivation. Duration is 3–4 months. All positions paid. Open to college sophomores, college juniors, college seniors, graduate students.
Benefits Formal training, job counseling, possible full-time employment, willing to complete paperwork for educational credit, willing to provide letters of recommendation, training on professional text-editing system.
Contact Write, call, fax, or e-mail Mr. Vincent Scaturro, Human Resources Representative. Phone: 610-964-4218. Fax: 610-964-2928. E-mail: vscaturro@cahners.com. In-person interview required. Applicants must submit a cover letter, resume. Applications are accepted continuously. World Wide Web: http://www.chilton.net.

CAPE COD LIFE
PO Box 1385
Pocasset, Massachusetts 02559-1385

General Information Publisher of Cape Cod Life, a bimonthly regional lifestyle magazine designed to capture the unique spirit of Cape Cod, Martha's Vineyard, and Nantucket; also publishes annual Cape Cod Home, Living and Gardening on the Cape and Islands. Established in 1979. Number of employees: 19. Number of internship applications received each year: 20.
Internships Available ▶ *1–2 editorial interns:* responsibilities include performing editorial tasks including research, fact checking, proofreading, editing, and writing. Candidates should have ability to work independently, organizational skills, personal interest in the field, written communication skills, knowledge of or interest in the region (Cape Cod, Martha's Vineyard, and Nantucket). Duration is flexible. Unpaid. Open to college freshmen, college sophomores, college juniors, college seniors.
Benefits Possible full-time employment, willing to complete paperwork for educational credit, willing to provide letters of recommendation.
Contact Write or e-mail Mr. Robert Ostergaard, Associate Editor. E-mail: capelife@capecodlife.com. In-person interview required. Applicants must submit a cover letter, resume, three personal references. Application deadline: March 27 for summer. World Wide Web: http://www.capecodlife.com.

CARIBBEAN TRAVEL AND LIFE MAGAZINE
460 North Orlando, Suite 200
Winter Park, Florida 32789

General Information Four-color consumer publication specializing in the Caribbean, the Bahamas, and Bermuda.
Internships Available ▶ *Advertising interns:* responsibilities include light clerical work, advertising prospecting from other magazines and media kit requests, helping with department mailings, coordinating with international team of sales representatives, learning advertising software, and updating advertiser records. ▶ *Editorial interns:* responsibilities include fact checking, researching photos, assisting with office and clerical work, researching articles, and writing; interns get their own byline. Duration for all positions is flexible. All positions are unpaid. Open to high school students, high school seniors, recent high school graduates, college freshmen, college sophomores, college juniors, college seniors, recent college graduates, graduate students, law students, law school graduates, career changers, individuals reentering the workforce.

Contact Write Sue Whitney, Managing Editor. Applicants must submit a cover letter, resume. Applications are accepted continuously.

CHARLESBRIDGE PUBLISHING
85 Main Street
Watertown, Massachusetts 02472

General Information Publisher of school books that help children use reason and creative thinking to learn and solve problems, as well as trade fiction and nonfiction picture books. Established in 1979. Number of employees: 30. Number of internship applications received each year: 100.
Internships Available ▶ *4 editorial assistants:* responsibilities include researching, editing, proofreading, writing, and analyzing manuscripts. Candidates should have analytical skills, editing skills, organizational skills, research skills, writing skills. ▶ *1 graphic arts assistant:* responsibilities include creating black and white line drawings, designing layouts, communicating with illustrators, evaluating the graphic potential of stories, and researching accuracy of illustrations. Candidates should have ability to work independently, ability to work with others, research skills, self-motivation, experience in graphic arts. Duration for all positions is 1 semester. All positions are unpaid. Open to college juniors, college seniors, recent college graduates, graduate students, career changers, individuals reentering the workforce.
Benefits Willing to complete paperwork for educational credit, willing to provide letters of recommendation.
Contact Write, call, or e-mail Ms. Elena Dworkin Wright, Managing Editor. Phone: 617-926-0329 Ext. 140. E-mail: schooleditorial@charlesbridge.com. In-person interview recommended. Applicants must submit a cover letter, resume, writing sample. Applications are accepted continuously.

THE CHRONICLE OF THE HORSE
108 The Plains Road, PO Box 46
Middleburg, Virginia 20118

General Information Weekly sport horse magazine with primary focus on news and additional articles on horse care, rider profiles, and how-to information on all English horse sports and breeding. Established in 1937. Number of employees: 20. Number of internship applications received each year: 25.
Internships Available ▶ *3–4 editorial interns:* responsibilities include proofreading, editing, writing, and working on special projects/assignments. Duration is 3–4 months. $6 per hour. International applications accepted.
Benefits Names of contacts, possible full-time employment, travel reimbursement, willing to complete paperwork for educational credit, willing to provide letters of recommendation.
Contact Write or call Beth Rasin, Assistant Editor, 108 The Plains Road, PO Box 46, Middleburg, Virginia 20118. Phone: 540-687-6341. In-person interview required. Applicants must submit a cover letter, resume, writing sample. Applications are accepted continuously.

CONGRESSIONAL QUARTERLY, INC.
1414 22nd Street, NW
Washington, District of Columbia 20037

General Information Company that publishes accurate, timely, and objective information on Congress and national politics; services include a weekly magazine and research reports, daily, weekly, and annual publications, and an on-line product "CQ. Com" as well as books and directories. Number of internship applications received each year: 200.
Internships Available ▶ *Interns:* responsibilities include working on the news media service and performing duties in the editorial, marketing, and advertising departments. Candidates should have computer skills, knowledge of field, office skills, oral communication skills, strong interpersonal skills, writing skills. Duration is 3 months. Position available as unpaid or paid. Open to college freshmen, college sophomores, college juniors,

college seniors, recent college graduates, graduate students, law students, career changers, individuals reentering the workforce. International applications accepted.
Benefits Names of contacts, opportunity to attend seminars/workshops, willing to complete paperwork for educational credit, willing to provide letters of recommendation.
Contact Write, fax, or e-mail Annette M. Billings, Human Resources Manager. Fax: 202-293-1487. E-mail: abillings@cq.com. No phone calls. Applicants must submit a cover letter, resume, three writing samples. Applications are accepted continuously.

CONNECTICUT MAGAZINE
35 Nutmeg Drive
Trumbull, Connecticut 06611

General Information General interest regional magazine with a circulation of 90,000. Established in 1971. Number of employees: 26. Unit of Communications International, New York, New York. Number of internship applications received each year: 75.
Internships Available ▶ *2–4 editorial interns:* responsibilities include working on monthly calendar and dining guide sections, checking facts, researching, typing correspondence, answering phones, and taking responsibility for various special project tasks. Candidates should have editing skills, oral communication skills, organizational skills, personal interest in the field, self-motivation, writing skills. Duration is 1 semester. Unpaid. Open to college freshmen, college sophomores, college juniors, college seniors, recent college graduates, graduate students, career changers, individuals reentering the workforce. International applications accepted.
Benefits Job counseling, names of contacts, willing to act as a professional reference, willing to complete paperwork for educational credit, willing to provide letters of recommendation.
Contact Write, call, fax, or e-mail Jill Pirozzoli, Editorial Assistant. Phone: 203-380-6600 Ext. 329. Fax: 203-380-6612. E-mail: ctmaga@pcnet.com. In-person interview recommended. Applicants must submit a cover letter, resume, 2-3 writing samples. Applications are accepted continuously. World Wide Web: http://www.connecticutmag.com.

DAVID R. GODINE, PUBLISHER, INC.
9 Hamilton Place
Boston, Massachusetts 02108

General Information Book publisher specializing in high-quality books on art, typography, and photography, as well as poetry, fiction, reprints of classics, and children's literature; publishes 25 titles per year. Established in 1970. Number of employees: 6. Number of internship applications received each year: 50.
Internships Available ▶ *3 interns:* responsibilities include general office work to assist with publicity, editing, and sales duties. Candidates should have editing skills, oral communication skills, organizational skills, plan to pursue career in field, written communication skills, Quark Xpress, Photoshop, and HTML skills. Duration is 4 months minimum (20-25 hours per week minimum). Unpaid. Open to college juniors, college seniors, recent college graduates, graduate students. International applications accepted.
Benefits Formal training, job counseling, names of contacts, on-the-job training, opportunity to attend seminars/workshops, willing to act as a professional reference, willing to complete paperwork for educational credit, willing to provide letters of recommendation, accessible by subway.
Contact Write Carl W. Scarbrough, Director of Publicity. Phone: 617-451-9600 Ext. 24. In-person interview recommended. Applicants must submit a cover letter, resume. Application deadline: March 1 for summer, June 1 for fall, October 1 for spring. World Wide Web: http://www.godine.com.

ENERGIZE, INC.
5450 Wissahickon Avenue
Philadelphia, Pennsylvania 19144

General Information Training, consulting, and publishing firm that specializes in volunteerism and assists international, national, state, and local organizations in developing citizen participation programs; publishes and distributes more than 65 books via a direct mailing catalog and a major Web site. Established in 1977. Number of employees: 5. Number of internship applications received each year: 10.

Internships Available ▶ *1–2 interns:* responsibilities include print and cyberspace marketing; research, editorial, and reporting duties. Candidates should have computer skills, personal interest in the field, research skills, writing skills. Duration is flexible. Unpaid. Open to college freshmen, college sophomores, college juniors, college seniors, recent college graduates, graduate students, career changers, individuals reentering the workforce. International applications accepted.

Benefits Job counseling, names of contacts, on-the-job training, opportunity to attend seminars/workshops, willing to act as a professional reference, willing to complete paperwork for educational credit, willing to provide letters of recommendation.

Contact Write or e-mail Ms. Susan J. Ellis, President. E-mail: susan@energizeinc.com. In-person interview required. Applicants must submit a cover letter, resume. Applications are accepted continuously. World Wide Web: http://www.energizeinc.com.

ENTERTAINMENT DESIGN AND LIGHTING DIMENSIONS MAGAZINES
32 West 18th Street, 11th Floor
New York, New York 10011-4612

General Information Publisher of leading trade magazines for the entertainment technology industry, covering all aspects of sound, lighting, set design, costume, architectural and themed entertainment applications. Established in 1967. Number of employees: 33. Division of Intertec Publishing Corporation, Overland Park, Kansas. Number of internship applications received each year: 35.

Internships Available ▶ *1 publishing/editorial intern:* responsibilities include supporting promotions and marketing projects, assisting with production, circulation, and advertising activities, and providing support for editorial projects and activities. Candidates should have college courses in field, computer skills, editing skills, office skills, oral communication skills, research skills, strong interpersonal skills, writing skills, personal interest in field preferred. Duration is 8–10 weeks. minimum wage to $10 per hour. Open to recent high school graduates, college freshmen, college sophomores, college juniors, college seniors, recent college graduates, graduate students, individuals reentering the workforce. ▶ *1–12 trade show interns:* responsibilities include assisting with on-site crew support of annual Lighting Dimensions International exposition. Candidates should have ability to work independently, knowledge of field, office skills, oral communication skills, organizational skills, strong interpersonal skills. Duration is 1-10 days during October or November. $35 per day, including accomodation. Open to high school seniors, recent high school graduates, college freshmen, college sophomores, college juniors, college seniors, recent college graduates, graduate students, individuals reentering the workforce.

Benefits Names of contacts, on-the-job training, opportunity to attend seminars/workshops, willing to complete paperwork for educational credit.

Contact Write or fax Internship Coordinator. Fax: 212-229-2084. No phone calls. In-person interview recommended. Applicants must submit a cover letter, letter of recommendation, resume, if applicable. Application deadline: May 15 for summer. World Wide Web: http://www.etenyc.net.

ENTERTAINMENT WEEKLY
1675 Broadway
New York, New York 10019

General Information Weekly magazine covering popular entertainment. Established in 1990. Number of employees: 200. Subsidiary of Time, Inc., New York, New York. Number of internship applications received each year: 500.

Internships Available ▶ *1 art intern:* responsibilities include assisting design editors in various tasks and maintaining art archives. Candidates should have ability to work independently, computer skills, office skills, organizational skills, personal interest in the field, self-motivation, strong interpersonal skills. Duration is 3–5 months. ▶ *4–5 editorial interns:* responsibilities include assisting editors in various tasks, such as inputting stories, transcribing interviews, running copy, and handling reader mail. Candidates should have ability to work independently, computer skills, editing skills, office skills, oral communication skills, organizational skills, self-motivation, strong interpersonal skills, written communication skills, love of entertainment. Duration is 3–5 months. ▶ *1 photo intern:* responsibilities include assisting photo editors in various tasks such as obtaining photos, contacting photographers, and maintaining archives. Candidates should have ability to work independently, office skills, organizational skills, self-motivation, strong interpersonal skills. Duration is 3 months (approximate). All positions paid at $8 per hour. Open to college juniors, college seniors, recent college graduates, graduate students.

Benefits Possible full-time employment, willing to act as a professional reference, willing to complete paperwork for educational credit.

Contact Write or fax Ms. Annabel Bentley, Director of Research Services. Fax: 212-522-6104. In-person interview required. Applicants must submit a cover letter, resume, 4-5 previously published clips. Application deadline: February 15 for summer, June 1 for fall, October 15 for spring.

E/THE ENVIRONMENTAL MAGAZINE
28 Knight Street
Norwalk, Connecticut 06851

General Information Magazine serving as a clearinghouse of information, news, and commentary on environmental issues, geared toward both the general public and dedicated environmentalists for the purpose of promoting environmental awareness and activism. Established in 1990. Number of employees: 6. Number of internship applications received each year: 30.

Internships Available ▶ *4 advertising interns:* responsibilities include assisting in advertisement sales, handling mailings, proofing ads, and computer work. Duration is flexible. ▶ *2 circulation interns:* responsibilities include assisting with the promotion and sales of the magazine. Duration is flexible. ▶ *4 editorial interns:* responsibilities include keying articles, proofreading, responding to editorial phone calls, correspondence, and performing library and phone research; will have opportunity to write and publish articles, possible travel for stories, Internet research, and conducting product reviews. Duration is 2 months minimum. All positions are unpaid. Open to college freshmen, college sophomores, college juniors, college seniors, recent college graduates, graduate students. International applications accepted.

Benefits Names of contacts, opportunity to attend seminars/workshops, possible full-time employment, travel reimbursement, willing to complete paperwork for educational credit, willing to provide letters of recommendation.

Contact Write, call, fax, or e-mail Jennifer Bogo, Assistant Editor. Phone: 203-854-5559 Ext. 108. Fax: 203-866-0602. E-mail: emagazine@prodigy.net. In-person interview recommended. Applicants must submit a cover letter, resume, writing sample. Applications are accepted continuously. World Wide Web: http://www.emagazine.com.

F & W PUBLICATIONS, INC.
1507 Dana Avenue
Cincinnati, Ohio 45207

General Information Book and magazine publisher of self-help materials in the art, writing, crafts, design,and woodworking fields. Established in 1910. Number of employees: 300. Number of internship applications received each year: 150.
Internships Available ▶ *8–10 editorial assistants:* responsibilities include copyediting, proofreading, and researching. Candidates should have computer skills, editing skills, organizational skills, plan to pursue career in field, writing skills. Duration is 10–12 weeks. ▶ *3–4 marketing/advertising assistants:* responsibilities include copywriting, researching, and planning mailings. Candidates should have analytical skills, computer skills, organizational skills, plan to pursue career in field, writing skills. Duration is 10-12 weeks (May to August or June to September). ▶ *1 new media assistant:* responsibilities include updating Web page content, assisting in e-mail newsletter. Candidates should have college courses in field, computer skills, HTML and Web page design experience. Duration is 10-12 weeks (May to August or June to September). ▶ *1–2 production assistants:* responsibilities include analyzing circulation programs, coordinating published and printed materials. Candidates should have computer skills, office skills, oral communication skills, organizational skills, personal interest in the field, interest in print production. Duration is 10-12 weeks (May to August or June to September). All positions paid at $300 per week. Open to college juniors, graduate students, students returning to school after internship ends (required).
Benefits Housing at a cost, job counseling, on-the-job training, possible full-time employment, willing to complete paperwork for educational credit.
Contact Write Gail Schrodt, Human Resources Manager. No phone calls. In-person interview recommended. Applicants must submit a cover letter, resume, 1-3 samples of work (design interns). Application deadline: December 31 for summer.

FANTAGRAPHICS BOOKS, INC.
7563 Lake City Way, NE
Seattle, Washington 98115

General Information Publisher of original comic books and book collections, book collections of classic comic strips and underground comic books, and a trade magazine about the comics industry. Established in 1976. Number of employees: 40. Number of internship applications received each year: 50.
Internships Available ▶ *3–4 editorial interns:* responsibilities include typesetting, proofreading, copyediting, writing copy, and assisting in promotional work. Duration is variable. ▶ *1–2 promotion/marketing interns:* responsibilities include writing press releases and general office work related to publicity, public relations, and marketing. Duration is 2–3 months. Candidates for all positions should have computer skills, editing skills, knowledge of field, office skills, organizational skills, personal interest in the field, written communication skills. All positions are unpaid. Open to high school students, high school seniors, recent high school graduates, college freshmen, college sophomores, college juniors, college seniors, recent college graduates, graduate students, law students, career changers, individuals reentering the workforce, must be 18 or older. International applications accepted.
Benefits Names of contacts, possible full-time employment, willing to complete paperwork for educational credit, willing to provide letters of recommendation.
Contact Write Anthony Pulsipher, Internship Coordinator. Applicants must submit a cover letter, resume. Applications are accepted continuously.

FARRAR, STRAUS, AND GIROUX
19 Union Square West
New York, New York 10003

General Information General trade-book publisher. Established in 1946. Number of employees: 100. Number of internship applications received each year: 500.

Internships Available ▶ *Interns:* responsibilities include working in different departments. Duration is flexible. Unpaid. Open to college freshmen, college sophomores, college juniors, college seniors, recent college graduates, graduate students, career changers.
Benefits Possible full-time employment, willing to complete paperwork for educational credit, willing to provide letters of recommendation.
Contact Write or call Ms. Peggy Miller, Office Manager. Phone: 212-741-6900. In-person interview required. Applications are accepted continuously.

FOREIGN AFFAIRS MAGAZINE
58 East 68th Street
New York, New York 10021

General Information Bimonthly journal devoted to international affairs and U.S. foreign policy. Established in 1922. Number of employees: 15. Number of internship applications received each year: 200.
Internships Available ▶ *1 academic-year intern:* responsibilities include editing, proofreading, and layout for articles to be published in magazine; research and fact checking; writing press releases; assisting with art acquisition; archiving; screening unsolicited manuscripts. Candidates should have analytical skills, editing skills, personal interest in the field, self-motivation, strong interpersonal skills, writing skills. Duration is 10 months. $450 per week. Open to college seniors, recent college graduates, graduate students, law students. ▶ *4 semester interns:* responsibilities include copy editing and proofreading, fact-checking, screening unsolicited manuscripts, and assisting editors. Candidates should have ability to work independently, editing skills, personal interest in the field, research skills, strong interpersonal skills, writing skills. Duration is 3 months. Unpaid. Open to college juniors, college seniors, recent college graduates, graduate students, law students. ▶ *1 summer intern:* responsibilities include editing, proofreading, and layout for articles to be published in magazine; research and fact checking; writing press releases; assisting with art acquisition; archiving; screening unsolicited manuscripts. Candidates should have analytical skills, editing skills, oral communication skills, personal interest in the field, strong interpersonal skills, written communication skills. Duration is 10 weeks. $300 per week. Open to college seniors, recent college graduates, graduate students, law students. International applications accepted.
Benefits Formal training, health insurance, names of contacts, opportunity to attend seminars/workshops, possible full-time employment, willing to act as a professional reference, willing to provide letters of recommendation, attendance at Council on Foreign Relations events.
Contact Write Warren Bass, Associate Editor. Applicants must submit a cover letter, resume, three writing samples, three letters of recommendation. Application deadline: mid-March for summer and academic year; start of semester for semester interns. World Wide Web: http://www.foreignaffairs.org.

FRIENDS JOURNAL
1216 Arch Street 2A
Philadelphia, Pennsylvania 19107

General Information Monthly religious periodical with emphasis on social action, spiritual nurturing, news/features, poetry, and book reviews. Established in 1955. Number of employees: 10. Number of internship applications received each year: 4.
Internships Available ▶ *1–3 editorial assistants:* responsibilities include writing, editing, working on the computer, possible Web site work, and office tasks. Candidates should have ability to work independently, computer skills, editing skills, organizational skills, self-motivation, written communication skills. ▶ *1–3 office assistants:* responsibilities include assisting with development and circulation tasks, and assisting editors. Candidates should have ability to work independently, ability to work with others, computer skills, office skills, organizational skills, self-motivation. Duration for all positions is 4-23 days per month. All positions

Friends Journal (continued)

are unpaid. Open to college juniors, college seniors, recent college graduates, graduate students, career changers.
Benefits Names of contacts, on-the-job training, possible full-time employment, willing to act as a professional reference, willing to provide letters of recommendation.
Contact Write or e-mail Susan Corson-Finnerty, Editor-Manager, 1216 Arch Street, 2A, Philadelphia, Pennsylvania 19027. E-mail: friendsjnl@aol.com. No phone calls. In-person interview recommended. Applicants must submit a resume, two personal references, 2-3 writing samples, and letter of interest. Applications are accepted continuously.

FRIENDS OF THE NATIONAL ZOO, COMMUNICATIONS OFFICE
National Zoological Park
Washington, District of Columbia 20008

General Information Office that publishes *ZooGoer*, a bimonthly magazine for members of Friends of the National Zoo (FONZ), and handles media relations. Established in 1889. Number of employees: 60. Number of internship applications received each year: 30.
Internships Available ▶ *1–2 communications interns:* responsibilities include writing, researching, editing, and general office work. Candidates should have ability to work with others, college courses in field, computer skills, editing skills, research skills, writing skills. Duration is 10 weeks (40 hours per week). Unpaid. Open to college sophomores, college juniors, college seniors, recent college graduates, graduate students. International applications accepted.
Benefits Job counseling, names of contacts, willing to complete paperwork for educational credit, willing to provide letters of recommendation.
Contact Write Mr. Robert Moll, Associate Editor, National Zoological Park, Washington, District of Columbia 20008. No phone calls. In-person interview recommended. Applicants must submit a formal organization application, cover letter, resume, three writing samples. Application deadline: January 15 for spring, April 15 for summer, June 15 for fall, October 15 for winter. World Wide Web: http://www.fonz.org.

FUTURE PRESS
Box 444, Prince Street Station
New York, New York 10012-0008

General Information Nonprofit organization that produces alternative materials and literature (books, prints, audios, videos, and film). Established in 1977. Number of employees: 1. Number of internship applications received each year: 50.
Internships Available ▶ *8–10 interns:* responsibilities include collaborating with a productive full-time artist/writer (usually Richard Kostelanetz) in the project-centered production of books, videotapes, films, holograms, and audiotapes for exhibition and production. Candidates should have ability to work independently, computer skills, editing skills, plan to pursue career in field, self-motivation, desire to complete a project that should prominently display the intern's name. Duration is flexible. Unpaid. Open to college sophomores, college juniors, college seniors, recent college graduates, career changers. International applications accepted.
Benefits Job counseling, names of contacts, on-the-job training, possible full-time employment, willing to complete paperwork for educational credit, willing to provide letters of recommendation, projects on which interns can put their names.
Contact Write Mr. Richard Kostelanetz, Director of Literature and Media. No phone calls. In-person interview recommended. Applicants must submit a cover letter, resume. Applications are accepted continuously.

THE GAZETTE COMPANY
PO Box 511, 500 Third Avenue, SE
Cedar Rapids, Iowa 52406

General Information Multi-media company. Established in 1883. Number of employees: 900. Number of internship applications received each year: 200.
Internships Available ▶ *2–3 KCRG-TV News interns:* responsibilities include shadowing reporters, assignment editors, photographers, and producers through the television news gathering process. Will learn all aspects of news, but will also focus on intern's interest. Candidates should have ability to work independently, ability to work with others, college courses in field, oral communication skills, organizational skills, self-motivation. Duration is 1 semester. Unpaid. Open to college juniors, college seniors. ▶ *2 advertising interns:* responsibilities include planning and conducting sales presentations, coordinating ad designs and layouts, providing customer service, and working with classified and display advertising. Candidates should have ability to work independently, college courses in field, computer skills, oral communication skills, plan to pursue career in field, written communication skills. Duration is 3 months in summer. $6 per hour. Open to college sophomores, college juniors. ▶ *3 news reporting interns:* responsibilities include working in newsroom. Candidates should have ability to work independently, college courses in field, computer skills, knowledge of field, plan to pursue career in field, written communication skills. Duration is 3 months in fall, spring, or summer. $8 per hour. Open to college sophomores, juniors, or seniors enrolled in journalism or journalism related programs. ▶ *3 photo interns:* responsibilities include taking photos. Candidates should have ability to work independently, ability to work with others, college courses in field, knowledge of field, oral communication skills, plan to pursue career in field, self-motivation. Duration is 3 months in fall, spring, or summer. $8 per hour. Open to college sophomores, recent college graduates, college juniors and seniors enrolled in photojournalism or journalism related program. ▶ *1 public relations intern:* responsibilities include assisting with "Newspaper in Education" projects and events, attending editor's coffees, assisting with "In Your Neighborhood" projects, in-house promotions, and other related efforts. Candidates should have ability to work independently, computer skills, knowledge of field, oral communication skills, personal interest in the field, strong interpersonal skills. Duration is 1 summer. $7 per hour. Open to college sophomores, college juniors. International applications accepted.
Benefits Possible full-time employment, willing to complete paperwork for educational credit, willing to provide letters of recommendation.
Contact Write, fax, or e-mail Trish Thoms, Human Resources Employment Manager. Fax: 319-368-8834. E-mail: gazcohr@fyiowa.com. No phone calls. Applicants must submit a cover letter, resume, at least 3 writing samples. Application deadline: January 1 for summer, March 31 for advertising positions, May 1 for fall, October 1 for winter.

HANLEY-WOOD, INC.
One Thomas Circle, NW, Suite 600
Washington, District of Columbia 20005

General Information Publisher of business and consumer media for the residential construction and design industry. Number of employees: 400.
Internships Available ▶ *1–5 intern assistants:* responsibilities include writing product blurbs for magazines, providing research for features, copy editing, proofreading, and a variety of administrative tasks related to editorial process. Candidates should have major in journalism (preferred). Duration is 2-3 months in summer. $10 per hour. Open to college juniors, college seniors, recent college graduates, graduate students. International applications accepted.
Benefits Formal training, opportunity to attend seminars/workshops, possible full-time employment, willing to complete paperwork for educational credit.
Contact Write, fax, or e-mail Mr. Paul Kitzke, Editorial Director. Fax: 202-785-1974. E-mail: pkitzke@hanley-wood.com. No phone

calls. Telephone interview required. Applicants must submit a resume, initial letter outlining career goals and why internship would be useful. Applications are accepted continuously. World Wide Web: http://www.hanley-wood.com.

HARPER'S MAGAZINE FOUNDATION
666 Broadway
New York, New York 10012

General Information Magazine publisher. Established in 1850. Number of employees: 35. Number of internship applications received each year: 100.
Internships Available ▶ *4 editorial interns:* responsibilities include assisting a section editor (Readings, Forum, or Articles and Annotations), participating in the general tasks required to run a magazine, and working on the Harper's Index. Candidates should have computer skills, personal interest in the field, research skills, writing skills. Duration is varied from term to term. ▶ *1 promotion intern:* responsibilities include working closely with the Vice President of Corporate and Public Affairs and the Promotion Manager on editorial publicity, special events, advertising promotions, phone research and follow up, compiling lists, copying, faxing, typing, mailing, and calling messengers. Duration is flexible. All positions are unpaid. Open to college freshmen, college sophomores, college juniors, college seniors, recent college graduates, graduate students. International applications accepted.
Benefits Formal training, names of contacts, possible full-time employment, willing to complete paperwork for educational credit, willing to provide letters of recommendation.
Contact Write, call, fax, or e-mail Donovan Hohn, Assistant Editor. Phone: 212-614-6500. Fax: 212-228-5889. E-mail: donovan@harpers.org. In person interview required. Applicants must submit a formal organization application, resume. Application deadline: February 15 for summer, June 15 for fall, October 15 for winter. World Wide Web: http://www.harpers.org.

THE HEARST BOOK GROUP, AVON BOOKS, WILLIAM MORROW & COMPANY
1350 Avenue of the Americas
New York, New York 10019

General Information Publisher of hardcover fiction, nonfiction, adult, mass market, children's, lifestyle, and cookbooks. Established in 1926. Number of employees: 300. Division of The Hearst Corporation, Charlotte, North Carolina. Number of internship applications received each year: 200.
Internships Available ▶ *6–10 summer interns:* responsibilities include working in a structured program with rotating functions in various departments and divisions. Candidates should have office skills, oral communication skills, personal interest in the field, self-motivation, strong interpersonal skills, written communication skills. Duration is 10 weeks. $300 per week. Open to college juniors, graduate students.
Benefits Possible full-time employment.
Contact Write or fax Audrey Altschul, Manager, Human Resources. Fax: 212-261-6518. No phone calls. In-person interview required. Applicants must submit a cover letter, resume. Application deadline: March 15. World Wide Web: http://www.hearstcorp.com, http://www.avonbooks.com, http://www.williammorrow.com.

HILL STREET PRESS
191 East Broad Street, Suite 209
Athens, Georgia 30605-2848

General Information Independent publisher of literary and trade fiction and nonfiction related to the diverse American South. Established in 1998. Number of employees: 4. Number of internship applications received each year: 40.
Internships Available ▶ *4–5 editorial interns:* responsibilities include evaluating unsolicited manuscripts, proofreading editorial research, technical preparation of manuscripts, drafting rejection letters, general office duties, and product development. Candidates should have ability to work independently, computer skills, editing skills, office skills, research skills, self-motivation, interest in the literature of the American South. ▶ *2 marketing assistants:* responsibilities include maintaining databases and Web sites, developing review lists, production of advertising copy, mass mailings, special events publicity. Candidates should have computer skills, office skills, organizational skills, research skills, strong interpersonal skills, writing skills. Duration for all positions is 1 semester. All positions are unpaid. Open to college sophomores, college juniors, college seniors, recent college graduates, graduate students, career changers.
Benefits Names of contacts, on-the-job training, willing to act as a professional reference, willing to complete paperwork for educational credit, willing to provide letters of recommendation.
Contact Write, fax, or e-mail Patrick Allen, Senior Editor, 191 East Broad Street, Suite 209, Athens, Georgia 30605-2848. Fax: 706-613-7204. E-mail: allen@hillstreetpress.com. No phone calls. In-person interview required. Applicants must submit a cover letter, resume, two writing samples. Applications are accepted continuously. World Wide Web: http://www.hillstreetpress.com.

HISPANIC LINK JOURNALISM FOUNDATION
1420 N Street, NW
Washington, District of Columbia 20005

General Information News service based in Washington, D.C., that publishes the national newsweekly *Hispanic Link Weekly Report* (in English) and syndicates 3 columns weekly (in English and Spanish) through the Los Angeles Times syndicate to approximately 70 newspapers and magazines in the United States and Latin America. Established in 1980. Number of employees: 3. Number of internship applications received each year: 40.
Internships Available ▶ *1–2 fellowships:* responsibilities include writing for *Hispanic Link Weekly Report* and other media outlets. Candidates should have analytical skills, oral communication skills, plan to pursue career in field, research skills, written communication skills. Duration is 1 year. $20,000 stipend for duration of internship. Open to college seniors, recent college graduates, graduate students, career changers, anyone interested regardless of education. ▶ *1–2 reporting interns:* responsibilities include a variety of tasks ranging from office and basic media training to full reporting, editing, and marketing training. Candidates should have personal interest in the field, plan to pursue career in field. Duration is flexible. Unpaid. Open to anyone interested regardless of education. International applications accepted.
Benefits Formal training, health insurance, job counseling, names of contacts, on-the-job training, travel reimbursement, willing to act as a professional reference, willing to complete paperwork for educational credit, willing to provide letters of recommendation, direct contact with potential employers provided (for paid interns only).
Contact Write, call, fax, or e-mail Hector Ericksen-Mendoza, Executive Director. Phone: 202-234-0280. Fax: 202-234-4090. E-mail: zapoteco@aol.com. Telephone interview required. Applicants must submit a formal organization application, cover letter, resume, three personal references, 3-10 writing clips. Application deadline: January 1 for winter/spring, May 1 for summer/fall.

HOUGHTON MIFFLIN COMPANY
College/School Division, 222 Berkeley Street
Boston, Massachusetts 02116-3764

General Information Publisher of textbooks, educational software, fiction, non-fiction, and reference works. Established in 1834.
Internships Available ▶ *12 interns:* responsibilities include working in the editorial, marketing, software development, or production and design department as an editorial assistant. Candidates should have computer skills, oral communication skills, written communication skills. Duration is 3 months (June-August), 35 hours per week. Paid. Open to college sophomores, college juniors, college seniors. International applications accepted.

Houghton Mifflin Company (continued)

Benefits Opportunity to attend seminars/workshops, possible full-time employment, willing to complete paperwork for educational credit.

Contact Write or e-mail Monica Ringle, College Division Intern Coordinator. E-mail: monica_ringle@hmco.com. No phone calls. In-person interview recommended. Applicants must submit a cover letter, resume. Application deadline: April 1. World Wide Web: http://www.hmco.com/college/division/internship.html.

HUNTER HOUSE, INC., PUBLISHERS
PO Box 2914
Alameda, California 94501-0914

General Information Independent book publishing company that specializes in health, social issues, self-help/psychology, and women's issues. Established in 1978. Number of employees: 7. Number of internship applications received each year: 20.

Internships Available ▶ *1–4 editorial interns:* responsibilities include copy editing manuscripts, proofreading page proofs, confirming resource information for particular books, compiling contacts, drafting letters, soliciting endorsements for upcoming books, logging and helping to evaluate manuscript submissions, and conducting library and bookstore research. Candidates should have computer skills, editing skills, plan to pursue career in field, research skills, written communication skills. Open to college freshmen, college sophomores, college juniors, college seniors, recent college graduates, career changers. ▶ *1 editorial/marketing intern:* responsibilities include following one project through editorial finalization and then working on the same book in marketing and publicity. Candidates should have ability to work independently, ability to work with others, computer skills, editing skills, experience in the field, personal interest in the field, research skills, written communication skills. Open to college freshmen, college sophomores, college juniors, college seniors, individuals reentering the workforce. ▶ *1 marketing intern:* responsibilities include compiling lists of contacts who will review the book, researching direct mail lists, writing promotional copy, updating marketing database, organizing direct mailings. Candidates should have analytical skills, computer skills, oral communication skills, self-motivation, strong interpersonal skills, written communication skills. Open to college juniors, college seniors, recent college graduates, individuals reentering the workforce. ▶ *1 publicity intern:* responsibilities include writing, designing, and mailing promotional new book announcement fliers; choosing relevant media for newly released books and mailing review copies to this list; assisting with book radio, television, and print interviews for authors; helping to write and mail press kits; contacting book stores to schedule and organize author events and signings. Candidates should have computer skills, experience in the field, oral communication skills, self-motivation, written communication skills. Open to college sophomores, college juniors, college seniors, recent college graduates, individuals reentering the workforce. ▶ *1 publisher's assistant intern:* responsibilities include assisting the publisher with business analysis and modeling, long-term plans and project schedules, and with daily activities related to operations and book acquisitions. Candidates should have ability to work with others, analytical skills, computer skills, office skills, organizational skills, research skills, literacy with either spreadsheets, databases, and scheduling software or Internet and HTML. Open to college seniors, recent college graduates, graduate students, career changers, individuals reentering the workforce. Duration for all positions is 3 months minimum, 16-20 hours per week. All positions are unpaid. International applications accepted.

Benefits Names of contacts, on-the-job training, willing to complete paperwork for educational credit, willing to provide letters of recommendation.

Contact Write, fax, or e-mail Internship Coordinator. Fax: 510-865-4295. E-mail: hhi@hunterhouse.com. No phone calls. In-person interview recommended. Applicants must submit a formal organization application, cover letter, resume, two personal references, 2-3 writing samples. Applications are accepted continuously. World Wide Web: http://www.hunterhouse.com/.

ISLAND PRESS
1718 Connecticut Avenue, NW, Suite 300
Washington, District of Columbia 20009

General Information Nonprofit publisher of books about the environment for professionals, students, and general readers. Established in 1978. Number of employees: 20. Number of internship applications received each year: 50.

Internships Available ▶ *1 general intern:* responsibilities include handling all communications through front office and general/operational support for all departments as needed. Candidates should have ability to work independently, computer skills, oral communication skills, organizational skills, personal interest in the field, self-motivation, strong interpersonal skills, interest in publishing and/or environment preferred. Duration is 20 hours per week (flexible). Open to high school students, high school seniors, recent high school graduates, college freshmen, college sophomores, college juniors, college seniors, recent college graduates, graduate students, law students, career changers, individuals reentering the workforce. ▶ *1 publicity intern:* responsibilities include researching press contracts, assisting in publicity campaign execution, responsible for all book review receipts and distribution in-house and to authors, general department support. Candidates should have ability to work independently, computer skills, oral communication skills, organizational skills, self-motivation, written communication skills, sense of humor, ability to juggle multiple tasks. Duration is 4 months minimum (longer preferred); 20 hours per week (flexible). Open to college sophomores, college juniors, college seniors, recent college graduates, individuals reentering the workforce. All positions available as unpaid or paid. International applications accepted.

Benefits On-the-job training, possible full-time employment, willing to act as a professional reference, willing to complete paperwork for educational credit, willing to provide letters of recommendation, stipend for publicity interns to cover transportation costs.

Contact Write, fax, or e-mail Human Resources. Phone: 202-232-7933. Fax: 202-234-1328. E-mail: info@islandpress.org. In-person interview recommended. Applicants must submit a cover letter, resume, writing sample. Applications are accepted continuously. World Wide Web: http://www.islandpress.org.

IVAN R. DEE, PUBLISHER
1332 North Halstead Street
Chicago, Illinois 60622-2694

General Information Book publisher. Established in 1987. Number of employees: 5. Unit of National Book Network, Lanham, Maryland. Number of internship applications received each year: 100.

Internships Available ▶ *2–4 general internships in publishing:* responsibilities include proofreading, general operational duties, sales, marketing, and general correspondence. Candidates should have analytical skills, computer skills, office skills, oral communication skills, self-motivation, written communication skills. Unpaid. ▶ *1–2 informations systems interns:* responsibilities include maintaining databases and updating information, editing and maintaining Web site. Candidates should have analytical skills, computer skills, knowledge of field, office skills, self-motivation. Position available as unpaid or paid. Duration for all positions is 1 semester. Open to college juniors, college seniors, recent college graduates, graduate students. International applications accepted.

Benefits Opportunity to attend seminars/workshops, willing to act as a professional reference, willing to complete paperwork for educational credit, willing to provide letters of recommendation.

Contact Write, fax, or e-mail Maureen Ryan, Operations Manager. Fax: 312-787-6269. E-mail: elephant@ivandee.com. In-person interview recommended. Applicants must submit a cover letter, resume. Applications are accepted continuously. World Wide Web: http://www.ivandee.com.

JOHN WILEY & SONS, INC.
605 Third Avenue
New York, New York 10158

General Information Largest and oldest independent publishing company in North America. Established in 1807. Number of employees: 850. Number of internship applications received each year: 300.

Internships Available ▶ *2 editorial assistants:* responsibilities include assisting product development, conducting market research and comparative analysis on competing books, and contacting professors as potential reviewers for manuscripts. Candidates should have ability to work independently, analytical skills, computer skills, knowledge of field, office skills, oral communication skills, organizational skills, personal interest in the field, self-motivation, strong interpersonal skills. Duration is 9 weeks in summer. $300 per week. ▶ *2–4 information technology interns:* responsibilities include software/hardware trouble shooting, basic network wiring, light applications development, and basic support call responding. Candidates should have ability to work independently, computer skills, declared college major in field, experience in the field, office skills, oral communication skills, plan to pursue career in field, self-motivation, strong interpersonal skills, writing skills, knowledge of Word, Lotus, NT/Novell Server, Sun Solaris, Unix, and databases. Duration is June to August (9 weeks). $350 per week. ▶ *2 marketing assistants:* responsibilities include building a database of target sales opportunities, conducting telephone research, assisting in preparation of material for national sales meeting, and Internet marketing. Candidates should have ability to work independently, analytical skills, computer skills, office skills, oral communication skills, organizational skills, plan to pursue career in field, self-motivation, strong interpersonal skills, writing skills. Duration is 9 weeks in summer. $300 per week. ▶ *1 new technology assistant:* responsibilities include assisting with research, development, and/or pilot implementation including new publishing technologies; Internet research, Web development, project tracking, and Web site quality assurance. Candidates should have ability to work independently, analytical skills, college courses in field, computer skills, knowledge of field, office skills, oral communication skills, organizational skills, plan to pursue career in field, research skills, self-motivation, strong interpersonal skills, writing skills. Duration is 9 weeks in summer. $300 per week. Open to college juniors.

Benefits Names of contacts, on-the-job training, opportunity to attend seminars/workshops, possible full-time employment, willing to act as a professional reference, willing to provide letters of recommendation.

Contact Write or fax Internship Coordinator. Fax: 212-850-6049. No phone calls. In-person interview required. Applicants must submit a cover letter, resume. Application deadline: February 1. World Wide Web: http://www.wiley.com.

LIBRARY JOURNAL MAGAZINE
245 West 17th Street
New York, New York 10011-5300

General Information A trade magazine that provides news and book reviews for public and academic libraries. Established in 1876.

Internships Available ▶ *1–2 book review interns:* responsibilities include opening and sorting mail, proofreading copy, inputting galleys into book review database, answering phone calls, faxing review status reports. Candidates should have ability to work independently, editing skills, office skills, oral communication skills, self-motivation, writing skills. Duration is 3–4 months. Position available as unpaid or at $6–$8 per hour. Open to college juniors, college seniors.

Benefits Opportunity to write book reviews and news briefs with a published byline.

Contact Call, fax, or e-mail Heather McCormack, Assistant Editor, 245 West 17th Street, New York, New York 10011-5300. Phone: 212-463-6818. Fax: 212-463-6734. E-mail: hmccormack@cahners.com. In-person interview required. Applicants must submit a cover letter, resume, two writing samples. Application

deadline: April 30 for summer, July 31 for fall, December 15 for spring. World Wide Web: http://www.libraryjournal.com.

LOS ANGELES MAGAZINE
11100 Santa Monica Boulevard, 7th Floor
Los Angeles, California 90025

General Information City magazine that focuses on local issues, problems, people, trends, events, and lifestyles, and shows options and opportunities available in the southern California area. Established in 1960. Number of employees: 50. Unit of ABC/Capital Cities Publishing, New York, New York. Number of internship applications received each year: 50.

Internships Available ▶ *4–6 editorial interns:* responsibilities include fact checking, researching, and performing basic clerical duties. Candidates should have ability to work independently, oral communication skills, plan to pursue career in field, research skills, writing skills. Duration is 2–3 months. Unpaid. Open to college juniors, college seniors.

Benefits Willing to complete paperwork for educational credit, willing to provide letters of recommendation.

Contact Write, fax, or e-mail Mr. Eric Mercado, Research Editor. Fax: 310-312-2285. E-mail: emercado@mindspring.com. No phone calls. In-person interview recommended. Applicants must submit a cover letter, resume, writing sample. Application deadline: April 1 for summer, July 31 for fall, October 31 for winter, December 1 for spring.

MCCALL'S MAGAZINE
375 Lexington Avenue, 9th Floor
New York, New York 10017

General Information Monthly women's service magazine. Established in 1876. Number of employees: 50. Unit of G & J USA Publishing, New York, New York. Number of internship applications received each year: 100.

Internships Available ▶ *2 articles interns:* responsibilities include performing research and writing activities and secretarial duties. Duration is 3 months. Position available as unpaid or at $6 per hour for summer, credit during school year. Open to college freshmen, college sophomores, college juniors, college seniors, recent college graduates, graduate students. ▶ *1–2 beauty interns:* responsibilities include research and selection of products for editorial shoots and general secretarial duties. Candidates should have ability to work independently, ability to work with others, oral communication skills, organizational skills, personal interest in the field, written communication skills. Unpaid. Open to college freshmen, college sophomores, college juniors, college seniors, recent college graduates. ▶ *1–2 fashion interns:* responsibilities include selecting and preparing merchandise for shoots and general secretarial work. Candidates should have ability to work independently, ability to work with others, office skills, oral communication skills, organizational skills, self-motivation. Unpaid. Open to college freshmen, college sophomores, college juniors, college seniors, graduate students. ▶ *1–2 food interns:* responsibilities include assisting in test kitchens, researching recipes, and secretarial duties. Candidates should have ability to work independently, ability to work with others, office skills, oral communication skills, organizational skills, personal interest in the field, self-motivation, written communication skills. Position available as unpaid or at $6 per hour for summer, credit during school year. Open to college freshmen, college sophomores, college juniors, college seniors, recent college graduates, graduate students. ▶ *Intersession internships:* responsibilities include assisting in the articles, food, fashion, and beauty departments over intersession breaks. Duration is minimum of 4 weeks. Position available as unpaid or paid. Open to college freshmen, college sophomores, college juniors, college seniors, recent college graduates, graduate students.

Benefits Names of contacts, possible full-time employment, willing to complete paperwork for educational credit, willing to provide letters of recommendation, reimbursement of travel expenses and free lunch in lieu of hourly pay for year-round interns.

McCall's Magazine (continued)
Contact Write Cybele Eidenschenk, Features Editor. In-person interview recommended. Applicants must submit a cover letter, resume, work and school references (letters not necessary, just phone numbers), 2-3 writing samples. Application deadline: March 1 for summer, October 1 for spring; continuous for year-round positions.

MIDDLE EAST RESEARCH AND INFORMATION PROJECT, INC. (MERIP)
1500 Massachusetts Avenue, NW, Suite 119
Washington, District of Columbia 20005

General Information Nonprofit organization seeking to educate the public about the contemporary Middle East in such areas as peace, human rights, and social justice; major program is the Middle East Report, a quarterly magazine that provides an independent look at the region and U.S. policy. Established in 1971. Number of employees: 4. Number of internship applications received each year: 80.
Internships Available ▶ *1 administrative intern:* responsibilities include assisting in the development and implementation of promotion and fund-raising strategies, expanding and maintaining the database, and coordinating mailings to donors. ▶ *1 editorial intern:* responsibilities include assisting the editorial staff in producing the Middle East Report; may include light research, proofreading, inputting copy, making corrections, and formatting articles for typesetting. Candidates should have background in journalism or publications. Open to college juniors, college seniors, recent college graduates, career changers, individuals reentering the workforce. ▶ *1 educational outreach intern:* responsibilities include organizing outreach program to teachers and students. ▶ *1 media outreach intern:* responsibilities include helping Media Outreach Director prepare material for journalists, maintaining database of media professionals, and assisting with conference preparations. Candidates should have prior experience with media. Duration for all positions is flexible. All positions are unpaid. International applications accepted.
Benefits Job counseling, names of contacts, opportunity to attend seminars/workshops, willing to act as a professional reference, willing to complete paperwork for educational credit, willing to provide letters of recommendation, opportunity to hear summer lunch speakers.
Contact Write or call Intern Coordinator. Phone: 202-223-3677. In-person interview recommended. Applicants must submit a cover letter, resume, writing sample. Application deadline: January 15 for summer. World Wide Web: http://www.merip.org.

MIDMARCH ARTS PRESS
300 Riverside Drive
New York, New York 10025

General Information Publisher of books and periodicals predominantly on women in the arts. Established in 1972. Number of employees: 4. Number of internship applications received each year: 160.
Internships Available ▶ *2 general interns:* responsibilities include writing, reading, handling correspondence, and assisting with publication of books. Candidates should have ability to work independently, computer skills, declared college major in field, editing skills, personal interest in the field, self-motivation, writing skills. Duration is 3 months or longer. Unpaid. Open to college sophomores, college juniors, college seniors, recent college graduates, graduate students. International applications accepted.
Benefits Names of contacts, on-the-job training, willing to act as a professional reference, willing to complete paperwork for educational credit, willing to provide letters of recommendation.
Contact Write Ms. C. Hulkower, Manager. No phone calls. In-person interview required. Applicants must submit a cover letter, resume. Applications are accepted continuously.

MILWAUKEE MAGAZINE
417 East Chicago Street
Milwaukee, Wisconsin 53202

General Information Magazine that entertains readers, keeps them informed on important regional issues and helps them get the most from their city. Established in 1979. Number of employees: 35. Subsidiary of Quad/Graphics Inc., Sussex, Wisconsin. Number of internship applications received each year: 25.
Internships Available ▶ *1–2 editorial interns:* responsibilities include researching special projects, reporting, and some writing. Candidates should have analytical skills, experience in the field, self-motivation, strong interpersonal skills, written communication skills, demonstrated interest in magazine journalism is highly recommended. Duration is 1 semester. Unpaid. Open to college sophomores, college juniors, college seniors, recent college graduates, career changers.
Benefits Names of contacts, on-the-job training, willing to act as a professional reference, willing to complete paperwork for educational credit, willing to provide letters of recommendation, possibility of part-time or freelance employment.
Contact Write or e-mail Mr. Stephen Filmanowicz, Senior Editor. E-mail: milmag@qgraph.com. No phone calls. In-person interview recommended. Applicants must submit a cover letter, resume, 3-5 writing samples. Application deadline: March 1 for summer.

MOMENT MAGAZINE
4710 41st Street, NW
Washington, District of Columbia 20016

General Information Independent Jewish bimonthly magazine that covers political, artistic, social, religious, and cultural issues affecting the Jewish world. Established in 1975. Number of employees: 20. Unit of Jewish Educational Ventures. Number of internship applications received each year: 40.
Internships Available ▶ *1–2 editorial assistants:* responsibilities include proofreading, writing, performing administrative tasks, researching, and fact checking. Candidates should have ability to work independently, ability to work with others, computer skills, office skills, oral communication skills, personal interest in the field, research skills, written communication skills. Duration is 3 months minimum (15-20 hours per week). Position available as unpaid or paid. Open to college sophomores, college juniors, college seniors, recent college graduates. International applications accepted.
Benefits Names of contacts, willing to complete paperwork for educational credit, willing to provide letters of recommendation.
Contact Write, call, fax, or e-mail Judy Horowitz, Internship Coordinator. Phone: 202-364-3300. Fax: 202-364-2636. E-mail: operations@bib-arch.org. In-person interview recommended. Applicants must submit a cover letter, resume. Applications are accepted continuously.

MOSBY, INC.
11830 Westline Industrial Drive
St. Louis, Missouri 63146

General Information Publisher of medical/health science textbooks, reference books, and journals and producer of videos, multimedia products, and seminars/conferences. Established in 1906. Number of employees: 1,600. Subsidiary of Harcourt Health Sciences, Chestnut Hill, Massachusetts. Number of internship applications received each year: 50.
Internships Available ▶ *Editorial interns:* responsibilities include reviewing manuscripts, phone surveying reviewers and synopsizing comments, obtaining copyright permissions, arranging for freelance photographers, and working for an editor responsible for developing a manuscript for a text or reference book in the health science field. ▶ *Marketing interns:* responsibilities include copywriting and/or editing. ▶ *Production interns:* responsibilities include dealing with print vendors, cost containment, quality control, and electronic product development. Duration for all

positions is flexible. All positions available as unpaid or paid. Open to college freshmen, college sophomores, college juniors, college seniors.
Benefits Possible full-time employment, willing to complete paperwork for educational credit.
Contact Write, fax, or e-mail Kelly Arnold, Recruiter. Fax: 314-432-0779. E-mail: kelly.arnold@mosby.com. No phone calls. In-person interview required. Applicants must submit a cover letter, resume. Applications are accepted continuously. World Wide Web: http://www.mosby.com.

MOTHER JONES MAGAZINE
731 Market Street, Suite 600
San Francisco, California 94103

General Information Magazine that specializes in investigative reporting and political analysis. Established in 1976. Number of employees: 25. Number of internship applications received each year: 500.
Internships Available ▶ *6–10 editorial interns:* responsibilities include fact checking and reporting support, research, and reporting assistance on investigative research projects. Candidates should have editing skills, research skills, writing skills. Duration is 4 months (minimum). $100 per month stipend; after 4 months, interns are reviewed for the Mother Jones fellowship which requires an additional 8-month commitment and pays a larger stipend. Open to recent college graduates, graduate students. International applications accepted.
Benefits Names of contacts, opportunity to attend seminars/workshops, willing to complete paperwork for educational credit, willing to provide letters of recommendation.
Contact Write, fax, or e-mail Internship Coordinator. Fax: 415-665-6696. E-mail: kratz@motherjones.com. No phone calls. In-person interview recommended. Applicants must submit a cover letter, resume, three writing samples, three personal references. Applications are accepted continuously. World Wide Web: http://www.motherjones.com.

NATIONAL BUSINESS SERVICES
1100 Wheeler Way
Langhorne, Pennsylvania 19047

General Information Trade publisher of information services (magazines, catalogs, and information directories) for the promotional products industry. Established in 1950. Number of employees: 450. Number of internship applications received each year: 50.
Internships Available ▶ *1 editorial intern:* responsibilities include assisting in research, phone interviews, writing, and survey analysis. Candidates should have editing skills, office skills, oral communication skills, personal interest in the field, self-motivation, written communication skills. ▶ *1 programming intern:* responsibilities include hardware and software support and involvement in CD-rom and World Wide Web product development. Candidates should have computer skills, oral communication skills, organizational skills, personal interest in the field, self-motivation, strong interpersonal skills. All positions paid at $8 per hour.
Benefits Possible full-time employment, willing to complete paperwork for educational credit, employment verification provided.
Contact Write or fax Intern Recruitment Director, Human Resources Department. Fax: 215-750-3686. No phone calls. In-person interview required. Applicants must submit a resume. Applications are accepted continuously. World Wide Web: http://users.aol.com/hrnbs.

NATIONAL JOURNAL
1501 M Street, NW
Washington, District of Columbia 20005

General Information Weekly magazine devoted to covering national politics and federal policy. Established in 1968. Number

of employees: 150. Unit of National Journal Group, Inc., Washington, District of Columbia. Number of internship applications received each year: 300.
Internships Available ▶ *3 editorial interns:* responsibilities include researching, reporting, and writing. Candidates should have oral communication skills, self-motivation, strong interpersonal skills, writing skills. Duration is 1–3 semesters. Position available as unpaid or at $275–$325 per week. Open to recent college graduates. International applications accepted.
Benefits Health insurance, willing to complete paperwork for educational credit, willing to provide letters of recommendation, access to library.
Contact Write or call Mr. Michael Wright, Executive Editor. Phone: 202-739-8434. Applicants must submit a cover letter, resume, six writing samples. Application deadline: March 1 for summer, July 1 for fall, October 1 for spring.

NATIONAL NEWS BUREAU
PO Box 43039
Philadelphia, Pennsylvania 19129

General Information Organization that handles the syndication of feature materials for newspapers, periodicals, and magazines. Established in 1979. Number of employees: 14. Number of internship applications received each year: 200.
Internships Available ▶ *4–8 interns:* responsibilities include interviewing and reviewing and writing travel stories. Candidates should have ability to work independently, self-motivation, strong interpersonal skills. Duration is 1 semester. dependent upon the intern's needs. Open to recent high school graduates, college freshmen, college sophomores, college juniors, college seniors, recent college graduates, graduate students, career changers. International applications accepted.
Benefits Formal training, free housing, health insurance, names of contacts, on-the-job training, opportunity to attend seminars/workshops, possible full-time employment, travel reimbursement, willing to complete paperwork for educational credit, willing to provide letters of recommendation.
International Internships Available.
Contact Write or e-mail Mr. Harry J. Katz, Publisher. E-mail: hjaykatz@aol.com. No phone calls. In-person interview required. Applicants must submit a cover letter, resume, copy of valid passport and/or driver's license. Applications are accepted continuously.

NEW MOON PUBLISHING
PO Box 3620
Duluth, Minnesota 55803-3620

General Information Magazine publishing. Established in 1992. Number of employees: 11. Number of internship applications received each year: 8.
Internships Available ▶ *1–3 editorial interns:* responsibilities include writing, researching, editing, and acquiring material; maintaining files; inputting submissions; researching and securing artwork; working with Girls Editorial Board; working with adult and girl contributors; contributing to planning and organizing of upcoming themes. Candidates should have ability to work independently, analytical skills, computer skills, editing skills, oral communication skills, organizational skills, personal interest in the field, research skills, self-motivation, strong interpersonal skills, strong leadership ability, writing skills, commitment to girls' and women's issues. Duration is flexible, at least 16 hours per week. Unpaid. Open to all. International applications accepted.
Benefits Names of contacts, willing to act as a professional reference, willing to complete paperwork for educational credit, willing to provide letters of recommendation.
Contact Write, call, or e-mail Bridget Grosser, Managing Editor. Phone: 218-725-5507. E-mail: bridgetg@newmoon.org. In-person interview recommended. Applicants must submit a cover letter, resume, three writing samples. Application deadline: March 1 for summer; continuous for fall, winter, and spring. World Wide Web: http://www.newmoon.org.

THE NEW REPUBLIC
1220 19th Street, NW, Suite 600
Washington, District of Columbia 20036

General Information Weekly journal of opinion. Established in 1914. Number of employees: 40. Number of internship applications received each year: 200.
Internships Available ▶ *3–5 reporters/researchers:* responsibilities include reading unsolicited manuscripts, proofreading, checking facts, handling editor's correspondence, periodic phone coverage, running errands, and writing short articles and editorials. Candidates should have ability to work independently, analytical skills, editing skills, office skills, oral communication skills, personal interest in the field, research skills, self-motivation, strong interpersonal skills, writing skills. Duration is 3–9 months. $300 per week. Open to college freshmen, college sophomores, college juniors, college seniors, recent college graduates, graduate students, law students. International applications accepted.
Benefits Job counseling, names of contacts, possible full-time employment, willing to act as a professional reference, willing to provide letters of recommendation, opportunity to attend lunches with prominent political figures.
Contact Write, fax, or e-mail Internship Coordinator. Fax: 202-331-0275. E-mail: admissions@tnr.com. No phone calls. Applicants must submit a cover letter, resume, two letters of recommendation, in-person or telephone interview for finalists, 3-5 writing samples. Application deadline: March 1. World Wide Web: http://www.thenewrepublic.com.

NEWSWEEK
251 West 57th Street
New York, New York 10019

General Information Major weekly news magazine. Established in 1933. Number of employees: 400. Unit of Washington Post Company.
Internships Available ▶ *10–12 editorial interns:* responsibilities include fact-checking, researching, reporting, and copy flow tasks. Candidates should have ability to work independently, ability to work with others, research skills, experience on school paper or other internships, writing and reporting skills. ▶ *2 photo interns.* ▶ *1 public relations intern:* responsibilities include writing press releases, fielding media calls, and updating biographies of press editors and correspondents. Duration for all positions is 13 weeks. All positions paid at $540 per week. Open to college juniors, college seniors, recent college graduates, graduate students. International applications accepted.
Benefits Possible full-time employment, opportunity to attend editorial meetings and luncheons with editors.
Contact Write Abigail Kuflik, Deputy Chief of Correspondents. Applicants must submit a cover letter, resume, names and phone numbers of 2 references, 5 published writing samples (editorial positions), 2 writing samples (public relations positions). Application deadline: January 7. World Wide Web: http://www.newsweek.com.

THE PARIS REVIEW
541 East 72nd Street
New York, New York 10021

General Information International literary quarterly that publishes fiction, poetry, interviews, art portfolios, and essays. Established in 1953. Number of employees: 8.
Internships Available ▶ *1–3 editorial assistants:* responsibilities include various editing and office duties. Duration is 3 months minimum. Unpaid. Open to college juniors, college seniors, recent college graduates, graduate students. International applications accepted.
Benefits Formal training, names of contacts, possible full-time employment, willing to complete paperwork for educational credit, willing to provide letters of recommendation.
Contact Write Stephen Clark, Associate Editor. No phone calls. In-person interview required. Applicants must submit a cover letter, resume. Applications are accepted continuously. World Wide Web: http://www.parisreview.com.

PASSEGGIATA PRESS
PO Box 636
Pueblo, Colorado 81002

General Information Specialist book publisher of non-Western creative literature and studies including criticism, literary history, biography, and bibliography. Established in 1973. Number of employees: 2. Number of internship applications received each year: 5.
Internships Available ▶ *1 editorial assistant:* responsibilities include performing clerical work, proofreading, answering phones, researching interests of and dealing with authors and visitors, compiling tables and graphs, editing, doing page proofs, writing blurb copy, and making flyers and mini-catalogues for special events. Candidates should have ability to work independently, ability to work with others, college courses in field, computer skills, editing skills, office skills, oral communication skills, personal interest in the field. Duration is 3–6 months. Unpaid. Open to college juniors, college seniors, recent college graduates. International applications accepted.
Benefits Formal training, job counseling, names of contacts, on-the-job training, possible full-time employment, willing to complete paperwork for educational credit, willing to provide letters of recommendation.
Contact Write, call, or fax Dr. Donald E. Herdeck, President,, or Leanna Hanks, Assoiciate Publisher. Phone: 719-544-1038. Fax: 719-546-7880. Telephone interview required. Applicants must submit a cover letter, resume. Applications are accepted continuously. World Wide Web: http://members.aol.com/Passeggia/passeggiata.htm.

PENGUIN PUTNAM, INC.
375 Hudson Street
New York, New York 10014

General Information Book publishing company of hardcover, paperback, and children's books. Established in 1838. Number of employees: 800. Number of internship applications received each year: 100.
Internships Available ▶ *1–2 art department interns:* responsibilities include paste and mechanical work, light design work, corrections, and packaging of originals; also some light clerical work involved in the day-to-day operations of the office. Candidates should have computer skills, office skills, oral communication skills, personal interest in the field, strong interpersonal skills. ▶ *4–6 editorial interns:* responsibilities include reading and evaluating unsolicited manuscripts, drafting and sending rejection letters, and research. Candidates should have editing skills, oral communication skills, personal interest in the field, self-motivation, strong interpersonal skills, writing skills. ▶ *3–5 publishing department interns:* responsibilities include working on various projects in departments such as subsidiary rights, contracts, and publicity. Candidates should have editing skills, office skills, oral communication skills, personal interest in the field, strong interpersonal skills, writing skills. Duration for all positions is 1 summer. All positions are unpaid. Open to college freshmen, college sophomores, college juniors, college seniors. International applications accepted.
Benefits Willing to complete paperwork for educational credit, $7 per day stipend.
Contact Write or e-mail Alison Conlon, Internship. E-mail: aconlon@penguinputnam.com. In-person interview required. Applicants must submit a cover letter, resume, proof that academic credit will be granted from home institution for internship (letter will suffice). Applications are accepted continuously. World Wide Web: http://www.penguinputnam.com.

PENOBSCOT BAY PRESS
PO Box 36
Stonington, Maine 04681

General Information Publisher of books, computer graphics, and 3 weekly newspapers. Established in 1964. Number of employees: 20. Number of internship applications received each year: 40.

Internships Available ▶ *1 advertising intern:* responsibilities include assisting with sales, research, filing, and design. Candidates should have ability to work independently, ability to work with others, oral communication skills, organizational skills, personal interest in the field, self-motivation. Position available as unpaid or at minimum wage or stipend. Open to high school seniors, recent high school graduates, college freshmen, college sophomores, college juniors, college seniors. ▶ *1 editorial intern:* responsibilities include writing, researching, filing, photographing, and performing production and clerical duties. Candidates should have ability to work independently, ability to work with others, personal interest in the field, self-motivation, writing skills. stipends are offered. Open to high school students, high school seniors, recent high school graduates, college freshmen, college sophomores, college juniors, college seniors. Duration for all positions is June to August. International applications accepted.
Benefits Names of contacts, on-the-job training, willing to act as a professional reference, willing to complete paperwork for educational credit, willing to provide letters of recommendation.
Contact Write Mr. Nat Barrows, Publisher. In-person interview recommended. Applicants must submit a cover letter, resume, portfolio, 6 writing samples. Applications are accepted continuously.

PHILADELPHIA MAGAZINE
1818 Market Street, 36th Floor
Philadelphia, Pennsylvania 19103

General Information City magazine covering local politics, news, and entertainment. Number of employees: 50. Unit of Metro Corporation, New York, New York. Number of internship applications received each year: 200.
Internships Available ▶ *4–5 art interns:* responsibilities include assisting designers, photographers, and stylists. Candidates should have ability to work independently, knowledge of field. Open to college freshmen, college sophomores, college juniors, college seniors, recent college graduates. ▶ *6–7 editorial interns:* responsibilities include assisting writers with research, functioning as a general editorial assistant, fact checking, reporting, and writing brief articles. Candidates should have ability to work independently, oral communication skills, organizational skills, research skills, strong interpersonal skills. Open to college freshmen, college sophomores, college juniors, college seniors, recent college graduates, graduate students, career changers. Duration for all positions is 1 semester or summer. All positions are unpaid. International applications accepted.
Benefits Job counseling, names of contacts, possible full-time employment, willing to act as a professional reference, willing to complete paperwork for educational credit, willing to provide letters of recommendation.
Contact Write or e-mail Richard Rys, Research Editor, 1818 Market Street, 36th Floor, Phildadelphia, Pennsylvania 19103. E-mail: rrys@phillymag.com. No phone calls. In-person interview recommended. Applicants must submit a cover letter, resume, 3-5 writing samples (preferably published). Application deadline: March 1 for summer, August 15 for fall, December 1 for spring. World Wide Web: http://www.phillymag.com.

PHILLIPS PUBLISHING INTERNATIONAL, INC.
7811 Montrose Road
Potomac, Maryland 20854

General Information A diverse publisher of newsletters, magazines, Web sites, and directories serving both the business-to-business and consumer markets. Established in 1974. Number of employees: 1,000. Number of internship applications received each year: 100.
Internships Available ▶ *Interns:* responsibilities include assisting in the editorial, marketing, or various other departments; gaining exposure to the publishing industry. Position available as unpaid or paid. Open to high school students, high school seniors, recent high school graduates, college freshmen, college sophomores, college juniors, college seniors, recent college graduates, graduate students.

Benefits On-the-job training, possible full-time employment, willing to act as a professional reference, willing to complete paperwork for educational credit, willing to provide letters of recommendation.
Contact Write, call, fax, or e-mail Debbie Cohen, Human Resources Manager. Phone: 301-340-2100 Ext. 6180. Fax: 301-424-0245. E-mail: dcohen@phillips.com. In-person interview recommended. Applicants must submit a cover letter, resume. Applications are accepted continuously. World Wide Web: http://www.phillips.com.

PRIMEDIA SPECIAL INTEREST PUBLICATIONS
6405 Flank Drive
Harrisburg, Pennsylvania 17112

General Information Publisher of over 50 special interest consumer magazines and related books and products. Topics include history, collectibles, healthy lifestyles, and outdoor/recreation skills. Established in 1986. Number of employees: 120. Division of PRIMEDIA, Inc., New York, New York. Number of internship applications received each year: 25.
Internships Available ▶ *1 marketing communications intern:* responsibilities include writing promotion copy, assisting with design and print production of promotion pieces, researching projects, assisting with mailings and routine promotion tasks, proofreading, assisting with special event planning, and working with other media, including video, audio, and slides. Candidates should have ability to work independently, ability to work with others, college courses in field, computer skills, office skills, writing skills. Duration is 1 semester. $500 per duration of internship. Open to college freshmen, college sophomores, college juniors, college seniors, recent college graduates, graduate students. International applications accepted.
Benefits On-the-job training, possible full-time employment, willing to complete paperwork for educational credit.
Contact Write, fax, or e-mail Ms. Beth A. Feltenberger, Marketing Communications Manager. Fax: 717-540-6706. E-mail: bethf@cowles.com. No phone calls. In-person interview recommended. Applicants must submit a cover letter, resume, three writing samples, portfolio (if available). Applications are accepted continuously. World Wide Web: http://www.cowles.com.

RANDOM HOUSE, INC.
201 East 50th Street- Mail Drop 15-2
New York, New York 10022

General Information General trade book publisher. Established in 1925. Number of internship applications received each year: 1,000.
Internships Available ▶ *7 summer interns:* responsibilities include working in one of the five major publishing groups. Candidates should have editing skills, knowledge of field, oral communication skills, plan to pursue career in field, written communication skills. Duration is 10 weeks. $300 per week. Open to college juniors.
Benefits Job counseling, possible full-time employment.
Contact Write Internship Coordinator, Human Resources, 201 East 50th Street—Mail Drop 15-2, New York, New York 10022. No phone calls. In-person interview required. Applicants must submit a cover letter, resume. Application deadline: March 31 for summer. World Wide Web: http://www.randomhouse.com.

THE READER'S DIGEST ASSOCIATION
Reader's Digest Road
Pleasantville, New York 10570

General Information Publisher and direct mail marketer. Established in 1922. Number of employees: 1,500. Number of internship applications received each year: 50.
Internships Available ▶ *1 Select Editions editorial intern:* responsibilities include providing support to the Select Editions editorial staff, reading prospective books, providing synopsis, and general editorial support work. Candidates should have ability to work independently, ability to work with others, computer skills, organizational skills, plan to pursue career in field, written com-

The Reader's Digest Association (continued)

munication skills. Duration is 8–10 weeks. ▶ *2–4 accounting interns:* responsibilities include providing accounting and financial support to a variety of areas. Candidates should have analytical skills, college courses in field, computer skills, plan to pursue career in field, self-motivation, strong interpersonal skills. Duration is 10–12 weeks. ▶ *Programmers:* responsibilities include providing systems support to a variety of technical departments. Candidates should have college courses in field, computer skills, plan to pursue career in field, self-motivation, strong interpersonal skills. All positions paid at $450–$475 per week. Open to college sophomores, college juniors.
Benefits Possible full-time employment.
Contact Write Susan Hynson, Recruitment Manager, Reader's Digest Road, Pleasantville, New York 10570. No phone calls. In-person interview required. Applicants must submit a cover letter, resume. Applications are accepted continuously. World Wide Web: http://www.readersdigest.com.

RESOURCE PUBLICATIONS, INC.
160 East Virginia Street, Suite 290
San Jose, California 95112-5876

General Information Communications firm dealing in resources for ministry, education, and personal growth. Established in 1973. Number of employees: 29. Number of internship applications received each year: 100.
Internships Available ▶ *1 accounting intern:* responsibilities include assisting with operations analysis and development of management reports for special projects. Candidates should have ability to work with others, computer skills, office skills, organizational skills, research skills, written communication skills. Duration is 10–12 weeks. Unpaid. Open to college juniors, college seniors, recent college graduates. ▶ *1 advertising intern:* responsibilities include developing all aspects of special projects in display advertising sales and marketing. Candidates should have ability to work independently, oral communication skills, organizational skills, strong interpersonal skills, written communication skills. Duration is 10 weeks. commission. ▶ *1 design intern:* responsibilities include designing book covers and layouts for brochures and advertisements. Candidates should have ability to work independently, ability to work with others, college courses in field, computer skills, knowledge of field, written communication skills. Duration is 10–12 weeks. $500 per duration of internship. Open to college juniors, college seniors. ▶ *1 editorial intern:* responsibilities include performing copy editing and product packaging/production projects. Candidates should have computer skills, editing skills, organizational skills, research skills, written communication skills. Duration is 10–12 weeks. Position available as unpaid or paid. Open to high school students. ▶ *1 marketing intern:* responsibilities include conducting market research, developing literature, and planning and executing promotional efforts. Candidates should have oral communication skills, organizational skills, plan to pursue career in field, written communication skills. Duration is 10–12 weeks. Unpaid. Open to high school students, college juniors, college seniors, recent college graduates, graduate students, individuals reentering the workforce. ▶ *1 sales intern:* responsibilities include planning and executing sales campaigns via telephone, exhibits, formal sales conferences, and related activities. Candidates should have experience in the field, knowledge of field, oral communication skills, organizational skills, strong interpersonal skills, written communication skills. Duration is 10–12 weeks. Position available as unpaid or at $8–$10 per hour. Open to college juniors, college seniors, recent college graduates, graduate students, career changers, individuals reentering the workforce.
Benefits On-the-job training, possible full-time employment, willing to act as a professional reference, willing to complete paperwork for educational credit, willing to provide letters of recommendation, commissions on sales.
Contact Write, fax, or e-mail Mr. William Burns, Publisher. Fax: 408-287-8748. E-mail: info@rpinet.com. No phone calls. In-person interview required. Applicants must submit a cover letter, resume. Applications are accepted continuously. World Wide Web: http://www.rpinet.com/.

RODALE PRESS, INC.
33 East Minor Street
Emmaus, Pennsylvania 18098

General Information Publisher of books and magazines focused on healthy, active living. Established in 1930. Number of employees: 1,150. Number of internship applications received each year: 500.
Internships Available ▶ *40–50 interns:* responsibilities include writing, editing, research, marketing, statistics, and public relations. Candidates should have computer skills, organizational skills, personal interest in the field, strong interpersonal skills, writing skills. Duration is 11 weeks. $425–$600 per week. Open to college sophomores, college juniors, recent college graduates, graduate students.
Benefits Formal training, job counseling, meals at a cost, names of contacts, on-the-job training, opportunity to attend seminars/workshops, possible full-time employment, willing to act as a professional reference, willing to complete paperwork for educational credit, willing to provide letters of recommendation.
Contact Write, fax, or e-mail Megan Bower, Human Resources Associate, 33 East Minor Street, Emmaus, Pennsylvania 18098. Fax: 610-967-9209. E-mail: mbower1@rodalepress.com. In-person interview recommended. Applicants must submit a cover letter, resume, three writing samples, portfolio if applicable. Application deadline: February 28 for summer; continuous for all other positions. World Wide Web: http://www.rodalepress.com.

ROOTS MAGAZINE
2625 Alcatraz Avenue #174
Berkley, California 84705

General Information People entertainment magazine. Number of employees: 8. Number of internship applications received each year: 20.
Internships Available ▶ *Interns:* responsibilities include assisting in various departments of the magazine such as writing, editing, photojournalism, graphics/typesetting, and advertising/marketing. Candidates should have ability to work independently, computer skills, editing skills, experience in the field, knowledge of field, oral communication skills, personal interest in the field, plan to pursue career in field, strong interpersonal skills, writing skills. Duration is open. Unpaid. Open to recent high school graduates, college freshmen, college sophomores, college juniors, college seniors.
Contact Write, call, fax, or e-mail Mahogany/PEP, Office Manager, 2625 Alcatraz Avenue, #174, Berkeley, California 94705. Phone: 510-549-52655. Fax: 510-841-7950. E-mail: rootsmag2@aol.com. Applications are accepted continuously. World Wide Web: http://www.rootspub.com.

RUNNING PRESS
125 South 22nd Street
Philadelphia, Pennsylvania 19103

General Information General book publisher mainly of nonfiction, children's titles, art books, and literature. Established in 1972. Number of employees: 70. Number of internship applications received each year: 30.
Internships Available ▶ *1–2 acquisitions interns:* responsibilities include communicating with authors and agents, assisting with requests for reprints, pulling information from contracts, and inputting data into a database. Candidates should have ability to work with others, office skills, personal interest in the field, self-motivation, writing skills. Open to college freshmen, college sophomores, college juniors, college seniors, recent college graduates, graduate students, law students. ▶ *1–2 assistants to Associate Publisher:* responsibilities include working with the Associate Publisher as well as with the editorial, sales, production, legal and publicity departments. Candidates should have computer skills, personal interest in the field, research skills, strong interpersonal skills, writing skills. Duration is flexible. Open to college freshmen, college sophomores, college juniors, college seniors, recent college graduates. ▶ *2 design interns:* responsibilities include developing design concepts, scanning

artwork, doing layout and design for book pages, and researching illustrator/photographer candidates. Candidates should have college courses in field, computer skills, oral communication skills, personal interest in the field, self-motivation, knowledge of Quark Xpress and Photoshop. Duration is flexible. Open to college sophomores, college juniors, college seniors. ▶ *3–4 editorial interns:* responsibilities include assisting with general editorial work. Candidates should have computer skills, editing skills, oral communication skills, personal interest in the field, research skills, writing skills. Duration is 12 weeks. Open to college sophomores, college juniors, college seniors, recent college graduates. ▶ *1 production intern:* responsibilities include assisting in daily administrative duties in the production department including some communication with vendors; distribution and/or trafficking materials; coordinating bound galleys; some data entry on computer. Candidates should have ability to work with others, computer skills, office skills, organizational skills, personal interest in the field, writing skills. Duration is 3–4 months. Open to college sophomores, college juniors, college seniors, recent college graduates, graduate students, law students. ▶ *2–3 publicity interns:* responsibilities include providing support to Publicity Director, Publicist and Publicity Assistant; handling publicity campaign for assigned title(s):- drafting pitch letter, press release, organizing mailing, making follow-up calls to media to pitch title(s), and clipping and filing reviews. Candidates should have computer skills, oral communication skills, personal interest in the field, self-motivation, strong interpersonal skills, written communication skills. Duration is 12 weeks. Open to college sophomores, college juniors, college seniors, recent college graduates, graduate students. ▶ *1–2 special sales interns:* responsibilities include assisting with day-to-day operations of the special sales department including order taking, customer service, and computer work. Candidates should have computer skills, oral communication skills, personal interest in the field, self-motivation, writing skills. Duration is 12 weeks. Open to college sophomores, college juniors, college seniors, recent college graduates, graduate students. All positions are unpaid.
Benefits Willing to complete paperwork for educational credit, willing to provide letters of recommendation, hands-on experience.
Contact Write or fax Internship Coordinator. Fax: 215-568-2919. In-person interview required. Applicants must submit a cover letter, resume, writing sample. Application deadline: April 1 for summer (May—August), August 1 for fall (September—December), December 1 for winter/spring (January—April). World Wide Web: http://www.runningpress.com.

SAN DIEGO COMMUNITY NEWSPAPER GROUP
4645 Cass Street
San Diego, California 92169

General Information Publisher of four community newspapers and assorted specialty publications. Established in 1988. Number of employees: 50. Division of Mannis Communications, Inc., San Diego, California. Number of internship applications received each year: 50.
Internships Available ▶ *Editorial interns:* responsibilities include researching and compiling information for editorials and articles, putting together calendars and obituaries, and occasionally gathering editorial information for the senior editor. Candidates should have ability to work independently, ability to work with others, computer skills, office skills, oral communication skills, written communication skills, knowledge of Associated Press style guidelines. Duration is 9–12 weeks. Unpaid. Open to college freshmen, college sophomores, college juniors, college seniors, recent college graduates, career changers, individuals reentering the workforce. International applications accepted.
Benefits Names of contacts, on-the-job training, possible full-time employment, willing to act as a professional reference, willing to complete paperwork for educational credit, willing to provide letters of recommendation.
Contact Write, fax, or e-mail Kristen Collier, Senior Editor, PO Box 9550, San Diego, California 92169. Fax: 619-271-9325. E-mail: sdnews@san.rr.com. No phone calls. In-person interview recommended. Applicants must submit a formal organization application, cover letter, resume, 1-3 writing samples, 1-3 personal

references, and a letter of recommendation (optional). Applications are accepted continuously. World Wide Web: http://www.sdnews.com.

THE SAN DIEGO UNION-TRIBUNE
350 Camino de la Reina
San Diego, California 92108

General Information Publishing and information services. Number of employees: 1,000. Unit of Copley Newspapers, Inc., La Jolla, California. Number of internship applications received each year: 250.
Internships Available ▶ *Interns:* responsibilities include working as professional reporter, photographer, page designer, and copy editor. Candidates should have experience in the field, plan to pursue career in field, research skills, self-motivation, writing skills, fluency in a second language that is spoken in San Diego. Duration is 10–12 weeks. Position available as unpaid or at $460 per week for 2 summer interns; academic interns throughout the year are unpaid. Open to college juniors, college seniors, recent college graduates, graduate students. International applications accepted.
Benefits On-the-job training, opportunity to attend seminars/workshops, willing to complete paperwork for educational credit.
Contact Write, call, or e-mail Carol Goodhue, Training and Development Coordinator, PO Box 120191, San Diego, California 92112-0191. Phone: 619-293-1261. E-mail: carol.goodhue@uniontrib.com. Telephone interview required. Applicants must submit a cover letter, resume, 6 writing samples. Application deadline: November 15 for summer; continuous for unpaid academic interns during the school year. World Wide Web: http://www.uniontrib.com.

SCHNEIDER PUBLISHING
13274 Fiji Way, Suite 116
Marina del Rey, California 90292

General Information Magazine publisher. Established in 1988. Number of employees: 9. Number of internship applications received each year: 50.
Internships Available ▶ *1–3 office assistants:* responsibilities include flexible duties depending on the intern's interest and experience; general assistance with office tasks. Candidates should have ability to work independently, analytical skills, editing skills, office skills, oral communication skills, organizational skills, personal interest in the field, research skills, self-motivation, strong interpersonal skills, writing skills, experience with computers (desirable). Duration is flexible. Position available as unpaid or at $6 per hour. Open to high school seniors, recent high school graduates, college freshmen, college sophomores, college juniors, college seniors, recent college graduates, graduate students. International applications accepted.
Benefits On-the-job training, possible full-time employment, willing to act as a professional reference, willing to complete paperwork for educational credit, willing to provide letters of recommendation, small stipend.
Contact Fax or e-mail Ann Shepphird, Managing Editor, 13274 Fiji Way, Suite 416, Marina del Rey, California 90292. Fax: 310-577-3715. E-mail: ann@schneiderpublishing.com. No phone calls. In-person interview recommended. Applicants must submit a cover letter, resume. Applications are accepted continuously.

SCIENCE NEWS MAGAZINE
1719 N Street, NW
Washington, District of Columbia 20036

General Information Weekly newsmagazine covering science. Established in 1922. Number of employees: 20. Unit of Science Service, Inc., Washington, District of Columbia. Number of internship applications received each year: 80.
Internships Available ▶ *3 science writer interns:* responsibilities include researching and writing short news stories and longer features for weekly magazine. Candidates should have ability to work independently, plan to pursue career in field, research skills, self-motivation, writing skills. Duration is 3 months. $1,650

Science News Magazine (continued)

per month. Open to college seniors, recent college graduates, graduate students, career changers. International applications accepted.
Benefits Job counseling, names of contacts, on-the-job training, willing to act as a professional reference, willing to complete paperwork for educational credit, willing to provide letters of recommendation, opportunity to write/publish stories.
Contact E-mail Internship Coordinator. E-mail: scinews@sciserv.org. Applicants must submit a cover letter, resume, at least 3 examples of journalistic writing. Application deadline: February 1 for summer, June 15 for fall, October 15 for spring. World Wide Web: http://www.sciencenews.org.

SEVENTEEN MAGAZINE
850 Third Avenue, 9th Floor
New York, New York 10022

General Information Publisher of magazine. Established in 1944. Number of employees: 50. Unit of PRIMEDIA Magazines, New York, New York. Number of internship applications received each year: 500.
Internships Available ▶ *2–4 academic year interns:* responsibilities include assisting in various departments. Candidates should have ability to work independently, office skills, oral communication skills, research skills, self-motivation, written communication skills. Duration is 1 semester. Unpaid. Open to high school students, high school seniors, college freshmen, college sophomores, college juniors, college seniors, graduate students. ▶ *2–4 summer fashion/style interns:* responsibilities include assisting fashion, market, model editors and stylists; calling manufacturers; typing purchase orders and "merch" sheets; packing and unpacking merchandise; maintaining order in closets; and helping out during fashion presentations and model fittings. Candidates should have ability to work independently, ability to work with others, office skills, organizational skills, personal interest in the field, self-motivation. Duration is 1 semester. Position available as unpaid or at $250 per week. Open to high school students, high school seniors, recent high school graduates, college freshmen, college sophomores, college juniors, college seniors, recent college graduates. ▶ *5–10 summer journalism interns:* responsibilities include working within the features department assisting editors in researching, fact-checking, and writing articles; reviewing submissions and clips for story ideas. Candidates should have office skills, oral communication skills, research skills, self-motivation, strong interpersonal skills, written communication skills. Duration is June to August. Position available as unpaid or at $250 per week. Open to high school students, high school seniors, recent high school graduates, college freshmen, college sophomores, college juniors, college seniors, recent college graduates. International applications accepted.
Benefits Willing to complete paperwork for educational credit.
Contact Write or fax Micheline Wolf, Internship Coordinator, 850 Third Avenue, 9th Floor, New York, New York 10022. Fax: 212-407-9899. No phone calls. Applicants must submit a cover letter, resume. Application deadline: March 15 for summer, July 1 for fall, October 15 for spring.

SMITHSONIAN INSTITUTION PRESS
470 L'Enfant Plaza, Suite 7100
Washington, District of Columbia 20560-0950

General Information Publishing arm of the Smithsonian Institution that annually produces 300 publications relating to Smithsonian collections and research interests. Established in 1846. Number of employees: 38. Unit of Smithsonian Institution, Washington, District of Columbia. Number of internship applications received each year: 20.
Internships Available ▶ *1–2 Smithsonian contributions and studies series interns:* responsibilities include proofing, editing, and coding files for upload to Web site, as well as proofing and editing of manuscripts in progress. Candidates should have college courses in field, computer skills, editing skills, knowledge of field, self-motivation, written communication skills. Open to college sophomores, college juniors, college seniors, recent college

graduates, graduate students. ▶ *1–2 acquisitions interns:* responsibilities include working on development of books on scholarly subjects for adults, researching the locations of outstanding photographs and illustrations for manuscripts, assisting with the correlation and preparation for publication of book projects. Candidates should have computer skills, office skills, personal interest in the field, research skills, strong interpersonal skills, written communication skills. Open to college sophomores, college juniors, college seniors, recent college graduates. ▶ *1–2 marketing interns:* responsibilities include assisting marketing staff with preparing print advertisements, flyers, and brochures for direct mail, publicity kits, sales kits, and jacket copy; sending books out for review by media and course adoption. Candidates should have ability to work with others, computer skills, office skills, oral communication skills, writing skills. Open to college sophomores, college juniors, college seniors, recent college graduates. Duration for all positions is 8–12 weeks. All positions are unpaid. International applications accepted.
Benefits Job counseling, names of contacts, opportunity to attend seminars/workshops, possible full-time employment, willing to complete paperwork for educational credit, willing to provide letters of recommendation, one-on-one professional mentor-student involvement.
Contact Write or e-mail Ms. Anne Garvey, Internship Coordinator. E-mail: agarvey@sipress.si.edu. In-person interview recommended. Applicants must submit a formal organization application, resume, academic transcripts, two letters of recommendation, personal essay. Application deadline: April 1 for summer, July 1 for fall, October 1 for spring. World Wide Web: http://www.si.edu/.

SOUTHERN PROGRESS CORPORATION
PO Box 2581
Birmingham, Alabama 35202

General Information Magazine and book publisher that specializes in lifestyle publications. Established in 1886. Number of employees: 1,200. Subsidary of Time Warner, Inc., New York, New York. Number of internship applications received each year: 300.
Internships Available ▶ *1–2 accounting interns:* responsibilities include general accounting functions. Candidates should have analytical skills, computer skills, declared college major in field, knowledge of field, organizational skills. Duration is 3–5 months. ▶ *4–6 advertising interns:* responsibilities include writing ad copy, selecting promotional items, assisting sales team with sales calls. Candidates should have ability to work independently, ability to work with others, college courses in field, organizational skills, personal interest in the field, written communication skills. Duration is 3–5 months. ▶ *9–12 editorial interns:* responsibilities include writing, proofreading, editing, and research. Candidates should have ability to work with others, editing skills, experience in the field, personal interest in the field, research skills, writing skills. Duration is 3–5 months. ▶ *1–2 graphic design interns:* responsibilities include designing promotional material for advertising department. Candidates should have ability to work independently, computer skills, declared college major in field, knowledge of field, organizational skills. Duration is 3–5 months. ▶ *1 information systems intern:* responsibilities include working on help desk, computer programming. Candidates should have ability to work with others, analytical skills, college courses in field, computer skills, knowledge of field, strong interpersonal skills. Duration is 3–5 months. ▶ *2–4 marketing interns:* responsibilities include maintaining vendor performance records, report tracking, and special research projects. Candidates should have analytical skills, computer skills, knowledge of field, organizational skills, personal interest in the field, research skills. Duration is 3–5 months. ▶ *1–2 test kitchens interns:* responsibilities include preparing recipes for taste testing and photography. Candidates should have ability to work independently, ability to work with others, knowledge of field, culinary arts degree preferred. Duration is 8–10 weeks. All positions paid at $8 per hour. Open to college juniors, college seniors, recent college graduates, graduate students.
Benefits Job counseling, names of contacts, on-the-job training, opportunity to attend seminars/workshops, possible full-

time employment, willing to complete paperwork for educational credit, willing to provide letters of recommendation, reimbursement of work-related travel expenses.
Contact Write Ms. Dru Harris, Human Resources Assistant. In-person interview required. Applicants must submit a cover letter, resume, letter of recommendation, 3-5 writing samples. Application deadline: March 1 for summer, October 1 for winter/spring.

TIKKUN MAGAZINE
26 Fell Street
San Francisco, California 94102

General Information Bimonthly Jewish critique of politics, culture, and society; influence is not limited to the Jewish population. Established in 1986. Number of employees: 5. Unit of Institute for Labor and Mental Health. Number of internship applications received each year: 30.
Internships Available ▶ *3–6 editorial, production, and publishing interns:* responsibilities include reading unsolicited manuscripts; writing evaluations and rejection letters; handling author correspondence; proofreading galleys; performing independent research projects; assisting with production of magazine; soliciting advertising; organizing outside conferences, lectures, seminars, and teach-ins; and assisting in office administration. Candidates should have oral communication skills, personal interest in the field, self-motivation, written communication skills. Duration is flexible; prefer a commitment of at least three months. Unpaid. Open to college freshmen, college sophomores, college juniors, college seniors, recent college graduates, graduate students, law students, career changers, individuals reentering the workforce. International applications accepted.
Benefits Job counseling, names of contacts, possible full-time employment, willing to complete paperwork for educational credit, willing to provide letters of recommendation, free books, free admission to local cultural events including films, lectures, and readings.
Contact Write, call, or e-mail Jo Ellen Green Kaiser, Managing Editor. Phone: 415-575-1200. E-mail: magazine@tikkun.org. In-person interview recommended. Applicants must submit a cover letter, resume. Applications are accepted continuously. World Wide Web: http://www.tikkun.org.

WASHINGTONIAN MAGAZINE
1828 L Street, NW, Suite 200
Washington, District of Columbia 20036

General Information General interest magazine that focuses on the people and issues of Washington, DC. Established in 1965. Number of employees: 60. Number of internship applications received each year: 250.
Internships Available ▶ *1–3 advertising/account executive interns:* responsibilities include phone sales and updating and researching ad files. Candidates should have ability to work independently, computer skills, oral communication skills, personal interest in the field, self-motivation, strong interpersonal skills. Duration is 3–5 months. approximately $5 per hour. Open to college freshmen, college sophomores, college juniors, college seniors. ▶ *1 art intern:* responsibilities include assisting with production, and in-house design assignments using photoshop and Quark Xpress. Candidates should have college courses in field, computer skills, oral communication skills, personal interest in the field, strong interpersonal skills. Duration is 2–3 months. Unpaid. Open to college freshmen, college sophomores, college juniors, college seniors, graduate students. ▶ *2–3 editorial assistants/interns:* responsibilities include fact checking, research, and writing. Candidates should have personal interest in the field, research skills, written communication skills. Duration is 3–9 months. $6 per hour. Open to college juniors, college seniors, recent college graduates, graduate students. International applications accepted.
Benefits Names of contacts, opportunity to attend seminars/workshops, willing to act as a professional reference, willing to complete paperwork for educational credit, willing to provide letters of recommendation.

Contact Write or e-mail Ms. Alicia Abell, Staff Editor. E-mail: aabell@washingtonian.com. No phone calls. In-person interview recommended. Applicants must submit a cover letter, resume, three writing samples. Application deadline: February 15 for summer, July 15 for 9-month editorial assistants. World Wide Web: http://www.washingtonian.com.

WELT PUBLISHING COMPANY
1413 K Street, NW, Suite 1400
Washington, District of Columbia 20005

General Information Business comprised of several regional newsletters that focus on financial, economic, political, and technical developments throughout the world. Established in 1972. Number of employees: 2. Number of internship applications received each year: 50.
Internships Available ▶ *1 research associate–Africa:* responsibilities include attending press conferences, developing stories, researching, writing, and promotional and general office work. Candidates should have writing skills, background in African studies. ▶ *1 research associate–CIS/Eastern Europe:* responsibilities include attending press conferences, developing stories, researching, writing, and promotional and general office work. Candidates should have writing skills, background in Soviet studies. ▶ *1 research associate–China:* responsibilities include attending press conferences, developing stories, researching, writing, and promotional and general office work. Candidates should have writing skills. ▶ *1 research associate–Latin America:* responsibilities include attending press conferences, developing stories, researching, writing, and promotional and general office work. Candidates should have writing skills, background in Latin American studies. ▶ *1–3 research associates:* responsibilities include attending press conferences, developing stories, researching, writing, and promotional and general office work. Candidates should have writing skills. Duration for all positions is flexible. All positions are unpaid. Open to college seniors, recent college graduates.
Benefits Willing to complete paperwork for educational credit.
Contact Write or call Mr. Leo Welt, Publisher. Phone: 202-371-0555. In-person interview recommended. Applications are accepted continuously.

WILSON QUARTERLY
1 Woodrow Wilson Plaza, 1300 Pennsylvania Avenue, NW
Washington, District of Columbia 20523

General Information General interest quarterly magazine focusing on humanities-related topics and providing a comprehensive survey of the latest scholarly research in a broad range of subject areas. Established in 1976. Number of employees: 7. Subsidiary of Woodrow Wilson International Center for Scholars, Washington, District of Columbia. Number of internship applications received each year: 200.
Internships Available ▶ *3 editorial interns:* responsibilities include fact checking, background and art research, phone work, and some basic office duties, including delivering packages and photocopying. Candidates should have ability to work independently, office skills, oral communication skills, organizational skills, research skills, written communication skills. Duration is 4 months. $400–$800 per month. Open to college freshmen, college sophomores, college juniors, college seniors, recent college graduates. International applications accepted.
Benefits Job counseling, names of contacts, willing to complete paperwork for educational credit, willing to provide letters of recommendation, reimbursement of expenses related to editorial research.
Contact Write, call, or e-mail Mr. James Carman, Managing Editor. Phone: 202-691-4200. E-mail: wq@wwic.si.edu. Applicants must submit a cover letter, resume, three personal references. Application deadline: March 15 for summer, July 15 for fall, October 15 for spring. World Wide Web: http://wwics.si.edu/wq.

RADIO BROADCASTING

KEUN/KJJB RADIO
330 West Laurel Avenue
Eunice, Louisiana 70535

General Information Radio and cable television programming. Established in 1952. Number of employees: 8. Number of internship applications received each year: 5.

Internships Available ▶ *2 interns:* responsibilities include camera work, radio work, and public relations. Candidates should have ability to work independently, computer skills, plan to pursue career in field, self-motivation, writing skills. Duration is 3–12 months. Open to high school seniors, recent high school graduates, college freshmen, college sophomores, college juniors, college seniors, recent college graduates, graduate students, individuals reentering the workforce. ▶ *1–2 news interns:* responsibilities include learning news gathering, writing, reporting, and production. Candidates should have ability to work independently, ability to work with others, personal interest in the field, self-motivation, writing skills. Duration is 3-6 months. Open to high school seniors, recent high school graduates, college juniors, college seniors, recent college graduates, career changers, individuals reentering the workforce. All positions are unpaid. International applications accepted.

Benefits Job counseling, names of contacts, opportunity to attend seminars/workshops, possible full-time employment, willing to complete paperwork for educational credit, willing to provide letters of recommendation.

Contact Write or fax Mr. Karl Rene De Rouen, President and General Manager, PO Box 1049, 330 West Laurel Avenue, Eunice, Louisiana 70535. Fax: 318-457-3081. Applicants must submit a formal organization application, resume. Applications are accepted continuously.

KJNP AM-FM RADIO-TV
2501 Mission Road, PO Box 56359
North Pole, Alaska 99705-1359

General Information Christian radio and television station spreading the gospel of Jesus Christ throughout Alaska and the Northern Hemisphere. Established in 1967. Number of employees: 21. Unit of Evangelistic Missionary Fellowship, Lakewood, Colorado. Number of internship applications received each year: 4.

Internships Available ▶ *1 TV technician:* responsibilities include taking meter readings on transmitter; airing prerecorded programs (entails cueing and rewinding tapes before airing) directly off the satellite, commercials, public service announcements, and interlude tapes between programs; maintaining TV log; and monitoring all equipment in control room during air time. Candidates should have ability to work independently, ability to work with others, self-motivation. Duration is 3 months minimum. Open to recent high school graduates, college freshmen, college sophomores, college juniors, college seniors, recent college graduates, graduate students, law students, career changers, individuals reentering the workforce. ▶ *1 camera operator:* responsibilities include operating cameras for live public service format program, preparing set to go on the air, escorting guests to the set, and helping out in other areas of the station. Candidates should have ability to work with others. Duration is flexible. Open to high school students, high school seniors, recent high school graduates, college freshmen, college sophomores, college juniors, college seniors, recent college graduates, graduate students, law students, career changers, individuals reentering the workforce. ▶ *Engineering interns:* responsibilities include maintaining electronic equipment and calibrating transmitters. Candidates should have ability to work independently, ability to work with others, self-motivation. Duration is flexible. Open to recent high school graduates, college freshmen, college sophomores, college juniors, college seniors, recent college graduates, graduate students, law students, career changers, individuals reentering the workforce. ▶ *Maintenance interns:* responsibilities include maintaining grounds and buildings, cutting wood, removing snow in winter, and some carpentry work. Candidates should have ability to work independently, ability to work with others. Duration is flexible. Open to high school students, high school seniors, recent high school graduates, college freshmen, college sophomores, college juniors, college seniors, recent college graduates, graduate students, law students, career changers, individuals reentering the workforce. ▶ *1 radio technician:* responsibilities include making sure stations are on the air, following and keeping logs for both the AM and FM stations, answering the lobby telephone, and helping out in other areas of the station. Candidates should have ability to work with others, oral communication skills. Duration is 1 year. Open to high school seniors, recent high school graduates, college freshmen, college sophomores, college juniors, college seniors, recent college graduates, graduate students, law students, career changers, individuals reentering the workforce. ▶ *1 receptionist intern:* responsibilities include answering 5 incoming telephone lines and intercom calls, greeting guests and tourists, directing calls to proper departments, monitoring AM/FM/TV, answering 2-way system, keeping coffee and hot water supplied, keeping lobby area clean, typing Trapline Chatter messages that are aired over radio, and performing office work. Candidates should have ability to work with others, oral communication skills, self-motivation, written communication skills. Duration is flexible. Open to recent high school graduates, college freshmen, college sophomores, college juniors, college seniors, recent college graduates, graduate students, law students, career changers, individuals reentering the workforce. All positions are unpaid. International applications accepted.

Benefits Free housing, on-the-job training, willing to complete paperwork for educational credit, willing to provide letters of recommendation.

Contact Write, call, fax, or e-mail Ms. Julie K. Beaver, Secretary to President/Director. Phone: 907-488-2216. Fax: 907-488-5246. E-mail: kjnp@mosquitonet.com. Applicants must submit a formal organization application, three professional references. Applications are accepted continuously. World Wide Web: http://www.mosquitonet.com/~kjnp.

NEWS RADIO WGST
1819 Peachtree Road, Suite 700
Atlanta, Georgia 30309

General Information News/talk radio station. Established in 1929. Number of employees: 100. Unit of Clear Channel Communications, San Antonio, Texas.

Internships Available ▶ *1–5 news department interns:* responsibilities include taking in network feeds, carting, labeling, and channeling the feeds appropriately; taking in reporter feeds; making police and fire checks; pursuing news tape; and writing news copy. Duration is 1 semester. ▶ *2–3 programming department interns:* responsibilities include assisting on remote broadcasts, dubbing public service announcements, helping to disseminate programming information to other departments, and screening calls for talk show. Duration is 3 months. ▶ *2–3 promotions department interns:* responsibilities include writing public service and promotional announcements, working on database projects, contacting contest winners, and assisting with weekend and evening remote broadcasts. Duration is 3 months. All positions are unpaid. Open to high school students, high school seniors, recent high school graduates, college freshmen, college sophomores, college juniors, college seniors, recent college graduates, graduate students.

Benefits Possible full-time employment, willing to complete paperwork for educational credit, willing to provide letters of recommendation.

Contact Write, fax, or e-mail Ken Charles, Director of Programming and News. Fax: 404-367-1100. E-mail: kcharles@wgst.com. No phone calls. In-person interview required. Applicants must submit a cover letter, resume. Applications are accepted continuously. World Wide Web: http://www.wgst.com.

93XRT/THE SCORE RADIO; WSCR/THE SCORE RADIO
4949 West Belmont Avenue
Chicago, Illinois 60641

General Information Major commercial radio stations. Established in 1972. Number of employees: 130. Number of internship applications received each year: 25.

Internships Available ▶ *1 FM93XRT programming department intern:* responsibilities include maintaining the record library, maintaining weekly trade publications, and assisting in special events. Candidates should have college courses in field, oral communication skills, strong interpersonal skills, written communication skills. Duration is flexible. ▶ *5 Score sports radio interns:* responsibilities include assisting in production, research, promotion, guest booking, and remote broadcasts. Candidates should have college courses in field, knowledge of field, oral communication skills, strong interpersonal skills, written communication skills. Duration is 3 months minimum. ▶ *5 promotion department interns:* responsibilities include gaining experience in promotions, marketing, public relations, and special event management. Candidates should have college courses in field, oral communication skills, strong interpersonal skills, written communication skills. Duration is flexible. Open to college freshmen, college sophomores, college juniors, college seniors. All positions are unpaid.

Benefits Names of contacts, on-the-job training, possible full-time employment, willing to complete paperwork for educational credit, willing to provide letters of recommendation.

Contact Write or call John Farneda (for FM programming), Mike Alzamora (for AM programming). Phone: 773-777-1700. In-person interview recommended. Applicants must submit a cover letter, resume. Applications are accepted continuously. World Wide Web: http://www.wxrt.com.

SHADOW BROADCAST SERVICES
201 Route 17 North, 9th Floor
Rutherford, New Jersey 07070

General Information Traffic, news, sports, weather, and programming services. Established in 1977. Number of employees: 100. Division of Westwood One Radio Network, Mutual Broadcasting System, Arlington, Virginia. Number of internship applications received each year: 30.

Internships Available ▶ *7–14 sports interns:* responsibilities include keeping up on sports scores and times, faxing stations, and informing announcers of sports information. ▶ *7–14 traffic interns:* responsibilities include phone calls, faxing, writing, collecting information, and listening for information. Candidates for all positions should have ability to work independently, ability to work with others, oral communication skills, personal interest in the field, writing skills. Duration for all positions is 6-week program throughout the year. All positions paid at $50 per duration of internship. Open to college freshmen, college sophomores, college juniors, college seniors, graduate students. International applications accepted.

Benefits Possible full-time employment, willing to act as a professional reference, willing to complete paperwork for educational credit, willing to provide letters of recommendation.

Contact Write, call, or fax Erin Fitzgerald, Intern Coordinator. Phone: 201-939-1888. Fax: 201-939-3683. In-person interview recommended. Applicants must submit a resume. Applications are accepted continuously.

WALK FM/AM
66 Colonial Drive
Patchogue, New York 11772

General Information Commercial FM/AM radio station offering programming to Long Island's adult audiences. Established in 1951. Number of employees: 40. Unit of Chancellor Media, Dallas, Texas. Number of internship applications received each year: 30.

Internships Available ▶ *2–5 news department interns:* responsibilities include assisting with information gathering, news writing, and traffic coordination. Candidates should have ability to work independently, ability to work with others, analytical skills, computer skills, editing skills, knowledge of field, oral communication skills, organizational skills, personal interest in the field, research skills, self-motivation, writing skills. Duration is 8–12 weeks. ▶ *2–12 promotion department interns:* responsibilities include assisting at station and with public appearances, meeting and greeting, and helping set up and breakdown sound equipment. Candidates should have oral communication skills, personal interest in the field, self-motivation, strong interpersonal skills, clean personal appearance, must be available to work weekends. Duration is 6 weeks. All positions are unpaid. Open to recent high school graduates, college freshmen, college sophomores, college juniors, college seniors, recent college graduates.

Benefits Job counseling, names of contacts, possible full-time employment, willing to complete paperwork for educational credit, willing to provide letters of recommendation.

Contact Write, call, or fax Priscilla Lee, Promotion Director, PO Box 230, Patchogue, New York 11772. Phone: 516-475-5200. Fax: 516-475-9016. In-person interview recommended. Applicants must submit a resume. Application deadline: June 30 for summer; continuous for positions during the academic year.

WAXQ-Q104.3
1180 Avenue of the Americas
New York, New York 10036

General Information Station that markets classic rock to tri-state area. Established in 1996. Number of employees: 50. Unit of Chancellor Media Corporation, New York, New York. Number of internship applications received each year: 150.

Internships Available ▶ *1 15 interns:* responsibilities include general office work, assisting in areas of promotion and programming, research, on-site interaction, production. Candidates should have college courses in field, computer skills, office skills, oral communication skills, strong interpersonal skills, writing skills. Duration is 1 semester. Unpaid. Open to college sophomores, college juniors, college seniors. International applications accepted.

Benefits Possible full-time employment, willing to complete paperwork for educational credit, willing to provide letters of recommendation.

Contact Write, call, fax, or e-mail Dan Mathers, Sales Promotion Coordinator. Phone: 212-575-1043. Fax: 212-302-7814. E-mail: dmathers@classicq104.com. In-person interview required. Applicants must submit a cover letter, resume. Applications are accepted continuously. World Wide Web: http://www.classicq104.com.

WBEB-FM (B101.1)
10 Presidential Boulevard
Bala Cynwyd, Pennsylvania 19004

General Information Adult contemporary radio station. Established in 1963. Number of employees: 45. Number of internship applications received each year: 100.

Internships Available ▶ *2–3 interns:* responsibilities include participating in the operation of a major market radio station in the promotion, sales, public service, production, research, traffic, and business departments. Candidates should have ability to work independently, ability to work with others, college courses in field, computer skills, office skills, personal interest in the field. Duration is 3 months minimum. Unpaid. Open to college freshmen, college sophomores, college juniors, college seniors.

Benefits Job counseling, names of contacts, possible full-time employment, willing to complete paperwork for educational credit, willing to provide letters of recommendation, reimbursement of work-related travel expenses.

Contact Write, call, or fax Ms. Karen Creely, Internship Coordinator. Phone: 610-667-8400. Fax: 610-667-6795. In-person interview required. Applicants must submit a cover letter, resume. Applications are accepted continuously. World Wide Web: http://www.b101radio.com.

WCEV-AM
5356 West Belmont Avenue
Chicago, Illinois 60641

General Information Multi-ethnic radio station broadcasting in 12 languages. Established in 1979. Number of employees: 45. Number of internship applications received each year: 30.
Internships Available ▶ *1 programming intern:* responsibilities include performing on-air duties in English and providing general assistance in programming department. Candidates should have computer skills, oral communication skills, organizational skills, personal interest in the field, strong interpersonal skills, written communication skills. Open to college freshmen, college sophomores, college juniors, college seniors, recent college graduates, graduate students, law students, career changers. ▶ *1 sales intern:* responsibilities include working with station sales manager on campaigns and station promotions. Candidates should have oral communication skills, personal interest in the field, strong interpersonal skills, written communication skills. Open to college juniors, college seniors, recent college graduates, graduate students, law students, career changers. Duration for all positions is 3 months. All positions are unpaid.
Benefits Job counseling, on-the-job training, possible full-time employment, willing to act as a professional reference, willing to complete paperwork for educational credit, willing to provide letters of recommendation.
Contact Write or call Ms. Lucyna Migala, Vice President and Program Director. Phone: 773-282-6700. In-person interview required. Applicants must submit a resume. Applications are accepted continuously.

WCTC-AM/WMGQ-FM
78 Veronica Avenue
Somerset, New Jersey 08873

General Information WCTC-AM is a news/talk station serving the central New Jersey area. WMGQ-FM is a stereo music station featuring adult contemporary programming. Established in 1946. Number of employees: 50. Unit of Greater Media, Inc., New Brunswick, New Jersey.
Internships Available ▶ *1 news reporter:* responsibilities include gathering and writing news stories. Duration is 1 semester. Unpaid. Open to college juniors, college seniors, recent college graduates, graduate students.
Benefits Job counseling, names of contacts, possible full-time employment, willing to complete paperwork for educational credit, willing to provide letters of recommendation.
Contact Write Maribell Lytle, Administrative Assistant. In-person interview required. Applicants must submit a cover letter, resume, writing sample. Applications are accepted continuously.

THE WESTWOOD ONE RADIO NETWORKS
1675 Broadway, 17th Floor
New York, New York 10019

General Information America's largest radio network, providing over 150 news, sports, music, talk, and entertainment programs; features; live events; 24-hour formats, and shadow broadcast services. Number of employees: 125. Number of internship applications received each year: 20.
Internships Available ▶ *2–4 artist relations/programming interns:* responsibilities include working in the programming and production departments; contacting artist representatives, including publicists and record company personnel; researching the artists being interviewed, including assembling and reviewing artist biographies and other source material. Candidates should have office skills, oral communication skills, organizational skills, self-motivation, strong interpersonal skills, written communication skills. Unpaid. Open to college freshmen, college sophomores, college juniors, college seniors. International applications accepted.

Benefits Job counseling, names of contacts, possible full-time employment, willing to act as a professional reference, willing to complete paperwork for educational credit, willing to provide letters of recommendation, $50 stipend.
Contact Write, call, fax, or e-mail Pam Green, Director of Artist Relations. Phone: 212-641-3088. Fax: 212-641-3085. E-mail: ww1pgreen@aol.com. In-person interview required. Applicants must submit a cover letter, resume. Applications are accepted continuously. World Wide Web: http://www.westwoodone.com.

WFLK-FM/WYLF-AM
481 Hamilton Street
Geneva, New York 14456

General Information AM and FM radio stations. Established in 1988. Number of employees: 20. Unit of M. B. Communications, Penn Yan, New York.
Internships Available ▶ *1–3 programming interns:* responsibilities include performing a variety of duties including general office and some computer and production work. Open to college freshmen, college sophomores, college juniors, college seniors. ▶ *1–3 research sales interns:* responsibilities include conducting phone research and putting together media packages. Open to high school students, high school seniors, recent high school graduates, college freshmen, college sophomores, college juniors, college seniors, recent college graduates, graduate students, law students, career changers, individuals reentering the workforce. Duration for all positions is flexible. All positions are unpaid.
Benefits Formal training, possible full-time employment, willing to complete paperwork for educational credit.
Contact Write, call, or fax Mr. Russ Kimble, President. Phone: 315-781-1101. Fax: 315-781-6666. In-person interview required. Applications are accepted continuously. World Wide Web: http://www.flare.net/k101.

WGIR RADIO–KNIGHT QUALITY STATION
Box 610
Manchester, New Hampshire 03105

General Information AM news/talk radio station; broadcasts the Boston Bruins, the New England Patriots, and the Boston Red Sox. Established in 1941. Number of employees: 45. Division of Atlantic Star, New York, New York. Number of internship applications received each year: 10.
Internships Available ▶ *1–4 news department interns:* responsibilities include recording news feeds, covering press conferences, writing news copy, working assignment desk, making police checks, and monitoring the competition. Candidates should have ability to work with others, computer skills, oral communication skills, plan to pursue career in field, writing skills. Open to college freshmen, college sophomores, college juniors, college seniors, recent college graduates, graduate students. ▶ *3–6 production interns:* responsibilities include copy production. Candidates should have ability to work independently, college courses in field, computer skills, editing skills, knowledge of field, personal interest in the field, plan to pursue career in field, research skills, self-motivation, writing skills. Open to college freshmen, college sophomores, college juniors, college seniors, recent college graduates, graduate students, law students, career changers. ▶ *3–6 promotions interns:* responsibilities include coordinating events. Candidates should have ability to work independently, oral communication skills, organizational skills, self-motivation, strong interpersonal skills, strong leadership ability. Open to college freshmen, college sophomores, college juniors, college seniors, recent college graduates, graduate students, law students, career changers. ▶ *1–4 sports interns:* responsibilities include covering local sporting events and producing local sports talk show. Candidates should have computer skills, knowledge of field, oral communication skills, plan to pursue career in field, strong interpersonal skills, written communication skills. Open to college freshmen, college sophomores, college juniors, college seniors, recent college graduates, graduate students. Duration for all positions is 3–6 months. All positions are unpaid. International applications accepted.

Benefits Willing to complete paperwork for educational credit, willing to provide letters of recommendation.
Contact Write or fax Mr. Dan Pierce, Program Director. Fax: 603-625-9255. No phone calls. In-person interview required. Applicants must submit a cover letter, resume. Applications are accepted continuously. World Wide Web: http://www.am610.wgir.com.

WGN-RADIO 720
435 North Michigan
Chicago, Illinois 60611

General Information Radio station featuring a progressive and flexible full-service news and talk format. Established in 1924. Number of employees: 100. Unit of Tribune Company, Chicago, Illinois. Number of internship applications received each year: 2,000.
Internships Available ▶ *1 network intern:* responsibilities include preparing programs for distribution to affiliates, answering phones, and assisting in specific projects. Candidates should have ability to work independently, ability to work with others, computer skills, editing skills, organizational skills, written communication skills. Open to college sophomores, college juniors, college seniors, recent college graduates, graduate students, law students, career changers, individuals reentering the workforce. ▶ *2 news interns:* responsibilities include answering phones, researching and writing stories, taking feeds, and assisting with major event coverage. Candidates should have analytical skills, computer skills, editing skills, plan to pursue career in field, self-motivation, written communication skills. Open to college sophomores, college juniors, college seniors, recent college graduates, graduate students, law students, career changers, individuals reentering the workforce. ▶ *2 programming interns:* responsibilities include booking guests, generating ideas, screening phones, producing audio, editing, completing promotional and programming paperwork, maintaining computerized music library, and completing special projects. Candidates should have editing skills, experience in the field, plan to pursue career in field, research skills, strong interpersonal skills, written communication skills. Open to college sophomores, college juniors, college seniors, recent college graduates, graduate students, law students, career changers, individuals reentering the workforce. ▶ *1 promotion intern:* responsibilities include preparing weekly press releases, writing and scheduling promotional announcements, working promotional events, writing for monthly listener newsletter, and compiling and editing community calendar newspaper column. Candidates should have ability to work independently, computer skills, knowledge of field, plan to pursue career in field, strong interpersonal skills, writing skills. Open to college sophomores, college juniors, college seniors, recent college graduates, graduate students, career changers, individuals reentering the workforce. ▶ *1 sports intern:* responsibilities include covering sports events; answering phones; and researching, writing, and producing stories. Candidates should have editing skills, experience in the field, plan to pursue career in field, research skills, self-motivation, strong interpersonal skills. Open to college sophomores, college juniors, college seniors, recent college graduates, graduate students, career changers, individuals reentering the workforce. Duration for all positions is 14 weeks. All positions are unpaid. International applications accepted.
Benefits Formal training, job counseling, names of contacts, opportunity to attend seminars/workshops, possible full-time employment, willing to act as a professional reference, willing to complete paperwork for educational credit, willing to provide letters of recommendation, $75 per week travel stipend.
Contact Write or e-mail Randy Eccles, Assistant Program Director. E-mail: randyeccles@wgnradio.com. No phone calls. In-person interview required. Applicants must submit a cover letter, resume. Application deadline: January 1 for spring, April 1 for summer, October 1 for winter. World Wide Web: http://wgnradio.com.

WGRD RADIO/CENTRAL STAR COMMUNICATIONS, INC.
38 West Fulton Street, Suite 200
Grand Rapids, Michigan 49503

General Information Modern rock radio station. Established in 1950. Number of employees: 29. Unit of Capstar Broadcasting Partners, Austin, Texas. Number of internship applications received each year: 20.
Internships Available ▶ *1–2 business interns:* responsibilities include banking, filing, data entry, accounting, accounts receivable, accounts payable. Candidates should have analytical skills, computer skills, office skills, oral communication skills, organizational skills, self-motivation. Duration is 1 semester. Open to college freshmen, college sophomores, college juniors, college seniors, graduate students. ▶ *1–2 morning show interns:* responsibilities include gathering news, traffic, weather, and school closings; handling board operations and remote attendance; tracking break times; and keeping commercial logs. Candidates should have computer skills, editing skills, oral communication skills, research skills, strong interpersonal skills. Duration is 1 semester. Open to high school seniors, recent high school graduates, college freshmen, college sophomores, college juniors, college seniors, graduate students. ▶ *3–5 programming interns:* responsibilities include helping disc jockeys in studio, helping at events and with playlists, possible production help. Candidates should have ability to work independently, oral communication skills, organizational skills, personal interest in the field, self-motivation, strong interpersonal skills, strong leadership ability, flexibility. Duration is 1–3 semesters. Open to high school seniors, recent high school graduates, college freshmen, college sophomores, college juniors, college seniors, graduate students. ▶ *2–3 promotions interns:* responsibilities include doing weekly playlists, faxing newsletters, performing database maintenance, handling remote attendance, updating concert calendar, writing liners and promos, and making sure the van is ready for remotes. Candidates should have ability to work independently, ability to work with others, computer skills, oral communication skills, personal interest in the field. Duration is 1 semester. Open to high school seniors, recent high school graduates, college freshmen, college sophomores, college juniors, college seniors. ▶ *1–2 sales interns:* responsibilities include writing sales proposals, analyzing rating data, and writing commercial copy. Candidates should have ability to work with others, analytical skills, computer skills, oral communication skills, plan to pursue career in field, written communication skills. Duration is 1 semester. Open to college juniors, college seniors, graduate students. All positions are unpaid. International applications accepted.
Benefits On-the-job training, possible full-time employment, willing to act as a professional reference, willing to complete paperwork for educational credit, willing to provide letters of recommendation.
Contact Write, call, or fax Todd Kangus, Promotions Director. Phone: 616-459-4111. Fax: 616-454-5530. In-person interview required. Applicants must submit a formal organization application. Applications are accepted continuously.

WJXA 92.9 FM/WRMX 96.3 FM
504 Rosedale Avenue
Nashville, Tennessee 37211

General Information Commercial radio station featuring soft rock and oldies music. Established in 1948. Number of employees: 50. Number of internship applications received each year: 50.
Internships Available ▶ *2 accounting/general business interns:* responsibilities include working on spread sheets, filing, accounts payable, accounts receivable, word processing. Duration is flexible. Open to recent high school graduates, college freshmen, career changers. ▶ *2 promotions interns:* responsibilities include assisting promotions director with internal and external sales promotions and station-involved events. Duration is 8 weeks. ▶ *1 retail marketing intern:* responsibilities include assisting retail marketing director. All positions are unpaid. International applications accepted.

WJXA 92.9 FM/WRMX 96.3 FM (continued)

Benefits Names of contacts, on-the-job training, possible full-time employment, willing to complete paperwork for educational credit, willing to provide letters of recommendation.
Contact Write Sharon Short, Business Manager, PO Box 40596, Nashville, Tennessee 37204. No phone calls. In-person interview recommended. Applicants must submit a formal organization application, resume, writing sample, two personal references, two letters of recommendation. Applications are accepted continuously.

WKXL–AM/FM RADIO
37 Redington Road, PO Box 875
Concord, New Hampshire 03302-0875

General Information Commercial radio stations with full-service format serving the over-30 audience in the capital city region of south central New Hampshire with a heavy emphasis on news, talk, sports, and community affairs. Established in 1946. Number of employees: 11. Number of internship applications received each year: 6.
Internships Available ► *1 news department intern:* responsibilities include assisting in covering, writing, editing, and rewriting local and state news. Candidates should have ability to work with others, college courses in field, oral communication skills, personal interest in the field, writing skills. ► *1 sales department intern:* responsibilities include assisting sales manager with sales, research, sales service, and promotions. Candidates should have major in communications or marketing. Duration for all positions is 3 months minimum. All positions are unpaid. Open to college sophomores, college juniors, college seniors, recent college graduates, graduate students.
Benefits Job counseling, names of contacts, willing to complete paperwork for educational credit, willing to provide letters of recommendation.
Contact Write, call, fax, or e-mail Mr. Richard W. Osborne, President and General Manager. Phone: 603-225-5521. Fax: 603-224-6404. E-mail: wkxlnews@juno.com. In-person interview required. Applicants must submit a cover letter, resume. Applications are accepted continuously.

WMAL, INC.
4400 Jenifer Street, NW
Washington, District of Columbia 20015

General Information Organization which includes three radio stations. WRQX-FM is an easy listening, adult contemporary station. WJZW-AM is a jazz station. WMAL-FM is a major market news station featuring news, talk, weather, and traffic reporting. Number of internship applications received each year: 20.
Internships Available ► *Advertising sales interns:* responsibilities include assisting with proposals, researching clients, organizing and producing proposals, and accompanying sales staff on presentations. ► *Advertising/promotion interns:* responsibilities include coordinating contests, writing promotions and press releases, assisting in designing print ads, researching promotional opportunities, and attending promotions. ► *News interns:* responsibilities include operating newsroom computer system, conducting research and story checks, performing telephone interviews, and typing. ► *Programming interns:* responsibilities include assisting programming department with day-to-day operations of the station including talent management, promotions, and station management; acting as a liaison to other affiliate stations; and assisting public service direction in working with listeners and producers on program development. Duration for all positions is 1 semester. All positions are unpaid. Open to college juniors, college seniors. International applications accepted.
Benefits Names of contacts, opportunity to attend seminars/workshops, possible full-time employment, willing to complete paperwork for educational credit, willing to provide letters of recommendation.

Contact Write or call Intern Coordinator. Phone: 202-686-3100. In-person interview required. Applicants must submit a formal organization application, cover letter, resume, example of work. Applications are accepted continuously.

WMMR-FM
1 Bala Plaza
Bala-Cynwyd, Pennsylvania 19004

General Information Album-oriented rock station providing entertainment, music, news, and public affairs programming to eastern Pennsylvania, New Jersey, and Delaware. Established in 1968. Number of employees: 45. Unit of Greater Media, Inc., New Brunswick, New Jersey. Number of internship applications received each year: 200.
Internships Available ► *5–7 programming/promotions interns:* responsibilities include producing music research tapes and entering data into Lotus 1-2-3, pulling and filing music, assisting the traffic and continuity department, answering correspondence, handling phone requests and giveaways, and preparing broadcast packs for remote broadcasts. Duration is flexible. Unpaid. Open to individuals receiving college credit.
Benefits Names of contacts, possible full-time employment, willing to complete paperwork for educational credit, willing to provide letters of recommendation.
Contact Write, call, or fax Mike von Flotow, Intern Coordinator. Phone: 610-771-9752. Fax: 610-771-9667. In-person interview required. Applicants must submit a cover letter, resume. Applications are accepted continuously.

WOPP-AM
1101 Cameron Road
Opp, Alabama 36467

General Information Commercial radio station broadcasting music, news, weather, and sports. Established in 1980. Number of employees: 4. Number of internship applications received each year: 20.
Internships Available ► *2 news interns:* responsibilities include gathering news. Candidates should have computer skills, oral communication skills, plan to pursue career in field, research skills, strong interpersonal skills, written communication skills. Duration is 3 months. ► *1 production intern:* responsibilities include producing promos and some commercials. Candidates should have ability to work independently, computer skills, editing skills, oral communication skills, personal interest in the field, writing skills. ► *1 sales intern:* responsibilities include selling and writing ads. Candidates should have knowledge of field, office skills, plan to pursue career in field, self-motivation, writing skills. All positions are unpaid. International applications accepted.
Benefits Opportunity to attend seminars/workshops, possible full-time employment, willing to complete paperwork for educational credit, willing to provide letters of recommendation, sales interns earn commission and are reimbuesed gas money.
Contact Write, fax, or e-mail Mr. Robert H. Boothe, General Manager. Fax: 334-493-4546. E-mail: wopp@wopp.com. No phone calls. Applicants must submit a resume, four personal references. Applications are accepted continuously. World Wide Web: http://www.wopp.com.

WOR RADIO
1440 Broadway
New York, New York 10018

General Information Radio station. Established in 1989. Number of employees: 120. Division of Buckley Broadcasting, Greenwich, Connecticut.
Internships Available ► *8–10 radio station interns:* responsibilities include assisting station personnel with hands-on jobs in any of the following departments: programming, engineering, or marketing. Candidates should have college courses in field, knowledge of field, self-motivation, strong interpersonal skills, writing skills. Duration is 1 semester (requires 2 full days per

week in fall and spring semesters and 3 full days per week in summer). Unpaid. Open to college juniors, college seniors, graduate students.

Benefits Opportunity to attend seminars/workshops, willing to complete paperwork for educational credit, willing to provide letters of recommendation, stipend of $10 per day for reimbursement of work-related travel expenses.

Contact Write or fax Ms. Judy Pasch, Director of Personnel. Fax: 212-575-2109. Applicants must submit a cover letter, resume, letter from university advisor that individual will receive college credit for internship. Applications are accepted continuously.

WXPN-FM 88.5, MEMBER SUPPORTED COMMERCIAL FREE MUSIC RADIO
3905 Spruce Street
Philadelphia, Pennsylvania 19104

General Information Member supported public radio station featuring an alternative adult acoustic music format; produces "The World Cafe" and "Kid's Corner" as well as a variety of local specialty programs. Established in 1945. Number of employees: 35. Unit of University of Pennsylvania, Philadelphia, Pennsylvania.

Internships Available ▶ *1 Amazon country assistant (gay and lesbian programming):* responsibilities include editing and producing feature pieces with on-air possibilities, organizing announcements for calendar segments, acting as public relations liaison between program and gay and lesbian community. Candidates should have ability to work independently, editing skills, strong interpersonal skills, writing skills, knowledge of gay and lesbian community is helpful, but not required. Duration is 1 school year or summer. Open to college freshmen, college sophomores, college juniors, college seniors, graduate students, any interested individuals. ▶ *1 Kid's Corner associate producer:* responsibilities include assisting in producing live children's talk radio program, working with producer to develop show segments, assisting with promotional campaigns. Candidates should have ability to work independently, computer skills, office skills, oral communication skills, self-motivation, strong interpersonal skills, familiarity with Internet and news groups. Duration is ongoing. Open to college freshmen, college sophomores, college juniors, college seniors, graduate students. ▶ *1–6 Q'Zine assistants (gay and lesbian program):* responsibilities include assisting with all facets of the program including production, programming, promotions, community outreach, research, and reporting. Candidates should have ability to work independently, oral communication skills, personal interest in the field, strong interpersonal skills, written communication skills, knowledge of and/or connection to gay and lesbian community is helpful. Duration is 1 school year or summer. Open to college freshmen, college sophomores, college juniors, college seniors, any interested individuals. ▶ *1–2 Web site assistants:* responsibilities include assisting Web site provider to update site information, assisting in managing e-mail replies, compiling on-line resource lists. Candidates should have ability to work independently, computer skills, editing skills, writing skills, familiarity with Internet/Web/on-line production skills, knowledge of WXPN music and artists. Duration is 1 school year or summer. Open to college freshmen, college sophomores, college juniors, college seniors, recent college graduates, graduate students. ▶ *1–2 development department assistants:* responsibilities include assisting with marketing, development and fund-raising programs; includes research, organizing, compiling information; possibly assisting with Major Donor program and working with WXPN alumni. Candidates should have computer skills, oral communication skills, organizational skills, research skills, self-motivation, strong interpersonal skills, writing skills. Duration is flexible. Open to college freshmen, college sophomores, college juniors, college seniors, graduate students. ▶ *1–2 news and public affairs assistants:* responsibilities include working as news stringer, attending local press conferences, logging and editing interviews, writing news stories and public affairs copy, and possibility of on-air work. Candidates should have ability to work independently, computer skills, oral communication skills, research skills, self-motivation, writing skills, tape editing ability is a plus. Duration is 8–10 weeks. Open to college freshmen,

college sophomores, college juniors, college seniors, graduate students. ▶ *1–4 production assistants:* responsibilities include assisting with taping and editing using digital and analog techniques, assisting with production of special broadcasts and live performances, assisting with editing and mixing of recordings and promotional spots, maintaining data information on computer. Candidates should have ability to work independently, computer skills, experience in the field, self-motivation, some experience with 2-track editing, recording, and live radio production preferred. Duration is ongoing. Open to college freshmen, college sophomores, college juniors, college seniors, graduate students. ▶ *1–4 programming assistants:* responsibilities include working closely with music director and assistant music director in all aspects of programming for both local and syndicated music programs; some research, writing, and contact with record labels and promoters. Candidates should have ability to work independently, computer skills, organizational skills, strong interpersonal skills, interest and/or knowledge of artists and music played on WXPN. Duration is ongoing. Open to college freshmen, college sophomores, college juniors, college seniors, graduate students. ▶ *1 public service announcement assistant:* responsibilities include writing copy for on-air use; processing, evaluating, and organizing all incoming material. Candidates should have ability to work with others, computer skills, self-motivation, writing skills. Duration is ongoing. Open to college freshmen, college sophomores, college juniors, college seniors, graduate students. ▶ *1–2 research assistants:* responsibilities include assisting general manager for programming to organize and implement audience research; helping with statistical analysis of research; assisting in creating reports, charts, and graphics. Candidates should have ability to work independently, research skills, spreadsheet and graphics software knowledge, knowledge of WXPN music, college courses in marketing. Duration is 1 school year or summer. Open to college freshmen, college sophomores, college juniors, college seniors, graduate students. ▶ *1–4 special events assistants:* responsibilities include acting as public relations liaison between WXPN, record labels, and local media; providing support to coordinate events; assisting in developing promotional campaigns. Candidates should have oral communication skills, organizational skills, strong interpersonal skills, written communication skills, knowledge of WXPN music and artists. Duration is 1 school year or summer. Open to college freshmen, college sophomores, college juniors, college seniors, graduate students. ▶ *10–15 sports on-air and production assistants:* responsibilities include writing copy, editing tape, and producing segments (live and taped) for University of Pennsylvania football and basketball games; conducting interviews and doing on-air segments; traveling with teams; covering other local sports teams. Candidates should have ability to work independently, computer skills, oral communication skills, strong interpersonal skills, written communication skills, willingness to learn radio production, personal interest in University of Pennsylvania sports. Duration is 1 school year. Open to college freshmen, college sophomores, college juniors, college seniors, graduate students. All positions are unpaid.

Benefits Formal training, names of contacts, willing to act as a professional reference, willing to complete paperwork for educational credit, willing to provide letters of recommendation.

Contact Write, call, or fax Shen Shellenberger, Volunteer Coordinator. Phone: 215-573-3340. Fax: 215-573-2152. In-person interview recommended. Applicants must submit a formal organization application, three personal references. Applications are accepted continuously. World Wide Web: http://www.xpn.org.

SOFTWARE PUBLISHERS

DST SYSTEMS, INC.
333 West 11th Street
Kansas City, Missouri 64105

General Information Developer of software for the financial services industry and is the leader in automated record keep-

DST Systems, Inc. (continued)

ing for the mutual fund industry. Established in 1969. Number of employees: 6,000. Number of internship applications received each year: 150.

Internships Available ▶ *20–25 computer programmers:* responsibilities include testing, research, programming, and analysis. Candidates should have ability to work independently, analytical skills, college courses in field, computer skills, knowledge of field, oral communication skills, plan to pursue career in field, self-motivation, strong interpersonal skills, 1 semester of COBOL or C++; minimum GPA of 3.0. Duration is 3–6 months. $14–$17 per hour. Open to college sophomores, college juniors, college seniors, career changers. International applications accepted.

Benefits Formal training, on-the-job training, possible full-time employment, tuition assistance, willing to complete paperwork for educational credit.

Contact Write, call, fax, or e-mail Tara Jacobs, Human Resources Recruiter, 333 West 11th Street, Kansas City, Missouri 64105. Phone: 800-874-0174. Fax: 816-435-8618. E-mail: tmjacobs@dstsystems.com. Telephone interview required. Applicants must submit a formal organization application, resume, academic transcripts, cover letter (preferred). Applications are accepted continuously. World Wide Web: http://www.dstsystems.com.

ELECTRONIC ARTS
209 Redwood Shores Parkway
Redwood City, California 94065-1175

General Information Interactive entertainment software company. Established in 1982. Number of employees: 800. Number of internship applications received each year: 500.

Internships Available ▶ *6–12 computer graphic artists:* responsibilities include producing bit map graphics, 3D shapes and computer animation by creating new art and/or retouching existing art. Candidates should have ability to work with others, college courses in field, computer skills, knowledge of field, self-motivation, knowledge of 3D graphics programs. $2,050–$2,306 per month. Open to college juniors, college seniors, graduate students. ▶ *15–25 software engineers:* responsibilities include programming specific features into the game; testing, debugging, and documenting code contributions. Candidates should have ability to work with others, analytical skills, college courses in field, computer skills, plan to pursue career in field, knowledge of C and C++, gaming industry experience. $2,562–$2,990 per month. Open to college juniors, college seniors, graduate students, those with one year remaining in school. Duration for all positions is 3 months. International applications accepted.

Benefits On-the-job training, opportunity to attend seminars/workshops, willing to act as a professional reference, willing to complete paperwork for educational credit, willing to provide letters of recommendation, mandated disability plan, health club membership, housing stipend.

Contact E-mail Kim Capps-Tanaka, University Relations Manager, 209 Redwood Shores Parkway, Redwood City, California 94065-1175. E-mail: interns@ea.com. In-person interview recommended. Applicants must submit a resume, portfolio, additional requirements located on Web site. Application deadline: February 28 for summer. World Wide Web: http://www.ea.com.

SYBASE, INC.
6425 Christie Avenue, 5th Floor
Emeryville, California 94608

General Information Sixth largest software company in the world with annual sales totaling over 1 billion dollars. Established in 1984. Number of employees: 800. Number of internship applications received each year: 1,000.

Internships Available ▶ *15–20 business interns:* responsibilities include various duties in advertising, customer relations, creative services, direct marketing, education marketing, field sales, global sales and marketing, marketing events, human resources, product marketing, promotions and programs, support renewal, tradeshow marketing, or worldwide references. Candidates should have analytical skills, computer skills, oral communication skills, self-motivation, strong interpersonal skills, written communication

skills. $10–$15 per hour. ▶ *8–10 technical interns:* responsibilities include various duties in information systems, release engineering, software development, software quality assurance engineering, technical support, or Web services. Candidates should have computer skills, knowledge of field, oral communication skills, personal interest in the field, self-motivation, strong interpersonal skills. $12–$18 per hour. Duration for all positions is 1–2 semesters. Open to college freshmen, college sophomores, college juniors, college seniors, graduate students. International applications accepted.

Benefits Formal training, names of contacts, on-the-job training, opportunity to attend seminars/workshops, possible full-time employment, willing to act as a professional reference, willing to complete paperwork for educational credit, willing to provide letters of recommendation, holiday pay and flex time.

International Internships Available.

Contact E-mail Min Lee, University Relations. E-mail: university_relations@sybase.com. No phone calls. In-person interview recommended. Applicants must submit a cover letter, resume. Applications are accepted continuously. World Wide Web: http://www.sybase.com/careers/college/.

TELECOMMUNICATIONS

AERIAL COMMUNICATIONS, INC.
8410 West Bryn Mawr Avenue, Suite1100
Chicago, Illinois 60631-340

General Information Telecommunications company supplying wireless personal communication services. Established in 1995. Number of employees: 2,000.

Internships Available ▶ *Engineering interns:* responsibilities include working in engineering department on various projects. Candidates should have ability to work independently, analytical skills, college courses in field, computer skills, knowledge of field, plan to pursue career in field. Open to college freshmen, college sophomores, college juniors, college seniors, recent college graduates, graduate students, career changers, individuals reentering the workforce. ▶ *Human resources interns.* Candidates should have ability to work with others, computer skills, office skills, oral communication skills, plan to pursue career in field, strong interpersonal skills. Open to college freshmen, college sophomores, college juniors, college seniors, recent college graduates, career changers, individuals reentering the workforce. ▶ *Information technology interns:* responsibilities include working on various projects in information technology department. Candidates should have ability to work independently, college courses in field, computer skills, knowledge of field, plan to pursue career in field. Open to college freshmen, college sophomores, college juniors, college seniors, recent college graduates, career changers, individuals reentering the workforce. Duration for all positions is flexible. All positions paid at $8–$12 per hour. International applications accepted.

Benefits Formal training, job counseling, on-the-job training, opportunity to attend seminars/workshops, possible full-time employment, travel reimbursement, willing to act as a professional reference, willing to complete paperwork for educational credit, willing to provide letters of recommendation.

Contact Write, fax, or e-mail Intern Coordinator, 8410 West Bryn Mawr Avenue, Suite 1100, Chicago, Illinois 60631-340. Fax: 773-399-4192. E-mail: aerialhr@aerial1.com. No phone calls. In-person interview recommended. Applicants must submit a resume, business and/or academic references. Applications are accepted continuously. World Wide Web: http://www.aerial1.com.

BELL ATLANTIC MOBILE
180 Washington Valley Road
Bedminster, New Jersey 07921

General Information Communication business and headquarters for a cellular phone company. Established in 1987. Number of employees: 30,000. Number of internship applications received each year: 16.

Internships Available ▶ *6–12 health and fitness specialists:* responsibilities include opening and closing the facility; stress testing, creating motivational programs, orientations, motivating others to achieve a healthy lifestyle. Candidates should have college courses in field, oral communication skills, plan to pursue career in field, self-motivation, strong interpersonal skills. Duration is 3 to 6 months (flexible). $1,000 per duration of internship. Open to college juniors, college seniors, recent college graduates, graduate students, career changers. International applications accepted.

Benefits Formal training, job counseling, on-the-job training, possible full-time employment, willing to act as a professional reference, willing to complete paperwork for educational credit, willing to provide letters of recommendation.

Contact Write, call, fax, or e-mail Mark Monteyne, Health Promotion Wellness Director, 180 Washington Valley Road, Bedminster, New Jersey 07921. Phone: 908-306-7198. Fax: 908-306-4229. E-mail: mmonteyn@mobile.bam.com. Telephone interview required. Applicants must submit a resume, academic transcripts. Applications are accepted continuously.

GEOSPATIAL INFORMATION AND TECHNOLOGY ASSOCIATION (GITA)
14456 East Evans Avenue
Aurora, Colorado 80014-1409

General Information Educational association serving professionals using geospatial information and technology in infrastructure-based industries (utilities, telecom, local government). Established in 1979. Number of employees: 11.

Internships Available ▶ *9 GITA interns:* responsibilities include working with GITA corporate members, using their geospatial information and technology skills in the workplace at their facilities. Interns may also find their own internship opportunities. Candidates should have college courses in field, knowledge of field, personal interest in the field, plan to pursue career in field. Duration is dependent on internship arranged. Paid. Open to college juniors, college seniors, graduate students. International applications accepted.

Benefits Names of contacts, on-the-job training.

International Internships Available.

Contact Write, call, fax, or e-mail Rosemarie Seemann, GITA, 14456 East Evans Avenue, Aurora, Colorado 80014. Phone: 303-337-0513. Fax: 303-337-1001. E-mail: rseemann@gita.org. Applicants must submit a formal organization application, cover letter, academic transcripts, three personal references, three letters of recommendation. Application deadline: December 15 for summer. World Wide Web: http://www.gita.org.

GTE CORPORATION
700 Hidden Ridge
Irving, Texas 75038

General Information Telecommunications organization that specializes in providing voice, video, and data products and services; core competencies lie in local and long distance service. Established in 1918. Number of employees: 3,000. Number of internship applications received each year: 10,000.

Internships Available ▶ *200–250 nontechnical college interns:* responsibilities include assisting in various nontechnical departments, such as accounting, finance, human resources, marketing/sales/sales support, or public affairs. Candidates should have ability to work independently, ability to work with others, analytical skills, college courses in field, computer skills, knowledge of field, oral communication skills, organizational skills, personal interest in the field, self-motivation, strong interpersonal skills, strong leadership ability, written communication skills. ▶ *250–300 technical college interns:* responsibilities include assisting in various technical departments, such as information technology, network operations, product development and sales, or operations research. Candidates should have ability to work independently, analytical skills, college courses in field, computer skills, knowledge of field, office skills, oral communication skills, organizational skills, personal interest in the field, research skills, self-motivation, strong interpersonal skills, strong leadership abil-

ity, writing skills, coursework in either computer engineering, computer science, electrical engineering, managment information systems, or telecommunications. Duration for all positions is 1 summer. All positions paid. Open to college sophomores, college juniors, college seniors, graduate students.

Benefits On-the-job training, opportunity to attend seminars/workshops, possible full-time employment, travel reimbursement, willing to complete paperwork for educational credit.

Contact Write, fax, or e-mail College Intern Program. Fax: 972-719-1529. E-mail: intern.program@telops.gte.com. No phone calls. In-person interview recommended. Applicants must submit a cover letter, resume. Application deadline: March 1 for summer; on-campus interviews conducted until mid-March. World Wide Web: http://www.gte.com.

SPRINT CORPORATION
2330 Shawnee-Mission Parkway
Westwood, Kansas 66205

General Information Diversified telecommunications company providing global voice, data, and videoconferencing services and related products. Established in 1986. Number of employees: 55,000. Number of internship applications received each year: 1,500.

Internships Available ▶ *300 interns I, II, III, and IV.* Candidates should have analytical skills, computer skills, office skills, oral communication skills, organizational skills, self-motivation, strong interpersonal skills, written communication skills. Duration is 1 summer or 1 semester. Paid. Open to high school seniors, recent high school graduates, college freshmen, college sophomores, college juniors, college seniors, graduate students, law students, individuals reentering the workforce. ▶ *20 staff associate interns:* responsibilities include working throughout company in international, marketing, treasury, engineering, strategic, or local telephone company departments. Candidates should have ability to work independently, self-motivation, strong interpersonal skills, strong leadership ability. Duration is 2–3 months. $4,500 per month. Open to graduate students in top-level MBA programs. International applications accepted.

Benefits Formal training, job counseling, names of contacts, on-the-job training, opportunity to attend seminars/workshops, possible full-time employment, travel reimbursement, willing to act as a professional reference, willing to provide letters of recommendation.

Contact Write, call, fax, or e-mail University Relations. Phone: 877-361-7300. Fax: 913-624-2467. E-mail: internship.program@mail.sprint.com. In-person interview recommended. Applicants must submit a formal organization application, cover letter, resume, personal reference, drug screen and background checks required. Applications are accepted continuously. World Wide Web: http://www.sprint.com/hr.

TELEVISION BROADCASTING

ABC NEWS NIGHTLINE
1717 DeSales Street, NW
Washington, District of Columbia 20036

General Information Television news, broadcast journalism. Established in 1980. Number of employees: 30. Number of internship applications received each year: 300.

Internships Available ▶ *3–5 interns:* responsibilities include helping to manage the enormous flow of information that comes in the office every day; participating in all editorial conferences with access to all areas of the broadcast. Candidates should have oral communication skills, personal interest in the field, self-motivation, strong interpersonal skills, written communication skills. Duration is 1 semester (flexible). Unpaid. Open to college juniors, college seniors. International applications accepted.

ABC News Nightline (continued)

Benefits Names of contacts, on-the-job training, opportunity to attend seminars/workshops, willing to act as a professional reference, willing to complete paperwork for educational credit, willing to provide letters of recommendation, occasional free meals, some travel reimbursement.

Contact Write, call, fax, or e-mail Lara Bontempo, Intern Director, 1717 DeSales Street, NW, Washington, District of Columbia 20036. Phone: 202-222-7000. Fax: 202-222-7680. E-mail: niteline@abcnews.com. Applicants must submit a formal organization application, cover letter, resume, three personal references, two letters of recommendation, letter from university confirming eligibility to receive credit. Application deadline: March 15 for summer, July 1 for fall, October 1 for winter, November 15 for spring semester I; February 1 for spring semester II. World Wide Web: http://www.abcnews.com.

ACADEMY OF TELEVISION ARTS AND SCIENCES
5220 Lankershim Boulevard
North Hollywood, California 91601-3109

General Information Service and awards organization that presents the annual primetime Emmy awards; provides activities for television industry members; and fosters competition for college students in the form of a paid summer internship program which places students with Los Angeles-based television stations, production companies, studios, and other television-related venues. Established in 1946. Number of internship applications received each year: 1,050.

Internships Available ▶ *27–29 interns:* responsibilities include working as an intern in one of 27 categories: Agency, Animation-Traditional, Animation-Computer Generated, Art Direction, Broadcast Advertising and Promotion, Business Affairs, Casting, Children's Programming and Development, Cinematography, Commercials, Costume Design, Development, Documentary/Reality Production, Editing, Entertainment News, Episodic Series, Movies for Television, Music, Network Programming Management, Production Management, Public Relations and Publicity, Sound, Syndication/Distribution, Television Directing-Single Camera, Television Directing-Multi-Camera, Television Scriptwriting, and Videotape Post Production. Candidates should have college courses in field, knowledge of field, oral communication skills, plan to pursue career in field, self-motivation, written communication skills. Duration is 8 weeks. $2,000 per duration of internship. Open to college freshmen, college sophomores, college juniors, college seniors, recent college graduates, graduate students, law students.

Benefits Job counseling, opportunity to attend seminars/workshops, willing to act as a professional reference, willing to provide letters of recommendation, $400 housing/travel supplement for non-L.A. County residents.

Contact Write, call, or e-mail Internships. Phone: 818-754-2830. E-mail: internships@emmys.org. Applicants must submit a formal organization application, cover letter, resume, academic transcripts, writing sample, three letters of recommendation, videotaped interview if selected as a finalist, portfolio may be required (depending on category). Application deadline: March 10 for summer. World Wide Web: http://www.emmys.org.

BLACK ENTERTAINMENT TELEVISION
One BET Plaza, 1900 W Place, NE
Washington, District of Columbia 20018

General Information Telecommunications company consisting of cable network channel, 2 magazines, pay per view channel, and other venues of mass communication. Established in 1980. Number of employees: 450. Number of internship applications received each year: 600.

Internships Available ▶ *40–60 interns:* responsibilities include various duties according to departmental needs. Candidates should have computer skills, oral communication skills, organizational skills, plan to pursue career in field, strong interpersonal skills. Duration is 1 semester. Unpaid. Open to

high school seniors, college freshmen, college sophomores, college juniors, college seniors, graduate students, law students. International applications accepted.

Benefits On-the-job training, possible full-time employment, willing to complete paperwork for educational credit.

Contact Write, call, or fax Internship Coordinator, One BET Plaza 1900 W Place, NE, Washington, District of Columbia 20018. Phone: 202-608-2020. Fax: 202-608-2589. In-person interview recommended. Applicants must submit a formal organization application, cover letter, resume, academic transcripts, three letters of recommendation, verification from school that internship is for academic credit. Application deadline: March 27 for summer, July 3 for fall, November 13 for spring. World Wide Web: http://www.msbet.com.

CABLEVISION OF RARITAN VALLEY, CABLEVISION 6
275 Centennial, CN 6805
Piscataway, New Jersey 08855-6805

General Information Cable company that provides an assortment of cable services to its local community. Established in 1973. Number of employees: 260. Unit of Cablevision, Woodbury, New York. Number of internship applications received each year: 20.

Internships Available ▶ *5–10 television interns:* responsibilities include production work on news, sports, documentaries, and talk shows; operating camera, audio, and tape equipment, acting as floor manager; performing some technical directing, producing, and editing; and writing news and doing voice overs. Candidates should have ability to work independently, ability to work with others, college courses in field, plan to pursue career in field, self-motivation, writing skills. Duration is 1 semester (according to school guidelines). Unpaid. Open to high school seniors, college freshmen, college sophomores, college juniors, college seniors. International applications accepted.

Benefits On-the-job training, opportunity to attend seminars/workshops, possible full-time employment, willing to complete paperwork for educational credit, willing to provide letters of recommendation, assistance with making resume tape, hands-on experience.

Contact Write or call Mr. David Garb, Internship Coordinator. Phone: 732-457-0131 Ext. 6005. In-person interview recommended. Applicants must submit a cover letter, resume, school's guidelines for internships. Application deadline: May 1 for summer, August 1 for fall, December 1 for spring.

CABLEVISION OF SOUTHERN WESTCHESTER
47 Purdy Street
Harrison, New York 10528

General Information Company that provides local programming for cable in Westchester, broadcasting news, sports, talk shows, and medical shows in the studio and on location. Number of employees: 325. Unit of Cablevision, Bethpage, New York. Number of internship applications received each year: 250.

Internships Available ▶ *Interns.* Candidates should have ability to work with others, college courses in field, knowledge of field, plan to pursue career in field, strong interpersonal skills. Duration is 1 semester. Unpaid. Open to college freshmen, college sophomores, college juniors, college seniors. International applications accepted.

Benefits On-the-job training, possible full-time employment, willing to complete paperwork for educational credit, willing to provide letters of recommendation.

Contact Write, call, fax, or e-mail Myles Rich, Production Manager. Phone: 914-835-5543. Fax: 914-835-5098. E-mail: mrich@cablevision.com. In-person interview recommended. Applicants must submit a cover letter, resume. Applications are accepted continuously.

CBS, INC.
1170 Soldiers Field Road
Boston, Massachusetts 02134

General Information Broadcast television and AM–FM radio stations serving the Boston area. Established in 1921. Number of employees: 300. Affiliate of CBS, Inc., New York, New York, New York, New York.

Internships Available ▶ *1–3 BZ Productions interns:* responsibilities include learning how commercials and promotional spots are made, field and studio production skills, post production techniques, and an overview of writing, directing, producing and editing; learning the terminology and uses of production equipment, logging and labeling tapes, and organizing production office, working closely with the TV Sales Department. Days needed: Monday-Friday. Candidates should have knowledge of field, oral communication skills, organizational skills, personal interest in the field, self-motivation, strong interpersonal skills. Unpaid. ▶ *1 CBS Boston: management information systems intern:* responsibilities include working with the Director of Information Technology who designs, installs, and maintains computers and network operations for WBZ-TV, WBZ NewsRadio, and WODS-FM; assisting in "help desk" type functions: installing PCs, supporting sales and news users on software/hardware problems or questions; learning computer hardware/software, some networking components and theory, and end-user support skills. Days needed: Monday-Friday. Candidates should have computer skills, knowledge of field, organizational skills, personal interest in the field, self-motivation, strong interpersonal skills. Unpaid. ▶ *1 CBS Boston: news media (Web) intern:* responsibilities include assisting Webmaster in site development, design, and upkeep (computer knowledge a must); learning how Web site content is maintained and updated; using HTML; helping design graphics for the site; learning how ad space is used by the sales departments; answering or forwarding numerous daily e-mail requests; developing skills in current Web design/publishing software, including Adobe Photoshop, Allair HomeSite, Netscape Navigator/Communicator, Microsoft Internet Explorer, and Microsoft Office. Days needed: Monday—Friday. Candidates should have computer skills, knowledge of field, personal interest in the field, self-motivation, strong interpersonal skills. Unpaid. ▶ *1 WBZ Newsradio: news intern:* responsibilities include assisting WBZ NewsRadio news department in news gathering, writing, audio production, and administration. Days needed: Monday-Friday 8am-11pm, plus possible weekend work (flexible). Candidates should have oral communication skills, personal interest in the field, research skills, self-motivation, strong interpersonal skills, written communication skills. Unpaid. ▶ *1 WBZ Newsradio: programming intern:* responsibilities include assisting with radio programming administrative tasks, working on special projects, learning use of radio broadcast equipment. Days needed: Monday-Friday 9:30am-6pm (flexible), some weekend work. Candidates should have oral communication skills, organizational skills, personal interest in the field, research skills, self-motivation, written communication skills. Unpaid. ▶ *1–2 WBZ newsradio promotions interns:* responsibilities include assisting the Promotions Director and Promotions Coordinator with the creation, development, and execution of promotions for advertising clients of WBZ NewsRadio; assisting at on-site remote station events; coordinating the scheduling of on-air prize giveaways and mailing out prizes and release forms to contest winners; using Microsoft Word 6.0 to prepare promotion proposals for use in sales presentations; writing on-air radio contest copy; scheduling air time for promotions; attending sales meetings and sales calls when appropriate; and general administrative tasks like typing, faxing, filing, sorting mail and answering phones. Days needed: Monday-Friday (prefer Monday, Wednesday, Friday) plus special events. Candidates should have ability to work independently, computer skills, oral communication skills, organizational skills, self-motivation, strong interpersonal skills, written communication skills. Unpaid. ▶ *1–4 WBZ-TV News: Assignment Desk interns:* responsibilities include assisting assignment editors, reporters, and producers in gathering news stories, pre-interviewing, researching, viewing/logging tapes, and extensive phone work to help cultivate news stories. Days needed: weekdays, nights, weekends (varies). Candidates should have oral communication skills, personal interest in the field, research skills, self-motivation, strong interpersonal skills, ability to work in a hectic environment. Unpaid. ▶ *1–3 WBZ-TV News: I-Team interns:* responsibilities include documenting research, pre-interviewing subjects, taking telephone tips, researching and developing tips, and logging tapes. Days needed: Monday-Friday. Candidates should have ability to work independently, computer skills, office skills, oral communication skills, personal interest in the field, research skills, strong interpersonal skills, written communication skills. Unpaid. ▶ *1–4 WBZ-TV News: News 4 This Morning interns:* responsibilities include researching topics for interviews, escorting guests and preparing the greenroom, and assisting production on live remotes. Days needed: Monday-Friday 5am-1pm. Candidates should have personal interest in the field, research skills, self-motivation, strong interpersonal skills, written communication skills. Unpaid. ▶ *1 WBZ-TV: marketing/creative services intern:* responsibilities include learning how a TV station uses their own air to achieve strategic marketing goals and objectives; learning the logistics and language of promotion; gaining a working knowledge of television production, from the creative writing process, to field producing, to post production in the edit room; learning how to develop and execute news topicals, news serials, and public service announcement. Days needed: Monday-Friday. Candidates should have computer skills, office skills, oral communication skills, personal interest in the field, strong interpersonal skills, writing skills. Unpaid. ▶ *1–2 WODS-FM: promotions interns:* responsibilities include assisting in contest administration, event coordination and execution, and special projects. Days needed: Monday-Friday, plus special events. Candidates should have ability to work independently, computer skills, oral communication skills, organizational skills, self-motivation, strong interpersonal skills, written communication skills. Unpaid. ▶ *1 public relations intern:* responsibilities include writing and maintaining updated biographies, photos, and press materials; tracking station press coverage for monthly reports; scheduling speaking engagements for talent; coordinating publicity elements of special events and broadcasts including telethons, network, and syndication talent visits; assisting in planning and execution of photo shoots; distributing press releases to media and maintaining the media database; updating and coordinating materials for the station's Web site with the Webmaster. Days needed: Monday—Friday. Candidates should have ability to work independently, computer skills, oral communication skills, personal interest in the field, strong interpersonal skills, written communication skills. Unpaid. Duration for all positions is 1 semester. Open to college sophomores, college juniors, college seniors, graduate students. International applications accepted.

Benefits Opportunity to attend seminars/workshops, willing to complete paperwork for educational credit, willing to provide letters of recommendation.

Contact Write, call, or fax CBS Boston Internship Program. Phone: 617-787-7000. Fax: 617-787-5769. In-person interview recommended. Applicants must submit a resume, academic transcripts, formal application, portion of which must be completed by intern/faculty advisor. Applications are accepted continuously. World Wide Web: http://www.wbz.com.

CBS NEWS, INC.
2020 M Street, NW
Washington, District of Columbia 20036

General Information A world-wide news organization serving the CBS Television and Radio Networks with regularly scheduled news and public affairs broadcasts and special reports. Established in 1966. Subsidiary of Westinghouse Electric Company, Pittsburgh, Pennsylvania. Number of internship applications received each year: 500.

Internships Available ▶ *Production interns:* responsibilities include working in various broadcast and support departments, including CBS This Morning, Evening News, 48 Hours, public relations, CBS promotions, CBS production, Sunday Morning/Weekend News, NewsPath, and Up to the Minute. Candidates should have computer skills, declared college major in field, knowledge of field, oral communication skills, writing skills. Dura-

CBS News, Inc. (continued)

tion is 1 semester. Unpaid. Open to college juniors, college seniors, graduate students, law students. International applications accepted.

Benefits On-the-job training, opportunity to attend seminars/ workshops, willing to act as a professional reference, willing to complete paperwork for educational credit.

Contact Write or e-mail Ms. Eldra Rodriguez-Gillman, Director of Professional Advancement and Internships. E-mail: eig@ cbsnews.com. No phone calls. Applicants must submit a cover letter, resume, academic transcripts, two letters of recommendation. Application deadline: first-come, first-served basis.

CHILDREN'S TELEVISION WORKSHOP
One Lincoln Plaza
New York, New York 10023

General Information Not-for-profit company using media to educate children and families worldwide; sponsors programs for traditional and new media; engages in publishing, product licensing, and community outreach; producer of Sesame Street. Established in 1969. Number of employees: 450. Number of internship applications received each year: 500.

Internships Available ▶ *20–30 interns:* responsibilities include working in areas of magazines/publishing, events, human resources, new show projects, research, video/technical operations, creative classroom, international television, library/records management, publicity, school publishing, and promotions. Candidates should have college courses in field, computer skills, oral communication skills, personal interest in the field, strong interpersonal skills, written communication skills. Duration is 1 semester. Position available as unpaid or paid. Open to college freshmen, college sophomores, college juniors, college seniors, recent college graduates, graduate students, law students, career changers. International applications accepted.

Benefits Opportunity to attend seminars/workshops, willing to complete paperwork for educational credit, willing to provide letters of recommendation.

Contact Write, call, fax, or e-mail Leo A. Munoz, Senior Human Resources Associate. Phone: 212-875-6813. Fax: 212-875-6088. E-mail: leo.munoz@ctw.org. In-person interview recommended. Applicants must submit a cover letter, resume. Applications are accepted continuously. World Wide Web: http://www.ctw.org.

CNN AMERICA, INC.
820 1st Street, NE
Washington, District of Columbia 20002

General Information Cable news network offering 24 hours of news and information programming daily. Established in 1980. Number of employees: 300. Unit of Turner Broadcasting System, Inc., Atlanta, Georgia. Number of internship applications received each year: 500.

Internships Available ▶ *15–20 alternate interns:* responsibilities include assisting with production needs, conducting research, and learning about booking guests and show research. Open to college juniors, college seniors, graduate students. ▶ *5–10 rotation interns:* responsibilities include assisting writers, producers, video librarians, and field crews. Open to college juniors, college seniors. Candidates for all positions should have ability to work independently, college courses in field, oral communication skills, plan to pursue career in field, self-motivation, strong interpersonal skills. Duration for all positions is 12–15 weeks. All positions are unpaid. International applications accepted.

Benefits Formal training, names of contacts, opportunity to attend seminars/workshops, willing to complete paperwork for educational credit.

International Internships Available in London, United Kingdom.

Contact Write, call, or e-mail Ms. Virginia Umrani, Intern Coordinator. Phone: 202-515-2916. E-mail: ginny.umrani@turner. com. Applicants must submit a formal organization application, cover letter, resume, academic transcripts, two letters of recommendation, 1- to 2-page essay. Application deadline: March 1 for summer, July 1 for fall, October 1 for holiday, November 1 for spring.

COMCAST SPORTSNET
3601 South Broad Street
Philadelphia, Pennsylvania 19148

General Information Cable television sports network. Unit of Comcast-Spectacor, Philadelphia, Pennsylvania.

Internships Available ▶ *1–3 market research interns:* responsibilities include designing, conducting, and interpreting random sample surveys to determine viewer perceptions and preferences, organizing Nielsen ratings data, and developing internal system for interpretation and presentation. Candidates should have oral communication skills, organizational skills, written communication skills, ability to use MS Word (or WordPerfect), MS Excel, and cc:Mail. Duration is January to May. Open to college juniors and seniors or graduate students, working for academic credit. ▶ *10 network sports interns:* responsibilities include logging games, selecting highlights, filing tapes, and pulling scripts. Candidates should have self-motivation, strong interpersonal skills, knowledge of sports and degree track in broadcast communications, sports communications, sports management, or related fields (preferred). Duration is 1 semester in fall, spring, or summer. Open to college freshmen, college sophomores, college juniors, college seniors. ▶ *1–2 operations/production interns:* responsibilities include assisting show director, studio crew, and control room in all aspects of daily production. Candidates should have self-motivation, strong interpersonal skills, academic coursework that emphasizes production side of broadcast communications industry, ability to work mornings, nights, and/or weekends. Duration is 1 semester. Open to college students pursuing degrees in broadcast communications. ▶ *3 programming/ production interns:* responsibilities include screening and logging taped programming to prepare for editing; detail work to procure footage from external sources; helping to line up guests for appearances; preparing, copying, and distributing programming information internally; and researching background and details for local shows. Candidates should have oral communication skills, organizational skills, written communication skills, ability to use word processing and spreadsheet applications. Duration is 1 semester in fall, spring, or summer. Open to college juniors and seniors or graduate students, working for academic credit. ▶ *1 promotions intern:* responsibilities include assisting Promotions Producer in writing, producing, and editing on-air promos; writing and distributing drop-in copy for live events; and performing clerical duties as needed. Candidates should have oral communication skills, organizational skills, personal interest in the field, written communication skills, professional phone skills, ability to use Microsoft Word (or WordPerfect), Excel, and cc: Mail. Duration is 1 semester. Open to college juniors and seniors or graduate students, working for academic credit. ▶ *1 public relations intern:* responsibilities include proofing, editing, and faxing press releases; managing photo file; maintaining media contact list and making follow-up media calls; assisting with Web site maintenance; accompanying Public Relations Director on various assignments, and clipping, filing, and disseminating Comcast SportsNet articles. Candidates should have oral communication skills, written communication skills, ability to use Microsoft Office or WordPerfect 5.1/6.0, database management experience (preferred). Duration is 1 semester in fall, spring, or summer. Open to college juniors and seniors or graduate students, working for academic credit. All positions are unpaid.

Benefits Names of contacts, possible full-time employment, willing to complete paperwork for educational credit, excellent experience in the sports and entertainment industry.

Contact Write Internship Program, Human Resources Department. No phone calls. In-person interview required. Applicants must submit a formal organization application, resume, cover letter indicating reasons for choosing a particular internship and the qualities or attributes that will help make a contribution, faculty recommendation form (sent with application). Application deadline: at least 2 months prior to intended start date. World Wide Web: http://www.comcast-spectacor.com.

COMEDY CENTRAL
1775 Broadway, 10th Floor
New York, New York 10019

General Information Advertiser-supported basic cable comedy service. Established in 1991. Number of employees: 250. Unit of Time Warner and Viacom, New York, New York. Number of internship applications received each year: 200.
Internships Available ▶ *1 affiliate relations intern:* responsibilities include supporting affiliate sales group. Candidates should have computer skills, oral communication skills, self-motivation, strong interpersonal skills, written communication skills. Open to college freshmen, college sophomores, college juniors, college seniors. ▶ *2 corporate communication interns:* responsibilities include assisting in day to day public relations effort/events; maintaining network press digest; updating press releases, and executive and talent bio photo files; maintaining press tape library; general office support; coordinating press kits. ▶ *1 human resources intern:* responsibilities include assisting in development of Human Resources administrative filing system, assisting in various Human Resources projects, providing general office support, assisting in development of recruitment database. ▶ *1–2 on-air promotions interns:* responsibilities include providing general office support, assisting at external shoots and screenings, helping production assistants, assisting on occasional off-lining. ▶ *1–2 on-line interns:* responsibilities include providing on-line administration, responding to all on-line correspondence, and organizing on-line archives. Candidates should have analytical skills, computer skills, oral communication skills, strong interpersonal skills, written communication skills. Open to college freshmen, college sophomores, college juniors, college seniors. ▶ *4–5 production interns:* responsibilities include providing basic office support, copying and labeling various programs for other departments, helping organize program cart sheets, and maintaining prop closet and reel library. Candidates should have ability to work independently, computer skills, oral communication skills, self-motivation, strong interpersonal skills, written communication skills. Open to college freshmen, college sophomores, college juniors, college seniors. ▶ *1–2 programming/development interns:* responsibilities include providing general office support, reviewing treatments (scripts and submission), handling all correspondence. Candidates should have ability to work independently, computer skills, oral communication skills, self-motivation, strong interpersonal skills, written communication skills. Open to college freshmen, college sophomores, college juniors, college seniors. ▶ *1 sales research intern:* responsibilities include providing basic office support and working with Nielsen database. Duration for all positions is 1 semester. All positions are unpaid.
Benefits On-the-job training, possible full-time employment, willing to act as a professional reference, willing to complete paperwork for educational credit, willing to provide letters of recommendation, small travel stipend, opportunity to attend show tapings and planned intern trips.
Contact Write or fax Human Resources Coordinator. Fax: 212-767-4257. No phone calls. In-person interview required. Applicants must submit a cover letter, resume, verification of school credit for internship. Applications are accepted continuously. World Wide Web: http://www.comedycentral.com.

COSMOS BROADCASTING CORPORATION
PO Box 32970
Louisville, Kentucky 40232

General Information Broadcast commercial television station. Established in 1948. Number of employees: 145. Affiliate of NBC-TV, New York, New York. Number of internship applications received each year: 50.
Internships Available ▶ *2 news interns:* responsibilities include working with professional staff in all technical areas, writing, and production. Candidates should have computer skills, oral communication skills, personal interest in the field, self-motivation, written communication skills. Position available as unpaid or at minimum wage in summertime; unpaid during other seasons. ▶ *2 production interns:* responsibilities include operating cameras, running teleprompter, lighting, and moving props. Candidates should have ability to work independently, ability to work with others, computer skills, oral communication skills, self-motivation. minimum wage. Duration for all positions is 8–12 weeks. Open to college seniors.
Benefits Willing to complete paperwork for educational credit, willing to provide letters of recommendation.
Contact Write Ms. Kathy Faulkner, Personnel Coordinator. No phone calls. In-person interview recommended. Applicants must submit a formal organization application, resume, academic transcripts. Applications are accepted continuously. World Wide Web: http://www.wave3.com.

C-SPAN
400 North Capitol Street, NW, Suite 650
Washington, District of Columbia 20001

General Information Provides audience access to live gavel-to-gavel proceedings of the U.S. House of Representatives and the U.S. Senate, and to other forums where public policy is discussed, debated, and decided, without editing, commentary, or analysis and with a balanced presentation of points-of-view. Established in 1979. Number of employees: 250. Number of internship applications received each year: 300.
Internships Available ▶ *2 "Washington Journal" interns:* responsibilities include developing specific live and taped programs for morning program, the $ITWashington Journal; greeting guests, setting up studio/green room, follow-up with guests, research. Candidates should have computer skills, oral communication skills, personal interest in the field, self-motivation, strong interpersonal skills. ▶ *2 affiliate and community relations interns:* responsibilities include supporting targeted community marketing efforts to cable companies across the country. Candidates should have ability to work independently, oral communication skills, personal interest in the field, strong interpersonal skills, written communication skills. ▶ *2 assignment desk interns:* responsibilities include soliciting and gathering information about events on Capitol Hill and around the nation, and coordinating all logistical and technical requirements to cover these events. Candidates should have ability to work independently, ability to work with others, oral communication skills, organizational skills, personal interest in the field, self-motivation. ▶ *2 creative services interns:* responsibilities include providing creative direction and developing support materials that promote the network to cable operators, educators, and viewers; generating ads and publications. Candidates should have computer skills, editing skills, organizational skills, personal interest in the field, self-motivation, writing skills. ▶ *2 educational and marketing services interns:* responsibilities include developing educational materials and outreach programs. Candidates should have computer skills, office skills, oral communication skills, personal interest in the field, self-motivation, written communication skills. ▶ *2 field producers:* responsibilities include developing programming ideas by researching specific areas of government, its history and the process, as well as coordinating logistical aspects required in production. Candidates should have analytical skills, computer skills, organizational skills, personal interest in the field, research skills, self-motivation. ▶ *2 field production interns:* responsibilities include handling audio, lighting, and camera operation for events that take place in and around Washington D.C., and executing set-up and breakdown of equipment. Candidates should have ability to work independently, personal interest in the field, self-motivation, strong interpersonal skills, strong leadership ability. ▶ *2 media relations interns:* responsibilities include communicating C-SPAN's mission, programming, style, and content to national media outlets. Candidates should have computer skills, office skills, organizational skills, personal interest in the field, research skills, self-motivation. ▶ *2 new media interns:* responsibilities include developing and managing contracts and initiating business relationships relating to C-SPAN products, videotapes, transcripts, and online services. Candidates should have computer skills, editing skills, organizational skills, personal interest in the field, research skills, writing skills. ▶ *2 programming operations editorial interns:* responsibilities include working with producers in developing daily schedule, tracking House and Senate floor debate, script-writing, voice overs,

C-Span (continued)

scheduling breaks, coordinating final programming that airs on C-Span. Candidates should have computer skills, oral communication skills, personal interest in the field, self-motivation, strong interpersonal skills. ▶ *2 programming operations technical interns:* responsibilities include technical aspects of setting the networks on-air, including program direction, master control, camera, lighting, audio and on-air promotions. Candidates should have ability to work with others, knowledge of field, oral communication skills, personal interest in the field, self-motivation, strong leadership ability. ▶ *2 radio interns:* responsibilities include broadcasting a mix of daily programs similar in style to those found on the C-SPAN television networks, including congressional hearings, speeches, debates, and forum discussions. Candidates should have ability to work independently, computer skills, editing skills, oral communication skills, organizational skills, personal interest in the field, research skills, self-motivation, strong interpersonal skills, writing skills. Duration for all positions is 10 weeks. All positions are unpaid. Open to college juniors, college seniors. International applications accepted.
Benefits Job counseling, names of contacts, possible full-time employment, willing to complete paperwork for educational credit.
Contact Write, call, or fax Melanie Van Wicklin, Human Resources Specialist, 400 North Capitol Street, NW Suite 650, Washington, District of Columbia 20001. Phone: 202-626-4851. Fax: 202-737-3323. Applicants must submit a cover letter, resume. Applications are accepted continuously. World Wide Web: http://www.c-span.org.

GREATER DAYTON PUBLIC TELEVISION, WPTD-TV/WPTO-TV
110 South Jefferson Street
Dayton, Ohio 45402-2415

General Information Television station comprising 2 public broadcasting stations: WPTD and WPTO. Established in 1959. Number of employees: 50. Number of internship applications received each year: 15.
Internships Available ▶ *3–4 interns:* responsibilities include working in areas of production, engineering, or marketing/administration. Duration is flexible. $6 per hour. Open to college freshmen, college sophomores, college juniors, college seniors. International applications accepted.
Benefits Formal training, names of contacts, possible full-time employment, willing to complete paperwork for educational credit, willing to provide letters of recommendation.
Contact Write or fax Ms. Brenda Bathgate, Office and Personnel Manager. Fax: 937-220-1642. No phone calls. In-person interview required. Applicants must submit a cover letter, resume. Applications are accepted continuously. World Wide Web: http://www.gdpt.org.

GREATER MEDIA CABLE
95 Higgins Street
Worcester, Massachusetts 01606

General Information Cable company servicing 22 central Massachusetts communities. Established in 1975. Number of employees: 175. Unit of Greater Media, Inc., New Brunswick, New Jersey. Number of internship applications received each year: 30.
Internships Available ▶ *4–5 advertising production assistants:* responsibilities include lighting, setting up equipment, editing, producing, scriptwriting, and maintaining sets. ▶ *1 community affairs assistant:* responsibilities include writing newsletters, conducting company tours, attending meetings, writing press releases, and dealing with the public. Candidates should have computer skills, editing skills, oral communication skills, plan to pursue career in field, strong interpersonal skills, written communication skills. ▶ *4–5 production assistants for news:* responsibilities include running camera and audio, writing scripts, editing, co-producing, directing, and floor directing. Candidates should have ability to work with others, college courses in field, computer skills, experience in the field, personal interest in the field, self-

motivation. Duration for all positions is flexible. All positions are unpaid. Open to college juniors, college seniors.
Benefits Possible full-time employment, willing to complete paperwork for educational credit.
Contact Write, call, or fax Leslie Parella, Internship Coordinator. Phone: 508-853-1515. Fax: 508-854-5065. In-person interview recommended. Applicants must submit a cover letter, resume, two letters of recommendation. Application deadline: May 1 for summer; first come, first serve for all deadlines, August 1 for fall, December 1 for spring.

HOME BOX OFFICE
1100 Avenue of the Americas
New York, New York 10036

General Information Subscriber-based cable television channel. Established in 1972. Number of employees: 2,000. Unit of Time Warner, Inc., New York, New York. Number of internship applications received each year: 1,000.
Internships Available ▶ *50–75 communications interns:* responsibilities include duties relating to all areas of communications including production, original programming, advertising, marketing, finance, computers, human resources, public relations, accounting, and photography. Candidates should have computer skills, oral communication skills, personal interest in the field, strong interpersonal skills, writing skills. Duration is 10 weeks. $500 per duration of internship. Open to college sophomores, college juniors, college seniors. International applications accepted.
Benefits Possible full-time employment, willing to complete paperwork for educational credit, willing to provide letters of recommendation, $500 stipend upon completion of internship.
Contact Write Christine Buderman, Internship Coordinator. No phone calls. In-person interview required. Applicants must submit a cover letter, resume, formal letter from college or university stating that internship is being done for educational credit. Applications are accepted continuously. World Wide Web: http://www.HBO.com.

ISN SPORTS
10220 South Bensley Avenue
Chicago, Illinois 60617-5730

General Information Nonprofit sports broadcasting organization geared toward covering amateur (high school and college) sports. Established in 1998. Number of employees: 4. Number of internship applications received each year: 5.
Internships Available ▶ *2–4 color analysts:* responsibilities include assisting the ISN play-by-play team in live-event game commentary, using knowledge of the sport being presented to highlight certain details and nuances of the broadcast. Candidates should have ability to work with others, analytical skills, oral communication skills, research skills, strong interpersonal skills, written communication skills. ▶ *12–16 field/sideline reporters:* responsibilities include reporting on specific details related to a particular sports broadcast, and researching and reporting on other athletics-related stories for ISN-based shows. Candidates should have ability to work independently, oral communication skills, self-motivation, strong interpersonal skills, writing skills. Duration for all positions is 1 year. All positions are unpaid. Open to high school students, recent high school graduates, college freshmen, college sophomores, college juniors, college seniors, recent college graduates.
Benefits Names of contacts, on-the-job training, opportunity to attend seminars/workshops, willing to act as a professional reference, willing to provide letters of recommendation.
Contact Call or e-mail Alvin Washington, Jr., Coordinator/Shooting Stars, 10220 South Bensley Avenue, Chicago, Illinois 60617-5730. Phone: 773-302-9715. E-mail: isnsports@cnnsimail.com. Applicants must submit a formal organization application, resume. Application deadline: June 1. World Wide Web: http://members.tripod.com/isnsports.

THE JIM HENSON COMPANY
117 East 69th Street
New York, New York 10021

General Information Independent multimedia company that focuses on television and film production, international and domestic licensing and publishing, public relations, archives and exhibits, and design services. Established in 1958. Number of employees: 125. Branch of The Jim Henson Company, Los Angeles, California. Number of internship applications received each year: 400.

Internships Available ▶ *Jim Henson Foundation interns:* responsibilities include assembling press kits, answering telephones, faxing, copying, running errands, and filing. Candidates should have computer skills, office skills, oral communication skills, organizational skills, personal interest in the field, self-motivation, strong interpersonal skills, interest in development/fund-raising, theater background preferred. ▶ *Archives/photo library interns:* responsibilities include assisting with photo shoot plans, answering telephones, faxing, copying, running errands, and filing. Candidates should have computer skills, office skills, oral communication skills, organizational skills, personal interest in the field, self-motivation, strong interpersonal skills, library or archival background preferred. ▶ *Licensing interns:* responsibilities include assembling marketing kits, answering telephones, faxing, copying, running errands, and filing. Candidates should have computer skills, office skills, oral communication skills, organizational skills, personal interest in the field, self-motivation, strong interpersonal skills, interest in business and marketing knowledge preferred. ▶ *Pre-production interns:* responsibilities include copying and issuing scripts, working with numbers, answering telephones, faxing, copying, running errands, and filing. Candidates should have computer skills, office skills, oral communication skills, organizational skills, personal interest in the field, self-motivation, strong interpersonal skills. ▶ *Public relations interns:* responsibilities include maintaining and preparing monthly clippings package, answering telephones, faxing, copying, running errands, and filing. Candidates should have computer skills, office skills, oral communication skills, organizational skills, personal interest in the field, self-motivation, strong interpersonal skills. ▶ *Publishing interns:* responsibilities include answering telephones, faxing, copying, running errands, and filing. Candidates should have computer skills, office skills, oral communication skills, organizational skills, self-motivation, strong interpersonal skills, interest in editing and research. ▶ *Studio interns:* responsibilities include video and audio dubbing, working with storage facilities, assisting in productions or editing, answering telephones, faxing, copying, running errands, and filing. Candidates should have personal interest in the field, high energy. Duration for all positions is at least two full days per week, as needed. All positions are unpaid. Open to college freshmen, college sophomores, college juniors, college seniors, must be eligible to receive college credit.

Benefits Possible full-time employment, willing to act as a professional reference, willing to complete paperwork for educational credit, willing to provide letters of recommendation.

Contact Write Shefali Kothari, Internship Coordinator. No phone calls. In-person interview required. Applicants must submit a cover letter, resume. Application deadline: March 30 for summer, July 30 for fall, November 30 for spring. World Wide Web: http://www.henson.com.

JONES COMMUNICATIONS, INC.
12345G Sunrise Valley Drive
Reston, Virginia 20191

General Information Television studio and mobile unit providing locally produced television programming for a cable television community channel. Established in 1970. Number of employees: 28. Unit of Jones Intercable, Inc., Denver, Colorado. Number of internship applications received each year: 20.

Internships Available ▶ *3 TV production interns:* responsibilities include learning camera editing and possibly directing. Candidates should have ability to work independently, ability to work with others, personal interest in the field, self-motivation. Duration is 1 semester. Unpaid. Open to high school students, high school seniors, recent high school graduates, college freshmen, college sophomores, college juniors, college seniors, recent college graduates, graduate students, career changers, individuals reentering the workforce.

Benefits On-the-job training, willing to act as a professional reference, willing to complete paperwork for educational credit, willing to provide letters of recommendation.

Contact Write or call Mr. Thomas F. Bartelt, Community Programming Manager. Phone: 703-758-8099. In-person interview recommended. Applicants must submit a cover letter, resume. Applications are accepted continuously.

KCRA-TV
3 Television Circle
Sacramento, California 95814

General Information Commercial broadcast television station. Established in 1945. Number of employees: 175. Unit of Hearst-Argyle Television, Inc., New York, New York. Number of internship applications received each year: 180.

Internships Available ▶ *2 commercial production assistants:* responsibilities include production of commercial spots, promotions, public service announcements, and some special programming. Candidates should have college courses in field, computer skills, editing skills, personal interest in the field, research skills, self-motivation. Duration is 1 semester. Open to college freshmen, college sophomores, college juniors, college seniors, recent college graduates, graduate students. ▶ *2 community relations assistants:* responsibilities include providing clerical support for public relations functions and KCRA-TV scholarship program, preparing community calendar, and assisting in production of public affairs programming. Candidates should have ability to work independently, computer skills, office skills, organizational skills, writing skills. Duration is 1 semester. Open to college sophomores, college juniors, college seniors, recent college graduates, graduate students. ▶ *1 consumer reporter assistant:* responsibilities include researching stories, setting up locations, accompanying reporters on assignment, and researching case files and records. Candidates should have college courses in field, computer skills, personal interest in the field, research skills, self-motivation, written communication skills. Duration is 1 semester. Open to college juniors, college seniors, recent college graduates, graduate students. ▶ *3 editing assistants:* responsibilities include working with the engineering supervisor and staff in transferring video and audio reports to master library tapes. Candidates should have ability to work with others, computer skills, oral communication skills, organizational skills, personal interest in the field, self-motivation. Duration is 1 semester. Open to college freshmen, college sophomores, college juniors, college seniors, recent college graduates, graduate students. ▶ *8 general news assistants:* responsibilities include working at the assignment desk answering reporters' phones, researching stories, accompanying reporters and/or photographers on assignments, and assisting news producers with production chores. Candidates should have college courses in field, computer skills, editing skills, personal interest in the field, research skills, written communication skills. Duration is 1 semester. Open to college sophomores, college juniors, college seniors, recent college graduates, graduate students. ▶ *1 graphics assistant:* responsibilities include working with art department in non-broadcast artwork including sales prices, printwork, set building and design, and computer graphics. Candidates should have college courses in field, computer skills, editing skills, plan to pursue career in field, self-motivation. Duration is 1 semester. Open to college sophomores, college juniors, college seniors, recent college graduates, graduate students. ▶ *2 news producer assistants:* responsibilities include performing news production functions including tearing scripts, recording and logging news feeds, answering telephones, researching news stories, and writing. Candidates should have ability to work independently, ability to work with others, computer skills, personal interest in the field, research skills, self-motivation. Duration is 1 semester. Open to college sophomores, college juniors, college seniors, recent college graduates, graduate students. ▶ *2 news special projects interns:*

KCRA-TV (continued)

responsibilities include researching story ideas and assisting reporters and photographers in researching information for series and special projects. Candidates should have college courses in field, computer skills, organizational skills, personal interest in the field, research skills, self-motivation. Duration is 1 semester. Open to college sophomores, college juniors, college seniors, recent college graduates, graduate students. ▶ *1 promotions assistant:* responsibilities include assisting with production of on-air promotional spots including field, studio, and post production work; creating outside media work (newspaper ads and radio spots); and producing public service announcements. Candidates should have ability to work with others, college courses in field, computer skills, plan to pursue career in field, self-motivation. Duration is 8–10 weeks. Open to college sophomores, college juniors, college seniors, recent college graduates, graduate students. ▶ *1 sales marketing assistant:* responsibilities include working on sales research, typing rough formats for sales promotion information; opportunities to accompany account executives on sales calls. Candidates should have computer skills, office skills, organizational skills, personal interest in the field, self-motivation, strong interpersonal skills, writing skills. Duration is 1 semester. Open to college sophomores, college juniors, college seniors, recent college graduates, graduate students. ▶ *3 sports assistants:* responsibilities include compiling scores, researching stories and game information, monitoring televised games, and accompanying reporter and photographer in the field. Duration is 1 semester. Open to college sophomores, college juniors, college seniors, recent college graduates, graduate students. All positions are unpaid. International applications accepted.

Benefits On-the-job training, possible full-time employment, travel reimbursement, willing to act as a professional reference, willing to complete paperwork for educational credit, willing to provide letters of recommendation.
Contact Write, call, fax, or e-mail Mr. Dave Kaylor, News Operation Manager/Internship Director. Phone: 916-325-3320. Fax: 916-441-4050. E-mail: dkaylor@hearstsc.com. In-person interview recommended. Application deadline: May 31 for summer, August 8 for fall, December 5 for spring.

KET, THE KENTUCKY NETWORK
600 Cooper Drive
Lexington, Kentucky 40502

General Information Statewide public television network. Established in 1968. Number of employees: 200. Number of internship applications received each year: 100.
Internships Available ▶ *20–30 interns:* responsibilities include performing tasks assigned by the KET supervisor. Candidates should have oral communication skills, self-motivation, strong interpersonal skills, written communication skills. Duration is 1 semester. Unpaid. Open to college juniors, college seniors, graduate students.
Benefits Formal training, on-the-job training, possible full-time employment, willing to complete paperwork for educational credit, willing to provide letters of recommendation.
Contact Write, call, fax, or e-mail Ms. Jan Mullaney, Volunteer Services Administrator. Phone: 606-258-7232. Fax: 606-258-7393. E-mail: jmullaney@ket.org. In-person interview required. Applicants must submit a resume, 3-5 writing samples for communication interns. Application deadline: April 15 for summer, December 1 for spring. World Wide Web: http://www.ket.org.

KGW-TV
1501 Southwest Jefferson Street
Portland, Oregon 97201

General Information Television station airing sunrise, noon, 5 p.m., 6 p.m.,11 p.m., and weekend news shows; produces local commercials. Established in 1946. Number of employees: 160. Unit of A. H. Belo Corporation, Dallas, Texas. Number of internship applications received each year: 50.
Internships Available ▶ *1–2 creative services interns:* responsibilities include assisting with station promotions or commercial

production, and with coordination of station events. Candidates should have ability to work with others, college courses in field, office skills, oral communication skills, personal interest in the field, self-motivation, written communication skills. ▶ *3–6 news interns:* responsibilities include gaining an understanding of TV news through assisting with story setup, dispatching crews, writing newscasts, and assisting producers, reporters, and photographers with news production. Candidates should have college courses in field, oral communication skills, plan to pursue career in field, self-motivation, written communication skills. ▶ *Sports interns:* responsibilities include working with sports staff in preparation of daily sportcasts. Candidates should have ability to work independently, college courses in field, oral communication skills, personal interest in the field, self-motivation, strong interpersonal skills, written communication skills. Duration for all positions is 1 quarter or semester. All positions are unpaid. Open to undergraduates who are eligible for college credit; juniors and seniors preferred. International applications accepted.
Benefits Names of contacts, willing to complete paperwork for educational credit.
Contact Write, fax, or e-mail Ms. Kathy Copeland, Human Resource Director. Fax: 503-226-4573. E-mail: kathyc@kgw.com. No phone calls. In-person interview recommended. Applicants must submit a formal organization application, cover letter, resume. Applications are accepted continuously. World Wide Web: http://www.kgw.com.

KIDSNET
6856 Eastern Avenue, NW, Suite 208
Washington, District of Columbia 20012

General Information Informational clearinghouse database for children's audio, video, radio, and television programs. Established in 1983. Number of employees: 5. Number of internship applications received each year: 40.
Internships Available ▶ *2–3 research interns:* responsibilities include marketing; fulfilling subscriber requests; updating and maintaining computer database; preparing, editing, and distributing monthly publication; working with on-line services; assisting in grant application process; preparing for participation in national, regional, and local conferences, workshops, and charter member and board meetings. Candidates should have analytical skills, computer skills, editing skills, oral communication skills, organizational skills, written communication skills. Duration is 2–4 months. Unpaid. Open to college sophomores, college juniors, college seniors.
Benefits Opportunity to attend seminars/workshops, possible full-time employment, willing to complete paperwork for educational credit, willing to provide letters of recommendation.
Contact Write, call, fax, or e-mail Matthew Smith, Research Manager. Phone: 202-291-1400. Fax: 202-882-7315. E-mail: kidsnet@aol.com. In-person interview recommended. Applicants must submit writing sample. Applications are accepted continuously. World Wide Web: http://www.kidsnet.org.

KOIN-TV
222 Southwest Columbia Street
Portland, Oregon 97201

General Information Television station. Established in 1953. Number of employees: 175. Number of internship applications received each year: 50.
Internships Available ▶ *News interns:* responsibilities include exposure to all aspects of news preparation. ▶ *Production interns:* responsibilities include exposure to all phases of production, including studio, field, and post-production. Duration for all positions is flexible (summer only). All positions are unpaid. Open to recent high school graduates, college freshmen, college sophomores, college juniors, college seniors, recent college graduates.
Benefits Willing to complete paperwork for educational credit.
Contact Write, call, or fax Allison Brown, Internship Coordinator. Phone: 503-464-0600. Fax: 503-464-0655. In-person interview

recommended. Applicants must submit a formal organization application, cover letter, resume. Application deadline: May 15 for summer.

KOTV
PO Box 6
Tulsa, Oklahoma 74101

General Information Television station that produces local news and public affairs programs. Established in 1947. Number of employees: 130. Unit of A.H. Belo Corporation, Dallas, Texas. Number of internship applications received each year: 10.
Internships Available ▶ *4 newsroom interns:* responsibilities include assisting reporters, photographers, and associate producers; editing; and operating teleprompter. ▶ *2 production interns:* responsibilities include running studio camera, assisting technical director with pre- and post-production work, and operating the teleprompter. ▶ *2 sports interns:* responsibilities include assisting sports department in shooting and editing stories and in the production of a sports newscast. Duration for all positions is 1 semester. All positions are unpaid. Open to high school students, high school seniors, recent high school graduates, college freshmen, college sophomores, college juniors, college seniors, recent college graduates, graduate students, law students, career changers, individuals reentering the workforce.
Benefits Formal training, willing to complete paperwork for educational credit, willing to provide letters of recommendation.
Contact Write, call, fax, or e-mail Mr. Michael McCardel, Political Reporter. Phone: 918-599-1420. Fax: 918-584-5513. E-mail: mmccardel@kotv.com. Applicants must submit a cover letter, resume. Applications are accepted continuously. World Wide Web: http://www.kotv.com.

KQED INC.
2601 Mariposa Street
San Francisco, California 94110

General Information Public broadcasting company that includes KQED-TV and KQED-FM. Established in 1954. Number of employees: 167. Number of internship applications received each year: 100.
Internships Available ▶ *KQED FM The California Report interns:* responsibilities include helping program producers, host, and reporters; and assisting in research, reporting, sound gathering, and writing. Candidates should have minimum GPA of 2.5; major in journalism, broadcasting, or communications; fluency in foreign languages is helpful. Duration is minimum of 3 months (2-3 days per week). Open to college juniors, college seniors, graduate students. ▶ *KQED Media Education Project interns:* responsibilities include working at the Center for Education and Lifelong Learning on such tasks as writing/editing publications, researching media, dubbing videotapes, and developing educational workshops. Candidates should have ability to work independently, computer skills, oral communication skills, research skills, written communication skills, minimum GPA of 2.5, experience with PC or Macintosh word processing and desktop publishing applications, Spanish skills a plus. Duration is flexible, minimum of 15 hours per week. Open to college juniors, college seniors, graduate students. ▶ *KQED TV Center for Education and Lifelong Learning (CELL) interns:* responsibilities include assisting in workshop recruitment for the Sesame Street Preschool Educational Program (PEP), evaluating children's video, designing and producing a monthly newsletter, dubbing video tapes, implementing educational activities, and general office support. Candidates should have minimum GPA of 2.5, major in early education or child development, knowledge of Spanish a plus. Duration is flexible (minimum of 15 hours per week and 1 weekend day per month). Open to college juniors, college seniors, graduate students. ▶ *KQED TV Web interns:* responsibilities include participating in maintenance and development of the CELL Web site, researching and updating content, assisting program development staff and Web manager. Candidates should have ability to work independently, oral communication skills, written communication skills, minimum GPA of 2.5, strong computer skills including HTML programming, desktop publish-

ing, and telecommunications. Duration is flexible, typically 4 months in spring, fall, or summer. Open to college juniors, college seniors, graduate students. ▶ *KQED TV program publicity interns:* responsibilities include assisiting the Publicist, filing program information and press clips, proofreading, research, writing, and organizing and preparing mailings. Candidates should have oral communication skills, organizational skills, self-motivation, writing skills, minimun GPA of 2.5, attention to detail, flexibility, Macintosh and/or PC proficiency, humor and enthusiasm. Duration is 1 semester (15-20 hours per week). Open to college juniors, college seniors, graduate students. ▶ *KQED communications/community affairs interns:* responsibilities include researching, writing, preparing mailings, contacting community organizations for various outreach projects promoting KQED and special events, and helping to organize teleconferences. Candidates should have computer skills, oral communication skills, organizational skills, self-motivation, writing skills, minimum GPA of 2.5, strong English and grammar skills, Macintosh and/or PC skills preferable. Duration is 4 months, minimum of 12 hours per week. Open to college juniors, college seniors, graduate students. ▶ *KQED educational services interns:* responsibilities include working in KQED's Center for Education and Lifelong Learning, writing and editing publications, doing audience research, developing educational content, and facilitating outreach activities. Candidates should have ability to work independently, computer skills, oral communication skills, research skills, self-motivation, written communication skills, major in education or related experience (preferred), Spanish skills a plus, knowledge of word processing and desktop publishing is desirable, minimum GPA of 2.5. Duration is flexible, minimum of 15 hours. Open to college juniors, college seniors, graduate students. ▶ *KQED human resources interns:* responsibilities include developing effective communication techniques, HTML Web maintenance, events planning, employee relations, diversity training, benefits administration, recruiting, and customer services. Candidates should have computer skills, oral communication skills, organizational skills, self-motivation, writing skills, minimum GPA of 2.5, major in liberal arts, strong English/grammatical skills. Duration is flexible (16-24 hours per week); typically 4 months in spring, fall, or summer. Open to college juniors, college seniors, graduate students. ▶ *KQED-FM Forum/public affairs interns:* responsibilities include conducting preliminary background and research for the Forum staff, conducting phone calls and outreach interviews, pre-screening, and assisting the producer. Candidates should have plan to pursue career in field, minimum GPA of 2.5, previous journalism experience (preferred). Duration is May to September with additional 2 months possible. Open to college sophomores, college juniors, college seniors, graduate students. ▶ *KQED-FM news interns:* responsibilities include researching, reporting, sound gathering, producing news and feature stories, and attending seminars and workshops on a variety of topics. Candidates should have minimum GPA of 2.5; major in journalism, communications, or broadcasting or strong writing experience. Duration is 4 months, minimum of 16-24 hours per week. Open to college juniors, college seniors, graduate students. All positions are unpaid. International applications accepted.

Benefits Formal training, job counseling, names of contacts, opportunity to attend seminars/workshops, willing to complete paperwork for educational credit.

Contact Write, fax, or e-mail Mr. Michael Dorame, Human Resources Coordinator. Fax: 415-553-2183. E-mail: hr@kqed. org. No phone calls. In-person interview recommended. Applicants must submit a cover letter, resume, proof of eligibility to receive college credit; women and minorities strongly encouraged to apply. Application deadline: March 21 for KQED-FM Forum/public affairs, summer position; continuous applications for all other positions. World Wide Web: http://www.kqed.org/HR.

KSDK NEWS CHANNEL 5
1000 Market Street
St. Louis, Missouri 63101

General Information NBC-affiliated news source for St. Louis. Established in 1947. Number of employees: 155. Unit of Gannett News Service, Arlington, Virginia. Number of internship applications received each year: 800.
Internships Available ▶ *1 assignment desk intern:* responsibilities include answering phones and making calls. Candidates should have ability to work independently, knowledge of field, oral communication skills, self-motivation, strong interpersonal skills, written communication skills. Duration is flexible by semester. ▶ *1 program intern:* responsibilities include assisting with production of *Show Me St. Louis*. Candidates should have computer skills, oral communication skills, self-motivation, strong interpersonal skills, strong leadership ability, written communication skills. Duration is flexible. ▶ *1 special projects intern:* responsibilities include working on various programs including entertainment and other series acting, working as reporters' assistants, and working with producers. Candidates should have ability to work independently, computer skills, oral communication skills, plan to pursue career in field, self-motivation, strong interpersonal skills, written communication skills. Duration is flexible by semester. ▶ *1 sports intern.* Candidates should have ability to work independently, knowledge of field, oral communication skills, self-motivation, strong interpersonal skills, written communication skills. Duration is flexible by semester. All positions are unpaid. Open to college freshmen, college sophomores, college juniors, college seniors, graduate students. International applications accepted.
Benefits Formal training, job counseling, names of contacts, opportunity to attend seminars/workshops, possible full-time employment, willing to act as a professional reference, willing to complete paperwork for educational credit, willing to provide letters of recommendation.
Contact Write, call, or fax Ava Ehrlich, News Planning Manager. Phone: 314-444-5120. Fax: 314-444-5164. In-person interview recommended. Applicants must submit a cover letter, resume, academic transcripts, three writing samples. Application deadline: April 15 for fall, April 15 for summer, December 1 for winter.

KUED-TV
101 Wasatch Drive, University of Utah
Salt Lake City, Utah 84112

General Information Television station whose goal is to be a vital community resource in the areas of public discourse, education, community service, and the arts by providing alternative, noncommercial television programs that educate, enlighten, and entertain. Established in 1958. Number of employees: 75. Unit of University of Utah, Salt Lake City, Utah. Number of internship applications received each year: 10.
Internships Available ▶ *1 intern:* responsibilities include performing studio and field production lighting, audio work, off- and on-line editing, and rotating among administrative, development, and creative services departments. Candidates should have personal interest in the field. Duration is 1 summer. $1,500 per duration of internship. Open to college juniors, college seniors. International applications accepted.
Benefits Formal training.
Contact Write or e-mail Christy Dunn, Human Resources Manager. E-mail: cdunn@media.utah.edu. No phone calls. In-person interview required. Applicants must submit a cover letter, resume. Application deadline: April 24 for summer. World Wide Web: http://www.media.utah.edu.

KVIE-TV
PO Box 6, 2595 Capitol Oaks Drive
Sacramento, California 95833

General Information Public television station serving the nation's 21st-largest media market covering Sacramento, California, and 28 surrounding counties; striving to educate, enlighten, and entertain its viewers and members. Established in 1959. Number of employees: 91. Number of internship applications received each year: 30.
Internships Available ▶ *3–5 production interns:* responsibilities include assisting with productions and membership drives. Candidates should have computer skills, office skills, oral communication skills, strong interpersonal skills, written communication skills. ▶ *3–5 research/production interns:* responsibilities include office work and researching for productions and membership drives. Candidates should have ability to work with others, computer skills, office skills, oral communication skills, written communication skills. ▶ *1–2 special events interns:* responsibilities include assisting with organizing and implementing special events and on-air auctions. Duties include: follow-up with donors, speakers, and vendors; solicitation of items for auction(s); preparing written correspondence; helping with set-up and tear-down of events; and graphic and Web design. Candidates should have ability to work with others, computer skills, office skills, oral communication skills, organizational skills, written communication skills. Duration for all positions is flexible. All positions are unpaid. Open to college freshmen, college sophomores, college juniors, college seniors, recent college graduates, graduate students. International applications accepted.
Benefits Formal training, job counseling, names of contacts, on-the-job training, possible full-time employment, willing to complete paperwork for educational credit, willing to provide letters of recommendation, reimbursement of work-related travel expenses.
Contact Write, call, fax, or e-mail Ms. Lillian Nelson, Volunteer Intern Coordinator. Phone: 916-923-7474 Ext. 6482. Fax: 916-929-7215. E-mail: lnelson@kvie.org. In-person interview required. Applicants must submit a cover letter, resume. Applications are accepted continuously.

MARIN 31
1111 Anderson Drive
San Rafael, California 94901

General Information Public access and local origination facility where professional and nonprofessional community programming is produced. Established in 1976. Number of employees: 5. Department of TCI, San Rafael, California. Number of internship applications received each year: 20.
Internships Available ▶ *4–8 access interns:* responsibilities include assisting access coordinator and programming. Duration is flexible; minimum of 140 hours per semester required. ▶ *4–6 productions interns:* responsibilities include working for staff productions, overseeing automated playback system, office maintenance, and working as part of crew on public access production. Duration is 1 flexible; minimum of 140 hours per semester. Candidates for all positions should have ability to work independently, ability to work with others, organizational skills, personal interest in the field. All positions are unpaid. Open to high school seniors, recent high school graduates, college freshmen, college sophomores, college juniors, college seniors, recent college graduates, graduate students, career changers, individuals reentering the workforce.
Benefits Job counseling, opportunity to attend seminars/workshops, willing to complete paperwork for educational credit, willing to provide letters of recommendation, informal training in television production.
Contact Write or call Ms. Jennifer Kloepping, Community Access Coordinator. Phone: 415-459-5260 Ext. 1242. In-person interview recommended. Applicants must submit a formal organization application, two personal references. Application deadline: May 15 for summer, August 15 for fall, December 15 for spring. World Wide Web: http://marin.org/npo/marin31.

MEDIA ONE
27800 Franklin Road
Southfield, Michigan 48034

General Information Cable television local programming department producing local origination programming. Established in 1981. Number of internship applications received each year: 10.

Internships Available ▶ *2 local programming interns:* responsibilities include learning video production, editing, and camera work. Duration is 3-4 months minimum. Unpaid. Open to college freshmen, college sophomores, college juniors, college seniors, recent college graduates, graduate students, law students, career changers, individuals reentering the workforce. International applications accepted.

Benefits Formal training, opportunity to attend seminars/workshops, willing to complete paperwork for educational credit, willing to provide letters of recommendation.

Contact Write, call, or fax Production Supervisor. Phone: 248-353-3905. Fax: 248-353-0141. In-person interview required. Applicants must submit a cover letter, resume. Applications are accepted continuously.

MEDIA ONE OF NEW ENGLAND
257 Chestnut Street
Needham, Massachusetts 02492

General Information Local programming department of Media One of New England providing video training and local programming to communities in Massachusetts and New Hampshire. Established in 1980. Number of employees: 20. Unit of Media One, Northeast Region, Andover, Massachusetts. Number of internship applications received each year: 200.

Internships Available ▶ *30 television production interns:* responsibilities include working on video production crews. Candidates should have ability to work independently, ability to work with others, computer skills, editing skills, oral communication skills, self-motivation, written communication skills. Duration is 3–5 months. Unpaid. Open to college freshmen, college sophomores, college juniors, college seniors, recent college graduates, graduate students, law students, career changers, individuals reentering the workforce. International applications accepted.

Benefits Names of contacts, on-the-job training, opportunity to attend seminars/workshops, possible full-time employment, willing to act as a professional reference, willing to complete paperwork for educational credit, willing to provide letters of recommendation.

Contact Write, fax, or e-mail Peter Strzetelski, Regional Manager of Quality Assurance. Fax: 781-449-6910. E-mail: pstrzetelski@mediaone.com. In-person interview recommended. Applicants must submit a cover letter, resume. Application deadline: July 1 for fall, November 1 for spring.

MONTGOMERY COMMUNITY TELEVISION
7548 Standish Place
Rockville, Maryland 20855

General Information Independent nonprofit organization that operates 2 cable channels, produces original programming, and provides television production training and facilities for residents of Montgomery County, Maryland. Established in 1985. Number of employees: 70. Number of internship applications received each year: 100.

Internships Available ▶ *2–3 news interns:* responsibilities include writing on-air copy, researching, editing, and field-producing stories under strict deadlines. Candidates should have ability to work with others, declared college major in field, knowledge of field, oral communication skills, self-motivation, written communication skills. Open to college juniors, college seniors, recent college graduates, graduate students. ▶ *1–2 operations interns:* responsibilities include assisting with all electronic equipment repair and maintenance. Candidates should have ability to work independently, ability to work with others, college courses in field, knowledge of field, plan to pursue career in field, self-motivation. Open to college juniors, college seniors, recent college graduates. ▶ *1 photographer intern:* responsibilities include assisting department staff in collection of visual elements and the integration of those elements into pieces for a daily news program. Candidates should have ability to work with others, college courses in field, knowledge of field, office skills, plan to pursue career in field. Open to college juniors, college seniors, recent college graduates, graduate students. ▶ *1–2 production interns:* responsibilities include assisting in all phases of produc-

tion for field and studio productions for weekly television programs by researching, organizing, editing, and performing clerical duties as needed. Candidates should have college courses in field, oral communication skills, organizational skills, self-motivation, strong interpersonal skills, written communication skills. Open to college juniors, college seniors, recent college graduates. ▶ *1–2 production interns:* responsibilities include assisting producer and hosts of programs, researching and booking guests, assisting with studio lighting and teleprompter, and preparing scripts. Candidates should have college courses in field, editing skills, oral communication skills, research skills, self-motivation, written communication skills. Open to college juniors, college seniors, recent college graduates, graduate students. ▶ *1–2 programming interns:* responsibilities include assisting the programming department with clerical, videotape preparation, and character generator duties. Candidates should have ability to work independently, ability to work with others, computer skills, editing skills, office skills, personal interest in the field. Open to college freshmen, college sophomores, college juniors, college seniors, recent college graduates. ▶ *1 public relations intern:* responsibilities include assisting in marketing, public relations, and community outreach efforts. Candidates should have ability to work independently, computer skills, oral communication skills, personal interest in the field, self-motivation, strong interpersonal skills, written communication skills. Open to college juniors, college seniors, recent college graduates, graduate students. Duration for all positions is 1 semester. All positions are unpaid. International applications accepted.

Benefits Job counseling, names of contacts, on-the-job training, opportunity to attend seminars/workshops, possible full-time employment, willing to complete paperwork for educational credit, willing to provide letters of recommendation.

Contact Write or fax Internship Coordinator. Fax: 301-294-7476. In-person interview required. Applicants must submit a cover letter, resume, 2-3 personal references. Application deadline: April 30 for summer, September 15 for fall, December 1 for spring.

NBC 10
10 Monument Road
Bala Cynwyd, Pennsylvania 19004

General Information Television station serving the greater Philadelphia region. Established in 1948. Number of employees: 275. Number of internship applications received each year: 150.

Internships Available ▶ *Interns:* responsibilities include working in news, sales, research, press relations, community relations, finance, and employee relations. Candidates should have ability to work independently, computer skills, oral communication skills, organizational skills, research skills, self-motivation, strong interpersonal skills, written communication skills. Duration is 13 weeks (35.40 hours per week or part-time). Unpaid. Open to college juniors, college seniors, graduate students, those taking internship for college credit only.

Benefits Willing to complete paperwork for educational credit.

Contact Mr. Antoine Murray, Manager, Community Relations. E-mail: antoine.murray@nbc.com. No phone calls. In-person interview recommended. Applicants must submit a cover letter, resume, application found on Web site (this is the only way applications will be accepted). Applications are accepted continuously. World Wide Web: http://www.nbc10.com.

NBC4
30 Rockefeller Plaza, Suite 687–E1
New York, New York 10112

General Information Television broadcasting station. Established in 1941. Number of employees: 35. Number of internship applications received each year: 35.

Internships Available ▶ *20–25 NEWS-4 interns:* responsibilities include gathering information, researching stories, working in the field on remotes, and performing field and library research. Duration is one summer or semester. ▶ *3–4 creative services interns:* responsibilities include assisting on-air administrator, producers/

NBC4 (continued)

writers, managers, and directors in all facets of pre- and post-production; tagging network and syndicated promotions, and assisting with major campaign work. ▶ *1 finance and administrative intern*. Duration is one summer or semester. ▶ *1 press and publicity intern*: responsibilities include gathering press clippings, researching, writing, maintaining biographies, and assisting with NBC speakers bureau. Duration is one summer or semester. ▶ *Research/marketing interns*: responsibilities include analyzing daily station ratings and sweeps rating books; assisting sales department with special projects, and helping to develop sales promotions. Duration is one summer or semester. ▶ *2 sales interns*. ▶ *1–2 station relations interns*: responsibilities include organizing and producing daily public service announcements and assisting in the production of studio and remote shows. Candidates should have ability to work with others, oral communication skills, organizational skills, personal interest in the field, research skills, written communication skills. Duration is one summer or semester. ▶ *Traffic operations interns*. Duration is one summer or semester. All positions are unpaid. Open to college freshmen, college sophomores, college juniors, college seniors.

Benefits Opportunity to attend seminars/workshops, willing to act as a professional reference, willing to complete paperwork for educational credit, willing to provide letters of recommendation, reimbursement of reasonable travel expenses, opportunity to interact with professionals in all departments.

Contact Write, fax, or e-mail Ms. Millie Quiles, Internship Coordinator, 30 Rockefeller Plaza, suite 687-E1, New York, New York 10012. Fax: 212-664-6449. E-mail: millie.quiles@nbc.com. In-person interview required. Applicants must submit a cover letter, resume, some documentation showing academic credit will be received for the internship experience. Applications are accepted continuously.

NOVA (WGBH)
125 Western Avenue
Boston, Massachusetts 02134

General Information Public Broadcasting System science series produced for television in Boston. Unit of WGBH Educational Foundation, Boston, Massachusetts.

Internships Available ▶ *1 NOVA Online intern*: responsibilities include telephone and library research, stock photo research, converting video and photographic material to digital media, manipulating that media in Photoshop, reading and answering e-mail, and generally assisting the personnel in the department. Duration is 1 semester in fall (15-20 hours per week). Open to full-time students. ▶ *3 WGBH Science Unit interns*: responsibilities include telephone and library research; acquired footage research, film library maintenance, dubbing and logging of tapes, assisting with studio and field work, general office assistance, and possibly off-line editing and location shooting. Duration is 1 semester in fall, spring, or summer (15-20 hours per week). All positions are unpaid.

Benefits Names of contacts, on-the-job training, possible full-time employment, willing to act as a professional reference, willing to complete paperwork for educational credit.

Contact Write Human Resources Department, (INT-99), 125 Western Avenue, Boston, Massachusetts 02134. No phone calls. In-person interview recommended. Applicants must submit a resume. Applications are accepted continuously. World Wide Web: http://www.wgbh.org/wgbh/jobs/internships/novaintern.html.

SMOKY HILLS PUBLIC TELEVISION/KOOD & KSWK
Box 9
Bunker Hill, Kansas 67626

General Information Public television station featuring quality educational and cultural programming. Established in 1982. Number of employees: 25. Number of internship applications received each year: 5.

Internships Available ▶ *1–2 engineering interns*: responsibilities include learning operation of video, audio, and remote control equipment. Candidates should have ability to work independently, college courses in field, computer skills, knowledge of field, organizational skills, plan to pursue career in field, self-motivation, strong interpersonal skills. Open to college freshmen, college sophomores, college juniors, college seniors. ▶ *1 marketing/advertising intern*: responsibilities include assisting in coordination of special events, press releases, community relations and integration, and nonprofit fund-raising projects. Candidates should have ability to work independently, ability to work with others, college courses in field, computer skills, oral communication skills, writing skills. Open to college sophomores, college juniors, college seniors, recent college graduates, graduate students. ▶ *1–2 production/directors and videographers*: responsibilities include assisting in all areas of production, preproduction planning, shooting, editing graphics, live shows, and pledge drives. Candidates should have ability to work independently, college courses in field, computer skills, knowledge of field, personal interest in the field, strong interpersonal skills, writing skills. Open to college sophomores, college juniors, college seniors. ▶ *1 public relations intern*: responsibilities include assisting in production of monthly program guide, helping design brochures and other publications, writing and editing news releases and articles, assisting with advertising through various mediums, and helping plan promotional and special events. Candidates should have ability to work independently, college courses in field, computer skills, office skills, oral communication skills, plan to pursue career in field, research skills, strong interpersonal skills, writing skills. Open to high school seniors, college freshmen, college sophomores, college juniors, college seniors. Duration for all positions is flexible. All positions are unpaid. International applications accepted.

Benefits Formal training, names of contacts, possible full-time employment, willing to complete paperwork for educational credit, willing to provide letters of recommendation.

Contact Write or e-mail Ms. Mary Pat Waymaster, Director of Broadcasting. E-mail: marypat_waymaster@kood.pbs.org. In-person interview required. Applicants must submit a cover letter, resume, three personal references. Application deadline: April 1 for summer, November 1 for spring; continuous for other positions. World Wide Web: http://www.pbs.org/shptv.

TWIN CITIES PUBLIC TELEVISION, INC.
172 East Fourth Street
St. Paul, Minnesota 55101

General Information Public television station. Established in 1957. Number of employees: 157. Number of internship applications received each year: 75.

Internships Available ▶ *1 advertising intern*: responsibilities include writing press releases and handling viewer inquiries and promotional publicity. Candidates should have computer skills, research skills, writing skills. Duration is one quarter. ▶ *1 edit intern*: responsibilities include learning digitizing low-resoluting video into the AVID system, proofing messages in the Halo character generator, and general assisting. Candidates should have computer skills, editing skills. Duration is one quarter. ▶ *1 membership intern*: responsibilities include developing skills working on projects related to membership drives. Candidates should have computer skills, office skills. Duration is one quarter. ▶ *6–12 production interns*: responsibilities include dubbing and logging of tapes, finding props, researching, and other miscellaneous duties. Candidates should have ability to work with others, research skills. Duration is 3 months. All positions are unpaid. Open to college freshmen, college sophomores, college juniors, college seniors. International applications accepted.

Benefits Willing to complete paperwork for educational credit, willing to provide letters of recommendation.

Contact Write or fax Mr. Walter Ritter, Human Resources Specialist. Fax: 651-229-1408. E-mail: elatzer@ktca.org. No phone calls. Applicants must submit a cover letter, resume. Application deadline: February 1 for spring, May 1 for summer, November 1 for winter.

WBAL-TV
3800 Hooper Avenue
Baltimore, Maryland 21211

General Information   Commercial, VHF, NBC-affiliated television station. Established in 1948. Number of employees: 130. Unit of Hearst Argyle Corporation, New York, New York. Number of internship applications received each year: 100.

Internships Available ► *10 TV news interns:* responsibilities include assisting news personnel. Candidates should have ability to work independently, analytical skills, college courses in field, computer skills, editing skills, experience in the field, office skills, oral communication skills, organizational skills, plan to pursue career in field, research skills, self-motivation, strong interpersonal skills, writing skills. ► *4 TV promotion interns:* responsibilities include assisting promotion personnel. Candidates should have ability to work independently, computer skills, plan to pursue career in field, self-motivation, strong interpersonal skills, writing skills. ► *2 marketing research interns:* responsibilities include working with marketing director on marketing plans for sales department and assisting account executives with market research. Candidates should have ability to work independently, computer skills, oral communication skills, plan to pursue career in field, research skills, self-motivation, strong interpersonal skills, writing skills. ► *2 production interns:* responsibilities include pulling file tapes, writing script for commercials, going on location, and watching the editing process. Candidates should have ability to work independently, computer skills, office skills, oral communication skills, organizational skills, personal interest in the field, research skills, self-motivation, strong interpersonal skills, writing skills. ► *2–4 programming interns:* responsibilities include booking 60-minute talk show on local issues, lining up audience for live taping, performing research, and handling audience and guests at taping. Candidates should have ability to work independently, computer skills, experience in the field, office skills, oral communication skills, organizational skills, personal interest in the field, plan to pursue career in field, research skills, self-motivation, strong interpersonal skills, writing skills. ► *1 public affairs intern:* responsibilities include helping with day-to-day running of office, writing FCC quarterly report, and helping with sponsorships. Candidates should have ability to work independently, computer skills, office skills, oral communication skills, organizational skills, plan to pursue career in field, research skills, self-motivation, strong interpersonal skills, writing skills. ► *6 sports interns:* responsibilities include working with sports director to cover local sports, pull tapes, and write copy. Candidates should have ability to work independently, computer skills, knowledge of field, oral communication skills, plan to pursue career in field, research skills, self-motivation, strong interpersonal skills, writing skills. Duration for all positions is 12 weeks, May-September or September-December; or 16 weeks, January-May. All positions are unpaid. Open to college juniors, college seniors, graduate students. International applications accepted.

Benefits Names of contacts, possible full-time employment, willing to complete paperwork for educational credit, willing to provide letters of recommendation.

Contact Write Ms. Wanda Draper, Public Affairs Director. In-person interview recommended. Applicants must submit a formal organization application, cover letter, resume, two personal references, two letters of recommendation. Application deadline: April 15 for summer, August 15 for fall, December 12 for winter. World Wide Web: http://www.wbaltv.com.

WBCC-TV
1519 Clearlake Road
Cocoa, Florida 32922

General Information   Broadcast television station providing educational programming. Established in 1988. Number of employees: 20. Unit of Brevard Community College, Cocoa, Florida.

Internships Available ► *3–5 production assistants:* responsibilities include assisting television production personnel with producing programming, talk shows, specials, promos, and other spots;

operations (studio and field); editing; audio production; lighting; set construction; and tape library organization. Candidates should have ability to work with others, editing skills, knowledge of field, plan to pursue career in field, self-motivation. Duration is 120 hours. Open to recent high school graduates, college freshmen, college sophomores, recent college graduates, graduate students. ► *1–3 production management assistants:* responsibilities include assisting with charting productions, planning projects, scheduling productions, writing scripts, and working closely with producers, editors, and studio producers to complete projects. Candidates should have ability to work independently, ability to work with others, editing skills, knowledge of field, personal interest in the field, self-motivation. Duration is 1 semester. Open to high school seniors, recent high school graduates, college freshmen, college sophomores, recent college graduates, graduate students, career changers, individuals reentering the workforce. ► *1–3 television engineer assistants:* responsibilities include assisting in the maintenance of television equipment and installation of broadcast equipment in production studios, maintaining satellite operation, and developing off-site television facilities. Candidates should have ability to work independently, ability to work with others, analytical skills, knowledge of field, oral communication skills, personal interest in the field, self-motivation. Duration is 1 semester. Open to high school seniors, recent high school graduates, college freshmen, college sophomores, recent college graduates, graduate students, career changers, individuals reentering the workforce. All positions are unpaid. International applications accepted.

Benefits Names of contacts, on-the-job training, possible full-time employment, willing to act as a professional reference, willing to complete paperwork for educational credit, willing to provide letters of recommendation.

Contact Write, fax, or e-mail Ms. Beverly Payne, Intern Coordinator. Fax: 407-634-3724. E-mail: payneb@brevard.cc.fl.us. No phone calls. In-person interview required. Applicants must submit a cover letter, resume, academic transcripts, portfolio, two letters of recommendation. Applications are accepted continuously. World Wide Web: http://www.brevard.cc.fl.us/wbcc.

WCHS-TV
1301 Piedmont Road
Charleston, West Virginia 25301

General Information   Commercial television station broadcasting in a competitive top-50 market. Established in 1958. Number of employees: 100. Unit of Sinclair Broadcast Group, Baltimore, Maryland. Number of internship applications received each year: 40.

Internships Available ► *6–15 news interns:* responsibilities include performing off-air reporting duties such as gathering and writing news stories and running the teleprompter. Candidates should have college courses in field, computer skills, editing skills, plan to pursue career in field, strong interpersonal skills, writing skills. Duration is 200 hours. Unpaid. Open to college freshmen, college sophomores, college juniors, college seniors, recent college graduates, graduate students, law students, career changers, individuals reentering the workforce. International applications accepted.

Benefits Willing to complete paperwork for educational credit, willing to provide letters of recommendation.

Contact Write, call, or fax Ms. Lisa McClure, Administrative Assistant. Phone: 304-345-4115. Fax: 304-345-1849. In-person interview recommended. Applications are accepted continuously. World Wide Web: http://www.wchstv.com.

WCIU-TV CHANNEL 26
26 North Halsted
Chicago, Illinois 60661

General Information   Independent television broadcasting station that features some local production. Established in 1964. Number of employees: 100. Unit of Weigel Broadcasting, Chicago, Illinois. Number of internship applications received each year: 100.

WCIU-TV Channel 26 (continued)

Internships Available ▶ *1 newsroom intern.* Candidates should have ability to work with others, editing skills, experience in the field, self-motivation, writing skills. ▶ *1–3 programming/production assistants:* responsibilities include working on on-air productions and taping. Candidates should have ability to work with others, editing skills, oral communication skills, self-motivation, writing skills. ▶ *1 public relations intern:* responsibilities include developing promotion campaigns. Candidates should have ability to work with others, editing skills, oral communication skills, self-motivation, writing skills. Duration for all positions is 10-15 weeks (20-40 hours per week). All positions are unpaid. Open to college freshmen, college sophomores, college juniors.
Benefits Possible full-time employment, willing to complete paperwork for educational credit.
Contact Write or fax Ms. Lilli Scheye, Internship Coordinator, 28 North Halsted, Chicago, Illinois 60661. Fax: 312-705-2656. No phone calls. In-person interview required. Applicants must submit a cover letter, resume, writing sample, two personal references. Applications are accepted continuously.

WDAF-TV
3030 Summit
Kansas City, Missouri 64108

General Information FOX affiliate that provides diverse programming, including sports and entertainment, with emphasis on local news. Established in 1949. Number of employees: 250. Unit of News Corporation, Los Angeles, California. Number of internship applications received each year: 40.
Internships Available ▶ *1–2 art/graphics interns:* responsibilities include working on AVA Paintbox or Macintosh. Candidates should have ability to work independently, college courses in field, computer skills, oral communication skills, self-motivation. Duration is one summer or one semester. ▶ *1–2 community relations/public relations interns:* responsibilities include writing and producing public service announcements, helping with events, writing press releases, assisting in field and studio shoots, and performing clerical responsibilities. Candidates should have ability to work independently, college courses in field, computer skills, organizational skills, strong interpersonal skills, writing skills. Duration is one summer or one semester. ▶ *1–3 creative services interns:* responsibilities include writing on-air voice-over copy, assisting in field and studio shoots, editing, producing audio carts, and performing various other duties. Candidates should have ability to work independently, college courses in field, computer skills, oral communication skills, self-motivation, writing skills. Duration is 1 semester. ▶ *3–5 news interns:* responsibilities include performing various duties. Candidates should have computer skills, oral communication skills, plan to pursue career in field, self-motivation, strong interpersonal skills, writing skills. Duration is one summer or one semester. ▶ *1–2 sales interns:* responsibilities include assisting account executives, going on sales calls, and performing various other duties. Candidates should have computer skills, knowledge of field, oral communication skills, self-motivation, strong interpersonal skills, writing skills. Duration is one summer or one semester. All positions are unpaid. Open to college juniors, college seniors. International applications accepted.
Benefits Job counseling, names of contacts, possible full-time employment, willing to complete paperwork for educational credit, willing to provide letters of recommendation.
Contact Write or fax Gail Lang, Human Resources. Fax: 816-932-9193. In-person interview required. Applicants must submit a cover letter, resume. Applications are accepted continuously. World Wide Web: http://www.wdaftv4.com.

WDBJ TELEVISION, INC.
2001 Colonial Avenue
Roanoke, Virginia 24015

General Information CBS affiliate with a potential viewing audience of over 1 million each week in portions of Virginia, West Virginia, and North Carolina. Established in 1955. Number of employees: 130. Unit of Schurz Communications, Inc., South Bend, Indiana. Number of internship applications received each year: 25.
Internships Available ▶ *1 engineering intern:* responsibilities include assisting with master control and maintenance observation. ▶ *1 marketing intern:* responsibilities include assisting with research, data gathering, compilation, and computer operation. ▶ *1–2 news interns:* responsibilities include assisting with reporting and producing. ▶ *1–2 production interns:* responsibilities include learning camera techniques, lighting, audio, tape editing, studio set-up, electronic field production, and character generator. Duration for all positions is flexible. All positions are unpaid. Open to college juniors, college seniors. International applications accepted.
Benefits Possible full-time employment, willing to complete paperwork for educational credit.
Contact Write, call, or fax Ms. Monica L. Taylor, Personnel Manager. Phone: 540-344-7000. Fax: 540-344-5097. In-person interview required. Applicants must submit a formal organization application, cover letter, resume, letter of recommendation. Applications are accepted continuously. World Wide Web: http://www.wdbj7.com.

WDCA-TV
5202 River Road
Bethesda, Maryland 20816

General Information Television station. Established in 1966. Number of employees: 63. Unit of Paramount Stations Group, Los Angeles, California. Number of internship applications received each year: 50.
Internships Available ▶ *1 film editing intern:* responsibilities include editing films for content and length. Candidates should have ability to work independently, ability to work with others, declared college major in field, editing skills, experience in the field, self-motivation. Duration is 12–15 weeks. ▶ *1 production intern:* responsibilities include operating teleprompter, floor direction, and providing production assistance. Candidates should have ability to work independently, college courses in field, editing skills, experience in the field, plan to pursue career in field, self-motivation. Duration is 1 semester. ▶ *2 promotions interns:* responsibilities include working with and learning about various promotional vehicles and interrelating with other departments and the local media. Candidates should have ability to work with others, declared college major in field, knowledge of field, oral communication skills, organizational skills, writing skills. Duration is 1 semester. ▶ *1 public affairs programming intern:* responsibilities include assisting with production of "Community Calendar" and assisting in production of station program and public service announcements. Candidates should have ability to work with others, declared college major in field, organizational skills, personal interest in the field, research skills, written communication skills. Duration is 1 semester. ▶ *1–2 sales/research interns:* responsibilities include learning to read ratings books and overnight rating reports, attending sales meetings and presentations. Candidates should have ability to work with others, college courses in field, declared college major in field, oral communication skills, personal interest in the field, plan to pursue career in field, research skills, self-motivation, strong interpersonal skills. Duration is 1 semester. All positions available as unpaid or at $6 per hour. Open to college juniors, college seniors. International applications accepted.
Benefits Names of contacts, on-the-job training, possible full-time employment, willing to act as a professional reference, willing to complete paperwork for educational credit, willing to provide letters of recommendation.
Contact Write, call, or fax Nancy Krantz, Internship Coordinator. Phone: 301-986-9322. Fax: 301-654-3517. In-person interview recommended. Applicants must submit a formal organization application, cover letter, resume. Application deadline: April 15 for summer (paid), May 15 for summer (unpaid), September 15 for fall. World Wide Web: http://www.upn20wdca.com.

WDCQ-TV
1961 Delta Road
University Center, Michigan 48710

General Information Professional TV and radio stations (PBS and NPR) providing academic preparation for work in telecommunications industry. Established in 1964. Number of employees: 30. Unit of Delta College, University Center, Michigan.
Internships Available ▶ *1–2 TV field/studio production interns:* responsibilities include assisting in producing and editing on-air productions. ▶ *1 radio intern:* responsibilities include on-air programming, fund-raising on-air, and assisting with production of audio tapes. Duration for all positions is 4–6 months. All positions available as unpaid or paid. Open to college freshmen, college sophomores, college juniors, college seniors.
Benefits Formal training, job counseling, names of contacts, willing to complete paperwork for educational credit, willing to provide letters of recommendation.
Contact Write or call Mr. Kent Wieland, Production Manager, Delta Broadcasting. Phone: 517-686-9350. Applicants must submit a cover letter, resume. Applications are accepted continuously. World Wide Web: http://www.delta.edu/~tvradio.

WDIV-TV
550 West Lafayette Boulevard
Detroit, Michigan 48226

General Information Commercial television station. Number of employees: 200. Unit of Post-Newsweek Stations, Hartford, Connecticut. Number of internship applications received each year: 250.
Internships Available ▶ *5–8 news department interns:* responsibilities include assisting in areas including assignment desk, sports, and special projects. ▶ *2–3 programming department interns:* responsibilities include assisting producers with field and studio shoots, research, writing scripts, screening and logging tapes, audience booking, organizing edit sessions, and researching and gathering materials for editorials and documentaries. Candidates for all positions should have college courses in field, oral communication skills, plan to pursue career in field, self-motivation, written communication skills. Duration for all positions is 1 semester. All positions are unpaid. Open to college juniors, college seniors, graduate students.
Benefits On-the-job training, willing to complete paperwork for educational credit.
Contact Write or fax Barbara Zielinski, Human Resource Adminstrator, 550, West Lafayette Boulevard, Detroit, Michigan 48226. Fax: 313-222-0417. No phone calls. In-person interview required. Applicants must submit a formal organization application. Application deadline: April 1 for summer; continuous for academic year.

WEWS-TV 5
3001 Euclid Avenue
Cleveland, Ohio 44115

General Information Television station. Established in 1947. Number of employees: 209. Unit of Scripps Howard Company, Cincinnati, Ohio. Number of internship applications received each year: 175.
Internships Available ▶ *3–4 "The Morning Exchange" interns:* responsibilities include answering phones, filing, booking guests, assisting with remote shows, and helping field-produce live shots. Candidates should have ability to work independently, computer skills, oral communication skills, organizational skills, research skills, self-motivation, strong interpersonal skills, strong leadership ability, writing skills. Open to college juniors, college seniors, graduate students. ▶ *1 Akron News Bureau intern:* responsibilities include working as the assignment desk editor in Akron. Candidates should have ability to work independently, oral communication skills, self-motivation, strong interpersonal skills, written communication skills. Open to college sophomores, college juniors, graduate students, law students. ▶ *1 Connie's Kids intern:* responsibilities include working with the anchor, Connie Dieken, researching events geared towards kids and families. Segment is

aired weekdays, during 5:00 PM news. Candidates should have ability to work independently, computer skills, oral communication skills, organizational skills, research skills, self-motivation, strong interpersonal skills, writing skills. Open to college juniors, college seniors, graduate students. ▶ *3–6 Team 5 investigators:* responsibilities include conducting phone work, giving referrals to viewers who call helpline, accompanying field reporters, and assisting the investigative team with research. Candidates should have ability to work independently, oral communication skills, organizational skills, research skills, self-motivation, strong interpersonal skills, strong leadership ability, written communication skills, interest in investigative and consumer reporting and producing. Open to college juniors, college seniors, graduate students, law students. ▶ *3 editing interns:* responsibilities include working with editors, receiving and cataloging video materials from all over the world, and learning to edit stories that are to appear on the air. Candidates should have ability to work independently, oral communication skills, self-motivation, strong interpersonal skills. Open to college juniors, college seniors, graduate students, law students. ▶ *6–8 news assignment desk interns:* responsibilities include answering phone calls, placing calls to local law enforcement or story contacts, and communicating with field news crews. Candidates should have ability to work independently, computer skills, oral communication skills, organizational skills, research skills, self-motivation, strong interpersonal skills, strong leadership ability. Open to college juniors, college seniors, graduate students, law students. ▶ *1 production intern.* Candidates should have oral communication skills, self-motivation, strong interpersonal skills. Open to college juniors, college seniors, graduate students. ▶ *3 promotion interns:* responsibilities include assisting with the coordination of station events and special projects, answering viewer calls and letters, sending out promotional materials, writing movie promos, scheduling and maintaining public service announcements, and performing general office duties. Candidates should have ability to work independently, computer skills, oral communication skills, organizational skills, plan to pursue career in field, self-motivation, strong interpersonal skills, strong leadership ability, written communication skills. Open to college juniors, college seniors, graduate students. ▶ *1 sales intern:* responsibilities include typing, filing, checking sales orders, assisting the sales managers on special projects, assisting the account executives, and occasionally accompanying account executives on sales calls. Candidates should have computer skills, office skills, organizational skills, self-motivation, strong interpersonal skills. Open to college juniors, college seniors, graduate students. ▶ *3 sports interns:* responsibilities include clearing the sports wires, shot-sheeting and timing interviews, monitoring afternoon sports feeds, helping keep the sports director informed on breaking events, and periodically accompanying the sports producer on stories. Candidates should have ability to work independently, oral communication skills, self-motivation, strong interpersonal skills, written communication skills, knowledge of sports helpful. Open to college juniors, college seniors, graduate students, law students. Duration for all positions is 1 quarter or semester. All positions are unpaid. International applications accepted.
Benefits Possible full-time employment, willing to complete paperwork for educational credit, hands-on experience.
Contact Write or fax Ms. Moreen Bailey, Community Affairs Director. Fax: 216-361-1762. In-person interview required. Applicants must submit a cover letter, resume. Applications are accepted continuously. World Wide Web: http://www.newsnets.com.

WFLA-TV
905 East Jackson Street
Tampa, Florida 33601

General Information NBC affiliate in the 14th-largest market in the U.S. Established in 1955. Number of employees: 215. Unit of Media General, Richmond, Virginia. Number of internship applications received each year: 100.
Internships Available ▶ *1–3 bureau interns:* responsibilities include working with segment producers, reporters, and photographers in areas such as health, consumer, business,

WFLA-TV (continued)

features; helping in research and story development. Candidates should have ability to work independently, college courses in field, computer skills, oral communication skills, plan to pursue career in field, research skills, self-motivation, writing skills. Open to college juniors, college seniors. ▶ *1 computer/interactive intern:* responsibilities include working with our on-line producer on computer journalism aspects of our newscasts. Candidates should have ability to work independently, ability to work with others, college courses in field, knowledge of field, personal interest in the field, research skills, self-motivation, strong interpersonal skills, strong leadership ability, written communication skills. Open to college juniors, college seniors, graduate students. ▶ *1–2 franchise interns:* responsibilities include working with segment producers, reporters, and photographers in areas such as health, consumer, business, features; helping in research and story development. Candidates should have ability to work independently, ability to work with others, college courses in field, computer skills, oral communication skills, personal interest in the field, plan to pursue career in field, research skills, self-motivation, writing skills. Open to college juniors, college seniors. ▶ *5 news interns:* responsibilities include working assignment desk, editing, producing news, and performing fieldwork. Candidates should have ability to work independently, ability to work with others, college courses in field, oral communication skills, personal interest in the field, plan to pursue career in field, self-motivation, writing skills. Open to college juniors, college seniors. ▶ *2 sports interns:* responsibilities include editing and performing fieldwork tasks. Candidates should have ability to work independently, college courses in field, computer skills, editing skills, oral communication skills, organizational skills, personal interest in the field, plan to pursue career in field, self-motivation, strong interpersonal skills, writing skills. Open to college juniors, college seniors. ▶ *1–2 weather interns:* responsibilities include working with meterologists on daily newscasts and special reports. Candidates should have ability to work independently, college courses in field, computer skills, personal interest in the field, plan to pursue career in field, self-motivation, writing skills. Open to college juniors, college seniors, graduate students. Duration for all positions is 1 semester. All positions are unpaid. International applications accepted.
Benefits On-the-job training, willing to act as a professional reference, willing to complete paperwork for educational credit, willing to provide letters of recommendation.
Contact Write, call, fax, or e-mail Ms. Elisa Berkowitz, Night Assignment Manager. Phone: 813-221-5788. Fax: 813-275-8819. E-mail: eberkowitz@wfla.com. In-person interview recommended. Applicants must submit a resume, academic transcripts, writing sample, personal reference, letter of recommendation. Application deadline: February 1 for summer, November 1 for spring. World Wide Web: http://www.wfla.com.

WGAL 8 (TV)
1300 Columbia Avenue
Lancaster, Pennsylvania 17604-7127

General Information Television station, affiliated with NBC, emphasizing news, public affairs, and programming. Established in 1949. Number of employees: 150. Unit of Hearst-Argyle Television, Inc., New York, New York. Number of internship applications received each year: 100.
Internships Available ▶ *1–2 12:30 LIVE show interns:* responsibilities include working as a production assistant for daily half-hour LIVE program and interaction with audience. Candidates should have ability to work independently, oral communication skills, organizational skills, research skills, self-motivation, strong interpersonal skills, writing skills, video editing skills, phone skills, ability to learn studio camera operation. ▶ *1 creative services intern:* responsibilities include working as production assistant on commercial, promotional, and public service announcement shoots; and updating Web site data. Candidates should have computer skills, declared college major in field, oral communication skills, organizational skills, personal interest in the field, self-motivation, strong interpersonal skills, writing skills, audio and video editing skills, knowledge of field cameras. ▶ *4–6 news interns:*

responsibilities include accompanying reporters and assisting the assignment editor and newscast producers. Candidates should have ability to work independently, oral communication skills, organizational skills, strong leadership ability, writing skills. ▶ *1 program department intern:* responsibilities include working as a production assistant for program department producer, assisting with two local programs taped each week. Candidates should have ability to work with others, computer skills, organizational skills, personal interest in the field, research skills, self-motivation, strong interpersonal skills, writing skills, video editing skills. ▶ *1–2 sports interns:* responsibilities include assisting department staff. Candidates should have ability to work independently, declared college major in field, knowledge of field, oral communication skills, personal interest in the field, self-motivation, strong interpersonal skills, writing skills, video editing skills. ▶ *2–3 weather interns:* responsibilities include preparing weather data and learning about broadcasting. Candidates should have ability to work independently, ability to work with others, analytical skills, computer skills, declared college major in field, oral communication skills, organizational skills, self-motivation, written communication skills. Duration for all positions is 1 semester. All positions are unpaid. Open to college juniors, college seniors, graduate students, applicants must attend school or have home residence in viewing area.
Benefits On-the-job training, possible full-time employment, willing to complete paperwork for educational credit.
Contact Write, call, fax, or e-mail Ms. Edi Young, Community Affairs Coordinator. Phone: 717-393-5851 Ext. 283. Fax: 717-393-9484. E-mail: news8@wgal.com. In-person interview required. Applicants must submit a cover letter, resume. Application deadline: up to one year in advance, particularly for summer positions. World Wide Web: http://www.wgal.com.

WHAS-TV
520 West Chestnut Street
Louisville, Kentucky 40202

General Information ABC network affiliate television station in top 50 market. Established in 1950. Number of employees: 150. Unit of A. H. Belo Corporation, Dallas, Texas. Number of internship applications received each year: 50.
Internships Available ▶ *4–6 television news interns:* responsibilities include working with reporter/photographer team, writing and researching stories for news, and observing all aspects of news operation. ▶ *2–3 television production interns:* responsibilities include working with TV production staff in preparation for daily newscast. ▶ *1 television sales intern:* responsibilities include working with sales staff and going out on calls with account executives, learning rating structures, and participating in sales meetings. ▶ *1–2 television sports interns:* responsibilities include accompanying sports staff on stories, helping gather sports information, and possibly covering assignments. Duration for all positions is flexible. All positions are unpaid. Open to college juniors, college seniors.
Benefits Job counseling, names of contacts, possible full-time employment, willing to complete paperwork for educational credit, willing to provide letters of recommendation.
Contact Write or call Ms. Cynthia Vaughan, Human Resources Manager. Phone: 502-582-7701. In-person interview recommended. Applicants must submit a formal organization application, cover letter, resume. Application deadline: April 1 for spring, August 1 for fall, November 15 for winter. World Wide Web: http://www.whas11.com.

WHYY, INC.
Independence Mall West, 150 North Sixth Street
Philadelphia, Pennsylvania 19106

General Information Public television and radio station. Number of employees: 175. Number of internship applications received each year: 200.
Internships Available ▶ *1–2 Radio Times interns:* responsibilities include assisting staff with radio production duties and with library research relating to upcoming interview guests on the local public affairs program produced by WHYY-FM. Candidates

should have ability to work independently, ability to work with others, college courses in field, computer skills, editing skills, research skills. Open to college sophomores, college juniors, college seniors. ▶ *1–3 TV news interns for "Twelve Tonight"*: responsibilities include assisting the news and editorial staff with monitoring scanners and 2-way radio calls, performing clerical duties, and preparing stories to air in the Wilmington, Delaware office. Candidates should have ability to work with others, college courses in field, computer skills, research skills, writing skills. Open to college sophomores, college juniors, college seniors. ▶ *2–5 TV production interns*: responsibilities include assisting staff with library research and related duties, assisting with operating character generator/teleprompter, logging tapes, typing and filing scripts, and performing general office duties. Candidates should have ability to work with others, college courses in field, computer skills, editing skills, research skills, self-motivation, writing skills. Open to college sophomores, college juniors, college seniors. ▶ *1–2 Voices in the Family interns*. Candidates should have ability to work with others, college courses in field, computer skills, editing skills, research skills, strong interpersonal skills. Open to college sophomores, college juniors, college seniors. ▶ *2–3 WHYY-FM news interns*: responsibilities include assisting reporters with writing broadcast copy, handling phone calls, setting up interviews, and gathering research material and sound bites for broadcast. Candidates should have ability to work independently, college courses in field, computer skills, editing skills, research skills, writing skills. Open to college juniors, college seniors. ▶ *1–3 development/fund-raising interns*: responsibilities include assisting staff with choosing premiums for pledge drives, calling to obtain samples, writing and designing premium brochures, assisting with market research, and updating reports using Lotus 1-2-3. Candidates should have ability to work independently, ability to work with others, computer skills, office skills, oral communication skills, writing skills. Open to college sophomores, college juniors, college seniors. ▶ *1 foundation/ grants research intern*: responsibilities include assisting grants writer in establishing a coordinated and unified approach to soliciting support for WHYY, researching the many funding services to which WHYY could apply, and composing brief profiles of potential donors. Candidates should have ability to work independently, computer skills, research skills, self-motivation, writing skills. Open to college sophomores, college juniors, college seniors. ▶ *1 marketing intern*: responsibilities include assisting marketing/sales representatives with database research for client presentations, performing market research and audience research projects, and assisting with administrative duties as needed. Candidates should have ability to work independently, ability to work with others, computer skills, office skills, oral communication skills, research skills. ▶ *1–2 member services interns*: responsibilities include responding to member service calls and requests, assisting with premium shipments and inventory maintenance, assisting with fundraisers, and performing general office duties. Candidates should have ability to work independently, ability to work with others, computer skills, oral communication skills, self-motivation, writing skills. Open to college sophomores, college juniors, college seniors. ▶ *1–2 public information/public relations interns*: responsibilities include assisting publicists with writing press releases and pieces for company newsletter, updating mailing lists and press clips, and assisting with special events and promotional activities. Candidates should have ability to work with others, college courses in field, computer skills, editing skills, writing skills. Open to college sophomores, college juniors, college seniors. Duration for all positions is 1 semester. All positions are unpaid.

Benefits Possible full-time employment, willing to complete paperwork for educational credit.

Contact Write, call, fax, or e-mail Ms. Sandra Chatfield, Volunteer Coordinator. Phone: 215-351-1261. Fax: 215-574-1477. E-mail: schatfield@whyy.org. In-person interview recommended. Applicants must submit a formal organization application, cover letter, resume, writing sample. Applications are accepted continuously. World Wide Web: http://www.WHYY.org.

WJBK-TV
Box 2000
Southfield, Michigan 48037

General Information Television station. Number of employees: 220. Division of Fox Television Stations, Inc., Los Angeles, California. Number of internship applications received each year: 100.

Internships Available ▶ *1 community service intern*: responsibilities include helping in the actual production of public service announcements for community groups, contacting and preinterviewing guests, and producing videotapes and other visuals. Candidates should have college courses in field, oral communication skills, strong interpersonal skills, writing skills. Duration is minimum 12 weeks at 15 hours per week. ▶ *2 creative services interns*: responsibilities include working in marketing, advertising, or public relations; writing ad copy; and aiding with scheduling promotional materials. Candidates should have ability to work with others, college courses in field, office skills, oral communication skills, self-motivation, written communication skills. Duration is minimum 12 weeks at 15 hours per week. ▶ *1 graphics intern*: responsibilities include working with state-of-the-art equipment and learning typesetting, keylining, photographic reproduction methods, set design, and on-air graphics. Candidates should have ability to work independently, computer skills, experience in the field, oral communication skills, plan to pursue career in field, major in arts. Duration is minimum 12 weeks at 15 hours per week. ▶ *1 human resources intern*: responsibilities include assisting the Director of Human Resources with employee recruiting procedures, applicant tracking, wage/salary and benefits administration, and policy and procedure updates. Candidates should have ability to work independently, computer skills, oral communication skills, organizational skills, personal interest in the field, strong interpersonal skills. Duration is 12 weeks at 15 hours per week. ▶ *10–12 news interns*: responsibilities include working on assignment, specialty reporting, making recommendations for coverage, conducting extensive research for potential stories, and working closely with medical and consumer reporters. Candidates should have computer skills, oral communication skills, self-motivation, strong interpersonal skills. Duration is minimum 12 weeks at 15 hours per week. ▶ *1 program intern*: responsibilities include assisting in all levels of production, learning control room procedures, and special events programming. Candidates should have ability to work with others, college courses in field, oral communication skills, self-motivation. Duration is minimum 12 weeks at 15 hours per week. ▶ *1 public relations intern*: responsibilities include assisting in coordinating speaking engagements and personal appearances for on-air talent, and coordinating special events. Candidates should have office skills, strong interpersonal skills, writing skills. Duration is minimum 12 weeks at 15 hours per week. ▶ *1 research intern*: responsibilities include learning how to use ratings data for a variety of applications, becoming familiar with various PC software programs, and aiding in the preparation of persuasive sales pieces, marketing presentations, and competitive monitor reports. Candidates should have ability to work independently, analytical skills, college courses in field, computer skills, oral communication skills, personal interest in the field, research skills, self-motivation, written communication skills. Duration is minimum 12 weeks at 15 hours per week. ▶ *1 sales/marketing intern*: responsibilities include working with Fox 2 account executives to learn the difference between direct and agency accounts and the different sales approach for each, going out on sales calls with account executives, attending commercial shoots and edits, and learning how to coordinate both station events and client functions. Candidates should have ability to work independently, ability to work with others, college courses in field, computer skills, oral communication skills, organizational skills, personal interest in the field, written communication skills. Duration is 12 weeks at 15 hours per week. ▶ *4 sports interns*: responsibilities include assisting sports director and staff, working at sports events to provide help as needed. Candidates should have oral communication skills, organizational skills, personal interest in the field, strong interpersonal skills. Duration is

WJBK-TV (continued)

minimum 12 weeks at 15 hours per week. All positions are unpaid. Open to college juniors, college seniors, graduate students.

Benefits Willing to complete paperwork for educational credit.
Contact Write Ms. Valerie Poma, Intern Coordinator. In-person interview required. Portfolio for graphics interns. Application deadline: March 10 for summer, July 10 for fall, November 10 for winter.

WLRN PUBLIC RADIO AND TELEVISION
172 Northeast 15th Street
Miami, Florida 33132

General Information Public radio and television station.
Internships Available ▶ *3–5 interns:* responsibilities include working in TV production, radio, public relations, and technical aspects of radio and TV. Duration is 1 semester. Unpaid. Open to college freshmen, college sophomores, college juniors, college seniors.
Benefits Possible full-time employment, willing to complete paperwork for educational credit.
Contact Write, call, or fax Ms. Carmen Salman, Communications Director. Phone: 305-995-1717. Fax: 305-995-2299. Applicants must submit a cover letter, resume. Applications are accepted continuously. World Wide Web: http://www.wlrn.org.

WMAR-TV
6400 York Road
Baltimore, Maryland 21212

General Information Television station affiliate of ABC network. Established in 1948. Number of employees: 200. Unit of Scripps Howard Company, Cincinnati, Ohio. Number of internship applications received each year: 150.
Internships Available ▶ *1 creative services intern:* responsibilities include assisting promotion producers for news and entertainment promotion. ▶ *1 graphics intern:* responsibilities include assisting in art/graphics department. ▶ *3 news interns:* responsibilities include assisting in all aspects of news, reporting, producing, writing, and assignment functions. ▶ *1 public affairs intern:* responsibilities include assisting with public service announcements and production of local public affairs programs. ▶ *1 sales intern:* responsibilities include working on development of sales promotions and presentations and possibly in research. ▶ *1 sports/production intern:* responsibilities include covering area sports events. Candidates for all positions should have ability to work independently, college courses in field, computer skills, oral communication skills, strong interpersonal skills, writing skills. Duration for all positions is 1 semester. All positions are unpaid. Open to college juniors, college seniors, graduate students, applicants must be eligible for course credit for internship.
Benefits Willing to complete paperwork for educational credit.
Contact Write Ms. Brenda O. Mustian, Internship Coordinator. No phone calls. In-person interview required. Applicants must submit a formal organization application, writing sample. Application deadline: January 1 for spring, May 1 for summer, September 1 for fall.

WNYW-FOX TELEVISION
205 East 67th Street
New York, New York 10021

General Information Television station with a hands-on training program for individuals interested in obtaining experience in various fields of TV broadcasting. Established in 1986. Number of employees: 330. Unit of Fox, Inc., Los Angeles, California. Number of internship applications received each year: 1,000.
Internships Available ▶ *35–40 interns:* responsibilities include working in one of the following departments depending on intern's interest: human resources, sales, traffic, 10 o'clock/evening news, "Good Day New York", programming, or newsroom research. Duration is flexible. Unpaid. Open to college juniors, college seniors. International applications accepted.

Benefits Opportunity to attend seminars/workshops, willing to complete paperwork for educational credit, $5 per day travel stipend.
Contact Write or call Ms. Iris Sierra, Human Resources Manager. Phone: 212-452-5700. In-person interview required. Applicants must submit a cover letter, resume. Applications are accepted continuously.

WOND-WMGM RADIO/WMGM-TV (NBC)
1601 New Road
Linwood, New Jersey 08221

General Information TV and radio broadcasting station. Established in 1950. Number of employees: 100. Number of internship applications received each year: 40.
Internships Available ▶ *Interns:* responsibilities include various tasks, depending on the position. Duration is flexible. Unpaid. Open to college freshmen, college sophomores, college juniors, college seniors. International applications accepted.
Benefits Job counseling, names of contacts, possible full-time employment, willing to complete paperwork for educational credit, willing to provide letters of recommendation.
Contact Write, fax, or e-mail Ms. Jane B. Stark, General Manager for Television. Fax: 609-927-7014. E-mail: wmgmtv@acy.digex. net. No phone calls. In-person interview recommended. Applicants must submit a cover letter, resume. Applications are accepted continuously. World Wide Web: http://www.acy.digex.net/wmgmtv.

WPEC-TV 12
1100 Fairfield Drive
West Palm Beach, Florida 33407

General Information CBS affiliate television station. Established in 1973. Number of employees: 140. Unit of Freedom Communications, West Palm Beach, Florida. Number of internship applications received each year: 40.
Internships Available ▶ *Interns:* responsibilities include performing tasks similar to entry-level positions in newsroom, some graphic artwork, and community relations. Duration is flexible. Unpaid. Open to college sophomores, college juniors, college seniors. International applications accepted.
Benefits Names of contacts, possible full-time employment, willing to complete paperwork for educational credit, willing to provide letters of recommendation.
Contact Write or fax Lawrence Ganns, Assistant News Director. Phone: 561-844-1212. Fax: 561-842-1212. In-person interview recommended. Applicants must submit a formal organization application, cover letter, resume. Applications are accepted continuously.

WPRI-TV/WNAC-TV
25 Catamore Boulevard
East Providence, Rhode Island 02914

General Information Broadcast television station that handles news, commercial production, and promotion. Established in 1954. Number of employees: 123. Affiliate of Clear Channel Communications, San Antonio, Texas. Number of internship applications received each year: 50.
Internships Available ▶ *1 business interns:* responsibilities include billing, filing, copying payables and collections, organizing files, handling incoming and outgoing mail, and distributing traffic logs and faxes. Candidates should have computer skills, office skills, organizational skills, strong interpersonal skills, written communication skills. Duration is 1 semester. Open to college juniors, college seniors. ▶ *1–2 engineering interns:* responsibilities include operation of videotape machines and audio equipment; dubbing commercials, television shows, and public service announcements. Candidates should have ability to work with others, computer skills, declared college major in field, editing skills, knowledge of field, self-motivation. Duration is 1 semester. Open to college sophomores, college juniors, college seniors. ▶ *4–8 news interns:* responsibilities include assisting producer in newsroom work. Candidates should have computer skills, oral

communication skills, self-motivation, strong interpersonal skills, writing skills. Duration is 3–4 months. Open to college sophomores, college juniors, college seniors. ▶ *4–8 production interns:* responsibilities include working in studio and assisting with lighting, sets, and camera work. Candidates should have college courses in field, computer skills, plan to pursue career in field, research skills, self-motivation, strong interpersonal skills, writing skills. Duration is 1 semester. Open to college sophomores, college juniors, college seniors. ▶ *1–2 production producer interns:* responsibilities include rough scriptwriting for commercials. Candidates should have computer skills, editing skills, research skills, self-motivation, strong interpersonal skills, writing skills. Duration is 1 semester. Open to college sophomores, college juniors, college seniors. ▶ *Programming interns:* responsibilities include organizing tapes for daily air on both stations, maintaining the film library, organizing incoming information from both networks, and distributing and answering view mail. Candidates should have ability to work independently, computer skills, editing skills, research skills, self-motivation, strong interpersonal skills, writing skills. Duration is 1 semester. Open to college juniors, college seniors. ▶ *2–4 promotion interns:* responsibilities include assisting producer and writing. Candidates should have computer skills, research skills, self-motivation, strong interpersonal skills, writing skills. Duration is 1 semester. Open to college sophomores, college juniors, college seniors. ▶ *Public affairs interns:* responsibilities include researching and writing public service announcements, updating the WPRI/WNAC—TV Web site, reviewing incoming public service announcements and doing post-production on them. Candidates should have ability to work independently, computer skills, editing skills, research skills, strong interpersonal skills, writing skills. Duration is 1 semester. Open to college juniors, college seniors. ▶ *Research and marketing interns:* responsibilities include preparing charts and graphs using Neilsen information for sales and station use, preparing presentations for account executives. Candidates should have ability to work independently, computer skills, organizational skills, research skills, strong interpersonal skills, written communication skills. Duration is 1 semester. Open to college juniors, college seniors. ▶ *Sports interns:* responsibilities include learning to write for sports broadcasting, editing and archiving sports highlights, and charting games and incoming video feeds. Candidates should have ability to work independently, computer skills, editing skills, knowledge of field, plan to pursue career in field, strong interpersonal skills, writing skills. Duration is 1 semester. Open to college juniors, college seniors. All positions are unpaid. International applications accepted.

Benefits Formal training, on-the-job training, possible full-time employment, willing to complete paperwork for educational credit, willing to provide letters of recommendation.

Contact Write or call Mr. Richard Lynch, Internship Coordinator. Phone: 401-438-7200. In-person interview required. Applicants must submit a cover letter, resume, 2-3 writing samples. Application deadline: January 1 for spring, May 1 for summer, September 1 for fall. World Wide Web: http://www.wpri.com.

WPTA-TV
PO Box 2121, 3401 Butler Road
Ft. Wayne, Indiana 46808

General Information Television broadcast facility. Established in 1957. Number of employees: 100. Division of Granite Broadcasting, New York, New York. Number of internship applications received each year: 20.

Internships Available ▶ *1 community affairs intern:* responsibilities include learning and applying skills related to production of public service announcements, organizational skills related to community projects. Candidates should have ability to work independently, ability to work with others, computer skills, knowledge of field, self-motivation. ▶ *2–3 news production assistants:* responsibilities include working with news producers, reporters in learning skills for producing news stories. Candidates should have ability to work independently, computer skills, editing skills, plan to pursue career in field, self-motivation, writing skills. ▶ *2–3 production department assistants:* responsibilities include working with producers, directors, and photographers in produc-

tion of news and programming. Candidates should have ability to work independently, ability to work with others, computer skills, plan to pursue career in field, self-motivation. Duration for all positions is flexible. All positions are unpaid. Open to college sophomores, college juniors, college seniors.

Benefits On-the-job training, willing to act as a professional reference.

Contact Write Jan D'Italia, Director of Programming. No phone calls. Applicants must submit a cover letter, submit letter from college providing criteria and approval for college credit. Applications are accepted continuously.

WPVI-TV
4100 City Line Avenue
Philadelphia, Pennsylvania 19131

General Information Television station with news department that broadcasts local news 4 hours per day Monday through Fridays on weekends, plus an additional 5 to 7 hours weekly of other local shows. Established in 1948. Number of employees: 220. Unit of American Broadcasting Company, Inc., New York, New York. Number of internship applications received each year: 100.

Internships Available ▶ *1–2 "Philly After Midnight" interns:* responsibilities include booking guests and generating theme for weekday show. Candidates should have ability to work with others, personal interest in the field, self-motivation, strong interpersonal skills, eligibility to receive academic credit. Open to college juniors, college seniors. ▶ *1–2 creative services interns:* responsibilities include assisting with press releases, program schedules, and on-air promotions. Candidates should have personal interest in the field, self-motivation, strong interpersonal skills, eligibility to receive academic credit. Open to college juniors, college seniors. ▶ *6–8 news department interns:* responsibilities include serving as production assistants to newscast, segment producers, and assignment editor. Candidates should have personal interest in the field, self-motivation, strong interpersonal skills, eligibility to receive academic credit. Open to college juniors, college seniors. ▶ *3–5 public affairs department interns:* responsibilities include working as production assistants to producers, photographers, and editors working on the magazine shows "Prime Time", "Visions", "Fast Forward", and a variety of other studio programs. Candidates should have personal interest in the field, self-motivation, strong interpersonal skills, eligibility to receive academic credit. Open to college juniors, college seniors, graduate students. Duration for all positions is 1 semester. All positions are unpaid.

Benefits Job counseling, names of contacts, willing to complete paperwork for educational credit, willing to provide letters of recommendation.

Contact Write, call, or fax Ms. Linda Munich, Director of Public Affairs or Ms. Catherine Simonds, News Room Supervisor. Phone: 215-878-9700. Fax: 215-581-4515. In-person interview required. Applicants must submit a formal organization application, cover letter, resume, signature of academic advisor or school representative. Applications are accepted continuously. World Wide Web: http://www.wpvi.com.

WTVE-TV
1729 North 11th Street
Reading, Pennsylvania 19604

General Information Commercial broadcast station and video production house. Established in 1982. Number of employees: 25. Affiliate of Telemundo, Miami, Florida. Number of internship applications received each year: 10.

Internships Available ▶ *4–6 production assistants:* responsibilities include assisting in portable and studio camera operating, lighting setup, editing, operating master control, managing equipment, and scriptwriting. Candidates should have ability to work with others, editing skills, knowledge of field, oral communication skills, research skills, self-motivation, written communication skills. Duration is flexible. Unpaid. Open to high school seniors, recent high school graduates, college freshmen,

WTVE-TV (continued)

college sophomores, college juniors, college seniors, individuals reentering the workforce. International applications accepted.
Benefits On-the-job training, willing to complete paperwork for educational credit, willing to provide letters of recommendation.
Contact Write Kimberley G. Bradley, Production Manager. In-person interview required. Applicants must submit a resume. Applications are accepted continuously.

WTVF NEWS
474 James Robertson Parkway
Nashville, Tennessee 37219

General Information CBS television affiliate that produces and airs local newscasts, current events, entertainment, and public service shows. Number of employees: 160. Unit of Landmark Community, Norfolk, Virginia. Number of internship applications received each year: 60.
Internships Available ▶ *1–4 Newschannel 5+ interns:* responsibilities include scheduling guests, camera operation, some editing, answering phones, greeting guests, limited writing, switcher operation, graphics and audio tasks. Candidates should have ability to work independently, editing skills, oral communication skills, plan to pursue career in field, strong interpersonal skills. Duration is 1 semester. Open to college sophomores, college juniors, college seniors. ▶ *4–5 Talk of the Town interns:* responsibilities include answering viewer calls and letters, assisting with studio floor direction, typing daily show lists, assisting guests on outside remotes, and filling recipe requests. Candidates should have oral communication skills, organizational skills, strong interpersonal skills. Duration is 1 semester. Open to college freshmen, college sophomores, college juniors, college seniors. ▶ *10–15 news department interns:* responsibilities include answering phones, making beat calls, calling to verify facts, writing stories and logging video feeds, going out with reporters and photographers on stories, editing videotape, and ripping scripts. Candidates should have oral communication skills, plan to pursue career in field, self-motivation, strong interpersonal skills, written communication skills. Duration is length of school term. Open to college freshmen, college sophomores, college juniors, college seniors. ▶ *1–4 promotions interns:* responsibilities include writing promos for news and other locally produced shows, editing and shooting videotape, and assisting in marketing and promoting shows on the air. Candidates should have editing skills, experience in the field, oral communication skills, strong interpersonal skills, writing skills. Duration is 1 semester. Open to college sophomores, college juniors, college seniors. All positions are unpaid. International applications accepted.
Benefits Names of contacts, possible full-time employment, willing to complete paperwork for educational credit, willing to provide letters of recommendation.
Contact Write, call, or fax Ms. Susan Niland, Special Projects Coordinator, Tuwanda Coleman, Talk of the Town interns' contact. Phone: 615-248-5281. Fax: 615-244-9883. In-person interview recommended. Applicants must submit a cover letter, resume. Applications are accepted continuously. World Wide Web: http://www.newchannel5.com.

W*USA-TV
4100 Wisconsin Avenue, NW
Washington, District of Columbia 20016

General Information CBS affiliate commercial broadcast television station in Washington, D.C., offering local news and programming. Established in 1949. Number of employees: 230. Unit of Gannett Co., Inc., Arlington, Virginia. Number of internship applications received each year: 400.
Internships Available ▶ *1 "Eyewitness Sports" intern:* responsibilities include coordinating video footage of sports highlights for

sports department and assisting producers with story production. Candidates should have ability to work independently, analytical skills, personal interest in the field, research skills, self-motivation, strong interpersonal skills. ▶ *1 consumer unit intern ("9 Wants You to Know"):* responsibilities include researching stories, attending shoots with reporter or producer, logging video tapes and observing the editing process, assisting with handling viewer-calls and incoming story ideas. Candidates should have ability to work independently, computer skills, organizational skills. ▶ *1 news assignment desk intern:* responsibilities include assisting assignment editors and reporters in story research. Candidates should have ability to work independently, computer skills, organizational skills, plan to pursue career in field, research skills, self-motivation. ▶ *1 sales and research intern:* responsibilities include working with the sales department by assisting in tracking program viewing, market, and economic data; and developing presentations for station personnel and advertisers. Candidates should have ability to work independently, computer skills, personal interest in the field, research skills, self-motivation, strong interpersonal skills, enrollment in business degree program. Duration for all positions is flexible. All positions are unpaid. Open to college juniors, college seniors, graduate students. International applications accepted.
Benefits Opportunity to attend seminars/workshops, possible full-time employment, willing to complete paperwork for educational credit, free parking.
Contact Write, call, fax, or e-mail Sarah Chang, Producer. Phone: 202-895-5810. Fax: 202-363-9734. E-mail: schang@wusatv3.gannett. com. In-person interview required. Applicants must submit a resume, letter stating eligibility to earn college credits. Application deadline: March 15 for summer and fall, October 31 for winter, October 15 for spring. World Wide Web: http://www. wusatv.com.

WXIX-TV 19
19 Broadcast Plaza, 635 West 7th Street
Cincinnati, Ohio 45203

General Information Broadcasting station offering the Cincinnati TV market a variety of entertainment programming including the Fox network and local programming and news. Established in 1968. Number of employees: 132. Unit of Raycom Media, Inc., Montgomery, Alabama. Number of internship applications received each year: 200.
Internships Available ▶ *1 community affairs intern:* responsibilities include assisting with viewer calls and letters, community calendar, public service announcements, program and audience analysis, and program preparation for on-air, including screening. ▶ *3–4 news interns:* responsibilities include going on stories with photographers and reporters, writing, performing follow-up research, survey projects, and various tasks in the newsroom. ▶ *1 promotion and production intern:* responsibilities include writing promotional on-air copy, attending planning meetings, maintaining press relations, and scheduling daily logs. Candidates for all positions should have major in journalism/ broadcasting. Duration for all positions is flexible. All positions are unpaid. Open to college juniors, college seniors. International applications accepted.
Benefits Names of contacts, opportunity to attend seminars/ workshops, possible full-time employment, willing to complete paperwork for educational credit, willing to provide letters of recommendation, assistance with resume preparation.
Contact Write or e-mail Ms. Jenny Wagner, Human Resources Supervisor. E-mail: jwagner@raycommedia.com. No phone calls. In-person interview required. Applicants must submit a formal organization application, cover letter, resume. Applications are accepted continuously.

MANUFACTURING

GENERAL

ABB VETCO GRAY, INC.
12221 North Houston Rosslyn Road
Houston, Texas 77086

General Information Manufacturer of oil production equipment. Number of employees: 800. Number of internship applications received each year: 100.
Internships Available ► *5 mechanical engineer co-ops:* responsibilities include assisting engineer departments, some work with design programs, and exposure to manufacturing environment. Candidates should have college courses in field, computer skills, oral communication skills, plan to pursue career in field, strong interpersonal skills, written communication skills. Duration is a minimum of 2 15-week terms (spring, summer, fall, winter). $12–$14 per hour. Open to college sophomores, college juniors, college seniors. International applications accepted.
Benefits On-the-job training, possible full-time employment, tuition assistance, willing to act as a professional reference, willing to complete paperwork for educational credit, willing to provide letters of recommendation.
Contact Write, call, fax, or e-mail Brad McSherry, Senior Human Resources Generalist. Phone: 281-405-5687. Fax: 281-878-5155. E-mail: brad.mcsherry@usvgi.mail.abb.com. In-person interview required. Applicants must submit a resume, academic transcripts. Applications are accepted continuously. World Wide Web: http://www.abbvetcogray.com.

AIR PRODUCTS AND CHEMICALS, INC.
7201 Hamilton Boulevard
Allentown, Pennsylvania 18195-1501

General Information International supplier of industrial gases and related equipment, and specialty and performance chemicals. Established in 1940. Number of employees: 16,000. Number of internship applications received each year: 2,500.
Internships Available ► *6–8 MBA (financial or commercial) interns:* responsibilities include financial analysis, market analysis, sales and marketing strategies, make vs. buy analysis, customer contract analysis, sales and marketing plans, and competitive analysis. Candidates should have analytical skills, college degree in related field, computer skills, plan to pursue career in field, strong interpersonal skills, strong leadership ability. Duration is 2–3 months. Open to graduate students. ► *10 computer science/information technology specialists:* responsibilities include client-server development, data architecture/access, customer service, network and desktop support, telecommunications, Web development. Candidates should have ability to work independently, college courses in field, computer skills, strong interpersonal skills. Duration is 3–9 months. Open to college sophomores, college juniors, college seniors. ► *8 design engineers:* responsibilities include designing entire facilities or plant components, including heat exchangers and process piping, and generating specifications for equipment purchases. Candidates should have ability to work independently, college courses in field, computer skills, strong interpersonal skills. Duration is 3–9 months. Open to college sophomores, college juniors, college seniors. ► *2 development engineers:* responsibilities include developing new processes and equipment for markets. Candidates should have ability to work with others, college courses in field, computer

skills, self-motivation, strong interpersonal skills. Duration is 3–9 months. Open to college sophomores, college juniors, college seniors. ► *10 manufacturing/operations engineers:* responsibilities include performing all phases of manufacturing and plant operations at one of ten locations. Candidates should have ability to work independently, college courses in field, computer skills, strong interpersonal skills. Duration is 3–9 months. Open to college sophomores, college juniors, college seniors. ► *8 process engineers:* responsibilities include applying engineering principles to the design, development, and operation of chemical process plants, air separation systems, natural gas liquefaction, and various cryogenic and noncryogenic processes. Candidates should have college courses in field, computer skills, self-motivation, strong interpersonal skills. Duration is 3–9 months. Open to college sophomores, college juniors, college seniors. ► *6–7 research engineers:* responsibilities include conducting research in cryogenic and noncryogenic separation technologies, liquid natural gas processing, polymers, plastics, industrial and performance chemicals, catalysts, and nitrogenous fertilizers. Candidates should have ability to work independently, college courses in field, computer skills, strong interpersonal skills. Duration is 3–9 months. Open to college sophomores, college juniors, college seniors. ► *3 safety engineers:* responsibilities include ensuring company is applying the highest degree of technology to optimize safety in the lab and field environment. Candidates should have ability to work independently, college courses in field, computer skills, strong interpersonal skills. Duration is 3–9 months. Open to college sophomores, college juniors, college seniors. All positions paid.
Benefits Formal training, job counseling, meals at a cost, names of contacts, opportunity to attend seminars/workshops, possible full-time employment, travel reimbursement, willing to complete paperwork for educational credit, access to fitness center.
Contact Write J. Doug Moyer, University Relations. No phone calls. In-person interview recommended. Applicants must submit a formal organization application, cover letter, resume, academic transcripts. Application deadline: February 1 for summer (recommended), September 1 for spring (recommended). World Wide Web: http://www.airproducts.com.

ALLIANT TECHSYSTEMS
600 Second Sreet, NE
Hopkins, Minnesota 55343-8384

General Information Prime supplier of aerospace and defense technologies to the U.S. and its allies specializing in propulsion systems, conventional and smart munitions, composite structures, and unmanned vehicles. Number of employees: 900. Number of internship applications received each year: 200.
Internships Available ► *5–10 student engineering interns.* Candidates should have ability to work independently, ability to work with others, college courses in field, computer skills, oral communication skills, self-motivation. Duration is 10–20 weeks. $10–$16 per hour. Open to college freshmen, college sophomores, college juniors, college seniors, law students. International applications accepted.
Benefits Formal training, on-the-job training, opportunity to attend seminars/workshops, possible full-time employment, travel reimbursement, willing to act as a professional reference.
Contact Write or fax Ruth Modine, Human Resources Administrator, 600 Second Street, NE, Hopkins, Minnesota 55343-8384. Fax:

Alliant Techsystems (continued)

612-931-5953. No phone calls. Applicants must submit a cover letter, resume, academic transcripts. Applications are accepted continuously. World Wide Web: http://www.ATK.com.

APPLE COMPUTER, INC.
1 Infinite Loop, MS 38-3CE
Cupertino, California 95014

General Information   Computer company whose mission is to bring the best personal computing products and support to students, educators, designers, scientists, engineers, business persons, and consumers in 140 countries around the world. Established in 1977. Number of employees: 8,000. Number of internship applications received each year: 6,000.
Internships Available   ▶ *3–5 finance interns.* Candidates should have ability to work independently, ability to work with others, analytical skills, college courses in field, experience in the field, oral communication skills, written communication skills. Duration is 3–4 months. Open to college juniors, college seniors, graduate students. ▶ *10–15 hardware engineering interns.* Candidates should have ability to work independently, ability to work with others, college courses in field, computer skills, experience in the field, organizational skills, self-motivation. Duration is 3–4 months. Open to college sophomores, college juniors, graduate students, college seniors enrolled in graduate programs. ▶ *3–4 information systems and technology interns.* Candidates should have ability to work independently, ability to work with others, college courses in field, computer skills, experience in the field, oral communication skills. Duration is 3–4 months. Open to college sophomores, college juniors, graduate students, college seniors enrolled in graduate programs. ▶ *3–5 marketing interns.* Candidates should have ability to work independently, ability to work with others, computer skills, experience in the field, oral communication skills. Duration is 3 months. Open to college seniors, graduate students. ▶ *3–6 systems software engineering interns.* Candidates should have ability to work independently, ability to work with others, college courses in field, computer skills, experience in the field, oral communication skills. Duration is 3–4 months. Open to college sophomores, college juniors, graduate students, college seniors enrolled in graduate programs. All positions paid. International applications accepted.
Benefits   Health insurance, opportunity to attend seminars/workshops, possible full-time employment, training.
Contact   E-mail Ms. Alicia L. Inafuku, College Relations Specialist. E-mail: inafuk.a@apple.com or applejobs@apple.com. No phone calls. Telephone interview required. Applicants must submit a resume. Applications are accepted continuously. World Wide Web: http://www.apple.com.

BIC CORPORATION
500 Bic Drive
Milford, Connecticut 06460

General Information   Manufacturer of writing instruments, lighters, and shavers. Established in 1958. Number of employees: 900. Subsidiary of Societe Bic, Clichy, France. Number of internship applications received each year: 30.
Internships Available   ▶ *Interns:* responsibilities include assisting in various departments (marketing, manufacturing, engineering, information technology, or accounting/finance) according to applicant's abilities and departmental needs. Candidates should have computer skills, knowledge of field, oral communication skills, self-motivation, strong interpersonal skills, written communication skills. Duration is flexible. Paid. Open to college juniors, college seniors, recent college graduates, graduate students. International applications accepted.
Benefits   Health insurance, job counseling, on-the-job training, possible full-time employment, travel reimbursement, access to company store and company activities, breakfast and lunch at cost.
Contact   Write, call, fax, or e-mail Paul Moyher, Human Resources Manager. Phone: 203-783-2741. Fax: 203-783-2200. E-mail: jobs@bicworld.com. In-person interview required. Applicants must submit a cover letter, resume, three personal references. Applications are accepted continuously. World Wide Web: http://www.bicworld.com.

THE BOEING COMPANY
PO Box 3707, MS 6H-PR
Seattle, Washington 98124

General Information   The Boeing Company is the largest aerospace company in the world: a global enterprise that designs, produces, and supports commercial airplanes, defense systems, and civil and defense space systems. Established in 1916. Number of employees: 200,000. Number of internship applications received each year: 10,000.
Internships Available   ▶ *Business interns:* responsibilities include procurement, finance, and accounting. Candidates should have ability to work independently, analytical skills, computer skills, knowledge of field, oral communication skills, organizational skills, personal interest in the field, strong interpersonal skills, writing skills, major in business-related field. Duration is 1 summer; 6 months for co-ops. Open to college juniors, college seniors, graduate students. ▶ *Computer science interns:* responsibilities include computer systems programming and software analysis. Candidates should have ability to work independently, ability to work with others, computer skills, oral communication skills, personal interest in the field, writing skills, major in computing. Duration is 1 summer for interns; 6 months for co-ops. Open to college sophomores, college juniors, college seniors and graduate students who are not graduating following semester. ▶ *Engineering interns:* responsibilities include working with a lead engineer in design, engineering labs, or supporting manufacturing. Candidates should have analytical skills, knowledge of field, oral communication skills, personal interest in the field, strong interpersonal skills, writing skills, major in engineering. Duration is 1 summer for interns; 6 months for co-ops. Open to college juniors, college seniors, college seniors and graduate students who are not graduating following semester. All positions paid. International applications accepted.
Benefits   Formal training, health insurance, opportunity to attend seminars/workshops, possible full-time employment, travel reimbursement, access to recreation and fitness facilities.
Contact   Write, call, fax, or e-mail Laura Sycamore, Recruitment Manager. Phone: 425-965-4004. Fax: 425-234-2568. E-mail: submit.resume@boeing.com. Applicants must submit a resume, application materials as specified on Web site: www.boeing.com/employment. Applications are accepted continuously. World Wide Web: http://www.boeing.com.

THE BOEING COMPANY -ST. LOUIS
PO Box 516, Mailcode S2761740
St. Louis, Missouri 63166-0516

General Information   Defense contractor and producer of military aircraft and missiles. Number of employees: 22,000. Division of The Boeing Company, Seattle, Washington. Number of internship applications received each year: 3,000.
Internships Available   ▶ *EE/CS/CE interns:* responsibilities include working on a variety of assignments such as mission systems software designing programs, testing operational flight programs for avionic systems, and supporting flight test and hardware integration. Candidates should have ability to work with others, analytical skills, college courses in field, computer skills, oral communication skills, self-motivation. $440–$475 per week. ▶ *5–10 IE interns:* responsibilities include working on a variety of assignments including production methods engineering, liaison engineering, human factors, and strategic modernization. Candidates should have analytical skills, oral communication skills, organizational skills, personal interest in the field, self-motivation, strong interpersonal skills. $440–$475 per week. ▶ *10–30 ME/AE interns:* responsibilities include working on a variety of assignments including flight test engineering, structural definition, liaison engineering, and design development. Candidates should have ability to work with others, computer skills, declared college major in field, oral communication skills, personal interest in the field, self-motivation. $440–$475 per week. ▶ *5–25*

business administration interns: responsibilities include working on a variety of assignments including accounting contracts and pricing, logistics, estimating, and business operations. Candidates should have analytical skills, computer skills, oral communication skills, personal interest in the field, self-motivation, written communication skills. $370–$405 per week. Duration for all positions is 1–13 weeks. Open to college juniors, college seniors.

Benefits Formal training, free housing, job counseling, on-the-job training, opportunity to attend seminars/workshops, possible full-time employment, travel reimbursement, tuition assistance, willing to complete paperwork for educational credit.

Contact Write, fax, or e-mail Sheila R. Lake, Administrator, Student Development Programs. Fax: 314-234-6107. E-mail: sheila.r.lake@boeing.com. Applicants must submit a resume, academic transcripts. Application deadline: February 1 for summer. World Wide Web: http://www.boeing.com.

CAROLYN RAY
578 Nepperhan Avenue
Yonkers, New York 10701

General Information Manufacturer of fabrics and wallcoverings for interior designers and architects. Established in 1979. Number of employees: 4. Number of internship applications received each year: 20.

Internships Available ▶ *1–2 general assistants:* responsibilities include sample-making, clerical, customer service, studio production, maintenance, and organization. Candidates should have ability to work independently, ability to work with others, oral communication skills, organizational skills, personal interest in the field, self-motivation. Duration is flexible. Unpaid. Open to high school students, high school seniors, recent high school graduates, college freshmen, college sophomores, college juniors, college seniors, recent college graduates, graduate students, career changers, individuals reentering the workforce. International applications accepted.

Benefits Job counseling, names of contacts, opportunity to attend seminars/workshops, possible full-time employment, willing to act as a professional reference, willing to complete paperwork for educational credit, willing to provide letters of recommendation, reimbursement of local travel expenses.

Contact Write, fax, or e-mail Noelle Mills, Internship Coordinator. Fax: 914-476-0677. E-mail: carolyn-ray@msn.com. In-person interview recommended. Applicants must submit a cover letter, resume, portfolio. Applications are accepted continuously.

CONSOLIDATED PAPERS, INC.
231 First Avenue North, PO Box 8050
Wisconsin Rapids, Wisconsin 54495-8050

General Information Specialist in the coated paper, corrugated paper, medium weight coated ground wood publication paper, and high quality pulp manufacturing industry. Established in 1894. Number of employees: 7,000. Number of internship applications received each year: 50.

Internships Available ▶ *Environmental engineers.* Duration is 3–9 months. $12–$14 per hour. Open to college sophomores, college juniors, college seniors. ▶ *Forestry assistants.* Duration is 3–6 months. $10–$11 per hour. Open to college sophomores, college juniors, college seniors, recent college graduates, graduate students. ▶ *Industrial engineers.* Duration is 3–9 months. $12–$14 per hour. Open to college sophomores, college juniors, college seniors. ▶ *Information systems interns.* Duration is 3–6 months. $10–$14 per hour. Open to college sophomores, college juniors, college seniors. ▶ *Paper science engineers.* Duration is 3–9 months. $13–$14 per hour. Open to college sophomores, college juniors, college seniors. ▶ *Research interns.* Duration is 6–9 months. $15–$18 per hour. Open to college juniors, college seniors, graduate students. ▶ *Risk control management interns.* Duration is 3 months. $13 per hour (varies depending on experience/education).

Benefits Job counseling, names of contacts, possible full-time employment, travel reimbursement, willing to complete paperwork for educational credit, willing to provide letters of recommendation.

Contact Write, fax, or e-mail Bill Loock, Human Resources/Employment. Fax: 715-422-4000. E-mail: bill.loock@conpapers.com. No phone calls. Applicants must submit a cover letter, resume. Application deadline: April 1 for summer; continuous for other positions. World Wide Web: http://www.consolidatedpapers.com.

CORNING INCORPORATED
One Riverfront Plaza
Corning, New York 14831

General Information Creator of leading-edge technologies for the fastest growing segments of the world's economy. Established in 1851. Number of employees: 7,000. Number of internship applications received each year: 500.

Internships Available ▶ *50–70 engineering interns.* Candidates should have ability to work with others, computer skills, declared college major in field, oral communication skills, personal interest in the field, plan to pursue career in field, research skills, self-motivation, strong interpersonal skills. Duration is 3 months. contingent upon class status (freshman, sophomore, junior, senior, or graduate student). Open to college freshmen, college sophomores, college juniors, college seniors, recent college graduates, students attending a Corning key campus preferred. International applications accepted.

Benefits Housing at a cost, on-the-job training, opportunity to attend seminars/workshops, possible full-time employment, travel reimbursement, willing to act as a professional reference, willing to provide letters of recommendation.

Contact Write or e-mail John P. Carvana, University Relations Manager, One Riverfront Plaza, Corning, New York 14831. E-mail: carvanajp@corning.com. In-person interview recommended. Applicants must submit a cover letter, resume. Applications are accepted continuously. World Wide Web: http://www.corning.com.

CURTIS INSTRUMENTS
200 Kisco Avenue
Mt. Kisco, New York 10549

General Information Developer of instrumentation for automotive and industrial vehicles as well as instrumentation and power conversion products for the electric vehicle market. Number of employees: 163. Number of internship applications received each year: 25.

Internships Available ▶ *1–3 accounting/clerical interns:* responsibilities include assisting as needed on special projects in the accounting department. Candidates should have analytical skills, computer skills, office skills, oral communication skills, personal interest in the field, self-motivation, strong interpersonal skills, written communication skills. ▶ *1–3 engineering interns:* responsibilities include entry level electrical engineering. Candidates should have ability to work independently, analytical skills, college courses in field, computer skills, experience in the field, oral communication skills, self-motivation, strong interpersonal skills, written communication skills. Duration for all positions is 3 months. All positions paid at $8–$10 per hour. Open to college sophomores, college juniors, college seniors.

Benefits On-the-job training.

Contact Write, fax, or e-mail Human Resources Generalist. Fax: 914-666-2188. E-mail: reidc@curtisinst.com. No phone calls. Applicants must submit a cover letter, resume. Application deadline: May 1 for summer; continuous for academic year. World Wide Web: http://www.curtisinst.com.

DESIGNTECH INTERNATIONAL
7955 Cameron Brown Court
Springfield, Virginia 22153

General Information Company that develops and markets innovative consumer electronic products designed to enhance, protect, and simplify the lives of consumers. Established in 1986. Number of employees: 75. Number of internship applications received each year: 150.

Designtech International (continued)

Internships Available ▶ *2–4 engineering interns:* responsibilities include involvement with design of new products, primarily in the telephone accessory and auto security areas. Candidates should have ability to work independently, analytical skills, college courses in field, computer skills, knowledge of field, self-motivation. Open to college seniors, recent college graduates, graduate students. ▶ *2–3 marketing interns:* responsibilities include developing and packaging material for new products, public relations campaigns, sales analyses, and marketing programs. Candidates should have ability to work independently, analytical skills, computer skills, knowledge of field, writing skills. Open to college juniors, college seniors, recent college graduates, graduate students. ▶ *2–3 operations and finance interns:* responsibilities include working on projects involving manufacturing processes, inventory controls, and financial analysis. Candidates should have ability to work independently, ability to work with others, analytical skills, college courses in field, experience in the field, written communication skills. Open to college seniors, recent college graduates, graduate students. Duration for all positions is 3–12 months. All positions paid at $500–$1,000 per month. International applications accepted.

Benefits Formal training, free housing, names of contacts, possible full-time employment, travel reimbursement, willing to complete paperwork for educational credit, willing to provide letters of recommendation.

International Internships Available in Stockholm, Sweden.

Contact Write, call, fax, or e-mail Lisa Wright, Marketing Manager. Phone: 703-866-2000. Fax: 703-866-2001. E-mail: lisa@designtech-intl.com. In-person interview recommended. Applicants must submit a formal organization application, cover letter, resume. Applications are accepted continuously. World Wide Web: http://www.designtech-intl.com.

ELIZABETH DOW
155 6th Avenue, 4th Floor
New York, New York 10013

General Information Manufacturer of handpainted wallcoverings and interior decorative painting. Established in 1992. Number of employees: 14. Number of internship applications received each year: 750.

Internships Available ▶ *10–12 Elizabeth Dow Ltd. interns:* responsibilities include sampling, painting, studio work (art and design internships); Macintosh skills, database entry, followup (marketing/managerial internships). Candidates should have ability to work independently, ability to work with others, oral communication skills, organizational skills, personal interest in the field, self-motivation. Duration is flexible. Position available as unpaid or at $5 per hour minimum. Open to high school students, high school seniors, recent high school graduates, college freshmen, college sophomores, college juniors, college seniors, recent college graduates, graduate students, career changers, individuals reentering the workforce. ▶ *2 accounting interns:* responsibilities include invoicing and cost analysis. Candidates should have college courses in field, computer skills, knowledge of field, office skills, personal interest in the field, research skills, self-motivation. Position available as unpaid or paid. Open to college freshmen, college sophomores, college juniors, college seniors, recent college graduates, graduate students. International applications accepted.

Benefits Possible full-time employment, willing to act as a professional reference, willing to complete paperwork for educational credit, willing to provide letters of recommendation.

Contact Write, call, fax, or e-mail Xavier Santana, Internship Coordinator. Phone: 212-463-0144. Fax: 212-463-0824. E-mail: edowltd@aol.com. In-person interview recommended. Applicants must submit a cover letter, resume, personal reference, two letters of recommendation, portfolio (optional). Application deadline: continuous, but as early as possible for summer.

ENERGIZER (EVEREADY) BATTERY COMPANY
25225 Detroit Road, PO Box 450777
Westlake, Ohio 44145

General Information World's largest manufacturer of dry-cell batteries and flashlights; a global leader in the business of providing portable power. Established in 1890. Number of employees: 16,000. Number of internship applications received each year: 25.

Internships Available ▶ *Mechancial engineer co-ops:* responsibilities include assuring well-designed production equipment is available when needed and that it operates efficiently; planning, organizing, and controlling procurement and installation of projects. ▶ *Operation supervisors:* responsibilities include leading production and/or maintenance workers assigned to unit by assuring efficient operation of equipment, maintaining product quality standards, controlling cost, and maintaining employee safety and morale. ▶ *Quality engineers:* responsibilities include involvement with quality standards of various products, control systems used to maintain them, technical problems in the manufacturing process, and selection of raw materials. Candidates for all positions should have college courses in field, experience in the field. Duration for all positions is 1 semester or quarter (minimum). All positions paid at dependent on experience. Open to college juniors, college seniors.

Benefits On-the-job training, possible full-time employment.

Contact Write, fax, or e-mail Recruiting Manager. Fax: 440-835-7837. E-mail: recruitwl@energizer.com. No phone calls. In-person interview recommended. Applicants must submit a formal organization application, cover letter, resume, academic transcripts. Applications are accepted continuously. World Wide Web: http://www.energizer.com.

GOODE SKI TECHNOLOGIES
7340 Highland Road
Waterford, Michigan 48327

General Information Manufacturer of composite ski poles and waterskis.

Internships Available ▶ *1 marketing/public relations intern:* responsibilities include assisting the director of communications with advertising, marketing, and public relations tasks. Candidates should have college courses in field, declared college major in field. Duration is flexible. Position available as unpaid or paid. Open to college juniors, college seniors, recent college graduates, graduate students.

Contact Write, call, fax, or e-mail Bob Ortlieb, Director of Communications, 7340 Highland Road, Waterfront, Michigan 48327. Phone: 888-464-6633. Fax: 248-666-3492. E-mail: goode@goode.com. Applicants must submit a resume. Applications are accepted continuously. World Wide Web: http://www.goode.com.

HALLMARK CARDS, INC.
2501 McGee, #112
Kansas City, Missouri 64108-2516

General Information Personal expression company that designs, manufactures, and distributes greeting cards as well as albums, Christmas ornaments, collectibles, gift wrap, partyware, and related products. Established in 1910. Number of employees: 6,000. Number of internship applications received each year: 1,500.

Internships Available ▶ *1–5 financial analysts:* responsibilities include assisting with cash management, financial plans, forecasts, internal auditing, and other projects that may be individual or team based. Candidates should have analytical skills, college courses in field, computer skills, plan to pursue career in field, self-motivation, strong interpersonal skills. Duration is 10-12 weeks in summer. ▶ *10–12 information technology analysts:* responsibilities include applying technical training (including programming) to solve problems in specific business area: troubleshooting, implementation, needs analysis, design/program minor systems. Candidates should have college courses in field, oral communication skills, organizational skills, strong interpersonal skills, strong leadership ability. Duration is 10-12 weeks in

summer. ▶ *5–10 manufacturing interns:* responsibilities include working with industrial, mechanical, and electrical engineering staff; assisting in productivity improvement efforts in a variety of plant operations. Candidates should have analytical skills, college courses in field, oral communication skills, plan to pursue career in field, strong interpersonal skills, strong leadership ability. Duration is 10–12 weeks. ▶ *1–5 marketing associates:* responsibilities include assisting with strategic product development and product management by gathering, analyzing, and evaluating information. Candidates should have analytical skills, college courses in field, computer skills, oral communication skills, plan to pursue career in field, strong interpersonal skills, strong leadership ability. Duration is 10–12 weeks in summer. All positions paid. Open to college juniors, graduate students.
Benefits Job counseling, on-the-job training, possible full-time employment, travel reimbursement, 50% discount on most Hallmark products in company store (20% discount at Halls Plaza, Halls Crown Center, and associated stores), business travel accident insurance, paid holidays.
Contact Write or fax College Relations. Fax: 816-274-4299. No phone calls. Applicants must submit a cover letter, resume. Application deadline: January 15 for summer. World Wide Web: http://www.hallmark.com.

INTERNATIONAL FLAVORS & FRAGRANCES
521 West 57th Street
New York, New York 10019

General Information Manufacturer of flavors, fragrances and aroma chemicals. Number of employees: 170. Number of internship applications received each year: 15.
Internships Available ▶ *1 fragrance evaluation intern:* responsibilities include helping with brochure preparation, samples distribution, classification, and bottles preparation. Candidates should have ability to work independently, ability to work with others, office skills, organizational skills, self-motivation. Duration is 1 year. Position available as unpaid or paid. Open to high school students, high school seniors, recent high school graduates. ▶ *1–3 marketing interns:* responsibilities include market analysis, working on MS Word. Candidates should have ability to work with others, computer skills, office skills, oral communication skills, personal interest in the field, written communication skills. Duration is 2–6 months. $15 per day. Open to college freshmen, college sophomores, college juniors, college seniors, career changers. ▶ *1–2 public relations/advertising interns:* responsibilities include assisting director of advertising and public relations with all department functions including both administrative and corporate responsibilities. Candidates should have ability to work independently, computer skills, editing skills, office skills, oral communication skills, organizational skills, plan to pursue career in field, research skills, self-motivation, strong interpersonal skills, strong leadership ability, writing skills, major in advertising, marketing, or communications. Duration is flexible. $250 per week. Open to college freshmen, college sophomores, college juniors, college seniors, recent college graduates. International applications accepted.
Benefits On-the-job training, travel reimbursement, willing to act as a professional reference, willing to complete paperwork for educational credit, willing to provide letters of recommendation, meal allowance.
Contact Write, call, or fax Ms. Kashmira Palkhivala, Director, Human Resources. Phone: 212-708-7217. Fax: 212-708-7119. In-person interview recommended. Applicants must submit a formal organization application, cover letter, resume. Applications are accepted continuously.

INTERNATIONAL PAPER
6400 Poplar Avenue, Department PI
Memphis, Tennessee 38197

General Information Paper manufacturer and producer of products such as business communications, specialty industrial, photographic, and commercial and magazine printing papers; food packaging; corrugated containers; pulp; and films; also involved in oil and gas exploration and real estate. Established in 1898. Number of employees: 2,100. Number of internship applications received each year: 400.
Internships Available ▶ *85 engineering interns:* responsibilities include working in manufacturing facilities; placements available in various U.S. locations. Candidates should have ability to work with others, college courses in field, oral communication skills, plan to pursue career in field, written communication skills. Duration is 3 months. Paid. Open to college freshmen, college sophomores, college juniors, college seniors, graduate students. International applications accepted.
Benefits Formal training, job counseling, names of contacts, opportunity to attend seminars/workshops, possible full-time employment, travel reimbursement, willing to complete paperwork for educational credit, willing to provide letters of recommendation, paid holidays for summer interns.
Contact Write, fax, or e-mail Liz Hancher, Recruiting Coordinator. Fax: 901-763-6055. E-mail: liz.hancher@ipaper.com. In-person interview recommended. Applicants must submit a cover letter, resume. Applications are accepted continuously. World Wide Web: http://www.ipaper.com.

INVACARE CORPORATION
One Invacare Way
Elyria, Ohio 44036

General Information Manufacturer of durable medical equipment and home health-care products. Established in 1979. Number of employees: 1,600. Number of internship applications received each year: 50.
Internships Available ▶ *4–6 engineering interns:* responsibilities include assisting on design, manufacturing, testing, and new product development. Candidates should have ability to work independently, analytical skills, computer skills, declared college major in field, oral communication skills, organizational skills, plan to pursue career in field, self-motivation, strong interpersonal skills, writing skills. $10-$13 per hour for undergraduates; graduate student salary depends on experience. ▶ *1–2 finance/accounting interns:* Candidates should have ability to work independently, ability to work with others, analytical skills, computer skills, declared college major in field, oral communication skills, organizational skills, plan to pursue career in field, written communication skills. $10-$13 per hour for undergraduates; graduate student salary depends on experience. Duration for all positions is flexible. Open to college sophomores, college juniors, college seniors, graduate students.
Benefits Formal training, health insurance, job counseling, on-the-job training, opportunity to attend seminars/workshops, possible full-time employment, willing to act as a professional reference, willing to complete paperwork for educational credit, willing to provide letters of recommendation, travel reimbursement for initial interview.
Contact Write, fax, or e-mail Ruth Conway, Human Resources Manager, One Invacare Way, Elyria, Ohio 44036. Fax: 440-365-7480. E-mail: rconway@invacare.com. No phone calls. In-person interview required. Applicants must submit a cover letter, resume, academic transcripts. Applications are accepted continuously. World Wide Web: http://www.invacare.com.

KIMBERLY-CLARK CORPORATION
2100 Winchester Road
Neenah, Wisconsin 54956-0999

General Information Manufacturer of personal care, consumer tissue, and away-from-home products. Established in 1872. Number of employees: 5,044. Number of internship applications received each year: 800.
Internships Available ▶ *20–30 MIS interns (business systems):* responsibilities include modifying and maintaining production outputs; maintaining the project team documentation library which includes screen hierarchies, program index list, JCL index list, production support call lists, and program library; performing program moves to the production environment; developing test data, executing tests, and verifying test results; developing personal computer solutions to business problems; and apply-

Kimberly-Clark Corporation (continued)

ing Windows95 knowledge to accomplish tasks. Candidates should have ability to work independently, college courses in field, computer skills, oral communication skills, plan to pursue career in field, research skills, self-motivation, strong interpersonal skills, strong leadership ability, written communication skills, working knowledge of at least one programming language. Duration is 3 months in summer (locations: Neenah, WI; Roswell, GA; Knoxville, TN). $16 per hour. Open to college juniors. ▶ *20–30 MIS interns (computer services):* responsibilities include testing new desktop and server software; evaluating various desktop, server, and network configurations and performance; developing applications to improve productivity of their support teams; assisting with the administration of Netware file servers; documenting LAN/WAN network configurations; generating Internet/Intranet statistical reports. Candidates should have ability to work independently, college courses in field, oral communication skills, plan to pursue career in field, research skills, self-motivation, strong interpersonal skills, strong leadership ability, written communication skills, working knowledge of Windows 95, NT, UNIX, or Novell. Duration is 3 months in summer (locations: Neenah, WI; Roswell, GA; Knoxville, TN). $16 per hour. Open to college juniors. ▶ *20 electrical engineering co-ops:* responsibilities include application of electrical engineering skills to a manufacturing environment working with automated manufacturing equipment including programmable controllers, analog and digital motor controllers and discrete control hardware. Candidates should have declared college major in field, oral communication skills, self-motivation, strong interpersonal skills, written communication skills, minimum GPA of 3.0, completed basic circuits course. Duration is 3–6 months. $14–$20 per hour. Open to college sophomores, college juniors, college seniors. ▶ *20 mechanical engineering co-ops:* responsibilities include applying mechanical engineering skills to a manufacturing environment through CAD design, familiarization with plant safety, documentation, and participation on a project team. Candidates should have declared college major in field, oral communication skills, self-motivation, strong interpersonal skills, written communication skills, minimum GPA of 3.0, completed basic drafting course. Duration is 3–6 months. $14–$19 per hour. Open to college sophomores, college juniors, college seniors. ▶ *10–30 research and development co-ops:* responsibilities include product, process, or materials development. Candidates should have college courses in field, computer skills, oral communication skills, organizational skills, plan to pursue career in field, self-motivation, strong interpersonal skills, strong leadership ability, written communication skills. Duration is at least 3 semesters, normally alternating with school terms. $14–$20 per hour. Open to college freshmen, college sophomores. ▶ *10–40 research and development interns:* responsibilities include product, process, or materials development. Candidates should have college courses in field, computer skills, oral communication skills, organizational skills, plan to pursue career in field, self-motivation, strong interpersonal skills, strong leadership ability, written communication skills. Duration is 10-12 weeks in summer. $14–$20 per hour. Open to college sophomores, college juniors.
Benefits Formal training, on-the-job training, opportunity to attend seminars/workshops, possible full-time employment.
Contact Write, call, fax, or e-mail Kay Keberlein, Recruiting Assistant. Phone: 920-721-2602. Fax: 920-721-4219. E-mail: kkeber@kcc.com. In-person interview recommended. Applicants must submit a cover letter, resume, academic transcripts. Application deadline: February 1 for summer; continuous for co-op positions. World Wide Web: http://www.kimberly-clark.com.

KRAFT FOODS, INC.
Three Lakes Drive
Northfield, Illinois 60093

General Information Consumer packaged goods company. Number of employees: 4,000. Subsidiary of Phillip Morris, New York, New York. Number of internship applications received each year: 400.
Internships Available ▶ *12–15 assistant brand manager summer interns:* responsibilities include marketing project encompassing

marketing analysis, design, and execution; summary presentation to supervisors at conclusion. Candidates should have ability to work independently, oral communication skills, self-motivation, strong interpersonal skills, strong leadership ability, written communication skills. Duration is 12 weeks. Paid. Open to graduate students. ▶ *20–25 assistant research scientist summer interns.* Candidates should have ability to work independently, analytical skills, declared college major in field, oral communication skills, plan to pursue career in field, research skills, self-motivation, strong interpersonal skills, written communication skills. Duration is 3 months. Paid. Open to college juniors, college seniors, graduate students. ▶ *5–10 financial associates.* Candidates should have ability to work independently, analytical skills, computer skills, declared college major in field, oral communication skills, plan to pursue career in field, self-motivation, strong interpersonal skills, written communication skills. Duration is 3 months. Paid. Open to college juniors, graduate students. ▶ *4–6 human resources summer interns.* Candidates should have ability to work independently, analytical skills, college courses in field, computer skills, knowledge of field, oral communication skills, organizational skills, personal interest in the field, plan to pursue career in field, self-motivation, strong interpersonal skills, writing skills. Duration is 3 months. Paid. Open to college juniors, graduate students.
Benefits Formal training, housing at a cost, on-the-job training, opportunity to attend seminars/workshops, possible full-time employment, travel reimbursement, willing to act as a professional reference, willing to complete paperwork for educational credit, willing to provide letters of recommendation.
Contact Write Caroline Carlson, Associate Manager—University Relations, Three Lakes Drive, Northfield, Illinois 60093. No phone calls. In-person interview required. Applicants must submit a formal organization application, resume, three personal references, drug test required. Application deadline: February 1 for summer. World Wide Web: http://www.kraftfoods.com/careers.

LA TEMPESTA
439 Littlefield Avenue
South San Francisco, California 94080

General Information Bakery and confections manufacturer. Established in 1983. Number of employees: 75. Unit of Horizon Holdings, Inc., San Francisco, California.
Internships Available ▶ *1–4 interns:* responsibilities include information systems, sales, marketing, package design, software development, and Web page design; duties dependent upon experience and interest of intern. Candidates should have computer skills, oral communication skills, personal interest in the field, self-motivation, strong interpersonal skills, strong leadership ability. Duration is flexible. $5–$8 per hour. Open to high school seniors, recent high school graduates, college freshmen, college sophomores, college juniors, college seniors, recent college graduates, graduate students, career changers, individuals reentering the workforce.
Benefits Formal training, job counseling, names of contacts, on-the-job training, opportunity to attend seminars/workshops, possible full-time employment, travel reimbursement, willing to act as a professional reference, willing to complete paperwork for educational credit, willing to provide letters of recommendation.
Contact Write, call, fax, or e-mail Karen Hunt, Vice President of Sales, 439 Littlefield Avenue, South San Francisco, California 94050. Phone: 800-762-8330. Fax: 650-873-1190. E-mail: khunt@latempesta.com. In-person interview required. Applicants must submit a cover letter, resume, portfolio, four personal references, three letters of recommendation, 8 writing samples. Applications are accepted continuously.

LIPO CHEMICALS, INC.
207 19th Avenue
Paterson, New Jersey 07504

General Information Manufacturer and distributor of raw materials for the personal care industry. Established in 1960. Number of employees: 90. Number of internship applications received each year: 15.

Internships Available ▶ *1–5 interns:* responsibilities include assisting department with necessary projects. Candidates should have computer skills, office skills, oral communication skills, personal interest in the field, self-motivation, strong interpersonal skills. Duration is flexible. $250 per week. Open to college juniors, college seniors, graduate students. International applications accepted.

Benefits Names of contacts, on-the-job training, opportunity to attend seminars/workshops, possible full-time employment, willing to act as a professional reference, willing to complete paperwork for educational credit, willing to provide letters of recommendation.

Contact Write or fax Steven Young, Human Resources Manager, or Kathleen Carroll, Human Resources Assistant. Fax: 973-345-6343. In-person interview recommended. Applicants must submit a formal organization application, cover letter, resume, 1 or more professional references. Applications are accepted continuously. World Wide Web: http://www.lipochemicals.com.

MOTOROLA (ARIZONA SEMICONDUCTOR PRODUCTS SECTOR)
2200 West Broadway Road, MD: M375/AZ09
Mesa, Arizona 85202

General Information Electronics manufacturing. Number of employees: 11,000. Division of Motorola, Schaumburg, Illinois. Number of internship applications received each year: 40.

Internships Available ▶ *1–3 wellness interns:* responsibilities include design, development, marketing, implementation, and evaluation of wellness programs for 11,000 Motorola SPS employees, and assisting with day-to-day wellness program activities. Candidates should have ability to work with others, college courses in field, computer skills, personal interest in the field, plan to pursue career in field, an understanding of wellness as a healthy balance of optimal physical, emotional, social, intellectual, occupational, and spiritual well-being. Duration is made to meet specific educational requirements (300-720 hours). Unpaid. Open to college seniors, recent college graduates, graduate students.

Benefits Formal training, meals at a cost, names of contacts, on-the-job training, opportunity to attend seminars/workshops, willing to act as a professional reference, willing to complete paperwork for educational credit, willing to provide letters of recommendation.

Contact Write, call, or e-mail Phil McNett, Program Manager. Phone: 480-655-3617. E-mail: rkf890@email.sps.mot.com. Telephone interview required. Applicants must submit a cover letter, resume. Applications are accepted continuously.

NATIONAL STARCH AND CHEMICAL COMPANY
10 Finderne Avenue
Bridgewater, New Jersey 08807

General Information Leading manufacturer of adhesives, specialty chemicals, resins, electronic materials, and specialty food and industrial starches. Established in 1895. Number of employees: 1,200. Unit of Imperial Chemical Industries, Wilmington, Delaware. Number of internship applications received each year: 1,000.

Internships Available ▶ *15–20 summer interns:* responsibilities include working at World Headquarters in Bridgewater, NJ, or at one of our major manufacturing plants in Indiana, Illinois, North Carolina, South Carolina, or Missouri. Candidates should have analytical skills, computer skills, oral communication skills, organizational skills, personal interest in the field, research skills, self-motivation, strong interpersonal skills, strong leadership ability, written communication skills, major in chemistry, chemical engineering, food science, MIS/CIS, polymer science, or material science. Duration is 3 months. competitive salary. Open to college sophomores, college juniors, college seniors, graduate students.

Benefits On-the-job training, opportunity to attend seminars/workshops, possible full-time employment, travel reimbursement.

Contact Write, fax, or e-mail Colleen Twill, College Relations Manager, 10 Finderne Avenue, Bridgewater, New Jersey 08807.

Fax: 908-685-6956. E-mail: nsc.recruit@nstarch.com. No phone calls. In-person interview required. Applicants must submit a cover letter, resume, academic transcripts. Application deadline: February 28. World Wide Web: http://www.nationalstarch.com.

NEW HOLLAND INC.
500 Diller Avenue, PO Box 1895
New Holland, Pennsylvania 17557-0903

General Information Manufacturer of agricultural and industrial equipment. Established in 1895. Number of employees: 1,800. Unit of Fiat, Turin, Italy. Number of internship applications received each year: 500.

Internships Available ▶ *Interns:* responsibilities include working in field of interest: accounting, engineering, finance, human resources, logistics, product evaluation, programming, purchasing, sales, service, or service parts. Candidates should have computer skills, oral communication skills, strong interpersonal skills, written communication skills, personal transportation; agricultural background a plus. Duration is 3 months (average). $400–$450 per week. Open to college sophomores, college juniors, college seniors, graduate students. International applications accepted.

Benefits Housing at a cost, on-the-job training, opportunity to attend seminars/workshops, possible full-time employment, travel reimbursement, willing to act as a professional reference, willing to complete paperwork for educational credit, willing to provide letters of recommendation.

Contact Write, fax, or e-mail Ted S. Lyon, Recruiting and Diversity Manager. Fax: 717-355-3650. E-mail: tlyon1@newholland.com. No phone calls. In-person interview recommended. Applicants must submit a formal organization application, cover letter, resume, academic transcripts. Applications are accepted continuously. World Wide Web: http://www.newholland.com/na.

NIKE
One Bowerman Drive, Gray Oaks Building
Beaverton, Oregon 97005

General Information Designer and marketer of athletic footwear, apparel, and accessories. Established in 1972. Number of employees: 20,000. Number of internship applications received each year: 1,200.

Internships Available ▶ *40–150 interns:* responsibilities include working in the areas of sports marketing, information technology, finance/accounting, apparel, research, design and development, retail, customer service, sales, production, human resources, legal, marketing, corporate communication, and equipment. Candidates should have computer skills, office skills, strong interpersonal skills, written communication skills. Duration is 10 weeks. $9–$17 per hour. Open to college juniors, college seniors, recent college graduates, graduate students, law students. International applications accepted.

Benefits Housing at a cost, on-the-job training, opportunity to attend seminars/workshops, possible full-time employment, travel reimbursement, willing to complete paperwork for educational credit, $1,000 stipend towards living expenses.

International Internships Available in China; Hong Kong; Netherlands.

Contact E-mail Human Resource Service Center, Nike Internship Program, One Bowerman Drive, Gray Oaks Building, Beaverton, Oregon 97005. Phone: 800-890-6453. E-mail: jobs@nike.com. No phone calls. Telephone interview required. Applicants must submit a cover letter, resume, academic transcripts, portfolio for design internships. Application deadline: January 15 for summer. World Wide Web: http://www.nikebiz.com.

OSHKOSH B'GOSH, INC.
112 Otter Avenue, PO Box 300
Oshkosh, Wisconsin 54902

General Information Manufacturer, marketer, and retailer of children's wear and menswear. Established in 1895. Number of employees: 400. Number of internship applications received each year: 25.

Internships Available ▶ *1–3 associate merchandisers:* responsibilities include coordinating and developing new and existing sales aids; assisting merchandise manager in development of seasonal lot numbers forecasts, analysis of seasonal product costing, and work with designers and artists in all aspects of line development. Candidates should have ability to work independently, ability to work with others, analytical skills, college courses in field, computer skills, declared college major in field, oral communication skills, plan to pursue career in field, self-motivation, written communication skills. $11 per hour. Open to college juniors, college seniors, recent college graduates, graduate students. ▶ *1 import associates:* responsibilities include working with factory, agent, and mill to replicate desired fabric; implementing and maintaining tracking system; and ensuring on-time delivery of salesman samples. Candidates should have ability to work independently, ability to work with others, analytical skills, college courses in field, computer skills, office skills, oral communication skills, organizational skills, plan to pursue career in field, self-motivation, written communication skills. $11 per hour. Open to college juniors, college seniors, recent college graduates, graduate students. ▶ *1 product development associates:* responsibilities include gathering information needed from suppliers; completing purchasing and shipping tasks; organizing and maintaining all fabric, color, and documentation systems. Candidates should have ability to work independently, ability to work with others, analytical skills, college courses in field, computer skills, declared college major in field, office skills, oral communication skills, organizational skills, plan to pursue career in field, research skills, self-motivation, writing skills. $11 per hour. Open to college juniors, college seniors, recent college graduates. ▶ *1 programmer intern:* responsibilities include coding, testing, and debugging programs under direct supervision; maintaining and documenting programs. Candidates should have ability to work independently, ability to work with others, analytical skills, college courses in field, computer skills, editing skills, knowledge of field, oral communication skills, organizational skills, plan to pursue career in field, research skills, writing skills. $9–$10 per hour. Open to college juniors, college seniors. Duration for all positions is 10–12 weeks. International applications accepted.

Benefits Free housing, on-the-job training, opportunity to attend seminars/workshops, possible full-time employment, travel reimbursement, willing to act as a professional reference, willing to complete paperwork for educational credit, willing to provide letters of recommendation.

Contact Write, fax, or e-mail Brent Frederick, Recruiting Specialist. Fax: 920-232-2744. E-mail: fbrent@bgosh.com. In-person interview recommended. Applicants must submit a cover letter, resume, portfolio, personal reference. Applications are accepted continuously. World Wide Web: http://www.oshkoshbgosh.com.

OWENS CORNING WORLD HEADQUARTERS
One Owens Corning Parkway
Toledo, Ohio 43659

General Information Manufacturing company providing complete building material systems, pipe systems, and advanced glass fiber used in more than 40,000 composite end-use applications. Established in 1938. Number of employees: 1,000. Number of internship applications received each year: 1,500.

Internships Available ▶ *1–3 engineering interns:* responsibilities include working in chemical, mechanical, ceramic, and manufacturing technology. Candidates should have ability to work independently, analytical skills, college courses in field, oral communication skills, organizational skills, self-motivation, strong interpersonal skills, written communication skills, technical expertise. $1,733–$2,687 per month. Open to college juniors,

college seniors. ▶ *1–10 finance interns:* responsibilities include working in the area of audit, business analysis, tax, external reporting, and corporate accounting. Candidates should have ability to work independently, ability to work with others, analytical skills, college courses in field, computer skills, knowledge of field, oral communication skills, organizational skills, self-motivation, writing skills, major in accounting or finance. $1,907–$2,253 per month. Open to college juniors, college seniors. ▶ *1–3 sales interns:* responsibilities include working in specific geographic area within 200-300 miles radius of Toledo, analyzing the market, identifying major general contractors, determining products they are purchasing and why they are purchasing them. Candidates should have ability to work independently, analytical skills, college courses in field, declared college major in field, knowledge of field, oral communication skills, organizational skills, self-motivation, written communication skills, ability to establish relationships. $1,647–$1,907 per month. Open to college juniors, college seniors, MBA students specializing in marketing. Duration for all positions is one summer. International applications accepted.

Benefits On-the-job training, possible full-time employment, travel reimbursement, possibility of relocation or housing assistance.

Contact Maureen J. Comes, Staffing Consultant. No phone calls. In-person interview required. Applicants must submit a formal organization application, resume. Applications are accepted continuously. World Wide Web: http://www.owenscorning.com.

PELLA CORPORATION
102 Main Street
Pella, Iowa 50219

General Information World's second largest manufacturer of Pella windows and doors. Established in 1925. Number of employees: 6,500.

Internships Available ▶ *Accounting interns.* ▶ *Engineering interns.* ▶ *Information technology interns.* ▶ *Marketing interns.* Duration for all positions is flexible. All positions paid at $2,400–$3,000 per duration of internship. Open to college juniors, college seniors.

Benefits On-the-job training, possible full-time employment, willing to act as a professional reference, willing to provide letters of recommendation, health and dental insurance, holiday pay.

Contact Write, fax, or e-mail Tim Harn, Staffing Administrator, 102 Main Street, Pella, Iowa 50219. Phone: 515-628-6072. Fax: 515-628-6550. E-mail: tjharn@pella.com. No phone calls. Applicants must submit a resume, academic transcripts. Applications are accepted continuously. World Wide Web: http://www.pella.com.

P. H. GLATFELTER COMPANY
228 South Main Street
Spring Grove, Pennsylvania 17362

General Information Manufacturer of high-quality writing and technical specialty papers. Established in 1864. Number of employees: 4,000. Number of internship applications received each year: 200.

Internships Available ▶ *4 process engineers:* responsibilities include performing investigative/experimental programs, developing background in assigned areas, and maintaining related records and equipment. ▶ *4 research chemists:* responsibilities include developing new technologies and investigating research projects. Candidates for all positions should have enrollment in chemical engineering program. Duration for all positions is flexible. All positions paid. Open to college juniors, college seniors, recent college graduates, graduate students.

Benefits Job counseling, names of contacts, possible full-time employment, travel reimbursement, willing to complete paperwork for educational credit, willing to provide letters of recommendation.

Contact Write, fax, or e-mail Ken Ross, Employee Relations Manager. Fax: 717-225-6834. E-mail: kross@glatfelter.com. No phone calls. In-person interview required. Applicants must submit a cover letter, resume. Application deadline: December 31 for summer. World Wide Web: http://www.glatfelter.com.

POTLATCH CORPORATION
805 Mill Road
Lewiston, Idaho 83501

General Information Forestry products company. Established in 1995. Number of employees: 2. Unit of Industrial Relations, Spokane, Washington. Number of internship applications received each year: 30.

Internships Available ▶ *1–2 preventive health and wellness interns.* Candidates should have ability to work independently, analytical skills, college courses in field, college degree in related field, computer skills, editing skills, knowledge of field, office skills, oral communication skills, organizational skills, personal interest in the field, plan to pursue career in field, research skills, self-motivation, strong interpersonal skills, strong leadership ability, writing skills. Duration is 4 months. $1,000 per month. Open to college seniors, graduate students. International applications accepted.

Benefits Formal training, names of contacts, on-the-job training, opportunity to attend seminars/workshops, willing to act as a professional reference, willing to complete paperwork for educational credit, willing to provide letters of recommendation.

Contact Write or call Donna Russell-Cook, Corporate Manager, PO Box 1016, Lewiston, Idaho 83501. Phone: 208-799-1025. In-person interview recommended. Applicants must submit a formal organization application, cover letter, resume, writing sample, letter of recommendation. Applications are accepted continuously.

PRINCE UPHOLSTERY
115 Bruce Avenue
Stratford, Connecticut 06497

General Information Professional upholsterers working on commercial furniture and specializing in antique furniture. Established in 1975. Number of employees: 3. Number of internship applications received each year: 2.

Internships Available ▶ *2 experienced stitchers:* responsibilities include professionally stitching, sewing and/or mending upholstery fabrics for residential designers in furnitures, antique custom upholstery and cornices. Candidates should have ability to work independently, ability to work with others, knowledge of field, oral communication skills, organizational skills, personal interest in the field, self-motivation. ▶ *2 upholsterer trainees:* responsibilities include reporting to assigned master upholsterer for daily work/training method in step-by-step procedures on furniture upholstery; advance methodology; antique upholstery. Candidates should have ability to work independently, ability to work with others, experience in the field, oral communication skills, organizational skills, self-motivation. Duration for all positions is 3 months to 3 years. All positions paid at $500–$600 per month. Open to recent high school graduates, career changers, individuals reentering the workforce. International applications accepted.

Benefits Formal training, names of contacts, opportunity to attend seminars/workshops, possible full-time employment, willing to complete paperwork for educational credit, willing to provide letters of recommendation.

Contact Write, call, or fax Prince Dailey, Owner. Phone: 203-375-6270. Fax: 203-377-5207. In-person interview recommended. Applications are accepted continuously.

RAYONIER
1177 Summer Street
Stamford, Connecticut 06905

General Information Global forest products manufacturing corporation with 2300 employees worldwide and annual sales of $1.1 billion. Established in 1926. Number of employees: 85.

Internships Available ▶ *1 accounting intern:* responsibilities include reconciliations; accounts payable review and input; check printing; pension and savings plan audit reports and 5500's (tax forms); closure reserve analysis and reporting; consolidation report generation; balance sheet and income statement analysis. Candidates should have ability to work independently, ability to work with others, college courses in field, computer skills, declared college major in field, knowledge of field, oral communication skills, plan to pursue career in field, self-motivation, written communication skills. $500 minimum per week. Open to college juniors. ▶ *2 information systems interns:* responsibilities include assisting corporate network engineer; assisting with client installs and performing special assignments; assisting in applications and Internet/Intranet projects. Candidates should have ability to work independently, analytical skills, computer skills, declared college major in field, knowledge of field, oral communication skills, plan to pursue career in field, research skills, self-motivation, strong interpersonal skills, written communication skills. $750 minimum per week. Open to college sophomores, college juniors. Duration for all positions is 1 summer and Christmas school break.

Benefits Names of contacts, on-the-job training, travel reimbursement, willing to act as a professional reference, willing to complete paperwork for educational credit, willing to provide letters of recommendation.

Contact Write, fax, or e-mail Cynthia Kabbe, Employee Relations Administration, 1177 Summer Street, Stamford, Connecticut 06905. Fax: 203-964-4528. E-mail: cynthia.kabbe@ rayonier.com. No phone calls. In-person interview required. Applicants must submit a cover letter, resume. Applications are accepted continuously. World Wide Web: http://www.rayonier.com.

SUSQUEHANNA PFALTZGRAFF COMPANY
140 East Market Street
York, Pennsylvania 17401

General Information Privately-held, diversified media and dinnerware manufacturing company. Established in 1811. Number of employees: 2,000. Number of internship applications received each year: 40.

Internships Available ▶ *1–5 accounting interns:* responsibilities include assisting in preparing financial statements, business forecasting, product costing, and the monthly closing. Candidates should have analytical skills, computer skills, declared college major in field, oral communication skills, strong interpersonal skills, written communication skills. Duration is 10–12 weeks. ▶ *1–3 computer programmers:* responsibilities include writing computer programs for various projects and needs. Candidates should have ability to work independently, analytical skills, computer skills, declared college major in field, plan to pursue career in field. Duration is 12 weeks. ▶ *1–3 marketing interns:* responsibilities include assisting marketing manager with special projects. Candidates should have computer skills, declared college major in field, oral communication skills, strong interpersonal skills, written communication skills. Duration is 12 weeks. All positions paid at $8 per hour. Open to college juniors, college seniors, recent college graduates. International applications accepted.

Benefits On-the-job training, possible full-time employment, willing to act as a professional reference, willing to complete paperwork for educational credit.

Contact Write, fax, or e-mail Carol Hensel, Human Resources Administrator, 140 East Market Street, York, Pennsylvania 17401. Fax: 717-852-2594. E-mail: corp.hr@suspfz.com. No phone calls. In-person interview required. Applicants must submit a cover letter, resume. Applications are accepted continuously.

THE TORRINGTON COMPANY
59 Field Street
Torrington, Connecticut 06790

General Information Company that designs, develops, manufactures, and sells antifriction needle, roller and ball bearings, diversified precision metal components, and sub-assemblies. Established in 1866. Number of employees: 1,000. Unit of Ingersoll-Rand, Woodcliff Lake, New Jersey. Number of internship applications received each year: 50.

Internships Available ▶ *3–5 computer science/MIS interns:* responsibilities include assisting with project assignments in areas such as application, development, hardware/software, database administra-

The Torrington Company (continued)

tion, and network support. Opportunities exist in finance, human resources, sales, logistics, business systems, and manufacturing facilities. Candidates should have analytical skills, college courses in field, computer skills, strong interpersonal skills, strong leadership ability. $11–$15 per hour. Open to college sophomores, college juniors, college seniors. ▶ *10–12 mechanical engineering interns:* responsibilities include assisting with project assignments in areas such as mechanical design, manufacturing engineering, or special projects. Candidates should have college courses in field, computer skills, declared college major in field, knowledge of field, plan to pursue career in field, strong interpersonal skills. $11–$14 per hour. Open to college sophomores, college juniors. Duration for all positions is 3–4 months.

Benefits Job counseling, names of contacts, on-the-job training, possible full-time employment, travel reimbursement, willing to complete paperwork for educational credit, willing to provide letters of recommendation.

Contact Write, fax, or e-mail Mr. Kenneth M. Keane, Manager, Professional Recruiting. Fax: 423-977-6849. E-mail: keanek@ torrington.com. No phone calls. In-person interview required. Applicants must submit a cover letter, resume, academic transcripts. Applications are accepted continuously. World Wide Web: http://www.torrington.com.

TRACY WATTS MILLINERY
305 West 20th Street
New York, New York 10011

General Information Millinery studio that produces hat collections for high-end retailers and custom costumes work. Established in 1993. Number of employees: 2. Number of internship applications received each year: 10.

Internships Available ▶ *2 intern/assistants:* responsibilities include hand-finishing production, running errands to garment district, and answering telephone. Candidates should have ability to work independently, computer skills, personal interest in the field, self-motivation, strong interpersonal skills. Duration is minimum 2 months in summer. Unpaid. Open to college freshmen, college sophomores, college juniors, college seniors, recent college graduates, career changers. International applications accepted.

Benefits Job counseling, meals at a cost, names of contacts, possible full-time employment, willing to complete paperwork for educational credit, willing to provide letters of recommendation, exposure to retail buyers and fashion magazine editors, learning costume and millinery production techniques.

Contact Write or e-mail Ms. Tracy Watts, Owner. E-mail: tracywatts@ vcn.com. In-person interview required. Applicants must submit a cover letter, resume, portfolio. Applications are accepted continuously. World Wide Web: http://www.tracywatts.com.

TRANS-LUX CORPORATION
110 Richards Avenue
Norwalk, Connecticut 06854

General Information Leading manufacturer, distributor, and servicer of real-time electronic information displays for use in both the indoor and outdoor markets; owner of movie theater chain in southwest United States. Established in 1920. Number of employees: 225. Number of internship applications received each year: 20.

Internships Available ▶ *3 accounting interns:* responsibilities include assisting the accounting department with general accounting duties, which may include account analysis, consolidation of bank requisitions, and preparation of property tax returns. Candidates should have analytical skills, college courses in field, computer skills, knowledge of field, personal interest in the field, retail-oriented background. Position available as unpaid or at $8–$10 per hour. Open to college sophomores, college juniors, college seniors, recent college graduates, graduate students. ▶ *1–3 engineering department interns:* responsibilities include assisting the engineering department with hardware and software design projects, design completion, prototyping, and other functions or special projects. Candidates should have ability to work

independently, ability to work with others, analytical skills, college courses in field, computer skills, knowledge of field, oral communication skills, organizational skills, personal interest in the field, self-motivation. Position available as unpaid or at $12–$15 per hour. Open to college juniors, college seniors, recent college graduates, graduate students. ▶ *1–3 human resources department interns:* responsibilities include assisting a busy human resources department by performing a variety of entry-level professional duties. Candidates should have ability to work independently, analytical skills, computer skills, office skills, oral communication skills, organizational skills, personal interest in the field, research skills, self-motivation, strong interpersonal skills, writing skills. Position available as unpaid or paid. Open to college juniors, college seniors, recent college graduates, graduate students. ▶ *1–3 manufacturing timestudy interns:* responsibilities include determining standards for the sub-assemblies and final assemblies of our manufacturing process. Other duties may include serving as back-up bidder for FC's. Candidates should have ability to work with others, analytical skills, knowledge of field, personal interest in the field, research skills. $12–$15 per hour. Open to college juniors, college seniors, recent college graduates, graduate students. Duration for all positions is flexible. International applications accepted.

Benefits Job counseling, names of contacts, on-the-job training, opportunity to attend seminars/workshops, possible full-time employment, willing to act as a professional reference, willing to complete paperwork for educational credit, willing to provide letters of recommendation, daily stipend for work-related travel and lunch for human resources interns (academic year interns).

Contact Write, fax, or e-mail Katie Domville, Human Resources Generalist. Fax: 203-857-0299. E-mail: employment@trans-lux. com. Telephone interview required. Applicants must submit a formal organization application, cover letter, resume. Applications are accepted continuously. World Wide Web: http://www. trans-lux.com.

WEYERHAEUSER
PO Box 2999
Tacoma, Washington 98477-2999

General Information International forest products company that grows and harvests timber; produces and sells wood and paper products. Established in 1900. Number of employees: 4,000. Number of internship applications received each year: 1,000.

Internships Available ▶ *Timberlands program interns:* responsibilities include working with teams responsible for hands-on implementation of business and stewardship strategies. Candidates should have ability to work independently, ability to work with others, computer skills, declared college major in field, knowledge of field. Duration is 3–6 months. Paid. Open to college juniors, college seniors and graduate students who are returning to school for at least one quarter following internship. ▶ *12–16 controllership development interns:* responsibilities include accounting. Candidates should have ability to work with others, college courses in field, computer skills, declared college major in field, plan to pursue career in field, willingness to relocate, minimum GPA of 3.2. Duration is 6 months. $12 per hour. Open to college juniors, college seniors who are returning to school for at least one quarter following internship. ▶ *3–5 corporate research and development MBA interns:* responsibilities include working with Commercial Development group at Weyerhaeuser Technology Center. Candidates should have college degree in related field, computer skills, oral communication skills, organizational skills, research skills, strong interpersonal skills. Duration is 3 months. Paid. Open to graduate students. ▶ *6–8 engineering interns:* responsibilities include gaining experience in pulp and paper, project engineering design and construction (joint program with Harris Group and J.H. Kelly, Inc.). Candidates should have declared college major in field, minimum GPA of 3.0. Duration is 3 months (2 summers required). Paid. Open to college sophomores. ▶ *60–65 information technology interns:* responsibilities include performing meaningful, technically challenging work in a specific IT function such as applicatioin development, Web design, project management, or technical support. Candidates should have computer skills, declared college major in field, plan to pursue career in field, strong interpersonal skills, minimum GPA of 3.2. Duration is 6–8 months. Paid. Open to college sophomores, college juniors, college seniors, graduate students. ▶ *6–8 pulp, paper, and packaging research and development interns:* responsibilities include working in Technology Center. Candidates should have computer skills, declared college major in field, oral communication skills, plan to pursue career in field, research skills, strong interpersonal skills. Duration is 3 months. Paid. Open to graduate students. ▶ *15–20 technology research and development interns:* responsibilities include working with Weyerhaeuser Technology research and development organizations to transfer and implement new and improved technologies; may involve time at mill sites. Candidates should have declared college major in field, minimum GPA of 3.2. Duration is 3–6 months. Paid. Open to college juniors, college seniors, graduate students.

Benefits Formal training, job counseling, names of contacts, on-the-job training, opportunity to attend seminars/workshops, possible full-time employment, travel reimbursement, willing to act as a professional reference, willing to complete paperwork for educational credit, willing to provide letters of recommendation, health insurance for 6 month interns only.

Contact Write, call, fax, or e-mail Debra Barton, College Relations Representative, College Relations, Mail Stop CCB5D7, PO Box 2999, Tacoma, Washington 98477-2999. Phone: 253-924-2602. Fax: 253-924-4151. E-mail: college@wdni.com. In-person interview recommended. Applicants must submit a formal organization application, cover letter, resume, academic transcripts, three personal references. Applications are accepted continuously. World Wide Web: http://www.weyerhaeuser.com.

PHARMACEUTICAL AND MEDICINE MANUFACTURING

ALZA CORPORATION
PO Box 10950
Palo Alto, California 94303-0802

General Information A research-based pharmaceutical company with leading drug delivery technologies. The company applies its delivery technologies to develop pharmaceutical products with enhanced therapeutic value for its own portfolio and for many of the world's leading pharmaceutical companies. Established in 1968. Number of employees: 2,000. Number of internship applications received each year: 300.

Internships Available ▶ *15 summer interns:* responsibilities include working in biology, chemical engineering, chemistry, computer science, or business (MBAs). For more information refer to the Web site. Duration is 3 months. variable depending on education. Open to college freshmen, college sophomores, college juniors, college seniors, graduate students. International applications accepted.

Benefits Meals at a cost, on-the-job training, opportunity to attend seminars/workshops, possible full-time employment, willing to act as a professional reference, willing to complete paperwork for educational credit, willing to provide letters of recommendation.

Contact Write, call, fax, or e-mail Human Resources. Phone: 650-494-5319. Fax: 650-494-5656. E-mail: jobs@alza.com. In-person interview recommended. Applicants must submit a cover letter, resume. Applications are accepted continuously. World Wide Web: http://www.alza.com.

BRISTOL-MYERS SQUIBB- CENTER FOR HEALTH AND FITNESS
Route 206, PO Box 4000
Princeton, New Jersey 08540

General Information Fortune-100, internationally-based company engaged in research, manufacturing, and marketing of pharmaceutical products.

Internships Available ▶ *1 intern:* responsibilities include daily interaction with center participants on such topics as safe exercise practices and equipment use, assisting with design and administration of health promotion programs, and helping with office tasks. Candidates should have college courses in field, computer skills, oral communication skills, strong interpersonal skills, strong leadership ability, enrollment in an exercise physiology program or related health sciences program. Duration is flexible. Unpaid. Open to college sophomores, college juniors, college seniors, recent college graduates, graduate students, only those students who can get academic credit for internship.

Benefits On-the-job training, opportunity to attend seminars/workshops, willing to complete paperwork for educational credit, willing to provide letters of recommendation.

Contact Write, call, or fax Ms. Vanda Soldati, Intern Coordinator. Phone: 609-252-6400. Fax: 609-252-6758. Applicants must submit a cover letter, resume. Application deadline: March for summer, July for fall, November for spring.

MERCK RESEARCH LABORATORIES
126 East Lincoln Avenue, PO Box 2000
Rahway, New Jersey 07065

General Information Pharmaceutical corporation dedicated to the discovery and development of drugs to benefit the population. Established in 1890. Number of employees: 5,000. Number of internship applications received each year: 500.

Internships Available ▶ *75–100 summer interns:* responsibilities include hands-on research throughout research labs. Duration is 12–14 weeks. $500–$600 per week. Open to college juniors, graduate students.

Benefits Housing at a cost, meals at a cost, opportunity to attend seminars/workshops, possible full-time employment, travel reimbursement.

Contact Write, fax, or e-mail Andie Pagoulatos, Human Resources Manager, 126 East Lincoln Avenue, RY80-A3, Rahway, New Jersey 07065. Fax: 732-594-3844. E-mail: andie_pagoulatos@merck.com. No phone calls. Telephone interview required. Applicants must submit a cover letter, resume. Application deadline: February 15. World Wide Web: http://www.merck.com.

PROCYON PHARMACEUTICALS, INC.
165 New Boston Street
Woburn, Massachusetts 01801

General Information Pharmaceutical research firm involved in discovery and development of drugs for use in human therapy. Established in 1983. Number of employees: 8. Number of internship applications received each year: 15.

Internships Available ▶ *4–7 molecular pharmacology interns:* responsibilities include learning and carrying out binding and/or catalytic assays on Protein Kinase C-related enzymes, data manipulation and interpretation. Candidates should have ability to work independently, self-motivation, strong interpersonal skills, strong leadership ability, college major in chemistry, biology, or biochemistry. Duration is minimum of 10-12 weeks. Unpaid. Open to college freshmen, college sophomores, college juniors, college seniors, recent college graduates, graduate students. International applications accepted.

Benefits Formal training, on-the-job training, possible full-time employment, willing to act as a professional reference, willing to complete paperwork for educational credit, willing to provide letters of recommendation, exposure to leading-edge biomedical research in an exciting area of molecular pharmacology.

Contact Write, call, fax, or e-mail Dr. Paul E. Driedger, President. Phone: 781-935-3900. Fax: 781-938-5420. E-mail: driedger@procyonpharm.com. In-person interview required. Applicants

Procyon Pharmaceuticals, Inc. (continued)

must submit a cover letter, resume, academic transcripts, GPA for college science courses. Application deadline: May 1 for summer; continuous for year-round positions.

SMITHKLINE BEECHAM
One Franklin Plaza, PO Box 7929
Philadelphia, Pennsylvania 19101

General Information   Health-care company that discovers, develops, manufactures, and markets pharmaceuticals; over-the-counter (OTC) medicines; consumer health-care products; and clinical laboratory testing services. Established in 1989. Number of employees: 54,000. Number of internship applications received each year: 1,000.

Internships Available ▶ *10 MBA summer interns:* responsibilities include assisting in marketing, human resources, finance, operations, or computer information systems. Duration is 10–12 weeks. $1,100–$1,300 per month. Open to students enrolled in an MBA program. ▶ *65–90 undergraduate summer interns:* responsibilities include working in research and development (sciences) or commercial departments (marketing, human resources, finance). Candidates should have ability to work independently, college courses in field, computer skills, knowledge of field, research skills, written communication skills. Duration is 10–14 weeks. $11–$15 per hour. Open to college freshmen, college sophomores, college juniors, graduate students. International applications accepted.

Benefits Formal training, opportunity to attend seminars/workshops, possible full-time employment, willing to complete paperwork for educational credit, willing to provide letters of recommendation, 1/2 day company orientation, detailed department orientation, travel reimbursement provided for MBA summer interns only.

Contact Write or e-mail Ms. Trish Shafer, Administrator, United States University Relations. E-mail: patriciashafer@sb.com. No phone calls. Applicants must submit a cover letter, resume. Application deadline: February 1 for undergraduate program, February 15 for MBA program. World Wide Web: http://www.sb.com.

OTHER SERVICES

BUSINESS, PROFESSIONAL, LABOR, POLITICAL, AND OTHER ORGANIZATIONS

AFRICA POLICY INFORMATION CENTER
110 Maryland Avenue, NE, Suite 509
Washington, District of Columbia 20002

General Information Nonprofit educational organization with the primary objective of widening policy debate in the United States around African issues and the U.S. role in Africa, by providing accessible policy-relevant information and analysis usable by a wide range of groups and individuals. Established in 1978. Number of employees: 5. Number of internship applications received each year: 40.

Internships Available ▶ *1–4 legislative and research assistants:* responsibilities include researching and drafting background text for upcoming publications, working with partners in the Advocacy Network for Africa (ADNA) or in other coalitions, participating in community education and grassroots initiatives, and researching sources for the Africa Policy Web site. Candidates should have college courses in field, computer skills, knowledge of field, oral communication skills, self-motivation, written communication skills. Duration is 2–12 months. Unpaid. Open to college juniors, college seniors, recent college graduates, graduate students, law students, career changers. International applications accepted.

Benefits Names of contacts, opportunity to attend seminars/workshops, willing to act as a professional reference, willing to complete paperwork for educational credit, willing to provide letters of recommendation.

Contact Write, call, fax, or e-mail Sarah Godfrey, Administrative Assistant. Phone: 202-546-7961. Fax: 202-546-1545. E-mail: sarahg@africapolicy.org. In-person interview recommended. Applicants must submit a formal organization application, cover letter, resume, writing sample, two letters of recommendation, three letters of recommendation, 1- to 2-page essay describing goals and objectives in seeking an internship with APIC. Application deadline: March 15 for summer, July 15 for fall, November 15 for spring. World Wide Web: http://www. africapolicy.org.

ALASKA CIVIL LIBERTIES UNION
PO Box 201844
Anchorage, Alaska 99520-1844

General Information Nonprofit, non-partisan organization dedicated to protecting the guarantees of civil liberties in the Bill of Rights and Alaska Constitution through public education, litigation, and political lobbying. Established in 1983. Number of employees: 3. Affiliate of American Civil Liberties Union, New York, New York. Number of internship applications received each year: 4.

Internships Available ▶ *1 law clerk:* responsibilities include researching and drafting legal memoranda, assisting volunteer attorneys with filing pleadings, monitoring legislative committee hearings, and researching/ drafting testimony and position

papers on legislation affecting civil liberties. Candidates should have ability to work independently, analytical skills, oral communication skills, research skills, writing skills. Duration is quarter or semester (flexible with duration). Unpaid. Open to law students. International applications accepted.

Benefits Names of contacts, willing to act as a professional reference, willing to complete paperwork for educational credit, willing to provide letters of recommendation, free housing (when available).

Contact Write or e-mail Jennifer Rudinger, Executive Director, PO Box 201844, Anchorage, Alaska 99520-1844. E-mail: akclu@ alaska.net. In-person interview recommended. Applicants must submit a cover letter, resume, academic transcripts. Applications are accepted continuously. World Wide Web: http://www. aclu.org.

AMERICAN ACADEMY OF PEDIATRICS (AAP)
141 Northwest Point Boulevard
Elk Grove Village, Illinois 60007-1098

General Information Nonprofit medical association dedicated to the health, safety, and well-being of infants, children, adolescents, and young adults. Established in 1930. Number of employees: 300. Number of internship applications received each year: 9.

Internships Available ▶ *1 public relations intern:* responsibilities include interviewing doctors, writing news releases, and updating media database. ▶ *1 sections intern (Department of Education):* responsibilities include developing a new executive committee member orientation packet, developing a new member packet, organizing the design of a sections booth for AAP national meetings, working with the Division of Public Relations to organize writing of press releases; assisting in the planning of orientation sessions for the annual meeting and re-formatting and updating the sections resource manual. Duration for all positions is flexible. All positions are unpaid. Open to college freshmen, college sophomores, college juniors, college seniors, recent college graduates, graduate students. International applications accepted.

Benefits Willing to complete paperwork for educational credit.

Contact Fax or e-mail Kathryn Walter, Human Resource Generalist, 141 Norhtwest Point Boulevard, Elk Grove Village, Illinois 60007-1098. Fax: 847-228-5099. E-mail: resumes@aap.org. No phone calls. In-person interview required. Applicants must submit a cover letter, resume, writing sample. Applications are accepted continuously.

AMERICAN ASSOCIATION OF ADVERTISING AGENCIES
405 Lexington Avenue, 18th Floor
New York, New York 10174-1801

General Information National trade association of the advertising industry with more than 500 members nationwide. Established in 1917. Number of employees: 65. Number of internship applications received each year: 300.

Internships Available ▶ *70–90 multicultural advertising intern program:* responsibilities include performing duties in account management, art direction, interactive technologies, copywriting, research, broadcast production, graphic design, traffic, print product, and media in New York, Chicago, Boston, Detroit, Dallas, Seattle, Philadelphia, Portland, Los Angeles, or San Francisco.

Candidates should have computer skills, knowledge of field, oral communication skills, organizational skills, plan to pursue career in field, research skills, strong interpersonal skills, written communication skills. Duration is 10 weeks. $350–$400 per week. Open to college juniors, college seniors, graduate students.
Benefits Housing at a cost, names of contacts, opportunity to attend seminars/workshops, possible full-time employment, willing to act as a professional reference, willing to provide letters of recommendation, 60% payment of housing and transportation costs.
Contact Write, call, or fax Rhonda Jackman, Manager of Diversity Services. Phone: 800-676-9333. Fax: 212-573-8968. In-person interview required. Applicants must submit a formal organization application, resume, academic transcripts, two letters of recommendation, creative art and writing samples (if applying for art/copywriting positions). Application deadline: January 22 for summer. World Wide Web: http://www.commercepark.com/ AAAA/MAIP.

AMERICAN ASSOCIATION OF UNIVERSITY WOMEN EDUCATIONAL FOUNDATION
1111 16th Street, NW
Washington, District of Columbia 20036-4873

General Information Foundation that provides funding for educational programs that directly benefit women and girls; groundbreaking research on gender bias in schools; fellowships and grants for outstanding women from around the globe; and vital community action projects. Established in 1881. Number of employees: 28. Unit of AAUW, Washington, District of Columbia. Number of internship applications received each year: 30.
Internships Available ▶ *1 Eleanor Roosevelt teacher fellowships and community action grants intern:* responsibilities include assisting with the management and assessment of funding programs. ▶ *1 communications intern:* responsibilities include assisting the Coordinator with monitoring and managing the flow of materials between the two staffs; editing and writing articles, press releases, and creative briefs for meetings; and other programmatic, technical, and administrative projects. ▶ *2 development interns:* responsibilities include working with the staff to analyze contribution systems, determine donor trends, research potential funders, and write text for proposals, donor profiles, and publications. ▶ *1 gender equity research intern:* responsibilities include assisting in the coordination of commissioned research reports currently in production. ▶ *1 higher education fellowships intern:* responsibilities include working with the Senior Program Officer on program assessment projects and the development of a major Colleges of Teacher Education initiative. ▶ *1 international fellowships intern:* responsibilities include assisting the Senior Program Officer with assessment and evaluation efforts. ▶ *1 multicultural initiatives and higher education intern:* responsibilities include assisting the Associate Director and Coordinator of Multicultural Initiatives and the Program Officer for Career Development Grants and Selected Professions Fellowships to assess grant programs; researching and writing articles on minority women in higher education; and coordinating conferences and meetings. Duration for all positions is flexible. All positions are unpaid. Open to college freshmen, college sophomores, college juniors, college seniors, recent college graduates, graduate students. International applications accepted.
Benefits Formal training, job counseling, names of contacts, opportunity to attend seminars/workshops, possible full-time employment, travel reimbursement, willing to complete paperwork for educational credit, willing to provide letters of recommendation, small stipend, computer courses on all levels, career development lunches, networking opportunities.
Contact Write, call, fax, or e-mail Shelley Johnson, Intern Coordinator. Phone: 202-785-7700. Fax: 202-872-1425. E-mail: helpline@aauw.org. In-person interview recommended. Applicants must submit a cover letter, resume, writing sample. Applications are accepted continuously. World Wide Web: http://www.aauw.org.

AMERICAN COUNCIL FOR THE UNITED NATIONS UNIVERSITY
4421 Garrison Street, NW
Washington, District of Columbia 20016

General Information Nonprofit corporation that provides support for the United Nations University (UNU), an autonomous organization of the United Nations that focuses intellectual resources on world problems as a global, decentralized, non-degree granting, postgraduate research institution, and manages the Millenium project on futures research and global change. Established in 1976. Number of employees: 3. Unit of United Nations University, Tokyo, Japan. Number of internship applications received each year: 100.
Internships Available ▶ *5–10 Millennium Project interns:* responsibilities include assisting with research in social and technological fields, entering data, attending meetings and conferences, reviewing and reading documents, and helping develop studies. Candidates should have analytical skills, computer skills, editing skills, organizational skills, research skills, writing skills. Duration is 2.5 months to 1 year (preferably full-time for 1 semester). Open to college juniors, college seniors, recent college graduates, graduate students, law students, career changers, individuals reentering the workforce, preference given to graduate students. ▶ *1–3 Web master's assistants:* responsibilities include maintaining and improving Web site, assisting global research on future of global change, attending conferences, and finding the best ideas and experts. Candidates should have analytical skills, computer skills, editing skills, organizational skills, research skills, writing skills. Duration is 2.5 months to 1 year (preferably full-time for 1 semester). Open to college juniors, college seniors, recent college graduates, graduate students, career changers, individuals reentering the workforce. ▶ *1–2 general interns:* responsibilities include providing liaison services between U.S. research institutions and the United Nations University programs. Candidates should have computer skills, editing skills, office skills, oral communication skills, organizational skills, self-motivation. Duration is flexible, but prefer full-time for one semester. Open to college juniors, college seniors, recent college graduates, graduate students, law students, career changers, individuals reentering the workforce, preference given to graduate students. All positions are unpaid. International applications accepted.
Benefits Formal training, job counseling, names of contacts, on-the-job training, opportunity to attend seminars/workshops, possible full-time employment, travel reimbursement, willing to act as a professional reference, willing to complete paperwork for educational credit, willing to provide letters of recommendation.
International Internships Available in Buenos Aires, Argentina; Beijing, China; Cairo, Egypt; MaDurai, India; Tokyo, Japan; Moscow, Russian Federation; London, United Kingdom.
Contact Write, call, fax, or e-mail Jerome C. Glenn, Executive Director. Phone: 202-686-5179. Fax: 202-686-5179. E-mail: jglenn@ igc.org. In-person interview recommended. Applicants must submit a cover letter, resume. Applications are accepted continuously. World Wide Web: http://www.millennium-project. org.

AMERICAN FOREIGN SERVICE ASSOCIATION AND COALITION FOR AMERICAN LEADERSHIP ABROAD
2101 E Street, NW
Washington, District of Columbia 20037

General Information Professional association and labor union representing members of the U.S. Foreign Service in labor-management relations, in promoting and advancing the diplomatic profession, and securing popular support for an active and effective U.S. foreign policy. Established in 1924. Number of employees: 25.
Internships Available ▶ *1 advocacy and legislative affairs intern:* responsibilities include drafting letters to Congress and opinion leaders, calling congressional staff members, and working with community leaders. ▶ *1 journalist/research assistant:* responsibilities include assisting in research and writing for the Foreign Service Journal. ▶ *1 legislative affairs intern:* responsibilities include

helping maintain database, analyzing and summarizing legislation, attending hearings, working with grassroots and coalition organizations, and helping develop and implement legislative strategy. ▶ *1 public affairs intern:* responsibilities include interviewing Foreign Service personnel, drafting articles and other materials, and placing articles in newspapers and magazines. ▶ *1 publications marketing/advertising intern:* responsibilities include helping design and create a marketing campaign. Duration for all positions is 1 semester. All positions paid. Open to college freshmen, college sophomores, college juniors, college seniors.
Benefits Willing to complete paperwork for educational credit, stipends available.
Contact Write, call, fax, or e-mail Intern Coordinator. Phone: 202-338-4045. Fax: 202-338-6820. E-mail: asfa@asfa.org. In-person interview required. Applicants must submit a cover letter, resume, writing sample. Applications are accepted continuously. World Wide Web: http://www.afsa.org.

AMERICAN ISRAEL PUBLIC AFFAIRS COMMITTEE (AIPAC)
440 First Street, NW, Suite 600
Washington, District of Columbia 20001

General Information Bipartisan organization that lobbies Congress and the Administration on legislation that affects the U.S.-Israel relationship. Established in 1954. Number of employees: 80. Number of internship applications received each year: 300.
Internships Available ▶ *10–25 interns:* responsibilities include a variety of tasks and positions, including research, writing, public relations, legislative work, and event planning. Candidates should have computer skills, office skills, oral communication skills, research skills, writing skills, knowledge of/interest in the Middle-East. Duration is flexible. Position available as unpaid or at stipend for summer, full-time work. Open to college freshmen, college sophomores, college juniors, college seniors, recent college graduates, graduate students.
Benefits Willing to complete paperwork for educational credit.
Contact Write, call, fax, or e-mail Mr. Steven Bocknek, Internship Coordinator. Phone: 202-639-5200. Fax: 202-347-4918. E-mail: steve_bocknek@aipac.org. Applicants must submit a cover letter, resume, writing sample, two letters of recommendation. Application deadline: January 15 for spring, April 1 for summer, September 15 for fall, December 1 for winter. World Wide Web: http://www.aipac.org.

AMERICAN JUDICATURE SOCIETY
180 North Michigan Avenue, Suite 600
Chicago, Illinois 60601

General Information Society that strives to maintain and enhance the independence and effectiveness of the judicial system. Established in 1913. Number of employees: 24. Number of internship applications received each year: 50.
Internships Available ▶ *1–2 law clerks:* responsibilities include legal research and writing, and assisting in the publication of various journals/newsletters. Candidates should have analytical skills, computer skills, editing skills, research skills, writing skills. Open to law students. ▶ *1–2 research assistants:* responsibilities include library research, writing reports, and collating and cataloging information. Candidates should have analytical skills, college courses in field, computer skills, office skills, research skills, writing skills. Open to college juniors, college seniors. Duration for all positions is 2–3 months. All positions are unpaid. International applications accepted.
Benefits On-the-job training, possible full-time employment, willing to act as a professional reference, willing to complete paperwork for educational credit, willing to provide letters of recommendation.
Contact Write or e-mail Seth S. Andersen, Director, Hunter Center for Judicial Selection, 180 North Michigan Avenue Suite 600, Chicago, Illinois 60601. E-mail: sandersen@ajs.org. No phone calls. In-person interview required. Applicants must submit a cover letter, resume, writing sample, three personal references. Application deadline: April 1 for summer, August 1 for fall, December 1 for spring. World Wide Web: http://www.ajs.org.

AMERICAN LEGISLATIVE EXCHANGE COUNCIL
910 17th Street, NW, 5th Floor
Washington, District of Columbia 20006

General Information National bipartisan membership organization of state legislators dedicated to the principles of free enterprise, limited government, tax limitation, and effective educational and judicial institutions. Established in 1973. Number of employees: 30. Number of internship applications received each year: 200.
Internships Available ▶ *8–12 research assistants:* responsibilities include assisting a legislative director by tracking the progress of state legislation, performing research requests for legislators and corporate representatives, assisting in writing issue papers, and preparing for meetings, seminars, and workshops. Candidates should have ability to work independently, computer skills, research skills, self-motivation, writing skills. Duration is 3–5 months. Unpaid. Open to college freshmen, college sophomores, college juniors, college seniors, recent college graduates, graduate students, law students. International applications accepted.
Benefits Opportunity to attend seminars/workshops, possible full-time employment, travel reimbursement, willing to complete paperwork for educational credit, willing to provide letters of recommendation, compensation for lunch expenses.
Contact Write, call, fax, or e-mail Ms. Anne Singer, Intern Coordinator. Phone: 202-466-3800. Fax: 202-466-3801. E-mail: asinger@alec.org. In-person interview recommended. Applicants must submit a formal organization application, cover letter, resume, writing sample, two letters of recommendation. Application deadline: April 15 for summer, December 1 for spring. World Wide Web: http://www.alec.org.

AMERICAN MANAGEMENT ASSOCIATION
1601 Broadway, 11th Floor
New York, New York 10019

General Information Not-for-profit, membership-based organization providing a wide variety of services and training in the fields of business and management. Established in 1923. Number of employees: 300. Number of internship applications received each year: 300.
Internships Available ▶ *1–2 AMA periodicals interns:* responsibilities include working on various monthly and quarterly publications and working with fairs, workshops, and meetings. Candidates should have ability to work independently, ability to work with others, college courses in field, computer skills, editing skills, office skills, oral communication skills, organizational skills, plan to pursue career in field, research skills, written communication skills. Open to high school seniors, college juniors, college seniors, graduate students. ▶ *1–2 AMACOM books interns:* responsibilities include assisting in the production, proofreading, editing, and layout of publications; doing research and management analysis. Candidates should have ability to work independently, ability to work with others, college courses in field, computer skills, oral communication skills, organizational skills, plan to pursue career in field, research skills, written communication skills. Open to high school seniors, college juniors, college seniors, graduate students. ▶ *1–2 CMD interns:* responsibilities include coordinating and assisting in the creative marketing of brochures, notebooks, and promotion for AMA seminars, researching and compiling data on different seminars, and analyzing trends. Candidates should have ability to work independently, ability to work with others, analytical skills, college courses in field, computer skills, oral communication skills, organizational skills, plan to pursue career in field, research skills, written communication skills. Open to college juniors, college seniors, graduate students. ▶ *1–2 human resources interns:* responsibilities include analyzing personnel reports, researching new laws, assisting with various human resources audits, and compiling information for human resources reports. Candidates should have ability to work independently, ability to work with others, analytical skills, college courses in field, computer skills, oral communication skills, organizational skills, plan to pursue career in field, written communication skills. Open to high school seniors, college juniors, college seniors, graduate students. ▶ *1*

American Management Association (continued)

market research intern: responsibilities include conducting competitive analysis, survey data review, and statistics. Candidates should have ability to work independently, ability to work with others, analytical skills, college courses in field, oral communication skills, organizational skills, plan to pursue career in field, research skills, written communication skills, knowledge of SAS and SPSS, customer service experience a plus. Open to college seniors, graduate students. ▶ *1–2 marketing interns:* responsibilities include researching and compiling information for new product development and performing market analysis. Candidates should have ability to work independently, ability to work with others, analytical skills, college courses in field, computer skills, oral communication skills, plan to pursue career in field, research skills, written communication skills. Open to college juniors, college seniors, graduate students. Duration for all positions is 3–6 months. All positions paid at $5 per hour. International applications accepted.

Benefits Formal training, job counseling, names of contacts, opportunity to attend seminars/workshops, willing to complete paperwork for educational credit, willing to provide letters of recommendation, opportunity to attend two AMA complimentary seminars.

Contact Write, call, fax, or e-mail Ms. Martha S. Medina, Senior Human Resources Coordinator. Phone: 212-903-8021. Fax: 212-903-8163. E-mail: martha_medina@amanet.org. In-person interview recommended. Applicants must submit a cover letter, resume, 1 academic and 1 professional letter of recommendation. Applications are accepted continuously. World Wide Web: http://www.amanet.org.

THE AMERICAN-SCANDINAVIAN FOUNDATION
15 East 65 Street
New York, New York 10021

General Information Nonprofit organization founded to develop and promote educational and cultural exchange between the United States and the Scandinavian countries of Denmark, Finland, Iceland, Norway, and Sweden. Established in 1910. Number of employees: 15. Number of internship applications received each year: 60.

Internships Available ▶ *5–10 TEFL positions (Finland):* responsibilities include teaching English as a foreign language to Finns at a variety of age levels in Finnish public schools, institutes, or private firms. Candidates should have college degree in related field, declared college major in field, experience in the field, plan to pursue career in field, college major and/or college degree in related field. Duration is 2–10 months. $734–$918 per month. Open to college juniors, college seniors, recent college graduates, graduate students. ▶ *1–5 agricultural positions (Finland):* responsibilities include assisting in the daily work on small family farms. Candidates should have college degree in related field, declared college major in field, plan to pursue career in field, college major and/or college degree in related field. Duration is 2–3 months. $291–$341 per month. Open to college juniors, college seniors, recent college graduates, graduate students. ▶ *20–30 engineering interns (Scandinavia):* responsibilities include computer programming, performing entry-level engineering fieldwork, and assisting with projects. Candidates should have college courses in field, knowledge of field. Duration is 2–6 months. $6–$12 per hour. Open to college juniors, college seniors, graduate students.

Benefits Health insurance, international cultural experience, assistance in obtaining work permits for those who have found their own internships.

International Internships Available in Finland; Sweden.

Contact Write, call, or e-mail Exchange Division, ASF. Phone: 212-879-9779. E-mail: training@amscan.org. Applicants must submit a formal organization application, resume, academic transcripts, letter of recommendation. Application deadline: February 1 for TOEFL positions, December 31 for engineering positions. Fees: $50. World Wide Web: http://www.amscan.org.

AMERICAN SOCIETY OF INTERNATIONAL LAW
2223 Massachusetts Avenue, NW
Washington, District of Columbia 20008

General Information Professional organization that engages in the exploration of international legal issues, including economic and private transactions, the environment, armed conflicts, human rights, dispute resolution, space, and the United Nations system. Established in 1906. Number of employees: 18. Number of internship applications received each year: 150.

Internships Available ▶ *1 American Journal of International Law publication assistant:* responsibilities include keeping records for the "Books Received" section of the American Journal of International Law, responding to reprint permissions requests, bluebooking footnotes in book review section. Candidates should have ability to work with others, computer skills, editing skills, organizational skills, bluebooking skills. Duration is year-round on semester basis, including summer. Open to law students. ▶ *1–4 International Legal Materials legal interns:* responsibilities include obtaining texts of treaties, court decisions, national legislation, resolutions of international organizations, and reports for International Legal Materials; law students write analytical summaries of documents; all interns assist in proofreading and editing process. Candidates should have ability to work independently, analytical skills, college courses in field, editing skills, research skills, writing skills. Duration is year-round on semester basis, including summer. Open to law students. ▶ *1 financial office assistant:* responsibilities include assisting the financial officer with the financial functions of the Society. Candidates should have college courses in field, computer skills, office skills, organizational skills, self-motivation. Duration is 8–10 weeks. Open to college juniors, college seniors. ▶ *1 library/research assistant:* responsibilities include helping to maintain the ASIL Web site; assisting staff and the Washington legal community with their information needs; and general library activities. Candidates should have ability to work independently, ability to work with others, computer skills, office skills, oral communication skills, research skills, writing skills. Duration is 1 semester. Open to college sophomores, college juniors, college seniors, graduate students, law students, individuals reentering the workforce. ▶ *1 proceedings assistant:* responsibilities include bluebooking citations for the proceedings, a compilation of the papers, discussions, and speeches given at the Society's annual meeting; desktop publishing/formatting of the texts. Candidates should have ability to work independently, computer skills, editing skills, organizational skills, research skills, strong bluebooking and citation checking skills. Duration is 1 semester. Open to law students. ▶ *1–3 sales and marketing assistants:* responsibilities include assisting in the promotion of the Society's programs and publications; conducting market research; assisting in the development and implementation of marketing strategies. Candidates should have computer skills, oral communication skills, organizational skills, research skills, strong interpersonal skills, written communication skills. Duration is 1 semester. Open to college juniors, college seniors, graduate students, law students. All positions are unpaid. International applications accepted.

Benefits Opportunity to attend seminars/workshops, possible full-time employment, willing to act as a professional reference, willing to complete paperwork for educational credit, willing to provide letters of recommendation, assistance with development of legal analysis skills.

Contact Write, call, or fax Internship Coordinator. Phone: 202-939-6000. Fax: 202-797-7133. In-person interview recommended. Applicants must submit a cover letter, resume, abstracting exercise, references after interview. Application deadline: April 10 for summer, July 1 for fall, November 1 for spring. World Wide Web: http://www.asil.org.

AMERICAN SOCIETY OF MAGAZINE EDITORS
919 Third Avenue, 22nd Floor
New York, New York 10022

General Information Professional society for senior magazine editors that provides a forum for the discussion of matters of mutual concern. Established in 1963. Number of employees: 3.

Unit of Magazine Publishers of America, New York, New York. Number of internship applications received each year: 175.
Internships Available ▶ *40 editorial interns:* responsibilities include performing entry-level editorial tasks. Candidates should have college courses in field, editing skills, knowledge of field, plan to pursue career in field, writing skills, previous magazine experience. Duration is 10 weeks. $325 per week stipend. Open to college juniors.
Benefits Names of contacts, opportunity to attend seminars/workshops, willing to provide letters of recommendation, distribution of resumes to ASME members.
Contact Write or e-mail Marlene Kahan, Executive Director. E-mail: asme@magazine.org. No phone calls. Applicants must submit a formal organization application, cover letter, resume, three writing samples, letter of recommendation. Application deadline: December 15 for summer.

AMIDEAST
1730 M Street, NW, Suite 1100
Washington, District of Columbia 20036

General Information Private nonprofit organization promoting cooperation and understanding between Americans and the people of the Middle East and North Africa through education and development programs. Established in 1951. Number of employees: 45. Number of internship applications received each year: 100.
Internships Available ▶ *1 editorial research intern:* responsibilities include assisting in writing, researching, and marketing of quarterly professional periodical and other resources for overseas educational advisers and organizing and maintaining advising resource collections. Duration is flexible. ▶ *1 intern for special projects-short-term training:* responsibilities include researching short-term training programs, responding to trainees' requests, maintaining accurate records, corresponding with trainers and the field offices, and providing general program support. Duration is 1 month. ▶ *1 public relations/fund-raising intern:* responsibilities include researching international companies and compiling information to support fund-raising, public relations, and marketing products and services; researching, writing, and proofreading newsletters, annual report, flyers, and press releases; updating computerized mailing/donor lists. Duration is flexible. ▶ *1–4 publications interns:* responsibilities include researching, writing, editing, and producing educational materials; processing publications orders; and developing and implementing marketing activities. Duration is flexible (3 months minimum). ▶ *1 study abroad intern:* responsibilities include researching markets, developing advertisements and promotional materials, preparing mass mailings, and responding to requests for information. Duration is 1 semester. All positions available as unpaid or paid. Open to college freshmen, college sophomores, college juniors, college seniors.
Benefits Willing to complete paperwork for educational credit, willing to provide letters of recommendation.
Contact Write or e-mail Ms. May-Paulle Didon, Personnel Director, 170 M Street, NW, Suite 1100, Washington, District of Columbia 20036. E-mail: personnel@amideast.org. In-person interview recommended. Applicants must submit a cover letter, resume. Applications are accepted continuously. World Wide Web: http://www.amideast.org.

ARIZONA FOOD MARKETING ALLIANCE
120 East Pierce Street
Phoenix, Arizona 85004

General Information Nonprofit organization dedicated to effectively representing the Arizona retail food industry regarding interests in governmental, educational, business, or social issues that impact the industry. Established in 1943. Number of employees: 3. Number of internship applications received each year: 10.
Internships Available ▶ *1 publication intern:* responsibilities include writing, editing, photographing, and designing newsletters, brochures, flyers, and a monthly full-color magazine. Dura-

tion is 1 semester. $4–$6 per hour. Open to college sophomores, college juniors, college seniors, recent college graduates, graduate students.
Benefits Names of contacts, travel reimbursement, willing to complete paperwork for educational credit, willing to provide letters of recommendation.
Contact Write, call, or fax Richard Jennings, President, 120 East Pierce Street, Pheonix, Arizona 85004. Phone: 602-252-9761. Fax: 602-252-9021. In-person interview recommended. Applicants must submit a resume, writing sample. Applications are accepted continuously.

ASHOKA: INNOVATORS FOR THE PUBLIC
1700 North Moore Street, Suite 1920
Arlington, Virginia 22209-1903

General Information International nonprofit organization presenting fellowships to individuals with creative ideas for social change in Asia, Latin America, Central Europe, and Africa. Established in 1980. Number of employees: 40. Number of internship applications received each year: 100.
Internships Available ▶ *Interns:* responsibilities include working in areas of development, fellowship support services, finance, research, computers, and administration; working in offices dealing with Latin America, Asia, Central Europe, and Africa. Candidates should have ability to work independently, ability to work with others, computer skills, oral communication skills, research skills, self-motivation, writing skills, language ability a plus (French, Spanish, Portuguese, Thai or other Asian language). Duration is flexible (minimum of 12 hours per week preferred). Unpaid. Open to high school students, high school seniors, recent high school graduates, college freshmen, college sophomores, college juniors, college seniors, recent college graduates, graduate students, law students, career changers, individuals reentering the workforce. International applications accepted.
Benefits Names of contacts, opportunity to attend seminars/workshops, possible full-time employment, willing to complete paperwork for educational credit, willing to provide letters of recommendation.
Contact Write, fax, or e-mail Madeleine Carmichael, Intern Coordinator. Phone: 703-527-8300. Fax: 703-527-8383. E-mail: fdesk@ashoka.org. In-person interview recommended. Applicants must submit a cover letter, resume, two letters of recommendation. Applications are accepted continuously. World Wide Web: http://www.ashoka.org.

ASIAN AMERICAN ECONOMIC DEVELOPMENT ENTERPRISES, INC. (AAEDE)
216 West Garvey Avenue, Unit E
Monterey Park, California 91754

General Information Nonprofit organization aiding small business owners in the community via workshops and individual consultation; also provides the community with job fairs and volunteer opportunities. Established in 1977. Number of employees: 4. Number of internship applications received each year: 40.
Internships Available ▶ *1–2 community liaisons:* responsibilities include contacting various media and community organizations by sending out press releases, compiling press kits, arranging radio and television interviews, and making new media and association contacts for AAEDE. Candidates should have oral communication skills, organizational skills, self-motivation, writing skills. Position available as unpaid or paid. ▶ *2–3 conference coordinator assistants:* responsibilities include participating in all aspects of conference planning, including design and selection of invitations, sponsorship, speaker arrangements, lecture materials, lecture hall preparation, volunteer recruitment, and room set-up planning. Candidates should have ability to work with others, oral communication skills, organizational skills, self-motivation, creative and detail-oriented nature. Position available as unpaid or paid. ▶ *2–3 newsletter publication assistants:* responsibilities include gathering and evaluating information for newsletter, writing articles, editing submissions, reporting on community events, supporting design and layout, compiling

Asian American Economic Development Enterprises, Inc. (AAEDE) (continued)
graphic boards, interacting with the printer, and assisting with bulk mail. Candidates should have ability to work independently, ability to work with others, computer skills, editing skills, research skills, writing skills. Unpaid. ▶ *2–3 research/special project assistants:* responsibilities include gathering and evaluating business and/or demographic information for programs and grant applications, attending community meetings, evaluating proposals, and interacting with small business clients. Candidates should have analytical skills, computer skills, oral communication skills, research skills, writing skills, foreign language skills and business experience helpful. Unpaid. Duration for all positions is 8-12 hours per week. Open to college freshmen, college sophomores, college juniors, college seniors, graduate students.
Benefits Opportunity to attend seminars/workshops, willing to act as a professional reference, willing to complete paperwork for educational credit, willing to provide letters of recommendation.
Contact Write, call, fax, or e-mail Ms. Julia Hong, Program Manager, 216 West Garvey Avenue, Unit E, Monterey Park, California 91754. Phone: 626-572-7021. Fax: 626-572-6533. E-mail: julia@aaede.org. In-person interview recommended. Applicants must submit a cover letter, resume. Applications are accepted continuously. World Wide Web: http://www.aaede.org.

THE ASSOCIATED BLIND, INC.
110 William Street, Ninth Floor
New York, New York 10038

General Information Nonprofit organization that develops projects to enhance the lives of blind and visually impaired adults. Established in 1938. Number of employees: 12. Number of internship applications received each year: 100.
Internships Available ▶ *6–8 computer and Web development interns.* Candidates should have ability to work independently, analytical skills, computer skills, experience in the field, office skills, oral communication skills, organizational skills, personal interest in the field, research skills, self-motivation, strong interpersonal skills, strong leadership ability, writing skills, fluency in HTML coding, experience in SQL server, proficient in another low-level programming language such as C, C++. ▶ *6–8 finance-accounting department/marketing interns:* responsibilities include researching potential corporate partners, marketing new products via the Internet, developing and maintaining new databases, producing weekly statements on existing projects, and developing future programs. Candidates should have ability to work independently, analytical skills, computer skills, experience in the field, office skills, oral communication skills, organizational skills, personal interest in the field, research skills, self-motivation, strong interpersonal skills, strong leadership ability, writing skills. Duration for all positions is 2–3 months. All positions paid at $75 per week. Open to college freshmen, college sophomores, college juniors, college seniors, recent college graduates, graduate students. International applications accepted.
Benefits On-the-job training, opportunity to attend seminars/workshops, willing to complete paperwork for educational credit, willing to provide letters of recommendation.
Contact Write, fax, or e-mail Mr. Gerard Mawn, Chief Financial Officer, 110 William Street, 9th Floor, New York, New York 10038. Fax: 212-766-6809. E-mail: gerard_tab@altavista.net. In-person interview required. Applicants must submit a formal organization application, cover letter, resume, three personal references, three letters of recommendation. Application deadline: April 15 for summer, August 15 for fall, December 15 for winter. World Wide Web: http://www.tabinc.org.

ASTA FOUNDATION
1101 King Street
Alexandria, Virginia 22314

General Information Organization that encourages professionalism in the travel and tourism industry by offering financial aid to students and funding research in the tourism field. Established in 1982. Number of employees: 2. Affiliate of American Society of Travel Agents, Inc., Alexandria, Virginia. Number of internship applications received each year: 5.

Internships Available ▶ *1 Ayuso scholarship fellow:* responsibilities include attending a travel and trade show in Madrid, Spain for 10 days, utilizing knowledge of the Spanish language in order to interview Spanish tourism officials and to facilitate show functions. Candidates should have college courses in field, experience in the field, oral communication skills, plan to pursue career in field, written communication skills, ability to speak and read Spanish at a working level. Duration is 10 days in January. Paid expenses during 10-day stay in Madrid. Open to college juniors, college seniors, recent college graduates, graduate students, individuals with at least 2 years of college credit or work experience in the travel and tourism industry. International applications accepted.
Benefits Free housing, free meals, health insurance, names of contacts, on-the-job training, travel reimbursement.
International Internships Available in Madrid, Spain.
Contact Write, fax, or e-mail ASTA Foundation. Fax: 703-684-8319. E-mail: myriaml@astahq.com. No phone calls. Applicants must submit a formal organization application, academic transcripts, personal reference, letter of recommendation, 500-word essay in English and Spanish. Application deadline: July 28 for January. World Wide Web: http://www.astanet.com.

ATLANTIC AND PACIFIC EXCHANGE PROGRAM
1630 Crescent Place, NW, Suite 305
Washington, District of Columbia 20009

General Information Nonprofit organization that arranges study tours for professionals from the U.S., the Netherlands, China, and Japan. Established in 1981. Number of employees: 2. Unit of Atlantic and Pacific Exchange Program, Rotterdam, Netherlands. Number of internship applications received each year: 20.
Internships Available ▶ *2–3 program coordinators:* responsibilities include arranging study tours, developing contacts, and researching the backgrounds of professional participants. Candidates should have ability to work independently, computer skills, office skills, oral communication skills, research skills, writing skills. Duration is 12–16 weeks. Unpaid. Open to college juniors, college seniors, recent college graduates, graduate students. International applications accepted.
Benefits Names of contacts, willing to complete paperwork for educational credit, willing to provide letters of recommendation.
International Internships Available in Rotterdam, Netherlands.
Contact Write or fax Kathy Foster, Program Officer, 1630 Crescent Place, NW, Washington, District of Columbia 20009. Fax: 202-728-0715. No phone calls. In-person interview recommended. Applicants must submit a cover letter, resume, writing sample. Applications are accepted continuously.

ATLANTIC COUNCIL OF THE UNITED STATES
910 17th Street, NW, Suite 1000
Washington, District of Columbia 20006

General Information National, nonprofit, nonpartisan center for the formation of foreign policy. Established in 1961. Number of employees: 40. Number of internship applications received each year: 250.
Internships Available ▶ *15–20 John A. Baker interns:* responsibilities include scholarly research, administrative and/or office tasks, computer entry and application, weekly Intern Discussion Series roundtables, and a research project. Candidates should have computer skills, knowledge of field, office skills, personal interest in the field, research skills, written communication skills. Duration is 1 summer or semester. Unpaid. Open to college freshmen, college sophomores, college juniors, college seniors, recent college graduates, graduate students. International applications accepted.
Benefits Job counseling, names of contacts, opportunity to attend seminars/workshops, possible full-time employment, willing to complete paperwork for educational credit, willing to provide letters of recommendation, weekly intern discussion series roundtables.
Contact Write, fax, or e-mail Internship Coordinator. Fax: 202-463-7241. E-mail: internships@acus.org. No phone calls. Applicants must submit a cover letter, resume, academic transcripts, writ-

ing sample, two letters of recommendation. Application deadline: available on Web site. World Wide Web: http://www.acus.org.

BASS AND HOWES, INC.
1818 N Street, NW, Suite 450
Washington, District of Columbia 20036

General Information Public policy and public affairs consulting firm focusing on health and social welfare issues—particularly those of concern to women and their families. Established in 1986. Number of employees: 18. Number of internship applications received each year: 75.

Internships Available ▶ *1–2 interns:* responsibilities include providing logistical and administrative support for clients and programs; working with program staff and clients to prepare and finalize memoranda, reports, letters, minutes, etc.; attending meetings, hearings, or conferences on an as-needed basis; assisting with planning and logistics for conferences, meetings, and symposia; and research and retrieval of information from Internet and other sources. Candidates should have ability to work independently, computer skills, office skills, oral communication skills, organizational skills, personal interest in the field, research skills, self-motivation, strong interpersonal skills, writing skills. $750–$1,000 per month. Open to college sophomores, college juniors, college seniors, recent college graduates.

Benefits Names of contacts, opportunity to attend seminars/workshops, willing to act as a professional reference, willing to provide letters of recommendation.

Contact Write, fax, or e-mail Sara Chenault, Senior Program Associate, 1818 N Street, NW, Suite 450, Washington, District of Columbia 20036. Fax: 202-530-2901. E-mail: schenault@basshowes.com. No phone calls. Telephone interview required. Applicants must submit a cover letter, resume, writing sample, three personal references. Applications are accepted continuously.

BENTON FOUNDATION
1634 Eye Street, NW
Washington, District of Columbia 20007

General Information A private, nonpartisan foundation whose goal is to promote public interest in communications tools, applications, and policies. Established in 1948. Number of employees: 35. Number of internship applications received each year: 25.

Internships Available ▶ *1–3 communications policy and practice interns:* responsibilities include assisting in the publication of Benton's daily on-line news service and other reports and publications. Candidates should have ability to work independently, knowledge of field, research skills, self-motivation, written communication skills. Paid. Open to graduate students. International applications accepted.

Benefits On-the-job training, opportunity to attend seminars/workshops, willing to complete paperwork for educational credit.

Contact Write or e-mail Rachel Anderson, Communications Policy and Practice Associate. E-mail: rachel@benton.org. No phone calls. In-person interview recommended. Applicants must submit a cover letter, resume. Applications are accepted continuously. World Wide Web: http://www.benton.org.

BRAZILIAN-AMERICAN CHAMBER OF COMMERCE, INC.
509 Madison Avenue, 3rd Floor
New York, New York 10022

General Information Bilateral trade association aiming at fostering better business relations between Brazil and the US. Established in 1969. Number of employees: 5. Number of internship applications received each year: 6.

Internships Available ▶ *2–3 membership marketing interns:* responsibilities include contacting potential members over the phone, researching for our annual publication, and handling business information requests. Candidates should have oral communication skills, organizational skills, self-motivation, strong interpersonal skills, written communication skills. Duration is

June to August (minimum 25 hours per week). $500 stipend per month. Open to college seniors, graduate students.

Benefits Job counseling, names of contacts, on-the-job training, opportunity to attend seminars/workshops, willing to act as a professional reference, willing to complete paperwork for educational credit, willing to provide letters of recommendation.

Contact Write, fax, or e-mail Sueli Bonaparte, Executive Director, 509 Madison Avenue, 3rd Floor, New York, New York 10022. Fax: 212-751-7692. E-mail: membership@brazilcham.com. No phone calls. In-person interview required. Applicants must submit a cover letter, resume, academic transcripts, writing sample, letter of recommendation. Application deadline: May 15. World Wide Web: http://www.brazilcham.com.

BUSINESS EXECUTIVES FOR NATIONAL SECURITY
1717 Pennsylvania Avenue, NW, Suite 350
Washington, District of Columbia 20006-4603

General Information National nonpartisan association of business leaders working to improve national security by promoting better management of defense dollars, advocating measures to make the economy stronger, and finding ways to prevent the use of weapons of mass destruction. Established in 1982. Number of employees: 20. Number of internship applications received each year: 100.

Internships Available ▶ *3 research interns:* responsibilities include researching national security issues, attending congressional hearings, and researching background materials and related publications. Duration is 3 months. $35 per day. Open to college juniors, college seniors, recent college graduates, graduate students. International applications accepted.

Benefits Names of contacts, opportunity to attend seminars/workshops, willing to provide letters of recommendation.

Contact Write, fax, or e-mail Dr. Zach Selden, Intern Coordinator. Fax: 202-296-2490. E-mail: zselden@bens.org. Applicants must submit a cover letter, resume, writing sample. Application deadline: March 30 for summer, July 30 for fall, November 15 for spring. World Wide Web: http://www.bens.org.

CANADIAN EMBASSY
501 Pennsylvania Avenue, NW
Washington, District of Columbia 20001

General Information An embassy that provides students the opportunity for involvement in governmental affairs to gain a general understanding of the Canada/U.S. bilateral relationship. Established in 1936. Number of employees: 250. Number of internship applications received each year: 400.

Internships Available ▶ *2–5 economics interns:* responsibilities include working in areas such as energy, trade, science, defense, and OLIFI. Duration is January to December. Open to college sophomores, college juniors, college seniors, recent college graduates, graduate students, law students. ▶ *2–5 politics interns:* responsibilities include working in congressional relations and the environment. Duration is January to December. Open to college juniors, college seniors, recent college graduates, graduate students, law students. ▶ *5 public affairs interns:* responsibilities include working in areas such as relations, special events, cultural relations, press, and publications. Duration is 1 semester. Open to college sophomores, college juniors, college seniors, recent college graduates, graduate students. Candidates for all positions should have ability to work with others, computer skills, oral communication skills, organizational skills, research skills, written communication skills. All positions are unpaid.

Benefits Job counseling, names of contacts, opportunity to attend seminars/workshops, willing to complete paperwork for educational credit, willing to provide letters of recommendation, networking opportunities, access to gym.

Contact Write, call, fax, or e-mail Ingrid S. Summa, Intern Coordinator. Phone: 202-682-1740 Ext. 7530. Fax: 202-682-7791. E-mail: ingrid.summa@dfait-maeci.gc.ca. Telephone interview required. Applicants must submit a cover letter, resume, academic transcripts, writing sample, three letters of recommendation.

Canadian Embassy (continued)
Application deadline: March 15 for summer, July 15 for fall, November 15 for winter/spring. World Wide Web: http://www.cdnemb-washdc.org.

CARIBBEAN LATIN AMERICAN ACTION
1818 N Street, NW, #500
Washington, District of Columbia 20036

General Information Organization that promotes economic development in the Caribbean basin countries. Established in 1978. Number of employees: 12. Number of internship applications received each year: 35.

Internships Available ▶ *1–4 interns:* responsibilities include researching, writing, editing, conference planning, acting as a congressional liaison, and making regional contacts. Candidates should have ability to work independently, oral communication skills, research skills, self-motivation, written communication skills, Spanish fluency. Duration is 1 semester. Unpaid. Open to college freshmen, college sophomores, college juniors, college seniors, graduate students. International applications accepted.

Benefits Names of contacts, possible full-time employment, willing to complete paperwork for educational credit, willing to provide letters of recommendation.

Contact Write, call, fax, or e-mail Intern Coordinator. Phone: 202-466-7464. Fax: 202-822-0075. E-mail: info@claa.org. In-person interview recommended. Applicants must submit a formal organization application, cover letter, resume, academic transcripts, writing sample. Application deadline: April 15 for summer, August 15 for fall, November 15 for spring. World Wide Web: http://www.claa.org.

CAUX SCHOLARS PROGRAM
1156 15th Street, NW, Suite 910
Washington, District of Columbia 20005

General Information Program that trains young adults in the theory and practice of conflict transformation in the international context. Established in 1991. Number of employees: 6. Unit of Moral Re-Armament, Washington, District of Columbia. Number of internship applications received each year: 30.

Internships Available ▶ *1 Caux Scholars Program intern:* responsibilities include mailing information, working on production of reports and brochures, helping with mailings, maintaining database, handling phone and written inquiries, and attending Executive Committee and Advisory Board meetings. Candidates should have computer skills, office skills, personal interest in the field, self-motivation, strong interpersonal skills, written communication skills. Duration is flexible, generally fall to summer. ▶ *1 Moral Re-Armament intern:* responsibilities include answering telephone, responding to inquiries, mailings, conference/meeting arrangements, database maintenance, and arranging programs for international guests. Candidates should have ability to work with others, computer skills, office skills, oral communication skills, self-motivation, written communication skills. Duration is flexible. All positions are unpaid. Open to college juniors, college seniors, recent college graduates, graduate students. International applications accepted.

Benefits Job counseling, names of contacts, opportunity to attend seminars/workshops, travel reimbursement, willing to complete paperwork for educational credit, willing to provide letters of recommendation, housing may be provided at no cost, optional 4½ week course in Switzerland at cost of $1975.

International Internships Available in Australia; United Kingdom.

Contact Write, call, fax, or e-mail Evelyn Ruffin, Program Director. Phone: 202-872-9077. Fax: 202-872-9137. E-mail: cauxsp@aol.com. In-person interview recommended. Applicants must submit a formal organization application, cover letter, resume, essay, and either 2 personal references or 2 letters of recommendation. Application deadline: April 1 for summer. Fees: $25. World Wide Web: http://members.aol.com/cauxsp/web/cspweb.htm.

CDS INTERNATIONAL, INC.
871 United Nations Plaza, 15th Floor
New York, New York 10017-1814

General Information Organization that prepares college students and recent graduates for the challenges of international business by combining in-depth language training with on-the-job experience in another country. Programs are currently offered for Americans wishing to go to Europe and for Europeans seeking experience in the U.S. Established in 1968. Number of employees: 17. Number of internship applications received each year: 200.

Internships Available ▶ *10 Bayer summer program interns:* responsibilities include working in chemistry and engineering fields. Candidates should have college courses in field, knowledge of field, oral communication skills, plan to pursue career in field. Duration is 3 months. compensation to offset living expenses; limited stipends available for 1-month language course. Open to college juniors, college seniors. ▶ *60 Congress-Bundestag Youth Exchange for Young Professionals participants:* responsibilities include 2 months of German language training, 4 months at an institution of higher education, and a 5-month internship; interns live with host families in Germany. Candidates should have knowledge of field, plan to pursue career in field, sincere intercultural interest paired with interest, goals, and experience in a business, technical, or vocational field. Duration is 1 year (July-July). Position available as unpaid or paid. Open to recent high school graduates, college freshmen, college sophomores, college juniors, college seniors, recent college graduates, U.S. citizens between 18 and 24 years old. ▶ *Career training for Germans in the U.S.* Candidates should have college degree in related field, declared college major in field, knowledge of field, oral communication skills, plan to pursue career in field, strong interpersonal skills. Duration is 3–18 months. Position available as unpaid or paid. Open to college juniors, college seniors, recent college graduates, young professionals. ▶ *Independent work abroad program interns.* Candidates should have college courses in field, experience in the field, oral communication skills, strong interpersonal skills. Duration is 6–18 months. DM 1500 per month (approximate). Open to college juniors, college seniors, recent college graduates, young professionals. ▶ *20–30 interns.* Candidates should have college courses in field, experience in the field, knowledge of field, oral communication skills, plan to pursue career in field. Duration is 6–18 months. DM 1500 per month (average); limited stipends available for one-month language course. Open to college juniors, college seniors, recent college graduates, young professionals. ▶ *5–10 summer program interns.* Candidates should have college courses in field, knowledge of field, oral communication skills, strong interpersonal skills. Duration is 3 months. compensation to offset living expenses; 500-1,000 Deutsch Marks. Open to college juniors, college seniors. International applications accepted.

Benefits Formal training, willing to complete paperwork for educational credit, willing to provide letters of recommendation, opportunity to live and work in another country, assistance in securing necessary work and residency permits, unpaid interns receive stipends for necessities.

International Internships Available in Germany.

Contact Write, call, fax, or e-mail Program Assistant. Phone: 212-497-3500. Fax: 212-497-3535. E-mail: info@cdsintl.org. In-person interview recommended. Applicants must submit a formal organization application, resume, academic transcripts, personal reference, 2 personal references or letters of recommendation, academic transcripts for some positions, in-person interview required for Congress-Bundestag Youth Exchange for Young Professionals. Application deadline: February 15 for Bayer summer interns, continuous for other positions, December 15 for Congress—Bundestag Youth Exchange for Young Professionals. World Wide Web: http://www.cdsintl.org.

CENTER FOR COMMUNICATION, INC.
271 Madison Avenue, Suite 700
New York, New York 10016

General Information Nonprofit organization that encourages university students to meet professionals in communications

industries by sponsoring seminars featuring workers in print and broadcast journalism, book and magazine publishing, advertising, public relations, and new technologies. Established in 1980. Number of employees: 6. Number of internship applications received each year: 30.
Internships Available ▶ *Interns:* responsibilities include researching senior topics; collecting newsclips; compiling suggested reading lists; helping to promote, support, and publicize activities; and participating in all aspects of production of seminars. Candidates should have ability to work independently, computer skills, personal interest in the field, research skills, strong interpersonal skills. $250 per spring or fall internship (2 days per week); $500 per summer internship (4 days per week). Open to college sophomores, college juniors, college seniors. International applications accepted.
Benefits Names of contacts, opportunity to attend seminars/workshops, willing to complete paperwork for educational credit, willing to provide letters of recommendation.
Contact Write, call, fax, or e-mail Marilyn Jessup, Assistant Director. Phone: 212-686-5005. Fax: 212-686-6393. E-mail: info@cencom.org. In-person interview required. Applicants must submit a cover letter, resume. Applications are accepted continuously. World Wide Web: http://www.cencom.org.

CENTER FOR FOLKLIFE & CULTURAL HERITAGE
955 L'Enfant Plaza, Suite 2600
Washington, District of Columbia 20560

General Information Center that engages in cultural conservation and representation activities that promote continuity, integrity, and equity for traditional ethnic, tribal, regional, minority, and working-class cultures in the U.S. and abroad through scholarly research, professional advocacy, and public programs. Established in 1967. Number of employees: 35. Unit of Smithsonian Institution, Washington, District of Columbia. Number of internship applications received each year: 200.
Internships Available ▶ *1–25 interns:* responsibilities include organizing and handling written, audio and visual documentation and logistics for public programs, educational resources, publications, and recordings; performing computer input for archivist, following up field work by organizing and compiling reports and documentation, following up with potential participants by securing necessary information related to festival presentation, and acquiring and disseminating information from and to festival staff. Candidates should have ability to work with others, office skills, organizational skills, personal interest in the field, self-motivation, strong interpersonal skills. Duration is 1–12 months. Unpaid. Open to high school students, high school seniors, recent high school graduates, college freshmen, college sophomores, college juniors, college seniors, recent college graduates, graduate students, law students, career changers, individuals reentering the workforce. International applications accepted.
Benefits Names of contacts, on-the-job training, opportunity to attend seminars/workshops, willing to act as a professional reference, willing to complete paperwork for educational credit, willing to provide letters of recommendation.
Contact Write, call, fax, or e-mail Ms. Arlene Reiniger, Program Specialist, Intern Coordinator, 955 L'Enfant Plaza, Suite 2600, Washington, District of Columbia 20560. Phone: 202-287-3259. Fax: 202-287-7217. E-mail: arlene@folklife.si.edu. Applicants must submit a formal organization application, academic transcripts, writing sample, two letters of recommendation. Application deadline: March 15 for summer; continuous for other seasons.

CENTER FOR STRATEGIC & INTERNATIONAL STUDIES
1800 K Street, NW
Washington, District of Columbia 20006

General Information Public policy research organization dedicated to analysis and policy impact. Established in 1962. Number of employees: 200. Number of internship applications received each year: 600.

Internships Available ▶ *2 Anne Armstrong Leadership Awards interns:* responsibilities include research, data collection, and administrative duties. Candidates should have declared college major in field, oral communication skills, research skills, strong leadership ability, writing skills, written communication skills, minimum GPA of 3.5 in area of concentration. Duration is 3 months. $3,000 per duration of internship. Open to college sophomores, college juniors, college seniors. ▶ *3–5 international affairs for minority students interns:* responsibilities include research, data collection, and administrative duties. Candidates should have ability to work independently, computer skills, office skills, oral communication skills, research skills, written communication skills. Duration is 3 months. $6,000 per duration of internship. Open to college sophomores, college juniors, college seniors, graduate students. ▶ *40–50 interns:* responsibilities include research, data collection, and administrative duties. Candidates should have ability to work independently, computer skills, experience in the field, personal interest in the field, writing skills. Duration is 3–9 months. Unpaid. Open to college sophomores, college juniors, college seniors, recent college graduates, graduate students, law students. International applications accepted.
Benefits Job counseling, opportunity to attend seminars/workshops, possible full-time employment, travel reimbursement, willing to complete paperwork for educational credit, willing to provide letters of recommendation.
Contact Write or fax Pat Owens, Intern Coordinator. Fax: 202-775-3199. No phone calls. Applicants must submit a cover letter, resume, 1 writing sample (10 pages or less). Application deadline: March 1 for summer, August 15 for fall, December 1 for spring.

CENTER FOR STUDENT MISSIONS
27302 Calle Arroyo
San Juan Capistrano, California 92675

General Information Organization that facilitates Christian mission and service trips in several urban locations throughout the U.S. and Canada. Established in 1988. Number of employees: 3. Number of internship applications received each year: 50.
Internships Available ▶ *30–40 city hosts:* responsibilities include hosting and leading suburban and rural church youth groups during their short-term mission and service trips (two to six days) in the inner-cities of Chicago; Washington, DC; Houston; Los Angeles; Toronto; San Francisco; and Nashville. Candidates should have ability to work independently, oral communication skills, strong interpersonal skills, strong leadership ability, youth ministry experience or desire for experience, and strong Christian faith. Duration is 3–8 months. Paid. Open to college sophomores, college juniors, college seniors, recent college graduates, graduate students, career changers.
Benefits Free housing, free meals, on-the-job training, possible full-time employment, willing to act as a professional reference, willing to complete paperwork for educational credit, willing to provide letters of recommendation.
International Internships Available in Toronto, Canada.
Contact Call, fax, or e-mail Kyle Becchetti, Director of Ministries, 27302 Calle Arroyo, San Juan Capistrano, California 92675. Phone: 949-248-8200. Fax: 949-248-7753. E-mail: csm@gospelcom.net. In-person interview required. Applicants must submit a formal organization application, four personal references. Applications are accepted continuously. World Wide Web: http://www.csm.org.

CENTRAL CITY AIDS NETWORK
2020 Ingleside Avenue
Macon, Georgia 31204-2028

General Information Non-profit AIDS service organization. Established in 1985. Number of employees: 3. Number of internship applications received each year: 4.
Internships Available ▶ *1 case management intern:* responsibilities include training under permanent case manager, attending and maintaining client relationships, and participating in support group management. Candidates should have ability to work

Central City AIDS Network (continued)

independently, college courses in field, oral communication skills, organizational skills, self-motivation, written communication skills. Duration is 6–8 weeks. Unpaid. Open to college juniors, career changers, individuals reentering the workforce. **Benefits** On-the-job training, willing to act as a professional reference, willing to complete paperwork for educational credit, willing to provide letters of recommendation.
Contact Write, call, or e-mail Johnny Fambro, Executive Director, 2020 Ingleside Avenue, Macon, Georgia 31204-2028. Phone: 912-750-8080. E-mail: rainbow@mindspring.com. In-person interview required. Applicants must submit a cover letter, resume, letter of recommendation. Applications are accepted continuously. World Wide Web: http://www.mindspring.com/~RAINBOW.

CITIZENS FOR PARTICIPATION IN POLITICAL ACTION (CPPAX)
25 West Street, 4th Floor
Boston, Massachusetts 02111

General Information Multi-issue, progressive grassroots political organization with a current focus on economic democracy, including fair taxes, adequate human services, cuts in military budget, economic and labor rights issues, campaign finance reform, reform of managed health-care system, and public education funding. Established in 1962. Number of employees: 3. Number of internship applications received each year: 60.
Internships Available ▶ *1–2 economic democracy interns:* responsibilities include researching, writing, and organizing for a fair economy and assisting with campaign for single-payer national health-care plan. ▶ *1–2 electoral action interns:* responsibilities include researching and organizing candidates and ballot questions concentrating on campaign finance reform. ▶ *1–2 events planning interns:* responsibilities include planning annual membership convention and other events throughout the year. ▶ *1–2 fund-raising interns:* responsibilities include aiding development staff in all areas of grassroots fund-raising and researching and writing grant proposals. ▶ *1–2 peace and new priorities interns:* responsibilities include performing congressional research, member organizing for peace, and organizing campaign for the rights of oppressed people in Burma. ▶ *1–2 publications interns:* responsibilities include researching, writing, and producing publications. Duration for all positions is flexible. All positions are unpaid. Open to high school students, high school seniors, recent high school graduates, college freshmen, college sophomores, college juniors, college seniors, recent college graduates, graduate students, law students, career changers, individuals reentering the workforce. International applications accepted.
Benefits Travel reimbursement, willing to complete paperwork for educational credit, willing to provide letters of recommendation.
Contact Write, call, fax, or e-mail Ms. Debbie Nichelson, Administrative Director. Phone: 617-426-3040. Fax: 617-426-8389. E-mail: cppax@cppax.org. In-person interview recommended. Applicants must submit a cover letter, resume. Applications are accepted continuously. World Wide Web: http://www.cppax.com.

COMMUNICATING FOR AGRICULTURE, SCHOLARSHIP, AND EDUCATION FOUNDATION
112 East Lincoln Avenue
Fergus Falls, Minnesota 56537

General Information Foundation that provides an opportunity for people from other countries to learn agriculture, horticulture, and agribusiness in the U.S. and for U.S. citizens to be trained on farms in Europe, South America, Central America, Australia, and New Zealand. Established in 1985. Number of employees: 7. Unit of Communicating for Agriculture, Inc., Fergus Falls, Minnesota. Number of internship applications received each year: 150.
Internships Available ▶ *50–100 trainees:* responsibilities include taking an active role in the business operations of a farm, ranch, horticulture site, or business while living with host family. Candidates should have experience in the field, oral communica-

tion skills, personal interest in the field, self-motivation, strong interpersonal skills. Duration is 3–18 months. $350 to $600 per month. Open to recent high school graduates, college freshmen, college sophomores, college juniors, college seniors, recent college graduates, graduate students. International applications accepted.
Benefits Formal training, free housing, free meals, health insurance, opportunity to attend seminars/workshops, willing to complete paperwork for educational credit.
International Internships Available.
Contact Write, call, fax, or e-mail Ms. Barbara Nelson, CAEP Director. Phone: 218-739-3241. Fax: 218-739-3832. E-mail: bnelson@cainc.org. In-person interview recommended. Applicants must submit a formal organization application, resume, two letters of recommendation. Application deadline: January 1 for spring and for consideration for grant money, March 1 for summer, June 1 for fall. Fees: $425. World Wide Web: http://cainc.org/exchange/caep.htm.

CONGRESSIONAL HISPANIC CAUCUS INSTITUTE
504 C Street, NE
Washington, District of Columbia 20002

General Information Organization that educates the U.S. Hispanic population on the function of the American political system. Established in 1978. Number of employees: 9. Number of internship applications received each year: 400.
Internships Available ▶ *12–14 CHCI Fellows:* responsibilities include gaining hands-on work experience in the nation's capital in a placement selected by intern according to his or her interests or field of study; may include placements on Capitol Hill in federal agencies, community-based organizations, national advocacy organizations, and Washington-based media groups. Candidates should have analytical skills, oral communication skills, written communication skills, interest in career in public policy; community involvement and participation through public service; minimum GPA of 3.0. Duration is 9 months (early September—late May). $1550 monthly stipend. Open to recent college graduates, graduate students. ▶ *30 summer interns:* responsibilities include administrative duties, researching, monitoring, and answering constituent mail. Candidates should have oral communication skills, self-motivation, strong leadership ability, written communication skills, minimum GPA of 3.0; active interest and participation in community affairs; solid work ethic. Duration is 8 weeks. $2000 stipend. Open to college freshmen, college sophomores, college juniors, college seniors.
Benefits Opportunity to attend seminars/workshops, willing to complete paperwork for educational credit, round-trip airfare to and from D.C., free housing for summer positions, health insurance benefits for CHCI fellows.
Contact Write, call, fax, or e-mail Ms. Patricia Zavala, Programs Coordinator. Phone: 800-EXCEL-DC. Fax: 202-546-2143. E-mail: chci@chci.org. Telephone interview required. Applicants must submit a formal organization application, resume, academic transcripts, 3 references (1 from a professor, 1 from a community leader and 1 from an employer), response to essay questions on application. Application deadline: January 29 for summer interns, March 19 for CHCI fellows. World Wide Web: http://www.chci.org.

CO-OP AMERICA
1612 K Street, Suite 600
Washington, District of Columbia 20006

General Information National nonprofit membership association that links socially responsible businesses and consumers in a national network. Established in 1982. Number of employees: 25.
Internships Available ▶ *1 "National Green Pages" advertising intern:* responsibilities include assisting with research and selection of businesses to be targeted for ads and corporate sponsorships, soliciting and closing ad sales leads, and attending meetings and training sessions. Candidates should have excellent telephone and communication skills, Excel and Microsoft Word skills, and experience or interest in developing advertising sales

skills. Duration is flexible (minimum 20 hours per week) in spring or summer. $100 per month stipend. Open to individuals with at least 2 years of college or relevant work experience. ▶ *2–3 Internet marketing interns:* responsibilities include Web marketing, design, and programming; research and development of e-mail communications strategy; analysis of the effectiveness of different electronic marketing efforts. Candidates should have ability to work independently, ability to work with others, computer skills, editing skills, oral communication skills, writing skills, familiarity with Internet and World Wide Web, aptitude in public relations or marketing. Duration is 10 weeks, flexible hours (30 hours per week minimum). $200 per week stipend (through the Everett Public Service Internship Program). Open to college freshmen, college sophomores, college juniors, college seniors, recent college graduates, graduate students, career changers, individuals reentering the workforce. ▶ *1 WoodWise assistant:* responsibilities include conducting reasearch on American wood use, deforestation, new consumer choices for environmentally friendly substitutes for wood, and more; researching wood and forests; relationship building; campaign planning; and outreach and information dissemination. Position located in Washington, D.C. or San Francisco, CA. Candidates should have ability to work independently, ability to work with others, oral communication skills, written communication skills, flexibility, commitment to environmental and social change movement, familiarity and patience with aging office equipment, and ability to cope with staff in remote locations. $100 per month stipend. ▶ *1 corporate accountability/shareholder advocacy network intern:* responsibilities include researching organizations involved in promoting corporate social and environmental responsibility and determining their involvement in the shareholder advocacy process, gathering and organizing data from ally organizations on the behaviors of corporations they track, developing information for the Shareholder Advocacy Network Web site, and assisting with preparation and production of mailings to forum members. Candidates should have ability to work independently, ability to work with others, computer skills, organizational skills, writing skills. Duration is flexible (minimum 30 hours per week). $100 per month stipend. Open to individuals with at least 2 years of college or relevant work experience. ▶ *1 executive department intern (public education/media/public relations management):* responsibilities include shaping and implementing public education campaigns and putting together press kits and consumer action guides, research, report writing, correspondence, project coordination, grant research, and database management. Candidates should have ability to work independently, ability to work with others, oral communication skills, written communication skills, familiarity with Microsoft Word and Access or willingness to learn, commitment to environmental and social change. Duration is 10 weeks, 17-35 hours per week (flexible). $100 per month stipend. Open to college freshmen, college sophomores, college juniors, college seniors, recent college graduates, graduate students, career changers, individuals reentering the workforce. ▶ *1 foundation fund-raising intern:* responsibilities include research, strategic planning, communications with funders, and proposal and report writing. Candidates should have ability to work independently, oral communication skills, strong interpersonal skills, written communication skills, interest in learning how a progressive organization develops financial support from foundations, familiarity with Microsoft Word (or willingness to learn). Duration is 12 weeks. $100 per month stipend. ▶ *2–3 magazine and publications interns:* responsibilities include working on *National Green Pages* or *Co-op America Quarterly,* research, writing, editing, proofing, assisting in planning and production of publications, gathering art work and photos, and data entry. Candidates should have computer skills, editing skills, organizational skills, writing skills, excellent telephone skills, detail oriented. Duration is 10 weeks from late May to early August. $100 per month stipend or $200 per week (for 2 paid interns). Open to college freshmen, college sophomores, college juniors, college seniors, recent college graduates, graduate students, career changers, individuals reentering the workforce. ▶ *1 marketing analysis intern:* responsibilities include researching and analyzing potential markets for membership growth, researching markets similar to Co-op America's to locate mailing lists that are available and

appropriate for rental. Candidates should have organizational skills, facility with numbers, desire to learn the details of nonprofit marketing. Duration is 10 weeks. $100 per month stipend. Open to those with 2 years of college or relevant work experience. ▶ *Publications interns:* responsibilities include assisting with research, writing, and design of *Co-Op America Quarterly, Boycott Action News, Real Money,* and *National Green Pages* (during summer). Duration is 2–4 months. $100 per month stipend or $200 per week (for one paid intern). Open to college students and graduates. ▶ *1 research intern:* responsibilities include compiling information on topics of interest to members; researching answers to new topics as they arise; researching, writing, and editing fact sheets and information packets; and creating a "referrals list" of sources for information on other subjects. Candidates should have ability to work independently, ability to work with others, oral communication skills, written communication skills, familiarity with Internet and other research methods, love of research, and familiarity with (or willingness to learn) Microsoft Word. Duration is 12 weeks, flexible. $100 per month stipend. ▶ *1 socially responsible business research intern:* responsibilities include compiling information submitted by companies on their social and environmental policies and practices, interviewing prospective members about their practices, entering gathered information into database, presenting research to new member review committee, and reviewing and updating new member review policy. Candidates should have computer skills, oral communication skills, organizational skills, strong leadership ability, general familiarity with a broad range of social justice and environmental issues, interest in learning about socially responsible business practices. Duration is April to August (dates flexible). $50 per month stipend. International applications accepted.
Benefits Course credit, free lunches for summer interns.
Contact Write or fax Rafael Salomon, Internship Coordinator, 1612 K Street, Suite 600, Washington, District of Columbia 20006. Fax: 202-331-8166. Applicants must submit a cover letter, resume, short writing sample for Web interns. Applications are accepted continuously. World Wide Web: http://www.coopamerica.org.

COUNCIL ON FOREIGN RELATIONS
58 East 68th Street
New York, New York 10021

General Information Nonprofit organization dedicated to the study of international relations and foreign policy in the United States. Established in 1921. Number of employees: 140. Number of internship applications received each year: 500.
Internships Available ▶ *1–3 Studies Department interns:* responsibilities include providing general administrative support, preparing materials for meetings (including invitations), assisting with research. Candidates should have knowledge of field, office skills, organizational skills, research skills, strong interpersonal skills, written communication skills. Duration is 1–2 semesters. Position available as unpaid or at $8 per hour. Open to college juniors, college seniors. ▶ *1–3 Washington, D.C. interns:* responsibilities include supporting staff members with day-to-day office duties, providing research support which can be geared towards intern's academic interests. Candidates should have ability to work independently, computer skills, declared college major in field, office skills, oral communication skills, organizational skills. Duration is 1 semester. Unpaid. Open to college freshmen, college sophomores, college juniors, college seniors. ▶ *1–2 corporate program interns:* responsibilities include researching companies that may be interested in joining the Corporate Program, setting up appointments with potential members, assisting with conference planning, and database maintenance. Candidates should have computer skills, declared college major in field, office skills, research skills, strong interpersonal skills, written communication skills. Duration is 1 semester. Unpaid. Open to college freshmen, college sophomores, college juniors, college seniors. ▶ *1 development intern:* responsibilities include initial prospect research and indentification of potential funders, proofreading and editing proposals, gathering information on foundations, and database maintenance. Candidates should have computer skills, declared college major in field, organizational skills, research skills, strong interpersonal skills, written com-

Council on Foreign Relations (continued)

munication skills. Duration is 1 semester. Unpaid. Open to college freshmen, college sophomores, college juniors, college seniors. ▶ *1 human resources intern:* responsibilities include processing response letters to candidates, placing job postings and advertisements, helping with logistics for staff events, updating files on salary histories, and special projects. Candidates should have computer skills, declared college major in field, office skills, oral communication skills, organizational skills, written communication skills. Duration is 1 semester. Unpaid. Open to college freshmen, college sophomores, college juniors, college seniors. ▶ *1 publications intern:* responsibilities include all aspects of editorial and production process, laying out text, help in maintaining Council's online service, and some clerical work. Candidates should have declared college major in field, editing skills, office skills, organizational skills, writing skills. Duration is 1 semester. Unpaid. Open to college freshmen, college sophomores, college juniors, college seniors. International applications accepted.

Benefits Names of contacts, possible full-time employment, travel reimbursement, willing to complete paperwork for educational credit, willing to provide letters of recommendation, access to Council's private library and opportunity to sit in on foreign policy discussion groups.

Contact Write or fax Internship Coordinator. Fax: 212-734-1493. No phone calls. In-person interview required. Applicants must submit a cover letter, resume. Applications are accepted continuously. World Wide Web: http://www.foreignrelations.org.

COUNCIL ON HEMISPHERIC AFFAIRS
1444 I Street, NW, Suite 211
Washington, District of Columbia 20005

General Information Research and information organization that analyzes and monitors diplomatic, economic, social, political, trade, environmental, drug, and military trends in U.S.-Latin American relations. Established in 1975. Number of employees: 19. Number of internship applications received each year: 500.

Internships Available ▶ *12–15 research associates:* responsibilities include research, writing, and by-line publishing of articles on pressing regional topics as well as some light administrative duties. Candidates should have ability to work with others, analytical skills, computer skills, oral communication skills, research skills, written communication skills. Duration is 16 weeks or 13 weeks in summer. Unpaid. Open to high school seniors, recent high school graduates, college freshmen, college sophomores, college juniors, college seniors, recent college graduates, graduate students, law students, career changers, individuals reentering the workforce, academics on sabbatical, retirees. International applications accepted.

Benefits Formal training, job counseling, names of contacts, on-the-job training, opportunity to attend seminars/workshops, possible full-time employment, willing to act as a professional reference, willing to complete paperwork for educational credit, willing to provide letters of recommendation, occasional meals and recreational trips.

Contact Write, call, fax, or e-mail Secretary for Internships. Phone: 202-393-3322. Fax: 202-216-9193. E-mail: coha@coha.org. In-person interview recommended. Applicants must submit a formal organization application, cover letter, resume, academic transcripts, writing sample, two letters of recommendation. Applications are accepted continuously. World Wide Web: http://www.coha.org.

CROHN'S AND COLITIS FOUNDATION OF AMERICA
386 Park Avenue South
New York, New York 10016

General Information Foundation whose mission is to stimulate and encourage innovative basic biomedical and clinical research

of inflammatory bowel disease. Established in 1967. Number of employees: 35. Number of internship applications received each year: 12.

Internships Available ▶ *1–16 student research fellowship awards:* responsibilities include conducting full-time research with mentor investigating a subject relevant to inflammatory bowel disease. Candidates should have major in a medical field. Duration is 10 weeks in the spring. $2,500 per duration of internship. Open to college juniors, college seniors, recent college graduates, graduate students.

Benefits Opportunity to attend seminars/workshops, willing to act as a professional reference, willing to complete paperwork for educational credit, willing to provide letters of recommendation.

Contact Write, call, fax, or e-mail Research and Education Department. Phone: 800-932-2423. Fax: 212-779-4098. E-mail: info@ccfa.org. Applicants must submit a formal organization application. Application deadline: February 1. World Wide Web: http://www.ccfa.org.

DEALERS ELECTION ACTION COMMITTEE
8400 Westpark Drive
McLean, Virginia 22102

General Information Political action committee for the National Automobile Dealers Association. Established in 1975. Number of employees: 4. Department of National Automobile Dealers Association, McLean, Virginia. Number of internship applications received each year: 5.

Internships Available ▶ *1 intern:* responsibilities include helping with revision of promotional materials, assisting with production of mailings, assisting with drafting of fund-raising copy and correspondence, conducting political and legislative research on congressional members in database, compiling statistics and comparison lists for DEAC fund-raising, conducting contributor research at the Federal Election Commission, assisting with editing/proofing of mailing lists, answering miscellaneous correspondence, trouble shooting for DEAC contributor requests, updating congressional database, and assisting with other administrative tasks as assigned. Candidates should have ability to work independently, computer skills, office skills, organizational skills, research skills, written communication skills. Duration is 6–12 weeks. small stipend available. Open to college sophomores, college juniors, college seniors. International applications accepted.

Benefits Opportunity to attend seminars/workshops, willing to complete paperwork for educational credit, willing to provide letters of recommendation.

Contact Write Mr. Gregory V. Knopp, Director. No phone calls. In-person interview recommended. Applicants must submit a cover letter, resume, academic transcripts, writing sample, two personal references. Applications are accepted continuously.

DELEGATION OF THE EUROPEAN COMMISSION
2300 M Street, Suite 300
Washington, District of Columbia 20037

General Information Office that provides information on all aspects of the European Union to the American public, either directly or through various networks, and seeks to further communication and understanding between the European Union and the United States. Established in 1954. Number of employees: 90. Number of internship applications received each year: 500.

Internships Available ▶ *2 Europe Magazine interns:* responsibilities include designing and implementing projects to boost sales, subscriptions, and advertising. Candidates should have ability to work with others, computer skills, knowledge of field, plan to pursue career in field. Duration is 5 months. Open to college seniors, recent college graduates. ▶ *1 academic affairs intern:* responsibilities include researching and providing information on the European Union to the academic community; updating and creating new content for Delegation Web site, planning of academic events and programs; conducting research for Delegation staff in topics concerning European Union-U.S. relations. Candidates should have ability to work independently, analytical skills, college courses in field, computer skills, knowledge of field, office skills, oral communication skills, organizational skills, research skills, self-motivation, strong interpersonal skills, writing skills. Duration is 3-5 months in fall, spring, or summer. Open to college juniors, college seniors, recent college graduates. ▶ *1 agricultural intern:* responsibilities include carrying out in-depth research of U.S. food industry and agriculture sectors; preparing reports, summaries, analyses, and graphs for presentation to Brussels officials; may also monitor and assess U.S. legislation relating to trade and agriculture and make summary reports where necessary. Candidates should have ability to work with others, computer skills, personal interest in the field, research skills, writing skills. Duration is 3-5 months in fall, spring, or summer. Open to college seniors, recent college graduates, graduate students. ▶ *1 audiovisual department intern:* responsibilities include assisting in maintaining video archives, screening and writing descriptions of programs produced in Brussels, and assignments related to cultural projects and exhibitions. Candidates should have college courses in field, computer skills, oral communication skills, written communication skills, background in design, photography, broadcast journalism, or European Union course work a plus. Duration is 3-5 months in fall, spring, or summer. Open to college juniors, college seniors, recent college graduates. ▶ *1 development section intern:* responsibilities include summaries of World Bank or other documents, compilation of statistics and information on European Union development programs, research on issues affecting foreign policy in developing countries, reports on Congressional hearings, conferences, or seminars. Candidates should have ability to work with others, college courses in field, computer skills, personal interest in the field, research skills, written communication skills, background in economics, development economics, or international affairs experience in developing countries. Duration is 3-5 months in fall, spring, or summer. Open to college juniors, college seniors, recent college graduates, graduate students. ▶ *1 economic/financial section intern:* responsibilities include monitoring macroeconomic developments in the U.S. with an emphasis on quantitative research; specific research projects undertaken in relation to monetary, fiscal, or labor market policies. Candidates should have ability to work with others, college courses in field, computer skills, personal interest in the field, research skills, written communication skills. Duration is 3-5 months in fall, spring, or summer. Open to college juniors, college seniors, recent college graduates, graduate students. ▶ *1 political section intern:* responsibilities include following Congressional hearings and conducting research on a given subject. Candidates should have ability to work with others, college courses in field, computer skills, personal interest in the field, research skills, written communication skills, prior training in or familiarity with U.S. foreign policy and the congressional process desirable. Duration is 3-5 months in fall, spring, or summer. Open to college juniors, college seniors, recent college graduates, graduate students. ▶ *3 public inquiries interns:* responsibilities include researching and providing information on the European Union to the business community, government agencies, and international organizations. Candidates should have ability to work with others, college courses in field, computer skills, oral communication skills, research skills. Duration is 3-5 months in fall, spring, or summer. Open to college juniors, college seniors, recent college graduates, graduate students. ▶ *1 science, technology, and education section intern:* responsibilities include analyses of specific aspects of the U.S. R&D system in order to prepare summaries and reports; and monitoring and assessing U.S. legislative developments related to science and technology policy. Candidates should have ability to work with others, college courses in field, computer skills, personal interest in the field, research skills, written communication skills. Duration is 3-5 months in fall, spring, or summer. Open to college juniors, college seniors, recent college graduates, graduate students. ▶ *1 speakers' bureau intern:* responsibilities include working on research projects. Candidates should have ability to work with others, computer skills, oral communication skills, personal interest in the field, written communication skills, journalism experience helpful. Duration is 5 months. Open to college seniors, recent college graduates. ▶ *1 trade section intern:* responsibilities include carrying out projects, writing notes and attending and reporting on meetings with U.S. agencies and Congressional hearings. Candidates should have ability to work with others, college courses in field, computer skills, personal interest in the field, research skills, written communication skills, basic knowledge of international trade issues. Duration is 3-5 months in fall, spring, or summer. Open to college juniors, college seniors, recent college graduates, graduate students. ▶ *1 transport, energy, and environment intern:* responsibilities include monitoring and assessing U.S. legislative developments related to environment and energy. Candidates should have ability to work with others, college courses in field, computer skills, personal interest in the field, research skills, written communication skills, knowledge of and interest in European Union-United States environment/energy policies and the U.S. Congressional process essential. Duration is 3-5 months in fall, spring, or summer. Open to college juniors, college seniors, recent college graduates, graduate students. All positions are unpaid. International applications accepted.

Benefits Names of contacts, willing to complete paperwork for educational credit, willing to provide letters of recommendation. **Contact** Write, call, fax, or e-mail Ms. Julie Calaz, Assistant, Academic Affairs. Phone: 202-862-9500. Fax: 202-429-1766. E-mail: julie.calaz@delusw.cec.eu.int. Telephone interview required. Applicants must submit a formal organization application, cover letter, resume, academic transcripts. Application deadline: February 28 for summer, May 31 for fall, October 15 for spring. World Wide Web: http://www.eurunion.org.

DEMOCRATIC CONGRESSIONAL CAMPAIGN COMMITTEE
430 South Capitol Street, SE, 2nd Floor
Washington, District of Columbia 20003

General Information National political party committee organized to elect Democrats to the U.S. House of Representatives and be a dominant factor in Washington politics. Number of employees: 75. Number of internship applications received each year: 100. **Internships Available** ▶ *1 administration intern:* responsibilities include assisting with the business and financial management of the Democratic party while learning corporate management skills and federal elections law requirements and procedures. ▶ *2 communications interns:* responsibilities include helping with the daily operations of the press office including production of daily news summary for distribution to various congressional offices, the production of news releases, and arrangement of press conferences. ▶ *1 finance intern:* responsibilities include assisting with fund-raising efforts to raise the money used to operate the DCCC and contribute to the Democratic candidates. ▶ *2 marketing membership interns:* responsibilities include responding to constituent needs. ▶ *15 political/research interns:* responsibilities include assisting the research and political staff with mailings and member research requests, database and candidate file maintenance, analyzing the important issues of the upcoming election cycle, and researching the opposition. Duration for all positions is minimum of 4 weeks. All positions are unpaid. Open to high school students, high school seniors, recent high school graduates, college freshmen, college sophomores, college juniors, college seniors, recent college graduates. International applications accepted.

Benefits Names of contacts, opportunity to attend seminars/workshops, willing to complete paperwork for educational credit, willing to provide letters of recommendation, opportunity to attend fund-raisers.

Contact Write, call, fax, or e-mail Ms. Jacqui Vaughn, Intern Coordinator. Phone: 202-485-3413. Fax: 202-485-3536. E-mail: vaughn@dccc.org. In-person interview recommended. Applicants must submit a cover letter, resume, academic transcripts. Applications are accepted continuously. World Wide Web: http://www.dccc.org.

DEMOCRATIC NATIONAL COMMITTEE
430 South Capital Street, SE
Washington, District of Columbia 20003

General Information Administrative body of the Democratic Party whose primary job is to organize the national convention and assist state and local organizations with the election of candidates. Established in 1848. Number of employees: 175. Number of internship applications received each year: 300.
Internships Available ▶ *Interns.* Duration is 2–3 months. Unpaid. Open to college freshmen, college sophomores, college juniors, college seniors. International applications accepted.
Benefits Formal training, job counseling, opportunity to attend seminars/workshops, possible full-time employment, willing to complete paperwork for educational credit, willing to provide letters of recommendation.
Contact Write, call, or fax Nancy Ginesta, Intern Coordinator. Phone: 202-863-3139. Fax: 202-863-8105. Applicants must submit a formal organization application, resume, academic transcripts, letter of recommendation. Application deadline: April 15 for summer, July 30 for fall, November 15 for spring. World Wide Web: http://www.democrats.org.

DEMOCRATIC SENATORIAL CAMPAIGN COMMITTEE
430 South Capitol Street, SE
Washington, District of Columbia 20003

General Information Organization that supports and assists Democratic candidates running for the U.S. Senate. Established in 1959. Number of employees: 25. Number of internship applications received each year: 200.
Internships Available ▶ *Interns:* responsibilities include providing administrative support to the political, finance, research, or press departments. Duration is 1 semester or summer. Unpaid. Open to college freshmen, college sophomores, college juniors, college seniors, recent college graduates.
Benefits Names of contacts, opportunity to attend seminars/workshops, possible full-time employment, willing to complete paperwork for educational credit, willing to provide letters of recommendation.
Contact Write, call, fax, or e-mail Dan Freedberg, Intern Coordinator. Phone: 202-224-2447. Fax: 202-485-3120. E-mail: info@dscc.org. Applicants must submit a cover letter, resume. Applications are accepted continuously. World Wide Web: http://www.dscc.org.

EIGHT MILE BOULEVARD ASSOCIATION
15565 Northland Drive, Suite 604 West
Southfield, Michigan 48075

General Information A nonprofit economic development organization whose mission is to revitalize and promote an urban corridor.
Internships Available ▶ *Public relations/community planning interns:* responsibilities include coordinating special events, publications, and fund-raising. Duration is 2 semesters (minimum). minimum wage. Open to college juniors, college seniors, graduate students.
Contact Write, fax, or e-mail Sharlan Douglas, Executive Director, 15565 Northland Drive, Suite 604 West, Southfield, Michigan 48075. Fax: 248-559-2447. E-mail: douglas@eightmile.org. Applicants must submit a cover letter, resume. Applications are accepted continuously. World Wide Web: http://www.eightmile.org.

ELIZABETH GLASER PEDIATRIC AIDS FOUNDATION
2950 31st Street, Suite 125
Santa Monica, California 90405

General Information Foundation providing funds for research programs related to pediatric HIV/AIDS and motivating participants to consider future careers in this field. Established in 1989.

Number of employees: 25. Branch of Elizabeth Glaser Pediatric AIDS Foundation, New York, New York. Number of internship applications received each year: 100.
Internships Available ▶ *50 interns:* responsibilities include performing independent research in basic medical, clinical, epidemiological, or psychosocial areas relating to pediatric AIDS. Duration is 320 hours (minimum of 4 hours per week). $2000 stipend upon completion. Open to high school seniors, college freshmen, college sophomores, college juniors, college seniors, graduate students, medical school students. International applications accepted.
Benefits Job counseling, names of contacts.
International Internships Available.
Contact Write, call, fax, or e-mail Mr. Chris Hudnall, Resource Coordinator. Phone: 310-314-1459. Fax: 310-314-1469. E-mail: chris@pedaids.org. Applicants must submit a formal organization application, resume, academic transcripts, letter of sponsorship from M.D., Ph.D., or LCSW, statement of purpose from applicant, documentation from school registrar of full-time educational status, abbreviated curriculum vitae of sponsor. Application deadline: end of March.

EMIGRE MEMORIAL GERMAN INTERNSHIP PROGRAMS
PO Box 345
Durham, New Hampshire 03824

General Information Program sending students from non-German speaking countries to work in German Parliaments. Established in 1965. Number of employees: 1. Number of internship applications received each year: 25.
Internships Available ▶ *3–6 Deutscher Bundestag in Berlin interns:* responsibilities include work-study in the administrative, legislative research, and political areas of the Parliament. Candidates should have ability to work independently, college courses in field, editing skills, knowledge of field, oral communication skills, plan to pursue career in field, research skills, self-motivation, strong interpersonal skills, written communication skills, high fluency in German. Duration is 3 months. variable stipend. Open to college seniors, recent college graduates, graduate students, law students. ▶ *5–10 Landtage interns:* responsibilities include work-study in German legislatures. Candidates should have ability to work independently, college courses in field, editing skills, experience in the field, oral communication skills, organizational skills, plan to pursue career in field, research skills, self-motivation, strong interpersonal skills, written communication skills, high fluency in German. Duration is flexible. Position available as unpaid or at stipend of $200—$2,000 per internship. Open to college sophomores, college juniors, college seniors, recent college graduates, graduate students, career changers. International applications accepted.
Benefits Names of contacts, on-the-job training, opportunity to attend seminars/workshops, willing to provide letters of recommendation, possibility of free housing.
International Internships Available in Berlin, Germany; Dresden, Germany; Erfurt, Germany; Mainz, Germany; Schwerin, Germany; Wiesbaden, Germany.
Contact Write George K. Romoser, Director. No phone calls. In-person interview recommended. Applicants must submit a formal organization application, cover letter, resume, academic transcripts, three letters of recommendation, in-person interview required for finalists. Application deadline: January 10. Fees: $50.

ESQUEL GROUP FOUNDATION
1003 K Street, NW, Suite 800
Washington, District of Columbia 20001-4425

General Information Foundation that promotes civil society development in Latin America. Established in 1984. Number of employees: 5. Unit of Grupo Esquel (Regional Network), Washington, District of Columbia. Number of internship applications received each year: 15.
Internships Available ▶ *3–4 interns.* Candidates should have ability to work independently, computer skills, oral communication skills, personal interest in the field, research skills, written com-

munication skills, knowledge of Microsoft Word, advanced knowledge of Spanish and/or Portuguese (preferred). Duration is 3–6 months. Unpaid. Open to college sophomores, college juniors, college seniors, recent college graduates, graduate students, law students, career changers, people with work experience even if no college. International applications accepted.

Benefits Job counseling, names of contacts, on-the-job training, opportunity to attend seminars/workshops, willing to act as a professional reference, willing to complete paperwork for educational credit, willing to provide letters of recommendation, proposal development/fund-raising experience.

International Internships Available in Argentina; Bolivia; Peru, Brazil; Ecuador; Uruguay.

Contact Write, fax, or e-mail Marisol Pages, Executive Director, 1003 K Street, NW, Suite 800, Washington, District of Columbia 20001-4425. Fax: 202-347-1797. E-mail: info@esquel.org. In-person interview recommended. Applicants must submit a cover letter, resume, writing samples in English and Spanish or Portuguese. Application deadline: March 15 for summer, June 15 for fall, September 15 for spring. Deadlines are for college students; continuous for other applicants. World Wide Web: http://www. esquel.org.

ETHICS AND PUBLIC POLICY CENTER
1015 15th Street, NW, Suite 900
Washington, District of Columbia 20005

General Information Public policy center established to clarify and reinforce the bond between the Judeo-Christian moral tradition and the public debate over domestic and foreign policy issues. Established in 1976. Number of employees: 30. Number of internship applications received each year: 50.

Internships Available ▶ *1–5 center project interns:* responsibilities include performing library research, reading and summarizing results, attending seminars related to projects, and typing and organizing research. Candidates should have computer skills, editing skills, research skills, strong interpersonal skills, writing skills. Duration is 3–6 months. Open to college freshmen, college sophomores, college juniors, college seniors, recent college graduates, graduate students, individuals reentering the workforce. ▶ *1 law and society project intern:* responsibilities include performing library research, reading and summarizing results, attending seminars related to projects, and typing and organizing research. Candidates should have editing skills, personal interest in the field, research skills, strong interpersonal skills, writing skills. Duration is 1 semester. Open to college juniors, college seniors, recent college graduates, graduate students, law students. ▶ *1 media intern:* responsibilities include conducting background research and press relations for project covering "Religion and Society" and giving administrative support. Candidates should have computer skills, editing skills, oral communication skills, research skills, strong interpersonal skills, writing skills. Duration is 3–6 months. Open to college freshmen, college sophomores, college juniors, college seniors, recent college graduates. ▶ *1–5 neuroscience projects interns:* responsibilities include performing library research, reading and editing manuscripts, attending seminars related to the project, and typing and organizing research. Duration is 3–6 months. Open to college seniors, recent college graduates, graduate students. All positions are unpaid. International applications accepted.

Benefits Names of contacts, opportunity to attend seminars/workshops, possible full-time employment, willing to complete paperwork for educational credit, reimbursement of daily travel expenses.

Contact Write, call, or fax Intern Coordinator. Phone: 202-682-1200. Fax: 202-408-0632. Applicants must submit a cover letter, resume. Applications are accepted continuously. World Wide Web: http://www.eppc.org.

FARM SANCTUARY
3100 Aikens Road
Watkins Glen, New York 14891

General Information National nonprofit organization dedicated to ending animal agriculture abuses through public education programs, legislation, farm animal cruelty investigations, and campaigns in addition to running shelters that provide 24-hour emergency rescue, rehabilitation, and permanent care for hundreds of animals. Established in 1986. Number of employees: 17. Number of internship applications received each year: 200.

Internships Available ▶ *4–6 interns:* responsibilities include basic animal/barn maintenance, office work, and conducting educational tours. Candidates should have ability to work independently, ability to work with others, personal interest in the field, self-motivation, commitment to vegetarianism. Duration is 1–3 months. Unpaid. Open to high school students, high school seniors, recent high school graduates, college freshmen, college sophomores, college juniors, college seniors, recent college graduates, graduate students, law students, career changers, individuals reentering the workforce. International applications accepted.

Benefits Free housing, job counseling, names of contacts, possible full-time employment, willing to complete paperwork for educational credit, willing to provide letters of recommendation.

Contact Write, call, fax, or e-mail Intern Coordinator, PO Box 150, Watkins Glen, New York 14891. Phone: 607-583-2225. Fax: 607-583-2041. E-mail: educate@farmsanctuary.org. Telephone interview required. Applicants must submit a formal organization application, two letters of recommendation. Applications are accepted continuously. World Wide Web: http://www. farmsanctuary.org.

FOOD AND ALLIED SERVICE TRADES DEPARTMENT, AFL-CIO
815 16th Street, NW
Washington, District of Columbia 20006

General Information Labor organization that provides research support services for affiliated unions. Established in 1975. Number of employees: 20. Unit of AFL-CIO, Washington, District of Columbia. Number of internship applications received each year: 100.

Internships Available ▶ *3 interns:* responsibilities include researching and analyzing information on private and public corporations for organizing and bargaining purposes, identifying and educating workers on health hazards in the workplace, assisting in preparation of testimony and comments for regulatory agencies, researching and writing reports, and researching and contributing to media programs. Candidates should have ability to work independently, personal interest in the field, research skills, writing skills. Duration is 1–14 weeks. $100 per week. Open to college freshmen, college sophomores, college juniors, college seniors, graduate students, law students. International applications accepted.

Benefits Job counseling, names of contacts, on-the-job training, opportunity to attend seminars/workshops, possible full-time employment, willing to act as a professional reference, willing to complete paperwork for educational credit, willing to provide letters of recommendation.

Contact Write, fax, or e-mail Mr. Jeffrey L. Fiedler, President. Fax: 202-737-7208. E-mail: fast@igc.org. Applicants must submit a cover letter, resume, writing sample. Applications are accepted continuously. World Wide Web: http://www.fastaflcio.org.

FOREIGN POLICY ASSOCIATION
470 Park Avenue South, 2nd Floor, North
New York, New York 10016-6819

General Information National, nonprofit organization that educates Americans about significant world issues by providing impartial, nonpartisan publications, programs, and forums to increase public awareness of international matters. Established in 1918. Number of employees: 26. Number of internship applications received each year: 500.

Internships Available ▶ *2–4 editorial interns:* responsibilities include assisting with fact checking, resource lists, and updates for publications and performing minimal clerical tasks. Candidates should have computer skills, editing skills, personal interest in the field, research skills, self-motivation, written communication skills. Duration is 8–10 weeks. Unpaid. Open to college

Foreign Policy Association (continued)

juniors, college seniors, recent college graduates. ▶ *1–2 sales and fulfillment interns:* responsibilities include data entry with microsoft access, assistance with promotional mailings, and minimal clerical tasks. Candidates should have ability to work independently, analytical skills, computer skills, self-motivation. Duration is flexible. Position available as unpaid or paid. Open to college freshmen, college sophomores, career changers, individuals reentering the workforce. International applications accepted. **Benefits** Job counseling, names of contacts, on-the-job training, possible full-time employment, travel reimbursement, willing to act as a professional reference, willing to complete paperwork for educational credit, willing to provide letters of recommendation, free admission to events and free publications. **Contact** Write or fax Director of appropriate department, 470 Park Avenue South, 2nd Floor, North, New York, New York 10016-6819. Fax: 212-481-9275. No phone calls. In-person interview recommended. Applicants must submit a cover letter, resume. Applications are accepted continuously. World Wide Web: http://www.fpa.org.

GERMAN AMERICAN BUSINESS COUNCIL
1413 K Street, NW, Suite 1400
Washington, District of Columbia 20005

General Information Nonprofit organization aimed at improving relations between the business communities of Germany and the U.S. Established in 1991. Number of employees: 2. Number of internship applications received each year: 50.
Internships Available ▶ *1–3 administrative/research assistants:* responsibilities include attending business events, luncheons, and breakfast; preparation of events; organizational work; and independent projects. Candidates should have computer skills, office skills, oral communication skills, organizational skills, personal interest in the field, written communication skills. Duration is flexible. Unpaid. Open to college freshmen, college sophomores, college juniors, college seniors, recent college graduates, graduate students. International applications accepted. **Benefits** Willing to complete paperwork for educational credit. **Contact** Write or fax Mr. Leo Welt, Executive Director, 1413 K Street, NW, Suite 1400, Washington, District of Columbia 20005. Fax: 202-408-9369. Telephone interview required. Applicants must submit a cover letter, resume. Applications are accepted continuously. World Wide Web: http://www.washgabc.com.

THE HANSARD SOCIETY FOR PARLIAMENTARY GOVERNMENT
St. Philips Building North, Sheffield Street
London WC2A 2EX United Kingdom

General Information Program that brings overseas students into contact with the political process in Britain and enables them to meet and learn from its leading figures. Established in 1944. Number of employees: 8. Number of internship applications received each year: 70.
Internships Available ▶ *16 research assistants (political):* responsibilities include acting as research assistant to member of Parliament, lobby group, or associated political organization. Candidates should have college courses in field, oral communication skills, personal interest in the field, self-motivation, strong interpersonal skills, written communication skills. Duration is 1 or 2 semesters, 3 days per week. Unpaid. Open to college freshmen, college sophomores, college juniors, college seniors, recent college graduates, graduate students. International applications accepted. **Benefits** Housing at a cost, meals at a cost, opportunity to attend seminars/workshops, willing to act as a professional reference, willing to complete paperwork for educational credit, willing to provide letters of recommendation.
International Internships Available.
Contact Write, call, fax, or e-mail Penny O'Hara, Programme Manager. Phone: 44-171955 6250. Fax: 44-171 955 7492. E-mail: hansard@lse.ac.uk. Applicants must submit a formal organization application, cover letter, academic transcripts, writing sample,

personal reference, letter of recommendation. Applications are accepted continuously. World Wide Web: http://www.hansard-society.org.uk.

HERBERT SCOVILLE, JR. PEACE FELLOWSHIP
110 Maryland Avenue, NE, Suite 409
Washington, District of Columbia 20002

General Information Fellowship named for the late Dr. Herbert Scoville Jr., a longtime nuclear arms control activist in both government and private life who devoted special attention to encouraging young people interested in arms control and disarmament issues; brings 2-4 fellows per semester to Washington, D.C., to serve as project assistants at one of 21 arms control/disarmament groups. Established in 1987. Number of employees: 1. Number of internship applications received each year: 60.
Internships Available ▶ *2–4 Scoville Peace fellows:* responsibilities include serving as special project assistant and working on research and/or advocacy in the field of peace and security. Candidates should have ability to work with others, oral communication skills, personal interest in the field, plan to pursue career in field, research skills, written communication skills. Duration is 4–6 months. stipend of $1500 per month. Open to recent college graduates, graduate students, career changers.
Benefits Health insurance, travel reimbursement.
Contact Call or e-mail Mr. Paul Revsine, Program Director/Scoville Peace Fellowship. Phone: 202-543-4100 Ext. 124. E-mail: scoville@clw.org. In-person interview required. Applicants must submit a cover letter, resume, two personal references, two letters of recommendation, 2 essays with requirements that can be obtained by accessing Web site or calling for information. Application deadline: March 15 for fall, October 15 for spring. World Wide Web: http://www.scoville.org.

HILLEL OF NEW YORK
381 Park Avenue South, Suite 613
New York, New York 10016

General Information Jewish university student organization. Number of employees: 10. Division of Hillel, The Foundation for Jewish Campus Life, Washington, District of Columbia. Number of internship applications received each year: 175.
Internships Available ▶ *1–5 Jewish communal service interns.* Candidates should have ability to work independently, computer skills, oral communication skills, organizational skills, self-motivation, strong interpersonal skills, strong leadership ability, written communication skills. $1,300–$1,500 per duration of internship. Open to college freshmen, college sophomores, college juniors. ▶ *1–5 accounting interns.* Candidates should have ability to work independently, computer skills, self-motivation, strong interpersonal skills, strong leadership ability, written communication skills. $1,300–$1,500 per duration of internship. Open to college freshmen, college sophomores, college juniors. ▶ *1–5 education interns.* Candidates should have ability to work independently, computer skills, oral communication skills, self-motivation, strong interpersonal skills, strong leadership ability, writing skills. $1,300–$1,500 per duration of internship. Open to college freshmen, college sophomores, college juniors. ▶ *1–5 event planning interns.* Candidates should have ability to work independently, computer skills, oral communication skills, self-motivation, strong interpersonal skills, strong leadership ability, written communication skills. $1,200–$1,500 per duration of internship. Open to college freshmen, college sophomores, college juniors. ▶ *1–5 finance interns.* Candidates should have ability to work independently, computer skills, oral communication skills, self-motivation, strong interpersonal skills, strong leadership ability. $1,300–$1,500 per duration of internship. ▶ *1–5 information systems interns.* Candidates should have ability to work independently, computer skills, self-motivation, strong interpersonal skills, strong leadership ability, written communication skills. $1,300–$1,500 per duration of internship. Open to college freshmen, college sophomores, college juniors. ▶ *1–5 journalism interns.* Candidates should have ability to work independently, computer skills, editing skills, oral communication skills, self-motivation, strong interpersonal skills, strong leadership ability,

written communication skills. $1,300–$1,500 per duration of internship. Open to college freshmen, college sophomores, college juniors. ▶ *1–5 law interns.* Candidates should have ability to work independently, computer skills, research skills, self-motivation, strong interpersonal skills, strong leadership ability, written communication skills. $1,300–$1,500 per duration of internship. Open to college freshmen, college sophomores, college juniors. ▶ *1–5 museum interns.* Candidates should have ability to work independently, computer skills, oral communication skills, self-motivation, strong interpersonal skills, strong leadership ability, written communication skills. $1,300–$1,500 per duration of internship. Open to college freshmen, college sophomores, college juniors. ▶ *1–5 psychology interns.* Candidates should have ability to work independently, computer skills, strong interpersonal skills, strong leadership ability, written communication skills. $1,300–$1,500 per duration of internship. Open to college freshmen, college sophomores, college juniors. ▶ *1–5 public relations/marketing interns.* Candidates should have ability to work independently, computer skills, oral communication skills, self-motivation, strong interpersonal skills, strong leadership ability, written communication skills. $1,300–$1,500 per duration of internship. Open to college freshmen, college sophomores, college juniors. ▶ *1–5 social work interns.* Candidates should have ability to work independently, computer skills, self-motivation, strong interpersonal skills, strong leadership ability, written communication skills. $1,300–$1,500 per duration of internship. Open to college freshmen, college sophomores, college juniors. Duration for all positions is first week of June–first week of August. International applications accepted.

Benefits Formal training, job counseling, names of contacts, on-the-job training, opportunity to attend seminars/workshops, possible full-time employment, willing to complete paperwork for educational credit, willing to provide letters of recommendation.

Contact Write, call, or e-mail Simon Amiel, Director of Regional Programs. Phone: 212-696-1590 Ext. 206. E-mail: amiels.hillel@jon.cjfny.org. In-person interview recommended. Applicants must submit a formal organization application, resume, academic transcripts, writing sample, two letters of recommendation. Application deadline: March 6. World Wide Web: http://www.hillel.org.

HOOPS OF HOPE BASKETBALL MINISTRY
5510 Jennifer Lane
Colorado Springs, Colorado 80917

General Information Organization that conducts basketball clinics and ball-handling exhibitions as a way to share the Christian gospel. Established in 1996. Number of employees: 1. Number of internship applications received each year: 2.

Internships Available ▶ *Administrative assistants:* responsibilities include all administrative details plus assisting in basketball clinics and ball-handling exhibitions. Candidates should have ability to work independently, ability to work with others, oral communication skills, personal interest in the field, self-motivation, some basketball skills. Duration is 4–6 weeks. Unpaid. Open to college freshmen, college sophomores, college juniors, college seniors, recent college graduates, graduate students, career changers, individuals reentering the workforce.

Benefits On-the-job training, possible full-time employment, willing to act as a professional reference, willing to complete paperwork for educational credit, willing to provide letters of recommendation.

Contact Write, call, fax, or e-mail Rev. Brent W. Fuqua, Director, 5510 Jennifer Lane, Colorado Springs, Colorado 80917. Phone: 719-573-5647. Fax: 719-573-5952. E-mail: brent@hoops.org. Telephone interview required. Applicants must submit a formal organization application, cover letter, resume, three personal references. Applications are accepted continuously. World Wide Web: http://www.hoops.org.

HOSTELLING INTERNATIONAL–AMERICAN YOUTH HOSTELS
733 15th Street, NW, Suite 840
Washington, District of Columbia 20005

General Information Nonprofit organization dedicated to helping all people gain a greater understanding of the world and its people through the development and operation of hostels and coordination of educational and recreational programs. Established in 1934. Number of employees: 37. Unit of International Youth Hostel Federation, United Kingdom. Number of internship applications received each year: 150.

Internships Available ▶ *1–4 HI-AYH hostel interns:* responsibilities include educational program development, designing materials and displays, and working with local volunteers. Candidates should have ability to work with others, college courses in field, oral communication skills, research skills, writing skills, knowledge of languages, travel experience. Duration is 1 semester. Position available as unpaid or at $100–$150 per week. Open to college freshmen, college sophomores, college juniors, college seniors, recent college graduates, graduate students. ▶ *2–4 HI-AYH national office interns:* responsibilities include developing program models, researching nonprofit models, working with regional and hostel volunteers and staff, and updating publications and Web site. Candidates should have office skills, oral communication skills, organizational skills, personal interest in the field, strong interpersonal skills, writing skills, experience in research and proposal development. Duration is minimum of 12 weeks. $150 per week stipend and housing offered. Open to college seniors, recent college graduates, graduate students. ▶ *1 environmental program coordinator:* responsibilities include upgrading program materials, developing new program components, revising certification manual, and updating educational materials. Candidates should have declared college major in field, editing skills, research skills, self-motivation, writing skills. Duration is varied. $150 per week stipend and housing offered. Open to college seniors, recent college graduates, graduate students. ▶ *2–30 regional HI-AYH council offices interns:* responsibilities include assisting with program development, marketing, and special events. Candidates should have ability to work independently, declared college major in field, oral communication skills, written communication skills, major in education, marketing, nonprofit administration, or recreation desired, travel experience a plus. Duration is 1 semester. $100–$150 per week. Open to college sophomores, college juniors, college seniors, recent college graduates, graduate students. International applications accepted.

Benefits Opportunity to attend seminars/workshops, willing to act as a professional reference, willing to complete paperwork for educational credit, willing to provide letters of recommendation, stipends and housing provided for some positions.

Contact Write, fax, or e-mail Internship Coordinator. Fax: 202-783-6171. E-mail: rcolby@hiayh.org. No phone calls. Applicants must submit a cover letter, resume, two letters of recommendation. Application deadline: February 1 for spring, May 22 for summer, September 1 for winter. World Wide Web: http://www.hiayh.org.

HOUSTON INTERNATIONAL PROTOCOL ALLIANCE
901 Bagby, Suite 100
Houston, Texas 77002

General Information Nonprofit organization that serves as the protocol office for the city of Houston, working closely with the mayor's office to serve the local consular corps, visiting dignitaries, and the Sister City program. Established in 1983. Number of employees: 5. Department of Greater Houston Convention & Visitors Bureau, Houston, Texas. Number of internship applications received each year: 40.

Internships Available ▶ *1–15 protocol interns:* responsibilities include research, event coordination, day-to-day administrative tasks, special projects, and drafting correspondence. Candidates should have organizational skills, personal interest in the field, research skills, self-motivation, strong interpersonal skills, writ-

Houston International Protocol Alliance (continued)

ten communication skills. Duration is 3-6 months with option of extending past six months. Unpaid. Open to college freshmen, college sophomores, college juniors, college seniors, recent college graduates, graduate students. International applications accepted.

Benefits Job counseling, names of contacts, willing to act as a professional reference, willing to complete paperwork for educational credit, willing to provide letters of recommendation, free parking.

Contact Write, call, or fax Ms. Kathleen Silva, Sister Cities Coordinator/Protocol Officer. Phone: 713-227-3395. Fax: 713-227-3399. In-person interview recommended. Applicants must submit a cover letter, resume, writing sample. Application deadline: April 15 for summer, July 15 for fall, November 15 for spring.

INSTITUTE FOR HEALTH POLICY SOLUTIONS, INC.
1444 Eye Street, NW, Suite 900
Washington, District of Columbia 20005

General Information Independent, not-for-profit organization that identifies, analyzes, and develops strategies to solve health care system problems. Established in 1992. Number of employees: 10. Number of internship applications received each year: 20.

Internships Available ▶ *Interns:* responsibilities include assisting senior staff on a health care system improvement project, such as coordinating public and private health insurance coverage for uninsured children; information and counseling for consumer choice of health plans; or policy and technical assistance for developing consumer choice health purchasing groups. Candidates should have computer skills, oral communication skills, personal interest in the field, research skills, written communication skills. Duration is flexible (minimum of 4 months). Paid. Open to college freshmen, college sophomores, college juniors, college seniors, graduate students.

Benefits Hands-on experience.

Contact Write Jannis L. Warren, Director of Project Operations. No phone calls. Applicants must submit a cover letter, resume, academic transcripts, writing sample, two personal references, dates of availability. Application deadline: February 15 for summer. World Wide Web: http://www.ihps.org.

INSTITUTE OF CULTURAL AFFAIRS
4220 North 25th Street, Suite 4
Phoenix, Arizona 85016

General Information Nonprofit organization promoting social innovation through participation and community building with ICA's technology of participation (ToP Trademark) participatory approach to leadership with organizations, neighborhoods, and schools. Established in 1973. Number of employees: 14. Unit of Institute of Cultural Affairs International, Brussels, Belgium. Number of internship applications received each year: 6.

Internships Available ▶ *1–2 Hispanic services interns:* responsibilities include assisting the Director in Small Community Development along the Arizona-Mexico border; assisting with neighborhood project implementation, facilitation, and fund-raising. Candidates should have ability to work with others, computer skills, personal interest in the field, self-motivation, bilingual English/Spanish required, flexibility to work some evenings and/or weekends. Duration is 1–2 years. Position available as unpaid or at stipend of $900—$1000 per month. Open to college juniors, college seniors, recent college graduates, graduate students. ▶ *2–3 community youth development interns:* responsibilities include gathering interest by working with national and international participants to focus, conference, recruit, and register participants; establishing and leading events. Candidates should have oral communication skills, personal interest in the field, strong interpersonal skills, strong leadership ability, writing skills. Duration is 3–18 months. Position available as unpaid or at stipend of $900—$1000 per month. Open to college juniors, college seniors, recent college graduates, graduate students. ▶ *1–2 neighborhood partnership interns:* responsibilities include

working to assist senior staff in developing neighborhood partnerships in Phoenix, project administration and documentation, supporting local project implementation, helping with facilitation work with nonprofit neighborhood groups, recruiting participants, and helping with fund-raising. Candidates should have ability to work with others, computer skills, personal interest in the field, self-motivation, bilingual English/Spanish preferred, flexibility to work some evenings and/or weekends. Duration is 6–24 months. Position available as unpaid or at stipend of $900—$1000 per month. Open to college juniors, college seniors, recent college graduates, graduate students. ▶ *2 short-term interns:* responsibilities include working to support ICA trainers, facilitators, and field office representatives in marketing, fund-raising, program set-up and documentation, and administration in various locations across the U.S. Candidates should have ability to work with others, computer skills, plan to pursue career in field, self-motivation. Duration is 3 months minimum. Unpaid. Open to college sophomores, college juniors, college seniors, recent college graduates, graduate students. International applications accepted.

Benefits Formal training, housing at a cost, meals at a cost, names of contacts, on-the-job training, opportunity to attend seminars/workshops, possible full-time employment, willing to act as a professional reference, willing to complete paperwork for educational credit, willing to provide letters of recommendation, opportunity to develop skills with facilitation methods.

International Internships Available.

Contact Write, call, fax, or e-mail James Wiegel, Educational Partnership Coordinator. Phone: 800-742-4032. Fax: 602-954-0563. E-mail: icaphoenix@igc.apc.org. In-person interview recommended. Applicants must submit a cover letter, resume. Applications are accepted continuously. World Wide Web: http://www.ica-usa.org.

INTERHEMISPHERIC RESOURCE CENTER (IRC)
PO Box 4506
Albuquerque, New Mexico 87196-4506

General Information Nonprofit research institute that focuses on U.S. relations with the Third World. Established in 1979. Number of employees: 12. Number of internship applications received each year: 10.

Internships Available ▶ *2–4 researchers:* responsibilities include doing library research, interviewing, performing on-line computer searches, compiling information, synopsizing, and writing. Candidates should have ability to work independently, computer skills, oral communication skills, personal interest in the field, research skills, self-motivation, written communication skills. Duration is 12 weeks. Unpaid. Open to college juniors, college seniors, recent college graduates, graduate students. International applications accepted.

Benefits Formal training, opportunity to attend seminars/workshops, willing to complete paperwork for educational credit, willing to provide letters of recommendation, free housing (not guaranteed).

Contact Write, fax, or e-mail Ms. Debra Preusch, Director, PO Box 2176, Silver City, New Mexico 88062. Fax: 505-388-8619. E-mail: resourcetr@igc.apc.org. Applicants must submit a resume, writing sample, personal reference, two letters of recommendation. Applications are accepted continuously. World Wide Web: http://www.zianet.com/irc1.

INTERNATIONAL ASSOCIATION TO UNITE THE DEMOCRACIES
502 H Street, SW
Washington, District of Columbia 20024-2726

General Information Association with a history of commitment and support for world order and democracy. Established in 1940. Number of internship applications received each year: 30.

Internships Available ▶ *1–3 interns:* responsibilities include designing own program based on individual interests and abilities, such as serving as congressional liaison promoting AUD's conferences, building coalitions with other nongovernmental

organizations, finding and drafting applications to foundations for conference funding, and writing and editing for bimonthly newsletter. Candidates should have college courses in field, computer skills, editing skills, research skills, writing skills. Unpaid. Open to college sophomores, college juniors, college seniors, recent college graduates. International applications accepted.
Benefits Free housing, opportunity to attend seminars/workshops, willing to complete paperwork for educational credit.
Contact Write, fax, or e-mail Capt. Tom Hudgens, President. Fax: 202-544-3742. E-mail: atunite@aol.com. Applicants must submit a cover letter, resume. Applications are accepted continuously. World Wide Web: http://www.iaud.org.

INTERNATIONAL CENTER
731 8th Street, SE
Washington, District of Columbia 20003

General Information Organization that conducts programs of research; hosts foreign visitors; publishes briefing books to inform the press, Congress, U.S. Government officials, and the public of the impact of American policies abroad; and focuses on international development issues, particularly sustainable, small-scale development projects involving tree planting. Established in 1977. Number of employees: 12. Number of internship applications received each year: 100.
Internships Available ▶ *4–5 Russia Commission interns:* responsibilities include assisting with all programs of the Commission on U.S.-Russian relations, hosting foreign visitors, conducting translations, and assisting with international business and marketing projects. Duration is 3–4 months. ▶ *2–3 Viet Nam Trade Council interns:* responsibilities include assisting with all aspects of the U.S.-Viet Nam Trade Council, hosting foreign officials in D.C., organizing meetings and conferences, conducting research, and compiling statistics for briefing books. Candidates should have ability to work independently, ability to work with others, computer skills, knowledge of field, oral communication skills, organizational skills, personal interest in the field, strong leadership ability, writing skills. Open to college juniors, college seniors, recent college graduates, graduate students. ▶ *6 new forests project interns:* responsibilities include conducting research, writing project proposals, translating documents into Spanish/French, packaging tree seeds for worldwide distribution, and assisting with fund-raising projects. Candidates should have ability to work independently, ability to work with others, computer skills, oral communication skills, research skills, written communication skills. Open to college freshmen, college sophomores, college juniors, college seniors, recent college graduates, graduate students, law students. All positions are unpaid. International applications accepted.
Benefits Names of contacts, opportunity to attend seminars/workshops, possible full-time employment, travel reimbursement, willing to complete paperwork for educational credit, willing to provide letters of recommendation.
Contact Write, call, fax, or e-mail Erick Toledo, Intern Coordinator. Phone: 202-547-3800. Fax: 202-546-4784. E-mail: icnfp@erols.com. In-person interview recommended. Applicants must submit a cover letter, resume, writing sample. Application deadline: March 31 for summer, June 15 for fall, November 15 for spring. World Wide Web: http://www.internationalcenter.com.

INTERNATIONAL COMMITTEE OF LAWYERS FOR TIBET
2288 Fulton #312
Berkeley, California 94704

General Information Nonprofit membership group promoting self-determination for the Tibetan people and advocating human rights, environmental protection, and peaceful resolution through legal research, analysis, and education. Established in 1989. Number of employees: 2. Number of internship applications received each year: 30.
Internships Available ▶ *Interns:* responsibilities include general organizational assistance, research, writing, and editing. Candidates should have ability to work independently, research skills, writ-

ing skills. Duration is flexible; full time in summer, part time during school semester. Unpaid. Open to college freshmen, college sophomores, college juniors, college seniors, graduate students, law students. International applications accepted.
Benefits Job counseling, names of contacts, willing to complete paperwork for educational credit, willing to provide letters of recommendation.
Contact Write, call, fax, or e-mail Ms. Janice Mantell, Executive Director. Phone: 510-486-0588. Fax: 510-548-3785. E-mail: iclt@igc.org. In-person interview recommended. Applicants must submit a resume, 1 writing sample (optional). Applications are accepted continuously. World Wide Web: http://www.tibeticlt.org.

INTERNATIONAL FOUNDATION OF EMPLOYEE BENEFIT PLANS
18700 West Bluemound Road, PO Box 69
Brookfield, Wisconsin 53008-0069

General Information Nonprofit educational association serving the employee benefits industry as an information clearinghouse. Established in 1954. Number of employees: 135. Number of internship applications received each year: 1,000.
Internships Available ▶ *200 interns:* responsibilities include assisting with diverse duties in employee benefits and benefit administration. Duration is usually 2 consecutive summers (between sophomore/junior year and junior/senior year). $7–$12 per hour. Open to college sophomores. International applications accepted.
Benefits Formal training, job counseling, opportunity to attend seminars/workshops, possible full-time employment, willing to complete paperwork for educational credit, willing to provide letters of recommendation, use of all services of the Foundation, including the library.
International Internships Available in Toronto, Canada.
Contact Write, call, fax, or e-mail Margie Trede, Administrative Supervisor. Phone: 414-786-6710 Ext. 8218. Fax: 414-786-8670. E-mail: margiet@ifebp.org. In-person interview required. Application deadline: March 15. World Wide Web: http://www.ifebp.org.

INTERNATIONAL LABOR OFFICE
1828 L Street, NW
Washington, District of Columbia 20036

General Information Specialized agency of the United Nations that brings together governments, workers, and employers to improve working conditions, generate employment, and promote human rights. Established in 1919. Number of employees: 10. Number of internship applications received each year: 250.
Internships Available ▶ *Marketing/publications interns:* responsibilities include composing marketing brochures and flyers, writing book notices, selecting media to solicit book reviews, and creating awareness of ILO publications as part of the Marketing/Publications Unit. ▶ *Technical information/library interns:* responsibilities include drafting replies to inquiries, assisting in the maintenance of information documents and publications collection, and providing materials to constituency and the general public. Duration for all positions is flexible. All positions are unpaid. Open to college freshmen, college sophomores, college juniors, college seniors.
Benefits Opportunity to attend seminars/workshops, travel reimbursement, willing to complete paperwork for educational credit.
Contact Write Ms. Karen Dogan, Recruitment Officer. No phone calls. Applicants must submit a resume, letter of interest stating dates of availability. Applications are accepted continuously. World Wide Web: http://www.us.ilo.org.

INTERNATIONAL TRADE ADMINISTRATION
14th Street and Constitution Avenue, NW, Room 4809
Washington, District of Columbia 20230

General Information International trade organization that assists small and medium-sized businesses in exporting overseas;

International Trade Administration (continued)

formulates and implements U.S. foreign trade policy. Established in 1980. Number of employees: 1,745. Unit of United States Department of Commerce, Washington, District of Columbia. Number of internship applications received each year: 300.
Internships Available ▶ *1 student career experience program intern:* responsibilities include assisting with advising on international economic policy, administering international trade treaties, monitoring imports and exports, promoting exports, and many other trade-related functions. Candidates should have ability to work with others, college degree in related field, computer skills, oral communication skills, written communication skills, U.S. citizenship. Duration is 4–24 months. $9–$13 per hour. ▶ *1 student temporary employment program intern:* responsibilities include assisting with advising on international economic policy, administering international trade treaties, monitoring imports and exports, promoting exports, and many other trade-related functions. Candidates should have ability to work with others, computer skills, oral communication skills, written communication skills, U.S. citizenship. Duration is 3–12 months. $9–$13 per hour. ▶ *30–40 volunteer interns:* responsibilities include assisting with advising on international economic policy, administering international trade treaties, monitoring imports and exports, promoting exports, and many other trade-related functions. Candidates should have U.S. citizenship. Duration is flexible. Unpaid. Open to high school students, college freshmen, college sophomores, college juniors, college seniors, graduate students, law students.
Benefits Formal training, health insurance, possible full-time employment, willing to complete paperwork for educational credit, willing to provide letters of recommendation.
Contact Write, call, or fax Renee Beaty, Human Resources Office. Phone: 202-482-3301. Fax: 202-482-1903. Applicants must submit a resume, academic transcripts. Applications are accepted continuously.

INTERNATIONAL VOLUNTARY SERVICES, INC.
1601 Connecticut Avenue, NW, Suite 402D
Washington, District of Columbia 20009

General Information Private voluntary organization that provides technical assistance to local organizations in the developing world. Established in 1953. Number of employees: 3. Number of internship applications received each year: 150.
Internships Available ▶ *1–2 Andes program interns:* responsibilities include keeping track of field activities, summarizing reports, and fund-raising. Candidates should have ability to work independently, computer skills, oral communication skills, personal interest in the field, writing skills, fluency in Spanish (preferred). Duration is 1–9 months. Open to college juniors, college seniors, recent college graduates, graduate students, law students. ▶ *1 program intern:* responsibilities include keeping track of field activities, summarizing reports, and fund-raising. Candidates should have ability to work independently, computer skills, oral communication skills, personal interest in the field, writing skills, fluency in spanish (preferred). Open to college juniors, college seniors, recent college graduates, graduate students. All positions are unpaid. International applications accepted.
Benefits Job counseling, names of contacts, on-the-job training, opportunity to attend seminars/workshops, willing to act as a professional reference, willing to complete paperwork for educational credit, willing to provide letters of recommendation, small transportation stipend.
Contact Write, fax, or e-mail Anne Shirk, Executive Director, 1601 Connecticut Avneue, NW, Suite 402D, Washington, District of Columbia 20009. Fax: 202-387-4291. E-mail: ivs.inc@erols. com. No phone calls. In-person interview recommended. Applicants must submit a cover letter, resume, personal reference. Applications are accepted continuously.

IREX
1616 H Street
Washington, District of Columbia 20006

General Information Company that designs and implements programs to foster interaction between specialists from Central

and Eastern Europe, Eurasia, Mongolia, and East Asia. Established in 1968. Number of employees: 91. Number of internship applications received each year: 100.
Internships Available ▶ *Central and Eastern European programs interns:* responsibilities include assisting in program management, research, and/or general office duties. Candidates should have computer skills, knowledge of field, office skills, organizational skills, personal interest in the field. Position available as unpaid or at $8–$12 per hour. Open to college juniors, college seniors, recent college graduates, graduate students, law students, career changers. ▶ *1–2 NIS Division interns:* responsibilities include assisting with U.S. and Foreign Fellowship Exchange Programs. Candidates should have computer skills, office skills, oral communication skills, personal interest in the field, self-motivation, written communication skills. Position available as unpaid or paid. Open to college sophomores, college juniors, college seniors, recent college graduates, graduate students. International applications accepted.
Benefits Names of contacts, on-the-job training, opportunity to attend seminars/workshops, possible full-time employment, willing to complete paperwork for educational credit, willing to provide letters of recommendation.
International Internships Available in Moscow, Russian Federation.
Contact Write, fax, or e-mail Florence Prugnaud, Human Resources Specialist. Fax: 202-628-8189. E-mail: hr@irex.org. No phone calls. Applicants must submit a cover letter, resume, writing sample. Applications are accepted continuously. World Wide Web: http://www.irex.org.

ISAR: INITIATIVE FOR SOCIAL ACTION AND RENEWAL EURASIA
1601 Connecticut Avenue, NW, Suite 301
Washington, District of Columbia 20009

General Information Nonprofit, nongovernmental organization that supports environmental groups and projects in the former Soviet Union. Established in 1983. Number of employees: 12. Number of internship applications received each year: 75.
Internships Available ▶ *Interns:* responsibilities include focusing on individual projects, answering telephones, filing, entering data, and processing requests for information. Candidates should have editing skills, knowledge of field, office skills, personal interest in the field, writing skills. Duration is 3 months. Unpaid. Open to college freshmen, college sophomores, college juniors, college seniors, recent college graduates, graduate students.
Benefits Job counseling, names of contacts, opportunity to attend seminars/workshops, possible full-time employment, willing to complete paperwork for educational credit, willing to provide letters of recommendation, office training, reimbursement of local travel expenses to and from ISAR.
Contact Write Alice Hengesbach, Office Manager. No phone calls. In-person interview recommended. Applicants must submit a cover letter, resume. Applications are accepted continuously. World Wide Web: http://www.isar.org.

ISRAEL POLICY FORUM
1030 15th Street, NW, Suite 850
Washington, District of Columbia 20005

General Information Independent leadership institution involved in advocacy and education about the Middle East peace process. Established in 1993. Number of employees: 8. Division of Israel Policy Forum, New York, New York. Number of internship applications received each year: 70.
Internships Available ▶ *1–2 interns/research assistants:* responsibilities include doing research and administrative work, helping with national programs, editing, proofing, writing. Candidates should have computer skills, knowledge of field, organizational skills, plan to pursue career in field, research skills, strong interpersonal skills, writing skills. Duration is September to May. $1,000 per month. ▶ *1–2 interns/research assistants (summer):* responsibilities include doing research and administrative work, helping with national programs, editing, proofing, writing. Candidates should have computer skills, knowledge of field,

organizational skills, personal interest in the field, research skills, strong interpersonal skills, writing skills. Duration is May to August. Paid. Open to recent high school graduates, college freshmen, college sophomores, college juniors, college seniors, recent college graduates, graduate students, law students. International applications accepted.

Benefits Job counseling, names of contacts, on-the-job training, opportunity to attend seminars/workshops, willing to act as a professional reference, willing to complete paperwork for educational credit, willing to provide letters of recommendation, stipends.

Contact Write, call, fax, or e-mail Esther Lederman, Assistant Director, 1030 15th Street, NW, Suite 850, Washington, District of Columbia 20005. Phone: 202-842-1700. Fax: 202-842-1722. E-mail: elederman@ipforum.org. In-person interview recommended. Applicants must submit a cover letter, resume, writing sample, 2—3 personal references. Applications are accepted continuously. World Wide Web: http://www.peacepulse. org.

JAMESTOWN FOUNDATION
1528 18th Street, NW
Washington, District of Columbia 20036

General Information Nonprofit organization specializing in increasing Western understanding of the former Soviet Union through the monitoring of political, economic, and social trends. Established in 1983. Number of employees: 10. Number of internship applications received each year: 30.

Internships Available ▶ *1–4 research assistants:* responsibilities include providing administrative and research support for Foundation staff. Duration is 1 semester. Unpaid. Open to college freshmen, college sophomores, college juniors, college seniors.

Benefits Job counseling, opportunity to attend seminars/workshops, willing to complete paperwork for educational credit, willing to provide letters of recommendation.

Contact Write, call, fax, or e-mail Erin Long, Director of Communications. Phone: 202-483-8888. Fax: 202-483-8337. E-mail: long@jamestown.org. In-person interview recommended. Applicants must submit a cover letter, resume. Applications are accepted continuously. World Wide Web: http://www.jamestown.org.

JAPAN-AMERICA SOCIETY OF WASHINGTON, DC
1020 19th Street, LL #40
Washington, District of Columbia 20036

General Information Organization dedicated to promoting a better understanding between Japan and the United States through programs and services. Established in 1957. Number of employees: 4. Number of internship applications received each year: 10.

Internships Available ▶ *1 Cherry Blossom Festival intern:* responsibilities include coordinating various artistic functions. Open to college freshmen, college sophomores, college juniors, college seniors, recent college graduates. ▶ *1 Japan Bowl intern:* responsibilities include coordinating national student competition. Open to college freshmen, college sophomores, college juniors, college seniors, graduate students. ▶ *2–3 interns:* responsibilities include various office duties in membership programs and services. Open to college freshmen, college sophomores, college juniors, college seniors, graduate students. ▶ *1 press intern:* responsibilities include working on all programs. Open to college freshmen, college sophomores, college juniors, college seniors, graduate students. ▶ *1 publishing intern:* responsibilities include typing, editing, and other various duties in publishing the *Washington-Japan Journal.* Open to college freshmen, college sophomores, college juniors, college seniors, graduate students. Duration for all positions is minimum of 8 weeks. All positions are unpaid. International applications accepted.

Benefits Job counseling, names of contacts, opportunity to attend seminars/workshops, possible full-time employment, travel reimbursement, willing to complete paperwork for educational credit, willing to provide letters of recommendation.

Contact Write or fax Betty Taira, Office Manager. Fax: 202-833-2456. No phone calls. In-person interview required. Applicants must submit a cover letter, resume. Applications are accepted continuously. World Wide Web: http://www.us-japan.org.

JAPAN-AMERICA STUDENT CONFERENCE, INC.
2nd Floor, 606 18th Street, NW
Washington, District of Columbia 20006-5202

General Information 30-day exchange program for 40 Japanese and 40 American university students; alternates annually between Japan and the United States; freshman to Ph.D. levels. Established in 1934. Number of employees: 3.

Internships Available ▶ *1–3 interns:* responsibilities include fund-raising, general administrative duties, coordinating alumni activities, acting as university liaison, and working with database and other computer systems. Candidates should have ability to work with others, computer skills, office skills, organizational skills, personal interest in the field, research skills. Duration is flexible. Unpaid. Open to college freshmen, college sophomores, college juniors, college seniors, recent college graduates, graduate students, law students, career changers, individuals reentering the workforce. International applications accepted.

Contact Write, call, fax, or e-mail Ms. Gretchen Hobbs Donaldson, Executive Director, 2nd Floor, 606 18th Street, NW, Washington, District of Columbia 20006-5202. Phone: 202-289-4231. Fax: 202-789-8265. E-mail: jascinc@jasc.org. Applicants must submit a cover letter, resume. Applications are accepted continuously. World Wide Web: http://www.jasc.org.

KOREA ECONOMIC INSTITUTE OF AMERICA
1101 Vermont Avenue, Suite 401
Washington, District of Columbia 20005

General Information Institute that promotes economic dialogue and understanding between the United States and Korea. Established in 1982. Number of employees: 7. Unit of Korea Institute for International Economics Policy, Seoul, Republic of Korea. Number of internship applications received each year: 70.

Internships Available ▶ *1–2 research associates:* responsibilities include following legislative initiatives and international news developments to assist in the preparation of short reports for transmission to Korea; assisting with the preparations for various KEI-sponsored conferences and the annual visit by members of the Korean National Assembly; assisting with transmission of daily news articles; responding to requests for information; and researching special publication requests. Candidates should have computer skills, knowledge of field, organizational skills, self-motivation, strong interpersonal skills, writing skills. Duration is full spring, summer, or fall terms. Unpaid. Open to college sophomores, college juniors, college seniors, graduate students. International applications accepted.

Benefits Names of contacts, opportunity to attend seminars/workshops, willing to act as a professional reference, willing to complete paperwork for educational credit, willing to provide letters of recommendation.

Contact Write, fax, or e-mail Ms. Caroline G. Cooper, Director of Congressional Affairs. Fax: 202-371-0692. E-mail: cgc@keia.com. No phone calls. Telephone interview required. Applicants must submit a cover letter, resume, writing sample, letter of recommendation. Application deadline: April 15 for summer, August 1 for fall, December 1 for spring. World Wide Web: http://www.keia.com.

LAFAYETTE URBAN ENTERPRISE ASSOCIATION
422 Main Street
Lafayette, Indiana 47901

General Information Independent, nonpartisan, nonprofit organization established to direct zone activities and reinvestment. Established in 1993. Number of employees: 2. Number of internship applications received each year: 1.

Internships Available ▶ *1 community development intern:* responsibilities include assisting the executive director with design, implementa-

Lafayette Urban Enterprise Association *(continued)*

tion, and administration of community projects and organizational programs; interacting with zone businesses and residents to gather information for LUEA projects and programs; creating spreadsheets and generating reports for zone programs; writing, editing, and revising press releases and articles for publications such as the quarterly newsletter, IN THE ZONE; creating presentational media; Web site maintenance; and general administrative support duties. Candidates should have ability to work independently, ability to work with others, computer skills, office skills, oral communication skills, writing skills. Duration is 1 semester or longer. $6–$7 per hour. Open to college freshmen, college sophomores, college juniors, college seniors, recent college graduates, graduate students. International applications accepted.
Benefits Job counseling, names of contacts, on-the-job training, willing to act as a professional reference, willing to complete paperwork for educational credit, willing to provide letters of recommendation.
Contact Write, fax, or e-mail Dennis Carson, Executive Director. Fax: 765-742-2129. E-mail: info@luea.org. No phone calls. In-person interview recommended. Applicants must submit a cover letter, resume. Application deadline: March 1 for summer, July 1 for fall, November 1 for spring. World Wide Web: http://www.luea.org.

L. A. WORKS
351 South La Brea Avenue, Suite 202
Los Angeles, California 90036

General Information Nonprofit organization revitalizing Los Angeles by making it easy for busy people to get involved in volunteer service projects. Established in 1991. Number of employees: 6. Number of internship applications received each year: 15.
Internships Available ▶ *2–5 special events/volunteer programs assistants:* responsibilities include helping to plan and implement large-scale volunteer service projects and ongoing (smaller) volunteer projects, helping to research potential project sites, planning tasks, and recruiting volunteers. Candidates should have ability to work independently, computer skills, oral communication skills, organizational skills, strong interpersonal skills, written communication skills. Duration is flexible. Unpaid. Open to high school seniors, recent high school graduates, college freshmen, college sophomores, college juniors, college seniors, recent college graduates, graduate students, law students, career changers, individuals reentering the workforce. International applications accepted.
Benefits Formal training, job counseling, on-the-job training, opportunity to attend seminars/workshops, possible full-time employment, willing to act as a professional reference, willing to complete paperwork for educational credit, willing to provide letters of recommendation.
Contact Write, call, fax, or e-mail Julie Rajan, Executive Director. Phone: 323-936-1340. Fax: 323-936-1454. E-mail: laworks@deltanet.com. In-person interview recommended. Applicants must submit a cover letter, resume, two writing samples, two personal references. Applications are accepted continuously. World Wide Web: http://www.la-volunteer.org.

LAWYERS ALLIANCE FOR WORLD SECURITY /COMMITTEE FOR NATIONAL SECURITY
1901 Pennsylvania Avenue, NW, Suite 201
Washington, District of Columbia 20006

General Information Nonprofit, nonpartisan membership organization focused on arms control; defense budget; and chemical, nuclear, and biological weaponry. Established in 1981. Number of employees: 7. Number of internship applications received each year: 100.
Internships Available ▶ *2–3 project associates:* responsibilities include conducting research and tracking legislative issues, editing, and correspondence. Candidates should have ability to work independently, analytical skills, oral communication skills, personal interest in the field, research skills, self-motivation, writ-

ten communication skills, some experience and college courses in international relations, history, and disarmament desirable. Duration is 3–4 months. $150 per month stipend. Open to college juniors, college seniors, recent college graduates, graduate students, law students. International applications accepted.
Benefits Job counseling, names of contacts, opportunity to attend seminars/workshops, possible full-time employment, willing to act as a professional reference, willing to complete paperwork for educational credit, willing to provide letters of recommendation, $150 transportation stipend.
Contact Write, call, fax, or e-mail Ms. Leonor Tomero, Intern Coordinator. Phone: 202-745-2450. Fax: 202-667-0444. E-mail: disarmament@lawscns.org. In-person interview recommended. Applicants must submit a cover letter, resume, academic transcripts, two letters of recommendation, 3- to 5-page writing sample. Application deadline: March 15 for summer (recommended deadline), July 15 for fall (recommended deadline), October 20 for spring (recommended deadline). World Wide Web: http://www.lawscns.org.

LEGACY INTERNATIONAL'S GLOBAL YOUTH VILLAGE
1020 Legacy Drive
Bedford, Virginia 24523

General Information International youth training program, in a camp setting. It focuses on cross-cultural understanding and leadership training and offers workshops in conflict resolution, the arts, ESOL, international relations, business training, and more. Established in 1979. Number of employees: 5. Number of internship applications received each year: 40.
Internships Available ▶ *12–17 counselors/program specialists:* responsibilities include live-in cabin counseling plus other duties pending the applicant's skills. Candidates should have ability to work with others, oral communication skills, organizational skills, personal interest in the field, strong interpersonal skills, strong leadership ability, cross-cultural communication skills. Duration is 9 weeks June to August. Position available as unpaid or at $1,300 per duration of internship. Open to college sophomores, college juniors, college seniors, recent college graduates, graduate students, career changers, individuals reentering the workforce. International applications accepted.
Benefits Formal training, free housing, free meals, health insurance, names of contacts, on-the-job training, possible full-time employment, willing to act as a professional reference, willing to complete paperwork for educational credit, willing to provide letters of recommendation, laundry service, small stipend or travel reimbursement based on qualifications.
Contact Write, fax, or e-mail Paul Harvey, Staff Director. Fax: 540-297-1860. E-mail: staff@legacyintl.org. No phone calls. In-person interview recommended. Applicants must submit a formal organization application, resume, 2-3 professional references with phone/fax numbers. Applications are accepted continuously. World Wide Web: http://www.legacyintl.org/gyvhome.htm.

LEGISLATIVE SERVICE COMMISSION, RIFFE CENTER FOR GOVERNMENT AND THE ARTS
77 South High Street, 9th Floor
Columbus, Ohio 43266-0342

General Information Non-partisan organization providing the members of the Ohio General Assembly with legal, bill-drafting, and research services, as well as other support services. Established in 1953. Number of employees: 106. Number of internship applications received each year: 250.
Internships Available ▶ *22 legislative interns:* responsibilities include providing general staff assistance to legislators including assisting with constituent work; performing legislative research; writing press releases, newspaper columns, and speeches; attending committee meetings. Candidates should have ability to work independently, oral communication skills, self-motivation, strong interpersonal skills, written communication skills. ▶ *2 telecommunications interns:* responsibilities include working in Ohio State House telecommunications studio; working as production

assistants and with video production, editing, audio, floor directing, and lighting; and conducting studio tours for the public. Candidates should have college degree in related field, oral communication skills, self-motivation, strong interpersonal skills, written communication skills, video production experience. Duration for all positions is 13 months (December 1 to December 31 of the following year). All positions paid at $21,500–$23,500 per year. Open to individuals with at least a bachelor's degree by start of internship. International applications accepted.
Benefits Formal training, health insurance, names of contacts, on-the-job training, opportunity to attend seminars/workshops, possible full-time employment, willing to act as a professional reference, willing to provide letters of recommendation, leave time.
Contact Write or call Internship Coordinator. Phone: 614-466-3615. In-person interview required. Applicants must submit a formal organization application, resume, academic transcripts, three letters of recommendation, 2-4-page autobiographical statement. Application deadline: April 15 for legislative positions, May 31 for telecommunications positions. World Wide Web: http://www.lsc.state.oh.us.

MEDIA WATCH
PO Box 618
Santa Cruz, California 95061-0618

General Information Organization that challenges the biases found in commercial media. Established in 1984. Number of internship applications received each year: 10.
Internships Available ▶ *Management assistants:* responsibilities include performing office duties, including accounts payable, accounts receivable, checking incoming mail, helping to write newsletters, answering phones, and assisting with product protests and boycott campaigns. Candidates should have office skills, oral communication skills, personal interest in the field, strong interpersonal skills, writing skills. Duration is flexible. Unpaid. Open to high school seniors, recent high school graduates, college freshmen, college sophomores, college juniors, college seniors, recent college graduates, graduate students, career changers, individuals reentering the workforce. International applications accepted.
Benefits On-the-job training, willing to act as a professional reference, willing to complete paperwork for educational credit, willing to provide letters of recommendation.
Contact Write, call, fax, or e-mail Ann Simonton, Media Watch Director. Phone: 831-423-6355. Fax: 831-423-6355. E-mail: mwatch@cruzio.com. Applicants must submit a cover letter, resume. Applications are accepted continuously. World Wide Web: http://www.mediawatch.com.

MERIDIAN INTERNATIONAL CENTER–EDUCATIONAL AND VISITOR SERVICES
1630 Crescent Place, NW
Washington, District of Columbia 20009

General Information Service promoting international understanding through exchange of people. ideas, and the arts. Educational and Visitor Services division offers training, conferences, and services for international visitors and Americans sponsored by the United States government and foreign government or private corporation. Established in 1960. Number of employees: 90. Number of internship applications received each year: 50.
Internships Available ▶ *1–2 visitor services assistants:* responsibilities include working with volunteer corps, acting as a liaison between international visitors and volunteers, scheduling cultural events, assiting in conferences and workshops, and maintaining records. Candidates should have ability to work independently, ability to work with others, computer skills, office skills, oral communication skills, written communication skills. Duration is flexible. Unpaid. Open to high school students, recent high school graduates, college freshmen, college sophomores, college juniors, college seniors, recent college graduates, graduate students. International applications accepted.
Benefits Formal training, job counseling, names of contacts, on-the-job training, opportunity to attend seminars/workshops,

possible full-time employment, willing to act as a professional reference, willing to complete paperwork for educational credit, willing to provide letters of recommendation.
Contact Write or fax Intern Coordinator. Fax: 202-667-1475. No phone calls. In-person interview recommended. Applicants must submit a cover letter, resume. Applications are accepted continuously. World Wide Web: http://www.meridian.org.

THE MIDDLE EAST INSTITUTE
1761 N Street, NW
Washington, District of Columbia 20036

General Information Nonprofit organization dedicated to improving public knowledge and understanding of the politics, economics, cultures, languages, and religions of the Middle East, North Africa, Caucasus, and Central Asia; publishing the Middle East Journal; teaching Arabic, Hebrew, Persian, and Turkish languages; presenting cultural and political programs; and operating the Keiser Library. Established in 1946. Number of employees: 15. Number of internship applications received each year: 150.
Internships Available ▶ *1 development intern:* responsibilities include helping maintain records and increasing fund-raising activities. Candidates should have ability to work independently, computer skills, office skills, organizational skills, research skills, strong interpersonal skills. Open to college freshmen, college sophomores, college juniors, college seniors, recent college graduates. ▶ *1 language intern:* responsibilities include maintaining relations between language students and the institute, and recording finances. Candidates should have oral communication skills, organizational skills, strong interpersonal skills, written communication skills. Open to college freshmen, college sophomores, college juniors, college seniors, recent college graduates. ▶ *1–2 library interns:* responsibilities include compiling bibliographies, researching topics for patrons, answering telephone inquiries on the Middle East, and writing for the Institute's newsletter. Candidates should have ability to work independently, computer skills, office skills, oral communication skills, research skills, strong interpersonal skills, written communication skills. Open to college freshmen, college sophomores, college juniors, college seniors, recent college graduates. ▶ *2–3 programs interns:* responsibilities include research for conferences and seminars, helping to administer public events, writing newsletter about public events, and correspondence. Candidates should have ability to work independently, oral communication skills, research skills, strong interpersonal skills, written communication skills. Open to college freshmen, college sophomores, college juniors, college seniors, recent college graduates, graduate students. ▶ *3–4 publication interns:* responsibilities include proofreading book reviews, helping compile the journal's "Bibliography of Periodical Literature," drafting book annotations for publication in the Middle East Journal, and maintaining 2 databases. Candidates should have ability to work independently, computer skills, organizational skills, plan to pursue career in field, writing skills. Open to college freshmen, college sophomores, college juniors, college seniors, recent college graduates, graduate students. Duration for all positions is 1 semester. All positions are unpaid. International applications accepted.
Benefits Names of contacts, opportunity to attend seminars/workshops, willing to complete paperwork for educational credit, willing to provide letters of recommendation, 1 language course tuition-free, 1 year free membership in organization, reimbursement of local travel expenses.
Contact Write, call, fax, or e-mail Leslie Hunter, Internship Coordinator. Phone: 202-785-0191. Fax: 202-331-8861. E-mail: asted@mideasti.org. In-person interview recommended. Applicants must submit a cover letter, resume, academic transcripts, writing sample, letter of recommendation. Application deadline: April 1 for summer, August 1 for fall, December 1 for spring. World Wide Web: http://www.mideasti.org.

MINNESOTA INTERNATIONAL CENTER
711 East River Road
Minneapolis, Minnesota 55455

General Information Nonprofit community organization with a mission of promoting international exchange and understanding between Minnesotans and the world. Established in 1953. Number of employees: 17. Number of internship applications received each year: 100.

Internships Available ▶ *1–2 Twin Cities International Citizen Awards interns:* responsibilities include assisting in all aspects of implementing the awards event, including communications, public relations, Web site, mailings, and meeting and greeting. Candidates should have computer skills, oral communication skills, written communication skills, experience in international affairs or public relations. Duration is late April to early October. ▶ *8 administration/volunteer management interns:* responsibilities include assisting administrative manager in recruiting volunteers, and managing volunteer correspondence and record maintenance; maintaining board correspondence and record keeping; and providing administrative support for program staff. Candidates should have ability to work independently, computer skills, editing skills, office skills, oral communication skills, organizational skills, research skills, self-motivation, strong interpersonal skills, writing skills. Duration is 10–12 weeks. ▶ *6–8 intercultural program interns:* responsibilities include calling MIC volunteers to find dinner hospitality, general office tasks, maintaining database, and assisting with other program and activity arrangements. Candidates should have oral communication skills, stong phone skills. Duration is 10–12 weeks. ▶ *4 international classroom connection interns:* responsibilities include contacting international speakers, confirming and arranging appointments, arranging volunteer escorts, entering data, and general administrative assistance. Candidates should have ability to work independently, computer skills, editing skills, office skills, oral communication skills, organizational skills, research skills, self-motivation, strong interpersonal skills, writing skills. Duration is 10–12 weeks. ▶ *4 professional exchange program interns:* responsibilities include arranging and confirming appointments for international visitors, maintaining files and records on a database, and performing general clerical work. Candidates should have computer skills, office skills, oral communication skills, organizational skills, research skills, strong interpersonal skills, writing skills. Duration is 10–12 weeks. ▶ *4 world affairs education program interns:* responsibilities include assisting event registration, maintaining information files, doing telephone follow-up on event publicity, assisting in mailing announcements on events, performing general clerical work, doing research on topic areas, preparation of educational materials for events, and assisting with registration at events. Candidates should have ability to work independently, computer skills, office skills, oral communication skills, organizational skills, personal interest in the field, research skills, self-motivation, strong interpersonal skills, writing skills, flexibility. Duration is 10–12 weeks. All positions are unpaid. Open to college juniors, college seniors, recent college graduates, graduate students. International applications accepted.

Benefits Job counseling, names of contacts, opportunity to attend seminars/workshops, willing to complete paperwork for educational credit, willing to provide letters of recommendation.

Contact Write Lauren Hill, Intern Coordinator. In-person interview recommended. Applicants must submit a cover letter, resume. Applications are accepted continuously. World Wide Web: http://www.micglobe.org.

MOBILITY INTERNATIONAL USA
PO Box 10767
Eugene, Oregon 97440

General Information Organization that promotes and facilitates international exchange, leadership training, and disability rights seminars for individuals from around the world with disabilities. Established in 1981. Number of employees: 12. Unit of Mobility International, Belgium. Number of internship applications received each year: 40.

Internships Available ▶ *2–3 clearinghouse on disability and exchange research interns:* responsibilities include research related to providing and updating information and referral materials and systems on international exchange organizations and disability resources. Candidates should have computer skills, organizational skills, research skills, writing skills, experience in international and disabilities issues. Duration is 2–6 months. ▶ *1–2 international development interns:* responsibilities include assisting international development staff with implementation of MIUSA's new international development and disability program, project support, responding to information requests, development of training materials and documents. Candidates should have computer skills, organizational skills, self-motivation, strong interpersonal skills, international experience, experience in disability. ▶ *2–4 international exchange interns:* responsibilities include assisting with implementation of MIUSA inbound international exchange programs, assisting with recreational activities, performing general office duties, international correspondence, fund-raising, and language translation/interpreting if applicable. Candidates should have strong interpersonal skills, strong leadership ability, disability and cross-cultural experience. Duration is 3–6 months. ▶ *2–3 public relations interns:* responsibilities include assisting public relations staff with press releases, updating publications, community speaking, recruitment and membership, fund-raising, article writing, publicity at conferences, working on new publications, newsletter articles, and international exchange resources. Candidates should have oral communication skills, strong interpersonal skills, written communication skills, international experience, experience in field of disability. Duration is 2-6 months (part or full-time). All positions are unpaid. Open to college juniors, college seniors, recent college graduates, graduate students, people with disabilities. International applications accepted.

Benefits Names of contacts, on-the-job training, opportunity to attend seminars/workshops, willing to complete paperwork for educational credit, willing to provide letters of recommendation, stipends available for 6-month positions.

Contact Write, fax, or e-mail Internship Coordinator. Fax: 541-343-6812. E-mail: exchange@miusa.org. No phone calls. In-person interview recommended. Applicants must submit a cover letter, resume, two letters of recommendation, completion of MIUSA intern application questionnaire. Applications are accepted continuously. World Wide Web: http://www.miusa.org.

NATIONAL ASSOCIATION FOR COMMUNITY MEDIATION
1527 New Hampshire Avenue, NW
Washington, District of Columbia 20036

General Information An organization of community mediation programs and volunteer mediations whose goals are to provide a compelling voice in policy-making, legislative arenas and network support. Established in 1994. Number of employees: 5. Number of internship applications received each year: 10.

Internships Available ▶ *2 interns:* responsibilities include researching, information gathering, networking, maintaining communication with related national organizations, creating a profile of state mediation associations and activities in their states, and additional administrative and clerical tasks as needed. Candidates should have ability to work independently, computer skills, oral communication skills, research skills, strong interpersonal skills, written communication skills. Unpaid. Open to college seniors, recent college graduates, graduate students, law students, law school graduates. International applications accepted.

Benefits Names of contacts, on-the-job training, opportunity to attend seminars/workshops, willing to act as a professional reference, willing to complete paperwork for educational credit, willing to provide letters of recommendation.

Contact Write, call, fax, or e-mail Larry Ray, Executive Director, 1527 New Hampshire Avenue, NW, Washington, District of Columbia 20036. Phone: 202-667-9700 Ext. 224. Fax: 202-667-8629. E-mail: nafcm@nafcm.org. Telephone interview required. Applicants must submit a cover letter, resume, three personal references. Applications are accepted continuously. World Wide Web: http://www.nafcm.org.

NATIONAL ASSOCIATION OF COLLEGIATE DIRECTORS OF ATHLETICS (NACDA)
24651 Detroit Road
Westlake, Ohio 44145

General Information The largest association of collegiate athletics administrators with a membership of more than 6,100 individuals and more than 1,600 institutions throughout the United States, Canada, and Mexico. Established in 1965. Number of employees: 10. Number of internship applications received each year: 50.

Internships Available ▶ *3–4 10-month interns:* responsibilities include assisting with a wide range of activities and duties, including one of NACDA's main undertakings, its annual convention, which requires months of preparation to make the event successful. Duration is 10 months. ▶ *4 summer interns:* responsibilities include assisting with a wide range of activities and duties, including one of NACDA's main undertakings, its annual convention, which requires months of preparation to make the event successful. Duration is May to August. Candidates for all positions should have computer skills, oral communication skills, plan to pursue career in field, strong interpersonal skills, written communication skills. All positions paid at $100 per week. Open to college freshmen, college sophomores, college juniors, college seniors, recent college graduates, graduate students, career changers, individuals reentering the workforce. International applications accepted.

Benefits Willing to act as a professional reference, willing to complete paperwork for educational credit, willing to provide letters of recommendation.

Contact Write, call, or e-mail Becky Parke, Administrative Assistant, PO Box 16428, Cleveland, Ohio 44116. Phone: 440-892-4000. E-mail: bparke@nacda.com. Applicants must submit a cover letter, resume. Applications are accepted continuously. World Wide Web: http://www.nacda.com.

NATIONAL CENTER FOR PUBLIC POLICY RESEARCH
777 North Capitol Street, NE, Suite 803
Washington, District of Columbia 20002-4239

General Information Resource center for conservative activists, journalists, and policymakers that seeks to promote enlightened and reasoned debate on diverse public policy issues; dedicated to the principles of a strong defense, free competitive enterprise, and individual liberty. Established in 1982. Number of employees: 7. Number of internship applications received each year: 200.

Internships Available ▶ *3–5 research assistants:* responsibilities include researching a topic of interest concerning U.S. domestic policy and/or international relations, performing clerical and other standard office duties. Candidates should have ability to work independently, ability to work with others, organizational skills, research skills, self-motivation, writing skills. Duration is flexible. $6–$7 per hour. Open to college freshmen, college sophomores, college juniors, college seniors, recent college graduates. International applications accepted.

Benefits Job counseling, names of contacts, opportunity to attend seminars/workshops, willing to complete paperwork for educational credit, willing to provide letters of recommendation.

Contact Write, call, fax, or e-mail David Almasi, Director of Publications and Media Relations, 777 North Capitol Street, NE, Suite 803, Washington, District of Columbia 20002-4239. Phone: 202-371-1400 Ext. 106. Fax: 202-408-7773. E-mail: info@nationalcenter.org. Applicants must submit a formal organization application, cover letter, resume, writing sample, personal reference. Applications are accepted continuously. World Wide Web: http://www.nationalcenter.org.

NATIONAL COUNCIL FOR INTERNATIONAL VISITORS
1420 K Street, NW, Suite 800
Washington, District of Columbia 20005-2401

General Information A national nonprofit network of 97 community volunteer organizations and 17 national program agencies dedicated to improving international understanding and friendship through professional and personal exchange programs. Established in 1961. Number of employees: 4. Number of internship applications received each year: 70.

Internships Available ▶ *1–3 program interns:* responsibilities include assisting in the preparation of various resource materials, assisting in writing articles for newsletters and other publications, promoting various organizational conferences, helping establish links between NCIV community affiliates and their congressional representatives, and aiding in communications between the national organization and its membership. Candidates should have ability to work independently, computer skills, editing skills, office skills, self-motivation, writing skills. Duration is 1–2 semesters. $500 per duration of internship. Open to college sophomores, college juniors, college seniors, recent college graduates, graduate students. International applications accepted.

Benefits Job counseling, names of contacts, opportunity to attend seminars/workshops, willing to act as a professional reference, willing to complete paperwork for educational credit, willing to provide letters of recommendation, $500 stipend to U.S. citizens upon completion of internship.

Contact Write, fax, or e-mail Paul Binkley, Program Associate. Fax: 202-289-4625. E-mail: pbinkley@nciv.org. No phone calls. In-person interview recommended. Applicants must submit a cover letter, resume, writing sample, two personal references. Applications are accepted continuously. World Wide Web: http://www.nciv.org.

NATIONAL COUNCIL ON US–ARAB RELATIONS
1140 Connecticut Avenue, NW, Suite 1210
Washington, District of Columbia 20036

General Information Nonprofit organization dedicated to improving American knowledge and understanding of the Arab world through study, visits abroad, and other educational programs. Established in 1983. Number of employees: 12.

Internships Available ▶ *Interns:* responsibilities include performing clerical work and database entry, and assisting with the coordination of seminars and study abroad. Candidates should have office skills, personal interest in the field, written communication skills. Duration is 3 months in summer. Unpaid. Open to high school students, high school seniors, recent high school graduates, college freshmen, college sophomores, college juniors, college seniors, recent college graduates, graduate students, law students, career changers, individuals reentering the workforce.

Benefits Job counseling, names of contacts, opportunity to attend seminars/workshops, possible full-time employment, willing to complete paperwork for educational credit, willing to provide letters of recommendation.

Contact Write, call, fax, or e-mail Program Coordinator. Phone: 202-293-0801. Fax: 202-293-0903. E-mail: info@ncusar.org. In-person interview recommended. Applicants must submit a formal organization application, cover letter, resume, academic transcripts, writing sample, two letters of recommendation, 1-page autobiographical statement. Applications are accepted continuously. World Wide Web: http://www.ncusar.org.

NATIONAL INSTITUTE FOR PUBLIC POLICY
3031 Javier Road, Suite 300
Fairfax, Virginia 22031

General Information Organization that provides historically based strategic analysis, policy research, and education in the international security field. Established in 1981. Number of employees: 15. Number of internship applications received each year: 50.

Internships Available ▶ *1–2 research support interns:* responsibilities include researching and writing educational materials, assisting with editing the journal *Comparative Strategy*, and assisting with organizing conferences. Candidates should have college courses in field, knowledge of field, personal interest in the field, research skills. Duration is flexible. Position available as unpaid or paid. Open to recent college graduates, graduate students.

National Institute for Public Policy (continued)
Benefits Job counseling, names of contacts, opportunity to attend seminars/workshops, possible full-time employment, willing to complete paperwork for educational credit, willing to provide letters of recommendation.
Contact Write, call, or fax Mr. John J. Kohout, Vice President. Phone: 703-698-0563. Fax: 703-698-0566. In-person interview required. Applicants must submit a resume, writing sample. Applications are accepted continuously.

NATIONAL SOCIETY OF FUND RAISING EXECUTIVES
1101 King Street, Suite 700
Alexandria, Virginia 22314-2967

General Information Organization that advocates development and growth of fund-raising professionals working to advance philanthropy and volunteerism and to promote high ethical standards in the fund-raising profession. Established in 1960. Number of employees: 39. Number of internship applications received each year: 10.
Internships Available ▶ *1–2 library assistants:* responsibilities include researching and performing data entry and some phone work. Candidates should have computer skills, office skills, oral communication skills, organizational skills, research skills, strong interpersonal skills. Duration is up to 1 year. Unpaid. Open to recent high school graduates, college freshmen, college sophomores, college juniors, college seniors, career changers, individuals reentering the workforce.
Benefits Names of contacts, possible full-time employment, willing to complete paperwork for educational credit, willing to provide letters of recommendation.
Contact Write, call, fax, or e-mail Jan Alfieri, Senior Coordinator-NSFRE Resource Center. Phone: 703-519-8458. Fax: 703-684-0540. E-mail: jalfieri@nsfre.org. In-person interview required. Applicants must submit a resume. Applications are accepted continuously. World Wide Web: http://www.nsfre.org.

NATIONAL TREASURY EMPLOYEES UNION
901 E Street, NW, Suite 600
Washington, District of Columbia 20004

General Information Union of federal government employees representing the employee interests on Capitol Hill, in court, in negotiations, and in the news media. Established in 1938. Number of employees: 60. Number of internship applications received each year: 20.
Internships Available ▶ *1 public relations intern:* responsibilities include using computer software, desktop publishing and graphic designs. ▶ *1 staff writer intern:* responsibilities include developing written materials. Duration for all positions is flexible. All positions paid. Open to college juniors, college seniors, recent college graduates, graduate students.
Benefits Names of contacts, willing to complete paperwork for educational credit, willing to provide letters of recommendation.
Contact Write, call, or fax Mr. Jim Watkins, Director of Public Relations. Phone: 202-783-4444. Fax: 202-508-3771. In-person interview recommended. Applicants must submit a cover letter, resume. Applications are accepted continuously. World Wide Web: http://www.nteu.org.

NATIONAL TRUST FOR HISTORIC PRESERVATION
1785 Massachusetts Avenue, NW
Washington, District of Columbia 20036

General Information Nonprofit organization providing leadership, education, and advocacy to save America's diverse historic places and revitalize its communities. Established in 1949. Number of employees: 300. Number of internship applications received each year: 200.
Internships Available ▶ *15 programs, fund-raising, communications interns:* responsibilities include performing a variety of research projects on preservation issues and initiatives. Candidates should have ability to work independently, computer skills, office skills, personal interest in the field, research skills, written com-

munication skills. Duration is 8 weeks in summer. Unpaid. Open to college sophomores, college juniors, college seniors, recent college graduates, graduate students, law students, career changers, individuals reentering the workforce. International applications accepted.
Benefits Job counseling, names of contacts, opportunity to attend seminars/workshops, willing to complete paperwork for educational credit, willing to provide letters of recommendation, field trips, flexible work schedules.
Contact Write or fax Mr. David B. Field, Intern Coordinator. Fax: 202-588-6059. Telephone interview required. Applicants must submit a cover letter, resume. Application deadline: March 15. World Wide Web: http://www.nthp.org.

NETWORK IN SOLIDARITY WITH THE PEOPLE OF GUATEMALA
1830 Connecticut Avenue, NW
Washington, District of Columbia 20009

General Information Organization that educates North Americans to work for justice in Guatemala, to support Guatemala's grass roots movement, and to reorient U.S. policy towards Guatemala. Established in 1981. Number of employees: 3. Number of internship applications received each year: 10.
Internships Available ▶ *Human rights network interns:* responsibilities include alerting individuals, local committees, and national organizations to human rights emergencies in Guatemala, and activating network to generate faxes, telexes, and phone calls. Candidates should have ability to work independently, ability to work with others, editing skills, written communication skills. Duration is 3 months. Unpaid. Open to college sophomores, college juniors, college seniors, recent college graduates, graduate students, law students, career changers, individuals reentering the workforce. ▶ *1–3 legislative work interns:* responsibilities include monitoring U.S. government activity related to Guatemala, promoting grass roots initiatives toward a positive U.S. relationship with Guatemala. Candidates should have analytical skills, computer skills, editing skills, knowledge of field, writing skills. Duration is 1 semester. Unpaid. Open to college freshmen, college sophomores, college juniors, college seniors, recent college graduates, graduate students, career changers, individuals reentering the workforce. ▶ *1–2 solidarity update interns:* responsibilities include preparing the bulletin that provides news, action suggestions, and resources to get involved in supporting the people of Guatemala. Candidates should have analytical skills, computer skills, editing skills, organizational skills, writing skills. Duration is 1 semester. Unpaid. Open to college sophomores, college juniors, college seniors, recent college graduates, graduate students, career changers, individuals reentering the workforce. ▶ *1–2 tour interns:* responsibilities include bringing representatives of Guatemala's popular movement to speak to communities across the United States, coordinating national speaking tours, developing promotional resources, tracking and distributing material aid raised (fall only). Candidates should have knowledge of field, oral communication skills, organizational skills, written communication skills. Duration is August to November. Position available as unpaid or paid. Open to college seniors, recent college graduates, graduate students. International applications accepted.
Benefits Names of contacts, on-the-job training, opportunity to attend seminars/workshops, willing to act as a professional reference, willing to complete paperwork for educational credit, willing to provide letters of recommendation.
Contact Write, call, fax, or e-mail Amy E. Johnson, National Organizer. Phone: 202-518-7638. Fax: 202-223-8221. E-mail: nisgua@igc.apc.org. In-person interview recommended. Applicants must submit a formal organization application, resume, writing sample. Applications are accepted continuously. World Wide Web: http://www.nisgua.org.

NEW YORK COMMITTEE FOR OCCUPATIONAL SAFETY AND HEALTH
275 Seventh Avenue
New York, New York 10001

General Information Organization of labor unions and safety and health activists that provides training programs, educational materials, and technical assistance. Established in 1979. Number of employees: 9. Number of internship applications received each year: 10.

Internships Available ▶ *Interns:* responsibilities include performing duties in the areas of research, legislative work, training, and technical assistance. Candidates should have ability to work independently, computer skills, organizational skills, research skills, self-motivation, written communication skills. Unpaid. Open to college juniors, college seniors, recent college graduates, graduate students.

Benefits Job counseling, names of contacts, opportunity to attend seminars/workshops, possible full-time employment, travel reimbursement, willing to provide letters of recommendation.

Contact Write, call, fax, or e-mail Joel Shufro, Director. Phone: 212-627-3900. Fax: 212-627-9812. E-mail: nycosh@compuserve.com. In-person interview recommended. Applicants must submit a cover letter, resume, writing sample, two personal references. Applications are accepted continuously.

NICARAGUAN NETWORK EDUCATION FUND
1247 E Street, SE
Washington, District of Columbia 20003

General Information National grassroots organization whose goal is to develop ties between the peoples of the United States and Nicaragua. Established in 1979. Number of employees: 4. Program of Alliance for Global Justice, Washington, District of Columbia. Number of internship applications received each year: 30.

Internships Available ▶ *1–2 program interns:* responsibilities include responding to program requests, campaigning for labor rights, implementing organization programs, human rights advocacy work, assisting in designing educational or fund-raising programs, communicating with local grassroots affiliates/organizations; and assisting with writing research and production of monthly newsletter. Candidates should have ability to work independently, oral communication skills, personal interest in the field, self-motivation, strong interpersonal skills, written communication skills. Duration is flexible. Unpaid. Open to college sophomores, college juniors, college seniors, recent college graduates, graduate students. International applications accepted.

Benefits Formal training, job counseling, names of contacts, opportunity to attend seminars/workshops, willing to complete paperwork for educational credit, willing to provide letters of recommendation, job performance reviews provided.

Contact Write, call, fax, or e-mail Ms. Melinda St. Louis, Intern Coordinator. Phone: 202-544-9355. Fax: 202-544-9359. E-mail: nicanet@igc.org. Applicants must submit a cover letter, resume, writing sample, personal reference. Applications are accepted continuously.

NON-PROFIT HOUSING ASSOCIATION OF NORTHERN CALIFORNIA
369 Pine Street, Suite 350
San Francisco, California 94104

General Information Association of nonprofit housing developers in Northern California. Established in 1979. Number of employees: 6. Number of internship applications received each year: 10.

Internships Available ▶ *1 writer/researcher:* responsibilities include researching relevant housing issues such as child development, education, and need for affordable housing, and producing written work on the subject. Candidates should have ability to work independently, analytical skills, college courses in field, computer skills, editing skills, experience in the field, office skills, oral communication skills, plan to pursue career in field, research skills, self-motivation, strong interpersonal skills, writing skills. Duration is dependent upon availability. Position available as unpaid or at a variable stipend. Open to graduate students. International applications accepted.

Benefits Job counseling, on-the-job training, opportunity to attend seminars/workshops, possible full-time employment, travel reimbursement, willing to act as a professional reference, willing to complete paperwork for educational credit, willing to provide letters of recommendation, commuter benefit.

Contact Write Dianne J. Spaulding, Executive Director. No phone calls. In-person interview required. Applicants must submit a cover letter, resume. Applications are accepted continuously. World Wide Web: http://www.nonprofithousing.org.

NORTHEAST–MIDWEST INSTITUTE
218 D Street, SE
Washington, District of Columbia 20003

General Information Nonprofit research and public education organization that develops public policy, provides technical assistance, sponsors regional conferences, and distributes publications. Established in 1977. Number of employees: 18. Number of internship applications received each year: 25.

Internships Available ▶ *1 congressional affairs intern:* responsibilities include assisting with Capitol Hill briefings and public relations. ▶ *1 economic analysis intern:* responsibilities include gathering and analyzing economic and demographic information and assisting in the coordination of congressional briefings and events. ▶ *1 economic development intern:* responsibilities include assisting research for reuse of industrial sites, organizing forums for members of Congress, and preparing statements and case studies of noteworthy projects. ▶ *1 environmental intern:* responsibilities include researching and analyzing pollution prevention options, open technology initiatives, and best management practices for diverse industrial sectors. Candidates for all positions should have computer skills, office skills, oral communication skills, research skills, writing skills. Duration for all positions is flexible. All positions are unpaid. Open to college freshmen, college sophomores, college juniors, college seniors, recent college graduates, graduate students, law students, career changers. International applications accepted.

Benefits Names of contacts, opportunity to attend seminars/workshops, willing to provide letters of recommendation, reimbursement of local travel expenses.

Contact Write, fax, or e-mail Joanna Stover, Director of Administration. Fax: 202-544-0043. E-mail: jstover@nemw.org. No phone calls. In-person interview recommended. Applicants must submit a cover letter, resume, academic transcripts, writing sample. Applications are accepted continuously. World Wide Web: http://www.nemw.org.

NX CORPORATION
1272 Great Neck Road, Suite 220
Virginia Beach, Virginia 23454

General Information Firm engaged in export trade and international marketing and management services. Established in 1997. Number of employees: 6. Number of internship applications received each year: 300.

Internships Available ▶ *1–4 marketing assistants:* responsibilities include developing marketing plans; working on marketing techniques, product research, export trade, and management. Candidates should have computer skills, knowledge of field, oral communication skills, self-motivation, writing skills. Duration is 3 months to 1 year. Unpaid. Open to college juniors, college seniors, recent college graduates, graduate students. International applications accepted.

Benefits Formal training, job counseling, on-the-job training, opportunity to attend seminars/workshops, possible full-time employment, willing to act as a professional reference, willing to complete paperwork for educational credit, willing to provide letters of recommendation.

International Internships Available in China.

Contact Write, call, fax, or e-mail Dr. Ryan Gaskins, President and CEO, 1272 Great Neck Road, Suite 220, Virginia Beach,

NX Corporation (continued)
Virginia 23454. Phone: 757-496-4055. Fax: 757-496-4834. E-mail: rgaskins@nxcorporation.com. In-person interview recommended. Applicants must submit a cover letter, resume. Applications are accepted continuously. World Wide Web: http://www.nxcorporation.com.

OHIO LEGISLATIVE SERVICE COMMISSION
77 South High Street, Ninth Floor
Columbus, Ohio 43215

General Information Research and service agency providing wide variety of legal and administrative services to the Ohio legislative branch of state government. Number of employees: 135. Number of internship applications received each year: 250.
Internships Available ▶ *22 legislative intern:* responsibilities include legislative and administrative support to members of the Ohio General Assembly. Candidates should have analytical skills, oral communication skills, self-motivation, strong interpersonal skills, written communication skills. Duration is 13 months-December 1 to December 31 the following year. Open to recent college graduates, graduate students, law students. ▶ *2 legislative telecommunications internship:* responsibilities include assisting in production of televised sessions, committee hearings, and educational productions of the Ohio General Assembly. Candidates should have ability to work independently, knowledge of field, oral communication skills, strong interpersonal skills, written communication skills. Duration is 13 months-December 1 to December 31 of the following year. Open to recent college graduates, graduate students. All positions paid at $21,500–$23,500 per year.
Benefits Formal training, health insurance, on-the-job training, opportunity to attend seminars/workshops, possible full-time employment.
Contact Write or call Melissa Dangaran, Intern Program Administrator, 77 South High Street, Ninth Floor, Columbus, Ohio 43215. Phone: 614-466-3615. In-person interview required. Applicants must submit a formal organization application, resume, academic transcripts, writing sample, three letters of recommendation. Application deadline: April 15 for legislative interns, May 31 for legislative telecommunications interns.

PEOPLE TO PEOPLE INTERNATIONAL
501 East Armour Boulevard
Kansas City, Missouri 64109

General Information Nonprofit organization that specializes in cultural and educational exchanges; destination availability varies from year to year. Established in 1956. Number of employees: 15. Number of internship applications received each year: 50.
Internships Available ▶ *Interns:* responsibilities include working in virtually any field; positions available in Australia, United Kingom, Italy, Denmark, Ireland, Kenya, Argentina, South Africa, Germany, and Russia. Candidates should have ability to work independently, knowledge of field, organizational skills, self-motivation, strong interpersonal skills, flexibility, $1,875 tuition. Duration is 2 months. Unpaid. Open to college juniors, college seniors, recent college graduates, graduate students, law students. International applications accepted.
Benefits Health insurance, housing at a cost, willing to complete paperwork for educational credit.
International Internships Available in Argentina; Australia; Denmark; Germany; Ireland; Italy; Kenya; Russian Federation; South Africa; United Kingdom.
Contact Write, call, fax, or e-mail Ines Dahne-Steuber, Internship Coordinator. Phone: 816-531-4701. Fax: 816-561-7502. E-mail: internships@ptpi.org. Telephone interview required. Applicants must submit a formal organization application, cover letter, resume, academic transcripts, letter of recommendation. Application deadline: 3 months prior to internship. World Wide Web: http://www.ptpi.org.

PUBLIC FORUM INSTITUTE
1215 17th Street, NW
Washington, District of Columbia 20036

General Information Nonpartisan, independent public policy group specializing in the development of public forums to debate major issues on the national agenda and maintaining a strong emphasis on social security and budget issues, trade, energy, and economic policy. Established in 1978. Number of employees: 14. Number of internship applications received each year: 200.

Internships Available ▶ *2 congressional policy forum interns:* responsibilities include researching speakers issued for policy forums, attending congressional hearings, and working on survey reports. Duration is flexible. Unpaid. ▶ *1–2 media associates:* responsibilities include reporting to communication director, writing press/reporter research, press conferences, pitching position development, public policy editorial development. Candidates should have computer skills, plan to pursue career in field, self-motivation, strong interpersonal skills, written communication skills. Duration is 2–3 months. Unpaid. Open to high school students, high school seniors, recent high school graduates, college freshmen, college sophomores, college juniors, college seniors, recent college graduates, graduate students, law students, career changers, individuals reentering the workforce. ▶ *1–2 public affairs associates:* responsibilities include working with Senior Vice President for Business Development; proposal writing, team presentations, corporate research, and new ideas creation. Candidates should have oral communication skills, plan to pursue career in field, self-motivation, strong interpersonal skills, written communication skills. Duration is 1–3 months. Position available as unpaid or at $1,000 per month. Open to high school students, high school seniors, recent high school graduates, college freshmen, college sophomores, college juniors, college seniors, recent college graduates, graduate students, career changers, business school students. ▶ *4 summer associates:* responsibilities include joining a team of 3 professional staff and being fully integrated into the activities of that team; working primarily on national public policy summits. Candidates should have ability to work independently, computer skills, organizational skills, personal interest in the field, self-motivation, strong interpersonal skills. Unpaid. Open to college freshmen, college sophomores, college juniors, college seniors, individuals reentering the workforce. ▶ *2–3 summer project associates:* responsibilities include public policy event planning for congressional summits on topical issues; grassroots public relations and outreach work (no phone answering/mail handling). Candidates should have computer skills, oral communication skills, organizational skills, self-motivation, strong interpersonal skills. Duration is 2–3 months. Unpaid. Open to high school students, high school seniors, recent high school graduates, college freshmen, college sophomores, college juniors. ▶ *1 technology associate:* responsibilities include teaching technological skills to technology savvy people looking to broaden their skills. Candidates should have ability to work independently, computer skills, experience in the field, self-motivation. Duration is 1–4 months. Unpaid. Open to high school students, high school seniors, recent high school graduates, college freshmen, college sophomores, college juniors, college seniors, recent college graduates, graduate students, law students, career changers, individuals reentering the workforce. International applications accepted.

Benefits Names of contacts, on-the-job training, opportunity to attend seminars/workshops, possible full-time employment, willing to act as a professional reference, willing to complete paperwork for educational credit, willing to provide letters of recommendation.

Contact Write, call, fax, or e-mail Anne Neel, Vice President. Phone: 202-467-2774. Fax: 202-547-1893. E-mail: anne@publicforuminstitute.com. In-person interview recommended. Applicants must submit a formal organization application, cover letter, two personal references. Applications are accepted continuously. World Wide Web: http://www.publicforuminstitute.com.

QUAKER UNITED NATIONS OFFICE
777 United Nations Plaza, 5th Floor
New York, New York 10017

General Information Organization that represents the world body of the Religious Society of Friends (Quakers) at the United Nations. Established in 1948. Number of employees: 4. Number of internship applications received each year: 65.

Internships Available ► *2 QUNO interns:* responsibilities include providing program and administrative office support for staff by following the schedule of meetings and stream of documents around the activities of the General Assembly; monitoring, researching, and interpreting one or more substantial issues of interest to intern and QUNO; and assisting with office tasks, such as mailings, filing, phones, and assisting visitors. Candidates should have college courses in field, office skills, oral communication skills, organizational skills, personal interest in the field, writing skills. Duration is 1 year. $14,500 per year. Open to recent college graduates. International applications accepted.

Benefits Health insurance, opportunity to attend seminars/workshops, travel reimbursement, willing to act as a professional reference, willing to provide letters of recommendation, 12 days vacation.

Contact Write, call, fax, or e-mail David Jackman, Associate Representative. Phone: 212-682-2745. Fax: 212-983-0034. E-mail: qunony@pipeline.com. In-person interview recommended. Applicants must submit a formal organization application, cover letter, resume, writing sample, four letters of recommendation. Application deadline: February 11. World Wide Web: http://www.afsc.org/quno.htm.

RADIO FREE EUROPE/RADIO LIBERTY FUND
1201 Connecticut Avenue, NW
Washington, District of Columbia 20036

General Information Independent news and information broadcasting corporation whose goal is to encourage a constructive dialogue with the peoples of Eastern Europe and the former Soviet Union by enhancing their knowledge of development in the world at large and in their own countries. Established in 1976. Number of internship applications received each year: 100.

Internships Available ► *5–6 broadcast journalism interns:* responsibilities include reporting and writing. Candidates should have journalism experience. Duration is 10 weeks. Position available as unpaid or paid. Open to recent college graduates, graduate students.

Benefits Willing to complete paperwork for educational credit, housing with kitchen provided, per diem travel arrangements, daily stipend.

International Internships Available in Prague, Czech Republic.

Contact Write or call RFE/RL, Inc. Attn: Intern Program. Phone: 202-457-6900. Applicants must submit a formal organization application, cover letter, resume, two writing samples, audio or visual samples as needed. Application deadline: November 1. World Wide Web: http://www.rferl.org.

REPORTERS COMMITTEE FOR FREEDOM OF THE PRESS
1815 North Fort Myer Drive, Suite 900
Arlington, Virginia 22209

General Information Organization that helps reporters around the country gather and cover the news and advises them about First Amendment and freedom of information rights. Established in 1970. Number of employees: 9. Number of internship applications received each year: 75.

Internships Available ► *1 broadcast intern:* responsibilities include covering media law issues that affect broadcasters such as cameras in courtrooms. Part-time applicants will be considered. Duration is 1 semester. ► *1 press at home/press abroad intern:* responsibilities include assisting in editing publications, covering legal issues that involve journalists but do not fall within traditional media law categories, and covering legal problems encountered by American journalists abroad. Duration is flexible. Open to college juniors, college seniors, recent college gradu-

ates, graduate students, law students, career changers. Candidates for all positions should have editing skills, personal interest in the field, self-motivation, strong interpersonal skills, writing skills. All positions are unpaid. International applications accepted.

Benefits Formal training, on-the-job training, opportunity to attend seminars/workshops, willing to act as a professional reference, willing to complete paperwork for educational credit, willing to provide letters of recommendation, stipend available.

Contact Write, call, or e-mail Ms. Rebecca Daugherty, Internship Coordinator, 1815 North Fort Meyer Drive, Suite 900, Arlington, Virginia 22209. Phone: 703-807-2100. E-mail: rcfp@rcfp.org. Applicants must submit a cover letter, resume, writing sample. Application deadline: January 31 for summer, March 31 for fall, October 31 for winter/spring.

ROBERT BOSCH FOUNDATION FELLOWSHIP PROGRAM, CDS INTERNATIONAL, INC.
871 United Nations Plaza, 15th Floor
New York, New York 10017

General Information Fellowship program in Germany for American citizens in the following fields: business, economics, journalism, law, mass communications, political science, and public affairs/public policy. Established in 1968. Number of employees: 18. Number of internship applications received each year: 130.

Internships Available ► *20 executive level interns:* responsibilities include performing various duties dependent upon field of specialization. Candidates should have ability to work independently, analytical skills, experience in the field, oral communication skills, personal interest in the field, strong leadership ability. Duration is 9 months. stipend of DM 3500 per month. Open to recent college graduates, graduate students, law students.

Benefits Health insurance, opportunity to attend seminars/workshops, travel reimbursement, German language training.

International Internships Available in Germany.

Contact Write, call, fax, or e-mail Ms. Elfriede Andros, Program Officer. Phone: 212-497-3500. Fax: 212-497-3535. E-mail: eandros@cdsintl.org. In-person interview required. Applicants must submit a formal organization application, resume, academic transcripts, two letters of recommendation, statement of purpose. Application deadline: October 15 for September the following year. World Wide Web: http://www.cdsintl.org.

SAN FRANCISCO CHAMBER OF COMMERCE
465 California Street, 9th Floor
San Francisco, California 94104

General Information Nonprofit membership organization that seeks to attract, develop, and retain business in San Francisco and provide programs for its members and the business community. Established in 1911. Number of employees: 49. Number of internship applications received each year: 100.

Internships Available ► *Human resources department interns:* responsibilities include assisting in the personnel, training, and administration work of the human resources department. Candidates should have computer skills, office skills, oral communication skills, organizational skills, strong interpersonal skills, familiarity with Microsoft Office applications. Open to college seniors, recent college graduates, graduate students, career changers. ► *3 international interns:* responsibilities include assisting with market research inquiries and special projects. Candidates should have ability to work independently, ability to work with others, computer skills, office skills, oral communication skills, writing skills. Open to college juniors, college seniors, recent college graduates, graduate students, law students, career changers. ► *1 journalism intern:* responsibilities include writing for newsletters (writing assignments vary depending on skill), proofreading all publications, and researching for various publications. Candidates should have computer skills, editing skills, oral communication skills, research skills, writing skills. ► *1–2 programs/general business interns:* responsibilities include assisting with development and implementation of programs including research, correspondence, data, and information management. Candidates should have ability to work with oth-

San Francisco Chamber of Commerce (continued)

ers, computer skills, office skills, organizational skills, writing skills. Open to college juniors, college seniors, recent college graduates, graduate students, law students, career changers. ▶ *2 special events interns:* responsibilities include assisting with event organization. Candidates should have ability to work with others, computer skills, office skills, oral communication skills, writing skills. Open to college juniors, college seniors, recent college graduates, graduate students, law students, career changers. Duration for all positions is flexible. All positions are unpaid. International applications accepted.

Benefits Job counseling, names of contacts, opportunity to attend seminars/workshops, possible full-time employment, willing to complete paperwork for educational credit, willing to provide letters of recommendation, networking opportunities.

Contact Write Ms. Rhonda Scott, Human Resources/Facilities Manager. No phone calls. In-person interview required. Applicants must submit a cover letter, resume. Applications are accepted continuously. World Wide Web: http://www.sfchamber.com.

SEARCH FOR COMMON GROUND
1601 Connecticut Avenue, NW, Suite 200
Washington, District of Columbia 20009

General Information Nonprofit organization that specializes in domestic and international conflict resolution. Established in 1982. Number of employees: 35.

Internships Available ▶ *Interns:* responsibilities include planning conferences; making travel arrangments; administrative support; and researching, writing, editing, and proofreading on any of the following projects: Search for Common Ground in Macedonia, Burundi, Angola, or Middle East; Ukranian Mediation Group; Initiative for Peace and Cooperation in the Middle East; Islamic Western Dialogue and Cooperation Program; Commond Ground Network for Life and Choice; Search for Common Ground on Race; Common Ground Productions (radio and television production); and Bulletin for Regional Cooperation in the Middle East (newsletter). Candidates should have editing skills, office skills, oral communication skills, organizational skills, personal interest in the field, research skills, self-motivation, strong interpersonal skills, strong leadership ability, writing skills, experience living in a mentioned international area or speaking its language is helpful. Duration is generally 3-4 months, but possibly longer. Unpaid. Open to college freshmen, college sophomores, college juniors, college seniors, recent college graduates, graduate students, career changers. International applications accepted.

Benefits Names of contacts, opportunity to attend seminars/workshops, possible full-time employment, willing to complete paperwork for educational credit, willing to provide letters of recommendation.

Contact Write, call, or e-mail Susan Koscis, Vice President of Operations, 1601 Connecticut Avenue, NW Suite 200, Washington, District of Columbia 20009. Phone: 202-265-4300. E-mail: search@sfcg.org. In-person interview recommended. Applicants must submit a cover letter, resume. Applications are accepted continuously.

SOCIETY FOR INTERNATIONAL DEVELOPMENT–WASHINGTON CHAPTER
1875 Connecticut Avenue, NW, Suite 720
Washington, District of Columbia 20009-5728

General Information Nonpolitical, nonprofit membership organization with over 75 chapters around the world providing ways in which those interested in development can exchange ideas, information, and experience with others. Established in 1957. Number of employees: 5. Unit of Society for International Development International, Rome, Italy. Number of internship applications received each year: 200.

Internships Available ▶ *2–4 interns:* responsibilities include writing for newsletter, serving as liaison with SID work groups, organizing program and events, attending informational and educational programs, promoting SID among prospective members, and assisting with general office duties. Duration is 1 semester.

Unpaid. Open to college juniors, college seniors, recent college graduates, graduate students. International applications accepted.

Benefits Names of contacts, opportunity to attend seminars/workshops, willing to complete paperwork for educational credit, willing to provide letters of recommendation.

Contact Write, call, fax, or e-mail Andrea S. Camoens, Executive Director. Phone: 202-884-8590. Fax: 202-884-8499. E-mail: sid@aed.org. In-person interview recommended. Applicants must submit a resume, writing sample, three personal references. Applications are accepted continuously.

SPORTING GOODS MANUFACTURERS ASSOCIATION
1625 K Street, NW, Suite 900
Washington, District of Columbia 20006

General Information Trade association that promotes sports participation for all people and fosters sports products industry growth. Established in 1906. Number of employees: 3. Number of internship applications received each year: 15.

Internships Available ▶ *1 intern:* responsibilities include performing legislative research, attending Congressional hearings, handling oral and written public inquiries, and event planning. Candidates should have ability to work independently, ability to work with others, computer skills, knowledge of field, office skills, oral communication skills, writing skills. Duration is 3–5 months. $5 per hour. Open to college juniors, college seniors. International applications accepted.

Benefits Opportunity to attend seminars/workshops, travel reimbursement, willing to complete paperwork for educational credit, willing to provide letters of recommendation.

Contact Write or fax Thomas Cove, Vice President. Fax: 202-296-7462. No phone calls. In-person interview required. Applicants must submit a cover letter, resume. Applications are accepted continuously. World Wide Web: http://www.sportlink.com.

UNITED NATIONS ASSOCIATION OF THE USA
801 2nd Avenue
New York, New York 10017

General Information Nonprofit, nonpartisan, national organization dedicated to strengthening the United Nations system and to enhancing U.S. participation in the United Nations and other international institutions. Established in 1964. Number of employees: 55. Number of internship applications received each year: 350.

Internships Available ▶ *1 Council of Organizations intern:* responsibilities include assisting the liaison of the UNAUSA and performing research. Candidates should have computer skills, office skills, organizational skills, clerical skills. Unpaid. Open to college freshmen, college sophomores, college juniors, college seniors. ▶ *2 Division for Corporate Affairs interns:* responsibilities include writing, researching, and compiling information on United Nations purchasing activities and United Nations agency mandates. Unpaid. Open to college juniors, college seniors, recent college graduates, graduate students, law students. ▶ *6 Model UN interns:* responsibilities include researching the global issues and the work of the United Nations and adapting this information for use by the public, collecting materials for distribution to chapters, preparing responses to public inquiries, or assisting with outreach programs, researching and writing background papers about international issues, and assisting with the development of international affairs-related programs for youth. Candidates should have editing skills, oral communication skills, research skills, strong leadership ability, writing skills. Unpaid. Open to high school students, high school seniors, recent high school graduates, college freshmen, college sophomores, college juniors, college seniors, recent college graduates, graduate students. ▶ *3 communication department interns:* responsibilities include working with media relations and public affairs. Candidates should have computer skills, editing skills, oral communication skills, research skills, strong interpersonal skills, writing skills. Unpaid. Open to college seniors, recent college graduates, graduate students. ▶ *1 development intern.* Candidates should have computer

skills, office skills, research skills, clerical skills. Unpaid. Open to college freshmen, college sophomores, college juniors, college seniors. ▶ *4 policy studies department interns:* responsibilities include researching and writing for one of four policy studies programs. Candidates should have computer skills, editing skills, oral communication skills, research skills, writing skills. Position available as unpaid or paid. Open to college seniors, recent college graduates, graduate students, law students. Duration for all positions is flexible. International applications accepted.
Benefits Job counseling, names of contacts, opportunity to attend seminars/workshops, possible full-time employment, willing to complete paperwork for educational credit, willing to provide letters of recommendation.
International Internships Available.
Contact Write, call, or e-mail Mr. John Gagain, Intern Coordinator. Phone: 212-697-3232. E-mail: modelun@unausa.org. Applicants must submit a formal organization application, cover letter, resume, two writing samples. Application deadline: March 15 for summer, July 15 for fall, November 15 for spring. World Wide Web: http://www.unausa.org.

UNIVERSITY OF MARYLAND/CENTER FOR INTERNATIONAL DEVELOPMENT AND CONFLICT MANAGEMENT
Room 0145, Tydings Hall
College Park, Maryland 20742-7231

General Information Research center and think tank focusing on issues of ethnopolitical conflict, conflict management, and development of a broadly democratic political culture. Established in 1982. Number of employees: 20. Unit of University of Maryland University College, College Park, Maryland. Number of internship applications received each year: 15.
Internships Available ▶ *4–8 research assistants:* responsibilities include identification and/or mapping of minority groups and international organizations worldwide; tracking and analyzing international and intranational events from on-line sources; Web site development; or working on minorities-at-risk, conflict management, the Bahai Chair, or other special projects. Candidates should have analytical skills, oral communication skills, personal interest in the field, research skills, self-motivation, written communication skills. Duration is 2–12 months. Unpaid. Open to college juniors, college seniors, recent college graduates, graduate students, career changers. International applications accepted.
Benefits Names of contacts, on-the-job training, opportunity to attend seminars/workshops, willing to complete paperwork for educational credit, willing to provide letters of recommendation.
Contact Call, fax, or e-mail Dr. John Davies, Research Coordinator. Phone: 301-314-7709. Fax: 301-314-9256. E-mail: jdavies@cidcm1.umd.edu. Telephone interview required. Applicants must submit a cover letter, resume. Applications are accepted continuously. World Wide Web: http://www.bsos.umd.edu/cidcm.

UNREPRESENTED NATIONS AND PEOPLES ORGANIZATION AMERICAS COORDINATION OFFICE
444 North Capitol Street, NW, Suite 846
Washington, District of Columbia 20001-1570

General Information An international human rights organization serving as a forum for occupied nations, indigenous peoples, minorities, and oppressed majorities. Established in 1991. Number of employees: 1. Unit of Secretariat, The Hague, Netherlands. Number of internship applications received each year: 50.
Internships Available ▶ *1–5 interns:* responsibilities include working closely with director to maintain continuity of operations and relations and correspondence with the public. Candidates should have ability to work independently, office skills, organizational skills, personal interest in the field, strong interpersonal skills, written communication skills. Duration is flexible. Unpaid. Open to college freshmen, college sophomores, college juniors, college seniors, recent college graduates. International applications accepted.

Benefits Formal training, job counseling, names of contacts, willing to complete paperwork for educational credit, willing to provide letters of recommendation, experience in nonprofit administration and management, networking opportunities.
International Internships Available in The Hague, Netherlands.
Contact Write, call, fax, or e-mail Karen E. Onthank, Executive Director. Phone: 202-637-0475. Fax: 202-637-0585. E-mail: unposf@igc.apc.org. In-person interview recommended. Applicants must submit a cover letter, resume, writing sample, three personal references. Applications are accepted continuously. World Wide Web: http://www.unpo.org.

U.S.-AFRICA FREE ENTERPRISE EDUCATION FOUNDATION
400 North Tampa Street, Suite 1120
Tampa, Florida 33602

General Information Nonprofit education organization. Established in 1996. Number of employees: 4. Number of internship applications received each year: 25.
Internships Available ▶ *1–3 U.S.-Africa research assistants:* responsibilities include assisting foundation staff with a wide variety of projects relating to Africa, performing research, office duties, assisting with organizing conferences and seminars. Candidates should have office skills, personal interest in the field, research skills, strong interpersonal skills, strong leadership ability. Duration is 10-15 hours per week. Unpaid. Open to college seniors.
Benefits Formal training, names of contacts, opportunity to attend seminars/workshops, willing to act as a professional reference, willing to complete paperwork for educational credit, willing to provide letters of recommendation.
Contact Write, call, fax, or e-mail Nischal H. Patel, Director, Research and Community Outreach, 400 North Tampa Street, Suite 1120, Tampa, Florida 33602. Phone: 813-301-8723. Fax: 813-301-9301. E-mail: npatel@usafrica.com. In-person interview required. Applicants must submit a formal organization application, cover letter, resume, two writing samples, two personal references, two letters of recommendation. Applications are accepted continuously. World Wide Web: http://www.usafrica.com.

US/ICOMOS (INTERNATIONAL COUNCIL ON MONUMENTS AND SITES)
401 F Street, NW, Room 331
Washington, District of Columbia 20001-2728

General Information International nongovernmental organization composed of 90 national committees and 15 international specialized committees which form a worldwide alliance for the preservation and protection of historic buildings, districts, and sites. Established in 1965.
Internships Available ▶ *International summer interns:* responsibilities include learning about preservation policies, methods and techniques; internships are located abroad in countries such as: Australia, France, Ghana, Great Britain, Jordan, Lithuania, Poland, Russia, Slovak Republic, Turkey, Chile, Croatia, and Romania (varies year to year). Candidates should have knowledge of field, personal interest in the field, language ability (preferred but not necessary for all positions), college degree in history, archaeology, architecture, historic conservation, or a related field. Duration is 12 weeks (June through August). a variable stipend. Open to graduate students, professionals 22-35 years old with a background in historic preservation/conservation. International applications accepted.
Benefits Travel reimbursement, travel grants.
International Internships Available.
Contact Write, call, fax, or e-mail Ellen Delage, Program Director. Phone: 202-842-1862. Fax: 202-842-1861. E-mail: edelage@usicomos.org. Applicants must submit a formal organization application, resume, two letters of recommendation, examples of work, 500-word essay describing the reasons for wanting to participate in the program. Application deadline: February 15. World Wide Web: http://www.icomos.org/usicomos.

U.S. OLYMPIC COMMITTEE
One Olympic Plaza
Colorado Springs, Colorado 80909-5760

General Information Nonprofit sports organization promoting sports in the U.S. and sending teams to the Olympics. Established in 1978. Number of employees: 500. Number of internship applications received each year: 750.
Internships Available ▶ *25 Colorado Spring, Colorado interns:* responsibilities include working in broadcasting, sports administration, sport science, accounting, journalism and public relations, computer science, or marketing department. Candidates should have ability to work independently, college courses in field, computer skills, knowledge of field, plan to pursue career in field, written communication skills. Duration is 1 semester. ▶ *5 Lake Pacid, New York interns:* responsibilities include performing duties related to the chosen area of interest. Candidates should have ability to work independently, college courses in field, computer skills, knowledge of field, plan to pursue career in field, written communication skills. ▶ *3 Lake Placid, New York interns:* responsibilities include working in sports administration or sport science department. Candidates should have ability to work independently, college courses in field, computer skills, oral communication skills, plan to pursue career in field, written communication skills. Duration is 1 semester. ▶ *3 San Diego, California interns:* responsibilities include administrative duties or sport science activities. Candidates should have ability to work independently, college courses in field, computer skills, knowledge of field, plan to pursue career in field, written communication skills. Duration is 1 semester. All positions paid at housing, meals, and pay combined equal minimum wage. Open to college juniors, college seniors, graduate students.
Benefits On-the-job training, opportunity to attend seminars/workshops, possible full-time employment, willing to act as a professional reference, willing to complete paperwork for educational credit.
Contact Write, call, fax, or e-mail Manager of Intern Program. Phone: 719-632-5551 Ext. 2597. Fax: 719-578-4817. E-mail: internprog@usoc.org. Telephone interview required. Applicants must submit a formal organization application, cover letter, resume, academic transcripts, six writing samples for journalism positions. Application deadline: February 15 for summer, June 1 for fall, October 1 for winter/spring. World Wide Web: http://www.olympic-usa.org.

U.S. TERM LIMITS
1125 15th Street, #501
Washington, District of Columbia 20005

General Information Non-partisan issue advocacy organization. Established in 1992. Number of employees: 15. Number of internship applications received each year: 30.
Internships Available ▶ *4–5 interns.* Paid. International applications accepted.
Benefits On-the-job training, opportunity to attend seminars/workshops, willing to act as a professional reference, willing to complete paperwork for educational credit, willing to provide letters of recommendation.
Contact Write, call, fax, or e-mail Dave Mohel, Director of Congressional Affairs, 1125 15th Street, NW, Suite # 501, Washington, District of Columbia 20005. Phone: 800-733-6440. Fax: 202-463-3210. E-mail: resume@ustermlimits.org. Applicants must submit a cover letter, resume. Applications are accepted continuously. World Wide Web: http://www.ustermlimits.org.

US-UKRAINE FOUNDATION
733 15th Street, NW, Suite 1026
Washington, District of Columbia 20005

General Information Nonprofit non-governmental organization, established to facilitate democratic development free market reform, and to enhance human rights in Ukraine. Established in 1991. Number of employees: 13. Number of internship applications received each year: 40.
Internships Available ▶ *1 intern:* responsibilities include reporting on congressional hearings and other events, Web site maintenance, office management, and program support. Other responsibilities depend upon interests and skills of intern. Candidates should have ability to work with others, computer skills, office skills, personal interest in the field, self-motivation, written communication skills. Duration is flexible (usually one summer or one semester). Unpaid. Open to college freshmen, college sophomores, college juniors, college seniors, recent college graduates, graduate students. International applications accepted.
Benefits On-the-job training, opportunity to attend seminars/workshops, willing to act as a professional reference, willing to complete paperwork for educational credit, willing to provide letters of recommendation.
Contact Write, fax, or e-mail Keren Mandell or Sarah Potts, Program Assistants, 733 15th Street, NW, Suite 1026, Washington, District of Columbia 20005. Fax: 202-347-4267. E-mail: usuf@usukraine.org. In-person interview recommended. Applicants must submit a cover letter, resume. Applications are accepted continuously. World Wide Web: http://www.usukraine.org.

VISIONS IN ACTION
2710 Ontario Road, NW
Washington, District of Columbia 20009

General Information Nonprofit organization that places volunteers with other nonprofit organizations, development organizations, research institutes, health centers, and the progressive press in the countries of Uganda, Tanzania, South Africa, Zimbabwe, Burkina Faso and Mexico. Established in 1988. Number of employees: 14. Number of internship applications received each year: 100.
Internships Available ▶ *20–30 U.S. office interns:* responsibilities include working in areas of recruitment, international administraton, public relations, finance, fund-raising, research, Internet, newsletter, or conference organizing. Candidates should have computer skills, office skills, oral communication skills, organizational skills, research skills, written communication skills. Duration is 3 months. Open to college freshmen, college sophomores, college juniors, college seniors, recent college graduates, graduate students, law students, career changers, individuals reentering the workforce. ▶ *50–100 community development workers:* responsibilities include working with communities in low-income areas. Candidates should have oral communication skills, organizational skills, personal interest in the field, strong interpersonal skills, written communication skills. Duration is 6–12 months. Open to college juniors, college seniors, recent college graduates, graduate students, law students, career changers. ▶ *10–20 democratization trainers/election monitors:* responsibilities include training voters on their rights and voting procedures, monitoring elections, leading voting workshops, and observing ballot counting. Candidates should have ability to work with others, analytical skills, oral communication skills, organizational skills, personal interest in the field, strong interpersonal skills. Duration is 6–12 months. Open to college juniors, college seniors, recent college graduates, graduate students, law students, career changers. ▶ *30–60 health professionals:* responsibilities include working in a clinic, lab, or hospital. Candidates should have analytical skills, knowledge of field, personal interest in the field, strong interpersonal skills. Duration is 6–12 months. Open to college juniors, college seniors, recent college graduates, graduate students, law students, career changers. ▶ *30–60 journalists:* responsibilities include working for a newspaper, magazine, or radio/television station. Candidates should have ability to work independently, knowledge of field, oral communication skills, research skills, writing skills. Duration is 6–12 months. Open to college juniors, college seniors, recent college graduates, graduate students, law students, career changers. ▶ *50–100 program assistants:* responsibilities include writing, research, administration and organizing office-based assistance in areas of human rights, environment, children, women, housing, social work, or democratization. Candidates should have ability to work with others, computer skills, office skills, oral communication skills, personal interest in the field,

written communication skills. Duration is 6–12 months. Open to college juniors, college seniors, recent college graduates, graduate students, law students, career changers. ▶ *40–80 project managers:* responsibilities include managing rural and urban development projects. Candidates should have knowledge of field, oral communication skills, organizational skills, strong leadership ability, written communication skills. Duration is 6–12 months. Open to college juniors, college seniors, recent college graduates, graduate students, law students, career changers. ▶ *40–80 public health educators:* responsibilities include performing research, educating, and designing communication material. Candidates should have office skills, oral communication skills, personal interest in the field, strong interpersonal skills, written communication skills. Duration is 6–12 months. Open to college juniors, college seniors, recent college graduates, graduate students, law students, career changers. ▶ *40–80 researchers:* responsibilities include assisting with research in either a natural or social science discipline. Candidates should have analytical skills, computer skills, office skills, research skills, writing skills. Duration is 6–12 months. Open to college juniors, college seniors, recent college graduates, graduate students, law students, career changers. ▶ *30–60 youth group coordinators:* responsibilities include leading community service projects, sports, and vocational training. Candidates should have ability to work with others, oral communication skills, organizational skills, personal interest in the field, self-motivation, strong leadership ability. Duration is 6–12 months. Open to college juniors, college seniors, recent college graduates, graduate students, law students, career changers. All positions are unpaid. International applications accepted.
Benefits Formal training, job counseling, names of contacts, on-the-job training, opportunity to attend seminars/workshops, possible full-time employment, willing to act as a professional reference, willing to complete paperwork for educational credit, willing to provide letters of recommendation, small monthly stipend of $50-$100.
International Internships Available in Burkina Faso; Mexico; South Africa; Uganda; United Republic of Tanzania; Zimbabwe.
Contact Write, call, fax, or e-mail Dr. Shaun Skelton, Director. Phone: 202-625-7402. Fax: 202-625-2353. E-mail: visions@igc.apc. org. Telephone interview required. Applicants must submit a formal organization application, resume, two letters of recommendation. Application deadline: April 10 for July 10th departure, June 1 for September 1st departure, July 1 for October 1st departure, October 10 for January 10th departure. Fees: $45. World Wide Web: http://www.visionsinaction.org.

VOLUNTEERS IN ASIA
PO Box 4543
Stanford, California 94309

General Information Private, nonprofit, nonsectarian organization dedicated to increasing understanding between the United States and Asia. Established in 1963. Number of employees: 10. Number of internship applications received each year: 40.
Internships Available ▶ *2–4 volunteer English resource in Indonesia:* responsibilities include assisting non-government organization, editing brochures and periodicals in English, providing English language support to the organization. Candidates should have experience in the field, personal interest in the field. Duration is 2 years. ▶ *20–30 volunteer English teachers in Asia:* responsibilities include English language instruction at tertiary level. Candidates should have at least one course in language of host country, ESL training. Duration is 1–2 years. All positions paid at living stipend. Open to college seniors, recent college graduates, career changers, individuals with bachelor's degree. International applications accepted.
Benefits Formal training, health insurance, possible full-time employment, willing to provide letters of recommendation, scholarships to cover participation fee, transportation to host country, stipend to cover cost of living including room and board.
International Internships Available in China; Indonesia; Lao People's Democratic Republic; Viet Nam.

Contact Write, call, fax, or e-mail Kim Yap, Program Director. Phone: 650-723-3228. Fax: 650-725-1805. E-mail: volasia@volasia. org. In-person interview required. Applicants must submit a formal organization application, participation fee upon acceptance of $1350 for 1 year, $950 for 2 years, participation in training program March-May (4 weekends) in San Francisco. Application deadline: early February. World Wide Web: http://www. volasia.org.

WALLED LAKE DOWNTOWN DEVELOPMENT AUTHORITY
500 North Pontiac Trail, Suite B
Walled Lake, Michigan 48390

General Information Partnership between the city of Walled Lake and businesses in the downtown district. It is in charge of marketing the downtown, recruiting new businesses, and retaining the community's current businesses.
Internships Available ▶ *1 intern:* responsibilities include a wide variety of tasks including special events planning, attending trade shows, photography, database management, public service, and marketing. Duration is flexible. Unpaid. Open to college juniors, college seniors.
Contact Write, call, fax, or e-mail Tracy White, Director, 500 North Pontiac Trail, Suite 8, Walled Lake, Michigan 48390. Phone: 248-926-9004. Fax: 248-926-9029. E-mail: wldda@flash. net. Applicants must submit a cover letter, resume, three personal references. Applications are accepted continuously. World Wide Web: http://www.walledlake.com.

THE WINANT AND CLAYTON VOLUNTEERS, INC.
109 East 50th Street
New York, New York 10022

General Information International reciprocal exchange program between the U.S. and the U.K. Established in 1948. Number of internship applications received each year: 75.
Internships Available ▶ *20 volunteers:* responsibilities include working in youth clubs, centers for the homeless, rehabilitation and drug-crisis centers, and programs for the elderly. Duration is 9 weeks. Unpaid. Open to U.S. citizens 18 or older.
Benefits Free housing, 2 weeks independent travel, opportunity to see United Kingdom and live and work in another culture, small stipend available (paid in pounds). Applicant is responsible for airfare.
International Internships Available in United Kingdom.
Contact Write, call, or fax Ms. Nanette Rousseau, Coordinator of Volunteers. Phone: 212-378-0271. Fax: 212-378-0281. Applicants must submit a formal organization application, cover letter, resume. Application deadline: January 31. Fees: $35. World Wide Web: http://www.voicenet.com/~mjmcc/.

WOMEN'S CAMPAIGN FUND
734 15th Street, Suite 500
Washington, District of Columbia 20005

General Information Political action committee. Established in 1974. Number of employees: 6.
Internships Available ▶ *1 communications intern:* responsibilities include political research and writing, developing and updating the Web page, writing press releases, and providing follow-up to media contacts. Candidates should have computer skills, office skills, plan to pursue career in field, research skills, self-motivation, written communication skills. ▶ *1 development intern:* responsibilities include assisting development director with all aspects of fund-raising, including event planning and high donor solicitation, maintaining and updating contributor lists and databases, and processing of direct mail campaign and contributions. Candidates should have computer skills, knowledge of field, office skills, personal interest in the field, strong interpersonal skills, written communication skills. ▶ *1 political intern:* responsibilities include political research and tracking, event planning, list development for candidate fund-raising activities, and providing administrative support. Candidates should have ability to work independently, ability to work with others,

Women's Campaign Fund (continued)
office skills, personal interest in the field, writing skills. Duration for all positions is 3 months. All positions paid at $6 per hour. Open to college freshmen, college sophomores, college juniors, college seniors, recent college graduates. International applications accepted.
Benefits On-the-job training, willing to provide letters of recommendation.
Contact Write, call, fax, or e-mail Angela A. Morris, Intern Coordinator, 734 15th Street, Suite 500, Washington, District of Columbia 20005. Phone: 202-393-8164. Fax: 202-393-0649. E-mail: womenscampaignfund@erols.com. In-person interview recommended. Applicants must submit a cover letter, resume. Applications are accepted continuously.

WOMEN'S INSTITUTE FOR FREEDOM OF THE PRESS
3306 Ross Place, NW
Washington, District of Columbia 20008-3332

General Information Institute dedicated to researching and publishing new ideas and perspectives on expanding the communications system to make it more democratic, especially to increase the communication of women with each other and with the general public. Established in 1972. Number of employees: 2. Number of internship applications received each year: 20.
Internships Available ▶ *2 archives interns:* responsibilities include categorizing historic women's papers for research. Candidates should have ability to work independently, analytical skills, organizational skills, personal interest in the field, written communication skills. Open to high school students, high school seniors, recent high school graduates, college freshmen, college sophomores, college juniors, college seniors, recent college graduates, graduate students, law students, career changers, individuals reentering the workforce. ▶ *2–4 computer/online specialists:* responsibilities include surveying current uses of electronic communications for women's issues and equality, including management of web site and new uses of computer video and audio. Candidates should have ability to work independently, analytical skills, computer skills, knowledge of field, organizational skills, personal interest in the field. Open to high school students, high school seniors, recent high school graduates, college freshmen, college sophomores, college juniors, college seniors, recent college graduates, graduate students, law students, career changers, individuals reentering the workforce, computer technologists. ▶ *1–2 public relations interns:* responsibilities include devising publicity programs for WIFP publications. Candidates should have ability to work independently, organizational skills, personal interest in the field, research skills, written communication skills. Open to high school students, high school seniors, recent high school graduates, college freshmen, college sophomores, college juniors, college seniors, recent college graduates, graduate students, law students, career changers, individuals reentering the workforce. ▶ *1–5 writers:* responsibilities include writing articles on WIFP work and ongoing projects. Candidates should have analytical skills, organizational skills, personal interest in the field, self-motivation, written communication skills. Open to high school students, high school seniors, recent high school graduates, college freshmen, college sophomores, college juniors, college seniors, recent college graduates, graduate students, law students, career changers, individuals reentering the workforce. Duration for all positions is flexible. All positions are unpaid. International applications accepted.
Benefits Opportunity to attend seminars/workshops, willing to act as a professional reference, willing to complete paperwork for educational credit, willing to provide letters of recommendation.
Contact Write, call, fax, or e-mail Dr. Donna Allen, President. Phone: 202-966-7783. Fax: 202-966-7783. E-mail: wifponline@igc.apc.org. Applicants must submit a cover letter, resume. Applications are accepted continuously. World Wide Web: http://www.igc.org/wifp/.

WORLD AFFAIRS COUNCILS OF AMERICA
1726 M Street, NW, Suite 800
Washington, District of Columbia 20036

General Information Nongovernmental, nonprofit, nonpartisan organization composed of over 100 independent world affairs councils and affiliated educational institutions located throughout the U.S. whose purpose is to improve the quality of citizen education in international affairs. Established in 1960. Number of employees: 2. Number of internship applications received each year: 25.
Internships Available ▶ *1–3 general interns:* responsibilities include locating speakers on a wide range of topics connected with world affairs (foreign policy, environmental issues, and defense), maintaining records on World Affairs Councils and updating information on an ongoing basis, handling telephone inquiries regarding the work of the WACs, and updating the database of information, embassies, and think tanks. Candidates should have ability to work with others, computer skills, editing skills, organizational skills, personal interest in the field, writing skills. Duration is 1 semester. Unpaid. Open to college sophomores, college juniors, college seniors.
Benefits Job counseling, names of contacts, willing to complete paperwork for educational credit, willing to provide letters of recommendation.
Contact Write or e-mail Cori Welbourn, Internship Coordinator. E-mail: ncwao@aol.com. Applicants must submit a cover letter, resume, writing sample. Applications are accepted continuously.

WORLD FEDERALIST ASSOCIATION
418 Seventh Street, SE
Washington, District of Columbia 20003

General Information Organization working to transform the United Nations into a democratic world federation capable of protecting the environment, abolishing war, and protecting human rights. Established in 1947. Number of employees: 10. Number of internship applications received each year: 100.
Internships Available ▶ *4–6 staff assistants:* responsibilities include assisting in public outreach, writing and editing newsletters, assisting with lobbying activities, pitching events to the media, conducting policy research, and assisting with the monthly activist program. Candidates should have ability to work independently, computer skills, editing skills, oral communication skills, organizational skills, personal interest in the field, research skills, self-motivation, strong interpersonal skills, strong leadership ability, writing skills. Duration is 1 semester. $10 per day. Open to college freshmen, college sophomores, college juniors, college seniors, recent college graduates. International applications accepted.
Benefits Formal training, opportunity to attend seminars/workshops, possible full-time employment, willing to act as a professional reference, willing to complete paperwork for educational credit, willing to provide letters of recommendation, networking with other peace/justice organizations both nationally and internationally.
Contact Write or fax Internship Coordinator. Fax: 202-546-3749. No phone calls. In-person interview recommended. Applicants must submit a cover letter, resume, writing sample. Applications are accepted continuously. World Wide Web: http://www.wfa.org.

WORLD FEDERALIST MOVEMENT
United Nations Office, 777 United Nations Plaza
New York, New York 10017

General Information Educational organization dedicated to promoting international order and an effective United Nations. Established in 1947. Number of employees: 6. Number of internship applications received each year: 20.
Internships Available ▶ *1 Betsy Dana scholar:* responsibilities include assisting with office work and research, gathering United Nations documents, writing reports, and meeting with nongovernmental representatives and United Nations officials and personnel. Duration is 10 weeks. $1,000 per duration of

internship. Open to college freshmen, college sophomores, college juniors, college seniors, recent college graduates, graduate students. International applications accepted.
Benefits Names of contacts, opportunity to attend seminars/workshops, willing to complete paperwork for educational credit, willing to provide letters of recommendation.
Contact Write, call, fax, or e-mail Mr. Bill Pace, Executive Director. Phone: 212-599-1320. Fax: 212-599-1332. E-mail: wfm@igc.apc.org. In-person interview required. Applicants must submit a cover letter, resume, letter of recommendation. Applications are accepted continuously. World Wide Web: http://www.worldfederalist.org.

YOUTH SERVICE AMERICA
1101 15th Street, NW, Suite 200
Washington, District of Columbia 20005-5002

General Information Resource center and the premier alliance of 200+ organizations committed to increasing the quantity and quality of opportunities for young Americans to serve locally, nationally, or globally.
Internships Available ▶ *Fund for Social Entrepreneurs interns:* responsibilities include assisting in the organization of professional development retreats for the Fund members, helping in the development of an alumni program, and producing a national newsletter on the work of the Fund and its entrepreneurs. Candidates should have computer skills, oral communication skills, organizational skills, self-motivation, written communication skills, interest in community service and youth involvement, ability to manage several tasks at once, sense of humor. ▶ *National Service Affiliates Program interns:* responsibilities include assisting in writing and editing the National Service Briefing, recruiting new members, helping to organize the Faces of Youth Service national speakers' bureau, and assisting with the development policy and funding section of SERVEnet. Candidates should have computer skills, oral communication skills, organizational skills, self-motivation, written communication skills, interest in community service and youth involvement, ability to manage several tasks at once, sense of humor. ▶ *National Youth Service Day interns:* responsibilities include assisting with public relations strategy development, putting together media kits, development of the Toolkit (Web site section of SERVEnet), outreach to thousands of communities and local organizations, and marketing outreach to other national nonprofit organizations. Candidates should have computer skills, oral communication skills, organizational skills, self-motivation, written communication skills, interest in community service and youth involvement, ability to manage several tasks at once, sense of humor. ▶ *President's Student Service Awards interns:* responsibilities include developing a database of activities and implementation, writing news articles to promote the program, assisting in the development of marketing strategies, making outreach calls, and maintaining the Web site for awards. Candidates should have computer skills, oral communication skills, organizational skills, self-motivation, written communication skills, interest in community service and youth involvement, ability to manage several tasks at once, sense of humor. ▶ *SERVEnet interns:* responsibilities include assisting the Managing Editor and Webmaster with building Web site content and graphics, writing articles for various sections of SERVEnet, conducting research, developing marketing plans, and helping to organize the SERVEnet ambassadors/community mapping initiative. Candidates should have computer skills, oral communication skills, organizational skills, self-motivation, written communication skills, interest in community service and youth involvement, ability to manage several tasks at once, sense of humor. ▶ *Development interns:* responsibilities include producing monthly YSA updates for board members, funders, and major donors; researching potential funders, responding to requests for information, and performing administrative support. Candidates should have computer skills, oral communication skills, organizational skills, self-motivation, written communication skills, interest in community and youth involvement, ability to manage several tasks at once, sense of humor. ▶ *Finance/administrative interns:* responsibilities include inputting AR and AP data, tracking invoices, and perform-

ing administrative tasks for accounting activities. Candidates should have computer skills, oral communication skills, organizational skills, self-motivation, written communication skills, interest in community and youth involvement, ability to manage several tasks at once, sense of humor. All positions are unpaid.
Contact Write, call, fax, or e-mail Shannon Maynard, Internship Programs, 1101 15th Street, NW, Suite 200, Washington, District of Columbia 20005-5002. Phone: 202-296-4030. Fax: 202-296-4030. E-mail: shannon@ysa.org. Applicants must submit a cover letter, resume. Applications are accepted continuously. World Wide Web: http://www.servenet.org.

ENVIRONMENT, CONSERVATION, AND WILDLIFE ORGANIZATIONS

ALLIANCE FOR THE WILD ROCKIES
PO Box 8731
Missoula, Montana 59807

General Information Organization whose aim is to preserve and protect the remaining wilderness and biodiversity of the Northern Rockies bio-region by empowering regional conservationists and informing the public about the loss of wildlands. Established in 1988. Number of employees: 4. Number of internship applications received each year: 30.
Internships Available ▶ *2 ecosystem defense interns:* responsibilities include administering the Forest Watch program that includes reviewing timber sale, mining, and other development proposals; and filing written appeals when necessary. Candidates should have ability to work with others, computer skills, office skills, oral communication skills, writing skills, legal background. ▶ *1–2 outreach/education interns:* responsibilities include staffing AWR office, supervising volunteers, and public outreach. Candidates should have ability to work with others, computer skills, knowledge of field, office skills, oral communication skills, writing skills, experience in advocacy. Duration for all positions is 1–2 semesters. All positions are unpaid. Open to high school students, high school seniors, recent high school graduates, college freshmen, college sophomores, college juniors, college seniors, recent college graduates, graduate students, law students, career changers, individuals reentering the workforce. International applications accepted.
Benefits Formal training, job counseling, names of contacts, opportunity to attend seminars/workshops, possible full-time employment, travel reimbursement, willing to complete paperwork for educational credit, willing to provide letters of recommendation.
Contact Write Bob Clark, Outreach Director. No phone calls. Applicants must submit a cover letter, resume, writing sample. Applications are accepted continuously. World Wide Web: http://www.wildrockies.org/awr.

AMERICAN FORESTS
910 17th Street, NW, Suite 600
Washington, District of Columbia 20006

General Information Organization dedicated to ensuring the benefits of trees and forests for future generations. Established in 1875. Number of employees: 30. Number of internship applications received each year: 300.
Internships Available ▶ *1 communications/publications intern:* responsibilities include research and writing articles and press releases. Duration is flexible. ▶ *1 marketing intern-D.C.:* responsibilities include developing partnerships for tree planting. Duration is flexible. ▶ *1–2 policy interns:* responsibilities include writing and research. Duration is flexible. ▶ *1 policy research intern:*

American Forests (continued)

responsibilities include assisting with planning of policy and workshops. Duration is 8–10 weeks. ▶ *2 program services interns:* responsibilities include developing partnerships for tree planting. Duration is flexible. ▶ *1 urban forestry intern:* responsibilities include research and acting as community liaison. Duration is flexible. All positions paid at $50 per week. Open to college sophomores, college juniors, college seniors, recent college graduates, graduate students. International applications accepted.

Benefits Opportunity to attend seminars/workshops, possible full-time employment, willing to complete paperwork for educational credit, willing to provide letters of recommendation, opportunity to write for publications and present own seminar. **Contact** Write or fax Lu Rose, Vice President of Administration. Fax: 202-955-4588. No phone calls. In-person interview recommended. Applicants must submit a cover letter, resume, writing sample. Applications are accepted continuously. World Wide Web: http://www.amfor.org.

AMERICAN HORTICULTURAL SOCIETY
7931 East Boulevard Drive
Alexandria, Virginia 22308-1300

General Information Society that promotes excellence in horticulture through information, education, training, publications, and leadership. Established in 1922. Number of employees: 26. Number of internship applications received each year: 25.

Internships Available ▶ *6–8 horticultural interns:* responsibilities include maintaining plant collections, displays, and test gardens and working in gardening information offices. Candidates should have ability to work independently, plan to pursue career in field, research skills, self-motivation, strong interpersonal skills. Duration is 3–9 months. $7 per hour. Open to college freshmen, college sophomores, college juniors, college seniors, recent college graduates, graduate students, career changers.

Benefits Job counseling, names of contacts, on-the-job training, opportunity to attend seminars/workshops, travel reimbursement, willing to act as a professional reference, willing to complete paperwork for educational credit, willing to provide letters of recommendation, job lists provided when available. **Contact** Write, call, or fax Patrick Larkin, Director of Horticulture. Phone: 703-768-5700. Fax: 703-768-8700. In-person interview recommended. Applicants must submit a formal organization application, resume, academic transcripts, three personal references. Applications are accepted continuously. World Wide Web: http://www.ahs.org.

AMERICAN WIND ENERGY ASSOCIATION
122 C Street, NW, 4th Floor
Washington, District of Columbia 20001

General Information Organization working to further the development of wind energy as a clean and reliable energy alternative. Established in 1974. Number of employees: 14. Number of internship applications received each year: 50.

Internships Available ▶ *1–2 general office assistants/membership interns:* responsibilities include working on the annual conference and various seminars, and general office work. Candidates should have ability to work independently, analytical skills, computer skills, office skills, organizational skills, writing skills. stipend depending on hours worked. Open to college freshmen, college sophomores, college juniors, college seniors. ▶ *1–2 international interns:* responsibilities include writing, editing, researching, and reviewing materials; assisting and performing general office duties. Candidates should have computer skills, office skills, personal interest in the field, research skills, writing skills. stipend depending on hours worked. Open to college freshmen, college sophomores, college juniors, college seniors, graduate students, law students. ▶ *1–2 publications/communications interns:* responsibilities include writing, editing, and reviewing materials; filling orders for general and specific information; and performing general office duties. Candidates should have computer skills, editing skills, office skills, personal interest in the field, research skills, writing skills. stipend depending on hours worked. Open to college freshmen, college sophomores,

college juniors, college seniors, graduate students, law students. Duration for all positions is flexible. International applications accepted.

Benefits Names of contacts, opportunity to attend seminars/workshops, possible full-time employment, willing to complete paperwork for educational credit, willing to provide letters of recommendation. **Contact** Write, call, fax, or e-mail Joy Diggs, Internship Program Manager, PO Box 75428, Washington, District of Columbia 20013-0428. Phone: 202-383-2500. Fax: 202-383-2505. E-mail: joy_diggs@awea.org. In-person interview recommended. Applicants must submit a cover letter, resume. Applications are accepted continuously. World Wide Web: http://www.igc.apc.org/awea/.

ANACOSTIA WATERSHED SOCIETY
4302 Baltimore Avenue
Bladensburg, Maryland 20710

General Information Small environmental group whose purpose is to restore the Anacostia River, an urban river in Washington, D.C., by organizing volunteers to perform stream cleanups, tree planting, and water quality monitoring. Established in 1989. Number of employees: 5. Number of internship applications received each year: 1.

Internships Available ▶ *1–2 assistant project managers:* responsibilities include organizing volunteers to perform stream cleanups, water quality monitoring, newsletter writing, and tree planting. Candidates should have ability to work independently, ability to work with others, computer skills, office skills, personal interest in the field, writing skills. Duration is 1–3 semesters. Unpaid. Open to college sophomores, college juniors, college seniors. International applications accepted.

Benefits Formal training, opportunity to attend seminars/workshops, willing to complete paperwork for educational credit, willing to provide letters of recommendation. **Contact** Write, call, fax, or e-mail Mr. James Connolly, Executive Director. Phone: 301-699-6204. Fax: 301-699-3317. E-mail: jim@anacostiaws.org. In-person interview recommended. Applicants must submit a cover letter, resume. Applications are accepted continuously. World Wide Web: http://www.anacostiaws.org.

ANIMAL LEGAL DEFENSE FUND
127 Fourth Street
Petaluma, California 94952-3005

General Information National nonprofit public interest law organization dedicated to protecting animals and establishing their legal rights through litigation.

Internships Available ▶ *2 Eleanor Seiling Legal Clerkship interns:* responsibilities include legal research and preparation of pleadings in cases currently being handled by ALDF. Placement is in ALDF's Rockville, Maryland office. Duration is 10 weeks in summer. $3,500 per duration of internship. Open to second-year law students. **Contact** Write, call, or fax Ms. Joyce Tischler, Executive Director, 127 Fourth Street, Petaluma, California 94952-3005. Phone: 707-769-7771 Ext. 17. Fax: 707-769-0785. Applicants must submit a resume, writing sample. Application deadline: November 30.

THE ANTARCTICA PROJECT
PO Box 76920
Washington, District of Columbia 20013

General Information Organization working to preserve Antarctica by educating the public and governments on Antarctic issues. Established in 1982. Number of employees: 2. Number of internship applications received each year: 30.

Internships Available ▶ *3–6 interns:* responsibilities include assisting in running office, conducting research and writing on a variety of conservation issues, helping communicate with members. Candidates should have ability to work independently, declared college major in field, knowledge of field, oral communication skills, self-motivation, written communication skills. Duration is 1 semester. Unpaid. International applications accepted.

Benefits Opportunity to attend seminars/workshops, willing to complete paperwork for educational credit, willing to provide letters of recommendation.
Contact Write, fax, or e-mail Office Manager. Fax: 202-234-2482. E-mail: antarctica@igc.org. No phone calls. In-person interview recommended. Applicants must submit a cover letter, resume, writing sample. Applications are accepted continuously.

APOSTLE ISLANDS NATIONAL LAKESHORE
Route 1, Box 4
Bayfield, Wisconsin 54814

General Information Twenty-one islands in Lake Superior off the Northern tip of Wisconsin, offering hiking and camping in a wilderness setting. Established in 1970. Number of employees: 50. Number of internship applications received each year: 40.
Internships Available ▶ *Interpreter interns:* responsibilities include giving guided walks and talks, and staffing visitor centers. Candidates should have ability to work independently, analytical skills, office skills, oral communication skills, organizational skills, self-motivation, strong interpersonal skills, strong leadership ability, writing skills. Duration is flexible. Unpaid. Open to college freshmen, college sophomores, college juniors, college seniors, recent college graduates, graduate students, law students, career changers. International applications accepted.
Benefits Free housing, on-the-job training, willing to provide letters of recommendation.
Contact Write or call Margaret D. Ludwig, Volunteer Coordinator. Phone: 715-779-3397 Ext. 105. Telephone interview required. Applicants must submit a cover letter, resume, personal reference. Application deadline: March 5 for summer. World Wide Web: http://www.nps.gov/apis.

ASPEN CENTER FOR ENVIRONMENTAL STUDIES
100 Puppy Smith Street
Aspen, Colorado 81611

General Information Private nonprofit environmental education center located within the Hallam Lake Nature Reserve whose mission is to inspire a life-long commitment to the preservation of the natural world by educating for environmental stewardship, and conserving and restoring the balance of natural communities. Established in 1968. Number of employees: 11. Number of internship applications received each year: 150.
Internships Available ▶ *12 summer naturalist interns:* responsibilities include leading off-site interpretive hikes at the Maroon Bells, Snowmass, and on top of Aspen Mountain, teaching environmental education programs, maintaining trails, rehabilitating injured animals, caring for resident birds of prey. Candidates should have ability to work with others, college courses in field, experience in the field, oral communication skills, personal interest in the field, self-motivation. Duration is June through September. $125 per week. Open to college juniors, college seniors, recent college graduates, graduate students. International applications accepted.
Benefits Formal training, free housing, on-the-job training, possible full-time employment, willing to act as a professional reference, willing to complete paperwork for educational credit, willing to provide letters of recommendation, tuition-free participation in Natural Field School courses.
Contact Write, call, fax, or e-mail Internship Coordinator, 100 Puppy Street, Aspen, Colorado 81611. Phone: 970-925-5756. Fax: 970-925-4819. E-mail: acesone@rof.net. Applicants must submit a formal organization application, resume, in-person or telephone interview for qualified applicants. Application deadline: March 1. World Wide Web: http://www.aspen.com/aces.

AUDUBON NATURALIST SOCIETY
8940 Jones Mill Road
Chevy Chase, Maryland 20815

General Information Independent, nonprofit, environmental education and conservation organization serving the metropolitan Washington, D.C. region. Established in 1897. Number of employees: 30. Number of internship applications received each year: 100.
Internships Available ▶ *7 environmental education interns:* responsibilities include coteaching children's classes in environmental education, maintaining a classroom, assisting with the upkeep of a 40-acre wildlife sanctuary, and undertaking an independent project. Candidates should have ability to work independently, ability to work with others, personal interest in the field, self-motivation, strong leadership ability, experience working with children. Duration is 3 months in summer, spring, or fall. $1,200–$2,400 per duration of internship. Open to college sophomores, college juniors, college seniors, recent college graduates, graduate students, career changers. International applications accepted.
Benefits Formal training, free housing, names of contacts, opportunity to attend seminars/workshops, willing to complete paperwork for educational credit, willing to provide letters of recommendation.
Contact Write or call Children's Program Coordinator. Phone: 301-652-9188 Ext. 3007. In-person interview recommended. Applicants must submit a formal organization application, cover letter, resume, two letters of recommendation. Application deadline: February 1 for spring, April 10 for summer, August 1 for fall.

AULLWOOD AUDUBON CENTER AND FARM
1000 Aullwood Road
Dayton, Ohio 45414

General Information Nature center and organic farm dedicated to educating the public about environmental issues through the presentation of formal and informal tours. Established in 1957. Number of employees: 16. Unit of National Audubon Society, New York, New York. Number of internship applications received each year: 70.
Internships Available ▶ *Administrative assistant interns:* responsibilities include fiscal planning; networking with other Audubon groups; tracking projects; teaching; and participating in meetings, activities, and special events. Candidates should have computer skills, office skills, oral communication skills, written communication skills. Open to college sophomores, college juniors, college seniors, recent college graduates, graduate students. ▶ *Environmental education interns:* responsibilities include teaching youth and school groups, assisting with educational program development and teaching materials preparation, and involvement with all aspects of operations. Candidates should have college courses in field, experience in the field, oral communication skills. Open to college sophomores, college juniors, college seniors, recent college graduates, graduate students. ▶ *Maintenance interns:* responsibilities include working in close contact with the maintenance staff in dealing with special problems of the sanctuary. Candidates should have knowledge of field, experience with power equipment, experience with vehicle maintenance. Open to college sophomores, college juniors, college seniors, recent college graduates. ▶ *Museum store interns:* responsibilities include contacts with suppliers, assisting with daily store operations. Candidates should have ability to work independently, computer skills, office skills, organizational skills. Open to college sophomores, college juniors, college seniors, recent college graduates, graduate students. Duration for all positions is flexible. All positions paid at $70 per week. International applications accepted.
Benefits Formal training, free housing, job counseling, names of contacts, opportunity to attend seminars/workshops, possible full-time employment, willing to complete paperwork for educational credit, willing to provide letters of recommendation.
Contact Write, call, fax, or e-mail Mr. John A. Wilson, Intern Coordinator. Phone: 937-890-7360. Fax: 937-890-2382. E-mail: aullwood@gemair.com. Applicants must submit a formal organization application. Applications are accepted continuously. World Wide Web: http://www.audubon.org/local/sanctuary/aullwood.

BARRIER ISLAND ENVIRONMENTAL EDUCATION CENTER
2810 Seabrook Island Road
John's Island, South Carolina 29455

General Information Resident environmental education center serving elementary and middle school students in 3- or 5-day sessions; subjects include marine biology, forest ecology, sensory awareness, and Indian life. Established in 1981. Number of employees: 15. Division of Saint Christopher Camp and Conference Center, John's Island, South Carolina. Number of internship applications received each year: 4.

Internships Available ▶ *1–2 naturalist interns.* Candidates should have ability to work independently, college courses in field, computer skills, declared college major in field, experience in the field, oral communication skills, organizational skills, plan to pursue career in field, self-motivation, strong interpersonal skills, strong leadership ability, writing skills. ▶ *1–2 teaching interns:* responsibilities include performing tasks similar to those of regular teaching staff in the morning and afternoon, leading afternoon recreation activities, running evening programs, and working on a new curriculum. Candidates should have ability to work independently, college courses in field, computer skills, experience in the field, oral communication skills, organizational skills, plan to pursue career in field, self-motivation, strong interpersonal skills, strong leadership ability. Duration for all positions is flexible by semester (August to May). All positions paid at $75–$100 per week. Open to college juniors. International applications accepted.

Benefits Free housing, free meals, names of contacts, on-the-job training, possible full-time employment, willing to complete paperwork for educational credit, willing to provide letters of recommendation.

Contact Write Mr. Jim Koenig, Director. In-person interview recommended. Applicants must submit a formal organization application, cover letter, resume, academic transcripts, personal reference, two letters of recommendation. Application deadline: May 1.

BLACKWATER NATIONAL WILDLIFE REFUGE
2145 Key Wallace Drive
Cambridge, Maryland 21613

General Information Refuge providing a resting and feeding area for migratory waterfowl, habitat for threatened and endangered species (bald eagle, Delmarva fox squirrel), and recreation for the public. Established in 1933. Number of employees: 25. Unit of Fish & Wildlife Service Region V, Hadley, Massachusetts.

Internships Available ▶ *1 fall intern:* responsibilities include greeting the public, answering questions, showing films in the auditorium, acting as cashier, giving orientation talks to youth groups, assisting with wetland environmental education programs, preparing and presenting refuge slide program, guiding bus and trail tours, and answering letters and information requests. Duration is 16 weeks. Open to college freshmen, college sophomores, college juniors, college seniors, recent college graduates, graduate students, career changers, individuals reentering the workforce. ▶ *1 summer intern:* responsibilities include greeting the public, answering questions, showing films in the auditorium, acting as cashier, giving orientation talks to youth groups, assisting with wetland environmental education programs, preparing and presenting refuge slide program, guiding bus and trail tours, and answering letters and information requests. Duration is 12 weeks. Open to college freshmen, college sophomores, college juniors, college seniors, recent college graduates, graduate students, career changers. Candidates for all positions should have ability to work independently, computer skills, oral communication skills, plan to pursue career in field, self-motivation, strong interpersonal skills, written communication skills. All positions paid at stipend of $15–$24 per day depending on budget. International applications accepted.

Benefits Free housing, names of contacts, on-the-job training, opportunity to attend seminars/workshops, willing to act as a

professional reference, willing to complete paperwork for educational credit, willing to provide letters of recommendation.

Contact Write, call, fax, or e-mail Ms. Maggie Briggs, Outdoor Recreation Planner. Phone: 410-228-2677. Fax: 410-228-3261. E-mail: r5rw-bwnwr@mail.fws.gov. In-person interview recommended. Applicants must submit a formal organization application, resume, three personal references. Application deadline: March 31 for summer.

BOISE NATIONAL FOREST, MOUNTAIN HOME RANGER DISTRICT
2180 American Legion Boulevard
Mountain Home, Idaho 83647

General Information National forest. Number of employees: 30. Unit of Boise National Forest, Boise, Idaho. Number of internship applications received each year: 25.

Internships Available ▶ *1 wildlife volunteer:* responsibilities include conducting wildlife and habitat inventories for bald eagle and elk calving surveys, manipulating vegetation, planting shrubs, and installing water developments for improvement of fish and wildlife habitats. Candidates should have ability to work with others, computer skills, knowledge of field, oral communication skills, self-motivation, written communication skills. Duration is 3 to 4 months in the summer. $18 per day. Open to college freshmen, college sophomores, college juniors, college seniors, recent college graduates, graduate students, career changers, individuals reentering the workforce. International applications accepted.

Benefits Names of contacts, willing to complete paperwork for educational credit, willing to provide letters of recommendation, small stipend available.

Contact Write or call Ms. Jill Holderman, Wildlife Biologist. Phone: 208-587-7961. Applicants must submit a formal organization application, resume. Applications are accepted continuously.

BOWMAN'S HILL WILDFLOWER PRESERVE
River Road, PO Box 685
New Hope, Pennsylvania 18938-0685

General Information Natural preserve that grows, cares for, and exhibits a living collection of Pennsylvania's native plants and provides educational programs, exhibits, and literature centered on regional flora. Established in 1934. Number of employees: 7. Number of internship applications received each year: 60.

Internships Available ▶ *2 preserve interns:* responsibilities include leading tours and field trips, growing wildflowers, assisting with nursery operations, collecting and storing seeds, maintaining plant collection and trail system, completing an assigned project, maintaining a daily journal, weeding, planting, pruning, and performing trail work. Candidates should have knowledge of field, oral communication skills, plan to pursue career in field, self-motivation, strong interpersonal skills. Duration is 10 weeks (extensions possible). $6 per hour. Open to college freshmen, college sophomores, college juniors, college seniors, recent college graduates, graduate students, career changers. International applications accepted.

Benefits Formal training, housing at a cost, names of contacts, on-the-job training, opportunity to attend seminars/workshops, possible full-time employment, willing to act as a professional reference, willing to complete paperwork for educational credit, willing to provide letters of recommendation.

Contact Write, call, fax, or e-mail Intern Coordinator. Phone: 215-862-2924. Fax: 215-862-1846. E-mail: internship@bhwp.org. In-person interview recommended. Applicants must submit a formal organization application, resume, three personal references. Application deadline: March 1. World Wide Web: http://www.bhwp.org.

BRUKNER NATURE CENTER
5995 Horseshoe Bend Road
Troy, Ohio 45373

General Information Nature center whose mission is to provide environmental education and wildlife rehabilitation. Established in 1974. Number of employees: 9. Number of internship applications received each year: 75.
Internships Available ▶ *2–3 education/wildlife rehab assistants:* responsibilities include learning and participating in all phases of operation, assisting in the care of native Ohio wildlife, and providing programs for schools using live animals. Candidates should have ability to work independently, oral communication skills, personal interest in the field, self-motivation, strong interpersonal skills. Duration is 3–9 months. $75 per week. Open to college seniors, recent college graduates, graduate students.
Benefits Free housing, job counseling, names of contacts, on-the-job training, opportunity to attend seminars/workshops, possible full-time employment, willing to act as a professional reference, willing to complete paperwork for educational credit, willing to provide letters of recommendation.
Contact Write or e-mail Ms. Debra K. Brill, Administrative Director. E-mail: brukner@juno.com. Telephone interview required. Applicants must submit a cover letter, resume. Applications are accepted continuously.

BUREAU OF LAND MANAGEMENT, UNCOMPAHGRE FIELD OFFICE
2505 South Townsend Avenue
Montrose, Colorado 81401

General Information Federal agency responsible for management of 270 million acres of public lands and resources including recreation, range, timber, wildlife, wild horses, minerals, watershed, fish, wilderness, and natural, scientific, and cultural aspects. Established in 1934. Number of employees: 20. Unit of United States Department of Interior, Washington, District of Columbia. Number of internship applications received each year: 10.
Internships Available ▶ *1–4 recreation interns:* responsibilities include conducting commercial and private boat checks, collecting user fees, providing visitor services, patrolling recreation and wilderness areas, collecting wilderness resources use statistics, installing signs, posting vehicle closures, performing maintenance, and working with students on environmental education programs. Duration is 3–6 months. ▶ *1–4 wildlife interns:* responsibilities include collecting a variety of natural resource data and implementing research protection projects. Duration is 4–6 months. All positions available as unpaid or paid. Open to college juniors, college seniors, recent college graduates.
Benefits Job counseling, names of contacts, opportunity to attend seminars/workshops, travel reimbursement, willing to complete paperwork for educational credit, willing to provide letters of recommendation.
Contact Write, call, fax, or e-mail Ms. Karen Tucker, Recreation Planner (for recreation positions), or Ms. Amanda Clements, Ecologist (for wildlife positions). Phone: 970-240-5300. Fax: 970-240-5367. E-mail: karentucker@co.blm.gov or amandaclements@co.blm.gov. In-person interview recommended. Applicants must submit a resume. Application deadline: March 15. World Wide Web: http://www.co.blm.gov/ubra.html.

CAMPUS ECOLOGY, NATIONAL WILDLIFE FEDERATION
8925 Leesburg Pike
Vienna, Virginia 22184

General Information Organization that supports practical conservation projects on college and university campuses by assisting with project implementation, providing training, and documenting lessons learned nationally. Established in 1936. Number of employees: 250. Number of internship applications received each year: 60.
Internships Available ▶ *4 field coordinators (Atlanta, GA; Portland, OR; Ann Arbor, MI; Montpelier, VT):* responsibilities include coordinating on-site Campus Ecology training clinics and managing enrolled campus projects within the region; assisting with field and national office activities and special projects. One position available at each of the following locations: Atlanta, GA; Portland, OR; Ann Arbor, MI; Montpelier, VT. Candidates should have ability to work independently, knowledge of field, oral communication skills, personal interest in the field, self-motivation, written communication skills. Duration is September to May. $275 per week. Open to recent college graduates. ▶ *2–4 special projects interns:* responsibilities include assistance with various projects, possibly including resource development, research, database development, and Web maintenance. Candidates should have ability to work independently, office skills, personal interest in the field, research skills, writing skills. Duration is flexible. Unpaid. Open to high school students, high school seniors, recent high school graduates, college freshmen, college sophomores, college juniors, college seniors, recent college graduates, graduate students, law students, career changers, individuals reentering the workforce. International applications accepted.
Benefits On-the-job training, opportunity to attend seminars/workshops, travel reimbursement, willing to act as a professional reference, willing to complete paperwork for educational credit, willing to provide letters of recommendation.
Contact Write or e-mail Lydia Wicker, Assistant Coordinator, 8925 Leesburg Pike, Vienna, Virginia 22184. E-mail: wicker@nwf.org. No phone calls. Telephone interview required. Applicants must submit a cover letter, resume, two personal references, three letters of recommendation. Applications are accepted continuously. World Wide Web: http://www.nwf.org/campus.

CARIBBEAN CONSERVATION CORPORATION
4424 Northwest 13th Street, Suite A1
Gainesville, Florida 32609

General Information Organization that is dedicated to the conservation of sea turtles and related marine and coastal wildlife through research, training, advocacy, education, and protection of natural areas. Established in 1959. Number of employees: 9. Number of internship applications received each year: 200.
Internships Available ▶ *4–6 birding research assistants:* responsibilities include study of migrant and neotropical birds, working with volunteer groups including supervising and educating volunteers in avian behavior and research methodology. Candidates should have oral communication skills, organizational skills, research skills, strong interpersonal skills, background/experience with birds preferred. Duration is minimum of 2 months. ▶ *8 green turtle research assistants:* responsibilities include assisting scientists with research on the Green turtle, monitoring turtle nesting beach, tagging turtles and recording data, working with volunteer groups on turtle projects, and educating tourists about turtles. Candidates should have oral communication skills, plan to pursue career in field, research skills, strong interpersonal skills, background/experience with turtles preferred. Duration is minimum of 2 months, beginning in June, ending in late October. ▶ *4–6 leatherback turtle research assistants:* responsibilities include assisting scientists with research on the Leatherback turtle, monitoring turtle nesting beach, tagging turtles and recording data, working with volunteer groups on turtle projects, and educating tourists about turtles. Candidates should have oral communication skills, plan to pursue career in field, research skills, strong interpersonal skills, background/experience with turtles preferred, ability to speak English and Spanish at conversational levels. Duration is 2 months or more, beginning in March, ending in late May. All positions are unpaid. Open to recent college graduates, graduate students, career changers. International applications accepted.
Benefits Formal training, free housing, free meals, willing to complete paperwork for educational credit, willing to provide letters of recommendation.
International Internships Available in Costa Rica.
Contact Write, fax, or e-mail Dan Evans, Program Coordinator. Fax: 352-375-2449. E-mail: resprog@cccturtle.org. No phone calls. Telephone interview required. Applicants must submit a formal organization application, cover letter, resume, three personal

Caribbean Conservation Corporation (continued)

references. Application deadline: April 1 for green turtle research assistants, December 31 for leatherback turtle research assistants; continuous for birding research assistants. World Wide Web: http://www.cccturtle.org.

CAROLINA RAPTOR CENTER, INC.
PO Box 16443
Charlotte, North Carolina 28297

General Information   Nonprofit organization that exists to provide public education on the importance of raptors; to care for sick, injured, and orphaned raptors; and to conduct and contribute research about raptors. Established in 1981. Number of employees: 8. Number of internship applications received each year: 20.

Internships Available   ▶ *3–5 environmental educators:* responsibilities include assisting with the care of trained birds of prey, presenting programs at Raptor Center and elsewhere, and helping with displays and exhibits. Candidates should have ability to work independently, oral communication skills, personal interest in the field, strong interpersonal skills, writing skills. Open to high school students, high school seniors, recent high school graduates, college freshmen, college sophomores, college juniors, college seniors, recent college graduates, graduate students, career changers. ▶ *1–3 environmental nonprofit administration interns:* responsibilities include working with public relations, bookkeeping, and desktop publishing; assisting with volunteer coordination; some public speaking; and assisting with administration of a nonprofit wildlife conservation organization. Candidates should have ability to work independently, oral communication skills, organizational skills, strong interpersonal skills, written communication skills. Open to high school seniors, recent high school graduates, college freshmen, college sophomores, college juniors, college seniors, recent college graduates, graduate students, career changers, individuals reentering the workforce. ▶ *1–3 raptor care interns:* responsibilities include caring for, feeding, and training nonreleasable raptors. Candidates should have ability to work independently, ability to work with others, organizational skills, personal interest in the field, self-motivation. Open to high school students, high school seniors, recent high school graduates, college freshmen, college sophomores, college juniors, college seniors, recent college graduates, graduate students, career changers, individuals reentering the workforce. ▶ *3–5 raptor rehabilitators:* responsibilities include assisting with care, feeding, and releasing to the wild injured and orphaned raptors. Candidates should have ability to work independently, ability to work with others, organizational skills, personal interest in the field, self-motivation, written communication skills. Open to high school students, high school seniors, recent high school graduates, college freshmen, college sophomores, college juniors, college seniors, recent college graduates, graduate students, career changers, individuals reentering the workforce. Duration for all positions is minimum of 120 hours. All positions are unpaid. International applications accepted.

Benefits   Names of contacts, on-the-job training, opportunity to attend seminars/workshops, willing to complete paperwork for educational credit, willing to provide letters of recommendation.

Contact   Write or fax Lori Sparkman, Volunteer Coordinator. Fax: 704-875-8814. No phone calls. In-person interview recommended. Applicants must submit a formal organization application, cover letter, resume, three personal references. Applications are accepted continuously. Fees: $10. World Wide Web: http://www.charweb.org/organizations/science/raptorcenter/index.html.

CARRYING CAPACITY NETWORK
2000 P Street, NW, Suite 240
Washington, District of Columbia 20036

General Information   Informational network striving to make the public aware of such issues as environmental degradation, resource conservation, and population stabilization. Established in 1989. Number of employees: 6. Number of internship applications received each year: 175.

Internships Available   ▶ *1–2 staff/program assistants:* responsibilities include providing general office support, giving telephone assistance, maintaining the database, offering membership and research support, working on independent projects, and assisting with staff projects. Duration is 3 months minimum. $7 per hour. International applications accepted.

Benefits   Opportunity to attend seminars/workshops, possible full-time employment, willing to complete paperwork for educational credit, willing to provide letters of recommendation.

Contact   Write, fax, or e-mail Kathleen McNeilly, Associate Director. Fax: 202-296-4609. E-mail: ccn@us.net. No phone calls. In-person interview recommended. Applications are accepted continuously. World Wide Web: http://www.carryingcapacity.org.

CENTER FOR HEALTH, ENVIRONMENT AND JUSTICE
PO Box 6806
Falls Church, Virginia 22040

General Information   Organization that assists grassroots citizens' groups in the fight against pollution. Established in 1981. Number of employees: 10. Number of internship applications received each year: 50.

Internships Available   ▶ *1–2 development interns:* responsibilities include assisting with all aspects of development including grant writing, prospect research, and major donor activities. Candidates should have ability to work independently, editing skills, knowledge of field, oral communication skills, organizational skills, personal interest in the field, plan to pursue career in field, self-motivation, strong interpersonal skills, strong leadership ability, writing skills. Unpaid. Open to college seniors, recent college graduates, graduate students, career changers, individuals reentering the workforce. ▶ *1–5 grassroots organizing interns:* responsibilities include assisting with a variety of tasks including communication with local communities and answering phone inquiries. Candidates should have ability to work independently, analytical skills, oral communication skills, organizational skills, plan to pursue career in field, self-motivation, strong interpersonal skills, strong leadership ability. Position available as unpaid or paid. Open to college freshmen, college sophomores, college juniors, college seniors, recent college graduates, graduate students, career changers, individuals reentering the workforce. ▶ *1–2 journalism interns:* responsibilities include researching and updating a guidebook, working with editor of quarterly magazine. Candidates should have ability to work independently, computer skills, editing skills, organizational skills, personal interest in the field, plan to pursue career in field, self-motivation, strong interpersonal skills, strong leadership ability, writing skills. Unpaid. Open to college juniors, college seniors, graduate students, career changers, individuals reentering the workforce. ▶ *4–6 national campaign organizing interns:* responsibilities include working on and helping with organizing two national campaigns: Stop Dioxin Exposure Campaign and Health Care Without Harm Campaign. Candidates should have ability to work independently, analytical skills, computer skills, editing skills, office skills, oral communication skills, organizational skills, plan to pursue career in field, research skills, self-motivation, strong interpersonal skills, strong leadership ability, writing skills. Position available as unpaid or paid. Open to college juniors, college seniors, recent college graduates, graduate students, law students, career changers, individuals reentering the workforce. ▶ *1–3 nonprofit management interns:* responsibilities include assisting with a variety of tasks including marketing, public relations, schedule coordinating, and other activities. Candidates should have ability to work independently, computer skills, office skills, oral communication skills, organizational skills, plan to pursue career in field, self-motivation, strong interpersonal skills, strong leadership ability. Unpaid. Open to college seniors, recent college graduates, graduate students, career changers, individuals reentering the workforce. ▶ *1–4 research interns:* responsibilities include researching, compiling, and distributing information to activists in response to written and telephone inquiries. Candidates should have ability to work independently, analytical skills, computer skills, organizational skills, plan to pursue career in

field, research skills, self-motivation, strong interpersonal skills, strong leadership ability, writing skills. Unpaid. Open to college sophomores, college juniors, college seniors, recent college graduates, graduate students, career changers, individuals reentering the workforce. ▶ *2 research interns:* responsibilities include assisting with projects. Candidates should have ability to work independently, analytical skills, computer skills, editing skills, organizational skills, plan to pursue career in field, research skills, self-motivation, strong interpersonal skills, strong leadership ability, writing skills. Unpaid. ▶ *1–3 science interns:* responsibilities include compiling toxicity profiles on common chemicals found at contaminated sites. Candidates should have ability to work independently, ability to work with others, analytical skills, computer skills, plan to pursue career in field, research skills, self-motivation, written communication skills. Position available as unpaid or paid. Open to college juniors, college seniors, recent college graduates, graduate students, career changers, individuals reentering the workforce. Duration for all positions is flexible. International applications accepted.
Benefits Formal training, job counseling, names of contacts, opportunity to attend seminars/workshops, possible full-time employment, willing to complete paperwork for educational credit, willing to provide letters of recommendation, small transportation stipend.
Contact Write or e-mail Ms. Barbara Sullivan, Administrator of Personnel and Interns. E-mail: cchw@essential.org or barbaras@essential.org. No phone calls. In-person interview recommended. Applicants must submit a cover letter, resume. Application deadline: May 15 for summer, October 1 for fall. World Wide Web: http://www.essential.org/cchw.

CENTER FOR URBAN HORTICULTURE/WASHINGTON PARK ARBORETUM
University of Washington, Box 354115
Seattle, Washington 98195-4115

General Information Division within college whose mission is research, teaching, and public service in urban horticulture with programs that center on urban plant selection, placement, restoration, and management. Established in 1980. Number of employees: 40. Unit of College of Forest Resources, University of Washington, Seattle, Washington. Number of internship applications received each year: 20.
Internships Available ▶ *1–2 curatorial interns:* responsibilities include assisting with the maintenance and management of plant materials in the 200-acre Washington Park Arboretum and with record keeping of plant successions. Candidates should have declared college major in field, knowledge of field, plan to pursue career in field, willingness to work outdoors. Duration is 1 summer. Paid. ▶ *1–2 public education for adults interns:* responsibilities include planning, coordinating, and implementing public symposium and outreach curriculum; writing and editing newsletters; developing interpretive displays; leading tours; and co-instructing public courses. Candidates should have plan to pursue career in field. Duration is 8–12 weeks. Paid. ▶ *1–2 public education for youth interns:* responsibilities include planning and coordinating school tours and curriculum and working with youth projects and activities. Duration is 8–12 weeks. Paid. Open to college freshmen, college sophomores, college juniors, college seniors, graduate students. International applications accepted.
Benefits Formal training, opportunity to attend seminars/workshops, possible full-time employment, willing to complete paperwork for educational credit, willing to provide letters of recommendation.
Contact Write, call, or fax Mr. Dave Stockdale, Education Director. Phone: 206-685-8033. Fax: 206-685-2692. Applicants must submit a cover letter, resume, two personal references. Application deadline: February 28 for summer.

CENTRAL WISCONSIN ENVIRONMENTAL STATION/UNIVERSITY OF WISCONSIN–STEVENS POINT
10186 County Road MM
Amherst Junction, Wisconsin 54407

General Information Environmental station that provides a foundation for appreciation and understanding of our environment and develops the skills and attitudes needed to deal with present and future environmental problems. Established in 1975. Number of employees: 15. Unit of University of Wisconsin–Stevens Point, Stevens Point, Wisconsin. Number of internship applications received each year: 20.
Internships Available ▶ *3–4 environmental education interns:* responsibilities include providing instruction in environmental studies for groups of K-12 students, directing K-12 programs one day per week, being involved in a variety of administrative responsibilities, working with weekend groups, and performing other duties as necessary. Candidates should have oral communication skills, personal interest in the field, self-motivation, strong interpersonal skills, written communication skills, understanding of ecological concepts. Duration is 1 semester. $1,500 per semester. Open to college juniors, college seniors, recent college graduates, graduate students, career changers. International applications accepted.
Benefits Formal training, on-the-job training, opportunity to attend seminars/workshops, willing to act as a professional reference, willing to complete paperwork for educational credit, willing to provide letters of recommendation, some meals provided, possible housing allowance.
Contact Write, call, or e-mail Patty Dreier, Director. Phone: 715-824-2428. E-mail: pdreier@uwsp.edu. In-person interview recommended. Applicants must submit a formal organization application, cover letter, resume, academic transcripts, three personal references. Application deadline: July 1 for fall, December 1 for spring. World Wide Web: http://www.uwsp.edu/acad/cnr/affil/cwes/index/htm.

CHATTAHOOCHEE/OCONEE NATIONAL FOREST
1755 Cleveland Highway
Gainesville, Georgia 30501

General Information Forest service whose purpose is caring for the land and serving the people. Number of employees: 200. Unit of United States Forest Service, Washington, District of Columbia. Number of internship applications received each year: 25.
Internships Available ▶ *2 interpreters:* responsibilities include providing visitors with information. ▶ *2 recreation assistants:* responsibilities include developing recreational programs. Candidates should have major in outdoor education. Duration for all positions is 10 weeks. All positions are unpaid. Open to college freshmen, college sophomores, college juniors, college seniors.
Benefits Names of contacts, opportunity to attend seminars/workshops, possible full-time employment, willing to complete paperwork for educational credit, willing to provide letters of recommendation.
Contact Write, call, or fax Ms. Luana W. Kitchens, Human Resources Program Manager. Phone: 770-536-0541. Fax: 770-534-4411. Applicants must submit a cover letter, resume. Application deadline: April 1. World Wide Web: http://www.fs.fed.us.

CHATTANOOGA NATURE CENTER
400 Garden Road
Chattanooga, Tennessee 37419

General Information Wildlife rehabilitation and nature center seeking to lead its community toward greater understanding, appreciation, and enjoyment of the natural world through educational programs and a hospital specializing in the rehabilitation and care of birds of prey. Established in 1979. Number of employees: 14. Number of internship applications received each year: 30.

Chattanooga Nature Center (continued)

Internships Available ▶ *4–6 Chattanooga environmental youth corps:* responsibilities include hands-on experience with service projects around the community (many in parks or natural areas); planning, implementing, and evaluating projects; leading younger students. Candidates should have ability to work independently, ability to work with others, analytical skills, oral communication skills, organizational skills, strong leadership ability. Duration is available year-round. $6–$7 per hour. Open to recent high school graduates, college freshmen, college sophomores, college juniors, college seniors, recent college graduates. ▶ *1 administration and development intern:* responsibilities include working in management, development, and education programs, and with CNC part-timers throughout community (working closely with director and director of development). Candidates should have ability to work independently, ability to work with others, oral communication skills, self-motivation, strong leadership ability, written communication skills. Duration is 1 summer. Position available as unpaid or at $6–$7 per hour. Open to college sophomores, college juniors, college seniors, recent college graduates. ▶ *1 education intern:* responsibilities include working with the director of education to develop, implement, schedule, and evaluate new programs for K-12 groups as well as public programs. Working with K-12 and university personnel. Candidates should have ability to work independently, computer skills, oral communication skills, organizational skills, self-motivation, strong interpersonal skills, strong leadership ability, writing skills. Duration is available fall, spring, and summer. $6–$7 per hour. Open to college juniors, college seniors, graduate students. ▶ *1–2 environmental interpreter interns:* responsibilities include training and teaching outdoor education and environmental education classes/programs to students in grades K-12 in the field and in the schools. Candidates should have knowledge of field, oral communication skills, personal interest in the field, self-motivation, strong interpersonal skills. Duration is April-October (possibly year-round). Position available as unpaid or at $6–$7 per hour. Open to college freshmen, college sophomores, college juniors, college seniors, recent college graduates, graduate students. ▶ *1 horticulture intern:* responsibilities include designing theme garden plots on property, working with garden spot "adopting" groups, planning horticultural areas around property, and working with other community gardening groups. Candidates should have ability to work independently, analytical skills, oral communication skills, organizational skills, personal interest in the field, self-motivation, strong interpersonal skills, strong leadership ability. Duration is available fall, spring, and summer. $6–$7 per hour. Open to college sophomores, college juniors, college seniors, graduate students. ▶ *1 interpretive planning intern:* responsibilities include developing an interpretive plan for CNC under guidance of staff (especially non-personal interpretive plan). Candidates should have college courses in field, computer skills, knowledge of field, self-motivation, written communication skills. Duration is 1 summer. Position available as unpaid or at $6–$7 per hour. Open to college juniors, college seniors, graduate students. ▶ *1–3 wildlife rehabilitation interns:* responsibilities include assisting with animal-care activities (feeding, cage-cleaning, and exercising); assisting with environmental and interpretation programs through public speaking and education; researching; planning new projects; and working with the endangered red wolves, bobcats, and other predators. Candidates should have ability to work with others, college courses in field, knowledge of field, oral communication skills, personal interest in the field, self-motivation. Duration is year-round. Position available as unpaid or at $6–$7 per hour. Open to college freshmen, college sophomores, college juniors, college seniors, graduate students. International applications accepted.

Benefits On-the-job training, opportunity to attend seminars/workshops, possible full-time employment, willing to act as a professional reference, willing to complete paperwork for educational credit, willing to provide letters of recommendation, stipends available.

Contact Write, call, fax, or e-mail Jim Petruzzi, Executive Director. Phone: 423-821-1160. Fax: 423-821-1702. E-mail: cncdirec@vol.com. In-person interview recommended. Applicants must submit a formal organization application, cover letter, resume, 2-3 let-

ters of recommendation. Application deadline: April 15 for summer, November 1 for spring. World Wide Web: http://www.chattanooga.net/nature/.

CHEQUAMEGON NATIONAL FOREST, THE GREAT DIVIDE DISTRICT
PO Box 896
Hayward, Wisconsin 54843

General Information National forest focusing on natural resource management and emphasizing multiple use and conservation of resources such as wildlife, recreation, timber, wilderness, water, and soil. Established in 1905. Number of employees: 20. Unit of United States Forest Service, Washington, District of Columbia. Number of internship applications received each year: 30.

Internships Available ▶ *2 resort naturalists:* responsibilities include developing, promoting, and delivering interpretive programs in a resort setting; giving campfire talks; teaching outdoor skills; and arranging demonstrations and programs using local individuals. Candidates should have ability to work independently, knowledge of field, oral communication skills, organizational skills, personal interest in the field, self-motivation, strong interpersonal skills, strong leadership ability, writing skills. $100–$125 per week. Open to college juniors, college seniors, recent college graduates, graduate students, career changers, individuals reentering the workforce. ▶ *1 wilderness ranger intern:* responsibilities include working in the Rainbow Lake and Porcupine Wilderness areas, meeting with the public, constructing new trails, maintaining campsites, and engaging in other resource management projects. Candidates should have ability to work independently, ability to work with others, knowledge of field, oral communication skills, personal interest in the field, self-motivation, strong leadership ability. Position available as unpaid or at $100–$125 per week. Open to college juniors, college seniors, recent college graduates, graduate students. Duration for all positions is June to September. International applications accepted.

Benefits Formal training, free meals, names of contacts, on-the-job training, opportunity to attend seminars/workshops, willing to act as a professional reference, willing to complete paperwork for educational credit, willing to provide letters of recommendation.

Contact Write, call, or fax Ms. Kathy M. Moe, Resort Naturalist Coordinator. Phone: 715-634-4821. Fax: 715-634-3769. Telephone interview required. Applicants must submit a cover letter, resume. Applications are accepted continuously.

CHESAPEAKE WILDLIFE SANCTUARY
17308 Queen Anne Bridge Road
Bowie, Maryland 20716-9053

General Information Nonprofit wildlife rehabilitation center that rescues and treats an average of 10,000 injured and orphaned animals annually, providing intensive, hands-on training and experience to individuals who wish to pursue a career in wildlife, veterinary medicine, or related fields. Established in 1980. Number of employees: 13. Number of internship applications received each year: 150.

Internships Available ▶ *1–3 administration interns:* responsibilities include preparation of grant proposals to support our land trust, oiled wildlife, or intern and volunteer programs; fundraising; and computer training. Candidates should have ability to work independently, computer skills, office skills, oral communication skills, organizational skills, self-motivation, strong interpersonal skills, written communication skills. Duration is 3–12 months. Open to recent high school graduates, college freshmen, college sophomores, college juniors, college seniors, recent college graduates, graduate students, law students, career changers, individuals reentering the workforce. ▶ *5–25 avian interns:* responsibilities include recordkeeping, rehabilitation, cleaning cages and equipment, and rearing of a variety of birds; assisting with the sanctuary's regional oiled wildlife emergency response program. Candidates should have ability to work independently, oral communication skills, personal interest in the field, self-motivation, strong interpersonal skills, professional attitude. Duration is 3–12 months. Open to high school seniors, recent high school graduates, college freshmen, college sophomores, college juniors, college seniors, recent college graduates, graduate students, law students, career changers, individuals reentering the workforce, individuals 16 or older. ▶ *2–5 large mammals interns:* responsibilities include recordkeeping, rehabilitation, rearing, feeding, cleaning, health checks, and medical treatment of white-tailed deer. Candidates should have ability to work independently, ability to work with others, oral communication skills, personal interest in the field, self-motivation, strong interpersonal skills, professional attitude. Duration is 3–12 months. Open to high school seniors, recent high school graduates, college freshmen, college sophomores, college juniors, college seniors, recent college graduates, graduate students, career changers. ▶ *2–4 small mammals interns:* responsibilities include recordkeeping, cleaning, feeding, and rehabilitation focusing on hand-rearing and care of small mammals (squirrels, rabbits, opossums, groundhogs, and other animals). Candidates should have ability to work independently, ability to work with others, oral communication skills, personal interest in the field, self-motivation, professional attitude. Duration is 3–12 months. Open to high school seniors, recent high school graduates, college freshmen, college sophomores, college juniors, college seniors, recent college graduates, graduate students, law students, career changers, individuals reentering the workforce. ▶ *1–3 veterinary interns:* responsibilities include recordkeeping and treatment of injured wildlife, medical treatment of trauma cases, and design of treatment protocols. Candidates should have ability to work independently, ability to work with others, knowledge of field, oral communication skills, strong leadership ability, written communication skills. Duration is 1 month to 1 year. Open to 3rd or 4th-year veterinary students. ▶ *1–5 wildlife education interns:* responsibilities include design and presentation of on- and off-site educational programs for the public, and docent training programs. Candidates should have ability to work independently, ability to work with others, oral communication skills, personal interest in the field, self-motivation, written communication skills. Duration is 3–12 months. Open to college freshmen, college sophomores, college juniors, college seniors, recent college graduates, graduate students. All positions are unpaid. International applications accepted.

Benefits Housing at a cost, job counseling, names of contacts, on-the-job training, opportunity to attend seminars/workshops, possible full-time employment, willing to act as a professional reference, willing to complete paperwork for educational credit, willing to provide letters of recommendation, possibility of merit-based scholarship following internship.

Contact Write, call, fax, or e-mail Marla Rosenthal, Intern Coordinator, 17308 Queen Anne Bridge Road, Bowie, Maryland 20716-9033. Phone: 301-390-7011. Fax: 301-249-3511. E-mail: cheswild@erols.com. Telephone interview required. Applicants must submit a formal organization application, resume, academic transcripts, two letters of recommendation, 2-page essay stating goals for internship, send a self-addressed stamped envelope requesting application form. Applications are accepted continuously. World Wide Web: http://www.chesapeakewildlife.org.

CINCINNATI NATURE CENTER
4949 Tealtown Road
Milford, Ohio 45150

General Information Private nonprofit environmental education center with three sites including two farms and one large natural area totalling 1,425 acres. Established in 1966. Number of employees: 30. Number of internship applications received each year: 20.

Internships Available ▶ *1–2 environmental education interns:* responsibilities include teaching youth from pre-school through high school about environmental concepts in a natural or farm setting using a hands-on, experiential approach; assisting with special events; developing and conducting programs for the general public. Duration is one semester (35 hours per week). ▶ *2–4 farm educators:* responsibilities include teaching youth from pre-school through high school about environmental concepts on an educational farm; assisting with special events, garden-

ing, livestock care, and public programs. Duration is 1 semester. Candidates for all positions should have college courses in field, oral communication skills, personal interest in the field, self-motivation, strong interpersonal skills, written communication skills. All positions paid at $100 per week. Open to college freshmen, college sophomores, college juniors, college seniors, recent college graduates, graduate students, career changers, individuals reentering the workforce. International applications accepted.

Benefits Free housing, on-the-job training, opportunity to attend seminars/workshops, willing to act as a professional reference, willing to complete paperwork for educational credit, willing to provide letters of recommendation, $15 per week gas reimbursement if the internship takes place at a site other than where housing is offered.

Contact Write, call, fax, or e-mail Connie Brockman, Education Director, 4949 Tealtown Road, Milford, Ohio 45150. Phone: 513-965-4891. Fax: 513-831-8052. E-mail: cbrockman@cincynature.org. In-person interview recommended. Applicants must submit a cover letter, resume, two letters of recommendation, one essay on environmental philosophy. Application deadline: August 1 for fall, December 1 for spring.

CISPUS LEARNING CENTER
2142 Cispus Road
Randle, Washington 98377-9305

General Information Outdoor education learning facility used by school groups for environmental education; offers teacher training and a challenge course. Established in 1981. Number of employees: 22. Unit of Association of Washington School Principals, Olympia, Washington. Number of internship applications received each year: 24.

Internships Available ▶ *1–3 challenge course facilitators:* responsibilities include facilitating groups on the challenge ropes course. Candidates should have ability to work independently, oral communication skills, organizational skills, personal interest in the field, strong interpersonal skills, strong leadership ability. Duration is 12–16 weeks. $250–$1,000 per month. Open to college seniors, recent college graduates, graduate students, career changers, individuals reentering the workforce. ▶ *1 park host:* responsibilities include serving as a liaison between management and visitors. Candidates should have ability to work with others, oral communication skills, organizational skills, strong interpersonal skills, strong leadership ability. Duration is 4–12 weeks. Unpaid. Open to recent college graduates, career changers. ▶ *2–6 professional services volunteers:* responsibilities include business planning, writing newsletters, and developing curriculum. Candidates should have computer skills, oral communication skills, personal interest in the field, self-motivation, strong interpersonal skills, written communication skills. Duration is 2–4 weeks. Unpaid. Open to college juniors, college seniors, career changers, individuals reentering the workforce. ▶ *1–2 student leadership facilitators:* responsibilities include working with the summer student leadership program, assisting with facilitating groups of student body offices in small group learning sessions, assisting in general administration of the program. Candidates should have declared college major in field, oral communication skills, organizational skills, personal interest in the field, self-motivation, strong interpersonal skills, strong leadership ability, major in education preferred. Duration is 6–8 weeks. Unpaid. Open to college juniors, college seniors, recent college graduates. International applications accepted.

Benefits Free housing, free meals, on-the-job training, possible full-time employment, willing to act as a professional reference, willing to complete paperwork for educational credit, willing to provide letters of recommendation, orientation.

Contact Write, call, or e-mail Mr. Martin E. Fortin, Director. Phone: 360-497-7131. E-mail: fortin@myhome.net. Applicants must submit a cover letter, evidence of coordination with a college or university. Applications are accepted continuously. World Wide Web: http://www.cispus.org.

CLARKE ENVIRONMENTAL MOSQUITO MANAGEMENT, INC.
159 North Garden Avenue
Roselle, Illinois 60172

General Information   Largest and oldest professional mosquito control contractor in the United States. Established in 1946. Number of employees: 140. Number of internship applications received each year: 200.

Internships Available   ▶ *4 biological science interns (arbovirus surveillance technician and field inspector positions):* responsibilities include obtaining blood samples from wild birds to test for St. Louis Encephalitis. Candidates should have ability to work independently, ability to work with others, experience in the field, organizational skills, personal interest in the field. Duration is May to August. $8 per hour. Open to anyone 18 years of age or older. ▶ *2 environmental science interns:* responsibilities include stocking of mosquitofish and performing inspections. Candidates should have ability to work independently, ability to work with others, organizational skills, personal interest in the field, good map skills. Duration is 3 May to August. $8 per hour. Open to anyone 18 years of age or older. ▶ *1 geography intern:* responsibilities include working with cartography records to develop map files. Candidates should have ability to work independently, ability to work with others, college courses in field, experience in the field, knowledge of field, oral communication skills, self-motivation. Duration is 1 summer. $8 per hour. Open to anyone 18 years of age or older. ▶ *4 life science interns:* responsibilities include collecting adult and larval mosquito for identification and monitoring of mosquito populations. Candidates should have ability to work independently, experience in the field, organizational skills, self-motivation. Duration is May to August. $8 per hour. Open to anyone 18 years of age or older. ▶ *2 research and development interns:* responsibilities include helping research and development staff test new products for mosquito control. Candidates should have ability to work independently, ability to work with others, analytical skills, computer skills, knowledge of field, organizational skills, strong interpersonal skills. Duration is May to August. $8 per hour. Open to anyone over 18 years of age. ▶ *1 sales and marketing intern:* responsibilities include scheduling and coordinating the comfort package crews, assisting sales and marketing with special events and comfort packages, data entry, and customer service. Candidates should have ability to work independently, computer skills, knowledge of field, office skills, organizational skills, self-motivation, strong customer service skills. Duration is 3-4 months from May to August. $8 per hour. Open to anyone 18 years of age or older. International applications accepted.

Benefits   Possible full-time employment, willing to complete paperwork for educational credit, willing to provide letters of recommendation.

Contact   Write, call, fax, or e-mail Ms. Kara Kokotas, Seasonal Human Resources. Phone: 800-323-5727. Fax: 630-894-1774. E-mail: clarke@cmosquito.com. In-person interview required. Applicants must submit two letters of recommendation, call for a formal application. Application deadline: April 1 for summer. Fees: $4. World Wide Web: http://www.cmosquito.com.

CLIMATE INSTITUTE
333½ Pennsylvania Avenue, SE
Washington, District of Columbia 20003-1148

General Information   Organization serving as a link between scientists and policymakers on the issues of climate change and stratospheric ozone depletion. Established in 1986. Number of employees: 8. Number of internship applications received each year: 30.

Internships Available   ▶ *2–5 research assistants:* responsibilities include assisting with projects and office operations and supporting fund-raising activities. Candidates should have ability to work independently, ability to work with others, office skills, research skills, writing skills. Duration is flexible. Unpaid. Open to high school students, high school seniors, recent high school graduates, college freshmen, college sophomores, college juniors, college seniors, recent college graduates, graduate students, law students, career changers, individuals reentering the workforce. International applications accepted.

Benefits   Job counseling, names of contacts, opportunity to attend seminars/workshops, possible full-time employment, willing to act as a professional reference, willing to complete paperwork for educational credit, willing to provide letters of recommendation.

Contact   Write, fax, or e-mail Michele Pena, Director of Programs. Fax: 202-547-0111. E-mail: mpena@climate.org. In-person interview recommended. Applicants must submit a cover letter, resume, writing sample. Applications are accepted continuously. World Wide Web: http://www.climate.org.

CLINIC FOR THE REHABILITATION OF WILDLIFE (C.R.O.W.)
PO Box 150
Sanibel Island, Florida 33957

General Information   Nonprofit wildlife veterinary hospital dedicated to the rescue, medical, surgical, and rehabilitative care of the injured, ill, and orphaned native and migratory wildlife of Lee County. Established in 1968. Number of employees: 5. Number of internship applications received each year: 100.

Internships Available   ▶ *2 externs:* responsibilities include participating on medical and rehabilitative team. Candidates should have background in natural science and/or veterinary field; animal experience required. Duration is 6–8 weeks. Unpaid. Open to college juniors, college seniors, recent college graduates, graduate students. ▶ *1 fellow:* responsibilities include carrying out clinical duties such as patient examination, diagnosis, anesthesia, assistance in surgery, patient records, and environmental education; preparing special outreach programs for school-age children; giving public tours of the facility. Candidates should have prior externship with C.R.O.W. preferred; background in natural science/veterinary field; experience with animals. Duration is 6 months. stipend of $500 per month. Open to college freshmen, college sophomores, college juniors, college seniors, recent college graduates, graduate students.

Benefits   Free housing, willing to complete paperwork for educational credit, full benefits provided for fellows positions.

Contact   Write or e-mail Externships-CROW. E-mail: crowclinic@aol.com. No phone calls. Applicants must submit a formal organization application, resume, academic transcripts, 2 recommendations (1 must be from a veterinarian). Application deadline: 1 year in advance. World Wide Web: http://www.crowclinic.org.

CLYDE E. BUCKLEY WILDLIFE SANCTUARY
1305 Germany Road
Frankfort, Kentucky 40601

General Information   Sanctuary working to teach the public about the environment through hands-on experience and to encourage the potential of native flora and fauna through sound wildlife management. Established in 1967. Number of employees: 3. Unit of National Audubon Society, New York, New York. Number of internship applications received each year: 30.

Internships Available   ▶ *6 sanctuary operations interns:* responsibilities include assisting with nature interpretation, environmental education, wildlife management, research, caretaking, maintenance, administration, exhibits, photography, gift shop operations, fund-raising, and creative writing. Candidates should have ability to work independently, ability to work with others, computer skills, knowledge of field, oral communication skills, self-motivation. Duration is 10 weeks. $100 per week. Open to college freshmen, college sophomores, college juniors, college seniors, recent college graduates, graduate students, career changers, individuals reentering the workforce.

Benefits   Formal training, free housing, opportunity to attend seminars/workshops, willing to complete paperwork for educational credit, worker's compensation, utilities, uniforms.

Contact   Write, call, or fax Mr. Tim Williams, Sanctuary Manager. Phone: 606-873-5711. Fax: 606-873-5711. Applicants must submit a resume, two personal references, letter describing why you want the internship and what you could add to our programs. Also include your interests and hobbies. Application deadline: February 15 for spring, May 15 for summer, August 15 for fall.

COLORADO WILDLIFE FEDERATION
445 Union Boulevard, Suite 302
Lakewood, Colorado 80228-1243

General Information Conservation education organization that focuses on issues affecting Colorado's wildlife and conservation programs for children. Established in 1953. Number of employees: 3. Affiliate of National Wildlife Federation, Vienna, Virginia. Number of internship applications received each year: 10.

Internships Available ▶ *1–4 education interns:* responsibilities include visiting 2nd through 8th grade classrooms in the Denver metropolitan area to bring conservation education programming to students. Candidates should have oral communication skills, personal interest in the field, self-motivation, strong interpersonal skills, ability to work with children. Duration is September to June (9am to 3pm weekdays). Position available as unpaid or at $7 per hour. Open to college freshmen, college sophomores, college juniors, college seniors, recent college graduates, career changers, individuals reentering the workforce. ▶ *1 issues research intern:* responsibilities include researching conservation issues as assigned and preparing summaries for board of directors review; preparing issues statements for board of directors approval. Candidates should have ability to work independently, analytical skills, oral communication skills, personal interest in the field, research skills, written communication skills. Duration is year-round. Unpaid. Open to college freshmen, college sophomores, college juniors, college seniors, recent college graduates, graduate students. ▶ *1–3 office assistant/member relations interns:* responsibilities include updating CWF member records, corresponding with members, preparing mailings to update members on CWF actions, preparing member acknowledgment mailings, and assisting with phone inquires. Candidates should have ability to work independently, computer skills, office skills, oral communication skills, organizational skills, self-motivation. Duration is year-round. Unpaid. Open to college freshmen, college sophomores, college juniors, college seniors, recent college graduates, career changers, individuals reentering the workforce. International applications accepted.
Benefits Job counseling, names of contacts, on-the-job training, opportunity to attend seminars/workshops, willing to complete paperwork for educational credit, willing to provide letters of recommendation, mileage reimbursement for delivering programs.
Contact Write or fax Tanya Smart, Manager of Education Programs. Fax: 303-987-0200. No phone calls. In-person interview required. Applicants must submit a cover letter, resume. Applications are accepted continuously. World Wide Web: http://www.coloradowildlife.com.

COMMUNITY ENVIRONMENTAL CENTER
43-10 11th Street
Long Island City, New York 11101

General Information Energy conservation and environmental education not-for-profit center. Established in 1994. Number of employees: 30. Number of internship applications received each year: 40.
Internships Available ▶ *1–2 construction management interns (technical services):* responsibilities include developing construction management documentation, quality management, and performing field inspections. Candidates should have ability to work independently, computer skills, experience in the field, oral communication skills, self-motivation, writing skills, major or degree in construction management or related field; must be able to travel. Duration is 3–6 months. Position available as unpaid or at $12 per hour. Open to college seniors, recent college graduates, graduate students. ▶ *1–2 energy interns (technical services):* responsibilities include developing heating distribution and system specifications, performing building performance analyses, assisting in construction management and designing, and conducting energy audits. Candidates should have ability to work

independently, oral communication skills, organizational skills, personal interest in the field, writing skills, written communication skills, degree or major in energy or mechanical engineering or related field; experience in doing energy audits on buildings; must be able to travel. Duration is 3–6 months. Position available as unpaid or at $12 per hour. Open to college seniors, recent college graduates, graduate students. ▶ *1–2 information services assistants:* responsibilities include research of urban environmental issues; preparation of informational materials, including writing, editing, and layout; miscellaneous projects (e.g., educational programs, technical analyses, policy). Candidates should have ability to work independently, ability to work with others, editing skills, personal interest in the field, research skills, writing skills. Duration is one semester or one summer. Position available as unpaid or at $8 per hour. Open to college sophomores, college juniors, college seniors.
Benefits On-the-job training, opportunity to attend seminars/workshops, possible full-time employment, willing to act as a professional reference, willing to complete paperwork for educational credit, willing to provide letters of recommendation.
Contact Write, call, fax, or e-mail Lynn Grace, Director of External Communications/Youth Programs, 43-10 11th Street, Long Island City, New York 11101. Phone: 718-784-1444 Ext. 107. Fax: 718-784-8347. E-mail: cec@dti.net. In-person interview required. Applicants must submit a cover letter, resume. Applications are accepted continuously.

CONSERVANCY, INC.
1450 Merrihue Drive
Naples, Florida 34102

General Information Locally based, nonprofit conservation organization whose efforts are primarily focused on ecological research, environmental protection, and environmental education. The Conservancy operates 2 nature centers, a wildlife rehabilitation clinic, and offers many environmental programs and activities for the public. Established in 1964. Number of employees: 42. Number of internship applications received each year: 200.
Internships Available ▶ *1 Museum of Natural History/Naples Nature Center conservation associate:* responsibilities include working in museum research and exhibit interpretation, exhibit design, outdoors on nature trails, and delivering programs. Candidates should have ability to work independently, computer skills, knowledge of field, oral communication skills, strong interpersonal skills. Duration is 6–9 months. Open to college juniors, college seniors, recent college graduates, graduate students. ▶ *1 environmental land acquisition and policy conservation associate:* responsibilities include assisting in purchasing conservation land, research in water resource management, and the biology of endangered and threatened species. Candidates should have ability to work independently, oral communication skills, research skills, self-motivation, strong interpersonal skills, written communication skills. Duration is 6 months. Open to recent college graduates, graduate students. ▶ *1 environmental policy intern:* responsibilities include assisting all aspects of research and investigation of environmental issues. Candidates should have ability to work independently, oral communication skills, self-motivation, strong interpersonal skills, written communication skills. Duration is 3–6 months. Open to recent college graduates, graduate students, law students. ▶ *1 environmental science conservation associate:* responsibilities include working on current field and/or office projects. Candidates should have analytical skills, college degree in related field, oral communication skills, plan to pursue career in field, research skills, written communication skills. Duration is 3–9 months. Open to recent college graduates, graduate students, law students. ▶ *2–4 naturalist conservation associates (Briggs):* responsibilities include teaching middle school children beach and estuarine ecology programs and assisting and leading adult wilderness excursions. Candidates should have ability to work independently, college courses in field, knowledge of field, oral communication skills, organizational skills, personal interest in the field, strong interpersonal skills, physical ability to hike and canoe. Duration is 3–9 months. Open to college juniors, college seniors, recent college graduates, graduate students. ▶ *School programs conservation associates:*

Conservancy, Inc. (continued)

responsibilities include teaching the natural science of Florida ecology to preschool, elementary school, and middle school children. Candidates should have ability to work independently, college courses in field, oral communication skills, personal interest in the field, self-motivation, strong interpersonal skills, experience with children. Duration is 6–9 months. Open to college juniors, college seniors, recent college graduates, graduate students. ▶ *Sea turtle research conservation associates:* responsibilities include monitoring and recording loggerhead sea turtle nesting information, measuring and tagging nesting turtles, and securing the nest. Candidates should have ability to work independently, college degree in related field, oral communication skills, self-motivation, strong interpersonal skills. Duration is May 1 to August 15 or May 1 to October 14. Open to recent college graduates, graduate students. ▶ *4–6 summer camp conservation associates (5 at Naples, 1 at Briggs):* responsibilities include teaching the natural science of Florida ecology to preschool, elementary school, and middle school children. Candidates should have ability to work independently, oral communication skills, self-motivation, strong interpersonal skills, a favorable attitude towards children. Duration is 3 months. Open to college juniors, college seniors, recent college graduates, graduate students. ▶ *4 wildlife rehabilitation conservation associates:* responsibilities include assisting in care and treatment of injured, sick, and orphaned Florida wildlife and cleaning and maintaining facilities. Candidates should have ability to work independently, ability to work with others, college courses in field, experience in the field, self-motivation, strong interpersonal skills. Duration is 6–9 months. Open to college juniors, college seniors, recent college graduates, graduate students. All positions paid at $100 weekly cost-of-living allowance. International applications accepted.
Benefits Formal training, free housing, on-the-job training, opportunity to attend seminars/workshops, possible full-time employment, willing to act as a professional reference, willing to complete paperwork for educational credit, willing to provide letters of recommendation, uniform shirts furnished, accident insurance.
Contact Write, call, fax, or e-mail Ms. Sharon Truluck, Human Resources Director. Phone: 941-262-0304. Fax: 941-262-0672. E-mail: humanresources@conservancy.org. Telephone interview required. Applicants must submit a formal organization application, cover letter, resume, academic transcripts, three personal references, three letters of recommendation. Applications are accepted continuously. World Wide Web: http://www.conservancy.org.

CORKSCREW SWAMP SANCTUARY
375 Sanctuary Road
Naples, Florida 34120

General Information 11,000-acre wilderness area in southwest Florida providing preservation, protection, and public education; home to old-growth bald cypress forest and Florida's largest nesting colony of endangered wood storks. Established in 1954. Number of employees: 8. Number of internship applications received each year: 200.
Internships Available ▶ *4 naturalists:* responsibilities include resource management fieldwork, facilities maintenance, environmental education and interpretation tasks, and staffing of visitor center. Duration is 6 months. $150 per week. Open to college freshmen, college sophomores, college juniors, college seniors, recent college graduates, graduate students, career changers.
Benefits Formal training, free housing, job counseling, names of contacts, on-the-job training, willing to complete paperwork for educational credit, willing to provide letters of recommendation, job lists provided when available, $50 allowance for necessary clothing/uniform.
Contact Write, fax, or e-mail Mr. Andrew Mackie, Assistant Manager. Fax: 941-348-9155. E-mail: amackie@audubon.org. No phone calls. Telephone interview required. Applicants must submit a cover letter, resume, three personal references. Applications are accepted continuously. World Wide Web: http://www.audubon.org.

DAHLEM ENVIRONMENTAL EDUCATION CENTER
7117 South Jackson Road
Jackson, Michigan 49201

General Information Center that promotes understanding of ecological and environmental principles by providing the knowledge and skills for developing and maintaining a quality environment; activities include school and public programs, workshops, classes, summer ecology camps, special events, research, and a newsletter. Established in 1973. Number of employees: 12. Unit of Jackson Community College, Jackson, Michigan. Number of internship applications received each year: 50.
Internships Available ▶ *3–4 ecology camp counselors:* responsibilities include selecting and implementing environmental education activities and preparing, taking inventory of, and caring for camp equipment. Candidates should have knowledge of field, oral communication skills, organizational skills, strong interpersonal skills, strong leadership ability. Duration is 2–3 months. Open to college seniors, recent college graduates, graduate students, classroom teachers. ▶ *10–12 naturalists/interns:* responsibilities include organizing, conducting, and evaluating school and youth-group field experiences and assisting with projects that may include animal care, exhibit design and construction, writing news releases, working in the visitor center and gift shop, leading public programs, and/or preparing educational materials. Candidates should have college courses in field, oral communication skills, personal interest in the field, strong interpersonal skills, written communication skills, experience working with children. Duration is 3–4 months. Open to college juniors, college seniors, recent college graduates, graduate students, career changers. ▶ *1–2 wildlife biologists/naturalists:* responsibilities include coordinating a community-oriented restoration program for the eastern bluebird, monitoring and keeping accurate records for 400 nestboxes, and providing on-site supervision and assistance to volunteers and property owners. Candidates should have ability to work with others, college courses in field, knowledge of field, oral communication skills, organizational skills, research skills. Duration is 5–6 months. Open to college seniors, recent college graduates, graduate students, career changers. All positions paid at $206 per week.
Benefits Formal training, free housing, job counseling, names of contacts, opportunity to attend seminars/workshops, willing to act as a professional reference, willing to complete paperwork for educational credit, willing to provide letters of recommendation, scholarships for professional growth, travel reimbursement for wildlife biologists/naturalists.
Contact Write, call, or fax Ms. Diane Valen, Program Coordinator. Phone: 517-782-3453. Fax: 517-782-3441. Telephone interview required. Applicants must submit a formal organization application, cover letter, resume, three personal references. Application deadline: February 1 for wildlife biologists, February 15 for spring naturalists, April 1 for ecology camp counselors, July 1 for fall naturalists.

DEEP PORTAGE CONSERVATION RESERVE
2197 Nature Center Drive, NW
Hackensack, Minnesota 56452

General Information 6000-acre forest and conservation education center that conducts programs in environmental education. Established in 1973. Number of employees: 16. Number of internship applications received each year: 40.
Internships Available ▶ *5 instructor interns:* responsibilities include teaching environmental education. Duration is 3–6 months. Open to college freshmen, college sophomores, college juniors, college seniors, graduate students, career changers, individuals reentering the workforce. ▶ *5 naturalist interns:* responsibilities include leading groups, teaching, and hosting interpretive center. Duration is 12 weeks in summer. Open to college freshmen, college sophomores, college juniors, college seniors, recent college graduates, graduate students, career changers, individuals reentering the workforce. All positions paid at $150 per week. International applications accepted.

Benefits Formal training, free housing, free meals, job counseling, names of contacts, opportunity to attend seminars/workshops, possible full-time employment, willing to complete paperwork for educational credit, willing to provide letters of recommendation.
Contact Write, call, fax, or e-mail Dale Yerger, Director. Phone: 218-682-2325. Fax: 218-682-3121. E-mail: portage@uslink.net. In-person interview recommended. Applicants must submit a resume, three personal references. Applications are accepted continuously. World Wide Web: http://www.deep-portage.org.

DELAWARE NATURE SOCIETY (ASHLAND NATURE CENTER)
PO Box 700, Brackenville and Barley Mill Road
Hockessin, Delaware 19707

General Information Environmental education and advocacy organization. Established in 1964. Number of employees: 70. Number of internship applications received each year: 5.
Internships Available ▶ *1–3 environmental education interns:* responsibilities include teaching and co-teaching children's classes and leading or assisting with field trips. Candidates should have ability to work with others, knowledge of field, personal interest in the field, ability to work with children, outdoor skills. Duration is 1–3 months. Position available as unpaid or at $2,000 for 3-month internship. Open to college juniors, college seniors, recent college graduates, graduate students, career changers. International applications accepted.
Benefits Formal training, on-the-job training, opportunity to attend seminars/workshops, possible full-time employment, willing to act as a professional reference, willing to complete paperwork for educational credit, willing to provide letters of recommendation.
Contact Write, call, fax, or e-mail Karen Travers, Members Programs Coordinator, PO Box 700, Hockessin, Delaware 19707. Phone: 302-239-2334 Ext. 15. Fax: 302-239-2473. E-mail: karen@dnsashland.org. In-person interview required. Applicants must submit a formal organization application, cover letter, resume, two personal references, two letters of recommendation. Applications are accepted continuously. World Wide Web: http://www.dca.net/naturesociety.

DELAWARE WATER GAP NATIONAL RECREATION AREA
294 Old Milford Road
Milford, Pennsylvania 18337

General Information Organization devoted to conserving scenery, natural and historic objects, and wildlife for the enjoyment of future generations. Established in 1965. Number of employees: 100. Unit of United States National Park Service, Washington, District of Columbia. Number of internship applications received each year: 15.
Internships Available ▶ *1 geographic information systems laboratory assistant:* responsibilities include developing and implementing various software tools to facilitate spatial data creation, managing and analyzing within a GIS, assisting in development of GIS analytical procedure, and assisting in development of network communications. Candidates should have ability to work independently, ability to work with others, college courses in field, computer skills, organizational skills, self-motivation. Duration is 12–14 weeks. Open to college sophomores, college juniors, college seniors, recent college graduates, graduate students, career changers, individuals reentering the workforce. ▶ *1 resource assistant:* responsibilities include assisting with divisional activities that may include wildlife, fisheries, vegetation monitoring/management, trails development, water resources planning, wetland studies, and cultural landscape. Candidates should have ability to work independently, ability to work with others, college courses in field, computer skills, knowledge of field, oral communication skills, self-motivation, written communication skills. Duration is 3 months minimum. Open to college juniors, college seniors, recent college graduates, graduate students. ▶ *2 water quality assistants:* responsibilities include measuring water quality in streams and rivers, maintaining and

calibrating equipment, performing data entry, and analyzing data. Candidates should have ability to work independently, ability to work with others, analytical skills, computer skills, knowledge of field, organizational skills. Duration is 12 weeks. Open to college juniors, college seniors, recent college graduates, graduate students. All positions are unpaid. International applications accepted.
Benefits Free housing, job counseling, names of contacts, willing to complete paperwork for educational credit, willing to provide letters of recommendation, worker's compensation, potential stipend.
Contact Write or fax Denise Cooke, Acting Chief, Division of Research and Resource Planning. Phone: 570-296-6952 Ext. 16. Fax: 570-296-4706. In-person interview recommended. Applicants must submit a cover letter, resume. Application deadline: February 15 for spring/summer, November 1 for winter. World Wide Web: http://www.nps.gov/dewa.

EDUCATIONAL COMMUNICATIONS, INC.; ECONEWS TELEVISION; ENVIRONMENTAL DIRECTIONS RADIO; ECOLOGY CENTER OF SOUTHERN CALIFORNIA; PROJECT ECOTOURISM, COMPENDIOM
PO Box 351419
Los Angeles, California 90035-9119

General Information Environmental broadcasting and conservation organization specializing in ecological activism. Established in 1958. Unit of Educational Communications, Idyllwild, California. Number of internship applications received each year: 50.
Internships Available ▶ *Interns:* responsibilities include working in a variety of areas including ecological and environmental activism, administration, networking, organizing research, fundraising, public speaking, membership development, writing, producing, editing, directing, television and radio production, distribution, publishing, journalism, and broadcasting. Candidates should have ability to work independently, ability to work with others, editing skills, personal interest in the field, self-motivation, writing skills. Duration is flexible. Unpaid. Open to high school students, high school seniors, recent high school graduates, college freshmen, college sophomores, college juniors, college seniors, recent college graduates, graduate students, law students, career changers, individuals reentering the workforce. International applications accepted.
Benefits Job counseling, names of contacts, on-the-job training, opportunity to attend seminars/workshops, willing to act as a professional reference, willing to complete paperwork for educational credit, willing to provide letters of recommendation, referrals provided, opportunity to produce and host own television and radio shows.
International Internships Available.
Contact Write, call, or e-mail Leslie Lewis, Administrative Assistant. Phone: 310-559-9160. E-mail: ecnp@aol.com. Telephone interview required. Applicants must submit a cover letter, resume, writing sample, demo tape if applying for television editing position. Applications are accepted continuously. World Wide Web: http://home.earthlink.net/~dragonflight/ecoprojects.htm.

EL MALPAIS NATIONAL CONSERVATION AREA AND NATIONAL MONUMENT
2001 East Santa Fe Avenue
Grants, New Mexico 87020

General Information Area designated by Congress to preserve the natural geology and cultural resources surrounding Grant's Lava Flows; land includes 2 wilderness areas. Number of employees: 5. Unit of Bureau of Land Management, Rio Puerco Resource Area, Albuquerque, New Mexico. Number of internship applications received each year: 12.
Internships Available ▶ *1–2 backcountry rangers:* responsibilities include patrolling NCA backcountry/wilderness by vehicle or on foot, keeping a written patrol log, writing reports, providing visitors with accurate information, giving guided tours, assisting with maintenance, and staffing visitor center. ▶ *1–2 visitor informa-*

El Malpais National Conservation Area and National Monument (continued)

tion specialists: responsibilities include staffing the visitor center desk, responding to visitor questions, selling Cooperating Association books and materials, patrolling NCA by vehicle or on foot, keeping a written patrol log, writing reports as necessary, giving guided tours, and assisting with maintenance. Candidates for all positions should have computer skills, oral communication skills, personal interest in the field, strong interpersonal skills, written communication skills. Duration for all positions is 3 months (flexible). All positions are unpaid.

Benefits Free housing, willing to complete paperwork for educational credit, willing to provide letters of recommendation.

Contact Write or call Ms. Karen Davis, Volunteer Coordinator/Park Ranger. Phone: 505-287-7911. Applicants must submit a formal organization application, resume, two personal references. Applications are accepted continuously.

THE ENVIRONMENTAL CAREERS ORGANIZATION
179 South Street
Boston, Massachusetts 02111

General Information Environmental career development organization. Established in 1972. Number of employees: 39. Unit of The Environmental Careers Organization National Office, Boston, Massachusetts. Number of internship applications received each year: 25,000.

Internships Available ▶ *600–700 ECO associates:* responsibilities include various duties determined by position. Each position description is listed at www.eco.org. Duration is varies; 6 months to 2 years. $400–$700 per week. Open to college sophomores, college juniors, college seniors, recent college graduates, graduate students, law students, dependent upon position. International applications accepted.

Benefits Health insurance, opportunity to attend seminars/workshops.

Contact ECO Recruiters. Applicants must submit a cover letter, resume, other requirements are needed for certain positions; check the Web site for details. Applications are accepted continuously. World Wide Web: http://www.eco.org.

ENVIRONMENTAL DEFENSE FUND
257 Park Avenue South
New York, New York 10010

General Information Nonprofit national advocacy organization with over 300,000 members, working to develop economical and viable solutions to tough environmental problems. Established in 1967. Number of employees: 74. Number of internship applications received each year: 100.

Internships Available ▶ *4–8 environmental interns:* responsibilities include working on issues involving fisheries management, land use issues integrated with issues of air pollution and traffic congestion, legislative issues, policy/legal research, and policy analysis. Duration is 8–10 weeks. ▶ *1–2 political science interns:* responsibilities include working on biotechnology issues; mass transit improvement including issues of historic preservation, environmental equity, energy use, air and noise pollution. Duration is 10 weeks in summer. All positions available as unpaid or paid. Open to recent college graduates, graduate students, law students, career changers.

Benefits Names of contacts, opportunity to attend seminars/workshops, travel reimbursement, willing to complete paperwork for educational credit, willing to provide letters of recommendation.

Contact Write, call, fax, or e-mail Maxine Adams, Internship Coordinator, 257 Park Avenue, New York, New York 10010. Phone: 212-505-2100. Fax: 212-505-0892. E-mail: maxine_adams@edf.org. In-person interview recommended. Applicants must submit a cover letter, resume, academic transcripts, writing sample, two letters of recommendation. Application deadline: March 31.

ENVIRONMENTAL LAW INSTITUTE (ELI)
1616 P Street, NW, Suite 200
Washington, District of Columbia 20036

General Information National nonprofit research and education center that advances environmental protection, domestically and abroad, by improving law, policy, and management. Established in 1969. Number of employees: 60. Number of internship applications received each year: 150.

Internships Available ▶ *1–3 research interns:* responsibilities include working directly with ELI lawyers, economists, and scientists to conduct research on natural resource protection and pollution prevention, conducting library and internet research; attending and reporting on outside events, reviewing and summarizing scholarly material; assisting with preparation for environmental training courses; conducting telephone interviews; and performing various administrative tasks. Candidates should have analytical skills, oral communication skills, personal interest in the field, research skills, strong interpersonal skills, written communication skills. Duration is 1 semester (fall, spring, summer); or occasionally for shorter periods of time between semesters (e.g. January or May). Unpaid. Open to college sophomores, college juniors, college seniors, recent college graduates.

Benefits Job counseling, names of contacts, opportunity to attend seminars/workshops, possible full-time employment, willing to act as a professional reference, willing to complete paperwork for educational credit, willing to provide letters of recommendation, stipend for local commuting expenses.

Contact Write, call, fax, or e-mail Jill van Berg, Director, Research Intern Program. Phone: 202-939-3837. Fax: 202-939-3868. E-mail: vanberg@eli.org. In-person interview recommended. Applicants must submit a cover letter, resume, writing sample, three personal references, grade point average. Applications are accepted continuously. World Wide Web: http://www.eli.org.

ENVIRONMENTAL RESOURCE CENTER
PO Box 819, 411 East Sixth Street
Ketchum, Idaho 83340

General Information Nonprofit organization dedicated to providing resources and educational programs to the public about local, regional, and global environmental issues; acts as umbrella organization for local groups such as Sun Valley Avalanche Center, Wood River Valley Conservation Forum, and the Wood River Action Plan. Established in 1989. Number of employees: 2. Number of internship applications received each year: 30.

Internships Available ▶ *1–2 communications/events assistants:* responsibilities include helping with general office and program work; working on individual projects such as the organization of summer events, volunteers, and press work; and researching and writing environmental "fact sheets". Candidates should have ability to work with others, computer skills, oral communication skills, personal interest in the field, strong interpersonal skills, written communication skills. Duration is 10 weeks in summer (minimum 20 hours per week). Unpaid. Open to college freshmen, college sophomores, college juniors, college seniors, recent college graduates, graduate students, law students, career changers, individuals reentering the workforce. International applications accepted.

Benefits Formal training, job counseling, names of contacts, on-the-job training, opportunity to attend seminars/workshops, possible full-time employment, willing to act as a professional reference, willing to complete paperwork for educational credit, willing to provide letters of recommendation, assistance in finding housing.

Contact Write, call, fax, or e-mail Molly Goodyear, Executive Director. Phone: 208-726-4333. Fax: 208-726-1531. E-mail: erc@micron.net. In person interview recommended. Applicants must submit a cover letter, resume, personal reference. Application deadline: May 1.

ERIE NATIONAL WILDLIFE REFUGE
11296 Wood Duck Lane
Guys Mills, Pennsylvania 16327

General Information Refuge established under the authority of the Migratory Bird Conservation Act for use as a sanctuary or any other management purpose for migratory birds; provides a nesting, resting, and feeding area for waterfowl and a habitat for other species while providing the public with environmental education and recreation. Established in 1959. Number of employees: 7. Number of internship applications received each year: 50.

Internships Available ▶ *1 biologist:* responsibilities include conducting surveys, data collection, and working on a particular project. Candidates should have ability to work independently, ability to work with others, computer skills, knowledge of field, research skills, self-motivation. Open to high school students, high school seniors, recent high school graduates, college freshmen, college sophomores, college juniors, college seniors, recent college graduates, individuals reentering the workforce. ▶ *1 clerical worker:* responsibilities include working in office and providing clerical assistance. Candidates should have ability to work with others, computer skills, knowledge of field, office skills, organizational skills, self-motivation. Open to high school students, high school seniors, recent high school graduates, college freshmen, college sophomores, college juniors, college seniors, recent college graduates, career changers, individuals reentering the workforce. ▶ *1 computer technician:* responsibilities include entering data and providing computer assistance to the staff. Candidates should have ability to work independently, ability to work with others, computer skills, experience in the field, organizational skills, self-motivation. Open to high school students, high school seniors, recent high school graduates, college freshmen, college sophomores, college juniors, college seniors, recent college graduates, graduate students, career changers, individuals reentering the workforce. ▶ *1 interpreter:* responsibilities include staffing visitor center and conducting programs. Candidates should have ability to work independently, ability to work with others, computer skills, knowledge of field, oral communication skills, self-motivation. ▶ *1 maintenance worker:* responsibilities include working on trails, buildings, and grounds. Candidates should have ability to work independently, ability to work with others, experience in the field, organizational skills, self-motivation. Open to high school students, high school seniors, recent high school graduates, college freshmen, college sophomores, college juniors, college seniors, recent college graduates, graduate students, career changers, individuals reentering the workforce. Duration for all positions is variable. All positions are unpaid. International applications accepted.

Benefits Job counseling, names of contacts, willing to complete paperwork for educational credit, willing to provide letters of recommendation.

Contact Write, call, or e-mail Ms. Janet A. Marvin, Volunteer Coordinator. Phone: 814-789-3585. E-mail: r5rw_ernwr@mail.fws. gov. In-person interview recommended. Applications are accepted continuously.

EXOTIC FELINE BREEDING COMPOUND, INC.
HCR 1, Box 84
Rosamond, California 93560

General Information Nonprofit organization dedicated to the preservation and propagation of rare and endangered felines through breeding, research, and education. Established in 1977. Number of employees: 7. Number of internship applications received each year: 2.

Internships Available ▶ *1–3 keepers:* responsibilities include cleaning cages, behavioral observation and completion of health charts, dietary preparation, assisting in medical procedures, educational talks with public, and office procedures. Candidates should have ability to work independently, ability to work with others, analytical skills, declared college major in field, personal interest in the field, plan to pursue career in field. Duration is flexible. Unpaid. Open to college freshmen, college sophomores,

college juniors, college seniors, recent college graduates, graduate students. International applications accepted.

Benefits Housing at a cost, on-the-job training, willing to act as a professional reference, willing to complete paperwork for educational credit, willing to provide letters of recommendation.

Contact Write, call, fax, or e-mail Sandra Masek, General Manager, HCR 1, Box 84, Rosamond, California 93560. Phone: 661-256-3793. Fax: 661-256-6867. E-mail: info@cathouse-fcc.org. Applicants must submit a cover letter, resume, letter of recommendation. Applications are accepted continuously. World Wide Web: http://http://www.cathouse-fcc.org.

FAIRVIEW LAKE ENVIRONMENTAL EDUCATION CENTER–YMCA
1035 Fairview Lake Road
Newton, New Jersey 07860

General Information Residential facility that offers a hands-on approach to education and presents all-age courses dealing with life sciences, ecology, and technical wilderness skills. Established in 1915. Number of employees: 40. Branch of Metropolitan YMCA of the Oranges, West Orange, New Jersey. Number of internship applications received each year: 10.

Internships Available ▶ *1–2 fall naturalist interns:* responsibilities include participating in training, observing courses, teaching, aiding in maintenance, designing displays, and submitting paperwork. Duration is 3 months. Open to college juniors, college seniors, recent college graduates, graduate students. ▶ *2 recreational interns:* responsibilities include teaching, participating in training including team building, challenge, boating, archery, and hiking. Duration is 3 months. Open to college freshmen, college sophomores, college juniors, college seniors, recent college graduates, graduate students. ▶ *1–3 spring naturalist interns:* responsibilities include participating in training, observing courses, teaching, aiding in maintenance, designing displays, and submitting paperwork. Duration is 5 months. Open to college juniors, college seniors, recent college graduates, graduate students. Candidates for all positions should have college courses in field, oral communication skills, personal interest in the field, strong interpersonal skills. All positions paid at $125 per week. International applications accepted.

Benefits Formal training, free housing, free meals, opportunity to attend seminars/workshops, possible full-time employment, willing to complete paperwork for educational credit, willing to provide letters of recommendation, opportunity to receive certifications in first aid, CPR, and lifeguarding.

Contact Write, call, or fax Ms. Christina Henriksen, Environmental Education Director. Phone: 973-383-9282. Fax: 973-383-6386. In-person interview recommended. Applicants must submit a cover letter, resume. Applications are accepted continuously.

FARM AND WILDERNESS FOUNDATION
263 Farm and Wilderness Road
Plymouth, Vermont 05056

General Information Quaker-based foundation operating 6 summer camps, a retreat center, a school-year outdoor education program, and a year-round work crew. Established in 1939. Number of employees: 25. Number of internship applications received each year: 30.

Internships Available ▶ *2 carpentry interns:* responsibilities include working in maintenance and carpentry. Candidates should have ability to work independently, ability to work with others, personal interest in the field, self-motivation, some experience helpful. Duration is 3–8 months. Open to college freshmen, college sophomores, college juniors, college seniors, recent college graduates, graduate students, career changers, individuals reentering the workforce. ▶ *2 farm interns:* responsibilities include working in organic farming and gardening. Candidates should have ability to work independently, ability to work with others, oral communication skills, personal interest in the field, self-motivation. Duration is 8 months. Open to college freshmen, college sophomores, college juniors, college seniors, recent college graduates, graduate students, individuals reentering the workforce. ▶ *2 maintenance interns:* responsibilities include open-

Farm and Wilderness Foundation (continued)

ing, maintaining, and closing seasonal utilities, vehicle fleet, and buildings of an extensive physical plant. Candidates should have ability to work independently, personal interest in the field, self-motivation, strong interpersonal skills, some experience helpful. Duration is 3–8 months. Open to college freshmen, college sophomores, college juniors, college seniors, recent college graduates, graduate students, career changers, individuals reentering the workforce. ▶ *4 outdoor education interns:* responsibilities include instructing outdoor education day programs, school groups, and some adult special-need groups. Candidates should have oral communication skills, organizational skills, plan to pursue career in field, strong interpersonal skills, strong leadership ability, interest in teaching ages 3 to adult. Duration is 10 weeks. Open to college sophomores, college juniors, college seniors, recent college graduates, graduate students, individuals reentering the workforce. ▶ *1 retreat center caretaker:* responsibilities include responding to needs of groups in residence, scheduling and outreach to interested groups, and caretaking facilities. Candidates should have ability to work independently, office skills, oral communication skills, self-motivation, strong interpersonal skills, ability to keep facilities clean and orderly. Duration is 1 year. Open to college juniors, college seniors, recent college graduates, graduate students, career changers, individuals reentering the workforce. All positions paid at $150–$170 per week. International applications accepted.

Benefits Free housing, free meals, on-the-job training, willing to complete paperwork for educational credit, willing to provide letters of recommendation, worker's compensation.

Contact Write Taz Squire, Resource Manager. No phone calls. Telephone interview required. Applicants must submit a formal organization application, cover letter, resume, two personal references. Application deadline: January 1 for spring/fall; contiunous for outdoor education positions. World Wide Web: http://www.fandw.org.

FENTON RANCH
26473 Highway 126
Jemez Springs, New Mexico 87025

General Information Residential facility that houses the environmental education program for a private elementary school, Manzano Day School. Established in 1974. Number of employees: 5. Unit of Manzano Day School, Albuquerque, New Mexico. Number of internship applications received each year: 30.

Internships Available ▶ *1 environmental education intern (spring):* responsibilities include teaching environmental education programs to elementary-aged children, designing curriculum, facilitating freetime, keeping journals, supervising meals, and playing with children outdoors. Candidates should have ability to work independently, oral communication skills, organizational skills, personal interest in the field, self-motivation, strong interpersonal skills, strong leadership ability. Duration is 7 weeks (early April-late May). ▶ *2 environmental education interns (fall):* responsibilities include teaching environmental education to elementary-aged students, designing curriculum, facilitating freetime, keeping journals, meals, and playing with children outdoors. Candidates should have ability to work independently, oral communication skills, organizational skills, personal interest in the field, strong interpersonal skills, strong leadership ability. Duration is 11 weeks (mid-August-late October). All positions paid at $150–$200 per week. Open to college sophomores, college juniors, college seniors, recent college graduates, graduate students, career changers. International applications accepted.

Benefits Free housing, free meals, on-the-job training, travel reimbursement, willing to act as a professional reference, willing to provide letters of recommendation.

Contact Write or e-mail Stephanie Stansbury, Fenton Director, 1801 Central Avenue NW, Albuquerque, New Mexico 87104. E-mail: ss@mds.k12.nm.us. Telephone interview required. Applicants must submit a formal organization application, cover letter, resume, three personal references. Applications are accepted continuously.

FERNWOOD NATURE CENTER
13988 Range Line Road
Niles, Michigan 49120

General Information Nature Center and botanic garden working to educate people about the natural environment and to create environmental awareness and appreciation. Established in 1963. Number of employees: 15. Number of internship applications received each year: 25.

Internships Available ▶ *2 intern naturalists (spring term, fall term):* responsibilities include leading nature walks for children, teaching classes, and maintaining trails and displays. Candidates should have college courses in field, experience in the field, oral communication skills, personal interest in the field, strong interpersonal skills, experience or interest in working with children. Duration is 10–12 weeks. $6 per hour. Open to college juniors, college seniors, recent college graduates, graduate students, career changers, individuals reentering the workforce. ▶ *1 seasonal naturalist:* responsibilities include leading nature walks for children, teaching classes, trail maintenance, assisting in display work, and supervising and training of interns and volunteers. Candidates should have college degree in related field, experience in the field, oral communication skills, personal interest in the field, strong interpersonal skills, experience with children. Duration is 8 months. $6 per hour. Open to recent college graduates, graduate students, career changers, individuals reentering the workforce.

Benefits Formal training, housing at a cost, job counseling, names of contacts, on-the-job training, opportunity to attend seminars/workshops, travel reimbursement, willing to act as a professional reference, willing to complete paperwork for educational credit, willing to provide letters of recommendation.

Contact Write Ms. Wendy Jones, Head Naturalist. In-person interview recommended. Applicants must submit a cover letter, resume, three personal references. Application deadline: February 1 for seasonal naturalist, February 1 for spring, July 1 for fall.

FIVE RIVERS ENVIRONMENTAL EDUCATION CENTER
5 Rivers Center, Game Farm Road
Delmar, New York 12054

General Information Environmental center providing education programs to the public and schools. Established in 1973. Number of employees: 5. Unit of New York State Department of Environmental Conservation, Albany, New York. Number of internship applications received each year: 75.

Internships Available ▶ *8 naturalist interns:* responsibilities include teaching environmental programs and conducting other projects. Candidates should have college courses in field, oral communication skills, personal interest in the field, self-motivation, strong interpersonal skills, written communication skills. Duration is 10–12 weeks. $100 per week. Open to college freshmen, college sophomores, college juniors, college seniors, recent college graduates, graduate students, career changers, individuals reentering the workforce.

Benefits Formal training, free housing, job counseling, names of contacts, opportunity to attend seminars/workshops, travel reimbursement, willing to complete paperwork for educational credit, willing to provide letters of recommendation, worker's compensation.

Contact Write or call Ms. Anita Sanchez, Senior Environmental Educator. Phone: 518-475-0291. In-person interview recommended. Applicants must submit a formal organization application, resume, three personal references. Applications are accepted continuously.

FIVE RIVERS METROPARKS
1375 East Siebenthaler Avenue
Dayton, Ohio 45414

General Information Park agency with a total of 10,000 acres and annual visitation of approximately 5 million people that manages 20 facilities for public education, outdoor recreation, and protection of natural resources. Established in 1963. Number of employees: 90. Number of internship applications received each year: 30.

Internships Available ▶ *1 Carriage Hill agriculture intern/apprentice:* responsibilities include assisting with farm chores, animal care, agricultural work, and general park maintenance. Candidates should have ability to work independently, ability to work with others, oral communication skills, personal interest in the field, self-motivation. Duration is 3–9 months. $6 per hour (32 hours per week). ▶ *1 Carriage Hill restoration intern:* responsibilities include conducting major and minor repairs to historic structures and reconstructions and assisting with general farm maintenance and farm chores. Candidates should have ability to work independently, ability to work with others, personal interest in the field, research skills, self-motivation. Duration is 3–9 months. $6 per hour (32 hours per week). ▶ *1 Cox Arboretum intern:* responsibilities include planning and implementing educational programs, monitoring plant hotline, and working with staff and volunteers on horticulturally related projects. Candidates should have ability to work independently, oral communication skills, personal interest in the field, self-motivation, strong interpersonal skills, written communication skills. Duration is 9-12 months normally, 3-month summer position possible. $6 per hour (32 hours per week). ▶ *1–2 Germantown MetroPark interns/apprentices:* responsibilities include working in all phases of nature center programming and facility upkeep; conducting walks, workshops, and tours; and staffing the nature center. Candidates should have ability to work independently, ability to work with others, knowledge of field, oral communication skills, personal interest in the field, self-motivation. Duration is 3–12 months. $6 per hour (32 hours per week). ▶ *1 North MetroPark/apprentice:* responsibilities include leading natural history-oriented interpretive walks, workshops, and school programs; assisting with special events; and caring for some wild animals, primarily reptiles. Candidates should have ability to work independently, ability to work with others, knowledge of field, oral communication skills, personal interest in the field, self-motivation. Duration is 9–12 9-12 months; 3-month summer position considered if opening exists. $6 per hour (32 hours per week). ▶ *1 Possum Creek farm intern/apprentice:* responsibilities include leading tours of nature trail, barn, and farm animal area; assisting with weekend programs and special events; caring for farm animals; and performing some farm maintenance. Candidates should have ability to work independently, ability to work with others, oral communication skills, personal interest in the field, self-motivation, written communication skills. Duration is 3–12 months. $6 per hour (32 hours per week). ▶ *1 Wegerzyn adult education intern:* responsibilities include assisting chief of horticultural education in planning and implementing adult gardening programs, special seminars, workshops and professional horticulture training programs. Candidates should have ability to work independently, ability to work with others, oral communication skills, personal interest in the field, self-motivation, written communication skills. Duration is 3–9 months. $6 per hour (32 hours per week). ▶ *1 Wegerzyn youth program intern/apprentice:* responsibilities include developing educational materials and activities; planning and presenting programs for youth, school groups, and families; maintaining the Children's Discovery Garden. Candidates should have ability to work independently, oral communication skills, personal interest in the field, self-motivation, strong interpersonal skills. Duration is 3–12 months. $6 per hour (32 hours per week). ▶ *1–2 Wesleyan MetroPark naturalist interns:* responsibilities include leading natural history-related walks, workshops, and tours; working in all phases of nature center programming and upkeep; staffing the nature center; and animal care. Candidates should have ability to work independently, knowledge of field, oral communication skills, personal interest in the field, self-motivation, strong interpersonal skills, ability and interest in working with inner-city youth. Duration is 3–12 months. $6 per hour (32 hours per week). Open to college freshmen, college sophomores, college juniors, college seniors, recent college graduates, graduate students, career changers, individuals reentering the workforce.

Benefits Job counseling, names of contacts, on-the-job training, opportunity to attend seminars/workshops, possible full-time employment, willing to act as a professional reference, willing to complete paperwork for educational credit, housing provided at no cost at some sites.

Contact Write Ms. Lyn Modic, Chief of Education. In-person interview recommended. Applicants must submit a formal organization application, cover letter, resume, three personal references. Applications are accepted continuously. World Wide Web: http://www.metroparks.org.

FLORIDA PARK SERVICE
3900 Commonwealth Boulevard, MS 535
Tallahassee, Florida 32399

General Information Organization that manages 151 state parks. Established in 1935. Number of employees: 1,080. Division of Department of Environmental Protection, Tallahassee, Florida. Number of internship applications received each year: 10.

Internships Available ▶ *10–20 interns:* responsibilities include providing general assistance in the state park system; specific interests and assignments can be accommodated. Candidates should have ability to work with others, knowledge of field, oral communication skills, personal interest in the field, plan to pursue career in field. Duration is flexible. Unpaid. Open to high school students, recent high school graduates, college freshmen, college sophomores, college juniors, college seniors, recent college graduates, graduate students, career changers, individuals reentering the workforce. International applications accepted.

Benefits Formal training, job counseling, names of contacts, on-the-job training, possible full-time employment, travel reimbursement, willing to act as a professional reference, willing to complete paperwork for educational credit, willing to provide letters of recommendation, housing may be provided, camping may be available.

Contact Write, call, fax, or e-mail Mr. Phillip A. Werndli, Volunteer Coordinator, 3900 Commonwealth Boulevard, MS 535, Tallahassee, Florida 32399. Phone: 850-488-8243. Fax: 850-414-1624. E-mail: werndli_p@epic6.dep.state.fl.us. In-person interview required. Applicants must submit a formal organization application, cover letter, resume. Applications are accepted continuously. World Wide Web: http://www.dep.state.fl.us/parks/.

FRIENDS OF THE EARTH
1025 Vermont Avenue, NW, Suite 300
Washington, District of Columbia 20005

General Information Independent global advocacy organization working to protect the Earth from environmental disaster; preserve biological, cultural, and ethnic diversity; and empower citizens and help them develop an effective voice in decisions affecting their environment and lives. Established in 1969. Number of employees: 30. Number of internship applications received each year: 250.

Internships Available ▶ *6 fellowships:* responsibilities include Working with project directors from Eco-Team, Global Team, Journalism, Communications and Marketing Team, and Protect the Planet Team in researching, writing, lobbying, and assisting with administrative support on a variety of topics, including taxation and consumption, corporate accountability, water resource protection, ozone layer protection, Northwest rivers and wetlands, trade and international banking/monetary policy. Duration is 6 months. $800–$1,000 per month. ▶ *5–10 interns:* responsibilities include working with project directors from Eco-Team, Global Team, Journalism, Communications and Marketing Team, and Protect the Planet Team in researching, writing, lobbying, and assisting with administrative support on a variety of topics, including consumption and taxation, corporate accountability, water resource protection, ozone layer protection, Northwest rivers and wetlands, trade and international banking/monetary policy. Duration is 3–6 months. Unpaid. Candidates for all positions should have ability to work independently, computer skills, knowledge of field, oral communication skills, research skills, written communication skills. Open to recent college graduates, graduate students, law students. International applications accepted.

Friends of the Earth (continued)

Benefits Names of contacts, on-the-job training, travel reimbursement, willing to complete paperwork for educational credit, willing to provide letters of recommendation.

Contact Write or fax Jill Diskan, Fellowship Coordinator. Fax: 202-783-0444. No phone calls. Applicants must submit a cover letter, resume. Applications are accepted continuously. World Wide Web: http://www.foe.org/FOE.

FUND FOR ANIMALS, INC.
8121 Georgia Avenue, Suite 301
Silver Spring, Maryland 20910

General Information Nonprofit animal protection organization that focuses on companion animal and wildlife issues. Established in 1967. Number of employees: 10. Number of internship applications received each year: 30.

Internships Available ▶ *1–5 interns:* responsibilities include performing a variety of tasks in the legal, legislative, outreach, campaign, and administrative departments. Duration is 3 months minimum. $500 per duration of internship. Open to high school students, high school seniors, recent high school graduates, college freshmen, college sophomores, college juniors, college seniors, recent college graduates, graduate students, law students, career changers, individuals reentering the workforce. International applications accepted.

Benefits Formal training, opportunity to attend seminars/workshops, travel reimbursement, willing to complete paperwork for educational credit, willing to provide letters of recommendation.

Contact Write, call, fax, or e-mail Mr. Peter Petersan, Outreach Coordinator. Phone: 301-585-2591. Fax: 301-585-2595. E-mail: ppetersan@fund.org. In-person interview recommended. Applicants must submit a cover letter, resume. Applications are accepted continuously. World Wide Web: http://www.fund.org.

GARDEN IN THE WOODS
180 Hemenway Road
Framingham, Massachusetts 01701-2699

General Information Headquarters and botanical garden of the New England Wild Flower Society , a private, nonprofit organization dedicated to the conservation of temperate North American plants; offers programs in education, horticulture, research, habitat preservation, and conservation advocacy. Established in 1931. Number of employees: 15. Unit of New England Wild Flower Society, Framingham, Massachusetts. Number of internship applications received each year: 30.

Internships Available ▶ *1 garden maintenance and development intern:* responsibilities include general maintenance duties in a garden setting, rigorous physical labor, native plant identification, and standard horticultural practices. Candidates should have ability to work independently, ability to work with others, experience in the field, personal interest in the field, self-motivation. ▶ *1 plant conservation intern:* responsibilities include garden maintenance and construction, standard horticultural practices, native plant identification, record-keeping, native plant propagation, seed collection, public information duties, and plant conservation work. Candidates should have ability to work independently, ability to work with others, experience in the field, personal interest in the field, self-motivation. ▶ *2 propagation and nursery management interns:* responsibilities include native plant identification, native plant propagation, seed collection, production and sales, and public information duties. Candidates should have ability to work independently, ability to work with others, knowledge of field, personal interest in the field, self-motivation. Duration for all positions is 6 months (April–September). All positions paid at $200 per week. Open to college juniors, college seniors, recent college graduates, graduate students, career changers, individuals reentering the workforce.

Benefits Formal training, free housing, names of contacts, opportunity to attend seminars/workshops, willing to complete paperwork for educational credit, willing to provide letters of recommendation, worker's compensation.

Contact Write, call, fax, or e-mail Pattie Scheuring, Horticulturist. Phone: 508-877-7630 Ext. 3403. Fax: 508-877-3658. E-mail: scheuring@newfs.org. In-person interview recommended. Applicants must submit a resume, two letters of recommendation, application (can be downloaded from Web site). Application deadline: February 15. Fees: $8. World Wide Web: http://www.newfs.org/~newfs/.

GEORGE WASHINGTON & JEFFERSON NATIONAL FORESTS
5162 Valley Pointe Parkway
Roanoke, Virginia 24019-3050

General Information Organization responsible for the management of the George Washington and Jefferson National Forests, including recreation, wildlife, timber, wilderness, watershed, range, and cultural resources. Established in 1940. Number of employees: 364. Number of internship applications received each year: 45.

Internships Available ▶ *2–3 cultural resources interns:* responsibilities include preserving different areas, making signs/display boards, and performing archaeological duties. Candidates should have experience in the field, personal interest in the field, self-motivation, strong interpersonal skills. Duration is 1–3 months. Open to college freshmen, college sophomores, college juniors, college seniors, recent college graduates, graduate students, career changers. ▶ *1–2 range interns:* responsibilities include making surveys of species/animals in the forest. Candidates should have ability to work independently, knowledge of field, personal interest in the field, plan to pursue career in field, self-motivation. Duration is 1–3 months. Open to college freshmen, college sophomores, college juniors, college seniors, recent college graduates, graduate students, career changers. ▶ *2–4 recreation interns:* responsibilities include acting as campground host, performing recreational surveys, and making small repairs. Candidates should have knowledge of field, oral communication skills, personal interest in the field, self-motivation, strong interpersonal skills. Duration is 1–4 months. Open to college freshmen, college sophomores, college juniors, college seniors, recent college graduates, graduate students, career changers. ▶ *1–2 timber interns:* responsibilities include making surveys of species/animals in the forest. Candidates should have ability to work with others, knowledge of field, personal interest in the field, plan to pursue career in field, self-motivation. Duration is 1–3 months. Open to college sophomores, college juniors, college seniors, recent college graduates, graduate students, career changers. ▶ *1–3 wildlife interns:* responsibilities include hiking, living independently, and monitoring wilderness. Candidates should have ability to work independently, knowledge of field, plan to pursue career in field, self-motivation, strong interpersonal skills. Duration is 4 months. Open to college freshmen, college sophomores, college juniors, college seniors, recent college graduates, graduate students, career changers. All positions available as unpaid or paid. International applications accepted.

Benefits Formal training, job counseling, names of contacts, on-the-job training, possible full-time employment, travel reimbursement, willing to complete paperwork for educational credit, willing to provide letters of recommendation.

Contact Write, call, or fax Mr. Paul Paradzinski, Human Resources Coordinator. Phone: 540-265-5244. Fax: 540-265-5145. In-person interview recommended. Applications are accepted continuously.

GEORGIA 4-H ENVIRONMENTAL EDUCATION PROGRAM
350 Rock Eagle Road
Eatonton, Georgia 31024

General Information Environmental education center that services school-age children from the southeast during the school year, instructing the students and teachers in eco-specific lessons. Established in 1979. Number of employees: 50. Unit of University of Georgia, College of Agricultural and Environmental Science, Athens, Georgia, Athens, Georgia. Number of internship applications received each year: 100.

Internships Available ▶ *Jekyll Island interns:* responsibilities include teaching marine science and environmental education classes, providing leadership to school groups participating in the program, and conducting evening programs. Candidates should have oral communication skills, strong interpersonal skills, strong leadership ability, science-related background. Duration is 9 months. $180 per week. ▶ *Rock-Eagle interns:* responsibilities include teaching interdisciplinary outdoor and environmental education classes in history and the sciences. Candidates should have oral communication skills, strong interpersonal skills, strong leadership ability, written communication skills, science-related background. Duration is 3 months in fall; 4 months in spring. $180 per week. ▶ *Tybee Island 4-H Center interns:* responsibilities include teaching interdisciplinary outdoor and environmental education classes, providing leadership to school groups participating in the program, conducting evening programs, and maintaining teaching laboratories at Coastal Barrier Island. Candidates should have ability to work independently, oral communication skills, strong interpersonal skills, strong leadership ability, written communication skills. Duration is 2 months in fall, 5 months in spring. $130–$150 per week. ▶ *4 Wahsega 4-H Center interns:* responsibilities include teaching interdisciplinary outdoor and environmental education classes, providing leadership to school groups participating in the program, and maintaining teaching laboratories. Candidates should have oral communication skills, self-motivation, strong interpersonal skills, strong leadership ability. Duration is 2 months in fall, 3 months in spring. $150–$180 per week. Open to college juniors, college seniors.

Benefits Formal training, free housing, free meals, health insurance, names of contacts, possible full-time employment, willing to complete paperwork for educational credit, willing to provide letters of recommendation.

Contact Write, call, fax, or e-mail Cheryl Thompsen, Environmental Education Coordinator. Phone: 706-484-2834. Fax: 706-484-2888. E-mail: cthompse@uga.edu. Applicants must submit a cover letter, resume, three personal references. Applications are accepted continuously.

GLACIER INSTITUTE
PO Box 7457
Kalispell, Montana 59904

General Information Outdoor education organization dedicated to raising awareness for and appreciation of Glacier National Park and its surroundings. Established in 1983. Number of employees: 4. Number of internship applications received each year: 50.

Internships Available ▶ *1 assistant program director:* responsibilities include assisting in management of the environmental education facility including overseeing food preparation and purchase, and some teaching. Candidates should have ability to work independently, oral communication skills, organizational skills, self-motivation, strong interpersonal skills. Duration is 7 months. Paid. Open to recent college graduates, career changers. ▶ *2 interns:* responsibilities include providing administrative and field backup to instructors teaching college level courses in and around Glacier National Park, and teaching a basic outdoor education curriculum in a day camp setting. Candidates should have oral communication skills, organizational skills, personal interest in the field, self-motivation, strong interpersonal skills. Duration is 3 months. $175 per month. Open to college juniors, college seniors, recent college graduates, graduate students, career changers. ▶ *4 interns/teachers:* responsibilities include teaching an environmental education curriculum to fifth and sixth graders in a residential setting. Candidates should have ability to work independently, oral communication skills, personal interest in the field, self-motivation, strong interpersonal skills. Duration is 2-3 months in spring or fall. $175 per month. Open to college juniors, college seniors, recent college graduates, career changers. ▶ *2–3 teachers/naturalists:* responsibilities include teaching an environmental education curriculum to fifth and sixth graders in a residential setting; and assisting in instruction and administrative duties for summer camps, elderhostels, writing workshops, and teacher training workshops. Candidates should have ability to work independently, oral communication skills, personal interest in the field, self-motivation, strong

interpersonal skills. Duration is 7 months. $375 per month. Open to recent college graduates, graduate students. International applications accepted.

Benefits Formal training, free housing, free meals, on-the-job training, opportunity to attend seminars/workshops, possible full-time employment, willing to act as a professional reference, willing to complete paperwork for educational credit, willing to provide letters of recommendation.

Contact Write, call, fax, or e-mail Program Director. Phone: 406-755-1211. Fax: 406-755-7154. E-mail: glacinst@digisys.net. Telephone interview required. Applicants must submit a formal organization application, resume, writing sample, personal reference. Application deadline: January 31 for spring, March 1 for summer, March 1 for fall. World Wide Web: http://www.digisys.net/glacinst.

GLEN HELEN OUTDOOR EDUCATION CENTER
1075 State Route 343
Yellow Springs, Ohio 45387

General Information Residential environmental education center for elementary school-age children. Established in 1956. Number of employees: 7. Unit of Antioch University, Yellow Springs, Ohio. Number of internship applications received each year: 40.

Internships Available ▶ *10 naturalist interns:* responsibilities include planning and leading small groups of elementary school–age students in residential environmental education programs. Candidates should have ability to work independently, personal interest in the field, self-motivation, strong interpersonal skills, strong leadership ability. Duration is 1 semester. $250 per month. Open to college juniors, college seniors, recent college graduates, graduate students, career changers. International applications accepted.

Benefits Formal training, free housing, free meals, job counseling, names of contacts, on-the-job training, opportunity to attend seminars/workshops, tuition assistance, willing to complete paperwork for educational credit, willing to provide letters of recommendation, opportunity to purchase health insurance.

Contact Write, call, fax, or e-mail Mr. Gilbert DiSanto, Assistant Director. Phone: 937-767-7648. Fax: 937-767-6655. E-mail: gdisanto@antioch-college.edu. In-person interview recommended. Applicants must submit a formal organization application, academic transcripts. Applications are accepted continuously.

GLOBAL RESPONSE
PO Box 7490, 3546 Old Pearl Street
Boulder, Colorado 80306-7490

General Information Environmental action and education network. Established in 1990. Number of employees: 3. Number of internship applications received each year: 20.

Internships Available ▶ *1–3 Webmasters:* responsibilities include maintaining and updating Web site on an ongoing basis, developing strategies for fund-raising on the Internet and publicizing Web site. Candidates should have ability to work independently, computer skills, self-motivation. Duration is minimum of 3 months, at least 8 hours per week. ▶ *1–3 administrative assistants:* responsibilities include organizing and maintaining files on environmental topics, organizations, and monthly publications; answering phones; preparing materials for Board members; maintaining membership database; and generating spreadsheets. Duration is minimum of 3 months, at least 8 hours per week. ▶ *1–3 assistant volunteer coordinators:* responsibilities include organizing volunteers for temporary and long-term tasks; recruiting, interviewing, and evaluating volunteers; supervising volunteer activities; assisting in scheduling volunteers for special events; and working closely with volunteer organizations. Duration is minimum of 3 months, at least 8 hours per week. ▶ *1–3 e-mail administrators:* responsibilities include managing Listserv account, facilitating member subscriptions and unsubscriptions, investigating direct e-mail possibilities, and coordinating treatment of e-mail and conventional membership. Duration is minimum of 3 months, at least 8 hours per week. ▶ *1–3 freelance journalists:* responsibilities include writing articles about Global Response

Global Response (continued)

members and activities and submitting them to a variety of periodicals for publication. Candidates should have ability to work independently, editing skills, research skills, self-motivation, writing skills. Duration is minimum of 3 months, at least 8 hours per week. ▶ *1–3 fund-raising assistants:* responsibilities include assisting Executive Director with grant proposals, research, and follow-up; developing strategies and materials for generating corporate donations; assisting in membership donation appeals; and organizing special gift planning. Duration is minimum of 3 months, at least 8 hours per week. ▶ *1–3 materials editors:* responsibilities include reviewing and editing the organization's marketing, education, and in-house documents. Duration is minimum of 3 months, at least 8 hours per day. ▶ *1–3 outreach coordinators:* responsibilities include writing press releases and articles, and developing and publicizing materials for the purpose of outreach and fostering collaboration with three target groups; youth, high school students, and adults. Duration is minimum of 3 months, at least 8 hours per day. ▶ *1–3 research associates:* responsibilities include researching environmental topics (such as deforestation, nuclear energy, oceans, and mining) in order to develop new actions or researching past actions and campaigns to update membership and the board and developing strategies to gauge effectiveness of letter-writing. Duration is minimum of 3 months, at least 8 hours per week. ▶ *1–3 special events coordinators:* responsibilities include compiling a calendar of outreach events, developing strategies for outreach, and cultivating contacts with collaborating organizations to develop events. Duration is minimum of 3 months, at least 8 hours per week. All positions are unpaid. Open to high school students, high school seniors, recent high school graduates, college freshmen, college sophomores, college juniors, college seniors, recent college graduates, graduate students, law students, career changers, individuals reentering the workforce. International applications accepted.

Benefits On-the-job training, willing to act as a professional reference, willing to complete paperwork for educational credit, willing to provide letters of recommendation.

Contact Write, call, fax, or e-mail Susan Kamins, Intern Recruitment, PO Box 7490, Boulder, Colorado 80303. Phone: 303-444-0306. Fax: 303-449-9794. E-mail: globresponse@igc.org. In-person interview recommended. Applicants must submit a cover letter, resume, writing sample, GPA (if applicable). Applications are accepted continuously. World Wide Web: http://www.globalresponse.org.

GOLDEN GATE NATIONAL RECREATION AREA
Fort Mason, Building 201
San Francisco, California 94123

General Information Organization that seeks to conserve the scenery, cultural objects, and wildlife near San Francisco for the enjoyment of future generations. Established in 1972. Number of employees: 500. Unit of United States National Park Service, Washington, District of Columbia. Number of internship applications received each year: 100.

Internships Available ▶ *2–5 community outreach interns:* responsibilities include inspiring others to become involved with Golden Gate National Recreation Area by recruiting volunteers from diverse communities or giving presentations to community groups; helping create and distribute volunteer newsletters, updating volunteer database, and helping with special events. Candidates should have ability to work independently, oral communication skills, self-motivation, strong interpersonal skills, written communication skills. Duration is 6–8 months. Open to individuals 18 or older. ▶ *5–10 environmental education interns:* responsibilities include assisting park rangers in presenting education programs to visiting school children and researching topics for programs. Candidates should have ability to work independently, ability to work with others, oral communication skills, personal interest in the field, self-motivation. Duration is 3–9 months (no summers). Open to college freshmen, college sophomores, college juniors, college seniors, recent college graduates, graduate students, individuals reentering the workforce, individuals 18 or older. ▶ *10–20 historical/cultural interpreta-*

tion interns: responsibilities include assisting park rangers in roving patrols, spot interpretation, researching and developing individual program, collecting weather data, and operating visitor center; selected sites have period costume interpretation possibilities. Candidates should have ability to work independently, ability to work with others, oral communication skills, personal interest in the field, self-motivation, ability to relate to a diverse visiting public. Duration is 3–12 months. Open to recent high school graduates, recent college graduates, career changers, individuals reentering the workforce, individuals 18 or older. ▶ *10–20 natural resource management interns:* responsibilities include restoring habitats, monitoring vegetation and wildlife, assisting in native plant nursery operations, and performing duties pertaining to aquatics and hydrology. Candidates should have ability to work independently, ability to work with others, personal interest in the field, self-motivation, enthusiasm, willingness to work with small groups, willingness to work occasionally around children. Duration is 6–12 months. Open to individuals 18 or older. ▶ *1–4 public relations/communication interns:* responsibilities include assisting with press releases and weekly electronic newsletter; designing and updating park fact sheets; arranging press interviews and news filming within the park, as well as dealing with the public. Candidates should have ability to work independently, computer skills, oral communication skills, personal interest in the field, self-motivation, written communication skills. Duration is 6–8 months. Open to individuals 18 or older. ▶ *1–2 roads and trails interns:* responsibilities include controlling erosion, building trail structures (crib walls, water bars, cable steps) and hauling materials as a trail worker; trail inventory to measure and describe "social trails" (unofficial trails cut by the visiting public). Candidates should have personal interest in the field, self-motivation, strong interpersonal skills, enthusiasm, strong body. Duration is 6–8 months. Open to individuals 18 or older. All positions paid at $15 per day (for out-of-pocket expenses). International applications accepted.

Benefits Formal training, names of contacts, opportunity to attend seminars/workshops, possible full-time employment, willing to complete paperwork for educational credit, willing to provide letters of recommendation, out-of-pocket expenses provided on limited basis, free housing for full-time interns.

Contact Write, call, fax, or e-mail Terry Kreidler, Volunteer Coordinator. Phone: 415-561-4325. Fax: 415-561-4320. E-mail: volunteer@ggnpa.org. In-person interview recommended. Applicants must submit a formal organization application, cover letter and resume recommended. Applications are accepted continuously. World Wide Web: http://www.nps.gov/goga/volprog.htm.

GREAT VALLEY NATURE CENTER
PO Box 82
Devault, Pennsylvania 19432

General Information Center that provides environmental education and recreational experience for school children, organized groups, and the general public. Established in 1974. Number of employees: 10. Number of internship applications received each year: 40.

Internships Available ▶ *3–6 teachers:* responsibilities include teaching educational programs to school groups, proposing exhibits, and caring for the animals. Candidates should have ability to work independently, knowledge of field, oral communication skills, personal interest in the field, strong interpersonal skills. Duration is flexible. $100 per week. Open to recent high school graduates, college freshmen, college sophomores, college juniors, college seniors, recent college graduates, graduate students, career changers, individuals reentering the workforce. International applications accepted.

Benefits Possibility of free housing.

Contact Write, call, fax, or e-mail Mr. Tom Pascocello, Director. Phone: 610-935-9777. Fax: 610-935-9777. E-mail: gvncee@nni.com. Applicants must submit a cover letter, resume. Applications are accepted continuously.

GREEN MOUNTAIN CLUB
4711 Waterbury-Stowe Road
Waterbury Center, Vermont 05677

General Information Organization that promotes hiking in the Green Mountains, maintains trails, and protects the Long Trail Corridor. Established in 1910. Number of employees: 12. Number of internship applications received each year: 100.

Internships Available ▶ *Backcountry site managers:* responsibilities include collecting data on overnight site design and layout, waste management, water quality, and structural integrity. Unpaid. ▶ *3 education programs interns:* responsibilities include developing displays, brochures, presentations, and slide shows on the social, ecological, and physical aspects of the Long Trail System and its management. Candidates should have computer skills, editing skills, experience in the field, office skills, organizational skills, self-motivation, writing skills. Duration is 1–6 months. Unpaid. Open to recent high school graduates, college freshmen, college sophomores, college juniors, college seniors, recent college graduates, graduate students, career changers, individuals reentering the workforce. ▶ *15–20 shelter caretakers:* responsibilities include maintaining shelters, composting, maintaining trails, and interacting with the public. Candidates should have ability to work independently, oral communication skills, personal interest in the field, self-motivation, strong interpersonal skills. Duration is mid-May to mid-October. $200 per week (to start). Open to individuals 18 years and over. ▶ *7–10 summit caretakers:* responsibilities include educating the public on mountain ecology and mountain safety. Candidates should have ability to work independently, oral communication skills, personal interest in the field, self-motivation, strong interpersonal skills. Duration is mid-May to mid-October. $200 per week (to start). Open to individuals 18 years and over. ▶ *Trail crew interns:* responsibilities include building bridges and brush trails and performing light construction and drainage work. Candidates should have ability to work independently, ability to work with others, self-motivation. Duration is flexible. Unpaid. Open to individuals 18 years and over. International applications accepted.

Benefits Job counseling, names of contacts, on-the-job training, opportunity to attend seminars/workshops, possible full-time employment, travel reimbursement, tuition assistance, willing to complete paperwork for educational credit, willing to provide letters of recommendation, office space, computer use, possible housing.

Contact Write, call, or e-mail Mr. Dave Hardy, Director of Field Programs. Phone: 802-244-7037. E-mail: gmcdave@sover.net. In-person interview recommended. Applicants must submit a resume. Applications are accepted continuously. World Wide Web: http://www.greenmountainclub.org.

HAWTHORNE VALLEY FARM VISITING STUDENTS PROGRAM
327CR 21C
Ghent, New York 12075

General Information Residential farm/environmental education program that features a day school, a dairy farm, and a vegetable garden. Established in 1972. Number of employees: 7. Branch of Rudolph Steiner Educational and Farm Association, Ghent, New York. Number of internship applications received each year: 20.

Internships Available ▶ *3–4 interns:* responsibilities include baking bread, pressing cider, gardening, feeding animals, and planning and implementing outdoor programs for elementary school children. Candidates should have oral communication skills, organizational skills, personal interest in the field, self-motivation, strong interpersonal skills, strong leadership ability, maturity, experience working with children. Duration is 3–18 months. $200 per month stipend. Open to college freshmen, college sophomores, college juniors, college seniors, recent college graduates, graduate students, career changers, individuals reentering the workforce.

Benefits Formal training, free housing, free meals, opportunity to attend seminars/workshops, possible full-time employment, willing to act as a professional reference, willing to complete paperwork for educational credit, willing to provide letters of

recommendation, opportunity to observe Waldorf school classes K—12, participate in biodynamic agriculture and community cultural events.

Contact Write, call, fax, or e-mail Ruth Bruns, Executive Director, 327CR21C, Ghent, New York 12075. Phone: 518-672-4790. Fax: 518-672-7608. E-mail: vsp@taconic.net. In-person interview recommended. Applicants must submit a formal organization application, cover letter, resume, 3 personal references showing work with children. Application deadline: January 1 for spring, August 29 for fall.

HEAL THE BAY
2701 Ocean Park Boulevard, Suite 150
Santa Monica, California 90405

General Information Nonprofit environmental organization dedicated to making Santa Monica Bay and Southern California coastal waters safe and healthy again for people and marine life. Established in 1985. Number of employees: 20. Number of internship applications received each year: 20.

Internships Available ▶ *15–20 interns:* responsibilities include doing research and fieldwork in science, law and policy, community programs, development, and communications. Candidates should have oral communication skills, organizational skills, written communication skills. Duration is minimum 8-10 hours per week. Unpaid. Open to those who are of college age and above. International applications accepted.

Benefits Formal training, names of contacts, on-the-job training, opportunity to attend seminars/workshops, possible full-time employment, willing to act as a professional reference, willing to complete paperwork for educational credit, willing to provide letters of recommendation, opportunity to co-author a final report or study, dynamic and stimulating work environment.

Contact Write, call, fax, or e-mail Haan-Fawn Chau, Community Outreach Coordinator, 2701 Ocean Park Boulevard, Santa Monica, California 90405. Phone: 310-581-4188 Ext. 122. Fax: 310-581-4195. E-mail: hfchau@healthebay.org. In-person interview recommended. Applicants must submit a cover letter, resume, letter of recommendation. Applications are accepted continuously. World Wide Web: http://www.healthebay.org.

IDAHO RIVERS UNITED
PO Box 633
Boise, Idaho 83701

General Information Citizens' nonprofit river conservation organization working on wild and scenic rivers, water policy, and salmon restoration. Established in 1987. Number of employees: 8. Number of internship applications received each year: 50.

Internships Available ▶ *1 conservation assistant:* responsibilities include duties related to intern's interests and abilities, primarily helping director and assistant director with hydropower, wild and scenic issues, and salmon restoration. Candidates should have analytical skills, personal interest in the field, research skills, written communication skills, organization/campaign mobilization skills. Duration is 1 summer. $800 per month. Open to high school students, high school seniors, recent high school graduates, college freshmen, college sophomores, college juniors, college seniors, recent college graduates, graduate students, law students, career changers, individuals reentering the workforce. International applications accepted.

Benefits Names of contacts, opportunity to attend seminars/workshops, travel reimbursement, willing to complete paperwork for educational credit, willing to provide letters of recommendation.

Contact Write or e-mail Mr. Bill Sedivy, Executive Director. E-mail: irua@idahorivers.org. No phone calls. In-person interview recommended. Applicants must submit a resume, letter of interest (can be e-mailed). Applications are accepted continuously. World Wide Web: http://www.idahorivers.org.

ILLINOIS NATURE PRESERVES COMMISSION
524 South Second, Lincoln Tower Plaza
Springfield, Illinois 62701-1787

General Information Organization whose goal is to preserve Illinois' biodiversity by establishing a system of nature preserves. Established in 1963. Number of employees: 16. Number of internship applications received each year: 6.
Internships Available ▶ *2 volunteers:* responsibilities include performing various duties that can be customized to the volunteer's career interests, including working on special projects. Duration is 1 semester. Unpaid. Open to college freshmen, college sophomores, college juniors, college seniors, recent college graduates, graduate students. International applications accepted.
Benefits Job counseling, names of contacts, opportunity to attend seminars/workshops, willing to complete paperwork for educational credit, willing to provide letters of recommendation, liability insurance.
Contact Write, call, fax, or e-mail Randy Heidorn, Deputy Director for Stewardship, 524 South Second Lincoln Tower Plaza, Springfield, Illinois 62701-1787. Phone: 217-785-8686. Fax: 217-785-6040. E-mail: rheidorn@dnrmail.state.il.us. Applicants must submit a cover letter, resume. Applications are accepted continuously. World Wide Web: http://dnr.state.il.us/inpc/natpre.htm.

INTERNATIONAL CRANE FOUNDATION
PO Box 447
Baraboo, Wisconsin 53913

General Information Nonprofit foundation dedicated to the preservation of cranes and the wetlands on which they depend. Established in 1973. Number of employees: 27. Number of internship applications received each year: 200.
Internships Available ▶ *2 aviculture associates:* responsibilities include caring for and breeding cranes, completing 1 independent project under the supervision of a full-time employee, and supervising the volunteer chick parent program with emphasis on chick rearing. Candidates should have ability to work independently, ability to work with others, computer skills, knowledge of field, oral communication skills, personal interest in the field, research skills, self-motivation. $600 per month. Open to college juniors, college seniors, recent college graduates. ▶ *3 aviculture interns:* responsibilities include caring for and breeding cranes and completing an independent project under the supervision of a full-time employee; internships start March 1, June 1, September 1, and December 1. Candidates should have ability to work independently, ability to work with others, computer skills, knowledge of field, oral communication skills, personal interest in the field, self-motivation. $325 per month. Open to individuals 18 years or older with appropriate skills. Duration for all positions is 6 months. International applications accepted.
Benefits Free housing, names of contacts, on-the-job training, possible full-time employment, willing to complete paperwork for educational credit, willing to provide letters of recommendation.
Contact Write or e-mail Mr. Scott Swengel, Curator of Birds. E-mail: sswe.icf@baraboo.com. No phone calls. Applicants must submit a cover letter, resume, three letters of recommendation, telephone interview if selected as a finalist. Application deadline: January 1 for spring/summer, April 1 for summer/fall, July 1 for fall/winter, October 1 for winter/spring. World Wide Web: http://www.baraboo.com/bus/icf/whowhat.htm.

JACKSON HOLE CONSERVATION ALLIANCE
PO Box 2728
Jackson, Wyoming 83001

General Information Local nonprofit membership organization dedicated to protecting Jackson Hole's wildlife, scenery, and open spaces through land-use planning, citizen involvement and natural resource conservation. Established in 1979. Number of employees: 8. Number of internship applications received each year: 200.

Internships Available ▶ *2–4 project interns:* responsibilities include working on an independent project of mutual interest to both the intern and the alliance; helping with the day-to-day office administration of a nonprofit grassroots organization; assisting at meetings and special events; coordinating volunteers; maintaining community contacts; working on land-use planning and resource conservation issues; organizing fund-raising events, educational forums, and field trips. Candidates should have ability to work independently, computer skills, experience in the field, oral communication skills, organizational skills, written communication skills. $400 per month. Open to college juniors, college seniors, recent college graduates, graduate students, law students, career changers, individuals reentering the workforce. International applications accepted.
Benefits Names of contacts, opportunity to attend seminars/workshops, possible full-time employment, travel reimbursement, willing to act as a professional reference, willing to complete paperwork for educational credit, willing to provide letters of recommendation.
Contact Write, call, fax, or e-mail Ms. Heather Thomas, Outreach Coordinator. Phone: 307-733-9417. Fax: 307-733-9008. E-mail: heather@jhalliance.com. In-person interview recommended. Applicants must submit a cover letter, resume. Application deadline: April 1 for summer, October 15 for winter. World Wide Web: http://www.jhalliance.com.

JACKSON HOLE LAND TRUST
PO Box 2897
Jackson, Wyoming 83001

General Information Trust that was organized to protect open space on private land in Jackson Hole through voluntary nongovernmental means. Established in 1981. Number of employees: 7. Number of internship applications received each year: 60.
Internships Available ▶ *1–2 project interns:* responsibilities include providing program work and office support including reception and typing duties and working on projects that may involve research, protection, stewardship, or fund-raising. Candidates should have oral communication skills, organizational skills, personal interest in the field, research skills, written communication skills, Geographic Information System (GIS) experience. Duration is 3 months minimum in spring, summer, winter, or fall. $350 per month. Open to college freshmen, college sophomores, college juniors, college seniors, recent college graduates, graduate students, law students.
Benefits On-the-job training, willing to act as a professional reference, willing to complete paperwork for educational credit, willing to provide letters of recommendation.
Contact Write, call, fax, or e-mail Mr. Mark Berry, Intern Coordinator. Phone: 307-733-4707. Fax: 307-733-4144. E-mail: jhlt@wyoming.com. In-person interview recommended. Applicants must submit a cover letter, resume, writing sample. Applications are accepted continuously. World Wide Web: http://www.jhlandtrust.org.

KAUA'I NATIONAL WILDLIFE REFUGE COMPLEX
PO Box 1128
Kilauea, Hawaii 96754

General Information A complex of refuges that promote conservation of wildlife, habitat, environmental education, interpretation, and historic integrity. Established in 1985. Number of employees: 12. Unit of Hawaiian and Pacific Islands National Wildlife Refuge Complex, Honolulu, Hawaii. Number of internship applications received each year: 30.
Internships Available ▶ *1–3 biological interns:* responsibilities include working on census and survey projects and conducting habitat management activities. Candidates should have ability to work independently, ability to work with others, analytical skills, computer skills, plan to pursue career in field, self-motivation. Open to college juniors, college seniors, recent college graduates, graduate students, career changers. ▶ *1 public use intern:* responsibilities include greeting, orienting, and educating visiting public and school groups at visitor center. Candidates

should have ability to work independently, oral communication skills, plan to pursue career in field, strong interpersonal skills, writing skills. Open to college juniors, college seniors, recent college graduates, graduate students, individuals reentering the workforce. Duration for all positions is 3 months. All positions paid at $125 per week stipend.
Benefits Formal training, free housing, job counseling, names of contacts, on-the-job training, travel reimbursement, willing to act as a professional reference, willing to complete paperwork for educational credit, willing to provide letters of recommendation.
Contact Write, call, fax, or e-mail David Aplin, Outdoor Recreation Planner. Phone: 808-828-1413. Fax: 808-828-6634. E-mail: dave_aplin@mail.fws.gov. In-person interview recommended. Applicants must submit a cover letter, resume. Applications are accepted continuously.

LAND TRUST ALLIANCE
1319 F Street, NW, Suite 501
Washington, District of Columbia 20004

General Information National organization of local and regional land conservation groups providing information, education and technical assistance, public policy advocacy, and public education. Established in 1982. Number of employees: 23. Number of internship applications received each year: 200.
Internships Available ▶ *1 Land Trust Research intern:* responsibilities include researching and providing a wide array of information products and services to constituents. Candidates should have ability to work with others, oral communication skills, personal interest in the field, research skills, self-motivation, written communication skills. $1,000 per month. Open to college seniors, recent college graduates, graduate students, law students, career changers, individuals reentering the workforce. ▶ *Interns:* responsibilities include database research, networking with land trusts in the United States and Canada, library research, culling and organizing information into marketable formats, responding to requests for information from individuals and organizations, land trust database management and organization. Duration is flexible. small stipend occasionally available for special projects. ▶ *Public policy interns:* responsibilities include working with the public policy director on policy issues of concern to land conservationists. Candidates should have oral communication skills, written communication skills. Position available as unpaid or at dependent on funding. International applications accepted.
Benefits Job counseling, names of contacts, on-the-job training, opportunity to attend seminars/workshops, possible full-time employment, willing to act as a professional reference, willing to complete paperwork for educational credit, willing to provide letters of recommendation.
Contact Write, fax, or e-mail Rene Wiesner, Information Services Manager, 1319 F Street, NW, Suite 501, Washington, District of Columbia 20004. Fax: 202-638-4730. E-mail: rwiesner@lta.org. In-person interview required. Applicants must submit a cover letter, resume, 3-4 personal references, and a writing sample for advanced candidates. Applications are accepted continuously. World Wide Web: http://www.lta.org.

LA SABRANENQUE
Rue de la Tour de l'Oume
Saint Victor la Coste 30290 France

General Information Nonprofit organization focusing on preservation of rural habitat through volunteer projects involving restoration and reconstruction using traditional techniques at villages, houses, and natural sites. Established in 1969. Number of employees: 3. Number of internship applications received each year: 100.
Internships Available ▶ *10–12 restoration volunteers:* responsibilities include performing work related to the reconstruction of medieval buildings. Candidates should have personal interest in the field. Duration is 2–3 weeks. Unpaid. Open to high school seniors, recent high school graduates, college freshmen, college sophomores, college juniors, college seniors, recent col-

lege graduates, graduate students, law students, career changers, individuals reentering the workforce. International applications accepted.
Benefits Housing at a cost, meals at a cost, willing to complete paperwork for educational credit, opportunity to visit region.
International Internships Available in St. Victor La Coste, France; Altamura and Grallo, Italy.
Contact Write, call, or e-mail Ms. Jacqueline Simon, U.S. Correspondent. Phone: 716-836-8698. E-mail: sabranenque@wanadoo.fr. Applicants must submit a formal organization application. Applications are accepted continuously. World Wide Web: http://sabranenque.com.

LEAGUE OF CONSERVATION VOTERS
1707 L Street, NW, Suite 750
Washington, District of Columbia 20036

General Information Bipartisan political arm of the environmental community. Established in 1970. Number of employees: 30. Number of internship applications received each year: 250.
Internships Available ▶ *Communications interns:* responsibilities include researching stories for news reporters, drafting press releases, and assisting with media relations and media plans. Candidates should have ability to work independently, ability to work with others, college courses in field, personal interest in the field, plan to pursue career in field, research skills, self-motivation, written communication skills. ▶ *Political interns:* responsibilities include researching Congressional voting records and enviromental legislation, studying and reporting on Congressional candidates. Candidates should have ability to work independently, ability to work with others, college courses in field, personal interest in the field, plan to pursue career in field, research skills, written communication skills. Duration for all positions is 6 months. All positions paid at $950 monthly stipend. Open to recent college graduates, graduate students, law students, career changers. International applications accepted.
Benefits Opportunity to attend seminars/workshops, possible full-time employment, travel reimbursement, willing to act as a professional reference, willing to provide letters of recommendation.
Contact Write or fax Lydia Vermilye, Intern Coordinator, 1707 L Street, NW, Suite 750, Washington, District of Columbia 20036. Fax: 202-835-0491. No phone calls. In-person interview required. Applicants must submit a cover letter, resume, writing sample, three personal references, telephone or in-person interview. Applications are accepted continuously. World Wide Web: http://www.lcv.org.

LINSLY OUTDOOR CENTER
2425 Route 168
Georgetown, Pennsylvania 15043

General Information Outdoor center that builds teamwork, self-esteem, and trust through a variety of programs which provide adventure, environmental education, and a unique outdoor experience for groups of all ages. Established in 1987. Number of employees: 8. Unit of Linsly School, Wheeling, West Virginia. Number of internship applications received each year: 100.
Internships Available ▶ *6 instructors/interns:* responsibilities include teaching and developing adventure, challenge, and environmental education programs for all age groups, supervising day and evening programs, and assisting in daily operations. Candidates should have ability to work independently, organizational skills, self-motivation, strong interpersonal skills, strong leadership ability. Duration is 3-4 months in spring, summer, or fall. $150–$170 per week. Open to college freshmen, college sophomores, college juniors, college seniors, recent college graduates, graduate students, career changers. International applications accepted.
Benefits Formal training, free housing, free meals, names of contacts, possible full-time employment, willing to act as a professional reference, willing to complete paperwork for educational credit, willing to provide letters of recommendation.
Contact Write, call, or e-mail Gregg Somerhalder, Director. Phone: 724-899-2100. E-mail: loc1@timesnet.net. In-person

Linsly Outdoor Center (continued)

interview recommended. Applicants must submit a cover letter, resume, three personal references. Applications are accepted continuously.

LONG LAKE CONSERVATION CENTER
Route 2, Box 2550
Palisade, Minnesota 56469

General Information Residential conservation/environmental education facility providing activities and learning units designed to heighten and enhance students' appreciation of and sensitivity toward the environment. Established in 1963. Number of employees: 18. Unit of Aitkin County Parks Commission, Aitkin, Minnesota. Number of internship applications received each year: 50.
Internships Available ► *4–8 naturalist interns:* responsibilities include teaching, leading adolescents in environmental education programs and activities, and supervising groups of students. Candidates should have oral communication skills, organizational skills, personal interest in the field, strong interpersonal skills, written communication skills. Duration is 3–12 months. $100 per week. Open to college freshmen, college sophomores, college juniors, college seniors, recent college graduates, graduate students, career changers, individuals reentering the workforce. International applications accepted.
Benefits Free housing, free meals, job counseling, names of contacts, on-the-job training, willing to act as a professional reference, willing to complete paperwork for educational credit, willing to provide letters of recommendation.
Contact Write, call, fax, or e-mail Pam Carlson, Administrative Coordinator. Phone: 800-450-5522. Fax: 218-768-2309. E-mail: llcc@mlecmn.net. Applicants must submit a formal organization application, cover letter, resume, academic transcripts, letter of recommendation. Applications are accepted continuously. World Wide Web: http://www.llcc.org.

MANTI–LA SAL NATIONAL FOREST, MONTICELLO RANGER DISTRICT
PO Box 820
Monticello, Utah 84535

General Information Ranger district, located on a mountain range on the Colorado Plateau in a small community near Moab, Utah, that manages numerous Anasazi ruins and the Dark Canyon Wilderness. Number of employees: 15. District of Manti–La Sal National Forest, Price, Utah. Number of internship applications received each year: 25.
Internships Available ► *2 archaeological assistants:* responsibilities include assisting with office and fieldwork including surveying, identifying, and recording archaeological sites and ruins. Candidates should have ability to work with others, college courses in field, office skills, plan to pursue career in field, research skills, self-motivation, writing skills, driver's license. Duration is 6–12 weeks. Unpaid. Open to recent high school graduates, college freshmen, college sophomores, college juniors, college seniors, recent college graduates, graduate students, career changers, individuals reentering the workforce. ► *2–3 recreation site maintenance interns:* responsibilities include making public contacts, providing information, and collecting and evaluating visitor use data. Candidates should have ability to work independently, oral communication skills, strong interpersonal skills, written communication skills, driver's license. Duration is 3–4 months. Position available as unpaid or paid. Open to individuals 18 years or older. ► *2 wilderness rangers:* responsibilities include making public contacts, providing information, and collecting and evaluating visitor use data. Candidates should have good physical condition (hiking). Position available as unpaid or paid. Open to college freshmen, college sophomores, college juniors, college seniors, recent college graduates, graduate students, career changers, individuals reentering the workforce. International applications accepted.

Benefits Free housing, job counseling, on-the-job training, willing to complete paperwork for educational credit, willing to provide letters of recommendation, possible subsistence reimbursement.
Contact Write, call, or e-mail Ms. Leigh Ann Hunt, District Archaeologist. Phone: 801-587-2041. E-mail: hunt_leighann/r4_m.l@fs.fed.us. Informal application required. Application deadline: April 30 for summer.

MASSACHUSETTS AUDUBON SOCIETY
South Great Road
Lincoln, Massachusetts 01773

General Information Environmental organization with programs in conservation, education, and advocacy. Established in 1896. Number of employees: 190.
Internships Available ► *Advocacy interns:* responsibilities include assisting with the development and research of several protection issues. Duration is 1 semester. Position available as unpaid or paid. ► *Coastal bird program assistants:* responsibilities include monitoring nesting success, conducting experimental protection measures, greeting island visitors, and enforcing sanctuary regulations. Duration is 1 summer. Position available as unpaid or paid. ► *Day camp counselors:* responsibilities include participating in scheduled precamp training activities; conducting, planning, and preparing materials for daily activities; and protecting the physical and emotional welfare of the campers. Duration is 1 summer. $6–$7 per hour. ► *Education interns:* responsibilities include assisting and conducting formal interpretive and environmental education programs at various sanctuaries. Duration is 1 semester. Position available as unpaid or paid. ► *Intern/plover management assistants:* responsibilities include installing predator-proof fencing; assisting with banding activities; and monitoring, managing, and protecting nesting areas of terns and piping plovers on Cape Cod. Duration is 5 months. Position available as unpaid or paid. ► *Marketing interns:* responsibilities include helping to write press releases and public service announcements; assisting with ongoing projects. Duration is 1 semester. Position available as unpaid or paid. ► *Research assistants:* responsibilities include monitoring breeding behavior, performing data entry and management, and trapping and banding adult and juvenile terns. Duration is 3–4 months. Position available as unpaid or paid. Open to college freshmen, college sophomores, college juniors, college seniors, recent college graduates, graduate students. International applications accepted.
Benefits Possible full-time employment, willing to complete paperwork for educational credit.
Contact Write Ms. Claudia Veitch, Director of Human Resources. In-person interview recommended. Applicants must submit a cover letter, resume. Applications are accepted continuously. World Wide Web: http://www.massaudubon.org.

MAX MCGRAW WILDLIFE FOUNDATION
PO Box 9
Dundee, Illinois 60118

General Information Environmental organization dedicated to the conservation of wildlife and fishery resources providing education directed mainly at kindergarten through sixth grades, and teacher education. Established in 1962. Number of employees: 47. Number of internship applications received each year: 35.
Internships Available ► *2 conservation education assistants:* responsibilities include planning and presenting programs for children and adults, leading tours, creating educational materials, and assisting education staff as needed. Candidates should have computer skills, knowledge of field, office skills, oral communication skills, strong interpersonal skills, written communication skills, coursework in the biological/environmental sciences. Duration is February through November or March through October. $850 per month. Open to college juniors, college seniors, recent college graduates, graduate students, career changers.
Benefits Formal training, free housing, job counseling, names of contacts, on-the-job training, opportunity to attend seminars/

workshops, willing to act as a professional reference, willing to complete paperwork for educational credit, willing to provide letters of recommendation.
Contact Write, call, fax, or e-mail David Guritz, Manager, Conservation Education. Phone: 847-428-2240. Fax: 847-741-8157. E-mail: mcgrawed@aol.com. Applicants must submit a cover letter, resume. Application deadline: January 15 for 10-month interns, February 15 for 8-month interns.

MERCK FOREST AND FARMLAND CENTER
Box 86, Route 315
Rupert, Vermont 05768

General Information Center that teaches about land stewardship and sustainability by providing programs, access, and demonstrations on over 3130 acres of working farm and forest land. Established in 1950. Number of employees: 12. Number of internship applications received each year: 50.
Internships Available ▶ *1–4 resource assistants:* responsibilities include environmental education, farm chores, forest and trail management, Visitor Center duties, and seasonal work such as maple sugaring, lambing, organic gardening, and public programs. Candidates should have ability to work independently, ability to work with others, personal interest in the field, self-motivation. Duration is 4 months. $65 per week. Open to high school students, high school seniors, recent high school graduates, college freshmen, college sophomores, college juniors, college seniors, recent college graduates, graduate students, law students, career changers, individuals reentering the workforce. International applications accepted.
Benefits Free housing, on-the-job training, opportunity to attend seminars/workshops, willing to complete paperwork for educational credit, willing to provide letters of recommendation, leadership skills, free organic farm products.
Contact Write, call, fax, or e-mail Ann Budreski, Teacher Naturalist. Phone: 802-394-7836. Fax: 802-394-2519. E-mail: merck@vermontel.com. In-person interview recommended. Applicants must submit a cover letter, resume. Application deadline: March 1 for summer, August 1 for fall, December 1 for spring. World Wide Web: http://www.merckforest.org.

MONONGAHELA NATIONAL FOREST, WHITE SULPHUR DISTRICT
410 East Main Street
White Sulphur Springs, West Virginia 24986

General Information National forest dedicated to land management and public services. Number of employees: 3. Unit of Monongahela National Forest.
Internships Available ▶ *1–6 gate attendants/hosts:* responsibilities include greeting campers, maintaining grounds, and cleaning. Duration is May-August. Unpaid. Open to high school students, high school seniors, recent high school graduates, college freshmen, college sophomores, college juniors, college seniors, recent college graduates, graduate students, law students, career changers, individuals reentering the workforce. International applications accepted.
Benefits Willing to complete paperwork for educational credit.
Contact Write or fax Jim Miller, Forestry Technician, 410 East Main Street, White Sulpur Springs, West Virginia 24986. Fax: 304-536-1897. No phone calls. Telephone interview required. Applicants must submit a cover letter, resume, two personal references, two letters of recommendation. Application deadline: April 1.

MONTANA WILDLIFE FEDERATION
PO Box 1175
Helena, Montana 59624

General Information Statewide grassroots conservation organization working to protect and enhance wildlife, habitat, and wildlife values; lobbies state and federal agencies, the state legislature, and the congressional delegation to affect policy and management decisions. Established in 1935. Number of employees:

5. Affiliate of National Wildlife Federation, Missoula, Montana. Number of internship applications received each year: 40.
Internships Available ▶ *1–2 legislative interns:* responsibilities include assisting the MWF lobbyist during state legislative years; researching bills pertinent to MWF work; organizing grassroots support, in some cases testifying; organizing press coverage and developing voting record. Candidates should have ability to work with others, computer skills, oral communication skills, organizational skills, research skills, written communication skills. ▶ *1–2 program coordinators:* responsibilities include maintaining grassroots activist database, managing phonetree operation, writing editorials and letters to the editor, managing the phone fundraising program including personnel management; working with the Education Committee on special projects and event planning. Candidates should have computer skills, office skills, oral communication skills, organizational skills, research skills, written communication skills. Duration for all positions is 5–6 months. All positions paid at $500–$1,000 per month. Open to college freshmen, college sophomores, college juniors, college seniors, recent college graduates, graduate students, law students, career changers, individuals reentering the workforce.
Benefits Formal training, job counseling, names of contacts, on-the-job training, opportunity to attend seminars/workshops, possible full-time employment, willing to act as a professional reference, willing to complete paperwork for educational credit, willing to provide letters of recommendation, assistance in locating housing.
Contact Write or e-mail Mr. Tony Jewett, Executive Director. E-mail: tjewett@desktop.org. In-person interview recommended. Applicants must submit a cover letter, resume, three personal references. Application deadline: January 15 for fall, April 15 for summer. World Wide Web: http://www.montanawildlife.net.

MOUNTAIN TRAIL OUTDOOR SCHOOL
PO Box 250
Hendersonville, North Carolina 28793-0250

General Information Outdoor school that educates and inspires students of all ages to protect the natural and human environment. Established in 1991. Number of employees: 12. Unit of Kanuga Conference Center, Hendersonville, North Carolina. Number of internship applications received each year: 120.
Internships Available ▶ *2–4 outdoor environmental education interns:* responsibilities include teaching natural history classes, environmental awareness, and adventure activities, and assisting with training and program development. Candidates should have knowledge of field, oral communication skills, organizational skills, personal interest in the field, strong interpersonal skills, strong leadership ability, experience and/or desire to work with youth. Duration is 2–3 months. $150 per week. Open to college freshmen, college sophomores, college juniors, college seniors, recent college graduates, graduate students. International applications accepted.
Benefits Formal training, free housing, free meals, job counseling, names of contacts, on-the-job training, possible full-time employment, willing to complete paperwork for educational credit, willing to provide letters of recommendation.
Contact Write, call, or e-mail Paul Bockoven, Director, Outdoor Education. Phone: 828-692-9136. Fax: 828-696-3589. E-mail: kanuga@ecunet.org. Telephone interview required. Applicants must submit a formal organization application, cover letter, resume, three letters of recommendation. Application deadline: January 5 for spring, April 1 for summer. World Wide Web: http://www.kanuga.org.

NACUL CENTER FOR ECOLOGICAL ARCHITECTURE
592 Main Street
Amherst, Massachusetts 01002

General Information Center that researches and develops ecological architecture designs including sustainable communities, solar buildings, and other socially responsible projects. Established in 1970. Number of employees: 4. Number of internship applications received each year: 25.

Nacul Center for Ecological Architecture (continued)

Internships Available ▶ *3–6 architectural interns:* responsibilities include drafting, researching, model building, office work, photography, and design. Candidates should have college courses in field, computer skills, personal interest in the field, self-motivation. Duration is 3–12 months. Unpaid. Open to college freshmen, college sophomores, college juniors, college seniors, recent college graduates, graduate students. International applications accepted.

Benefits Formal training, opportunity to attend seminars/workshops, possible full-time employment, willing to complete paperwork for educational credit.

Contact Write, call, fax, or e-mail Mr. Tullio Inglese, Director. Phone: 413-256-8025. Fax: 413-253-2451. E-mail: nacul@crocker.com. In-person interview recommended. Applicants must submit a formal organization application, resume, portfolio. Applications are accepted continuously.

NAGS HEAD WOODS ECOLOGICAL PRESERVE
701 West Ocean Acres Drive
Kill Devil Hills, North Carolina 27948

General Information Nature preserve owned by The Nature Conservancy whose mission is to protect and preserve the diversity of plants, animals, and natural communities in this maritime forest preserve. Established in 1977. Number of employees: 4. Branch of The Nature Conservancy, Arlington, Virginia. Number of internship applications received each year: 50.

Internships Available ▶ *2 naturalist/outdoor education interns:* responsibilities include designing and implementing an interpretive program that targets the educational needs of the preserve, guiding kayak and field trips, leading sessions of EcoCamp, maintaining and assisting in the development of interpretive exhibits and publications. Candidates should have experience in the field, oral communication skills, plan to pursue career in field, strong interpersonal skills, good physical condition desirable; first aid and CPR certification. Duration is late May to early September. $6–$8 per hour. Open to college freshmen, college sophomores, college juniors, college seniors, recent college graduates, graduate students. ▶ *1 research intern:* responsibilities include providing specific research for the biohydrology project. Candidates should have college degree in related field, experience in the field, knowledge of field, self-motivation, strong interpersonal skills. Duration is May to September for 2 years. $7–$8 per hour. Open to graduate students, graduate students working on thesis. Research done for this project should be part of graduate thesis. International applications accepted.

Benefits Free housing, names of contacts, on-the-job training, willing to complete paperwork for educational credit, willing to provide letters of recommendation.

Contact Write, call, fax, or e-mail Ms. Tracy Triggs-Matthews, Environmental Educational Coordinator. Phone: 252-441-2525. Fax: 252-441-1271. E-mail: tmatthew@nhwoods.org. Applicants must submit a cover letter, resume, three personal references. Application deadline: February. World Wide Web: http://www.tnc.org.

NATIONAL AQUARIUM IN BALTIMORE
Pier 3, 501 East Pratt Street
Baltimore, Maryland 21202

General Information State-of-the-art aquatic institution dedicated to the conservation and preservation of the environment. Established in 1981. Number of employees: 250. Number of internship applications received each year: 200.

Internships Available ▶ *20–40 interns:* responsibilities include working in audiovisual, horticulture, marine education, herpetology, membership publications, public relations, marine mammal training, library, chemistry/water quality, development or marketing, or aiding aquarists and aviculturists. Candidates should have ability to work with others, college courses in field, knowledge of field, personal interest in the field, plan to pursue career in field. Duration is 120 hours. Unpaid. Open to college freshmen, college sophomores, college juniors, college seniors. International applications accepted.

Benefits Names of contacts, opportunity to attend seminars/workshops, willing to act as a professional reference, willing to complete paperwork for educational credit, willing to provide letters of recommendation, uniform, 20% discount at gift shop and on food service.

Contact Write, call, fax, or e-mail Stacy Sties, Intern Coordinator. Phone: 410-576-8236. Fax: 410-659-0116. E-mail: intern@aqua.org. In-person interview recommended. Applicants must submit a formal organization application, academic transcripts. Application deadline: April 1 for summer, November 1 for spring (January start). World Wide Web: http://www.aqua.org.

NATIONAL AUDUBON SOCIETY
Francis Beidler Forest, 336 Sanctuary Road
Harleyville, South Carolina 29448

General Information Wildlife sanctuary encompassing large stand of virgin cypress/tupelo swamp forest. Established in 1977. Number of employees: 3. Unit of National Audubon Society, New York, New York. Number of internship applications received each year: 75.

Internships Available ▶ *2 naturalist interns:* responsibilities include performing environmental interpretation, guiding canoe trips, and office work. ▶ *2 naturalist/warden interns:* responsibilities include performing environmental interpretation, guiding canoe trips, and miscellaneous maintenance. Candidates for all positions should have ability to work independently, ability to work with others, experience in the field, oral communication skills, plan to pursue career in field, self-motivation. Duration for all positions is 12–14 weeks. All positions paid at $150 per week. Open to college seniors, recent college graduates, graduate students, law students, career changers, individuals reentering the workforce.

Benefits Free housing, job counseling, names of contacts, on-the-job training, possible full-time employment, willing to act as a professional reference, willing to complete paperwork for educational credit, willing to provide letters of recommendation.

Contact Write, call, fax, or e-mail Mr. Michael Dawson, Assistant Manager. Phone: 843-462-2150. Fax: 843-462-2713. E-mail: mdawson@audubon.org. Telephone interview required. Applicants must submit a cover letter, resume, three personal references. Application deadline: January 1 for spring, April 15 for summer, July 15 for fall. World Wide Web: http://www.pride-net.com/swamp/.

NATIONAL CAPITAL REGION–ROCK CREEK PARK
3545 Williamsburg Lane, NW
Washington, District of Columbia 20008

General Information Service devoted to the preservation of land, historic landscapes, and wildlife for enjoyment and education of the public. Established in 1890. Number of employees: 100. Unit of United States Department of Interior, Washington, District of Columbia.

Internships Available ▶ *1–2 assistant curators:* responsibilities include care and cataloging of park archives including flora and fauna, photos, and other materials relating to park history. ▶ *1 historian:* responsibilities include researching and cataloging information. ▶ *1–3 interpreters/educators:* responsibilities include interpreting historic sites and/or natural environment, preparing programs, researching, assisting with planetarium operation and animal care. ▶ *1 librarian:* responsibilities include installation of library cataloging system, replacing books, and deleting out-of-date volumes. ▶ *2–4 maintenance workers:* responsibilities include maintaining grounds and facilities. ▶ *1 resource management specialist:* responsibilities include maintaining and monitoring natural resources for public use. ▶ *1–3 visitor information specialists:* responsibilities include answering telephones, typing, filing, taking reservations, bookstore sales, updating bulletin board, and preparing monthly activity guide. Duration for all positions is flexible. All positions are unpaid. Open to high school students, high school seniors, recent high school gradu-

ates, college freshmen, college sophomores, college juniors, college seniors, recent college graduates, graduate students, law students, career changers, individuals reentering the workforce.
Benefits Formal training, job counseling, names of contacts, opportunity to attend seminars/workshops, possible full-time employment, willing to complete paperwork for educational credit, willing to provide letters of recommendation, small stipend occasionally available, limited housing available.
Contact Write, call, fax, or e-mail Mr. Dwight Madison, Volunteer Coordinator. Phone: 202-426-6829. Fax: 202-426-1823. E-mail: dwight_madison@nps.gov. In-person interview recommended. Applicants must submit a cover letter, resume. Applications are accepted continuously. World Wide Web: http://www.nps.gov/rocr.

NATIONAL ENVIRONMENTAL TRUST
1200 18th Street, NW, 5th Floor
Washington, District of Columbia 20036

General Information Nonprofit, non-partisan organization that provides public education campaign expertise and communication services on national environmental issues; NET retains a staff experienced in media relations, advertising, issue campaign management, government affairs, federal environmental law, communications, and research. Established in 1994. Number of employees: 35. Number of internship applications received each year: 600.
Internships Available ▶ *1 climate change intern:* responsibilities include researching legislation; drafting legislative briefs; attending/reporting on seminars and press conferences; researching/reporting on legislative histories; working with businesses, advocacy groups, Congress, and the administration. Candidates should have ability to work independently, analytical skills, computer skills, editing skills, oral communication skills, organizational skills, personal interest in the field, research skills, self-motivation, strong interpersonal skills, writing skills. Duration is flexible. Open to college juniors, college seniors, recent college graduates, graduate students. ▶ *1 government affairs and policy intern:* responsibilities include research on legislative and environmental policy issues, maintaining legislative files, attending hearings and briefings, and assisting in distributing information to Congressional offices. Candidates should have ability to work independently, analytical skills, computer skills, editing skills, oral communication skills, organizational skills, personal interest in the field, plan to pursue career in field, research skills, self-motivation, strong interpersonal skills, writing skills, interest in public policy, conservation, and environmental protection efforts. Open to college seniors, recent college graduates, graduate students. ▶ *1 grassroots outreach intern:* responsibilities include assisting coordination of in-state field organizers; helping expand supportive coalitions; writing/creating sample materials; assisting and coordinating public education forums and press conferences; monitoring coalition-building, press work, and public education. Candidates should have ability to work independently, analytical skills, computer skills, editing skills, experience in the field, office skills, oral communication skills, organizational skills, personal interest in the field, research skills, self-motivation, strong interpersonal skills, strong leadership ability, writing skills, creative planning skills, previous volunteer experience on a political campaign or as an activist. Open to college juniors, college seniors, recent college graduates, graduate students. ▶ *1 information systems intern:* responsibilities include focusing on the Internet, software installation, FTP, e-mail listserver administration, database, graphic design, and assisting staff. Candidates should have ability to work independently, ability to work with others, computer skills, experience in the field, office skills, oral communication skills, personal interest in the field, self-motivation, Macintosh experience preferred. Open to college seniors, recent college graduates, graduate students. ▶ *1 nonprofit organization administration intern:* responsibilities include supporting the administration and executive offices; researching special assignments in human resources, benefits, budgeting, and accounting; participating in and observing management of the organization; database management; clerical tasks. Candidates should have ability to work independently, computer

skills, office skills, oral communication skills, organizational skills, self-motivation, strong interpersonal skills, written communication skills. Open to college juniors, college seniors, recent college graduates, graduate students. ▶ *2 press relations interns:* responsibilities include conducting research for radio, TV, and print media; organizing media events and pitching stories to talk radio and print media; tracking legislation and press coverage; researching bills; and attending hearings. Candidates should have ability to work independently, analytical skills, computer skills, editing skills, experience in the field, office skills, oral communication skills, organizational skills, personal interest in the field, research skills, self-motivation, strong interpersonal skills, writing skills. Open to college seniors, recent college graduates, graduate students. ▶ *1 research intern:* responsibilities include generating reports, data tables, and writing data analyses; reporting on both local and national levels on issues such as right-to-know, pollution prevention, and air quality. Candidates should have ability to work independently, analytical skills, college courses in field, computer skills, organizational skills, research skills, self-motivation, strong interpersonal skills, written communication skills, strong numeric ability; experience in database software; background in environmental science, engineering, chemistry, or biology a plus. Open to college juniors, college seniors, recent college graduates, graduate students. All positions available as unpaid or paid. International applications accepted.
Benefits Job counseling, names of contacts, on-the-job training, opportunity to attend seminars/workshops, willing to act as a professional reference, willing to complete paperwork for educational credit, willing to provide letters of recommendation, stipend.
Contact Write, fax, or e-mail Ryan Young, Internship Coordinator, 1200 18th Street, NW, 5th Floor, Washington, District of Columbia 20036. Fax: 202-887-8877. E-mail: ryoung@environet.org. Applicants must submit a cover letter, resume. Application deadline: March 15 for summer, June 30 for fall, October 31 for spring. World Wide Web: http://www.environet.org.

NATIONAL PARKS AND CONSERVATION ASSOCIATION
1776 Massachusetts Avenue, NW
Washington, District of Columbia 20036

General Information National environmental organization dedicated to protecting and enhancing the national park system. Established in 1919. Number of employees: 75. Number of internship applications received each year: 75.
Internships Available ▶ *1 Hastings Journalism intern:* responsibilities include research and writing related to National Park resource protection, supporting conservation policy staff, completing individual project(s). Candidates should have college courses in field, oral communication skills, research skills, self-motivation, strong interpersonal skills, written communication skills. Duration is 2–3 months. $3,000 per duration of internship. Open to college seniors, recent college graduates, graduate students, law students. ▶ *1–3 policy interns:* responsibilities include researching issues pertaining to natural and cultural resource policies and providing research support for staff. Candidates should have oral communication skills, personal interest in the field, research skills, self-motivation, strong interpersonal skills, written communication skills. Duration is 10–14 weeks. $6–$10 per hour. Open to college seniors, recent college graduates, graduate students, law students, career changers. International applications accepted.
Benefits Names of contacts, possible full-time employment, willing to act as a professional reference, willing to complete paperwork for educational credit, willing to provide letters of recommendation.
Contact Write, call, fax, or e-mail W. Neil Evans, Program Manager. Phone: 202-223-6722 Ext. 117. Fax: 202-659-8183. E-mail: natpark@aol.com. Telephone interview required. Applicants must submit a cover letter, resume, writing sample, three personal references. Application deadline: March 15 for summer, July 15 for fall, October 1 for winter. World Wide Web: http://www.npca.org.

NATIONAL WILDLIFE FEDERATION
1400 16th Street, NW, Suite 501
Washington, District of Columbia 20036-2266

General Information Nation's largest nonprofit conservation education organization. Established in 1936. Number of internship applications received each year: 500.

Internships Available ▶ *8 interns:* responsibilities include researching environmental policy issues; attending Congressional hearings, briefings, and seminars; lobbying on environmental legislation; and routine office work. Areas covered include endangered habitat water quality, wetlands, land stewardship, international development, and sustainable communities. Candidates should have ability to work with others, college degree in related field, experience in the field, oral communication skills, writing skills, interest in environmental issues, volunteer experience valued. Duration is 24 weeks. $275 per week. Open to recent college graduates, graduate students. International applications accepted.

Benefits Formal training, health insurance, names of contacts, willing to complete paperwork for educational credit, willing to provide letters of recommendation.

Contact Write, fax, or e-mail Resources Conservation Internship Program, 1400 16th Street, NW, Suite 501, Washington, District of Columbia 20036-2266. Fax: 202-797-6646. E-mail: washingtonl@nwf.org. No phone calls. Applicants must submit a cover letter, resume, writing sample, three personal references. Application deadline: March 15 for July positions, September 15 for January positions. World Wide Web: http://www.nwf.org/nwf.

NATURE CONSERVANCY, INTERNATIONAL HEADQUARTERS
4245 North Fairfax Drive, Suite 100
Arlington, Virginia 22203

General Information International conservation organization committed to preserving natural biological diversity by finding and protecting lands and waters. Established in 1951. Number of employees: 450.

Internships Available ▶ *Interns:* responsibilities include duties that depend on the organization's needs and the specific interests of the intern. Refer to Web site for most up-to-date information. Candidates should have knowledge of field, personal interest in the field, plan to pursue career in field, self-motivation. Duration is flexible. Position available as unpaid or at variable. Open to recent high school graduates, college freshmen, college sophomores, college juniors, college seniors, recent college graduates, graduate students, law students, career changers, individuals reentering the workforce. International applications accepted.

Benefits Possible full-time employment, travel reimbursement, willing to complete paperwork for educational credit, willing to provide letters of recommendation, social security, worker's compensation (for paid positions).

Contact Write, fax, or e-mail Laura Jarrell, Employment Specialist. Fax: 703-841-7292. E-mail: ljarrell@tnc.org. No phone calls. In-person interview required. Applicants must submit a cover letter, resume, 3 or 4 references (professional preferred). Applications are accepted continuously. World Wide Web: http://www.tnc.org.

NATURE CONSERVANCY, NORTH CAROLINA CHAPTER
4011 University Drive, Suite 201
Durham, North Carolina 27707

General Information Conservation organization that seeks to preserve plants, animals, and natural communities by protecting lands and waters. Established in 1977. Number of employees: 35. Number of internship applications received each year: 70.

Internships Available ▶ *1–2 Nags Head Woods environmental education interns:* responsibilities include leading educational field trips, assisting with an environmental education camp for K-12 children, maintaining and repairing trails, preparing reports, assisting with monitoring, posting boundaries, removing invasive species, assisting with prescribed fires, interacting with the public, and generally contributing to the maintenance and security of one or more nature preserves (the Mountains District of Western North Carolina, the Southeast Coastal Plain District, or the Nags Head Woods preserve on the Outer Banks). An internship report is required at the end of the term of employment. Duration is 6 months (May through October). Open to college juniors, college seniors, recent college graduates, graduate students. ▶ *2–6 interns:* responsibilities include leading educational field trips, assisting with environmental education, maintaining and repairing trails, preparing reports, assisting with monitoring, posting boundaries, removing invasive species, assisting with prescribed fires, interacting with the public, and generally contributing to the maintenance and security of one or more nature preserves (the Mountains District of Western North Carolina, the Southeast Coastal Plain District, or the Nags Head Woods preserve on the Outer Banks). An internship report is required at the end of the term of employment. Duration is 3-4 months in summer. ▶ *1–2 mountains seasonal ecologists:* responsibilities include leading educational field trips, assisting with environmental education, maintaining and repairing trails, preparing reports, assisting with monitoring, posting boundaries, removing invasive species, assisting with prescribed fires, interacting with the public, and generally contributing to the maintenance and security of one or more nature preserves (the Mountains District of Western North Carolina, the Southeast Coastal Plain District, or the Nags Head Woods preserve on the Outer Banks). An internship report is required at the end of the term of employment. Duration is 6 months (May through October). Open to college juniors, college seniors, recent college graduates, graduate students. ▶ *1–2 southeastern coastal plain interns:* responsibilities include leading educational field trips, assisting with environmental education, maintaining and repairing trails, preparing reports, assisting with monitoring, posting boundaries, removing invasive species, assisting with prescribed fires, interacting with the public, and generally contributing to the maintenance and security of one or more nature preserves (the Mountains District of Western North Carolina, the Southeast Coastal Plain District, or the Nags Head Woods preserve on the Outer Banks). An internship report is required at the end of the term of employment. Duration is 6 months (May through October). Open to college juniors, college seniors, recent college graduates, graduate students. All positions paid at $7–$8 per hour. International applications accepted.

Benefits Formal training, names of contacts, travel reimbursement, willing to complete paperwork for educational credit, willing to provide letters of recommendation.

Contact Write, call, fax, or e-mail Margaret Fields, Internship Coordinator. Phone: 919-403-8558. Fax: 919-403-0379. E-mail: mfields@tnc.org. Applicants must submit a cover letter, resume, personal reference, telephone interview for finalists. Application deadline: February 15 for summer. World Wide Web: http://www.tnc.org.

NEW ENGLAND SMALL FARM INSTITUTE/ NORTHEAST WORKERS ON ORGANIC FARMS
PO Box 608, 275 Jackson Street
Belchertown, Massachusetts 01007

General Information Small farm demonstration and training center that manages public farmland and advocates for sustainable agriculture in New England. Established in 1978. Number of employees: 3. Number of internship applications received each year: 200.

Internships Available ▶ *70 farm apprentices/Northeast Workers on Organic Farms(NEWOOF):* responsibilities include farm work; specific responsibilities vary at each farm. Candidates should have ability to work independently, ability to work with others, personal interest in the field, self-motivation, ability to do hard physical work and work with flexible schedule. Duration is 1 growing season. Open to college freshmen, college sophomores, college juniors, college seniors, recent college graduates, career changers. ▶ *General interns.* Candidates should have ability to work independently, ability to work with others, computer skills, editing skills, organizational skills, personal interest in the field, research skills, self-motivation, writing skills. Duration is flexible. Open to college juniors, college seniors, recent college graduates, graduate students, career changers. All positions available as unpaid or paid.

Benefits Names of contacts, on-the-job training, opportunity to attend seminars/workshops, travel reimbursement, willing to complete paperwork for educational credit, willing to provide letters of recommendation.

Contact Write, call, fax, or e-mail Kathryn Ruhf, Co-Director. Phone: 413-323-4531. Fax: 413-323-9594. E-mail: nesfi@igc.org. In-person interview recommended. Applicants must submit a cover letter, resume, two personal references, two letters of recommendation. Applications are accepted continuously.

NEW JERSEY SCHOOL OF CONSERVATION
One Wapalanne Road
Branchville, New Jersey 07826

General Information School that is dedicated to developing a knowledge of how natural systems operate that will in turn foster and cultivate the development of an environmentally sound value system which incorporates ethical, aesthetic, and economic elements. Established in 1949. Number of employees: 35. Unit of Montclair State University, Upper Montclair, New Jersey. Number of internship applications received each year: 25.

Internships Available ▶ *4 graduate teaching interns:* responsibilities include teaching small groups of students and teachers environmentally based interdisciplinary courses in sciences, social sciences, humanities, and outdoor pursuits; and working with faculty and fellows to develop teaching techniques. Candidates should have ability to work independently, knowledge of field, oral communication skills, personal interest in the field, self-motivation, strong interpersonal skills, strong leadership ability, written communication skills. Duration is 10 months. $1,500 per duration of internship. Open to recent college graduates, graduate students, career changers, individuals reentering the workforce. International applications accepted.

Benefits Free housing, free meals, job counseling, opportunity to attend seminars/workshops, willing to act as a professional reference, willing to complete paperwork for educational credit, willing to provide letters of recommendation, 3 graduate-level academic credits.

Contact Write, call, or fax Dr. John J. Kirk, Director. Phone: 973-948-4900. Fax: 973-948-5131. In-person interview recommended. Applicants must submit a formal organization application, cover letter, resume, academic transcripts, two letters of recommendation. Application deadline: April 15.

NICOLET NATIONAL FOREST, EAGLE RIVER-FLORENCE RANGER DISTRICT
PO Box 1809
Eagle River, Wisconsin 54521

General Information District providing management and administration of recreation areas and wilderness. Established in 1897. Number of employees: 35. Number of internship applications received each year: 25.

Internships Available ▶ *4 outdoor recreation interns:* responsibilities include assisting with the operation and maintenance of 14 campgrounds; includes wilderness management, trail operation and maintenance. Duration is 65 days. ▶ *1 trails coordinator-wilderness ranger intern:* responsibilities include assisting in the operation and maintenance of all recreation trails inside and outside of the three designated wildernesses, conducting trail condition surveys, and recommending trail rehabilitation and other actions needed to provide for public safety and enjoyment of the trails. Duration is 65–150 days. Candidates for all positions should have ability to work independently, ability to work with others, personal interest in the field, self-motivation. All positions paid at $20 per day. Open to high school students, high school seniors, recent high school graduates, college freshmen, college sophomores, college juniors, college seniors, recent college graduates, graduate students, law students, career changers, individuals reentering the workforce.

Benefits Free housing, on-the-job training, willing to act as a professional reference, willing to complete paperwork for educational credit, willing to provide letters of recommendation, uniform provided, work-related travel expenses reimbursed, stipend.

Contact Write, call, or fax Mr. Jeff Herrett, Assistant District Ranger. Phone: 715-479-2827. Fax: 715-479-6407. Applicants must submit a cover letter, resume. Application deadline: March 31 for summer.

NORTH CAROLINA BOTANICAL GARDEN
Campus Box 3375, Totten Center, UNC-CH
Chapel Hill, North Carolina 27599-3375

General Information Regional center for research, conservation, and interpretation of plants, particularly those native to the southeastern U.S., as well as horticultural plants with traditional uses or those of special botanical interest. Established in 1960. Number of employees: 25. Unit of The University of North Carolina at Chapel Hill, Chapel Hill, North Carolina. Number of internship applications received each year: 35.

Internships Available ▶ *3 gardening interns:* responsibilities include working with southeastern U.S. plants in a variety of display settings and native and exotic species in the Hubbard Herb Garden and Coker Arboretum, working with endangered species and fern culture, record keeping, seed collecting, cleaning, distribution, and providing interpretive services to the visiting public. Candidates should have ability to work independently, computer skills, personal interest in the field, self-motivation, strong interpersonal skills. Duration is 7–8 months. $8 per hour. Open to recent high school graduates, college freshmen, college sophomores, college juniors, college seniors, recent college graduates, graduate students, law students, career changers, individuals reentering the workforce. International applications accepted.

Benefits Job counseling, names of contacts, opportunity to attend seminars/workshops, possible full-time employment, willing to act as a professional reference, willing to complete paperwork for educational credit, willing to provide letters of recommendation.

Contact Write, call, fax, or e-mail Mr. James L. Ward, Curator, Campus Box 3375, Trotten Center, UNC-OH, Chapel Hill, North Carolina 27599-3375. Phone: 919-962-0522. Fax: 919-962-3531. E-mail: wardjl@email.unc.edu. In-person interview recommended. Applicants must submit a formal organization application, cover letter, resume, three personal references. Application deadline: February 14.

NORTH CASCADES INSTITUTE
2105 State Route 20
Sedro Woolley, Washington 98284-9394

General Information Environmental education organization dedicated to increasing understanding and appreciation of the natural, historical, and cultural landscapes of the Pacific Northwest through field seminars, school programs, watershed education, summer camps, and more. Established in 1986. Number of employees: 12. Number of internship applications received each year: 40.

Internships Available ▶ *1–2 administrative interns:* responsibilities include assisting program coordinator or director and writing, editing, telephoning, mailing, and database work. Candidates should have ability to work independently, ability to work with others, oral communication skills, personal interest in the field, self-motivation, written communication skills. Duration is 3 months. ▶ *15–20 environmental education interns:* responsibilities include assisting with environmental education programs for youth. Candidates should have oral communication skills, personal interest in the field, self-motivation, strong interpersonal skills, written communication skills. Duration is 9–20 weeks. ▶ *1–2 program interns:* responsibilities include assisting program coordinator with admissions, enrollment, registration, and publicity. Candidates should have ability to work independently, oral communication skills, self-motivation, strong interpersonal skills, written communication skills. Duration is 2–4 months. All

North Cascades Institute (continued)

positions are unpaid. Open to college juniors, college seniors, recent college graduates, graduate students. International applications accepted.

Benefits Formal training, job counseling, names of contacts, on-the-job training, opportunity to attend seminars/workshops, willing to act as a professional reference, willing to complete paperwork for educational credit, willing to provide letters of recommendation, first aid training, housing and meals provided for some internships.

Contact Write, call, fax, or e-mail Tracie Johannessen, Program Director. Phone: 360-856-5700 Ext. 240. Fax: 360-856-1934. E-mail: nci@ncascades.org. In-person interview recommended. Applicants must submit a formal organization application, cover letter, resume, three personal references. Applications are accepted continuously. World Wide Web: http://ncascades.org/nci/.

NORTHWEST COALITION FOR ALTERNATIVES TO PESTICIDES
PO Box 1393
Eugene, Oregon 97440

General Information Nonprofit 5-state grassroots membership organization that works to protect people and the environment by advancing healthy solutions to pest problems. Established in 1977. Number of employees: 9. Number of internship applications received each year: 100.

Internships Available ▶ *1–2 information services/program assistants:* responsibilities include researching and writing articles for NCAP's quarterly Journal of Pesticide Reform and responding to requests for information. Candidates should have ability to work independently, computer skills, office skills, oral communication skills, organizational skills, personal interest in the field, research skills, self-motivation, strong interpersonal skills, writing skills. Duration is flexible. Unpaid. Open to high school students, high school seniors, recent high school graduates, college freshmen, college sophomores, college juniors, college seniors, recent college graduates, graduate students, law students, career changers, individuals reentering the workforce. International applications accepted.

Benefits Names of contacts, willing to complete paperwork for educational credit, willing to provide letters of recommendation.

Contact Write or e-mail Ms. Pollyanna Lind, Information Services Coordinator. E-mail: info@pesticide.org. In-person interview recommended. Applicants must submit a cover letter, resume. Applications are accepted continuously. World Wide Web: http://www.efn.org/~ncap.

NUCLEAR INFORMATION AND RESOURCE SERVICE
1424 16th Street, NW, Suite 404
Washington, District of Columbia 20036

General Information Organization that assists citizens and communities concerned with the dangers of nuclear power and radioactive waste by promoting safe energy and energy alternatives. Established in 1978. Number of employees: 7. Number of internship applications received each year: 75.

Internships Available ▶ *1 activist support intern.* ▶ *1 computer systems intern:* responsibilities include helping run and improve NIRS Web site, improving and operating NIRS e-mail and Internet capabilities, and designing and building databases. Candidates should have computer skills, personal interest in the field, strong interpersonal skills. ▶ *1 publications intern.* Candidates should have ability to work with others, oral communication skills, research skills, writing skills. ▶ *Radioactive waste interns.* Candidates should have ability to work independently, experience in the field, oral communication skills, personal interest in the field, strong interpersonal skills, written communication skills. ▶ *1 reactor watchdog intern.* Candidates should have ability to work independently, ability to work with others, oral communication skills, personal interest in the field. Duration for all positions is flexible. All positions are unpaid. Open to high school students, high school seniors, recent high school graduates, college fresh-

men, college sophomores, college juniors, college seniors, recent college graduates, graduate students, law students, career changers, individuals reentering the workforce.

Benefits Names of contacts, opportunity to attend seminars/workshops, possible full-time employment, willing to complete paperwork for educational credit, willing to provide letters of recommendation.

Contact Write or e-mail Administrative Coordinator. E-mail: nirsnet@igc.apc.org. No phone calls. Applicants must submit a resume, writing sample. Applications are accepted continuously. World Wide Web: http://www.nirs.org.

OREGON MUSEUM OF SCIENCE AND INDUSTRY SCIENCE CAMPS
7171 Southwest Quarry Avenue
Redmond, Oregon 97756

General Information Organization that teaches natural history, outdoor skills, and environmental science to students of all ages. Established in 1951. Number of employees: 50. Division of Oregon Museum of Science and Industry, Portland, Oregon. Number of internship applications received each year: 30.

Internships Available ▶ *8 naturalist interns:* responsibilities include reviewing available curriculum and becoming proficient in teaching those subjects, developing and organizing program materials and displays, aiding in logistics for field programs, and being a positive role model for students. Candidates should have knowledge of field, organizational skills, personal interest in the field, self-motivation, strong interpersonal skills, strong leadership ability. Duration is 3 months. $15–$20 per day. Open to college juniors, college seniors, recent college graduates, graduate students. International applications accepted.

Benefits Free housing, free meals, on-the-job training, possible full-time employment, willing to act as a professional reference, willing to complete paperwork for educational credit, willing to provide letters of recommendation.

Contact Write, call, fax, or e-mail Mr. Joseph Jones, Director, OMSI Science Camps. Phone: 541-548-5473. Fax: 541-504-8365. E-mail: omsicamp@transport.com. In-person interview recommended. Applicants must submit a formal organization application, cover letter, resume, letter of recommendation. Applications are accepted continuously. World Wide Web: http://www.omsi.com.

PACIFIC ENVIRONMENT AND RESOURCES CENTER
1440 Broadway, Suite 306
Oakland, California 94612

General Information Nonprofit organization employing grassroots activism and environmental advocacy, committed to global environmental improvement projects around the Pacific Rim. Established in 1987. Number of employees: 9. Number of internship applications received each year: 20.

Internships Available ▶ *Administrative interns:* responsibilities include letter writing, typing, organizing files and information, answering phones, filling requests for information, assisting with mailings and databases, and helping with other miscellaneous tasks. Candidates should have ability to work independently, ability to work with others, computer skills, office skills, oral communication skills, organizational skills, research skills, writing skills. Duration is 3 months. ▶ *Independent project interns:* responsibilities include working with a project director on an issue that relates to a PERC project. Candidates should have ability to work independently, analytical skills, oral communication skills, research skills, self-motivation, writing skills. Duration is 4 months. ▶ *Project assistants:* responsibilities include researching and summarizing information on a particular subject of interest to the intern and relevant to a PERC project. Candidates should have ability to work independently, oral communication skills, organizational skills, research skills, self-motivation, written communication skills. Duration is 3–9 months. All positions are unpaid. Open to college freshmen, college sophomores, col-

lege juniors, college seniors, recent college graduates, graduate students, career changers, individuals reentering the workforce. International applications accepted.
Benefits Job counseling, names of contacts, possible full-time employment, travel reimbursement, willing to act as a professional reference, willing to complete paperwork for educational credit, willing to provide letters of recommendation, opportunity to work with experts, structured supervision, opportunity to learn about global environmental issues.
Contact Write, fax, or e-mail David Gordon, Intern Coordinator. Fax: 510-251-8838. E-mail: perc@igc.apc.org. No phone calls. In-person interview recommended. Applicants must submit a cover letter, resume. Applications are accepted continuously. World Wide Web: http://www.pacenv.org.

PAYETTE NATIONAL FOREST, MCCALL RANGER DISTRICT
PO Box 1026
McCall, Idaho 83638

General Information Forest service that cares for the land and serves the people. Established in 1905. Number of employees: 21. Number of internship applications received each year: 5.
Internships Available ▶ *Recreation assistants:* responsibilities include assisting with campground, trailhead and dispersed site maintenance. $60–$80 per week. Open to recent high school graduates, college freshmen, college sophomores, college juniors, college seniors, recent college graduates, graduate students, law students, individuals reentering the workforce. ▶ *1–3 trail maintenance volunteers:* responsibilities include working with small crew constructing and maintaining trails in steep terrain while camping out. Position available as unpaid or at $60–$80 per week. Open to recent high school graduates, college freshmen, college sophomores, college juniors, college seniors, recent college graduates, graduate students, law students, career changers, individuals reentering the workforce. Candidates for all positions should have ability to work independently, ability to work with others, self-motivation. Duration for all positions is 3-4 months in summer. International applications accepted.
Benefits Free housing, on-the-job training, willing to act as a professional reference, willing to provide letters of recommendation.
Contact Write, call, fax, or e-mail Beth Ludvigsen, Recreation Staff Assistant. Phone: 208-634-0400. Fax: 208-634-0433. E-mail: eludvig/r4,payette@ls.fed.us. Applicants must submit a resume. Applications are accepted continuously. World Wide Web: http://www.mccall.net/pnf.

PEACE VALLEY NATURE CENTER
170 Chapman Road
Doylestown, Pennsylvania 18901

General Information Center that promotes environmental awareness through a variety of educational experiences; serves as a wildlife sanctuary where citizens of southeast Pennsylvania can enjoy natural beauty. Established in 1975. Number of employees: 4. Unit of Bucks County Department of Parks and Recreation, Langhorne, Pennsylvania. Number of internship applications received each year: 10.
Internships Available ▶ *2 naturalist interns:* responsibilities include observing and teaching environmental education programs to children of all ages, completing and presenting an approved project, writing a newsletter article on a natural history topic, filling out weekly diary, assisting in all aspects of nature center operations. Candidates should have ability to work independently, knowledge of field, oral communication skills, personal interest in the field, plan to pursue career in field, self-motivation, strong interpersonal skills, strong leadership ability, writing skills. Duration is 10–12 weeks. $75 per week. Open to college freshmen, college sophomores, college juniors, college seniors, recent college graduates, graduate students, career changers.
Benefits Formal training, free housing, names of contacts, on-the-job training, opportunity to attend seminars/workshops, willing to act as a professional reference, willing to complete paperwork for educational credit, willing to provide letters of recommendation.

Contact Write, call, or fax Craig Olsen, Assistant Naturalist. Phone: 215-345-7860. Fax: 215-345-4529. In-person interview recommended. Applicants must submit a formal organization application, cover letter, resume, two personal references. Application deadline: February 15 for spring, April 15 for summer, August 15 for fall.

PLANET DRUM FOUNDATION
PO Box 31251
San Francisco, California 94131

General Information Nonprofit ecological education organization promoting the ideas of bioregionalism and urban sustainability through publications, workshops, lectures, performances, and hands-on environmental work. Established in 1973. Number of employees: 8. Number of internship applications received each year: 1.
Internships Available ▶ *Green City assistants:* responsibilities include making over-the-phone referrals to individuals and groups, maintaining the VolNet database, managing bulk mail parties, drafting descriptions of VolNet groups' activities for Calendar listings, planning monthly Workshop/Workdays, attending other groups' work parties and events, administrative assistant to the GC Coordinator, research and developing International GC Network, maintaining and expanding urban sustainability library. ▶ *1 Green City grassroots community organizer:* responsibilities include researching creek locations, recruiting and working with local San Francisco activists, determining portions of creeks to be restored, organizing the community around the sites, planning and publicizing the project kick off. ▶ *1 Green City sustainability researcher:* responsibilities include organizing information and resource materials in current library, gathering new resource materials, contacting organizations to determine if they want to be part of the Green City Network. ▶ *Administrative assistants:* responsibilities include running Planet Drum's office, acting as assistant to the Director, arranging appointments, conducting research, sorting archival materials, organizing the library, responding to telephone requests, and leading bulk mail parties. ▶ *Art and design assistants:* responsibilities include helping with the design and layout for Raise the Stakes, the Green City Calendar, flyers, notices to members, project photo albums, displays for tabling, and Web page; taking photos. ▶ *Bioregional association assistants:* responsibilities include expanding outreach and helping design a publicity campaign, assisting in planning a membership or Board of Directors' meeting, working on documenting and disseminating the results of this meeting, helping to organize a Resources Database. ▶ *Editorial assistants:* responsibilities include helping with Raise the Stakes, Planet Drum's international bi-annual review, The Green City Calendar, and bi-monthly publication, which lists daily, Bay Area environmental work parties and seminars. Interns will also research hot urban topics and stories, distribution potential, and how to expand the calendar's usefulness. ▶ *Education and action assistants:* responsibilities include helping to plan, coordinate, and lead Education + Action projects; documenting and evaluating these activities. ▶ *Fund-raising assistants:* responsibilities include researching funding sources, drafting the Annual Report and grant reports, assisting with member outreach, soliciting donations for E+A and Workshop/Workday projects. ▶ *Outreach/membership assistants:* responsibilities include assisting with distributing Planet Drum publications to bookstores, distributors, schools, and members, plus researching new distribution possibilities; promoting new publications to libraries, schools, stores, and reviewers, plus compiling publicity for press kits; processing information requests; managing and updating membership database; and designing, producing, and editing membership mailings. Duration for all positions is 3 months minimum at 20 hours per week. All positions are unpaid. International applications accepted.
Benefits Names of contacts, opportunity to attend seminars/workshops, willing to complete paperwork for educational credit, willing to provide letters of recommendation, access to library, hands-on experience, small stipend for local travel, opportunity to complete a project.

Planet Drum Foundation (continued)

Contact Write, call, fax, or e-mail Judy Goldhaft, Administrative Coordinator. Phone: 415-285-6556. Fax: 415-285-6563. E-mail: planetdrum@ipc.org. In-person interview recommended. Applicants must submit a formal organization application, resume. Applications are accepted continuously.

POCONO ENVIRONMENTAL EDUCATION CENTER
RR 2 Box 1010
Dingmans Ferry, Pennsylvania 18328

General Information Center that advances environmental awareness, knowledge, and skills through education. Established in 1968. Number of employees: 24. Number of internship applications received each year: 700.

Internships Available ▶ *1 development intern:* responsibilities include assisting Director of Development with management of membership and volunteer services, coordinating special events, and researching funding sources. Candidates should have ability to work independently, analytical skills, computer skills, knowledge of field, office skills, organizational skills, personal interest in the field, research skills, self-motivation, written communication skills. Open to college juniors, college seniors, recent college graduates, graduate students, career changers, individuals reentering the workforce. ▶ *6–10 environmental education instructors:* responsibilities include teaching environment/outdoor education to people of all ages, developing programs and activities, performing daily operations and procedures, and assisting with support services. Candidates should have ability to work independently, college courses in field, computer skills, knowledge of field, office skills, organizational skills, personal interest in the field, self-motivation, strong interpersonal skills. Open to college juniors, college seniors, recent college graduates, graduate students. ▶ *1 program planning intern:* responsibilities include scheduling group's program/activities; coordinating cabins, facilities, staff, and food-service arrangements; designing weekly schedules; and teaching environment/outdoor education to people of all ages. Candidates should have ability to work independently, ability to work with others, analytical skills, knowledge of field, office skills, oral communication skills, organizational skills, personal interest in the field, self-motivation. Open to college juniors, college seniors, recent college graduates, graduate students. ▶ *1 public relations intern:* responsibilities include writing press releases, designing layout for promotional materials, maintaining a darkroom, and assisting with programs and activities. Candidates should have ability to work independently, computer skills, editing skills, knowledge of field, oral communication skills, personal interest in the field, self-motivation, strong interpersonal skills, writing skills. Open to college juniors, college seniors, recent college graduates, graduate students. Duration for all positions is 6–10 months. All positions available as unpaid or at $500–$800 per month. International applications accepted.

Benefits Formal training, free housing, free meals, job counseling, names of contacts, on-the-job training, opportunity to attend seminars/workshops, tuition assistance, willing to act as a professional reference, willing to complete paperwork for educational credit, willing to provide letters of recommendation.

Contact Write, call, fax, or e-mail Ms. Florence Mauro, Director. Phone: 570-828-2319. Fax: 570-828-9695. E-mail: peec@ptd.net. In-person interview recommended. Applicants must submit a cover letter, resume, two personal references. Application deadline: February 1 for summer, June 1 for fall, October 1 for winter/spring. World Wide Web: http://www.peec.org.

POK-O-MACCREADY OUTDOOR EDUCATION CENTER
112 Reber Road North
Willsboro, New York 12996

General Information Outdoor education center in the Adirondacks that allows children in grades 5–12 to participate in activities such as pond study, pioneer living, rock climbing, cross-country skiing, winter camping, environmental study, and overnight hikes. Established in 1905. Number of employees: 10. Number of internship applications received each year: 12.

Internships Available ▶ *1 Native American culture interns:* responsibilities include teaching classes in Native American culture including hunting and gathering techniques, hide tanning, crafts, spirituality, primitive tools and technology, wild edibles, and Native American shelter construction. Candidates should have ability to work independently, oral communication skills, self-motivation, strong interpersonal skills, strong leadership ability. Duration is 1–3 months. Open to college freshmen, college sophomores, college juniors, college seniors, recent college graduates, career changers. ▶ *1 animal care intern:* responsibilities include taking care of oxen team, horses, chickens, and sheep, and using them to teach children about animals. Candidates should have personal interest in the field, self-motivation, strong interpersonal skills. Duration is 4–6 weeks. Open to college freshmen, college sophomores, college juniors, college seniors, recent college graduates, career changers, individuals reentering the workforce. ▶ *1 environmental studies intern:* responsibilities include teaching and working in Wildlife Activity Center. Candidates should have oral communication skills, personal interest in the field, self-motivation, strong interpersonal skills, strong leadership ability. Duration is 1–3 months. Open to college freshmen, college sophomores, college juniors, college seniors, recent college graduates, career changers. ▶ *1 winter camping intern:* responsibilities include taking students on winter camping expedition in the high peaks of the Adirondack Mountains. Candidates should have experience in the field, oral communication skills, personal interest in the field, self-motivation, strong interpersonal skills, strong leadership ability. Duration is 4–6 weeks. Open to college freshmen, college sophomores, college juniors, college seniors, recent college graduates, career changers. All positions paid at $100 per month. International applications accepted.

Benefits Formal training, free housing, free meals, health insurance, possible full-time employment, willing to complete paperwork for educational credit.

International Internships Available in Australia.

Contact Write, call, or fax Mr. Drew Canning, Director. Phone: 518-963-7967. Fax: 518-963-4165. Applicants must submit a cover letter, resume. Applications are accepted continuously. World Wide Web: http://members.aol.com/POKOMAC.

POWDER RIVER BASIN RESOURCE COUNCIL
PO Box 1178
Douglas, Wyoming 82633

General Information Nonprofit membership conservation/agriculture organization promoting stewardship of Wyoming's natural resources and quality of life through organizing, public education, and lobbying. Established in 1973. Number of employees: 7. Number of internship applications received each year: 50.

Internships Available ▶ *1–2 project assistants:* responsibilities include assisting with research; compiling information; drafting materials connected with resource issues such as water development, energy development, waste management, and sustainable agriculture; evaluating conservation policies; and increasing citizen involvement in decision making. Candidates should have ability to work independently, ability to work with others, research skills, self-motivation, writing skills, written communication skills. Duration is 3 months. Unpaid. Open to college freshmen, college sophomores, college juniors, college seniors, recent college graduates, graduate students, law students, career changers, individuals reentering the workforce. International applications accepted.

Benefits Formal training, free housing, free meals, housing at a cost, names of contacts, willing to complete paperwork for educational credit, willing to provide letters of recommendation, staff car for travel.

Contact Write, call, fax, or e-mail Ms. Vickie Goodwin, Co-Director. Phone: 307-358-5002. Fax: 307-358-6771. E-mail: doprbre@coffey.com. In-person interview recommended. Applicants must submit a cover letter, resume, three personal references, one-page writing sample. Applications are accepted continuously.

PUBLIC CITIZEN'S CRITICAL MASS ENERGY PROJECT
215 Pennsylvania Avenue, SE
Washington, District of Columbia 20003

General Information Project which opposes nuclear power and promotes cleaner, safer energy alternatives; researches and writes studies on energy issues, lobbies Congress, monitors relevant federal and state agencies, initiates litigation, and works with press and citizen groups. Established in 1974. Number of employees: 7. Unit of Public Citizen, Washington, District of Columbia. Number of internship applications received each year: 40.

Internships Available ▶ *2–4 interns:* responsibilities include researching and writing reports on energy-related policy or legal matters, helping in a lobbying campaign, working with the media and/or providing assistance to local safe energy organizations, performing some administrative tasks, and helping with organizing. Candidates should have ability to work independently, computer skills, oral communication skills, organizational skills, personal interest in the field, research skills, self-motivation, strong interpersonal skills, strong leadership ability, writing skills. Duration is over 10 weeks (indefinite). Position available as unpaid or paid. Open to college sophomores, college juniors, college seniors, recent college graduates, graduate students, law students, career changers, individuals reentering the workforce. International applications accepted.

Benefits Names of contacts, on-the-job training, opportunity to attend seminars/workshops, willing to complete paperwork for educational credit, willing to provide letters of recommendation.

Contact Write, fax, or e-mail Wenonah Hauter, Director. Fax: 202-547-7392. E-mail: cmep@citizen.org. No phone calls. In-person interview recommended. Applicants must submit a cover letter, resume, writing sample. Application deadline: April 15 for summer, August 1 for fall, November 15 for spring; ongoing applications also considered. World Wide Web: http://www.citizen.org/CMEP.

QUEENS COLLEGE CENTER FOR ENVIRONMENTAL TEACHING AND RESEARCH
Caumsett State Park, 31 Lloyd Harbor Road
Huntington, New York 11743

General Information Residential environmental and outdoor education center. Established in 1979. Number of employees: 8. Number of internship applications received each year: 75.

Internships Available ▶ *1–5 naturalist interns:* responsibilities include teaching environmental and outdoor education topics to various ages/grade levels during residential overnight programs, day programs, and classroom visits; animal care; and house support. Candidates should have oral communication skills, organizational skills, personal interest in the field, plan to pursue career in field, strong interpersonal skills, strong leadership ability, written communication skills. $50–$100 per week. Open to college sophomores, college juniors, college seniors, recent college graduates, graduate students, career changers. ▶ *2 interns:* responsibilities include preparing and presenting lessons in environmental education to all age groups, presenting live animal presentation and outreach programs, visiting other environmental centers, and caring for in-house raptors and reptiles. Duration is 1 semester. $50 per week. Open to college freshmen, college sophomores, college juniors, college seniors, recent college graduates, graduate students, law students. International applications accepted.

Benefits Free housing, free meals, job counseling, names of contacts, on-the-job training, opportunity to attend seminars/workshops, possible full-time employment, willing to complete paperwork for educational credit, willing to provide letters of recommendation.

Contact Write, fax, or e-mail Program Director. Fax: 516-421-3557. E-mail: susan.ohandley@rcn.com. Applicants must submit a cover letter, resume. Applications are accepted continuously.

RAIN FOREST ACTION NETWORK
221 Pine Street, Suite 500
San Francisco, California 94104

General Information Organization working to protect the Earth's rainforests and support the rights of their inhabitants through education, grassroots organizing, and nonviolent direct action. Established in 1985. Number of employees: 22. Number of internship applications received each year: 200.

Internships Available ▶ *30–50 interns:* responsibilities include working in media operations, database coordination, campaign administration, library assistance, executive administration, development assistance or research. Candidates should have ability to work independently, ability to work with others, organizational skills, personal interest in the field, self-motivation, desire to save the rainforests of the world. Duration is flexible (3 months minimum). Unpaid. Open to recent high school graduates, college freshmen, college sophomores, college juniors, college seniors, recent college graduates, graduate students, law students, career changers, individuals reentering the workforce. International applications accepted.

Benefits On-the-job training, opportunity to attend seminars/workshops, travel reimbursement, willing to act as a professional reference, willing to complete paperwork for educational credit, willing to provide letters of recommendation.

Contact Write, call, fax, or e-mail Adrienne L. Blum, Volunteer and Intern Program Director. Phone: 415-398-4404. Fax: 415-398-2732. E-mail: helpran@ran.org. In-person interview recommended. Applicants must submit a formal organization application, resume, writing sample. Applications are accepted continuously. World Wide Web: http://www.ran.org.

RANDALL DAVEY AUDUBON CENTER
PO Box 9314
Santa Fe, New Mexico 87504

General Information Environmental education center; advocate for environmental issues that effect the southwest United States. Established in 1983. Number of employees: 5. Field office of National Audubon Society, New York, New York. Number of internship applications received each year: 30.

Internships Available ▶ *1–3 environmental education interns:* responsibilities include assisting in planning and teaching environmental education classes for students, staffing the visitor center, leading interpretive walks, assisting with the maintenance of building and grounds, assisting with newsletter writing and production, and doing an independent project. Candidates should have ability to work independently, oral communication skills, plan to pursue career in field, self-motivation, strong interpersonal skills. Duration is 3 months. $75 per week. Open to college freshmen, college sophomores, college juniors, college seniors, recent college graduates, graduate students, career changers, individuals reentering the workforce. International applications accepted.

Benefits Formal training, free housing, job counseling, names of contacts, on-the-job training, opportunity to attend seminars/workshops, willing to act as a professional reference, willing to complete paperwork for educational credit, willing to provide letters of recommendation.

Contact Write, call, or e-mail Ms. Janie Chodosh, Education Specialist. Phone: 505-983-4609. E-mail: rdac@trail.com. Telephone interview required. Applicants must submit a cover letter, resume, 3 personal references or letters of recommendation. Application deadline: March 15 for summer (tentative), June 24 for fall (tentative), November 24 for spring (tentative). World Wide Web: http://www.audubon.org/.

RENEW AMERICA
1200 18th Street, NW, Suite 1100
Washington, District of Columbia 20036

General Information Organization that seeks to identify and verify successful environmental programs and releases this information to foster the rapid, efficient expansion of success-

Renew America (continued)

ful environmental programs. Established in 1978. Number of employees: 3. Number of internship applications received each year: 200.

Internships Available ▶ *1–2 research assistants:* responsibilities include researching, writing, providing administrative support, assisting with telephone work, and performing outreach tasks to environmental and other organizations. Candidates should have ability to work independently, ability to work with others, computer skills, oral communication skills, self-motivation, written communication skills. Duration is 3–6 months. Position available as unpaid or paid. Open to college juniors, college seniors, recent college graduates, graduate students.

Benefits Names of contacts, opportunity to attend seminars/workshops, possible full-time employment, willing to complete paperwork for educational credit, willing to provide letters of recommendation, possible stipend.

Contact Write, fax, or e-mail Internship Coordinator. Fax: 202-721-1545. E-mail: renewamerica@counterpart.org. No phone calls. In-person interview recommended. Applicants must submit a cover letter, resume. Applications are accepted continuously. World Wide Web: http://www.crest.org/renew_america.

RIVERBEND ENVIRONMENTAL EDUCATION CENTER
1950 Spring Mill Road
Gladwyne, Pennsylvania 19035-1000

General Information Environmental education center emphasizing awareness and appreciation of the environment. Established in 1974. Number of employees: 6. Number of internship applications received each year: 150.

Internships Available ▶ *3 Riverbend Exploration Camp environmental education interns:* responsibilities include attending 1½-week training session, assisting staff with summer day camp, greeting and speaking with public visitors, leading nature walks, assisting with upkeep and cleaning of facilities. Candidates should have ability to work independently, ability to work with others, college courses in field, plan to pursue career in field, self-motivation, strong interpersonal skills. Duration is 10 weeks. Open to college sophomores, college juniors, college seniors, recent college graduates. ▶ *3 seasonal environmental education interns:* responsibilities include teaching classes in schools, organized groups, and public; maintaining teaching areas; planning and preparing classes and public programs from assigned environmental concepts; assisting in developing and revising classes and programs; maintaining small animal cages; assisting with promotion of programs via press releases, newsletter, and articles; assisting with development and implementation of large public events; and assisting with office duties. Candidates should have ability to work independently, college courses in field, plan to pursue career in field, self-motivation, strong interpersonal skills. Duration is January-June, June-September, or September-December (40 hours per week). Open to college sophomores, college juniors, college seniors, recent college graduates, individuals reentering the workforce. All positions paid at $200 per week. International applications accepted.

Benefits Formal training, free housing, job counseling, names of contacts, on-the-job training, opportunity to attend seminars/workshops, possible full-time employment, willing to act as a professional reference, willing to complete paperwork for educational credit, willing to provide letters of recommendation, introduction to administration of other environmental centers, opportunity to visit other environmental centers in the region.

Contact Write, call, fax, or e-mail Ms. Stacy Olitsky, Director of Education. Phone: 610-527-5234. Fax: 610-527-5234. E-mail: rvrbend@aol.com. In-person interview recommended. Applicants must submit a formal organization application, cover letter, resume, academic transcripts, writing sample, three personal references. Applications are accepted continuously. World Wide Web: http://www.gladwynepa.com/riverbend/.

SAFARI CLUB INTERNATIONAL
4800 West Gates Pass Road
Tucson, Arizona 85745

General Information Nonprofit organization working for conservation of wildlife through education of people and hunters through programs sponsored by the International Wildlife Museum (IWM) and the American Wilderness Leadership School (AWLS). Established in 1971. Number of employees: 80. Number of internship applications received each year: 4.

Internships Available ▶ *1–2 American Wilderness Leadership School interns (AWLS):* responsibilities include assisting staff with outdoor education classes/conservation education, assisting with the facilitation of outdoor experiences at school, attending AWLS work weekend and staff training. Candidates should have knowledge of field, organizational skills, self-motivation, strong interpersonal skills, strong leadership ability. Duration is 4–5 months. ▶ *1–2 International Wildlife Museum interns (IWM):* responsibilities include facilitating interpretive tours and outreach programs, facilitating junior docent programs, assisting with research and development, and marketing of IWM exhibits and educational programs. Candidates should have knowledge of field, oral communication skills, organizational skills, self-motivation, strong interpersonal skills, strong leadership ability. Duration is 3–4 months. ▶ *1–2 educational interns:* responsibilities include assisting educational staff with preparing, implementing and maintaining SCI programs; assisting with advertising and promoting SCI's mission and programs; assisting with administrative duties of education department. Candidates should have ability to work independently, computer skills, oral communication skills, self-motivation, writing skills. Duration is 3–4 months. All positions available as unpaid or at $150–$250 per week. Open to college sophomores, college juniors, college seniors, recent college graduates, graduate students. International applications accepted.

Benefits Names of contacts, opportunity to attend seminars/workshops, willing to act as a professional reference, willing to complete paperwork for educational credit, willing to provide letters of recommendation, free housing and meals for May-September AWLS interns, and $600 maximum travel reimbursement.

Contact Write, call, or e-mail Donald J. Brown, Internship Supervisor. Phone: 520-620-1220. E-mail: dbrown@safariclub.org. Telephone interview required. Applicants must submit a cover letter, resume, personal reference, essay of 100 words or less describing goals. Application deadline: March 1 for summer (May-September) at AWLS, March 1 for summer (May-August) at SCR-/IWM, August 1 for fall (October-December) at SCI-IWM, November 1 for winter (January-March) at SCI/IWM. World Wide Web: http://www.safariclub.org.

SALT RIVER PROJECT (SRP)–PROJECT EMPLOYEES RECREATION ASSOCIATION (PERA)
PO Box 52025
Phoenix, Arizona 85072-2025

General Information Private club for Salt River Project employees and their immediate families. Established in 1952. Number of employees: 25. Division of Salt River Project, Tempe, Arizona. Number of internship applications received each year: 15.

Internships Available ▶ *Recreation interns:* responsibilities include working in the fitness center; assisting with facility booking, snack bar operations, maintenance, bartending, and special events; assembling 2 educational classes; working on promotional flyers and billings; overseeing the recreational aids; and assisting with swimming pool. Candidates should have ability to work with others, computer skills, knowledge of field, organizational skills, plan to pursue career in field, self-motivation. Duration is flexible. $75 per week. Open to recent high school graduates, college freshmen, college sophomores, college juniors, college seniors, recent college graduates, graduate students, career changers, individuals reentering the workforce. International applications accepted.

Benefits Formal training, job counseling, names of contacts, opportunity to attend seminars/workshops, possible full-time

employment, willing to complete paperwork for educational credit, willing to provide letters of recommendation, use of facility (store, fitness, pool).
Contact Write, call, or fax Ms. Shawna Collins, Facilities Supervisor Assistant. Phone: 602-236-5782. Fax: 602-236-5920. In-person interview recommended. Applicants must submit a formal organization application, cover letter, resume. Applications are accepted continuously.

SAN FRANCISCO BAY NATIONAL WILDLIFE REFUGE COMPLEX
PO Box 524
Newark, California 94560

General Information Refuge whose mission is to protect, enhance, and maximize natural resources and educate the public on the value of those resources. Established in 1972. Number of employees: 25. Number of internship applications received each year: 12.
Internships Available ▶ *8 environmental education assistants:* responsibilities include conducting workshops for teachers and helping environmental education specialists conduct field trips for elementary school classes. Candidates should have ability to work independently, knowledge of field, oral communication skills, organizational skills, self-motivation, strong interpersonal skills. Duration is 3–4 months. Open to college juniors, college seniors, recent college graduates, graduate students, career changers, individuals reentering the workforce. ▶ *6 resource management/biology interns:* responsibilities include monitoring and surveying endangered species, habitat restoration work, data entry, and report writing. Candidates should have ability to work independently, ability to work with others, computer skills, declared college major in field, experience in the field, research skills. Duration is 3–5 months. Open to college juniors, college seniors, recent college graduates, graduate students, career changers. All positions paid at $50 per week. International applications accepted.
Benefits Free housing, on-the-job training, travel reimbursement, willing to complete paperwork for educational credit, willing to provide letters of recommendation, accident insurance.
Contact Write or e-mail Kim Aichele, Volunteer Coordinator, PO Box 324, Newark, California 84560. E-mail: kim_aichele@ mail.fws.gov. No phone calls. Submit application through the Student Conservation Association, 603-543-1700. Applications are accepted continuously. World Wide Web: http://www.r1.fws.gov/ sfbnwr/sfbnwr.html.

SAN JUAN/RIO GRANDE NATIONAL FOREST
1803 West Highway 160
Monte Vista, Colorado 81144

General Information Natural resource agency that stresses multiple use of its resources and manages Bureau of Land Management lands. Number of employees: 200. Number of internship applications received each year: 150.
Internships Available ▶ *2–7 interdisciplinary-botany/geology/ hydrology interns:* responsibilities include survey work and site-specific project work in the field. Candidates should have ability to work independently, ability to work with others, experience in the field, oral communication skills, personal interest in the field, self-motivation. Duration is 3 months. Open to high school seniors, recent high school graduates, college freshmen, college sophomores, college juniors, college seniors, recent college graduates, graduate students, law students, career changers. ▶ *3–5 interpretive hosts:* responsibilities include talking to visitors and interacting with the public. Candidates should have ability to work independently, oral communication skills, self-motivation, strong interpersonal skills. Duration is 3 months. Open to high school seniors, recent high school graduates, college freshmen, college sophomores, college juniors, college seniors, recent college graduates, graduate students, law students, career changers, individuals reentering the workforce. ▶ *3–5 range conservation interns:* responsibilities include noxious weed inventory and control and identifying plants. Candidates should have ability to work independently, ability to work with others, knowledge

of field, oral communication skills, personal interest in the field, self-motivation. Duration is 3 months. Open to college freshmen, college sophomores, college juniors, college seniors, recent college graduates, graduate students, law students, career changers. ▶ *3–4 timber crew members:* responsibilities include land use location, surveys, and road and trail inventories. Candidates should have ability to work independently, ability to work with others, knowledge of field, oral communication skills, personal interest in the field, self-motivation. Duration is 3 months. Open to college freshmen, college sophomores, college juniors, college seniors, recent college graduates, graduate students, law students, career changers. ▶ *2–4 wilderness rangers:* responsibilities include hiking and camping in wilderness areas, contacting users, and gathering information. Candidates should have ability to work independently, ability to work with others, experience in the field, oral communication skills, personal interest in the field, self-motivation. Duration is 3 months. Open to high school seniors, recent high school graduates, college freshmen, college sophomores, college juniors, college seniors, recent college graduates, graduate students, law students, career changers. ▶ *2–4 wildlife technicians:* responsibilities include inventorying or monitoring wildlife and habitat. Candidates should have ability to work independently, ability to work with others, knowledge of field, oral communication skills, personal interest in the field, self-motivation. Duration is 2–3 months. Open to college freshmen, college sophomores, college juniors, college seniors, recent college graduates, graduate students, law students, career changers. All positions are unpaid.
Benefits Formal training, free housing, job counseling, names of contacts, on-the-job training, opportunity to attend seminars/ workshops, willing to complete paperwork for educational credit, willing to provide letters of recommendation, possible stipend for incidental expenses.
Contact Write, call, or fax Volunteer Coordinator. Phone: 719-852-5941. Fax: 719-852-6250. Applicants must submit a cover letter, resume, three personal references. Application deadline: April 15 for summer interns (flexible); continuous for other positions.

SARETT NATURE CENTER
2300 Benton Center Road
Benton Harbor, Michigan 49022

General Information Nature center designed to provide environmental education for the surrounding school districts as well as an outlet for natural history education of the general public. Established in 1970. Number of employees: 8. Unit of Michigan Audubon Society, Lansing, Michigan. Number of internship applications received each year: 20.
Internships Available ▶ *2 naturalist interns:* responsibilities include teaching diverse natural history programs to school groups primarily preschool through sixth grade, leading interpretive nature walks, and teaching cross-country skiing. Candidates should have ability to work independently, ability to work with others, knowledge of field, oral communication skills. Duration is 3–5 months. $100 per week. Open to college sophomores, college juniors, college seniors, recent college graduates.
Benefits Housing at a cost, job counseling, names of contacts, on-the-job training, opportunity to attend seminars/workshops, willing to complete paperwork for educational credit, willing to provide letters of recommendation.
Contact Write or call Dianne Braybrook, Chief Naturalist. Phone: 616-927-4832. Applicants must submit a cover letter, resume, three personal references. Applications are accepted continuously.

SAVE AMERICA'S FORESTS
4 Library Court, SE
Washington, District of Columbia 20003

General Information Environmental and forest protection education and lobbying organization. Established in 1989.
Internships Available ▶ *Interns:* responsibilities include research, writing, office tasks, lobbying, organizing for legislation. Candidates should have analytical skills, office skills, oral communication skills, strong interpersonal skills, writing skills. Duration is 1

Save America's Forests (continued)

semester. housing stipend available. Open to college sophomores, college juniors, college seniors, recent college graduates, graduate students, law students.

Contact Write or call Internship Coordinator, 4 Library Court, SE, Washington, District of Columbia 20003. Phone: 202-544-9219. Telephone interview required. Applicants must submit a cover letter, resume, two writing samples, 2 personal references or letters of recommendation. Applications are accepted continuously. World Wide Web: http://www.saveamericasforests.org.

SAVE THE SOUND, INC.
185 Magee Avenue
Stamford, Connecticut 06902

General Information   Environmental, nonprofit organization dedicated to the protection, restoration, and appreciation of Long Island Sound and its watershed through programs in education, research, and advocacy. Established in 1972. Number of employees: 11. Number of internship applications received each year: 60.

Internships Available ▶ *1 habitat restoration field intern:* responsibilities include conducting field surveys (from land and water) at selected sites around the Long Island Sound to identify stormwater and sewer outfalls and other sources of pollution and habitat degradation, and collecting data to assess the impact of those sources on nearby coastal habitats. Candidates should have B.S. degree in marine science, biology, ecology, environmental science or a related field preferred; upper-level undergraduates with appropriate course work/work experience will be considered; must have valid driver's license, transportation and valid Connecticut or New York Safe Boating Certificate; some computer-related experience is required. Duration is 10 weeks from May to September for 20 to 30 hours per week. $1000 stipend plus reimbursement for approved travel costs. ▶ *1–2 marketing assistants:* responsibilities include assisting in the development of a three-year public relations plan for Save the Sound. Candidates should have ability to work with others, computer skills, office skills, oral communication skills, writing skills. Duration is flexible. Unpaid. Open to college freshmen, college sophomores, college juniors, college seniors, recent college graduates, graduate students, career changers. ▶ *1 membership database assistant:* responsibilities include inputting membership data into the database and maintaining current membership information. Candidates should have ability to work independently, computer skills, office skills, organizational skills, self-motivation. Duration is flexible. Unpaid. Open to high school seniors, recent high school graduates, college freshmen, college sophomores, college juniors, college seniors, career changers. ▶ *1 nonprofit management intern:* responsibilities include assisting in the expansion of the fund-raising capabilities for Save the Sound; specific projects will be geared toward intern's experience. Candidates should have ability to work with others, computer skills, editing skills, office skills, organizational skills, writing skills. Duration is 3 months minimum. Unpaid. Open to college juniors, college seniors, recent college graduates, graduate students. ▶ *1 research data processor:* responsibilities include collecting and inputting data into database/spreadsheet program to be used for water quality analysis and the eelgrass restoration project. Candidates should have ability to work independently, computer skills, office skills, organizational skills, self-motivation. Duration is flexible. Unpaid. Open to college freshmen, college sophomores, college juniors, college seniors, recent college graduates, graduate students, career changers. ▶ *1–2 research interns:* responsibilities include identifying algae from water samples in lab and analyzing pigment content and nutrients of samples to track algae blooms. Candidates should have ability to work independently, analytical skills, knowledge of field, personal interest in the field, basic understanding of lab skills and science-related topics. Duration is flexible. Unpaid. Open to college freshmen, college sophomores, college juniors, college seniors, recent college graduates, graduate students, career changers. ▶ *1–2 volunteer coordinator assistants:* responsibilities include helping coordinate volunteer activities around the Sound,

recruiting and placing volunteers, and assembling support materials for volunteers. Candidates should have ability to work with others, computer skills, office skills, oral communication skills, strong leadership ability, writing skills, basic understanding of lab skills and science-related topics. Duration is flexible. Unpaid. Open to high school seniors, college freshmen, college sophomores, college juniors, college seniors, recent college graduates, career changers. International applications accepted.

Benefits Opportunity to attend seminars/workshops, willing to act as a professional reference, willing to complete paperwork for educational credit, willing to provide letters of recommendation.

Contact Write, fax, or e-mail Jenniffer Hanson, Internship Coordinator. Fax: 203-967-2677. E-mail: savethesound@snet.net. In-person interview recommended. Applicants must submit a formal organization application, cover letter, resume, writing sample, 3 references, list of applicable course work for habitat restoration position. Application deadline: April 1 for habitat restoration field intern; continuous for all others. World Wide Web: http://www.savethesound.org.

SCENIC AMERICA
801 Pennsylvania Avenue, SE, #300
Washington, District of Columbia 20003

General Information   Organization that educates the public about the need to protect and improve the visual environment through research and technical assistance to local and state activists and concerned citizens. Established in 1978. Number of employees: 8. Number of internship applications received each year: 60.

Internships Available ▶ *2 public policy programs and communications interns:* responsibilities include providing assistance to supervisor in a range of duties, including drafing fact sheets, newsletter articles, and correspondence, attending meetings, and completing various administrative tasks. Candidates should have ability to work independently, ability to work with others, computer skills, oral communication skills, self-motivation, writing skills. Duration is 10 weeks. $800 per duration of internship. Open to college freshmen, college sophomores, college juniors, college seniors, recent college graduates, graduate students, law students, career changers, individuals reentering the workforce. International applications accepted.

Benefits Names of contacts, on-the-job training, opportunity to attend seminars/workshops, willing to act as a professional reference, willing to complete paperwork for educational credit, willing to provide letters of recommendation.

Contact Write Mr. Frank Vespe, Vice President. In-person interview recommended. Applicants must submit a cover letter, resume, writing sample, three personal references. Applications are accepted continuously. World Wide Web: http://www.scenic.org.

SHARON AUDUBON CENTER
325 Cornwall Bridge Road
Sharon, Connecticut 06069

General Information   A 890-acre sanctuary providing environmental education, wildlife rehabilitation, and nature enjoyment. Established in 1961. Number of employees: 6. Unit of National Audubon Society, New York, New York. Number of internship applications received each year: 100.

Internships Available ▶ *2 environmental education interns:* responsibilities include teaching a wide variety of environmental and natural history topics to on-site and outreach audiences, assisting with curriculum development and exhibits, rehabilitating injured and orphaned birds, and participating in many other facets of a nature center's day-to-day operations. Candidates should have oral communication skills, personal interest in the field, self-motivation, strong interpersonal skills, strong leadership ability. Duration is 3 months. $100 per week. Open to college juniors, college seniors, recent college graduates, graduate students. International applications accepted.

Benefits Free housing, names of contacts, opportunity to attend seminars/workshops, willing to complete paperwork for educational credit, willing to provide letters of recommendation, worker's compensation, Audubon Summer Camp scholarship eligibility. **Contact** Write, call, fax, or e-mail Mr. Scott Heth, Manager. Phone: 860-364-0520. Fax: 860-364-5792. E-mail: sheth@audubon. org. In-person interview recommended. Applicants must submit a cover letter, resume, three personal references. Applications are accepted continuously.

SHAVER'S CREEK ENVIRONMENTAL CENTER, PENNSYLVANIA STATE UNIVERSITY
508A Keller Building
University Park, Pennsylvania 16802

General Information Center providing exemplary day and residential environmental education and outdoor adventure programming. Established in 1976. Number of employees: 15. Unit of Division of Continuing and Distance Education, Pennsylvania State University, University Park, Pennsylvania. Number of internship applications received each year: 75.
Internships Available ▶ *4–6 environmental education interns:* responsibilities include participating in all aspects of the center's operation which may include summer camps, school programs, visitor center operations, live animal care and handling, public natural and cultural history walks, volunteer training and supervision, adventure and recreational programs, weekend festivals and events, teacher and pre-teacher workshops, team building programs, curriculum and program development, and writing articles for newsletter. Candidates should have organizational skills, plan to pursue career in field, self-motivation, strong interpersonal skills, strong leadership ability, background in education or natural sciences helpful. Duration is January to May, June to August, or September to December. $125–$150 per week. Open to college freshmen, college sophomores, college juniors, college seniors, recent college graduates, career changers. International applications accepted.
Benefits Formal training, free housing, on-the-job training, opportunity to attend seminars/workshops, willing to act as a professional reference, willing to complete paperwork for educational credit, willing to provide letters of recommendation, assistance with resume preparation, access to the Internet.
Contact Write, call, fax, or e-mail Doug Wentzel, Intern Coordinator. Phone: 814-863-2000. Fax: 814-865-2706. E-mail: shaverscreek@ cde.psu.edu. Telephone interview required. Applicants must submit a formal organization application, resume, three personal references, 3 letters of recommendation (international applicants only). Application deadline: March 1 for summer, July 1 for fall, November 1 for spring. World Wide Web: http://www.outreach. psu.edu/shaverscreek/.

SIERRA CLUB
408 C Street, NE
Washington, District of Columbia 20002

General Information Organization dedicated to the preservation and enjoyment of our environment. Established in 1892. Number of employees: 30. Unit of Sierra Club, San Francisco, California. Number of internship applications received each year: 200.
Internships Available ▶ *1 computer support intern:* responsibilities include providing computer support to Sierra Club field staff, working with computer systems manager, and learning how nonprofit organizations use computer programs in their work. Candidates should have ability to work independently, analytical skills, computer skills, experience in the field, oral communication skills, strong interpersonal skills. Duration is 1 semester. Open to college freshmen, college sophomores, college juniors, college seniors, recent college graduates, graduate students, individuals reentering the workforce. ▶ *10 issue-oriented interns:* responsibilities include performing research on a specific environmental issue (public lands and wilderness, toxics and environmental quality, energy and global warming, population, human rights, trade) to be used in the education of the public and Congress; attending congressional hearings, meetings with other environmental groups, and other strategy sessions; and other administrative duties. Candidates should have ability to

work independently, computer skills, oral communication skills, research skills, writing skills, written communication skills. Duration is 3–4 months. Open to college sophomores, college juniors, college seniors, recent college graduates, graduate students, law students, career changers. ▶ *3 media interns:* responsibilities include helping set up press conferences, issue press releases, and ensuring that journalists receive timely information; writing op-ed articles to newspapers on environmental issues. Candidates should have ability to work independently, computer skills, editing skills, oral communication skills, written communication skills, ability to work in a busy office. Duration is 1 semester. Open to college sophomores, college juniors, college seniors, recent college graduates, graduate students. ▶ *3 political interns:* responsibilities include helping with the endorsement process of individuals running for Congress and checking voting records. Candidates should have ability to work with others, computer skills, oral communication skills, research skills, strong interpersonal skills, written communication skills. Duration is 1 semester. Open to college sophomores, college juniors, college seniors, recent college graduates, graduate students, law students. All positions are unpaid. International applications accepted.
Benefits Names of contacts, opportunity to attend seminars/workshops, possible full-time employment, willing to act as a professional reference, willing to complete paperwork for educational credit, willing to provide letters of recommendation, 6 summer college stipends.
Contact Write Annette Henkin, Intern Coordinator. Applicants must submit a cover letter, resume, writing sample. Applications are accepted continuously.

SLIDE RANCH
2025 Shoreline Highway
Muir Beach, California 94965

General Information Environmental farm and wilderness-based teaching center; serves wide variety of schools, organizations, and families from both the local affluent area and also from low-income, urban, under-served populations. Established in 1970. Number of employees: 14. Number of internship applications received each year: 100.
Internships Available ▶ *10 teacher-in-residence:* responsibilities include planning lessons and teaching groups and families, gardening, caring for various farm animals, and various community responsibilities. Candidates should have ability to work with others, oral communication skills, personal interest in the field, self-motivation, strong interpersonal skills, experience and interest in community living situation, educational skills. Duration is January to August or September to December. $200 per month. Open to college juniors, college seniors, recent college graduates, graduate students, law students, career changers, individuals reentering the workforce, anyone with interest in outdoor education. International applications accepted.
Benefits Formal training, free housing, free meals, names of contacts, on-the-job training, opportunity to attend seminars/workshops, possible full-time employment, willing to act as a professional reference, willing to complete paperwork for educational credit, willing to provide letters of recommendation, scholarships available for low-income applicants.
Contact Write, call, or fax Jason S. Reisinger, Head Teacher. Phone: 415-381-6155 Ext. 201. Fax: 415-381-5762. In-person interview recommended. Applicants must submit a cover letter, resume, three personal references, personal statement. Application deadline: June 30 for fall, October 31 for spring/summer. World Wide Web: http://www.igc.org/slideranch.

SOCIETY OF AMERICAN FORESTERS
5400 Grosvenor Lane
Bethesda, Maryland 20814

General Information Professional organization founded to advance the science, education, technology, and practice of forestry. Established in 1900. Number of employees: 29. Number of internship applications received each year: 8.

Society of American Foresters (continued)

Internships Available ▶ *1 Henry Clepper Forest Policy intern:* responsibilities include preparing background reports on current resource issues; assisting, preparing, and developing recommendations to Congress; monitoring federal environmental and natural resources legislation; providing liaison support with environmental and natural resource organizations. Candidates should have ability to work independently, knowledge of field, oral communication skills, research skills, self-motivation, written communication skills. Duration is 6 months starting July or January. $1,000 per month. Open to college seniors, recent college graduates, graduate students.

Benefits Names of contacts, opportunity to attend seminars/workshops, travel reimbursement, willing to provide letters of recommendation, association with established professionals in SAF and other organizations.

Contact Write Director, Forest Policy. Applicants must submit a cover letter, resume, academic transcripts, writing sample, 1-3 personal references. Application deadline: April 15 for fall, October 15 for spring. World Wide Web: http://www.safnet.org.

SOMERSET COUNTY PARK COMMISSION ENVIRONMENTAL EDUCATION CENTER
190 Lord Stirling Road
Basking Ridge, New Jersey 07920

General Information Environmental education center/park providing leisure learning opportunities for the public, schools, and scouting groups. Established in 1971. Number of employees: 15. Unit of Somerset County Park Commission, North Branch, New Jersey. Number of internship applications received each year: 50.

Internships Available ▶ *3–4 conservation crew members:* responsibilities include assisting the maintenance department with trail maintenance and repair, landscaping, and various outdoor assignments. Candidates should have ability to work with others, personal interest in the field, self-motivation, trailwork experience and experience with hand tools preferred. Duration is 8 weeks. $7 per hour. Open to high school students, high school seniors, recent high school graduates, college freshmen, college sophomores, college juniors, college seniors, recent college graduates, graduate students, career changers, individuals reentering the workforce. ▶ *7 seasonal naturalists:* responsibilities include assisting in presentation of environmental projects and teaching various kinds of environmental programs. Candidates should have knowledge of field, oral communication skills, personal interest in the field, strong interpersonal skills, environmental education background preferred. Duration is 10–12 weeks. $8 per hour. Open to college freshmen, college sophomores, college juniors, college seniors, recent college graduates, graduate students, career changers, individuals reentering the workforce.

Benefits Job counseling, names of contacts, possible full-time employment, willing to act as a professional reference, willing to complete paperwork for educational credit, willing to provide letters of recommendation.

Contact Write, call, or fax Kurt Bender, Environmental Science Supervisor. Phone: 908-766-2489. Fax: 908-766-2687. In-person interview recommended. Applicants must submit a formal organization application, cover letter, resume. Application deadline: April 30.

SOUTHERN RESEARCH STATION
200 W.T. Weaver Boulevard, PO Box 2680
Asheville, North Carolina 28802

General Information One of seven forest service research stations in the U.S., this organization manages forest land and conducts research in biology, forestry, global warming, and forest genetics and economics. Unit of USDA Forest Service, Asheville, North Carolina.

Internships Available ▶ *20 conservation education interns:* responsibilities include teaching children in inner cities about conservation concepts, recycling, and water quality. Candidates should

have declared college major in natural science, agriculture, forestry, urban forestry, or education; ability to work with children. Duration is July 1 through August 15. $8–$11 per hour. Open to individuals currently enrolled in a college program.

Contact Write, call, or e-mail Rod Kindlund, Public Affairs Officer. Phone: 828-259-0560. Fax: 828-257-4840. E-mail: rkindlund@srs.fs.usda.gov. Applicants must submit a formal organization application, resume, academic transcripts. Application deadline: July 1. World Wide Web: http://www.srs.fs.fed.us.

SOUTHFACE ENERGY INSTITUTE
241 Pine Street
Atlanta, Georgia 30308

General Information Private nonprofit energy and environmental education and research organization concentrating on energy efficient and sustainable building practices, community design, alternative energy technologies, sustainable landscaping, and urban wildlife habitat development. Established in 1978. Number of employees: 13. Number of internship applications received each year: 300.

Internships Available ▶ *12–16 interns:* responsibilities include assisting staff with ongoing activities; working on special projects, such as hands-on workshops or government-sponsored projects; and working on independent projects. Candidates should have oral communication skills, research skills, self-motivation, strong interpersonal skills, written communication skills, enthusiasm about being involved in a wide variety of projects, computer skills useful. Duration is 3–6 months. $335 per month. Open to college freshmen, college sophomores, college juniors, college seniors, recent college graduates, graduate students, career changers, individuals reentering the workforce. International applications accepted.

Benefits Free housing, names of contacts, opportunity to attend seminars/workshops, possible full-time employment, travel reimbursement, willing to complete paperwork for educational credit, willing to provide letters of recommendation.

Contact Write, call, fax, or e-mail Ms. Gretchen Gigley, Internship Coordinator. Phone: 404-872-3549 Ext. 119. Fax: 404-872-5009. E-mail: gretchen@southface.org. In-person interview recommended. Applicants must submit a formal organization application, resume, two personal references, statement of intent. Applications are accepted continuously. World Wide Web: http://www.southface.org.

STUDENT CONSERVATION ASSOCIATION (SCA)
PO Box 550
Charlestown, New Hampshire 03603

General Information Nonprofit organization that places volunteers year-round in expense-paid conservation projects in national parks, national historic sites, forests, and wildlife refuges nationwide. Established in 1957. Number of employees: 75. Number of internship applications received each year: 5,000.

Internships Available ▶ *100 conservation associates:* responsibilities include resource management duties ranging from wildlife ecology, forestry, and environmental education to archeology and historical interpretation. Duration is 6–12 months. ▶ *1,500 resource assistants:* responsibilities include resource management duties ranging from wildlife ecology, forestry, and environmental education to archaeology and historical interpretation. Duration is 12–16 weeks. Candidates for all positions should have ability to work independently, ability to work with others, self-motivation, qualifications as specified on Web site. All positions are unpaid. Open to recent high school graduates, college freshmen, college sophomores, college juniors, college seniors, recent college graduates, graduate students, law students, career changers, individuals reentering the workforce, minimum age of 18 years. International applications accepted.

Benefits Formal training, free housing, travel reimbursement, food and uniform stipend, living expenses stipend, conservation associates are eligible for Americorps educational awards.

Contact Write, call, fax, or e-mail Recruitment Office. Phone: 603-543-1700. Fax: 603-543-1828. E-mail: internships@sca-inc.org. Telephone interview required. Applicants must submit a formal organization application, academic transcripts, two letters of recommendation, additional requirements on searchable database at Web site. Applications are accepted continuously. Fees: $10. World Wide Web: http://www.sca-inc.org.

SURFRIDER FOUNDATION
122 South El Camino Real, #67
San Clemente, California 92672

General Information Nonprofit environmental organization dedicated to the protection, preservation and restoration of the world's oceans, waves, and beaches through conservation, activism, research, and education. Established in 1984. Number of employees: 10. Number of internship applications received each year: 50.
Internships Available ▶ *Chapter interns/volunteers:* responsibilities include working in local communities with chapter leaders on local issues; areas available include administrative, public relations/media, legal counsel, membership services, events/fundraisers, literature distribution, newletter publication, research. Candidates should have oral communication skills, organizational skills, personal interest in the field, strong interpersonal skills, strong leadership ability. Open to high school seniors, recent high school graduates, college freshmen, college sophomores, college juniors, college seniors, recent college graduates, law students. ▶ *4 national interns/volunteers:* responsibilities include working in Southern California area in administrative chapter development, events/fundraisers, legislative analysis, program research, cataloging and archiving, public speaking, report writing, newsletter, or membership development. Candidates should have ability to work with others, computer skills, office skills, oral communication skills, organizational skills, personal interest in the field. Open to high school seniors, recent high school graduates, college freshmen, college sophomores, college juniors, college seniors, recent college graduates, graduate students, law students. Duration for all positions is flexible. All positions are unpaid. International applications accepted.
Benefits Possible full-time employment, willing to act as a professional reference, willing to complete paperwork for educational credit, willing to provide letters of recommendation.
Contact Write or e-mail Josh Wright, Member Services. E-mail: jwright@surfrider.org. No phone calls. In-person interview recommended. Applicants must submit a formal organization application, resume. Applications are accepted continuously. World Wide Web: http://www.surfrider.org.

TENNESSEE VALLEY AUTHORITY LAND BETWEEN THE LAKES
100 Van Morgan Drive
Golden Pond, Kentucky 42211

General Information Agency providing outdoor recreation and environmental education in a managed natural setting to strengthen environmental responsibility among customers and communicate TVA's environmental leadership role. Established in 1963. Number of employees: 106. Unit of Tennessee Valley Authority, Knoxville, Tennessee. Number of internship applications received each year: 50.
Internships Available ▶ *3 environmental education interns:* responsibilities include working with foresters, wildlife biologists, and ecologists in a recreational setting. Candidates should have ability to work independently, college courses in field, computer skills, knowledge of field, oral communication skills, written communication skills. Duration is 12–16 weeks. $175 per week. Open to recent college graduates. ▶ *1 graphic design apprentice:* responsibilities include designing a variety of printed materials, operating copy camera, maintaining equipment, and assisting client sections with 2- and 3-dimensional interpretive media. Candidates should have college courses in field, computer skills, knowledge of field, oral communication skills, self-motivation, written communication skills. Duration is 1 year. $175 per week. Open to recent college graduates. ▶ *1 living history interpretation apprentice:* responsibilities include daily interpretation in period dress on farm site, designing and testing interpretive programs, and conducting research projects. Candidates

should have college courses in field, computer skills, knowledge of field, oral communication skills, research skills, self-motivation. Duration is 1 year. $175 per week. Open to recent college graduates. ▶ *2 natural history interpretation apprentices:* responsibilities include assisting in the daily operation of the Nature Station and providing information about natural resources to the public. Candidates should have college courses in field, computer skills, knowledge of field, oral communication skills, strong interpersonal skills, written communication skills. Duration is 1 year. $175 per week. Open to recent college graduates. ▶ *1 outdoor recreation administration apprentice:* responsibilities include assisting the Special Events Coordinator with planning, coordinating, and monitoring recreational activities. Candidates should have college courses in field, computer skills, knowledge of field, oral communication skills, organizational skills, self-motivation, strong interpersonal skills, written communication skills. Duration is 1 year. $175 per week. Open to recent college graduates. ▶ *6–8 outdoor recreation interns:* responsibilities include creating, planning, conducting, and evaluating recreation and environmental programs in a campground setting. Candidates should have ability to work independently, college courses in field, computer skills, knowledge of field, oral communication skills, organizational skills, written communication skills. Duration is flexible. $125 per week. Open to college juniors, college seniors. ▶ *1 photography apprentice:* responsibilities include shooting black-and-white, color, slide, and print film; developing; writing cut lines for press releases; producing audiovisual shows; and covering media assignments. Candidates should have college courses in field, computer skills, knowledge of field, office skills, oral communication skills, written communication skills. Duration is 1 year. $175 per week. Open to recent college graduates. ▶ *1 public relations apprentice:* responsibilities include maintaining liaison with tourism organizations and promoting LBL by writing press releases and magazine articles. Candidates should have college courses in field, computer skills, knowledge of field, oral communication skills, writing skills. Duration is 1 year. $175 per week. Open to recent college graduates. ▶ *2 recreation apprentices:* responsibilities include assisting in creating, planning, and conducting recreational programs in family campgrounds. Candidates should have ability to work independently, college courses in field, computer skills, knowledge of field, oral communication skills, organizational skills, self-motivation, strong interpersonal skills, strong leadership ability, written communication skills. Duration is 1 year. $175 per week. Open to recent college graduates. ▶ *2 resource management apprentices:* responsibilities include promoting and planning educational programs for teachers, communities, and day-use school groups. Candidates should have ability to work independently, college courses in field, computer skills, knowledge of field, strong interpersonal skills, writing skills. Duration is 1 year. $175 per week. Open to recent college graduates. ▶ *1 waste management apprentice:* responsibilities include conducting inventory and analyzing solid waste. Candidates should have analytical skills, college courses in field, computer skills, knowledge of field, office skills, written communication skills. Duration is 1 year. $175 per week. Open to recent college graduates. International applications accepted.
Benefits Formal training, free housing, job counseling, names of contacts, on-the-job training, opportunity to attend seminars/workshops, travel reimbursement, willing to complete paperwork for educational credit, willing to provide letters of recommendation, worker's compensation, assistance with resume preparation.
Contact Write, call, fax, or e-mail Ms. Jo Travis, Intern/Apprentice Coordinator. Phone: 502-924-2075. Fax: 502-924-2060. E-mail: jbtravis@tva.gov. In-person interview recommended. Applicants must submit a formal organization application, resume, academic transcripts. Applications are accepted continuously. World Wide Web: http://www.lbl.org.

THREE LAKES NATURE CENTER AND AQUARIUM
400 Sausiluta Drive
Richmond, Virginia 23227

General Information Facility providing environmental education in many areas through visitation, public and school programs,

Three Lakes Nature Center and Aquarium (continued)

and group tours. Established in 1992. Number of employees: 4. Subsidiary of Henrico County Division of Recreation and Parks, Richmond, Virginia. Number of internship applications received each year: 10.

Internships Available ▶ *2 nature center interns:* responsibilities include participating in all aspects of nature center operation including program planning and implementation, exhibit design and fabrication, and animal care and maintenance. Candidates should have ability to work independently, oral communication skills, organizational skills, personal interest in the field, self-motivation, strong leadership ability. Duration is flexible. Unpaid. Open to college freshmen, college sophomores, college juniors, college seniors, graduate students. International applications accepted.

Benefits Formal training, names of contacts, willing to provide letters of recommendation.

Contact Write, call, or e-mail Mr. Tom Thorp, Nature Coordinator. Phone: 804-261-8230. E-mail: tt-threelakes@juno.com. In-person interview recommended. Applicants must submit a cover letter, resume. Applications are accepted continuously.

TREES FOR TOMORROW NATURAL RESOURCES EDUCATION CENTER
519 Sheridan Street East
Eagle River, Wisconsin 54521

General Information Natural resource education center teaching fourth graders through adults about the wise use and management of forests, wildlife, and water and soil resources. Established in 1944. Number of employees: 17. Number of internship applications received each year: 50.

Internships Available ▶ *4 instructor naturalists:* responsibilities include teaching groups ranging from fourth graders to adults about the importance of conserving natural resourses (forests, wildlife, water, soil, and energy) through hands-on activities and guided tours of managed forest areas and industries. Candidates should have ability to work independently, oral communication skills, self-motivation, strong interpersonal skills, written communication skills. Duration is 10 months (August 30-June 5). $500–$550 per month. Open to college juniors, college seniors, recent college graduates, graduate students, law students, career changers, individuals reentering the workforce. International applications accepted.

Benefits Formal training, free housing, free meals, names of contacts, on-the-job training, possible full-time employment, willing to complete paperwork for educational credit, willing to provide letters of recommendation.

Contact Write, call, or e-mail Ms. Sandy Lotto, Internship Coordinator. Phone: 800-838-9472. E-mail: trees@nnex.net. Applicants must submit a cover letter, resume, three personal references. Application deadline: June 1. World Wide Web: http://www.treesfortomorrow.com.

TREES NEW YORK
51 Chambers Street, Suite 1412 A
New York, New York 10007

General Information Nonprofit dedicated to the preservation, improvement, and increase of New York's urban forest, through advocacy education, publishing, and direct community service. Number of employees: 5.

Internships Available ▶ *Interns.* Candidates should have interest in urban forestry, forestry, nonprofit management, and environmental studies (these applicants will be given priority). Unpaid. Open to college freshmen, college sophomores, college juniors, college seniors, recent college graduates, graduate students, career changers, individuals reentering the workforce. International applications accepted.

Benefits Names of contacts, willing to complete paperwork for educational credit, willing to provide letters of recommendation, Citizen Pruner course available at no charge.

Contact Write, call, fax, or e-mail Susan Gooberman, Program Director, 51 Chambers Street, Suite 1412A, New York, New York 10007. Phone: 212-227-1887. Fax: 212-732-5325. E-mail: treesny@

treesny.com. Applicants must submit a resume, cover letter indicating preference in time frame. Applications are accepted continuously. World Wide Web: http://www.treesny.com.

TRUSTEES OF RESERVATIONS, WESTERN REGION
PO Box 792
Stockbridge, Massachusetts 01262

General Information Organization that preserves properties of scenic, historical, and ecological value throughout Massachusetts for public use and enjoyment. Established in 1891. Number of employees: 11. Unit of Trustees of Reservations, Beverly, Massachusetts. Number of internship applications received each year: 30.

Internships Available ▶ *1–3 historic site administrators:* responsibilities include working with the historic house administrator to gain professional experience in the daily administration of historic properties. Candidates should have ability to work independently, oral communication skills, self-motivation, strong interpersonal skills, written communication skills. Duration is 10–15 weeks. Position available as unpaid or at $1,400 per duration of internship. Open to college juniors, college seniors, recent college graduates, graduate students. International applications accepted.

Benefits Free housing, willing to act as a professional reference, willing to complete paperwork for educational credit, willing to provide letters of recommendation.

Contact Write or call Lisa Anderson, Site Administrator. Phone: 413-298-3239. In-person interview recommended. Applicants must submit a cover letter, resume. Application deadline: March 15 for summer.

TURNBULL NATIONAL WILDLIFE REFUGE
26010 South Smith Road
Cheney, Washington 99004-9326

General Information Refuge and breeding ground for migratory birds and other wildlife. Established in 1937. Number of employees: 7. Unit of United States Fish and Wildlife Service, Portland, Oregon, Portland, Oregon. Number of internship applications received each year: 10.

Internships Available ▶ *1 biological aide:* responsibilities include assisting with wildlife and habitat monitoring and bird banding. Candidates should have ability to work independently, ability to work with others, college courses in field, research skills, self-motivation. Duration is 4 months (beginning May 1). Position available as unpaid or paid. Open to college juniors, college seniors, recent college graduates, individuals reentering the workforce. ▶ *1–2 environmental education assistants:* responsibilities include conducting environmental education activities for refuge visitors, assisting groups in conducting field study activities, and preparing and presenting programs on wildlife, wildflowers, and ecology. Candidates should have oral communication skills, personal interest in the field, self-motivation, strong interpersonal skills, written communication skills. Duration is 3 months. Unpaid. Possible stipend of $50 per week. Open to college freshmen, college sophomores, college juniors, college seniors, recent college graduates, graduate students, individuals reentering the workforce. International applications accepted.

Benefits Job counseling, names of contacts, on-the-job training, willing to act as a professional reference, willing to complete paperwork for educational credit, willing to provide letters of recommendation, free housing if available.

Contact Write, call, fax, or e-mail Ms. Nancy J. Curry, Refuge Manager. Phone: 509-235-4723. Fax: 509-235-4703. E-mail: nancy_curry@fws.gov. Telephone interview required. Applicants must submit a cover letter, resume, personal reference, letter of recommendation. Application deadline: March 1 for spring, May 1 for summer, August 1 for fall. World Wide Web: http://www.r1.fws.gov/turnbull/turnbull.html.

TURTLE MOUNTAIN ENVIRONMENTAL LEARNING CENTER
#2 Lake Metigoshe State Park
Bottineau, North Dakota 58318

General Information Environmental education program for diverse age groups that emphasizes learning in an outdoor environment. Established in 1985. Number of employees: 2. Unit of Lake Metigoshe State Park, Bottineau, North Dakota. Number of internship applications received each year: 20.

Internships Available ▶ *2 naturalist interns:* responsibilities include facilitating group activities and discussions in teaching environmental awareness. Candidates should have ability to work independently, ability to work with others, oral communication skills, personal interest in the field, self-motivation, desire to share nature with all age groups. Duration is April 1 to June 5, May 25 to September 5, August 25 to November 1. $5 per hour. Open to college freshmen, college sophomores, college juniors, college seniors, recent college graduates, career changers, individuals reentering the workforce. International applications accepted.

Benefits Free housing, names of contacts, on-the-job training, opportunity to attend seminars/workshops, willing to act as a professional reference, willing to complete paperwork for educational credit, willing to provide letters of recommendation, reimbursement of work-related travel expenses, uniforms provided.

Contact Write, call, fax, or e-mail Angie Becker, TMELC Coordinator. Phone: 701-263-4514. Fax: 701-263-4648. E-mail: tmelc@state.nd.us. Applicants must submit a cover letter, resume, academic transcripts, three personal references, telephone interview if selected. Application deadline: February 28 for spring, April 1 for summer. World Wide Web: http://www.state.nd.us/ndparks/Parks/Metigoshe/TMELC.htm.

UNIVERSITY OF RHODE ISLAND, ENVIRONMENTAL EDUCATION CENTER
W. Alton Jones Campus, 401 Victory Highway
West Greenwich, Rhode Island 02817

General Information Organization dedicated to educating school-age children about the environment, ecology, cultural history, farming, and group building. Established in 1964. Number of employees: 20. Department of University of Rhode Island, Kingston, Rhode Island. Number of internship applications received each year: 15.

Internships Available ▶ *3–5 field teachers/naturalists:* responsibilities include planning and teaching outdoor lessons in forest and wetland ecology, team building, outdoor skills, environmental issues, farming, and Native American and pioneer history on 2300-acre wilderness campus; teaching outdoor lessons in farming, animal care, gardening, and pioneer history on 300-acre historic farm. Candidates should have knowledge of field, oral communication skills, personal interest in the field, strong interpersonal skills, strong leadership ability. Duration is 4–9 months. stipend of $175 per week minimum . Open to college freshmen, college sophomores, college juniors, college seniors, recent college graduates, graduate students. ▶ *1 student camp nurse:* responsibilities include assisting RN in injury and illness assessment, dispensing medicaton, and operating camp infirmary. Candidates should have declared college major in field, knowledge of field, oral communication skills, self-motivation, strong interpersonal skills. Duration is mid-June to mid-August. $200–$250 per week. Open to college sophomores, college juniors, college seniors, recent college graduates, graduate students. ▶ *16 summer camp naturalists/counselors:* responsibilities include leading campers ages 8-14 during seven six-day residential camping programs; counselors may teach up to seven themes or lead natural and cultural history and sensory awareness, canoeing, no-trace camping and survival skills, conservation activities, and new games. Candidates should have ability to work with others, knowledge of field, oral communication skills, strong leadership ability, CPR and first aid. Duration is 9 weeks (mid-June to mid-August). stipend of approximately $150 per week. Open to high school seniors, recent high school graduates, college freshmen, college sophomores, college juniors, college seniors, recent

college graduates, graduate students. ▶ *10–12 teen expedition leaders:* responsibilities include leading week-long sessions of the Teen Expeditions program, planning and implementing canoeing, kayaking, backpacking, and rock climbing trips for participants ages 12-17. Candidates should have ability to work with others, experience in the field, oral communication skills, organizational skills, self-motivation, strong leadership ability, strong skills in at least one of the following: canoeing, kayaking, backpacking, or rock climbing. Duration is mid-June to late August. stipend of $185 per week minimum. Open to college juniors, college seniors, recent college graduates, graduate students. International applications accepted.

Benefits Formal training, free housing, free meals, on-the-job training, willing to act as a professional reference, willing to complete paperwork for educational credit, willing to provide letters of recommendation.

Contact Write, call, fax, or e-mail Mr. John Jacques, Manager. Phone: 401-397-3304 Ext. 6043. Fax: 401-397-3293. E-mail: urieec@etal.uri.edu. In-person interview recommended. Applicants must submit a formal organization application, cover letter, resume, personal reference, three personal references. Application deadline: January 15 for spring, May 15 for summer, July 15 for fall, November 15 for winter/spring. World Wide Web: http://www.uri.edu/ajc.

UPHAM WOODS 4-H ENVIRONMENTAL CENTER
N194 County Road North
Wisconsin Dells, Wisconsin 53965

General Information Youth camp and environmental education facility where youth and adults gain first-hand experience in natural sciences, citizenship, and group living. Established in 1941. Number of employees: 7. Number of internship applications received each year: 20.

Internships Available ▶ *2 teaching naturalists:* responsibilities include teaching awareness and appreciation of environment, camp operations, and nature center operations; assisting with upkeep; and working on exhibits. Candidates should have ability to work with others, oral communication skills, personal interest in the field, written communication skills. Duration is 12–52 weeks. $2,400–$10,400 per duration of internship. Open to college sophomores, college juniors, college seniors, recent college graduates, graduate students. International applications accepted.

Benefits Free housing, job counseling, names of contacts, willing to complete paperwork for educational credit, willing to provide letters of recommendation, most meals provided.

Contact Write, call, fax, or e-mail Bob Nichols, Director. Phone: 608-254-6461. Fax: 608-253-7140. E-mail: bob.nichols@ces.uwex.edu. In-person interview recommended. Applicants must submit a cover letter, resume. Application deadline: February 1 for spring, March 1 for summer, November 1 for winter.

U.S. FOREST SERVICE, PIKE AND SAN ISABEL FORESTS, SOUTH PARK DISTRICT
PO Box 219
Fairplay, Colorado 80440

General Information National forest district with 4 broad missions: research, international forestry, state and private forestry, and managing forest resources in a way that will best meet the needs of its visitors without impairing the productivity of the land. Established in 1891. Number of employees: 40. Unit of Pike & San Isabel National Forests, Pueblo, Colorado. Number of internship applications received each year: 40.

Internships Available ▶ *2–4 naturalists/interpreters:* responsibilities include developing and conducting interpretive programs at Wilkerson Pass and 21 campgrounds; writing news releases; assisting with the maintenance of the interpretive center; operating book sales outlet; providing visitor information; and conducting independent projects such as creating publications, fliers, children's programs, photography exhibits, and district projects. Candidates should have ability to work independently, computer skills, oral communication skills, organizational skills, plan to pursue career in field, self-motivation, strong interpersonal skills,

U.S. Forest Service, Pike and San Isabel Forests, South Park District (continued)
writing skills. Duration is end of May-end of September, 2 months minimum. Position available as unpaid or at $70 per week (40 hours per week). Open to recent high school graduates, college freshmen, college sophomores, college juniors, college seniors, recent college graduates, graduate students, law students, career changers, individuals reentering the workforce, individuals 18 years or older. International applications accepted.

Benefits Formal training, free housing, job counseling, names of contacts, opportunity to attend seminars/workshops, tuition assistance, willing to complete paperwork for educational credit, willing to provide letters of recommendation, specific information on USFS hiring methods and applications.

International Internships Available in United Kingdom.

Contact Write or call Becky Anderson, Interpretive Specialist. Phone: 719-836-2031. Applicants must submit a cover letter, resume, writing sample, volunteer application. Application deadline: March applications preferred.

VERMONT INSTITUTE OF NATURAL SCIENCE
27023 Church Hill Road
Woodstock, Vermont 05091-9642

General Information Institute specializing in environmental education, avian research, and raptor rehabilitation. Established in 1974. Number of employees: 30. Number of internship applications received each year: 40.

Internships Available ▶ *1–2 environmental education interns:* responsibilities include coordinating and teaching on- and off-site school programs, presenting informal visitor educational talks, scheduling and training volunteers, writing, and answering nature-related phone calls, opportunities for animal care/handling (reptiles/raptors). Candidates should have ability to work independently, college courses in field, computer skills, knowledge of field, oral communication skills, organizational skills, personal interest in the field, self-motivation, strong interpersonal skills, writing skills, driver's license. Duration is 4–6 months. Position available as unpaid or paid. Open to college freshmen, college sophomores, college juniors, college seniors, recent college graduates, graduate students, law students, career changers, individuals reentering the workforce. International applications accepted.

Benefits On-the-job training, opportunity to attend seminars/workshops, willing to act as a professional reference, willing to complete paperwork for educational credit, willing to provide letters of recommendation, possibility of free housing.

Contact Write, call, fax, or e-mail Marcia Whitney, Director of Education. Phone: 802-457-2779. Fax: 802-457-1053. E-mail: mwhitney@sover.net. In-person interview recommended. Applicants must submit a cover letter, resume, 1-3 letters of recommendation or reference contact information. Application deadline: April for summer (when offered), June for August/September-December, October for December/January-May/June. World Wide Web: http://www.vinsweb.org.

VERMONT RAPTOR CENTER
Church Hill Road, RR 2, Box 532
Woodstock, Vermont 05091-9720

General Information Living museum of birds of prey and rehabilitation facility for all birds. Established in 1987. Number of employees: 7. Branch of Vermont Institute of Natural Science, Woodstock, Vermont. Number of internship applications received each year: 100.

Internships Available ▶ *2–4 environmental education center interns:* responsibilities include natural history outreach programs, leading day camps, writing articles, and curriculum development. Candidates should have ability to work independently, experience in the field, oral communication skills, personal interest in the field, strong interpersonal skills, written communication skills. $250 per month. ▶ *2–4 raptor center interns:* responsibilities include assisting with monitoring health of raptors, and general operation of center. Candidates should have knowledge of field, oral communication skills, personal interest in the field, plan to pursue career in field, strong interpersonal skills. Unpaid.

Duration for all positions is 3–5 months. Open to college freshmen, college sophomores, college juniors, college seniors, recent college graduates, graduate students, law students, career changers, individuals reentering the workforce. International applications accepted.

Benefits Formal training, names of contacts, on-the-job training, opportunity to attend seminars/workshops, willing to act as a professional reference, willing to complete paperwork for educational credit, willing to provide letters of recommendation.

Contact Write or e-mail Mr. Mike Cox, Raptor Center Director. E-mail: vtraptct@sover.net. In-person interview recommended. Applicants must submit a cover letter, resume, two letters of recommendation. Application deadline: March 1 for summer, June 1 for fall, October 1 for spring.

VOLUNTEERS FOR OUTDOOR COLORADO
600 South Marion Parkway
Denver, Colorado 80209

General Information Organization that seeks to instill a personal sense of responsibility for the stewardship of Colorado's public lands, working in partnership with federal, state, and local land management agencies and other nonprofits to organize 25 to 1300 volunteers on projects statewide, year-round. Established in 1984. Number of employees: 7. Number of internship applications received each year: 25.

Internships Available ▶ *200–230 clearinghouse internships:* responsibilities include working for federal, state, and local management agencies or other nonprofit agencies in backcountry, environmental education, recreation, botany, or research/field work. Duration is flexible. Position available as unpaid or paid. Open to high school students, high school seniors, recent high school graduates, college freshmen, college sophomores, college juniors, college seniors, recent college graduates, graduate students, law students, career changers, individuals reentering the workforce. ▶ *1 outreach intern:* responsibilities include supporting the operations of the clearinghouse and training programs by responding to volunteer requests, attending volunteer/community fairs, and assisting with outreach efforts. Candidates should have ability to work independently, ability to work with others, computer skills, knowledge of field, oral communication skills, organizational skills, writing skills, knowledge of Windows (helpful); major in natural resource management, nonprofit management, education, or liberal arts preferred. Duration is January to mid-June or longer. Unpaid. Open to college juniors, college seniors, recent college graduates, graduate students, career changers, individuals reentering the workforce. ▶ *1 projects intern:* responsibilities include working with projects director to implement volunteer projects, completing office work, writing and editing newsletters, attending evening committee meetings, and helping orchestrate weekend projects. Candidates should have ability to work with others, computer skills, oral communication skills, organizational skills, personal interest in the field, self-motivation, strong leadership ability, writing skills, own transportation and physical stamina (capable of lifting 50 pounds); major in outdoor recreation, nonprofit management, liberal arts, or environmental studies preferred. Duration is March to mid-May, up to 20 hours per week; mid-May to August, 40 hours per week; September to mid-October, 15-20 hours per week. Unpaid. Open to college juniors, college seniors, recent college graduates, graduate students, career changers. International applications accepted.

Benefits Names of contacts, on-the-job training, travel reimbursement, willing to complete paperwork for educational credit, stipend and mileage reimbursement for outreach and projects interns, possible stipend and housing and training reimbursement for clearinghouse interns.

Contact Write, call, fax, or e-mail Clearinghouse Coordinator. Phone: 303-715-1010. Fax: 303-715-1212. E-mail: voc@voc.org. In-person interview recommended. Applicants must submit a cover letter, resume, personal reference. Application deadline: February 15 for projects intern, November 15 for outreach intern; continuous for clearinghouse positions. World Wide Web: http://www.voc.org.

WESTWOOD HILLS NATURE CENTER
8300 West Franklin Avenue
St. Louis Park, Minnesota 55426

General Information Nature center providing natural history and environmental education programs to school groups, families, preschoolers, seniors, and adults in an outdoor setting that develops an awareness and appreciation of the natural world. Established in 1980. Number of employees: 12. Unit of City of St. Louis Park Parks and Recreation Department, St. Louis Park, Minnesota. Number of internship applications received each year: 10.

Internships Available ▶ *1 naturalist intern:* responsibilities include conducting school program curriculum, assisting in general public programming, and completing a special project designed by the intern. Candidates should have college courses in field, knowledge of field, oral communication skills, plan to pursue career in field, strong interpersonal skills. Duration is 12 weeks. $1,200 per duration of internship. Open to college juniors, college seniors, recent college graduates, graduate students, career changers. International applications accepted.

Benefits Free housing, names of contacts, on-the-job training, opportunity to attend seminars/workshops, willing to complete paperwork for educational credit, willing to provide letters of recommendation.

Contact Write, call, fax, or e-mail Mr. Mark Oestreich, Senior Naturalist. Phone: 612-924-2543. Fax: 612-797-9691. E-mail: moestreich@stlouispark.org. Telephone interview required. Applicants must submit a formal organization application. Application deadline: January 1 for spring, April 1 for summer, November 1 for winter. World Wide Web: http://www.stlpark.k12.mn.us/default.html.

WETLANDS INSTITUTE
1075 Stone Harbor Boulevard
Stone Harbor, New Jersey 08247-1424

General Information Private nonprofit organization dedicated to public education and scientific research concerning intertidal salt marshes and other coastal ecosystems. Established in 1969. Number of employees: 17. Number of internship applications received each year: 60.

Internships Available ▶ *2 aquarist interns:* responsibilities include maintaining aquariums in exhibit building, collecting specimens, and interpreting exhibits for visitors. Candidates should have ability to work independently, college courses in field, experience in the field, personal interest in the field, self-motivation. Duration is year-round. Open to college freshmen, college sophomores, college juniors, college seniors, recent college graduates, graduate students, career changers, individuals reentering the workforce. ▶ *2–6 environmental education interns:* responsibilities include teaching summer nature classes and assisting with public programs. Candidates should have knowledge of field, oral communication skills, self-motivation, strong interpersonal skills, written communication skills. Duration is 3 months. Open to college freshmen, college sophomores, college juniors, college seniors, recent college graduates, graduate students, career changers, individuals reentering the workforce. ▶ *1 exhibit intern:* responsibilities include creating and changing exhibits for small discovery room and other exhibit areas. Candidates should have college courses in field, experience in the field, oral communication skills, personal interest in the field, art and design skills. Duration is May to September. Open to college freshmen, college sophomores, college juniors, college seniors, recent college graduates, graduate students, career changers, individuals reentering the workforce. ▶ *1 public relations intern:* responsibilities include conducting exit surveys of visitors, writing and distributing press releases, and soliciting donations. Candidates should have computer skills, oral communication skills, personal interest in the field, self-motivation, strong interpersonal skills, written communication skills. Duration is flexible. Open to college freshmen, college sophomores, college juniors, college seniors, recent college graduates, graduate students, career changers, individuals reentering the workforce. ▶ *5–15 research interns:* responsibilities include assisting visiting researchers with

projects. Candidates should have college courses in field, computer skills, experience in the field, personal interest in the field, self-motivation. Duration is May to August/September. Open to college freshmen, college sophomores, college juniors, college seniors, recent college graduates, graduate students, career changers. All positions are unpaid. International applications accepted.

Benefits Formal training, opportunity to attend seminars/workshops, willing to act as a professional reference, willing to complete paperwork for educational credit, willing to provide letters of recommendation, housing is available.

Contact Write, call, or fax Ms. Charlotte A. McDevitt, Coordinator of Interns. Phone: 609-368-1211. Fax: 609-368-3871. In-person interview recommended. Applicants must submit a formal organization application, resume, academic transcripts, personal reference, letter of recommendation, letter stating personal goals. Application deadline: March 1 for summer, September 1 for fall, December 1 for spring.

WHITE SANDS NATIONAL MONUMENT
PO Box 1086
Holloman A.F.B., New Mexico 88330

General Information National monument that preserves the world's largest gypsum dunefield. Established in 1933. Number of employees: 24. Unit of United States National Park Service, Washington, District of Columbia. Number of internship applications received each year: 3.

Internships Available ▶ *1 environmental interpretation intern:* responsibilities include performing interpretive ranger duties, developing and presenting talks, conducting nature walks and slide programs, staffing information desk, and performing roving interpretation on bike and on foot. Candidates should have college courses in field, oral communication skills, self-motivation, strong interpersonal skills, written communication skills. Duration is 12-14 weeks in spring, fall, or winter. Unpaid. Open to college juniors, college seniors, recent college graduates, graduate students, career changers. ▶ *1 geology interpretation intern:* responsibilities include performing interpretive ranger duties; developing and presenting programs on geology and ecology of the dunes; staffing information desk; developing exhibits/informational brochures. Candidates should have college courses in field, oral communication skills, self-motivation, strong interpersonal skills, written communication skills, major in geology or earth science education. Duration is 12-14 weeks in summer. Unpaid. Open to college juniors, college seniors, graduate students. International applications accepted.

Benefits Formal training, free housing, job counseling, names of contacts, on-the-job training, travel reimbursement, willing to act as a professional reference, willing to complete paperwork for educational credit, willing to provide letters of recommendation, $50 per week food reimbursement for environmental interpretation positions.

Contact Write, call, fax, or e-mail Mr. John Mangimeli, Volunteer Coordinator. Phone: 505-679-2599 Ext. 230. Fax: 505-479-4333. E-mail: john_mangimeli@nps.gov. Applicants must submit a formal organization application, resume, academic transcripts, two letters of recommendation, materials through Student Conservation Association application process (603)543-1700. Application deadline: January 1 for spring (March—late May), March 1 for summer (mid-May—mid-August), August 1 for fall (October—December), September 1 for winter (mid-December—early March). World Wide Web: http://www.nps.gov/whsa.

WILDERNESS WATCH
PO Box 9175
Missoula, Montana 59807

General Information National organization committed to stewardship of the areas protected in the National Wilderness Preservation System and the Wild and Scenic Rivers System providing education programs, provoking public involvement, and offering professional criticism or support of agency actions regarding wilderness and rivers. Uses litigation to uphold the

Wilderness Watch (continued)

Wilderness Acts as a course of last resort. Established in 1989. Number of employees: 3. Number of internship applications received each year: 25.

Internships Available ▶ *General assistant/issues activists:* responsibilities include performing research and writing on issues pertaining to the Wilderness and Wild and Scenic Rivers Systems. ▶ *Wilderness interns:* responsibilities include assisting in program and fund-raising activities and expanding WW's membership and presence through public participation throughout the Rocky Mountains and elsewhere. Duration for all positions is flexible. All positions are unpaid. Open to high school students, high school seniors, recent high school graduates, college freshmen, college sophomores, college juniors, college seniors, recent college graduates, graduate students, law students, career changers, individuals reentering the workforce. International applications accepted.

Benefits Willing to act as a professional reference, willing to complete paperwork for educational credit.

Contact Write, call, fax, or e-mail George Nickas, Executive Director. Phone: 406-542-2048. Fax: 406-542-7714. E-mail: wild@wildernesswatch.org. Applicants must submit a cover letter, resume. Applications are accepted continuously. World Wide Web: http://www.wildernesswatch.org.

WILDLIFE CONSERVATION SOCIETY
Education Department, Bronx Zoo, 2300 Southern Boulevard
Bronx, New York 10460-1099

General Information Society devoted to the conservation of wildlife and habitats through conservation, education, and science. Established in 1895. Number of employees: 200. Number of internship applications received each year: 200.

Internships Available ▶ *2–6 fall teaching interns:* responsibilities include assisting staff in teaching school groups who come to the zoo by demonstrating live animals, using audio visual equipment, and lecturing. Candidates should have ability to work independently, knowledge of field, oral communication skills, strong interpersonal skills, experience working with children. Duration is 20 weeks. $8–$10 per hour. Open to recent college graduates, graduate students. ▶ *2–6 spring teaching interns:* responsibilities include assisting staff in teaching school groups who come to the zoo by demonstrating live animals, using audio visual equipment, and lecturing. Candidates should have ability to work independently, knowledge of field, oral communication skills, strong interpersonal skills, experience working with children. Duration is 20 weeks. $8–$10 per hour. Open to recent college graduates, graduate students. ▶ *6–10 summer teaching interns:* responsibilities include helping to run an environmentally based summer camp at the zoo, leading children in crafts, games, songs, and demonstrating live animals. Candidates should have knowledge of field, oral communication skills, strong interpersonal skills, experience working with children. Duration is 10 weeks. $6–$10 per hour. Open to college juniors, college seniors, recent college graduates, graduate students. International applications accepted.

Benefits Formal training, willing to complete paperwork for educational credit.

Contact Write or fax Ms. Ilyssa Gillman, Internship Coordinator, Education Department, Bronx Zoo 2300 Southern Boulevard, Bronx, New York 10460-1099. Fax: 718-733-4460. No phone calls. In-person interview required. Applicants must submit a cover letter, resume, letter of recommendation, application from Web site (preferred). Applications are accepted continuously. World Wide Web: http://www.wcs.org.

WILDLIFE SOCIETY
5410 Grosvenor Lane
Bethesda, Maryland 20814-2197

General Information Society whose mission is to enhance the scientific, technical, managerial, and educational capabilities and

achievements of wildlife professionals. Established in 1937. Number of employees: 9. Number of internship applications received each year: 15.

Internships Available ▶ *1 policy intern:* responsibilities include researching conservation issues, preparing background information for use in testimony or comments, attending briefings and hearings, writing for and assisting with the preparation of publications, and assisting with the routine activities of the society. Candidates should have college courses in field, knowledge of field, research skills, self-motivation, writing skills. Duration is 6 months. $1,000 per month. Open to college freshmen, college sophomores, college juniors, college seniors, recent college graduates, graduate students. International applications accepted.

Benefits Health insurance, willing to provide letters of recommendation.

Contact Write or e-mail Thomas M. Franklin, Wildlife Policy Director. E-mail: tws@wildlife.org. In-person interview recommended. Applicants must submit a cover letter, resume, academic transcripts, two writing samples, three personal references. Applications are accepted continuously. World Wide Web: http://ns.us.net/wildlife/welcome.html.

WOLF RIDGE ENVIRONMENTAL LEARNING CENTER
6282 Cranberry Road
Finland, Minnesota 55603

General Information Residential environmental school for students of all ages; mission is to teach stewardship, promote a quality environment through educational programs, and awaken the natural curiosity of the human mind. Established in 1971. Number of employees: 40. Number of internship applications received each year: 50.

Internships Available ▶ *15 student naturalists:* responsibilities include teaching ecology, cultural history, and recreation classes; participating in diplomatic liaison relationships; participating in seminars; conducting formal evening slide presentations; enrolling in a post-baccalaureate program in environmental education offered through the University of Minnesota, Duluth. Candidates should have oral communication skills, plan to pursue career in field, strong interpersonal skills, strong leadership ability, written communication skills. Duration is 10 months. Unpaid. Open to recent college graduates, graduate students, career changers. International applications accepted.

Benefits Formal training, free housing, free meals, job counseling, names of contacts, on-the-job training, opportunity to attend seminars/workshops, tuition assistance, willing to act as a professional reference, willing to complete paperwork for educational credit, willing to provide letters of recommendation, full tuition scholarship for post-baccalaureate certificate in environmental education through University of Minnesota, Duluth.

Contact Write, call, fax, or e-mail Ms. Terry McLaughlin, Director of Naturalist Training. Phone: 218-353-7414. Fax: 218-353-7762. E-mail: mail@wolf-ridge.org. Telephone interview required. Applicants must submit a formal organization application, cover letter, resume, academic transcripts, three personal references. Application deadline: March 31. World Wide Web: http://www.wolf-ridge.org.

WOOD LAKE NATURE CENTER
735 Lake Shore Drive
Richfield, Minnesota 55423

General Information Natural area with 150 acres of fields, woods, marsh, and private prairie preserved by the city of Richfield to give children and adults a place to explore, observe, and learn about the natural world. Established in 1970. Number of employees: 14. Division of City of Richfield, Recreation Services, Richfield, Minnesota. Number of internship applications received each year: 50.

Internships Available ▶ *1–3 naturalist interns:* responsibilities include leading environmental education activities for individuals of all ages. Candidates should have college courses in field, knowledge of field, oral communication skills, plan to pursue

career in field, self-motivation, strong interpersonal skills. Duration is flexible; 9 weeks or more. Position available as unpaid or at $1200 per internship if intern works 40 hours per week. Open to college juniors, college seniors, recent college graduates, graduate students, law students, career changers, individuals reentering the workforce. ▶ *1 summer professional intern:* responsibilities include teaching classes and supervising volunteers, exhibit design, animal care. Candidates should have ability to work independently, knowledge of field, oral communication skills, plan to pursue career in field, self-motivation, strong interpersonal skills. Duration is June through August. Paid. Open to college juniors, college seniors, recent college graduates, graduate students, career changers, individuals reentering the workforce. International applications accepted.
Benefits Formal training, job counseling, names of contacts, on-the-job training, opportunity to attend seminars/workshops, willing to act as a professional reference, willing to complete paperwork for educational credit, willing to provide letters of recommendation.
Contact Write, call, fax, or e-mail Mr. Tom Moffatt, Naturalist Intern Coordinator. Phone: 612-861-9365. Fax: 612-861-9367. E-mail: tmoffatt@ci.richfield.mn.us. In-person interview recommended. Applicants must submit a formal organization application, cover letter, resume, academic transcripts, three personal references. Application deadline: February 1 for spring, April 1 for summer, August 1 for fall, December 1 for winter. World Wide Web: http://www.ci.richfield.mn.us/RecreationServices/WoodLake/.

WORLD STEWARDSHIP INSTITUTE
409 Mendocino Avenue, Suite A
Santa Rosa, California 95401-8513

General Information Organization striving to cultivate environmental stewardship using and synthesizing different ethical approaches to the environment.
Internships Available ▶ *Interns:* responsibilities include various tasks depending on the intern's skills and interests. Jobs include running programs, foreign language communication, editing the newsletter, selling raffle tickets, or administrative support. Duration is flexible. Unpaid. Open to college juniors, college seniors, graduate students.
Contact Write, call, fax, or e-mail Ed Castellini, Executive Director, 409 Mendocino Avenue, Suite A, Santa Rosa, California 95401-8513. Phone: 707-573-3160. Fax: 707-578-7702. E-mail: wsi@ecostewards.org. Applicants must submit a resume. Applications are accepted continuously. World Wide Web: http://www.ecostewards.org.

YMCA BECKET–CHIMNEY CORNERS OUTDOOR CENTER
748 Hamilton Road
Becket, Massachusetts 01223

General Information 1200-acre outdoor center in Berkshire Mountains serving over 10,000 guests annually in retreat, environmental education, adventure, and family camp programs. Established in 1903. Number of employees: 350. Number of internship applications received each year: 30.
Internships Available ▶ *Program instructors:* responsibilities include leading recreation and education programs; providing general support and administrative procedures specific to the outdoor center programs. Candidates should have ability to work with others, personal interest in the field, strong leadership ability. Duration is 2–12 months. $125–$175 per week. Open to recent high school graduates, college freshmen, college sophomores, college juniors, college seniors, individuals reentering the workforce. International applications accepted.
Benefits Formal training, free housing, free meals, job counseling, names of contacts, on-the-job training, opportunity to attend seminars/workshops, possible full-time employment, willing to act as a professional reference, willing to complete paperwork for educational credit, willing to provide letters of recommendation, free use of the facility when not working.

Contact Write, call, fax, or e-mail Eric Grimes, Director of Environmental Education. Phone: 413-623-8991. Fax: 413-623-5890. E-mail: bccymca@bcn.net. Telephone interview required. Applicants must submit a formal organization application, cover letter, resume, three personal references. Applications are accepted continuously.

YMCA CAMP KERN
5291 State Route 350
Oregonia, Ohio 45054

General Information Camp operating as a residential outdoor education center. Established in 1910. Number of employees: 35. Branch of Dayton YMCA, Dayton, Ohio. Number of internship applications received each year: 5.
Internships Available ▶ *1 fall naturalist intern:* responsibilities include teaching and leading activities dealing with natural history, pioneer, and Native American topics. Duration is 3–4 months. ▶ *1 spring naturalist intern:* responsibilities include teaching and leading activities dealing with natural history, pioneer, and Native American topics. Duration is 4 months. Candidates for all positions should have oral communication skills, personal interest in the field, self-motivation, strong interpersonal skills, desire to work with children. All positions paid at $100 per week. Open to high school students, high school seniors, recent high school graduates, college freshmen, college sophomores, college juniors, college seniors, recent college graduates, graduate students, law students, career changers, individuals reentering the workforce. International applications accepted.
Benefits Free housing, free meals, names of contacts, opportunity to attend seminars/workshops, possible full-time employment, willing to complete paperwork for educational credit, willing to provide letters of recommendation.
Contact Write, call, fax, or e-mail Mr. Gary Saxton, Director of Outdoor Education. Phone: 513-932-3756. Fax: 513-932-8607. E-mail: kernouted@yahoo.com. In-person interview recommended. Applicants must submit a cover letter, resume. Applications are accepted continuously.

YMCA CAMP WIDJIWAGAN'S ENVIRONMENTAL EDUCATION PROGRAM
3788 North Arm Road
Ely, Minnesota 55731-9604

General Information Educational facility that uses a wilderness-based program to teach about the environment. Established in 1973. Number of employees: 18. Unit of YMCA Camp Widjiwagan. Number of internship applications received each year: 15.
Internships Available ▶ *2–4 naturalist interns:* responsibilities include leading students in grades 4–9, helping co-lead small group activities for 10 students, serving in program support roles, and assisting with curriculum as part of independent intern project development. Candidates should have ability to work with others, oral communication skills, organizational skills, personal interest in the field, self-motivation, strong interpersonal skills. Duration is 1 semester. $120–$160 per month. Open to college sophomores, college juniors, college seniors, recent college graduates.
Benefits Free meals, willing to complete paperwork for educational credit, willing to provide letters of recommendation, extensive training and staff development, possibility of seasonal, full-time employment.
Contact Write or call Ms. Karen Pick, Program Director-Camp Widjiwagan. Phone: 218-365-2117. Applicants must submit a formal organization application, resume, personal reference, letter of recommendation. Application deadline: June 10 for fall, August 15 for winter. World Wide Web: http://www.mtn.org/widji.

ZERO POPULATION GROWTH
1400 16th Street, NW, Suite 320
Washington, District of Columbia 20036

General Information A national nonprofit membership organization that works to mobilize broad public support for a sustain-

Zero Population Growth (continued)

able balance of the earth's people, environment, and resources. Established in 1968. Number of employees: 40. Number of internship applications received each year: 70.

Internships Available ▶ *1–2 Zero 24—7 radio interns:* responsibilities include assisting with programming, responding to audience mail, assisting with technical operation, and possibly some "on-air" work. Candidates should have computer skills, editing skills, knowledge of field, oral communication skills, organizational skills, personal interest in the field. Duration is flexible. Unpaid. Open to college freshmen, college sophomores, college juniors, college seniors, recent college graduates, graduate students. ▶ *1 field and outreach fellow:* responsibilities include grass roots organizing, coordinating exhibits, and public speaking. Candidates should have editing skills, knowledge of field, oral communication skills, organizational skills, strong interpersonal skills. Duration is January 1 to June 15 or July 1 to December 15; unpaid positions of flexible duration also available. $549 bi-weekly. Open to recent college graduates, graduate students. ▶ *1–2 fundraising interns:* responsibilities include researching for fundraising and developing proposals. Candidates should have ability to work independently, analytical skills, computer skills, organizational skills. Duration is flexible. Unpaid. Open to college freshmen, college sophomores, college juniors, college seniors, recent college graduates, graduate students. ▶ *1–2 government relations fellows:* responsibilities include monitoring legislation and influencing public policy. Candidates should have ability to work independently, ability to work with others, oral communication skills, personal interest in the field, self-motivation, written communication skills. Duration is 5½ months each, January to June and July to December. $549 bi-weekly. Open to recent college graduates, graduate students. ▶ *1–2 media/communications fellows:* responsibilities include researching, writing, and marketing publications and general media work. Candidates should have computer skills, editing skills, office skills, personal interest in the field, research skills, writing skills. Duration is 5½ months each, January to June and July to December. $549 bi-weekly. Open to recent college graduates, graduate students. ▶ *1–2 population education fellows:* responsibilities include developing and marketing teaching materials and teacher training. Candidates should have ability to work independently, editing skills, organizational skills, personal interest in the field, research skills, written communication skills. Duration is 5½ months each, January to June and July to December. $549 bi-weekly. Open to recent college graduates, graduate students. ▶ *1–2 research fellows:* responsibilities include researching and writing reports and maintaining library. Candidates should have ability to work independently, analytical skills, computer skills, editing skills, research skills, writing skills. Duration is 5½ months each, January to June and July to December. Position available as unpaid or at $549 bi-weekly. Open to recent college graduates. International applications accepted.

Benefits Health insurance, job counseling, on-the-job training, possible full-time employment, willing to act as a professional reference, willing to complete paperwork for educational credit, willing to provide letters of recommendation.

Contact Write or e-mail Jay Keller, National Field Director, ZPG Internship Program, 1400 15th Street, NW, Suite 320, Washington, District of Columbia 20036. E-mail: jay@zpg.org. Applicants must submit a cover letter, resume, 3 reference names, titles, and phone numbers, 2 writing samples (3-5 pages total). Application deadline: April 15 for July-December positions, October 1 for January-June positions. World Wide Web: http://www.zpg. org.

SOCIAL ADVOCACY ORGANIZATIONS

ADC RESEARCH INSTITUTE
4201 Connecticut Avenue, NW, Suite 300
Washington, District of Columbia 20008

General Information Grassroots civil rights organization that defends the rights of Arab-Americans and promotes Arab heritage. Established in 1980. Number of employees: 10.

Internships Available ▶ *Education interns:* responsibilities include working closely with Director of Educational Programs in mobilizing grassroots network of ADC chapters campaigning for Arab-American issues, responding to requests from educators and activists, and developing lesson plans. Candidates should have knowledge of field, writing skills, written communication skills. Duration is 1-2 semesters or 10-week summer term. Position available as unpaid or at $800 for graduate students and $500 for undergraduates during summer term; prorated during semester. Open to college sophomores, college juniors, college seniors, recent college graduates, graduate students. ▶ *1–2 information systems interns:* responsibilities include organizing Internet workshop, and assisting in all aspects of registration process for national convention. Candidates should have ability to work independently, computer skills, knowledge of field, oral communication skills, research skills. Duration is flexible. Position available as unpaid or paid. Open to college sophomores, college juniors, college seniors, recent college graduates, graduate students. ▶ *Legal interns:* responsibilities include working closely with attorney on immigration law, civil and human rights law, international law, and treaties; screening new cases as they come into the office; legal research; drafting client letters and press releases. Candidates should have 1-2 years of law school. Duration is 1-2 semesters or 10-week summer term. Position available as unpaid or at $800 for 10-week summer term, prorated during semester. Open to graduate students, law students. ▶ *Media and publications interns:* responsibilities include writing articles for ADC Times; conducting research; producing and/or updating publications; helping write, edit, and design Annual Activity Report; maintaining video book library and filing system; monitoring media; responding to public and media information requests. Candidates should have knowledge of field, writing skills. Duration is 1-2 semesters or 10-week summer term. Position available as unpaid or at $800 for graduate students and $500 for undergraduates during summer term; prorated during semester. Open to college sophomores, college juniors, college seniors, recent college graduates, graduate students. ▶ *Organizing and special events interns:* responsibilities include assisting the director with work involving the national network of local chapters, organizing regional conferences, monitoring and mobilizing activists to work on projects, and assisting with planning ADC's National Convention in Washington, D.C. Candidates should have computer skills, knowledge of field, oral communication skills, organizational skills, written communication skills. Duration is 1-2 semesters or 10-week summer term. Position available as unpaid or at $800 for graduate students and $500 for undergraduates during summer; prorated during semester. Open to college sophomores, college juniors, college seniors, recent college graduates, graduate students. ▶ *Summer interns:* responsibilities include attending meetings and conferences of government officials; emphasis on educational programs located around Washington, D.C.; working with legal, media, education, and organizing departments in relation to projects and campaigns. Candidates should have knowledge of field, writing skills. Duration is 10 weeks. Position available as unpaid or at $500 stipend for undergraduates, $800 stipend for graduate and law students. Open to college sophomores, college juniors, college seniors, recent college graduates, graduate students, law students. International applications accepted.

Benefits Names of contacts, opportunity to attend seminars/ workshops, willing to complete paperwork for educational credit, willing to provide letters of recommendation, one day per week

of leadership development skills for summer interns, introduction to Washington, assistance with locating roommates and/or housing, opportunity to attend meetings with Congress, administration officials, Arab embassies, and American organizations.
Contact Write, call, or fax Mr. Marvin Wingfield, Director of Educational Programs. Phone: 202-244-2990. Fax: 202-244-3196. Applicants must submit a cover letter, resume, academic transcripts, two letters of recommendation, 2-page essay. Application deadline: March 30 for summer.

AFRICA FUND–AMERICAN COMMITTEE ON AFRICA
50 Broad Street, Suite 711
New York, New York 10004-2307

General Information Organization that supports reconstruction, development, and democracy in Africa. Established in 1966. Number of employees: 8. Number of internship applications received each year: 200.
Internships Available ▶ *1–4 interns:* responsibilities include performing office work and special tasks. Candidates should have ability to work independently, computer skills, office skills, oral communication skills, organizational skills, personal interest in the field, research skills, self-motivation, strong interpersonal skills, writing skills. Duration is flexible. Unpaid. Open to college freshmen, college sophomores, college juniors, college seniors, recent college graduates, graduate students, career changers. International applications accepted.
Benefits Opportunity to attend seminars/workshops, willing to complete paperwork for educational credit, willing to provide letters of recommendation.
Contact Write or fax Muadi B. Dibinga, Director of Finance and Administration. Fax: 212-785-1078. No phone calls. Telephone interview required. Applicants must submit a formal organization application, cover letter, resume, writing sample, three personal references. Application deadline: April 1 for summer, July 1 for fall.

ALBANY COUNTY SAFE PROJECT
312 Steele
Laramie, Wyoming 82070

General Information Advocacy for victims of domestic violence and sexual assault. Established in 1980. Number of employees: 8. Number of internship applications received each year: 5.
Internships Available ▶ *2–10 volunteer interns:* responsibilities include working with staff to determine a new project, developing the project, and implementing it in the community. Direct service projects are available. Candidates should have ability to work independently, computer skills, office skills, oral communication skills, personal interest in the field, self-motivation, strong interpersonal skills, completion of SAFE Project 40-hour training or equivalent. Duration is 1–2 semesters. Unpaid. Open to college sophomores, college juniors, college seniors, recent college graduates, graduate students, law students, individuals reentering the workforce. International applications accepted.
Benefits Formal training, on-the-job training, opportunity to attend seminars/workshops, possible full-time employment, willing to act as a professional reference, willing to complete paperwork for educational credit, willing to provide letters of recommendation.
Contact Write, call, fax, or e-mail Teresa C. Wroe, Executive Director, PO Box 665, Laramie, Wyoming 82073. Phone: 307-742-7273. Fax: 307-745-4510. E-mail: safeproject@vcn.com. In-person interview required. Applicants must submit a cover letter, resume, three personal references. Applications are accepted continuously.

ALLIANCE FOR GLOBAL JUSTICE
1247 E Street, SE
Washington, District of Columbia 20003

General Information Progressive, grassroots organization that works for social change through a variety of projects. The Alliance brings together different organizations to promote a cross-fertilization of ideas and build a broader base of support to work together to defend the human and economic rights of

people throughout the world. Established in 1998. Number of employees: 7. Number of internship applications received each year: 30.
Internships Available ▶ *2–3 program interns:* responsibilities include writing and researching articles for newsletters, lobbying work, monitoring campaigns, organizing conferences, attending meetings, and some general office and clerical tasks. Candidates should have ability to work independently, computer skills, personal interest in the field, self-motivation, strong interpersonal skills, writing skills, knowledge of Latin American issues; Spanish ability helpful. Duration is flexible (8 weeks minimum). Unpaid. Open to college sophomores, college juniors, college seniors, recent college graduates, graduate students. International applications accepted.
Benefits On-the-job training, opportunity to attend seminars/workshops, willing to act as a professional reference, willing to complete paperwork for educational credit, willing to provide letters of recommendation.
Contact Write, call, fax, or e-mail Melinda St. Louis, Intern Coordinator, 1247 E Street, SE, Washington, District of Columbia 20003. Phone: 202-544-9355. Fax: 202-544-9359. E-mail: agj@igc.org. Telephone interview required. Applicants must submit a cover letter, resume, writing sample. Applications are accepted continuously.

ALLIANCE FOR HEALTH REFORM
1900 L Street, NW, Suite 512
Washington, District of Columbia 20036

General Information Nonpartisan, not-for-profit organization that strives to educate news media and others about issues in health reform. Established in 1991. Number of employees: 7. Number of internship applications received each year: 50.
Internships Available ▶ *2–3 interns:* responsibilities include locating, cataloging, and securing reprint permission for articles, charts, reports, and other material by building and maintaining media lists; calling editors, reporters, and producers; researching all aspects of health reform; and performing general administrative work and seminar logistics. Candidates should have ability to work with others, college courses in field, oral communication skills, organizational skills, personal interest in the field, research skills, written communication skills. Duration is 2 months minimum. Unpaid. Open to college freshmen, college sophomores, college juniors, college seniors, recent college graduates, graduate students, law students, career changers, individuals reentering the workforce. International applications accepted.
Benefits Opportunity to attend seminars/workshops, willing to complete paperwork for educational credit, willing to provide letters of recommendation.
Contact Write or fax Ms. Nancy Peavy, Director of Operations. Fax: 202-466-5625. In-person interview recommended. Applicants must submit a cover letter, resume, academic transcripts, writing sample. Application deadline: March 1. World Wide Web: http://www.allhealth.org.

ALLIANCE FOR JUSTICE
2000 P Street, NW, Suite 712
Washington, District of Columbia 20036

General Information An association of national, regional, and local organizations working for public interest to provide equal access to government forums for all groups and individuals. Established in 1979. Number of employees: 17. Number of internship applications received each year: 100.
Internships Available ▶ *3–4 Everett interns:* responsibilities include general office duties, working mostly with First Monday Coordinator on First Monday event held the first Monday in October of each year. Candidates should have ability to work with others, computer skills, oral communication skills, organizational skills, research skills, written communication skills. Duration is May to August. $200 per week. Open to college freshmen, college sophomores, college juniors, college seniors, graduate students, law students. International applications accepted.

Alliance for Justice (continued)

Benefits Names of contacts, on-the-job training, opportunity to attend seminars/workshops, willing to act as a professional reference, willing to complete paperwork for educational credit, willing to provide letters of recommendation.
Contact Write, fax, or e-mail Alicia Holmes, Director of Administration. Fax: 202-822-6068. E-mail: alliance@afj.org. In-person interview recommended. Applicants must submit a cover letter, resume, writing sample. Applications are accepted continuously. World Wide Web: http://www.afj.org.

AMERICAN CIVIL LIBERTIES UNION OF PENNSYLVANIA
125 South Ninth Street, Suite 701
Philadelphia, Pennsylvania 19105-1161

General Information Nonprofit nationwide membership organization whose sole purpose is to preserve the basic rights and freedoms guaranteed to all Americans by the Constitution. Established in 1948. Number of employees: 9. Affiliate of American Civil Liberties Union, New York, New York. Number of internship applications received each year: 30.
Internships Available ▶ *Public education interns:* responsibilities include planning, developing, and organizing the American Civil Liberties Union's public education initiatives and coordinating with local schools, students, and youth groups to promote civil liberties with youth. Candidates should have ability to work independently, ability to work with others, oral communication skills, organizational skills, self-motivation, strong interpersonal skills, strong leadership ability. Duration is a year or a semester. Unpaid. Open to high school students, high school seniors, recent high school graduates, college freshmen, college sophomores, college juniors, college seniors, recent college graduates, graduate students, law students, career changers, individuals reentering the workforce.
Benefits Willing to provide letters of recommendation.
Contact Write, call, fax, or e-mail Jonna Revitz, Internship Coordinator, PO Box 1161, Philadelphia, Pennsylvania 19105-1161. Phone: 215-592-1513 Ext. 222. Fax: 215-592-1343. E-mail: aclupubed@aol.com. In-person interview recommended. Applicants must submit a cover letter, resume, personal reference, at least one writing sample, where applicable. Application deadline: April 10. World Wide Web: http://www.aclupa.org.

AMERICAN COMMITTEE ON AFRICA/THE AFRICA FUND
50 Broad Street, Suite 711
New York, New York 10004

General Information The Africa Fund works for a positive U.S. policy toward Africa and supports African human rights, democracy, and development. Established in 1966. Number of employees: 7. Number of internship applications received each year: 100.
Internships Available ▶ *Interns:* responsibilities include monitoring and clipping publications; answering phones; photocopying requested materials; assisting with the production of publications; participating in staff meetings, meetings with visiting African leaders, and various sessions with other organizations, such as the United Nations. Assignments are to one of major ongoing projects: Women in Africa, Democracy in Africa, Labor Unions, and Human Rights. Candidates should have personal interest in the field. Duration is flexible. Unpaid. Open to college freshmen, college sophomores, college juniors, college seniors, recent college graduates, graduate students, law students.
Benefits Willing to complete paperwork for educational credit.
Contact Write, call, fax, or e-mail Internship Program. Phone: 212-785-1024. Fax: 212-785-1078. E-mail: africafund@igc.org. In-person interview recommended. Applicants must submit a formal organization application, writing sample, two personal references. Application deadline: April 1 for summer, July 1 for fall. World Wide Web: http://www.prairienet.org/acas/afund. html.

AMERICAN FORUM IN WASHINGTON
National Press Building, 529 14th Street, NW, Suite 840
Washington, District of Columbia 20045-1203

General Information Progressive nonprofit media organization that publishes articles on quality of life issues and provides a resource for progressives to disseminate social commentary to the media. Established in 1981. Number of employees: 6. Number of internship applications received each year: 60.
Internships Available ▶ *2–4 media interns:* responsibilities include tracking article usage through extensive media contact; researching and compiling information for reports; preparing and distributing media packets to print, radio, and television outlets; building databases; and providing administrative support. Candidates should have ability to work independently, computer skills, personal interest in the field, research skills, strong interpersonal skills, writing skills. Duration is minimum 14 hours per week. Unpaid. Open to recent high school graduates, college freshmen, college sophomores, college juniors, college seniors, recent college graduates, graduate students, career changers.
Benefits Names of contacts, willing to complete paperwork for educational credit, willing to provide letters of recommendation.
Contact Write, call, fax, or e-mail Intern Coordinator, National Press Building 529 14th Street, NW, Suite 840, Washington, District of Columbia 20045-1203. Phone: 202-638-1431. Fax: 202-638-1434. E-mail: forum@forum-media.org. In-person interview recommended. Applicants must submit a cover letter, resume. Applications are accepted continuously.

AMERICAN HUMANE ASSOCIATION
63 Inverness Drive East
Englewood, Colorado 80112

General Information National organization dedicated to identifying and preventing the causes of animal and child abuse and neglect; provides advocacy, research, training, technical assistance, and other services in the areas of animal and child protection. Established in 1877. Number of employees: 60.
Internships Available ▶ *1 editorial intern:* responsibilities include writing and editing for national magazines and other marketing/direct mail promotions. Candidates should have college courses in field, computer skills, editing skills, plan to pursue career in field, self-motivation, writing skills. Duration is 3–6 months. Unpaid. Open to college freshmen, college sophomores, college juniors, college seniors, recent college graduates, graduate students. ▶ *2 marketing interns:* responsibilities include project management of a range of existing cause marketing programs with corporate sponsors, evaluating market opportunities, and creating proposals. Duration is flexible. Position available as unpaid or paid. ▶ *2 public relations interns:* responsibilities include preparing press releases and articles, contacting media, using on-line services to create mailing lists, and participating in campaign/event planning. Duration is flexible. Unpaid. International applications accepted.
Benefits Possible full-time employment, willing to complete paperwork for educational credit, willing to provide letters of recommendation, stipend may be available.
Contact Write, call, or fax Intern Coordinator. Phone: 303-792-9900. Fax: 303-792-5333. In-person interview recommended. Applicants must submit a cover letter, resume, 2 personal references/letters of recommendation. Applications are accepted continuously. World Wide Web: http://www.americanhumane. org.

AMERICAN JEWISH CONGRESS, GOVERNMENTAL AND PUBLIC AFFAIRS OFFICE
2027 Massachusetts Avenue, NW
Washington, District of Columbia 20036

General Information National community relations organization dedicated to protecting the religious, civil, political, and economic rights of all Americans. Established in 1918. Number of employees: 3. Unit of American Jewish Congress, New York, New York. Number of internship applications received each year: 50.

Internships Available ▶ *3–4 legislative interns:* responsibilities include attending and reporting on Congressional committee hearings and interest group coalition meetings and performing administrative duties. Duration is 3 months minimum. Unpaid. Open to college freshmen, college sophomores, college juniors, college seniors, recent college graduates. International applications accepted.

Benefits Names of contacts, opportunity to attend seminars/ workshops, possible full-time employment, travel reimbursement, willing to complete paperwork for educational credit, willing to provide letters of recommendation.

International Internships Available in Jerusalem, Israel.

Contact Write, call, fax, or e-mail David Harris, Director. Phone: 202-332-4001. Fax: 202-387-3434. E-mail: washrep@ajcongress. org. Telephone interview required. Applicants must submit a formal organization application, cover letter, resume, writing sample. Applications are accepted continuously. World Wide Web: http://www.ajcongress.org.

AMERICANS FOR DEMOCRATIC ACTION
1625 K Street, NW, Suite 210
Washington, District of Columbia 20006

General Information Nation's oldest liberal lobbying group combining grassroots organizing with lobbying on various issues at local, state, and national levels. Established in 1947. Number of employees: 10. Number of internship applications received each year: 100.

Internships Available ▶ *4–10 legislative interns:* responsibilities include researching, writing, helping with mailings, and following one or two issues on Capitol Hill. Candidates should have ability to work independently, computer skills, personal interest in the field, strong interpersonal skills, written communication skills. Duration is flexible. Unpaid. Open to high school students, high school seniors, recent high school graduates, college freshmen, college sophomores, college juniors, college seniors, recent college graduates, graduate students, law students, career changers, individuals reentering the workforce. International applications accepted.

Benefits Names of contacts, opportunity to attend seminars/ workshops, possible full-time employment, willing to act as a professional reference, willing to complete paperwork for educational credit, willing to provide letters of recommendation.

Contact Write, call, fax, or e-mail Valerie Dulk, Special Assistant to the Director. Phone: 202-785-5980. Fax: 202-785-5969. E-mail: adaction@ix.netcom.com. In-person interview recommended. Applicants must submit a cover letter, resume, writing sample. Application deadline: May 1 for summer, August 1 for fall, December 1 for spring. World Wide Web: http://adaction.org.

AMERICAN WOMAN'S ECONOMIC DEVELOPMENT CORPORATION
71 Vanderbilt Avenue
New York, New York 10169

General Information Not-for-profit organization that provides training, counseling, and technical assistance to women who own or would like start their own businesses. Established in 1976. Number of employees: 15. Number of internship applications received each year: 100.

Internships Available ▶ *1 administration intern:* responsibilities include supporting assistant to executive secretary of President and CEO. Candidates should have ability to work independently, computer skills, self-motivation, strong interpersonal skills, written communication skills. ▶ *1–2 development assistants:* responsibilities include researching and identifying potential funders and grants writing. Candidates should have ability to work independently, computer skills, editing skills, oral communication skills, strong interpersonal skills, writing skills. Duration is flexible. ▶ *1–2 program coordinators:* responsibilities include working with training or counseling director on program logistics, including assisting with registration, mailings and publicity, and interfacing with

clients and instructors. Candidates should have ability to work independently, computer skills, oral communication skills, self-motivation, strong interpersonal skills, written communication skills. Duration is flexible. All positions are unpaid. Open to college freshmen, college sophomores, college juniors, college seniors. International applications accepted.

Benefits Opportunity to attend seminars/workshops, willing to act as a professional reference, willing to complete paperwork for educational credit, willing to provide letters of recommendation.

Contact Write or fax Ms. Roseanne Antonucci, Chief Operating Officer. Fax: 212-692-9296. No phone calls. In-person interview required. Applicants must submit a cover letter, resume, three personal references, telephone interview acceptable for out-of-town candidates. Application deadline: March 30 for summer; continuous for fall, winter and spring. World Wide Web: http:// www.womenconnect.com/awed.

AMNESTY INTERNATIONAL, MIDWEST REGION
53 West Jackson, Suite 1162
Chicago, Illinois 60604-3607

General Information Grassroots international human rights organization that trains and organizes membership, functions as a liaison with the media, and organizes fundraising and special events. Established in 1961. Number of employees: 8. Unit of Amnesty International USA, New York, New York. Number of internship applications received each year: 50.

Internships Available ▶ *1–2 administrative interns:* responsibilities include working in a not-for-profit office environment, organizing various information such as international reports, country specific materials (written and audio-visual) and other office duties. Candidates should have ability to work independently, ability to work with others, analytical skills, computer skills, editing skills, office skills, oral communication skills, organizational skills, personal interest in the field, self-motivation, writing skills. Duration is 3 to 6 months (2-3 days a week). Open to high school students, high school seniors, recent high school graduates, college freshmen, college sophomores, college juniors, college seniors. ▶ *1 computer communications intern:* responsibilities include establishing list-serves in the office and working with members in the Midwest on Web site construction. Candidates should have ability to work independently, analytical skills, computer skills, editing skills, experience in the field, knowledge of field, office skills, oral communication skills, organizational skills, personal interest in the field, self-motivation, writing skills. Duration is 2–3 months. Open to high school students, high school seniors, recent high school graduates, college freshmen, college sophomores, college juniors, college seniors, recent college graduates, graduate students, law students. ▶ *1 death penalty abolition intern:* responsibilities include working with Deputy Director on death penalty related projects in region. Candidates should have ability to work independently, computer skills, editing skills, office skills, oral communication skills, organizational skills, personal interest in the field, research skills, self-motivation, strong interpersonal skills, strong leadership ability, writing skills. Duration is 3–4 months. Open to high school students, high school seniors, recent high school graduates, college freshmen, college sophomores, college juniors, college seniors, recent college graduates, graduate students, law students. ▶ *1–2 desktop materials publishing interns:* responsibilities include producing regional quarterly newsletter which is mailed to approximately 500-600 people, over-seeing the printing/mailing and producing of other materials such as brochures, flyers, and announcements. Candidates should have ability to work independently, computer skills, editing skills, organizational skills, writing skills, knowledge of Windows. Duration is 1 to 6 months (2-3 days a week). Open to high school students, high school seniors, recent high school graduates, college freshmen, college sophomores, college juniors, college seniors, recent college graduates, career changers. ▶ *2–3 human rights education interns:* responsibilities include assisting in the development of human rights materials for various ages, educational groups and educators. Candidates should have ability to work independently, ability to work with others, computer skills, editing skills, office skills, oral communication skills, organizational skills, personal interest in the field, research skills,

Amnesty International, Midwest Region (continued)

self-motivation, written communication skills. Duration is 1–12 months. Open to high school students, high school seniors, recent high school graduates, college freshmen, college sophomores, college juniors, college seniors, recent college graduates. ▶ *1–2 media interns:* responsibilities include working with media and special events coordinator. Candidates should have ability to work independently, computer skills, knowledge of field, office skills, oral communication skills, organizational skills, personal interest in the field, self-motivation, strong interpersonal skills, writing skills. Duration is flexible. Open to high school seniors, recent high school graduates, college freshmen, college sophomores, college juniors, college seniors, recent college graduates, graduate students. ▶ *1–2 membership servicing interns:* responsibilities include maintaining and recruiting members by managing lists, phone, and e-mail; developing and sending membership information; contacting group coordinators, data entry, and assistance in event planning. Candidates should have ability to work independently, computer skills, editing skills, office skills, oral communication skills, organizational skills, personal interest in the field, research skills, self-motivation, strong interpersonal skills, writing skills. Duration is 3–6 months. Open to high school students, high school seniors, recent high school graduates, college freshmen, college sophomores, college juniors, college seniors, recent college graduates, graduate students, law students. ▶ *1 women's human rights intern:* responsibilities include attending Women's Convention Coalition meetings, assisting in passing resolution through city council, arranging Alderman visits, outreach to ally organizations answering general requests, mailings help, and general office work. Candidates should have ability to work independently, computer skills, office skills, oral communication skills, organizational skills, personal interest in the field, research skills, self-motivation, strong interpersonal skills, written communication skills. Duration is 1–6 months. Open to college freshmen, college sophomores, college juniors, college seniors, recent college graduates, graduate students, law students, career changers. All positions are unpaid. International applications accepted.

Benefits Opportunity to attend seminars/workshops, travel reimbursement, willing to complete paperwork for educational credit, willing to provide letters of recommendation.

International Internships Available.

Contact Write, call, fax, or e-mail Ms. Audrey Randall, Office Administrator. Phone: 312-427-6382. Fax: 312-427-2589. E-mail: arandall@aiusa.org. In-person interview recommended. Applicants must submit a formal organization application, cover letter, resume, two personal references, 1-2 letters of recommendation. Applications are accepted continuously. World Wide Web: http://www.amnesty-usa.org.

AMNESTY INTERNATIONAL USA
322 Eighth Avenue
New York, New York 10001

General Information Nonprofit human rights organization working on behalf of prisoners of conscience and political prisoners and for an end to torture and execution with prior work authorization. Established in 1961. Number of employees: 69. Number of internship applications received each year: 5.

Internships Available ▶ *Interns:* responsibilities include working in the areas of death penalty abolition, country coordination groups and actions, women outreach, local national program, membership development, fund-raising, communications, and executive unit. Duration is flexible. Position available as unpaid or paid. International applications accepted.

Benefits Travel reimbursement, willing to complete paperwork for educational credit.

Contact Write or fax Darryle Johnson, Internship Coordinator. Fax: 212-627-1451. No phone calls. In-person interview required. Applicants must submit a cover letter, resume. Applications are accepted continuously. World Wide Web: http://www.amnesty-usa.org.

AMNESTY INTERNATIONAL USA, REFUGEE PROGRAM
500 Sansome Street, Suite 615
San Francisco, California 94111-3222

General Information An independent worldwide movement working impartially for the release of prisoners of conscience; fair, prompt trials for political prisoners; and an end to torture and executions. Established in 1961. Number of employees: 4. Unit of Amnesty International USA, New York, New York. Number of internship applications received each year: 50.

Internships Available ▶ *3–4 research interns:* responsibilities include researching political asylum cases in appropriate Amnesty International country files, annotating and analyzing information, photocopying information and sending to asylum applicant or representative, answering phones, keeping up filing material, answering questions on Amnesty International and its refugee concerns, and working on other projects assigned in office. Candidates should have analytical skills, computer skills, office skills, self-motivation, strong interpersonal skills, written communication skills. Duration is 3-6 months (2 days per week). Unpaid. Open to recent high school graduates, college freshmen, college sophomores, college juniors, college seniors, recent college graduates, graduate students, law students, career changers, individuals reentering the workforce. International applications accepted.

Benefits Travel reimbursement, willing to complete paperwork for educational credit, willing to provide letters of recommendation, opportunity to attend seminars, workshops, and political asylum hearings.

International Internships Available.

Contact Write or fax Coleen Liebmann, Refugee Program Assistant, 500 Sansome Street, Suite 615, San Francisco, California 94111-3222. Fax: 415-291-8722. In-person interview recommended. Applicants must submit a formal organization application, resume, writing sample. Applications are accepted continuously. World Wide Web: http://www.io.org/amnesty.

AMNESTY INTERNATIONAL USA, WASHINGTON OFFICE
600 Pennsylvania Avenue, SE, 5th Floor
Washington, District of Columbia 20003

General Information Organization conducting a worldwide movement working impartially for the release of prisoners of conscience, fair and prompt trials for political prisoners, and an end to torture and executions. Established in 1961. Number of employees: 32. Unit of Amnesty International USA, New York, New York. Number of internship applications received each year: 500.

Internships Available ▶ *2 African affairs interns:* responsibilities include monitoring and providing information on developments in the region. Candidates should have ability to work independently, computer skills, office skills, oral communication skills, organizational skills, personal interest in the field, research skills, strong interpersonal skills, writing skills. Unpaid. Open to college freshmen, college sophomores, college juniors, college seniors, recent college graduates, graduate students, law students, career changers. ▶ *2 Asian affairs interns:* responsibilities include monitoring and providing information on developments in the region. Candidates should have ability to work independently, computer skills, office skills, oral communication skills, organizational skills, personal interest in the field, research skills, strong interpersonal skills, writing skills. Unpaid. Open to college freshmen, college sophomores, college juniors, college seniors, recent college graduates, graduate students, law students, career changers. ▶ *2 European/Middle Eastern affairs interns:* responsibilities include monitoring and providing information on developments in the region. Candidates should have ability to work independently, computer skills, office skills, oral communication skills, organizational skills, personal interest in the field, research skills, strong interpersonal skills, writing skills. Paid. Open to college freshmen, college sophomores, college juniors, college seniors, recent college graduates, graduate students, law students, career changers. ▶ *1–2 Human Rights and* *the Environment interns:* responsibilities include providing research on cases involving environmental and human rights violations and assisting in grassroots organizing strategies. Candidates should have ability to work independently, computer skills, office skills, oral communication skills, organizational skills, personal interest in the field, research skills, strong interpersonal skills, writing skills. Unpaid. Open to college freshmen, college sophomores, college juniors, college seniors, recent college graduates, graduate students. ▶ *2 Latin American affairs interns:* responsibilities include monitoring and providing information on developments in the region. Candidates should have ability to work independently, computer skills, office skills, oral communication skills, organizational skills, personal interest in the field, research skills, strong interpersonal skills, writing skills. Unpaid. Open to college freshmen, college sophomores, college juniors, college seniors, recent college graduates, graduate students. ▶ *1–2 Program to Abolish the Death Penalty interns:* responsibilities include assisting in creating training materials for organizing against the death penalty, and providing research on the death penalty and related issues in the U.S. and internationally. Candidates should have ability to work independently, computer skills, office skills, oral communication skills, organizational skills, personal interest in the field, research skills, strong interpersonal skills, writing skills. Unpaid. Open to college freshmen, college sophomores, college juniors, college seniors, recent college graduates, graduate students. ▶ *2 campaign interns:* responsibilities include assisting with all aspects of campaigns and crisis response including planning, materials preparation, event coordination, and evaluation. Candidates should have ability to work independently, computer skills, office skills, oral communication skills, organizational skills, personal interest in the field, research skills, strong interpersonal skills, writing skills. Unpaid. Open to college freshmen, college sophomores, college juniors, college seniors, recent college graduates, graduate students. ▶ *2 co-group interns:* responsibilities include assisting in the recruitment, training, and servicing of volunteer country specialists. Candidates should have ability to work independently, computer skills, office skills, oral communication skills, organizational skills, personal interest in the field, strong interpersonal skills, writing skills. Unpaid. Open to college freshmen, college sophomores, college juniors, college seniors, recent college graduates, graduate students. ▶ *1 legislative affairs intern:* responsibilities include assisting the Legislative Council in tracking the progress of, and developing support for, legislation and treaties of concern to AIUSA. Candidates should have ability to work independently, computer skills, office skills, oral communication skills, organizational skills, personal interest in the field, strong interpersonal skills, writing skills. Unpaid. Open to college freshmen, college sophomores, college juniors, college seniors, recent college graduates, graduate students. ▶ *2 media relations intern:* responsibilities include assisting the press officer with all aspects of work to ensure media coverage of human rights issues. Candidates should have ability to work independently, computer skills, office skills, oral communication skills, organizational skills, personal interest in the field, strong interpersonal skills, writing skills. Unpaid. Open to college freshmen, college sophomores, college juniors, college seniors, recent college graduates, graduate students. ▶ *3–4 mid-Atlantic regional office interns:* responsibilities include working to mobilize, motivate and support AIUSA members in their efforts to publicize worldwide human rights abuses and work for an end to them. Candidates should have ability to work independently, computer skills, office skills, oral communication skills, organizational skills, personal interest in the field, research skills, strong interpersonal skills, writing skills. Unpaid. Open to college freshmen, college sophomores, college juniors, college seniors, recent college graduates, graduate students. ▶ *3–4 national field program interns:* responsibilities include assisting in the coordination of national training programs and the development of activists tools, assisting in grassroots organizing strategies. Candidates should have ability to work independently, office skills, oral communication skills, organizational skills, personal interest in the field, research skills, strong interpersonal skills, writing skills. Unpaid. Open to college freshmen, college sophomores, college juniors, college seniors, recent college

graduates, graduate students. Duration for all positions is minimum of 3 months. International applications accepted.
Benefits Job counseling, names of contacts, opportunity to attend seminars/workshops, travel reimbursement, willing to act as a professional reference, willing to complete paperwork for educational credit, willing to provide letters of recommendation.
Contact Write, call, fax, or e-mail Oneida Khalsa, Office Manager, 600 Pennsylvania Avenue, SE 5th Floor, Washington, District of Columbia 20003. Phone: 202-544-0200. Fax: 202-546-7142. E-mail: okhalsa@aiusa.org. Telephone interview required. Applicants must submit a cover letter, resume, writing sample, two letters of recommendation. Applications are accepted continuously. World Wide Web: http://amnesty-usa.org.

ANIMAL PROTECTION INSTITUTE
2831 Fruitrigde Road
Sacramento, California 95820

General Information Animal advocacy organization. Established in 1968. Number of employees: 20. Number of internship applications received each year: 25.
Internships Available ▶ *1–2 animal advocacy interns:* responsibilities include assisting program and legal staff with advocacy campaigns by conducting research, writing publications, drafting member action alerts, and lobbying public officials. Candidates should have ability to work independently, analytical skills, plan to pursue career in field, research skills, strong interpersonal skills, written communication skills. Duration is 40 hours per week during summer; variable during school year. Position available as unpaid or at $7-$10 per hour for summer positions only. Open to college juniors, college seniors, recent college graduates, graduate students, law students.
Benefits On-the-job training, opportunity to attend seminars/workshops, possible full-time employment, travel reimbursement, willing to act as a professional reference, willing to complete paperwork for educational credit, willing to provide letters of recommendation.
Contact Write, fax, or e-mail Dena Jones, Program Director, PO Box 22505, Sacramento, California 95822. Fax: 916-731-4467. E-mail: djones@gvn.net. No phone calls. In-person interview recommended. Applicants must submit a cover letter, resume, writing sample, three personal references. Application deadline: March 15 for summer; continuous for school year. World Wide Web: http://www.api4animals.org.

ARAB AMERICAN INSTITUTE
918 16th Street, NW, #601
Washington, District of Columbia 20006

General Information Organization that nurtures and encourages direct participation of Arab Americans in political and civic life in the U.S. Established in 1985. Number of employees: 10. Number of internship applications received each year: 15.
Internships Available ▶ *8–12 interns:* responsibilities include assisting in Public Affairs or Organizing departments, setting up meetings, assisting with logistics of special events, helping the Institute build its action network, some clerical work, research, and writing. Candidates should have ability to work independently, computer skills, knowledge of field, office skills, research skills. Duration is minimum 6 weeks in winter, spring, summer, or fall. $600–$700 per month. Open to college freshmen, college sophomores, college juniors, college seniors, recent college graduates, graduate students. International applications accepted.
Benefits Opportunity to attend seminars/workshops, possible full-time employment, willing to complete paperwork for educational credit, willing to provide letters of recommendation.
Contact Write, call, fax, or e-mail Dianne L. Davidson, Office Manager. Phone: 202-429-9210. Fax: 202-429-9214. E-mail: ddavidson@arab-aai.org. In-person interview recommended. Applicants must submit a cover letter, resume, writing sample. Application deadline: April 1 for summer; continuous for others.

THE ARMS CONTROL ASSOCIATION
1726 M Street, NW, Suite 201
Washington, District of Columbia 20036

General Information Independent research organization dedicated to raising public knowledge of arms control and related national security issues. Established in 1971. Number of employees: 8. Number of internship applications received each year: 100.

Internships Available ▶ *1 editorial assistant:* responsibilities include proofreading, editing, and layout; some clerical duties. Candidates should have ability to work with others, computer skills, editing skills, office skills, writing skills. Duration is 8–10 weeks. Open to college freshmen, college sophomores, college juniors, college seniors, recent college graduates, graduate students. ▶ *1–4 general interns:* responsibilities include research support and clerical duties. Candidates should have ability to work independently, computer skills, office skills, personal interest in the field, research skills, self-motivation. Duration is 1 semester. Open to college freshmen, college sophomores, college juniors, college seniors, recent college graduates, graduate students, law students. All positions paid at $30–$50 per week.

Benefits Job counseling, meals at a cost, names of contacts, opportunity to attend seminars/workshops, possible full-time employment, travel reimbursement, willing to act as a professional reference, willing to complete paperwork for educational credit, willing to provide letters of recommendation.

Contact Write, call, fax, or e-mail Craig Cerniello, Senior Research Analyst and Intern Coordinator. Phone: 202-463-8270. Fax: 202-463-8273. E-mail: craig@armscontrol.org. In-person interview recommended. Applicants must submit a cover letter, resume, 1 writing sample (3-5 pages). Applications are accepted continuously. World Wide Web: http://www.armscontrol.org.

ASSOCIATION FOR WOMEN IN SCIENCE (AWIS)
1200 New York Avenue, NW, Suite 650
Washington, District of Columbia 20005

General Information Nonprofit organization whose mission is to expand education and employment opportunities in science for girls and women. Established in 1971. Number of employees: 7. Number of internship applications received each year: 150.

Internships Available ▶ *Interns:* responsibilities include helping to develop chapter activities and plan AWIS events, assisting with grant proposal writing, legislative analysis, assisting with magazine production, membership services, research, and obtaining resources/statistics on issues of women in science. Candidates should have ability to work independently, office skills, research skills, strong interpersonal skills, written communication skills. Duration is 2-4 months (year-round). Paid. Open to college freshmen, college sophomores, college juniors, college seniors, recent college graduates, graduate students.

Benefits Opportunity to attend seminars/workshops, willing to complete paperwork for educational credit, willing to provide letters of recommendation.

Contact Write or e-mail Deborah Morman, Intern Coordinator, 1200 New York Avenue, NW, Suite 650, Washington, District of Columbia 20005. E-mail: awis@awis.org. Applicants must submit a cover letter, resume. Applications are accepted continuously. World Wide Web: http://www.awis.org.

ASTRAEA NATIONAL LESBIAN ACTION FOUNDATION
116 East 16th Street, 7th Floor
New York, New York 10003

General Information The leading source of financial support for organizations that serve or directly address issues related to lesbians and which actively promote an end to political injustices.

Internships Available ▶ *1 grants program intern:* responsibilities include processing applications, entering applicant information into database, corresponding with applicants to get additional information, preparing applications for the grants panel. Candidates should have ability to work with others, computer skills, office skills, oral communication skills, personal interest in the field, written communication skills. Duration is September to December, or February to May. Unpaid. Open to college freshmen, college sophomores, college juniors, college seniors.

Benefits On-the-job training, travel reimbursement, willing to act as a professional reference, willing to complete paperwork for educational credit, willing to provide letters of recommendation.

Contact Write or fax Internship Coordinator, 116 East 16th Street, New York, New York 10003. Fax: 212-982-3321. No phone calls. In-person interview required. Applicants must submit a cover letter, resume. Application deadline: February 5 for spring, September 17 for fall. World Wide Web: http://www.astrea.com.

THE AUDRE LORDE PROJECT
85 South Oxford Street
Brooklyn, New York 11217

General Information Center to promote and ensure the physical, mental, spiritual, and political health of lesbian, gay, bisexual, two spirits and transgender people of color communities in the New York City area. Programs include: women's organizing; police violence, immigrant rights and education; HIV/AIDS; library and archives; arts and culture; rap discussion groups for men, women, and youth. Established in 1993. Number of employees: 8. Number of internship applications received each year: 20.

Internships Available ▶ *1 coalition development intern:* responsibilities include working with coalition of 25 community-based HIV service providers, facilitating and planning meetings, and developing outreach materials. Candidates should have ability to work independently, oral communication skills, self-motivation, strong interpersonal skills, written communication skills, commitment to organization's mission and principles, multilingual proficiency (strongly desired). Duration is minimum 10 to 15 hours per week for at least 3 months. Open to high school students, high school seniors, recent high school graduates, college freshmen, college sophomores, college juniors, college seniors, recent college graduates, graduate students, law students, career changers, individuals reentering the workforce. ▶ *1 development assistant:* responsibilities include working directly with executive director and fund-raising committee to develop and implement creative strategies for sustainable fund-raising. Will include correspondence with donors, researching prospective funding streams, and donor data management. Candidates should have computer skills, oral communication skills, strong interpersonal skills, writing skills, commitment to organization's mission and principles. Duration is minimum 10 to 16 hours per week for at least 3 months. ▶ *1 library/archives intern:* responsibilities include evaluating and cataloging materials for collection, working with library volunteers, corresponding with donors, donor database management, developing and managing a system to accept archive and library materials from individual and organizational donors, and creating a system that would provide public access to the resources. Candidates should have organizational skills, experience working with archive and library materials, and commitment to organization's mission and principles. Duration is 10 to 16 hours per week for at least 3 months. Open to high school students, high school seniors, recent high school graduates, college freshmen, college sophomores, college juniors, college seniors, recent college graduates, graduate students, law students, career changers, individuals reentering the workforce. ▶ *1 newsletter production intern:* responsibilities include helping to produce quarterly newsletter by typing, editing, fact-checking, soliciting articles and photographs, and assisting in design and layout. Candidates should have ability to work independently, computer skills, oral communication skills, strong interpersonal skills, written communication skills, commitment to organization's mission and principles familiarity with Adobe Photoshop and QuarkXpress software. Duration is minimum 10 to 16 hours per week for at least 3 months. Open to high school students, high school seniors, recent high school graduates, college freshmen, college sophomores, college juniors, college seniors, recent college graduates, graduate students, law students, career changers, individuals reentering the workforce. ▶ *1 reception, information and referral specialist:* responsibilities include greeting and

directing visitors, volunteers and participants; providing information, referrals, support, and crisis intervention to callers and walk-ins; supervising volunteers; organizing and maintaining files and databases; and providing clerical and administrative support to staff. Candidates should have crisis management skills; proven ability working with multi-racial, multi-ethnic, and multi-gendered communities; commitment to organization's mission and principles; ability to work independently and with others; some knowledge of computers. Duration is 3-month minimum; Monday to Friday from 12-4. Open to high school students, high school seniors, recent high school graduates, college freshmen, college sophomores, college juniors, college seniors, recent college graduates, graduate students, law students, career changers, individuals reentering the workforce. ▶ *1 video production intern:* responsibilities include assisting in oral history interviews, transcribing audiotape and videotape, editing footage, providing training for audiovisual skills, and supporting fund-raising efforts. Candidates should have ability to work independently, experience in the field, oral communication skills, strong interpersonal skills, writing skills, commitment to organization's mission and principles. Duration is 3-month minimum. Open to high school students, high school seniors, recent high school graduates, college freshmen, college sophomores, college juniors, college seniors, recent college graduates, graduate students, law students, career changers, individuals reentering the workforce. All positions are unpaid. International applications accepted.
Benefits Names of contacts, opportunity to attend seminars/workshops, willing to act as a professional reference, willing to complete paperwork for educational credit, willing to provide letters of recommendation, hands-on community organizing experience.
Contact Write, call, or e-mail Raymond L. Costantino, Volunteer and Facilities Coordinator, 85 South Oxford Street, Brooklyn, New York 11217. Phone: 718-596-0342 Ext. 12. E-mail: alpinfo@alp.org. In-person interview recommended. Applicants must submit a formal organization application, resume, three personal references, writing sample depending on proposed project. Applications are accepted continuously.

BETTER GOVERNMENT ASSOCIATION
28 East Jackson Boulevard, Suite 1900
Chicago, Illinois 60604

General Information Nationally recognized public interest organization that collaborates with local and national print and broadcast news organizations to investigate waste, corruption, and inefficiency in government. Established in 1923. Number of employees: 7. Number of internship applications received each year: 150.
Internships Available ▶ *7–10 interns:* responsibilities include conducting background research, interviews, litigation searches, surveillance, and administrative duties. Candidates should have ability to work independently, ability to work with others, analytical skills, research skills, self-motivation, desire to work in the public interest. Open to college juniors, college seniors, recent college graduates, graduate students, law students. ▶ *1–3 legal interns:* responsibilities include researching analyzing, and developing legal theory; investigating waste fraud and corruption in government; and performing general office duties. Candidates should have analytical skills, declared college major in field, organizational skills, personal interest in the field, research skills, self-motivation. Open to law students. Duration for all positions is flexible. All positions are unpaid. International applications accepted.
Benefits Possible full-time employment, willing to act as a professional reference, willing to complete paperwork for educational credit, leadership skills.
Contact Write, call, or fax Mr. James Newcomb, Director of Development. Phone: 312-427-8330. Fax: 312-427-8340. Telephone interview required. Applicants must submit a cover letter, resume. Application deadline: January 15 for spring, May 30 for summer, September 1 for fall. World Wide Web: http://www.bgawatchdog.org.

BREAD FOR THE WORLD AND BREAD FOR THE WORLD INSTITUTE
1100 Wayne Avenue, Suite 1000
Silver Spring, Maryland 20910

General Information A nonprofit anti-hunger advocacy organization that addresses U.S. public policy affecting the hungry. Established in 1974. Number of employees: 50. Number of internship applications received each year: 100.

Internships Available ▶ *1–2 annual hunger report interns:* responsibilities include assisting with publishing a major reference guide on global hunger. Candidates should have ability to work independently, analytical skills, computer skills, editing skills, knowledge of field, oral communication skills, organizational skills, personal interest in the field, research skills, self-motivation, strong interpersonal skills, strong leadership ability, writing skills. Duration is 3 months or 1-2 years. Unpaid. ▶ *1 church relations intern:* responsibilities include carrying out promotional efforts to churches and denominational representatives in support of BFW legislation. Candidates should have ability to work independently, computer skills, knowledge of field, office skills, oral communication skills, organizational skills, personal interest in the field, self-motivation, strong interpersonal skills, writing skills. Duration is 8–10 weeks. Unpaid. ▶ *1–3 development interns:* responsibilities include assisting with fund-raising for both the general budget and special projects. Candidates should have ability to work independently, computer skills, office skills, oral communication skills, personal interest in the field, self-motivation, strong interpersonal skills, writing skills. Duration is 3 months or 1-2 years. Unpaid. ▶ *1 domestic hunger issues intern:* responsibilities include assisting with developing and communicating policy and legislative strategy on domestic hunger issues. Candidates should have ability to work independently, analytical skills, college courses in field, computer skills, editing skills, knowledge of field, oral communication skills, personal interest in the field, research skills, self-motivation, strong interpersonal skills, writing skills. Duration is 3 months or 1-2 years. Unpaid. ▶ *1 human resources intern.* Candidates should have ability to work independently, college courses in field, computer skills, oral communication skills, plan to pursue career in field, self-motivation, strong interpersonal skills, written communication skills. Duration is 3 months or 1 year. Unpaid. Open to college freshmen, college sophomores, college juniors, college seniors, recent college graduates, graduate students, career changers. ▶ *1 international hunger issues intern:* responsibilities include assisting with research and lobbying support. Candidates should have ability to work independently, computer skills, editing skills, knowledge of field, oral communication skills, organizational skills, personal interest in the field, plan to pursue career in field, research skills, self-motivation, strong interpersonal skills, strong leadership ability, writing skills. Duration is 3 months or 1-2 years. Unpaid. ▶ *1 media intern:* responsibilities include using a variety of media to fulfill objectives. Candidates should have ability to work independently, computer skills, knowledge of field, oral communication skills, personal interest in the field, self-motivation, strong interpersonal skills, writing skills. Duration is 3 months or 1-2 years. Unpaid. ▶ *1–3 organizing interns:* responsibilities include assisting with building a strong grassroots lobbying network by working on specific projects or in a specific region of the country. Candidates should have ability to work independently, computer skills, knowledge of field, oral communication skills, organizational skills, personal interest in the field, self-motivation, strong interpersonal skills, writing skills. Duration is 3 months or 1-2 years. Unpaid. ▶ *1–5 stipend interns:* responsibilities include serving in any capacity where needed in any of the above positions. Candidates should have ability to work independently, computer skills, office skills, oral communication skills, personal interest in the field, self-motivation, strong interpersonal skills, written communication skills. Duration is 1 year. $15,700 per year plus medical and dental benefits. International applications accepted.

Benefits Job counseling, names of contacts, opportunity to attend seminars/workshops, possible full-time employment, will-

Bread for the World and Bread for the World Institute (continued)

ing to complete paperwork for educational credit, willing to provide letters of recommendation, reimbursement of work-related travel expenses.
Contact Write, call, or e-mail Ms. Katherine Simmons, Human Resources Manager. Phone: 301-608-2400. E-mail: bread@igc.org or human.resources@bread.org. Applicants must submit a formal organization application, cover letter, resume, academic transcripts, writing sample, three letters of recommendation. Application deadline: April 1 for summer, July 1 for fall, November 1 for winter and spring. World Wide Web: http://www.bread.org.

CARAL-CALIFORNIA ABORTION & REPRODUCTIVE RIGHTS ACTION LEAGUE
330 Townsend Street, Suite 204
San Francisco, California 94107

General Information Political lobbying, educational organization dedicated to creating and sustaining a constituency that uses the political process to guarantee the full range of reproductive rights to all women . Established in 1978. Number of employees: 10. Affiliate of National Abortion and Reproductive Rights Action League, Washington, District of Columbia. Number of internship applications received each year: 25.
Internships Available ▶ *1 Hospital Project intern:* responsibilities include assisting with research and writing for a project designed to expand access to abortion services at hospitals. Candidates should have ability to work independently, analytical skills, oral communication skills, research skills, written communication skills, strong commitment to reproductive rights and access to healthcare for all women. Duration is May to August. Unpaid. Open to college freshmen, college sophomores, college juniors, college seniors, recent college graduates. ▶ *1–3 Web site interns:* responsibilities include maintenance of political Web site, updating news and events in newsletter, possibly working with on-line database, and working on the graphic image. Candidates should have computer skills, oral communication skills, organizational skills, personal interest in the field, self-motivation, strong interpersonal skills, writing skills. Duration is 3–12 months. Unpaid. Open to high school seniors, recent high school graduates, college freshmen, college sophomores, college juniors, college seniors, recent college graduates, graduate students, law students, career changers. ▶ *1–3 Women of Color Organizing Project interns:* responsibilities include developing educational material, organizing collaborations with women of color health organizations, and organizing events. Candidates should have computer skills, oral communication skills, self-motivation, strong interpersonal skills, writing skills. Duration is 3 or more months. Position available as unpaid or at stipend. Open to high school students, high school seniors, recent high school graduates, college freshmen, college sophomores, college juniors, college seniors, recent college graduates, graduate students, law students, career changers, individuals reentering the workforce. ▶ *1–3 fund-raising interns:* responsibilities include in-kind donation solicitation, planning annual event, coordinating reception and developing volunteers. Candidates should have ability to work with others, computer skills, oral communication skills, organizational skills, self-motivation, written communication skills. Duration is 3–6 months. Unpaid. Open to high school students, high school seniors, recent high school graduates, college freshmen, college sophomores, college juniors, college seniors, recent college graduates, graduate students, law students, career changers, individuals reentering the workforce. ▶ *1–3 political organizing interns:* responsibilities include coordinating volunteers, supervising and directing campaign strategy implementation, legislative alert organizing, event work, and writing. Candidates should have ability to work independently, ability to work with others, computer skills, oral communication skills, personal interest in the field, self-motivation, written communication skills. Duration is 3–12 months. Unpaid. Open to high school students, high school seniors, recent high school graduates, college freshmen, college sophomores, college juniors, college seniors, recent college graduates, graduate students, law students, individuals reentering the workforce. International applications accepted.

Benefits Formal training, names of contacts, on-the-job training, opportunity to attend seminars/workshops, possible full-time employment, travel reimbursement, willing to act as a professional reference, willing to complete paperwork for educational credit, willing to provide letters of recommendation, $100 travel stipend.
Contact Write, call, fax, or e-mail Meryl Block, Political Organizer, 330 Townsend Street Suite 204, San Francisco, California 94107. Phone: 415-546-7211. Fax: 415-546-7634. E-mail: caral@aol.com. In-person interview recommended. Applicants must submit a cover letter, resume, three personal references. Applications are accepted continuously. World Wide Web: http://www.caral.org.

THE CARTER CENTER
One Copenhill, 453 Freedom Parkway
Atlanta, Georgia 30307

General Information Nonprofit organization, founded by Jimmy and Rosalynn Carter, dedicated to resolving conflicts, promoting democracy, and fighting disease, hunger, poverty, and oppression throughout the world. Established in 1982. Number of employees: 200. Unit of Emory University, Atlanta, Georgia.
Internships Available ▶ *Interns:* responsibilities include duties focusing on issues concerning democratization and development, global health, and urban revitalization, including some office administration. Duration is minimum of 15 hours per week for at least one semester. Unpaid. ▶ *Summer graduate assistants:* responsibilities include duties focusing on issues concerning democratization and development, global health, and urban revitalization. Duration is 1 summer. Paid. ▶ *Volunteers.* Duration is flexible. Unpaid. Open to college juniors, college seniors, recent college graduates, graduate students. International applications accepted.
Benefits Formal training, job counseling, names of contacts, opportunity to attend seminars/workshops, willing to complete paperwork for educational credit, willing to provide letters of recommendation.
Contact Write, call, or fax Internship Coordinator. Phone: 404-420-5151. Fax: 404-420-5196. Applicants must submit a formal organization application, cover letter, resume, academic transcripts, writing sample, two letters of recommendation, short essay. Application deadline: March 15 for summer, June 15 for fall, October 15 for spring. World Wide Web: http://www.cartercenter.org.

CENTER FOR CAMPUS ORGANIZING
165 Friend Street #1
Boston, Massachusetts 02125-2025

General Information National clearinghouse that promotes progressive activism and investigative journalism on campuses. Established in 1990. Number of employees: 4. Number of internship applications received each year: 60.
Internships Available ▶ *1 affirmative action student intern:* responsibilities include researching and writing on affirmative action, leading workshops and trainings on affirmative action, and travelling to conferences. Candidates should have ability to work with others, computer skills, oral communication skills, personal interest in the field, research skills, writing skills. approximately $6 per hour. Open to recent high school graduates, college freshmen, college sophomores, college juniors, college seniors, recent college graduates, graduate students, law students. ▶ *1–2 campus activist resource creation interns:* responsibilities include creating and distributing "action sheets" for students working on issues of multicultural curriculum reform, challenging the bell curve, establishing a women's rights or multicultural center. Candidates should have ability to work independently, computer skills, editing skills, personal interest in the field, written communication skills. Position available as unpaid or at $6–$7 per hour. Open to high school students, high school seniors, recent high school graduates, college freshmen, college sophomores, college juniors, college seniors, recent college graduates, graduate students, law students, career changers, individuals reentering the workforce. ▶ *1–2 campus newspaper network interns:* responsibilities include assisting with the layout

and design of the Center's publications. Candidates should have ability to work independently, computer skills, editing skills, experience in the field, personal interest in the field, written communication skills. Position available as unpaid or at $6–$7 per hour. Open to high school seniors, recent high school graduates, college freshmen, college sophomores, college juniors, college seniors, recent college graduates, graduate students, law students, career changers, individuals reentering the workforce.
▶ *1–3 campus organizing interns:* responsibilities include assisting with center's organizing work. Candidates should have ability to work independently, oral communication skills, personal interest in the field, self-motivation, strong interpersonal skills. Position available as unpaid or at $6–$7 per hour. Open to high school seniors, recent high school graduates, college freshmen, college sophomores, college juniors, college seniors, recent college graduates, graduate students, law students, career changers, individuals reentering the workforce. ▶ *1–2 research interns:* responsibilities include helping to maintain active records and listing of right-wing foundations. Candidates should have ability to work independently, computer skills, personal interest in the field, research skills, written communication skills. Position available as unpaid or at $6–$7 per hour. Open to high school seniors, recent high school graduates, college freshmen, college sophomores, college juniors, college seniors, recent college graduates, graduate students, law students, career changers, individuals reentering the workforce. ▶ *1–2 student labor solidarity interns:* responsibilities include building networks of student-labor activists, implementing one student labor campaign, campus visits, and leading workshops. Candidates should have computer skills, oral communication skills, personal interest in the field, strong interpersonal skills. approximately $6 per hour. Open to high school students, high school seniors, recent high school graduates, college freshmen, college sophomores, college juniors, college seniors, recent college graduates, graduate students, law students, career changers, individuals reentering the workforce. Duration for all positions is 2–6 months. International applications accepted.
Benefits Names of contacts, on-the-job training, opportunity to attend seminars/workshops, possible full-time employment, willing to act as a professional reference, willing to complete paperwork for educational credit, willing to provide letters of recommendation.
Contact Write, fax, or e-mail Bill Capowski, Executive Director. Fax: 617-725-2873. E-mail: cco@igc.org. No phone calls. Applicants must submit a formal organization application, cover letter, resume. Applications are accepted continuously. World Wide Web: http://www.cco.org.

CENTER FOR POLICY ALTERNATIVES
1875 Connecticut Avenue, NW, Suite 710
Washington, District of Columbia 20009

General Information Organization that provides state policymakers with effective alternative models on cutting-edge issues, promotes informed leadership among public officials and advocates, and provides assistance and public education. Established in 1974. Number of employees: 20. Number of internship applications received each year: 300.
Internships Available ▶ *7–10 interns:* responsibilities include research, writing, and administrative work. Candidates should have research skills, writing skills. Duration is flexible. Unpaid. Open to college freshmen, college sophomores, college juniors, college seniors, recent college graduates, graduate students. International applications accepted.
Benefits Opportunity to attend seminars/workshops, possible full-time employment, willing to complete paperwork for educational credit.
Contact Write or call Internship Coodinator. Phone: 202-387-6030. Applicants must submit a cover letter, resume, writing sample (4-5 pages, maximum). Applications are accepted continuously. World Wide Web: http://www.cfpa.org.

CENTER FOR THE STUDY OF CONFLICT, INC.
5846 Bellona Avenue
Baltimore, Maryland 21212

General Information Center that performs research on abstract conflict resolution, applies the findings on how to stop violence at all levels, and distributes the results. Established in 1982. Number of employees: 2. Number of internship applications received each year: 10.
Internships Available ▶ *2 research assistants:* responsibilities include library research, copyediting, writing, fund-raising, and office work, including typing. Candidates should have ability to work independently, computer skills, editing skills, research skills, self-motivation, writing skills. Duration is flexible. Unpaid. Open to college freshmen, college sophomores, college juniors, college seniors, recent college graduates, graduate students, law students, career changers, individuals reentering the workforce. International applications accepted.
Benefits Names of contacts, on-the-job training, willing to act as a professional reference, willing to complete paperwork for educational credit, willing to provide letters of recommendation.
Contact Write or call Dr. Richard Wendell Fogg, Director. Phone: 410-323-7656. Application materials which are obtained by calling or writing. Applications are accepted continuously.

CENTER FOR THE STUDY OF SOCIAL STRUCTURES
2502 Orella Street
Santa Barbara, California 93105-3899

General Information Nonprofit organization working to change the social structure of the American government to form kinder and freer government. It believes that all early childhood and college education should be free; drugs should be decriminalized and heavily taxed; and less money should be spent on the military. Established in 1981.
Internships Available ▶ *Interns/volunteers:* responsibilities include duties as listed on the Web site. Duration is flexible. Unpaid. Open to anyone interested.
Contact Fax or e-mail William B. Hackett, Director/Founder, 2502 Orella Street, Santa Barbara, California 93105-3899. Fax: 805-687-0082. E-mail: center@rain.org. Applicants must submit a resume, letter explaining how the applicant could contribute to the organization. Applications are accepted continuously. World Wide Web: http://www.rain.org/~center.

CENTER FOR WAR, PEACE, AND THE NEWS MEDIA AT NEW YORK UNIVERSITY
418 Lafayette Street, Suite 554
New York, New York 10003

General Information University-based public policy organization that focuses on improving press coverage of international political and security affairs. Established in 1985. Number of employees: 45. Number of internship applications received each year: 40.
Internships Available ▶ *3–5 interns:* responsibilities include library research, collecting and analyzing academic articles, creating clipping files, maintaining and developing outreach programs, and general administrative duties. Candidates should have ability to work independently, ability to work with others, oral communication skills, organizational skills, self-motivation. Duration is 1 semester. Unpaid. Open to college sophomores, college juniors, college seniors, recent college graduates, graduate students. International applications accepted.
Benefits Names of contacts, willing to complete paperwork for educational credit, willing to provide letters of recommendation, stipends for transportation.
Contact Write or e-mail Internship Coordinator, 418 Lafayette Street, Sutie 554, New York, New York 10003. E-mail: war.peace.news@nyu.edu. No phone calls. In-person interview required. Applicants must submit a cover letter, resume, writing sample. Applications are accepted continuously.

CHAMBER OF COMMERCE OF THE UNITED STATES
1615 H Street, NW
Washington, District of Columbia 20062

General Information Business federation dedicated to advancing human progress through an economic, political, and social system based on individual freedom, incentive, initiative, opportunity, and responsibility. Established in 1912. Number of employees: 350. Number of internship applications received each year: 200.

Internships Available ▶ *GAIN/Grassroots Action interns:* responsibilities include conducting candidate research, issue research and tracking; writing; editing; marketing; handling meeting planning; Internet promotion and logistics. Duration is flexible. ▶ *Accounting interns:* responsibilities include conducting financial analysis and reporting; recording receivables and payables. Duration is flexible. ▶ *Art interns:* responsibilities include producing commercial art, layout, and design for magazine. Duration is flexible. ▶ *Congressional affairs, international interns:* responsibilities include tracking regulations, legislation, and political activities; attending congressional hearings and task force meetings. Duration is flexible. ▶ *Domestic policy interns:* responsibilities include completing business/government policy projects related to employee relations issues, legal and regulatory affairs matters, and small business practices. Duration is flexible. ▶ *Human resources interns:* responsibilities include assisting with recruiting, testing, and employment procedures. Duration is flexible. ▶ *Magazine marketing interns:* responsibilities include preparing media kits, conducting market research, handling ancillary product fulfillment, and writing press releases. ▶ *Media relations interns:* responsibilities include preparing news releases, arranging and attending press sessions, arranging interviews, and researching press coverage. Duration is flexible. ▶ *Membership interns:* responsibilities include conducting market research, writing, editing, and fund-raising. Duration is flexible. ▶ *Planning and marketing interns:* responsibilities include researching and writing for variety of publications associated with international issues, economic policy, legislation, and regulations. Duration is flexible. ▶ *Publishing interns:* responsibilities include marketing; conducting research; assisting with strategic planning, membership, and sales promotion writing. Duration is flexible. All positions are unpaid. International applications accepted.

Benefits Possible full-time employment, willing to provide letters of recommendation, allowance for local transportation costs.

Contact Write or fax Robert Brown, Internship Coordinator. Fax: 202-463-5799. Applicants must submit a cover letter, resume, writing sample. Application deadline: March 31 for summer, May 31 for fall, November 30 for winter/spring. World Wide Web: http://www.uschamber.org.

CHICAGO FOUNDATION FOR WOMEN
230 West Superior, Suite 400
Chicago, Illinois 60610-3536

General Information Foundation dedicated to increasing resources and opportunities for women and girls; the Foundation has awarded over $4 million to hundreds of programs serving women and girls in the greater Chicago area. Established in 1985. Number of employees: 18. Number of internship applications received each year: 50.

Internships Available ▶ *1 Jessica Eve Patt intern:* responsibilities include assisting with special projects and administrative support in development department, interacting with leaders in women's philanthropic and social service advocacy community. Duration is 12–24 months. $8 per hour. Open to high school students, high school seniors, recent high school graduates, college freshmen, college sophomores, college juniors, college seniors, recent college graduates, graduate students, law students, career changers, individuals reentering the workforce. International applications accepted.

Benefits Names of contacts, opportunity to attend seminars/workshops, possible full-time employment, travel reimbursement, willing to complete paperwork for educational credit, willing to provide letters of recommendation.

Contact Write or fax Candace Anderson, Internship Coordinator, 230 West Superior, Suite 400, Chicago, Illinois 60610-3636. Fax: 312-266-0990. No phone calls. In-person interview required. Applicants must submit a cover letter, resume. Applications are accepted continuously.

CHILDREN'S DEFENSE FUND
25 E Street, NW
Washington, District of Columbia 20001

General Information Advocacy organization that exists to provide a strong voice for children. Goals are achieved by educating the public about children's needs and encouraging preventive investment in children before they get sick, get into trouble, drop out of school, or suffer from family breakdown. Established in 1969. Number of employees: 110. Number of internship applications received each year: 450.

Internships Available ▶ *60–100 interns:* responsibilities include duties from general office tasks to extensive researching and writing. Candidates should have ability to work with others, computer skills, office skills, organizational skills, personal interest in the field, flexibility. Duration is varied. Unpaid. Open to high school students, high school seniors, recent high school graduates, college freshmen, college sophomores, college juniors, college seniors, recent college graduates, graduate students, law students, career changers, individuals reentering the workforce.

Benefits Travel reimbursement, willing to complete paperwork for educational credit.

Contact Write or e-mail Herman Piper, Office of Interns and Volunteers. E-mail: hpiper@childrensdefense.org. Applicants must submit a formal organization application. Applications are accepted continuously. World Wide Web: http://www.childrensdefense.org.

CITIZENS FOR A SOUND ECONOMY AND CSE FOUNDATION
1250 H Street, NW, Suite 700
Washington, District of Columbia 20005

General Information Organization working to educate and mobilize citizens to promote market-based solutions for public policy issues such as tax and budget policy, trade policy, and regulatory policy. Established in 1984. Number of employees: 70. Number of internship applications received each year: 200.

Internships Available ▶ *1 development intern:* responsibilities include writing and researching. Candidates should have office skills, oral communication skills, personal interest in the field, writing skills, written communication skills. Duration is flexible. Open to college freshmen, college sophomores, college juniors, college seniors. ▶ *3 grassroots interns:* responsibilities include mobilizing citizens at grassroots level and communicating with volunteers. Candidates should have college courses in field, computer skills, experience in the field, office skills, oral communication skills, personal interest in the field, strong interpersonal skills. Duration is May to September, daily schedule can be flexible. Open to college juniors, college seniors, recent college graduates, graduate students. ▶ *1 policy tax and budget intern:* responsibilities include writing and researching. Candidates should have college courses in field, oral communication skills, personal interest in the field, research skills, self-motivation, written communication skills. Duration is flexible. Open to college freshmen, college sophomores, college juniors, college seniors. ▶ *1 policy trade intern:* responsibilities include writing, researching, and attending hearings. Candidates should have knowledge of field, oral communication skills, research skills, self-motivation, writing skills. Duration is flexible. Open to college freshmen, college sophomores, college juniors, college seniors. ▶ *1 public relations intern:* responsibilities include assisting with press conferences, special events, op-ed and article placement, and event follow-up. Candidates should have oral communication skills, personal interest in the field, self-motivation, strong interpersonal skills, writing skills. Duration is flexible. Open to college freshmen, college sophomores, college juniors, college seniors. ▶ *1 regulatory intern:* responsibilities include writing, researching, and attending hearings on regulatory issues. Candidates should have

editing skills, knowledge of field, oral communication skills, personal interest in the field, research skills, self-motivation, written communication skills. Duration is flexible. Open to college freshmen, college sophomores, college juniors, college seniors. All positions are unpaid. International applications accepted.
Benefits Opportunity to attend seminars/workshops, willing to complete paperwork for educational credit, willing to provide letters of recommendation.
Contact Write, call, fax, or e-mail Lila Chan, Intern Coordinator. Phone: 202-783-3870. Fax: 202-783-4687. E-mail: chan@cse.org. In-person interview recommended. Applicants must submit a cover letter, resume, writing sample, letter of recommendation. Applications are accepted continuously. World Wide Web: http://www.cse.org.

CITIZENS FOR TAX JUSTICE
1311 L Street, NW
Washington, District of Columbia 20005

General Information Research and advocacy organization. Established in 1979. Number of employees: 9. Number of internship applications received each year: 40.
Internships Available ▶ *3 research interns:* responsibilities include research, writing, representing organization at coalition meetings. Candidates should have analytical skills, computer skills, editing skills, knowledge of field, office skills, oral communication skills, organizational skills, personal interest in the field, research skills, self-motivation, strong interpersonal skills, strong leadership ability, writing skills. $210 per week. Open to recent high school graduates, college freshmen, college sophomores, college juniors, college seniors, recent college graduates, graduate students, law students. International applications accepted.
Benefits Names of contacts, opportunity to attend seminars/workshops, possible full-time employment, willing to act as a professional reference, willing to complete paperwork for educational credit, willing to provide letters of recommendation.
Contact Write, fax, or e-mail Tyson Slocum, Policy Analyst, 1311 L Street, NW, Washington, District of Columbia 20005. Fax: 202-638-3486. E-mail: tslocum@ctj.org. No phone calls. Telephone interview required. Applicants must submit a cover letter, resume, writing sample, three personal references. Applications are accepted continuously. World Wide Web: http://www.ctj.org.

CITIZENS' NETWORK FOR FOREIGN AFFAIRS
1111 19th Street, NW, Suite 900
Washington, District of Columbia 20036

General Information Nonprofit organization working to inform U.S. citizens of America's role in the developing world. Established in 1986. Number of employees: 16. Number of internship applications received each year: 500.
Internships Available ▶ *4 interns:* responsibilities include administrative duties and researching, attending, and reporting on meetings. Candidates should have ability to work independently, computer skills, knowledge of field, research skills, self-motivation, written communication skills. Duration is flexible. $1,000 per month. Open to college juniors, college seniors, recent college graduates. International applications accepted.
Benefits Formal training, job counseling, names of contacts, on-the-job training, opportunity to attend seminars/workshops, possible full-time employment, willing to complete paperwork for educational credit, willing to provide letters of recommendation.
Contact Write, call, fax, or e-mail Mr. Jack W. Swartwood, Director of Operations. Phone: 202-296-3920. Fax: 202-296-3948. E-mail: intern@cnfa.org. Applicants must submit a cover letter, resume, writing sample. Application deadline: March 15 for summer, July 15 for fall, November 15 for spring. World Wide Web: http://www.cnfa.com.

COMMITTEE FOR A UNIFIED INDEPENDENT PARTY
225 Broadway, Suite 2010
New York, New York 10007

General Information Founded to promote democratic reform and growth of independent politics, this organization has developed a successful model of youth voter registration and education, so that young people can enter the political process as full participants. Established in 1994. Number of employees: 3. Number of internship applications received each year: 10.
Internships Available ▶ *4–10 assistant field organizers:* responsibilities include voter outreach campaigns that include youth-oriented voter registration and education drives, field organizing, and administrative support. Candidates should have ability to work with others, office skills, oral communication skills, written communication skills. Duration is 2–6 months. Open to high school students, high school seniors, recent high school graduates, college freshmen, college sophomores, college juniors, college seniors, law students. ▶ *1–2 nonprofit development assistants:* responsibilities include learning nuts and bolts of fund-raising for election reform, advocacy organization, direct mailing, fund-raising, prospecting, donor relations, campaign development, and systems management. Candidates should have ability to work independently, office skills, oral communication skills, strong interpersonal skills, writing skills, course work in finance or management helpful. Duration is 3–6 months. Open to recent high school graduates, college freshmen, college sophomores, college juniors, college seniors, recent college graduates, graduate students, law students, career changers. ▶ *1–3 political research assistants:* responsibilities include political research, communications, administrative support. Candidates should have ability to work independently, computer skills, office skills, oral communication skills, organizational skills, research skills, self-motivation, strong interpersonal skills, strong leadership ability, writing skills. Duration is 3–6 months. Open to high school seniors, college freshmen, college sophomores, college juniors, college seniors, recent college graduates, graduate students, law students. ▶ *2–4 public relations specialists:* responsibilities include participating in designated projects and providing administrative support, such as maintaining press files, following up on press releases, creating media lists, assisting with outreach campaigns; researching new media trends, and electronically distributing advisory press releases. Candidates should have ability to work with others, computer skills, office skills, oral communication skills, personal interest in the field, written communication skills. Duration is 3–6 months. Open to high school seniors, recent high school graduates, college freshmen, college sophomores, college juniors, college seniors, recent college graduates, individuals reentering the workforce. All positions are unpaid. International applications accepted.
Benefits Opportunity to attend seminars/workshops, willing to act as a professional reference, willing to complete paperwork for educational credit, willing to provide letters of recommendation.
Contact Write, call, fax, or e-mail Sarah Lyons, Manager of Media and Public Relations, 225 Broadway Suite 2010, New York, New York 10007. Phone: 212-803-1880. Fax: 212-803-1899. E-mail: slyons@cuip.org. In-person interview required. Applicants must submit a cover letter. Applications are accepted continuously. World Wide Web: http://www.cuip.org.

COMMON CAUSE
1250 Connecticut Avenue, NW
Washington, District of Columbia 20036

General Information Nonprofit, nonpartisan citizens' campaign finance reform lobbying group working to promote honesty, accountability, and ethics in government. Established in 1970. Number of employees: 40. Number of internship applications received each year: 150.
Internships Available ▶ *1 campaign finance research intern:* responsibilities include helping staff collect and analyze reports of political contributions to candidates and political parties, and gathering research materials regarding PACs and other large political donors. Candidates should have ability to work

Common Cause (continued)

independently, computer skills, knowledge of field, organizational skills, research skills, self-motivation. Open to college freshmen, college sophomores, college juniors, college seniors, recent college graduates, graduate students. ▶ *20–25 grassroots interns:* responsibilities include organizing grassroots effort. Candidates should have oral communication skills, strong interpersonal skills. Open to high school students, high school seniors, recent high school graduates, college freshmen, college sophomores, college juniors, college seniors, recent college graduates, graduate students, law students. ▶ *1 issue mail intern:* responsibilities include issuing mail correspondence and assisting the governing board representative. Candidates should have ability to work independently, computer skills, editing skills, oral communication skills, writing skills. Open to college freshmen, college sophomores, college juniors, college seniors, recent college graduates, graduate students. ▶ *2–3 legislative policy interns:* responsibilities include assisting lobbying staff and researching issues development. Candidates should have analytical skills, computer skills, oral communication skills, organizational skills, strong interpersonal skills, written communication skills. Open to college freshmen, college sophomores, college juniors, college seniors, recent college graduates, graduate students, law students. ▶ *2 media communication interns:* responsibilities include assisting in producing, proofing, and editing press releases; booking radio talk shows; answering requests for information. Candidates should have editing skills, oral communication skills, personal interest in the field, strong interpersonal skills. Open to college freshmen, college sophomores, college juniors, college seniors, recent college graduates, graduate students. ▶ *1 membership and fund-raising intern:* responsibilities include assisting membership/fund-raising staff. Candidates should have ability to work with others, office skills, oral communication skills, personal interest in the field. Open to college freshmen, college sophomores, college juniors, college seniors, recent college graduates, graduate students. All positions are unpaid. International applications accepted.
Benefits Job counseling, opportunity to attend seminars/workshops, willing to act as a professional reference, willing to complete paperwork for educational credit, willing to provide letters of recommendation, daily travel expenses paid.
Contact Write, call, fax, or e-mail Chad Ramsey, Washington Connection Coordinator. Phone: 202-833-1200. Fax: 202-659-3716. E-mail: cramsey@commoncause.org. Applicants must submit a formal organization application, writing sample. Applications are accepted continuously. World Wide Web: http://www.commoncause.org.

COMMUNITY NUTRITION INSTITUTE (CNI)
910 17th Street NW, Suite 413
Washington, District of Columbia 20006

General Information Nonprofit advocacy organization specializing in public policy regarding food safety and the Federal Food Assistance Programs.
Internships Available ▶ *1 intern:* responsibilities include writing for newsletter and attending press conferences and hearings; keeping in touch with grass roots and nonprofit alliance of organizations; reporting on federal nutrition policy. Duration is 1 summer or 1-2 semesters. Unpaid. Open to college freshmen, college sophomores, college juniors, college seniors, recent college graduates.
Benefits Travel reimbursement, willing to complete paperwork for educational credit.
Contact Write, call, fax, or e-mail Editor. Phone: 202-776-0595. Fax: 202-776-0599. E-mail: cni@unidial.com. Applicants must submit a cover letter, resume, writing sample. Applications are accepted continuously.

THE CONGRESSIONAL HUNGER CENTER
229½ Pennsylvania Avenue
Washington, District of Columbia 20003

General Information Nonprofit organization that fights hunger by developing leaders. Affiliate of Americorps Vista.

Internships Available ▶ *20 Mickey Leland Hunger fellows:* responsibilities include working for a grassroots antihunger organization (6 months) and then a national nonprofit, specialing in hunger/poverty policy (6 months). Duration is 1 year. Paid. ▶ *Interns:* responsibilities include working on one of several projects, depending on the intern's interests. Duration is flexible. Position available as unpaid or paid. Open to individuals 18 years of age or older.
Benefits Health insurance.
Contact Write, call, fax, or e-mail Amanda Harrod, Program Director, Mickey Leland Hunger Fellows Program, 229½ Pennsylvania Avenue, SE, Washington, District of Columbia 20003. Phone: 202-547-7022 Ext. 17. Fax: 202-547-7575. E-mail: nohungr@aol.com. Applicants must submit a resume, formal application on Web site. Application deadline: January 30. World Wide Web: http://www.hungercenter.org.

THE CONSERVATIVE CAUCUS, INC.
450 Maple Avenue East, Suite 309
Vienna, Virginia 22180

General Information Organization dedicated to grassroots lobbying for conservative policies at the federal level. Established in 1974. Number of employees: 25. Number of internship applications received each year: 10.
Internships Available ▶ *1–2 interns:* responsibilities include researching government documents, helping set up press conferences, or working on petitions. Candidates should have ability to work independently, office skills, personal interest in the field, research skills, written communication skills. Duration is flexible. Unpaid. Open to high school students, high school seniors, recent high school graduates, college freshmen, college sophomores, college juniors, college seniors, recent college graduates, graduate students, law students, career changers, individuals reentering the workforce. International applications accepted.
Benefits Names of contacts, opportunity to attend seminars/workshops, possible full-time employment, willing to complete paperwork for educational credit, willing to provide letters of recommendation.
Contact Write Mr. Charles Orndorff, Administrative Vice Chairman. Applicants must submit a formal organization application, resume, personal reference. Application deadline: March 15 for summer, July 15 for fall, October 15 for winter. World Wide Web: http://www.conservativeusa.org.

CONSUMER ENERGY COUNCIL OF AMERICA RESEARCH FOUNDATION
2000 L Street, NW, Suite 802
Washington, District of Columbia 20036

General Information Research and policy organization that promotes consumer interests in policy issues, conducts research, and builds coalitions between public and private sectors; issues include utility industry restructuring, telecommunications policy, pricing policies; publishes The Quad Report, a monthly newsletter that focuses on demand-side management, energy efficiency, and energy policy. Established in 1973. Number of employees: 5. Number of internship applications received each year: 200.
Internships Available ▶ *2–5 research assistants:* responsibilities include researching policies, drafting letters, tracking legislation, reviewing literature, compiling and analyzing data, preparing tables and charts, editing, proofreading, assisting in drafting proposals and general office work, and assisting in project development. Candidates should have ability to work independently, analytical skills, computer skills, editing skills, office skills, oral communication skills, organizational skills, research skills, self-motivation, strong interpersonal skills, strong leadership ability, writing skills. Duration is flexible. Position available as unpaid or paid. Open to college sophomores, college juniors, college seniors, recent college graduates, graduate students. International applications accepted.
Benefits Job counseling, names of contacts, on-the-job training, opportunity to attend seminars/workshops, possible full-time employment, travel reimbursement, willing to act as a

professional reference, willing to complete paperwork for educational credit, willing to provide letters of recommendation, stipends may be available based on project funding.
Contact Write, fax, or e-mail Ellen Berman, President. Fax: 202-659-0407. E-mail: cecarf@hotmail.com. No phone calls. In-person interview recommended. Applicants must submit a cover letter, resume, academic transcripts or GPA, 3 in-depth writing samples, 3 letters of recommendation from professors or employers. Applications are accepted continuously. World Wide Web: http://www.cecarf.org.

CONSUMER FEDERATION OF AMERICA
1424 16th Street, NW, Suite 604
Washington, District of Columbia 20036

General Information Nonprofit public interest organization seeking to advocate the consumer interest in the areas of product safety, telecommunications, protection against consumer scams, advertising, insurance, real estate, banking, health care, and utility deregulation before Congress, federal regulatory agencies, and the courts. Established in 1967. Number of employees: 15. Number of internship applications received each year: 50.
Internships Available ▶ *6 general interns:* responsibilities include research, working on legislation, attending occasional coalition meetings and briefings on Capitol Hill, as well as working with regulatory agencies. Candidates should have office skills, organizational skills, personal interest in the field, research skills. Duration is 1 semester. $25 weekly stipend for undergraduates working full-time, $50 weekly stipend for graduates and law students working full-time. Open to college freshmen, college sophomores, college juniors, college seniors, recent college graduates, graduate students, law students. International applications accepted.
Benefits Names of contacts, opportunity to attend seminars/workshops, travel reimbursement, willing to act as a professional reference, willing to complete paperwork for educational credit, willing to provide letters of recommendation.
Contact Write or call Ms. Jackie Balser, Director of Administration. Phone: 202-387-6121. Applicants must submit a cover letter, resume, writing sample. Applications are accepted continuously. World Wide Web: http://www.consumerfed.org.

CONSUMERS FOR WORLD TRADE
2000 L Street, NW, Suite 200
Washington, District of Columbia 20036

General Information Association that advocates for freer trade policy and educates the American public about trade's effects on consumers. Established in 1978. Number of employees: 2. Number of internship applications received each year: 50.
Internships Available ▶ *1 Students for World Trade coordinator:* responsibilities include working with Students for World Trade, assisting with discussion materials (writing/distributing), arranging meetings, and assisting with member drives. Candidates should have computer skills, oral communication skills, self-motivation, strong interpersonal skills, strong leadership ability. Duration is 2–9 months. $2,000 per duration of internship. Open to college sophomores, college juniors, college seniors. ▶ *2–4 legislative fellows:* responsibilities include assisting in the areas of fund-raising, publications, membership development, research, editing, and administration. Candidates should have ability to work with others, analytical skills, computer skills, personal interest in the field, research skills, written communication skills. Duration is 2–12 months. Unpaid. Open to college freshmen, college sophomores, college juniors, college seniors, graduate students. International applications accepted.
Benefits Names of contacts, opportunity to attend seminars/workshops, willing to act as a professional reference, willing to complete paperwork for educational credit, willing to provide letters of recommendation, opportunity to attend U.S. Committees and trade hearings.
Contact Write, fax, or e-mail Intern Coordinator. Fax: 202-416-1734. E-mail: interns@cwt.org. Applicants must submit a cover letter, resume, writing sample, interview (either in-person or telephone). Applications are accepted continuously. World Wide Web: http://www.cwt.org.

CORO SOUTHERN CALIFORNIA
811 Wilshire Boulevard, Suite 1025
Los Angeles, California 90017-2624

General Information Conducts research, education, and training in public affairs; participants' learning comes from their experiences in field assignments, interviews, and projects with diverse organizations. Established in 1942. Number of employees: 12. Affiliate of The Coro Foundation, Berkeley, California. Number of internship applications received each year: 100.
Internships Available ▶ *12 Coro program in public affairs fellows:* responsibilities include working a minimum of 1600 hours over 9.5 months in 6 field assignments of public affairs (government, business, labor unions, non-profit, media, and political campaigns); dozens of group interviews, 2 projects, 2-3 three-day retreats, and bi-weekly seminars. Candidates should have ability to work independently, analytical skills, computer skills, editing skills, office skills, oral communication skills, organizational skills, personal interest in the field, research skills, self-motivation, strong interpersonal skills, strong leadership ability, writing skills. Duration is September-June. Position available as unpaid or paid. Open to college seniors, recent college graduates, graduate students, law students, career changers, individuals reentering the workforce. International applications accepted.
Benefits Formal training, names of contacts, on-the-job training, opportunity to attend seminars/workshops, possible full-time employment, willing to act as a professional reference, willing to complete paperwork for educational credit, willing to provide letters of recommendation, monthly stipends available based on financial need (ranging from $400-$1500).
Contact Write, call, fax, or e-mail Larry Labrado, Program Manager, 811 Wilshire Boulevard, Suite 1025, Los Angeles, California 90017-2624. Phone: 213-623-1234 Ext. 15. Fax: 213-680-0079. E-mail: llabrado@coro.org. In-person interview required. Applicants must submit a formal organization application, academic transcripts, two writing samples, four letters of recommendation, all finalists must participate in a selection event in late March/early April. Application deadline: February 1. Fees: $50. World Wide Web: http://www.coro.org.

COUNCIL FOR A LIVABLE WORLD
110 Maryland Avenue, NE, Suite 409
Washington, District of Columbia 20002

General Information Organization founded by Leo Szilard and other pioneers of nuclear weapons to stop the nuclear arms race. Has prepared an agenda for action advocating the reduction of danger posed by weapons of mass destruction , the strengthening and reform of multilateral conflict resolution and peacekeeping, and the revision of the military budget to meet current circumstances. Established in 1980. Number of employees: 14. Number of internship applications received each year: 90.
Internships Available ▶ *Coalition to Reduce Nuclear Dangers interns.* Candidates should have computer skills, oral communication skills, personal interest in the field, research skills, self-motivation, written communication skills. Duration is 3 months. $500 per month. Open to college juniors, college seniors, recent college graduates, graduate students. ▶ *2 interns:* responsibilities include assisting with research, writing factsheets, networking at meetings, attending debates, and sharing daily administrative duties. Candidates should have ability to work independently, analytical skills, computer skills, editing skills, knowledge of field, office skills, personal interest in the field, self-motivation, written communication skills. Duration is flexible. Position available as unpaid or paid. Open to college sophomores, college juniors, college seniors, recent college graduates, graduate students, law students, career changers, individuals reentering the workforce. International applications accepted.
Benefits Job counseling, opportunity to attend seminars/workshops, travel reimbursement, willing to complete paperwork for educational credit, willing to provide letters of recommendation.

Council for a Livable World (continued)

Contact Write, call, fax, or e-mail Paul Revsine, Intern Coordinator. Phone: 202-543-4100. Fax: 202-543-6297. E-mail: clw@clw.org. In-person interview recommended. Applicants must submit a cover letter, resume, writing sample, two letters of recommendation. Application deadline: February 15 for summer positions, continuous for others. World Wide Web: http://www.clw.org/clw/intern.html.

COUNCIL FOR URBAN ECONOMIC DEVELOPMENT
1730 K Street, NW, Suite 700
Washington, District of Columbia 20006

General Information Nonprofit membership association that serves public and private sector practitioners in economic development and provides information to its members to help improve local economies. Established in 1967. Number of employees: 30. Number of internship applications received each year: 25.
Internships Available ▶ *5–8 interns:* responsibilities include assisting with research project on urban economic-related topics, tracking legislation, writing newsletter articles, and completing survey analyses. Candidates should have ability to work independently, editing skills, organizational skills, plan to pursue career in field, research skills, writing skills. Duration is flexible (minimum commitment of 2 months). $800–$1,000 per month. Open to college juniors, college seniors, recent college graduates, graduate students, Ph.D. candidates. International applications accepted.
Benefits Names of contacts, on-the-job training, opportunity to attend seminars/workshops, possible full-time employment, willing to act as a professional reference, willing to complete paperwork for educational credit, willing to provide letters of recommendation, practical work experience, opportunity to have work published.
Contact Write or e-mail Courtney Anderson, Economic Development Analyst. E-mail: canderson@urbandevelopment.com. Applicants must submit a cover letter, resume, writing sample. Application deadline: second week of March for summer. World Wide Web: http://www.cued.org.

COUNCIL ON ECONOMIC PRIORITIES
30 Irving Place
New York, New York 10003

General Information Public interest organization that monitors and reports on corporate social responsibility in order to improve social and environmental performance. Established in 1969. Number of employees: 19. Number of internship applications received each year: 200.
Internships Available ▶ *Corporate accountability and environmental research interns:* responsibilities include research, data entry, report writing, and some clerical duties. ▶ *1 international security research intern (London):* responsibilities include research, data entry, and some clerical duties. ▶ *Marketing/public relations interns:* responsibilities include writing letters and press releases, generating lists for book sales, and phone work. Duration for all positions is 10 weeks. All positions available as unpaid or paid. Open to high school seniors, college freshmen, college sophomores, college juniors, college seniors, graduate students.
Benefits Job counseling, opportunity to attend seminars/workshops, possible full-time employment, willing to complete paperwork for educational credit, willing to provide letters of recommendation, college work-study credit.
International Internships Available in London, United Kingdom.
Contact Write, fax, or e-mail Mr. Tom Knowlton, Chief Operating Officer. Fax: 212-420-0988. E-mail: ksmith@cepnyc.org. No phone calls. In-person interview recommended. Applicants must submit a resume, academic transcripts, writing sample. Application deadline: March 15. World Wide Web: http://www.cepnyc.org.

THE DEVELOPMENT GAP
927 15th Street
Washington, District of Columbia 20005

General Information Organization that works for grassroots input into economic policymaking, and organizes opposition to imposition of economic policy from Washington. Established in 1977. Number of employees: 7. Number of internship applications received each year: 60.
Internships Available ▶ *4–8 interns:* responsibilities include conducting research and writing reports on the impact of World Bank/IMF programs; assisting with organizing events. Candidates should have experience in the field, oral communication skills, personal interest in the field, research skills, self-motivation, written communication skills. Duration is flexible. Unpaid. Open to recent college graduates, graduate students, career changers. International applications accepted.
Benefits Names of contacts, on-the-job training, opportunity to attend seminars/workshops, willing to act as a professional reference, willing to complete paperwork for educational credit, willing to provide letters of recommendation, reimbursement of local transportation expenses.
Contact Write, fax, or e-mail Tony Avirgan, Communications Coordinator. Fax: 202-898-1612. E-mail: dgap@ige.org. In-person interview recommended. Applicants must submit a cover letter, resume, academic transcripts, writing sample. Applications are accepted continuously. World Wide Web: http://www.igc.org/dgap.

FAMILIES U.S.A. FOUNDATION
1334 G Street, NW, 3rd Floor
Washington, District of Columbia 20005

General Information National health-care consumer advocacy organization engaged in the fight for affordable health and long-term care for all American families in areas including policy research, field organizing, lobbying, and media operations. Established in 1982. Number of employees: 30. Number of internship applications received each year: 300.
Internships Available ▶ *1 field Internet intern:* responsibilities include working with more than 200 state and local organizations that are involved in consumer health issues, helping provide a wide array of technical assistance to these groups on issues such as Medicaid and managed care, and using innovative on-line and teleconferencing techniques to communicate with these groups. Candidates should have ability to work independently, ability to work with others, computer skills, knowledge of field, office skills, written communication skills. Open to college juniors, college seniors, recent college graduates, graduate students, law students, individuals reentering the workforce. ▶ *1 field organizing intern:* responsibilities include working with more than 200 state and local organizations that are involved in consumer health issues, helping provide a wide array of tachnical assistance to these groups on issues such as Medicaid and managed care, and using innovative on-line and teleconferencing techniques to communicate with these groups. Candidates should have ability to work independently, oral communication skills, organizational skills, personal interest in the field, self-motivation, written communication skills. Open to college juniors, college seniors, recent college graduates, graduate students, law students, individuals reentering the workforce. ▶ *1 government affairs intern:* responsibilities include attending and reporting on hearings related to health-care reform and income security issues for seniors, possibly accompanying lobbyists on Congressional visits, writing issue briefs, helping with mass mailings. Candidates should have ability to work independently, analytical skills, oral communication skills, organizational skills, self-motivation, written communication skills. Open to college seniors, recent college graduates, graduate students, law students. ▶ *2 health policy interns:* responsibilities include engaging in health policy research on issues such as consumer protections in managed care, the devolution of federal health programs such as Medicare and Medicaid, access and affordability issues, and analysis of federal and state health care legislation. Candidates should have ability to work independently, editing skills, personal interest in the

field, research skills, self-motivation, written communication skills. Open to college seniors, recent college graduates, graduate students. ▶ *1 media intern:* responsibilities include contacting media, interviewing individuals with health care stories, helping with media events, and monitoring media. Candidates should have ability to work independently, oral communication skills, organizational skills, personal interest in the field, strong interpersonal skills, written communication skills. Open to college sophomores, college juniors, college seniors, recent college graduates, career changers, individuals reentering the workforce. Duration for all positions is one semester (possibly longer if internship successful). All positions paid at $6 per hour. International applications accepted.
Benefits On-the-job training, opportunity to attend seminars/workshops, willing to act as a professional reference, willing to complete paperwork for educational credit, willing to provide letters of recommendation.
Contact Write, fax, or e-mail Nefretiri Cooley, Internship Program Coordinator, 1334 G Street, NW, 3rd Floor, Washington, District of Columbia 20005. Fax: 202-347-2417. E-mail: intern@familiesusa. org. No phone calls. Telephone interview required. Applicants must submit a cover letter, resume, three personal references, writing sample (3-5 pages). Application deadline: March 15 for summer, June 30 for fall, October 15 for winter/spring. World Wide Web: http://www.familiesusa.org.

FARM SANCTUARY–WEST
19080 Newville Road
Orland, California 95963

General Information National nonprofit organization dedicated to ending animal agricultural abuses through public education programs, legislation, farm animal cruelty investigations, and campaigns, in addition to providing shelters for rescuing, rehabilitating, and caring directly for animals. Established in 1993. Number of employees: 6. Branch of Farm Sanctuary, Watkins Glen, New York. Number of internship applications received each year: 200.
Internships Available ▶ *Interns:* responsibilities include basic animal and barn maintenance, office work, and conducting educational tours. Candidates should have ability to work with others, personal interest in the field, self-motivation, commitment to vegetarianism. Duration is 1–3 months. Unpaid. Open to high school students, high school seniors, recent high school graduates, college freshmen, college sophomores, college juniors, college seniors, recent college graduates, graduate students, law students, career changers, individuals reentering the workforce. International applications accepted.
Benefits Free housing, job counseling, names of contacts, possible full-time employment, willing to complete paperwork for educational credit, willing to provide letters of recommendation.
Contact Write, call, fax, or e-mail Intern Coordinator, PO Box 150, Watkins Glen, New York 14891. Phone: 607-583-2225. Fax: 607-583-2041. E-mail: educate@farmsanctuary.org. Telephone interview required. Applicants must submit a formal organization application. Applications are accepted continuously. World Wide Web: http://www.farmsanctuary.org.

FEDERALLY EMPLOYED WOMEN
1400 Eye Street, NW, Suite 425
Washington, District of Columbia 20005

General Information Nonprofit, nonpartisan international membership organization representing more than 1 million women employed by the federal government and the U.S. Military; attempts to eliminate sexual harassment and discrimination and enhance career opportunities for women in government. Established in 1968. Number of employees: 6. Number of internship applications received each year: 60.
Internships Available ▶ *1 legislative assistant:* responsibilities include researching and monitoring legislative activities, coordinating grassroots lobbying efforts, representing the national organization in coalition campaigns, and developing written communication material for the newsletter. Candidates should have computer skills. Duration is flexible. Unpaid. Open to college freshmen,

college sophomores, college juniors, college seniors, recent college graduates, graduate students. International applications accepted.
Benefits Job counseling, names of contacts, opportunity to attend seminars/workshops, travel reimbursement, willing to complete paperwork for educational credit, willing to provide letters of recommendation.
Contact Write, call, fax, or e-mail Ms. Cheryl Anthony-Epps, Legislative Representative. Phone: 202-898-0994. Fax: 202-898-0998. E-mail: legrep@few.org. In-person interview recommended. Applicants must submit a cover letter, resume. Applications are accepted continuously. World Wide Web: http://www.few.org.

FEDERATION FOR AMERICAN IMMIGRATION REFORM
1666 Connectict Avenue, NW, #400
Washington, District of Columbia 20009

General Information Nonprofit public education organization. Established in 1979. Number of employees: 25. Number of internship applications received each year: 100.
Internships Available ▶ *1 government relations intern:* responsibilities include tracking and analyzing legislation; conducting research; distributing information to Hill staff; assisting with Hill mailings; attending, taking notes, and reporting on Hill committee hearings; filing, faxing, and some general office duties. Candidates should have ability to work independently, knowledge of field, oral communication skills, personal interest in the field, self-motivation, written communication skills. Duration is 12–16 weeks. $7 per hour. Open to college sophomores, college juniors, college seniors, recent college graduates, graduate students, law students. ▶ *1 law intern:* responsibilities include heavy research, primarily in the areas of immigration law, constitutional law and administrative law, writing briefs, editing, and cite checking law review articles. Candidates should have ability to work independently, analytical skills, college courses in field, declared college major in field, organizational skills, written communication skills. Duration is 12-16 weeks during summer. $10 per hour. Open to college sophomores, college juniors, college seniors, recent college graduates, graduate students, law students. ▶ *1 media relations intern:* responsibilities include updating the media database; scheduling radio shows; faxing background material to television radio, and print press; maintaining the video library; attending and helping plan press conferences; filing and writing articles for the newsletter. Candidates should have ability to work independently, college courses in field, oral communication skills, personal interest in the field, self-motivation, written communication skills. Duration is 3–6 months. $7 per hour. Open to college sophomores, college juniors, college seniors, recent college graduates, graduate students, law students. ▶ *1 membership development/fund-raising intern:* responsibilities include coordination and production of 6-month appreciation gift mailings, assisting with round table meeting planning, drafting articles for the monthly newsletter, and assisting with major donor mailings. Candidates should have ability to work independently, office skills, organizational skills, plan to pursue career in field, self-motivation, written communication skills. Duration is 12–16 weeks. $7 per hour. Open to college sophomores, college juniors, college seniors, recent college graduates, graduate students. International applications accepted.
Benefits Job counseling, on-the-job training, opportunity to attend seminars/workshops, possible full-time employment, travel reimbursement, willing to act as a professional reference, willing to complete paperwork for educational credit, willing to provide letters of recommendation.
Contact Write, fax, or e-mail Jennie McAllister, Intern Coordinator. Fax: 202-387-3447. E-mail: fair@fairus.org. In-person interview recommended. Applicants must submit a cover letter, resume, writing sample, 2—3 personal references. Application deadline: April 30 for summer, July 1 for fall; continuous for winter/spring positions. World Wide Web: http://www.fairus.org.

THE FORD FOUNDATION
320 East 43rd Street
New York, New York 10017

General Information Private nonprofit philanthropic institution dedicated to advancing the well-being of people around the world by strengthening democratic values, reducing poverty and injustice, promoting international cooperation, and advancing human achievement. Established in 1936. Number of employees: 400.

Internships Available ▶ *16–20 program assistants:* responsibilities include assisting in program work: monitoring new developments, reviewing proposals, meeting with grantees, preparing related documents, monitoring and closing grants, helping organize meetings, and providing administrative support; researching and writing assignments; team projects. Candidates should have computer skills, experience in the field, research skills, strong leadership ability, writing skills, strong interest in field. Duration is 2 years (full-time). $35,000 per year. Open to individuals with recent master's or law degree (conferred no earlier than September 1998 and no later than August 2000).

Benefits Health insurance, travel reimbursement, vacation, opportunity to learn about world of philanthropy and the not-for-profit sector.

Contact Program Assistantship Program, c/o Office of Human Resources. E-mail: pgmast@fordfound.org. No phone calls. In-person interview required. Applicants must submit a formal organization application, academic transcripts, personal reference, letter of recommendation, essays as specified in application (posted on Web site). Application deadline: December for September, 2000. World Wide Web: http://www.fordfound.org.

FRIENDS COMMITTEE ON NATIONAL LEGISLATION
245 Second Street, NE
Washington, District of Columbia 20002

General Information Lobbying organization guided by Quaker religious beliefs that attempts to bring spiritual values to public policy decisions. Established in 1943. Number of employees: 22. Number of internship applications received each year: 30.

Internships Available ▶ *3 legislative interns:* responsibilities include attending coalition meetings, answering constituent phone calls and letters, contributing to FCNL's newsletter, writing issue papers, drafting documents and letters for legislative advocacy, preparing FCNL's weekly legislative action message, and performing general administrative work. Candidates should have ability to work independently, analytical skills, computer skills, editing skills, office skills, oral communication skills, organizational skills, personal interest in the field, research skills, self-motivation, strong interpersonal skills, writing skills. Duration is 11 months. $1,100 per month. Open to recent college graduates, graduate students, law students. International applications accepted.

Benefits Health insurance, on-the-job training, opportunity to attend seminars/workshops, possible full-time employment, willing to act as a professional reference, willing to complete paperwork for educational credit, willing to provide letters of recommendation.

Contact Write, fax, or e-mail Internship Coordinator. Fax: 202-547-6019. E-mail: fcnl@fcnl.org. No phone calls. Telephone interview required. Applicants must submit a formal organization application, academic transcripts, four personal references. Application deadline: applicants for September through July position must apply between January 1 and March 1. World Wide Web: http://www.fcnl.org.

FRIENDS FOR A NON-VIOLENT WORLD
1929 South 5th Street
Minneapolis, Minnesota 55454

General Information Organization that provides education about non-violence and peacemaking. Established in 1981. Number of employees: 3. Number of internship applications received each year: 15.

Internships Available ▶ *2 summer interns:* responsibilities include coordinating one major project such as organizing our week-long summer camp; office work; participation in study group. Candidates should have knowledge of field, office skills, organizational skills, self-motivation, strong interpersonal skills, passion for non-violence. Duration is June 15-August 30. $1,475 per duration of internship. Open to college freshmen, college sophomores, college juniors, college seniors, recent college graduates, graduate students, law students, career changers, individuals reentering the workforce. International applications accepted.

Benefits Formal training, on-the-job training, opportunity to attend seminars/workshops, willing to act as a professional reference, willing to complete paperwork for educational credit, willing to provide letters of recommendation, support from mentors.

Contact Write, call, fax, or e-mail Michael Bischoff, Executive Director, 1929 South 5th Street, Minneapolis, Minnesota 55454. Phone: 612-321-9787. Fax: 612-321-9788. E-mail: fnvw@mm.com. Applicants must submit a cover letter, resume, three personal references, telephone interview or in-person interview. Application deadline: April 1. World Wide Web: http://www.mm.com/fnvw.

GAY AND LESBIAN VICTORY FUND
1012 14th Street, NW, 10th Floor
Washington, District of Columbia 20005

General Information National donor network committed to electing qualified, openly gay and lesbian candidates to public office. Established in 1991. Number of employees: 8. Number of internship applications received each year: 20.

Internships Available ▶ *Interns:* responsibilities include duties coincident with interest and experience of applicant; positions available in the areas of media relations, fund-raising, campaign management, and research. Candidates should have ability to work independently, ability to work with others, oral communication skills, self-motivation, written communication skills, confidentiality. Duration is flexible. Position available as unpaid or at $7–$8 per hour. Open to high school students, high school seniors, recent high school graduates, college freshmen, college sophomores, college juniors, college seniors, recent college graduates, graduate students, career changers, individuals reentering the workforce. International applications accepted.

Benefits Job counseling, names of contacts, possible full-time employment, willing to complete paperwork for educational credit, willing to provide letters of recommendation, networking opportunities, possible stipend.

Contact Write, call, fax, or e-mail Intern Coordinator. Phone: 202-842-8679. Fax: 202-289-3863. E-mail: victoryf@aol.com. Telephone interview required. Applicants must submit a cover letter, resume, writing sample, 4 personal references including phone numbers. Applications are accepted continuously. World Wide Web: http://www.victoryfund.org.

GLOBAL EXCHANGE
2017 Mission Street, Room 303
San Francisco, California 94110

General Information Nonprofit research, education, action center devoted to international human rights. Established in 1988. Number of employees: 30. Number of internship applications received each year: 130.

Internships Available ▶ *2 alternative trade interns:* responsibilities include overseeing craft booth at Bay Area fairs and festivals, and researching and writing materials about country conditions and alternative trade. Candidates should have ability to work independently, oral communication skills, personal interest in the field, self-motivation, strong interpersonal skills. Duration is 4–12 weeks. Unpaid. Open to college freshmen, college sophomores, college juniors, college seniors, recent college graduates, career changers. ▶ *4 campaign program interns:* responsibilities include organizing and promoting campaign to end Cold War against Cuba and campaign to promote peace in Mexico. Candidates should have ability to work independently, analytical skills, editing skills, organizational skills, research skills, self-motivation, strong leadership ability, writing skills. Duration is 4–12 weeks. Unpaid. Open to college seniors, recent college graduates, graduate students. ▶ *2 fund-raising interns:* responsibilities include researching private and corporate foundations, developing ways to reach new members, and cultivating existing members. Candidates should have computer skills, office skills, oral communication skills, organizational skills, personal interest in the field, self-motivation, writing skills. Duration is 4–12 weeks. Unpaid. Open to college juniors, college seniors, recent college graduates, career changers. ▶ *4 human rights interns:* responsibilities include organizing around the issues of human rights, corporate accountability, and the global economy. Candidates should have ability to work independently, analytical skills, organizational skills, personal interest in the field, plan to pursue career in field, research skills, self-motivation, strong interpersonal skills, strong leadership ability, written communication skills. Duration is 4–12 months. Position available as unpaid or at $800 per month. Open to recent college graduates, graduate students, law students. ▶ *2 media interns:* responsibilities include writing and distributing promotional articles on the work of Global Exchange, developing media contacts, developing and distributing promotional materials for Global Exchange Speakers Bureau. Candidates should have computer skills, editing skills, oral communication skills, research skills, strong interpersonal skills, writing skills. Duration is 8–10 weeks. Unpaid. Open to college juniors, college seniors, recent college graduates, graduate students, career changers. ▶ *2 publications assistants:* responsibilities include writing and distributing promotional articles and developing media contacts. Candidates should have computer skills, editing skills, research skills, self-motivation, writing skills. Duration is 4–12 weeks. Unpaid. Open to college seniors, recent college graduates, graduate students, career changers. ▶ *2 reality tours interns:* responsibilities include developing information packets about areas to be visited (Cuba, Vietnam, Mexico, Brazil, Central America), inputting data, producing flyers, answering phones, typing, and mailing. Candidates should have computer skills, office skills, oral communication skills, organizational skills, research skills, writing skills. Duration is 1–6 months. Unpaid. Open to college sophomores, college juniors. ▶ *2 research interns:* responsibilities include researching areas such as President Clinton's foreign policy, condition of world hunger, and policies of U.S. Agency for International Development and compiling a directory of resources on the grassroots internationalist movement, as well as researching global economic issues and specific multinational companies. Candidates should have analytical skills, computer skills, office skills, research skills, self-motivation, writing skills. Duration is 4–12 weeks. Unpaid. Open to college seniors, recent college graduates, graduate students. International applications accepted.

Benefits Names of contacts, on-the-job training, opportunity to attend seminars/workshops, willing to complete paperwork for educational credit, willing to provide letters of recommendation.

International Internships Available in San Cristobal de las Casas, Mexico.

Contact Write or e-mail Ms. Kirsten Moller, Administrative Director. E-mail: info@globalexchange.org. No phone calls. In-person interview recommended. Applicants must submit a formal organization application, cover letter, resume, two letters of recommendation. Application deadline: April 1 for summer positions; continuous for other positions. World Wide Web: http://www.globalexchange.org.

HEARTS AND MINDS NETWORK
3074 Broadway
New York, New York 10027

General Information Nonprofit public service organization that promotes volunteering and self help for a wide range of issues. It provides the public with information on racism, poverty, the environment, addictions, human rights, and other important topics through its Web site, magazine, and public service ad campaigns. Established in 1996. Number of employees: 40. Number of internship applications received each year: 100.

Internships Available ▶ *10 Internet/Web site interns:* responsibilities include possible Web site editing, design, management, or promotion. Candidates should have ability to work independently, ability to work with others, computer skills, knowledge of field, self-motivation. Open to high school seniors, recent high school graduates, college freshmen, college sophomores, college juniors, college seniors, recent college graduates, graduate students, law students, career changers, individuals reentering the workforce. ▶ *3 accounting and financial management interns:* responsibilities include bookkeeping, accounting, analysis and reporting, or socially-responsible investing. Candidates should have ability to work independently, ability to work with others, computer skills, knowledge of field, personal interest in the field, self-motivation. Open to high school seniors, recent high school graduates, college freshmen, college sophomores, college juniors, college seniors, recent college graduates, graduate students, law students, career changers, individuals reentering the workforce. ▶ *4 ad sales:* responsibilities include selling ads for the Web site and/or print publications. Candidates should have ability to work independently, computer skills, personal interest in the field, self-motivation, strong interpersonal skills. Open to high school seniors, recent high school graduates, college freshmen, college sophomores, college juniors, college seniors, recent college graduates, graduate students, law students, career changers, individuals reentering the workforce. ▶ *5 advertising interns:* responsibilities include working on public-service ad campaigns regarding the environment, homelessness, addictions, child abuse, and other important issues; working on campaigns to promote Hearts and Minds publications. Candidates should have oral communication skills, personal interest in the field, self-motivation, strong interpersonal skills, written communication skills. Open to high school seniors, recent high school graduates, college freshmen, college sophomores, college juniors, college seniors, recent college graduates, graduate students, law students, career changers, individuals reentering the workforce. ▶ *4 computers/technical support interns:* responsibilities include providing technical support for computers, printers, software, year 2000 compliance, phones, and Web site. Candidates should have ability to work independently, computer skills, personal interest in the field, self-motivation, strong interpersonal skills. Open to high school seniors, recent high school graduates, college freshmen, college sophomores, college juniors, college seniors, recent college graduates, graduate students, law students, career changers, individuals reentering the workforce. ▶ *29 creative and design interns:* responsibilities include arts management, creative writing, fine art, illustration, or photography for Web site, campaigns, or print publications (15 positions); art direction and graphic design for Web site, ad campaigns, or print publications (10 positions); or doing promotional writing for Web site, ad campaigns, or print publications (4 positions). Candidates should have ability to work independently, computer skills, self-motivation, strong interpersonal skills, design skills. Open to high school seniors, recent high school graduates, college freshmen, college sophomores, college juniors, college seniors, recent college graduates, graduate students, law students, career changers, individuals reentering the workforce. ▶ *10 fund-raising/events planning interns:* responsibilities include fund-raising through direct mailing; corporate, foundation, or personal solicitation; and planned giving (7 positions). Planning cultural and fund-raising events (3 positions). Candidates should have ability to work independently, computer skills, oral communication skills, self-motivation, strong interpersonal skills. Open to high school seniors, recent high school graduates, college freshmen, college sophomores, college juniors, college seniors, recent college graduates, graduate students, law students, career changers, individuals reentering the workforce. ▶ *8 general interns:* responsibilities include working in any combination of other position offerings. Candidates should have ability to work with others, computer skills, self-motivation. Open to high school seniors, recent high school graduates, college freshmen, college sophomores, college juniors, college seniors, recent college graduates, graduate students, law students, career changers, individuals reentering the workforce. ▶ *15 journalism interns:* responsibilities include research, writing, and editing articles. Candidates should have ability to work independently, computer skills, personal interest in the field, self-motivation, strong interpersonal skills. Open to high school seniors, recent high

Hearts and Minds Network (continued)

school graduates, college freshmen, college sophomores, college juniors, college seniors, recent college graduates, graduate students, law students, career changers, individuals reentering the workforce. ▶ *5 law and regulatory compliance interns:* responsibilities include possible employee, volunteer, member, and government relations; advice on copyrights; avoiding libel, liability, and other legal exposure; regulatory compliance. Candidates should have ability to work independently, self-motivation, strong interpersonal skills. Open to high school seniors, recent high school graduates, college freshmen, college sophomores, college juniors, college seniors, recent college graduates, graduate students, law students, career changers, individuals reentering the workforce. ▶ *7 marketing and publishing interns:* responsibilities include circulation promotion, production, direct mailing, and/or other marketing activities. Candidates should have ability to work independently, computer skills, personal interest in the field, self-motivation, strong interpersonal skills. Open to high school seniors, recent high school graduates, college freshmen, college sophomores, college juniors, college seniors, recent college graduates, graduate students, law students, career changers, individuals reentering the workforce. ▶ *4 marketing research interns:* responsibilities include strategic planning, surveys, and focus groups to evaluate effectiveness of organization. Candidates should have ability to work independently, analytical skills, computer skills, personal interest in the field, strong interpersonal skills. Open to high school seniors, recent high school graduates, college freshmen, college sophomores, college juniors, college seniors, recent college graduates, graduate students, law students, career changers, individuals reentering the workforce. ▶ *7 office interns:* responsibilities include office management, phone calls, photocopying, running errands, faxing, word processing, and desk top publishing. Candidates should have ability to work independently, ability to work with others, computer skills, personal interest in the field, self-motivation. Open to high school seniors, recent high school graduates, college freshmen, college sophomores, college juniors, college seniors, recent college graduates, graduate students, law students, career changers, individuals reentering the workforce. ▶ *3 personnel/volunteer recruitment and relations interns:* responsibilities include recruiting, communicating, and supervising volunteers and interns at the office and all over the world (via phone and e-mail). Candidates should have ability to work independently, computer skills, personal interest in the field, self-motivation, strong interpersonal skills. Open to recent high school graduates, college freshmen, college sophomores, college juniors, college seniors, recent college graduates, graduate students, law students, career changers, individuals reentering the workforce, high school juniors and seniors. ▶ *15 public relations interns:* responsibilities include contact with major media (newspapers, magazines, radio, television, and Internet), editing/writing articles, press releases, and other marketing materials. Candidates should have ability to work independently, ability to work with others, oral communication skills, self-motivation, written communication skills. Open to high school seniors, recent high school graduates, college freshmen, college sophomores, college juniors, college seniors, recent college graduates, graduate students, law students, career changers, individuals reentering the workforce. Duration for all positions is 2 weeks (minimum). All positions are unpaid. International applications accepted.

Benefits Job counseling, names of contacts, on-the-job training, opportunity to attend seminars/workshops, willing to act as a professional reference, willing to complete paperwork for educational credit, willing to provide letters of recommendation, advice on resume and cover letter, cooperation for independent study.

Contact Write, call, fax, or e-mail Intern/Volunteer Manager. Phone: 212-280-0333. Fax: 212-280-0336. E-mail: help@change.net. Cover letter, resume, in-person interview helpful, portfolio helpful for (graphic design, writing, art, and photography applicants). Applications are accepted continuously. World Wide Web: http://www.change.net.

HELEN WOODWARD ANIMAL CENTER
6461 El Apajo Road, PO Box 64
Rancho Santa Fe, California 92067

General Information Animal related activities: education, animal adoption animal assisted therapy. Established in 1973. Number of employees: 70. Number of internship applications received each year: 10.
Internships Available ▶ *1–2 events marketing assistants:* responsibilities include assisting with planning and event logistics, implementation, assisting with planning and acquisition of underwriting and auction donations, and following through with clerical details of event. Candidates should have oral communication skills, organizational skills, research skills, self-motivation, strong interpersonal skills, written communication skills. Open to recent high school graduates, college freshmen, college sophomores, college juniors, college seniors, recent college graduates, graduate students, law students, law school graduates, career changers, individuals reentering the workforce. ▶ *1–2 public relations assistants:* responsibilities include writing articles for newsletter or press releases (graphics desktop and programs), clerical and computer work, and market research projects. Candidates should have ability to work independently, college courses in field, research skills, self-motivation, written communication skills. Open to college sophomores, college juniors, college seniors, communications, journalism, marketing or English majors. Duration for all positions is 6 months. All positions are unpaid. International applications accepted.
Benefits Formal training, on-the-job training, references and letters or recommendations if intern's performance is satisfactory.
Contact Write, call, fax, or e-mail Amy Holt Bennett, Volunteer Coordinator, PO Box 64, Rancho Sante Fe, California 92067. Phone: 619-756-4117 Ext. 305. Fax: 619-756-1466. E-mail: amyb@animalcenter.org. In-person interview required. Applicants must submit a formal organization application, writing samples and portfolio for some positions. Applications are accepted continuously. World Wide Web: http://www.animalcenter.org.

INTERNATIONAL HUMAN RIGHTS LAW GROUP
1200 18th Street, NW, Suite 602
Washington, District of Columbia 20036

General Information Nonprofit organization of human rights and legal professionals engaged in human rights advocacy, litigation, and training around the world. Established in 1978. Number of employees: 21. Number of internship applications received each year: 200.
Internships Available ▶ *6–8 legal/graduate interns:* responsibilities include assisting attorneys in program work; legal research projects; writing, summarizing, and analyzing reports. Candidates should have ability to work independently, analytical skills, experience in the field, research skills, self-motivation, writing skills. Open to graduate students, law students, career changers. ▶ *2–3 undergraduate interns:* responsibilities include researching, writing, and administrative duties. Candidates should have oral communication skills, personal interest in the field, research skills, self-motivation, strong interpersonal skills, writing skills. Open to college sophomores, college juniors, college seniors, recent college graduates. Duration for all positions is 10 weeks. All positions are unpaid. International applications accepted.
Benefits Names of contacts, opportunity to attend seminars/workshops, willing to act as a professional reference, willing to complete paperwork for educational credit, willing to provide letters of recommendation, great opportunity to learn how human rights organization works.
International Internships Available in Bosnia and Herzegovina; Cambodia.
Contact Write or fax Internship Coordinator, 1200 18th Street, NW, Suite 602, Washington, District of Columbia 20036. Fax: 202-822-4606. No phone calls. Telephone interview required. Applicants must submit a cover letter, resume, three letters of recommendation, 5-page writing sample. Application deadline: March 1 for summer, August 31 for fall, December 31 for spring.

INTERNS FOR PEACE
475 Riverside Drive, 16th Floor
New York, New York 10115-0109

General Information Organization that trains for conflict resolution through community work in Israel and the Middle East. Established in 1976. Number of employees: 20. Number of internship applications received each year: 120.

Internships Available ▶ *12 interns:* responsibilities include performing duties designed to bring groups together through community work in Israel and the Middle East; helping to design community development activities that meet mutual interests of Jews and Arabs in six principal areas: women, education, sports, arts, community and business. Candidates should have plan to pursue a career in intergroup relations, advanced language skills in Hebrew or Abrabic. Duration is 12 months. $500 stipend per month. Open to recent college graduates, individuals reentering the workforce. International applications accepted.

Benefits Formal training, free housing, health insurance, job counseling, names of contacts, opportunity to attend seminars/workshops, possible full-time employment, willing to complete paperwork for educational credit, willing to provide letters of recommendation, reimbursement of work-related travel expenses.

Contact Write, call, or fax Karen Wald Cohen, North American Director. Phone: 212-870-2226. Fax: 212-870-2911. In-person interview required. Applicants must submit a cover letter, resume. Applications are accepted continuously.

JAPAN PACIFIC RESOURCE NETWORK
310 8th Street #305
Oakland, California 94607

General Information Nonprofit educational organization to promote nonprofit activities, civil rights, and corporate social responsibility in the US and Japan. Established in 1985. Number of employees: 5. Number of internship applications received each year: 20.

Internships Available ▶ *Administrative interns:* responsibilities include assisting executive director and administrative assistant with office work and the organization's projects. Candidates should have computer skills, office skills, oral communication skills, self-motivation, strong interpersonal skills, writing skills. ▶ *Research interns:* responsibilities include assisting a senior researcher and other staff with research projects. Candidates should have ability to work with others, computer skills, editing skills, research skills, self-motivation, writing skills. Duration for all positions is minimum 3 months. All positions are unpaid. Open to college freshmen, college sophomores, college juniors, college seniors, recent college graduates, graduate students, law students, career changers. International applications accepted.

Benefits On-the-job training, opportunity to attend seminars/workshops, willing to provide letters of recommendation.

International Internships Available in Tokyo, Japan.

Contact Write, call, fax, or e-mail Hiroshi Kashiwagi, Executive Director. Phone: 510-891-9045. Fax: 510-891-9047. E-mail: jprnusa@earthlink.net. In-person interview recommended. Applicants must submit a cover letter, resume, writing sample. Applications are accepted continuously. World Wide Web: http://www.jprn.org.

JOBS WITH JUSTICE
501 Third Street, NW
Washington, District of Columbia 20001-2797

General Information National coalition of labor unions and religious, civil rights, women's, student, farm, and community organizations working together at the local level to defend and expand the rights of working people. Established in 1989.

Internships Available ▶ *Jobs with justice interns:* responsibilities include organizing student-labor outreach, assisting national staff in providing support services to local coalitions, helping in preparation for trainings, and general administrative support. Candidates should have ability to work with others, self-motivation, interest in the labor movement and/or issues affecting working people, desktop publishing and database experi-

ence a plus. Duration is summer, spring, or fall semester (full- or part-time). Position available as unpaid or at small stipend (depending on need).

Benefits Willing to complete paperwork for educational credit.

Contact Write, call, or fax Laura Bogle, 501 Third Street, NW, Washington, District of Columbia 20001. Phone: 202-434-1106. Fax: 202-434-1477. Applicants must submit a cover letter, resume. Applications are accepted continuously. World Wide Web: http://www.jwj.org.

JUSTACT: YOUTH ACTION FOR GLOBAL JUSTICE
333 Valencia Street, Suite 101
San Francisco, California 94103

General Information Nonprofit organization that links students to organizations and grassroots movements working for sustainable and just communities around the world. Established in 1983. Number of employees: 9. Number of internship applications received each year: 50.

Internships Available ▶ *3 Bike Aid fellows:* responsibilities include arranging educational exchanges, host stays, and community service projects for Bike-Aid, a cross-country bicycle ride during the summer. Candidates should have self-motivation, strong interpersonal skills, strong leadership ability. Duration is 3–6 months. Position available as unpaid or paid. Open to high school students, high school seniors, recent high school graduates, college freshmen, college sophomores, college juniors, college seniors, recent college graduates. ▶ *1–2 Bike-Aid public relations and outreach intern:* responsibilities include publicity for Bike-Aid by updating and managing media and recruitment, creating press releases, and assisting in the national publicity campaign. Candidates should have oral communication skills, organizational skills, writing skills. Duration is 2–6 months. Unpaid. Open to high school students, high school seniors, recent high school graduates, college freshmen, college sophomores, college juniors, college seniors, recent college graduates. ▶ *1–3 Global Links newsletter interns:* responsibilities include coordinating the production of newsletter "Global Links;" designing layout; writing, researching, and editing articles. Candidates should have editing skills, knowledge of field, research skills, writing skills. Duration is 2–6 months. Unpaid. Open to high school students, high school seniors, recent high school graduates, college freshmen, college sophomores, college juniors, college seniors, recent college graduates. ▶ *1–3 Webmaster interns:* responsibilities include maintaining JustAct's Web site, researching to create links to other relevant Web sites. Candidates should have computer skills. Duration is 2–6 months. Unpaid. Open to high school students, high school seniors, recent high school graduates, college freshmen, college sophomores, college juniors, college seniors, recent college graduates. ▶ *1–3 alternative opportunities clearinghouse interns:* responsibilities include assisting in compiling information on international non-governmental organizations and responding to information requests from individuals seeking international internships. Candidates should have computer skills, knowledge of field, office skills, research skills, strong interpersonal skills. Duration is 2–6 months. Unpaid. Open to high school seniors, recent high school graduates, college freshmen, college sophomores, college juniors, college seniors, recent college graduates. ▶ *1–2 alumni and donor relations interns:* responsibilities include working with Executive Director to promote greater alumni involvement in JustAct; assisting with foundation outreach; and helping in conceptualizing, planning, and implementing fund-raising events. Candidates should have computer skills, experience in the field, organizational skills, self-motivation, strong interpersonal skills, written communication skills. Duration is 2–6 months. Unpaid. Open to college freshmen, college sophomores, college juniors, college seniors, recent college graduates, career changers. ▶ *1–3 education and organizing interns:* responsibilities include compiling training materials and resources for students; researching, writing, and editing educational materials to facilitate campus activism; and coorganizing national speaking tours, conferences, and education camps. Candidates should have editing skills, organizational skills, research skills, writing skills. Duration is 2–6 months. Unpaid. Open to high school seniors, recent high school gradu-

ates, college freshmen, college sophomores, college juniors, college seniors, recent college graduates. ▶ *2 educational resource interns:* responsibilities include coordinating educational materials for student network; subject areas include leadership development, student organizing, and global education. Candidates should have ability to work independently, analytical skills, research skills, self-motivation, written communication skills. Duration is 2–6 months. Unpaid. Open to high school students, high school seniors, recent high school graduates, college freshmen, college sophomores, college juniors, college seniors, recent college graduates. ▶ *2 media assistants:* responsibilities include writing press releases, conducting mailings and follow-up, compiling national media database, helping coordinate national media plan, and compiling past media materials. Candidates should have ability to work independently, computer skills, office skills, oral communication skills, personal interest in the field, strong interpersonal skills, written communication skills, knowledge of media or experience with outreach. Duration is 2–6 months. Unpaid. Open to high school students, high school seniors, recent high school graduates, college freshmen, college sophomores, college juniors, college seniors, recent college graduates. ▶ *1–3 office operations interns:* responsibilities include assisting operations manager; responding to information requests by telephone, mail, and Internet; updating database; troubleshooting office equipment and computer problems. Candidates should have ability to work independently, computer skills, office skills, oral communication skills, organizational skills, research skills, attention to detail. Duration is 2–6 months. Unpaid. Open to college freshmen, college sophomores, college juniors, college seniors, recent college graduates. International applications accepted.
Benefits Job counseling, names of contacts, on-the-job training, possible full-time employment, willing to complete paperwork for educational credit, willing to provide letters of recommendation, biweekly field trips to other nonprofit organizations, guest speakers.
Contact Write, call, fax, or e-mail Sahar Khoury, Office Internship Coordinator. Phone: 415-431-4204. Fax: 415-431-5953. E-mail: sahar@justact.org. Telephone interview required. Applicants must submit a formal organization application, cover letter, resume. Application deadline: April 1 for summer interns; continuous for other positions. World Wide Web: http://www.justact.org.

KID PROTECTION NETWORK
PO Box 516
Middle Sield, Colorado 06455

General Information Nonprofit organization campaigning to keep streets safe for all children.
Internships Available ▶ *Interns:* responsibilities include coordinating the development of a Kid Protection Network chapter, at local level, with the proper officials. Duration is flexible. Unpaid. Open to anyone interested.
Contact Write, call, fax, or e-mail Michael E. Cluney, President, PO Box 516, Middle Sield, Colorado 06455. Phone: 860-349-8170. Fax: 860-349-8170. E-mail: mcluney@wesleyan.edu. Applications are accepted continuously. World Wide Web: http://www.researchsvcs.com/kpn.

KOREAN AMERICAN COALITION
3421 West Eighth Street
Los Angeles, California 90005

General Information Nonprofit community advocacy organization. Established in 1983. Number of employees: 15. Number of internship applications received each year: 80.
Internships Available ▶ *4–6 corporate interns:* responsibilities include working with KAC and a designated multinational corporation. Candidates should have college courses in field, knowledge of field, oral communication skills, self-motivation, strong interpersonal skills, written communication skills. $1000 stipend per duration of internship. Open to college sophomores, college juniors, non-graduating college seniors. ▶ *1–4 legal interns:* responsibilities include working in law office 4 days per week and KAC office 1 day per week. Candidates should have computer skills, knowledge of field, office skills, oral communication skills, personal interest in the field, self-motivation, strong interpersonal skills, written communication skills. $1000 stipend per duration of internship. Open to college freshmen, college sophomores, college juniors. ▶ *2–5 media interns:* responsibilities include working with KAC and local news service. Candidates should have knowledge of field, office skills, oral communication skills, strong interpersonal skills, writing skills, written communication skills. $1000 stipend per duration of internship. Open to college freshmen, college sophomores, college juniors, non-graduating college seniors. ▶ *2–4 political interns:* responsibilities include working with KAC and a local political office in various functions. Candidates should have knowledge of field, office skills, oral communication skills, self-motivation, strong interpersonal skills, writing skills. $1000 stipend per duration of internship. Open to college freshmen, college sophomores, college juniors, non-graduating college seniors. Duration for all positions is 2 months.
Benefits Names of contacts, opportunity to attend seminars/workshops, possible full-time employment, willing to complete paperwork for educational credit, willing to provide letters of recommendation.
Contact Write, call, or e-mail Minah Park, Program Coordinator. Phone: 213-365-5999. E-mail: kacla1983@aol.com. Telephone interview required. Applicants must submit a formal organization application, resume, academic transcripts, two letters of recommendation, 2 essays. Application deadline: February 29 for summer. Fees: $5.

LATINO CIVIL RIGHTS CENTER
2701 Ontario Road, NW, 2nd Floor
Washington, District of Columbia 20009

General Information Community-based organization that advocates on behalf of Hispanics in the Washington metropolitan area. Established in 1991. Number of employees: 4. Number of internship applications received each year: 10.
Internships Available ▶ *1–2 administrative assistants:* responsibilities include fund-raising assistance, member and volunteer recruitment, marketing and media relations, database management, and general office support. Candidates should have ability to work independently, computer skills, organizational skills, self-motivation, strong interpersonal skills. Open to high school seniors, recent high school graduates, college freshmen, college sophomores, college juniors. ▶ *1–3 community liaison:* responsibilities include attending meetings in the community, documenting incidents, conducting needs assessments, and generating reports; conducting workshops (naturalization, voter), and political forums (candidates). Candidates should have ability to work independently, oral communication skills, organizational skills, self-motivation, strong interpersonal skills, written communication skills. Open to college juniors, college seniors, recent college graduates, graduate students. ▶ *1 public policy and legislative analyst:* responsibilities include assisting executive director in conducting research on immigration, welfare, and education policy concerning Latinos in the metropolitan Washington area. Candidates should have ability to work independently, organizational skills, research skills, self-motivation, writing skills, written communication skills. Open to college juniors, college seniors, graduate students, law students. ▶ *1 public relations intern:* responsibilities include developing government relations program; writing newsletter; developing relations with English and Latino press; writing press releases, news advisories, and letters to the media; developing relations with Latino student organizations at colleges in the Washington area. Candidates should have ability to work independently, oral communication skills, self-motivation, strong interpersonal skills, written communication skills. Open to college freshmen, college sophomores, college juniors, college seniors. ▶ *1–2 training assistants:* responsibilities include helping recruit and coordinate training of parents for PODER—a parents leadership program whose workshops aim to increase understanding of the public school system, to increase parental involvement, and to teach advocacy skills. Candidates should have oral communication skills, organizational skills, self-

motivation, strong interpersonal skills, writing skills. Open to college freshmen, college sophomores, college juniors, college seniors, recent college graduates, graduate students, law students, career changers. Duration for all positions is 1 semester. All positions are unpaid. International applications accepted.

Benefits Formal training, job counseling, names of contacts, opportunity to attend seminars/workshops, willing to complete paperwork for educational credit, willing to provide letters of recommendation, tickets to Latino cultural events.

Contact Write, call, or fax Mr. Mario Acosta-Velez, Executive Director. Phone: 202-332-1053. Fax: 202-483-7460. In-person interview recommended. Applicants must submit a formal organization application, cover letter, resume, writing sample. Application deadline: May 15 for summer, November 15 for spring.

LAWYERS' COMMITTEE FOR CIVIL RIGHTS UNDER LAW
1401 New York Avenue, 4th Floor
Washington, District of Columbia 20005

General Information Civil rights litigation and advocacy organization. Established in 1963. Number of employees: 29. Number of internship applications received each year: 300.

Internships Available ▶ *10–15 law student interns:* responsibilities include legal research and writing, assisting attorneys with case investigation and trial preparation, working with civil rights and/or community based organizations, interviewing clients and witnesses. Candidates should have ability to work independently, ability to work with others, personal interest in the field, research skills, writing skills, evidence of community service or civil rights interest. Open to law students. ▶ *2–3 undergraduate interns:* responsibilities include assisting administrative and attorney employees with administrative tasks, desktop publishing, non-legal writing and research, filing, and some clerical work. Candidates should have ability to work independently, ability to work with others, office skills, personal interest in the field, self-motivation, evidence of community service or civil rights interest. Open to college freshmen, college sophomores, college juniors, college seniors, recent college graduates, graduate students, career changers, individuals reentering the workforce. Duration for all positions is flexible. All positions are unpaid. International applications accepted.

Benefits Names of contacts, on-the-job training, opportunity to attend seminars/workshops, possible full-time employment, travel reimbursement, willing to act as a professional reference, willing to complete paperwork for educational credit, willing to provide letters of recommendation.

Contact Write, call, fax, or e-mail Teresa Ferrante, Intern Coordinator. Phone: 202-662-8600. Fax: 202-783-0857. E-mail: interncoordinator@lawyerscomm.org. In-person interview recommended. Applicants must submit a cover letter, resume, writing sample, 2-3 personal references. World Wide Web: http://www.lawyerscomm.org.

LOS ANGELES LAKERS
Great Western Forum, PO Box 10
Inglewood, California 90306

General Information Group that serves as the liaison between the organization, media, and public. Established in 1961. Number of employees: 7. Unit of California Sports, Inc. Number of internship applications received each year: 50.

Internships Available ▶ *5 public relations interns:* responsibilities include addressing the media's questions regarding team's players' credentials, statistics, and quotes; answering telephone calls; distributing information and material to the public; handling general office work. Candidates should have ability to work with others, oral communication skills, organizational skills, personal interest in the field, strong interpersonal skills, written communication skills. Duration is 1 season. $6 per hour. Open to college juniors, college seniors. International applications accepted.

Benefits Formal training, free meals, names of contacts, possible full-time employment, willing to complete paperwork for educational credit, willing to provide letters of recommendation.

Contact Write or fax John Black, Director of Public Relations. Fax: 310-419-3235. No phone calls. In-person interview required. Applicants must submit a cover letter, resume, documentation from college or university that internship is being done for college credit. Applications are accepted continuously.

MARCH OF DIMES BIRTH DEFECTS FOUNDATION, OFFICE OF GOVERNMENT AFFAIRS
1901 L Street, NW, Suite 200
Washington, District of Columbia 20036

General Information Nonprofit organization that is dedicated to the prevention of birth defects through research, public health education, advocacy, and community service. Established in 1938. Number of employees: 8. Unit of National Office March of Dimes, White Plains, New York. Number of internship applications received each year: 25.

Internships Available ▶ *1–2 school-year interns:* responsibilities include assisting with monitoring, tracking, and reporting on public policy issues; researching and drafting letters, position papers, testimony, and legislative updates; attending and monitoring congressional hearings, markups, and meetings; and providing general office support. Duration is 1 semester. Open to college sophomores, college juniors, college seniors, recent college graduates, graduate students. ▶ *1–2 summer interns:* responsibilities include assisting with monitoring, tracking, and reporting on public policy issues; researching and drafting letters, position papers, testimony, and legislative updates; attending and monitoring congressional hearings, markups, and meetings; and providing general office support. Duration is 1–3 months. Candidates for all positions should have knowledge of field, personal interest in the field, research skills, self-motivation, strong interpersonal skills, writing skills. All positions available as unpaid or paid.

Benefits Willing to complete paperwork for educational credit.

Contact Write Ms. Elizabeth Barnhart, Director of Office Administration, 1901 L Street, NW, Suite 200, Washington, District of Columbia 20036. No phone calls. In-person interview recommended. Applicants must submit a cover letter, resume, writing sample, three letters of recommendation. Applications are accepted continuously. World Wide Web: http://www.modimes.org.

MASSACHUSETTS PUBLIC INTEREST RESEARCH GROUPS
29 Temple Place
Boston, Massachusetts 02111-1305

General Information Nonprofit, nonpartisan organization involved in research, organizing, and advocacy for statewide environmental and consumer protection reforms. Established in 1972. Number of employees: 25. Number of internship applications received each year: 50.

Internships Available ▶ *2–5 advocacy/organizing/research interns:* responsibilities include conducting research, preparing investigative reports, drafting public education materials, working with media and coalition groups to build support for issues through public education programs, representing MASSPIRG on specific issues to coalition and other local organizations, and preparing testimony for government hearings on pending legislation. Candidates should have ability to work with others, computer skills, organizational skills, personal interest in the field, self-motivation, written communication skills. Duration is flexible. Unpaid. Open to college freshmen, college sophomores, college juniors, college seniors, recent college graduates, law students, career changers. International applications accepted.

Benefits Names of contacts, opportunity to attend seminars/workshops, possible full-time employment, willing to act as a professional reference, willing to complete paperwork for educational credit, willing to provide letters of recommendation.

Contact Write, call, fax, or e-mail Kim Nelson, Program Administrator. Phone: 617-292-4800. Fax: 617-292-8067. E-mail:

masspirg@pirg.org. In-person interview recommended. Applicants must submit a cover letter, resume. Applications are accepted continuously. World Wide Web: http://www.pirg.org.

MEDIA ALLIANCE
814 Mission Street, Suite 205
San Francisco, California 94103

General Information Nonprofit organization of media professionals and members of the general public that offers a wide variety of programs that reflect its commitment to the principles of excellence, ethics, diversity, and accountability in all aspects of the media in the interests of peace, justice, and social responsibility. Established in 1977. Number of employees: 9. Number of internship applications received each year: 30.
Internships Available ▶ *1–3 interns:* responsibilities include marketing, research, programming, computer work, general office work, and organizing events. Duration is flexible. $100–$300 per month. Open to high school students, high school seniors, recent high school graduates, college freshmen, college sophomores, college juniors, college seniors, recent college graduates, graduate students, law students, career changers, individuals reentering the workforce. International applications accepted.
Benefits Formal training, names of contacts, opportunity to attend seminars/workshops, willing to complete paperwork for educational credit, willing to provide letters of recommendation, job-listing service (lists approximately 300 jobs/internships per month).
Contact Write, call, fax, or e-mail Elton Bradman, Internship Director. Phone: 415-546-6334 Ext. 301. Fax: 415-546-6218. E-mail: eltonb@media-alliance.org. In-person interview recommended. Applicants must submit a cover letter, resume. Application deadline: call or e-mail for specifics. World Wide Web: http://www.media-alliance.org.

METRO FAMILY YMCA
2831 Southwest Barbur Boulevard
Portland, Oregon 97201

General Information Organization that promotes Christian principles through programs that build healthy bodies, minds, and spirits for all. Established in 1977. Number of employees: 140. Unit of YMCA of Columbia-Willamette, Portland, Oregon. Number of internship applications received each year: 12.
Internships Available ▶ *4 adult health/fitness/cardiac rehabilitation interns:* responsibilities include teaching land and water classes; and overseeing weight room, cardiovascular and health education, social events, and program operations. Candidates should have college courses in field, oral communication skills, personal interest in the field, plan to pursue career in field, strong interpersonal skills. Duration is 10 weeks or 1 semester (36-40 hours per week). Open to college freshmen, college sophomores, college juniors, college seniors, recent college graduates, graduate students, career changers. ▶ *4 child care program interns:* responsibilities include assisting teachers, teaching students, and performing administrative duties. Candidates should have declared college major in field, experience in the field, personal interest in the field, strong interpersonal skills, strong leadership ability. Duration is 10 weeks or 1 semester. Open to college sophomores, college juniors, college seniors. ▶ *1 corporate site intern:* responsibilities include assisting program directors at corporate health and fitness sites; teaching fitness; and conducting weight orientations, health education, and incentive programs. Candidates should have college courses in field, experience in the field, oral communication skills, self-motivation, strong interpersonal skills, strong leadership ability. Duration is 1 semester. Open to college juniors, college seniors. ▶ *4 youth sports and aquatics interns:* responsibilities include assisting program director in youth sports program and for special events, coordinating programs, performing administrative duties, and teaching. Candidates should have college courses in field, oral communication skills, personal interest in the field, strong interpersonal skills, strong leadership ability. Duration is 10 weeks or 1

semester. Open to college freshmen, college sophomores, college juniors, college seniors, recent college graduates, graduate students. All positions are unpaid. International applications accepted.
Benefits Formal training, job counseling, names of contacts, on-the-job training, opportunity to attend seminars/workshops, possible full-time employment, willing to complete paperwork for educational credit, willing to provide letters of recommendation.
Contact Write Jane Loverin, Associate Executive Director. No phone calls. In-person interview recommended. Applicants must submit a cover letter, resume. Application deadline: March 1 for spring, May 1 for summer, August 1 for fall, November 1 for winter.

METRO JUSTICE OF ROCHESTER
36 St. Paul Street, Room 112
Rochester, New York 14604

General Information Multi-issue community organization focusing on economic justice, antiracism, Latin American solidarity, health care, labor, women's issues, and environmental issues. Established in 1965. Number of employees: 3. Number of internship applications received each year: 10.
Internships Available ▶ *2–3 interns:* responsibilities include assisting with a substantial research project that aids the community in some way. Duration is 1 semester. Unpaid. Open to college sophomores, college juniors, college seniors, recent college graduates, graduate students.
Benefits Willing to complete paperwork for educational credit, willing to provide letters of recommendation.
Contact Write, call, fax, or e-mail Mr. William Appel, Organizer. Phone: 716-325-2560. Fax: 716-325-2561. E-mail: metroj@frontiernet.net. In-person interview recommended. Applicants must submit a cover letter, resume. Applications are accepted continuously.

MID-SOUTH PEACE AND JUSTICE CENTER
PO Box 11428
Memphis, Tennessee 38111-0428

General Information Grassroots organization that advocates and educates people in peace and justice issues. Established in 1982. Number of employees: 1. Number of internship applications received each year: 10.
Internships Available ▶ *Central America coordinator interns:* responsibilities include assisting with the coordination of programs and volunteers working on Central American issues, doing research, organizing events, and working with volunteers. ▶ *Community Reinvestment Act researchers:* responsibilities include researching the lending records of local financial institutions using their Home Mortgage Disclosure Data, helping to prepare the information for the public, and preparing challenges for the files of local financial institutions. ▶ *South Africa interns:* responsibilities include working with community groups to create and maintain a pen-pal program between Memphis and the Red Location (sister community outside Port Elizabeth, South Africa). ▶ *Alternative public spending outreach coordinators:* responsibilities include working with community organizations and general public about the need to change federal spending priorities. ▶ *Disarmament interns:* responsibilities include researching information on issues related to U.S. conventional arms sales and/or nuclear non-proliferation and using this information to write articles, educate the public, and/or lobbying efforts. ▶ *Environmental justice interns:* responsibilities include researching impact of toxics, pollution, and waste on Memphis, particularly on the African-American community, creating educational materials, and helping to design an outreach program. ▶ *Health reform interns:* responsibilities include accessing the state program (TennCare), doing educational work, and organizing advocacy work. ▶ *Independent interns.* ▶ *Media watch interns:* responsibilities include performing an in-depth analysis of news coverage. ▶ *Office manager interns:* responsibilities include coordinating the overall operations of the office. ▶ *Tax reform interns:* responsibilities include working with community groups for fair taxation to educate the public about the current regressive structure of the Tennessee tax system. ▶ *Youth and nonviolence interns:* responsibili-

473 ties include working with pledge of nonviolence in public schools and community. Duration for all positions is flexible. All positions are unpaid. International applications accepted.
Benefits On-the-job training, willing to act as a professional reference, willing to complete paperwork for educational credit, willing to provide letters of recommendation, willing to work with intern to find affordable housing.
Contact Write, call, fax, or e-mail Mr. Bill Akin, Program Director. Phone: 901-452-6997. Fax: 901-452-7029. E-mail: pax@magibox. net. Applicants must submit a formal organization application, three personal references. Applications are accepted continuously.

MOTHERS' VOICES
165 West 46th Street, Suite 701
New York, New York 10036

General Information The only national, grassroots, nonprofit organization working to mobilize mothers to educate and advocate about sexual health and HIV/AIDS prevention. Established in 1991. Number of employees: 8. Number of internship applications received each year: 10.
Internships Available ▶ *1–2 community programs associates:* responsibilities include assisting Community Programs Director in the planning, assessment, implementation, and evaluation of sexual health and HIV prevention education and advocacy programs; writing proposals; community organizing and networking. Candidates should have ability to work independently, oral communication skills, plan to pursue career in field, research skills, self-motivation, written communication skills, basic understanding of sexual health and HIV. Duration is flexible. Position available as unpaid or at $10 per hour (if funding permits). Open to college seniors, recent college graduates, graduate students. International applications accepted.
Benefits Job counseling, on-the-job training, opportunity to attend seminars/workshops, willing to act as a professional reference, willing to complete paperwork for educational credit, willing to provide letters of recommendation.
Contact Write, call, fax, or e-mail Lori Rolleri, Director of Community Programs. Phone: 212-730-2777. Fax: 212-730-4378. E-mail: lrolleri@mvoices.org. In-person interview required. Applicants must submit a cover letter, resume, writing sample, three personal references. Applications are accepted continuously. World Wide Web: http://www.mvoices.org.

NATIONAL ABORTION AND REPRODUCTIVE RIGHTS ACTION LEAGUE OF OHIO
760 East Broad Street
Columbus, Ohio 43201

General Information Political lobbying organization, education foundation, grassroots organization. Established in 1979. Number of employees: 4. Affiliate of National Abortion and Reproductive Rights Action League, Washington, District of Columbia. Number of internship applications received each year: 5.
Internships Available ▶ *5 interns:* responsibilities include assisting with educational, grass roots organizing, and lobbying projects; providing staff support as needed. Candidates should have ability to work independently, organizational skills, personal interest in the field, research skills, strong interpersonal skills, writing skills. Duration is unlimited. Unpaid. Open to high school seniors, recent high school graduates, college freshmen, college sophomores, college juniors, college seniors, recent college graduates.
Benefits On-the-job training, opportunity to attend seminars/workshops, willing to act as a professional reference, willing to complete paperwork for educational credit, willing to provide letters of recommendation.
Contact Call or e-mail Jon Strange, State Organizer, 760 East Broad Street, Columbus, Ohio 43201. Phone: 614-221-2594. E-mail: naralohio@juno.com. In-person interview required. Applicants must submit a cover letter, resume. Applications are accepted continuously. World Wide Web: http://www.rascalnut. com/naral-ohio.

NATIONAL ASIAN PACIFIC AMERICAN LEGAL CONSORTIUM
1140 Connecticut Avenue, NW, Suite 1200
Washington, District of Columbia 20036

General Information Civil rights organization that advances the legal and civil rights of Asian-Pacific Americans through litigation, advocacy, public education, and public policy development. Established in 1991. Number of employees: 8. Number of internship applications received each year: 100.
Internships Available ▶ *1 law student intern:* responsibilities include assisting the executive director and legal staff on special research projects; writing policy statements, legislative alerts, and news articles; reviewing and assisting in preparation of amicus briefs; attending congressional hearings and representing NAPALC at coalition meetings; some administrative work. Candidates should have analytical skills, computer skills, editing skills, organizational skills, research skills, writing skills. Duration is 1 semester. Open to law students. ▶ *3 undergraduate and graduate interns:* responsibilities include assisting consortium's executive director, associate director, and legal staff on special research projects; writing legislative alerts, press releases, and news articles; attending congressional hearings and representing NAPALC at coalition meetings; performing some administrative work. Candidates should have ability to work with others, computer skills, editing skills, research skills, writing skills. Duration is 10 weeks or 1 semester. Open to college juniors, college seniors, graduate students. All positions are unpaid.
Benefits Names of contacts, on-the-job training, opportunity to attend seminars/workshops, travel reimbursement, willing to complete paperwork for educational credit, willing to provide letters of recommendation.
Contact Write, call, fax, or e-mail Ms. Ronda Coleman, Program Assistant NAPALC, 1140 Connecticut Avenue, NW Suite 1200, Washington, District of Columbia 20036. Phone: 202-296-2300. Fax: 202-296-2318. E-mail: rcoleman@napalc.org. Telephone interview required. Applicants must submit a cover letter, resume, academic transcripts, one 2- to 5-page writing sample. Application deadline: March 15 for summer, August 15 for fall, November 15 for winter/spring. World Wide Web: http://www.napalc.org.

NATIONAL CAMPAIGN FOR FREEDOM OF EXPRESSION
918 F Street, NW, Suite 609
Washington, District of Columbia 20004

General Information Educational and advocacy network of artists, arts organizations, audience members, and concerned citizens formed to protect and extend freedom of artistic expression and fight censorship throughout the United States. Established in 1990. Number of employees: 4. Number of internship applications received each year: 20.
Internships Available ▶ *2 interns:* responsibilities include assisting program staff and the Executive Director; providing support to artists; collecting, researching, and producing the *NCFE Quarterly*; organizing and maintaining Congressional, coalition, and censorship incident databases; administrative tasks; retrieval and distribution of information in daily and weekly publications. Candidates should have computer skills, office skills, personal interest in the field, research skills, self-motivation, writing skills. Duration is flexible. Unpaid. Open to high school students, high school seniors, recent high school graduates, college freshmen, college sophomores, college juniors, college seniors, recent college graduates. International applications accepted.
Benefits Opportunity to attend seminars/workshops, willing to act as a professional reference, willing to complete paperwork for educational credit, willing to provide letters of recommendation.
Contact Write, call, fax, or e-mail Michelle Coffey, Program Director, 918 F Street, NW, Suite 609, Washington, District of Columbia 20004. Phone: 202-393-2787. Fax: 202-347-7376. E-mail: mcoffey@ncfe.net. In-person interview recommended. Applicants must submit a cover letter, resume, writing sample. Applications are accepted continuously. World Wide Web: http://www. ncfe.net.

Peterson's Internships 2000

NATIONAL CENTER FOR FAIR AND OPEN TESTING (FAIRTEST)
342 Broadway
Cambridge, Massachusetts 02139

General Information Public education and advocacy organization fighting race, gender, and class bias in standardized exams and promoting assessment methods that are fair, accurate, and educationally sound. Established in 1985. Number of employees: 4. Number of internship applications received each year: 25.

Internships Available ▶ *1–2 Denise Carty-Bennia interns:* responsibilities include researching and writing for a current project or campaign related to civil rights and educational testing, preparing a report on test coaching, and researching challenges to tests and test misuses. Duration is 1 summer. Position available as unpaid or at $500–$1,500 per duration of internship. Open to college juniors, college seniors, graduate students, individuals reentering the workforce.

Benefits Names of contacts, willing to complete paperwork for educational credit, willing to provide letters of recommendation.

Contact Write Ms. Jennifer Griffis, Office Manager. Applicants must submit a cover letter, resume, writing sample. Applications are accepted continuously.

NATIONAL CLEARINGHOUSE ON MARITAL AND DATE RAPE
2325 Oak Street
Berkeley, California 94708

General Information Library and research center that compiles and provides information on date and marital rape cases and on legislation and media publication on these subjects; representatives are available as consultants, speakers, and organizers for campaigns for political and social change for women. Established in 1978. Number of employees: 10. Number of internship applications received each year: 120.

Internships Available ▶ *Health interns:* responsibilities include training in media coverage of issues, cases, and statistics. Candidates should have ability to work with others, office skills, oral communication skills, personal interest in the field, self-motivation, written communication skills. Duration is minimum of 1 summer, semester, or January term. Open to high school seniors, recent high school graduates, college freshmen, college sophomores, college juniors, college seniors, recent college graduates, graduate students, law students, career changers, individuals reentering the workforce, any high school graduate. ▶ *Journalism interns:* responsibilities include filling phone and written media requests for information on the organization and the issues through the use of a twenty-year archive, and calling courts, legislators, shelters, and media for information. Candidates should have editing skills, office skills, oral communication skills, personal interest in the field, writing skills, written communication skills. Duration is minimum of 1 summer, semester, or January term. Open to high school seniors, recent high school graduates, college freshmen, college sophomores, college juniors, college seniors, recent college graduates, graduate students, law students, career changers, individuals reentering the workforce, any high school graduate. ▶ *Office and library assistants:* responsibilities include analyzing, sorting, filing, and integrating materials. Candidates should have ability to work with others, computer skills, office skills, oral communication skills, organizational skills, written communication skills. Duration is minimum of 1 summer, semester, or January term. Open to high school seniors, recent high school graduates, college freshmen, college sophomores, college juniors, college seniors, recent college graduates, graduate students, law students, career changers, individuals reentering the workforce, any high school graduate. ▶ *Psychology/counseling interns:* responsibilities include studying social basis and victim/survivor reaction to marital and date rape and answering letters and information requests from victims/survivors. Candidates should have ability to work independently, oral communication skills, personal interest in the field, self-motivation, strong interpersonal skills, written communication skills. Duration is minimum of 1 summer, semester, or January term. Open to high school seniors, recent

high school graduates, college freshmen, college sophomores, college juniors, college seniors, recent college graduates, graduate students, law students, career changers, individuals reentering the workforce. ▶ *Publicity/office coordinators:* responsibilities include making promotional and outreach calls, taking messages, handling inquiries, writing correspondence, and filing. Candidates should have ability to work independently, ability to work with others, computer skills, office skills, oral communication skills, written communication skills. Duration is minimum of 1 summer, semester, or January term. Open to high school seniors, recent high school graduates, college freshmen, college sophomores, college juniors, college seniors, recent college graduates, graduate students, law students, career changers, individuals reentering the workforce, any high school graduate. ▶ *Women's studies interns:* responsibilities include covering court cases and legislation. Candidates should have ability to work with others, office skills, oral communication skills, personal interest in the field, self-motivation, written communication skills. Duration is 1 summer or semester minimum. Open to high school seniors, recent high school graduates, college freshmen, college sophomores, college juniors, college seniors, recent college graduates, graduate students, law students, career changers, individuals reentering the workforce, any high school graduate. All positions are unpaid. International applications accepted.

Benefits Job counseling, names of contacts, opportunity to attend seminars/workshops, willing to act as a professional reference, willing to complete paperwork for educational credit, willing to provide letters of recommendation, referrals to agencies, films, lectures, theater, protests, free meals provided during work, networking possibilities, housing at a cost provided during summer only.

Contact Write or e-mail Laura X, Director. E-mail: laurax@gte.net. No phone calls. Cover letter indicating skills and interests, telephone interview for finalists; see Web site for application process information. Applications are accepted continuously. World Wide Web: http://ncmdr.org.

NATIONAL COMMITTEE FOR RESPONSIVE PHILANTHROPY
2001 S Street, NW, Suite 620
Washington, District of Columbia 20009

General Information Organization committed to making philanthropy more responsive to the economically, socially, and politically disenfranchised. Established in 1976. Number of employees: 11. Number of internship applications received each year: 50.

Internships Available ▶ *2 program/administration interns (Washington, DC):* responsibilities include grass roots lobbying; performing research through periodicals, libraries, and especially telephone surveys; various administrative tasks; assisting media director with press releases and phone calls to reporters; coordinating conferences; assisting fund-raising director. Candidates should have analytical skills, computer skills, self-motivation, writing skills. Duration is 3–12 months. $6–$8 per hour. Open to recent college graduates, graduate students. International applications accepted.

Benefits Health insurance, on-the-job training, opportunity to attend seminars/workshops, possible full-time employment, willing to act as a professional reference, willing to complete paperwork for educational credit, willing to provide letters of recommendation.

Contact Write, call, fax, or e-mail Kate Conover, Vice President. Phone: 202-387-9177. Fax: 202-332-5084. E-mail: kate@ncrp.org. In-person interview recommended. Applicants must submit a cover letter, resume, three personal references. Applications are accepted continuously. World Wide Web: http://www.ncrp.org.

NATIONAL CONSUMERS LEAGUE
1701 K Street, NW, Suite 1200
Washington, District of Columbia 20006

General Information Private nonprofit membership organization that uses a 3-pronged approach of research, education, and advocacy in providing information for consumers and workers. Established in 1899. Number of employees: 23. Number of internship applications received each year: 50.

Internships Available ▶ *2 interns:* responsibilities include working on issues in food and drug safety, health care, child labor, consumer fraud, financial services, or telecommunications. Duration is minimum of 8 weeks. Unpaid. Open to college juniors, college seniors, recent college graduates, graduate students, law students, career changers, individuals reentering the workforce. International applications accepted.

Benefits Job counseling, names of contacts, opportunity to attend seminars/workshops, willing to complete paperwork for educational credit, willing to provide letters of recommendation, opportunity to contribute to League publications.

Contact Write, call, fax, or e-mail Ms. Sara Cooper, Executive Vice President. Phone: 202-835-3323. Fax: 202-835-0747. E-mail: nclncl@aol.com. Applicants must submit a formal organization application, writing sample. Applications are accepted continuously. World Wide Web: http://www.nclnet.org.

NATIONAL COUNCIL FOR RESEARCH ON WOMEN
11 Hanover Square
New York, New York 10005

General Information A working alliance of centers and individuals actively involved in feminist research, policy analysis, advocacy, and innovative programs for women and girls. Established in 1981. Number of employees: 6. Number of internship applications received each year: 50.

Internships Available ▶ *3 interns:* responsibilities include administrative duties, such as database maintenance, fulfilling orders, mail merges, and organization. Interns will also network with others in the field, get an introduction to nonprofits, and gain access to women-centered goings-on around New York City. Candidates should have ability to work independently, analytical skills, organizational skills, personal interest in the field, strong interpersonal skills. Duration is full-time (1 position); part-time, 2-3 days per week (2 positions). $10 per day for subway and lunch. Open to high school seniors, recent high school graduates, college freshmen, college sophomores, college juniors, college seniors. International applications accepted.

Benefits Opportunity to attend seminars/workshops, willing to complete paperwork for educational credit, willing to provide letters of recommendation.

Contact Write, call, fax, or e-mail Tejal Jesrani, Administrative Coordinator, 11 Hanover Square, 20th Floor, New York, New York 10005. Phone: 212-785-7335. Fax: 212-785-7350. E-mail: tjesrani@ncrw.org. In-person interview recommended. Applicants must submit a resume, writing sample, two personal references. Applications are accepted continuously. World Wide Web: http://www.ncrw.org.

NATIONAL COUNCIL OF JEWISH WOMEN-LEGISTLATIVE OFFICE
1707 L Street, NW, Suite 950
Washington, District of Columbia 20036

General Information Legislative branch office of a large membership organization with a service and advocacy mission. Number of employees: 4. Branch of National Council of Jewish Women, New York, New York.

Internships Available ▶ *2 legislative interns:* responsibilities include assisting staff with substantive hands-on lobbying and tracking legislative issues. Candidates should have analytical skills, computer skills, personal interest in the field, research skills, writing skills, progressive stance on social issues. Duration is flexible. Unpaid. Open to college sophomores, college juniors, college seniors, recent college graduates, graduate students. International applications accepted.

Benefits Formal training, job counseling, opportunity to attend seminars/workshops, travel reimbursement, willing to act as a professional reference, willing to complete paperwork for educational credit, willing to provide letters of recommendation.

Contact Write or e-mail Jody Rabham, Associate Director, 1707 L Street, NW, Suite 950, Washington, District of Columbia 20036.

E-mail: ncjwdc@aol.com. Applicants must submit a cover letter, resume, writing sample, personal reference. Applications are accepted continuously.

NATIONAL CRIME PREVENTION COUNCIL
1700 K Street, NW, 2nd Floor
Washington, District of Columbia 20006

General Information Organization that helps focus the power of the individual and the community in the fight against crime. Established in 1980. Number of employees: 61. Number of internship applications received each year: 7.

Internships Available ▶ *3 interns:* responsibilities include working in any of the following programs: communities, research, press relations, public service, policing, prevention, education, state services, human resources, finance, and production. Candidates should have ability to work independently, ability to work with others, college courses in field, computer skills, knowledge of field, office skills, oral communication skills, personal interest in the field, research skills, self-motivation, writing skills. $7 per hour. Open to high school students, college freshmen, college sophomores, college juniors, college seniors, recent college graduates, graduate students, law students. International applications accepted.

Benefits Opportunity to attend seminars/workshops, possible full-time employment, travel reimbursement, willing to act as a professional reference, willing to complete paperwork for educational credit, willing to provide letters of recommendation.

Contact Write, call, fax, or e-mail LeAnn Logue, Personnel Assistant. Phone: 202-261-4149. Fax: 202-296-1356. E-mail: logue@ncpc.org. Telephone interview required. Applicants must submit a cover letter, resume. Application deadline: March 31 for summer, November 30 for spring. World Wide Web: http://www.weprevent.org.

NATIONAL CRIMINAL JUSTICE ASSOCIATION
444 North Capitol Street, NW, Suite 618
Washington, District of Columbia 20001

General Information Nonprofit, membership-based criminal justice association representing state and local government interests in public safety and crime control to Congress, federal executive, private and public agencies. Established in 1971. Number of employees: 9. Number of internship applications received each year: 30.

Internships Available ▶ *1 graduate intern:* responsibilities include researching, writing, and developing a quarterly policy report; and assisting staff with grant projects. Candidates should have analytical skills, editing skills, knowledge of field, research skills, self-motivation, writing skills. Open to graduate students. ▶ *1–2 undergraduate interns:* responsibilities include researching and writing articles for the monthly association newsletter; attending hearings, press conferences, and Supreme Court sessions; administrative and clerical work; and assisting staff with grant projects. Candidates should have ability to work independently, analytical skills, editing skills, research skills, self-motivation, writing skills. Open to college sophomores, college juniors, college seniors. Duration for all positions is fall, spring, or summer. All positions are unpaid.

Benefits On-the-job training, opportunity to attend seminars/workshops, willing to act as a professional reference, willing to complete paperwork for educational credit, willing to provide letters of recommendation.

Contact Write, call, fax, or e-mail Lisa Doyle Moran, Associate Director, 444 North Capitol Street, Suite 618, Washington, District of Columbia 20001. Phone: 202-624-1440. Fax: 202-508-3859. E-mail: ncja@sso.org. In-person interview required. Applicants must submit a cover letter, resume, academic transcripts, writing sample, 3 personal references or 3 letters of recommendation. Applications are accepted continuously. World Wide Web: http://www.sso.org/ncja.

NATIONAL ORGANIZATION FOR VICTIM ASSISTANCE (NOVA)
1757 Park Road, NW
Washington, District of Columbia 20010

General Information Private, nonprofit, 501(c)(3) organization of victim and witness assistance programs and practitioners, criminal justice agencies and professionals, mental health professionals researchers, former victims and survivors, and others committed to the recognition and implementation of victim rights and services. Established in 1975. Number of employees: 9.

Internships Available ► *Legislative assistants/lobbyists:* responsibilities include assisting in monitoring proposed federal legislation and promoting passage of designated bills to assist victims of crime. Candidates should have ability to work with others, oral communication skills, personal interest in the field, written communication skills. ► *Victim advocates:* responsibilities include working directly with victims of crime by phone, mail, or in person; and possibility of participating in a 40-hour victim advocacy training to learn crisis intervention. Candidates should have oral communication skills, personal interest in the field, strong interpersonal skills, writing skills, written communication skills. Duration for all positions is flexible. All positions are unpaid. Open to college freshmen, college sophomores, college juniors, college seniors, recent college graduates, graduate students, law students, career changers, individuals reentering the workforce. International applications accepted.

Benefits Formal training, names of contacts, on-the-job training, opportunity to attend seminars/workshops, willing to act as a professional reference, willing to complete paperwork for educational credit, willing to provide letters of recommendation, flexible hours, input in designing the internship, development of long-lasting skills, friendly atmosphere.

Contact Write, call, fax, or e-mail Melanie A. Merola, Volunteer Coordinator, 1757 Park Road, NW, Washington, District of Columbia 20010. Phone: 202-232-6682. Fax: 202-462-2255. E-mail: melanie@try_nova.org. In-person interview recommended. Applicants must submit a cover letter, resume. Applications are accepted continuously. World Wide Web: http://www.try-nova.org.

NATIONAL ORGANIZATION FOR WOMEN (NATIONAL ACTION CENTER)
1000 16th Street, NW, Suite 700
Washington, District of Columbia 20036

General Information Feminist organization working to ensure full equality for women and to end discrimination. Established in 1966. Number of employees: 35. Number of internship applications received each year: 200.

Internships Available ► *1–2 Internet/LAN interns:* responsibilities include assisting in programming and maintaining NOW's Web page and working with membership services. Candidates should have ability to work with others, computer skills, experience in the field, organizational skills, research skills, self-motivation. Duration is 1 semester. Open to college freshmen, college sophomores, college juniors, college seniors, recent college graduates, graduate students. ► *1 comptroller assistant:* responsibilities include maintaining a nonprofit organization's cash flow by assisting comptroller in daily book maintenance and organizing for yearly audit. Candidates should have ability to work independently, analytical skills, college courses in field, computer skills, office skills, organizational skills. Duration is 1 semester. Open to college sophomores, college juniors, college seniors, recent college graduates. ► *1–2 direct mail/marketing interns:* responsibilities include researching, writing, creating ads, working on product catalog, grant writing and research. Candidates should have ability to work independently, computer skills, research skills, strong interpersonal skills, written communication skills. Duration is 1 semester. Open to recent high school graduates, college freshmen, college sophomores, college juniors, college seniors, recent college graduates, graduate students, individuals reentering the workforce. ► *1–4 field organizing interns:* responsibilities include working on special projects in areas such as welfare rights, lesbian rights, racial diversity, violence against women, and state and chapter development. Candidates should have ability to work with others, oral communication skills, organizational skills, personal interest in the field, written communication skills. Duration is 1 semester. Open to high school seniors, recent high school graduates, college freshmen, college sophomores, college juniors, college seniors, recent college graduates, graduate students. ► *1–3 government relations interns:* responsibilities include lobbying, attending meetings, and performing legislative research and writing. Candidates should have ability to work independently, analytical skills, organizational skills, self-motivation, strong interpersonal skills, written communication skills. Duration is 14 weeks. Open to college sophomores, college juniors, college seniors, recent college graduates, graduate students. ► *1–3 legal interns:* responsibilities include researching, writing, analysis, and policy drafts. Candidates should have analytical skills, knowledge of field, oral communication skills, organizational skills, research skills, self-motivation. Duration is 8–10 weeks. Open to law students. ► *1–2 political action interns:* responsibilities include assisting NOW in PAC organizing, meeting with candidates, candidate research, processing endorsement requests, and managing Federal Election Commission materials. Candidates should have analytical skills, computer skills, organizational skills, self-motivation, strong interpersonal skills, written communication skills. Duration is 1 semester. Open to college freshmen, college sophomores, college juniors, college seniors, recent college graduates. ► *2–4 press/communications interns:* responsibilities include researching and writing articles for the *National NOW Times,* assisting in maintaining press clippings, drafting press releases. Candidates should have editing skills, research skills, self-motivation, strong interpersonal skills, writing skills. Duration is 1 semester. Open to high school seniors, recent high school graduates, college freshmen, college sophomores, college juniors, college seniors, recent college graduates, graduate students, individuals reentering the workforce. All positions are unpaid. International applications accepted.

Benefits Names of contacts, on-the-job training, opportunity to attend seminars/workshops, possible full-time employment, willing to act as a professional reference, willing to complete paperwork for educational credit, willing to provide letters of recommendation, formal training in grassroots organizing, field trips.

Contact Write, call, fax, or e-mail AnitaMarie Murano, Intern/Volunteer Coordinator. Phone: 202-331-0066. Fax: 202-785-8576. E-mail: volunt@now.org. In-person interview recommended. Applicants must submit a formal organization application, cover letter, resume, 1-2 letters of recommendation. Application deadline: March 15 for summer, July 15 for fall, November 27 for spring. World Wide Web: http://www.now.org.

NATIONAL PARTNERSHIP FOR WOMEN AND FAMILIES
1875 Connecticut Avenue, NW, Suite 710
Washington, District of Columbia 20009

General Information Nonprofit, nonpartisan organization that uses public education and advocacy to promote fairness in the workplace, quality health care, and policies that help women and men meet the dual demands of work and family. Founded as the Women's Legal Defense Fund, the National Partnership has grown from a small group of volunteers into one of the nation's most powerful and effective advocates for women and families. Working with business, government, unions, nonprofit organizations, and the media, the National Partnership is a voice of fairness, a source for solutions, and a force for change. Established in 1971. Number of employees: 28. Number of internship applications received each year: 250.

Internships Available ► *1 Action Council and membership intern:* responsibilities include membership recruitment and fundraising; expanding the National Partnership's membership in the Action Council through implementation of small fundraising events, creation of fund-raising solicitations, follow-up of pledges, and administrative duties associated with the daily operations of the development department; conducting research regarding current and potential major donors. Candidates should have ability to work independently, computer skills, oral communication skills, organizational skills, research skills, written communication skills. Duration is 8-10 weeks (10-20 hours per week during academic year; full-time during summer). Open to college freshmen, college sophomores, college juniors, college seniors, recent college graduates, graduate students. ▶ *1 annual luncheon intern:* responsibilities include assisting in the production of the annual luncheon, including coordinating invitation and follow-up mailings to guests, tracking responses, assisting with logistics, and other luncheon related duties. Candidates should have ability to work independently, computer skills, oral communication skills, organizational skills, research skills, written communication skills. Duration is 8-10 weeks (10-20 hours per week during academic year; full-time during summer). Open to college freshmen, college sophomores, college juniors, college seniors, recent college graduates, graduate students. ▶ *Communications interns:* responsibilities include researching, writing, and assisting with quarterly newsletter production, attending inside and outside meetings and press events, responding to requests for information from the media and public, producing and distributing daily clip packets, and maintaining filing systems. Candidates should have ability to work independently, computer skills, oral communication skills, organizational skills, research skills, written communication skills. Duration is 8-10 weeks (10-20 hours per week during academic year; full-time during summer). Open to college freshmen, college sophomores, college juniors, college seniors, recent college graduates, graduate students. ▶ *1–2 law clerks for health care program:* responsibilities include assisting with the National Partnership's advocacy efforts to improve women's access to affordable, quality health care; researching and analyzing women's health issues, monitoring federal and state legislation, and attending and reporting back to staff about relevant congressional hearings, briefings, and other meetings. Candidates should have ability to work independently, editing skills, research skills, self-motivation, writing skills, background in women's health. Duration is 8-10 weeks (10-20 hours per week during academic year; full time during summer). Open to graduate students, law students. ▶ *1–2 law clerks for work and family program:* responsibilities include assisting the National Partnership's advocacy efforts in the areas of equal employment opportunities, family friendly workplace policy, expansion of the Family and Medical Leave Act, and employment barriers affecting low-income women; working on ensuring effective enforcement of federal agencies responsible for enforcing anti-discrimination laws, and attending and reporting back to staff about relevant congressional hearings, briefings, and other meetings. Candidates should have ability to work independently, editing skills, research skills, self-motivation, writing skills. Duration is 8-10 weeks (10-20 hours per week during academic year; full-time during summer). Open to law students. ▶ *1–2 law clerks for workplace fairness:* responsibilities include assisting the National Partnership's advocacy efforts in the areas of equal employment opportunities, employment barries affecting low-income women, and the civil rights impact of welfare reform; legal research and writing in support of our monitoring of EEO enforcement; advocacy of broader laws and legal interpretations; amicus litigation; coalition advocacy; and public education about laws and proposals in this area. Candidates should have ability to work independently, editing skills, research skills, self-motivation, writing skills. Duration is 8-10 weeks (10-20 hours per week during academic year; full-time during summer). Open to law students. ▶ *1–2 work and family interns:* responsibilities include assisting with the National Partnership's advocacy efforts in the areas of equal employment opportunities, family-friendly workplace policy, expansion of the Family and Medical Leave Act, and barriers affecting low-income women; ensuring effective enforcement of federal agencies responsible for enforcing anti-discrimination laws, monitoring and developing legislative initiatives on employment issues, and public education. Candidates should have ability to work independently, computer skills, oral communication skills, organizational skills, research skills, written communication skills. Duration is 8-10 weeks (10-20 hours per week during academic year; full-time during summer). Open to college freshmen, college sophomores, college juniors, college seniors, recent college graduates, graduate students. ▶ *1–2*

workplace fairness interns: responsibilities include assisting with the National Partnership's advocacy efforts in the areas of equal employment opportunities, such as affirmative action; employment barriers affecting low-income women, particiularly welfare recipients; and the civil rights impact of welfare policy changes at the national and state levels. Interns will also assist in monitoring enforcement of federal anti-discrimination laws, advocating for legislation on employment issues, representation of the National Partnership in coalitions, research and writing, and educating the public about laws and proposals in the area, including developing factsheets and other informational materials. Candidates should have ability to work independently, computer skills, office skills, oral communication skills, organizational skills, research skills, written communication skills. Duration is 8-10 weeks (10-20 hours per week during academic year; full time during summer). Open to college freshmen, college sophomores, college juniors, college seniors, recent college graduates, graduate students. All positions are unpaid. International applications accepted.

Benefits Job counseling, names of contacts, willing to complete paperwork for educational credit, willing to provide letters of recommendation.

Contact Write, call, fax, or e-mail Ms. Antoinette Allsbrooks, Director of Administration. Phone: 202-986-2600. Fax: 202-986-2539. E-mail: amallsbrooks@nationalpartnership.org. Applicants must submit a resume, academic transcripts, writing sample, references. Application deadline: March 15 for summer; continuous for spring/fall. World Wide Web: http://www.nationalpartnership.org.

NATIONAL SPACE SOCIETY
600 Pennsylvania Avenue, SE, Suite 201
Washington, District of Columbia 20003

General Information Grassroots organization dedicated to public education and advocacy of the civilian space program; publishes a bimonthly magazine, lobbies Congress, and conducts educational and media programs. Established in 1974. Number of employees: 8. Number of internship applications received each year: 20.

Internships Available ▶ *1 administrative assistant:* responsibilities include assisting staff in everyday duties. Duration is flexible. ▶ *1 editorial assistant:* responsibilities include editing and writing. Duration is 3–6 flexible. ▶ *1 electronic networks assistant:* responsibilities include communicating with the public on the Internet, commercial computer networks, and WWW home page. Duration is flexible. ▶ *1 financial/accounting assistant:* responsibilities include assisting with office management. Duration is flexible. ▶ *1 political assistant:* responsibilities include writing and reporting on congressional/administrative space policy. Duration is flexible. ▶ *1 research assistant:* responsibilities include researching and writing technical/political/social articles for bimonthly publication. Duration is flexible. All positions are unpaid. Open to college freshmen, college sophomores, college juniors, college seniors, recent college graduates. International applications accepted.

Benefits Names of contacts, opportunity to attend seminars/workshops, possible full-time employment, willing to complete paperwork for educational credit, willing to provide letters of recommendation, membership.

Contact Write, call, fax, or e-mail Office Manager. Phone: 202-543-1900. Fax: 202-546-4189. E-mail: nsshq@nss.org. Applicants must submit a cover letter, resume, writing sample. Applications are accepted continuously. World Wide Web: http://www.nss.org.

NATIONAL TAXPAYERS UNION
108 North Alfred Street
Alexandria, Virginia 22314

General Information Public interest group that works for tax relief, constitutional limits on taxes and spending, taxpayers' rights, and reduction of government waste. Established in 1969. Number of employees: 15. Number of internship applications received each year: 100.

National Taxpayers Union (continued)

Internships Available ▶ *2 legislative aides:* responsibilities include assisting lobbying staff with mailings, visits to legislators, and calls to congressional aides. Candidates should have knowledge of field, office skills, oral communication skills, personal interest in the field, strong interpersonal skills, written communication skills. Position available as unpaid or at $180 per week. ▶ *2 policy/editorial assistants:* responsibilities include conducting long-term research on fiscal policy issues and writing and editing newsletter copy. Candidates should have ability to work independently, analytical skills, editing skills, personal interest in the field, research skills, writing skills. Position available as unpaid or at $180 per week. ▶ *2 researchers:* responsibilities include researching cost impact of fiscal policies. Candidates should have computer skills, office skills, oral communication skills, research skills, strong interpersonal skills. Position available as unpaid or at $180 per week. Duration for all positions is minimum of 10 weeks. Open to college sophomores, college juniors, college seniors, graduate students, law students. International applications accepted.

Benefits Names of contacts, opportunity to attend seminars/workshops, willing to complete paperwork for educational credit, willing to provide letters of recommendation.

Contact Write, fax, or e-mail Jeff Dircksen, Director of Internships. Fax: 703-683-5722. E-mail: dircksen@ntu.org. Telephone interview required. Applicants must submit a cover letter, resume, two writing samples, personal reference. Applications are accepted continuously. World Wide Web: http://www.ntu.org.

NATIONAL TRAINING AND INFORMATION CENTER
810 North Milwaukee
Chicago, Illinois 60622

General Information Resource center for grassroots neighborhood groups, providing training in community, organizing and focusing on issues such as housing, reinvestment, safe neighborhoods, and education. Established in 1972. Number of employees: 18. Number of internship applications received each year: 30.

Internships Available ▶ *2 community organizing interns:* responsibilities include researching domestic policy, attending night and weekend meetings in Chicago neighborhoods, writing, and supporting staff as directed. Candidates should have oral communication skills, personal interest in the field, strong interpersonal skills, strong leadership ability. Duration is 3–6 months. Unpaid. Open to high school students, high school seniors, recent high school graduates, college freshmen, college sophomores, college juniors, college seniors, recent college graduates, graduate students, law students, career changers, individuals reentering the workforce. International applications accepted.

Benefits Formal training, job counseling, names of contacts, on-the-job training, opportunity to attend seminars/workshops, possible full-time employment, willing to act as a professional reference, willing to complete paperwork for educational credit, willing to provide letters of recommendation.

Contact Write, fax, or e-mail Mr. Shel Trapp, Staff Director. Fax: 312-243-7044. E-mail: ntic@dls.net. No phone calls. Applicants must submit a cover letter, resume. Applications are accepted continuously.

NATIONAL WHISTLEBLOWER CENTER
3238 P Street, NW
Washington, District of Columbia 20007

General Information Nonprofit educational and advocacy organization committed to environmental protection, nuclear safety, government accountability, and protecting the rights of employee whistle blowers. Established in 1988.

Internships Available ▶ *Law clerks:* responsibilities include significant legal research and writing projects, assisting at trials, and performing all the work of an associate attorney. Duration is 10 weeks (minimum). Unpaid. Open to law students.

Benefits Willing to complete paperwork for educational credit, one-on-one supervision from an attorney.

Contact Write, call, fax, or e-mail Joyce Claro, Internship Coordinator, 3238 P Street, NW, Washington, District of Columbia 20007. Phone: 202-342-6980. Fax: 202-342-6984. E-mail: whistle@ whistleblowers.org. Telephone interview required. Applicants must submit a cover letter, resume. Applications are accepted continuously. World Wide Web: http://www.whistleblowers.org.

NATIONAL WOMEN'S HEALTH NETWORK
514 10th Street, NW, Suite 400
Washington, District of Columbia 20004

General Information Organization that provides information on women's health issues and advocates for women's health by functioning as a watchdog over federal agencies. Established in 1975. Number of employees: 5. Number of internship applications received each year: 200.

Internships Available ▶ *5 women's health advocacy interns:* responsibilities include working in the clearinghouse and on special projects, attending meetings and conferences. Candidates should have oral communication skills, organizational skills, personal interest in the field, self-motivation, strong interpersonal skills, written communication skills. Duration is 3 months minimum. Position available as unpaid or at $80 per week. Open to high school students, high school seniors, recent high school graduates, college freshmen, college sophomores, college juniors, college seniors, recent college graduates, graduate students, law students, career changers, individuals reentering the workforce. International applications accepted.

Benefits Names of contacts, opportunity to attend seminars/workshops, willing to act as a professional reference, willing to complete paperwork for educational credit, willing to provide letters of recommendation.

Contact Write, call, or fax Ms. Brooke Grandle, Clearinghouse and Intern Coordinator. Phone: 202-347-1140. Fax: 202-347-1168. Telephone interview required. Applicants must submit a cover letter, resume, writing sample. Application deadline: continuous for spring and fall, March 15 for summer.

NATIONAL WOMEN'S POLITICAL CAUCUS
1630 Connecticut Avenue, NW, Suite 201
Washington, District of Columbia 20006

General Information National bipartisan grassroots organization dedicated to the advancement of women through appointed and elected public office; operates a nonprofit, leadership development, education, and research arm and conducts extensive training seminars designed to train women for potential candidacy. Established in 1971. Number of employees: 12. Number of internship applications received each year: 250.

Internships Available ▶ *1–2 development interns:* responsibilities include coordinating major fund-raising events, creating high donor materials, and dealing with major financiers and donors. ▶ *1–2 membership interns:* responsibilities include working as member services liaisons and assisting national field director in grassroots organizing and development of state and local caucuses. ▶ *1 office of the President intern:* responsibilities include working with the President's or Executive Director's assistant in making travel arrangements, scheduling, and attending meetings on behalf of the President. ▶ *1–2 political department interns:* responsibilities include tracking political races and evaluating women candidates for NWPC endorsements. ▶ *Press office interns:* responsibilities include assisting with coordinating contact with national and local media, and promoting NWPC and President. ▶ *Special events interns:* responsibilities include assisting with the coordination of various aspects of the NWPC's special events, including Exceptional Merit Medal Awards, Good Guys, Coalition for Women's Appointments, and training. Duration for all positions is one semester, 4-5 days per week. All positions are unpaid. International applications accepted.

Benefits Names of contacts, opportunity to attend seminars/workshops, possible full-time employment, willing to complete paperwork for educational credit, willing to provide letters of recommendation, opportunity to gain leadership skills.

Contact Write or call Anita Nunez, Intern Coordinator. Phone: 202-785-1100. Applicants must submit a cover letter, resume, writing sample. Applications are accepted continuously.

NATIONAL YOUTH & MILITARISM PROGRAM, AMERICAN FRIENDS SERVICE COMMITTEE
1501 Cherry Street
Philadelphia, Pennsylvania 19102

General Information Quaker organization committed to peace and social justice. Conducts public education campaigns and supports grassroots organizing on issues involving youth, war, and peace. Established in 1917. Number of employees: 150. Unit of American Friends Service Committee, Philadelphia, Pennsylvania. Number of internship applications received each year: 40.
Internships Available ▶ *1 Jim Bristol youth and militarism fellow:* responsibilities include working for social change on a national level. Candidates should have ability to work with others, computer skills, experience in the field, oral communication skills, personal interest in the field, written communication skills. Duration is 1 year. $14,000 per year. International applications accepted.
Benefits Health insurance, on-the-job training, opportunity to attend seminars/workshops, possible full-time employment, travel reimbursement, willing to act as a professional reference, willing to provide letters of recommendation.
Contact Write, call, or e-mail Jim Bristol, Fellowship Recruiter, 1501 Cherry Street, Philadelphia, Pennsylvania 19102. Phone: 215-241-7107. E-mail: tmaguire@afsc.org. In-person interview required. Applicants must submit a formal organization application, cover letter, resume. Application deadline: April 1. World Wide Web: http://www.afsc.org/youthmil.htm.

NETWORK
801 Pennsylvania Avenue, SE, Suite 460
Washington, District of Columbia 20003

General Information A national Catholic social justice lobby whose members seek to influence national legislation for health-care reform, affordable housing, economic conversion, deficit reduction, and global collaboration for equitable and sustainable development. Established in 1971. Number of employees: 12. Number of internship applications received each year: 10.
Internships Available ▶ *3 associates:* responsibilities include representing staff at coalition meetings, conveying legislative information to staff, lobbying, activating grass roots organizing, and assisting with administrative work. Candidates should have ability to work with others, computer skills, oral communication skills, personal interest in the field, self-motivation, written communication skills. Duration is 11 months. $6,000 per duration of internship. Open to recent college graduates, career changers, individuals reentering the workforce.
Benefits Names of contacts, opportunity to attend seminars/workshops, possible full-time employment, willing to complete paperwork for educational credit, willing to provide letters of recommendation, partial health benefits for paid internships.
Contact Write, call, fax, or e-mail Ms. Linda Rich, Associate Coordinator. Phone: 202-547-5556. Fax: 202-547-5510. E-mail: lrich@networklobby.org. Telephone interview required. Applicants must submit a formal organization application. Application deadline: February 1. World Wide Web: http://www.networklobby.org.

THE NETWORK OF EAST-WEST WOMEN
1601 Connecticut Avenue, NW, Suite 603
Washington, District of Columbia 20009

General Information Communication network that links over 2,000 women's advocates in more than 30 countries in the former Soviet Union and Eastern and Central Europe.
Internships Available ▶ *Interns:* responsibilities include researching and writing on a variety of women's advocacy projects, translation, project coordination, media relations, and general administration. Duration is 1–2 semesters. Unpaid. Open to college freshmen, college sophomores, college juniors, college seniors, graduate students. International applications accepted.
Benefits Names of contacts, opportunity to attend seminars/workshops, willing to complete paperwork for educational credit, willing to provide letters of recommendation.
Contact Write, call, fax, or e-mail Erin Barclay, Executive Director, 1601 Connecticut Avenue, NW, Suite 603, Washington, District of Columbia 20009. Phone: 202-265-3585. Fax: 205-265-3508. E-mail: eastwest@neww.org. Applicants must submit a resume, personal reference, cover letter that describes applicant's language skills, computer skills, nature of interest in women's issues, and how you hope to benefit from this internship. Applications are accepted continuously. World Wide Web: http://www.neww.org.

NEW PARTY
88 Third Avenue, Suite 313
Brooklyn, New York 11217

General Information Grassroots political party focusing on issues of economic justice, democratic political reform, and investment in education and children.
Internships Available ▶ *Interns:* responsibilities include working at national office in Brooklyn, or for field offices in New York, Boston, Washington, DC, St. Paul, Milwaukee, Madison, Little Rock, Chicago, and Missoula; assisting with electoral campaigns, planning, fund-raising, canvassing, direct mailing, and administrative duties. Duration is flexible. $100 per week. Open to high school students, high school seniors, recent high school graduates, college freshmen, college sophomores, college juniors, college seniors, recent college graduates, graduate students, law students, career changers, individuals reentering the workforce.
Benefits Possible full-time employment, willing to complete paperwork for educational credit.
Contact Write, call, or fax Intern Director. Phone: 718-246-3713. Fax: 718-246-3718. Applicants must submit a cover letter, resume. Applications are accepted continuously. World Wide Web: http://www.newparty.org.

NEW YORK PUBLIC INTEREST RESEARCH GROUP
107 Washington Avenue
Albany, New York 12210

General Information Nonpartisan, not-for-profit research and advocacy organization established and directed by New York state college and university students that works for consumer protection, environmental preservation, and reform in health care, education, and government. Established in 1973. Number of employees: 60. Number of internship applications received each year: 60.
Internships Available ▶ *6–10 legislative associates:* responsibilities include researching issues, tracking legislation, organizing public support, and advocating positions in the New York legislature. Candidates should have ability to work independently, ability to work with others, oral communication skills, self-motivation, strong leadership ability, writing skills. Duration is 1 semester. $400 per month. Open to college juniors, college seniors, graduate students. International applications accepted.
Benefits Formal training, names of contacts, opportunity to attend seminars/workshops, possible full-time employment, travel reimbursement, willing to complete paperwork for educational credit, willing to provide letters of recommendation.
Contact Write, call, or fax Mr. Blair Horner, Legislative Director. Phone: 518-436-0876. Fax: 518-432-6178. E-mail: bhorner@nypirg.org. In-person interview recommended. Applicants must submit a formal organization application, writing sample. Application deadline: November 1.

9 TO 5, NATIONAL ASSOCIATION OF WORKING WOMEN
231 West Wisconsin Avenue, Suite 900
Milwaukee, Wisconsin 53203-2308

General Information Advocacy group for women addressing issues including job problem counseling, policy advising, research

9 to 5, National Association of Working Women (continued)

and education, sexual harassment, and health and safety; internship opportunities available in Wisconsin and Georgia. Established in 1973. Number of employees: 25. Number of internship applications received each year: 100.

Internships Available ▶ *2 interns:* responsibilities include assisting on Job Problem hot line, organizing members, assisting with research materials and publications, assembling and mailing membership packets, and doing clerical work. Duration is flexible. Unpaid. Open to high school students, high school seniors, recent high school graduates, college freshmen, college sophomores, college juniors, college seniors, recent college graduates, graduate students, law students, career changers, individuals reentering the workforce. International applications accepted.

Benefits Names of contacts, willing to complete paperwork for educational credit, willing to provide letters of recommendation.

Contact Write, fax, or e-mail Teresa Ragland, Office Administrator. Fax: 414-272-2870. E-mail: naww9to5@execpc.com. In-person interview recommended. Applicants must submit a cover letter, resume. Applications are accepted continuously.

NORTH CAROLINA CENTER FOR PUBLIC POLICY RESEARCH
PO Box 430
Raleigh, North Carolina 27602

General Information Public policy research center that studies state government policies and procedures and attempts to educate the public. Established in 1977. Number of employees: 6.

Internships Available ▶ *2 research interns:* responsibilities include keeping up with legislation, writing and researching articles, and performing data entry. Candidates should have personal interest in the field, plan to pursue career in field, research skills, writing skills. Duration is 10 weeks. Position available as unpaid or paid. Open to college juniors, college seniors, recent college graduates, graduate students. International applications accepted.

Benefits Willing to act as a professional reference, willing to complete paperwork for educational credit, willing to provide letters of recommendation.

Contact Write, call, fax, or e-mail Policy Analyst. Phone: 919-832-2839. Fax: 919-832-2847. E-mail: rosebud@nando.net. In-person interview recommended. Applicants must submit a resume, academic transcripts, writing sample. Application deadline: March 31 for summer; continuous for all other positions. World Wide Web: http://www.nando.net/insider/nccppr.

NORTH HIGHLANDS CHILDRENS COALITION
5428 Watt Avenue
North Highlands, California 95660

General Information Child advocacy organization. Established in 1994. Number of employees: 10. Number of internship applications received each year: 2.

Internships Available ▶ *1–5 after-school program assistants:* responsibilities include organizing parents and children to interact and play together at Friday night program, and assisting director in after-school day program. Candidates should have ability to work independently, oral communication skills, self-motivation, strong interpersonal skills. Open to high school students, high school seniors, recent high school graduates, college freshmen, college sophomores, college juniors, college seniors, recent college graduates, graduate students, law students, career changers, individuals reentering the workforce. ▶ *1–5 community liaisons:* responsibilities include working with community businesses and the NHCC to develop partnerships which enable resource sharing. Candidates should have ability to work independently, oral communication skills, organizational skills, self-motivation, strong interpersonal skills. Open to high school seniors, recent high school graduates, college freshmen, college sophomores, college juniors, college seniors, recent college graduates, graduate students, law students, career changers, individuals reentering the workforce. All positions are unpaid.

Benefits On-the-job training, opportunity to attend seminars/workshops, willing to act as a professional reference.

Contact Write, call, fax, or e-mail Linda Andersen, Project Coordinator, 5428 Watt Avenue, #300, North Highlands, California 95660. Phone: 916-339-9252. Fax: 916-339-9271. E-mail: hn5755@handsnet.org. Applicants must submit a cover letter. Applications are accepted continuously.

OLDER WOMEN'S LEAGUE
666 11th Street, NW, Suite 700
Washington, District of Columbia 20001

General Information National membership organization that strives to improve the status and quality of life for women, midlife and older. Established in 1980. Number of employees: 12.

Internships Available ▶ *1 organizing and advocacy intern.* Candidates should have strong interest in women's issues and a positive attitude. Duration is flexible. Open to college freshmen, college sophomores, college juniors, college seniors, recent college graduates, career changers, individuals reentering the workforce, non-traditional students. ▶ *1 public policy and research intern.* Candidates should have strong interest in women's issues, and a positive attitude. Duration is flexible (minimum 16 hours per week). Open to college freshmen, college sophomores, college juniors, college seniors, recent college graduates, graduate students, career changers, individuals reentering the workforce, non-traditional students. All positions are unpaid. International applications accepted.

Benefits Names of contacts, opportunity to attend seminars/workshops, travel reimbursement, willing to complete paperwork for educational credit, willing to provide letters of recommendation, willing to design special projects to match intern's academic targets.

Contact Write, call, or fax Kellye McIntosh, Field Services Director, 666 11th Street, NW, Suite 700, Washington, District of Columbia 20001. Phone: 800-825-3695. Fax: 202-638-2356. In-person interview recommended. Applicants must submit a formal organization application, resume, personal reference. Applications are accepted continuously. World Wide Web: http://www.owl-national.org.

ORGANIZATION OF CHINESE AMERICANS
1001 Connecticut Avenue, NW, Suite 707
Washington, District of Columbia 20036

General Information National nonprofit advocacy organization of concerned Chinese Americans dedicated to securing social justice, equal opportunity, and equal treatment of Chinese Americans. Established in 1973. Number of employees: 4. Number of internship applications received each year: 80.

Internships Available ▶ *1–4 Congressional interns:* responsibilities include attending subcommittee hearings, tracking legislation, research, writing articles and press releases, and office duties. Candidates should have ability to work independently, ability to work with others, analytical skills, computer skills, editing skills, office skills, oral communication skills, self-motivation, strong leadership ability, writing skills. Paid. ▶ *1–4 OCA national office interns:* responsibilities include writing press releases and articles; attending meetings. Candidates should have ability to work independently, analytical skills, computer skills, editing skills, office skills, oral communication skills, organizational skills, research skills, self-motivation, strong interpersonal skills, writing skills. Paid. ▶ *1–4 government interns:* responsibilities include attending subcommittee hearings, tracking legislation, research, writing articles and press releases, and office duties. Candidates should have ability to work independently, ability to work with others, analytical skills, editing skills, oral communication skills, research skills, self-motivation, strong leadership ability, writing skills. Paid. Duration for all positions is 10 weeks. Open to college freshmen, college sophomores, college juniors, college seniors.

Benefits Opportunity to attend seminars/workshops, willing to complete paperwork for educational credit, stipend of $2000.

Contact Write, call, fax, or e-mail Daphne Kwok, Executive Director. Phone: 202-223-5500. Fax: 202-296-0540. E-mail: oca@

ocanatl.org. Telephone interview required. Applicants must submit a formal organization application, cover letter, resume, academic transcripts, three personal references, essay (typed and double-spaced) explaining interest in internship. Application deadline: March 15 for summer, July 15 for fall, November 15 for spring. World Wide Web: http://www.ocanatl.org.

OVARIAN CANCER NATIONAL ALLIANCE
1627 K Street, NW, 12th Floor
Washington, District of Columbia 20006

General Information Nonprofit organization working at the national level to increase public and professional understanding of ovarian cancer and to advocate for increased research for more effective diagnostics and treatment. This is an opportunity to get in on the ground floor of a burgeoning nonprofit organization. Established in 1997. Number of employees: 3. Number of internship applications received each year: 10.
Internships Available ▶ *Staff assistants:* responsibilities include working closely with the Executive and Assistant Directors; handling consumer correspondence, data entry, statistics, and information gathering; outreach; and representing the Alliance at meetings. Candidates should have computer skills, personal interest in the field, interest in women's and health issues. Unpaid. Open to college freshmen, college sophomores, college juniors, college seniors, recent college graduates, career changers.
Benefits Opportunity to attend seminars/workshops, willing to act as a professional reference, willing to complete paperwork for educational credit, willing to provide letters of recommendation.
Contact Write, call, fax, or e-mail Ann Kolker, Executive Director. Phone: 202-331-1332. Fax: 202-293-1990. E-mail: ovarian@aol.com. In-person interview recommended. Applicants must submit a resume, two personal references. Applications are accepted continuously. World Wide Web: http://www.ovariancancer.org.

PARTNERS FOR LIVABLE COMMUNITIES
1429 21st Street, NW
Washington, District of Columbia 20036

General Information Nonprofit organization working to improve the livability of communities by promoting quality of life, economic development, and social equity. Established in 1978. Number of employees: 10. Number of internship applications received each year: 25.
Internships Available ▶ *2–4 interns:* responsibilities include assisting in research, writing, event coordinating, and information management. Candidates should have ability to work independently, ability to work with others, computer skills, editing skills, organizational skills, personal interest in the field, research skills, self-motivation, written communication skills. Duration is flexible. Position available as unpaid or paid. Open to college sophomores, college juniors, college seniors, recent college graduates, graduate students. International applications accepted.
Benefits Willing to complete paperwork for educational credit, willing to provide letters of recommendation.
Contact Write, call, or e-mail Hannah Roberts, Program Officer. Phone: 202-887-5990. E-mail: partners@livable.com. In-person interview recommended. Applicants must submit a cover letter, resume, 1-2 writing samples. Application deadline: April 1 for summer, August 10 for fall, December 10 for spring.

PEACE ACTION
1819 H Street, NW, Room 420
Washington, District of Columbia 20006

General Information Grassroots peace and justice organization that seeks to promote global security by converting to a peace economy and stopping the nuclear arms race and conventional arms trade. Established in 1957. Number of employees: 15. Number of internship applications received each year: 100.
Internships Available ▶ *1–2 organizing department interns:* responsibilities include assisting with event organizing, research, writing, desk top publishing, Web publishing, some administra-

tive work. ▶ *1–2 policy department interns:* responsibilities include research, writing, desktop and Web publishing, coalition meetings, some event organizing, and administrative work. Candidates for all positions should have ability to work independently, ability to work with others, computer skills, organizational skills, personal interest in the field, written communication skills. Duration for all positions is 3 months. All positions are unpaid. Open to high school seniors, recent high school graduates, college freshmen, college sophomores, college juniors, college seniors, recent college graduates, graduate students, law students, career changers, individuals reentering the workforce. International applications accepted.
Benefits Job counseling, names of contacts, on-the-job training, opportunity to attend seminars/workshops, possible full-time employment, travel reimbursement, willing to complete paperwork for educational credit, willing to provide letters of recommendation.
Contact Write, call, fax, or e-mail Jim Bridgman, Internship Coordinator. Phone: 202-862-9740 Ext. 3041. Fax: 202-862-9762. E-mail: jbridgman@peace-action.org. In-person interview recommended. Applicants must submit a formal organization application, cover letter, resume, writing sample, 2-3 personal references. Applications are accepted continuously. World Wide Web: http://www.peace-action.org.

PEACE BRIGADES INTERNATIONAL/USA
1904 Franklin Street, Suite 505
Oakland, California 94612

General Information Peace and human rights organization with projects in seven countries specializing in the promotion of human rights, protection of human rights activists, and nonviolent conflict resolution. Established in 1981. Number of employees: 2. Number of internship applications received each year: 30.
Internships Available ▶ *Human rights interns:* responsibilities include coordinating emergency alerts, organizing special events, translating, and assisting with fund-raising. Candidates should have ability to work independently, ability to work with others, computer skills, office skills, organizational skills, writing skills, proficiency in French or Spanish. ▶ *Journalism interns:* responsibilities include writing feature articles and opinion-editorials, helping with publication of newsletter, desktop publishing. Candidates should have ability to work independently, editing skills, organizational skills, writing skills, proficiency in French or Spanish. ▶ *Media/public relations interns:* responsibilities include cultivating media contacts, arranging speaking tours, and writing feature articles and opinion-editorials. Candidates should have computer skills, personal interest in the field, research skills, self-motivation, writing skills, proficiency in French or Spanish. Duration for all positions is at least 10-15 hours per week. All positions are unpaid. Open to college freshmen, college sophomores, college juniors, college seniors, recent college graduates, graduate students, law students, career changers, individuals reentering the workforce. International applications accepted.
Benefits On-the-job training, opportunity to attend seminars/workshops, willing to act as a professional reference, willing to provide letters of recommendation.
International Internships Available in Canada; Colombia; Croatia; Haiti; Mexico; Yugoslavia.
Contact Write, call, fax, or e-mail Peter Stanga, Co-Director, 1904 Franklin Street, Suite 505, Oakland, California 94612. Phone: 510-663-2362. Fax: 510-663-2364. E-mail: pbiusa@igc.org. In-person interview recommended. Applicants must submit a cover letter, resume. Applications are accepted continuously. World Wide Web: http://www.igc.org/pbi/index/html.

PEACE LINKS USA
666 11th Street, NW, Suite 202
Washington, District of Columbia 20001

General Information A grassroots network of women who are dedicated to a peaceful future, locally and globally. Established in 1982. Number of employees: 6. Number of internship applications received each year: 40.

Peace Links USA (continued)

Internships Available ▶ *1 Pen Pals for Peace intern:* responsibilities include administering Russia-America correspondence program, logging incoming requests for pen pals, matching Russians and Americans, handling general correspondence, and some general administrative tasks. Candidates should have ability to work independently, computer skills, office skills, personal interest in the field, self-motivation, written communication skills, advanced knowledge of Russian language. Duration is 1 semester. $7–$10 per hour. Open to college juniors, college seniors, recent college graduates. ▶ *1 Safe Schools intern:* responsibilities include assisting field director in managing program, assembling promotional and informational materials on program, providing logistical support for *Listen Up* events, and some general administrative duites. Candidates should have college courses in field, oral communication skills, organizational skills, plan to pursue career in field, writing skills, ability and desire to work with youth. Duration is 1 semester. Position available as unpaid or at $7–$10 per hour. Open to college juniors, college seniors, recent college graduates, graduate students. ▶ *1 administrative intern:* responsibilities include providing support to many areas, with opportunity to concentrate on one of the following specific programs: international "Citizen Diplomacy" exchanges, nuclear disaramament, or nonprofit development. Also responsible for assembling press and informational packets, photocopying, faxing, and handling correspondence with Peace Links board and Congressional spouses. Candidates should have self-motivation, willingness to learn Microsoft Office software on Windows-based computers, especially Microsoft Access database software. Unpaid. Open to undergraduate liberal arts majors. International applications accepted.

Benefits On-the-job training, opportunity to attend seminars/workshops, possible full-time employment, willing to act as a professional reference, willing to complete paperwork for educational credit, willing to provide letters of recommendation.

Contact Write Ian Chelsey, Program Assistant. In-person interview recommended. Applicants must submit a cover letter, resume, two letters of recommendation. Applications are accepted continuously. World Wide Web: http://www.peacelinksusa.org.

PEACE OFFERINGS/PROJECT OF THE SOCIAL JUSTICE CENTER OF ALBANY
33 Central Avenue
Albany, New York 12210

General Information Umbrella organization of sixteen different peace and justice groups concerned with issues from nuclear disarmament to the environment. Established in 1982. Number of employees: 2.

Internships Available ▶ *1 intern:* responsibilities include working on a specific project. Duration is 3 months. ▶ *2–4 peace offering interns:* responsibilities include outreach and referral for member organizations, performing day-to-day operations and program work centered on public education and promotion of store mission regarding the sale of crafts by indigenous peoples, and fair trade support activities. Duration is 1 semester. All positions are unpaid. Open to high school students, high school seniors, recent high school graduates, college freshmen, college sophomores, college juniors, college seniors, recent college graduates, graduate students, individuals reentering the workforce. International applications accepted.

Benefits Willing to complete paperwork for educational credit, willing to provide letters of recommendation.

Contact Write or call Kimberly Manning, Coordinator. Phone: 518-434-4037. In-person interview recommended. Applicants must submit a cover letter, resume, 1 academic and 1 personal reference. Application deadline: semester prior to internship semester.

PEOPLE FOR THE AMERICAN WAY FOUNDATION
2000 M Street, NW, #400
Washington, District of Columbia 20036

General Information A nonprofit 300,000-member, progressive, nonpartisan, constitutional liberties organization. Established in 1980. Number of employees: 65. Number of internship applications received each year: 300.

Internships Available ▶ *5–10 interns:* responsibilities include writing; grassroots organizing; researching; monitoring legislation; and performing media relations, marketing, and development work. Candidates should have ability to work with others, computer skills, knowledge of field, oral communication skills, plan to pursue career in field, written communication skills. Duration is 2–12 months. $8–$10 per hour. Open to high school students, high school seniors, recent high school graduates, college freshmen, college sophomores, college juniors, college seniors, recent college graduates, graduate students, law students, career changers, individuals reentering the workforce. International applications accepted.

Benefits Opportunity to attend seminars/workshops, possible full-time employment, willing to act as a professional reference, willing to complete paperwork for educational credit, willing to provide letters of recommendation.

Contact Write, call, fax, or e-mail Ms. Judy Green, Senior Vice President. Phone: 202-467-2306. Fax: 202-293-2672. E-mail: jgreen@pfaw.org. Telephone interview required. Applicants must submit a cover letter, resume. Applications are accepted continuously. World Wide Web: http://www.pfaw.org.

PEOPLE MAKING A DIFFERENCE THROUGH COMMUNITY SERVICE, INC.
PO Box 120189
Boston, Massachusetts 02112-0189

General Information Organizes one-day community service projects that assist other charitable groups in the greater Boston area. Established in 1992. Number of employees: 1. Number of internship applications received each year: 1.

Internships Available ▶ *1–2 development assistants:* responsibilities include assisting Board development committee with biannual appeals and special events for grassroots support. Candidates should have computer skills, knowledge of field, office skills, organizational skills, self-motivation. Open to college seniors, recent college graduates, graduate students, career changers. ▶ *1–3 program assistants:* responsibilities include assisting with all aspects of service program: volunteer recruitment, project development, planning, evaluation, participation, and fundraising. Candidates should have ability to work with others, computer skills, experience in the field, organizational skills, personal interest in the field, self-motivation. Open to college juniors, college seniors, recent college graduates, graduate students. Duration for all positions is flexible. All positions are unpaid.

Benefits Names of contacts, on-the-job training, willing to act as a professional reference, willing to complete paperwork for educational credit, willing to provide letters of recommendation.

Contact Write, call, or e-mail Lori Tsuruda, Founder and Executive Director. Phone: 617-437-8871. E-mail: lori@pmd.org. In-person interview recommended. Applicants must submit a cover letter, resume, academic transcripts, two letters of recommendation, participation in at least one PMD community service project prior to application (offered on a weekly basis). Applications are accepted continuously. World Wide Web: http://www.pmd.org.

PHILADELPHIA LESBIAN AND GAY TASKFORCE
1616 Walnut Street, Suite 1005
Philadelphia, Pennsylvania 19103-5310

General Information Public interest organization dedicated to the civil, human, and constitutional rights of lesbian and gay people, focusing on research, public policy, advocacy, direct service, and litigation. Established in 1978. Number of employees: 2. Number of internship applications received each year: 6.

Internships Available ▶ *1 broadcast communications intern:* responsibilities include performing research and statistical analysis and offering clerical support. Candidates should have ability to work independently, analytical skills, computer skills, office skills, oral communication skills, organizational skills, research skills, written communication skills. Open to college juniors, college seniors, recent college graduates, graduate students. ▶ *2 education interns:* responsibilities include performing research and statistical analysis and offering clerical support. Candidates should have ability to work independently, ability to work with others, computer skills, office skills, oral communication skills, research skills, written communication skills. Open to college seniors, recent college graduates, graduate students, law students. ▶ *2 law interns:* responsibilities include performing research and offering clerical support. Candidates should have ability to work independently, computer skills, declared college major in field, office skills, oral communication skills, research skills, writing skills. Duration for all positions is ongoing. All positions are unpaid.

Benefits Names of contacts, on-the-job training, opportunity to attend seminars/workshops, possible full-time employment, travel reimbursement, willing to provide letters of recommendation.

Contact Write, call, fax, or e-mail Ms. Rita Addessa, Executive Director. Phone: 215-772-2000. Fax: 215-772-2004. E-mail: plgtf@ op.net. In-person interview required. Applicants must submit a cover letter, resume, writing sample. Applications are accepted continuously. World Wide Web: http://www.op.net/plgtf.

PHYSICIANS FOR HUMAN RIGHTS
100 Boylston Street, Suite 702
Boston, Massachusetts 02116

General Information Organization that examines health effects of human rights violations and applies methods of medical research to the documentation of those violations. Established in 1986. Number of employees: 14. Number of internship applications received each year: 30.

Internships Available ▶ *1–4 interns (in Boston and DC offices):* responsibilities include researching cases of health professionals and others whose international human rights are violated, assisting in organization of advocacy actions and educational events on health and human rights, drafting letters and background materials, and researching topics of special interest to the organization in the field of health and human rights. Candidates should have ability to work independently, ability to work with others, computer skills, personal interest in the field, writing skills. Duration is minimum 2 months. Unpaid. Open to recent high school graduates, college freshmen, college sophomores, college juniors, college seniors, recent college graduates. International applications accepted.

Benefits Names of contacts, opportunity to attend seminars/ workshops, willing to complete paperwork for educational credit.

Contact Write or e-mail Lori Maida, Director of Finance and Administration. E-mail: phrusa@phrusa.org. No phone calls. In-person interview recommended. Applicants must submit a cover letter, resume, writing sample, two letters of recommendation. Application deadline: March 1 for summer; continuous for other positions. World Wide Web: http://www.phrusa.org/.

PHYSICIANS FOR SOCIAL RESPONSIBILITY
1101 14th Street, NW, Suite 700
Washington, District of Columbia 20005

General Information Organization of health-care professionals and other concerned citizens working to prevent nuclear war and dedicated to the elimination of weapons of mass destruction, the preservation of a sustainable environment, and the reduction of violence and its causes. Recipient of 1985 Nobel Peace Prize. Established in 1961. Number of employees: 20. Number of internship applications received each year: 200.

Internships Available ▶ *1 environmental health intern:* responsibilities include researching and writing on national and international environmental health issues such as global climate change and persistent toxic pollutants. Candidates should have ability to work independently, oral communication skills, research

skills, self-motivation, strong interpersonal skills, written communication skills. Duration is 3 months or more (6 months to 1 year preferred). Open to college juniors, college seniors, recent college graduates, graduate students. ▶ *1–2 security program interns:* responsibilities include research, writing and related tasks in the field of nuclear weapons. Candidates should have analytical skills, computer skills, personal interest in the field, research skills, self-motivation, writing skills. Duration is 3 months or more. Open to college freshmen, college sophomores, college juniors, college seniors, recent college graduates, graduate students, law students. ▶ *1 violence prevention intern:* responsibilities include research into violence, especially gun violence, from both public health and criminal justice perspectives; outreach to physicians, medical students, other health professionals; update and develop activist materials and Web site . Candidates should have ability to work independently, computer skills, oral communication skills, research skills, self-motivation, strong interpersonal skills, written communication skills, familiarity with/interest in public health and public policy. Duration is 3 months or more. Open to college juniors, college seniors, recent college graduates, graduate students. All positions paid at $200 per week. International applications accepted.

Benefits Names of contacts, possible full-time employment, willing to complete paperwork for educational credit, willing to provide letters of recommendation.

Contact Write, fax, or e-mail Alyson Michael, Coordinator. Fax: 202-898-0172. E-mail: psrnatl@igc.apc.org. No phone calls. Telephone interview required. Applicants must submit a cover letter, resume, writing sample. Application deadline: March 15 for summer, July 15 for fall, November 15 for spring. World Wide Web: http://www.psr.org.

THE POPULATION INSTITUTE
107 2nd Street, NE
Washington, District of Columbia 20002

General Information Nonprofit grassroots organization specializing in the link between international populations and environmental issues. Established in 1969. Number of employees: 13. Number of internship applications received each year: 50.

Internships Available ▶ *1 World Population Awareness Week coordinator:* responsibilities include organizing events and establishing network of contacts for this officially sponsored week. Candidates should have ability to work independently, computer skills, editing skills, oral communication skills, organizational skills, self-motivation, strong interpersonal skills, strong leadership ability, writing skills. Duration is 6 months in the fall session only. Open to college freshmen, college sophomores, college juniors, college seniors, recent college graduates, graduate students, those 21 to 25 years old only. ▶ *1–2 field coordinators:* responsibilities include planning and implementing trips around the nation for the president of the Institute and maintaining contact with educators and community organizations. Candidates should have ability to work independently, computer skills, office skills, oral communication skills, organizational skills, self-motivation, strong interpersonal skills, strong leadership ability, writing skills. Duration is 6 months. Open to college freshmen, college sophomores, college juniors, college seniors, recent college graduates, graduate students, age requirement 21 to 25 only. ▶ *1 media coordinator:* responsibilities include maintaining a press list, acting as liaison with media, writing, reporting, proofreading, and editing. Candidates should have ability to work independently, college degree in related field, computer skills, editing skills, oral communication skills, research skills, self-motivation, strong interpersonal skills, writing skills. Duration is 6 months. Open to college freshmen, college sophomores, college juniors, college seniors, recent college graduates, graduate students, those 21 to 25 years old only. ▶ *1–2 public policy staff assistants:* responsibilities include assisting with legislative alerts and informing legislators and key staff about population issues. Candidates should have ability to work independently, analytical skills, college courses in field, college degree in related field, computer skills, oral communication skills, organizational skills, self-motivation, strong interpersonal skills, strong leadership ability. Duration is 6 months. Open to college freshmen, col-

The Population Institute (continued)

lege sophomores, college juniors, college seniors, recent college graduates, graduate students, those 21 to 25 years old only. All positions paid at $1,200 per month. International applications accepted.

Benefits Formal training, names of contacts, on-the-job training, willing to act as a professional reference, willing to complete paperwork for educational credit, willing to provide letters of recommendation, health and dental coverage.

Contact Write, call, fax, or e-mail Education Coordinator. Phone: 202-544-3300. Fax: 202-544-0068. E-mail: web@populationinstitute. org. In-person interview required. Applicants must submit a cover letter, resume, academic transcripts, three letters of recommendation. Application deadline: April 1 for July—December session, September 1 for January—June session. World Wide Web: http://www.populationinstitute.org.

PROGRESSIVE ACTION NETWORK (EAST COAST AND MIDWEST INTERNS)
1341 G Street, NW, Suite 600
Washington, District of Columbia 20005

General Information Network providing stable funding for progressive political organizations, mobilizing mass numbers of people to participate in the political process, and developing activism and membership development careers. Established in 1978. Number of employees: 2. Number of internship applications received each year: 50.

Internships Available ▶ *25–50 field and phone outreach staff interns:* responsibilities include educating and fund-raising by phone or by doing neighborhood outreach. Candidates should have analytical skills, oral communication skills, personal interest in the field, self-motivation, strong interpersonal skills, ability to learn quickly, desire to work with people. Duration is from 2 months to long-term career. $9-11 per hour, plus bonus (either full-time or part-time). Open to high school seniors, recent high school graduates, college freshmen, college sophomores, college juniors, college seniors, recent college graduates, graduate students, law students, career changers, individuals reentering the workforce. International applications accepted.

Benefits Formal training, health insurance, opportunity to attend seminars/workshops, possible full-time employment, travel reimbursement, willing to act as a professional reference, willing to complete paperwork for educational credit, willing to provide letters of recommendation, relocation opportunity, career placement.

Contact Write, call, fax, or e-mail Paula Barvin, Regional Director, New Jersey Citizen Action, 556 Haddon Avenue, Collingswood, New Jersey 08108. Phone: 609-869-0007. Fax: 609-869-0111. E-mail: pbarvin@aol.com. In-person interview recommended. Applicants must submit a cover letter, resume. Application deadline: June 1 for summer, August 1 for fall.

PROGRESSIVE ACTION NETWORK (WEST COAST INTERNS)
1341 G Street, NW, Suite 600
Washington, District of Columbia 20005

General Information Network providing stable funding for progressive political organizations, mobilizing mass numbers of people to participate in the political process, and developing activism and membership development careers. Established in 1978. Affiliate of Citizen Action and Clean Water Action. Number of internship applications received each year: 300.

Internships Available ▶ *Field and phone outreach organizers:* responsibilities include community outreach, education, fund-raising, and membership acquisition. Candidates should have ability to work independently, oral communication skills, self-motivation, strong interpersonal skills. Duration is flexible. Position available as unpaid or at $8—$11 per hour plus bonus. Open to high school students, high school seniors, recent high school graduates, college freshmen, college sophomores, college juniors, college seniors, recent college graduates, graduate students, law students, law school graduates, career changers, individuals reentering the workforce. ▶ *25–50 field and phone*

outreach staff interns: responsibilities include educating and fund-raising by phone or by doing neighborhood outreach. Candidates should have oral communication skills, personal interest in the field, self-motivation, strong interpersonal skills, ability to learn quickly, desire to work with people. Duration is from 2 months to long-term career. $9-11 per hour, plus bonus (either full-time or part-time). Open to high school seniors, recent high school graduates, college freshmen, college sophomores, college juniors, college seniors, recent college graduates, graduate students, law students, career changers, individuals reentering the workforce. International applications accepted.

Benefits Formal training, health insurance, opportunity to attend seminars/workshops, possible full-time employment, travel reimbursement, willing to act as a professional reference, willing to complete paperwork for educational credit, willing to provide letters of recommendation, relocation opportunity, career placement.

Contact Write, call, or fax Lori Schroyer Hazelchild, Regional Director, Washington Citizen Action, 100 South King Street, Seattle, Washington 98104. Phone: 206-389-0050. Fax: 206-389-0049. In-person interview recommended. Applicants must submit a cover letter, resume. Applications are accepted continuously.

PUBLIC CITIZEN'S CONGRESS WATCH
215 Pennsylvania Avenue, SE
Washington, District of Columbia 20003

General Information Consumer organization concerned with lobbying, organizing, and researching consumer rights and government and corporate accountability. Established in 1971. Number of employees: 25. Unit of Public Citizen, Washington, District of Columbia. Number of internship applications received each year: 25.

Internships Available ▶ *2–4 research interns:* responsibilities include researching legislation, making phone calls to Congress, organizing conferences and rallies, and assisting with office duties. Duration is 3–4 months. Unpaid. Open to high school students, high school seniors, recent high school graduates, college freshmen, college sophomores, college juniors, college seniors, recent college graduates, graduate students. International applications accepted.

Benefits Formal training, possible full-time employment, travel reimbursement, willing to complete paperwork for educational credit.

Contact Write or fax Maura Kealey, Deputy Director. Fax: 202-547-7392. In-person interview recommended. Applicants must submit a cover letter, resume, writing sample. Applications are accepted continuously.

PUBLIC LEADERSHIP EDUCATION NETWORK (PLEN)
1001 Connecticut Avenue, NW, Suite 900
Washington, District of Columbia 20036-5507

General Information National consortium of women's and other colleges that runs public policy programs and places students in organizations working with public policy. Established in 1978. Number of employees: 3. Number of internship applications received each year: 30.

Internships Available ▶ *12–20 women and public policy interns:* responsibilities include performing various duties, including research, writing reports, and attending hearings. Candidates should have knowledge of field, office skills, oral communication skills, organizational skills, personal interest in the field, research skills, written communication skills. Duration is 1 semester. Position available as unpaid or paid. Open to college freshmen, college sophomores, college juniors, college seniors, recent college graduates, graduate students. International applications accepted.

Benefits Formal training, housing at a cost, job counseling, names of contacts, on-the-job training, opportunity to attend seminars/workshops, willing to act as a professional reference, willing to complete paperwork for educational credit, willing to provide letters of recommendation, opportunity to attend classes focusing on women and public policy.

Contact Write, call, or e-mail Ms. Sharon Stoneback, Executive Director. Phone: 202-872-1585. E-mail: plen@plen.org. In-person interview recommended. Applicants must submit a formal organization application, cover letter, resume, writing sample, letter of recommendation. Application deadline: March 1 for summer, June 30 for fall, November 1 for spring. Fees: $40. World Wide Web: http://www.plen.org.

RELIGIOUS ACTION CENTER OF REFORM JUDAISM
2027 Massachusetts Avenue, NW
Washington, District of Columbia 20036

General Information Organization that advocates social justice and religious liberty, serves as a Reform Jewish movement advocate in the nation's capital, and monitors legislation of concern to American Jewish communities. Established in 1961. Number of employees: 20. Unit of Union of American Hebrew Congregations, New York, New York. Number of internship applications received each year: 30.
Internships Available ▶ *6 legislative assistants:* responsibilities include representing the Center in various coalitions, monitoring legislation, participating in visits to offices of senators and representatives, preparing educational and programmatic materials for congregations, and performing administrative work. Candidates should have ability to work with others, personal interest in the field, plan to pursue career in field, self-motivation, strong leadership ability, written communication skills. Duration is 1 year. $1,300 per month. Open to recent college graduates. International applications accepted.
Benefits Health insurance, names of contacts, opportunity to attend seminars/workshops, travel reimbursement, willing to provide letters of recommendation.
Contact Write, call, or e-mail Mark Pelavin, Associate Director. Phone: 202-387-2800. E-mail: mpelavin@vahc.org. Applicants must submit a formal organization application, resume, two letters of recommendation. Application deadline: March 1. World Wide Web: http://www.rj.org/rac.

RESULTS
440 First Street, NW, Suite 450
Washington, District of Columbia 20001

General Information Grassroots citizens lobbying group working to create the political will to end hunger and poverty.
Internships Available ▶ *1 administrative intern:* responsibilities include office support and communications. Duration is flexible. small stipend. ▶ *1 development intern:* responsibilities include research into fund-raising and compiling material for donors. Duration is flexible. small stipend. ▶ *1 legislative intern:* responsibilities include research and grassroots support. Duration is flexible. small stipend. ▶ *1 summer conference intern:* responsibilities include supporting the annual conference for volunteers in Washington. Duration is 1 summer. Position available as unpaid or paid. Open to college freshmen, college sophomores, college juniors, college seniors, graduate students.
Benefits Formal training, on-the-job training, travel reimbursement, willing to act as a professional reference, willing to complete paperwork for educational credit, willing to provide letters of recommendation, health insurance (sometimes available).
Contact Write, call, fax, or e-mail Janet Hughes, Administrator, 440 First Street, NW, Suite 450, Washington, District of Columbia 20001. Phone: 202-783-7100. Fax: 202-783-2818. E-mail: results@resultsusa.org. Applicants must submit a cover letter, resume, writing sample. Applications are accepted continuously. World Wide Web: http://www.resultsusa.org.

THE RUTHERFORD INSTITUTE
PO Box 7482
Charlottesville, Virginia 22906-7482

General Information Nonprofit, legal and educational civil liberties organization specializing in the defense of constitutional and human rights. Established in 1982. Number of employees: 50. Number of internship applications received each year: 65.

Internships Available ▶ *5–12 summer interns:* responsibilities include participation in an intensive course in constitutional law, and providing research and writing for litigation in state and federal courts and for educational resources. Candidates should have analytical skills, personal interest in the field, research skills, self-motivation, writing skills. Duration is 8–10 weeks. Position available as unpaid or at $350 per week. Open to law students. International applications accepted.
Benefits On-the-job training, opportunity to attend seminars/workshops, possible full-time employment, willing to complete paperwork for educational credit, willing to provide letters of recommendation, housing stipend of $300 per month.
Contact Write or e-mail Jean-Marc Gadoury, Legal Resource Manager, PO Box 7482, Charlottesville, Virginia 22906-7482. E-mail: jgadoury@rutherford.org. Applicants must submit a cover letter, resume, writing sample, two personal references. Application deadline: January 1. World Wide Web: http://www.rutherford.org.

SEATTLE YOUTH INVOLVEMENT NETWORK
172 20th Avenue
Seattle, Washington 98122

General Information SYIN advocates with youth in order to create positive changes in the community through civic involvement, leadership development, and volunteer service. Established in 1992. Number of employees: 7. Number of internship applications received each year: 5.
Internships Available ▶ *1–2 fund-raising interns:* responsibilities include assisting with grant writing, special events, and other fund-raising activities. Candidates should have ability to work independently, computer skills, office skills, organizational skills, strong interpersonal skills, writing skills, some interest or experience in fundraising. ▶ *1 program intern:* responsibilities include working with youth to design and implement forums, service projects, publications, and activities in the community. Candidates should have ability to work independently, computer skills, organizational skills, strong interpersonal skills, strong leadership ability, written communication skills. Duration for all positions is flexible. All positions are unpaid. Open to high school students, high school seniors, recent high school graduates, college freshmen, college sophomores, college juniors, college seniors, recent college graduates, graduate students, law students, career changers, individuals reentering the workforce. International applications accepted.
Benefits Names of contacts, on-the-job training, possible full-time employment, willing to act as a professional reference, willing to complete paperwork for educational credit, willing to provide letters of recommendation.
Contact Write, fax, or e-mail Jamie Flaxman, Executive Director, 172 20th Avenue, Seattle, Washington 98122. Fax: 206-323-8731. E-mail: jamie@seattleyouth.org. No phone calls. In-person interview recommended. Applicants must submit a cover letter, resume, criminal records check required. Applications are accepted continuously. World Wide Web: http://www.seattleyouth.org.

SELF-HELP CREDIT UNION
301 West Main Street
Durham, North Carolina 27701

General Information Organization that creates ownership opportunities and wealth among North Carolina's disadvantaged populations through loans and technical assistance to home and business owners. Established in 1980. Number of employees: 75. Number of internship applications received each year: 25.
Internships Available ▶ *9–12 interns:* responsibilities include working in various positions. Candidates should have ability to work independently, analytical skills, computer skills, editing skills, oral communication skills, personal interest in the field, research skills, self-motivation, strong interpersonal skills, writing skills. Duration is 8–10 weeks. $8–$9 per hour. Open to college sophomores, college juniors, college seniors, graduate students, law students.

Self-Help Credit Union (continued)

Benefits On-the-job training, willing to complete paperwork for educational credit, willing to provide letters of recommendation. **Contact** Write, call, or fax Lyle M. Jones, Executive Staff. Phone: 919-956-4400. Fax: 919-956-4600. Applicants must submit a cover letter, resume, writing sample. Applications are accepted continuously. World Wide Web: http://www.self-help.org.

SENIOR ACTION NETWORK
1370 Mission Street, Third Floor
San Francisco, California 94103

General Information Grassroots advocacy organization passionately devoted to issues which affect senior communities. Its mission is to organize and empower seniors and influence public policy.
Internships Available ▶ *1 community organizer's assistant:* responsibilities include working on various issues relating to improvement of quality of life for seniors, including healthcare, crime prevention, and housing. Open to college juniors, college seniors, recent college graduates, graduate students. ▶ *1 office assistant:* responsibilities include administrative duties. Open to 16 years of age and older. Duration for all positions is flexible. All positions are unpaid.
Contact Write, call, fax, or e-mail Executive Director, 1370 Mission Street, 3rd Floor, San Francisco, California 94103. Phone: 415-863-2033. Fax: 415-703-0186. E-mail: sfsan@hotmail.com. Applicants must submit a cover letter, resume. Applications are accepted continuously.

SOUTHEAST ASIA RESOURCE ACTION CENTER
1628 16th Street, NW, 3rd Floor
Washington, District of Columbia 20009-3099

General Information SEARAC is a national voice for Southeast Asian communities in the U.S., primarily Cambodian, Laotian, and Vietnamese. SEARAC's mission is to facilitate the integration of Southeast Asian refugees and immigrants into mainstream American society through public education, leadership development, advocacy, and community empowerment. Established in 1979. Number of employees: 9. Number of internship applications received each year: 50.
Internships Available ▶ *1 intern:* responsibilities include conducting research, assisting public education and advocacy efforts, responding to requests for information, attending public meetings, contributing articles for publication, and administrative duties. Candidates should have computer skills, editing skills, office skills, oral communication skills, organizational skills, plan to pursue career in field, research skills, self-motivation, strong interpersonal skills, strong leadership ability, written communication skills, multicultural sensitivity, interest in community and public service, knowledge of Southeast Asia, knowledge of immigrant issues. Duration is 1 semester. Unpaid. Open to college sophomores, college juniors, college seniors, recent college graduates, graduate students, law students, career changers. International applications accepted.
Benefits Names of contacts, opportunity to attend seminars/workshops, willing to complete paperwork for educational credit, willing to provide letters of recommendation.
Contact Write, call, fax, or e-mail Dr. W.R. Niedzwiecki, Director of Programs and Resource Development, 1628 16th Street, NW, 3rd Floor, Washington, District of Columbia 20009-3099. Phone: 202-667-4690. Fax: 202-667-6449. E-mail: max@searac.org. In-person interview recommended. Applicants must submit a cover letter, resume. Applications are accepted continuously. World Wide Web: http://www.searac.org.

SPEAK OUT
PO Box 99096
Emeryville, California 94662

General Information Nonprofit national speakers and artists agency, providing 200 speakers and artists who address issues of social, economic, and political justice, working primarily through campuses and community groups. Established in 1990. Number of employees: 4. Affiliate of Institute for Democratic Education and Culture, Oakland, California. Number of internship applications received each year: 10.
Internships Available ▶ *Interns:* responsibilities include working alongside staff members on specific projects, setting up speaking engagements, coordinating tour schedules, working on publicity campaigns and grant writing, and performing some basic office work. Duration is minimum of one month commitment. Unpaid. International applications accepted.
Benefits Names of contacts, on-the-job training, willing to act as a professional reference, willing to complete paperwork for educational credit, willing to provide letters of recommendation.
Contact Write, call, fax, or e-mail Jean Caiani, Co-Director. Phone: 510-601-0182. Fax: 510-601-0183. E-mail: speakout@igc.org. Applicants must submit a formal organization application. Applications are accepted continuously. World Wide Web: http://www.vida.com/speakout.

SPRING VALLEY BRUDERHOF
Route 381 North
Farmington, Pennsylvania 15437

General Information Christian community engaging in community service, publishing, farming, and manufacturing. Established in 1920. Number of employees: 300. Number of internship applications received each year: 10.
Internships Available ▶ *6–10 co-workers:* responsibilities include voluntary service; jobs may include cooking, cleaning, washing dishes, gardening, carpentry, and child care. Candidates should have ability to work with others, personal interest in the field, self-motivation, desire to live in community. Duration is 6–12 weeks. Unpaid. Open to high school seniors, recent high school graduates, college freshmen, college sophomores, college juniors, college seniors, recent college graduates, graduate students, law students, career changers, individuals reentering the workforce. International applications accepted.
Benefits Free housing, free meals, on-the-job training, opportunity to attend seminars/workshops, willing to complete paperwork for educational credit, willing to provide letters of recommendation.
International Internships Available in Nonnington, United Kingdom; Robertsbridge, United Kingdom.
Contact Write, call, fax, or e-mail Sam Hine, Member, PO Box 260, Farmington, Pennsylvania 15437. Phone: 724-329-1100. Fax: 724-329-0914. E-mail: shine@bruderhof.com. Telephone interview required. Applicants must submit a formal organization application, personal reference. Application deadline: May 15 for summer. World Wide Web: http://www.bruderhof.org.

STUDENT PUGWASH USA
815 15th Street, NW, Suite 814
Washington, District of Columbia 20005

General Information National nonprofit educational organization that provides a wide range of activities for university and select high school students to promote the socially responsible application of science and technology. Established in 1979. Number of employees: 5. Number of internship applications received each year: 15.
Internships Available ▶ *1–2 summer interns:* responsibilities include helping plan and organize national conference; researching science, technology, and society issues; providing general support for nationwide chapter program; possibility of publishing issue brief. Candidates should have computer skills, knowledge of field, research skills, self-motivation, strong interpersonal skills, written communication skills. Duration is 3–4 months. $6 per hour. Open to recent high school graduates, college freshmen, college sophomores, college juniors, college seniors, recent college graduates, graduate students, law students.
Benefits Formal training, job counseling, names of contacts, opportunity to attend seminars/workshops, possible full-time employment, willing to complete paperwork for educational credit, willing to provide letters of recommendation.
Contact Write or call Associate Director. Phone: 202-393-6555. In-person interview recommended. Applicants must submit a

cover letter, resume, writing sample. Application deadline: April 15 for summer (recommended). World Wide Web: http://www. spusa.org/pugwash/.

THIRD MILLENNIUM: ADVOCATES FOR THE FUTURE, INC.
121 Avenue of the Americas, Suite 505
New York, New York 10013

General Information National, nonprofit, advocacy, and educational organization started by young Americans concerned about the long-term future of the US. The purpose is to redirect America's political focus from the next election cycle to the next generation cycle, addressing the issues of the national debt, crime, the environment, race relations, and health-care from a generational perspective. Established in 1993. Number of employees: 6. Number of internship applications received each year: 30.
Internships Available ▶ *5 general interns:* responsibilities include researching grants, writing press releases, researching congressional testimony, and administrative work. Candidates should have ability to work independently, oral communication skills, personal interest in the field, research skills, self-motivation, written communication skills. ▶ *3 project assistants:* responsibilities include working one-on-one with project directors to organize and execute symposia, parties, or educational programs. Candidates should have ability to work with others, computer skills, office skills, oral communication skills, organizational skills, written communication skills. Duration for all positions is flexible. All positions are unpaid. Open to college freshmen, college sophomores, college juniors, college seniors, recent college graduates. International applications accepted.
Benefits Names of contacts, opportunity to attend seminars/ workshops, possible full-time employment, travel reimbursement, willing to act as a professional reference, willing to complete paperwork for educational credit, willing to provide letters of recommendation, opportunity to write op-ed pieces and meet future leaders.
Contact Write, call, fax, or e-mail Arlynda Boyer, Director of Operations. Phone: 212-226-2077. Fax: 212-966-6940. E-mail: arlyndab@juno.com. Applicants must submit a cover letter, resume. Applications are accepted continuously. World Wide Web: http://www.thirdmil.org.

20/20 VISION
1828 Jefferson Place, NW
Washington, District of Columbia 20036

General Information Nonprofit lobbying and citizen education organization whose goal is to revitalize democracy by creating persistent, strategic citizen action, persuading decision-makers to protect the earth by reducing militarism, and preserving the environment. Established in 1986. Number of employees: 8. Number of internship applications received each year: 200.
Internships Available ▶ *1 fellowship:* responsibilities include attending congressional hearings, floor debates, and coalition meetings to obtain current legislative information and help disseminate it to grassroots contacts in monthly legislative updates; working with staff to support grassroots outreach program including helping with creation of new local projects; helping to develop, implement, and coordinate a creative national promotion strategy; and responding to inquiries from the press and other organizations. Candidates should have ability to work with others, computer skills, oral communication skills, personal interest in the field, research skills, writing skills. Duration is 12 months minimum. $1,200 per month. Open to recent college graduates, graduate students. ▶ *1–3 interns:* responsibilities include assisting with general office responsibilities and working on specific projects within the legislation, media, field, development, promotion, and membership departments as priorities dictate. Candidates should have ability to work independently, oral communication skills, self-motivation, strong interpersonal skills, written communication skills. Duration is 2-3 months

minimum. Unpaid. Open to college freshmen, college sophomores, college juniors, college seniors, recent college graduates. International applications accepted.
Benefits Job counseling, names of contacts, travel reimbursement, willing to complete paperwork for educational credit, willing to provide letters of recommendation.
Contact Write, call, fax, or e-mail Intern Coordinator. Phone: 202-833-2020. Fax: 202-833-5307. E-mail: vision@2020vision.org. In-person interview recommended. Applicants must submit a cover letter, resume, personal reference. Application deadline: March 31 for fellowship position and summer interns; continuous for fall, winter, and spring. World Wide Web: http://www. 2020vision.org.

UNION INSTITUTE–OFFICE FOR SOCIAL RESPONSIBILITY
1710 Rhode Island Avenue, NW, Suite 1100
Washington, District of Columbia 20036-3007

General Information Organization that heightens critical consciousness through the combination of directed scholarship and service. Established in 1985. Number of employees: 8.
Internships Available ▶ *1–2 interns:* responsibilities include assisting staff in various projects, including planning and making arrangements for conferences/seminars; preparation of major reports on nonprofit sector issues; developing new contacts; and occasional administrative duties. Duration is 2 months minimum. Unpaid. Open to college freshmen, college sophomores, college juniors, college seniors, recent college graduates, graduate students. International applications accepted.
Benefits Job counseling, names of contacts, willing to complete paperwork for educational credit, willing to provide letters of recommendation, possibility of small stipend.
Contact Write, call, or fax Internship Coordinator, 1710 Rhode Island Avenue, NW Suite 1100, Washington, District of Columbia 20039-3007. Phone: 202-496-1630. Fax: 202-496-1635. In-person interview recommended. Applicants must submit a cover letter, resume, writing sample, two personal references. Applications are accepted continuously. World Wide Web: http://www.tui. edu/~OSR/osr.htm.

UNITED STATES COMMITTEE FOR REFUGEES
1717 Massachusetts Avenue, NW, Suite 200
Washington, District of Columbia 20036

General Information Private, nonprofit public information and advocacy organization that is devoted to the protection of refugees, asylum seekers, and internally displaced people. Established in 1958. Number of employees: 10. Department of Immigration and Refugee Services of America, Washington, District of Columbia. Number of internship applications received each year: 350.
Internships Available ▶ *1 communications/media intern:* responsibilities include assisting communications officer in forging links with the media; database management; tracking organization; answering inquiries from the media about refugees; attending meetings; and drafting correspondence. Candidates should have oral communication skills, plan to pursue career in field, research skills, self-motivation, writing skills. Duration is minimum of 12 weeks. $75 per month part time (20-35 hours); $100 per month full time (35+ hours). ▶ *1 fund-raising/development intern:* responsibilities include researching potential funding sources, assisting with direct mail campaigns, attending meetings on behalf of development staff, working with donor database, and tracking success of USCR's campaigns/advocacy. Candidates should have oral communication skills, organizational skills, self-motivation, strong interpersonal skills, written communication skills. Duration is minimum of 12 weeks. $75 per month part time (20-35 hours); $100 per month full time (35+ hours) . ▶ *4 research interns:* responsibilities include performing research and writing, attending meetings and congressional hearings, and providing administrative support. Candidates should have ability to work independently, oral communication skills, personal interest in the field, research skills, writing skills. Duration is minimum 12 weeks. $75 per month part time (20-35 hours); $100 per month full time (35+

United States Committee for Refugees (continued)
hours). Open to college freshmen, college sophomores, college juniors, college seniors, recent college graduates, graduate students, law students, career changers. International applications accepted.
Benefits Names of contacts, travel reimbursement, willing to complete paperwork for educational credit, willing to provide letters of recommendation.
Contact Write, call, or fax Internship Coordinator, 1717 Massachusetts Avenue, NW Suite 200, Washington, District of Columbia 20036. Phone: 202-797-2105. Fax: 202-347-2460. In-person interview recommended. Applicants must submit a cover letter, resume, one 3- to 5-page writing sample. Application deadline: April 15 for summer, August 1 for fall, December 15 for winter/spring. World Wide Web: http://www.refugees.org.

U.S.–ASIA INSTITUTE
232 East Capitol Street, NE
Washington, District of Columbia 20003

General Information Private, non-governmental organization that promotes dialogue on international issues of common interest to the United States and participating Asian nations. Established in 1979. Number of employees: 3. Number of internship applications received each year: 80.
Internships Available ▶ *1–2 staff assistants:* responsibilities include assisting staff in organizing various programs, performing research and office work, and attending and reporting on congressional hearings, seminars, and workshops. Candidates should have editing skills, knowledge of field, office skills, personal interest in the field, research skills, self-motivation. Duration is 3 months minimum (preferred). Unpaid. Open to college juniors, college seniors, graduate students. International applications accepted.
Benefits Opportunity to attend seminars/workshops, possible full-time employment, willing to complete paperwork for educational credit, willing to provide letters of recommendation.
Contact Write or call Ms. Miki Yagi, Program Director, 232 East Capitol Street, NE, Washington, District of Columbia 20003. Phone: 202-544-3181. In-person interview recommended. Applicants must submit a cover letter, resume, academic transcripts, 1 writing sample (3-4 pages). Application deadline: March 15 for summer, July 15 for fall, December 15 for spring.

U.S. PUBLIC INTEREST RESEARCH GROUP (PIRG)
218 D Street, SE
Washington, District of Columbia 20003

General Information National lobbying office for network of statewide consumer, environmental, and campaign finance reform public interest watchdog organizations. Established in 1983. Number of employees: 25. Number of internship applications received each year: 100.
Internships Available ▶ *1–3 field interns:* responsibilities include Coordinating media events, assisting in preparing news releases, coordinating grass roots campaign activities, and working with campaign offices. Candidates should have ability to work independently, oral communication skills, organizational skills, strong interpersonal skills, written communication skills. Duration is usually one semester. ▶ *4–8 legislative interns:* responsibilities include conducting research, preparing investigative reports, coordinating media events, coordinating grass roots campaigns, monitoring legislation, coordinating coalitions. Candidates should have oral communication skills, organizational skills, self-motivation, strong interpersonal skills, written communication skills. Duration is 1 semester. All positions are unpaid. Open to college freshmen, college sophomores, college juniors, college seniors, recent college graduates. International applications accepted.
Benefits Opportunity to attend seminars/workshops, possible full-time employment, willing to act as a professional reference, willing to complete paperwork for educational credit, willing to provide letters of recommendation, various trainings, brown bag lunch discussions.

Contact Write, call, fax, or e-mail Rick Trilsch, Internship Coordinator. Phone: 202-546-9707. Fax: 202-546-2461. E-mail: uspirg@pirg.org. In-person interview recommended. Applicants must submit a cover letter, resume, 1- to 3-page writing sample. Applications are accepted continuously. World Wide Web: http://www.pirg.org.

U.S. SERVAS, INC.
11 John Street, Suite 407
New York, New York 10038

General Information Cultural exchange and peace organization created to give people the opportunity to have a short homestay with hosts in other cultures. Servas strives for peace through education and the understanding of cultural differences both in the U.S. and abroad. Established in 1948. Number of employees: 3. Unit of Servas, International, New York, New York. Number of internship applications received each year: 2.
Internships Available ▶ *1–2 administrative interns:* responsibilities include data entry, filing, customer service, phones, letter writing, e-mail, problem solving, and various small projects; opportunity for research. Candidates should have ability to work with others, office skills, oral communication skills, self-motivation, writing skills, a personal interest in the field (helpful). Duration is 1–6 months. Unpaid. Open to high school students, high school seniors, recent high school graduates, college freshmen, college sophomores, college juniors, college seniors, recent college graduates, graduate students, law students, career changers, individuals reentering the workforce, senior citizens. International applications accepted.
Benefits Names of contacts, opportunity to attend seminars/workshops, possible full-time employment, willing to act as a professional reference, willing to complete paperwork for educational credit, willing to provide letters of recommendation, $4 per day lunch stipend, $3 per day transportation stipend.
Contact Write, call, fax, or e-mail Tori Napier, Intern Coordinator/Program Officer. Phone: 212-267-0252. Fax: 212-267-0292. E-mail: usservas@servas.org. In-person interview recommended. Applicants must submit a formal organization application, cover letter, resume, letter of introduction. Applications are accepted continuously. World Wide Web: http://servas.org.

VANGUARD COMMUNICATIONS
1019 19th Street, NW, Suite 1200
Washington, District of Columbia 20036-5105

General Information Company that develops and implements advocacy communications campaigns to help resolve the world's most pressing problems, such as the environment, energy, healthcare, issues concerning women and children, human rights, civil liberties, reproductive choice, and education. Number of employees: 20.
Internships Available ▶ *Interns:* responsibilities include drafting and distributing press releases, monitoring client news coverage, media database maintenance, assisting in news release production, contacting reporters, editing correspondence, and assisting office personnel. Candidates should have office skills, oral communication skills, strong interpersonal skills, written communication skills, previous work/internships experience and knowledge of Microsoft Word preferred; major in mass communications, public relations, journalism, or related subject required. Unpaid. Open to college freshmen, college sophomores, college juniors, college seniors, graduate students.
Benefits Willing to complete paperwork for educational credit.
Contact Write, call, fax, or e-mail Scott Ward, Senior Account Executive, 1019 19th Street, NW, Suite 120, Washington, District of Columbia 20036-5105. Phone: 202-331-4323. Fax: 202-331-0420. E-mail: sward@vancomm.com. Applicants must submit a resume, cover letter. Applications are accepted continuously. World Wide Web: http://www.vancomm.com.

THE VEGETARIAN RESOURCE GROUP
PO Box 1463
Baltimore, Maryland 21203

General Information Public interest group that educates the public about the various aspects of vegetarianism, including health, environment, and ethics. Established in 1982. Number of employees: 8. Number of internship applications received each year: 20.

Internships Available ▶ *1–2 interns:* responsibilities include writing for *The Vegetarian Journal* and performing research, outreach work, and clerical duties. Candidates should have ability to work independently, ability to work with others, organizational skills, personal interest in the field, self-motivation, written communication skills. Duration is 1–16 weeks. Unpaid. Open to high school students, high school seniors, recent high school graduates, college freshmen, college sophomores, college juniors, college seniors, recent college graduates, graduate students, law students, career changers, individuals reentering the workforce. International applications accepted.

Benefits Free housing, names of contacts, opportunity to attend seminars/workshops, possible full-time employment, travel reimbursement, willing to complete paperwork for educational credit, willing to provide letters of recommendation.

Contact Write Mr. Charles Stahler. In-person interview required. Applicants must submit a cover letter, resume, writing sample. Applications are accepted continuously. World Wide Web: http://www.vrg.org.

VIRGINIA AFFILIATE OF THE NATIONAL ABORTION AND REPRODUCTIVE RIGHTS ACTION LEAGUE
PO Box 489
Falls Church, Virginia 22040

General Information Political lobbying organization for reproductive rights. Number of employees: 1. Affiliate of National Abortion and Reproductive Rights Action League, Washington, District of Columbia. Number of internship applications received each year: 5.

Internships Available ▶ *1–3 field organizers:* responsibilities include coordinating recruitment of new members, activists, and grass roots fund-raising events. Candidates should have oral communication skills, personal interest in the field, self-motivation, strong interpersonal skills, willingness to work evenings. Duration is 12 weeks. Open to high school students, high school seniors, recent high school graduates, college freshmen, college sophomores, college juniors, college seniors, recent college graduates, graduate students, career changers, individuals reentering the workforce. ▶ *1–3 media/public relations interns:* responsibilities include contacting press secretaries of local, state, and federal elected officials; writing and updating press releases and editorials; and planning and initiating media coverage for VANARAL events. Candidates should have ability to work independently, personal interest in the field, writing skills. Open to high school students, high school seniors, recent high school graduates, college freshmen, college sophomores, college juniors, college seniors, recent college graduates, graduate students, career changers, individuals reentering the workforce. ▶ *1–3 on-line organizers:* responsibilities include coordinating outreach through the Internet, maintaining and updating Web page, and answering e-mail correspondence. Candidates should have ability to work independently, personal interest in the field, writing skills, knowledge of or willingness to learn HTML. Open to high school seniors, recent high school graduates, college freshmen, college sophomores, college juniors, college seniors, recent college graduates, graduate students, career changers, individuals reentering the workforce. ▶ *1–3 youth organizers:* responsibilities include outreach to high school and college students, serving as a liaison with student groups, coordinating youth organizing activities. Candidates should have ability to work with others, oral communication skills, personal interest in the field, self-motivation. Open to high school students, high school seniors,

recent high school graduates, college freshmen, college sophomores, college juniors, college seniors, recent college graduates. All positions are unpaid.

Benefits On-the-job training, willing to act as a professional reference, willing to complete paperwork for educational credit, willing to provide letters of recommendation, possible opportunity to attend seminars/workshops.

Contact Write, call, fax, or e-mail C. Lee, Executive Director. Phone: 703-532-3448. Fax: 703-532-1982. E-mail: vanaral@erols.com. Applicants must submit a cover letter, resume, 1 short writing sample. Applications are accepted continuously. World Wide Web: http://www.erols.com/vanaral.

WASHINGTON OFFICE ON LATIN AMERICA
1630 Connecticut Avenue, NW
Washington, District of Columbia 20009

General Information Nongovernmental organization aiming to help shape foreign policy that advances human rights, political, and economic development in Latin America. Established in 1974. Number of employees: 16. Number of internship applications received each year: 150.

Internships Available ▶ *6 interns:* responsibilities include monitoring U.S. foreign policy and events in the region, assisting administrative staff with clerical duties, and actively participating in day-to-day operations of human rights organization. Duration is 1 semester or summer. Unpaid. Open to college freshmen, college sophomores, college juniors, college seniors, recent college graduates. International applications accepted.

Benefits Job counseling, names of contacts, possible full-time employment, willing to complete paperwork for educational credit, willing to provide letters of recommendation.

Contact Write, call, or fax Internship Coordinator. Phone: 202-797-2171. Fax: 202-797-2172. E-mail: wola@wola.org. In-person interview recommended. Applicants must submit a cover letter, resume, writing sample, two personal references, telephone interview for finalists only. Applications are accepted continuously. World Wide Web: http://www.wola.org.

WASHINGTON PEACE CENTER
1801 Columbia Road, NW, Suite104
Washington, District of Columbia 20009

General Information Multi-issue, grassroots, anti-racist organization working for nonviolent social change through education and action. Established in 1963. Number of employees: 1. Number of internship applications received each year: 100.

Internships Available ▶ *1–3 interns:* responsibilities include developing programs and materials in support of educational events and direct actions, community outreach and development to further social justice initiatives such as economic literacy, anti-racism education, and anti-military campaigns. Candidates should have ability to work independently, ability to work with others, computer skills, writing skills, commitment to social justice. Duration is 1 semester. Unpaid. Open to high school seniors, recent high school graduates, college freshmen, college sophomores, college juniors, college seniors, recent college graduates, graduate students. International applications accepted.

Benefits Opportunity to attend seminars/workshops, willing to act as a professional reference, willing to complete paperwork for educational credit, willing to provide letters of recommendation.

Contact Write, call, or fax Luci Murphy, Coordinator, 1801 Columbia Road, NW, Suite 104, Washington, District of Columbia 20009. Phone: 202-234-2000. Fax: 202-234-7064. E-mail: peacecent@aol.com. In-person interview recommended. Applicants must submit a cover letter, resume, personal history in social justice activism and/or social service projects. Application deadline: April 1 for summer; continuous for remainder of year, November 1 for spring.

WEST VIRGINIA KIDS COUNT FUND
1031 Quarrier Street, Suite 313
Charleston, West Virginia 25301

General Information Advocacy group that seeks to improve the lives of West Virginia's at-risk children by mobilizing the private and public sectors to create prevention and early intervention programs, policies, and strategies; creates and maintains a statewide network of child advocates; and collects, analyzes, and disseminates information about at-risk children to the public through the media. Established in 1989. Number of employees: 4. Number of internship applications received each year: 2.

Internships Available ▶ *1 communications intern:* responsibilities include writing fact sheets, media releases, compiling information, organizing media contacts, compiling media results, working on desktop publishing and Web site maintenance. Candidates should have ability to work with others, analytical skills, computer skills, oral communication skills, plan to pursue career in field, research skills, written communication skills. ▶ *1 social work intern:* responsibilities include compiling community resources for manuals, writing special reports, and scanning media articles. Candidates should have analytical skills, computer skills, oral communication skills, plan to pursue career in field, research skills, strong interpersonal skills, written communication skills. Duration for all positions is flexible. All positions are unpaid. Open to college juniors, college seniors, graduate students.

Benefits Names of contacts, opportunity to attend seminars/workshops, travel reimbursement, willing to complete paperwork for educational credit, willing to provide letters of recommendation, networking opportunities with professionals in the field.

Contact Write Jeff Crist, Director of Communications. In-person interview recommended. Applications are accepted continuously. World Wide Web: http://www.wvkidscountfund.org.

WIDER OPPORTUNITIES FOR WOMEN, INC.
815 15th Street, NW, Suite 916
Washington, District of Columbia 20005-3104

General Information Organization that works nationally and in Washington, D.C., to achieve economic self-sufficiency for women through public policy advocacy and program service delivery. Established in 1964. Number of employees: 13. Number of internship applications received each year: 100.

Internships Available ▶ *2–4 community service delivery/employment training interns:* responsibilities include case management, evaluation, administration, and organizing. Candidates should have ability to work with others, computer skills, oral communication skills, organizational skills, personal interest in the field, self-motivation. Duration is flexible. ▶ *1–3 public policy interns:* responsibilities include researching and analyzing public policies for their impact on women's employment and training; representing WOW at briefings, hearings, and other meetings relating to legislative agenda; State Organizing for Family Economic Self-Sufficiency Projects; updating grassroots network of women's employment training organizations on legislation and soliciting their support when necessary. Candidates should have analytical skills, computer skills, personal interest in the field, research skills, self-motivation, written communication skills. Duration is 2 months minimum. ▶ *1–3 resource development interns:* responsibilities include newsletter writing and layout; maintaining resource library; developing graphic/photo stock library of women performing non-traditional jobs; researching, writing, and layout to update existing publications. Candidates should have computer skills, personal interest in the field, research skills, self-motivation, writing skills. Duration is flexible. Open to college sophomores, college juniors, college seniors, recent college graduates, graduate students. All positions are unpaid. International applications accepted.

Benefits Job counseling, names of contacts, willing to complete paperwork for educational credit, willing to provide letters of recommendation, assistance with resume preparation, stipend of $10 per day to cover transportation and lunch.

Contact Write, fax, or e-mail Internship Coordinator. Fax: 202-638-4885. E-mail: info@w-o-w.org. In-person interview

recommended. Applicants must submit a cover letter, resume, writing sample. Applications are accepted continuously. World Wide Web: http://www.w-o-w.org.

WOMEN'S ACTION FOR NEW DIRECTIONS/ WOMEN LEGISLATORS' LOBBY
110 Maryland Avenue, NE, Suite 205
Washington, District of Columbia 20002

General Information National membership organization aiming to empower women to get politically involved. Established in 1980. Number of employees: 6. Number of internship applications received each year: 50.

Internships Available ▶ *1 assistant to WILL director:* responsibilities include researching, assisting with lobbying, preparing and editing reports on issues related to violence against women, and women's issues in general; mailing press and member communications; organizing conference and seminars for women state legislators; phoning women state legislators; and offering general office support. ▶ *1 assistant to director of policy and program:* responsibilities include researching; assisting and supporting lobbying; preparing and editing reports on issues related to arms control, military budget, and nuclear issues; mailing press and member communications; attending congressional hearings; and offering general office support. Candidates for all positions should have computer skills, oral communication skills, organizational skills, self-motivation, strong interpersonal skills, written communication skills. Duration for all positions is 3–12 months. All positions paid at small stipend. International applications accepted.

Benefits Formal training, job counseling, names of contacts, opportunity to attend seminars/workshops, willing to complete paperwork for educational credit, willing to provide letters of recommendation.

Contact Write or e-mail Kimberly Robson, Director of Policy and Programs. E-mail: wand@wand.org. No phone calls. In-person interview recommended. Applicants must submit a resume, writing sample. Applications are accepted continuously. World Wide Web: http://www.wand.org.

WOMEN'S HISTORY LIBRARY
2325 Oak Street
Berkeley, California 94708

General Information Center that actively documented the first six years of the women's movement (1968-1974) and has acted as a networking center since 1974. Established in 1968. Number of employees: 5.

Internships Available ▶ *Collection development interns:* responsibilities include cataloging and organizing materials, responding to research requests, conducting research, and aiding in telephone referrals. Candidates should have ability to work independently, ability to work with others, analytical skills, editing skills, office skills, oral communication skills, organizational skills, personal interest in the field, self-motivation, written communication skills. ▶ *Office support/library support interns:* responsibilities include tracking documents and cataloging information for clipping archives, handling phones and correspondence, and researching documents for callers who request information on sexual assault. Candidates should have office skills, oral communication skills, organizational skills, self-motivation, strong interpersonal skills, written communication skills. ▶ *Outreach coordinators:* responsibilities include contacting individuals and organizations about internships and publications using database, e-mail, phone, and fax; collecting and logging information from other organizations, libraries, and colleges. Candidates should have office skills, oral communication skills, self-motivation, strong interpersonal skills, written communication skills. ▶ *Volunteer and intern administrative assistants:* responsibilities include recruiting; keeping track of intake forms, interview schedules, and training times; much phone work, filing, voicemail, and e-mail; being a friendly phone and office host when people are new; and making regular alerts about community events. Candidates should have office skills, oral communication skills, organizational skills, self-motivation, strong interpersonal skills, written communication skills. Duration for all positions is one summer or one semester minimum. All positions are unpaid. Open to high school seniors, recent high school graduates, college freshmen, college sophomores, college juniors, college seniors, recent college graduates, graduate students, law students, career changers, individuals reentering the workforce. International applications accepted.

Benefits Job counseling, names of contacts, on-the-job training, opportunity to attend seminars/workshops, willing to complete paperwork for educational credit, willing to provide letters of recommendation, referrals provided, housing provided (summer only), free meals while working.

Contact Write, fax, or e-mail Laura X, Director. Fax: 510-524-7768. E-mail: laurax@gte.net. No phone calls. Applicants must submit a cover letter, telephone interview after submission of letter stating skills and interests (see Web site for further information). Applications are accepted continuously. World Wide Web: http://members.aol.com/ncmdr/index.html.

WOMEN'S INTERNATIONAL LEAGUE FOR PEACE AND FREEDOM
1213 Race Street
Philadelphia, Pennsylvania 19107-1691

General Information Organization devoted to ending sexism, racism, classism, oppression, militarism, and all forms of violence. Established in 1915. Number of employees: 8. Division of Women's International League for Peace and Freedom, Geneva, Switzerland. Number of internship applications received each year: 100.

Internships Available ▶ *1–2 development interns:* responsibilities include working with development director and staff on funding WILPF national political campaign; includes coordinating, fund-raising, appeal letters, and grant research. Candidates should have ability to work independently, ability to work with others, oral communication skills, organizational skills, research skills, writing skills. Open to high school seniors, recent high school graduates, college freshmen, college sophomores, college juniors, college seniors, recent college graduates, graduate students, law students, career changers, individuals reentering the workforce. ▶ *1 executive and administrative assistant:* responsibilities include helping with board and branch liaison work and developing relations between WILPF and other national organizations. Candidates should have ability to work independently, oral communication skills, personal interest in the field, research skills, self-motivation, writing skills. Open to recent high school graduates, college freshmen, college sophomores, college juniors, college seniors, recent college graduates, graduate students, career changers, individuals reentering the workforce. ▶ *1–3 membership assistants:* responsibilities include helping members organize new branches and strengthen existing branches and participating in all phases of campaigning from keeping records to bringing in new members. Candidates should have ability to work independently, oral communication skills, self-motivation, strong interpersonal skills, written communication skills, leadership ability. Open to high school seniors, recent high school graduates, college freshmen, college sophomores, college juniors, college seniors, recent college graduates, graduate students, law students, career changers, individuals reentering the workforce. ▶ *1 publications assistant:* responsibilities include assisting the editor in locating and soliciting copy, editing news, researching and writing stories, checking facts, and using desktop publishing programs. Candidates should have ability to work independently,

computer skills, editing skills, oral communication skills, research skills, writing skills. Open to college freshmen, college sophomores, college juniors, college seniors, recent college graduates, graduate students, career changers, individuals reentering the workforce. Duration for all positions is 12 weeks (minimum 20 hours per week). All positions available as unpaid or at $160 per week.

Benefits Formal training, on-the-job training, opportunity to attend seminars/workshops, possible full-time employment, willing to act as a professional reference, willing to complete paperwork for educational credit, willing to provide letters of recommendation.

International Internships Available in Geneva, Switzerland.

Contact Write, call, fax, or e-mail Chris Morin, Leadership/Outreach Coordinator. Phone: 215-563-7110. Fax: 215-563-5527. E-mail: wilpf@wilpf.org. In-person interview recommended. Applicants must submit a cover letter, resume, writing sample. Application deadline: May 1 for summer, August 1 for fall, December 1 for spring. World Wide Web: http://www.wilpf.org.

WOMEN STRIKE FOR PEACE
110 Maryland Avenue, NE, Suite 102
Washington, District of Columbia 20002

General Information Women's organization involved in education and in lobbying Congress on issues of peace and disarmament. Established in 1961. Number of internship applications received each year: 25.

Internships Available ▶ *2 general interns:* responsibilities include helping with newsletter production, covering coalition meetings, and working to lobby Congress. Duration is flexible. Unpaid. Open to college freshmen, college sophomores, college juniors, college seniors, recent college graduates. International applications accepted.

Benefits Names of contacts, opportunity to attend seminars/workshops, willing to complete paperwork for educational credit, willing to provide letters of recommendation.

Contact Write or call Ms. Edith Villastrigo, National Legislative Coordinator, 110 Maryland Avenue, NE, Suite 102, Washington, District of Columbia 20002. Phone: 202-543-2660. In-person interview recommended. Applicants must submit a cover letter, resume, writing sample. Applications are accepted continuously.

THE YOUNG WOMEN'S PROJECT
923 F Street, NW, 3rd Floor
Washington, District of Columbia 20004

General Information A national mulitcultural organization that develops and supports young women leaders and organizations through leadership training, technical assistance, and community-based action.

Internships Available ▶ *Interns:* responsibilities include 20 to 30 percent administrative work and 70 to 80 percent project work. Project work is determined by the intern's skills and interest. Refer to the Web site for more information. Candidates should have ability to work independently, ability to work with others, computer skills, oral communication skills, self-motivation, written communication skills, good listening skills, an interest in women's issues and lives. Duration is 3–6 months. Position available as unpaid or paid.

Contact Write or fax Interns. Fax: 202-393-0065. Applicants must submit a resume, writing sample, cover letter. Application deadline: May 30 for summer; continuous for remainder of year. World Wide Web: http://www.tidalwave.net/~ywp.

PROFESSIONAL, SCIENTIFIC, AND TECHNICAL SERVICES

GENERAL

A. E. SCHWARTZ & ASSOCIATES
PO Box 79228
Waverley, Massachusetts 02479-9998

General Information Comprehensive training and consulting organization offering over 40 management and professional training programs to managers and support staff nationally and internationally. Established in 1982. Number of employees: 12. Number of internship applications received each year: 1,200.

Internships Available ▶ *1 HTML/JAVA/CGI programmer:* responsibilities include assisting in programming and managing commericial Web sites, trainingconsortium.com and aeschwartz.com. Candidates should have ability to work independently, ability to work with others, college courses in field, computer skills, personal interest in the field, self-motivation. Duration is flexible, minimum 16-24 hours per week. stipend of up to $250 per 16 weeks. Open to college juniors, college seniors, recent college graduates, graduate students, career changers, individuals reentering the workforce. ▶ *3 IBM software specialists:* responsibilities include learning and teaching all Windows software packages, converting and constructing databases (Internet emphasis), performing desktop publishing using graphics software, and researching new products. Candidates should have ability to work independently, computer skills, declared college major in field, organizational skills, personal interest in the field, self-motivation. Duration is flexible (minimum 16-24 hours weekly). stipend of up to $250 per 16 weeks. Open to college juniors, college seniors, recent college graduates, graduate students, career changers, individuals reentering the workforce. ▶ *1 Internet marketing intern:* responsibilities include assisting in managing and creating marketing venues of commercial Web sites, including bulk e-mail, preferred business partnerships, auto-responders, bounty agreements, etc. Candidates should have ability to work independently, ability to work with others, personal interest in the field, self-motivation, writing skills. Duration is flexible, minimum 16-24 hours per week. stipend of up to $250 per 16 weeks. Open to college juniors, college seniors, recent college graduates, graduate students, career changers. ▶ *2 graphic designers:* responsibilities include creating new design concepts; designing flyers, book covers, sales materials, catalog and exhibit materials including specialty and promotional items; writing, editing and copy editing; providing camera- ready output and overseeing printing; Internet Web design. Candidates should have ability to work independently, analytical skills, computer skills, declared college major in field, organizational skills, written communication skills. Duration is flexible (minimum 16-24 hours weekly). stipend of up to $250 per 16 weeks. Open to college juniors, college seniors, recent college graduates, graduate students, career changers, individuals reentering the workforce. ▶ *2 public relations interns:* responsibilities include arranging media coverage; networking with organizations to arrange media coverage for special projects; writing letters, articles, and press releases; and placing advertisements and directory listings. Candidates should have ability to work independently, oral communication skills, personal interest in the field, self-motivation, strong interpersonal skills, written communication skills. Dura-

tion is flexible (minimum 16-24 hours weekly). stipend of up to $250 per 16 weeks. Open to college juniors, college seniors, recent college graduates, graduate students, career changers, individuals reentering the workforce. ▶ *2 publishing editors:* responsibilities include writing, and editing. Candidates should have ability to work with others, analytical skills, editing skills, organizational skills, written communication skills. Duration is flexible (minimum 16-24 hours weekly). stipend of up to $250 per 16 weeks. Open to college juniors, college seniors, recent college graduates, graduate students, career changers, individuals reentering the workforce. ▶ *3-5 sales/marketing interns:* responsibilities include assisting in telemarketing to potential clients, networking with sponsoring organizations to arrange programs, developing contacts, researching new distribution avenues (Internet emphasis), developing and maintaining computer systems for mail projects, placing advertisements, and handling correspondence. Candidates should have ability to work independently, ability to work with others, oral communication skills, organizational skills, personal interest in the field, self-motivation. Duration is flexible (minimum 16-24 hours weekly). stipend of up to $250 per 16 weeks. Open to college juniors, college seniors, recent college graduates, graduate students, career changers, individuals reentering the workforce. ▶ *6 writers/editors:* responsibilities include assisting in the writing, editing, and copy editing of new and existing materials; researching supplemental information; writing articles for training and management journals; and compiling, writing, and editing manuscripts and training manuals. Candidates should have ability to work with others, analytical skills, editing skills, organizational skills, written communication skills. Duration is flexible, minimum 16-24 hours weekly. stipend of up to $250 per 16 weeks. Open to college juniors, college seniors, recent college graduates, graduate students, career changers, individuals reentering the workforce. International applications accepted.

Benefits Formal training, on-the-job training, possible full-time employment, willing to act as a professional reference, willing to complete paperwork for educational credit, willing to provide letters of recommendation, opportunity to attend seminars/workshops/meetings.

Contact Write, fax, or e-mail Mr. Andrew E. Schwartz, President. Fax: 617-926-0660. E-mail: aes@aeschwartz.com. In-person interview recommended. Applicants must submit a cover letter, resume, two writing samples, 3 personal and professional references (names and numbers). Applications are accepted continuously. World Wide Web: http://www.aeschwartz.com.

ANIMAL BEHAVIOR CENTER OF NEW YORK
89-10 Eliot Avenue
Rego Park, New York 11374

General Information Not-for-profit applied animal behavior treatment and teaching center. Established in 1992. Number of employees: 18. Subsidiary of American Foundation for Animal Rescue, Inc., Rego Park, New York. Number of internship applications received each year: 100.

Internships Available ▶ *6-12 clinical behavior therapist interns:* responsibilities include lectures, case studies, videotape, training dogs, instruction (private and group), rounds, off-site trips to veterinarian hospitals and shelters. Candidates should have ability to work independently, analytical skills, oral communication skills, personal interest in the field, plan to pursue career in field, strong interpersonal skills. Duration is 5–6 weeks. Unpaid. Open to recent high school graduates, college freshmen, college sophomores, college juniors, college seniors, recent college graduates, graduate students, career changers, individuals reentering the workforce. International applications accepted. **Benefits** Formal training, housing at a cost, job counseling, on-the-job training, opportunity to attend seminars/workshops, possible full-time employment, willing to act as a professional reference, willing to complete paperwork for educational credit, willing to provide letters of recommendation. **Contact** Write, call, fax, or e-mail Robert DeFranco, Executive Director. Phone: 718-205-0200. Fax: 718-651-7681. E-mail: abcny@canines.com. In-person interview recommended. Applicants must submit a formal organization application. Applications are accepted continuously. Fees: $50. World Wide Web: http://www.canines.com.

CORPORATE FITNESS MIDWEST, INC.
11469 Olive Boulevard #251
St. Louis, Missouri 63141

General Information Corporate fitness/wellness management and consulting company that sets up, plans, and manages on-site corporate fitness wellness centers. Established in 1991. Number of employees: 15. Number of internship applications received each year: 20.
Internships Available ▶ *1–2 interns.* Candidates should have ability to work independently, computer skills, plan to pursue career in field, strong interpersonal skills, written communication skills. Duration is 10–14 weeks. $50–$100 per week. Open to college juniors, college seniors, graduate students. International applications accepted.
Benefits Job counseling, on-the-job training, willing to act as a professional reference, willing to complete paperwork for educational credit, willing to provide letters of recommendation. **Contact** Write, fax, or e-mail Harold Denlow, President, 11469 Olive Boulevard #251, St. Louis, Missouri 63141. Fax: 314-994-1545. E-mail: info@welltech.com. In-person interview recommended. Applicants must submit a cover letter, resume, two writing samples, two personal references, work samples that demonstrates talents and accomplishments. Applications are accepted continuously. World Wide Web: http://www.welltech.com.

THE CORPORATE RESPONSE GROUP, INC.
1101 17th Street, NW, Suite 1200
Washington, District of Columbia 20036

General Information Worldwide crisis management consulting firm. Established in 1986. Number of employees: 30. Number of internship applications received each year: 100.
Internships Available ▶ *4–6 crisis management research interns:* responsibilities include researching crisis management cases, conducting interviews for crisis management survey, administrative tasks, and participating in product development activities. Candidates should have ability to work independently, computer skills, oral communication skills, organizational skills, research skills, written communication skills. Duration is 2–3 months. ▶ *1 marketing intern:* responsibilities include gathering information, personnel identification, annual reports, and news articles for Corporate Response Group. Candidates should have ability to work independently, oral communication skills, organizational skills, research skills, written communication skills. Duration is determined by applicant's availability. All positions are unpaid. Open to college freshmen, college sophomores, college juniors, college seniors. International applications accepted.
Benefits Formal training, possible full-time employment, willing to act as a professional reference, willing to complete paperwork for educational credit, willing to provide letters of recommendation.
Contact Write, fax, or e-mail Rena L. Shooman, Internship Coordinator. Fax: 202-467-0513. E-mail: rshooman@crgdc.com.

Telephone interview required. Applicants must submit a cover letter, resume. Applications are accepted continuously. World Wide Web: http://www.crgdc.com.

CUE DATA SERVICES, INC.
165 Beal Street, Suite 1
Hingham, Massachusetts 02043

General Information Information technology consulting firm providing interim consulting services to Fortune 500 companies from coast to coast. Established in 1994. Number of employees: 19. Number of internship applications received each year: 5.
Internships Available ▶ *2–3 account representative trainees:* responsibilities include developing new clients from Fortune 500/1000 industries, expanding current client penetration, and recruiting candidates for client accounts. ▶ *2–3 recruiter trainees:* responsibilities include sourcing candidates, qualifying candidates, negotiating contracts, and assembling necessary documentation. Candidates for all positions should have ability to work independently, analytical skills, computer skills, oral communication skills, organizational skills, plan to pursue career in field, research skills, self-motivation, strong interpersonal skills, strong leadership ability, written communication skills. Duration for all positions is 8 weeks. All positions available as unpaid or paid. Open to college seniors, recent college graduates.
Benefits Formal training, job counseling, on-the-job training, opportunity to attend seminars/workshops, possible full-time employment, willing to act as a professional reference, willing to complete paperwork for educational credit, willing to provide letters of recommendation.
Contact Write, call, fax, or e-mail Martin J. Gallagher, Recruiting Manager, 165 Beal Street, Suite 1, Hingham, Massachusetts 02043. Phone: 781-749-3675. Fax: 781-749-0515. E-mail: resume@cuedata.com. In-person interview recommended. Applicants must submit a cover letter, resume, three personal references, three letters of recommendation. Applications are accepted continuously. World Wide Web: http://www.cuedata.com.

DELOITTE & TOUCHE
10 Westport Road
Wilton, Connecticut 06897

General Information One of the world's leading professional services firms that provides accounting and auditing, management consulting, and tax services. Established in 1895. Number of employees: 30,000. Unit of Deloitte Touche Tohmatsu, New York, New York. Number of internship applications received each year: 10,000.
Internships Available ▶ *400–600 business assurance and advisory (audit) interns:* responsibilities include preparation of audit workpapers, communicating with the client, and analysis of issues pertaining to specific areas of an audit; special projects as assigned. Candidates should have analytical skills, oral communication skills, organizational skills, strong leadership ability, written communication skills. $750–$1,000 per week. Open to college sophomores, college juniors, college seniors, graduate students. ▶ *50–100 enterprise risk services interns:* responsibilities include providing support to large corporate clients in a range of industry and technology control consulting services such as control assessments, network and PC systems security, and business process and application control implementation; providing internal audit services. Candidates should have analytical skills, computer skills, oral communication skills, organizational skills, strong leadership ability, written communication skills. $750–$1,000 per week. Open to college juniors, college seniors, graduate students. ▶ *25–50 human capital advisory services interns:* responsibilities include working with a team of consultants providing consultant services to Fortune 500 companies in areas of human resources strategies, compensation, human resources communications, actuarial, benefits, and global human resources strategies. Candidates should have analytical skills, computer skills, oral communication skills, organizational skills, strong leadership ability, written communication skills. $750–$1,000 per week. Open to college juniors, college seniors, graduate students. ▶ *50–100 management solutions and services interns:* responsibili-

Deloitte & Touche (continued)

ties include working with team of consultants providing consulting services to middle-market and emerging growth companies in areas of information management, operations management, and financial services consulting. Candidates should have analytical skills, computer skills, oral communication skills, organizational skills, strong leadership ability, written communication skills. $750–$1,000 per week. Open to college juniors, college seniors, graduate students. ▶ *200–250 tax services interns:* responsibilities include working within tax career tracks of generalist, specialist, and creative tax services consultant; working with tax teams. Candidates should have analytical skills, computer skills, oral communication skills, research skills, strong leadership ability, written communication skills. $750–$1,150 per week. Open to college juniors, graduate students, law students. Duration for all positions is 10–12 weeks. International applications accepted. **Benefits** Formal training, on-the-job training, opportunity to attend seminars/workshops, possible full-time employment, willing to complete paperwork for educational credit, holiday and illness pay, networking, participation in national SELECT internship conference, building of technical skills, laptop computer provided.
International Internships Available in Australia; Netherlands; South Africa; United Kingdom.
Contact Write or fax Internship Coordinator, Recruiting Director at office of interest, locations listed on web site, Wilton, Connecticut 06897. No phone calls. In-person interview required. Applicants must submit a resume. Application deadline: January 31 for summer; continuous for other seasons. World Wide Web: http://www.us.deloitte.com.

EASTMONT COMPUTING CENTER
7200 Bancroft Avenue, Suite 209
Oakland, California 94605

General Information Organization that provides free computer training and access to community members (includes Internet access, Microsoft, Apple, Adobe, etc.).
Internships Available ▶ *2–4 hardware/technical support interns:* responsibilities include troubleshooting, system administration, network administration, and LAN. ▶ *2 office assistants:* responsibilities include filing, word processing, and other administrative duties. ▶ *4–6 teaching interns:* responsibilities include teaching application use and technical skills. Duration for all positions is flexible. All positions paid at $12 per hour.
Contact Write, call, fax, or e-mail Jabari Adisa, Administrator, 7200 Bancroft Avenue, Suite 209, Oakland, California 94605. Phone: 510-382-0555. Fax: 510-382-1050. E-mail: ecc@eastmont. net. Applicants must submit a resume. Applications are accepted continuously. World Wide Web: http://www.eastmont.net.

HEWITT ASSOCIATES LLC
100 Half Day Road
Lincolnshire, Illinois 60069

General Information Consulting firm specializing in human resource solutions that help clients get the most from the design, financing, communication, administration, and delivery of human resources, compensation, and benefit plans. Established in 1940. Number of employees: 9,000.
Internships Available ▶ *12–20 actuarial consultants:* responsibilities include using analytical and communication skills to help clients address various employee benefit issues, pension valuations, merger and acquisition strategy, union negotiation support, design of executive retirement plans, and financial analysis of health care benefits. Candidates should have ability to work independently, analytical skills, plan to pursue career in field, self-motivation, strong interpersonal skills. ▶ *10–25 business analysts:* responsibilities include working on teams delivering pension, 401(k), or health and welfare benefits to clients' employees; testing the computer systems which support the benefit plans, researching client problems, benefit calculations, and analyzing data. Candidates should have ability to work independently, ability to work with others, analytical skills, self-motivation, detail orientation and flexibility. ▶ *3–5 information systems interns:*

responsibilities include formulating and recommending strategies for the use of computer and communications technology to support all of the practices within Hewitt Associates, including Peoplesoft, Lotus Notes, and internal systems. Candidates should have ability to work independently, ability to work with others, analytical skills, knowledge of field, SQL, C++, Visual Basic, Windows NT, Access, networking, and database administration experience. ▶ *10–20 programmer analysts:* responsibilities include working on teams to deliver the technology which administers clients' benefit plans, tailoring Hewitt's customized systems and software to clients' requirements, developing system specifications, customizing programs, converting data, and designing and implementing interactive systems such as voice-response and Internet. Candidates should have ability to work independently, ability to work with others, analytical skills, self-motivation, COBOL, JCL knowledge. Duration for all positions is 10–12 weeks. All positions paid. Open to individuals entering senior year of college. International applications accepted.
Benefits Free housing, free meals, on-the-job training, opportunity to attend seminars/workshops, possible full-time employment, willing to act as a professional reference, willing to complete paperwork for educational credit, willing to provide letters of recommendation.
Contact Write or fax College Recruiting, 100 Half Day Road, Lincolnshire, Illinois 60069. Fax: 847-295-0679. E-mail: careers@ hewitt.com. No phone calls. In-person interview required. Applicants must submit a cover letter, resume, academic transcripts. Application deadline: January 15 for summer. World Wide Web: http://www.hewitt.com.

JEFFERSON GOVERNMENT RELATIONS
1341 G Street, NW, Suite 1000
Washington, District of Columbia 20005

General Information Professional services firm bringing talent and depth to many areas, including congressional relations, regulatory affairs, health care, federal marketing, crisis communications, infrastructure and cities, and state and local public affairs. Established in 1987. Number of employees: 25. Number of internship applications received each year: 200.
Internships Available ▶ *1–5 interns:* responsibilities include reporting to group supervisors, conducting professional and administrative duties, and conducting research for current clients or new business activity. Depending upon internship selected, opportunities exist for entry–level accounting duties, human resource management, government relations, and healthcare. Candidates should have analytical skills, college courses in field, oral communication skills, plan to pursue career in field, research skills, written communication skills. Duration is 2–4 months. Unpaid. Open to high school seniors, college freshmen, college sophomores, college juniors, college seniors, recent college graduates, graduate students, law students. International applications accepted.
Benefits Names of contacts, willing to complete paperwork for educational credit, willing to provide letters of recommendation, $100 per month transportation reimbursement.
Contact Write, call, fax, or e-mail Ms. Andrea Whetzel, Executive Assistant. Phone: 202-626-8227. Fax: 202-626-8593. E-mail: awhetzel@jeffersongr.com. In-person interview recommended. Applicants must submit a cover letter, resume, academic transcripts, writing sample. Application deadline: April 30 for summer; continuous for others.

OFFICE OF INFORMATION TECHNOLOGY, SMITHSONIAN INSTITUTION
Arts and Industries Building, 900 Jefferson Drive, SW, Room 2224
Washington, District of Columbia 20560-0433

General Information Unit that provides the Smithsonian's central computing and telecommunications services and training as well as leadership in information technology. Unit of Smithsonian Institution, Washington, District of Columbia.
Internships Available ▶ *Interns:* responsibilities include providing technical support to several mainframe systems and network

servers doing computer training, helping to maintain e-mail and Web services, assisting with image scanning and the development of multimedia documents. Candidates should have interest in computer help desk operations, e-mail, programming languages, or network design. Duration is flexible. Position available as unpaid or paid. International applications accepted.
Benefits Willing to complete paperwork for educational credit, practical experience with information technology services unit.
Contact Write, call, fax, or e-mail Sherri Manning, Internship Coordinator. Phone: 202-786-2311. Fax: 202-633-9466. E-mail: smanning@oit.si.edu. Applicants must submit a formal organization application, cover letter, resume, academic transcripts, personal reference, essay. Applications are accepted continuously. World Wide Web: http://www.si.edu/organiza/offices/oit/start.htm.

OFFICE OF SPONSORED PROJECTS, SMITHSONIAN INSTITUTION
955 L'Enfant Plaza, Suite 7400
Washington, District of Columbia 20560-0903

General Information Unit that provides assistance to Smithsonian staff who are seeking, or have obtained, grants or other external funding for sponsored projects. Unit of Smithsonian Institution, Washington, District of Columbia.
Internships Available ▶ *Grants and contract administration interns:* responsibilities include helping research, curatorial, and educational staff find funding, prepare proposals, and administer grants and contracts. Duration is variable (minimum 2 months, 10-15 hours per week). Unpaid. Open to high school students, high school seniors, recent high school graduates, college freshmen, college sophomores, college juniors, college seniors, recent college graduates, graduate students, law students, career changers, individuals reentering the workforce. International applications accepted.
Benefits Willing to complete paperwork for educational credit.
Contact Write, call, fax, or e-mail Karen Otiji. Phone: 202-287-3793. Fax: 202-287-3707. E-mail: kareno@osp.si.edu. Applicants must submit a formal organization application, resume, academic transcripts, personal reference, essay, cover letter indicating proposed internship dates and internship objectives. Applications are accepted continuously. World Wide Web: http://www.si.edu.

PERFORMANCE RESEARCH
25 Mill Street, Queen Anne Square
Newport, Rhode Island 02840

General Information Market research firm specializing in quantitatively evaluating the effectiveness of sports and special event sponsorships. Established in 1986. Number of employees: 8. Number of internship applications received each year: 400.
Internships Available ▶ *1–2 market research interns:* responsibilities include travel and data collecting at sporting events, conducting personal interviews, performing data entry, designing surveys, and generating reports. Candidates should have computer skills, oral communication skills, self-motivation, strong interpersonal skills, writing skills, some experience with word-processing and graphics applications on the computer (preferred). Duration is 12–15 weeks. Unpaid. International applications accepted.
Benefits Job counseling, names of contacts, possible full-time employment, travel reimbursement, willing to complete paperwork for educational credit, willing to provide letters of recommendation, stipend paid upon completion of internship.
Contact Write or fax Ms. Nicole Alio, Internship Coordinator, 25 Milll Street, Queen Anne Square, Newport, Rhode Island 02840. Fax: 401-848-0110. In-person interview required. Applicants must submit a cover letter, resume, writing sample. Application deadline: February 1 for spring, April 1 for summer, July 1 for fall, November 1 for winter. World Wide Web: http://www.performanceresearch.com.

PIONEER HI-BRED INTERNATIONAL
400 Locust Street, Suite 700, PO Box 14454
Des Moines, Iowa 50306-3454

General Information World leader in the discovery, development, and delivery of elite crop genetics. Established in 1926. Number of employees: 1,500. Number of internship applications received each year: 300.
Internships Available ▶ *50 interns.* Duration is 3 months. $9 per hour, plus a $1000 stipend if returning to school. Open to college sophomores, college juniors, college seniors. International applications accepted.
Benefits Formal training, free meals, on-the-job training, opportunity to attend seminars/workshops, possible full-time employment, tuition assistance, willing to act as a professional reference, willing to complete paperwork for educational credit, willing to provide letters of recommendation.
International Internships Available.
Contact E-mail Dr. Judy Winkelpleck, Director, Workforce Strategies. Fax: 515-334-6555. E-mail: winkelpleck@phibred.com. No phone calls. In-person interview recommended. Applicants must submit a formal organization application, cover letter, academic transcripts, portfolio, writing sample, personal reference, letter of recommendation, resume that can be scanned. Application deadline: April 1 for summer. World Wide Web: http://www.pioneer.com.

PRO-FOUND SOFTWARE, INC.
500 Frank W. Burr Boulevard, Glenpointe Centre West
Teaneck, New Jersey 07666

General Information Technology consulting firm specializing in software development and system connectivity. Established in 1989. Number of employees: 6. Number of internship applications received each year: 1,000.
Internships Available ▶ *2 software consultants:* responsibilities include working with senior professionals and industry-leading clients in all aspects of software development from requirements definition through design and implementation. Candidates should have ability to work independently, ability to work with others, college courses in field, computer skills, experience in the field, personal interest in the field. Duration is 3–12 months. $500–$650 per week. Open to college sophomores, college juniors, college seniors, recent college graduates, graduate students. International applications accepted.
Benefits Opportunity to attend seminars/workshops, possible full-time employment, willing to complete paperwork for educational credit, willing to provide letters of recommendation, opportunity to co-publish articles and utilize and extend cutting-edge tools and components in software laboratory.
Contact Write, call, fax, or e-mail William Frenkel, Principal. Phone: 201-928-0400. Fax: 201-928-1122. E-mail: wfrenkel@pro.found.com. In-person interview recommended. Applicants must submit a cover letter, resume. Applications are accepted continuously. World Wide Web: http://www.pro-found.com.

ROSENBLUTH INTERNATIONAL
2401 Walnut Street
Philadelphia, Pennsylvania 19103-4390

General Information Travel management company offering comprehensive corporate, vacation, and meeting travel services. Established in 1892. Number of employees: 4,500. Number of internship applications received each year: 300.
Internships Available ▶ *1–2 corporate communications interns:* responsibilities include researching media interview topics; writing and assisting with distribution of news releases; writing articles for associate and client newsletters, Web site, and corporate biographies; assisting with collateral, video, and CD production. Candidates should have ability to work with others, college courses in field, experience in the field, research skills, self-motivation, writing skills. Duration is 1 semester. Open to college freshmen, college sophomores, college juniors, college seniors, recent college graduates, graduate students, career changers, individuals reentering the workforce. ▶ *1 corporate*

Rosenbluth International (continued)

strategies intern: responsibilities include providing assistance with analysis, review, and interpretation of corporate airline agreements; preparing reports and making recommendations to enhance reporting. Candidates should have college courses in field, computer skills, oral communication skills, research skills, written communication skills. Duration is 1 semester. Open to college freshmen, college sophomores, college juniors, college seniors, recent college graduates, graduate students. ▶ *1–2 human resources interns:* responsibilities include assisting human resources associates in all aspects of human resources and completing special projects, reviewing resumes and reference works, preparing letters/memos, and working on projects as needed. Candidates should have computer skills, knowledge of field, oral communication skills, organizational skills, personal interest in the field, self-motivation. Duration is 1 semester. Open to college freshmen, college sophomores, college juniors, college seniors, recent college graduates, graduate students, career changers, individuals reentering the workforce. ▶ *Information systems interns:* responsibilities include developing detailed project to collect inventory information, designing database and retrieval system, implementing automated inventory management software, establishing administrative procedures, and other related tasks. Candidates should have college courses in field, computer skills, knowledge of field, oral communication skills, written communication skills. Duration is 1 semester. Open to college freshmen, college sophomores, college juniors, college seniors, recent college graduates, graduate students. ▶ *1–2 marketing interns:* responsibilities include ongoing maintenance of marketing client database; assisting with creation, distribution, collection, and analysis of customer data; and assisting with distribution of all internal and external communication. Candidates should have college courses in field, computer skills, knowledge of field, research skills, self-motivation. Duration is 1 semester. Open to college freshmen, college sophomores, college juniors, college seniors, recent college graduates, graduate students, career changers, individuals reentering the workforce. ▶ *1–2 reservations interns:* responsibilities include assisting with projects from support/customer service, reservations, and hotel immigration; updating client profiles; assisting with reservations and customer satisfaction surveys; dealing with customer services issues; managing and monitoring calls; and working closely with hotels to negotiate rates. Candidates should have ability to work with others, computer skills, knowledge of field, self-motivation. Open to college freshmen, college sophomores, college juniors, college seniors, recent college graduates, graduate students, career changers, individuals reentering the workforce. ▶ *1 strategy analyst intern:* responsibilities include maintaining DACODA database which analyzes long-term travel strategies for clients to maximize cost savings; assisting with maintaining and developing progressive and profitable relationships with preferred airline, hotel, car rental, and computer reservation system suppliers on a global level. Candidates should have college courses in field, computer skills, knowledge of field, organizational skills, self-motivation. Duration is 1 semester. Open to college juniors, college seniors, recent college graduates, graduate students. All positions are unpaid. International applications accepted.

Benefits On-the-job training, opportunity to attend seminars/workshops, possible full-time employment, willing to act as a professional reference, willing to complete paperwork for educational credit, willing to provide letters of recommendation, daily stipend to contribute toward lunch or parking for some positions.

Contact Write, call, fax, or e-mail Gloria Miller, Internship Coordinator. Phone: 215-977-5429. Fax: 215-977-4444. E-mail: gmiller@rosenbluth.com. In-person interview required. Applicants must submit a formal organization application, cover letter, resume, academic transcripts, two letters of recommendation, one writing sample (corporate communications internship only). Application deadline: May 15 for summer, September 15 for fall, December 15 for spring. World Wide Web: http://www.rosenbluth.com.

SQUIER KNAPP OCHS DUNN
511 Second Street, NE
Washington, District of Columbia 20002

General Information Political consulting firm specializing in communications/media. The Communications Company (affiliate) does consulting for corporations and associations. Established in 1969. Number of employees: 35. Number of internship applications received each year: 50.

Internships Available ▶ *Staff assistants:* responsibilities include assisting in production, candidate, issue, and media research; light administrative work. Candidates should have ability to work independently, office skills, oral communication skills, research skills, strong interpersonal skills. Duration is 1 semester. $6 per hour. Open to college freshmen, college sophomores, college juniors, college seniors. International applications accepted.

Benefits On-the-job training, possible full-time employment, willing to act as a professional reference, willing to complete paperwork for educational credit, willing to provide letters of recommendation.

Contact Write, call, or fax Christina Lisi, Administrative Assistant. Phone: 202-547-4970. Fax: 202-543-6911. In-person interview recommended. Applicants must submit a cover letter, resume, writing sample, 1—2 personal references. Applications are accepted continuously.

STUDENT WORKS PAINTING
1505 East 17th Street, Suite 210
Santa Ana, California 92705

General Information Organization providing training and financial support for students to organize and operate an independent house-painting business. Established in 1981. Number of employees: 2,000. Number of internship applications received each year: 8,000.

Internships Available ▶ *600 branch managers:* responsibilities include recruiting and training a 6-9 person team; marketing, pricing, and selling services; production, quality and cost control, and collections; and promoting ethical business practices; positions available in Colorado, Texas, Washington, Idaho, California, Oregon, Arizona, Utah, and North Carolina. Duration is April—September (part-time in spring, full-time in summer). $7,000 per duration of internship. Open to college freshmen, college sophomores, college juniors, college seniors. International applications accepted.

Benefits Formal training, free meals, job counseling, on-the-job training, opportunity to attend seminars/workshops, possible full-time employment, tuition assistance, willing to complete paperwork for educational credit, willing to provide letters of recommendation, scholarships, trip to Cabo San Lucas, special training workshops for top producers, multiple business contacts.

Contact Write, call, fax, or e-mail Matthew Stewart, Vice President. Phone: 714-564-7900. Fax: 714-564-8725. E-mail: swpainting@aol.com. Applicants must submit a formal organization application, resume, 3 in-person interviews. Application deadline: April 1. World Wide Web: http://www.collegeworks.com.

ADVERTISING AND PUBLIC RELATIONS

ABRAMSON LABUS VAN DE VELDE
1275 K Street, NW, Suite 300
Washington, District of Columbia 20005

General Information Full-service advertising agency. Established in 1965. Number of employees: 45. Number of internship applications received each year: 300.

Internships Available ▶ *4–6 interns:* responsibilities include working on various tasks within 7 departments (creative, client services, media, new business, account planning, entertainment, and accounting). Candidates should have analytical skills,

computer skills, organizational skills, plan to pursue career in field, self-motivation, strong interpersonal skills. Duration is 3–4 months. Unpaid. Open to college sophomores, college juniors, college seniors, recent college graduates, graduate students. International applications accepted.
Benefits Names of contacts, possible full-time employment, willing to complete paperwork for educational credit, opportunity to attend press screenings of movies and receive promotional items.
Contact Write, fax, or e-mail Jason Lang, Internship Coordinator, 1275 E Street, NW, Suite 500, Washington, District of Columbia 20005. Fax: 202-789-2596. E-mail: jlang@alvweb.com. No phone calls. In-person interview recommended. Applicants must submit a cover letter, resume, specific essay (must call or e-mail for topic). Application deadline: February 15 for summer, May 15 for fall, September 15 for spring. World Wide Web: http://www.alvweb.com.

AIGNER ASSOCIATES PR/SPECIAL EVENTS, INC.
250 Everett Street
Boston, Massachusetts 02134

General Information Public relations and special events agency. Established in 1984. Number of employees: 8. Number of internship applications received each year: 80.
Internships Available ▶ *4 account coordinators:* responsibilities include assisting with media contacts, office support, writing, and helping with special event production. ▶ *2 assistant business managers:* responsibilities include assisting with general business management and financial affairs. Candidates should have interest in business. Duration for all positions is 1 semester. All positions are unpaid. Open to college freshmen, college sophomores, college juniors, college seniors.
Benefits Names of contacts, possible full-time employment, willing to complete paperwork for educational credit, willing to provide letters of recommendation.
Contact Write, call, fax, or e-mail Mr. John White, Assistant Account Executive. Phone: 617-254-9500. Fax: 617-254-3700. E-mail: jwhite@aignerassoc.com. In-person interview required. Applicants must submit a cover letter, resume, two writing samples. Application deadline: February 1 for spring, June 1 for summer, October 1 for fall.

AMWAY CORPORATION
7575 Fulton Street East
Ada, Michigan 49355-0001

General Information One of the world's largest network marketing companies, marketing products and services through independent distributors in the U.S. and more than 60 other countries and territories. Established in 1959. Number of employees: 5,000. Number of internship applications received each year: 600.
Internships Available ▶ *50 summer interns:* responsibilities include working in any of the following departments: accounting, marketing, chemistry, biology, chemical and electrical engineering, and/or purchasing. Candidates should have declared college major in field, minimum GPA of 3.0. Duration is 12-13 weeks. minimum of $11 per hour. Open to college juniors, graduate students, college seniors still to complete a term or semester.
Benefits Travel reimbursement, willing to complete paperwork for educational credit, discounts on Amway products.
Contact Write, fax, or e-mail Pam Powers, College Relations Coordinator. Fax: 616-787-5675. E-mail: pam_powers@amway.com. No phone calls. In-person interview required. Applicants must submit a cover letter, resume, academic transcripts. Application deadline: January 31 for January 31 (recommended). World Wide Web: http://www.amway.com.

ANNE SCHWAB'S MODEL STORE
906 D Street, NE
Washington, District of Columbia 20002

General Information Modeling and casting agency, booking professional talent, makeup artists and sytlists; communications company producing advertising, marketing, public relations, and event planning for companies large and small. Established in 1980. Number of employees: 2. Number of internship applications received each year: 100.
Internships Available ▶ *1 special assistant to the President:* responsibilities include interviewing talent; handling client bookings; making arrangements for travel and wardrobe; accompanying owner to photo shoots, TV bookings, fashion shows, and parties; and assisting with events planning and writing/advertising services. Candidates should have ability to work independently, analytical skills, computer skills, office skills, oral communication skills, organizational skills, self-motivation, strong interpersonal skills, strong leadership ability, writing skills. Duration is 1 semester. Unpaid. Open to high school students, high school seniors, recent high school graduates, college freshmen, college sophomores, college juniors, college seniors, recent college graduates, graduate students, law students, career changers, individuals reentering the workforce.
Benefits Job counseling, names of contacts, on-the-job training, willing to act as a professional reference, willing to complete paperwork for educational credit, willing to provide letters of recommendation, lunch provided.
Contact Write, call, fax, or e-mail Ms. Anne Schwab, President. Phone: 202-333-3560. Fax: 202-544-2856. E-mail: crmgtser@aol.com. In-person interview recommended. Applicants must submit a cover letter, resume. Applications are accepted continuously.

BERNSTEIN-REIN ADVERTISING
4600 Madison, Suite 1500
Kansas City, Missouri 64112

General Information Full-service advertising agency. Established in 1964. Number of employees: 260. Number of internship applications received each year: 150.
Internships Available ▶ *1–2 account management interns:* responsibilities include attending internal strategy meetings, coordinating daily operations of accounts, and writing conference reports. Candidates should have college courses in field, knowledge of field, office skills, oral communication skills, organizational skills, personal interest in the field, plan to pursue career in field, written communication skills. ▶ *1–2 creative interns:* responsibilities include working as a copywriter or art director; conceiving and executing print, outdoor, and broadcast advertising; creating logos and taglines; selecting talent; and attending commercial shoots and edits. Candidates should have ability to work with others, college courses in field, computer skills, knowledge of field, personal interest in the field, writing skills, graphic design/art experience. ▶ *1 market research intern:* responsibilities include designing questionnaires, observing focus groups and field data collection, researching secondary sources, obtaining bids from vendors, and assisting in report generation. Candidates should have analytical skills, computer skills, knowledge of field, oral communication skills, research skills, writing skills. ▶ *1–2 media interns:* responsibilities include researching media, targeting markets, developing budgets, projecting ratings, assisting in post-buy analyses, attending meetings with national media representatives, and researching new media trends. Candidates should have analytical skills, computer skills, knowledge of field, office skills, organizational skills, research skills. ▶ *1 public relations intern:* responsibilities include providing media relations, including media list and press kit development; planning and coordinating special events; conducting research; drafting proposals. Candidates should have computer skills, editing skills, knowledge of field, oral communication skills, organizational skills, written communication skills. Duration for all positions is June to August. All positions paid at $6 per hour. Open to college students entering their senior year.
Benefits On-the-job training, possible full-time employment, willing to complete paperwork for educational credit.
Contact Write, fax, or e-mail Julie Truman, Assistant Manager of Human Resources. Fax: 816-531-5708. E-mail: human_res@bradv.com. No phone calls. In-person interview required. Applicants must submit a formal organization application, cover letter, resume, writing sample, three personal references. Application deadline: February 15.

BOZELL WORLDWIDE ADVERTISING AND PUBLIC RELATIONS
13801 FNB Parkway
Omaha, Nebraska 68154

General Information Full service advertising and public relations firm. Established in 1921. Number of employees: 120. Unit of True North Communications, Chicago, Illinois. Number of internship applications received each year: 75.

Internships Available ▶ *5–8 advertising and public relations interns:* responsibilities include working closely with advertising and public relations professionals, assisting with client projects, and working on a team to develop a complete campaign for client. Candidates should have ability to work with others, knowledge of field, oral communication skills, personal interest in the field, self-motivation, written communication skills, relevant course work or professional experience. Duration is 12 weeks in summer. $6 per hour. Open to college sophomores, college juniors, college seniors, recent college graduates, graduate students. International applications accepted.

Benefits Possible full-time employment, willing to complete paperwork for educational credit, willing to provide letters of recommendation.

Contact Write, fax, or e-mail Jan Sammons, Internship Coordinator. Fax: 402-965-4333. E-mail: jsammons@omaha.bozell.com. No phone calls. In-person interview recommended. Applicants must submit a formal organization application, cover letter, resume, academic transcripts, writing sample, letter of recommendation, portfolio for creative positions. Application deadline: February 14. World Wide Web: http://www.bozell.com.

BROWN-MILLER COMMUNICATIONS
1330 Arnold Drive, Suite 252
Martinez, California 94553

General Information Full-service public relations agency serving the food, wine, and agriculture industries; emphasizes creativity, strong writing skills, thorough research, and persistent work. Established in 1987. Number of employees: 5. Number of internship applications received each year: 50.

Internships Available ▶ *1 account coordinator:* responsibilities include writing press releases and magazine articles, answering phones and making media calls, coordinating special events, preparing monthly activity reports, supervising account timelines, tracking press clippings, coordinating product mailing, performing database updates, running errands, researching, and filing. Candidates should have college courses in field, computer skills, oral communication skills, personal interest in the field, self-motivation, writing skills. Duration is 1 semester. Unpaid. Open to individuals with two years of college-related course experience in public relations, journalism, English, or communications. International applications accepted.

Benefits Job counseling, travel reimbursement, willing to complete paperwork for educational credit, willing to provide letters of recommendation, writing and editing skills enhancement, exposure to media relations.

Contact Write, fax, or e-mail Ms. Sharron Faaborg, Internship Coordinator. Fax: 925-370-9811. E-mail: bmc@dnai.com. No phone calls. In-person interview recommended. Applicants must submit a cover letter, resume, two writing samples. Applications are accepted continuously. World Wide Web: http://www.dnai.com/~bmc.

BSMG WORLDWIDE
640 5th Avenue
New York, New York 10019

General Information Full-service communications agency. Established in 1980. Number of employees: 170. Division of True North Communications, Chicago, Illinois. Number of internship applications received each year: 250.

Internships Available ▶ *2–3 consulting interns:* responsibilities include conducting research for and interacting with clients, evaluating communications efforts and recommending tactics to reach target audiences, and executing projects. Candidates should have ability to work independently, analytical skills, oral communication skills, strong interpersonal skills, written communication skills. Open to college juniors, college seniors, recent college graduates, graduate students, law students. ▶ *2–3 public relations interns:* responsibilities include writing, researching, and performing media relations activities. Candidates should have ability to work independently, ability to work with others, plan to pursue career in field, research skills, self-motivation, written communication skills. Open to college juniors, college seniors, recent college graduates, graduate students. ▶ *1–2 research interns:* responsibilities include writing and testing of surveys, compiling case studies, conducting secondary research, compiling data gathered from primary research. Candidates should have ability to work independently, ability to work with others, analytical skills, computer skills, personal interest in the field, research skills. Open to college juniors, college seniors, recent college graduates, graduate students. Duration for all positions is 3 months. All positions paid at $8–$9 per hour. International applications accepted.

Benefits Job counseling, names of contacts, on-the-job training, opportunity to attend seminars/workshops, possible full-time employment, willing to act as a professional reference, willing to complete paperwork for educational credit, willing to provide letters of recommendation.

Contact Write, fax, or e-mail Michelle Hunt, Human Resources Associate. Fax: 212-445-8095. E-mail: mhunt@bsmg.com. No phone calls. In-person interview recommended. Applicants must submit a cover letter, resume, writing sample. Application deadline: March 31 for summer, November 30 for winter. World Wide Web: http://www.bsmgworldwide.com.

BSMG WORLDWIDE- MARKETING COMMUNICATIONS
625 North Michigan Avenue, 25th Floor
Chicago, Illinois 60611-3110

General Information Public relations firm. Number of employees: 120.

Internships Available ▶ *14–18 interns:* responsibilities include working on 2-3 accounts, compiling media lists, pitching, market research, vendor coordination, writing, editing, and daily clip reports. Candidates should have major in journalism, communications, public relations, or related fields. Duration is 3 months. Paid. Open to college seniors. International applications accepted.

Benefits Names of contacts, on-the-job training, possible full-time employment, willing to act as a professional reference, willing to complete paperwork for educational credit, willing to provide letters of recommendation.

Contact Write, call, or fax Katy Lauler, Intern Coordinator, 625 North Michigan Avenue, 25th Floor, Chicago, Illinois 60611-3110. Phone: 312-988-2320. Fax: 312-988-2200. In-person interview required. Applicants must submit a cover letter, resume, test for writing and proofreading skills. Applications are accepted continuously. World Wide Web: http://www.bsmg.com.

BURSON-MARSTELLER
230 Park Avenue South
New York, New York 10003

General Information Global perception management firm focused on delivering measurable business results to its clients through a full range of consulting and communications disciplines. Established in 1953. Number of employees: 400. Unit of Young and Rubicam, New York, New York.

Internships Available ▶ *15–25 public relations interns:* responsibilities include working as part of a team, creating media lists, writing press materials, pitching stories to media, helping with logistics and staffing of press conferences and/or special events, conducting research, and monitoring media; positions also available in Chicago, DC, and California. Candidates should have oral communication skills, personal interest in the field, written communication skills, minimum GPA of 3.0 or equivalent, participation in extracurricular activities. Duration is 10 weeks. Paid. Open to college seniors, recent college graduates.

Benefits Opportunity to attend seminars/workshops, possible full-time employment.
Contact E-mail Ronni Goldman, Human Resources Associate. E-mail: internships@bm.com. No phone calls. Applicants must submit a cover letter, resume, academic transcripts, 2 essays on assigned topics. Application deadline: March 1. World Wide Web: http://www.bursonmarsteller.com.

CAIRNS & ASSOCIATES
3 Park Avenue, 14th Floor
New York, New York 10016

General Information Full service public relations and integrated marketing agency. Established in 1983. Number of employees: 47. Number of internship applications received each year: 1,000.
Internships Available ▶ *2–5 interns:* responsibilities include preparing media lists and coordinating press mailings, contacting editors and television producers, maintaining press clippings, preparing client reports, writing press materials, and conducting research projects. Candidates should have knowledge of field, oral communication skills, personal interest in the field, research skills, self-motivation, written communication skills. Duration is 1 semester. $5 per hour. Open to college sophomores, college juniors. International applications accepted.
Benefits Job counseling, names of contacts, on-the-job training, opportunity to attend seminars/workshops, possible full-time employment, willing to complete paperwork for educational credit, willing to provide letters of recommendation, participation in mentor program.
Contact Write or fax Jackie Widrow, or Avra Goldstone, Intern Coordinators. Fax: 212-421-9799. No phone calls. In-person interview required. Applicants must submit a cover letter, resume. Application deadline: March 15 for summer.

CANAAN PUBLIC RELATIONS
114 East 32nd Street, Suite 801
New York, New York 10016

General Information Full Service public relations firm. Established in 1977. Number of employees: 8.
Internships Available ▶ *2 interns:* responsibilities include assisting account executive, preparing press kits, editing, writing, and helping plan events. Candidates should have office skills, oral communication skills, self-motivation, strong interpersonal skills, written communication skills. Duration is flexible. $15 per day. International applications accepted.
Benefits Formal training, names of contacts, opportunity to attend seminars/workshops, possible full-time employment, travel reimbursement, willing to complete paperwork for educational credit, willing to provide letters of recommendation.
Contact Write or fax Jed Canaan, President, 114 East 32nd Street, New York, New York 10016. Fax: 212-223-3737. In-person interview required. Applicants must submit a cover letter, resume. Applications are accepted continuously.

COLLEGE CONNECTIONS/ HALSTEAD COMMUNICATIONS
329 East 82nd Street
New York, New York 10028

General Information Company providing public relations for education and non-profit organizations. Established in 1980. Number of employees: 8. Number of internship applications received each year: 250.
Internships Available ▶ *1 public relations intern:* responsibilities include writing pitch letters and press releases, pitching stories to print and broadcast media, word processing, and compiling and updating databases and general mailing lists. Candidates should have computer skills, office skills, oral communication skills, personal interest in the field, self-motivation, written communication skills. Duration is 1 semester. Position available as unpaid or at $8–$10 per hour. Open to college juniors, college seniors, recent college graduates.
Benefits Job counseling, names of contacts, on-the-job training, opportunity to attend seminars/workshops, possible full-

time employment, travel reimbursement, willing to act as a professional reference, willing to complete paperwork for educational credit, willing to provide letters of recommendation.
Contact Write, call, fax, or e-mail Wendy Wilkinson, Internship Coordinator. Phone: 212-734-2190. Fax: 212-517-7284. E-mail: intern@halsteadpr.com. In-person interview recommended. Applicants must submit a cover letter, resume, writing sample. Application deadline: March 31 for summer, August 31 for fall, December 15 for spring. World Wide Web: http://www.halsteadpr.com.

CONE, INC.
90 Canal Street
Boston, Massachusetts 02114

General Information Public relations/communications firm that seeks to find true alignments between companies and their customers and create programs and communications to build image, understanding, and sales. Established in 1980. Number of employees: 60. Number of internship applications received each year: 100.
Internships Available ▶ *10 account management interns:* responsibilities include engaging in all aspects of strategic marketing communications while linked to a team through which the intern will be exposed to all areas of account management. Candidates should have ability to work with others, college courses in field, computer skills, plan to pursue career in field, self-motivation, written communication skills. Open to college freshmen, college sophomores, college juniors, college seniors, graduate students. ▶ *1 human resources intern:* responsibilities include performing diverse human resources functions including: intern/employee development training and workshops, employee benefits, intern administration, scanning and reviewing resumes, sitting in on interviews, and other administrative functions. Candidates should have ability to work independently, computer skills, oral communication skills, organizational skills, plan to pursue career in field, strong interpersonal skills, written communication skills. Open to college freshmen, college sophomores, college juniors, college seniors. Duration for all positions is 3 months. All positions are unpaid. International applications accepted.
Benefits Formal training, job counseling, names of contacts, opportunity to attend seminars/workshops, willing to complete paperwork for educational credit, willing to provide letters of recommendation, assistance with resume preparation and interviews, networking opportunities, free transportation pass for interns working 3 days a week.
Contact Write or fax Karen Taylor, Intern Coordinator. Fax: 617-523-3955. In-person interview required. Applicants must submit a cover letter, resume. Application deadline: April 1 for summer, June 1 for fall, November 1 for spring. World Wide Web: http://www.conenet.com.

C. PAUL LUONGO COMPANY, PUBLIC RELATIONS AND MARKETING
441 Stuart Street
Boston, Massachusetts 02116

General Information Public relations firm and marketing agency that offers corporate, product, and financial publicity consulting and marketing communications services throughout the U.S. and Canada. Established in 1964. Number of employees: 6. Number of internship applications received each year: 100.
Internships Available ▶ *1–2 assistants to President:* responsibilities include new business and media research, telephone contacts. Candidates should have ability to work independently, analytical skills, computer skills, editing skills, office skills, oral communication skills, organizational skills, research skills, self-motivation, strong interpersonal skills, strong leadership ability, writing skills. Duration is 3–6 months. Open to recent high school graduates, college freshmen, college sophomores, college juniors, college seniors, recent college graduates, graduate students, law students, career changers, individuals reentering the workforce. ▶ *1 intern:* responsibilities include performing a variety of public relations activities. Candidates should have abil-

C. Paul Luongo Company, Public Relations and Marketing (continued)

ity to work independently, analytical skills, computer skills, editing skills, office skills, oral communication skills, organizational skills, research skills, self-motivation, strong interpersonal skills, writing skills. Duration is 3 months minimum. Open to high school seniors, college freshmen, college sophomores, college juniors, college seniors, recent college graduates, graduate students, law students, career changers, individuals reentering the workforce. All positions are unpaid.

Benefits Formal training, job counseling, names of contacts, on-the-job training, possible full-time employment, willing to act as a professional reference, willing to complete paperwork for educational credit, willing to provide letters of recommendation.

Contact Write or call Mr. C. Paul Luongo, President. Phone: 617-266-4210. In-person interview recommended. Applicants must submit a cover letter, resume. Applications are accepted continuously.

CREAMER, DICKSON, BASFORD
350 Hudson Street, 5th Floor
New York, New York 10014

General Information Public relations agency providing full-service communications services including media relations, special events, strategic planning and research, creative services, corporate management, and crisis management. Number of employees: 75. Number of internship applications received each year: 1,000.

Internships Available ▶ *Interns:* responsibilities include writing press materials, pitching stories, researching and fact-checking, and coordinating special events. Duration is 3 months in fall, summer, or spring. Position available as unpaid or paid. Open to college juniors, college seniors, recent college graduates, graduate students, career changers. International applications accepted.

Benefits Formal training, names of contacts, opportunity to attend seminars/workshops, possible full-time employment, travel reimbursement, willing to complete paperwork for educational credit, willing to provide letters of recommendation.

Contact Write, call, or fax Ms. Meghan Selway or Ms. Amanda Aldridge, Intern Coordinators. Phone: 212-367-6814. Fax: 212-367-7154. In-person interview required. Applicants must submit a cover letter, resume, writing sample. Applications are accepted continuously. World Wide Web: http://www.cdbpr.com.

CRESWELL, MUNSELL, FULTZ, & ZIRBEL
600 East Court Avenue
Des Moines, Iowa 50309

General Information Public relations/advertising firm that provides creative solutions for specialized markets. Established in 1939. Number of employees: 75. Affiliate of Young and Rubicam, New York, New York. Number of internship applications received each year: 100.

Internships Available ▶ *1 advertising intern:* responsibilities include performing duties in the creative, account management, media, production, and database departments. Candidates should have ability to work with others, college courses in field, computer skills, experience in the field, office skills, self-motivation. ▶ *1 computer graphic design intern:* responsibilities include layout, concept development, and brainstorming. Candidates should have ability to work with others, college courses in field, computer skills, experience in the field, self-motivation, Quark Xpress and Photoshop skills. ▶ *1 copy intern:* responsibilities include copywriting, concept development, and brainstorming. Candidates should have analytical skills, college courses in field, experience in the field, self-motivation, strong interpersonal skills, writing skills. ▶ *1 public relations intern:* responsibilities include writing, assisting account managers on projects, and handling media relations. Candidates should have ability to work with others, college courses in field, experience in the field, organizational skills, self-motivation, writing skills. Duration for all positions is flexible. All positions available as unpaid or at $300 per week. Open to college juniors, college seniors.

Benefits Formal training, opportunity to attend seminars/workshops, possible full-time employment, willing to complete paperwork for educational credit, reimbursement of business-related travel expenses.

Contact Write, fax, or e-mail Sue Caley, Senior Vice President/Human Resource Manager. Fax: 515-246-3592. E-mail: sue_caley@cmfz.com. No phone calls. In-person interview required. Applicants must submit a cover letter, resume, academic transcripts, writing sample, portfolio (after reaching interview stage). Applications are accepted continuously. World Wide Web: http://www.cmfz.com.

CROMARTY AND COMPANY
110 West 40th Street, Suite 405
New York, New York 10018

General Information Theatrical press agency serving a wide range of Broadway, off-Broadway, music, and dance clients by handling publicity needs. Established in 1987. Number of employees: 5. Number of internship applications received each year: 200.

Internships Available ▶ *1–2 interns:* responsibilities include assisting press agents in all aspects of publicity, including writing and mailing press releases and other materials, attending opening nights and interviews, and assisting in the office. Candidates should have ability to work independently, ability to work with others, college courses in field, computer skills, editing skills, knowledge of field, office skills, oral communication skills, organizational skills, plan to pursue career in field, self-motivation, written communication skills. Duration is 4 months. $50–$100 per week. Open to college freshmen, college sophomores, college juniors, college seniors, recent college graduates, graduate students, career changers, individuals reentering the workforce. International applications accepted.

Benefits Names of contacts, possible full-time employment, travel reimbursement, willing to complete paperwork for educational credit, willing to provide letters of recommendation, reimbursement for lunch on work days, small stipend.

Contact Write, fax, or e-mail Alice Cromarty, Internship Coordinator. Fax: 212-302-1257. E-mail: alicec@cromarty.com. No phone calls. In-person interview recommended. Applicants must submit a cover letter, resume, writing sample. Application deadline: April 1 for summer, September 1 for fall, November 1 for winter.

DYE VAN MOL AND LAWRENCE
209 Seventh Avenue North
Nashville, Tennessee 37219

General Information Full-service marketing and communications firm that specializes in national, regional, and local public relations and community activities. Established in 1980. Number of employees: 80. Number of internship applications received each year: 50.

Internships Available ▶ *3–6 interns:* responsibilities include performing research and writing, arranging special events and meetings, and calling the media. Candidates should have ability to work with others, oral communication skills, organizational skills, research skills, self-motivation, writing skills. Duration is 3-5 months in fall, spring, or summer. $6 per hour. Open to college freshmen, college sophomores, college juniors, college seniors, recent college graduates, graduate students.

Benefits Formal training, names of contacts, willing to complete paperwork for educational credit, willing to provide letters of recommendation.

Contact Write, call, fax, or e-mail Ms. Jennifer Alexander, Account Executive. Phone: 615-244-1818. Fax: 615-780-3302. E-mail: jennifer.alexander@dvl.com. In-person interview required. Applicants must submit a formal organization application, cover letter, resume. Applications are accepted continuously. World Wide Web: http://www.dvl.com.

DYKEMAN ASSOCIATES, INC.
4115 Rawlins
Dallas, Texas 75219

General Information Full–service marketing, public relations, and video production firm. Established in 1974. Number of employees: 5. Number of internship applications received each year: 75.
Internships Available ▶ *3–4 interns:* responsibilities include assisting with production of collateral materials, video production, and ad preparation; compiling media lists; contacting media; setting up programs for speakers; creating proposals for business prospects; and monitoring presentations to clients. Candidates should have analytical skills, college courses in field, computer skills, organizational skills, plan to pursue career in field, self-motivation, writing skills, dependability. Duration is 1 semester to 1 year. $8.50 per hour in barter dollars. Open to college juniors, college seniors, recent college graduates, graduate students. International applications accepted.
Benefits Formal training, job counseling, names of contacts, on-the-job training, opportunity to attend seminars/workshops, possible full-time employment, willing to complete paperwork for educational credit, willing to provide letters of recommendation, job listings, barter dollars (in lieu of cash) for salary. **Contact** Write, fax, or e-mail Ms. Alice Dykeman, President/CEO. Fax: 214-528-0241. E-mail: adykeman@airmail.net. No phone calls. In-person interview recommended. Applicants must submit a cover letter, resume, four writing samples, two personal references, two letters of recommendation. Application deadline: March 15 for summer, June 15 for fall, November 15 for spring. World Wide Web: http://www.dykemanassoc.com.

THE EDELMAN GROUP
420 Lexington Avenue, Suite 1706
New York, New York 10170

General Information Firm that specializes in design, advertising, and marketing for corporate clients. Established in 1982. Number of employees: 9. Number of internship applications received each year: 25.
Internships Available ▶ *1 accounting assistant:* responsibilities include invoicing, billing, and reconciling accounts. Candidates should have ability to work independently, oral communication skills, organizational skills, personal interest in the field. Open to college freshmen, college sophomores, college juniors, college seniors, recent college graduates. ▶ *1–2 graphic design interns:* responsibilities include photo research, preparing artwork for presentation, and some design work. Candidates should have ability to work independently, ability to work with others, personal interest in the field, plan to pursue career in field, self-motivation, previous study of design and/or fine art. Duration is flexible. Open to college freshmen, college sophomores, college juniors, college seniors, recent college graduates. ▶ *1 receptionist:* responsibilities include answering telephone calls from clients and using fax and copying machines. Candidates should have office skills, oral communication skills, written communication skills. Open to college freshmen, college sophomores, college juniors, college seniors. ▶ *1 sales assistant:* responsibilities include assisting salesperson with research, lead qualification, and telemarketing. Candidates should have computer skills, oral communication skills, personal interest in the field, research skills, self-motivation, strong interpersonal skills. Duration is flexible. Open to college freshmen, college sophomores, college juniors, college seniors. All positions are unpaid. International applications accepted.
Benefits Formal training, possible full-time employment, travel reimbursement, willing to complete paperwork for educational credit, willing to provide letters of recommendation.
Contact Write or e-mail Michelle Callot, Senior Art Director, 420 Lexington Avenue, Suite 1706, New York, New York 10170. E-mail: michelle@edelmangroup.com. No phone calls. In-person interview recommended. Applicants must submit a portfolio. Applications are accepted continuously. World Wide Web: http://www.edelmangroup.com.

EISNER, PETROU, AND ASSOCIATES
927 15th Street, NW, Suite 900
Washington, District of Columbia 20005

General Information Full-service marketing communications agency specializing in travel/tourism/hospitality, health care, business-to-business public relations, and special events. Established in 1986. Number of employees: 16. Unit of Eisner and Associates, Baltimore, Maryland. Number of internship applications received each year: 50.
Internships Available ▶ *1–3 interns:* responsibilities include performing research, special events planning and implementation, and assisting in media relations and client contact. Candidates should have declared college major in field, knowledge of field, oral communication skills, organizational skills, strong interpersonal skills, written communication skills. Duration is 1 semester. Position available as unpaid or at credit for college or stipend. Open to college juniors, college seniors. International applications accepted.
Benefits Names of contacts, opportunity to attend seminars/workshops, possible full-time employment, travel reimbursement, willing to complete paperwork for educational credit, willing to provide letters of recommendation.
Contact Write Debbi Malamud, Senior Account Executive, 927 15th Street, NW, Suite 900, Washington, District of Columbia 20005. In-person interview recommended. Applicants must submit a cover letter, resume, writing sample. Application deadline: April 1 for summer, October 1 for spring.

ELKMAN/ALEXANDER AND PARTNERS
2 Penn Center Plaza, 1500 JFK Boulevard, Suite 1500
Philadelphia, Pennsylvania 19102

General Information Full-service marketing communications agency that offers advertising, public relations, media planning, and market research services to regional and national clients. Established in 1954. Number of employees: 40.
Internships Available ▶ *1–2 advertising/account management interns:* responsibilities include developing a marketing plan, interacting with other departments, and analyzing competition. ▶ *1 market research intern:* responsibilities include collecting data, preparing evaluations, interviewing, field checks, and writing reports. ▶ *1–2 media interns:* responsibilities include research and analysis. ▶ *1–2 public relations interns:* responsibilities include media and library research, writing publicity material, compiling and analyzing news clips, coordinating special events, and organizing projects and mailings. Duration for all positions is flexible (summer, winter, or spring). All positions are unpaid. Open to college freshmen, college sophomores, college juniors, college seniors.
Benefits Formal training, job counseling, names of contacts, opportunity to attend seminars/workshops, possible full-time employment, willing to complete paperwork for educational credit, willing to provide letters of recommendation, guidelines on how to set-up portfolio and interview assistance provided, reimbursement of work-related travel expenses.
Contact Write, call, or fax Internship Coordinator, 2 Penn Center Plaza 1500 JFK Boulevard, Suite 1500, Philadelphia, Pennsylvania 19102. Phone: 215-557-1570. Fax: 215-557-1577. In-person interview required. Applicants must submit a cover letter, resume. Applications are accepted continuously.

FENTON COMMUNICATIONS
1320 18th Street, NW, 5th Floor
Washington, District of Columbia 20036

General Information Issue-oriented public relations firm committed to representing socially responsible clients. Established in 1981. Number of employees: 50. Number of internship applications received each year: 200.
Internships Available ▶ *4 full-time public relations interns:* responsibilities include assisting with administrative support, developing media lists, monitoring media coverage, and distributing press materials. Candidates should have ability to work with others, office skills, oral communication skills, personal interest in the

Fenton Communications (continued)

field, written communication skills. Duration is 1 semester. small stipend available. Open to college freshmen, college sophomores, college juniors, college seniors, recent college graduates, graduate students. International applications accepted.
Benefits Formal training, job counseling, willing to complete paperwork for educational credit, willing to provide letters of recommendation, opportunity to attend press conferences.
Contact Write, call, or e-mail Ms. Stacia Tipton, Intern Coordinator. Phone: 202-822-5200. E-mail: stacia@fenton.com. In-person interview required. Applicants must submit a cover letter, resume. Applications are accepted continuously. World Wide Web: http://www.fenton.com.

FORTUNE PUBLIC RELATIONS
2319 California Street
Berkeley, California 94703

General Information Restaurant , hospitality, and food products public relations firm. Established in 1986. Number of employees: 2. Number of internship applications received each year: 20.
Internships Available ▶ *2 publicist trainees:* responsibilities include copywriting, client contact, press kit design and production, media list development, media follow-up calls, and general office duties. Candidates should have ability to work independently, computer skills, knowledge of field, oral communication skills, writing skills. Duration is flexible. Unpaid. Open to college seniors, recent college graduates, graduate students, career changers, individuals reentering the workforce. International applications accepted.
Benefits Job counseling, names of contacts, opportunity to attend seminars/workshops, willing to act as a professional reference, willing to complete paperwork for educational credit, willing to provide letters of recommendation, possibility of part-time employment.
Contact Write, call, fax, or e-mail Tom Walton, Co-owner. Phone: 510-548-1097. Fax: 510-841-7006. E-mail: fortunepr@aol.com. In-person interview recommended. Applications are accepted continuously. World Wide Web: http://www.fortunepublicrelations.com.

FRANCO PUBLIC RELATIONS GROUP
400 Renaissance Center, Suite 1050
Detroit, Michigan 48243

General Information Organization that specializes in public relations counseling, graphics design/illustration, art studio work, corporate video production, and Web-site communications. Established in 1964. Number of employees: 30. Number of internship applications received each year: 100.
Internships Available ▶ *1–2 public relations interns:* responsibilities include researching, writing, editing, and assembling public relations case studies. Candidates should have oral communication skills, self-motivation, strong interpersonal skills, strong leadership ability, written communication skills. Duration is 3 months in summer, fall, or winter. $6 per day. Open to college freshmen, college sophomores, college juniors, college seniors. International applications accepted.
Benefits Names of contacts, possible full-time employment, willing to complete paperwork for educational credit, willing to provide letters of recommendation, reimbursement of work-related travel expenses, parking pass.
Contact Write, call, fax, or e-mail Tracey E. Kilbey, Account Executive. Phone: 313-567-5074. Fax: 313-567-4486. E-mail: kilbey@franco.com. Applicants must submit a cover letter, resume, writing sample. Applications are accepted continuously. World Wide Web: http://www.franco.com.

FRANKLIN ADVERTISING ASSOCIATES, INC.
51 Winchester Street
Newton, Massachusetts 02461

General Information Full-service advertising agency providing print advertising and collateral support to a wide variety of clients

from banks to resort properties to high-tech companies. Established in 1970. Number of employees: 5. Number of internship applications received each year: 100.
Internships Available ▶ *1 art department intern:* responsibilities include participating in all phases of art department work including design, layout, typesetting, and mechanical preparation of all advertisements and collateral materials. Candidates should have college courses in field, computer skills, oral communication skills, organizational skills, personal interest in the field, strong interpersonal skills. ▶ *1–2 general advertising interns:* responsibilities include being exposed to daily operations of agency, including maintaining magazine/newspaper research library and client research files, copywriting, taking part in traffic function, and providing receptionist relief. Candidates should have computer skills, oral communication skills, organizational skills, strong interpersonal skills, strong leadership ability, written communication skills. Duration for all positions is one summer or one semester. All positions are unpaid. Open to college freshmen, college sophomores, college juniors, college seniors. International applications accepted.
Benefits Willing to complete paperwork for educational credit, willing to provide letters of recommendation.
Contact Write, call, fax, or e-mail Lottie Smith, Intern Coordinator. Phone: 617-244-8368. Fax: 617-244-5897. E-mail: franklin@tp.net. In-person interview required. Applicants must submit a cover letter, resume. Applications are accepted continuously.

HILL AND KNOWLTON, INC.
466 Lexington Avenue, 3rd Floor
New York, New York 10017

General Information Headquarters of global public relations firm. Established in 1927. Number of employees: 200. Number of internship applications received each year: 450.
Internships Available ▶ *Fall/winter interns:* responsibilities include working on assignments and attending regular employee seminars and office events. Duration is flexible. ▶ *10–12 summer interns:* responsibilities include working with one or two supervisors as part of their account teams; exposure to practice specialties within the public relations profession such as media relations, financial relations, marketing and crisis communications, and health care; researching; preparing and presenting proposals. Duration is mid-June to mid-August (8-10 week minimum). Candidates for all positions should have oral communication skills, organizational skills, personal interest in the field, written communication skills, previous academic or work experience in public relations field helpful. All positions paid at $7 per hour. Open to college juniors, college seniors, recent college graduates, graduate students. International applications accepted.
Benefits Formal training, opportunity to attend seminars/workshops, possible full-time employment, willing to complete paperwork for educational credit, willing to provide letters of recommendation.
Contact Write Rebecca Moatz, Internship Coordinator. Applicants must submit a cover letter, resume, two writing samples. Application deadline: February 28 for summer, July 30 for fall, October 15 for winter. World Wide Web: http://www.hillandknowlton.com.

JACKSINA COMPANY
1501 Broadway, Suite 1508
New York, New York 10036

General Information Publicity, public relations, and marketing company whose expertise is concentrated in the entertainment field with specific attention to the promoting, publicizing, and marketing of Broadway shows and films; also works in the music industry. Established in 1978. Number of employees: 2. Number of internship applications received each year: 50.
Internships Available ▶ *2–4 assistants to account executives:* responsibilities include working in areas including public relations, marketing, film production, and television development. Candidates should have office skills, oral communication skills, organizational skills, personal interest in the field, strong interpersonal skills, written communication skills. Position avail-

able as unpaid or paid. Open to college sophomores, college juniors, college seniors, recent college graduates, graduate students. ▶ *1–2 general assistants:* responsibilities include assisting in all areas within the organization. Candidates should have ability to work independently, office skills, oral communication skills, personal interest in the field, self-motivation, strong interpersonal skills, written communication skills. Unpaid. Duration for all positions is 3–6 months. International applications accepted.

Benefits Free meals, job counseling, on-the-job training, opportunity to attend seminars/workshops, possible full-time employment, travel reimbursement, willing to act as a professional reference, willing to complete paperwork for educational credit, willing to provide letters of recommendation.

Contact Write, call, or fax Judy Jacksina, President. Phone: 212-221-8361. Fax: 212-221-8369. Applicants must submit a resume. Applications are accepted continuously.

JAY RAY ADS & PUBLIC RELATIONS; JACOBSON, RAY, MCLAUGHLIN, FILLIPS ADVERTISING AND PUBLIC RELATIONS
535 East Dock Street, Suite 205
Tacoma, Washington 98402-4616

General Information Full-service advertising, public relations, and marketing agency. Established in 1970. Number of employees: 18. Number of internship applications received each year: 20.

Internships Available ▶ *1 advertising/public relations intern:* responsibilities include handling assignments in media planning and scheduling; performing media and market research and account coordination; assisting with photography, radio, TV production, promotions, public relations events, projects, and new business research. Candidates should have college courses in field, computer skills, oral communication skills, organizational skills, plan to pursue career in field, self-motivation, phone skills, writing skills (preferred). Duration is 5–16 weeks. Unpaid. Open to college juniors, college seniors, recent college graduates, graduate students, career changers. International applications accepted.

Benefits Names of contacts, opportunity to attend seminars/workshops, travel reimbursement, willing to complete paperwork for educational credit, willing to provide letters of recommendation.

Contact Write or e-mail Kathleen Deakins, Vice President, Client Services. E-mail: kdeakins@jayray.com. In-person interview recommended. Applicants must submit a cover letter, resume, three personal references. Applications are accepted continuously.

KCSA
800 Second Avenue
New York, New York 10017

General Information Public relations agency specializing in public and investor relations, corporate communications, and marketing communications. Established in 1969. Number of employees: 65. Number of internship applications received each year: 250.

Internships Available ▶ *3–5 public relations interns:* responsibilities include working with various groups. Candidates should have ability to work with others, computer skills, oral communication skills, personal interest in the field, self-motivation, written communication skills. Duration is flexible. Unpaid. Open to college sophomores, college juniors, college seniors. International applications accepted.

Benefits Formal training, job counseling, on-the-job training, possible full-time employment, travel reimbursement, willing to complete paperwork for educational credit, willing to provide letters of recommendation.

Contact Write, call, fax, or e-mail Joseph A. Mansi, Managing Partner. Phone: 212-682-6300. Fax: 212-697-0910. E-mail: jmansi@kcsa.com. In-person interview required. Applicants must submit a cover letter, resume. Applications are accepted continuously. World Wide Web: http://www.kcsa.com.

KELMAN AND BURDITCH
118½ South La Brea Avenue
Los Angeles, California 90036

General Information Public relations firm representing a variety of entertainment and tourism accounts, including international resorts and hotels, airlines, and one nonprofit educational organization. Established in 1992. Number of employees: 6. Number of internship applications received each year: 100.

Internships Available ▶ *1–3 public relations assistants:* responsibilities include writing, researching, and performing telephone follow-up. Candidates should have ability to work independently, computer skills, office skills, oral communication skills, organizational skills, personal interest in the field, self-motivation, strong interpersonal skills. Duration is 2–12 months. Unpaid. Open to college freshmen, college sophomores, college juniors, college seniors, recent college graduates, graduate students, law students, career changers, individuals reentering the workforce. International applications accepted.

Benefits Job counseling, names of contacts, on-the-job training, willing to complete paperwork for educational credit, willing to provide letters of recommendation.

Contact Write or fax Ms. Deborah Kelman, President. Fax: 323-932-1425. No phone calls. In-person interview recommended. Applicants must submit a cover letter, resume. Applications are accepted continuously.

KETCHUM PUBLIC RELATIONS
292 Madison Avenue
New York, New York 10017

General Information Public relations firm specializing in corporate and investor relations, food and consumer marketing, employee communications, and media relations. Established in 1923. Number of employees: 150. Number of internship applications received each year: 500.

Internships Available ▶ *Interns:* responsibilities include planning and conducting promotion, publicity, and media contact; positions available in Atlanta, GA; Chicago, IL; Dallas, TX; Los Angeles, CA; Miami, FL; New York, NY; Pittsburgh, PA; San Francisco, CA; and Washington, DC. Candidates should have ability to work with others, declared college major in field, editing skills, organizational skills, personal interest in the field, writing skills. Duration is 8–10 weeks. $250–$350 per week. Open to college juniors, college seniors, recent college graduates, graduate students. International applications accepted.

Benefits Formal training, on-the-job training, opportunity to attend seminars/workshops, possible full-time employment, willing to complete paperwork for educational credit, internships available in 9 locations.

Contact Write, fax, or e-mail Heather Cohen, Corporate Communications Coordinator/National Internship Coordinator. Fax: 212-448-4488. E-mail: heather.cohen@ketchum.com. No phone calls. In-person interview required. Applicants must submit a cover letter, resume, 2—3 writing samples, indication of placement location(s) preferred. Application deadline: March 1 for summer. World Wide Web: http://www.ketchum.com.

KNOLL AND COMPANY, INC.
110 Southwest Yamhill, Suite 300
Portland, Oregon 97204

General Information Full-service advertising, public relations, direct marketing, and design firm. Established in 1954. Number of employees: 16. Number of internship applications received each year: 50.

Internships Available ▶ *4 interns:* responsibilities include assisting all agency departments in day-to-day projects and performing independent library research. Candidates should have editing skills, plan to pursue career in field, research skills, self-motivation, strong interpersonal skills, writing skills. Duration is 3 months. $500 per duration of internship.

Benefits Names of contacts, willing to complete paperwork for educational credit, willing to provide letters of recommendation.

Knoll and Company, Inc. (continued)

Contact Write, fax, or e-mail Jane Baker, Senior Account Manager, 110 Southwest Yamhill, Suite 300, Portland, Oregon 97204. Fax: 503-273-8007. E-mail: jane@knol.com. No phone calls. In-person interview recommended. Applicants must submit a cover letter, resume, personal reference. Applications are accepted continuously. World Wide Web: http://www.knol.com.

LIGGETT-STASHOWER PUBLIC RELATIONS
1228 Euclid Avenue
Cleveland, Ohio 44115

General Information Public relations division of one of the largest communications firms in the Midwest, serving clients nationwide. Established in 1980. Number of employees: 150. Unit of Liggett-Stashower Inc., Cleveland, Ohio. Number of internship applications received each year: 15.

Internships Available ▶ *1–2 public relations interns:* responsibilities include managing media relations, assisting print editors and broadcast journalists on telephone, and assisting, as needed, on general assignments. Candidates should have computer skills, knowledge of field, oral communication skills, plan to pursue career in field, writing skills, formal education in public relations. Duration is 1 summer or fall semester. minimum wage stipend. Open to college juniors, college seniors.

Benefits Formal training, names of contacts, on-the-job training, opportunity to attend seminars/workshops, willing to act as a professional reference, willing to complete paperwork for educational credit, willing to provide letters of recommendation.

Contact Write, fax, or e-mail Ms. Marilyn Casey, Vice President. Fax: 216-736-8118. E-mail: mcasey@liggett.com. No phone calls. In-person interview required. Applicants must submit a cover letter, resume, portfolio, writing sample. Application deadline: March 1 for summer, August 1 for fall. World Wide Web: http://www.liggett.com.

LINDY PROMOTIONS, INC.
4343 Montgomery Avenue, Suite 5
Bethesda, Maryland 20814

General Information Promotions and event planning company. Number of employees: 6. Number of internship applications received each year: 400.

Internships Available ▶ *1–4 marketing interns:* responsibilities include various administrative duties, grassroots marketing in DC metropolitan area, writing press releases, helping with planning and execution of events, assisting with mailings, advertising sales for monthly newsletter. Candidates should have ability to work independently, computer skills, office skills, organizational skills, personal interest in the field, research skills, self-motivation, strong interpersonal skills, strong leadership ability, writing skills. Duration is 3–4 months. Unpaid. Open to college sophomores, college juniors, college seniors.

Benefits Names of contacts, on-the-job training, possible full-time employment, willing to act as a professional reference, willing to complete paperwork for educational credit, willing to provide letters of recommendation.

Contact Write, fax, or e-mail Jennifer Fouts, Assistant Event Coordinator, 4343 Montgomery Avenue, Suite #5, Bethesda, Maryland 20814. Fax: 301-652-7714. E-mail: jenifouts@lindypromo.com. In-person interview recommended. Applicants must submit a cover letter, resume. World Wide Web: http://www.lindypromo.com.

MAKOVSKY AND COMPANY, INC.
575 Lexington Avenue, 15th Floor
New York, New York 10022

General Information Mid-size public relations agency providing a full range of public relations services for clients nationwide, with major divisions in technology, health and industrial, and financial services/investor relations.

Internships Available ▶ *2–3 interns:* responsibilities include assisting with planning campaigns, researching, writing, placing publicity with editors, and working, if appropriate, with clients. Dura-

tion is 4 months in fall and/or spring or 3 months in summer. $750 per month (summer); fall and spring positions pay hourly wages. Open to college juniors, college seniors, recent college graduates.

Benefits Opportunity to attend seminars/workshops, possible full-time employment, willing to complete paperwork for educational credit, willing to provide letters of recommendation.

Contact Write or fax Internship Coordinator, 575 Lexington Avenue, 15th Floor, New York, New York 10022. Fax: 212-751-9710. In-person interview required. Applicants must submit a cover letter, resume, three writing samples. Application deadline: March 1 for summer.

MALLORY FACTOR, INC.
555 Madison Avenue
New York, New York 10022

General Information Boutique and stylized independent public relations firms with divisions in investor relations, marketing communications, special events, and issues management. Established in 1976. Number of employees: 11. Number of internship applications received each year: 60.

Internships Available ▶ *1–2 interns:* responsibilities include writing and editing press releases, arranging meetings and events, compiling press kits and media lists, and conducting research. Duration is flexible; positions available throughout the year. Unpaid. Open to college freshmen, college sophomores, college juniors, college seniors, recent college graduates, graduate students.

Benefits Job counseling, possible full-time employment, willing to complete paperwork for educational credit, willing to provide letters of recommendation.

Contact Write, call, fax, or e-mail Richard Aaron, President. Phone: 212-350-0000. Fax: 212-350-0001. E-mail: mfipr@aol.com. In-person interview recommended. Applicants must submit a resume. Applications are accepted continuously.

MARINA MAHER COMMUNICATIONS
830 Third Avenue, 12th Floor
New York, New York 10022

General Information Integrated marketing communications agency. Established in 1983. Number of employees: 50. Number of internship applications received each year: 300.

Internships Available ▶ *Public relations interns:* responsibilities include supporting account team with research, press events, administrative duties, and account work. Duration is 1 semester. $6 per hour. Open to college freshmen, college sophomores, college juniors, college seniors. International applications accepted.

Benefits Job counseling, possible full-time employment, willing to complete paperwork for educational credit, willing to provide letters of recommendation.

Contact Write or fax Internship Coordinator, 830 Third Avenue, 12th Floor, New York, New York 10022. Fax: 212-355-6318. No phone calls. Applicants must submit a cover letter, resume. Applications are accepted continuously.

THE MARTIN AGENCY
One Shockoe Plaza
Richmond, Virginia 23219-4132

General Information Agency providing unified, multi-disciplined communications in a workplace generating creativity, accomplishment, and personal growth. Established in 1965. Number of employees: 450. Unit of The Interpublic Agency Network.

Internships Available ▶ *15 student workshop interns:* responsibilities include participating in seminars on various aspects about the advertising business; case project; real-life, real-client situation. Duration is 8 days in either January or June. Unpaid. Open to college freshmen, college sophomores, college juniors, college seniors, recent college graduates going on directly to graduate school. International applications accepted.

Benefits Opportunity to attend seminars/workshops, certificate of completion, networking opportunities.

Contact Write, call, fax, or e-mail Erika Willis, Student Workshop Coordinator. Phone: 804-698-8269. Fax: 804-698-8245. E-mail: willise@mail.martinagency.com. Applicants must submit a formal organization application, cover letter, resume. Application deadline: April 15 for June session, November 16 for January session. World Wide Web: http://www.martinagency.com.

MILLER SHANDWICK TECHNOLOGIES
1888 Century Park East, Suite 920
Los Angeles, California 90067

General Information Publicity agency. Number of employees: 16. Unit of Shandwick North America, Inc., New York, New York. Number of internship applications received each year: 100.
Internships Available ▶ *4–6 interns:* responsibilities include doing research on the Internet, updating the media contact database, preparing press clip books, and maintaining schedules and activity reports. Candidates should have ability to work with others, college courses in field, computer skills, oral communication skills, plan to pursue career in field, written communication skills. Duration is flexible. Position available as unpaid or paid. Open to college juniors, college seniors. International applications accepted.
Benefits Formal training, on-the-job training, opportunity to attend seminars/workshops, possible full-time employment, willing to complete paperwork for educational credit, willing to provide letters of recommendation.
Contact Write, call, or fax Human Resources Department/ Internship Coordinator, 1888 Century Park East, 5th Floor, Los Angeles, California 90067. Phone: 310-201-6606. Fax: 310-284-2070. In-person interview required. Applicants must submit a cover letter, resume. Applications are accepted continuously.

MORTON DENNIS WAX & ASSOCIATES, INC.
1560 Broadway
New York, New York 10036

General Information Organization that provides public relations/ marketing for entertainment, communications, and allied industries. Established in 1956. Number of employees: 2. Number of internship applications received each year: 40.
Internships Available ▶ *2–4 film distribution/marketing interns:* responsibilities include writing and researching press releases, stories, and media marketing plans; contacting clients and the media; researching the marketing of foreign films; creating marketing mailing lists; and performing general office duties. Duration is 2–6 months. ▶ *3 public relations/marketing interns:* responsibilities include writing and researching press releases, stories, and media marketing plans and contacting clients and media. Duration is 1–6 months. Candidates for all positions should have ability to work independently, computer skills, office skills, oral communication skills, self-motivation, writing skills. All positions are unpaid. Open to college freshmen, college sophomores, college juniors, college seniors. International applications accepted.
Benefits Names of contacts, possible full-time employment, willing to act as a professional reference, willing to complete paperwork for educational credit, willing to provide letters of recommendation.
Contact Write Ms. Sandra Wax, Vice President. No phone calls. Applicants must submit a cover letter, resume. Applications are accepted continuously.

M. SILVER ASSOCIATES, INC.
747 Third Avenue, 23rd Floor
New York, New York 10017-2803

General Information Public relations/marketing communications consultants to travel, consumer, and tourism industries worldwide. Established in 1960. Number of employees: 27. Number of internship applications received each year: 200.
Internships Available ▶ *1–2 fall/winter/spring interns:* responsibilities include assisting account group with daily workload necessary to serving clients; attending staff/creative meetings; conducting on-line research; writing press releases; preparing and

disseminating press releases, press kits, and photographs; using ACT database to initiate, track, and report on media contact; assisting with press trip invitations, itineraries, and trips. Candidates should have college courses in field, computer skills, declared college major in field, experience in the field, oral communication skills, organizational skills, written communication skills. Duration is 1 semester. $6–$8 per hour. ▶ *2–3 summer interns:* responsibilities include assisting account group with daily work load necessary to serving clients; attending staff/creative meetings; conducting on-line research; writing press releases; preparing and disseminating press releases, press kits, and photographs; using ACT database to initiate, track, and report on media contact; assisting with press trip invitations, itineraries, and trips. Candidates should have college courses in field, computer skills, experience in the field, oral communication skills, organizational skills, written communication skills, declared major in communications/public relations. Duration is 3 months. $200 per week. Open to college sophomores, college juniors, college seniors.
Benefits Job counseling, names of contacts, on-the-job training, possible full-time employment, travel reimbursement, willing to act as a professional reference, willing to complete paperwork for educational credit, willing to provide letters of recommendation, opportunity to attend staff meetings/creative sessions and to be a fully participating accounts group member.
Contact Write, fax, or e-mail Vivian DiMare, Internship Coordinator. Fax: 212-754-6698. E-mail: vdimare@msilver.com. In-person interview recommended. Applicants must submit a cover letter, resume, academic transcripts, 1 or 2 letters of recommendation. Application deadline: April 1 for summer, July 1 for fall, October 1 for winter, December 1 for spring.

NATIONAL CANCER INSTITUTE, OFFICE OF CANCER COMMUNICATIONS
Building 31, Room 10A28, 9000 Rockville Pike
Bethesda, Maryland 20892-2580

General Information Organization responsible for developing and managing communications activities of the National Cancer Institute and disseminating information to the public, the press, and health professionals. Established in 1937. Number of employees: 55. Unit of National Institute of Health, Bethesda, Maryland. Number of internship applications received each year: 30.
Internships Available ▶ *1–3 Web site development interns:* responsibilities include developing new and innovative communications products. ▶ *1–3 cancer information service interns:* responsibilities include assisting in program management, quality assurance, staff training, program evaluation, and publicity and promotion activities. ▶ *1–3 health promotion and social marketing interns:* responsibilities include planning, developing, evaluating, and promoting education and information programs to target audiences, preparing and carrying out national education campaigns, and pre-testing and evaluating health education materials. ▶ *1–3 patient education interns:* responsibilities include assisting with the design, implementation, promotion, and evaluation of comprehensive education programs for cancer patients and their families; preparing needs assessment tools; determining target audience information; conducting literature reviews; preparing educational materials; and providing feedback on program plans. ▶ *1–3 science writing interns:* responsibilities include handling inquiries from reporters, writing news and feature articles and fact sheets for the press and public, and attending scientific meetings. Candidates for all positions should have ability to work with others, analytical skills, college courses in field, oral communication skills, organizational skills, written communication skills. Duration for all positions is 6 months-1 year. All positions paid at $1,500 per month. Open to graduate students.
Benefits Formal training, health insurance, opportunity to attend seminars/workshops, willing to complete paperwork for educational credit, reimbursement of on-the-job travel expenses.
Contact Write, call, fax, or e-mail Ms. Maggie Bartlett, Internship Director, Building 31, Room 10A25, 9000 Rockville Pike, Bethesda, Maryland 20892-2580. Phone: 301-496-4394. Fax: 301-496-7096. E-mail: m4b@box-m.nnih.gov. Telephone interview

National Cancer Institute, Office of Cancer Communications (continued)
required. Applicants must submit a formal organization application, cover letter, resume, academic transcripts, two writing samples, 1 personal reference from advisor/Dean, 1 letter of recommendation from Dean. Application deadline: April 1 for July—December term, October 1 for January—June term. World Wide Web: http://www.nci.nih.gov.

NORTH CAROLINA AMATEUR SPORTS
PO Box 12727
Research Triangle Park, North Carolina 27709

General Information Organization that promotes the Olympic movement through amateur sports, produces the State Games of North Carolina, sponsors state conferences on the Olympic movement and amateur sports, and attracts national and international events and conferences to North Carolina. Established in 1983. Number of employees: 5. Number of internship applications received each year: 30.
Internships Available ▶ *1 media/promotions intern:* responsibilities include working with newspapers, radio, and television to promote events; recording and distributing sporting event results to local newspapers, AP, and UPI; and assisting with program layout. Candidates should have ability to work with others, computer skills, editing skills, oral communication skills, self-motivation, written communication skills. $150–$200 per week. ▶ *1 operations intern:* responsibilities include acquiring facilities, providing communications needs, procuring equipment, assisting with the medical and concession plans, and venue set up. Candidates should have ability to work independently, ability to work with others, oral communication skills, organizational skills, self-motivation, written communication skills. $150–$200 per week. ▶ *1 special events intern:* responsibilities include working with events cohosted by North Carolina Amateur Sports. Candidates should have ability to work independently, office skills, oral communication skills, personal interest in the field, self-motivation, written communication skills. Position available as unpaid or paid. ▶ *1 special projects intern:* responsibilities include handling all monies involved with event entry fees and working with accountant and auditor on organization's finances. Candidates should have ability to work independently, ability to work with others, computer skills, organizational skills, self-motivation, written communication skills. $150–$200 per week. ▶ *1 volunteer coordinator:* responsibilities include recruiting, training, supervising, and assigning 1000–2000 volunteers that work with the State Games. Candidates should have computer skills, oral communication skills, organizational skills, self-motivation, strong interpersonal skills, written communication skills. $150–$200 per week. Duration for all positions is 8–10 weeks. Open to college freshmen, college sophomores, college juniors, college seniors, recent college graduates, graduate students.
Benefits Job counseling, names of contacts, opportunity to attend seminars/workshops, possible full-time employment, travel reimbursement, willing to act as a professional reference, willing to complete paperwork for educational credit, willing to provide letters of recommendation.
Contact Write, fax, or e-mail Linda Smith, Director of Operations. Fax: 919-361-2559. E-mail: ncas@interpath.com. No phone calls. In-person interview recommended. Applicants must submit a formal organization application, cover letter, resume. Application deadline: February 15 for summer. World Wide Web: http://www.ncsports.org.

THE PETE SANDERS GROUP
1560 Broadway, Suite 1101
New York, New York 10036

General Information Public relations firm specializing in entertainment and fashion, with such clients as the Broadway Musical "Chicago" and Tommy Hilfiger. Established in 1990. Number of employees: 5. Number of internship applications received each year: 40.
Internships Available ▶ *2 press interns:* responsibilities include direct contact with the media, setting up and supervising press interviews, editing press releases, assisting in special events planning, and general office duties. Candidates should have ability to work independently, computer skills, editing skills, office skills, oral communication skills, personal interest in the field, self-motivation, strong interpersonal skills, writing skills, major in communications, journalism, theater, or English. Duration is 8 weeks minimum (generally 1 semester or winter break). Unpaid. Open to college sophomores, college juniors, college seniors. International applications accepted.
Benefits Free meals, on-the-job training, opportunity to attend seminars/workshops, possible full-time employment, travel reimbursement, willing to act as a professional reference, willing to complete paperwork for educational credit, willing to provide letters of recommendation, some complimentary theater tickets.
Contact Write, call, or fax Glenna Freedman, 1560 Broadway, Suite 1101, New York, New York 10036. Phone: 212-730-0067. Fax: 212-730-0394. In-person interview recommended. Applicants must submit a cover letter, resume. Application deadline: February 28 for summer, September 2 for winter, December 30 for spring.

PORTER NOVELLI
220 East 42nd Street
New York, New York 10017

General Information Marketing-based public relations firm with divisions for healthcare, consumer, business-to-business, and media relations. Established in 1972. Number of employees: 150. Unit of Omnicon-New York, New York, New York.
Internships Available ▶ *Assistant account executives:* responsibilities include media contact, press materials, researching special events, brainstorming, media coverage, and administrative duties. Candidates should have writing skills, major in communications preferred. Duration is 3 months. $300 per week. Open to college juniors, college seniors, recent college graduates, graduate students. International applications accepted.
Benefits Opportunity to attend seminars/workshops, possible full-time employment, willing to complete paperwork for educational credit.
Contact Write, call, fax, or e-mail Frank Sole, Human Resources. Phone: 212-601-8000. Fax: 212-601-8101. E-mail: fsole@porternovelli.com. In-person interview required. Applicants must submit a cover letter, resume, writing test. Application deadline: March 15 for summer; continuous for all other seasons. World Wide Web: http://www.porternovelli.com.

QUALLY AND COMPANY, INC.
2238 Central Street
Evanston, Illinois 60201-1457

General Information Full-service integrated advertising agency specializing in new product development, new product introductions, and repositioning of existing products and services. Established in 1979. Number of employees: 4. Number of internship applications received each year: 300.
Internships Available ▶ *2 account executives:* responsibilities include assisting with new and existing business. Candidates should have ability to work independently, analytical skills, college courses in field, computer skills, editing skills, experience in the field, office skills, oral communication skills, organizational skills, plan to pursue career in field, research skills, self-motivation, strong interpersonal skills, strong leadership ability, written communication skills. Duration is 3–6 months. Open to college juniors, college seniors, recent college graduates, graduate students, law students, career changers. ▶ *2–3 art directors:* responsibilities include performing art, design, production, and general tasks. Candidates should have ability to work independently, analytical skills, computer skills, editing skills, personal interest in the field, self-motivation. Duration is 3–9 months. ▶ *2 copywriters:* responsibilities include performing various writing assignments and general tasks. Candidates should have ability to work independently, ability to work with others, analytical skills, college courses in field, computer skills, editing skills, knowledge of field, organizational skills, plan to pursue career in field, research skills, self-motivation, written communication skills.

Duration is 3–6 months. Open to college juniors, college seniors, recent college graduates, graduate students, law students, career changers. ▶ *2–3 graphic designers:* responsibilities include assisting with art direction and production and performing general tasks. Candidates should have ability to work independently, ability to work with others, analytical skills, college courses in field, computer skills, organizational skills, plan to pursue career in field, self-motivation. Duration is 3–6 months. Open to college juniors, college seniors, recent college graduates, graduate students, career changers. ▶ *2 new business development interns:* responsibilities include assisting with new business development, direct mail, account service, and public relations. Candidates should have ability to work independently, oral communication skills, personal interest in the field, self-motivation, strong interpersonal skills. Duration is 3–6 months. Open to college juniors, college seniors, recent college graduates, graduate students, law students, career changers. ▶ *1 research intern:* responsibilities include researching for new and existing businesses and performing general tasks. Candidates should have analytical skills, computer skills, organizational skills, personal interest in the field, research skills, written communication skills. Duration is 3–6 months. Open to college juniors, college seniors, recent college graduates, graduate students, law students, career changers. All positions are unpaid. International applications accepted.
Benefits Formal training, job counseling, names of contacts, on-the-job training, opportunity to attend seminars/workshops, possible full-time employment, willing to act as a professional reference, willing to complete paperwork for educational credit, willing to provide letters of recommendation, networking opportunities.
Contact Write or call Mr. Robert Qually, President. Phone: 847-864-6316. In-person interview recommended. Applicants must submit a cover letter, resume, portfolio, three personal references, three letters of recommendation, 10 writing samples. Application deadline: nine months in advance of desired internship.

RENEE SALL ASSOCIATES, INC.
Cali Corporate Center, 50 Tice Boulevard
Woodcliff Lake, New Jersey 07675

General Information Public relations firm servicing a wide variety of interests including consumer products, professionals, business-to-business services, and nonprofit organizations. Established in 1986. Number of employees: 5.
Internships Available ▶ *Office assistants:* responsibilities include performing clerical work and assisting account executives in all aspects of public relations. Duration is year-round. Unpaid. Open to college freshmen, college sophomores, college juniors, college seniors. International applications accepted.
Benefits Willing to complete paperwork for educational credit, willing to provide letters of recommendation.
Contact Write Director of Internships, Cali Corporate Center 50 Tice Boulevard, Woodcliff Lake, New Jersey 07675. No phone calls. In-person interview required. Applications are accepted continuously.

RESNICK COMMUNICATIONS
1528 Walnut Street
Philadelphia, Pennsylvania 19102

General Information Communications firm working with innovative individuals and organizations, offering customized personal service to both corporate and nonprofit clients in all phases of growth and development. Established in 1986. Number of employees: 3. Number of internship applications received each year: 10.
Internships Available ▶ *2–4 interns:* responsibilities include working in public relations, marketing, and communications. Candidates should have ability to work independently, ability to work with others, computer skills, oral communication skills, personal interest in the field, written communication skills. Duration is one semester or one summer. Unpaid. Open to high school seniors, recent high school graduates, college freshmen, college

sophomores, college juniors, college seniors, recent college graduates, career changers, individuals reentering the workforce. International applications accepted.
Benefits Job counseling, names of contacts, on-the-job training, opportunity to attend seminars/workshops, possible full-time employment, travel reimbursement, willing to act as a professional reference, willing to complete paperwork for educational credit, willing to provide letters of recommendation.
Contact Write, call, fax, or e-mail Melanie Johnson, Associate. Phone: 215-893-0204. Fax: 215-893-0311. E-mail: prres@aol.com. In-person interview required. Applicants must submit a cover letter, resume. Applications are accepted continuously.

THE ROCKEY COMPANY
2121 Fifth Avenue
Seattle, Washington 98121

General Information Public relations and public affairs firm that provides counsel to a wide range of industries including timber, aerospace, health care, sports, entertainment, and manufacturing. Established in 1962. Number of employees: 35. Number of internship applications received each year: 100.
Internships Available ▶ *Public relations interns:* responsibilities include working directly with account executives on many different accounts and developing different studies and areas of expertise. Candidates should have ability to work with others, oral communication skills, organizational skills, self-motivation, writing skills. Duration is 10–12 weeks. Unpaid. Open to college juniors, college seniors, recent college graduates.
Benefits Formal training, opportunity to attend seminars/workshops, possible full-time employment, travel reimbursement, stipend for completing successful internship.
Contact Write Katy Strausborger, Intern Coordinator. No phone calls. In-person interview required. Applicants must submit a cover letter, resume, two writing samples. Applications are accepted continuously. World Wide Web: http://www.rockey-seattle.com.

ROGERS & COWAN, INC.
1888 Century Park East, 5th Floor
Los Angeles, California 90067

General Information Publicity agency. Established in 1950. Number of employees: 75. Unit of Shandwick North America, Inc., New York, New York. Number of internship applications received each year: 150.
Internships Available ▶ *15–20 interns:* responsibilities include assisting publicists with research, writing copy for news releases and feature stories, helping coordinate photo shoots, and aiding in the organization and preparation of special client events. Candidates should have ability to work with others, college courses in field, computer skills, oral communication skills, plan to pursue career in field, written communication skills. Duration is flexible. Unpaid. Open to college freshmen, college sophomores, college juniors, college seniors. International applications accepted.
Benefits Possible full-time employment, willing to complete paperwork for educational credit, willing to provide letters of recommendation.
Contact Write, call, or fax Internship Coordinator, Human Resource Department. Phone: 310-201-8808. Fax: 310-284-2070. In-person interview required. Applicants must submit a cover letter, resume. Applications are accepted continuously.

ROGERS & COWAN- NY
475 Park Avenue South, 32nd Floor
New York, New York 10016

General Information Publicity agency. Established in 1950. Number of employees: 25. Unit of Shandwick North America, Inc., New York, New York. Number of internship applications received each year: 150.
Internships Available ▶ *15–20 interns:* responsibilities include assisting publicists with research, writing copy for news releases and feature stories, helping coordinate photo shoots, and aid-

Rogers & Cowan- NY (continued)

ing in the organization and preperation of special client events. Candidates should have ability to work with others, college courses in field, computer skills, oral communication skills, plan to pursue career in field, written communication skills. Duration is flexible. Unpaid. Open to college freshmen, college sophomores, college juniors, college seniors. International applications accepted.

Benefits Possible full-time employment, willing to complete paperwork for educational credit, willing to provide letters of recommendation.

Contact Write, call, or fax Human Resources Department/Internship Coordinator, 1888 Century Park East, 5th Floor, Los Angeles, California 90067. Phone: 310-201-8808. Fax: 310-284-2070. In-person interview required. Applicants must submit a cover letter, resume. Applications are accepted continuously.

ROSEN GROUP
30 West 26th Street
New York, New York 10010

General Information Public relations firm specializing in media, publishing, and liquor promotions. Established in 1984. Number of employees: 8. Number of internship applications received each year: 50.

Internships Available ▶ *2 office interns:* responsibilities include writing, copying, and performing phone work and research. Candidates should have ability to work with others, oral communication skills, personal interest in the field, plan to pursue career in field, strong interpersonal skills, writing skills. Duration is 1 semester. $6–$7 per hour. Open to college juniors, college seniors, recent college graduates.

Benefits On-the-job training, possible full-time employment, travel reimbursement, willing to complete paperwork for educational credit, willing to provide letters of recommendation.

Contact Write Ms. Lori Rosen, President. In-person interview required. Applicants must submit a cover letter, resume. Applications are accepted continuously.

RUDER FINN, INC.
301 East 57th Street
New York, New York 10022

General Information Full-service independently owned public relations agency that has survey research, design, arts and communication, consumer products, visual technology, and other subsidiaries. Established in 1948. Number of employees: 250. Number of internship applications received each year: 500.

Internships Available ▶ *3–5 summer interns:* responsibilities include assisting an account team. Candidates should have computer skills, office skills, oral communication skills, organizational skills, self-motivation, strong interpersonal skills, written communication skills. Duration is 2–3 months. $10 per hour. Open to college juniors. ▶ *12–15 trainees:* responsibilities include assisting the account team. Candidates should have computer skills, editing skills, office skills, oral communication skills, organizational skills, personal interest in the field, self-motivation, strong interpersonal skills, writing skills. Duration is 4 months. salary is equivalent to $19,000 per year. Open to college seniors, recent college graduates, graduate students, law students, career changers.

Benefits Formal training, names of contacts, opportunity to attend seminars/workshops, possible full-time employment, willing to provide letters of recommendation.

Contact Write, call, fax, or e-mail Ms. Deidra Degn, Coordinator Executive Training/Intern Program. Phone: 212-593-6332. Fax: 212-715-1659. E-mail: degnd@ruderfinn.com. In-person interview recommended. Applicants must submit a formal organization application, resume, academic transcripts, two writing samples, three personal references, 2 writing assignments. Application deadline: April 1 for summer (June-October), August 1 for fall (October-February), December 1 for spring (February-June). World Wide Web: http://www.ruderfinn.com.

SALES & MARKETING GROUP
911 Main Street, Suite 2400
Kansas City, Missouri 64105

General Information North American field marketing and sales service company which develops and executes field marketing events, product training seminars, retail promotions, and sales/mechandising coverage for Fortune 500 clients. Established in 1986. Number of employees: 350. Subsidiary of Mosaic Group, Inc., Toronto, Ontario, Canada.

Internships Available ▶ *Field managers-in-training:* responsibilities include building the client program and enhancing brand presence and image in a manner that ensures achievement of both client and S&MG business goals and objectives through effective management of the execution of team objectives and overall team performace, communications, and development of personnel. Candidates should have organizational skills, plan to pursue career in field, self-motivation, strong interpersonal skills, strong leadership ability, problem-solving skills. Duration is 3–6 months. Based on experience. Open to recent college graduates, graduate students. ▶ *Field marketing coordinator interns:* responsibilities include building the client program and enhancing brand presence and image in a manner that ensures achievement of both client and S&MG business goals and objectives through effective management of the execution of team objectives and overall team performance, communication, and development of personnel. Candidates should have oral communication skills, organizational skills, personal interest in the field, self-motivation, strong interpersonal skills, strong leadership ability. Duration is part-time for program duration and/or full-time during summer. $8–$11 per hour. Open to college freshmen, college sophomores, college juniors, college seniors, recent college graduates, graduate students, individuals reentering the workforce. International applications accepted.

Benefits Formal training, on-the-job training, opportunity to attend seminars/workshops, possible full-time employment, travel reimbursement, willing to complete paperwork for educational credit, scholarship opportunity.

Contact Write, call, fax, or e-mail Internship Coordinator, 911 Main Street, Suite 2400, Kansas City, Missouri 64105. Phone: 816-472-9100. Fax: 816-472-1899. E-mail: hrdept@samg.com. In-person interview required. Applicants must submit a formal organization application, resume. Applications are accepted continuously. World Wide Web: http://www.samg.com.

SALLY FISCHER PUBLIC RELATIONS
315 West 57th Street, Suite 407
New York, New York 10019

General Information Small public relations firm specializing in the areas of design, fashion, food, publishing, and entertainment. Established in 1989. Number of employees: 7. Number of internship applications received each year: 75.

Internships Available ▶ *3–4 interns:* responsibilities include direct involvement in all aspects of public relations, including special events, media relations, client relations, and writing. Candidates should have editing skills, oral communication skills, personal interest in the field, research skills, writing skills. Open to high school seniors, college freshmen, college sophomores, college juniors, college seniors, career changers, individuals reentering the workforce. ▶ *2–4 junior-publicist trainees:* responsibilities include direct hands-on experience, working with clients as well as a team with employees, planning strategies, writing press releases, contacting the media. Candidates should have editing skills, oral communication skills, personal interest in the field, research skills, writing skills. Open to high school seniors, recent high school graduates, college freshmen, college sophomores, college juniors, college seniors, recent college graduates, career changers, individuals reentering the workforce. ▶ *1–2 research assistants.* Candidates should have computer skills, organizational skills, research skills, self-motivation, writing skills. Open to high school seniors, recent high school graduates, college freshmen, college sophomores, college juniors, college seniors, recent college graduates, career changers, individuals reentering the workforce. Duration for all positions is flexible. All positions are unpaid. International applications accepted.

Benefits Names of contacts, possible full-time employment, travel reimbursement, willing to complete paperwork for educational credit, willing to provide letters of recommendation.

Contact Write, call, fax, or e-mail Sally Fischer, President. Phone: 212-246-2977. Fax: 212-246-8116. E-mail: sallyfpr@aol.com. In-person interview recommended. Applicants must submit a cover letter, resume. Applications are accepted continuously. World Wide Web: http://www.sallyfpr.com.

SAVVY MANAGEMENT
80 Fourth Avenue, Suite 800
New York, New York 10003

General Information Small public relations agency that represents clients in the tabletop, gift and decorative accessories, bridal, publishing, fashion, cookware, and special events industries. Established in 1978. Number of employees: 17. Number of internship applications received each year: 500.

Internships Available ▶ *1–4 interns:* responsibilities include writing press releases, pitch letters, backgrounders, and biographies; researching media lists; phoning editors and producers to secure media placements; producing press kits; coordinating mailing; retrieving clips; producing events; and interacting with clients. Candidates should have knowledge of field, oral communication skills, personal interest in the field, self-motivation, strong interpersonal skills, strong leadership ability, writing skills. Duration is flexible. Unpaid. Open to college juniors, college seniors, recent college graduates.

Benefits Job counseling, names of contacts, possible full-time employment, willing to complete paperwork for educational credit, willing to provide letters of recommendation, daily stipend of $20.

Contact Write, call, fax, or e-mail Mr. Peter Morgan, Internship Coordinator. Phone: 212-477-1717. Fax: 212-477-1736. E-mail: savvypr@inch.com. In-person interview required. Applicants must submit a cover letter, resume. Applications are accepted continuously.

SHANDWICK
8400 Normandale Lake Boulevard, Suite 500
Bloomington, Minnesota 55437

General Information Public relations and marketing communications firm. Established in 1981. Number of employees: 175. Subsidiary of Shandwick International, London, United Kingdom. Number of internship applications received each year: 500.

Internships Available ▶ *Public relations interns.* Candidates should have college courses in field, computer skills, editing skills, oral communication skills, strong interpersonal skills, written communication skills. Duration is 3–6 months. $10 per hour. Open to recent college graduates.

Benefits Opportunity to attend seminars/workshops, possible full-time employment, travel reimbursement.

Contact Write JoAnn Manthey, Senior Human Resources Representative. No phone calls. In-person interview required. Applicants must submit a cover letter, resume, writing sample. Applications are accepted continuously.

SHIRLEY HERZ ASSOCIATES
165 West 46th Street, Suite 910
New York, New York 10036

General Information Public relations firm for Broadway and off-Broadway shows, projects, and institutions. Established in 1972. Number of employees: 5. Number of internship applications received each year: 200.

Internships Available ▶ *3–5 interns:* responsibilities include aiding five press agents, answering phones, and writing press releases. Candidates should have ability to work with others, computer skills, office skills, oral communication skills, organizational skills, research skills, self-motivation, written communication skills. Duration is 1 semester. Unpaid. Open to recent

high school graduates, college freshmen, college sophomores, college juniors, college seniors. International applications accepted.

Benefits Formal training, free meals, possible full-time employment, travel reimbursement, willing to complete paperwork for educational credit, willing to provide letters of recommendation.

Contact Write, call, or fax Vanessa Meza, Intern Coordinator. Phone: 212-221-8466. Fax: 212-921-8023. In-person interview required. Applicants must submit a cover letter, resume. Applications are accepted continuously.

SILVERMAN MEDIA & MARKETING GROUP, INC.
185 Madison Avenue, Suite 1602
New York, New York 10016

General Information Media and marketing company specializing in public relations, integrated marketing, special event creation and management, celebrity representation, and Internet communications. Focus is on sports, entertainment, nonprofit, travel, special events, TV shows, home video, automotive, and new product publicity and promotion. Established in 1984. Number of employees: 6. Number of internship applications received each year: 200.

Internships Available ▶ *1–3 public relations assistants:* responsibilities include assisting with media research and contact, phone work, event and account coordination, writing of press releases, and general office duties. Candidates should have office skills, oral communication skills, plan to pursue career in field, self-motivation, strong interpersonal skills, written communication skills. Duration is 3–4 months. Unpaid. Open to college freshmen, college sophomores, college juniors, college seniors, recent college graduates, graduate students, law students, career changers, individuals reentering the workforce.

Benefits Job counseling, names of contacts, on-the-job training, possible full-time employment, travel reimbursement, willing to act as a professional reference, willing to complete paperwork for educational credit, willing to provide letters of recommendation.

Contact Write or fax Mr. Ira H. Silverman, President. Fax: 212-686-8742. No phone calls. In-person interview required. Applicants must submit a cover letter, resume, photo at time of interview to attach to resume. Application deadline: March 15 for summer; continuous for year-round interns.

SMITHSONIAN OFFICE OF PUBLIC AFFAIRS
1000 Jefferson Drive, SW, Room 354
Washington, District of Columbia 20560-0033

General Information Office of the Smithsonian that informs the public and staff through publications and media relations about exhibitions, programs, and research activities. Unit of Smithsonian Institution, Washington, District of Columbia.

Internships Available ▶ *Media relations interns:* responsibilities include updating mailing lists of journalists, newspapers and magazines, and others; organizing materials and filling information kits for journalists; and writing news releases and other informational materials. ▶ *Publications interns:* responsibilities include writing features, news stories, and column items. Candidates should have research skills, writing skills, interviewing skills. Duration for all positions is flexible. All positions are unpaid. Open to high school students, college freshmen, college sophomores, college juniors, college seniors, recent college graduates, graduate students. International applications accepted.

Benefits Willing to act as a professional reference, willing to complete paperwork for educational credit.

Contact Write, call, or fax Catherine Maree, Intern Coordinator. Phone: 202-357-2627 Ext. 100. Fax: 202-786-2377. Applicants must submit a formal organization application, academic transcripts, personal reference, essay, by-lined writing samples for publications positions. Applications are accepted continuously. World Wide Web: http://www.si.edu.

SPORTS ILLUSTRATED, COMMUNICATIONS DEPARTMENT
1271 Avenue of the Americas
New York, New York 10020

General Information Department responsible for all public relations and publicity for Sports Illustrated, Sports Illustrated for Kids, and Sports Illustrated for Women. Established in 1954. Number of employees: 500. Unit of Time, Inc., New York, New York. Number of internship applications received each year: 250.

Internships Available ▶ *1–4 communications interns:* responsibilities include assisting the communications staff in all areas of publicity, including media relations and special events. Candidates should have ability to work independently, ability to work with others, computer skills, knowledge of field, office skills, oral communication skills, self-motivation. Duration is 1–4 months. Unpaid. Open to college juniors, college seniors.

Benefits Job counseling, names of contacts, opportunity to attend seminars/workshops, possible full-time employment, travel reimbursement, willing to complete paperwork for educational credit, willing to provide letters of recommendation.

Contact Write, fax, or e-mail Rick McCabe, Publicity Coordinator. Fax: 212-522-4832. E-mail: rick_mccabe@timeinc.com. No phone calls. In-person interview recommended. Applicants must submit a cover letter, resume, 1-3 writing samples. Application deadline: April 1 for summer, July 1 for fall, November 1 for spring. World Wide Web: http://www.cnnsi.com.

TCI MEDIA SERVICES
1030 Higgins Road, Suite 100
Park Ridge, Illinois 60068

General Information Cable advertising company that sells local air time on cable networks such as CNN, ESPN, and BET, and produces commercials. Number of employees: 140. Unit of TCI, Denver, Colorado. Number of internship applications received each year: 40.

Internships Available ▶ *6 TV production interns:* responsibilities include assisting in location and studio production of commercials, set-up and breakdown of all equipment, and audio monitoring. Candidates should have knowledge of field, plan to pursue career in field, strong interpersonal skills. Duration is flexible. ▶ *6 copywriting interns:* responsibilities include assisting producers and writing ad copy. Candidates should have computer skills, knowledge of field, personal interest in the field, plan to pursue career in field, writing skills. Duration is 3–6 months. ▶ *Marketing and sales research interns:* responsibilities include implementing and producing advertising proposals, developing sales presentations, marketing related products, and promotional events. Duration is flexible. All positions are unpaid. Open to college juniors, college seniors, recent college graduates, graduate students.

Benefits Willing to complete paperwork for educational credit, willing to provide letters of recommendation.

Contact Write, call, fax, or e-mail Mr. Terry Cantwell, Production Manager. Phone: 847-384-5022. Fax: 847-292-0164. E-mail: cantwell.terry@tci.com. In-person interview required. Applicants must submit a resume. Applications are accepted continuously.

TERRIE WILLIAMS AGENCY
1500 Broadway, Suite 502
New York, New York 10036

General Information Full-service firm that specializes in public relations, media relations, and special event planning for entertainment, sports, political, and corporate figures and conglomerates in the United States and abroad. Established in 1988. Number of employees: 10. Number of internship applications received each year: 200.

Internships Available ▶ *1–4 public relations interns:* responsibilities include writing and researching for newsletters and press releases, developing press kits, and assisting with campaigns. Candidates should have computer skills, knowledge of field, office skills, organizational skills, self-motivation, strong interpersonal skills, written communication skills. Duration is 12 weeks. Unpaid.

Open to college freshmen, college sophomores, college juniors, college seniors, recent college graduates, graduate students, law students, career changers, individuals reentering the workforce. International applications accepted.

Benefits Job counseling, names of contacts, on-the-job training, possible full-time employment, travel reimbursement, willing to act as a professional reference, willing to complete paperwork for educational credit, willing to provide letters of recommendation.

Contact Write Terrie Williams, President. No phone calls. In-person interview recommended. Applicants must submit a cover letter, resume, two personal references, 2-3 writing samples. Application deadline: May 30 for summer, June 30 for fall/winter.

TMP WORLDWIDE
1500 Walnut Street, Suite 1300
Philadelphia, Pennsylvania 19102

General Information Creative agency that deals with yellow page advertising, recruitment advertising, and interactive direct response marketing. Established in 1967. Number of employees: 17. Division of TMP Worldwide, New York, New York. Number of internship applications received each year: 60.

Internships Available ▶ *2–3 interns:* responsibilities include assisting account executives with marketing research, recommendations, demographic reports, dealer maintenance, marketing surveys, updating orders, copying, and some filing. Candidates should have ability to work independently, ability to work with others, computer skills, office skills, organizational skills, plan to pursue career in field. Duration is 1 semester. $10 per day. Open to high school seniors, recent high school graduates, college freshmen, college sophomores, college juniors, college seniors, recent college graduates. International applications accepted.

Benefits On-the-job training, possible full-time employment, willing to act as a professional reference, willing to complete paperwork for educational credit, willing to provide letters of recommendation.

Contact Write, call, fax, or e-mail Nancy Burr, Senior Account Executive. Phone: 215-985-2700 Ext. 20. Fax: 215-985-2704. E-mail: nburr@tmp.com. In-person interview recommended. Applicants must submit a resume, letter of interest (preferred). Applications are accepted continuously. World Wide Web: http://www.tmp.com.

UNIVERSITY DIRECTORIES
88 VilCom Center
Chapel Hill, North Carolina 27514

General Information Publisher of campus telephone directories. Established in 1974. Number of employees: 30. Unit of The Village Companies, Chapel Hill, North Carolina. Number of internship applications received each year: 75.

Internships Available ▶ *200–300 sales interns.* Candidates should have ability to work independently, oral communication skills, self-motivation, strong interpersonal skills, strong leadership ability. Duration is 10 weeks. commission. Open to college freshmen, college sophomores, college juniors, college seniors, recent college graduates, graduate students. International applications accepted.

Benefits Formal training, job counseling, names of contacts, opportunity to attend seminars/workshops, possible full-time employment, willing to complete paperwork for educational credit, willing to provide letters of recommendation.

Contact Write, call, fax, or e-mail Yvonne Knutson, National Recruiting Manager. Phone: 919-968-0225. Fax: 919-968-8513. E-mail: yknutson@vilcom.com. In-person interview recommended. Applicants must submit a cover letter, resume. Applications are accepted continuously. World Wide Web: http://www.universitydirectories.com.

VAL-PAK DIRECT MARKETING SYSTEMS, INC.
8605 Largo Lakes Drive
Largo, Florida 33773

General Information Direct mail advertising company. Established in 1968. Number of employees: 1,500. Number of internship applications received each year: 10.

Internships Available ▶ *1–10 advertising sales assistants:* responsibilities include assisting sales representatives with sales calls, proofs, collections, customer service, layout designs, and research. Candidates should have ability to work independently, college courses in field, editing skills, oral communication skills, organizational skills, personal interest in the field, research skills, self-motivation, strong interpersonal skills, strong leadership ability, writing skills, experience in field preferred. Duration is flexible. Position available as unpaid or paid. Open to college juniors, college seniors, recent college graduates, career changers, individuals reentering the workforce.

Benefits On-the-job training, possible full-time employment, willing to act as a professional reference, willing to complete paperwork for educational credit, willing to provide letters of recommendation.

Contact Write, call, fax, or e-mail Linda Finn, Recruiting Supervisor, 8605 Largo Lakes Drive, Largo, Florida 33773. Phone: 800-294-1455. Fax: 727-391-2710. E-mail: linda_finn@valpak.com. In-person interview recommended. Applicants must submit a formal organization application, cover letter, resume, three personal references. Applications are accepted continuously. World Wide Web: http://www.valpak.com.

ARCHITECTURAL, ENGINEERING, AND DESIGN SERVICES

ALSTOM DRIVES & CONTROLS INC.
301 Alpha Drive
Pittsburgh, Pennsylvania 15238

General Information International electrical engineering firm providing turnkey automation services, primarily in the metal industries. Number of employees: 275. Subsidiary of Alstom, France. Number of internship applications received each year: 50.

Internships Available ▶ *1–10 commissioning engineering interns:* responsibilities include assisting senior-level engineers with testing and installation of projects at customer worksites, primarily steel mills; locations throughout U.S.(requires extensive travel). Candidates should have ability to work with others, analytical skills, college courses in field, computer skills, declared college major in field, knowledge of field, oral communication skills, organizational skills, personal interest in the field, plan to pursue career in field, research skills, self-motivation, written communication skills, college degree in related field (for recent college graduate applicants only). Open to college juniors, college seniors, recent college graduates, graduate students. ▶ *1–10 electrical engineering interns:* responsibilities include assisting senior-level engineer with defined projects. Candidates should have ability to work independently, ability to work with others, analytical skills, college courses in field, computer skills, knowledge of field, oral communication skills, organizational skills, plan to pursue career in field, research skills, self-motivation, writing skills, college degree in related field (for college graduate applicants only). Open to college juniors, college seniors, recent college graduates. Duration for all positions is 6–12 months. All positions paid at $10–$14 per hour. International applications accepted.

Benefits Formal training, on-the-job training, possible full-time employment, travel reimbursement, willing to act as a professional reference, willing to complete paperwork for educational credit, willing to provide letters of recommendation.

Contact Write, fax, or e-mail Susan Shuster, Human Resources Generalist, 301 Alpha Drive, Pittsburgh, Pennsylvania 15238. Fax: 412-963-3212. E-mail: shuster@cegelec.com. No phone calls. In-person interview required. Applicants must submit a cover letter, resume, academic transcripts, three personal references. Applications are accepted continuously. World Wide Web: http://www.alstom.com.

AMERICAN & INTERNATIONAL DESIGNS, INC.
1752 Hylan Boulevard
Staten Island, New York 10305

General Information Interior design firm that specializes in restaurant, healthcare, medical, and corporate facilities. Established in 1980. Number of employees: 5. Number of internship applications received each year: 120.

Internships Available ▶ *3–4 CAD operator:* responsibilities include drawing floor plans, furniture plans, tile plans, window elevations, and general drafting and plotting. Candidates should have college courses in field, computer skills, declared college major in field, experience in the field, organizational skills, plan to pursue career in field. Duration is 8–10 weeks. Open to college juniors, college seniors, recent college graduates, graduate students. ▶ *2–4 administrative interns:* responsibilities include working directly with the administrator, assisting in minutes of meetings, project management, and expiditing and tracking interior design projects. Duration is 1–2 months or semesters. Open to high school seniors, recent high school graduates. ▶ *1 advertising assistant.* Duration is 3–8 weeks. Open to college seniors, recent college graduates. ▶ *2 bookkeeper/accounting assistants:* responsibilities include assisting in maintaining financial books for 3 divisions, preparing budgets, and keeping intern time sheets. Candidates should have ability to work independently, analytical skills, college courses in field, experience in the field, office skills, organizational skills. Duration is 6–10 weeks. Open to college sophomores, college juniors, college seniors, recent college graduates, graduate students. ▶ *2 computer and technical information interns:* responsibilities include researching new products, assisting in training on new software, installing updates, reviewing all equipment and new contracts, maintaining supplies, and Web site development. Candidates should have ability to work with others, college degree in related field, experience in the field, office skills, organizational skills, research skills. Duration is 4–6 weeks. Open to college juniors, college seniors, recent college graduates, graduate students. ▶ *3 graphic design interns:* responsibilities include designing graphics for collateral materials, brochures, inserts, press kits, tear sheets, Web site, mailings, and presentations. Candidates should have ability to work independently, ability to work with others, computer skills, experience in the field, organizational skills, research skills, writing skills. Duration is 8–12 weeks. Open to college sophomores, college juniors, college seniors, recent college graduates, graduate students, individuals reentering the workforce. ▶ *5–10 junior interior designer interns:* responsibilities include working with design team to develop and design new restaurants and health care facilities. Candidates should have ability to work with others, college courses in field, computer skills, office skills, organizational skills, plan to pursue career in field. Duration is 6–8 weeks. Open to college juniors, college seniors, recent college graduates, graduate students. ▶ *2 librarian interns:* responsibilities include maintaining 4 libraries, updating all literature, coordinating samples, distributing information to all in-house staff, updating presentation boards, and maintaining photo library. Candidates should have ability to work independently, computer skills, office skills, oral communication skills, organizational skills, strong interpersonal skills. Duration is 6 weeks. Open to high school seniors, recent high school graduates, college freshmen, college sophomores, college juniors, college seniors, recent college graduates. ▶ *2–4 marketing information interns:* responsibilities include launching new products and services for the health care industries, organizing and developing press kits, attending trade shows and local seminars, coordinating and purchasing mailing lists, assisting in the development of collateral material for information requests. Candidates should have ability to work independently, college courses in field,

American & International Designs, Inc. (continued)

computer skills, oral communication skills, strong interpersonal skills, written communication skills. Duration is 3–8 weeks. Open to college juniors, college seniors, recent college graduates, graduate students. ▶ *2 personnel assistants:* responsibilities include maintaining and updating procedures manual, reviewing general procedures with staff, reviewing time sheets, developing daily schedules, preparing letters of recommendation, assisting in job placements, and working with principles. Candidates should have computer skills, office skills, oral communication skills, strong interpersonal skills, strong leadership ability. Duration is 8–10 weeks. Open to recent high school graduates, college freshmen, college juniors, college seniors. ▶ *4 photographer interns.* Candidates should have ability to work independently, ability to work with others, analytical skills, college courses in field, computer skills, editing skills, plan to pursue career in field. Duration is 3–12 weeks. Open to college seniors, recent college graduates. ▶ *4 public relations interns:* responsibilities include organizing and developing case studies of recent completed jobs, writing public relations news about company and products, vendor public relations, and attending and promoting grand openings. Candidates should have ability to work independently, computer skills, oral communication skills, plan to pursue career in field, research skills, written communication skills. Duration is 6–8 weeks. Open to college juniors, college seniors, recent college graduates, graduate students. All positions are unpaid. International applications accepted.
Benefits Formal training, free meals, job counseling, on-the-job training, opportunity to attend seminars/workshops, possible full-time employment, travel reimbursement, willing to act as a professional reference, willing to complete paperwork for educational credit, willing to provide letters of recommendation.
Contact Write or fax April Falconneti, Internship Coordinator. Fax: 718-370-2705. No phone calls. In-person interview recommended. Applicants must submit a formal organization application, resume, personal reference, portfolio (occasionally). Application deadline: January 30 for spring, May 1 for summer, July 15 for fall, September 15 for winter. World Wide Web: http://www.designamericanyc.com.

AMERICAN STANDARDS TESTING BUREAU, INC.
40 Water Street
New York, New York 10004

General Information Technical and management consulting firm. Established in 1916. Number of employees: 900. Number of internship applications received each year: 1,000.
Internships Available ▶ *3–6 interns:* responsibilities include performing duties consistent with intern's interests and skills. Candidates should have computer skills, organizational skills, self-motivation, strong interpersonal skills, writing skills, declared college major in engineering (particularly welcome). Duration is 1 semester. Position available as unpaid or paid. Open to college freshmen, college sophomores, college juniors, college seniors, recent college graduates, graduate students, career changers, individuals reentering the workforce.
Benefits Health insurance, possible full-time employment, willing to complete paperwork for educational credit, willing to provide letters of recommendation.
Contact Write, fax, or e-mail Dr. John Zimmerman, Director of Staffing. Fax: 212-825-2250. E-mail: worldteck@aol.com. No phone calls. In-person interview required. Applicants must submit a resume. Applications are accepted continuously.

BURNS AND MCDONNELL
9400 Ward Parkway
Kansas City, Missouri 64114

General Information Consulting firm for engineering, architectural, and environmental projects. Established in 1898. Number of employees: 1,400.
Internships Available ▶ *3–5 civil engineering interns:* responsibilities include assisting senior engineers with projects. ▶ *3–5 electrical engineering interns:* responsibilities include assisting senior electrical engineers with lighting, electrical instruments and

control, and a variety of other duties. ▶ *1–3 environmental engineer interns:* responsibilities include assisting senior engineer with waste management and water and air pollution control projects. ▶ *3–5 mechanical engineering interns:* responsibilities include assisting senior engineers with HVAC, piping, and plumbing projects. Duration for all positions is 1 summer. All positions paid. Open to college freshmen, college sophomores, college juniors, college seniors. International applications accepted.
Benefits Job counseling, names of contacts, opportunity to attend seminars/workshops, possible full-time employment, travel reimbursement, willing to complete paperwork for educational credit, willing to provide letters of recommendation.
Contact Write, call, fax, or e-mail Ms. Melissa Hragyil, Intern Coordinator. Phone: 816-822-3129. Fax: 816-822-3516. E-mail: mhragy@burnsmcd.com. Applicants must submit a resume, academic transcripts. Applications are accepted continuously. World Wide Web: http://www.burnsmcd.com.

DATA GENERAL CORPORATION
4400 Computer Drive
Westboro, Massachusetts 01580

General Information A major supplier of storage and enterprise computing solutions. Products include CLARiiON full fibre channel storage systems, high-end NT and UNIX based AViiON servers, and related software and services. Established in 1968. Number of employees: 3,000.
Internships Available ▶ *5–10 engineering co-ops:* responsibilities include code and test development and expanding product's compatibility with various operating systems running on Aviion hardware. Candidates should have ability to work independently, analytical skills, college courses in field, computer skills, knowledge of field, oral communication skills, strong interpersonal skills. ▶ *4–6 firmware development interns:* responsibilities include developing NT qualification test plans, automating firmware qualification to expedite process, integrating test process with Data General/UX and/or NT based application, and developing firmware for integration testing on new PCI controllers. Candidates should have ability to work independently, analytical skills, college courses in field, computer skills, knowledge of field, oral communication skills, strong interpersonal skills. ▶ *10–15 software development interns:* responsibilities include working on projects involving coding, testing, Web page development, and network management; position located at Research Triangle Park, NC. Candidates should have ability to work independently, ability to work with others, analytical skills, college courses in field, computer skills, knowledge of field, oral communication skills, plan to pursue career in field. ▶ *2–4 software quality assurance interns:* responsibilities include integrating a variety of hardware and software. Candidates should have ability to work independently, college courses in field, computer skills, knowledge of field, strong interpersonal skills. ▶ *2–5 systems engineering interns:* responsibilities include working on schematic capture, simulation, systems configuration, loading, running, and debugging bios, diagnostic programs, and NT and UNIX operating systems. Candidates should have ability to work independently, analytical skills, college courses in field, computer skills, knowledge of field, self-motivation, strong interpersonal skills. Duration for all positions is 3–6 months. All positions paid at $14–$25 per hour. Open to college sophomores, college juniors, college seniors, recent college graduates, graduate students. International applications accepted.
Benefits Possible full-time employment, willing to complete paperwork for educational credit, vacation and sick time, paid holidays.
Contact Write or fax Sandy Bradshaw, Corporate Staffing Manager. Fax: 508-898-4686. No phone calls. In-person interview required. Applicants must submit a cover letter, resume. Applications are accepted continuously. World Wide Web: http://www.dg.com.

ELLIS/NAEYAERT/GENHEIMER ASSOCIATES, INC.
888 West Big Beaver, Suite 1000
Troy, Michigan 48084

General Information Full-service architectural engineering planning firm that serves commercial, governmental, health care, and industrial clients throughout the Midwest. Established in 1962. Number of employees: 110. Number of internship applications received each year: 100.

Internships Available ▶ *1–2 architecture co-ops:* responsibilities include learning and applying basic CADD skills to office standard drafting procedures. The internship also offers the opportunity to gain exposure and familarity with basic construction materials and methods through drafting, training, and field opportunities. Candidates should have ability to work with others, analytical skills, computer skills, declared college major in field, oral communication skills, plan to pursue career in field. $9–$12 per hour. ▶ *1 civil engineer co-op:* responsibilities include helping design site layouts, grading and utilities including storm and sanitary sewers and watermains, CADD drafting and field measuring. Candidates should have ability to work with others, analytical skills, computer skills, declared college major in field, oral communication skills, personal interest in the field. $11–$14 per hour. ▶ *1–2 electrical engineer co-ops:* responsibilities include assisting engineers in field data collection, calculations, sketching, code research and other research. Candidates should have ability to work with others, analytical skills, computer skills, declared college major in field, oral communication skills, personal interest in the field. $11–$14 per hour. ▶ *2 facilities management co-ops:* responsibilities include performing basic CAD/CAFM design applications (AutoCAD Rel.14.01), assisting in preparing limited calculations (e.g. builidng areas, space/department allocations, etc.), and assisting in gathering dimensionally accurate on-site data for CAD applications. Candidates should have ability to work with others, computer skills, oral communication skills, plan to pursue career in field, declared college major in related field. $9–$12 per hour. ▶ *2 mechanical engineer co-ops:* responsibilities include developing basic understanding of building design as it relates to mechanical engineering, performing limited mechanical engineering design calculations, and developing familiarity with engineering drawings and specifications. Candidates should have ability to work with others, analytical skills, computer skills, declared college major in field, oral communication skills, personal interest in the field. $11–$14 per hour. ▶ *1 structural engineer co-op:* responsibilities include assisting in preparation of project structural analysis and design, construction documents (manual and/or CAD), and project written documentation; assisting in gathernig on-site data and developing an understanding of the design process. Candidates should have ability to work with others, analytical skills, computer skills, declared college major in field, oral communication skills, personal interest in the field. $11–$14 per hour. Duration for all positions is 3 months (minimum). Open to college juniors, college seniors.

Benefits Health insurance, on-the-job training, opportunity to attend seminars/workshops, possible full-time employment, travel reimbursement, willing to act as a professional reference, willing to complete paperwork for educational credit, willing to provide letters of recommendation, sick and personal days, vacation, life insurance.

Contact Write, call, fax, or e-mail Carolyn C. Palmer, Vice President. Phone: 248-244-8700. Fax: 248-244-2080. E-mail: cpalmer@enga.com. In-person interview recommended. Applicants must submit a cover letter, resume. Applications are accepted continuously. World Wide Web: http://www.enga.com.

FLUOR DANIEL
3353 Michelson Drive
Irvine, California 92698

General Information International engineering, procurement, construction, maintenance and diversified services company providing a broad range of technical services to more than 700 clients on over 2,200 projects in more than 50 countries.

Established in 1890. Number of employees: 2,300. Subsidiary of Fluor Corporation, Irvine, California. Number of internship applications received each year: 700.

Internships Available ▶ *20 interns:* responsibilities include working as needed in various departments, including engineering (mechical, chemical, electrical) project controls, procurement, or human resources support. Candidates should have ability to work independently, college courses in field, computer skills, plan to pursue career in field, self-motivation, strong interpersonal skills. Duration is 3 months. $1,685–$2,930 per month. Open to college sophomores, college juniors, graduate students, college seniors only if going to graduate school.

Benefits Formal training, health insurance, names of contacts, on-the-job training, opportunity to attend seminars/workshops, possible full-time employment, willing to act as a professional reference, willing to complete paperwork for educational credit, willing to provide letters of recommendation.

Contact Write, fax, or e-mail Kendra Miller, College Relations Coordinator. Fax: 949-975-5639. E-mail: kendra.miller@fluordaniel.com. No phone calls. Applicants must submit a resume. Application deadline: March 1 for summer. World Wide Web: http://www.fluordaniel.com.

GME CONSULTANTS
14000 21st Avenue North
Minneapolis, Minnesota 55447

General Information Geotechnical engineering consulting firm. Established in 1981. Number of employees: 65. Number of internship applications received each year: 10.

Internships Available ▶ *4 field services technicians:* responsibilities include working with civil engineering technicians. Candidates should have college courses in field, knowledge of field, self-motivation, strong interpersonal skills. Duration is 4–6 months. $10 per hour. Open to recent high school graduates, college freshmen, college sophomores, college juniors, college seniors, recent college graduates, graduate students, individuals reentering the workforce. International applications accepted.

Benefits On-the-job training, opportunity to attend seminars/workshops, possible full-time employment.

Contact Write William Donahue, Field Services Coordinator. No phone calls. In-person interview recommended. Applicants must submit a resume, three personal references, letter of recommendation. Applications are accepted continuously. World Wide Web: http://www.gmeconsultants.com.

KINGSBURY CORPORATION
80 Laurel Street
Keene, New Hampshire 03431

General Information Engineering manufacturing firm which designs, manufacturers, and assembles high-production machining systems. Established in 1894. Number of employees: 270. Number of internship applications received each year: 6.

Internships Available ▶ *1–4 interns:* responsibilities include assisting in the various departments of corporation depending on need. Duration is one summer. Paid. Open to college juniors, college seniors.

Benefits On-the-job training, possible full-time employment.

Contact Write Dianne Tisdale, Manager, Human Resources, 80 Laurel Street, Keene, New Hampshire 03431. No phone calls. In-person interview recommended. Applicants must submit a formal organization application, cover letter, resume, academic transcripts. Applications are accepted continuously.

PROGRAM FOR WOMEN IN SCIENCE AND ENGINEERING
Iowa State University, 210 Lab of Mechanics
Ames, Iowa 50011-2131

General Information Program working to increase the number of women in science and engineering. Established in 1986. Number of employees: 5. Unit of Iowa State University of Science and Technology, Ames, Iowa. Number of internship applications received each year: 100.

Program for Women in Science and Engineering (continued)

Internships Available ▶ *20–40 high school interns:* responsibilities include working on an independent research project under the supervision of science or engineering faculty or staff. Candidates should have ability to work with others, plan to pursue career in field, self-motivation. Duration is 6 weeks. $1,250 per duration of internship. Open to individuals between junior and senior year in high school. ▶ *30–45 undergraduate interns:* responsibilities include working on an independent research project under the supervision of science or engineering faculty or staff. Candidates should have ability to work with others, college courses in field, knowledge of field, plan to pursue career in field, self-motivation. Duration is 8 weeks. $2,500 per duration of internship. Open to college freshmen, college sophomores, college juniors. International applications accepted.
Benefits Housing at a cost, meals at a cost, opportunity to attend seminars/workshops, willing to provide letters of recommendation, opportunity to be part of state-of-the-art scientific research.
Contact Write, call, fax, or e-mail Dr. Krishna Athreya, Coordinator. Phone: 515-294-4317. Fax: 515-294-8627. E-mail: pwse@iastate.edu. Applicants must submit a formal organization application, academic transcripts, writing sample, two personal references, two letters of recommendation. Application deadline: January 31 for summer. World Wide Web: http://www.iastate.edu/~pwse_info/.

RENAISSANCE MULTIMEDIA
90 John Street, Suite 309
New York, New York 10038

General Information Digital communications company with two specialties within multimedia production: development of corporate Web sites and the creation of multimedia sales presentations utilizing animation, sound, video, graphics, and text. Established in 1993. Number of employees: 15.
Internships Available ▶ *2 interns:* responsibilities include assisting in either digital production or marketing/sales. Candidates should have HTML, Photoshop, and scanning skills (preferred). Duration is flexible. Position available as unpaid or paid. Open to high school students, high school seniors, recent high school graduates, college freshmen, college sophomores, college juniors, college seniors, recent college graduates, graduate students, law students, career changers, individuals reentering the workforce.
Benefits Willing to complete paperwork for educational credit, willing to provide letters of recommendation.
Contact Write, fax, or e-mail Ken Matthews, Internship Coordinator. Fax: 212-619-0054. E-mail: ken@rcac.com. No phone calls. In-person interview required. Applicants must submit a resume, letter of recommendation. Applications are accepted continuously. World Wide Web: http://www.rcac.com.

SHIVE-HATTERY, INC.
115 3rd Street, SE, 9th Floor
Cedar Rapids, Iowa 52401

General Information Engineering and architectural consulting firm. Established in 1962.
Internships Available ▶ *Interns:* responsibilities include working in any of the following engineering areas: civil, mechanical, electrical, or architectural; duties may include land survey, CAD design, or going to actual job sites. Candidates should have ability to work independently, analytical skills, computer skills, declared college major in field, editing skills, knowledge of field, office skills, oral communication skills, organizational skills, personal interest in the field, research skills, self-motivation, strong interpersonal skills, strong leadership ability, writing skills. Duration is flexible. Paid. Open to college juniors, college seniors.
Benefits On-the-job training, opportunity to attend seminars/workshops, possible full-time employment, travel reimbursement, willing to complete paperwork for educational credit, worker's compensation.
Contact Write, fax, or e-mail Gloria J. Frost, Vice President/Director of Human Resources, 115 3rd Street, SE, 9th Floor,

Cedar Rapids, Iowa 52401. Fax: 319-362-2883. E-mail: gfrost@shive-hattery.com. No phone calls. In-person interview required. Applicants must submit a formal organization application, resume. Applications are accepted continuously. World Wide Web: http://www.shive-hattery.com.

TELLABS
1000 Remington Boulevard, MS 147
Bolingbrook, Illinois 60440

General Information Global designer and manufacturer of telecommunications equipment. Established in 1975. Number of employees: 3,000. Number of internship applications received each year: 400.
Internships Available ▶ *5–10 PC support interns.* Candidates should have college courses in field, college degree in related field, computer skills, oral communication skills, written communication skills. $10–$16 per hour. Open to college sophomores, college juniors, college seniors. ▶ *5–8 VLSI designers.* Candidates should have computer skills, declared college major in field, oral communication skills, written communication skills, minimum 3.5 GPA. $12–$20 per hour. Open to college juniors, college seniors, graduate students. ▶ *8–10 Web site development interns.* Candidates should have college courses in field, computer skills, oral communication skills, written communication skills. $12–$18 per hour. Open to college juniors, college seniors. ▶ *15–20 hardware design/test interns.* Candidates should have computer skills, declared college major in field, oral communication skills, written communication skills. $12–$18 per hour. Open to college sophomores, college juniors, college seniors, graduate students. ▶ *2–5 human resources interns.* Candidates should have computer skills, declared college major in field, oral communication skills, plan to pursue career in field, strong interpersonal skills, written communication skills. $12–$15 per hour. Open to college seniors, graduate students. ▶ *3–4 mechanical design interns.* Candidates should have computer skills, declared college major in field, oral communication skills, written communication skills. $12–$18 per hour. Open to college juniors, college seniors. ▶ *4–6 research interns (telecommunications and optics).* Candidates should have declared college major in field, oral communication skills, research skills, written communication skills, knowledge of hardware, software, telecommunications, and optics. $18–$21 per hour. Open to graduate students. ▶ *40–50 software development interns.* Candidates should have college courses in field, oral communication skills, written communication skills, knowledge of C, C++, UNIX. $12–$18 per hour. Open to college sophomores, college juniors, college seniors, graduate students. ▶ *10–15 software testing interns.* Candidates should have college courses in field, oral communication skills, written communication skills, knowledge of C, C++, UNIX. $12–$18 per hour. Open to college sophomores, college juniors, college seniors, graduate students. ▶ *3–4 systems engineering interns.* Candidates should have college courses in field, computer skills, declared college major in field, oral communication skills, written communication skills, knowledge of hardware and software. $12–$18 per hour. Open to college juniors, college seniors. Duration for all positions is 12–15 weeks.
Benefits Opportunity to attend seminars/workshops, possible full-time employment, willing to complete paperwork for educational credit, housing provided for interns more than 60 miles from home.
Contact Write, fax, or e-mail Tellabs College Relations Department PI00. Fax: 630-378-5620. E-mail: interns@tellabs.com. No phone calls. Telephone interview required. Applicants must submit a cover letter, resume. Application deadline: April 1 for summer. World Wide Web: http://www.tellabs.com.

VOGT-NEM, INC.
4000 DuPont Circle, Suite 400
Louisville, Kentucky 40207

General Information Engineering and manufacturing firm specializing in heat recovery steam generators for the power industry on a worldwide scale. Established in 1996. Number of employees: 130. Number of internship applications received each year: 15.

Internships Available ▶ *1–2 staff support interns:* responsibilities include code calculations, reviewing mechanical designs. Candidates should have ability to work independently, analytical skills, college courses in field, computer skills, office skills, oral communication skills, personal interest in the field, research skills, strong interpersonal skills, written communication skills. Duration is 1 year. $36,000—$38,000 per year. ▶ *2–4 thermal design interns:* responsibilities include developing designs for proposals; preparing master documents. Candidates should have ability to work independently, analytical skills, college courses in field, computer skills, oral communication skills, organizational skills, plan to pursue career in field, research skills, self-motivation, strong interpersonal skills, writing skills. Duration is 2 years. $37,000-$39,000 per year. Open to recent college graduates, graduate students. International applications accepted.

Benefits Formal training, health insurance, on-the-job training, opportunity to attend seminars/workshops, possible full-time employment, travel reimbursement, tuition assistance, willing to act as a professional reference, willing to complete paperwork for educational credit, willing to provide letters of recommendation.

Contact Write, fax, or e-mail Virginia McCombs, Director of Human Resources, 4000 DuPont Circle, Suite 400, Louisville, Kentucky 40207. Fax: 502-899-4690. E-mail: hr@vogt_nem.com. No phone calls. In-person interview required. Applicants must submit a formal organization application, cover letter, resume, academic transcripts, three personal references. Applications are accepted continuously. World Wide Web: http://www.vogt-nem.com.

WASHINGTON INTERNSHIPS FOR STUDENTS OF ENGINEERING (WISE)
400 Commonwealth Drive
Warrendale, Pennsylvania 15096-0001

General Information A program set-up to match engineering students with suitable internships. The seven engineering societies that sponsor WISE are: AICHE, ANS, ASCE, ASME, IEEE, NSPE and SAE (which acts as the program administrator). Established in 1980. Number of internship applications received each year: 75.

Internships Available ▶ *13–15 WISE interns:* responsibilities include researching and completing a paper on a current and topical engineering related public policy issue; meeting with congressional committees, executive office departments, and corporate government affairs offices daily. Candidates should have ability to work independently, research skills, self-motivation, strong leadership ability, writing skills, membership in an engineering society (required by most of the sponsoring societies). Duration is June to August (10 weeks). $1800 stipend. Open to college juniors.

Benefits Free housing, travel reimbursement, interaction with leaders in Congress and administration, industry, and prominent non-governmental organizations.

Contact Write, call, fax, or e-mail Anne Hickox. Phone: 714-776-4841 Ext. 7476. Fax: 724-776-2103. E-mail: anne@sae.org. Applicants must submit a formal organization application, academic transcripts, two writing samples, 2 personal references and/or 2 letters of recommendation. Application deadline: December 1. World Wide Web: http://www.wise-intern.org.

WOLF CREEK NUCLEAR OPERATING CORPORATION
1550 Oxen Lane, PO Box 411
Burlington, Kansas 66839-0411

General Information Commercial nuclear electric power generating station. Established in 1987. Number of employees: 1,000. Number of internship applications received each year: 20.

Internships Available ▶ *1–4 engineering trainees:* responsibilities include assisting engineers in daily operations of nuclear power plant; assigned projects as needed to complete mission of work group. Candidates should have ability to work with others, analytical skills, college courses in field, computer skills, oral communication skills, personal interest in the field, self-motivation, written communication skills. Duration is 7 months. $12 per hour. Open to college juniors, college seniors.

Benefits On-the-job training, opportunity to attend seminars/workshops, possible full-time employment, travel reimbursement.

Contact Write, fax, or e-mail David O. Reynolds, Human Resource Specialist. Fax: 316-364-4186. E-mail: dareyno@wcnoc.com. No phone calls. Applicants must submit a cover letter, resume, academic transcripts. Application deadline: February 28 for summer/fall, September 30 for spring/summer.

LEGAL SERVICES

AMERICAN BAR ASSOCIATION
740 15th Street, NW
Washington, District of Columbia 20005

General Information National voluntary association of attorneys with primary goals of professional and public service as well as the improvement of the judicial system. Established in 1878. Number of employees: 180. Field office of American Bar Association, Chicago, Illinois.

Internships Available ▶ *2–4 Center for Immigration Law and Representation interns:* responsibilities include doing various tasks in immigration benefits and procedures including interviewing, legal research, and case preparation, in either Washington, D.C. or Harlingen, Texas. Duration is 1 semester or 1 summer (for Washington, DC interns) 2-3 months (Harlingen, TX interns). Position available as unpaid or at stipends available for Texas interns. Open to law students. ▶ *Central and East European Law Initiative interns:* responsibilities include researching, writing, and legal assessments (lawyers). Candidates should have ability to work independently, self-motivation, strong interpersonal skills, writing skills, training/experience in international affairs preferred. Duration is 15 hours per week minimum during school year; full-time in summer. Unpaid. Open to college freshmen, college sophomores, college juniors, college seniors, law students, attorneys. ▶ *6 Commission on Mental and Physical Disability Law interns.* Duration is fall, spring, or summer semester. Position available as unpaid or paid. Open to college freshmen, college sophomores, college juniors, college seniors, law students. ▶ *1 Division for Media Relations and Public Affairs intern:* responsibilities include participating in press briefings, news conferences, strategic planning, event publicity, interview placements, and other duties. Candidates should have demonstrated interest in public relations. Duration is one academic term (part-time). Unpaid. Open to college sophomores, college juniors, college seniors. ▶ *6 Government Public Sector Lawyers Division interns:* responsibilities include helping on the division's publications, assisting in award program, and a wide variety of clerical and administrative tasks. Candidates should have self-motivation, strong leadership ability. Duration is 1 semester or 1 summer. Unpaid. Open to college juniors, college seniors, law students. ▶ *1–3 Governmental Affairs Office interns:* responsibilities include working with the staff, conducting research, and writing memoranda on legislative and policy issues. Candidates should have research skills, writing skills. Duration is part-time during school year; full-time during summer. Unpaid. Open to college freshmen, college sophomores, college juniors, college seniors. ▶ *1 Immigration and Pro Bono Development intern.* Candidates should have immigration law experience/coursework. Duration is 10-20 hours per week for length of school year. Unpaid. Open to law students in second or third year. ▶ *1–5 Public Services Division interns:* responsibilities include compiling information for directories and other databases; coordinating survey development, distribution, and results; assisting with mailings, copying, and faxing. Duration is 8–10 weeks. Position available as unpaid or paid. Open to college freshmen, college sophomores, college juniors, college seniors, law students, undergraduates and first-year law students (project internships only); second and third-year law

American Bar Association (continued)

students (eligible for 1 Public Service Summer Internship). ▶ *6 Section of Dispute Resolution interns:* responsibilities include various tasks in mediation, arbitration, and other non-litigious forms of dispute resolution. Unpaid. Open to college freshmen, college sophomores, college juniors, college seniors. ▶ *1–4 Section of Individual Rights and Responsibilities interns:* responsibilities include conducting legal research; assisting in monitoring state and federal legislative developments on various civil rights, civil liberties, and human rights issues; and writing newsletter articles for the Section newsletter. Candidates should have personal interest in the field, research skills, writing skills. Duration is 1 semester. Unpaid. Open to college juniors, college seniors, law students. ▶ *1–4 Section of International Law and Practice interns:* responsibilities include conducting legal research; assisting in monitoring state and federal legislative developments on various civil rights, civil liberties, and human rights issues; and writing newsletter articles for the Section. Candidates should have personal interest in the field. Duration is 1 academic term or summer. Unpaid. Open to college freshmen, college sophomores, college juniors, college seniors. ▶ *1 Standing Committee on Law and National Security intern:* responsibilities include assisting with daily operation of standing committee business, responding to requests, organizing monthly breakfast meeting, and other tasks as necessary. Duration is 2-3 days per week. Unpaid. Open to college freshmen, college sophomores, college juniors, college seniors, graduate students. International applications accepted. **Benefits** Opportunity to attend seminars/workshops, possible full-time employment, willing to act as a professional reference, willing to complete paperwork for educational credit, willing to provide letters of recommendation. **Contact** Write, call, or fax Internship Coordinator. Phone: 202-662-1010. Fax: 202-662-1032. Applicants must submit a cover letter, resume. Applications are accepted continuously. World Wide Web: http://www.abanet.org.

AMERICAN BAR ASSOCIATION- CENTRAL AND EAST EUROPEAN LAW INITIATIVE (CEELI)
740 15th Street, NW
Washington, District of Columbia 20005

General Information Program which provides legal reform in Central and Eastern Europe and former Soviet states. Established in 1990. Number of employees: 35. Unit of American Bar Association, Chicago, Illinois. Number of internship applications received each year: 400.
Internships Available ▶ *6 legal assessments analysts:* responsibilities include organizing and managing legal assessment projects. Specifically, analysts will organize panels of legal experts to comment on draft legislation from CEE and NIS governments, and will draft comprehensive analysis of the legislation based on experts' comments. Candidates should have analytical skills, computer skills, organizational skills, personal interest in the field, strong interpersonal skills, writing skills. Open to law students, attorneys. ▶ *2 legal research interns:* responsibilities include receiving training in basic legal research, responding to research requests from CEELI liaisons and staff, researching legal, political, and economic conditions in CEE and WIS countries. Candidates should have ability to work independently, analytical skills, computer skills, personal interest in the field, research skills, self-motivation. Open to college freshmen, college sophomores, college juniors, college seniors, recent college graduates, graduate students, law students. Duration for all positions is year-round, minimum 10-week commitment for at least 15 hours per week. All positions are unpaid. International applications accepted.
Benefits Opportunity to attend seminars/workshops, willing to act as a professional reference, willing to complete paperwork for educational credit, willing to provide letters of recommendation, access to internal ABA job postings for full-time employment.
Contact Write, fax, or e-mail Simon Conte, Associate Director, Legall Assessments and Research. Fax: 202-662-1597. E-mail: sconte@abaceeli.org. In-person interview recommended. Applicants

must submit a cover letter, resume, writing sample. Applications are accepted continuously. World Wide Web: http://www.abanet.org/ceeli.

AYUDA, INC.
1736 Columbia Road, NW
Washington, District of Columbia 20009

General Information Nonprofit community-based agency that provides legal assistance with immigration and domestic violence matters to the low-income, foreign-born population of Washington. Established in 1971. Number of employees: 17. Number of internship applications received each year: 500.
Internships Available ▶ *5–8 domestic violence legal assistants:* responsibilities include conducting initial interviews with battered women, drafting legal documents, preparing clients for trial, conducting case investigations, assisting at counsel table during trial, and accompanying the police when clients need assistance. Candidates should have experience in the field, oral communication skills, plan to pursue career in field, strong interpersonal skills, proficiency in Spanish. Open to college sophomores, college juniors, college seniors, recent college graduates, graduate students, law students. ▶ *5–8 immigration legal assistants:* responsibilities include working in areas of political asylum, naturalization, relative petition, adjustment of status, advance parole, and suspension of deportation. Candidates should have ability to work independently, organizational skills, plan to pursue career in field, research skills, writing skills, proficiency in Spanish. Open to college freshmen, college sophomores, college juniors, college seniors, recent college graduates, graduate students, law students. ▶ *5–8 policy interns:* responsibilities include conducting research on issues affecting battered immigrant women, tracking legislation, providing technical assistance to Congress, translating outreach materials, and fielding calls from shelter workers and attorneys. Candidates should have ability to work independently, editing skills, plan to pursue career in field, research skills, writing skills. Open to college freshmen, college sophomores, college juniors, college seniors, recent college graduates, graduate students, law students. ▶ *1–2 public relations interns:* responsibilities include drafting grant proposals, creating annual report, developing media contacts, and working on fund-raising projects. Candidates should have ability to work independently, computer skills, editing skills, office skills, self-motivation, strong interpersonal skills, writing skills. Open to college freshmen, college sophomores, college juniors, college seniors, recent college graduates, graduate students, law students. Duration for all positions is 10–12 weeks. All positions are unpaid. International applications accepted.
Benefits Opportunity to attend seminars/workshops, willing to complete paperwork for educational credit, willing to provide letters of recommendation, help in obtaining fellowships.
Contact Write, call, fax, or e-mail Ms. Rachel Kaufman, Volunteer Coordinator. Phone: 202-387-4848. Fax: 202-387-0324. E-mail: immayuda@erols.com. In-person interview recommended. Applicants must submit a formal organization application, cover letter, resume, writing sample, 2 to 3 personal references. Application deadline: January 15 for spring, March 15 for summer, September 1 for fall.

THE BECKET FUND FOR RELIGIOUS LIBERTY
2000 Pennsylvania Avenue, NW, Suite 3580
Washington, District of Columbia 20006

General Information Nonpartisan, economical public-interest law firm that protects religious liberty and defends the free expression of all religious traditions. Established in 1993. Number of employees: 8.
Internships Available ▶ *1 computer intern:* responsibilities include updating Web site, network administration, Internet research, and editing Web newsletter. Candidates should have computer skills, writing skills. Open to college freshmen, college sophomores, college juniors, college seniors, recent college graduates, graduate students, law students, career changers. ▶ *2–3 interns:* responsibilities include compiling and researching news stories, assisting with research (legal and academic), assisting in writing

and editing newsletter, writing radio copy, and providing general litigation support. Candidates should have personal interest in the field, research skills, self-motivation, writing skills. Open to college freshmen, college sophomores, college juniors, college seniors, recent college graduates, graduate students, law students, career changers, individuals reentering the workforce. Duration for all positions is flexible. All positions are unpaid. International applications accepted.
Benefits On-the-job training, possible full-time employment, willing to act as a professional reference, willing to complete paperwork for educational credit, willing to provide letters of recommendation.
International Internships Available in Oxford, United Kingdom.
Contact Write, fax, or e-mail Megan Donley, Staff Attorney/Public Affairs. Fax: 202-955-0090. E-mail: megan@becketfund.org. In-person interview recommended. Applicants must submit a cover letter, resume, two personal references, 1 writing sample recommended. Applications are accepted continuously. World Wide Web: http://www.becketfund.org.

BET TZEDEK LEGAL SERVICES
145 South Fairfax Avenue, Suite 200
Los Angeles, California 90036

General Information Legal services organization providing free legal services to poor and low-income residents of Los Angeles County, focusing primarily on senior citizens. Established in 1973. Number of employees: 44. Number of internship applications received each year: 100.
Internships Available ▶ *1–3 human resources/volunteer coordination interns:* responsibilities include assisting with recruitment of staff and volunteers, arranging appointments with applicants for staff and volunteer placements, assisting in composing recruitment and advertising materials, maintaining personnel records and benefit materials, collating employee orientation and termination documents, maintaining database of staff and volunteers, coordinating meetings and events, and assisting in administrative projects as needed. Candidates should have computer skills, office skills, oral communication skills, organizational skills, strong interpersonal skills, writing skills, basic clerical skills, typing of 35 WPM and ability to use word processing software. Must have good command of English. Duration is 10-12 weeks (8 hours per week). Open to college freshmen, college sophomores, college juniors, college seniors, recent college graduates, graduate students, career changers, individuals reentering the workforce. ▶ *1–2 marketing/development interns:* responsibilities include assisting in special event production, direct mail solicitation, and telephone follow-up. Candidates should have ability to work independently, computer skills, office skills, organizational skills, strong interpersonal skills, writing skills, good phone skills and high-energy, people-oriented disposition. Duration is 10-12 weeks (20 hours per week during summer; 8 hours per week during academic year). Open to college sophomores, college juniors, college seniors, recent college graduates, graduate students, career changers. ▶ *1–2 nonprofit fund accounting interns:* responsibilities include working hands-on with computerized accounts payable and receivable documentation, assisting in the input and accounting functions specific to nonprofit organizations with multiple funding sources, receiving training in the use and function of spreadsheet applications, organizing data for review and taking part in the data analysis process. Candidates should have ability to work with others, office skills, oral communication skills, organizational skills, general accounting and/or bookkeeping background (helpful), 10-key experience, moderate typing skills, familiarity with computers. Duration is 10-12 weeks (8 hours per week). Open to college freshmen, college sophomores, college juniors, college seniors, recent college graduates, graduate students, career changers, individuals reentering the workforce. ▶ *7–9 prescreeners/legal assistants:* responsibilities include prescreening clients by phone for financial and case type eligibility, making appropriate referrals, conducting in-person interviews, writing letters on behalf of clients, and other client advocacy under the direction of supervising attorneys. Candidates should have ability to work independently, analytical skills, oral communication skills, plan to pursue career in field, strong interpersonal skills,

written communication skills, demonstrable commitment to community service, understanding of the problems of the poor. Duration is 11-12 weeks (20 hours per week during summer, 8 hours per week during academic year). Open to college freshmen, college sophomores, college juniors, recent college graduates, college seniors (during academic year only). All positions are unpaid. International applications accepted.
Benefits Formal training, on-the-job training, willing to act as a professional reference, willing to complete paperwork for educational credit, willing to provide letters of recommendation.
Contact Write, call, or fax Ms. Robin Sommerstein, Personnel Director/Volunteer Coordinator. Phone: 323-939-0506. Fax: 323-939-1040. In-person interview recommended. Applicants must submit a cover letter, resume. Application deadline: April 15 for summer, September 10 for fall. World Wide Web: http://www.comquest.com/bet-tzedek.

CENTER FOR INTERNATIONAL LEGAL STUDIES
Schweigmuhlweg 6B
Salzburg Austria

General Information Legal publication, research, and training institute. The center's essential purpose is the promotion of information dissemination and the administration of postgraduate programs. Established in 1976. Number of employees: 17. Number of internship applications received each year: 60.
Internships Available ▶ *International law interns:* responsibilities include a variety of legal work. Duration is 1 semester. $800–$1,000 per month. Open to graduate students. ▶ *Summer externs:* responsibilities include a variety of legal work. Duration is 1 month. Unpaid. Open to law students. International applications accepted.
Benefits Free housing, free meals, on-the-job training, willing to complete paperwork for educational credit.
International Internships Available.
Contact Write or e-mail Andrea Kinaver, Schweigmuhlueg 6B, Salzburg 5020 Australia. E-mail: akincils@ping.at. Applicants must submit a resume, academic transcripts, two letters of recommendation, statement of interest. Applications are accepted continuously. Fees: $300. World Wide Web: http://www.cils.org.

COUNCIL FOR COURT EXCELLENCE
1150 Connecticut Avenue, NW, Suite 620
Washington, District of Columbia 20036-4104

General Information Nonprofit, nonpartisan civic organization working to improve the administration of justice in local and federal courts. Activities include public education about courts, tracking federal and local legislation concerning courts, and studies and analyses of aspects of the judicial branch. Established in 1982. Number of employees: 6. Number of internship applications received each year: 60.
Internships Available ▶ *3 interns:* responsibilities include assisting in development and progress of selected projects. Candidates should have computer skills, office skills, research skills, strong interpersonal skills, written communication skills. Duration is 1 semester. Unpaid. Open to college freshmen, college sophomores, college juniors, college seniors, recent college graduates, graduate students, law students. International applications accepted.
Benefits Job counseling, names of contacts, opportunity to attend seminars/workshops, possible full-time employment, travel reimbursement, willing to complete paperwork for educational credit, willing to provide letters of recommendation.
Contact Write or call Ms. Priscilla Skillman, Assistant Director, 1150 Connecticut Avenue, NW Suite 620, Washington, District of Columbia 20036-4104. Phone: 202-785-5917. In-person interview recommended. Applicants must submit a cover letter, resume, writing sample. Applications are accepted continuously. World Wide Web: http://www.courtexcellence.org.

GEORGETOWN UNIVERSITY LAW CENTER–CRIMINAL JUSTICE CLINIC
111 F Street, NW
Washington, District of Columbia 20001-2095

General Information Clinic that provides representation to indigent criminal defendants in District of Columbia. Number of employees: 18. Number of internship applications received each year: 400.

Internships Available ▶ *10 investigative interns:* responsibilities include meeting investigative needs of 2 clinic attorneys in all aspects of investigations, including assessing government's cases, interviewing potential witnesses, gathering relevant paperwork, serving subpoenas, collecting evidence, and other field work. Candidates should have oral communication skills, organizational skills, self-motivation, strong interpersonal skills, strong leadership ability. Duration is 1 semester or summer. Unpaid. Open to college freshmen, college sophomores, college juniors, college seniors, recent college graduates, graduate students, law students. International applications accepted.

Benefits Formal training, names of contacts, on-the-job training, opportunity to attend seminars/workshops, travel reimbursement, willing to act as a professional reference, willing to complete paperwork for educational credit, willing to provide letters of recommendation.

Contact Write, call, fax, or e-mail Keri Salzillo, Investigations Supervisor. Phone: 202-662-9575. Fax: 202-662-9681. E-mail: salzillk@law.georgetown.edu. Telephone interview required. Applicants must submit a formal organization application, two personal references. Application deadline: March 15 for 1st round fall, April 1 for summer, July 1 for 2nd round fall, December 1 for spring.

HALT- AN ORGANIZATION OF AMERICANS FOR LEGAL REFORM
1612 K Street, NW, Suite 510
Washington, District of Columbia 20006

General Information National nonprofit membership organization dedicated to making the civil legal system more accessible, less costly, and more equitable. Established in 1978. Number of employees: 8. Number of internship applications received each year: 200.

Internships Available ▶ *1–6 interns:* responsibilities include working in all aspects of organization on projects including writing book reviews for newsletter, attending congressional hearings, conducting national surveys, providing background information, writing press releases, coordinating conferences, grant writing, and other duties. Candidates should have research skills, writing skills. Duration is flexible. Position available as unpaid or paid. Open to high school seniors, recent high school graduates, college freshmen, college sophomores, college juniors, college seniors, recent college graduates, graduate students, law students. International applications accepted.

Benefits Possible full-time employment, willing to act as a professional reference, willing to complete paperwork for educational credit, willing to provide letters of recommendation.

Contact Write, call, fax, or e-mail Joyce McGee, Internship Coordinator. Phone: 202-887-8255. Fax: 202-887-9699. E-mail: halt@halt.org. In-person interview recommended. Applicants must submit a cover letter, resume, writing sample. Application deadline: March 31 for summer, August 31 for fall, November 30 for spring. World Wide Web: http://www.halt.org.

HOUSE OF RUTH DOMESTIC VIOLENCE LEGAL CLINIC
2201 Argonne Drive
Baltimore, Maryland 21218

General Information Organization that provides legal information and legal representation in civil cases, accompanies victims of domestic violence to court and offers other assistance, and provides training sessions and workshops to the legal system and the community. Established in 1977. Number of employees: 17. Number of internship applications received each year: 20.

Internships Available ▶ *1–3 legal advocates:* responsibilities include research, legal writing, and other duties. Interns may choose to work in the Baltimore City office (main office) answering incoming calls from victims seeking legal relief from domestic violence and providing accompaniment to victims during trial; or interns may aide staff attorneys at the District Court House or the Prince George's County Office. Candidates should have interest in victim's rights and women's issues, speaking skills, interest in public interest law. Unpaid. Open to law students. International applications accepted.

Benefits Opportunity to attend seminars/workshops, willing to complete paperwork for educational credit, reimbursement of court-related expenses (mileage and parking).

Contact Write, call, or fax Twilah Shipley, Esq., Managing Attorney (main office), (410)554-8463; Laura Kniaz, Managing Attorney (Baltimore City District Court House), (410)385-2263;. Phone: 410-554-8463. Fax: 410-243-3014. In-person interview recommended. Applicants must submit a cover letter, resume, personal reference. Application deadline: 3 months before semester/term of interest.

JUDICIAL INTERNSHIP PROGRAM, SUPREME COURT OF THE UNITED STATES
Office of the Administrative Assistant to the Chief Justice, Room 5
Washington, District of Columbia 20543

General Information Office that aids the Chief Justice in fulfilling nonadjudicatory responsibilities. Established in 1972. Number of internship applications received each year: 150.

Internships Available ▶ *1–3 judicial interns:* responsibilities include performing routine office tasks which include clipping, categorizing, and filing articles; monitoring research on the federal judicial system; helping prepare memoranda, correspondence, and background research for articles and speeches. Candidates should have ability to work with others, analytical skills, oral communication skills, research skills, self-motivation, written communication skills, some course work in constitutional law or the Supreme Court. Duration is 1 semester. Unpaid. Open to college juniors, college seniors, recent college graduates. International applications accepted.

Benefits $1000 stipend may be available for interns who are returning to academic studies.

Contact Write, call, or fax Christie S. Warren, Judicial Fellow. Phone: 202-479-3415. Fax: 202-479-3484. Applicants must submit a formal organization application, resume, academic transcripts, writing sample, three letters of recommendation, candidate statement describing experience, skills, and reason for application, and essay of 2 pages or more. Application deadline: March 10 for summer, June 1 for fall, October 10 for winter.

KOHN, KOHN AND COLAPINTO, P.C.
3233 P Street, NW
Washington, District of Columbia 20007-2756

General Information Public interest law firm specializing in representation of whistle blowers. The firm represents numerous employees who were fired or retaliated against for making disclosures regarding nuclear safety, corporate or government misconduct, environmental protection or health and safety violations.

Internships Available ▶ *Legal interns:* responsibilities include significant legal research and writing projects, assisting at trials, and performing all the work of an associate attorney. Unpaid. Open to law students.

Benefits Willing to complete paperwork for educational credit, one-on-one supervision from an attorney.

Contact Write, call, fax, or e-mail Joyce Claro, Internship Coordinator. Phone: 202-342-6980. Fax: 202-342-6984. E-mail: jc@kkc.com. Telephone interview required. Applicants must submit a resume, cover letter. Applications are accepted continuously. World Wide Web: http://www.whistleblowers.org.

LAMBDA LEGAL DEFENSE AND EDUCATION FUND, INC.
6030 Wilshire Boulevard, Suite 200
Los Angeles, California 90036-3617

General Information National organization committed to achieving full recognition of the civil rights of lesbians, gay men and people with HIV/AIDS through impact litigation, education, and public policy work. Established in 1973. Number of employees: 5. Branch of Lambda Legal Defense and Education Fund, Inc., New York, New York. Number of internship applications received each year: 1.
Internships Available ▶ *1–3 interns:* responsibilities include handling intake of callers, researching legal matters and classifying them into subject-matter files, utilizing programs such as Lexis or Westlaw. Candidates should have ability to work with others, computer skills, personal interest in the field, research skills, self-motivation. Duration is one summer. Unpaid. Open to law students.
Benefits Willing to act as a professional reference, willing to provide letters of recommendation.
Contact Write Myron Quon, Esq. Applicants must submit a formal organization application, cover letter, resume. Applications are accepted continuously. World Wide Web: http://www.lambdalegal.org.

LAMBDA LEGAL DEFENSE AND EDUCATION FUND, INC. (MIDWEST REGION)
11 East Adams, Suite 1008
Chicago, Illinois 60603-6303

General Information National organization committed to achieving full recognition of the civil rights of lesbians, gay men and people with HIV/AIDS through impact litigation, education and public policy work. Established in 1973. Number of employees: 7. Branch of Lambda Legal Defense and Education Fund, Inc., New York, New York.
Internships Available ▶ *1 fund-raising intern:* responsibilities include assisting with the functions of the fund-raising department; heavy clerical work and data entry; assisting in planning and execution of special events. Candidates should have ability to work independently, computer skills, office skills, oral communication skills, organizational skills, self-motivation, strong interpersonal skills, written communication skills. Duration is 1 semester. Unpaid. Open to college seniors, recent college graduates, graduate students, career changers. ▶ *1–2 intake interns:* responsibilities include speaking with callers about potential legal issues, assisting them in identifying key facts and recording vital information for attorneys to review, connecting callers to legal and social services in their area as appropriate. Candidates should have computer skills, oral communication skills, personal interest in the field, self-motivation, strong interpersonal skills, written communication skills. Duration is 6-8 hours per week (variable number of weeks). Unpaid. Open to college sophomores, college juniors, college seniors, recent college graduates, graduate students, career changers. ▶ *1–3 legal interns:* responsibilities include working with lawyers on legal research projects, preparing written memoranda of work, and assisting in briefs and filings for state and federal courts. Candidates should have ability to work independently, analytical skills, oral communication skills, personal interest in the field, research skills, written communication skills. Duration is 10–12 weeks. Position available as unpaid or at school-year interns are paid approximately $10 per hour; summer intern stipends vary, depending on available funding. Open to law students. International applications accepted.
Benefits Names of contacts, on-the-job training, willing to act as a professional reference, willing to provide letters of recommendation, completion of paperwork for educational credit for legal internship only.
Contact Write, call, fax, or e-mail RoiAnn Phillips, Program Assistant. Phone: 312-663-4413. Fax: 312-663-4307. E-mail: lldefmro@aol.com. In-person interview required. Applicants must submit a cover letter, resume, 1 writing sample required for legal intern-

ship only; 2—3 personal references. Application deadline: January 1 for summer legal interns; continuous for others. World Wide Web: http://www.lambdalegal.org.

LEGAL AID OF THE CENTRAL COAST
21 Carr Street
Watsonville, California 95076

General Information Law office funded by federal, state, county, and city government, providing free legal advice to qualifying low-income people in the areas of unemployment, housing, welfare law, debtor rights, and education. Established in 1968. Number of employees: 13. Number of internship applications received each year: 50.
Internships Available ▶ *12 legal interns:* responsibilities include handling case work, conducting client intake, advising and referral, preparing legal materials, and working closely with staff attorneys; special research projects are also possible. Duration is 2 quarters. Unpaid. Open to college freshmen, college sophomores, college juniors, college seniors, recent college graduates, graduate students, law students. International applications accepted.
Benefits Willing to complete paperwork for educational credit, willing to provide letters of recommendation, 3–4 hours of lectures on law and forms, one-on-one supervision by an attorney.
Contact Write, call, fax, or e-mail Shirley Conner, Intern Coordinator. Phone: 831-724-2253. Fax: 831-724-7530. E-mail: lac1@earthlink.net. In-person interview recommended. Applicants must submit a cover letter, resume. Applications are accepted continuously.

THE LEGAL AID SOCIETY, CRIMINAL DEFENSE DIVISION
49 Thomas Street, 2nd Floor
New York, New York 10013

General Information Organization that provides free legal assistance to indigent clients in all areas of the law, including criminal defense, juvenile, appeals, and civil. Established in 1876. Number of employees: 250. Division of Legal Aid Society, New York, New York. Number of internship applications received each year: 200.
Internships Available ▶ *30–40 investigator interns:* responsibilities include locating, interviewing, and taking written statements from witnesses in the field; background checks and research; serving subpoenas; and assisting attorneys in preparing for court. Candidates should have ability to work independently, oral communication skills, personal interest in the field, strong interpersonal skills, written communication skills, commitment to community service and advocacy for the indigent. ▶ *10–15 juvenile rights division interns:* responsibilities include working with attorneys in all aspects of investigations, post-sentencing placement, and advocacy work. Candidates should have ability to work independently, oral communication skills, personal interest in the field, strong interpersonal skills, written communication skills. Duration for all positions is 1–2 semesters. All positions are unpaid. Open to college sophomores, college juniors, college seniors, recent college graduates, graduate students, law students. International applications accepted.
Benefits Formal training, job counseling, opportunity to attend seminars/workshops, possible full-time employment, willing to act as a professional reference, willing to complete paperwork for educational credit, willing to provide letters of recommendation.
Contact Write, call, fax, or e-mail Peter Lane, Investigative Projects Director, 49 Thomas Street, 2nd Floor, New York, New York 10015. Phone: 212-298-5001. Fax: 212-693-1149. E-mail: plane@legal-aid.org. In-person interview recommended. Applicants must submit a formal organization application, resume, two personal references, two letters of recommendation. Application deadline: January 9 for spring, March 31 for summer, September 11 for fall. World Wide Web: http://www.legal-aid.org.

LEGAL SERVICES FOR PRISONERS WITH CHILDREN
100 McAllister Street
San Francisco, California 94102

General Information Organization that provides training, technical assistance, advocacy, and litigation support to legal service offices and to prisoners, their families, and advocates throughout California. Established in 1978. Number of employees: 5. Number of internship applications received each year: 100.

Internships Available ▶ *Interns:* responsibilities include handling client intake, responding to requests for assistance from prisoners and their families, conducting legal research, and writing. Candidates should have ability to work independently, ability to work with others, oral communication skills, personal interest in the field, research skills, written communication skills. Duration is flexible. Unpaid. Open to college juniors, college seniors, recent college graduates, graduate students, law students. International applications accepted.

Benefits Job counseling, names of contacts, travel reimbursement, willing to act as a professional reference, willing to complete paperwork for educational credit, willing to provide letters of recommendation.

Contact Write or e-mail Karen Shain, Administrative Director. E-mail: lspc@igc.org. No phone calls. Applicants must submit a cover letter, resume, writing sample. Applications are accepted continuously.

MADISON COUNTY PROBATION AND COURT SERVICES DEPARTMENT
157 North Main, Suite 312
Edwardsville, Illinois 62025

General Information Criminal justice organization that provides courts with information regarding sentencing and victim compensation. Number of employees: 135. Number of internship applications received each year: 25.

Internships Available ▶ *2 detention home interns:* responsibilities include providing education and recreation to children and being responsible for their welfare. Candidates should have ability to work with others, computer skills, oral communication skills, self-motivation, major in human services preferred. Open to college juniors or seniors (seniors preferred). ▶ *1 human resources/training assistant:* responsibilities include working with the human services administrator by assisting with training issues and research evaluations of department programs. Candidates should have ability to work independently, knowledge of field, organizational skills, research skills, self-motivation, written communication skills. Open to college seniors. ▶ *2 juvenile and adult probation interns:* responsibilities include assisting probation officer in all phases of job. Candidates should have ability to work with others, computer skills, oral communication skills, self-motivation, major in human services preferred. Open to college juniors or seniors (seniors preferred). Duration for all positions is 1 semester. All positions are unpaid. International applications accepted.

Benefits Opportunity to attend seminars/workshops, possible full-time employment, willing to act as a professional reference, willing to complete paperwork for educational credit.

Contact Write, call, or fax Richard Asperger, Human Services Administrator. Phone: 618-692-6255. Fax: 618-656-4591. In-person interview required. Applicants must submit a formal organization application, three personal references, documentation from professor that intern is doing work for course credit. Application deadline: May 1 for summer semester, December 1 for winter/spring semester.

MIGRANT LEGAL ACTION PROGRAM
PO Box 53308
Washington, District of Columbia 20009

General Information National support and advocacy center providing legal representation to migrant and seasonal farm workers nationwide concerning employment conditions, health,

housing, education, wages, public benefits, and general welfare. Established in 1970. Number of employees: 5. Number of internship applications received each year: 120.

Internships Available ▶ *2 law student interns:* responsibilities include legal research and writing under the supervision of a staff attorney. Open to law students. ▶ *1 undergraduate intern:* responsibilities include assisting staff in a variety of research, writing, and some clerical duties. Open to college sophomores, college juniors, college seniors, recent college graduates. Candidates for all positions should have ability to work independently, ability to work with others, oral communication skills, research skills, self-motivation, written communication skills. Duration for all positions is 1-2 semesters or summer. All positions are unpaid.

Benefits Names of contacts, opportunity to attend seminars/workshops, willing to complete paperwork for educational credit, willing to provide letters of recommendation.

Contact Write Mr. Roger C. Rosenthal, Executive Director. In-person interview recommended. Applicants must submit a cover letter, resume, writing sample, two personal references. Application deadline: March 1 for summer, August 15 for fall, October 1 for spring.

MONTGOMERY COUNTY COMMUNITY CORRECTIONS
11651 Nebel Street
Rockville, Maryland 20852

General Information Agency that provides effective community correctional alternatives between probation/parole supervision and security confinement for male and female adult offenders. Established in 1972. Number of employees: 60. Unit of Montgomery County Department of Corrections and Rehabilitation, Rockville, Maryland. Number of internship applications received each year: 100.

Internships Available ▶ *4 CART interns:* responsibilities include working in the Community Accountability and Treatment Services Program, verifying participant's whereabouts; collecting and testing urine; assisting in group treatment facilitation of life skills and substance-abuse education; performing crisis intervention; and assisting in home visits in the community. Candidates should have ability to work independently, oral communication skills, personal interest in the field, self-motivation, strong interpersonal skills. Duration is minimum 4 months, maximum 1 year. $5.15 per hour (24 hours per week). Open to college juniors, college seniors, recent college graduates, graduate students, law students, career changers, individuals reentering the workforce. ▶ *2 IPSA interns:* responsibilities include working in the Intervention Program for Substance Abusers; assisting in screening, placement, and case management; supervising and checking community service work; collecting and testing urine; monitoring attendance; and assisting in developing community service projects. Candidates should have declared college major in field, oral communication skills, personal interest in the field, self-motivation, strong interpersonal skills. Duration is minimum 4 months, maximum 1 year. $5.15 per hour (24 hours per week). Open to college juniors, college seniors, recent college graduates, graduate students, law students, career changers, individuals reentering the workforce. ▶ *2 PTSU interns:* responsibilities include working in the Pre-Trial Services Unit checking arrest histories, assisting assessment case workers with interviews and verifications, helping defendants obtain information, collecting and testing urine, assisting supervision staff in conducting seminars, maintaining referral resource book, and reminding defendants of court appearances. Candidates should have ability to work independently, oral communication skills, personal interest in the field, self-motivation, strong interpersonal skills. Duration is minimum 4 months, maximum 1 year. $5 per hour. Open to college juniors, recent college graduates, graduate students, law students, career changers. ▶ *6 PreRelease Center interns:* responsibilities include supervising adult offenders residing in a community correctional facility preparing for release and recreational trips, collecting and testing urine, coordinating employment, performing resident verifications, and participating as a treatment team member. Candidates should have oral

communication skills, personal interest in the field, self-motivation, strong interpersonal skills, written communication skills. Duration is 4–12 months. $5 per hour. Open to college juniors, college seniors, recent college graduates, graduate students, law students, career changers, individuals reentering the workforce. International applications accepted.
Benefits Formal training, free housing, free meals, job counseling, on-the-job training, opportunity to attend seminars/workshops, possible full-time employment, willing to act as a professional reference, willing to complete paperwork for educational credit, willing to provide letters of recommendation.
Contact Write, call, fax, or e-mail Ms. Jane S. Sachs, Supervisor, Administration and Training. Phone: 301-468-4200. Fax: 301-468-4420. E-mail: corectns.sachsj@co.mo.md.us. In-person interview recommended. Applicants must submit a formal organization application. Applications are accepted continuously.

NATIVE AMERICAN RIGHTS FUND
1506 Broadway
Boulder, Colorado 80302

General Information Nonprofit law firm that represents tribes and individuals on tribal issues such as land, water, and recognition. Established in 1970. Number of employees: 40. Number of internship applications received each year: 50.
Internships Available ▶ *5 law clerks:* responsibilities include conducting legal research and writing projects on issues of Indian law, procedure, and policy (work setting is either Boulder, Colorado; Anchorage, Alaska; or Washington, DC). Candidates should have ability to work with others, college courses in field, plan to pursue career in field, research skills, written communication skills. Duration is 10–12 weeks. $15 per hour. Open to second-year law students.
Benefits Names of contacts, willing to complete paperwork for educational credit, willing to provide letters of recommendation.
Contact Write, call, or fax Ms. Tracy A. Labin, Staff Attorney/Law Clerk Supervisor. Phone: 303-447-8760. Fax: 303-443-7776. Applicants must submit a cover letter, resume, academic transcripts, writing sample, three letters of recommendation. Application deadline: November 30 for summer law clerks. World Wide Web: http://www.narf.org.

NEW YORK STATE BAR ASSOCIATION
One Elk Street
Albany, New York 12207

General Information Official organization of lawyers in New York that strives to aid the administration of justice, promote legal reforms, and apply legal knowledge and experience for public benefit. Established in 1876. Number of employees: 110. Number of internship applications received each year: 20.
Internships Available ▶ *1 public relations intern:* responsibilities include writing news releases, preparing backgrounders, scripting broadcast public service announcements, assisting with special events, learning how to conduct research through databases, handling requests for materials produced by the department and available to the public, writing news and feature stories for the monthly newspaper and the staff publication, and assisting with photography. Candidates should have ability to work independently, computer skills, knowledge of field, office skills, personal interest in the field, research skills, writing skills, major in journalism or public relations preferred. Duration is 10 weeks. Position available as unpaid or at $7 per hour for summer interns; during other times of the year interns are not paid. Open to college juniors who are residents of northeastern United States.
Benefits Formal training, job counseling, opportunity to attend seminars/workshops, travel reimbursement, willing to complete paperwork for educational credit, willing to provide letters of recommendation.
Contact Write or e-mail Mr. Brad Carr, Director of Media Services and Public Affairs. E-mail: bcarr@nysba.org. No phone calls. In-person interview required. Applicants must submit a

cover letter, resume, three writing samples. Application deadline: April 1 for summer; continuous for all other positions. World Wide Web: http://www.nysba.org.

NOW LEGAL DEFENSE AND EDUCATION FUND
395 Hudson Street, 5th Floor
New York, New York 10014

General Information Public interest law and policy office working to expand women's rights. Established in 1970. Number of employees: 20. Number of internship applications received each year: 400.
Internships Available ▶ *6–8 legal interns (New York City):* responsibilities include performing legal research and writing and assisting with litigation and legislative projects. Candidates should have editing skills, oral communication skills, research skills, self-motivation, writing skills. Duration is 10 weeks in summer. $350 per week. Open to law students. ▶ *1–2 legal interns (Washington, D.C.):* responsibilities include performing legal research and writing and assisting with legislative and policy analysis. $350 per week. Open to law students. ▶ *1 public policy intern:* responsibilities include researching public policy involving economics analysis, assembling and interpreting social science data and applied research on women's rights, and writing informational hand-outs and publications. Candidates should have computer skills, editing skills, oral communication skills, research skills, writing skills. Duration is 10 weeks in summer. $350 per week. Open to graduate students, graduate students majoring in public policy. ▶ *2–5 undergraduate summer and semester interns:* responsibilities include working in the areas of fund-raising/development, media/communications/World Wide Web, intake, and judicial education at both the New York and D.C. offices. Candidates should have computer skills, editing skills, oral communication skills, research skills, writing skills. Duration is varied, depending on internship. Position available as unpaid or at $180 per week during summer. Open to college freshmen, college sophomores, college juniors, college seniors. International applications accepted.
Benefits Names of contacts, on-the-job training, opportunity to attend seminars/workshops, possible full-time employment, willing to act as a professional reference, willing to complete paperwork for educational credit, willing to provide letters of recommendation.
Contact Write, fax, or e-mail JuliAna Grant, Program Associate/Intern Coordinator. Fax: 212-226-1066. E-mail: jgrant@nowldef.org. No phone calls. In-person interview recommended. Applicants must submit a cover letter, resume, writing sample, three personal references. Application deadline: February 1 for summer (undergraduates and first-year law students); January 2 (summer second- and third-year law students); continuous for all other positions. World Wide Web: http://www.nowldef.org.

OFFICE OF GENERAL COUNSEL
1600 Defense, Pentagon
Washington, District of Columbia 20301-1600

General Information Office that advises high-level policymakers in the Office of the Secretary of Defense and works closely with senior attorneys and policymakers from the military departments and with officials from the Departments of Justice, State, and Treasury and other government agencies. Number of employees: 80. Unit of Office of the Secretary of Defense, Washington, District of Columbia. Number of internship applications received each year: 200.
Internships Available ▶ *10–13 summer interns:* responsibilities include assisting with drafting and commenting on legislation, regulations, Congressional testimony, litigation materials, and legal opinions and assisting with the formulation of Department of Defense legal policy on topics of current interest. Candidates should have ability to work independently, ability to work with others, oral communication skills, plan to pursue career in field, research skills, written communication skills. Duration is 10–13 weeks. $470–$575 per week. Open to law students.

Office of General Counsel (continued)

Benefits Job counseling, names of contacts, willing to complete paperwork for educational credit, willing to provide letters of recommendation.
Contact Write, call, or e-mail Kimberly Lenzer, Internship Coordinator. Phone: 703-697-9342. E-mail: lenzerk@osdgc.osd. mil. Applicants must submit a cover letter, resume, writing sample, optional form (OF)6-12, statement of class rank and law school transcripts for 2nd-year law students. Application deadline: January 10 for first-year law students, November 22 for second-year law students.

OFFICE OF THE CORPORATION COUNSEL
441 Fourth Steet, NW, Room 1060, North
Washington, District of Columbia 20001

General Information Legal branch of the District of Colombia government handling legal matters involving juvenile delinquency, appeals, government fraud, adult crimes (selected), child abuse, domestic violence, child support, mental health, personnel, civil litigation, legislation, finance, and general government operations. Established in 1853. Number of employees: 450. Agency of District of Columbia Government, Washington, District of Columbia. Number of internship applications received each year: 300.
Internships Available ▶ *200–225 legal interns:* responsibilities include assisting in all aspects of legal work, including preparation for hearings and trials, courtroom assistance, research, drafting and delivering documents, contacting witnesses, making evidence available, obtaining updates on cases and laws, providing information to the opposing counsel, and general office duties. Candidates should have analytical skills, oral communication skills, organizational skills, self-motivation, strong interpersonal skills, written communication skills. Duration is 8–12 weeks. Unpaid. Open to college sophomores, college juniors, college seniors, graduate students, law students.
Benefits Job counseling, names of contacts, on-the-job training, opportunity to attend seminars/workshops, willing to complete paperwork for educational credit, willing to provide letters of recommendation.
Contact Write or call Ms. Natalie Nash, Internship Coordinator. Phone: 202-724-5648. Telephone interview required. Applicants must submit a cover letter, resume, writing sample, two letters of recommendation, indication of dates and hours available and list of interests. Applications are accepted continuously.

PUBLIC DEFENDER SERVICE
633 Indiana Avenue, NW
Washington, District of Columbia 20004

General Information Service that provides criminal defense for indigent clients of the District of Columbia. Established in 1970. Number of employees: 150. Number of internship applications received each year: 600.
Internships Available ▶ *25–30 case assistants:* responsibilities include working with a staff trial attorney, interviewing witnesses, taking statements, photographing crime scenes, and assisting attorney with trial preparations. Candidates should have ability to work with others, analytical skills, oral communication skills, organizational skills, personal interest in the field, strong interpersonal skills. Duration is 12 weeks. Unpaid. ▶ *5 fellowship investigators:* responsibilities include working with a staff trial attorney, interviewing witnesses, taking statements, photographing crime scenes, and assisting attorney with trial preparations. Candidates should have ability to work independently, experience in the field, oral communication skills, self-motivation, strong interpersonal skills, written communication skills. Duration is 16 weeks. $1,000 per duration of internship. ▶ *80 investigators:* responsibilities include working with a staff trial attorney, interviewing witnesses, taking statements, and assisting the attorney with trial preparations. Candidates should have ability to work independently, analytical skills, personal interest in the field, self-motivation, strong interpersonal skills. Duration is 12–16 weeks. Unpaid. Open to college freshmen, college sophomores, college juniors, college seniors, recent college

graduates, graduate students, law students, career changers, individuals reentering the workforce. International applications accepted.
Benefits Formal training, housing at a cost, names of contacts, on-the-job training, opportunity to attend seminars/workshops, possible full-time employment, travel reimbursement, willing to act as a professional reference, willing to complete paperwork for educational credit, willing to provide letters of recommendation.
Contact Write, call, fax, or e-mail Kesha Taylor, Internship Coordinator. Phone: 800-341-2582. Fax: 202-626-8437. E-mail: pdsclip@hotmail.com. Telephone interview required. Applicants must submit a formal organization application, cover letter, resume, 2 personal references or 2 letters of recommendation. Application deadline: February 16 for fall, April 1 for summer, December 1 for spring; those meeting application deadlines receive priority, but applications may be continuous.

PUBLIC DEFENDER SERVICE FOR THE DISTRICT OF COLUMBIA, MENTAL HEALTH DIVISION
St. Elizabeths Hospital, Cottage 2
Washington, District of Columbia 20032

General Information Independent government public interest law office that specializes in representing indigent clients facing civil and criminal commitment to D.C. area mental institutions. Established in 1970. Number of employees: 11. Number of internship applications received each year: 70.
Internships Available ▶ *14 investigators:* responsibilities include interviewing clients and witnesses, helping attorneys prepare cases for court, documenting all investigations, gathering and organizing medical and legal records, executing subpoenas, and testifying in court. ▶ *2 social work interns:* responsibilities include assisting social worker in securing necessary social services for clients. Candidates for all positions should have ability to work independently, oral communication skills, organizational skills, self-motivation, strong interpersonal skills, written communication skills. Duration for all positions is 10-12 weeks minimum (2 days per week to full-time). All positions are unpaid. Open to college freshmen, college sophomores, college juniors, college seniors, recent college graduates, graduate students, law students, career changers.
Benefits Formal training, on-the-job training, opportunity to attend seminars/workshops, willing to act as a professional reference, willing to complete paperwork for educational credit, willing to provide letters of recommendation, reimbursement of work-related travel expenses.
Contact Write or fax Carolyn Slenska-Gemble, Chief Investigator, St. Elizabeths Hospital., Cottage 2, Washington, District of Columbia 20032. Fax: 202-562-2529. In-person interview recommended. Applicants must submit a cover letter, resume, two letters of recommendation, one 3—4 page writing sample. Application deadline: March 30 for summer; continuous for all other positions.

RICHARD P. DIEGUEZ, ATTORNEY AND COUNSELLOR AT LAW
192 Garden Street, Suite 2
Roslyn Heights, New York 11577-1012

General Information Entertainment law practice and entertainment industry educational organization. Established in 1987. Number of employees: 2. Number of internship applications received each year: 100.
Internships Available ▶ *2–4 law clerks:* responsibilities include assisting with client intake, file maintenance, legal research, investigation, negotiation, and contract review. Candidates should have analytical skills, office skills, oral communication skills, organizational skills, research skills, writing skills. Open to college juniors, college seniors, recent college graduates, graduate students, law students, career changers. ▶ *2–4 management assistants:* responsibilities include developing and implementing marketing and promotional campaigns for entertainment industry educational organization; industry research; phone contact with producers, publishers, recording artists, managers, agents, and media. Candidates should have ability to work independently,

oral communication skills, organizational skills, self-motivation, strong interpersonal skills, strong leadership ability. Open to high school students, high school seniors, recent high school graduates, college freshmen, college sophomores, college juniors, college seniors, recent college graduates, graduate students, career changers, individuals reentering the workforce. Duration for all positions is flexible. All positions are unpaid. International applications accepted.

Benefits Job counseling, names of contacts, on-the-job training, opportunity to attend seminars/workshops, willing to act as a professional reference, willing to complete paperwork for educational credit, willing to provide letters of recommendation, hands-on experience.

Contact Write or e-mail Richard P. Dieguez, Esq., Attorney. E-mail: rpdieguez@rpdieguez.com. In-person interview recommended. Applicants must submit a cover letter, resume, academic transcripts, writing sample, three personal references, additional requirements found on Web site at http://www.RPDieguez.com/internships.html. Applications are accepted continuously. World Wide Web: http://www.RPDieguez.com.

SAN FRANCISCO NEIGHBORHOOD LEGAL ASSISTANCE FOUNDATION
225 Bush Street, 7th Floor
San Francisco, California 94104

General Information Foundation that provides free legal representation and counseling to low-income clients in the areas of landlord-tenant disputes, public assistance benefits, and domestic violence. Established in 1967. Number of employees: 29. Number of internship applications received each year: 200.

Internships Available ▶ *5–8 law clerks:* responsibilities include assisting attorneys and representing clients. Candidates should have ability to work independently, ability to work with others, computer skills, oral communication skills, writing skills, written communication skills, eligibility for college work-study and willingness to commit to working at least 2 semesters. Duration is 6–12 months. $10 per hour. ▶ *8–12 volunteer law clerks:* responsibilities include assisting attorneys and representing clients. Candidates should have ability to work independently, ability to work with others, computer skills, oral communication skills, writing skills. Duration is 3–12 months. Unpaid. Open to law students. International applications accepted.

Benefits Willing to complete paperwork for educational credit, willing to provide letters of recommendation.

Contact Write Mr. Robert P. Capistrano, Director of Litigation. No phone calls. In-person interview recommended. Applicants must submit a resume, writing sample. Application deadline: February 1 for summer, July 1 for fall, November 1 for spring.

STUDENT PRESS LAW CENTER
1815 North Fort Meyer Drive
Arlington, Virginia 22209

General Information Nonprofit corporation that provides free legal assistance to student journalists and advisers and publishes materials explaining students' First Amendment rights. Established in 1974. Number of employees: 3. Number of internship applications received each year: 85.

Internships Available ▶ *2 journalism interns:* responsibilities include writing, editing, and laying out the "Report". $1,750 stipend for full-semester interns, $750 stipend for summer interns. Open to college sophomores, college juniors, college seniors, recent college graduates, graduate students. ▶ *2 media law interns:* responsibilities include researching and writing opinions and articles and making client contact. $2,000 stipend for full-semester interns, $750 stipend for summer interns. Open to law students. Duration for all positions is 1 semester or summer. International applications accepted.

Benefits Job counseling, opportunity to attend seminars/workshops, willing to complete paperwork for educational credit, willing to provide letters of recommendation.

Contact Write, call, or e-mail Mr. Mark Goodman, Executive Director. Phone: 703-807-1904. E-mail: splc@splc.org. Applicants must submit a cover letter, resume, two writing samples, two personal references. Applications are accepted continuously. World Wide Web: http://www.splc.org.

THISTLEDEW CAMP
62741 County Road 551
Togo, Minnesota 55723

General Information Residential correctional camp for juvenile males; offers short-term program for nonserious offenders including a special education program, work experience, recreation, and a comprehensive high-adventure portion. Established in 1955. Number of employees: 56. Unit of Minnesota Department of Corrections, St. Paul, Minnesota. Number of internship applications received each year: 15.

Internships Available ▶ *2–3 challenge interns:* responsibilities include assisting director of high adventure challenge program including training of students on high ropes course, rock climbing, helping in supervision of a 3-day solo experience, and participating in 2 or 3-week long wilderness treks; possible modes of travel are canoeing, backpacking, or cross-country skiing. $412 per duration of internship. ▶ *2–3 residential interns:* responsibilities include assisting professional staff with counseling and report writing and working some afternoons and evenings helping to supervise students on work and recreational activities; also includes involvement in a week-long wilderness expedition with a graduating group. $412 stipend per internship. ▶ *2–3 school interns:* responsibilities include assisting professional staff in providing treatment and education to juvenile boys ages 13 to 17 years. $412 stipend per internship. Candidates for all positions should have ability to work with others. Duration for all positions is 12 weeks. Open to college juniors, college seniors. International applications accepted.

Benefits Formal training, free housing, free meals, names of contacts, on-the-job training, opportunity to attend seminars/workshops, possible full-time employment, willing to complete paperwork for educational credit, willing to provide letters of recommendation.

Contact Write, call, or fax Gisele Place, Personnel Aide. Phone: 218-376-4411. Fax: 218-376-4548. In-person interview recommended. Applicants must submit a formal organization application, cover letter, resume, two personal references. Applications are accepted continuously.

UNITED STATES DISTRICT COURT FOR THE DISTRICT OF COLUMBIA
333 Constitution Avenue, NW, Room 1824
Washington, District of Columbia 20001

General Information Office that provides non-judicial support to judges, the courts, and the public. Established in 1801. Number of employees: 70. Number of internship applications received each year: 100.

Internships Available ▶ *2–4 interns:* responsibilities include gathering data for analysis, writing reports and recommendations, preparing charts and graphs, summarizing research findings, conducting interviews, and assisting with clerical tasks. Candidates should have ability to work independently, analytical skills, computer skills, oral communication skills, strong interpersonal skills, written communication skills. Duration is 1 semester. Unpaid. Open to college freshmen, college sophomores, college juniors, college seniors, graduate students majoring in court administration. International applications accepted.

Benefits Formal training, job counseling, names of contacts, opportunity to attend seminars/workshops, possible full-time employment, willing to complete paperwork for educational credit, willing to provide letters of recommendation, informal career and academic advice.

Contact Write, call, fax, or e-mail Ms. Teresa Salazar, Intern Coordinator. Phone: 202-354-3016. Fax: 202-354-3023. E-mail: teresa_salazar@dcd.uscourts.gov. In-person interview recommended. Applicants must submit a cover letter, resume, writing sample. Application deadline: January 15 for spring, March 15 for summer, September 15 for fall/winter.

VICTIM-WITNESS ASSISTANCE PROGRAM–OFFICE OF THE DISTRICT ATTORNEY, COUNTY OF LOS ANGELES
Volunteer Services, 3220 Rosemead Boulevard, Second Floor
El Monte, California 91731

General Information Provides a broad range of services to victims and witnesses of crime. Established in 1977. Number of employees: 150. Number of internship applications received each year: 100.
Internships Available ▶ *Student interns/volunteers:* responsibilities include contacting victims; providing resource referrals; explaining court procedures; providing court escort; providing case status and disposition; notifying families; assisting victims with information about obtaining crime reports, witness fees, property return; arranging for restitution or translation; assisting children, elderly and handicapped. Candidates should have analytical skills, oral communication skills, personal interest in the field, self-motivation, strong interpersonal skills, written communication skills. Duration is 1 summer, 6 months, or 1 year. Unpaid. Open to college freshmen, college sophomores, college juniors, college seniors, recent college graduates, graduate students, law students, career changers, individuals over 18 years of age.
Benefits Formal training, health insurance, job counseling, names of contacts, opportunity to attend seminars/workshops, possible full-time employment, willing to complete paperwork for educational credit, willing to provide letters of recommendation.
Contact Call Pamela Calder, Assistant Program Administrator/ Volunteer Services. Phone: 626-572-6364. In-person interview required. Applicants must submit a formal organization application, two personal references. Application deadline: January 2 for spring, April 1 for summer, November 1 for winter.

WASHINGTON AREA LAWYERS FOR THE ARTS
815 15th Street, NW, Suite 900
Washington, District of Columbia 20005

General Information Organization that provides legal assistance to artists. Number of employees: 4. Number of internship applications received each year: 100.
Internships Available ▶ *1–25 art law interns:* responsibilities include counseling artists/clients by telephone and helping them discern their legal needs; preparing summaries of facts, issues, and applicable laws for the Director of Legal Services; possibly sitting in on client consultations. ▶ *1–25 paralegal interns:* responsibilities include fielding calls from artists, corresponding with artists and members, and assisting with the day-to-day tasks of the organization. Candidates for all positions should have ability to work independently, college courses in field, computer skills, knowledge of field, oral communication skills, research skills. Duration for all positions is 1–4 months. All positions are unpaid. Open to college juniors, college seniors, recent college graduates, graduate students, law students. International applications accepted.
Benefits Formal training, job counseling, on-the-job training, opportunity to attend seminars/workshops, willing to act as a professional reference, willing to complete paperwork for educational credit, willing to provide letters of recommendation.
Contact Write, call, fax, or e-mail Paige Totaro, Director of Legal Services, 815 15th Street, NW, Suite 900, Washington, District of Columbia 20005. Phone: 202-393-2826 Ext. 22. Fax: 202-393-4444. E-mail: ptotaro@thewala.org. In-person interview required. Applicants must submit a cover letter, resume. Applications are accepted continuously. World Wide Web: http://www.thewala.org.

WASHINGTON LEGAL FOUNDATION
2009 Massachusetts Avenue, NW
Washington, District of Columbia 20036

General Information Public interest law firm advocating free enterprise and working to restore balance to the judiciary through original litigation and distribution of multiple publications.

Established in 1977. Number of employees: 20. Number of internship applications received each year: 100.
Internships Available ▶ *Interns:* responsibilities include researching, marketing, entering data, and filing. Duration is flexible. Unpaid. Open to high school students, high school seniors, recent high school graduates, college freshmen, college sophomores, college juniors, college seniors, recent college graduates, graduate students, law students, career changers, individuals reentering the workforce. International applications accepted.
Benefits Names of contacts, possible full-time employment, willing to complete paperwork for educational credit, willing to provide letters of recommendation.
Contact Write Ms. Constance Claffey Larcher, President and Executive Director. No phone calls. In-person interview required. Applicants must submit a cover letter, resume. Applications are accepted continuously. World Wide Web: http://www.wlf.org.

SCIENTIFIC RESEARCH AND DEVELOPMENT SERVICES

AMERICAN ASSOCIATION FOR THE ADVANCEMENT OF SCIENCE
1200 New York Avenue, NW, #102
Washington, District of Columbia 20005

General Information Federation of scientific and engineering societies with nearly 300 affiliated organizations, comprised of scientists, engineers, educators, policymakers, and interested citizens. Established in 1848. Number of employees: 300. Number of internship applications received each year: 50.
Internships Available ▶ *2 science newswriting interns:* responsibilities include reporting, writing, obtaining photos, performing office duties, and page layout. Candidates should have ability to work with others, editing skills, knowledge of field, oral communication skills, organizational skills, personal interest in the field, research skills, written communication skills. Duration is less than 6 months. $8 per hour. Open to college juniors, college seniors, recent college graduates, graduate students. International applications accepted.
Benefits Opportunity to attend seminars/workshops, possible full-time employment, willing to complete paperwork for educational credit.
Contact Write or fax Dawn Graf, Human Resources Specialist. Fax: 202-682-1630. No phone calls. In-person interview required. Applicants must submit a cover letter, resume, writing sample. Applications are accepted continuously. World Wide Web: http://www.aaas.org.

AMERICAN GEOGRAPHICAL SOCIETY
120 Wall Street, Suite 100
New York, New York 10005

General Information Organization that encourages geographical research and field work and makes it available to policy makers, the media, and the public to reduce geographical illiteracy in the United States; publishes scholarly journal, a magazine, and a newsletter; and maintains programs of educational travel, volunteer teaching, economic geography, and geographic information service and speakers. Established in 1851. Number of employees: 4. Number of internship applications received each year: 35.
Internships Available ▶ *3–6 editorial, research, and/or administrative interns.* Candidates should have ability to work independently, computer skills, oral communication skills, self-motivation, strong interpersonal skills, writing skills. Duration is 10 weeks. Unpaid.

Open to college freshmen, college sophomores, college juniors, college seniors, recent college graduates, graduate students. International applications accepted.

Benefits Formal training, job counseling, names of contacts, on-the-job training, willing to act as a professional reference, willing to complete paperwork for educational credit, willing to provide letters of recommendation.

Contact Write, call, fax, or e-mail Ms. Mary Lynne Bird, Executive Director. Phone: 212-422-5456. Fax: 212-422-5480. E-mail: amgeosoc@earthlink.net. In-person interview recommended. Applicants must submit a cover letter, resume, writing sample, letter of recommendation. Applications are accepted continuously.

THE AMERIND FOUNDATION, INC.
PO Box 400
Dragoon, Arizona 85609

General Information Archaeological research facility and museum focusing on Native American cultures. Established in 1937. Number of employees: 10. Number of internship applications received each year: 100.

Internships Available ▶ *1–6 interns:* responsibilities include performing archaeological research or working on museum-related programs. Candidates should have ability to work independently, ability to work with others, college courses in field, plan to pursue career in field, self-motivation. Duration is up to 1 year. stipend. Open to college freshmen, college sophomores, college juniors, college seniors, recent college graduates, graduate students. International applications accepted.

Benefits Free housing, job counseling, names of contacts, on-the-job training, possible full-time employment, willing to complete paperwork for educational credit, willing to provide letters of recommendation.

Contact Write, call, fax, or e-mail Dr. Anne I. Woosley, Director. Phone: 520-586-3666. Fax: 520-586-4679. E-mail: woosley@amerind.org. Applicants must submit a cover letter, resume, academic transcripts, two personal references, brief statement of purpose. Applications are accepted continuously. World Wide Web: http://www.amerind.org.

ARGONNE NATIONAL LABORATORY, DIVISION OF EDUCATIONAL PROGRAMS
9700 South Cass Avenue
Argonne, Illinois 60439

General Information Laboratory conducting research in a wide variety of disciplines including biological, environmental, medical, and materials sciences and ceramics, chemistry, physics, engineering, computer science, mathematics, and reactor and energy technologies. Number of employees: 3,500. Number of internship applications received each year: 600.

Internships Available ▶ *80–120 interns:* responsibilities include working on a research project with a staff scientist. Candidates should have ability to work with others, oral communication skills, research skills, self-motivation, written communication skills. Duration is 1 semester. $350 per week. Open to college sophomores, college juniors, college seniors, recent college graduates.

Benefits Free housing, opportunity to attend seminars/workshops, travel reimbursement.

Contact Write, call, fax, or e-mail Ms. Lisa Reed, Administrative Assistant. Phone: 630-252-3366. Fax: 630-252-3193. E-mail: lreed@dep.anl.gov. Applicants must submit a formal organization application, academic transcripts, three letters of recommendation. Application deadline: February 1 for summer, March 15 for fall, October 15 for spring. World Wide Web: http://www.dep.anl.gov.

ARKENSTONE, INC.
NASA Ames Moffett Complex, Building 23, PO Box 215
Moffett Field, California 94035-0215

General Information Nonprofit developer of adaptive technology for people with disabilities. Established in 1989. Number of employees: 35. Number of internship applications received each year: 20.

Internships Available ▶ *1–3 marketing interns:* responsibilities include working with people with disabilities, mainly over the telephone, to assess their needs and help develop adaptive technology tools for them. Candidates should have computer skills, oral communication skills, personal interest in the field, self-motivation, strong interpersonal skills, written communication skills. Open to college freshmen, college sophomores, college juniors, college seniors, recent college graduates. ▶ *1–3 software interns:* responsibilities include programming and testing for reading systems and other adaptive tools for people with disabilities. Candidates should have analytical skills, computer skills, personal interest in the field, research skills, self-motivation, programming experience. Open to college sophomores, college juniors, college seniors, recent college graduates, graduate students, individuals with disabilities are encouraged to apply. Duration for all positions is 1 summer or 1 semester. All positions available as unpaid or paid. International applications accepted.

Benefits On-the-job training, possible full-time employment, willing to act as a professional reference, willing to provide letters of recommendation.

Contact Write, fax, or e-mail J. Fruchterman, Chief Executive Officer, NASA Ames Moffett Complex, Building 23, PO Box 215, Moffett Field, California 94035-0215. Fax: 650-603-8887. E-mail: jim@arkenstone.org. No phone calls. Telephone interview required. Applicants must submit a cover letter, resume, writing sample, two letters of recommendation. Applications are accepted continuously. World Wide Web: http://www.arkenstone.org.

BAXTER INTERNATIONAL
1 Baxter Parkway
Deerfield, Illinois 60015

General Information Worldwide leader in technologies related to the blood and circulatory system. Established in 1931. Number of employees: 1,300. Number of internship applications received each year: 1,000.

Internships Available ▶ *40–60 interns:* responsibilities include working in finance, engineering, human resources, research and development, marketing, and law. Candidates should have ability to work independently, analytical skills, computer skills, oral communication skills, organizational skills, self-motivation, strong interpersonal skills, strong leadership ability, writing skills. Duration is 3 months (May to August). salary depends on years at school, field, or degree. Open to college sophomores, college juniors, recent college graduates, graduate students, law students, individuals reentering the workforce. International applications accepted.

Benefits Housing at a cost, meals at a cost, on-the-job training, opportunity to attend seminars/workshops, possible full-time employment, travel reimbursement, willing to complete paperwork for educational credit, willing to provide letters of recommendation.

International Internships Available in Salzburg, Austria; Brussels, Belgium; Paris, France; Munich, Germany; Rome, Italy; Tokyo, Japan; Singapore.

Contact Write, fax, or e-mail Ana M. Trbojevich, Manager, Global College Relations, 1 Baxter Parkway, Deefield, Illinois 60015. Fax: 847-948-4494. E-mail: trbojea@baxter.com. No phone calls. In-person interview required. Applicants must submit a cover letter, resume, academic transcripts. Application deadline: March 1 for summer. World Wide Web: http://www.baxter.com.

BERMUDA BIOLOGICAL STATION FOR RESEARCH, INC.
17 Biological Lane
Ferry Reach, St. George's GE01 Bermuda

General Information Research and education center for oceanography, marine biology, and global climate change. Established in 1903. Number of employees: 100. Number of internship applications received each year: 300.
Internships Available ► *10 graduate interns:* responsibilities include conducting research with technical staff or independently. Candidates should have acceptance into graduate program by recognized university; thesis proposal must have been approved by advisor at that university; must have faculty supervisor at BBSR and approved funding. Duration is 3 months to 3 years. Unpaid. Open to graduate students. ► *8 open ocean and subtropical research experience interns:* responsibilities include conducting independent research project. Candidates should have ability to work independently, college courses in field, knowledge of field, research skills, strong interpersonal skills. Duration is August to November only. room and board is deducted from salary of $265 per week. Open to college juniors, college seniors. ► *Volunteer interns:* responsibilities include working 40 hours per week in lab of scientist who pays intern's room and board. Candidates should have computer skills, knowledge of field, organizational skills, personal interest in the field, self-motivation, strong interpersonal skills. Duration is 3-4 months; 3-5 positions per session, 3 sessions per year. Unpaid. Open to college juniors, college seniors, recent college graduates, graduate students. International applications accepted.
Benefits Opportunity to attend seminars/workshops, possible full-time employment, willing to act as a professional reference, willing to complete paperwork for educational credit, willing to provide letters of recommendation, free room and board for volunteer interns.
International Internships Available in St. George's, Bermuda.
Contact Write, call, fax, or e-mail Anne Kermode, Education Secretary, 17 Biological Lane, Ferry Reach, St. George's GEO1 Bermuda. Phone: 441-297-1880 Ext. 238. Fax: 441-297-1919. E-mail: akermo@bbsr.edu. Telephone interview required. Applicants must submit a formal organization application, cover letter, resume, academic transcripts, two personal references, two letters of recommendation. Application deadline: February 1 for summer, March 1 for research experience (fall); no application deadline for graduate interns, June 1 for fall, October 1 for spring. World Wide Web: http://www.bbsr.edu/.

CENTER FOR STRATEGIC AND BUDGETARY ASSESSMENTS
1730 Rhode Island Avenue, NW, Suite 912
Washington, District of Columbia 20036

General Information Organization that analyzes the defense budget, military strategy, and policies, and other issues and educates the media, government, and public on these issues. Established in 1983. Number of employees: 12. Number of internship applications received each year: 200.
Internships Available ► *1–2 research assistants:* responsibilities include supporting staff research, performing office and administrative tasks. Candidates should have ability to work independently, computer skills, knowledge of field, office skills, oral communication skills, written communication skills. Duration is 10–12 weeks. $260–$285 per week. Open to college juniors, college seniors, recent college graduates, graduate students.
Benefits Names of contacts, opportunity to attend seminars/workshops, willing to complete paperwork for educational credit, willing to provide letters of recommendation.
Contact Write, call, fax, or e-mail Erwin A. Godoy, Intern Coordinator, 1730 Rhode Island Avenue, NW Suite 912, Washington, District of Columbia 20036. Phone: 202-331-7990. Fax: 202-331-8019. E-mail: godoy@csbahome.com. Applicants must submit a cover letter, resume, writing sample of 3-4 pages. Application deadline: April 15 for summer, August 1 for fall, November 15 for spring. World Wide Web: http://www.csbahome.com.

CENTER FOR WOMEN POLICY STUDIES (CWPS)
1211 Connecticut Avenue, NW, Suite 312
Washington, District of Columbia 20036

General Information Public policy research and advocacy organization that advances the rights of women. Established in 1972. Number of employees: 12. Number of internship applications received each year: 150.
Internships Available ► *1–3 policy research/administrative assistants:* responsibilities include assisting with library research, fact checking, data entry, and supporting administrative staff and various programs. Candidates should have computer skills, knowledge of field, personal interest in the field, research skills, writing skills. Duration is 2–3 months. Unpaid. Open to college juniors, college seniors, recent college graduates, graduate students, career changers, individuals reentering the workforce. International applications accepted.
Benefits Opportunity to attend seminars/workshops, willing to complete paperwork for educational credit, willing to provide letters of recommendation.
Contact Write or fax Internship Coordinator. Fax: 202-296-8962. No phone calls. In-person interview recommended. Applicants must submit a cover letter, resume. Applications are accepted continuously. World Wide Web: http://www.centerwomenpolicy.org.

CENTER OF CONCERN
1225 Otis Street, NE
Washington, District of Columbia 20017

General Information Social justice research organization. Established in 1971. Number of employees: 15. Number of internship applications received each year: 100.
Internships Available ► *2–3 Global Women's Project interns:* responsibilities include research and communication on women's activities around the world. Candidates should have ability to work independently, analytical skills, college courses in field, computer skills, knowledge of field, office skills, organizational skills, research skills, written communication skills. Open to college sophomores, college juniors, college seniors, recent college graduates, graduate students. ► *2–3 foreign aid and international financial institutions project interns:* responsibilities include monitoring relevant congressional activities, drafting memos summarizing legislative developments, attending meetings, and assisting with library research and general support work. Candidates should have ability to work independently, ability to work with others, college courses in field, computer skills, editing skills, knowledge of field, office skills, oral communication skills, organizational skills, research skills, self-motivation, written communication skills. Open to college sophomores, college juniors, college seniors, recent college graduates, graduate students, law students. ► *1 fund-raising intern:* responsibilities include general fund-raising duties. Candidates should have ability to work independently, computer skills, oral communication skills, organizational skills, written communication skills. Open to college sophomores, college juniors, college seniors, recent college graduates, graduate students. ► *1 global justice education intern:* responsibilities include assisting with outreach to schools and dissemination of educational materials for elementary and secondary schools. Candidates should have ability to work independently, computer skills, oral communication skills, organizational skills, written communication skills. Open to college sophomores, college juniors, college seniors, recent college graduates, graduate students. ► *2–3 international economics research interns:* responsibilities include surveying literature; and assisting with research, networking, and general support on economic issues. Candidates should have ability to work independently, college courses in field, computer skills, knowledge of field, office skills, oral communication skills, research skills, self-motivation, strong interpersonal skills, written communication skills. Open to college seniors, recent college graduates, graduate students. ► *1 public relations intern:* responsibilities include assisting in media contact, developing and placing press release and news stories, and assisting in developing and implementing marketing strategies for publications. Candidates

should have ability to work independently, computer skills, editing skills, office skills, oral communication skills, written communication skills. Open to college sophomores, college juniors, college seniors, recent college graduates, graduate students. Duration for all positions is flexible. All positions are unpaid. International applications accepted.

Benefits Free meals, names of contacts, opportunity to attend seminars/workshops, travel reimbursement, willing to act as a professional reference, willing to complete paperwork for educational credit, willing to provide letters of recommendation, exposure to international networks and Washington, D.C. international development community.

Contact Write, fax, or e-mail Mark Torma, Administrative Coordinator. Fax: 202-832-9494. E-mail: mtorma@coc.org. No phone calls. Telephone interview required. Applicants must submit a cover letter, resume, writing sample. Applications are accepted continuously. World Wide Web: http://www.coc.org/coc.

CENTER ON POLICY ATTITUDES
1779 Massachusetts Avenue, NW, Suite 510
Washington, District of Columbia 20036

General Information Research organization, think tank, and public opinion polling organization, devoted to the study of public and elite attitudes on foreign and domestic public policy. Established in 1992. Number of employees: 10. Affiliate of University of Maryland, College Park, College Park, Maryland. Number of internship applications received each year: 200.

Internships Available ▶ *1 Web site intern:* responsibilities include assisting the Webmaster in maintaining and updating COPA's Web site, and assisting in small research tasks as needed. Candidates should have ability to work independently, ability to work with others, computer skills, editing skills, research skills, writing skills. Open to college juniors, college seniors, recent college graduates. ▶ *1–2 office interns:* responsibilities include assisting in office support by filing; maintaining database mailing lists and press lists; maintaining press clippings; and assisting on small research projects as needed. Candidates should have ability to work with others, computer skills, office skills, organizational skills, personal interest in the field, research skills. Open to college sophomores, college juniors, college seniors, recent college graduates. Duration for all positions is 1 semester. All positions paid at $7 per hour. International applications accepted.

Benefits Opportunity to attend seminars/workshops, possible full-time employment, travel reimbursement, willing to act as a professional reference, willing to provide letters of recommendation.

Contact Write, fax, or e-mail Karin Johnston, Assistant Director, 1779 Massachusetts Avenue, NW, Suite 510, Washington, District of Columbia 20036. Fax: 202-232-1159. E-mail: kjohnston@his.com. Applicants must submit a cover letter, resume. Applications are accepted continuously. World Wide Web: http://www.policyattitudes.org.

COMMITTEE FOR ECONOMIC DEVELOPMENT
2000 L Street, NW, Suite 700
Washington, District of Columbia 20036

General Information Nonprofit, nonpartisan, business-sponsored, policy organization involving 250 of the nation's business and education leaders who develop in-depth studies that are distributed to Congress, the Administration, and state, local, and public- and private-sector leaders. Established in 1942. Number of employees: 12. Number of internship applications received each year: 50.

Internships Available ▶ *4 research interns:* responsibilities include researching prospective legislation, attending and summarizing meetings and hearings, and compiling statistics and other data in connection with CED publications and studies in progress. Candidates should have analytical skills, computer skills, research skills, writing skills, college courses in economics. Duration is flexible. $1,000 per duration of internship. Open to college sophomores, college juniors, college seniors, recent college graduates. International applications accepted.

Benefits Opportunity to attend seminars/workshops, travel reimbursement, willing to complete paperwork for educational credit, willing to provide letters of recommendation, opportunity to attend congressional hearings.

Contact Write, call, fax, or e-mail Mr. Chris Dreibelbis, Intern Coordinator. Phone: 202-296-5860. Fax: 202-223-0776. E-mail: chris.dreibelbis@ced.org. Applicants must submit a cover letter, resume, academic transcripts, writing sample. Application deadline: March 20 for summer; applications accepted continuously for all others. World Wide Web: http://www.ced.org.

CONGRESSIONAL RESEARCH SERVICE, LM 205
Library of Congress, 101 Independence Avenue, SE
Washington, District of Columbia 20540-7000

General Information Organization that works exclusively for Congress conducting research, analyzing legislation, and providing information at the request of committees, members, and their staffs. Established in 1946. Number of employees: 760. Unit of Library of Congress, Washington, District of Columbia. Number of internship applications received each year: 1,000.

Internships Available ▶ *10–20 reference and library services interns:* responsibilities include performing reference duties in response to inquiries related to public policy; assisting in the development, planning, and coordinating of seminars; briefing programs for members of Congress and their staffs. Candidates should have analytical skills, research skills, writing skills, some background in policy issues involving defense, foreign policy, environmental topics, taxes, and the economy. Duration is 3–12 months. Unpaid. Open to college freshmen, college sophomores, college juniors, college seniors, recent college graduates, graduate students.

Benefits Job counseling, opportunity to attend seminars/workshops, willing to act as a professional reference, willing to complete paperwork for educational credit.

Contact Write or e-mail Warren W. Lenhart, CRS Management Specialist, Library of Congress 101 Independence Avenue, SE, Washington, District of Columbia 20540-7000. E-mail: wlenhart@crs.loc.gov. Applicants must submit a cover letter, resume. Applications are accepted continuously. World Wide Web: http://www.loc.gov/crsinfo.

COSANTI FOUNDATION-ARCOSANTI WORKSHOP
HC 74, Box 4136
Mayer, Arizona 86333

General Information Nonprofit, public educational foundation devoted to the support of Paolo Soleri's architectural and urban planning research. Established in 1962. Number of employees: 64. Number of internship applications received each year: 135.

Internships Available ▶ *1–7 agriculture/landscaping interns:* responsibilities include application of organic gardening and landscaping and permaculture on a 25.5-acre site, leading new workshop participants in daily activities, and site assessemnt and design. Candidates should have ability to work independently, ability to work with others, oral communication skills, personal interest in the field, self-motivation, strong leadership ability. Duration is 1–6 months. ▶ *1–6 arcosanti woodworking interns:* responsibilities include fabrication of cabinetry and furniture, assisting in ongoing construction of prototype arcology, and leading new workshop participants in daily projects. Candidates should have ability to work independently, personal interest in the field, self-motivation, strong interpersonal skills, mathematical aptitude. Duration is 3–6 months. ▶ *1–6 bronze foundry interns:* responsibilities include fabrication of bronze wind bells, made on site, working in all phases of fabrication from raw metal to patina using the sand cast method. Candidates should have ability to work independently, oral communication skills, personal interest in the field, self-motivation, strong interpersonal skills. Duration is 3–6 months. ▶ *1–2 ceramics department interns:* responsibilities include working in all stages of production of ceramic wind bells using the silt casting method. Candidates should have ability to work independently, oral communication skills, personal interest in the field, self-motivation, strong

Cosanti Foundation-Arcosanti Workshop (continued)

interpersonal skills. Duration is 3–12 months. ▶ *1–6 construction crew leaders/interns:* responsibilities include assisting in all phases of construction of prototype arcology, leading a small construction crew of workshop participants in designing/building the on site operation. Candidates should have ability to work with others, experience in the field, oral communication skills, organizational skills, self-motivation, strong leadership ability. Duration is 3–6 months. ▶ *Planning department interns:* responsibilities include drafting of structural and architectural details both on paper and computer, some designing/building, and working in a small designing/building office. Candidates should have ability to work with others, computer skills, oral communication skills, self-motivation, written communication skills, drafting experience. Duration is 3–6 months. ▶ *1–30 workshop participants:* responsibilities include helping in the construction of Arcosanti, a prototype for an energy-efficient town combining architectural and ecological concepts. Candidates should have ability to work independently, ability to work with others, oral communication skills, organizational skills, personal interest in the field, self-motivation. Duration is 1–5 weeks. All positions available as unpaid or at $5 per hour. Open to individuals over 18 years. International applications accepted.

Benefits Formal training, free housing, free meals, housing at a cost, names of contacts, on-the-job training, opportunity to attend seminars/workshops, possible full-time employment, willing to complete paperwork for educational credit, willing to provide letters of recommendation, partial stipend on meals.

Contact Write, call, fax, or e-mail Teri Grinlinton, Workshop Coordinator. Phone: 520-632-7135 Ext. 233. Fax: 520-632-6229. E-mail: terigrin@getnet.com. Applicants must submit a formal organization application, cover letter, resume, three personal references, $400 for 1-week seminar, $800 for 5 weeks, $50 registration fee. Application deadline: 2 weeks before workshop or 5 weeks before internship. Fees: $50. World Wide Web: http://www.arcosanti.org.

CROW CANYON ARCHAEOLOGICAL CENTER
23390 County Road K
Cortez, Colorado 81321

General Information Archaeological Center initiates and conducts significant archaeological research in the Southwest and shares the results through innovative public and professional education, open communication with Native Americans, and partnerships with institutions having common interests. Established in 1983. Number of employees: 50. Number of internship applications received each year: 100.

Internships Available ▶ *3–6 education interns:* responsibilities include assisting in teaching lay participants ranging in age from 4th graders to senior citizens about anthropological/archaeological concepts and methods, serving as docent at excavation sites and assisting in planning and implementing field trips, developing lesson plan or research project. Candidates should have knowledge of field, oral communication skills, research skills, self-motivation, strong interpersonal skills. Duration is 8–11 weeks. Open to college juniors, college seniors, recent college graduates, graduate students. ▶ *2 environmental archaeology interns:* responsibilities include archaeobotanical analysis of macrofossil and flotation samples, identification of ethnobotanical samples, analysis of ongoing modern ecological projects designed to help interpret the archaeobotanical record. Candidates should have ability to work independently, analytical skills, experience in the field, plan to pursue career in field, research skills, self-motivation. Duration is 8–11 weeks. Open to college juniors, college seniors, recent college graduates, graduate students. ▶ *4 field interns:* responsibilities include excavating and recording architectural and non-architectural contexts, mapping with a total station, site photography, instructing and supervising lay participants in basic excavation techniques and archaeological concepts. Candidates should have ability to work independently, ability to work with others, experience in the field, oral communication skills, organizational skills, research skills. Duration is 12 weeks. ▶ *4 lab interns:* responsibilities include processing, cataloging, and analyzing a variety of

archaeological samples, artifacts, maps and other records; collections and database management; maintenance of a small research library; instructing and supervising lay participants ranging in age from 4th graders to senior citizens in laboratory research. Candidates should have analytical skills, computer skills, experience in the field, organizational skills, strong interpersonal skills. Duration is 11–12 weeks. Open to college juniors, college seniors, recent college graduates, graduate students. All positions are unpaid. International applications accepted.

Benefits Free housing, free meals, names of contacts, on-the-job training, possible full-time employment, travel reimbursement, willing to act as a professional reference, willing to complete paperwork for educational credit, willing to provide letters of recommendation, modest weekly stipend, training in archaeological field and laboratory techniques, experiential teaching program.

Contact Write or e-mail Internship Coordinator. E-mail: interns@ crowcanyon.org. No phone calls. Applicants must submit a formal organization application, three personal references, telephone interview on occasion. Application deadline: February 15 for spring education, March 1 for research, March 15 for summer education, June 1 for fall education. World Wide Web: http://www.crowcanyon.org.

ECONOMIC STRATEGY INSTITUTE
1401 H Street, NW, Suite 750
Washington, District of Columbia 20005

General Information Nonprofit public policy research organization specializing in international trade issues. Established in 1989. Number of employees: 20. Number of internship applications received each year: 150.

Internships Available ▶ *1–10 research assistants:* responsibilities include assisting research associates and senior staff with trade policy research, performing general office duties, and assisting with publications. Candidates should have ability to work independently, computer skills, oral communication skills, research skills, writing skills. Duration is 3-4 months in summer or anytime during the academic year. Unpaid. Open to college freshmen, college sophomores, college juniors, college seniors, recent college graduates, graduate students, law students, career changers, individuals reentering the workforce. International applications accepted.

Benefits Opportunity to attend seminars/workshops, possible full-time employment, willing to provide letters of recommendation.

Contact Write Intern Coordinator. No phone calls. In-person interview recommended. Applicants must submit a cover letter, resume, writing sample. Applications are accepted continuously. World Wide Web: http://www.econstrat.org.

EDUCATIONAL TESTING SERVICE
Rosedale Road
Princeton, New Jersey 08541

General Information Private educational measurement institution and leader in educational research that develops and administers achievement and admission tests. Established in 1948. Number of employees: 2,000. Number of internship applications received each year: 80.

Internships Available ▶ *1 Center for Performance Assessment Postdoctoral Award Scholar:* responsibilities include independent research for the Center for Performance Assessment. Candidates should have knowledge of field. Duration is 1 year. $35,000 per duration of internship. Open to individuals who hold doctorate degree in fields related to assessment. ▶ *3 ETS Postdoctoral Fellowship Award Program interns:* responsibilities include conducting intern's own original research at ETS in fields relevant to education, psychology, psychometrics, statistics, computer science, linguistics, testing, minority issues, or policy research. Candidates should have academic scholarship with relevance to ETS research mission. Duration is 1 year. $35,000 per duration of internship. Open to doctoral-level scholars. ▶ *1 National Assessment for Educational Progress visiting scholar:* responsibilities include independent research, with access to senior NAEP staff and other ETS scientists; research should address either important educational

policy issues or measurement issues which affect the efficiency of NAEP. Candidates should have knowledge of field, oral communication skills, written communication skills, studies focused on issues concerning the education of minority students encouraged, academic leadership skills. Duration is 10 months. salary commensurate with experience. Open to doctoral-level scholars with evidence of scholarship. ▶ *1 TOEFL 2000 Postdoctoral Fellowship Award Program intern:* responsibilities include independent research and development efforts. Duration is 1 year. $35,000 per duration of internship. Open to individuals who hold a doctorate degree in linguistics or similiar discipline. ▶ *8–12 summer program in research for graduate students:* responsibilities include independent research with access to a mentor in fields relevant to education, psychology, psychometrics, statistics, computer science, linguistics, testing, minority issues, or policy research. Candidates should have computer skills, oral communication skills, research skills, written communication skills, scholarship with relevance to ETS mission. Duration is 8 weeks. $3,500 per duration of internship. Open to doctoral students who have completed one year of full-time graduate study. International applications accepted.
Benefits Housing at a cost, opportunity to attend seminars/workshops, possible full-time employment, travel reimbursement, willing to provide letters of recommendation, reimbursement of roundtrip travel expenses, and minimal compensation if accompanied by spouse or child.
Contact Write, call, fax, or e-mail Ms. Linda J. DeLauro, Fellowship Program Administrator, Rosedale Road, Mail Stop 16T, Princeton, New Jersey 08541. Phone: 609-734-1806. Fax: 609-497-6032. E-mail: ldelauro@ets.org. Applicants must submit a resume, academic transcripts, two personal references, three letters of recommendation, additional requirements vary by program (contact ETS for specifics). Application deadline: February 1. World Wide Web: http://www.ets.org.

FEMINIST MAJORITY AND FEMINIST MAJORITY FOUNDATION
8105 West Third Street, Suite 1
Los Angeles, California 90048

General Information Nonprofit research and advocacy organizations dedicated to promoting equality for women. Established in 1987. Number of employees: 10. Number of internship applications received each year: 150.
Internships Available ▶ *5–10 interns:* responsibilities include researching, writing, analyzing policy, organizing demonstrations and pro-choice rock-and-roll concerts, and clinic defense. Candidates should have ability to work independently, ability to work with others, knowledge of field, self-motivation, strong leadership ability, written communication skills. Duration is 2 months minimum. Unpaid. Open to college freshmen, college sophomores, college juniors, college seniors, recent college graduates, graduate students, law students. International applications accepted.
Benefits Job counseling, names of contacts, on-the-job training, possible full-time employment, willing to complete paperwork for educational credit, willing to provide letters of recommendation.
Contact Write or fax Diana Garcia, Internship Coordinator. Fax: 323-653-2689. Applicants must submit a cover letter, resume, writing sample, two personal references, telephone or in-person interview for finalists. Applications are accepted continuously. World Wide Web: http://www.feminist.org.

FEMINIST MAJORITY AND FEMINIST MAJORITY FOUNDATION
1600 Wilson Boulevard, Suite 801
Arlington, Virginia 22209

General Information Nonprofit research and advocacy organizations dedicated to promoting equality for women. Established in 1987. Number of employees: 20. Number of internship applications received each year: 150.
Internships Available ▶ *4–10 interns:* responsibilities include monitoring press conferences and congressional hearings; researching, writing, analyzing policy, and organizing demonstra-

tions; constructing and updating Web site; advocacy on women's rights violations outside of the U.S. Duration is 2 months minimum. stipend of $70 per week. Open to college freshmen, college sophomores, college juniors, college seniors. International applications accepted.
Benefits Names of contacts, willing to complete paperwork for educational credit, willing to provide letters of recommendation, computer training provided.
Contact Write, call, or e-mail Sarah Boonin, Coordinator, Campus Programs. Phone: 703-522-2214. Fax: 703-522-2219. E-mail: sboonin@feminist.org. Telephone interview required. Applicants must submit a cover letter, resume, writing sample, two personal references. Applications are accepted continuously. World Wide Web: http://www.feminist.org.

FOREIGN POLICY RESEARCH INSTITUTE
1528 Walnut Street, Suite 610
Philadelphia, Pennsylvania 19102

General Information Independent nonprofit organization devoted to scholarly research and public education on international affairs and publishes an academic quarterly journal. Established in 1955. Number of employees: 10. Number of internship applications received each year: 75.
Internships Available ▶ *1–2 administrative assistants:* responsibilities include general office assistance, conference preparation, public relations, development. Candidates should have computer skills, knowledge of field, office skills, organizational skills, personal interest in the field. Open to recent high school graduates, college freshmen, college sophomores, college juniors, college seniors, recent college graduates, graduate students. ▶ *1 editorial assistant:* responsibilities include proofreading, fact-checking, assisting in publication of FPRI's journal of world affairs, Orbis. Candidates should have computer skills, editing skills, knowledge of field, organizational skills, personal interest in the field. Open to college freshmen, college sophomores, college juniors, college seniors, recent college graduates, graduate students. ▶ *4–6 research assistants:* responsibilities include maintaining data files, conducting literature searches, compiling indices, general office/research help. Candidates should have computer skills, knowledge of field, organizational skills, personal interest in the field, research skills, writing skills. Open to college freshmen, college sophomores, college juniors, college seniors, recent college graduates, graduate students. Duration for all positions is 1 semester. All positions available as unpaid or paid. International applications accepted.
Benefits Opportunity to attend seminars/workshops, use of library resources, pay for those eligible for Pennsylvania state work-study only.
Contact Write, call, fax, or e-mail Keith A. Alt, Internship Coordinator. Phone: 215-732-3774 Ext. 204. Fax: 215-732-4401. E-mail: fpri@aol.com. Applicants must submit a cover letter, resume, writing sample, two letters of recommendation. Application deadline: April 1 for summer, December 1 for spring. World Wide Web: http://www.fpri.org.

FRONTIER EDUCATION CENTER
HCR 65, Box 98
Ojo Sarco, New Mexico 87521

General Information Research and advocacy organization focused on health-related frontier issues. Established in 1997. Number of employees: 2.
Internships Available ▶ *1 research assistant:* responsibilities include conducting research, compiling data, writing reports. Candidates should have ability to work independently, analytical skills, computer skills, oral communication skills, organizational skills, research skills, written communication skills, knowledge of Geographic Information System software. Position available as unpaid or at $8–$12 per hour. Open to college juniors, college seniors, recent college graduates, graduate students. International applications accepted.
Benefits On-the-job training, willing to act as a professional reference, willing to complete paperwork for educational credit, willing to provide letters of recommendation.

Frontier Education Center (continued)

Contact Write or e-mail Carol Miller, President, HCR 65 Box 98, Ojo Sarco, New Mexico 87521. E-mail: frontierus@roadrunner. com. No phone calls. Telephone interview required. Applicants must submit a cover letter, resume, writing sample, two letters of recommendation. Applications are accepted continuously.

HARVARD-SMITHSONIAN CENTER FOR ASTROPHYSICS–SMITHSONIAN ASTROPHYSICAL OBSERVATORY
60 Garden Street, Mail Stop 83
Cambridge, Massachusetts 02138

General Information Observatory dedicated to increasing knowledge through discovery and explanation of the physical processes that determine the nature and evolution of the universe. Established in 1890. Number of employees: 600. Unit of Smithsonian Institution, Washington, District of Columbia. Number of internship applications received each year: 250.
Internships Available ▶ *10–12 research interns:* responsibilities include working with scientists or individual research projects in diverse areas: observational and theoretical cosmology, extragalactic and galactic astronomy, interstellar medium and star formation, laboratory astrophysics, supernovae and supernovae remnants, and planetary science. Candidates should have ability to work independently, ability to work with others, analytical skills, computer skills, self-motivation, written communication skills, interest in physical science career. Duration is 10 weeks. $300 per week. Open to college freshmen, college sophomores, college juniors, college seniors not graduating that spring.
Benefits Free housing, job counseling, names of contacts, travel reimbursement, willing to complete paperwork for educational credit, willing to provide letters of recommendation.
Contact Write or e-mail Tania Ruiz, SAO Summer Intern Program. E-mail: intern@cfa.harvard.edu. No phone calls. Applicants must submit academic transcripts, two letters of recommendation, essay. Application deadline: February 11. World Wide Web: http://www.harvard.edu/REU.

HEALTH AND MEDICINE POLICY RESEARCH GROUP
332 South Michigan Avenue, Suite 500
Chicago, Illinois 60604

General Information Nonprofit organization that does policy research work on health care issues that affect the poor women, children, and the general population. Established in 1980. Number of employees: 6. Number of internship applications received each year: 30.
Internships Available ▶ *1–4 policy interns:* responsibilities include policy research, policy writing, office administration, and conference development. Candidates should have ability to work independently, analytical skills, college courses in field, computer skills, editing skills, knowledge of field, office skills, oral communication skills, organizational skills, personal interest in the field, plan to pursue career in field, research skills, self-motivation, strong interpersonal skills, writing skills. Duration is dependent on intern's availability. Unpaid. Open to college freshmen, college sophomores, college juniors, college seniors, recent college graduates, graduate students, law students. International applications accepted.
Benefits Names of contacts, on-the-job training, opportunity to attend seminars/workshops, willing to act as a professional reference, willing to provide letters of recommendation.
Contact Write, call, fax, or e-mail Margie Schaps, Executive Director, 332 South Michigan Avenue, Suite 500, Chicago, Illinois 60604. Phone: 312-922-8057. Fax: 312-922-6861. E-mail: hmprg@aol.com. In-person interview recommended. Applicants must submit a cover letter, resume, writing sample, personal reference. Application deadline: January 1 for spring, April 1 for summer, October 1 for winter. World Wide Web: http://www.hmprg.org.

HEALTH RISK MANAGEMENT GROUP
1711 N Street, NW, Suite 1000
Washington, District of Columbia 20036

General Information Public health research organization. Established in 1983. Number of employees: 25. Number of internship applications received each year: 50.
Internships Available ▶ *1–5 research assistants:* responsibilities include obtaining information from libraries and government organizations, critically reviewing scientific articles, keywording library articles, writing reports, attending conferences, creating tables and forms, reviewing newspapers, making presentations, and assisting researchers as needed with scientific support work. Candidates should have ability to work with others, analytical skills, college courses in field, computer skills, research skills, writing skills. Duration is 6 months or more. $10 per hour. Open to college freshmen, college sophomores, college juniors, college seniors, recent college graduates, graduate students, law students. International applications accepted.
Benefits Opportunity to attend seminars/workshops, possible full-time employment, willing to provide letters of recommendation.
Contact Write, fax, or e-mail Polly M. Thibodeau, Research Assistant Coordinator. Fax: 202-296-7576. E-mail: polly@hesgroup. com. No phone calls. In-person interview recommended. Applicants must submit a cover letter, resume, academic transcripts, writing sample. Applications are accepted continuously.

HERITAGE FOUNDATION
214 Massachusetts Avenue, NE
Washington, District of Columbia 20002

General Information Conservative think tank whose mission is to formulate and promote public policies based on the principles of free enterprise, limited government, individual freedom, traditional American values, and a strong national defense. Number of employees: 160. Number of internship applications received each year: 700.
Internships Available ▶ *40–50 academic year interns:* responsibilities include performing a variety of research and administrative assignments, attending public lectures and conferences, and assisting with computer and other projects. Duration is 1–10 weeks. $8 per day expense stipend. ▶ *40–50 summer interns:* responsibilities include performing a variety of research and administrative assignments, attending public lectures and conferences, and assisting with computer and other projects. Duration is 10 weeks. Position available as unpaid or at $250 per week. Candidates for all positions should have ability to work independently, ability to work with others, computer skills, research skills, self-motivation, writing skills. Open to college juniors, college seniors, recent college graduates. International applications accepted.
Benefits Formal training, job counseling, names of contacts, opportunity to attend seminars/workshops, possible full-time employment, travel reimbursement, willing to complete paperwork for educational credit, willing to provide letters of recommendation.
Contact Write Melissa Naudin, Intern Coordinator. Applicants must submit a cover letter, resume, writing sample, letter of recommendation. Application deadline: March 1 for summer, August 1 for fall, December 1 for spring. World Wide Web: http://www.heritage.org.

INSTITUTE FOR POLICY STUDIES
733 15th Street, NW, Suite 1020
Washington, District of Columbia 20005

General Information Progressive, nonprofit, public policy research institute that conducts research and public outreach on a range of domestic and foreign policy issues. Established in 1963. Number of employees: 20. Number of internship applications received each year: 300.
Internships Available ▶ *1 Crisis of Childhood in America Project intern:* responsibilities include researching the role of heredity in shaping personality and behavior and children's needs, the role of government in family policy, and the effects of changes in the workplace on childcare. Candidates should have ability

to work independently, ability to work with others, oral communication skills, personal interest in the field, research skills, writing skills, background in children's issues, experience in social science and database management. Duration is flexible. Open to college freshmen, college sophomores, college juniors, college seniors, graduate students, law students. ▶ *1 Cuba Project intern:* responsibilities include conducting research and assisting with writing, editing, and office work. Candidates should have ability to work independently, ability to work with others, editing skills, office skills, oral communication skills, personal interest in the field, research skills, writing skills, political science and Latin American studies coursework; Spanish language skills. Duration is 8–10 weeks. Open to college freshmen, college sophomores, college juniors, college seniors, graduate students, law students. ▶ *1 Global Communities Project intern:* responsibilities include doing extensive library research and checking of facts in areas of interest such as anti-apartheid divestment ordinances, nuclear-free zones, sister cities, and local military conversion efforts. Candidates should have ability to work independently, oral communication skills, personal interest in the field, research skills, self-motivation, writing skills, background or interest in constitutional law, international affairs, and progressive politics. Duration is flexible. Open to college freshmen, college sophomores, college juniors, college seniors, graduate students, law students. ▶ *1 Global Economic Integration Project intern:* responsibilities include producing policy papers related to issues including changes in the international division of labor, the global job crisis, and the enforcement of international labor rights; monitoring the social and environmental impact of the North American Free Trade Agreement. Candidates should have ability to work independently, ability to work with others, oral communication skills, personal interest in the field, research skills, self-motivation, writing skills. Open to college freshmen, college sophomores, college juniors, college seniors, graduate students, law students. ▶ *1 Human Rights Award Event intern:* responsibilities include marketing and planning the annual fall event marking the presentation of the international and domestic human rights award to a distinguished group or individual, engaging in extensive networking with the human rights community in Washington, D.C. Candidates should have ability to work independently, oral communication skills, organizational skills, personal interest in the field, self-motivation, strong interpersonal skills, strong leadership ability, writing skills. Duration is flexible. Open to college freshmen, college sophomores, college juniors, college seniors, graduate students, law students. ▶ *1–3 Miriam Pemlserton Economic Conversion Project interns:* responsibilities include research, writing, organizing, and dealing with administrative hassles related to the conversion of military resources to civilian use. Candidates should have ability to work independently, ability to work with others, oral communication skills, research skills, written communication skills. Duration is flexible. Open to college freshmen, college sophomores, college juniors, college seniors, recent college graduates, graduate students, law students, career changers. ▶ *1 Public Trust Research/Action intern:* responsibilities include participating in progressive politics and debates. Candidates should have ability to work independently, ability to work with others, computer skills, personal interest in the field, research skills, self-motivation, writing skills, knowledge of Internet a plus. Duration is flexible. Open to college freshmen, college sophomores, college juniors, college seniors, graduate students, law students. ▶ *1 Social Action Leadership School for Activists intern:* responsibilities include coordinating training sessions and engaging in extensive outreach to the activist community. Candidates should have ability to work with others, oral communication skills, organizational skills, personal interest in the field, strong leadership ability, writing skills. Duration is flexible. Open to college freshmen, college sophomores, college juniors, college seniors, graduate students, law students. ▶ *1 Sustainable Communities Project intern:* responsibilities include establishing a journal on sustainability. Candidates should have ability to work independently, ability to work with others, oral communication skills, organizational skills, personal interest in the field, research skills, writing skills, familiarity with environmental issues. Duration is flexible. Open to college freshmen, college sophomores, college juniors, college seniors, gradu-

ate students, law students. ▶ *1 Sustainable Energy and Environment Network intern:* responsibilities include researching and writing independent projects. Candidates should have ability to work independently, personal interest in the field, research skills, self-motivation, writing skills, background in gender studies, environmental issues, micro credit, or activities of the Bretton Woods Institutions. Duration is flexible. Open to college freshmen, college sophomores, college juniors, college seniors, graduate students, law students. ▶ *1 biographical researcher:* responsibilities include doing extensive library and archival research on the Hiroshima project, the biography of the family of MacGeorge Bundy, the Cold War, the Vietnam War, nuclear weapons, and arms control. Candidates should have ability to work independently, personal interest in the field, research skills, self-motivation, writing skills. Duration is 1 semester. Open to college freshmen, college sophomores, college juniors, college seniors, graduate students, law students. ▶ *1 corporate accountability/national tax policy/feminist agenda project intern:* responsibilities include assisting in the writing of briefing papers and articles intended to apply a liberal analysis to tax policy, and to promote more responsible corporate behavior with respect to pay equity and prevention of sexual harassment, and working jointly with Center for Advancement of Public Policy on these issues. Candidates should have ability to work independently, ability to work with others, oral communication skills, personal interest in the field, research skills, writing skills. Duration is flexible. Open to college freshmen, college sophomores, college juniors, college seniors, graduate students, law students. All positions are unpaid. International applications accepted.
Benefits Job counseling, names of contacts, opportunity to attend seminars/workshops, possible full-time employment, willing to complete paperwork for educational credit, willing to provide letters of recommendation.
Contact Write, fax, or e-mail Ms. Dorian Lipscombe, Office Manager. Fax: 202-387-7915. E-mail: dorian@igc.org. No phone calls. Applicants must submit a formal organization application, cover letter, resume, academic transcripts, writing sample, personal reference. Applications are accepted continuously.

INSTITUTE FOR SOUTHERN STUDIES
PO Box 531
Durham, North Carolina 27702

General Information Regional research and publications organization that supports community-based research and investigative journalism; publisher of Southern Exposure Magazine. Established in 1970. Number of employees: 5. Number of internship applications received each year: 15.
Internships Available ▶ *1–3 "Southern Exposure" journalism interns:* responsibilities include assisting with editing, layout, and production of a quarterly magazine focused on social change in the southern U.S.; some opportunities for writing articles. Candidates should have ability to work independently, computer skills, editing skills, strong interpersonal skills, written communication skills, interest in social change movements. ▶ *1–3 research interns:* responsibilities include assisting research staff as they engage in community-based research to promote long-term positive social change in the southern U.S. Candidates should have ability to work independently, analytical skills, personal interest in the field, research skills, writing skills, written communication skills. Open to college freshmen, college sophomores, college juniors, college seniors, recent college graduates, graduate students, law students, career changers. Duration for all positions is 2–6 months. All positions available as unpaid or paid. International applications accepted.
Benefits Names of contacts, possible full-time employment, willing to act as a professional reference, willing to complete paperwork for educational credit, willing to provide letters of recommendation.
Contact Write, call, fax, or e-mail Rev. Aqueelah As-Salaam, Executive Director. Phone: 919-419-8311 Ext. 24. Fax: 919-419-8315. E-mail: aqueell@aol.com. Telephone interview required. Applicants must submit a cover letter, resume. Applications are accepted continuously. World Wide Web: http://www.i4south.org.

INSTITUTE OF ECOSYSTEM STUDIES (IES)
Box R
Millbrook, New York 12545-0178

General Information Ecological research and education institute. Established in 1983. Number of employees: 100. Number of internship applications received each year: 200.

Internships Available ▶ *8–10 research experiences for undergraduates interns:* responsibilities include working closely with a mentor scientist, developing and conducting an independent ecological research project and writing a paper for an Institute publication, and presenting results at a formal symposium. Duration is 3 months. $3,000 per duration of internship. Open to college freshmen, college sophomores, college juniors, first semester seniors.

Benefits Housing at a cost, names of contacts, opportunity to attend seminars/workshops, possible full-time employment, willing to complete paperwork for educational credit, willing to provide letters of recommendation.

Contact Write, call, fax, or e-mail Stephanie Shoemaker, REU Program Coordinator. Phone: 914-677-7645. Fax: 914-677-6455. E-mail: shoemakers@ecostudies.org. Applicants must submit a formal organization application, resume. Application deadline: February 15 for summer. World Wide Web: http://www.ecostudies.org.

INTERHEMISPHERIC RESOURCE CENTER
PO Box 2178
Silver City, New Mexico 88062

General Information Private, nonprofit research and analysis policy institute producing books, policy reports, and periodicals on U.S. foreign relations, as well as sponsoring popular education projects. Established in 1979. Number of employees: 14. Number of internship applications received each year: 100.

Internships Available ▶ *1–4 research interns:* responsibilities include working with staff writers compiling information on U.S. foreign policy and the U.S.-Mexico border. Candidates should have ability to work independently, computer skills, knowledge of field, personal interest in the field, research skills, written communication skills. Duration is 1 semester. Unpaid. Open to college freshmen, college sophomores, college juniors, college seniors, recent college graduates, graduate students. International applications accepted.

Benefits Free housing, on-the-job training, opportunity to attend seminars/workshops, possible full-time employment, willing to complete paperwork for educational credit, willing to provide letters of recommendation.

Contact Write, call, fax, or e-mail Ms. Debra Preusch, Director. Phone: 505-388-0208. Fax: 505-388-0619. E-mail: irc1@zianet.com. Telephone interview required. Applicants must submit a cover letter, resume, writing sample, 3 letters of recommendation, including 2 from professors. Applications are accepted continuously. World Wide Web: http://www.zianet.com/irc1.

INTERNATIONAL RESEARCH AND EVALUATION
21098 IRE Control Center
Eagan, Minnesota 55121-0098

General Information Private, nonpartisan, interdisciplinary research company that collects, indexes, stores, synthesizes, retrieves, and disseminates information on-line and on-demand. Established in 1972. Number of employees: 119. Number of internship applications received each year: 53.

Internships Available ▶ *3–8 interactive multimedia platform interns:* responsibilities include securing input and scanning and embedding data into user–friendly multimedia platforms. Candidates should have analytical skills, knowledge of field, plan to pursue career in field, self-motivation. Duration is 3 months. $9–$20 per hour. Open to recent high school graduates, college freshmen, college sophomores, college juniors, college seniors, recent college graduates, graduate students. International applications accepted.

Benefits Formal training, health insurance, opportunity to attend seminars/workshops, possible full-time employment, willing to complete paperwork for educational credit.

Contact Write Valantina Voight, Internship Director. E-mail: ireittn@gte.net. No phone calls. In-person interview required. Applicants must submit a cover letter, academic transcripts. Applications are accepted continuously.

INVESTOR RESPONSIBILITY RESEARCH CENTER
1350 Connecticut Avenue, NW, Suite 700
Washington, District of Columbia 20036-1701

General Information Not-for-profit research organization that reports to nearly 500 institutional investors on a wide range of questions relating to the role of business in society. Established in 1972.

Internships Available ▶ *4–6 research interns:* responsibilities include writing reports or articles; compiling databases on selected topics; and working on surveys concerning stockholders, questions relating to social responsibility, and corporate governance issues. Duration is flexible. Position available as unpaid or paid. Open to students receiving credit. International applications accepted.

Contact Write or fax Internship Program, 1350 Connecticut Avenue, NW Suite 700, Washington, District of Columbia 20036-1701. Fax: 202-833-3555. No phone calls. In-person interview recommended. Applicants must submit a cover letter, resume, writing sample. Applications are accepted continuously.

JAPAN ECONOMIC INSTITUTE
1000 Connecticut Avenue, NW, Suite 211
Washington, District of Columbia 20036

General Information Nonprofit research organization devoted to disseminating information and objective analysis on the Japanese economy and U.S.-Japan political and economic relations. Established in 1957. Number of employees: 13. Number of internship applications received each year: 10.

Internships Available ▶ *1 intern:* responsibilities include providing general research support by attending Congressional hearings, doing library research, and gathering data; and assisting media outreach director with press releases and media database. Candidates should have ability to work independently, analytical skills, college courses in field, computer skills, knowledge of field, oral communication skills, research skills, self-motivation, strong interpersonal skills, written communication skills. Duration is 12 weeks. Unpaid. Open to college freshmen, college sophomores, college juniors.

Benefits Opportunity to attend seminars/workshops, willing to complete paperwork for educational credit, willing to provide letters of recommendation.

Contact Write Barbara Wanner, Senior Political Analyst and Intern Supervisor, 1000 Connecticut Avenue, NW Suite 211, Washington, District of Columbia 20036. In-person interview recommended. Applicants must submit a cover letter, resume, academic transcripts, 1 writing sample (up to 5 pages). Application deadline: March 31 for summer, July 31 for fall, November 30 for spring.

JOSEPH HENRY PAPERS, SMITHSONIAN INSTITUTION
Arts and Industries Building 2188, 900 Jefferson Drive, SW
Washington, District of Columbia 20560-0429

General Information Historical documentary editing project preparing a 15-volume selective letterpress edition of the papers of Joseph Henry (1797-1878), an eminent American physicist, professor at Princeton University, and the first Secretary of the Smithsonian Institution. Established in 1967. Number of employees: 4. Division of Smithsonian Institution, Washington, District of Columbia. Number of internship applications received each year: 25.

Internships Available ▶ *1–3 research interns:* responsibilities include conducting historical research on selected or assigned topics relating to documents or themes to be treated in current or future volumes of *The Papers of Joseph Henry*. Candidates should have ability to work independently, ability to work with others, personal interest in the field, research skills, self-motivation, written communication skills. Duration is 2–3 months. Unpaid. Open to college sophomores, college juniors, college seniors, recent college graduates, graduate students, career changers. International applications accepted.

Benefits Health insurance, job counseling, opportunity to attend seminars/workshops, willing to act as a professional reference, willing to complete paperwork for educational credit, willing to provide letters of recommendation, use of research facilities, 20% discount at museum store, stipends may be available.

Contact Write, call, fax, or e-mail Mr. Marc Rothenberg, Internship Coordinator/Editor, Arts and Industries Building 2188 900 Jefferson Drive, SW, Washington, District of Columbia 20560-0429. Phone: 202-357-1421 Ext. 18. Fax: 202-786-2878. E-mail: rothenbergm@osia.si.edu. Applicants must submit a formal organization application, academic transcripts, writing sample, letter of recommendation. Application deadline: April 1 for summer. World Wide Web: http://www.si.edu/archives/ihd/jhp.

KENNAN INSTITUTE FOR ADVANCED RUSSIAN STUDIES
1300 Pennsylvania Avenue, NW
Washington, District of Columbia 20523

General Information Institute that sponsors domestic and foreign scholars to conduct research in residence on topics related to the former Soviet Union. Established in 1974. Number of employees: 6. Program of Woodrow Wilson International Center for Scholars, Washington, District of Columbia. Number of internship applications received each year: 40.

Internships Available ▶ *10–15 research interns:* responsibilities include providing research assistance for a scholar in residence, conducting research, translating, editing, some photocopying, summarizing research articles, compiling bibliographies, and writing reports. Candidates should have ability to work independently, editing skills, knowledge of field, organizational skills, research skills, Russian language ability. Duration is 3–9 months. $52 per week. Open to college juniors, college seniors, recent college graduates, graduate students, law students. ▶ *1 staff intern:* responsibilities include providing assistance to various staff members, organizing and maintaining library, and researching assignments. Candidates should have ability to work independently, college courses in field, office skills, organizational skills, Russian or Ukrainian language skills. Duration is 3 months minimum. $4 per hour.

Benefits Opportunity to attend seminars/workshops, willing to complete paperwork for educational credit, willing to provide letters of recommendation.

Contact Write, call, fax, or e-mail Mr. Joseph Dresen, Intern Coordinator, 1300 Pennsylvania Avenue, NW, Washington, District of Columbia 20523. Phone: 202-691-4245. Fax: 202-691-4247. E-mail: dresenjo@wwic.si.edu. In-person interview recommended. Applicants must submit a cover letter, resume. Applications are accepted continuously. World Wide Web: http://wwics.si.edu/PROGRAMS/REGION/KENNAN/KENNAN.HTM.

LAMONT-DOHERTY EARTH OBSERVATORY
Room 103A Oceanography
Palisades, New York 10964

General Information Organization involved in geological, oceanographic, environmental, and climatic research. Established in 1948. Number of employees: 550. Number of internship applications received each year: 170.

Internships Available ▶ *14–20 summer interns:* responsibilities include undertaking research projects in oceanography, marine geophysics, geochemistry, and geology. Candidates should have analytical skills, computer skills, knowledge of field, personal interest in the field, written communication skills, 2 semesters of calculus. Duration is 10 weeks. $2,420 per duration of internship. Open to college sophomores, college juniors.

Benefits Free housing, names of contacts, opportunity to attend seminars/workshops, willing to complete paperwork for educational credit, willing to provide letters of recommendation, travel reimbursement (for travel over 200 miles).

Contact Write or e-mail Dr. Dallas Abbott, Summer Internship Program Director. E-mail: dallas@ldeo.columbia.edu. No phone calls. Applicants must submit a cover letter, academic transcripts, writing sample, three personal references, two letters of recommendation. Application deadline: March 10 for summer. World Wide Web: http://www.ldeo.columbia.edu/~dallas/abbott_sum.html.

LAWRENCE LIVERMORE NATIONAL LABORATORY, UNDERGRADUATE SUMMER INSTITUTE
PO Box 808, L-353
Livermore, California 94551-0808

General Information Research facility providing scientific and technological expertise; dedicated to global security, the environment, and the future scientific needs of the nation. Established in 1985. Number of employees: 8,000. Number of internship applications received each year: 100.

Internships Available ▶ *30–34 interns:* responsibilities include attending lectures on fusion, lasers, computational modeling, physics, chemistry, engineering, and national security. Candidates should have major in applied science field, experience in a lab science setting in previous summers is preferred. Duration is 2 weeks in August. daily allowance for living expenses (amount varies) in addition to $500 stipend. Open to students who will be beginning their senior year of college in the fall following the internship.

Benefits Free housing, free meals, opportunity to attend seminars/workshops, travel reimbursement, opportunity to work on small research projects.

Contact Write, call, fax, or e-mail Kathleen Poeckert, Undergraduate Summer Institute Administrative Chair. Phone: 925-423-7709. Fax: 925-422-2644. E-mail: poeckert1@llnl.gov. Applicants must submit a formal organization application, cover letter, resume, academic transcripts, three personal references. Application deadline: February 28. World Wide Web: http://www.llnl.gov/usi/.

LIBRARY OF CONGRESS–CONGRESSIONAL RESEARCH SERVICE
CRS/LM-205
Washington, District of Columbia 20540-7000

General Information Service that provides objective, nonpartisan research, analysis, and reference services to members and committees of Congress and their staff. Research divisions are American law; domestic social policy; foreign affairs, defense and trade; government and finance; information research, resources, science, and industry. Number of employees: 700. Number of internship applications received each year: 1,000.

Internships Available ▶ *East and South Asian issues interns:* responsibilities include working with analysts on issues surrounding policy and economic and political developments in East and South Asia. Candidates should have research skills, writing skills, knowledge of computer and statistical skills are a plus. Open to college seniors, graduate students, professionals. ▶ *Europe/Eurasia issues interns:* responsibilities include working with analysts to cover the European and Central Asian countries in their regions, including Germany, France, Britain, Russia, Ukraine, Kosovo, and Bosnia. Candidates should have research skills, writing skills, knowledge of computer and statistical skills are a plus. Open to college seniors, graduate students, professionals. ▶ *Latin-American, Middle-Eastern, and African issues interns:* responsibilities include working with analysts to cover politics and economics in the three regions. Candidates should have research skills, writing skills, knowledge of computer and statistical skills are a plus. Open to college seniors, graduate students, professionals. ▶ *1 agricultural and food issues intern:* responsibilities include assisting analysts in providing Congress with information on and analyses of domestic farm policy, the programs and policies of the U.S. Department of Agriculture, and agricultural trade.

Library of Congress–Congressional Research Service (continued)

Candidates should have research skills, writing skills, knowledge of computer and statistical skills are a plus. Open to college seniors and graduate students in the social, biological or physical sciences. ▶ *1 children's health insurance issues intern:* responsibilities include assisting on a project to analyze state plan materials submitted during the implementation of the State Children's Health Program (S-CHIP). Candidates should have computer skills, research skills, writing skills, background in health and/or social policy is preferred. Duration is 3–12 months. Open to undergraduates or graduate students in the social sciences or public policy. ▶ *Defense resources issues interns:* responsibilities include working with analysts and specialists to provide support to Congress as it considers the annual defense authorization and appropriations bills, and helping to provide expertise on military base closures in the U.S., participation by DOD in peacekeeping operations, and issues involving the U.S. intelligence community. Candidates should have research skills, writing skills, knowledge of computer and statistical skills are a plus. Open to college seniors, graduate students, professionals. ▶ *1 endangered species and ecology issues intern:* responsibilities include working on issues relating to reauthorization and funding of the Endangered Species Act, management and funding of National Wildlife Refuges, and control and impact of invasive species. Candidates should have research skills, writing skills, knowledge of word processing. Open to college graduates, graduate students, or professionals in the biological or ecological sciences. ▶ *1 energy and minerals issues intern:* responsibilities include assisting analysts in providing Congress with information on and analyses of energy resources, energy security, energy-related environmental effects, electric utilities, mineral resources, nuclear waste disposal, and nuclear proliferation. Candidates should have research skills, writing skills, knowledge of computer and statistical skills are a plus. Open to college seniors or graduate students in the social, biological, or physical sciences. ▶ *1 environmental policy issues intern:* responsibilities include assisting analysts in providing Congress with information on and analyses of environmental quality and policies related to assessing, restoring, maintaining, and implementing programs administered by the Environmental Protection Agency. Candidates should have research skills, writing skills, knowledge of computer and statistical skills are a plus. Open to graduate students in the social, biological, or physical sciences. ▶ *1 federal lands and multiple use management issues intern:* responsibilities include helping in preparing responses to requests from Congress members and committees on management planning for the National Forest System and Bureau of Land Management's public lands; implementation of plans and activities; and the resulting uses and outputs, land and resource conditions, and economic and environmental effects. Candidates should have research skills, writing skills, knowledge of computer and statistical skills are a plus. Open to college graduates, graduate students, or professionals in the social, biological, or physical sciences. ▶ *Foreign and trade policy management issues interns:* responsibilities include working with analysts on issues such as U.S. foreign aid programs; strategies and resources allocations; State Department budget, management, and embassy security; foreign affairs; agency reorganization issues; debt reduction initiatives for poor countries; public diplomacy and international broadcasting; and legislation on foreign relations. Candidates should have research skills, writing skills, knowledge of computer and statistical skills are a plus. Open to college seniors, graduate students, professionals. ▶ *1 telecommunications policy issues intern:* responsibilities include working on policy-relevant research of interest to the intern and on projects in response to Congressional requests, including alternative telecommunications delivery systems, competition in developing markets, and the changing telecommunications market structures. Candidates should have research skills, writing skills, knowledge of computer and statistical skills are a plus. Open to graduate students, postgraduates, and professionals in economics or a related field. All positions are unpaid. International applications accepted.

Benefits Opportunity to attend seminars/workshops, willing to act as a professional reference, willing to complete paperwork for educational credit, willing to provide letters of recommendation.

Contact Write or fax Warren W. Lenhart, Management Specialist. Fax: 202-707-2615. Applicants must submit a cover letter, resume, academic transcripts (optional). Applications are accepted continuously. World Wide Web: http://www.loc.gov/crsinfo.

LINCOLN LABORATORY, MASSACHUSETTS INSTITUTE OF TECHNOLOGY
244 Wood Street
Lexington, Massachusetts 02420-9108

General Information Research and development center whose primary focus is in the field of advanced electronics; research includes space surveillance, tactical systems, satellite communications, and radar and air traffic control systems. Established in 1951. Number of employees: 2,250. Number of internship applications received each year: 40.

Internships Available ▶ *15 summer technical assistants:* responsibilities include designing hardware, conducting scientific programming, and offering technical support. Candidates should have minimum 3.0 GPA; major in physics or mathematics. Duration is 10 weeks. Paid. Open to college juniors and seniors who are minority members (African Americans, Puerto Ricans, Mexican Americans, Native Americans).

Benefits Formal training, housing at a cost, job counseling, opportunity to attend seminars/workshops, possible full-time employment, travel reimbursement, willing to provide letters of recommendation.

Contact Write, call, fax, or e-mail Mr. Paul F. Hezel, 844 Wood Street, Lexington, Massachusetts 02420-9108. Phone: 781-981-7048. Fax: 781-981-7086. E-mail: hezel@ll.mit.edu. Applicants must submit a formal organization application, cover letter, resume, academic transcripts, two letters of recommendation. Application deadline: February 15. World Wide Web: http://www.ll.mit.edu.

LUNAR AND PLANETARY INSTITUTE
3600 Bay Area Boulevard
Houston, Texas 77058-1113

General Information Institute whose goal is to facilitate methods for the distribution of results of current research in planetary science to the worldwide scientific community. Established in 1968. Number of employees: 60. Unit of Universities Space Research Association, Columbia, Maryland. Number of internship applications received each year: 130.

Internships Available ▶ *10–12 interns:* responsibilities include participating actively in lunar/planetary research with scientists at the institute and the NASA Johnson Space Center in such areas as cosmic dust characterization, meteorite fall statistics, planetary rigolith studies, Mars soil analog chemistry, trace element partitioning studies, volcano morphology characterization, planetary volcanism and thermal histories, thermal and mechanical modeling of planetary interiors, database management systems, and search for micro-organisms in geologic samples. Candidates should have ability to work independently, college courses in field, computer skills, declared college major in field, experience in the field, plan to pursue career in field, 50 semester hours of credit. Duration is 10 weeks. $350 per week. Open to college sophomores, college juniors, college seniors, recent college graduates. International applications accepted.

Benefits Housing at a cost, opportunity to attend seminars/workshops, up to $1000 travel allowance.

Contact Write, fax, or e-mail Ms. Cecilia M. Hoelscher, Intern Program Administrator. Fax: 281-486-2132. E-mail: hoelscher@lpi.jsc.nasa.gov. Applicants must submit a cover letter, academic transcripts, three letters of recommendation, biographical sketch, including goals, career plans, scientific interests, reason for application, major field of study. Application deadline: February 4 for summer. World Wide Web: http://cass.jsc.nasa.gov/lpiintern.html.

MARIA MITCHELL OBSERVATORY
3 Vestal Street
Nantucket, Massachusetts 02554

General Information Observatory that runs an active, diverse program in astronomical research and an educational outreach program. Established in 1908. Number of employees: 7. Unit of Maria Mitchell Association, Nantucket, Massachusetts. Number of internship applications received each year: 100.

Internships Available ▶ *6 summer research assistants:* responsibilities include performing scientific research and participating in public and educational programs. Candidates should have computer skills, oral communication skills, personal interest in the field, plan to pursue career in field, research skills, self-motivation. Duration is 10–15 weeks. $1,100 per month. Open to college freshmen, college sophomores, college juniors, college seniors, must be U.S. citizen or have permanent residency.

Benefits Free housing, job counseling, names of contacts, on-the-job training, opportunity to attend seminars/workshops, travel reimbursement, tuition assistance, willing to complete paperwork for educational credit, willing to provide letters of recommendation.

Contact Write, call, fax, or e-mail Dr. Vladimir Strelnitski, Director. Phone: 508-228-9273. Fax: 508-228-1031. E-mail: vladimir@mmo.org. Telephone interview required. Applicants must submit a formal organization application, cover letter, resume, academic transcripts, three letters of recommendation. Application deadline: February 15. World Wide Web: http://www.mmo.org.

MELPOMENE INSTITUTE FOR WOMEN'S HEALTH RESEARCH
1010 University Avenue
St. Paul, Minnesota 55104

General Information Organization helping girls and women of all ages to link physical activity and health through research, education, and publication.

Internships Available ▶ *3–6 interns:* responsibilities include a variety of assignments in health research, marketing/public relations, or computer projects depending on intern's background and interests. Candidates should have ability to work independently, computer skills, experience in the field, oral communication skills, personal interest in the field, writing skills, experience with Macintosh computers is helpful but not required. Duration is 13-15 weeks (10-12 hours per week). Unpaid. Open to college freshmen, college sophomores, college juniors, college seniors, recent college graduates, graduate students, career changers, individuals reentering the workforce.

Benefits On-the-job training, real chance to contribute to research on women's health, small stipend.

Contact Write, call, fax, or e-mail Renee Carey, Intern Coordinator, 1010 University Avenue, St. Paul, Minnesota 55104. Phone: 651-642-1951. Fax: 651-642-1871. E-mail: melpomen@skypoint.com. Applicants must submit a formal organization application, cover letter, resume. Application deadline: April 1 for summer; continuous for remainder of year. World Wide Web: http://www.melpomene.org.

MOTE MARINE LABORATORY
1600 Ken Thompson Parkway
Sarasota, Florida 34236

General Information Independent nonprofit organization dedicated to research in marine and environmental sciences. Established in 1955. Number of employees: 100. Number of internship applications received each year: 300.

Internships Available ▶ *2–5 business interns:* responsibilities include business and financial duties, including bookkeeping, accounts payable, and accounts receivable. Candidates should have ability to work independently, ability to work with others, computer skills, office skills, organizational skills, personal interest in the field, plan to pursue career in field, self-motivation. Open to college juniors, college seniors. ▶ *2–3 communications interns:* responsibilities include press release writing, preparation of articles for newsletters and magazines, and office assistance. Candidates should have ability to work with others, college courses in field, computer skills, editing skills, written communication skills. Open to college sophomores, college juniors, college seniors, recent college graduates. ▶ *2–5 development office interns:* responsibilities include administrative duties in marketing/development office. Candidates should have ability to work independently, college courses in field, computer skills, office skills, oral communication skills, personal interest in the field, plan to pursue career in field, self-motivation, strong interpersonal skills, written communication skills. Open to college juniors, college seniors. ▶ *2–5 education interns:* responsibilities include assisting as instructors and designing education program. Candidates should have ability to work independently, ability to work with others, college courses in field, oral communication skills, plan to pursue career in field, strong leadership ability. Open to college sophomores, college juniors, college seniors, recent college graduates. ▶ *20–50 research interns:* responsibilities include various duties depending on assigned research area, such as tissue processing, sediment and water analysis, animal monitoring, data entry, and report writing. Candidates should have ability to work independently, college courses in field, plan to pursue career in field, research skills, self-motivation. Open to recent high school graduates, college sophomores, college juniors, college seniors. Duration for all positions is 8–16 weeks. All positions are unpaid. International applications accepted.

Benefits Housing at a cost, on-the-job training, opportunity to attend seminars/workshops, willing to act as a professional reference, willing to complete paperwork for educational credit, willing to provide letters of recommendation, free aquarium admission, gift shop discount.

Contact Write, call, fax, or e-mail Andrea Davis, Coordinator of Intern/Volunteer Services. Phone: 941-388-4441. Fax: 941-388-4312. E-mail: adavis@mote.org. Applicants must submit a formal organization application, academic transcripts, writing sample. Applications are accepted continuously. World Wide Web: http://www.mote.org.

NATIONAL ASTRONOMY AND IONOSPHERE CENTER (NAIC)
Cornell University, 504 Space Sciences Building
Ithaca, New York 14853-6801

General Information Center for atmospheric sciences, radar, and radio astronomy that operates the world's largest single dish radio telescope located in Puerto Rico. Established in 1963. Number of employees: 135. Unit of Cornell University. Number of internship applications received each year: 175.

Internships Available ▶ *8–10 summer research assistants:* responsibilities include participation in research projects such as searches for pulsars; studies of galaxies, giant stars, or interstellar medium; investigation of ionized portions of the earth's atmosphere; mapping planets or other members of the solar system; and developing projects for instrumentation or software. Candidates should have ability to work independently, ability to work with others, college courses in field, computer skills, knowledge of field, research skills, self-motivation. Duration is 10 weeks. $1,470 per month. Open to college freshmen, college sophomores, college juniors.

Benefits Formal training, housing at a cost, meals at a cost, opportunity to attend seminars/workshops, travel reimbursement, willing to complete paperwork for educational credit, willing to provide letters of recommendation.

Contact Write, fax, or e-mail Ms. Jill Morrison, Administrative Assistant, Cornell University 504 Space Sciences Building, Ithaca, New York 14853-6801. Fax: 607-255-8803. E-mail: jtm14@cornell.edu. Applicants must submit a formal organization application, cover letter, academic transcripts, three letters of recommendation. Application deadline: February 15. World Wide Web: http://www.naic.edu.

NATIONAL CENTER FOR ECONOMIC AND SECURITY ALTERNATIVES
2000 P Street, NW, Suite 330
Washington, District of Columbia 20036-6923

General Information Nonprofit research organization. Established in 1977. Number of employees: 8. Number of internship applications received each year: 100.

Internships Available ▶ *2–3 Third Way interns:* responsibilities include conducting research on innovative economic institutions which increase community economic stability, for example local currencies, worker-owned firms, and community development corporations. Candidates should have ability to work independently, personal interest in the field, research skills, writing skills. Unpaid. Open to college freshmen, college sophomores, college juniors, college seniors, recent college graduates, graduate students, career changers. ▶ *1–2 War and Economy in the 20th Century interns:* responsibilities include researching and writing on the economic effects of war and military spending on the U.S. economy in the 20th century, focusing particularly on Keynesian effects. Candidates should have ability to work independently, college courses in field, knowledge of field, research skills, self-motivation, written communication skills. Position available as unpaid or paid. Open to college juniors, college seniors, recent college graduates, graduate students. ▶ *3–4 good society interns:* responsibilities include research into theoretical and/or practical elements of a new political economic system that would support the core values of equality, democracy, community, and liberty. Candidates should have ability to work independently, knowledge of field, personal interest in the field, research skills, self-motivation, writing skills. Unpaid. Open to college freshmen, college sophomores, college juniors, college seniors, recent college graduates, graduate students, career changers. Duration for all positions is 3–4 months. International applications accepted.

Benefits Names of contacts, on-the-job training, opportunity to attend seminars/workshops, possible full-time employment, willing to act as a professional reference, willing to complete paperwork for educational credit, willing to provide letters of recommendation, opportunity to do professional-level research.

Contact Write, call, or fax Intern Coordinator. Phone: 202-835-1150. Fax: 202-835-1150. In-person interview recommended. Applicants must submit a cover letter, resume, three personal references, 1-2 writing samples. Applications are accepted continuously. World Wide Web: http://www.ncesa.org.

NATIONAL CENTER FOR TOXICOLOGICAL RESEARCH (NCTR)
3900 NCTR Road
Jefferson, Arkansas 72079

General Information Center that conducts peer-reviewed biological research relevant to the current and future needs of the Food and Drug Administration. Established in 1971. Number of employees: 600. Unit of Food and Drug Administration, Rockville, Maryland. Number of internship applications received each year: 55.

Internships Available ▶ *8–10 student interns:* responsibilities include participating part-time on-site at NCTR in biological research experiments under the mentorship of an NCTR scientist (while full-time student at an accredited college or university). Candidates should have ability to work independently, ability to work with others, analytical skills, college courses in field, editing skills, oral communication skills, plan to pursue career in field, research skills, self-motivation, writing skills. Duration is 1 year. $12,800—$20,735 stipend per year (part-time). Open to college sophomores, college juniors, college seniors, recent college graduates, graduate students, students must be from local area. ▶ *15–17 summer student research program interns:* responsibilities include conducting biological research studies (may involve laboratory animals, probably rodents), preparing written reports, and making an oral presentation of research results under mentorship of an NCTR scientist. Candidates should have ability to work independently, ability to work with others, analytical skills, college courses in field, oral communication skills, research

skills, self-motivation, writing skills. Duration is 3 months. $1392—$2658 stipend per month. Open to college freshmen, college sophomores, college juniors, college seniors, recent college graduates, graduate students, pre-postdoctoral students.

Benefits On-the-job training, opportunity to attend seminars/workshops.

Contact Write, call, fax, or e-mail Pat Pressley, Program Assistant, Oak Ridge Institute for Science and Education (ORISE), Oak Ridge, Tennessee 37831-0117. Phone: 423-241-5654. Fax: 423-241-5219. E-mail: presslep@orau.gov. Applicants must submit a formal organization application, cover letter, academic transcripts, three personal references, three letters of recommendation. Application deadline: March 1 for summer student research program; continuous for student interns. World Wide Web: http://www.nctr.fda.gov.

NATIONAL OPINION RESEARCH CENTER
1155 East 60th Street
Chicago, Illinois 60637

General Information Social science research center that studies health, education, labor, alcohol and drug abuse, and other areas of public policy interest; located at University of Chicago. Established in 1941. Number of employees: 500. Number of internship applications received each year: 175.

Internships Available ▶ *12–15 summer interns:* responsibilities include assisting project staff in coding, editing, and data entry of questionnaires; preparing interviewer training materials; sampling; questionnaire design; and instrument testing. Candidates should have ability to work with others, analytical skills, college courses in field, personal interest in the field, writing skills. Duration is 10 weeks. $8–$10 per hour. Open to college juniors, college seniors, graduate students. International applications accepted.

Benefits Possible full-time employment, willing to complete paperwork for educational credit.

Contact Write, call, fax, or e-mail Ms. Linda Sharp, Human Resources Associate. Phone: 773-256-6053. Fax: 773-753-7808. E-mail: sharp-linda@norcmail.uchicago.edu. Telephone interview required. Applicants must submit a cover letter, resume, 5-page writing sample. Application deadline: April 15. World Wide Web: http://www.norc.uchicago.edu.

NATIONAL SECURITY ARCHIVE, THE GEORGE WASHINGTON UNIVERSITY
Gelman Library, Suite 701, 2130 H Street, NW
Washington, District of Columbia 20037

General Information Nonprofit research institute, library, and publisher providing scholars, journalists, librarians, students, and other researchers with unclassified and declassified government documents for research and informed debate. Established in 1985. Number of employees: 25. Number of internship applications received each year: 150.

Internships Available ▶ *5–10 interns:* responsibilities include performing library and archival research; building chronology of events; obtaining, ordering, and cataloging government documents; and entering computer data. Candidates should have ability to work independently, college courses in field, computer skills, knowledge of field, research skills, writing skills. Duration is 2 months. Unpaid. Open to college freshmen, college sophomores, college juniors, college seniors, recent college graduates, graduate students. International applications accepted.

Benefits Possible full-time employment, willing to complete paperwork for educational credit, willing to provide letters of recommendation.

Contact Write, call, fax, or e-mail Ms. Sue Bechtel, Administrator. Phone: 202-994-7000. Fax: 202-994-7005. E-mail: sbechtel@gwu.edu. Applicants must submit a cover letter, resume, writing sample. Application deadline: March 15 for summer (suggested), July 15 for fall (suggested), December 1 for spring (suggested). World Wide Web: http://www.seas.gwu.edu/nsarchive.

OAK RIDGE INSTITUTE FOR SCIENCE AND EDUCATION (ORISE)
MS36, PO Box 117
Oak Ridge, Tennessee 37831-0117

General Information   Organization that conducts multi-disciplinary science and engineering internships. Established in 1946. Number of employees: 500. Unit of United States Department of Energy, Washington, District of Columbia.
Internships Available   ▶ *Professional interns (graduate students):* responsibilities include participating in fossil energy-related research in the areas of chemistry, computer science, engineering, environmental sciences, geology, mathematics, physics, and statistics at any of the following sites: Savannah River Site, Federal Energy Technology Center, or Oak Ridge National Lab. $350–$871 per week. Open to graduate students. ▶ *Professional interns (undergraduate):* responsibilities include participating in fossil energy-related research in the areas of chemistry, computer science, engineering, environmental sciences, geology, mathematics, physics, and statistics at any of the following sites: Savannah River, Pittsburgh Energy Technology Center, or Oak Ridge National Lab. $250–$703 per week. Open to college freshmen, college sophomores, college juniors, college seniors, college graduates with BS received no longer than 2 years ago. ▶ *Technology interns:* responsibilities include research in the areas of chemistry, physics, engineering, mathematics, computer science, safety, and health at either of the following sites: Oak Ridge National Lab or Pittsburgh Energy Technology Center. $300 per week. Open to college sophomores at 2-year colleges. Duration for all positions is 3–18 months.
Benefits   Travel reimbursement, possible tuition assistance for off-campus students only.
Contact   Write, call, fax, or e-mail Kathy Ketner, Project Manager or Cheryl Terry, Program Specialist, Program Specialist. Phone: 423-576-3427. Fax: 423-241-5220. E-mail: ketnerk@orau.gov or terryc@orau.gov. Applicants must submit a formal organization application, academic transcripts, two letters of recommendation. Application deadline: February 15 for summer, June 1 for fall, October 1 for spring. World Wide Web: http://www.orau.gov/orise.htm.

PRESBYTERIAN CHURCH (USA), DEPARTMENT OF HISTORY
425 Lombard Street
Philadelphia, Pennsylvania 19147-1516

General Information   Archives that collect and preserve official records and personal papers of the Presbyterian Church, serve the administrative needs of the Presbyterian Church, and provide access to academic and other researchers. Established in 1852. Number of employees: 25. Unit of Presbyterian Church (USA), Louisville, Kentucky. Number of internship applications received each year: 1.
Internships Available   ▶ *1 archives department intern:* responsibilities include processing archival collections and assisting with reference questions. Candidates should have ability to work independently, college courses in field, organizational skills, personal interest in the field, research skills, written communication skills. Duration is flexible. Unpaid. Open to college freshmen, college sophomores, college juniors, college seniors, graduate students, career changers. International applications accepted.
Benefits   On-the-job training, willing to act as a professional reference, willing to complete paperwork for educational credit, willing to provide letters of recommendation.
Contact   Write Margery N. Sly, Deputy Director. In-person interview recommended. Applicants must submit a cover letter, resume, three personal references. Applications are accepted continuously. World Wide Web: http://www.pcusa.org.

PROCTER & GAMBLE COMPANY
Miami Valley Laboratories, Box 538707
Cincinnati, Ohio 45253-8707

General Information   International, technically based company engaged in the research, development, manufacture, and sale of consumer products in beauty care, cosmetics and fragrances, food and beverage, health care, laundry and cleaning, paper, and pharmaceuticals. Established in 1837. Number of employees: 95,000. Unit of Procter and Gamble, Cincinnati, Ohio. Number of internship applications received each year: 100.
Internships Available   ▶ *15–25 doctoral summer interns:* responsibilities include performing duties as full-time researcher at one corporate technical center in Cincinnati. Candidates should have ability to work with others, analytical skills, knowledge of field, oral communication skills, plan to pursue career in field, strong leadership ability, written communication skills. Duration is 10–12 weeks. $750 per week. Open to graduate students, graduating seniors going on to graduate school.
Benefits   Formal training, opportunity to attend seminars/workshops, travel reimbursement, local transportation from housing to work site, affordable university housing available.
Contact   Write or e-mail Brenda Cromer, Recruiting Coordinator, Miami Valley Laboratories Box 538707, Cincinnati, Ohio 45253-8707. Fax: 513-627-2266. E-mail: cromer.bh@pg.com. No phone calls. Applicants must submit a formal organization application, cover letter, resume, two letters of recommendation. Application deadline: March 1. World Wide Web: http://www.pg.com/careers.

RAND
1700 Main Street, PO Box 2138
Santa Monica, California 90407-2138

General Information   Private, nonprofit institution for research and analysis on issues affecting national security and the public welfare. Established in 1948. Number of employees: 1,100. Number of internship applications received each year: 200.
Internships Available   ▶ *20–25 summer interns:* responsibilities include conducting research related to dissertation and discussing problems of mutual interest with RAND researchers. Positions available in Santa Monica, CA and Washington, DC. Candidates should have ability to work independently, ability to work with others, analytical skills, oral communication skills, research skills, written communication skills. Duration is 3 months. Paid. Open to graduate students. International applications accepted.
Benefits   Names of contacts, on-the-job training, opportunity to attend seminars/workshops, possible full-time employment, travel reimbursement, willing to complete paperwork for educational credit, willing to provide letters of recommendation, opportunity to use self-written report for future portfolio/vitae.
Contact   Write, fax, or e-mail Director, Graduate Student Summer Intern Program. Fax: 310-393-4818. E-mail: keating@rand.org. Applicants must submit a cover letter, resume. Application deadline: February 1. World Wide Web: http://www.rand.org.

SDV/ACCI
21144 Mission Boulevard
Hayward, California 94541-2010

General Information   Research and software development company that provides services to the state of California, utility companies, and the federal government. Established in 1986. Number of employees: 20. Number of internship applications received each year: 30.
Internships Available   ▶ *2–3 proposal assistants:* responsibilities include assisting in marketing and human resources departments. ▶ *2–3 research assistants:* responsibilities include providing project assistance to senior level consultant. ▶ *2–3 systems administrative assistants:* responsibilities include assisting in-house systems administrator to develop or maintain systems applications and hardware. Duration for all positions is flexible. All positions paid at $7–$10 per hour. Open to high school students, high school seniors, recent high school graduates, college freshmen, college sophomores, college juniors, college seniors, recent college graduates, graduate students, career changers, individuals reentering the workforce. International applications accepted.
Benefits   Formal training, job counseling, names of contacts, opportunity to attend seminars/workshops, possible full-time

SDV/ACCI (continued)

employment, travel reimbursement, tuition assistance, willing to complete paperwork for educational credit, willing to provide letters of recommendation.

Contact Write or e-mail Penny Robinson, Director of Client Services. E-mail: acci@hothire.com. No phone calls. In-person interview required. Applicants must submit a resume. Applications are accepted continuously. World Wide Web: http://www.hothire.com.

SMITHSONIAN ENVIRONMENTAL RESEARCH CENTER
647 Contees Wharf Road, PO Box 28
Edgewater, Maryland 21037

General Information Research facility that advances stewardship of the biosphere through interdisciplinary research and educational outreach. SERC's scientists study a variety of interconnected ecosystems at the Center's primary research site in Maryland, and at affiliated sites around the world. Established in 1965. Number of employees: 80. Branch of Smithsonian Institution, Washington, District of Columbia. Number of internship applications received each year: 200.

Internships Available ▶ *1–4 environmental and ecology education interns:* responsibilities include conducting nature trail tours on Center's trails, leading group on canoe trips along tidal wetlands, assisting education staff with teacher workshops and environmental education programs. Candidates should have ability to work with others, college courses in field, computer skills, oral communication skills, plan to pursue career in field, self-motivation. Open to college sophomores, college juniors, college seniors, recent college graduates, graduate students. ▶ *1–4 environmental engineering interns:* responsibilities include assisting SERC engineers in the fields of computers, micrometeorology, nutrient and water flows, and light in ecosystems. Candidates should have ability to work independently, ability to work with others, analytical skills, college courses in field, computer skills, plan to pursue career in field, research skills. Open to college freshmen, college sophomores, college juniors, college seniors, recent college graduates, graduate students. ▶ *Environmental research interns:* responsibilities include working on a specific project under the supervision of the Center's professional staff. Projects include terrestrial and estuarine environmental research and are tailored to provide the maximum educational benefit to each participant. Candidates should have ability to work independently, ability to work with others, analytical skills, college courses in field, computer skills, plan to pursue career in field, research skills. Open to college freshmen, college sophomores, college juniors, college seniors, recent college graduates, graduate students. Duration for all positions is 10–16 weeks. All positions paid at $240–$300 per week. International applications accepted.

Benefits Housing at a cost, names of contacts, on-the-job training, opportunity to attend seminars/workshops, possible full-time employment, willing to complete paperwork for educational credit, willing to provide letters of recommendation, access to the Smithsonian Institution, availability of cooking and utensils.

Contact Write, call, or e-mail Ms. Anita Chapa, Fellowship Coordinator, PO Box 28, Edgewater, Maryland 21037. Phone: 301-261-4190 Ext. 217. E-mail: intern@serc.si.edu. Applicants must submit a formal organization application, academic transcripts, two letters of recommendation, personal essay. Application deadline: March 1 for summer (priority consideration), November 1 for spring (priority consideration). World Wide Web: http://www.serc.si.edu.

SMITHSONIAN TROPICAL RESEARCH INSTITUTE
Arts and Industries Building, 900 Jefferson Drive, SW, Suite 2207
Washington, District of Columbia 20560

General Information A center for basic research on tropical ecosystems that includes modern labs and a network of field stations located in the Republic of Panama. Unit of Smithsonian Institution, Washington, District of Columbia.

Internships Available ▶ *Interns:* responsibilities include working at marine or terrestrial research stations on projects that match interns interests and future career goals. Duration is flexible. Position available as unpaid or at stipend support available occasionally on a limited basis. Open to individuals completing undergraduate studies or beginning graduate studies in areas related to the interests of STRI staff. International applications accepted.

Benefits Willing to complete paperwork for educational credit.

International Internships Available in Panama.

Contact Write Internship Coordinator, Office of Education. Applicants must submit a formal organization application, resume, academic transcripts, personal reference, letter outlining interests, qualifications, and how you will pay for travel to Panama and room and board expenses while working there. Applications are accepted continuously. World Wide Web: http://www.si.edu/stri.

SOUTHWEST RESEARCH INSTITUTE (SWRI)
6220 Culebra Road
San Antonio, Texas 78238-5166

General Information An institute that researches and develops technology in science and engineering fields. Established in 1947. Number of employees: 2,600. Number of internship applications received each year: 2,000.

Internships Available ▶ *75 analysts:* responsibilities include assisting senior-level analysts on current projects. Candidates should have ability to work independently, college courses in field, computer skills, oral communication skills, self-motivation, strong interpersonal skills, strong leadership ability. Open to college sophomores, college juniors, college seniors, graduate students. ▶ *75 engineers:* responsibilities include assisting senior-level engineers on current projects. Candidates should have ability to work independently, college courses in field, oral communication skills, strong interpersonal skills, written communication skills. Open to college sophomores, college juniors, college seniors. ▶ *10–15 scientists:* responsibilities include assisting senior-level scientists on current projects. Candidates should have ability to work independently, college courses in field, computer skills, oral communication skills, strong interpersonal skills, written communication skills. Open to college sophomores, college juniors, college seniors. Duration for all positions is flexible. All positions paid at $11–$15 per hour.

Benefits Formal training, job counseling, names of contacts, possible full-time employment, travel reimbursement, willing to complete paperwork for educational credit, willing to provide letters of recommendation, competitive salaries based on semester hours completed and payment for relocation.

Contact Write, call, fax, or e-mail Ms. Marilyn Martin, Student Employment Coordinator. Phone: 210-522-2223. Fax: 210-522-3990. E-mail: mmartin@swri.org. Applicants must submit a formal organization application, academic transcripts. Applications are accepted continuously. World Wide Web: http://www.swri.org.

UNIVERSITY RESEARCH EXPEDITIONS PROGRAM (UREP)
University of California, Davis
Davis, California 95616

General Information Organization that matches members of the general public with University of California academics on field research projects worldwide. Established in 1976. Number of employees: 10. Unit of University of California, Davis, Davis, California. Number of internship applications received each year: 300.

Internships Available ▶ *200–300 UREP researchers:* responsibilities include working in one of the many unique programs offered by UREP; examples from last summer's projects include archaeological digs in Ireland and Peru, rain forest ecology in Ecuador and Costa Rica, and animal studies in Central and South America. Candidates should have ability to work with others, personal interest in the field, good overall health. Duration is 2–3 weeks. Unpaid. Open to recent high school graduates, college freshmen, college sophomores, college juniors, college

seniors, recent college graduates, graduate students, law students, career changers, individuals reentering the workforce, individuals 16 years of age and older. International applications accepted.
Benefits Formal training, willing to provide letters of recommendation, limited partial scholarships available.
International Internships Available.
Contact Write, call, fax, or e-mail Jean Colvin, Program Director. Phone: 530-752-0692. Fax: 530-752-0681. E-mail: urep@ucdavis. edu. Applicants must submit a formal organization application. Applications are accepted continuously. Fees: $200. World Wide Web: http://www.urep.ucdavis.edu.

THE URBAN INSTITUTE
2100 M Street, NW
Washington, District of Columbia 20037

General Information Private nonprofit, nonpartisan public policy research organization. Established in 1968. Number of employees: 357. Number of internship applications received each year: 200.
Internships Available ► *5–15 temporary research assistants:* responsibilities include assisting senior researchers in public policy research, data gathering, literature reviews, telephone survey work, and statistical analyses using a software package such as SAS or SPSS. Candidates should have analytical skills, college courses in field, computer skills, plan to pursue career in field, research skills, writing skills. Duration is flexible. $9–$14 per hour. Open to college freshmen, college sophomores, college juniors, college seniors, graduate students. International applications accepted.
Benefits On-the-job training, opportunity to attend seminars/ workshops, possible full-time employment, willing to act as a professional reference, willing to complete paperwork for educational credit, willing to provide letters of recommendation.
Contact Write, fax, or e-mail Internship Coordinator, Personnel Office. Fax: 202-887-5189. E-mail: resumes@ui.urban.org. No phone calls. In-person interview recommended. Applicants must submit a formal organization application, cover letter, resume, academic transcripts, writing sample, two personal references. Applications are accepted continuously. World Wide Web: http:// www.urban.org.

WASHINGTON INSTITUTE FOR NEAR EAST POLICY
1828 L Street, NW, Suite 1050
Washington, District of Columbia 20036

General Information Research institute that analyzes U.S. policy in the Middle East. Established in 1985. Number of employees: 25. Number of internship applications received each year: 150.
Internships Available ► *4–5 research assistants:* responsibilities include preparing reports and assisting with seminars and conferences. Candidates should have ability to work with others, analytical skills, college courses in field, research skills, writing skills, written communication skills. Duration is 1 year. $18,000–$24,000 per year. Open to recent college graduates.
► *1–8 research interns:* responsibilities include carrying out directed research and administrative duties, including at seminars. Duration is flexible (at least 4 days per week preferred). Position available as unpaid or paid. Open to college freshmen, college sophomores, college juniors, college seniors, recent college graduates, graduate students. International applications accepted.
Benefits Health insurance, opportunity to attend seminars/ workshops, possible full-time employment, willing to act as a professional reference, willing to complete paperwork for educational credit, willing to provide letters of recommendation, training, job counseling for research assistants.
Contact Write or e-mail Patrick Clawson, Director for Research. E-mail: patrickc@washingtoninstitute.org. In-person interview recommended. Applicants must submit a cover letter, resume, writing sample, explanation of knowledge of Middle East suggested. Application deadline: January 1 for spring, March 1 for research assistants, April 1 for summer. World Wide Web: http://www.washingtoninstitute.org.

WOMEN'S POLICY, INC.
409 12th Street, SW, Suite 705
Washington, District of Columbia 20024

General Information Political research and publications organization. Established in 1995. Number of employees: 4. Number of internship applications received each year: 30.
Internships Available ► *2–3 interns.* Candidates should have ability to work independently, ability to work with others, office skills, organizational skills, research skills, written communication skills. Duration is flexible. Unpaid. Open to college sophomores, college juniors, college seniors, recent college graduates, graduate students. International applications accepted.
Benefits Names of contacts, on-the-job training, opportunity to attend seminars/workshops, willing to act as a professional reference, willing to complete paperwork for educational credit, willing to provide letters of recommendation, opportunity to attend projects and events with congressional caucus for women's issues.
Contact Write, call, fax, or e-mail Whitney Painter or Jennifer Lockwood-Shabat, 409 12th Street, SW, Suite 705, Washington, District of Columbia 20024. Phone: 202-554-2323. Fax: 202-554-2346. E-mail: wpic@erols.com. In-person interview recommended. Applicants must submit a cover letter, resume, writing sample. Application deadline: April 1 for summer, August 1 for fall, November 15 for winter/spring. World Wide Web: http://orgs. womenconnect.com/wpi.

YOUTH POLICY INSTITUTE
1333 Green Court Street, NW
Washington, District of Columbia 20005

General Information Organization that performs research and analysis of public and private sector issues, curriculum development, and magazine publishing. Number of employees: 3. Number of internship applications received each year: 150.
Internships Available ► *2–3 research assistants:* responsibilities include learning the corps methodology and applying it to a topic of intern's choice, some office administration and layout of a semi-monthly publication. Duration is 6–12 months. Position available as unpaid or paid. Open to college juniors, college seniors, recent college graduates, graduate students, law students. International applications accepted.
Benefits Formal training, possible full-time employment, willing to complete paperwork for educational credit, willing to provide letters of recommendation.
Contact Write, call, fax, or e-mail David L. Hackett, Executive Director. Phone: 202-638-2144. Fax: 202-638-2325. E-mail: corpsnet@ mnsinc.com. In-person interview required. Applicants must submit a cover letter, resume. Applications are accepted continuously.

PUBLIC ADMINISTRATION

GENERAL

ALASKA STATE PARKS
3901 C Street, Suite 1200
Anchorage, Alaska 99503

General Information State agency that maintains parks and provides outdoor recreation facilities. Established in 1970. Number of employees: 184. Division of State of Alaska Department of Natural Resources, Anchorage, Alaska. Number of internship applications received each year: 100.
Internships Available ▶ *5–50 interns:* responsibilities include various duties at park facilities depending on current needs and intern's abilities. Candidates should have ability to work independently, ability to work with others, college courses in field, knowledge of field, personal interest in the field, self-motivation. Duration is 1 summer. Unpaid. Open to college freshmen, college sophomores, college juniors, college seniors, recent college graduates, individuals reentering the workforce, individuals age 18 or older.
Benefits Free housing, on-the-job training, willing to complete paperwork for educational credit, expense allowance to cover food costs.
Contact Write, call, fax, or e-mail Volunteer Coordinator. Phone: 907-269-8708. Fax: 907-269-8907. E-mail: volunteer@dnr.state.ak. us. Telephone interview required. Applicants must submit a formal organization application, cover letter, resume, academic transcripts, personal reference, three letters of recommendation. Application deadline: April 1 for summer, August 1 for winter. World Wide Web: http://www.dnr.state.ak.us/parks/vip.

AUSTRALIAN EMBASSY
1601 Massachusetts Avenue, NW
Washington, District of Columbia 20036

General Information Liaison office that monitors Congress and reports U.S. political developments to Australia. Established in 1946. Number of employees: 350. Unit of Department of Foreign Affairs and Trade, Canberra, Australia. Number of internship applications received each year: 200.
Internships Available ▶ *3 ANZACC (Australian, New Zealand, American Chamber of Commerce) interns:* responsibilities include assisting with the planning and organizing of ANZACC's annual conference, performing research and answering questions from the regional Chambers, assisting with the production of the ANZACC newsletter, performing general administrative duties. Candidates should have ability to work independently, organizational skills, personal interest in the field, research skills, self-motivation, writing skills. Open to college juniors, college seniors, recent college graduates, graduate students. ▶ *3 congressional liaison/ public diplomacy interns:* responsibilities include conducting research on domestic politics, congressional activities, and administration policies; attending and reporting on hearings and press conferences; performing various tasks for the Public Affairs and Cultural Affairs offices; performing general administrative duties. Candidates should have ability to work independently, organizational skills, personal interest in the field, research skills, strong interpersonal skills, writing skills. Open to college sophomores, college juniors, college seniors, recent college

graduates, graduate students. Duration for all positions is one semester or summer. All positions are unpaid. International applications accepted.
Benefits Willing to complete paperwork for educational credit, willing to provide letters of recommendation, opportunity to attend seminars/workshops/congressional hearings.
Contact Write or call Elizabeth A. McKenna, Internship Coordinator. Phone: 202-797-3071. Applicants must submit a cover letter, resume. Application deadline: April 1 for summer, July 1 for fall, December 1 for spring. World Wide Web: http://www.austemb.org/.

BUREAU OF LAND MANAGEMENT, COOS BAY DISTRICT, UMPQUA RESOURCE AREA
1300 Airport Lane
North Bend, Oregon 97459

General Information Federal agency that manages natural resources on over 270 million acres of public lands for the people of the United States; employs people in many fields including natural resources, administration, and computer resources. Established in 1946. Number of employees: 200. Unit of Bureau of Land Management, Washington, District of Columbia. Number of internship applications received each year: 10.
Internships Available ▶ *2–6 interpretive education interns:* responsibilities include developing and implementing interpretive and environmental education programs; developing interpretive exhibit, brochures, and panels; and assisting staff. Candidates should have ability to work independently, ability to work with others, oral communication skills, organizational skills, personal interest in the field, writing skills, written communication skills. $75 weekly stipend. Open to recent high school graduates, college freshmen, college sophomores, college juniors, college seniors, recent college graduates, graduate students, law students, career changers, individuals reentering the workforce, must be 18 years or older. ▶ *5–8 seasonal recreation technical interns:* responsibilities include operating the park entrance station, performing day-to-day maintenance, giving group tours and formal presentations to the public. Candidates should have ability to work independently, ability to work with others, oral communication skills, organizational skills, personal interest in the field, written communication skills. $75 weekly stipend. Open to recent high school graduates, college freshmen, college sophomores, college juniors, college seniors, recent college graduates, graduate students, law students, career changers, individuals reentering the workforce, those 18 years or older only. ▶ *1–6 summer natural resource interns:* responsibilities include giving small group tours and presentations, working in the gift shop, developing educational programs, creating displays, and maintaining site. Candidates should have ability to work with others, oral communication skills, personal interest in the field, self-motivation. $75 weekly stipend. Open to recent high school graduates, college freshmen, college sophomores, college juniors, college seniors, recent college graduates, graduate students, law students, career changers, individuals reentering the workforce, must be 18 years or older. Duration for all positions is May to September (flexible). International applications accepted.
Benefits Formal training, free housing, job counseling, names of contacts, on-the-job training, opportunity to attend seminars/workshops, willing to act as a professional reference, willing to complete paperwork for educational credit, willing to provide

letters of recommendation, reimbursement of on-site travel expenses, preference to volunteers for regular positions.
Contact Write, call, fax, or e-mail Mr. Robert Golden, Park Manager. Phone: 541-756-0100. Fax: 541-751-4303. E-mail: robert_golden@or.blm.gov. Applicants must submit a cover letter, resume, three personal references. Applications are accepted continuously.

BUREAU OF LAND MANAGEMENT, PRICE FIELD OFFICE
125 South, 600 West
Price, Utah 84501

General Information Federal agency responsible for managing and administering the use of public lands located primarily in the western United States and Alaska. Established in 1946. Number of employees: 30. Number of internship applications received each year: 4.
Internships Available ▶ *2–4 recreation/archaeology interns:* responsibilities include taking inventory of use and users of Nine Mile Canyon, developing and providing interpretive information to visitors, participating in inventory and recording of cultural sites, monitoring impact of visitation on cultural sites, light maintenance of recreation facilities, and identifying need for facilities development. Candidates should have ability to work independently, oral communication skills, personal interest in the field, research skills, self-motivation. Duration is 5 weeks or 6 months beginning in April. Open to college freshmen, college sophomores, college juniors, college seniors, recent college graduates, graduate students, career changers, individuals reentering the workforce. ▶ *2 recreation/paleontology interns:* responsibilities include taking inventory of recreation use and users, developing and providing educational information to visitors, participating in discovery and recording of fossil sites, monitoring impacts of visitation on paleontological sites, performing light maintenance of recreation facilities, identifying future development needs, and working with CEU Prehistoric Museum in laboratory and field preparation of specimens. Candidates should have ability to work independently, oral communication skills, personal interest in the field, self-motivation. Duration is Easter through Labor Day (or 8-week time frames). Open to college freshmen, college sophomores, college juniors, college seniors, recent college graduates, graduate students, career changers, individuals reentering the workforce, retirees. ▶ *2–6 river ranger/recreation interns:* responsibilities include conducting compliance checks of private and commercial river runners; monitoring resource conditions. Candidates should have ability to work independently, analytical skills, oral communication skills, self-motivation, strong interpersonal skills, writing skills. Duration is 2–6 months. Open to college freshmen, college sophomores, college juniors, college seniors, recent college graduates, graduate students, career changers, individuals reentering the workforce, retirees. All positions paid at $18 per day. International applications accepted.
Benefits Free housing, job counseling, names of contacts, on-the-job training, opportunity to attend seminars/workshops, possible full-time employment, willing to act as a professional reference, willing to complete paperwork for educational credit, willing to provide letters of recommendation, worker's compensation.
Contact Write, call, fax, or e-mail Mr. Dennis J. Willis, Recreation Planner. Phone: 435-636-3622. Fax: 435-636-3657. E-mail: dwillis@ ut.blm.gov. Telephone interview required. Applicants must submit a formal organization application, cover letter. Applications are accepted continuously. World Wide Web: http://www.blm.gov/ utah/.

BUREAU OF LAND MANAGEMENT, SAN JUAN FIELD OFFICE
PO Box 7
Monticello, Utah 84535

General Information Federal agency responsible for multiple use management of public lands. Established in 1946. Number of employees: 20. Number of internship applications received each year: 20.

Internships Available ▶ *1–3 Grand Gulch ranger assistants:* responsibilities include providing information to visitors in the Grand Gulch area, conducting foot patrols into remote canyons, light clean-up and maintenance of campsites and ranger station, and assisting with the protection of Anasazi archaeological sites by providing visitors with information on site stewardship and the value of archaeological sites. ▶ *1–3 San Juan River ranger assistants:* responsibilities include contacting boaters at launch areas for the San Juan River, accompanying river rangers on rafting patrols of the river, light clean-up and maintenance at launch areas and along the river, and assisting with inventories of resource conditions along the river. Candidates for all positions should have ability to work independently, ability to work with others, oral communication skills. Duration for all positions is 4 weeks minimum. All positions are unpaid. Open to recent high school graduates, college freshmen, college sophomores, college juniors, college seniors, recent college graduates, graduate students, law students, career changers, individuals reentering the workforce. International applications accepted.
Benefits Formal training, free housing, job counseling, names of contacts, on-the-job training, willing to complete paperwork for educational credit, willing to provide letters of recommendation, opportunity to work in a scenic area with rich archaeological resources, food allowance of $12 per day.
Contact Write, call, fax, or e-mail Ms. Robin Fehlau, Outdoor Recreation Planner. Phone: 435-587-2141. Fax: 435-587-1503. E-mail: rfehlau@ut.blm.gov. In-person interview recommended. Applicants must submit a resume. Applications are accepted continuously. World Wide Web: http://www.blm.gov/utah/ monticello.

CALIFORNIA SENATE ASSOCIATES PROGRAM
6000 J Street
Sacramento, California 95819-6081

General Information Program administered by California State University, Sacramento. Established in 1974. Number of internship applications received each year: 300.
Internships Available ▶ *18 Senate associate fellows:* responsibilities include being assigned to the personal or committee staff of a senate member; working as part of the team; and performing tasks that run the gamut of legislative activity, including research and bill analysis, constituent casework, and other administrative duties. Candidates should have analytical skills, oral communication skills, organizational skills, strong interpersonal skills, written communication skills. Duration is 11 months. $1,792 per month. Open to college seniors, recent college graduates, graduate students, law students, career changers, individuals reentering the workforce. International applications accepted.
Benefits Formal training, on-the-job training, tuition assistance, health and dental benefits, enrollment fees provided, 12 graduate credits from the Government Department at CSUS, opportunity to attend seminars.
Contact Write, call, fax, or e-mail Mr. Dan Friedlander, Director, Senate Associates Program Center for California Studies, CSUS. Phone: 916-278-6906. Fax: 916-278-5199. E-mail: calstudies@ csus.edu. In-person interview required. Applicants must submit a formal organization application, academic transcripts, two writing samples, two letters of recommendation. Application deadline: February for fall. World Wide Web: http://www.csus.edu/calst.

CALIFORNIA STATE ASSEMBLY AND EXECUTIVE FELLOWSHIP, SENATE ASSOCIATES, AND JUDICIAL ADMINISTRATION FELLOWSHIP PROGRAMS
Center for California Studies, CSU Sacramento, 6000 J Street
Sacramento, California 95819-6081

General Information Public policy, public service, and curricular support unit devoted to promoting the understanding of California's history, cultures, and public policies. Established in 1957. Number of employees: 10. Unit of California State University, Sacramento, Sacramento, California. Number of internship applications received each year: 1,000.

California State Assembly and Executive Fellowship, Senate Associates, and Judicial Administration Fellowship Programs (continued)

Internships Available ▶ *18 Assembly fellows:* responsibilities include assuming the role of a professional staff team member in Assembly branch of California's state government and accepting responsibility and challenging assignments. ▶ *18 Senate associates:* responsibilities include assuming the role of a professional staff team member in Senate branch of California's state government and accepting responsibility and challenging assignments. ▶ *18 executive fellows:* responsibilities include assuming the role of a professional staff team member in the executive branch of California's state government and accepting responsibility and challenging assignments. ▶ *5 judicial administration fellows:* responsibilities include assuming the role of a professional staff team member in Judicial branch of California's state government and accepting responsibility and challenging assignments. Candidates for all positions should have ability to work with others, knowledge of field, oral communication skills, personal interest in the field, written communication skills. Duration for all positions is 11–12 months. All positions paid at $1,792 per month. Open to college seniors, recent college graduates, graduate students, law students, career changers, must have completed 4-year degree by August. International applications accepted.
Benefits Formal training, health insurance, opportunity to attend seminars/workshops, dental and vision care, 12 units of graduate credit for fellows who fulfill academic requirements.
Contact Write, call, fax, or e-mail Fellowship Program Coordinator. Phone: 916-278-6906. Fax: 916-278-5199. E-mail: calstudies@csus. edu. In-person interview required. Applicants must submit a formal organization application, academic transcripts, writing sample, three letters of recommendation. Application deadline: February for Assembly, Executive, and Senate positions; January for Judicial positions. World Wide Web: http://www.csus. edu/calst.

CENTER FOR NATIONAL POLICY
1 Massachusetts Avenue, NW, Suite 333
Washington, District of Columbia 20001-1401

General Information Public policy organization committed to the idea of a vital public sector. Established in 1981. Number of employees: 15. Number of internship applications received each year: 200.
Internships Available ▶ *Interns:* responsibilities include assisting in policy research, event planning, publicity, and general office support work. Duration is 3 months. stipend. Open to college freshmen, college sophomores, college juniors, college seniors, recent college graduates, graduate students, law students, career changers, individuals reentering the workforce.
Benefits Job counseling, names of contacts, willing to complete paperwork for educational credit, willing to provide letters of recommendation.
Contact Write Ms. Jill Hanauer, Vice President. No phone calls. Telephone interview required. Applicants must submit a cover letter, resume, writing sample. Applications are accepted continuously. World Wide Web: http://www.cnponline.org.

CENTRAL INTELLIGENCE AGENCY
PO Box 12727
Arlington, Virginia 22209-8727

General Information Agency involved in information collection, processing, analysis, and reporting. Established in 1947.
Internships Available ▶ *Graduate studies interns:* responsibilities include becoming acquainted with professional intelligence analysts and participating in substantive agency work. Duration is flexible. $15–$20 per hour. Open to college seniors, graduate students. ▶ *Student trainees:* responsibilities include participating in substantive agency assignments commensurate with intern's academic training and ability. Candidates should have declared college major in field, self-motivation, strong leadership ability, written communication skills. Duration is 3 semesters. $10–$15 per hour. Open to college sophomores. ▶ *Summer internships:* responsibilities include working with professionals and viewing the role of the agency while gaining work experience. Candidates

should have declared college major in field. Duration is 1 summer (minimum of 90 days). $10–$15 per hour. Open to college sophomores, college juniors.
Benefits Formal training, health insurance, names of contacts, opportunity to attend seminars/workshops, possible full-time employment, travel reimbursement, willing to complete paperwork for educational credit, vacation and sick days accrual.
Contact Write Personnel Representative. Applicants must submit a cover letter, resume, formal application provided following review of cover letter/resume. Application deadline: April 1 for fall, August 1 for spring, November 1 for summer. World Wide Web: http://www.cia.gov.

CITY OF CHICAGO, DEPARTMENT OF PERSONNEL
City Hall, Room 1100, 121 North LaSalle Street
Chicago, Illinois 60602

General Information Municipal government. Number of employees: 42,000. Number of internship applications received each year: 500.
Internships Available ▶ *140–160 summer interns:* responsibilities include performing duties under supervision required to assist in various city departments; specific duties will vary depending upon individual department's needs. Candidates should have ability to work independently, analytical skills, college courses in field, computer skills, editing skills, knowledge of field, office skills, oral communication skills, organizational skills, plan to pursue career in field, research skills, self-motivation, strong interpersonal skills, strong leadership ability, writing skills. Duration is 10 weeks. $6–$10 per hour. Open to college freshmen, college sophomores, college juniors, college seniors, graduate students, law students. International applications accepted.
Benefits Formal training, job counseling, on-the-job training, opportunity to attend seminars/workshops, possible full-time employment, willing to act as a professional reference, willing to complete paperwork for educational credit, willing to provide letters of recommendation.
Contact Write Wesley J. Morgan, Director of Recruitment. In-person interview required. Applicants must submit a formal organization application, cover letter, resume, academic transcripts. Application deadline: May 29.

CITY OF DETROIT-OUTREACH ACTIVITIES UNIT
2 Woodward Avenue, Room 314, City County Building
Detroit, Michigan 48226

General Information Internship program that offers college students an opportunity to receive paid work experience in their area of study. Unit of City of Detroit–Human Resources Department, Detroit, Michigan. Number of internship applications received each year: 60.
Internships Available ▶ *1–20 interns:* responsibilities include performing varied tasks depending upon position and department requirements. Duration is 9 weeks. Position available as unpaid or at $8–$10 per hour. Open to college freshmen, college sophomores, college juniors, college seniors, graduate students. International applications accepted.
Benefits Opportunity to attend seminars/workshops, possible full-time employment, willing to complete paperwork for educational credit, willing to provide letters of recommendation.
Contact Write or fax Mary K. Shanks-Allen, Internship Coordinator. Fax: 313-224-3410. In-person interview required. Applicants must submit a cover letter, resume, academic transcripts. Application deadline: April 15 for summer. World Wide Web: http://www.ci. detroit.mi.us.

CITY OF FORT COLLINS UTILITY WELLNESS PROGRAM
700 Wood Street
Fort Collins, Colorado 80522

General Information Provider of electric power, water, wastewater, stormwater, and street services to the community. Established in 1930. Number of employees: 500. Division of City of Fort Collins Municipality, Fort Collins, Colorado. Number of internship applications received each year: 12.

Internships Available ▶ *1–2 wellness interns:* responsibilities include working in exercise room and orientation, resource library upkeep, health education, exercise testing, program planning and implementation, group exercise leadership. Candidates should have ability to work with others, knowledge of field, oral communication skills, plan to pursue career in field, self-motivation, written communication skills. Duration is variable, depending on university schedules. $6–$10 per hour. Open to high school seniors, recent high school graduates, college seniors, graduate students, individuals reentering the workforce. International applications accepted.

Benefits Job counseling, opportunity to attend seminars/workshops, willing to act as a professional reference, willing to complete paperwork for educational credit, willing to provide letters of recommendation, flexible schedule, possibility of part-time employment.

Contact Write or e-mail Maureen Balzer, Utility Services Wellness Coordinator, 700 Wood Street, Fort Collins, Colorado 80522. Phone: 970-221-6349. E-mail: mbalzer@ci.fort-collins.co.us. In-person interview recommended. Applicants must submit a formal organization application, cover letter, resume, writing sample. Application deadline: April 1 for summer (recommended deadline), June 1 for fall (recommended deadline), October 1 for winter (recommended deadline).

CITY OF HOONAH, DEPARTMENT OF PARKS AND RECREATION
1 Harbor Drive, PO Box 360
Hoonah, Alaska 99829

General Information Parks and recreation department running youth-oriented programs. Established in 1997. Number of employees: 4. Department of City of Hoonah, Hoonah, Alaska. Number of internship applications received each year: 30.

Internships Available ▶ *1 youth recreation assistant:* responsibilities include working one-on-one with youth at a drop-in recreation center and other sites, both indoor and outdoor sports and crafts activities; prevention education, working with at-risk, native youth. Candidates should have ability to work independently, ability to work with others, college courses in field, knowledge of field, oral communication skills. Duration is 12–14 weeks. $350 per month. Open to college juniors, college seniors, recent college graduates, graduate students, law students, career changers, individuals reentering the workforce. International applications accepted.

Benefits Free housing, names of contacts, on-the-job training, travel reimbursement, willing to act as a professional reference, willing to complete paperwork for educational credit, willing to provide letters of recommendation.

Contact Write or e-mail David Paperman, Director, PO Box 360, Hoohan, Alaska 99829. E-mail: paperman@hoonah.net. Telephone interview required. Applicants must submit a formal organization application, cover letter, resume. Application deadline: April 1 for summer, September 1 for winter, November 1 for spring.

CITY OF LEWISVILLE
1197 West Main
Lewisville, Texas 75067

General Information Municipal government. Number of employees: 549. Number of internship applications received each year: 10.

Internships Available ▶ *1 administrative intern:* responsibilities include administrative duties in city manager's office; analyses and reports. Candidates should have ability to work independently, ability to work with others, analytical skills, college degree in related field, computer skills, oral communication skills, plan to pursue career in field, research skills, self-motivation, writing skills. Duration is up to one year. $8 per hour. Open to graduate students. International applications accepted.

Benefits On-the-job training, opportunity to attend seminars/workshops, possible full-time employment, travel reimbursement, willing to act as a professional reference.

Contact Write, call, or fax Melinda Galler, Human Resources Manager, 1197 West Main, Lewisville, Texas 75067. Phone: 972-219-3452. Fax: 972-219-5005. In-person interview required. Applicants must submit a formal organization application. Applications are accepted continuously. World Wide Web: http://www.cityoflewisville.com.

CITY OF LONG BEACH, DEPARTMENT OF HUMAN RESOURCES AND AFFIRMATIVE ACTION
333 West Ocean Boulevard, 13th Floor
Long Beach, California 90802

General Information Municipal government with a city manager and mayor-appointed council consisting of 22 city departments including non-city manager departments. Established in 1897. Number of employees: 4,176. Number of internship applications received each year: 100.

Internships Available ▶ *2 management assistants:* responsibilities include activities varying with an intern's experience and city needs; typical past internships have involved assisting in implementation and evaluation of City's Neighborhood Improvement Strategy, preparing and making public presentations of City plans and proposals, evaluating impact of state and federal legislation on the City, preparing reports for the Mayor and City Council, assisting community service organizations, and preparing departmental budgets. Duration is 1 year. Paid. Open to recent college graduates, graduate students, individuals who have completed a master's degree in public administration, business administration, or related field by end of July. International applications accepted.

Benefits Health insurance, possible full-time employment, executive leave (5 days per calendar year), life insurance.

Contact Write, call, fax, or e-mail Management Assistant Program, 333 West Ocean Boulevard 13th Floor, Long Beach, California 90802. Phone: 562-570-6915. Fax: 562-570-6107. E-mail: lymccra@ci.long-beach.ca.us. Applicants must submit a resume, academic transcripts, three personal references, 3-5 page statement describing career goals and the reason for application. Application deadline: January 31. World Wide Web: http://www.ci.long-beach.ca.us.

CITY OF NEW YORK/PARKS & RECREATION
830 Fifth Avenue
New York, New York 10021

General Information Local government agency responsible for 27,000 acres of green space; oversees cultural, athletic, and social events. Number of employees: 2,275. Number of internship applications received each year: 650.

Internships Available ▶ *150–200 interns:* responsibilities include working in the areas of public administration, recreation, environmental science, computer operations, photography, architecture, landscape architecture, engineering, urban planning, revenue, accounting, and forestry; locations in all five boroughs. Candidates should have college courses in field, oral communication skills, organizational skills, self-motivation, strong interpersonal skills, written communication skills. Duration is flexible. Position available as unpaid or paid. Open to high school students, high school seniors, recent high school graduates, college freshmen, college sophomores, college juniors, college seniors, recent college graduates, graduate students, law students. International applications accepted.

Benefits On-the-job training, opportunity to attend seminars/workshops, possible full-time employment, travel reimbursement, willing to act as a professional reference, willing to complete paperwork for educational credit, willing to provide letters of recommendation, participation in monthly speaker series, some stipends available for federal work-study participants.

Contact Write, call, fax, or e-mail Kasia Pindak, Internship Coordinator, 830 Fifth Avenue, New York, New York 97103. Phone: 212-360-1349. Fax: 212-360-1387. E-mail: ggiulian@parklan.nycnet.ci.nyc.us. In-person interview required. Applicants

City of New York/Parks & Recreation (continued)

must submit a cover letter, resume, academic transcripts, 1-3 writing samples (on specific occasions). Applications are accepted continuously. World Wide Web: http://www.nycparks.org.

CITY OF PHOENIX, BUDGET AND RESEARCH DEPARTMENT
200 West Washington Street, 14th Floor
Phoenix, Arizona 85003-1611

General Information Department that assists in allocation of city resources to provide efficient, effective, and economical municipal services; develops the city's annual budget and capital improvement program by monitoring expenditures and revenues; and conducts management research analysis. Established in 1913. Number of employees: 29. Department of City of Phoenix, Phoenix, Arizona.

Internships Available ▶ *3 management interns:* responsibilities include conducting municipal research and analysis of administrative and organizational problems, policies, and practices and providing staff assistance for city council and subcommittees. Candidates should have satisfactory completion of all courses for a master's degree in public or business administration or a closely related field by July 1. Duration is 1 year. $27,851 per year. Open to graduate students, law students, career changers, individuals reentering the workforce. International applications accepted.

Benefits Formal training, health insurance, job counseling, names of contacts, opportunity to attend seminars/workshops, possible full-time employment, tuition assistance, dental insurance.

Contact Write Cecile Pettle, Budget and Research Director. In-person interview required. Applicants must submit a formal organization application, cover letter, academic transcripts, writing sample, three letters of recommendation. Application deadline: January. World Wide Web: http://www.ci.phoenix.az.us.

CITY OF SAN LEANDRO
Civic Center, 835 East 14th Street
San Leandro, California 94577

General Information The City Manager Division is responsible for the overall administration and supervision of city activities and provides professional staff support and guidance to the City Council. Established in 1812. Number of employees: 401. Number of internship applications received each year: 20.

Internships Available ▶ *1 Wesley McClure Graduate Management intern:* responsibilities include tracking state and federal legislation, drafting legislation letters on behalf of the Mayor and City Council, working with various city departments on specific projects, and providing administrative support to the City Manager's office. Candidates should have ability to work independently, analytical skills, computer skills, plan to pursue career in field, strong interpersonal skills, written communication skills. Duration is 9 months. $8–$12 per hour. Open to graduate students, recent graduate school graduates. International applications accepted.

Benefits Job counseling, on-the-job training, opportunity to attend seminars/workshops, possible full-time employment, willing to act as a professional reference, willing to complete paperwork for educational credit, willing to provide letters of recommendation.

Contact Write or call Jacqui Diaz, Interim Assistant to the City Manager. Phone: 510-577-3353. In-person interview recommended. Applicants must submit a formal organization application, resume, three personal references. Application deadline: May 14. World Wide Web: http://www.ci.san-leandro.ca.us.

CONGRESSIONAL MANAGEMENT FOUNDATION
513 Capitol Court, NE, Suite 300
Washington, District of Columbia 20002

General Information Nonprofit, nonpartisan organization dedicated to helping Congress become a better-managed, more effective institution by tailoring private sector management tools to the congressional environment. Established in 1977. Number of employees: 6. Number of internship applications received each year: 100.

Internships Available ▶ *2–4 interns:* responsibilities include assisting professional staff in all aspects of current projects including research, writing, survey tabulation and analysis, and general office support. Candidates should have computer skills, oral communication skills, personal interest in the field, self-motivation, strong interpersonal skills, written communication skills. Duration is minimum of 3 months. Unpaid. Open to college sophomores, college juniors, college seniors, recent college graduates, graduate students. International applications accepted.

Benefits Job counseling, names of contacts, opportunity to attend seminars/workshops, willing to act as a professional reference, willing to complete paperwork for educational credit, willing to provide letters of recommendation.

Contact Write Ms. Kathy Bainbridge, Executive Assistant. Telephone interview required. Applicants must submit a cover letter, resume, writing sample. Application deadline: March 15 for summer, July 1 for fall, November 1 for spring. World Wide Web: http://www.cmfweb.org.

CONGRESSMAN BILL THOMAS
2208 Rayburn House Office Building
Washington, District of Columbia 20515

General Information Republican U.S. Congressman serving the 21st Congressional District of California; Chairman of House Administration Committee and Chairman of Subcommittee on Health, Ways, and Means. Number of employees: 8. Number of internship applications received each year: 150.

Internships Available ▶ *10 interns:* responsibilities include legislative research and basic office duties. Duration is 6 weeks minimum. Position available as unpaid or paid. Open to college freshmen, college sophomores, college juniors, college seniors.

Benefits Opportunity to attend seminars/workshops, possible full-time employment, willing to complete paperwork for educational credit, willing to provide letters of recommendation.

Contact Write, call, or fax Cathy Abernathy, Chief of Staff. Phone: 202-225-2915. Fax: 202-225-2908. Applicants must submit a cover letter, resume, writing sample. Applications are accepted continuously.

CONGRESSMAN GEORGE E. BROWN, JR.
2300 Rayburn Building
Washington, District of Columbia 20515

General Information Congressman. Number of employees: 11. Number of internship applications received each year: 125.

Internships Available ▶ *1–2 general interns:* responsibilities include answering phones, writing constituent mail, researching projects of interest to the Congressman, and working on special tasks as assigned. Duration is 2–4 months. Unpaid. Open to college freshmen, college sophomores, college juniors, college seniors, recent college graduates, graduate students, law students, career changers, individuals reentering the workforce.

Benefits Names of contacts, willing to complete paperwork for educational credit, willing to provide letters of recommendation.

Contact Write or fax Robert Armenta, Intern Coordinator. Fax: 202-225-8671. Applicants must submit a cover letter, resume, writing sample. Applications are accepted continuously. World Wide Web: http://www.house.gov/georgebrown.

CONGRESSMAN MICHAEL BILIRAKIS
2369 Rayburn House Office Building
Washington, District of Columbia 20515

General Information Congressional office. Established in 1982. Number of employees: 10. Number of internship applications received each year: 20.

Internships Available ▶ *1–3 legislative interns:* responsibilities include assisting legislative staff with daily operations from running errands to attending legislative hearings. Candidates should have ability to work with others, computer skills, research skills,

self-motivation, writing skills. Duration is 6 weeks minimum. Unpaid. Open to college freshmen, college sophomores, college juniors, college seniors, recent college graduates, graduate students, law students.
Benefits Names of contacts, opportunity to attend seminars/workshops, willing to complete paperwork for educational credit, willing to provide letters of recommendation.
Contact Write, call, fax, or e-mail Christy Stefadouros, Staff Assistant/Intern Coordinator. Phone: 202-225-5755. Fax: 202-225-4085. E-mail: fl09@mail.house.gov. In-person interview recommended. Applicants must submit a cover letter, resume, writing sample, 3 letters of recommendation or personal references. Application deadline: January 1 for spring, April 1 for summer, August 1 for fall. World Wide Web: http://www.house.gov/bilirakis.

CONGRESSWOMAN DIANA DEGETTE
U.S. House of Representatives, Room 1339 Longworth
Washington, District of Columbia 20515

General Information Democratic U.S. Congresswoman serving the 1st Congressional District of Colorado. Established in 1997. Number of employees: 8. Number of internship applications received each year: 50.
Internships Available ▶ *1–5 interns:* responsibilities include assisting staff, answering phones, opening mail, conducting research, answering letters, and attending meetings and hearings. Candidates should have ability to work independently, office skills, oral communication skills, personal interest in the field, research skills, self-motivation, writing skills. Duration is minimum of 8 weeks. Unpaid. Open to recent high school graduates, college freshmen, college sophomores, college juniors, college seniors, recent college graduates, graduate students, law students, career changers, individuals reentering the workforce.
Benefits Job counseling, meals at a cost, names of contacts, on-the-job training, opportunity to attend seminars/workshops, willing to act as a professional reference, willing to complete paperwork for educational credit, willing to provide letters of recommendation, opportunity to observe how Congress works and take part in legislative initiatives.
Contact Write, call, or fax Mr. Peter Irvine, Intern Coordinator, U.S. House of Representatives, Room 1339 Longworth, Washington, District of Columbia 20515. Phone: 202-225-4431. Fax: 202-225-5657. In-person interview recommended. Applicants must submit a cover letter, resume, writing sample. Applications are accepted continuously. World Wide Web: http://www.house.gov/degette.

CONGRESSWOMAN SLAUGHTER
2347 Rayburn House Office Building, (NY-28)
Washington, District of Columbia 20515

General Information Democratic member of the United States House of Representatives. Established in 1986. Number of employees: 11. Unit of United States House of Representatives, Washington, District of Columbia. Number of internship applications received each year: 20.
Internships Available ▶ *2 interns:* responsibilities include drafting constituent letters, attending committee hearings, administrative duties, research projects. Candidates should have oral communication skills, organizational skills, research skills, strong interpersonal skills, writing skills, interest in government/legislative process. Unpaid. Open to college freshmen, college sophomores, college juniors, college seniors, recent college graduates. International applications accepted.
Benefits Opportunity to attend seminars/workshops, willing to complete paperwork for educational credit, willing to provide letters of recommendation.
Contact Write Josh Farrelman, Staff Assistant. Telephone interview required. Applicants must submit a formal organization application, cover letter, resume, academic transcripts, writing sample, two letters of recommendation. Application deadline: January 15 for spring, March 30 for summer, July 31 for fall. World Wide Web: http://www.house.gov/slaughter/.

DEMOCRATIC CAUCUS OF THE HOUSE OF REPRESENTATIVES
Room 149 State House, 200 West Washington Street
Indianapolis, Indiana 46204-2786

General Information Group consists of the collective membership of state representatives affiliated with the Democratic Party of the House of Representatives. Number of employees: 75. Unit of State of Indiana, Indiana. Number of internship applications received each year: 70.
Internships Available ▶ *15 constituent/caucus services interns:* responsibilities include working with a full-time legislative assistant in support of 3 or 4 state representatives, drafting constituent letters, conducting legislative and constituent problem research, attending committee meetings, summarizing legislation, and preparing material for newsletters. ▶ *3 media services interns:* responsibilities include working with the caucus media director in assisting all Democratic state representatives with media relations, research, writing news releases, setting up press conferences, taping and sending radio feeds, and coordinating photograph sessions with visiting constituents. ▶ *1 ways and means intern:* responsibilities include assisting the Democratic fiscal analyst in working for the chief Democratic member of the Ways and Means Committee and following meetings of the Committee. Duration for all positions is 5 months. All positions paid at $225 per week. Open to college juniors, college seniors, recent college graduates, graduate students.
Benefits Possible full-time employment, willing to complete paperwork for educational credit.
Contact Write, call, fax, or e-mail Mr. Judson R. Kring, Director, Room 149 State House 200 West Washington Street, Indianapolis, Indiana 46204-2786. Phone: 317-232-9655. Fax: 317-233-8184. E-mail: jkring@iga.state.in.us. In-person interview required. Applicants must submit a cover letter, resume. Application deadline: October 15. World Wide Web: http://www.state.in.us/legislative/house_democrats.

DEPARTMENT OF CITYWIDE ADMINISTRATIVE SERVICES
1 Center Street, 24th Floor, Rooms 24-25
New York, New York 10007

General Information Program addressing issues in New York City government. Established in 1969. Number of employees: 6. Number of internship applications received each year: 250.
Internships Available ▶ *25 government interns:* responsibilities include assisting with administrative problem solving, research and policy consultation; planning direct service delivery; and attending weekly seminars that examine crucial issues facing city government. Duration is 10 weeks. $3,000 per duration of internship. Open to college juniors, college seniors, law students. ▶ *25 urban fellows:* responsibilities include assisting with policy analysis and review, direct service delivery, fieldwork, and computer applications; and working in areas such as human services, criminal justice, health, housing, transportation, and economic development. Duration is 9 months. $ 3,000 for summer, $21,000 for 9 months. Open to recent college graduates, graduate students.
Benefits Job counseling, names of contacts, opportunity to attend seminars/workshops, possible full-time employment, willing to provide letters of recommendation.
Contact Write, call, or fax Ms. Barbara Simmons, Director of Fellowship Programs, 1 Center Street, 24th Floor, Rooms 24-25, New York, New York 10007. Phone: 212-669-3695. Fax: 212-669-3688. Applicants must submit a formal organization application, cover letter, resume, academic transcripts, two writing samples. Application deadline: January 15.

DEPARTMENT OF FAMILY SERVICES, MENTAL HEALTH AUTHORITY DIVISION, PRINCE GEORGE'S COUNTY
5012 Rhode Island
Hyattsville, Maryland 20781

General Information   Government agency responsible for planning, monitoring, evaluating and funding public mental health programs and services. Established in 1992. Number of employees: 10. Number of internship applications received each year: 1.
Internships Available   ▶ *1–2 social work interns:* responsibilities include researching, convening meetings (focus groups and interagency), evaluating programs, and preparing reports. Candidates should have ability to work independently, college courses in field, oral communication skills, strong interpersonal skills, written communication skills. Duration is 1 year. Unpaid. Open to college juniors, college seniors, recent college graduates, graduate students, career changers, individuals reentering the workforce. International applications accepted.
Benefits   Names of contacts, on-the-job training, opportunity to attend seminars/workshops, possible full-time employment, travel reimbursement, willing to act as a professional reference, willing to complete paperwork for educational credit, willing to provide letters of recommendation.
Contact   Write, call, or fax Terezie S. Bohrer, Director. Phone: 301-985-3890. Fax: 301-985-3889. In-person interview required. Applicants must submit a cover letter, resume. Applications are accepted continuously.

ECONOMIC RESEARCH SERVICE, US DEPARTMENT OF AGRICULTURE
1800 M Street, NW
Washington, District of Columbia 20036-5831

General Information   Federal agency that provides economic and social science research and analysis for use by decision makers in areas relating to agriculture, food, natural resources, and rural America. Established in 1961. Number of employees: 520. Unit of United States Department of Agriculture, Washington, District of Columbia. Number of internship applications received each year: 150.
Internships Available   ▶ *1–3 computer specialists:* responsibilities include assisting in development of agency Internet or Intranet services; assisting in development of Windows database application programs; assisting in the development and validation of relational databases; and assisting in the development of standard system operating procedures. Candidates should have analytical skills, college courses in field, computer skills, declared college major in field, knowledge of field, personal interest in the field, knowledge of Internet technologies, client-server databases, or Visual C++. Duration is flexible within period of May to August. $8-$12 per hour, depending on education level. ▶ *15–20 economics assistants/economists:* responsibilities include assisting economists in developing and presenting economic research and analysis, conducting literature searches, collecting and analyzing information using a variety of software packages to develop spreadsheets, creating graphics and text for documents. Candidates should have analytical skills, college courses in field, computer skills, knowledge of field, research skills. Duration is negotiable within period of May to August. $8.60 to $18 per hour, depending on education level. Open to college sophomores, college juniors, college seniors, graduate students, must be continuing students (enrolled in school in fall).
Benefits   Opportunity to attend seminars/workshops, willing to complete paperwork for educational credit, computer training, public transit subsidy.
Contact   Write, call, fax, or e-mail Victoria Smith, Assistant to the Administrator, 1800 M Street, NW, Room 4151, Washington, District of Columbia 20036-5831. Phone: 202-694-5004. Fax: 202-694-5757. E-mail: vsmith@econ.ag.gov. Applicants must submit a formal organization application, resume, academic transcripts, two personal references. Application deadline: March 1. World Wide Web: http://www.econ.ag.gov.

FEDERAL EMERGENCY MANAGEMENT AGENCY (F.E.M.A.)
500 C Street, SW, Room 816
Washington, District of Columbia 20472

General Information   Agency that coordinates federal efforts to respond to disasters declared by the President and provides resources for disaster preparedness and training. Established in 1979. Number of employees: 5,000. Number of internship applications received each year: 70.
Internships Available   ▶ *1–3 computer assistants:* responsibilities include assisting in the development and implementation of geographic information systems programs. Open to college sophomores, college juniors, college seniors, graduate students. ▶ *10–20 program assistants:* responsibilities include performing duties related to disaster preparedness and training, accounting, and liaison work between local, state, and federal governments. Open to college sophomores, college juniors, college seniors, graduate students. ▶ *1–2 public affairs assistants:* responsibilities include preparing daily news clip summaries, assisting in preparing media briefs, and receiving and directing media inquiries. Candidates should have college courses in field, computer skills, experience in the field, oral communication skills, research skills, written communication skills. Duration is 1 semester. Open to college sophomores, college juniors, college seniors, graduate students, law students. All positions are unpaid.
Benefits   Job counseling, names of contacts, on-the-job training, opportunity to attend seminars/workshops, willing to complete paperwork for educational credit, willing to provide letters of recommendation.
Contact   Write Ms. Sheryl Withers, Personnel Management Specialist. In-person interview recommended. Applicants must submit a resume, academic transcripts. Applications are accepted continuously. World Wide Web: http://www.fema.gov.

FEDERAL RESERVE BANK OF NEW YORK
33 Liberty Street
New York, New York 10045

General Information   One of the 12 regional banks which along with the Federal Reserve Board in Washington, D.C., comprise the Federal Reserve System, and are responsible for implementing the nation's monetary policy through a variety of techniques including buying and selling U.S. Government securities in the open market. Established in 1913. Number of employees: 3,400. Number of internship applications received each year: 800.
Internships Available   ▶ *12 graduate summer analysts.* Candidates should have analytical skills, computer skills, oral communication skills, plan to pursue career in field, written communication skills. $1,100 per week. Open to students pursuing master's degree in business, economics, finance, public policy, or related disciplines. ▶ *12 undergraduate summer interns.* Candidates should have computer skills, declared college major in field, oral communication skills, research skills, self-motivation. Paid. Open to students who have completed junior year of college by beginning of internship. Duration for all positions is 10–12 weeks.
Benefits   Formal training, meals at a cost, on-the-job training, opportunity to attend seminars/workshops, possible full-time employment, willing to act as a professional reference, willing to complete paperwork for educational credit, willing to provide letters of recommendation.
Contact   Write, call, or fax Internship Coordinator. Phone: 212-720-2000. Fax: 212-720-7594. In-person interview recommended. Applicants must submit a formal organization application, cover letter, resume, academic transcripts, writing sample. Application deadline: January 31 for summer. World Wide Web: http://www.ny.frb.org.

FEDERAL RESERVE BOARD OF GOVERNORS
20th & Constitution Avenue, NW, M.S. 129
Washington, District of Columbia 20551

General Information   Central banking system of the U.S. whose primary function is the formulation of monetary policy to foster stable economic conditions and long-term economic growth.

Established in 1913. Number of employees: 1,650. Number of internship applications received each year: 100.

Internships Available ▶ *Division of Banking Supervision and Regulation interns:* responsibilities include helping to support the operations of the division. Candidates should have major in finance, economics, or a related discipline. Duration is approximately June 1 to September 1. Unpaid. Open to college sophomores, college juniors, college seniors. ▶ *Division of Information Resources Management interns:* responsibilities include writing and testing software, assisting with hardware and software installation, designing Web pages and PowerPoint presentations, writing documentation for applications being developed or modified, performing routine office functions. Candidates should have major in computer science, economics, finance, business administration, or a related discipline. Duration is approximately June 1 to September 1. Position available as unpaid or paid. Open to college students who have completed their sophomore, junior, or senior year. ▶ *Division of Research and Statistics/Division of Monetary Affairs interns:* responsibilities include research projects according to individual interests, aptitude, and experience (graduate students); assisting in research projects conducted by economists at the Board (undergraduates). Duration is approximately June 1 to September 1 (paid interns) or 10-12 weeks in summer (unpaid interns). Position available as unpaid or paid. Open to graduate students working toward doctoral degrees in economics and undergraduates majoring in economics, finance, mathematics, statistics, or computer science.

Benefits Formal training, names of contacts, opportunity to attend seminars/workshops, possible full-time employment, willing to complete paperwork for educational credit, willing to provide letters of recommendation.

Contact Write Recruitment Section, 20th & Constitution Avenue, NW M.S. 129, Washington, District of Columbia 20551. No phone calls. Applicants must submit a resume, academic transcripts, cover letter and 3 letters of recommendation (Division of Banking Supervision and Regulation), 3 letters of academic reference (Division of Research and Statistics/Division of Monetary Affairs). Application deadline: March 31 for Division of Banking Supervision and Regulation; end of first week in March for Division of Information Resources Management, March 15 for Division of Research and Statistics/ Division of Monetary Affairs. World Wide Web: http://www.federalreserve.gov.

FINNEGAN FOUNDATION
3600 Raymond Street
Reading, Pennsylvania 19605

General Information Foundation that provides practical training in government and politics by offering internships in Harrisburg, Pennsylvania. Established in 1961. Number of employees: 1. Number of internship applications received each year: 50.

Internships Available ▶ *5–10 interns:* responsibilities include various positions in the many departments of state government. Candidates should have ability to work with others, analytical skills, research skills, self-motivation, writing skills. Duration is 8–10 weeks. Paid. Open to college freshmen, college sophomores, college juniors, college seniors. International applications accepted.

Benefits Opportunity to attend seminars/workshops, willing to act as a professional reference, willing to complete paperwork for educational credit, willing to provide letters of recommendation.

Contact Write, call, fax, or e-mail William C. Baer, Administrator. Phone: 610-921-3070. Fax: 610-921-3075. E-mail: bbam200@aol.com. Applicants must submit a formal organization application, cover letter, academic transcripts, personal reference, letter of recommendation, essay on varied topics. Application deadline: February for summer. World Wide Web: http:////members.aol.com/JAFINNEGAN.

GOVERNOR'S OFFICE, STATE OF CALIFORNIA
State Capitol
Sacramento, California 95814

General Information Responsible for administering all aspects of the executive branch of the State of California. Number of employees: 130.

Internships Available ▶ *1 advance intern:* responsibilities include managing the logistics of the Governor's schedule, including determining where an event will be held and the Governor's responsibilities for the event. Candidates should have organizational skills, strong interpersonal skills, strong leadership ability. ▶ *1 appointments intern:* responsibilities include assisting in evaluating potential governmental appointees. Candidates should have ability to work independently, ability to work with others, computer skills, office skills, organizational skills, written communication skills. ▶ *1 cabinet office intern:* responsibilities include working in the office that serves as the liaison between the Governor and the 11 cabinet secretaries and 39 department directors. Candidates should have ability to work independently, computer skills, office skills, oral communication skills, organizational skills, strong interpersonal skills, writing skills. ▶ *1–2 communications/press relations interns:* responsibilities include writing and releasing statements to the press and scheduling media interviews and press conferences. Candidates should have ability to work independently, analytical skills, office skills, organizational skills, written communication skills. Open to high school students, high school seniors, recent high school graduates, college freshmen, college sophomores, college juniors, college seniors, recent college graduates, graduate students, law students, career changers, individuals reentering the workforce. ▶ *1–2 constituent affairs interns:* responsibilities include tallying opinions, providing assistance to constituents, and managing the public phone lines and all constituent correspondence. Candidates should have computer skills, office skills, oral communication skills, strong interpersonal skills, writing skills. ▶ *1 executive intern:* responsibilities include assisting staff members in the governor's private office. Candidates should have editing skills, office skills, oral communication skills, organizational skills, strong interpersonal skills, written communication skills. ▶ *1 legal intern:* responsibilities include assisting with providing in-house counsel for the Governor and his staff. ▶ *1–2 legislative interns:* responsibilities include tracking legislation and compiling information necessary for the Governor to make decisions on bills. Candidates should have ability to work independently, analytical skills, computer skills, research skills, self-motivation, writing skills. ▶ *1 scheduling intern:* responsibilities include organizing and finalizing the Governor's schedule. Candidates should have computer skills, office skills, organizational skills, strong interpersonal skills. ▶ *1 special projects intern:* responsibilities include scheduling, planning, and advancing the First Lady's engagements. ▶ *1 speech writing intern:* responsibilities include assisting with researching and writing speeches, public service announcements, radio addresses, resolutions, and letters to constituents from the Governor. Candidates should have oral communication skills, research skills, self-motivation, strong interpersonal skills, writing skills. Duration for all positions is 10–15 weeks. All positions are unpaid. International applications accepted.

Benefits Opportunity to attend seminars/workshops, possible full-time employment, willing to complete paperwork for educational credit, willing to provide letters of recommendation, parking.

Contact Write, call, or fax Deborah Slon, Director, Constituent Affairs. Phone: 916-445-2841. Fax: 916-445-4633. In-person interview recommended. Applicants must submit a formal organization application, cover letter, resume, letter of recommendation. Application deadline: February 19 for winter/spring, April 30 for summer. World Wide Web: http://www.ca.gov/s/governor.

HOUSE EDUCATIONAL PROGRAMS
B57 State Office Building
St. Paul, Minnesota 55155

General Information Office that provides means by which students can gain experience through working with legislators

House Educational Programs (continued)

to facilitate legislative process. Established in 1975. Number of employees: 1. Unit of Minnesota House of Representatives, St. Paul, Minnesota. Number of internship applications received each year: 75.

Internships Available ▶ *75–100 interns:* responsibilities include research, corresponding, writing news releases, designing or compiling surveys, telephoning, providing constituent services, monitoring committee meetings, or following the status of a bill. Candidates should have ability to work with others, office skills, oral communication skills, personal interest in the field, research skills, written communication skills. Duration is 3–5 months. Unpaid. Open to college freshmen, college sophomores, college juniors, college seniors, recent college graduates, graduate students, law students, career changers, individuals reentering the workforce. International applications accepted.

Benefits Opportunity to attend seminars/workshops, willing to complete paperwork for educational credit.

Contact Write, call, fax, or e-mail Andrew H. Carter, Assistant Sergeant -at- Arms. Phone: 651-296-7452. Fax: 651-215-3903. E-mail: andrew.carter@house.leg.state.mn.us. Applicants must submit a formal organization application. Application deadline: October 1. World Wide Web: http://www.houseleg.state.mn.us.

ILLINOIS LEGISLATIVE STAFF INTERNSHIP PROGRAM
University of Illinois, PO Box 19243
Springfield, Illinois 62794-9243

General Information Program providing experience in a legislative environment. Established in 1963. Number of employees: 254. Number of internship applications received each year: 100.

Internships Available ▶ *20 partisan staff interns:* responsibilities include researching issues, drafting bills, analyzing bills and agency budget requests to prepare for committee and floor action; providing general staff work for the party they serve. Candidates should have oral communication skills, written communication skills. Duration is October to August (10½ months). ▶ *3 research interns:* responsibilities include researching a variety of questions on public issues for legislators. Candidates should have oral communication skills, research skills, writing skills, written communication skills. Duration is September to July. ▶ *1 science writing intern:* responsibilities include answering a variety of inquiries from legislators and publishing articles on scientific topics in legislative newsletter. Candidates should have college degree in related field, oral communication skills, research skills, writing skills, written communication skills. Duration is September to July (10½ months). All positions paid at $1,850 per month. Open to college seniors, recent college graduates, graduate students, law students.

Benefits Health insurance, opportunity to attend seminars/workshops, possible full-time employment, tuition assistance, willing to complete paperwork for educational credit, 8 hours of graduate credit.

Contact Write, call, fax, or e-mail Dr. Kent Redfield, Coordinator. Phone: 217-206-6602. Fax: 217-206-6542. E-mail: aldrich.ann@uis.edu. In-person interview required. Applicants must submit a formal organization application, resume, academic transcripts, writing sample, three letters of recommendation. Application deadline: March 1. World Wide Web: http://www.uis.edu/~redfield/.

INTERNATIONAL BUSINESS–GOVERNMENT COUNSELORS, INC. (IBC)
818 Connecticut Avenue, NW, 12th, Floor
Washington, District of Columbia 20006

General Information International government relations firm that provides research and analysis to clients from major international corporations. Established in 1972. Number of employees: 20. Number of internship applications received each year: 30.

Internships Available ▶ *3 interns:* responsibilities include attending congressional hearings and other trade-related meetings, and performing basic research on a variety of issues and providing written summaries. Candidates should have ability to work

independently, computer skills, knowledge of field, research skills, strong interpersonal skills, written communication skills. Duration is 3 months (flexible). Unpaid. Open to college juniors, college seniors, recent college graduates, graduate students, law students. International applications accepted.

Benefits Job counseling, on-the-job training, opportunity to attend seminars/workshops, willing to complete paperwork for educational credit, willing to provide letters of recommendation.

Contact Write or e-mail Ms. Mary Fromyer, Intern Supervisor, 818 Connecticut Avenue, NW 12th Floor, Washington, District of Columbia 20006. E-mail: mfromyer@ibgc.com. In-person interview recommended. Applicants must submit a cover letter, resume, writing sample. Applications are accepted continuously. World Wide Web: http://www.ibgc.com.

INTERNATIONAL CITY/COUNTY MANAGEMENT ASSOCIATION
777 North Capitol Street, NE, Suite 500
Washington, District of Columbia 20002-4201

General Information Association that promotes and supports professional management of local governments; advocates the council-manager form of government and collects and publishes data and information on local government, primarily in the U.S. Established in 1914. Number of employees: 120. Number of internship applications received each year: 200.

Internships Available ▶ *Environmental program interns:* responsibilities include working on grant- and contract-funded environmental projects; assisting with meetings, workshops, and conference planning; and preparing articles and case studies on local government environmental issues. ▶ *Inquiry service interns:* responsibilities include receiving and responding to requests for information, reading and abstracting new documents to be added to database, and working on special research, writing, and general projects involving other departments. ▶ *International interns:* responsibilities include assisting with recruiting for overseas assignments; researching and writing for quarterly newsletter, arranging seminars, study tours, and on-the-job training for overseas officials. ▶ *Management information publications and urban management interns:* responsibilities include researching and writing brief descriptions of local government programs, making phone calls to collect information for the Software Reference Guide, and helping assemble mailings. Duration for all positions is flexible. All positions paid at $9–$11 per hour.

Benefits Opportunity to attend seminars/workshops, willing to complete paperwork for educational credit.

Contact Write, call, fax, or e-mail Mark Mohan, Manager, Inquiry Services, 777 North Capitol Street, NE Suite 500, Washington, District of Columbia 20002-4201. Phone: 202-962-3587. Fax: 202-962-3500. E-mail: mmohan@icma.org. In-person interview recommended. Applicants must submit a cover letter, resume. Applications are accepted continuously.

INTERNATIONAL TRADE ADMINISTRATION, U.S. AND FOREIGN COMMERCIAL SERVICE
2012 HCHB, 14th and Constitution Avenue, NW
Washington, District of Columbia 20230

General Information International network of commercial specialists in 70 countries that promotes the export of U.S. goods and services. Established in 1980. Number of employees: 1,600. Unit of United States Department of Commerce, Washington, District of Columbia. Number of internship applications received each year: 50.

Internships Available ▶ *2 certified trade missions interns:* responsibilities include working with private sector organizers of trade missions to provide promotion and logistical support overseas. Candidates should have computer skills, oral communication skills, strong interpersonal skills, written communication skills. ▶ *2–4 international buyer program interns:* responsibilities include assisting project officer to coordinate worldwide promotion of selected U.S. trade shows. Candidates should have ability to work with others, computer skills, oral communication skills, strong interpersonal skills, written communication skills. ▶ *4 matchmaker program interns:* responsibilities include assisting project manag-

ers to plan, organize, and recruit small to medium size U.S. companies for participation in overseas trade missions. Candidates should have computer skills, oral communication skills, strong interpersonal skills, written communication skills. ▶ *2–3 multi-state/catalog exhibition program interns:* responsibilities include assisting project managers to plan, organize, and recruit small to medium size U.S. companies to participate in catalog show exhibitions designed to penetrate foreign markets. Candidates should have computer skills, oral communication skills, strong interpersonal skills, written communication skills. ▶ *2–4 trade fair certification interns:* responsibilities include helping program staff review and select international trade shows for support by U.S. Department of Commerce overseas staff and coordinating domestic promotion of shows to potential exhibitors. Candidates should have computer skills, oral communication skills, strong interpersonal skills, written communication skills. Duration for all positions is year-round. All positions are unpaid. Open to college freshmen, college sophomores, college juniors, college seniors, graduate students.
Benefits On-the-job training, willing to act as a professional reference, willing to complete paperwork for educational credit, willing to provide letters of recommendation, international marketing experience.
Contact Write, call, fax, or e-mail Ms. Molly Costa, Manager Matchmaker Program FCS/EDS. Phone: 202-482-0692. Fax: 202-482-0178. E-mail: molly.costa@mail.doc.gov. Telephone interview required. Applicants must submit a formal organization application, cover letter. Applications are accepted continuously. World Wide Web: http://www.ita.doc.gov/doctm/doctm.html.

KANSAS CITY LANDMARKS COMMISSION
414 East 12th Street, 26th Floor
Kansas City, Missouri 64106

General Information City preservation planning commission. Established in 1970. Number of employees: 4. Number of internship applications received each year: 10.
Internships Available ▶ *1 preservation intern:* responsibilities include support to preservation/landmarks staff; duties may include photograhy, archival research, historic resources survey, data entry, and analysis of data. Candidates should have ability to work independently, college courses in field, knowledge of field, office skills, oral communication skills, plan to pursue career in field, research skills, self-motivation, strong interpersonal skills, writing skills, GIS (Geographic Information Systems) skills. Duration is 2–3 months. salary varies with level of education. Open to students enrolled in degree program. International applications accepted.
Benefits Willing to act as a professional reference, willing to complete paperwork for educational credit, willing to provide letters of recommendation.
Contact Write, call, fax, or e-mail Alma Hubbard, Administrator, 414 East 12th Street, 26th Floor, Kansas City, Missouri 64106. Phone: 816-274-2555. Fax: 816-274-1879. E-mail: alma_hubbard@kcmo.org. Telephone interview required. Applicants must submit a cover letter, resume. Application deadline: March 1 for summer. World Wide Web: http://www.kcmo.org.

MICHIGAN HOUSE OF REPRESENTATIVES–REPUBLICAN CAUCUS SERVICES
PO Box 30014
Lansing, Michigan 48909-7514

General Information State legislative office that provides services in media relations, research, legislative analysis, and planning events. Established in 1833. Number of employees: 1,000. Unit of Michigan Legislature, Lansing, Michigan, Lansing, Michigan. Number of internship applications received each year: 100.
Internships Available ▶ *1–10 central staff interns:* responsibilities include answering constituent concerns, assisting with district events and media relations, and performing detailed analysis of legislation. Candidates should have ability to work independently, ability to work with others, computer skills, office skills, oral communication skills, personal interest in the field, written communication skills. ▶ *1–30 representative staff interns:* responsibili-

ties include scheduling, tracking legislation, and performing general office duties. Candidates should have office skills, oral communication skills, personal interest in the field, self-motivation, strong interpersonal skills, written communication skills. Duration for all positions is 1 semester. All positions are unpaid. Open to high school students, high school seniors, recent high school graduates, college freshmen, college sophomores, college juniors, college seniors. International applications accepted.
Benefits Names of contacts, possible full-time employment, willing to complete paperwork for educational credit, willing to provide letters of recommendation.
Contact Write, call, or fax Gary Muentener, Communications Analyst. Phone: 517-373-8930. Fax: 517-373-8402. In-person interview recommended. Applicants must submit a formal organization application, cover letter, resume. Applications are accepted continuously.

MICHIGAN STATE DEPARTMENT OF CIVIL SERVICE
400 South Pine Street
Lansing, Michigan 48909

General Information State government merit system administering all government operations. Established in 1946. Number of internship applications received each year: 1,200.
Internships Available ▶ *1,000 State of Michigan student interns:* responsibilities include working with engineers, doctors, attorneys, social workers, chemists, conservation officers, animal health inspectors, and other state job categories, such as information technology, accounting, and marketing. Duration is flexible. $10–$12 per hour. Open to college freshmen, college sophomores, college juniors, college seniors. International applications accepted.
Benefits Possible full-time employment, travel reimbursement, referrals provided.
Contact Write, call, or fax Ms. Peggy Price, Human Resources Services- Student Programs. Phone: 517-335-0300. Fax: 517-373-3867. Applicants must submit a formal organization application, cover letter, resume. Applications are accepted continuously. World Wide Web: http://www.state.mi.us/mdcs/index.htm.

MISSOURI LEGISLATIVE INTERN PROGRAM
State Capitol
Jefferson City, Missouri 65101

General Information Program that selects the best students in related fields at Missouri institutions of higher education and provides interns an opportunity to gain valuable practical experience in the government process. Established in 1972. Unit of Missouri State Government, Jefferson City, Missouri. Number of internship applications received each year: 115.
Internships Available ▶ *40–50 legislative interns:* responsibilities include working with legislators and their staff. Candidates should have ability to work with others, computer skills, oral communication skills, organizational skills, research skills, written communication skills. Duration is 1 semester (part-time and full-time); January to mid-May. Unpaid. Open to college juniors, college seniors, recent college graduates, graduate students, law students. International applications accepted.
Benefits Opportunity to attend seminars/workshops, willing to act as a professional reference, willing to complete paperwork for educational credit, willing to provide letters of recommendation.
Contact Write or call Representative Deleta Williams, at 573-751-2272 or Representative Mary Lou Sallee at 573-751-2205. In-person interview required. Applicants must submit a formal organization application, cover letter, resume, academic transcripts, three letters of recommendation. Application deadline: December 1 for spring.

MONTANA LEGISLATIVE COUNCIL
Room 138, State Capitol
Helena, Montana 59620

General Information   Council that provides legislating services. Established in 1957. Number of employees: 47. Unit of Montana Legislature, Helena, Montana. Number of internship applications received each year: 11.
Internships Available   ▶ *11 interns:* responsibilities include assisting legislators. Duration is 4 months in one legislative session. Unpaid. Open to college juniors and seniors in a Montana school.
Benefits   On-the-job training, willing to complete paperwork for educational credit.
Contact   Montana Unit of Higher Education, Room 138 State Capitol, Helena, Montana 59620. No phone calls. Applications should be sent to intern coordinator at Montana school. Application deadline: October 15 for winter. World Wide Web: http://www.state.mt.us.

MONTGOMERY COUNTY COMMISSION FOR WOMEN
255 North Washington Street
Rockville, Maryland 20850

General Information   Government unit that conducts research and advocacy activities for women's issues and operates a counseling and career center primarily for women. Number of employees: 20. Department of Montgomery County Government, Rockville, Maryland.
Internships Available   ▶ *6–7 counseling interns.* Duration is flexible. Unpaid. Open to individuals enrolled in a graduate-level program for counseling or social work and are using this experience as part of a formal practicum or internship approved by their university for credit. International applications accepted.
Benefits   On-the-job training, opportunity to attend seminars/workshops, willing to act as a professional reference, willing to complete paperwork for educational credit, willing to provide letters of recommendation, supervision for university-based practica and internships.
Contact   Write or fax Elma Rambo, Internship Coordinator, 255 North Washington Street, Rockville, Maryland 20850. Phone: 301-279-1800. Fax: 301-279-1318. In-person interview required. Applicants must submit a resume, personal reference, letter of interest that indicates time of availability. Applications are accepted continuously. World Wide Web: http://www.co.mo.md.us/cfw.

NATIONAL ARCHIVES AND RECORD ADMINISTRATION, STAFF DEVELOPMENT SERVICES
National Archives at College Park, 8601 Adelphi Road, Room 1510
College Park, Maryland 20740-6001

General Information   Custodian of noncurrent federal government records of continuing value, relating to all federal government activities from 1789 to the present. Established in 1935. Number of employees: 2,000. Unit of United States Federal Government, Washington, District of Columbia. Number of internship applications received each year: 25.
Internships Available   ▶ *1–20 archival interns:* responsibilities include working with textual or nontextual documents such as photographs, motion pictures, maps, and electronic records; performing basic preservation activities, preparing finding aids, responding to reference inquiries, or developing outreach programs/products. Candidates should have ability to work independently, ability to work with others, oral communication skills, organizational skills, research skills, written communication skills. ▶ *1–5 nonarchival interns:* responsibilities include a variety of administrative functions such as facilities management, policy development, and auditing activities. Candidates should have ability to work independently, ability to work with others, oral communication skills, written communication skills. Duration for all positions is 160 hours minimum. All positions are

unpaid. Open to college freshmen, college sophomores, college juniors, college seniors, recent college graduates, graduate students. International applications accepted.
Benefits   On-the-job training, willing to complete paperwork for educational credit, willing to provide letters of recommendation.
Contact   Write, call, fax, or e-mail Ms. Mary Rephlo, Staff Development Officer. Phone: 301-713-7390 Ext. 260. Fax: 301-713-7342. E-mail: mary.rephlo@arch2.nara.gov. Telephone interview required. Applicants must submit a cover letter, resume, academic transcripts, letter of recommendation. Applications are accepted continuously. World Wide Web: http://www.nara.gov/professional/intern/intern.html.

NATIONAL REPUBLICAN SENATORIAL COMMITTEE
425 2nd Street, NE
Washington, District of Columbia 20002

General Information   Republican senatorial committee that works to elect Republican candidates to the U.S. Senate. Number of employees: 70.
Internships Available   ▶ *Accounting interns:* responsibilities include performing entry-level work in accounting department. ▶ *Administrative interns:* responsibilities include assisting with general administrative tasks. ▶ *Communications interns:* responsibilities include writing press releases, attending meetings, and completing general administrative tasks. ▶ *Finance division interns:* responsibilities include performing various duties within finance division and fund-raising. ▶ *Political interns:* responsibilities include providing general support for all Senate races. ▶ *Research interns:* responsibilities include providing support to research staff and performing opposition research and data entry tasks. Duration for all positions is flexible, 1 month minimum. All positions are unpaid. Open to college freshmen, college sophomores, college juniors, college seniors, recent college graduates, graduate students. International applications accepted.
Benefits   Job counseling, opportunity to attend seminars/workshops, possible full-time employment, willing to complete paperwork for educational credit, willing to provide letters of recommendation.
Contact   Write Intern Coordinator. No phone calls. Applicants must submit a formal organization application, cover letter, resume, writing sample, three personal references, letters of recommendation helpful. Applications are accepted continuously. World Wide Web: http://www.nrsc.org.

NATIONAL SECURITY AGENCY
9800 Savage Road, Attention: S232, Suite 6840
Fort George G. Meade, Maryland 20755-6840

General Information   Federal government agency that coordinates certain domestic and foreign communications challenges, including the collection of foreign secure communications and the protection of U.S. secure communications. Established in 1952. Number of internship applications received each year: 1,100.
Internships Available   ▶ *10–25 computer science interns:* responsibilities include performing a variety of programming and analysis functions, including systems design, computer security research, systems programming, computer security systems design, applications analysis, application, and evaluation. Candidates should have ability to work independently, ability to work with others, college courses in field, knowledge of field, personal interest in the field, minimum GPA of 3.0 preferred. $12 per hour. Open to college juniors. ▶ *10–15 electronic computer engineering interns:* responsibilities include working as part of a small team to develop advanced communication security and foreign signals intelligence collection and processing systems, including fundamental research through advanced development, small to large system design and prototype development, developmental test and evaluation, field installation, and operational support. Candidates should have ability to work independently, ability to work with others, college courses in field, minimum GPA of 3.0 preferred. $12 per hour. Open to college juniors, graduate students. ▶ *25–35 mathematics interns:* responsibilities include using advanced concepts to solve cryptologic problems and help-

ing develop and evaluate code and cipher systems. Candidates should have ability to work independently, ability to work with others, college courses in field, personal interest in the field. $12–$17 per hour. Open to college juniors, graduate students, exceptional mathematics students in their freshman or sophomore years of college. Duration for all positions is June through August 31.
Benefits Opportunity to attend seminars/workshops, possible full-time employment, travel reimbursement, willing to complete paperwork for educational credit, annual and sick leave.
Contact Write, fax, or e-mail Cecile O'Connor, Personnel Officer. Fax: 410-859-4593. E-mail: njobs@fggm.osis.gov. In-person interview required. Applicants must submit a resume, academic transcripts, security processing required, letters of recommendation necessary if applicant is a math student. Application deadline: October 15 for summer mathematics interns; November 15 for all others. World Wide Web: http://www.nsa.gov.

NATIONAL SECURITY AGENCY CO-OP PROGRAM
9800 Savage Road
Fort George G. Meade, Maryland 20755

General Information Federal government agency that coordinates certain domestic and foreign communications challenges, including the collection of foreign secure communications and the protection of U.S. secure communications. Established in 1952.
Internships Available ▶ *Computer engineers:* responsibilities include designing, developing, and implementing software systems, database management, real-time systems, networking, and distributed processing systems. ▶ *Computer scientists:* responsibilities include designing and implementing software systems such as database management systems, real-time systems, management information systems, networking, and distributed processing systems. ▶ *Electrical engineer interns:* responsibilities include designing, developing, and evaluating electronic communications system (optics, lasers, acoustics, and microprocessing). Duration for all positions is minimum of 3 semesters. All positions paid at $21,060–$26,532 per year. Open to college freshmen, college sophomores.
Benefits Health insurance, possible full-time employment, travel reimbursement, tuition assistance.
Contact Write, call, or fax Co-op Manager, 9800 Savage Road, Attn: S232 Suite 6840, Fort George G. Meade, Maryland 20755. Phone: 800-962-9398. Fax: 410-854-4593. In-person interview required. Applicants must submit a resume, academic transcripts. Applications are accepted continuously. World Wide Web: http://www.nsa.gov.

NEW YORK CITY SCHOOL CONSTRUCTION AUTHORITY
30-30 Thomson Avenue
Long Island City, New York 11101

General Information New York City school construction authority created by the state legislature to build, renovate, and expand schools in New York City. Established in 1989. Number of employees: 650. Number of internship applications received each year: 25.
Internships Available ▶ *1–10 field supervisors:* responsibilities include mentoring and supervising 30-35 high school juniors, and acting as liaison between SCA and outside firms (travel is required throughout the five boroughs). Candidates should have ability to work independently, computer skills, office skills, oral communication skills, strong interpersonal skills. Duration is June to August. $10–$12 per hour. Open to recent high school graduates, college freshmen, college sophomores. ▶ *20–30 work-study interns:* responsibilities include administrative, clerical duties, and CAD. Candidates should have ability to work independently, computer skills, editing skills, office skills, oral communication skills, organizational skills, personal interest in the field, self-motivation, strong interpersonal skills, writing skills. Duration is September—June (20-25 hours per week). Position available as unpaid or at $6 per hour for high school students; $8 per hour for college students. Open to high school seniors, college freshmen, college sophomores, college juniors.

Benefits On-the-job training, possible full-time employment, willing to act as a professional reference, willing to complete paperwork for educational credit, willing to provide letters of recommendation.
Contact Write, fax, or e-mail Luz Rodriguez, Human Resources Specialist, 30-30 Thomson Avenue, Long Island City, New York 11101. Fax: 718-472-8299. E-mail: lrodriguez@nycsca.org. In-person interview required. Applicants must submit a formal organization application, cover letter, resume, academic transcripts, letter of recommendation. Application deadline: March 1 for summer. World Wide Web: http://www.ci.nyc.ny.us.

NEW YORK STATE ASSEMBLY INTERNSHIP PROGRAM
104-A Legislative Office Building
Albany, New York 12248

General Information Program that seeks to provide experiential learning for students, and services to elected members and staff of the New York State Assembly. Established in 1971. Number of employees: 6. Unit of New York State Assembly, Albany, New York. Number of internship applications received each year: 190.
Internships Available ▶ *10 graduate interns:* responsibilities include performing research necessary to the development of legislative issues for standing committees and commission offices. Candidates should have C+ average, strong interest in state government. Duration is January to June. $11,500 per duration of internship. Open to students within one year of graduating from graduate school and recent graduates from graduate school. ▶ *150 session interns:* responsibilities include participating in the daily operation of a state legislator's office; attending Assembly sessions, committee meetings, and public hearings; and researching proposed legislation and constituent problems. Candidates should have C+ average, interest in state government. Duration is January to mid-May. $3,000 per duration of internship. Open to college juniors, college seniors, college sophomores of exceptional academic standing. International applications accepted.
Benefits Health insurance, names of contacts, on-the-job training, opportunity to attend seminars/workshops, possible full-time employment, willing to complete paperwork for educational credit, willing to provide letters of recommendation.
Contact Write, call, fax, or e-mail James A. Murphy, Director. Phone: 518-455-4704. Fax: 518-455-4705. E-mail: intern@assembly.state.ny.us. Applicants must submit a formal organization application, cover letter, resume, academic transcripts, writing sample, personal reference, 3 letters of recommendation (including 1 personal). Application deadline: November 1. World Wide Web: http://assembly.state.ny.us:/internship/.

NEW YORK STATE COUNCIL ON THE ARTS
915 Broadway
New York, New York 10010

General Information State agency engaged in the funding of nonprofit cultural organizations. Established in 1960. Number of employees: 40. Unit of State of New York, Albany, New York. Number of internship applications received each year: 15.
Internships Available ▶ *Staff support services interns:* responsibilities include a variety of clerical work, including writing, drafting, and data entry; directing staff support services; recruiting and working with placement institutions; and serving as staff representative to agency and outside entities. Duration is flexible. Unpaid. Open to college freshmen, college sophomores, college juniors, college seniors, graduate students, individuals reentering the workforce.
Benefits Willing to complete paperwork for educational credit.
Contact Write, call, or fax Ms. Marnee Geller, Personnel Associate. Phone: 212-387-7008. Fax: 212-387-7164. In-person interview required. Applicants must submit a cover letter, resume. Applications are accepted continuously.

NEW YORK STATE SENATE STUDENT PROGRAMS OFFICE
State Capitol, Room 416, 90 South Swan Street
Albany, New York 12247

General Information Program promoting public service career options with the legislature. Established in 1965. Number of employees: 2. Unit of New York State Senate-The State Legislature, Albany, New York. Number of internship applications received each year: 120.

Internships Available ▶ *1 Richard J. Roth Journalism Fellow:* responsibilities include researching and writing in Senate press office. Candidates should have analytical skills, editing skills, oral communication skills, research skills, written communication skills, New York residency. Duration is approximately 10 months (September through late July/early August of the next year). $25,000 stipend for duration of fellowship. Open to recent college graduates, graduate students. ▶ *1 Richard Wiebe Public Service Fellow:* responsibilities include expert-level participation in the routines and specialty areas of a legislative office, including research, analysis, synthesis, and legislative and/or constituent casework. Candidates should have analytical skills, editing skills, oral communication skills, research skills, written communication skills, New York residency, enrollment in a New York university. Duration is approximately 10 months (September through late July/early August of the next year). $25,000 stipend for duration of fellowship. Open to graduate students, law students. ▶ *9 legislative fellows:* responsibilities include expert-level participation in the routines and specialty areas of a legislative office, including research, analysis, synthesis, and legislative and/or constituent casework. Candidates should have analytical skills, editing skills, oral communication skills, research skills, written communication skills, New York residency, enrollment in a New York university. Duration is approximately 10 months (September through late July/early August of the next year). $25,000 stipend for duration of fellowship. Open to graduate students, law students. ▶ *61 session assistants:* responsibilities include assisting with legislative routines, analyses, and representation. Candidates should have analytical skills, editing skills, oral communication skills, research skills, written communication skills, New York residency, enrollment in a New York college or university. Duration is approximately 4 months (January through late April/early May). $3000 stipend for duration of internship. Open to college sophomores, college juniors, college seniors.

Benefits Formal training, health insurance, job counseling, names of contacts, on-the-job training, opportunity to attend seminars/workshops, possible full-time employment, willing to complete paperwork for educational credit, willing to provide letters of recommendation, willing to complete any necessary paperwork for an intern to receive a loan deferment, where possible.

Contact Write, call, fax, or e-mail Dr. Russell J. Williams, Director, State Capitol, Room 416, 90 South Swan Street, Albany, New York 12247. Phone: 518-455-2611. Fax: 518-426-6827. E-mail: students@senate.state.ny.us. In-person interview required. Applicants must submit a formal organization application, resume, academic transcripts, four writing samples, three letters of recommendation, indication of preferred areas of placement, 3 academic references. Application deadline: May 5 for graduate fellows, October 26 for undergraduates.

OFFICE OF CONSUMER AFFAIRS AND BUSINESS REGULATION
One Ashburton Place, Room 1411
Boston, Massachusetts 02108

General Information Oversees nine state agencies including the divisions of banks, insurance, telecommunications and energy, and other regulated industries and professions. Number of internship applications received each year: 250.

Internships Available ▶ *Consumer information specialists:* responsibilities include answering consumer questions and receiving training in consumer protection laws, assisting in research, and working on investigation and undercover testing of alleged unfair business practices. Candidates should have analytical skills, oral communication skills, organizational skills, strong leadership ability, written communication skills. Duration is 3–6 months. Position available as unpaid or at $8 per hour. Open to college freshmen, college sophomores, college juniors, college seniors, graduate students.

Benefits Willing to complete paperwork for educational credit.

Contact Write, call, fax, or e-mail Andrea Faia, Intern Coordinator. Phone: 617-727-7755. Fax: 617-227-6094. E-mail: andrea.faia@state.ma.us. Applicants must submit a cover letter, resume. Applications are accepted continuously. World Wide Web: http://www.state.ma.us/consumer/.

OFFICE OF LABOR RELATIONS AND COLLECTIVE BARGAINING (OLRCB)
441 Fourth Street, NW, Suite 200-South
Washington, District of Columbia 20001

General Information Agency that represents the Mayor of the District of Columbia in all aspects of collective bargaining and labor relations. Established in 1979. Number of employees: 10. Branch of Office of Personnel, Washington, District of Columbia. Number of internship applications received each year: 20.

Internships Available ▶ *1–4 labor relations interns:* responsibilities include assisting staff in contract negotiations, arbitration case presentations, and representational proceedings with public employees union on behalf of the Mayor and city agencies. Candidates should have ability to work independently, college courses in field, computer skills, knowledge of field, oral communication skills, personal interest in the field, research skills, self-motivation, strong interpersonal skills, written communication skills. Duration is 2–5 months. Unpaid. Open to college sophomores, college juniors, college seniors, recent college graduates, graduate students, law students, career changers, individuals reentering the workforce. International applications accepted.

Benefits Formal training, job counseling, names of contacts, on-the-job training, opportunity to attend seminars/workshops, willing to act as a professional reference, willing to complete paperwork for educational credit, willing to provide letters of recommendation.

Contact Write, call, fax, or e-mail Veronica M. Harris, Intern Coordinator. Phone: 202-724-4953. Fax: 202-727-6887. E-mail: olrcb@hotmail.com. In-person interview recommended. Applicants must submit a cover letter, resume, one 8- to 10-page writing sample. Applications are accepted continuously.

OFFICE OF LEGISLATIVE RESEARCH AND GENERAL COUNSEL
436 State Capitol Building
Salt Lake City, Utah 84114

General Information Office that provides professional staff sources to the state legislature. Established in 1948. Number of employees: 53. Unit of Utah State Legislature, Salt Lake City, Utah. Number of internship applications received each year: 45.

Internships Available ▶ *50–65 legislature interns:* responsibilities include providing staff and research services to individual legislators. Candidates should have ability to work independently, analytical skills, computer skills, office skills, oral communication skills, personal interest in the field, research skills, self-motivation, strong interpersonal skills, written communication skills. Duration is 45 days. $800 stipend per internship. Open to college juniors, college seniors, preference given to students from Utah Colleges.

Benefits Class credit.

Contact Write or fax Jerry D. Howe, Internship Director at Universities in Utah, 436 State Capitol Building, Salt Lake City, Utah 89114. Fax: 801-538-1712. No phone calls. Applicants must submit a resume, academic transcripts, writing sample, three personal references. Application deadline: December 1.

OFFICE OF MANAGEMENT AND BUDGET (OMB)
725 17th Street, NW
Washington, District of Columbia 20503

General Information U.S. federal government agency. Established in 1970. Number of employees: 518. Unit of Executive Office of the President, Washington, District of Columbia. Number of internship applications received each year: 200.
Internships Available ▶ *30–45 policy analysts:* responsibilities include providing assistance to senior analysts on public policy issues (budget, management, legislation, regulation). Candidates should have analytical skills, college courses in field, organizational skills, research skills, self-motivation, writing skills. Duration is 2–4 months. $5,000–$9,000 per duration of internship. Open to graduate students, law students.
Benefits Formal training, job counseling, names of contacts, on-the-job training, opportunity to attend seminars/workshops, possible full-time employment, willing to act as a professional reference, willing to complete paperwork for educational credit, willing to provide letters of recommendation.
Contact Write, call, fax, or e-mail Steve Weigler, Deputy to the Associate Director for Administration, 725 17th Street, NW, Washington, District of Columbia 20503. Phone: 202-395-4855. Fax: 202-395-3504. E-mail: stephen_a_weigler@eop.gov. In-person interview recommended. Applicants must submit a cover letter, resume, academic transcripts, writing sample. Applications are accepted continuously. World Wide Web: http://www.whitehouse.gov/whitehouse/eop/omb.

OFFICE OF THE U.S. TRADE REPRESENTATIVE
600 17th Street, NW
Washington, District of Columbia 20508

General Information Agency responsible for monitoring U.S. trade relations and trade policy with other nations. Number of employees: 175. Number of internship applications received each year: 300.
Internships Available ▶ *Interns:* responsibilities include researching, writing, analyzing, studying statistics, briefing books, reporting on hearings and meetings, preparing responses to correspondence, conducting research for reports such as "Update of U.S.-Japan Trade Issues", organizing materials for advisory committee hearings, investigating the impact of changes on a country's political economy, compiling data for a report on the discrepancies between U.S. and Taiwan trade statistics, and drafting economic profiles of various countries. Duration is 3–12 months. Unpaid.
Benefits Willing to complete paperwork for educational credit, opportunity to gain leadership skills.
International Internships Available in Geneva, Switzerland.
Contact Write, call, or fax Ms. Deborah Tidwell, Human Resources Assistant. Phone: 202-395-7360. Fax: 202-395-9677. Applicants must submit a cover letter, resume. Application deadline: March 15 for summer, August 15 for fall, November 30 for spring. World Wide Web: http://www.ustr.gov.

OFFICE OF U.S. SENATOR JEFF BINGAMAN
United States Senate
Washington, District of Columbia 20510

General Information U.S. Senate office. Number of employees: 50. Number of internship applications received each year: 30.
Internships Available ▶ *3–6 fall and spring interns:* responsibilities include writing letters, conducting research, and greeting constituents. Duration is 4 months. Unpaid. ▶ *10–16 summer interns:* responsibilities include wiring letters, conducting research, and greeting constituents. Duration is 6 weeks. Position available as unpaid or at $600 per duration of internship. Candidates for all positions should have computer skills, office skills, oral communication skills, self-motivation, strong interpersonal skills, writing skills. Open to undergraduates who are residents of New Mexico or attending college in New Mexico. International applications accepted.
Benefits On-the-job training, opportunity to attend seminars/workshops, willing to act as a professional reference, willing to complete paperwork for educational credit, willing to provide letters of recommendation, possibility of paid housing (summer interns).
Contact Write, call, or e-mail David Pike, Intern Coordinator. Phone: 202-224-5521. E-mail: david_pike@bingaman.senate.gov. Applicants must submit a formal organization application, resume, writing sample, three letters of recommendation. Application deadline: March 31 for summer; continuous for fall and spring. World Wide Web: http://www.senate.gov/~bingaman.

OHIO STATE PARKS
1952 Belcher, Building C-3
Columbus, Ohio 43224

General Information State agency overseeing the operation of 73 state parks. Established in 1949. Number of employees: 5,700. Division of Ohio Department of Natural Resources, Columbus, Ohio. Number of internship applications received each year: 10.
Internships Available ▶ *100–200 adopt-a-trail volunteers:* responsibilities include adopting a trail to maintain on a regular basis. Candidates should have ability to work independently, ability to work with others, knowledge of field, oral communication skills, personal interest in the field, self-motivation. Duration is flexible, up to 1 year. Open to high school students, high school seniors, recent high school graduates, college freshmen, college sophomores, college juniors, college seniors, recent college graduates, graduate students, law students, career changers. ▶ *100–300 campground hosts:* responsibilities include welcoming people and performing public relations work, helping maintain campgrounds, and leading group activities. Candidates should have ability to work independently, analytical skills, oral communication skills, organizational skills, personal interest in the field, self-motivation, strong interpersonal skills, strong leadership ability. Duration is up to 6 months (April 1 to October 31). Open to college juniors, college seniors, recent college graduates, career changers, retired people, avid campers. ▶ *Green teens:* responsibilities include working in state parks, assisting staff with interpretive programs, trail maintenance, leading with youth groups on hiking trips, and light maintenance. Candidates should have ability to work independently, oral communication skills, personal interest in the field, self-motivation, strong interpersonal skills. Duration is flexible, can be year-round depending on projects. Open to high school students, individuals 12 to 18 years of age with parental permission. ▶ *200–400 groups volunteers:* responsibilities include working with groups such as the camera club, garden club, horseman's groups, and scouts in trail maintenance and park beautification. Candidates should have ability to work independently, college courses in field, knowledge of field, oral communication skills, personal interest in the field, self-motivation, strong interpersonal skills, strong leadership ability. Duration is flexible, up to 1 year. Open to high school students, recent high school graduates, college freshmen, college sophomores, college juniors, college seniors, recent college graduates, graduate students, law students, career changers. ▶ *Individual volunteers-in-parks:* responsibilities include a wide variety of work opportunities in state parks and nature centers designed to meet the needs of the individual and the park/nature center. Candidates should have ability to work independently, knowledge of field, oral communication skills, personal interest in the field, self-motivation, strong interpersonal skills. Duration is flexible; can be year-round. Open to recent high school graduates, college freshmen, college sophomores, college juniors, college seniors, recent college graduates, graduate students, career changers, individuals reentering the workforce. All positions are unpaid. International applications accepted.
Benefits Formal training, housing at a cost, job counseling, on-the-job training, opportunity to attend seminars/workshops, willing to act as a professional reference, willing to complete paperwork for educational credit, willing to provide letters of recommendation, worker's compensation, opportunity to learn first-hand about careers in natural resources and parks.
Contact Write, call, fax, or e-mail Mr. Jim Henahan, Volunteer Coordinator. Phone: 614-265-6561. Fax: 614-261-8407. E-mail: jim.henahan@dnr.state.oh.us. In-person interview recommended.

Ohio State Parks (continued)

Applicants must submit a formal organization application, cover letter, resume, three letters of recommendation. Applications are accepted continuously. World Wide Web: http://www.state. ohio.us/odnr/parks.

OREGON ARTS COMMISSION
775 Summer Street, NE
Salem, Oregon 97310

General Information State agency providing grants and services to not-for-profit arts organizations and artists in Oregon. Established in 1967. Number of employees: 5. Unit of State of Oregon, Oregon. Number of internship applications received each year: 10.

Internships Available ▶ *1–2 fall, spring, or summer interns:* responsibilities include assisting with grants administration, special projects, and programming administration. Candidates should have ability to work with others, analytical skills, computer skills, office skills, oral communication skills, written communication skills. Duration is 3–6 months. Unpaid. Open to graduate students.

Benefits Job counseling, names of contacts, willing to complete paperwork for educational credit, willing to provide letters of recommendation.

Contact Write, call, fax, or e-mail Mr. Michael Faison, Assistant Director. Phone: 503-986-0086. Fax: 503-986-0260. E-mail: michael. b.faison@state.or.us. In-person interview recommended. Applicants must submit a cover letter, resume. Applications are accepted continuously. World Wide Web: http://art.econ.state.or.us.

OVERSEAS PRIVATE INVESTMENT CORPORATION (OPIC)
1100 New York Avenue
Washington, District of Columbia 20527

General Information Self-sustaining federal agency that encourages private investment in 140 developing nations and contributes substantially to the growth of the U.S. economy; also helps less developed nations expand their economies. Established in 1971. Number of employees: 200. Number of internship applications received each year: 300.

Internships Available ▶ *Congressional and intergovernmental affairs legislative interns:* responsibilities include responding to telephone and written communications; conducting research; collecting data; preparing papers on various issues; monitoring congressional activities of interest to the corporation; preparing summary of hearings, markups, and floor action. Candidates should have ability to work independently, personal interest in the field, research skills, self-motivation, strong interpersonal skills, written communication skills. Open to college juniors, college seniors. ▶ *11–12 finance department interns:* responsibilities include performing financial analysis for projects, researching policy issues, and preparing economic and political risk analyses by country. Candidates should have ability to work independently, oral communication skills, organizational skills, self-motivation, written communication skills, academic concentration or work experience in finance, experience in spreadsheet and computer modeling. Open to graduate students. ▶ *1 financial management and statutory review intern (worker rights/economic analysis and research office):* responsibilities include assisting in preparation of in-depth reports on worker rights conditions (especially in OPIC-eligible countries), assisting in reviewing individual projects proposed for OPIC insurance and finance with respect to potential worker rights violations, and attending congressional hearings and other public meetings. Candidates should have ability to work independently, analytical skills, oral communication skills, research skills, writing skills, experience/background in human or labor rights/ relations. Open to graduate students. ▶ *4–5 financial management and statutory review interns:* responsibilities include researching and analyzing the effects of proposed overseas investments on the economies of the host country and the United States; in-depth research on particular sectors or on investment opportunities in designated countries or regions; or monitoring projects to ascertain actual effects on U.S. economy,

host country, or environment. Candidates should have ability to work independently, ability to work with others, oral communication skills, research skills, self-motivation, writing skills, academic background in economics and international affairs. Open to graduate students. ▶ *1–2 financial management and statutory review interns (environmental policy office):* responsibilities include performing research and analysis of projects upon host country environment and worker safety issues or analyzing environmental conditions included in OPIC environmental assessments, assisting in monitoring investor compliance, and integrating international and domestic policy considerations into environmental assessments (policy office positions). Candidates should have analytical skills, experience in the field, knowledge of field, oral communication skills, research skills, written communication skills, background in environmental sciences, engineering, or management (environmental position); background in international environmental law and policy (policy officer position). Open to college seniors for the environmental office position; graduate students for the policy office position. ▶ *3–4 financial management and statutory review interns (treasury office):* responsibilities include working in either the credit review section (conducting credit reviews of outstanding loans and assisting in project analysis and spreading of financial statements) or in the capital markets section (maintaining a database tracking and analyzing information related to international project finance and investment fund transactions). Candidates should have ability to work independently, ability to work with others, analytical skills, knowledge of field, exposure/experience in credit and financial statement analysis and Excel spreadsheet experience for the credit review position; academic concentrations in finance, accounting, or management information systems, interest in financial markets and banking knowledge of Excel, Word, and Access for the capital markets position. Open to graduate students for the credit review section; college juniors and seniors for the capital markets section. ▶ *3–4 insurance department interns:* responsibilities include performing insurance portfolio analysis, conducting research on underwriting issues and selected topics in international investment, assisting insurance officers with contract amendments and country risk profiles, and undertaking business development and market research tasks. Candidates should have analytical skills, computer skills, oral communication skills, research skills, written communication skills, background in international affairs, business, and economics. Open to graduate students. ▶ *1 investment development department (communications office) intern:* responsibilities include drafting press releases, editing articles for publication, answering telephone queries, helping organize news conferences, monitoring media coverage of OPIC, and assisting with a variety of other public information duties. Candidates should have ability to work independently, ability to work with others, oral communication skills, writing skills, major or experience in journalism, public relations, or related field preferred. Open to college freshmen, college sophomores, college juniors, college seniors. ▶ *Investment development department interns:* responsibilities include working in either the protocol and special initiatives office (assisting with development and implementation of prodecures on protocol matters for foreign dignitaries; conducting research on assigned topics dealing with protocol issues; general office duties), or in the marketing/outreach office (identifying industry sectors, markets, and potential clients to support OPIC business development efforts; composing and mailing promotional material; telemarketing). Candidates should have ability to work independently, ability to work with others, computer skills, oral communication skills, written communication skills, detail-oriented and major in communications, marketing, or public relations preferred for former position; knowledge of Power Point and database systems required for latter (Word and Excel experience helpful). Open to college freshmen, college sophomores, college juniors, college seniors. ▶ *5–6 investment development department interns (Russia, Asia, Central and Eastern Europe, Africa, Middle East, or Latin America):* responsibilities include developing investment project profiles and researching investment opportunities and other marketing development activities; direct marketing and telemarketing activities; planning round-table discussions, attending meetings, and working

on special projects. Candidates should have ability to work independently, ability to work with others, computer skills, oral communication skills, personal interest in the field, written communication skills, background in international finance and affairs, background in area studies and language preferred. Open to college juniors, college seniors, graduate students. ▶ *2 investment funds department interns:* responsibilities include analyzing and reviewing materials on venture capital/private equity fund proposals, designing and modifying financial models, preparing written reports on current funds, researching new financial structures and investment vehicles, and performing due diligence on proposed funds. Candidates should have ability to work independently, ability to work with others, experience in the field, personal interest in the field, research skills, computer modeling and spreadsheet experience, some experience in venture capital, direct equity, or investment banking, and a strong desire to expand that experience. Open to graduate students. ▶ *2–3 management services department interns:* responsibilities include working in any of the following three areas: human resources management (reviewing applications, intern activities, recordkeeping, and research on employment and benefits); information resource management; or library management (reference services in business, economics, law, finance, and marketing). Candidates should have analytical skills, college courses in field, oral communication skills, personal interest in the field, written communication skills, experience with Microsoft Windows, Word, Excel, and Power Point programs in a Novell Net Ware/ Microsoft Windows NT environment; experience in development of applications using Visual Basic with Access/SQL server database helpful for information resource position; skill in using Dialog, Lexis/Nexis, or other on-line business services desired for library internship. Open to college juniors, college seniors, graduate students. Duration for all positions is 1-2 semesters or 1 summer. All positions available as unpaid or paid.
Benefits On-the-job training, opportunity to attend seminars/ workshops, willing to complete paperwork for educational credit, possible salary for summer term.
Contact Write or call Mary Festa, Intern Program Officer. Phone: 202-336-8683. In-person interview recommended. Applicants must submit a formal organization application, cover letter, resume, academic transcripts, one short analytical writing sample. Application deadline: March 30 for summer; continuous for other positions. World Wide Web: http://www.opic.gov.

PENNSYLVANIA DEPARTMENT OF TRANSPORTATION, BUREAU OF PERSONNEL
555 Walnut Street, 9th Floor, Forum Place
Harrisburg, Pennsylvania 17101-1900

General Information State agency responsible for the planning, design, construction, and maintenance of Pennsylvania's multimodal transportation system. Established in 1903. Number of employees: 11,850. Number of internship applications received each year: 500.
Internships Available ▶ *300–500 engineering interns:* responsibilities include technical duties such as project inspection, materials sampling and testing, construction diary, and plans preparation. Candidates should have ability to work independently, oral communication skills, strong interpersonal skills, written communication skills. Duration is 6 months. $8 per hour. Open to college freshmen, college sophomores, college juniors, college seniors, graduate students. International applications accepted.
Benefits Possible full-time employment, travel reimbursement, willing to complete paperwork for educational credit.
Contact Write or call Ms. Diana Hershey, College Relations Coordinator. Phone: 717-783-2680. In-person interview recommended. Personal data sheet with resume attached. Applications are accepted continuously. World Wide Web: http://www.dot.state.pa.us.

SAN MATEO COUNTY PLANNING AND BUILDING DIVISION
455 County Center
Redwood City, California 94063

General Information Government division that regulates land use and development in unincorporated San Mateo county. Established in 1856. Number of employees: 50. Division of County of San Mateo, Redwood City, California. Number of internship applications received each year: 15.
Internships Available ▶ *3–5 research interns:* responsibilities include assisting with literature and telephone surveys, organizing and interpreting data, writing letters and reports, and some clerical work on a variety of projects in Long Range Planning and Current Planning departments. Candidates should have analytical skills, oral communication skills, personal interest in the field, research skills, written communication skills. Duration is 10 weeks to 1 year. Unpaid. Open to college juniors, college seniors, recent college graduates, graduate students, career changers. International applications accepted.
Benefits Names of contacts, on-the-job training, opportunity to attend seminars/workshops, willing to complete paperwork for educational credit, willing to provide letters of recommendation.
Contact Write, call, fax, or e-mail Mr. Jim Eggemeyer, Internship Coordinator. Phone: 650-363-4852. Fax: 650-363-4849. E-mail: pln*jeggemeyer@co.sanmateo.ca.us. In-person interview recommended. Applicants must submit a cover letter, resume. Applications are accepted continuously. World Wide Web: http://www.co.sanmateo.ca.us.

SECURITIES AND EXCHANGE COMMISSION
6432 General Green Way
Alexandria, Virginia 22312

General Information Commission that regulates national securities markets, stockbrokers, investment companies, and investment advisors and prescribes certain disclosure requirements for companies that issue stocks and securities to the public. Number of employees: 2,800. Number of internship applications received each year: 200.
Internships Available ▶ *Advanced commitment program interns:* responsibilities include providing legal research and other assistance to staff attorneys. Duration is maximum of 14 months. Paid. Open to third-year law students, graduating LOM students, recent graduates now serving as law clerks at appellate level. ▶ *Research assistants:* responsibilities include providing research and other assistance to professional staff members. Duration is 8-12 weeks in summer. Paid. Open to college freshmen, college sophomores, college juniors, college seniors. ▶ *Student observer program interns:* responsibilities include assisting attorneys in research and memoranda of legal cases. Duration is 10 weeks. Unpaid. Open to third-year law students. ▶ *Summer honors program interns:* responsibilities include participating in topical seminars on various aspects of federal securities laws, taking part in a series of educational lectures and meetings, and working with an assigned attorney on a variety of projects. Duration is 10 weeks. Unpaid. Open to first and second-year law students. ▶ *20 summer law student program.* Duration is 8-10 weeks. Paid. Open to first and second-year law students.
Benefits Formal training, job counseling, names of contacts, opportunity to attend seminars/workshops, possible full-time employment, travel reimbursement, willing to complete paperwork for educational credit, willing to provide letters of recommendation.
Contact Write Marcia Spillane or Derek Childress (legal positions), Personnel Management Specialists. No phone calls. In-person interview recommended. Applicants must submit a formal organization application, cover letter, resume, academic transcripts. Application deadline: 7—8 weeks before beginning of semester for student observer program, continuous for research assistants, February 13 for summer law student program, March 13 for summer honors program, November 1 for advanced commitment program. World Wide Web: http://www.sec.gov/asec/secjobs.htm.

SENATE REPUBLICAN POLICY COMMITTEE
347 Russell Senate Office Building
Washington, District of Columbia 20510

General Information Committee that assists U.S. Senators and their staffs in aspects of the legislative process, distributes legislative background papers, and provides closed-circuit broadcasting of Senate Floor activities. Established in 1946. Number of employees: 18. Unit of United States Senate, Washington, District of Columbia. Number of internship applications received each year: 75.

Internships Available ▶ *3–4 legislative interns:* responsibilities include assisting the RPC staff with a full range of office tasks; answering phones and providing general clerical assistance, as well as conducting legislative research to assist in the compilation of policy papers and other timely projects. Candidates should have computer skills, editing skills, knowledge of field, office skills, oral communication skills, organizational skills, personal interest in the field, research skills, self-motivation, strong interpersonal skills, writing skills. Duration is 1–2 semesters. $892 per month. Open to college juniors, college seniors.

Benefits Names of contacts, opportunity to attend seminars/workshops, willing to complete paperwork for educational credit, willing to provide letters of recommendation.

Contact Write or call Mr. Wes Harris, Administrative Director. Phone: 202-224-2946. Telephone interview required. Applicants must submit a formal organization application, cover letter, resume, writing sample, three letters of recommendation, one 3-to 5-page writing sample. Application deadline: March 15 for summer, July 1 for fall, November 30 for spring. World Wide Web: http://www.senate.gov/~rpc.

SENATOR JAMES M. INHOFE
453 Russell Senate Office Building
Washington, District of Columbia 20510

General Information Congressional office representing the State of Oklahoma. Established in 1994. Number of employees: 24. Number of internship applications received each year: 30.

Internships Available ▶ *2–6 spring/fall interns:* responsibilities include administrative duties, correspondence, attending hearings, preparing reports, and running errands. Duration is 10 weeks. Unpaid. Open to college juniors, college seniors, recent college graduates, law students. ▶ *10–15 summer interns:* responsibilities include administrative duties, correspondence, attending hearings, preparing reports, and running errands. Duration is 6 weeks. Position available as unpaid or at $800 per duration of internship. Open to college juniors, college seniors, recent college graduates. Candidates for all positions should have editing skills, office skills, oral communication skills, personal interest in the field, research skills, strong interpersonal skills, strong leadership ability, writing skills. International applications accepted.

Benefits Opportunity to attend seminars/workshops, willing to act as a professional reference, willing to complete paperwork for educational credit, willing to provide letters of recommendation.

Contact Write, call, or e-mail Cathey Cravens, Intern Coordinator. Phone: 202-224-4721. E-mail: cathey_cravens@inhofe.senate.gov. Applicants must submit a formal organization application, cover letter, resume, academic transcripts, writing sample, three personal references, three letters of recommendation. Application deadline: March 15 for summer, August 15 for fall, December 15 for spring. World Wide Web: http://www.senate.gov/~inhofe/.

SENATOR LARRY E. CRAIG
United States Senate
Washington, District of Columbia 20510-1203

General Information Personal office of Republican Senator from Idaho. Number of employees: 22. Number of internship applications received each year: 30.

Internships Available ▶ *5–6 legislative interns:* responsibilities include working with legislative correspondent to research issues; composing correspondence; attending committee hearings; sitting in and taking notes on meetings; and completing small projects; may also include opening, sorting, and delivering mail; answering phone; greeting constituents; running errands; and other clerical duties. Candidates should have ability to work independently, computer skills, oral communication skills, organizational skills, personal interest in the field, research skills, self-motivation, strong interpersonal skills, written communication skills. Duration is 1 semester. $800 per month. Open to college freshmen, college sophomores, college juniors, college seniors, recent college graduates, graduate students, law students, preference given to Idaho students. International applications accepted.

Benefits On-the-job training, willing to act as a professional reference, willing to complete paperwork for educational credit, willing to provide letters of recommendation, DC political experience for Idaho students.

Contact Write, call, or e-mail Pat Olsen, Administrative Director. Phone: 202-224-2752. E-mail: pat_olsen@craig.senate.gov. In-person interview recommended. Applicants must submit a formal organization application, resume, academic transcripts, 1-2 writing samples and 2-3 personal references. Application deadline: March 15 for summer (May—August), July 1 for fall (September—December), November 15 for spring (January—May). World Wide Web: http://craig.senate.gov.

SONOMA COUNTY ECONOMIC DEVELOPMENT BOARD
401 College Avenue, Suite D
Santa Rosa, California 95401-5119

General Information Government body charged with enhancing the local economy and quality of life. Established in 1957. Number of employees: 10. Department of County of Sonoma, Santa Rosa, California. Number of internship applications received each year: 100.

Internships Available ▶ *4 economic vitality fellows.* Candidates should have ability to work independently, oral communication skills, self-motivation, strong interpersonal skills, writing skills. Duration is 1 year, beginning in either winter or summer (2 positions each term). $2,700 per month. Open to recent college graduates, graduate students, law students. International applications accepted.

Benefits Formal training, job counseling, names of contacts, on-the-job training, opportunity to attend seminars/workshops, possible full-time employment, travel reimbursement, willing to act as a professional reference, willing to complete paperwork for educational credit, willing to provide letters of recommendation, chance to work with leaders in business, government, and education.

Contact Write Ben G. Stone, Coordinator, 401 College Avenue, Suite D, Santa Rosa, California 95401-5119. No phone calls. In-person interview required. Applicants must submit a cover letter, resume, academic transcripts, 3-page writing sample. Application deadline: February 15 for summer-to-summer (1 year) fellowship, September 15 for winter-to-winter (1 year) fellowship.

SOUTH DAKOTA LEGISLATURE–LEGISLATIVE RESEARCH COUNCIL
500 East Capitol
Pierre, South Dakota 57501-5070

General Information Legislative service agency that provides nonpartisan research and legal services to the 105 members of the South Dakota legislature. Established in 1951. Number of employees: 24. Number of internship applications received each year: 30.

Internships Available ▶ *22 legislative interns:* responsibilities include serving as partisan staff to legislators, conducting research on issues facing the legislature, tracking and responding to legislators' constituent requests, monitoring and summarizing legislative meetings and legislation, and performing general office administration. Candidates should have office skills, organizational skills, research skills, self-motivation, strong interpersonal skills, writing skills. Duration is 7–8 weeks. $1,960–$2,240 per duration of internship. Open to college freshmen,

college sophomores, college juniors, college seniors, graduate students, law students. International applications accepted.
Benefits Names of contacts, willing to act as a professional reference, willing to complete paperwork for educational credit, willing to provide letters of recommendation.
Contact Write Mr. David Ortbahn, Principal Research Analyst. In-person interview recommended. Application deadline: October 15 for winter (January to March). World Wide Web: http://www.state.sd.us/state/legis/lrc.htm.

STATE OF MINNESOTA, DEPARTMENT OF EMPLOYEE RELATIONS
200 Centennial Office Building, 658 Cedar Street
St. Paul, Minnesota 55155

General Information Department of Employee Relations oversees the State Employee Health Promotion Program which provides consultations and resources to help state agencies develop policies/programs that promote healthy lifestyles and better health among employees and their families. Number of employees: 46,000. Number of internship applications received each year: 15.
Internships Available ▶ *1 Minnesota State Employee Health Promotion Program intern.* Candidates should have ability to work independently, ability to work with others, college degree in related field, computer skills, personal interest in the field, self-motivation. Position available as unpaid or paid. Open to college juniors, college seniors, recent college graduates, graduate students. International applications accepted.
Benefits Opportunity to attend seminars/workshops, travel reimbursement, willing to act as a professional reference, willing to complete paperwork for educational credit, willing to provide letters of recommendation, parking expenses covered.
Contact Write, call, fax, or e-mail John F. Hogan, Health Promotion Specialist. Phone: 651-296-5843. Fax: 651-296-5445. E-mail: john.hogan@state.mn.us. In-person interview recommended. Applicants must submit a cover letter, resume, three personal references. Applications are accepted continuously. World Wide Web: http://www.doer.state.mn.us/ei-schpp.htm.

UNITED STATES SECRET SERVICE
1800 G Street, NW, Room 912
Washington, District of Columbia 20223

General Information Government office of investigative and protective operations. Established in 1865. Number of employees: 4,800. Unit of United States Department of Treasury, Washington, District of Columbia. Number of internship applications received each year: 130.
Internships Available ▶ *20–30 student volunteer interns:* responsibilities include assisting agents with various tasks and administrative duties. Candidates should have ability to work with others, college courses in field, office skills, plan to pursue career in field. Duration is 1 semester. Unpaid. Open to college freshmen, college sophomores, college juniors, college seniors, graduate students.
Benefits Job counseling, names of contacts, willing to provide letters of recommendation.
Contact Write, call, or fax Velina S. Sutton, Internship Coordinator, 1800 G Street, NW, Room 912, Washington, District of Columbia 20223. Phone: 202-435-5800. Fax: 202-435-5613. In-person interview recommended. Applicants must submit a cover letter, resume, background check. Application deadline: January 10 for summer, April 14 for fall, August 15 for spring. World Wide Web: http://www.jobweb.org/employer/ussecret.htm.

U.S. SENATOR DIANNE FEINSTEIN
11111 Santa Monica Boulevard, Suite 915
Los Angeles, California 90025

General Information One of the four district offices representing Senator Feinstein in the state of California. Established in 1992. Number of employees: 8. Number of internship applications received each year: 20.

Internships Available ▶ *5–10 interns:* responsibilities include research, drafting letters to constituents, drafting memos to the Senator, attending events on behalf of the Senator, administrative work. Candidates should have ability to work independently, computer skills, knowledge of field, oral communication skills, research skills, self-motivation, strong interpersonal skills, writing skills. Duration is flexible (25 hours per week). Unpaid. Open to high school seniors, recent high school graduates, college freshmen, college sophomores, college juniors, college seniors. International applications accepted.
Benefits Names of contacts, on-the-job training, opportunity to attend seminars/workshops, possible full-time employment, travel reimbursement, willing to act as a professional reference, willing to complete paperwork for educational credit, willing to provide letters of recommendation.
Contact Write or call Juliette Aldarondo, Intern Coordinator, 11111 Santa Monica Boulevard, Suite 915, Los Angeles, California 90025. Phone: 310-914-7300. In-person interview recommended. Applicants must submit a formal organization application, cover letter, resume, writing sample, three personal references. Applications are accepted continuously. World Wide Web: http://www.senate.gov/~feinstein/.

U.S. SENATOR MAX BAUCUS
511 Hart Building
Washington, District of Columbia 20510

General Information Represents state of Montana in U.S. Senate. Established in 1978. Number of employees: 25.
Internships Available ▶ *4–5 administrative/legislative interns:* responsibilities include writing statements, attending hearings and briefings, and researching legislation. Duration is 1 semester or 1 summer. Unpaid. Open to college freshmen, college sophomores, college juniors, college seniors, recent college graduates, graduate students, law students.
Benefits Job counseling, on-the-job training, opportunity to attend seminars/workshops, possible full-time employment, willing to act as a professional reference, willing to complete paperwork for educational credit, willing to provide letters of recommendation.
Contact Write or call Ms. Nancy Hadley, Intern Coordinator. Phone: 202-224-2651. Applicants must submit a formal organization application, two personal references. Applications are accepted continuously.

VERMONT STATE PARKS DIVISION
103 South Main Street
Waterbury, Vermont 05671

General Information Division that plans, maintains, operates, designs, and constructs a system of state parks. Established in 1924. Number of employees: 5. Division of Department of Forests, Parks, and Recreation, Waterbury, Vermont. Number of internship applications received each year: 5.
Internships Available ▶ *1–2 interns:* responsibilities include designing and conducting programs focused on the operation of a state park system. Candidates should have ability to work independently, organizational skills, self-motivation, strong interpersonal skills, writing skills, written communication skills. Duration is flexible. Unpaid. Open to college seniors, recent college graduates, graduate students. International applications accepted.
Benefits Job counseling, names of contacts, opportunity to attend seminars/workshops, travel reimbursement, willing to complete paperwork for educational credit, willing to provide letters of recommendation.
Contact Write Mr. Larry Simino, Director of State Parks. No phone calls. In-person interview required. Applicants must submit a cover letter, resume, three personal references, three letters of recommendation. Application deadline: March 1 for summer; continuous for academic year. World Wide Web: http://www.state.vt.us/anr/fpr/parks/.

VIRGINIA OFFICE OF VOLUNTEERISM
730 East Broad Street
Richmond, Virginia 23219-1849

General Information Provider of information, training, and technical assistance to public and nonprofit organizations which mobilize volunteers to meet community needs. Established in 1974. Number of employees: 6. Unit of Virginia Department of Social Services, Division of Community Programs and Resources, Richmond, Virginia. Number of internship applications received each year: 3.

Internships Available ▶ *1 Virginia Youth Service Council publications coordinator:* responsibilities include entering text and designing layout for the council newsletter and other publications, updating and maintaining the database and coordinating mailings, attending 1 to 2 VYSC meetings, and working with VA COOL to redesign a brochure. Candidates should have ability to work independently, editing skills, organizational skills, personal interest in the field, written communication skills, knowledge of Pagemaker, MS Windows, MS Word, MS Access and MS Excel. Duration is flexible (5 to 10 hours per week). Open to high school seniors, recent high school graduates, college freshmen, college sophomores, college juniors, college seniors, recent college graduates, individuals reentering the workforce. ▶ *1–2 project assistants:* responsibilities include working with small staff to assist leaders of volunteer and community service programs. Candidates should have ability to work independently, ability to work with others, computer skills, organizational skills, personal interest in the field, self-motivation. Duration is flexible. Open to high school students, high school seniors, recent high school graduates, college freshmen, college sophomores, college juniors, college seniors, recent college graduates, graduate students, law students, career changers, individuals reentering the workforce. ▶ *1–2 research assistants:* responsibilities include helping to streamline volunteerism research library. Candidates should have ability to work independently, analytical skills, computer skills, organizational skills, self-motivation, writing skills. Duration is flexible. Open to high school students, high school seniors, recent high school graduates, college freshmen, college sophomores, college juniors, college seniors, recent college graduates, graduate students, law students, career changers, individuals reentering the workforce. All positions are unpaid. International applications accepted.

Benefits Names of contacts, opportunity to attend seminars/workshops, possible full-time employment, travel reimbursement, willing to act as a professional reference, willing to complete paperwork for educational credit, willing to provide letters of recommendation.

Contact Write, call, fax, or e-mail Director. Phone: 804-692-1950. Fax: 804-692-1999. E-mail: llb2@email1.dss.state.va.us. In-person interview recommended. Applicants must submit a cover letter, resume, writing sample. Application deadline: February 28 for spring, May 31 for summer, September 30 for fall. World Wide Web: http://www.dss.state.va.us.

THE WHITE HOUSE INTERNSHIP PROGRAM
Old Executive Office Building, Room 84
Washington, District of Columbia 20502

General Information Program responding to the President's call for active participation in government by providing students with an opportunity to learn through service in the Executive Office of the President. Division of Executive Office of the President, Washington, District of Columbia. Number of internship applications received each year: 2,000.

Internships Available ▶ *225 interns:* responsibilities include working in various departments, assisting in the operations of press conferences, briefings, and public events. Candidates should have various skills, dependent upon office placement. Duration is 15–17 weeks. Unpaid. Open to college freshmen, college sophomores, college juniors, college seniors, recent college graduates, graduate students, law students, U.S. citizens at least 18 years old.

Benefits Formal training, job counseling, on-the-job training, opportunity to attend seminars/workshops, possible full-time employment, willing to act as a professional reference, willing to complete paperwork for educational credit, willing to provide letters of recommendation, speaker series, tour series, workshops.

Contact Write, call, or fax Alison Kolwaite, Director, Internship Program. Phone: 202-456-2742. Fax: 202-456-5123. Telephone interview required. Applicants must submit a formal organization application, cover letter, resume, academic transcripts, writing sample, two letters of recommendation. Application deadline: March 1 for summer, June 25 for fall (early decision deadline; applications accepted on a rolling basis thereafter), November 1 for spring (early decision deadline; applications accepted on a rolling basis thereafter).

YOUTH ADVOCACY AND INVOLVEMENT OFFICE, NORTH CAROLINA DEPARTMENT OF ADMINISTRATION
217 West Jones Street
Raleigh, North Carolina 27603

General Information State government agency that serves as an advocate for children and youth. Seeks to enhance the quality of life for North Carolina's children and youth through policy reviews, legislative recommendations, and positive intervention through leadership educational opportunities. Established in 1977. Number of employees: 12. Division of North Carolina Department of Administration, Raleigh, North Carolina. Number of internship applications received each year: 350.

Internships Available ▶ *100 interns.* Candidates should have oral communication skills, personal interest in the field, strong interpersonal skills, written communication skills. Duration is 10 weeks. $7 per hour. Open to college juniors and seniors who are North Carolina residents.

Benefits Formal training, job counseling, names of contacts, opportunity to attend seminars/workshops, willing to complete paperwork for educational credit, willing to provide letters of recommendation.

Contact Write, call, or fax Karen Bass, Internship Coordinator. Phone: 919-733-9296. Fax: 919-733-1461. In-person interview recommended. Applicants must submit a formal organization application, cover letter, resume, academic transcripts. Application deadline: January 25 for summer. World Wide Web: http://www.doa.state.nc.us/doa/yaio/intern.htm.

REAL ESTATE AND RENTAL AND LEASING

GENERAL

AVIS RENT A CAR SYSTEM, INC.
900 Old Country Road
Garden City, New York 11530

General Information Global leader in car rental services, with a worldwide repution for excellence in customer satisfaction, quality performance, employee involvement, financial strength and innovation; covers over 140 nations through more than 4800 worldwide locations. Established in 1946. Number of employees: 700. Number of internship applications received each year: 50.
Internships Available ▶ *Account managers:* responsibilities include planning sales strategies, negotiating rates and contract terms, and leading project work that will involve research, documentation, and presentations. Candidates should have computer skills, oral communication skills, self-motivation, strong interpersonal skills, strong leadership ability, written communication skills. Duration is 1 year minimum. Open to college sophomores, college juniors, college seniors. ▶ *General interns:* responsibilities include various duties based on requesting department. Candidates should have analytical skills, oral communication skills, organizational skills, personal interest in the field, self-motivation, strong interpersonal skills, strong leadership ability. Duration is flexible. Open to college freshmen, college sophomores, college juniors, college seniors, graduate students. ▶ *Management interns:* responsibilities include all basic rental and car preparation responsibilities in all operations, including indirect supervision of employees. Candidates should have oral communication skills, personal interest in the field, self-motivation, strong interpersonal skills, strong leadership ability. Duration is 1 year minimum. Open to college sophomores, college juniors. All positions paid at $8–$12 per hour.
Benefits Formal training, on-the-job training, opportunity to attend seminars/workshops, possible full-time employment, willing to act as a professional reference, willing to complete paperwork for educational credit, willing to provide letters of recommendation.
Contact Write, fax, or e-mail Sam Ojofeitimi, Manager of College Relations, 900 Old Country Road, Garden City, New York 11530. Fax: 516-222-6677. E-mail: sojofeit@avis.com. No phone calls. In-person interview required. Applicants must submit a formal organization application, cover letter, resume, three personal references, letter of recommendation, 1 writing sample may be required. Application deadline: March 1 for summer, December 1 for spring. World Wide Web: http://www.avis.com.

INSTITUTE OF REAL ESTATE MANAGEMENT FOUNDATION (IREM)
430 North Michigan Avenue
Chicago, Illinois 60611

General Information Foundation that provides resources for the betterment of real estate management, including quality education, publications, research, and other services. Established in 1977. Number of employees: 1. Number of internship applications received each year: 30.
Internships Available ▶ *15–30 interns with property management firms nationwide:* responsibilities include performing duties subject to the needs of the real estate management firm and the interest and skills of the intern. Candidates should have college degree in related field, computer skills, oral communication skills, plan to pursue career in field, strong interpersonal skills. Duration is 1 summer. Paid. Open to college sophomores, college juniors, college seniors, recent college graduates, graduate students. International applications accepted.
Benefits Possible full-time employment, willing to act as a professional reference, willing to complete paperwork for educational credit, willing to provide letters of recommendation, possible housing (free or at cost).
Contact Write, call, fax, or e-mail Ms. Lorraine Arbetter, Foundation Coordinator. Phone: 312-329-6008. Fax: 312-410-7908. E-mail: larbette@irem.org. In-person interview recommended. Applicants must submit a formal organization application, cover letter, resume, 2 letters of recommendation in scaled envelopes marked "confidential". Application deadline: March 1. World Wide Web: http://www.irem.org.

PREIT-RUBIN, INC.
200 South Broad Street
Philadelphia, Pennsylvania 19102

General Information Real estate management/development of commerical, multi-family, and retail properties. Established in 1997. Number of employees: 125. Affiliate of Pennsylvania Real Estate Investment Trust (PREIT), Philadelphia, Pennsylvania. Number of internship applications received each year: 50.
Internships Available ▶ *2–3 accounting interns:* responsibilities include assisting controllers with various accounting functions. Candidates should have ability to work independently, computer skills, knowledge of field, oral communication skills, organizational skills, personal interest in the field, plan to pursue career in field, strong interpersonal skills, written communication skills. Duration is flexible, but mainly the summer months (May to August). $9–$10 per hour. Open to college sophomores, college juniors, college seniors. ▶ *1–2 associate interns/financial analysts:* responsibilities include working on specific projects as assigned by the CFO, using analytical abilities. Candidates should have ability to work independently, analytical skills, computer skills, oral communication skills, personal interest in the field, strong interpersonal skills, written communication skills, bachelor's degree (minimum) required. Duration is flexible. fair with market value. Open to recent college graduates, graduate students, career changers, individuals reentering the workforce. International applications accepted.
Benefits On-the-job training, possible full-time employment, willing to act as a professional reference, willing to complete paperwork for educational credit, willing to provide letters of recommendation.
Contact Write, fax, or e-mail Jacquelyne Berry Batista, Human Resources Generalist. Fax: 215-546-3766. E-mail: batistaj@preit.com. No phone calls. In-person interview required. Applicants must submit a cover letter, resume. Applications are accepted continuously. World Wide Web: http://www.preit.com.

RETAIL TRADE

GENERAL

AUTOMOTIVE RESTORATION, INC.
1785 Barnum Avenue
Stratford, Connecticut 06497

General Information Antique and classic automobile restoration shop that performs panel fabrication, woodwork, upholstery, body, paint, and mechanical work; includes management, appraisal, and evaluation. Number of employees: 30. Number of internship applications received each year: 5.
Internships Available ► *1–4 apprentices:* responsibilities include assisting tradespeople in areas including panel fabrication, photography, research, documentation, upholstery, older vehicle mechanics, race mechanics, paint/body, assembly/detail, and woodwork. $6–$15 per hour commensurate with experience and ability. ► *1–2 general office interns:* responsibilities include bookkeeping, invoicing, research, documentation, and business management. $6–$15 per hour, commensurate with experience and ability. Duration for all positions is 6–12 months. Open to high school students, high school seniors, recent high school graduates, college freshmen, college sophomores, college juniors, college seniors, recent college graduates, graduate students, law students, career changers, individuals reentering the workforce. International applications accepted.
Benefits Names of contacts, possible full-time employment, willing to complete paperwork for educational credit, willing to provide letters of recommendation.
Contact Write, call, fax, or e-mail Mr. Kent Bain, President. Phone: 203-377-6745. Fax: 203-386-0486. E-mail: bainks@msn.com. In-person interview recommended. Applicants must submit a cover letter, resume. Applications are accepted continuously. World Wide Web: http://www.automotiverestorationinc.org.

BARNEYS NEW YORK
575 Fifth Avenue
New York, New York 10017

General Information Retail organization that sells high quality clothes, accessories, and gifts. Established in 1923. Number of employees: 1,000. Number of internship applications received each year: 200.
Internships Available ► *Buying interns:* responsibilities include using the STS database system to input purchase orders information, input and monitor distributions, input and check transfers, and input and check price changes; tracking sales and preparing reports; checking daily on the status of outstanding purchase orders. Candidates should have ability to work independently, ability to work with others, computer skills, oral communication skills, organizational skills, plan to pursue career in field.
► *1 corporate human resources intern:* responsibilities include assisting in the preparation of various training projects, assisting the directors of human resources in various projects, assisting in the publication and distribution of BNY newsletter. Candidates should have ability to work with others, organizational skills, personal interest in the field, self-motivation, writing skills. ► *1–2 display interns:* responsibilities include assisting with the production of the seasonal Display Fashion Directive, assisting display staff in-store with the installation of display windows, hands-on experience with store displays management and store functions. Candidates should have ability to work independently, organizational

skills, plan to pursue career in field, self-motivation, strong interpersonal skills. ► *1 fashion merchandising intern:* responsibilities include helping to prepare seasonal fashion directive, calling new vendors, updating vendor press kits, keeping merchandise closet and presentation room in order, organizing files, communicating with buyers, steaming merchandise on photoshoots, scheduling appointments, and analyzing information pertaining to mailers. Candidates should have ability to work independently, ability to work with others, oral communication skills, personal interest in the field, self-motivation, written communication skills.
► *1–2 graphic design interns:* responsibilities include assisting in the creation, preparation, and publication of small-space advertising; working on design projects to support image campaign, warehouse sales, store openings, and in-state selling and promotional activities. Candidates should have ability to work independently, ability to work with others, knowledge of field, organizational skills, knowledge of QuarkXpress, Illustrator, and PhotoShop; preference given to majors in advertising and marketing communications or advertising design and computer graphics. ► *1 human resources intern (store):* responsibilities include managing and coordinating applicant pool, organizing and tracking all new hires and current employees on the human resources system, assisting human resources manager on various training programs. Candidates should have ability to work independently, ability to work with others, office skills, oral communication skills, organizational skills, plan to pursue career in field, strong interpersonal skills, strong leadership ability. ► *1–2 media/ marketing interns:* responsibilities include assisting in the research, compilation, evaluation, and reconciliation of media/marketing information necessary for planning. Candidates should have ability to work independently, oral communication skills, organizational skills, plan to pursue career in field, self-motivation, written communication skills. ► *1 merchandise planning intern:* responsibilities include compiling, organizing, and tracking weekly ready-to-wear receipts by department; tracking sales and preparing reports; gaining knowledge of the relationship between the planning and the buying offices. Candidates should have ability to work independently, ability to work with others, analytical skills, computer skills, organizational skills, personal interest in the field, self-motivation. ► *Publicity interns:* responsibilities include assisting with fashion presentations, special events, photo shoots, editorial credits, and merchandise. Candidates should have ability to work independently, ability to work with others, oral communication skills, organizational skills, plan to pursue career in field, self-motivation, writing skills, fluency in French or Japanese a plus. ► *1 studio services intern:* responsibilities include greeting clients, creating correspondence to clients, checking in all merchandise, making appointments for new clients, assisting shoppers, and packaging and preparing merchandise for delivery. Duration for all positions is one summer or one semester. All positions are unpaid. Open to college sophomores, college juniors, college seniors, graduate students. International applications accepted.

Benefits Job counseling, names of contacts, opportunity to attend seminars/workshops, possible full-time employment, willing to act as a professional reference, willing to complete paperwork for educational credit, willing to provide letters of recommendation, store discount, travel/meal stipend.

Contact Write, call, or fax Internship Coordinator; Corporate Human Resources, 575 Fifth Avenue, 11th Floor, New York, New York 10017. Phone: 212-450-8740. Fax: 212-450-8489. In-person interview required. Applicants must submit a formal organization application, cover letter, resume, portfolio. Applications are accepted continuously.

BMW OF NORTH AMERICA, INC.
300 Chestnut Ridge Road
Woodcliff Lake, New Jersey 07675-7731

General Information Wholesaler and distributor of automobiles, motorcycles, and parts. Established in 1976. Number of employees: 800. Unit of BMW, AG, Munich, Germany. Number of internship applications received each year: 400.

Internships Available ▶ *6 summer interns:* responsibilities include positions in sales, engineering, finance, distribution, marketing, administration, and service. Duration is 3 months minimum. Paid. Open to college juniors, college seniors. International applications accepted.

Benefits Formal training, job counseling, names of contacts, on-the-job training, travel reimbursement, willing to complete paperwork for educational credit, willing to provide letters of recommendation.

Contact Write or fax Human Resources Department, PO Box 8271, Haledon, New Jersey 07538. Fax: 201-307-0992. No phone calls. In-person interview required. Applicants must submit a cover letter, resume. Application deadline: March 1.

GRANDY FARM MARKET
PO Box 673
Grandy, North Carolina 27939

General Information Retail outlet for fruits and vegetables, frozen yogurt, and baked goods. Established in 1987. Number of employees: 25.

Internships Available ▶ *2 retail produce trainees:* responsibilities include carrying out various tasks and responsibilities involved in the retail of fresh produce and baked goods. Duties are similar to those in a supermarket, but in a farm market atmosphere. Candidates should have personal interest in the field, self-motivation, strong interpersonal skills. $5–$6 per hour. Open to recent high school graduates, college freshmen, college sophomores, college juniors, college seniors, recent college graduates. International applications accepted.

Benefits Free housing, meals at a cost, on-the-job training, willing to act as a professional reference, willing to complete paperwork for educational credit, willing to provide letters of recommendation.

Contact Write or call Colon Grandy, Owner. Phone: 252-453-2658. Telephone interview required. Applicants must submit a formal organization application, resume, academic transcripts, three personal references, letter of recommendation. Application deadline: April 30.

THE HOME DEPOT, CORPORATE OFFICE
2455 Paces Ferry Road
Atlanta, Georgia 30339

General Information Retailer of hardware, home improvement, and garden/patio supplies. Established in 1979. Number of employees: 4,000. Number of internship applications received each year: 40.

Internships Available ▶ *8–12 building better health interns:* responsibilities include assisting in coordination of wellness events, facility supervision, instruction of fitness and nutrition classes, writing articles for newsletters, promoting wellness program through incentive and motivational programs, and coordinating community resources in the field. Candidates should have ability to work independently, knowledge of field, oral communication skills, self-motivation, strong interpersonal skills, written communication skills. Paid. Open to college juniors, college seniors, recent college graduates, graduate students, career changers. International applications accepted.

Benefits Free meals, job counseling, on-the-job training, willing to act as a professional reference, willing to complete paperwork for educational credit, willing to provide letters of recommendation, stipend opportunity.

Contact Write, call, or e-mail Linda Welch, Corporate Wellness Coordinator, The Home Depot, 2455 Paces Ferry Road, Atlanta, Georgia 30339. Phone: 770-433-8211 Ext. 18489. E-mail: linda_welch@homedepot.com. In-person interview recommended. Applicants must submit a formal organization application, resume. Applications are accepted continuously.

LANDS' END
5 Lands' End Lane
Dodgeville, Wisconsin 53585

General Information A direct merchant of traditionally-styled classic casualwear for the family and products for bed and bath. Accessories are offered to customers through regular mailing of catalogs and through the Internet. Established in 1963. Number of employees: 8,000. Number of internship applications received each year: 1,000.

Internships Available ▶ *2–4 art directors:* responsibilities include assisting with the layout and design of the catalogs; coordinating laydown shoots, editing film, and working with revision; learning the catalog creative process by working with experienced art directors. Candidates should have ability to work independently, college courses in field, self-motivation, strong interpersonal skills, strong leadership ability. Duration is 6 months. $10 per hour. ▶ *4–6 information services:* responsibilities include developing programs and documentation, coding, testing, and debugging programs, and developing specifications and test plans. Candidates should have college courses in field, computer skills, self-motivation, strong interpersonal skills, strong leadership ability. Duration is 3 or 6 months. $15 per hour. ▶ *1–2 internet development interns:* responsibilities include designing layouts for the internet using the Mac, understanding of HTML markup language, taking projects through the creative cycle from conception and design to find electronic authoring. Candidates should have ability to work independently, college courses in field, computer skills, self-motivation, strong interpersonal skills, strong leadership ability. Duration is 3–6 months. $10–$15 per hour. ▶ *2–4 inventory interns:* responsibilities include pre-season planning and forecasting, extensive sales trend analysis, learning inventory concepts and strategies for direct marketing, and tracking the manufacturing process. Candidates should have ability to work independently, analytical skills, self-motivation, strong interpersonal skills, strong leadership ability. Duration is 3 months. $10 per hour. ▶ *2–3 merchandising interns:* responsibilities include assisting merchants in driving specific categories through product development, developing competitive analysis for team reviews, understanding the levers that affect the business. Candidates should have analytical skills, college courses in field, plan to pursue career in field, self-motivation, strong interpersonal skills. Duration is 3 months. $10 per hour. ▶ *5–10 operations management interns:* responsibilities include providing managerial support in distribution centers, taking on a leadership role within call centers operations, and coaching and developing an interal work force. Candidates should have ability to work independently, college courses in field, self-motivation, strong interpersonal skills, strong leadership ability. Duration is June to December. $10 per hour. ▶ *2–4 quality interns:* responsibilities include assisting with product and specification development, fit evaluation, and testing of fabrics. Candidates should have ability to work independently, college courses in field, self-motivation, strong interpersonal skills, strong leadership ability, background in clothing and textiles. Duration is 3 months. $10 per hour. ▶ *2–4 retail store management interns:* responsibilities include assisting with store operations including merchandising, monitoring inventory levels, accountability for overall operations, and setting up and executing store and advertising plans. Candidates should have ability to work independently, experience in the field, self-motivation, strong interpersonal skills, strong leadership ability. Duration is 3 months. $10 per hour. Open to college juniors, college seniors.

Benefits Formal training, job counseling, on-the-job training, opportunity to attend seminars/workshops, possible full-time employment, travel reimbursement, willing to complete paperwork for educational credit, willing to provide letters of recom-

Lands' End (continued)

mendation, clothing/merchandise discounts, access to on-site fitness facility, payment of housing security deposit.
Contact Write, call, fax, or e-mail Stephanie Bennett, Recruitment and Development Specialist, 5 Lands End Lane, Dodgeville, Wisconsin 53595. Phone: 608-935-4928. Fax: 608-935-4831. E-mail: sdbenne@landsend.com. In-person interview recommended. Applicants must submit a resume, portfolio, video conference (where applicable), on-line application, 2-3 writing samples (for certain positions). Application deadline: March 1 for summer, August 1 for fall, December 1 for spring. World Wide Web: http://www.de.landsend.com.

MAURICES, INC.
105 West Superior Street
Duluth, Minnesota 55802

General Information Nationwide retailer. Established in 1931.
Internships Available ▶ *Programming interns:* responsibilities include assisting in the development of mainframe and PC systems to support retail business applications. Candidates should have computer skills, information systems degree or major. Duration is 6 months. Paid. Open to college freshmen, college sophomores, college juniors, college seniors, recent college graduates.
Benefits Names of contacts, willing to complete paperwork for educational credit, willing to provide letters of recommendation.
Contact Write or e-mail Human Resources Department. E-mail: human_resources@maurices.inrg.com. No phone calls. Applicants must submit a cover letter, resume. Applications are accepted continuously.

METROPOLITAN WATER DISTRICT OF SOUTHERN CALIFORNIA
700 North Alameda Street
Los Angeles, California 90012

General Information Water wholesaler. Established in 1928. Number of employees: 1,000. Number of internship applications received each year: 200.
Internships Available ▶ *1 publications intern (photography):* responsibilities include assisting with photography for public information material produced by Metropolitan. Interns will also learn about maintaining photo archives, and will perform identification, labeling and cataloging activities. Candidates should have experience in the field, oral communication skills, personal interest in the field, plan to pursue career in field, strong interpersonal skills. ▶ *1 publications intern (writing):* responsibilities include assisting with the writing of public information material produced by Metropolitan, including project and general information brochures, an internal company newsletter, and a general interest magazine. Candidates should have computer skills, editing skills, plan to pursue career in field, research skills, writing skills. Duration for all positions is 3–6 months. All positions paid at $10 per hour. Open to college juniors, college seniors, graduate students. International applications accepted.
Benefits Meals at a cost, names of contacts, opportunity to attend seminars/workshops, possible full-time employment, travel reimbursement, willing to act as a professional reference, willing to complete paperwork for educational credit, willing to provide letters of recommendation.
Contact Write, call, fax, or e-mail Monica Schwarze, Public Affairs Representative, 700 North Alameda Street, Los Angeles, California 90012. Phone: 213-217-6487. Fax: 213-217-6500. E-mail: mschwarze@mwd.dst.ca.us. In-person interview required. Applicants must submit a cover letter, resume, three writing samples, letter of recommendation. Applications are accepted continuously. World Wide Web: http://www.mwd.dst.ca.us.

ON CAMPUS MARKETING
4630 Montgomery Avenue, Suite 300
Bethesda, Maryland 20814

General Information Direct mail marketing firm which sells useful products and services to college students and groups. Established in 1988. Number of employees: 45. Number of internship applications received each year: 100.
Internships Available ▶ *1 human resources intern:* responsibilities include helping the human resources department with candidate tracking, reference checks, calling back to give information, setting up interviews, other administrative duties, and special projects. Candidates should have computer skills, office skills, oral communication skills, personal interest in the field, strong interpersonal skills. $25–$50 per week. ▶ *1–3 information technology interns:* responsibilities include updating Web page, creation on Web links, Access database work, and talking with clients on information technology issues. Candidates should have analytical skills, college courses in field, computer skills, experience in the field, knowledge of field, office skills. $25–$50 per week. ▶ *1–3 marketing (school management) interns:* responsibilities include assisting account managers with day-to-day client contact using database and spreadsheet applications to run reports and create correspondence. Candidates should have ability to work independently, ability to work with others, analytical skills, computer skills, oral communication skills, organizational skills, self-motivation. $25–$50 per week. ▶ *1–3 marketing interns:* responsibilities include assisting in conference logistics and purchasing, organizing and doing inventory on marketing supplies, and executing administrative detail for marketing plans and promotion. Candidates should have ability to work with others, computer skills, office skills, research skills, self-motivation, written communication skills. $25–$50 per week. ▶ *1–2 production interns:* responsibilities include using the Internet, proofreading, and assisting in direct mail print production. Candidates should have ability to work independently, computer skills, editing skills, office skills, organizational skills, self-motivation. $25–$50 per week. Open to high school students, high school seniors, college freshmen, college sophomores, college juniors, college seniors.
Benefits Names of contacts, on-the-job training, possible full-time employment, willing to act as a professional reference, willing to complete paperwork for educational credit, willing to provide letters of recommendation.
Contact Write, fax, or e-mail Emma Eastwood, Recruiter, 4630 Montgomery Avenue, Suite 300, Bethesda, Maryland 20814. Fax: 301-652-1480. E-mail: emma@ocmemail.com. In-person interview recommended. Applicants must submit a formal organization application, cover letter, resume. Application deadline: April 1 for summer, July 1 for fall, November 15 for spring. World Wide Web: http://www.oncampusmarketing.com.

RICH'S/LAZARUS/GOLDSMITH'S DEPARTMENT STORES
223 Perimeter Center Parkway
Atlanta, Georgia 30346

General Information Traditional retail department store that emphasizes dynamic store environments, diverse merchandise selection, and superior customer service. Established in 1867. Number of employees: 20,000. Unit of Federated Department Stores, Inc., Cincinnati, Ohio. Number of internship applications received each year: 200.
Internships Available ▶ *Sales management interns:* responsibilities include management, visual merchandising, human resources, business analysis, and store-line support exposure. Duration is 10 weeks. $8 per hour. Open to college sophomores, college juniors, college seniors. International applications accepted.
Benefits Formal training, possible full-time employment, willing to complete paperwork for educational credit.
Contact Write, call, fax, or e-mail Tim Ferenchik, Manager, College Relations. Phone: 770-913-5528. Fax: 770-913-5114. E-mail: tferenchick@fds.com. In-person interview required. Applicants must submit a resume. Applications are accepted continuously. World Wide Web: http://www.federated-fds.com.

SHERWIN-WILLIAMS
10740 C Broadway Avenue
Garfield Heights, Ohio 44125

General Information Company specializing in the sale of paint coatings and related products to wholesale and commercial markets. Established in 1866. Number of employees: 3,000. Unit of Sherwin-Williams Company, Cleveland, Ohio.
Internships Available ▶ *30–50 summer interns:* responsibilities include servicing customers, performing basic administrative tasks such as processing audit applications, receiving payments on accounts, processing paperwork, performing tasks assigned by manager. Candidates should have oral communication skills, personal interest in the field, self-motivation, strong interpersonal skills, interests in sales as a career. Duration is 10–12 weeks. $8–$9 per hour. Open to college sophomores, college juniors, college seniors. International applications accepted.
Benefits Formal training, names of contacts, on-the-job training, possible full-time employment, willing to complete paperwork for educational credit, management training program.
Contact Write or fax Tony Dolejs, Human Resources Manager. Fax: 216-341-1032. No phone calls. In-person interview required. Applicants must submit a formal organization application, cover letter, resume. Applications are accepted continuously. World Wide Web: http://www.sherwin.com.

SMITHSONIAN INSTITUTION RETAIL
955 L'Enfant Plaza, Suite 8000
Washington, District of Columbia 20024

General Information Central coordinating unit for museum shop and catalogue sales. Unit of Smithsonian Institution, Washington, District of Columbia.
Internships Available ▶ *Interns:* responsibilities include assisting in operation of museum gift shops and the catalogue sales departments. Candidates should have interest in retail merchandising, marketing, and sales. Duration is flexible. Position available as unpaid or paid. Open to college freshmen, college sophomores, college juniors, college seniors. International applications accepted.
Benefits Willing to complete paperwork for educational credit.
Contact Write Central Referral Service, Arts and Industries Building, 900 Jefferson Drive, SW, Washington, District of Columbia 20560-0427. Standard Smithsonian intern application (must be done through Central Referral Service). Application deadline: February 15 for summer, June 15 for fall, October 15 for spring.

THE SOUTHWESTERN COMPANY
PO Box 305140
Nashville, Tennessee 37230

General Information Summer work program for college students. Established in 1868.
Internships Available ▶ *4,000 student sales interns.* Duration is 12 weeks. Paid. Open to college freshmen, college sophomores, college juniors, college seniors, recent college graduates. International applications accepted.
Benefits Formal training, job counseling, names of contacts, possible full-time employment, willing to complete paperwork for educational credit, willing to provide letters of recommendation, access to full-service placement office.
Contact Write Melanie Yappen, Corporate Recruiting Manager. In-person interview recommended. Applicants must submit a formal organization application, cover letter, resume. Application deadline: June 1. World Wide Web: http://www.southwestern.com.

STEIN MART
1200 Riverplace Boulevard
Jacksonville, Florida 32207

General Information Fashion retail store. Established in 1909. Number of employees: 15,000. Number of internship applications received each year: 50.
Internships Available ▶ *1–3 buying office corporate interns:* responsibilities include working with buyers and vendors to purchase and distribute merchandise to the stores. Candidates should have ability to work independently, analytical skills, college courses in field, computer skills, editing skills, knowledge of field, office skills, oral communication skills, organizational skills, plan to pursue career in field, research skills, self-motivation, strong interpersonal skills, strong leadership ability, writing skills. Open to college seniors. ▶ *5–20 store interns:* responsibilities include working in the retail store, learning merchandising and sales techniques. Candidates should have ability to work independently, college courses in field, knowledge of field, oral communication skills, organizational skills, plan to pursue career in field, self-motivation, strong interpersonal skills, strong leadership ability, written communication skills. Open to college juniors, college seniors. Duration for all positions is 8–12 weeks. All positions paid at $7 per hour.
Benefits Job counseling, on-the-job training, willing to complete paperwork for educational credit.
Contact Write, fax, or e-mail Internship Coordinator, 1200 Riverplace Boulevard, Jacksonville, Florida 32207. Fax: 904-346-1297. E-mail: hr@steinmart.com. No phone calls. In-person interview required. Applicants must submit a formal organization application, cover letter, resume. Applications are accepted continuously. World Wide Web: http://www.steinmart.com.

TJX COMPANIES INC./T.J. MAXX & MARSHALLS DIVISIONS
770 Cochituate Road
Framingham, Massachusetts 01701

General Information World's largest off-price retailer, with divisions including T.J. Maxx, Marshalls, Homegoods, A.J. Wright, Winners (Canada), and T.K. Maxx (United Kingdom). Established in 1977. Number of employees: 2,000. Number of internship applications received each year: 200.
Internships Available ▶ *6–10 allocation analysts:* responsibilities include assisting with decisions regarding the allocation of merchandise, analyzing sales trends, and acting as a liaison between the distribution centers and the buyers. Candidates should have analytical skills, computer skills, knowledge of field, oral communication skills, organizational skills, plan to pursue career in field, research skills, strong interpersonal skills, written communication skills. Duration is 12 weeks. Paid. Open to college juniors, college seniors.
Benefits Job counseling, on-the-job training, possible full-time employment, willing to complete paperwork for educational credit.
Contact Write, fax, or e-mail Staffing Specialist, Department INT 2000, 770 Cochituate Road, Framingham, Massachusetts 01701. Fax: 508-390-2650. E-mail: jobs@tjx.com. No phone calls. In-person interview required. Applicants must submit a formal organization application, cover letter, resume, two personal references, math and/or typing tests (for certain positions). Application deadline: March 21 for summer. World Wide Web: http://www.tjx.com.

TRANSPORTATION

GENERAL

AMERICA WEST AIRLINES
4000 East Sky Harbor Boulevard
Phoenix, Arizona 85034

General Information Major airline providing scheduled air service. Established in 1983. Number of employees: 11,000. Number of internship applications received each year: 100.
Internships Available ► *Interns:* responsibilities include working in public relations, communications, marketing, sales, or finance. Duration is flexible. Position available as unpaid or at up to $1500 per month. Open to college freshmen, college sophomores, college juniors, college seniors, graduate students. International applications accepted.
Benefits Willing to complete paperwork for educational credit, travel stipend.
Contact Write, fax, or e-mail Internship Coordinator, 4000 East Sky Harbor Boulevard, Phoenix, Arizona 55034. Fax: 602-693-8813. E-mail: employment@americawest.com. No phone calls. In-person interview required. Applicants must submit a cover letter, resume. Applications are accepted continuously. World Wide Web: http://www.americawest.com.

ARKANSAS BEST CORPORATION
3801 Old Greenwood Road, PO Box 10048
Fort Smith, Arkansas 72917-0048

General Information Holding company with subsidiaries engaged in worldwide freight transportation and distribution services, truck tire remanufacturing, and information services. Established in 1935. Number of employees: 15,055. Number of internship applications received each year: 100.
Internships Available ► *6–10 programmers/analysts:* responsibilities include analyzing, designing, and programming computer applications systems. Candidates should have analytical skills, college courses in field, computer skills, oral communication skills, strong interpersonal skills. Duration is flexible. $2,500–$2,700 per month. Open to college juniors, college seniors, graduate students.
Benefits Formal training, on-the-job training, opportunity to attend seminars/workshops, possible full-time employment, willing to complete paperwork for educational credit.
Contact Write, call, fax, or e-mail Mr. Timothy R. Harmon, Account Analyst. Phone: 501-784-8573. Fax: 501-784-8599. E-mail: tim.harmon@data-tronics.com. In-person interview required. Applicants must submit a formal organization application, cover letter, resume, academic transcripts. Applications are accepted continuously. World Wide Web: http://www.ARKBEST.com.

UTILITIES

GENERAL

AMERITECH NETWORK SERVICES
45 Erieview Plaza
Cleveland, Ohio 44114-1814

General Information Organization responsible for the planning, designing, construction, and maintenance of the telecommunication network, and installing and maintaining communication services to customers. Number of internship applications received each year: 200.

Internships Available ▶ *Management trainees:* responsibilities include telecommunications engineering, installation, switch technologies, and operator services (both technical and supervisory). Candidates should have analytical skills, computer skills, organizational skills, personal interest in the field, self-motivation, strong interpersonal skills, strong leadership ability, verbal skills. Duration is 3 months. $1650 per month (minimum). Open to college sophomores, graduate students, college juniors preferred.

Benefits Job counseling, names of contacts, on-the-job training, opportunity to attend seminars/workshops, possible full-time employment, travel reimbursement.

Contact Write or fax Human Resources Staffing Manager, Ameritech Managment Staffing Center, 2000 Ameritech Drive, Room 2F29A, Hoffman Estates, Illinois 60195. Fax: 847-248-9029. No phone calls. In-person interview recommended. Applicants must submit a formal organization application, resume. Applications are accepted continuously. World Wide Web: http://www.ameritech.com.

ASSOCIATED ELECTRIC COOPERATIVE, INC.
2814 South Golden Avenue, PO Box 754
Springfield, Missouri 65801-0754

General Information Electric utility (bulk supplier). Established in 1961. Number of employees: 125. Number of internship applications received each year: 20.

Internships Available ▶ *1 editorial/photography intern:* responsibilities include taking photos; assisting with interviews; helping write, research, proofread, and edit articles/news releases; handling most darkroom work; and conducting reader surveys. Candidates should have computer skills, editing skills, research skills, strong interpersonal skills, writing skills, college courses or experience in field. Duration is 1 summer. $6–$8 per hour. ▶ *1–3 engineering aides:* responsibilities include transmission planning/distribution for cooperative systems, planning load demands, looking for efficient ways to use current resource, making million-dollar decisions. Candidates should have analytical skills, computer skills, knowledge of field, plan to pursue career in field, strong interpersonal skills, college courses in power engineering. Duration is 1 summer, possible Christmas break. $8–$14 per hour. ▶ *1–3 programming aides:* responsibilities include developing designs and specifications for complex software applications (business and engineering disciplines) or support and expansion of existing mission-critical databases (real-time programming). Candidates should have college courses in field, computer skills, knowledge of field, plan to pursue career in field, strong interpersonal skills, major in computer science or electrical engineering. Duration is 1 summer. $8–$14 per hour. Open to college sophomores, college juniors, college seniors. International applications accepted.

Benefits On-the-job training, possible full-time employment, willing to act as a professional reference, willing to complete paperwork for educational credit, willing to provide letters of recommendation.

Contact Write, call, fax, or e-mail Cynthia Bryan, Senior Human Resourses Assistant, 2814 South Golden Avenue, PO Box 754, Springfield, Missouri 65801-0754. Phone: 417-881-1204. Fax: 417-885-9252. E-mail: cbryan@acci.org. In-person interview recommended. Applicants must submit a formal organization application, resume, academic transcripts, three personal references, portfolio and writing samples required for editorial/photographic intern. Application deadline: May 1 for summer. World Wide Web: http://www.aeci.org.

FIELD OF INTEREST INDEX

Key

The list below shows you how fields of interest are organized in this index. Find the categories in the index that best match your interests to find out which companies offer internships in those areas.

Architecture and Engineering
Engineers

Arts, Design, Entertainment, Media, and Sports
Artists and Related Workers
Communications and Media
Performers and Entertainers
Public Relations Specialists

Business and Financial Operations
Accountants and Auditors
Business Operations Specialists
Financial Specialists
Human Resources, Training, and Labor Relations
Specialists

Community and Social Services
Recreation Workers

Computer and Mathematical
Computer Specialists

Education, Training, and Library

Farming, Fishing, and Forestry

Food Preparation and Serving

Health
Health Service Coordinators

Installation, Maintenance, and Repair

Law

Life, Physical, and Social Sciences
Social Scientists

Office and Administration

Personal Care and Service
Transportation, Tourism, and Lodging Attendants

Production

Sales

Transportation and Material Moving Occupations

Arts, Design, Entertainment, Media, and Sports

Community and Social Services

Education, Training, and Library

Farming, Fishing, and Forestry

GEOGRAPHIC INDEX

INTERNATIONAL INTERNSHIPS INDEX

EMPLOYER INDEX

ACADEMIC LEVEL REQUIRED INDEX

Monongahela National Forest, White Sulphur District 429
NAFSA 195
National Campaign for Freedom of Expression 473
National Capital Region–Rock Creek Park 430
National Council on US–Arab Relations 395
National Crime Prevention Council 475
National Museum of American History 95
National Science Foundation 196
National Training and Information Center 478
National Women's Health Network 478
The New Conservatory Theatre Center 144
New Dramatists 50
New Haven Advocate 308
New Party 479
News Radio WGST 332
Nicolet National Forest, Eagle River-Florence Ranger District 433
9 to 5, National Association of Working Women 479
North Carolina State Parks and Recreation, Jockey's Ridge State Park 100
North Highlands Childrens Coalition 480
Northwest Coalition for Alternatives to Pesticides 434
Nuclear Information and Resource Service 434
Office of Historic Alexandria 103
Office of Sponsored Projects, Smithsonian Institution 495
Ohio State Parks 553
Old Post Office Tower, National Park Service 104
On Campus Marketing 562
Oxfam America 267
Paper Mill Playhouse 147
Partos Company 296
Pasadena Historical Museum 105
Pathfinders 268
Peace Offerings/Project of the Social Justice Center of Albany 482
Pennsylvania State Parks, Greenwood Furnace State Park 106
Penobscot Bay Press 326
People for the American Way Foundation 482
Phillips Publishing International, Inc. 327
Pioneer Playhouse 148
The Poetry Project at St. Mark's Church 107
Prevent Blindness Ohio 224
Primark 291
Progressive Action Network (West Coast Interns) 484
Project Open Hand Atlanta 270
Public Citizen's Congress Watch 484
Public Forum Institute 398
Pulse Ensemble Theatre 149

Queens Theater in the Park 173
Renaissance Multimedia 514
Resource Publications, Inc. 328
Rhode Island Commission on State Government Internships 36
Richard P. Dieguez, Attorney and Counsellor at Law 522
Rock Bridge Memorial State Park 108
Roundabout Theatre Company, Inc. 150
Sam Houston National Forest 110
San Diego Youth and Community Services 272
Scott County Family YMCA 273
SDV/ACCI 537
Seattle Opera Association 151
Seattle Youth Involvement Network 485
Seventeen Magazine 330
Siuslaw National Forest, Waldport Ranger District–Cape Perpetua Scenic Area 111
Smithsonian Office of Public Affairs 509
Somerset County Park Commission Environmental Education Center 442
South Street Seaport Museum 112
South Wood County YMCA 274
Spanish Education Development Center 200
Summerbridge National 202
Teen Line 276
Theatre De La Jeune Lune 154
The Theatre-Studio, Inc. 154
Tommy Boy Music 298
Touch of Nature Environmental Center 276
United Nations Association of the USA 400
United Way of Howard County 278
United Way of Waco 278
Untitled Theater Company #61 155
U.S. Servas, Inc. 488
The Vegetarian Resource Group 489
The Village Voice 312
Virginia Affiliate of the National Abortion and Reproductive Rights Action League 489
Virginia Office of Volunteerism 558
Visual Art Exchange 53
Volunteer Center of San Francisco 281
Volunteers for Outdoor Colorado 446
Washington Legal Foundation 524
WFLK-FM/WYLF-AM 334
Wilderness Watch 447
Williamstown Theater Festival 157
Wolf Trap Foundation for the Performing Arts 158
Women's Institute for Freedom of the Press 404
Women's Project and Productions 159
Women's Sports Foundation 205
World Game Institute 206
Yeshiva University Museum 121
Y.E.S. to Jobs 38
YMCA Camp Kern 449
YMCA of Greater West Chester 285

YWCA of Wake County, Inc. 288

HIGH SCHOOL SENIORS
Accredited Care, Inc. 215
Accuracy in Media 290
Affiliated Sante Group and the Rock Creek Foundation 226
AIM for the Handicapped 176
Albany Institute of History and Art 55
Allegheny Portage Railroad National Historic Site 56
Alliance for the Wild Rockies 405
Alternative House 228
Alternative Museum 56
Alternatives Federal Credit Union 209
American & International Designs, Inc. 511
American Association of Overseas Studies 29
American Civil Liberties Union of Pennsylvania 452
American Lung Association of Central Florida 216
American Lung Association of the District of Columbia (ALADC) 217
American Management Association 373
Americans for Democratic Action 453
American Visions Magazine 314
American Youth Work Center/ Youth Today 299
Amnesty International, Midwest Region 453
The Andy Warhol Museum 57
Anne Schwab's Model Store 497
Apple Art Gallery 40
Archive of Contemporary Music 161
Arden Theatre Company 125
Ash Lawn–Highland Summer Festival 126
Ashoka: Innovators for the Public 375
Association for Experiential Education (AEE) 178
Association of Independent Video and Filmmakers–Foundation for Independent Video and Film 292
The Audre Lorde Project 456
Automotive Restoration, Inc. 560
Ballet Internationale 127
Battery Dance Company 127
Big Brothers Big Sisters-Niagara County, Inc. 230
Big Brothers/Big Sisters of Meriden/Wallingford 232
Big Brothers/Big Sisters of North Alabama 232
Big Brothers Big Sisters of Salem County 233
Big Brothers/Big Sisters of the Fox Valley 233
Black Entertainment Television 340
Booker T. Washington National Monument 60
Boston YWCA 234
Boulder County AIDS Project 235
Boys and Girls Club of Albany 235

COLLEGE JUNIORS

INTERNATIONAL APPLICANTS ACCEPTED INDEX

PAID INTERNSHIPS INDEX

POSSIBILITY OF PERMANENT EMPLOYMENT INDEX

Notes

Notes

Notes

Notes

Peterson's gives you everything you need to start a lifetime of learning!

At **petersons.com** you can

- Explore graduate programs
- Discover distance learning programs
- Find out how to finance your education
- Search for career opportunities

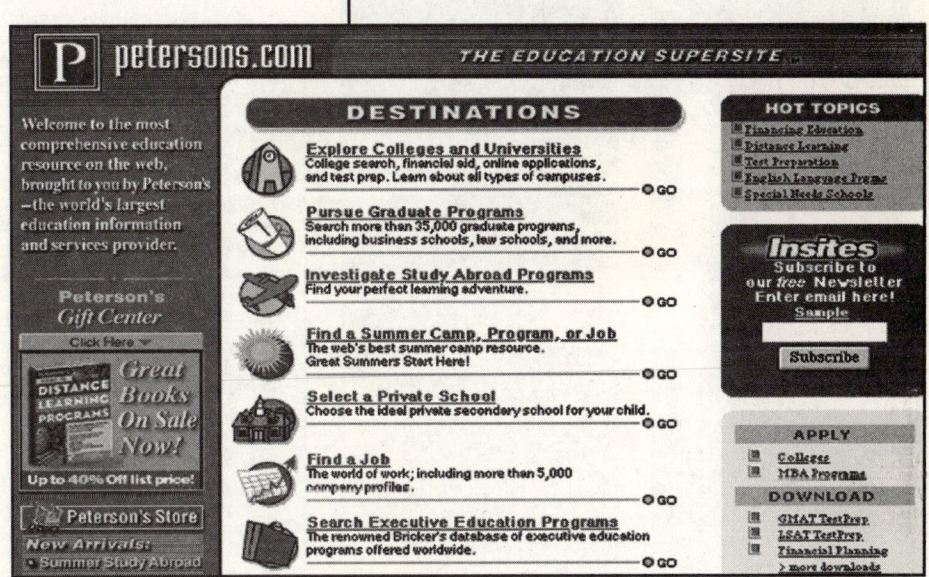

Looking for advice on finding the right graduate program? Look no further than the **Enrollment Message Center at petersons.com!**

- Explore program options by discipline
- E-mail program contacts for more information
- Best of all—**It's FREE**

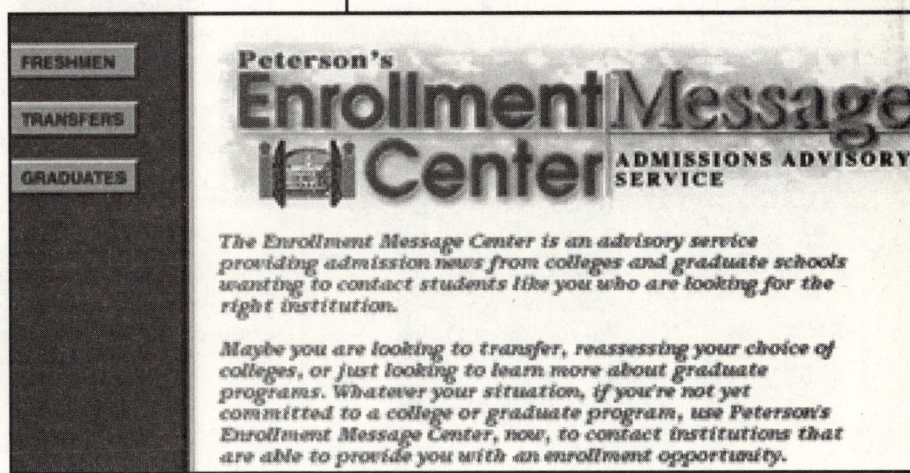

And it's all just a mouse click away!

PETERSON'S
Princeton, New Jersey
www.petersons.com

Keyword on AOL: Petersons
1-800-338-3282

The Right Advice. The Right Tools. The Right Choice.

Logic & Reading Review for the GRE*, GMAT*, LSAT*, MCAT*
Hone skills required for top-notch performance with extensive preparation in logic games, analysis, and reading comprehension.
ISBN 0-7689-0229-0, $16.95 pb/$24.95 CAN, July 1999

Graduate Schools in the U.S. 1999
This overview of programs is the first tool a student needs to make the education decision of a lifetime. Includes CD with practice GRE and financial aid information.
ISBN 0-7689-0207-X, with CD, $24.95 pb/$36.95 CAN/£17.99 UK, January 1999

U.S. and Canadian Medical Schools 1999
Profiles of 400 accredited M.D. and combined medical degree programs in the U.S., Canada, and Puerto Rico. Plus—a full-length MCAT and financial aid options.
ISBN 0-7689-0150-2, $24.95 pb/$34.95 CAN/£17.99 UK, 1998

The Insider's Guide to Medical Schools
Profiles all 148 accredited medical colleges in the U.S., giving a student's view of each school, advice on medical school, and articles on managing medical studies.
ISBN 0-7689-0203-7, $21.95 pb/$32.95 CAN/£16.99 UK, June 1999

Law Schools 2000
The essential guide to legal education—everything prospective law students really need to know. Comprehensive coverage of all 181 nationally accredited U.S. law schools and a practice LSAT on CD.
ISBN 0-7689-0290-8, with CD, $24.95 pb/$36.95 CAN/£17.99 UK, December 1999

MBA Programs 2000
A grad school essential! Details over 900 business schools offering full-time, part-time, joint-degree, dual-degree, international, and executive MBA programs.
ISBN 0-7689-0262-2, $26.95 pb/$39.95 CAN/£17.99 UK, October 1999

GRE* Success 2000
The only comprehensive test prep for both the written and computerized GRE format.
ISBN 0-7689-0240-1, with CD, $16.95 pb/$24.95 CAN/£14.99 UK, July 1999

LSAT* Success 2000
Inside advice on handling the essay and test questions from a designer of the LSAT.
ISBN 0-7689-0224-X, with CD, $16.95 pb/$24.95 CAN/£14.99 UK, July 1999

Gold Standard MCAT*
Delivers intensive coverage of science and math concepts and features practice exams.
ISBN 0-7689-0192-8, $44.95 pb/£37.00 UK, January 1999

GMAT* Success 2000
Results-oriented tips, strategies, and review for all content areas of the GMAT.
ISBN 0-7689-0233-9, with CD, $16.95/$24.95 CAN/£14.99 UK, July 1999

Financing Graduate School
Expert advice on securing assistantships, fellowships, loans, and internships.
ISBN 1-56079-638-3, $16.95 pb/$23.95 CAN/£12.99 UK, 1996

Grants for Graduate & Postdoctoral Study
Identify 1,900 grants, scholarships, and fellowships in this key guide.
ISBN 0-7689-0019-0, $32.95 pb/$45.95 CAN, 1998

How to Write a Winning Personal Statement for Graduate and Professional School
Exclusive tips from admissions officers at the nation's top graduate schools.
ISBN 1-56079-855-6 $12.95 pb/$17.95 CAN/£9.99 UK, 1997

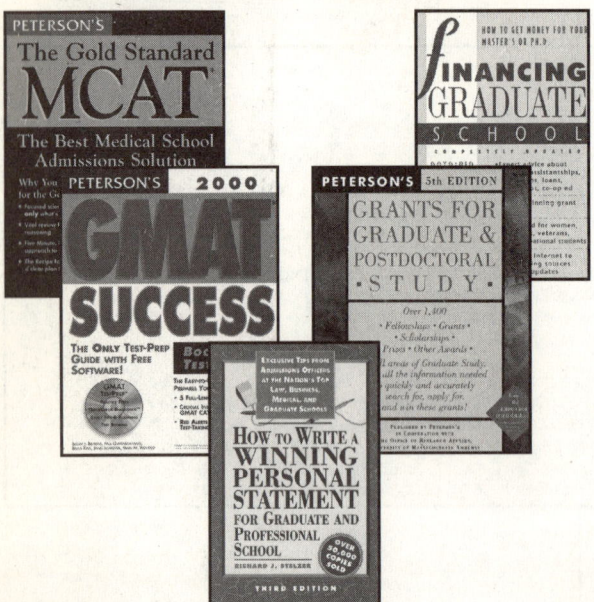

At fine bookstores near you.

**To order direct, call 1-800-338-3282
Or fax your order to 609-243-9150**

To order on line, access our Web site at http://bookstore.petersons.com

PETERSON'S
Princeton, New Jersey
www.petersons.com
Keyword on AOL: Petersons

*GRE is a registered trademark of Educational Testing Service, LSAT is a registered trademark of the Law School Admission Service, MCAT is a registered trademark of the Association of American Medical Colleges, and GMAT is a registered trademark of the